Y0-BDE-062

America's
Top-Rated Cities:
A Statistical Handbook

Volume 2

2015

Twenty-Second Edition

America's
Top-Rated Cities:
A Statistical Handbook

Volume 2: Western Region

A Universal Reference Book

Grey House
Publishing

PUBLISHER: Leslie Mackenzie
EDITORIAL DIRECTOR: Laura Mars
EDITOR: David Garoogian

RESEARCHER & WRITER: Sebastian Marturana
PRODUCTION MANAGER: Kristen Thatcher
MARKETING DIRECTOR: Jessica Moody

A Universal Reference Book
Grey House Publishing, Inc.
4919 Route 22
Amenia, NY 12501
518.789.8700
Fax 845.373.6390
www.greyhouse.com
e-mail: books @greyhouse.com

Twenty-second Edition
Printed in Canada

Publisher's Cataloging-in-Publication Data
(Prepared by The Donohue Group, Inc.)

America's top-rated cities. Vol. II, Western region : a statistical handbook. — 1992-

  v. : ill. ; cm.
  Annual, 1995-
  Irregular, 1992-1993
  ISSN: 1082-7102

1. Cities and towns--Ratings--Western States--Statistics--Periodicals. 2. Cities and towns--Western States--Statistics--Periodicals. 3. Social indicators--Western States--Periodicals. 4. Quality of life--Western States--Statistics--Periodicals. 5. Western States--Social conditions--Statistics--Periodicals. I. Title: America's top rated cities. II. Title: Western region

HT123.5.S6 A44
307.76/0973/05
95644648

4-Volume Set   ISBN: 978-1-61925-552-4
Volume 1   ISBN: 978-1-61925-553-1
Volume 2   **ISBN: 978-1-61925-554-8**
Volume 3   ISBN: 978-1-61925-555-5
Volume 4   ISBN: 978-1-61925-556-2

Boulder, Colorado

Colorado Springs, Colorado

Denver, Colorado

Eugene, Oregon

Fort Collins, Colorado

Honolulu, Hawaii

Las Vegas, Nevada

Los Angeles, California

Reno, Nevada

Sacramento, California

Salem, Oregon

Salt Lake City, Utah

Seattle, Washington

Spokane, Washington

Introduction

This twenty-second edition of *America's Top-Rated Cities* is a concise, statistical, 4-volume work identifying America's top-rated cities with populations of at least 100,000. It profiles 100 cities that have received high marks for business and living from prominent sources such as *Forbes, U.S. News & World Report, BusinessWeek, Inc., Fortune, Men's Health, The Wall Street Journal, Cosmopolitan,* and *CNNMoney.*

Each volume covers a different region of the country—Southern, Western, Central and Eastern—and includes a detailed Table of Contents, City Chapters, Appendices, and Maps. Each City Chapter incorporates information from hundreds of resources to create the following major sections:

- **Background**—lively narrative of significant, up-to-date news for both businesses and residents. These combine historical facts with current developments, "known-for" annual events, and climate data.
- **Rankings**—fun-to-read, bulleted survey results from over 300 books, magazines, and online articles, ranging from general (Great Places to Live), to specific (Best Cities for Newlyweds), and everything in between.
- **Statistical Tables**—122 tables and detailed topics—several new and expanded—that offer an unparalleled view of each city's Business and Living Environments. They are carefully organized with data that is easy to read and understand.
- **Appendices**—five in all, follow each volume of City Chapters. These range from listings of Metropolitan Statistical Areas to Comparative Statistics for all 100 cities.

This new edition of *America's Top-Rated Cities* includes cities that not only surveyed well, but ranked highest using our unique weighting system. We looked at violent crime, property crime, population growth, median household income, housing affordability, poverty, educational attainment, and unemployment. You'll find that a number of American cities remain "top-rated" despite less-than-stellar numbers. Miami, for example, is known for high crime and unemployment, but also for its unique location—as both a valuable business port and popular vacation spot. New York and Los Angeles have relatively low high school graduation rates, but both of these cities make up for it in other ways. A final consideration is location—we strive to include as many states in the country as possible.

Part of this year's city criteria is that it be the "primary" city in a given metropolitan area. For example, if the metro area is Raleigh-Cary, NC, we would consider Raleigh, not Cary. This allows for a more equitable core city to core city comparison. In general, the core city of a metro area is defined as having substantial influence on neighboring cities.

The following five cities have never before appeared as a top-rated city:
- SOUTHERN: Tyler, TX; Palm Bay, FL
- CENTRAL: Springfield, IL
- EASTERN: Roanoke, VA; Winston-Salem, NC

The following city has regained its top-city status after being removed from the list for several years:
- WESTERN: Sacramento, CA

Praise for previous editions:

> "...[ATRC] has...proven its worth to a wide audience...from businesspeople and corporations planning to launch, relocate, or expand their operations to market researchers, real estate professionals, urban planners, job-seekers, students...interested in...reliable, attractively presented statistical information about larger U.S. cities."
> —ARBA

> "...For individuals or businesses looking to relocate, this resource conveniently reports rankings from more than 300 sources for the top 100 US cities. Recommended..."
> —Choice

> "...While patrons are becoming increasingly comfortable locating statistical data online, there is still something to be said for the ease associated with such a compendium of otherwise scattered data. A well-organized and appropriate update..."
> —Library Journal

BACKGROUND

Each city begins with an informative Background that combines history with current events. These narratives often reflect changes that have occurred during the past year, and touch on the city's environment, politics, employment, cultural offerings, and climate, often including interesting trivia. For example: The unique craft of cowboy boot making is demonstrated at the Abilene Historical Museum; Peregrine Falcons were rehabilitated and released into the wild from Boise City's World Center for Birds of Prey; Gainesville is home to a 6,800 square-foot living Butterfly Rainforest, and Grand Rapids was the first city to introduce fluoride into its drinking water in 1945.

RANKINGS

This section has rankings from a possible 316 books, articles, and reports. For easy reference, these Rankings are categorized into 16 topics including Business/Finance, Dating/Romance, and Health/Fitness.

The Rankings are presented in an easy-to-read, bulleted format and include results from both annual surveys and one-shot studies. **Fastest-Growing Wages . . . Most Well-Read . . . Most Playful . . . Most Wired. . . Healthiest for Women . . . Best for Minority Entrepreneurs . . . Safest . . . Best to Grow Old . . . Most Polite . . . Best for Moviemakers . . . Most Frugal . . . Noisiest . . . Most Vegetarian-Friendly . . . Least Stressful . . . Hottest Cities of the Future . . . Most Political . . . Most Charitable . . . Most Tax Friendly . . . Best for Telecommuters . . . Best for Singles . . . Gayest . . . Best for Dogs . . . Most Tattooed . . . Best for Wheelchair Users,** and more.

Sources for these Rankings include both well-known magazines and other media, including *Forbes, Fortune, Inc. Magazine, Working Mother, BusinessWeek, Kiplinger's Personal Finance, Men's Journal,* and *Travel + Leisure,* as well as resources not as well known, such as the *Asthma & Allergy Foundation of America, Christopher & Dana Reeve Foundation, The Advocate, Black Enterprise, National Civic League, The National Coalition for the Homeless, MovieMaker Magazine, Center for Digital Government, U.S. Conference of Mayors,* and the *Milken Institute.*

Since rankings cover a variety of geographic areas-metropolitan statistical areas, metropolitan divisions, cities, etc.- rankings can apply to one or all of these areas; see Appendix B for full geographic definitions.

STATISTICAL TABLES

Each city chapter includes a possible 122 tables and detailed topics—68 in BUSINESS and 54 in LIVING. Over 90% of statistical data has been updated. New topics include *Disability Status.* Expanded topics include the addition of gender and gender identity bias to *Hate Crimes* and best medical schools to *Higher Education.*

Business Environment includes hard facts and figures on 10 topics, including City Finances, Demographics, Income, Economy, Employment, and Taxes. *Living Environment* includes 11 topics, such as Cost of Living, Housing, Health, Education, Safety, Recreation, and Climate.

To compile the Statistical Tables, our editors have again turned to a wide range of sources, some well known, such as the *U.S. Census Bureau, U.S. Environmental Protection Agency, Bureau of Labor Statistics, Centers for Disease Control and Prevention,* and the *Federal Bureau of Investigation,* and some more obscure, like *The Council for Community and Economic Research, Texas Transportation Institute,* and *Federation of Tax Administrators.*

APPENDICES: Data for all cities appear in all volumes.
- **Appendix A**—*Comparative Statistics*
- **Appendix B**—*Metropolitan Area Definitions*
- **Appendix C**—*Government Type and County*
- **Appendix D**—*Chambers of Commerce and Economic Development Organizations*
- **Appendix E**—*State Departments of Labor and Employment*

Material provided by public and private agencies and organizations was supplemented by original research, numerous library sources and Internet sites. *America's Top-Rated Cities, 2015,* is designed for a wide range of readers: private individuals considering relocating a residence or business; professionals considering expanding their businesses or changing careers; corporations considering relocation, opening up additional offices or creating new divisions; government agencies; general and market researchers; real estate consultants; human resource personnel; urban planners; investors; and urban government students.

Customers who purchase the four-volume set receive free online access to *America's Top-Rated Cities* to: download city reports; sort and rank by 50-plus data points; and access data for 200 more cities than in the print version.

AMERICA'S TOP-RATED CITIES

CBSA: Core Base Statistical Area

- ○ Top Rated City
- STATE
- East Region
- Central Region
- West Region
- South Region

©Larry Mandelin 2014

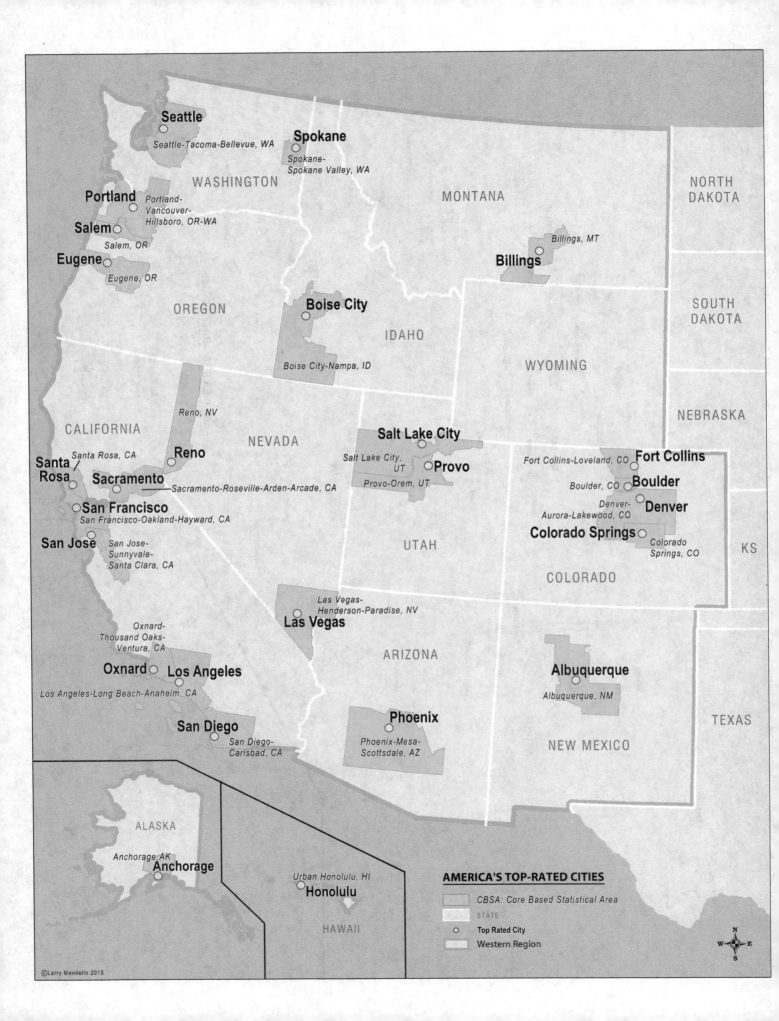

Seattle
Seattle-Tacoma-Bellevue, WA

Spokane
Spokane-Spokane Valley, WA

WASHINGTON

MONTANA

NORTH DAKOTA

Portland
Portland-Vancouver-Hillsboro, OR-WA

Salem
Salem, OR

Eugene
Eugene, OR

OREGON

Boise City
Boise City-Nampa, ID

IDAHO

Billings
Billings, MT

WYOMING

SOUTH DAKOTA

NEBRASKA

Reno, NV

CALIFORNIA

Santa Rosa, CA

Santa Rosa

Reno

Sacramento
Sacramento-Roseville-Arden-Arcade, CA

San Francisco
San Francisco-Oakland-Hayward, CA

San Jose
San Jose-Sunnyvale-Santa Clara, CA

NEVADA

Salt Lake City
Salt Lake City, UT

Provo
Provo-Orem, UT

UTAH

Fort Collins-Loveland, CO

Boulder, CO

Denver-Aurora-Lakewood, CO

Fort Collins

Boulder

Denver

Colorado Springs
Colorado Springs, CO

COLORADO

KS

Oxnard-Thousand Oaks-Ventura, CA

Oxnard

Los Angeles
Los Angeles-Long Beach-Anaheim, CA

San Diego
San Diego-Carlsbad, CA

Las Vegas
Las Vegas-Henderson-Paradise, NV

ARIZONA

Phoenix
Phoenix-Mesa-Scottsdale, AZ

Albuquerque
Albuquerque, NM

NEW MEXICO

TEXAS

ALASKA

Anchorage, AK

Anchorage

Urban Honolulu, HI

Honolulu

HAWAII

AMERICA'S TOP-RATED CITIES

CBSA: Core Based Statistical Area

STATE

○ Top Rated City

Western Region

©Larry Mandelin 2015

N
W E
S

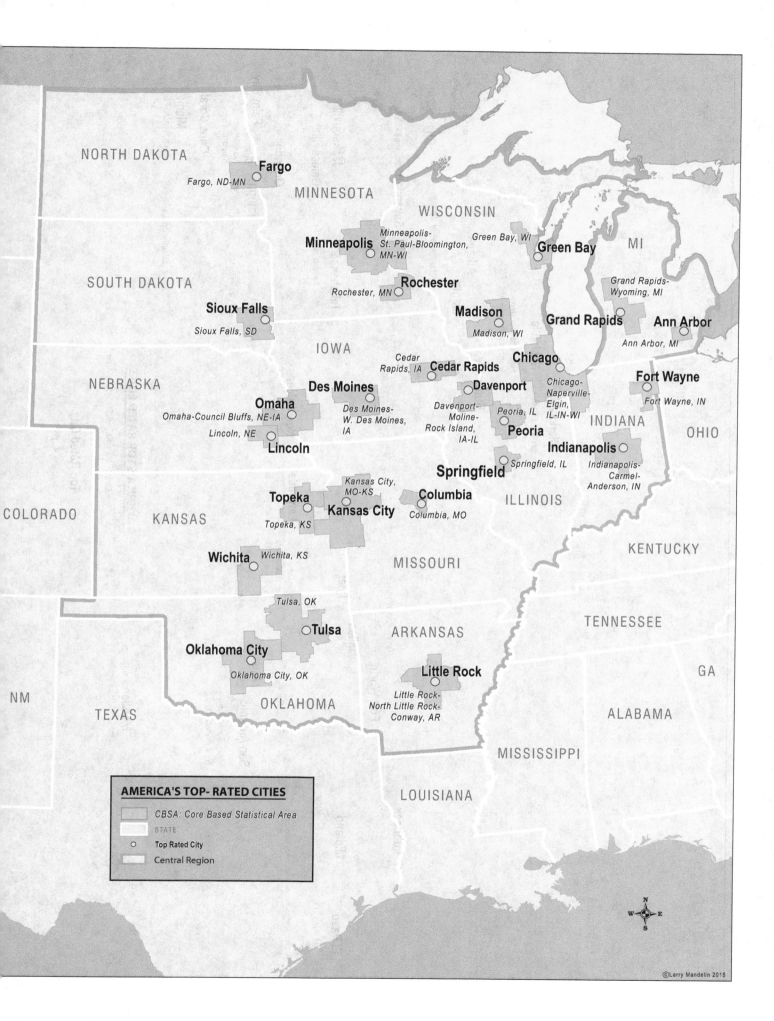

AMERICA'S TOP- RATED CITIES

CBSA: Core Based Statistical Area
STATE
○ Top Rated City
Central Region

NORTH DAKOTA

Fargo
Fargo, ND-MN

MINNESOTA

Minneapolis
Minneapolis-
St. Paul-Bloomington,
MN-WI

WISCONSIN

Green Bay, WI

Green Bay

MI

SOUTH DAKOTA

Rochester
Rochester, MN

Grand Rapids-
Wyoming, MI

Sioux Falls
Sioux Falls, SD

Madison
Madison, WI

Grand Rapids

Ann Arbor
Ann Arbor, MI

IOWA

Cedar
Rapids, IA

Cedar Rapids

Chicago

Fort Wayne
Fort Wayne, IN

NEBRASKA

Des Moines

Davenport

Chicago-
Naperville-
Elgin,
IL-IN-WI

Omaha
Omaha-Council Bluffs, NE-IA

Des Moines-
W. Des Moines,
IA

Davenport-
Moline-
Rock Island,
IA-IL

Peoria, IL

INDIANA

OHIO

Lincoln, NE

Peoria

Lincoln

Indianapolis

Springfield

Springfield, IL

Indianapolis-
Carmel-
Anderson, IN

Kansas City,
MO-KS

Columbia

ILLINOIS

Topeka

Columbia, MO

COLORADO

Kansas City

KENTUCKY

KANSAS

Topeka, KS

MISSOURI

Wichita
Wichita, KS

Tulsa, OK

TENNESSEE

Tulsa

GA

ARKANSAS

NM

Oklahoma City

Little Rock

ALABAMA

Oklahoma City, OK

Little Rock-
North Little Rock-
Conway, AR

TEXAS

OKLAHOMA

MISSISSIPPI

LOUISIANA

N
W   E
S

©Larry Mandelin 2015

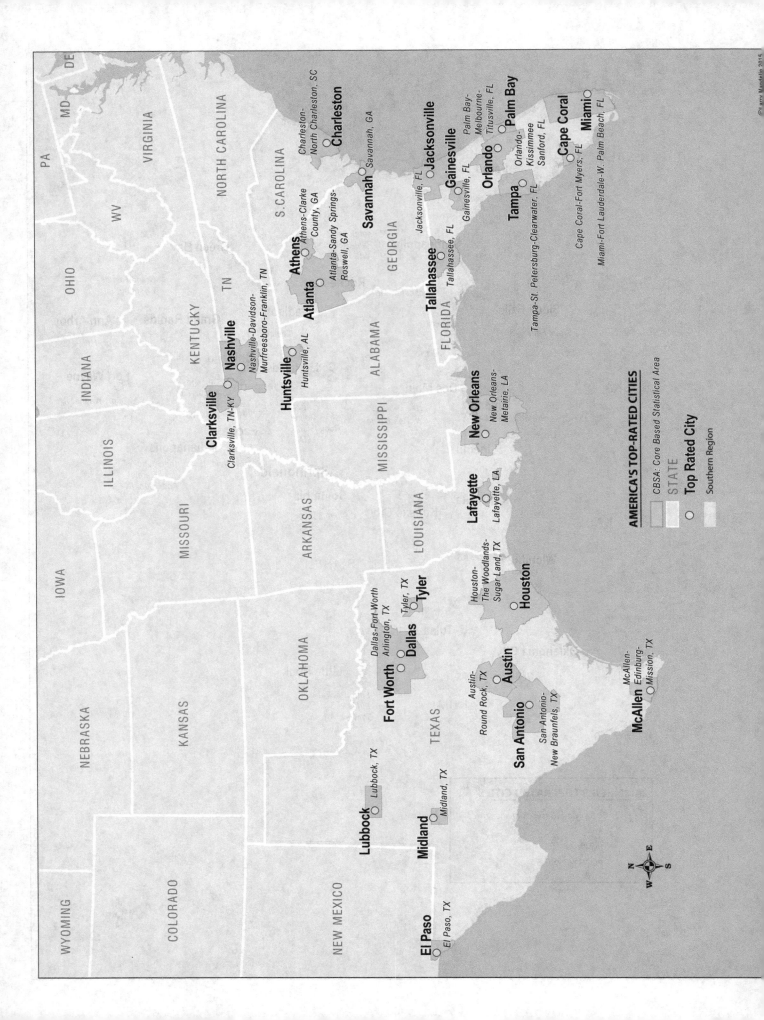

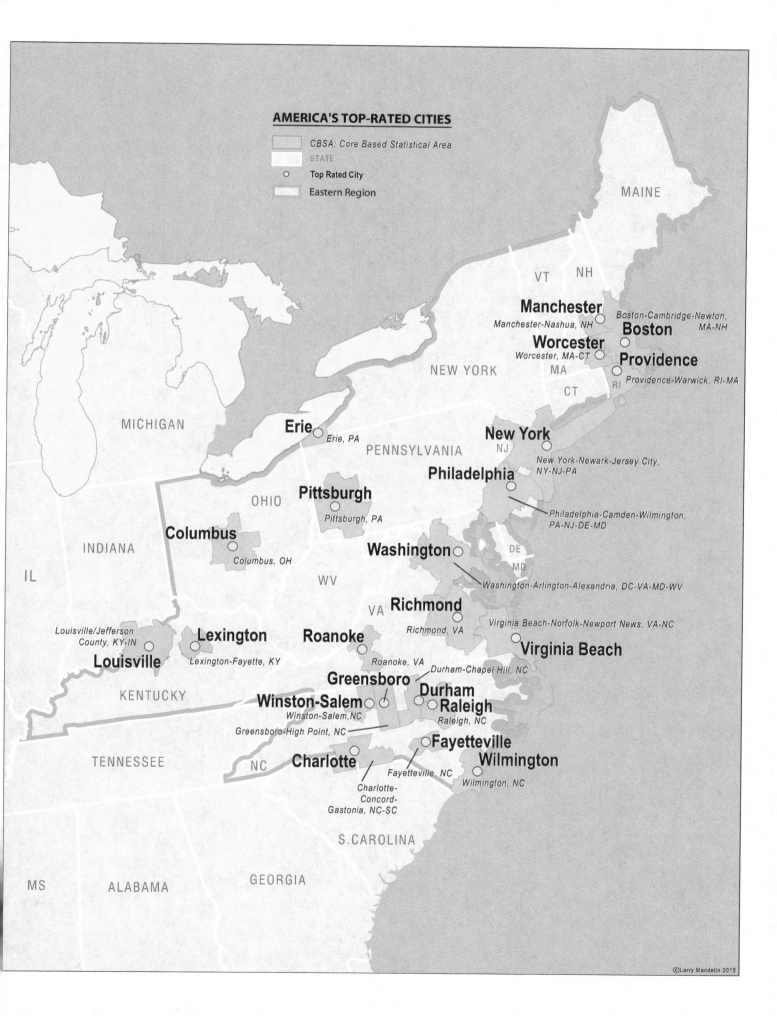

AMERICA'S TOP-RATED CITIES

CBSA: Core Based Statistical Area
STATE
○ Top Rated City
Eastern Region

MAINE

VT NH

Manchester
Manchester-Nashua, NH

Boston-Cambridge-Newton, MA-NH

Boston ○

Worcester
Worcester, MA-CT

Providence ○
Providence-Warwick, RI-MA

MA
CT
RI

NEW YORK

MICHIGAN

Erie ○
Erie, PA

PENNSYLVANIA

NJ

New York ○
New York-Newark-Jersey City, NY-NJ-PA

Philadelphia
Philadelphia-Camden-Wilmington, PA-NJ-DE-MD

OHIO

Pittsburgh ○
Pittsburgh, PA

Columbus ○
Columbus, OH

INDIANA

DE
MD

WV

Washington ○
Washington-Arlington-Alexandria, DC-VA-MD-WV

IL

VA

Richmond ○
Richmond, VA

Virginia Beach-Norfolk-Newport News, VA-NC

Louisville/Jefferson County, KY-IN

Lexington ○
Lexington-Fayette, KY

Roanoke ○
Roanoke, VA

Virginia Beach ○

Louisville ○

Durham-Chapel Hill, NC

KENTUCKY

Greensboro ○
Winston-Salem ○
Winston-Salem, NC

Durham ○
Raleigh ○
Raleigh, NC

Greensboro-High Point, NC

Fayetteville ○

TENNESSEE

NC

Charlotte ○
Charlotte-Concord-Gastonia, NC-SC

Fayetteville, NC

Wilmington ○
Wilmington, NC

S.CAROLINA

MS ALABAMA GEORGIA

©Larry Mandelin 2015

Albuquerque, New Mexico

Background

Pueblo Indians originally inhabited what is now the Albuquerque metropolitan area. In the sixteenth century, Spaniards began pushing up from Mexico in search of riches, but it was not until 1706 that they founded the settlement, naming it after the viceroy of New Spain, San Francisco Xavier de Albuquerque, a duke whose permission was needed to set up the town. Eventually, the city's name would lose a consonant and become Albuquerque. The city earned the sobriquet "Duke City" because of its namesake.

In the early nineteenth century, Mexico secured her independence from Spanish rule and allowed Americans to enter the province of New Mexico to trade. During the Mexican War of the 1840s, Americans under the command of General Stephen Kearny captured the town, and New Mexico was transferred to the United States in the Treaty of Guadalupe Hidalgo, ending the war.

During the Civil War, Confederates held the town for a few weeks, eventually surrendering it to a besieging Union army. After the war, the railroad arrived in 1880, bringing with it people and business. In 1891 the town received a city charter. Albuquerque became an important site for tuberculosis sanatoriums during the next few decades because of the healing nature of the dry desert air.

World War II had a great impact on Albuquerque, as Kirtland Air Force Base became an important site for the making of the atomic bomb. Sandia National Laboratories was founded in the city after the war, and was important in defense-related research during the Cold War.

The defense industry is of prime significance to Albuquerque. Institutions once dedicated to defense research are now involved in applying such technology to the private sector, making the city a perfect place for high-tech concerns. In addition to Sandia, the city hosts a branch of the Air Force Research Laboratories and the Los Alamos National Laboratory. Biotech and semiconductor industries also have had a positive impact on the city's economy.

Albuquerque and New Mexico have many programs to assist business. The state has property taxes that are among the lowest in the nation.

More traditional forms of making a living are still present, as the city is located in an area where ranchers raise sheep and other livestock.

Albuquerque is also a critical transportation center for the American Southwest, with two major interstates that intersect there. Its airport, Albuquerque International Sunport, is served by seven major commercial carriers and at least five commuter airlines. A recent expansion included an "aerotropolis" of state-of-the-art manufacturing and shipping facilities and Mesa del Sol, a mixed-used development site on 20 square miles of land, connected to the airport by light-rail and a commuter rail line that also serves the region. The New Mexico Rail Runner Express system began operation in July 2006; in 2010, the train's new Wi-Fi network became operational. An 11-mile bus service, Rapid Ride, was so popular that a new Green Line of service was added. Interestingly, the city was voted one of the most walkable American cities in 2011.

There are various venues for higher education located in Albuquerque, the most significant of which is the University of New Mexico.

There are festive events scheduled throughout the year. The annual International Albuquerque International Balloon Fiesta has become a "must" for residents and visitors alike. The city is also home to the annual Gathering of Nations Powwow, an international event featuring over 3,000 indigenous Native American dancers and singers representing more than 500 tribes from Canada and the United States.

Albuquerque enjoys a dry, arid climate, with plenty of sunshine, low humidity, and scant rainfall. More than three-fourths of the daylight hours have sunshine, summer and winter. As in all desert climates, temperatures can fluctuate widely between day and night, all year round. Precipitation is meager during the winter, more abundant in summer with afternoon and evening thunderstorms.

Rankings

General Rankings

- The U.S. Conference of Mayors and Waste Management sponsor the City Livability Awards Program. The awards recognize and honor mayors for exemplary leadership in developing and implementing specific programs that improve the quality of life in America's cities. Albuquerque was one of 17 second round finalists in the large cities (population 100,000 or more) category. *U.S. Conference of Mayors, "2015 City Livability Awards"*

Business/Finance Rankings

- The Brookings Institution ranked the 50 largest cities in the U.S. based on income inequality. Albuquerque was ranked #41. (#1 = greatest ineqality). Criteria: the cities were ranked based on the "95/20 ratio," a figure representing the income at which a household earns more than 95 percent of all other households, divided by the income at which a household earns more than only 20 percent of all other households. *Brookings Institution, "Income Inequality in America's 50 Largest Cities, 2007-2013," March 17, 2015*

- Albuquerque was ranked #89 out of 100 metro areas in terms of economic performance (#1 = best) during the recession and recovery from trough quarter through the second quarter of 2013. Criteria: percent change in employment; percentage point change in unemployment rate; percent change in gross metropolitan product; percent change in House Price Index. *Brookings Institution, MetroMonitor: Tracking Economic Recession and Recovery in America's 100 Largest Metropolitan Areas, September 2013*

- The Albuquerque metro area appeared on the Milken Institute "2013 Best Performing Cities" list. Rank: #179 out of 200 large metro areas. Criteria: job growth; wage and salary growth; high-tech output growth. *Milken Institute, "Best-Performing Cities 2014," January 2015*

- *Forbes* ranked the 200 most populous metro areas to determine the nation's "Best Places for Business and Careers." The Albuquerque metro area was ranked #166. Criteria: costs (business and living); job growth (past and projected); income growth; educational attainment (college and high school); projected economic growth; cultural and recreational opportunities; net migration patterns; number of highly ranked colleges. *Forbes, "The Best Places for Business and Careers 2014," July 23, 2014*

Culture/Performing Arts Rankings

- Albuquerque was selected as one of the ten best large U.S. cities in which to be a moviemaker. Of cities with a population over 400,000, the city was ranked #8. Criteria: film community; access to new films; access to equipment; cost of living; tax incentives. *MovieMaker Magazine, "Best Places to Live and Work as a Moviemaker: 2013," January 22, 2015*

- Albuquerque was selected as one of America's top cities for the arts. The city ranked #7 in the big city (population 500,000 and over) category. Criteria: readers' top choices for arts travel destinations based on the richness and variety of visual arts sites, activities and events. *American Style, "2012 Top 25 Arts Destinations," June 2012*

Dating/Romance Rankings

- Of the 100 U.S. cities surveyed by *Men's Health* in its quest to identify the nation's best cities for dating and forming relationships, Albuquerque was ranked #57 for online dating (#1 = best). *Men's Health, "The Best and Worst Cities for Online Dating," January 30, 2013*

Education Rankings

- Personal finance website *WalletHub* analyzed the 150 largest U.S. metropolitan statistical areas to determine where the most educated Americans are choosing to settle. Criteria: educational attainment; percentage of workers with jobs in computer, engineering, and science fields; quality and size of each metro area's universities. Albuquerque was ranked #46 (#1 = most educated city). *www.WalletHub.com, "2014's Most and Least Educated Cities*

- Albuquerque was selected as one of America's most literate cities. The city ranked #45 out of the 77 largest U.S. cities. Criteria: number of booksellers; library resources; Internet resources; educational attainment; periodical publishing resources; newspaper circulation. *Central Connecticut State University, "America's Most Literate Cities, 2014," April 8, 2015*

Environmental Rankings

- The Albuquerque metro area came in at #90 for the relative comfort of its climate on Sperling's list of "chill cities," as measured by the Sperling Heat Index. All 361 metro areas are included. Criteria included daytime high temperatures, nighttime low temperatures, dew point, and relative humidity at the high temperatures. *www.bertsperling.com, "Sperling's Chill Cities," July 18, 2013*

- Sperling's BestPlaces assessed 379 metropolitan areas of the United States for the likelihood of dangerously extreme weather events or earthquakes. In general the Southeast and South-Central regions have the highest risk of weather extremes and earthquakes, while the Pacific Northwest enjoys the lowest risk. Of the least risky metropolitan areas, the Albuquerque metro area was ranked #115. *www.bestplaces.net, "Safest Places from Natural Disasters," April 2011*

- The Albuquerque metro area was identified as one of nine cities running out of water by *24/7 Wall St.* The area ranked #8. Based on data provided by the U.S. Drought Monitor, a joint program produced by academic and government organizations, *24/7 Wall St.* identified large U.S. urban areas that have been under persistent, serious drought for months. *24/7 Wall St., "Nine Cities Running Out of Water," August 1, 2013*

- Albuquerque was highlighted as one of the top 25 cleanest metro areas for year-round particle pollution (Annual PM 2.5) in the U.S. during 2011 through 2013. The area ranked #16. *American Lung Association, State of the Air 2015*

Food/Drink Rankings

- *Men's Health* ranked 100 major U.S. cities in terms of alcohol intoxication. Albuquerque ranked #62 (#1 = most sober).Criteria: binge drinking; alcohol-related traffic accidents, arrests, and fatalities. *Men's Health, "The Drunkest Cities in America," November 19, 2013*

Health/Fitness Rankings

- Albuquerque was selected as one of the 25 fittest cities in America by *Men's Fitness Online*. It ranked #3 out of America's 50 largest cities. Criteria: fitness centers and sport stores; nutrition; sports participation; TV viewing; overweight/sedentary; junk food; air quality; geography; commute; parks and open space; city recreational facilities; access to healthcare; motivation; mayor and city initiatives; state obesity initiatives. *Men's Fitness, "The Fittest and Fattest Cities in America," March 5, 2012*

- Albuquerque was identified as a "2013 Spring Allergy Capital." The area ranked #79 out of 100. Three groups of factors were used to identify the most severe cities for people with allergies during the spring season: annual pollen levels; medicine utilization; access to board-certified allergists. *Asthma and Allergy Foundation of America, "Spring Allergy Capitals 2013"*

- Albuquerque was identified as a "2013 Fall Allergy Capital." The area ranked #82 out of 100. Three groups of factors were used to identify the most severe cities for people with allergies during the fall season: annual pollen levels; medicine utilization; access to board-certified allergists. *Asthma and Allergy Foundation of America, "Fall Allergy Capitals 2013"*

- Albuquerque was identified as a "2013 Asthma Capital." The area ranked #94 out of the nation's 100 largest metropolitan areas. Twelve factors were used to identify the most challenging places to live for people with asthma: estimated prevalence; self-reported prevalence; crude death rate for asthma; annual pollen score; annual air quality; public smoking laws; number of board-certified asthma specialists; school inhaler access laws; rescue medication use; controller medication use; uninsured rate; poverty rate. *Asthma and Allergy Foundation of America, "Asthma Capitals 2013"*

- *Men's Health* ranked 100 major U.S. cities in terms of the best and worst cities for men. Albuquerque ranked #59. Criteria: thirty-three data points were examined covering health, fitness, and quality of life. *Men's Health, "The Best & Worst Cities for Men 2014," December 6, 2013*

- The Albuquerque metro area appeared in the 2013 Gallup-Healthways Well-Being Index. The area ranked #97 out of 189. The Gallup-Healthways Well-Being Index score is an average of six sub-indexes, which individually examine life evaluation, emotional health, work environment, physical health, healthy behaviors, and access to basic necessities. Results are based on telephone interviews conducted as part of the Gallup-Healthways Well-Being Index survey January 2–December 29, 2012, and January 2–December 30, 2013, with a random sample of 531,630 adults, aged 18 and older, living in metropolitan areas in the 50 U.S. states and the District of Columbia. *Gallup-Healthways, "State of American Well-Being," March 25, 2014*

- Albuquerque was selected as one of the "20 Most Livable U.S. Cities for Wheelchair Users" by the Christopher & Dana Reeve Foundation. The city ranked #2. Criteria: Medicaid eligibility and spending; access to physicians and rehabilitation facilities; access to fitness facilities and recreation; access to paratransit; percentage of people living with disabilities who are employed; clean air; climate. *Christopher & Dana Reeve Foundation, "20 Most Livable U.S. Cities for Wheelchair Users," July 26, 2010*

Pet Rankings

- Albuquerque was selected as one of the best cities for dogs by real estate website Estately.com. The city was ranked #6. Criteria: weather; walkability; yard sizes; dog activities; meetup groups; availability of dogsitters. *Estately.com, "17 Best U.S. Cities for Dogs," May 14, 2013*

Real Estate Rankings

- Albuquerque was ranked #187 out of 275 metro areas in terms of house price appreciation in 2014 (#1 = highest rate). *Federal Housing Finance Agency, House Price Index, 4th Quarter 2014*

- Albuquerque was ranked #130 out of 226 metro areas in terms of housing affordability in 2014 by the National Association of Home Builders (#1 = most affordable). The NAHB-Wells Fargo Housing Opportunity Index (HOI) for a given area is defined as the share of homes sold in that area that would have been affordable to a family earning the local median income, based on standard mortgage underwriting criteria. *National Association of Home Builders®, NAHB-Wells Fargo Housing Opportunity Index, 4th Quarter 2014*

Safety Rankings

- Symantec, in partnership with Sperling's BestPlaces, ranked the 50 largest cities in the U.S. in terms of their vulnerability to cybercrime. The city ranked #41. Criteria: number of cyberattacks and potential infections; level of Internet access; expenditures on smartphones and computer hardware/software; wireless hotspots; broadband connectivity; Internet usage; online purchases. *Symantec, "Riskiest Online Cities of 2012" February 15, 2012*

- Allstate ranked the 200 largest cities in America in terms of driver safety. Albuquerque ranked #126. Allstate researchers analyzed internal property damage claims over a two-year period from January 2011 to December 2012. A weighted average of the two-year numbers determined the annual percentages. *Allstate, "Allstate America's Best Drivers Report, 2014"*

- Albuquerque was identified as one of the least disaster-proof places in the U.S. in terms of its vulnerability to natural and non-natural disasters. The city ranked #1 out of 5. Rankings are based on the U.S. Center for Disease Control's Cities Readiness Initiative (CRI). As part of the CRI, the CDC and state public health personnel assess local emergency-management plans, protocols and capabilities for 72 Metropolitan Statistical Areas and four non-MSA large cities. *Forbes, "America's Most and Least Disaster-Proof Cities," December 12, 2011*

- The National Insurance Crime Bureau ranked 380 metro areas in the U.S. in terms of per capita rates of vehicle theft. The Albuquerque metro area ranked #20 (#1 = highest rate). Criteria: number of vehicle theft offenses per 100,000 inhabitants in 2012. *National Insurance Crime Bureau, "Hot Spots 2012," June 26, 2013*

Seniors/Retirement Rankings

- From its Best Cities for Successful Aging indexes, the Milken Institute generated rankings for metropolitan areas, weighing data in eight categories—health care, wellness, living arrangements, transportation, financial characteristics, education and employment opportunities, community engagement, and overall livability. The Albuquerque metro area was ranked #67 overall in the large metro area category. *Milken Institute, "Best Cities for Successful Aging, 2014"*

- Albuquerque was chosen in the "Big City" category of CNNMoney's list of the 25 best places to retire." Criteria include: type of location (big city, small town, resort area, college town); median home prices; top state income tax rate. *CNNMoney, "25 Best Places to Retire," December 17, 2012*

- *U.S. News & World Report* listed the best places to retire on an income of $40,000 per year. Albuquerque was among the ten cities selected. Criteria: low cost of living; affordable housing; quality of life; accessible major medical facilities; services for seniors; educational institutions; outdoor recreational activities. *U.S. News & World Report, "Best Places to Retire for Under $40,000," October 15, 2012*

- Albuquerque was identified as one of the most popular places to retire by *Topretirements.com*. The list reflects the 100 cities (out of 900+ total cities reviewed) that visitors to the website are most interested in for retirement. *Topretirements.com, "Most Popular Places to Retire for 2014," February 25, 2014*

Sports/Recreation Rankings

- Albuquerque was chosen as a bicycle friendly community by the League of American Bicyclists. A "Bicycle Friendly Community" welcomes cyclists by providing safe accommodation for cycling and encouraging people to bike for transportation and recreation. There are four award levels: Platinum; Gold; Silver; and Bronze. The community achieved an award level of Bronze. *League of American Bicyclists, "Bicycle Friendly Community Master List," Fall 2013*

- Albuquerque was chosen as one of America's best cities for bicycling. The city ranked #20 out of 50. Criteria: robust cycling infrastructure; vibrant bike culture. The editors only considered cities with populations of 95,000 or more. *Bicycling, "America's Top 50 Bike-Friendly Cities," May 23, 2012*

Women/Minorities Rankings

- *Women's Health* examined U.S. cities and identified the 100 best cities for women. Albuquerque was ranked #36. Criteria: 30 categories were examined from obesity and breast cancer rates to commuting times and hours spent working out. *Women's Health, "Best Cities for Women 2012"*

Miscellaneous Rankings

- Albuquerque was selected as a 2013 Digital Cities Survey winner. The city ranked #7 in the large city (250,000 or more population) category. The survey examined and assessed how city governments are utilizing information technology to operate and deliver quality service to their customers and citizens. Survey questions focused on implementation and adoption of online service delivery; planning and governance; and the infrastructure and architecture that make the transformation to digital government possible. *Center for Digital Government, "2013 Digital Cities Survey," November 7, 2013*

- The National Alliance to End Homelessness ranked the 100 most populous metro areas in terms the rate of homelessness. The Albuquerque metro area ranked #28. Criteria: number of homeless people per 10,000 population in 2011. *National Alliance to End Homelessness, The State of Homelessness in America 2012*

Business Environment

CITY FINANCES

City Government Finances

Component	2012 ($000)	2012 ($ per capita)
Total Revenues	1,070,256	1,961
Total Expenditures	1,016,998	1,863
Debt Outstanding	2,091,765	3,832
Cash and Securities[1]	1,432,688	2,625

Note: (1) Cash and security holdings of a government at the close of its fiscal year, including those of its dependent agencies, utilities, and liquor stores.
Source: U.S Census Bureau, State & Local Government Finances 2012

City Government Revenue by Source

Source	2012 ($000)	2012 ($ per capita)
General Revenue		
From Federal Government	51,884	95
From State Government	227,126	416
From Local Governments	3,481	6
Taxes		
Property	135,440	248
Sales and Gross Receipts	216,151	396
Personal Income	0	0
Corporate Income	0	0
Motor Vehicle License	0	0
Other Taxes	16,210	30
Current Charges	248,192	455
Liquor Store	0	0
Utility	119,102	218
Employee Retirement	0	0

Source: U.S Census Bureau, State & Local Government Finances 2012

City Government Expenditures by Function

Function	2012 ($000)	2012 ($ per capita)	2012 (%)
General Direct Expenditures			
Air Transportation	56,041	103	5.5
Corrections	0	0	0.0
Education	0	0	0.0
Employment Security Administration	0	0	0.0
Financial Administration	15,248	28	1.5
Fire Protection	71,001	130	7.0
General Public Buildings	24,654	45	2.4
Governmental Administration, Other	17,273	32	1.7
Health	27,878	51	2.7
Highways	73,027	134	7.2
Hospitals	0	0	0.0
Housing and Community Development	36,045	66	3.5
Interest on General Debt	26,831	49	2.6
Judicial and Legal	4,432	8	0.4
Libraries	13,290	24	1.3
Parking	5,203	10	0.5
Parks and Recreation	109,641	201	10.8
Police Protection	162,415	298	16.0
Public Welfare	25,177	46	2.5
Sewerage	42,183	77	4.1
Solid Waste Management	48,972	90	4.8
Veterans' Services	0	0	0.0
Liquor Store	0	0	0.0
Utility	189,645	347	18.6
Employee Retirement	0	0	0.0

Source: U.S Census Bureau, State & Local Government Finances 2012

DEMOGRAPHICS

Population Growth

Area	1990 Census	2000 Census	2010 Census	Population Growth (%) 1990-2000	Population Growth (%) 2000-2010
City	388,375	448,607	545,852	15.5	21.7
MSA[1]	599,416	729,649	887,077	21.7	21.6
U.S.	248,709,873	281,421,906	308,745,538	13.2	9.7

Note: (1) Figures cover the Albuquerque, NM Metropolitan Statistical Area—see Appendix B for areas included
Source: U.S. Census Bureau, Census 1990, 2000, 2010

Household Size

Area	One	Two	Three	Four	Five	Six	Seven or More	Average Household Size
City	32.4	32.8	15.3	11.5	5.0	2.2	0.8	2.46
MSA[1]	29.5	33.8	15.3	12.1	5.6	2.5	1.2	2.59
U.S.	27.7	33.6	15.7	13.1	6.0	2.3	1.5	2.64

Note: (1) Figures cover the Albuquerque, NM Metropolitan Statistical Area—see Appendix B for areas included
Source: U.S. Census Bureau, 2011-2013 American Community Survey 3-Year Estimates

Race

Area	White Alone[2] (%)	Black Alone[2] (%)	Asian Alone[2] (%)	AIAN[3] Alone[2] (%)	NHOPI[4] Alone[2] (%)	Other Race Alone[2] (%)	Two or More Races (%)
City	72.0	3.5	2.6	4.2	0.1	13.7	3.9
MSA[1]	71.8	2.8	1.9	5.5	0.1	14.1	3.8
U.S.	73.9	12.6	5.0	0.8	0.2	4.7	2.9

Note: (1) Figures cover the Albuquerque, NM Metropolitan Statistical Area—see Appendix B for areas included; (2) Alone is defined as not being in combination with one or more other races; (3) American Indian and Alaska Native; (4) Native Hawaiian and Other Pacific Islander
Source: U.S. Census Bureau, 2011-2013 American Community Survey 3-Year Estimates

Hispanic or Latino Origin

Area	Total (%)	Mexican (%)	Puerto Rican (%)	Cuban (%)	Other (%)
City	46.9	26.2	0.5	0.6	19.6
MSA[1]	47.4	25.6	0.4	0.4	21.0
U.S.	16.9	10.8	1.6	0.6	3.8

Note: Persons of Hispanic or Latino origin can be of any race; (1) Figures cover the Albuquerque, NM Metropolitan Statistical Area—see Appendix B for areas included
Source: U.S. Census Bureau, 2011-2013 American Community Survey 3-Year Estimates

Segregation

Type	Segregation Indices[1] 1990	2000	2010	2010 Rank[2]	Percent Change 1990-2000	1990-2010	2000-2010
Black/White	38.0	32.0	30.9	99	-6.0	-7.1	-1.1
Asian/White	25.7	28.1	28.5	93	2.4	2.9	0.4
Hispanic/White	40.5	39.8	36.4	79	-0.8	-4.1	-3.4

Note: All figures cover the Metropolitan Statistical Area—see Appendix B for areas included; Figures are based on an analysis of 1990, 2000, and 2010 Census Decennial Census tract data by William H. Frey, Brookings Institution and the University of Michigan Social Science Data Analysis Network. In this analysis all racial groups (whites, blacks, and asians) are non-Hispanic members of those races. Hispanics are shown as a separate category;
(1) Segregation Indices are Dissimilarity Indices that measure the degree to which the minority group is distributed differently than whites across census tracts. They range from 0 (complete integration) to 100 (complete segregation) where the value indicates the percentage of the minority group that needs to move to be distributed exactly like whites; (2) Ranges from 1 (most segregated) to 102 (least segregated); n/a not available.
Source: www.CensusScope.org

Ancestry

Area	German	Irish	English	American	Italian	Polish	French[2]	Scottish	Dutch
City	10.4	7.4	6.7	4.0	3.2	1.2	2.0	1.7	1.0
MSA[1]	10.6	7.2	6.8	4.8	3.1	1.5	1.8	1.6	1.0
U.S.	14.9	10.8	8.0	7.4	5.5	3.0	2.7	1.7	1.4

Note: Figures are the percentage of the total population reporting a particular ancestry. The nine most commonly reported ancestries in the U.S. are shown. Figures include multiple ancestries (e.g. if a person reported being Irish and Italian, they were included in both columns); (1) Figures cover the Albuquerque, NM Metropolitan Statistical Area—see Appendix B for areas included; (2) Excludes Basque
Source: U.S. Census Bureau, 2011-2013 American Community Survey 3-Year Estimates

Foreign-Born Population

Area	Percent of Population Born in								
	Any Foreign Country	Mexico	Asia	Europe	Carribean	South America	Central America[2]	Africa	Canada
City	10.6	6.0	2.2	1.0	0.4	0.4	0.3	0.2	0.2
MSA[1]	9.6	6.0	1.6	0.8	0.3	0.3	0.3	0.1	0.1
U.S.	13.0	3.7	3.8	1.5	1.2	0.9	1.0	0.6	0.3

Note: (1) Figures cover the Albuquerque, NM Metropolitan Statistical Area—see Appendix B for areas included; (2) Excludes Mexico.
Source: U.S. Census Bureau, 2011-2013 American Community Survey 3-Year Estimates

Marital Status

Area	Never Married	Now Married[2]	Separated	Widowed	Divorced
City	35.7	43.1	1.9	5.2	14.0
MSA[1]	33.9	45.4	1.8	5.3	13.6
U.S.	32.7	48.1	2.2	6.0	11.0

Note: Figures are percentages and cover the population 15 years of age and older; (1) Figures cover the Albuquerque, NM Metropolitan Statistical Area—see Appendix B for areas included; (2) Excludes separated
Source: U.S. Census Bureau, 2011-2013 American Community Survey 3-Year Estimates

Disability Status

Area	All Ages	Under 18 Years Old	18 to 64 Years Old	65 Years and Over
City	12.8	4.0	10.8	39.2
MSA[1]	13.3	4.0	11.6	38.6
U.S.	12.3	4.1	10.2	36.3

Note: Figures show percent of the civilian noninstitutionalized population that reported having a disability. Disability status is determined from from six types of difficulty: vision, hearing, cognitive, ambulatory, self-care, and independent living. For children under 5 years old, hearing and vision difficulty are used to determine disability status. For children between the ages of 5 and 14, disability status is determined from hearing, vision, cognitive, ambulatory, and self-care difficulties. For people aged 15 years and older, they are considered to have a disability if they have difficulty with any one of the six difficulty types; (1) Figures cover the Albuquerque, NM Metropolitan Statistical Area—see Appendix B for areas included.
Source: U.S. Census Bureau, 2011-2013 American Community Survey 3-Year Estimates

Age

Area	Percent of Population									Median Age
	Under Age 5	Age 5–19	Age 20–34	Age 35–44	Age 45–54	Age 55–64	Age 65–74	Age 75–84	Age 85+	
City	6.7	19.3	23.1	12.7	13.3	12.0	7.1	4.0	1.8	35.6
MSA[1]	6.5	20.1	21.2	12.5	13.8	12.7	7.7	4.0	1.6	36.9
U.S.	6.4	19.9	20.7	12.9	14.1	12.3	7.6	4.2	1.9	37.4

Note: (1) Figures cover the Albuquerque, NM Metropolitan Statistical Area—see Appendix B for areas included
Source: U.S. Census Bureau, 2011-2013 American Community Survey 3-Year Estimates

Gender

Area	Males	Females	Males per 100 Females
City	269,222	285,083	94.4
MSA[1]	443,025	457,019	96.9
U.S.	154,451,010	159,410,713	96.9

Note: (1) Figures cover the Albuquerque, NM Metropolitan Statistical Area—see Appendix B for areas included
Source: U.S. Census Bureau, 2011-2013 American Community Survey 3-Year Estimates

Religious Groups by Family

Area	Catholic	Baptist	Non-Den.	Methodist[2]	Lutheran	LDS[3]	Pente-costal	Presby-terian[4]	Muslim[5]	Judaism
MSA[1]	27.2	3.8	4.2	1.5	1.0	2.4	1.5	1.1	0.2	0.3
U.S.	19.1	9.3	4.0	4.0	2.3	2.0	1.9	1.6	0.8	0.7

Note: Figures are the number of adherents as a percentage of the total population; (1) Figures cover the Albuquerque, NM Metropolitan Statistical Area—see Appendix B for areas included; (2) Methodist/Pietist; (3) Latter Day Saints; (4) Reformed; (5) Figures are estimates
Source: Association of Statisticians of American Religious Bodies, 2010 U.S. Religion Census: Religious Congregations & Membership Study

Religious Groups by Tradition

Area	Catholic	Evangelical Protestant	Mainline Protestant	Other Tradition	Black Protestant	Orthodox
MSA[1]	27.2	11.3	3.3	3.9	0.2	0.2
U.S.	19.1	16.2	7.3	4.3	1.6	0.3

Note: Figures are the number of adherents as a percentage of the total population; (1) Figures cover the Albuquerque, NM Metropolitan Statistical Area—see Appendix B for areas included
Source: Association of Statisticians of American Religious Bodies, 2010 U.S. Religion Census: Religious Congregations & Membership Study

ECONOMY

Gross Metropolitan Product

Area	2012	2013	2014	2015	Rank[2]
MSA[1]	38.8	39.9	41.5	43.3	62

Note: Figures are in billions of dollars; (1) Figures cover the Albuquerque, NM Metropolitan Statistical Area—see Appendix B for areas included; (2) Rank is based on 2015 data and ranges from 1 to 363
Source: The U.S. Conference of Mayors, U.S. Metro Economies: GMP and Employment 2013-2015, June 2014

Economic Growth

Area	2010-12 (%)	2013 (%)	2014 (%)	2015 (%)	Rank[2]
MSA[1]	0.6	1.2	2.2	2.7	220
U.S.	2.1	2.0	2.3	3.2	–

Note: Figures are real gross metropolitan product (GMP) growth rates and represent annual average percent change; (1) Figures cover the Albuquerque, NM Metropolitan Statistical Area—see Appendix B for areas included; (2) Rank is based on 2015 data and ranges from 1 to 363
Source: The U.S. Conference of Mayors, U.S. Metro Economies: GMP and Employment 2013-2015, June 2014

Metropolitan Area Exports

Area	2008	2009	2010	2011	2012	2013	Rank[2]
MSA[1]	474.9	357.6	519.9	951.9	1,790.6	1,389.6	129

Note: Figures are in millions of dollars; (1) Figures cover the Albuquerque, NM Metropolitan Statistical Area—see Appendix B for areas included; (2) Rank is based on 2013 data and ranges from 1 to 387
Source: U.S. Department of Commerce, International Trade Administration, Office of Trade & Industry Information, Manufacturing & Services, data extracted April 3, 2015

Building Permits

Area	Single-Family			Multi-Family			Total		
	2013	2014	Pct. Chg.	2013	2014	Pct. Chg.	2013	2014	Pct. Chg.
City	434	1,110	155.8	1,040	306	-70.6	1,474	1,416	-3.9
MSA[1]	1,456	2,128	46.2	1,150	415	-63.9	2,606	2,543	-2.4
U.S.	620,802	634,597	2.2	370,020	411,766	11.3	990,822	1,046,363	5.6

Note: (1) Figures cover the Albuquerque, NM Metropolitan Statistical Area—see Appendix B for areas included; Figures represent new, privately-owned housing units authorized (unadjusted data); All permit data are based on estimates with imputation.
Source: U.S. Census Bureau, Manufacturing, Mining, and Construction Statistics, Building Permits, 2013, 2014

Bankruptcy Filings

Area	Business Filings			Nonbusiness Filings		
	2013	2014	% Chg.	2013	2014	% Chg.
Bernalillo County	64	50	-21.9	1,668	1,399	-16.1
U.S.	33,212	26,983	-18.8	1,038,720	909,812	-12.4

Note: Business filings include Chapter 7, Chapter 11, Chapter 12, and Chapter 13; Nonbusiness filings include Chapter 7, Chapter 11, and Chapter 13
Source: Administrative Office of the U.S. Courts, Business and Nonbusiness Bankruptcy, County Cases Commenced by Chapter of the Bankruptcy Code, During the 12- Month Period Ending December 31, 2013 and Business and Nonbusiness Bankruptcy, County Cases Commenced by Chapter of the Bankruptcy Code, During the 12- Month Period Ending December 31, 2014

Housing Vacancy Rates

Area	Gross Vacancy Rate[2] (%)			Year-Round Vacancy Rate[3] (%)			Rental Vacancy Rate[4] (%)			Homeowner Vacancy Rate[5] (%)		
	2012	2013	2014	2012	2013	2014	2012	2013	2014	2012	2013	2014
MSA[1]	7.1	8.4	8.6	6.5	7.7	7.3	5.1	7.8	7.5	2.2	2.4	1.9
U.S.	13.8	13.6	13.4	10.8	10.7	10.4	8.7	8.3	7.6	2.0	2.0	1.9

Note: (1) Figures cover the Albuquerque, NM Metropolitan Statistical Area—see Appendix B for areas included; (2) The percentage of the total housing inventory that is vacant; (3) The percentage of the housing inventory (excluding seasonal units) that is year-round vacant; (4) The percentage of rental inventory that is vacant for rent; (5) The percentage of homeowner inventory that is vacant for sale
Source: U.S. Census Bureau, Housing Vacancies and Homeownership Annual Statistics: 2014

INCOME

Income

Area	Per Capita ($)	Median Household ($)	Average Household ($)
City	26,403	46,668	63,418
MSA[1]	25,525	47,754	64,396
U.S.	27,884	52,176	72,897

Note: (1) Figures cover the Albuquerque, NM Metropolitan Statistical Area—see Appendix B for areas included
Source: U.S. Census Bureau, 2011-2013 American Community Survey 3-Year Estimates

Household Income Distribution

Area	Percent of Households Earning							
	Under $15,000	$15,000 -24,999	$25,000 -34,999	$35,000 -49,999	$50,000 -74,999	$75,000 -99,000	$100,000 -149,999	$150,000 and up
City	15.2	12.1	11.3	13.9	18.0	11.4	11.4	6.7
MSA[1]	15.0	12.1	11.1	13.6	18.1	11.3	11.6	7.3
U.S.	13.0	10.9	10.3	13.6	17.9	11.9	12.7	9.6

Note: (1) Figures cover the Albuquerque, NM Metropolitan Statistical Area—see Appendix B for areas included
Source: U.S. Census Bureau, 2011-2013 American Community Survey 3-Year Estimates

Poverty Rate

Area	All Ages	Under 18 Years Old	18 to 64 Years Old	65 Years and Over
City	18.6	26.1	17.9	8.1
MSA[1]	19.3	27.2	18.2	9.9
U.S.	15.9	22.4	14.8	9.5

Note: Figures are percentage of people whose income during the past 12 months was below the poverty level; (1) Figures cover the Albuquerque, NM Metropolitan Statistical Area—see Appendix B for areas included
Source: U.S. Census Bureau, 2011-2013 American Community Survey 3-Year Estimates

EMPLOYMENT

Labor Force and Employment

Area	Civilian Labor Force			Workers Employed		
	Dec. 2013	Dec. 2014	% Chg.	Dec. 2013	Dec. 2014	% Chg.
City	269,058	268,681	-0.1	253,374	255,366	0.8
MSA[1]	415,650	414,520	-0.3	389,105	391,974	0.7
U.S.	154,408,000	155,521,000	0.7	144,423,000	147,190,000	1.9

Note: Data is not seasonally adjusted and covers workers 16 years of age and older; (1) Figures cover the Albuquerque, NM Metropolitan Statistical Area—see Appendix B for areas included
Source: Bureau of Labor Statistics, Local Area Unemployment Statistics

Unemployment Rate

Area	2014											
	Jan.	Feb.	Mar.	Apr.	May	Jun.	Jul.	Aug.	Sep.	Oct.	Nov.	Dec.
City	6.3	6.2	6.1	5.5	5.7	6.6	6.4	6.0	5.7	5.5	5.3	5.0
MSA[1]	6.9	6.7	6.6	6.1	6.3	7.2	7.1	6.6	6.2	5.9	5.8	5.4
U.S.	7.0	7.0	6.8	5.9	6.1	6.3	6.5	6.3	5.7	5.5	5.5	5.4

Note: Data is not seasonally adjusted and covers workers 16 years of age and older; (1) Figures cover the Albuquerque, NM Metropolitan Statistical Area—see Appendix B for areas included
Source: Bureau of Labor Statistics, Local Area Unemployment Statistics

Employment by Occupation

Occupation Classification	City (%)	MSA[1] (%)	U.S. (%)
Management, Business, Science, and Arts	40.8	38.9	36.2
Natural Resources, Construction, and Maintenance	8.3	9.5	9.0
Production, Transportation, and Material Moving	7.3	8.2	12.1
Sales and Office	23.8	24.0	24.4
Service	19.8	19.5	18.3

Note: Figures cover employed civilians 16 years of age and older; (1) Figures cover the Albuquerque, NM Metropolitan Statistical Area—see Appendix B for areas included
Source: U.S. Census Bureau, 2011-2013 American Community Survey 3-Year Estimates

Employment by Industry

Sector	MSA[1]		U.S.
	Number of Employees	Percent of Total	Percent of Total
Construction, Mining, and Logging	21,300	5.6	5.0
Education and Health Services	61,200	16.0	15.5
Financial Activities	18,000	4.7	5.7
Government	83,300	21.7	15.8
Information	7,800	2.0	2.0
Leisure and Hospitality	39,900	10.4	10.3
Manufacturing	16,400	4.3	8.7
Other Services	11,800	3.1	4.0
Professional and Business Services	57,400	15.0	13.8
Retail Trade	43,900	11.5	11.4
Transportation, Warehousing, and Utilities	10,200	2.7	3.9
Wholesale Trade	11,900	3.1	4.2

Note: Figures are non-farm employment as of December 2014. Figures are not seasonally adjusted and include workers 16 years of age and older; (1) Figures cover the Albuquerque, NM Metropolitan Statistical Area—see Appendix B for areas included; n/a not available
Source: Bureau of Labor Statistics, Current Employment Statistics, Employment, Hours, and Earnings

Occupations with Greatest Projected Employment Growth: 2012 – 2022

Occupation[1]	2012 Employment	2022 Projected Employment	Numeric Employment Change	Percent Employment Change
Personal Care Aides	20,500	30,950	10,450	51.0
Combined Food Preparation and Serving Workers, Including Fast Food	15,720	20,080	4,360	27.8
Retail Salespersons	29,070	32,850	3,780	13.0
Waiters and Waitresses	16,410	19,210	2,800	17.0
Secretaries and Administrative Assistants, Except Legal, Medical, and Executive	20,750	23,380	2,630	12.7
Elementary School Teachers, Except Special Education	8,810	11,240	2,430	27.6
Home Health Aides	5,330	7,740	2,410	45.4
Registered Nurses	16,140	18,370	2,230	13.8
General and Operations Managers	15,980	17,970	1,990	12.5
Customer Service Representatives	13,540	15,360	1,820	13.4

Note: Projections cover New Mexico; (1) Sorted by numeric employment change
Source: www.projectionscentral.com, State Occupational Projections, 2012–2022 Long-Term Projections

Fastest Growing Occupations: 2012 – 2022

Occupation[1]	2012 Employment	2022 Projected Employment	Numeric Employment Change	Percent Employment Change
Personal Care Aides	20,500	30,950	10,450	51.0
Home Health Aides	5,330	7,740	2,410	45.4
Occupational Therapy Assistants	220	320	100	43.0
Interpreters and Translators	350	490	140	42.3
Diagnostic Medical Sonographers	310	430	120	39.7
Information Security Analysts	340	470	130	37.8
Health Technologists and Technicians, All Other	550	730	180	33.1
Physical Therapist Aides	300	400	100	32.6
Market Research Analysts and Marketing Specialists	950	1,250	300	31.8
Physical Therapist Assistants	350	460	110	31.3

Note: Projections cover New Mexico; (1) Sorted by percent employment change and excludes occupations with numeric employment change less than 100
Source: www.projectionscentral.com, State Occupational Projections, 2012–2022 Long-Term Projections

Average Wages

Occupation	$/Hr.	Occupation	$/Hr.
Accountants and Auditors	30.53	Maids and Housekeeping Cleaners	9.06
Automotive Mechanics	19.82	Maintenance and Repair Workers	17.34
Bookkeepers	17.21	Marketing Managers	43.67
Carpenters	18.35	Nuclear Medicine Technologists	35.06
Cashiers	10.07	Nurses, Licensed Practical	23.04
Clerks, General Office	12.62	Nurses, Registered	32.08
Clerks, Receptionists/Information	12.30	Nursing Assistants	13.56
Clerks, Shipping/Receiving	14.19	Packers and Packagers, Hand	9.38
Computer Programmers	47.67	Physical Therapists	42.05
Computer Systems Analysts	35.95	Postal Service Mail Carriers	25.32
Computer User Support Specialists	21.40	Real Estate Brokers	n/a
Cooks, Restaurant	10.54	Retail Salespersons	11.93
Dentists	90.64	Sales Reps., Exc. Tech./Scientific	25.47
Electrical Engineers	51.12	Sales Reps., Tech./Scientific	32.08
Electricians	20.63	Secretaries, Exc. Legal/Med./Exec.	15.01
Financial Managers	52.39	Security Guards	13.09
First-Line Supervisors/Managers, Sales	17.47	Surgeons	n/a
Food Preparation Workers	10.11	Teacher Assistants	9.80
General and Operations Managers	47.54	Teachers, Elementary School	21.10
Hairdressers/Cosmetologists	12.41	Teachers, Secondary School	22.80
Internists	n/a	Telemarketers	10.63
Janitors and Cleaners	10.84	Truck Drivers, Heavy/Tractor-Trailer	18.93
Landscaping/Groundskeeping Workers	11.39	Truck Drivers, Light/Delivery Svcs.	14.78
Lawyers	43.13	Waiters and Waitresses	10.44

Note: Wage data covers the Albuquerque, NM Metropolitan Statistical Area—see Appendix B for areas included; Hourly wages for elementary/secondary school teachers and teacher assistants were calculated by the editors from annual wage data assuming a 40 hour work week; n/a not available.
Source: Bureau of Labor Statistics, Metro Area Occupational Employment and Wage Estimates, May 2014

TAXES

State Corporate Income Tax Rates

State	Tax Rate (%)	Income Brackets ($)	Num. of Brackets	Financial Institution Tax Rate (%)[a]	Federal Income Tax Ded.
New Mexico	4.8 - 6.9 (s)	500,000 - 1 mil.	3	4.8 - 6.9 (s)	No

Note: Tax rates as of January 1, 2015; (a) Rates listed are the corporate income tax rate applied to financial institutions or excise taxes based on income. Some states have other taxes based upon the value of deposits or shares; (s) New Mexico tax rates are scheduled to decrease for tax year 2016.
Source: Federation of Tax Administrators, "State Corporate Income Tax Rates, 2015"

State Individual Income Tax Rates

State	Tax Rate (%)	Income Brackets ($)	Num. of Brackets	Personal Exempt. ($)[1] Single	Personal Exempt. ($)[1] Dependents	Fed. Inc. Tax Ded.
New Mexico	1.7 - 4.9	5,500 - 16,001 (p)	4	4,000 (d)	4,000 (d)	No

Note: Tax rates as of January 1, 2015; Local- and county-level taxes are not included; n/a not applicable; (1) Married joint filers generally receive double the single exemption; (d) These states use the personal exemption amounts provided in the federal Internal Revenue Code; (p) The income brackets reported for New Mexico are for single individuals. For married couples filing jointly, the same tax rates apply to income brackets ranging from $8,000 to $24,000.
Source: Federation of Tax Administrators, "State Individual Income Tax Rates, 2015"

Various State and Local Tax Rates

State	State and Local Sales and Use (%)	State Sales and Use (%)	Gasoline[1] (¢/gal.)	Cigarette[2] ($/pack)	Spirits[3] ($/gal.)	Wine[4] ($/gal.)	Beer[5] ($/gal.)
New Mexico	7.0	5.13 (c)	18.88	1.66	6.06	1.70	0.41

Note: All tax rates as of January 1, 2015; (1) The American Petroleum Institute has developed a methodology for determining the average tax rate on a gallon of fuel. Rates may include any of the following: excise taxes, environmental fees, storage tank fees, other fees or taxes, general sales tax, and local taxes. In states where gasoline is subject to the general sales tax, or where the fuel tax is based on the average sale price, the average rate determined by API is sensitive to changes in the price of gasoline. States that fully or partially apply general sales taxes to gasoline: CA, CO, GA, IL, IN, MI, NY; (2) The federal excise tax of $1.0066 per pack and local taxes are not included; (3) Rates are those applicable to off-premise sales of 40% alcohol by volume (a.b.v.) distilled spirits in 750ml containers. Local excise taxes are excluded; (4) Rates are those applicable to off-premise sales of 11% a.b.v. non-carbonated wine in 750ml containers; (5) Rates are those applicable to off-premise sales of 4.7% a.b.v. beer in 12 ounce containers; (c) The sales taxes in Hawaii, New Mexico, and South Dakota have broad bases that include many business-to-business services.
Source: Tax Foundation, 2015 Facts & Figures: How Does Your State Compare?

State Business Tax Climate Index Rankings

State	Overall Rank	Corporate Tax Index Rank	Individual Income Tax Index Rank	Sales Tax Index Rank	Unemployment Insurance Tax Index Rank	Property Tax Index Rank
New Mexico	38	35	35	45	10	1

Note: The index is a measure of how each state's tax laws affect economic performance. The lower the rank, the more favorable a state's tax system is for business. States without a given tax are given a ranking of 1. The scores/rankings for the District of Columbia do not affect other states. The 2015 index represents the tax climate as of July 1, 2014.
Source: Tax Foundation, State Business Tax Climate Index 2015

COMMERCIAL UTILITIES

Typical Monthly Electric Bills

Area	Commercial Service ($/month)		Industrial Service ($/month)	
	1,500 kWh	40 kW demand 14,000 kWh	1,000 kW demand 200,000 kWh	50,000 kW demand 32,500,000 kWh
City	n/a	n/a	n/a	n/a
Average[1]	201	1,653	26,124	2,639,743

Note: Figures are based on annualized 2014 rates; (1) Average based on 180 utilities surveyed; n/a not available
Source: Edison Electric Institute, Typical Bills and Average Rates Report, Summer 2014

TRANSPORTATION

Means of Transportation to Work

Area	Car/Truck/Van Drove Alone	Car/Truck/Van Car-pooled	Public Transportation Bus	Public Transportation Subway	Public Transportation Railroad	Bicycle	Walked	Other Means	Worked at Home
City	79.6	9.7	1.7	0.0	0.1	1.3	2.1	1.5	3.8
MSA[1]	80.0	9.6	1.3	0.0	0.3	1.0	1.9	1.6	4.4
U.S.	76.4	9.6	2.6	1.8	0.6	0.6	2.8	1.3	4.3

Note: Figures are percentages and cover workers 16 years of age and older; (1) Figures cover the Albuquerque, NM Metropolitan Statistical Area—see Appendix B for areas included
Source: U.S. Census Bureau, 2011-2013 American Community Survey 3-Year Estimates

Travel Time to Work

Area	Less Than 10 Minutes	10 to 19 Minutes	20 to 29 Minutes	30 to 44 Minutes	45 to 59 Minutes	60 to 89 Minutes	90 Minutes or More
City	11.5	36.8	28.7	16.5	3.1	2.0	1.4
MSA[1]	11.9	32.4	25.7	19.7	5.5	3.1	1.7
U.S.	13.3	29.7	20.9	20.2	7.7	5.7	2.6

Note: Figures are percentages and include workers 16 years old and over; (1) Figures cover the Albuquerque, NM Metropolitan Statistical Area—see Appendix B for areas included
Source: U.S. Census Bureau, 2011-2013 American Community Survey 3-Year Estimates

Travel Time Index

Area	1985	1990	1995	2000	2005	2010	2011
Urban Area[1]	1.06	1.10	1.15	1.17	1.16	1.10	1.10
Average[2]	1.09	1.14	1.16	1.19	1.23	1.18	1.18

Note: Travel Time Index—the ratio of travel time in the peak period to the travel time at free-flow conditions. For example, a value of 1.30 indicates a 20-minute free-flow trip takes 26 minutes in the peak. Free-flow speeds (60 mph on freeways and 35 mph on principal arterials) are used as the comparison threshold; (1) Covers the Albuquerque NM urban area; (2) average of 498 urban areas
Source: Texas Transportation Institute, Urban Mobility Report 2012, December 2012

Public Transportation

Agency Name / Mode of Transportation	Vehicles Operated in Maximum Service	Annual Unlinked Passenger Trips (in thous.)	Annual Passenger Miles (in thous.)
ABQ Ride			
Bus (directly operated)	131	12,906.2	45,300.9
Demand Response (directly operated)	54	244.1	2,330.5

Source: Federal Transit Administration, National Transit Database, 2013

Air Transportation

Airport Name and Code / Type of Service	Passenger Airlines[1]	Passenger Enplanements	Freight Carriers[2]	Freight (lbs.)
Albuquerque International (ABQ)				
Domestic service (U.S. carriers - 2014)	23	2,341,855	12	85,579,622
International service (U.S. carriers - 2013)	3	117	0	0

Note: (1) Includes all U.S.-based major, minor and commuter airlines that carried at least one passenger during the year; (2) Includes all U.S.-based airlines and freight carriers that transported at least one lb. of freight during the year.
Source: Bureau of Transportation Statistics, The Intermodal Transportation Database, Air Carriers: T-100 Domestic Market (U.S. Carriers), 2014; Bureau of Transportation Statistics, The Intermodal Transportation Database, Air Carriers: T-100 International Market (U.S. Carriers), 2013

Other Transportation Statistics

Major Highways:	I-25; I-40
Amtrak Service:	Yes
Major Waterways/Ports:	None

Source: Amtrak.com; Google Maps

BUSINESSES

Major Business Headquarters

Company Name	Rankings	
	Fortune[1]	Forbes[2]
No companies listed	-	-

Note: (1) Fortune 500—companies that produce a 10-K are ranked 1 to 500 based on 2013 revenue; (2) all private companies with at least $2 billion in annual revenue through the end of their most current fiscal year are ranked 1 to 221; companies listed are headquartered in the city; dashes indicate no ranking
Source: Fortune, "Fortune 500," June 16, 2014; Forbes, "America's Largest Private Companies," November 5, 2014

Fast-Growing Businesses

According to *Inc.*, Albuquerque is home to one of America's 500 fastest-growing private companies: **InkSoft** (#179). Criteria: must be an independent, privately-held, for-profit, U.S. corporation, proprietorship or partnership; revenues must be at least $100,000 in 2010 and $2 million in 2013; must have four-year operating/sales history. Holding companies, regulated banks, and utilities were excluded. *Inc., "America's 500 Fastest-Growing Private Companies," September 2014*

Minority Business Opportunity

Albuquerque is home to 19 companies which are on the *Hispanic Business* 500 list (500 largest U.S. Hispanic-owned companies based on 2012 revenue): **Manuel Lujan Insurance** (#61); **Roses Southwest Papers** (#80); **Applied Technology Associates** (#127); **Holman's USA** (#136); **L&M Technologies** (#178); **Integrated Control Systems** (#197); **ADC** (#231); **San Bar Construction Corp.** (#242); **Service Electric Company** (#247); **Captiva Group** (#266); **Molzen Corbin** (#298); **Ray's Flooring Specialists** (#302); **Star Paving Co.** (#306); **Sparkle Maintenance** (#318); **Apache Construction Co.** (#319); **GenQuest** (#358); **Fiore Industries** (#378); **Sabio Systems** (#421); **Queston Construction** (#444). Companies included must show at least 51 percent ownership by Hispanic U.S. citizens, and must maintain headquarters in one of the 50 states or Washington, D.C. *Hispanic Business, "Hispanic Business 500," June 20, 2013*

Albuquerque is home to one company which is on the *Hispanic Business* Fastest-Growing 100 list (greatest sales growth from 2008 to 2012): **Applied Technology Associates** (#94). Companies included must show at least 51 percent ownership by Hispanic U.S. citizens, and must maintain headquarters in one of the 50 states or Washington, D.C. In addition, companies must have minimum revenues of $200,000 for calendar year 2008. *Hispanic Business, June 20, 2013*

Minority- and Women-Owned Businesses

Group	All Firms		Firms with Paid Employees			
	Firms	Sales ($000)	Firms	Sales ($000)	Employees	Payroll ($000)
Asian	1,738	574,140	460	530,694	4,242	112,480
Black	912	297,162	45	276,321	928	27,301
Hispanic	10,291	2,799,414	1,690	2,538,011	19,254	553,758
Women	14,187	2,349,306	1,822	2,010,087	16,711	456,681
All Firms	44,460	48,200,294	11,462	46,862,334	237,916	8,087,404

Note: Figures cover firms located in the city; minority- and women-owned business are defined as firms in which the corresponding group own 51% or more of the stock or equity of the company
Source: U.S. Census Bureau, 2007 Economic Census, Survey of Business Owners (2012 Survey of Business Owners data will be released starting in June 2015)

HOTELS & CONVENTION CENTERS

Hotels/Motels

Area	5 Star		4 Star		3 Star		2 Star		1 Star		Not Rated	
	Num.	Pct.[3]	Num.	Pct.[3]	Num.	Pct.[3]	Num.	Pct.[3]	Num.	Pct.[3]	Num.	Pct.[3]
City[1]	0	0.0	3	2.3	38	29.2	84	64.6	4	3.1	1	0.8
Total[2]	166	0.9	1,264	7.0	5,718	31.8	9,340	52.0	411	2.3	1,070	6.0

Note: (1) Figures cover Albuquerque and vicinity; (2) Figures cover all 100 cities in this book; (3) Percentage of hotels which have a given star rating; Star ratings are determined by expedia.com and offer an indication of the general quality of a particular hotel.
Source: expedia.com, April 2, 2015

Major Convention Centers

Name	Overall Space (sq. ft.)	Exhibit Space (sq. ft.)	Meeting Space (sq. ft.)	Meeting Rooms
Albuquerque Convention Center	n/a	272,746	n/a	37

Note: Table includes convention centers located in the Albuquerque, NM metro area; n/a not available
Source: Original research

Living Environment

COST OF LIVING

Cost of Living Index

Composite Index	Groceries	Housing	Utilities	Trans-portation	Health Care	Misc. Goods/Services
92.1	95.1	77.3	89.2	101.1	97.4	100.7

Note: The Cost of Living Index measures regional differences in the cost of consumer goods and services, excluding taxes and non-consumer expenditures, for professional and managerial households in the top income quintile. It is based on more than 50,000 prices covering almost 60 different items for which prices are collected three times a year by chambers of commerce, economic development organizations or university applied economic centers in each participating urban area. The numbers shown should be read as a percentage above or below the national average of 100. For example, a value of 115.4 in the groceries column indicates that grocery prices are 15.4% higher than the national average. Small differences in the index numbers should not be interpreted as significant; Figures cover the Rio Rancho NM urban area.
Source: The Council for Community and Economic Research, ACCRA Cost of Living Index, 2014

Grocery Prices

Area[1]	T-Bone Steak ($/pound)	Frying Chicken ($/pound)	Whole Milk ($/half gal.)	Eggs ($/dozen)	Orange Juice ($/64 oz.)	Coffee ($/11.5 oz.)
City[2]	10.88	1.06	2.52	2.04	3.48	4.79
Avg.	10.40	1.37	2.40	1.99	3.46	4.27
Min.	8.48	0.93	1.37	1.30	2.83	2.99
Max.	14.20	2.44	3.62	4.02	6.42	6.96

Note: (1) Values for the local area are compared with the average, minimum and maximum values for all 308 areas in the Cost of Living Index; (2) Figures cover the Rio Rancho NM urban area; **T-Bone Steak** *(price per pound);* **Frying Chicken** *(price per pound, whole fryer);* **Whole Milk** *(half gallon carton);* **Eggs** *(price per dozen, Grade A, large);* **Orange Juice** *(64 oz. Tropicana or Florida Natural);* **Coffee** *(11.5 oz. can, vacuum-packed, Maxwell House, Hills Bros, or Folgers).*
Source: The Council for Community and Economic Research, ACCRA Cost of Living Index, 2014

Housing and Utility Costs

Area[1]	New Home Price ($)	Apartment Rent ($/month)	All Electric ($/month)	Part Electric ($/month)	Other Energy ($/month)	Telephone ($/month)
City[2]	234,773	747	-	103.86	59.10	22.15
Avg.	305,838	919	181.00	93.66	73.14	27.95
Min.	183,142	480	112.00	42.06	23.42	17.16
Max.	1,358,576	3,851	594.00	180.03	440.99	40.42

Note: (1) Values for the local area are compared with the average, minimum and maximum values for all 308 areas in the Cost of Living Index; (2) Figures cover the Rio Rancho NM urban area; **New Home Price** *(2,400 sf living area, 8,000 sf lot, in urban area with full utilities);* **Apartment Rent** *(950 sf 2 bedroom/1.5 or 2 bath, unfurnished, excluding all utilities except water);* **All Electric** *(average monthly cost for an all-electric home);* **Part Electric** *(average monthly cost for a part-electric home);* **Other Energy** *(average monthly cost for natural gas, fuel oil, coal, wood, and any other forms of energy except electricity);* **Telephone** *(price includes basic monthly rate for a private residential line plus additional local usage charges incurred by a family of four).*
Source: The Council for Community and Economic Research, ACCRA Cost of Living Index, 2014

Health Care, Transportation, and Other Costs

Area[1]	Doctor ($/visit)	Dentist ($/visit)	Optometrist ($/visit)	Gasoline ($/gallon)	Beauty Salon ($/visit)	Men's Shirt ($)
City[2]	96.44	93.30	99.33	3.28	25.89	33.77
Avg.	102.86	87.89	97.66	3.44	34.37	26.74
Min.	67.47	65.78	51.18	3.00	17.43	12.79
Max.	173.50	150.14	235.00	4.33	64.28	49.50

Note: (1) Values for the local area are compared with the average, minimum and maximum values for all 308 areas in the Cost of Living Index; (2) Figures cover the Rio Rancho NM urban area; **Doctor** *(general practitioners routine exam of an established patient);* **Dentist** *(adult teeth cleaning and periodic oral examination);* **Optometrist** *(full vision eye exam for established adult patient);* **Gasoline** *(one gallon regular unleaded, national brand, including all taxes, cash price at self-service pump if available);* **Beauty Salon** *(woman's shampoo, trim, and blow-dry);* **Men's Shirt** *(cotton/polyester dress shirt, pinpoint weave, long sleeves).*
Source: The Council for Community and Economic Research, ACCRA Cost of Living Index, 2014

HOUSING

House Price Index (HPI)

Area	National Ranking[2]	Quarterly Change (%)	One-Year Change (%)	Five-Year Change (%)
MSA[1]	187	0.19	3.13	-4.10
U.S.[3]	–	1.35	4.91	11.59

Note: The HPI is a weighted repeat sales index. It measures average price changes in repeat sales or refinancings on the same properties. This information is obtained by reviewing repeat mortgage transactions on single-family properties whose mortgages have been purchased or securitized by Fannie Mae or Freddie Mac in January 1975; (1) Albuquerque Metropolitan Statistical Area—see Appendix B for areas included; (2) Rankings are based on annual percentage change for all metro areas containing at least 15,000 transactions over the last 10 years and ranges from 1 to 275; (3) figures based on a weighted average of Census Division estimates using a seasonally adjusted, purchase-only index; all figures are for the period ending December 31, 2014
Source: Federal Housing Finance Agency, House Price Index, February 26, 2015

Median Single-Family Home Prices

Area	2012	2013	2014p	Percent Change 2013 to 2014
MSA[1]	170.3	174.3	177.6	1.9
U.S. Average	177.2	197.4	209.0	5.9

Note: Figures are median sales prices of existing single-family homes in thousands of dollars; (p) preliminary; n/a not available; (1) Albuquerque, NM Metropolitan Statistical Area—see Appendix B for areas included
Source: National Association of Realtors, Median Sales Price of Existing Single-Family Homes for Metropolitan Areas, 4th Quarter 2014

Qualifying Income Based on Median Sales Price of Existing Single-Family Homes

Area	With 5% Down ($)	With 10% Down ($)	With 20% Down ($)
MSA[1]	38,940	36,891	32,792
U.S. Average	45,863	43,449	38,621

Note: Figures are preliminary; Qualifying income is based on a mortgage rate of 4.0%. Monthly principal and interest payment is limited to 25% of income; n/a not available; (1) Albuquerque, NM Metropolitan Statistical Area—see Appendix B for areas included
Source: National Association of Realtors, Qualifying Income Based on Median Sales Price of Existing Single-Family Homes for Metropolitan Areas, 4th Quarter 2014

Median Apartment Condo-Coop Home Prices

Area	2012	2013	2014p	Percent Change 2013 to 2014
MSA[1]	n/a	n/a	n/a	n/a
U.S. Average	173.7	194.9	205.1	5.2

Note: Figures are median sales prices of existing apartment condo-coop homes in thousands of dollars; (p) preliminary; n/a not available; (1) Albuquerque, NM Metropolitan Statistical Area—see Appendix B for areas included
Source: National Association of Realtors, Median Sales Price of Existing Apartment Condo-Coop Homes for Metropolitan Areas, 4th Quarter 2014

Gross Monthly Rent

Area	Under $200	$200 -299	$300 -499	$500 -749	$750 -999	$1,000 -1,499	$1,500 and up	Median ($)
City	1.7	2.5	8.6	32.3	26.9	23.0	5.0	786
MSA[1]	1.4	2.4	8.9	30.6	27.4	23.6	5.7	800
U.S.	1.7	3.2	7.8	22.1	24.3	26.0	14.9	900

Note: Figures are percentages except for Median; Gross rent is the contract rent plus the estimated average monthly cost of utilities (electricity, gas, and water and sewer) and fuels (oil, coal, kerosene, wood, etc.) if these are paid by the renter (or paid for the renter by someone else); (1) Figures cover the Albuquerque, NM Metropolitan Statistical Area—see Appendix B for areas included
Source: U.S. Census Bureau, 2011-2013 American Community Survey 3-Year Estimates

Homeownership Rate

Area	2007 (%)	2008 (%)	2009 (%)	2010 (%)	2011 (%)	2012 (%)	2013 (%)	2014 (%)
MSA[1]	70.5	68.2	65.7	65.5	67.1	62.8	65.9	64.4
U.S.	68.1	67.8	67.4	66.9	66.1	65.4	65.1	64.5

Note: (1) Figures cover the Albuquerque, NM Metropolitan Statistical Area—see Appendix B for areas included
Source: U.S. Census Bureau, Housing Vacancies and Homeownership Annual Statistics: 2014

Year Housing Structure Built

Area	2010 or Later	2000 -2009	1990 -1999	1980 -1989	1970 -1979	1960 -1969	1950 -1959	1940 -1949	Before 1940	Median Year
City	0.6	18.3	15.1	15.1	20.5	10.5	12.4	4.5	3.1	1980
MSA[1]	0.7	19.4	17.8	17.2	18.6	9.4	9.9	3.7	3.3	1983
U.S.	0.9	15.0	13.9	13.8	15.8	11.0	10.9	5.4	13.3	1976

Note: Figures are percentages except for Median Year; (1) Figures cover the Albuquerque, NM Metropolitan Statistical Area—see Appendix B for areas included
Source: U.S. Census Bureau, 2011-2013 American Community Survey 3-Year Estimates

HEALTH

Health Risk Data

Category	MSA[1] (%)	U.S. (%)
Adults aged 18–64 who have any kind of health care coverage	76.4	79.6
Adults who reported being in good or excellent health	82.3	83.1
Adults who are current smokers	18.7	19.6
Adults who are heavy drinkers[2]	5.4	6.1
Adults who are binge drinkers[3]	14.1	16.9
Adults who are overweight (BMI 25.0 - 29.9)	34.4	35.8
Adults who are obese (BMI 30.0 - 99.8)	25.1	27.6
Adults who participated in any physical activities in the past month	81.1	77.1
Adults 50+ who have ever had a sigmoidoscopy or colonoscopy	67.8	67.3
Women aged 40+ who have had a mammogram within the past two years	69.7	74.0
Men aged 40+ who have had a PSA test within the past two years	40.7	45.2
Adults aged 65+ who have had flu shot within the past year	60.1	60.1
Adults who always wear a seatbelt	96.9	93.8

Note: Data as of 2012 unless otherwise noted; (1) Figures cover the Albuquerque, NM Metropolitan Statistical Area—see Appendix B for areas included; (2) Heavy drinkers are classified as males having more than two drinks per day or females having more than one drink per day; (3) Binge drinkers are classified as males having five or more drinks on one occasion or females having four or more drinks on one occasion
Source: Centers for Disease Control and Prevention, Behaviorial Risk Factor Surveillance System, SMART: Selected Metropolitan/Micropolitan Area Risk Trends, 2012 (Note: the CDC has discontinued this dataset but will be releasing a replacement in late 2015)

Chronic Health Indicators

Category	MSA[1] (%)	U.S. (%)
Adults who have ever been told they had a heart attack	3.8	4.5
Adults who have ever been told they had a stroke	2.7	2.9
Adults who have been told they currently have asthma	9.8	8.9
Adults who have ever been told they have arthritis	22.9	25.7
Adults who have ever been told they have diabetes[2]	8.7	9.7
Adults who have ever been told they had skin cancer	5.6	5.7
Adults who have ever been told they had any other types of cancer	5.9	6.5
Adults who have ever been told they have COPD	6.5	6.2
Adults who have ever been told they have kidney disease	3.6	2.5
Adults who have ever been told they have a form of depression	21.2	18.0

Note: Data as of 2012 unless otherwise noted; (1) Figures cover the Albuquerque, NM Metropolitan Statistical Area—see Appendix B for areas included; (2) Figures do not include pregnancy-related, borderline, or pre-diabetes
Source: Centers for Disease Control and Prevention, Behaviorial Risk Factor Surveillance System, SMART: Selected Metropolitan/Micropolitan Area Risk Trends, 2012 (Note: the CDC has discontinued this dataset but will be releasing a replacement in late 2015)

Mortality Rates for the Top 10 Causes of Death in the U.S.

ICD-10[a] Sub-Chapter	ICD-10[a] Code	Age-Adjusted Mortality Rate[1] per 100,000 population	
		County[2]	U.S.
Malignant neoplasms	C00-C97	144.3	166.2
Ischaemic heart diseases	I20-I25	92.7	105.7
Other forms of heart disease	I30-I51	32.1	49.3
Chronic lower respiratory diseases	J40-J47	41.7	42.1
Organic, including symptomatic, mental disorders	F01-F09	42.3	38.1
Cerebrovascular diseases	I60-I69	32.8	37.0
Other external causes of accidental injury	W00-X59	43.9	26.9
Other degenerative diseases of the nervous system	G30-G31	21.4	25.6
Diabetes mellitus	E10-E14	25.6	21.3
Hypertensive diseases	I10-I15	21.2	19.4

Note: (a) ICD-10 = International Classification of Diseases 10th Revision; (1) Mortality rates are a three year average covering 2011-2013; (2) Figures cover Bernalillo County
Source: Centers for Disease Control and Prevention, National Center for Health Statistics. Compressed Mortality File 1999-2013 on CDC WONDER Online Database, released October 2014. Data are compiled from the Compressed Mortality File 1999-2013, Series 20 No. 2S, 2014.

Mortality Rates for Selected Causes of Death

ICD-10[a] Sub-Chapter	ICD-10[a] Code	Age-Adjusted Mortality Rate[1] per 100,000 population	
		County[2]	U.S.
Assault	X85-Y09	5.7	5.2
Diseases of the liver	K70-K76	24.7	13.2
Human immunodeficiency virus (HIV) disease	B20-B24	1.2	2.2
Influenza and pneumonia	J09-J18	12.9	15.4
Intentional self-harm	X60-X84	20.1	12.5
Malnutrition	E40-E46	*0.5	0.9
Obesity and other hyperalimentation	E65-E68	3.4	1.8
Renal failure	N17-N19	10.5	13.1
Transport accidents	V01-V99	12.0	11.7
Viral hepatitis	B15-B19	4.1	2.2

Note: (a) ICD-10 = International Classification of Diseases 10th Revision; (1) Mortality rates are a three year average covering 2011-2013; (2) Figures cover Bernalillo County; (*) Unreliable data as per CDC
Source: Centers for Disease Control and Prevention, National Center for Health Statistics. Compressed Mortality File 1999-2013 on CDC WONDER Online Database, released October 2014. Data are compiled from the Compressed Mortality File 1999-2013, Series 20 No. 2S, 2014.

Health Insurance Coverage

Area	With Health Insurance	With Private Health Insurance	With Public Health Insurance	Without Health Insurance	Population Under Age 18 Without Health Insurance
City	84.2	59.5	35.2	15.8	6.2
MSA[1]	83.8	58.3	36.1	16.2	6.6
U.S.	85.2	65.2	31.0	14.8	7.3

Note: Figures are percentages that cover the civilian noninstitutionalized population; (1) Figures cover the Albuquerque, NM Metropolitan Statistical Area—see Appendix B for areas included
Source: U.S. Census Bureau, 2011-2013 American Community Survey 3-Year Estimates

Number of Medical Professionals

Area[1]	MDs[2]	DOs[2,3]	Dentists	Podiatrists	Chiropractors	Optometrists
Local (number)	2,820	134	504	55	154	107
Local (rate[4])	419.0	19.9	74.7	8.1	22.8	15.9
U.S. (rate[4])	270.0	20.2	63.1	5.7	25.2	14.9

Note: Data as of 2013 unless noted; (1) Local data covers Bernalillo County; (2) Data as of 2012 and includes all active, non-federal physicians; (3) Doctor of Osteopathic Medicine; (4) rate per 100,000 population
Source: U.S. Department of Health and Human Services, Health Resources and Services Administration, Bureau of Health Professions, Area Resource File (ARF) 2013-2014

EDUCATION

Public School District Statistics

District Name	Schls	Pupils	Pupil/ Teacher Ratio	Minority Pupils[1] (%)	Free Lunch Eligible[2] (%)	IEP[3] (%)
Albuquerque Public Schools	161	94,083	15.2	78.1	59.9	14.8

Note: Table includes school districts with 2,000 or more students; (1) Percentage of students that are not non-Hispanic white; (2) Percentage of students that are eligible for the free lunch program; (3) Percentage of students that have an Individualized Education Program.
Source: U.S. Department of Education, National Center for Education Statistics, Common Core of Data, Local Education Agency (School District) Universe Survey: School Year 2012-2013; U.S. Department of Education, National Center for Education Statistics, Common Core of Data, Public Elementary/Secondary School Universe Survey: School Year 2012-2013

Highest Level of Education

Area	Less than H.S.	H.S. Diploma	Some College, No Deg.	Associate Degree	Bachelor's Degree	Master's Degree	Prof. School Degree	Doctorate Degree
City	10.8	23.3	24.4	8.0	18.7	10.2	2.3	2.3
MSA[1]	12.5	25.1	24.2	8.1	16.9	9.2	2.0	2.0
U.S.	13.7	28.0	21.2	7.9	18.2	7.7	1.9	1.3

Note: Figures cover persons age 25 and over; (1) Figures cover the Albuquerque, NM Metropolitan Statistical Area—see Appendix B for areas included
Source: U.S. Census Bureau, 2011-2013 American Community Survey 3-Year Estimates

Educational Attainment by Race

Area	High School Graduate or Higher (%)					Bachelor's Degree or Higher (%)				
	Total	White	Black	Asian	Hisp.[2]	Total	White	Black	Asian	Hisp.[2]
City	89.2	91.4	90.8	82.8	80.2	33.6	37.3	30.3	44.9	18.6
MSA[1]	87.5	89.9	91.1	83.9	77.7	30.1	33.8	30.6	44.5	16.4
U.S.	86.3	88.3	83.1	85.7	64.0	29.1	30.4	18.8	50.7	13.7

Note: Figures shown cover persons 25 years old and over; (1) Figures cover the Albuquerque, NM Metropolitan Statistical Area—see Appendix B for areas included; (2) People of Hispanic origin can be of any race
Source: U.S. Census Bureau, 2011-2013 American Community Survey 3-Year Estimates

School Enrollment by Grade and Control

Area	Preschool (%)		Kindergarten (%)		Grades 1 - 4 (%)		Grades 5 - 8 (%)		Grades 9 - 12 (%)	
	Public	Private	Public	Private	Public	Private	Public	Private	Public	Private
City	57.0	43.0	90.0	10.0	89.8	10.2	88.3	11.7	88.8	11.2
MSA[1]	61.8	38.2	89.1	10.9	90.7	9.3	89.4	10.6	89.7	10.3
U.S.	57.7	42.3	87.9	12.1	89.9	10.1	90.0	10.0	90.7	9.3

Note: Figures shown cover persons 3 years old and over; (1) Figures cover the Albuquerque, NM Metropolitan Statistical Area—see Appendix B for areas included
Source: U.S. Census Bureau, 2011-2013 American Community Survey 3-Year Estimates

Average Salaries of Public School Classroom Teachers

Area	2013-14		2014-15		Percent Change 2013-14 to 2014-15	Percent Change 2004-05 to 2014-15
	Dollars	Rank[1]	Dollars	Rank[1]		
NEW MEXICO	45,727	43	46,003	44	0.60	16.8
U.S. Average	56,610	–	57,379	–	1.36	20.8

Note: (1) State rank ranges from 1 to 51 where 1 indicates highest salary.
Source: National Education Association, Rankings & Estimates: Rankings of the States 2014 and Estimates of School Statistics 2015, March 2015

Higher Education

Four-Year Colleges			Two-Year Colleges			Medical Schools[1]	Law Schools[2]	Voc/ Tech[3]
Public	Private Non-profit	Private For-profit	Public	Private Non-profit	Private For-profit			
1	0	8	2	0	2	1	1	5

Note: Figures cover institutions located within the city limits and include main campuses only; (1) includes schools accredited by the Liaison Committee on Medical Education and the American Osteopathic Association's Commission on Osteopathic College Accreditation; (2) includes ABA-accredited schools, schools with provisional ABA accreditation, and state accredited schools; (3) includes all schools with programs that are less than 2 years.
Source: National Center for Education Statistics, Integrated Postsecondary Education System (IPEDS), 2013-14; Association of American Medical Colleges, Member List, May 1, 2015; American Osteopathic Association, Member List, May 1, 2015; Law School Admission Council, Official Guide to ABA-Approved Law Schools Online, May 1, 2015; Wikipedia, List of Medical Schools in the United States, May 1, 2015; Wikipedia, List of Law Schools in the United States, May 1, 2015

According to *U.S. News & World Report*, the Albuquerque, NM metro area is home to one of the best national universities in the U.S.: **University of New Mexico** (#189). The indicators used to capture academic quality fall into a number of categories: assessment by administrators at peer institutions; retention of students; faculty resources; student selectivity; financial resources; alumni giving; high school counselor ratings of colleges; and graduation rate. *U.S. News & World Report*, *"America's Best Colleges 2015"*

According to *U.S. News & World Report*, the Albuquerque, NM metro area is home to one of the top 100 law schools in the U.S.: **University of New Mexico** (#71). The rankings are based on a weighted average of 12 measures of quality: peer assessment score; assessment score by lawyers/judges; median LSAT scores; median undergrad GPA; acceptance rate; employment rates for graduates; placement success; bar passage rate; faculty resources; expenditures per student; student/faculty ratio; and library resources. *U.S. News & World Report*, *"America's Best Graduate Schools, Law, 2016"*

PRESIDENTIAL ELECTION

2012 Presidential Election Results

Area	Obama (%)	Romney (%)	Other (%)
Bernalillo County	55.6	39.3	5.1
U.S.	51.0	47.2	1.8

Note: Results may not add to 100% due to rounding
Source: Dave Leip's Atlas of U.S. Presidential Elections

EMPLOYERS

Major Employers

Company Name	Industry
Central New Mexico Community College	Vocational schools
City of Albuquerque	City and town managers' office
City of Albuquerque Police Department	Municipal police
Fish and Wildlife Service, United States	Fish and wildlife conservation agency, government
Jack Henry & Associates	Computers
Laguna Development Corporation	Grocery stores, independent
Mediplex of Massachusetts	Nursing home, exc skilled & intermediate care facility
Sandia Corporation	Noncommercial research organizations
The Boeing Company	Aircraft
United States Department of Energy	Energy development and conservation agency, government
United States Department of the Air Force	Testing laboratories
University of New Mexico	University
University of New Mexico Hospital	General medical and surgical hospitals
USAF	Air force
Veterans Health Administration	Administration of veterans' affiars
Veterans Hospital	General medical and surgical hospitals

Note: Companies shown are located within the Albuquerque, NM Metropolitan Statistical Area.
Source: Hoovers.com; Wikipedia

PUBLIC SAFETY

Crime Rate

Area	All Crimes	Violent Crimes				Property Crimes		
		Murder	Forcible Rape	Robbery	Aggrav. Assault	Burglary	Larceny -Theft	Motor Vehicle Theft
City	6,244.7	6.6	78.7	187.4	502.2	1,307.3	3,624.2	538.4
Suburbs[1]	3,575.1	4.6	38.9	56.0	589.9	886.3	1,754.3	245.0
Metro[2]	5,226.0	5.9	63.5	137.3	535.7	1,146.7	2,910.6	426.4
U.S.	3,098.6	4.5	25.2	109.1	229.1	610.0	1,899.4	221.3

Note: Figures are crimes per 100,000 population; (1) All areas within the metro area that are located outside the city limits; (2) Figures cover the Albuquerque, NM Metropolitan Statistical Area—see Appendix B for areas included
Source: FBI Uniform Crime Reports, 2013

Hate Crimes

Area	Number of Quarters Reported	Number of Incidents per Bias Motivation						
		Race	Religion	Sexual Orientation	Ethnicity	Disability	Gender	Gender Identity
City	4	5	1	4	0	0	0	0
U.S.	4	2,871	1,031	1,233	655	83	18	31

Source: Federal Bureau of Investigation, Hate Crime Statistics 2013

Identity Theft Consumer Complaints

Area	Complaints	Complaints per 100,000 Population	Rank[2]
MSA[1]	897	99.4	63
U.S.	332,646	104.3	-

Note: (1) Figures cover the Albuquerque, NM Metropolitan Statistical Area—see Appendix B for areas included; (2) Rank ranges from 1 to 380 where 1 indicates greatest number of identity theft complaints per 100,000 population
Source: Federal Trade Commission, Consumer Sentinel Network Data Book for January–December 2014

Fraud and Other Consumer Complaints

Area	Complaints	Complaints per 100,000 Population	Rank[2]
MSA[1]	4,402	487.6	27
U.S.	2,250,205	705.7	-

Note: (1) Figures cover the Albuquerque, NM Metropolitan Statistical Area—see Appendix B for areas included; (2) Rank ranges from 1 to 380 where 1 indicates greatest number of identity theft complaints per 100,000 population
Source: Federal Trade Commission, Consumer Sentinel Network Data Book for January–December 2014

RECREATION

Culture

Dance[1]	Theatre[1]	Instrumental Music[1]	Vocal Music[1]	Series and Festivals	Museums and Art Galleries[2]	Zoos and Aquariums[3]
2	6	2	1	2	50	1

Note: (1) Professional perfoming groups; (2) Based on organizations with SIC code 8412; (3) AZA-accredited
Source: The Grey House Performing Arts Directory, 2015-16; Association of Zoos & Aquariums, AZA Member Zoos & Aquariums, April 2015; www.AccuLeads.com, April 2015

Professional Sports Teams

Team Name	League	Year Established
No teams are located in the metro area		

Source: Wikipedia, Major Professional Sports Teams of the United States and Canada, April 2015

CLIMATE

Average and Extreme Temperatures

Temperature	Jan	Feb	Mar	Apr	May	Jun	Jul	Aug	Sep	Oct	Nov	Dec	Yr.
Extreme High (°F)	69	76	85	89	98	105	105	101	100	91	77	72	105
Average High (°F)	47	53	61	71	80	90	92	89	83	72	57	48	70
Average Temp. (°F)	35	40	47	56	65	75	79	76	70	58	45	36	57
Average Low (°F)	23	27	33	41	50	59	65	63	56	44	31	24	43
Extreme Low (°F)	-17	-5	8	19	28	40	52	50	37	21	-7	-7	-17

Note: Figures cover the years 1948-1992
Source: National Climatic Data Center, International Station Meteorological Climate Summary, 9/96

Average Precipitation/Snowfall/Humidity

Precip./Humidity	Jan	Feb	Mar	Apr	May	Jun	Jul	Aug	Sep	Oct	Nov	Dec	Yr.
Avg. Precip. (in.)	0.4	0.4	0.5	0.4	0.5	0.5	1.4	1.5	0.9	0.9	0.4	0.5	8.5
Avg. Snowfall (in.)	3	2	2	1	Tr	0	0	0	Tr	Tr	1	3	11
Avg. Rel. Hum. 5am (%)	68	64	55	48	48	45	60	65	61	60	63	68	59
Avg. Rel. Hum. 5pm (%)	41	33	25	20	19	18	27	30	29	29	35	43	29

Note: Figures cover the years 1948-1992; Tr = Trace amounts (<0.05 in. of rain; <0.5 in. of snow)
Source: National Climatic Data Center, International Station Meteorological Climate Summary, 9/96

Weather Conditions

Temperature			Daytime Sky			Precipitation		
10°F & below	32°F & below	90°F & above	Clear	Partly cloudy	Cloudy	0.01 inch or more precip.	0.1 inch or more snow/ice	Thunder-storms
4	114	65	140	161	64	60	9	38

Note: Figures are average number of days per year and cover the years 1948-1992
Source: National Climatic Data Center, International Station Meteorological Climate Summary, 9/96

HAZARDOUS WASTE

Superfund Sites

Albuquerque has three hazardous waste sites on the EPA's Superfund Final National Priorities List: **AT&SF (Albuquerque); Fruit Avenue Plume; South Valley**. There are a total of 1,322 Superfund sites on the list in the U.S. *U.S. Environmental Protection Agency, Final National Priorities List, April 14, 2015*

AIR & WATER QUALITY

Air Quality Trends: Ozone

	2004	2005	2006	2007	2008	2009	2010	2011	2012	2013
MSA[1]	0.071	0.074	0.071	0.070	0.066	0.065	0.066	0.070	0.070	0.068

Note: (1) Data covers the Albuquerque, NM Metropolitan Statistical Area—see Appendix B for areas included. The values shown are the composite ozone concentration averages among trend sites based on the highest fourth daily maximum 8-hour concentration in parts per million. These trends are based on sites having an adequate record of monitoring data during the trend period. Data from exceptional events are included. Source: U.S. Environmental Protection Agency, Air Quality Monitoring Information, "Air Quality Trends by City, 2000-2013"

Air Quality Index

Area	Percent of Days when Air Quality was...[2]					AQI Statistics[2]	
	Good	Moderate	Unhealthy for Sensitive Groups	Unhealthy	Very Unhealthy	Maximum	Median
MSA[1]	64.1	35.3	0.5	0.0	0.0	105	47

Note: (1) Data covers the Albuquerque, NM Metropolitan Statistical Area—see Appendix B for areas included; (2) Based on 365 days with AQI data in 2014. Air Quality Index (AQI) is an index for reporting daily air quality. EPA calculates the AQI for five major air pollutants regulated by the Clean Air Act: ground-level ozone, particle pollution (aka particulate matter), carbon monoxide, sulfur dioxide, and nitrogen dioxide. The AQI runs from 0 to 500. The higher the AQI value, the greater the level of air pollution and the greater the health concern. There are six AQI categories: "Good" AQI is between 0 and 50. Air quality is considered satisfactory; "Moderate" AQI is between 51 and 100. Air quality is acceptable; "Unhealthy for Sensitive Groups" When AQI values are between 101 and 150, members of sensitive groups may experience health effects; "Unhealthy" When AQI values are between 151 and 200 everyone may begin to experience health effects; "Very Unhealthy" AQI values between 201 and 300 trigger a health alert; "Hazardous" AQI values over 300 trigger warnings of emergency conditions (not shown).
Source: U.S. Environmental Protection Agency, Air Quality Index Report, 2014

Air Quality Index Pollutants

Area	Percent of Days when AQI Pollutant was...[2]					
	Carbon Monoxide	Nitrogen Dioxide	Ozone	Sulfur Dioxide	Particulate Matter 2.5	Particulate Matter 10
MSA[1]	0.0	1.1	57.3	0.8	20.0	20.8

Note: (1) Data covers the Albuquerque, NM Metropolitan Statistical Area—see Appendix B for areas included; (2) Based on 365 days with AQI data in 2014. The Air Quality Index (AQI) is an index for reporting daily air quality. EPA calculates the AQI for five major air pollutants regulated by the Clean Air Act: ground-level ozone, particle pollution (also known as particulate matter), carbon monoxide, sulfur dioxide, and nitrogen dioxide. The AQI runs from 0 to 500. The higher the AQI value, the greater the level of air pollution and the greater the health concern.
Source: U.S. Environmental Protection Agency, Air Quality Index Report, 2014

Maximum Air Pollutant Concentrations: Particulate Matter, Ozone, CO and Lead

	Particulate Matter 10 (ug/m^3)	Particulate Matter 2.5 Wtd AM (ug/m^3)	Particulate Matter 2.5 24-Hr (ug/m^3)	Ozone (ppm)	Carbon Monoxide (ppm)	Lead (ug/m^3)
MSA[1] Level	155	8.7	19	0.072	1	0.01
NAAQS[2]	150	15	35	0.075	9	0.15
Met NAAQS[2]	No	Yes	Yes	Yes	Yes	Yes

Note: (1) Data covers the Albuquerque, NM Metropolitan Statistical Area—see Appendix B for areas included; Data from exceptional events are included; (2) National Ambient Air Quality Standards; ppm = parts per million; ug/m^3 = micrograms per cubic meter; n/a not available.
Concentrations: Particulate Matter 10 (coarse particulate)—highest second maximum 24-hour concentration; Particulate Matter 2.5 Wtd AM (fine particulate)—highest weighted annual mean concentration; Particulate Matter 2.5 24-Hour (fine particulate)—highest 98th percentile 24-hour concentration; Ozone—highest fourth daily maximum 8-hour concentration; Carbon Monoxide—highest second maximum non-overlapping 8-hour concentration; Lead—maximum running 3-month average
Source: U.S. Environmental Protection Agency, Air Quality Monitoring Information, "Air Quality Statistics by City, 2013"

Maximum Air Pollutant Concentrations: Nitrogen Dioxide and Sulfur Dioxide

	Nitrogen Dioxide AM (ppb)	Nitrogen Dioxide 1-Hr (ppb)	Sulfur Dioxide AM (ppb)	Sulfur Dioxide 1-Hr (ppb)	Sulfur Dioxide 24-Hr (ppb)
MSA[1] Level	12	45	n/a	4	n/a
NAAQS[2]	53	100	30	75	140
Met NAAQS[2]	Yes	Yes	n/a	Yes	n/a

Note: (1) Data covers the Albuquerque, NM Metropolitan Statistical Area—see Appendix B for areas included; Data from exceptional events are included; (2) National Ambient Air Quality Standards; ppm = parts per million; ug/m^3 = micrograms per cubic meter; n/a not available.
Concentrations: Nitrogen Dioxide AM—highest arithmetic mean concentration; Nitrogen Dioxide 1-Hr—highest 98th percentile 1-hour daily maximum concentration; Sulfur Dioxide AM—highest annual mean concentration; Sulfur Dioxide 1-Hr—highest 99th percentile 1-hour daily maximum concentration; Sulfur Dioxide 24-Hr—highest second maximum 24-hour concentration
Source: U.S. Environmental Protection Agency, Air Quality Monitoring Information, "Air Quality Statistics by City, 2013"

Drinking Water

Water System Name	Pop. Served	Primary Water Source Type	Violations[1]	
			Health Based	Monitoring/ Reporting
Albuquerque Water System	601,983	Surface	0	0

Note: (1) Based on violation data from January 1, 2014 to December 31, 2014 (includes unresolved violations from earlier years)

Source: U.S. Environmental Protection Agency, Office of Ground Water and Drinking Water, Safe Drinking Water Information System (based on data extracted January 27, 2015)

Anchorage, Alaska

Background

Anchorage, in south central Alaska, is the state's largest city and a center for the state's communication, transportation, health care, and finance industries. Originally powered by the railroads and the fishing industry, Anchorage's economy has in more recent times been closely tied to petroleum production, which accounts for more than 22 percent of the nation's oil reserves.

This modern city lies in a spectacular natural setting, with the Chugach Mountain Range across its eastern skyline and the waters of the Cook Inlet to the west. The city boasts all the advantages of a dynamic urban center, while its residents enjoy a natural environment that teems with bear, moose, caribou, fox, eagles, wolves, dall sheep, orcas, and beluga whales.

The city is young, having been incorporated in 1920, and grew slowly for the next several decades. During World War II, when airfields and roads were constructed to aid in the war effort, the population expanded dramatically; by 1946, Anchorage was home to more than 40,000 people.

In 1964, the region was hit by the strongest earthquake ever to strike North America. There was extensive damage and some loss of life, but the city was quickly rebuilt; in fact, reconstruction was so prompt, efficient, and successful that many look back on the period with considerable civic pride. Earthquakes are not uncommon to the region, with a moderate 5.7 event occurring in Anchorage in January 2009.

In 1951, Anchorage International Airport, which is now Ted Stevens International Airport (ANC), was completed, and the city became vital to the emerging air transport industry as new routes were created. Ted Stevens International Airport flies more than 560 transcontinental cargo flights each week and is the busiest cargo airport in the country. Elmendorf Air Force Base at the northeast end of town, and Anchorage's pioneering development of "bush" aviation, which serves the entire interior of Alaska, further testify to the importance of air travel to the city's development. Also located at the airport are Fort Richardson Army Post and Kulis Air National Guard Base that together employ 8,500.

Oil in Alaska was first discovered in 1957, and 17 oil companies subsequently set up headquarters in Anchorage, giving the city a tremendous economic boost. In 1968, the large North Slope field was discovered, Anchorage was again a major beneficiary. With the completion of the Trans-Alaskan Pipeline System in 1977, Anchorage entered into its contemporary period of sustained population growth and dynamic economic development.

Alaska's tourism industry accounts for more than 30,000 statewide jobs and an estimated economic impact of nearly $80 million in Anchorage alone.

The city's cultural amenities include the Anchorage Museum at Rasmuson Center and the Alaska Aviation Heritage Museum, which chronicles the story of Alaska's early and pioneering air transport system. Near the city is the Potter Section House Railway Museum, which pays homage to the state's vital rail industry. The city also boasts the Alaska Center for the Performing Arts and the Alaska Botanical Garden. Delaney Park, also known as the Park Strip, is a venerable and valued recreational resource in the city's business district, and its ongoing improvement looks toward a year-round "Central Park" for Anchorage. The Alaska State Fair has been recognized as one of the Top 100 Events in North America.

Because of its long summer days and relatively mild temperatures, Anchorage is called "The City of Lights and Flowers," and is adorned in summer throughout the municipality with open, grassy expanses and flowers. The season brings out a friendly competition among the city's residents, who plant along streets, in parks, private gardens, window boxes, and lobbies.

The natural environment of Anchorage is spectacular, and at nearby Portage Glacier, one can watch the glacier "calving," as huge blocks of ice crash into the lake below. Anchorage is also located at one end of the famous annual Iditarod Trail Sled Dog Race.

The city is an educational center with two universities and many technical, vocational, and private schools. A campus of the University of Alaska has been in Anchorage since 1954, and the city is also home to Alaska Pacific University.

The weather in Anchorage, contrary to what many believe, is not savagely cold. It is tempered by the city's location on the coast and by the Alaska Mountain Range, which acts as a barrier to very cold air from the north. Snow season lasts from October to May. Summers can bring fog and rain.

Rankings

General Rankings

- The editors of *Kiplinger's Personal Finance Magazine* chose the ten best cities of manageable size (less than a million residents) with a sound job market, reasonably priced homes, good schools, and access to excellent healthcare facilities. The Anchorage metro area earned the #9 spot on the *Kiplinger's* list. *www.kiplinger.com, "10 Great Places to Live," July 2013*

- Anchorage was selected as one of America's best cities by *Bloomberg Businessweek*. The city ranked #49 out of 50. Criteria: leisure attributes (the number of restaurants, bars, libraries, museums, professional sports teams, and park acres by population); educational attributes (public school performance, the number of colleges, and graduate degree holders); economic factors (2011 income and June and July 2012 unemployment); crime; and air quality. *Bloomberg BusinessWeek, "America's Best Cities," September 26, 2012*

- Anchorage was selected as one the best places to live in America by *Outside Magazine*. The city ranked #4. Criteria included nearby adventure, healthy eating options, bike lanes, green spaces, number of outfitters and bike shops, miles of trails, median income, and unemployment rate. *Outside Magazine, "Outside's Best 16 Best Places to Live in the U.S. 2014," September 2014*

Business/Finance Rankings

- Analysts for the business website 24/7 Wall Street looked at the local government report "Tax Rates and Tax Burdens in the District of Columbia—A Nationwide Comparison" to determine where a family of three at two different income levels would pay the least and the most in state and local taxes. Among the ten cities with the lowest state and local tax burdens was Anchorage, at #2. *247wallst.com, American Cities with the Highest (and Lowest) Taxes, February 25, 2013*

- Using data from the Council for Community and Economic Research's 2013 Annual Report, NerdWallet ranked the 100 U.S. cities with the most expensive cost of living. Cities in California and in the Northeast topped the list. Of the cities with the highest cost of living, Anchorage ranked #23. *NerdWallet.com, "Most Expensive Cities in America," June 4, 2014*

- The Anchorage metro area appeared on the Milken Institute "2013 Best Performing Cities" list. Rank: #74 out of 200 large metro areas. Criteria: job growth; wage and salary growth; high-tech output growth. *Milken Institute, "Best-Performing Cities 2014," January 2015*

- *Forbes* ranked the 200 most populous metro areas to determine the nation's "Best Places for Business and Careers." The Anchorage metro area was ranked #53. Criteria: costs (business and living); job growth (past and projected); income growth; educational attainment (college and high school); projected economic growth; cultural and recreational opportunities; net migration patterns; number of highly ranked colleges. *Forbes, "The Best Places for Business and Careers 2014," July 23, 2014*

Children/Family Rankings

- Anchorage was chosen as one of America's 100 best communities for young people. The winners were selected based upon detailed information provided about each community's efforts to fulfill five essential promises critical to the well-being of young people: caring adults who are actively involved in their lives; safe places in which to learn and grow; a healthy start toward adulthood; an effective education that builds marketable skills; and opportunities to help others. *America's Promise Alliance, "100 Best Communities for Young People, 2012"*

Dating/Romance Rankings

- Of the 100 U.S. cities surveyed by *Men's Health* in its quest to identify the nation's best cities for dating and forming relationships, Anchorage was ranked #61 for online dating (#1 = best). *Men's Health, "The Best and Worst Cities for Online Dating," January 30, 2013*

Education Rankings

- Personal finance website *WalletHub* analyzed the 150 largest U.S. metropolitan statistical areas to determine where the most educated Americans are choosing to settle. Criteria: educational attainment; percentage of workers with jobs in computer, engineering, and science fields; quality and size of each metro area's universities. Anchorage was ranked #18 (#1 = most educated city). *www.WalletHub.com, "2014's Most and Least Educated Cities*

- Anchorage was selected as one of America's most literate cities. The city ranked #58 out of the 77 largest U.S. cities. Criteria: number of booksellers; library resources; Internet resources; educational attainment; periodical publishing resources; newspaper circulation. *Central Connecticut State University, "America's Most Literate Cities, 2014," April 8, 2015*

Environmental Rankings

- The Weather Channel determined the nation's snowiest cities, based on the National Oceanic and Atmospheric Administration's 30-year average snowfall data. Among cities with a population of at least 100,000, the #6-ranked city was Anchorage *weather.com, America's 20 Snowiest Major Cities, February 3, 2014*

- The Anchorage metro area came in at #1 for the relative comfort of its climate on Sperling's list of "chill cities," as measured by the Sperling Heat Index. All 361 metro areas are included. Criteria included daytime high temperatures, nighttime low temperatures, dew point, and relative humidity at the high temperatures. *www.bertsperling.com, "Sperling's Chill Cities," July 18, 2013*

- Sperling's BestPlaces assessed 379 metropolitan areas of the United States for the likelihood of dangerously extreme weather events or earthquakes. In general the Southeast and South-Central regions have the highest risk of weather extremes and earthquakes, while the Pacific Northwest enjoys the lowest risk. Of the least risky metropolitan areas, the Anchorage metro area was ranked #71. *www.bestplaces.net, "Safest Places from Natural Disasters," April 2011*

- *The Daily Beast* identifed the snowiest among the 100 largest U.S. cities, looking at average snowfall per month from December 2011 through March 2012 and from December 1, 2012 to December 21, 2012. Number of days with maximum and minimum temperatures of 32 degrees or less contributed to the rankings. Anchorage ranked #1. *The Daily Beast, "25 Snowiest Cities in America," December 21, 2012*

- Anchorage was highlighted as one of the top 25 cleanest metro areas for year-round particle pollution (Annual PM 2.5) in the U.S. during 2011 through 2013. The area ranked #10. *American Lung Association, State of the Air 2015*

Food/Drink Rankings

- For the Gallup-Healthways Well-Being Index, researchers interviewed at least 300 adults in each of 189 metropolitan areas on residents' access to affordable fresh produce. The Anchorage metro area was found to be among the ten communities with the least accessible and affordable produce. *www.gallup.com, "In Anchorage, Access to Fruits and Vegetables Remains Lowest," April 8, 2014*

- *Men's Health* ranked 100 major U.S. cities in terms of alcohol intoxication. Anchorage ranked #61 (#1 = most sober).Criteria: binge drinking; alcohol-related traffic accidents, arrests, and fatalities. *Men's Health, "The Drunkest Cities in America," November 19, 2013*

Health/Fitness Rankings

- *Men's Health* ranked 100 major U.S. cities in terms of the best and worst cities for men. Anchorage ranked #26. Criteria: thirty-three data points were examined covering health, fitness, and quality of life. *Men's Health, "The Best & Worst Cities for Men 2014," December 6, 2013*

- The Anchorage metro area appeared in the 2013 Gallup-Healthways Well-Being Index. The area ranked #84 out of 189. The Gallup-Healthways Well-Being Index score is an average of six sub-indexes, which individually examine life evaluation, emotional health, work environment, physical health, healthy behaviors, and access to basic necessities. Results are based on telephone interviews conducted as part of the Gallup-Healthways Well-Being Index survey January 2–December 29, 2012, and January 2–December 30, 2013, with a random sample of 531,630 adults, aged 18 and older, living in metropolitan areas in the 50 U.S. states and the District of Columbia. *Gallup-Healthways, "State of American Well-Being," March 25, 2014*

Real Estate Rankings

- Anchorage was ranked #248 out of 275 metro areas in terms of house price appreciation in 2014 (#1 = highest rate). *Federal Housing Finance Agency, House Price Index, 4th Quarter 2014*

- Anchorage was ranked #120 out of 226 metro areas in terms of housing affordability in 2014 by the National Association of Home Builders (#1 = most affordable). The NAHB-Wells Fargo Housing Opportunity Index (HOI) for a given area is defined as the share of homes sold in that area that would have been affordable to a family earning the local median income, based on standard mortgage underwriting criteria. *National Association of Home Builders®, NAHB-Wells Fargo Housing Opportunity Index, 4th Quarter 2014*

Safety Rankings

- Allstate ranked the 200 largest cities in America in terms of driver safety. Anchorage ranked #131. Allstate researchers analyzed internal property damage claims over a two-year period from January 2011 to December 2012. A weighted average of the two-year numbers determined the annual percentages. *Allstate, "Allstate America's Best Drivers Report, 2014"*

- The National Insurance Crime Bureau ranked 380 metro areas in the U.S. in terms of per capita rates of vehicle theft. The Anchorage metro area ranked #86 (#1 = highest rate). Criteria: number of vehicle theft offenses per 100,000 inhabitants in 2012. *National Insurance Crime Bureau, "Hot Spots 2012," June 26, 2013*

Seniors/Retirement Rankings

- From its Best Cities for Successful Aging indexes, the Milken Institute generated rankings for metropolitan areas, weighing data in eight categories—health care, wellness, living arrangements, transportation, financial characteristics, education and employment opportunities, community engagement, and overall livability. The Anchorage metro area was ranked #44 overall in the small metro area category. *Milken Institute, "Best Cities for Successful Aging, 2014"*

Sports/Recreation Rankings

- Anchorage was chosen as a bicycle friendly community by the League of American Bicyclists. A "Bicycle Friendly Community" welcomes cyclists by providing safe accommodation for cycling and encouraging people to bike for transportation and recreation. There are four award levels: Platinum; Gold; Silver; and Bronze. The community achieved an award level of Silver. *League of American Bicyclists, "Bicycle Friendly Community Master List," Fall 2013*

- Anchorage was chosen as one of America's best cities for bicycling. The city ranked #46 out of 50. Criteria: robust cycling infrastructure; vibrant bike culture. The editors only considered cities with populations of 95,000 or more. *Bicycling, "America's Top 50 Bike-Friendly Cities," May 23, 2012*

Women/Minorities Rankings

- *Women's Health* examined U.S. cities and identified the 100 best cities for women. Anchorage was ranked #26. Criteria: 30 categories were examined from obesity and breast cancer rates to commuting times and hours spent working out. *Women's Health, "Best Cities for Women 2012"*

Miscellaneous Rankings

- Anchorage appeared on *Travel + Leisure's* list of America's least attractive people. Criteria: cities were selected by readers in their annual America's Favorite Cities survey. The city ranked #4 out of 10. *Travel + Leisure, "America's Most and Least Attractive People," November 2013*

Business Environment

CITY FINANCES

City Government Finances

Component	2012 ($000)	2012 ($ per capita)
Total Revenues	1,492,131	5,113
Total Expenditures	1,554,149	5,326
Debt Outstanding	1,789,000	6,130
Cash and Securities[1]	1,081,964	3,708

Note: (1) Cash and security holdings of a government at the close of its fiscal year, including those of its dependent agencies, utilities, and liquor stores.
Source: U.S Census Bureau, State & Local Government Finances 2012

City Government Revenue by Source

Source	2012 ($000)	2012 ($ per capita)
General Revenue		
From Federal Government	49,698	170
From State Government	522,432	1,790
From Local Governments	0	0
Taxes		
Property	484,644	1,661
Sales and Gross Receipts	40,749	140
Personal Income	0	0
Corporate Income	0	0
Motor Vehicle License	9,878	34
Other Taxes	11,367	39
Current Charges	137,122	470
Liquor Store	0	0
Utility	189,958	651
Employee Retirement	5,365	18

Source: U.S Census Bureau, State & Local Government Finances 2012

City Government Expenditures by Function

Function	2012 ($000)	2012 ($ per capita)	2012 (%)
General Direct Expenditures			
Air Transportation	4,433	15	0.3
Corrections	0	0	0.0
Education	665,196	2,279	42.8
Employment Security Administration	0	0	0.0
Financial Administration	22,646	78	1.5
Fire Protection	90,763	311	5.8
General Public Buildings	4,140	14	0.3
Governmental Administration, Other	21,904	75	1.4
Health	26,823	92	1.7
Highways	74,081	254	4.8
Hospitals	0	0	0.0
Housing and Community Development	0	0	0.0
Interest on General Debt	35,273	121	2.3
Judicial and Legal	7,996	27	0.5
Libraries	25,429	87	1.6
Parking	5,536	19	0.4
Parks and Recreation	21,024	72	1.4
Police Protection	123,926	425	8.0
Public Welfare	0	0	0.0
Sewerage	40,222	138	2.6
Solid Waste Management	22,852	78	1.5
Veterans' Services	0	0	0.0
Liquor Store	0	0	0.0
Utility	275,640	945	17.7
Employee Retirement	27,366	94	1.8

Source: U.S Census Bureau, State & Local Government Finances 2012

DEMOGRAPHICS

Population Growth

Area	1990 Census	2000 Census	2010 Census	Population Growth (%) 1990-2000	Population Growth (%) 2000-2010
City	226,338	260,283	291,826	15.0	12.1
MSA[1]	266,021	319,605	380,821	20.1	19.2
U.S.	248,709,873	281,421,906	308,745,538	13.2	9.7

Note: (1) Figures cover the Anchorage, AK Metropolitan Statistical Area—see Appendix B for areas included
Source: U.S. Census Bureau, Census 1990, 2000, 2010

Household Size

Area	Persons in Household (%) One	Two	Three	Four	Five	Six	Seven or More	Average Household Size
City	26.3	33.1	17.1	13.0	5.7	2.6	2.2	2.77
MSA[1]	25.2	34.1	16.7	13.0	5.8	2.8	2.3	2.80
U.S.	27.7	33.6	15.7	13.1	6.0	2.3	1.5	2.64

Note: (1) Figures cover the Anchorage, AK Metropolitan Statistical Area—see Appendix B for areas included
Source: U.S. Census Bureau, 2011-2013 American Community Survey 3-Year Estimates

Race

Area	White Alone[2] (%)	Black Alone[2] (%)	Asian Alone[2] (%)	AIAN[3] Alone[2] (%)	NHOPI[4] Alone[2] (%)	Other Race Alone[2] (%)	Two or More Races (%)
City	65.9	6.0	8.4	6.7	2.1	1.4	9.5
MSA[1]	70.3	4.8	6.7	6.4	1.7	1.3	8.8
U.S.	73.9	12.6	5.0	0.8	0.2	4.7	2.9

Note: (1) Figures cover the Anchorage, AK Metropolitan Statistical Area—see Appendix B for areas included;
(2) Alone is defined as not being in combination with one or more other races; (3) American Indian and Alaska Native; (4) Native Hawaiian and Other Pacific Islander
Source: U.S. Census Bureau, 2011-2013 American Community Survey 3-Year Estimates

Hispanic or Latino Origin

Area	Total (%)	Mexican (%)	Puerto Rican (%)	Cuban (%)	Other (%)
City	8.3	4.5	1.2	0.2	2.3
MSA[1]	7.3	4.1	1.1	0.2	2.0
U.S.	16.9	10.8	1.6	0.6	3.8

Note: Persons of Hispanic or Latino origin can be of any race; (1) Figures cover the Anchorage, AK Metropolitan Statistical Area—see Appendix B for areas included
Source: U.S. Census Bureau, 2011-2013 American Community Survey 3-Year Estimates

Segregation

Type	Segregation Indices[1] 1990	2000	2010	2010 Rank[2]	Percent Change 1990-2000	1990-2010	2000-2010
Black/White	n/a	n/a	n/a	n/a	n/a	n/a	n/a
Asian/White	n/a	n/a	n/a	n/a	n/a	n/a	n/a
Hispanic/White	n/a	n/a	n/a	n/a	n/a	n/a	n/a

Note: All figures cover the Metropolitan Statistical Area—see Appendix B for areas included; Figures are based on an analysis of 1990, 2000, and 2010 Census Decennial Census tract data by William H. Frey, Brookings Institution and the University of Michigan Social Science Data Analysis Network. In this analysis all racial groups (whites, blacks, and asians) are non-Hispanic members of those races. Hispanics are shown as a separate category;
(1) Segregation Indices are Dissimilarity Indices that measure the degree to which the minority group is distributed differently than whites across census tracts. They range from 0 (complete integration) to 100 (complete segregation) where the value indicates the percentage of the minority group that needs to move to be distributed exactly like whites; (2) Ranges from 1 (most segregated) to 102 (least segregated); n/a not available.
Source: www.CensusScope.org

Ancestry

Area	German	Irish	English	American	Italian	Polish	French[2]	Scottish	Dutch
City	16.7	10.1	8.6	5.7	3.2	1.8	2.8	3.0	1.7
MSA[1]	18.1	10.8	8.7	5.6	3.2	1.9	3.0	3.0	1.8
U.S.	14.9	10.8	8.0	7.4	5.5	3.0	2.7	1.7	1.4

Note: Figures are the percentage of the total population reporting a particular ancestry. The nine most commonly reported ancestries in the U.S. are shown. Figures include multiple ancestries (e.g. if a person reported being Irish and Italian, they were included in both columns); (1) Figures cover the Anchorage, AK Metropolitan Statistical Area—see Appendix B for areas included; (2) Excludes Basque
Source: U.S. Census Bureau, 2011-2013 American Community Survey 3-Year Estimates

Foreign-Born Population

Area	Percent of Population Born in								
	Any Foreign Country	Mexico	Asia	Europe	Carribean	South America	Central America[2]	Africa	Canada
City	9.4	0.9	5.6	1.1	0.4	0.3	0.2	0.3	0.3
MSA[1]	8.1	0.7	4.5	1.2	0.3	0.2	0.2	0.3	0.3
U.S.	13.0	3.7	3.8	1.5	1.2	0.9	1.0	0.6	0.3

Note: (1) Figures cover the Anchorage, AK Metropolitan Statistical Area—see Appendix B for areas included; (2) Excludes Mexico.
Source: U.S. Census Bureau, 2011-2013 American Community Survey 3-Year Estimates

Marital Status

Area	Never Married	Now Married[2]	Separated	Widowed	Divorced
City	35.3	47.4	1.6	3.6	12.1
MSA[1]	33.4	49.0	1.6	3.7	12.3
U.S.	32.7	48.1	2.2	6.0	11.0

Note: Figures are percentages and cover the population 15 years of age and older; (1) Figures cover the Anchorage, AK Metropolitan Statistical Area—see Appendix B for areas included; (2) Excludes separated
Source: U.S. Census Bureau, 2011-2013 American Community Survey 3-Year Estimates

Disability Status

Area	All Ages	Under 18 Years Old	18 to 64 Years Old	65 Years and Over
City	9.8	2.9	9.1	37.5
MSA[1]	10.2	3.0	9.5	38.1
U.S.	12.3	4.1	10.2	36.3

Note: Figures show percent of the civilian noninstitutionalized population that reported having a disability. Disability status is determined from from six types of difficulty: vision, hearing, cognitive, ambulatory, self-care, and independent living. For children under 5 years old, hearing and vision difficulty are used to determine disability status. For children between the ages of 5 and 14, disability status is determined from hearing, vision, cognitive, ambulatory, and self-care difficulties. For people aged 15 years and older, they are considered to have a disability if they have difficulty with any one of the six difficulty types; (1) Figures cover the Anchorage, AK Metropolitan Statistical Area—see Appendix B for areas included.
Source: U.S. Census Bureau, 2011-2013 American Community Survey 3-Year Estimates

Age

Area	Percent of Population									Median Age
	Under Age 5	Age 5–19	Age 20–34	Age 35–44	Age 45–54	Age 55–64	Age 65–74	Age 75–84	Age 85+	
City	7.5	20.5	25.4	12.9	14.0	11.7	5.2	2.2	0.7	32.7
MSA[1]	7.5	21.1	23.9	13.0	14.2	12.0	5.3	2.3	0.7	33.2
U.S.	6.4	19.9	20.7	12.9	14.1	12.3	7.6	4.2	1.9	37.4

Note: (1) Figures cover the Anchorage, AK Metropolitan Statistical Area—see Appendix B for areas included
Source: U.S. Census Bureau, 2011-2013 American Community Survey 3-Year Estimates

Gender

Area	Males	Females	Males per 100 Females
City	151,980	146,404	103.8
MSA[1]	200,581	191,444	104.8
U.S.	154,451,010	159,410,713	96.9

Note: (1) Figures cover the Anchorage, AK Metropolitan Statistical Area—see Appendix B for areas included
Source: U.S. Census Bureau, 2011-2013 American Community Survey 3-Year Estimates

Religious Groups by Family

Area	Catholic	Baptist	Non-Den.	Methodist[2]	Lutheran	LDS[3]	Pente-costal	Presby-terian[4]	Muslim[5]	Judaism
MSA[1]	6.9	5.0	6.4	1.4	1.9	5.1	1.9	0.7	0.2	0.1
U.S.	19.1	9.3	4.0	4.0	2.3	2.0	1.9	1.6	0.8	0.7

Note: Figures are the number of adherents as a percentage of the total population; (1) Figures cover the Anchorage, AK Metropolitan Statistical Area—see Appendix B for areas included; (2) Methodist/Pietist; (3) Latter Day Saints; (4) Reformed; (5) Figures are estimates
Source: Association of Statisticians of American Religious Bodies, 2010 U.S. Religion Census: Religious Congregations & Membership Study

Religious Groups by Tradition

Area	Catholic	Evangelical Protestant	Mainline Protestant	Other Tradition	Black Protestant	Orthodox
MSA[1]	6.9	15.7	3.6	6.8	0.3	0.6
U.S.	19.1	16.2	7.3	4.3	1.6	0.3

Note: Figures are the number of adherents as a percentage of the total population; (1) Figures cover the Anchorage, AK Metropolitan Statistical Area—see Appendix B for areas included
Source: Association of Statisticians of American Religious Bodies, 2010 U.S. Religion Census: Religious Congregations & Membership Study

ECONOMY

Gross Metropolitan Product

Area	2012	2013	2014	2015	Rank[2]
MSA[1]	28.6	29.3	30.4	31.8	83

Note: Figures are in billions of dollars; (1) Figures cover the Anchorage, AK Metropolitan Statistical Area—see Appendix B for areas included; (2) Rank is based on 2015 data and ranges from 1 to 363
Source: The U.S. Conference of Mayors, U.S. Metro Economies: GMP and Employment 2013-2015, June 2014

Economic Growth

Area	2010-12 (%)	2013 (%)	2014 (%)	2015 (%)	Rank[2]
MSA[1]	1.6	1.1	1.1	3.7	54
U.S.	2.1	2.0	2.3	3.2	–

Note: Figures are real gross metropolitan product (GMP) growth rates and represent annual average percent change; (1) Figures cover the Anchorage, AK Metropolitan Statistical Area—see Appendix B for areas included; (2) Rank is based on 2015 data and ranges from 1 to 363
Source: The U.S. Conference of Mayors, U.S. Metro Economies: GMP and Employment 2013-2015, June 2014

Metropolitan Area Exports

Area	2008	2009	2010	2011	2012	2013	Rank[2]
MSA[1]	245.8	213.9	n/a	n/a	416.4	518.0	211

Note: Figures are in millions of dollars; (1) Figures cover the Anchorage, AK Metropolitan Statistical Area—see Appendix B for areas included; (2) Rank is based on 2013 data and ranges from 1 to 387
Source: U.S. Department of Commerce, International Trade Administration, Office of Trade & Industry Information, Manufacturing & Services, data extracted April 3, 2015

Building Permits

Area	Single-Family			Multi-Family			Total		
	2013	2014	Pct. Chg.	2013	2014	Pct. Chg.	2013	2014	Pct. Chg.
City	475	572	20.4	58	198	241.4	533	770	44.5
MSA[1]	500	671	34.2	76	216	184.2	576	887	54.0
U.S.	620,802	634,597	2.2	370,020	411,766	11.3	990,822	1,046,363	5.6

Note: (1) Figures cover the Anchorage, AK Metropolitan Statistical Area—see Appendix B for areas included; Figures represent new, privately-owned housing units authorized (unadjusted data); All permit data are based on estimates with imputation.
Source: U.S. Census Bureau, Manufacturing, Mining, and Construction Statistics, Building Permits, 2013, 2014

Bankruptcy Filings

Area	Business Filings			Nonbusiness Filings		
	2013	2014	% Chg.	2013	2014	% Chg.
Anchorage Borough	19	17	-10.5	268	210	-21.6
U.S.	33,212	26,983	-18.8	1,038,720	909,812	-12.4

Note: Business filings include Chapter 7, Chapter 11, Chapter 12, and Chapter 13; Nonbusiness filings include Chapter 7, Chapter 11, and Chapter 13
Source: Administrative Office of the U.S. Courts, Business and Nonbusiness Bankruptcy, County Cases Commenced by Chapter of the Bankruptcy Code, During the 12- Month Period Ending December 31, 2013 and Business and Nonbusiness Bankruptcy, County Cases Commenced by Chapter of the Bankruptcy Code, During the 12- Month Period Ending December 31, 2014

Housing Vacancy Rates

Area	Gross Vacancy Rate[2] (%)			Year-Round Vacancy Rate[3] (%)			Rental Vacancy Rate[4] (%)			Homeowner Vacancy Rate[5] (%)		
	2012	2013	2014	2012	2013	2014	2012	2013	2014	2012	2013	2014
MSA[1]	n/a	n/a	n/a	n/a	n/a	n/a	n/a	n/a	n/a	n/a	n/a	n/a
U.S.	13.8	13.6	13.4	10.8	10.7	10.4	8.7	8.3	7.6	2.0	2.0	1.9

Note: (1) Figures cover the Anchorage, AK Metropolitan Statistical Area—see Appendix B for areas included; (2) The percentage of the total housing inventory that is vacant; (3) The percentage of the housing inventory (excluding seasonal units) that is year-round vacant; (4) The percentage of rental inventory that is vacant for rent; (5) The percentage of homeowner inventory that is vacant for sale; n/a not available
Source: U.S. Census Bureau, Housing Vacancies and Homeownership Annual Statistics: 2014

INCOME

Income

Area	Per Capita ($)	Median Household ($)	Average Household ($)
City	35,769	76,159	96,249
MSA[1]	34,228	74,830	93,213
U.S.	27,884	52,176	72,897

Note: (1) Figures cover the Anchorage, AK Metropolitan Statistical Area—see Appendix B for areas included
Source: U.S. Census Bureau, 2011-2013 American Community Survey 3-Year Estimates

Household Income Distribution

Area	Percent of Households Earning							
	Under $15,000	$15,000 -24,999	$25,000 -34,999	$35,000 -49,999	$50,000 -74,999	$75,000 -99,000	$100,000 -149,999	$150,000 and up
City	5.5	6.2	6.3	12.9	18.1	15.2	19.1	16.7
MSA[1]	6.2	6.7	6.4	12.2	18.6	15.4	19.0	15.5
U.S.	13.0	10.9	10.3	13.6	17.9	11.9	12.7	9.6

Note: (1) Figures cover the Anchorage, AK Metropolitan Statistical Area—see Appendix B for areas included
Source: U.S. Census Bureau, 2011-2013 American Community Survey 3-Year Estimates

Poverty Rate

Area	All Ages	Under 18 Years Old	18 to 64 Years Old	65 Years and Over
City	7.7	10.6	7.0	4.2
MSA[1]	8.2	11.1	7.5	4.3
U.S.	15.9	22.4	14.8	9.5

Note: Figures are percentage of people whose income during the past 12 months was below the poverty level; (1) Figures cover the Anchorage, AK Metropolitan Statistical Area—see Appendix B for areas included
Source: U.S. Census Bureau, 2011-2013 American Community Survey 3-Year Estimates

EMPLOYMENT

Labor Force and Employment

Area	Civilian Labor Force			Workers Employed		
	Dec. 2013	Dec. 2014	% Chg.	Dec. 2013	Dec. 2014	% Chg.
City	161,364	162,186	0.5	153,539	154,675	0.7
MSA[1]	206,084	206,927	0.4	194,694	196,055	0.7
U.S.	154,408,000	155,521,000	0.7	144,423,000	147,190,000	1.9

Note: Data is not seasonally adjusted and covers workers 16 years of age and older; (1) Figures cover the Anchorage, AK Metropolitan Statistical Area—see Appendix B for areas included
Source: Bureau of Labor Statistics, Local Area Unemployment Statistics

Unemployment Rate

Area	2014											
	Jan.	Feb.	Mar.	Apr.	May	Jun.	Jul.	Aug.	Sep.	Oct.	Nov.	Dec.
City	5.4	5.7	5.5	5.3	5.2	5.6	5.0	4.9	4.9	4.7	4.8	4.6
MSA[1]	6.2	6.5	6.3	6.0	5.8	6.2	5.6	5.4	5.4	5.2	5.4	5.3
U.S.	7.0	7.0	6.8	5.9	6.1	6.3	6.5	6.3	5.7	5.5	5.5	5.4

Note: Data is not seasonally adjusted and covers workers 16 years of age and older; (1) Figures cover the Anchorage, AK Metropolitan Statistical Area—see Appendix B for areas included
Source: Bureau of Labor Statistics, Local Area Unemployment Statistics

Employment by Occupation

Occupation Classification	City (%)	MSA[1] (%)	U.S. (%)
Management, Business, Science, and Arts	39.0	38.0	36.2
Natural Resources, Construction, and Maintenance	9.1	10.6	9.0
Production, Transportation, and Material Moving	9.3	9.4	12.1
Sales and Office	25.0	24.5	24.4
Service	17.6	17.5	18.3

Note: Figures cover employed civilians 16 years of age and older; (1) Figures cover the Anchorage, AK Metropolitan Statistical Area—see Appendix B for areas included
Source: U.S. Census Bureau, 2011-2013 American Community Survey 3-Year Estimates

Employment by Industry

Sector	MSA[1]		U.S.
	Number of Employees	Percent of Total	Percent of Total
Construction	9,900	5.5	4.4
Education and Health Services	29,600	16.5	15.5
Financial Activities	8,400	4.7	5.7
Government	35,800	20.0	15.8
Information	4,500	2.5	2.0
Leisure and Hospitality	18,800	10.5	10.3
Manufacturing	2,300	1.3	8.7
Mining and Logging	3,800	2.1	0.6
Other Services	7,000	3.9	4.0
Professional and Business Services	20,700	11.6	13.8
Retail Trade	22,000	12.3	11.4
Transportation, Warehousing, and Utilities	11,300	6.3	3.9
Wholesale Trade	4,800	2.7	4.2

Note: Figures are non-farm employment as of December 2014. Figures are not seasonally adjusted and include workers 16 years of age and older; (1) Figures cover the Anchorage, AK Metropolitan Statistical Area—see Appendix B for areas included
Source: Bureau of Labor Statistics, Current Employment Statistics, Employment, Hours, and Earnings

Occupations with Greatest Projected Employment Growth: 2012 – 2022

Occupation[1]	2012 Employment	2022 Projected Employment	Numeric Employment Change	Percent Employment Change
Personal Care Aides	3,970	5,010	1,040	26.0
Retail Salespersons	10,600	11,630	1,030	9.7
Registered Nurses	4,980	5,970	990	20.0
Cashiers	8,750	9,430	680	7.7
Combined Food Preparation and Serving Workers, Including Fast Food	5,600	6,260	660	11.8
Office Clerks, General	6,800	7,420	620	9.2
Home Health Aides	2,340	2,950	610	26.0
Office and Administrative Support Workers, All Other	4,500	5,110	610	13.5
Janitors and Cleaners, Except Maids and Housekeeping Cleaners	5,560	6,120	560	10.0
Meat, Poultry, and Fish Cutters and Trimmers	7,530	8,030	500	6.6

Note: Projections cover Alaska; (1) Sorted by numeric employment change
Source: www.projectionscentral.com, State Occupational Projections, 2012–2022 Long-Term Projections

Fastest Growing Occupations: 2012 – 2022

Occupation[1]	2012 Employment	2022 Projected Employment	Numeric Employment Change	Percent Employment Change
Dental Hygienists	570	730	160	27.8
Dental Assistants	1,080	1,370	290	27.0
Home Health Aides	2,340	2,950	610	26.0
Personal Care Aides	3,970	5,010	1,040	26.0
Medical Assistants	1,130	1,420	290	25.7
Mental Health and Substance Abuse Social Workers	520	640	120	25.0
Healthcare Support Workers, All Other	1,140	1,420	280	24.3
Family and General Practitioners	400	500	100	24.1
Medical Secretaries	510	630	120	23.7
Radiologic Technologists	440	540	100	22.2

Note: Projections cover Alaska; (1) Sorted by percent employment change and excludes occupations with numeric employment change less than 100
Source: www.projectionscentral.com, State Occupational Projections, 2012–2022 Long-Term Projections

Average Wages

Occupation	$/Hr.	Occupation	$/Hr.
Accountants and Auditors	38.15	Maids and Housekeeping Cleaners	11.80
Automotive Mechanics	23.62	Maintenance and Repair Workers	22.16
Bookkeepers	21.70	Marketing Managers	43.16
Carpenters	31.91	Nuclear Medicine Technologists	n/a
Cashiers	12.05	Nurses, Licensed Practical	25.37
Clerks, General Office	20.64	Nurses, Registered	41.46
Clerks, Receptionists/Information	15.67	Nursing Assistants	17.75
Clerks, Shipping/Receiving	18.30	Packers and Packagers, Hand	13.44
Computer Programmers	38.79	Physical Therapists	48.61
Computer Systems Analysts	37.89	Postal Service Mail Carriers	25.82
Computer User Support Specialists	25.59	Real Estate Brokers	42.45
Cooks, Restaurant	14.45	Retail Salespersons	12.99
Dentists	105.67	Sales Reps., Exc. Tech./Scientific	28.46
Electrical Engineers	53.37	Sales Reps., Tech./Scientific	37.22
Electricians	37.67	Secretaries, Exc. Legal/Med./Exec.	16.96
Financial Managers	57.37	Security Guards	14.72
First-Line Supervisors/Managers, Sales	20.58	Surgeons	n/a
Food Preparation Workers	11.77	Teacher Assistants	17.70
General and Operations Managers	52.07	Teachers, Elementary School	33.20
Hairdressers/Cosmetologists	15.62	Teachers, Secondary School	33.30
Internists	87.17	Telemarketers	n/a
Janitors and Cleaners	13.96	Truck Drivers, Heavy/Tractor-Trailer	26.53
Landscaping/Groundskeeping Workers	15.76	Truck Drivers, Light/Delivery Svcs.	18.71
Lawyers	57.05	Waiters and Waitresses	13.45

Note: Wage data covers the Anchorage, AK Metropolitan Statistical Area—see Appendix B for areas included; Hourly wages for elementary/secondary school teachers and teacher assistants were calculated by the editors from annual wage data assuming a 40 hour work week; n/a not available.
Source: Bureau of Labor Statistics, Metro Area Occupational Employment and Wage Estimates, May 2014

TAXES

State Corporate Income Tax Rates

State	Tax Rate (%)	Income Brackets ($)	Num. of Brackets	Financial Institution Tax Rate (%)[a]	Federal Income Tax Ded.
Alaska	0 - 9.4	25,000 - 222,000	10	0 - 9.4	No

Note: Tax rates as of January 1, 2015; (a) Rates listed are the corporate income tax rate applied to financial institutions or excise taxes based on income. Some states have other taxes based upon the value of deposits or shares.
Source: Federation of Tax Administrators, "State Corporate Income Tax Rates, 2015"

State Individual Income Tax Rates

State	Tax Rate (%)	Income Brackets ($)	Num. of Brackets	Personal Exempt. ($)[1] Single	Personal Exempt. ($)[1] Dependents	Fed. Inc. Tax Ded.
Alaska	None	–	–	–	–	–

Note: Tax rates as of January 1, 2015; Local- and county-level taxes are not included; n/a not applicable; (1) Married joint filers generally receive double the single exemption
Source: Federation of Tax Administrators, "State Individual Income Tax Rates, 2015"

Various State and Local Tax Rates

State	State and Local Sales and Use (%)	State Sales and Use (%)	Gasoline[1] (¢/gal.)	Cigarette[2] ($/pack)	Spirits[3] ($/gal.)	Wine[4] ($/gal.)	Beer[5] ($/gal.)
Alaska	None	None	11.3	2.00	12.80 (f)	2.50	1.07

Note: All tax rates as of January 1, 2015; (1) The American Petroleum Institute has developed a methodology for determining the average tax rate on a gallon of fuel. Rates may include any of the following: excise taxes, environmental fees, storage tank fees, other fees or taxes, general sales tax, and local taxes. In states where gasoline is subject to the general sales tax, or where the fuel tax is based on the average sale price, the average rate determined by API is sensitive to changes in the price of gasoline. States that fully or partially apply general sales taxes to gasoline: CA, CO, GA, IL, IN, MI, NY; (2) The federal excise tax of $1.0066 per pack and local taxes are not included; (3) Rates are those applicable to off-premise sales of 40% alcohol by volume (a.b.v.) distilled spirits in 750ml containers. Local excise taxes are excluded; (4) Rates are those applicable to off-premise sales of 11% a.b.v. non-carbonated wine in 750ml containers; (5) Rates are those applicable to off-premise sales of 4.7% a.b.v. beer in 12 ounce containers; (f) Different rates are also applicable according to alcohol content, place of production, size of container, or place purchased (on- or off-premise or onboard airlines).
Source: Tax Foundation, 2015 Facts & Figures: How Does Your State Compare?

State Business Tax Climate Index Rankings

State	Overall Rank	Corporate Tax Index Rank	Individual Income Tax Index Rank	Sales Tax Index Rank	Unemployment Insurance Tax Index Rank	Property Tax Index Rank
Alaska	4	30	1	5	24	32

Note: The index is a measure of how each state's tax laws affect economic performance. The lower the rank, the more favorable a state's tax system is for business. States without a given tax are given a ranking of 1. The scores/rankings for the District of Columbia do not affect other states. The 2015 index represents the tax climate as of July 1, 2014.
Source: Tax Foundation, State Business Tax Climate Index 2015

COMMERCIAL UTILITIES

Typical Monthly Electric Bills

Area	Commercial Service ($/month)		Industrial Service ($/month)	
	1,500 kWh	40 kW demand 14,000 kWh	1,000 kW demand 200,000 kWh	50,000 kW demand 32,500,000 kWh
City	n/a	n/a	n/a	n/a
Average[1]	201	1,653	26,124	2,639,743

Note: Figures are based on annualized 2014 rates; (1) Average based on 180 utilities surveyed; n/a not available
Source: Edison Electric Institute, Typical Bills and Average Rates Report, Summer 2014

TRANSPORTATION

Means of Transportation to Work

Area	Car/Truck/Van Drove Alone	Car/Truck/Van Car-pooled	Public Transportation Bus	Public Transportation Subway	Public Transportation Railroad	Bicycle	Walked	Other Means	Worked at Home
City	74.4	12.1	2.2	0.0	0.0	1.2	3.4	2.8	4.0
MSA[1]	73.8	12.4	2.0	0.0	0.0	1.0	3.1	3.5	4.3
U.S.	76.4	9.6	2.6	1.8	0.6	0.6	2.8	1.3	4.3

Note: Figures are percentages and cover workers 16 years of age and older; (1) Figures cover the Anchorage, AK Metropolitan Statistical Area—see Appendix B for areas included
Source: U.S. Census Bureau, 2011-2013 American Community Survey 3-Year Estimates

Travel Time to Work

Area	Less Than 10 Minutes	10 to 19 Minutes	20 to 29 Minutes	30 to 44 Minutes	45 to 59 Minutes	60 to 89 Minutes	90 Minutes or More
City	15.3	44.4	22.1	12.0	2.8	1.4	1.9
MSA[1]	15.0	41.1	20.7	11.8	4.5	4.4	2.4
U.S.	13.3	29.7	20.9	20.2	7.7	5.7	2.6

Note: Figures are percentages and include workers 16 years old and over; (1) Figures cover the Anchorage, AK Metropolitan Statistical Area—see Appendix B for areas included
Source: U.S. Census Bureau, 2011-2013 American Community Survey 3-Year Estimates

Travel Time Index

Area	1985	1990	1995	2000	2005	2010	2011
Urban Area[1]	1.18	1.18	1.18	1.18	1.21	1.18	1.18
Average[2]	1.09	1.14	1.16	1.19	1.23	1.18	1.18

Note: Travel Time Index—the ratio of travel time in the peak period to the travel time at free-flow conditions. For example, a value of 1.30 indicates a 20-minute free-flow trip takes 26 minutes in the peak. Free-flow speeds (60 mph on freeways and 35 mph on principal arterials) are used as the comparison threshold; (1) Covers the Anchorage AK urban area; (2) average of 498 urban areas
Source: Texas Transportation Institute, Urban Mobility Report 2012, December 2012

Public Transportation

Agency Name / Mode of Transportation	Vehicles Operated in Maximum Service	Annual Unlinked Passenger Trips (in thous.)	Annual Passenger Miles (in thous.)
Anchorage Public Transportation Dept. (People Mover)			
Bus (directly operated)	44	3,986.9	19,307.3
Demand Response (purchased transportation)	42	184.0	922.9

Source: Federal Transit Administration, National Transit Database, 2013

Air Transportation

Airport Name and Code / Type of Service	Passenger Airlines[1]	Passenger Enplanements	Freight Carriers[2]	Freight (lbs.)
Anchorage International (ANC)				
Domestic service (U.S. carriers - 2014)	25	2,319,343	31	1,235,124,278
International service (U.S. carriers - 2013)	5	1,699	12	305,383,324

Note: (1) Includes all U.S.-based major, minor and commuter airlines that carried at least one passenger during the year; (2) Includes all U.S.-based airlines and freight carriers that transported at least one lb. of freight during the year.
Source: Bureau of Transportation Statistics, The Intermodal Transportation Database, Air Carriers: T-100 Domestic Market (U.S. Carriers), 2014; Bureau of Transportation Statistics, The Intermodal Transportation Database, Air Carriers: T-100 International Market (U.S. Carriers), 2013

Other Transportation Statistics

Major Highways:	None
Amtrak Service:	No
Major Waterways/Ports:	Gulf of Alaska

Source: Amtrak.com; Google Maps

BUSINESSES

Major Business Headquarters

Company Name	Rankings	
	Fortune[1]	Forbes[2]
No companies listed	-	-

Note: (1) Fortune 500—companies that produce a 10-K are ranked 1 to 500 based on 2013 revenue; (2) all private companies with at least $2 billion in annual revenue through the end of their most current fiscal year are ranked 1 to 221; companies listed are headquartered in the city; dashes indicate no ranking
Source: Fortune, "Fortune 500," June 16, 2014; Forbes, "America's Largest Private Companies," November 5, 2014

Minority- and Women-Owned Businesses

Group	All Firms		Firms with Paid Employees			
	Firms	Sales ($000)	Firms	Sales ($000)	Employees	Payroll ($000)
Asian	1,415	331,168	397	290,202	2,836	66,437
Black	680	72,101	87	54,292	1,030	22,278
Hispanic	825	121,023	141	91,944	930	28,512
Women	8,063	1,665,467	1,288	1,492,529	9,775	335,936
All Firms	26,726	42,963,995	6,947	42,051,422	112,855	5,330,369

Note: Figures cover firms located in the city; minority- and women-owned business are defined as firms in which the corresponding group own 51% or more of the stock or equity of the company
Source: U.S. Census Bureau, 2007 Economic Census, Survey of Business Owners (2012 Survey of Business Owners data will be released starting in June 2015)

**HOTELS &
CONVENTION
CENTERS**

Hotels/Motels

Area	5 Star		4 Star		3 Star		2 Star		1 Star		Not Rated	
	Num.	Pct.[3]	Num.	Pct.[3]	Num.	Pct.[3]	Num.	Pct.[3]	Num.	Pct.[3]	Num.	Pct.[3]
City[1]	0	0.0	2	2.3	24	27.9	44	51.2	3	3.5	13	15.1
Total[2]	166	0.9	1,264	7.0	5,718	31.8	9,340	52.0	411	2.3	1,070	6.0

Note: (1) Figures cover Anchorage and vicinity; (2) Figures cover all 100 cities in this book; (3) Percentage of hotels which have a given star rating; Star ratings are determined by expedia.com and offer an indication of the general quality of a particular hotel.
Source: expedia.com, April 2, 2015

Major Convention Centers

Name	Overall Space (sq. ft.)	Exhibit Space (sq. ft.)	Meeting Space (sq. ft.)	Meeting Rooms
Dena'ina Civic and Convention Center	n/a	50,000	n/a	n/a

Note: Table includes convention centers located in the Anchorage, AK metro area; n/a not available
Source: Original research

Living Environment

COST OF LIVING

Cost of Living Index

Composite Index	Groceries	Housing	Utilities	Trans-portation	Health Care	Misc. Goods/ Services
128.1	123.0	157.0	97.2	105.0	139.8	122.1

Note: The Cost of Living Index measures regional differences in the cost of consumer goods and services, excluding taxes and non-consumer expenditures, for professional and managerial households in the top income quintile. It is based on more than 50,000 prices covering almost 60 different items for which prices are collected three times a year by chambers of commerce, economic development organizations or university applied economic centers in each participating urban area. The numbers shown should be read as a percentage above or below the national average of 100. For example, a value of 115.4 in the groceries column indicates that grocery prices are 15.4% higher than the national average. Small differences in the index numbers should not be interpreted as significant; Figures cover the Anchorage AK urban area.
Source: The Council for Community and Economic Research, ACCRA Cost of Living Index, 2014

Grocery Prices

Area[1]	T-Bone Steak ($/pound)	Frying Chicken ($/pound)	Whole Milk ($/half gal.)	Eggs ($/dozen)	Orange Juice ($/64 oz.)	Coffee ($/11.5 oz.)
City[2]	11.85	1.39	2.53	2.29	4.54	5.49
Avg.	10.40	1.37	2.40	1.99	3.46	4.27
Min.	8.48	0.93	1.37	1.30	2.83	2.99
Max.	14.20	2.44	3.62	4.02	6.42	6.96

Note: (1) Values for the local area are compared with the average, minimum and maximum values for all 308 areas in the Cost of Living Index; (2) Figures cover the Anchorage AK urban area; **T-Bone Steak** (price per pound); **Frying Chicken** (price per pound, whole fryer); **Whole Milk** (half gallon carton); **Eggs** (price per dozen, Grade A, large); **Orange Juice** (64 oz. Tropicana or Florida Natural); **Coffee** (11.5 oz. can, vacuum-packed, Maxwell House, Hills Bros, or Folgers).
Source: The Council for Community and Economic Research, ACCRA Cost of Living Index, 2014

Housing and Utility Costs

Area[1]	New Home Price ($)	Apartment Rent ($/month)	All Electric ($/month)	Part Electric ($/month)	Other Energy ($/month)	Telephone ($/month)
City[2]	493,524	1,280	-	82.78	85.24	26.34
Avg.	305,838	919	181.00	93.66	73.14	27.95
Min.	183,142	480	112.00	42.06	23.42	17.16
Max.	1,358,576	3,851	594.00	180.03	440.99	40.42

Note: (1) Values for the local area are compared with the average, minimum and maximum values for all 308 areas in the Cost of Living Index; (2) Figures cover the Anchorage AK urban area; **New Home Price** (2,400 sf living area, 8,000 sf lot, in urban area with full utilities); **Apartment Rent** (950 sf 2 bedroom/1.5 or 2 bath, unfurnished, excluding all utilities except water); **All Electric** (average monthly cost for an all-electric home); **Part Electric** (average monthly cost for a part-electric home); **Other Energy** (average monthly cost for natural gas, fuel oil, coal, wood, and any other forms of energy except electricity); **Telephone** (price includes basic monthly rate for a private residential line plus additional local usage charges incurred by a family of four).
Source: The Council for Community and Economic Research, ACCRA Cost of Living Index, 2014

Health Care, Transportation, and Other Costs

Area[1]	Doctor ($/visit)	Dentist ($/visit)	Optometrist ($/visit)	Gasoline ($/gallon)	Beauty Salon ($/visit)	Men's Shirt ($)
City[2]	167.20	129.47	164.89	3.76	48.53	27.39
Avg.	102.86	87.89	97.66	3.44	34.37	26.74
Min.	67.47	65.78	51.18	3.00	17.43	12.79
Max.	173.50	150.14	235.00	4.33	64.28	49.50

Note: (1) Values for the local area are compared with the average, minimum and maximum values for all 308 areas in the Cost of Living Index; (2) Figures cover the Anchorage AK urban area; **Doctor** (general practitioners routine exam of an established patient); **Dentist** (adult teeth cleaning and periodic oral examination); **Optometrist** (full vision eye exam for established adult patient); **Gasoline** (one gallon regular unleaded, national brand, including all taxes, cash price at self-service pump if available); **Beauty Salon** (woman's shampoo, trim, and blow-dry); **Men's Shirt** (cotton/polyester dress shirt, pinpoint weave, long sleeves).
Source: The Council for Community and Economic Research, ACCRA Cost of Living Index, 2014

HOUSING

House Price Index (HPI)

Area	National Ranking[2]	Quarterly Change (%)	One-Year Change (%)	Five-Year Change (%)
MSA[1]	248	-1.16	1.26	7.37
U.S.[3]	–	1.35	4.91	11.59

Note: The HPI is a weighted repeat sales index. It measures average price changes in repeat sales or refinancings on the same properties. This information is obtained by reviewing repeat mortgage transactions on single-family properties whose mortgages have been purchased or securitized by Fannie Mae or Freddie Mac in January 1975; (1) Anchorage Metropolitan Statistical Area—see Appendix B for areas included; (2) Rankings are based on annual percentage change for all metro areas containing at least 15,000 transactions over the last 10 years and ranges from 1 to 275; (3) figures based on a weighted average of Census Division estimates using a seasonally adjusted, purchase-only index; all figures are for the period ending December 31, 2014
Source: Federal Housing Finance Agency, House Price Index, February 26, 2015

Median Single-Family Home Prices

Area	2012	2013	2014p	Percent Change 2013 to 2014
MSA[1]	n/a	n/a	n/a	n/a
U.S. Average	177.2	197.4	209.0	5.9

Note: Figures are median sales prices of existing single-family homes in thousands of dollars; (p) preliminary; n/a not available; (1) Anchorage, AK Metropolitan Statistical Area—see Appendix B for areas included
Source: National Association of Realtors, Median Sales Price of Existing Single-Family Homes for Metropolitan Areas, 4th Quarter 2014

Qualifying Income Based on Median Sales Price of Existing Single-Family Homes

Area	With 5% Down ($)	With 10% Down ($)	With 20% Down ($)
MSA[1]	n/a	n/a	n/a
U.S. Average	45,863	43,449	38,621

Note: Figures are preliminary; Qualifying income is based on a mortgage rate of 4.0%. Monthly principal and interest payment is limited to 25% of income; n/a not available; (1) Anchorage, AK Metropolitan Statistical Area—see Appendix B for areas included
Source: National Association of Realtors, Qualifying Income Based on Median Sales Price of Existing Single-Family Homes for Metropolitan Areas, 4th Quarter 2014

Median Apartment Condo-Coop Home Prices

Area	2012	2013	2014p	Percent Change 2013 to 2014
MSA[1]	n/a	n/a	n/a	n/a
U.S. Average	173.7	194.9	205.1	5.2

Note: Figures are median sales prices of existing apartment condo-coop homes in thousands of dollars; (p) preliminary; n/a not available; (1) Anchorage, AK Metropolitan Statistical Area—see Appendix B for areas included
Source: National Association of Realtors, Median Sales Price of Existing Apartment Condo-Coop Homes for Metropolitan Areas, 4th Quarter 2014

Gross Monthly Rent

Area	Under $200	$200 -299	$300 -499	$500 -749	$750 -999	$1,000 -1,499	$1,500 and up	Median ($)
City	0.5	0.6	3.9	8.7	22.8	35.4	28.0	1,150
MSA[1]	0.7	0.7	4.0	9.3	23.1	35.1	27.2	1,137
U.S.	1.7	3.2	7.8	22.1	24.3	26.0	14.9	900

Note: Figures are percentages except for Median; Gross rent is the contract rent plus the estimated average monthly cost of utilities (electricity, gas, and water and sewer) and fuels (oil, coal, kerosene, wood, etc.) if these are paid by the renter (or paid for the renter by someone else); (1) Figures cover the Anchorage, AK Metropolitan Statistical Area—see Appendix B for areas included
Source: U.S. Census Bureau, 2011-2013 American Community Survey 3-Year Estimates

Homeownership Rate

Area	2007 (%)	2008 (%)	2009 (%)	2010 (%)	2011 (%)	2012 (%)	2013 (%)	2014 (%)
MSA[1]	n/a	n/a	n/a	n/a	n/a	n/a	n/a	n/a
U.S.	68.1	67.8	67.4	66.9	66.1	65.4	65.1	64.5

Note: (1) Figures cover the Anchorage, AK Metropolitan Statistical Area—see Appendix B for areas included; n/a not available
Source: U.S. Census Bureau, Housing Vacancies and Homeownership Annual Statistics: 2014

Year Housing Structure Built

Area	2010 or Later	2000 -2009	1990 -1999	1980 -1989	1970 -1979	1960 -1969	1950 -1959	1940 -1949	Before 1940	Median Year
City	0.6	13.8	11.2	24.4	29.5	12.2	6.3	1.7	0.4	1980
MSA[1]	1.0	19.1	12.8	24.7	25.5	9.9	5.0	1.5	0.5	1983
U.S.	0.9	15.0	13.9	13.8	15.8	11.0	10.9	5.4	13.3	1976

Note: Figures are percentages except for Median Year; (1) Figures cover the Anchorage, AK Metropolitan Statistical Area—see Appendix B for areas included
Source: U.S. Census Bureau, 2011-2013 American Community Survey 3-Year Estimates

HEALTH

Health Risk Data

Category	MSA[1] (%)	U.S. (%)
Adults aged 18–64 who have any kind of health care coverage	80.9	79.6
Adults who reported being in good or excellent health	86.3	83.1
Adults who are current smokers	18.1	19.6
Adults who are heavy drinkers[2]	6.6	6.1
Adults who are binge drinkers[3]	17.2	16.9
Adults who are overweight (BMI 25.0 - 29.9)	39.8	35.8
Adults who are obese (BMI 30.0 - 99.8)	25.3	27.6
Adults who participated in any physical activities in the past month	83.4	77.1
Adults 50+ who have ever had a sigmoidoscopy or colonoscopy	63.9	67.3
Women aged 40+ who have had a mammogram within the past two years	73.2	74.0
Men aged 40+ who have had a PSA test within the past two years	42.7	45.2
Adults aged 65+ who have had flu shot within the past year	54.5	60.1
Adults who always wear a seatbelt	96.2	93.8

Note: Data as of 2012 unless otherwise noted; (1) Figures cover the Anchorage, AK Metropolitan Statistical Area—see Appendix B for areas included; (2) Heavy drinkers are classified as males having more than two drinks per day or females having more than one drink per day; (3) Binge drinkers are classified as males having five or more drinks on one occasion or females having four or more drinks on one occasion
Source: Centers for Disease Control and Prevention, Behavioral Risk Factor Surveillance System, SMART: Selected Metropolitan/Micropolitan Area Risk Trends, 2012 (Note: the CDC has discontinued this dataset but will be releasing a replacement in late 2015)

Chronic Health Indicators

Category	MSA[1] (%)	U.S. (%)
Adults who have ever been told they had a heart attack	2.6	4.5
Adults who have ever been told they had a stroke	2.2	2.9
Adults who have been told they currently have asthma	10.0	8.9
Adults who have ever been told they have arthritis	21.7	25.7
Adults who have ever been told they have diabetes[2]	7.8	9.7
Adults who have ever been told they had skin cancer	2.7	5.7
Adults who have ever been told they had any other types of cancer	4.2	6.5
Adults who have ever been told they have COPD	4.5	6.2
Adults who have ever been told they have kidney disease	2.2	2.5
Adults who have ever been told they have a form of depression	18.0	18.0

Note: Data as of 2012 unless otherwise noted; (1) Figures cover the Anchorage, AK Metropolitan Statistical Area—see Appendix B for areas included; (2) Figures do not include pregnancy-related, borderline, or pre-diabetes
Source: Centers for Disease Control and Prevention, Behaviorial Risk Factor Surveillance System, SMART: Selected Metropolitan/Micropolitan Area Risk Trends, 2012 (Note: the CDC has discontinued this dataset but will be releasing a replacement in late 2015)

Mortality Rates for the Top 10 Causes of Death in the U.S.

ICD-10[a] Sub-Chapter	ICD-10[a] Code	Age-Adjusted Mortality Rate[1] per 100,000 population	
		County[2]	U.S.
Malignant neoplasms	C00-C97	161.6	166.2
Ischaemic heart diseases	I20-I25	72.7	105.7
Other forms of heart disease	I30-I51	47.8	49.3
Chronic lower respiratory diseases	J40-J47	35.6	42.1
Organic, including symptomatic, mental disorders	F01-F09	54.1	38.1
Cerebrovascular diseases	I60-I69	38.0	37.0
Other external causes of accidental injury	W00-X59	36.3	26.9
Other degenerative diseases of the nervous system	G30-G31	24.8	25.6
Diabetes mellitus	E10-E14	22.7	21.3
Hypertensive diseases	I10-I15	13.2	19.4

Note: (a) ICD-10 = International Classification of Diseases 10th Revision; (1) Mortality rates are a three year average covering 2011-2013; (2) Figures cover Anchorage Borough
Source: Centers for Disease Control and Prevention, National Center for Health Statistics. Compressed Mortality File 1999-2013 on CDC WONDER Online Database, released October 2014. Data are compiled from the Compressed Mortality File 1999-2013, Series 20 No. 2S, 2014.

Mortality Rates for Selected Causes of Death

ICD-10[a] Sub-Chapter	ICD-10[a] Code	Age-Adjusted Mortality Rate[1] per 100,000 population	
		County[2]	U.S.
Assault	X85-Y09	5.9	5.2
Diseases of the liver	K70-K76	19.0	13.2
Human immunodeficiency virus (HIV) disease	B20-B24	*1.7	2.2
Influenza and pneumonia	J09-J18	11.2	15.4
Intentional self-harm	X60-X84	18.1	12.5
Malnutrition	E40-E46	*2.3	0.9
Obesity and other hyperalimentation	E65-E68	*2.4	1.8
Renal failure	N17-N19	9.4	13.1
Transport accidents	V01-V99	9.1	11.7
Viral hepatitis	B15-B19	3.3	2.2

Note: (a) ICD-10 = International Classification of Diseases 10th Revision; (1) Mortality rates are a three year average covering 2011-2013; (2) Figures cover Anchorage Borough; (*) Unreliable data as per CDC
Source: Centers for Disease Control and Prevention, National Center for Health Statistics. Compressed Mortality File 1999-2013 on CDC WONDER Online Database, released October 2014. Data are compiled from the Compressed Mortality File 1999-2013, Series 20 No. 2S, 2014.

Health Insurance Coverage

Area	With Health Insurance	With Private Health Insurance	With Public Health Insurance	Without Health Insurance	Population Under Age 18 Without Health Insurance
City	83.1	67.9	23.9	16.9	11.1
MSA[1]	82.3	66.6	24.6	17.7	11.6
U.S.	85.2	65.2	31.0	14.8	7.3

Note: Figures are percentages that cover the civilian noninstitutionalized population; (1) Figures cover the Anchorage, AK Metropolitan Statistical Area—see Appendix B for areas included
Source: U.S. Census Bureau, 2011-2013 American Community Survey 3-Year Estimates

Number of Medical Professionals

Area[1]	MDs[2]	DOs[2,3]	Dentists	Podiatrists	Chiropractors	Optometrists
Local (number)	927	82	314	13	141	73
Local (rate[4])	310.4	27.5	104.1	4.3	46.7	24.2
U.S. (rate[4])	270.0	20.2	63.1	5.7	25.2	14.9

Note: Data as of 2013 unless noted; (1) Local data covers Anchorage (B) Borough; (2) Data as of 2012 and includes all active, non-federal physicians; (3) Doctor of Osteopathic Medicine; (4) rate per 100,000 population
Source: U.S. Department of Health and Human Services, Health Resources and Services Administration, Bureau of Health Professions, Area Resource File (ARF) 2013-2014

EDUCATION

Public School District Statistics

District Name	Schls	Pupils	Pupil/ Teacher Ratio	Minority Pupils[1] (%)	Free Lunch Eligible[2] (%)	IEP[3] (%)
Anchorage School District	97	48,790	17.0	54.9	34.5	14.2

Note: Table includes school districts with 2,000 or more students; (1) Percentage of students that are not non-Hispanic white; (2) Percentage of students that are eligible for the free lunch program; (3) Percentage of students that have an Individualized Education Program.
Source: U.S. Department of Education, National Center for Education Statistics, Common Core of Data, Local Education Agency (School District) Universe Survey: School Year 2012-2013; U.S. Department of Education, National Center for Education Statistics, Common Core of Data, Public Elementary/Secondary School Universe Survey: School Year 2012-2013

Highest Level of Education

Area	Less than H.S.	H.S. Diploma	Some College, No Deg.	Associate Degree	Bachelor's Degree	Master's Degree	Prof. School Degree	Doctorate Degree
City	7.5	24.5	27.3	8.3	20.3	8.4	2.4	1.3
MSA[1]	7.5	26.2	28.1	8.4	18.8	7.6	2.2	1.2
U.S.	13.7	28.0	21.2	7.9	18.2	7.7	1.9	1.3

Note: Figures cover persons age 25 and over; (1) Figures cover the Anchorage, AK Metropolitan Statistical Area—see Appendix B for areas included
Source: U.S. Census Bureau, 2011-2013 American Community Survey 3-Year Estimates

Educational Attainment by Race

Area	High School Graduate or Higher (%)					Bachelor's Degree or Higher (%)				
	Total	White	Black	Asian	Hisp.[2]	Total	White	Black	Asian	Hisp.[2]
City	92.5	95.9	86.0	76.0	87.8	32.4	37.8	22.4	22.0	22.9
MSA[1]	92.5	95.2	86.0	75.9	88.1	29.7	33.5	21.9	21.7	22.6
U.S.	86.3	88.3	83.1	85.7	64.0	29.1	30.4	18.8	50.7	13.7

Note: Figures shown cover persons 25 years old and over; (1) Figures cover the Anchorage, AK Metropolitan Statistical Area—see Appendix B for areas included; (2) People of Hispanic origin can be of any race
Source: U.S. Census Bureau, 2011-2013 American Community Survey 3-Year Estimates

School Enrollment by Grade and Control

Area	Preschool (%)		Kindergarten (%)		Grades 1 - 4 (%)		Grades 5 - 8 (%)		Grades 9 - 12 (%)	
	Public	Private	Public	Private	Public	Private	Public	Private	Public	Private
City	41.1	58.9	91.3	8.7	92.5	7.5	93.1	6.9	91.4	8.6
MSA[1]	47.7	52.3	89.9	10.1	91.0	9.0	90.8	9.2	90.9	9.1
U.S.	57.7	42.3	87.9	12.1	89.9	10.1	90.0	10.0	90.7	9.3

Note: Figures shown cover persons 3 years old and over; (1) Figures cover the Anchorage, AK Metropolitan Statistical Area—see Appendix B for areas included
Source: U.S. Census Bureau, 2011-2013 American Community Survey 3-Year Estimates

Average Salaries of Public School Classroom Teachers

Area	2013-14		2014-15		Percent Change 2013-14 to 2014-15	Percent Change 2004-05 to 2014-15
	Dollars	Rank[1]	Dollars	Rank[1]		
ALASKA	65,891	7	66,755	7	1.31	27.3
U.S. Average	56,610	–	57,379	–	1.36	20.8

Note: (1) State rank ranges from 1 to 51 where 1 indicates highest salary.
Source: National Education Association, Rankings & Estimates: Rankings of the States 2014 and Estimates of School Statistics 2015, March 2015

Higher Education

Four-Year Colleges			Two-Year Colleges			Medical Schools[1]	Law Schools[2]	Voc/Tech[3]
Public	Private Non-profit	Private For-profit	Public	Private Non-profit	Private For-profit			
1	1	1	0	0	1	0	0	0

Note: Figures cover institutions located within the city limits and include main campuses only; (1) includes schools accredited by the Liaison Committee on Medical Education and the American Osteopathic Association's Commission on Osteopathic College Accreditation; (2) includes ABA-accredited schools, schools with provisional ABA accreditation, and state accredited schools; (3) includes all schools with programs that are less than 2 years.
Source: National Center for Education Statistics, Integrated Postsecondary Education System (IPEDS), 2013-14; Association of American Medical Colleges, Member List, May 1, 2015; American Osteopathic Association, Member List, May 1, 2015; Law School Admission Council, Official Guide to ABA-Approved Law Schools Online, May 1, 2015; Wikipedia, List of Medical Schools in the United States, May 1, 2015; Wikipedia, List of Law Schools in the United States, May 1, 2015

PRESIDENTIAL ELECTION

2012 Presidential Election Results

Area	Obama (%)	Romney (%)	Other (%)
Alaska Districts 18–32	41.5	54.5	4.0
U.S.	51.0	47.2	1.8

Note: Results may not add to 100% due to rounding
Source: Dave Leip's Atlas of U.S. Presidential Elections

EMPLOYERS

Major Employers

Company Name	Industry
Ahtna Technical Services	Building maintenance services
Akima Logistics Services	General warehousing and storage
Alaska Native Tribal Health Consortium	General medical and surgical hospitals
Alaskan Professional Employers	Employee leasing service
ASRC Energy Services	Oil and gas field services
AT&T Alas.com	Telephone communication, except radio
BP Transportation (Alaska)	Crude petroleum production
Bureau of Land Management	Information bureau
Federal Aviation Administration	Aircraft regulating agencies
Federal Express Corporation	Air cargo carrier, scheduled
Fish and Wildlife Service, United States	Fish and wildlife conservation agency, government
Galen Hospital Alaska	General medical and surgical hospitals
Indian Health Service	General medical and surgical hospitals
Municipality of Anchorage	Mayors' office
Nabors Alaska Drilling	Drilling oil and gas wells
United States Department of the Air Force	Air force
USPHS AK Native Medical Center	General medical and surgical hospitals

Note: Companies shown are located within the Anchorage, AK Metropolitan Statistical Area.
Source: Hoovers.com; Wikipedia

PUBLIC SAFETY

Crime Rate

Area	All Crimes	Violent Crimes				Property Crimes		
		Murder	Forcible Rape	Robbery	Aggrav. Assault	Burglary	Larceny -Theft	Motor Vehicle Theft
City	4,831.1	4.7	136.2	174.3	497.9	440.1	3,287.6	290.2
Suburbs[1]	7,133.4	6.6	72.9	39.7	291.4	529.9	5,808.7	384.2
Metro[2]	4,941.6	4.8	133.2	167.9	488.0	444.4	3,408.6	294.7
U.S.	3,098.6	4.5	25.2	109.1	229.1	610.0	1,899.4	221.3

Note: Figures are crimes per 100,000 population; (1) All areas within the metro area that are located outside the city limits; (2) Figures cover the Anchorage, AK Metropolitan Statistical Area—see Appendix B for areas included
Source: FBI Uniform Crime Reports, 2013

Hate Crimes

Area	Number of Quarters Reported	Number of Incidents per Bias Motivation						
		Race	Religion	Sexual Orientation	Ethnicity	Disability	Gender	Gender Identity
City	4	8	0	0	0	0	0	0
U.S.	4	2,871	1,031	1,233	655	83	18	31

Source: Federal Bureau of Investigation, Hate Crime Statistics 2013

Identity Theft Consumer Complaints

Area	Complaints	Complaints per 100,000 Population	Rank[2]
MSA[1]	317	80.0	125
U.S.	332,646	104.3	-

Note: (1) Figures cover the Anchorage, AK Metropolitan Statistical Area—see Appendix B for areas included; (2) Rank ranges from 1 to 380 where 1 indicates greatest number of identity theft complaints per 100,000 population
Source: Federal Trade Commission, Consumer Sentinel Network Data Book for January–December 2014

Fraud and Other Consumer Complaints

Area	Complaints	Complaints per 100,000 Population	Rank[2]
MSA[1]	1,691	426.9	97
U.S.	2,250,205	705.7	-

Note: (1) Figures cover the Anchorage, AK Metropolitan Statistical Area—see Appendix B for areas included; (2) Rank ranges from 1 to 380 where 1 indicates greatest number of identity theft complaints per 100,000 population
Source: Federal Trade Commission, Consumer Sentinel Network Data Book for January–December 2014

RECREATION

Culture

Dance[1]	Theatre[1]	Instrumental Music[1]	Vocal Music[1]	Series and Festivals	Museums and Art Galleries[2]	Zoos and Aquariums[3]
2	4	2	3	2	16	0

Note: (1) Professional perfoming groups; (2) Based on organizations with SIC code 8412; (3) AZA-accredited
Source: The Grey House Performing Arts Directory, 2015-16; Association of Zoos & Aquariums, AZA Member Zoos & Aquariums, April 2015; www.AccuLeads.com, April 2015

Professional Sports Teams

Team Name	League	Year Established
No teams are located in the metro area		

Source: Wikipedia, Major Professional Sports Teams of the United States and Canada, April 2015

CLIMATE

Average and Extreme Temperatures

Temperature	Jan	Feb	Mar	Apr	May	Jun	Jul	Aug	Sep	Oct	Nov	Dec	Yr.
Extreme High (°F)	50	48	51	65	77	85	82	82	73	61	53	48	85
Average High (°F)	22	25	33	43	55	62	65	63	55	41	28	22	43
Average Temp. (°F)	15	18	25	36	47	55	59	57	48	35	22	16	36
Average Low (°F)	8	11	17	28	39	47	51	49	41	28	15	10	29
Extreme Low (°F)	-34	-26	-24	-4	17	33	36	31	19	-5	-21	-30	-34

Note: Figures cover the years 1953-1995
Source: National Climatic Data Center, International Station Meteorological Climate Summary, 9/96

Average Precipitation/Snowfall/Humidity

Precip./Humidity	Jan	Feb	Mar	Apr	May	Jun	Jul	Aug	Sep	Oct	Nov	Dec	Yr.
Avg. Precip. (in.)	0.8	0.8	0.7	0.6	0.7	1.0	1.9	2.4	2.7	1.9	1.1	1.1	15.7
Avg. Snowfall (in.)	10	12	10	5	Tr	0	0	0	Tr	8	12	15	71
Avg. Rel. Hum. 6am (%)	74	74	72	75	73	74	80	84	84	78	78	78	77
Avg. Rel. Hum. 3pm (%)	73	67	57	54	50	55	62	64	64	67	74	76	64

Note: Figures cover the years 1953-1995; Tr = Trace amounts (<0.05 in. of rain; <0.5 in. of snow)
Source: National Climatic Data Center, International Station Meteorological Climate Summary, 9/96

Weather Conditions

	Temperature			Daytime Sky			Precipitation		
	0°F & below	32°F & below	65°F & above	Clear	Partly cloudy	Cloudy	0.01 inch or more precip.	0.1 inch or more snow/ice	Thunder-storms
	32	194	41	50	115	200	113	49	2

Note: Figures are average number of days per year and cover the years 1953-1995
Source: National Climatic Data Center, International Station Meteorological Climate Summary, 9/96

HAZARDOUS WASTE

Superfund Sites

Anchorage has two hazardous waste sites on the EPA's Superfund Final National Priorities List: **Elmendorf Air Force Base**; **Fort Richardson (USARMY)**. There are a total of 1,322 Superfund sites on the list in the U.S. *U.S. Environmental Protection Agency, Final National Priorities List, April 14, 2015*

AIR & WATER QUALITY

Air Quality Trends: Ozone

	2004	2005	2006	2007	2008	2009	2010	2011	2012	2013
MSA[1]	n/a	n/a	n/a	n/a	n/a	n/a	n/a	n/a	n/a	n/a

Note: (1) Data covers the Anchorage, AK Metropolitan Statistical Area—see Appendix B for areas included; n/a not available. The values shown are the composite ozone concentration averages among trend sites based on the highest fourth daily maximum 8-hour concentration in parts per million. These trends are based on sites having an adequate record of monitoring data during the trend period. Data from exceptional events are included.
Source: U.S. Environmental Protection Agency, Air Quality Monitoring Information, "Air Quality Trends by City, 2000-2013"

Air Quality Index

Area	Percent of Days when Air Quality was...[2]					AQI Statistics[2]	
	Good	Moderate	Unhealthy for Sensitive Groups	Unhealthy	Very Unhealthy	Maximum	Median
MSA[1]	67.4	29.0	2.7	0.5	0.3	231	34

Note: (1) Data covers the Anchorage, AK Metropolitan Statistical Area—see Appendix B for areas included; (2) Based on 365 days with AQI data in 2014. Air Quality Index (AQI) is an index for reporting daily air quality. EPA calculates the AQI for five major air pollutants regulated by the Clean Air Act: ground-level ozone, particle pollution (aka particulate matter), carbon monoxide, sulfur dioxide, and nitrogen dioxide. The AQI runs from 0 to 500. The higher the AQI value, the greater the level of air pollution and the greater the health concern. There are six AQI categories: "Good" AQI is between 0 and 50. Air quality is considered satisfactory; "Moderate" AQI is between 51 and 100. Air quality is acceptable; "Unhealthy for Sensitive Groups" When AQI values are between 101 and 150, members of sensitive groups may experience health effects; "Unhealthy" When AQI values are between 151 and 200 everyone may begin to experience health effects; "Very Unhealthy" AQI values between 201 and 300 trigger a health alert; "Hazardous" AQI values over 300 trigger warnings of emergency conditions (not shown).
Source: U.S. Environmental Protection Agency, Air Quality Index Report, 2014

Air Quality Index Pollutants

Area	Percent of Days when AQI Pollutant was...[2]					
	Carbon Monoxide	Nitrogen Dioxide	Ozone	Sulfur Dioxide	Particulate Matter 2.5	Particulate Matter 10
MSA[1]	0.3	0.0	14.8	0.0	55.1	29.9

Note: (1) Data covers the Anchorage, AK Metropolitan Statistical Area—see Appendix B for areas included; (2) Based on 365 days with AQI data in 2014. The Air Quality Index (AQI) is an index for reporting daily air quality. EPA calculates the AQI for five major air pollutants regulated by the Clean Air Act: ground-level ozone, particle pollution (also known as particulate matter), carbon monoxide, sulfur dioxide, and nitrogen dioxide. The AQI runs from 0 to 500. The higher the AQI value, the greater the level of air pollution and the greater the health concern.
Source: U.S. Environmental Protection Agency, Air Quality Index Report, 2014

Maximum Air Pollutant Concentrations: Particulate Matter, Ozone, CO and Lead

	Particulate Matter 10 (ug/m³)	Particulate Matter 2.5 Wtd AM (ug/m³)	Particulate Matter 2.5 24-Hr (ug/m³)	Ozone (ppm)	Carbon Monoxide (ppm)	Lead (ug/m³)
MSA[1] Level	120	6.4	28	n/a	4	n/a
NAAQS[2]	150	15	35	0.075	9	0.15
Met NAAQS[2]	Yes	Yes	Yes	n/a	Yes	n/a

Note: (1) Data covers the Anchorage, AK Metropolitan Statistical Area—see Appendix B for areas included; Data from exceptional events are included; (2) National Ambient Air Quality Standards; ppm = parts per million; ug/m³ = micrograms per cubic meter; n/a not available.
Concentrations: Particulate Matter 10 (coarse particulate)—highest second maximum 24-hour concentration; Particulate Matter 2.5 Wtd AM (fine particulate)—highest weighted annual mean concentration; Particulate Matter 2.5 24-Hour (fine particulate)—highest 98th percentile 24-hour concentration; Ozone—highest fourth daily maximum 8-hour concentration; Carbon Monoxide—highest second maximum non-overlapping 8-hour concentration; Lead—maximum running 3-month average
Source: U.S. Environmental Protection Agency, Air Quality Monitoring Information, "Air Quality Statistics by City, 2013"

Maximum Air Pollutant Concentrations: Nitrogen Dioxide and Sulfur Dioxide

	Nitrogen Dioxide AM (ppb)	Nitrogen Dioxide 1-Hr (ppb)	Sulfur Dioxide AM (ppb)	Sulfur Dioxide 1-Hr (ppb)	Sulfur Dioxide 24-Hr (ppb)
MSA[1] Level	n/a	n/a	n/a	n/a	n/a
NAAQS[2]	53	100	30	75	140
Met NAAQS[2]	n/a	n/a	n/a	n/a	n/a

Note: (1) Data covers the Anchorage, AK Metropolitan Statistical Area—see Appendix B for areas included; Data from exceptional events are included; (2) National Ambient Air Quality Standards; ppm = parts per million; ug/m³ = micrograms per cubic meter; n/a not available.
Concentrations: Nitrogen Dioxide AM—highest arithmetic mean concentration; Nitrogen Dioxide 1-Hr—highest 98th percentile 1-hour daily maximum concentration; Sulfur Dioxide AM—highest annual mean concentration; Sulfur Dioxide 1-Hr—highest 99th percentile 1-hour daily maximum concentration; Sulfur Dioxide 24-Hr—highest second maximum 24-hour concentration
Source: U.S. Environmental Protection Agency, Air Quality Monitoring Information, "Air Quality Statistics by City, 2013"

Drinking Water

Water System Name	Pop. Served	Primary Water Source Type	Violations[1] Health Based	Violations[1] Monitoring/ Reporting
MOA Municipality of Anchorage	221,351	Surface	0	0

Note: (1) Based on violation data from January 1, 2014 to December 31, 2014 (includes unresolved violations from earlier years)
Source: U.S. Environmental Protection Agency, Office of Ground Water and Drinking Water, Safe Drinking Water Information System (based on data extracted January 27, 2015)

Billings, Montana

Background

Established in 1882 in Montana Territory, Billings is the largest city in the state. Located in the Yellowstone Valley, it was once home to prehistoric hunters and the Crow Indians. In 1806, William Clark (of the Lewis and Clark expedition) visited the area and inscribed his name on a pillar in 1806. Shortly after the city's establishment, it prospered as a rail hub by the Northern Pacific Railroad, which came to be known as Clark's Fork Bottom. Billings' location on the Yellowstone River made it a natural central point for traveling steamboats.

Shortly following Billings' settlement, entrepreneur Herman Clark arrived and announced ambitious plans to house 20,000 residents, build nearly a dozen sawmills, roads, and most importantly a massive railroad system. Clark's dream became a reality when the city added a transcontinental railroad in 1883 and had a growing population of 1,500 by 1888. In 1909, the Great Northern Railway laid tracks through Billings and congress passed the Enlarged Homestead act, allowing settlers to lay claims to 320 acres of farmlands. This encouraged more growth, and settlers from around the world arrived in Billings.

Throughout the early half of the 20th Century, Billings established itself as an industrial metropolis in Yellowstone Valley. By 1910, the population had peaked above 10,000 and the city included banks, hotels, shopping districts and government buildings. The discovery of oil and natural gas in the area helped Billings to propel itself into the post-war era of the 1940s and 50s. Due to its oil boom, the city secured a dominant role in the energy industry throughout the 1970s and onward. In the 1970s and 80s, while the rest of the country was experiencing a severe economic recession, Billings constructed the first high rise buildings in Montana and welcomed a handful of development companies to construct local shopping districts and residential areas.

Even in the 1990s, Billings continued to grow by expanding its I-90 corridor, welcoming large hotel chains and Fortune 500 corporations. This trend continued into the 21st century, as companies like GE and Wells Fargo aided in the development of Billings' downtown business district, resulting in Skypoint, the city's highest elevated building and observation point. The rapid pace of construction coupled with low tax rates placed Billings at the top of a number of "best cities" lists. Today, Billings maintains high levels of employment, construction, and investments in the local community.

There is no lack of local flavor and attractions in Billings. The Western Romance Company offers wagons, horses, and equipment for visitors who wish to explore like the cowboys did. For kids and families, Billings offers multiple nearby water parks like Big Splash, the Amusement Park Drive In, and local sports teams like the Billings Mustangs baseball team. Cultural attractions are abundant in the Downtown Historic District, with local theaters and museums, notably the Yellowstone Art Museum and the Billings Symphony Orchestra.

Billings also boasts stunning geography, nestled between the Yellowstone Valley and the Yellowstone River. The surrounding Bighorn and Pyror Mountains help create its desirable semi-arid climate with hot summers and tepid winters.

Rankings

General Rankings

- The editors of *Kiplinger's Personal Finance Magazine* chose the ten best cities of manageable size (less than a million residents) with a sound job market, reasonably priced homes, good schools, and access to excellent healthcare facilities. The Billings metro area earned the #6 spot on the *Kiplinger's* list. *www.kiplinger.com, "10 Great Places to Live," July 2013*

Business/Finance Rankings

- The Billings metro area appeared on the Milken Institute "2013 Best Performing Cities" list. Rank: #50 out of 179 small metro areas. Criteria: job growth; wage and salary growth; high-tech output growth.*Milken Institute, "Best-Performing Cities 2014," January 2015*
- *Forbes* ranked 184 smaller metro areas to determine the nation's "Best Small Places for Business and Careers." The Billings metro area was ranked #40. Criteria: costs (business and living); job growth (past and projected); income growth; educational attainment (college and high school); projected economic growth; cultural and recreational opportunities; net migration patterns; number of highly ranked colleges. *Forbes, "The Best Small Places for Business and Careers 2014," July 23, 2014*

Dating/Romance Rankings

- Of the 100 U.S. cities surveyed by *Men's Health* in its quest to identify the nation's best cities for dating and forming relationships, Billings was ranked #81 for online dating (#1 = best). *Men's Health, "The Best and Worst Cities for Online Dating," January 30, 2013*
- Billings was selected as one of the most romantic cities in America by Amazon.com. The city ranked #17 of 20. Criteria: cities with 100,000 or more residents were ranked on their per capita sales of romance novels and relationship books, romantic comedy movies, romantic music, and sexual wellness products. *Amazon.com, "Top 20 Most Romantic Cities in America," February 5, 2015*

Environmental Rankings

- The Weather Channel determined the nation's snowiest cities, based on the National Oceanic and Atmospheric Administration's 30-year average snowfall data. Among cities with a population of at least 100,000, the #14-ranked city was Billings *weather.com, America's 20 Snowiest Major Cities, February 3, 2014*
- The Billings metro area came in at #47 for the relative comfort of its climate on Sperling's list of "chill cities," as measured by the Sperling Heat Index. All 361 metro areas are included. Criteria included daytime high temperatures, nighttime low temperatures, dew point, and relative humidity at the high temperatures. *www.bertsperling.com, "Sperling's Chill Cities," July 18, 2013*
- Sperling's BestPlaces assessed 379 metropolitan areas of the United States for the likelihood of dangerously extreme weather events or earthquakes. In general the Southeast and South-Central regions have the highest risk of weather extremes and earthquakes, while the Pacific Northwest enjoys the lowest risk. Of the least risky metropolitan areas, the Billings metro area was ranked #22. *www.bestplaces.net, "Safest Places from Natural Disasters," April 2011*

Food/Drink Rankings

- *Men's Health* ranked 100 major U.S. cities in terms of alcohol intoxication. Billings ranked #94 (#1 = most sober).Criteria: binge drinking; alcohol-related traffic accidents, arrests, and fatalities. *Men's Health, "The Drunkest Cities in America," November 19, 2013*

Health/Fitness Rankings

- For the Gallup-Healthways Well-Being Index, researchers asked at least 300 adult residents in each of 189 U.S. metropolitan areas how satisfied they were with the metro area in which they lived. The Billings metro area was among the top ten for residents' satisfaction. *www.gallup.com, "City Satisfaction Highest in Fort Collins-Loveland, Colo.," April 11, 2014*

- *Men's Health* ranked 100 major U.S. cities in terms of the best and worst cities for men. Billings ranked #52. Criteria: thirty-three data points were examined covering health, fitness, and quality of life. *Men's Health, "The Best & Worst Cities for Men 2014," December 6, 2013*

- The Billings metro area appeared in the 2013 Gallup-Healthways Well-Being Index. The area ranked #15 out of 189. The Gallup-Healthways Well-Being Index score is an average of six sub-indexes, which individually examine life evaluation, emotional health, work environment, physical health, healthy behaviors, and access to basic necessities. Results are based on telephone interviews conducted as part of the Gallup-Healthways Well-Being Index survey January 2–December 29, 2012, and January 2–December 30, 2013, with a random sample of 531,630 adults, aged 18 and older, living in metropolitan areas in the 50 U.S. states and the District of Columbia. *Gallup-Healthways, "State of American Well-Being," March 25, 2014*

Real Estate Rankings

- Billings was ranked #154 out of 275 metro areas in terms of house price appreciation in 2014 (#1 = highest rate). *Federal Housing Finance Agency, House Price Index, 4th Quarter 2014*

Safety Rankings

- The National Insurance Crime Bureau ranked 380 metro areas in the U.S. in terms of per capita rates of vehicle theft. The Billings metro area ranked #38 (#1 = highest rate). Criteria: number of vehicle theft offenses per 100,000 inhabitants in 2012. *National Insurance Crime Bureau, "Hot Spots 2012," June 26, 2013*

Seniors/Retirement Rankings

- From its Best Cities for Successful Aging indexes, the Milken Institute generated rankings for metropolitan areas, weighing data in eight categories—health care, wellness, living arrangements, transportation, financial characteristics, education and employment opportunities, community engagement, and overall livability. The Billings metro area was ranked #18 overall in the small metro area category. *Milken Institute, "Best Cities for Successful Aging, 2014"*

- *Forbes* selected the Billings metro area as one of 25 "Best Places for a Working Retirement." Criteria: affordability; improving, above-average economies and job prospects; and a favorable tax climate for retirees. *Forbes.com, "Best Places for a Working Retirement in 2013," February 4, 2013*

Sports/Recreation Rankings

- Billings was chosen as a bicycle friendly community by the League of American Bicyclists. A "Bicycle Friendly Community" welcomes cyclists by providing safe accommodation for cycling and encouraging people to bike for transportation and recreation. There are four award levels: Platinum; Gold; Silver; and Bronze. The community achieved an award level of Bronze. *League of American Bicyclists, "Bicycle Friendly Community Master List," Fall 2013*

Women/Minorities Rankings

- *Women's Health* examined U.S. cities and identified the 100 best cities for women. Billings was ranked #30. Criteria: 30 categories were examined from obesity and breast cancer rates to commuting times and hours spent working out. *Women's Health, "Best Cities for Women 2012"*

Business Environment

CITY FINANCES

City Government Finances

Component	2012 ($000)	2012 ($ per capita)
Total Revenues	163,439	1,569
Total Expenditures	150,128	1,441
Debt Outstanding	108,184	1,039
Cash and Securities[1]	163,109	1,566

Note: (1) Cash and security holdings of a government at the close of its fiscal year, including those of its dependent agencies, utilities, and liquor stores.
Source: U.S Census Bureau, State & Local Government Finances 2012

City Government Revenue by Source

Source	2012 ($000)	2012 ($ per capita)
General Revenue		
From Federal Government	11,434	110
From State Government	14,427	138
From Local Governments	980	9
Taxes		
Property	30,654	294
Sales and Gross Receipts	0	0
Personal Income	0	0
Corporate Income	0	0
Motor Vehicle License	2,016	19
Other Taxes	5,475	53
Current Charges	47,622	457
Liquor Store	0	0
Utility	24,183	232
Employee Retirement	0	0

Source: U.S Census Bureau, State & Local Government Finances 2012

City Government Expenditures by Function

Function	2012 ($000)	2012 ($ per capita)	2012 (%)
General Direct Expenditures			
Air Transportation	13,348	128	8.9
Corrections	0	0	0.0
Education	0	0	0.0
Employment Security Administration	0	0	0.0
Financial Administration	1,225	12	0.8
Fire Protection	15,000	144	10.0
General Public Buildings	1,500	14	1.0
Governmental Administration, Other	3,098	30	2.1
Health	769	7	0.5
Highways	20,500	197	13.7
Hospitals	0	0	0.0
Housing and Community Development	3,410	33	2.3
Interest on General Debt	2,200	21	1.5
Judicial and Legal	1,500	14	1.0
Libraries	2,823	27	1.9
Parking	2,312	22	1.5
Parks and Recreation	4,106	39	2.7
Police Protection	19,518	187	13.0
Public Welfare	0	0	0.0
Sewerage	15,605	150	10.4
Solid Waste Management	10,292	99	6.9
Veterans' Services	0	0	0.0
Liquor Store	0	0	0.0
Utility	28,776	276	19.2
Employee Retirement	0	0	0.0

Source: U.S Census Bureau, State & Local Government Finances 2012

DEMOGRAPHICS

Population Growth

Area	1990 Census	2000 Census	2010 Census	Population Growth (%) 1990-2000	Population Growth (%) 2000-2010
City	81,812	89,847	104,170	9.8	15.9
MSA[1]	121,499	138,904	158,050	14.3	13.8
U.S.	248,709,873	281,421,906	308,745,538	13.2	9.7

Note: (1) Figures cover the Billings, MT Metropolitan Statistical Area—see Appendix B for areas included
Source: U.S. Census Bureau, Census 1990, 2000, 2010

Household Size

Area	Persons in Household (%) One	Two	Three	Four	Five	Six	Seven or More	Average Household Size
City	32.3	35.5	13.8	10.5	5.9	1.3	0.8	2.38
MSA[1]	29.8	37.1	13.4	11.5	5.6	1.5	1.0	2.44
U.S.	27.7	33.6	15.7	13.1	6.0	2.3	1.5	2.64

Note: (1) Figures cover the Billings, MT Metropolitan Statistical Area—see Appendix B for areas included
Source: U.S. Census Bureau, 2011-2013 American Community Survey 3-Year Estimates

Race

Area	White Alone[2] (%)	Black Alone[2] (%)	Asian Alone[2] (%)	AIAN[3] Alone[2] (%)	NHOPI[4] Alone[2] (%)	Other Race Alone[2] (%)	Two or More Races (%)
City	89.0	1.1	1.1	4.4	0.1	1.7	2.7
MSA[1]	90.7	0.8	0.8	3.9	0.1	1.4	2.4
U.S.	73.9	12.6	5.0	0.8	0.2	4.7	2.9

Note: (1) Figures cover the Billings, MT Metropolitan Statistical Area—see Appendix B for areas included; (2) Alone is defined as not being in combination with one or more other races; (3) American Indian and Alaska Native; (4) Native Hawaiian and Other Pacific Islander
Source: U.S. Census Bureau, 2011-2013 American Community Survey 3-Year Estimates

Hispanic or Latino Origin

Area	Total (%)	Mexican (%)	Puerto Rican (%)	Cuban (%)	Other (%)
City	5.5	3.9	0.4	0.0	1.1
MSA[1]	4.9	3.8	0.3	0.0	0.8
U.S.	16.9	10.8	1.6	0.6	3.8

Note: Persons of Hispanic or Latino origin can be of any race; (1) Figures cover the Billings, MT Metropolitan Statistical Area—see Appendix B for areas included
Source: U.S. Census Bureau, 2011-2013 American Community Survey 3-Year Estimates

Segregation

Type	Segregation Indices[1] 1990	2000	2010	2010 Rank[2]	Percent Change 1990-2000	Percent Change 1990-2010	Percent Change 2000-2010
Black/White	n/a	n/a	n/a	n/a	n/a	n/a	n/a
Asian/White	n/a	n/a	n/a	n/a	n/a	n/a	n/a
Hispanic/White	n/a	n/a	n/a	n/a	n/a	n/a	n/a

Note: All figures cover the Metropolitan Statistical Area—see Appendix B for areas included; Figures are based on an analysis of 1990, 2000, and 2010 Census Decennial Census tract data by William H. Frey, Brookings Institution and the University of Michigan Social Science Data Analysis Network. In this analysis all racial groups (whites, blacks, and asians) are non-Hispanic members of those races. Hispanics are shown as a separate category;
(1) Segregation Indices are Dissimilarity Indices that measure the degree to which the minority group is distributed differently than whites across census tracts. They range from 0 (complete integration) to 100 (complete segregation) where the value indicates the percentage of the minority group that needs to move to be distributed exactly like whites; (2) Ranges from 1 (most segregated) to 102 (least segregated); n/a not available.
Source: www.CensusScope.org

Ancestry

Area	German	Irish	English	American	Italian	Polish	French[2]	Scottish	Dutch
City	26.2	12.1	9.8	14.5	3.7	2.0	3.2	2.4	1.8
MSA[1]	28.1	11.8	10.0	15.2	3.1	1.9	3.0	2.6	2.0
U.S.	14.9	10.8	8.0	7.4	5.5	3.0	2.7	1.7	1.4

Note: Figures are the percentage of the total population reporting a particular ancestry. The nine most commonly reported ancestries in the U.S. are shown. Figures include multiple ancestries (e.g. if a person reported being Irish and Italian, they were included in both columns); (1) Figures cover the Billings, MT Metropolitan Statistical Area—see Appendix B for areas included; (2) Excludes Basque
Source: U.S. Census Bureau, 2011-2013 American Community Survey 3-Year Estimates

Foreign-Born Population

Area	Percent of Population Born in								
	Any Foreign Country	Mexico	Asia	Europe	Carribean	South America	Central America[2]	Africa	Canada
City	n/a	n/a	n/a	n/a	n/a	n/a	n/a	n/a	n/a
MSA[1]	n/a	n/a	n/a	n/a	n/a	n/a	n/a	n/a	n/a
U.S.	13.0	3.7	3.8	1.5	1.2	0.9	1.0	0.6	0.3

Note: (1) Figures cover the Billings, MT Metropolitan Statistical Area—see Appendix B for areas included; (2) Excludes Mexico.
Source: U.S. Census Bureau, 2011-2013 American Community Survey 3-Year Estimates

Marital Status

Area	Never Married	Now Married[2]	Separated	Widowed	Divorced
City	30.5	45.8	1.3	6.7	15.7
MSA[1]	27.5	50.1	1.3	6.4	14.7
U.S.	32.7	48.1	2.2	6.0	11.0

Note: Figures are percentages and cover the population 15 years of age and older; (1) Figures cover the Billings, MT Metropolitan Statistical Area—see Appendix B for areas included; (2) Excludes separated
Source: U.S. Census Bureau, 2011-2013 American Community Survey 3-Year Estimates

Disability Status

Area	All Ages	Under 18 Years Old	18 to 64 Years Old	65 Years and Over
City	13.8	5.0	11.6	36.8
MSA[1]	14.1	5.5	11.9	37.1
U.S.	12.3	4.1	10.2	36.3

Note: Figures show percent of the civilian noninstitutionalized population that reported having a disability. Disability status is determined from from six types of difficulty: vision, hearing, cognitive, ambulatory, self-care, and independent living. For children under 5 years old, hearing and vision difficulty are used to determine disability status. For children between the ages of 5 and 14, disability status is determined from hearing, vision, cognitive, ambulatory, and self-care difficulties. For people aged 15 years and older, they are considered to have a disability if they have difficulty with any one of the six difficulty types; (1) Figures cover the Billings, MT Metropolitan Statistical Area—see Appendix B for areas included.
Source: U.S. Census Bureau, 2011-2013 American Community Survey 3-Year Estimates

Age

Area	Percent of Population									Median Age
	Under Age 5	Age 5–19	Age 20–34	Age 35–44	Age 45–54	Age 55–64	Age 65–74	Age 75–84	Age 85+	
City	6.6	18.7	21.6	12.0	13.3	12.9	7.8	4.7	2.5	37.4
MSA[1]	6.3	19.1	19.3	12.1	14.1	13.8	8.0	4.7	2.3	39.0
U.S.	6.4	19.9	20.7	12.9	14.1	12.3	7.6	4.2	1.9	37.4

Note: (1) Figures cover the Billings, MT Metropolitan Statistical Area—see Appendix B for areas included
Source: U.S. Census Bureau, 2011-2013 American Community Survey 3-Year Estimates

Gender

Area	Males	Females	Males per 100 Females
City	51,432	55,776	92.2
MSA[1]	79,631	83,411	95.5
U.S.	154,451,010	159,410,713	96.9

Note: (1) Figures cover the Billings, MT Metropolitan Statistical Area—see Appendix B for areas included
Source: U.S. Census Bureau, 2011-2013 American Community Survey 3-Year Estimates

Religious Groups by Family

Area	Catholic	Baptist	Non-Den.	Methodist[2]	Lutheran	LDS[3]	Pentecostal	Presbyterian[4]	Muslim[5]	Judaism
MSA[1]	12.1	2.5	3.8	2.1	6.1	4.9	4.1	1.8	<0.1	0.1
U.S.	19.1	9.3	4.0	4.0	2.3	2.0	1.9	1.6	0.8	0.7

Note: Figures are the number of adherents as a percentage of the total population; (1) Figures cover the Billings, MT Metropolitan Statistical Area—see Appendix B for areas included; (2) Methodist/Pietist; (3) Latter Day Saints; (4) Reformed; (5) Figures are estimates
Source: Association of Statisticians of American Religious Bodies, 2010 U.S. Religion Census: Religious Congregations & Membership Study

Religious Groups by Tradition

Area	Catholic	Evangelical Protestant	Mainline Protestant	Other Tradition	Black Protestant	Orthodox
MSA[1]	12.1	13.7	8.2	5.2	0.1	0.1
U.S.	19.1	16.2	7.3	4.3	1.6	0.3

Note: Figures are the number of adherents as a percentage of the total population; (1) Figures cover the Billings, MT Metropolitan Statistical Area—see Appendix B for areas included
Source: Association of Statisticians of American Religious Bodies, 2010 U.S. Religion Census: Religious Congregations & Membership Study

ECONOMY

Gross Metropolitan Product

Area	2012	2013	2014	2015	Rank[2]
MSA[1]	8.5	8.7	8.9	9.4	205

Note: Figures are in billions of dollars; (1) Figures cover the Billings, MT Metropolitan Statistical Area—see Appendix B for areas included; (2) Rank is based on 2015 data and ranges from 1 to 363
Source: The U.S. Conference of Mayors, U.S. Metro Economies: GMP and Employment 2013-2015, June 2014

Economic Growth

Area	2010-12 (%)	2013 (%)	2014 (%)	2015 (%)	Rank[2]
MSA[1]	4.2	1.0	1.6	2.7	220
U.S.	2.1	2.0	2.3	3.2	—

Note: Figures are real gross metropolitan product (GMP) growth rates and represent annual average percent change; (1) Figures cover the Billings, MT Metropolitan Statistical Area—see Appendix B for areas included; (2) Rank is based on 2015 data and ranges from 1 to 363
Source: The U.S. Conference of Mayors, U.S. Metro Economies: GMP and Employment 2013-2015, June 2014

Metropolitan Area Exports

Area	2008	2009	2010	2011	2012	2013	Rank[2]
MSA[1]	88.6	70.7	86.7	102.1	141.4	139.8	326

Note: Figures are in millions of dollars; (1) Figures cover the Billings, MT Metropolitan Statistical Area—see Appendix B for areas included; (2) Rank is based on 2013 data and ranges from 1 to 387
Source: U.S. Department of Commerce, International Trade Administration, Office of Trade & Industry Information, Manufacturing & Services, data extracted April 3, 2015

Building Permits

Area	Single-Family			Multi-Family			Total		
	2013	2014	Pct. Chg.	2013	2014	Pct. Chg.	2013	2014	Pct. Chg.
City	481	473	-1.7	558	132	-76.3	1,039	605	-41.8
MSA[1]	974	517	-46.9	1,128	134	-88.1	2,102	651	-69.0
U.S.	620,802	634,597	2.2	370,020	411,766	11.3	990,822	1,046,363	5.6

*Note: (1) Figures cover the Billings, MT Metropolitan Statistical Area—see Appendix B for areas included;
Figures represent new, privately-owned housing units authorized (unadjusted data); All permit data are based
on estimates with imputation.
Source: U.S. Census Bureau, Manufacturing, Mining, and Construction Statistics, Building Permits, 2013, 2014*

Bankruptcy Filings

Area	Business Filings			Nonbusiness Filings		
	2013	2014	% Chg.	2013	2014	% Chg.
Yellowstone County	13	17	30.8	296	263	-11.1
U.S.	33,212	26,983	-18.8	1,038,720	909,812	-12.4

*Note: Business filings include Chapter 7, Chapter 11, Chapter 12, and Chapter 13; Nonbusiness filings include
Chapter 7, Chapter 11, and Chapter 13
Source: Administrative Office of the U.S. Courts, Business and Nonbusiness Bankruptcy, County Cases
Commenced by Chapter of the Bankruptcy Code, During the 12- Month Period Ending December 31, 2013 and
Business and Nonbusiness Bankruptcy, County Cases Commenced by Chapter of the Bankruptcy Code, During
the 12- Month Period Ending December 31, 2014*

Housing Vacancy Rates

Area	Gross Vacancy Rate[2] (%)			Year-Round Vacancy Rate[3] (%)			Rental Vacancy Rate[4] (%)			Homeowner Vacancy Rate[5] (%)		
	2012	2013	2014	2012	2013	2014	2012	2013	2014	2012	2013	2014
MSA[1]	n/a	n/a	n/a	n/a	n/a	n/a	n/a	n/a	n/a	n/a	n/a	n/a
U.S.	13.8	13.6	13.4	10.8	10.7	10.4	8.7	8.3	7.6	2.0	2.0	1.9

*Note: (1) Figures cover the Billings, MT Metropolitan Statistical Area—see Appendix B for areas included; (2)
The percentage of the total housing inventory that is vacant; (3) The percentage of the housing inventory
(excluding seasonal units) that is year-round vacant; (4) The percentage of rental inventory that is vacant for
rent; (5) The percentage of homeowner inventory that is vacant for sale; n/a not available
Source: U.S. Census Bureau, Housing Vacancies and Homeownership Annual Statistics: 2014*

INCOME

Income

Area	Per Capita ($)	Median Household ($)	Average Household ($)
City	27,024	47,196	64,341
MSA[1]	27,609	50,472	66,897
U.S.	27,884	52,176	72,897

*Note: (1) Figures cover the Billings, MT Metropolitan Statistical Area—see Appendix B for areas included
Source: U.S. Census Bureau, 2011-2013 American Community Survey 3-Year Estimates*

Household Income Distribution

Area	Percent of Households Earning							
	Under $15,000	$15,000 -24,999	$25,000 -34,999	$35,000 -49,999	$50,000 -74,999	$75,000 -99,000	$100,000 -149,999	$150,000 and up
City	14.5	12.3	10.3	15.0	18.4	11.5	11.2	6.7
MSA[1]	13.2	11.4	10.4	14.5	19.1	12.7	12.0	6.8
U.S.	13.0	10.9	10.3	13.6	17.9	11.9	12.7	9.6

*Note: (1) Figures cover the Billings, MT Metropolitan Statistical Area—see Appendix B for areas included
Source: U.S. Census Bureau, 2011-2013 American Community Survey 3-Year Estimates*

Poverty Rate

Area	All Ages	Under 18 Years Old	18 to 64 Years Old	65 Years and Over
City	15.2	19.6	14.8	10.2
MSA[1]	12.8	16.3	12.4	9.1
U.S.	15.9	22.4	14.8	9.5

Note: Figures are percentage of people whose income during the past 12 months was below the poverty level; (1) Figures cover the Billings, MT Metropolitan Statistical Area—see Appendix B for areas included
Source: U.S. Census Bureau, 2011-2013 American Community Survey 3-Year Estimates

EMPLOYMENT

Labor Force and Employment

Area	Civilian Labor Force			Workers Employed		
	Dec. 2013	Dec. 2014	% Chg.	Dec. 2013	Dec. 2014	% Chg.
City	56,312	56,686	0.7	54,003	54,802	1.5
MSA[1]	85,366	85,903	0.6	81,779	82,995	1.5
U.S.	154,408,000	155,521,000	0.7	144,423,000	147,190,000	1.9

Note: Data is not seasonally adjusted and covers workers 16 years of age and older; (1) Figures cover the Billings, MT Metropolitan Statistical Area—see Appendix B for areas included
Source: Bureau of Labor Statistics, Local Area Unemployment Statistics

Unemployment Rate

Area	2014											
	Jan.	Feb.	Mar.	Apr.	May	Jun.	Jul.	Aug.	Sep.	Oct.	Nov.	Dec.
City	4.5	4.3	4.4	3.5	3.3	3.9	3.6	3.6	3.3	3.2	3.4	3.3
MSA[1]	4.6	4.4	4.5	3.6	3.4	3.9	3.7	3.6	3.3	3.2	3.6	3.4
U.S.	7.0	7.0	6.8	5.9	6.1	6.3	6.5	6.3	5.7	5.5	5.5	5.4

Note: Data is not seasonally adjusted and covers workers 16 years of age and older; (1) Figures cover the Billings, MT Metropolitan Statistical Area—see Appendix B for areas included
Source: Bureau of Labor Statistics, Local Area Unemployment Statistics

Employment by Occupation

Occupation Classification	City (%)	MSA[1] (%)	U.S. (%)
Management, Business, Science, and Arts	33.2	31.8	36.2
Natural Resources, Construction, and Maintenance	9.9	11.9	9.0
Production, Transportation, and Material Moving	9.7	10.8	12.1
Sales and Office	26.0	26.1	24.4
Service	21.3	19.4	18.3

Note: Figures cover employed civilians 16 years of age and older; (1) Figures cover the Billings, MT Metropolitan Statistical Area—see Appendix B for areas included
Source: U.S. Census Bureau, 2011-2013 American Community Survey 3-Year Estimates

Employment by Industry

Sector	MSA[1]		U.S.
	Number of Employees	Percent of Total	Percent of Total
Construction, Mining, and Logging	n/a	n/a	5.0
Education and Health Services	14,200	17.0	15.5
Financial Activities	n/a	n/a	5.7
Government	9,800	11.7	15.8
Information	n/a	n/a	2.0
Leisure and Hospitality	10,500	12.5	10.3
Manufacturing	n/a	n/a	8.7
Other Services	n/a	n/a	4.0
Professional and Business Services	8,700	10.4	13.8
Retail Trade	n/a	n/a	11.4
Transportation, Warehousing, and Utilities	n/a	n/a	3.9
Wholesale Trade	n/a	n/a	4.2

Note: Figures are non-farm employment as of December 2014. Figures are not seasonally adjusted and include workers 16 years of age and older; (1) Figures cover the Billings, MT Metropolitan Statistical Area—see Appendix B for areas included; n/a not available
Source: Bureau of Labor Statistics, Current Employment Statistics, Employment, Hours, and Earnings

Occupations with Greatest Projected Employment Growth: 2012 – 2022

Occupation[1]	2012 Employment	2022 Projected Employment	Numeric Employment Change	Percent Employment Change
Retail Salespersons	13,950	16,680	2,730	19.6
Combined Food Preparation and Serving Workers, Including Fast Food	10,650	12,940	2,290	21.5
Bookkeeping, Accounting, and Auditing Clerks	11,340	13,350	2,010	17.7
Registered Nurses	8,780	10,560	1,780	20.4
Secretaries and Administrative Assistants, Except Legal, Medical, and Executive	10,500	12,210	1,710	16.3
Waiters and Waitresses	8,960	10,440	1,480	16.5
Cashiers	14,680	16,130	1,450	9.8
Personal Care Aides	6,350	7,680	1,330	20.8
Maids and Housekeeping Cleaners	5,930	7,250	1,320	22.2
Heavy and Tractor-Trailer Truck Drivers	7,070	8,320	1,250	17.7

Note: Projections cover Montana; (1) Sorted by numeric employment change
Source: www.projectionscentral.com, State Occupational Projections, 2012–2022 Long-Term Projections

Fastest Growing Occupations: 2012 – 2022

Occupation[1]	2012 Employment	2022 Projected Employment	Numeric Employment Change	Percent Employment Change
Veterinary Technologists and Technicians	410	580	170	38.9
Roustabouts, Oil and Gas	700	960	260	36.8
Rotary Drill Operators, Oil and Gas	290	400	110	36.4
Aircraft Mechanics and Service Technicians	360	480	120	33.4
Software Developers, Systems Software	410	550	140	33.2
Medical Secretaries	2,160	2,850	690	32.2
Surgical Technologists	410	540	130	32.1
Physician Assistants	430	560	130	31.7
Market Research Analysts and Marketing Specialists	570	750	180	31.4
Wellhead Pumpers	590	780	190	31.4

Note: Projections cover Montana; (1) Sorted by percent employment change and excludes occupations with numeric employment change less than 100
Source: www.projectionscentral.com, State Occupational Projections, 2012–2022 Long-Term Projections

Average Wages

Occupation	$/Hr.	Occupation	$/Hr.
Accountants and Auditors	29.56	Maids and Housekeeping Cleaners	10.18
Automotive Mechanics	20.43	Maintenance and Repair Workers	15.40
Bookkeepers	16.29	Marketing Managers	n/a
Carpenters	19.33	Nuclear Medicine Technologists	n/a
Cashiers	10.05	Nurses, Licensed Practical	19.04
Clerks, General Office	14.68	Nurses, Registered	31.34
Clerks, Receptionists/Information	13.27	Nursing Assistants	12.31
Clerks, Shipping/Receiving	13.31	Packers and Packagers, Hand	11.20
Computer Programmers	27.50	Physical Therapists	35.01
Computer Systems Analysts	35.04	Postal Service Mail Carriers	25.15
Computer User Support Specialists	21.03	Real Estate Brokers	22.10
Cooks, Restaurant	10.31	Retail Salespersons	13.67
Dentists	73.25	Sales Reps., Exc. Tech./Scientific	25.53
Electrical Engineers	36.65	Sales Reps., Tech./Scientific	n/a
Electricians	28.93	Secretaries, Exc. Legal/Med./Exec.	14.85
Financial Managers	55.25	Security Guards	11.70
First-Line Supervisors/Managers, Sales	19.30	Surgeons	n/a
Food Preparation Workers	9.55	Teacher Assistants	13.70
General and Operations Managers	47.00	Teachers, Elementary School	24.10
Hairdressers/Cosmetologists	18.62	Teachers, Secondary School	26.70
Internists	n/a	Telemarketers	13.17
Janitors and Cleaners	12.51	Truck Drivers, Heavy/Tractor-Trailer	23.71
Landscaping/Groundskeeping Workers	11.85	Truck Drivers, Light/Delivery Svcs.	17.24
Lawyers	35.98	Waiters and Waitresses	9.33

Note: Wage data covers the Billings, MT Metropolitan Statistical Area—see Appendix B for areas included;
Hourly wages for elementary/secondary school teachers and teacher assistants were calculated by the editors
from annual wage data assuming a 40 hour work week; n/a not available.
Source: Bureau of Labor Statistics, Metro Area Occupational Employment and Wage Estimates, May 2014

TAXES

State Corporate Income Tax Rates

State	Tax Rate (%)	Income Brackets ($)	Num. of Brackets	Financial Institution Tax Rate (%)[a]	Federal Income Tax Ded.
Montana	6.75 (p)	Flat rate	1	6.75 (p)	No

Note: Tax rates as of January 1, 2015; (a) Rates listed are the corporate income tax rate applied to financial institutions or excise taxes based on income. Some states have other taxes based upon the value of deposits or shares; (p) Montana levies a 7% tax on taxpayers using water's edge combination. The minimum tax per corporation is $50; the $50 minimum applies to each corporation included on a combined tax return. Taxpayers with gross sales in Montana of $100,000 or less maypay an alternative tax of 0.5% on such sales, instead of the net income tax.
Source: Federation of Tax Administrators, "State Corporate Income Tax Rates, 2015"

State Individual Income Tax Rates

State	Tax Rate (%)	Income Brackets ($)	Num. of Brackets	Personal Exempt. ($)[1] Single	Dependents	Fed. Inc. Tax Ded.
Montana (a)	1.0 - 6.9	2,800 - 17,100	7	2,280	2,280	Yes (n)

Note: Tax rates as of January 1, 2015; Local- and county-level taxes are not included; n/a not applicable; (1) Married joint filers generally receive double the single exemption; (a) 17 states have statutory provision for automatically adjusting to the rate of inflation the dollar values of the income tax brackets, standard deductions, and/or personal exemptions. Massachusetts, Michigan, and Nebraska index the personal exemptiononly. Oregon does not index the income brackets for $125,000 and over. Maine has suspended indexing for 2014 and 2015; (n) The deduction for federal income tax is limited to $5,000 for individuals and $10,000 for joint returns in Missouri and Montana, and to $6,350 for all filers in Oregon.
Source: Federation of Tax Administrators, "State Individual Income Tax Rates, 2015"

Various State and Local Tax Rates

State	State and Local Sales and Use (%)	State Sales and Use (%)	Gasoline[1] (¢/gal.)	Cigarette[2] ($/pack)	Spirits[3] ($/gal.)	Wine[4] ($/gal.)	Beer[5] ($/gal.)
Montana	None	None (d)	27.75	1.70	9.74 (g)	1.06	0.14

Note: All tax rates as of January 1, 2015; (1) The American Petroleum Institute has developed a methodology for determining the average tax rate on a gallon of fuel. Rates may include any of the following: excise taxes, environmental fees, storage tank fees, other fees or taxes, general sales tax, and local taxes. In states where gasoline is subject to the general sales tax, or where the fuel tax is based on the average sale price, the average rate determined by API is sensitive to changes in the price of gasoline. States that fully or partially apply general sales taxes to gasoline: CA, CO, GA, IL, IN, MI, NY; (2) The federal excise tax of $1.0066 per pack and local taxes are not included; (3) Rates are those applicable to off-premise sales of 40% alcohol by volume (a.b.v.) distilled spirits in 750ml containers. Local excise taxes are excluded; (4) Rates are those applicable to off-premise sales of 11% a.b.v. non-carbonated wine in 750ml containers; (5) Rates are those applicable to off-premise sales of 4.7% a.b.v. beer in 12 ounce containers; (d) Due to data limitations, the table does not include sales taxes in local resort areas in Montana; (g) States where the government controls sales. In these "control states," products are subject to ad valorem mark-up and excise taxes. The excise tax rate is calculated using a methodology developed by the Distilled Spirits Council of the United States.
Source: Tax Foundation, 2015 Facts & Figures: How Does Your State Compare?

State Business Tax Climate Index Rankings

State	Overall Rank	Corporate Tax Index Rank	Individual Income Tax Index Rank	Sales Tax Index Rank	Unemployment Insurance Tax Index Rank	Property Tax Index Rank
Montana	6	18	20	3	18	8

Note: The index is a measure of how each state's tax laws affect economic performance. The lower the rank, the more favorable a state's tax system is for business. States without a given tax are given a ranking of 1. The scores/rankings for the District of Columbia do not affect other states. The 2015 index represents the tax climate as of July 1, 2014.
Source: Tax Foundation, State Business Tax Climate Index 2015

COMMERCIAL UTILITIES

Typical Monthly Electric Bills

Area	Commercial Service ($/month)		Industrial Service ($/month)	
	1,500 kWh	40 kW demand 14,000 kWh	1,000 kW demand 200,000 kWh	50,000 kW demand 32,500,000 kWh
City	n/a	n/a	n/a	n/a
Average[1]	201	1,653	26,124	2,639,743

Note: Figures are based on annualized 2014 rates; (1) Average based on 180 utilities surveyed; n/a not available
Source: Edison Electric Institute, Typical Bills and Average Rates Report, Summer 2014

TRANSPORTATION

Means of Transportation to Work

Area	Car/Truck/Van Drove Alone	Car/Truck/Van Car-pooled	Public Transportation Bus	Public Transportation Subway	Public Transportation Railroad	Bicycle	Walked	Other Means	Worked at Home
City	78.5	10.5	1.1	0.0	0.0	1.2	3.6	0.9	4.1
MSA[1]	78.7	10.8	1.0	0.0	0.0	0.9	3.5	1.0	4.0
U.S.	76.4	9.6	2.6	1.8	0.6	0.6	2.8	1.3	4.3

Note: Figures are percentages and cover workers 16 years of age and older; (1) Figures cover the Billings, MT Metropolitan Statistical Area—see Appendix B for areas included
Source: U.S. Census Bureau, 2011-2013 American Community Survey 3-Year Estimates

Travel Time to Work

Area	Less Than 10 Minutes	10 to 19 Minutes	20 to 29 Minutes	30 to 44 Minutes	45 to 59 Minutes	60 to 89 Minutes	90 Minutes or More
City	19.6	51.2	19.2	5.0	1.8	1.2	2.0
MSA[1]	18.2	43.6	22.6	9.0	2.4	1.7	2.5
U.S.	13.3	29.7	20.9	20.2	7.7	5.7	2.6

Note: Figures are percentages and include workers 16 years old and over; (1) Figures cover the Billings, MT Metropolitan Statistical Area—see Appendix B for areas included
Source: U.S. Census Bureau, 2011-2013 American Community Survey 3-Year Estimates

Travel Time Index

Area	1985	1990	1995	2000	2005	2010	2011
Urban Area[1]	n/a	n/a	n/a	n/a	n/a	n/a	n/a
Average[2]	1.09	1.14	1.16	1.19	1.23	1.18	1.18

Note: Travel Time Index—the ratio of travel time in the peak period to the travel time at free-flow conditions. For example, a value of 1.30 indicates a 20-minute free-flow trip takes 26 minutes in the peak. Free-flow speeds (60 mph on freeways and 35 mph on principal arterials) are used as the comparison threshold; (1) Data for the Billings, MT urban area was not available; (2) average of 498 urban areas
Source: Texas Transportation Institute, Urban Mobility Report 2012, December 2012

Public Transportation

Agency Name / Mode of Transportation	Vehicles Operated in Maximum Service	Annual Unlinked Passenger Trips (in thous.)	Annual Passenger Miles (in thous.)
Billings Metropolitan Transit (Billings MET Transit)			
Bus (directly operated)	20	609.2	2,344.1
Demand Response (directly operated)	11	53.6	395.7

Source: Federal Transit Administration, National Transit Database, 2013

Air Transportation

Airport Name and Code / Type of Service	Passenger Airlines[1]	Passenger Enplanements	Freight Carriers[2]	Freight (lbs.)
Logan International (BIL)				
Domestic service (U.S. carriers - 2014)	14	419,745	7	27,929,957
International service (U.S. carriers - 2013)	1	18	0	0

Note: (1) Includes all U.S.-based major, minor and commuter airlines that carried at least one passenger during the year; (2) Includes all U.S.-based airlines and freight carriers that transported at least one lb. of freight during the year.
Source: Bureau of Transportation Statistics, The Intermodal Transportation Database, Air Carriers: T-100 Domestic Market (U.S. Carriers), 2014; Bureau of Transportation Statistics, The Intermodal Transportation Database, Air Carriers: T-100 International Market (U.S. Carriers), 2013

Other Transportation Statistics

Major Highways:	I-90; I-94; SR-87
Amtrak Service:	No
Major Waterways/Ports:	Yellowstone River

Source: Amtrak.com; Google Maps

BUSINESSES

Major Business Headquarters

Company Name	Rankings	
	Fortune[1]	Forbes[2]
No companies listed	-	-

Note: (1) Fortune 500—companies that produce a 10-K are ranked 1 to 500 based on 2013 revenue; (2) all private companies with at least $2 billion in annual revenue through the end of their most current fiscal year are ranked 1 to 221; companies listed are headquartered in the city; dashes indicate no ranking
Source: Fortune, "Fortune 500," June 16, 2014; Forbes, "America's Largest Private Companies," November 5, 2014

Minority- and Women-Owned Businesses

Group	All Firms		Firms with Paid Employees			
	Firms	Sales ($000)	Firms	Sales ($000)	Employees	Payroll ($000)
Asian	122	30,909	24	29,099	152	6,409
Black	58	15,535	16	12,804	21	1,297
Hispanic	(s)	(s)	(s)	(s)	(s)	(s)
Women	3,122	402,079	585	334,328	3,706	72,251
All Firms	11,697	15,961,953	3,724	15,598,880	59,722	1,967,731

Note: Figures cover firms located in the city; minority- and women-owned business are defined as firms in which the corresponding group own 51% or more of the stock or equity of the company; (s) estimates are suppressed when publication standards are not met
Source: U.S. Census Bureau, 2007 Economic Census, Survey of Business Owners (2012 Survey of Business Owners data will be released starting in June 2015)

HOTELS & CONVENTION CENTERS

Hotels/Motels

Area	5 Star		4 Star		3 Star		2 Star		1 Star		Not Rated	
	Num.	Pct.[3]	Num.	Pct.[3]	Num.	Pct.[3]	Num.	Pct.[3]	Num.	Pct.[3]	Num.	Pct.[3]
City[1]	0	0.0	1	2.6	8	20.5	29	74.4	0	0.0	1	2.6
Total[2]	166	0.9	1,264	7.0	5,718	31.8	9,340	52.0	411	2.3	1,070	6.0

Note: (1) Figures cover Billings and vicinity; (2) Figures cover all 100 cities in this book; (3) Percentage of hotels which have a given star rating; Star ratings are determined by expedia.com and offer an indication of the general quality of a particular hotel.
Source: expedia.com, April 2, 2015

Major Convention Centers

Name	Overall Space (sq. ft.)	Exhibit Space (sq. ft.)	Meeting Space (sq. ft.)	Meeting Rooms
Billings Convention Center	50,000	n/a	n/a	n/a

Note: Table includes convention centers located in the Billings, MT metro area; n/a not available
Source: Original research

Living Environment

COST OF LIVING

Cost of Living Index

Composite Index	Groceries	Housing	Utilities	Trans-portation	Health Care	Misc. Goods/Services
n/a	n/a	n/a	n/a	n/a	n/a	n/a

Note: The Cost of Living Index measures regional differences in the cost of consumer goods and services, excluding taxes and non-consumer expenditures, for professional and managerial households in the top income quintile. It is based on more than 50,000 prices covering almost 60 different items for which prices are collected three times a year by chambers of commerce, economic development organizations or university applied economic centers in each participating urban area. The numbers shown should be read as a percentage above or below the national average of 100. For example, a value of 115.4 in the groceries column indicates that grocery prices are 15.4% higher than the national average. Small differences in the index numbers should not be interpreted as significant; n/a not available.
Source: The Council for Community and Economic Research, ACCRA Cost of Living Index, 2014

Grocery Prices

Area[1]	T-Bone Steak ($/pound)	Frying Chicken ($/pound)	Whole Milk ($/half gal.)	Eggs ($/dozen)	Orange Juice ($/64 oz.)	Coffee ($/11.5 oz.)
City[2]	n/a	n/a	n/a	n/a	n/a	n/a
Avg.	10.40	1.37	2.40	1.99	3.46	4.27
Min.	8.48	0.93	1.37	1.30	2.83	2.99
Max.	14.20	2.44	3.62	4.02	6.42	6.96

Note: (1) Values for the local area are compared with the average, minimum and maximum values for all 308 areas in the Cost of Living Index; (2) Figures cover the Billings MT urban area; n/a not available; **T-Bone Steak** *(price per pound);* **Frying Chicken** *(price per pound, whole fryer);* **Whole Milk** *(half gallon carton);* **Eggs** *(price per dozen, Grade A, large);* **Orange Juice** *(64 oz. Tropicana or Florida Natural);* **Coffee** *(11.5 oz. can, vacuum-packed, Maxwell House, Hills Bros, or Folgers).*
Source: The Council for Community and Economic Research, ACCRA Cost of Living Index, 2014

Housing and Utility Costs

Area[1]	New Home Price ($)	Apartment Rent ($/month)	All Electric ($/month)	Part Electric ($/month)	Other Energy ($/month)	Telephone ($/month)
City[2]	n/a	n/a	n/a	n/a	n/a	n/a
Avg.	305,838	919	181.00	93.66	73.14	27.95
Min.	183,142	480	112.00	42.06	23.42	17.16
Max.	1,358,576	3,851	594.00	180.03	440.99	40.42

Note: (1) Values for the local area are compared with the average, minimum and maximum values for all 308 areas in the Cost of Living Index; (2) Figures cover the Billings MT urban area; n/a not available; **New Home Price** *(2,400 sf living area, 8,000 sf lot, in urban area with full utilities);* **Apartment Rent** *(950 sf 2 bedroom/1.5 or 2 bath, unfurnished, excluding all utilities except water);* **All Electric** *(average monthly cost for an all-electric home);* **Part Electric** *(average monthly cost for a part-electric home);* **Other Energy** *(average monthly cost for natural gas, fuel oil, coal, wood, and any other forms of energy except electricity);* **Telephone** *(price includes basic monthly rate for a private residential line plus additional local usage charges incurred by a family of four).*
Source: The Council for Community and Economic Research, ACCRA Cost of Living Index, 2014

Health Care, Transportation, and Other Costs

Area[1]	Doctor ($/visit)	Dentist ($/visit)	Optometrist ($/visit)	Gasoline ($/gallon)	Beauty Salon ($/visit)	Men's Shirt ($)
City[2]	n/a	n/a	n/a	n/a	n/a	n/a
Avg.	102.86	87.89	97.66	3.44	34.37	26.74
Min.	67.47	65.78	51.18	3.00	17.43	12.79
Max.	173.50	150.14	235.00	4.33	64.28	49.50

Note: (1) Values for the local area are compared with the average, minimum and maximum values for all 308 areas in the Cost of Living Index; (2) Figures cover the Billings MT urban area; n/a not available; **Doctor** *(general practitioners routine exam of an established patient);* **Dentist** *(adult teeth cleaning and periodic oral examination);* **Optometrist** *(full vision eye exam for established adult patient);* **Gasoline** *(one gallon regular unleaded, national brand, including all taxes, cash price at self-service pump if available);* **Beauty Salon** *(woman's shampoo, trim, and blow-dry);* **Men's Shirt** *(cotton/polyester dress shirt, pinpoint weave, long sleeves).*
Source: The Council for Community and Economic Research, ACCRA Cost of Living Index, 2014

HOUSING

House Price Index (HPI)

Area	National Ranking[2]	Quarterly Change (%)	One-Year Change (%)	Five-Year Change (%)
MSA[1]	154	-1.43	3.86	11.67
U.S.[3]	–	1.35	4.91	11.59

Note: The HPI is a weighted repeat sales index. It measures average price changes in repeat sales or refinancings on the same properties. This information is obtained by reviewing repeat mortgage transactions on single-family properties whose mortgages have been purchased or securitized by Fannie Mae or Freddie Mac in January 1975; (1) Billings Metropolitan Statistical Area—see Appendix B for areas included; (2) Rankings are based on annual percentage change for all metro areas containing at least 15,000 transactions over the last 10 years and ranges from 1 to 275; (3) figures based on a weighted average of Census Division estimates using a seasonally adjusted, purchase-only index; all figures are for the period ending December 31, 2014
Source: Federal Housing Finance Agency, House Price Index, February 26, 2015

Median Single-Family Home Prices

Area	2012	2013	2014p	Percent Change 2013 to 2014
MSA[1]	n/a	n/a	n/a	n/a
U.S. Average	177.2	197.4	209.0	5.9

Note: Figures are median sales prices of existing single-family homes in thousands of dollars; (p) preliminary; n/a not available; (1) Billings, MT Metropolitan Statistical Area—see Appendix B for areas included
Source: National Association of Realtors, Median Sales Price of Existing Single-Family Homes for Metropolitan Areas, 4th Quarter 2014

Qualifying Income Based on Median Sales Price of Existing Single-Family Homes

Area	With 5% Down ($)	With 10% Down ($)	With 20% Down ($)
MSA[1]	n/a	n/a	n/a
U.S. Average	45,863	43,449	38,621

Note: Figures are preliminary; Qualifying income is based on a mortgage rate of 4.0%. Monthly principal and interest payment is limited to 25% of income; n/a not available; (1) Billings, MT Metropolitan Statistical Area—see Appendix B for areas included
Source: National Association of Realtors, Qualifying Income Based on Median Sales Price of Existing Single-Family Homes for Metropolitan Areas, 4th Quarter 2014

Median Apartment Condo-Coop Home Prices

Area	2012	2013	2014p	Percent Change 2013 to 2014
MSA[1]	n/a	n/a	n/a	n/a
U.S. Average	173.7	194.9	205.1	5.2

Note: Figures are median sales prices of existing apartment condo-coop homes in thousands of dollars; (p) preliminary; n/a not available; (1) Billings, MT Metropolitan Statistical Area—see Appendix B for areas included
Source: National Association of Realtors, Median Sales Price of Existing Apartment Condo-Coop Homes for Metropolitan Areas, 4th Quarter 2014

Gross Monthly Rent

Area	Under $200	$200 -299	$300 -499	$500 -749	$750 -999	$1,000 -1,499	$1,500 and up	Median ($)
City	2.5	3.4	10.3	38.5	23.3	15.8	6.2	718
MSA[1]	2.4	3.2	11.1	38.9	23.0	15.1	6.2	711
U.S.	1.7	3.2	7.8	22.1	24.3	26.0	14.9	900

Note: Figures are percentages except for Median; Gross rent is the contract rent plus the estimated average monthly cost of utilities (electricity, gas, and water and sewer) and fuels (oil, coal, kerosene, wood, etc.) if these are paid by the renter (or paid for the renter by someone else); (1) Figures cover the Billings, MT Metropolitan Statistical Area—see Appendix B for areas included
Source: U.S. Census Bureau, 2011-2013 American Community Survey 3-Year Estimates

Homeownership Rate

Area	2007 (%)	2008 (%)	2009 (%)	2010 (%)	2011 (%)	2012 (%)	2013 (%)	2014 (%)
MSA[1]	n/a	n/a	n/a	n/a	n/a	n/a	n/a	n/a
U.S.	68.1	67.8	67.4	66.9	66.1	65.4	65.1	64.5

Note: (1) Figures cover the Billings, MT Metropolitan Statistical Area—see Appendix B for areas included; n/a not available
Source: U.S. Census Bureau, Housing Vacancies and Homeownership Annual Statistics: 2014

Year Housing Structure Built

Area	2010 or Later	2000 -2009	1990 -1999	1980 -1989	1970 -1979	1960 -1969	1950 -1959	1940 -1949	Before 1940	Median Year
City	1.4	14.7	10.3	11.6	20.1	10.1	16.1	6.7	8.8	1974
MSA[1]	1.5	16.1	11.2	12.1	21.1	8.3	12.9	5.7	11.1	1976
U.S.	0.9	15.0	13.9	13.8	15.8	11.0	10.9	5.4	13.3	1976

Note: Figures are percentages except for Median Year; (1) Figures cover the Billings, MT Metropolitan Statistical Area—see Appendix B for areas included
Source: U.S. Census Bureau, 2011-2013 American Community Survey 3-Year Estimates

HEALTH

Health Risk Data

Category	MSA[1] (%)	U.S. (%)
Adults aged 18–64 who have any kind of health care coverage	80.0	79.6
Adults who reported being in good or excellent health	84.6	83.1
Adults who are current smokers	20.0	19.6
Adults who are heavy drinkers[2]	9.1	6.1
Adults who are binge drinkers[3]	22.5	16.9
Adults who are overweight (BMI 25.0 - 29.9)	38.5	35.8
Adults who are obese (BMI 30.0 - 99.8)	23.3	27.6
Adults who participated in any physical activities in the past month	78.6	77.1
Adults 50+ who have ever had a sigmoidoscopy or colonoscopy	67.0	67.3
Women aged 40+ who have had a mammogram within the past two years	71.4	74.0
Men aged 40+ who have had a PSA test within the past two years	43.8	45.2
Adults aged 65+ who have had flu shot within the past year	66.6	60.1
Adults who always wear a seatbelt	87.8	93.8

Note: Data as of 2012 unless otherwise noted; (1) Figures cover the Billings, MT Metropolitan Statistical Area—see Appendix B for areas included; (2) Heavy drinkers are classified as males having more than two drinks per day or females having more than one drink per day; (3) Binge drinkers are classified as males having five or more drinks on one occasion or females having four or more drinks on one occasion
Source: Centers for Disease Control and Prevention, Behaviorial Risk Factor Surveillance System, SMART: Selected Metropolitan/Micropolitan Area Risk Trends, 2012 (Note: the CDC has discontinued this dataset but will be releasing a replacement in late 2015)

Chronic Health Indicators

Category	MSA[1] (%)	U.S. (%)
Adults who have ever been told they had a heart attack	4.4	4.5
Adults who have ever been told they had a stroke	2.6	2.9
Adults who have been told they currently have asthma	8.3	8.9
Adults who have ever been told they have arthritis	30.1	25.7
Adults who have ever been told they have diabetes[2]	8.1	9.7
Adults who have ever been told they had skin cancer	8.4	5.7
Adults who have ever been told they had any other types of cancer	6.5	6.5
Adults who have ever been told they have COPD	6.5	6.2
Adults who have ever been told they have kidney disease	1.8	2.5
Adults who have ever been told they have a form of depression	22.5	18.0

Note: Data as of 2012 unless otherwise noted; (1) Figures cover the Billings, MT Metropolitan Statistical Area—see Appendix B for areas included; (2) Figures do not include pregnancy-related, borderline, or pre-diabetes
Source: Centers for Disease Control and Prevention, Behaviorial Risk Factor Surveillance System, SMART: Selected Metropolitan/Micropolitan Area Risk Trends, 2012 (Note: the CDC has discontinued this dataset but will be releasing a replacement in late 2015)

Mortality Rates for the Top 10 Causes of Death in the U.S.

ICD-10[a] Sub-Chapter	ICD-10[a] Code	Age-Adjusted Mortality Rate[1] per 100,000 population	
		County[2]	U.S.
Malignant neoplasms	C00-C97	168.3	166.2
Ischaemic heart diseases	I20-I25	72.2	105.7
Other forms of heart disease	I30-I51	62.9	49.3
Chronic lower respiratory diseases	J40-J47	53.9	42.1
Organic, including symptomatic, mental disorders	F01-F09	39.6	38.1
Cerebrovascular diseases	I60-I69	40.0	37.0
Other external causes of accidental injury	W00-X59	18.4	26.9
Other degenerative diseases of the nervous system	G30-G31	35.3	25.6
Diabetes mellitus	E10-E14	17.6	21.3
Hypertensive diseases	I10-I15	16.0	19.4

Note: (a) ICD-10 = International Classification of Diseases 10th Revision; (1) Mortality rates are a three year average covering 2011-2013; (2) Figures cover Yellowstone County
Source: Centers for Disease Control and Prevention, National Center for Health Statistics. Compressed Mortality File 1999-2013 on CDC WONDER Online Database, released October 2014. Data are compiled from the Compressed Mortality File 1999-2013, Series 20 No. 2S, 2014.

Mortality Rates for Selected Causes of Death

ICD-10[a] Sub-Chapter	ICD-10[a] Code	Age-Adjusted Mortality Rate[1] per 100,000 population	
		County[2]	U.S.
Assault	X85-Y09	*3.9	5.2
Diseases of the liver	K70-K76	15.7	13.2
Human immunodeficiency virus (HIV) disease	B20-B24	Suppressed	2.2
Influenza and pneumonia	J09-J18	13.1	15.4
Intentional self-harm	X60-X84	23.1	12.5
Malnutrition	E40-E46	Suppressed	0.9
Obesity and other hyperalimentation	E65-E68	Suppressed	1.8
Renal failure	N17-N19	9.5	13.1
Transport accidents	V01-V99	13.9	11.7
Viral hepatitis	B15-B19	*2.1	2.2

Note: (a) ICD-10 = International Classification of Diseases 10th Revision; (1) Mortality rates are a three year average covering 2011-2013; (2) Figures cover Yellowstone County; (*) Unreliable data as per CDC
Source: Centers for Disease Control and Prevention, National Center for Health Statistics. Compressed Mortality File 1999-2013 on CDC WONDER Online Database, released October 2014. Data are compiled from the Compressed Mortality File 1999-2013, Series 20 No. 2S, 2014.

Health Insurance Coverage

Area	With Health Insurance	With Private Health Insurance	With Public Health Insurance	Without Health Insurance	Population Under Age 18 Without Health Insurance
City	83.3	65.1	30.8	16.7	10.4
MSA[1]	83.7	67.1	29.4	16.3	10.3
U.S.	85.2	65.2	31.0	14.8	7.3

Note: Figures are percentages that cover the civilian noninstitutionalized population; (1) Figures cover the Billings, MT Metropolitan Statistical Area—see Appendix B for areas included
Source: U.S. Census Bureau, 2011-2013 American Community Survey 3-Year Estimates

Number of Medical Professionals

Area[1]	MDs[2]	DOs[2,3]	Dentists	Podiatrists	Chiropractors	Optometrists
Local (number)	516	30	128	11	50	37
Local (rate[4])	339.7	19.8	83.1	7.1	32.5	24.0
U.S. (rate[4])	270.0	20.2	63.1	5.7	25.2	14.9

Note: Data as of 2013 unless noted; (1) Local data covers Yellowstone County; (2) Data as of 2012 and includes all active, non-federal physicians; (3) Doctor of Osteopathic Medicine; (4) rate per 100,000 population
Source: U.S. Department of Health and Human Services, Health Resources and Services Administration, Bureau of Health Professions, Area Resource File (ARF) 2013-2014

EDUCATION

Public School District Statistics

District Name	Schls	Pupils	Pupil/ Teacher Ratio	Minority Pupils[1] (%)	Free Lunch Eligible[2] (%)	IEP[3] (%)
Billings Elementary	26	11,145	17.2	23.7	32.4	10.7
Billings High School	3	5,220	17.9	17.0	17.8	11.8

Note: Table includes school districts with 2,000 or more students; (1) Percentage of students that are not non-Hispanic white; (2) Percentage of students that are eligible for the free lunch program; (3) Percentage of students that have an Individualized Education Program.
Source: U.S. Department of Education, National Center for Education Statistics, Common Core of Data, Local Education Agency (School District) Universe Survey: School Year 2012-2013; U.S. Department of Education, National Center for Education Statistics, Common Core of Data, Public Elementary/Secondary School Universe Survey: School Year 2012-2013

Highest Level of Education

Area	Less than H.S.	H.S. Diploma	Some College, No Deg.	Associate Degree	Bachelor's Degree	Master's Degree	Prof. School Degree	Doctorate Degree
City	7.4	29.5	26.8	7.3	20.1	5.8	2.0	1.1
MSA[1]	7.7	31.1	26.6	7.1	19.4	5.2	1.9	0.9
U.S.	13.7	28.0	21.2	7.9	18.2	7.7	1.9	1.3

Note: Figures cover persons age 25 and over; (1) Figures cover the Billings, MT Metropolitan Statistical Area—see Appendix B for areas included
Source: U.S. Census Bureau, 2011-2013 American Community Survey 3-Year Estimates

Educational Attainment by Race

Area	High School Graduate or Higher (%)					Bachelor's Degree or Higher (%)				
	Total	White	Black	Asian	Hisp.[2]	Total	White	Black	Asian	Hisp.[2]
City	92.6	93.5	n/a	n/a	82.6	29.0	30.3	n/a	n/a	12.5
MSA[1]	92.3	92.9	n/a	n/a	79.7	27.4	28.3	n/a	n/a	11.5
U.S.	86.3	88.3	83.1	85.7	64.0	29.1	30.4	18.8	50.7	13.7

Note: Figures shown cover persons 25 years old and over; (1) Figures cover the Billings, MT Metropolitan Statistical Area—see Appendix B for areas included; (2) People of Hispanic origin can be of any race
Source: U.S. Census Bureau, 2011-2013 American Community Survey 3-Year Estimates

School Enrollment by Grade and Control

Area	Preschool (%)		Kindergarten (%)		Grades 1 - 4 (%)		Grades 5 - 8 (%)		Grades 9 - 12 (%)	
	Public	Private	Public	Private	Public	Private	Public	Private	Public	Private
City	45.4	54.6	90.3	9.7	94.6	5.4	91.2	8.8	91.2	8.8
MSA[1]	44.8	55.2	91.7	8.3	95.0	5.0	90.4	9.6	89.5	10.5
U.S.	57.7	42.3	87.9	12.1	89.9	10.1	90.0	10.0	90.7	9.3

Note: Figures shown cover persons 3 years old and over; (1) Figures cover the Billings, MT Metropolitan Statistical Area—see Appendix B for areas included
Source: U.S. Census Bureau, 2011-2013 American Community Survey 3-Year Estimates

Average Salaries of Public School Classroom Teachers

Area	2013-14		2014-15		Percent Change 2013-14 to 2014-15	Percent Change 2004-05 to 2014-15
	Dollars	Rank[1]	Dollars	Rank[1]		
MONTANA	49,893	28	50,999	27	2.22	32.5
U.S. Average	56,610	–	57,379	–	1.36	20.8

Note: (1) State rank ranges from 1 to 51 where 1 indicates highest salary.
Source: National Education Association, Rankings & Estimates: Rankings of the States 2014 and Estimates of School Statistics 2015, March 2015

Higher Education

	Four-Year Colleges			Two-Year Colleges			Medical Schools[1]	Law Schools[2]	Voc/Tech[3]
Public	Private Non-profit	Private For-profit	Public	Private Non-profit	Private For-profit			
1	1	0	0	0	1	0	0	0

Note: Figures cover institutions located within the city limits and include main campuses only; (1) includes schools accredited by the Liaison Committee on Medical Education and the American Osteopathic Association's Commission on Osteopathic College Accreditation; (2) includes ABA-accredited schools, schools with provisional ABA accreditation, and state accredited schools; (3) includes all schools with programs that are less than 2 years.
Source: National Center for Education Statistics, Integrated Postsecondary Education System (IPEDS), 2013-14; Association of American Medical Colleges, Member List, May 1, 2015; American Osteopathic Association, Member List, May 1, 2015; Law School Admission Council, Official Guide to ABA-Approved Law Schools Online, May 1, 2015; Wikipedia, List of Medical Schools in the United States, May 1, 2015; Wikipedia, List of Law Schools in the United States, May 1, 2015

PRESIDENTIAL ELECTION

2012 Presidential Election Results

Area	Obama (%)	Romney (%)	Other (%)
Yellowstone County	38.4	58.9	2.8
U.S.	51.0	47.2	1.8

Note: Results may not add to 100% due to rounding
Source: Dave Leip's Atlas of U.S. Presidential Elections

EMPLOYERS

Major Employers

Company Name	Industry
Beall Trailers of Montana	Tanks, standard or custom fabricated: metal plate
Billings Clinic	General medical and surgical hospitals
Bureau of Land Management	Land management agency, government
Employee Benefit Management Services	Med. insurance claim processing, contract or fee basis
EXXON Mobil Corporation	Nonaromatic chemical products
First Interstate Bank	State commercial banks
Interstate Brands Corporation	Bread, cake, and related products
Montana Dept of Environmental Quality	Air, water, and solid waste management
Montana State University-Billings	Colleges and universities
Sears, Roebuck and Co	Department stores
St John's Lutheran Ministries	Skilled nursing care facilities
St Vincent Healthcare Foundation	General medical and surgical hospitals
St Vincent Hospital Auxilliary	Charitable organization
SYSCO Montana	Groceries and related products
Wal-Mart Stores	Department stores, discount
Yellowstone Boys and Girls Ranch	Emotionally disturbed home
Yellowstone City-County Health Department	Medical service organization

Note: Companies shown are located within the Billings, MT Metropolitan Statistical Area.
Source: Hoovers.com; Wikipedia

PUBLIC SAFETY

Crime Rate

Area	All Crimes	Violent Crimes				Property Crimes		
		Murder	Forcible Rape	Robbery	Aggrav. Assault	Burglary	Larceny -Theft	Motor Vehicle Theft
City	5,532.4	3.7	36.2	75.1	218.9	917.4	3,779.2	501.8
Suburbs[1]	1,868.7	0.0	17.5	5.3	115.7	380.4	1,155.2	194.6
Metro[2]	4,264.6	2.4	29.7	51.0	183.2	731.6	2,871.2	395.5
U.S.	3,098.6	4.5	25.2	109.1	229.1	610.0	1,899.4	221.3

Note: Figures are crimes per 100,000 population; (1) All areas within the metro area that are located outside the city limits; (2) Figures cover the Billings, MT Metropolitan Statistical Area—see Appendix B for areas included
Source: FBI Uniform Crime Reports, 2013

Hate Crimes

Area	Number of Quarters Reported	Number of Incidents per Bias Motivation						
		Race	Religion	Sexual Orientation	Ethnicity	Disability	Gender	Gender Identity
City	4	5	1	1	0	0	0	0
U.S.	4	2,871	1,031	1,233	655	83	18	31

Source: Federal Bureau of Investigation, Hate Crime Statistics 2013

Identity Theft Consumer Complaints

Area	Complaints	Complaints per 100,000 Population	Rank[2]
MSA[1]	110	66.5	212
U.S.	332,646	104.3	-

Note: (1) Figures cover the Billings, MT Metropolitan Statistical Area—see Appendix B for areas included; (2) Rank ranges from 1 to 380 where 1 indicates greatest number of identity theft complaints per 100,000 population
Source: Federal Trade Commission, Consumer Sentinel Network Data Book for January–December 2014

Fraud and Other Consumer Complaints

Area	Complaints	Complaints per 100,000 Population	Rank[2]
MSA[1]	576	348.3	236
U.S.	2,250,205	705.7	-

Note: (1) Figures cover the Billings, MT Metropolitan Statistical Area—see Appendix B for areas included; (2) Rank ranges from 1 to 380 where 1 indicates greatest number of identity theft complaints per 100,000 population
Source: Federal Trade Commission, Consumer Sentinel Network Data Book for January–December 2014

RECREATION

Culture

Dance[1]	Theatre[1]	Instrumental Music[1]	Vocal Music[1]	Series and Festivals	Museums and Art Galleries[2]	Zoos and Aquariums[3]
0	1	2	1	1	12	0

Note: (1) Professional perfoming groups; (2) Based on organizations with SIC code 8412; (3) AZA-accredited
Source: The Grey House Performing Arts Directory, 2015-16; Association of Zoos & Aquariums, AZA Member Zoos & Aquariums, April 2015; www.AccuLeads.com, April 2015

Professional Sports Teams

Team Name	League	Year Established
No teams are located in the metro area		

Source: Wikipedia, Major Professional Sports Teams of the United States and Canada, April 2015

CLIMATE

Average and Extreme Temperatures

Temperature	Jan	Feb	Mar	Apr	May	Jun	Jul	Aug	Sep	Oct	Nov	Dec	Yr.
Extreme High (°F)	68	72	79	90	95	105	105	105	103	90	77	69	105
Average High (°F)	32	38	45	57	67	77	86	85	72	61	45	36	59
Average Temp. (°F)	23	29	35	46	56	65	72	71	60	49	36	27	47
Average Low (°F)	14	19	25	34	44	52	58	57	47	37	26	18	36
Extreme Low (°F)	-28	-28	-19	9	14	32	41	35	22	-7	-22	-32	-32

Note: Figures cover the years 1948-1995
Source: National Climatic Data Center, International Station Meteorological Climate Summary, 9/96

Average Precipitation/Snowfall/Humidity

Precip./Humidity	Jan	Feb	Mar	Apr	May	Jun	Jul	Aug	Sep	Oct	Nov	Dec	Yr.
Avg. Precip. (in.)	0.8	0.6	1.1	1.8	2.4	2.1	1.1	0.9	1.3	1.1	0.8	0.7	14.6
Avg. Snowfall (in.)	10	7	10	9	2	Tr	0	Tr	1	4	7	9	59
Avg. Rel. Hum. 5am (%)	64	66	69	68	71	72	64	61	64	63	65	64	66
Avg. Rel. Hum. 5pm (%)	56	53	48	42	42	41	32	30	37	42	53	56	44

Note: Figures cover the years 1948-1995; Tr = Trace amounts (<0.05 in. of rain; <0.5 in. of snow)
Source: National Climatic Data Center, International Station Meteorological Climate Summary, 9/96

Weather Conditions

	Temperature			Daytime Sky			Precipitation		
	5°F & below	32°F & below	90°F & above	Clear	Partly cloudy	Cloudy	0.01 inch or more precip.	0.1 inch or more snow/ice	Thunder-storms
	25	149	29	75	163	127	97	41	27

Note: Figures are average number of days per year and cover the years 1948-1995
Source: National Climatic Data Center, International Station Meteorological Climate Summary, 9/96

HAZARDOUS WASTE

Superfund Sites

Billings has one hazardous waste site on the EPA's Superfund Final National Priorities List: **Lockwood Solvent Ground Water Plume**. There are a total of 1,322 Superfund sites on the list in the U.S. *U.S. Environmental Protection Agency, Final National Priorities List, April 14, 2015*

AIR & WATER QUALITY

Air Quality Trends: Ozone

	2004	2005	2006	2007	2008	2009	2010	2011	2012	2013
MSA[1]	n/a	n/a	n/a	n/a	n/a	n/a	n/a	n/a	n/a	n/a

Note: (1) Data covers the Billings, MT Metropolitan Statistical Area—see Appendix B for areas included; n/a not available. The values shown are the composite ozone concentration averages among trend sites based on the highest fourth daily maximum 8-hour concentration in parts per million. These trends are based on sites having an adequate record of monitoring data during the trend period. Data from exceptional events are included.
Source: U.S. Environmental Protection Agency, Air Quality Monitoring Information, "Air Quality Trends by City, 2000-2013"

Air Quality Index

Area	Percent of Days when Air Quality was...[2]					AQI Statistics[2]	
	Good	Moderate	Unhealthy for Sensitive Groups	Unhealthy	Very Unhealthy	Maximum	Median
MSA[1]	81.4	16.4	2.2	0.0	0.0	125	27

Note: (1) Data covers the Billings, MT Metropolitan Statistical Area—see Appendix B for areas included; (2) Based on 365 days with AQI data in 2014. Air Quality Index (AQI) is an index for reporting daily air quality. EPA calculates the AQI for five major air pollutants regulated by the Clean Air Act: ground-level ozone, particle pollution (aka particulate matter), carbon monoxide, sulfur dioxide, and nitrogen dioxide. The AQI runs from 0 to 500. The higher the AQI value, the greater the level of air pollution and the greater the health concern. There are six AQI categories: "Good" AQI is between 0 and 50. Air quality is considered satisfactory; "Moderate" AQI is between 51 and 100. Air quality is acceptable; "Unhealthy for Sensitive Groups" When AQI values are between 101 and 150, members of sensitive groups may experience health effects; "Unhealthy" When AQI values are between 151 and 200 everyone may begin to experience health effects; "Very Unhealthy" AQI values between 201 and 300 trigger a health alert; "Hazardous" AQI values over 300 trigger warnings of emergency conditions (not shown).
Source: U.S. Environmental Protection Agency, Air Quality Index Report, 2014

Air Quality Index Pollutants

Area	Percent of Days when AQI Pollutant was...[2]					
	Carbon Monoxide	Nitrogen Dioxide	Ozone	Sulfur Dioxide	Particulate Matter 2.5	Particulate Matter 10
MSA[1]	0.0	0.0	0.0	43.8	56.2	0.0

Note: (1) Data covers the Billings, MT Metropolitan Statistical Area—see Appendix B for areas included; (2) Based on 365 days with AQI data in 2014. The Air Quality Index (AQI) is an index for reporting daily air quality. EPA calculates the AQI for five major air pollutants regulated by the Clean Air Act: ground-level ozone, particle pollution (also known as particulate matter), carbon monoxide, sulfur dioxide, and nitrogen dioxide. The AQI runs from 0 to 500. The higher the AQI value, the greater the level of air pollution and the greater the health concern.
Source: U.S. Environmental Protection Agency, Air Quality Index Report, 2014

Maximum Air Pollutant Concentrations: Particulate Matter, Ozone, CO and Lead

	Particulate Matter 10 (ug/m^3)	Particulate Matter 2.5 Wtd AM (ug/m^3)	Particulate Matter 2.5 24-Hr (ug/m^3)	Ozone (ppm)	Carbon Monoxide (ppm)	Lead (ug/m^3)
MSA[1] Level	n/a	n/a	n/a	n/a	n/a	n/a
NAAQS[2]	150	15	35	0.075	9	0.15
Met NAAQS[2]	n/a	n/a	n/a	n/a	n/a	n/a

Note: (1) Data covers the Billings, MT Metropolitan Statistical Area—see Appendix B for areas included; Data from exceptional events are included; (2) National Ambient Air Quality Standards; ppm = parts per million; ug/m^3 = micrograms per cubic meter; n/a not available.
Concentrations: Particulate Matter 10 (coarse particulate)—highest second maximum 24-hour concentration; Particulate Matter 2.5 Wtd AM (fine particulate)—highest weighted annual mean concentration; Particulate Matter 2.5 24-Hour (fine particulate)—highest 98th percentile 24-hour concentration; Ozone—highest fourth daily maximum 8-hour concentration; Carbon Monoxide—highest second maximum non-overlapping 8-hour concentration; Lead—maximum running 3-month average
Source: U.S. Environmental Protection Agency, Air Quality Monitoring Information, "Air Quality Statistics by City, 2013"

Maximum Air Pollutant Concentrations: Nitrogen Dioxide and Sulfur Dioxide

	Nitrogen Dioxide AM (ppb)	Nitrogen Dioxide 1-Hr (ppb)	Sulfur Dioxide AM (ppb)	Sulfur Dioxide 1-Hr (ppb)	Sulfur Dioxide 24-Hr (ppb)
MSA[1] Level	n/a	n/a	n/a	48	n/a
NAAQS[2]	53	100	30	75	140
Met NAAQS[2]	n/a	n/a	n/a	Yes	n/a

Note: (1) Data covers the Billings, MT Metropolitan Statistical Area—see Appendix B for areas included; Data from exceptional events are included; (2) National Ambient Air Quality Standards; ppm = parts per million; ug/m^3 = micrograms per cubic meter; n/a not available.
Concentrations: Nitrogen Dioxide AM—highest arithmetic mean concentration; Nitrogen Dioxide 1-Hr—highest 98th percentile 1-hour daily maximum concentration; Sulfur Dioxide AM—highest annual mean concentration; Sulfur Dioxide 1-Hr—highest 99th percentile 1-hour daily maximum concentration; Sulfur Dioxide 24-Hr—highest second maximum 24-hour concentration
Source: U.S. Environmental Protection Agency, Air Quality Monitoring Information, "Air Quality Statistics by City, 2013"

Drinking Water

Water System Name	Pop. Served	Primary Water Source Type	Violations[1] Health Based	Violations[1] Monitoring/ Reporting
City of Billings	114,000	Surface	0	0

Note: (1) Based on violation data from January 1, 2014 to December 31, 2014 (includes unresolved violations from earlier years)
Source: U.S. Environmental Protection Agency, Office of Ground Water and Drinking Water, Safe Drinking Water Information System (based on data extracted January 27, 2015)

Boise City, Idaho

Background

Boise (boy-see) is the capital and largest city in Idaho, lying along the Boise River adjacent to the foothills of the Rocky Mountains. The city is located south and west of the western slopes of the Rockies, and is the site of a great system of natural warm water springs.

Boise's spectacular natural location is its first and most obvious attraction, and this, coupled with its dynamic economic growth in recent decades, makes Boise an altogether remarkable city. The splendor of its surroundings, together with an average 18-minute drive to work, has allowed the city to combine pleasure and efficiency in an enviable mix.

French-Canadian trappers were familiar with Boise and its environs by 1811, and the name of the city is an Anglicization of the French Les Bois—the trees. The first substantial European settlement dates to 1863 when, in the spring of that year, I.M. Coston built from pegged driftwood a great house that served as a hub for the activities of prospectors, traders, and Native Americans. In the same year, the U.S. Army built Fort Boise, and considerable deposits of gold and silver were discovered in the area. The U.S. Assay Office in Boise, in 1870-71 alone, is said to have valuated more than $75 million in precious metals.

The area is rich in gold rush lore, and six miles above Boise, on the south side of the river, there may even be buried treasure from that era. The eastbound stagecoach from Boise was said to have been waylaid by a robber who, though wounded in the attack by a resourceful passenger, managed to drag off a strongbox filled with $50,000 in gold. The robber died of his wounds and was discovered the next day, but he had apparently buried his loot. No one has ever located it.

The Boise area was subsequently developed for farming, as crops of grains, vegetables, and fruits, replaced the mines as its source of wealth. It became the territorial capital of Idaho in 1864 and the state capital in 1890. Education was served with the opening of a university in 1932, which became Boise State University in 1974 and now enrolls almost 20,000 students.

The city's natural setting offers a great range of outdoor activities that are pursued energetically by its citizens. Its rivers, mountains, deserts, and lakes offer world-class skiing, hiking, camping, kayaking, river rafting, hunting, and fishing. Bike paths run throughout the city and into Boise's large outdoor trail network, the Boise River Greenbelt. Recreational wilderness exists extensively just outside the city's limits. The Word Center for Birds of Prey is located on the city's southern frontier, and is the site of the Peregrine Falcon's rehabilitation and release into the wild.

Many large regional, national, and international companies are headquartered in Boise, including plus major call centers for DIRECTV and T-Mobile.

The city produces high- and low-tech products and everything in between: software, computer components, steel and sheet metal products, mobile homes, lumber products, farm machinery, packed meats, and processed foods. Increasingly an advanced technological center, it continues to serve as a trading center for the greater agricultural region.

By virtue of its history and geographical character, the city can be considered a presence on the Pacific Rim. In a more tangible vein, Boise, with ten airlines operating at its airport, is conveniently tied to the wider world.

Boise's Basque community, numbering about 15,000, is the largest in the United States and the third largest in the world outside Argentina and the Basque Country in Spain and France. A large Basque festival known as Jaialdi is held once every five years, most recently in 2010. Boise (along with Valley and Boise Counties) hosted the 2009 Special Olympics World Winter Games. More than 2,500 athletes from over 100 countries participated.

The city is protected by the mountains to the north in such a way that it is largely unbothered by the extreme blizzards that affect eastern Idaho and parts of neighboring states. Boise, and this section of western Idaho generally, are affected by climatic influences from the Pacific Ocean and exhibits an unusually mild climate for this latitude. Summers can be hot, but nights are almost always cool, and sunshine generally prevails.

Rankings

General Rankings

- Among the 50 largest U.S. cities, Boise City placed #11 in Vocativ's "semi-exhaustive, mostly scientific" city Livability Index for people aged 35 and under. Average salary, unemployment rates, rents, and other living costs were considered, along with crime rates, weather, public transportation, access to music and sports, and "lifestyle metrics" such as the price of dinner at Buffalo Wild Wings and an ounce of high-quality weed. *vocative.com, "The Livability Index: The Best U.S. Cities for People 35 and Under," December 9, 2014*

- Boise City was selected as one of America's best river towns by *Outside Magazine*. Criteria: cost of living; cultural vibrancy; job prospects; environmental stewardship; access to the outdoors. *Outside Magazine, "Best River Towns 2012," October 2012*

- In their second annual survey, analysts for the small- and mid-sized city lifestyle site Livability.com looked at data for more than 2,000 U.S. cities to determine the rankings for Livability's "Top 100 Best Places to Live" in 2015. Boise City ranked #9. Criteria: vibrant economy; low cost of living; abundant lifestyle amenities. *Livability.com, "Top 100 Best Places to Live 2015"*

Business/Finance Rankings

- Boise City was the #4-ranked city for savers, according to the finance site GoBankingRates, which considered the prospects for for people trying to save money, looking at sales tax, median home and condo value, median monthly rent, median income, unemployment rates, and gas prices in the nation's 100 largest cities. *www.gobankingrates.com, "Best Cities for Saving Money," February 23, 2015*

- Boise City was the city ranked #4 among the nation's 100 largest cities for most difficult conditions for savers, according to the finance site GOBankingRates. Criteria: sales tax; median home and condo values; median monthly rent; median income; unemployment rate; and gas prices. *www.gobankingrates.com, "Worst Cities for Saving Money," February 23, 2015*

- Looking at February 2012–2013, 24/7 Wall Street's analysts focused on metro areas where jobs were being added at a faster rate than the labor force was growing to identify the metro areas with the biggest real declines in unemployment. The #5 metro area for gains posted in employment was the Boise City metro area. *247wallst.com, "Cities Where Unemployment Has Fallen the Most," April 16, 2013*

- The Boise City metro area was identified as having one of the largest percentage of home workers in the U.S. The area ranked #9, according to the business website 24/7 Wall Street, which based its conclusions on data from the U.S. Census Bureau and the Bureau of Labor Statistics. *247wallst.com, "Cities Where the Most Americans Work from Home," March 18, 2013*

- *Forbes* ranked the largest metro areas in the U.S. in terms of the "Best Cities for Young Professionals." The Boise City metro area ranked #6 out of 15. Criteria: job growth; unemployment rate; median salary of college graduates age 24 to 34; cost of living; number of small businesses per capita; number of large companies; percentage of population 25 years of age and older with college degrees. *Forbes.com, "America's 15 Best Cities for Young Professionals," August 18, 2014*

- Boise City was ranked #18 out of 100 metro areas in terms of economic performance (#1 = best) during the recession and recovery from trough quarter through the second quarter of 2013. Criteria: percent change in employment; percentage point change in unemployment rate; percent change in gross metropolitan product; percent change in House Price Index. *Brookings Institution, MetroMonitor: Tracking Economic Recession and Recovery in America's 100 Largest Metropolitan Areas, September 2013*

- The Boise City metro area appeared on the Milken Institute "2013 Best Performing Cities" list. Rank: #81 out of 200 large metro areas. Criteria: job growth; wage and salary growth; high-tech output growth. *Milken Institute, "Best-Performing Cities 2014," January 2015*

- *Forbes* ranked the 200 most populous metro areas to determine the nation's "Best Places for Business and Careers." The Boise City metro area was ranked #27. Criteria: costs (business and living); job growth (past and projected); income growth; educational attainment (college and high school); projected economic growth; cultural and recreational opportunities; net migration patterns; number of highly ranked colleges. *Forbes, "The Best Places for Business and Careers 2014," July 23, 2014*

Children/Family Rankings

- *Forbes* analyzed data on the 100 largest metropolitan areas in the United States to compile its 2014 list of the ten "Best Cities for Raising a Family." The Boise City metro area was ranked #7. Criteria: median income; overall cost of living; housing affordability; commuting delays; percentage of families owning homes; crime rate; education quality (mainly test scores). *Forbes, "The Best Cities for Raising a Family," April 16, 2014*

- Boise City was identified as one of the best cities for raising a family by *24/7 Wall St.* The city ranked #9. The nation's 100 largest cities were evaluated on the following criteria: large public outdoor spaces; top hospitals; strong schools; low unemployment; high educational attainment; low violent crime rates. *24/7 Wall St., "The 10 Best U.S. Cities for Raising a Family," January 13, 2012*

Dating/Romance Rankings

- Of the 100 U.S. cities surveyed by *Men's Health* in its quest to identify the nation's best cities for dating and forming relationships, Boise City was ranked #45 for online dating (#1 = best). *Men's Health, "The Best and Worst Cities for Online Dating," January 30, 2013*

Education Rankings

- Personal finance website *WalletHub* analyzed the 150 largest U.S. metropolitan statistical areas to determine where the most educated Americans are choosing to settle. Criteria: educational attainment; percentage of workers with jobs in computer, engineering, and science fields; quality and size of each metro area's universities. Boise City was ranked #60 (#1 = most educated city). *www.WalletHub.com, "2014's Most and Least Educated Cities*

Environmental Rankings

- The Boise City metro area came in at #73 for the relative comfort of its climate on Sperling's list of "chill cities," as measured by the Sperling Heat Index. All 361 metro areas are included. Criteria included daytime high temperatures, nighttime low temperatures, dew point, and relative humidity at the high temperatures. *www.bertsperling.com, "Sperling's Chill Cities," July 18, 2013*

- Sperling's BestPlaces assessed 379 metropolitan areas of the United States for the likelihood of dangerously extreme weather events or earthquakes. In general the Southeast and South-Central regions have the highest risk of weather extremes and earthquakes, while the Pacific Northwest enjoys the lowest risk. Of the least risky metropolitan areas, the Boise City metro area was ranked #31. *www.bestplaces.net, "Safest Places from Natural Disasters," April 2011*

- *The Daily Beast* identifed the snowiest among the 100 largest U.S. cities, looking at average snowfall per month from December 2011 through March 2012 and from December 1, 2012 to December 21, 2012. Number of days with maximum and minimum temperatures of 32 degrees or less contributed to the rankings. Boise City ranked #25. *The Daily Beast, "25 Snowiest Cities in America," December 21, 2012*

- Boise City was highlighted as one of the 25 metro areas most polluted by short-term particle pollution (24-hour PM 2.5) in the U.S. during 2011 through 2013. The area ranked #23. *American Lung Association, State of the Air 2015*

Food/Drink Rankings

- *Men's Health* ranked 100 major U.S. cities in terms of alcohol intoxication. Boise City ranked #53 (#1 = most sober).Criteria: binge drinking; alcohol-related traffic accidents, arrests, and fatalities. *Men's Health, "The Drunkest Cities in America," November 19, 2013*

Health/Fitness Rankings

- Boise City was identified as a "2013 Spring Allergy Capital." The area ranked #99 out of 100. Three groups of factors were used to identify the most severe cities for people with allergies during the spring season: annual pollen levels; medicine utilization; access to board-certified allergists. *Asthma and Allergy Foundation of America, "Spring Allergy Capitals 2013"*

- Boise City was identified as a "2013 Fall Allergy Capital." The area ranked #93 out of 100. Three groups of factors were used to identify the most severe cities for people with allergies during the fall season: annual pollen levels; medicine utilization; access to board-certified allergists. *Asthma and Allergy Foundation of America, "Fall Allergy Capitals 2013"*

- Boise City was identified as a "2013 Asthma Capital." The area ranked #98 out of the nation's 100 largest metropolitan areas. Twelve factors were used to identify the most challenging places to live for people with asthma: estimated prevalence; self-reported prevalence; crude death rate for asthma; annual pollen score; annual air quality; public smoking laws; number of board-certified asthma specialists; school inhaler access laws; rescue medication use; controller medication use; uninsured rate; poverty rate. *Asthma and Allergy Foundation of America, "Asthma Capitals 2013"*

- *Men's Health* ranked 100 major U.S. cities in terms of the best and worst cities for men. Boise City ranked #11. Criteria: thirty-three data points were examined covering health, fitness, and quality of life. *Men's Health, "The Best & Worst Cities for Men 2014," December 6, 2013*

- The Boise City metro area appeared in the 2013 Gallup-Healthways Well-Being Index. The area ranked #91 out of 189. The Gallup-Healthways Well-Being Index score is an average of six sub-indexes, which individually examine life evaluation, emotional health, work environment, physical health, healthy behaviors, and access to basic necessities. Results are based on telephone interviews conducted as part of the Gallup-Healthways Well-Being Index survey January 2–December 29, 2012, and January 2–December 30, 2013, with a random sample of 531,630 adults, aged 18 and older, living in metropolitan areas in the 50 U.S. states and the District of Columbia. *Gallup-Healthways, "State of American Well-Being," March 25, 2014*

Real Estate Rankings

- The Boise City metro area was identified as one of the top 20 housing markets to invest in for 2015 by *Forbes*. The area ranked #8. Criteria: strong population and job growth; relatively low home prices which are below equilibrium home price (EHP). The EHP is what the average price for a market should be, if speculation, weird distortions in local income, and other factors (like the housing collapse) weren't present in the market. *Forbes.com, "Best Buy Cities: Where to Invest in Housing in 2015," January 9, 2015*

- Boise City was ranked #65 out of 275 metro areas in terms of house price appreciation in 2014 (#1 = highest rate). *Federal Housing Finance Agency, House Price Index, 4th Quarter 2014*

- Boise City was ranked #167 out of 226 metro areas in terms of housing affordability in 2014 by the National Association of Home Builders (#1 = most affordable). The NAHB-Wells Fargo Housing Opportunity Index (HOI) for a given area is defined as the share of homes sold in that area that would have been affordable to a family earning the local median income, based on standard mortgage underwriting criteria. *National Association of Home Builders®, NAHB-Wells Fargo Housing Opportunity Index, 4th Quarter 2014*

Safety Rankings

- In search of the nation's safest cities, Business Insider looked at the FBI's preliminary Uniform Crime Report, excluding localities with fewer than 200,000 residents. To judge by its low murder, rape, and robbery data, Boise City made the 20 safest cities list, at #7. *www.businessinsider.com, "The 20 Safest Cities in America," July 25, 2013*

- Farmers Insurance, in partnership with Sperling's BestPlaces, ranked metro areas in the U.S. and identified the "Most Secure Places to Live." The Boise City metro area ranked #11 out of the top 20 in the large metro area category (500,000 or more residents). Criteria: economic stability; crime statistics; extreme weather; risk of natural disasters; housing depreciation; foreclosures; air quality; environmental hazards; life expectancy; motor vehicle fatalities; and employment numbers. *Farmers Insurance Group of Companies, "Most Secure U.S. Places to Live in the U.S.," June 25, 2013*

- Allstate ranked the 200 largest cities in America in terms of driver safety. Boise City ranked #3. Allstate researchers analyzed internal property damage claims over a two-year period from January 2011 to December 2012. A weighted average of the two-year numbers determined the annual percentages. *Allstate, "Allstate America's Best Drivers Report, 2014"*

- The National Insurance Crime Bureau ranked 380 metro areas in the U.S. in terms of per capita rates of vehicle theft. The Boise City metro area ranked #315 (#1 = highest rate). Criteria: number of vehicle theft offenses per 100,000 inhabitants in 2012. *National Insurance Crime Bureau, "Hot Spots 2012," June 26, 2013*

Seniors/Retirement Rankings

- From its Best Cities for Successful Aging indexes, the Milken Institute generated rankings for metropolitan areas, weighing data in eight categories—health care, wellness, living arrangements, transportation, financial characteristics, education and employment opportunities, community engagement, and overall livability. The Boise City metro area was ranked #22 overall in the large metro area category. *Milken Institute, "Best Cities for Successful Aging, 2014"*

- Boise City made the 2014 *Forbes* list of "25 Best Places to Retire." Criteria include: housing and living costs; tax climate for retirees; weather and air quality; crime rates; doctor availability; active-lifestyle rankings for walkability, bicycling and volunteering. *Forbes.com, "The Best Places to Retire in 2014," January 16, 2014*

Sports/Recreation Rankings

- Boise City was chosen as one of America's best cities for bicycling. The city ranked #30 out of 50. Criteria: robust cycling infrastructure; vibrant bike culture. The editors only considered cities with populations of 95,000 or more. *Bicycling, "America's Top 50 Bike-Friendly Cities," May 23, 2012*

Transportation Rankings

- NerdWallet surveyed average annual car insurance premiums in 125 U.S. cities to identify the least expensive U.S. cities in which to insure a car. Locations without no-fault insurance laws was a strong determinant. Boise City came in at #6 for the least expensive rates. *www.nerdwallet.com, "Best Cities for Cheap Car Insurance," February 3, 2014*

Women/Minorities Rankings

- Movoto chose five objective criteria to identify the best places for professional women among the largest 100 American cities. Boise City was among the top ten, at #10, based on commute time, recent job growth, unemployment rank, professional women's groups per capita, and average earnings adjusted for the cost of living. *www.movoto.com, "These Are America's Best Cities for Professional Women," March 5, 2014*

- *Women's Health* examined U.S. cities and identified the 100 best cities for women. Boise City was ranked #4. Criteria: 30 categories were examined from obesity and breast cancer rates to commuting times and hours spent working out. *Women's Health, "Best Cities for Women 2012"*

Miscellaneous Rankings

- According to the World Giving Index, the United States is the fifth most generous nation in the world. The finance and lifestyle site NerdWallet looked for the U.S. cities that topped the list in donating money and time to good causes. The Boise City metro area proved to be the #9-ranked metro area, judged by culture of volunteerism, depth of commitment in terms of volunteer hours per year, and monetary contributions. *www.nerdwallet.com, "Most Generous Cities," September 22, 2013*

- The National Alliance to End Homelessness ranked the 100 most populous metro areas in terms the rate of homelessness. The Boise City metro area ranked #58. Criteria: number of homeless people per 10,000 population in 2011. *National Alliance to End Homelessness, The State of Homelessness in America 2012*

Business Environment

CITY FINANCES

City Government Finances

Component	2012 ($000)	2012 ($ per capita)
Total Revenues	271,992	1,322
Total Expenditures	267,812	1,302
Debt Outstanding	79,674	387
Cash and Securities[1]	159,202	774

Note: (1) Cash and security holdings of a government at the close of its fiscal year, including those of its dependent agencies, utilities, and liquor stores.
Source: U.S Census Bureau, State & Local Government Finances 2012

City Government Revenue by Source

Source	2012 ($000)	2012 ($ per capita)
General Revenue		
From Federal Government	8,567	42
From State Government	17,255	84
From Local Governments	0	0
Taxes		
Property	107,504	523
Sales and Gross Receipts	5,575	27
Personal Income	0	0
Corporate Income	0	0
Motor Vehicle License	0	0
Other Taxes	4,623	22
Current Charges	114,243	555
Liquor Store	0	0
Utility	0	0
Employee Retirement	0	0

Source: U.S Census Bureau, State & Local Government Finances 2012

City Government Expenditures by Function

Function	2012 ($000)	2012 ($ per capita)	2012 (%)
General Direct Expenditures			
Air Transportation	24,500	119	9.1
Corrections	0	0	0.0
Education	0	0	0.0
Employment Security Administration	0	0	0.0
Financial Administration	7,800	38	2.9
Fire Protection	40,706	198	15.2
General Public Buildings	1,560	8	0.6
Governmental Administration, Other	7,801	38	2.9
Health	0	0	0.0
Highways	2,505	12	0.9
Hospitals	0	0	0.0
Housing and Community Development	6,338	31	2.4
Interest on General Debt	1,693	8	0.6
Judicial and Legal	6,618	32	2.5
Libraries	9,604	47	3.6
Parking	0	0	0.0
Parks and Recreation	20,407	99	7.6
Police Protection	45,150	220	16.9
Public Welfare	0	0	0.0
Sewerage	28,419	138	10.6
Solid Waste Management	24,013	117	9.0
Veterans' Services	0	0	0.0
Liquor Store	0	0	0.0
Utility	0	0	0.0
Employee Retirement	0	0	0.0

Source: U.S Census Bureau, State & Local Government Finances 2012

DEMOGRAPHICS

Population Growth

Area	1990 Census	2000 Census	2010 Census	Population Growth (%) 1990-2000	Population Growth (%) 2000-2010
City	144,317	185,787	205,671	28.7	10.7
MSA[1]	319,596	464,840	616,561	45.4	32.6
U.S.	248,709,873	281,421,906	308,745,538	13.2	9.7

Note: (1) Figures cover the Boise City-Nampa, ID Metropolitan Statistical Area—see Appendix B for areas included
Source: U.S. Census Bureau, Census 1990, 2000, 2010

Household Size

Area	One	Two	Three	Four	Five	Six	Seven or More	Average Household Size
City	30.6	35.0	16.4	11.1	4.5	1.9	0.6	2.39
MSA[1]	24.1	34.7	15.5	13.9	6.8	3.0	1.8	2.71
U.S.	27.7	33.6	15.7	13.1	6.0	2.3	1.5	2.64

Note: (1) Figures cover the Boise City, ID Metropolitan Statistical Area—see Appendix B for areas included
Source: U.S. Census Bureau, 2011-2013 American Community Survey 3-Year Estimates

Race

Area	White Alone[2] (%)	Black Alone[2] (%)	Asian Alone[2] (%)	AIAN[3] Alone[2] (%)	NHOPI[4] Alone[2] (%)	Other Race Alone[2] (%)	Two or More Races (%)
City	89.6	1.2	3.6	0.7	0.2	1.4	3.4
MSA[1]	91.6	0.7	2.0	0.6	0.2	2.1	2.8
U.S.	73.9	12.6	5.0	0.8	0.2	4.7	2.9

Note: (1) Figures cover the Boise City, ID Metropolitan Statistical Area—see Appendix B for areas included; (2) Alone is defined as not being in combination with one or more other races; (3) American Indian and Alaska Native; (4) Native Hawaiian and Other Pacific Islander
Source: U.S. Census Bureau, 2011-2013 American Community Survey 3-Year Estimates

Hispanic or Latino Origin

Area	Total (%)	Mexican (%)	Puerto Rican (%)	Cuban (%)	Other (%)
City	7.6	6.3	0.2	0.1	1.1
MSA[1]	12.8	10.9	0.3	0.1	1.5
U.S.	16.9	10.8	1.6	0.6	3.8

Note: Persons of Hispanic or Latino origin can be of any race; (1) Figures cover the Boise City, ID Metropolitan Statistical Area—see Appendix B for areas included
Source: U.S. Census Bureau, 2011-2013 American Community Survey 3-Year Estimates

Segregation

Type	Segregation Indices[1] 1990	2000	2010	2010 Rank[2]	Percent Change 1990-2000	Percent Change 1990-2010	Percent Change 2000-2010
Black/White	31.6	26.8	30.2	101	-4.8	-1.4	3.4
Asian/White	19.2	23.4	27.6	95	4.1	8.4	4.3
Hispanic/White	41.1	39.0	36.2	80	-2.1	-4.9	-2.8

Note: All figures cover the Metropolitan Statistical Area—see Appendix B for areas included; Figures are based on an analysis of 1990, 2000, and 2010 Census Decennial Census tract data by William H. Frey, Brookings Institution and the University of Michigan Social Science Data Analysis Network. In this analysis all racial groups (whites, blacks, and asians) are non-Hispanic members of those races. Hispanics are shown as a separate category;
(1) Segregation Indices are Dissimilarity Indices that measure the degree to which the minority group is distributed differently than whites across census tracts. They range from 0 (complete integration) to 100 (complete segregation) where the value indicates the percentage of the minority group that needs to move to be distributed exactly like whites; (2) Ranges from 1 (most segregated) to 102 (least segregated); n/a not available.
Source: www.CensusScope.org

Ancestry

Area	German	Irish	English	American	Italian	Polish	French[2]	Scottish	Dutch
City	18.0	10.5	14.2	6.9	4.6	1.8	2.5	3.8	2.2
MSA[1]	17.0	8.8	13.9	10.4	3.3	1.5	2.2	3.2	2.0
U.S.	14.9	10.8	8.0	7.4	5.5	3.0	2.7	1.7	1.4

Note: Figures are the percentage of the total population reporting a particular ancestry. The nine most commonly reported ancestries in the U.S. are shown. Figures include multiple ancestries (e.g. if a person reported being Irish and Italian, they were included in both columns); (1) Figures cover the Boise City, ID Metropolitan Statistical Area—see Appendix B for areas included; (2) Excludes Basque
Source: U.S. Census Bureau, 2011-2013 American Community Survey 3-Year Estimates

Foreign-Born Population

Area	Any Foreign Country	Mexico	Asia	Europe	Carribean	South America	Central America[2]	Africa	Canada
City	7.4	1.4	3.3	1.5	0.0	0.1	0.3	0.4	0.4
MSA[1]	6.6	2.8	1.6	1.1	0.0	0.2	0.2	0.2	0.3
U.S.	13.0	3.7	3.8	1.5	1.2	0.9	1.0	0.6	0.3

Note: (1) Figures cover the Boise City, ID Metropolitan Statistical Area—see Appendix B for areas included; (2) Excludes Mexico.
Source: U.S. Census Bureau, 2011-2013 American Community Survey 3-Year Estimates

Marital Status

Area	Never Married	Now Married[2]	Separated	Widowed	Divorced
City	33.1	47.2	0.9	4.8	14.1
MSA[1]	27.5	53.8	1.2	4.8	12.6
U.S.	32.7	48.1	2.2	6.0	11.0

Note: Figures are percentages and cover the population 15 years of age and older; (1) Figures cover the Boise City, ID Metropolitan Statistical Area—see Appendix B for areas included; (2) Excludes separated
Source: U.S. Census Bureau, 2011-2013 American Community Survey 3-Year Estimates

Disability Status

Area	All Ages	Under 18 Years Old	18 to 64 Years Old	65 Years and Over
City	11.3	4.1	9.4	36.0
MSA[1]	11.6	4.5	10.0	36.2
U.S.	12.3	4.1	10.2	36.3

Note: Figures show percent of the civilian noninstitutionalized population that reported having a disability. Disability status is determined from from six types of difficulty: vision, hearing, cognitive, ambulatory, self-care, and independent living. For children under 5 years old, hearing and vision difficulty are used to determine disability status. For children between the ages of 5 and 14, disability status is determined from hearing, vision, cognitive, ambulatory, and self-care difficulties. For people aged 15 years and older, they are considered to have a disability if they have difficulty with any one of the six difficulty types; (1) Figures cover the Boise City, ID Metropolitan Statistical Area—see Appendix B for areas included.
Source: U.S. Census Bureau, 2011-2013 American Community Survey 3-Year Estimates

Age

Area	Under Age 5	Age 5–19	Age 20–34	Age 35–44	Age 45–54	Age 55–64	Age 65–74	Age 75–84	Age 85+	Median Age
City	5.9	18.7	23.9	13.3	13.9	12.6	6.5	3.4	1.7	36.0
MSA[1]	7.0	22.7	20.4	13.5	13.1	11.4	7.0	3.4	1.4	34.9
U.S.	6.4	19.9	20.7	12.9	14.1	12.3	7.6	4.2	1.9	37.4

Note: (1) Figures cover the Boise City, ID Metropolitan Statistical Area—see Appendix B for areas included
Source: U.S. Census Bureau, 2011-2013 American Community Survey 3-Year Estimates

Gender

Area	Males	Females	Males per 100 Females
City	104,867	107,013	98.0
MSA[1]	318,282	320,228	99.4
U.S.	154,451,010	159,410,713	96.9

Note: (1) Figures cover the Boise City, ID Metropolitan Statistical Area—see Appendix B for areas included
Source: U.S. Census Bureau, 2011-2013 American Community Survey 3-Year Estimates

Religious Groups by Family

Area	Catholic	Baptist	Non-Den.	Methodist[2]	Lutheran	LDS[3]	Pente-costal	Presby-terian[4]	Muslim[5]	Judaism
MSA[1]	8.0	2.9	4.2	2.1	1.2	15.9	2.3	0.6	0.1	0.1
U.S.	19.1	9.3	4.0	4.0	2.3	2.0	1.9	1.6	0.8	0.7

Note: Figures are the number of adherents as a percentage of the total population; (1) Figures cover the Boise City-Nampa, ID Metropolitan Statistical Area—see Appendix B for areas included; (2) Methodist/Pietist; (3) Latter Day Saints; (4) Reformed; (5) Figures are estimates
Source: Association of Statisticians of American Religious Bodies, 2010 U.S. Religion Census: Religious Congregations & Membership Study

Religious Groups by Tradition

Area	Catholic	Evangelical Protestant	Mainline Protestant	Other Tradition	Black Protestant	Orthodox
MSA[1]	8.0	13.0	4.4	16.7	<0.1	0.1
U.S.	19.1	16.2	7.3	4.3	1.6	0.3

Note: Figures are the number of adherents as a percentage of the total population; (1) Figures cover the Boise City-Nampa, ID Metropolitan Statistical Area—see Appendix B for areas included
Source: Association of Statisticians of American Religious Bodies, 2010 U.S. Religion Census: Religious Congregations & Membership Study

ECONOMY

Gross Metropolitan Product

Area	2012	2013	2014	2015	Rank[2]
MSA[1]	27.5	28.3	29.5	31.1	85

Note: Figures are in billions of dollars; (1) Figures cover the Boise City, ID Metropolitan Statistical Area—see Appendix B for areas included; (2) Rank is based on 2015 data and ranges from 1 to 363
Source: The U.S. Conference of Mayors, U.S. Metro Economies: GMP and Employment 2013-2015, June 2014

Economic Growth

Area	2010-12 (%)	2013 (%)	2014 (%)	2015 (%)	Rank[2]
MSA[1]	1.3	1.5	2.7	3.4	88
U.S.	2.1	2.0	2.3	3.2	–

Note: Figures are real gross metropolitan product (GMP) growth rates and represent annual average percent change; (1) Figures cover the Boise City, ID Metropolitan Statistical Area—see Appendix B for areas included; (2) Rank is based on 2015 data and ranges from 1 to 363
Source: The U.S. Conference of Mayors, U.S. Metro Economies: GMP and Employment 2013-2015, June 2014

Metropolitan Area Exports

Area	2008	2009	2010	2011	2012	2013	Rank[2]
MSA[1]	3,851.2	2,849.7	3,647.7	4,131.5	4,088.2	3,657.9	68

Note: Figures are in millions of dollars; (1) Figures cover the Boise City, ID Metropolitan Statistical Area—see Appendix B for areas included; (2) Rank is based on 2013 data and ranges from 1 to 387
Source: U.S. Department of Commerce, International Trade Administration, Office of Trade & Industry Information, Manufacturing & Services, data extracted April 3, 2015

Building Permits

Area	Single-Family			Multi-Family			Total		
	2013	2014	Pct. Chg.	2013	2014	Pct. Chg.	2013	2014	Pct. Chg.
City	498	467	-6.2	222	793	257.2	720	1,260	75.0
MSA[1]	3,522	3,481	-1.2	843	1,702	101.9	4,365	5,183	18.7
U.S.	620,802	634,597	2.2	370,020	411,766	11.3	990,822	1,046,363	5.6

*Note: (1) Figures cover the Boise City, ID Metropolitan Statistical Area—see Appendix B for areas included;
Figures represent new, privately-owned housing units authorized (unadjusted data); All permit data are based
on estimates with imputation.*
Source: U.S. Census Bureau, Manufacturing, Mining, and Construction Statistics, Building Permits, 2013, 2014

Bankruptcy Filings

Area	Business Filings			Nonbusiness Filings		
	2013	2014	% Chg.	2013	2014	% Chg.
Ada County	60	47	-21.7	1,494	1,177	-21.2
U.S.	33,212	26,983	-18.8	1,038,720	909,812	-12.4

*Note: Business filings include Chapter 7, Chapter 11, Chapter 12, and Chapter 13; Nonbusiness filings include
Chapter 7, Chapter 11, and Chapter 13*
*Source: Administrative Office of the U.S. Courts, Business and Nonbusiness Bankruptcy, County Cases
Commenced by Chapter of the Bankruptcy Code, During the 12- Month Period Ending December 31, 2013 and
Business and Nonbusiness Bankruptcy, County Cases Commenced by Chapter of the Bankruptcy Code, During
the 12- Month Period Ending December 31, 2014*

Housing Vacancy Rates

Area	Gross Vacancy Rate[2] (%)			Year-Round Vacancy Rate[3] (%)			Rental Vacancy Rate[4] (%)			Homeowner Vacancy Rate[5] (%)		
	2012	2013	2014	2012	2013	2014	2012	2013	2014	2012	2013	2014
MSA[1]	n/a	n/a	n/a	n/a	n/a	n/a	n/a	n/a	n/a	n/a	n/a	n/a
U.S.	13.8	13.6	13.4	10.8	10.7	10.4	8.7	8.3	7.6	2.0	2.0	1.9

*Note: (1) Figures cover the Boise City, ID Metropolitan Statistical Area—see Appendix B for areas included; (2)
The percentage of the total housing inventory that is vacant; (3) The percentage of the housing inventory
(excluding seasonal units) that is year-round vacant; (4) The percentage of rental inventory that is vacant for
rent; (5) The percentage of homeowner inventory that is vacant for sale; n/a not available*
Source: U.S. Census Bureau, Housing Vacancies and Homeownership Annual Statistics: 2014

INCOME

Income

Area	Per Capita ($)	Median Household ($)	Average Household ($)
City	27,616	46,757	65,336
MSA[1]	23,630	48,755	63,335
U.S.	27,884	52,176	72,897

Note: (1) Figures cover the Boise City, ID Metropolitan Statistical Area—see Appendix B for areas included
Source: U.S. Census Bureau, 2011-2013 American Community Survey 3-Year Estimates

Household Income Distribution

Area	Percent of Households Earning							
	Under $15,000	$15,000 -24,999	$25,000 -34,999	$35,000 -49,999	$50,000 -74,999	$75,000 -99,000	$100,000 -149,999	$150,000 and up
City	13.7	11.5	12.1	15.5	17.1	11.6	10.6	7.8
MSA[1]	12.3	11.2	11.9	15.6	20.2	12.1	10.4	6.3
U.S.	13.0	10.9	10.3	13.6	17.9	11.9	12.7	9.6

Note: (1) Figures cover the Boise City, ID Metropolitan Statistical Area—see Appendix B for areas included
Source: U.S. Census Bureau, 2011-2013 American Community Survey 3-Year Estimates

Poverty Rate

Area	All Ages	Under 18 Years Old	18 to 64 Years Old	65 Years and Over
City	15.9	18.9	16.6	6.3
MSA[1]	16.2	20.7	15.7	8.9
U.S.	15.9	22.4	14.8	9.5

Note: Figures are percentage of people whose income during the past 12 months was below the poverty level;
(1) Figures cover the Boise City, ID Metropolitan Statistical Area—see Appendix B for areas included
Source: U.S. Census Bureau, 2011-2013 American Community Survey 3-Year Estimates

EMPLOYMENT

Labor Force and Employment

Area	Civilian Labor Force			Workers Employed		
	Dec. 2013	Dec. 2014	% Chg.	Dec. 2013	Dec. 2014	% Chg.
City	115,170	115,344	0.2	110,221	111,964	1.6
MSA[1]	312,188	313,572	0.4	296,477	300,918	1.5
U.S.	154,408,000	155,521,000	0.7	144,423,000	147,190,000	1.9

Note: Data is not seasonally adjusted and covers workers 16 years of age and older; (1) Figures cover the Boise City, ID Metropolitan Statistical Area—see Appendix B for areas included
Source: Bureau of Labor Statistics, Local Area Unemployment Statistics

Unemployment Rate

Area	2014											
	Jan.	Feb.	Mar.	Apr.	May	Jun.	Jul.	Aug.	Sep.	Oct.	Nov.	Dec.
City	4.8	4.6	4.4	4.1	3.9	4.1	4.0	4.1	3.7	3.4	3.3	2.9
MSA[1]	5.7	5.4	5.2	4.7	4.4	4.6	4.6	4.7	4.2	4.0	4.2	4.0
U.S.	7.0	7.0	6.8	5.9	6.1	6.3	6.5	6.3	5.7	5.5	5.5	5.4

Note: Data is not seasonally adjusted and covers workers 16 years of age and older; (1) Figures cover the Boise City, ID Metropolitan Statistical Area—see Appendix B for areas included
Source: Bureau of Labor Statistics, Local Area Unemployment Statistics

Employment by Occupation

Occupation Classification	City (%)	MSA[1] (%)	U.S. (%)
Management, Business, Science, and Arts	42.6	36.4	36.2
Natural Resources, Construction, and Maintenance	5.9	9.7	9.0
Production, Transportation, and Material Moving	7.8	10.6	12.1
Sales and Office	26.6	26.1	24.4
Service	17.2	17.3	18.3

Note: Figures cover employed civilians 16 years of age and older; (1) Figures cover the Boise City, ID Metropolitan Statistical Area—see Appendix B for areas included
Source: U.S. Census Bureau, 2011-2013 American Community Survey 3-Year Estimates

Employment by Industry

Sector	MSA[1]		U.S.
	Number of Employees	Percent of Total	Percent of Total
Construction, Mining, and Logging	17,600	6.2	5.0
Education and Health Services	43,200	15.1	15.5
Financial Activities	16,000	5.6	5.7
Government	45,300	15.9	15.8
Information	4,400	1.5	2.0
Leisure and Hospitality	26,400	9.2	10.3
Manufacturing	24,900	8.7	8.7
Other Services	10,200	3.6	4.0
Professional and Business Services	40,200	14.1	13.8
Retail Trade	34,700	12.2	11.4
Transportation, Warehousing, and Utilities	9,100	3.2	3.9
Wholesale Trade	13,500	4.7	4.2

Note: Figures are non-farm employment as of December 2014. Figures are not seasonally adjusted and include workers 16 years of age and older; (1) Figures cover the Boise City, ID Metropolitan Statistical Area—see Appendix B for areas included; n/a not available
Source: Bureau of Labor Statistics, Current Employment Statistics, Employment, Hours, and Earnings

Occupations with Greatest Projected Employment Growth: 2012 – 2022

Occupation[1]	2012 Employment	2022 Projected Employment	Numeric Employment Change	Percent Employment Change
Retail Salespersons	21,290	25,580	4,290	20.1
Customer Service Representatives	15,620	19,010	3,390	21.7
Registered Nurses	12,280	15,510	3,230	26.4
Combined Food Preparation and Serving Workers, Including Fast Food	9,860	13,080	3,220	32.6
Personal Care Aides	8,200	11,300	3,100	37.8
Cashiers	14,780	17,070	2,290	15.5
Waiters and Waitresses	10,000	12,160	2,160	21.6
General and Operations Managers	10,970	13,000	2,030	18.5
Nursing Assistants	7,630	9,450	1,820	23.9
Cooks, Restaurant	5,510	7,280	1,770	32.2

Note: Projections cover Idaho; (1) Sorted by numeric employment change
Source: www.projectionscentral.com, State Occupational Projections, 2012–2022 Long-Term Projections

Fastest Growing Occupations: 2012 – 2022

Occupation[1]	2012 Employment	2022 Projected Employment	Numeric Employment Change	Percent Employment Change
Insulation Workers, Floor, Ceiling, and Wall	150	250	100	74.5
Diagnostic Medical Sonographers	420	630	210	50.8
Drywall and Ceiling Tile Installers	680	990	310	45.6
Brickmasons and Blockmasons	230	330	100	43.4
Tile and Marble Setters	370	530	160	41.8
Home Health Aides	2,330	3,300	970	41.6
Cardiovascular Technologists and Technicians	270	370	100	39.8
Physical Therapist Assistants	370	510	140	37.8
Personal Care Aides	8,200	11,300	3,100	37.8
Nursing Instructors and Teachers, Postsecondary	270	370	100	37.5

Note: Projections cover Idaho; (1) Sorted by percent employment change and excludes occupations with numeric employment change less than 100
Source: www.projectionscentral.com, State Occupational Projections, 2012–2022 Long-Term Projections

Average Wages

Occupation	$/Hr.	Occupation	$/Hr.
Accountants and Auditors	31.21	Maids and Housekeeping Cleaners	10.54
Automotive Mechanics	19.95	Maintenance and Repair Workers	15.46
Bookkeepers	16.67	Marketing Managers	51.47
Carpenters	16.83	Nuclear Medicine Technologists	n/a
Cashiers	10.18	Nurses, Licensed Practical	20.09
Clerks, General Office	13.70	Nurses, Registered	29.51
Clerks, Receptionists/Information	12.93	Nursing Assistants	11.14
Clerks, Shipping/Receiving	13.54	Packers and Packagers, Hand	12.24
Computer Programmers	31.15	Physical Therapists	36.62
Computer Systems Analysts	37.77	Postal Service Mail Carriers	24.83
Computer User Support Specialists	20.70	Real Estate Brokers	n/a
Cooks, Restaurant	9.81	Retail Salespersons	12.38
Dentists	85.84	Sales Reps., Exc. Tech./Scientific	28.69
Electrical Engineers	44.74	Sales Reps., Tech./Scientific	30.79
Electricians	22.22	Secretaries, Exc. Legal/Med./Exec.	14.58
Financial Managers	48.15	Security Guards	13.16
First-Line Supervisors/Managers, Sales	18.16	Surgeons	n/a
Food Preparation Workers	9.20	Teacher Assistants	11.90
General and Operations Managers	39.82	Teachers, Elementary School	24.50
Hairdressers/Cosmetologists	11.79	Teachers, Secondary School	24.20
Internists	n/a	Telemarketers	12.08
Janitors and Cleaners	10.63	Truck Drivers, Heavy/Tractor-Trailer	18.12
Landscaping/Groundskeeping Workers	12.63	Truck Drivers, Light/Delivery Svcs.	14.55
Lawyers	50.07	Waiters and Waitresses	8.96

Note: Wage data covers the Boise City-Nampa, ID Metropolitan Statistical Area—see Appendix B for areas included; Hourly wages for elementary/secondary school teachers and teacher assistants were calculated by the editors from annual wage data assuming a 40 hour work week; n/a not available.
Source: Bureau of Labor Statistics, Metro Area Occupational Employment and Wage Estimates, May 2014

TAXES

State Corporate Income Tax Rates

State	Tax Rate (%)	Income Brackets ($)	Num. of Brackets	Financial Institution Tax Rate (%)[a]	Federal Income Tax Ded.
Idaho	7.4 (h)	Flat rate	1	7.4 (h)	No

Note: Tax rates as of January 1, 2015; (a) Rates listed are the corporate income tax rate applied to financial institutions or excise taxes based on income. Some states have other taxes based upon the value of deposits or shares; (h) Idaho's minimum tax on a corporation is $20. The $10 Permanent Building Fund Tax must be paid by each corporation in a unitary group filing a combined return. Taxpayers with gross sales in Idaho under $100,000, and with no property or payroll in Idaho, may elect to pay 1% on such sales (instead of the tax on net income).
Source: Federation of Tax Administrators, "State Corporate Income Tax Rates, 2015"

State Individual Income Tax Rates

State	Tax Rate (%)	Income Brackets ($)	Num. of Brackets	Personal Exempt. ($)[1] Single	Personal Exempt. ($)[1] Dependents	Fed. Inc. Tax Ded.
Idaho (a)	1.6 - 7.4	1,429 - 10,718 (b)	7	4,000 (d)	4,000 (d)	No

Note: Tax rates as of January 1, 2015; Local- and county-level taxes are not included; n/a not applicable; (1) Married joint filers generally receive double the single exemption; (a) 17 states have statutory provision for automatically adjusting to the rate of inflation the dollar values of the income tax brackets, standard deductions, and/or personal exemptions. Massachusetts, Michigan, and Nebraska index the personal exemption only. Oregon does not index the income brackets for $125,000 and over. Maine has suspended indexing for 2014 and 2015; (b) For joint returns, taxes are twice the tax on half the couple's income; (d) These states use the personal exemption amounts provided in the federal Internal Revenue Code.
Source: Federation of Tax Administrators, "State Individual Income Tax Rates, 2015"

Various State and Local Tax Rates

State	State and Local Sales and Use (%)	State Sales and Use (%)	Gasoline[1] (¢/gal.)	Cigarette[2] ($/pack)	Spirits[3] ($/gal.)	Wine[4] ($/gal.)	Beer[5] ($/gal.)
Idaho	6.0	6.0	25	0.57	10.90 (g)	0.45	0.15 (p)

Note: All tax rates as of January 1, 2015; (1) The American Petroleum Institute has developed a methodology for determining the average tax rate on a gallon of fuel. Rates may include any of the following: excise taxes, environmental fees, storage tank fees, other fees or taxes, general sales tax, and local taxes. In states where gasoline is subject to the general sales tax, or where the fuel tax is based on the average sale price, the average rate determined by API is sensitive to changes in the price of gasoline. States that fully or partially apply general sales taxes to gasoline: CA, CO, GA, IL, IN, MI, NY; (2) The federal excise tax of $1.0066 per pack and local taxes are not included; (3) Rates are those applicable to off-premise sales of 40% alcohol by volume (a.b.v.) distilled spirits in 750ml containers. Local excise taxes are excluded; (4) Rates are those applicable to off-premise sales of 11% a.b.v. non-carbonated wine in 750ml containers; (5) Rates are those applicable to off-premise sales of 4.7% a.b.v. beer in 12 ounce containers; (g) States where the government controls sales. In these "control states," products are subject to ad valorem mark-up and excise taxes. The excise tax rate is calculated using a methodology developed by the Distilled Spirits Council of the United States; (p) Local excise taxes are excluded.
Source: Tax Foundation, 2015 Facts & Figures: How Does Your State Compare?

State Business Tax Climate Index Rankings

State	Overall Rank	Corporate Tax Index Rank	Individual Income Tax Index Rank	Sales Tax Index Rank	Unemployment Insurance Tax Index Rank	Property Tax Index Rank
Idaho	19	21	24	22	46	3

Note: The index is a measure of how each state's tax laws affect economic performance. The lower the rank, the more favorable a state's tax system is for business. States without a given tax are given a ranking of 1. The scores/rankings for the District of Columbia do not affect other states. The 2015 index represents the tax climate as of July 1, 2014.
Source: Tax Foundation, State Business Tax Climate Index 2015

COMMERCIAL UTILITIES

Typical Monthly Electric Bills

Area	Commercial Service ($/month)		Industrial Service ($/month)	
	1,500 kWh	40 kW demand 14,000 kWh	1,000 kW demand 200,000 kWh	50,000 kW demand 32,500,000 kWh
City	178	954	15,992	n/a
Average[1]	201	1,653	26,124	2,639,743

Note: Figures are based on annualized 2014 rates; (1) Average based on 180 utilities surveyed; n/a not available
Source: Edison Electric Institute, Typical Bills and Average Rates Report, Summer 2014

TRANSPORTATION

Means of Transportation to Work

Area	Car/Truck/Van		Public Transportation			Bicycle	Walked	Other Means	Worked at Home
	Drove Alone	Car-pooled	Bus	Subway	Railroad				
City	78.9	7.6	0.7	0.0	0.0	2.5	3.2	1.4	5.6
MSA[1]	79.0	8.7	0.4	0.0	0.0	1.1	2.0	1.9	6.8
U.S.	76.4	9.6	2.6	1.8	0.6	0.6	2.8	1.3	4.3

Note: Figures are percentages and cover workers 16 years of age and older; (1) Figures cover the Boise City, ID Metropolitan Statistical Area—see Appendix B for areas included
Source: U.S. Census Bureau, 2011-2013 American Community Survey 3-Year Estimates

Travel Time to Work

Area	Less Than 10 Minutes	10 to 19 Minutes	20 to 29 Minutes	30 to 44 Minutes	45 to 59 Minutes	60 to 89 Minutes	90 Minutes or More
City	17.3	44.9	24.2	9.7	1.3	1.3	1.3
MSA[1]	14.4	34.8	26.3	17.6	3.8	2.0	1.2
U.S.	13.3	29.7	20.9	20.2	7.7	5.7	2.6

Note: Figures are percentages and include workers 16 years old and over; (1) Figures cover the Boise City, ID Metropolitan Statistical Area—see Appendix B for areas included
Source: U.S. Census Bureau, 2011-2013 American Community Survey 3-Year Estimates

Travel Time Index

Area	1985	1990	1995	2000	2005	2010	2011
Urban Area[1]	1.02	1.04	1.04	1.07	1.09	1.06	1.06
Average[2]	1.09	1.14	1.16	1.19	1.23	1.18	1.18

Note: Travel Time Index—the ratio of travel time in the peak period to the travel time at free-flow conditions. For example, a value of 1.30 indicates a 20-minute free-flow trip takes 26 minutes in the peak. Free-flow speeds (60 mph on freeways and 35 mph on principal arterials) are used as the comparison threshold; (1) Covers the Boise ID urban area; (2) average of 498 urban areas
Source: Texas Transportation Institute, Urban Mobility Report 2012, December 2012

Public Transportation

Agency Name / Mode of Transportation	Vehicles Operated in Maximum Service	Annual Unlinked Passenger Trips (in thous.)	Annual Passenger Miles (in thous.)
ValleyRide			
Bus (directly operated)	38	1,454.1	9,175.4
Demand Response (directly operated)	15	46.2	368.6

Source: Federal Transit Administration, National Transit Database, 2013

Air Transportation

Airport Name and Code / Type of Service	Passenger Airlines[1]	Passenger Enplanements	Freight Carriers[2]	Freight (lbs.)
Boise Air Terminal-Gowen Field (BOI)				
Domestic service (U.S. carriers - 2014)	18	1,376,976	9	38,093,883
International service (U.S. carriers - 2013)	2	108	0	0

Note: (1) Includes all U.S.-based major, minor and commuter airlines that carried at least one passenger during the year; (2) Includes all U.S.-based airlines and freight carriers that transported at least one lb. of freight during the year.
Source: Bureau of Transportation Statistics, The Intermodal Transportation Database, Air Carriers: T-100 Domestic Market (U.S. Carriers), 2014; Bureau of Transportation Statistics, The Intermodal Transportation Database, Air Carriers: T-100 International Market (U.S. Carriers), 2013

Other Transportation Statistics

Major Highways:	I-84
Amtrak Service:	Bus connection
Major Waterways/Ports:	None

Source: Amtrak.com; Google Maps

BUSINESSES

Major Business Headquarters

Company Name	Rankings	
	Fortune[1]	Forbes[2]
Albertsons	-	11
JR Simplot	-	63
Micron Technology	302	-
WinCo Foods	-	68

Note: (1) Fortune 500—companies that produce a 10-K are ranked 1 to 500 based on 2013 revenue; (2) all private companies with at least $2 billion in annual revenue through the end of their most current fiscal year are ranked 1 to 221; companies listed are headquartered in the city; dashes indicate no ranking
Source: Fortune, "Fortune 500," June 16, 2014; Forbes, "America's Largest Private Companies," November 5, 2014

Fast-Growing Businesses

According to *Inc.*, Boise City is home to one of America's 500 fastest-growing private companies: **Ataraxis** (#112). Criteria: must be an independent, privately-held, for-profit, U.S. corporation, proprietorship or partnership; revenues must be at least $100,000 in 2010 and $2 million in 2013; must have four-year operating/sales history. Holding companies, regulated banks, and utilities were excluded. *Inc.*, *"America's 500 Fastest-Growing Private Companies," September 2014*

Minority- and Women-Owned Businesses

Group	All Firms		Firms with Paid Employees			
	Firms	Sales ($000)	Firms	Sales ($000)	Employees	Payroll ($000)
Asian	334	87,192	127	78,909	818	12,425
Black	115	10,503	8	6,281	47	702
Hispanic	447	35,995	104	30,376	465	8,701
Women	6,314	730,171	849	606,840	5,526	146,859
All Firms	24,611	47,523,495	6,802	46,786,667	173,758	7,366,058

Note: Figures cover firms located in the city; minority- and women-owned business are defined as firms in which the corresponding group own 51% or more of the stock or equity of the company
Source: U.S. Census Bureau, 2007 Economic Census, Survey of Business Owners (2012 Survey of Business Owners data will be released starting in June 2015)

HOTELS & CONVENTION CENTERS

Hotels/Motels

Area	5 Star		4 Star		3 Star		2 Star		1 Star		Not Rated	
	Num.	Pct.[3]	Num.	Pct.[3]	Num.	Pct.[3]	Num.	Pct.[3]	Num.	Pct.[3]	Num.	Pct.[3]
City[1]	0	0.0	1	1.3	21	27.6	50	65.8	1	1.3	3	3.9
Total[2]	166	0.9	1,264	7.0	5,718	31.8	9,340	52.0	411	2.3	1,070	6.0

Note: (1) Figures cover Boise City and vicinity; (2) Figures cover all 100 cities in this book; (3) Percentage of hotels which have a given star rating; Star ratings are determined by expedia.com and offer an indication of the general quality of a particular hotel.
Source: expedia.com, April 2, 2015

Major Convention Centers

Name	Overall Space (sq. ft.)	Exhibit Space (sq. ft.)	Meeting Space (sq. ft.)	Meeting Rooms
Boise Centre on the Grove	n/a	45,000	n/a	n/a

Note: Table includes convention centers located in the Boise City, ID metro area; n/a not available
Source: Original research

Living Environment

COST OF LIVING

Cost of Living Index

Composite Index	Groceries	Housing	Utilities	Trans-portation	Health Care	Misc. Goods/Services
94.5	93.3	86.0	88.8	106.0	103.9	98.6

Note: The Cost of Living Index measures regional differences in the cost of consumer goods and services, excluding taxes and non-consumer expenditures, for professional and managerial households in the top income quintile. It is based on more than 50,000 prices covering almost 60 different items for which prices are collected three times a year by chambers of commerce, economic development organizations or university applied economic centers in each participating urban area. The numbers shown should be read as a percentage above or below the national average of 100. For example, a value of 115.4 in the groceries column indicates that grocery prices are 15.4% higher than the national average. Small differences in the index numbers should not be interpreted as significant; Figures cover the Boise ID urban area.
Source: The Council for Community and Economic Research, ACCRA Cost of Living Index, 2014

Grocery Prices

Area[1]	T-Bone Steak ($/pound)	Frying Chicken ($/pound)	Whole Milk ($/half gal.)	Eggs ($/dozen)	Orange Juice ($/64 oz.)	Coffee ($/11.5 oz.)
City[2]	8.98	1.29	1.72	1.35	3.52	4.75
Avg.	10.40	1.37	2.40	1.99	3.46	4.27
Min.	8.48	0.93	1.37	1.30	2.83	2.99
Max.	14.20	2.44	3.62	4.02	6.42	6.96

Note: (1) Values for the local area are compared with the average, minimum and maximum values for all 308 areas in the Cost of Living Index; (2) Figures cover the Boise ID urban area; **T-Bone Steak** *(price per pound);* **Frying Chicken** *(price per pound, whole fryer);* **Whole Milk** *(half gallon carton);* **Eggs** *(price per dozen, Grade A, large);* **Orange Juice** *(64 oz. Tropicana or Florida Natural);* **Coffee** *(11.5 oz. can, vacuum-packed, Maxwell House, Hills Bros, or Folgers).*
Source: The Council for Community and Economic Research, ACCRA Cost of Living Index, 2014

Housing and Utility Costs

Area[1]	New Home Price ($)	Apartment Rent ($/month)	All Electric ($/month)	Part Electric ($/month)	Other Energy ($/month)	Telephone ($/month)
City[2]	266,916	730	-	83.64	65.94	24.98
Avg.	305,838	919	181.00	93.66	73.14	27.95
Min.	183,142	480	112.00	42.06	23.42	17.16
Max.	1,358,576	3,851	594.00	180.03	440.99	40.42

Note: (1) Values for the local area are compared with the average, minimum and maximum values for all 308 areas in the Cost of Living Index; (2) Figures cover the Boise ID urban area; **New Home Price** *(2,400 sf living area, 8,000 sf lot, in urban area with full utilities);* **Apartment Rent** *(950 sf 2 bedroom/1.5 or 2 bath, unfurnished, excluding all utilities except water);* **All Electric** *(average monthly cost for an all-electric home);* **Part Electric** *(average monthly cost for a part-electric home);* **Other Energy** *(average monthly cost for natural gas, fuel oil, coal, wood, and any other forms of energy except electricity);* **Telephone** *(price includes basic monthly rate for a private residential line plus additional local usage charges incurred by a family of four).*
Source: The Council for Community and Economic Research, ACCRA Cost of Living Index, 2014

Health Care, Transportation, and Other Costs

Area[1]	Doctor ($/visit)	Dentist ($/visit)	Optometrist ($/visit)	Gasoline ($/gallon)	Beauty Salon ($/visit)	Men's Shirt ($)
City[2]	123.82	83.40	110.75	3.48	28.39	30.38
Avg.	102.86	87.89	97.66	3.44	34.37	26.74
Min.	67.47	65.78	51.18	3.00	17.43	12.79
Max.	173.50	150.14	235.00	4.33	64.28	49.50

Note: (1) Values for the local area are compared with the average, minimum and maximum values for all 308 areas in the Cost of Living Index; (2) Figures cover the Boise ID urban area; **Doctor** *(general practitioners routine exam of an established patient);* **Dentist** *(adult teeth cleaning and periodic oral examination);* **Optometrist** *(full vision eye exam for established adult patient);* **Gasoline** *(one gallon regular unleaded, national brand, including all taxes, cash price at self-service pump if available);* **Beauty Salon** *(woman's shampoo, trim, and blow-dry);* **Men's Shirt** *(cotton/polyester dress shirt, pinpoint weave, long sleeves).*
Source: The Council for Community and Economic Research, ACCRA Cost of Living Index, 2014

HOUSING

House Price Index (HPI)

Area	National Ranking[2]	Quarterly Change (%)	One-Year Change (%)	Five-Year Change (%)
MSA[1]	65	0.31	7.45	8.86
U.S.[3]	–	1.35	4.91	11.59

Note: The HPI is a weighted repeat sales index. It measures average price changes in repeat sales or refinancings on the same properties. This information is obtained by reviewing repeat mortgage transactions on single-family properties whose mortgages have been purchased or securitized by Fannie Mae or Freddie Mac in January 1975; (1) Boise City Metropolitan Statistical Area—see Appendix B for areas included; (2) Rankings are based on annual percentage change for all metro areas containing at least 15,000 transactions over the last 10 years and ranges from 1 to 275; (3) figures based on a weighted average of Census Division estimates using a seasonally adjusted, purchase-only index; all figures are for the period ending December 31, 2014
Source: Federal Housing Finance Agency, House Price Index, February 26, 2015

Median Single-Family Home Prices

Area	2012	2013	2014p	Percent Change 2013 to 2014
MSA[1]	138.7	163.7	172.9	5.6
U.S. Average	177.2	197.4	209.0	5.9

Note: Figures are median sales prices of existing single-family homes in thousands of dollars; (p) preliminary; n/a not available; (1) Boise City, ID Metropolitan Statistical Area—see Appendix B for areas included
Source: National Association of Realtors, Median Sales Price of Existing Single-Family Homes for Metropolitan Areas, 4th Quarter 2014

Qualifying Income Based on Median Sales Price of Existing Single-Family Homes

Area	With 5% Down ($)	With 10% Down ($)	With 20% Down ($)
MSA[1]	38,457	36,433	32,385
U.S. Average	45,863	43,449	38,621

Note: Figures are preliminary; Qualifying income is based on a mortgage rate of 4.0%. Monthly principal and interest payment is limited to 25% of income; n/a not available; (1) Boise City, ID Metropolitan Statistical Area—see Appendix B for areas included
Source: National Association of Realtors, Qualifying Income Based on Median Sales Price of Existing Single-Family Homes for Metropolitan Areas, 4th Quarter 2014

Median Apartment Condo-Coop Home Prices

Area	2012	2013	2014p	Percent Change 2013 to 2014
MSA[1]	n/a	n/a	n/a	n/a
U.S. Average	173.7	194.9	205.1	5.2

Note: Figures are median sales prices of existing apartment condo-coop homes in thousands of dollars; (p) preliminary; n/a not available; (1) Boise City, ID Metropolitan Statistical Area—see Appendix B for areas included
Source: National Association of Realtors, Median Sales Price of Existing Apartment Condo-Coop Homes for Metropolitan Areas, 4th Quarter 2014

Gross Monthly Rent

Area	Under $200	$200 -299	$300 -499	$500 -749	$750 -999	$1,000 -1,499	$1,500 and up	Median ($)
City	0.7	2.0	8.7	34.0	30.3	19.1	5.2	779
MSA[1]	1.0	2.8	9.1	31.6	29.0	22.5	3.9	789
U.S.	1.7	3.2	7.8	22.1	24.3	26.0	14.9	900

Note: Figures are percentages except for Median; Gross rent is the contract rent plus the estimated average monthly cost of utilities (electricity, gas, and water and sewer) and fuels (oil, coal, kerosene, wood, etc.) if these are paid by the renter (or paid for the renter by someone else); (1) Figures cover the Boise City, ID Metropolitan Statistical Area—see Appendix B for areas included
Source: U.S. Census Bureau, 2011-2013 American Community Survey 3-Year Estimates

Homeownership Rate

Area	2007 (%)	2008 (%)	2009 (%)	2010 (%)	2011 (%)	2012 (%)	2013 (%)	2014 (%)
MSA[1]	n/a	n/a	n/a	n/a	n/a	n/a	n/a	n/a
U.S.	68.1	67.8	67.4	66.9	66.1	65.4	65.1	64.5

Note: (1) Figures cover the Boise City, ID Metropolitan Statistical Area—see Appendix B for areas included; n/a not available
Source: U.S. Census Bureau, Housing Vacancies and Homeownership Annual Statistics: 2014

Year Housing Structure Built

Area	2010 or Later	2000 -2009	1990 -1999	1980 -1989	1970 -1979	1960 -1969	1950 -1959	1940 -1949	Before 1940	Median Year
City	0.7	12.6	22.2	14.6	22.4	7.7	8.0	4.7	7.0	1980
MSA[1]	1.2	27.9	22.2	10.4	18.1	5.4	5.1	3.7	5.9	1991
U.S.	0.9	15.0	13.9	13.8	15.8	11.0	10.9	5.4	13.3	1976

Note: Figures are percentages except for Median Year; (1) Figures cover the Boise City, ID Metropolitan Statistical Area—see Appendix B for areas included
Source: U.S. Census Bureau, 2011-2013 American Community Survey 3-Year Estimates

HEALTH

Health Risk Data

Category	MSA[1] (%)	U.S. (%)
Adults aged 18–64 who have any kind of health care coverage	76.3	79.6
Adults who reported being in good or excellent health	85.9	83.1
Adults who are current smokers	16.0	19.6
Adults who are heavy drinkers[2]	5.6	6.1
Adults who are binge drinkers[3]	15.1	16.9
Adults who are overweight (BMI 25.0 - 29.9)	33.6	35.8
Adults who are obese (BMI 30.0 - 99.8)	28.1	27.6
Adults who participated in any physical activities in the past month	81.5	77.1
Adults 50+ who have ever had a sigmoidoscopy or colonoscopy	70.0	67.3
Women aged 40+ who have had a mammogram within the past two years	62.8	74.0
Men aged 40+ who have had a PSA test within the past two years	44.9	45.2
Adults aged 65+ who have had flu shot within the past year	51.1	60.1
Adults who always wear a seatbelt	91.0	93.8

Note: Data as of 2012 unless otherwise noted; (1) Figures cover the Boise City-Nampa, ID Metropolitan Statistical Area—see Appendix B for areas included; (2) Heavy drinkers are classified as males having more than two drinks per day or females having more than one drink per day; (3) Binge drinkers are classified as males having five or more drinks on one occasion or females having four or more drinks on one occasion
Source: Centers for Disease Control and Prevention, Behaviorial Risk Factor Surveillance System, SMART: Selected Metropolitan/Micropolitan Area Risk Trends, 2012 (Note: the CDC has discontinued this dataset but will be releasing a replacement in late 2015)

Chronic Health Indicators

Category	MSA[1] (%)	U.S. (%)
Adults who have ever been told they had a heart attack	2.6	4.5
Adults who have ever been told they had a stroke	3.2	2.9
Adults who have been told they currently have asthma	7.3	8.9
Adults who have ever been told they have arthritis	24.3	25.7
Adults who have ever been told they have diabetes[2]	7.3	9.7
Adults who have ever been told they had skin cancer	7.6	5.7
Adults who have ever been told they had any other types of cancer	6.5	6.5
Adults who have ever been told they have COPD	5.1	6.2
Adults who have ever been told they have kidney disease	1.7	2.5
Adults who have ever been told they have a form of depression	20.0	18.0

Note: Data as of 2012 unless otherwise noted; (1) Figures cover the Boise City-Nampa, ID Metropolitan Statistical Area—see Appendix B for areas included; (2) Figures do not include pregnancy-related, borderline, or pre-diabetes
Source: Centers for Disease Control and Prevention, Behaviorial Risk Factor Surveillance System, SMART: Selected Metropolitan/Micropolitan Area Risk Trends, 2012 (Note: the CDC has discontinued this dataset but will be releasing a replacement in late 2015)

Mortality Rates for the Top 10 Causes of Death in the U.S.

ICD-10[a] Sub-Chapter	ICD-10[a] Code	Age-Adjusted Mortality Rate[1] per 100,000 population	
		County[2]	U.S.
Malignant neoplasms	C00-C97	148.6	166.2
Ischaemic heart diseases	I20-I25	80.0	105.7
Other forms of heart disease	I30-I51	45.9	49.3
Chronic lower respiratory diseases	J40-J47	42.1	42.1
Organic, including symptomatic, mental disorders	F01-F09	56.9	38.1
Cerebrovascular diseases	I60-I69	30.5	37.0
Other external causes of accidental injury	W00-X59	25.2	26.9
Other degenerative diseases of the nervous system	G30-G31	28.6	25.6
Diabetes mellitus	E10-E14	18.6	21.3
Hypertensive diseases	I10-I15	15.4	19.4

Note: (a) ICD-10 = International Classification of Diseases 10th Revision; (1) Mortality rates are a three year average covering 2011-2013; (2) Figures cover Ada County
Source: Centers for Disease Control and Prevention, National Center for Health Statistics. Compressed Mortality File 1999-2013 on CDC WONDER Online Database, released October 2014. Data are compiled from the Compressed Mortality File 1999-2013, Series 20 No. 2S, 2014.

Mortality Rates for Selected Causes of Death

ICD-10[a] Sub-Chapter	ICD-10[a] Code	Age-Adjusted Mortality Rate[1] per 100,000 population	
		County[2]	U.S.
Assault	X85-Y09	*1.6	5.2
Diseases of the liver	K70-K76	11.7	13.2
Human immunodeficiency virus (HIV) disease	B20-B24	Suppressed	2.2
Influenza and pneumonia	J09-J18	9.7	15.4
Intentional self-harm	X60-X84	15.6	12.5
Malnutrition	E40-E46	*0.9	0.9
Obesity and other hyperalimentation	E65-E68	1.6	1.8
Renal failure	N17-N19	7.5	13.1
Transport accidents	V01-V99	8.7	11.7
Viral hepatitis	B15-B19	2.2	2.2

Note: (a) ICD-10 = International Classification of Diseases 10th Revision; (1) Mortality rates are a three year average covering 2011-2013; (2) Figures cover Ada County; (*) Unreliable data as per CDC
Source: Centers for Disease Control and Prevention, National Center for Health Statistics. Compressed Mortality File 1999-2013 on CDC WONDER Online Database, released October 2014. Data are compiled from the Compressed Mortality File 1999-2013, Series 20 No. 2S, 2014.

Health Insurance Coverage

Area	With Health Insurance	With Private Health Insurance	With Public Health Insurance	Without Health Insurance	Population Under Age 18 Without Health Insurance
City	86.4	72.9	24.5	13.6	7.0
MSA[1]	84.7	68.1	27.2	15.3	7.4
U.S.	85.2	65.2	31.0	14.8	7.3

Note: Figures are percentages that cover the civilian noninstitutionalized population; (1) Figures cover the Boise City, ID Metropolitan Statistical Area—see Appendix B for areas included
Source: U.S. Census Bureau, 2011-2013 American Community Survey 3-Year Estimates

Number of Medical Professionals

Area[1]	MDs[2]	DOs[2,3]	Dentists	Podiatrists	Chiropractors	Optometrists
Local (number)	1,138	84	332	14	211	74
Local (rate[4])	278.3	20.5	79.7	3.4	50.7	17.8
U.S. (rate[4])	270.0	20.2	63.1	5.7	25.2	14.9

Note: Data as of 2013 unless noted; (1) Local data covers Ada County; (2) Data as of 2012 and includes all active, non-federal physicians; (3) Doctor of Osteopathic Medicine; (4) rate per 100,000 population
Source: U.S. Department of Health and Human Services, Health Resources and Services Administration, Bureau of Health Professions, Area Resource File (ARF) 2013-2014

EDUCATION

Public School District Statistics

District Name	Schls	Pupils	Pupil/ Teacher Ratio	Minority Pupils[1] (%)	Free Lunch Eligible[2] (%)	IEP[3] (%)
Boise Independent District	50	25,750	17.6	21.8	38.2	10.4

Note: Table includes school districts with 2,000 or more students; (1) Percentage of students that are not non-Hispanic white; (2) Percentage of students that are eligible for the free lunch program; (3) Percentage of students that have an Individualized Education Program.
Source: U.S. Department of Education, National Center for Education Statistics, Common Core of Data, Local Education Agency (School District) Universe Survey: School Year 2012-2013; U.S. Department of Education, National Center for Education Statistics, Common Core of Data, Public Elementary/Secondary School Universe Survey: School Year 2012-2013

Highest Level of Education

Area	Less than H.S.	H.S. Diploma	Some College, No Deg.	Associate Degree	Bachelor's Degree	Master's Degree	Prof. School Degree	Doctorate Degree
City	5.9	20.5	25.8	9.0	24.7	10.2	2.4	1.6
MSA[1]	10.0	25.2	26.7	8.3	20.4	6.8	1.6	1.0
U.S.	13.7	28.0	21.2	7.9	18.2	7.7	1.9	1.3

Note: Figures cover persons age 25 and over; (1) Figures cover the Boise City, ID Metropolitan Statistical Area—see Appendix B for areas included
Source: U.S. Census Bureau, 2011-2013 American Community Survey 3-Year Estimates

Educational Attainment by Race

Area	High School Graduate or Higher (%)					Bachelor's Degree or Higher (%)				
	Total	White	Black	Asian	Hisp.[2]	Total	White	Black	Asian	Hisp.[2]
City	94.1	95.0	n/a	82.1	81.4	38.9	39.4	n/a	50.2	17.9
MSA[1]	90.0	90.9	91.0	83.3	63.2	29.9	30.3	25.3	48.4	10.4
U.S.	86.3	88.3	83.1	85.7	64.0	29.1	30.4	18.8	50.7	13.7

Note: Figures shown cover persons 25 years old and over; (1) Figures cover the Boise City, ID Metropolitan Statistical Area—see Appendix B for areas included; (2) People of Hispanic origin can be of any race
Source: U.S. Census Bureau, 2011-2013 American Community Survey 3-Year Estimates

School Enrollment by Grade and Control

Area	Preschool (%)		Kindergarten (%)		Grades 1 - 4 (%)		Grades 5 - 8 (%)		Grades 9 - 12 (%)	
	Public	Private	Public	Private	Public	Private	Public	Private	Public	Private
City	52.4	47.6	92.8	7.2	92.6	7.4	93.3	6.7	92.8	7.2
MSA[1]	47.1	52.9	90.3	9.7	92.9	7.1	94.1	5.9	93.6	6.4
U.S.	57.7	42.3	87.9	12.1	89.9	10.1	90.0	10.0	90.7	9.3

Note: Figures shown cover persons 3 years old and over; (1) Figures cover the Boise City, ID Metropolitan Statistical Area—see Appendix B for areas included
Source: U.S. Census Bureau, 2011-2013 American Community Survey 3-Year Estimates

Average Salaries of Public School Classroom Teachers

Area	2013-14		2014-15		Percent Change 2013-14 to 2014-15	Percent Change 2004-05 to 2014-15
	Dollars	Rank[1]	Dollars	Rank[1]		
IDAHO	44,465	49	45,218	48	1.69	10.7
U.S. Average	56,610	–	57,379	–	1.36	20.8

Note: (1) State rank ranges from 1 to 51 where 1 indicates highest salary.
Source: National Education Association, Rankings & Estimates: Rankings of the States 2014 and Estimates of School Statistics 2015, March 2015

Higher Education

Four-Year Colleges			Two-Year Colleges			Medical Schools[1]	Law Schools[2]	Voc/ Tech[3]
Public	Private Non-profit	Private For-profit	Public	Private Non-profit	Private For-profit			
1	2	2	0	0	6	0	1	1

Note: Figures cover institutions located within the city limits and include main campuses only; (1) includes schools accredited by the Liaison Committee on Medical Education and the American Osteopathic Association's Commission on Osteopathic College Accreditation; (2) includes ABA-accredited schools, schools with provisional ABA accreditation, and state accredited schools; (3) includes all schools with programs that are less than 2 years.
Source: National Center for Education Statistics, Integrated Postsecondary Education System (IPEDS), 2013-14; Association of American Medical Colleges, Member List, May 1, 2015; American Osteopathic Association, Member List, May 1, 2015; Law School Admission Council, Official Guide to ABA-Approved Law Schools Online, May 1, 2015; Wikipedia, List of Medical Schools in the United States, May 1, 2015; Wikipedia, List of Law Schools in the United States, May 1, 2015

According to *U.S. News & World Report*, the Boise City, ID metro area is home to one of the best liberal arts colleges in the U.S.: **College of Idaho** (#159). The indicators used to capture academic quality fall into a number of categories: assessment by administrators at peer institutions; retention of students; faculty resources; student selectivity; financial resources; alumni giving; high school counselor ratings of colleges; and graduation rate. *U.S. News & World Report, "America's Best Colleges 2015"*

PRESIDENTIAL ELECTION

2012 Presidential Election Results

Area	Obama (%)	Romney (%)	Other (%)
Ada County	42.7	54.0	3.2
U.S.	51.0	47.2	1.8

Note: Results may not add to 100% due to rounding
Source: Dave Leip's Atlas of U.S. Presidential Elections

EMPLOYERS

Major Employers

Company Name	Industry
Albertson's	Grocery stores
American Drug Stores	Drug stores
Blue Cross of Idaho Health Service	Hospital and medical service plans
Boise State University	Colleges and universities
Bureau of Land Management	Land management agency, government
Hewlett-Packard Company	Computers
Idaho Division of Military	National security
Kit Manufacturing Company	Travel trailers and campers
Lactalis American Group	Cheese; natural and processed
Micron Technology	Semiconductors and related devices
MK Capital Corporation	Bridge, tunnel, and elevated highway construction
Morrison-Knudsen Engineers	Bridge construction
Motivepower	Railroad car rebuilding
Saint Alphonsus Regional Medical Center	General medical and surgical hospitals
St Luke's Health System	General medical and surgical hospitals
St Luke's Regional Medical Center	Hospital, affiliated with ama residency
URS Energy & Construction	Bridge, tunnel, and elevated highway construction
Veterans Health Administration	Administration of veterans' affairs
Washington Closure Co	Environmental cleanup services
Washington Group International	Equipment rental and leasing
Wells Fargo Bank	National commercial banks
Young Men's Christian Assn of Boise	Youth organizations

Note: Companies shown are located within the Boise City, ID Metropolitan Statistical Area.
Source: Hoovers.com; Wikipedia

PUBLIC SAFETY

Crime Rate

Area	All Crimes	Violent Crimes				Property Crimes		
		Murder	Forcible Rape	Robbery	Aggrav. Assault	Burglary	Larceny -Theft	Motor Vehicle Theft
City	2,492.0	1.4	57.4	21.0	200.2	384.9	1,727.7	99.4
Suburbs[1]	1,644.6	0.7	43.8	9.0	143.2	340.9	1,034.1	72.9
Metro[2]	1,925.0	0.9	48.3	13.0	162.1	355.5	1,263.5	81.7
U.S.	3,098.6	4.5	25.2	109.1	229.1	610.0	1,899.4	221.3

Note: Figures are crimes per 100,000 population; (1) All areas within the metro area that are located outside the city limits; (2) Figures cover the Boise City, ID Metropolitan Statistical Area—see Appendix B for areas included
Source: FBI Uniform Crime Reports, 2013

Hate Crimes

Area	Number of Quarters Reported	Number of Incidents per Bias Motivation						
		Race	Religion	Sexual Orientation	Ethnicity	Disability	Gender	Gender Identity
City	4	8	1	4	0	0	0	0
U.S.	4	2,871	1,031	1,233	655	83	18	31

Source: Federal Bureau of Investigation, Hate Crime Statistics 2013

Identity Theft Consumer Complaints

Area	Complaints	Complaints per 100,000 Population	Rank[2]
MSA[1]	433	66.6	209
U.S.	332,646	104.3	-

Note: (1) Figures cover the Boise City, ID Metropolitan Statistical Area—see Appendix B for areas included; (2) Rank ranges from 1 to 380 where 1 indicates greatest number of identity theft complaints per 100,000 population
Source: Federal Trade Commission, Consumer Sentinel Network Data Book for January–December 2014

Fraud and Other Consumer Complaints

Area	Complaints	Complaints per 100,000 Population	Rank[2]
MSA[1]	2,748	422.6	102
U.S.	2,250,205	705.7	-

Note: (1) Figures cover the Boise City, ID Metropolitan Statistical Area—see Appendix B for areas included; (2) Rank ranges from 1 to 380 where 1 indicates greatest number of identity theft complaints per 100,000 population
Source: Federal Trade Commission, Consumer Sentinel Network Data Book for January–December 2014

RECREATION

Culture

Dance[1]	Theatre[1]	Instrumental Music[1]	Vocal Music[1]	Series and Festivals	Museums and Art Galleries[2]	Zoos and Aquariums[3]
4	3	3	3	2	19	1

Note: (1) Professional perfoming groups; (2) Based on organizations with SIC code 8412; (3) AZA-accredited
Source: The Grey House Performing Arts Directory, 2015-16; Association of Zoos & Aquariums, AZA Member Zoos & Aquariums, April 2015; www.AccuLeads.com, April 2015

Professional Sports Teams

Team Name	League	Year Established
No teams are located in the metro area		

Source: Wikipedia, Major Professional Sports Teams of the United States and Canada, April 2015

CLIMATE

Average and Extreme Temperatures

Temperature	Jan	Feb	Mar	Apr	May	Jun	Jul	Aug	Sep	Oct	Nov	Dec	Yr.
Extreme High (°F)	63	70	81	92	98	105	111	110	101	94	74	65	111
Average High (°F)	36	44	53	62	71	80	90	88	78	65	48	38	63
Average Temp. (°F)	29	36	42	49	58	66	74	73	63	52	40	31	51
Average Low (°F)	22	27	31	37	44	52	58	57	48	39	30	23	39
Extreme Low (°F)	-17	-15	6	19	22	31	35	34	23	11	-3	-25	-25

Note: Figures cover the years 1948-1995
Source: National Climatic Data Center, International Station Meteorological Climate Summary, 9/96

Average Precipitation/Snowfall/Humidity

Precip./Humidity	Jan	Feb	Mar	Apr	May	Jun	Jul	Aug	Sep	Oct	Nov	Dec	Yr.
Avg. Precip. (in.)	1.4	1.1	1.2	1.2	1.2	0.9	0.3	0.3	0.6	0.7	1.4	1.4	11.8
Avg. Snowfall (in.)	7	4	2	1	Tr	Tr	0	0	0	Tr	2	6	22
Avg. Rel. Hum. 7am (%)	81	80	75	69	65	59	48	50	58	67	77	81	68
Avg. Rel. Hum. 4pm (%)	68	58	45	35	34	29	22	23	28	36	55	67	42

Note: Figures cover the years 1948-1995; Tr = Trace amounts (<0.05 in. of rain; <0.5 in. of snow)
Source: National Climatic Data Center, International Station Meteorological Climate Summary, 9/96

Weather Conditions

Temperature			Daytime Sky			Precipitation		
5°F & below	32°F & below	90°F & above	Clear	Partly cloudy	Cloudy	0.01 inch or more precip.	0.1 inch or more snow/ice	Thunder-storms
6	124	45	106	133	126	91	22	14

Note: Figures are average number of days per year and cover the years 1948-1995
Source: National Climatic Data Center, International Station Meteorological Climate Summary, 9/96

HAZARDOUS WASTE

Superfund Sites

Boise City has no sites on the EPA's Superfund Final National Priorities List. There are a total of 1,322 Superfund sites on the list in the U.S. *U.S. Environmental Protection Agency, Final National Priorities List, April 14, 2015*

AIR & WATER QUALITY

Air Quality Trends: Ozone

	2004	2005	2006	2007	2008	2009	2010	2011	2012	2013
MSA[1]	n/a	n/a	n/a	n/a	n/a	n/a	n/a	n/a	n/a	n/a

Note: (1) Data covers the Boise City, ID Metropolitan Statistical Area—see Appendix B for areas included; n/a not available. The values shown are the composite ozone concentration averages among trend sites based on the highest fourth daily maximum 8-hour concentration in parts per million. These trends are based on sites having an adequate record of monitoring data during the trend period. Data from exceptional events are included.
Source: U.S. Environmental Protection Agency, Air Quality Monitoring Information, "Air Quality Trends by City, 2000-2013"

Air Quality Index

Area	Percent of Days when Air Quality was...[2]					AQI Statistics[2]	
	Good	Moderate	Unhealthy for Sensitive Groups	Unhealthy	Very Unhealthy	Maximum	Median
MSA[1]	87.9	11.8	0.0	0.3	0.0	156	37

Note: (1) Data covers the Boise City, ID Metropolitan Statistical Area—see Appendix B for areas included; (2) Based on 365 days with AQI data in 2014. Air Quality Index (AQI) is an index for reporting daily air quality. EPA calculates the AQI for five major air pollutants regulated by the Clean Air Act: ground-level ozone, particle pollution (aka particulate matter), carbon monoxide, sulfur dioxide, and nitrogen dioxide. The AQI runs from 0 to 500. The higher the AQI value, the greater the level of air pollution and the greater the health concern. There are six AQI categories: "Good" AQI is between 0 and 50. Air quality is considered satisfactory; "Moderate" AQI is between 51 and 100. Air quality is acceptable; "Unhealthy for Sensitive Groups" When AQI values are between 101 and 150, members of sensitive groups may experience health effects; "Unhealthy" When AQI values are between 151 and 200 everyone may begin to experience health effects; "Very Unhealthy" AQI values between 201 and 300 trigger a health alert; "Hazardous" AQI values over 300 trigger warnings of emergency conditions (not shown).
Source: U.S. Environmental Protection Agency, Air Quality Index Report, 2014

Air Quality Index Pollutants

Area	Percent of Days when AQI Pollutant was...[2]					
	Carbon Monoxide	Nitrogen Dioxide	Ozone	Sulfur Dioxide	Particulate Matter 2.5	Particulate Matter 10
MSA[1]	0.3	18.4	63.0	0.0	10.4	7.9

Note: (1) Data covers the Boise City, ID Metropolitan Statistical Area—see Appendix B for areas included; (2) Based on 365 days with AQI data in 2014. The Air Quality Index (AQI) is an index for reporting daily air quality. EPA calculates the AQI for five major air pollutants regulated by the Clean Air Act: ground-level ozone, particle pollution (also known as particulate matter), carbon monoxide, sulfur dioxide, and nitrogen dioxide. The AQI runs from 0 to 500. The higher the AQI value, the greater the level of air pollution and the greater the health concern.
Source: U.S. Environmental Protection Agency, Air Quality Index Report, 2014

Maximum Air Pollutant Concentrations: Particulate Matter, Ozone, CO and Lead

	Particulate Matter 10 (ug/m^3)	Particulate Matter 2.5 Wtd AM (ug/m^3)	Particulate Matter 2.5 24-Hr (ug/m^3)	Ozone (ppm)	Carbon Monoxide (ppm)	Lead (ug/m^3)
MSA[1] Level	99	13	89	0.074	1	n/a
NAAQS[2]	150	15	35	0.075	9	0.15
Met NAAQS[2]	Yes	Yes	No	Yes	Yes	n/a

Note: (1) Data covers the Boise City, ID Metropolitan Statistical Area—see Appendix B for areas included; Data from exceptional events are included; (2) National Ambient Air Quality Standards; ppm = parts per million; ug/m³ = micrograms per cubic meter; n/a not available.
Concentrations: Particulate Matter 10 (coarse particulate)—highest second maximum 24-hour concentration; Particulate Matter 2.5 Wtd AM (fine particulate)—highest weighted annual mean concentration; Particulate Matter 2.5 24-Hour (fine particulate)—highest 98th percentile 24-hour concentration; Ozone—highest fourth daily maximum 8-hour concentration; Carbon Monoxide—highest second maximum non-overlapping 8-hour concentration; Lead—maximum running 3-month average
Source: U.S. Environmental Protection Agency, Air Quality Monitoring Information, "Air Quality Statistics by City, 2013"

Maximum Air Pollutant Concentrations: Nitrogen Dioxide and Sulfur Dioxide

	Nitrogen Dioxide AM (ppb)	Nitrogen Dioxide 1-Hr (ppb)	Sulfur Dioxide AM (ppb)	Sulfur Dioxide 1-Hr (ppb)	Sulfur Dioxide 24-Hr (ppb)
MSA[1] Level	11	n/a	n/a	n/a	n/a
NAAQS[2]	53	100	30	75	140
Met NAAQS[2]	Yes	n/a	n/a	n/a	n/a

Note: (1) Data covers the Boise City, ID Metropolitan Statistical Area—see Appendix B for areas included; Data from exceptional events are included; (2) National Ambient Air Quality Standards; ppm = parts per million; ug/m³ = micrograms per cubic meter; n/a not available.
Concentrations: Nitrogen Dioxide AM—highest arithmetic mean concentration; Nitrogen Dioxide 1-Hr—highest 98th percentile 1-hour daily maximum concentration; Sulfur Dioxide AM—highest annual mean concentration; Sulfur Dioxide 1-Hr—highest 99th percentile 1-hour daily maximum concentration; Sulfur Dioxide 24-Hr—highest second maximum 24-hour concentration
Source: U.S. Environmental Protection Agency, Air Quality Monitoring Information, "Air Quality Statistics by City, 2013"

Drinking Water

Water System Name	Pop. Served	Primary Water Source Type	Violations[1]	
			Health Based	Monitoring/ Reporting
United Water Idaho	214,000	Surface	2	0

Note: (1) Based on violation data from January 1, 2014 to December 31, 2014 (includes unresolved violations from earlier years)
Source: U.S. Environmental Protection Agency, Office of Ground Water and Drinking Water, Safe Drinking Water Information System (based on data extracted January 27, 2015)

Boulder, Colorado

Background

Boulder lies at the foot of the Rocky Mountains in Boulder County. It is the eighth largest city in Colorado, with 27.8 square miles. Tourism is a major industry in Boulder, which offers spectacular views from its elevation of 5,430 feet and many outdoor recreation opportunities in over 31,000 acres of open space.

Boulder Valley originally was home to the Southern Arapahoe tribe. The first white settlement was established by gold miners in 1858 near the entrance to Boulder Canyon at Red Rocks. In 1859, the Boulder City Town Company was formed. The town's first schoolhouse was built in 1860, and in 1874, the University of Colorado opened.

Boulder was incorporated as a town in 1871 and as a city in 1882. By 1890, the railroad provided service from Boulder to Golden, Denver, and the western mining camps. In 1905, amidst a weakening economy, Boulder began promoting tourism to boost its finances. The city raised money to construct a first-class hotel, which was completed in 1908 and named Hotel Boulderado.

Although tourism remained strong until the late 1930s, it had begun to decline by World War II. However, the U.S. Navy's Japanese language school, housed at the city's University of Colorado, proved to be an impressive introduction to the area, and many people later returned to Boulder as students, professionals, and veterans attending the university on the GI Bill. Consequently, Boulder's population grew from 12,958 in 1940 to 20,000 in 1950. To accommodate this huge increase, new public buildings, highways, residential areas, and shopping centers developed, spurring further economic expansion.

Many major tech companies have operations in Boulder, as does NOAA, the National Oceanic and Atmospheric Administration.

Boulder is home to the University of Colorado, which houses a research park that includes corporate tenants such as Qwest. Cultural venues in the city include the Boulder Dushanbe Teahouse, a gift to the city from its sister city of Dushanbe in Tajikistan, and the Pearl Street Mall, an open-air walkway that was the city's original downtown and is today rich with restaurants, cafes, bookstores, and street entertainers. Boulder offers many scenic opportunities for outdoor activities, with parks, recreation areas, and hiking trails. The city boasts hundreds of miles of bike trails, lanes and paths as a part of their renowned network of citywide bikeways. In 2008, Boulder was recognized by the League of American Bicyclists for being a leading bicyclist-friendly city.

Keeping with Boulder's tradition of outdoor recreation, each Memorial Day, over 50,000 runners, joggers, walkers and wheelers participate in the "Bolder Boulder," a popular race that lures more than 100,000 spectators.

Annual attractions include the Creek Festival in May, Art Fair in July, Fall Festival, and Lights of December Parade. The annual Boulder International Film Festival (BIFF) is held in February. Since its creation in 2005, BIFF has created a name for itself in the international film community.

Like the rest of Colorado, Boulder enjoys a cool, dry highland continental climate. In winter, the mountains to the west shield the city from the coldest temperatures. Humidity is generally low. Winter storms moving east from the Pacific drop most of their moisture on the mountains to the west, while summer precipitation comes from scattered thunderstorms.

Rankings

General Rankings

- Boulder was selected as one the best places to live in America by *Outside Magazine*. The city ranked #10. Criteria included nearby adventure, healthy eating options, bike lanes, green spaces, number of outfitters and bike shops, miles of trails, median income, and unemployment rate. *Outside Magazine, "Outside's Best 16 Best Places to Live in the U.S. 2014," September 2014*

- Boulder was selected as one of the best places to live in the United States by *Money* magazine. The city ranked #23 out of 50. This year's list focused on cities with populations of 50,000 to 300,000. Beginning with a pool of 781 candidates, editors looked at more than 50 metrics, from local economy and housing market to schools and healthcare—and then sent reporters to look for a sense of community and other intangibles. *Money, "Best Places to Live: America's Best Small Towns, 2013" September, 2013*

- In their second annual survey, analysts for the small- and mid-sized city lifestyle site Livability.com looked at data for more than 2,000 U.S. cities to determine the rankings for Livability's "Top 100 Best Places to Live" in 2015. Boulder ranked #4. Criteria: vibrant economy; low cost of living; abundant lifestyle amenities. *Livability.com, "Top 100 Best Places to Live 2015"*

Business/Finance Rankings

- Measuring indicators of "tolerance"—the nonjudgmental environment that "attracts open-minded and new-thinking kinds of people"— as well as concentrations of technological and economic innovators, analysts identified the most creative American metro areas. On the resulting 2012 Creativity Index, the Boulder metro area placed #1. *www.thedailybeast.com, "Boulder, Ann Arbor, Tucson & More: 20 Most Creative U.S. Cities," June 26, 2012*

- The Boulder metro area was identified as having one of the largest percentage of home workers in the U.S. The area ranked #1, according to the business website 24/7 Wall Street, which based its conclusions on data from the U.S. Census Bureau and the Bureau of Labor Statistics. *247wallst.com, "Cities Where the Most Americans Work from Home," March 18, 2013*

- CareerBliss, an employment and careers website, analyzed U.S. Bureau of Labor Statistics data, more than 30,000 company reviews from employees and former employees, and job openings over a 12-month period to arrive at its list of the best and worst places in the United States to look for a job. Boulder was #1 among the worst places. *CareerBliss.com, "CareerBliss 2013 Best and Worst Cities to Find a Job," January 8, 2013*

- Boulder was identified as one of "America's Hardest-Working Towns." The city ranked #16 out of 25. Criteria: average hours worked per capita; willingness to work during personal time; number of dual income households; local employment rate. *Parade, "What is America's Hardest-Working Town?," April 15, 2012*

- The Boulder metro area appeared on the Milken Institute "2013 Best Performing Cities" list. Rank: #13 out of 200 large metro areas. Criteria: job growth; wage and salary growth; high-tech output growth. *Milken Institute, "Best-Performing Cities 2014," January 2015*

- *Forbes* ranked the 200 most populous metro areas to determine the nation's "Best Places for Business and Careers." The Boulder metro area was ranked #23. Criteria: costs (business and living); job growth (past and projected); income growth; educational attainment (college and high school); projected economic growth; cultural and recreational opportunities; net migration patterns; number of highly ranked colleges. *Forbes, "The Best Places for Business and Careers 2014," July 23, 2014*

Culture/Performing Arts Rankings

- Boulder was selected as one of America's top cities for the arts. The city ranked #14 in the mid-sized city (population 100,000 to 499,999) category. Criteria: readers' top choices for arts travel destinations based on the richness and variety of visual arts sites, activities and events. *American Style, "2012 Top 25 Arts Destinations," June 2012*

Dating/Romance Rankings

- Boulder ranked #7 among cities congenial to singles, according to Kiplinger, which searched for "dating scenes as financially attractive as they are romantically promising." High percentages of unmarried people, above-average household incomes, and cost-of-living factors determined the rankings. *Kiplinger.com, "10 Best Cities for Singles," February 2014*

Education Rankings

- Based on a Brookings Institution study, *24/7 Wall St*. identified the ten U.S. metropolitan areas with the most average patent filings per million residents between 2007 and 2011. Boulder ranked #5. *24/7 Wall St., "America's Most Innovative Cities," February 1, 2013*

- The Boulder metro area was selected as one of America's most innovative cities" by *The Business Insider*. The metro area was ranked #5 out of 20. Criteria: patents per capita. *The Business Insider, "The 20 Most Innovative Cities in the U.S.," February 1, 2013*

- Boulder was identified as one of "Smartest Cities in America" by the brain-training website *Lumosity* using data from three million of its own users. The metro area ranked #16 out of 50. Criteria: users' brain performance index scores, considering core cognitive abilities such as memory, processing speed, flexibility, attention and problem-solving. *Lumosity, " Smartest Cities in America," June 25, 2013*

Environmental Rankings

- The Weather Channel determined the nation's snowiest cities, based on the National Oceanic and Atmospheric Administration's 30-year average snowfall data. Among cities with a population of at least 100,000, the #5-ranked city was Boulder *weather.com, America's 20 Snowiest Major Cities, February 3, 2014*

- The Boulder metro area came in at #6 for the relative comfort of its climate on Sperling's list of "chill cities," as measured by the Sperling Heat Index. All 361 metro areas are included. Criteria included daytime high temperatures, nighttime low temperatures, dew point, and relative humidity at the high temperatures. *www.bertsperling.com, "Sperling's Chill Cities," July 18, 2013*

- Sperling's BestPlaces assessed 379 metropolitan areas of the United States for the likelihood of dangerously extreme weather events or earthquakes. In general the Southeast and South-Central regions have the highest risk of weather extremes and earthquakes, while the Pacific Northwest enjoys the lowest risk. Of the least risky metropolitan areas, the Boulder metro area was ranked #119. *www.bestplaces.net, "Safest Places from Natural Disasters," April 2011*

Food/Drink Rankings

- For the Gallup-Healthways Well-Being Index, researchers interviewed at least 300 adults in each of 189 metropolitan areas on residents' access to affordable fresh produce. The Boulder metro area was found to be among the top ten communities for affordable produce accessibility. *www.gallup.com, "In Anchorage, Access to Fruits and Vegetables Remains Lowest," April 8, 2014*

- Boulder was selected as one of America's 10 most vegan-friendly cities. The city was ranked #9. *People for the Ethical Treatment of Animals, "Top Vegan-Friendly Cities of 2013," June 11, 2013*

Health/Fitness Rankings

- For the Gallup-Healthways Well-Being Index, researchers asked at least 300 adult residents in each of 189 U.S. metropolitan areas how satisfied they were with the metro area in which they lived. The Boulder metro area was among the top ten for residents' satisfaction. *www.gallup.com, "City Satisfaction Highest in Fort Collins-Loveland, Colo.," April 11, 2014*

- Analysts who tracked obesity rates in 189 of the nation's metro areas found that the Boulder metro area was one of the ten communities where residents were least likely to be obese, defined as a BMI score of 30 or above. *www.gallup.com, "Boulder, Colo., Residents Still Least Likely to Be Obese," April 4, 2014*

- The Boulder metro area appeared in the 2013 Gallup-Healthways Well-Being Index. The area ranked #2 out of 189. The Gallup-Healthways Well-Being Index score is an average of six sub-indexes, which individually examine life evaluation, emotional health, work environment, physical health, healthy behaviors, and access to basic necessities. Results are based on telephone interviews conducted as part of the Gallup-Healthways Well-Being Index survey January 2–December 29, 2012, and January 2–December 30, 2013, with a random sample of 531,630 adults, aged 18 and older, living in metropolitan areas in the 50 U.S. states and the District of Columbia. *Gallup-Healthways, "State of American Well-Being," March 25, 2014*

Real Estate Rankings

- The Boulder metro area was identified as one of the nations's 20 hottest housing markets in 2015. Criteria: listing views relative to the number of listings. The area ranked #14. *Realtor.com, "These Are the 20 Hottest Housing Markets in the U.S. Right Now," April 8, 2015*

- The Boulder metro area was identified as one of the nation's 20 hottest housing markets in 2015.Criteria: median number of days homes were spending on the market in March 2015. The area ranked #6. *Realtor.com, "These Are the 20 Hottest Housing Markets in the U.S. Right Now," April 8, 2015*

- Boulder was ranked #34 out of 275 metro areas in terms of house price appreciation in 2014 (#1 = highest rate). *Federal Housing Finance Agency, House Price Index, 4th Quarter 2014*

- The Boulder metro area was identified as one of the 10 best condo markets in the U.S. in 2014. The area ranked #1 out of 66 markets with a price appreciation of 19.9%. Criteria: year-over-year change of median sales price of existing apartment condo-coop homes between the 4th quarter of 2013 and the 4th quarter of 2014. *National Association of Realtors®, Median Sales Price of Existing Apartment Condo-Coop Homes for Metropolitan Areas, 4th Quarter 2014*

- The Boulder metro area was identified as one of the 20 least affordable housing markets in the U.S. in 2014. The area ranked #15 out of 178 markets. Criteria: whether or not a typical family could qualify for a mortgage loan on a typical home. *National Association of Realtors®, Affordability Index of Existing Single-Family Homes for Metropolitan Areas, 2014*

- Boulder was ranked #148 out of 226 metro areas in terms of housing affordability in 2014 by the National Association of Home Builders (#1 = most affordable). The NAHB-Wells Fargo Housing Opportunity Index (HOI) for a given area is defined as the share of homes sold in that area that would have been affordable to a family earning the local median income, based on standard mortgage underwriting criteria. *National Association of Home Builders®, NAHB-Wells Fargo Housing Opportunity Index, 4th Quarter 2014*

Safety Rankings

- Farmers Insurance, in partnership with Sperling's BestPlaces, ranked metro areas in the U.S. and identified the "Most Secure Places to Live." The Boulder metro area ranked #5 out of the top 20 in the mid-size city category (150,000 to 500,000 residents). Criteria: economic stability; crime statistics; extreme weather; risk of natural disasters; housing depreciation; foreclosures; air quality; environmental hazards; life expectancy; motor vehicle fatalities; and employment numbers. *Farmers Insurance Group of Companies, "Most Secure U.S. Places to Live in the U.S.," June 25, 2013*

- The National Insurance Crime Bureau ranked 380 metro areas in the U.S. in terms of per capita rates of vehicle theft. The Boulder metro area ranked #285 (#1 = highest rate). Criteria: number of vehicle theft offenses per 100,000 inhabitants in 2012. *National Insurance Crime Bureau, "Hot Spots 2012," June 26, 2013*

Seniors/Retirement Rankings

- From its Best Cities for Successful Aging indexes, the Milken Institute generated rankings for metropolitan areas, weighing data in eight categories—health care, wellness, living arrangements, transportation, financial characteristics, education and employment opportunities, community engagement, and overall livability. The Boulder metro area was ranked #26 overall in the small metro area category. *Milken Institute, "Best Cities for Successful Aging, 2014"*

Sports/Recreation Rankings

- Boulder was chosen as a bicycle friendly community by the League of American Bicyclists. A "Bicycle Friendly Community" welcomes cyclists by providing safe accommodation for cycling and encouraging people to bike for transportation and recreation. There are four award levels: Platinum; Gold; Silver; and Bronze. The community achieved an award level of Platinum. *League of American Bicyclists, "Bicycle Friendly Community Master List," Fall 2013*

- Boulder was chosen as one of America's best cities for bicycling. The city ranked #3 out of 50. Criteria: robust cycling infrastructure; vibrant bike culture. The editors only considered cities with populations of 95,000 or more. *Bicycling, "America's Top 50 Bike-Friendly Cities," May 23, 2012*

Miscellaneous Rankings

- Boulder was selected as a 2013 Digital Cities Survey winner. The city ranked #8 in the small city (75,000 to 124,999 population) category. The survey examined and assessed how city governments are utilizing information technology to operate and deliver quality service to their customers and citizens. Survey questions focused on implementation and adoption of online service delivery; planning and governance; and the infrastructure and architecture that make the transformation to digital government possible. *Center for Digital Government, "2013 Digital Cities Survey," November 7, 2013*

- Of the American metro areas that allow medical or recreational use of marijuana, the Boulder metro area was identified by CNBC editors as one of the most livable for marijuana lovers. Criteria included the Sperling's BestPlaces assessment of marijuana-friendly cities in terms of sound economy, cultural diversity, and a healthy population, plus cost-of-living index and high-quality schools. *www.cnbc.com, "The Best Cities to Live for Marijuana Lovers," February 5, 2014*

- According to the World Giving Index, the United States is the fifth most generous nation in the world. The finance and lifestyle site NerdWallet looked for the U.S. cities that topped the list in donating money and time to good causes. The Boulder metro area proved to be the #5-ranked metro area, judged by culture of volunteerism, depth of commitment in terms of volunteer hours per year, and monetary contributions. *www.nerdwallet.com, "Most Generous Cities," September 22, 2013*

Business Environment

CITY FINANCES

City Government Finances

Component	2012 ($000)	2012 ($ per capita)
Total Revenues	243,671	2,502
Total Expenditures	226,981	2,331
Debt Outstanding	155,717	1,599
Cash and Securities[1]	170,461	1,750

Note: (1) Cash and security holdings of a government at the close of its fiscal year, including those of its dependent agencies, utilities, and liquor stores.
Source: U.S Census Bureau, State & Local Government Finances 2012

City Government Revenue by Source

Source	2012 ($000)	2012 ($ per capita)
General Revenue		
From Federal Government	2,615	27
From State Government	13,808	142
From Local Governments	0	0
Taxes		
Property	29,218	300
Sales and Gross Receipts	110,326	1,133
Personal Income	0	0
Corporate Income	0	0
Motor Vehicle License	0	0
Other Taxes	10,517	108
Current Charges	39,616	407
Liquor Store	0	0
Utility	23,403	240
Employee Retirement	770	8

Source: U.S Census Bureau, State & Local Government Finances 2012

City Government Expenditures by Function

Function	2012 ($000)	2012 ($ per capita)	2012 (%)
General Direct Expenditures			
Air Transportation	1,688	17	0.7
Corrections	0	0	0.0
Education	0	0	0.0
Employment Security Administration	0	0	0.0
Financial Administration	5,178	53	2.3
Fire Protection	16,295	167	7.2
General Public Buildings	0	0	0.0
Governmental Administration, Other	8,755	90	3.9
Health	0	0	0.0
Highways	36,107	371	15.9
Hospitals	0	0	0.0
Housing and Community Development	19,804	203	8.7
Interest on General Debt	5,284	54	2.3
Judicial and Legal	3,961	41	1.7
Libraries	7,233	74	3.2
Parking	6,332	65	2.8
Parks and Recreation	40,034	411	17.6
Police Protection	45,367	466	20.0
Public Welfare	0	0	0.0
Sewerage	11,585	119	5.1
Solid Waste Management	0	0	0.0
Veterans' Services	0	0	0.0
Liquor Store	0	0	0.0
Utility	15,442	159	6.8
Employee Retirement	1,099	11	0.5

Source: U.S Census Bureau, State & Local Government Finances 2012

DEMOGRAPHICS

Population Growth

Area	1990 Census	2000 Census	2010 Census	Population Growth (%) 1990-2000	Population Growth (%) 2000-2010
City	87,737	94,673	97,385	7.9	2.9
MSA[1]	208,898	269,758	294,567	29.1	9.2
U.S.	248,709,873	281,421,906	308,745,538	13.2	9.7

Note: (1) Figures cover the Boulder, CO Metropolitan Statistical Area—see Appendix B for areas included
Source: U.S. Census Bureau, Census 1990, 2000, 2010

Household Size

Area	Persons in Household (%) One	Two	Three	Four	Five	Six	Seven or More	Average Household Size
City	33.1	36.1	16.0	10.3	3.7	0.7	0.2	2.26
MSA[1]	28.2	36.1	15.4	13.2	5.1	1.5	0.6	2.44
U.S.	27.7	33.6	15.7	13.1	6.0	2.3	1.5	2.64

Note: (1) Figures cover the Boulder, CO Metropolitan Statistical Area—see Appendix B for areas included
Source: U.S. Census Bureau, 2011-2013 American Community Survey 3-Year Estimates

Race

Area	White Alone[2] (%)	Black Alone[2] (%)	Asian Alone[2] (%)	AIAN[3] Alone[2] (%)	NHOPI[4] Alone[2] (%)	Other Race Alone[2] (%)	Two or More Races (%)
City	89.4	0.8	4.5	0.2	0.0	2.0	3.0
MSA[1]	88.3	1.0	4.1	0.5	0.1	3.2	2.9
U.S.	73.9	12.6	5.0	0.8	0.2	4.7	2.9

Note: (1) Figures cover the Boulder, CO Metropolitan Statistical Area—see Appendix B for areas included; (2) Alone is defined as not being in combination with one or more other races; (3) American Indian and Alaska Native; (4) Native Hawaiian and Other Pacific Islander
Source: U.S. Census Bureau, 2011-2013 American Community Survey 3-Year Estimates

Hispanic or Latino Origin

Area	Total (%)	Mexican (%)	Puerto Rican (%)	Cuban (%)	Other (%)
City	8.3	5.9	0.3	0.3	1.8
MSA[1]	13.6	10.8	0.3	0.2	2.3
U.S.	16.9	10.8	1.6	0.6	3.8

Note: Persons of Hispanic or Latino origin can be of any race; (1) Figures cover the Boulder, CO Metropolitan Statistical Area—see Appendix B for areas included
Source: U.S. Census Bureau, 2011-2013 American Community Survey 3-Year Estimates

Segregation

Type	Segregation Indices[1] 1990	2000	2010	2010 Rank[2]	Percent Change 1990-2000	1990-2010	2000-2010
Black/White	n/a	n/a	n/a	n/a	n/a	n/a	n/a
Asian/White	n/a	n/a	n/a	n/a	n/a	n/a	n/a
Hispanic/White	n/a	n/a	n/a	n/a	n/a	n/a	n/a

Note: All figures cover the Metropolitan Statistical Area—see Appendix B for areas included; Figures are based on an analysis of 1990, 2000, and 2010 Census Decennial Census tract data by William H. Frey, Brookings Institution and the University of Michigan Social Science Data Analysis Network. In this analysis all racial groups (whites, blacks, and asians) are non-Hispanic members of those races. Hispanics are shown as a separate category;
(1) Segregation Indices are Dissimilarity Indices that measure the degree to which the minority group is distributed differently than whites across census tracts. They range from 0 (complete integration) to 100 (complete segregation) where the value indicates the percentage of the minority group that needs to move to be distributed exactly like whites; (2) Ranges from 1 (most segregated) to 102 (least segregated); n/a not available.
Source: www.CensusScope.org

Ancestry

Area	German	Irish	English	American	Italian	Polish	French[2]	Scottish	Dutch
City	22.4	14.0	12.9	5.1	6.6	4.1	4.4	3.1	2.0
MSA[1]	22.4	13.6	13.5	5.5	5.8	3.8	4.0	3.4	2.3
U.S.	14.9	10.8	8.0	7.4	5.5	3.0	2.7	1.7	1.4

Note: Figures are the percentage of the total population reporting a particular ancestry. The nine most commonly reported ancestries in the U.S. are shown. Figures include multiple ancestries (e.g. if a person reported being Irish and Italian, they were included in both columns); (1) Figures cover the Boulder, CO Metropolitan Statistical Area—see Appendix B for areas included; (2) Excludes Basque
Source: U.S. Census Bureau, 2011-2013 American Community Survey 3-Year Estimates

Foreign-Born Population

Area	Percent of Population Born in								
	Any Foreign Country	Mexico	Asia	Europe	Carribean	South America	Central America[2]	Africa	Canada
City	9.7	1.8	3.6	3.0	0.1	0.4	0.1	0.1	0.4
MSA[1]	10.5	3.7	3.2	2.3	0.1	0.3	0.3	0.3	0.4
U.S.	13.0	3.7	3.8	1.5	1.2	0.9	1.0	0.6	0.3

Note: (1) Figures cover the Boulder, CO Metropolitan Statistical Area—see Appendix B for areas included; (2) Excludes Mexico.
Source: U.S. Census Bureau, 2011-2013 American Community Survey 3-Year Estimates

Marital Status

Area	Never Married	Now Married[2]	Separated	Widowed	Divorced
City	55.7	32.8	0.7	2.7	8.1
MSA[1]	37.2	47.7	1.1	3.5	10.6
U.S.	32.7	48.1	2.2	6.0	11.0

Note: Figures are percentages and cover the population 15 years of age and older; (1) Figures cover the Boulder, CO Metropolitan Statistical Area—see Appendix B for areas included; (2) Excludes separated
Source: U.S. Census Bureau, 2011-2013 American Community Survey 3-Year Estimates

Disability Status

Area	All Ages	Under 18 Years Old	18 to 64 Years Old	65 Years and Over
City	6.7	1.4	5.4	25.4
MSA[1]	8.3	2.9	7.0	26.7
U.S.	12.3	4.1	10.2	36.3

Note: Figures show percent of the civilian noninstitutionalized population that reported having a disability. Disability status is determined from from six types of difficulty: vision, hearing, cognitive, ambulatory, self-care, and independent living. For children under 5 years old, hearing and vision difficulty are used to determine disability status. For children between the ages of 5 and 14, disability status is determined from hearing, vision, cognitive, ambulatory, and self-care difficulties. For people aged 15 years and older, they are considered to have a disability if they have difficulty with any one of the six difficulty types; (1) Figures cover the Boulder, CO Metropolitan Statistical Area—see Appendix B for areas included.
Source: U.S. Census Bureau, 2011-2013 American Community Survey 3-Year Estimates

Age

Area	Percent of Population									Median Age
	Under Age 5	Age 5–19	Age 20–34	Age 35–44	Age 45–54	Age 55–64	Age 65–74	Age 75–84	Age 85+	
City	3.9	19.8	36.0	10.7	10.5	9.4	5.4	2.7	1.5	27.8
MSA[1]	5.3	19.9	23.7	13.3	14.1	12.5	6.5	3.2	1.4	35.8
U.S.	6.4	19.9	20.7	12.9	14.1	12.3	7.6	4.2	1.9	37.4

Note: (1) Figures cover the Boulder, CO Metropolitan Statistical Area—see Appendix B for areas included
Source: U.S. Census Bureau, 2011-2013 American Community Survey 3-Year Estimates

Gender

Area	Males	Females	Males per 100 Females
City	51,017	50,854	100.3
MSA[1]	153,103	152,181	100.6
U.S.	154,451,010	159,410,713	96.9

Note: (1) Figures cover the Boulder, CO Metropolitan Statistical Area—see Appendix B for areas included
Source: U.S. Census Bureau, 2011-2013 American Community Survey 3-Year Estimates

Religious Groups by Family

Area	Catholic	Baptist	Non-Den.	Methodist[2]	Lutheran	LDS[3]	Pente-costal	Presby-terian[4]	Muslim[5]	Judaism
MSA[1]	20.1	2.4	4.8	1.8	3.1	3.0	0.5	2.0	0.1	0.8
U.S.	19.1	9.3	4.0	4.0	2.3	2.0	1.9	1.6	0.8	0.7

Note: Figures are the number of adherents as a percentage of the total population; (1) Figures cover the Boulder, CO Metropolitan Statistical Area—see Appendix B for areas included; (2) Methodist/Pietist; (3) Latter Day Saints; (4) Reformed; (5) Figures are estimates
Source: Association of Statisticians of American Religious Bodies, 2010 U.S. Religion Census: Religious Congregations & Membership Study

Religious Groups by Tradition

Area	Catholic	Evangelical Protestant	Mainline Protestant	Other Tradition	Black Protestant	Orthodox
MSA[1]	20.1	9.8	6.5	4.9	<0.1	0.2
U.S.	19.1	16.2	7.3	4.3	1.6	0.3

Note: Figures are the number of adherents as a percentage of the total population; (1) Figures cover the Boulder, CO Metropolitan Statistical Area—see Appendix B for areas included
Source: Association of Statisticians of American Religious Bodies, 2010 U.S. Religion Census: Religious Congregations & Membership Study

ECONOMY

Gross Metropolitan Product

Area	2012	2013	2014	2015	Rank[2]
MSA[1]	20.3	21.1	21.8	22.9	107

Note: Figures are in billions of dollars; (1) Figures cover the Boulder, CO Metropolitan Statistical Area—see Appendix B for areas included; (2) Rank is based on 2015 data and ranges from 1 to 363
Source: The U.S. Conference of Mayors, U.S. Metro Economies: GMP and Employment 2013-2015, June 2014

Economic Growth

Area	2010-12 (%)	2013 (%)	2014 (%)	2015 (%)	Rank[2]
MSA[1]	3.7	2.4	1.9	2.9	172
U.S.	2.1	2.0	2.3	3.2	–

Note: Figures are real gross metropolitan product (GMP) growth rates and represent annual average percent change; (1) Figures cover the Boulder, CO Metropolitan Statistical Area—see Appendix B for areas included; (2) Rank is based on 2015 data and ranges from 1 to 363
Source: The U.S. Conference of Mayors, U.S. Metro Economies: GMP and Employment 2013-2015, June 2014

Metropolitan Area Exports

Area	2008	2009	2010	2011	2012	2013	Rank[2]
MSA[1]	891.7	727.2	1,058.7	946.7	1,128.0	1,046.0	153

Note: Figures are in millions of dollars; (1) Figures cover the Boulder, CO Metropolitan Statistical Area—see Appendix B for areas included; (2) Rank is based on 2013 data and ranges from 1 to 387
Source: U.S. Department of Commerce, International Trade Administration, Office of Trade & Industry Information, Manufacturing & Services, data extracted April 3, 2015

Building Permits

Area	Single-Family			Multi-Family			Total		
	2013	2014	Pct. Chg.	2013	2014	Pct. Chg.	2013	2014	Pct. Chg.
City	89	104	16.9	789	504	-36.1	878	608	-30.8
MSA[1]	591	560	-5.2	1,034	811	-21.6	1,625	1,371	-15.6
U.S.	620,802	634,597	2.2	370,020	411,766	11.3	990,822	1,046,363	5.6

*Note: (1) Figures cover the Boulder, CO Metropolitan Statistical Area—see Appendix B for areas included;
Figures represent new, privately-owned housing units authorized (unadjusted data); All permit data are based
on estimates with imputation.*
Source: U.S. Census Bureau, Manufacturing, Mining, and Construction Statistics, Building Permits, 2013, 2014

Bankruptcy Filings

Area	Business Filings			Nonbusiness Filings		
	2013	2014	% Chg.	2013	2014	% Chg.
Boulder County	46	33	-28.3	708	544	-23.2
U.S.	33,212	26,983	-18.8	1,038,720	909,812	-12.4

*Note: Business filings include Chapter 7, Chapter 11, Chapter 12, and Chapter 13; Nonbusiness filings include
Chapter 7, Chapter 11, and Chapter 13*
*Source: Administrative Office of the U.S. Courts, Business and Nonbusiness Bankruptcy, County Cases
Commenced by Chapter of the Bankruptcy Code, During the 12- Month Period Ending December 31, 2013 and
Business and Nonbusiness Bankruptcy, County Cases Commenced by Chapter of the Bankruptcy Code, During
the 12- Month Period Ending December 31, 2014*

Housing Vacancy Rates

Area	Gross Vacancy Rate[2] (%)			Year-Round Vacancy Rate[3] (%)			Rental Vacancy Rate[4] (%)			Homeowner Vacancy Rate[5] (%)		
	2012	2013	2014	2012	2013	2014	2012	2013	2014	2012	2013	2014
MSA[1]	n/a	n/a	n/a	n/a	n/a	n/a	n/a	n/a	n/a	n/a	n/a	n/a
U.S.	13.8	13.6	13.4	10.8	10.7	10.4	8.7	8.3	7.6	2.0	2.0	1.9

*Note: (1) Figures cover the Boulder, CO Metropolitan Statistical Area—see Appendix B for areas included; (2)
The percentage of the total housing inventory that is vacant; (3) The percentage of the housing inventory
(excluding seasonal units) that is year-round vacant; (4) The percentage of rental inventory that is vacant for
rent; (5) The percentage of homeowner inventory that is vacant for sale; n/a not available*
Source: U.S. Census Bureau, Housing Vacancies and Homeownership Annual Statistics: 2014

INCOME

Income

Area	Per Capita ($)	Median Household ($)	Average Household ($)
City	37,315	57,012	88,752
MSA[1]	37,871	69,260	93,227
U.S.	27,884	52,176	72,897

Note: (1) Figures cover the Boulder, CO Metropolitan Statistical Area—see Appendix B for areas included
Source: U.S. Census Bureau, 2011-2013 American Community Survey 3-Year Estimates

Household Income Distribution

Area	Percent of Households Earning							
	Under $15,000	$15,000 -24,999	$25,000 -34,999	$35,000 -49,999	$50,000 -74,999	$75,000 -99,000	$100,000 -149,999	$150,000 and up
City	16.7	9.2	8.9	10.4	14.7	9.8	12.5	17.9
MSA[1]	10.9	8.0	7.8	11.3	15.4	12.2	16.3	18.2
U.S.	13.0	10.9	10.3	13.6	17.9	11.9	12.7	9.6

Note: (1) Figures cover the Boulder, CO Metropolitan Statistical Area—see Appendix B for areas included
Source: U.S. Census Bureau, 2011-2013 American Community Survey 3-Year Estimates

Poverty Rate

Area	All Ages	Under 18 Years Old	18 to 64 Years Old	65 Years and Over
City	23.8	8.8	29.2	6.0
MSA[1]	14.5	13.2	16.3	5.9
U.S.	15.9	22.4	14.8	9.5

Note: Figures are percentage of people whose income during the past 12 months was below the poverty level;
(1) Figures cover the Boulder, CO Metropolitan Statistical Area—see Appendix B for areas included
Source: U.S. Census Bureau, 2011-2013 American Community Survey 3-Year Estimates

EMPLOYMENT

Labor Force and Employment

Area	Civilian Labor Force			Workers Employed		
	Dec. 2013	Dec. 2014	% Chg.	Dec. 2013	Dec. 2014	% Chg.
City	59,422	59,883	0.8	56,735	58,038	2.3
MSA[1]	175,574	177,034	0.8	167,341	171,184	2.3
U.S.	154,408,000	155,521,000	0.7	144,423,000	147,190,000	1.9

Note: Data is not seasonally adjusted and covers workers 16 years of age and older; (1) Figures cover the
Boulder, CO Metropolitan Statistical Area—see Appendix B for areas included
Source: Bureau of Labor Statistics, Local Area Unemployment Statistics

Unemployment Rate

Area	2014											
	Jan.	Feb.	Mar.	Apr.	May	Jun.	Jul.	Aug.	Sep.	Oct.	Nov.	Dec.
City	5.0	5.1	4.8	4.2	4.0	4.5	4.4	3.8	3.3	3.3	3.5	3.1
MSA[1]	5.1	5.2	5.0	4.2	4.0	4.3	4.2	3.8	3.4	3.3	3.4	3.3
U.S.	7.0	7.0	6.8	5.9	6.1	6.3	6.5	6.3	5.7	5.5	5.5	5.4

Note: Data is not seasonally adjusted and covers workers 16 years of age and older; (1) Figures cover the
Boulder, CO Metropolitan Statistical Area—see Appendix B for areas included
Source: Bureau of Labor Statistics, Local Area Unemployment Statistics

Employment by Occupation

Occupation Classification	City (%)	MSA[1] (%)	U.S. (%)
Management, Business, Science, and Arts	55.7	52.8	36.2
Natural Resources, Construction, and Maintenance	2.7	5.2	9.0
Production, Transportation, and Material Moving	5.0	6.7	12.1
Sales and Office	19.5	19.9	24.4
Service	17.1	15.4	18.3

Note: Figures cover employed civilians 16 years of age and older; (1) Figures cover the Boulder, CO
Metropolitan Statistical Area—see Appendix B for areas included
Source: U.S. Census Bureau, 2011-2013 American Community Survey 3-Year Estimates

Employment by Industry

Sector	MSA[1]		U.S.
	Number of Employees	Percent of Total	Percent of Total
Construction, Mining, and Logging	5,000	2.8	5.0
Education and Health Services	23,200	12.9	15.5
Financial Activities	7,600	4.2	5.7
Government	35,800	20.0	15.8
Information	8,200	4.6	2.0
Leisure and Hospitality	18,500	10.3	10.3
Manufacturing	17,700	9.9	8.7
Other Services	5,800	3.2	4.0
Professional and Business Services	32,700	18.2	13.8
Retail Trade	17,300	9.7	11.4
Transportation, Warehousing, and Utilities	1,800	1.0	3.9
Wholesale Trade	5,600	3.1	4.2

Note: Figures are non-farm employment as of December 2014. Figures are not seasonally adjusted and include
workers 16 years of age and older; (1) Figures cover the Boulder, CO Metropolitan Statistical Area—see
Appendix B for areas included; n/a not available
Source: Bureau of Labor Statistics, Current Employment Statistics, Employment, Hours, and Earnings

Occupations with Greatest Projected Employment Growth: 2012 – 2022

Occupation[1]	2012 Employment	2022 Projected Employment	Numeric Employment Change	Percent Employment Change
Combined Food Preparation and Serving Workers, Including Fast Food	60,670	77,380	16,710	27.5
Secretaries and Administrative Assistants, Except Legal, Medical, and Executive	63,150	77,880	14,730	23.3
Retail Salespersons	79,300	94,000	14,700	18.5
Customer Service Representatives	45,990	59,210	13,220	28.8
Registered Nurses	42,200	53,270	11,070	26.2
General and Operations Managers	42,170	52,340	10,170	24.1
Accountants and Auditors	33,870	43,490	9,620	28.4
Personal Care Aides	16,940	26,210	9,270	54.7
Janitors and Cleaners, Except Maids and Housekeeping Cleaners	36,300	45,470	9,170	25.3
Business Operations Specialists, All Other	42,990	51,450	8,460	19.7

Note: Projections cover Colorado; (1) Sorted by numeric employment change
Source: www.projectionscentral.com, State Occupational Projections, 2012–2022 Long-Term Projections

Fastest Growing Occupations: 2012 – 2022

Occupation[1]	2012 Employment	2022 Projected Employment	Numeric Employment Change	Percent Employment Change
Service Unit Operators, Oil, Gas, and Mining	3,520	6,290	2,770	78.4
Derrick Operators, Oil and Gas	630	1,110	480	76.0
Rotary Drill Operators, Oil and Gas	1,280	2,200	920	71.5
Roustabouts, Oil and Gas	2,770	4,710	1,940	70.2
Interpreters and Translators	1,510	2,550	1,040	68.5
Petroleum Engineers	1,500	2,500	1,000	66.9
Pump Operators, Except Wellhead Pumpers	700	1,160	460	64.9
Helpers—Brickmasons, Blockmasons, Stonemasons, and Tile and Marble Setters	200	320	120	61.3
Insulation Workers, Mechanical	420	680	260	61.2
Information Security Analysts	1,240	1,960	720	57.8

Note: Projections cover Colorado; (1) Sorted by percent employment change and excludes occupations with numeric employment change less than 100
Source: www.projectionscentral.com, State Occupational Projections, 2012–2022 Long-Term Projections

Average Wages

Occupation	$/Hr.	Occupation	$/Hr.
Accountants and Auditors	36.66	Maids and Housekeeping Cleaners	9.78
Automotive Mechanics	20.61	Maintenance and Repair Workers	18.72
Bookkeepers	18.94	Marketing Managers	70.60
Carpenters	19.33	Nuclear Medicine Technologists	37.63
Cashiers	11.16	Nurses, Licensed Practical	22.06
Clerks, General Office	19.42	Nurses, Registered	34.99
Clerks, Receptionists/Information	14.09	Nursing Assistants	13.61
Clerks, Shipping/Receiving	15.58	Packers and Packagers, Hand	10.50
Computer Programmers	45.70	Physical Therapists	35.24
Computer Systems Analysts	42.22	Postal Service Mail Carriers	25.32
Computer User Support Specialists	26.32	Real Estate Brokers	31.66
Cooks, Restaurant	11.59	Retail Salespersons	14.72
Dentists	89.92	Sales Reps., Exc. Tech./Scientific	38.65
Electrical Engineers	47.38	Sales Reps., Tech./Scientific	36.38
Electricians	22.87	Secretaries, Exc. Legal/Med./Exec.	17.54
Financial Managers	66.19	Security Guards	15.25
First-Line Supervisors/Managers, Sales	24.57	Surgeons	103.98
Food Preparation Workers	10.82	Teacher Assistants	15.50
General and Operations Managers	62.75	Teachers, Elementary School	26.90
Hairdressers/Cosmetologists	15.89	Teachers, Secondary School	27.30
Internists	101.78	Telemarketers	12.13
Janitors and Cleaners	13.26	Truck Drivers, Heavy/Tractor-Trailer	21.50
Landscaping/Groundskeeping Workers	13.43	Truck Drivers, Light/Delivery Svcs.	16.76
Lawyers	59.33	Waiters and Waitresses	11.02

Note: Wage data covers the Boulder, CO Metropolitan Statistical Area—see Appendix B for areas included; Hourly wages for elementary/secondary school teachers and teacher assistants were calculated by the editors from annual wage data assuming a 40 hour work week; n/a not available.
Source: Bureau of Labor Statistics, Metro Area Occupational Employment and Wage Estimates, May 2014

TAXES

State Corporate Income Tax Rates

State	Tax Rate (%)	Income Brackets ($)	Num. of Brackets	Financial Institution Tax Rate (%)[a]	Federal Income Tax Ded.
Colorado	4.63	Flat rate	1	4.63	No

Note: Tax rates as of January 1, 2015; (a) Rates listed are the corporate income tax rate applied to financial institutions or excise taxes based on income. Some states have other taxes based upon the value of deposits or shares.
Source: Federation of Tax Administrators, "State Corporate Income Tax Rates, 2015"

State Individual Income Tax Rates

State	Tax Rate (%)	Income Brackets ($)	Num. of Brackets	Personal Exempt. ($)[1] Single	Dependents	Fed. Inc. Tax Ded.
Colorado	4.63	Flat rate	1	4,000 (d)	4,000 (d)	No

Note: Tax rates as of January 1, 2015; Local- and county-level taxes are not included; n/a not applicable; (1) Married joint filers generally receive double the single exemption; (d) These states use the personal exemption amounts provided in the federal Internal Revenue Code.
Source: Federation of Tax Administrators, "State Individual Income Tax Rates, 2015"

Various State and Local Tax Rates

State	State and Local Sales and Use (%)	State Sales and Use (%)	Gasoline[1] (¢/gal.)	Cigarette[2] ($/pack)	Spirits[3] ($/gal.)	Wine[4] ($/gal.)	Beer[5] ($/gal.)
Colorado	8.845	2.90	22	0.84	2.28	0.32	0.08

Note: All tax rates as of January 1, 2015; (1) The American Petroleum Institute has developed a methodology for determining the average tax rate on a gallon of fuel. Rates may include any of the following: excise taxes, environmental fees, storage tank fees, other fees or taxes, general sales tax, and local taxes. In states where gasoline is subject to the general sales tax, or where the fuel tax is based on the average sale price, the average rate determined by API is sensitive to changes in the price of gasoline. States that fully or partially apply general sales taxes to gasoline: CA, CO, GA, IL, IN, MI, NY; (2) The federal excise tax of $1.0066 per pack and local taxes are not included; (3) Rates are those applicable to off-premise sales of 40% alcohol by volume (a.b.v.) distilled spirits in 750ml containers. Local excise taxes are excluded; (4) Rates are those applicable to off-premise sales of 11% a.b.v. non-carbonated wine in 750ml containers; (5) Rates are those applicable to off-premise sales of 4.7% a.b.v. beer in 12 ounce containers.
Source: Tax Foundation, 2015 Facts & Figures: How Does Your State Compare?

State Business Tax Climate Index Rankings

State	Overall Rank	Corporate Tax Index Rank	Individual Income Tax Index Rank	Sales Tax Index Rank	Unemployment Insurance Tax Index Rank	Property Tax Index Rank
Colorado	20	12	16	43	35	22

Note: The index is a measure of how each state's tax laws affect economic performance. The lower the rank, the more favorable a state's tax system is for business. States without a given tax are given a ranking of 1. The scores/rankings for the District of Columbia do not affect other states. The 2015 index represents the tax climate as of July 1, 2014.
Source: Tax Foundation, State Business Tax Climate Index 2015

COMMERCIAL UTILITIES

Typical Monthly Electric Bills

Area	Commercial Service ($/month)		Industrial Service ($/month)	
	1,500 kWh	40 kW demand 14,000 kWh	1,000 kW demand 200,000 kWh	50,000 kW demand 32,500,000 kWh
City	198	1,525	28,386	2,329,788
Average[1]	201	1,653	26,124	2,639,743

Note: Figures are based on annualized 2014 rates; (1) Average based on 180 utilities surveyed
Source: Edison Electric Institute, Typical Bills and Average Rates Report, Summer 2014

TRANSPORTATION

Means of Transportation to Work

Area	Car/Truck/Van		Public Transportation			Bicycle	Walked	Other Means	Worked at Home
	Drove Alone	Car-pooled	Bus	Subway	Railroad				
City	51.3	5.2	9.0	0.1	0.0	10.8	10.5	1.6	11.5
MSA[1]	64.1	8.0	5.5	0.0	0.0	4.4	5.1	1.8	11.1
U.S.	76.4	9.6	2.6	1.8	0.6	0.6	2.8	1.3	4.3

Note: Figures are percentages and cover workers 16 years of age and older; (1) Figures cover the Boulder, CO Metropolitan Statistical Area—see Appendix B for areas included
Source: U.S. Census Bureau, 2011-2013 American Community Survey 3-Year Estimates

Travel Time to Work

Area	Less Than 10 Minutes	10 to 19 Minutes	20 to 29 Minutes	30 to 44 Minutes	45 to 59 Minutes	60 to 89 Minutes	90 Minutes or More
City	20.8	42.7	16.2	11.4	4.9	2.5	1.5
MSA[1]	15.7	34.5	21.1	16.7	6.3	4.0	1.6
U.S.	13.3	29.7	20.9	20.2	7.7	5.7	2.6

Note: Figures are percentages and include workers 16 years old and over; (1) Figures cover the Boulder, CO Metropolitan Statistical Area—see Appendix B for areas included
Source: U.S. Census Bureau, 2011-2013 American Community Survey 3-Year Estimates

Travel Time Index

Area	1985	1990	1995	2000	2005	2010	2011
Urban Area[1]	1.08	1.10	1.18	1.19	1.18	1.18	1.18
Average[2]	1.09	1.14	1.16	1.19	1.23	1.18	1.18

*Note: Travel Time Index—the ratio of travel time in the peak period to the travel time at free-flow conditions.
For example, a value of 1.30 indicates a 20-minute free-flow trip takes 26 minutes in the peak. Free-flow speeds
(60 mph on freeways and 35 mph on principal arterials) are used as the comparison threshold; (1) Covers the
Boulder CO urban area; (2) average of 498 urban areas
Source: Texas Transportation Institute, Urban Mobility Report 2012, December 2012*

Public Transportation

Agency Name / Mode of Transportation	Vehicles Operated in Maximum Service	Annual Unlinked Passenger Trips (in thous.)	Annual Passenger Miles (in thous.)
Community Transit Network			
Bus (directly operated)	452	52,111.9	276,564.2
Bus (purchased transportation)	367	24,236.8	124,350.8
Demand Response (directly operated)	8	56.0	733.7
Demand Response (purchased transportation)	362	1,174.3	9,927.0
Light Rail (directly operated)	139	23,773.8	201,995.3

*Note: n/a not available
Source: City of Boulder, www.bouldercolorado.gov*

Air Transportation

Airport Name and Code / Type of Service	Passenger Airlines[1]	Passenger Enplanements	Freight Carriers[2]	Freight (lbs.)
Denver International (40 miles) (DEN)				
Domestic service (U.S. carriers - 2014)	29	24,875,236	19	209,229,037
International service (U.S. carriers - 2013)	12	655,399	3	611,491

*Note: (1) Includes all U.S.-based major, minor and commuter airlines that carried at least one passenger during
the year; (2) Includes all U.S.-based airlines and freight carriers that transported at least one lb. of freight during
the year.
Source: Bureau of Transportation Statistics, The Intermodal Transportation Database, Air Carriers: T-100
Domestic Market (U.S. Carriers), 2014; Bureau of Transportation Statistics, The Intermodal Transportation
Database, Air Carriers: T-100 International Market (U.S. Carriers), 2013*

Other Transportation Statistics

Major Highways:	SR-36 connecting to I-25, I-70 and I-76
Amtrak Service:	No
Major Waterways/Ports:	None

Source: Amtrak.com; Google Maps

BUSINESSES

Major Business Headquarters

Company Name	Rankings	
	Fortune[1]	Forbes[2]
No companies listed	-	-

*Note: (1) Fortune 500—companies that produce a 10-K are ranked 1 to 500
based on 2013 revenue; (2) all private companies with at least $2 billion in
annual revenue through the end of their most current fiscal year are ranked 1 to
221; companies listed are headquartered in the city; dashes indicate no ranking
Source: Fortune, "Fortune 500," June 16, 2014; Forbes, "America's Largest
Private Companies," November 5, 2014*

Fast-Growing Businesses

According to *Inc.*, Boulder is home to four of America's 500 fastest-growing private companies:
Minute Key (#11); **Clean Energy Collective** (#194); **Tax Guard** (#207); **SendGrid** (#233).
Criteria: must be an independent, privately-held, for-profit, U.S. corporation, proprietorship or
partnership; revenues must be at least $100,000 in 2010 and $2 million in 2013; must have
four-year operating/sales history. Holding companies, regulated banks, and utilities were excluded.
Inc., "America's 500 Fastest-Growing Private Companies," September 2014

According to Deloitte, Boulder is home to two of North America's 500 fastest-growing high-technology companies: **Rally** (#232); **Array Biopharma** (#419). Companies are ranked by percentage growth in revenue over a five-year period. Criteria for inclusion: company must be headquartered within North America; must own proprietary intellectual property or proprietary technology that contributes to a significant portion of the company's operating revenue, or devote a significant proportion of revenues to research and development of technology; must have been in business for a minumum of five years with 2009 operating revenues of at least $50,000 USD/CD and 2013 operating revenues of at least $5 million USD/CD. *Deloitte Touche Tohmatsu, 2014 Technology Fast 500*[TM]

Minority Business Opportunity

Boulder is home to one company which is on the *Hispanic Business* 500 list (500 largest U.S. Hispanic-owned companies based on 2012 revenue): **KIRA** (#109). Companies included must show at least 51 percent ownership by Hispanic U.S. citizens, and must maintain headquarters in one of the 50 states or Washington, D.C. *Hispanic Business, "Hispanic Business 500," June 20, 2013*

Minority- and Women-Owned Businesses

Group	All Firms		Firms with Paid Employees			
	Firms	Sales ($000)	Firms	Sales ($000)	Employees	Payroll ($000)
Asian	304	135,831	98	126,651	933	20,421
Black	86	21,745	16	18,546	285	6,350
Hispanic	324	64,376	92	59,990	544	14,621
Women	4,923	532,099	919	408,550	4,467	119,646
All Firms	16,762	16,610,865	4,853	16,023,312	71,677	3,680,870

Note: Figures cover firms located in the city; minority- and women-owned business are defined as firms in which the corresponding group own 51% or more of the stock or equity of the company
Source: U.S. Census Bureau, 2007 Economic Census, Survey of Business Owners (2012 Survey of Business Owners data will be released starting in June 2015)

HOTELS & CONVENTION CENTERS

Hotels/Motels

Area	5 Star		4 Star		3 Star		2 Star		1 Star		Not Rated	
	Num.	Pct.[3]	Num.	Pct.[3]	Num.	Pct.[3]	Num.	Pct.[3]	Num.	Pct.[3]	Num.	Pct.[3]
City[1]	0	0.0	3	3.6	29	34.5	46	54.8	4	4.8	2	2.4
Total[2]	166	0.9	1,264	7.0	5,718	31.8	9,340	52.0	411	2.3	1,070	6.0

Note: (1) Figures cover Boulder and vicinity; (2) Figures cover all 100 cities in this book; (3) Percentage of hotels which have a given star rating; Star ratings are determined by expedia.com and offer an indication of the general quality of a particular hotel.
Source: expedia.com, April 2, 2015

Major Convention Centers

Name	Overall Space (sq. ft.)	Exhibit Space (sq. ft.)	Meeting Space (sq. ft.)	Meeting Rooms

There are no major convention centers located in the metro area
Source: Original research

Living Environment

COST OF LIVING

Cost of Living Index

Composite Index	Groceries	Housing	Utilities	Trans-portation	Health Care	Misc. Goods/ Services
n/a	n/a	n/a	n/a	n/a	n/a	n/a

Note: The Cost of Living Index measures regional differences in the cost of consumer goods and services, excluding taxes and non-consumer expenditures, for professional and managerial households in the top income quintile. It is based on more than 50,000 prices covering almost 60 different items for which prices are collected three times a year by chambers of commerce, economic development organizations or university applied economic centers in each participating urban area. The numbers shown should be read as a percentage above or below the national average of 100. For example, a value of 115.4 in the groceries column indicates that grocery prices are 15.4% higher than the national average. Small differences in the index numbers should not be interpreted as significant; n/a not available.
Source: The Council for Community and Economic Research, ACCRA Cost of Living Index, 2014

Grocery Prices

Area[1]	T-Bone Steak ($/pound)	Frying Chicken ($/pound)	Whole Milk ($/half gal.)	Eggs ($/dozen)	Orange Juice ($/64 oz.)	Coffee ($/11.5 oz.)
City[2]	n/a	n/a	n/a	n/a	n/a	n/a
Avg.	10.40	1.37	2.40	1.99	3.46	4.27
Min.	8.48	0.93	1.37	1.30	2.83	2.99
Max.	14.20	2.44	3.62	4.02	6.42	6.96

Note: (1) Values for the local area are compared with the average, minimum and maximum values for all 308 areas in the Cost of Living Index; (2) Figures cover the Boulder CO urban area; n/a not available; **T-Bone Steak** (price per pound); **Frying Chicken** (price per pound, whole fryer); **Whole Milk** (half gallon carton); **Eggs** (price per dozen, Grade A, large); **Orange Juice** (64 oz. Tropicana or Florida Natural); **Coffee** (11.5 oz. can, vacuum-packed, Maxwell House, Hills Bros, or Folgers).
Source: The Council for Community and Economic Research, ACCRA Cost of Living Index, 2014

Housing and Utility Costs

Area[1]	New Home Price ($)	Apartment Rent ($/month)	All Electric ($/month)	Part Electric ($/month)	Other Energy ($/month)	Telephone ($/month)
City[2]	n/a	n/a	n/a	n/a	n/a	n/a
Avg.	305,838	919	181.00	93.66	73.14	27.95
Min.	183,142	480	112.00	42.06	23.42	17.16
Max.	1,358,576	3,851	594.00	180.03	440.99	40.42

Note: (1) Values for the local area are compared with the average, minimum and maximum values for all 308 areas in the Cost of Living Index; (2) Figures cover the Boulder CO urban area; n/a not available; **New Home Price** (2,400 sf living area, 8,000 sf lot, in urban area with full utilities); **Apartment Rent** (950 sf 2 bedroom/1.5 or 2 bath, unfurnished, excluding all utilities except water); **All Electric** (average monthly cost for an all-electric home); **Part Electric** (average monthly cost for a part-electric home); **Other Energy** (average monthly cost for natural gas, fuel oil, coal, wood, and any other forms of energy except electricity); **Telephone** (price includes basic monthly rate for a private residential line plus additional local usage charges incurred by a family of four).
Source: The Council for Community and Economic Research, ACCRA Cost of Living Index, 2014

Health Care, Transportation, and Other Costs

Area[1]	Doctor ($/visit)	Dentist ($/visit)	Optometrist ($/visit)	Gasoline ($/gallon)	Beauty Salon ($/visit)	Men's Shirt ($)
City[2]	n/a	n/a	n/a	n/a	n/a	n/a
Avg.	102.86	87.89	97.66	3.44	34.37	26.74
Min.	67.47	65.78	51.18	3.00	17.43	12.79
Max.	173.50	150.14	235.00	4.33	64.28	49.50

Note: (1) Values for the local area are compared with the average, minimum and maximum values for all 308 areas in the Cost of Living Index; (2) Figures cover the Boulder CO urban area; n/a not available; **Doctor** (general practitioners routine exam of an established patient); **Dentist** (adult teeth cleaning and periodic oral examination); **Optometrist** (full vision eye exam for established adult patient); **Gasoline** (one gallon regular unleaded, national brand, including all taxes, cash price at self-service pump if available); **Beauty Salon** (woman's shampoo, trim, and blow-dry); **Men's Shirt** (cotton/polyester dress shirt, pinpoint weave, long sleeves).
Source: The Council for Community and Economic Research, ACCRA Cost of Living Index, 2014

HOUSING

House Price Index (HPI)

Area	National Ranking[2]	Quarterly Change (%)	One-Year Change (%)	Five-Year Change (%)
MSA[1]	34	1.67	9.27	19.39
U.S.[3]	–	1.35	4.91	11.59

Note: The HPI is a weighted repeat sales index. It measures average price changes in repeat sales or refinancings on the same properties. This information is obtained by reviewing repeat mortgage transactions on single-family properties whose mortgages have been purchased or securitized by Fannie Mae or Freddie Mac in January 1975; (1) Boulder Metropolitan Statistical Area—see Appendix B for areas included; (2) Rankings are based on annual percentage change for all metro areas containing at least 15,000 transactions over the last 10 years and ranges from 1 to 275; (3) figures based on a weighted average of Census Division estimates using a seasonally adjusted, purchase-only index; all figures are for the period ending December 31, 2014
Source: Federal Housing Finance Agency, House Price Index, February 26, 2015

Median Single-Family Home Prices

Area	2012	2013	2014p	Percent Change 2013 to 2014
MSA[1]	383.7	371.8	390.7	5.1
U.S. Average	177.2	197.4	209.0	5.9

Note: Figures are median sales prices of existing single-family homes in thousands of dollars; (p) preliminary; n/a not available; (1) Boulder, CO Metropolitan Statistical Area—see Appendix B for areas included
Source: National Association of Realtors, Median Sales Price of Existing Single-Family Homes for Metropolitan Areas, 4th Quarter 2014

Qualifying Income Based on Median Sales Price of Existing Single-Family Homes

Area	With 5% Down ($)	With 10% Down ($)	With 20% Down ($)
MSA[1]	93,835	88,896	79,019
U.S. Average	45,863	43,449	38,621

Note: Figures are preliminary; Qualifying income is based on a mortgage rate of 4.0%. Monthly principal and interest payment is limited to 25% of income; n/a not available; (1) Boulder, CO Metropolitan Statistical Area—see Appendix B for areas included
Source: National Association of Realtors, Qualifying Income Based on Median Sales Price of Existing Single-Family Homes for Metropolitan Areas, 4th Quarter 2014

Median Apartment Condo-Coop Home Prices

Area	2012	2013	2014p	Percent Change 2013 to 2014
MSA[1]	217.5	193.4	231.8	19.9
U.S. Average	173.7	194.9	205.1	5.2

Note: Figures are median sales prices of existing apartment condo-coop homes in thousands of dollars; (p) preliminary; n/a not available; (1) Boulder, CO Metropolitan Statistical Area—see Appendix B for areas included
Source: National Association of Realtors, Median Sales Price of Existing Apartment Condo-Coop Homes for Metropolitan Areas, 4th Quarter 2014

Gross Monthly Rent

Area	Under $200	$200 -299	$300 -499	$500 -749	$750 -999	$1,000 -1,499	$1,500 and up	Median ($)
City	0.5	1.6	1.5	7.6	26.3	31.0	31.5	1,173
MSA[1]	0.8	1.6	2.3	9.1	26.0	35.0	25.3	1,120
U.S.	1.7	3.2	7.8	22.1	24.3	26.0	14.9	900

Note: Figures are percentages except for Median; Gross rent is the contract rent plus the estimated average monthly cost of utilities (electricity, gas, and water and sewer) and fuels (oil, coal, kerosene, wood, etc.) if these are paid by the renter (or paid for the renter by someone else); (1) Figures cover the Boulder, CO Metropolitan Statistical Area—see Appendix B for areas included
Source: U.S. Census Bureau, 2011-2013 American Community Survey 3-Year Estimates

Homeownership Rate

Area	2007 (%)	2008 (%)	2009 (%)	2010 (%)	2011 (%)	2012 (%)	2013 (%)	2014 (%)
MSA[1]	n/a	n/a	n/a	n/a	n/a	n/a	n/a	n/a
U.S.	68.1	67.8	67.4	66.9	66.1	65.4	65.1	64.5

Note: (1) Figures cover the Boulder, CO Metropolitan Statistical Area—see Appendix B for areas included; n/a not available
Source: U.S. Census Bureau, Housing Vacancies and Homeownership Annual Statistics: 2014

Year Housing Structure Built

Area	2010 or Later	2000 -2009	1990 -1999	1980 -1989	1970 -1979	1960 -1969	1950 -1959	1940 -1949	Before 1940	Median Year
City	1.2	9.8	9.8	16.9	23.6	18.2	9.1	2.1	9.3	1975
MSA[1]	0.8	13.9	19.9	17.0	21.9	11.8	5.3	1.7	7.7	1981
U.S.	0.9	15.0	13.9	13.8	15.8	11.0	10.9	5.4	13.3	1976

Note: Figures are percentages except for Median Year; (1) Figures cover the Boulder, CO Metropolitan Statistical Area—see Appendix B for areas included
Source: U.S. Census Bureau, 2011-2013 American Community Survey 3-Year Estimates

HEALTH

Health Risk Data

Category	MSA[1] (%)	U.S. (%)
Adults aged 18–64 who have any kind of health care coverage	79.3	79.6
Adults who reported being in good or excellent health	90.5	83.1
Adults who are current smokers	13.5	19.6
Adults who are heavy drinkers[2]	5.8	6.1
Adults who are binge drinkers[3]	15.4	16.9
Adults who are overweight (BMI 25.0 - 29.9)	31.5	35.8
Adults who are obese (BMI 30.0 - 99.8)	14.8	27.6
Adults who participated in any physical activities in the past month	90.8	77.1
Adults 50+ who have ever had a sigmoidoscopy or colonoscopy	68.0	67.3
Women aged 40+ who have had a mammogram within the past two years	63.1	74.0
Men aged 40+ who have had a PSA test within the past two years	33.9	45.2
Adults aged 65+ who have had flu shot within the past year	72.2	60.1
Adults who always wear a seatbelt	95.3	93.8

Note: Data as of 2012 unless otherwise noted; (1) Figures cover the Boulder, CO Metropolitan Statistical Area—see Appendix B for areas included; (2) Heavy drinkers are classified as males having more than two drinks per day or females having more than one drink per day; (3) Binge drinkers are classified as males having five or more drinks on one occasion or females having four or more drinks on one occasion
Source: Centers for Disease Control and Prevention, Behaviorial Risk Factor Surveillance System, SMART: Selected Metropolitan/Micropolitan Area Risk Trends, 2012 (Note: the CDC has discontinued this dataset but will be releasing a replacement in late 2015)

Chronic Health Indicators

Category	MSA[1] (%)	U.S. (%)
Adults who have ever been told they had a heart attack	n/a	4.5
Adults who have ever been told they had a stroke	n/a	2.9
Adults who have been told they currently have asthma	6.3	8.9
Adults who have ever been told they have arthritis	23.0	25.7
Adults who have ever been told they have diabetes[2]	3.4	9.7
Adults who have ever been told they had skin cancer	7.2	5.7
Adults who have ever been told they had any other types of cancer	6.0	6.5
Adults who have ever been told they have COPD	2.4	6.2
Adults who have ever been told they have kidney disease	n/a	2.5
Adults who have ever been told they have a form of depression	18.3	18.0

Note: Data as of 2012 unless otherwise noted; n/a not available; (1) Figures cover the Boulder, CO Metropolitan Statistical Area—see Appendix B for areas included; (2) Figures do not include pregnancy-related, borderline, or pre-diabetes
Source: Centers for Disease Control and Prevention, Behaviorial Risk Factor Surveillance System, SMART: Selected Metropolitan/Micropolitan Area Risk Trends, 2012 (Note: the CDC has discontinued this dataset but will be releasing a replacement in late 2015)

Mortality Rates for the Top 10 Causes of Death in the U.S.

ICD-10[a] Sub-Chapter	ICD-10[a] Code	Age-Adjusted Mortality Rate[1] per 100,000 population	
		County[2]	U.S.
Malignant neoplasms	C00-C97	119.6	166.2
Ischaemic heart diseases	I20-I25	62.2	105.7
Other forms of heart disease	I30-I51	37.4	49.3
Chronic lower respiratory diseases	J40-J47	32.9	42.1
Organic, including symptomatic, mental disorders	F01-F09	42.5	38.1
Cerebrovascular diseases	I60-I69	30.4	37.0
Other external causes of accidental injury	W00-X59	41.2	26.9
Other degenerative diseases of the nervous system	G30-G31	24.2	25.6
Diabetes mellitus	E10-E14	8.7	21.3
Hypertensive diseases	I10-I15	6.8	19.4

Note: (a) ICD-10 = International Classification of Diseases 10th Revision; (1) Mortality rates are a three year average covering 2011-2013; (2) Figures cover Boulder County
Source: Centers for Disease Control and Prevention, National Center for Health Statistics. Compressed Mortality File 1999-2013 on CDC WONDER Online Database, released October 2014. Data are compiled from the Compressed Mortality File 1999-2013, Series 20 No. 2S, 2014.

Mortality Rates for Selected Causes of Death

ICD-10[a] Sub-Chapter	ICD-10[a] Code	Age-Adjusted Mortality Rate[1] per 100,000 population	
		County[2]	U.S.
Assault	X85-Y09	*1.1	5.2
Diseases of the liver	K70-K76	12.7	13.2
Human immunodeficiency virus (HIV) disease	B20-B24	Suppressed	2.2
Influenza and pneumonia	J09-J18	12.4	15.4
Intentional self-harm	X60-X84	17.4	12.5
Malnutrition	E40-E46	*2.2	0.9
Obesity and other hyperalimentation	E65-E68	Suppressed	1.8
Renal failure	N17-N19	6.1	13.1
Transport accidents	V01-V99	6.9	11.7
Viral hepatitis	B15-B19	*1.6	2.2

Note: (a) ICD-10 = International Classification of Diseases 10th Revision; (1) Mortality rates are a three year average covering 2011-2013; (2) Figures cover Boulder County; (*) Unreliable data as per CDC
Source: Centers for Disease Control and Prevention, National Center for Health Statistics. Compressed Mortality File 1999-2013 on CDC WONDER Online Database, released October 2014. Data are compiled from the Compressed Mortality File 1999-2013, Series 20 No. 2S, 2014.

Health Insurance Coverage

Area	With Health Insurance	With Private Health Insurance	With Public Health Insurance	Without Health Insurance	Population Under Age 18 Without Health Insurance
City	92.0	85.0	14.2	8.0	7.1
MSA[1]	89.4	79.2	18.8	10.6	6.8
U.S.	85.2	65.2	31.0	14.8	7.3

Note: Figures are percentages that cover the civilian noninstitutionalized population; (1) Figures cover the Boulder, CO Metropolitan Statistical Area—see Appendix B for areas included
Source: U.S. Census Bureau, 2011-2013 American Community Survey 3-Year Estimates

Number of Medical Professionals

Area[1]	MDs[2]	DOs[2,3]	Dentists	Podiatrists	Chiropractors	Optometrists
Local (number)	1,104	71	284	14	208	72
Local (rate[4])	361.4	23.2	91.5	4.5	67.0	23.2
U.S. (rate[4])	270.0	20.2	63.1	5.7	25.2	14.9

Note: Data as of 2013 unless noted; (1) Local data covers Boulder County; (2) Data as of 2012 and includes all active, non-federal physicians; (3) Doctor of Osteopathic Medicine; (4) rate per 100,000 population
Source: U.S. Department of Health and Human Services, Health Resources and Services Administration, Bureau of Health Professions, Area Resource File (ARF) 2013-2014

EDUCATION

Public School District Statistics

District Name	Schls	Pupils	Pupil/ Teacher Ratio	Minority Pupils[1] (%)	Free Lunch Eligible[2] (%)	IEP[3] (%)
Boulder Valley SD No. RE2	56	30,041	17.6	29.7	15.7	0.0

Note: Table includes school districts with 2,000 or more students; (1) Percentage of students that are not non-Hispanic white; (2) Percentage of students that are eligible for the free lunch program; (3) Percentage of students that have an Individualized Education Program.
Source: U.S. Department of Education, National Center for Education Statistics, Common Core of Data, Local Education Agency (School District) Universe Survey: School Year 2012-2013; U.S. Department of Education, National Center for Education Statistics, Common Core of Data, Public Elementary/Secondary School Universe Survey: School Year 2012-2013

Highest Level of Education

Area	Less than H.S.	H.S. Diploma	Some College, No Deg.	Associate Degree	Bachelor's Degree	Master's Degree	Prof. School Degree	Doctorate Degree
City	3.5	7.2	11.8	3.9	35.3	23.7	5.1	9.6
MSA[1]	6.2	12.6	17.2	5.6	31.1	18.1	3.4	5.7
U.S.	13.7	28.0	21.2	7.9	18.2	7.7	1.9	1.3

Note: Figures cover persons age 25 and over; (1) Figures cover the Boulder, CO Metropolitan Statistical Area—see Appendix B for areas included
Source: U.S. Census Bureau, 2011-2013 American Community Survey 3-Year Estimates

Educational Attainment by Race

Area	High School Graduate or Higher (%)					Bachelor's Degree or Higher (%)				
	Total	White	Black	Asian	Hisp.[2]	Total	White	Black	Asian	Hisp.[2]
City	96.5	97.6	n/a	96.0	70.0	73.6	75.8	n/a	68.2	39.1
MSA[1]	93.8	95.1	86.8	95.0	62.3	58.3	60.0	38.1	69.9	21.8
U.S.	86.3	88.3	83.1	85.7	64.0	29.1	30.4	18.8	50.7	13.7

Note: Figures shown cover persons 25 years old and over; (1) Figures cover the Boulder, CO Metropolitan Statistical Area—see Appendix B for areas included; (2) People of Hispanic origin can be of any race
Source: U.S. Census Bureau, 2011-2013 American Community Survey 3-Year Estimates

School Enrollment by Grade and Control

Area	Preschool (%)		Kindergarten (%)		Grades 1 - 4 (%)		Grades 5 - 8 (%)		Grades 9 - 12 (%)	
	Public	Private	Public	Private	Public	Private	Public	Private	Public	Private
City	24.7	75.3	85.4	14.6	86.0	14.0	86.2	13.8	93.2	6.8
MSA[1]	42.9	57.1	92.9	7.1	90.1	9.9	91.7	8.3	95.2	4.8
U.S.	57.7	42.3	87.9	12.1	89.9	10.1	90.0	10.0	90.7	9.3

Note: Figures shown cover persons 3 years old and over; (1) Figures cover the Boulder, CO Metropolitan Statistical Area—see Appendix B for areas included
Source: U.S. Census Bureau, 2011-2013 American Community Survey 3-Year Estimates

Average Salaries of Public School Classroom Teachers

Area	2013-14		2014-15		Percent Change 2013-14 to 2014-15	Percent Change 2004-05 to 2014-15
	Dollars	Rank[1]	Dollars	Rank[1]		
COLORADO	49,615	31	49,828	34	0.43	13.4
U.S. Average	56,610	–	57,379	–	1.36	20.8

Note: (1) State rank ranges from 1 to 51 where 1 indicates highest salary.
Source: National Education Association, Rankings & Estimates: Rankings of the States 2014 and Estimates of School Statistics 2015, March 2015

Higher Education

Four-Year Colleges			Two-Year Colleges			Medical Schools[1]	Law Schools[2]	Voc/ Tech[3]
Public	Private Non-profit	Private For-profit	Public	Private Non-profit	Private For-profit			
1	2	1	0	1	0	0	1	2

Note: Figures cover institutions located within the city limits and include main campuses only; (1) includes schools accredited by the Liaison Committee on Medical Education and the American Osteopathic Association's Commission on Osteopathic College Accreditation; (2) includes ABA-accredited schools, schools with provisional ABA accreditation, and state accredited schools; (3) includes all schools with programs that are less than 2 years.
Source: National Center for Education Statistics, Integrated Postsecondary Education System (IPEDS), 2013-14; Association of American Medical Colleges, Member List, May 1, 2015; American Osteopathic Association, Member List, May 1, 2015; Law School Admission Council, Official Guide to ABA-Approved Law Schools Online, May 1, 2015; Wikipedia, List of Medical Schools in the United States, May 1, 2015; Wikipedia, List of Law Schools in the United States, May 1, 2015

According to *U.S. News & World Report*, the Boulder, CO metro area is home to one of the best national universities in the U.S.: **University of Colorado-Boulder** (#88). The indicators used to capture academic quality fall into a number of categories: assessment by administrators at peer institutions; retention of students; faculty resources; student selectivity; financial resources; alumni giving; high school counselor ratings of colleges; and graduation rate. *U.S. News & World Report, "America's Best Colleges 2015"*

According to *U.S. News & World Report*, the Boulder, CO metro area is home to one of the top 100 law schools in the U.S.: **University of Colorado-Boulder** (#40). The rankings are based on a weighted average of 12 measures of quality: peer assessment score; assessment score by lawyers/judges; median LSAT scores; median undergrad GPA; acceptance rate; employment rates for graduates; placement success; bar passage rate; faculty resources; expenditures per student; student/faculty ratio; and library resources. *U.S. News & World Report, "America's Best Graduate Schools, Law, 2016"*

PRESIDENTIAL ELECTION

2012 Presidential Election Results

Area	Obama (%)	Romney (%)	Other (%)
Boulder County	69.7	27.9	2.4
U.S.	51.0	47.2	1.8

Note: Results may not add to 100% due to rounding
Source: Dave Leip's Atlas of U.S. Presidential Elections

EMPLOYERS

Major Employers

Company Name	Industry
Agilent Technologies	Instruments to measure electricity
America's Note Network	Mortgage bankers and loan correspondents
Ball Aerospace & Technologies Corp.	Search and navigation equipment
Ball Corporation	Space research and technology
Corden Pharma Colorado	Pharmaceutical preparations
County of Boulder	Sheriffs' office
Crispin Porter Bogusky	Business services at non-commercial site
Health Carechain	Medical field-related associations
IBM	Magnetic storage devices, computer
IBM	Computer related consulting services
Lockheed Martin Corporation	Search and navigation equipment
Micro Motion	Liquid meters
National Oceanic and Atmospheric Admin	Environmental protection agency, government
Natl Inst of Standards & Technology	Commercial physical research
Qualcomm Incorporated	Integrated circuits, semiconductor networks
Staffing Solutions Southwest	Temporary help service
The Regents of the University of Colorado	Noncommercial research organizations
The Regents of the University of Colorado	Libraries
Tyco Healthcare Group	Medical instruments & equipment, blood & bone work
University Corp for Atmospheric Research	Noncommercial research organizations
University of Colorado	Colleges and universities
Wall Street On Demand	Financial services
Whole Foods Market	Grocery stores

Note: Companies shown are located within the Boulder, CO Metropolitan Statistical Area.
Source: Hoovers.com; Wikipedia

PUBLIC SAFETY

Crime Rate

Area	All Crimes	Violent Crimes				Property Crimes		
		Murder	Forcible Rape	Robbery	Aggrav. Assault	Burglary	Larceny -Theft	Motor Vehicle Theft
City	3,078.9	0.0	37.0	38.9	136.1	595.2	2,174.5	97.2
Suburbs[1]	2,202.8	1.0	59.8	16.4	134.9	298.8	1,579.7	112.3
Metro[2]	2,493.1	0.6	52.2	23.8	135.3	397.0	1,776.8	107.3
U.S.	3,098.6	4.5	25.2	109.1	229.1	610.0	1,899.4	221.3

Note: Figures are crimes per 100,000 population; (1) All areas within the metro area that are located outside the city limits; (2) Figures cover the Boulder, CO Metropolitan Statistical Area—see Appendix B for areas included
Source: FBI Uniform Crime Reports, 2013

Hate Crimes

Area	Number of Quarters Reported	Number of Incidents per Bias Motivation						
		Race	Religion	Sexual Orientation	Ethnicity	Disability	Gender	Gender Identity
City	4	0	0	0	0	0	0	0
U.S.	4	2,871	1,031	1,233	655	83	18	31

Source: Federal Bureau of Investigation, Hate Crime Statistics 2013

Identity Theft Consumer Complaints

Area	Complaints	Complaints per 100,000 Population	Rank[2]
MSA[1]	227	73.2	167
U.S.	332,646	104.3	-

Note: (1) Figures cover the Boulder, CO Metropolitan Statistical Area—see Appendix B for areas included; (2) Rank ranges from 1 to 380 where 1 indicates greatest number of identity theft complaints per 100,000 population
Source: Federal Trade Commission, Consumer Sentinel Network Data Book for January–December 2014

Fraud and Other Consumer Complaints

Area	Complaints	Complaints per 100,000 Population	Rank[2]
MSA[1]	1,279	412.5	117
U.S.	2,250,205	705.7	-

Note: (1) Figures cover the Boulder, CO Metropolitan Statistical Area—see Appendix B for areas included; (2) Rank ranges from 1 to 380 where 1 indicates greatest number of identity theft complaints per 100,000 population
Source: Federal Trade Commission, Consumer Sentinel Network Data Book for January–December 2014

RECREATION

Culture

Dance[1]	Theatre[1]	Instrumental Music[1]	Vocal Music[1]	Series and Festivals	Museums and Art Galleries[2]	Zoos and Aquariums[3]
2	3	3	0	8	21	0

Note: (1) Professional perfoming groups; (2) Based on organizations with SIC code 8412; (3) AZA-accredited
Source: The Grey House Performing Arts Directory, 2015-16; Association of Zoos & Aquariums, AZA Member Zoos & Aquariums, April 2015; www.AccuLeads.com, April 2015

Professional Sports Teams

Team Name	League	Year Established
No teams are located in the metro area		

Source: Wikipedia, Major Professional Sports Teams of the United States and Canada, April 2015

CLIMATE

Average and Extreme Temperatures

Temperature	Jan	Feb	Mar	Apr	May	Jun	Jul	Aug	Sep	Oct	Nov	Dec	Yr.
Extreme High (°F)	73	76	84	90	93	102	103	100	97	89	79	75	103
Average High (°F)	43	47	52	62	71	81	88	86	77	67	52	45	64
Average Temp. (°F)	30	34	39	48	58	67	73	72	63	52	39	32	51
Average Low (°F)	16	20	25	34	44	53	59	57	48	37	25	18	37
Extreme Low (°F)	-25	-25	-10	-2	22	30	43	41	17	3	-8	-25	-25

Note: Figures cover the years 1948-1992
Source: National Climatic Data Center, International Station Meteorological Climate Summary, 9/96

Average Precipitation/Snowfall/Humidity

Precip./Humidity	Jan	Feb	Mar	Apr	May	Jun	Jul	Aug	Sep	Oct	Nov	Dec	Yr.
Avg. Precip. (in.)	0.6	0.6	1.3	1.7	2.5	1.7	1.9	1.5	1.1	1.0	0.9	0.6	15.5
Avg. Snowfall (in.)	9	7	14	9	2	Tr	0	0	2	4	9	8	63
Avg. Rel. Hum. 5am (%)	62	65	67	66	70	68	67	68	66	63	66	63	66
Avg. Rel. Hum. 5pm (%)	49	44	40	35	38	34	34	34	32	34	47	50	39

Note: Figures cover the years 1948-1992; Tr = Trace amounts (<0.05 in. of rain; <0.5 in. of snow)
Source: National Climatic Data Center, International Station Meteorological Climate Summary, 9/96

Weather Conditions

Temperature			Daytime Sky			Precipitation		
10°F & below	32°F & below	90°F & above	Clear	Partly cloudy	Cloudy	0.01 inch or more precip.	0.1 inch or more snow/ice	Thunder-storms
24	155	33	99	177	89	90	38	39

Note: Figures are average number of days per year and cover the years 1948-1992
Source: National Climatic Data Center, International Station Meteorological Climate Summary, 9/96

HAZARDOUS WASTE

Superfund Sites

Boulder has one hazardous waste site on the EPA's Superfund Final National Priorities List: **Marshall Landfill**. There are a total of 1,322 Superfund sites on the list in the U.S. *U.S. Environmental Protection Agency, Final National Priorities List, April 14, 2015*

**AIR & WATER
QUALITY**

Air Quality Trends: Ozone

	2004	2005	2006	2007	2008	2009	2010	2011	2012	2013
MSA[1]	0.068	0.076	0.082	0.085	0.076	0.073	0.072	0.076	0.076	0.079

Note: (1) Data covers the Boulder, CO Metropolitan Statistical Area—see Appendix B for areas included. The values shown are the composite ozone concentration averages among trend sites based on the highest fourth daily maximum 8-hour concentration in parts per million. These trends are based on sites having an adequate record of monitoring data during the trend period. Data from exceptional events are included.
Source: U.S. Environmental Protection Agency, Air Quality Monitoring Information, "Air Quality Trends by City, 2000-2013"

Air Quality Index

Area	Percent of Days when Air Quality was...[2]					AQI Statistics[2]	
	Good	Moderate	Unhealthy for Sensitive Groups	Unhealthy	Very Unhealthy	Maximum	Median
MSA[1]	84.3	15.2	0.6	0.0	0.0	126	41

Note: (1) Data covers the Boulder, CO Metropolitan Statistical Area—see Appendix B for areas included; (2) Based on 362 days with AQI data in 2014. Air Quality Index (AQI) is an index for reporting daily air quality. EPA calculates the AQI for five major air pollutants regulated by the Clean Air Act: ground-level ozone, particle pollution (aka particulate matter), carbon monoxide, sulfur dioxide, and nitrogen dioxide. The AQI runs from 0 to 500. The higher the AQI value, the greater the level of air pollution and the greater the health concern. There are six AQI categories: "Good" AQI is between 0 and 50. Air quality is considered satisfactory; "Moderate" AQI is between 51 and 100. Air quality is acceptable; "Unhealthy for Sensitive Groups" When AQI values are between 101 and 150, members of sensitive groups may experience health effects; "Unhealthy" When AQI values are between 151 and 200 everyone may begin to experience health effects; "Very Unhealthy" AQI values between 201 and 300 trigger a health alert; "Hazardous" AQI values over 300 trigger warnings of emergency conditions (not shown).
Source: U.S. Environmental Protection Agency, Air Quality Index Report, 2014

Air Quality Index Pollutants

Area	Percent of Days when AQI Pollutant was...[2]					
	Carbon Monoxide	Nitrogen Dioxide	Ozone	Sulfur Dioxide	Particulate Matter 2.5	Particulate Matter 10
MSA[1]	0.0	0.0	92.0	0.0	7.7	0.3

Note: (1) Data covers the Boulder, CO Metropolitan Statistical Area—see Appendix B for areas included; (2) Based on 362 days with AQI data in 2014. The Air Quality Index (AQI) is an index for reporting daily air quality. EPA calculates the AQI for five major air pollutants regulated by the Clean Air Act: ground-level ozone, particle pollution (also known as particulate matter), carbon monoxide, sulfur dioxide, and nitrogen dioxide. The AQI runs from 0 to 500. The higher the AQI value, the greater the level of air pollution and the greater the health concern.
Source: U.S. Environmental Protection Agency, Air Quality Index Report, 2014

Maximum Air Pollutant Concentrations: Particulate Matter, Ozone, CO and Lead

	Particulate Matter 10 (ug/m^3)	Particulate Matter 2.5 Wtd AM (ug/m^3)	Particulate Matter 2.5 24-Hr (ug/m^3)	Ozone (ppm)	Carbon Monoxide (ppm)	Lead (ug/m^3)
MSA[1] Level	51	7.1	23	0.079	n/a	n/a
NAAQS[2]	150	15	35	0.075	9	0.15
Met NAAQS[2]	Yes	Yes	Yes	No	n/a	n/a

Note: (1) Data covers the Boulder, CO Metropolitan Statistical Area—see Appendix B for areas included; Data from exceptional events are included; (2) National Ambient Air Quality Standards; ppm = parts per million; ug/m^3 = micrograms per cubic meter; n/a not available.
Concentrations: Particulate Matter 10 (coarse particulate)—highest second maximum 24-hour concentration; Particulate Matter 2.5 Wtd AM (fine particulate)—highest weighted annual mean concentration; Particulate Matter 2.5 24-Hour (fine particulate)—highest 98th percentile 24-hour concentration; Ozone—highest fourth daily maximum 8-hour concentration; Carbon Monoxide—highest second maximum non-overlapping 8-hour concentration; Lead—maximum running 3-month average
Source: U.S. Environmental Protection Agency, Air Quality Monitoring Information, "Air Quality Statistics by City, 2013"

Maximum Air Pollutant Concentrations: Nitrogen Dioxide and Sulfur Dioxide

	Nitrogen Dioxide AM (ppb)	Nitrogen Dioxide 1-Hr (ppb)	Sulfur Dioxide AM (ppb)	Sulfur Dioxide 1-Hr (ppb)	Sulfur Dioxide 24-Hr (ppb)
MSA[1] Level	n/a	n/a	n/a	n/a	n/a
NAAQS[2]	53	100	30	75	140
Met NAAQS[2]	n/a	n/a	n/a	n/a	n/a

Note: (1) Data covers the Boulder, CO Metropolitan Statistical Area—see Appendix B for areas included; Data from exceptional events are included; (2) National Ambient Air Quality Standards; ppm = parts per million; ug/m³ = micrograms per cubic meter; n/a not available.
Concentrations: Nitrogen Dioxide AM—highest arithmetic mean concentration; Nitrogen Dioxide 1-Hr—highest 98th percentile 1-hour daily maximum concentration; Sulfur Dioxide AM—highest annual mean concentration; Sulfur Dioxide 1-Hr—highest 99th percentile 1-hour daily maximum concentration; Sulfur Dioxide 24-Hr—highest second maximum 24-hour concentration
Source: U.S. Environmental Protection Agency, Air Quality Monitoring Information, "Air Quality Statistics by City, 2013"

Drinking Water

Water System Name	Pop. Served	Primary Water Source Type	Violations[1] Health Based	Violations[1] Monitoring/ Reporting
City of Boulder	166,080	Surface	0	0

Note: (1) Based on violation data from January 1, 2014 to December 31, 2014 (includes unresolved violations from earlier years)
Source: U.S. Environmental Protection Agency, Office of Ground Water and Drinking Water, Safe Drinking Water Information System (based on data extracted January 27, 2015)

Colorado Springs, Colorado

Background

Colorado Springs is the seat of El Paso County in central Colorado and sits at the foot of Pike's Peak. A dynamic and growing city, its economy is based on health care, high-tech manufacturing, tourism, and sports, with strong employment links to nearby military installations. With such an economic base and gorgeous surroundings, it is no wonder that Colorado Springs ranks as one of the fastest-growing cities in the country.

In 1806, Lieutenant Zebulon Pike visited the site and the mountain that now bears his name, but true settlement did not begin in earnest until gold was discovered in 1859 and miners flooded into the area.

In 1871, General William Jackson Palmer, a railroad tycoon, purchased the site for $10,000 and began promoting the area as a health and recreation resort. Pike's Peak was already well known as a scenic landmark, and very soon the Garden of the Gods, Seven Falls, Cheyenne Mountain, and Manitou Springs were also widely known as spectacular natural sites. The extraordinary nature of the natural environment has long been celebrated, but perhaps the highest testimonial came from Katherine Lee Bates, who, after a trip to Pike's Peak in 1893, wrote "America the Beautiful."

The planned community of Colorado Springs was incorporated in 1876. As a resort, it was wildly successful, hosting the likes of Oscar Wilde and John D. Rockefeller. It became a special favorite of English visitors, one of whom made the claim that there were two "civilized" places between the Atlantic and the Pacific—Chicago and Colorado Springs.

The English were so enamored of the place, in fact, that it came to be called "Little London," as English visitors settled in the area, introducing golf, cricket, polo, and fox hunting; but since there were no local foxes, an artificial scent was spread out for the hounds, or sometimes a coyote was substituted. Several sumptuous hotels were built during this period, as was an elegantly appointed opera house.

In 1891, gold was again discovered, and the city's population tripled to 35,000 in the following decade. Sufficient gold deposits allowed a lucky few to amass considerable fortunes and build huge houses north of the city. However, not all of the newly minted millionaires were inclined toward conspicuous display; Winfield Scott Stratton, "Midas of the Rockies," bruised emerging aesthetic sensibilities by constructing a crude wooden frame house near the business district.

After the 1890s rush ended, Colorado Springs resumed a more measured pace of growth. During and after World War II, though, the town again saw considerable development as Fort Carson and the Peterson Air Force Base were established, followed by the North American Aerospace Defense Command (NORAD) and the U.S. Air Force Academy in the 1950s. Today NORAD is primarily concerned with the tracking of ICBMs, and celebrated its 51st anniversary in 2009. The city's military connection has contributed in large part to the economic base of the area, and to the presence of a highly educated and technically skilled workforce. In late 2008, Fort Carson became the home station of the 4th Infantry Division, nearly doubling the population of the base.

Colorado Springs is the site of the headquarters of the United States Olympics Committee, which maintains an important Olympic training center there. It is also home to the World Figure Skating Museum and Hall of Fame and the Pro Rodeo Hall of Fame and Museum of the American Cowboy.

The city hosts several institutions of higher learning, including Colorado College (1874), the U.S. Air Force Academy (1954), a campus of the University of Colorado (1965), and Nazarene Bible College (1967). Cultural amenities include the Fine Arts Center and Theatreworks at the University of Colorado.

The region enjoys four seasons, with plenty of sunshine—300 days each year. Rainfall is relatively minimal, but snow can pile up.

Rankings

General Rankings

- Colorado Springs was selected as one of America's best cities by *Bloomberg Businessweek*. The city ranked #36 out of 50. Criteria: leisure attributes (the number of restaurants, bars, libraries, museums, professional sports teams, and park acres by population); educational attributes (public school performance, the number of colleges, and graduate degree holders); economic factors (2011 income and June and July 2012 unemployment); crime; and air quality. *Bloomberg BusinessWeek, "America's Best Cities," September 26, 2012*

Business/Finance Rankings

- The Brookings Institution ranked the 50 largest cities in the U.S. based on income inequality. Colorado Springs was ranked #49. (#1 = greatest ineqality). Criteria: the cities were ranked based on the "95/20 ratio," a figure representing the income at which a household earns more than 95 percent of all other households, divided by the income at which a household earns more than only 20 percent of all other households. *Brookings Institution, "Income Inequality in America's 50 Largest Cities, 2007-2013," March 17, 2015*

- Colorado Springs was ranked #63 out of 100 metro areas in terms of economic performance (#1 = best) during the recession and recovery from trough quarter through the second quarter of 2013. Criteria: percent change in employment; percentage point change in unemployment rate; percent change in gross metropolitan product; percent change in House Price Index. *Brookings Institution, MetroMonitor: Tracking Economic Recession and Recovery in America's 100 Largest Metropolitan Areas, September 2013*

- The finance site *24/7 Wall St.* identified the metropolitan areas that have the smallest and largest pay disparities between men and women, comparing the median earnings for the past 12 months of both men and women working full-time in the country's 100 largest metropolitan statistical areas. Of the ten worst-paying metros for women, the Colorado Springs metro area ranked #9. *24/7 Wall St., "The Best (and Worst) Paying Cities for Women," March 6, 2015*

- The Colorado Springs metro area was identified as one of the most affordable metropolitan areas in America by *Forbes*. The area ranked #11 out of 20. Criteria: the 100 largest metro areas in the U.S. were analyzed based on the National Association of Home Builders/Wells Fargo Housing Affordability Index and Sperling's Best Places' cost-of-living index. Some major cities were omitted for lack of data. *Forbes.com, "America's Most Affordable Cities in 2015," March 12, 2015*

- The Colorado Springs metro area appeared on the Milken Institute "2013 Best Performing Cities" list. Rank: #90 out of 200 large metro areas. Criteria: job growth; wage and salary growth; high-tech output growth. *Milken Institute, "Best-Performing Cities 2014," January 2015*

- *Forbes* ranked the 200 most populous metro areas to determine the nation's "Best Places for Business and Careers." The Colorado Springs metro area was ranked #29. Criteria: costs (business and living); job growth (past and projected); income growth; educational attainment (college and high school); projected economic growth; cultural and recreational opportunities; net migration patterns; number of highly ranked colleges. *Forbes, "The Best Places for Business and Careers 2014," July 23, 2014*

Children/Family Rankings

- Colorado Springs was selected as one of the best cities for families to live by *Parenting* magazine. The city ranked #2 out of 100. Criteria: education ratings; FBI crime statistics, Bureau of Labor statistics, U.S. Census data. *Parenting.com, " Top Ten Best Cities for Families 2014"*

Culture/Performing Arts Rankings

- Colorado Springs was selected as one of America's top cities for the arts. The city ranked #22 in the mid-sized city (population 100,000 to 499,999) category. Criteria: readers' top choices for arts travel destinations based on the richness and variety of visual arts sites, activities and events. *American Style, "2012 Top 25 Arts Destinations," June 2012*

Dating/Romance Rankings

- Of the 100 U.S. cities surveyed by *Men's Health* in its quest to identify the nation's best cities for dating and forming relationships, Colorado Springs was ranked #27 for online dating (#1 = best). *Men's Health, "The Best and Worst Cities for Online Dating," January 30, 2013*

Education Rankings

- Colorado Springs was identified as one of America's "smartest" metropolitan areas by *The Business Journals*. The area ranked #10 out of 10. Criteria: percentage of adults (25 and older) with high school diplomas, bachelor's degrees and graduate degrees. *The Business Journals, "Where the Brainpower Is: Exclusive U.S. Rankings, Insights," February 27, 2014*

- Personal finance website *WalletHub* analyzed the 150 largest U.S. metropolitan statistical areas to determine where the most educated Americans are choosing to settle. Criteria: educational attainment; percentage of workers with jobs in computer, engineering, and science fields; quality and size of each metro area's universities. Colorado Springs was ranked #8 (#1 = most educated city). *www.WalletHub.com, "2014's Most and Least Educated Cities*

- Colorado Springs was selected as one of America's most literate cities. The city ranked #32 out of the 77 largest U.S. cities. Criteria: number of booksellers; library resources; Internet resources; educational attainment; periodical publishing resources; newspaper circulation. *Central Connecticut State University, "America's Most Literate Cities, 2014," April 8, 2015*

Environmental Rankings

- The Colorado Springs metro area came in at #7 for the relative comfort of its climate on Sperling's list of "chill cities," as measured by the Sperling Heat Index. All 361 metro areas are included. Criteria included daytime high temperatures, nighttime low temperatures, dew point, and relative humidity at the high temperatures. *www.bertsperling.com, "Sperling's Chill Cities," July 18, 2013*

- Sperling's BestPlaces assessed 379 metropolitan areas of the United States for the likelihood of dangerously extreme weather events or earthquakes. In general the Southeast and South-Central regions have the highest risk of weather extremes and earthquakes, while the Pacific Northwest enjoys the lowest risk. Of the least risky metropolitan areas, the Colorado Springs metro area was ranked #109. *www.bestplaces.net, "Safest Places from Natural Disasters," April 2011*

- *The Daily Beast* identifed the snowiest among the 100 largest U.S. cities, looking at average snowfall per month from December 2011 through March 2012 and from December 1, 2012 to December 21, 2012. Number of days with maximum and minimum temperatures of 32 degrees or less contributed to the rankings. Colorado Springs ranked #18. *The Daily Beast, "25 Snowiest Cities in America," December 21, 2012*

- The Colorado Springs metro area was identified as one of nine cities running out of water by *24/7 Wall St.* The area ranked #4. Based on data provided by the U.S. Drought Monitor, a joint program produced by academic and government organizations, *24/7 Wall St.* identified large U.S. urban areas that have been under persistent, serious drought for months. *24/7 Wall St., "Nine Cities Running Out of Water," August 1, 2013*

- Colorado Springs was highlighted as one of the top 25 cleanest metro areas for short-term particle pollution (24-hour PM 2.5) in the U.S. during 2011 through 2013. Monitors in these cities reported no days with unhealthful PM 2.5 levels. *American Lung Association, State of the Air 2015*

Food/Drink Rankings

- *Men's Health* ranked 100 major U.S. cities in terms of alcohol intoxication. Colorado Springs ranked #76 (#1 = most sober).Criteria: binge drinking; alcohol-related traffic accidents, arrests, and fatalities. *Men's Health, "The Drunkest Cities in America," November 19, 2013*

Health/Fitness Rankings

- The Colorado Springs metro area was identified as one of the worst cities for bed bugs in America by pest control company Orkin. The area ranked #42 out of 50 based on the number of bed bug treatments Orkin performed from January to December 2013. *Orkin, "Chicago Tops Bed Bug Cities List for Second Year in a Row," January 16, 2014*

- Colorado Springs was selected as one of the 25 fittest cities in America by *Men's Fitness Online*. It ranked #13 out of America's 50 largest cities. Criteria: fitness centers and sport stores; nutrition; sports participation; TV viewing; overweight/sedentary; junk food; air quality; geography; commute; parks and open space; city recreational facilities; access to healthcare; motivation; mayor and city initiatives; state obesity initiatives. *Men's Fitness, "The Fittest and Fattest Cities in America," March 5, 2012*

- Colorado Springs was identified as a "2013 Spring Allergy Capital." The area ranked #89 out of 100. Three groups of factors were used to identify the most severe cities for people with allergies during the spring season: annual pollen levels; medicine utilization; access to board-certified allergists. *Asthma and Allergy Foundation of America, "Spring Allergy Capitals 2013"*

- Colorado Springs was identified as a "2013 Fall Allergy Capital." The area ranked #97 out of 100. Three groups of factors were used to identify the most severe cities for people with allergies during the fall season: annual pollen levels; medicine utilization; access to board-certified allergists. *Asthma and Allergy Foundation of America, "Fall Allergy Capitals 2013"*

- Colorado Springs was identified as a "2013 Asthma Capital." The area ranked #85 out of the nation's 100 largest metropolitan areas. Twelve factors were used to identify the most challenging places to live for people with asthma: estimated prevalence; self-reported prevalence; crude death rate for asthma; annual pollen score; annual air quality; public smoking laws; number of board-certified asthma specialists; school inhaler access laws; rescue medication use; controller medication use; uninsured rate; poverty rate. *Asthma and Allergy Foundation of America, "Asthma Capitals 2013"*

- *Men's Health* ranked 100 major U.S. cities in terms of the best and worst cities for men. Colorado Springs ranked #23. Criteria: thirty-three data points were examined covering health, fitness, and quality of life. *Men's Health, "The Best & Worst Cities for Men 2014," December 6, 2013*

- Colorado Springs was selected as one of the best metropolitan areas for hospital care in America by *HealthGrades.com*. The rankings are based on a comprehensive study of patient death and complication rates in the nation's nearly 5,000 hospitals. Hospitals performing in the top 5% nationwide across 26 different medical procedures and diagnoses were identified. *HealthGrades.com* then ranked cities by the highest percentage of these Distinguished Hospitals for Clinical Excellence™. The Colorado Springs metro area ranked #28. *HealthGrades.com, "America's Top 50 Cities for Hospital Care," January 21, 2012*

- The Colorado Springs metro area appeared in the 2013 Gallup-Healthways Well-Being Index. The area ranked #58 out of 189. The Gallup-Healthways Well-Being Index score is an average of six sub-indexes, which individually examine life evaluation, emotional health, work environment, physical health, healthy behaviors, and access to basic necessities. Results are based on telephone interviews conducted as part of the Gallup-Healthways Well-Being Index survey January 2–December 29, 2012, and January 2–December 30, 2013, with a random sample of 531,630 adults, aged 18 and older, living in metropolitan areas in the 50 U.S. states and the District of Columbia. *Gallup-Healthways, "State of American Well-Being," March 25, 2014*

Pet Rankings

- Colorado Springs was selected as one of the best cities for dogs by real estate website Estately.com. The city was ranked #11. Criteria: weather; walkability; yard sizes; dog activities; meetup groups; availability of dogsitters. *Estately.com, "17 Best U.S. Cities for Dogs," May 14, 2013*

Real Estate Rankings

- Colorado Springs was ranked #147 out of 275 metro areas in terms of house price appreciation in 2014 (#1 = highest rate). *Federal Housing Finance Agency, House Price Index, 4th Quarter 2014*

- Colorado Springs was ranked #83 out of 226 metro areas in terms of housing affordability in 2014 by the National Association of Home Builders (#1 = most affordable). The NAHB-Wells Fargo Housing Opportunity Index (HOI) for a given area is defined as the share of homes sold in that area that would have been affordable to a family earning the local median income, based on standard mortgage underwriting criteria. *National Association of Home Builders®, NAHB-Wells Fargo Housing Opportunity Index, 4th Quarter 2014*

Safety Rankings

- Symantec, in partnership with Sperling's BestPlaces, ranked the 50 largest cities in the U.S. in terms of their vulnerability to cybercrime. The city ranked #20. Criteria: number of cyberattacks and potential infections; level of Internet access; expenditures on smartphones and computer hardware/software; wireless hotspots; broadband connectivity; Internet usage; online purchases. *Symantec, "Riskiest Online Cities of 2012" February 15, 2012*

- Allstate ranked the 200 largest cities in America in terms of driver safety. Colorado Springs ranked #14. Allstate researchers analyzed internal property damage claims over a two-year period from January 2011 to December 2012. A weighted average of the two-year numbers determined the annual percentages. *Allstate, "Allstate America's Best Drivers Report, 2014"*

- The National Insurance Crime Bureau ranked 380 metro areas in the U.S. in terms of per capita rates of vehicle theft. The Colorado Springs metro area ranked #60 (#1 = highest rate). Criteria: number of vehicle theft offenses per 100,000 inhabitants in 2012. *National Insurance Crime Bureau, "Hot Spots 2012," June 26, 2013*

Seniors/Retirement Rankings

- From its Best Cities for Successful Aging indexes, the Milken Institute generated rankings for metropolitan areas, weighing data in eight categories—health care, wellness, living arrangements, transportation, financial characteristics, education and employment opportunities, community engagement, and overall livability. The Colorado Springs metro area was ranked #49 overall in the large metro area category. *Milken Institute, "Best Cities for Successful Aging, 2014"*

- Colorado Springs was identified as one of the most popular places to retire by *Topretirements.com*. The list reflects the 100 cities (out of 900+ total cities reviewed) that visitors to the website are most interested in for retirement. *Topretirements.com, "Most Popular Places to Retire for 2014," February 25, 2014*

Sports/Recreation Rankings

- Colorado Springs was chosen as a bicycle friendly community by the League of American Bicyclists. A "Bicycle Friendly Community" welcomes cyclists by providing safe accommodation for cycling and encouraging people to bike for transportation and recreation. There are four award levels: Platinum; Gold; Silver; and Bronze. The community achieved an award level of Silver. *League of American Bicyclists, "Bicycle Friendly Community Master List," Fall 2013*

- Colorado Springs was chosen as one of America's best cities for bicycling. The city ranked #31 out of 50. Criteria: robust cycling infrastructure; vibrant bike culture. The editors only considered cities with populations of 95,000 or more. *Bicycling, "America's Top 50 Bike-Friendly Cities," May 23, 2012*

Transportation Rankings

- Colorado Springs appeared on *Trapster.com's* list of the 10 most-active U.S. cities for speed traps. The city ranked #9 of 10. *Trapster.com* is a community platform accessed online and via smartphone app that alerts drivers to traps, hazards and other traffic issues nearby. *Trapster.com, "Speeders Beware: Cities With the Most Speed Traps," February 10, 2012*

Women/Minorities Rankings

- *24/7 Wall St.* compared median earnings over a 12-month period for men and women who worked full-time, year-round, and employment composition by sector to identify the worst-paying cities for women. Of the largest 100 U.S. metropolitan areas, Colorado Springs was ranked #6 in pay disparity. *24/7 Wall St., "The Worst-Paying Cities for Women," March 8, 2013*

- *Women's Health* examined U.S. cities and identified the 100 best cities for women. Colorado Springs was ranked #29. Criteria: 30 categories were examined from obesity and breast cancer rates to commuting times and hours spent working out. *Women's Health, "Best Cities for Women 2012"*

Miscellaneous Rankings

- The watchdog site Charity Navigator conducts an annual study of charities in the nation's major markets both to analyze statistical differences in their financial, accountability, and transparency practices and to track year-to-year variations in individual communities. The Colorado Springs metro area was ranked #21 among the 30 metro markets. *www.charitynavigator.org, "Metro Market Study 2013," June 1, 2013*

- According to the World Giving Index, the United States is the fifth most generous nation in the world. The finance and lifestyle site NerdWallet looked for the U.S. cities that topped the list in donating money and time to good causes. The Colorado Springs metro area proved to be the #12-ranked metro area, judged by culture of volunteerism, depth of commitment in terms of volunteer hours per year, and monetary contributions. *www.nerdwallet.com, "Most Generous Cities," September 22, 2013*

- The National Alliance to End Homelessness ranked the 100 most populous metro areas in terms the rate of homelessness. The Colorado Springs metro area ranked #45. Criteria: number of homeless people per 10,000 population in 2011. *National Alliance to End Homelessness, The State of Homelessness in America 2012*

Business Environment

CITY FINANCES

City Government Finances

Component	2012 ($000)	2012 ($ per capita)
Total Revenues	1,776,361	4,266
Total Expenditures	1,661,146	3,989
Debt Outstanding	2,643,758	6,349
Cash and Securities[1]	550,132	1,321

Note: (1) Cash and security holdings of a government at the close of its fiscal year, including those of its dependent agencies, utilities, and liquor stores.
Source: U.S Census Bureau, State & Local Government Finances 2012

City Government Revenue by Source

Source	2012 ($000)	2012 ($ per capita)
General Revenue		
From Federal Government	38,905	93
From State Government	20,739	50
From Local Governments	6,050	15
Taxes		
Property	22,617	54
Sales and Gross Receipts	190,932	459
Personal Income	0	0
Corporate Income	0	0
Motor Vehicle License	0	0
Other Taxes	871	2
Current Charges	669,206	1,607
Liquor Store	0	0
Utility	756,287	1,816
Employee Retirement	0	0

Source: U.S Census Bureau, State & Local Government Finances 2012

City Government Expenditures by Function

Function	2012 ($000)	2012 ($ per capita)	2012 (%)
General Direct Expenditures			
Air Transportation	32,718	79	2.0
Corrections	0	0	0.0
Education	0	0	0.0
Employment Security Administration	0	0	0.0
Financial Administration	38,620	93	2.3
Fire Protection	40,725	98	2.5
General Public Buildings	0	0	0.0
Governmental Administration, Other	3,277	8	0.2
Health	1,210	3	0.1
Highways	84,597	203	5.1
Hospitals	515,359	1,238	31.0
Housing and Community Development	4,878	12	0.3
Interest on General Debt	26,641	64	1.6
Judicial and Legal	5,881	14	0.4
Libraries	0	0	0.0
Parking	2,367	6	0.1
Parks and Recreation	20,900	50	1.3
Police Protection	88,661	213	5.3
Public Welfare	0	0	0.0
Sewerage	37,923	91	2.3
Solid Waste Management	0	0	0.0
Veterans' Services	0	0	0.0
Liquor Store	0	0	0.0
Utility	692,752	1,664	41.7
Employee Retirement	0	0	0.0

Source: U.S Census Bureau, State & Local Government Finances 2012

DEMOGRAPHICS

Population Growth

Area	1990 Census	2000 Census	2010 Census	Population Growth (%)	
				1990-2000	2000-2010
City	283,798	360,890	416,427	27.2	15.4
MSA[1]	409,482	537,484	645,613	31.3	20.1
U.S.	248,709,873	281,421,906	308,745,538	13.2	9.7

Note: (1) Figures cover the Colorado Springs, CO Metropolitan Statistical Area—see Appendix B for areas included
Source: U.S. Census Bureau, Census 1990, 2000, 2010

Household Size

Area	Persons in Household (%)							Average Household Size
	One	Two	Three	Four	Five	Six	Seven or More	
City	29.1	34.1	15.0	13.3	5.4	2.1	1.1	2.53
MSA[1]	25.7	35.0	15.6	14.2	6.0	2.3	1.2	2.63
U.S.	27.7	33.6	15.7	13.1	6.0	2.3	1.5	2.64

Note: (1) Figures cover the Colorado Springs, CO Metropolitan Statistical Area—see Appendix B for areas included
Source: U.S. Census Bureau, 2011-2013 American Community Survey 3-Year Estimates

Race

Area	White Alone[2] (%)	Black Alone[2] (%)	Asian Alone[2] (%)	AIAN[3] Alone[2] (%)	NHOPI[4] Alone[2] (%)	Other Race Alone[2] (%)	Two or More Races (%)
City	80.2	6.2	2.9	0.6	0.3	5.0	4.8
MSA[1]	81.6	5.8	2.7	0.6	0.3	3.8	5.1
U.S.	73.9	12.6	5.0	0.8	0.2	4.7	2.9

Note: (1) Figures cover the Colorado Springs, CO Metropolitan Statistical Area—see Appendix B for areas included; (2) Alone is defined as not being in combination with one or more other races; (3) American Indian and Alaska Native; (4) Native Hawaiian and Other Pacific Islander
Source: U.S. Census Bureau, 2011-2013 American Community Survey 3-Year Estimates

Hispanic or Latino Origin

Area	Total (%)	Mexican (%)	Puerto Rican (%)	Cuban (%)	Other (%)
City	17.1	11.2	0.9	0.2	4.7
MSA[1]	15.3	9.5	1.1	0.2	4.5
U.S.	16.9	10.8	1.6	0.6	3.8

Note: Persons of Hispanic or Latino origin can be of any race; (1) Figures cover the Colorado Springs, CO Metropolitan Statistical Area—see Appendix B for areas included
Source: U.S. Census Bureau, 2011-2013 American Community Survey 3-Year Estimates

Segregation

Type	Segregation Indices[1]				Percent Change		
	1990	2000	2010	2010 Rank[2]	1990-2000	1990-2010	2000-2010
Black/White	44.6	43.3	39.3	92	-1.3	-5.3	-4.0
Asian/White	28.5	25.2	24.1	98	-3.2	-4.3	-1.1
Hispanic/White	27.8	31.5	30.3	95	3.7	2.5	-1.3

Note: All figures cover the Metropolitan Statistical Area—see Appendix B for areas included; Figures are based on an analysis of 1990, 2000, and 2010 Census Decennial Census tract data by William H. Frey, Brookings Institution and the University of Michigan Social Science Data Analysis Network. In this analysis all racial groups (whites, blacks, and asians) are non-Hispanic members of those races. Hispanics are shown as a separate category;
(1) Segregation Indices are Dissimilarity Indices that measure the degree to which the minority group is distributed differently than whites across census tracts. They range from 0 (complete integration) to 100 (complete segregation) where the value indicates the percentage of the minority group that needs to move to be distributed exactly like whites; (2) Ranges from 1 (most segregated) to 102 (least segregated); n/a not available.
Source: www.CensusScope.org

Ancestry

Area	German	Irish	English	American	Italian	Polish	French[2]	Scottish	Dutch
City	22.4	13.0	10.2	5.8	5.8	2.4	3.0	2.9	2.1
MSA[1]	22.2	13.2	10.1	6.3	5.4	2.6	3.2	2.9	2.1
U.S.	14.9	10.8	8.0	7.4	5.5	3.0	2.7	1.7	1.4

Note: Figures are the percentage of the total population reporting a particular ancestry. The nine most commonly reported ancestries in the U.S. are shown. Figures include multiple ancestries (e.g. if a person reported being Irish and Italian, they were included in both columns); (1) Figures cover the Colorado Springs, CO Metropolitan Statistical Area—see Appendix B for areas included; (2) Excludes Basque
Source: U.S. Census Bureau, 2011-2013 American Community Survey 3-Year Estimates

Foreign-Born Population

Area	Any Foreign Country	Mexico	Asia	Europe	Carribean	South America	Central America[2]	Africa	Canada
City	8.2	2.5	2.1	1.7	0.3	0.4	0.5	0.4	0.3
MSA[1]	7.1	1.8	2.0	1.7	0.3	0.3	0.4	0.3	0.3
U.S.	13.0	3.7	3.8	1.5	1.2	0.9	1.0	0.6	0.3

Note: (1) Figures cover the Colorado Springs, CO Metropolitan Statistical Area—see Appendix B for areas included; (2) Excludes Mexico.
Source: U.S. Census Bureau, 2011-2013 American Community Survey 3-Year Estimates

Marital Status

Area	Never Married	Now Married[2]	Separated	Widowed	Divorced
City	29.3	51.0	2.0	4.6	12.9
MSA[1]	28.1	53.9	1.8	4.3	11.9
U.S.	32.7	48.1	2.2	6.0	11.0

Note: Figures are percentages and cover the population 15 years of age and older; (1) Figures cover the Colorado Springs, CO Metropolitan Statistical Area—see Appendix B for areas included; (2) Excludes separated
Source: U.S. Census Bureau, 2011-2013 American Community Survey 3-Year Estimates

Disability Status

Area	All Ages	Under 18 Years Old	18 to 64 Years Old	65 Years and Over
City	12.0	4.2	10.8	36.2
MSA[1]	11.6	4.3	10.7	34.1
U.S.	12.3	4.1	10.2	36.3

Note: Figures show percent of the civilian noninstitutionalized population that reported having a disability. Disability status is determined from from six types of difficulty: vision, hearing, cognitive, ambulatory, self-care, and independent living. For children under 5 years old, hearing and vision difficulty are used to determine disability status. For children between the ages of 5 and 14, disability status is determined from hearing, vision, cognitive, ambulatory, and self-care difficulties. For people aged 15 years and older, they are considered to have a disability if they have difficulty with any one of the six difficulty types; (1) Figures cover the Colorado Springs, CO Metropolitan Statistical Area—see Appendix B for areas included.
Source: U.S. Census Bureau, 2011-2013 American Community Survey 3-Year Estimates

Age

Area	Under Age 5	Age 5–19	Age 20–34	Age 35–44	Age 45–54	Age 55–64	Age 65–74	Age 75–84	Age 85+	Median Age
City	7.1	20.3	23.6	12.4	13.8	11.4	6.4	3.6	1.4	34.0
MSA[1]	7.0	21.4	22.7	12.6	14.0	11.6	6.4	3.3	1.1	34.1
U.S.	6.4	19.9	20.7	12.9	14.1	12.3	7.6	4.2	1.9	37.4

Note: (1) Figures cover the Colorado Springs, CO Metropolitan Statistical Area—see Appendix B for areas included
Source: U.S. Census Bureau, 2011-2013 American Community Survey 3-Year Estimates

Gender

Area	Males	Females	Males per 100 Females
City	215,263	218,356	98.6
MSA[1]	335,926	333,190	100.8
U.S.	154,451,010	159,410,713	96.9

Note: (1) Figures cover the Colorado Springs, CO Metropolitan Statistical Area—see Appendix B for areas included
Source: U.S. Census Bureau, 2011-2013 American Community Survey 3-Year Estimates

Religious Groups by Family

Area	Catholic	Baptist	Non-Den.	Methodist[2]	Lutheran	LDS[3]	Pente-costal	Presby-terian[4]	Muslim[5]	Judaism
MSA[1]	8.4	4.3	7.4	2.4	2.0	3.0	1.1	2.1	0.1	0.1
U.S.	19.1	9.3	4.0	4.0	2.3	2.0	1.9	1.6	0.8	0.7

Note: Figures are the number of adherents as a percentage of the total population; (1) Figures cover the Colorado Springs, CO Metropolitan Statistical Area—see Appendix B for areas included; (2) Methodist/Pietist; (3) Latter Day Saints; (4) Reformed; (5) Figures are estimates
Source: Association of Statisticians of American Religious Bodies, 2010 U.S. Religion Census: Religious Congregations & Membership Study

Religious Groups by Tradition

Area	Catholic	Evangelical Protestant	Mainline Protestant	Other Tradition	Black Protestant	Orthodox
MSA[1]	8.4	15.2	5.4	3.7	0.4	0.1
U.S.	19.1	16.2	7.3	4.3	1.6	0.3

Note: Figures are the number of adherents as a percentage of the total population; (1) Figures cover the Colorado Springs, CO Metropolitan Statistical Area—see Appendix B for areas included
Source: Association of Statisticians of American Religious Bodies, 2010 U.S. Religion Census: Religious Congregations & Membership Study

ECONOMY

Gross Metropolitan Product

Area	2012	2013	2014	2015	Rank[2]
MSA[1]	28.0	28.6	29.6	31.2	84

Note: Figures are in billions of dollars; (1) Figures cover the Colorado Springs, CO Metropolitan Statistical Area—see Appendix B for areas included; (2) Rank is based on 2015 data and ranges from 1 to 363
Source: The U.S. Conference of Mayors, U.S. Metro Economies: GMP and Employment 2013-2015, June 2014

Economic Growth

Area	2010-12 (%)	2013 (%)	2014 (%)	2015 (%)	Rank[2]
MSA[1]	2.1	0.7	1.8	3.1	134
U.S.	2.1	2.0	2.3	3.2	–

Note: Figures are real gross metropolitan product (GMP) growth rates and represent annual average percent change; (1) Figures cover the Colorado Springs, CO Metropolitan Statistical Area—see Appendix B for areas included; (2) Rank is based on 2015 data and ranges from 1 to 363
Source: The U.S. Conference of Mayors, U.S. Metro Economies: GMP and Employment 2013-2015, June 2014

Metropolitan Area Exports

Area	2008	2009	2010	2011	2012	2013	Rank[2]
MSA[1]	1,932.4	1,281.1	1,193.1	1,118.7	1,044.6	1,065.4	149

Note: Figures are in millions of dollars; (1) Figures cover the Colorado Springs, CO Metropolitan Statistical Area—see Appendix B for areas included; (2) Rank is based on 2013 data and ranges from 1 to 387
Source: U.S. Department of Commerce, International Trade Administration, Office of Trade & Industry Information, Manufacturing & Services, data extracted April 3, 2015

Building Permits

Area	Single-Family			Multi-Family			Total		
	2013	2014	Pct. Chg.	2013	2014	Pct. Chg.	2013	2014	Pct. Chg.
City	n/a	n/a	n/a	n/a	n/a	n/a	n/a	n/a	n/a
MSA[1]	2,885	2,662	-7.7	702	1,011	44.0	3,587	3,673	2.4
U.S.	620,802	634,597	2.2	370,020	411,766	11.3	990,822	1,046,363	5.6

Note: (1) Figures cover the Colorado Springs, CO Metropolitan Statistical Area—see Appendix B for areas included; Figures represent new, privately-owned housing units authorized (unadjusted data); All permit data are based on estimates with imputation.
Source: U.S. Census Bureau, Manufacturing, Mining, and Construction Statistics, Building Permits, 2013, 2014

Bankruptcy Filings

Area	Business Filings			Nonbusiness Filings		
	2013	2014	% Chg.	2013	2014	% Chg.
El Paso County	51	40	-21.6	2,641	2,126	-19.5
U.S.	33,212	26,983	-18.8	1,038,720	909,812	-12.4

Note: Business filings include Chapter 7, Chapter 11, Chapter 12, and Chapter 13; Nonbusiness filings include Chapter 7, Chapter 11, and Chapter 13
Source: Administrative Office of the U.S. Courts, Business and Nonbusiness Bankruptcy, County Cases Commenced by Chapter of the Bankruptcy Code, During the 12- Month Period Ending December 31, 2013 and Business and Nonbusiness Bankruptcy, County Cases Commenced by Chapter of the Bankruptcy Code, During the 12- Month Period Ending December 31, 2014

Housing Vacancy Rates

Area	Gross Vacancy Rate[2] (%)			Year-Round Vacancy Rate[3] (%)			Rental Vacancy Rate[4] (%)			Homeowner Vacancy Rate[5] (%)		
	2012	2013	2014	2012	2013	2014	2012	2013	2014	2012	2013	2014
MSA[1]	n/a	n/a	n/a	n/a	n/a	n/a	n/a	n/a	n/a	n/a	n/a	n/a
U.S.	13.8	13.6	13.4	10.8	10.7	10.4	8.7	8.3	7.6	2.0	2.0	1.9

Note: (1) Figures cover the Colorado Springs, CO Metropolitan Statistical Area—see Appendix B for areas included; (2) The percentage of the total housing inventory that is vacant; (3) The percentage of the housing inventory (excluding seasonal units) that is year-round vacant; (4) The percentage of rental inventory that is vacant for rent; (5) The percentage of homeowner inventory that is vacant for sale; n/a not available
Source: U.S. Census Bureau, Housing Vacancies and Homeownership Annual Statistics: 2014

INCOME

Income

Area	Per Capita ($)	Median Household ($)	Average Household ($)
City	28,854	53,619	72,046
MSA[1]	29,097	57,110	75,630
U.S.	27,884	52,176	72,897

Note: (1) Figures cover the Colorado Springs, CO Metropolitan Statistical Area—see Appendix B for areas included
Source: U.S. Census Bureau, 2011-2013 American Community Survey 3-Year Estimates

Household Income Distribution

Area	Percent of Households Earning							
	Under $15,000	$15,000 -24,999	$25,000 -34,999	$35,000 -49,999	$50,000 -74,999	$75,000 -99,000	$100,000 -149,999	$150,000 and up
City	10.6	11.1	10.5	14.2	18.7	12.8	13.5	8.8
MSA[1]	9.4	10.0	9.8	14.1	19.3	13.4	14.5	9.7
U.S.	13.0	10.9	10.3	13.6	17.9	11.9	12.7	9.6

Note: (1) Figures cover the Colorado Springs, CO Metropolitan Statistical Area—see Appendix B for areas included
Source: U.S. Census Bureau, 2011-2013 American Community Survey 3-Year Estimates

Poverty Rate

Area	All Ages	Under 18 Years Old	18 to 64 Years Old	65 Years and Over
City	14.1	19.1	13.3	8.2
MSA[1]	12.1	16.1	11.4	7.3
U.S.	15.9	22.4	14.8	9.5

Note: Figures are percentage of people whose income during the past 12 months was below the poverty level;
(1) Figures cover the Colorado Springs, CO Metropolitan Statistical Area—see Appendix B for areas included
Source: U.S. Census Bureau, 2011-2013 American Community Survey 3-Year Estimates

EMPLOYMENT

Labor Force and Employment

Area	Civilian Labor Force			Workers Employed		
	Dec. 2013	Dec. 2014	% Chg.	Dec. 2013	Dec. 2014	% Chg.
City	215,051	214,044	-0.5	200,273	203,493	1.6
MSA[1]	317,531	315,991	-0.5	295,202	299,942	1.6
U.S.	154,408,000	155,521,000	0.7	144,423,000	147,190,000	1.9

Note: Data is not seasonally adjusted and covers workers 16 years of age and older; (1) Figures cover the
Colorado Springs, CO Metropolitan Statistical Area—see Appendix B for areas included
Source: Bureau of Labor Statistics, Local Area Unemployment Statistics

Unemployment Rate

Area	2014											
	Jan.	Feb.	Mar.	Apr.	May	Jun.	Jul.	Aug.	Sep.	Oct.	Nov.	Dec.
City	7.4	7.2	7.2	6.5	5.8	6.1	5.9	5.5	5.0	4.7	4.9	4.9
MSA[1]	7.6	7.4	7.3	6.5	5.9	6.2	6.0	5.5	5.0	4.8	5.0	5.1
U.S.	7.0	7.0	6.8	5.9	6.1	6.3	6.5	6.3	5.7	5.5	5.5	5.4

Note: Data is not seasonally adjusted and covers workers 16 years of age and older; (1) Figures cover the
Colorado Springs, CO Metropolitan Statistical Area—see Appendix B for areas included
Source: Bureau of Labor Statistics, Local Area Unemployment Statistics

Employment by Occupation

Occupation Classification	City (%)	MSA[1] (%)	U.S. (%)
Management, Business, Science, and Arts	40.5	40.6	36.2
Natural Resources, Construction, and Maintenance	7.7	8.4	9.0
Production, Transportation, and Material Moving	8.1	8.1	12.1
Sales and Office	24.6	24.0	24.4
Service	19.1	18.8	18.3

Note: Figures cover employed civilians 16 years of age and older; (1) Figures cover the Colorado Springs, CO
Metropolitan Statistical Area—see Appendix B for areas included
Source: U.S. Census Bureau, 2011-2013 American Community Survey 3-Year Estimates

Employment by Industry

Sector	MSA[1] Number of Employees	MSA[1] Percent of Total	U.S. Percent of Total
Construction, Mining, and Logging	14,100	5.3	5.0
Education and Health Services	34,700	13.1	15.5
Financial Activities	16,100	6.1	5.7
Government	49,400	18.6	15.8
Information	6,800	2.6	2.0
Leisure and Hospitality	32,400	12.2	10.3
Manufacturing	11,900	4.5	8.7
Other Services	15,600	5.9	4.0
Professional and Business Services	42,000	15.8	13.8
Retail Trade	32,100	12.1	11.4
Transportation, Warehousing, and Utilities	4,700	1.8	3.9
Wholesale Trade	5,200	2.0	4.2

Note: Figures are non-farm employment as of December 2014. Figures are not seasonally adjusted and include
workers 16 years of age and older; (1) Figures cover the Colorado Springs, CO Metropolitan Statistical
Area—see Appendix B for areas included; n/a not available
Source: Bureau of Labor Statistics, Current Employment Statistics, Employment, Hours, and Earnings

Occupations with Greatest Projected Employment Growth: 2012 – 2022

Occupation[1]	2012 Employment	2022 Projected Employment	Numeric Employment Change	Percent Employment Change
Combined Food Preparation and Serving Workers, Including Fast Food	60,670	77,380	16,710	27.5
Secretaries and Administrative Assistants, Except Legal, Medical, and Executive	63,150	77,880	14,730	23.3
Retail Salespersons	79,300	94,000	14,700	18.5
Customer Service Representatives	45,990	59,210	13,220	28.8
Registered Nurses	42,200	53,270	11,070	26.2
General and Operations Managers	42,170	52,340	10,170	24.1
Accountants and Auditors	33,870	43,490	9,620	28.4
Personal Care Aides	16,940	26,210	9,270	54.7
Janitors and Cleaners, Except Maids and Housekeeping Cleaners	36,300	45,470	9,170	25.3
Business Operations Specialists, All Other	42,990	51,450	8,460	19.7

Note: Projections cover Colorado; (1) Sorted by numeric employment change
Source: www.projectionscentral.com, State Occupational Projections, 2012–2022 Long-Term Projections

Fastest Growing Occupations: 2012 – 2022

Occupation[1]	2012 Employment	2022 Projected Employment	Numeric Employment Change	Percent Employment Change
Service Unit Operators, Oil, Gas, and Mining	3,520	6,290	2,770	78.4
Derrick Operators, Oil and Gas	630	1,110	480	76.0
Rotary Drill Operators, Oil and Gas	1,280	2,200	920	71.5
Roustabouts, Oil and Gas	2,770	4,710	1,940	70.2
Interpreters and Translators	1,510	2,550	1,040	68.5
Petroleum Engineers	1,500	2,500	1,000	66.9
Pump Operators, Except Wellhead Pumpers	700	1,160	460	64.9
Helpers—Brickmasons, Blockmasons, Stonemasons, and Tile and Marble Setters	200	320	120	61.3
Insulation Workers, Mechanical	420	680	260	61.2
Information Security Analysts	1,240	1,960	720	57.8

Note: Projections cover Colorado; (1) Sorted by percent employment change and excludes occupations with numeric employment change less than 100
Source: www.projectionscentral.com, State Occupational Projections, 2012–2022 Long-Term Projections

Average Wages

Occupation	$/Hr.	Occupation	$/Hr.
Accountants and Auditors	31.59	Maids and Housekeeping Cleaners	9.60
Automotive Mechanics	20.26	Maintenance and Repair Workers	17.93
Bookkeepers	16.46	Marketing Managers	66.67
Carpenters	21.37	Nuclear Medicine Technologists	n/a
Cashiers	10.46	Nurses, Licensed Practical	21.39
Clerks, General Office	15.97	Nurses, Registered	31.03
Clerks, Receptionists/Information	13.32	Nursing Assistants	12.49
Clerks, Shipping/Receiving	14.48	Packers and Packagers, Hand	10.75
Computer Programmers	37.28	Physical Therapists	36.99
Computer Systems Analysts	46.56	Postal Service Mail Carriers	25.15
Computer User Support Specialists	23.66	Real Estate Brokers	n/a
Cooks, Restaurant	11.63	Retail Salespersons	13.47
Dentists	100.65	Sales Reps., Exc. Tech./Scientific	32.60
Electrical Engineers	50.76	Sales Reps., Tech./Scientific	36.45
Electricians	22.45	Secretaries, Exc. Legal/Med./Exec.	15.92
Financial Managers	66.96	Security Guards	13.45
First-Line Supervisors/Managers, Sales	23.33	Surgeons	113.24
Food Preparation Workers	10.18	Teacher Assistants	11.90
General and Operations Managers	54.42	Teachers, Elementary School	22.10
Hairdressers/Cosmetologists	12.65	Teachers, Secondary School	22.40
Internists	n/a	Telemarketers	11.94
Janitors and Cleaners	12.21	Truck Drivers, Heavy/Tractor-Trailer	18.92
Landscaping/Groundskeeping Workers	12.34	Truck Drivers, Light/Delivery Svcs.	14.73
Lawyers	53.13	Waiters and Waitresses	9.56

Note: Wage data covers the Colorado Springs, CO Metropolitan Statistical Area—see Appendix B for areas included; Hourly wages for elementary/secondary school teachers and teacher assistants were calculated by the editors from annual wage data assuming a 40 hour work week; n/a not available.
Source: Bureau of Labor Statistics, Metro Area Occupational Employment and Wage Estimates, May 2014

TAXES

State Corporate Income Tax Rates

State	Tax Rate (%)	Income Brackets ($)	Num. of Brackets	Financial Institution Tax Rate (%)[a]	Federal Income Tax Ded.
Colorado	4.63	Flat rate	1	4.63	No

Note: Tax rates as of January 1, 2015; (a) Rates listed are the corporate income tax rate applied to financial institutions or excise taxes based on income. Some states have other taxes based upon the value of deposits or shares.
Source: Federation of Tax Administrators, "State Corporate Income Tax Rates, 2015"

State Individual Income Tax Rates

State	Tax Rate (%)	Income Brackets ($)	Num. of Brackets	Personal Exempt. ($)[1] Single	Personal Exempt. ($)[1] Dependents	Fed. Inc. Tax Ded.
Colorado	4.63	Flat rate	1	4,000 (d)	4,000 (d)	No

Note: Tax rates as of January 1, 2015; Local- and county-level taxes are not included; n/a not applicable; (1) Married joint filers generally receive double the single exemption; (d) These states use the personal exemption amounts provided in the federal Internal Revenue Code.
Source: Federation of Tax Administrators, "State Individual Income Tax Rates, 2015"

Various State and Local Tax Rates

State	State and Local Sales and Use (%)	State Sales and Use (%)	Gasoline[1] (¢/gal.)	Cigarette[2] ($/pack)	Spirits[3] ($/gal.)	Wine[4] ($/gal.)	Beer[5] ($/gal.)
Colorado	7.63	2.90	22	0.84	2.28	0.32	0.08

Note: All tax rates as of January 1, 2015; (1) The American Petroleum Institute has developed a methodology for determining the average tax rate on a gallon of fuel. Rates may include any of the following: excise taxes, environmental fees, storage tank fees, other fees or taxes, general sales tax, and local taxes. In states where gasoline is subject to the general sales tax, or where the fuel tax is based on the average sale price, the average rate determined by API is sensitive to changes in the price of gasoline. States that fully or partially apply general sales taxes to gasoline: CA, CO, GA, IL, IN, MI, NY; (2) The federal excise tax of $1.0066 per pack and local taxes are not included; (3) Rates are those applicable to off-premise sales of 40% alcohol by volume (a.b.v.) distilled spirits in 750ml containers. Local excise taxes are excluded; (4) Rates are those applicable to off-premise sales of 11% a.b.v. non-carbonated wine in 750ml containers; (5) Rates are those applicable to off-premise sales of 4.7% a.b.v. beer in 12 ounce containers.
Source: Tax Foundation, 2015 Facts & Figures: How Does Your State Compare?

State Business Tax Climate Index Rankings

State	Overall Rank	Corporate Tax Index Rank	Individual Income Tax Index Rank	Sales Tax Index Rank	Unemployment Insurance Tax Index Rank	Property Tax Index Rank
Colorado	20	12	16	43	35	22

Note: The index is a measure of how each state's tax laws affect economic performance. The lower the rank, the more favorable a state's tax system is for business. States without a given tax are given a ranking of 1. The scores/rankings for the District of Columbia do not affect other states. The 2015 index represents the tax climate as of July 1, 2014.
Source: Tax Foundation, State Business Tax Climate Index 2015

COMMERCIAL UTILITIES

Typical Monthly Electric Bills

Area	Commercial Service ($/month)		Industrial Service ($/month)	
	1,500 kWh	40 kW demand 14,000 kWh	1,000 kW demand 200,000 kWh	50,000 kW demand 32,500,000 kWh
City	n/a	n/a	n/a	n/a
Average[1]	201	1,653	26,124	2,639,743

Note: Figures are based on annualized 2014 rates; (1) Average based on 180 utilities surveyed; n/a not available
Source: Edison Electric Institute, Typical Bills and Average Rates Report, Summer 2014

TRANSPORTATION

Means of Transportation to Work

Area	Car/Truck/Van Drove Alone	Car/Truck/Van Car-pooled	Public Transportation Bus	Public Transportation Subway	Public Transportation Railroad	Bicycle	Walked	Other Means	Worked at Home
City	79.5	10.3	0.9	0.0	0.0	0.6	2.1	1.3	5.3
MSA[1]	77.5	10.4	0.7	0.0	0.0	0.4	4.1	1.1	5.8
U.S.	76.4	9.6	2.6	1.8	0.6	0.6	2.8	1.3	4.3

Note: Figures are percentages and cover workers 16 years of age and older; (1) Figures cover the Colorado Springs, CO Metropolitan Statistical Area—see Appendix B for areas included
Source: U.S. Census Bureau, 2011-2013 American Community Survey 3-Year Estimates

Travel Time to Work

Area	Less Than 10 Minutes	10 to 19 Minutes	20 to 29 Minutes	30 to 44 Minutes	45 to 59 Minutes	60 to 89 Minutes	90 Minutes or More
City	13.3	38.3	27.2	14.5	2.7	2.5	1.5
MSA[1]	13.0	35.4	25.9	16.7	4.5	2.9	1.6
U.S.	13.3	29.7	20.9	20.2	7.7	5.7	2.6

Note: Figures are percentages and include workers 16 years old and over; (1) Figures cover the Colorado Springs, CO Metropolitan Statistical Area—see Appendix B for areas included
Source: U.S. Census Bureau, 2011-2013 American Community Survey 3-Year Estimates

Travel Time Index

Area	1985	1990	1995	2000	2005	2010	2011
Urban Area[1]	1.03	1.04	1.09	1.18	1.18	1.13	1.13
Average[2]	1.09	1.14	1.16	1.19	1.23	1.18	1.18

Note: Travel Time Index—the ratio of travel time in the peak period to the travel time at free-flow conditions. For example, a value of 1.30 indicates a 20-minute free-flow trip takes 26 minutes in the peak. Free-flow speeds (60 mph on freeways and 35 mph on principal arterials) are used as the comparison threshold; (1) Covers the Colorado Springs CO urban area; (2) average of 498 urban areas
Source: Texas Transportation Institute, Urban Mobility Report 2012, December 2012

Public Transportation

Agency Name / Mode of Transportation	Vehicles Operated in Maximum Service	Annual Unlinked Passenger Trips (in thous.)	Annual Passenger Miles (in thous.)
Colorado Springs Transit System			
Bus (purchased transportation)	30	2,669.3	14,697.3
Demand Response (purchased transportation)	85	271.6	1,584.5
Vanpool (directly operated)	32	50.9	3,462.8

Source: Federal Transit Administration, National Transit Database, 2013

Air Transportation

Airport Name and Code / Type of Service	Passenger Airlines[1]	Passenger Enplanements	Freight Carriers[2]	Freight (lbs.)
City of Colorado Springs Municipal (COS)				
Domestic service (U.S. carriers - 2014)	13	614,075	2	13,631,621
International service (U.S. carriers - 2013)	0	0	0	0

Note: (1) Includes all U.S.-based major, minor and commuter airlines that carried at least one passenger during the year; (2) Includes all U.S.-based airlines and freight carriers that transported at least one lb. of freight during the year.
Source: Bureau of Transportation Statistics, The Intermodal Transportation Database, Air Carriers: T-100 Domestic Market (U.S. Carriers), 2014; Bureau of Transportation Statistics, The Intermodal Transportation Database, Air Carriers: T-100 International Market (U.S. Carriers), 2013

Other Transportation Statistics

Major Highways:	I-25
Amtrak Service:	Bus connection
Major Waterways/Ports:	None

Source: Amtrak.com; Google Maps

BUSINESSES

Major Business Headquarters

Company Name	Rankings	
	Fortune[1]	Forbes[2]
No companies listed	-	-

Note: (1) Fortune 500—companies that produce a 10-K are ranked 1 to 500 based on 2013 revenue; (2) all private companies with at least $2 billion in annual revenue through the end of their most current fiscal year are ranked 1 to 221; companies listed are headquartered in the city; dashes indicate no ranking
Source: Fortune, "Fortune 500," June 16, 2014; Forbes, "America's Largest Private Companies," November 5, 2014

Fast-Growing Businesses

According to *Inc.*, Colorado Springs is home to one of America's 500 fastest-growing private companies: **Themesoft** (#469). Criteria: must be an independent, privately-held, for-profit, U.S. corporation, proprietorship or partnership; revenues must be at least $100,000 in 2010 and $2 million in 2013; must have four-year operating/sales history. Holding companies, regulated banks, and utilities were excluded. *Inc., "America's 500 Fastest-Growing Private Companies," September 2014*

According to Deloitte, Colorado Springs is home to one of North America's 500 fastest-growing high-technology companies: **Cherwell Software** (#102). Companies are ranked by percentage growth in revenue over a five-year period. Criteria for inclusion: company must be headquartered within North America; must own proprietary intellectual property or proprietary technology that contributes to a significant portion of the company's operating revenue, or devote a significant proportion of revenues to research and development of technology; must have been in business for a minumum of five years with 2009 operating revenues of at least $50,000 USD/CD and 2013 operating revenues of at least $5 million USD/CD. *Deloitte Touche Tohmatsu, 2014 Technology Fast 500*[TM]

Minority- and Women-Owned Businesses

Group	All Firms		Firms with Paid Employees			
	Firms	Sales ($000)	Firms	Sales ($000)	Employees	Payroll ($000)
Asian	1,422	296,184	370	259,767	2,180	49,218
Black	1,108	41,563	48	19,675	322	7,302
Hispanic	2,040	325,147	325	288,389	2,072	62,148
Women	12,933	1,527,256	1,833	1,280,462	12,859	327,221
All Firms	41,019	38,769,299	10,051	37,456,398	181,328	7,036,810

Note: Figures cover firms located in the city; minority- and women-owned business are defined as firms in which the corresponding group own 51% or more of the stock or equity of the company
Source: U.S. Census Bureau, 2007 Economic Census, Survey of Business Owners (2012 Survey of Business Owners data will be released starting in June 2015)

HOTELS & CONVENTION CENTERS

Hotels/Motels

Area	5 Star		4 Star		3 Star		2 Star		1 Star		Not Rated	
	Num.	Pct.[3]	Num.	Pct.[3]	Num.	Pct.[3]	Num.	Pct.[3]	Num.	Pct.[3]	Num.	Pct.[3]
City[1]	1	0.8	4	3.3	32	26.7	73	60.8	2	1.7	8	6.7
Total[2]	166	0.9	1,264	7.0	5,718	31.8	9,340	52.0	411	2.3	1,070	6.0

Note: (1) Figures cover Colorado Springs and vicinity; (2) Figures cover all 100 cities in this book; (3) Percentage of hotels which have a given star rating; Star ratings are determined by expedia.com and offer an indication of the general quality of a particular hotel.
Source: expedia.com, April 2, 2015

The Colorado Springs, CO metro area is home to one of the best hotels in the U.S. according to *Travel & Leisure*: **The Broadmoor**. Criteria: service; location; rooms; food; and value. The list includes the top 236 hotels in the U.S. *Travel & Leisure, "T+L 500, The World's Best Hotels 2015"*

Major Convention Centers

Name	Overall Space (sq. ft.)	Exhibit Space (sq. ft.)	Meeting Space (sq. ft.)	Meeting Rooms

There are no major convention centers located in the metro area
Source: Original research

Living Environment

COST OF LIVING

Cost of Living Index

Composite Index	Groceries	Housing	Utilities	Trans-portation	Health Care	Misc. Goods/ Services
97.2	93.3	98.4	93.9	98.5	104.0	97.4

Note: The Cost of Living Index measures regional differences in the cost of consumer goods and services, excluding taxes and non-consumer expenditures, for professional and managerial households in the top income quintile. It is based on more than 50,000 prices covering almost 60 different items for which prices are collected three times a year by chambers of commerce, economic development organizations or university applied economic centers in each participating urban area. The numbers shown should be read as a percentage above or below the national average of 100. For example, a value of 115.4 in the groceries column indicates that grocery prices are 15.4% higher than the national average. Small differences in the index numbers should not be interpreted as significant; Figures cover the Colorado Springs CO urban area.
Source: The Council for Community and Economic Research, ACCRA Cost of Living Index, 2014

Grocery Prices

Area[1]	T-Bone Steak ($/pound)	Frying Chicken ($/pound)	Whole Milk ($/half gal.)	Eggs ($/dozen)	Orange Juice ($/64 oz.)	Coffee ($/11.5 oz.)
City[2]	10.56	1.09	2.00	2.07	3.14	4.64
Avg.	10.40	1.37	2.40	1.99	3.46	4.27
Min.	8.48	0.93	1.37	1.30	2.83	2.99
Max.	14.20	2.44	3.62	4.02	6.42	6.96

Note: (1) Values for the local area are compared with the average, minimum and maximum values for all 308 areas in the Cost of Living Index; (2) Figures cover the Colorado Springs CO urban area; **T-Bone Steak** *(price per pound);* **Frying Chicken** *(price per pound, whole fryer);* **Whole Milk** *(half gallon carton);* **Eggs** *(price per dozen, Grade A, large);* **Orange Juice** *(64 oz. Tropicana or Florida Natural);* **Coffee** *(11.5 oz. can, vacuum-packed, Maxwell House, Hills Bros, or Folgers).*
Source: The Council for Community and Economic Research, ACCRA Cost of Living Index, 2014

Housing and Utility Costs

Area[1]	New Home Price ($)	Apartment Rent ($/month)	All Electric ($/month)	Part Electric ($/month)	Other Energy ($/month)	Telephone ($/month)
City[2]	285,348	963	-	73.42	61.97	31.64
Avg.	305,838	919	181.00	93.66	73.14	27.95
Min.	183,142	480	112.00	42.06	23.42	17.16
Max.	1,358,576	3,851	594.00	180.03	440.99	40.42

Note: (1) Values for the local area are compared with the average, minimum and maximum values for all 308 areas in the Cost of Living Index; (2) Figures cover the Colorado Springs CO urban area; **New Home Price** *(2,400 sf living area, 8,000 sf lot, in urban area with full utilities);* **Apartment Rent** *(950 sf 2 bedroom/1.5 or 2 bath, unfurnished, excluding all utilities except water);* **All Electric** *(average monthly cost for an all-electric home);* **Part Electric** *(average monthly cost for a part-electric home);* **Other Energy** *(average monthly cost for natural gas, fuel oil, coal, wood, and any other forms of energy except electricity);* **Telephone** *(price includes basic monthly rate for a private residential line plus additional local usage charges incurred by a family of four).*
Source: The Council for Community and Economic Research, ACCRA Cost of Living Index, 2014

Health Care, Transportation, and Other Costs

Area[1]	Doctor ($/visit)	Dentist ($/visit)	Optometrist ($/visit)	Gasoline ($/gallon)	Beauty Salon ($/visit)	Men's Shirt ($)
City[2]	115.00	90.05	107.03	3.32	34.60	23.58
Avg.	102.86	87.89	97.66	3.44	34.37	26.74
Min.	67.47	65.78	51.18	3.00	17.43	12.79
Max.	173.50	150.14	235.00	4.33	64.28	49.50

Note: (1) Values for the local area are compared with the average, minimum and maximum values for all 308 areas in the Cost of Living Index; (2) Figures cover the Colorado Springs CO urban area; **Doctor** *(general practitioners routine exam of an established patient);* **Dentist** *(adult teeth cleaning and periodic oral examination);* **Optometrist** *(full vision eye exam for established adult patient);* **Gasoline** *(one gallon regular unleaded, national brand, including all taxes, cash price at self-service pump if available);* **Beauty Salon** *(woman's shampoo, trim, and blow-dry);* **Men's Shirt** *(cotton/polyester dress shirt, pinpoint weave, long sleeves).*
Source: The Council for Community and Economic Research, ACCRA Cost of Living Index, 2014

HOUSING

House Price Index (HPI)

Area	National Ranking[2]	Quarterly Change (%)	One-Year Change (%)	Five-Year Change (%)
MSA[1]	147	-0.33	4.01	4.01
U.S.[3]	–	1.35	4.91	11.59

Note: The HPI is a weighted repeat sales index. It measures average price changes in repeat sales or refinancings on the same properties. This information is obtained by reviewing repeat mortgage transactions on single-family properties whose mortgages have been purchased or securitized by Fannie Mae or Freddie Mac in January 1975; (1) Colorado Springs Metropolitan Statistical Area—see Appendix B for areas included; (2) Rankings are based on annual percentage change for all metro areas containing at least 15,000 transactions over the last 10 years and ranges from 1 to 275; (3) figures based on a weighted average of Census Division estimates using a seasonally adjusted, purchase-only index; all figures are for the period ending December 31, 2014

Source: Federal Housing Finance Agency, House Price Index, February 26, 2015

Median Single-Family Home Prices

Area	2012	2013	2014P	Percent Change 2013 to 2014
MSA[1]	201.6	216.8	222.3	2.5
U.S. Average	177.2	197.4	209.0	5.9

Note: Figures are median sales prices of existing single-family homes in thousands of dollars; (p) preliminary; n/a not available; (1) Colorado Springs, CO Metropolitan Statistical Area—see Appendix B for areas included
Source: National Association of Realtors, Median Sales Price of Existing Single-Family Homes for Metropolitan Areas, 4th Quarter 2014

Qualifying Income Based on Median Sales Price of Existing Single-Family Homes

Area	With 5% Down ($)	With 10% Down ($)	With 20% Down ($)
MSA[1]	49,445	46,842	41,638
U.S. Average	45,863	43,449	38,621

Note: Figures are preliminary; Qualifying income is based on a mortgage rate of 4.0%. Monthly principal and interest payment is limited to 25% of income; n/a not available; (1) Colorado Springs, CO Metropolitan Statistical Area—see Appendix B for areas included
Source: National Association of Realtors, Qualifying Income Based on Median Sales Price of Existing Single-Family Homes for Metropolitan Areas, 4th Quarter 2014

Median Apartment Condo-Coop Home Prices

Area	2012	2013	2014P	Percent Change 2013 to 2014
MSA[1]	130.4	137.6	146.0	6.1
U.S. Average	173.7	194.9	205.1	5.2

Note: Figures are median sales prices of existing apartment condo-coop homes in thousands of dollars; (p) preliminary; n/a not available; (1) Colorado Springs, CO Metropolitan Statistical Area—see Appendix B for areas included
Source: National Association of Realtors, Median Sales Price of Existing Apartment Condo-Coop Homes for Metropolitan Areas, 4th Quarter 2014

Gross Monthly Rent

Area	Under $200	$200 -299	$300 -499	$500 -749	$750 -999	$1,000 -1,499	$1,500 and up	Median ($)
City	0.5	1.6	5.9	28.2	24.2	28.5	11.1	881
MSA[1]	0.4	1.5	5.3	25.1	22.7	32.5	12.4	937
U.S.	1.7	3.2	7.8	22.1	24.3	26.0	14.9	900

Note: Figures are percentages except for Median; Gross rent is the contract rent plus the estimated average monthly cost of utilities (electricity, gas, and water and sewer) and fuels (oil, coal, kerosene, wood, etc.) if these are paid by the renter (or paid for the renter by someone else); (1) Figures cover the Colorado Springs, CO Metropolitan Statistical Area—see Appendix B for areas included
Source: U.S. Census Bureau, 2011-2013 American Community Survey 3-Year Estimates

Homeownership Rate

Area	2007 (%)	2008 (%)	2009 (%)	2010 (%)	2011 (%)	2012 (%)	2013 (%)	2014 (%)
MSA[1]	n/a	n/a	n/a	n/a	n/a	n/a	n/a	n/a
U.S.	68.1	67.8	67.4	66.9	66.1	65.4	65.1	64.5

Note: (1) Figures cover the Colorado Springs, CO Metropolitan Statistical Area—see Appendix B for areas included; n/a not available
Source: U.S. Census Bureau, Housing Vacancies and Homeownership Annual Statistics: 2014

Year Housing Structure Built

Area	2010 or Later	2000 -2009	1990 -1999	1980 -1989	1970 -1979	1960 -1969	1950 -1959	1940 -1949	Before 1940	Median Year
City	0.9	18.3	15.1	19.6	18.9	11.2	7.6	2.2	6.2	1982
MSA[1]	1.3	21.1	16.6	18.5	17.9	10.1	6.9	1.9	5.7	1984
U.S.	0.9	15.0	13.9	13.8	15.8	11.0	10.9	5.4	13.3	1976

Note: Figures are percentages except for Median Year; (1) Figures cover the Colorado Springs, CO Metropolitan Statistical Area—see Appendix B for areas included
Source: U.S. Census Bureau, 2011-2013 American Community Survey 3-Year Estimates

HEALTH

Health Risk Data

Category	MSA[1] (%)	U.S. (%)
Adults aged 18–64 who have any kind of health care coverage	80.9	79.6
Adults who reported being in good or excellent health	87.3	83.1
Adults who are current smokers	17.9	19.6
Adults who are heavy drinkers[2]	4.3	6.1
Adults who are binge drinkers[3]	12.8	16.9
Adults who are overweight (BMI 25.0 - 29.9)	34.4	35.8
Adults who are obese (BMI 30.0 - 99.8)	21.1	27.6
Adults who participated in any physical activities in the past month	83.4	77.1
Adults 50+ who have ever had a sigmoidoscopy or colonoscopy	73.3	67.3
Women aged 40+ who have had a mammogram within the past two years	70.3	74.0
Men aged 40+ who have had a PSA test within the past two years	42.9	45.2
Adults aged 65+ who have had flu shot within the past year	62.0	60.1
Adults who always wear a seatbelt	95.0	93.8

Note: Data as of 2012 unless otherwise noted; (1) Figures cover the Colorado Springs, CO Metropolitan Statistical Area—see Appendix B for areas included; (2) Heavy drinkers are classified as males having more than two drinks per day or females having more than one drink per day; (3) Binge drinkers are classified as males having five or more drinks on one occasion or females having four or more drinks on one occasion
Source: Centers for Disease Control and Prevention, Behaviorial Risk Factor Surveillance System, SMART: Selected Metropolitan/Micropolitan Area Risk Trends, 2012 (Note: the CDC has discontinued this dataset but will be releasing a replacement in late 2015)

Chronic Health Indicators

Category	MSA[1] (%)	U.S. (%)
Adults who have ever been told they had a heart attack	2.7	4.5
Adults who have ever been told they had a stroke	1.8	2.9
Adults who have been told they currently have asthma	7.8	8.9
Adults who have ever been told they have arthritis	23.5	25.7
Adults who have ever been told they have diabetes[2]	8.6	9.7
Adults who have ever been told they had skin cancer	4.4	5.7
Adults who have ever been told they had any other types of cancer	5.7	6.5
Adults who have ever been told they have COPD	4.6	6.2
Adults who have ever been told they have kidney disease	2.3	2.5
Adults who have ever been told they have a form of depression	17.7	18.0

Note: Data as of 2012 unless otherwise noted; (1) Figures cover the Colorado Springs, CO Metropolitan Statistical Area—see Appendix B for areas included; (2) Figures do not include pregnancy-related, borderline, or pre-diabetes
Source: Centers for Disease Control and Prevention, Behaviorial Risk Factor Surveillance System, SMART: Selected Metropolitan/Micropolitan Area Risk Trends, 2012 (Note: the CDC has discontinued this dataset but will be releasing a replacement in late 2015)

Mortality Rates for the Top 10 Causes of Death in the U.S.

ICD-10[a] Sub-Chapter	ICD-10[a] Code	Age-Adjusted Mortality Rate[1] per 100,000 population	
		County[2]	U.S.
Malignant neoplasms	C00-C97	146.6	166.2
Ischaemic heart diseases	I20-I25	81.3	105.7
Other forms of heart disease	I30-I51	34.4	49.3
Chronic lower respiratory diseases	J40-J47	45.7	42.1
Organic, including symptomatic, mental disorders	F01-F09	52.3	38.1
Cerebrovascular diseases	I60-I69	37.4	37.0
Other external causes of accidental injury	W00-X59	36.5	26.9
Other degenerative diseases of the nervous system	G30-G31	19.5	25.6
Diabetes mellitus	E10-E14	17.8	21.3
Hypertensive diseases	I10-I15	16.1	19.4

Note: (a) ICD-10 = International Classification of Diseases 10th Revision; (1) Mortality rates are a three year average covering 2011-2013; (2) Figures cover El Paso County
Source: Centers for Disease Control and Prevention, National Center for Health Statistics. Compressed Mortality File 1999-2013 on CDC WONDER Online Database, released October 2014. Data are compiled from the Compressed Mortality File 1999-2013, Series 20 No. 2S, 2014.

Mortality Rates for Selected Causes of Death

ICD-10[a] Sub-Chapter	ICD-10[a] Code	Age-Adjusted Mortality Rate[1] per 100,000 population	
		County[2]	U.S.
Assault	X85-Y09	5.4	5.2
Diseases of the liver	K70-K76	13.8	13.2
Human immunodeficiency virus (HIV) disease	B20-B24	*0.7	2.2
Influenza and pneumonia	J09-J18	12.0	15.4
Intentional self-harm	X60-X84	20.9	12.5
Malnutrition	E40-E46	*0.6	0.9
Obesity and other hyperalimentation	E65-E68	2.3	1.8
Renal failure	N17-N19	6.8	13.1
Transport accidents	V01-V99	11.2	11.7
Viral hepatitis	B15-B19	2.1	2.2

Note: (a) ICD-10 = International Classification of Diseases 10th Revision; (1) Mortality rates are a three year average covering 2011-2013; (2) Figures cover El Paso County; (*) Unreliable data as per CDC
Source: Centers for Disease Control and Prevention, National Center for Health Statistics. Compressed Mortality File 1999-2013 on CDC WONDER Online Database, released October 2014. Data are compiled from the Compressed Mortality File 1999-2013, Series 20 No. 2S, 2014.

Health Insurance Coverage

Area	With Health Insurance	With Private Health Insurance	With Public Health Insurance	Without Health Insurance	Population Under Age 18 Without Health Insurance
City	86.0	69.3	28.4	14.0	6.9
MSA[1]	87.1	72.0	26.7	12.9	6.7
U.S.	85.2	65.2	31.0	14.8	7.3

Note: Figures are percentages that cover the civilian noninstitutionalized population; (1) Figures cover the Colorado Springs, CO Metropolitan Statistical Area—see Appendix B for areas included
Source: U.S. Census Bureau, 2011-2013 American Community Survey 3-Year Estimates

Number of Medical Professionals

Area[1]	MDs[2]	DOs[2,3]	Dentists	Podiatrists	Chiropractors	Optometrists
Local (number)	1,196	177	633	25	248	143
Local (rate[4])	185.2	27.4	96.6	3.8	37.8	21.8
U.S. (rate[4])	270.0	20.2	63.1	5.7	25.2	14.9

Note: Data as of 2013 unless noted; (1) Local data covers El Paso County; (2) Data as of 2012 and includes all active, non-federal physicians; (3) Doctor of Osteopathic Medicine; (4) rate per 100,000 population
Source: U.S. Department of Health and Human Services, Health Resources and Services Administration, Bureau of Health Professions, Area Resource File (ARF) 2013-2014

EDUCATION

Public School District Statistics

District Name	Schls	Pupils	Pupil/ Teacher Ratio	Minority Pupils[1] (%)	Free Lunch Eligible[2] (%)	IEP[3] (%)
Academy School District No. 20	32	23,973	16.6	25.0	9.0	0.0
Cheyenne Mountain SD No. 12	9	4,651	15.5	24.3	11.4	0.0
Harrison, School District No. 2	24	10,775	15.5	66.2	60.7	0.0
School District No. 11	60	29,032	17.0	47.2	44.9	0.0
School District No. 3	16	9,297	17.7	48.0	32.0	0.0

Note: Table includes school districts with 2,000 or more students; (1) Percentage of students that are not non-Hispanic white; (2) Percentage of students that are eligible for the free lunch program; (3) Percentage of students that have an Individualized Education Program.
Source: U.S. Department of Education, National Center for Education Statistics, Common Core of Data, Local Education Agency (School District) Universe Survey: School Year 2012-2013; U.S. Department of Education, National Center for Education Statistics, Common Core of Data, Public Elementary/Secondary School Universe Survey: School Year 2012-2013

Best High Schools

According to *The Daily Beast*, Colorado Springs is home to three of the best high schools in the U.S.: **Cheyenne Mountain High School** (#378); **Rampart High School** (#547); **Air Academy High School** (#577); *The Daily Beast* used six indicators culled from school surveys to compare public high schools in the U.S., with graduation and college acceptance rates weighed most heavily. Other criteria included: college-level courses/exams and SAT/ACT scores. *The Daily Beast, "Top High Schools 2014"*

Highest Level of Education

Area	Less than H.S.	H.S. Diploma	Some College, No Deg.	Associate Degree	Bachelor's Degree	Master's Degree	Prof. School Degree	Doctorate Degree
City	6.7	20.9	25.0	10.7	22.3	11.1	1.9	1.3
MSA[1]	6.1	21.5	26.1	11.3	21.5	10.6	1.7	1.3
U.S.	13.7	28.0	21.2	7.9	18.2	7.7	1.9	1.3

Note: Figures cover persons age 25 and over; (1) Figures cover the Colorado Springs, CO Metropolitan Statistical Area—see Appendix B for areas included
Source: U.S. Census Bureau, 2011-2013 American Community Survey 3-Year Estimates

Educational Attainment by Race

Area	High School Graduate or Higher (%)					Bachelor's Degree or Higher (%)				
	Total	White	Black	Asian	Hisp.[2]	Total	White	Black	Asian	Hisp.[2]
City	93.3	95.0	91.7	86.1	79.2	36.6	39.2	22.9	35.9	16.4
MSA[1]	93.9	95.3	92.8	84.3	82.1	35.1	37.2	22.6	35.2	17.1
U.S.	86.3	88.3	83.1	85.7	64.0	29.1	30.4	18.8	50.7	13.7

Note: Figures shown cover persons 25 years old and over; (1) Figures cover the Colorado Springs, CO Metropolitan Statistical Area—see Appendix B for areas included; (2) People of Hispanic origin can be of any race
Source: U.S. Census Bureau, 2011-2013 American Community Survey 3-Year Estimates

School Enrollment by Grade and Control

Area	Preschool (%)		Kindergarten (%)		Grades 1 - 4 (%)		Grades 5 - 8 (%)		Grades 9 - 12 (%)	
	Public	Private	Public	Private	Public	Private	Public	Private	Public	Private
City	59.5	40.5	89.5	10.5	93.0	7.0	93.4	6.6	93.1	6.9
MSA[1]	62.2	37.8	90.7	9.3	93.3	6.7	92.9	7.1	93.4	6.6
U.S.	57.7	42.3	87.9	12.1	89.9	10.1	90.0	10.0	90.7	9.3

Note: Figures shown cover persons 3 years old and over; (1) Figures cover the Colorado Springs, CO Metropolitan Statistical Area—see Appendix B for areas included
Source: U.S. Census Bureau, 2011-2013 American Community Survey 3-Year Estimates

Average Salaries of Public School Classroom Teachers

Area	2013-14		2014-15		Percent Change 2013-14 to 2014-15	Percent Change 2004-05 to 2014-15
	Dollars	Rank[1]	Dollars	Rank[1]		
COLORADO	49,615	31	49,828	34	0.43	13.4
U.S. Average	56,610	–	57,379	–	1.36	20.8

Note: (1) State rank ranges from 1 to 51 where 1 indicates highest salary.
Source: National Education Association, Rankings & Estimates: Rankings of the States 2014 and Estimates of School Statistics 2015, March 2015

Higher Education

Four-Year Colleges			Two-Year Colleges			Medical Schools[1]	Law Schools[2]	Voc/ Tech[3]
Public	Private Non-profit	Private For-profit	Public	Private Non-profit	Private For-profit			
1	4	6	1	1	8	0	0	2

Note: Figures cover institutions located within the city limits and include main campuses only; (1) includes schools accredited by the Liaison Committee on Medical Education and the American Osteopathic Association's Commission on Osteopathic College Accreditation; (2) includes ABA-accredited schools, schools with provisional ABA accreditation, and state accredited schools; (3) includes all schools with programs that are less than 2 years.
Source: National Center for Education Statistics, Integrated Postsecondary Education System (IPEDS), 2013-14; Association of American Medical Colleges, Member List, May 1, 2015; American Osteopathic Association, Member List, May 1, 2015; Law School Admission Council, Official Guide to ABA-Approved Law Schools Online, May 1, 2015; Wikipedia, List of Medical Schools in the United States, May 1, 2015; Wikipedia, List of Law Schools in the United States, May 1, 2015

According to *U.S. News & World Report*, the Colorado Springs, CO metro area is home to two of the best liberal arts colleges in the U.S.: **Colorado College** (#27); **United States Air Force Academy** (#27). The indicators used to capture academic quality fall into a number of categories: assessment by administrators at peer institutions; retention of students; faculty resources; student selectivity; financial resources; alumni giving; high school counselor ratings of colleges; and graduation rate. *U.S. News & World Report, "America's Best Colleges 2015"*

PRESIDENTIAL ELECTION

2012 Presidential Election Results

Area	Obama (%)	Romney (%)	Other (%)
El Paso County	38.1	59.4	2.5
U.S.	51.0	47.2	1.8

Note: Results may not add to 100% due to rounding
Source: Dave Leip's Atlas of U.S. Presidential Elections

EMPLOYERS

Major Employers

Company Name	Industry
Agilent Technologies	Instruments to measure electricity
Air Force, United States Dept of the	Air force
Broadmoor Hotel	Hotels and motels
Catholic Health Initiatives Colorado	Charitable organization
Centura Health Corporation	General medical and surgical hospitals
CISCO Systems	Data conversion equipment, media-to-media: computer
Direct Checks Unlimited	Checkbooks
Hewlett-Packard Company	Computer rental and leasing
ITT Federal Services Intl Corp	Electrical or electronic engineering
Lockheed Martin Corporation	Search and navigation equipment
Lockheed Martin Corporation	Acceleration indicators & systems components, aerospace
Lockheed Martin Corporation	Defense systems and equipment
Lockheed Martin Corporation	Engineering services
Memorial Health System	General medical and surgical hospitals
United States Department of Defense	National security, federal government
World Radio Missionary Fellowship	Nonchurch religious organizations
YMCA of The Pikes Peak Region	Recreation association

Note: Companies shown are located within the Colorado Springs, CO Metropolitan Statistical Area.
Source: Hoovers.com; Wikipedia

PUBLIC SAFETY

Crime Rate

Area	All Crimes	Violent Crimes				Property Crimes		
		Murder	Forcible Rape	Robbery	Aggrav. Assault	Burglary	Larceny -Theft	Motor Vehicle Theft
City	4,601.6	6.0	84.8	95.8	247.4	854.4	2,871.1	442.1
Suburbs[1]	1,921.2	6.6	52.7	19.0	173.5	429.3	1,115.3	124.8
Metro[2]	3,643.2	6.2	73.4	68.4	221.0	702.4	2,243.3	328.7
U.S.	3,098.6	4.5	25.2	109.1	229.1	610.0	1,899.4	221.3

Note: Figures are crimes per 100,000 population; (1) All areas within the metro area that are located outside the city limits; (2) Figures cover the Colorado Springs, CO Metropolitan Statistical Area—see Appendix B for areas included
Source: FBI Uniform Crime Reports, 2013

Hate Crimes

Area	Number of Quarters Reported	Number of Incidents per Bias Motivation							
		Race	Religion	Sexual Orientation	Ethnicity	Disability	Gender	Gender Identity
City	4	3	1	2	1	0	0	0
U.S.	4	2,871	1,031	1,233	655	83	18	31

Source: Federal Bureau of Investigation, Hate Crime Statistics 2013

Identity Theft Consumer Complaints

Area	Complaints	Complaints per 100,000 Population	Rank[2]
MSA[1]	660	97.3	67
U.S.	332,646	104.3	-

Note: (1) Figures cover the Colorado Springs, CO Metropolitan Statistical Area—see Appendix B for areas included; (2) Rank ranges from 1 to 380 where 1 indicates greatest number of identity theft complaints per 100,000 population
Source: Federal Trade Commission, Consumer Sentinel Network Data Book for January–December 2014

Fraud and Other Consumer Complaints

Area	Complaints	Complaints per 100,000 Population	Rank[2]
MSA[1]	5,204	767.2	3
U.S.	2,250,205	705.7	-

Note: (1) Figures cover the Colorado Springs, CO Metropolitan Statistical Area—see Appendix B for areas included; (2) Rank ranges from 1 to 380 where 1 indicates greatest number of identity theft complaints per 100,000 population
Source: Federal Trade Commission, Consumer Sentinel Network Data Book for January–December 2014

RECREATION

Culture

Dance[1]	Theatre[1]	Instrumental Music[1]	Vocal Music[1]	Series and Festivals	Museums and Art Galleries[2]	Zoos and Aquariums[3]
1	0	1	2	2	35	1

Note: (1) Professional perfoming groups; (2) Based on organizations with SIC code 8412; (3) AZA-accredited
Source: The Grey House Performing Arts Directory, 2015-16; Association of Zoos & Aquariums, AZA Member Zoos & Aquariums, April 2015; www.AccuLeads.com, April 2015

Professional Sports Teams

Team Name	League	Year Established
No teams are located in the metro area		

Source: Wikipedia, Major Professional Sports Teams of the United States and Canada, April 2015

CLIMATE

Average and Extreme Temperatures

Temperature	Jan	Feb	Mar	Apr	May	Jun	Jul	Aug	Sep	Oct	Nov	Dec	Yr.
Extreme High (°F)	71	72	78	87	93	99	98	97	94	86	78	75	99
Average High (°F)	41	44	51	61	68	79	85	81	75	63	49	41	62
Average Temp. (°F)	29	32	39	48	55	66	71	69	61	50	37	30	49
Average Low (°F)	17	20	26	34	42	52	57	55	48	36	24	17	36
Extreme Low (°F)	-20	-19	-3	8	22	36	48	39	22	7	-5	-24	-24

Note: Figures cover the years 1948-1993
Source: National Climatic Data Center, International Station Meteorological Climate Summary, 9/96

Average Precipitation/Snowfall/Humidity

Precip./Humidity	Jan	Feb	Mar	Apr	May	Jun	Jul	Aug	Sep	Oct	Nov	Dec	Yr.
Avg. Precip. (in.)	0.3	0.4	1.3	1.3	2.6	2.1	2.6	3.4	1.0	0.9	0.6	0.5	17.0
Avg. Snowfall (in.)	6	6	10	5	2	0	0	0	Tr	3	7	8	48
Avg. Rel. Hum. 5am (%)	57	60	62	62	69	67	66	71	66	59	60	59	63
Avg. Rel. Hum. 5pm (%)	48	43	39	34	39	36	36	43	36	36	45	52	41

Note: Figures cover the years 1948-1993; Tr = Trace amounts (<0.05 in. of rain; <0.5 in. of snow)
Source: National Climatic Data Center, International Station Meteorological Climate Summary, 9/96

Weather Conditions

Temperature			Daytime Sky			Precipitation		
10°F & below	32°F & below	90°F & above	Clear	Partly cloudy	Cloudy	0.01 inch or more precip.	0.1 inch or more snow/ice	Thunder-storms
21	161	18	108	157	100	98	33	49

Note: Figures are average number of days per year and cover the years 1948-1993
Source: National Climatic Data Center, International Station Meteorological Climate Summary, 9/96

HAZARDOUS WASTE

Superfund Sites

Colorado Springs has no sites on the EPA's Superfund Final National Priorities List. There are a total of 1,322 Superfund sites on the list in the U.S. *U.S. Environmental Protection Agency, Final National Priorities List, April 14, 2015*

AIR & WATER QUALITY

Air Quality Trends: Ozone

	2004	2005	2006	2007	2008	2009	2010	2011	2012	2013
MSA[1]	0.070	0.077	0.072	0.072	0.070	0.060	0.068	0.074	0.075	0.074

Note: (1) Data covers the Colorado Springs, CO Metropolitan Statistical Area—see Appendix B for areas included. The values shown are the composite ozone concentration averages among trend sites based on the highest fourth daily maximum 8-hour concentration in parts per million. These trends are based on sites having an adequate record of monitoring data during the trend period. Data from exceptional events are included.
Source: U.S. Environmental Protection Agency, Air Quality Monitoring Information, "Air Quality Trends by City, 2000-2013"

Air Quality Index

Area	Percent of Days when Air Quality was...[2]					AQI Statistics[2]	
	Good	Moderate	Unhealthy for Sensitive Groups	Unhealthy	Very Unhealthy	Maximum	Median
MSA[1]	84.9	14.8	0.3	0.0	0.0	104	42

Note: (1) Data covers the Colorado Springs, CO Metropolitan Statistical Area—see Appendix B for areas included; (2) Based on 365 days with AQI data in 2014. Air Quality Index (AQI) is an index for reporting daily air quality. EPA calculates the AQI for five major air pollutants regulated by the Clean Air Act: ground-level ozone, particle pollution (aka particulate matter), carbon monoxide, sulfur dioxide, and nitrogen dioxide. The AQI runs from 0 to 500. The higher the AQI value, the greater the level of air pollution and the greater the health concern. There are six AQI categories: "Good" AQI is between 0 and 50. Air quality is considered satisfactory; "Moderate" AQI is between 51 and 100. Air quality is acceptable; "Unhealthy for Sensitive Groups" When AQI values are between 101 and 150, members of sensitive groups may experience health effects; "Unhealthy" When AQI values are between 151 and 200 everyone may begin to experience health effects; "Very Unhealthy" AQI values between 201 and 300 trigger a health alert; "Hazardous" AQI values over 300 trigger warnings of emergency conditions (not shown).
Source: U.S. Environmental Protection Agency, Air Quality Index Report, 2014

Air Quality Index Pollutants

Area	Percent of Days when AQI Pollutant was...[2]					
	Carbon Monoxide	Nitrogen Dioxide	Ozone	Sulfur Dioxide	Particulate Matter 2.5	Particulate Matter 10
MSA[1]	0.0	0.0	86.6	11.2	2.2	0.0

Note: (1) Data covers the Colorado Springs, CO Metropolitan Statistical Area—see Appendix B for areas included; (2) Based on 365 days with AQI data in 2014. The Air Quality Index (AQI) is an index for reporting daily air quality. EPA calculates the AQI for five major air pollutants regulated by the Clean Air Act: ground-level ozone, particle pollution (also known as particulate matter), carbon monoxide, sulfur dioxide, and nitrogen dioxide. The AQI runs from 0 to 500. The higher the AQI value, the greater the level of air pollution and the greater the health concern.
Source: U.S. Environmental Protection Agency, Air Quality Index Report, 2014

Maximum Air Pollutant Concentrations: Particulate Matter, Ozone, CO and Lead

	Particulate Matter 10 (ug/m³)	Particulate Matter 2.5 Wtd AM (ug/m³)	Particulate Matter 2.5 24-Hr (ug/m³)	Ozone (ppm)	Carbon Monoxide (ppm)	Lead (ug/m³)
MSA[1] Level	52	6	18	0.074	2	n/a
NAAQS[2]	150	15	35	0.075	9	0.15
Met NAAQS[2]	Yes	Yes	Yes	Yes	Yes	n/a

Note: (1) Data covers the Colorado Springs, CO Metropolitan Statistical Area—see Appendix B for areas included; Data from exceptional events are included; (2) National Ambient Air Quality Standards; ppm = parts per million; ug/m³ = micrograms per cubic meter; n/a not available.
Concentrations: Particulate Matter 10 (coarse particulate)—highest second maximum 24-hour concentration; Particulate Matter 2.5 Wtd AM (fine particulate)—highest weighted annual mean concentration; Particulate Matter 2.5 24-Hour (fine particulate)—highest 98th percentile 24-hour concentration; Ozone—highest fourth daily maximum 8-hour concentration; Carbon Monoxide—highest second maximum non-overlapping 8-hour concentration; Lead—maximum running 3-month average
Source: U.S. Environmental Protection Agency, Air Quality Monitoring Information, "Air Quality Statistics by City, 2013"

Maximum Air Pollutant Concentrations: Nitrogen Dioxide and Sulfur Dioxide

	Nitrogen Dioxide AM (ppb)	Nitrogen Dioxide 1-Hr (ppb)	Sulfur Dioxide AM (ppb)	Sulfur Dioxide 1-Hr (ppb)	Sulfur Dioxide 24-Hr (ppb)
MSA[1] Level	n/a	n/a	n/a	58	n/a
NAAQS[2]	53	100	30	75	140
Met NAAQS[2]	n/a	n/a	n/a	Yes	n/a

Note: (1) Data covers the Colorado Springs, CO Metropolitan Statistical Area—see Appendix B for areas included; Data from exceptional events are included; (2) National Ambient Air Quality Standards; ppm = parts per million; ug/m³ = micrograms per cubic meter; n/a not available.
Concentrations: Nitrogen Dioxide AM—highest arithmetic mean concentration; Nitrogen Dioxide 1-Hr—highest 98th percentile 1-hour daily maximum concentration; Sulfur Dioxide AM—highest annual mean concentration; Sulfur Dioxide 1-Hr—highest 99th percentile 1-hour daily maximum concentration; Sulfur Dioxide 24-Hr—highest second maximum 24-hour concentration
Source: U.S. Environmental Protection Agency, Air Quality Monitoring Information, "Air Quality Statistics by City, 2013"

Drinking Water

Water System Name	Pop. Served	Primary Water Source Type	Violations[1]	
			Health Based	Monitoring/ Reporting
Colorado Springs Utilities	418,096	Surface	0	0

Note: (1) Based on violation data from January 1, 2014 to December 31, 2014 (includes unresolved violations from earlier years)
Source: U.S. Environmental Protection Agency, Office of Ground Water and Drinking Water, Safe Drinking Water Information System (based on data extracted January 27, 2015)

Denver, Colorado

Background

From almost anywhere in Denver, you can command a breathtaking view of the 14,000-foot Rocky Mountains. However, the early settlers of Denver were not attracted to the city because of its vistas; they were there in search of gold.

In 1858, there were rumors that gold had been discovered in Cherry Creek, one of the waterways on which Denver stands. Although prospectors came and went without much luck, later it was discovered that there really was gold, and silver as well. By 1867, Denver had been established.

Today, Denver, with its sparkling, dramatic skyline of glass and steel towers, bears little resemblance to the dusty frontier village of the nineteenth century. With an excellent location, the "Mile High City" has become a manufacturing, distribution, and transportation center that serves not only the western regions of the United States, but the entire nation. Denver is also home to many companies that are engaged in alternative fuel research and development.

Denver has been the host city of the Democratic National Convention twice: first in 1908 and again in 2008. The city also hosted the international G7 (now G8) summit in 1997. These events bolstered Denver's international reputation both on a political and socioeconomic level.

The massively renovated Colorado Convention Center—now 584,000 square feet—is a magnet for regional and national conferences and shows, and is enhanced by the 5,000 seat Wells Fargo Theatre and new Light Rail Train Station. Major construction is underway at the historic Denver Union Station, which will operate as a mixed-use retail and multi-modal transportation hub. Another architecturally interesting building is the Jeppesen Terminal at Denver's airport, the largest international hub in the United States. The unique roof is made of heat- and light-reflecting tension fabric. The airport is huge, with 53 square miles and 6 million square feet of public space and 93 gates.

The city is also home to a lively cultural, recreational, and educational scene. There are concerts at the Boettcher Concert Hall of the Denver Center for the Performing Arts, seasonal drives through the Denver Mountain Park Circle Drive, and skiing and hiking the Rockies just 90 minutes away. Other area attractions include the Denver Museum of Nature and Science, the Colorado History Museum, and the Denver Art Museum, which increased its exhibition space in 2006 with the dramatic new Frederick C. Hamilton building designed by Daniel Libeskind. Opposite the museum, a new condominium complex, Museum Residences, also by Libeskind, recently opened it sales office.

The city has developed a 12-year, $4.7 billion public transportation expansion plan, FasTracks, for the Denver-Aurora and Boulder Metropolitan Areas, developed by the Regional Transportation District. The plan calls for six light rail and diesel commuter rail lines with a combined length of 119 miles to be opened between 2013 and 2016.

The city also has its share of offbeat, distinctive places to have fun including the hip Capitol Hill district, which offers small music venues and dank bars that appeal to University of Denver students. Sports fans have the Colorado Avalanche hockey team, the Denver Nuggets basketball team, the Colorado Rockies baseball team, and the Denver Broncos football team. The city also has the Six Flags Elitch Gardens amusement park.

The Denver Zoo is open year-round and houses nearly 4,000 animals representing 700 species, including the okapi, red-bellied lemur, Amur leopard, black rhino, and Siberian tiger. In recent years, the zoo has been implementing features of a master modernization plan of habitats. Most recently was the completion of Predator Ridge, home to 14 African species of mammals, birds and reptiles, and an indoor tropical rain forest.

The University of Denver, Community College of Denver, Metropolitan State College, and the University of Colorado at Denver are only a few of the many excellent educational opportunities available in the city.

Denver's invigorating climate matches much of the central Rocky Mountain region, without the frigidly cold mornings of the higher elevations during winter, or the hot afternoons of summer at lower altitudes. Extreme cold and heat are generally short-lived. Low relative humidity, light precipitation, and abundant sunshine characterize Denver's weather. Spring is the cloudiest, wettest, and windiest season, while autumn is the most pleasant. Air pollution, known locally as the "brown cloud," which the city has spent decades combating, continues to be a problem.

Rankings

General Rankings

- Denver appeared on *Business Insider's* list of the "15 Hottest American Cities for 2015." Criteria: job and population growth; demographics; affordability; livability; residents' health and welfare; technological innovation; sustainability; culture favoring youth and creativity. *www.businessinsider.com, "The Fifteen Hottest American Cities for 2015," November 19, 2014*

- The Denver metro area was identified as one of America's fastest-growing areas in terms of population and economy by *Forbes*. The area ranked #6 out of 20. The 100 most populous metro areas in the U.S. were evaluated on the following criteria: estimated population growth; job growth; gross metropolitan product growth; unemployment; median salaries for college-educated workers. *Forbes, "America's Fastest-Growing Cities 2015," January 27, 2015*

- Denver was identified as one of America's fastest-growing major metropolitan areas in terms of population growth by CNNMoney.com. The area ranked #6 out of 10. Criteria: population growth between July 2012 and July 2013. *CNNMoney, "10 Fastest-Growing Cities," March 28, 2014*

- Among the 50 largest U.S. cities, Denver placed #4 in Vocativ's "semi-exhaustive, mostly scientific" city Livability Index for people aged 35 and under. Average salary, unemployment rates, rents, and other living costs were considered, along with crime rates, weather, public transportation, access to music and sports, and "lifestyle metrics" such as the price of dinner at Buffalo Wild Wings and an ounce of high-quality weed. *vocative.com, "The Livability Index: The Best U.S. Cities for People 35 and Under," December 9, 2014*

- Denver was selected as one of America's best cities by *Bloomberg Businessweek*. The city ranked #6 out of 50. Criteria: leisure attributes (the number of restaurants, bars, libraries, museums, professional sports teams, and park acres by population); educational attributes (public school performance, the number of colleges, and graduate degree holders); economic factors (2011 income and June and July 2012 unemployment); crime; and air quality. *Bloomberg BusinessWeek, "America's Best Cities," September 26, 2012*

Business/Finance Rankings

- The personal finance site NerdWallet scored the nation's 50 largest American cities according to how friendly a business climate they offer to would-be entrepreneurs. Criteria included access to funding, human capital, local economy, and business-friendliness as judged by small business owners. On the resulting list of most welcoming cities, Denver ranked #9. *www.nerdwallet.com, "Best Cities to Start a Business," May 7, 2014*

- The editors of *Kiplinger's Personal Finance Magazine* named Denver to their list of ten of the best metro areas for start-ups. The area rank #9.Criteria: well-educated workforce; low living costs for self-employed people, as measured by the Council for Community and Economic Research; a strong existing community of small business; low unemployment; low business costs. *www.kiplinger.com, "10 Great Cities for Starting a Business," October 2014*

- The finance website Wall St. Cheat Sheet reported on the prospects for high-wage job creation in the nation's largest metro areas over the next five years and ranked them accordingly, drawing on in-depth analysis by CareerBuilder and Economic Modeling Specialists International (EMSI). The Denver metro area placed #8 on the Wall St. Cheat Sheet list. *wallstcheatsheet.com, "Top 10 Cities for High-Wage Job Growth," December 8, 2013*

- Based on metro area social media reviews, the employment opinion group Glassdoor surveyed 50 of the largest U.S. metro areas on measures including compensation and benefits, satisfaction with management, business outlook, and number of employers hiring. The Denver metro area was ranked #49 in overall employee satisfaction. *www.glassdoor.com, "Employment Satisfaction Report Card by City," June 13, 2014*

- In a survey of economic confidence in the nation's 50 largest metropolitan areas conducted January–December 2014, the Denver metro area placed #8, according to Gallup's 2014 Economic Confidence Index. *Gallup, "San Jose and San Francisco Lead in Economic Confidence," March 19, 2015*

- Using data from the Council for Community and Economic Research's 2013 Annual Report, NerdWallet ranked the 100 U.S. cities with the most expensive cost of living. Cities in California and in the Northeast topped the list. Of the cities with the highest cost of living, Denver ranked #56. *NerdWallet.com, "Most Expensive Cities in America," June 4, 2014*

- The financial literacy site NerdWallet.com set out to identify the 10 most promising cities for job seekers, analyzing data for the nation's 100 largest cities. Denver was ranked #5. Criteria: job availability; workforce growth; affordability. *NerdWallet.com, "Best Cities for Job Seekers in 2015," January 12, 2015*

- The Brookings Institution ranked the 50 largest cities in the U.S. based on income inequality. Denver was ranked #17. (#1 = greatest ineqality). Criteria: the cities were ranked based on the "95/20 ratio," a figure representing the income at which a household earns more than 95 percent of all other households, divided by the income at which a household earns more than only 20 percent of all other households. *Brookings Institution, "Income Inequality in America's 50 Largest Cities, 2007-2013," March 17, 2015*

- *Forbes* ranked the largest metro areas in the U.S. in terms of the "Best Cities for Young Professionals." The Denver metro area ranked #9 out of 15. Criteria: job growth; unemployment rate; median salary of college graduates age 24 to 34; cost of living; number of small businesses per capita; number of large companies; percentage of population 25 years of age and older with college degrees. *Forbes.com, "America's 15 Best Cities for Young Professionals," August 18, 2014*

- Denver was ranked #33 out of 100 metro areas in terms of economic performance (#1 = best) during the recession and recovery from trough quarter through the second quarter of 2013. Criteria: percent change in employment; percentage point change in unemployment rate; percent change in gross metropolitan product; percent change in House Price Index. *Brookings Institution, MetroMonitor: Tracking Economic Recession and Recovery in America's 100 Largest Metropolitan Areas, September 2013*

- The Denver metro area was identified as one of the most debt-ridden places in America by the finance site Credit.com. The metro area was ranked #7. Criteria: residents' average personal debt load and average credit scores. *Credit.com, "The Most Debt-Ridden Cities," May 1, 2014*

- Denver was identified as one of America's most frugal metro areas by *Coupons.com*. The city ranked #9 out of 25. Criteria: online coupon usage. *Coupons.com, "Top 25 Most Frugal Cities of 2013," April 10, 2014*

- Denver was identified as one of America's most frugal metro areas by *Coupons.com*. The city ranked #17 out of 25. Criteria: Grocery IQ and coupons.com mobile app usage. *Coupons.com, "Top 25 Most On-the-Go Frugal Cities of 2013," April 10, 2014*

- Denver was identified as one of the best cities for college graduates to find work—and live. The city ranked #11 out of 15. Criteria: job availability; average salary; average rent. *CareerBuilder.com, "15 Best Cities for College Grads to Find Work—and Live," June 5, 2012*

- The Denver metro area appeared on the Milken Institute "2013 Best Performing Cities" list. Rank: #12 out of 200 large metro areas. Criteria: job growth; wage and salary growth; high-tech output growth. *Milken Institute, "Best-Performing Cities 2014," January 2015*

- *Forbes* ranked the 200 most populous metro areas to determine the nation's "Best Places for Business and Careers." The Denver metro area was ranked #4. Criteria: costs (business and living); job growth (past and projected); income growth; educational attainment (college and high school); projected economic growth; cultural and recreational opportunities; net migration patterns; number of highly ranked colleges. *Forbes, "The Best Places for Business and Careers 2014," July 23, 2014*

Culture/Performing Arts Rankings

- Denver was selected as one of America's top cities for the arts. The city ranked #14 in the big city (population 500,000 and over) category. Criteria: readers' top choices for arts travel destinations based on the richness and variety of visual arts sites, activities and events. *American Style, "2012 Top 25 Arts Destinations," June 2012*

Dating/Romance Rankings

- Of the 100 U.S. cities surveyed by *Men's Health* in its quest to identify the nation's best cities for dating and forming relationships, Denver was ranked #2 for online dating (#1 = best). *Men's Health, "The Best and Worst Cities for Online Dating," January 30, 2013*

- Denver was selected as one of the best cities for post grads by *Rent.com*. The city ranked #3 of 10. Criteria: millenial population; jobs per capita; unemployment rate; median rent; number of bars and restaurants; access to nightlife and entertainment. *Rent.com, "Top 10 Best Cities for Post Grads," April 3, 2015*

Education Rankings

- Personal finance website *WalletHub* analyzed the 150 largest U.S. metropolitan statistical areas to determine where the most educated Americans are choosing to settle. Criteria: educational attainment; percentage of workers with jobs in computer, engineering, and science fields; quality and size of each metro area's universities. Denver was ranked #28 (#1 = most educated city). *www.WalletHub.com, "2014's Most and Least Educated Cities*

- The real estate website *MovoTo.com* selected Denver as one of the "Nerdiest Cities in America." The city ranked #10 among the top 10 derived from data on the 50 most populous cities in the United States. Criteria: Number of annual comic book, video game, anime, and sci-fi/fantasy conventions; people per comic book store, video game store, and traditional gaming store; people per LARPing ("live action role-playing") group; people per science museum. Also factored in: distance to the nearest Renaissance faire. *MovoTo.com, "The 10 Nerdiest Cities in America," April 10, 2013*

- Denver was selected as one of America's most literate cities. The city ranked #7 out of the 77 largest U.S. cities. Criteria: number of booksellers; library resources; Internet resources; educational attainment; periodical publishing resources; newspaper circulation. *Central Connecticut State University, "America's Most Literate Cities, 2014," April 8, 2015*

Environmental Rankings

- The Weather Channel determined the nation's snowiest cities, based on the National Oceanic and Atmospheric Administration's 30-year average snowfall data. Among cities with a population of at least 100,000, the #17-ranked city was Denver *weather.com, America's 20 Snowiest Major Cities, February 3, 2014*

- The Denver metro area came in at #29 for the relative comfort of its climate on Sperling's list of "chill cities," as measured by the Sperling Heat Index. All 361 metro areas are included. Criteria included daytime high temperatures, nighttime low temperatures, dew point, and relative humidity at the high temperatures. *www.bertsperling.com, "Sperling's Chill Cities," July 18, 2013*

- Sperling's BestPlaces assessed 379 metropolitan areas of the United States for the likelihood of dangerously extreme weather events or earthquakes. In general the Southeast and South-Central regions have the highest risk of weather extremes and earthquakes, while the Pacific Northwest enjoys the lowest risk. Of the least risky metropolitan areas, the Denver metro area was ranked #214. *www.bestplaces.net, "Safest Places from Natural Disasters," April 2011*

- *The Daily Beast* identifed the snowiest among the 100 largest U.S. cities, looking at average snowfall per month from December 2011 through March 2012 and from December 1, 2012 to December 21, 2012. Number of days with maximum and minimum temperatures of 32 degrees or less contributed to the rankings. Denver ranked #4. *The Daily Beast, "25 Snowiest Cities in America," December 21, 2012*

- The U.S. Environmental Protection Agency (EPA) released a list of large U.S. metropolitan areas with the most ENERGY STAR certified buildings in 2014. The Denver metro area was ranked #9 out of 25. *U.S. Environmental Protection Agency, "Top Cities With the Most ENERGY STAR Certified Buildings in 2014," March 25, 2015*

- The Denver metro area was identified as one of the snowiest major metropolitan areas in the U.S. by *Forbes*. The metro area ranked #1 out of 10. Criteria: average annual snowfall. *Forbes, "America's Snowiest Cities," January 12, 2011*

- Denver was highlighted as one of the 25 most ozone-polluted metro areas in the U.S. during 2011 through 2013. The area ranked #13. *American Lung Association, State of the Air 2015*

Food/Drink Rankings

- *Men's Health* ranked 100 major U.S. cities in terms of alcohol intoxication. Denver ranked #83 (#1 = most sober).Criteria: binge drinking; alcohol-related traffic accidents, arrests, and fatalities. *Men's Health, "The Drunkest Cities in America," November 19, 2013*

- Denver was identified as one of the most vegetarian-friendly cities in America by GrubHub.com, the nation's largest food ordering service. The city ranked #9 out of 10. Criteria: percentage of vegetarian restaurants. *GrubHub.com, "Top Vegetarian-Friendly Cities," July 18, 2012*

Health/Fitness Rankings

- Analysts who tracked obesity rates in the nation's largest metro areas (those with populations above one million) found that the Denver metro area was one of the ten major metros where residents were least likely to be obese, defined as a BMI score of 30 or above. *www.gallup.com, "Boulder, Colo., Residents Still Least Likely to Be Obese," April 4, 2014*

- Analysts who tracked obesity rates in 189 of the nation's metro areas found that the Denver metro area was one of the ten communities where residents were least likely to be obese, defined as a BMI score of 30 or above. *www.gallup.com, "Boulder, Colo., Residents Still Least Likely to Be Obese," April 4, 2014*

- For each of the 50 most populous metro areas in the United States, the American College of Sports Medicine's American Fitness Index evaluated infrastructure, community assets, and policies that encourage healthy and fit lifestyles, including preventive health behaviors, levels of chronic disease conditions, health care access, and community resources and policies that support physical activity. The Denver metro area ranked #5 for "community fitness." Personal health indicators were considered as well as community and environmental indicators. *www.americanfitnessindex.org, "ACSM American Fitness Index Health and Community Fitness Status of the 50 Largest Metropolitan Areas," May 2013*

- The Denver metro area was identified as one of the worst cities for bed bugs in America by pest control company Orkin. The area ranked #9 out of 50 based on the number of bed bug treatments Orkin performed from January to December 2013. *Orkin, "Chicago Tops Bed Bug Cities List for Second Year in a Row," January 16, 2014*

- Denver was identified as one of 15 cities with the highest increase in bed bug activity in the U.S. by pest control provider Terminix. The city ranked #10.Criteria: cities with the largest percentage gains in bed bug customer calls from January–May 2013 compared to the same time period in 2012. *Terminix, "Cities with Highest Increases in Bed Bug Activity," July 9, 2013*

- Denver was selected as one of the 25 fittest cities in America by *Men's Fitness Online*. It ranked #7 out of America's 50 largest cities. Criteria: fitness centers and sport stores; nutrition; sports participation; TV viewing; overweight/sedentary; junk food; air quality; geography; commute; parks and open space; city recreational facilities; access to healthcare; motivation; mayor and city initiatives; state obesity initiatives. *Men's Fitness, "The Fittest and Fattest Cities in America," March 5, 2012*

- Denver was identified as a "2013 Spring Allergy Capital." The area ranked #91 out of 100. Three groups of factors were used to identify the most severe cities for people with allergies during the spring season: annual pollen levels; medicine utilization; access to board-certified allergists. *Asthma and Allergy Foundation of America, "Spring Allergy Capitals 2013"*

- Denver was identified as a "2013 Fall Allergy Capital." The area ranked #94 out of 100. Three groups of factors were used to identify the most severe cities for people with allergies during the fall season: annual pollen levels; medicine utilization; access to board-certified allergists. *Asthma and Allergy Foundation of America, "Fall Allergy Capitals 2013"*

- Denver was identified as a "2013 Asthma Capital." The area ranked #84 out of the nation's 100 largest metropolitan areas. Twelve factors were used to identify the most challenging places to live for people with asthma: estimated prevalence; self-reported prevalence; crude death rate for asthma; annual pollen score; annual air quality; public smoking laws; number of board-certified asthma specialists; school inhaler access laws; rescue medication use; controller medication use; uninsured rate; poverty rate. *Asthma and Allergy Foundation of America, "Asthma Capitals 2013"*

- *Men's Health* ranked 100 major U.S. cities in terms of the best and worst cities for men. Denver ranked #25. Criteria: thirty-three data points were examined covering health, fitness, and quality of life. *Men's Health, "The Best & Worst Cities for Men 2014," December 6, 2013*

- Denver was selected as one of the best metropolitan areas for hospital care in America by *HealthGrades.com*. The rankings are based on a comprehensive study of patient death and complication rates in the nation's nearly 5,000 hospitals. Hospitals performing in the top 5% nationwide across 26 different medical procedures and diagnoses were identified. *HealthGrades.com* then ranked cities by the highest percentage of these Distinguished Hospitals for Clinical Excellence™. The Denver metro area ranked #39. *HealthGrades.com, "America's Top 50 Cities for Hospital Care," January 21, 2012*

- The Denver metro area appeared in the 2013 Gallup-Healthways Well-Being Index. The area ranked #18 out of 189. The Gallup-Healthways Well-Being Index score is an average of six sub-indexes, which individually examine life evaluation, emotional health, work environment, physical health, healthy behaviors, and access to basic necessities. Results are based on telephone interviews conducted as part of the Gallup-Healthways Well-Being Index survey January 2–December 29, 2012, and January 2–December 30, 2013, with a random sample of 531,630 adults, aged 18 and older, living in metropolitan areas in the 50 U.S. states and the District of Columbia. *Gallup-Healthways, "State of American Well-Being," March 25, 2014*

- The Denver metro area was identified as one of "America's Most Stressful Cities" by *Sperling's BestPlaces*. The metro area ranked #19 out of 50. Criteria: unemployment rate; suicide rate; commute time; mental health; poor rest; alcohol use; violent crime rate; property crime rate; cloudy days annually. *Sperling's BestPlaces, www.BestPlaces.net, "Stressful Cities 2012*

- Denver was selected as one of the "20 Most Livable U.S. Cities for Wheelchair Users" by the Christopher & Dana Reeve Foundation. The city ranked #4. Criteria: Medicaid eligibility and spending; access to physicians and rehabilitation facilities; access to fitness facilities and recreation; access to paratransit; percentage of people living with disabilities who are employed; clean air; climate. *Christopher & Dana Reeve Foundation, "20 Most Livable U.S. Cities for Wheelchair Users," July 26, 2010*

Pet Rankings

- Denver was selected as one of the best cities for dogs by real estate website Estately.com. The city was ranked #16. Criteria: weather; walkability; yard sizes; dog activities; meetup groups; availability of dogsitters. *Estately.com, "17 Best U.S. Cities for Dogs," May 14, 2013*

Real Estate Rankings

- On the list compiled by Penske Truck Rental, the Denver metro area was named the #7 moving destination in 2014, based on one-way consumer truck rental reservations made through Penske's website and reservations call center. *blog.gopenske.com, "Penske Truck Rental's 2014 Top Moving Destinations List," February 4, 2015*

- The Denver metro area appeared on Realtor.com's list of the hottest housing markets to watch in 2015. Criteria: strong housing growth; affordable prices; and fast-paced sales. *Realtor.com®, "Top 10 Hot Housing Markets to Watch in 2015," December 4, 2014*

- Using data from the housing-market research firm RealtyTrac, Yahoo! Finance researchers listed the housing markets in which housing affordability is deteriorating most, factoring in interest rates as well as median home prices. The Denver metro area was among the least affordable housing markets according to the percentage difference in the income required to buy a home in December 2013 as opposed to in December 2012. *news.yahoo.com, "10 Cities Where Ordinary People Can No Longer Afford Homes," March 5, 2014*

- The Denver metro area was identified as one of the nations's 20 hottest housing markets in 2015. Criteria: listing views relative to the number of listings. The area ranked #4. *Realtor.com, "These Are the 20 Hottest Housing Markets in the U.S. Right Now," April 8, 2015*

- The Denver metro area was identified as one of the nation's 20 hottest housing markets in 2015.Criteria: median number of days homes were spending on the market in March 2015. The area ranked #4. *Realtor.com, "These Are the 20 Hottest Housing Markets in the U.S. Right Now," April 8, 2015*

- The Denver metro area was identified as one of the top 20 housing markets to invest in for 2015 by *Forbes*. The area ranked #7. Criteria: strong population and job growth; relatively low home prices which are below equilibrium home price (EHP). The EHP is what the average price for a market should be, if speculation, weird distortions in local income, and other factors (like the housing collapse) weren't present in the market. *Forbes.com, "Best Buy Cities: Where to Invest in Housing in 2015," January 9, 2015*

- Denver was ranked #24 out of 275 metro areas in terms of house price appreciation in 2014 (#1 = highest rate). *Federal Housing Finance Agency, House Price Index, 4th Quarter 2014*

- The Denver metro area was identified as one of the 15 worst housing markets for the next five years." Criteria: projected annualized change in home prices between the fourth quarter 2012 and the fourth quarter 2017. *The Business Insider, "The 15 Worst Housing Markets for the Next Five Years," May 22, 2013*

- The Denver metro area was identified as one of the 20 least affordable housing markets in the U.S. in 2014. The area ranked #19 out of 178 markets. Criteria: whether or not a typical family could qualify for a mortgage loan on a typical home. *National Association of Realtors®, Affordability Index of Existing Single-Family Homes for Metropolitan Areas, 2014*

- Denver was ranked #161 out of 226 metro areas in terms of housing affordability in 2014 by the National Association of Home Builders (#1 = most affordable). The NAHB-Wells Fargo Housing Opportunity Index (HOI) for a given area is defined as the share of homes sold in that area that would have been affordable to a family earning the local median income, based on standard mortgage underwriting criteria. *National Association of Home Builders®, NAHB-Wells Fargo Housing Opportunity Index, 4th Quarter 2014*

Safety Rankings

- Symantec, in partnership with Sperling's BestPlaces, ranked the 50 largest cities in the U.S. in terms of their vulnerability to cybercrime. The city ranked #6. Criteria: number of cyberattacks and potential infections; level of Internet access; expenditures on smartphones and computer hardware/software; wireless hotspots; broadband connectivity; Internet usage; online purchases. *Symantec, "Riskiest Online Cities of 2012" February 15, 2012*

- Allstate ranked the 200 largest cities in America in terms of driver safety. Denver ranked #88. Allstate researchers analyzed internal property damage claims over a two-year period from January 2011 to December 2012. A weighted average of the two-year numbers determined the annual percentages. *Allstate, "Allstate America's Best Drivers Report, 2014"*

- The National Insurance Crime Bureau ranked 380 metro areas in the U.S. in terms of per capita rates of vehicle theft. The Denver metro area ranked #50 (#1 = highest rate). Criteria: number of vehicle theft offenses per 100,000 inhabitants in 2012. *National Insurance Crime Bureau, "Hot Spots 2012," June 26, 2013*

Seniors/Retirement Rankings

- From its Best Cities for Successful Aging indexes, the Milken Institute generated rankings for metropolitan areas, weighing data in eight categories—health care, wellness, living arrangements, transportation, financial characteristics, education and employment opportunities, community engagement, and overall livability. The Denver metro area was ranked #11 overall in the large metro area category. *Milken Institute, "Best Cities for Successful Aging, 2014"*

- Denver was identified as one of the most popular places to retire by *Topretirements.com*. The list reflects the 100 cities (out of 900+ total cities reviewed) that visitors to the website are most interested in for retirement. *Topretirements.com, "Most Popular Places to Retire for 2014," February 25, 2014*

Sports/Recreation Rankings

- According to the personal finance website NerdWallet, the Denver metro area, at #8, is one of the nation's top dozen metro areas for sports fans. Criteria included the presence of all four major sports—MLB, NFL, NHL, and NBA, fan enthusiasm (as measured by game attendance), ticket affordability, and "sports culture," that is, number of sports bars. *www.nerdwallet.com, "Best Cities for Sports Fans," May 5, 2013*

- *24/7 Wall St.* analysts isolated the ten cities that spent the most public money per capita on sports stadiums, according to 2010 data. Denver ranked #6. *24/7 Wall St., "Cities Paying the Most for Sports Teams," January 30, 2013*

- Denver was selected as one of "America's Most Miserable Sports Cities" by *Forbes*. The city was ranked #10. Criteria: postseason losses; years since last title; ratio of cumulative seasons to championships won. Contenders were limited to cities with at least 75 total seasons of NFL, NBA, NHL and MLB play. *Forbes, "America's Most Miserable Sports Cities," July 31, 2013*

- Denver was chosen as a bicycle friendly community by the League of American Bicyclists. A "Bicycle Friendly Community" welcomes cyclists by providing safe accommodation for cycling and encouraging people to bike for transportation and recreation. There are four award levels: Platinum; Gold; Silver; and Bronze. The community achieved an award level of Silver. *League of American Bicyclists, "Bicycle Friendly Community Master List," Fall 2013*

- Denver was chosen as one of America's best cities for bicycling. The city ranked #14 out of 50. Criteria: robust cycling infrastructure; vibrant bike culture. The editors only considered cities with populations of 95,000 or more. *Bicycling, "America's Top 50 Bike-Friendly Cities," May 23, 2012*

Women/Minorities Rankings

- To determine the best metro areas for working women, the personal finance website NerdWallet considered city size as well as relevant economic metrics—high salaries, narrow pay differential by gender, prevalence of women in the highest-paying industries, and population growth over 2010–2012. Of the large U.S. cities examined, the Denver metro area held the #7 position. *www.nerdwallet.com, "Best Places for Women in the Workforce," May 19, 2013*

- *Women's Health* examined U.S. cities and identified the 100 best cities for women. Denver was ranked #25. Criteria: 30 categories were examined from obesity and breast cancer rates to commuting times and hours spent working out. *Women's Health, "Best Cities for Women 2012"*

- Denver was selected as one of the best cities for young Latinos in 2013 by mun2, a national cable television broadcast network. The city ranked #3. Criteria: U.S. cities with populations over 500,000 residents were evaluated on the following criteria: number of young latinos; jobs; friendliness; cost of living; fun. *mun2.tv, "Best Cities for Young Latinos 2013"*

Miscellaneous Rankings

- Denver was selected as a 2013 Digital Cities Survey winner. The city ranked #7 in the large city (250,000 or more population) category. The survey examined and assessed how city governments are utilizing information technology to operate and deliver quality service to their customers and citizens. Survey questions focused on implementation and adoption of online service delivery; planning and governance; and the infrastructure and architecture that make the transformation to digital government possible. *Center for Digital Government, "2013 Digital Cities Survey," November 7, 2013*

- The watchdog site Charity Navigator conducts an annual study of charities in the nation's major markets both to analyze statistical differences in their financial, accountability, and transparency practices and to track year-to-year variations in individual communities. The Denver metro area was ranked #22 among the 30 metro markets. *www.charitynavigator.org, "Metro Market Study 2013," June 1, 2013*

- Business Insider reports on the 2013 Trick-or-Treat Index compiled by the real estate site Zillow, which used its own Home Value Index and Walk Score along with population density and local crime stats to determine that Denver ranked #15 for "how much candy it gives out versus how far kids have to walk to get it." Zillow also zeroes in on the best neighborhoods in its top 20 cities. *www.businessinsider.com, "These Are the Best Cities for Trick-or-Treating," October 15, 2013*

- Denver was selected as one of America's funniest cities by the Humor Research Lab at the University of Colorado. The city ranked #8 out of 10. Criteria: frequency of visits to comedy websites; number of comedy clubs per square mile; traveling comedians' ratings of each city's comedy-club audiences; number of famous comedians born in each city per capita; number of famous funny tweeters living in each city per capita; number of comedy radio stations available in each city; frequency of humor-related web searches originating in each city. *The New York Times, "So These Professors Walk Into a Comedy Club…," April 20, 2014*

- Mars Chocolate North America, the makers of COMBOS®, in partnership with Sperling's BestPlaces, ranked 50 major metro areas in terms of their "manliness." The Denver metro area ranked #34. Criteria: number of professional sports teams; number of nearby NASCAR tracks and racing events; manly lifestyle; concentration of manly retail stores; manly occupations per capita; salty snack sales; "Board of Manliness" rankings. *Mars Chocolate North America, "America's Manliest Cities 2012"*

- Denver was selected as one of "America's Best Cities for Hipsters" by *Travel + Leisure*. The city was ranked #6 out of 20. Criteria: live music; coffee bars; independent boutiques; best microbrews; offbeat and tech-savvy locals. *Travel + Leisure, "America's Best Cities for Hipsters," November 2013*

- The National Alliance to End Homelessness ranked the 100 most populous metro areas in terms the rate of homelessness. The Denver metro area ranked #30. Criteria: number of homeless people per 10,000 population in 2011. *National Alliance to End Homelessness, The State of Homelessness in America 2012*

- The financial education website CreditDonkey compiled a list of the ten "best" cities of the future, based on percentage of housing built in 1990 or later, population change since 2010, and construction jobs as a percentage of population. Also considered were two more futuristic criteria: number of DeLorean cars available for purchase and number of spaceport companies and proposed spaceports. Denver was scored #5. *www.creditDonkey.com, "In the Future, Almost All of America's 'Best' Cities Will Be on the West Coast, Report Says," February 14, 2014*

Business Environment

CITY FINANCES

City Government Finances

Component	2012 ($000)	2012 ($ per capita)
Total Revenues	3,219,266	5,364
Total Expenditures	3,032,694	5,053
Debt Outstanding	7,039,435	11,729
Cash and Securities[1]	3,278,519	5,463

Note: (1) Cash and security holdings of a government at the close of its fiscal year, including those of its dependent agencies, utilities, and liquor stores.
Source: U.S Census Bureau, State & Local Government Finances 2012

City Government Revenue by Source

Source	2012 ($000)	2012 ($ per capita)
General Revenue		
From Federal Government	1,907	3
From State Government	288,557	481
From Local Governments	186,645	311
Taxes		
Property	386,539	644
Sales and Gross Receipts	632,011	1,053
Personal Income	0	0
Corporate Income	0	0
Motor Vehicle License	17,140	29
Other Taxes	72,235	120
Current Charges	1,147,201	1,911
Liquor Store	0	0
Utility	256,814	428
Employee Retirement	21,832	36

Source: U.S Census Bureau, State & Local Government Finances 2012

City Government Expenditures by Function

Function	2012 ($000)	2012 ($ per capita)	2012 (%)
General Direct Expenditures			
Air Transportation	394,851	658	13.0
Corrections	138,032	230	4.6
Education	0	0	0.0
Employment Security Administration	0	0	0.0
Financial Administration	77,119	128	2.5
Fire Protection	112,010	187	3.7
General Public Buildings	46,197	77	1.5
Governmental Administration, Other	71,108	118	2.3
Health	52,415	87	1.7
Highways	155,204	259	5.1
Hospitals	0	0	0.0
Housing and Community Development	116,553	194	3.8
Interest on General Debt	289,291	482	9.5
Judicial and Legal	60,039	100	2.0
Libraries	30,959	52	1.0
Parking	0	0	0.0
Parks and Recreation	195,292	325	6.4
Police Protection	225,208	375	7.4
Public Welfare	168,723	281	5.6
Sewerage	79,805	133	2.6
Solid Waste Management	6,751	11	0.2
Veterans' Services	0	0	0.0
Liquor Store	0	0	0.0
Utility	256,103	427	8.4
Employee Retirement	153,200	255	5.1

Source: U.S Census Bureau, State & Local Government Finances 2012

DEMOGRAPHICS

Population Growth

Area	1990 Census	2000 Census	2010 Census	Population Growth (%) 1990-2000	Population Growth (%) 2000-2010
City	467,153	554,636	600,158	18.7	8.2
MSA[1]	1,666,935	2,179,296	2,543,482	30.7	16.7
U.S.	248,709,873	281,421,906	308,745,538	13.2	9.7

Note: (1) Figures cover the Denver-Aurora-Broomfield, CO Metropolitan Statistical Area—see Appendix B for areas included
Source: U.S. Census Bureau, Census 1990, 2000, 2010

Household Size

Area	Persons in Household (%) One	Two	Three	Four	Five	Six	Seven or More	Average Household Size
City	40.6	31.5	12.0	8.3	4.2	2.0	1.4	2.30
MSA[1]	29.6	33.3	15.0	12.8	5.5	2.3	1.4	2.56
U.S.	27.7	33.6	15.7	13.1	6.0	2.3	1.5	2.64

Note: (1) Figures cover the Denver-Aurora-Lakewood, CO Metropolitan Statistical Area—see Appendix B for areas included
Source: U.S. Census Bureau, 2011-2013 American Community Survey 3-Year Estimates

Race

Area	White Alone[2] (%)	Black Alone[2] (%)	Asian Alone[2] (%)	AIAN[3] Alone[2] (%)	NHOPI[4] Alone[2] (%)	Other Race Alone[2] (%)	Two or More Races (%)
City	75.0	9.9	3.5	1.0	0.1	7.0	3.4
MSA[1]	81.9	5.6	3.8	0.8	0.1	4.4	3.5
U.S.	73.9	12.6	5.0	0.8	0.2	4.7	2.9

Note: (1) Figures cover the Denver-Aurora-Lakewood, CO Metropolitan Statistical Area—see Appendix B for areas included; (2) Alone is defined as not being in combination with one or more other races; (3) American Indian and Alaska Native; (4) Native Hawaiian and Other Pacific Islander
Source: U.S. Census Bureau, 2011-2013 American Community Survey 3-Year Estimates

Hispanic or Latino Origin

Area	Total (%)	Mexican (%)	Puerto Rican (%)	Cuban (%)	Other (%)
City	31.2	26.3	0.6	0.2	4.0
MSA[1]	22.7	18.1	0.5	0.1	3.9
U.S.	16.9	10.8	1.6	0.6	3.8

Note: Persons of Hispanic or Latino origin can be of any race; (1) Figures cover the Denver-Aurora-Lakewood, CO Metropolitan Statistical Area—see Appendix B for areas included
Source: U.S. Census Bureau, 2011-2013 American Community Survey 3-Year Estimates

Segregation

Type	Segregation Indices[1] 1990	2000	2010	2010 Rank[2]	Percent Change 1990-2000	Percent Change 1990-2010	Percent Change 2000-2010
Black/White	64.8	64.2	62.6	31	-0.5	-2.2	-1.6
Asian/White	29.5	32.3	33.4	83	2.9	3.9	1.1
Hispanic/White	46.7	50.3	48.8	31	3.6	2.1	-1.5

Note: All figures cover the Metropolitan Statistical Area—see Appendix B for areas included; Figures are based on an analysis of 1990, 2000, and 2010 Census Decennial Census tract data by William H. Frey, Brookings Institution and the University of Michigan Social Science Data Analysis Network. In this analysis all racial groups (whites, blacks, and asians) are non-Hispanic members of those races. Hispanics are shown as a separate category;
(1) Segregation Indices are Dissimilarity Indices that measure the degree to which the minority group is distributed differently than whites across census tracts. They range from 0 (complete integration) to 100 (complete segregation) where the value indicates the percentage of the minority group that needs to move to be distributed exactly like whites; (2) Ranges from 1 (most segregated) to 102 (least segregated); n/a not available.
Source: www.CensusScope.org

Ancestry

Area	German	Irish	English	American	Italian	Polish	French[2]	Scottish	Dutch
City	14.9	10.1	7.8	3.3	4.2	2.5	2.5	2.2	1.4
MSA[1]	19.7	11.9	9.9	5.1	5.3	2.7	2.8	2.4	1.6
U.S.	14.9	10.8	8.0	7.4	5.5	3.0	2.7	1.7	1.4

Note: Figures are the percentage of the total population reporting a particular ancestry. The nine most commonly reported ancestries in the U.S. are shown. Figures include multiple ancestries (e.g. if a person reported being Irish and Italian, they were included in both columns); (1) Figures cover the Denver-Aurora-Lakewood, CO Metropolitan Statistical Area—see Appendix B for areas included; (2) Excludes Basque
Source: U.S. Census Bureau, 2011-2013 American Community Survey 3-Year Estimates

Foreign-Born Population

Area	Percent of Population Born in								
	Any Foreign Country	Mexico	Asia	Europe	Carribean	South America	Central America[2]	Africa	Canada
City	15.8	9.0	2.8	1.4	0.2	0.4	0.5	1.2	0.3
MSA[1]	12.1	5.5	2.9	1.5	0.1	0.4	0.4	0.9	0.3
U.S.	13.0	3.7	3.8	1.5	1.2	0.9	1.0	0.6	0.3

Note: (1) Figures cover the Denver-Aurora-Lakewood, CO Metropolitan Statistical Area—see Appendix B for areas included; (2) Excludes Mexico.
Source: U.S. Census Bureau, 2011-2013 American Community Survey 3-Year Estimates

Marital Status

Area	Never Married	Now Married[2]	Separated	Widowed	Divorced
City	41.8	38.5	2.3	4.4	13.0
MSA[1]	31.9	49.5	1.8	4.3	12.5
U.S.	32.7	48.1	2.2	6.0	11.0

Note: Figures are percentages and cover the population 15 years of age and older; (1) Figures cover the Denver-Aurora-Lakewood, CO Metropolitan Statistical Area—see Appendix B for areas included; (2) Excludes separated
Source: U.S. Census Bureau, 2011-2013 American Community Survey 3-Year Estimates

Disability Status

Area	All Ages	Under 18 Years Old	18 to 64 Years Old	65 Years and Over
City	9.8	2.7	8.1	35.7
MSA[1]	9.3	3.2	7.8	32.4
U.S.	12.3	4.1	10.2	36.3

Note: Figures show percent of the civilian noninstitutionalized population that reported having a disability. Disability status is determined from from six types of difficulty: vision, hearing, cognitive, ambulatory, self-care, and independent living. For children under 5 years old, hearing and vision difficulty are used to determine disability status. For children between the ages of 5 and 14, disability status is determined from hearing, vision, cognitive, ambulatory, and self-care difficulties. For people aged 15 years and older, they are considered to have a disability if they have difficulty with any one of the six difficulty types; (1) Figures cover the Denver-Aurora-Lakewood, CO Metropolitan Statistical Area—see Appendix B for areas included.
Source: U.S. Census Bureau, 2011-2013 American Community Survey 3-Year Estimates

Age

Area	Percent of Population									Median Age
	Under Age 5	Age 5–19	Age 20–34	Age 35–44	Age 45–54	Age 55–64	Age 65–74	Age 75–84	Age 85+	
City	7.0	16.3	28.6	15.3	11.7	10.5	5.8	3.1	1.6	34.0
MSA[1]	6.7	19.9	21.9	14.7	14.1	11.9	6.4	3.1	1.4	36.0
U.S.	6.4	19.9	20.7	12.9	14.1	12.3	7.6	4.2	1.9	37.4

Note: (1) Figures cover the Denver-Aurora-Lakewood, CO Metropolitan Statistical Area—see Appendix B for areas included
Source: U.S. Census Bureau, 2011-2013 American Community Survey 3-Year Estimates

Gender

Area	Males	Females	Males per 100 Females
City	317,325	317,360	100.0
MSA[1]	1,318,148	1,329,879	99.1
U.S.	154,451,010	159,410,713	96.9

Note: (1) Figures cover the Denver-Aurora-Lakewood, CO Metropolitan Statistical Area—see Appendix B for areas included
Source: U.S. Census Bureau, 2011-2013 American Community Survey 3-Year Estimates

Religious Groups by Family

Area	Catholic	Baptist	Non-Den.	Methodist[2]	Lutheran	LDS[3]	Pentecostal	Presbyterian[4]	Muslim[5]	Judaism
MSA[1]	16.1	3.0	4.6	1.7	2.1	2.4	1.2	1.6	0.6	0.6
U.S.	19.1	9.3	4.0	4.0	2.3	2.0	1.9	1.6	0.8	0.7

Note: Figures are the number of adherents as a percentage of the total population; (1) Figures cover the Denver-Aurora-Broomfield, CO Metropolitan Statistical Area—see Appendix B for areas included; (2) Methodist/Pietist; (3) Latter Day Saints; (4) Reformed; (5) Figures are estimates
Source: Association of Statisticians of American Religious Bodies, 2010 U.S. Religion Census: Religious Congregations & Membership Study

Religious Groups by Tradition

Area	Catholic	Evangelical Protestant	Mainline Protestant	Other Tradition	Black Protestant	Orthodox
MSA[1]	16.1	11.1	4.5	4.6	0.4	0.3
U.S.	19.1	16.2	7.3	4.3	1.6	0.3

Note: Figures are the number of adherents as a percentage of the total population; (1) Figures cover the Denver-Aurora-Broomfield, CO Metropolitan Statistical Area—see Appendix B for areas included
Source: Association of Statisticians of American Religious Bodies, 2010 U.S. Religion Census: Religious Congregations & Membership Study

ECONOMY

Gross Metropolitan Product

Area	2012	2013	2014	2015	Rank[2]
MSA[1]	167.9	174.8	182.6	192.6	18

Note: Figures are in billions of dollars; (1) Figures cover the Denver-Aurora-Lakewood, CO Metropolitan Statistical Area—see Appendix B for areas included; (2) Rank is based on 2015 data and ranges from 1 to 363
Source: The U.S. Conference of Mayors, U.S. Metro Economies: GMP and Employment 2013-2015, June 2014

Economic Growth

Area	2010-12 (%)	2013 (%)	2014 (%)	2015 (%)	Rank[2]
MSA[1]	2.1	2.8	2.6	3.8	47
U.S.	2.1	2.0	2.3	3.2	–

Note: Figures are real gross metropolitan product (GMP) growth rates and represent annual average percent change; (1) Figures cover the Denver-Aurora-Lakewood, CO Metropolitan Statistical Area—see Appendix B for areas included; (2) Rank is based on 2015 data and ranges from 1 to 363
Source: The U.S. Conference of Mayors, U.S. Metro Economies: GMP and Employment 2013-2015, June 2014

Metropolitan Area Exports

Area	2008	2009	2010	2011	2012	2013	Rank[2]
MSA[1]	4,633.5	4,309.8	4,990.9	3,771.3	3,355.8	3,618.4	69

Note: Figures are in millions of dollars; (1) Figures cover the Denver-Aurora-Lakewood, CO Metropolitan Statistical Area—see Appendix B for areas included; (2) Rank is based on 2013 data and ranges from 1 to 387
Source: U.S. Department of Commerce, International Trade Administration, Office of Trade & Industry Information, Manufacturing & Services, data extracted April 3, 2015

Building Permits

Area	Single-Family			Multi-Family			Total		
	2013	2014	Pct. Chg.	2013	2014	Pct. Chg.	2013	2014	Pct. Chg.
City	1,284	1,710	33.2	4,586	4,248	-7.4	5,870	5,958	1.5
MSA[1]	6,965	8,064	15.8	8,510	7,703	-9.5	15,475	15,767	1.9
U.S.	620,802	634,597	2.2	370,020	411,766	11.3	990,822	1,046,363	5.6

Note: (1) Figures cover the Denver-Aurora-Lakewood, CO Metropolitan Statistical Area—see Appendix B for areas included; Figures represent new, privately-owned housing units authorized (unadjusted data); All permit data are based on estimates with imputation.
Source: U.S. Census Bureau, Manufacturing, Mining, and Construction Statistics, Building Permits, 2013, 2014

Bankruptcy Filings

Area	Business Filings			Nonbusiness Filings		
	2013	2014	% Chg.	2013	2014	% Chg.
Denver County	126	69	-45.2	2,829	2,203	-22.1
U.S.	33,212	26,983	-18.8	1,038,720	909,812	-12.4

Note: Business filings include Chapter 7, Chapter 11, Chapter 12, and Chapter 13; Nonbusiness filings include Chapter 7, Chapter 11, and Chapter 13
Source: Administrative Office of the U.S. Courts, Business and Nonbusiness Bankruptcy, County Cases Commenced by Chapter of the Bankruptcy Code, During the 12- Month Period Ending December 31, 2013 and Business and Nonbusiness Bankruptcy, County Cases Commenced by Chapter of the Bankruptcy Code, During the 12- Month Period Ending December 31, 2014

Housing Vacancy Rates

Area	Gross Vacancy Rate[2] (%)			Year-Round Vacancy Rate[3] (%)			Rental Vacancy Rate[4] (%)			Homeowner Vacancy Rate[5] (%)		
	2012	2013	2014	2012	2013	2014	2012	2013	2014	2012	2013	2014
MSA[1]	6.3	6.3	6.1	5.9	5.5	5.1	4.7	5.3	3.3	1.5	1.2	0.8
U.S.	13.8	13.6	13.4	10.8	10.7	10.4	8.7	8.3	7.6	2.0	2.0	1.9

Note: (1) Figures cover the Denver-Aurora-Lakewood, CO Metropolitan Statistical Area—see Appendix B for areas included; (2) The percentage of the total housing inventory that is vacant; (3) The percentage of the housing inventory (excluding seasonal units) that is year-round vacant; (4) The percentage of rental inventory that is vacant for rent; (5) The percentage of homeowner inventory that is vacant for sale
Source: U.S. Census Bureau, Housing Vacancies and Homeownership Annual Statistics: 2014

INCOME

Income

Area	Per Capita ($)	Median Household ($)	Average Household ($)
City	33,654	50,728	75,906
MSA[1]	33,364	62,229	83,895
U.S.	27,884	52,176	72,897

Note: (1) Figures cover the Denver-Aurora-Lakewood, CO Metropolitan Statistical Area—see Appendix B for areas included
Source: U.S. Census Bureau, 2011-2013 American Community Survey 3-Year Estimates

Household Income Distribution

Area	Percent of Households Earning							
	Under $15,000	$15,000 -24,999	$25,000 -34,999	$35,000 -49,999	$50,000 -74,999	$75,000 -99,000	$100,000 -149,999	$150,000 and up
City	14.6	10.4	10.7	13.5	16.6	11.3	11.4	11.4
MSA[1]	9.7	8.5	9.1	12.8	18.4	13.2	15.5	12.8
U.S.	13.0	10.9	10.3	13.6	17.9	11.9	12.7	9.6

Note: (1) Figures cover the Denver-Aurora-Lakewood, CO Metropolitan Statistical Area—see Appendix B for areas included
Source: U.S. Census Bureau, 2011-2013 American Community Survey 3-Year Estimates

Poverty Rate

Area	All Ages	Under 18 Years Old	18 to 64 Years Old	65 Years and Over
City	18.7	28.3	16.9	11.2
MSA[1]	12.6	17.6	11.5	7.3
U.S.	15.9	22.4	14.8	9.5

Note: Figures are percentage of people whose income during the past 12 months was below the poverty level; (1) Figures cover the Denver-Aurora-Lakewood, CO Metropolitan Statistical Area—see Appendix B for areas included
Source: U.S. Census Bureau, 2011-2013 American Community Survey 3-Year Estimates

EMPLOYMENT

Labor Force and Employment

Area	Civilian Labor Force			Workers Employed		
	Dec. 2013	Dec. 2014	% Chg.	Dec. 2013	Dec. 2014	% Chg.
City	364,755	371,168	1.8	343,595	356,126	3.6
MSA[1]	1,470,470	1,497,400	1.8	1,386,478	1,437,876	3.7
U.S.	154,408,000	155,521,000	0.7	144,423,000	147,190,000	1.9

Note: Data is not seasonally adjusted and covers workers 16 years of age and older; (1) Figures cover the Denver-Aurora-Lakewood, CO Metropolitan Statistical Area—see Appendix B for areas included
Source: Bureau of Labor Statistics, Local Area Unemployment Statistics

Unemployment Rate

Area	2014											
	Jan.	Feb.	Mar.	Apr.	May	Jun.	Jul.	Aug.	Sep.	Oct.	Nov.	Dec.
City	6.2	6.1	6.0	5.2	4.8	4.9	4.7	4.5	4.1	3.9	4.0	4.1
MSA[1]	6.1	6.1	5.9	5.2	4.8	4.9	4.8	4.5	4.0	3.9	4.0	4.0
U.S.	7.0	7.0	6.8	5.9	6.1	6.3	6.5	6.3	5.7	5.5	5.5	5.4

Note: Data is not seasonally adjusted and covers workers 16 years of age and older; (1) Figures cover the Denver-Aurora-Lakewood, CO Metropolitan Statistical Area—see Appendix B for areas included
Source: Bureau of Labor Statistics, Local Area Unemployment Statistics

Employment by Occupation

Occupation Classification	City (%)	MSA[1] (%)	U.S. (%)
Management, Business, Science, and Arts	43.8	41.6	36.2
Natural Resources, Construction, and Maintenance	7.1	8.3	9.0
Production, Transportation, and Material Moving	8.2	8.8	12.1
Sales and Office	22.8	25.0	24.4
Service	18.0	16.4	18.3

Note: Figures cover employed civilians 16 years of age and older; (1) Figures cover the Denver-Aurora-Lakewood, CO Metropolitan Statistical Area—see Appendix B for areas included
Source: U.S. Census Bureau, 2011-2013 American Community Survey 3-Year Estimates

Employment by Industry

Sector	MSA[1]		U.S.
	Number of Employees	Percent of Total	Percent of Total
Construction, Mining, and Logging	95,100	6.9	5.0
Education and Health Services	173,800	12.6	15.5
Financial Activities	99,600	7.2	5.7
Government	190,800	13.9	15.8
Information	44,000	3.2	2.0
Leisure and Hospitality	147,900	10.8	10.3
Manufacturing	66,600	4.8	8.7
Other Services	53,500	3.9	4.0
Professional and Business Services	245,200	17.8	13.8
Retail Trade	135,600	9.9	11.4
Transportation, Warehousing, and Utilities	53,300	3.9	3.9
Wholesale Trade	68,600	5.0	4.2

Note: Figures are non-farm employment as of December 2014. Figures are not seasonally adjusted and include workers 16 years of age and older; (1) Figures cover the Denver-Aurora-Lakewood, CO Metropolitan Statistical Area—see Appendix B for areas included; n/a not available
Source: Bureau of Labor Statistics, Current Employment Statistics, Employment, Hours, and Earnings

Occupations with Greatest Projected Employment Growth: 2012 – 2022

Occupation[1]	2012 Employment	2022 Projected Employment	Numeric Employment Change	Percent Employment Change
Combined Food Preparation and Serving Workers, Including Fast Food	60,670	77,380	16,710	27.5
Secretaries and Administrative Assistants, Except Legal, Medical, and Executive	63,150	77,880	14,730	23.3
Retail Salespersons	79,300	94,000	14,700	18.5
Customer Service Representatives	45,990	59,210	13,220	28.8
Registered Nurses	42,200	53,270	11,070	26.2
General and Operations Managers	42,170	52,340	10,170	24.1
Accountants and Auditors	33,870	43,490	9,620	28.4
Personal Care Aides	16,940	26,210	9,270	54.7
Janitors and Cleaners, Except Maids and Housekeeping Cleaners	36,300	45,470	9,170	25.3
Business Operations Specialists, All Other	42,990	51,450	8,460	19.7

Note: Projections cover Colorado; (1) Sorted by numeric employment change
Source: www.projectionscentral.com, State Occupational Projections, 2012–2022 Long-Term Projections

Fastest Growing Occupations: 2012 – 2022

Occupation[1]	2012 Employment	2022 Projected Employment	Numeric Employment Change	Percent Employment Change
Service Unit Operators, Oil, Gas, and Mining	3,520	6,290	2,770	78.4
Derrick Operators, Oil and Gas	630	1,110	480	76.0
Rotary Drill Operators, Oil and Gas	1,280	2,200	920	71.5
Roustabouts, Oil and Gas	2,770	4,710	1,940	70.2
Interpreters and Translators	1,510	2,550	1,040	68.5
Petroleum Engineers	1,500	2,500	1,000	66.9
Pump Operators, Except Wellhead Pumpers	700	1,160	460	64.9
Helpers—Brickmasons, Blockmasons, Stonemasons, and Tile and Marble Setters	200	320	120	61.3
Insulation Workers, Mechanical	420	680	260	61.2
Information Security Analysts	1,240	1,960	720	57.8

Note: Projections cover Colorado; (1) Sorted by percent employment change and excludes occupations with numeric employment change less than 100
Source: www.projectionscentral.com, State Occupational Projections, 2012–2022 Long-Term Projections

Average Wages

Occupation	$/Hr.	Occupation	$/Hr.
Accountants and Auditors	37.01	Maids and Housekeeping Cleaners	10.24
Automotive Mechanics	20.60	Maintenance and Repair Workers	19.12
Bookkeepers	19.12	Marketing Managers	67.90
Carpenters	20.42	Nuclear Medicine Technologists	38.70
Cashiers	10.56	Nurses, Licensed Practical	23.98
Clerks, General Office	17.84	Nurses, Registered	34.76
Clerks, Receptionists/Information	15.02	Nursing Assistants	14.69
Clerks, Shipping/Receiving	16.05	Packers and Packagers, Hand	11.03
Computer Programmers	46.46	Physical Therapists	36.46
Computer Systems Analysts	46.48	Postal Service Mail Carriers	25.20
Computer User Support Specialists	27.55	Real Estate Brokers	40.15
Cooks, Restaurant	11.63	Retail Salespersons	12.90
Dentists	79.78	Sales Reps., Exc. Tech./Scientific	34.55
Electrical Engineers	46.18	Sales Reps., Tech./Scientific	47.66
Electricians	23.46	Secretaries, Exc. Legal/Med./Exec.	18.22
Financial Managers	73.42	Security Guards	14.70
First-Line Supervisors/Managers, Sales	20.81	Surgeons	115.12
Food Preparation Workers	10.87	Teacher Assistants	13.30
General and Operations Managers	64.10	Teachers, Elementary School	25.60
Hairdressers/Cosmetologists	13.60	Teachers, Secondary School	27.10
Internists	104.45	Telemarketers	14.69
Janitors and Cleaners	11.61	Truck Drivers, Heavy/Tractor-Trailer	22.34
Landscaping/Groundskeeping Workers	13.64	Truck Drivers, Light/Delivery Svcs.	16.52
Lawyers	65.99	Waiters and Waitresses	10.01

Note: Wage data covers the Denver-Aurora-Broomfield, CO Metropolitan Statistical Area—see Appendix B for areas included; Hourly wages for elementary/secondary school teachers and teacher assistants were calculated by the editors from annual wage data assuming a 40 hour work week; n/a not available.
Source: Bureau of Labor Statistics, Metro Area Occupational Employment and Wage Estimates, May 2014

TAXES

State Corporate Income Tax Rates

State	Tax Rate (%)	Income Brackets ($)	Num. of Brackets	Financial Institution Tax Rate (%)[a]	Federal Income Tax Ded.
Colorado	4.63	Flat rate	1	4.63	No

Note: Tax rates as of January 1, 2015; (a) Rates listed are the corporate income tax rate applied to financial institutions or excise taxes based on income. Some states have other taxes based upon the value of deposits or shares.
Source: Federation of Tax Administrators, "State Corporate Income Tax Rates, 2015"

State Individual Income Tax Rates

State	Tax Rate (%)	Income Brackets ($)	Num. of Brackets	Personal Exempt. ($)[1] Single	Dependents	Fed. Inc. Tax Ded.
Colorado	4.63	Flat rate	1	4,000 (d)	4,000 (d)	No

Note: Tax rates as of January 1, 2015; Local- and county-level taxes are not included; n/a not applicable; (1) Married joint filers generally receive double the single exemption; (d) These states use the personal exemption amounts provided in the federal Internal Revenue Code.
Source: Federation of Tax Administrators, "State Individual Income Tax Rates, 2015"

Various State and Local Tax Rates

State	State and Local Sales and Use (%)	State Sales and Use (%)	Gasoline[1] (¢/gal.)	Cigarette[2] ($/pack)	Spirits[3] ($/gal.)	Wine[4] ($/gal.)	Beer[5] ($/gal.)
Colorado	7.65	2.90	22	0.84	2.28	0.32	0.08

Note: All tax rates as of January 1, 2015; (1) The American Petroleum Institute has developed a methodology for determining the average tax rate on a gallon of fuel. Rates may include any of the following: excise taxes, environmental fees, storage tank fees, other fees or taxes, general sales tax, and local taxes. In states where gasoline is subject to the general sales tax, or where the fuel tax is based on the average sale price, the average rate determined by API is sensitive to changes in the price of gasoline. States that fully or partially apply general sales taxes to gasoline: CA, CO, GA, IL, IN, MI, NY; (2) The federal excise tax of $1.0066 per pack and local taxes are not included; (3) Rates are those applicable to off-premise sales of 40% alcohol by volume (a.b.v.) distilled spirits in 750ml containers. Local excise taxes are excluded; (4) Rates are those applicable to off-premise sales of 11% a.b.v. non-carbonated wine in 750ml containers; (5) Rates are those applicable to off-premise sales of 4.7% a.b.v. beer in 12 ounce containers.
Source: Tax Foundation, 2015 Facts & Figures: How Does Your State Compare?

State Business Tax Climate Index Rankings

State	Overall Rank	Corporate Tax Index Rank	Individual Income Tax Index Rank	Sales Tax Index Rank	Unemployment Insurance Tax Index Rank	Property Tax Index Rank
Colorado	20	12	16	43	35	22

Note: The index is a measure of how each state's tax laws affect economic performance. The lower the rank, the more favorable a state's tax system is for business. States without a given tax are given a ranking of 1. The scores/rankings for the District of Columbia do not affect other states. The 2015 index represents the tax climate as of July 1, 2014.
Source: Tax Foundation, State Business Tax Climate Index 2015

COMMERCIAL REAL ESTATE

Office Market

Market Area	Inventory (sq. ft.)	Vacancy Rate (%)	Under Construction (sq. ft.)	YTD Net Absorption (sq. ft.)	Total Average Asking Rent ($/sq. ft./year)
Denver	92,382,550	14.4	1,727,049	1,524,689	23.63
National	4,745,108,508	14.3	71,190,461	51,084,126	27.40

Source: Newmark Grubb Knight Frank, National Office Market Report, 4th Quarter 2014

Industrial/Warehouse/R&D Market

Market Area	Inventory (sq. ft.)	Vacancy Rate (%)	Under Construction (sq. ft.)	YTD Net Absorption (sq. ft.)	Total Average Asking Rent ($/sq. ft./year)
Denver	176,278,681	3.8	2,232,867	4,236,371	7.70
National	14,238,613,765	7.2	134,387,407	185,246,438	5.64

Source: Newmark Grubb Knight Frank, National Industrial Market Report, 4th Quarter 2014

COMMERCIAL UTILITIES

Typical Monthly Electric Bills

Area	Commercial Service ($/month)		Industrial Service ($/month)	
	1,500 kWh	40 kW demand 14,000 kWh	1,000 kW demand 200,000 kWh	50,000 kW demand 32,500,000 kWh
City	198	1,525	28,386	2,329,788
Average[1]	201	1,653	26,124	2,639,743

Note: Figures are based on annualized 2014 rates; (1) Average based on 180 utilities surveyed
Source: Edison Electric Institute, Typical Bills and Average Rates Report, Summer 2014

TRANSPORTATION

Means of Transportation to Work

Area	Car/Truck/Van		Public Transportation			Bicycle	Walked	Other Means	Worked at Home
	Drove Alone	Car-pooled	Bus	Subway	Railroad				
City	69.6	8.8	6.0	0.6	0.2	2.4	4.8	1.3	6.3
MSA[1]	75.9	9.0	3.7	0.4	0.2	1.0	2.2	1.2	6.4
U.S.	76.4	9.6	2.6	1.8	0.6	0.6	2.8	1.3	4.3

Note: Figures are percentages and cover workers 16 years of age and older; (1) Figures cover the Denver-Aurora-Lakewood, CO Metropolitan Statistical Area—see Appendix B for areas included
Source: U.S. Census Bureau, 2011-2013 American Community Survey 3-Year Estimates

Travel Time to Work

Area	Less Than 10 Minutes	10 to 19 Minutes	20 to 29 Minutes	30 to 44 Minutes	45 to 59 Minutes	60 to 89 Minutes	90 Minutes or More
City	9.9	30.2	24.8	23.1	6.5	3.9	1.5
MSA[1]	9.1	26.1	23.8	25.4	8.7	5.0	1.9
U.S.	13.3	29.7	20.9	20.2	7.7	5.7	2.6

Note: Figures are percentages and include workers 16 years old and over; (1) Figures cover the Denver-Aurora-Lakewood, CO Metropolitan Statistical Area—see Appendix B for areas included
Source: U.S. Census Bureau, 2011-2013 American Community Survey 3-Year Estimates

Travel Time Index

Area	1985	1990	1995	2000	2005	2010	2011
Urban Area[1]	1.10	1.12	1.21	1.29	1.31	1.27	1.27
Average[2]	1.09	1.14	1.16	1.19	1.23	1.18	1.18

Note: Travel Time Index—the ratio of travel time in the peak period to the travel time at free-flow conditions. For example, a value of 1.30 indicates a 20-minute free-flow trip takes 26 minutes in the peak. Free-flow speeds (60 mph on freeways and 35 mph on principal arterials) are used as the comparison threshold; (1) Covers the Denver-Aurora CO urban area; (2) average of 498 urban areas
Source: Texas Transportation Institute, Urban Mobility Report 2012, December 2012

Public Transportation

Agency Name / Mode of Transportation	Vehicles Operated in Maximum Service	Annual Unlinked Passenger Trips (in thous.)	Annual Passenger Miles (in thous.)
Denver Regional Transportation District (RTD)			
Bus (directly operated)	452	52,111.9	276,564.2
Bus (purchased transportation)	367	24,236.8	124,350.8
Demand Response (directly operated)	8	56.0	733.7
Demand Response (purchased transportation)	362	1,174.3	9,927.0
Light Rail (directly operated)	139	23,773.8	201,995.3

Source: Federal Transit Administration, National Transit Database, 2013

Air Transportation

Airport Name and Code / Type of Service	Passenger Airlines[1]	Passenger Enplanements	Freight Carriers[2]	Freight (lbs.)
Denver International (DEN)				
Domestic service (U.S. carriers - 2014)	29	24,875,236	19	209,229,037
International service (U.S. carriers - 2013)	12	655,399	3	611,491

Note: (1) Includes all U.S.-based major, minor and commuter airlines that carried at least one passenger during the year; (2) Includes all U.S.-based airlines and freight carriers that transported at least one lb. of freight during the year.
Source: Bureau of Transportation Statistics, The Intermodal Transportation Database, Air Carriers: T-100 Domestic Market (U.S. Carriers), 2014; Bureau of Transportation Statistics, The Intermodal Transportation Database, Air Carriers: T-100 International Market (U.S. Carriers), 2013

Other Transportation Statistics

Major Highways:	I-25; I-70; I-76
Amtrak Service:	Yes
Major Waterways/Ports:	None

Source: Amtrak.com; Google Maps

BUSINESSES

Major Business Headquarters

Company Name	Rankings	
	Fortune[1]	Forbes[2]
DaVita HealthCare Partners	230	-
Gates Corporation	-	168
Leprino Foods	-	177
ProBuild Holdings	-	98

Note: (1) Fortune 500—companies that produce a 10-K are ranked 1 to 500 based on 2013 revenue; (2) all private companies with at least $2 billion in annual revenue through the end of their most current fiscal year are ranked 1 to 221; companies listed are headquartered in the city; dashes indicate no ranking Source: Fortune, "Fortune 500," June 16, 2014; Forbes, "America's Largest Private Companies," November 5, 2014

Fast-Growing Businesses

According to *Inc.*, Denver is home to three of America's 500 fastest-growing private companies: **Stoneside Blinds & Shades** (#220); **Phidiax** (#317); **Swiftpage** (#440). Criteria: must be an independent, privately-held, for-profit, U.S. corporation, proprietorship or partnership; revenues must be at least $100,000 in 2010 and $2 million in 2013; must have four-year operating/sales history. Holding companies, regulated banks, and utilities were excluded. *Inc., "America's 500 Fastest-Growing Private Companies," September 2014*

According to *Fortune*, Denver is home to one of the 100 fastest-growing companies in the world: **Kodiak Oil & Gas** (#5). Companies were ranked by their revenue growth rate; their EPS growth rate; and their three-year annualized total return to investors for the period ending June 30, 2014. Criteria for inclusion: a company, foreign or domestic, must trade on a major U.S. stock exchange; must file quarterly reports with the SEC; must have a minimum market capitalization of $250 million; must have a stock price of at least $5 on June 30, 2014; must have been trading continuously since June 30, 2010; must have revenue and net income for the four quarters ended on or before April 30, 2014, of at least $50 million and $10 million, respectively; and must have posted a compound annual growth in revenue and earnings per share of at least 20% annually over the three years ending on or before April 30, 2014. Real estate investment trusts, limited-liability companies, limited parterships, business development companies, closed end investment firms, and companies that lost money in the quarter ending April 30, 2014 were excluded. *Fortune, "100 Fastest-Growing Companies," August 28, 2014*

According to *Initiative for a Competitive Inner City (ICIC)*, Denver is home to one of America's 100 fastest-growing "inner city" companies: **CAM Services** (#91). Criteria for inclusion: company must be headquartered in or have 51 percent or more of its physical operations in an economically distressed urban area; must be an independent, for-profit corporation, partnership or proprietorship; must have 10 or more employees and have a five-year sales history that includes sales of at least $200,000 in the base year and at least $1 million in the current year with no decrease in sales over the two most recent years. This year, for the first time in the list's 16-year history, the Inner City 100 consists of 10 fast-growing businesses in 10 industry categories. Companies were ranked overall by revenue growth over the five-year period between 2009 and 2013 as well as within their respective industry categories. *Initiative for a Competitive Inner City (ICIC), "Inner City 100 Companies, 2014"*

According to Deloitte, Denver is home to one of North America's 500 fastest-growing high-technology companies: **Junction Solutions** (#495). Companies are ranked by percentage growth in revenue over a five-year period. Criteria for inclusion: company must be headquartered within North America; must own proprietary intellectual property or proprietary technology that contributes to a significant portion of the company's operating revenue, or devote a significant proportion of revenues to research and development of technology; must have been in business for a minumum of five years with 2009 operating revenues of at least $50,000 USD/CD and 2013 operating revenues of at least $5 million USD/CD. *Deloitte Touche Tohmatsu, 2014 Technology Fast 500™*

Minority Business Opportunity

Denver is home to one company which is on the *Black Enterprise* Industrial/Service 100 list (100 largest companies based on gross sales): **RTL Networks** (#99). Criteria: operational in previous calendar year; at least 51% black-owned and manufactures/owns the product it sells or provides industrial or consumer services. Brokerages, real estate firms and firms that provide professional services are not eligible. *Black Enterprise, B.E. 100s, 2014*

Denver is home to five companies which are on the *Hispanic Business* 500 list (500 largest U.S. Hispanic-owned companies based on 2012 revenue): **Mike Shaw Automotive Group** (#22); **Venoco** (#23); **Alpine Buick GMC** (#129); **Istonish** (#336); **The Idea Marketing** (#482). Companies included must show at least 51 percent ownership by Hispanic U.S. citizens, and must maintain headquarters in one of the 50 states or Washington, D.C. *Hispanic Business, "Hispanic Business 500," June 20, 2013*

Denver is home to one company which is on the *Hispanic Business* Fastest-Growing 100 list (greatest sales growth from 2008 to 2012): **Mike Shaw Automotive** (#87). Companies included must show at least 51 percent ownership by Hispanic U.S. citizens, and must maintain headquarters in one of the 50 states or Washington, D.C. In addition, companies must have minimum revenues of $200,000 for calendar year 2008. *Hispanic Business, June 20, 2013*

Minority- and Women-Owned Businesses

Group	All Firms		Firms with Paid Employees			
	Firms	Sales ($000)	Firms	Sales ($000)	Employees	Payroll ($000)
Asian	2,498	800,497	834	744,502	6,198	148,319
Black	2,922	289,901	265	227,986	2,260	59,624
Hispanic	5,893	1,099,027	824	894,252	7,765	231,497
Women	20,354	4,462,192	3,023	3,949,844	22,574	750,709
All Firms	67,500	107,004,756	17,531	104,443,789	393,770	20,209,927

Note: Figures cover firms located in the city; minority- and women-owned business are defined as firms in which the corresponding group own 51% or more of the stock or equity of the company
Source: U.S. Census Bureau, 2007 Economic Census, Survey of Business Owners (2012 Survey of Business Owners data will be released starting in June 2015)

HOTELS & CONVENTION CENTERS

Hotels/Motels

Area	5 Star		4 Star		3 Star		2 Star		1 Star		Not Rated	
	Num.	Pct.[3]	Num.	Pct.[3]	Num.	Pct.[3]	Num.	Pct.[3]	Num.	Pct.[3]	Num.	Pct.[3]
City[1]	2	0.7	17	6.1	103	36.9	138	49.5	6	2.2	13	4.7
Total[2]	166	0.9	1,264	7.0	5,718	31.8	9,340	52.0	411	2.3	1,070	6.0

Note: (1) Figures cover Denver and vicinity; (2) Figures cover all 100 cities in this book; (3) Percentage of hotels which have a given star rating; Star ratings are determined by expedia.com and offer an indication of the general quality of a particular hotel.
Source: expedia.com, April 2, 2015

The Denver-Aurora-Lakewood, CO metro area is home to one of the best hotels in the U.S. according to *Travel & Leisure*: **Four Seasons Hotel Denver**. Criteria: service; location; rooms; food; and value. The list includes the top 236 hotels in the U.S. *Travel & Leisure, "T+L 500, The World's Best Hotels 2015"*

Major Convention Centers

Name	Overall Space (sq. ft.)	Exhibit Space (sq. ft.)	Meeting Space (sq. ft.)	Meeting Rooms
Colorado Convention Center	2,200,000	584,000	100,000	63

Note: Table includes convention centers located in the Denver-Aurora-Lakewood, CO metro area; n/a not available
Source: Original research

Living Environment

COST OF LIVING

Cost of Living Index

Composite Index	Groceries	Housing	Utilities	Trans- portation	Health Care	Misc. Goods/ Services
107.2	98.2	123.8	97.9	101.4	103.7	102.3

Note: The Cost of Living Index measures regional differences in the cost of consumer goods and services, excluding taxes and non-consumer expenditures, for professional and managerial households in the top income quintile. It is based on more than 50,000 prices covering almost 60 different items for which prices are collected three times a year by chambers of commerce, economic development organizations or university applied economic centers in each participating urban area. The numbers shown should be read as a percentage above or below the national average of 100. For example, a value of 115.4 in the groceries column indicates that grocery prices are 15.4% higher than the national average. Small differences in the index numbers should not be interpreted as significant; Figures cover the Denver CO urban area.
Source: The Council for Community and Economic Research, ACCRA Cost of Living Index, 2014

Grocery Prices

Area[1]	T-Bone Steak ($/pound)	Frying Chicken ($/pound)	Whole Milk ($/half gal.)	Eggs ($/dozen)	Orange Juice ($/64 oz.)	Coffee ($/11.5 oz.)
City[2]	10.29	1.35	2.05	2.10	3.66	5.13
Avg.	10.40	1.37	2.40	1.99	3.46	4.27
Min.	8.48	0.93	1.37	1.30	2.83	2.99
Max.	14.20	2.44	3.62	4.02	6.42	6.96

Note: (1) Values for the local area are compared with the average, minimum and maximum values for all 308 areas in the Cost of Living Index; (2) Figures cover the Denver CO urban area; **T-Bone Steak** *(price per pound);* **Frying Chicken** *(price per pound, whole fryer);* **Whole Milk** *(half gallon carton);* **Eggs** *(price per dozen, Grade A, large);* **Orange Juice** *(64 oz. Tropicana or Florida Natural);* **Coffee** *(11.5 oz. can, vacuum-packed, Maxwell House, Hills Bros, or Folgers).*
Source: The Council for Community and Economic Research, ACCRA Cost of Living Index, 2014

Housing and Utility Costs

Area[1]	New Home Price ($)	Apartment Rent ($/month)	All Electric ($/month)	Part Electric ($/month)	Other Energy ($/month)	Telephone ($/month)
City[2]	377,658	1,158	-	96.13	68.50	27.60
Avg.	305,838	919	181.00	93.66	73.14	27.95
Min.	183,142	480	112.00	42.06	23.42	17.16
Max.	1,358,576	3,851	594.00	180.03	440.99	40.42

Note: (1) Values for the local area are compared with the average, minimum and maximum values for all 308 areas in the Cost of Living Index; (2) Figures cover the Denver CO urban area; **New Home Price** *(2,400 sf living area, 8,000 sf lot, in urban area with full utilities);* **Apartment Rent** *(950 sf 2 bedroom/1.5 or 2 bath, unfurnished, excluding all utilities except water);* **All Electric** *(average monthly cost for an all-electric home);* **Part Electric** *(average monthly cost for a part-electric home);* **Other Energy** *(average monthly cost for natural gas, fuel oil, coal, wood, and any other forms of energy except electricity);* **Telephone** *(price includes basic monthly rate for a private residential line plus additional local usage charges incurred by a family of four).*
Source: The Council for Community and Economic Research, ACCRA Cost of Living Index, 2014

Health Care, Transportation, and Other Costs

Area[1]	Doctor ($/visit)	Dentist ($/visit)	Optometrist ($/visit)	Gasoline ($/gallon)	Beauty Salon ($/visit)	Men's Shirt ($)
City[2]	120.48	85.30	99.71	3.46	36.43	29.58
Avg.	102.86	87.89	97.66	3.44	34.37	26.74
Min.	67.47	65.78	51.18	3.00	17.43	12.79
Max.	173.50	150.14	235.00	4.33	64.28	49.50

Note: (1) Values for the local area are compared with the average, minimum and maximum values for all 308 areas in the Cost of Living Index; (2) Figures cover the Denver CO urban area; **Doctor** *(general practitioners routine exam of an established patient);* **Dentist** *(adult teeth cleaning and periodic oral examination);* **Optometrist** *(full vision eye exam for established adult patient);* **Gasoline** *(one gallon regular unleaded, national brand, including all taxes, cash price at self-service pump if available);* **Beauty Salon** *(woman's shampoo, trim, and blow-dry);* **Men's Shirt** *(cotton/polyester dress shirt, pinpoint weave, long sleeves).*
Source: The Council for Community and Economic Research, ACCRA Cost of Living Index, 2014

HOUSING

House Price Index (HPI)

Area	National Ranking[2]	Quarterly Change (%)	One-Year Change (%)	Five-Year Change (%)
MSA[1]	24	1.73	10.18	24.67
U.S.[3]	–	1.35	4.91	11.59

Note: The HPI is a weighted repeat sales index. It measures average price changes in repeat sales or refinancings on the same properties. This information is obtained by reviewing repeat mortgage transactions on single-family properties whose mortgages have been purchased or securitized by Fannie Mae or Freddie Mac in January 1975; (1) Denver-Aurora-Lakewood Metropolitan Statistical Area—see Appendix B for areas included; (2) Rankings are based on annual percentage change for all metro areas containing at least 15,000 transactions over the last 10 years and ranges from 1 to 275; (3) figures based on a weighted average of Census Division estimates using a seasonally adjusted, purchase-only index; all figures are for the period ending December 31, 2014
Source: Federal Housing Finance Agency, House Price Index, February 26, 2015

Median Single-Family Home Prices

Area	2012	2013	2014p	Percent Change 2013 to 2014
MSA[1]	252.4	280.6	310.2	10.5
U.S. Average	177.2	197.4	209.0	5.9

Note: Figures are median sales prices of existing single-family homes in thousands of dollars; (p) preliminary; n/a not available; (1) Denver-Aurora-Lakewood, CO Metropolitan Statistical Area—see Appendix B for areas included
Source: National Association of Realtors, Median Sales Price of Existing Single-Family Homes for Metropolitan Areas, 4th Quarter 2014

Qualifying Income Based on Median Sales Price of Existing Single-Family Homes

Area	With 5% Down ($)	With 10% Down ($)	With 20% Down ($)
MSA[1]	69,179	65,538	58,256
U.S. Average	45,863	43,449	38,621

Note: Figures are preliminary; Qualifying income is based on a mortgage rate of 4.0%. Monthly principal and interest payment is limited to 25% of income; n/a not available; (1) Denver-Aurora-Lakewood, CO Metropolitan Statistical Area—see Appendix B for areas included
Source: National Association of Realtors, Qualifying Income Based on Median Sales Price of Existing Single-Family Homes for Metropolitan Areas, 4th Quarter 2014

Median Apartment Condo-Coop Home Prices

Area	2012	2013	2014p	Percent Change 2013 to 2014
MSA[1]	n/a	n/a	n/a	n/a
U.S. Average	173.7	194.9	205.1	5.2

Note: Figures are median sales prices of existing apartment condo-coop homes in thousands of dollars; (p) preliminary; n/a not available; (1) Denver-Aurora-Lakewood, CO Metropolitan Statistical Area—see Appendix B for areas included
Source: National Association of Realtors, Median Sales Price of Existing Apartment Condo-Coop Homes for Metropolitan Areas, 4th Quarter 2014

Gross Monthly Rent

Area	Under $200	$200 -299	$300 -499	$500 -749	$750 -999	$1,000 -1,499	$1,500 and up	Median ($)
City	2.7	4.2	4.5	23.1	25.7	25.9	13.9	889
MSA[1]	1.4	2.4	3.2	18.9	26.4	31.9	15.8	977
U.S.	1.7	3.2	7.8	22.1	24.3	26.0	14.9	900

Note: Figures are percentages except for Median; Gross rent is the contract rent plus the estimated average monthly cost of utilities (electricity, gas, and water and sewer) and fuels (oil, coal, kerosene, wood, etc.) if these are paid by the renter (or paid for the renter by someone else); (1) Figures cover the Denver-Aurora-Lakewood, CO Metropolitan Statistical Area—see Appendix B for areas included
Source: U.S. Census Bureau, 2011-2013 American Community Survey 3-Year Estimates

Homeownership Rate

Area	2007 (%)	2008 (%)	2009 (%)	2010 (%)	2011 (%)	2012 (%)	2013 (%)	2014 (%)
MSA[1]	69.5	66.9	65.3	65.7	63.0	61.8	61.0	61.9
U.S.	68.1	67.8	67.4	66.9	66.1	65.4	65.1	64.5

Note: (1) Figures cover the Denver-Aurora-Lakewood, CO Metropolitan Statistical Area—see Appendix B for areas included
Source: U.S. Census Bureau, Housing Vacancies and Homeownership Annual Statistics: 2014

Year Housing Structure Built

Area	2010 or Later	2000 -2009	1990 -1999	1980 -1989	1970 -1979	1960 -1969	1950 -1959	1940 -1949	Before 1940	Median Year
City	1.3	13.8	6.9	8.5	14.0	11.9	16.0	7.0	20.6	1965
MSA[1]	0.9	18.6	15.7	15.2	19.0	10.4	10.0	3.1	7.2	1980
U.S.	0.9	15.0	13.9	13.8	15.8	11.0	10.9	5.4	13.3	1976

Note: Figures are percentages except for Median Year; (1) Figures cover the Denver-Aurora-Lakewood, CO Metropolitan Statistical Area—see Appendix B for areas included
Source: U.S. Census Bureau, 2011-2013 American Community Survey 3-Year Estimates

HEALTH

Health Risk Data

Category	MSA[1] (%)	U.S. (%)
Adults aged 18–64 who have any kind of health care coverage	79.0	79.6
Adults who reported being in good or excellent health	85.0	83.1
Adults who are current smokers	18.0	19.6
Adults who are heavy drinkers[2]	7.5	6.1
Adults who are binge drinkers[3]	21.6	16.9
Adults who are overweight (BMI 25.0 - 29.9)	35.5	35.8
Adults who are obese (BMI 30.0 - 99.8)	20.1	27.6
Adults who participated in any physical activities in the past month	82.9	77.1
Adults 50+ who have ever had a sigmoidoscopy or colonoscopy	68.0	67.3
Women aged 40+ who have had a mammogram within the past two years	70.5	74.0
Men aged 40+ who have had a PSA test within the past two years	41.8	45.2
Adults aged 65+ who have had flu shot within the past year	68.3	60.1
Adults who always wear a seatbelt	94.2	93.8

Note: Data as of 2012 unless otherwise noted; (1) Figures cover the Denver-Aurora, CO Metropolitan Statistical Area—see Appendix B for areas included; (2) Heavy drinkers are classified as males having more than two drinks per day or females having more than one drink per day; (3) Binge drinkers are classified as males having five or more drinks on one occasion or females having four or more drinks on one occasion
Source: Centers for Disease Control and Prevention, Behaviorial Risk Factor Surveillance System, SMART: Selected Metropolitan/Micropolitan Area Risk Trends, 2012 (Note: the CDC has discontinued this dataset but will be releasing a replacement in late 2015)

Chronic Health Indicators

Category	MSA[1] (%)	U.S. (%)
Adults who have ever been told they had a heart attack	3.0	4.5
Adults who have ever been told they had a stroke	1.8	2.9
Adults who have been told they currently have asthma	9.6	8.9
Adults who have ever been told they have arthritis	21.6	25.7
Adults who have ever been told they have diabetes[2]	7.4	9.7
Adults who have ever been told they had skin cancer	6.0	5.7
Adults who have ever been told they had any other types of cancer	5.9	6.5
Adults who have ever been told they have COPD	4.5	6.2
Adults who have ever been told they have kidney disease	2.0	2.5
Adults who have ever been told they have a form of depression	17.3	18.0

Note: Data as of 2012 unless otherwise noted; (1) Figures cover the Denver-Aurora, CO Metropolitan Statistical Area—see Appendix B for areas included; (2) Figures do not include pregnancy-related, borderline, or pre-diabetes
Source: Centers for Disease Control and Prevention, Behaviorial Risk Factor Surveillance System, SMART: Selected Metropolitan/Micropolitan Area Risk Trends, 2012 (Note: the CDC has discontinued this dataset but will be releasing a replacement in late 2015)

Mortality Rates for the Top 10 Causes of Death in the U.S.

ICD-10[a] Sub-Chapter	ICD-10[a] Code	Age-Adjusted Mortality Rate[1] per 100,000 population	
		County[2]	U.S.
Malignant neoplasms	C00-C97	159.5	166.2
Ischaemic heart diseases	I20-I25	79.5	105.7
Other forms of heart disease	I30-I51	41.6	49.3
Chronic lower respiratory diseases	J40-J47	46.4	42.1
Organic, including symptomatic, mental disorders	F01-F09	33.3	38.1
Cerebrovascular diseases	I60-I69	32.3	37.0
Other external causes of accidental injury	W00-X59	44.8	26.9
Other degenerative diseases of the nervous system	G30-G31	33.5	25.6
Diabetes mellitus	E10-E14	19.2	21.3
Hypertensive diseases	I10-I15	18.4	19.4

Note: (a) ICD-10 = International Classification of Diseases 10th Revision; (1) Mortality rates are a three year average covering 2011-2013; (2) Figures cover Denver County
Source: Centers for Disease Control and Prevention, National Center for Health Statistics. Compressed Mortality File 1999-2013 on CDC WONDER Online Database, released October 2014. Data are compiled from the Compressed Mortality File 1999-2013, Series 20 No. 2S, 2014.

Mortality Rates for Selected Causes of Death

ICD-10[a] Sub-Chapter	ICD-10[a] Code	Age-Adjusted Mortality Rate[1] per 100,000 population	
		County[2]	U.S.
Assault	X85-Y09	6.2	5.2
Diseases of the liver	K70-K76	22.2	13.2
Human immunodeficiency virus (HIV) disease	B20-B24	3.1	2.2
Influenza and pneumonia	J09-J18	13.9	15.4
Intentional self-harm	X60-X84	16.1	12.5
Malnutrition	E40-E46	*1.0	0.9
Obesity and other hyperalimentation	E65-E68	1.4	1.8
Renal failure	N17-N19	12.5	13.1
Transport accidents	V01-V99	8.7	11.7
Viral hepatitis	B15-B19	3.5	2.2

Note: (a) ICD-10 = International Classification of Diseases 10th Revision; (1) Mortality rates are a three year average covering 2011-2013; (2) Figures cover Denver County; (*) Unreliable data as per CDC
Source: Centers for Disease Control and Prevention, National Center for Health Statistics. Compressed Mortality File 1999-2013 on CDC WONDER Online Database, released October 2014. Data are compiled from the Compressed Mortality File 1999-2013, Series 20 No. 2S, 2014.

Health Insurance Coverage

Area	With Health Insurance	With Private Health Insurance	With Public Health Insurance	Without Health Insurance	Population Under Age 18 Without Health Insurance
City	83.4	60.8	30.0	16.6	8.9
MSA[1]	85.3	69.4	24.5	14.7	8.9
U.S.	85.2	65.2	31.0	14.8	7.3

Note: Figures are percentages that cover the civilian noninstitutionalized population; (1) Figures cover the Denver-Aurora-Lakewood, CO Metropolitan Statistical Area—see Appendix B for areas included
Source: U.S. Census Bureau, 2011-2013 American Community Survey 3-Year Estimates

Number of Medical Professionals

Area[1]	MDs[2]	DOs[2,3]	Dentists	Podiatrists	Chiropractors	Optometrists
Local (number)	3,563	163	424	43	199	93
Local (rate[4])	562.1	25.7	65.4	6.6	30.7	14.3
U.S. (rate[4])	270.0	20.2	63.1	5.7	25.2	14.9

Note: Data as of 2013 unless noted; (1) Local data covers Denver County; (2) Data as of 2012 and includes all active, non-federal physicians; (3) Doctor of Osteopathic Medicine; (4) rate per 100,000 population
Source: U.S. Department of Health and Human Services, Health Resources and Services Administration, Bureau of Health Professions, Area Resource File (ARF) 2013-2014

Best Hospitals

According to *U.S. News*, the Denver-Aurora-Lakewood, CO metro area is home to four of the best hospitals in the U.S.: **Craig Hospital** (1 specialty); **National Jewish Health, Denver-University of Colorado Hospital** (1 specialty); **Porter Adventist Hospital** (1 specialty); **University of Colorado Hospital** (8 specialties). The hospitals listed were nationally ranked in at least one adult specialty. Only 144 hospitals nationwide were nationally ranked in one or more specialties. Seventeen hospitals in the U.S. made the Honor Roll with high scores in at least six specialties. *U.S. News Online, "America's Best Children's Hospitals 2014-15"*

According to *U.S. News*, the Denver-Aurora-Lakewood, CO metro area is home to one of the best children's hospitals in the U.S.: **Children's Hospital Colorado** (Honor Roll/9 specialties). The hospital listed was highly ranked in at least one pediatric specialty. Eighty-nine children's hospitals in the U.S. were nationally ranked in at least one specialty. Ten children's hospitals in the U.S. made the Honor Roll with high scores in at least three specialties. *U.S. News Online, "America's Best Children's Hospitals 2014-15"*

EDUCATION

Public School District Statistics

District Name	Schls	Pupils	Pupil/ Teacher Ratio	Minority Pupils[1] (%)	Free Lunch Eligible[2] (%)	IEP[3] (%)
Denver, School District No. 1	173	83,377	16.9	79.4	64.9	0.0
Mapleton, School District No. 1	16	8,051	20.2	70.7	58.7	0.0
State Charter School Institute	26	11,756	21.0	54.3	39.7	0.0

Note: Table includes school districts with 2,000 or more students; (1) Percentage of students that are not non-Hispanic white; (2) Percentage of students that are eligible for the free lunch program; (3) Percentage of students that have an Individualized Education Program.
Source: U.S. Department of Education, National Center for Education Statistics, Common Core of Data, Local Education Agency (School District) Universe Survey: School Year 2012-2013; U.S. Department of Education, National Center for Education Statistics, Common Core of Data, Public Elementary/Secondary School Universe Survey: School Year 2012-2013

Best High Schools

According to *The Daily Beast*, Denver is home to two of the best high schools in the U.S.: **D'Evelyn Jr./Sr. High School** (#55); **East High School** (#531); *The Daily Beast* used six indicators culled from school surveys to compare public high schools in the U.S., with graduation and college acceptance rates weighed most heavily. Other criteria included: college-level courses/exams and SAT/ACT scores. *The Daily Beast, "Top High Schools 2014"*

Highest Level of Education

Area	Less than H.S.	H.S. Diploma	Some College, No Deg.	Associate Degree	Bachelor's Degree	Master's Degree	Prof. School Degree	Doctorate Degree
City	13.9	18.2	18.4	5.3	26.9	11.5	3.9	1.9
MSA[1]	10.1	20.8	21.8	7.7	25.5	10.3	2.5	1.4
U.S.	13.7	28.0	21.2	7.9	18.2	7.7	1.9	1.3

Note: Figures cover persons age 25 and over; (1) Figures cover the Denver-Aurora-Lakewood, CO Metropolitan Statistical Area—see Appendix B for areas included
Source: U.S. Census Bureau, 2011-2013 American Community Survey 3-Year Estimates

Educational Attainment by Race

Area	High School Graduate or Higher (%)					Bachelor's Degree or Higher (%)				
	Total	White	Black	Asian	Hisp.[2]	Total	White	Black	Asian	Hisp.[2]
City	86.1	88.5	87.3	76.8	60.8	44.1	49.4	23.9	46.8	11.0
MSA[1]	89.9	91.5	89.5	84.7	66.3	39.7	41.7	25.3	46.7	13.0
U.S.	86.3	88.3	83.1	85.7	64.0	29.1	30.4	18.8	50.7	13.7

Note: Figures shown cover persons 25 years old and over; (1) Figures cover the Denver-Aurora-Lakewood, CO Metropolitan Statistical Area—see Appendix B for areas included; (2) People of Hispanic origin can be of any race
Source: U.S. Census Bureau, 2011-2013 American Community Survey 3-Year Estimates

School Enrollment by Grade and Control

Area	Preschool (%)		Kindergarten (%)		Grades 1 - 4 (%)		Grades 5 - 8 (%)		Grades 9 - 12 (%)	
	Public	Private	Public	Private	Public	Private	Public	Private	Public	Private
City	58.9	41.1	88.4	11.6	88.7	11.3	86.8	13.2	90.2	9.8
MSA[1]	56.1	43.9	90.4	9.6	92.9	7.1	91.6	8.4	92.6	7.4
U.S.	57.7	42.3	87.9	12.1	89.9	10.1	90.0	10.0	90.7	9.3

Note: Figures shown cover persons 3 years old and over; (1) Figures cover the Denver-Aurora-Lakewood, CO Metropolitan Statistical Area—see Appendix B for areas included
Source: U.S. Census Bureau, 2011-2013 American Community Survey 3-Year Estimates

Average Salaries of Public School Classroom Teachers

Area	2013-14		2014-15		Percent Change 2013-14 to 2014-15	Percent Change 2004-05 to 2014-15
	Dollars	Rank[1]	Dollars	Rank[1]		
COLORADO	49,615	31	49,828	34	0.43	13.4
U.S. Average	56,610	–	57,379	–	1.36	20.8

Note: (1) State rank ranges from 1 to 51 where 1 indicates highest salary.
Source: National Education Association, Rankings & Estimates: Rankings of the States 2014 and Estimates of School Statistics 2015, March 2015

Higher Education

Four-Year Colleges			Two-Year Colleges			Medical Schools[1]	Law Schools[2]	Voc/ Tech[3]
Public	Private Non-profit	Private For-profit	Public	Private Non-profit	Private For-profit			
2	7	8	1	0	6	0	1	4

Note: Figures cover institutions located within the city limits and include main campuses only; (1) includes schools accredited by the Liaison Committee on Medical Education and the American Osteopathic Association's Commission on Osteopathic College Accreditation; (2) includes ABA-accredited schools, schools with provisional ABA accreditation, and state accredited schools; (3) includes all schools with programs that are less than 2 years.
Source: National Center for Education Statistics, Integrated Postsecondary Education System (IPEDS), 2013-14; Association of American Medical Colleges, Member List, May 1, 2015; American Osteopathic Association, Member List, May 1, 2015; Law School Admission Council, Official Guide to ABA-Approved Law Schools Online, May 1, 2015; Wikipedia, List of Medical Schools in the United States, May 1, 2015; Wikipedia, List of Law Schools in the United States, May 1, 2015

According to *U.S. News & World Report*, the Denver-Aurora-Lakewood, CO metro area is home to two of the best national universities in the U.S.: **Colorado School of Mines** (#88); **University of Denver** (#88). The indicators used to capture academic quality fall into a number of categories: assessment by administrators at peer institutions; retention of students; faculty resources; student selectivity; financial resources; alumni giving; high school counselor ratings of colleges; and graduation rate. *U.S. News & World Report*, *"America's Best Colleges 2015"*

According to *U.S. News & World Report*, the Denver-Aurora-Lakewood, CO metro area is home to one of the top 100 law schools in the U.S.: **University of Denver (Sturm)** (#67). The rankings are based on a weighted average of 12 measures of quality: peer assessment score; assessment score by lawyers/judges; median LSAT scores; median undergrad GPA; acceptance rate; employment rates for graduates; placement success; bar passage rate; faculty resources; expenditures per student; student/faculty ratio; and library resources. *U.S. News & World Report*, *"America's Best Graduate Schools, Law, 2016"*

According to *U.S. News & World Report*, the Denver-Aurora-Lakewood, CO metro area is home to one of the top 75 medical schools for research in the U.S.: **University of Colorado** (#35). The rankings are based on a weighted average of 11 measures of quality: quality assessment; peer assessment score; assessment score by residency directors; research activity; total research activity; average research activity per faculty member; student selectivity; median MCAT total score; median undergraduate GPA; acceptance rate; and faculty resources. *U.S. News & World Report*, *"America's Best Graduate Schools, Medical, 2016"*

PRESIDENTIAL ELECTION

2012 Presidential Election Results

Area	Obama (%)	Romney (%)	Other (%)
Denver County	73.5	24.4	2.1
U.S.	51.0	47.2	1.8

Note: Results may not add to 100% due to rounding
Source: Dave Leip's Atlas of U.S. Presidential Elections

EMPLOYERS

Major Employers

Company Name	Industry
Arvada House Preservation	Apartment building operators
Centura Health Corporation	General medical and surgical hospitals
Colorado Department of Transportation	Regulation, administration of transportation
County of Jefferson	County commissioner
DISH Network Corporation	Cable and other pay television services
Gart Bros Sporting Goods Company	Sporting goods and bicycle shops
HCA-Healthone	General medical and surgical hospitals
IBM	Printers, computer
Level 3 Communications	Telephone communication, except radio
Lockheed Martin Corporation	Space vehicles, complete
Lockheed Martin Corporation	Aircraft
Lockheed Martin Corporation	Search and navigation equipment
Mormon Church	Mormon Church
MWH/Fni Joint Venture	Engineering services
Newmont Gold Company	Gold ores mining
Noodles and Company	Eating places
Strasburg Telephone Company	Telephone communication, except radio
Synergy Services	Payroll accounting service
TW Telecom Holdings	Telephone communication, except radio
Western Union Financial Services	Electronic funds transfer network, including switching

Note: Companies shown are located within the Denver-Aurora-Lakewood, CO Metropolitan Statistical Area.
Source: Hoovers.com; Wikipedia

Best Companies to Work For

PCL Construction, headquartered in Denver, is among "The 100 Best Companies to Work For." To pick the best companies, *Fortune* partnered with the Great Place to Work Institute. Two-thirds of a company's score is based on the results of the Institute's Trust Index survey, which is sent to a random sample of employees from each company. The questions related to attitudes about management's credibility, job satisfaction, and camaraderie. The other third of the scoring is based on the company's responses to the Institute's Culture Audit, which includes detailed questions about pay and benefit programs, and a series of open-ended questions about hiring practices, internal communication, training, recognition programs, and diversity efforts. Any company that is at least five years old with more than 1,000 U.S. employees is eligible. *Fortune, "The 100 Best Companies to Work For," 2015*

SquareTwo Financial, headquartered in Denver, is among the "100 Best Places to Work in IT." To qualify, companies, both public and private, had to have a minimum of 50 IT employees and were selected based on average salary and bonus increases, the percentage of IT staffers promoted, IT staff turnover rates, training and development programs, and the percentage of women and minorities in IT staff and management positions. In addition, *Computerworld* looked at retention efforts, programs for recognizing and rewarding outstanding performances, and benefits such as flextime, elder care and child care, and reimbursement for college tuition and the cost of pursuing technology certifications. *Computerworld, "100 Best Places to Work in IT 2014"*

PUBLIC SAFETY

Crime Rate

Area	All Crimes	Violent Crimes				Property Crimes		
		Murder	Forcible Rape	Robbery	Aggrav. Assault	Burglary	Larceny -Theft	Motor Vehicle Theft
City	4,283.3	6.2	79.2	174.4	370.0	757.8	2,358.5	537.3
Suburbs[1]	2,691.8	2.9	44.7	48.6	136.8	369.5	1,866.6	222.9
Metro[2]	3,075.3	3.7	53.0	78.9	193.0	463.1	1,985.1	298.6
U.S.	3,098.6	4.5	25.2	109.1	229.1	610.0	1,899.4	221.3

Note: Figures are crimes per 100,000 population; (1) All areas within the metro area that are located outside the city limits; (2) Figures cover the Denver-Aurora-Lakewood, CO Metropolitan Statistical Area—see Appendix B for areas included
Source: FBI Uniform Crime Reports, 2013

Hate Crimes

Area	Number of Quarters Reported	Number of Incidents per Bias Motivation						
		Race	Religion	Sexual Orientation	Ethnicity	Disability	Gender	Gender Identity
City	4	9	5	15	1	0	0	0
U.S.	4	2,871	1,031	1,233	655	83	18	31

Source: Federal Bureau of Investigation, Hate Crime Statistics 2013

Identity Theft Consumer Complaints

Area	Complaints	Complaints per 100,000 Population	Rank[2]
MSA[1]	2,440	90.5	87
U.S.	332,646	104.3	-

Note: (1) Figures cover the Denver-Aurora-Lakewood, CO Metropolitan Statistical Area—see Appendix B for areas included; (2) Rank ranges from 1 to 380 where 1 indicates greatest number of identity theft complaints per 100,000 population
Source: Federal Trade Commission, Consumer Sentinel Network Data Book for January–December 2014

Fraud and Other Consumer Complaints

Area	Complaints	Complaints per 100,000 Population	Rank[2]
MSA[1]	13,848	513.4	20
U.S.	2,250,205	705.7	-

Note: (1) Figures cover the Denver-Aurora-Lakewood, CO Metropolitan Statistical Area—see Appendix B for areas included; (2) Rank ranges from 1 to 380 where 1 indicates greatest number of identity theft complaints per 100,000 population
Source: Federal Trade Commission, Consumer Sentinel Network Data Book for January–December 2014

RECREATION

Culture

Dance[1]	Theatre[1]	Instrumental Music[1]	Vocal Music[1]	Series and Festivals	Museums and Art Galleries[2]	Zoos and Aquariums[3]
5	16	3	6	2	86	2

Note: (1) Professional perfoming groups; (2) Based on organizations with SIC code 8412; (3) AZA-accredited
Source: The Grey House Performing Arts Directory, 2015-16; Association of Zoos & Aquariums, AZA Member Zoos & Aquariums, April 2015; www.AccuLeads.com, April 2015

Professional Sports Teams

Team Name	League	Year Established
Colorado Avalanche	National Hockey League (NHL)	1995
Colorado Rapids	Major League Soccer (MLS)	1996
Colorado Rockies	Major League Baseball (MLB)	1993
Denver Broncos	National Football League (NFL)	1960
Denver Nuggets	National Basketball Association (NBA)	1967

Note: Includes teams located in the Denver-Aurora-Lakewood, CO Metropolitan Statistical Area.
Source: Wikipedia, Major Professional Sports Teams of the United States and Canada, April 2015

CLIMATE

Average and Extreme Temperatures

Temperature	Jan	Feb	Mar	Apr	May	Jun	Jul	Aug	Sep	Oct	Nov	Dec	Yr.
Extreme High (°F)	73	76	84	90	93	102	103	100	97	89	79	75	103
Average High (°F)	43	47	52	62	71	81	88	86	77	67	52	45	64
Average Temp. (°F)	30	34	39	48	58	67	73	72	63	52	39	32	51
Average Low (°F)	16	20	25	34	44	53	59	57	48	37	25	18	37
Extreme Low (°F)	-25	-25	-10	-2	22	30	43	41	17	3	-8	-25	-25

Note: Figures cover the years 1948-1992
Source: National Climatic Data Center, International Station Meteorological Climate Summary, 9/96

Average Precipitation/Snowfall/Humidity

Precip./Humidity	Jan	Feb	Mar	Apr	May	Jun	Jul	Aug	Sep	Oct	Nov	Dec	Yr.
Avg. Precip. (in.)	0.6	0.6	1.3	1.7	2.5	1.7	1.9	1.5	1.1	1.0	0.9	0.6	15.5
Avg. Snowfall (in.)	9	7	14	9	2	Tr	0	0	2	4	9	8	63
Avg. Rel. Hum. 5am (%)	62	65	67	66	70	68	67	68	66	63	66	63	66
Avg. Rel. Hum. 5pm (%)	49	44	40	35	38	34	34	34	32	34	47	50	39

Note: Figures cover the years 1948-1992; Tr = Trace amounts (<0.05 in. of rain; <0.5 in. of snow)
Source: National Climatic Data Center, International Station Meteorological Climate Summary, 9/96

Weather Conditions

Temperature			Daytime Sky			Precipitation		
10°F & below	32°F & below	90°F & above	Clear	Partly cloudy	Cloudy	0.01 inch or more precip.	0.1 inch or more snow/ice	Thunder-storms
24	155	33	99	177	89	90	38	39

Note: Figures are average number of days per year and cover the years 1948-1992
Source: National Climatic Data Center, International Station Meteorological Climate Summary, 9/96

HAZARDOUS WASTE

Superfund Sites

Denver has four hazardous waste sites on the EPA's Superfund Final National Priorities List: **Broderick Wood Products**; **Chemical Sales Co.**; **Denver Radium Site**; **Vasquez Boulevard and I-70**. There are a total of 1,322 Superfund sites on the list in the U.S. *U.S. Environmental Protection Agency, Final National Priorities List, April 14, 2015*

AIR & WATER QUALITY

Air Quality Trends: Ozone

	2004	2005	2006	2007	2008	2009	2010	2011	2012	2013
MSA[1]	0.068	0.075	0.080	0.079	0.075	0.070	0.072	0.078	0.080	0.080

Note: (1) Data covers the Denver-Aurora-Lakewood, CO Metropolitan Statistical Area—see Appendix B for areas included. The values shown are the composite ozone concentration averages among trend sites based on the highest fourth daily maximum 8-hour concentration in parts per million. These trends are based on sites having an adequate record of monitoring data during the trend period. Data from exceptional events are included.
Source: U.S. Environmental Protection Agency, Air Quality Monitoring Information, "Air Quality Trends by City, 2000-2013"

Air Quality Index

Area	Percent of Days when Air Quality was...[2]					AQI Statistics[2]	
	Good	Moderate	Unhealthy for Sensitive Groups	Unhealthy	Very Unhealthy	Maximum	Median
MSA[1]	45.2	51.8	2.7	0.3	0.0	152	51

Note: (1) Data covers the Denver-Aurora-Lakewood, CO Metropolitan Statistical Area—see Appendix B for areas included; (2) Based on 365 days with AQI data in 2014. Air Quality Index (AQI) is an index for reporting daily air quality. EPA calculates the AQI for five major air pollutants regulated by the Clean Air Act: ground-level ozone, particle pollution (aka particulate matter), carbon monoxide, sulfur dioxide, and nitrogen dioxide. The AQI runs from 0 to 500. The higher the AQI value, the greater the level of air pollution and the greater the health concern. There are six AQI categories: "Good" AQI is between 0 and 50. Air quality is considered satisfactory; "Moderate" AQI is between 51 and 100. Air quality is acceptable; "Unhealthy for Sensitive Groups" When AQI values are between 101 and 150, members of sensitive groups may experience health effects; "Unhealthy" When AQI values are between 151 and 200 everyone may begin to experience health effects; "Very Unhealthy" AQI values between 201 and 300 trigger a health alert; "Hazardous" AQI values over 300 trigger warnings of emergency conditions (not shown).
Source: U.S. Environmental Protection Agency, Air Quality Index Report, 2014

Air Quality Index Pollutants

Area	Percent of Days when AQI Pollutant was...[2]					
	Carbon Monoxide	Nitrogen Dioxide	Ozone	Sulfur Dioxide	Particulate Matter 2.5	Particulate Matter 10
MSA[1]	0.0	26.8	46.3	0.3	23.3	3.3

Note: (1) Data covers the Denver-Aurora-Lakewood, CO Metropolitan Statistical Area—see Appendix B for areas included; (2) Based on 365 days with AQI data in 2014. The Air Quality Index (AQI) is an index for reporting daily air quality. EPA calculates the AQI for five major air pollutants regulated by the Clean Air Act: ground-level ozone, particle pollution (also known as particulate matter), carbon monoxide, sulfur dioxide, and nitrogen dioxide. The AQI runs from 0 to 500. The higher the AQI value, the greater the level of air pollution and the greater the health concern.
Source: U.S. Environmental Protection Agency, Air Quality Index Report, 2014

Maximum Air Pollutant Concentrations: Particulate Matter, Ozone, CO and Lead

	Particulate Matter 10 (ug/m³)	Particulate Matter 2.5 Wtd AM (ug/m³)	Particulate Matter 2.5 24-Hr (ug/m³)	Ozone (ppm)	Carbon Monoxide (ppm)	Lead (ug/m³)
MSA[1] Level	97	8.2	23	0.085	3	0.02
NAAQS[2]	150	15	35	0.075	9	0.15
Met NAAQS[2]	Yes	Yes	Yes	No	Yes	Yes

Note: (1) Data covers the Denver-Aurora-Lakewood, CO Metropolitan Statistical Area—see Appendix B for areas included; Data from exceptional events are included; (2) National Ambient Air Quality Standards; ppm = parts per million; ug/m³ = micrograms per cubic meter; n/a not available.
Concentrations: Particulate Matter 10 (coarse particulate)—highest second maximum 24-hour concentration; Particulate Matter 2.5 Wtd AM (fine particulate)—highest weighted annual mean concentration; Particulate Matter 2.5 24-Hour (fine particulate)—highest 98th percentile 24-hour concentration; Ozone—highest fourth daily maximum 8-hour concentration; Carbon Monoxide—highest second maximum non-overlapping 8-hour concentration; Lead—maximum running 3-month average
Source: U.S. Environmental Protection Agency, Air Quality Monitoring Information, "Air Quality Statistics by City, 2013"

Maximum Air Pollutant Concentrations: Nitrogen Dioxide and Sulfur Dioxide

	Nitrogen Dioxide AM (ppb)	Nitrogen Dioxide 1-Hr (ppb)	Sulfur Dioxide AM (ppb)	Sulfur Dioxide 1-Hr (ppb)	Sulfur Dioxide 24-Hr (ppb)
MSA[1] Level	24	68	n/a	38	n/a
NAAQS[2]	53	100	30	75	140
Met NAAQS[2]	Yes	Yes	n/a	Yes	n/a

Note: (1) Data covers the Denver-Aurora-Lakewood, CO Metropolitan Statistical Area—see Appendix B for areas included; Data from exceptional events are included; (2) National Ambient Air Quality Standards; ppm = parts per million; ug/m³ = micrograms per cubic meter; n/a not available.
Concentrations: Nitrogen Dioxide AM—highest arithmetic mean concentration; Nitrogen Dioxide 1-Hr—highest 98th percentile 1-hour daily maximum concentration; Sulfur Dioxide AM—highest annual mean concentration; Sulfur Dioxide 1-Hr—highest 99th percentile 1-hour daily maximum concentration; Sulfur Dioxide 24-Hr—highest second maximum 24-hour concentration
Source: U.S. Environmental Protection Agency, Air Quality Monitoring Information, "Air Quality Statistics by City, 2013"

Drinking Water

Water System Name	Pop. Served	Primary Water Source Type	Violations[1] Health Based	Monitoring/ Reporting
Denver Water Board	1,000,000	Surface	0	0

Note: (1) Based on violation data from January 1, 2014 to December 31, 2014 (includes unresolved violations from earlier years)
Source: U.S. Environmental Protection Agency, Office of Ground Water and Drinking Water, Safe Drinking Water Information System (based on data extracted January 27, 2015)

Eugene, Oregon

Background

In 1846, Eugene F. Skinner, for whom the city is named, and his family settled in the lush Willamette Valley. In 1853, the town was named the seat of the newly created Lane County. The city was incorporated in 1862, and in 1876 the University of Oregon was established.

Eugene is Oregon's third-largest city and was a major processing and shipping center for lumber until the decline of the timber industry in the 1980s. Eugene's economy struggled for a time, but by the latter 1990s, recovery was in full swing.

The city now enjoys a diverse economic base, with 10,000 businesses in and around Eugene. Government, education, and health care remain the largest providers of jobs. The city's major employers include the state's two major universities—University of Oregon in Eugene and Oregon State University in Corvallis. The local economy is also considerably bolstered by many small and medium-sized businesses employing 20 or fewer workers. Many of the leading companies in natural and organic foods movement, found their start in Eugene, including The Organically Grown Company, Nancy's Yogurt, Yogi Tea, and Emerald Valley Kitchen.

Eugene Airport, also known as Mahlon Sweet Field, is owned and operated by the City of Eugene, and is the fifth-largest airport in the Pacific Northwest. In addition to commercial flights, it also has an expanded air cargo facility to serve the growing demands of the region. Airport improvements are being implemented in line with a Master Plan drawn up in 1990, which features both short and long-term needs. Most recently, a new 6,000-foot runway was completed, and several taxiways have been rehabilitated, allowing two aircraft to land or take off at the same time.

The Eugene/Springfield area boasts nearly 100 organizations and facilities providing performing, literary, ethnic, and visual arts activities. The state-of-the-art Hult Center is home to resident ballet, symphony, opera, and musical theater companies and also attracts top performers from around the world. There are seven area museums and over a dozen galleries featuring local, national, and international artists' work. The Science Factory Children's Museum & Planetarium is the second-largest facility of its kind in the Northwest, seating 125 under a 40-foot dome. The University of Oregon's natural history museum has been renovated and reopened.

Other fairs, festivals, and special events occur throughout the year, including the Lane County Fair, the Oregon Country Fair, Art and the Vineyard, the Asian Celebration, and the internationally acclaimed Oregon Bach Festival. The Lane County Ice Arena hosts world-class skaters, three Olympic Track and Field Trials, the Olympic Scientific Congress, the World Veterans' Championships, and the International Music Educator's Society.

Located in the famed South Willamette Valley wine country, Eugene is home to nine wineries and within easy reach of dozens more; there are more than 200 wineries in the entire Willamette Valley. The cool climate is particularly congenial to the early-ripening pinot noir grape, but chardonnay and pinot gris are also grown here.

In addition to the University of Oregon, several colleges are located in Eugene, such as Eugene Bible College, Northwest Christian College, and Lane Community College. The city offers a wide variety of restaurants such as Italian, German, and Thai, and plenty of shops, cinemas, and nightclubs.

According to a recent survey, friendly people, scenery/terrain, and outdoor recreation are three top reasons why residents like to live in Eugene.

The Coast Range, west of the city, acts as a barrier to coastal fog, but active storms cross with little hindrance. To the east, the Cascade Range, which lures skiers to the area, blocks all but the strongest continental air masses. When eastern air does flow into the valley during dry, hot summer weather, an extreme fire hazard can develop. In the winter, however, clear, sunny days and cool, frosty nights result. Temperatures are largely controlled by maritime air from the Pacific Ocean, so that long periods of extremely hot or cold weather never occur.

Rankings

General Rankings

- In their second annual survey, analysts for the small- and mid-sized city lifestyle site Livability.com looked at data for more than 2,000 U.S. cities to determine the rankings for Livability's "Top 100 Best Places to Live" in 2015. Eugene ranked #20. Criteria: vibrant economy; low cost of living; abundant lifestyle amenities. *Livability.com, "Top 100 Best Places to Live 2015"*

Business/Finance Rankings

- The Eugene metro area appeared on the Milken Institute "2013 Best Performing Cities" list. Rank: #147 out of 200 large metro areas. Criteria: job growth; wage and salary growth; high-tech output growth. *Milken Institute, "Best-Performing Cities 2014," January 2015*

- *Forbes* ranked the 200 most populous metro areas to determine the nation's "Best Places for Business and Careers." The Eugene metro area was ranked #74. Criteria: costs (business and living); job growth (past and projected); income growth; educational attainment (college and high school); projected economic growth; cultural and recreational opportunities; net migration patterns; number of highly ranked colleges. *Forbes, "The Best Places for Business and Careers 2014," July 23, 2014*

Education Rankings

- Personal finance website *WalletHub* analyzed the 150 largest U.S. metropolitan statistical areas to determine where the most educated Americans are choosing to settle. Criteria: educational attainment; percentage of workers with jobs in computer, engineering, and science fields; quality and size of each metro area's universities. Eugene was ranked #32 (#1 = most educated city). *www.WalletHub.com, "2014's Most and Least Educated Cities*

Environmental Rankings

- The Eugene metro area came in at #13 for the relative comfort of its climate on Sperling's list of "chill cities," as measured by the Sperling Heat Index. All 361 metro areas are included. Criteria included daytime high temperatures, nighttime low temperatures, dew point, and relative humidity at the high temperatures. *www.bertsperling.com, "Sperling's Chill Cities," July 18, 2013*

- Sperling's BestPlaces assessed 379 metropolitan areas of the United States for the likelihood of dangerously extreme weather events or earthquakes. In general the Southeast and South-Central regions have the highest risk of weather extremes and earthquakes, while the Pacific Northwest enjoys the lowest risk. Of the least risky metropolitan areas, the Eugene metro area was ranked #17. *www.bestplaces.net, "Safest Places from Natural Disasters," April 2011*

- Eugene was highlighted as one of the 25 metro areas most polluted by short-term particle pollution (24-hour PM 2.5) in the U.S. during 2011 through 2013. The area ranked #20. *American Lung Association, State of the Air 2015*

- Eugene was highlighted as one of the cleanest metro areas for ozone air pollution in the U.S. during 2011 through 2013. The list represents cities with no monitored ozone air pollution in unhealthful ranges. *American Lung Association, State of the Air 2015*

Health/Fitness Rankings

- Eugene was selected as one of the best metropolitan areas for hospital care in America by *HealthGrades.com*. The rankings are based on a comprehensive study of patient death and complication rates in the nation's nearly 5,000 hospitals. Hospitals performing in the top 5% nationwide across 26 different medical procedures and diagnoses were identified. *HealthGrades.com* then ranked cities by the highest percentage of these Distinguished Hospitals for Clinical Excellence™. The Eugene metro area ranked #44. *HealthGrades.com, "America's Top 50 Cities for Hospital Care," January 21, 2012*

- The Eugene metro area appeared in the 2013 Gallup-Healthways Well-Being Index. The area ranked #69 out of 189. The Gallup-Healthways Well-Being Index score is an average of six sub-indexes, which individually examine life evaluation, emotional health, work environment, physical health, healthy behaviors, and access to basic necessities. Results are based on telephone interviews conducted as part of the Gallup-Healthways Well-Being Index survey January 2–December 29, 2012, and January 2–December 30, 2013, with a random sample of 531,630 adults, aged 18 and older, living in metropolitan areas in the 50 U.S. states and the District of Columbia. *Gallup-Healthways, "State of American Well-Being," March 25, 2014*

Real Estate Rankings

- Using data from the housing-market research firm RealtyTrac, Yahoo! Finance researchers listed the housing markets in which housing affordability is deteriorating most, factoring in interest rates as well as median home prices. The Eugene metro area was among the least affordable housing markets according to the percentage difference in the income required to buy a home in December 2013 as opposed to in December 2012. *news.yahoo.com, "10 Cities Where Ordinary People Can No Longer Afford Homes," March 5, 2014*

- Eugene was ranked #135 out of 275 metro areas in terms of house price appreciation in 2014 (#1 = highest rate). *Federal Housing Finance Agency, House Price Index, 4th Quarter 2014*

- The Eugene metro area was identified as one of the 20 best housing markets in the U.S. in 2014. The area ranked #10 out of 178 markets with a home price appreciation of 12.7%. Criteria: year-over-year change of median sales price of existing single-family homes between the 4th quarter of 2013 and the 4th quarter of 2014. *National Association of Realtors®, Median Sales Price of Existing Single-Family Homes for Metropolitan Areas, 4th Quarter 2014*

- Eugene was ranked #170 out of 226 metro areas in terms of housing affordability in 2014 by the National Association of Home Builders (#1 = most affordable). The NAHB-Wells Fargo Housing Opportunity Index (HOI) for a given area is defined as the share of homes sold in that area that would have been affordable to a family earning the local median income, based on standard mortgage underwriting criteria. *National Association of Home Builders®, NAHB-Wells Fargo Housing Opportunity Index, 4th Quarter 2014*

Safety Rankings

- Allstate ranked the 200 largest cities in America in terms of driver safety. Eugene ranked #23. Allstate researchers analyzed internal property damage claims over a two-year period from January 2011 to December 2012. A weighted average of the two-year numbers determined the annual percentages. *Allstate, "Allstate America's Best Drivers Report, 2014"*

- The National Insurance Crime Bureau ranked 380 metro areas in the U.S. in terms of per capita rates of vehicle theft. The Eugene metro area ranked #67 (#1 = highest rate). Criteria: number of vehicle theft offenses per 100,000 inhabitants in 2012. *National Insurance Crime Bureau, "Hot Spots 2012," June 26, 2013*

Seniors/Retirement Rankings

- From its Best Cities for Successful Aging indexes, the Milken Institute generated rankings for metropolitan areas, weighing data in eight categories—health care, wellness, living arrangements, transportation, financial characteristics, education and employment opportunities, community engagement, and overall livability. The Eugene metro area was ranked #196 overall in the small metro area category. *Milken Institute, "Best Cities for Successful Aging, 2014"*

- Eugene was identified as one of the most popular places to retire by *Topretirements.com*. The list reflects the 100 cities (out of 900+ total cities reviewed) that visitors to the website are most interested in for retirement. *Topretirements.com, "Most Popular Places to Retire for 2014," February 25, 2014*

Sports/Recreation Rankings

- Eugene was chosen as a bicycle friendly community by the League of American Bicyclists. A "Bicycle Friendly Community" welcomes cyclists by providing safe accommodation for cycling and encouraging people to bike for transportation and recreation. There are four award levels: Platinum; Gold; Silver; and Bronze. The community achieved an award level of Gold. *League of American Bicyclists, "Bicycle Friendly Community Master List," Fall 2013*

- Eugene was chosen as one of America's best cities for bicycling. The city ranked #9 out of 50. Criteria: robust cycling infrastructure; vibrant bike culture. The editors only considered cities with populations of 95,000 or more. *Bicycling, "America's Top 50 Bike-Friendly Cities," May 23, 2012*

Business Environment

CITY FINANCES

City Government Finances

Component	2012 ($000)	2012 ($ per capita)
Total Revenues	552,544	3,538
Total Expenditures	534,222	3,420
Debt Outstanding	418,205	2,678
Cash and Securities[1]	271,246	1,737

Note: (1) Cash and security holdings of a government at the close of its fiscal year, including those of its dependent agencies, utilities, and liquor stores.
Source: U.S Census Bureau, State & Local Government Finances 2012

City Government Revenue by Source

Source	2012 ($000)	2012 ($ per capita)
General Revenue		
From Federal Government	7,763	50
From State Government	20,845	133
From Local Governments	16,732	107
Taxes		
Property	97,838	626
Sales and Gross Receipts	15,125	97
Personal Income	0	0
Corporate Income	0	0
Motor Vehicle License	0	0
Other Taxes	6,599	42
Current Charges	78,791	504
Liquor Store	0	0
Utility	287,427	1,840
Employee Retirement	0	0

Source: U.S Census Bureau, State & Local Government Finances 2012

City Government Expenditures by Function

Function	2012 ($000)	2012 ($ per capita)	2012 (%)
General Direct Expenditures			
Air Transportation	9,747	62	1.8
Corrections	0	0	0.0
Education	0	0	0.0
Employment Security Administration	0	0	0.0
Financial Administration	3,069	20	0.6
Fire Protection	31,297	200	5.9
General Public Buildings	39,430	252	7.4
Governmental Administration, Other	8,789	56	1.6
Health	0	0	0.0
Highways	6,444	41	1.2
Hospitals	0	0	0.0
Housing and Community Development	7,471	48	1.4
Interest on General Debt	2,208	14	0.4
Judicial and Legal	4,216	27	0.8
Libraries	10,288	66	1.9
Parking	3,781	24	0.7
Parks and Recreation	24,648	158	4.6
Police Protection	46,411	297	8.7
Public Welfare	0	0	0.0
Sewerage	33,934	217	6.4
Solid Waste Management	1,789	11	0.3
Veterans' Services	0	0	0.0
Liquor Store	0	0	0.0
Utility	279,707	1,791	52.4
Employee Retirement	0	0	0.0

Source: U.S Census Bureau, State & Local Government Finances 2012

DEMOGRAPHICS

Population Growth

Area	1990 Census	2000 Census	2010 Census	Population Growth (%)	
				1990-2000	2000-2010
City	118,073	137,893	156,185	16.8	13.3
MSA[1]	282,912	322,959	351,715	14.2	8.9
U.S.	248,709,873	281,421,906	308,745,538	13.2	9.7

Note: (1) Figures cover the Eugene-Springfield, OR Metropolitan Statistical Area—see Appendix B for areas included
Source: U.S. Census Bureau, Census 1990, 2000, 2010

Household Size

Area	Persons in Household (%)							Average Household Size
	One	Two	Three	Four	Five	Six	Seven or More	
City	33.0	36.1	15.6	9.4	3.9	1.3	0.7	2.30
MSA[1]	29.4	38.0	15.2	10.3	4.4	1.6	1.0	2.39
U.S.	27.7	33.6	15.7	13.1	6.0	2.3	1.5	2.64

Note: (1) Figures cover the Eugene, OR Metropolitan Statistical Area—see Appendix B for areas included
Source: U.S. Census Bureau, 2011-2013 American Community Survey 3-Year Estimates

Race

Area	White Alone[2] (%)	Black Alone[2] (%)	Asian Alone[2] (%)	AIAN[3] Alone[2] (%)	NHOPI[4] Alone[2] (%)	Other Race Alone[2] (%)	Two or More Races (%)
City	85.7	1.4	4.2	1.1	0.4	2.6	4.5
MSA[1]	88.4	1.0	2.6	1.1	0.3	2.4	4.3
U.S.	73.9	12.6	5.0	0.8	0.2	4.7	2.9

Note: (1) Figures cover the Eugene, OR Metropolitan Statistical Area—see Appendix B for areas included; (2) Alone is defined as not being in combination with one or more other races; (3) American Indian and Alaska Native; (4) Native Hawaiian and Other Pacific Islander
Source: U.S. Census Bureau, 2011-2013 American Community Survey 3-Year Estimates

Hispanic or Latino Origin

Area	Total (%)	Mexican (%)	Puerto Rican (%)	Cuban (%)	Other (%)
City	8.3	6.5	0.3	0.1	1.4
MSA[1]	7.8	6.3	0.3	0.1	1.2
U.S.	16.9	10.8	1.6	0.6	3.8

Note: Persons of Hispanic or Latino origin can be of any race; (1) Figures cover the Eugene, OR Metropolitan Statistical Area—see Appendix B for areas included
Source: U.S. Census Bureau, 2011-2013 American Community Survey 3-Year Estimates

Segregation

Type	Segregation Indices[1]				Percent Change		
	1990	2000	2010	2010 Rank[2]	1990-2000	1990-2010	2000-2010
Black/White	n/a	n/a	n/a	n/a	n/a	n/a	n/a
Asian/White	n/a	n/a	n/a	n/a	n/a	n/a	n/a
Hispanic/White	n/a	n/a	n/a	n/a	n/a	n/a	n/a

Note: All figures cover the Metropolitan Statistical Area—see Appendix B for areas included; Figures are based on an analysis of 1990, 2000, and 2010 Census Decennial Census tract data by William H. Frey, Brookings Institution and the University of Michigan Social Science Data Analysis Network. In this analysis all racial groups (whites, blacks, and asians) are non-Hispanic members of those races. Hispanics are shown as a separate category;
(1) Segregation Indices are Dissimilarity Indices that measure the degree to which the minority group is distributed differently than whites across census tracts. They range from 0 (complete integration) to 100 (complete segregation) where the value indicates the percentage of the minority group that needs to move to be distributed exactly like whites; (2) Ranges from 1 (most segregated) to 102 (least segregated); n/a not available.
Source: www.CensusScope.org

Ancestry

Area	German	Irish	English	American	Italian	Polish	French[2]	Scottish	Dutch
City	19.0	13.3	12.0	4.9	4.2	2.6	3.7	2.8	2.2
MSA[1]	19.0	13.6	12.0	5.9	4.2	2.3	3.4	3.0	2.3
U.S.	14.9	10.8	8.0	7.4	5.5	3.0	2.7	1.7	1.4

Note: Figures are the percentage of the total population reporting a particular ancestry. The nine most commonly reported ancestries in the U.S. are shown. Figures include multiple ancestries (e.g. if a person reported being Irish and Italian, they were included in both columns); (1) Figures cover the Eugene, OR Metropolitan Statistical Area—see Appendix B for areas included; (2) Excludes Basque
Source: U.S. Census Bureau, 2011-2013 American Community Survey 3-Year Estimates

Foreign-Born Population

Area	Percent of Population Born in								
	Any Foreign Country	Mexico	Asia	Europe	Carribean	South America	Central America[2]	Africa	Canada
City	7.9	2.0	3.5	1.1	0.1	0.2	0.2	0.2	0.4
MSA[1]	5.8	1.8	2.0	0.9	0.0	0.2	0.2	0.1	0.4
U.S.	13.0	3.7	3.8	1.5	1.2	0.9	1.0	0.6	0.3

Note: (1) Figures cover the Eugene, OR Metropolitan Statistical Area—see Appendix B for areas included; (2) Excludes Mexico.
Source: U.S. Census Bureau, 2011-2013 American Community Survey 3-Year Estimates

Marital Status

Area	Never Married	Now Married[2]	Separated	Widowed	Divorced
City	43.2	37.1	1.4	5.2	13.1
MSA[1]	33.3	45.1	1.6	5.9	14.1
U.S.	32.7	48.1	2.2	6.0	11.0

Note: Figures are percentages and cover the population 15 years of age and older; (1) Figures cover the Eugene, OR Metropolitan Statistical Area—see Appendix B for areas included; (2) Excludes separated
Source: U.S. Census Bureau, 2011-2013 American Community Survey 3-Year Estimates

Disability Status

Area	All Ages	Under 18 Years Old	18 to 64 Years Old	65 Years and Over
City	13.2	4.6	10.3	39.5
MSA[1]	15.6	5.4	13.1	37.9
U.S.	12.3	4.1	10.2	36.3

Note: Figures show percent of the civilian noninstitutionalized population that reported having a disability. Disability status is determined from from six types of difficulty: vision, hearing, cognitive, ambulatory, self-care, and independent living. For children under 5 years old, hearing and vision difficulty are used to determine disability status. For children between the ages of 5 and 14, disability status is determined from hearing, vision, cognitive, ambulatory, and self-care difficulties. For people aged 15 years and older, they are considered to have a disability if they have difficulty with any one of the six difficulty types; (1) Figures cover the Eugene, OR Metropolitan Statistical Area—see Appendix B for areas included.
Source: U.S. Census Bureau, 2011-2013 American Community Survey 3-Year Estimates

Age

Area	Percent of Population									Median Age
	Under Age 5	Age 5–19	Age 20–34	Age 35–44	Age 45–54	Age 55–64	Age 65–74	Age 75–84	Age 85+	
City	4.7	17.8	28.7	11.9	11.3	12.2	7.2	3.8	2.4	34.1
MSA[1]	5.0	17.8	22.3	11.4	12.8	14.4	9.1	4.8	2.2	39.1
U.S.	6.4	19.9	20.7	12.9	14.1	12.3	7.6	4.2	1.9	37.4

Note: (1) Figures cover the Eugene, OR Metropolitan Statistical Area—see Appendix B for areas included
Source: U.S. Census Bureau, 2011-2013 American Community Survey 3-Year Estimates

Gender

Area	Males	Females	Males per 100 Females
City	77,877	80,292	97.0
MSA[1]	174,253	180,485	96.5
U.S.	154,451,010	159,410,713	96.9

Note: (1) Figures cover the Eugene, OR Metropolitan Statistical Area—see Appendix B for areas included
Source: U.S. Census Bureau, 2011-2013 American Community Survey 3-Year Estimates

Religious Groups by Family

Area	Catholic	Baptist	Non-Den.	Methodist[2]	Lutheran	LDS[3]	Pente-costal	Presby-terian[4]	Muslim[5]	Judaism
MSA[1]	6.2	3.1	1.9	0.9	1.4	3.7	3.3	0.6	0.1	0.4
U.S.	19.1	9.3	4.0	4.0	2.3	2.0	1.9	1.6	0.8	0.7

Note: Figures are the number of adherents as a percentage of the total population; (1) Figures cover the Eugene-Springfield, OR Metropolitan Statistical Area—see Appendix B for areas included; (2) Methodist/Pietist; (3) Latter Day Saints; (4) Reformed; (5) Figures are estimates
Source: Association of Statisticians of American Religious Bodies, 2010 U.S. Religion Census: Religious Congregations & Membership Study

Religious Groups by Tradition

Area	Catholic	Evangelical Protestant	Mainline Protestant	Other Tradition	Black Protestant	Orthodox
MSA[1]	6.2	9.7	3.4	5.5	0.1	0.1
U.S.	19.1	16.2	7.3	4.3	1.6	0.3

Note: Figures are the number of adherents as a percentage of the total population; (1) Figures cover the Eugene-Springfield, OR Metropolitan Statistical Area—see Appendix B for areas included
Source: Association of Statisticians of American Religious Bodies, 2010 U.S. Religion Census: Religious Congregations & Membership Study

ECONOMY

Gross Metropolitan Product

Area	2012	2013	2014	2015	Rank[2]
MSA[1]	12.2	12.6	13.0	13.6	160

Note: Figures are in billions of dollars; (1) Figures cover the Eugene, OR Metropolitan Statistical Area—see Appendix B for areas included; (2) Rank is based on 2015 data and ranges from 1 to 363
Source: The U.S. Conference of Mayors, U.S. Metro Economies: GMP and Employment 2013-2015, June 2014

Economic Growth

Area	2010-12 (%)	2013 (%)	2014 (%)	2015 (%)	Rank[2]
MSA[1]	1.8	1.6	1.8	2.9	172
U.S.	2.1	2.0	2.3	3.2	–

Note: Figures are real gross metropolitan product (GMP) growth rates and represent annual average percent change; (1) Figures cover the Eugene, OR Metropolitan Statistical Area—see Appendix B for areas included; (2) Rank is based on 2015 data and ranges from 1 to 363
Source: The U.S. Conference of Mayors, U.S. Metro Economies: GMP and Employment 2013-2015, June 2014

Metropolitan Area Exports

Area	2008	2009	2010	2011	2012	2013	Rank[2]
MSA[1]	781.3	314.4	415.5	464.5	482.2	476.0	218

Note: Figures are in millions of dollars; (1) Figures cover the Eugene, OR Metropolitan Statistical Area—see Appendix B for areas included; (2) Rank is based on 2013 data and ranges from 1 to 387
Source: U.S. Department of Commerce, International Trade Administration, Office of Trade & Industry Information, Manufacturing & Services, data extracted April 3, 2015

Building Permits

Area	Single-Family			Multi-Family			Total		
	2013	2014	Pct. Chg.	2013	2014	Pct. Chg.	2013	2014	Pct. Chg.
City	182	224	23.1	733	808	10.2	915	1,032	12.8
MSA[1]	506	506	0.0	743	810	9.0	1,249	1,316	5.4
U.S.	620,802	634,597	2.2	370,020	411,766	11.3	990,822	1,046,363	5.6

Note: (1) Figures cover the Eugene, OR Metropolitan Statistical Area—see Appendix B for areas included; Figures represent new, privately-owned housing units authorized (unadjusted data); All permit data are based on estimates with imputation.
Source: U.S. Census Bureau, Manufacturing, Mining, and Construction Statistics, Building Permits, 2013, 2014

Bankruptcy Filings

Area	Business Filings			Nonbusiness Filings		
	2013	2014	% Chg.	2013	2014	% Chg.
Lane County	29	18	-37.9	1,174	1,025	-12.7
U.S.	33,212	26,983	-18.8	1,038,720	909,812	-12.4

Note: Business filings include Chapter 7, Chapter 11, Chapter 12, and Chapter 13; Nonbusiness filings include Chapter 7, Chapter 11, and Chapter 13
Source: Administrative Office of the U.S. Courts, Business and Nonbusiness Bankruptcy, County Cases Commenced by Chapter of the Bankruptcy Code, During the 12- Month Period Ending December 31, 2013 and Business and Nonbusiness Bankruptcy, County Cases Commenced by Chapter of the Bankruptcy Code, During the 12- Month Period Ending December 31, 2014

Housing Vacancy Rates

Area	Gross Vacancy Rate[2] (%)			Year-Round Vacancy Rate[3] (%)			Rental Vacancy Rate[4] (%)			Homeowner Vacancy Rate[5] (%)		
	2012	2013	2014	2012	2013	2014	2012	2013	2014	2012	2013	2014
MSA[1]	n/a	n/a	n/a	n/a	n/a	n/a	n/a	n/a	n/a	n/a	n/a	n/a
U.S.	13.8	13.6	13.4	10.8	10.7	10.4	8.7	8.3	7.6	2.0	2.0	1.9

Note: (1) Figures cover the Eugene, OR Metropolitan Statistical Area—see Appendix B for areas included; (2) The percentage of the total housing inventory that is vacant; (3) The percentage of the housing inventory (excluding seasonal units) that is year-round vacant; (4) The percentage of rental inventory that is vacant for rent; (5) The percentage of homeowner inventory that is vacant for sale; n/a not available
Source: U.S. Census Bureau, Housing Vacancies and Homeownership Annual Statistics: 2014

INCOME

Income

Area	Per Capita ($)	Median Household ($)	Average Household ($)
City	25,688	40,628	59,964
MSA[1]	23,915	41,936	57,134
U.S.	27,884	52,176	72,897

Note: (1) Figures cover the Eugene, OR Metropolitan Statistical Area—see Appendix B for areas included
Source: U.S. Census Bureau, 2011-2013 American Community Survey 3-Year Estimates

Household Income Distribution

Area	Percent of Households Earning							
	Under $15,000	$15,000 -24,999	$25,000 -34,999	$35,000 -49,999	$50,000 -74,999	$75,000 -99,000	$100,000 -149,999	$150,000 and up
City	22.0	11.3	11.3	14.0	17.2	8.1	10.0	6.2
MSA[1]	17.5	12.9	11.9	14.7	18.5	10.5	9.2	4.7
U.S.	13.0	10.9	10.3	13.6	17.9	11.9	12.7	9.6

Note: (1) Figures cover the Eugene, OR Metropolitan Statistical Area—see Appendix B for areas included
Source: U.S. Census Bureau, 2011-2013 American Community Survey 3-Year Estimates

Poverty Rate

Area	All Ages	Under 18 Years Old	18 to 64 Years Old	65 Years and Over
City	26.7	23.9	31.0	8.7
MSA[1]	22.0	25.2	24.4	8.5
U.S.	15.9	22.4	14.8	9.5

Note: Figures are percentage of people whose income during the past 12 months was below the poverty level; (1) Figures cover the Eugene, OR Metropolitan Statistical Area—see Appendix B for areas included
Source: U.S. Census Bureau, 2011-2013 American Community Survey 3-Year Estimates

EMPLOYMENT

Labor Force and Employment

Area	Civilian Labor Force			Workers Employed		
	Dec. 2013	Dec. 2014	% Chg.	Dec. 2013	Dec. 2014	% Chg.
City	77,207	78,708	1.9	72,364	74,184	2.5
MSA[1]	168,275	171,408	1.9	156,388	160,322	2.5
U.S.	154,408,000	155,521,000	0.7	144,423,000	147,190,000	1.9

Note: Data is not seasonally adjusted and covers workers 16 years of age and older; (1) Figures cover the Eugene, OR Metropolitan Statistical Area—see Appendix B for areas included
Source: Bureau of Labor Statistics, Local Area Unemployment Statistics

Unemployment Rate

Area	2014											
	Jan.	Feb.	Mar.	Apr.	May	Jun.	Jul.	Aug.	Sep.	Oct.	Nov.	Dec.
City	6.9	6.8	6.7	5.9	5.9	6.5	6.9	6.8	6.0	5.9	5.9	5.7
MSA[1]	7.8	7.9	7.7	6.9	6.6	7.0	7.3	7.3	6.6	6.7	6.7	6.5
U.S.	7.0	7.0	6.8	5.9	6.1	6.3	6.5	6.3	5.7	5.5	5.5	5.4

Note: Data is not seasonally adjusted and covers workers 16 years of age and older; (1) Figures cover the Eugene, OR Metropolitan Statistical Area—see Appendix B for areas included
Source: Bureau of Labor Statistics, Local Area Unemployment Statistics

Employment by Occupation

Occupation Classification	City (%)	MSA[1] (%)	U.S. (%)
Management, Business, Science, and Arts	40.1	34.3	36.2
Natural Resources, Construction, and Maintenance	5.9	8.0	9.0
Production, Transportation, and Material Moving	8.8	11.7	12.1
Sales and Office	24.9	25.4	24.4
Service	20.3	20.6	18.3

Note: Figures cover employed civilians 16 years of age and older; (1) Figures cover the Eugene, OR Metropolitan Statistical Area—see Appendix B for areas included
Source: U.S. Census Bureau, 2011-2013 American Community Survey 3-Year Estimates

Employment by Industry

Sector	MSA[1]		U.S.
	Number of Employees	Percent of Total	Percent of Total
Construction	5,600	3.7	4.4
Education and Health Services	23,700	15.7	15.5
Financial Activities	7,300	4.8	5.7
Government	30,600	20.3	15.8
Information	3,400	2.3	2.0
Leisure and Hospitality	15,100	10.0	10.3
Manufacturing	13,000	8.6	8.7
Mining and Logging	900	0.6	0.6
Other Services	4,800	3.2	4.0
Professional and Business Services	15,400	10.2	13.8
Retail Trade	21,400	14.2	11.4
Transportation, Warehousing, and Utilities	3,600	2.4	3.9
Wholesale Trade	6,000	4.0	4.2

Note: Figures are non-farm employment as of December 2014. Figures are not seasonally adjusted and include workers 16 years of age and older; (1) Figures cover the Eugene, OR Metropolitan Statistical Area—see Appendix B for areas included
Source: Bureau of Labor Statistics, Current Employment Statistics, Employment, Hours, and Earnings

Occupations with Greatest Projected Employment Growth: 2012 – 2022

Occupation[1]	2012 Employment	2022 Projected Employment	Numeric Employment Change	Percent Employment Change
Retail Salespersons	55,160	62,550	7,390	13.4
Combined Food Preparation and Serving Workers, Including Fast Food	35,480	42,020	6,540	18.4
Registered Nurses	30,680	35,640	4,960	16.2
Waiters and Waitresses	27,760	32,690	4,930	17.8
Janitors and Cleaners, Except Maids and Housekeeping Cleaners	24,200	28,670	4,470	18.4
Bookkeeping, Accounting, and Auditing Clerks	26,030	30,280	4,250	16.3
Customer Service Representatives	22,630	26,520	3,890	17.2
Medical Secretaries	12,380	16,170	3,790	30.6
Farmworkers and Laborers, Crop, Nursery, and Greenhouse	20,290	24,010	3,720	18.4
Secretaries and Administrative Assistants, Except Legal, Medical, and Executive	22,400	26,100	3,700	16.5

Note: Projections cover Oregon; (1) Sorted by numeric employment change
Source: www.projectionscentral.com, State Occupational Projections, 2012–2022 Long-Term Projections

Fastest Growing Occupations: 2012 – 2022

Occupation[1]	2012 Employment	2022 Projected Employment	Numeric Employment Change	Percent Employment Change
Skincare Specialists	300	470	170	57.2
Computer Numerically Controlled Machine Tool Programmers, Metal and Plastic	460	680	220	47.2
Roofers	1,960	2,740	780	39.5
Brickmasons and Blockmasons	460	640	180	38.9
Physician Assistants	930	1,290	360	38.7
Insulation Workers, Floor, Ceiling, and Wall	450	620	170	38.7
Fence Erectors	420	570	150	38.3
Diagnostic Medical Sonographers	470	650	180	38.2
Market Research Analysts and Marketing Specialists	2,390	3,290	900	37.8
Helpers—Brickmasons, Blockmasons, Stonemasons, and Tile and Marble Setters	270	380	110	37.4

Note: Projections cover Oregon; (1) Sorted by percent employment change and excludes occupations with numeric employment change less than 100
Source: www.projectionscentral.com, State Occupational Projections, 2012–2022 Long-Term Projections

Average Wages

Occupation	$/Hr.	Occupation	$/Hr.
Accountants and Auditors	29.42	Maids and Housekeeping Cleaners	10.36
Automotive Mechanics	17.85	Maintenance and Repair Workers	18.32
Bookkeepers	17.43	Marketing Managers	33.62
Carpenters	21.32	Nuclear Medicine Technologists	n/a
Cashiers	10.76	Nurses, Licensed Practical	22.53
Clerks, General Office	14.38	Nurses, Registered	38.61
Clerks, Receptionists/Information	13.22	Nursing Assistants	13.86
Clerks, Shipping/Receiving	15.02	Packers and Packagers, Hand	10.83
Computer Programmers	27.98	Physical Therapists	42.09
Computer Systems Analysts	36.63	Postal Service Mail Carriers	24.68
Computer User Support Specialists	21.02	Real Estate Brokers	32.09
Cooks, Restaurant	11.04	Retail Salespersons	13.26
Dentists	92.36	Sales Reps., Exc. Tech./Scientific	23.83
Electrical Engineers	42.35	Sales Reps., Tech./Scientific	37.87
Electricians	29.10	Secretaries, Exc. Legal/Med./Exec.	16.13
Financial Managers	43.83	Security Guards	12.67
First-Line Supervisors/Managers, Sales	18.18	Surgeons	n/a
Food Preparation Workers	10.61	Teacher Assistants	13.10
General and Operations Managers	40.22	Teachers, Elementary School	26.40
Hairdressers/Cosmetologists	12.34	Teachers, Secondary School	26.20
Internists	n/a	Telemarketers	n/a
Janitors and Cleaners	12.54	Truck Drivers, Heavy/Tractor-Trailer	19.12
Landscaping/Groundskeeping Workers	14.20	Truck Drivers, Light/Delivery Svcs.	17.16
Lawyers	42.01	Waiters and Waitresses	11.02

Note: Wage data covers the Eugene-Springfield, OR Metropolitan Statistical Area—see Appendix B for areas included; Hourly wages for elementary/secondary school teachers and teacher assistants were calculated by the editors from annual wage data assuming a 40 hour work week; n/a not available.
Source: Bureau of Labor Statistics, Metro Area Occupational Employment and Wage Estimates, May 2014

TAXES

State Corporate Income Tax Rates

State	Tax Rate (%)	Income Brackets ($)	Num. of Brackets	Financial Institution Tax Rate (%)[a]	Federal Income Tax Ded.
Oregon	6.6 - 7.6 (w)	1 million	2	6.6 - 7.6 (w)	No

Note: Tax rates as of January 1, 2015; (a) Rates listed are the corporate income tax rate applied to financial institutions or excise taxes based on income. Some states have other taxes based upon the value of deposits or shares; (w) Oregon's minimum tax for C corporations depends on the Oregon sales of the filing group. The minimum tax ranges from $150 for corporations with sales under $500,000, up to $100,000 for companies with sales of $100 million or above.
Source: Federation of Tax Administrators, "State Corporate Income Tax Rates, 2015"

State Individual Income Tax Rates

State	Tax Rate (%)	Income Brackets ($)	Num. of Brackets	Personal Exempt. ($)[1] Single	Personal Exempt. ($)[1] Dependents	Fed. Inc. Tax Ded.
Oregon (a)	5.0 - 9.9	3,350 -125,000 (b)	4	194 (c)	194 (c)	Yes (n)

Note: Tax rates as of January 1, 2015; Local- and county-level taxes are not included; n/a not applicable; (1) Married joint filers generally receive double the single exemption; (a) 17 states have statutory provision for automatically adjusting to the rate of inflation the dollar values of the income tax brackets, standard deductions, and/or personal exemptions. Massachusetts, Michigan, and Nebraska index the personal exemption only. Oregon does not index the income brackets for $125,000 and over. Maine has suspended indexing for 2014 and 2015; (b) For joint returns, taxes are twice the tax on half the couple's income; (c) The personal exemption takes the form of a tax credit instead of a deduction; (n) The deduction for federal income tax is limited to $5,000 for individuals and $10,000 for joint returns in Missouri and Montana, and to $6,350 for all filers in Oregon.
Source: Federation of Tax Administrators, "State Individual Income Tax Rates, 2015"

Various State and Local Tax Rates

State	State and Local Sales and Use (%)	State Sales and Use (%)	Gasoline[1] (¢/gal.)	Cigarette[2] ($/pack)	Spirits[3] ($/gal.)	Wine[4] ($/gal.)	Beer[5] ($/gal.)
Oregon	None	None	31.07	1.31	22.72 (g)	0.67	0.08

Note: All tax rates as of January 1, 2015; (1) The American Petroleum Institute has developed a methodology for determining the average tax rate on a gallon of fuel. Rates may include any of the following: excise taxes, environmental fees, storage tank fees, other fees or taxes, general sales tax, and local taxes. In states where gasoline is subject to the general sales tax, or where the fuel tax is based on the average sale price, the average rate determined by API is sensitive to changes in the price of gasoline. States that fully or partially apply general sales taxes to gasoline: CA, CO, GA, IL, IN, MI, NY; (2) The federal excise tax of $1.0066 per pack and local taxes are not included; (3) Rates are those applicable to off-premise sales of 40% alcohol by volume (a.b.v.) distilled spirits in 750ml containers. Local excise taxes are excluded; (4) Rates are those applicable to off-premise sales of 11% a.b.v. non-carbonated wine in 750ml containers; (5) Rates are those applicable to off-premise sales of 4.7% a.b.v. beer in 12 ounce containers; (g) States where the government controls sales. In these "control states," products are subject to ad valorem mark-up and excise taxes. The excise tax rate is calculated using a methodology developed by the Distilled Spirits Council of the United States.
Source: Tax Foundation, 2015 Facts & Figures: How Does Your State Compare?

State Business Tax Climate Index Rankings

State	Overall Rank	Corporate Tax Index Rank	Individual Income Tax Index Rank	Sales Tax Index Rank	Unemployment Insurance Tax Index Rank	Property Tax Index Rank
Oregon	12	36	31	4	30	15

Note: The index is a measure of how each state's tax laws affect economic performance. The lower the rank, the more favorable a state's tax system is for business. States without a given tax are given a ranking of 1. The scores/rankings for the District of Columbia do not affect other states. The 2015 index represents the tax climate as of July 1, 2014.
Source: Tax Foundation, State Business Tax Climate Index 2015

COMMERCIAL UTILITIES

Typical Monthly Electric Bills

Area	Commercial Service ($/month) 1,500 kWh	Commercial Service ($/month) 40 kW demand 14,000 kWh	Industrial Service ($/month) 1,000 kW demand 200,000 kWh	Industrial Service ($/month) 50,000 kW demand 32,500,000 kWh
City	n/a	n/a	n/a	n/a
Average[1]	201	1,653	26,124	2,639,743

Note: Figures are based on annualized 2014 rates; (1) Average based on 180 utilities surveyed; n/a not available
Source: Edison Electric Institute, Typical Bills and Average Rates Report, Summer 2014

TRANSPORTATION

Means of Transportation to Work

Area	Car/Truck/Van		Public Transportation			Bicycle	Walked	Other Means	Worked at Home
	Drove Alone	Car-pooled	Bus	Subway	Railroad				
City	65.7	8.2	3.9	0.0	0.0	8.0	7.0	0.9	6.4
MSA[1]	70.9	10.0	2.8	0.0	0.0	4.5	4.7	0.8	6.3
U.S.	76.4	9.6	2.6	1.8	0.6	0.6	2.8	1.3	4.3

Note: Figures are percentages and cover workers 16 years of age and older; (1) Figures cover the Eugene, OR Metropolitan Statistical Area—see Appendix B for areas included
Source: U.S. Census Bureau, 2011-2013 American Community Survey 3-Year Estimates

Travel Time to Work

Area	Less Than 10 Minutes	10 to 19 Minutes	20 to 29 Minutes	30 to 44 Minutes	45 to 59 Minutes	60 to 89 Minutes	90 Minutes or More
City	17.5	50.6	19.9	7.2	1.9	2.1	0.8
MSA[1]	17.0	43.5	21.7	11.0	2.8	2.6	1.3
U.S.	13.3	29.7	20.9	20.2	7.7	5.7	2.6

Note: Figures are percentages and include workers 16 years old and over; (1) Figures cover the Eugene, OR Metropolitan Statistical Area—see Appendix B for areas included
Source: U.S. Census Bureau, 2011-2013 American Community Survey 3-Year Estimates

Travel Time Index

Area	1985	1990	1995	2000	2005	2010	2011
Urban Area[1]	1.07	1.08	1.08	1.17	1.17	1.08	1.08
Average[2]	1.09	1.14	1.16	1.19	1.23	1.18	1.18

Note: Travel Time Index—the ratio of travel time in the peak period to the travel time at free-flow conditions. For example, a value of 1.30 indicates a 20-minute free-flow trip takes 26 minutes in the peak. Free-flow speeds (60 mph on freeways and 35 mph on principal arterials) are used as the comparison threshold; (1) Covers the Eugene OR urban area; (2) average of 498 urban areas
Source: Texas Transportation Institute, Urban Mobility Report 2012, December 2012

Public Transportation

Agency Name / Mode of Transportation	Vehicles Operated in Maximum Service	Annual Unlinked Passenger Trips (in thous.)	Annual Passenger Miles (in thous.)
Lane Transit District (LTD)			
Bus (directly operated)	76	8,569.2	34,088.6
Bus (purchased transportation)	1	15.9	667.4
Bus Rapid Transit (directly operated)	8	2,707.3	7,840.0
Demand Response (purchased transportation)	49	203.9	1,868.2
Demand Response Taxi (purchased transportation)	128	113.9	954.6
Vanpool (purchased transportation)	13	35.8	2,066.1

Source: Federal Transit Administration, National Transit Database, 2013

Air Transportation

Airport Name and Code / Type of Service	Passenger Airlines[1]	Passenger Enplanements	Freight Carriers[2]	Freight (lbs.)
Mahlon Sweet Field (EUG)				
Domestic service (U.S. carriers - 2014)	15	439,745	4	1,549,449
International service (U.S. carriers - 2013)	0	0	0	0

Note: (1) Includes all U.S.-based major, minor and commuter airlines that carried at least one passenger during the year; (2) Includes all U.S.-based airlines and freight carriers that transported at least one lb. of freight during the year.
Source: Bureau of Transportation Statistics, The Intermodal Transportation Database, Air Carriers: T-100 Domestic Market (U.S. Carriers), 2014; Bureau of Transportation Statistics, The Intermodal Transportation Database, Air Carriers: T-100 International Market (U.S. Carriers), 2013

Other Transportation Statistics

Major Highways:	I-5
Amtrak Service:	Yes
Major Waterways/Ports:	None

Source: Amtrak.com; Google Maps

BUSINESSES

Major Business Headquarters

Company Name	Rankings	
	Fortune[1]	Forbes[2]
No companies listed	-	-

Note: (1) Fortune 500—companies that produce a 10-K are ranked 1 to 500 based on 2013 revenue; (2) all private companies with at least $2 billion in annual revenue through the end of their most current fiscal year are ranked 1 to 221; companies listed are headquartered in the city; dashes indicate no ranking Source: Fortune, "Fortune 500," June 16, 2014; Forbes, "America's Largest Private Companies," November 5, 2014

Minority- and Women-Owned Businesses

Group	All Firms		Firms with Paid Employees			
	Firms	Sales ($000)	Firms	Sales ($000)	Employees	Payroll ($000)
Asian	373	76,187	126	57,921	821	14,696
Black	(s)	(s)	(s)	(s)	(s)	(s)
Hispanic	314	29,981	65	20,984	501	7,602
Women	4,985	578,400	696	481,629	4,008	119,043
All Firms	16,643	13,060,402	4,608	12,510,499	75,086	2,519,715

Note: Figures cover firms located in the city; minority- and women-owned business are defined as firms in which the corresponding group own 51% or more of the stock or equity of the company; (s) estimates are suppressed when publication standards are not met Source: U.S. Census Bureau, 2007 Economic Census, Survey of Business Owners (2012 Survey of Business Owners data will be released starting in June 2015)

HOTELS & CONVENTION CENTERS

Hotels/Motels

Area	5 Star		4 Star		3 Star		2 Star		1 Star		Not Rated	
	Num.	Pct.[3]	Num.	Pct.[3]	Num.	Pct.[3]	Num.	Pct.[3]	Num.	Pct.[3]	Num.	Pct.[3]
City[1]	0	0.0	1	1.7	11	18.6	41	69.5	4	6.8	2	3.4
Total[2]	166	0.9	1,264	7.0	5,718	31.8	9,340	52.0	411	2.3	1,070	6.0

Note: (1) Figures cover Eugene and vicinity; (2) Figures cover all 100 cities in this book; (3) Percentage of hotels which have a given star rating; Star ratings are determined by expedia.com and offer an indication of the general quality of a particular hotel.
Source: expedia.com, April 2, 2015

Major Convention Centers

Name	Overall Space (sq. ft.)	Exhibit Space (sq. ft.)	Meeting Space (sq. ft.)	Meeting Rooms
Lane County Convention Center	n/a	30,000	n/a	n/a

Note: Table includes convention centers located in the Eugene, OR metro area; n/a not available
Source: Original research

Living Environment

COST OF LIVING

Cost of Living Index

Composite Index	Groceries	Housing	Utilities	Trans-portation	Health Care	Misc. Goods/Services
n/a	n/a	n/a	n/a	n/a	n/a	n/a

Note: The Cost of Living Index measures regional differences in the cost of consumer goods and services, excluding taxes and non-consumer expenditures, for professional and managerial households in the top income quintile. It is based on more than 50,000 prices covering almost 60 different items for which prices are collected three times a year by chambers of commerce, economic development organizations or university applied economic centers in each participating urban area. The numbers shown should be read as a percentage above or below the national average of 100. For example, a value of 115.4 in the groceries column indicates that grocery prices are 15.4% higher than the national average. Small differences in the index numbers should not be interpreted as significant; n/a not available.
Source: The Council for Community and Economic Research, ACCRA Cost of Living Index, 2014

Grocery Prices

Area[1]	T-Bone Steak ($/pound)	Frying Chicken ($/pound)	Whole Milk ($/half gal.)	Eggs ($/dozen)	Orange Juice ($/64 oz.)	Coffee ($/11.5 oz.)
City[2]	n/a	n/a	n/a	n/a	n/a	n/a
Avg.	10.40	1.37	2.40	1.99	3.46	4.27
Min.	8.48	0.93	1.37	1.30	2.83	2.99
Max.	14.20	2.44	3.62	4.02	6.42	6.96

Note: (1) Values for the local area are compared with the average, minimum and maximum values for all 308 areas in the Cost of Living Index; (2) Figures cover the Eugene OR urban area; n/a not available; **T-Bone Steak** (price per pound); **Frying Chicken** (price per pound, whole fryer); **Whole Milk** (half gallon carton); **Eggs** (price per dozen, Grade A, large); **Orange Juice** (64 oz. Tropicana or Florida Natural); **Coffee** (11.5 oz. can, vacuum-packed, Maxwell House, Hills Bros, or Folgers).
Source: The Council for Community and Economic Research, ACCRA Cost of Living Index, 2014

Housing and Utility Costs

Area[1]	New Home Price ($)	Apartment Rent ($/month)	All Electric ($/month)	Part Electric ($/month)	Other Energy ($/month)	Telephone ($/month)
City[2]	n/a	n/a	n/a	n/a	n/a	n/a
Avg.	305,838	919	181.00	93.66	73.14	27.95
Min.	183,142	480	112.00	42.06	23.42	17.16
Max.	1,358,576	3,851	594.00	180.03	440.99	40.42

Note: (1) Values for the local area are compared with the average, minimum and maximum values for all 308 areas in the Cost of Living Index; (2) Figures cover the Eugene OR urban area; n/a not available; **New Home Price** (2,400 sf living area, 8,000 sf lot, in urban area with full utilities); **Apartment Rent** (950 sf 2 bedroom/1.5 or 2 bath, unfurnished, excluding all utilities except water); **All Electric** (average monthly cost for an all-electric home); **Part Electric** (average monthly cost for a part-electric home); **Other Energy** (average monthly cost for natural gas, fuel oil, coal, wood, and any other forms of energy except electricity); **Telephone** (price includes basic monthly rate for a private residential line plus additional local usage charges incurred by a family of four).
Source: The Council for Community and Economic Research, ACCRA Cost of Living Index, 2014

Health Care, Transportation, and Other Costs

Area[1]	Doctor ($/visit)	Dentist ($/visit)	Optometrist ($/visit)	Gasoline ($/gallon)	Beauty Salon ($/visit)	Men's Shirt ($)
City[2]	n/a	n/a	n/a	n/a	n/a	n/a
Avg.	102.86	87.89	97.66	3.44	34.37	26.74
Min.	67.47	65.78	51.18	3.00	17.43	12.79
Max.	173.50	150.14	235.00	4.33	64.28	49.50

Note: (1) Values for the local area are compared with the average, minimum and maximum values for all 308 areas in the Cost of Living Index; (2) Figures cover the Eugene OR urban area; n/a not available; **Doctor** (general practitioners routine exam of an established patient); **Dentist** (adult teeth cleaning and periodic oral examination); **Optometrist** (full vision eye exam for established adult patient); **Gasoline** (one gallon regular unleaded, national brand, including all taxes, cash price at self-service pump if available); **Beauty Salon** (woman's shampoo, trim, and blow-dry); **Men's Shirt** (cotton/polyester dress shirt, pinpoint weave, long sleeves).
Source: The Council for Community and Economic Research, ACCRA Cost of Living Index, 2014

HOUSING

House Price Index (HPI)

Area	National Ranking[2]	Quarterly Change (%)	One-Year Change (%)	Five-Year Change (%)
MSA[1]	135	-0.05	4.33	-0.31
U.S.[3]	–	1.35	4.91	11.59

Note: The HPI is a weighted repeat sales index. It measures average price changes in repeat sales or refinancings on the same properties. This information is obtained by reviewing repeat mortgage transactions on single-family properties whose mortgages have been purchased or securitized by Fannie Mae or Freddie Mac in January 1975; (1) Eugene Metropolitan Statistical Area—see Appendix B for areas included; (2) Rankings are based on annual percentage change for all metro areas containing at least 15,000 transactions over the last 10 years and ranges from 1 to 275; (3) figures based on a weighted average of Census Division estimates using a seasonally adjusted, purchase-only index; all figures are for the period ending December 31, 2014
Source: Federal Housing Finance Agency, House Price Index, February 26, 2015

Median Single-Family Home Prices

Area	2012	2013	2014p	Percent Change 2013 to 2014
MSA[1]	178.7	178.2	200.9	12.7
U.S. Average	177.2	197.4	209.0	5.9

Note: Figures are median sales prices of existing single-family homes in thousands of dollars; (p) preliminary; n/a not available; (1) Eugene, OR Metropolitan Statistical Area—see Appendix B for areas included
Source: National Association of Realtors, Median Sales Price of Existing Single-Family Homes for Metropolitan Areas, 4th Quarter 2014

Qualifying Income Based on Median Sales Price of Existing Single-Family Homes

Area	With 5% Down ($)	With 10% Down ($)	With 20% Down ($)
MSA[1]	47,401	44,906	39,917
U.S. Average	45,863	43,449	38,621

Note: Figures are preliminary; Qualifying income is based on a mortgage rate of 4.0%. Monthly principal and interest payment is limited to 25% of income; n/a not available; (1) Eugene, OR Metropolitan Statistical Area—see Appendix B for areas included
Source: National Association of Realtors, Qualifying Income Based on Median Sales Price of Existing Single-Family Homes for Metropolitan Areas, 4th Quarter 2014

Median Apartment Condo-Coop Home Prices

Area	2012	2013	2014p	Percent Change 2013 to 2014
MSA[1]	n/a	n/a	n/a	n/a
U.S. Average	173.7	194.9	205.1	5.2

Note: Figures are median sales prices of existing apartment condo-coop homes in thousands of dollars; (p) preliminary; n/a not available; (1) Eugene, OR Metropolitan Statistical Area—see Appendix B for areas included
Source: National Association of Realtors, Median Sales Price of Existing Apartment Condo-Coop Homes for Metropolitan Areas, 4th Quarter 2014

Gross Monthly Rent

Area	Under $200	$200 -299	$300 -499	$500 -749	$750 -999	$1,000 -1,499	$1,500 and up	Median ($)
City	1.4	2.1	7.8	25.8	26.8	25.4	10.7	864
MSA[1]	1.5	2.2	7.6	26.6	29.1	25.5	7.5	850
U.S.	1.7	3.2	7.8	22.1	24.3	26.0	14.9	900

Note: Figures are percentages except for Median; Gross rent is the contract rent plus the estimated average monthly cost of utilities (electricity, gas, and water and sewer) and fuels (oil, coal, kerosene, wood, etc.) if these are paid by the renter (or paid for the renter by someone else); (1) Figures cover the Eugene, OR Metropolitan Statistical Area—see Appendix B for areas included
Source: U.S. Census Bureau, 2011-2013 American Community Survey 3-Year Estimates

Homeownership Rate

Area	2007 (%)	2008 (%)	2009 (%)	2010 (%)	2011 (%)	2012 (%)	2013 (%)	2014 (%)
MSA[1]	n/a	n/a	n/a	n/a	n/a	n/a	n/a	n/a
U.S.	68.1	67.8	67.4	66.9	66.1	65.4	65.1	64.5

Note: (1) Figures cover the Eugene, OR Metropolitan Statistical Area—see Appendix B for areas included; n/a not available
Source: U.S. Census Bureau, Housing Vacancies and Homeownership Annual Statistics: 2014

Year Housing Structure Built

Area	2010 or Later	2000 -2009	1990 -1999	1980 -1989	1970 -1979	1960 -1969	1950 -1959	1940 -1949	Before 1940	Median Year
City	0.9	13.4	17.8	8.7	22.6	13.7	9.3	6.0	7.7	1976
MSA[1]	0.8	12.5	16.0	9.5	23.0	14.2	9.4	7.1	7.6	1975
U.S.	0.9	15.0	13.9	13.8	15.8	11.0	10.9	5.4	13.3	1976

Note: Figures are percentages except for Median Year; (1) Figures cover the Eugene, OR Metropolitan Statistical Area—see Appendix B for areas included
Source: U.S. Census Bureau, 2011-2013 American Community Survey 3-Year Estimates

HEALTH

Health Risk Data

Category	MSA[1] (%)	U.S. (%)
Adults aged 18–64 who have any kind of health care coverage	74.8	79.6
Adults who reported being in good or excellent health	84.5	83.1
Adults who are current smokers	17.1	19.6
Adults who are heavy drinkers[2]	7.5	6.1
Adults who are binge drinkers[3]	16.3	16.9
Adults who are overweight (BMI 25.0 - 29.9)	29.7	35.8
Adults who are obese (BMI 30.0 - 99.8)	30.6	27.6
Adults who participated in any physical activities in the past month	85.7	77.1
Adults 50+ who have ever had a sigmoidoscopy or colonoscopy	71.8	67.3
Women aged 40+ who have had a mammogram within the past two years	70.2	74.0
Men aged 40+ who have had a PSA test within the past two years	42.9	45.2
Adults aged 65+ who have had flu shot within the past year	49.9	60.1
Adults who always wear a seatbelt	n/a	93.8

Note: Data as of 2012 unless otherwise noted; n/a not available; (1) Figures cover the Eugene-Springfield, OR Metropolitan Statistical Area—see Appendix B for areas included; (2) Heavy drinkers are classified as males having more than two drinks per day or females having more than one drink per day; (3) Binge drinkers are classified as males having five or more drinks on one occasion or females having four or more drinks on one occasion
Source: Centers for Disease Control and Prevention, Behaviorial Risk Factor Surveillance System, SMART: Selected Metropolitan/Micropolitan Area Risk Trends, 2012 (Note: the CDC has discontinued this dataset but will be releasing a replacement in late 2015)

Chronic Health Indicators

Category	MSA[1] (%)	U.S. (%)
Adults who have ever been told they had a heart attack	3.4	4.5
Adults who have ever been told they had a stroke	2.3	2.9
Adults who have been told they currently have asthma	13.8	8.9
Adults who have ever been told they have arthritis	29.0	25.7
Adults who have ever been told they have diabetes[2]	8.7	9.7
Adults who have ever been told they had skin cancer	7.6	5.7
Adults who have ever been told they had any other types of cancer	5.0	6.5
Adults who have ever been told they have COPD	7.8	6.2
Adults who have ever been told they have kidney disease	2.4	2.5
Adults who have ever been told they have a form of depression	24.2	18.0

Note: Data as of 2012 unless otherwise noted; (1) Figures cover the Eugene-Springfield, OR Metropolitan Statistical Area—see Appendix B for areas included; (2) Figures do not include pregnancy-related, borderline, or pre-diabetes
Source: Centers for Disease Control and Prevention, Behaviorial Risk Factor Surveillance System, SMART: Selected Metropolitan/Micropolitan Area Risk Trends, 2012 (Note: the CDC has discontinued this dataset but will be releasing a replacement in late 2015)

Mortality Rates for the Top 10 Causes of Death in the U.S.

ICD-10[a] Sub-Chapter	ICD-10[a] Code	Age-Adjusted Mortality Rate[1] per 100,000 population	
		County[2]	U.S.
Malignant neoplasms	C00-C97	168.9	166.2
Ischaemic heart diseases	I20-I25	67.1	105.7
Other forms of heart disease	I30-I51	53.4	49.3
Chronic lower respiratory diseases	J40-J47	48.4	42.1
Organic, including symptomatic, mental disorders	F01-F09	45.7	38.1
Cerebrovascular diseases	I60-I69	37.4	37.0
Other external causes of accidental injury	W00-X59	36.9	26.9
Other degenerative diseases of the nervous system	G30-G31	36.3	25.6
Diabetes mellitus	E10-E14	23.3	21.3
Hypertensive diseases	I10-I15	17.5	19.4

Note: (a) ICD-10 = International Classification of Diseases 10th Revision; (1) Mortality rates are a three year average covering 2011-2013; (2) Figures cover Lane County
Source: Centers for Disease Control and Prevention, National Center for Health Statistics. Compressed Mortality File 1999-2013 on CDC WONDER Online Database, released October 2014. Data are compiled from the Compressed Mortality File 1999-2013, Series 20 No. 2S, 2014.

Mortality Rates for Selected Causes of Death

ICD-10[a] Sub-Chapter	ICD-10[a] Code	Age-Adjusted Mortality Rate[1] per 100,000 population	
		County[2]	U.S.
Assault	X85-Y09	2.6	5.2
Diseases of the liver	K70-K76	17.0	13.2
Human immunodeficiency virus (HIV) disease	B20-B24	*1.1	2.2
Influenza and pneumonia	J09-J18	8.4	15.4
Intentional self-harm	X60-X84	18.5	12.5
Malnutrition	E40-E46	Suppressed	0.9
Obesity and other hyperalimentation	E65-E68	2.9	1.8
Renal failure	N17-N19	7.4	13.1
Transport accidents	V01-V99	10.2	11.7
Viral hepatitis	B15-B19	4.0	2.2

Note: (a) ICD-10 = International Classification of Diseases 10th Revision; (1) Mortality rates are a three year average covering 2011-2013; (2) Figures cover Lane County; (*) Unreliable data as per CDC
Source: Centers for Disease Control and Prevention, National Center for Health Statistics. Compressed Mortality File 1999-2013 on CDC WONDER Online Database, released October 2014. Data are compiled from the Compressed Mortality File 1999-2013, Series 20 No. 2S, 2014.

Health Insurance Coverage

Area	With Health Insurance	With Private Health Insurance	With Public Health Insurance	Without Health Insurance	Population Under Age 18 Without Health Insurance
City	85.6	68.1	28.8	14.4	5.0
MSA[1]	85.0	64.5	34.7	15.0	5.9
U.S.	85.2	65.2	31.0	14.8	7.3

Note: Figures are percentages that cover the civilian noninstitutionalized population; (1) Figures cover the Eugene, OR Metropolitan Statistical Area—see Appendix B for areas included
Source: U.S. Census Bureau, 2011-2013 American Community Survey 3-Year Estimates

Number of Medical Professionals

Area[1]	MDs[2]	DOs[2,3]	Dentists	Podiatrists	Chiropractors	Optometrists
Local (number)	859	41	231	10	94	59
Local (rate[4])	242.3	11.6	64.9	2.8	26.4	16.6
U.S. (rate[4])	270.0	20.2	63.1	5.7	25.2	14.9

Note: Data as of 2013 unless noted; (1) Local data covers Lane County; (2) Data as of 2012 and includes all active, non-federal physicians; (3) Doctor of Osteopathic Medicine; (4) rate per 100,000 population
Source: U.S. Department of Health and Human Services, Health Resources and Services Administration, Bureau of Health Professions, Area Resource File (ARF) 2013-2014

EDUCATION

Public School District Statistics

District Name	Schls	Pupils	Pupil/ Teacher Ratio	Minority Pupils[1] (%)	Free Lunch Eligible[2] (%)	IEP[3] (%)
Bethel School District 52	12	5,930	26.0	29.2	50.5	17.8
Eugene School District 4J	36	17,029	23.5	30.2	32.2	15.0

Note: Table includes school districts with 2,000 or more students; (1) Percentage of students that are not non-Hispanic white; (2) Percentage of students that are eligible for the free lunch program; (3) Percentage of students that have an Individualized Education Program.
Source: U.S. Department of Education, National Center for Education Statistics, Common Core of Data, Local Education Agency (School District) Universe Survey: School Year 2012-2013; U.S. Department of Education, National Center for Education Statistics, Common Core of Data, Public Elementary/Secondary School Universe Survey: School Year 2012-2013

Highest Level of Education

Area	Less than H.S.	H.S. Diploma	Some College, No Deg.	Associate Degree	Bachelor's Degree	Master's Degree	Prof. School Degree	Doctorate Degree
City	6.1	18.8	29.0	7.8	22.0	10.6	2.5	3.2
MSA[1]	8.6	25.5	29.8	8.3	16.8	7.4	1.7	1.9
U.S.	13.7	28.0	21.2	7.9	18.2	7.7	1.9	1.3

Note: Figures cover persons age 25 and over; (1) Figures cover the Eugene, OR Metropolitan Statistical Area—see Appendix B for areas included
Source: U.S. Census Bureau, 2011-2013 American Community Survey 3-Year Estimates

Educational Attainment by Race

Area	High School Graduate or Higher (%)					Bachelor's Degree or Higher (%)				
	Total	White	Black	Asian	Hisp.[2]	Total	White	Black	Asian	Hisp.[2]
City	93.9	94.6	96.3	95.5	68.5	38.3	38.8	31.3	57.3	18.0
MSA[1]	91.4	92.2	94.2	87.3	69.5	27.9	28.2	30.0	45.7	14.2
U.S.	86.3	88.3	83.1	85.7	64.0	29.1	30.4	18.8	50.7	13.7

Note: Figures shown cover persons 25 years old and over; (1) Figures cover the Eugene, OR Metropolitan Statistical Area—see Appendix B for areas included; (2) People of Hispanic origin can be of any race
Source: U.S. Census Bureau, 2011-2013 American Community Survey 3-Year Estimates

School Enrollment by Grade and Control

Area	Preschool (%)		Kindergarten (%)		Grades 1 - 4 (%)		Grades 5 - 8 (%)		Grades 9 - 12 (%)	
	Public	Private	Public	Private	Public	Private	Public	Private	Public	Private
City	36.0	64.0	81.2	18.8	85.8	14.2	87.3	12.7	90.9	9.1
MSA[1]	53.0	47.0	83.8	16.2	89.4	10.6	89.7	10.3	92.8	7.2
U.S.	57.7	42.3	87.9	12.1	89.9	10.1	90.0	10.0	90.7	9.3

Note: Figures shown cover persons 3 years old and over; (1) Figures cover the Eugene, OR Metropolitan Statistical Area—see Appendix B for areas included
Source: U.S. Census Bureau, 2011-2013 American Community Survey 3-Year Estimates

Average Salaries of Public School Classroom Teachers

Area	2013-14		2014-15		Percent Change 2013-14 to 2014-15	Percent Change 2004-05 to 2014-15
	Dollars	Rank[1]	Dollars	Rank[1]		
OREGON	58,638	14	59,811	13	2.00	23.8
U.S. Average	56,610	–	57,379	–	1.36	20.8

Note: (1) State rank ranges from 1 to 51 where 1 indicates highest salary.
Source: National Education Association, Rankings & Estimates: Rankings of the States 2014 and Estimates of School Statistics 2015, March 2015

Higher Education

Four-Year Colleges			Two-Year Colleges			Medical Schools[1]	Law Schools[2]	Voc/Tech[3]
Public	Private Non-profit	Private For-profit	Public	Private Non-profit	Private For-profit			
1	2	0	1	1	0	0	1	0

Note: Figures cover institutions located within the city limits and include main campuses only; (1) includes schools accredited by the Liaison Committee on Medical Education and the American Osteopathic Association's Commission on Osteopathic College Accreditation; (2) includes ABA-accredited schools, schools with provisional ABA accreditation, and state accredited schools; (3) includes all schools with programs that are less than 2 years.
Source: National Center for Education Statistics, Integrated Postsecondary Education System (IPEDS), 2013-14; Association of American Medical Colleges, Member List, May 1, 2015; American Osteopathic Association, Member List, May 1, 2015; Law School Admission Council, Official Guide to ABA-Approved Law Schools Online, May 1, 2015; Wikipedia, List of Medical Schools in the United States, May 1, 2015; Wikipedia, List of Law Schools in the United States, May 1, 2015

According to *U.S. News & World Report*, the Eugene, OR metro area is home to one of the best national universities in the U.S.: **University of Oregon** (#106). The indicators used to capture academic quality fall into a number of categories: assessment by administrators at peer institutions; retention of students; faculty resources; student selectivity; financial resources; alumni giving; high school counselor ratings of colleges; and graduation rate. *U.S. News & World Report, "America's Best Colleges 2015"*

According to *U.S. News & World Report*, the Eugene, OR metro area is home to one of the top 100 law schools in the U.S.: **University of Oregon** (#82). The rankings are based on a weighted average of 12 measures of quality: peer assessment score; assessment score by lawyers/judges; median LSAT scores; median undergrad GPA; acceptance rate; employment rates for graduates; placement success; bar passage rate; faculty resources; expenditures per student; student/faculty ratio; and library resources. *U.S. News & World Report, "America's Best Graduate Schools, Law, 2016"*

PRESIDENTIAL ELECTION

2012 Presidential Election Results

Area	Obama (%)	Romney (%)	Other (%)
Lane County	59.7	36.4	3.9
U.S.	51.0	47.2	1.8

Note: Results may not add to 100% due to rounding
Source: Dave Leip's Atlas of U.S. Presidential Elections

EMPLOYERS

Major Employers

Company Name	Industry
Abby's	Pizzeria, chain
Arclin USA LLC	Plastics materials and resins
Bi-Mart Corporation	Miscellaneous general merchandise stores
County of Lane	Automotive maintenance equipment
Datalogic Adc	Magnetic ink and optical scanning devices
Datalogic Scanning	Calculating and accounting equipment
Farwest Steel Corporation	Fabricated structural metal
Lane Community College	Community college
Lane County School District #52	Public combined elementary and secondary school
Lane County School District 4J	Public elementary school
Market of Choice	Supermarkets, independent
McKenzie-Williamette Medical Services	General medical and surgical hospitals
Navistar RV	Motor homes
Oregon University System	University
Pacificsource Health Plans	Accident and health insurance carriers
Papé Material Handling	Industrial machinery and equipment
Peacehealth	Medical laboratories
Pinnacle Healthcare	Skilled nursing care facilities
S Butler-Rosboro Corporation	Glow lamp bulbs
Springfield School District 19	Public elementary and secondary schools
States Industries	Hardwood veneer and plywood
The Papé Group	Construction and mining machinery
Three Rivers Casino	Casino hotel
Timber Products Co. Limited Partnership	Plywood, softwood
University of Oregon	Colleges and universities

Note: Companies shown are located within the Eugene, OR Metropolitan Statistical Area.
Source: Hoovers.com; Wikipedia

PUBLIC SAFETY

Crime Rate

Area	All Crimes	Violent Crimes				Property Crimes		
		Murder	Forcible Rape	Robbery	Aggrav. Assault	Burglary	Larceny -Theft	Motor Vehicle Theft
City	5,250.5	0.0	42.9	123.0	87.7	971.0	3,642.3	383.6
Suburbs[1]	2,815.7	2.0	18.7	23.8	101.6	512.1	1,956.3	201.2
Metro[2]	3,898.7	1.1	29.5	67.9	95.4	716.2	2,706.3	282.3
U.S.	3,098.6	4.5	25.2	109.1	229.1	610.0	1,899.4	221.3

Note: Figures are crimes per 100,000 population; (1) All areas within the metro area that are located outside the city limits; (2) Figures cover the Eugene, OR Metropolitan Statistical Area—see Appendix B for areas included
Source: FBI Uniform Crime Reports, 2013

Hate Crimes

Area	Number of Quarters Reported	Number of Incidents per Bias Motivation						
		Race	Religion	Sexual Orientation	Ethnicity	Disability	Gender	Gender Identity
City	4	6	4	3	2	0	0	0
U.S.	4	2,871	1,031	1,233	655	83	18	31

Source: Federal Bureau of Investigation, Hate Crime Statistics 2013

Identity Theft Consumer Complaints

Area	Complaints	Complaints per 100,000 Population	Rank[2]
MSA[1]	290	81.4	119
U.S.	332,646	104.3	-

Note: (1) Figures cover the Eugene, OR Metropolitan Statistical Area—see Appendix B for areas included; (2) Rank ranges from 1 to 380 where 1 indicates greatest number of identity theft complaints per 100,000 population
Source: Federal Trade Commission, Consumer Sentinel Network Data Book for January–December 2014

Fraud and Other Consumer Complaints

Area	Complaints	Complaints per 100,000 Population	Rank[2]
MSA[1]	1,552	435.7	80
U.S.	2,250,205	705.7	-

Note: (1) Figures cover the Eugene, OR Metropolitan Statistical Area—see Appendix B for areas included; (2) Rank ranges from 1 to 380 where 1 indicates greatest number of identity theft complaints per 100,000 population
Source: Federal Trade Commission, Consumer Sentinel Network Data Book for January–December 2014

RECREATION

Culture

Dance[1]	Theatre[1]	Instrumental Music[1]	Vocal Music[1]	Series and Festivals	Museums and Art Galleries[2]	Zoos and Aquariums[3]
3	3	4	1	3	18	0

Note: (1) Professional perfoming groups; (2) Based on organizations with SIC code 8412; (3) AZA-accredited
Source: The Grey House Performing Arts Directory, 2015-16; Association of Zoos & Aquariums, AZA Member Zoos & Aquariums, April 2015; www.AccuLeads.com, April 2015

Professional Sports Teams

Team Name	League	Year Established
No teams are located in the metro area		

Source: Wikipedia, Major Professional Sports Teams of the United States and Canada, April 2015

CLIMATE

Average and Extreme Temperatures

Temperature	Jan	Feb	Mar	Apr	May	Jun	Jul	Aug	Sep	Oct	Nov	Dec	Yr.
Extreme High (°F)	67	69	77	86	93	102	105	108	103	94	76	68	108
Average High (°F)	46	51	55	61	67	74	82	82	76	64	53	47	63
Average Temp. (°F)	40	44	46	50	55	61	67	67	62	53	46	41	53
Average Low (°F)	33	35	37	39	43	48	51	51	48	42	38	35	42
Extreme Low (°F)	-4	-3	20	27	28	32	39	38	32	19	12	-12	-12

Note: Figures cover the years 1948-1992
Source: National Climatic Data Center, International Station Meteorological Climate Summary, 9/96

Average Precipitation/Snowfall/Humidity

Precip./Humidity	Jan	Feb	Mar	Apr	May	Jun	Jul	Aug	Sep	Oct	Nov	Dec	Yr.
Avg. Precip. (in.)	7.8	5.6	5.3	3.0	2.2	1.4	0.4	0.8	1.4	3.6	7.6	8.2	47.3
Avg. Snowfall (in.)	4	1	1	Tr	Tr	0	0	0	0	Tr	Tr	1	7
Avg. Rel. Hum. 7am (%)	91	92	91	88	84	81	78	82	88	93	93	92	88
Avg. Rel. Hum. 4pm (%)	79	73	64	57	54	49	38	39	44	61	79	84	60

Note: Figures cover the years 1948-1992; Tr = Trace amounts (<0.05 in. of rain; <0.5 in. of snow)
Source: National Climatic Data Center, International Station Meteorological Climate Summary, 9/96

Weather Conditions

Temperature			Daytime Sky			Precipitation		
32°F & below	45°F & below	90°F & above	Clear	Partly cloudy	Cloudy	0.01 inch or more precip.	0.1 inch or more snow/ice	Thunder-storms
54	233	15	75	115	175	136	4	3

Note: Figures are average number of days per year and cover the years 1948-1992
Source: National Climatic Data Center, International Station Meteorological Climate Summary, 9/96

HAZARDOUS WASTE

Superfund Sites

Eugene has no sites on the EPA's Superfund Final National Priorities List. There are a total of 1,322 Superfund sites on the list in the U.S. *U.S. Environmental Protection Agency, Final National Priorities List, April 14, 2015*

**AIR & WATER
QUALITY**

Air Quality Trends: Ozone

	2004	2005	2006	2007	2008	2009	2010	2011	2012	2013
MSA[1]	0.066	0.068	0.073	0.060	0.059	0.065	0.058	0.059	0.061	0.055

Note: (1) Data covers the Eugene, OR Metropolitan Statistical Area—see Appendix B for areas included. The values shown are the composite ozone concentration averages among trend sites based on the highest fourth daily maximum 8-hour concentration in parts per million. These trends are based on sites having an adequate record of monitoring data during the trend period. Data from exceptional events are included.
Source: U.S. Environmental Protection Agency, Air Quality Monitoring Information, "Air Quality Trends by City, 2000-2013"

Air Quality Index

Area	Percent of Days when Air Quality was...[2]					AQI Statistics[2]	
	Good	Moderate	Unhealthy for Sensitive Groups	Unhealthy	Very Unhealthy	Maximum	Median
MSA[1]	69.6	25.8	4.7	0.0	0.0	135	39

Note: (1) Data covers the Eugene, OR Metropolitan Statistical Area—see Appendix B for areas included; (2) Based on 365 days with AQI data in 2014. Air Quality Index (AQI) is an index for reporting daily air quality. EPA calculates the AQI for five major air pollutants regulated by the Clean Air Act: ground-level ozone, particle pollution (aka particulate matter), carbon monoxide, sulfur dioxide, and nitrogen dioxide. The AQI runs from 0 to 500. The higher the AQI value, the greater the level of air pollution and the greater the health concern. There are six AQI categories: "Good" AQI is between 0 and 50. Air quality is considered satisfactory; "Moderate" AQI is between 51 and 100. Air quality is acceptable; "Unhealthy for Sensitive Groups" When AQI values are between 101 and 150, members of sensitive groups may experience health effects; "Unhealthy" When AQI values are between 151 and 200 everyone may begin to experience health effects; "Very Unhealthy" AQI values between 201 and 300 trigger a health alert; "Hazardous" AQI values over 300 trigger warnings of emergency conditions (not shown).
Source: U.S. Environmental Protection Agency, Air Quality Index Report, 2014

Air Quality Index Pollutants

Area	Percent of Days when AQI Pollutant was...[2]					
	Carbon Monoxide	Nitrogen Dioxide	Ozone	Sulfur Dioxide	Particulate Matter 2.5	Particulate Matter 10
MSA[1]	0.0	0.0	26.0	0.0	74.0	0.0

Note: (1) Data covers the Eugene, OR Metropolitan Statistical Area—see Appendix B for areas included; (2) Based on 365 days with AQI data in 2014. The Air Quality Index (AQI) is an index for reporting daily air quality. EPA calculates the AQI for five major air pollutants regulated by the Clean Air Act: ground-level ozone, particle pollution (also known as particulate matter), carbon monoxide, sulfur dioxide, and nitrogen dioxide. The AQI runs from 0 to 500. The higher the AQI value, the greater the level of air pollution and the greater the health concern.
Source: U.S. Environmental Protection Agency, Air Quality Index Report, 2014

Maximum Air Pollutant Concentrations: Particulate Matter, Ozone, CO and Lead

	Particulate Matter 10 (ug/m^3)	Particulate Matter 2.5 Wtd AM (ug/m^3)	Particulate Matter 2.5 24-Hr (ug/m^3)	Ozone (ppm)	Carbon Monoxide (ppm)	Lead (ug/m^3)
MSA[1] Level	42	9.8	41	0.056	n/a	n/a
NAAQS[2]	150	15	35	0.075	9	0.15
Met NAAQS[2]	Yes	Yes	No	Yes	n/a	n/a

Note: (1) Data covers the Eugene, OR Metropolitan Statistical Area—see Appendix B for areas included; Data from exceptional events are included; (2) National Ambient Air Quality Standards; ppm = parts per million; ug/m^3 = micrograms per cubic meter; n/a not available.
Concentrations: Particulate Matter 10 (coarse particulate)—highest second maximum 24-hour concentration; Particulate Matter 2.5 Wtd AM (fine particulate)—highest weighted annual mean concentration; Particulate Matter 2.5 24-Hour (fine particulate)—highest 98th percentile 24-hour concentration; Ozone—highest fourth daily maximum 8-hour concentration; Carbon Monoxide—highest second maximum non-overlapping 8-hour concentration; Lead—maximum running 3-month average
Source: U.S. Environmental Protection Agency, Air Quality Monitoring Information, "Air Quality Statistics by City, 2013"

Maximum Air Pollutant Concentrations: Nitrogen Dioxide and Sulfur Dioxide

	Nitrogen Dioxide AM (ppb)	Nitrogen Dioxide 1-Hr (ppb)	Sulfur Dioxide AM (ppb)	Sulfur Dioxide 1-Hr (ppb)	Sulfur Dioxide 24-Hr (ppb)
MSA[1] Level	n/a	n/a	n/a	n/a	n/a
NAAQS[2]	53	100	30	75	140
Met NAAQS[2]	n/a	n/a	n/a	n/a	n/a

Note: (1) Data covers the Eugene, OR Metropolitan Statistical Area—see Appendix B for areas included; Data from exceptional events are included; (2) National Ambient Air Quality Standards; ppm = parts per million; ug/m³ = micrograms per cubic meter; n/a not available.
Concentrations: Nitrogen Dioxide AM—highest arithmetic mean concentration; Nitrogen Dioxide 1-Hr—highest 98th percentile 1-hour daily maximum concentration; Sulfur Dioxide AM—highest annual mean concentration; Sulfur Dioxide 1-Hr—highest 99th percentile 1-hour daily maximum concentration; Sulfur Dioxide 24-Hr—highest second maximum 24-hour concentration
Source: U.S. Environmental Protection Agency, Air Quality Monitoring Information, "Air Quality Statistics by City, 2013"

Drinking Water

Water System Name	Pop. Served	Primary Water Source Type	Violations[1] Health Based	Violations[1] Monitoring/ Reporting
Eugene Water & Electric Board	178,100	Surface	0	0

Note: (1) Based on violation data from January 1, 2014 to December 31, 2014 (includes unresolved violations from earlier years)
Source: U.S. Environmental Protection Agency, Office of Ground Water and Drinking Water, Safe Drinking Water Information System (based on data extracted January 27, 2015)

Fort Collins, Colorado

Background

At 4,985 feet, Fort Collins lies high in the eastern base of the Rocky Mountains' front range along the Cache la Poudre River about one hour from Denver. Although not quite as large as Denver, Fort Collins, home to Colorado State University and its own symphony orchestra, offers virtually everything its citizens need, all within a spectacular landscape.

Fort Collins owes its name to Colonel William Collins of the Civil War era, who was sent with a regiment of Union soldiers to guard farmers and ranchers scattered throughout the valley, and to provide security for the Overland Stage trail. Originally called Camp Collins, the place remained a military reservation until 1866 and was incorporated in 1879.

The early economy of the town depended first on lumber, and then on the raising of livestock and produce, with alfalfa, grain, and sugar beets as the chief crops. Sugar refiners, dairies, and meatpacking plants bolstered the wealth of the town, as did the products of mining and quarrying. Fort Collins is still the commercial center for a rich agricultural region that produces hay, barley, and sugar beets.

Colorado State University, the land grant University of Colorado, was established in Fort Collins in 1879, and offers innumerable cultural, economic, and educational benefits to residents. More than 24,000 students are enrolled at CSU, which is the largest employer in the city. CSU offers a world-class range of undergraduate and graduate programs, and is an internationally recognized center for forestry, agricultural science, veterinary medicine, and civil engineering.

Fort Collins' businesses produce motion-picture film, combustion engines, prefabricated metal buildings, arc welders and rods, cement products, dental hygiene appliances, and miscellaneous plastics. With fabulous scenery, a symphony orchestra, and all the attractions of Denver an hour away, Fort Collins offers an attractive site for relocation. For outdoor sporting enthusiasts, the area is irresistible. The town is only a few hours from Colorado's world-famous ski areas, and cross-country skiing is nearby.

The Fort Collins public school system, within the Poudre School District, is one of the area's largest employers. New construction in the Poudre School District has recently been completed with the opening of the city's 32nd elementary school. The city's public library system, Poudre River Public Libraries, now operates three branches.

Gateway Natural Area, 15 miles from Fort Collins, offers several recreation opportunities, including a quarter-mile nature trail and a designated boat launching area. Lakes are easily accessible for all water sports, and the Cache La Poudre River itself offers some of the best trout fishing in Colorado. For hunters, the area is a paradise, with ample supplies of antelope, black bear, deer, elk, mountain lion, and small game.

Fort Collins also offers a great range of cultural amenities. The city's Lincoln Center presents year-round performances by a variety of artists. Old Town, a historic downtown shopping district, hosts a number of large festivals each year. Fort Collins Symphony, the Larimer Chorale, Open Stage Theatre, and the Canyon Concert Ballet call Fort Collins their home. The city also cultivates the visual arts, with "Art in Public Places" sponsored by the city, and provides exhibits at the Lincoln Center, Fort Collins Museum, and private galleries.

Transportation in and around the city is convenient. The municipality operates its own bus service on 10 daily routes, and interstate bus service is available. Residents are served by three nearby airports, Fort Collins/Loveland Airport, Cheyenne Municipal Airport, and Denver International Airport, which is one of the nation's busiest airports.

Fort Collins features four distinct seasons and, though high in the foothills, is buffered from both summer and winter extremes of temperature. The most typical day in Fort Collins is warm and dry, and mild nights are the rule. The town enjoys 296 days per year of sun, and an annual snowfall of 51 inches. Rainfall is far less. Summers are comfortable, while winters are cold.

Rankings

General Rankings

- In their second annual survey, analysts for the small- and mid-sized city lifestyle site Livability.com looked at data for more than 2,000 U.S. cities to determine the rankings for Livability's "Top 100 Best Places to Live" in 2015. Fort Collins ranked #24. Criteria: vibrant economy; low cost of living; abundant lifestyle amenities. *Livability.com, "Top 100 Best Places to Live 2015"*

Business/Finance Rankings

- The Fort Collins metro area appeared on the Milken Institute "2013 Best Performing Cities" list. Rank: #17 out of 200 large metro areas. Criteria: job growth; wage and salary growth; high-tech output growth. *Milken Institute, "Best-Performing Cities 2014," January 2015*

- *Forbes* ranked the 200 most populous metro areas to determine the nation's "Best Places for Business and Careers." The Fort Collins metro area was ranked #5. Criteria: costs (business and living); job growth (past and projected); income growth; educational attainment (college and high school); projected economic growth; cultural and recreational opportunities; net migration patterns; number of highly ranked colleges. *Forbes, "The Best Places for Business and Careers 2014," July 23, 2014*

Education Rankings

- Fort Collins was identified as one of "Smartest Cities in America" by the brain-training website *Lumosity* using data from three million of its own users. The metro area ranked #47 out of 50. Criteria: users' brain performance index scores, considering core cognitive abilities such as memory, processing speed, flexibility, attention and problem-solving. *Lumosity, " Smartest Cities in America," June 25, 2013*

Environmental Rankings

- The Weather Channel determined the nation's snowiest cities, based on the National Oceanic and Atmospheric Administration's 30-year average snowfall data. Among cities with a population of at least 100,000, the #15-ranked city was Fort Collins *weather.com, America's 20 Snowiest Major Cities, February 3, 2014*

- The Fort Collins metro area came in at #16 for the relative comfort of its climate on Sperling's list of "chill cities," as measured by the Sperling Heat Index. All 361 metro areas are included. Criteria included daytime high temperatures, nighttime low temperatures, dew point, and relative humidity at the high temperatures. *www.bertsperling.com, "Sperling's Chill Cities," July 18, 2013*

- Sperling's BestPlaces assessed 379 metropolitan areas of the United States for the likelihood of dangerously extreme weather events or earthquakes. In general the Southeast and South-Central regions have the highest risk of weather extremes and earthquakes, while the Pacific Northwest enjoys the lowest risk. Of the least risky metropolitan areas, the Fort Collins metro area was ranked #169. *www.bestplaces.net, "Safest Places from Natural Disasters," April 2011*

- The U.S. Environmental Protection Agency (EPA) released a list of mid-size U.S. metropolitan areas with the most ENERGY STAR certified buildings in 2014. The Fort Collins metro area was ranked #9 out of 10. *U.S. Environmental Protection Agency, "Top Cities With the Most ENERGY STAR Certified Buildings in 2014," March 25, 2015*

- Fort Collins was highlighted as one of the 25 most ozone-polluted metro areas in the U.S. during 2011 through 2013. The area ranked #16. *American Lung Association, State of the Air 2015*

- Fort Collins was highlighted as one of the top 25 cleanest metro areas for short-term particle pollution (24-hour PM 2.5) in the U.S. during 2011 through 2013. Monitors in these cities reported no days with unhealthful PM 2.5 levels. *American Lung Association, State of the Air 2015*

Food/Drink Rankings

- For the Gallup-Healthways Well-Being Index, researchers interviewed at least 300 adults in each of 189 metropolitan areas on residents' access to affordable fresh produce. The Fort Collins metro area was found to be among the top ten communities for affordable produce accessibility. *www.gallup.com, "In Anchorage, Access to Fruits and Vegetables Remains Lowest," April 8, 2014*

Health/Fitness Rankings

- For the Gallup-Healthways Well-Being Index, researchers asked at least 300 adult residents in each of 189 U.S. metropolitan areas how satisfied they were with the metro area in which they lived. The Fort Collins metro area was among the top ten for residents' satisfaction. *www.gallup.com, "City Satisfaction Highest in Fort Collins-Loveland, Colo.," April 11, 2014*

- Analysts who tracked obesity rates in 189 of the nation's metro areas found that the Fort Collins metro area was one of the ten communities where residents were least likely to be obese, defined as a BMI score of 30 or above. *www.gallup.com, "Boulder, Colo., Residents Still Least Likely to Be Obese," April 4, 2014*

- The Fort Collins metro area appeared in the 2013 Gallup-Healthways Well-Being Index. The area ranked #3 out of 189. The Gallup-Healthways Well-Being Index score is an average of six sub-indexes, which individually examine life evaluation, emotional health, work environment, physical health, healthy behaviors, and access to basic necessities. Results are based on telephone interviews conducted as part of the Gallup-Healthways Well-Being Index survey January 2–December 29, 2012, and January 2–December 30, 2013, with a random sample of 531,630 adults, aged 18 and older, living in metropolitan areas in the 50 U.S. states and the District of Columbia. *Gallup-Healthways, "State of American Well-Being," March 25, 2014*

Real Estate Rankings

- Fort Collins was ranked #63 out of 275 metro areas in terms of house price appreciation in 2014 (#1 = highest rate). *Federal Housing Finance Agency, House Price Index, 4th Quarter 2014*

- Fort Collins was ranked #145 out of 226 metro areas in terms of housing affordability in 2014 by the National Association of Home Builders (#1 = most affordable). The NAHB-Wells Fargo Housing Opportunity Index (HOI) for a given area is defined as the share of homes sold in that area that would have been affordable to a family earning the local median income, based on standard mortgage underwriting criteria. *National Association of Home Builders®, NAHB-Wells Fargo Housing Opportunity Index, 4th Quarter 2014*

Safety Rankings

- Farmers Insurance, in partnership with Sperling's BestPlaces, ranked metro areas in the U.S. and identified the "Most Secure Places to Live." The Fort Collins metro area ranked #16 out of the top 20 in the mid-size city category (150,000 to 500,000 residents). Criteria: economic stability; crime statistics; extreme weather; risk of natural disasters; housing depreciation; foreclosures; air quality; environmental hazards; life expectancy; motor vehicle fatalities; and employment numbers. *Farmers Insurance Group of Companies, "Most Secure U.S. Places to Live in the U.S.," June 25, 2013*

- Allstate ranked the 200 largest cities in America in terms of driver safety. Fort Collins ranked #1. Allstate researchers analyzed internal property damage claims over a two-year period from January 2011 to December 2012. A weighted average of the two-year numbers determined the annual percentages. *Allstate, "Allstate America's Best Drivers Report, 2014"*

- The National Insurance Crime Bureau ranked 380 metro areas in the U.S. in terms of per capita rates of vehicle theft. The Fort Collins metro area ranked #321 (#1 = highest rate). Criteria: number of vehicle theft offenses per 100,000 inhabitants in 2012. *National Insurance Crime Bureau, "Hot Spots 2012," June 26, 2013*

Seniors/Retirement Rankings

- From its Best Cities for Successful Aging indexes, the Milken Institute generated rankings for metropolitan areas, weighing data in eight categories—health care, wellness, living arrangements, transportation, financial characteristics, education and employment opportunities, community engagement, and overall livability. The Fort Collins metro area was ranked #62 overall in the small metro area category. *Milken Institute, "Best Cities for Successful Aging, 2014"*

- Fort Collins was identified as one of the most popular places to retire by *Topretirements.com*. The list reflects the 100 cities (out of 900+ total cities reviewed) that visitors to the website are most interested in for retirement. *Topretirements.com, "Most Popular Places to Retire for 2014," February 25, 2014*

Sports/Recreation Rankings

- Fort Collins was chosen as a bicycle friendly community by the League of American Bicyclists. A "Bicycle Friendly Community" welcomes cyclists by providing safe accommodation for cycling and encouraging people to bike for transportation and recreation. There are four award levels: Platinum; Gold; Silver; and Bronze. The community achieved an award level of Platinum. *League of American Bicyclists, "Bicycle Friendly Community Master List," Fall 2013*

- Fort Collins was chosen as one of America's best cities for bicycling. The city ranked #11 out of 50. Criteria: robust cycling infrastructure; vibrant bike culture. The editors only considered cities with populations of 95,000 or more. *Bicycling, "America's Top 50 Bike-Friendly Cities," May 23, 2012*

Miscellaneous Rankings

- Fort Collins was selected as a 2013 Digital Cities Survey winner. The city ranked #5 in the mid-sized city (125,000 to 249,999 population) category. The survey examined and assessed how city governments are utilizing information technology to operate and deliver quality service to their customers and citizens. Survey questions focused on implementation and adoption of online service delivery; planning and governance; and the infrastructure and architecture that make the transformation to digital government possible. *Center for Digital Government, "2013 Digital Cities Survey," November 7, 2013*

- According to the World Giving Index, the United States is the fifth most generous nation in the world. The finance and lifestyle site NerdWallet looked for the U.S. cities that topped the list in donating money and time to good causes. The Fort Collins metro area proved to be the #7-ranked metro area, judged by culture of volunteerism, depth of commitment in terms of volunteer hours per year, and monetary contributions. *www.nerdwallet.com, "Most Generous Cities," September 22, 2013*

- Bustle.com, a news, entertainment, and lifestyle site for women, studied binge- and heavy drinking rates among nonalcoholics to determine the nation's ten "drunkest" cities. Fort Collins made the list, at #4. *www.bustle.com, "38 Million Americans Have a Problem with Alcohol: The 10 Drunkest American Cities," January 2014*

Business Environment

CITY FINANCES

City Government Finances

Component	2012 ($000)	2012 ($ per capita)
Total Revenues	367,793	2,554
Total Expenditures	368,388	2,558
Debt Outstanding	216,445	1,503
Cash and Securities[1]	368,432	2,559

*Note: (1) Cash and security holdings of a government at the close of its fiscal
year, including those of its dependent agencies, utilities, and liquor stores.*
Source: U.S Census Bureau, State & Local Government Finances 2012

City Government Revenue by Source

Source	2012 ($000)	2012 ($ per capita)
General Revenue		
From Federal Government	13,234	92
From State Government	5,089	35
From Local Governments	12,508	87
Taxes		
Property	17,742	123
Sales and Gross Receipts	103,832	721
Personal Income	0	0
Corporate Income	0	0
Motor Vehicle License	1,546	11
Other Taxes	2,449	17
Current Charges	57,083	396
Liquor Store	0	0
Utility	129,667	901
Employee Retirement	0	0

Source: U.S Census Bureau, State & Local Government Finances 2012

City Government Expenditures by Function

Function	2012 ($000)	2012 ($ per capita)	2012 (%)
General Direct Expenditures			
Air Transportation	0	0	0.0
Corrections	0	0	0.0
Education	0	0	0.0
Employment Security Administration	0	0	0.0
Financial Administration	32,214	224	8.7
Fire Protection	0	0	0.0
General Public Buildings	0	0	0.0
Governmental Administration, Other	0	0	0.0
Health	0	0	0.0
Highways	52,579	365	14.3
Hospitals	0	0	0.0
Housing and Community Development	0	0	0.0
Interest on General Debt	4,349	30	1.2
Judicial and Legal	0	0	0.0
Libraries	0	0	0.0
Parking	0	0	0.0
Parks and Recreation	48,528	337	13.2
Police Protection	31,780	221	8.6
Public Welfare	0	0	0.0
Sewerage	16,376	114	4.4
Solid Waste Management	0	0	0.0
Veterans' Services	0	0	0.0
Liquor Store	0	0	0.0
Utility	134,717	936	36.6
Employee Retirement	0	0	0.0

Source: U.S Census Bureau, State & Local Government Finances 2012

DEMOGRAPHICS

Population Growth

Area	1990 Census	2000 Census	2010 Census	Population Growth (%) 1990-2000	Population Growth (%) 2000-2010
City	89,555	118,652	143,986	32.5	21.4
MSA[1]	186,136	251,494	299,630	35.1	19.1
U.S.	248,709,873	281,421,906	308,745,538	13.2	9.7

Note: (1) Figures cover the Fort Collins-Loveland, CO Metropolitan Statistical Area—see Appendix B for areas included
Source: U.S. Census Bureau, Census 1990, 2000, 2010

Household Size

Area	Persons in Household (%) One	Two	Three	Four	Five	Six	Seven or More	Average Household Size
City	26.2	36.5	19.0	11.7	4.6	1.5	0.6	2.46
MSA[1]	25.4	39.4	16.1	12.2	4.7	1.6	0.7	2.45
U.S.	27.7	33.6	15.7	13.1	6.0	2.3	1.5	2.64

Note: (1) Figures cover the Fort Collins, CO Metropolitan Statistical Area—see Appendix B for areas included
Source: U.S. Census Bureau, 2011-2013 American Community Survey 3-Year Estimates

Race

Area	White Alone[2] (%)	Black Alone[2] (%)	Asian Alone[2] (%)	AIAN[3] Alone[2] (%)	NHOPI[4] Alone[2] (%)	Other Race Alone[2] (%)	Two or More Races (%)
City	89.6	1.2	2.9	0.4	0.2	2.0	3.7
MSA[1]	90.8	0.8	2.0	0.5	0.1	2.7	3.1
U.S.	73.9	12.6	5.0	0.8	0.2	4.7	2.9

Note: (1) Figures cover the Fort Collins, CO Metropolitan Statistical Area—see Appendix B for areas included;
(2) Alone is defined as not being in combination with one or more other races; (3) American Indian and Alaska Native; (4) Native Hawaiian and Other Pacific Islander
Source: U.S. Census Bureau, 2011-2013 American Community Survey 3-Year Estimates

Hispanic or Latino Origin

Area	Total (%)	Mexican (%)	Puerto Rican (%)	Cuban (%)	Other (%)
City	10.6	7.4	0.8	0.1	2.3
MSA[1]	10.8	8.1	0.4	0.1	2.2
U.S.	16.9	10.8	1.6	0.6	3.8

Note: Persons of Hispanic or Latino origin can be of any race; (1) Figures cover the Fort Collins, CO Metropolitan Statistical Area—see Appendix B for areas included
Source: U.S. Census Bureau, 2011-2013 American Community Survey 3-Year Estimates

Segregation

Type	Segregation Indices[1] 1990	2000	2010	2010 Rank[2]	Percent Change 1990-2000	1990-2010	2000-2010
Black/White	n/a	n/a	n/a	n/a	n/a	n/a	n/a
Asian/White	n/a	n/a	n/a	n/a	n/a	n/a	n/a
Hispanic/White	n/a	n/a	n/a	n/a	n/a	n/a	n/a

Note: All figures cover the Metropolitan Statistical Area—see Appendix B for areas included; Figures are based on an analysis of 1990, 2000, and 2010 Census Decennial Census tract data by William H. Frey, Brookings Institution and the University of Michigan Social Science Data Analysis Network. In this analysis all racial groups (whites, blacks, and asians) are non-Hispanic members of those races. Hispanics are shown as a separate category;
(1) Segregation Indices are Dissimilarity Indices that measure the degree to which the minority group is distributed differently than whites across census tracts. They range from 0 (complete integration) to 100 (complete segregation) where the value indicates the percentage of the minority group that needs to move to be distributed exactly like whites; (2) Ranges from 1 (most segregated) to 102 (least segregated); n/a not available.
Source: www.CensusScope.org

Ancestry

Area	German	Irish	English	American	Italian	Polish	French[2]	Scottish	Dutch
City	26.3	14.2	11.6	4.1	6.8	3.6	3.9	2.9	2.6
MSA[1]	28.2	13.9	12.6	4.7	5.8	3.1	4.0	3.1	2.5
U.S.	14.9	10.8	8.0	7.4	5.5	3.0	2.7	1.7	1.4

Note: Figures are the percentage of the total population reporting a particular ancestry. The nine most commonly reported ancestries in the U.S. are shown. Figures include multiple ancestries (e.g. if a person reported being Irish and Italian, they were included in both columns); (1) Figures cover the Fort Collins, CO Metropolitan Statistical Area—see Appendix B for areas included; (2) Excludes Basque
Source: U.S. Census Bureau, 2011-2013 American Community Survey 3-Year Estimates

Foreign-Born Population

Area	Percent of Population Born in								
	Any Foreign Country	Mexico	Asia	Europe	Carribean	South America	Central America[2]	Africa	Canada
City	6.1	1.2	2.5	1.2	0.1	0.4	0.2	0.2	0.3
MSA[1]	5.3	1.8	1.6	1.0	0.0	0.3	0.2	0.2	0.2
U.S.	13.0	3.7	3.8	1.5	1.2	0.9	1.0	0.6	0.3

Note: (1) Figures cover the Fort Collins, CO Metropolitan Statistical Area—see Appendix B for areas included; (2) Excludes Mexico.
Source: U.S. Census Bureau, 2011-2013 American Community Survey 3-Year Estimates

Marital Status

Area	Never Married	Now Married[2]	Separated	Widowed	Divorced
City	44.0	42.3	0.7	3.4	9.6
MSA[1]	33.6	50.9	1.0	4.0	10.5
U.S.	32.7	48.1	2.2	6.0	11.0

Note: Figures are percentages and cover the population 15 years of age and older; (1) Figures cover the Fort Collins, CO Metropolitan Statistical Area—see Appendix B for areas included; (2) Excludes separated
Source: U.S. Census Bureau, 2011-2013 American Community Survey 3-Year Estimates

Disability Status

Area	All Ages	Under 18 Years Old	18 to 64 Years Old	65 Years and Over
City	7.5	1.9	5.9	33.2
MSA[1]	9.4	2.8	7.4	30.7
U.S.	12.3	4.1	10.2	36.3

Note: Figures show percent of the civilian noninstitutionalized population that reported having a disability. Disability status is determined from from six types of difficulty: vision, hearing, cognitive, ambulatory, self-care, and independent living. For children under 5 years old, hearing and vision difficulty are used to determine disability status. For children between the ages of 5 and 14, disability status is determined from hearing, vision, cognitive, ambulatory, and self-care difficulties. For people aged 15 years and older, they are considered to have a disability if they have difficulty with any one of the six difficulty types; (1) Figures cover the Fort Collins, CO Metropolitan Statistical Area—see Appendix B for areas included.
Source: U.S. Census Bureau, 2011-2013 American Community Survey 3-Year Estimates

Age

Area	Percent of Population									Median Age
	Under Age 5	Age 5–19	Age 20–34	Age 35–44	Age 45–54	Age 55–64	Age 65–74	Age 75–84	Age 85+	
City	5.5	19.6	33.0	11.5	11.7	9.8	5.0	2.5	1.5	29.7
MSA[1]	5.6	19.1	24.6	12.0	13.0	12.9	7.5	3.8	1.7	35.6
U.S.	6.4	19.9	20.7	12.9	14.1	12.3	7.6	4.2	1.9	37.4

Note: (1) Figures cover the Fort Collins, CO Metropolitan Statistical Area—see Appendix B for areas included
Source: U.S. Census Bureau, 2011-2013 American Community Survey 3-Year Estimates

Gender

Area	Males	Females	Males per 100 Females
City	73,780	75,195	98.1
MSA[1]	154,721	155,883	99.3
U.S.	154,451,010	159,410,713	96.9

Note: (1) Figures cover the Fort Collins, CO Metropolitan Statistical Area—see Appendix B for areas included
Source: U.S. Census Bureau, 2011-2013 American Community Survey 3-Year Estimates

Religious Groups by Family

Area	Catholic	Baptist	Non-Den.	Methodist[2]	Lutheran	LDS[3]	Pentecostal	Presbyterian[4]	Muslim[5]	Judaism
MSA[1]	11.8	2.2	6.4	4.4	3.5	3.0	4.7	1.9	0.1	<0.1
U.S.	19.1	9.3	4.0	4.0	2.3	2.0	1.9	1.6	0.8	0.7

Note: Figures are the number of adherents as a percentage of the total population; (1) Figures cover the Fort Collins-Loveland, CO Metropolitan Statistical Area—see Appendix B for areas included; (2) Methodist/Pietist; (3) Latter Day Saints; (4) Reformed; (5) Figures are estimates
Source: Association of Statisticians of American Religious Bodies, 2010 U.S. Religion Census: Religious Congregations & Membership Study

Religious Groups by Tradition

Area	Catholic	Evangelical Protestant	Mainline Protestant	Other Tradition	Black Protestant	Orthodox
MSA[1]	11.8	18.8	5.9	4.0	<0.1	0.1
U.S.	19.1	16.2	7.3	4.3	1.6	0.3

Note: Figures are the number of adherents as a percentage of the total population; (1) Figures cover the Fort Collins-Loveland, CO Metropolitan Statistical Area—see Appendix B for areas included
Source: Association of Statisticians of American Religious Bodies, 2010 U.S. Religion Census: Religious Congregations & Membership Study

ECONOMY

Gross Metropolitan Product

Area	2012	2013	2014	2015	Rank[2]
MSA[1]	12.4	12.8	13.3	14.0	155

Note: Figures are in billions of dollars; (1) Figures cover the Fort Collins, CO Metropolitan Statistical Area—see Appendix B for areas included; (2) Rank is based on 2015 data and ranges from 1 to 363
Source: The U.S. Conference of Mayors, U.S. Metro Economies: GMP and Employment 2013-2015, June 2014

Economic Growth

Area	2010-12 (%)	2013 (%)	2014 (%)	2015 (%)	Rank[2]
MSA[1]	2.5	1.8	2.0	3.3	102
U.S.	2.1	2.0	2.3	3.2	–

Note: Figures are real gross metropolitan product (GMP) growth rates and represent annual average percent change; (1) Figures cover the Fort Collins, CO Metropolitan Statistical Area—see Appendix B for areas included; (2) Rank is based on 2015 data and ranges from 1 to 363
Source: The U.S. Conference of Mayors, U.S. Metro Economies: GMP and Employment 2013-2015, June 2014

Metropolitan Area Exports

Area	2008	2009	2010	2011	2012	2013	Rank[2]
MSA[1]	631.5	584.0	694.1	812.7	861.7	986.1	157

Note: Figures are in millions of dollars; (1) Figures cover the Fort Collins, CO Metropolitan Statistical Area—see Appendix B for areas included; (2) Rank is based on 2013 data and ranges from 1 to 387
Source: U.S. Department of Commerce, International Trade Administration, Office of Trade & Industry Information, Manufacturing & Services, data extracted April 3, 2015

Building Permits

Area	Single-Family			Multi-Family			Total		
	2013	2014	Pct. Chg.	2013	2014	Pct. Chg.	2013	2014	Pct. Chg.
City	612	742	21.2	779	410	-47.4	1,391	1,152	-17.2
MSA[1]	1,489	1,627	9.3	888	871	-1.9	2,377	2,498	5.1
U.S.	620,802	634,597	2.2	370,020	411,766	11.3	990,822	1,046,363	5.6

Note: (1) Figures cover the Fort Collins, CO Metropolitan Statistical Area—see Appendix B for areas included; Figures represent new, privately-owned housing units authorized (unadjusted data); All permit data are based on estimates with imputation.
Source: U.S. Census Bureau, Manufacturing, Mining, and Construction Statistics, Building Permits, 2013, 2014

Bankruptcy Filings

Area	Business Filings			Nonbusiness Filings		
	2013	2014	% Chg.	2013	2014	% Chg.
Larimer County	49	29	-40.8	1,077	857	-20.4
U.S.	33,212	26,983	-18.8	1,038,720	909,812	-12.4

Note: Business filings include Chapter 7, Chapter 11, Chapter 12, and Chapter 13; Nonbusiness filings include Chapter 7, Chapter 11, and Chapter 13
Source: Administrative Office of the U.S. Courts, Business and Nonbusiness Bankruptcy, County Cases Commenced by Chapter of the Bankruptcy Code, During the 12- Month Period Ending December 31, 2013 and Business and Nonbusiness Bankruptcy, County Cases Commenced by Chapter of the Bankruptcy Code, During the 12- Month Period Ending December 31, 2014

Housing Vacancy Rates

Area	Gross Vacancy Rate[2] (%)			Year-Round Vacancy Rate[3] (%)			Rental Vacancy Rate[4] (%)			Homeowner Vacancy Rate[5] (%)		
	2012	2013	2014	2012	2013	2014	2012	2013	2014	2012	2013	2014
MSA[1]	n/a	n/a	n/a	n/a	n/a	n/a	n/a	n/a	n/a	n/a	n/a	n/a
U.S.	13.8	13.6	13.4	10.8	10.7	10.4	8.7	8.3	7.6	2.0	2.0	1.9

Note: (1) Figures cover the Fort Collins, CO Metropolitan Statistical Area—see Appendix B for areas included; (2) The percentage of the total housing inventory that is vacant; (3) The percentage of the housing inventory (excluding seasonal units) that is year-round vacant; (4) The percentage of rental inventory that is vacant for rent; (5) The percentage of homeowner inventory that is vacant for sale; n/a not available
Source: U.S. Census Bureau, Housing Vacancies and Homeownership Annual Statistics: 2014

INCOME

Income

Area	Per Capita ($)	Median Household ($)	Average Household ($)
City	28,766	53,435	72,215
MSA[1]	30,422	57,316	74,915
U.S.	27,884	52,176	72,897

Note: (1) Figures cover the Fort Collins, CO Metropolitan Statistical Area—see Appendix B for areas included
Source: U.S. Census Bureau, 2011-2013 American Community Survey 3-Year Estimates

Household Income Distribution

Area	Percent of Households Earning							
	Under $15,000	$15,000 -24,999	$25,000 -34,999	$35,000 -49,999	$50,000 -74,999	$75,000 -99,000	$100,000 -149,999	$150,000 and up
City	13.8	11.2	8.6	13.5	17.3	13.1	13.4	9.2
MSA[1]	10.7	10.6	9.7	13.2	18.7	13.4	14.1	9.7
U.S.	13.0	10.9	10.3	13.6	17.9	11.9	12.7	9.6

Note: (1) Figures cover the Fort Collins, CO Metropolitan Statistical Area—see Appendix B for areas included
Source: U.S. Census Bureau, 2011-2013 American Community Survey 3-Year Estimates

Poverty Rate

Area	All Ages	Under 18 Years Old	18 to 64 Years Old	65 Years and Over
City	18.5	11.4	22.2	6.1
MSA[1]	14.0	13.0	16.1	5.0
U.S.	15.9	22.4	14.8	9.5

Note: Figures are percentage of people whose income during the past 12 months was below the poverty level; (1) Figures cover the Fort Collins, CO Metropolitan Statistical Area—see Appendix B for areas included
Source: U.S. Census Bureau, 2011-2013 American Community Survey 3-Year Estimates

EMPLOYMENT

Labor Force and Employment

Area	Civilian Labor Force			Workers Employed		
	Dec. 2013	Dec. 2014	% Chg.	Dec. 2013	Dec. 2014	% Chg.
City	86,406	87,583	1.4	82,460	84,643	2.6
MSA[1]	173,690	175,415	1.0	164,957	169,324	2.6
U.S.	154,408,000	155,521,000	0.7	144,423,000	147,190,000	1.9

Note: Data is not seasonally adjusted and covers workers 16 years of age and older; (1) Figures cover the Fort Collins, CO Metropolitan Statistical Area—see Appendix B for areas included
Source: Bureau of Labor Statistics, Local Area Unemployment Statistics

Unemployment Rate

Area	2014											
	Jan.	Feb.	Mar.	Apr.	May	Jun.	Jul.	Aug.	Sep.	Oct.	Nov.	Dec.
City	5.3	5.3	5.0	4.4	3.9	4.2	4.1	3.8	3.4	3.3	3.4	3.4
MSA[1]	5.6	5.6	5.3	4.5	4.1	4.3	4.2	3.9	3.4	3.4	3.5	3.5
U.S.	7.0	7.0	6.8	5.9	6.1	6.3	6.5	6.3	5.7	5.5	5.5	5.4

Note: Data is not seasonally adjusted and covers workers 16 years of age and older; (1) Figures cover the Fort Collins, CO Metropolitan Statistical Area—see Appendix B for areas included
Source: Bureau of Labor Statistics, Local Area Unemployment Statistics

Employment by Occupation

Occupation Classification	City (%)	MSA[1] (%)	U.S. (%)
Management, Business, Science, and Arts	44.6	42.1	36.2
Natural Resources, Construction, and Maintenance	6.0	8.4	9.0
Production, Transportation, and Material Moving	7.0	8.6	12.1
Sales and Office	24.3	23.5	24.4
Service	18.1	17.3	18.3

Note: Figures cover employed civilians 16 years of age and older; (1) Figures cover the Fort Collins, CO Metropolitan Statistical Area—see Appendix B for areas included
Source: U.S. Census Bureau, 2011-2013 American Community Survey 3-Year Estimates

Employment by Industry

Sector	MSA[1]		U.S.
	Number of Employees	Percent of Total	Percent of Total
Construction, Mining, and Logging	9,700	6.5	5.0
Education and Health Services	15,200	10.2	15.5
Financial Activities	6,300	4.2	5.7
Government	36,200	24.2	15.8
Information	2,500	1.7	2.0
Leisure and Hospitality	18,500	12.4	10.3
Manufacturing	12,600	8.4	8.7
Other Services	5,500	3.7	4.0
Professional and Business Services	19,200	12.8	13.8
Retail Trade	17,100	11.4	11.4
Transportation, Warehousing, and Utilities	3,000	2.0	3.9
Wholesale Trade	3,900	2.6	4.2

Note: Figures are non-farm employment as of December 2014. Figures are not seasonally adjusted and include workers 16 years of age and older; (1) Figures cover the Fort Collins, CO Metropolitan Statistical Area—see Appendix B for areas included; n/a not available
Source: Bureau of Labor Statistics, Current Employment Statistics, Employment, Hours, and Earnings

Occupations with Greatest Projected Employment Growth: 2012 – 2022

Occupation[1]	2012 Employment	2022 Projected Employment	Numeric Employment Change	Percent Employment Change
Combined Food Preparation and Serving Workers, Including Fast Food	60,670	77,380	16,710	27.5
Secretaries and Administrative Assistants, Except Legal, Medical, and Executive	63,150	77,880	14,730	23.3
Retail Salespersons	79,300	94,000	14,700	18.5
Customer Service Representatives	45,990	59,210	13,220	28.8
Registered Nurses	42,200	53,270	11,070	26.2
General and Operations Managers	42,170	52,340	10,170	24.1
Accountants and Auditors	33,870	43,490	9,620	28.4
Personal Care Aides	16,940	26,210	9,270	54.7
Janitors and Cleaners, Except Maids and Housekeeping Cleaners	36,300	45,470	9,170	25.3
Business Operations Specialists, All Other	42,990	51,450	8,460	19.7

Note: Projections cover Colorado; (1) Sorted by numeric employment change
Source: www.projectionscentral.com, State Occupational Projections, 2012–2022 Long-Term Projections

Fastest Growing Occupations: 2012 – 2022

Occupation[1]	2012 Employment	2022 Projected Employment	Numeric Employment Change	Percent Employment Change
Service Unit Operators, Oil, Gas, and Mining	3,520	6,290	2,770	78.4
Derrick Operators, Oil and Gas	630	1,110	480	76.0
Rotary Drill Operators, Oil and Gas	1,280	2,200	920	71.5
Roustabouts, Oil and Gas	2,770	4,710	1,940	70.2
Interpreters and Translators	1,510	2,550	1,040	68.5
Petroleum Engineers	1,500	2,500	1,000	66.9
Pump Operators, Except Wellhead Pumpers	700	1,160	460	64.9
Helpers—Brickmasons, Blockmasons, Stonemasons, and Tile and Marble Setters	200	320	120	61.3
Insulation Workers, Mechanical	420	680	260	61.2
Information Security Analysts	1,240	1,960	720	57.8

Note: Projections cover Colorado; (1) Sorted by percent employment change and excludes occupations with numeric employment change less than 100
Source: www.projectionscentral.com, State Occupational Projections, 2012–2022 Long-Term Projections

Average Wages

Occupation	$/Hr.	Occupation	$/Hr.
Accountants and Auditors	30.38	Maids and Housekeeping Cleaners	9.99
Automotive Mechanics	20.72	Maintenance and Repair Workers	17.29
Bookkeepers	17.74	Marketing Managers	67.14
Carpenters	19.23	Nuclear Medicine Technologists	n/a
Cashiers	10.12	Nurses, Licensed Practical	21.75
Clerks, General Office	15.89	Nurses, Registered	31.50
Clerks, Receptionists/Information	13.73	Nursing Assistants	13.68
Clerks, Shipping/Receiving	13.49	Packers and Packagers, Hand	9.53
Computer Programmers	43.50	Physical Therapists	34.13
Computer Systems Analysts	42.95	Postal Service Mail Carriers	25.41
Computer User Support Specialists	25.95	Real Estate Brokers	30.37
Cooks, Restaurant	11.24	Retail Salespersons	12.51
Dentists	67.22	Sales Reps., Exc. Tech./Scientific	28.50
Electrical Engineers	46.14	Sales Reps., Tech./Scientific	33.51
Electricians	22.15	Secretaries, Exc. Legal/Med./Exec.	16.40
Financial Managers	61.03	Security Guards	11.03
First-Line Supervisors/Managers, Sales	20.77	Surgeons	102.71
Food Preparation Workers	11.18	Teacher Assistants	12.70
General and Operations Managers	47.71	Teachers, Elementary School	23.60
Hairdressers/Cosmetologists	12.67	Teachers, Secondary School	23.80
Internists	n/a	Telemarketers	13.69
Janitors and Cleaners	11.76	Truck Drivers, Heavy/Tractor-Trailer	16.93
Landscaping/Groundskeeping Workers	13.24	Truck Drivers, Light/Delivery Svcs.	17.08
Lawyers	66.59	Waiters and Waitresses	10.10

Note: Wage data covers the Fort Collins-Loveland, CO Metropolitan Statistical Area—see Appendix B for areas included; Hourly wages for elementary/secondary school teachers and teacher assistants were calculated by the editors from annual wage data assuming a 40 hour work week; n/a not available.
Source: Bureau of Labor Statistics, Metro Area Occupational Employment and Wage Estimates, May 2014

TAXES

State Corporate Income Tax Rates

State	Tax Rate (%)	Income Brackets ($)	Num. of Brackets	Financial Institution Tax Rate (%)[a]	Federal Income Tax Ded.
Colorado	4.63	Flat rate	1	4.63	No

Note: Tax rates as of January 1, 2015; (a) Rates listed are the corporate income tax rate applied to financial institutions or excise taxes based on income. Some states have other taxes based upon the value of deposits or shares.
Source: Federation of Tax Administrators, "State Corporate Income Tax Rates, 2015"

State Individual Income Tax Rates

State	Tax Rate (%)	Income Brackets ($)	Num. of Brackets	Personal Exempt. ($)[1] Single	Personal Exempt. ($)[1] Dependents	Fed. Inc. Tax Ded.
Colorado	4.63	Flat rate	1	4,000 (d)	4,000 (d)	No

Note: Tax rates as of January 1, 2015; Local- and county-level taxes are not included; n/a not applicable; (1) Married joint filers generally receive double the single exemption; (d) These states use the personal exemption amounts provided in the federal Internal Revenue Code.
Source: Federation of Tax Administrators, "State Individual Income Tax Rates, 2015"

Various State and Local Tax Rates

State	State and Local Sales and Use (%)	State Sales and Use (%)	Gasoline[1] (¢/gal.)	Cigarette[2] ($/pack)	Spirits[3] ($/gal.)	Wine[4] ($/gal.)	Beer[5] ($/gal.)
Colorado	7.4	2.90	22	0.84	2.28	0.32	0.08

Note: All tax rates as of January 1, 2015; (1) The American Petroleum Institute has developed a methodology for determining the average tax rate on a gallon of fuel. Rates may include any of the following: excise taxes, environmental fees, storage tank fees, other fees or taxes, general sales tax, and local taxes. In states where gasoline is subject to the general sales tax, or where the fuel tax is based on the average sale price, the average rate determined by API is sensitive to changes in the price of gasoline. States that fully or partially apply general sales taxes to gasoline: CA, CO, GA, IL, IN, MI, NY; (2) The federal excise tax of $1.0066 per pack and local taxes are not included; (3) Rates are those applicable to off-premise sales of 40% alcohol by volume (a.b.v.) distilled spirits in 750ml containers. Local excise taxes are excluded; (4) Rates are those applicable to off-premise sales of 11% a.b.v. non-carbonated wine in 750ml containers; (5) Rates are those applicable to off-premise sales of 4.7% a.b.v. beer in 12 ounce containers.
Source: Tax Foundation, 2015 Facts & Figures: How Does Your State Compare?

State Business Tax Climate Index Rankings

State	Overall Rank	Corporate Tax Index Rank	Individual Income Tax Index Rank	Sales Tax Index Rank	Unemployment Insurance Tax Index Rank	Property Tax Index Rank
Colorado	20	12	16	43	35	22

Note: The index is a measure of how each state's tax laws affect economic performance. The lower the rank, the more favorable a state's tax system is for business. States without a given tax are given a ranking of 1. The scores/rankings for the District of Columbia do not affect other states. The 2015 index represents the tax climate as of July 1, 2014.
Source: Tax Foundation, State Business Tax Climate Index 2015

COMMERCIAL UTILITIES

Typical Monthly Electric Bills

Area	Commercial Service ($/month)		Industrial Service ($/month)	
	1,500 kWh	40 kW demand 14,000 kWh	1,000 kW demand 200,000 kWh	50,000 kW demand 32,500,000 kWh
City	n/a	n/a	n/a	n/a
Average[1]	201	1,653	26,124	2,639,743

Note: Figures are based on annualized 2014 rates; (1) Average based on 180 utilities surveyed; n/a not available
Source: Edison Electric Institute, Typical Bills and Average Rates Report, Summer 2014

TRANSPORTATION

Means of Transportation to Work

Area	Car/Truck/Van		Public Transportation			Bicycle	Walked	Other Means	Worked at Home
	Drove Alone	Car-pooled	Bus	Subway	Railroad				
City	71.2	7.9	1.3	0.0	0.0	7.4	4.0	1.3	6.8
MSA[1]	74.3	8.3	1.0	0.0	0.0	4.3	3.0	1.5	7.6
U.S.	76.4	9.6	2.6	1.8	0.6	0.6	2.8	1.3	4.3

Note: Figures are percentages and cover workers 16 years of age and older; (1) Figures cover the Fort Collins, CO Metropolitan Statistical Area—see Appendix B for areas included
Source: U.S. Census Bureau, 2011-2013 American Community Survey 3-Year Estimates

Travel Time to Work

Area	Less Than 10 Minutes	10 to 19 Minutes	20 to 29 Minutes	30 to 44 Minutes	45 to 59 Minutes	60 to 89 Minutes	90 Minutes or More
City	17.9	45.2	18.5	10.7	3.2	2.7	1.9
MSA[1]	16.0	38.5	19.8	13.8	5.1	4.5	2.3
U.S.	13.3	29.7	20.9	20.2	7.7	5.7	2.6

Note: Figures are percentages and include workers 16 years old and over; (1) Figures cover the Fort Collins, CO Metropolitan Statistical Area—see Appendix B for areas included
Source: U.S. Census Bureau, 2011-2013 American Community Survey 3-Year Estimates

Travel Time Index

Area	1985	1990	1995	2000	2005	2010	2011
Urban Area[1]	n/a	n/a	n/a	n/a	n/a	n/a	n/a
Average[2]	1.09	1.14	1.16	1.19	1.23	1.18	1.18

Note: Travel Time Index—the ratio of travel time in the peak period to the travel time at free-flow conditions. For example, a value of 1.30 indicates a 20-minute free-flow trip takes 26 minutes in the peak. Free-flow speeds (60 mph on freeways and 35 mph on principal arterials) are used as the comparison threshold; (1) Data for the Fort Collins, CO urban area was not available; (2) average of 498 urban areas
Source: Texas Transportation Institute, Urban Mobility Report 2012, December 2012

Public Transportation

Agency Name / Mode of Transportation	Vehicles Operated in Maximum Service	Annual Unlinked Passenger Trips (in thous.)	Annual Passenger Miles (in thous.)
Transfort			
Bus (directly operated)	26	2,214.9	7,211.9
Bus (purchased transportation)	4	21.1	30.8
Demand Response Taxi (purchased transportation)	8	34.1	154.5

Source: Federal Transit Administration, National Transit Database, 2013

Air Transportation

Airport Name and Code / Type of Service	Passenger Airlines[1]	Passenger Enplanements	Freight Carriers[2]	Freight (lbs.)
Denver International (60 miles) (DEN)				
Domestic service (U.S. carriers - 2014)	29	24,875,236	19	209,229,037
International service (U.S. carriers - 2013)	12	655,399	3	611,491

Note: (1) Includes all U.S.-based major, minor and commuter airlines that carried at least one passenger during the year; (2) Includes all U.S.-based airlines and freight carriers that transported at least one lb. of freight during the year.
Source: Bureau of Transportation Statistics, The Intermodal Transportation Database, Air Carriers: T-100 Domestic Market (U.S. Carriers), 2014; Bureau of Transportation Statistics, The Intermodal Transportation Database, Air Carriers: T-100 International Market (U.S. Carriers), 2013

Other Transportation Statistics

Major Highways:	I-25
Amtrak Service:	Bus connection
Major Waterways/Ports:	None

Source: Amtrak.com; Google Maps

BUSINESSES

Major Business Headquarters

Company Name	Rankings	
	Fortune[1]	Forbes[2]
No companies listed	-	-

Note: (1) Fortune 500—companies that produce a 10-K are ranked 1 to 500 based on 2013 revenue; (2) all private companies with at least $2 billion in annual revenue through the end of their most current fiscal year are ranked 1 to 221; companies listed are headquartered in the city; dashes indicate no ranking
Source: Fortune, "Fortune 500," June 16, 2014; Forbes, "America's Largest Private Companies," November 5, 2014

Fast-Growing Businesses

According to Deloitte, Fort Collins is home to one of North America's 500 fastest-growing high-technology companies: **Advanced Energy Industries** (#349). Companies are ranked by percentage growth in revenue over a five-year period. Criteria for inclusion: company must be headquartered within North America; must own proprietary intellectual property or proprietary technology that contributes to a significant portion of the company's operating revenue, or devote a significant proportion of revenues to research and development of technology; must have been in business for a minumum of five years with 2009 operating revenues of at least $50,000 USD/CD and 2013 operating revenues of at least $5 million USD/CD. *Deloitte Touche Tohmatsu, 2014 Technology Fast 500*[TM]

Minority- and Women-Owned Businesses

Group	All Firms		Firms with Paid Employees			
	Firms	Sales ($000)	Firms	Sales ($000)	Employees	Payroll ($000)
Asian	290	104,508	80	98,664	1,086	27,846
Black	93	5,047	6	3,468	62	2,148
Hispanic	564	46,054	(s)	(s)	(s)	(s)
Women	4,372	474,930	608	391,512	3,868	115,341
All Firms	14,921	11,436,748	3,866	10,959,813	57,564	2,139,714

Note: Figures cover firms located in the city; minority- and women-owned business are defined as firms in which the corresponding group own 51% or more of the stock or equity of the company; (s) estimates are suppressed when publication standards are not met
Source: U.S. Census Bureau, 2007 Economic Census, Survey of Business Owners (2012 Survey of Business Owners data will be released starting in June 2015)

HOTELS & CONVENTION CENTERS

Hotels/Motels

Area	5 Star		4 Star		3 Star		2 Star		1 Star		Not Rated	
	Num.	Pct.[3]	Num.	Pct.[3]	Num.	Pct.[3]	Num.	Pct.[3]	Num.	Pct.[3]	Num.	Pct.[3]
City[1]	0	0.0	0	0.0	18	22.0	61	74.4	2	2.4	1	1.2
Total[2]	166	0.9	1,264	7.0	5,718	31.8	9,340	52.0	411	2.3	1,070	6.0

Note: (1) Figures cover Fort Collins and vicinity; (2) Figures cover all 100 cities in this book; (3) Percentage of hotels which have a given star rating; Star ratings are determined by expedia.com and offer an indication of the general quality of a particular hotel.
Source: expedia.com, April 2, 2015

Major Convention Centers

Name	Overall Space (sq. ft.)	Exhibit Space (sq. ft.)	Meeting Space (sq. ft.)	Meeting Rooms

There are no major convention centers located in the metro area
Source: Original research

Living Environment

COST OF LIVING

Cost of Living Index

Composite Index	Groceries	Housing	Utilities	Trans-portation	Health Care	Misc. Goods/ Services
n/a	n/a	n/a	n/a	n/a	n/a	n/a

Note: The Cost of Living Index measures regional differences in the cost of consumer goods and services, excluding taxes and non-consumer expenditures, for professional and managerial households in the top income quintile. It is based on more than 50,000 prices covering almost 60 different items for which prices are collected three times a year by chambers of commerce, economic development organizations or university applied economic centers in each participating urban area. The numbers shown should be read as a percentage above or below the national average of 100. For example, a value of 115.4 in the groceries column indicates that grocery prices are 15.4% higher than the national average. Small differences in the index numbers should not be interpreted as significant; n/a not available.
Source: The Council for Community and Economic Research, ACCRA Cost of Living Index, 2014

Grocery Prices

Area[1]	T-Bone Steak ($/pound)	Frying Chicken ($/pound)	Whole Milk ($/half gal.)	Eggs ($/dozen)	Orange Juice ($/64 oz.)	Coffee ($/11.5 oz.)
City[2]	n/a	n/a	n/a	n/a	n/a	n/a
Avg.	10.40	1.37	2.40	1.99	3.46	4.27
Min.	8.48	0.93	1.37	1.30	2.83	2.99
Max.	14.20	2.44	3.62	4.02	6.42	6.96

Note: (1) Values for the local area are compared with the average, minimum and maximum values for all 308 areas in the Cost of Living Index; (2) Figures cover the Fort Collins CO urban area; n/a not available; **T-Bone Steak** (price per pound); **Frying Chicken** (price per pound, whole fryer); **Whole Milk** (half gallon carton); **Eggs** (price per dozen, Grade A, large); **Orange Juice** (64 oz. Tropicana or Florida Natural); **Coffee** (11.5 oz. can, vacuum-packed, Maxwell House, Hills Bros, or Folgers).
Source: The Council for Community and Economic Research, ACCRA Cost of Living Index, 2014

Housing and Utility Costs

Area[1]	New Home Price ($)	Apartment Rent ($/month)	All Electric ($/month)	Part Electric ($/month)	Other Energy ($/month)	Telephone ($/month)
City[2]	n/a	n/a	n/a	n/a	n/a	n/a
Avg.	305,838	919	181.00	93.66	73.14	27.95
Min.	183,142	480	112.00	42.06	23.42	17.16
Max.	1,358,576	3,851	594.00	180.03	440.99	40.42

Note: (1) Values for the local area are compared with the average, minimum and maximum values for all 308 areas in the Cost of Living Index; (2) Figures cover the Fort Collins CO urban area; n/a not available; **New Home Price** (2,400 sf living area, 8,000 sf lot, in urban area with full utilities); **Apartment Rent** (950 sf 2 bedroom/1.5 or 2 bath, unfurnished, excluding all utilities except water); **All Electric** (average monthly cost for an all-electric home); **Part Electric** (average monthly cost for a part-electric home); **Other Energy** (average monthly cost for natural gas, fuel oil, coal, wood, and any other forms of energy except electricity); **Telephone** (price includes basic monthly rate for a private residential line plus additional local usage charges incurred by a family of four).
Source: The Council for Community and Economic Research, ACCRA Cost of Living Index, 2014

Health Care, Transportation, and Other Costs

Area[1]	Doctor ($/visit)	Dentist ($/visit)	Optometrist ($/visit)	Gasoline ($/gallon)	Beauty Salon ($/visit)	Men's Shirt ($)
City[2]	n/a	n/a	n/a	n/a	n/a	n/a
Avg.	102.86	87.89	97.66	3.44	34.37	26.74
Min.	67.47	65.78	51.18	3.00	17.43	12.79
Max.	173.50	150.14	235.00	4.33	64.28	49.50

Note: (1) Values for the local area are compared with the average, minimum and maximum values for all 308 areas in the Cost of Living Index; (2) Figures cover the Fort Collins CO urban area; n/a not available; **Doctor** (general practitioners routine exam of an established patient); **Dentist** (adult teeth cleaning and periodic oral examination); **Optometrist** (full vision eye exam for established adult patient); **Gasoline** (one gallon regular unleaded, national brand, including all taxes, cash price at self-service pump if available); **Beauty Salon** (woman's shampoo, trim, and blow-dry); **Men's Shirt** (cotton/polyester dress shirt, pinpoint weave, long sleeves).
Source: The Council for Community and Economic Research, ACCRA Cost of Living Index, 2014

HOUSING

House Price Index (HPI)

Area	National Ranking[2]	Quarterly Change (%)	One-Year Change (%)	Five-Year Change (%)
MSA[1]	63	0.78	7.53	19.30
U.S.[3]	–	1.35	4.91	11.59

Note: The HPI is a weighted repeat sales index. It measures average price changes in repeat sales or refinancings on the same properties. This information is obtained by reviewing repeat mortgage transactions on single-family properties whose mortgages have been purchased or securitized by Fannie Mae or Freddie Mac in January 1975; (1) Fort Collins Metropolitan Statistical Area—see Appendix B for areas included; (2) Rankings are based on annual percentage change for all metro areas containing at least 15,000 transactions over the last 10 years and ranges from 1 to 275; (3) figures based on a weighted average of Census Division estimates using a seasonally adjusted, purchase-only index; all figures are for the period ending December 31, 2014
Source: Federal Housing Finance Agency, House Price Index, February 26, 2015

Median Single-Family Home Prices

Area	2012	2013	2014p	Percent Change 2013 to 2014
MSA[1]	n/a	n/a	n/a	n/a
U.S. Average	177.2	197.4	209.0	5.9

Note: Figures are median sales prices of existing single-family homes in thousands of dollars; (p) preliminary; n/a not available; (1) Fort Collins, CO Metropolitan Statistical Area—see Appendix B for areas included
Source: National Association of Realtors, Median Sales Price of Existing Single-Family Homes for Metropolitan Areas, 4th Quarter 2014

Qualifying Income Based on Median Sales Price of Existing Single-Family Homes

Area	With 5% Down ($)	With 10% Down ($)	With 20% Down ($)
MSA[1]	n/a	n/a	n/a
U.S. Average	45,863	43,449	38,621

Note: Figures are preliminary; Qualifying income is based on a mortgage rate of 4.0%. Monthly principal and interest payment is limited to 25% of income; n/a not available; (1) Fort Collins, CO Metropolitan Statistical Area—see Appendix B for areas included
Source: National Association of Realtors, Qualifying Income Based on Median Sales Price of Existing Single-Family Homes for Metropolitan Areas, 4th Quarter 2014

Median Apartment Condo-Coop Home Prices

Area	2012	2013	2014p	Percent Change 2013 to 2014
MSA[1]	n/a	n/a	n/a	n/a
U.S. Average	173.7	194.9	205.1	5.2

Note: Figures are median sales prices of existing apartment condo-coop homes in thousands of dollars; (p) preliminary; n/a not available; (1) Fort Collins, CO Metropolitan Statistical Area—see Appendix B for areas included
Source: National Association of Realtors, Median Sales Price of Existing Apartment Condo-Coop Homes for Metropolitan Areas, 4th Quarter 2014

Gross Monthly Rent

Area	Under $200	$200 -299	$300 -499	$500 -749	$750 -999	$1,000 -1,499	$1,500 and up	Median ($)
City	0.5	0.9	3.3	15.3	28.7	35.5	15.8	1,014
MSA[1]	0.7	1.4	3.6	18.3	28.6	34.1	13.3	979
U.S.	1.7	3.2	7.8	22.1	24.3	26.0	14.9	900

Note: Figures are percentages except for Median; Gross rent is the contract rent plus the estimated average monthly cost of utilities (electricity, gas, and water and sewer) and fuels (oil, coal, kerosene, wood, etc.) if these are paid by the renter (or paid for the renter by someone else); (1) Figures cover the Fort Collins, CO Metropolitan Statistical Area—see Appendix B for areas included
Source: U.S. Census Bureau, 2011-2013 American Community Survey 3-Year Estimates

Homeownership Rate

Area	2007 (%)	2008 (%)	2009 (%)	2010 (%)	2011 (%)	2012 (%)	2013 (%)	2014 (%)
MSA[1]	n/a	n/a	n/a	n/a	n/a	n/a	n/a	n/a
U.S.	68.1	67.8	67.4	66.9	66.1	65.4	65.1	64.5

Note: (1) Figures cover the Fort Collins, CO Metropolitan Statistical Area—see Appendix B for areas included; n/a not available
Source: U.S. Census Bureau, Housing Vacancies and Homeownership Annual Statistics: 2014

Year Housing Structure Built

Area	2010 or Later	2000 -2009	1990 -1999	1980 -1989	1970 -1979	1960 -1969	1950 -1959	1940 -1949	Before 1940	Median Year
City	0.9	20.3	21.7	17.4	20.4	8.0	3.4	2.0	5.8	1986
MSA[1]	1.5	20.3	20.7	14.3	21.6	8.3	4.0	2.2	7.3	1985
U.S.	0.9	15.0	13.9	13.8	15.8	11.0	10.9	5.4	13.3	1976

Note: Figures are percentages except for Median Year; (1) Figures cover the Fort Collins, CO Metropolitan Statistical Area—see Appendix B for areas included
Source: U.S. Census Bureau, 2011-2013 American Community Survey 3-Year Estimates

HEALTH

Health Risk Data

Category	MSA[1] (%)	U.S. (%)
Adults aged 18–64 who have any kind of health care coverage	80.8	79.6
Adults who reported being in good or excellent health	88.8	83.1
Adults who are current smokers	15.7	19.6
Adults who are heavy drinkers[2]	4.1	6.1
Adults who are binge drinkers[3]	18.0	16.9
Adults who are overweight (BMI 25.0 - 29.9)	32.7	35.8
Adults who are obese (BMI 30.0 - 99.8)	18.3	27.6
Adults who participated in any physical activities in the past month	87.6	77.1
Adults 50+ who have ever had a sigmoidoscopy or colonoscopy	71.0	67.3
Women aged 40+ who have had a mammogram within the past two years	68.3	74.0
Men aged 40+ who have had a PSA test within the past two years	48.2	45.2
Adults aged 65+ who have had flu shot within the past year	70.3	60.1
Adults who always wear a seatbelt	95.6	93.8

Note: Data as of 2012 unless otherwise noted; (1) Figures cover the Fort Collins-Loveland, CO Metropolitan Statistical Area—see Appendix B for areas included; (2) Heavy drinkers are classified as males having more than two drinks per day or females having more than one drink per day; (3) Binge drinkers are classified as males having five or more drinks on one occasion or females having four or more drinks on one occasion
Source: Centers for Disease Control and Prevention, Behaviorial Risk Factor Surveillance System, SMART: Selected Metropolitan/Micropolitan Area Risk Trends, 2012 (Note: the CDC has discontinued this dataset but will be releasing a replacement in late 2015)

Chronic Health Indicators

Category	MSA[1] (%)	U.S. (%)
Adults who have ever been told they had a heart attack	2.1	4.5
Adults who have ever been told they had a stroke	2.2	2.9
Adults who have been told they currently have asthma	6.1	8.9
Adults who have ever been told they have arthritis	19.8	25.7
Adults who have ever been told they have diabetes[2]	5.4	9.7
Adults who have ever been told they had skin cancer	6.6	5.7
Adults who have ever been told they had any other types of cancer	5.0	6.5
Adults who have ever been told they have COPD	4.5	6.2
Adults who have ever been told they have kidney disease	n/a	2.5
Adults who have ever been told they have a form of depression	17.6	18.0

Note: Data as of 2012 unless otherwise noted; n/a not available; (1) Figures cover the Fort Collins-Loveland, CO Metropolitan Statistical Area—see Appendix B for areas included; (2) Figures do not include pregnancy-related, borderline, or pre-diabetes
Source: Centers for Disease Control and Prevention, Behaviorial Risk Factor Surveillance System, SMART: Selected Metropolitan/Micropolitan Area Risk Trends, 2012 (Note: the CDC has discontinued this dataset but will be releasing a replacement in late 2015)

Mortality Rates for the Top 10 Causes of Death in the U.S.

ICD-10[a] Sub-Chapter	ICD-10[a] Code	Age-Adjusted Mortality Rate[1] per 100,000 population	
		County[2]	U.S.
Malignant neoplasms	C00-C97	130.3	166.2
Ischaemic heart diseases	I20-I25	62.0	105.7
Other forms of heart disease	I30-I51	44.8	49.3
Chronic lower respiratory diseases	J40-J47	31.0	42.1
Organic, including symptomatic, mental disorders	F01-F09	34.7	38.1
Cerebrovascular diseases	I60-I69	34.6	37.0
Other external causes of accidental injury	W00-X59	30.6	26.9
Other degenerative diseases of the nervous system	G30-G31	24.2	25.6
Diabetes mellitus	E10-E14	14.1	21.3
Hypertensive diseases	I10-I15	14.3	19.4

Note: (a) ICD-10 = International Classification of Diseases 10th Revision; (1) Mortality rates are a three year average covering 2011-2013; (2) Figures cover Larimer County
Source: Centers for Disease Control and Prevention, National Center for Health Statistics. Compressed Mortality File 1999-2013 on CDC WONDER Online Database, released October 2014. Data are compiled from the Compressed Mortality File 1999-2013, Series 20 No. 2S, 2014.

Mortality Rates for Selected Causes of Death

ICD-10[a] Sub-Chapter	ICD-10[a] Code	Age-Adjusted Mortality Rate[1] per 100,000 population	
		County[2]	U.S.
Assault	X85-Y09	*1.2	5.2
Diseases of the liver	K70-K76	11.6	13.2
Human immunodeficiency virus (HIV) disease	B20-B24	Suppressed	2.2
Influenza and pneumonia	J09-J18	10.4	15.4
Intentional self-harm	X60-X84	19.1	12.5
Malnutrition	E40-E46	Suppressed	0.9
Obesity and other hyperalimentation	E65-E68	*1.5	1.8
Renal failure	N17-N19	7.6	13.1
Transport accidents	V01-V99	7.9	11.7
Viral hepatitis	B15-B19	*1.1	2.2

Note: (a) ICD-10 = International Classification of Diseases 10th Revision; (1) Mortality rates are a three year average covering 2011-2013; (2) Figures cover Larimer County; (*) Unreliable data as per CDC
Source: Centers for Disease Control and Prevention, National Center for Health Statistics. Compressed Mortality File 1999-2013 on CDC WONDER Online Database, released October 2014. Data are compiled from the Compressed Mortality File 1999-2013, Series 20 No. 2S, 2014.

Health Insurance Coverage

Area	With Health Insurance	With Private Health Insurance	With Public Health Insurance	Without Health Insurance	Population Under Age 18 Without Health Insurance
City	89.8	79.8	18.7	10.2	3.7
MSA[1]	88.2	75.1	24.0	11.8	6.4
U.S.	85.2	65.2	31.0	14.8	7.3

Note: Figures are percentages that cover the civilian noninstitutionalized population; (1) Figures cover the Fort Collins, CO Metropolitan Statistical Area—see Appendix B for areas included
Source: U.S. Census Bureau, 2011-2013 American Community Survey 3-Year Estimates

Number of Medical Professionals

Area[1]	MDs[2]	DOs[2,3]	Dentists	Podiatrists	Chiropractors	Optometrists
Local (number)	719	75	237	13	157	63
Local (rate[4])	231.3	24.1	74.9	4.1	49.6	19.9
U.S. (rate[4])	270.0	20.2	63.1	5.7	25.2	14.9

Note: Data as of 2013 unless noted; (1) Local data covers Larimer County; (2) Data as of 2012 and includes all active, non-federal physicians; (3) Doctor of Osteopathic Medicine; (4) rate per 100,000 population
Source: U.S. Department of Health and Human Services, Health Resources and Services Administration, Bureau of Health Professions, Area Resource File (ARF) 2013-2014

EDUCATION

Public School District Statistics

District Name	Schls	Pupils	Pupil/ Teacher Ratio	Minority Pupils[1] (%)	Free Lunch Eligible[2] (%)	IEP[3] (%)
Poudre School District R-1	51	27,909	17.2	26.1	24.2	0.0

Note: Table includes school districts with 2,000 or more students; (1) Percentage of students that are not non-Hispanic white; (2) Percentage of students that are eligible for the free lunch program; (3) Percentage of students that have an Individualized Education Program.
Source: U.S. Department of Education, National Center for Education Statistics, Common Core of Data, Local Education Agency (School District) Universe Survey: School Year 2012-2013; U.S. Department of Education, National Center for Education Statistics, Common Core of Data, Public Elementary/Secondary School Universe Survey: School Year 2012-2013

Highest Level of Education

Area	Less than H.S.	H.S. Diploma	Some College, No Deg.	Associate Degree	Bachelor's Degree	Master's Degree	Prof. School Degree	Doctorate Degree
City	4.7	14.0	20.5	9.1	31.8	13.7	2.4	3.8
MSA[1]	5.4	18.6	23.6	8.9	27.2	11.6	2.1	2.7
U.S.	13.7	28.0	21.2	7.9	18.2	7.7	1.9	1.3

Note: Figures cover persons age 25 and over; (1) Figures cover the Fort Collins, CO Metropolitan Statistical Area—see Appendix B for areas included
Source: U.S. Census Bureau, 2011-2013 American Community Survey 3-Year Estimates

Educational Attainment by Race

Area	High School Graduate or Higher (%)					Bachelor's Degree or Higher (%)				
	Total	White	Black	Asian	Hisp.[2]	Total	White	Black	Asian	Hisp.[2]
City	95.3	96.1	87.5	96.0	75.7	51.7	52.8	23.5	65.2	25.9
MSA[1]	94.6	95.6	85.4	95.9	74.1	43.6	44.4	18.4	60.3	21.2
U.S.	86.3	88.3	83.1	85.7	64.0	29.1	30.4	18.8	50.7	13.7

Note: Figures shown cover persons 25 years old and over; (1) Figures cover the Fort Collins, CO Metropolitan Statistical Area—see Appendix B for areas included; (2) People of Hispanic origin can be of any race
Source: U.S. Census Bureau, 2011-2013 American Community Survey 3-Year Estimates

School Enrollment by Grade and Control

Area	Preschool (%)		Kindergarten (%)		Grades 1 - 4 (%)		Grades 5 - 8 (%)		Grades 9 - 12 (%)	
	Public	Private	Public	Private	Public	Private	Public	Private	Public	Private
City	31.5	68.5	92.1	7.9	90.1	9.9	90.1	9.9	97.4	2.6
MSA[1]	38.2	61.8	86.5	13.5	91.5	8.5	90.6	9.4	95.9	4.1
U.S.	57.7	42.3	87.9	12.1	89.9	10.1	90.0	10.0	90.7	9.3

Note: Figures shown cover persons 3 years old and over; (1) Figures cover the Fort Collins, CO Metropolitan Statistical Area—see Appendix B for areas included
Source: U.S. Census Bureau, 2011-2013 American Community Survey 3-Year Estimates

Average Salaries of Public School Classroom Teachers

Area	2013-14		2014-15		Percent Change 2013-14 to 2014-15	Percent Change 2004-05 to 2014-15
	Dollars	Rank[1]	Dollars	Rank[1]		
COLORADO	49,615	31	49,828	34	0.43	13.4
U.S. Average	56,610	–	57,379	–	1.36	20.8

Note: (1) State rank ranges from 1 to 51 where 1 indicates highest salary.
Source: National Education Association, Rankings & Estimates: Rankings of the States 2014 and Estimates of School Statistics 2015, March 2015

Higher Education

Four-Year Colleges			Two-Year Colleges			Medical Schools[1]	Law Schools[2]	Voc/ Tech[3]
Public	Private Non-profit	Private For-profit	Public	Private Non-profit	Private For-profit			
1	1	0	0	0	3	0	0	1

Note: Figures cover institutions located within the city limits and include main campuses only; (1) includes schools accredited by the Liaison Committee on Medical Education and the American Osteopathic Association's Commission on Osteopathic College Accreditation; (2) includes ABA-accredited schools, schools with provisional ABA accreditation, and state accredited schools; (3) includes all schools with programs that are less than 2 years.
Source: National Center for Education Statistics, Integrated Postsecondary Education System (IPEDS), 2013-14; Association of American Medical Colleges, Member List, May 1, 2015; American Osteopathic Association, Member List, May 1, 2015; Law School Admission Council, Official Guide to ABA-Approved Law Schools Online, May 1, 2015; Wikipedia, List of Medical Schools in the United States, May 1, 2015; Wikipedia, List of Law Schools in the United States, May 1, 2015

According to *U.S. News & World Report*, the Fort Collins, CO metro area is home to one of the best national universities in the U.S.: **Colorado State University** (#121). The indicators used to capture academic quality fall into a number of categories: assessment by administrators at peer institutions; retention of students; faculty resources; student selectivity; financial resources; alumni giving; high school counselor ratings of colleges; and graduation rate. *U.S. News & World Report, "America's Best Colleges 2015"*

PRESIDENTIAL ELECTION

2012 Presidential Election Results

Area	Obama (%)	Romney (%)	Other (%)
Larimer County	51.4	45.8	2.7
U.S.	51.0	47.2	1.8

Note: Results may not add to 100% due to rounding
Source: Dave Leip's Atlas of U.S. Presidential Elections

EMPLOYERS

Major Employers

Company Name	Industry
Advanced Energy Industrials	Special industry machinery
Anheuser Busch	Malt beverages
Animal and Plant Health Inspection	Management services
Aramark Corporation	Food/bars
Center Partners	Business services
City of Loveland	City and town managers office
Colorado State University	Colleges/universities
Contibeef	Beef cattle feedlots
Deere and Company	Farm machinery/equipment
Hach Company	Analytical instruments
Hewlett Packard Co	Electronic computers
Hewlett Packard Co	Tape storage units/computers
Medical Center of the Rockies	General medical/surgical hospitals
Poudre School District	Building cleaning service
Poudre Valley Health Systems	General medical/surgical hospitals
Woodward	Relays/industrial controls
Woodward	Governors/aircraft propeller feathering
Woodward	Aircraft engines/parts

Note: Companies shown are located within the Fort Collins, CO Metropolitan Statistical Area.
Source: Hoovers.com; Wikipedia

PUBLIC SAFETY

Crime Rate

Area	All Crimes	Violent Crimes				Property Crimes		
		Murder	Forcible Rape	Robbery	Aggrav. Assault	Burglary	Larceny -Theft	Motor Vehicle Theft
City	2,775.4	0.0	38.0	24.7	175.3	353.8	2,090.4	93.3
Suburbs[1]	1,985.6	1.2	48.8	17.5	106.7	243.0	1,503.9	64.5
Metro[2]	2,360.8	0.6	43.7	20.9	139.3	295.7	1,782.5	78.2
U.S.	3,098.6	4.5	25.2	109.1	229.1	610.0	1,899.4	221.3

Note: Figures are crimes per 100,000 population; (1) All areas within the metro area that are located outside the city limits; (2) Figures cover the Fort Collins, CO Metropolitan Statistical Area—see Appendix B for areas included
Source: FBI Uniform Crime Reports, 2013

Hate Crimes

Area	Number of Quarters Reported	Number of Incidents per Bias Motivation						
		Race	Religion	Sexual Orientation	Ethnicity	Disability	Gender	Gender Identity
City	4	0	0	0	0	0	0	0
U.S.	4	2,871	1,031	1,233	655	83	18	31

Source: Federal Bureau of Investigation, Hate Crime Statistics 2013

Identity Theft Consumer Complaints

Area	Complaints	Complaints per 100,000 Population	Rank[2]
MSA[1]	206	65.2	218
U.S.	332,646	104.3	-

Note: (1) Figures cover the Fort Collins, CO Metropolitan Statistical Area—see Appendix B for areas included; (2) Rank ranges from 1 to 380 where 1 indicates greatest number of identity theft complaints per 100,000 population
Source: Federal Trade Commission, Consumer Sentinel Network Data Book for January–December 2014

Fraud and Other Consumer Complaints

Area	Complaints	Complaints per 100,000 Population	Rank[2]
MSA[1]	1,416	448.1	64
U.S.	2,250,205	705.7	-

Note: (1) Figures cover the Fort Collins, CO Metropolitan Statistical Area—see Appendix B for areas included; (2) Rank ranges from 1 to 380 where 1 indicates greatest number of identity theft complaints per 100,000 population
Source: Federal Trade Commission, Consumer Sentinel Network Data Book for January–December 2014

RECREATION

Culture

Dance[1]	Theatre[1]	Instrumental Music[1]	Vocal Music[1]	Series and Festivals	Museums and Art Galleries[2]	Zoos and Aquariums[3]
1	2	2	2	0	8	0

Note: (1) Professional perfoming groups; (2) Based on organizations with SIC code 8412; (3) AZA-accredited
Source: The Grey House Performing Arts Directory, 2015-16; Association of Zoos & Aquariums, AZA Member Zoos & Aquariums, April 2015; www.AccuLeads.com, April 2015

Professional Sports Teams

Team Name	League	Year Established
No teams are located in the metro area		

Source: Wikipedia, Major Professional Sports Teams of the United States and Canada, April 2015

CLIMATE

Average and Extreme Temperatures

Temperature	Jan	Feb	Mar	Apr	May	Jun	Jul	Aug	Sep	Oct	Nov	Dec	Yr.
Extreme High (°F)	73	76	84	90	93	102	103	100	97	89	79	75	103
Average High (°F)	43	47	52	62	71	81	88	86	77	67	52	45	64
Average Temp. (°F)	30	34	39	48	58	67	73	72	63	52	39	32	51
Average Low (°F)	16	20	25	34	44	53	59	57	48	37	25	18	37
Extreme Low (°F)	-25	-25	-10	-2	22	30	43	41	17	3	-8	-25	-25

Note: Figures cover the years 1948-1992
Source: National Climatic Data Center, International Station Meteorological Climate Summary, 9/96

Average Precipitation/Snowfall/Humidity

Precip./Humidity	Jan	Feb	Mar	Apr	May	Jun	Jul	Aug	Sep	Oct	Nov	Dec	Yr.
Avg. Precip. (in.)	0.6	0.6	1.3	1.7	2.5	1.7	1.9	1.5	1.1	1.0	0.9	0.6	15.5
Avg. Snowfall (in.)	9	7	14	9	2	Tr	0	0	2	4	9	8	63
Avg. Rel. Hum. 5am (%)	62	65	67	66	70	68	67	68	66	63	66	63	66
Avg. Rel. Hum. 5pm (%)	49	44	40	35	38	34	34	34	32	34	47	50	39

Note: Figures cover the years 1948-1992; Tr = Trace amounts (<0.05 in. of rain; <0.5 in. of snow)
Source: National Climatic Data Center, International Station Meteorological Climate Summary, 9/96

Weather Conditions

Temperature			Daytime Sky			Precipitation		
10°F & below	32°F & below	90°F & above	Clear	Partly cloudy	Cloudy	0.01 inch or more precip.	0.1 inch or more snow/ice	Thunder-storms
24	155	33	99	177	89	90	38	39

Note: Figures are average number of days per year and cover the years 1948-1992
Source: National Climatic Data Center, International Station Meteorological Climate Summary, 9/96

HAZARDOUS WASTE

Superfund Sites

Fort Collins has no sites on the EPA's Superfund Final National Priorities List. There are a total of 1,322 Superfund sites on the list in the U.S. *U.S. Environmental Protection Agency, Final National Priorities List, April 14, 2015*

AIR & WATER QUALITY

Air Quality Trends: Ozone

	2004	2005	2006	2007	2008	2009	2010	2011	2012	2013
MSA[1]	0.069	0.076	0.077	0.074	0.071	0.066	0.072	0.073	0.077	0.074

Note: (1) Data covers the Fort Collins, CO Metropolitan Statistical Area—see Appendix B for areas included. The values shown are the composite ozone concentration averages among trend sites based on the highest fourth daily maximum 8-hour concentration in parts per million. These trends are based on sites having an adequate record of monitoring data during the trend period. Data from exceptional events are included.
Source: U.S. Environmental Protection Agency, Air Quality Monitoring Information, "Air Quality Trends by City, 2000-2013"

Air Quality Index

Area	Percent of Days when Air Quality was...[2]					AQI Statistics[2]	
	Good	Moderate	Unhealthy for Sensitive Groups	Unhealthy	Very Unhealthy	Maximum	Median
MSA[1]	74.2	24.7	1.1	0.0	0.0	116	45

Note: (1) Data covers the Fort Collins, CO Metropolitan Statistical Area—see Appendix B for areas included; (2) Based on 365 days with AQI data in 2014. Air Quality Index (AQI) is an index for reporting daily air quality. EPA calculates the AQI for five major air pollutants regulated by the Clean Air Act: ground-level ozone, particle pollution (aka particulate matter), carbon monoxide, sulfur dioxide, and nitrogen dioxide. The AQI runs from 0 to 500. The higher the AQI value, the greater the level of air pollution and the greater the health concern. There are six AQI categories: "Good" AQI is between 0 and 50. Air quality is considered satisfactory; "Moderate" AQI is between 51 and 100. Air quality is acceptable; "Unhealthy for Sensitive Groups" When AQI values are between 101 and 150, members of sensitive groups may experience health effects; "Unhealthy" When AQI values are between 151 and 200 everyone may begin to experience health effects; "Very Unhealthy" AQI values between 201 and 300 trigger a health alert; "Hazardous" AQI values over 300 trigger warnings of emergency conditions (not shown).
Source: U.S. Environmental Protection Agency, Air Quality Index Report, 2014

Air Quality Index Pollutants

Area	Percent of Days when AQI Pollutant was...[2]					
	Carbon Monoxide	Nitrogen Dioxide	Ozone	Sulfur Dioxide	Particulate Matter 2.5	Particulate Matter 10
MSA[1]	0.0	0.0	95.1	0.0	4.1	0.8

Note: (1) Data covers the Fort Collins, CO Metropolitan Statistical Area—see Appendix B for areas included;
(2) Based on 365 days with AQI data in 2014. The Air Quality Index (AQI) is an index for reporting daily air quality. EPA calculates the AQI for five major air pollutants regulated by the Clean Air Act: ground-level ozone, particle pollution (also known as particulate matter), carbon monoxide, sulfur dioxide, and nitrogen dioxide. The AQI runs from 0 to 500. The higher the AQI value, the greater the level of air pollution and the greater the health concern.
Source: U.S. Environmental Protection Agency, Air Quality Index Report, 2014

Maximum Air Pollutant Concentrations: Particulate Matter, Ozone, CO and Lead

	Particulate Matter 10 (ug/m³)	Particulate Matter 2.5 Wtd AM (ug/m³)	Particulate Matter 2.5 24-Hr (ug/m³)	Ozone (ppm)	Carbon Monoxide (ppm)	Lead (ug/m³)
MSA[1] Level	55	6.8	18	0.082	1	n/a
NAAQS[2]	150	15	35	0.075	9	0.15
Met NAAQS[2]	Yes	Yes	Yes	No	Yes	n/a

Note: (1) Data covers the Fort Collins, CO Metropolitan Statistical Area—see Appendix B for areas included; Data from exceptional events are included; (2) National Ambient Air Quality Standards; ppm = parts per million; ug/m³ = micrograms per cubic meter; n/a not available.
Concentrations: Particulate Matter 10 (coarse particulate)—highest second maximum 24-hour concentration; Particulate Matter 2.5 Wtd AM (fine particulate)—highest weighted annual mean concentration; Particulate Matter 2.5 24-Hour (fine particulate)—highest 98th percentile 24-hour concentration; Ozone—highest fourth daily maximum 8-hour concentration; Carbon Monoxide—highest second maximum non-overlapping 8-hour concentration; Lead—maximum running 3-month average
Source: U.S. Environmental Protection Agency, Air Quality Monitoring Information, "Air Quality Statistics by City, 2013"

Maximum Air Pollutant Concentrations: Nitrogen Dioxide and Sulfur Dioxide

	Nitrogen Dioxide AM (ppb)	Nitrogen Dioxide 1-Hr (ppb)	Sulfur Dioxide AM (ppb)	Sulfur Dioxide 1-Hr (ppb)	Sulfur Dioxide 24-Hr (ppb)
MSA[1] Level	n/a	n/a	n/a	n/a	n/a
NAAQS[2]	53	100	30	75	140
Met NAAQS[2]	n/a	n/a	n/a	n/a	n/a

Note: (1) Data covers the Fort Collins, CO Metropolitan Statistical Area—see Appendix B for areas included; Data from exceptional events are included; (2) National Ambient Air Quality Standards; ppm = parts per million; ug/m³ = micrograms per cubic meter; n/a not available.
Concentrations: Nitrogen Dioxide AM—highest arithmetic mean concentration; Nitrogen Dioxide 1-Hr—highest 98th percentile 1-hour daily maximum concentration; Sulfur Dioxide AM—highest annual mean concentration; Sulfur Dioxide 1-Hr—highest 99th percentile 1-hour daily maximum concentration; Sulfur Dioxide 24-Hr—highest second maximum 24-hour concentration
Source: U.S. Environmental Protection Agency, Air Quality Monitoring Information, "Air Quality Statistics by City, 2013"

Drinking Water

Water System Name	Pop. Served	Primary Water Source Type	Violations[1]	
			Health Based	Monitoring/ Reporting
City of Fort Collins	129,100	Surface	0	0

Note: (1) Based on violation data from January 1, 2014 to December 31, 2014 (includes unresolved violations from earlier years)
Source: U.S. Environmental Protection Agency, Office of Ground Water and Drinking Water, Safe Drinking Water Information System (based on data extracted January 27, 2015)

Honolulu, Hawaii

Background

Honolulu, whose name means "sheltered harbor," is the capital of Hawaii and the seat of Honolulu County. The city sits in one of the most famously attractive areas of the world, on the island of Oahu, home to the extinct volcano Diamond Head, Waikiki Beach, and two mountain ranges, the Koolau and the Waianae. Honolulu is the economic hub of Hawaii, a major seaport and, most importantly, home to a $10 billion tourist industry.

Traditionally home to a fishing and horticultural tribal groups, the Hawaiian islands were politically united under the reign of King Kamehameha I, who first moved his triumphant court to Waikiki and subsequently to a site in what is now downtown Honolulu (1804). It was during his time that the port became a center for the sandalwood trade, thus establishing the region as an international presence even before the political interventions of non-Hawaiians.

European activity dates from 1794, when the English sea captain William Brown entered Honolulu, dubbing it Fair Harbor. Two decades later, the first missionaries arrived. American Congregationalists were followed by French Catholics and, later, Mormons and Anglicans. By the end of the nineteenth century, non-Hawaiians owned most of the land. In 1898 Hawaii was annexed by the U.S.

As is true for many strategically located cities, the events of World War II had a profound effect on Honolulu. The Japanese attack on December 7, 1941, forever etched the name of Pearl Harbor into the national memory. During the war, existing military bases were expanded and new bases built, providing considerable economic stimuli. The Vietnam War also had a dramatic effect on Honolulu; by the end of the twentieth century, military families accounted for 10 percent of the population.

Today, the U.S. military employs more than 45,000 throughout the state. Fruit, primarily pineapple, processing and light manufacturing are also important to the economy. Aquaculture, which includes cultivated species of shellfish, finfish and algae, has grown in recent years, as has biotechnology.

Increasingly, however, tourism has been the private-sector mainstay of Honolulu's economy, with most of the millions of tourists who visit Hawaii annually coming through its port or airport. Honolulu is a required stop for any holiday ship cruising these waters, and it is also the center for the inter-island air services that ferry tourists to various resort locations.

The center of Honolulu's downtown district is dominated by the Iolani Palace, once home to Hawaii's original royal family. Nearby are the State Capitol Building and the State Supreme Court Building, known as Aliiolani Hall. The Aloha Tower Development Corporation, a state agency tasked with redeveloping underused state property, continues to modernize the mixed-use space in and around the Aloha Tower Complex along the city's piers.

In 2008 Honolulu residents voted to go forward with the proposed Honolulu High-Capacity Transit Corridor Project. The project details include building a rail line connecting Kapolei in West Oahu to the University of Hawaii at Manoa, and construction began in February 2011. Completion is planned in phases—East Kapolei to Aloha Stadium in 2017, and Aloha Stadium to Ala Moana in 2019.

Honolulu, as it has grown along the southern coast of Oahu, has established a mix of residential zones, with single-family dwellings and relatively small multi-unit buildings. The result is that large parts of what is a major metropolitan area feel like cozy neighborhoods. In fact, Honolulu is governed in part through the device of a Neighborhood Board System, which insures maximal local input with regard to planning decisions and city services.

Cultural amenities include the Bishop Museum, the Honolulu Academy of Arts, and the Contemporary Museum, which together offer world-class collections in Polynesian art and artifacts, Japanese, Chinese, and Korean art, and modern art from the world over. Honolulu also hosts a symphony orchestra, the oldest U.S. symphony orchestra west of the Rocky Mountains, which performs at the Neal S. Blaisdell Center.

Barack Obama, the United States' 44th president, is the first president from Hawaii. Obama was born in Honolulu, causing the city a fair amount of attention during the 2008 presidential election.

Honolulu's weather is subtropical, with temperatures moderated by the surrounding ocean and the trade winds. There are only slight variations in temperature from summer to winter. Rain is moderate, though heavier in summer, when it sometimes comes in the form of quick showers while the sun is shining—an effect known locally as "liquid sunshine."

Rankings

General Rankings

- Honolulu was selected as one of America's best cities by *Bloomberg Businessweek*. The city ranked #19 out of 50. Criteria: leisure attributes (the number of restaurants, bars, libraries, museums, professional sports teams, and park acres by population); educational attributes (public school performance, the number of colleges, and graduate degree holders); economic factors (2011 income and June and July 2012 unemployment); crime; and air quality. *Bloomberg BusinessWeek, "America's Best Cities," September 26, 2012*

- The human resources consulting firm Mercer ranked 230 cities worldwide in terms of overall quality of life. Honolulu ranked #36. Criteria: political, social, economic, and socio-cultural factors; medical and health considerations; schools and education; public services and transportation; recreation; consumer goods; housing; and natural environment. *Mercer, "Mercer 2015 Quality of Living Survey," March 4, 2015*

- In their second annual survey, analysts for the small- and mid-sized city lifestyle site Livability.com looked at data for more than 2,000 U.S. cities to determine the rankings for Livability's "Top 100 Best Places to Live" in 2015. Honolulu ranked #58. Criteria: vibrant economy; low cost of living; abundant lifestyle amenities. *Livability.com, "Top 100 Best Places to Live 2015"*

Business/Finance Rankings

- TransUnion ranked the nation's metro areas by average credit score, calculated on the VantageScore system, developed by the three major credit-reporting bureaus—TransUnion, Experian, and Equifax. The Honolulu metro area was among the ten cities with the highest collective credit score, meaning that its residents posed the lowest average consumer credit risk. *www.usatoday.com, "Metro Areas' Average Credit Rating Revealed," February 7, 2013*

- Using data from the Council for Community and Economic Research's 2013 Annual Report, NerdWallet ranked the 100 U.S. cities with the most expensive cost of living. Cities in California and in the Northeast topped the list. Of the cities with the highest cost of living, Honolulu ranked #3. *NerdWallet.com, "Most Expensive Cities in America," June 4, 2014*

- Honolulu was ranked #55 out of 100 metro areas in terms of economic performance (#1 = best) during the recession and recovery from trough quarter through the second quarter of 2013. Criteria: percent change in employment; percentage point change in unemployment rate; percent change in gross metropolitan product; percent change in House Price Index. *Brookings Institution, MetroMonitor: Tracking Economic Recession and Recovery in America's 100 Largest Metropolitan Areas, September 2013*

- For its annual survey of the "Most Expensive U.S. Cities to Live In," Kiplinger applied Cost of Living Index statistics developed by the Council for Community and Economic Research to U.S. Census Bureau population and median household income data for cities with populations above 50,000. In the resulting ranking, Honolulu ranked #2. *Kiplinger.com, "Most Expensive U.S. Cities to Live In," May 2014*

- The Honolulu metro area appeared on the Milken Institute "2013 Best Performing Cities" list. Rank: #99 out of 200 large metro areas. Criteria: job growth; wage and salary growth; high-tech output growth. *Milken Institute, "Best-Performing Cities 2014," January 2015*

- *Forbes* ranked the 200 most populous metro areas to determine the nation's "Best Places for Business and Careers." The Honolulu metro area was ranked #96. Criteria: costs (business and living); job growth (past and projected); income growth; educational attainment (college and high school); projected economic growth; cultural and recreational opportunities; net migration patterns; number of highly ranked colleges. *Forbes, "The Best Places for Business and Careers 2014," July 23, 2014*

- Mercer Human Resources Consulting ranked 211 urban areas worldwide in terms of cost-of-living. Honolulu ranked #97 (the lower the ranking, the higher the cost-of-living). The survey measured the comparative cost of over 200 items (such as housing, food, clothing, household goods, transportation, and entertainment) in each location.*Mercer, "2014 Cost of Living Survey," July 10, 2014*

Children/Family Rankings

- Honolulu was chosen as one of America's 100 best communities for young people. The winners were selected based upon detailed information provided about each community's efforts to fulfill five essential promises critical to the well-being of young people: caring adults who are actively involved in their lives; safe places in which to learn and grow; a healthy start toward adulthood; an effective education that builds marketable skills; and opportunities to help others. *America's Promise Alliance, "100 Best Communities for Young People, 2012"*

Dating/Romance Rankings

- Of the 100 U.S. cities surveyed by *Men's Health* in its quest to identify the nation's best cities for dating and forming relationships, Honolulu was ranked #60 for online dating (#1 = best). *Men's Health, "The Best and Worst Cities for Online Dating," January 30, 2013*

Education Rankings

- Personal finance website *WalletHub* analyzed the 150 largest U.S. metropolitan statistical areas to determine where the most educated Americans are choosing to settle. Criteria: educational attainment; percentage of workers with jobs in computer, engineering, and science fields; quality and size of each metro area's universities. Honolulu was ranked #29 (#1 = most educated city). *www.WalletHub.com, "2014's Most and Least Educated Cities*

- Honolulu was selected as one of America's most literate cities. The city ranked #16 out of the 77 largest U.S. cities. Criteria: number of booksellers; library resources; Internet resources; educational attainment; periodical publishing resources; newspaper circulation. *Central Connecticut State University, "America's Most Literate Cities, 2014," April 8, 2015*

Environmental Rankings

- The Honolulu metro area came in at #227 for the relative comfort of its climate on Sperling's list of "chill cities," as measured by the Sperling Heat Index. All 361 metro areas are included. Criteria included daytime high temperatures, nighttime low temperatures, dew point, and relative humidity at the high temperatures. *www.bertsperling.com, "Sperling's Chill Cities," July 18, 2013*

- Sperling's BestPlaces assessed 379 metropolitan areas of the United States for the likelihood of dangerously extreme weather events or earthquakes. In general the Southeast and South-Central regions have the highest risk of weather extremes and earthquakes, while the Pacific Northwest enjoys the lowest risk. Of the least risky metropolitan areas, the Honolulu metro area was ranked #43. *www.bestplaces.net, "Safest Places from Natural Disasters," April 2011*

- Honolulu was highlighted as one of the cleanest metro areas for ozone air pollution in the U.S. during 2011 through 2013. The list represents cities with no monitored ozone air pollution in unhealthful ranges. *American Lung Association, State of the Air 2015*

- Honolulu was highlighted as one of the top 25 cleanest metro areas for year-round particle pollution (Annual PM 2.5) in the U.S. during 2011 through 2013. The area ranked #23. *American Lung Association, State of the Air 2015*

Food/Drink Rankings

- For the Gallup-Healthways Well-Being Index, researchers interviewed at least 300 adults in each of 189 metropolitan areas on residents' access to affordable fresh produce. The Honolulu metro area was found to be among the ten communities with the least accessible and affordable produce. *www.gallup.com, "In Anchorage, Access to Fruits and Vegetables Remains Lowest," April 8, 2014*

- *Men's Health* ranked 100 major U.S. cities in terms of alcohol intoxication. Honolulu ranked #19 (#1 = most sober).Criteria: binge drinking; alcohol-related traffic accidents, arrests, and fatalities. *Men's Health, "The Drunkest Cities in America," November 19, 2013*

Health/Fitness Rankings

- For the Gallup-Healthways Well-Being Index, researchers asked at least 300 adult residents in each of 189 U.S. metropolitan areas how satisfied they were with the metro area in which they lived. The Honolulu metro area was among the top ten for residents' satisfaction. *www.gallup.com, "City Satisfaction Highest in Fort Collins-Loveland, Colo.," April 11, 2014*

- The Honolulu metro area was identified as one of the worst cities for bed bugs in America by pest control company Orkin. The area ranked #45 out of 50 based on the number of bed bug treatments Orkin performed from January to December 2013. *Orkin, "Chicago Tops Bed Bug Cities List for Second Year in a Row," January 16, 2014*

- Honolulu was selected as one of the 25 fittest cities in America by *Men's Fitness Online*. It ranked #10 out of America's 50 largest cities. Criteria: fitness centers and sport stores; nutrition; sports participation; TV viewing; overweight/sedentary; junk food; air quality; geography; commute; parks and open space; city recreational facilities; access to healthcare; motivation; mayor and city initiatives; state obesity initiatives. *Men's Fitness, "The Fittest and Fattest Cities in America," March 5, 2012*

- *Men's Health* ranked 100 major U.S. cities in terms of the best and worst cities for men. Honolulu ranked #37. Criteria: thirty-three data points were examined covering health, fitness, and quality of life. *Men's Health, "The Best & Worst Cities for Men 2014," December 6, 2013*

- Honolulu was selected as one of the best metropolitan areas for hospital care in America by *HealthGrades.com*. The rankings are based on a comprehensive study of patient death and complication rates in the nation's nearly 5,000 hospitals. Hospitals performing in the top 5% nationwide across 26 different medical procedures and diagnoses were identified. *HealthGrades.com* then ranked cities by the highest percentage of these Distinguished Hospitals for Clinical Excellence™. The Honolulu metro area ranked #33. *HealthGrades.com, "America's Top 50 Cities for Hospital Care," January 21, 2012*

- The Honolulu metro area appeared in the 2013 Gallup-Healthways Well-Being Index. The area ranked #4 out of 189. The Gallup-Healthways Well-Being Index score is an average of six sub-indexes, which individually examine life evaluation, emotional health, work environment, physical health, healthy behaviors, and access to basic necessities. Results are based on telephone interviews conducted as part of the Gallup-Healthways Well-Being Index survey January 2–December 29, 2012, and January 2–December 30, 2013, with a random sample of 531,630 adults, aged 18 and older, living in metropolitan areas in the 50 U.S. states and the District of Columbia. *Gallup-Healthways, "State of American Well-Being," March 25, 2014*

Real Estate Rankings

- Honolulu was ranked #97 out of 275 metro areas in terms of house price appreciation in 2014 (#1 = highest rate). *Federal Housing Finance Agency, House Price Index, 4th Quarter 2014*

- The Honolulu metro area was identified as one of the 20 least affordable housing markets in the U.S. in 2014. The area ranked #3 out of 178 markets. Criteria: whether or not a typical family could qualify for a mortgage loan on a typical home. *National Association of Realtors®, Affordability Index of Existing Single-Family Homes for Metropolitan Areas, 2014*

- Honolulu was ranked #212 out of 226 metro areas in terms of housing affordability in 2014 by the National Association of Home Builders (#1 = most affordable). The NAHB-Wells Fargo Housing Opportunity Index (HOI) for a given area is defined as the share of homes sold in that area that would have been affordable to a family earning the local median income, based on standard mortgage underwriting criteria. *National Association of Home Builders®, NAHB-Wells Fargo Housing Opportunity Index, 4th Quarter 2014*

Safety Rankings

- Symantec, in partnership with Sperling's BestPlaces, ranked the 50 largest cities in the U.S. in terms of their vulnerability to cybercrime. The city ranked #14. Criteria: number of cyberattacks and potential infections; level of Internet access; expenditures on smartphones and computer hardware/software; wireless hotspots; broadband connectivity; Internet usage; online purchases. *Symantec, "Riskiest Online Cities of 2012" February 15, 2012*

- Farmers Insurance, in partnership with Sperling's BestPlaces, ranked metro areas in the U.S. and identified the "Most Secure Places to Live." The Honolulu metro area ranked #18 out of the top 20 in the large metro area category (500,000 or more residents). Criteria: economic stability; crime statistics; extreme weather; risk of natural disasters; housing depreciation; foreclosures; air quality; environmental hazards; life expectancy; motor vehicle fatalities; and employment numbers. *Farmers Insurance Group of Companies, "Most Secure U.S. Places to Live in the U.S.," June 25, 2013*

- Allstate ranked the 200 largest cities in America in terms of driver safety. Honolulu ranked #140. Allstate researchers analyzed internal property damage claims over a two-year period from January 2011 to December 2012. A weighted average of the two-year numbers determined the annual percentages. *Allstate, "Allstate America's Best Drivers Report, 2014"*

- The National Insurance Crime Bureau ranked 380 metro areas in the U.S. in terms of per capita rates of vehicle theft. The Honolulu metro area ranked #69 (#1 = highest rate). Criteria: number of vehicle theft offenses per 100,000 inhabitants in 2012. *National Insurance Crime Bureau, "Hot Spots 2012," June 26, 2013*

Seniors/Retirement Rankings

- In addition to affordability, good employment prospects, low crime rates, and pleasant climate, the Huffington Post considered community strength, recreational opportunities, and other markers of stress-free living in its search for the best retirement destinations for those who appreciate peace and quiet. Among those on the list was Honolulu. *www.huffingtonpost.com, "Best Places to Retire: 10 Most Relaxing U.S. Cities to Enjoy Your Golden Years," April 2, 2013*

- The finance website CNNMoney surveyed small U.S. cities that offer exceptional urban amenities at a cost of living somewhat higher than for the top-ten locations but still affordable for retirees. Median home-price figures were supplied by the residential real-estate website Trulia. Honolulu was among the eight small cities singled out. *money.cnn.com, "Best Places to Retire with a Nice Nest Egg," October 28, 2013*

- From its Best Cities for Successful Aging indexes, the Milken Institute generated rankings for metropolitan areas, weighing data in eight categories—health care, wellness, living arrangements, transportation, financial characteristics, education and employment opportunities, community engagement, and overall livability. The Honolulu metro area was ranked #12 overall in the large metro area category. *Milken Institute, "Best Cities for Successful Aging, 2014"*

Transportation Rankings

- NerdWallet surveyed average annual car insurance premiums in 125 U.S. cities to identify the least expensive U.S. cities in which to insure a car. Locations with no-fault insurance laws was a strong determinant. Honolulu came in at #20 for the most expensive rates. *www.nerdwallet.com, "Best Cities for Cheap Car Insurance," February 3, 2014*

Women/Minorities Rankings

- *Women's Health* examined U.S. cities and identified the 100 best cities for women. Honolulu was ranked #20. Criteria: 30 categories were examined from obesity and breast cancer rates to commuting times and hours spent working out. *Women's Health, "Best Cities for Women 2012"*

- Honolulu was selected as one of the best cities for young Latinos in 2013 by mun2, a national cable television broadcast network. The city ranked #7. Criteria: U.S. cities with populations over 500,000 residents were evaluated on the following criteria: number of young latinos; jobs; friendliness; cost of living; fun. *mun2.tv, "Best Cities for Young Latinos 2013*

Miscellaneous Rankings

- Ink Army reported on a survey by the website TotalBeauty calculating the number of tattoo shops per 100,000 residents in order to determine the U.S. cities with the most tattoo acceptance. Honolulu took the #8 slot. *inkarmy.com, "Most Tattoo Friendly Cities in the United States," November 1, 2013*

- Business Insider reports on the 2013 Trick-or-Treat Index compiled by the real estate site Zillow, which used its own Home Value Index and Walk Score along with population density and local crime stats to determine that Honolulu ranked #3 for "how much candy it gives out versus how far kids have to walk to get it." Zillow also zeroes in on the best neighborhoods in its top 20 cities. *www.businessinsider.com, "These Are the Best Cities for Trick-or-Treating," October 15, 2013*

- Honolulu was selected as one of the most tattooed cities in America by *Lovelyish.com*. The city was ranked #8. Criteria: number of tattoo shops per capita. *Lovelyish.com, "Top Ten: Most Tattooed Cities in America," October 17, 2012*

- Honolulu was selected as one of "America's Best Cities for Hipsters" by *Travel + Leisure*. The city was ranked #17 out of 20. Criteria: live music; coffee bars; independent boutiques; best microbrews; offbeat and tech-savvy locals. *Travel + Leisure, "America's Best Cities for Hipsters," November 2013*

- The National Alliance to End Homelessness ranked the 100 most populous metro areas in terms the rate of homelessness. The Honolulu metro area ranked #5. Criteria: number of homeless people per 10,000 population in 2011. *National Alliance to End Homelessness, The State of Homelessness in America 2012*

Business Environment

CITY FINANCES

City Government Finances

Component	2012 ($000)	2012 ($ per capita)
Total Revenues	2,412,211	2,531
Total Expenditures	2,324,071	2,438
Debt Outstanding	4,701,881	4,933
Cash and Securities[1]	1,847,933	1,939

Note: (1) Cash and security holdings of a government at the close of its fiscal year, including those of its dependent agencies, utilities, and liquor stores.
Source: U.S Census Bureau, State & Local Government Finances 2012

City Government Revenue by Source

Source	2012 ($000)	2012 ($ per capita)
General Revenue		
From Federal Government	218,849	230
From State Government	95,055	100
From Local Governments	414	0
Taxes		
Property	813,319	853
Sales and Gross Receipts	341,519	358
Personal Income	0	0
Corporate Income	0	0
Motor Vehicle License	139,322	146
Other Taxes	22,280	23
Current Charges	525,888	552
Liquor Store	0	0
Utility	217,000	228
Employee Retirement	0	0

Source: U.S Census Bureau, State & Local Government Finances 2012

City Government Expenditures by Function

Function	2012 ($000)	2012 ($ per capita)	2012 (%)
General Direct Expenditures			
Air Transportation	0	0	0.0
Corrections	0	0	0.0
Education	0	0	0.0
Employment Security Administration	0	0	0.0
Financial Administration	34,225	36	1.5
Fire Protection	105,377	111	4.5
General Public Buildings	35,435	37	1.5
Governmental Administration, Other	30,893	32	1.3
Health	24,340	26	1.0
Highways	124,997	131	5.4
Hospitals	0	0	0.0
Housing and Community Development	57,942	61	2.5
Interest on General Debt	166,786	175	7.2
Judicial and Legal	23,540	25	1.0
Libraries	0	0	0.0
Parking	562	1	0.0
Parks and Recreation	118,723	125	5.1
Police Protection	242,433	254	10.4
Public Welfare	0	0	0.0
Sewerage	224,214	235	9.6
Solid Waste Management	242,963	255	10.5
Veterans' Services	0	0	0.0
Liquor Store	0	0	0.0
Utility	770,105	808	33.1
Employee Retirement	0	0	0.0

Source: U.S Census Bureau, State & Local Government Finances 2012

DEMOGRAPHICS

Population Growth

Area	1990 Census	2000 Census	2010 Census	Population Growth (%) 1990-2000	Population Growth (%) 2000-2010
City	376,465	371,657	337,256	-1.3	-9.3
MSA[1]	n/a	n/a	n/a	n/a	n/a
U.S.	248,709,873	281,421,906	308,745,538	13.2	9.7

Note: (1) Figures cover the Honolulu, HI Metropolitan Statistical Area—see Appendix B for areas included
Source: U.S. Census Bureau, Census 1990, 2000, 2010

Household Size

Area	Persons in Household (%) One	Two	Three	Four	Five	Six	Seven or More	Average Household Size
City	33.9	30.9	14.6	10.3	4.6	2.6	3.1	2.59
MSA[1]	23.7	30.1	17.1	14.1	7.2	3.4	4.3	3.04
U.S.	27.7	33.6	15.7	13.1	6.0	2.3	1.5	2.64

Note: (1) Figures cover the Urban Honolulu, HI Metropolitan Statistical Area—see Appendix B for areas included
Source: U.S. Census Bureau, 2011-2013 American Community Survey 3-Year Estimates

Race

Area	White Alone[2] (%)	Black Alone[2] (%)	Asian Alone[2] (%)	AIAN[3] Alone[2] (%)	NHOPI[4] Alone[2] (%)	Other Race Alone[2] (%)	Two or More Races (%)
City	18.0	1.9	54.2	0.1	8.1	0.7	17.1
MSA[1]	21.5	2.6	43.1	0.2	9.3	1.0	22.4
U.S.	73.9	12.6	5.0	0.8	0.2	4.7	2.9

Note: (1) Figures cover the Urban Honolulu, HI Metropolitan Statistical Area—see Appendix B for areas included; (2) Alone is defined as not being in combination with one or more other races; (3) American Indian and Alaska Native; (4) Native Hawaiian and Other Pacific Islander
Source: U.S. Census Bureau, 2011-2013 American Community Survey 3-Year Estimates

Hispanic or Latino Origin

Area	Total (%)	Mexican (%)	Puerto Rican (%)	Cuban (%)	Other (%)
City	6.0	1.6	2.1	0.1	2.1
MSA[1]	8.9	2.6	3.1	0.1	3.1
U.S.	16.9	10.8	1.6	0.6	3.8

Note: Persons of Hispanic or Latino origin can be of any race; (1) Figures cover the Urban Honolulu, HI Metropolitan Statistical Area—see Appendix B for areas included
Source: U.S. Census Bureau, 2011-2013 American Community Survey 3-Year Estimates

Segregation

Type	Segregation Indices[1] 1990	2000	2010	2010 Rank[2]	Percent Change 1990-2000	1990-2010	2000-2010
Black/White	43.4	41.4	36.9	95	-2.0	-6.4	-4.5
Asian/White	38.5	41.4	42.1	44	2.9	3.5	0.7
Hispanic/White	32.4	32.8	31.9	91	0.3	-0.5	-0.8

Note: All figures cover the Metropolitan Statistical Area—see Appendix B for areas included; Figures are based on an analysis of 1990, 2000, and 2010 Census Decennial Census tract data by William H. Frey, Brookings Institution and the University of Michigan Social Science Data Analysis Network. In this analysis all racial groups (whites, blacks, and asians) are non-Hispanic members of those races. Hispanics are shown as a separate category;
(1) Segregation Indices are Dissimilarity Indices that measure the degree to which the minority group is distributed differently than whites across census tracts. They range from 0 (complete integration) to 100 (complete segregation) where the value indicates the percentage of the minority group that needs to move to be distributed exactly like whites; (2) Ranges from 1 (most segregated) to 102 (least segregated); n/a not available.
Source: www.CensusScope.org

Ancestry

Area	German	Irish	English	American	Italian	Polish	French[2]	Scottish	Dutch
City	4.3	3.2	2.8	1.5	2.0	0.6	1.3	0.9	0.4
MSA[1]	5.2	4.0	3.3	1.5	2.0	0.8	1.1	0.8	0.6
U.S.	14.9	10.8	8.0	7.4	5.5	3.0	2.7	1.7	1.4

Note: Figures are the percentage of the total population reporting a particular ancestry. The nine most commonly reported ancestries in the U.S. are shown. Figures include multiple ancestries (e.g. if a person reported being Irish and Italian, they were included in both columns); (1) Figures cover the Urban Honolulu, HI Metropolitan Statistical Area—see Appendix B for areas included; (2) Excludes Basque
Source: U.S. Census Bureau, 2011-2013 American Community Survey 3-Year Estimates

Foreign-Born Population

Area	Any Foreign Country	Mexico	Asia	Europe	Carribean	South America	Central America[2]	Africa	Canada
City	27.8	0.2	23.2	1.1	0.1	0.2	0.0	0.1	0.3
MSA[1]	19.3	0.2	15.8	0.7	0.1	0.2	0.1	0.1	0.3
U.S.	13.0	3.7	3.8	1.5	1.2	0.9	1.0	0.6	0.3

Note: (1) Figures cover the Urban Honolulu, HI Metropolitan Statistical Area—see Appendix B for areas included; (2) Excludes Mexico.
Source: U.S. Census Bureau, 2011-2013 American Community Survey 3-Year Estimates

Marital Status

Area	Never Married	Now Married[2]	Separated	Widowed	Divorced
City	36.7	44.5	1.4	7.3	10.2
MSA[1]	33.8	50.2	1.3	6.2	8.6
U.S.	32.7	48.1	2.2	6.0	11.0

Note: Figures are percentages and cover the population 15 years of age and older; (1) Figures cover the Urban Honolulu, HI Metropolitan Statistical Area—see Appendix B for areas included; (2) Excludes separated
Source: U.S. Census Bureau, 2011-2013 American Community Survey 3-Year Estimates

Disability Status

Area	All Ages	Under 18 Years Old	18 to 64 Years Old	65 Years and Over
City	11.1	2.5	7.2	33.5
MSA[1]	10.6	3.0	7.6	34.1
U.S.	12.3	4.1	10.2	36.3

Note: Figures show percent of the civilian noninstitutionalized population that reported having a disability. Disability status is determined from from six types of difficulty: vision, hearing, cognitive, ambulatory, self-care, and independent living. For children under 5 years old, hearing and vision difficulty are used to determine disability status. For children between the ages of 5 and 14, disability status is determined from hearing, vision, cognitive, ambulatory, and self-care difficulties. For people aged 15 years and older, they are considered to have a disability if they have difficulty with any one of the six difficulty types; (1) Figures cover the Urban Honolulu, HI Metropolitan Statistical Area—see Appendix B for areas included.
Source: U.S. Census Bureau, 2011-2013 American Community Survey 3-Year Estimates

Age

Area	Under Age 5	Age 5–19	Age 20–34	Age 35–44	Age 45–54	Age 55–64	Age 65–74	Age 75–84	Age 85+	Median Age
City	5.4	14.9	22.7	12.6	13.5	13.0	8.3	6.0	3.6	40.5
MSA[1]	6.5	17.7	23.1	12.7	13.0	11.9	7.8	4.7	2.6	37.2
U.S.	6.4	19.9	20.7	12.9	14.1	12.3	7.6	4.2	1.9	37.4

Note: (1) Figures cover the Urban Honolulu, HI Metropolitan Statistical Area—see Appendix B for areas included
Source: U.S. Census Bureau, 2011-2013 American Community Survey 3-Year Estimates

Gender

Area	Males	Females	Males per 100 Females
City	170,480	174,427	97.7
MSA[1]	491,583	483,100	101.8
U.S.	154,451,010	159,410,713	96.9

Note: (1) Figures cover the Urban Honolulu, HI Metropolitan Statistical Area—see Appendix B for areas included
Source: U.S. Census Bureau, 2011-2013 American Community Survey 3-Year Estimates

Religious Groups by Family

Area	Catholic	Baptist	Non-Den.	Methodist[2]	Lutheran	LDS[3]	Pentecostal	Presbyterian[4]	Muslim[5]	Judaism
MSA[1]	18.2	1.9	2.2	0.8	0.3	5.1	4.2	1.5	<0.1	0.1
U.S.	19.1	9.3	4.0	4.0	2.3	2.0	1.9	1.6	0.8	0.7

Note: Figures are the number of adherents as a percentage of the total population; (1) Figures cover the Honolulu, HI Metropolitan Statistical Area—see Appendix B for areas included; (2) Methodist/Pietist; (3) Latter Day Saints; (4) Reformed; (5) Figures are estimates
Source: Association of Statisticians of American Religious Bodies, 2010 U.S. Religion Census: Religious Congregations & Membership Study

Religious Groups by Tradition

Area	Catholic	Evangelical Protestant	Mainline Protestant	Other Tradition	Black Protestant	Orthodox
MSA[1]	18.2	9.7	2.9	8.4	<0.1	<0.1
U.S.	19.1	16.2	7.3	4.3	1.6	0.3

Note: Figures are the number of adherents as a percentage of the total population; (1) Figures cover the Honolulu, HI Metropolitan Statistical Area—see Appendix B for areas included
Source: Association of Statisticians of American Religious Bodies, 2010 U.S. Religion Census: Religious Congregations & Membership Study

ECONOMY

Gross Metropolitan Product

Area	2012	2013	2014	2015	Rank[2]
MSA[1]	56.6	57.8	59.8	62.2	51

Note: Figures are in billions of dollars; (1) Figures cover the Urban Honolulu, HI Metropolitan Statistical Area—see Appendix B for areas included; (2) Rank is based on 2015 data and ranges from 1 to 363
Source: The U.S. Conference of Mayors, U.S. Metro Economies: GMP and Employment 2013-2015, June 2014

Economic Growth

Area	2010-12 (%)	2013 (%)	2014 (%)	2015 (%)	Rank[2]
MSA[1]	2.3	0.8	1.8	1.9	332
U.S.	2.1	2.0	2.3	3.2	–

Note: Figures are real gross metropolitan product (GMP) growth rates and represent annual average percent change; (1) Figures cover the Urban Honolulu, HI Metropolitan Statistical Area—see Appendix B for areas included; (2) Rank is based on 2015 data and ranges from 1 to 363
Source: The U.S. Conference of Mayors, U.S. Metro Economies: GMP and Employment 2013-2015, June 2014

Metropolitan Area Exports

Area	2008	2009	2010	2011	2012	2013	Rank[2]
MSA[1]	546.0	357.9	439.5	375.3	306.3	323.2	257

Note: Figures are in millions of dollars; (1) Figures cover the Urban Honolulu, HI Metropolitan Statistical Area—see Appendix B for areas included; (2) Rank is based on 2013 data and ranges from 1 to 387
Source: U.S. Department of Commerce, International Trade Administration, Office of Trade & Industry Information, Manufacturing & Services, data extracted April 3, 2015

Building Permits

Area	Single-Family			Multi-Family			Total		
	2013	2014	Pct. Chg.	2013	2014	Pct. Chg.	2013	2014	Pct. Chg.
City	n/a	n/a	n/a	n/a	n/a	n/a	n/a	n/a	n/a
MSA[1]	1,137	875	-23.0	1,504	703	-53.3	2,641	1,578	-40.2
U.S.	620,802	634,597	2.2	370,020	411,766	11.3	990,822	1,046,363	5.6

Note: (1) Figures cover the Urban Honolulu, HI Metropolitan Statistical Area—see Appendix B for areas included; Figures represent new, privately-owned housing units authorized (unadjusted data); All permit data are based on estimates with imputation.
Source: U.S. Census Bureau, Manufacturing, Mining, and Construction Statistics, Building Permits, 2013, 2014

Bankruptcy Filings

Area	Business Filings			Nonbusiness Filings		
	2013	2014	% Chg.	2013	2014	% Chg.
Honolulu County	54	44	-18.5	1,231	1,057	-14.1
U.S.	33,212	26,983	-18.8	1,038,720	909,812	-12.4

Note: Business filings include Chapter 7, Chapter 11, Chapter 12, and Chapter 13; Nonbusiness filings include Chapter 7, Chapter 11, and Chapter 13
Source: Administrative Office of the U.S. Courts, Business and Nonbusiness Bankruptcy, County Cases Commenced by Chapter of the Bankruptcy Code, During the 12- Month Period Ending December 31, 2013 and Business and Nonbusiness Bankruptcy, County Cases Commenced by Chapter of the Bankruptcy Code, During the 12- Month Period Ending December 31, 2014

Housing Vacancy Rates

Area	Gross Vacancy Rate[2] (%)			Year-Round Vacancy Rate[3] (%)			Rental Vacancy Rate[4] (%)			Homeowner Vacancy Rate[5] (%)		
	2012	2013	2014	2012	2013	2014	2012	2013	2014	2012	2013	2014
MSA[1]	10.2	10.9	12.3	8.8	8.6	10.2	6.3	6.0	5.6	1.3	0.9	1.1
U.S.	13.8	13.6	13.4	10.8	10.7	10.4	8.7	8.3	7.6	2.0	2.0	1.9

Note: (1) Figures cover the Urban Honolulu, HI Metropolitan Statistical Area—see Appendix B for areas included; (2) The percentage of the total housing inventory that is vacant; (3) The percentage of the housing inventory (excluding seasonal units) that is year-round vacant; (4) The percentage of rental inventory that is vacant for rent; (5) The percentage of homeowner inventory that is vacant for sale
Source: U.S. Census Bureau, Housing Vacancies and Homeownership Annual Statistics: 2014

INCOME

Income

Area	Per Capita ($)	Median Household ($)	Average Household ($)
City	30,378	59,490	77,842
MSA[1]	30,002	71,728	89,208
U.S.	27,884	52,176	72,897

Note: (1) Figures cover the Urban Honolulu, HI Metropolitan Statistical Area—see Appendix B for areas included
Source: U.S. Census Bureau, 2011-2013 American Community Survey 3-Year Estimates

Household Income Distribution

Area	Percent of Households Earning							
	Under $15,000	$15,000 -24,999	$25,000 -34,999	$35,000 -49,999	$50,000 -74,999	$75,000 -99,000	$100,000 -149,999	$150,000 and up
City	11.8	8.3	8.6	13.2	19.8	13.1	14.1	11.3
MSA[1]	8.5	6.3	7.0	11.7	18.9	14.2	19.1	14.5
U.S.	13.0	10.9	10.3	13.6	17.9	11.9	12.7	9.6

Note: (1) Figures cover the Urban Honolulu, HI Metropolitan Statistical Area—see Appendix B for areas included
Source: U.S. Census Bureau, 2011-2013 American Community Survey 3-Year Estimates

Poverty Rate

Area	All Ages	Under 18 Years Old	18 to 64 Years Old	65 Years and Over
City	12.3	16.8	11.9	9.4
MSA[1]	9.9	13.5	9.3	7.2
U.S.	15.9	22.4	14.8	9.5

Note: Figures are percentage of people whose income during the past 12 months was below the poverty level;
(1) Figures cover the Urban Honolulu, HI Metropolitan Statistical Area—see Appendix B for areas included
Source: U.S. Census Bureau, 2011-2013 American Community Survey 3-Year Estimates

EMPLOYMENT

Labor Force and Employment

Area	Civilian Labor Force			Workers Employed		
	Dec. 2013	Dec. 2014	% Chg.	Dec. 2013	Dec. 2014	% Chg.
City	460,385	469,161	1.9	442,022	452,749	2.4
MSA[1]	460,385	469,161	1.9	442,022	452,749	2.4
U.S.	154,408,000	155,521,000	0.7	144,423,000	147,190,000	1.9

Note: Data is not seasonally adjusted and covers workers 16 years of age and older; (1) Figures cover the
Urban Honolulu, HI Metropolitan Statistical Area—see Appendix B for areas included
Source: Bureau of Labor Statistics, Local Area Unemployment Statistics

Unemployment Rate

Area	2014											
	Jan.	Feb.	Mar.	Apr.	May	Jun.	Jul.	Aug.	Sep.	Oct.	Nov.	Dec.
City	4.4	4.2	4.1	4.0	4.0	4.6	4.1	3.9	4.1	3.9	3.9	3.5
MSA[1]	4.4	4.2	4.1	4.0	4.0	4.6	4.1	3.9	4.1	3.9	3.9	3.5
U.S.	7.0	7.0	6.8	5.9	6.1	6.3	6.5	6.3	5.7	5.5	5.5	5.4

Note: Data is not seasonally adjusted and covers workers 16 years of age and older; (1) Figures cover the
Urban Honolulu, HI Metropolitan Statistical Area—see Appendix B for areas included
Source: Bureau of Labor Statistics, Local Area Unemployment Statistics

Employment by Occupation

Occupation Classification	City (%)	MSA[1] (%)	U.S. (%)
Management, Business, Science, and Arts	36.2	35.7	36.2
Natural Resources, Construction, and Maintenance	6.7	9.2	9.0
Production, Transportation, and Material Moving	8.1	8.8	12.1
Sales and Office	26.1	25.1	24.4
Service	23.0	21.2	18.3

Note: Figures cover employed civilians 16 years of age and older; (1) Figures cover the Urban Honolulu, HI
Metropolitan Statistical Area—see Appendix B for areas included
Source: U.S. Census Bureau, 2011-2013 American Community Survey 3-Year Estimates

Employment by Industry

Sector	MSA[1]		U.S.
	Number of Employees	Percent of Total	Percent of Total
Construction, Mining, and Logging	24,300	5.2	5.0
Education and Health Services	63,200	13.4	15.5
Financial Activities	21,100	4.5	5.7
Government	100,700	21.4	15.8
Information	7,400	1.6	2.0
Leisure and Hospitality	68,900	14.6	10.3
Manufacturing	11,100	2.4	8.7
Other Services	21,000	4.5	4.0
Professional and Business Services	67,100	14.2	13.8
Retail Trade	50,100	10.6	11.4
Transportation, Warehousing, and Utilities	22,000	4.7	3.9
Wholesale Trade	14,500	3.1	4.2

Note: Figures are non-farm employment as of December 2014. Figures are not seasonally adjusted and include
workers 16 years of age and older; (1) Figures cover the Urban Honolulu, HI Metropolitan Statistical
Area—see Appendix B for areas included; n/a not available
Source: Bureau of Labor Statistics, Current Employment Statistics, Employment, Hours, and Earnings

Occupations with Greatest Projected Employment Growth: 2012 – 2022

Occupation[1]	2012 Employment	2022 Projected Employment	Numeric Employment Change	Percent Employment Change
Retail Salespersons	24,490	27,010	2,520	10.3
Combined Food Preparation and Serving Workers, Including Fast Food	16,320	18,720	2,400	14.7
Registered Nurses	10,370	12,170	1,800	17.4
Personal Care Aides	4,070	5,770	1,700	41.9
Carpenters	7,030	8,670	1,640	23.3
Maids and Housekeeping Cleaners	14,240	15,740	1,500	10.5
General and Operations Managers	10,610	11,880	1,270	12.0
Nursing Assistants	5,260	6,520	1,260	23.9
Janitors and Cleaners, Except Maids and Housekeeping Cleaners	12,410	13,650	1,240	10.0
Construction Laborers	4,110	5,270	1,160	28.2

Note: Projections cover Hawaii; (1) Sorted by numeric employment change
Source: www.projectionscentral.com, State Occupational Projections, 2012–2022 Long-Term Projections

Fastest Growing Occupations: 2012 – 2022

Occupation[1]	2012 Employment	2022 Projected Employment	Numeric Employment Change	Percent Employment Change
Personal Care Aides	4,070	5,770	1,700	41.9
Information Security Analysts	340	480	140	39.8
Home Health Aides	2,160	3,010	850	39.4
Helpers—Electricians	280	380	100	39.3
Skincare Specialists	480	640	160	34.2
Helpers—Carpenters	450	610	160	34.1
Cost Estimators	1,160	1,530	370	32.8
Market Research Analysts and Marketing Specialists	880	1,140	260	30.3
Cement Masons and Concrete Finishers	530	690	160	29.3
Construction Laborers	4,110	5,270	1,160	28.2

Note: Projections cover Hawaii; (1) Sorted by percent employment change and excludes occupations with numeric employment change less than 100
Source: www.projectionscentral.com, State Occupational Projections, 2012–2022 Long-Term Projections

Average Wages

Occupation	$/Hr.	Occupation	$/Hr.
Accountants and Auditors	29.42	Maids and Housekeeping Cleaners	15.83
Automotive Mechanics	21.49	Maintenance and Repair Workers	20.38
Bookkeepers	18.39	Marketing Managers	44.45
Carpenters	34.11	Nuclear Medicine Technologists	42.17
Cashiers	10.72	Nurses, Licensed Practical	23.19
Clerks, General Office	15.52	Nurses, Registered	43.39
Clerks, Receptionists/Information	13.84	Nursing Assistants	14.28
Clerks, Shipping/Receiving	16.27	Packers and Packagers, Hand	10.66
Computer Programmers	33.81	Physical Therapists	38.79
Computer Systems Analysts	38.30	Postal Service Mail Carriers	26.41
Computer User Support Specialists	23.78	Real Estate Brokers	72.67
Cooks, Restaurant	12.56	Retail Salespersons	12.09
Dentists	83.04	Sales Reps., Exc. Tech./Scientific	22.95
Electrical Engineers	41.55	Sales Reps., Tech./Scientific	34.42
Electricians	31.86	Secretaries, Exc. Legal/Med./Exec.	18.61
Financial Managers	48.00	Security Guards	13.23
First-Line Supervisors/Managers, Sales	22.63	Surgeons	n/a
Food Preparation Workers	10.93	Teacher Assistants	13.10
General and Operations Managers	49.10	Teachers, Elementary School	26.30
Hairdressers/Cosmetologists	18.81	Teachers, Secondary School	26.80
Internists	91.52	Telemarketers	12.13
Janitors and Cleaners	12.01	Truck Drivers, Heavy/Tractor-Trailer	20.79
Landscaping/Groundskeeping Workers	14.13	Truck Drivers, Light/Delivery Svcs.	14.96
Lawyers	50.53	Waiters and Waitresses	14.19

Note: Wage data covers the Honolulu, HI Metropolitan Statistical Area—see Appendix B for areas included; Hourly wages for elementary/secondary school teachers and teacher assistants were calculated by the editors from annual wage data assuming a 40 hour work week; n/a not available.
Source: Bureau of Labor Statistics, Metro Area Occupational Employment and Wage Estimates, May 2014

TAXES

State Corporate Income Tax Rates

State	Tax Rate (%)	Income Brackets ($)	Num. of Brackets	Financial Institution Tax Rate (%)[a]	Federal Income Tax Ded.
Hawaii	4.4 - 6.4 (g)	25,000 - 100,001	3	7.92 (g)	No

Note: Tax rates as of January 1, 2015; (a) Rates listed are the corporate income tax rate applied to financial institutions or excise taxes based on income. Some states have other taxes based upon the value of deposits or shares; (g) Hawaii taxes capital gains at 4%. Financial institutions pay a franchise tax of 7.92% of taxable income (in lieu of the corporate income tax and general excise taxes).
Source: Federation of Tax Administrators, "State Corporate Income Tax Rates, 2015"

State Individual Income Tax Rates

State	Tax Rate (%)	Income Brackets ($)	Num. of Brackets	Personal Exempt. ($)[1] Single	Personal Exempt. ($)[1] Dependents	Fed. Inc. Tax Ded.
Hawaii (w)	1.4 - 11.00	2,400 - 200,001 (b)	12	1,040	1,040	No

Note: Tax rates as of January 1, 2015; Local- and county-level taxes are not included; n/a not applicable; (1) Married joint filers generally receive double the single exemption; (b) For joint returns, taxes are twice the tax on half the couple's income; (w) Tax rates in the District of Columbia and Hawaii are scheduled to decrease for tax year 2016.
Source: Federation of Tax Administrators, "State Individual Income Tax Rates, 2015"

Various State and Local Tax Rates

State	State and Local Sales and Use (%)	State Sales and Use (%)	Gasoline[1] (¢/gal.)	Cigarette[2] ($/pack)	Spirits[3] ($/gal.)	Wine[4] ($/gal.)	Beer[5] ($/gal.)
Hawaii	4.5	4.0 (c)	45	3.20	5.98	1.38	0.93 (p)

Note: All tax rates as of January 1, 2015; (1) The American Petroleum Institute has developed a methodology for determining the average tax rate on a gallon of fuel. Rates may include any of the following: excise taxes, environmental fees, storage tank fees, other fees or taxes, general sales tax, and local taxes. In states where gasoline is subject to the general sales tax, or where the fuel tax is based on the average sale price, the average rate determined by API is sensitive to changes in the price of gasoline. States that fully or partially apply general sales taxes to gasoline: CA, CO, GA, IL, IN, MI, NY; (2) The federal excise tax of $1.0066 per pack and local taxes are not included; (3) Rates are those applicable to off-premise sales of 40% alcohol by volume (a.b.v.) distilled spirits in 750ml containers. Local excise taxes are excluded; (4) Rates are those applicable to off-premise sales of 11% a.b.v. non-carbonated wine in 750ml containers; (5) Rates are those applicable to off-premise sales of 4.7% a.b.v. beer in 12 ounce containers; (c) The sales taxes in Hawaii, New Mexico, and South Dakota have broad bases that include many business-to-business services; (p) Local excise taxes are excluded.
Source: Tax Foundation, 2015 Facts & Figures: How Does Your State Compare?

State Business Tax Climate Index Rankings

State	Overall Rank	Corporate Tax Index Rank	Individual Income Tax Index Rank	Sales Tax Index Rank	Unemployment Insurance Tax Index Rank	Property Tax Index Rank
Hawaii	30	9	37	15	28	12

Note: The index is a measure of how each state's tax laws affect economic performance. The lower the rank, the more favorable a state's tax system is for business. States without a given tax are given a ranking of 1. The scores/rankings for the District of Columbia do not affect other states. The 2015 index represents the tax climate as of July 1, 2014.
Source: Tax Foundation, State Business Tax Climate Index 2015

COMMERCIAL UTILITIES

Typical Monthly Electric Bills

Area	Commercial Service ($/month)		Industrial Service ($/month)	
	1,500 kWh	40 kW demand 14,000 kWh	1,000 kW demand 200,000 kWh	50,000 kW demand 32,500,000 kWh
City	551	4,489	76,086	9,569,154
Average[1]	201	1,653	26,124	2,639,743

Note: Figures are based on annualized 2014 rates; (1) Average based on 180 utilities surveyed
Source: Edison Electric Institute, Typical Bills and Average Rates Report, Summer 2014

TRANSPORTATION

Means of Transportation to Work

Area	Car/Truck/Van Drove Alone	Car/Truck/Van Car-pooled	Public Transportation Bus	Public Transportation Subway	Public Transportation Railroad	Bicycle	Walked	Other Means	Worked at Home
City	57.5	12.6	12.1	0.0	0.0	1.9	8.9	3.5	3.5
MSA[1]	64.4	14.8	8.0	0.0	0.0	1.2	5.2	2.9	3.5
U.S.	76.4	9.6	2.6	1.8	0.6	0.6	2.8	1.3	4.3

Note: Figures are percentages and cover workers 16 years of age and older; (1) Figures cover the Urban Honolulu, HI Metropolitan Statistical Area—see Appendix B for areas included
Source: U.S. Census Bureau, 2011-2013 American Community Survey 3-Year Estimates

Travel Time to Work

Area	Less Than 10 Minutes	10 to 19 Minutes	20 to 29 Minutes	30 to 44 Minutes	45 to 59 Minutes	60 to 89 Minutes	90 Minutes or More
City	8.4	35.9	24.7	22.0	5.0	3.2	0.8
MSA[1]	9.9	25.8	20.5	25.5	9.3	6.9	2.3
U.S.	13.3	29.7	20.9	20.2	7.7	5.7	2.6

Note: Figures are percentages and include workers 16 years old and over; (1) Figures cover the Urban Honolulu, HI Metropolitan Statistical Area—see Appendix B for areas included
Source: U.S. Census Bureau, 2011-2013 American Community Survey 3-Year Estimates

Travel Time Index

Area	1985	1990	1995	2000	2005	2010	2011
Urban Area[1]	1.20	1.32	1.34	1.30	1.36	1.36	1.36
Average[2]	1.09	1.14	1.16	1.19	1.23	1.18	1.18

Note: Travel Time Index—the ratio of travel time in the peak period to the travel time at free-flow conditions. For example, a value of 1.30 indicates a 20-minute free-flow trip takes 26 minutes in the peak. Free-flow speeds (60 mph on freeways and 35 mph on principal arterials) are used as the comparison threshold; (1) Covers the Honolulu HI urban area; (2) average of 498 urban areas
Source: Texas Transportation Institute, Urban Mobility Report 2012, December 2012

Public Transportation

Agency Name / Mode of Transportation	Vehicles Operated in Maximum Service	Annual Unlinked Passenger Trips (in thous.)	Annual Passenger Miles (in thous.)
City and County of Honolulu Dept. of Transportation Services (DTS)			
Bus (purchased transportation)	433	69,242.2	359,913.1
Demand Response (purchased transportation)	136	841.4	10,383.1
Demand Response Taxi (purchased transportation)	117	160.3	1,063.8

Source: Federal Transit Administration, National Transit Database, 2013

Air Transportation

Airport Name and Code / Type of Service	Passenger Airlines[1]	Passenger Enplanements	Freight Carriers[2]	Freight (lbs.)
Honolulu International (HNL)				
Domestic service (U.S. carriers - 2014)	17	6,987,416	20	342,754,034
International service (U.S. carriers - 2013)	5	1,049,451	9	130,581,296

Note: (1) Includes all U.S.-based major, minor and commuter airlines that carried at least one passenger during the year; (2) Includes all U.S.-based airlines and freight carriers that transported at least one lb. of freight during the year.
Source: Bureau of Transportation Statistics, The Intermodal Transportation Database, Air Carriers: T-100 Domestic Market (U.S. Carriers), 2014; Bureau of Transportation Statistics, The Intermodal Transportation Database, Air Carriers: T-100 International Market (U.S. Carriers), 2013

Other Transportation Statistics

Major Highways:	None
Amtrak Service:	No
Major Waterways/Ports:	Port of Honolulu

Source: Amtrak.com; Google Maps

BUSINESSES

Major Business Headquarters

Company Name	Rankings	
	Fortune[1]	Forbes[2]
No companies listed	-	-

Note: (1) Fortune 500—companies that produce a 10-K are ranked 1 to 500 based on 2013 revenue; (2) all private companies with at least $2 billion in annual revenue through the end of their most current fiscal year are ranked 1 to 221; companies listed are headquartered in the city; dashes indicate no ranking
Source: Fortune, "Fortune 500," June 16, 2014; Forbes, "America's Largest Private Companies," November 5, 2014

Fast-Growing Businesses

According to *Inc.*, Honolulu is home to one of America's 500 fastest-growing private companies: **Asentra Health** (#16). Criteria: must be an independent, privately-held, for-profit, U.S. corporation, proprietorship or partnership; revenues must be at least $100,000 in 2010 and $2 million in 2013; must have four-year operating/sales history. Holding companies, regulated banks, and utilities were excluded. *Inc., "America's 500 Fastest-Growing Private Companies," September 2014*

Minority- and Women-Owned Businesses

Group	All Firms		Firms with Paid Employees			
	Firms	Sales ($000)	Firms	Sales ($000)	Employees	Payroll ($000)
Asian	24,262	10,337,119	6,013	9,505,117	58,665	2,020,268
Black	373	155,621	51	148,102	1,143	58,161
Hispanic	1,133	138,484	111	114,435	1,275	32,060
Women	12,530	2,456,477	2,063	2,068,992	18,903	518,607
All Firms	42,030	46,813,051	11,887	45,343,943	250,071	9,395,949

Note: Figures cover firms located in the city; minority- and women-owned business are defined as firms in which the corresponding group own 51% or more of the stock or equity of the company
Source: U.S. Census Bureau, 2007 Economic Census, Survey of Business Owners (2012 Survey of Business Owners data will be released starting in June 2015)

**HOTELS &
CONVENTION
CENTERS**

Hotels/Motels

Area	5 Star		4 Star		3 Star		2 Star		1 Star		Not Rated	
	Num.	Pct.[3]	Num.	Pct.[3]	Num.	Pct.[3]	Num.	Pct.[3]	Num.	Pct.[3]	Num.	Pct.[3]
City[1]	5	4.5	17	15.5	56	50.9	26	23.6	1	0.9	5	4.5
Total[2]	166	0.9	1,264	7.0	5,718	31.8	9,340	52.0	411	2.3	1,070	6.0

Note: (1) Figures cover Honolulu and vicinity; (2) Figures cover all 100 cities in this book; (3) Percentage of hotels which have a given star rating; Star ratings are determined by expedia.com and offer an indication of the general quality of a particular hotel.
Source: expedia.com, April 2, 2015

The Urban Honolulu, HI metro area is home to three of the best hotels in the U.S. according to *Travel & Leisure*: **Halekulani**; **Royal Hawaiian, A Luxury Collection Resort**; **Trump International Hotel Waikiki Beach Walk**. Criteria: service; location; rooms; food; and value. The list includes the top 236 hotels in the U.S. *Travel & Leisure, "T+L 500, The World's Best Hotels 2015"*

The Urban Honolulu, HI metro area is home to two of the best hotels in the world according to *Condé Nast Traveler*: **Halekulani**; **The Royal Hawaiian (Luxury Collection)**. The selections are based on editors' picks. The list includes the top 25 hotels in the U.S. *Condé Nast Traveler, "Gold List 2015, The Top Hotels in the World"*

Major Convention Centers

Name	Overall Space (sq. ft.)	Exhibit Space (sq. ft.)	Meeting Space (sq. ft.)	Meeting Rooms
Hawaii Convention Center	1,100,000	200,000	138,869	47

Note: Table includes convention centers located in the Urban Honolulu, HI metro area; n/a not available
Source: Original research

Living Environment

COST OF LIVING

Cost of Living Index

Composite Index	Groceries	Housing	Utilities	Trans-portation	Health Care	Misc. Goods/ Services
174.3	154.3	266.1	214.5	125.7	112.0	116.6

Note: The Cost of Living Index measures regional differences in the cost of consumer goods and services, excluding taxes and non-consumer expenditures, for professional and managerial households in the top income quintile. It is based on more than 50,000 prices covering almost 60 different items for which prices are collected three times a year by chambers of commerce, economic development organizations or university applied economic centers in each participating urban area. The numbers shown should be read as a percentage above or below the national average of 100. For example, a value of 115.4 in the groceries column indicates that grocery prices are 15.4% higher than the national average. Small differences in the index numbers should not be interpreted as significant; Figures cover the Honolulu HI urban area.
Source: The Council for Community and Economic Research, ACCRA Cost of Living Index, 2014

Grocery Prices

Area[1]	T-Bone Steak ($/pound)	Frying Chicken ($/pound)	Whole Milk ($/half gal.)	Eggs ($/dozen)	Orange Juice ($/64 oz.)	Coffee ($/11.5 oz.)
City[2]	11.62	2.42	3.62	3.58	4.92	6.96
Avg.	10.40	1.37	2.40	1.99	3.46	4.27
Min.	8.48	0.93	1.37	1.30	2.83	2.99
Max.	14.20	2.44	3.62	4.02	6.42	6.96

*Note: (1) Values for the local area are compared with the average, minimum and maximum values for all 308 areas in the Cost of Living Index; (2) Figures cover the Honolulu HI urban area; **T-Bone Steak** (price per pound); **Frying Chicken** (price per pound, whole fryer); **Whole Milk** (half gallon carton); **Eggs** (price per dozen, Grade A, large); **Orange Juice** (64 oz. Tropicana or Florida Natural); **Coffee** (11.5 oz. can, vacuum-packed, Maxwell House, Hills Bros, or Folgers).*
Source: The Council for Community and Economic Research, ACCRA Cost of Living Index, 2014

Housing and Utility Costs

Area[1]	New Home Price ($)	Apartment Rent ($/month)	All Electric ($/month)	Part Electric ($/month)	Other Energy ($/month)	Telephone ($/month)
City[2]	752,644	2,975	498.00	-	-	28.95
Avg.	305,838	919	181.00	93.66	73.14	27.95
Min.	183,142	480	112.00	42.06	23.42	17.16
Max.	1,358,576	3,851	594.00	180.03	440.99	40.42

*Note: (1) Values for the local area are compared with the average, minimum and maximum values for all 308 areas in the Cost of Living Index; (2) Figures cover the Honolulu HI urban area; **New Home Price** (2,400 sf living area, 8,000 sf lot, in urban area with full utilities); **Apartment Rent** (950 sf 2 bedroom/1.5 or 2 bath, unfurnished, excluding all utilities except water); **All Electric** (average monthly cost for an all-electric home); **Part Electric** (average monthly cost for a part-electric home); **Other Energy** (average monthly cost for natural gas, fuel oil, coal, wood, and any other forms of energy except electricity); **Telephone** (price includes basic monthly rate for a private residential line plus additional local usage charges incurred by a family of four).*
Source: The Council for Community and Economic Research, ACCRA Cost of Living Index, 2014

Health Care, Transportation, and Other Costs

Area[1]	Doctor ($/visit)	Dentist ($/visit)	Optometrist ($/visit)	Gasoline ($/gallon)	Beauty Salon ($/visit)	Men's Shirt ($)
City[2]	110.28	92.34	142.51	4.21	52.93	37.57
Avg.	102.86	87.89	97.66	3.44	34.37	26.74
Min.	67.47	65.78	51.18	3.00	17.43	12.79
Max.	173.50	150.14	235.00	4.33	64.28	49.50

*Note: (1) Values for the local area are compared with the average, minimum and maximum values for all 308 areas in the Cost of Living Index; (2) Figures cover the Honolulu HI urban area; **Doctor** (general practitioners routine exam of an established patient); **Dentist** (adult teeth cleaning and periodic oral examination); **Optometrist** (full vision eye exam for established adult patient); **Gasoline** (one gallon regular unleaded, national brand, including all taxes, cash price at self-service pump if available); **Beauty Salon** (woman's shampoo, trim, and blow-dry); **Men's Shirt** (cotton/polyester dress shirt, pinpoint weave, long sleeves).*
Source: The Council for Community and Economic Research, ACCRA Cost of Living Index, 2014

HOUSING

House Price Index (HPI)

Area	National Ranking[2]	Quarterly Change (%)	One-Year Change (%)	Five-Year Change (%)
MSA[1]	97	1.94	5.54	20.20
U.S.[3]	–	1.35	4.91	11.59

Note: The HPI is a weighted repeat sales index. It measures average price changes in repeat sales or refinancings on the same properties. This information is obtained by reviewing repeat mortgage transactions on single-family properties whose mortgages have been purchased or securitized by Fannie Mae or Freddie Mac in January 1975; (1) Honolulu Metropolitan Statistical Area—see Appendix B for areas included; (2) Rankings are based on annual percentage change for all metro areas containing at least 15,000 transactions over the last 10 years and ranges from 1 to 275; (3) figures based on a weighted average of Census Division estimates using a seasonally adjusted, purchase-only index; all figures are for the period ending December 31, 2014
Source: Federal Housing Finance Agency, House Price Index, February 26, 2015

Median Single-Family Home Prices

Area	2012	2013	2014p	Percent Change 2013 to 2014
MSA[1]	628.8	661.5	682.8	3.2
U.S. Average	177.2	197.4	209.0	5.9

Note: Figures are median sales prices of existing single-family homes in thousands of dollars; (p) preliminary; n/a not available; (1) Urban Honolulu, HI Metropolitan Statistical Area—see Appendix B for areas included
Source: National Association of Realtors, Median Sales Price of Existing Single-Family Homes for Metropolitan Areas, 4th Quarter 2014

Qualifying Income Based on Median Sales Price of Existing Single-Family Homes

Area	With 5% Down ($)	With 10% Down ($)	With 20% Down ($)
MSA[1]	154,114	146,002	129,780
U.S. Average	45,863	43,449	38,621

Note: Figures are preliminary; Qualifying income is based on a mortgage rate of 4.0%. Monthly principal and interest payment is limited to 25% of income; n/a not available; (1) Urban Honolulu, HI Metropolitan Statistical Area—see Appendix B for areas included
Source: National Association of Realtors, Qualifying Income Based on Median Sales Price of Existing Single-Family Homes for Metropolitan Areas, 4th Quarter 2014

Median Apartment Condo-Coop Home Prices

Area	2012	2013	2014p	Percent Change 2013 to 2014
MSA[1]	319.2	338.1	346.5	2.5
U.S. Average	173.7	194.9	205.1	5.2

Note: Figures are median sales prices of existing apartment condo-coop homes in thousands of dollars; (p) preliminary; n/a not available; (1) Urban Honolulu, HI Metropolitan Statistical Area—see Appendix B for areas included
Source: National Association of Realtors, Median Sales Price of Existing Apartment Condo-Coop Homes for Metropolitan Areas, 4th Quarter 2014

Gross Monthly Rent

Area	Under $200	$200 -299	$300 -499	$500 -749	$750 -999	$1,000 -1,499	$1,500 and up	Median ($)
City	1.8	2.8	4.2	6.7	15.2	35.0	34.4	1,247
MSA[1]	1.3	2.0	3.2	5.3	10.9	27.5	49.8	1,497
U.S.	1.7	3.2	7.8	22.1	24.3	26.0	14.9	900

Note: Figures are percentages except for Median; Gross rent is the contract rent plus the estimated average monthly cost of utilities (electricity, gas, and water and sewer) and fuels (oil, coal, kerosene, wood, etc.) if these are paid by the renter (or paid for the renter by someone else); (1) Figures cover the Urban Honolulu, HI Metropolitan Statistical Area—see Appendix B for areas included
Source: U.S. Census Bureau, 2011-2013 American Community Survey 3-Year Estimates

Homeownership Rate

Area	2007 (%)	2008 (%)	2009 (%)	2010 (%)	2011 (%)	2012 (%)	2013 (%)	2014 (%)
MSA[1]	58.8	57.2	57.6	54.9	54.1	56.1	57.9	58.2
U.S.	68.1	67.8	67.4	66.9	66.1	65.4	65.1	64.5

Note: (1) Figures cover the Urban Honolulu, HI Metropolitan Statistical Area—see Appendix B for areas included
Source: U.S. Census Bureau, Housing Vacancies and Homeownership Annual Statistics: 2014

Year Housing Structure Built

Area	2010 or Later	2000 -2009	1990 -1999	1980 -1989	1970 -1979	1960 -1969	1950 -1959	1940 -1949	Before 1940	Median Year
City	0.9	7.1	8.2	10.6	26.5	22.2	13.4	5.6	5.4	1971
MSA[1]	1.2	11.1	12.6	12.8	24.9	19.0	11.1	4.1	3.3	1975
U.S.	0.9	15.0	13.9	13.8	15.8	11.0	10.9	5.4	13.3	1976

Note: Figures are percentages except for Median Year; (1) Figures cover the Urban Honolulu, HI Metropolitan Statistical Area—see Appendix B for areas included
Source: U.S. Census Bureau, 2011-2013 American Community Survey 3-Year Estimates

HEALTH

Health Risk Data

Category	MSA[1] (%)	U.S. (%)
Adults aged 18–64 who have any kind of health care coverage	87.8	79.6
Adults who reported being in good or excellent health	85.3	83.1
Adults who are current smokers	14.0	19.6
Adults who are heavy drinkers[2]	6.3	6.1
Adults who are binge drinkers[3]	17.4	16.9
Adults who are overweight (BMI 25.0 - 29.9)	32.0	35.8
Adults who are obese (BMI 30.0 - 99.8)	23.8	27.6
Adults who participated in any physical activities in the past month	81.4	77.1
Adults 50+ who have ever had a sigmoidoscopy or colonoscopy	65.8	67.3
Women aged 40+ who have had a mammogram within the past two years	77.5	74.0
Men aged 40+ who have had a PSA test within the past two years	34.1	45.2
Adults aged 65+ who have had flu shot within the past year	65.4	60.1
Adults who always wear a seatbelt	96.5	93.8

Note: Data as of 2012 unless otherwise noted; (1) Figures cover the Urban Honolulu, HI Metropolitan Statistical Area—see Appendix B for areas included; (2) Heavy drinkers are classified as males having more than two drinks per day or females having more than one drink per day; (3) Binge drinkers are classified as males having five or more drinks on one occasion or females having four or more drinks on one occasion
Source: Centers for Disease Control and Prevention, Behaviorial Risk Factor Surveillance System, SMART: Selected Metropolitan/Micropolitan Area Risk Trends, 2012 (Note: the CDC has discontinued this dataset but will be releasing a replacement in late 2015)

Chronic Health Indicators

Category	MSA[1] (%)	U.S. (%)
Adults who have ever been told they had a heart attack	3.1	4.5
Adults who have ever been told they had a stroke	3.1	2.9
Adults who have been told they currently have asthma	8.9	8.9
Adults who have ever been told they have arthritis	19.8	25.7
Adults who have ever been told they have diabetes[2]	7.8	9.7
Adults who have ever been told they had skin cancer	3.3	5.7
Adults who have ever been told they had any other types of cancer	5.1	6.5
Adults who have ever been told they have COPD	3.6	6.2
Adults who have ever been told they have kidney disease	3.6	2.5
Adults who have ever been told they have a form of depression	10.7	18.0

Note: Data as of 2012 unless otherwise noted; (1) Figures cover the Urban Honolulu, HI Metropolitan Statistical Area—see Appendix B for areas included; (2) Figures do not include pregnancy-related, borderline, or pre-diabetes
Source: Centers for Disease Control and Prevention, Behaviorial Risk Factor Surveillance System, SMART: Selected Metropolitan/Micropolitan Area Risk Trends, 2012 (Note: the CDC has discontinued this dataset but will be releasing a replacement in late 2015)

Mortality Rates for the Top 10 Causes of Death in the U.S.

ICD-10[a] Sub-Chapter	ICD-10[a] Code	Age-Adjusted Mortality Rate[1] per 100,000 population	
		County[2]	U.S.
Malignant neoplasms	C00-C97	133.8	166.2
Ischaemic heart diseases	I20-I25	64.2	105.7
Other forms of heart disease	I30-I51	61.2	49.3
Chronic lower respiratory diseases	J40-J47	15.9	42.1
Organic, including symptomatic, mental disorders	F01-F09	40.3	38.1
Cerebrovascular diseases	I60-I69	35.6	37.0
Other external causes of accidental injury	W00-X59	22.7	26.9
Other degenerative diseases of the nervous system	G30-G31	11.6	25.6
Diabetes mellitus	E10-E14	15.4	21.3
Hypertensive diseases	I10-I15	8.1	19.4

Note: (a) ICD-10 = International Classification of Diseases 10th Revision; (1) Mortality rates are a three year average covering 2011-2013; (2) Figures cover Honolulu County
Source: Centers for Disease Control and Prevention, National Center for Health Statistics. Compressed Mortality File 1999-2013 on CDC WONDER Online Database, released October 2014. Data are compiled from the Compressed Mortality File 1999-2013, Series 20 No. 2S, 2014.

Mortality Rates for Selected Causes of Death

ICD-10[a] Sub-Chapter	ICD-10[a] Code	Age-Adjusted Mortality Rate[1] per 100,000 population	
		County[2]	U.S.
Assault	X85-Y09	1.6	5.2
Diseases of the liver	K70-K76	10.0	13.2
Human immunodeficiency virus (HIV) disease	B20-B24	1.0	2.2
Influenza and pneumonia	J09-J18	23.2	15.4
Intentional self-harm	X60-X84	10.8	12.5
Malnutrition	E40-E46	0.6	0.9
Obesity and other hyperalimentation	E65-E68	1.3	1.8
Renal failure	N17-N19	10.9	13.1
Transport accidents	V01-V99	6.4	11.7
Viral hepatitis	B15-B19	2.0	2.2

Note: (a) ICD-10 = International Classification of Diseases 10th Revision; (1) Mortality rates are a three year average covering 2011-2013; (2) Figures cover Honolulu County
Source: Centers for Disease Control and Prevention, National Center for Health Statistics. Compressed Mortality File 1999-2013 on CDC WONDER Online Database, released October 2014. Data are compiled from the Compressed Mortality File 1999-2013, Series 20 No. 2S, 2014.

Health Insurance Coverage

Area	With Health Insurance	With Private Health Insurance	With Public Health Insurance	Without Health Insurance	Population Under Age 18 Without Health Insurance
City	93.2	75.8	31.5	6.8	2.6
MSA[1]	94.3	78.9	29.4	5.7	2.7
U.S.	85.2	65.2	31.0	14.8	7.3

Note: Figures are percentages that cover the civilian noninstitutionalized population; (1) Figures cover the Urban Honolulu, HI Metropolitan Statistical Area—see Appendix B for areas included
Source: U.S. Census Bureau, 2011-2013 American Community Survey 3-Year Estimates

Number of Medical Professionals

Area[1]	MDs[2]	DOs[2,3]	Dentists	Podiatrists	Chiropractors	Optometrists
Local (number)	3,160	134	889	29	160	207
Local (rate[4])	323.5	13.7	90.1	2.9	16.2	21.0
U.S. (rate[4])	270.0	20.2	63.1	5.7	25.2	14.9

Note: Data as of 2013 unless noted; (1) Local data covers Honolulu County; (2) Data as of 2012 and includes all active, non-federal physicians; (3) Doctor of Osteopathic Medicine; (4) rate per 100,000 population
Source: U.S. Department of Health and Human Services, Health Resources and Services Administration, Bureau of Health Professions, Area Resource File (ARF) 2013-2014

EDUCATION

Public School District Statistics

District Name	Schls	Pupils	Pupil/ Teacher Ratio	Minority Pupils[1] (%)	Free Lunch Eligible[2] (%)	IEP[3] (%)
Hawaii Department of Education	286	184,760	15.9	86.1	40.1	10.7

Note: Table includes school districts with 2,000 or more students; (1) Percentage of students that are not non-Hispanic white; (2) Percentage of students that are eligible for the free lunch program; (3) Percentage of students that have an Individualized Education Program.
Source: U.S. Department of Education, National Center for Education Statistics, Common Core of Data, Local Education Agency (School District) Universe Survey: School Year 2012-2013; U.S. Department of Education, National Center for Education Statistics, Common Core of Data, Public Elementary/Secondary School Universe Survey: School Year 2012-2013

Highest Level of Education

Area	Less than H.S.	H.S. Diploma	Some College, No Deg.	Associate Degree	Bachelor's Degree	Master's Degree	Prof. School Degree	Doctorate Degree
City	12.0	24.6	19.3	9.0	22.4	8.2	2.6	1.9
MSA[1]	9.5	26.4	21.7	10.3	21.2	7.4	2.3	1.4
U.S.	13.7	28.0	21.2	7.9	18.2	7.7	1.9	1.3

Note: Figures cover persons age 25 and over; (1) Figures cover the Urban Honolulu, HI Metropolitan Statistical Area—see Appendix B for areas included
Source: U.S. Census Bureau, 2011-2013 American Community Survey 3-Year Estimates

Educational Attainment by Race

Area	High School Graduate or Higher (%)					Bachelor's Degree or Higher (%)				
	Total	White	Black	Asian	Hisp.[2]	Total	White	Black	Asian	Hisp.[2]
City	88.0	96.6	95.6	84.6	93.1	35.0	51.5	33.0	33.3	27.0
MSA[1]	90.5	96.7	96.3	87.6	90.9	32.2	44.2	28.2	33.1	21.6
U.S.	86.3	88.3	83.1	85.7	64.0	29.1	30.4	18.8	50.7	13.7

Note: Figures shown cover persons 25 years old and over; (1) Figures cover the Urban Honolulu, HI Metropolitan Statistical Area—see Appendix B for areas included; (2) People of Hispanic origin can be of any race
Source: U.S. Census Bureau, 2011-2013 American Community Survey 3-Year Estimates

School Enrollment by Grade and Control

Area	Preschool (%)		Kindergarten (%)		Grades 1 - 4 (%)		Grades 5 - 8 (%)		Grades 9 - 12 (%)	
	Public	Private	Public	Private	Public	Private	Public	Private	Public	Private
City	41.3	58.7	86.7	13.3	81.9	18.1	80.8	19.2	74.1	25.9
MSA[1]	39.7	60.3	84.0	16.0	82.6	17.4	79.0	21.0	75.1	24.9
U.S.	57.7	42.3	87.9	12.1	89.9	10.1	90.0	10.0	90.7	9.3

Note: Figures shown cover persons 3 years old and over; (1) Figures cover the Urban Honolulu, HI Metropolitan Statistical Area—see Appendix B for areas included
Source: U.S. Census Bureau, 2011-2013 American Community Survey 3-Year Estimates

Average Salaries of Public School Classroom Teachers

Area	2013-14		2014-15		Percent Change 2013-14 to 2014-15	Percent Change 2004-05 to 2014-15
	Dollars	Rank[1]	Dollars	Rank[1]		
HAWAII	56,291	17	57,189	18	1.59	23.9
U.S. Average	56,610	–	57,379	–	1.36	20.8

Note: (1) State rank ranges from 1 to 51 where 1 indicates highest salary.
Source: National Education Association, Rankings & Estimates: Rankings of the States 2014 and Estimates of School Statistics 2015, March 2015

Higher Education

Four-Year Colleges			Two-Year Colleges			Medical Schools[1]	Law Schools[2]	Voc/ Tech[3]
Public	Private Non-profit	Private For-profit	Public	Private Non-profit	Private For-profit			
1	5	3	2	0	3	1	1	3

Note: Figures cover institutions located within the city limits and include main campuses only; (1) includes schools accredited by the Liaison Committee on Medical Education and the American Osteopathic Association's Commission on Osteopathic College Accreditation; (2) includes ABA-accredited schools, schools with provisional ABA accreditation, and state accredited schools; (3) includes all schools with programs that are less than 2 years.
Source: National Center for Education Statistics, Integrated Postsecondary Education System (IPEDS), 2013-14; Association of American Medical Colleges, Member List, May 1, 2015; American Osteopathic Association, Member List, May 1, 2015; Law School Admission Council, Official Guide to ABA-Approved Law Schools Online, May 1, 2015; Wikipedia, List of Medical Schools in the United States, May 1, 2015; Wikipedia, List of Law Schools in the United States, May 1, 2015

According to *U.S. News & World Report*, the Urban Honolulu, HI metro area is home to one of the best national universities in the U.S.: **University of Hawaii-Manoa** (#168). The indicators used to capture academic quality fall into a number of categories: assessment by administrators at peer institutions; retention of students; faculty resources; student selectivity; financial resources; alumni giving; high school counselor ratings of colleges; and graduation rate. *U.S. News & World Report, "America's Best Colleges 2015"*

According to *U.S. News & World Report*, the Urban Honolulu, HI metro area is home to one of the top 100 law schools in the U.S.: **University of Hawaii-Manoa (Richardson)** (#82). The rankings are based on a weighted average of 12 measures of quality: peer assessment score; assessment score by lawyers/judges; median LSAT scores; median undergrad GPA; acceptance rate; employment rates for graduates; placement success; bar passage rate; faculty resources; expenditures per student; student/faculty ratio; and library resources. *U.S. News & World Report, "America's Best Graduate Schools, Law, 2016"*

According to *U.S. News & World Report*, the Urban Honolulu, HI metro area is home to one of the top 75 medical schools for research in the U.S.: **University of Hawaii-Manoa (Burns)** (#74). The rankings are based on a weighted average of 11 measures of quality: quality assessment; peer assessment score; assessment score by residency directors; research activity; total research activity; average research activity per faculty member; student selectivity; median MCAT total score; median undergraduate GPA; acceptance rate; and faculty resources. *U.S. News & World Report, "America's Best Graduate Schools, Medical, 2016"*

PRESIDENTIAL ELECTION

2012 Presidential Election Results

Area	Obama (%)	Romney (%)	Other (%)
Honolulu County	68.9	29.8	1.3
U.S.	51.0	47.2	1.8

Note: Results may not add to 100% due to rounding
Source: Dave Leip's Atlas of U.S. Presidential Elections

EMPLOYERS

Major Employers

Company Name	Industry
City and County of Honolulu	General government/local government
City and County of Honolulu	Civil service/commission government
First Hawaiin Bank	State commercial banks
Hawaii Dept of Health	Administration of public health programs
Hawaii Dept of Transportation	Admin of transportation
Hawaii Mediacal Services Assoc	Hospital and medical service plans
Hawaii Pacific Health	General medical/surgical hospitals
Hawaiin Telecom	Local and long distance telephone
KYO YA Hotels and Resorts	Hotels/motels
Mormon Church	Misc denominational church
OAHU transit Services	Bus line operations
St Francis Healthcare Sys of Hawaii	Skilled nursing facility
State of Hawaii	Public order and safety/state gov't
The Boeing Company	Airplanes fixed or rotary wing
The Queens Medical Center	General medical/surgical hospitals
Trustess of the Estate of Bernice Bishop	Private elementary/secondary schools
University of Hawaii System	Colleges/universities

Note: Companies shown are located within the Urban Honolulu, HI Metropolitan Statistical Area.
Source: Hoovers.com; Wikipedia

PUBLIC SAFETY

Crime Rate

Area	All Crimes	Violent Crimes				Property Crimes		
		Murder	Forcible Rape	Robbery	Aggrav. Assault	Burglary	Larceny -Theft	Motor Vehicle Theft
City	n/a	n/a	n/a	n/a	n/a	n/a	n/a	n/a
Suburbs[1]	n/a	n/a	n/a	n/a	n/a	n/a	n/a	n/a
Metro[2]	n/a	n/a	n/a	n/a	n/a	n/a	n/a	n/a
U.S.	3,098.6	4.5	25.2	109.1	229.1	610.0	1,899.4	221.3

Note: Figures are crimes per 100,000 population; (1) All areas within the metro area that are located outside the city limits; (2) Figures cover the Urban Honolulu, HI Metropolitan Statistical Area—see Appendix B for areas included; n/a not available
Source: FBI Uniform Crime Reports, 2013

Hate Crimes

Area	Number of Quarters Reported	Number of Incidents per Bias Motivation						
		Race	Religion	Sexual Orientation	Ethnicity	Disability	Gender	Gender Identity
City	n/a	n/a	n/a	n/a	n/a	n/a	n/a	n/a
U.S.	4	2,871	1,031	1,233	655	83	18	31

Note: n/a not available.
Source: Federal Bureau of Investigation, Hate Crime Statistics 2013

Identity Theft Consumer Complaints

Area	Complaints	Complaints per 100,000 Population	Rank[2]
MSA[1]	404	41.1	356
U.S.	332,646	104.3	-

Note: (1) Figures cover the Urban Honolulu, HI Metropolitan Statistical Area—see Appendix B for areas included; (2) Rank ranges from 1 to 380 where 1 indicates greatest number of identity theft complaints per 100,000 population
Source: Federal Trade Commission, Consumer Sentinel Network Data Book for January–December 2014

Fraud and Other Consumer Complaints

Area	Complaints	Complaints per 100,000 Population	Rank[2]
MSA[1]	3,394	345.1	244
U.S.	2,250,205	705.7	-

Note: (1) Figures cover the Urban Honolulu, HI Metropolitan Statistical Area—see Appendix B for areas included; (2) Rank ranges from 1 to 380 where 1 indicates greatest number of identity theft complaints per 100,000 population
Source: Federal Trade Commission, Consumer Sentinel Network Data Book for January–December 2014

RECREATION

Culture

Dance[1]	Theatre[1]	Instrumental Music[1]	Vocal Music[1]	Series and Festivals	Museums and Art Galleries[2]	Zoos and Aquariums[3]
2	4	6	4	2	37	1

Note: (1) Professional perfoming groups; (2) Based on organizations with SIC code 8412; (3) AZA-accredited
Source: The Grey House Performing Arts Directory, 2015-16; Association of Zoos & Aquariums, AZA Member Zoos & Aquariums, April 2015; www.AccuLeads.com, April 2015

Professional Sports Teams

Team Name	League	Year Established
No teams are located in the metro area		

Source: Wikipedia, Major Professional Sports Teams of the United States and Canada, April 2015

CLIMATE

Average and Extreme Temperatures

Temperature	Jan	Feb	Mar	Apr	May	Jun	Jul	Aug	Sep	Oct	Nov	Dec	Yr.
Extreme High (°F)	87	88	89	89	93	92	92	93	94	94	93	89	94
Average High (°F)	80	80	81	82	84	86	87	88	88	86	84	81	84
Average Temp. (°F)	73	73	74	76	77	79	80	81	81	79	77	74	77
Average Low (°F)	66	66	67	69	70	72	73	74	73	72	70	67	70
Extreme Low (°F)	52	53	55	56	60	65	66	67	66	64	57	54	52

Note: Figures cover the years 1949-1990
Source: National Climatic Data Center, International Station Meteorological Climate Summary, 9/96

Average Precipitation/Snowfall/Humidity

Precip./Humidity	Jan	Feb	Mar	Apr	May	Jun	Jul	Aug	Sep	Oct	Nov	Dec	Yr.
Avg. Precip. (in.)	3.7	2.5	2.8	1.4	1.0	0.4	0.5	0.6	0.7	2.0	2.8	3.7	22.4
Avg. Snowfall (in.)	0	0	0	0	0	0	0	0	0	0	0	0	0
Avg. Rel. Hum. 5am (%)	82	80	78	77	76	75	75	75	76	78	79	80	78
Avg. Rel. Hum. 5pm (%)	66	64	62	61	60	58	58	58	60	63	66	66	62

Note: Figures cover the years 1949-1990; Tr = Trace amounts (<0.05 in. of rain; <0.5 in. of snow)
Source: National Climatic Data Center, International Station Meteorological Climate Summary, 9/96

Weather Conditions

Temperature			Daytime Sky			Precipitation		
32°F & below	45°F & below	90°F & above	Clear	Partly cloudy	Cloudy	0.01 inch or more precip.	0.1 inch or more snow/ice	Thunder-storms
0	0	23	25	286	54	98	0	7

Note: Figures are average number of days per year and cover the years 1949-1990
Source: National Climatic Data Center, International Station Meteorological Climate Summary, 9/96

HAZARDOUS WASTE

Superfund Sites

Honolulu has one hazardous waste site on the EPA's Superfund Final National Priorities List: **Del Monte Corp. (Oahu Plantation)**. There are a total of 1,322 Superfund sites on the list in the U.S.
U.S. Environmental Protection Agency, Final National Priorities List, April 14, 2015

**AIR & WATER
QUALITY**

Air Quality Trends: Ozone

	2004	2005	2006	2007	2008	2009	2010	2011	2012	2013
MSA[1]	0.046	0.042	0.040	0.033	0.041	0.048	0.047	0.046	0.043	0.047

Note: (1) Data covers the Urban Honolulu, HI Metropolitan Statistical Area—see Appendix B for areas included. The values shown are the composite ozone concentration averages among trend sites based on the highest fourth daily maximum 8-hour concentration in parts per million. These trends are based on sites having an adequate record of monitoring data during the trend period. Data from exceptional events are included.
Source: U.S. Environmental Protection Agency, Air Quality Monitoring Information, "Air Quality Trends by City, 2000-2013"

Air Quality Index

Area	Percent of Days when Air Quality was...[2]					AQI Statistics[2]	
	Good	Moderate	Unhealthy for Sensitive Groups	Unhealthy	Very Unhealthy	Maximum	Median
MSA[1]	97.5	2.2	0.0	0.3	0.0	195	27

Note: (1) Data covers the Urban Honolulu, HI Metropolitan Statistical Area—see Appendix B for areas included; (2) Based on 360 days with AQI data in 2014. Air Quality Index (AQI) is an index for reporting daily air quality. EPA calculates the AQI for five major air pollutants regulated by the Clean Air Act: ground-level ozone, particle pollution (aka particulate matter), carbon monoxide, sulfur dioxide, and nitrogen dioxide. The AQI runs from 0 to 500. The higher the AQI value, the greater the level of air pollution and the greater the health concern. There are six AQI categories: "Good" AQI is between 0 and 50. Air quality is considered satisfactory; "Moderate" AQI is between 51 and 100. Air quality is acceptable; "Unhealthy for Sensitive Groups" When AQI values are between 101 and 150, members of sensitive groups may experience health effects; "Unhealthy" When AQI values are between 151 and 200 everyone may begin to experience health effects; "Very Unhealthy" AQI values between 201 and 300 trigger a health alert; "Hazardous" AQI values over 300 trigger warnings of emergency conditions (not shown).
Source: U.S. Environmental Protection Agency, Air Quality Index Report, 2014

Air Quality Index Pollutants

Area	Percent of Days when AQI Pollutant was...[2]					
	Carbon Monoxide	Nitrogen Dioxide	Ozone	Sulfur Dioxide	Particulate Matter 2.5	Particulate Matter 10
MSA[1]	0.0	0.3	52.5	1.7	38.9	6.7

Note: (1) Data covers the Urban Honolulu, HI Metropolitan Statistical Area—see Appendix B for areas included; (2) Based on 360 days with AQI data in 2014. The Air Quality Index (AQI) is an index for reporting daily air quality. EPA calculates the AQI for five major air pollutants regulated by the Clean Air Act: ground-level ozone, particle pollution (also known as particulate matter), carbon monoxide, sulfur dioxide, and nitrogen dioxide. The AQI runs from 0 to 500. The higher the AQI value, the greater the level of air pollution and the greater the health concern.
Source: U.S. Environmental Protection Agency, Air Quality Index Report, 2014

Maximum Air Pollutant Concentrations: Particulate Matter, Ozone, CO and Lead

	Particulate Matter 10 (ug/m^3)	Particulate Matter 2.5 Wtd AM (ug/m^3)	Particulate Matter 2.5 24-Hr (ug/m^3)	Ozone (ppm)	Carbon Monoxide (ppm)	Lead (ug/m^3)
MSA[1] Level	39	6.2	13	0.051	1	0
NAAQS[2]	150	15	35	0.075	9	0.15
Met NAAQS[2]	Yes	Yes	Yes	Yes	Yes	Yes

Note: (1) Data covers the Urban Honolulu, HI Metropolitan Statistical Area—see Appendix B for areas included; Data from exceptional events are included; (2) National Ambient Air Quality Standards; ppm = parts per million; ug/m^3 = micrograms per cubic meter; n/a not available.
Concentrations: Particulate Matter 10 (coarse particulate)—highest second maximum 24-hour concentration; Particulate Matter 2.5 Wtd AM (fine particulate)—highest weighted annual mean concentration; Particulate Matter 2.5 24-Hour (fine particulate)—highest 98th percentile 24-hour concentration; Ozone—highest fourth daily maximum 8-hour concentration; Carbon Monoxide—highest second maximum non-overlapping 8-hour concentration; Lead—maximum running 3-month average
Source: U.S. Environmental Protection Agency, Air Quality Monitoring Information, "Air Quality Statistics by City, 2013"

Maximum Air Pollutant Concentrations: Nitrogen Dioxide and Sulfur Dioxide

	Nitrogen Dioxide AM (ppb)	Nitrogen Dioxide 1-Hr (ppb)	Sulfur Dioxide AM (ppb)	Sulfur Dioxide 1-Hr (ppb)	Sulfur Dioxide 24-Hr (ppb)
MSA[1] Level	3	23	n/a	9	n/a
NAAQS[2]	53	100	30	75	140
Met NAAQS[2]	Yes	Yes	n/a	Yes	n/a

Note: (1) Data covers the Urban Honolulu, HI Metropolitan Statistical Area—see Appendix B for areas included; Data from exceptional events are included; (2) National Ambient Air Quality Standards; ppm = parts per million; ug/m³ = micrograms per cubic meter; n/a not available.
Concentrations: Nitrogen Dioxide AM—highest arithmetic mean concentration; Nitrogen Dioxide 1-Hr—highest 98th percentile 1-hour daily maximum concentration; Sulfur Dioxide AM—highest annual mean concentration; Sulfur Dioxide 1-Hr—highest 99th percentile 1-hour daily maximum concentration; Sulfur Dioxide 24-Hr—highest second maximum 24-hour concentration
Source: U.S. Environmental Protection Agency, Air Quality Monitoring Information, "Air Quality Statistics by City, 2013"

Drinking Water

Water System Name	Pop. Served	Primary Water Source Type	Violations[1] Health Based	Violations[1] Monitoring/ Reporting
Honolulu-Windward-Pearl Harbor	676,358	Ground	0	0

Note: (1) Based on violation data from January 1, 2014 to December 31, 2014 (includes unresolved violations from earlier years)
Source: U.S. Environmental Protection Agency, Office of Ground Water and Drinking Water, Safe Drinking Water Information System (based on data extracted January 27, 2015)

Las Vegas, Nevada

Background

Upright citizens can accuse Las Vegas of many vices, but not of hypocrisy. Back in 1931, the city officials of this desert town, located 225 miles northeast of Los Angeles, saw gambling to be a growing popular pastime. To capitalize upon that trend, the city simply legalized it. Gambling, combined with spectacular, neon-lit entertainment, lures more than 36.4 million visitors a year to its more than 1,700 casinos and 140,000 hotel rooms.

Before Wayne Newton ever saw his name in lights or Siegfried and Roy made white tigers disappear, Las Vegas was a temporary stopping place for a diverse group of people. In the early 1880s, Las Vegas was a watering hole for those on the trail to California. Areas of the Las Vegas Valley contained artesian wells that supported extensive green meadows, or *vega* in Spanish, hence the name Las Vegas. In 1855 the area was settled by Mormon missionaries, but they left two years later. Finally, in the late 1800s, the land was used for ranching.

In the beginning of the twentieth century, the seeds of the present Las Vegas began to sprout. In 1905 the arrival of the Union Pacific Railroad sprinkled businesses, saloons, and gambling houses along it tracks; the city was formally founded on May 15, 1905. Then, during the Great Depression, men working on the nearby Hoover Dam spent their extra money in the establishments. Finally, gambling was legalized, hydroelectric power from the Hoover Dam lit the city in neon, and hotels began to compete for the brightest stars and the plushest surroundings. Las Vegas was an overnight success, luring many people with get-rich-quick dreams. The dream has thus far endured, and in 2005 the city celebrated its centennial with a suitably festive media blitz, many special events, and the world's largest birthday cake at 130,000 pounds.

Las Vegas is home to the World Series of Poker, which began in Texas in 1969. Winners can pocket close to $10 million.

For the past 25 years, senior citizens have constituted the fastest-growing segment of the Las Vegas population, as people over 60 years arrive to take advantage of the dry climate, reasonably priced housing, low property taxes, no sales tax, and plenty of entertainment. Today, the state leads the nation in growth of its senior citizen population, and this is expected to continue. Many programs exist to ensure their comfort and welfare, including quality economic, legal, and medical plans.

In 2005 the World Market Center opened. Intended to be the nation's preeminent furniture wholesale showroom and marketplace, it was built to compete with the current furniture market capital of High Point, North Carolina. In recent years, several megahotels and many smaller projects have been completed. At least $6 billion has been spent in hotel and casino construction. At the highest point of this activity, some 3,000 people moved to the city each month, most of them in construction and casino-related work. The new $3.7 million Durango Drive Improvement project has helped to ease traffic congestion with new ramps, a trails system underpass, new auxiliary lanes, and a new traffic signal system.

One of the more serious problems facing the fast-growing city is its diminishing water supply. Las Vegas uses approximately 350 gallons daily per person, more than any city in the world. The city has raised water rates and encourages conservation by homeowners and businesses through desert landscaping, which can reduce water use by as much as 80 percent.

Las Vegas is located near the center of a broad desert valley, which is almost surrounded by mountains ranging from 2,000 to 10,000 feet. The four seasons are well defined. Summers display desert conditions with extreme high temperatures, but nights are relatively cool due to the closeness of the mountains. For about two weeks almost every summer, warm, moist air predominates, causing higher-than-average humidity and scattered, sever thunderstorms. Winters are generally mild and pleasant with clear skies prevailing. Strong winds, associated with major storms, usually reach the valley from the southwest or through the pass from the northwest. Winds over 50 miles per hour are infrequent but, when they do occur, are the most troublesome of the elements because of the dust and sand they stir up.

Rankings

General Rankings

- The Las Vegas metro area was identified as one of America's fastest-growing areas in terms of population and economy by *Forbes*. The area ranked #18 out of 20. The 100 most populous metro areas in the U.S. were evaluated on the following criteria: estimated population growth; job growth; gross metropolitan product growth; unemployment; median salaries for college-educated workers. *Forbes, "America's Fastest-Growing Cities 2015," January 27, 2015*

Business/Finance Rankings

- TransUnion ranked the nation's metro areas by average credit score, calculated on the VantageScore system, developed by the three major credit-reporting bureaus—TransUnion, Experian, and Equifax. The Las Vegas metro area was among the ten cities with the lowest collective credit score, meaning that its residents posed the highest average consumer credit risk. *www.usatoday.com, "Metro Areas' Average Credit Rating Revealed," February 7, 2013*

- Building on the U.S. Department of Labor's Occupational Information Network Data Collection Program, the Brookings Institution defined STEM occupations and job opportunities for STEM workers at various levels of educational attainment. The Las Vegas metro area was one of the ten metro areas where workers in low-education-level STEM jobs earn the lowest relative wages. *www.brookings.edu, "The Hidden Stem Economy," June 10, 2013*

- Building on the U.S. Department of Labor's Occupational Information Network Data Collection Program, the Brookings Institution defined STEM occupations and job opportunities for STEM workers at various levels of educational attainment. The Las Vegas metro area was placed among the ten large metro areas with the lowest demand for high-level STEM knowledge. *www.brookings.edu, "The Hidden Stem Economy," June 10, 2013*

- Looking at February 2012–2013, 24/7 Wall Street's analysts focused on metro areas where jobs were being added at a faster rate than the labor force was growing to identify the metro areas with the biggest real declines in unemployment. The #3 metro area for gains posted in employment was the Las Vegas metro area. *247wallst.com, "Cities Where Unemployment Has Fallen the Most," April 16, 2013*

- Analysts for the business website 24/7 Wall Street looked at the local government report "Tax Rates and Tax Burdens in the District of Columbia—A Nationwide Comparison" to determine where a family of three at two different income levels would pay the least and the most in state and local taxes. Among the ten cities with the lowest state and local tax burdens was Las Vegas, at #10. *247wallst.com, American Cities with the Highest (and Lowest) Taxes, February 25, 2013*

- Based on metro area social media reviews, the employment opinion group Glassdoor surveyed 50 of the largest U.S. metro areas on measures including compensation and benefits, satisfaction with management, business outlook, and number of employers hiring. The Las Vegas metro area was ranked #48 in overall employee satisfaction. *www.glassdoor.com, "Employment Satisfaction Report Card by City," June 13, 2014*

- In a survey of economic confidence in the nation's 50 largest metropolitan areas conducted January–December 2014, the Las Vegas metro area placed #29, according to Gallup's 2014 Economic Confidence Index. *Gallup, "San Jose and San Francisco Lead in Economic Confidence," March 19, 2015*

- Using data from the Council for Community and Economic Research's 2013 Annual Report, NerdWallet ranked the 100 U.S. cities with the most expensive cost of living. Cities in California and in the Northeast topped the list. Of the cities with the highest cost of living, Las Vegas ranked #75. *NerdWallet.com, "Most Expensive Cities in America," June 4, 2014*

- The Brookings Institution ranked the 50 largest cities in the U.S. based on income inequality. Las Vegas was ranked #44. (#1 = greatest ineqality). Criteria: the cities were ranked based on the "95/20 ratio," a figure representing the income at which a household earns more than 95 percent of all other households, divided by the income at which a household earns more than only 20 percent of all other households. *Brookings Institution, "Income Inequality in America's 50 Largest Cities, 2007-2013," March 17, 2015*

- Las Vegas was ranked #19 out of 100 metro areas in terms of economic performance (#1 = best) during the recession and recovery from trough quarter through the second quarter of 2013. Criteria: percent change in employment; percentage point change in unemployment rate; percent change in gross metropolitan product; percent change in House Price Index. *Brookings Institution, MetroMonitor: Tracking Economic Recession and Recovery in America's 100 Largest Metropolitan Areas, September 2013*

- Las Vegas was identified as one of America's most frugal metro areas by *Coupons.com*. The city ranked #20 out of 25. Criteria: Grocery IQ and coupons.com mobile app usage. *Coupons.com, "Top 25 Most On-the-Go Frugal Cities of 2013," April 10, 2014*

- *Forbes* reports that Las Vegas was identified as one of the happiest cities to work in by CareerBliss.com, an online community for career advancement. The city ranked #3 out of 10. Criteria: work-life balance; an employee's relationship with his or her boss and co-workers; general work environment; compensation; opportunities for advancement; company culture; and resources. *Forbes.com, "The 10 Happiest and Unhappiest Cities to Work in Right Now," January 16, 2015*

- The Las Vegas metro area appeared on the Milken Institute "2013 Best Performing Cities" list. Rank: #144 out of 200 large metro areas. Criteria: job growth; wage and salary growth; high-tech output growth. *Milken Institute, "Best-Performing Cities 2014," January 2015*

- *Forbes* ranked the 200 most populous metro areas to determine the nation's "Best Places for Business and Careers." The Las Vegas metro area was ranked #111. Criteria: costs (business and living); job growth (past and projected); income growth; educational attainment (college and high school); projected economic growth; cultural and recreational opportunities; net migration patterns; number of highly ranked colleges. *Forbes, "The Best Places for Business and Careers 2014," July 23, 2014*

Culture/Performing Arts Rankings

- Las Vegas was selected as one of America's top cities for the arts. The city ranked #20 in the big city (population 500,000 and over) category. Criteria: readers' top choices for arts travel destinations based on the richness and variety of visual arts sites, activities and events. *American Style, "2012 Top 25 Arts Destinations," June 2012*

Dating/Romance Rankings

- Of the 100 U.S. cities surveyed by *Men's Health* in its quest to identify the nation's best cities for dating and forming relationships, Las Vegas was ranked #6 for online dating (#1 = best). *Men's Health, "The Best and Worst Cities for Online Dating," January 30, 2013*

- Las Vegas was selected as one of America's best cities for singles by the readers of *Travel + Leisure* in their annual "America's Favorite Cities" survey. The city was ranked #6 out of 20. Criteria included good-looking locals, cool shopping, and hipster-magnet coffee bars. *Travel + Leisure, "America's Best Cities for Singles," January 23, 2015*

- Las Vegas was selected as one of the most romantic cities in America by Amazon.com. The city ranked #11 of 20. Criteria: cities with 100,000 or more residents were ranked on their per capita sales of romance novels and relationship books, romantic comedy movies, romantic music, and sexual wellness products. *Amazon.com, "Top 20 Most Romantic Cities in America," February 5, 2015*

Education Rankings

- Personal finance website *WalletHub* analyzed the 150 largest U.S. metropolitan statistical areas to determine where the most educated Americans are choosing to settle. Criteria: educational attainment; percentage of workers with jobs in computer, engineering, and science fields; quality and size of each metro area's universities. Las Vegas was ranked #133 (#1 = most educated city). *www.WalletHub.com, "2014's Most and Least Educated Cities*

- The real estate website *MovoTo.com* selected Las Vegas as one of the "Nerdiest Cities in America." The city ranked #7 among the top 10 derived from data on the 50 most populous cities in the United States. Criteria: Number of annual comic book, video game, anime, and sci-fi/fantasy conventions; people per comic book store, video game store, and traditional gaming store; people per LARPing ("live action role-playing") group; people per science museum. Also factored in: distance to the nearest Renaissance faire. *MovoTo.com, "The 10 Nerdiest Cities in America," April 10, 2013*

- Las Vegas was selected as one of America's most literate cities. The city ranked #53 out of the 77 largest U.S. cities. Criteria: number of booksellers; library resources; Internet resources; educational attainment; periodical publishing resources; newspaper circulation. *Central Connecticut State University, "America's Most Literate Cities, 2014," April 8, 2015*

Environmental Rankings

- The Las Vegas metro area came in at #356 for the relative comfort of its climate on Sperling's list of "chill cities," as measured by the Sperling Heat Index. All 361 metro areas are included. Criteria included daytime high temperatures, nighttime low temperatures, dew point, and relative humidity at the high temperatures. *www.bertsperling.com, "Sperling's Chill Cities," July 18, 2013*

- Sperling's BestPlaces assessed 379 metropolitan areas of the United States for the likelihood of dangerously extreme weather events or earthquakes. In general the Southeast and South-Central regions have the highest risk of weather extremes and earthquakes, while the Pacific Northwest enjoys the lowest risk. Of the least risky metropolitan areas, the Las Vegas metro area was ranked #122. *www.bestplaces.net, "Safest Places from Natural Disasters," April 2011*

- Las Vegas was highlighted as one of the 25 most ozone-polluted metro areas in the U.S. during 2011 through 2013. The area ranked #9. *American Lung Association, State of the Air 2015*

Food/Drink Rankings

- *Men's Health* ranked 100 major U.S. cities in terms of alcohol intoxication. Las Vegas ranked #72 (#1 = most sober).Criteria: binge drinking; alcohol-related traffic accidents, arrests, and fatalities. *Men's Health, "The Drunkest Cities in America," November 19, 2013*

- Las Vegas was selected as one of America's 10 most vegan-friendly cities. The city was ranked #8. *People for the Ethical Treatment of Animals, "Top Vegan-Friendly Cities of 2013," June 11, 2013*

Health/Fitness Rankings

- For each of the 50 most populous metro areas in the United States, the American College of Sports Medicine's American Fitness Index evaluated infrastructure, community assets, and policies that encourage healthy and fit lifestyles, including preventive health behaviors, levels of chronic disease conditions, health care access, and community resources and policies that support physical activity. The Las Vegas metro area ranked #39 for "community fitness." Personal health indicators were considered as well as community and environmental indicators. *www.americanfitnessindex.org, "ACSM American Fitness Index Health and Community Fitness Status of the 50 Largest Metropolitan Areas," May 2013*

- Las Vegas was identified as one of 15 cities with the highest increase in bed bug activity in the U.S. by pest control provider Terminix. The city ranked #3.Criteria: cities with the largest percentage gains in bed bug customer calls from January–May 2013 compared to the same time period in 2012. *Terminix, "Cities with Highest Increases in Bed Bug Activity," July 9, 2013*

- Las Vegas was selected as one of the 25 fattest cities in America by *Men's Fitness Online*. It ranked #6 out of America's 50 largest cities. Criteria: fitness centers and sport stores; nutrition; sports participation; TV viewing; overweight/sedentary; junk food; air quality; geography; commute; parks and open space; city recreational facilities; access to healthcare; motivation; mayor and city initiatives; state obesity initiatives. *Men's Fitness, "The Fittest and Fattest Cities in America," March 5, 2012*

- Las Vegas was identified as a "2013 Spring Allergy Capital." The area ranked #55 out of 100. Three groups of factors were used to identify the most severe cities for people with allergies during the spring season: annual pollen levels; medicine utilization; access to board-certified allergists. *Asthma and Allergy Foundation of America, "Spring Allergy Capitals 2013"*

- Las Vegas was identified as a "2013 Fall Allergy Capital." The area ranked #70 out of 100. Three groups of factors were used to identify the most severe cities for people with allergies during the fall season: annual pollen levels; medicine utilization; access to board-certified allergists. *Asthma and Allergy Foundation of America, "Fall Allergy Capitals 2013"*

- Las Vegas was identified as a "2013 Asthma Capital." The area ranked #59 out of the nation's 100 largest metropolitan areas. Twelve factors were used to identify the most challenging places to live for people with asthma: estimated prevalence; self-reported prevalence; crude death rate for asthma; annual pollen score; annual air quality; public smoking laws; number of board-certified asthma specialists; school inhaler access laws; rescue medication use; controller medication use; uninsured rate; poverty rate. *Asthma and Allergy Foundation of America, "Asthma Capitals 2013"*

- *Men's Health* ranked 100 major U.S. cities in terms of the best and worst cities for men. Las Vegas ranked #76. Criteria: thirty-three data points were examined covering health, fitness, and quality of life. *Men's Health, "The Best & Worst Cities for Men 2014," December 6, 2013*

- The Las Vegas metro area appeared in the 2013 Gallup-Healthways Well-Being Index. The area ranked #144 out of 189. The Gallup-Healthways Well-Being Index score is an average of six sub-indexes, which individually examine life evaluation, emotional health, work environment, physical health, healthy behaviors, and access to basic necessities. Results are based on telephone interviews conducted as part of the Gallup-Healthways Well-Being Index survey January 2–December 29, 2012, and January 2–December 30, 2013, with a random sample of 531,630 adults, aged 18 and older, living in metropolitan areas in the 50 U.S. states and the District of Columbia. *Gallup-Healthways, "State of American Well-Being," March 25, 2014*

- The Las Vegas metro area was identified as one of "America's Most Stressful Cities" by *Sperling's BestPlaces*. The metro area ranked #2 out of 50. Criteria: unemployment rate; suicide rate; commute time; mental health; poor rest; alcohol use; violent crime rate; property crime rate; cloudy days annually. *Sperling's BestPlaces, www.BestPlaces.net, "Stressful Cities 2012*

Pet Rankings

- Las Vegas was selected as one of the best cities for dogs by real estate website Estately.com. The city was ranked #13. Criteria: weather; walkability; yard sizes; dog activities; meetup groups; availability of dogsitters. *Estately.com, "17 Best U.S. Cities for Dogs," May 14, 2013*

Real Estate Rankings

- On the list compiled by Penske Truck Rental, the Las Vegas metro area was named the #10 moving destination in 2014, based on one-way consumer truck rental reservations made through Penske's website and reservations call center. *blog.gopenske.com, "Penske Truck Rental's 2014 Top Moving Destinations List," February 4, 2015*

- The Las Vegas metro area was identified as #1 among the ten housing markets with the highest percentage of distressed property sales, based on the findings of the housing data website RealtyTrac. Criteria included being sold "short"—for less than the outstanding mortgage balance—or in a foreclosure auction, income and poverty figures, and unemployment data. *247wallst.com, "Cities Selling the Most Distressed Homes," January 23, 2014*

- Las Vegas was ranked #6 out of 275 metro areas in terms of house price appreciation in 2014 (#1 = highest rate). *Federal Housing Finance Agency, House Price Index, 4th Quarter 2014*

- The Las Vegas metro area was identified as one of the 20 best housing markets in the U.S. in 2014. The area ranked #5 out of 178 markets with a home price appreciation of 13.9%. Criteria: year-over-year change of median sales price of existing single-family homes between the 4th quarter of 2013 and the 4th quarter of 2014. *National Association of Realtors®, Median Sales Price of Existing Single-Family Homes for Metropolitan Areas, 4th Quarter 2014*

- The Las Vegas metro area was identified as one of the 10 best condo markets in the U.S. in 2014. The area ranked #3 out of 66 markets with a price appreciation of 18.9%. Criteria: year-over-year change of median sales price of existing apartment condo-coop homes between the 4th quarter of 2013 and the 4th quarter of 2014. *National Association of Realtors®, Median Sales Price of Existing Apartment Condo-Coop Homes for Metropolitan Areas, 4th Quarter 2014*

- Las Vegas was ranked #193 out of 226 metro areas in terms of housing affordability in 2014 by the National Association of Home Builders (#1 = most affordable). The NAHB-Wells Fargo Housing Opportunity Index (HOI) for a given area is defined as the share of homes sold in that area that would have been affordable to a family earning the local median income, based on standard mortgage underwriting criteria. *National Association of Home Builders®, NAHB-Wells Fargo Housing Opportunity Index, 4th Quarter 2014*

- The nation's largest metro areas were analyzed in terms of the percentage of households entering some stage of foreclosure in 2013. The Las Vegas metro area ranked #9 out of 10 (#1 = highest foreclosure rate). *RealtyTrac, "2013 Year-End U.S. Foreclosure Market Report™," January 16, 2014*

Safety Rankings

- Symantec, in partnership with Sperling's BestPlaces, ranked the 50 largest cities in the U.S. in terms of their vulnerability to cybercrime. The city ranked #11. Criteria: number of cyberattacks and potential infections; level of Internet access; expenditures on smartphones and computer hardware/software; wireless hotspots; broadband connectivity; Internet usage; online purchases. *Symantec, "Riskiest Online Cities of 2012" February 15, 2012*

- Allstate ranked the 200 largest cities in America in terms of driver safety. Las Vegas ranked #123. Allstate researchers analyzed internal property damage claims over a two-year period from January 2011 to December 2012. A weighted average of the two-year numbers determined the annual percentages. *Allstate, "Allstate America's Best Drivers Report, 2014"*

- The National Insurance Crime Bureau ranked 380 metro areas in the U.S. in terms of per capita rates of vehicle theft. The Las Vegas metro area ranked #27 (#1 = highest rate). Criteria: number of vehicle theft offenses per 100,000 inhabitants in 2012. *National Insurance Crime Bureau, "Hot Spots 2012," June 26, 2013*

Seniors/Retirement Rankings

- From its Best Cities for Successful Aging indexes, the Milken Institute generated rankings for metropolitan areas, weighing data in eight categories—health care, wellness, living arrangements, transportation, financial characteristics, education and employment opportunities, community engagement, and overall livability. The Las Vegas metro area was ranked #94 overall in the large metro area category. *Milken Institute, "Best Cities for Successful Aging, 2014"*

Sports/Recreation Rankings

- *Card Player* magazine scoured North America to identify the top five metropolitan areas where a player can access the types of games that make launching a poker career possible. The Las Vegas metro area ranked #3. *Card Player, "The Top Five Cities to Launch Your Poker Career," April 2, 2014*

Transportation Rankings

- NerdWallet surveyed average annual car insurance premiums in 125 U.S. cities to identify the least expensive U.S. cities in which to insure a car. Locations with no-fault insurance laws was a strong determinant. Las Vegas came in at #17 for the most expensive rates. *www.nerdwallet.com, "Best Cities for Cheap Car Insurance," February 3, 2014*

- Las Vegas appeared on *Trapster.com's* list of the 10 most-active U.S. cities for speed traps. The city ranked #4 of 10. *Trapster.com* is a community platform accessed online and via smartphone app that alerts drivers to traps, hazards and other traffic issues nearby. *Trapster.com, "Speeders Beware: Cities With the Most Speed Traps," February 10, 2012*

Women/Minorities Rankings

- *Women's Health* examined U.S. cities and identified the 100 best cities for women. Las Vegas was ranked #87. Criteria: 30 categories were examined from obesity and breast cancer rates to commuting times and hours spent working out. *Women's Health, "Best Cities for Women 2012"*

- Las Vegas was selected as one of the best cities for young Latinos in 2013 by mun2, a national cable television broadcast network. The city ranked #9. Criteria: U.S. cities with populations over 500,000 residents were evaluated on the following criteria: number of young latinos; jobs; friendliness; cost of living; fun. *mun2.tv, "Best Cities for Young Latinos 2013*

Miscellaneous Rankings

- Las Vegas was selected as a 2013 Digital Cities Survey winner. The city ranked #5 in the large city (250,000 or more population) category. The survey examined and assessed how city governments are utilizing information technology to operate and deliver quality service to their customers and citizens. Survey questions focused on implementation and adoption of online service delivery; planning and governance; and the infrastructure and architecture that make the transformation to digital government possible. *Center for Digital Government, "2013 Digital Cities Survey," November 7, 2013*

- Ink Army reported on a survey by the website TotalBeauty calculating the number of tattoo shops per 100,000 residents in order to determine the U.S. cities with the most tattoo acceptance. Las Vegas took the #2 slot. *inkarmy.com, "Most Tattoo Friendly Cities in the United States," November 1, 2013*

- Las Vegas appeared on *Travel + Leisure's* list of America's least attractive people. Criteria: cities were selected by readers in their annual America's Favorite Cities survey. The city ranked #3 out of 10. *Travel + Leisure, "America's Most and Least Attractive People," November 2013*

- The Las Vegas metro area was selected as one of "The Best U.S. Cities for Bargain Shopping" by *Forbes*. The area ranked #4 out of 10. Criteria: number of outlet stores; gross leasable retail space in major malls; low consumer price index; low sales tax rate. Indicators were examined in the nation's 50 largest metropolitan areas. *Forbes, "The Best U.S. Cities for Bargain Shopping," January 20, 2012*

- Mars Chocolate North America, the makers of COMBOS®, in partnership with Sperling's BestPlaces, ranked 50 major metro areas in terms of their "manliness." The Las Vegas metro area ranked #38. Criteria: number of professional sports teams; number of nearby NASCAR tracks and racing events; manly lifestyle; concentration of manly retail stores; manly occupations per capita; salty snack sales; "Board of Manliness" rankings. *Mars Chocolate North America, "America's Manliest Cities 2012"*

- Las Vegas was selected as one of the most tattooed cities in America by *Lovelyish.com*. The city was ranked #2. Criteria: number of tattoo shops per capita. *Lovelyish.com, "Top Ten: Most Tattooed Cities in America," October 17, 2012*

- The National Alliance to End Homelessness ranked the 100 most populous metro areas in terms the rate of homelessness. The Las Vegas metro area ranked #4. Criteria: number of homeless people per 10,000 population in 2011. *National Alliance to End Homelessness, The State of Homelessness in America 2012*

Business Environment

CITY FINANCES

City Government Finances

Component	2012 ($000)	2012 ($ per capita)
Total Revenues	801,628	1,373
Total Expenditures	876,797	1,502
Debt Outstanding	637,497	1,092
Cash and Securities[1]	601,567	1,031

Note: (1) Cash and security holdings of a government at the close of its fiscal year, including those of its dependent agencies, utilities, and liquor stores.
Source: U.S Census Bureau, State & Local Government Finances 2012

City Government Revenue by Source

Source	2012 ($000)	2012 ($ per capita)
General Revenue		
From Federal Government	40,802	70
From State Government	258,330	443
From Local Governments	108,493	186
Taxes		
Property	111,021	190
Sales and Gross Receipts	58,969	101
Personal Income	0	0
Corporate Income	0	0
Motor Vehicle License	0	0
Other Taxes	30,645	52
Current Charges	132,798	227
Liquor Store	0	0
Utility	0	0
Employee Retirement	0	0

Source: U.S Census Bureau, State & Local Government Finances 2012

City Government Expenditures by Function

Function	2012 ($000)	2012 ($ per capita)	2012 (%)
General Direct Expenditures			
Air Transportation	0	0	0.0
Corrections	44,663	77	5.1
Education	0	0	0.0
Employment Security Administration	0	0	0.0
Financial Administration	15,857	27	1.8
Fire Protection	123,031	211	14.0
General Public Buildings	76,869	132	8.8
Governmental Administration, Other	12,386	21	1.4
Health	3,247	6	0.4
Highways	60,624	104	6.9
Hospitals	0	0	0.0
Housing and Community Development	23,918	41	2.7
Interest on General Debt	30,764	53	3.5
Judicial and Legal	26,240	45	3.0
Libraries	0	0	0.0
Parking	3,789	6	0.4
Parks and Recreation	94,279	162	10.8
Police Protection	9,274	16	1.1
Public Welfare	907	2	0.1
Sewerage	111,819	192	12.8
Solid Waste Management	5,342	9	0.6
Veterans' Services	0	0	0.0
Liquor Store	0	0	0.0
Utility	13	< 1	< 0.1
Employee Retirement	0	0	0.0

Source: U.S Census Bureau, State & Local Government Finances 2012

DEMOGRAPHICS

Population Growth

Area	1990 Census	2000 Census	2010 Census	Population Growth (%) 1990-2000	Population Growth (%) 2000-2010
City	261,374	478,434	583,756	83.0	22.0
MSA[1]	741,459	1,375,765	1,951,269	85.5	41.8
U.S.	248,709,873	281,421,906	308,745,538	13.2	9.7

Note: (1) Figures cover the Las Vegas-Paradise, NV Metropolitan Statistical Area—see Appendix B for areas included
Source: U.S. Census Bureau, Census 1990, 2000, 2010

Household Size

Area	One	Two	Three	Four	Five	Six	Seven or More	Average Household Size
City	28.7	31.4	15.2	13.0	6.6	3.0	2.1	2.78
MSA[1]	27.8	32.0	15.4	13.1	6.7	3.2	2.0	2.79
U.S.	27.7	33.6	15.7	13.1	6.0	2.3	1.5	2.64

Note: (1) Figures cover the Las Vegas-Henderson-Paradise, NV Metropolitan Statistical Area—see Appendix B for areas included
Source: U.S. Census Bureau, 2011-2013 American Community Survey 3-Year Estimates

Race

Area	White Alone[2] (%)	Black Alone[2] (%)	Asian Alone[2] (%)	AIAN[3] Alone[2] (%)	NHOPI[4] Alone[2] (%)	Other Race Alone[2] (%)	Two or More Races (%)
City	65.3	11.6	6.6	0.6	0.6	10.9	4.4
MSA[1]	64.9	10.7	9.0	0.6	0.7	9.8	4.4
U.S.	73.9	12.6	5.0	0.8	0.2	4.7	2.9

Note: (1) Figures cover the Las Vegas-Henderson-Paradise, NV Metropolitan Statistical Area—see Appendix B for areas included; (2) Alone is defined as not being in combination with one or more other races; (3) American Indian and Alaska Native; (4) Native Hawaiian and Other Pacific Islander
Source: U.S. Census Bureau, 2011-2013 American Community Survey 3-Year Estimates

Hispanic or Latino Origin

Area	Total (%)	Mexican (%)	Puerto Rican (%)	Cuban (%)	Other (%)
City	31.7	24.5	0.9	0.9	5.3
MSA[1]	29.7	22.7	1.0	1.1	5.0
U.S.	16.9	10.8	1.6	0.6	3.8

Note: Persons of Hispanic or Latino origin can be of any race; (1) Figures cover the Las Vegas-Henderson-Paradise, NV Metropolitan Statistical Area—see Appendix B for areas included
Source: U.S. Census Bureau, 2011-2013 American Community Survey 3-Year Estimates

Segregation

Type	Segregation Indices[1] 1990	2000	2010	2010 Rank[2]	Percent Change 1990-2000	1990-2010	2000-2010
Black/White	49.0	40.4	37.6	94	-8.7	-11.5	-2.8
Asian/White	23.3	25.4	28.8	92	2.1	5.5	3.5
Hispanic/White	28.8	42.4	42.0	58	13.6	13.3	-0.4

Note: All figures cover the Metropolitan Statistical Area—see Appendix B for areas included; Figures are based on an analysis of 1990, 2000, and 2010 Census Decennial Census tract data by William H. Frey, Brookings Institution and the University of Michigan Social Science Data Analysis Network. In this analysis all racial groups (whites, blacks, and asians) are non-Hispanic members of those races. Hispanics are shown as a separate category;
(1) Segregation Indices are Dissimilarity Indices that measure the degree to which the minority group is distributed differently than whites across census tracts. They range from 0 (complete integration) to 100 (complete segregation) where the value indicates the percentage of the minority group that needs to move to be distributed exactly like whites; (2) Ranges from 1 (most segregated) to 102 (least segregated); n/a not available.
Source: www.CensusScope.org

Ancestry

Area	German	Irish	English	American	Italian	Polish	French[2]	Scottish	Dutch
City	9.8	8.2	5.7	3.8	6.2	2.3	2.2	1.3	0.7
MSA[1]	10.5	8.2	6.1	4.2	6.0	2.4	2.1	1.4	0.9
U.S.	14.9	10.8	8.0	7.4	5.5	3.0	2.7	1.7	1.4

Note: Figures are the percentage of the total population reporting a particular ancestry. The nine most commonly reported ancestries in the U.S. are shown. Figures include multiple ancestries (e.g. if a person reported being Irish and Italian, they were included in both columns); (1) Figures cover the Las Vegas-Henderson-Paradise, NV Metropolitan Statistical Area—see Appendix B for areas included; (2) Excludes Basque
Source: U.S. Census Bureau, 2011-2013 American Community Survey 3-Year Estimates

Foreign-Born Population

Area	Percent of Population Born in								
	Any Foreign Country	Mexico	Asia	Europe	Carribean	South America	Central America[2]	Africa	Canada
City	21.3	10.1	5.1	1.5	0.8	0.8	2.0	0.4	0.4
MSA[1]	21.8	9.0	6.7	1.7	0.9	0.7	1.8	0.6	0.4
U.S.	13.0	3.7	3.8	1.5	1.2	0.9	1.0	0.6	0.3

Note: (1) Figures cover the Las Vegas-Henderson-Paradise, NV Metropolitan Statistical Area—see Appendix B for areas included; (2) Excludes Mexico.
Source: U.S. Census Bureau, 2011-2013 American Community Survey 3-Year Estimates

Marital Status

Area	Never Married	Now Married[2]	Separated	Widowed	Divorced
City	33.1	43.3	3.1	5.5	15.0
MSA[1]	33.6	44.7	2.7	5.2	13.9
U.S.	32.7	48.1	2.2	6.0	11.0

Note: Figures are percentages and cover the population 15 years of age and older; (1) Figures cover the Las Vegas-Henderson-Paradise, NV Metropolitan Statistical Area—see Appendix B for areas included; (2) Excludes separated
Source: U.S. Census Bureau, 2011-2013 American Community Survey 3-Year Estimates

Disability Status

Area	All Ages	Under 18 Years Old	18 to 64 Years Old	65 Years and Over
City	12.7	3.9	11.2	36.6
MSA[1]	11.7	3.8	10.2	35.2
U.S.	12.3	4.1	10.2	36.3

Note: Figures show percent of the civilian noninstitutionalized population that reported having a disability. Disability status is determined from from six types of difficulty: vision, hearing, cognitive, ambulatory, self-care, and independent living. For children under 5 years old, hearing and vision difficulty are used to determine disability status. For children between the ages of 5 and 14, disability status is determined from hearing, vision, cognitive, ambulatory, and self-care difficulties. For people aged 15 years and older, they are considered to have a disability if they have difficulty with any one of the six difficulty types; (1) Figures cover the Las Vegas-Henderson-Paradise, NV Metropolitan Statistical Area—see Appendix B for areas included.
Source: U.S. Census Bureau, 2011-2013 American Community Survey 3-Year Estimates

Age

Area	Percent of Population									Median Age
	Under Age 5	Age 5–19	Age 20–34	Age 35–44	Age 45–54	Age 55–64	Age 65–74	Age 75–84	Age 85+	
City	6.8	20.5	20.6	14.2	13.6	11.3	7.7	4.1	1.4	36.6
MSA[1]	6.7	20.1	21.6	14.4	13.5	11.4	7.6	3.5	1.2	36.1
U.S.	6.4	19.9	20.7	12.9	14.1	12.3	7.6	4.2	1.9	37.4

Note: (1) Figures cover the Las Vegas-Henderson-Paradise, NV Metropolitan Statistical Area—see Appendix B for areas included
Source: U.S. Census Bureau, 2011-2013 American Community Survey 3-Year Estimates

Gender

Area	Males	Females	Males per 100 Females
City	301,119	294,787	102.1
MSA[1]	1,003,453	993,918	101.0
U.S.	154,451,010	159,410,713	96.9

Note: (1) Figures cover the Las Vegas-Henderson-Paradise, NV Metropolitan Statistical Area—see Appendix B for areas included
Source: U.S. Census Bureau, 2011-2013 American Community Survey 3-Year Estimates

Religious Groups by Family

Area	Catholic	Baptist	Non-Den.	Methodist[2]	Lutheran	LDS[3]	Pentecostal	Presbyterian[4]	Muslim[5]	Judaism
MSA[1]	18.1	3.0	3.1	0.4	0.7	6.4	1.5	0.2	0.1	0.3
U.S.	19.1	9.3	4.0	4.0	2.3	2.0	1.9	1.6	0.8	0.7

Note: Figures are the number of adherents as a percentage of the total population; (1) Figures cover the Las Vegas-Paradise, NV Metropolitan Statistical Area—see Appendix B for areas included; (2) Methodist/Pietist; (3) Latter Day Saints; (4) Reformed; (5) Figures are estimates
Source: Association of Statisticians of American Religious Bodies, 2010 U.S. Religion Census: Religious Congregations & Membership Study

Religious Groups by Tradition

Area	Catholic	Evangelical Protestant	Mainline Protestant	Other Tradition	Black Protestant	Orthodox
MSA[1]	18.1	7.7	1.4	7.6	0.4	0.4
U.S.	19.1	16.2	7.3	4.3	1.6	0.3

Note: Figures are the number of adherents as a percentage of the total population; (1) Figures cover the Las Vegas-Paradise, NV Metropolitan Statistical Area—see Appendix B for areas included
Source: Association of Statisticians of American Religious Bodies, 2010 U.S. Religion Census: Religious Congregations & Membership Study

ECONOMY

Gross Metropolitan Product

Area	2012	2013	2014	2015	Rank[2]
MSA[1]	95.6	98.7	103.2	109.5	34

Note: Figures are in billions of dollars; (1) Figures cover the Las Vegas-Henderson-Paradise, NV Metropolitan Statistical Area—see Appendix B for areas included; (2) Rank is based on 2015 data and ranges from 1 to 363
Source: The U.S. Conference of Mayors, U.S. Metro Economies: GMP and Employment 2013-2015, June 2014

Economic Growth

Area	2010-12 (%)	2013 (%)	2014 (%)	2015 (%)	Rank[2]
MSA[1]	1.3	1.8	2.9	4.0	29
U.S.	2.1	2.0	2.3	3.2	–

Note: Figures are real gross metropolitan product (GMP) growth rates and represent annual average percent change; (1) Figures cover the Las Vegas-Henderson-Paradise, NV Metropolitan Statistical Area—see Appendix B for areas included; (2) Rank is based on 2015 data and ranges from 1 to 363
Source: The U.S. Conference of Mayors, U.S. Metro Economies: GMP and Employment 2013-2015, June 2014

Metropolitan Area Exports

Area	2008	2009	2010	2011	2012	2013	Rank[2]
MSA[1]	1,167.7	1,022.7	1,187.8	1,667.6	1,811.5	2,008.2	100

Note: Figures are in millions of dollars; (1) Figures cover the Las Vegas-Henderson-Paradise, NV Metropolitan Statistical Area—see Appendix B for areas included; (2) Rank is based on 2013 data and ranges from 1 to 387
Source: U.S. Department of Commerce, International Trade Administration, Office of Trade & Industry Information, Manufacturing & Services, data extracted April 3, 2015

Building Permits

Area	Single-Family			Multi-Family			Total		
	2013	2014	Pct. Chg.	2013	2014	Pct. Chg.	2013	2014	Pct. Chg.
City	1,517	1,453	-4.2	0	0	-	1,517	1,453	-4.2
MSA[1]	7,067	6,809	-3.7	1,506	3,227	114.3	8,573	10,036	17.1
U.S.	620,802	634,597	2.2	370,020	411,766	11.3	990,822	1,046,363	5.6

Note: (1) Figures cover the Las Vegas-Henderson-Paradise, NV Metropolitan Statistical Area—see Appendix B for areas included; Figures represent new, privately-owned housing units authorized (unadjusted data); All permit data are based on estimates with imputation.
Source: U.S. Census Bureau, Manufacturing, Mining, and Construction Statistics, Building Permits, 2013, 2014

Bankruptcy Filings

Area	Business Filings			Nonbusiness Filings		
	2013	2014	% Chg.	2013	2014	% Chg.
Clark County	408	327	-19.9	10,814	8,554	-20.9
U.S.	33,212	26,983	-18.8	1,038,720	909,812	-12.4

Note: Business filings include Chapter 7, Chapter 11, Chapter 12, and Chapter 13; Nonbusiness filings include Chapter 7, Chapter 11, and Chapter 13
Source: Administrative Office of the U.S. Courts, Business and Nonbusiness Bankruptcy, County Cases Commenced by Chapter of the Bankruptcy Code, During the 12- Month Period Ending December 31, 2013 and Business and Nonbusiness Bankruptcy, County Cases Commenced by Chapter of the Bankruptcy Code, During the 12- Month Period Ending December 31, 2014

Housing Vacancy Rates

Area	Gross Vacancy Rate[2] (%)			Year-Round Vacancy Rate[3] (%)			Rental Vacancy Rate[4] (%)			Homeowner Vacancy Rate[5] (%)		
	2012	2013	2014	2012	2013	2014	2012	2013	2014	2012	2013	2014
MSA[1]	16.2	16.6	14.3	15.0	15.5	13.4	12.8	14.1	10.1	3.4	3.0	2.9
U.S.	13.8	13.6	13.4	10.8	10.7	10.4	8.7	8.3	7.6	2.0	2.0	1.9

Note: (1) Figures cover the Las Vegas-Henderson-Paradise, NV Metropolitan Statistical Area—see Appendix B for areas included; (2) The percentage of the total housing inventory that is vacant; (3) The percentage of the housing inventory (excluding seasonal units) that is year-round vacant; (4) The percentage of rental inventory that is vacant for rent; (5) The percentage of homeowner inventory that is vacant for sale
Source: U.S. Census Bureau, Housing Vacancies and Homeownership Annual Statistics: 2014

INCOME

Income

Area	Per Capita ($)	Median Household ($)	Average Household ($)
City	24,945	48,676	66,092
MSA[1]	25,354	50,498	67,454
U.S.	27,884	52,176	72,897

Note: (1) Figures cover the Las Vegas-Henderson-Paradise, NV Metropolitan Statistical Area—see Appendix B for areas included
Source: U.S. Census Bureau, 2011-2013 American Community Survey 3-Year Estimates

Household Income Distribution

Area	Percent of Households Earning							
	Under $15,000	$15,000 -24,999	$25,000 -34,999	$35,000 -49,999	$50,000 -74,999	$75,000 -99,000	$100,000 -149,999	$150,000 and up
City	12.9	11.3	11.3	15.6	18.8	11.8	11.0	7.3
MSA[1]	11.5	10.7	11.5	15.6	19.9	12.2	11.3	7.2
U.S.	13.0	10.9	10.3	13.6	17.9	11.9	12.7	9.6

Note: (1) Figures cover the Las Vegas-Henderson-Paradise, NV Metropolitan Statistical Area—see Appendix B for areas included
Source: U.S. Census Bureau, 2011-2013 American Community Survey 3-Year Estimates

Poverty Rate

Area	All Ages	Under 18 Years Old	18 to 64 Years Old	65 Years and Over
City	18.6	27.1	17.0	9.9
MSA[1]	16.3	23.5	15.0	9.2
U.S.	15.9	22.4	14.8	9.5

Note: Figures are percentage of people whose income during the past 12 months was below the poverty level; (1) Figures cover the Las Vegas-Henderson-Paradise, NV Metropolitan Statistical Area—see Appendix B for areas included
Source: U.S. Census Bureau, 2011-2013 American Community Survey 3-Year Estimates

EMPLOYMENT

Labor Force and Employment

Area	Civilian Labor Force			Workers Employed		
	Dec. 2013	Dec. 2014	% Chg.	Dec. 2013	Dec. 2014	% Chg.
City	288,653	293,421	1.7	263,230	272,820	3.6
MSA[1]	1,005,346	1,023,287	1.8	918,649	952,117	3.6
U.S.	154,408,000	155,521,000	0.7	144,423,000	147,190,000	1.9

Note: Data is not seasonally adjusted and covers workers 16 years of age and older; (1) Figures cover the Las Vegas-Henderson-Paradise, NV Metropolitan Statistical Area—see Appendix B for areas included
Source: Bureau of Labor Statistics, Local Area Unemployment Statistics

Unemployment Rate

Area	2014											
	Jan.	Feb.	Mar.	Apr.	May	Jun.	Jul.	Aug.	Sep.	Oct.	Nov.	Dec.
City	9.0	8.6	8.6	8.2	8.0	8.3	8.3	7.8	7.6	7.3	7.2	7.0
MSA[1]	8.8	8.5	8.4	8.0	7.8	8.0	8.0	7.6	7.4	7.1	7.0	7.0
U.S.	7.0	7.0	6.8	5.9	6.1	6.3	6.5	6.3	5.7	5.5	5.5	5.4

Note: Data is not seasonally adjusted and covers workers 16 years of age and older; (1) Figures cover the Las Vegas-Henderson-Paradise, NV Metropolitan Statistical Area—see Appendix B for areas included
Source: Bureau of Labor Statistics, Local Area Unemployment Statistics

Employment by Occupation

Occupation Classification	City (%)	MSA[1] (%)	U.S. (%)
Management, Business, Science, and Arts	27.5	26.3	36.2
Natural Resources, Construction, and Maintenance	8.2	8.0	9.0
Production, Transportation, and Material Moving	8.8	9.2	12.1
Sales and Office	25.6	26.0	24.4
Service	29.9	30.6	18.3

Note: Figures cover employed civilians 16 years of age and older; (1) Figures cover the Las Vegas-Henderson-Paradise, NV Metropolitan Statistical Area—see Appendix B for areas included
Source: U.S. Census Bureau, 2011-2013 American Community Survey 3-Year Estimates

Employment by Industry

Sector	MSA[1]		U.S.
	Number of Employees	Percent of Total	Percent of Total
Construction	48,300	5.4	4.4
Education and Health Services	83,500	9.3	15.5
Financial Activities	43,900	4.9	5.7
Government	98,400	10.9	15.8
Information	10,300	1.1	2.0
Leisure and Hospitality	280,700	31.1	10.3
Manufacturing	21,400	2.4	8.7
Mining and Logging	400	<0.1	0.6
Other Services	25,900	2.9	4.0
Professional and Business Services	118,400	13.1	13.8
Retail Trade	109,300	12.1	11.4
Transportation, Warehousing, and Utilities	39,100	4.3	3.9
Wholesale Trade	21,600	2.4	4.2

Note: Figures are non-farm employment as of December 2014. Figures are not seasonally adjusted and include workers 16 years of age and older; (1) Figures cover the Las Vegas-Henderson-Paradise, NV Metropolitan Statistical Area—see Appendix B for areas included
Source: Bureau of Labor Statistics, Current Employment Statistics, Employment, Hours, and Earnings

Occupations with Greatest Projected Employment Growth: 2012 – 2022

Occupation[1]	2012 Employment	2022 Projected Employment	Numeric Employment Change	Percent Employment Change
Combined Food Preparation and Serving Workers, Including Fast Food	29,300	35,950	6,650	22.7
Retail Salespersons	45,710	51,200	5,490	12.0
Carpenters	10,350	15,400	5,050	48.8
Construction Laborers	7,620	11,780	4,160	54.7
Waiters and Waitresses	37,760	41,880	4,120	10.9
Laborers and Freight, Stock, and Material Movers, Hand	18,250	21,670	3,420	18.7
Gaming Dealers	22,640	25,950	3,310	14.6
Personal Care Aides	8,020	11,090	3,070	38.2
Customer Service Representatives	16,580	19,620	3,040	18.3
Cooks, Restaurant	17,440	20,450	3,010	17.3

Note: Projections cover Nevada; (1) Sorted by numeric employment change
Source: www.projectionscentral.com, State Occupational Projections, 2012–2022 Long-Term Projections

Fastest Growing Occupations: 2012 – 2022

Occupation[1]	2012 Employment	2022 Projected Employment	Numeric Employment Change	Percent Employment Change
Helpers—Brickmasons, Blockmasons, Stonemasons, and Tile and Marble Setters	170	380	210	119.8
Helpers—Painters, Paperhangers, Plasterers, and Stucco Masons	90	200	110	113.8
Brickmasons and Blockmasons	470	970	500	104.4
Cement Masons and Concrete Finishers	1,200	2,250	1,050	87.3
Structural Iron and Steel Workers	530	980	450	86.3
Helpers—Carpenters	160	300	140	83.9
Glaziers	460	810	350	77.1
Crane and Tower Operators	280	470	190	68.5
Roofers	1,200	2,020	820	67.8
Helpers—Electricians	260	430	170	65.3

Note: Projections cover Nevada; (1) Sorted by percent employment change and excludes occupations with numeric employment change less than 100
Source: www.projectionscentral.com, State Occupational Projections, 2012–2022 Long-Term Projections

Average Wages

Occupation	$/Hr.	Occupation	$/Hr.
Accountants and Auditors	30.63	Maids and Housekeeping Cleaners	15.39
Automotive Mechanics	19.99	Maintenance and Repair Workers	22.63
Bookkeepers	18.00	Marketing Managers	55.16
Carpenters	23.76	Nuclear Medicine Technologists	36.22
Cashiers	10.72	Nurses, Licensed Practical	25.70
Clerks, General Office	15.19	Nurses, Registered	39.82
Clerks, Receptionists/Information	12.91	Nursing Assistants	16.84
Clerks, Shipping/Receiving	16.42	Packers and Packagers, Hand	11.10
Computer Programmers	38.46	Physical Therapists	68.02
Computer Systems Analysts	38.43	Postal Service Mail Carriers	25.25
Computer User Support Specialists	24.36	Real Estate Brokers	57.87
Cooks, Restaurant	14.21	Retail Salespersons	12.87
Dentists	62.06	Sales Reps., Exc. Tech./Scientific	30.00
Electrical Engineers	42.42	Sales Reps., Tech./Scientific	42.07
Electricians	27.13	Secretaries, Exc. Legal/Med./Exec.	17.97
Financial Managers	49.10	Security Guards	13.08
First-Line Supervisors/Managers, Sales	20.58	Surgeons	126.61
Food Preparation Workers	13.01	Teacher Assistants	15.50
General and Operations Managers	49.24	Teachers, Elementary School	25.20
Hairdressers/Cosmetologists	11.31	Teachers, Secondary School	25.60
Internists	84.91	Telemarketers	13.83
Janitors and Cleaners	14.03	Truck Drivers, Heavy/Tractor-Trailer	21.71
Landscaping/Groundskeeping Workers	12.39	Truck Drivers, Light/Delivery Svcs.	16.57
Lawyers	60.83	Waiters and Waitresses	11.33

Note: Wage data covers the Las Vegas-Paradise, NV Metropolitan Statistical Area—see Appendix B for areas included; Hourly wages for elementary/secondary school teachers and teacher assistants were calculated by the editors from annual wage data assuming a 40 hour work week; n/a not available.
Source: Bureau of Labor Statistics, Metro Area Occupational Employment and Wage Estimates, May 2014

TAXES

State Corporate Income Tax Rates

State	Tax Rate (%)	Income Brackets ($)	Num. of Brackets	Financial Institution Tax Rate (%)[a]	Federal Income Tax Ded.
Nevada	None	–	–	–	–

Note: Tax rates as of January 1, 2015; (a) Rates listed are the corporate income tax rate applied to financial institutions or excise taxes based on income. Some states have other taxes based upon the value of deposits or shares.
Source: Federation of Tax Administrators, "State Corporate Income Tax Rates, 2015"

State Individual Income Tax Rates

State	Tax Rate (%)	Income Brackets ($)	Num. of Brackets	Personal Exempt. ($)[1] Single	Dependents	Fed. Inc. Tax Ded.
Nevada	None	–	–	–	–	–

Note: Tax rates as of January 1, 2015; Local- and county-level taxes are not included; n/a not applicable; (1) Married joint filers generally receive double the single exemption
Source: Federation of Tax Administrators, "State Individual Income Tax Rates, 2015"

Various State and Local Tax Rates

State	State and Local Sales and Use (%)	State Sales and Use (%)	Gasoline[1] (¢/gal.)	Cigarette[2] ($/pack)	Spirits[3] ($/gal.)	Wine[4] ($/gal.)	Beer[5] ($/gal.)
Nevada	8.1	6.85	33.15	0.80	3.60 (f)	0.70	0.16

Note: All tax rates as of January 1, 2015; (1) The American Petroleum Institute has developed a methodology for determining the average tax rate on a gallon of fuel. Rates may include any of the following: excise taxes, environmental fees, storage tank fees, other fees or taxes, general sales tax, and local taxes. In states where gasoline is subject to the general sales tax, or where the fuel tax is based on the average sale price, the average rate determined by API is sensitive to changes in the price of gasoline. States that fully or partially apply general sales taxes to gasoline: CA, CO, GA, IL, IN, MI, NY; (2) The federal excise tax of $1.0066 per pack and local taxes are not included; (3) Rates are those applicable to off-premise sales of 40% alcohol by volume (a.b.v.) distilled spirits in 750ml containers. Local excise taxes are excluded; (4) Rates are those applicable to off-premise sales of 11% a.b.v. non-carbonated wine in 750ml containers; (5) Rates are those applicable to off-premise sales of 4.7% a.b.v. beer in 12 ounce containers; (f) Different rates are also applicable according to alcohol content, place of production, size of container, or place purchased (on- or off-premise or onboard airlines).
Source: Tax Foundation, 2015 Facts & Figures: How Does Your State Compare?

State Business Tax Climate Index Rankings

State	Overall Rank	Corporate Tax Index Rank	Individual Income Tax Index Rank	Sales Tax Index Rank	Unemployment Insurance Tax Index Rank	Property Tax Index Rank
Nevada	3	1	1	39	43	9

Note: The index is a measure of how each state's tax laws affect economic performance. The lower the rank, the more favorable a state's tax system is for business. States without a given tax are given a ranking of 1. The scores/rankings for the District of Columbia do not affect other states. The 2015 index represents the tax climate as of July 1, 2014.
Source: Tax Foundation, State Business Tax Climate Index 2015

COMMERCIAL REAL ESTATE

Office Market

Market Area	Inventory (sq. ft.)	Vacancy Rate (%)	Under Construction (sq. ft.)	YTD Net Absorption (sq. ft.)	Total Average Asking Rent ($/sq. ft./year)
Las Vegas	37,259,980	21.5	345,000	1,335,229	26.45
National	4,745,108,508	14.3	71,190,461	51,084,126	27.40

Source: Newmark Grubb Knight Frank, National Office Market Report, 4th Quarter 2014

Industrial/Warehouse/R&D Market

Market Area	Inventory (sq. ft.)	Vacancy Rate (%)	Under Construction (sq. ft.)	YTD Net Absorption (sq. ft.)	Total Average Asking Rent ($/sq. ft./year)
Las Vegas	101,062,194	9.7	1,064,203	4,038,647	6.57
National	14,238,613,765	7.2	134,387,407	185,246,438	5.64

Source: Newmark Grubb Knight Frank, National Industrial Market Report, 4th Quarter 2014

COMMERCIAL UTILITIES

Typical Monthly Electric Bills

Area	Commercial Service ($/month)		Industrial Service ($/month)	
	1,500 kWh	40 kW demand 14,000 kWh	1,000 kW demand 200,000 kWh	50,000 kW demand 32,500,000 kWh
City	135	1,198	22,791	2,541,003
Average[1]	201	1,653	26,124	2,639,743

Note: Figures are based on annualized 2014 rates; (1) Average based on 180 utilities surveyed
Source: Edison Electric Institute, Typical Bills and Average Rates Report, Summer 2014

TRANSPORTATION

Means of Transportation to Work

Area	Car/Truck/Van		Public Transportation			Bicycle	Walked	Other Means	Worked at Home
	Drove Alone	Car-pooled	Bus	Subway	Railroad				
City	78.1	11.4	3.9	0.0	0.0	0.4	1.7	1.4	3.0
MSA[1]	78.9	10.6	3.7	0.0	0.0	0.3	1.8	1.6	2.9
U.S.	76.4	9.6	2.6	1.8	0.6	0.6	2.8	1.3	4.3

Note: Figures are percentages and cover workers 16 years of age and older; (1) Figures cover the Las Vegas-Henderson-Paradise, NV Metropolitan Statistical Area—see Appendix B for areas included
Source: U.S. Census Bureau, 2011-2013 American Community Survey 3-Year Estimates

Travel Time to Work

Area	Less Than 10 Minutes	10 to 19 Minutes	20 to 29 Minutes	30 to 44 Minutes	45 to 59 Minutes	60 to 89 Minutes	90 Minutes or More
City	7.1	26.1	29.2	28.5	4.5	2.8	1.8
MSA[1]	8.3	29.0	29.5	24.6	4.3	2.6	1.8
U.S.	13.3	29.7	20.9	20.2	7.7	5.7	2.6

Note: Figures are percentages and include workers 16 years old and over; (1) Figures cover the Las Vegas-Henderson-Paradise, NV Metropolitan Statistical Area—see Appendix B for areas included
Source: U.S. Census Bureau, 2011-2013 American Community Survey 3-Year Estimates

Travel Time Index

Area	1985	1990	1995	2000	2005	2010	2011
Urban Area[1]	1.06	1.13	1.19	1.21	1.24	1.20	1.20
Average[2]	1.09	1.14	1.16	1.19	1.23	1.18	1.18

Note: Travel Time Index—the ratio of travel time in the peak period to the travel time at free-flow conditions. For example, a value of 1.30 indicates a 20-minute free-flow trip takes 26 minutes in the peak. Free-flow speeds (60 mph on freeways and 35 mph on principal arterials) are used as the comparison threshold; (1) Covers the Las Vegas NV urban area; (2) average of 498 urban areas
Source: Texas Transportation Institute, Urban Mobility Report 2012, December 2012

Public Transportation

Agency Name / Mode of Transportation	Vehicles Operated in Maximum Service	Annual Unlinked Passenger Trips (in thous.)	Annual Passenger Miles (in thous.)
Regional Transportation Commission of Southern Nevada (RTC)			
Bus (purchased transportation)	308	55,959.4	198,656.0
Bus Rapid Transit (purchased transportation)	16	4,377.6	21,912.9
Demand Response (purchased transportation)	330	1,367.3	14,913.6

Source: Federal Transit Administration, National Transit Database, 2013

Air Transportation

Airport Name and Code / Type of Service	Passenger Airlines[1]	Passenger Enplanements	Freight Carriers[2]	Freight (lbs.)
McCarran International (LAS)				
Domestic service (U.S. carriers - 2014)	32	18,762,415	16	89,997,240
International service (U.S. carriers - 2013)	9	15,567	2	170,002

Note: (1) Includes all U.S.-based major, minor and commuter airlines that carried at least one passenger during the year; (2) Includes all U.S.-based airlines and freight carriers that transported at least one lb. of freight during the year.
Source: Bureau of Transportation Statistics, The Intermodal Transportation Database, Air Carriers: T-100 Domestic Market (U.S. Carriers), 2014; Bureau of Transportation Statistics, The Intermodal Transportation Database, Air Carriers: T-100 International Market (U.S. Carriers), 2013

Other Transportation Statistics

Major Highways:	I-15
Amtrak Service:	Bus connection
Major Waterways/Ports:	None

Source: Amtrak.com; Google Maps

BUSINESSES

Major Business Headquarters

Company Name	Rankings	
	Fortune[1]	Forbes[2]
Caesars Entertainment Corporation	318	-
Las Vegas Sands Corp.	211	-
MGM Resorts International	287	-
Wynn Resorts	Limited	452

Note: (1) Fortune 500—companies that produce a 10-K are ranked 1 to 500 based on 2013 revenue; (2) all private companies with at least $2 billion in annual revenue through the end of their most current fiscal year are ranked 1 to 221; companies listed are headquartered in the city; dashes indicate no ranking
Source: Fortune, "Fortune 500," June 16, 2014; Forbes, "America's Largest Private Companies," November 5, 2014

Fast-Growing Businesses

According to *Inc.*, Las Vegas is home to two of America's 500 fastest-growing private companies: **Luxe Royale** (#272); **FreeRateUpdate.com** (#283). Criteria: must be an independent, privately-held, for-profit, U.S. corporation, proprietorship or partnership; revenues must be at least $100,000 in 2010 and $2 million in 2013; must have four-year operating/sales history. Holding companies, regulated banks, and utilities were excluded. *Inc.*, *"America's 500 Fastest-Growing Private Companies," September 2014*

According to *Fortune*, Las Vegas is home to one of the 100 fastest-growing companies in the world: **Las Vegas Sands** (#85). Companies were ranked by their revenue growth rate; their EPS growth rate; and their three-year annualized total return to investors for the period ending June 30, 2014. Criteria for inclusion: a company, foreign or domestic, must trade on a major U.S. stock exchange; must file quarterly reports with the SEC; must have a minimum market capitalization of $250 million; must have a stock price of at least $5 on June 30, 2014; must have been trading continuously since June 30, 2010; must have revenue and net income for the four quarters ended on or before April 30, 2014, of at least $50 million and $10 million, respectively; and must have posted a compound annual growth in revenue and earnings per share of at least 20% annually over the three years ending on or before April 30, 2014. Real estate investment trusts, limited-liability companies, limited parterships, business development companies, closed end investment firms, and companies that lost money in the quarter ending April 30, 2014 were excluded. *Fortune, "100 Fastest-Growing Companies," August 28, 2014*

Minority Business Opportunity

Las Vegas is home to one company which is on the *Hispanic Business* 500 list (500 largest U.S. Hispanic-owned companies based on 2012 revenue): **Local Leads HQ/NMCC Strategic Edge Profits** (#415). Companies included must show at least 51 percent ownership by Hispanic U.S. citizens, and must maintain headquarters in one of the 50 states or Washington, D.C. *Hispanic Business, "Hispanic Business 500," June 20, 2013*

Minority- and Women-Owned Businesses

Group	All Firms		Firms with Paid Employees			
	Firms	Sales ($000)	Firms	Sales ($000)	Employees	Payroll ($000)
Asian	5,710	1,037,064	804	856,837	5,412	184,775
Black	2,929	376,877	203	306,884	3,779	96,193
Hispanic	5,387	1,061,966	589	901,531	4,758	158,683
Women	16,073	3,984,163	1,673	3,402,002	14,667	503,397
All Firms	54,557	42,855,099	11,069	40,579,778	213,977	8,261,303

Note: Figures cover firms located in the city; minority- and women-owned business are defined as firms in which the corresponding group own 51% or more of the stock or equity of the company
Source: U.S. Census Bureau, 2007 Economic Census, Survey of Business Owners (2012 Survey of Business Owners data will be released starting in June 2015)

**HOTELS &
CONVENTION
CENTERS**

Hotels/Motels

Area	5 Star		4 Star		3 Star		2 Star		1 Star		Not Rated	
	Num.	Pct.[3]	Num.	Pct.[3]	Num.	Pct.[3]	Num.	Pct.[3]	Num.	Pct.[3]	Num.	Pct.[3]
City[1]	15	6.8	32	14.4	88	39.6	76	34.2	4	1.8	7	3.2
Total[2]	166	0.9	1,264	7.0	5,718	31.8	9,340	52.0	411	2.3	1,070	6.0

Note: (1) Figures cover Las Vegas and vicinity; (2) Figures cover all 100 cities in this book; (3) Percentage of hotels which have a given star rating; Star ratings are determined by expedia.com and offer an indication of the general quality of a particular hotel.
Source: expedia.com, April 2, 2015

The Las Vegas-Henderson-Paradise, NV metro area is home to eight of the best hotels in the U.S. according to *Travel & Leisure*: **ARIA, Las Vegas**; **Bellagio, Las Vegas**; **Encore Las Vegas**; **Four Seasons Hotel Las Vegas**; **Mandarin Oriental, Las Vegas**; **The Palazzo**; **The Venetian**; **Wynn Las Vegas**. Criteria: service; location; rooms; food; and value. The list includes the top 236 hotels in the U.S. *Travel & Leisure, "T+L 500, The World's Best Hotels 2015"*

The Las Vegas-Henderson-Paradise, NV metro area is home to three of the best hotels in the world according to *Condé Nast Traveler*: **Bellagio**; **The Cosmopolitan of Las Vegas**; **Wynn Las Vegas and Encore**. The selections are based on editors' picks. The list includes the top 25 hotels in the U.S. *Condé Nast Traveler, "Gold List 2015, The Top Hotels in the World"*

Major Convention Centers

Name	Overall Space (sq. ft.)	Exhibit Space (sq. ft.)	Meeting Space (sq. ft.)	Meeting Rooms
Cashman Center	483,000	98,100	n/a	12
Henderson Events Plaza	60,000	n/a	n/a	n/a
Las Vegas Convention Center	3,200,000	2,000,000	241,000	144
Mandalay Bay Convention Center	1,700,000	934,731	n/a	n/a
Sands Expo and Convention Center	1,800,000	n/a	n/a	n/a

Note: Table includes convention centers located in the Las Vegas-Henderson-Paradise, NV metro area; n/a not available
Source: Original research

Living Environment

COST OF LIVING

Cost of Living Index

Composite Index	Groceries	Housing	Utilities	Trans-portation	Health Care	Misc. Goods/Services
105.8	111.2	107.0	90.8	104.6	102.4	108.0

Note: The Cost of Living Index measures regional differences in the cost of consumer goods and services, excluding taxes and non-consumer expenditures, for professional and managerial households in the top income quintile. It is based on more than 50,000 prices covering almost 60 different items for which prices are collected three times a year by chambers of commerce, economic development organizations or university applied economic centers in each participating urban area. The numbers shown should be read as a percentage above or below the national average of 100. For example, a value of 115.4 in the groceries column indicates that grocery prices are 15.4% higher than the national average. Small differences in the index numbers should not be interpreted as significant; Figures cover the Las Vegas NV urban area.
Source: The Council for Community and Economic Research, ACCRA Cost of Living Index, 2014

Grocery Prices

Area[1]	T-Bone Steak ($/pound)	Frying Chicken ($/pound)	Whole Milk ($/half gal.)	Eggs ($/dozen)	Orange Juice ($/64 oz.)	Coffee ($/11.5 oz.)
City[2]	8.83	1.61	2.17	2.02	3.95	4.81
Avg.	10.40	1.37	2.40	1.99	3.46	4.27
Min.	8.48	0.93	1.37	1.30	2.83	2.99
Max.	14.20	2.44	3.62	4.02	6.42	6.96

*Note: (1) Values for the local area are compared with the average, minimum and maximum values for all 308 areas in the Cost of Living Index; (2) Figures cover the Las Vegas NV urban area; **T-Bone Steak** (price per pound); **Frying Chicken** (price per pound, whole fryer); **Whole Milk** (half gallon carton); **Eggs** (price per dozen, Grade A, large); **Orange Juice** (64 oz. Tropicana or Florida Natural); **Coffee** (11.5 oz. can, vacuum-packed, Maxwell House, Hills Bros, or Folgers).*
Source: The Council for Community and Economic Research, ACCRA Cost of Living Index, 2014

Housing and Utility Costs

Area[1]	New Home Price ($)	Apartment Rent ($/month)	All Electric ($/month)	Part Electric ($/month)	Other Energy ($/month)	Telephone ($/month)
City[2]	334,773	911	-	133.02	49.81	18.66
Avg.	305,838	919	181.00	93.66	73.14	27.95
Min.	183,142	480	112.00	42.06	23.42	17.16
Max.	1,358,576	3,851	594.00	180.03	440.99	40.42

*Note: (1) Values for the local area are compared with the average, minimum and maximum values for all 308 areas in the Cost of Living Index; (2) Figures cover the Las Vegas NV urban area; **New Home Price** (2,400 sf living area, 8,000 sf lot, in urban area with full utilities); **Apartment Rent** (950 sf 2 bedroom/1.5 or 2 bath, unfurnished, excluding all utilities except water); **All Electric** (average monthly cost for an all-electric home); **Part Electric** (average monthly cost for a part-electric home); **Other Energy** (average monthly cost for natural gas, fuel oil, coal, wood, and any other forms of energy except electricity); **Telephone** (price includes basic monthly rate for a private residential line plus additional local usage charges incurred by a family of four).*
Source: The Council for Community and Economic Research, ACCRA Cost of Living Index, 2014

Health Care, Transportation, and Other Costs

Area[1]	Doctor ($/visit)	Dentist ($/visit)	Optometrist ($/visit)	Gasoline ($/gallon)	Beauty Salon ($/visit)	Men's Shirt ($)
City[2]	114.52	88.96	98.47	3.57	49.06	43.20
Avg.	102.86	87.89	97.66	3.44	34.37	26.74
Min.	67.47	65.78	51.18	3.00	17.43	12.79
Max.	173.50	150.14	235.00	4.33	64.28	49.50

*Note: (1) Values for the local area are compared with the average, minimum and maximum values for all 308 areas in the Cost of Living Index; (2) Figures cover the Las Vegas NV urban area; **Doctor** (general practitioners routine exam of an established patient); **Dentist** (adult teeth cleaning and periodic oral examination); **Optometrist** (full vision eye exam for established adult patient); **Gasoline** (one gallon regular unleaded, national brand, including all taxes, cash price at self-service pump if available); **Beauty Salon** (woman's shampoo, trim, and blow-dry); **Men's Shirt** (cotton/polyester dress shirt, pinpoint weave, long sleeves).*
Source: The Council for Community and Economic Research, ACCRA Cost of Living Index, 2014

HOUSING

House Price Index (HPI)

Area	National Ranking[2]	Quarterly Change (%)	One-Year Change (%)	Five-Year Change (%)
MSA[1]	6	1.44	12.66	23.87
U.S.[3]	–	1.35	4.91	11.59

Note: The HPI is a weighted repeat sales index. It measures average price changes in repeat sales or refinancings on the same properties. This information is obtained by reviewing repeat mortgage transactions on single-family properties whose mortgages have been purchased or securitized by Fannie Mae or Freddie Mac in January 1975; (1) Las Vegas-Henderson-Paradise Metropolitan Statistical Area—see Appendix B for areas included; (2) Rankings are based on annual percentage change for all metro areas containing at least 15,000 transactions over the last 10 years and ranges from 1 to 275; (3) figures based on a weighted average of Census Division estimates using a seasonally adjusted, purchase-only index; all figures are for the period ending December 31, 2014
Source: Federal Housing Finance Agency, House Price Index, February 26, 2015

Median Single-Family Home Prices

Area	2012	2013	2014p	Percent Change 2013 to 2014
MSA[1]	134.1	173.8	198.0	13.9
U.S. Average	177.2	197.4	209.0	5.9

Note: Figures are median sales prices of existing single-family homes in thousands of dollars; (p) preliminary; n/a not available; (1) Las Vegas-Henderson-Paradise, NV Metropolitan Statistical Area—see Appendix B for areas included
Source: National Association of Realtors, Median Sales Price of Existing Single-Family Homes for Metropolitan Areas, 4th Quarter 2014

Qualifying Income Based on Median Sales Price of Existing Single-Family Homes

Area	With 5% Down ($)	With 10% Down ($)	With 20% Down ($)
MSA[1]	44,456	42,117	37,437
U.S. Average	45,863	43,449	38,621

Note: Figures are preliminary; Qualifying income is based on a mortgage rate of 4.0%. Monthly principal and interest payment is limited to 25% of income; n/a not available; (1) Las Vegas-Henderson-Paradise, NV Metropolitan Statistical Area—see Appendix B for areas included
Source: National Association of Realtors, Qualifying Income Based on Median Sales Price of Existing Single-Family Homes for Metropolitan Areas, 4th Quarter 2014

Median Apartment Condo-Coop Home Prices

Area	2012	2013	2014p	Percent Change 2013 to 2014
MSA[1]	62.7	84.7	100.7	18.9
U.S. Average	173.7	194.9	205.1	5.2

Note: Figures are median sales prices of existing apartment condo-coop homes in thousands of dollars; (p) preliminary; n/a not available; (1) Las Vegas-Henderson-Paradise, NV Metropolitan Statistical Area—see Appendix B for areas included
Source: National Association of Realtors, Median Sales Price of Existing Apartment Condo-Coop Homes for Metropolitan Areas, 4th Quarter 2014

Gross Monthly Rent

Area	Under $200	$200 -299	$300 -499	$500 -749	$750 -999	$1,000 -1,499	$1,500 and up	Median ($)
City	0.9	1.2	3.8	20.7	28.0	34.5	10.9	959
MSA[1]	0.5	0.7	2.7	18.7	29.2	34.4	13.9	985
U.S.	1.7	3.2	7.8	22.1	24.3	26.0	14.9	900

Note: Figures are percentages except for Median; Gross rent is the contract rent plus the estimated average monthly cost of utilities (electricity, gas, and water and sewer) and fuels (oil, coal, kerosene, wood, etc.) if these are paid by the renter (or paid for the renter by someone else); (1) Figures cover the Las Vegas-Henderson-Paradise, NV Metropolitan Statistical Area—see Appendix B for areas included
Source: U.S. Census Bureau, 2011-2013 American Community Survey 3-Year Estimates

Homeownership Rate

Area	2007 (%)	2008 (%)	2009 (%)	2010 (%)	2011 (%)	2012 (%)	2013 (%)	2014 (%)
MSA[1]	60.5	60.3	59.0	55.7	52.9	52.6	52.8	53.2
U.S.	68.1	67.8	67.4	66.9	66.1	65.4	65.1	64.5

Note: (1) Figures cover the Las Vegas-Henderson-Paradise, NV Metropolitan Statistical Area—see Appendix B for areas included
Source: U.S. Census Bureau, Housing Vacancies and Homeownership Annual Statistics: 2014

Year Housing Structure Built

Area	2010 or Later	2000 -2009	1990 -1999	1980 -1989	1970 -1979	1960 -1969	1950 -1959	1940 -1949	Before 1940	Median Year
City	1.1	24.1	32.4	17.8	11.0	7.3	4.9	1.1	0.4	1992
MSA[1]	1.3	34.3	27.9	15.3	12.5	5.2	2.6	0.7	0.3	1995
U.S.	0.9	15.0	13.9	13.8	15.8	11.0	10.9	5.4	13.3	1976

Note: Figures are percentages except for Median Year; (1) Figures cover the Las Vegas-Henderson-Paradise, NV Metropolitan Statistical Area—see Appendix B for areas included
Source: U.S. Census Bureau, 2011-2013 American Community Survey 3-Year Estimates

HEALTH

Health Risk Data

Category	MSA[1] (%)	U.S. (%)
Adults aged 18–64 who have any kind of health care coverage	69.4	79.6
Adults who reported being in good or excellent health	80.3	83.1
Adults who are current smokers	17.0	19.6
Adults who are heavy drinkers[2]	5.8	6.1
Adults who are binge drinkers[3]	13.8	16.9
Adults who are overweight (BMI 25.0 - 29.9)	36.5	35.8
Adults who are obese (BMI 30.0 - 99.8)	27.4	27.6
Adults who participated in any physical activities in the past month	78.1	77.1
Adults 50+ who have ever had a sigmoidoscopy or colonoscopy	59.2	67.3
Women aged 40+ who have had a mammogram within the past two years	66.4	74.0
Men aged 40+ who have had a PSA test within the past two years	50.1	45.2
Adults aged 65+ who have had flu shot within the past year	50.6	60.1
Adults who always wear a seatbelt	94.4	93.8

Note: Data as of 2012 unless otherwise noted; (1) Figures cover the Las Vegas-Paradise, NV Metropolitan Statistical Area—see Appendix B for areas included; (2) Heavy drinkers are classified as males having more than two drinks per day or females having more than one drink per day; (3) Binge drinkers are classified as males having five or more drinks on one occasion or females having four or more drinks on one occasion
Source: Centers for Disease Control and Prevention, Behaviorial Risk Factor Surveillance System, SMART: Selected Metropolitan/Micropolitan Area Risk Trends, 2012 (Note: the CDC has discontinued this dataset but will be releasing a replacement in late 2015)

Chronic Health Indicators

Category	MSA[1] (%)	U.S. (%)
Adults who have ever been told they had a heart attack	4.6	4.5
Adults who have ever been told they had a stroke	3.4	2.9
Adults who have been told they currently have asthma	7.1	8.9
Adults who have ever been told they have arthritis	23.5	25.7
Adults who have ever been told they have diabetes[2]	9.5	9.7
Adults who have ever been told they had skin cancer	4.4	5.7
Adults who have ever been told they had any other types of cancer	5.1	6.5
Adults who have ever been told they have COPD	7.7	6.2
Adults who have ever been told they have kidney disease	3.2	2.5
Adults who have ever been told they have a form of depression	15.4	18.0

Note: Data as of 2012 unless otherwise noted; (1) Figures cover the Las Vegas-Paradise, NV Metropolitan Statistical Area—see Appendix B for areas included; (2) Figures do not include pregnancy-related, borderline, or pre-diabetes
Source: Centers for Disease Control and Prevention, Behaviorial Risk Factor Surveillance System, SMART: Selected Metropolitan/Micropolitan Area Risk Trends, 2012 (Note: the CDC has discontinued this dataset but will be releasing a replacement in late 2015)

Mortality Rates for the Top 10 Causes of Death in the U.S.

ICD-10[a] Sub-Chapter	ICD-10[a] Code	Age-Adjusted Mortality Rate[1] per 100,000 population	
		County[2]	U.S.
Malignant neoplasms	C00-C97	165.4	166.2
Ischaemic heart diseases	I20-I25	87.4	105.7
Other forms of heart disease	I30-I51	86.1	49.3
Chronic lower respiratory diseases	J40-J47	50.0	42.1
Organic, including symptomatic, mental disorders	F01-F09	43.5	38.1
Cerebrovascular diseases	I60-I69	35.2	37.0
Other external causes of accidental injury	W00-X59	29.9	26.9
Other degenerative diseases of the nervous system	G30-G31	12.9	25.6
Diabetes mellitus	E10-E14	12.8	21.3
Hypertensive diseases	I10-I15	18.7	19.4

Note: (a) ICD-10 = International Classification of Diseases 10th Revision; (1) Mortality rates are a three year average covering 2011-2013; (2) Figures cover Clark County
Source: Centers for Disease Control and Prevention, National Center for Health Statistics. Compressed Mortality File 1999-2013 on CDC WONDER Online Database, released October 2014. Data are compiled from the Compressed Mortality File 1999-2013, Series 20 No. 2S, 2014.

Mortality Rates for Selected Causes of Death

ICD-10[a] Sub-Chapter	ICD-10[a] Code	Age-Adjusted Mortality Rate[1] per 100,000 population	
		County[2]	U.S.
Assault	X85-Y09	4.9	5.2
Diseases of the liver	K70-K76	15.5	13.2
Human immunodeficiency virus (HIV) disease	B20-B24	3.1	2.2
Influenza and pneumonia	J09-J18	19.6	15.4
Intentional self-harm	X60-X84	17.1	12.5
Malnutrition	E40-E46	0.4	0.9
Obesity and other hyperalimentation	E65-E68	0.9	1.8
Renal failure	N17-N19	16.8	13.1
Transport accidents	V01-V99	10.0	11.7
Viral hepatitis	B15-B19	3.0	2.2

Note: (a) ICD-10 = International Classification of Diseases 10th Revision; (1) Mortality rates are a three year average covering 2011-2013; (2) Figures cover Clark County
Source: Centers for Disease Control and Prevention, National Center for Health Statistics. Compressed Mortality File 1999-2013 on CDC WONDER Online Database, released October 2014. Data are compiled from the Compressed Mortality File 1999-2013, Series 20 No. 2S, 2014.

Health Insurance Coverage

Area	With Health Insurance	With Private Health Insurance	With Public Health Insurance	Without Health Insurance	Population Under Age 18 Without Health Insurance
City	76.7	58.7	27.3	23.3	16.6
MSA[1]	77.8	61.8	24.9	22.2	15.7
U.S.	85.2	65.2	31.0	14.8	7.3

Note: Figures are percentages that cover the civilian noninstitutionalized population; (1) Figures cover the Las Vegas-Henderson-Paradise, NV Metropolitan Statistical Area—see Appendix B for areas included
Source: U.S. Census Bureau, 2011-2013 American Community Survey 3-Year Estimates

Number of Medical Professionals

Area[1]	MDs[2]	DOs[2,3]	Dentists	Podiatrists	Chiropractors	Optometrists
Local (number)	3,440	501	1,140	73	387	236
Local (rate[4])	172.1	25.1	56.2	3.6	19.1	11.6
U.S. (rate[4])	270.0	20.2	63.1	5.7	25.2	14.9

Note: Data as of 2013 unless noted; (1) Local data covers Clark County; (2) Data as of 2012 and includes all active, non-federal physicians; (3) Doctor of Osteopathic Medicine; (4) rate per 100,000 population
Source: U.S. Department of Health and Human Services, Health Resources and Services Administration, Bureau of Health Professions, Area Resource File (ARF) 2013-2014

EDUCATION

Public School District Statistics

District Name	Schls	Pupils	Pupil/ Teacher Ratio	Minority Pupils[1] (%)	Free Lunch Eligible[2] (%)	IEP[3] (%)
Clark County School District	372	316,778	22.2	70.6	47.5	10.7

Note: Table includes school districts with 2,000 or more students; (1) Percentage of students that are not non-Hispanic white; (2) Percentage of students that are eligible for the free lunch program; (3) Percentage of students that have an Individualized Education Program.
Source: U.S. Department of Education, National Center for Education Statistics, Common Core of Data, Local Education Agency (School District) Universe Survey: School Year 2012-2013; U.S. Department of Education, National Center for Education Statistics, Common Core of Data, Public Elementary/Secondary School Universe Survey: School Year 2012-2013

Best High Schools

According to *The Daily Beast*, Las Vegas is home to one of the best high schools in the U.S.: **Las Vegas Academy of the Arts** (#507); *The Daily Beast* used six indicators culled from school surveys to compare public high schools in the U.S., with graduation and college acceptance rates weighed most heavily. Other criteria included: college-level courses/exams and SAT/ACT scores. *The Daily Beast, "Top High Schools 2014"*

Highest Level of Education

Area	Less than H.S.	H.S. Diploma	Some College, No Deg.	Associate Degree	Bachelor's Degree	Master's Degree	Prof. School Degree	Doctorate Degree
City	17.0	29.2	24.4	7.7	14.2	5.2	1.6	0.7
MSA[1]	15.9	29.5	25.0	7.5	14.8	5.0	1.5	0.7
U.S.	13.7	28.0	21.2	7.9	18.2	7.7	1.9	1.3

Note: Figures cover persons age 25 and over; (1) Figures cover the Las Vegas-Henderson-Paradise, NV Metropolitan Statistical Area—see Appendix B for areas included
Source: U.S. Census Bureau, 2011-2013 American Community Survey 3-Year Estimates

Educational Attainment by Race

Area	High School Graduate or Higher (%)					Bachelor's Degree or Higher (%)				
	Total	White	Black	Asian	Hisp.[2]	Total	White	Black	Asian	Hisp.[2]
City	83.0	85.6	85.8	89.5	59.2	21.7	23.1	16.8	39.0	7.4
MSA[1]	84.1	86.3	86.8	87.9	61.8	22.1	23.1	16.5	35.2	8.6
U.S.	86.3	88.3	83.1	85.7	64.0	29.1	30.4	18.8	50.7	13.7

Note: Figures shown cover persons 25 years old and over; (1) Figures cover the Las Vegas-Henderson-Paradise, NV Metropolitan Statistical Area—see Appendix B for areas included; (2) People of Hispanic origin can be of any race
Source: U.S. Census Bureau, 2011-2013 American Community Survey 3-Year Estimates

School Enrollment by Grade and Control

Area	Preschool (%)		Kindergarten (%)		Grades 1 - 4 (%)		Grades 5 - 8 (%)		Grades 9 - 12 (%)	
	Public	Private	Public	Private	Public	Private	Public	Private	Public	Private
City	50.7	49.3	86.9	13.1	92.9	7.1	91.9	8.1	94.7	5.3
MSA[1]	55.8	44.2	90.3	9.7	93.4	6.6	94.5	5.5	95.3	4.7
U.S.	57.7	42.3	87.9	12.1	89.9	10.1	90.0	10.0	90.7	9.3

Note: Figures shown cover persons 3 years old and over; (1) Figures cover the Las Vegas-Henderson-Paradise, NV Metropolitan Statistical Area—see Appendix B for areas included
Source: U.S. Census Bureau, 2011-2013 American Community Survey 3-Year Estimates

Average Salaries of Public School Classroom Teachers

Area	2013-14		2014-15		Percent Change 2013-14 to 2014-15	Percent Change 2004-05 to 2014-15
	Dollars	Rank[1]	Dollars	Rank[1]		
NEVADA	55,813	20	56,703	19	1.59	30.7
U.S. Average	56,610	–	57,379	–	1.36	20.8

Note: (1) State rank ranges from 1 to 51 where 1 indicates highest salary.
Source: National Education Association, Rankings & Estimates: Rankings of the States 2014 and Estimates of School Statistics 2015, March 2015

Higher Education

Four-Year Colleges			Two-Year Colleges			Medical Schools[1]	Law Schools[2]	Voc/ Tech[3]
Public	Private Non-profit	Private For-profit	Public	Private Non-profit	Private For-profit			
2	0	1	0	1	13	0	1	8

Note: Figures cover institutions located within the city limits and include main campuses only; (1) includes schools accredited by the Liaison Committee on Medical Education and the American Osteopathic Association's Commission on Osteopathic College Accreditation; (2) includes ABA-accredited schools, schools with provisional ABA accreditation, and state accredited schools; (3) includes all schools with programs that are less than 2 years.

Source: National Center for Education Statistics, Integrated Postsecondary Education System (IPEDS), 2013-14; Association of American Medical Colleges, Member List, May 1, 2015; American Osteopathic Association, Member List, May 1, 2015; Law School Admission Council, Official Guide to ABA-Approved Law Schools Online, May 1, 2015; Wikipedia, List of Medical Schools in the United States, May 1, 2015; Wikipedia, List of Law Schools in the United States, May 1, 2015

According to *U.S. News & World Report*, the Las Vegas-Henderson-Paradise, NV metro area is home to one of the top 100 law schools in the U.S.: **University of Nevada-Las Vegas** (#67). The rankings are based on a weighted average of 12 measures of quality: peer assessment score; assessment score by lawyers/judges; median LSAT scores; median undergrad GPA; acceptance rate; employment rates for graduates; placement success; bar passage rate; faculty resources; expenditures per student; student/faculty ratio; and library resources. *U.S. News & World Report, "America's Best Graduate Schools, Law, 2016"*

PRESIDENTIAL ELECTION

2012 Presidential Election Results

Area	Obama (%)	Romney (%)	Other (%)
Clark County	56.4	41.9	1.8
U.S.	51.0	47.2	1.8

Note: Results may not add to 100% due to rounding
Source: Dave Leip's Atlas of U.S. Presidential Elections

EMPLOYERS

Major Employers

Company Name	Industry
Barrick Gaming Operations	Casino hotel
City of Las vegas	Executive offices
Coast Casinos	Hotels/motels
Consolidated Electric	Electrical apparatus equipment
Donald J Laughlin	Gambling machines, coin operated
E-T-T	Slot machines
Gaughan South	Casino hotel
Las Vegas Sands	Casino hotel
M Arthur Gensler Jr & Associates	Architectual services
Nevada System of Higher Education	Colleges/universities
Nevada System of Higher Education	General medical/surgical hospitals
New Castle Corp	Casino hotel
New York - New York Hotel and Casino	Casino hotel
Paris Hotel Casino Resort	Casino hotel
Primm Casinos	Hotels/motels
Sam-Will	Casino hotel
Station Casinos	Hotels/motels
Station Casinos	Casino hotel
Stratosphere Gaming	Hotels/motels
Sunrise Hospitality and Medical Center	General medical/surgical hospitals
University Medical Center of Southern NV	General medical/surgical hospitals
Venetian Casino/Resort	Resort hotel

Note: Companies shown are located within the Las Vegas-Henderson-Paradise, NV Metropolitan Statistical Area.
Source: Hoovers.com; Wikipedia

Best Companies to Work For

Zappos.com, headquartered in Las Vegas, is among "The 100 Best Companies to Work For." To pick the best companies, *Fortune* partnered with the Great Place to Work Institute. Two-thirds of a company's score is based on the results of the Institute's Trust Index survey, which is sent to a random sample of employees from each company. The questions related to attitudes about management's credibility, job satisfaction, and camaraderie. The other third of the scoring is based on the company's responses to the Institute's Culture Audit, which includes detailed questions about pay and benefit programs, and a series of open-ended questions about hiring practices, internal communication, training, recognition programs, and diversity efforts. Any company that is at least five years old with more than 1,000 U.S. employees is eligible. *Fortune, "The 100 Best Companies to Work For," 2015*

One Nevada Credit Union, headquartered in Las Vegas, is among the "50 Best Employers for Workers Over 50." Criteria: recruiting practices; opportunities for training, education, and career development; workplace accommodations; alternative work options, such as flexible scheduling, job sharing, and phased retirement; employee health and pension benefits; and retiree benefits. Employers with at least 50 employees based in the U.S. are eligible, including for-profit companies, not-for-profit organizations, and government employers. *AARP, "2013 AARP Best Employers for Workers Over 50"*

Caesars Entertainment, headquartered in Las Vegas, is among the "100 Best Places to Work in IT." To qualify, companies, both public and private, had to have a minimum of 50 IT employees and were selected based on average salary and bonus increases, the percentage of IT staffers promoted, IT staff turnover rates, training and development programs, and the percentage of women and minorities in IT staff and management positions. In addition, *Computerworld* looked at retention efforts, programs for recognizing and rewarding outstanding performances, and benefits such as flextime, elder care and child care, and reimbursement for college tuition and the cost of pursuing technology certifications. *Computerworld, "100 Best Places to Work in IT 2014"*

PUBLIC SAFETY

Crime Rate

Area	All Crimes	Violent Crimes				Property Crimes		
		Murder	Forcible Rape	Robbery	Aggrav. Assault	Burglary	Larceny -Theft	Motor Vehicle Theft
City	3,954.9	6.5	47.0	271.4	433.2	985.4	1,769.3	442.2
Suburbs[1]	2,951.8	3.6	28.5	122.6	294.6	720.0	1,475.8	306.6
Metro[2]	3,694.8	5.7	42.2	232.8	397.3	916.5	1,693.2	407.0
U.S.	3,098.6	4.5	25.2	109.1	229.1	610.0	1,899.4	221.3

Note: Figures are crimes per 100,000 population; (1) All areas within the metro area that are located outside the city limits; (2) Figures cover the Las Vegas-Henderson-Paradise, NV Metropolitan Statistical Area—see Appendix B for areas included
Source: FBI Uniform Crime Reports, 2013

Hate Crimes

Area	Number of Quarters Reported	Number of Incidents per Bias Motivation						
		Race	Religion	Sexual Orientation	Ethnicity	Disability	Gender	Gender Identity
Area[1]	4	27	9	23	6	0	0	0
U.S.	4	2,871	1,031	1,233	655	83	18	31

Note: (1) Figures cover the Las Vegas Metropolitan Police Department.
Source: Federal Bureau of Investigation, Hate Crime Statistics 2013

Identity Theft Consumer Complaints

Area	Complaints	Complaints per 100,000 Population	Rank[2]
MSA[1]	2,068	102.0	57
U.S.	332,646	104.3	-

Note: (1) Figures cover the Las Vegas-Henderson-Paradise, NV Metropolitan Statistical Area—see Appendix B for areas included; (2) Rank ranges from 1 to 380 where 1 indicates greatest number of identity theft complaints per 100,000 population
Source: Federal Trade Commission, Consumer Sentinel Network Data Book for January–December 2014

Fraud and Other Consumer Complaints

Area	Complaints	Complaints per 100,000 Population	Rank[2]
MSA[1]	11,934	588.5	9
U.S.	2,250,205	705.7	-

Note: (1) Figures cover the Las Vegas-Henderson-Paradise, NV Metropolitan Statistical Area—see Appendix B for areas included; (2) Rank ranges from 1 to 380 where 1 indicates greatest number of identity theft complaints per 100,000 population

Source: Federal Trade Commission, Consumer Sentinel Network Data Book for January–December 2014

RECREATION

Culture

Dance[1]	Theatre[1]	Instrumental Music[1]	Vocal Music[1]	Series and Festivals	Museums and Art Galleries[2]	Zoos and Aquariums[3]
3	2	3	0	2	74	1

Note: (1) Professional perfoming groups; (2) Based on organizations with SIC code 8412; (3) AZA-accredited

Source: The Grey House Performing Arts Directory, 2015-16; Association of Zoos & Aquariums, AZA Member Zoos & Aquariums, April 2015; www.AccuLeads.com, April 2015

Professional Sports Teams

Team Name	League	Year Established
No teams are located in the metro area		

Source: Wikipedia, Major Professional Sports Teams of the United States and Canada, April 2015

CLIMATE

Average and Extreme Temperatures

Temperature	Jan	Feb	Mar	Apr	May	Jun	Jul	Aug	Sep	Oct	Nov	Dec	Yr.
Extreme High (°F)	77	87	91	99	109	115	116	116	113	103	87	77	116
Average High (°F)	56	62	69	78	88	99	104	102	94	81	66	57	80
Average Temp. (°F)	45	50	56	65	74	84	90	88	80	68	54	46	67
Average Low (°F)	33	38	43	51	60	69	76	74	66	54	41	34	53
Extreme Low (°F)	8	16	23	31	40	49	60	56	43	26	21	11	8

Note: Figures cover the years 1948-1990

Source: National Climatic Data Center, International Station Meteorological Climate Summary, 9/96

Average Precipitation/Snowfall/Humidity

Precip./Humidity	Jan	Feb	Mar	Apr	May	Jun	Jul	Aug	Sep	Oct	Nov	Dec	Yr.
Avg. Precip. (in.)	0.5	0.4	0.4	0.2	0.2	0.1	0.4	0.5	0.3	0.2	0.4	0.3	4.0
Avg. Snowfall (in.)	1	Tr	Tr	Tr	0	0	0	0	0	0	Tr	Tr	1
Avg. Rel. Hum. 7am (%)	59	52	41	31	26	20	26	31	30	36	47	56	38
Avg. Rel. Hum. 4pm (%)	32	25	20	15	13	10	14	16	16	18	26	31	20

Note: Figures cover the years 1948-1990; Tr = Trace amounts (<0.05 in. of rain; <0.5 in. of snow)

Source: National Climatic Data Center, International Station Meteorological Climate Summary, 9/96

Weather Conditions

Temperature			Daytime Sky			Precipitation		
10°F & below	32°F & below	90°F & above	Clear	Partly cloudy	Cloudy	0.01 inch or more precip.	0.1 inch or more snow/ice	Thunder-storms
< 1	37	134	185	132	48	27	2	13

Note: Figures are average number of days per year and cover the years 1948-1990

Source: National Climatic Data Center, International Station Meteorological Climate Summary, 9/96

HAZARDOUS WASTE

Superfund Sites

Las Vegas has no sites on the EPA's Superfund Final National Priorities List. There are a total of 1,322 Superfund sites on the list in the U.S. *U.S. Environmental Protection Agency, Final National Priorities List, April 14, 2015*

AIR & WATER QUALITY

Air Quality Trends: Ozone

	2004	2005	2006	2007	2008	2009	2010	2011	2012	2013
MSA[1]	0.078	0.082	0.081	0.081	0.074	0.072	0.071	0.074	0.077	0.073

Note: (1) Data covers the Las Vegas-Henderson-Paradise, NV Metropolitan Statistical Area—see Appendix B for areas included. The values shown are the composite ozone concentration averages among trend sites based on the highest fourth daily maximum 8-hour concentration in parts per million. These trends are based on sites having an adequate record of monitoring data during the trend period. Data from exceptional events are included.
Source: U.S. Environmental Protection Agency, Air Quality Monitoring Information, "Air Quality Trends by City, 2000-2013"

Air Quality Index

Area	Percent of Days when Air Quality was...[2]					AQI Statistics[2]	
	Good	Moderate	Unhealthy for Sensitive Groups	Unhealthy	Very Unhealthy	Maximum	Median
MSA[1]	46.3	51.8	1.6	0.3	0.0	158	51

Note: (1) Data covers the Las Vegas-Henderson-Paradise, NV Metropolitan Statistical Area—see Appendix B for areas included; (2) Based on 365 days with AQI data in 2014. Air Quality Index (AQI) is an index for reporting daily air quality. EPA calculates the AQI for five major air pollutants regulated by the Clean Air Act: ground-level ozone, particle pollution (aka particulate matter), carbon monoxide, sulfur dioxide, and nitrogen dioxide. The AQI runs from 0 to 500. The higher the AQI value, the greater the level of air pollution and the greater the health concern. There are six AQI categories: "Good" AQI is between 0 and 50. Air quality is considered satisfactory; "Moderate" AQI is between 51 and 100. Air quality is acceptable; "Unhealthy for Sensitive Groups" When AQI values are between 101 and 150, members of sensitive groups may experience health effects; "Unhealthy" When AQI values are between 151 and 200 everyone may begin to experience health effects; "Very Unhealthy" AQI values between 201 and 300 trigger a health alert; "Hazardous" AQI values over 300 trigger warnings of emergency conditions (not shown).
Source: U.S. Environmental Protection Agency, Air Quality Index Report, 2014

Air Quality Index Pollutants

Area	Percent of Days when AQI Pollutant was...[2]					
	Carbon Monoxide	Nitrogen Dioxide	Ozone	Sulfur Dioxide	Particulate Matter 2.5	Particulate Matter 10
MSA[1]	0.0	1.4	58.1	0.0	37.3	3.3

Note: (1) Data covers the Las Vegas-Henderson-Paradise, NV Metropolitan Statistical Area—see Appendix B for areas included; (2) Based on 365 days with AQI data in 2014. The Air Quality Index (AQI) is an index for reporting daily air quality. EPA calculates the AQI for five major air pollutants regulated by the Clean Air Act: ground-level ozone, particle pollution (also known as particulate matter), carbon monoxide, sulfur dioxide, and nitrogen dioxide. The AQI runs from 0 to 500. The higher the AQI value, the greater the level of air pollution and the greater the health concern.
Source: U.S. Environmental Protection Agency, Air Quality Index Report, 2014

Maximum Air Pollutant Concentrations: Particulate Matter, Ozone, CO and Lead

	Particulate Matter 10 (ug/m³)	Particulate Matter 2.5 Wtd AM (ug/m³)	Particulate Matter 2.5 24-Hr (ug/m³)	Ozone (ppm)	Carbon Monoxide (ppm)	Lead (ug/m³)
MSA[1] Level	169	10.1	26	0.082	3	0.01
NAAQS[2]	150	15	35	0.075	9	0.15
Met NAAQS[2]	No	Yes	Yes	No	Yes	Yes

Note: (1) Data covers the Las Vegas-Henderson-Paradise, NV Metropolitan Statistical Area—see Appendix B for areas included; Data from exceptional events are included; (2) National Ambient Air Quality Standards; ppm = parts per million; ug/m³ = micrograms per cubic meter; n/a not available.
Concentrations: Particulate Matter 10 (coarse particulate)—highest second maximum 24-hour concentration; Particulate Matter 2.5 Wtd AM (fine particulate)—highest weighted annual mean concentration; Particulate Matter 2.5 24-Hour (fine particulate)—highest 98th percentile 24-hour concentration; Ozone—highest fourth daily maximum 8-hour concentration; Carbon Monoxide—highest second maximum non-overlapping 8-hour concentration; Lead—maximum running 3-month average
Source: U.S. Environmental Protection Agency, Air Quality Monitoring Information, "Air Quality Statistics by City, 2013"

Maximum Air Pollutant Concentrations: Nitrogen Dioxide and Sulfur Dioxide

	Nitrogen Dioxide AM (ppb)	Nitrogen Dioxide 1-Hr (ppb)	Sulfur Dioxide AM (ppb)	Sulfur Dioxide 1-Hr (ppb)	Sulfur Dioxide 24-Hr (ppb)
MSA[1] Level	14	n/a	n/a	7	n/a
NAAQS[2]	53	100	30	75	140
Met NAAQS[2]	Yes	n/a	n/a	Yes	n/a

Note: (1) Data covers the Las Vegas-Henderson-Paradise, NV Metropolitan Statistical Area—see Appendix B for areas included; Data from exceptional events are included; (2) National Ambient Air Quality Standards; ppm = parts per million; ug/m³ = micrograms per cubic meter; n/a not available.
Concentrations: Nitrogen Dioxide AM—highest arithmetic mean concentration; Nitrogen Dioxide 1-Hr—highest 98th percentile 1-hour daily maximum concentration; Sulfur Dioxide AM—highest annual mean concentration; Sulfur Dioxide 1-Hr—highest 99th percentile 1-hour daily maximum concentration; Sulfur Dioxide 24-Hr—highest second maximum 24-hour concentration
Source: U.S. Environmental Protection Agency, Air Quality Monitoring Information, "Air Quality Statistics by City, 2013"

Drinking Water

Water System Name	Pop. Served	Primary Water Source Type	Violations[1] Health Based	Violations[1] Monitoring/ Reporting
Las Vegas Valley Water District	1,347,550	Surface	0	0

Note: (1) Based on violation data from January 1, 2014 to December 31, 2014 (includes unresolved violations from earlier years)
Source: U.S. Environmental Protection Agency, Office of Ground Water and Drinking Water, Safe Drinking Water Information System (based on data extracted January 27, 2015)

Los Angeles, California

Background

There is as much to say about Los Angeles as there are unincorporated and incorporated municipalities under its jurisdiction. The city is immense, and in the words of one of its residents, "If you want a life in LA, you need a car."

Los Angeles acquired its many neighborhoods and communities such as Hollywood, Glendale, Burbank, and Alhambra when those cities wanted to share in the water piped into Los Angeles from the Owens River. To obtain it, the cities were required to join the Los Angeles municipal system. Due to those annexations, Los Angeles is now one of the largest U.S. cities in both acreage and population. It is also one of the most racially diverse.

The city tries to connect the communities in its far-flung empire through a rather Byzantine system of freeways which gives Los Angeles its reputation as a congested, car-oriented culture, where people have to schedule their days around the three-hour rush hour.

Despite these challenges, Los Angeles is a city with a diversified economy and 325 days of sunshine a year. What was founded in 1781 as a sleepy pueblo of 44 people, with chickens roaming the footpaths, is now a city leading the nation in commerce, transportation, finance, and, especially, entertainment—with three-quarters of all motion pictures made in the United States still produced in the Los Angeles area, and headquarters of such major studios as MGM and Universal located in "municipalities" unto themselves.

Playa Vista, the first new community to be established on the Westside of Los Angeles in more than 50 years, is home to Electronic Arts, the world's leading video game publisher. Lincoln Properties is currently building office buildings totaling more than 820,000 square feet in the eastern portion of Playa Vista community known as "The Campus at Playa Vista." The National Basketball Association Clippers has a new training facility at the Campus, which is also home to a basketball-themed public park, a fitting way to celebrate the 2011 NBA champion Lakers.

The arts are center-stage in Los Angeles. The new home of the Getty Center and Museum, an architectural masterpiece designed by Richard Meier and built on a commanding hill, is a dramatic venue for visual arts and other events. The Los Angeles Opera, under the direction of Placido Domingo, offers a lively season of operas as well as recitals by such luminaries as Cecilia Bartoli and Renee Fleming. The Los Angeles Philharmonic now performs in the Walt Disney Concert Hall, dedicated in October of 2003. This hall was designed by Frank Gehry, famous as the architect of the Guggenheim Museum at Bilbao.

The downtown's first modern industrial park, The Los Angeles World Trade Center, is a 20-acre project that is downtown's only foreign trade zone.

Inland and up foothill slopes, both high and low temperatures become more extreme and the average relative humidity drops. Relative humidity is frequently high near the coast, but may be quite low along the foothills. Most rain falls November through March, while the summers are very dry. Destructive flash floods occasionally develop in and below some mountain canyons. Snow is often visible on the nearby mountains in the winter, but is extremely rare in the coastal basin. Thunderstorms are infrequent.

The climate of Los Angeles is normally pleasant and mild throughout the year, with unusual differences in temperature, humidity, cloudiness, fog, rain, and sunshine over fairly short distances in the metro area. Low clouds are common at night and in the morning along the coast during spring and summer. Near the foothills, clouds form later in the day and clear earlier. Annual percentages of fog and cloudiness are greatest near the ocean. Sunshine totals are highest on the inland side of the city.

At times, high concentrations of air pollution affect the Los Angeles coastal basin and adjacent areas, when lack of air movement combines with an atmospheric inversion. In the fall and winter, the Santa Ana winds pick up considerable amounts of dust and can blow strongly in the northern and eastern sections of the city and in outlying areas in the north and east; these rarely reach coastal sections of the city.

Rankings

General Rankings

- Among the 50 largest U.S. cities, Los Angeles placed #13 in Vocativ's "semi-exhaustive, mostly scientific" city Livability Index for people aged 35 and under. Average salary, unemployment rates, rents, and other living costs were considered, along with crime rates, weather, public transportation, access to music and sports, and "lifestyle metrics" such as the price of dinner at Buffalo Wild Wings and an ounce of high-quality weed. *vocative.com, "The Livability Index: The Best U.S. Cities for People 35 and Under," December 9, 2014*

- Los Angeles was selected as one of America's best cities by *Bloomberg Businessweek*. The city ranked #50 out of 50. Criteria: leisure attributes (the number of restaurants, bars, libraries, museums, professional sports teams, and park acres by population); educational attributes (public school performance, the number of colleges, and graduate degree holders); economic factors (2011 income and June and July 2012 unemployment); crime; and air quality. *Bloomberg BusinessWeek, "America's Best Cities," September 26, 2012*

- The human resources consulting firm Mercer ranked 230 cities worldwide in terms of overall quality of life. Los Angeles ranked #47. Criteria: political, social, economic, and socio-cultural factors; medical and health considerations; schools and education; public services and transportation; recreation; consumer goods; housing; and natural environment. *Mercer, "Mercer 2015 Quality of Living Survey," March 4, 2015*

Business/Finance Rankings

- Recognizing the sizeable percentage of American workers who are self-employed, NerdWallet editors assessed the country's cities according to percentage of freelancers, median rental costs, and affordability of median healthcare costs. By these criteria, Los Angeles placed #1 among the best cities for independent workers. *www.nerdwallet.com, "Best Cities for Freelancers," February 25, 2014*

- Building on the U.S. Department of Labor's Occupational Information Network Data Collection Program, the Brookings Institution defined STEM occupations and job opportunities for STEM workers at various levels of educational attainment. The Los Angeles metro area was one of the ten metro areas where workers in low-education-level STEM jobs earn the lowest relative wages. *www.brookings.edu, "The Hidden Stem Economy," June 10, 2013*

- Analysts for the business website 24/7 Wall Street looked at the local government report "Tax Rates and Tax Burdens in the District of Columbia—A Nationwide Comparison" to determine where a family of three at two different income levels would pay the least and the most in state and local taxes. Among the ten cities with the highest state and local tax burdens was Los Angeles, at #8. *247wallst.com, American Cities with the Highest (and Lowest) Taxes, February 25, 2013*

- Based on metro area social media reviews, the employment opinion group Glassdoor surveyed 50 of the largest U.S. metro areas on measures including compensation and benefits, satisfaction with management, business outlook, and number of employers hiring. The Los Angeles metro area was ranked #13 in overall employee satisfaction. *www.glassdoor.com, "Employment Satisfaction Report Card by City," June 13, 2014*

- In a survey of economic confidence in the nation's 50 largest metropolitan areas conducted January–December 2014, the Los Angeles metro area placed #11, according to Gallup's 2014 Economic Confidence Index. *Gallup, "San Jose and San Francisco Lead in Economic Confidence," March 19, 2015*

- Using data from the Council for Community and Economic Research's 2013 Annual Report, NerdWallet ranked the 100 U.S. cities with the most expensive cost of living. Cities in California and in the Northeast topped the list. Of the cities with the highest cost of living, Los Angeles ranked #19. *NerdWallet.com, "Most Expensive Cities in America," June 4, 2014*

- The Brookings Institution ranked the 50 largest cities in the U.S. based on income inequality. Los Angeles was ranked #9. (#1 = greatest ineqality). Criteria: the cities were ranked based on the "95/20 ratio," a figure representing the income at which a household earns more than 95 percent of all other households, divided by the income at which a household earns more than only 20 percent of all other households. *Brookings Institution, "Income Inequality in America's 50 Largest Cities, 2007-2013," March 17, 2015*

- MarketWatch shared a *24/7 Wall St.* analysis of the District of Columbia's Office of Revenue Analysis report on the estimated property, sales, auto, and income taxes paid in the largest city of each state in 2011. Of the U.S. cities with the highest tax burden, Los Angeles ranked #8. *Marketwatch.com, "10 U.S. Cities with the Highest Taxes," March 2, 2013*

- CareerBliss, an employment and careers website, analyzed U.S. Bureau of Labor Statistics data, more than 30,000 company reviews from employees and former employees, and job openings over a 12-month period to arrive at its list of the best and worst places in the United States to look for a job. Los Angeles was #1 among the best places. *CareerBliss.com, "CareerBliss 2013 Best and Worst Cities to Find a Job," January 8, 2013*

- Los Angeles was ranked #34 out of 100 metro areas in terms of economic performance (#1 = best) during the recession and recovery from trough quarter through the second quarter of 2013. Criteria: percent change in employment; percentage point change in unemployment rate; percent change in gross metropolitan product; percent change in House Price Index. *Brookings Institution, MetroMonitor: Tracking Economic Recession and Recovery in America's 100 Largest Metropolitan Areas, September 2013*

- The finance site *24/7 Wall St.* identified the metropolitan areas that have the smallest and largest pay disparities between men and women, comparing the median earnings for the past 12 months of both men and women working full-time in the country's 100 largest metropolitan statistical areas. Of the ten best-paying metros for women, the Los Angeles metro area ranked #2. *24/7 Wall St., "The Best (and Worst) Paying Cities for Women," March 6, 2015*

- Payscale.com ranked the 20 largest metro areas in terms of wage growth. The Los Angeles metro area ranked #7. Criteria: private-sector wage growth between the 1st quarter of 2014 and the 1st quarter of 2015. *PayScale, "Wage Trends by Metro Area," 1st Quarter, 2015*

- For its annual survey of the "Most Expensive U.S. Cities to Live In," Kiplinger applied Cost of Living Index statistics developed by the Council for Community and Economic Research to U.S. Census Bureau population and median household income data for cities with populations above 50,000. In the resulting ranking, Los Angeles ranked #9. *Kiplinger.com, "Most Expensive U.S. Cities to Live In," May 2014*

- Los Angeles was identified as one of "America's Hardest-Working Towns." The city ranked #13 out of 25. Criteria: average hours worked per capita; willingness to work during personal time; number of dual income households; local employment rate. *Parade, "What is America's Hardest-Working Town?," April 15, 2012*

- *Forbes* reports that Los Angeles was identified as one of the happiest cities to work in by CareerBliss.com, an online community for career advancement. The city ranked #6 out of 10. Criteria: work-life balance; an employee's relationship with his or her boss and co-workers; general work environment; compensation; opportunities for advancement; company culture; and resources. *Forbes.com, "The 10 Happiest and Unhappiest Cities to Work in Right Now," January 16, 2015*

- The Los Angeles metro area appeared on the Milken Institute "2013 Best Performing Cities" list. Rank: #42 out of 200 large metro areas. Criteria: job growth; wage and salary growth; high-tech output growth. *Milken Institute, "Best-Performing Cities 2014," January 2015*

- *Forbes* ranked the 200 most populous metro areas to determine the nation's "Best Places for Business and Careers." The Los Angeles metro area was ranked #117. Criteria: costs (business and living); job growth (past and projected); income growth; educational attainment (college and high school); projected economic growth; cultural and recreational opportunities; net migration patterns; number of highly ranked colleges. *Forbes, "The Best Places for Business and Careers 2014," July 23, 2014*

- Mercer Human Resources Consulting ranked 211 urban areas worldwide in terms of cost-of-living. Los Angeles ranked #62 (the lower the ranking, the higher the cost-of-living). The survey measured the comparative cost of over 200 items (such as housing, food, clothing, household goods, transportation, and entertainment) in each location. *Mercer, "2014 Cost of Living Survey," July 10, 2014*

Culture/Performing Arts Rankings

- Los Angeles was selected as one of the ten best large U.S. cities in which to be a moviemaker. Of cities with a population over 400,000, the city was ranked #2. Criteria: film community; access to new films; access to equipment; cost of living; tax incentives. *MovieMaker Magazine, "Best Places to Live and Work as a Moviemaker: 2013," January 22, 2015*

- Los Angeles was selected as one of America's top cities for the arts. The city ranked #11 in the big city (population 500,000 and over) category. Criteria: readers' top choices for arts travel destinations based on the richness and variety of visual arts sites, activities and events. *American Style, "2012 Top 25 Arts Destinations," June 2012*

Dating/Romance Rankings

- A *Cosmopolitan* magazine article surveyed the gender balance and other factors to arrive at a list of the best and worst cities for women to meet single guys. Los Angeles was #1 among the best for single women looking for dates. *www.cosmopolitan.com, "Working the Ratio," October 1, 2013*

- Gizmodo reported on data that Facebook collected on the best American cities for singles. Criteria included highest percentage of single people, the widest single female-to-single male ratio (and vice versa), and the best probability of relationship formation. Among the top 50 American population centers Los Angeles ranked #2. *gizmodo.com, "The Best Places to Find Hot Singles (According to Facebook)," February 13, 2014*

- Of the 100 U.S. cities surveyed by *Men's Health* in its quest to identify the nation's best cities for dating and forming relationships, Los Angeles was ranked #33 for online dating (#1 = best). *Men's Health, "The Best and Worst Cities for Online Dating," January 30, 2013*

- Los Angeles was selected as one of America's best cities for singles by the readers of *Travel + Leisure* in their annual "America's Favorite Cities" survey. The city was ranked #8 out of 20. Criteria included good-looking locals, cool shopping, and hipster-magnet coffee bars. *Travel + Leisure, "America's Best Cities for Singles," January 23, 2015*

- Los Angeles was selected as one of the best cities for single women by *Rent.com*. Criteria: high single male-to-female ratio. *Rent.com, "Top Cities for Single Women," March 7, 2013*

Education Rankings

- Personal finance website *WalletHub* analyzed the 150 largest U.S. metropolitan statistical areas to determine where the most educated Americans are choosing to settle. Criteria: educational attainment; percentage of workers with jobs in computer, engineering, and science fields; quality and size of each metro area's universities. Los Angeles was ranked #79 (#1 = most educated city). *www.WalletHub.com, "2014's Most and Least Educated Cities*

- Los Angeles was selected as one of America's most literate cities. The city ranked #63 out of the 77 largest U.S. cities. Criteria: number of booksellers; library resources; Internet resources; educational attainment; periodical publishing resources; newspaper circulation. *Central Connecticut State University, "America's Most Literate Cities, 2014," April 8, 2015*

Environmental Rankings

- CNNMoney based its list of the nation's ten most polluted cities on the annual State of the Air report prepared by the American Lung Association, which noted that the cities with the worst air pollution also had some of the highest incidences of heart and lung disease. At #4 (#1 = worst), Los Angeles was among those with the poorest air quality. *money.cnn.com, "10 Most Polluted Cities," April 24, 2013*

- The Los Angeles metro area came in at #148 for the relative comfort of its climate on Sperling's list of "chill cities," as measured by the Sperling Heat Index. All 361 metro areas are included. Criteria included daytime high temperatures, nighttime low temperatures, dew point, and relative humidity at the high temperatures. *www.bertsperling.com, "Sperling's Chill Cities," July 18, 2013*

- Sperling's BestPlaces assessed 379 metropolitan areas of the United States for the likelihood of dangerously extreme weather events or earthquakes. In general the Southeast and South-Central regions have the highest risk of weather extremes and earthquakes, while the Pacific Northwest enjoys the lowest risk. Of the least risky metropolitan areas, the Los Angeles metro area was ranked #183. *www.bestplaces.net, "Safest Places from Natural Disasters," April 2011*

- Los Angeles was identified as one of America's dirtiest metro areas by *Forbes*. The area ranked #17 out of 20. Criteria: air quality; water quality; toxic releases; superfund sites. *Forbes, "America's 20 Dirtiest Cities," December 10, 2012*

- The U.S. Environmental Protection Agency (EPA) released a list of large U.S. metropolitan areas with the most ENERGY STAR certified buildings in 2014. The Los Angeles metro area was ranked #2 out of 25. *U.S. Environmental Protection Agency, "Top Cities With the Most ENERGY STAR Certified Buildings in 2014," March 25, 2015*

- Los Angeles was highlighted as one of the 25 most ozone-polluted metro areas in the U.S. during 2011 through 2013. The area ranked #1. *American Lung Association, State of the Air 2015*

- Los Angeles was highlighted as one of the 25 metro areas most polluted by year-round particle pollution (Annual PM 2.5) in the U.S. during 2011 through 2013. The area ranked #5. *American Lung Association, State of the Air 2015*

- Los Angeles was highlighted as one of the 25 metro areas most polluted by short-term particle pollution (24-hour PM 2.5) in the U.S. during 2011 through 2013. The area ranked #5. *American Lung Association, State of the Air 2015*

Food/Drink Rankings

- According to Fodor's Travel, Los Angeles placed #5 among the best U.S. cities for food-truck cuisine. *www.fodors.com, "America's Best Food Truck Cities," December 20, 2013*

- *Men's Health* ranked 100 major U.S. cities in terms of alcohol intoxication. Los Angeles ranked #41 (#1 = most sober).Criteria: binge drinking; alcohol-related traffic accidents, arrests, and fatalities. *Men's Health, "The Drunkest Cities in America," November 19, 2013*

- Los Angeles was identified as one of the most vegetarian-friendly cities in America by GrubHub.com, the nation's largest food ordering service. The city ranked #8 out of 10. Criteria: percentage of vegetarian restaurants. *GrubHub.com, "Top Vegetarian-Friendly Cities," July 18, 2012*

- Los Angeles was selected as one of America's best cities for hamburgers by the readers of *Travel + Leisure* in their annual America's Favorite Cities survey. The city was ranked #10 out of 10. *Travel + Leisure, "America's Best Burger Cities," August 25, 2013*

- Los Angeles was selected as one of America's 10 most vegan-friendly cities. The city was ranked #3. *People for the Ethical Treatment of Animals, "Top Vegan-Friendly Cities of 2013," June 11, 2013*

- Angel Stadium of Anaheim (Los Angeles Angels' was selected as one of PETA's "Top 10 Vegetarian-Friendly Major League Ballparks" for 2013. The park ranked #5. *People for the Ethical Treatment of Animals, "Top 10 Vegetarian-Friendly Major League Ballparks, " June 12, 2013*

Health/Fitness Rankings

- Analysts who tracked obesity rates in the nation's largest metro areas (those with populations above one million) found that the Los Angeles metro area was one of the ten major metros where residents were least likely to be obese, defined as a BMI score of 30 or above. *www.gallup.com, "Boulder, Colo., Residents Still Least Likely to Be Obese," April 4, 2014*

- For each of the 50 most populous metro areas in the United States, the American College of Sports Medicine's American Fitness Index evaluated infrastructure, community assets, and policies that encourage healthy and fit lifestyles, including preventive health behaviors, levels of chronic disease conditions, health care access, and community resources and policies that support physical activity. The Los Angeles metro area ranked #29 for "community fitness." Personal health indicators were considered as well as community and environmental indicators. *www.americanfitnessindex.org, "ACSM American Fitness Index Health and Community Fitness Status of the 50 Largest Metropolitan Areas," May 2013*

- The Los Angeles metro area was identified as one of the worst cities for bed bugs in America by pest control company Orkin. The area ranked #2 out of 50 based on the number of bed bug treatments Orkin performed from January to December 2013. *Orkin, "Chicago Tops Bed Bug Cities List for Second Year in a Row," January 16, 2014*

- Los Angeles was identified as one of 15 cities with the highest increase in bed bug activity in the U.S. by pest control provider Terminix. The city ranked #11. Criteria: cities with the largest percentage gains in bed bug customer calls from January–May 2013 compared to the same time period in 2012. *Terminix, "Cities with Highest Increases in Bed Bug Activity," July 9, 2013*

- Los Angeles was selected as one of the 25 fattest cities in America by *Men's Fitness Online*. It ranked #9 out of America's 50 largest cities. Criteria: fitness centers and sport stores; nutrition; sports participation; TV viewing; overweight/sedentary; junk food; air quality; geography; commute; parks and open space; city recreational facilities; access to healthcare; motivation; mayor and city initiatives; state obesity initiatives. *Men's Fitness, "The Fittest and Fattest Cities in America," March 5, 2012*

- Los Angeles was identified as a "2013 Spring Allergy Capital." The area ranked #77 out of 100. Three groups of factors were used to identify the most severe cities for people with allergies during the spring season: annual pollen levels; medicine utilization; access to board-certified allergists. *Asthma and Allergy Foundation of America, "Spring Allergy Capitals 2013"*

- Los Angeles was identified as a "2013 Fall Allergy Capital." The area ranked #76 out of 100. Three groups of factors were used to identify the most severe cities for people with allergies during the fall season: annual pollen levels; medicine utilization; access to board-certified allergists. *Asthma and Allergy Foundation of America, "Fall Allergy Capitals 2013"*

- Los Angeles was identified as a "2013 Asthma Capital." The area ranked #46 out of the nation's 100 largest metropolitan areas. Twelve factors were used to identify the most challenging places to live for people with asthma: estimated prevalence; self-reported prevalence; crude death rate for asthma; annual pollen score; annual air quality; public smoking laws; number of board-certified asthma specialists; school inhaler access laws; rescue medication use; controller medication use; uninsured rate; poverty rate. *Asthma and Allergy Foundation of America, "Asthma Capitals 2013"*

- *Men's Health* ranked 100 major U.S. cities in terms of the best and worst cities for men. Los Angeles ranked #31. Criteria: thirty-three data points were examined covering health, fitness, and quality of life. *Men's Health, "The Best & Worst Cities for Men 2014," December 6, 2013*

- Los Angeles was selected as one of the best metropolitan areas for hospital care in America by *HealthGrades.com*. The rankings are based on a comprehensive study of patient death and complication rates in the nation's nearly 5,000 hospitals. Hospitals performing in the top 5% nationwide across 26 different medical procedures and diagnoses were identified. *HealthGrades.com* then ranked cities by the highest percentage of these Distinguished Hospitals for Clinical Excellence™. The Los Angeles metro area ranked #22. *HealthGrades.com, "America's Top 50 Cities for Hospital Care," January 21, 2012*

- The Los Angeles metro area appeared in the 2013 Gallup-Healthways Well-Being Index. The area ranked #43 out of 189. The Gallup-Healthways Well-Being Index score is an average of six sub-indexes, which individually examine life evaluation, emotional health, work environment, physical health, healthy behaviors, and access to basic necessities. Results are based on telephone interviews conducted as part of the Gallup-Healthways Well-Being Index survey January 2–December 29, 2012, and January 2–December 30, 2013, with a random sample of 531,630 adults, aged 18 and older, living in metropolitan areas in the 50 U.S. states and the District of Columbia. *Gallup-Healthways, "State of American Well-Being," March 25, 2014*

- The Los Angeles metro area was identified as one of "America's Most Stressful Cities" by *Sperling's BestPlaces*. The metro area ranked #14 out of 50. Criteria: unemployment rate; suicide rate; commute time; mental health; poor rest; alcohol use; violent crime rate; property crime rate; cloudy days annually. *Sperling's BestPlaces, www.BestPlaces.net, "Stressful Cities 2012*

Real Estate Rankings

- The Los Angeles metro area appeared on Realtor.com's list of the hottest housing markets to watch in 2015. Criteria: strong housing growth; affordable prices; and fast-paced sales. *Realtor.com®, "Top 10 Hot Housing Markets to Watch in 2015," December 4, 2014*

- Using data from the housing-market research firm RealtyTrac, Yahoo! Finance researchers listed the housing markets in which housing affordability is deteriorating most, factoring in interest rates as well as median home prices. The Los Angeles metro area was among the least affordable housing markets according to the percentage difference in the income required to buy a home in December 2013 as opposed to in December 2012. *news.yahoo.com, "10 Cities Where Ordinary People Can No Longer Afford Homes," March 5, 2014*

- The Los Angeles metro area was identified as one of the nation's 20 hottest housing markets in 2015.Criteria: median number of days homes were spending on the market in March 2015. The area ranked #8. *Realtor.com, "These Are the 20 Hottest Housing Markets in the U.S. Right Now," April 8, 2015*

- Los Angeles was ranked #56 out of 275 metro areas in terms of house price appreciation in 2014 (#1 = highest rate). *Federal Housing Finance Agency, House Price Index, 4th Quarter 2014*

- The Los Angeles metro area was identified as one of the 20 best housing markets in the U.S. in 2014. The area ranked #20 out of 178 markets with a home price appreciation of 10.8%. Criteria: year-over-year change of median sales price of existing single-family homes between the 4th quarter of 2013 and the 4th quarter of 2014. *National Association of Realtors®, Median Sales Price of Existing Single-Family Homes for Metropolitan Areas, 4th Quarter 2014*

- The Los Angeles metro area was identified as one of the 20 least affordable housing markets in the U.S. in 2014. The area ranked #5 out of 178 markets. Criteria: whether or not a typical family could qualify for a mortgage loan on a typical home. *National Association of Realtors®, Affordability Index of Existing Single-Family Homes for Metropolitan Areas, 2014*

- Los Angeles was ranked #223 out of 226 metro areas in terms of housing affordability in 2014 by the National Association of Home Builders (#1 = most affordable). The NAHB-Wells Fargo Housing Opportunity Index (HOI) for a given area is defined as the share of homes sold in that area that would have been affordable to a family earning the local median income, based on standard mortgage underwriting criteria. *National Association of Home Builders®, NAHB-Wells Fargo Housing Opportunity Index, 4th Quarter 2014*

Safety Rankings

- Symantec, in partnership with Sperling's BestPlaces, ranked the 50 largest cities in the U.S. in terms of their vulnerability to cybercrime. The city ranked #35. Criteria: number of cyberattacks and potential infections; level of Internet access; expenditures on smartphones and computer hardware/software; wireless hotspots; broadband connectivity; Internet usage; online purchases. *Symantec, "Riskiest Online Cities of 2012" February 15, 2012*

- Allstate ranked the 200 largest cities in America in terms of driver safety. Los Angeles ranked #188. Allstate researchers analyzed internal property damage claims over a two-year period from January 2011 to December 2012. A weighted average of the two-year numbers determined the annual percentages. *Allstate, "Allstate America's Best Drivers Report, 2014"*

- Los Angeles was identified as one of the safest large cities in America by CQ Press. All 32 cities with populations of 500,000 or more that reported crime rates in 2012 for murder, rape, robbery, aggravated assault, burglary, and motor vehicle thefts were ranked. The city ranked #5 out of the top 10. *CQ Press, City Crime Rankings 2014*

- The National Insurance Crime Bureau ranked 380 metro areas in the U.S. in terms of per capita rates of vehicle theft. The Los Angeles metro area ranked #29 (#1 = highest rate). Criteria: number of vehicle theft offenses per 100,000 inhabitants in 2012. *National Insurance Crime Bureau, "Hot Spots 2012," June 26, 2013*

Seniors/Retirement Rankings

- From its Best Cities for Successful Aging indexes, the Milken Institute generated rankings for metropolitan areas, weighing data in eight categories—health care, wellness, living arrangements, transportation, financial characteristics, education and employment opportunities, community engagement, and overall livability. The Los Angeles metro area was ranked #66 overall in the large metro area category. *Milken Institute, "Best Cities for Successful Aging, 2014"*

Sports/Recreation Rankings

- *Card Player* magazine scoured North America to identify the top five metropolitan areas where a player can access the types of games that make launching a poker career possible. The Los Angeles metro area ranked #1. *Card Player, "The Top Five Cities to Launch Your Poker Career," April 2, 2014*
- Los Angeles was chosen as one of America's best cities for bicycling. The city ranked #32 out of 50. Criteria: robust cycling infrastructure; vibrant bike culture. The editors only considered cities with populations of 95,000 or more. *Bicycling, "America's Top 50 Bike-Friendly Cities," May 23, 2012*

Transportation Rankings

- Business Insider presented a Walk Score ranking of public transportation in 316 U.S. cities and thousands of city neighborhoods in which Los Angeles earned the #9-ranked "Transit Score," awarded for frequency, type of route, and distance between stops. *www.businessinsider.com, "The US Cities with the Best Public Transportation Systems," January 30, 2014*
- NerdWallet surveyed average annual car insurance premiums in 125 U.S. cities to identify the least expensive U.S. cities in which to insure a car. Locations with no-fault insurance laws was a strong determinant. Los Angeles came in at #22 for the most expensive rates. *www.nerdwallet.com, "Best Cities for Cheap Car Insurance," February 3, 2014*
- Los Angeles appeared on *Trapster.com's* list of the 10 most-active U.S. cities for speed traps. The city ranked #2 of 10. *Trapster.com* is a community platform accessed online and via smartphone app that alerts drivers to traps, hazards and other traffic issues nearby. *Trapster.com, "Speeders Beware: Cities With the Most Speed Traps," February 10, 2012*
- Los Angeles was identified as one of the most congested metro areas in the U.S. The area ranked #2 out of 10. Criteria: yearly delay per auto commuter in hours. *Texas A&M Transportation Institute, "2012 Urban Mobility Report," December 2012*
- The Los Angeles metro area appeared on *Forbes* list of places with the most extreme commutes. The metro area ranked #5 out of 10. Criteria: average travel time; percentage of mega commuters. Mega-commuters travel more than 90 minutes and 50 miles each way to work. *Forbes.com, "The Cities with the Most Extreme Commutes," March 5, 2013*

Women/Minorities Rankings

- The Daily Beast surveyed the nation's cities for highest percentage of singles and lowest divorce rate, plus other measures, to determine "emotional intelligence"—happiness, confidence, kindness—which, researchers say, has a strong correlation with people's satisfaction with their romantic relationships. Los Angeles placed #21. *www.thedailybeast.com, "Best Cities to Find Love and Stay in Love," February 14, 2014*

- To determine the best metro areas for working women, the personal finance website NerdWallet considered city size as well as relevant economic metrics—high salaries, narrow pay differential by gender, prevalence of women in the highest-paying industries, and population growth over 2010–2012. Of the large U.S. cities examined, the Los Angeles metro area held the #6 position. *www.nerdwallet.com, "Best Places for Women in the Workforce," May 19, 2013*

- *Women's Health* examined U.S. cities and identified the 100 best cities for women. Los Angeles was ranked #45. Criteria: 30 categories were examined from obesity and breast cancer rates to commuting times and hours spent working out. *Women's Health, "Best Cities for Women 2012"*

- Los Angeles was selected as one of the best cities for young Latinos in 2013 by mun2, a national cable television broadcast network. The city ranked #5. Criteria: U.S. cities with populations over 500,000 residents were evaluated on the following criteria: number of young latinos; jobs; friendliness; cost of living; fun. *mun2.tv, "Best Cities for Young Latinos 2013*

Miscellaneous Rankings

- Los Angeles was selected as a 2013 Digital Cities Survey winner. The city ranked #9 in the large city (250,000 or more population) category. The survey examined and assessed how city governments are utilizing information technology to operate and deliver quality service to their customers and citizens. Survey questions focused on implementation and adoption of online service delivery; planning and governance; and the infrastructure and architecture that make the transformation to digital government possible. *Center for Digital Government, "2013 Digital Cities Survey," November 7, 2013*

- *Travel + Leisure* invited readers to rate cities on indicators such as aloofness, "smarty-pants residents," highbrow cultural offerings, high-end shopping, artisanal coffeehouses, conspicuous eco-consciousness, and more in order to identify the nation's snobbiest cities. Cities large and small made the list; among them was Los Angeles, at #16. *www.travelandleisure.com, "America's Snobbiest Cities, June 2013*

- The watchdog site Charity Navigator conducts an annual study of charities in the nation's major markets both to analyze statistical differences in their financial, accountability, and transparency practices and to track year-to-year variations in individual communities. The Los Angeles metro area was ranked #13 among the 30 metro markets. *www.charitynavigator.org, "Metro Market Study 2013," June 1, 2013*

- According to *Condé Nast Traveler* magazine's 2013 Readers' Choice Survey of American cities, Los Angeles was rated #6 (#1 = worst) among the ten most unfriendly. *www.cntraveler.com, "The Friendliest and Unfriendliest Cities in the U.S.," July 30, 2013*

- Ink Army reported on a survey by the website TotalBeauty calculating the number of tattoo shops per 100,000 residents in order to determine the U.S. cities with the most tattoo acceptance. Los Angeles took the #10 slot. *inkarmy.com, "Most Tattoo Friendly Cities in the United States," November 1, 2013*

- Business Insider reports on the 2013 Trick-or-Treat Index compiled by the real estate site Zillow, which used its own Home Value Index and Walk Score along with population density and local crime stats to determine that Los Angeles ranked #6 for "how much candy it gives out versus how far kids have to walk to get it." Zillow also zeroes in on the best neighborhoods in its top 20 cities. *www.businessinsider.com, "These Are the Best Cities for Trick-or-Treating," October 15, 2013*

- The Harris Poll's Happiness Index survey revealed that of the top ten U.S. markets, the Los Angeles metro area residents ranked #5 in happiness. Criteria included strong assent to positive statements and strong disagreement with negative ones, and degree of agreement with a series of statements about respondents' personal relationships and general outlook. The online survey was conducted between July 14 and July 30, 2013. *www.harrisinteractive.com, "Dallas/Fort Worth Is "Happiest" City among America's Top Ten Markets," September 4, 2013*

- Los Angeles was selected as one of America's funniest cities by the Humor Research Lab at the University of Colorado. The city ranked #7 out of 10. Criteria: frequency of visits to comedy websites; number of comedy clubs per square mile; traveling comedians' ratings of each city's comedy-club audiences; number of famous comedians born in each city per capita; number of famous funny tweeters living in each city per capita; number of comedy radio stations available in each city; frequency of humor-related web searches originating in each city. *The New York Times, "So These Professors Walk Into a Comedy Club…," April 20, 2014*

- Energizer Personal Care, the makers of Edge® shave gel, in partnership with Sperling's BestPlaces, ranked 50 major metro areas in terms of everyday irritations. The Los Angeles metro area ranked #6. Criteria: high male-to-female ratio; poor sports team performance and high ticket prices; slow traffic; lack of job availability; unaffordable housing; extreme weather; lack of nightlife and fitness options. *Energizer Personal Care, "Most Irritatng Cities for Guys," August 26, 2013*

- Mars Chocolate North America, the makers of COMBOS®, in partnership with Sperling's BestPlaces, ranked 50 major metro areas in terms of their "manliness." The Los Angeles metro area ranked #46. Criteria: number of professional sports teams; number of nearby NASCAR tracks and racing events; manly lifestyle; concentration of manly retail stores; manly occupations per capita; salty snack sales; "Board of Manliness" rankings. *Mars Chocolate North America, "America's Manliest Cities 2012"*

- Los Angeles was selected as one of the most tattooed cities in America by *Lovelyish.com*. The city was ranked #10. Criteria: number of tattoo shops per capita. *Lovelyish.com, "Top Ten: Most Tattooed Cities in America," October 17, 2012*

- Los Angeles was selected as one of "America's Best Cities for Hipsters" by *Travel + Leisure*. The city was ranked #15 out of 20. Criteria: live music; coffee bars; independent boutiques; best microbrews; offbeat and tech-savvy locals. *Travel + Leisure, "America's Best Cities for Hipsters," November 2013*

- The National Alliance to End Homelessness ranked the 100 most populous metro areas in terms the rate of homelessness. The Los Angeles metro area ranked #6. Criteria: number of homeless people per 10,000 population in 2011. *National Alliance to End Homelessness, The State of Homelessness in America 2012*

- The financial education website CreditDonkey compiled a list of the ten "best" cities of the future, based on percentage of housing built in 1990 or later, population change since 2010, and construction jobs as a percentage of population. Also considered were two more futuristic criteria: number of DeLorean cars available for purchase and number of spaceport companies and proposed spaceports. Los Angeles was scored #1. *www.creditDonkey.com, "In the Future, Almost All of America's 'Best' Cities Will Be on the West Coast, Report Says," February 14, 2014*

Business Environment

CITY FINANCES

City Government Finances

Component	2012 ($000)	2012 ($ per capita)
Total Revenues	14,016,535	3,696
Total Expenditures	15,611,941	4,116
Debt Outstanding	23,104,186	6,092
Cash and Securities[1]	41,433,774	10,925

Note: (1) Cash and security holdings of a government at the close of its fiscal year, including those of its dependent agencies, utilities, and liquor stores.
Source: U.S Census Bureau, State & Local Government Finances 2012

City Government Revenue by Source

Source	2012 ($000)	2012 ($ per capita)
General Revenue		
From Federal Government	454,129	120
From State Government	351,703	93
From Local Governments	41,622	11
Taxes		
Property	1,701,742	449
Sales and Gross Receipts	1,548,665	408
Personal Income	0	0
Corporate Income	0	0
Motor Vehicle License	0	0
Other Taxes	598,861	158
Current Charges	3,065,509	808
Liquor Store	0	0
Utility	3,976,313	1,048
Employee Retirement	765,769	202

Source: U.S Census Bureau, State & Local Government Finances 2012

City Government Expenditures by Function

Function	2012 ($000)	2012 ($ per capita)	2012 (%)
General Direct Expenditures			
Air Transportation	1,616,929	426	10.4
Corrections	0	0	0.0
Education	0	0	0.0
Employment Security Administration	0	0	0.0
Financial Administration	163,418	43	1.0
Fire Protection	445,927	118	2.9
General Public Buildings	0	0	0.0
Governmental Administration, Other	116,387	31	0.7
Health	228,768	60	1.5
Highways	705,275	186	4.5
Hospitals	0	0	0.0
Housing and Community Development	366,220	97	2.3
Interest on General Debt	528,119	139	3.4
Judicial and Legal	81,030	21	0.5
Libraries	107,054	28	0.7
Parking	30,815	8	0.2
Parks and Recreation	392,801	104	2.5
Police Protection	1,699,729	448	10.9
Public Welfare	0	0	0.0
Sewerage	482,057	127	3.1
Solid Waste Management	263,179	69	1.7
Veterans' Services	0	0	0.0
Liquor Store	0	0	0.0
Utility	4,892,506	1,290	31.3
Employee Retirement	2,041,375	538	13.1

Source: U.S Census Bureau, State & Local Government Finances 2012

DEMOGRAPHICS

Population Growth

Area	1990 Census	2000 Census	2010 Census	Population Growth (%)	
				1990-2000	2000-2010
City	3,487,671	3,694,820	3,792,621	5.9	2.6
MSA[1]	11,273,720	12,365,627	12,828,837	9.7	3.7
U.S.	248,709,873	281,421,906	308,745,538	13.2	9.7

Note: (1) Figures cover the Los Angeles-Long Beach-Santa Ana, CA Metropolitan Statistical Area—see Appendix B for areas included
Source: U.S. Census Bureau, Census 1990, 2000, 2010

Household Size

Area	Persons in Household (%)							Average Household Size
	One	Two	Three	Four	Five	Six	Seven or More	
City	30.3	27.9	15.4	13.2	7.1	3.2	2.8	2.84
MSA[1]	24.9	28.1	16.4	15.4	8.3	3.7	3.2	3.03
U.S.	27.7	33.6	15.7	13.1	6.0	2.3	1.5	2.64

Note: (1) Figures cover the Los Angeles-Long Beach-Anaheim, CA Metropolitan Statistical Area—see Appendix B for areas included
Source: U.S. Census Bureau, 2011-2013 American Community Survey 3-Year Estimates

Race

Area	White Alone[2] (%)	Black Alone[2] (%)	Asian Alone[2] (%)	AIAN[3] Alone[2] (%)	NHOPI[4] Alone[2] (%)	Other Race Alone[2] (%)	Two or More Races (%)
City	52.4	9.1	11.4	0.5	0.2	22.8	3.5
MSA[1]	56.1	6.8	15.0	0.5	0.3	17.7	3.7
U.S.	73.9	12.6	5.0	0.8	0.2	4.7	2.9

Note: (1) Figures cover the Los Angeles-Long Beach-Anaheim, CA Metropolitan Statistical Area—see Appendix B for areas included; (2) Alone is defined as not being in combination with one or more other races; (3) American Indian and Alaska Native; (4) Native Hawaiian and Other Pacific Islander
Source: U.S. Census Bureau, 2011-2013 American Community Survey 3-Year Estimates

Hispanic or Latino Origin

Area	Total (%)	Mexican (%)	Puerto Rican (%)	Cuban (%)	Other (%)
City	48.6	32.5	0.5	0.3	15.3
MSA[1]	44.8	34.9	0.5	0.4	9.0
U.S.	16.9	10.8	1.6	0.6	3.8

Note: Persons of Hispanic or Latino origin can be of any race; (1) Figures cover the Los Angeles-Long Beach-Anaheim, CA Metropolitan Statistical Area—see Appendix B for areas included
Source: U.S. Census Bureau, 2011-2013 American Community Survey 3-Year Estimates

Segregation

Type	Segregation Indices[1]				Percent Change		
	1990	2000	2010	2010 Rank[2]	1990-2000	1990-2010	2000-2010
Black/White	72.7	70.0	67.8	10	-2.8	-4.9	-2.1
Asian/White	43.5	47.9	48.4	12	4.4	4.9	0.5
Hispanic/White	60.3	62.5	62.2	2	2.2	1.9	-0.3

Note: All figures cover the Metropolitan Statistical Area—see Appendix B for areas included; Figures are based on an analysis of 1990, 2000, and 2010 Census Decennial Census tract data by William H. Frey, Brookings Institution and the University of Michigan Social Science Data Analysis Network. In this analysis all racial groups (whites, blacks, and asians) are non-Hispanic members of those races. Hispanics are shown as a separate category;
(1) Segregation Indices are Dissimilarity Indices that measure the degree to which the minority group is distributed differently than whites across census tracts. They range from 0 (complete integration) to 100 (complete segregation) where the value indicates the percentage of the minority group that needs to move to be distributed exactly like whites; (2) Ranges from 1 (most segregated) to 102 (least segregated); n/a not available.
Source: www.CensusScope.org

Ancestry

Area	German	Irish	English	American	Italian	Polish	French[2]	Scottish	Dutch
City	4.3	3.7	3.1	3.0	2.6	1.6	1.2	0.8	0.5
MSA[1]	6.0	4.9	4.3	3.5	3.0	1.3	1.4	1.0	0.7
U.S.	14.9	10.8	8.0	7.4	5.5	3.0	2.7	1.7	1.4

Note: Figures are the percentage of the total population reporting a particular ancestry. The nine most commonly reported ancestries in the U.S. are shown. Figures include multiple ancestries (e.g. if a person reported being Irish and Italian, they were included in both columns); (1) Figures cover the Los Angeles-Long Beach-Anaheim, CA Metropolitan Statistical Area—see Appendix B for areas included; (2) Excludes Basque
Source: U.S. Census Bureau, 2011-2013 American Community Survey 3-Year Estimates

Foreign-Born Population

Area									
	Any Foreign Country	Mexico	Asia	Europe	Carribean	South America	Central America[2]	Africa	Canada
City	38.6	13.9	11.1	2.4	0.3	1.1	8.6	0.7	0.3
MSA[1]	33.8	13.2	12.4	1.7	0.3	0.9	4.3	0.5	0.3
U.S.	13.0	3.7	3.8	1.5	1.2	0.9	1.0	0.6	0.3

Note: (1) Figures cover the Los Angeles-Long Beach-Anaheim, CA Metropolitan Statistical Area—see Appendix B for areas included; (2) Excludes Mexico.
Source: U.S. Census Bureau, 2011-2013 American Community Survey 3-Year Estimates

Marital Status

Area	Never Married	Now Married[2]	Separated	Widowed	Divorced
City	45.7	38.2	2.9	4.7	8.5
MSA[1]	39.8	44.0	2.6	5.0	8.6
U.S.	32.7	48.1	2.2	6.0	11.0

Note: Figures are percentages and cover the population 15 years of age and older; (1) Figures cover the Los Angeles-Long Beach-Anaheim, CA Metropolitan Statistical Area—see Appendix B for areas included; (2) Excludes separated
Source: U.S. Census Bureau, 2011-2013 American Community Survey 3-Year Estimates

Disability Status

Area	All Ages	Under 18 Years Old	18 to 64 Years Old	65 Years and Over
City	9.7	2.7	7.2	39.4
MSA[1]	9.3	2.7	6.8	36.5
U.S.	12.3	4.1	10.2	36.3

Note: Figures show percent of the civilian noninstitutionalized population that reported having a disability. Disability status is determined from from six types of difficulty: vision, hearing, cognitive, ambulatory, self-care, and independent living. For children under 5 years old, hearing and vision difficulty are used to determine disability status. For children between the ages of 5 and 14, disability status is determined from hearing, vision, cognitive, ambulatory, and self-care difficulties. For people aged 15 years and older, they are considered to have a disability if they have difficulty with any one of the six difficulty types; (1) Figures cover the Los Angeles-Long Beach-Anaheim, CA Metropolitan Statistical Area—see Appendix B for areas included.
Source: U.S. Census Bureau, 2011-2013 American Community Survey 3-Year Estimates

Age

Area										Median Age
	Under Age 5	Age 5–19	Age 20–34	Age 35–44	Age 45–54	Age 55–64	Age 65–74	Age 75–84	Age 85+	
City	6.5	18.7	25.4	14.8	13.3	10.5	5.9	3.4	1.6	34.6
MSA[1]	6.4	20.0	22.6	14.2	14.0	10.9	6.4	3.6	1.7	35.6
U.S.	6.4	19.9	20.7	12.9	14.1	12.3	7.6	4.2	1.9	37.4

Note: (1) Figures cover the Los Angeles-Long Beach-Anaheim, CA Metropolitan Statistical Area—see Appendix B for areas included
Source: U.S. Census Bureau, 2011-2013 American Community Survey 3-Year Estimates

Gender

Area	Males	Females	Males per 100 Females
City	1,914,874	1,937,942	98.8
MSA[1]	6,433,666	6,602,204	97.4
U.S.	154,451,010	159,410,713	96.9

Note: (1) Figures cover the Los Angeles-Long Beach-Anaheim, CA Metropolitan Statistical Area—see Appendix B for areas included
Source: U.S. Census Bureau, 2011-2013 American Community Survey 3-Year Estimates

Religious Groups by Family

Area	Catholic	Baptist	Non-Den.	Methodist[2]	Lutheran	LDS[3]	Pentecostal	Presbyterian[4]	Muslim[5]	Judaism
MSA[1]	33.8	2.8	3.6	1.1	0.7	1.7	1.8	0.9	0.7	1.0
U.S.	19.1	9.3	4.0	4.0	2.3	2.0	1.9	1.6	0.8	0.7

Note: Figures are the number of adherents as a percentage of the total population; (1) Figures cover the Los Angeles-Long Beach-Santa Ana, CA Metropolitan Statistical Area—see Appendix B for areas included; (2) Methodist/Pietist; (3) Latter Day Saints; (4) Reformed; (5) Figures are estimates
Source: Association of Statisticians of American Religious Bodies, 2010 U.S. Religion Census: Religious Congregations & Membership Study

Religious Groups by Tradition

Area	Catholic	Evangelical Protestant	Mainline Protestant	Other Tradition	Black Protestant	Orthodox
MSA[1]	33.8	9.0	2.4	4.6	0.9	0.6
U.S.	19.1	16.2	7.3	4.3	1.6	0.3

Note: Figures are the number of adherents as a percentage of the total population; (1) Figures cover the Los Angeles-Long Beach-Santa Ana, CA Metropolitan Statistical Area—see Appendix B for areas included
Source: Association of Statisticians of American Religious Bodies, 2010 U.S. Religion Census: Religious Congregations & Membership Study

ECONOMY

Gross Metropolitan Product

Area	2012	2013	2014	2015	Rank[2]
MSA[1]	765.7	792.2	822.9	865.2	2

Note: Figures are in billions of dollars; (1) Figures cover the Los Angeles-Long Beach-Anaheim, CA Metropolitan Statistical Area—see Appendix B for areas included; (2) Rank is based on 2015 data and ranges from 1 to 363
Source: The U.S. Conference of Mayors, U.S. Metro Economies: GMP and Employment 2013-2015, June 2014

Economic Growth

Area	2010-12 (%)	2013 (%)	2014 (%)	2015 (%)	Rank[2]
MSA[1]	2.1	2.3	2.3	3.3	102
U.S.	2.1	2.0	2.3	3.2	–

Note: Figures are real gross metropolitan product (GMP) growth rates and represent annual average percent change; (1) Figures cover the Los Angeles-Long Beach-Anaheim, CA Metropolitan Statistical Area—see Appendix B for areas included; (2) Rank is based on 2015 data and ranges from 1 to 363
Source: The U.S. Conference of Mayors, U.S. Metro Economies: GMP and Employment 2013-2015, June 2014

Metropolitan Area Exports

Area	2008	2009	2010	2011	2012	2013	Rank[2]
MSA[1]	59,985.6	51,528.4	62,167.6	72,688.9	75,007.5	76,305.7	3

Note: Figures are in millions of dollars; (1) Figures cover the Los Angeles-Long Beach-Anaheim, CA Metropolitan Statistical Area—see Appendix B for areas included; (2) Rank is based on 2013 data and ranges from 1 to 387
Source: U.S. Department of Commerce, International Trade Administration, Office of Trade & Industry Information, Manufacturing & Services, data extracted April 3, 2015

Building Permits

Area	Single-Family			Multi-Family			Total		
	2013	2014	Pct. Chg.	2013	2014	Pct. Chg.	2013	2014	Pct. Chg.
City	1,144	1,668	45.8	7,248	9,596	32.4	8,392	11,264	34.2
MSA[1]	7,509	8,300	10.5	17,689	18,650	5.4	25,198	26,950	7.0
U.S.	620,802	634,597	2.2	370,020	411,766	11.3	990,822	1,046,363	5.6

Note: (1) Figures cover the Los Angeles-Long Beach-Anaheim, CA Metropolitan Statistical Area—see Appendix B for areas included; Figures represent new, privately-owned housing units authorized (unadjusted data); All permit data are based on estimates with imputation.
Source: U.S. Census Bureau, Manufacturing, Mining, and Construction Statistics, Building Permits, 2013, 2014

Bankruptcy Filings

Area	Business Filings			Nonbusiness Filings		
	2013	2014	% Chg.	2013	2014	% Chg.
Los Angeles County	1,456	1,212	-16.8	37,662	29,341	-22.1
U.S.	33,212	26,983	-18.8	1,038,720	909,812	-12.4

Note: Business filings include Chapter 7, Chapter 11, Chapter 12, and Chapter 13; Nonbusiness filings include Chapter 7, Chapter 11, and Chapter 13
Source: Administrative Office of the U.S. Courts, Business and Nonbusiness Bankruptcy, County Cases Commenced by Chapter of the Bankruptcy Code, During the 12- Month Period Ending December 31, 2013 and Business and Nonbusiness Bankruptcy, County Cases Commenced by Chapter of the Bankruptcy Code, During the 12- Month Period Ending December 31, 2014

Housing Vacancy Rates

Area	Gross Vacancy Rate[2] (%)			Year-Round Vacancy Rate[3] (%)			Rental Vacancy Rate[4] (%)			Homeowner Vacancy Rate[5] (%)		
	2012	2013	2014	2012	2013	2014	2012	2013	2014	2012	2013	2014
MSA[1]	6.2	6.2	5.8	5.9	5.7	5.5	4.9	4.2	4.6	1.3	1.2	0.8
U.S.	13.8	13.6	13.4	10.8	10.7	10.4	8.7	8.3	7.6	2.0	2.0	1.9

Note: (1) Figures cover the Los Angeles-Long Beach-Anaheim, CA Metropolitan Statistical Area—see Appendix B for areas included; (2) The percentage of the total housing inventory that is vacant; (3) The percentage of the housing inventory (excluding seasonal units) that is year-round vacant; (4) The percentage of rental inventory that is vacant for rent; (5) The percentage of homeowner inventory that is vacant for sale
Source: U.S. Census Bureau, Housing Vacancies and Homeownership Annual Statistics: 2014

INCOME

Income

Area	Per Capita ($)	Median Household ($)	Average Household ($)
City	27,345	47,812	75,509
MSA[1]	28,785	58,569	84,766
U.S.	27,884	52,176	72,897

Note: (1) Figures cover the Los Angeles-Long Beach-Anaheim, CA Metropolitan Statistical Area—see Appendix B for areas included
Source: U.S. Census Bureau, 2011-2013 American Community Survey 3-Year Estimates

Household Income Distribution

Area	Percent of Households Earning							
	Under $15,000	$15,000 -24,999	$25,000 -34,999	$35,000 -49,999	$50,000 -74,999	$75,000 -99,000	$100,000 -149,999	$150,000 and up
City	15.9	12.3	10.4	13.0	15.8	10.2	11.3	11.0
MSA[1]	11.8	10.2	9.1	12.3	16.7	11.8	14.3	13.7
U.S.	13.0	10.9	10.3	13.6	17.9	11.9	12.7	9.6

Note: (1) Figures cover the Los Angeles-Long Beach-Anaheim, CA Metropolitan Statistical Area—see Appendix B for areas included
Source: U.S. Census Bureau, 2011-2013 American Community Survey 3-Year Estimates

Poverty Rate

Area	All Ages	Under 18 Years Old	18 to 64 Years Old	65 Years and Over
City	22.9	33.5	20.5	16.3
MSA[1]	17.4	24.7	15.7	12.2
U.S.	15.9	22.4	14.8	9.5

Note: Figures are percentage of people whose income during the past 12 months was below the poverty level; (1) Figures cover the Los Angeles-Long Beach-Anaheim, CA Metropolitan Statistical Area—see Appendix B for areas included
Source: U.S. Census Bureau, 2011-2013 American Community Survey 3-Year Estimates

EMPLOYMENT

Labor Force and Employment

Area	Civilian Labor Force			Workers Employed		
	Dec. 2013	Dec. 2014	% Chg.	Dec. 2013	Dec. 2014	% Chg.
City	2,001,203	2,023,204	1.1	1,820,275	1,862,132	2.3
MD[1]	4,988,880	5,047,001	1.2	4,562,492	4,667,406	2.3
U.S.	154,408,000	155,521,000	0.7	144,423,000	147,190,000	1.9

Note: Data is not seasonally adjusted and covers workers 16 years of age and older; (1) Figures cover the Los Angeles-Long Beach-Glendale, CA Metropolitan Division—see Appendix B for areas included
Source: Bureau of Labor Statistics, Local Area Unemployment Statistics

Unemployment Rate

Area	2014											
	Jan.	Feb.	Mar.	Apr.	May	Jun.	Jul.	Aug.	Sep.	Oct.	Nov.	Dec.
City	9.5	9.2	9.0	8.2	8.4	8.7	9.5	9.1	8.5	8.4	8.3	8.0
MD[1]	9.0	8.7	8.5	7.8	8.0	8.2	9.0	8.6	8.1	8.0	7.9	7.5
U.S.	7.0	7.0	6.8	5.9	6.1	6.3	6.5	6.3	5.7	5.5	5.5	5.4

Note: Data is not seasonally adjusted and covers workers 16 years of age and older; (1) Figures cover the Los Angeles-Long Beach-Glendale, CA Metropolitan Division—see Appendix B for areas included
Source: Bureau of Labor Statistics, Local Area Unemployment Statistics

Employment by Occupation

Occupation Classification	City (%)	MSA[1] (%)	U.S. (%)
Management, Business, Science, and Arts	35.7	36.3	36.2
Natural Resources, Construction, and Maintenance	8.1	7.6	9.0
Production, Transportation, and Material Moving	11.9	12.1	12.1
Sales and Office	23.2	25.1	24.4
Service	21.1	18.9	18.3

Note: Figures cover employed civilians 16 years of age and older; (1) Figures cover the Los Angeles-Long Beach-Anaheim, CA Metropolitan Statistical Area—see Appendix B for areas included
Source: U.S. Census Bureau, 2011-2013 American Community Survey 3-Year Estimates

Employment by Industry

Sector	MD[1]		U.S.
	Number of Employees	Percent of Total	Percent of Total
Construction	121,600	2.8	4.4
Education and Health Services	771,300	17.8	15.5
Financial Activities	210,800	4.9	5.7
Government	570,800	13.2	15.8
Information	200,400	4.6	2.0
Leisure and Hospitality	471,900	10.9	10.3
Manufacturing	364,500	8.4	8.7
Mining and Logging	4,600	0.1	0.6
Other Services	153,200	3.5	4.0
Professional and Business Services	617,400	14.3	13.8
Retail Trade	438,100	10.1	11.4
Transportation, Warehousing, and Utilities	168,100	3.9	3.9
Wholesale Trade	228,500	5.3	4.2

Note: Figures are non-farm employment as of December 2014. Figures are not seasonally adjusted and include workers 16 years of age and older; (1) Figures cover the Los Angeles-Long Beach-Glendale, CA Metropolitan Division—see Appendix B for areas included
Source: Bureau of Labor Statistics, Current Employment Statistics, Employment, Hours, and Earnings

Occupations with Greatest Projected Employment Growth: 2012 – 2022

Occupation[1]	2012 Employment	2022 Projected Employment	Numeric Employment Change	Percent Employment Change
Personal Care Aides	386,900	587,200	200,300	51.8
Combined Food Preparation and Serving Workers, Including Fast Food	286,000	362,400	76,400	26.7
Retail Salespersons	468,400	528,100	59,700	12.7
Laborers and Freight, Stock, and Material Movers, Hand	270,500	322,300	51,800	19.1
Waiters and Waitresses	246,100	290,300	44,200	18.0
Registered Nurses	254,500	297,400	42,900	16.9
General and Operations Managers	253,800	295,700	41,900	16.5
Secretaries and Administrative Assistants, Except Legal, Medical, and Executive	212,800	250,100	37,300	17.5
Cashiers	357,800	392,600	34,800	9.7
Cooks, Restaurant	116,900	150,600	33,700	28.8

Note: Projections cover California; (1) Sorted by numeric employment change
Source: www.projectionscentral.com, State Occupational Projections, 2012–2022 Long-Term Projections

Fastest Growing Occupations: 2012 – 2022

Occupation[1]	2012 Employment	2022 Projected Employment	Numeric Employment Change	Percent Employment Change
Economists	3,100	5,100	2,000	64.5
Helpers—Brickmasons, Blockmasons, Stonemasons, and Tile and Marble Setters	2,900	4,600	1,700	58.6
Brickmasons and Blockmasons	5,100	8,000	2,900	56.9
Insulation Workers, Floor, Ceiling, and Wall	1,600	2,500	900	56.3
Stonemasons	1,100	1,700	600	54.5
Insulation Workers, Mechanical	1,100	1,700	600	54.5
Personal Care Aides	386,900	587,200	200,300	51.8
Foresters	1,200	1,800	600	50.0
Terrazzo Workers and Finishers	1,100	1,600	500	45.5
Mechanical Door Repairers	1,100	1,600	500	45.5

Note: Projections cover California; (1) Sorted by percent employment change and excludes occupations with numeric employment change less than 100
Source: www.projectionscentral.com, State Occupational Projections, 2012–2022 Long-Term Projections

Average Wages

Occupation	$/Hr.	Occupation	$/Hr.
Accountants and Auditors	36.68	Maids and Housekeeping Cleaners	12.17
Automotive Mechanics	18.59	Maintenance and Repair Workers	20.92
Bookkeepers	20.19	Marketing Managers	68.97
Carpenters	26.08	Nuclear Medicine Technologists	48.08
Cashiers	10.49	Nurses, Licensed Practical	24.02
Clerks, General Office	15.32	Nurses, Registered	45.26
Clerks, Receptionists/Information	14.37	Nursing Assistants	14.15
Clerks, Shipping/Receiving	14.56	Packers and Packagers, Hand	10.44
Computer Programmers	43.18	Physical Therapists	42.21
Computer Systems Analysts	45.36	Postal Service Mail Carriers	26.10
Computer User Support Specialists	26.63	Real Estate Brokers	48.11
Cooks, Restaurant	11.48	Retail Salespersons	12.89
Dentists	70.52	Sales Reps., Exc. Tech./Scientific	30.21
Electrical Engineers	53.36	Sales Reps., Tech./Scientific	40.43
Electricians	28.71	Secretaries, Exc. Legal/Med./Exec.	18.49
Financial Managers	73.35	Security Guards	12.86
First-Line Supervisors/Managers, Sales	20.59	Surgeons	119.27
Food Preparation Workers	9.99	Teacher Assistants	14.20
General and Operations Managers	61.38	Teachers, Elementary School	34.60
Hairdressers/Cosmetologists	13.23	Teachers, Secondary School	35.30
Internists	84.61	Telemarketers	13.05
Janitors and Cleaners	13.07	Truck Drivers, Heavy/Tractor-Trailer	20.06
Landscaping/Groundskeeping Workers	13.57	Truck Drivers, Light/Delivery Svcs.	16.61
Lawyers	82.27	Waiters and Waitresses	11.81

Note: Wage data covers the Los Angeles-Long Beach-Glendale, CA Metropolitan Division—see Appendix B for areas included; Hourly wages for elementary/secondary school teachers and teacher assistants were calculated by the editors from annual wage data assuming a 40 hour work week; n/a not available.
Source: Bureau of Labor Statistics, Metro Area Occupational Employment and Wage Estimates, May 2014

TAXES

State Corporate Income Tax Rates

State	Tax Rate (%)	Income Brackets ($)	Num. of Brackets	Financial Institution Tax Rate (%)[a]	Federal Income Tax Ded.
California	8.84 (c)	Flat rate	1	10.84 (c)	No

Note: Tax rates as of January 1, 2015; (a) Rates listed are the corporate income tax rate applied to financial institutions or excise taxes based on income. Some states have other taxes based upon the value of deposits or shares; (c) Minimum tax is $800 in California, $100 in District of Columbia, $50 in North Dakota (banks), $500 in Rhode Island, $200 per location in South Dakota (banks), $100 in Utah, $250 in Vermont.
Source: Federation of Tax Administrators, "State Corporate Income Tax Rates, 2015"

State Individual Income Tax Rates

State	Tax Rate (%)	Income Brackets ($)	Num. of Brackets	Personal Exempt. ($)[1] Single	Personal Exempt. ($)[1] Dependents	Fed. Inc. Tax Ded.
California (a)	1.0 - 12.3 (f)	7,749- 519,687 (b)	9	108 (c)	333 (c)	No

Note: Tax rates as of January 1, 2015; Local- and county-level taxes are not included; n/a not applicable; (1) Married joint filers generally receive double the single exemption; (a) 17 states have statutory provision for automatically adjusting to the rate of inflation the dollar values of the income tax brackets, standard deductions, and/or personal exemptions. Massachusetts, Michigan, and Nebraska index the personal exemption only. Oregon does not index the income brackets for $125,000 and over. Maine has suspended indexing for 2014 and 2015; (b) For joint returns, taxes are twice the tax on half the couple's income; (c) The personal exemption takes the form of a tax credit instead of a deduction; (f) California imposes an additional 1% tax on taxable income over $1 million, making the maximum rate 13.3% over $1 million.
Source: Federation of Tax Administrators, "State Individual Income Tax Rates, 2015"

Various State and Local Tax Rates

State	State and Local Sales and Use (%)	State Sales and Use (%)	Gasoline[1] (¢/gal.)	Cigarette[2] ($/pack)	Spirits[3] ($/gal.)	Wine[4] ($/gal.)	Beer[5] ($/gal.)
California	9.0	7.50 (b)	45.39	0.87	3.30 (f)	0.20	0.20

Note: All tax rates as of January 1, 2015; (1) The American Petroleum Institute has developed a methodology for determining the average tax rate on a gallon of fuel. Rates may include any of the following: excise taxes, environmental fees, storage tank fees, other fees or taxes, general sales tax, and local taxes. In states where gasoline is subject to the general sales tax, or where the fuel tax is based on the average sale price, the average rate determined by API is sensitive to changes in the price of gasoline. States that fully or partially apply general sales taxes to gasoline: CA, CO, GA, IL, IN, MI, NY; (2) The federal excise tax of $1.0066 per pack and local taxes are not included; (3) Rates are those applicable to off-premise sales of 40% alcohol by volume (a.b.v.) distilled spirits in 750ml containers. Local excise taxes are excluded; (4) Rates are those applicable to off-premise sales of 11% a.b.v. non-carbonated wine in 750ml containers; (5) Rates are those applicable to off-premise sales of 4.7% a.b.v. beer in 12 ounce containers; (b) Three states levy mandatory, statewide, local add-on sales taxes at the state level: California (1%), Utah (1.25%), and Virginia (1%). We include these in their state sales taxes; (f) Different rates are also applicable according to alcohol content, place of production, size of container, or place purchased (on- or off-premise or onboard airlines).
Source: Tax Foundation, 2015 Facts & Figures: How Does Your State Compare?

State Business Tax Climate Index Rankings

State	Overall Rank	Corporate Tax Index Rank	Individual Income Tax Index Rank	Sales Tax Index Rank	Unemployment Insurance Tax Index Rank	Property Tax Index Rank
California	48	34	50	42	14	14

Note: The index is a measure of how each state's tax laws affect economic performance. The lower the rank, the more favorable a state's tax system is for business. States without a given tax are given a ranking of 1. The scores/rankings for the District of Columbia do not affect other states. The 2015 index represents the tax climate as of July 1, 2014.
Source: Tax Foundation, State Business Tax Climate Index 2015

COMMERCIAL REAL ESTATE

Office Market

Market Area	Inventory (sq. ft.)	Vacancy Rate (%)	Under Construction (sq. ft.)	YTD Net Absorption (sq. ft.)	Total Average Asking Rent ($/sq. ft./year)
Los Angeles	190,365,659	15.2	762,421	2,209,506	32.99
National	4,745,108,508	14.3	71,190,461	51,084,126	27.40

Source: Newmark Grubb Knight Frank, National Office Market Report, 4th Quarter 2014

Industrial/Warehouse/R&D Market

Market Area	Inventory (sq. ft.)	Vacancy Rate (%)	Under Construction (sq. ft.)	YTD Net Absorption (sq. ft.)	Total Average Asking Rent ($/sq. ft./year)
Los Angeles	985,231,942	1.6	2,922,826	4,737,787	7.44
National	14,238,613,765	7.2	134,387,407	185,246,438	5.64

Source: Newmark Grubb Knight Frank, National Industrial Market Report, 4th Quarter 2014

COMMERCIAL UTILITIES

Typical Monthly Electric Bills

Area	Commercial Service ($/month)		Industrial Service ($/month)	
	40 kW demand 5,000 kWh	500 kW demand 100,000 kWh	5,000 kW demand 1,500,000 kWh	70,000 kW demand 50,000,000 kWh
City	996	15,024	203,613	7,576,875

Note: Figures are based on rates in effect January 2, 2014
Source: Memphis Light, Gas and Water, 2014 Utility Bill Comparisons for Selected U.S. Cities

TRANSPORTATION

Means of Transportation to Work

Area	Car/Truck/Van		Public Transportation			Bicycle	Walked	Other Means	Worked at Home
	Drove Alone	Car-pooled	Bus	Subway	Railroad				
City	67.2	9.8	10.2	0.6	0.1	1.1	3.7	1.6	5.7
MSA[1]	73.9	10.1	5.4	0.3	0.2	0.9	2.7	1.3	5.1
U.S.	76.4	9.6	2.6	1.8	0.6	0.6	2.8	1.3	4.3

Note: Figures are percentages and cover workers 16 years of age and older; (1) Figures cover the Los Angeles-Long Beach-Anaheim, CA Metropolitan Statistical Area—see Appendix B for areas included
Source: U.S. Census Bureau, 2011-2013 American Community Survey 3-Year Estimates

Travel Time to Work

Area	Less Than 10 Minutes	10 to 19 Minutes	20 to 29 Minutes	30 to 44 Minutes	45 to 59 Minutes	60 to 89 Minutes	90 Minutes or More
City	7.2	24.3	20.3	26.9	9.5	8.6	3.2
MSA[1]	8.1	26.2	20.4	24.8	9.1	8.3	3.1
U.S.	13.3	29.7	20.9	20.2	7.7	5.7	2.6

Note: Figures are percentages and include workers 16 years old and over; (1) Figures cover the Los Angeles-Long Beach-Anaheim, CA Metropolitan Statistical Area—see Appendix B for areas included
Source: U.S. Census Bureau, 2011-2013 American Community Survey 3-Year Estimates

Travel Time Index

Area	1985	1990	1995	2000	2005	2010	2011
Urban Area[1]	1.22	1.40	1.35	1.38	1.41	1.37	1.37
Average[2]	1.09	1.14	1.16	1.19	1.23	1.18	1.18

Note: Travel Time Index—the ratio of travel time in the peak period to the travel time at free-flow conditions. For example, a value of 1.30 indicates a 20-minute free-flow trip takes 26 minutes in the peak. Free-flow speeds (60 mph on freeways and 35 mph on principal arterials) are used as the comparison threshold; (1) Covers the Los Angeles-Long Beach-Santa Ana CA urban area; (2) average of 498 urban areas
Source: Texas Transportation Institute, Urban Mobility Report 2012, December 2012

Public Transportation

Agency Name / Mode of Transportation	Vehicles Operated in Maximum Service	Annual Unlinked Passenger Trips (in thous.)	Annual Passenger Miles (in thous.)
Los Angeles Co. Metro Transportation Authority (LACMTA)			
Bus (directly operated)	1,739	336,447.0	1,386,574.9
Bus (purchased transportation)	121	13,938.6	52,176.7
Bus Rapid Transit (directly operated)	32	9,118.4	57,728.9
Heavy Rail (directly operated)	70	49,516.5	237,760.1
Light Rail (directly operated)	144	63,652.2	408,031.9
Vanpool (purchased transportation)	1,266	3,626.6	163,339.3
City of Los Angeles Department of Transportation (LADOT)			
Bus (purchased transportation)	169	24,242.6	34,949.7
Commuter Bus (purchased transportation)	83	2,063.7	34,389.3
Demand Response (purchased transportation)	99	212.5	1,040.0
Demand Response Taxi (purchased transportation)	9	101.0	196.6
LACMTA - Small Operators			
Bus (purchased transportation)	184	10,919.8	26,181.9
Demand Response (purchased transportation)	191	997.8	3,608.7
Demand Response Taxi (purchased transportation)	86	434.6	1,370.8

Source: Federal Transit Administration, National Transit Database, 2013

Air Transportation

Airport Name and Code / Type of Service	Passenger Airlines[1]	Passenger Enplanements	Freight Carriers[2]	Freight (lbs.)
Los Angeles International (LAX)				
Domestic service (U.S. carriers - 2014)	31	25,048,184	27	760,739,558
International service (U.S. carriers - 2013)	13	2,022,569	13	177,725,809

Note: (1) Includes all U.S.-based major, minor and commuter airlines that carried at least one passenger during the year; (2) Includes all U.S.-based airlines and freight carriers that transported at least one lb. of freight during the year.
Source: Bureau of Transportation Statistics, The Intermodal Transportation Database, Air Carriers: T-100 Domestic Market (U.S. Carriers), 2014; Bureau of Transportation Statistics, The Intermodal Transportation Database, Air Carriers: T-100 International Market (U.S. Carriers), 2013

Other Transportation Statistics

Major Highways:	I-10; I-5
Amtrak Service:	Yes
Major Waterways/Ports:	Port of Los Angeles

Source: Amtrak.com; Google Maps

BUSINESSES

Major Business Headquarters

Company Name	Rankings	
	Fortune[1]	Forbes[2]
AECOM Technology Corporation	332	-
CBRE Group	363	-
Capital Group Cos	-	49
Forever 21	-	118
Oaktree Capital Group	354	-
Occidental Petroleum Corporation	116	-
Reliance Steel & Aluminum Co.	299	-
Roll Global	-	134

Note: (1) Fortune 500—companies that produce a 10-K are ranked 1 to 500 based on 2013 revenue; (2) all private companies with at least $2 billion in annual revenue through the end of their most current fiscal year are ranked 1 to 221; companies listed are headquartered in the city; dashes indicate no ranking
Source: Fortune, "Fortune 500," June 16, 2014; Forbes, "America's Largest Private Companies," November 5, 2014

Fast-Growing Businesses

According to *Inc.*, Los Angeles is home to 17 of America's 500 fastest-growing private companies: **American Solar Direct** (#17); **EcoSense Lighting** (#59); **Fortress Gold Group (Sherman Oaks)** (#113); **AdColony** (#114); **Sky Zone Indoor Trampoline Park** (#152); **GrayPay (Encino)** (#157); **AudioMicro (Sherman Oaks)** (#164); **180Fusion** (#176); **Genzum Life Sciences** (#182); **Wren** (#215); **TNH Advanced Specialty Pharmacy (Van Nuys)** (#266); **Outdoor Tech** (#329); **Dope** (#356); **TK Media Direct (North Hollywood)** (#424); **I.T. Source** (#444); **The Doctor's Choice** (#453); **SeaSnax** (#479). Criteria: must be an independent, privately-held, for-profit, U.S. corporation, proprietorship or partnership; revenues must be at least $100,000 in 2010 and $2 million in 2013; must have four-year operating/sales history. Holding companies, regulated banks, and utilities were excluded. *Inc., "America's 500 Fastest-Growing Private Companies," September 2014*

According to *Fortune*, Los Angeles is home to one of the 100 fastest-growing companies in the world: **BBCN Bancorp** (#76). Companies were ranked by their revenue growth rate; their EPS growth rate; and their three-year annualized total return to investors for the period ending June 30, 2014. Criteria for inclusion: a company, foreign or domestic, must trade on a major U.S. stock exchange; must file quarterly reports with the SEC; must have a minimum market capitalization of $250 million; must have a stock price of at least $5 on June 30, 2014; must have been trading continuously since June 30, 2010; must have revenue and net income for the four quarters ended on or before April 30, 2014, of at least $50 million and $10 million, respectively; and must have posted a compound annual growth in revenue and earnings per share of at least 20% annually over the three years ending on or before April 30, 2014. Real estate investment trusts, limited-liability companies, limited parterships, business development companies, closed end investment firms, and companies that lost money in the quarter ending April 30, 2014 were excluded. *Fortune, "100 Fastest-Growing Companies," August 28, 2014*

According to *Initiative for a Competitive Inner City (ICIC)*, Los Angeles is home to two of America's 100 fastest-growing "inner city" companies: **Decor Interior Design** (#47); **Ace Exhibits** (#76). Criteria for inclusion: company must be headquartered in or have 51 percent or more of its physical operations in an economically distressed urban area; must be an independent, for-profit corporation, partnership or proprietorship; must have 10 or more employees and have a five-year sales history that includes sales of at least $200,000 in the base year and at least $1 million in the current year with no decrease in sales over the two most recent years. This year, for the first time in the list's 16-year history, the Inner City 100 consists of 10 fast-growing businesses in 10 industry categories. Companies were ranked overall by revenue growth over the five-year period between 2009 and 2013 as well as within their respective industry categories. *Initiative for a Competitive Inner City (ICIC), "Inner City 100 Companies, 2014"*

According to Deloitte, Los Angeles is home to seven of North America's 500 fastest-growing high-technology companies: **AudioMicro (Sherman Oaks)** (#28); **MarketShare** (#203); **BlackLine** (#225); **Chrome River Technologies** (#239); **Slickdeals (Hollywood)** (#311); **Broadvoice (Winnetka)** (#316); **Capstone Turbine Corporation (Chatsworth)** (#401). Companies are ranked by percentage growth in revenue over a five-year period. Criteria for inclusion: company must be headquartered within North America; must own proprietary intellectual property or proprietary technology that contributes to a significant portion of the company's operating revenue, or devote a significant proportion of revenues to research and development of technology; must have been in business for a minumum of five years with 2009 operating revenues of at least $50,000 USD/CD and 2013 operating revenues of at least $5 million USD/CD. *Deloitte Touche Tohmatsu, 2014 Technology Fast 500*^{TM}

Minority Business Opportunity

Los Angeles is home to one company which is on the *Black Enterprise* Industrial/Service 100 list (100 largest companies based on gross sales): **The Client Base Funding Group** (#64). Criteria: operational in previous calendar year; at least 51% black-owned and manufactures/owns the product it sells or provides industrial or consumer services. Brokerages, real estate firms and firms that provide professional services are not eligible. *Black Enterprise, B.E. 100s, 2014*

Los Angeles is home to one company which is on the *Black Enterprise* Bank 20 list (20 largest banks based on total assets, capital, deposits and loans, including mortgage-backed securities for the calendar year): **Broadway Financial Corp. (Broadway Federal Bank)** (#7). Only commercial banks or savings and loans that are classified by the Federal Reserve as black institutions and have been fully operational for the previous calendar year were considered. *Black Enterprise, B.E. 100s, 2014*

Los Angeles is home to 13 companies which are on the *Hispanic Business* 500 list (500 largest U.S. Hispanic-owned companies based on 2012 revenue): **TELACU Industries** (#55); **Jules and Associates** (#70); **Field Fresh Foods** (#115); **E.J. De La Rosa & Co.** (#147); **PromoShop** (#151); **Cordoba Corp.** (#217); **RBB Architects** (#220); **Avcogas Propane Sales and Service** (#276); **Quijote Corp.** (#282); **Executive Clothiers** (#367); **Art Lewin & Co. Custom Clothiers** (#375); **Art Lewin & Co. Bespoke Clothiers** (#384); **General Transistor Corp.** (#435). Companies included must show at least 51 percent ownership by Hispanic U.S. citizens, and must maintain headquarters in one of the 50 states or Washington, D.C. *Hispanic Business, "Hispanic Business 500," June 20, 2013*

Los Angeles is home to two companies which are on the *Hispanic Business* Fastest-Growing 100 list (greatest sales growth from 2008 to 2012): **Art Lewin & Co. Bespoke Clothiers** (#58); **Quijote Corp.** (#63). Companies included must show at least 51 percent ownership by Hispanic U.S. citizens, and must maintain headquarters in one of the 50 states or Washington, D.C. In addition, companies must have minimum revenues of $200,000 for calendar year 2008. *Hispanic Business, June 20, 2013*

Minority- and Women-Owned Businesses

Group	All Firms		Firms with Paid Employees			
	Firms	Sales ($000)	Firms	Sales ($000)	Employees	Payroll ($000)
Asian	61,606	25,468,797	17,779	23,159,723	116,912	3,326,715
Black	26,002	2,936,749	2,073	2,214,730	15,385	570,684
Hispanic	94,643	11,214,207	7,162	8,442,631	54,236	1,603,109
Women	136,579	21,535,185	15,674	17,247,176	99,164	3,688,050
All Firms	450,050	379,390,317	91,908	360,903,264	1,448,871	68,250,202

Note: Figures cover firms located in the city; minority- and women-owned business are defined as firms in which the corresponding group own 51% or more of the stock or equity of the company
Source: U.S. Census Bureau, 2007 Economic Census, Survey of Business Owners (2012 Survey of Business Owners data will be released starting in June 2015)

**HOTELS &
CONVENTION
CENTERS**

Hotels/Motels

Area	5 Star		4 Star		3 Star		2 Star		1 Star		Not Rated	
	Num.	Pct.[3]	Num.	Pct.[3]	Num.	Pct.[3]	Num.	Pct.[3]	Num.	Pct.[3]	Num.	Pct.[3]
City[1]	16	2.1	74	9.9	208	27.9	397	53.2	22	2.9	29	3.9
Total[2]	166	0.9	1,264	7.0	5,718	31.8	9,340	52.0	411	2.3	1,070	6.0

Note: (1) Figures cover Los Angeles and vicinity; (2) Figures cover all 100 cities in this book; (3) Percentage of hotels which have a given star rating; Star ratings are determined by expedia.com and offer an indication of the general quality of a particular hotel.
Source: expedia.com, April 2, 2015

The Los Angeles-Long Beach-Glendale, CA metro area is home to seven of the best hotels in the U.S. according to *Travel & Leisure*: **The Peninsula Beverly Hills; Beverly Hills Hotel & Bungalows; Beverly Wilshire (A Four Seasons Hotel); Four Seasons Hotel Westlake Village; Hotel Bel-Air; L'Ermitage Beverly Hills; Montage Beverly Hills.** Criteria: service; location; rooms; food; and value. The list includes the top 236 hotels in the U.S. *Travel & Leisure, "T+L 500, The World's Best Hotels 2015"*

The Los Angeles-Long Beach-Glendale, CA metro area is home to three of the best hotels in the world according to *Condé Nast Traveler*: **Chateau Marmont, West Hollywood; Shutters on the Beach, Santa Monica; Sunset Tower Hotel, West Hollywood.** The selections are based on editors' picks. The list includes the top 25 hotels in the U.S. *Condé Nast Traveler, "Gold List 2015, The Top Hotels in the World"*

Major Convention Centers

Name	Overall Space (sq. ft.)	Exhibit Space (sq. ft.)	Meeting Space (sq. ft.)	Meeting Rooms
Los Angeles Convention Center	n/a	720,000	147,000	64

Note: Table includes convention centers located in the Los Angeles-Long Beach-Anaheim, CA metro area; n/a not available
Source: Original research

Living Environment

COST OF LIVING

Cost of Living Index

Composite Index	Groceries	Housing	Utilities	Trans-portation	Health Care	Misc. Goods/ Services
134.7	104.5	204.1	112.4	112.0	112.1	106.1

Note: The Cost of Living Index measures regional differences in the cost of consumer goods and services, excluding taxes and non-consumer expenditures, for professional and managerial households in the top income quintile. It is based on more than 50,000 prices covering almost 60 different items for which prices are collected three times a year by chambers of commerce, economic development organizations or university applied economic centers in each participating urban area. The numbers shown should be read as a percentage above or below the national average of 100. For example, a value of 115.4 in the groceries column indicates that grocery prices are 15.4% higher than the national average. Small differences in the index numbers should not be interpreted as significant; Figures cover the Los Angeles-Long Beach CA urban area.
Source: The Council for Community and Economic Research, ACCRA Cost of Living Index, 2014

Grocery Prices

Area[1]	T-Bone Steak ($/pound)	Frying Chicken ($/pound)	Whole Milk ($/half gal.)	Eggs ($/dozen)	Orange Juice ($/64 oz.)	Coffee ($/11.5 oz.)
City[2]	9.88	1.53	2.51	2.46	3.20	5.09
Avg.	10.40	1.37	2.40	1.99	3.46	4.27
Min.	8.48	0.93	1.37	1.30	2.83	2.99
Max.	14.20	2.44	3.62	4.02	6.42	6.96

Note: (1) Values for the local area are compared with the average, minimum and maximum values for all 308 areas in the Cost of Living Index; (2) Figures cover the Los Angeles-Long Beach CA urban area; **T-Bone Steak** *(price per pound);* **Frying Chicken** *(price per pound, whole fryer);* **Whole Milk** *(half gallon carton);* **Eggs** *(price per dozen, Grade A, large);* **Orange Juice** *(64 oz. Tropicana or Florida Natural);* **Coffee** *(11.5 oz. can, vacuum-packed, Maxwell House, Hills Bros, or Folgers).*
Source: The Council for Community and Economic Research, ACCRA Cost of Living Index, 2014

Housing and Utility Costs

Area[1]	New Home Price ($)	Apartment Rent ($/month)	All Electric ($/month)	Part Electric ($/month)	Other Energy ($/month)	Telephone ($/month)
City[2]	574,972	2,289	-	112.12	69.90	33.30
Avg.	305,838	919	181.00	93.66	73.14	27.95
Min.	183,142	480	112.00	42.06	23.42	17.16
Max.	1,358,576	3,851	594.00	180.03	440.99	40.42

Note: (1) Values for the local area are compared with the average, minimum and maximum values for all 308 areas in the Cost of Living Index; (2) Figures cover the Los Angeles-Long Beach CA urban area; **New Home Price** *(2,400 sf living area, 8,000 sf lot, in urban area with full utilities);* **Apartment Rent** *(950 sf 2 bedroom/1.5 or 2 bath, unfurnished, excluding all utilities except water);* **All Electric** *(average monthly cost for an all-electric home);* **Part Electric** *(average monthly cost for a part-electric home);* **Other Energy** *(average monthly cost for natural gas, fuel oil, coal, wood, and any other forms of energy except electricity);* **Telephone** *(price includes basic monthly rate for a private residential line plus additional local usage charges incurred by a family of four).*
Source: The Council for Community and Economic Research, ACCRA Cost of Living Index, 2014

Health Care, Transportation, and Other Costs

Area[1]	Doctor ($/visit)	Dentist ($/visit)	Optometrist ($/visit)	Gasoline ($/gallon)	Beauty Salon ($/visit)	Men's Shirt ($)
City[2]	97.18	108.13	124.85	4.01	63.24	27.74
Avg.	102.86	87.89	97.66	3.44	34.37	26.74
Min.	67.47	65.78	51.18	3.00	17.43	12.79
Max.	173.50	150.14	235.00	4.33	64.28	49.50

Note: (1) Values for the local area are compared with the average, minimum and maximum values for all 308 areas in the Cost of Living Index; (2) Figures cover the Los Angeles-Long Beach CA urban area; **Doctor** *(general practitioners routine exam of an established patient);* **Dentist** *(adult teeth cleaning and periodic oral examination);* **Optometrist** *(full vision eye exam for established adult patient);* **Gasoline** *(one gallon regular unleaded, national brand, including all taxes, cash price at self-service pump if available);* **Beauty Salon** *(woman's shampoo, trim, and blow-dry);* **Men's Shirt** *(cotton/polyester dress shirt, pinpoint weave, long sleeves).*
Source: The Council for Community and Economic Research, ACCRA Cost of Living Index, 2014

HOUSING

House Price Index (HPI)

Area	National Ranking[2]	Quarterly Change (%)	One-Year Change (%)	Five-Year Change (%)
MD[1]	56	1.22	7.85	21.79
U.S.[3]	–	1.35	4.91	11.59

Note: The HPI is a weighted repeat sales index. It measures average price changes in repeat sales or refinancings on the same properties. This information is obtained by reviewing repeat mortgage transactions on single-family properties whose mortgages have been purchased or securitized by Fannie Mae or Freddie Mac in January 1975; (1) Los Angeles-Long Beach-Glendale Metropolitan Division—see Appendix B for areas included; (2) Rankings are based on annual percentage change for all metro areas containing at least 15,000 transactions over the last 10 years and ranges from 1 to 275; (3) figures based on a weighted average of Census Division estimates using a seasonally adjusted, purchase-only index; all figures are for the period ending December 31, 2014
Source: Federal Housing Finance Agency, House Price Index, February 26, 2015

Median Single-Family Home Prices

Area	2012	2013	2014p	Percent Change 2013 to 2014
MSA[1]	327.5	405.6	449.5	10.8
U.S. Average	177.2	197.4	209.0	5.9

Note: Figures are median sales prices of existing single-family homes in thousands of dollars; (p) preliminary; n/a not available; (1) Los Angeles-Long Beach-Anaheim, CA Metropolitan Statistical Area—see Appendix B for areas included
Source: National Association of Realtors, Median Sales Price of Existing Single-Family Homes for Metropolitan Areas, 4th Quarter 2014

Qualifying Income Based on Median Sales Price of Existing Single-Family Homes

Area	With 5% Down ($)	With 10% Down ($)	With 20% Down ($)
MSA[1]	99,087	93,872	83,442
U.S. Average	45,863	43,449	38,621

Note: Figures are preliminary; Qualifying income is based on a mortgage rate of 4.0%. Monthly principal and interest payment is limited to 25% of income; n/a not available; (1) Los Angeles-Long Beach-Anaheim, CA Metropolitan Statistical Area—see Appendix B for areas included
Source: National Association of Realtors, Qualifying Income Based on Median Sales Price of Existing Single-Family Homes for Metropolitan Areas, 4th Quarter 2014

Median Apartment Condo-Coop Home Prices

Area	2012	2013	2014p	Percent Change 2013 to 2014
MSA[1]	245.5	341.9	382.2	11.8
U.S. Average	173.7	194.9	205.1	5.2

Note: Figures are median sales prices of existing apartment condo-coop homes in thousands of dollars; (p) preliminary; n/a not available; (1) Los Angeles-Long Beach-Anaheim, CA Metropolitan Statistical Area—see Appendix B for areas included
Source: National Association of Realtors, Median Sales Price of Existing Apartment Condo-Coop Homes for Metropolitan Areas, 4th Quarter 2014

Gross Monthly Rent

Area	Under $200	$200 -299	$300 -499	$500 -749	$750 -999	$1,000 -1,499	$1,500 and up	Median ($)
City	0.7	2.5	3.1	9.0	20.8	35.4	28.5	1,172
MSA[1]	0.6	2.0	2.6	6.9	17.7	37.2	33.1	1,256
U.S.	1.7	3.2	7.8	22.1	24.3	26.0	14.9	900

Note: Figures are percentages except for Median; Gross rent is the contract rent plus the estimated average monthly cost of utilities (electricity, gas, and water and sewer) and fuels (oil, coal, kerosene, wood, etc.) if these are paid by the renter (or paid for the renter by someone else); (1) Figures cover the Los Angeles-Long Beach-Anaheim, CA Metropolitan Statistical Area—see Appendix B for areas included
Source: U.S. Census Bureau, 2011-2013 American Community Survey 3-Year Estimates

Homeownership Rate

Area	2007 (%)	2008 (%)	2009 (%)	2010 (%)	2011 (%)	2012 (%)	2013 (%)	2014 (%)
MSA[1]	52.3	52.1	50.4	49.7	50.1	49.9	48.7	49.0
U.S.	68.1	67.8	67.4	66.9	66.1	65.4	65.1	64.5

Note: (1) Figures cover the Los Angeles-Long Beach-Anaheim, CA Metropolitan Statistical Area—see Appendix B for areas included
Source: U.S. Census Bureau, Housing Vacancies and Homeownership Annual Statistics: 2014

Year Housing Structure Built

Area	2010 or Later	2000 -2009	1990 -1999	1980 -1989	1970 -1979	1960 -1969	1950 -1959	1940 -1949	Before 1940	Median Year
City	0.6	6.6	5.7	10.2	13.6	14.2	18.0	10.5	20.6	1961
MSA[1]	0.5	7.0	7.6	12.6	16.5	15.9	19.0	8.8	12.2	1966
U.S.	0.9	15.0	13.9	13.8	15.8	11.0	10.9	5.4	13.3	1976

Note: Figures are percentages except for Median Year; (1) Figures cover the Los Angeles-Long Beach-Anaheim, CA Metropolitan Statistical Area—see Appendix B for areas included
Source: U.S. Census Bureau, 2011-2013 American Community Survey 3-Year Estimates

HEALTH

Health Risk Data

Category	MD[1] (%)	U.S. (%)
Adults aged 18–64 who have any kind of health care coverage	68.3	79.6
Adults who reported being in good or excellent health	78.4	83.1
Adults who are current smokers	11.8	19.6
Adults who are heavy drinkers[2]	5.0	6.1
Adults who are binge drinkers[3]	16.3	16.9
Adults who are overweight (BMI 25.0 - 29.9)	34.3	35.8
Adults who are obese (BMI 30.0 - 99.8)	25.0	27.6
Adults who participated in any physical activities in the past month	78.5	77.1
Adults 50+ who have ever had a sigmoidoscopy or colonoscopy	62.0	67.3
Women aged 40+ who have had a mammogram within the past two years	78.5	74.0
Men aged 40+ who have had a PSA test within the past two years	39.8	45.2
Adults aged 65+ who have had flu shot within the past year	55.6	60.1
Adults who always wear a seatbelt	96.5	93.8

Note: Data as of 2012 unless otherwise noted; (1) Figures cover the Los Angeles-Long Beach-Glendale, CA Metropolitan Division—see Appendix B for areas included; (2) Heavy drinkers are classified as males having more than two drinks per day or females having more than one drink per day; (3) Binge drinkers are classified as males having five or more drinks on one occasion or females having four or more drinks on one occasion
Source: Centers for Disease Control and Prevention, Behaviorial Risk Factor Surveillance System, SMART: Selected Metropolitan/Micropolitan Area Risk Trends, 2012 (Note: the CDC has discontinued this dataset but will be releasing a replacement in late 2015)

Chronic Health Indicators

Category	MD[1] (%)	U.S. (%)
Adults who have ever been told they had a heart attack	3.1	4.5
Adults who have ever been told they had a stroke	2.0	2.9
Adults who have been told they currently have asthma	7.2	8.9
Adults who have ever been told they have arthritis	19.5	25.7
Adults who have ever been told they have diabetes[2]	10.6	9.7
Adults who have ever been told they had skin cancer	3.3	5.7
Adults who have ever been told they had any other types of cancer	4.4	6.5
Adults who have ever been told they have COPD	3.6	6.2
Adults who have ever been told they have kidney disease	2.6	2.5
Adults who have ever been told they have a form of depression	10.6	18.0

Note: Data as of 2012 unless otherwise noted; (1) Figures cover the Los Angeles-Long Beach-Glendale, CA Metropolitan Division—see Appendix B for areas included; (2) Figures do not include pregnancy-related, borderline, or pre-diabetes
Source: Centers for Disease Control and Prevention, Behaviorial Risk Factor Surveillance System, SMART: Selected Metropolitan/Micropolitan Area Risk Trends, 2012 (Note: the CDC has discontinued this dataset but will be releasing a replacement in late 2015)

Mortality Rates for the Top 10 Causes of Death in the U.S.

ICD-10[a] Sub-Chapter	ICD-10[a] Code	Age-Adjusted Mortality Rate[1] per 100,000 population	
		County[2]	U.S.
Malignant neoplasms	C00-C97	145.3	166.2
Ischaemic heart diseases	I20-I25	121.6	105.7
Other forms of heart disease	I30-I51	31.7	49.3
Chronic lower respiratory diseases	J40-J47	31.0	42.1
Organic, including symptomatic, mental disorders	F01-F09	19.9	38.1
Cerebrovascular diseases	I60-I69	34.4	37.0
Other external causes of accidental injury	W00-X59	13.0	26.9
Other degenerative diseases of the nervous system	G30-G31	26.3	25.6
Diabetes mellitus	E10-E14	22.8	21.3
Hypertensive diseases	I10-I15	21.4	19.4

Note: (a) ICD-10 = International Classification of Diseases 10th Revision; (1) Mortality rates are a three year average covering 2011-2013; (2) Figures cover Los Angeles County
Source: Centers for Disease Control and Prevention, National Center for Health Statistics. Compressed Mortality File 1999-2013 on CDC WONDER Online Database, released October 2014. Data are compiled from the Compressed Mortality File 1999-2013, Series 20 No. 2S, 2014.

Mortality Rates for Selected Causes of Death

ICD-10[a] Sub-Chapter	ICD-10[a] Code	Age-Adjusted Mortality Rate[1] per 100,000 population	
		County[2]	U.S.
Assault	X85-Y09	5.5	5.2
Diseases of the liver	K70-K76	14.5	13.2
Human immunodeficiency virus (HIV) disease	B20-B24	2.3	2.2
Influenza and pneumonia	J09-J18	22.1	15.4
Intentional self-harm	X60-X84	7.7	12.5
Malnutrition	E40-E46	0.4	0.9
Obesity and other hyperalimentation	E65-E68	1.3	1.8
Renal failure	N17-N19	9.2	13.1
Transport accidents	V01-V99	7.5	11.7
Viral hepatitis	B15-B19	2.6	2.2

Note: (a) ICD-10 = International Classification of Diseases 10th Revision; (1) Mortality rates are a three year average covering 2011-2013; (2) Figures cover Los Angeles County
Source: Centers for Disease Control and Prevention, National Center for Health Statistics. Compressed Mortality File 1999-2013 on CDC WONDER Online Database, released October 2014. Data are compiled from the Compressed Mortality File 1999-2013, Series 20 No. 2S, 2014.

Health Insurance Coverage

Area	With Health Insurance	With Private Health Insurance	With Public Health Insurance	Without Health Insurance	Population Under Age 18 Without Health Insurance
City	74.9	48.7	31.8	25.1	9.0
MSA[1]	79.2	56.0	29.5	20.8	8.4
U.S.	85.2	65.2	31.0	14.8	7.3

Note: Figures are percentages that cover the civilian noninstitutionalized population; (1) Figures cover the Los Angeles-Long Beach-Anaheim, CA Metropolitan Statistical Area—see Appendix B for areas included
Source: U.S. Census Bureau, 2011-2013 American Community Survey 3-Year Estimates

Number of Medical Professionals

Area[1]	MDs[2]	DOs[2,3]	Dentists	Podiatrists	Chiropractors	Optometrists
Local (number)	28,120	1,056	7,784	573	2,630	1,521
Local (rate[4])	281.9	10.6	77.4	5.7	26.2	15.1
U.S. (rate[4])	270.0	20.2	63.1	5.7	25.2	14.9

Note: Data as of 2013 unless noted; (1) Local data covers Los Angeles County; (2) Data as of 2012 and includes all active, non-federal physicians; (3) Doctor of Osteopathic Medicine; (4) rate per 100,000 population
Source: U.S. Department of Health and Human Services, Health Resources and Services Administration, Bureau of Health Professions, Area Resource File (ARF) 2013-2014

Best Hospitals

According to *U.S. News,* the Los Angeles-Long Beach-Glendale, CA metro area is home to 11 of the best hospitals in the U.S.: **Cedars-Sinai Medical Center** (Honor Roll/12 specialties); **City of Hope** (2 specialties); **Kaiser Permanente Los Angeles Medical Center** (2 specialties); **Keck Medical Center of USC** (2 specialties); **Long Beach Memorial Medical Center** (1 specialty); **Resnick Neuropsychiatric Hospital at UCLA** (1 specialty); **Santa Monica-UCLA Medical Center and Orthopedic Hospital** (1 specialty); **Stein and Doheny Eye Institutes, UCLA Medical Center** (1 specialty); **UCLA Medical Center** (Honor Roll/12 specialties); **USC Eye Institute-Keck Medical Center of USC** (1 specialty); **USC Norris Cancer Hospital-Keck Medical Center of USC** (1 specialty). The hospitals listed were nationally ranked in at least one adult specialty. Only 144 hospitals nationwide were nationally ranked in one or more specialties. Seventeen hospitals in the U.S. made the Honor Roll with high scores in at least six specialties. *U.S. News Online, "America's Best Children's Hospitals 2014-15"*

According to *U.S. News,* the Los Angeles-Long Beach-Glendale, CA metro area is home to two of the best children's hospitals in the U.S.: **Children's Hospital Los Angeles** (Honor Roll/10 specialties); **Mattel Children's Hospital UCLA** (8 specialties). The hospitals listed were highly ranked in at least one pediatric specialty. Eighty-nine children's hospitals in the U.S. were nationally ranked in at least one specialty. Ten children's hospitals in the U.S. made the Honor Roll with high scores in at least three specialties. *U.S. News Online, "America's Best Children's Hospitals 2014-15"*

EDUCATION

Public School District Statistics

District Name	Schls	Pupils	Pupil/ Teacher Ratio	Minority Pupils[1] (%)	Free Lunch Eligible[2] (%)	IEP[3] (%)
Los Angeles USD	978	655,455	23.6	90.8	54.4	12.6

Note: Table includes school districts with 2,000 or more students; (1) Percentage of students that are not non-Hispanic white; (2) Percentage of students that are eligible for the free lunch program; (3) Percentage of students that have an Individualized Education Program.
Source: U.S. Department of Education, National Center for Education Statistics, Common Core of Data, Local Education Agency (School District) Universe Survey: School Year 2012-2013; U.S. Department of Education, National Center for Education Statistics, Common Core of Data, Public Elementary/Secondary School Universe Survey: School Year 2012-2013

Best High Schools

According to *The Daily Beast,* Los Angeles is home to six of the best high schools in the U.S.: **Van Nuys High Magnets** (#278); **Granada Hills Charter High School** (#464); **Animo Jackie Robinson CHS** (#490); **Oscar De La Hoya Animo CHS** (#611); **Downtown Magnets High School** (#618); **Animo South Los Angeles CHS** (#687); *The Daily Beast* used six indicators culled from school surveys to compare public high schools in the U.S., with graduation and college acceptance rates weighed most heavily. Other criteria included: college-level courses/exams and SAT/ACT scores. *The Daily Beast, "Top High Schools 2014"*

Highest Level of Education

Area	Less than H.S.	H.S. Diploma	Some College, No Deg.	Associate Degree	Bachelor's Degree	Master's Degree	Prof. School Degree	Doctorate Degree
City	25.2	19.6	18.0	5.9	20.9	6.6	2.6	1.2
MSA[1]	21.5	20.0	19.9	7.1	20.6	7.2	2.4	1.3
U.S.	13.7	28.0	21.2	7.9	18.2	7.7	1.9	1.3

Note: Figures cover persons age 25 and over; (1) Figures cover the Los Angeles-Long Beach-Anaheim, CA Metropolitan Statistical Area—see Appendix B for areas included
Source: U.S. Census Bureau, 2011-2013 American Community Survey 3-Year Estimates

Educational Attainment by Race

Area	High School Graduate or Higher (%)					Bachelor's Degree or Higher (%)				
	Total	White	Black	Asian	Hisp.[2]	Total	White	Black	Asian	Hisp.[2]
City	74.8	79.1	86.2	89.5	51.2	31.3	36.6	23.0	51.7	9.8
MSA[1]	78.5	81.1	88.3	87.2	57.4	31.6	33.3	24.1	49.9	10.9
U.S.	86.3	88.3	83.1	85.7	64.0	29.1	30.4	18.8	50.7	13.7

Note: Figures shown cover persons 25 years old and over; (1) Figures cover the Los Angeles-Long Beach-Anaheim, CA Metropolitan Statistical Area—see Appendix B for areas included; (2) People of Hispanic origin can be of any race
Source: U.S. Census Bureau, 2011-2013 American Community Survey 3-Year Estimates

School Enrollment by Grade and Control

Area	Preschool (%)		Kindergarten (%)		Grades 1 - 4 (%)		Grades 5 - 8 (%)		Grades 9 - 12 (%)	
	Public	Private	Public	Private	Public	Private	Public	Private	Public	Private
City	61.5	38.5	86.7	13.3	89.1	10.9	88.8	11.2	89.5	10.5
MSA[1]	59.0	41.0	87.9	12.1	90.3	9.7	90.6	9.4	91.8	8.2
U.S.	57.7	42.3	87.9	12.1	89.9	10.1	90.0	10.0	90.7	9.3

Note: Figures shown cover persons 3 years old and over; (1) Figures cover the Los Angeles-Long Beach-Anaheim, CA Metropolitan Statistical Area—see Appendix B for areas included
Source: U.S. Census Bureau, 2011-2013 American Community Survey 3-Year Estimates

Average Salaries of Public School Classroom Teachers

Area	2013-14		2014-15		Percent Change 2013-14 to 2014-15	Percent Change 2004-05 to 2014-15
	Dollars	Rank[1]	Dollars	Rank[1]		
CALIFORNIA	71,396	4	72,535	4	1.59	25.9
U.S. Average	56,610	–	57,379	–	1.36	20.8

Note: (1) State rank ranges from 1 to 51 where 1 indicates highest salary.
Source: National Education Association, Rankings & Estimates: Rankings of the States 2014 and Estimates of School Statistics 2015, March 2015

Higher Education

Four-Year Colleges			Two-Year Colleges			Medical Schools[1]	Law Schools[2]	Voc/ Tech[3]
Public	Private Non-profit	Private For-profit	Public	Private Non-profit	Private For-profit			
2	20	14	6	5	12	2	5	30

Note: Figures cover institutions located within the city limits and include main campuses only; (1) includes schools accredited by the Liaison Committee on Medical Education and the American Osteopathic Association's Commission on Osteopathic College Accreditation; (2) includes ABA-accredited schools, schools with provisional ABA accreditation, and state accredited schools; (3) includes all schools with programs that are less than 2 years.
Source: National Center for Education Statistics, Integrated Postsecondary Education System (IPEDS), 2013-14; Association of American Medical Colleges, Member List, May 1, 2015; American Osteopathic Association, Member List, May 1, 2015; Law School Admission Council, Official Guide to ABA-Approved Law Schools Online, May 1, 2015; Wikipedia, List of Medical Schools in the United States, May 1, 2015; Wikipedia, List of Law Schools in the United States, May 1, 2015

According to U.S. News & World Report, the Los Angeles-Long Beach-Glendale, CA metro division is home to seven of the best national universities in the U.S.: **California Institute of Technology** (#10); **University of California-Los Angeles** (#23); **University of Southern California** (#25); **Pepperdine University** (#54); **Biola University** (#161); **University of La Verne** (#166); **Azusa Pacific University** (#173). The indicators used to capture academic quality fall into a number of categories: assessment by administrators at peer institutions; retention of students; faculty resources; student selectivity; financial resources; alumni giving; high school counselor ratings of colleges; and graduation rate. U.S. News & World Report, "America's Best Colleges 2015"

According to U.S. News & World Report, the Los Angeles-Long Beach-Glendale, CA metro division is home to seven of the best liberal arts colleges in the U.S.: **Pomona College** (#5); **Claremont McKenna College** (#8); **Harvey Mudd College** (#15); **Scripps College** (#24); **Pitzer College** (#35); **Occidental College** (#44); **Whittier College** (#133). The indicators used to capture academic quality fall into a number of categories: assessment by administrators at peer institutions; retention of students; faculty resources; student selectivity; financial resources; alumni giving; high school counselor ratings of colleges; and graduation rate. U.S. News & World Report, "America's Best Colleges 2015"

According to *U.S. News & World Report*, the Los Angeles-Long Beach-Glendale, CA metro division is home to four of the top 100 law schools in the U.S.: **University of California-Los Angeles** (#16); **University of Southern California (Gould)** (#20); **Pepperdine University** (#52); **Loyola Marymount University** (#75). The rankings are based on a weighted average of 12 measures of quality: peer assessment score; assessment score by lawyers/judges; median LSAT scores; median undergrad GPA; acceptance rate; employment rates for graduates; placement success; bar passage rate; faculty resources; expenditures per student; student/faculty ratio; and library resources. *U.S. News & World Report, "America's Best Graduate Schools, Law, 2016"*

According to *U.S. News & World Report*, the Los Angeles-Long Beach-Glendale, CA metro division is home to two of the top 75 medical schools for research in the U.S.: **University of California-Los Angeles (Geffen)** (#13); **University of Southern California (Keck)** (#31). The rankings are based on a weighted average of 11 measures of quality: quality assessment; peer assessment score; assessment score by residency directors; research activity; total research activity; average research activity per faculty member; student selectivity; median MCAT total score; median undergraduate GPA; acceptance rate; and faculty resources. *U.S. News & World Report, "America's Best Graduate Schools, Medical, 2016"*

According to *U.S. News & World Report*, the Los Angeles-Long Beach-Glendale, CA metro division is home to two of the top 75 business schools in the U.S.: **University of California-Los Angeles (Anderson)** (#15); **University of Southern California (Marshall)** (#25). The rankings are based on a weighted average of the following nine measures: quality assessment; peer assessment; recruiter assessment; placement success; mean starting salary and bonus; student selectivity; mean GMAT and GRE scores; mean undergraduate GPA; and acceptance rate. *U.S. News & World Report, "America's Best Graduate Schools, Business, 2016"*

PRESIDENTIAL ELECTION

2012 Presidential Election Results

Area	Obama (%)	Romney (%)	Other (%)
Los Angeles County	68.6	29.1	2.3
U.S.	51.0	47.2	1.8

Note: Results may not add to 100% due to rounding
Source: Dave Leip's Atlas of U.S. Presidential Elections

EMPLOYERS

Major Employers

Company Name	Industry
City of Los Angeles	General government
County of Los Angeles	General government
County of Los Angeles	Pubblic welfare administration: nonoperating, government
Decton	Employment agencies
Disney Enterprises	Motion picture production and distribution
Disney Worldwide Services	Telecommunication equipment repair (except telephones)
Electronic Arts	Home entertainment computer software
King Holding Corporation	Bolts, nuts, rivets, and washers
Securitas Security Services USA	Security guard service
Team-One Employment Specialists	Employment agencies
The Boeing Company	Aircraft
The Boeing Company	Aircraft engines and engine parts
The Walt Disney Company	Television broadcasting stations
UCLA Health System	Home health care services
UCLA Medical Group	Medical centers
University of California, Irvine	University
University of Southern California	Colleges and universities
Veterans Health Administration	Administration of veterans' affairs
Warner Bros. Entertainment	Motion picture and video production

Note: Companies shown are located within the Los Angeles-Long Beach-Anaheim, CA Metropolitan Statistical Area.
Source: Hoovers.com; Wikipedia

Best Companies to Work For

Cedars-Sinai Health System, headquartered in Los Angeles, is among the "100 Best Places to Work in IT." To qualify, companies, both public and private, had to have a minimum of 50 IT employees and were selected based on average salary and bonus increases, the percentage of IT staffers promoted, IT staff turnover rates, training and development programs, and the percentage of women and minorities in IT staff and management positions. In addition, *Computerworld* looked at retention efforts, programs for recognizing and rewarding outstanding performances, and benefits such as flextime, elder care and child care, and reimbursement for college tuition and the cost of pursuing technology certifications. *Computerworld, "100 Best Places to Work in IT 2014"*

PUBLIC SAFETY

Crime Rate

Area	All Crimes	Violent Crimes				Property Crimes		
		Murder	Forcible Rape	Robbery	Aggrav. Assault	Burglary	Larceny -Theft	Motor Vehicle Theft
City	2,639.2	6.5	19.7	203.3	196.6	405.5	1,436.9	370.8
Suburbs[1]	2,709.0	4.8	16.1	144.8	222.7	528.1	1,392.9	399.6
Metro[2]	2,682.0	5.4	17.5	167.5	212.6	480.6	1,410.0	388.5
U.S.	3,098.6	4.5	25.2	109.1	229.1	610.0	1,899.4	221.3

Note: Figures are crimes per 100,000 population; (1) All areas within the metro area that are located outside the city limits; (2) Figures cover the Los Angeles-Long Beach-Glendale, CA Metropolitan Division—see Appendix B for areas included
Source: FBI Uniform Crime Reports, 2013

Hate Crimes

Area	Number of Quarters Reported	Number of Incidents per Bias Motivation						
		Race	Religion	Sexual Orientation	Ethnicity	Disability	Gender	Gender Identity
City	4	41	29	33	9	0	0	2
U.S.	4	2,871	1,031	1,233	655	83	18	31

Source: Federal Bureau of Investigation, Hate Crime Statistics 2013

Identity Theft Consumer Complaints

Area	Complaints	Complaints per 100,000 Population	Rank[2]
MSA[1]	14,397	109.6	40
U.S.	332,646	104.3	-

Note: (1) Figures cover the Los Angeles-Long Beach-Anaheim, CA Metropolitan Statistical Area—see Appendix B for areas included; (2) Rank ranges from 1 to 380 where 1 indicates greatest number of identity theft complaints per 100,000 population
Source: Federal Trade Commission, Consumer Sentinel Network Data Book for January–December 2014

Fraud and Other Consumer Complaints

Area	Complaints	Complaints per 100,000 Population	Rank[2]
MSA[1]	52,933	403.1	130
U.S.	2,250,205	705.7	-

Note: (1) Figures cover the Los Angeles-Long Beach-Anaheim, CA Metropolitan Statistical Area—see Appendix B for areas included; (2) Rank ranges from 1 to 380 where 1 indicates greatest number of identity theft complaints per 100,000 population
Source: Federal Trade Commission, Consumer Sentinel Network Data Book for January–December 2014

RECREATION

Culture

Dance[1]	Theatre[1]	Instrumental Music[1]	Vocal Music[1]	Series and Festivals	Museums and Art Galleries[2]	Zoos and Aquariums[3]
13	45	11	8	14	164	2

Note: (1) Professional perfoming groups; (2) Based on organizations with SIC code 8412; (3) AZA-accredited
Source: The Grey House Performing Arts Directory, 2015-16; Association of Zoos & Aquariums, AZA Member Zoos & Aquariums, April 2015; www.AccuLeads.com, April 2015

Professional Sports Teams

Team Name	League	Year Established
Anaheim Ducks	National Hockey League (NHL)	1993
C.D. Chivas USA	Major League Soccer (MLS)	2004
Los Angeles Angels of Anaheim	Major League Baseball (MLB)	1961
Los Angeles Clippers	National Basketball Association (NBA)	1984
Los Angeles Dodgers	Major League Baseball (MLB)	1958
Los Angeles Galaxy	Major League Soccer (MLS)	1996
Los Angeles Kings	National Hockey League (NHL)	1967
Los Angeles Lakers	National Basketball Association (NBA)	1960

Note: Includes teams located in the Los Angeles-Long Beach-Anaheim, CA Metropolitan Statistical Area.
Source: Wikipedia, Major Professional Sports Teams of the United States and Canada, April 2015

CLIMATE

Average and Extreme Temperatures

Temperature	Jan	Feb	Mar	Apr	May	Jun	Jul	Aug	Sep	Oct	Nov	Dec	Yr.
Extreme High (°F)	88	92	95	102	97	104	97	98	110	106	101	94	110
Average High (°F)	65	66	65	67	69	72	75	76	76	74	71	66	70
Average Temp. (°F)	56	57	58	60	63	66	69	70	70	67	62	57	63
Average Low (°F)	47	49	50	53	56	59	63	64	63	59	52	48	55
Extreme Low (°F)	27	34	37	43	45	48	52	51	47	43	38	32	27

Note: Figures cover the years 1947-1990
Source: National Climatic Data Center, International Station Meteorological Climate Summary, 9/96

Average Precipitation/Snowfall/Humidity

Precip./Humidity	Jan	Feb	Mar	Apr	May	Jun	Jul	Aug	Sep	Oct	Nov	Dec	Yr.
Avg. Precip. (in.)	2.6	2.3	1.8	0.8	0.1	Tr	Tr	0.1	0.2	0.3	1.5	1.5	11.3
Avg. Snowfall (in.)	Tr	0	0	0	0	0	0	0	0	0	0	0	Tr
Avg. Rel. Hum. 7am (%)	69	72	76	76	77	80	80	81	80	76	69	67	75
Avg. Rel. Hum. 4pm (%)	60	62	64	64	66	67	67	68	67	66	61	60	64

Note: Figures cover the years 1947-1990; Tr = Trace amounts (<0.05 in. of rain; <0.5 in. of snow)
Source: National Climatic Data Center, International Station Meteorological Climate Summary, 9/96

Weather Conditions

Temperature			Daytime Sky			Precipitation		
10°F & below	32°F & below	90°F & above	Clear	Partly cloudy	Cloudy	0.01 inch or more precip.	0.1 inch or more snow/ice	Thunder-storms
0	< 1	5	131	125	109	34	0	1

Note: Figures are average number of days per year and cover the years 1947-1990
Source: National Climatic Data Center, International Station Meteorological Climate Summary, 9/96

HAZARDOUS WASTE

Superfund Sites

Los Angeles has four hazardous waste sites on the EPA's Superfund Final National Priorities List: **Del Amo; San Fernando Valley (Area 1); San Fernando Valley (Area 2); San Fernando Valley (Area 4)**. There are a total of 1,322 Superfund sites on the list in the U.S. *U.S. Environmental Protection Agency, Final National Priorities List, April 14, 2015*

AIR & WATER QUALITY

Air Quality Trends: Ozone

	2004	2005	2006	2007	2008	2009	2010	2011	2012	2013
MSA[1]	0.088	0.083	0.088	0.084	0.088	0.085	0.073	0.077	0.078	0.074

Note: (1) Data covers the Los Angeles-Long Beach-Anaheim, CA Metropolitan Statistical Area—see Appendix B for areas included. The values shown are the composite ozone concentration averages among trend sites based on the highest fourth daily maximum 8-hour concentration in parts per million. These trends are based on sites having an adequate record of monitoring data during the trend period. Data from exceptional events are included.
Source: U.S. Environmental Protection Agency, Air Quality Monitoring Information, "Air Quality Trends by City, 2000-2013"

Air Quality Index

Area	Percent of Days when Air Quality was...[2]					AQI Statistics[2]	
	Good	Moderate	Unhealthy for Sensitive Groups	Unhealthy	Very Unhealthy	Maximum	Median
MSA[1]	6.8	69.0	20.8	3.3	0.0	187	76

Note: (1) Data covers the Los Angeles-Long Beach-Anaheim, CA Metropolitan Statistical Area—see Appendix B for areas included; (2) Based on 365 days with AQI data in 2014. Air Quality Index (AQI) is an index for reporting daily air quality. EPA calculates the AQI for five major air pollutants regulated by the Clean Air Act: ground-level ozone, particle pollution (aka particulate matter), carbon monoxide, sulfur dioxide, and nitrogen dioxide. The AQI runs from 0 to 500. The higher the AQI value, the greater the level of air pollution and the greater the health concern. There are six AQI categories: "Good" AQI is between 0 and 50. Air quality is considered satisfactory; "Moderate" AQI is between 51 and 100. Air quality is acceptable; "Unhealthy for Sensitive Groups" When AQI values are between 101 and 150, members of sensitive groups may experience health effects; "Unhealthy" When AQI values are between 151 and 200 everyone may begin to experience health effects; "Very Unhealthy" AQI values between 201 and 300 trigger a health alert; "Hazardous" AQI values over 300 trigger warnings of emergency conditions (not shown).
Source: U.S. Environmental Protection Agency, Air Quality Index Report, 2014

Air Quality Index Pollutants

Area	Percent of Days when AQI Pollutant was...[2]					
	Carbon Monoxide	Nitrogen Dioxide	Ozone	Sulfur Dioxide	Particulate Matter 2.5	Particulate Matter 10
MSA[1]	1.1	4.9	33.7	0.0	58.9	1.4

Note: (1) Data covers the Los Angeles-Long Beach-Anaheim, CA Metropolitan Statistical Area—see Appendix B for areas included; (2) Based on 365 days with AQI data in 2014. The Air Quality Index (AQI) is an index for reporting daily air quality. EPA calculates the AQI for five major air pollutants regulated by the Clean Air Act: ground-level ozone, particle pollution (also known as particulate matter), carbon monoxide, sulfur dioxide, and nitrogen dioxide. The AQI runs from 0 to 500. The higher the AQI value, the greater the level of air pollution and the greater the health concern.
Source: U.S. Environmental Protection Agency, Air Quality Index Report, 2014

Maximum Air Pollutant Concentrations: Particulate Matter, Ozone, CO and Lead

	Particulate Matter 10 (ug/m^3)	Particulate Matter 2.5 Wtd AM (ug/m^3)	Particulate Matter 2.5 24-Hr (ug/m^3)	Ozone (ppm)	Carbon Monoxide (ppm)	Lead (ug/m^3)
MSA[1] Level	91	12.5	30	0.094	3	0.1
NAAQS[2]	150	15	35	0.075	9	0.15
Met NAAQS[2]	Yes	Yes	Yes	No	Yes	Yes

Note: (1) Data covers the Los Angeles-Long Beach-Anaheim, CA Metropolitan Statistical Area—see Appendix B for areas included; Data from exceptional events are included; (2) National Ambient Air Quality Standards; ppm = parts per million; ug/m^3 = micrograms per cubic meter; n/a not available.
Concentrations: Particulate Matter 10 (coarse particulate)—highest second maximum 24-hour concentration; Particulate Matter 2.5 Wtd AM (fine particulate)—highest weighted annual mean concentration; Particulate Matter 2.5 24-Hour (fine particulate)—highest 98th percentile 24-hour concentration; Ozone—highest fourth daily maximum 8-hour concentration; Carbon Monoxide—highest second maximum non-overlapping 8-hour concentration; Lead—maximum running 3-month average
Source: U.S. Environmental Protection Agency, Air Quality Monitoring Information, "Air Quality Statistics by City, 2013"

Maximum Air Pollutant Concentrations: Nitrogen Dioxide and Sulfur Dioxide

	Nitrogen Dioxide AM (ppb)	Nitrogen Dioxide 1-Hr (ppb)	Sulfur Dioxide AM (ppb)	Sulfur Dioxide 1-Hr (ppb)	Sulfur Dioxide 24-Hr (ppb)
MSA[1] Level	23	71	n/a	12	n/a
NAAQS[2]	53	100	30	75	140
Met NAAQS[2]	Yes	Yes	n/a	Yes	n/a

Note: (1) Data covers the Los Angeles-Long Beach-Anaheim, CA Metropolitan Statistical Area—see Appendix B for areas included; Data from exceptional events are included; (2) National Ambient Air Quality Standards; ppm = parts per million; ug/m^3 = micrograms per cubic meter; n/a not available.
Concentrations: Nitrogen Dioxide AM—highest arithmetic mean concentration; Nitrogen Dioxide 1-Hr—highest 98th percentile 1-hour daily maximum concentration; Sulfur Dioxide AM—highest annual mean concentration; Sulfur Dioxide 1-Hr—highest 99th percentile 1-hour daily maximum concentration; Sulfur Dioxide 24-Hr—highest second maximum 24-hour concentration
Source: U.S. Environmental Protection Agency, Air Quality Monitoring Information, "Air Quality Statistics by City, 2013"

Drinking Water

Water System Name	Pop. Served	Primary Water Source Type	Violations[1]	
			Health Based	Monitoring/ Reporting
LA Dept of Water & Power	3,894,439	Surface	0	0

Note: (1) Based on violation data from January 1, 2014 to December 31, 2014 (includes unresolved violations from earlier years)
Source: U.S. Environmental Protection Agency, Office of Ground Water and Drinking Water, Safe Drinking Water Information System (based on data extracted January 27, 2015)

Oxnard, California

Background

Oxnard is the largest city in southern California's Ventura County. The city sits on the Oxnard Plain, which is known for having some of the most fertile soil in the world. Because of this natural resource, Oxnard's major industry is agriculture. It is considered by many to be the strawberry capital of the world and hosts an annual California Strawberry Festival.

The area that is now Oxnard was originally inhabited by the Chumash Native American Tribe. The territory was then claimed for Spain by a Portuguese explorer in 1542. After the Mexican-American War, California became part of the United States, and its own state in 1850. Around this time that American settlers began to migrate to the area. These first Americans to live in the region were mostly farmers who took advantage of its rich soil to grow lima beans and barley.

The city of Oxnard was incorporated by the California State Legislature in 1903. It was named for Henry Oxnard, who had opened a large factory in the area in 1899. A railroad station was built in 1898, helping to grow the city's economy at the turn of the century. A public library paid for by steel tycoon Andrew Carnegie was built in Oxnard in 1907. The fact that the region possessed the only navigable port on the California coast between Los Angeles and San Francisco led to the founding of Point Mugu and Port Hueneme during World War II and established the region as a hub for the defense and communications industries.

After the War, Oxnard continued to expand and grow quickly. An influential developer named Martin Smith was responsible for the Wagon Wheel Junction, the Topa Financial Plaza, the Channel Islands Harbor, the Casa Sirena Resort, the Esplanade Shopping Mall, and numerous other projects. The city's expansion was so rapid, in fact, that many acres of prime agricultural land were annexed for development, especially during the 1970s and 1980s. This led to the creation in 1995 of an initiative called Save Open Space and Agricultural Resources (SOAR), which was founded by farmers, ranchers and other concerned citizens to preserve the land of the Oxnard Plain.

In addition to agriculture, other major segments of the city's economy include international trade, manufacturing, defense, and tourism. Port Hueneme is the only deep-water port between Los Angeles and San Francisco and has steadily exceeded the million-ton mark in general cargo tonnage since it first crossed that landmark number in the 1990s. In 2012-2013, the Port had its best fiscal year ever with 1.4 metric tons. Automobiles, heavy cargo, fresh produce, fertilizer, and fish and petroleum products helped to drive the increase. The port supports the transport of more than $7 billion in cargo and generates a $1 billion economic impact. Major trading partners include Austria, Brazil, Canada, Costa Rica, China, Ecuador, and numerous other countries throughout the world. Major companies that use the port include DelMonte and Chiquita.

Major companies with headquarters or regional operations centers in Oxnard include Vivitar, Haas Automation, Boss Audio, Proctor & Gamble and Sysco. The city is home to two U.S. Navy bases, Port Hueneme and NAS Point Mugo.

The Henry T. Oxnard District of the city's downtown area is on the National Register of Historic Places. The Historic Enhancement and Revitalization of Oxnard (HERO) was designed to promote historic preservation and guide new development of selected sites throughout Oxnard. RiverPark was developed in recent years, a large mixed-use community anchored by The Collection, with dining, shopping and offices. Riverpark is also home to a middle school, an elementary school, a police station, a fire station, numerous parks and five neighborhoods of homes, as well as individual residences.

Major attractions in the city include the Carnegie Art Museum, which was founded in 1907, the Murphy Auto Museum, Heritage Square, and the Oxnard Performing Arts Convention Center. In addition to Oxnard College, California Lutheran University, DeVry University, the University of La Verne—Ventura County, Charter College, and Channel Islands Bible College and Seminary all operate satellite campuses in the city. Oxnard is not home to any major professional sports teams, but the NFL's Dallas Cowboys hold their off-season training camp there.

Oxnard has a mild subtropical climate that typically produces cool, dry weather. Its climate is distinctive when compared to other southern California regions because its winters are usually slightly warmer than average and its summers are usually slightly cooler than average. This subtle difference contributes to the city's ideal conditions for agriculture.

Rankings

Business/Finance Rankings

- TransUnion ranked the nation's metro areas by average credit score, calculated on the VantageScore system, developed by the three major credit-reporting bureaus—TransUnion, Experian, and Equifax. The Oxnard metro area was among the ten cities with the highest collective credit score, meaning that its residents posed the lowest average consumer credit risk. *www.usatoday.com, "Metro Areas' Average Credit Rating Revealed," February 7, 2013*

- Building on the U.S. Department of Labor's Occupational Information Network Data Collection Program, the Brookings Institution defined STEM occupations and job opportunities for STEM workers at various levels of educational attainment. The Oxnard metro area was one of the ten metro areas where workers in low-education-level STEM jobs earn the lowest relative wages. *www.brookings.edu, "The Hidden Stem Economy," June 10, 2013*

- Oxnard was ranked #46 out of 100 metro areas in terms of economic performance (#1 = best) during the recession and recovery from trough quarter through the second quarter of 2013. Criteria: percent change in employment; percentage point change in unemployment rate; percent change in gross metropolitan product; percent change in House Price Index. *Brookings Institution, MetroMonitor: Tracking Economic Recession and Recovery in America's 100 Largest Metropolitan Areas, September 2013*

- The finance site *24/7 Wall St.* identified the metropolitan areas that have the smallest and largest pay disparities between men and women, comparing the median earnings for the past 12 months of both men and women working full-time in the country's 100 largest metropolitan statistical areas. Of the ten best-paying metros for women, the Oxnard metro area ranked #8. *24/7 Wall St., "The Best (and Worst) Paying Cities for Women," March 6, 2015*

- The Oxnard metro area appeared on the Milken Institute "2013 Best Performing Cities" list. Rank: #95 out of 200 large metro areas. Criteria: job growth; wage and salary growth; high-tech output growth. *Milken Institute, "Best-Performing Cities 2014," January 2015*

- *Forbes* ranked the 200 most populous metro areas to determine the nation's "Best Places for Business and Careers." The Oxnard metro area was ranked #131. Criteria: costs (business and living); job growth (past and projected); income growth; educational attainment (college and high school); projected economic growth; cultural and recreational opportunities; net migration patterns; number of highly ranked colleges. *Forbes, "The Best Places for Business and Careers 2014," July 23, 2014*

Education Rankings

- Personal finance website *WalletHub* analyzed the 150 largest U.S. metropolitan statistical areas to determine where the most educated Americans are choosing to settle. Criteria: educational attainment; percentage of workers with jobs in computer, engineering, and science fields; quality and size of each metro area's universities. Oxnard was ranked #50 (#1 = most educated city). *www.WalletHub.com, "2014's Most and Least Educated Cities*

Environmental Rankings

- The Oxnard metro area came in at #31 for the relative comfort of its climate on Sperling's list of "chill cities," as measured by the Sperling Heat Index. All 361 metro areas are included. Criteria included daytime high temperatures, nighttime low temperatures, dew point, and relative humidity at the high temperatures. *www.bertsperling.com, "Sperling's Chill Cities," July 18, 2013*

- Sperling's BestPlaces assessed 379 metropolitan areas of the United States for the likelihood of dangerously extreme weather events or earthquakes. In general the Southeast and South-Central regions have the highest risk of weather extremes and earthquakes, while the Pacific Northwest enjoys the lowest risk. Of the least risky metropolitan areas, the Oxnard metro area was ranked #143. *www.bestplaces.net, "Safest Places from Natural Disasters," April 2011*

Health/Fitness Rankings

- Oxnard was identified as a "2013 Spring Allergy Capital." The area ranked #90 out of 100. Three groups of factors were used to identify the most severe cities for people with allergies during the spring season: annual pollen levels; medicine utilization; access to board-certified allergists. *Asthma and Allergy Foundation of America, "Spring Allergy Capitals 2013"*

- Oxnard was identified as a "2013 Fall Allergy Capital." The area ranked #90 out of 100. Three groups of factors were used to identify the most severe cities for people with allergies during the fall season: annual pollen levels; medicine utilization; access to board-certified allergists. *Asthma and Allergy Foundation of America, "Fall Allergy Capitals 2013"*

- Oxnard was identified as a "2013 Asthma Capital." The area ranked #90 out of the nation's 100 largest metropolitan areas. Twelve factors were used to identify the most challenging places to live for people with asthma: estimated prevalence; self-reported prevalence; crude death rate for asthma; annual pollen score; annual air quality; public smoking laws; number of board-certified asthma specialists; school inhaler access laws; rescue medication use; controller medication use; uninsured rate; poverty rate. *Asthma and Allergy Foundation of America, "Asthma Capitals 2013"*

- The Oxnard metro area appeared in the 2013 Gallup-Healthways Well-Being Index. The area ranked #47 out of 189. The Gallup-Healthways Well-Being Index score is an average of six sub-indexes, which individually examine life evaluation, emotional health, work environment, physical health, healthy behaviors, and access to basic necessities. Results are based on telephone interviews conducted as part of the Gallup-Healthways Well-Being Index survey January 2–December 29, 2012, and January 2–December 30, 2013, with a random sample of 531,630 adults, aged 18 and older, living in metropolitan areas in the 50 U.S. states and the District of Columbia. *Gallup-Healthways, "State of American Well-Being," March 25, 2014*

Real Estate Rankings

- The Oxnard metro area was identified as one of the nation's 20 hottest housing markets in 2015.Criteria: median number of days homes were spending on the market in March 2015. The area ranked #14. *Realtor.com, "These Are the 20 Hottest Housing Markets in the U.S. Right Now," April 8, 2015*

- Oxnard was ranked #77 out of 275 metro areas in terms of house price appreciation in 2014 (#1 = highest rate). *Federal Housing Finance Agency, House Price Index, 4th Quarter 2014*

- Oxnard was ranked #213 out of 226 metro areas in terms of housing affordability in 2014 by the National Association of Home Builders (#1 = most affordable). The NAHB-Wells Fargo Housing Opportunity Index (HOI) for a given area is defined as the share of homes sold in that area that would have been affordable to a family earning the local median income, based on standard mortgage underwriting criteria. *National Association of Home Builders®, NAHB-Wells Fargo Housing Opportunity Index, 4th Quarter 2014*

Safety Rankings

- In search of the nation's safest cities, Business Insider looked at the FBI's preliminary Uniform Crime Report, excluding localities with fewer than 200,000 residents. To judge by its low murder, rape, and robbery data, Oxnard made the 20 safest cities list, at #16. *www.businessinsider.com, "The 20 Safest Cities in America," July 25, 2013*

- Allstate ranked the 200 largest cities in America in terms of driver safety. Oxnard ranked #100. Allstate researchers analyzed internal property damage claims over a two-year period from January 2011 to December 2012. A weighted average of the two-year numbers determined the annual percentages. *Allstate, "Allstate America's Best Drivers Report, 2014"*

- The National Insurance Crime Bureau ranked 380 metro areas in the U.S. in terms of per capita rates of vehicle theft. The Oxnard metro area ranked #109 (#1 = highest rate). Criteria: number of vehicle theft offenses per 100,000 inhabitants in 2012. *National Insurance Crime Bureau, "Hot Spots 2012," June 26, 2013*

Seniors/Retirement Rankings

- From its Best Cities for Successful Aging indexes, the Milken Institute generated rankings for metropolitan areas, weighing data in eight categories—health care, wellness, living arrangements, transportation, financial characteristics, education and employment opportunities, community engagement, and overall livability. The Oxnard metro area was ranked #77 overall in the large metro area category. *Milken Institute, "Best Cities for Successful Aging, 2014"*

Women/Minorities Rankings

- To determine the best metro areas for working women, the personal finance website NerdWallet considered city size as well as relevant economic metrics—high salaries, narrow pay differential by gender, prevalence of women in the highest-paying industries, and population growth over 2010–2012. Of the medium-sized U.S. cities examined, the Oxnard metro area held the #2 position. *www.nerdwallet.com, "Best Places for Women in the Workforce," May 19, 2013*

Miscellaneous Rankings

- According to the World Giving Index, the United States is the fifth most generous nation in the world. The finance and lifestyle site NerdWallet looked for the U.S. cities that topped the list in donating money and time to good causes. The Oxnard metro area proved to be the #8-ranked metro area, judged by culture of volunteerism, depth of commitment in terms of volunteer hours per year, and monetary contributions. *www.nerdwallet.com, "Most Generous Cities," September 22, 2013*

- The National Alliance to End Homelessness ranked the 100 most populous metro areas in terms the rate of homelessness. The Oxnard metro area ranked #22. Criteria: number of homeless people per 10,000 population in 2011. *National Alliance to End Homelessness, The State of Homelessness in America 2012*

Business Environment

CITY FINANCES

City Government Finances

Component	2012 ($000)	2012 ($ per capita)
Total Revenues	359,769	1,818
Total Expenditures	399,858	2,021
Debt Outstanding	484,295	2,447
Cash and Securities[1]	154,914	783

Note: (1) Cash and security holdings of a government at the close of its fiscal year, including those of its dependent agencies, utilities, and liquor stores.
Source: U.S Census Bureau, State & Local Government Finances 2012

City Government Revenue by Source

Source	2012 ($000)	2012 ($ per capita)
General Revenue		
From Federal Government	2,475	13
From State Government	37,827	191
From Local Governments	0	0
Taxes		
Property	68,250	345
Sales and Gross Receipts	39,539	200
Personal Income	0	0
Corporate Income	0	0
Motor Vehicle License	0	0
Other Taxes	8,058	41
Current Charges	134,419	679
Liquor Store	0	0
Utility	46,871	237
Employee Retirement	0	0

Source: U.S Census Bureau, State & Local Government Finances 2012

City Government Expenditures by Function

Function	2012 ($000)	2012 ($ per capita)	2012 (%)
General Direct Expenditures			
Air Transportation	0	0	0.0
Corrections	0	0	0.0
Education	0	0	0.0
Employment Security Administration	0	0	0.0
Financial Administration	7,957	40	2.0
Fire Protection	22,812	115	5.7
General Public Buildings	0	0	0.0
Governmental Administration, Other	12,128	61	3.0
Health	0	0	0.0
Highways	39,107	198	9.8
Hospitals	0	0	0.0
Housing and Community Development	14,101	71	3.5
Interest on General Debt	23,398	118	5.9
Judicial and Legal	0	0	0.0
Libraries	5,267	27	1.3
Parking	876	4	0.2
Parks and Recreation	33,074	167	8.3
Police Protection	68,449	346	17.1
Public Welfare	0	0	0.0
Sewerage	29,385	148	7.3
Solid Waste Management	41,058	207	10.3
Veterans' Services	0	0	0.0
Liquor Store	0	0	0.0
Utility	79,145	400	19.8
Employee Retirement	0	0	0.0

Source: U.S Census Bureau, State & Local Government Finances 2012

DEMOGRAPHICS

Population Growth

Area	1990 Census	2000 Census	2010 Census	Population Growth (%) 1990-2000	Population Growth (%) 2000-2010
City	143,271	170,358	197,899	18.9	16.2
MSA[1]	669,016	753,197	823,318	12.6	9.3
U.S.	248,709,873	281,421,906	308,745,538	13.2	9.7

Note: (1) Figures cover the Oxnard-Thousand Oaks-Ventura, CA Metropolitan Statistical Area—see Appendix B for areas included
Source: U.S. Census Bureau, Census 1990, 2000, 2010

Household Size

Area	Persons in Household (%) One	Two	Three	Four	Five	Six	Seven or More	Average Household Size
City	14.7	21.9	16.7	18.4	12.5	6.8	8.9	3.93
MSA[1]	20.7	30.5	17.3	16.0	8.3	3.7	3.5	3.08
U.S.	27.7	33.6	15.7	13.1	6.0	2.3	1.5	2.64

Note: (1) Figures cover the Oxnard-Thousand Oaks-Ventura, CA Metropolitan Statistical Area—see Appendix B for areas included
Source: U.S. Census Bureau, 2011-2013 American Community Survey 3-Year Estimates

Race

Area	White Alone[2] (%)	Black Alone[2] (%)	Asian Alone[2] (%)	AIAN[3] Alone[2] (%)	NHOPI[4] Alone[2] (%)	Other Race Alone[2] (%)	Two or More Races (%)
City	73.8	2.8	8.0	0.9	0.2	10.5	3.8
MSA[1]	77.7	1.8	6.9	0.6	0.1	8.4	4.3
U.S.	73.9	12.6	5.0	0.8	0.2	4.7	2.9

Note: (1) Figures cover the Oxnard-Thousand Oaks-Ventura, CA Metropolitan Statistical Area—see Appendix B for areas included; (2) Alone is defined as not being in combination with one or more other races; (3) American Indian and Alaska Native; (4) Native Hawaiian and Other Pacific Islander
Source: U.S. Census Bureau, 2011-2013 American Community Survey 3-Year Estimates

Hispanic or Latino Origin

Area	Total (%)	Mexican (%)	Puerto Rican (%)	Cuban (%)	Other (%)
City	73.8	69.7	0.4	0.1	3.6
MSA[1]	41.2	36.6	0.5	0.2	3.9
U.S.	16.9	10.8	1.6	0.6	3.8

Note: Persons of Hispanic or Latino origin can be of any race; (1) Figures cover the Oxnard-Thousand Oaks-Ventura, CA Metropolitan Statistical Area—see Appendix B for areas included
Source: U.S. Census Bureau, 2011-2013 American Community Survey 3-Year Estimates

Segregation

Type	Segregation Indices[1] 1990	2000	2010	2010 Rank[2]	Percent Change 1990-2000	Percent Change 1990-2010	Percent Change 2000-2010
Black/White	47.8	48.9	39.9	91	1.1	-7.9	-9.0
Asian/White	30.0	31.0	31.2	87	1.0	1.2	0.2
Hispanic/White	52.3	56.1	54.6	13	3.8	2.2	-1.6

Note: All figures cover the Metropolitan Statistical Area—see Appendix B for areas included; Figures are based on an analysis of 1990, 2000, and 2010 Census Decennial Census tract data by William H. Frey, Brookings Institution and the University of Michigan Social Science Data Analysis Network. In this analysis all racial groups (whites, blacks, and asians) are non-Hispanic members of those races. Hispanics are shown as a separate category;
(1) Segregation Indices are Dissimilarity Indices that measure the degree to which the minority group is distributed differently than whites across census tracts. They range from 0 (complete integration) to 100 (complete segregation) where the value indicates the percentage of the minority group that needs to move to be distributed exactly like whites; (2) Ranges from 1 (most segregated) to 102 (least segregated); n/a not available.
Source: www.CensusScope.org

Ancestry

Area	German	Irish	English	American	Italian	Polish	French[2]	Scottish	Dutch
City	4.1	3.4	2.4	1.5	1.7	0.5	0.9	0.6	0.5
MSA[1]	11.6	8.7	8.3	3.6	5.1	1.9	2.5	1.9	1.1
U.S.	14.9	10.8	8.0	7.4	5.5	3.0	2.7	1.7	1.4

Note: Figures are the percentage of the total population reporting a particular ancestry. The nine most commonly reported ancestries in the U.S. are shown. Figures include multiple ancestries (e.g. if a person reported being Irish and Italian, they were included in both columns); (1) Figures cover the Oxnard-Thousand Oaks-Ventura, CA Metropolitan Statistical Area—see Appendix B for areas included; (2) Excludes Basque
Source: U.S. Census Bureau, 2011-2013 American Community Survey 3-Year Estimates

Foreign-Born Population

Area	Percent of Population Born in								
	Any Foreign Country	Mexico	Asia	Europe	Carribean	South America	Central America[2]	Africa	Canada
City	n/a	n/a	n/a	n/a	n/a	n/a	n/a	n/a	n/a
MSA[1]	22.6	13.1	5.3	1.6	0.1	0.6	1.2	0.2	0.5
U.S.	13.0	3.7	3.8	1.5	1.2	0.9	1.0	0.6	0.3

Note: (1) Figures cover the Oxnard-Thousand Oaks-Ventura, CA Metropolitan Statistical Area—see Appendix B for areas included; (2) Excludes Mexico.
Source: U.S. Census Bureau, 2011-2013 American Community Survey 3-Year Estimates

Marital Status

Area	Never Married	Now Married[2]	Separated	Widowed	Divorced
City	38.3	45.5	2.7	4.4	9.1
MSA[1]	32.2	50.4	1.9	5.1	10.4
U.S.	32.7	48.1	2.2	6.0	11.0

Note: Figures are percentages and cover the population 15 years of age and older; (1) Figures cover the Oxnard-Thousand Oaks-Ventura, CA Metropolitan Statistical Area—see Appendix B for areas included; (2) Excludes separated
Source: U.S. Census Bureau, 2011-2013 American Community Survey 3-Year Estimates

Disability Status

Area	All Ages	Under 18 Years Old	18 to 64 Years Old	65 Years and Over
City	10.5	4.4	9.1	41.1
MSA[1]	10.2	3.9	7.8	35.2
U.S.	12.3	4.1	10.2	36.3

Note: Figures show percent of the civilian noninstitutionalized population that reported having a disability. Disability status is determined from from six types of difficulty: vision, hearing, cognitive, ambulatory, self-care, and independent living. For children under 5 years old, hearing and vision difficulty are used to determine disability status. For children between the ages of 5 and 14, disability status is determined from hearing, vision, cognitive, ambulatory, and self-care difficulties. For people aged 15 years and older, they are considered to have a disability if they have difficulty with any one of the six difficulty types; (1) Figures cover the Oxnard-Thousand Oaks-Ventura, CA Metropolitan Statistical Area—see Appendix B for areas included.
Source: U.S. Census Bureau, 2011-2013 American Community Survey 3-Year Estimates

Age

Area	Percent of Population									Median Age
	Under Age 5	Age 5–19	Age 20–34	Age 35–44	Age 45–54	Age 55–64	Age 65–74	Age 75–84	Age 85+	
City	8.6	22.8	25.2	13.5	11.8	9.4	5.0	2.8	1.0	30.5
MSA[1]	6.5	21.3	20.0	12.9	14.6	12.0	7.0	3.8	1.9	36.8
U.S.	6.4	19.9	20.7	12.9	14.1	12.3	7.6	4.2	1.9	37.4

Note: (1) Figures cover the Oxnard-Thousand Oaks-Ventura, CA Metropolitan Statistical Area—see Appendix B for areas included
Source: U.S. Census Bureau, 2011-2013 American Community Survey 3-Year Estimates

Gender

Area	Males	Females	Males per 100 Females
City	102,516	98,864	103.7
MSA[1]	414,557	420,323	98.6
U.S.	154,451,010	159,410,713	96.9

Note: (1) Figures cover the Oxnard-Thousand Oaks-Ventura, CA Metropolitan Statistical Area—see Appendix B for areas included
Source: U.S. Census Bureau, 2011-2013 American Community Survey 3-Year Estimates

Religious Groups by Family

Area	Catholic	Baptist	Non-Den.	Methodist[2]	Lutheran	LDS[3]	Pente-costal	Presby-terian[4]	Muslim[5]	Judaism
MSA[1]	28.2	1.9	4.1	1.1	1.5	2.5	1.3	0.7	0.4	0.7
U.S.	19.1	9.3	4.0	4.0	2.3	2.0	1.9	1.6	0.8	0.7

Note: Figures are the number of adherents as a percentage of the total population; (1) Figures cover the Oxnard-Thousand Oaks-Ventura, CA Metropolitan Statistical Area—see Appendix B for areas included; (2) Methodist/Pietist; (3) Latter Day Saints; (4) Reformed; (5) Figures are estimates
Source: Association of Statisticians of American Religious Bodies, 2010 U.S. Religion Census: Religious Congregations & Membership Study

Religious Groups by Tradition

Area	Catholic	Evangelical Protestant	Mainline Protestant	Other Tradition	Black Protestant	Orthodox
MSA[1]	28.2	8.9	2.7	4.5	0.2	0.2
U.S.	19.1	16.2	7.3	4.3	1.6	0.3

Note: Figures are the number of adherents as a percentage of the total population; (1) Figures cover the Oxnard-Thousand Oaks-Ventura, CA Metropolitan Statistical Area—see Appendix B for areas included
Source: Association of Statisticians of American Religious Bodies, 2010 U.S. Religion Census: Religious Congregations & Membership Study

ECONOMY

Gross Metropolitan Product

Area	2012	2013	2014	2015	Rank[2]
MSA[1]	39.1	39.7	41.3	43.5	61

Note: Figures are in billions of dollars; (1) Figures cover the Oxnard-Thousand Oaks-Ventura, CA Metropolitan Statistical Area—see Appendix B for areas included; (2) Rank is based on 2015 data and ranges from 1 to 363
Source: The U.S. Conference of Mayors, U.S. Metro Economies: GMP and Employment 2013-2015, June 2014

Economic Growth

Area	2010-12 (%)	2013 (%)	2014 (%)	2015 (%)	Rank[2]
MSA[1]	1.8	0.5	2.2	3.6	61
U.S.	2.1	2.0	2.3	3.2	–

Note: Figures are real gross metropolitan product (GMP) growth rates and represent annual average percent change; (1) Figures cover the Oxnard-Thousand Oaks-Ventura, CA Metropolitan Statistical Area—see Appendix B for areas included; (2) Rank is based on 2015 data and ranges from 1 to 363
Source: The U.S. Conference of Mayors, U.S. Metro Economies: GMP and Employment 2013-2015, June 2014

Metropolitan Area Exports

Area	2008	2009	2010	2011	2012	2013	Rank[2]
MSA[1]	2,579.1	2,483.8	2,611.2	2,919.8	2,854.6	2,893.9	82

Note: Figures are in millions of dollars; (1) Figures cover the Oxnard-Thousand Oaks-Ventura, CA Metropolitan Statistical Area—see Appendix B for areas included; (2) Rank is based on 2013 data and ranges from 1 to 387
Source: U.S. Department of Commerce, International Trade Administration, Office of Trade & Industry Information, Manufacturing & Services, data extracted April 3, 2015

Building Permits

Area	Single-Family			Multi-Family			Total		
	2013	2014	Pct. Chg.	2013	2014	Pct. Chg.	2013	2014	Pct. Chg.
City	94	71	-24.5	276	431	56.2	370	502	35.7
MSA[1]	430	536	24.7	571	778	36.3	1,001	1,314	31.3
U.S.	620,802	634,597	2.2	370,020	411,766	11.3	990,822	1,046,363	5.6

Note: (1) Figures cover the Oxnard-Thousand Oaks-Ventura, CA Metropolitan Statistical Area—see Appendix B for areas included; Figures represent new, privately-owned housing units authorized (unadjusted data); All permit data are based on estimates with imputation.
Source: U.S. Census Bureau, Manufacturing, Mining, and Construction Statistics, Building Permits, 2013, 2014

Bankruptcy Filings

Area	Business Filings			Nonbusiness Filings		
	2013	2014	% Chg.	2013	2014	% Chg.
Ventura County	101	84	-16.8	2,483	1,935	-22.1
U.S.	33,212	26,983	-18.8	1,038,720	909,812	-12.4

Note: Business filings include Chapter 7, Chapter 11, Chapter 12, and Chapter 13; Nonbusiness filings include Chapter 7, Chapter 11, and Chapter 13
Source: Administrative Office of the U.S. Courts, Business and Nonbusiness Bankruptcy, County Cases Commenced by Chapter of the Bankruptcy Code, During the 12- Month Period Ending December 31, 2013 and Business and Nonbusiness Bankruptcy, County Cases Commenced by Chapter of the Bankruptcy Code, During the 12- Month Period Ending December 31, 2014

Housing Vacancy Rates

Area	Gross Vacancy Rate[2] (%)			Year-Round Vacancy Rate[3] (%)			Rental Vacancy Rate[4] (%)			Homeowner Vacancy Rate[5] (%)		
	2012	2013	2014	2012	2013	2014	2012	2013	2014	2012	2013	2014
MSA[1]	5.5	7.4	8.4	4.6	5.6	8.1	2.3	5.3	2.5	0.5	1.7	2.1
U.S.	13.8	13.6	13.4	10.8	10.7	10.4	8.7	8.3	7.6	2.0	2.0	1.9

Note: (1) Figures cover the Oxnard-Thousand Oaks-Ventura, CA Metropolitan Statistical Area—see Appendix B for areas included; (2) The percentage of the total housing inventory that is vacant; (3) The percentage of the housing inventory (excluding seasonal units) that is year-round vacant; (4) The percentage of rental inventory that is vacant for rent; (5) The percentage of homeowner inventory that is vacant for sale
Source: U.S. Census Bureau, Housing Vacancies and Homeownership Annual Statistics: 2014

INCOME

Income

Area	Per Capita ($)	Median Household ($)	Average Household ($)
City	20,438	59,465	75,180
MSA[1]	32,489	75,536	97,897
U.S.	27,884	52,176	72,897

Note: (1) Figures cover the Oxnard-Thousand Oaks-Ventura, CA Metropolitan Statistical Area—see Appendix B for areas included
Source: U.S. Census Bureau, 2011-2013 American Community Survey 3-Year Estimates

Household Income Distribution

Area	Percent of Households Earning							
	Under $15,000	$15,000 -24,999	$25,000 -34,999	$35,000 -49,999	$50,000 -74,999	$75,000 -99,000	$100,000 -149,999	$150,000 and up
City	8.0	10.0	8.7	14.9	20.1	14.3	15.1	8.9
MSA[1]	7.2	7.7	7.1	11.1	16.5	13.6	18.4	18.3
U.S.	13.0	10.9	10.3	13.6	17.9	11.9	12.7	9.6

Note: (1) Figures cover the Oxnard-Thousand Oaks-Ventura, CA Metropolitan Statistical Area—see Appendix B for areas included
Source: U.S. Census Bureau, 2011-2013 American Community Survey 3-Year Estimates

Poverty Rate

Area	All Ages	Under 18 Years Old	18 to 64 Years Old	65 Years and Over
City	17.1	26.7	14.0	9.0
MSA[1]	11.6	17.4	10.3	7.0
U.S.	15.9	22.4	14.8	9.5

Note: Figures are percentage of people whose income during the past 12 months was below the poverty level; (1) Figures cover the Oxnard-Thousand Oaks-Ventura, CA Metropolitan Statistical Area—see Appendix B for areas included
Source: U.S. Census Bureau, 2011-2013 American Community Survey 3-Year Estimates

EMPLOYMENT

Labor Force and Employment

Area	Civilian Labor Force			Workers Employed		
	Dec. 2013	Dec. 2014	% Chg.	Dec. 2013	Dec. 2014	% Chg.
City	100,705	99,409	-1.3	92,898	92,730	-0.2
MSA[1]	432,764	427,575	-1.2	401,909	401,181	-0.2
U.S.	154,408,000	155,521,000	0.7	144,423,000	147,190,000	1.9

Note: Data is not seasonally adjusted and covers workers 16 years of age and older; (1) Figures cover the Oxnard-Thousand Oaks-Ventura, CA Metropolitan Statistical Area—see Appendix B for areas included
Source: Bureau of Labor Statistics, Local Area Unemployment Statistics

Unemployment Rate

Area	2014											
	Jan.	Feb.	Mar.	Apr.	May	Jun.	Jul.	Aug.	Sep.	Oct.	Nov.	Dec.
City	8.1	7.9	7.7	6.6	6.6	6.9	7.7	7.6	7.1	7.0	7.2	6.7
MSA[1]	7.5	7.3	7.1	6.1	6.1	6.4	7.0	7.0	6.6	6.4	6.6	6.2
U.S.	7.0	7.0	6.8	5.9	6.1	6.3	6.5	6.3	5.7	5.5	5.5	5.4

Note: Data is not seasonally adjusted and covers workers 16 years of age and older; (1) Figures cover the Oxnard-Thousand Oaks-Ventura, CA Metropolitan Statistical Area—see Appendix B for areas included
Source: Bureau of Labor Statistics, Local Area Unemployment Statistics

Employment by Occupation

Occupation Classification	City (%)	MSA[1] (%)	U.S. (%)
Management, Business, Science, and Arts	21.0	36.8	36.2
Natural Resources, Construction, and Maintenance	20.9	11.1	9.0
Production, Transportation, and Material Moving	16.2	9.9	12.1
Sales and Office	23.0	24.6	24.4
Service	18.9	17.6	18.3

Note: Figures cover employed civilians 16 years of age and older; (1) Figures cover the Oxnard-Thousand Oaks-Ventura, CA Metropolitan Statistical Area—see Appendix B for areas included
Source: U.S. Census Bureau, 2011-2013 American Community Survey 3-Year Estimates

Employment by Industry

| Sector | MSA[1] | | U.S. |
	Number of Employees	Percent of Total	Percent of Total
Construction	13,600	4.6	4.4
Education and Health Services	41,200	13.8	15.5
Financial Activities	18,500	6.2	5.7
Government	44,900	15.1	15.8
Information	5,600	1.9	2.0
Leisure and Hospitality	35,400	11.9	10.3
Manufacturing	30,300	10.2	8.7
Mining and Logging	1,300	0.4	0.6
Other Services	9,800	3.3	4.0
Professional and Business Services	36,300	12.2	13.8
Retail Trade	41,300	13.9	11.4
Transportation, Warehousing, and Utilities	6,400	2.2	3.9
Wholesale Trade	13,000	4.4	4.2

Note: Figures are non-farm employment as of December 2014. Figures are not seasonally adjusted and include workers 16 years of age and older; (1) Figures cover the Oxnard-Thousand Oaks-Ventura, CA Metropolitan Statistical Area—see Appendix B for areas included
Source: Bureau of Labor Statistics, Current Employment Statistics, Employment, Hours, and Earnings

Occupations with Greatest Projected Employment Growth: 2012 – 2022

Occupation[1]	2012 Employment	2022 Projected Employment	Numeric Employment Change	Percent Employment Change
Personal Care Aides	386,900	587,200	200,300	51.8
Combined Food Preparation and Serving Workers, Including Fast Food	286,000	362,400	76,400	26.7
Retail Salespersons	468,400	528,100	59,700	12.7
Laborers and Freight, Stock, and Material Movers, Hand	270,500	322,300	51,800	19.1
Waiters and Waitresses	246,100	290,300	44,200	18.0
Registered Nurses	254,500	297,400	42,900	16.9
General and Operations Managers	253,800	295,700	41,900	16.5
Secretaries and Administrative Assistants, Except Legal, Medical, and Executive	212,800	250,100	37,300	17.5
Cashiers	357,800	392,600	34,800	9.7
Cooks, Restaurant	116,900	150,600	33,700	28.8

Note: Projections cover California; (1) Sorted by numeric employment change
Source: www.projectionscentral.com, State Occupational Projections, 2012–2022 Long-Term Projections

Fastest Growing Occupations: 2012 – 2022

Occupation[1]	2012 Employment	2022 Projected Employment	Numeric Employment Change	Percent Employment Change
Economists	3,100	5,100	2,000	64.5
Helpers—Brickmasons, Blockmasons, Stonemasons, and Tile and Marble Setters	2,900	4,600	1,700	58.6
Brickmasons and Blockmasons	5,100	8,000	2,900	56.9
Insulation Workers, Floor, Ceiling, and Wall	1,600	2,500	900	56.3
Stonemasons	1,100	1,700	600	54.5
Insulation Workers, Mechanical	1,100	1,700	600	54.5
Personal Care Aides	386,900	587,200	200,300	51.8
Foresters	1,200	1,800	600	50.0
Terrazzo Workers and Finishers	1,100	1,600	500	45.5
Mechanical Door Repairers	1,100	1,600	500	45.5

Note: Projections cover California; (1) Sorted by percent employment change and excludes occupations with numeric employment change less than 100
Source: www.projectionscentral.com, State Occupational Projections, 2012–2022 Long-Term Projections

Average Wages

Occupation	$/Hr.	Occupation	$/Hr.
Accountants and Auditors	36.91	Maids and Housekeeping Cleaners	11.15
Automotive Mechanics	20.91	Maintenance and Repair Workers	19.73
Bookkeepers	21.42	Marketing Managers	71.68
Carpenters	24.04	Nuclear Medicine Technologists	47.69
Cashiers	11.80	Nurses, Licensed Practical	25.10
Clerks, General Office	15.59	Nurses, Registered	41.29
Clerks, Receptionists/Information	13.92	Nursing Assistants	14.21
Clerks, Shipping/Receiving	16.02	Packers and Packagers, Hand	11.19
Computer Programmers	48.02	Physical Therapists	41.46
Computer Systems Analysts	49.88	Postal Service Mail Carriers	25.87
Computer User Support Specialists	24.80	Real Estate Brokers	n/a
Cooks, Restaurant	12.52	Retail Salespersons	12.76
Dentists	59.61	Sales Reps., Exc. Tech./Scientific	n/a
Electrical Engineers	51.41	Sales Reps., Tech./Scientific	46.05
Electricians	27.04	Secretaries, Exc. Legal/Med./Exec.	18.59
Financial Managers	57.20	Security Guards	15.68
First-Line Supervisors/Managers, Sales	21.66	Surgeons	121.08
Food Preparation Workers	11.67	Teacher Assistants	14.70
General and Operations Managers	58.42	Teachers, Elementary School	33.30
Hairdressers/Cosmetologists	12.46	Teachers, Secondary School	33.30
Internists	99.51	Telemarketers	16.20
Janitors and Cleaners	14.13	Truck Drivers, Heavy/Tractor-Trailer	22.71
Landscaping/Groundskeeping Workers	13.29	Truck Drivers, Light/Delivery Svcs.	18.52
Lawyers	74.13	Waiters and Waitresses	11.45

Note: Wage data covers the Oxnard-Thousand Oaks-Ventura, CA Metropolitan Statistical Area—see Appendix B for areas included; Hourly wages for elementary/secondary school teachers and teacher assistants were calculated by the editors from annual wage data assuming a 40 hour work week; n/a not available.
Source: Bureau of Labor Statistics, Metro Area Occupational Employment and Wage Estimates, May 2014

TAXES

State Corporate Income Tax Rates

State	Tax Rate (%)	Income Brackets ($)	Num. of Brackets	Financial Institution Tax Rate (%)[a]	Federal Income Tax Ded.
California	8.84 (c)	Flat rate	1	10.84 (c)	No

Note: Tax rates as of January 1, 2015; (a) Rates listed are the corporate income tax rate applied to financial institutions or excise taxes based on income. Some states have other taxes based upon the value of deposits or shares; (c) Minimum tax is $800 in California, $100 in District of Columbia, $50 in North Dakota (banks), $500 in Rhode Island, $200 per location in South Dakota (banks), $100 in Utah, $250 in Vermont.
Source: Federation of Tax Administrators, "State Corporate Income Tax Rates, 2015"

State Individual Income Tax Rates

State	Tax Rate (%)	Income Brackets ($)	Num. of Brackets	Personal Exempt. ($)[1] Single	Personal Exempt. ($)[1] Dependents	Fed. Inc. Tax Ded.
California (a)	1.0 - 12.3 (f)	7,749- 519,687 (b)	9	108 (c)	333 (c)	No

Note: Tax rates as of January 1, 2015; Local- and county-level taxes are not included; n/a not applicable; (1) Married joint filers generally receive double the single exemption; (a) 17 states have statutory provision for automatically adjusting to the rate of inflation the dollar values of the income tax brackets, standard deductions, and/or personal exemptions. Massachusetts, Michigan, and Nebraska index the personal exemptiononly. Oregon does not index the income brackets for $125,000 and over. Maine has suspended indexing for 2014 and 2015; (b) For joint returns, taxes are twice the tax on half the couple's income; (c) The personal exemption takes the form of a tax credit instead of a deduction; (f) California imposes an additional 1% tax on taxable income over $1 million, making the maximum rate 13.3% over $1 million.
Source: Federation of Tax Administrators, "State Individual Income Tax Rates, 2015"

Various State and Local Tax Rates

State	State and Local Sales and Use (%)	State Sales and Use (%)	Gasoline[1] (¢/gal.)	Cigarette[2] ($/pack)	Spirits[3] ($/gal.)	Wine[4] ($/gal.)	Beer[5] ($/gal.)
California	8.0	7.50 (b)	45.39	0.87	3.30 (f)	0.20	0.20

Note: All tax rates as of January 1, 2015; (1) The American Petroleum Institute has developed a methodology for determining the average tax rate on a gallon of fuel. Rates may include any of the following: excise taxes, environmental fees, storage tank fees, other fees or taxes, general sales tax, and local taxes. In states where gasoline is subject to the general sales tax, or where the fuel tax is based on the average sale price, the average rate determined by API is sensitive to changes in the price of gasoline. States that fully or partially apply general sales taxes to gasoline: CA, CO, GA, IL, IN, MI, NY; (2) The federal excise tax of $1.0066 per pack and local taxes are not included; (3) Rates are those applicable to off-premise sales of 40% alcohol by volume (a.b.v.) distilled spirits in 750ml containers. Local excise taxes are excluded; (4) Rates are those applicable to off-premise sales of 11% a.b.v. non-carbonated wine in 750ml containers; (5) Rates are those applicable to off-premise sales of 4.7% a.b.v. beer in 12 ounce containers; (b) Three states levy mandatory, statewide, local add-on sales taxes at the state level: California (1%), Utah (1.25%), and Virginia (1%). We include these in their state sales taxes; (f) Different rates are also applicable according to alcohol content, place of production, size of container, or place purchased (on- or off-premise or onboard airlines).
Source: Tax Foundation, 2015 Facts & Figures: How Does Your State Compare?

State Business Tax Climate Index Rankings

State	Overall Rank	Corporate Tax Index Rank	Individual Income Tax Index Rank	Sales Tax Index Rank	Unemployment Insurance Tax Index Rank	Property Tax Index Rank
California	48	34	50	42	14	14

Note: The index is a measure of how each state's tax laws affect economic performance. The lower the rank, the more favorable a state's tax system is for business. States without a given tax are given a ranking of 1. The scores/rankings for the District of Columbia do not affect other states. The 2015 index represents the tax climate as of July 1, 2014.
Source: Tax Foundation, State Business Tax Climate Index 2015

COMMERCIAL UTILITIES

Typical Monthly Electric Bills

Area	Commercial Service ($/month)		Industrial Service ($/month)	
	1,500 kWh	40 kW demand 14,000 kWh	1,000 kW demand 200,000 kWh	50,000 kW demand 32,500,000 kWh
City	274	2,283	42,096	2,976,088
Average[1]	201	1,653	26,124	2,639,743

Note: Figures are based on annualized 2014 rates; (1) Average based on 180 utilities surveyed
Source: Edison Electric Institute, Typical Bills and Average Rates Report, Summer 2014

TRANSPORTATION

Means of Transportation to Work

Area	Car/Truck/Van		Public Transportation			Bicycle	Walked	Other Means	Worked at Home
	Drove Alone	Car-pooled	Bus	Subway	Railroad				
City	72.6	20.5	1.3	0.0	0.1	0.7	1.3	1.0	2.5
MSA[1]	76.7	12.7	0.9	0.0	0.3	0.7	2.0	1.0	5.6
U.S.	76.4	9.6	2.6	1.8	0.6	0.6	2.8	1.3	4.3

Note: Figures are percentages and cover workers 16 years of age and older; (1) Figures cover the Oxnard-Thousand Oaks-Ventura, CA Metropolitan Statistical Area—see Appendix B for areas included
Source: U.S. Census Bureau, 2011-2013 American Community Survey 3-Year Estimates

Travel Time to Work

Area	Less Than 10 Minutes	10 to 19 Minutes	20 to 29 Minutes	30 to 44 Minutes	45 to 59 Minutes	60 to 89 Minutes	90 Minutes or More
City	9.2	34.1	25.8	21.1	4.5	3.3	2.1
MSA[1]	13.6	31.3	20.8	19.3	6.5	5.5	2.8
U.S.	13.3	29.7	20.9	20.2	7.7	5.7	2.6

Note: Figures are percentages and include workers 16 years old and over; (1) Figures cover the Oxnard-Thousand Oaks-Ventura, CA Metropolitan Statistical Area—see Appendix B for areas included
Source: U.S. Census Bureau, 2011-2013 American Community Survey 3-Year Estimates

Travel Time Index

Area	1985	1990	1995	2000	2005	2010	2011
Urban Area[1]	1.02	1.02	1.05	1.07	1.10	1.10	1.10
Average[2]	1.09	1.14	1.16	1.19	1.23	1.18	1.18

Note: Travel Time Index—the ratio of travel time in the peak period to the travel time at free-flow conditions. For example, a value of 1.30 indicates a 20-minute free-flow trip takes 26 minutes in the peak. Free-flow speeds (60 mph on freeways and 35 mph on principal arterials) are used as the comparison threshold; (1) Covers the Oxnard CA urban area; (2) average of 498 urban areas
Source: Texas Transportation Institute, Urban Mobility Report 2012, December 2012

Public Transportation

Agency Name / Mode of Transportation	Vehicles Operated in Maximum Service	Annual Unlinked Passenger Trips (in thous.)	Annual Passenger Miles (in thous.)
Gold Coast Transit (SCAT)			
Bus (directly operated)	43	3,566.5	15,014.8
Demand Response (purchased transportation)	17	70.9	560.2

Source: Federal Transit Administration, National Transit Database, 2013

Air Transportation

Airport Name and Code / Type of Service	Passenger Airlines[1]	Passenger Enplanements	Freight Carriers[2]	Freight (lbs.)
Los Angeles International (65 miles) (LAX)				
Domestic service (U.S. carriers - 2014)	31	25,048,184	27	760,739,558
International service (U.S. carriers - 2013)	13	2,022,569	13	177,725,809
Oxnard Airport (OXR)				
Domestic service (U.S. carriers - 2014)	1	2	0	0
International service (U.S. carriers - 2013)	0	0	0	0

Note: (1) Includes all U.S.-based major, minor and commuter airlines that carried at least one passenger during the year; (2) Includes all U.S.-based airlines and freight carriers that transported at least one lb. of freight during the year.
Source: Bureau of Transportation Statistics, The Intermodal Transportation Database, Air Carriers: T-100 Domestic Market (U.S. Carriers), 2014; Bureau of Transportation Statistics, The Intermodal Transportation Database, Air Carriers: T-100 International Market (U.S. Carriers), 2013

Other Transportation Statistics

Major Highways:	SR-101
Amtrak Service:	Yes
Major Waterways/Ports:	Pacific Ocean

Source: Amtrak.com; Google Maps

BUSINESSES

Major Business Headquarters

Company Name	Rankings	
	Fortune[1]	Forbes[2]
No companies listed	-	-

Note: (1) Fortune 500—companies that produce a 10-K are ranked 1 to 500 based on 2013 revenue; (2) all private companies with at least $2 billion in annual revenue through the end of their most current fiscal year are ranked 1 to 221; companies listed are headquartered in the city; dashes indicate no ranking
Source: Fortune, "Fortune 500," June 16, 2014; Forbes, "America's Largest Private Companies," November 5, 2014

Fast-Growing Businesses

According to *Inc.*, Oxnard is home to one of America's 500 fastest-growing private companies: **KeVita Sparkling Probiotic Drinks** (#301). Criteria: must be an independent, privately-held, for-profit, U.S. corporation, proprietorship or partnership; revenues must be at least $100,000 in 2010 and $2 million in 2013; must have four-year operating/sales history. Holding companies, regulated banks, and utilities were excluded. *Inc.*, *"America's 500 Fastest-Growing Private Companies," September 2014*

According to *Fortune*, Oxnard is home to one of the 100 fastest-growing companies in the world: **CalAmp** (#10). Companies were ranked by their revenue growth rate; their EPS growth rate; and their three-year annualized total return to investors for the period ending June 30, 2014. Criteria for inclusion: a company, foreign or domestic, must trade on a major U.S. stock exchange; must file quarterly reports with the SEC; must have a minimum market capitalization of $250 million; must have a stock price of at least $5 on June 30, 2014; must have been trading continuously since June 30, 2010; must have revenue and net income for the four quarters ended on or before April 30, 2014, of at least $50 million and $10 million, respectively; and must have posted a compound annual growth in revenue and earnings per share of at least 20% annually over the three years ending on or before April 30, 2014. Real estate investment trusts, limited-liability companies, limited parterships, business development companies, closed end investment firms, and companies that lost money in the quarter ending April 30, 2014 were excluded. *Fortune, "100 Fastest-Growing Companies," August 28, 2014*

Minority- and Women-Owned Businesses

Group	All Firms		Firms with Paid Employees			
	Firms	Sales ($000)	Firms	Sales ($000)	Employees	Payroll ($000)
Asian	1,350	300,763	481	264,411	4,964	60,358
Black	252	19,686	48	12,932	240	4,852
Hispanic	4,317	413,782	447	260,320	2,334	56,725
Women	3,276	970,830	(s)	(s)	(s)	(s)
All Firms	11,119	10,926,771	2,594	10,562,135	51,444	1,791,197

Note: Figures cover firms located in the city; minority- and women-owned business are defined as firms in which the corresponding group own 51% or more of the stock or equity of the company; (s) estimates are suppressed when publication standards are not met
Source: U.S. Census Bureau, 2007 Economic Census, Survey of Business Owners (2012 Survey of Business Owners data will be released starting in June 2015)

HOTELS & CONVENTION CENTERS

Hotels/Motels

Area	5 Star		4 Star		3 Star		2 Star		1 Star		Not Rated	
	Num.	Pct.[3]	Num.	Pct.[3]	Num.	Pct.[3]	Num.	Pct.[3]	Num.	Pct.[3]	Num.	Pct.[3]
City[1]	4	4.3	3	3.2	25	26.6	56	59.6	1	1.1	5	5.3
Total[2]	166	0.9	1,264	7.0	5,718	31.8	9,340	52.0	411	2.3	1,070	6.0

Note: (1) Figures cover Oxnard and vicinity; (2) Figures cover all 100 cities in this book; (3) Percentage of hotels which have a given star rating; Star ratings are determined by expedia.com and offer an indication of the general quality of a particular hotel.
Source: expedia.com, April 2, 2015

The Oxnard-Thousand Oaks-Ventura, CA metro area is home to one of the best hotels in the U.S. according to *Travel & Leisure*: **Ojai Valley Inn & Spa**. Criteria: service; location; rooms; food; and value. The list includes the top 236 hotels in the U.S. *Travel & Leisure, "T+L 500, The World's Best Hotels 2015"*

The Oxnard-Thousand Oaks-Ventura, CA metro area is home to one of the best hotels in the world according to *Condé Nast Traveler*: **Ojai Valley Inn & Spa**. The selections are based on editors' picks. The list includes the top 25 hotels in the U.S. *Condé Nast Traveler, "Gold List 2015, The Top Hotels in the World"*

Major Convention Centers

Name	Overall Space (sq. ft.)	Exhibit Space (sq. ft.)	Meeting Space (sq. ft.)	Meeting Rooms
Oxnard Performing Arts & Convention Center	65,835	n/a	n/a	n/a

Note: Table includes convention centers located in the Oxnard-Thousand Oaks-Ventura, CA metro area; n/a not available
Source: Original research

Living Environment

COST OF LIVING

Cost of Living Index

Composite Index	Groceries	Housing	Utilities	Trans- portation	Health Care	Misc. Goods/ Services
n/a	n/a	n/a	n/a	n/a	n/a	n/a

Note: The Cost of Living Index measures regional differences in the cost of consumer goods and services, excluding taxes and non-consumer expenditures, for professional and managerial households in the top income quintile. It is based on more than 50,000 prices covering almost 60 different items for which prices are collected three times a year by chambers of commerce, economic development organizations or university applied economic centers in each participating urban area. The numbers shown should be read as a percentage above or below the national average of 100. For example, a value of 115.4 in the groceries column indicates that grocery prices are 15.4% higher than the national average. Small differences in the index numbers should not be interpreted as significant; n/a not available.
Source: The Council for Community and Economic Research, ACCRA Cost of Living Index, 2014

Grocery Prices

Area[1]	T-Bone Steak ($/pound)	Frying Chicken ($/pound)	Whole Milk ($/half gal.)	Eggs ($/dozen)	Orange Juice ($/64 oz.)	Coffee ($/11.5 oz.)
City[2]	n/a	n/a	n/a	n/a	n/a	n/a
Avg.	10.40	1.37	2.40	1.99	3.46	4.27
Min.	8.48	0.93	1.37	1.30	2.83	2.99
Max.	14.20	2.44	3.62	4.02	6.42	6.96

*Note: (1) Values for the local area are compared with the average, minimum and maximum values for all 308 areas in the Cost of Living Index; (2) Figures cover the Oxnard CA urban area; n/a not available; **T-Bone Steak** (price per pound); **Frying Chicken** (price per pound, whole fryer); **Whole Milk** (half gallon carton); **Eggs** (price per dozen, Grade A, large); **Orange Juice** (64 oz. Tropicana or Florida Natural); **Coffee** (11.5 oz. can, vacuum-packed, Maxwell House, Hills Bros, or Folgers).*
Source: The Council for Community and Economic Research, ACCRA Cost of Living Index, 2014

Housing and Utility Costs

Area[1]	New Home Price ($)	Apartment Rent ($/month)	All Electric ($/month)	Part Electric ($/month)	Other Energy ($/month)	Telephone ($/month)
City[2]	n/a	n/a	n/a	n/a	n/a	n/a
Avg.	305,838	919	181.00	93.66	73.14	27.95
Min.	183,142	480	112.00	42.06	23.42	17.16
Max.	1,358,576	3,851	594.00	180.03	440.99	40.42

*Note: (1) Values for the local area are compared with the average, minimum and maximum values for all 308 areas in the Cost of Living Index; (2) Figures cover the Oxnard CA urban area; n/a not available; **New Home Price** (2,400 sf living area, 8,000 sf lot, in urban area with full utilities); **Apartment Rent** (950 sf 2 bedroom/1.5 or 2 bath, unfurnished, excluding all utilities except water); **All Electric** (average monthly cost for an all-electric home); **Part Electric** (average monthly cost for a part-electric home); **Other Energy** (average monthly cost for natural gas, fuel oil, coal, wood, and any other forms of energy except electricity); **Telephone** (price includes basic monthly rate for a private residential line plus additional local usage charges incurred by a family of four).*
Source: The Council for Community and Economic Research, ACCRA Cost of Living Index, 2014

Health Care, Transportation, and Other Costs

Area[1]	Doctor ($/visit)	Dentist ($/visit)	Optometrist ($/visit)	Gasoline ($/gallon)	Beauty Salon ($/visit)	Men's Shirt ($)
City[2]	n/a	n/a	n/a	n/a	n/a	n/a
Avg.	102.86	87.89	97.66	3.44	34.37	26.74
Min.	67.47	65.78	51.18	3.00	17.43	12.79
Max.	173.50	150.14	235.00	4.33	64.28	49.50

*Note: (1) Values for the local area are compared with the average, minimum and maximum values for all 308 areas in the Cost of Living Index; (2) Figures cover the Oxnard CA urban area; n/a not available; **Doctor** (general practitioners routine exam of an established patient); **Dentist** (adult teeth cleaning and periodic oral examination); **Optometrist** (full vision eye exam for established adult patient); **Gasoline** (one gallon regular unleaded, national brand, including all taxes, cash price at self-service pump if available); **Beauty Salon** (woman's shampoo, trim, and blow-dry); **Men's Shirt** (cotton/polyester dress shirt, pinpoint weave, long sleeves).*
Source: The Council for Community and Economic Research, ACCRA Cost of Living Index, 2014

HOUSING

House Price Index (HPI)

Area	National Ranking[2]	Quarterly Change (%)	One-Year Change (%)	Five-Year Change (%)
MSA[1]	77	0.71	6.55	17.96
U.S.[3]	–	1.35	4.91	11.59

Note: The HPI is a weighted repeat sales index. It measures average price changes in repeat sales or refinancings on the same properties. This information is obtained by reviewing repeat mortgage transactions on single-family properties whose mortgages have been purchased or securitized by Fannie Mae or Freddie Mac in January 1975; (1) Oxnard-Thousand Oaks-Ventura Metropolitan Statistical Area—see Appendix B for areas included; (2) Rankings are based on annual percentage change for all metro areas containing at least 15,000 transactions over the last 10 years and ranges from 1 to 275; (3) figures based on a weighted average of Census Division estimates using a seasonally adjusted, purchase-only index; all figures are for the period ending December 31, 2014

Source: Federal Housing Finance Agency, House Price Index, February 26, 2015

Median Single-Family Home Prices

Area	2012	2013	2014p	Percent Change 2013 to 2014
MSA[1]	n/a	n/a	n/a	n/a
U.S. Average	177.2	197.4	209.0	5.9

Note: Figures are median sales prices of existing single-family homes in thousands of dollars; (p) preliminary; n/a not available; (1) Oxnard-Thousand Oaks-Ventura, CA Metropolitan Statistical Area—see Appendix B for areas included

Source: National Association of Realtors, Median Sales Price of Existing Single-Family Homes for Metropolitan Areas, 4th Quarter 2014

Qualifying Income Based on Median Sales Price of Existing Single-Family Homes

Area	With 5% Down ($)	With 10% Down ($)	With 20% Down ($)
MSA[1]	n/a	n/a	n/a
U.S. Average	45,863	43,449	38,621

Note: Figures are preliminary; Qualifying income is based on a mortgage rate of 4.0%. Monthly principal and interest payment is limited to 25% of income; n/a not available; (1) Oxnard-Thousand Oaks-Ventura, CA Metropolitan Statistical Area—see Appendix B for areas included

Source: National Association of Realtors, Qualifying Income Based on Median Sales Price of Existing Single-Family Homes for Metropolitan Areas, 4th Quarter 2014

Median Apartment Condo-Coop Home Prices

Area	2012	2013	2014p	Percent Change 2013 to 2014
MSA[1]	n/a	n/a	n/a	n/a
U.S. Average	173.7	194.9	205.1	5.2

Note: Figures are median sales prices of existing apartment condo-coop homes in thousands of dollars; (p) preliminary; n/a not available; (1) Oxnard-Thousand Oaks-Ventura, CA Metropolitan Statistical Area—see Appendix B for areas included

Source: National Association of Realtors, Median Sales Price of Existing Apartment Condo-Coop Homes for Metropolitan Areas, 4th Quarter 2014

Gross Monthly Rent

Area	Under $200	$200 -299	$300 -499	$500 -749	$750 -999	$1,000 -1,499	$1,500 and up	Median ($)
City	0.4	2.9	3.7	4.7	14.6	36.9	36.8	1,314
MSA[1]	0.7	2.1	3.2	4.7	9.6	32.3	47.4	1,462
U.S.	1.7	3.2	7.8	22.1	24.3	26.0	14.9	900

Note: Figures are percentages except for Median; Gross rent is the contract rent plus the estimated average monthly cost of utilities (electricity, gas, and water and sewer) and fuels (oil, coal, kerosene, wood, etc.) if these are paid by the renter (or paid for the renter by someone else); (1) Figures cover the Oxnard-Thousand Oaks-Ventura, CA Metropolitan Statistical Area—see Appendix B for areas included

Source: U.S. Census Bureau, 2011-2013 American Community Survey 3-Year Estimates

Homeownership Rate

Area	2007 (%)	2008 (%)	2009 (%)	2010 (%)	2011 (%)	2012 (%)	2013 (%)	2014 (%)
MSA[1]	71.4	71.7	73.1	67.1	67.0	66.1	66.8	64.5
U.S.	68.1	67.8	67.4	66.9	66.1	65.4	65.1	64.5

Note: (1) Figures cover the Oxnard-Thousand Oaks-Ventura, CA Metropolitan Statistical Area—see Appendix B for areas included
Source: U.S. Census Bureau, Housing Vacancies and Homeownership Annual Statistics: 2014

Year Housing Structure Built

Area	2010 or Later	2000 -2009	1990 -1999	1980 -1989	1970 -1979	1960 -1969	1950 -1959	1940 -1949	Before 1940	Median Year
City	0.4	14.1	10.3	11.0	21.2	21.0	15.0	4.5	2.6	1973
MSA[1]	0.4	11.3	10.8	16.7	23.2	20.6	10.5	2.9	3.6	1975
U.S.	0.9	15.0	13.9	13.8	15.8	11.0	10.9	5.4	13.3	1976

Note: Figures are percentages except for Median Year; (1) Figures cover the Oxnard-Thousand Oaks-Ventura, CA Metropolitan Statistical Area—see Appendix B for areas included
Source: U.S. Census Bureau, 2011-2013 American Community Survey 3-Year Estimates

HEALTH

Health Risk Data

Category	MSA[1] (%)	U.S. (%)
Adults aged 18–64 who have any kind of health care coverage	n/a	79.6
Adults who reported being in good or excellent health	n/a	83.1
Adults who are current smokers	n/a	19.6
Adults who are heavy drinkers[2]	n/a	6.1
Adults who are binge drinkers[3]	n/a	16.9
Adults who are overweight (BMI 25.0 - 29.9)	n/a	35.8
Adults who are obese (BMI 30.0 - 99.8)	n/a	27.6
Adults who participated in any physical activities in the past month	n/a	77.1
Adults 50+ who have ever had a sigmoidoscopy or colonoscopy	n/a	67.3
Women aged 40+ who have had a mammogram within the past two years	n/a	74.0
Men aged 40+ who have had a PSA test within the past two years	n/a	45.2
Adults aged 65+ who have had flu shot within the past year	n/a	60.1
Adults who always wear a seatbelt	n/a	93.8

Note: Data as of 2012 unless otherwise noted; n/a not available; (1) Figures cover the Oxnard-Thousand Oaks-Ventura, CA Metropolitan Statistical Area—see Appendix B for areas included; (2) Heavy drinkers are classified as males having more than two drinks per day or females having more than one drink per day; (3) Binge drinkers are classified as males having five or more drinks on one occasion or females having four or more drinks on one occasion
Source: Centers for Disease Control and Prevention, Behaviorial Risk Factor Surveillance System, SMART: Selected Metropolitan/Micropolitan Area Risk Trends, 2012 (Note: the CDC has discontinued this dataset but will be releasing a replacement in late 2015)

Chronic Health Indicators

Category	MSA[1] (%)	U.S. (%)
Adults who have ever been told they had a heart attack	n/a	4.5
Adults who have ever been told they had a stroke	n/a	2.9
Adults who have been told they currently have asthma	n/a	8.9
Adults who have ever been told they have arthritis	n/a	25.7
Adults who have ever been told they have diabetes[2]	n/a	9.7
Adults who have ever been told they had skin cancer	n/a	5.7
Adults who have ever been told they had any other types of cancer	n/a	6.5
Adults who have ever been told they have COPD	n/a	6.2
Adults who have ever been told they have kidney disease	n/a	2.5
Adults who have ever been told they have a form of depression	n/a	18.0

Note: Data as of 2012 unless otherwise noted; n/a not available; (1) Figures cover the Oxnard-Thousand Oaks-Ventura, CA Metropolitan Statistical Area—see Appendix B for areas included; (2) Figures do not include pregnancy-related, borderline, or pre-diabetes
Source: Centers for Disease Control and Prevention, Behaviorial Risk Factor Surveillance System, SMART: Selected Metropolitan/Micropolitan Area Risk Trends, 2012 (Note: the CDC has discontinued this dataset but will be releasing a replacement in late 2015)

Mortality Rates for the Top 10 Causes of Death in the U.S.

ICD-10[a] Sub-Chapter	ICD-10[a] Code	Age-Adjusted Mortality Rate[1] per 100,000 population	
		County[2]	U.S.
Malignant neoplasms	C00-C97	141.0	166.2
Ischaemic heart diseases	I20-I25	84.0	105.7
Other forms of heart disease	I30-I51	35.6	49.3
Chronic lower respiratory diseases	J40-J47	31.6	42.1
Organic, including symptomatic, mental disorders	F01-F09	23.1	38.1
Cerebrovascular diseases	I60-I69	34.6	37.0
Other external causes of accidental injury	W00-X59	21.8	26.9
Other degenerative diseases of the nervous system	G30-G31	32.4	25.6
Diabetes mellitus	E10-E14	16.6	21.3
Hypertensive diseases	I10-I15	27.1	19.4

Note: (a) ICD-10 = International Classification of Diseases 10th Revision; (1) Mortality rates are a three year average covering 2011-2013; (2) Figures cover Ventura County
Source: Centers for Disease Control and Prevention, National Center for Health Statistics. Compressed Mortality File 1999-2013 on CDC WONDER Online Database, released October 2014. Data are compiled from the Compressed Mortality File 1999-2013, Series 20 No. 2S, 2014.

Mortality Rates for Selected Causes of Death

ICD-10[a] Sub-Chapter	ICD-10[a] Code	Age-Adjusted Mortality Rate[1] per 100,000 population	
		County[2]	U.S.
Assault	X85-Y09	2.7	5.2
Diseases of the liver	K70-K76	12.1	13.2
Human immunodeficiency virus (HIV) disease	B20-B24	0.8	2.2
Influenza and pneumonia	J09-J18	10.3	15.4
Intentional self-harm	X60-X84	11.6	12.5
Malnutrition	E40-E46	*0.5	0.9
Obesity and other hyperalimentation	E65-E68	1.1	1.8
Renal failure	N17-N19	5.5	13.1
Transport accidents	V01-V99	9.2	11.7
Viral hepatitis	B15-B19	3.3	2.2

Note: (a) ICD-10 = International Classification of Diseases 10th Revision; (1) Mortality rates are a three year average covering 2011-2013; (2) Figures cover Ventura County; (*) Unreliable data as per CDC
Source: Centers for Disease Control and Prevention, National Center for Health Statistics. Compressed Mortality File 1999-2013 on CDC WONDER Online Database, released October 2014. Data are compiled from the Compressed Mortality File 1999-2013, Series 20 No. 2S, 2014.

Health Insurance Coverage

Area	With Health Insurance	With Private Health Insurance	With Public Health Insurance	Without Health Insurance	Population Under Age 18 Without Health Insurance
City	75.6	48.1	34.2	24.4	10.4
MSA[1]	83.8	66.4	26.9	16.2	7.6
U.S.	85.2	65.2	31.0	14.8	7.3

Note: Figures are percentages that cover the civilian noninstitutionalized population; (1) Figures cover the Oxnard-Thousand Oaks-Ventura, CA Metropolitan Statistical Area—see Appendix B for areas included
Source: U.S. Census Bureau, 2011-2013 American Community Survey 3-Year Estimates

Number of Medical Professionals

Area[1]	MDs[2]	DOs[2,3]	Dentists	Podiatrists	Chiropractors	Optometrists
Local (number)	1,821	71	671	43	288	125
Local (rate[4])	218.0	8.5	79.8	5.1	34.2	14.9
U.S. (rate[4])	270.0	20.2	63.1	5.7	25.2	14.9

Note: Data as of 2013 unless noted; (1) Local data covers Ventura County; (2) Data as of 2012 and includes all active, non-federal physicians; (3) Doctor of Osteopathic Medicine; (4) rate per 100,000 population
Source: U.S. Department of Health and Human Services, Health Resources and Services Administration, Bureau of Health Professions, Area Resource File (ARF) 2013-2014

EDUCATION

Public School District Statistics

District Name	Schls	Pupils	Pupil/ Teacher Ratio	Minority Pupils[1] (%)	Free Lunch Eligible[2] (%)	IEP[3] (%)
Ocean View	5	2,550	22.2	93.5	99.4	9.3
Oxnard	21	16,533	25.3	95.9	66.0	9.4
Oxnard Union High	10	16,780	26.6	84.0	55.5	10.3
Rio Elementary	8	4,692	26.5	95.0	62.3	8.1

Note: Table includes school districts with 2,000 or more students; (1) Percentage of students that are not non-Hispanic white; (2) Percentage of students that are eligible for the free lunch program; (3) Percentage of students that have an Individualized Education Program.
Source: U.S. Department of Education, National Center for Education Statistics, Common Core of Data, Local Education Agency (School District) Universe Survey: School Year 2012-2013; U.S. Department of Education, National Center for Education Statistics, Common Core of Data, Public Elementary/Secondary School Universe Survey: School Year 2012-2013

Highest Level of Education

Area	Less than H.S.	H.S. Diploma	Some College, No Deg.	Associate Degree	Bachelor's Degree	Master's Degree	Prof. School Degree	Doctorate Degree
City	34.7	21.2	20.4	7.8	11.7	3.1	0.7	0.4
MSA[1]	17.0	19.1	23.8	8.8	19.8	7.9	2.3	1.3
U.S.	13.7	28.0	21.2	7.9	18.2	7.7	1.9	1.3

Note: Figures cover persons age 25 and over; (1) Figures cover the Oxnard-Thousand Oaks-Ventura, CA Metropolitan Statistical Area—see Appendix B for areas included
Source: U.S. Census Bureau, 2011-2013 American Community Survey 3-Year Estimates

Educational Attainment by Race

Area	High School Graduate or Higher (%)					Bachelor's Degree or Higher (%)				
	Total	White	Black	Asian	Hisp.[2]	Total	White	Black	Asian	Hisp.[2]
City	65.3	62.2	86.9	87.9	51.8	15.9	14.6	19.4	32.1	8.2
MSA[1]	83.0	84.0	93.0	91.5	59.7	31.3	31.3	33.6	55.2	11.3
U.S.	86.3	88.3	83.1	85.7	64.0	29.1	30.4	18.8	50.7	13.7

Note: Figures shown cover persons 25 years old and over; (1) Figures cover the Oxnard-Thousand Oaks-Ventura, CA Metropolitan Statistical Area—see Appendix B for areas included; (2) People of Hispanic origin can be of any race
Source: U.S. Census Bureau, 2011-2013 American Community Survey 3-Year Estimates

School Enrollment by Grade and Control

Area	Preschool (%)		Kindergarten (%)		Grades 1 - 4 (%)		Grades 5 - 8 (%)		Grades 9 - 12 (%)	
	Public	Private	Public	Private	Public	Private	Public	Private	Public	Private
City	74.8	25.2	94.1	5.9	93.9	6.1	94.6	5.4	93.3	6.7
MSA[1]	53.3	46.7	90.2	9.8	91.1	8.9	90.2	9.8	90.2	9.8
U.S.	57.7	42.3	87.9	12.1	89.9	10.1	90.0	10.0	90.7	9.3

Note: Figures shown cover persons 3 years old and over; (1) Figures cover the Oxnard-Thousand Oaks-Ventura, CA Metropolitan Statistical Area—see Appendix B for areas included
Source: U.S. Census Bureau, 2011-2013 American Community Survey 3-Year Estimates

Average Salaries of Public School Classroom Teachers

Area	2013-14		2014-15		Percent Change 2013-14 to 2014-15	Percent Change 2004-05 to 2014-15
	Dollars	Rank[1]	Dollars	Rank[1]		
CALIFORNIA	71,396	4	72,535	4	1.59	25.9
U.S. Average	56,610	–	57,379	–	1.36	20.8

Note: (1) State rank ranges from 1 to 51 where 1 indicates highest salary.
Source: National Education Association, Rankings & Estimates: Rankings of the States 2014 and Estimates of School Statistics 2015, March 2015

Higher Education

Four-Year Colleges			Two-Year Colleges			Medical Schools[1]	Law Schools[2]	Voc/ Tech[3]
Public	Private Non-profit	Private For-profit	Public	Private Non-profit	Private For-profit			
0	0	1	1	0	0	0	0	3

Note: Figures cover institutions located within the city limits and include main campuses only; (1) includes schools accredited by the Liaison Committee on Medical Education and the American Osteopathic Association's Commission on Osteopathic College Accreditation; (2) includes ABA-accredited schools, schools with provisional ABA accreditation, and state accredited schools; (3) includes all schools with programs that are less than 2 years.
Source: National Center for Education Statistics, Integrated Postsecondary Education System (IPEDS), 2013-14; Association of American Medical Colleges, Member List, May 1, 2015; American Osteopathic Association, Member List, May 1, 2015; Law School Admission Council, Official Guide to ABA-Approved Law Schools Online, May 1, 2015; Wikipedia, List of Medical Schools in the United States, May 1, 2015; Wikipedia, List of Law Schools in the United States, May 1, 2015

According to *U.S. News & World Report,* the Oxnard-Thousand Oaks-Ventura, CA metro area is home to one of the best liberal arts colleges in the U.S.: **Thomas Aquinas College** (#77). The indicators used to capture academic quality fall into a number of categories: assessment by administrators at peer institutions; retention of students; faculty resources; student selectivity; financial resources; alumni giving; high school counselor ratings of colleges; and graduation rate. *U.S. News & World Report, "America's Best Colleges 2015"*

PRESIDENTIAL ELECTION

2012 Presidential Election Results

Area	Obama (%)	Romney (%)	Other (%)
Ventura County	51.7	46.1	2.2
U.S.	51.0	47.2	1.8

Note: Results may not add to 100% due to rounding
Source: Dave Leip's Atlas of U.S. Presidential Elections

EMPLOYERS

Major Employers

Company Name	Industry
Amgen	Biological produtcs, except diagnostic
Amgen Pharmaceuticals	Biotechnical research, noncommercial
Baxter Healthcare Corporation	Drugs, proprietaries, and sundries
California Department of Mental Health	Mental hospital, except for the mentally retarded
Central Purchasing	Hardware, nec
Community Memorial Health System	General medical and surgical hospitals
County of Ventura	Executive offices
Dignity Health	General medical and surgical hospitals
Farmers Group	Insurance agents, brokers, and service
GTE Corporation	Employment agencies
Haas Automation	Machine tools, metal cutting type
Kavlico Corporation	Relays and industrial controls
L-3 Services	Engineering services
Official Police Garage Assn of LA	Towing and tugboat service
Oxnard School District	Public and elementary secondary schools
Technicolor Thomson Group	Video, tape or disk reproduction
Truck Underwriters Association	Life insurance
US Navy	Primary care medical clinic
Xavient Information Systems	Business consulting, nec
Xmultiple	Connectors and terminals for electrical devices

Note: Companies shown are located within the Oxnard-Thousand Oaks-Ventura, CA Metropolitan Statistical Area.
Source: Hoovers.com; Wikipedia

PUBLIC SAFETY

Crime Rate

Area	All Crimes	Violent Crimes				Property Crimes		
		Murder	Forcible Rape	Robbery	Aggrav. Assault	Burglary	Larceny -Theft	Motor Vehicle Theft
City	2,825.8	7.4	4.9	161.9	147.1	480.8	1,696.0	327.7
Suburbs[1]	1,928.3	3.0	11.8	43.7	94.8	350.4	1,293.6	131.0
Metro[2]	2,144.6	4.0	10.1	72.2	107.4	381.8	1,390.5	178.4
U.S.	3,098.6	4.5	25.2	109.1	229.1	610.0	1,899.4	221.3

Note: Figures are crimes per 100,000 population; (1) All areas within the metro area that are located outside the city limits; (2) Figures cover the Oxnard-Thousand Oaks-Ventura, CA Metropolitan Statistical Area—see Appendix B for areas included
Source: FBI Uniform Crime Reports, 2013

Hate Crimes

Area	Number of Quarters Reported	Number of Incidents per Bias Motivation						
		Race	Religion	Sexual Orientation	Ethnicity	Disability	Gender	Gender Identity
City	4	0	0	1	0	0	0	0
U.S.	4	2,871	1,031	1,233	655	83	18	31

Source: Federal Bureau of Investigation, Hate Crime Statistics 2013

Identity Theft Consumer Complaints

Area	Complaints	Complaints per 100,000 Population	Rank[2]
MSA[1]	710	84.6	106
U.S.	332,646	104.3	-

Note: (1) Figures cover the Oxnard-Thousand Oaks-Ventura, CA Metropolitan Statistical Area—see Appendix B for areas included; (2) Rank ranges from 1 to 380 where 1 indicates greatest number of identity theft complaints per 100,000 population
Source: Federal Trade Commission, Consumer Sentinel Network Data Book for January–December 2014

Fraud and Other Consumer Complaints

Area	Complaints	Complaints per 100,000 Population	Rank[2]
MSA[1]	3,424	407.8	125
U.S.	2,250,205	705.7	-

Note: (1) Figures cover the Oxnard-Thousand Oaks-Ventura, CA Metropolitan Statistical Area—see Appendix B for areas included; (2) Rank ranges from 1 to 380 where 1 indicates greatest number of identity theft complaints per 100,000 population
Source: Federal Trade Commission, Consumer Sentinel Network Data Book for January–December 2014

RECREATION

Culture

Dance[1]	Theatre[1]	Instrumental Music[1]	Vocal Music[1]	Series and Festivals	Museums and Art Galleries[2]	Zoos and Aquariums[3]
0	0	0	0	0	7	0

Note: (1) Professional perfoming groups; (2) Based on organizations with SIC code 8412; (3) AZA-accredited
Source: The Grey House Performing Arts Directory, 2015-16; Association of Zoos & Aquariums, AZA Member Zoos & Aquariums, April 2015; www.AccuLeads.com, April 2015

Professional Sports Teams

Team Name	League	Year Established

No teams are located in the metro area
Source: Wikipedia, Major Professional Sports Teams of the United States and Canada, April 2015

CLIMATE

Average and Extreme Temperatures

Temperature	Jan	Feb	Mar	Apr	May	Jun	Jul	Aug	Sep	Oct	Nov	Dec	Yr.
Extreme High (°F)	90	89	99	100	96	100	93	97	100	105	98	89	105
Average High (°F)	64	64	64	65	66	69	71	73	73	71	69	65	68
Average Temp. (°F)	54	55	55	57	59	62	65	66	66	63	59	55	60
Average Low (°F)	45	45	46	48	52	54	57	59	58	53	48	45	51
Extreme Low (°F)	29	27	33	34	35	39	41	46	41	33	31	27	27

Note: Figures cover the years 1946-1995
Source: National Climatic Data Center, International Station Meteorological Climate Summary, 9/96

Average Precipitation/Snowfall/Humidity

Precip./Humidity	Jan	Feb	Mar	Apr	May	Jun	Jul	Aug	Sep	Oct	Nov	Dec	Yr.
Avg. Precip. (in.)	2.9	2.4	2.0	0.8	0.1	Tr	Tr	0.1	0.3	0.2	1.5	1.7	12.0
Avg. Snowfall (in.)	Tr	Tr	0	0	0	0	0	0	0	0	0	0	0
Avg. Rel. Hum. 7am (%)	68	75	80	81	82	84	87	88	86	79	69	67	79
Avg. Rel. Hum. 4pm (%)	61	64	67	68	70	71	71	71	70	69	63	61	67

Note: Figures cover the years 1946-1995; Tr = Trace amounts (<0.05 in. of rain; <0.5 in. of snow)
Source: National Climatic Data Center, International Station Meteorological Climate Summary, 9/96

Weather Conditions

Temperature			Daytime Sky			Precipitation		
10°F & below	32°F & below	90°F & above	Clear	Partly cloudy	Cloudy	0.01 inch or more precip.	0.1 inch or more snow/ice	Thunder-storms
0	1	2	114	155	96	34	< 1	1

Note: Figures are average number of days per year and cover the years 1946-1995
Source: National Climatic Data Center, International Station Meteorological Climate Summary, 9/96

HAZARDOUS WASTE

Superfund Sites

Oxnard has one hazardous waste site on the EPA's Superfund Final National Priorities List: **Halaco Engineering Company**. There are a total of 1,322 Superfund sites on the list in the U.S.
U.S. Environmental Protection Agency, Final National Priorities List, April 14, 2015

AIR & WATER QUALITY

Air Quality Trends: Ozone

	2004	2005	2006	2007	2008	2009	2010	2011	2012	2013
MSA[1]	0.084	0.080	0.081	0.075	0.079	0.079	0.074	0.074	0.071	0.068

Note: (1) Data covers the Oxnard-Thousand Oaks-Ventura, CA Metropolitan Statistical Area—see Appendix B for areas included. The values shown are the composite ozone concentration averages among trend sites based on the highest fourth daily maximum 8-hour concentration in parts per million. These trends are based on sites having an adequate record of monitoring data during the trend period. Data from exceptional events are included.
Source: U.S. Environmental Protection Agency, Air Quality Monitoring Information, "Air Quality Trends by City, 2000-2013"

Air Quality Index

Area	Percent of Days when Air Quality was...[2]					AQI Statistics[2]	
	Good	Moderate	Unhealthy for Sensitive Groups	Unhealthy	Very Unhealthy	Maximum	Median
MSA[1]	49.0	49.0	1.9	0.0	0.0	124	51

Note: (1) Data covers the Oxnard-Thousand Oaks-Ventura, CA Metropolitan Statistical Area—see Appendix B for areas included; (2) Based on 365 days with AQI data in 2014. Air Quality Index (AQI) is an index for reporting daily air quality. EPA calculates the AQI for five major air pollutants regulated by the Clean Air Act: ground-level ozone, particle pollution (aka particulate matter), carbon monoxide, sulfur dioxide, and nitrogen dioxide. The AQI runs from 0 to 500. The higher the AQI value, the greater the level of air pollution and the greater the health concern. There are six AQI categories: "Good" AQI is between 0 and 50. Air quality is considered satisfactory; "Moderate" AQI is between 51 and 100. Air quality is acceptable; "Unhealthy for Sensitive Groups" When AQI values are between 101 and 150, members of sensitive groups may experience health effects; "Unhealthy" When AQI values are between 151 and 200 everyone may begin to experience health effects; "Very Unhealthy" AQI values between 201 and 300 trigger a health alert; "Hazardous" AQI values over 300 trigger warnings of emergency conditions (not shown).
Source: U.S. Environmental Protection Agency, Air Quality Index Report, 2014

Air Quality Index Pollutants

Area	Percent of Days when AQI Pollutant was...[2]					
	Carbon Monoxide	Nitrogen Dioxide	Ozone	Sulfur Dioxide	Particulate Matter 2.5	Particulate Matter 10
MSA[1]	0.0	0.3	48.8	0.0	49.0	1.9

Note: (1) Data covers the Oxnard-Thousand Oaks-Ventura, CA Metropolitan Statistical Area—see Appendix B for areas included; (2) Based on 365 days with AQI data in 2014. The Air Quality Index (AQI) is an index for reporting daily air quality. EPA calculates the AQI for five major air pollutants regulated by the Clean Air Act: ground-level ozone, particle pollution (also known as particulate matter), carbon monoxide, sulfur dioxide, and nitrogen dioxide. The AQI runs from 0 to 500. The higher the AQI value, the greater the level of air pollution and the greater the health concern.
Source: U.S. Environmental Protection Agency, Air Quality Index Report, 2014

Maximum Air Pollutant Concentrations: Particulate Matter, Ozone, CO and Lead

	Particulate Matter 10 (ug/m^3)	Particulate Matter 2.5 Wtd AM (ug/m^3)	Particulate Matter 2.5 24-Hr (ug/m^3)	Ozone (ppm)	Carbon Monoxide (ppm)	Lead (ug/m^3)
MSA[1] Level	143	9.3	23	0.077	n/a	n/a
NAAQS[2]	150	15	35	0.075	9	0.15
Met NAAQS[2]	Yes	Yes	Yes	No	n/a	n/a

Note: (1) Data covers the Oxnard-Thousand Oaks-Ventura, CA Metropolitan Statistical Area—see Appendix B for areas included; Data from exceptional events are included; (2) National Ambient Air Quality Standards; ppm = parts per million; ug/m^3 = micrograms per cubic meter; n/a not available.
Concentrations: Particulate Matter 10 (coarse particulate)—highest second maximum 24-hour concentration; Particulate Matter 2.5 Wtd AM (fine particulate)—highest weighted annual mean concentration; Particulate Matter 2.5 24-Hour (fine particulate)—highest 98th percentile 24-hour concentration; Ozone—highest fourth daily maximum 8-hour concentration; Carbon Monoxide—highest second maximum non-overlapping 8-hour concentration; Lead—maximum running 3-month average
Source: U.S. Environmental Protection Agency, Air Quality Monitoring Information, "Air Quality Statistics by City, 2013"

Maximum Air Pollutant Concentrations: Nitrogen Dioxide and Sulfur Dioxide

	Nitrogen Dioxide AM (ppb)	Nitrogen Dioxide 1-Hr (ppb)	Sulfur Dioxide AM (ppb)	Sulfur Dioxide 1-Hr (ppb)	Sulfur Dioxide 24-Hr (ppb)
MSA[1] Level	9	37	n/a	n/a	n/a
NAAQS[2]	53	100	30	75	140
Met NAAQS[2]	Yes	Yes	n/a	n/a	n/a

Note: (1) Data covers the Oxnard-Thousand Oaks-Ventura, CA Metropolitan Statistical Area—see Appendix B for areas included; Data from exceptional events are included; (2) National Ambient Air Quality Standards; ppm = parts per million; ug/m^3 = micrograms per cubic meter; n/a not available.
Concentrations: Nitrogen Dioxide AM—highest arithmetic mean concentration; Nitrogen Dioxide 1-Hr—highest 98th percentile 1-hour daily maximum concentration; Sulfur Dioxide AM—highest annual mean concentration; Sulfur Dioxide 1-Hr—highest 99th percentile 1-hour daily maximum concentration; Sulfur Dioxide 24-Hr—highest second maximum 24-hour concentration
Source: U.S. Environmental Protection Agency, Air Quality Monitoring Information, "Air Quality Statistics by City, 2013"

Drinking Water

Water System Name	Pop. Served	Primary Water Source Type	Violations[1]	
			Health Based	Monitoring/ Reporting
Oxnard Water Dept.	200,855	Purchased Surface	0	0

Note: (1) Based on violation data from January 1, 2014 to December 31, 2014 (includes unresolved violations from earlier years)

Source: U.S. Environmental Protection Agency, Office of Ground Water and Drinking Water, Safe Drinking Water Information System (based on data extracted January 27, 2015)

Phoenix, Arizona

Background

Phoenix, the arid "Valley of the Sun," and the capital of Arizona, was named by the English soldier and prospector, "Lord Darell" Duppa for the mythical bird of ancient Greek/Phoenician lore. According to the legend, the Phoenix was a beautiful bird that destroyed itself with its own flames. When nothing remained but embers, it would rise again from the ashes, more awesome and beautiful than before. Like the romantic tale, Duppa hoped that his city of Phoenix would rise again from the mysteriously abandoned Hohokam village.

Many might agree that Phoenix fulfilled Duppa's wish. Within 15 years after its second founding in 1867, Phoenix had grown to be an important supply point for the mining districts of north-central Arizona, as well as an important trading site for farmers, cattlemen, and prospectors.

Around this time, Phoenix entered its Wild West phase, complete with stagecoaches, saloons, gambling houses, soldiers, cowboys, miners, and the pungent air of outlawry. Two public hangings near the end of the 1800s set a dramatic example, and helped turn the tide.

Today, Phoenix—Arizona's state capital—is just as exciting as ever, but more law-abiding, and many continue to be attracted to Phoenix's natural beauty. Despite occasional sprawling suburbs and shopping malls, the sophisticated blend of Spanish, Native American, and cowboy culture is obvious in the city's architecture, arts, and crafts. Downtown Phoenix underwent a major renaissance in the 1990s with the completion of a history museum, expanded art museum, new central library, Arizona Science Center, and a renovated concert hall. Today it also features the 20,000 square foot Musical Instrument Museum featuring musical instruments from around the world. More than 300 arts and entertainment venues are located in the Phoenix region, as well as five professional sports teams.

Phoenix is the country's sixth-largest city, with more than one million people, while the Phoenix metro area population has grown to nearly four million. This increase in population continues to make Phoenix an attractive location for companies that are expanding in the fields of electronics and communications. Renewable energy, biomedicine, advanced business services, manufacturing and distribution, aerospace and aviation, and emerging technologies from start-ups are key industries in the region. Insurance, healthcare, and technology companies expanded or opened new facilities in Phoenix in late 2013 and early 2014.

The Valley Metro Rail light rail, now 20 miles of eco-friendly transit, is in the midst of constructing or planning seven extensions that will create a 60-mile system by 2034.

Temperatures in Phoenix are mild in winter and very hot in summer. However, with the low humidity, the summer heat is somewhat more bearable than one might expect. Rainfall is slight and comes in two seasons. In winter rain comes on winds from the Pacific, ending by April. In summer, especially during July and August, there are severe thunderstorms from the southeast.

Rankings

General Rankings

- The Phoenix metro area was identified as one of America's fastest-growing areas in terms of population and economy by *Forbes*. The area ranked #11 out of 20. The 100 most populous metro areas in the U.S. were evaluated on the following criteria: estimated population growth; job growth; gross metropolitan product growth; unemployment; median salaries for college-educated workers. *Forbes, "America's Fastest-Growing Cities 2015," January 27, 2015*

- Phoenix was identified as one of America's fastest-growing major metropolitan areas in terms of population growth by CNNMoney.com. The area ranked #10 out of 10. Criteria: population growth between July 2012 and July 2013. *CNNMoney, "10 Fastest-Growing Cities," March 28, 2014*

- Phoenix was selected as one of America's best cities by *Bloomberg Businessweek*. The city ranked #44 out of 50. Criteria: leisure attributes (the number of restaurants, bars, libraries, museums, professional sports teams, and park acres by population); educational attributes (public school performance, the number of colleges, and graduate degree holders); economic factors (2011 income and June and July 2012 unemployment); crime; and air quality. *Bloomberg BusinessWeek, "America's Best Cities," September 26, 2012*

Business/Finance Rankings

- The finance website Wall St. Cheat Sheet reported on the prospects for high-wage job creation in the nation's largest metro areas over the next five years and ranked them accordingly, drawing on in-depth analysis by CareerBuilder and Economic Modeling Specialists International (EMSI). The Phoenix metro area placed #3 on the Wall St. Cheat Sheet list. *wallstcheatsheet.com, "Top 10 Cities for High-Wage Job Growth," December 8, 2013*

- Based on metro area social media reviews, the employment opinion group Glassdoor surveyed 50 of the largest U.S. metro areas on measures including compensation and benefits, satisfaction with management, business outlook, and number of employers hiring. The Phoenix metro area was ranked #46 in overall employee satisfaction. *www.glassdoor.com, "Employment Satisfaction Report Card by City," June 13, 2014*

- In its Competitive Alternatives report, consulting firm KPMG analyzed the 27 largest metropolitan statistical areas according to 26 cost components (such as taxes, labor costs, and utilities) and 30 non-cost-related variables (such as crime rates and number of universities). The business website 24/7 Wall Street examined the KPMG findings, adding to the mix current unemployment rates, GDP, median income, and employment decline during the last recession and "projected" recovery. It identified the Phoenix metro area as #10 among the ten best American cities for business. *247wallst.com, "Best American Cities for Business," April 4, 2012*

- In a survey of economic confidence in the nation's 50 largest metropolitan areas conducted January–December 2014, the Phoenix metro area placed #26, according to Gallup's 2014 Economic Confidence Index. *Gallup, "San Jose and San Francisco Lead in Economic Confidence," March 19, 2015*

- The Brookings Institution ranked the 50 largest cities in the U.S. based on income inequality. Phoenix was ranked #30. (#1 = greatest ineqality). Criteria: the cities were ranked based on the "95/20 ratio," a figure representing the income at which a household earns more than 95 percent of all other households, divided by the income at which a household earns more than only 20 percent of all other households. *Brookings Institution, "Income Inequality in America's 50 Largest Cities, 2007-2013," March 17, 2015*

- Phoenix was ranked #7 out of 100 metro areas in terms of economic performance (#1 = best) during the recession and recovery from trough quarter through the second quarter of 2013. Criteria: percent change in employment; percentage point change in unemployment rate; percent change in gross metropolitan product; percent change in House Price Index. *Brookings Institution, MetroMonitor: Tracking Economic Recession and Recovery in America's 100 Largest Metropolitan Areas, September 2013*

- Payscale.com ranked the 20 largest metro areas in terms of wage growth. The Phoenix metro area ranked #4. Criteria: private-sector wage growth between the 1st quarter of 2014 and the 1st quarter of 2015. *PayScale, "Wage Trends by Metro Area," 1st Quarter, 2015*

- The Phoenix metro area was identified as one of the most debt-ridden places in America by the finance site Credit.com. The metro area was ranked #6. Criteria: residents' average personal debt load and average credit scores. *Credit.com, "The Most Debt-Ridden Cities," May 1, 2014*

- Phoenix was identified as one of America's most frugal metro areas by *Coupons.com*. The city ranked #17 out of 25. Criteria: online coupon usage. *Coupons.com, "Top 25 Most Frugal Cities of 2013," April 10, 2014*

- Phoenix was identified as one of America's most frugal metro areas by *Coupons.com*. The city ranked #19 out of 25. Criteria: Grocery IQ and coupons.com mobile app usage. *Coupons.com, "Top 25 Most On-the-Go Frugal Cities of 2013," April 10, 2014*

- Phoenix was identified as one of the happiest cities for young professionals by *CareerBliss.com*, an online community for career advancement. The city ranked #9. Criteria: more than 45,000 young professionals were asked to rate key factors that affect workplace happiness including: work-life balance; compensation; company culture; overall work environment; company reputation; relationships with managers and co-workers; opportunities for growth; job resources; daily tasks; job autonomy. Young professionals are defined as having less than 10 years of work experience. *CareerBliss.com, "Happiest Cities for Young Professionals," April 26, 2013*

- The Phoenix metro area appeared on the Milken Institute "2013 Best Performing Cities" list. Rank: #65 out of 200 large metro areas. Criteria: job growth; wage and salary growth; high-tech output growth. *Milken Institute, "Best-Performing Cities 2014," January 2015*

- *Forbes* ranked the 200 most populous metro areas to determine the nation's "Best Places for Business and Careers." The Phoenix metro area was ranked #56. Criteria: costs (business and living); job growth (past and projected); income growth; educational attainment (college and high school); projected economic growth; cultural and recreational opportunities; net migration patterns; number of highly ranked colleges. *Forbes, "The Best Places for Business and Careers 2014," July 23, 2014*

Culture/Performing Arts Rankings

- Phoenix was selected as one of America's top cities for the arts. The city ranked #25 in the big city (population 500,000 and over) category. Criteria: readers' top choices for arts travel destinations based on the richness and variety of visual arts sites, activities and events. *American Style, "2012 Top 25 Arts Destinations," June 2012*

Dating/Romance Rankings

- A *Cosmopolitan* magazine article surveyed the gender balance and other factors to arrive at a list of the best and worst cities for women to meet single guys. Phoenix was #4 among the best for single women looking for dates. *www.cosmopolitan.com, "Working the Ratio," October 1, 2013*

- Of the 100 U.S. cities surveyed by *Men's Health* in its quest to identify the nation's best cities for dating and forming relationships, Phoenix was ranked #31 for online dating (#1 = best). *Men's Health, "The Best and Worst Cities for Online Dating," January 30, 2013*

- Phoenix was selected as one of the best cities for single women by *Rent.com*. Criteria: high single male-to-female ratio. *Rent.com, "Top Cities for Single Women," March 7, 2013*

- Phoenix was selected as one of "America's Best Cities for Dating" by *Yahoo! Travel*. Criteria: high proportion of singles; excellent dating venues and/or stunning natural settings. *Yahoo! Travel, "America's Best Cities for Dating," February 7, 2012*

Education Rankings

- Personal finance website *WalletHub* analyzed the 150 largest U.S. metropolitan statistical areas to determine where the most educated Americans are choosing to settle. Criteria: educational attainment; percentage of workers with jobs in computer, engineering, and science fields; quality and size of each metro area's universities. Phoenix was ranked #58 (#1 = most educated city). *www.WalletHub.com, "2014's Most and Least Educated Cities*

- Phoenix was selected as one of America's most literate cities. The city ranked #65 out of the 77 largest U.S. cities. Criteria: number of booksellers; library resources; Internet resources; educational attainment; periodical publishing resources; newspaper circulation. *Central Connecticut State University, "America's Most Literate Cities, 2014," April 8, 2015*

Environmental Rankings

- The Phoenix metro area came in at #359 for the relative comfort of its climate on Sperling's list of "chill cities," as measured by the Sperling Heat Index. All 361 metro areas are included. Criteria included daytime high temperatures, nighttime low temperatures, dew point, and relative humidity at the high temperatures. *www.bertsperling.com, "Sperling's Chill Cities," July 18, 2013*

- Sperling's BestPlaces assessed 379 metropolitan areas of the United States for the likelihood of dangerously extreme weather events or earthquakes. In general the Southeast and South-Central regions have the highest risk of weather extremes and earthquakes, while the Pacific Northwest enjoys the lowest risk. Of the least risky metropolitan areas, the Phoenix metro area was ranked #120. *www.bestplaces.net, "Safest Places from Natural Disasters," April 2011*

- The U.S. Environmental Protection Agency (EPA) released a list of large U.S. metropolitan areas with the most ENERGY STAR certified buildings in 2014. The Phoenix metro area was ranked #11 out of 25. *U.S. Environmental Protection Agency, "Top Cities With the Most ENERGY STAR Certified Buildings in 2014," March 25, 2015*

- Phoenix was highlighted as one of the 25 most ozone-polluted metro areas in the U.S. during 2011 through 2013. The area ranked #10. *American Lung Association, State of the Air 2015*

- Phoenix was highlighted as one of the 25 metro areas most polluted by short-term particle pollution (24-hour PM 2.5) in the U.S. during 2011 through 2013. The area ranked #12. *American Lung Association, State of the Air 2015*

Food/Drink Rankings

- *Men's Health* ranked 100 major U.S. cities in terms of alcohol intoxication. Phoenix ranked #81 (#1 = most sober).Criteria: binge drinking; alcohol-related traffic accidents, arrests, and fatalities. *Men's Health, "The Drunkest Cities in America," November 19, 2013*

Health/Fitness Rankings

- For each of the 50 most populous metro areas in the United States, the American College of Sports Medicine's American Fitness Index evaluated infrastructure, community assets, and policies that encourage healthy and fit lifestyles, including preventive health behaviors, levels of chronic disease conditions, health care access, and community resources and policies that support physical activity. The Phoenix metro area ranked #33 for "community fitness." Personal health indicators were considered as well as community and environmental indicators. *www.americanfitnessindex.org, "ACSM American Fitness Index Health and Community Fitness Status of the 50 Largest Metropolitan Areas," May 2013*

- The Phoenix metro area was identified as one of the worst cities for bed bugs in America by pest control company Orkin. The area ranked #28 out of 50 based on the number of bed bug treatments Orkin performed from January to December 2013. *Orkin, "Chicago Tops Bed Bug Cities List for Second Year in a Row," January 16, 2014*

- Phoenix was selected as one of the 25 fattest cities in America by *Men's Fitness Online*. It ranked #18 out of America's 50 largest cities. Criteria: fitness centers and sport stores; nutrition; sports participation; TV viewing; overweight/sedentary; junk food; air quality; geography; commute; parks and open space; city recreational facilities; access to healthcare; motivation; mayor and city initiatives; state obesity initiatives. *Men's Fitness, "The Fittest and Fattest Cities in America," March 5, 2012*

- Phoenix was identified as a "2013 Spring Allergy Capital." The area ranked #75 out of 100. Three groups of factors were used to identify the most severe cities for people with allergies during the spring season: annual pollen levels; medicine utilization; access to board-certified allergists. *Asthma and Allergy Foundation of America, "Spring Allergy Capitals 2013"*

- Phoenix was identified as a "2013 Fall Allergy Capital." The area ranked #72 out of 100. Three groups of factors were used to identify the most severe cities for people with allergies during the fall season: annual pollen levels; medicine utilization; access to board-certified allergists. *Asthma and Allergy Foundation of America, "Fall Allergy Capitals 2013"*

- Phoenix was identified as a "2013 Asthma Capital." The area ranked #56 out of the nation's 100 largest metropolitan areas. Twelve factors were used to identify the most challenging places to live for people with asthma: estimated prevalence; self-reported prevalence; crude death rate for asthma; annual pollen score; annual air quality; public smoking laws; number of board-certified asthma specialists; school inhaler access laws; rescue medication use; controller medication use; uninsured rate; poverty rate. *Asthma and Allergy Foundation of America, "Asthma Capitals 2013"*

- *Men's Health* ranked 100 major U.S. cities in terms of the best and worst cities for men. Phoenix ranked #34. Criteria: thirty-three data points were examined covering health, fitness, and quality of life. *Men's Health, "The Best & Worst Cities for Men 2014," December 6, 2013*

- Phoenix was selected as one of the best metropolitan areas for hospital care in America by *HealthGrades.com*. The rankings are based on a comprehensive study of patient death and complication rates in the nation's nearly 5,000 hospitals. Hospitals performing in the top 5% nationwide across 26 different medical procedures and diagnoses were identified. *HealthGrades.com* then ranked cities by the highest percentage of these Distinguished Hospitals for Clinical Excellence™. The Phoenix metro area ranked #2. *HealthGrades.com, "America's Top 50 Cities for Hospital Care," January 21, 2012*

- The Phoenix metro area appeared in the 2013 Gallup-Healthways Well-Being Index. The area ranked #51 out of 189. The Gallup-Healthways Well-Being Index score is an average of six sub-indexes, which individually examine life evaluation, emotional health, work environment, physical health, healthy behaviors, and access to basic necessities. Results are based on telephone interviews conducted as part of the Gallup-Healthways Well-Being Index survey January 2–December 29, 2012, and January 2–December 30, 2013, with a random sample of 531,630 adults, aged 18 and older, living in metropolitan areas in the 50 U.S. states and the District of Columbia. *Gallup-Healthways, "State of American Well-Being," March 25, 2014*

- The Phoenix metro area was identified as one of "America's Most Stressful Cities" by *Sperling's BestPlaces*. The metro area ranked #18 out of 50. Criteria: unemployment rate; suicide rate; commute time; mental health; poor rest; alcohol use; violent crime rate; property crime rate; cloudy days annually. *Sperling's BestPlaces, www.BestPlaces.net, "Stressful Cities 2012*

Pet Rankings

- Phoenix was selected as one of the best cities for dogs by real estate website Estately.com. The city was ranked #9. Criteria: weather; walkability; yard sizes; dog activities; meetup groups; availability of dogsitters. *Estately.com, "17 Best U.S. Cities for Dogs," May 14, 2013*

Real Estate Rankings

- On the list compiled by Penske Truck Rental, the Phoenix metro area was named the #4 moving destination in 2014, based on one-way consumer truck rental reservations made through Penske's website and reservations call center. *blog.gopenske.com, "Penske Truck Rental's 2014 Top Moving Destinations List," February 4, 2015*

- The Phoenix metro area appeared on Realtor.com's list of the hottest housing markets to watch in 2015. Criteria: strong housing growth; affordable prices; and fast-paced sales. *Realtor.com®, "Top 10 Hot Housing Markets to Watch in 2015," December 4, 2014*

- The Phoenix metro area was identified as one of the top 20 housing markets to invest in for 2015 by *Forbes*. The area ranked #11. Criteria: strong population and job growth; relatively low home prices which are below equilibrium home price (EHP). The EHP is what the average price for a market should be, if speculation, weird distortions in local income, and other factors (like the housing collapse) weren't present in the market. *Forbes.com, "Best Buy Cities: Where to Invest in Housing in 2015," January 9, 2015*

- Phoenix was ranked #68 out of 275 metro areas in terms of house price appreciation in 2014 (#1 = highest rate). *Federal Housing Finance Agency, House Price Index, 4th Quarter 2014*

- The Phoenix metro area was identified as one of the 15 worst housing markets for the next five years." Criteria: projected annualized change in home prices between the fourth quarter 2012 and the fourth quarter 2017. *The Business Insider, "The 15 Worst Housing Markets for the Next Five Years," May 22, 2013*

- Phoenix was ranked #147 out of 226 metro areas in terms of housing affordability in 2014 by the National Association of Home Builders (#1 = most affordable). The NAHB-Wells Fargo Housing Opportunity Index (HOI) for a given area is defined as the share of homes sold in that area that would have been affordable to a family earning the local median income, based on standard mortgage underwriting criteria. *National Association of Home Builders®, NAHB-Wells Fargo Housing Opportunity Index, 4th Quarter 2014*

Safety Rankings

- Symantec, in partnership with Sperling's BestPlaces, ranked the 50 largest cities in the U.S. in terms of their vulnerability to cybercrime. The city ranked #31. Criteria: number of cyberattacks and potential infections; level of Internet access; expenditures on smartphones and computer hardware/software; wireless hotspots; broadband connectivity; Internet usage; online purchases. *Symantec, "Riskiest Online Cities of 2012" February 15, 2012*

- Allstate ranked the 200 largest cities in America in terms of driver safety. Phoenix ranked #79. Allstate researchers analyzed internal property damage claims over a two-year period from January 2011 to December 2012. A weighted average of the two-year numbers determined the annual percentages. *Allstate, "Allstate America's Best Drivers Report, 2014"*

- The National Insurance Crime Bureau ranked 380 metro areas in the U.S. in terms of per capita rates of vehicle theft. The Phoenix metro area ranked #83 (#1 = highest rate). Criteria: number of vehicle theft offenses per 100,000 inhabitants in 2012. *National Insurance Crime Bureau, "Hot Spots 2012," June 26, 2013*

Seniors/Retirement Rankings

- From its Best Cities for Successful Aging indexes, the Milken Institute generated rankings for metropolitan areas, weighing data in eight categories—health care, wellness, living arrangements, transportation, financial characteristics, education and employment opportunities, community engagement, and overall livability. The Phoenix metro area was ranked #90 overall in the large metro area category. *Milken Institute, "Best Cities for Successful Aging, 2014"*

- Phoenix was identified as one of the most popular places to retire by *Topretirements.com*. The list reflects the 100 cities (out of 900+ total cities reviewed) that visitors to the website are most interested in for retirement. *Topretirements.com, "Most Popular Places to Retire for 2014," February 25, 2014*

Sports/Recreation Rankings

- According to the personal finance website NerdWallet, the Phoenix metro area, at #7, is one of the nation's top dozen metro areas for sports fans. Criteria included the presence of all four major sports—MLB, NFL, NHL, and NBA, fan enthusiasm (as measured by game attendance), ticket affordability, and "sports culture," that is, number of sports bars. *www.nerdwallet.com, "Best Cities for Sports Fans," May 5, 2013*

- The sports site Bleacher Report named Phoenix as one of the nation's top ten golf cities. Criteria included the concentration of public and private golf courses in a given city and the favored locations of PGA tour events. *BleacherReport.com, "Top 10 U.S. Cities for Golf," September 16, 2013*

- Phoenix was selected as one of "America's Most Miserable Sports Cities" by *Forbes*. The city was ranked #3. Criteria: postseason losses; years since last title; ratio of cumulative seasons to championships won. Contenders were limited to cities with at least 75 total seasons of NFL, NBA, NHL and MLB play. *Forbes, "America's Most Miserable Sports Cities," July 31, 2013*

Women/Minorities Rankings

- *Women's Health* examined U.S. cities and identified the 100 best cities for women. Phoenix was ranked #33. Criteria: 30 categories were examined from obesity and breast cancer rates to commuting times and hours spent working out. *Women's Health, "Best Cities for Women 2012"*

- Phoenix was selected as one of the best cities for young Latinos in 2013 by mun2, a national cable television broadcast network. The city ranked #11. Criteria: U.S. cities with populations over 500,000 residents were evaluated on the following criteria: number of young latinos; jobs; friendliness; cost of living; fun. *mun2.tv, "Best Cities for Young Latinos 2013*

Miscellaneous Rankings

- The watchdog site Charity Navigator conducts an annual study of charities in the nation's major markets both to analyze statistical differences in their financial, accountability, and transparency practices and to track year-to-year variations in individual communities. The Phoenix metro area was ranked #23 among the 30 metro markets. *www.charitynavigator.org, "Metro Market Study 2013," June 1, 2013*

- The Phoenix metro area was selected as one of "The Best U.S. Cities for Bargain Shopping" by *Forbes*. The area ranked #3 out of 10. Criteria: number of outlet stores; gross leasable retail space in major malls; low consumer price index; low sales tax rate. Indicators were examined in the nation's 50 largest metropolitan areas. *Forbes, "The Best U.S. Cities for Bargain Shopping," January 20, 2012*

- Mars Chocolate North America, the makers of COMBOS®, in partnership with Sperling's BestPlaces, ranked 50 major metro areas in terms of their "manliness." The Phoenix metro area ranked #25. Criteria: number of professional sports teams; number of nearby NASCAR tracks and racing events; manly lifestyle; concentration of manly retail stores; manly occupations per capita; salty snack sales; "Board of Manliness" rankings. *Mars Chocolate North America, "America's Manliest Cities 2012"*

- The National Alliance to End Homelessness ranked the 100 most populous metro areas in terms the rate of homelessness. The Phoenix metro area ranked #60. Criteria: number of homeless people per 10,000 population in 2011. *National Alliance to End Homelessness, The State of Homelessness in America 2012*

- The financial education website CreditDonkey compiled a list of the ten "best" cities of the future, based on percentage of housing built in 1990 or later, population change since 2010, and construction jobs as a percentage of population. Also considered were two more futuristic criteria: number of DeLorean cars available for purchase and number of spaceport companies and proposed spaceports. Phoenix was scored #8. *www.creditDonkey.com, "In the Future, Almost All of America's 'Best' Cities Will Be on the West Coast, Report Says," February 14, 2014*

Business Environment

CITY FINANCES

City Government Finances

Component	2012 ($000)	2012 ($ per capita)
Total Revenues	3,429,374	2,372
Total Expenditures	3,428,910	2,372
Debt Outstanding	8,278,032	5,726
Cash and Securities[1]	6,134,193	4,243

Note: (1) Cash and security holdings of a government at the close of its fiscal year, including those of its dependent agencies, utilities, and liquor stores.
Source: U.S Census Bureau, State & Local Government Finances 2012

City Government Revenue by Source

Source	2012 ($000)	2012 ($ per capita)
General Revenue		
From Federal Government	273,937	189
From State Government	537,940	372
From Local Governments	36,561	25
Taxes		
Property	226,323	157
Sales and Gross Receipts	710,455	491
Personal Income	0	0
Corporate Income	0	0
Motor Vehicle License	0	0
Other Taxes	50,307	35
Current Charges	875,572	606
Liquor Store	0	0
Utility	403,404	279
Employee Retirement	123,034	85

Source: U.S Census Bureau, State & Local Government Finances 2012

City Government Expenditures by Function

Function	2012 ($000)	2012 ($ per capita)	2012 (%)
General Direct Expenditures			
Air Transportation	457,296	316	13.3
Corrections	0	0	0.0
Education	23,813	16	0.7
Employment Security Administration	0	0	0.0
Financial Administration	20,077	14	0.6
Fire Protection	283,475	196	8.3
General Public Buildings	14,148	10	0.4
Governmental Administration, Other	18,923	13	0.6
Health	0	0	0.0
Highways	174,786	121	5.1
Hospitals	0	0	0.0
Housing and Community Development	193,952	134	5.7
Interest on General Debt	275,585	191	8.0
Judicial and Legal	47,376	33	1.4
Libraries	35,778	25	1.0
Parking	1,307	1	0.0
Parks and Recreation	194,968	135	5.7
Police Protection	471,353	326	13.7
Public Welfare	749	1	0.0
Sewerage	182,475	126	5.3
Solid Waste Management	111,781	77	3.3
Veterans' Services	0	0	0.0
Liquor Store	0	0	0.0
Utility	622,548	431	18.2
Employee Retirement	154,645	107	4.5

Source: U.S Census Bureau, State & Local Government Finances 2012

DEMOGRAPHICS

Population Growth

Area	1990 Census	2000 Census	2010 Census	Population Growth (%)	
				1990-2000	2000-2010
City	989,873	1,321,045	1,445,632	33.5	9.4
MSA[1]	2,238,480	3,251,876	4,192,887	45.3	28.9
U.S.	248,709,873	281,421,906	308,745,538	13.2	9.7

Note: (1) Figures cover the Phoenix-Mesa-Glendale, AZ Metropolitan Statistical Area—see Appendix B for areas included
Source: U.S. Census Bureau, Census 1990, 2000, 2010

Household Size

Area	Persons in Household (%)							Average Household Size
	One	Two	Three	Four	Five	Six	Seven or More	
City	28.8	30.2	15.0	13.0	6.8	3.4	2.7	2.83
MSA[1]	26.8	34.8	14.3	12.7	6.4	3.0	2.1	2.76
U.S.	27.7	33.6	15.7	13.1	6.0	2.3	1.5	2.64

Note: (1) Figures cover the Phoenix-Mesa-Scottsdale, AZ Metropolitan Statistical Area—see Appendix B for areas included
Source: U.S. Census Bureau, 2011-2013 American Community Survey 3-Year Estimates

Race

Area	White Alone[2] (%)	Black Alone[2] (%)	Asian Alone[2] (%)	AIAN[3] Alone[2] (%)	NHOPI[4] Alone[2] (%)	Other Race Alone[2] (%)	Two or More Races (%)
City	76.6	6.8	3.2	2.0	0.2	8.4	2.8
MSA[1]	80.5	5.1	3.4	2.2	0.2	5.6	2.9
U.S.	73.9	12.6	5.0	0.8	0.2	4.7	2.9

Note: (1) Figures cover the Phoenix-Mesa-Scottsdale, AZ Metropolitan Statistical Area—see Appendix B for areas included; (2) Alone is defined as not being in combination with one or more other races; (3) American Indian and Alaska Native; (4) Native Hawaiian and Other Pacific Islander
Source: U.S. Census Bureau, 2011-2013 American Community Survey 3-Year Estimates

Hispanic or Latino Origin

Area	Total (%)	Mexican (%)	Puerto Rican (%)	Cuban (%)	Other (%)
City	40.6	37.4	0.5	0.3	2.4
MSA[1]	29.8	26.8	0.6	0.2	2.2
U.S.	16.9	10.8	1.6	0.6	3.8

Note: Persons of Hispanic or Latino origin can be of any race; (1) Figures cover the Phoenix-Mesa-Scottsdale, AZ Metropolitan Statistical Area—see Appendix B for areas included
Source: U.S. Census Bureau, 2011-2013 American Community Survey 3-Year Estimates

Segregation

Type	Segregation Indices[1]				Percent Change		
	1990	2000	2010	2010 Rank[2]	1990-2000	1990-2010	2000-2010
Black/White	50.1	45.1	43.6	86	-5.0	-6.4	-1.5
Asian/White	28.1	30.1	32.7	85	2.0	4.6	2.6
Hispanic/White	48.6	52.2	49.3	28	3.5	0.7	-2.8

Note: All figures cover the Metropolitan Statistical Area—see Appendix B for areas included; Figures are based on an analysis of 1990, 2000, and 2010 Census Decennial Census tract data by William H. Frey, Brookings Institution and the University of Michigan Social Science Data Analysis Network. In this analysis all racial groups (whites, blacks, and asians) are non-Hispanic members of those races. Hispanics are shown as a separate category;
(1) Segregation Indices are Dissimilarity Indices that measure the degree to which the minority group is distributed differently than whites across census tracts. They range from 0 (complete integration) to 100 (complete segregation) where the value indicates the percentage of the minority group that needs to move to be distributed exactly like whites; (2) Ranges from 1 (most segregated) to 102 (least segregated); n/a not available.
Source: www.CensusScope.org

Ancestry

Area	German	Irish	English	American	Italian	Polish	French[2]	Scottish	Dutch
City	11.8	8.1	6.2	4.2	4.0	2.2	1.9	1.4	1.1
MSA[1]	14.4	9.4	8.3	6.4	4.6	2.6	2.3	1.7	1.4
U.S.	14.9	10.8	8.0	7.4	5.5	3.0	2.7	1.7	1.4

Note: Figures are the percentage of the total population reporting a particular ancestry. The nine most commonly reported ancestries in the U.S. are shown. Figures include multiple ancestries (e.g. if a person reported being Irish and Italian, they were included in both columns); (1) Figures cover the Phoenix-Mesa-Scottsdale, AZ Metropolitan Statistical Area—see Appendix B for areas included; (2) Excludes Basque
Source: U.S. Census Bureau, 2011-2013 American Community Survey 3-Year Estimates

Foreign-Born Population

Area	Percent of Population Born in								
	Any Foreign Country	Mexico	Asia	Europe	Carribean	South America	Central America[2]	Africa	Canada
City	20.1	13.1	3.0	1.5	0.3	0.4	0.8	0.7	0.4
MSA[1]	14.4	7.9	2.9	1.4	0.2	0.3	0.5	0.4	0.7
U.S.	13.0	3.7	3.8	1.5	1.2	0.9	1.0	0.6	0.3

Note: (1) Figures cover the Phoenix-Mesa-Scottsdale, AZ Metropolitan Statistical Area—see Appendix B for areas included; (2) Excludes Mexico.
Source: U.S. Census Bureau, 2011-2013 American Community Survey 3-Year Estimates

Marital Status

Area	Never Married	Now Married[2]	Separated	Widowed	Divorced
City	38.9	41.7	2.5	4.2	12.7
MSA[1]	33.3	47.5	1.9	5.0	12.3
U.S.	32.7	48.1	2.2	6.0	11.0

Note: Figures are percentages and cover the population 15 years of age and older; (1) Figures cover the Phoenix-Mesa-Scottsdale, AZ Metropolitan Statistical Area—see Appendix B for areas included; (2) Excludes separated
Source: U.S. Census Bureau, 2011-2013 American Community Survey 3-Year Estimates

Disability Status

Area	All Ages	Under 18 Years Old	18 to 64 Years Old	65 Years and Over
City	9.5	3.2	8.5	35.7
MSA[1]	10.3	3.2	8.5	32.6
U.S.	12.3	4.1	10.2	36.3

Note: Figures show percent of the civilian noninstitutionalized population that reported having a disability. Disability status is determined from from six types of difficulty: vision, hearing, cognitive, ambulatory, self-care, and independent living. For children under 5 years old, hearing and vision difficulty are used to determine disability status. For children between the ages of 5 and 14, disability status is determined from hearing, vision, cognitive, ambulatory, and self-care difficulties. For people aged 15 years and older, they are considered to have a disability if they have difficulty with any one of the six difficulty types; (1) Figures cover the Phoenix-Mesa-Scottsdale, AZ Metropolitan Statistical Area—see Appendix B for areas included.
Source: U.S. Census Bureau, 2011-2013 American Community Survey 3-Year Estimates

Age

Area	Percent of Population									Median Age
	Under Age 5	Age 5–19	Age 20–34	Age 35–44	Age 45–54	Age 55–64	Age 65–74	Age 75–84	Age 85+	
City	7.7	22.1	23.2	14.2	13.5	10.2	5.3	2.6	1.1	33.0
MSA[1]	7.0	21.3	21.1	13.5	13.0	11.0	7.6	4.0	1.6	35.5
U.S.	6.4	19.9	20.7	12.9	14.1	12.3	7.6	4.2	1.9	37.4

Note: (1) Figures cover the Phoenix-Mesa-Scottsdale, AZ Metropolitan Statistical Area—see Appendix B for areas included
Source: U.S. Census Bureau, 2011-2013 American Community Survey 3-Year Estimates

Gender

Area	Males	Females	Males per 100 Females
City	745,057	743,612	100.2
MSA[1]	2,151,086	2,175,269	98.9
U.S.	154,451,010	159,410,713	96.9

Note: (1) Figures cover the Phoenix-Mesa-Scottsdale, AZ Metropolitan Statistical Area—see Appendix B for areas included
Source: U.S. Census Bureau, 2011-2013 American Community Survey 3-Year Estimates

Religious Groups by Family

Area	Catholic	Baptist	Non-Den.	Methodist[2]	Lutheran	LDS[3]	Pente-costal	Presby-terian[4]	Muslim[5]	Judaism
MSA[1]	13.4	3.5	5.2	1.0	1.6	6.1	2.9	0.6	0.2	0.3
U.S.	19.1	9.3	4.0	4.0	2.3	2.0	1.9	1.6	0.8	0.7

Note: Figures are the number of adherents as a percentage of the total population; (1) Figures cover the Phoenix-Mesa-Glendale, AZ Metropolitan Statistical Area—see Appendix B for areas included; (2) Methodist/Pietist; (3) Latter Day Saints; (4) Reformed; (5) Figures are estimates
Source: Association of Statisticians of American Religious Bodies, 2010 U.S. Religion Census: Religious Congregations & Membership Study

Religious Groups by Tradition

Area	Catholic	Evangelical Protestant	Mainline Protestant	Other Tradition	Black Protestant	Orthodox
MSA[1]	13.4	13.2	2.6	7.8	0.2	0.3
U.S.	19.1	16.2	7.3	4.3	1.6	0.3

Note: Figures are the number of adherents as a percentage of the total population; (1) Figures cover the Phoenix-Mesa-Glendale, AZ Metropolitan Statistical Area—see Appendix B for areas included
Source: Association of Statisticians of American Religious Bodies, 2010 U.S. Religion Census: Religious Congregations & Membership Study

ECONOMY

Gross Metropolitan Product

Area	2012	2013	2014	2015	Rank[2]
MSA[1]	201.7	210.9	221.0	234.5	14

Note: Figures are in billions of dollars; (1) Figures cover the Phoenix-Mesa-Scottsdale, AZ Metropolitan Statistical Area—see Appendix B for areas included; (2) Rank is based on 2015 data and ranges from 1 to 363
Source: The U.S. Conference of Mayors, U.S. Metro Economies: GMP and Employment 2013-2015, June 2014

Economic Growth

Area	2010-12 (%)	2013 (%)	2014 (%)	2015 (%)	Rank[2]
MSA[1]	2.6	3.3	3.2	4.0	29
U.S.	2.1	2.0	2.3	3.2	–

Note: Figures are real gross metropolitan product (GMP) growth rates and represent annual average percent change; (1) Figures cover the Phoenix-Mesa-Scottsdale, AZ Metropolitan Statistical Area—see Appendix B for areas included; (2) Rank is based on 2015 data and ranges from 1 to 363
Source: The U.S. Conference of Mayors, U.S. Metro Economies: GMP and Employment 2013-2015, June 2014

Metropolitan Area Exports

Area	2008	2009	2010	2011	2012	2013	Rank[2]
MSA[1]	12,623.6	7,947.5	9,342.7	10,914.4	10,834.3	11,473.5	27

Note: Figures are in millions of dollars; (1) Figures cover the Phoenix-Mesa-Scottsdale, AZ Metropolitan Statistical Area—see Appendix B for areas included; (2) Rank is based on 2013 data and ranges from 1 to 387
Source: U.S. Department of Commerce, International Trade Administration, Office of Trade & Industry Information, Manufacturing & Services, data extracted April 3, 2015

Building Permits

Area	Single-Family			Multi-Family			Total		
	2013	2014	Pct. Chg.	2013	2014	Pct. Chg.	2013	2014	Pct. Chg.
City	1,673	1,608	-3.9	1,458	3,530	142.1	3,131	5,138	64.1
MSA[1]	12,959	11,557	-10.8	5,778	8,784	52.0	18,737	20,341	8.6
U.S.	620,802	634,597	2.2	370,020	411,766	11.3	990,822	1,046,363	5.6

Note: (1) Figures cover the Phoenix-Mesa-Scottsdale, AZ Metropolitan Statistical Area—see Appendix B for areas included; Figures represent new, privately-owned housing units authorized (unadjusted data); All permit data are based on estimates with imputation.
Source: U.S. Census Bureau, Manufacturing, Mining, and Construction Statistics, Building Permits, 2013, 2014

Bankruptcy Filings

Area	Business Filings			Nonbusiness Filings		
	2013	2014	% Chg.	2013	2014	% Chg.
Maricopa County	705	545	-22.7	15,679	13,283	-15.3
U.S.	33,212	26,983	-18.8	1,038,720	909,812	-12.4

Note: Business filings include Chapter 7, Chapter 11, Chapter 12, and Chapter 13; Nonbusiness filings include Chapter 7, Chapter 11, and Chapter 13
Source: Administrative Office of the U.S. Courts, Business and Nonbusiness Bankruptcy, County Cases Commenced by Chapter of the Bankruptcy Code, During the 12- Month Period Ending December 31, 2013 and Business and Nonbusiness Bankruptcy, County Cases Commenced by Chapter of the Bankruptcy Code, During the 12- Month Period Ending December 31, 2014

Housing Vacancy Rates

Area	Gross Vacancy Rate[2] (%)			Year-Round Vacancy Rate[3] (%)			Rental Vacancy Rate[4] (%)			Homeowner Vacancy Rate[5] (%)		
	2012	2013	2014	2012	2013	2014	2012	2013	2014	2012	2013	2014
MSA[1]	16.6	18.4	17.5	9.8	11.5	11.3	10.3	9.7	9.7	2.7	2.4	2.9
U.S.	13.8	13.6	13.4	10.8	10.7	10.4	8.7	8.3	7.6	2.0	2.0	1.9

Note: (1) Figures cover the Phoenix-Mesa-Scottsdale, AZ Metropolitan Statistical Area—see Appendix B for areas included; (2) The percentage of the total housing inventory that is vacant; (3) The percentage of the housing inventory (excluding seasonal units) that is year-round vacant; (4) The percentage of rental inventory that is vacant for rent; (5) The percentage of homeowner inventory that is vacant for sale
Source: U.S. Census Bureau, Housing Vacancies and Homeownership Annual Statistics: 2014

INCOME

Income

Area	Per Capita ($)	Median Household ($)	Average Household ($)
City	23,367	45,775	63,762
MSA[1]	26,247	51,923	70,448
U.S.	27,884	52,176	72,897

Note: (1) Figures cover the Phoenix-Mesa-Scottsdale, AZ Metropolitan Statistical Area—see Appendix B for areas included
Source: U.S. Census Bureau, 2011-2013 American Community Survey 3-Year Estimates

Household Income Distribution

Area	Percent of Households Earning							
	Under $15,000	$15,000 -24,999	$25,000 -34,999	$35,000 -49,999	$50,000 -74,999	$75,000 -99,000	$100,000 -149,999	$150,000 and up
City	15.0	12.1	11.4	15.1	17.5	10.9	10.9	7.2
MSA[1]	11.8	10.7	10.8	14.7	18.7	12.2	12.8	8.5
U.S.	13.0	10.9	10.3	13.6	17.9	11.9	12.7	9.6

Note: (1) Figures cover the Phoenix-Mesa-Scottsdale, AZ Metropolitan Statistical Area—see Appendix B for areas included
Source: U.S. Census Bureau, 2011-2013 American Community Survey 3-Year Estimates

Poverty Rate

Area	All Ages	Under 18 Years Old	18 to 64 Years Old	65 Years and Over
City	23.4	34.1	20.7	11.1
MSA[1]	17.4	25.2	16.1	8.0
U.S.	15.9	22.4	14.8	9.5

Note: Figures are percentage of people whose income during the past 12 months was below the poverty level; (1) Figures cover the Phoenix-Mesa-Scottsdale, AZ Metropolitan Statistical Area—see Appendix B for areas included
Source: U.S. Census Bureau, 2011-2013 American Community Survey 3-Year Estimates

EMPLOYMENT

Labor Force and Employment

Area	Civilian Labor Force			Workers Employed		
	Dec. 2013	Dec. 2014	% Chg.	Dec. 2013	Dec. 2014	% Chg.
City	729,162	750,178	2.9	683,046	707,507	3.6
MSA[1]	2,080,302	2,140,674	2.9	1,953,680	2,023,418	3.6
U.S.	154,408,000	155,521,000	0.7	144,423,000	147,190,000	1.9

Note: Data is not seasonally adjusted and covers workers 16 years of age and older; (1) Figures cover the Phoenix-Mesa-Scottsdale, AZ Metropolitan Statistical Area—see Appendix B for areas included
Source: Bureau of Labor Statistics, Local Area Unemployment Statistics

Unemployment Rate

Area	2014											
	Jan.	Feb.	Mar.	Apr.	May	Jun.	Jul.	Aug.	Sep.	Oct.	Nov.	Dec.
City	6.5	6.3	6.3	5.6	5.9	6.4	6.5	6.6	6.2	6.0	5.8	5.7
MSA[1]	6.3	6.2	6.2	5.5	5.8	6.2	6.3	6.4	6.0	5.8	5.6	5.5
U.S.	7.0	7.0	6.8	5.9	6.1	6.3	6.5	6.3	5.7	5.5	5.5	5.4

Note: Data is not seasonally adjusted and covers workers 16 years of age and older; (1) Figures cover the Phoenix-Mesa-Scottsdale, AZ Metropolitan Statistical Area—see Appendix B for areas included
Source: Bureau of Labor Statistics, Local Area Unemployment Statistics

Employment by Occupation

Occupation Classification	City (%)	MSA[1] (%)	U.S. (%)
Management, Business, Science, and Arts	33.2	35.9	36.2
Natural Resources, Construction, and Maintenance	9.5	8.6	9.0
Production, Transportation, and Material Moving	10.7	9.5	12.1
Sales and Office	26.3	27.1	24.4
Service	20.3	18.9	18.3

Note: Figures cover employed civilians 16 years of age and older; (1) Figures cover the Phoenix-Mesa-Scottsdale, AZ Metropolitan Statistical Area—see Appendix B for areas included
Source: U.S. Census Bureau, 2011-2013 American Community Survey 3-Year Estimates

Employment by Industry

Sector	MSA[1]		U.S.
	Number of Employees	Percent of Total	Percent of Total
Construction	96,700	5.1	4.4
Education and Health Services	278,300	14.6	15.5
Financial Activities	165,900	8.7	5.7
Government	242,400	12.7	15.8
Information	34,900	1.8	2.0
Leisure and Hospitality	202,700	10.6	10.3
Manufacturing	117,400	6.1	8.7
Mining and Logging	3,300	0.2	0.6
Other Services	66,300	3.5	4.0
Professional and Business Services	320,900	16.8	13.8
Retail Trade	235,800	12.3	11.4
Transportation, Warehousing, and Utilities	69,300	3.6	3.9
Wholesale Trade	78,600	4.1	4.2

Note: Figures are non-farm employment as of December 2014. Figures are not seasonally adjusted and include workers 16 years of age and older; (1) Figures cover the Phoenix-Mesa-Scottsdale, AZ Metropolitan Statistical Area—see Appendix B for areas included
Source: Bureau of Labor Statistics, Current Employment Statistics, Employment, Hours, and Earnings

Occupations with Greatest Projected Employment Growth: 2012 – 2022

Occupation[1]	2012 Employment	2022 Projected Employment	Numeric Employment Change	Percent Employment Change
Combined Food Preparation and Serving Workers, Including Fast Food	50,540	68,080	17,540	34.7
Customer Service Representatives	64,570	81,660	17,090	26.5
Retail Salespersons	88,270	102,400	14,130	16.0
Construction Laborers	28,290	42,000	13,710	48.5
Registered Nurses	48,660	61,130	12,470	25.6
Waiters and Waitresses	48,150	59,900	11,750	24.4
General and Operations Managers	46,340	57,660	11,320	24.4
Secretaries and Administrative Assistants, Except Legal, Medical, and Executive	45,880	56,340	10,460	22.8
Personal Care Aides	22,040	30,960	8,920	40.5
Office Clerks, General	49,260	58,180	8,920	18.1

Note: Projections cover Arizona; (1) Sorted by numeric employment change
Source: www.projectionscentral.com, State Occupational Projections, 2012–2022 Long-Term Projections

Fastest Growing Occupations: 2012 – 2022

Occupation[1]	2012 Employment	2022 Projected Employment	Numeric Employment Change	Percent Employment Change
Helpers—Brickmasons, Blockmasons, Stonemasons, and Tile and Marble Setters	370	610	240	65.9
Brickmasons and Blockmasons	840	1,370	530	63.5
Helpers—Electricians	790	1,280	490	61.6
Cement Masons and Concrete Finishers	4,000	6,210	2,210	55.2
Diagnostic Medical Sonographers	1,240	1,920	680	54.9
Tile and Marble Setters	1,370	2,130	760	54.9
Millwrights	400	610	210	54.7
Fence Erectors	370	570	200	54.5
Computer Numerically Controlled Machine Tool Programmers, Metal and Plastic	360	550	190	53.2
Solar Photovoltaic Installers	220	340	120	52.5

Note: Projections cover Arizona; (1) Sorted by percent employment change and excludes occupations with numeric employment change less than 100
Source: www.projectionscentral.com, State Occupational Projections, 2012–2022 Long-Term Projections

Average Wages

Occupation	$/Hr.	Occupation	$/Hr.
Accountants and Auditors	31.92	Maids and Housekeeping Cleaners	9.99
Automotive Mechanics	20.45	Maintenance and Repair Workers	17.50
Bookkeepers	17.99	Marketing Managers	57.16
Carpenters	19.02	Nuclear Medicine Technologists	37.02
Cashiers	10.25	Nurses, Licensed Practical	25.13
Clerks, General Office	15.98	Nurses, Registered	35.15
Clerks, Receptionists/Information	13.20	Nursing Assistants	13.85
Clerks, Shipping/Receiving	15.64	Packers and Packagers, Hand	11.08
Computer Programmers	39.60	Physical Therapists	40.31
Computer Systems Analysts	43.35	Postal Service Mail Carriers	25.45
Computer User Support Specialists	24.36	Real Estate Brokers	n/a
Cooks, Restaurant	11.20	Retail Salespersons	11.97
Dentists	64.84	Sales Reps., Exc. Tech./Scientific	28.59
Electrical Engineers	49.47	Sales Reps., Tech./Scientific	44.41
Electricians	21.77	Secretaries, Exc. Legal/Med./Exec.	16.47
Financial Managers	56.97	Security Guards	13.71
First-Line Supervisors/Managers, Sales	19.42	Surgeons	117.17
Food Preparation Workers	10.37	Teacher Assistants	11.80
General and Operations Managers	52.50	Teachers, Elementary School	21.00
Hairdressers/Cosmetologists	12.16	Teachers, Secondary School	23.60
Internists	84.25	Telemarketers	11.67
Janitors and Cleaners	10.94	Truck Drivers, Heavy/Tractor-Trailer	20.02
Landscaping/Groundskeeping Workers	11.61	Truck Drivers, Light/Delivery Svcs.	16.12
Lawyers	60.06	Waiters and Waitresses	10.41

Note: Wage data covers the Phoenix-Mesa-Glendale, AZ Metropolitan Statistical Area—see Appendix B for areas included; Hourly wages for elementary/secondary school teachers and teacher assistants were calculated by the editors from annual wage data assuming a 40 hour work week; n/a not available.
Source: Bureau of Labor Statistics, Metro Area Occupational Employment and Wage Estimates, May 2014

TAXES

State Corporate Income Tax Rates

State	Tax Rate (%)	Income Brackets ($)	Num. of Brackets	Financial Institution Tax Rate (%)[a]	Federal Income Tax Ded.
Arizona	6.0 (b)	Flat rate	1	6.0 (b)	No

Note: Tax rates as of January 1, 2015; (a) Rates listed are the corporate income tax rate applied to financial institutions or excise taxes based on income. Some states have other taxes based upon the value of deposits or shares; (b) Arizona minimum tax is $100. Tax rate is scheduled to decrease to 5.5% in tax years 2016.
Source: Federation of Tax Administrators, "State Corporate Income Tax Rates, 2015"

State Individual Income Tax Rates

State	Tax Rate (%)	Income Brackets ($)	Num. of Brackets	Personal Exempt. ($)[1]		Fed. Inc. Tax Ded.
				Single	Dependents	
Arizona	2.59 - 4.54	10,000 - 150,001 (b)	5	2,100	2,100	No

Note: Tax rates as of January 1, 2015; Local- and county-level taxes are not included; n/a not applicable; (1) Married joint filers generally receive double the single exemption; (b) For joint returns, taxes are twice the tax on half the couple's income.
Source: Federation of Tax Administrators, "State Individual Income Tax Rates, 2015"

Various State and Local Tax Rates

State	State and Local Sales and Use (%)	State Sales and Use (%)	Gasoline[1] (¢/gal.)	Cigarette[2] ($/pack)	Spirits[3] ($/gal.)	Wine[4] ($/gal.)	Beer[5] ($/gal.)
Arizona	8.3	5.60	19	2.00	3.00	0.84	0.16

Note: All tax rates as of January 1, 2015; (1) The American Petroleum Institute has developed a methodology for determining the average tax rate on a gallon of fuel. Rates may include any of the following: excise taxes, environmental fees, storage tank fees, other fees or taxes, general sales tax, and local taxes. In states where gasoline is subject to the general sales tax, or where the fuel tax is based on the average sale price, the average rate determined by API is sensitive to changes in the price of gasoline. States that fully or partially apply general sales taxes to gasoline: CA, CO, GA, IL, IN, MI, NY; (2) The federal excise tax of $1.0066 per pack and local taxes are not included; (3) Rates are those applicable to off-premise sales of 40% alcohol by volume (a.b.v.) distilled spirits in 750ml containers. Local excise taxes are excluded; (4) Rates are those applicable to off-premise sales of 11% a.b.v. non-carbonated wine in 750ml containers; (5) Rates are those applicable to off-premise sales of 4.7% a.b.v. beer in 12 ounce containers.
Source: Tax Foundation, 2015 Facts & Figures: How Does Your State Compare?

State Business Tax Climate Index Rankings

State	Overall Rank	Corporate Tax Index Rank	Individual Income Tax Index Rank	Sales Tax Index Rank	Unemployment Insurance Tax Index Rank	Property Tax Index Rank
Arizona	23	24	19	49	4	6

Note: The index is a measure of how each state's tax laws affect economic performance. The lower the rank, the more favorable a state's tax system is for business. States without a given tax are given a ranking of 1. The scores/rankings for the District of Columbia do not affect other states. The 2015 index represents the tax climate as of July 1, 2014.
Source: Tax Foundation, State Business Tax Climate Index 2015

COMMERCIAL REAL ESTATE

Office Market

Market Area	Inventory (sq. ft.)	Vacancy Rate (%)	Under Construction (sq. ft.)	YTD Net Absorption (sq. ft.)	Total Average Asking Rent ($/sq. ft./year)
Phoenix	73,158,945	22.0	1,651,845	1,866,667	21.26
National	4,745,108,508	14.3	71,190,461	51,084,126	27.40

Source: Newmark Grubb Knight Frank, National Office Market Report, 4th Quarter 2014

Industrial/Warehouse/R&D Market

Market Area	Inventory (sq. ft.)	Vacancy Rate (%)	Under Construction (sq. ft.)	YTD Net Absorption (sq. ft.)	Total Average Asking Rent ($/sq. ft./year)
Phoenix	282,103,805	11.4	2,054,269	5,142,897	6.36
National	14,238,613,765	7.2	134,387,407	185,246,438	5.64

Source: Newmark Grubb Knight Frank, National Industrial Market Report, 4th Quarter 2014

COMMERCIAL UTILITIES

Typical Monthly Electric Bills

Area	Commercial Service ($/month)		Industrial Service ($/month)	
	1,500 kWh	40 kW demand 14,000 kWh	1,000 kW demand 200,000 kWh	50,000 kW demand 32,500,000 kWh
City	256	1,765	26,672	1,939,150
Average[1]	201	1,653	26,124	2,639,743

Note: Figures are based on annualized 2014 rates; (1) Average based on 180 utilities surveyed
Source: Edison Electric Institute, Typical Bills and Average Rates Report, Summer 2014

TRANSPORTATION

Means of Transportation to Work

Area	Car/Truck/Van		Public Transportation			Bicycle	Walked	Other Means	Worked at Home
	Drove Alone	Car-pooled	Bus	Subway	Railroad				
City	75.0	12.0	3.5	0.1	0.1	0.7	1.9	2.1	4.7
MSA[1]	76.5	11.3	2.1	0.0	0.0	0.9	1.5	1.9	5.8
U.S.	76.4	9.6	2.6	1.8	0.6	0.6	2.8	1.3	4.3

Note: Figures are percentages and cover workers 16 years of age and older; (1) Figures cover the Phoenix-Mesa-Scottsdale, AZ Metropolitan Statistical Area—see Appendix B for areas included
Source: U.S. Census Bureau, 2011-2013 American Community Survey 3-Year Estimates

Travel Time to Work

Area	Less Than 10 Minutes	10 to 19 Minutes	20 to 29 Minutes	30 to 44 Minutes	45 to 59 Minutes	60 to 89 Minutes	90 Minutes or More
City	9.1	29.2	25.0	25.4	6.6	3.4	1.4
MSA[1]	9.9	27.2	23.4	24.8	8.6	4.6	1.5
U.S.	13.3	29.7	20.9	20.2	7.7	5.7	2.6

Note: Figures are percentages and include workers 16 years old and over; (1) Figures cover the Phoenix-Mesa-Scottsdale, AZ Metropolitan Statistical Area—see Appendix B for areas included
Source: U.S. Census Bureau, 2011-2013 American Community Survey 3-Year Estimates

Travel Time Index

Area	1985	1990	1995	2000	2005	2010	2011
Urban Area[1]	1.08	1.09	1.09	1.15	1.18	1.18	1.18
Average[2]	1.09	1.14	1.16	1.19	1.23	1.18	1.18

Note: Travel Time Index—the ratio of travel time in the peak period to the travel time at free-flow conditions. For example, a value of 1.30 indicates a 20-minute free-flow trip takes 26 minutes in the peak. Free-flow speeds (60 mph on freeways and 35 mph on principal arterials) are used as the comparison threshold; (1) Covers the Phoenix-Mesa AZ urban area; (2) average of 498 urban areas
Source: Texas Transportation Institute, Urban Mobility Report 2012, December 2012

Public Transportation

Agency Name / Mode of Transportation	Vehicles Operated in Maximum Service	Annual Unlinked Passenger Trips (in thous.)	Annual Passenger Miles (in thous.)
City of Phoenix Public Transit Dept. (Valley Metro)			
Bus (purchased transportation)	392	40,845.9	152,071.3
Demand Response (directly operated)	22	118.4	883.3
Demand Response (purchased transportation)	105	336.3	3,396.8
Phoenix - VPSI Inc.			
Vanpool (directly operated)	394	1,197.0	30,764.6

Source: Federal Transit Administration, National Transit Database, 2013

Air Transportation

Airport Name and Code / Type of Service	Passenger Airlines[1]	Passenger Enplanements	Freight Carriers[2]	Freight (lbs.)
Phoenix Sky Harbor International (PHX)				
Domestic service (U.S. carriers - 2014)	22	19,198,298	20	272,382,639
International service (U.S. carriers - 2013)	7	728,104	5	912,469

Note: (1) Includes all U.S.-based major, minor and commuter airlines that carried at least one passenger during the year; (2) Includes all U.S.-based airlines and freight carriers that transported at least one lb. of freight during the year.
Source: Bureau of Transportation Statistics, The Intermodal Transportation Database, Air Carriers: T-100 Domestic Market (U.S. Carriers), 2014; Bureau of Transportation Statistics, The Intermodal Transportation Database, Air Carriers: T-100 International Market (U.S. Carriers), 2013

Other Transportation Statistics

Major Highways:	I-10; I-17
Amtrak Service:	Bus connection
Major Waterways/Ports:	None

Source: Amtrak.com; Google Maps

BUSINESSES

Major Business Headquarters

Company Name	Rankings	
	Fortune[1]	Forbes[2]
Avnet	117	-
Freeport-McMoRan Copper & Gold	142	-
PetSmart	376	-
Republic Services	325	-
Shamrock Foods	-	185

Note: (1) Fortune 500—companies that produce a 10-K are ranked 1 to 500 based on 2013 revenue; (2) all private companies with at least $2 billion in annual revenue through the end of their most current fiscal year are ranked 1 to 221; companies listed are headquartered in the city; dashes indicate no ranking
Source: Fortune, "Fortune 500," June 16, 2014; Forbes, "America's Largest Private Companies," November 5, 2014

Fast-Growing Businesses

According to *Inc.*, Phoenix is home to one of America's 500 fastest-growing private companies: **WebPT** (#362). Criteria: must be an independent, privately-held, for-profit, U.S. corporation, proprietorship or partnership; revenues must be at least $100,000 in 2010 and $2 million in 2013; must have four-year operating/sales history. Holding companies, regulated banks, and utilities were excluded. *Inc., "America's 500 Fastest-Growing Private Companies," September 2014*

According to *Fortune*, Phoenix is home to one of the 100 fastest-growing companies in the world: **Cavco Industries** (#52). Companies were ranked by their revenue growth rate; their EPS growth rate; and their three-year annualized total return to investors for the period ending June 30, 2014. Criteria for inclusion: a company, foreign or domestic, must trade on a major U.S. stock exchange; must file quarterly reports with the SEC; must have a minimum market capitalization of $250 million; must have a stock price of at least $5 on June 30, 2014; must have been trading continuously since June 30, 2010; must have revenue and net income for the four quarters ended on or before April 30, 2014, of at least $50 million and $10 million, respectively; and must have posted a compound annual growth in revenue and earnings per share of at least 20% annually over the three years ending on or before April 30, 2014. Real estate investment trusts, limited-liability companies, limited parterships, business development companies, closed end investment firms, and companies that lost money in the quarter ending April 30, 2014 were excluded. *Fortune, "100 Fastest-Growing Companies," August 28, 2014*

According to Deloitte, Phoenix is home to one of North America's 500 fastest-growing high-technology companies: **Inilex** (#247). Companies are ranked by percentage growth in revenue over a five-year period. Criteria for inclusion: company must be headquartered within North America; must own proprietary intellectual property or proprietary technology that contributes to a significant portion of the company's operating revenue, or devote a significant proportion of revenues to research and development of technology; must have been in business for a minumum of five years with 2009 operating revenues of at least $50,000 USD/CD and 2013 operating revenues of at least $5 million USD/CD. *Deloitte Touche Tohmatsu, 2014 Technology Fast 500*[TM]

Minority Business Opportunity

Phoenix is home to five companies which are on the *Hispanic Business* 500 list (500 largest U.S. Hispanic-owned companies based on 2012 revenue): **Apodaca Wall Systems** (#300); **Hernandez Companies** (#408); **State Technology & Manufacturing** (#425); **Mi Ranchito Mexican Food Products** (#428); **Torres Marquez Communications** (#471). Companies included must show at least 51 percent ownership by Hispanic U.S. citizens, and must maintain headquarters in one of the 50 states or Washington, D.C. *Hispanic Business, "Hispanic Business 500," June 20, 2013*

Minority- and Women-Owned Businesses

Group	All Firms		Firms with Paid Employees			
	Firms	Sales ($000)	Firms	Sales ($000)	Employees	Payroll ($000)
Asian	4,173	1,441,105	1,240	1,301,808	8,257	229,530
Black	3,409	250,109	239	169,296	2,483	58,288
Hispanic	12,658	2,245,759	1,618	1,847,147	15,846	494,736
Women	30,006	6,885,198	4,152	6,036,357	44,707	1,451,500
All Firms	112,192	175,477,167	28,685	170,955,625	773,842	32,674,607

Note: Figures cover firms located in the city; minority- and women-owned business are defined as firms in which the corresponding group own 51% or more of the stock or equity of the company
Source: U.S. Census Bureau, 2007 Economic Census, Survey of Business Owners (2012 Survey of Business Owners data will be released starting in June 2015)

HOTELS & CONVENTION CENTERS

Hotels/Motels

Area	5 Star		4 Star		3 Star		2 Star		1 Star		Not Rated	
	Num.	Pct.[3]	Num.	Pct.[3]	Num.	Pct.[3]	Num.	Pct.[3]	Num.	Pct.[3]	Num.	Pct.[3]
City[1]	8	1.9	41	9.5	165	38.3	186	43.2	9	2.1	22	5.1
Total[2]	166	0.9	1,264	7.0	5,718	31.8	9,340	52.0	411	2.3	1,070	6.0

Note: (1) Figures cover Phoenix and vicinity; (2) Figures cover all 100 cities in this book; (3) Percentage of hotels which have a given star rating; Star ratings are determined by expedia.com and offer an indication of the general quality of a particular hotel.
Source: expedia.com, April 2, 2015

The Phoenix-Mesa-Scottsdale, AZ metro area is home to five of the best hotels in the U.S. according to *Travel & Leisure*: **The Boulders, A Waldorf Astoria Resort; Sanctuary on Camelback Mountain Resort & Spa; Hyatt Regency Scottsdale Resort and Spa at Gainey Ranch; Royal Palms Resort & Spa; The Phoenician, a Luxury Collection Resort**. Criteria: service; location; rooms; food; and value. The list includes the top 236 hotels in the U.S. *Travel & Leisure, "T+L 500, The World's Best Hotels 2015"*

Major Convention Centers

Name	Overall Space (sq. ft.)	Exhibit Space (sq. ft.)	Meeting Space (sq. ft.)	Meeting Rooms
Phoenix Convention Center	2,000,000	900,000	n/a	n/a

Note: Table includes convention centers located in the Phoenix-Mesa-Scottsdale, AZ metro area; n/a not available
Source: Original research

Living Environment

COST OF LIVING

Cost of Living Index

Composite Index	Groceries	Housing	Utilities	Trans-portation	Health Care	Misc. Goods/ Services
95.9	100.3	92.4	96.6	102.9	101.5	93.4

Note: The Cost of Living Index measures regional differences in the cost of consumer goods and services, excluding taxes and non-consumer expenditures, for professional and managerial households in the top income quintile. It is based on more than 50,000 prices covering almost 60 different items for which prices are collected three times a year by chambers of commerce, economic development organizations or university applied economic centers in each participating urban area. The numbers shown should be read as a percentage above or below the national average of 100. For example, a value of 115.4 in the groceries column indicates that grocery prices are 15.4% higher than the national average. Small differences in the index numbers should not be interpreted as significant; Figures cover the Phoenix AZ urban area.
Source: The Council for Community and Economic Research, ACCRA Cost of Living Index, 2014

Grocery Prices

Area[1]	T-Bone Steak ($/pound)	Frying Chicken ($/pound)	Whole Milk ($/half gal.)	Eggs ($/dozen)	Orange Juice ($/64 oz.)	Coffee ($/11.5 oz.)
City[2]	10.45	1.99	1.83	2.06	3.61	4.76
Avg.	10.40	1.37	2.40	1.99	3.46	4.27
Min.	8.48	0.93	1.37	1.30	2.83	2.99
Max.	14.20	2.44	3.62	4.02	6.42	6.96

*Note: (1) Values for the local area are compared with the average, minimum and maximum values for all 308 areas in the Cost of Living Index; (2) Figures cover the Phoenix AZ urban area; **T-Bone Steak** (price per pound); **Frying Chicken** (price per pound, whole fryer); **Whole Milk** (half gallon carton); **Eggs** (price per dozen, Grade A, large); **Orange Juice** (64 oz. Tropicana or Florida Natural); **Coffee** (11.5 oz. can, vacuum-packed, Maxwell House, Hills Bros, or Folgers).*
Source: The Council for Community and Economic Research, ACCRA Cost of Living Index, 2014

Housing and Utility Costs

Area[1]	New Home Price ($)	Apartment Rent ($/month)	All Electric ($/month)	Part Electric ($/month)	Other Energy ($/month)	Telephone ($/month)
City[2]	283,722	827	188.00	-	-	21.32
Avg.	305,838	919	181.00	93.66	73.14	27.95
Min.	183,142	480	112.00	42.06	23.42	17.16
Max.	1,358,576	3,851	594.00	180.03	440.99	40.42

*Note: (1) Values for the local area are compared with the average, minimum and maximum values for all 308 areas in the Cost of Living Index; (2) Figures cover the Phoenix AZ urban area; **New Home Price** (2,400 sf living area, 8,000 sf lot, in urban area with full utilities); **Apartment Rent** (950 sf 2 bedroom/1.5 or 2 bath, unfurnished, excluding all utilities except water); **All Electric** (average monthly cost for an all-electric home); **Part Electric** (average monthly cost for a part-electric home); **Other Energy** (average monthly cost for natural gas, fuel oil, coal, wood, and any other forms of energy except electricity); **Telephone** (price includes basic monthly rate for a private residential line plus additional local usage charges incurred by a family of four).*
Source: The Council for Community and Economic Research, ACCRA Cost of Living Index, 2014

Health Care, Transportation, and Other Costs

Area[1]	Doctor ($/visit)	Dentist ($/visit)	Optometrist ($/visit)	Gasoline ($/gallon)	Beauty Salon ($/visit)	Men's Shirt ($)
City[2]	105.67	98.33	76.00	3.42	25.00	21.66
Avg.	102.86	87.89	97.66	3.44	34.37	26.74
Min.	67.47	65.78	51.18	3.00	17.43	12.79
Max.	173.50	150.14	235.00	4.33	64.28	49.50

*Note: (1) Values for the local area are compared with the average, minimum and maximum values for all 308 areas in the Cost of Living Index; (2) Figures cover the Phoenix AZ urban area; **Doctor** (general practitioners routine exam of an established patient); **Dentist** (adult teeth cleaning and periodic oral examination); **Optometrist** (full vision eye exam for established adult patient); **Gasoline** (one gallon regular unleaded, national brand, including all taxes, cash price at self-service pump if available); **Beauty Salon** (woman's shampoo, trim, and blow-dry); **Men's Shirt** (cotton/polyester dress shirt, pinpoint weave, long sleeves).*
Source: The Council for Community and Economic Research, ACCRA Cost of Living Index, 2014

HOUSING

House Price Index (HPI)

Area	National Ranking[2]	Quarterly Change (%)	One-Year Change (%)	Five-Year Change (%)
MSA[1]	68	1.15	7.05	21.42
U.S.[3]	–	1.35	4.91	11.59

Note: The HPI is a weighted repeat sales index. It measures average price changes in repeat sales or refinancings on the same properties. This information is obtained by reviewing repeat mortgage transactions on single-family properties whose mortgages have been purchased or securitized by Fannie Mae or Freddie Mac in January 1975; (1) Phoenix-Mesa-Scottsdale Metropolitan Statistical Area—see Appendix B for areas included; (2) Rankings are based on annual percentage change for all metro areas containing at least 15,000 transactions over the last 10 years and ranges from 1 to 275; (3) figures based on a weighted average of Census Division estimates using a seasonally adjusted, purchase-only index; all figures are for the period ending December 31, 2014

Source: Federal Housing Finance Agency, House Price Index, February 26, 2015

Median Single-Family Home Prices

Area	2012	2013	2014p	Percent Change 2013 to 2014
MSA[1]	147.6	183.6	198.5	8.1
U.S. Average	177.2	197.4	209.0	5.9

Note: Figures are median sales prices of existing single-family homes in thousands of dollars; (p) preliminary; n/a not available; (1) Phoenix-Mesa-Scottsdale, AZ Metropolitan Statistical Area—see Appendix B for areas included

Source: National Association of Realtors, Median Sales Price of Existing Single-Family Homes for Metropolitan Areas, 4th Quarter 2014

Qualifying Income Based on Median Sales Price of Existing Single-Family Homes

Area	With 5% Down ($)	With 10% Down ($)	With 20% Down ($)
MSA[1]	44,017	41,700	37,067
U.S. Average	45,863	43,449	38,621

Note: Figures are preliminary; Qualifying income is based on a mortgage rate of 4.0%. Monthly principal and interest payment is limited to 25% of income; n/a not available; (1) Phoenix-Mesa-Scottsdale, AZ Metropolitan Statistical Area—see Appendix B for areas included

Source: National Association of Realtors, Qualifying Income Based on Median Sales Price of Existing Single-Family Homes for Metropolitan Areas, 4th Quarter 2014

Median Apartment Condo-Coop Home Prices

Area	2012	2013	2014p	Percent Change 2013 to 2014
MSA[1]	83.4	105.0	109.1	3.9
U.S. Average	173.7	194.9	205.1	5.2

Note: Figures are median sales prices of existing apartment condo-coop homes in thousands of dollars; (p) preliminary; n/a not available; (1) Phoenix-Mesa-Scottsdale, AZ Metropolitan Statistical Area—see Appendix B for areas included

Source: National Association of Realtors, Median Sales Price of Existing Apartment Condo-Coop Homes for Metropolitan Areas, 4th Quarter 2014

Gross Monthly Rent

Area	Under $200	$200 -299	$300 -499	$500 -749	$750 -999	$1,000 -1,499	$1,500 and up	Median ($)
City	0.8	1.2	6.5	28.0	28.0	27.2	8.2	861
MSA[1]	0.8	1.1	4.6	22.2	27.8	31.9	11.6	937
U.S.	1.7	3.2	7.8	22.1	24.3	26.0	14.9	900

Note: Figures are percentages except for Median; Gross rent is the contract rent plus the estimated average monthly cost of utilities (electricity, gas, and water and sewer) and fuels (oil, coal, kerosene, wood, etc.) if these are paid by the renter (or paid for the renter by someone else); (1) Figures cover the Phoenix-Mesa-Scottsdale, AZ Metropolitan Statistical Area—see Appendix B for areas included

Source: U.S. Census Bureau, 2011-2013 American Community Survey 3-Year Estimates

Homeownership Rate

Area	2007 (%)	2008 (%)	2009 (%)	2010 (%)	2011 (%)	2012 (%)	2013 (%)	2014 (%)
MSA[1]	70.8	70.2	69.8	66.5	63.3	63.1	62.2	61.9
U.S.	68.1	67.8	67.4	66.9	66.1	65.4	65.1	64.5

Note: (1) Figures cover the Phoenix-Mesa-Scottsdale, AZ Metropolitan Statistical Area—see Appendix B for areas included
Source: U.S. Census Bureau, Housing Vacancies and Homeownership Annual Statistics: 2014

Year Housing Structure Built

Area	2010 or Later	2000 -2009	1990 -1999	1980 -1989	1970 -1979	1960 -1969	1950 -1959	1940 -1949	Before 1940	Median Year
City	0.7	18.0	16.2	18.8	20.7	9.6	10.6	3.3	2.1	1982
MSA[1]	0.9	28.1	20.8	18.2	17.2	6.8	5.4	1.5	1.0	1990
U.S.	0.9	15.0	13.9	13.8	15.8	11.0	10.9	5.4	13.3	1976

Note: Figures are percentages except for Median Year; (1) Figures cover the Phoenix-Mesa-Scottsdale, AZ Metropolitan Statistical Area—see Appendix B for areas included
Source: U.S. Census Bureau, 2011-2013 American Community Survey 3-Year Estimates

HEALTH

Health Risk Data

Category	MSA[1] (%)	U.S. (%)
Adults aged 18–64 who have any kind of health care coverage	75.3	79.6
Adults who reported being in good or excellent health	83.2	83.1
Adults who are current smokers	16.9	19.6
Adults who are heavy drinkers[2]	5.0	6.1
Adults who are binge drinkers[3]	15.5	16.9
Adults who are overweight (BMI 25.0 - 29.9)	35.8	35.8
Adults who are obese (BMI 30.0 - 99.8)	25.3	27.6
Adults who participated in any physical activities in the past month	77.3	77.1
Adults 50+ who have ever had a sigmoidoscopy or colonoscopy	63.0	67.3
Women aged 40+ who have had a mammogram within the past two years	68.5	74.0
Men aged 40+ who have had a PSA test within the past two years	44.4	45.2
Adults aged 65+ who have had flu shot within the past year	54.1	60.1
Adults who always wear a seatbelt	94.3	93.8

Note: Data as of 2012 unless otherwise noted; (1) Figures cover the Phoenix-Mesa-Scottsdale, AZ Metropolitan Statistical Area—see Appendix B for areas included; (2) Heavy drinkers are classified as males having more than two drinks per day or females having more than one drink per day; (3) Binge drinkers are classified as males having five or more drinks on one occasion or females having four or more drinks on one occasion
Source: Centers for Disease Control and Prevention, Behaviorial Risk Factor Surveillance System, SMART: Selected Metropolitan/Micropolitan Area Risk Trends, 2012 (Note: the CDC has discontinued this dataset but will be releasing a replacement in late 2015)

Chronic Health Indicators

Category	MSA[1] (%)	U.S. (%)
Adults who have ever been told they had a heart attack	4.7	4.5
Adults who have ever been told they had a stroke	2.6	2.9
Adults who have been told they currently have asthma	8.6	8.9
Adults who have ever been told they have arthritis	23.8	25.7
Adults who have ever been told they have diabetes[2]	9.8	9.7
Adults who have ever been told they had skin cancer	6.5	5.7
Adults who have ever been told they had any other types of cancer	6.2	6.5
Adults who have ever been told they have COPD	5.5	6.2
Adults who have ever been told they have kidney disease	3.5	2.5
Adults who have ever been told they have a form of depression	18.2	18.0

Note: Data as of 2012 unless otherwise noted; (1) Figures cover the Phoenix-Mesa-Scottsdale, AZ Metropolitan Statistical Area—see Appendix B for areas included; (2) Figures do not include pregnancy-related, borderline, or pre-diabetes
Source: Centers for Disease Control and Prevention, Behaviorial Risk Factor Surveillance System, SMART: Selected Metropolitan/Micropolitan Area Risk Trends, 2012 (Note: the CDC has discontinued this dataset but will be releasing a replacement in late 2015)

Mortality Rates for the Top 10 Causes of Death in the U.S.

ICD-10[a] Sub-Chapter	ICD-10[a] Code	Age-Adjusted Mortality Rate[1] per 100,000 population	
		County[2]	U.S.
Malignant neoplasms	C00-C97	145.9	166.2
Ischaemic heart diseases	I20-I25	100.8	105.7
Other forms of heart disease	I30-I51	20.9	49.3
Chronic lower respiratory diseases	J40-J47	43.2	42.1
Organic, including symptomatic, mental disorders	F01-F09	22.6	38.1
Cerebrovascular diseases	I60-I69	28.4	37.0
Other external causes of accidental injury	W00-X59	31.2	26.9
Other degenerative diseases of the nervous system	G30-G31	41.8	25.6
Diabetes mellitus	E10-E14	23.8	21.3
Hypertensive diseases	I10-I15	24.5	19.4

Note: (a) ICD-10 = International Classification of Diseases 10th Revision; (1) Mortality rates are a three year average covering 2011-2013; (2) Figures cover Maricopa County
Source: Centers for Disease Control and Prevention, National Center for Health Statistics. Compressed Mortality File 1999-2013 on CDC WONDER Online Database, released October 2014. Data are compiled from the Compressed Mortality File 1999-2013, Series 20 No. 2S, 2014.

Mortality Rates for Selected Causes of Death

ICD-10[a] Sub-Chapter	ICD-10[a] Code	Age-Adjusted Mortality Rate[1] per 100,000 population	
		County[2]	U.S.
Assault	X85-Y09	5.4	5.2
Diseases of the liver	K70-K76	13.3	13.2
Human immunodeficiency virus (HIV) disease	B20-B24	1.7	2.2
Influenza and pneumonia	J09-J18	7.0	15.4
Intentional self-harm	X60-X84	15.6	12.5
Malnutrition	E40-E46	0.5	0.9
Obesity and other hyperalimentation	E65-E68	2.4	1.8
Renal failure	N17-N19	2.4	13.1
Transport accidents	V01-V99	10.5	11.7
Viral hepatitis	B15-B19	3.7	2.2

Note: (a) ICD-10 = International Classification of Diseases 10th Revision; (1) Mortality rates are a three year average covering 2011-2013; (2) Figures cover Maricopa County
Source: Centers for Disease Control and Prevention, National Center for Health Statistics. Compressed Mortality File 1999-2013 on CDC WONDER Online Database, released October 2014. Data are compiled from the Compressed Mortality File 1999-2013, Series 20 No. 2S, 2014.

Health Insurance Coverage

Area	With Health Insurance	With Private Health Insurance	With Public Health Insurance	Without Health Insurance	Population Under Age 18 Without Health Insurance
City	77.1	51.5	32.0	22.9	14.7
MSA[1]	82.6	61.5	31.0	17.4	12.0
U.S.	85.2	65.2	31.0	14.8	7.3

Note: Figures are percentages that cover the civilian noninstitutionalized population; (1) Figures cover the Phoenix-Mesa-Scottsdale, AZ Metropolitan Statistical Area—see Appendix B for areas included
Source: U.S. Census Bureau, 2011-2013 American Community Survey 3-Year Estimates

Number of Medical Professionals

Area[1]	MDs[2]	DOs[2,3]	Dentists	Podiatrists	Chiropractors	Optometrists
Local (number)	9,284	1,266	2,522	232	1,327	547
Local (rate[4])	235.5	32.1	62.8	5.8	33.1	13.6
U.S. (rate[4])	270.0	20.2	63.1	5.7	25.2	14.9

Note: Data as of 2013 unless noted; (1) Local data covers Maricopa County; (2) Data as of 2012 and includes all active, non-federal physicians; (3) Doctor of Osteopathic Medicine; (4) rate per 100,000 population
Source: U.S. Department of Health and Human Services, Health Resources and Services Administration, Bureau of Health Professions, Area Resource File (ARF) 2013-2014

Best Hospitals

According to *U.S. News,* the Phoenix-Mesa-Scottsdale, AZ metro area is home to four of the best hospitals in the U.S.: **Banner Estrella Medical Center** (1 specialty); **Banner Good Samaritan Medical Center** (1 specialty); **Mayo Clinic** (10 specialties); **St. Joseph's Hospital and Medical Center** (1 specialty). The hospitals listed were nationally ranked in at least one adult specialty. Only 144 hospitals nationwide were nationally ranked in one or more specialties. Seventeen hospitals in the U.S. made the Honor Roll with high scores in at least six specialties. *U.S. News Online, "America's Best Children's Hospitals 2014-15"*

According to *U.S. News,* the Phoenix-Mesa-Scottsdale, AZ metro area is home to one of the best children's hospitals in the U.S.: **Phoenix Children's Hospital** (4 specialties). The hospital listed was highly ranked in at least one pediatric specialty. Eighty-nine children's hospitals in the U.S. were nationally ranked in at least one specialty. Ten children's hospitals in the U.S. made the Honor Roll with high scores in at least three specialties. *U.S. News Online, "America's Best Children's Hospitals 2014-15"*

EDUCATION

Public School District Statistics

District Name	Schls	Pupils	Pupil/ Teacher Ratio	Minority Pupils[1] (%)	Free Lunch Eligible[2] (%)	IEP[3] (%)
Alhambra Elementary District	15	14,313	23.4	93.0	82.0	10.0
Balsz Elementary District	5	2,681	17.4	92.2	88.1	10.4
Cartwright Elementary District	20	18,928	19.7	95.8	99.7	10.4
Creighton Elementary District	10	6,715	19.4	93.3	63.9	10.9
Deer Valley Unified District	38	34,028	19.1	28.2	15.9	9.3
Fowler Elementary District	7	4,575	19.8	84.9	n/a	11.6
Isaac Elementary District	11	7,101	20.4	98.4	14.9	11.6
Madison Elementary District	8	5,910	20.2	51.4	22.3	9.3
Osborn Elementary District	5	3,046	19.2	87.9	4.2	17.9
Paradise Valley Unified District	49	32,919	18.8	38.6	n/a	12.7
Pendergast Elementary District	14	9,715	22.3	83.8	58.3	11.0
Phoenix Elementary District	14	7,189	17.7	95.1	72.7	11.3
Phoenix Union High School District	15	25,854	18.0	94.4	50.4	12.0
Portable Practical Educational Prep	2	5,206	n/a	35.6	43.9	12.7
Roosevelt Elementary District	20	9,960	22.7	96.9	12.2	12.0
Scottsdale Unified District	32	25,246	18.2	31.2	20.6	10.8

Note: Table includes school districts with 2,000 or more students; (1) Percentage of students that are not non-Hispanic white; (2) Percentage of students that are eligible for the free lunch program; (3) Percentage of students that have an Individualized Education Program.
Source: U.S. Department of Education, National Center for Education Statistics, Common Core of Data, Local Education Agency (School District) Universe Survey: School Year 2012-2013; U.S. Department of Education, National Center for Education Statistics, Common Core of Data, Public Elementary/Secondary School Universe Survey: School Year 2012-2013

Best High Schools

According to *The Daily Beast,* Phoenix is home to two of the best high schools in the U.S.: **Horizon Honors High School** (#107); **Shadow Mountain High School** (#573); *The Daily Beast* used six indicators culled from school surveys to compare public high schools in the U.S., with graduation and college acceptance rates weighed most heavily. Other criteria included: college-level courses/exams and SAT/ACT scores. *The Daily Beast, "Top High Schools 2014"*

Highest Level of Education

Area	Less than H.S.	H.S. Diploma	Some College, No Deg.	Associate Degree	Bachelor's Degree	Master's Degree	Prof. School Degree	Doctorate Degree
City	19.4	23.7	22.8	7.6	17.2	6.5	1.9	0.9
MSA[1]	13.6	23.9	25.1	8.4	18.7	7.5	1.8	1.1
U.S.	13.7	28.0	21.2	7.9	18.2	7.7	1.9	1.3

Note: Figures cover persons age 25 and over; (1) Figures cover the Phoenix-Mesa-Scottsdale, AZ Metropolitan Statistical Area—see Appendix B for areas included
Source: U.S. Census Bureau, 2011-2013 American Community Survey 3-Year Estimates

Educational Attainment by Race

Area	High School Graduate or Higher (%)					Bachelor's Degree or Higher (%)				
	Total	White	Black	Asian	Hisp.[2]	Total	White	Black	Asian	Hisp.[2]
City	80.6	82.3	86.2	83.8	56.7	26.5	28.0	16.5	51.2	8.7
MSA[1]	86.4	87.8	88.6	86.9	62.9	29.0	29.8	22.5	53.3	10.5
U.S.	86.3	88.3	83.1	85.7	64.0	29.1	30.4	18.8	50.7	13.7

Note: Figures shown cover persons 25 years old and over; (1) Figures cover the Phoenix-Mesa-Scottsdale, AZ Metropolitan Statistical Area—see Appendix B for areas included; (2) People of Hispanic origin can be of any race
Source: U.S. Census Bureau, 2011-2013 American Community Survey 3-Year Estimates

School Enrollment by Grade and Control

Area	Preschool (%)		Kindergarten (%)		Grades 1 - 4 (%)		Grades 5 - 8 (%)		Grades 9 - 12 (%)	
	Public	Private	Public	Private	Public	Private	Public	Private	Public	Private
City	57.3	42.7	92.8	7.2	94.1	5.9	94.1	5.9	93.7	6.3
MSA[1]	57.4	42.6	92.2	7.8	92.9	7.1	94.2	5.8	94.1	5.9
U.S.	57.7	42.3	87.9	12.1	89.9	10.1	90.0	10.0	90.7	9.3

Note: Figures shown cover persons 3 years old and over; (1) Figures cover the Phoenix-Mesa-Scottsdale, AZ Metropolitan Statistical Area—see Appendix B for areas included
Source: U.S. Census Bureau, 2011-2013 American Community Survey 3-Year Estimates

Average Salaries of Public School Classroom Teachers

Area	2013-14		2014-15		Percent Change 2013-14 to 2014-15	Percent Change 2004-05 to 2014-15
	Dollars	Rank[1]	Dollars	Rank[1]		
ARIZONA	45,335	45	45,406	47	0.16	13.4
U.S. Average	56,610	–	57,379	–	1.36	20.8

Note: (1) State rank ranges from 1 to 51 where 1 indicates highest salary.
Source: National Education Association, Rankings & Estimates: Rankings of the States 2014 and Estimates of School Statistics 2015, March 2015

Higher Education

Four-Year Colleges			Two-Year Colleges			Medical Schools[1]	Law Schools[2]	Voc/ Tech[3]
Public	Private Non-profit	Private For-profit	Public	Private Non-profit	Private For-profit			
1	5	20	4	0	7	1	1	11

Note: Figures cover institutions located within the city limits and include main campuses only; (1) includes schools accredited by the Liaison Committee on Medical Education and the American Osteopathic Association's Commission on Osteopathic College Accreditation; (2) includes ABA-accredited schools, schools with provisional ABA accreditation, and state accredited schools; (3) includes all schools with programs that are less than 2 years.
Source: National Center for Education Statistics, Integrated Postsecondary Education System (IPEDS), 2013-14; Association of American Medical Colleges, Member List, May 1, 2015; American Osteopathic Association, Member List, May 1, 2015; Law School Admission Council, Official Guide to ABA-Approved Law Schools Online, May 1, 2015; Wikipedia, List of Medical Schools in the United States, May 1, 2015; Wikipedia, List of Law Schools in the United States, May 1, 2015

According to *U.S. News & World Report*, the Phoenix-Mesa-Scottsdale, AZ metro area is home to one of the best national universities in the U.S.: **Arizona State University-Tempe** (#129). The indicators used to capture academic quality fall into a number of categories: assessment by administrators at peer institutions; retention of students; faculty resources; student selectivity; financial resources; alumni giving; high school counselor ratings of colleges; and graduation rate. *U.S. News & World Report*, "America's Best Colleges 2015"

According to *U.S. News & World Report*, the Phoenix-Mesa-Scottsdale, AZ metro area is home to one of the top 100 law schools in the U.S.: **Arizona State University (O'Connor)** (#26). The rankings are based on a weighted average of 12 measures of quality: peer assessment score; assessment score by lawyers/judges; median LSAT scores; median undergrad GPA; acceptance rate; employment rates for graduates; placement success; bar passage rate; faculty resources; expenditures per student; student/faculty ratio; and library resources. *U.S. News & World Report*, "America's Best Graduate Schools, Law, 2016"

According to *U.S. News & World Report*, the Phoenix-Mesa-Scottsdale, AZ metro area is home to one of the top 75 business schools in the U.S.: **Arizona State University (Carey)** (#30). The rankings are based on a weighted average of the following nine measures: quality assessment; peer assessment; recruiter assessment; placement success; mean starting salary and bonus; student selectivity; mean GMAT and GRE scores; mean undergraduate GPA; and acceptance rate. *U.S. News & World Report, "America's Best Graduate Schools, Business, 2016"*

PRESIDENTIAL ELECTION

2012 Presidential Election Results

Area	Obama (%)	Romney (%)	Other (%)
Maricopa County	43.1	54.9	2.0
U.S.	51.0	47.2	1.8

Note: Results may not add to 100% due to rounding
Source: Dave Leip's Atlas of U.S. Presidential Elections

EMPLOYERS

Major Employers

Company Name	Industry
Arizona Dept of Transportation	Regulation, administration of transportation
Arizona State University	University
Arizona State University	Libraries
Avnet	Electronic parts and equipment, nec
Carter & Burgess	Engineering services
Chase Bankcard Services	State commercial banks
City of Mesa	Executive offices
City of Phoenix	Administration of social and human resources
City of Phoenix	Executive offices
General Dynamics C4 Systems	Communications equipment, nec
Grand Canyon Education	Colleges and universities
Honeywell International	Aircraft engines and engine parts
Lockheed Martin Corporation	Search and navigation equipment
Paramount Building Solutions	Janitorial service, contract basis
Salt River Pima-Maricopa Indian Community	Gambling establishment
Scottsdale Healthcare Corp.	Hospital management
Scottsdale Healthcare Osborn Med Ctr	General medical and surgical hospitals
Swift Transportation Company	Trucking, except local
The Boeing Company	Helicopters
Veterans Health Administration	General medical and surgical hospitals

Note: Companies shown are located within the Phoenix-Mesa-Scottsdale, AZ Metropolitan Statistical Area.
Source: Hoovers.com; Wikipedia

PUBLIC SAFETY

Crime Rate

Area	All Crimes	Violent Crimes				Property Crimes		
		Murder	Forcible Rape	Robbery	Aggrav. Assault	Burglary	Larceny -Theft	Motor Vehicle Theft
City	4,631.9	7.9	42.3	215.2	366.5	1,114.9	2,462.0	423.1
Suburbs[1]	-1,815.2	3.3	22.8	63.2	178.3	531.2	2,093.0	n/a
Metro[2]	392.3	4.8	29.5	115.3	242.8	731.0	2,219.4	n/a
U.S.	3,098.6	4.5	25.2	109.1	229.1	610.0	1,899.4	221.3

Note: Figures are crimes per 100,000 population; (1) All areas within the metro area that are located outside the city limits; (2) Figures cover the Phoenix-Mesa-Scottsdale, AZ Metropolitan Statistical Area—see Appendix B for areas included
Source: FBI Uniform Crime Reports, 2013

Hate Crimes

Area	Number of Quarters Reported	Number of Incidents per Bias Motivation						
		Race	Religion	Sexual Orientation	Ethnicity	Disability	Gender	Gender Identity
City	3	40	12	14	14	1	0	0
U.S.	4	2,871	1,031	1,233	655	83	18	31

Source: Federal Bureau of Investigation, Hate Crime Statistics 2013

Identity Theft Consumer Complaints

Area	Complaints	Complaints per 100,000 Population	Rank[2]
MSA[1]	4,584	104.2	51
U.S.	332,646	104.3	-

Note: (1) Figures cover the Phoenix-Mesa-Scottsdale, AZ Metropolitan Statistical Area—see Appendix B for areas included; (2) Rank ranges from 1 to 380 where 1 indicates greatest number of identity theft complaints per 100,000 population
Source: Federal Trade Commission, Consumer Sentinel Network Data Book for January–December 2014

Fraud and Other Consumer Complaints

Area	Complaints	Complaints per 100,000 Population	Rank[2]
MSA[1]	21,698	493.3	25
U.S.	2,250,205	705.7	-

Note: (1) Figures cover the Phoenix-Mesa-Scottsdale, AZ Metropolitan Statistical Area—see Appendix B for areas included; (2) Rank ranges from 1 to 380 where 1 indicates greatest number of identity theft complaints per 100,000 population
Source: Federal Trade Commission, Consumer Sentinel Network Data Book for January–December 2014

RECREATION

Culture

Dance[1]	Theatre[1]	Instrumental Music[1]	Vocal Music[1]	Series and Festivals	Museums and Art Galleries[2]	Zoos and Aquariums[3]
1	1	2	4	1	66	1

Note: (1) Professional perfoming groups; (2) Based on organizations with SIC code 8412; (3) AZA-accredited
Source: The Grey House Performing Arts Directory, 2015-16; Association of Zoos & Aquariums, AZA Member Zoos & Aquariums, April 2015; www.AccuLeads.com, April 2015

Professional Sports Teams

Team Name	League	Year Established
Arizona Cardinals	National Football League (NFL)	1988
Arizona Diamondbacks	Major League Baseball (MLB)	1998
Phoenix Coyotes	National Hockey League (NHL)	1996
Phoenix Suns	National Basketball Association (NBA)	1968

Note: Includes teams located in the Phoenix-Mesa-Scottsdale, AZ Metropolitan Statistical Area.
Source: Wikipedia, Major Professional Sports Teams of the United States and Canada, April 2015

CLIMATE

Average and Extreme Temperatures

Temperature	Jan	Feb	Mar	Apr	May	Jun	Jul	Aug	Sep	Oct	Nov	Dec	Yr.
Extreme High (°F)	88	92	100	105	113	122	118	116	118	107	93	88	122
Average High (°F)	66	70	75	84	93	103	105	103	99	88	75	67	86
Average Temp. (°F)	53	57	62	70	78	88	93	91	85	74	62	54	72
Average Low (°F)	40	44	48	55	63	72	80	78	72	60	48	41	59
Extreme Low (°F)	17	22	25	37	40	51	66	61	47	34	27	22	17

Note: Figures cover the years 1948-1990
Source: National Climatic Data Center, International Station Meteorological Climate Summary, 9/96

Average Precipitation/Snowfall/Humidity

Precip./Humidity	Jan	Feb	Mar	Apr	May	Jun	Jul	Aug	Sep	Oct	Nov	Dec	Yr.
Avg. Precip. (in.)	0.7	0.6	0.8	0.3	0.1	0.1	0.8	1.0	0.7	0.6	0.6	0.9	7.3
Avg. Snowfall (in.)	Tr	Tr	0	0	0	0	0	0	0	0	0	Tr	Tr
Avg. Rel. Hum. 5am (%)	68	63	56	45	37	33	47	53	50	53	59	66	53
Avg. Rel. Hum. 5pm (%)	34	28	24	17	14	12	21	24	23	24	28	34	24

Note: Figures cover the years 1948-1990; Tr = Trace amounts (<0.05 in. of rain; <0.5 in. of snow)
Source: National Climatic Data Center, International Station Meteorological Climate Summary, 9/96

Weather Conditions

Temperature			Daytime Sky			Precipitation		
10°F & below	32°F & below	90°F & above	Clear	Partly cloudy	Cloudy	0.01 inch or more precip.	0.1 inch or more snow/ice	Thunder-storms
0	10	167	186	125	54	37	< 1	23

Note: Figures are average number of days per year and cover the years 1948-1990
Source: National Climatic Data Center, International Station Meteorological Climate Summary, 9/96

HAZARDOUS WASTE

Superfund Sites

Phoenix has one hazardous waste site on the EPA's Superfund Final National Priorities List: **Motorola, Inc. (52nd Street Plant)**. There are a total of 1,322 Superfund sites on the list in the U.S. *U.S. Environmental Protection Agency, Final National Priorities List, April 14, 2015*

AIR & WATER QUALITY

Air Quality Trends: Ozone

	2004	2005	2006	2007	2008	2009	2010	2011	2012	2013
MSA[1]	0.073	0.078	0.078	0.073	0.076	0.069	0.072	0.076	0.076	0.073

Note: (1) Data covers the Phoenix-Mesa-Scottsdale, AZ Metropolitan Statistical Area—see Appendix B for areas included. The values shown are the composite ozone concentration averages among trend sites based on the highest fourth daily maximum 8-hour concentration in parts per million. These trends are based on sites having an adequate record of monitoring data during the trend period. Data from exceptional events are included.
Source: U.S. Environmental Protection Agency, Air Quality Monitoring Information, "Air Quality Trends by City, 2000-2013"

Air Quality Index

Area	Percent of Days when Air Quality was...[2]					AQI Statistics[2]	
	Good	Moderate	Unhealthy for Sensitive Groups	Unhealthy	Very Unhealthy	Maximum	Median
MSA[1]	8.5	66.0	20.3	3.6	1.6	825	77

Note: (1) Data covers the Phoenix-Mesa-Scottsdale, AZ Metropolitan Statistical Area—see Appendix B for areas included; (2) Based on 365 days with AQI data in 2014. Air Quality Index (AQI) is an index for reporting daily air quality. EPA calculates the AQI for five major air pollutants regulated by the Clean Air Act: ground-level ozone, particle pollution (aka particulate matter), carbon monoxide, sulfur dioxide, and nitrogen dioxide. The AQI runs from 0 to 500. The higher the AQI value, the greater the level of air pollution and the greater the health concern. There are six AQI categories: "Good" AQI is between 0 and 50. Air quality is considered satisfactory; "Moderate" AQI is between 51 and 100. Air quality is acceptable; "Unhealthy for Sensitive Groups" When AQI values are between 101 and 150, members of sensitive groups may experience health effects; "Unhealthy" When AQI values are between 151 and 200 everyone may begin to experience health effects; "Very Unhealthy" AQI values between 201 and 300 trigger a health alert; "Hazardous" AQI values over 300 trigger warnings of emergency conditions (not shown).
Source: U.S. Environmental Protection Agency, Air Quality Index Report, 2014

Air Quality Index Pollutants

Area	Percent of Days when AQI Pollutant was...[2]					
	Carbon Monoxide	Nitrogen Dioxide	Ozone	Sulfur Dioxide	Particulate Matter 2.5	Particulate Matter 10
MSA[1]	0.0	1.6	19.7	0.0	20.5	58.1

Note: (1) Data covers the Phoenix-Mesa-Scottsdale, AZ Metropolitan Statistical Area—see Appendix B for areas included; (2) Based on 365 days with AQI data in 2014. The Air Quality Index (AQI) is an index for reporting daily air quality. EPA calculates the AQI for five major air pollutants regulated by the Clean Air Act: ground-level ozone, particle pollution (also known as particulate matter), carbon monoxide, sulfur dioxide, and nitrogen dioxide. The AQI runs from 0 to 500. The higher the AQI value, the greater the level of air pollution and the greater the health concern.
Source: U.S. Environmental Protection Agency, Air Quality Index Report, 2014

Maximum Air Pollutant Concentrations: Particulate Matter, Ozone, CO and Lead

	Particulate Matter 10 (ug/m³)	Particulate Matter 2.5 Wtd AM (ug/m³)	Particulate Matter 2.5 24-Hr (ug/m³)	Ozone (ppm)	Carbon Monoxide (ppm)	Lead (ug/m³)
MSA[1] Level	510	10.6	42	0.079	3	0.04
NAAQS[2]	150	15	35	0.075	9	0.15
Met NAAQS[2]	No	Yes	No	No	Yes	Yes

Note: (1) Data covers the Phoenix-Mesa-Scottsdale, AZ Metropolitan Statistical Area—see Appendix B for areas included; Data from exceptional events are included; (2) National Ambient Air Quality Standards; ppm = parts per million; ug/m³ = micrograms per cubic meter; n/a not available.
Concentrations: Particulate Matter 10 (coarse particulate)—highest second maximum 24-hour concentration; Particulate Matter 2.5 Wtd AM (fine particulate)—highest weighted annual mean concentration; Particulate Matter 2.5 24-Hour (fine particulate)—highest 98th percentile 24-hour concentration; Ozone—highest fourth daily maximum 8-hour concentration; Carbon Monoxide—highest second maximum non-overlapping 8-hour concentration; Lead—maximum running 3-month average
Source: U.S. Environmental Protection Agency, Air Quality Monitoring Information, "Air Quality Statistics by City, 2013"

Maximum Air Pollutant Concentrations: Nitrogen Dioxide and Sulfur Dioxide

	Nitrogen Dioxide AM (ppb)	Nitrogen Dioxide 1-Hr (ppb)	Sulfur Dioxide AM (ppb)	Sulfur Dioxide 1-Hr (ppb)	Sulfur Dioxide 24-Hr (ppb)
MSA[1] Level	25	63	n/a	9	n/a
NAAQS[2]	53	100	30	75	140
Met NAAQS[2]	Yes	Yes	n/a	Yes	n/a

Note: (1) Data covers the Phoenix-Mesa-Scottsdale, AZ Metropolitan Statistical Area—see Appendix B for areas included; Data from exceptional events are included; (2) National Ambient Air Quality Standards; ppm = parts per million; ug/m³ = micrograms per cubic meter; n/a not available.
Concentrations: Nitrogen Dioxide AM—highest arithmetic mean concentration; Nitrogen Dioxide 1-Hr—highest 98th percentile 1-hour daily maximum concentration; Sulfur Dioxide AM—highest annual mean concentration; Sulfur Dioxide 1-Hr—highest 99th percentile 1-hour daily maximum concentration; Sulfur Dioxide 24-Hr—highest second maximum 24-hour concentration
Source: U.S. Environmental Protection Agency, Air Quality Monitoring Information, "Air Quality Statistics by City, 2013"

Drinking Water

Water System Name	Pop. Served	Primary Water Source Type	Violations[1] Health Based	Violations[1] Monitoring/ Reporting
City of Phoenix	1,500,000	Surface	1	0

Note: (1) Based on violation data from January 1, 2014 to December 31, 2014 (includes unresolved violations from earlier years)
Source: U.S. Environmental Protection Agency, Office of Ground Water and Drinking Water, Safe Drinking Water Information System (based on data extracted January 27, 2015)

Portland, Oregon

Background

Portland is the kind of city that inspires civic pride and the desire to preserve. For who among us could be indifferent to the magnificent views of the Cascade Mountains, the mild climate, and the historical brick structures that blend so well with its more contemporary structures?

Nature is undisputedly "Queen" in Portland. The symbol of the city, she is embodied in Portlandia, a statue of an earth mother kneeling among her sculpture animal children. The number of activities, such as fishing, skiing, and hunting, as well as the number of outdoor zoological gardens, attest to the mindset of the typical Portlander. And to think that in 1845 Portland held the unromantic name of "Stumptown!"

For the concerned citizen looking for a place that espouses the ideals of the early 1990s television series *Northern Exposure,*Portland may be its real-world, big city counterpart. Portland is a major industrial and commercial center that can still boast clean air and water within its city limits as many of the factories use the electricity generated by mountain rivers; thus, little soot or smoke is belched out. The largest employers in the city are in the health services and Oregon State University.

Portland is a major cultural center, with art museums such as the Portland Art Museum and the Oregon Museum of Science and Industry, and fine educational institutions such as Reed College and the University of Portland. The site where Portland's PGE Park sports stadium now stands was first used for athletic competition in 1893, when the Multnomah Amateur Athletic Club rented a piece of Tanner Creek Gulch pasture there. More recently, in 2001, the PGE was given a $38.5 facelift, and now meets more contemporary tastes and standards, with accommodations that include a field level bar and grill and pavilion suites, all state-of-the-art and seismic code compliant.

The Portland area's regional government is referred to as Metro and includes 24 cities and parts of three counties. Established in the late 1970s, it is the nation's first and only elected regional government. It attempts to control growth by using its authority over land use, transportation, and the environment. This experiment in urban planning is designed to protect farms, forests, and open space. Portland today has a downtown area that caters to pedestrians and includes a heavily used city park where once there was a freeway. Visible from the air is a clear line against sprawl—with cities on one side and open spaces on the other.

Portland is Oregon's biggest city, and has long been considered a shining example of effective sprawl control. Urban planners and visiting city officials see Portland as a "role model for twenty-first century urban development." The city, with its seven-member Metro Council, faces the question of whether further growth will be more sprawling or more dense for Portland and other communities inside the UGB (urban growth boundary), with homebuilders and other advocates on one side of the debate and local officials on the other side.

Finally, Portland's well-organized mass-transit system makes living there all the more enjoyable; this is a city that takes history, progress, and environmental protection seriously. The Portland Streetcar recently added miles of track.

In 2000, the Portland Art Museum completed its "Program for the Millennium," a multi-stage expansion program that brought total exhibition space to 240,000 square feet. In 2005, restoration of the North Building, a former Masonic Temple, was completed. While preserving the historical integrity, the restoration provides space for the Portland Art Museum's Center for Modern and Contemporary Art.

Portland has a very definite winter rainfall climate, with the most rain falling October through May. The winter season is marked by relatively mild temperatures, cloudy skies, and rain with southeasterly surface winds predominating. Summer produces pleasant, mild temperatures with very little precipitation. Fall and spring are transitional. Fall and early winter bring the most frequent fog. Destructive storms are infrequent, with thunderstorms occurring once a month through the spring and summer.

Rankings

General Rankings

- Among the 50 largest U.S. cities, Portland placed #10 in Vocativ's "semi-exhaustive, mostly scientific" city Livability Index for people aged 35 and under. Average salary, unemployment rates, rents, and other living costs were considered, along with crime rates, weather, public transportation, access to music and sports, and "lifestyle metrics" such as the price of dinner at Buffalo Wild Wings and an ounce of high-quality weed. *vocative.com, "The Livability Index: The Best U.S. Cities for People 35 and Under," December 9, 2014*

- Portland was selected as one of America's best cities by *Bloomberg Businessweek*. The city ranked #5 out of 50. Criteria: leisure attributes (the number of restaurants, bars, libraries, museums, professional sports teams, and park acres by population); educational attributes (public school performance, the number of colleges, and graduate degree holders); economic factors (2011 income and June and July 2012 unemployment); crime; and air quality. *Bloomberg BusinessWeek, "America's Best Cities," September 26, 2012*

Business/Finance Rankings

- Measuring indicators of "tolerance"—the nonjudgmental environment that "attracts open-minded and new-thinking kinds of people"— as well as concentrations of technological and economic innovators, analysts identified the most creative American metro areas. On the resulting 2012 Creativity Index, the Portland metro area placed #13. *www.thedailybeast.com, "Boulder, Ann Arbor, Tucson & More: 20 Most Creative U.S. Cities," June 26, 2012*

- Portland was the #1-ranked city for savers, according to the finance site GoBankingRates, which considered the prospects for for people trying to save money, looking at sales tax, median home and condo value, median monthly rent, median income, unemployment rates, and gas prices in the nation's 100 largest cities. *www.gobankingrates.com, "Best Cities for Saving Money," February 23, 2015*

- Portland was the city ranked #1 among the nation's 100 largest cities for most difficult conditions for savers, according to the finance site GOBankingRates. Criteria: sales tax; median home and condo values; median monthly rent; median income; unemployment rate; and gas prices. *www.gobankingrates.com, "Worst Cities for Saving Money," February 23, 2015*

- Recognizing the sizeable percentage of American workers who are self-employed, NerdWallet editors assessed the country's cities according to percentage of freelancers, median rental costs, and affordability of median healthcare costs. By these criteria, Portland placed #2 among the best cities for independent workers. *www.nerdwallet.com, "Best Cities for Freelancers," February 25, 2014*

- The finance website Wall St. Cheat Sheet reported on the prospects for high-wage job creation in the nation's largest metro areas over the next five years and ranked them accordingly, drawing on in-depth analysis by CareerBuilder and Economic Modeling Specialists International (EMSI). The Portland metro area placed #10 on the Wall St. Cheat Sheet list. *wallstcheatsheet.com, "Top 10 Cities for High-Wage Job Growth," December 8, 2013*

- Based on metro area social media reviews, the employment opinion group Glassdoor surveyed 50 of the largest U.S. metro areas on measures including compensation and benefits, satisfaction with management, business outlook, and number of employers hiring. The Portland metro area was ranked #44 in overall employee satisfaction. *www.glassdoor.com, "Employment Satisfaction Report Card by City," June 13, 2014*

- In a survey of economic confidence in the nation's 50 largest metropolitan areas conducted January–December 2014, the Portland metro area placed #15, according to Gallup's 2014 Economic Confidence Index. *Gallup, "San Jose and San Francisco Lead in Economic Confidence," March 19, 2015*

- Using data from the Council for Community and Economic Research's 2013 Annual Report, NerdWallet ranked the 100 U.S. cities with the most expensive cost of living. Cities in California and in the Northeast topped the list. Of the cities with the highest cost of living, Portland ranked #31. *NerdWallet.com, "Most Expensive Cities in America," June 4, 2014*

- The financial literacy site NerdWallet.com set out to identify the 10 most promising cities for job seekers, analyzing data for the nation's 100 largest cities. Portland was ranked #8. Criteria: job availability; workforce growth; affordability. *NerdWallet.com, "Best Cities for Job Seekers in 2015," January 12, 2015*

- The Brookings Institution ranked the 50 largest cities in the U.S. based on income inequality. Portland was ranked #21. (#1 = greatest ineqality). Criteria: the cities were ranked based on the "95/20 ratio," a figure representing the income at which a household earns more than 95 percent of all other households, divided by the income at which a household earns more than only 20 percent of all other households. *Brookings Institution, "Income Inequality in America's 50 Largest Cities, 2007-2013," March 17, 2015*

- Portland was ranked #9 out of 100 metro areas in terms of economic performance (#1 = best) during the recession and recovery from trough quarter through the second quarter of 2013. Criteria: percent change in employment; percentage point change in unemployment rate; percent change in gross metropolitan product; percent change in House Price Index. *Brookings Institution, MetroMonitor: Tracking Economic Recession and Recovery in America's 100 Largest Metropolitan Areas, September 2013*

- The Portland metro area appeared on the Milken Institute "2013 Best Performing Cities" list. Rank: #16 out of 200 large metro areas. Criteria: job growth; wage and salary growth; high-tech output growth. *Milken Institute, "Best-Performing Cities 2014," January 2015*

- *Forbes* ranked the 200 most populous metro areas to determine the nation's "Best Places for Business and Careers." The Portland metro area was ranked #21. Criteria: costs (business and living); job growth (past and projected); income growth; educational attainment (college and high school); projected economic growth; cultural and recreational opportunities; net migration patterns; number of highly ranked colleges. *Forbes, "The Best Places for Business and Careers 2014," July 23, 2014*

- Mercer Human Resources Consulting ranked 211 urban areas worldwide in terms of cost-of-living. Portland ranked #166 (the lower the ranking, the higher the cost-of-living). The survey measured the comparative cost of over 200 items (such as housing, food, clothing, household goods, transportation, and entertainment) in each location.*Mercer, "2014 Cost of Living Survey," July 10, 2014*

Children/Family Rankings

- Portland was chosen as one of America's 100 best communities for young people. The winners were selected based upon detailed information provided about each community's efforts to fulfill five essential promises critical to the well-being of young people: caring adults who are actively involved in their lives; safe places in which to learn and grow; a healthy start toward adulthood; an effective education that builds marketable skills; and opportunities to help others. *America's Promise Alliance, "100 Best Communities for Young People, 2012"*

Culture/Performing Arts Rankings

- Portland was selected as one of the ten best large U.S. cities in which to be a moviemaker. Of cities with a population over 400,000, the city was ranked #9. Criteria: film community; access to new films; access to equipment; cost of living; tax incentives. *MovieMaker Magazine, "Best Places to Live and Work as a Moviemaker: 2013," January 22, 2015*

- Portland was selected as one of America's top cities for the arts. The city ranked #12 in the big city (population 500,000 and over) category. Criteria: readers' top choices for arts travel destinations based on the richness and variety of visual arts sites, activities and events. *American Style, "2012 Top 25 Arts Destinations," June 2012*

Dating/Romance Rankings

- Of the 100 U.S. cities surveyed by *Men's Health* in its quest to identify the nation's best cities for dating and forming relationships, Portland was ranked #63 for online dating (#1 = best). *Men's Health, "The Best and Worst Cities for Online Dating," January 30, 2013*

Education Rankings

- *Fast Company* magazine measured six key components of "smart" cities and three "drivers" for each component to reveal the top ten "Smartest Cities in North America." By these complex metrics, Portland ranked #8. *Fastcoexist.com, "The Top 10 Smartest Cities in North America," November 15, 2013*

- *Reader's Digest* analyzed data for 120 U.S. cities to arrive at a list of "America's 10 Sharpest Cities." Researchers looked at education level, eating and exercise habits, health conditions, and sociability factors calculated to build and maintain mental alertness into the upper decades of life. Portland ranked #6 on the list. *Reader's Digest, "America's 10 Sharpest Cities," October 2012*

- Personal finance website *WalletHub* analyzed the 150 largest U.S. metropolitan statistical areas to determine where the most educated Americans are choosing to settle. Criteria: educational attainment; percentage of workers with jobs in computer, engineering, and science fields; quality and size of each metro area's universities. Portland was ranked #24 (#1 = most educated city). *www.WalletHub.com, "2014's Most and Least Educated Cities*

- The real estate website *MovoTo.com* selected Portland as one of the "Nerdiest Cities in America." The city ranked #2 among the top 10 derived from data on the 50 most populous cities in the United States. Criteria: Number of annual comic book, video game, anime, and sci-fi/fantasy conventions; people per comic book store, video game store, and traditional gaming store; people per LARPing ("live action role-playing") group; people per science museum. Also factored in: distance to the nearest Renaissance faire. *MovoTo.com, "The 10 Nerdiest Cities in America," April 10, 2013*

- Portland was selected as one of America's most literate cities. The city ranked #11 out of the 77 largest U.S. cities. Criteria: number of booksellers; library resources; Internet resources; educational attainment; periodical publishing resources; newspaper circulation. *Central Connecticut State University, "America's Most Literate Cities, 2014," April 8, 2015*

Environmental Rankings

- The Portland metro area came in at #22 for the relative comfort of its climate on Sperling's list of "chill cities," as measured by the Sperling Heat Index. All 361 metro areas are included. Criteria included daytime high temperatures, nighttime low temperatures, dew point, and relative humidity at the high temperatures. *www.bertsperling.com, "Sperling's Chill Cities," July 18, 2013*

- Sperling's BestPlaces assessed 379 metropolitan areas of the United States for the likelihood of dangerously extreme weather events or earthquakes. In general the Southeast and South-Central regions have the highest risk of weather extremes and earthquakes, while the Pacific Northwest enjoys the lowest risk. Of the least risky metropolitan areas, the Portland metro area was ranked #19. *www.bestplaces.net, "Safest Places from Natural Disasters," April 2011*

- The U.S. Environmental Protection Agency (EPA) released a list of large U.S. metropolitan areas with the most ENERGY STAR certified buildings in 2014. The Portland metro area was ranked #23 out of 25. *U.S. Environmental Protection Agency, "Top Cities With the Most ENERGY STAR Certified Buildings in 2014," March 25, 2015*

Food/Drink Rankings

- According to Fodor's Travel, Portland placed #23 among the best U.S. cities for food-truck cuisine. *www.fodors.com, "America's Best Food Truck Cities," December 20, 2013*

- *Men's Health* ranked 100 major U.S. cities in terms of alcohol intoxication. Portland ranked #52 (#1 = most sober).Criteria: binge drinking; alcohol-related traffic accidents, arrests, and fatalities. *Men's Health, "The Drunkest Cities in America," November 19, 2013*

- Portland was selected as one of America's 10 most vegan-friendly cities. The city was ranked #2. *People for the Ethical Treatment of Animals, "Top Vegan-Friendly Cities of 2013," June 11, 2013*

Health/Fitness Rankings

- For each of the 50 most populous metro areas in the United States, the American College of Sports Medicine's American Fitness Index evaluated infrastructure, community assets, and policies that encourage healthy and fit lifestyles, including preventive health behaviors, levels of chronic disease conditions, health care access, and community resources and policies that support physical activity. The Portland metro area ranked #3 for "community fitness." Personal health indicators were considered as well as community and environmental indicators. *www.americanfitnessindex.org, "ACSM American Fitness Index Health and Community Fitness Status of the 50 Largest Metropolitan Areas," May 2013*

- Portland was selected as one of the 25 fittest cities in America by *Men's Fitness Online*. It ranked #1 out of America's 50 largest cities. Criteria: fitness centers and sport stores; nutrition; sports participation; TV viewing; overweight/sedentary; junk food; air quality; geography; commute; parks and open space; city recreational facilities; access to healthcare; motivation; mayor and city initiatives; state obesity initiatives. *Men's Fitness, "The Fittest and Fattest Cities in America," March 5, 2012*

- Portland was identified as a "2013 Spring Allergy Capital." The area ranked #98 out of 100. Three groups of factors were used to identify the most severe cities for people with allergies during the spring season: annual pollen levels; medicine utilization; access to board-certified allergists. *Asthma and Allergy Foundation of America, "Spring Allergy Capitals 2013"*

- Portland was identified as a "2013 Fall Allergy Capital." The area ranked #100 out of 100. Three groups of factors were used to identify the most severe cities for people with allergies during the fall season: annual pollen levels; medicine utilization; access to board-certified allergists. *Asthma and Allergy Foundation of America, "Fall Allergy Capitals 2013"*

- Portland was identified as a "2013 Asthma Capital." The area ranked #96 out of the nation's 100 largest metropolitan areas. Twelve factors were used to identify the most challenging places to live for people with asthma: estimated prevalence; self-reported prevalence; crude death rate for asthma; annual pollen score; annual air quality; public smoking laws; number of board-certified asthma specialists; school inhaler access laws; rescue medication use; controller medication use; uninsured rate; poverty rate. *Asthma and Allergy Foundation of America, "Asthma Capitals 2013"*

- *Men's Health* ranked 100 major U.S. cities in terms of the best and worst cities for men. Portland ranked #17. Criteria: thirty-three data points were examined covering health, fitness, and quality of life. *Men's Health, "The Best & Worst Cities for Men 2014," December 6, 2013*

- The Portland metro area appeared in the 2013 Gallup-Healthways Well-Being Index. The area ranked #57 out of 189. The Gallup-Healthways Well-Being Index score is an average of six sub-indexes, which individually examine life evaluation, emotional health, work environment, physical health, healthy behaviors, and access to basic necessities. Results are based on telephone interviews conducted as part of the Gallup-Healthways Well-Being Index survey January 2–December 29, 2012, and January 2–December 30, 2013, with a random sample of 531,630 adults, aged 18 and older, living in metropolitan areas in the 50 U.S. states and the District of Columbia. *Gallup-Healthways, "State of American Well-Being," March 25, 2014*

- The Portland metro area was identified as one of "America's Most Stressful Cities" by *Sperling's BestPlaces*. The metro area ranked #20 out of 50. Criteria: unemployment rate; suicide rate; commute time; mental health; poor rest; alcohol use; violent crime rate; property crime rate; cloudy days annually. *Sperling's BestPlaces, www.BestPlaces.net, "Stressful Cities 2012*

- Portland was selected as one of the "20 Most Livable U.S. Cities for Wheelchair Users" by the Christopher & Dana Reeve Foundation. The city ranked #5. Criteria: Medicaid eligibility and spending; access to physicians and rehabilitation facilities; access to fitness facilities and recreation; access to paratransit; percentage of people living with disabilities who are employed; clean air; climate. *Christopher & Dana Reeve Foundation, "20 Most Livable U.S. Cities for Wheelchair Users," July 26, 2010*

Pet Rankings

- Portland was selected as one of the best cities for dogs by real estate website Estately.com. The city was ranked #1. Criteria: weather; walkability; yard sizes; dog activities; meetup groups; availability of dogsitters. *Estately.com, "17 Best U.S. Cities for Dogs," May 14, 2013*

Real Estate Rankings

- Using data from the housing-market research firm RealtyTrac, Yahoo! Finance researchers listed the housing markets in which housing affordability is deteriorating most, factoring in interest rates as well as median home prices. The Portland metro area was among the least affordable housing markets according to the percentage difference in the income required to buy a home in December 2013 as opposed to in December 2012. *news.yahoo.com, "10 Cities Where Ordinary People Can No Longer Afford Homes," March 5, 2014*

- The Portland metro area was identified as one of the nation's 20 hottest housing markets in 2015.Criteria: median number of days homes were spending on the market in March 2015. The area ranked #16. *Realtor.com, "These Are the 20 Hottest Housing Markets in the U.S. Right Now," April 8, 2015*

- Portland was ranked #39 out of 275 metro areas in terms of house price appreciation in 2014 (#1 = highest rate). *Federal Housing Finance Agency, House Price Index, 4th Quarter 2014*

- The Portland metro area was identified as one of the 20 least affordable housing markets in the U.S. in 2014. The area ranked #17 out of 178 markets. Criteria: whether or not a typical family could qualify for a mortgage loan on a typical home. *National Association of Realtors®, Affordability Index of Existing Single-Family Homes for Metropolitan Areas, 2014*

- Portland was ranked #188 out of 226 metro areas in terms of housing affordability in 2014 by the National Association of Home Builders (#1 = most affordable). The NAHB-Wells Fargo Housing Opportunity Index (HOI) for a given area is defined as the share of homes sold in that area that would have been affordable to a family earning the local median income, based on standard mortgage underwriting criteria. *National Association of Home Builders®, NAHB-Wells Fargo Housing Opportunity Index, 4th Quarter 2014*

Safety Rankings

- Symantec, in partnership with Sperling's BestPlaces, ranked the 50 largest cities in the U.S. in terms of their vulnerability to cybercrime. The city ranked #16. Criteria: number of cyberattacks and potential infections; level of Internet access; expenditures on smartphones and computer hardware/software; wireless hotspots; broadband connectivity; Internet usage; online purchases. *Symantec, "Riskiest Online Cities of 2012" February 15, 2012*

- Farmers Insurance, in partnership with Sperling's BestPlaces, ranked metro areas in the U.S. and identified the "Most Secure Places to Live." The Portland metro area ranked #9 out of the top 20 in the large metro area category (500,000 or more residents). Criteria: economic stability; crime statistics; extreme weather; risk of natural disasters; housing depreciation; foreclosures; air quality; environmental hazards; life expectancy; motor vehicle fatalities; and employment numbers. *Farmers Insurance Group of Companies, "Most Secure U.S. Places to Live in the U.S.," June 25, 2013*

- Allstate ranked the 200 largest cities in America in terms of driver safety. Portland ranked #177. Allstate researchers analyzed internal property damage claims over a two-year period from January 2011 to December 2012. A weighted average of the two-year numbers determined the annual percentages. *Allstate, "Allstate America's Best Drivers Report, 2014"*

- Portland was identified as one of the safest large cities in America by CQ Press. All 32 cities with populations of 500,000 or more that reported crime rates in 2012 for murder, rape, robbery, aggravated assault, burglary, and motor vehicle thefts were ranked. The city ranked #7 out of the top 10. *CQ Press, City Crime Rankings 2014*

- The National Insurance Crime Bureau ranked 380 metro areas in the U.S. in terms of per capita rates of vehicle theft. The Portland metro area ranked #54 (#1 = highest rate). Criteria: number of vehicle theft offenses per 100,000 inhabitants in 2012. *National Insurance Crime Bureau, "Hot Spots 2012," June 26, 2013*

Seniors/Retirement Rankings

- In addition to affordability, good employment prospects, low crime rates, and pleasant climate, the Huffington Post considered community strength, recreational opportunities, and other markers of stress-free living in its search for the best retirement destinations for those who appreciate peace and quiet. Among those on the list was Portland. *www.huffingtonpost.com, "Best Places to Retire: 10 Most Relaxing U.S. Cities to Enjoy Your Golden Years," April 2, 2013*

- From its Best Cities for Successful Aging indexes, the Milken Institute generated rankings for metropolitan areas, weighing data in eight categories—health care, wellness, living arrangements, transportation, financial characteristics, education and employment opportunities, community engagement, and overall livability. The Portland metro area was ranked #34 overall in the large metro area category. *Milken Institute, "Best Cities for Successful Aging, 2014"*

- Portland was chosen in the "Big City" category of CNNMoney's list of the 25 best places to retire." Criteria include: type of location (big city, small town, resort area, college town); median home prices; top state income tax rate. *CNNMoney, "25 Best Places to Retire," December 17, 2012*

- Portland was identified as one of the most popular places to retire by *Topretirements.com*. The list reflects the 100 cities (out of 900+ total cities reviewed) that visitors to the website are most interested in for retirement. *Topretirements.com, "Most Popular Places to Retire for 2014," February 25, 2014*

Sports/Recreation Rankings

- The sports site Bleacher Report named Portland as one of the nation's top ten golf cities. Criteria included the concentration of public and private golf courses in a given city and the favored locations of PGA tour events. *BleacherReport.com, "Top 10 U.S. Cities for Golf," September 16, 2013*

- Portland was chosen as a bicycle friendly community by the League of American Bicyclists. A "Bicycle Friendly Community" welcomes cyclists by providing safe accommodation for cycling and encouraging people to bike for transportation and recreation. There are four award levels: Platinum; Gold; Silver; and Bronze. The community achieved an award level of Platinum. *League of American Bicyclists, "Bicycle Friendly Community Master List," Fall 2013*

- Portland was chosen as one of America's best cities for bicycling. The city ranked #1 out of 50. Criteria: robust cycling infrastructure; vibrant bike culture. The editors only considered cities with populations of 95,000 or more. *Bicycling, "America's Top 50 Bike-Friendly Cities," May 23, 2012*

Transportation Rankings

- Business Insider presented a Walk Score ranking of public transportation in 316 U.S. cities and thousands of city neighborhoods in which Portland earned the #10-ranked "Transit Score," awarded for frequency, type of route, and distance between stops. *www.businessinsider.com, "The US Cities with the Best Public Transportation Systems," January 30, 2014*

Women/Minorities Rankings

- *Women's Health* examined U.S. cities and identified the 100 best cities for women. Portland was ranked #32. Criteria: 30 categories were examined from obesity and breast cancer rates to commuting times and hours spent working out. *Women's Health, "Best Cities for Women 2012"*

Miscellaneous Rankings

- *Travel + Leisure* invited readers to rate cities on indicators such as aloofness, "smarty-pants residents," highbrow cultural offerings, high-end shopping, artisanal coffeehouses, conspicuous eco-consciousness, and more in order to identify the nation's snobbiest cities. Cities large and small made the list; among them was Portland, at #11. *www.travelandleisure.com, "America's Snobbiest Cities, June 2013*

- Of the American metro areas that allow medical or recreational use of marijuana, the Portland metro area was identified by CNBC editors as one of the most livable for marijuana lovers. Criteria included the Sperling's BestPlaces assessment of marijuana-friendly cities in terms of sound economy, cultural diversity, and a healthy population, plus cost-of-living index and high-quality schools. *www.cnbc.com, "The Best Cities to Live for Marijuana Lovers," February 5, 2014*

- The watchdog site Charity Navigator conducts an annual study of charities in the nation's major markets both to analyze statistical differences in their financial, accountability, and transparency practices and to track year-to-year variations in individual communities. The Portland metro area was ranked #12 among the 30 metro markets. *www.charitynavigator.org, "Metro Market Study 2013," June 1, 2013*

- Ink Army reported on a survey by the website TotalBeauty calculating the number of tattoo shops per 100,000 residents in order to determine the U.S. cities with the most tattoo acceptance. Portland took the #5 slot. *inkarmy.com, "Most Tattoo Friendly Cities in the United States," November 1, 2013*

- Business Insider reports on the 2013 Trick-or-Treat Index compiled by the real estate site Zillow, which used its own Home Value Index and Walk Score along with population density and local crime stats to determine that Portland ranked #9 for "how much candy it gives out versus how far kids have to walk to get it." Zillow also zeroes in on the best neighborhoods in its top 20 cities. *www.businessinsider.com, "These Are the Best Cities for Trick-or-Treating," October 15, 2013*

- Market analyst Scarborough Research surveyed adults who had done volunteer work over the previous 12 months to find out where volunteers are concentrated. The Portland metro area made the list for highest volunteer participation. *Scarborough Research, "Salt Lake City, UT; Minneapolis, MN; and Des Moines, IA Lend a Helping Hand," November 27, 2012*

- Portland was selected as one of America's funniest cities by the Humor Research Lab at the University of Colorado. The city ranked #5 out of 10. Criteria: frequency of visits to comedy websites; number of comedy clubs per square mile; traveling comedians' ratings of each city's comedy-club audiences; number of famous comedians born in each city per capita; number of famous funny tweeters living in each city per capita; number of comedy radio stations available in each city; frequency of humor-related web searches originating in each city. *The New York Times, "So These Professors Walk Into a Comedy Club…," April 20, 2014*

- Portland appeared on *Travel + Leisure's* list of America's most attractive people. Criteria: cities were selected by readers in their annual America's Favorite Cities survey. The city ranked #8 out of 10. *Travel + Leisure, "America's Most and Least Attractive People," November 2013*

- Mars Chocolate North America, the makers of COMBOS®, in partnership with Sperling's BestPlaces, ranked 50 major metro areas in terms of their "manliness." The Portland metro area ranked #32. Criteria: number of professional sports teams; number of nearby NASCAR tracks and racing events; manly lifestyle; concentration of manly retail stores; manly occupations per capita; salty snack sales; "Board of Manliness" rankings. *Mars Chocolate North America, "America's Manliest Cities 2012"*

- Portland was selected as one of the most tattooed cities in America by *Lovelyish.com*. The city was ranked #5. Criteria: number of tattoo shops per capita. *Lovelyish.com, "Top Ten: Most Tattooed Cities in America," October 17, 2012*

- Portland was selected as one of "America's Best Cities for Hipsters" by *Travel + Leisure*. The city was ranked #3 out of 20. Criteria: live music; coffee bars; independent boutiques; best microbrews; offbeat and tech-savvy locals. *Travel + Leisure, "America's Best Cities for Hipsters," November 2013*

- The National Alliance to End Homelessness ranked the 100 most populous metro areas in terms the rate of homelessness. The Portland metro area ranked #15. Criteria: number of homeless people per 10,000 population in 2011. *National Alliance to End Homelessness, The State of Homelessness in America 2012*

Business Environment

CITY FINANCES

City Government Finances

Component	2012 ($000)	2012 ($ per capita)
Total Revenues	1,434,053	2,457
Total Expenditures	1,553,610	2,661
Debt Outstanding	3,381,145	5,792
Cash and Securities[1]	721,205	1,235

Note: (1) Cash and security holdings of a government at the close of its fiscal year, including those of its dependent agencies, utilities, and liquor stores.
Source: U.S Census Bureau, State & Local Government Finances 2012

City Government Revenue by Source

Source	2012 ($000)	2012 ($ per capita)
General Revenue		
From Federal Government	43,616	75
From State Government	117,772	202
From Local Governments	105,104	180
Taxes		
Property	427,005	731
Sales and Gross Receipts	73,857	127
Personal Income	0	0
Corporate Income	0	0
Motor Vehicle License	0	0
Other Taxes	111,668	191
Current Charges	366,766	628
Liquor Store	0	0
Utility	134,993	231
Employee Retirement	270	0

Source: U.S Census Bureau, State & Local Government Finances 2012

City Government Expenditures by Function

Function	2012 ($000)	2012 ($ per capita)	2012 (%)
General Direct Expenditures			
Air Transportation	0	0	0.0
Corrections	0	0	0.0
Education	0	0	0.0
Employment Security Administration	0	0	0.0
Financial Administration	47,471	81	3.1
Fire Protection	96,689	166	6.2
General Public Buildings	4,765	8	0.3
Governmental Administration, Other	32,615	56	2.1
Health	0	0	0.0
Highways	178,177	305	11.5
Hospitals	0	0	0.0
Housing and Community Development	96,450	165	6.2
Interest on General Debt	97,596	167	6.3
Judicial and Legal	9,128	16	0.6
Libraries	0	0	0.0
Parking	8,269	14	0.5
Parks and Recreation	100,425	172	6.5
Police Protection	172,980	296	11.1
Public Welfare	0	0	0.0
Sewerage	255,131	437	16.4
Solid Waste Management	5,153	9	0.3
Veterans' Services	0	0	0.0
Liquor Store	0	0	0.0
Utility	171,002	293	11.0
Employee Retirement	101,773	174	6.6

Source: U.S Census Bureau, State & Local Government Finances 2012

DEMOGRAPHICS

Population Growth

Area	1990 Census	2000 Census	2010 Census	Population Growth (%)	
				1990-2000	2000-2010
City	485,833	529,121	583,776	8.9	10.3
MSA[1]	1,523,741	1,927,881	2,226,009	26.5	15.5
U.S.	248,709,873	281,421,906	308,745,538	13.2	9.7

Note: (1) Figures cover the Portland-Vancouver-Hillsboro, OR-WA Metropolitan Statistical Area—see Appendix B for areas included
Source: U.S. Census Bureau, Census 1990, 2000, 2010

Household Size

Area	Persons in Household (%)							Average Household Size
	One	Two	Three	Four	Five	Six	Seven or More	
City	35.1	33.8	14.4	10.0	3.8	1.7	1.2	2.34
MSA[1]	27.6	34.6	15.7	13.0	5.6	2.0	1.5	2.57
U.S.	27.7	33.6	15.7	13.1	6.0	2.3	1.5	2.64

Note: (1) Figures cover the Portland-Vancouver-Hillsboro, OR-WA Metropolitan Statistical Area—see Appendix B for areas included
Source: U.S. Census Bureau, 2011-2013 American Community Survey 3-Year Estimates

Race

Area	White Alone[2] (%)	Black Alone[2] (%)	Asian Alone[2] (%)	AIAN[3] Alone[2] (%)	NHOPI[4] Alone[2] (%)	Other Race Alone[2] (%)	Two or More Races (%)
City	77.8	6.1	7.6	0.7	0.5	2.9	4.4
MSA[1]	82.1	2.9	6.0	0.8	0.5	3.6	4.0
U.S.	73.9	12.6	5.0	0.8	0.2	4.7	2.9

Note: (1) Figures cover the Portland-Vancouver-Hillsboro, OR-WA Metropolitan Statistical Area—see Appendix B for areas included; (2) Alone is defined as not being in combination with one or more other races; (3) American Indian and Alaska Native; (4) Native Hawaiian and Other Pacific Islander
Source: U.S. Census Bureau, 2011-2013 American Community Survey 3-Year Estimates

Hispanic or Latino Origin

Area	Total (%)	Mexican (%)	Puerto Rican (%)	Cuban (%)	Other (%)
City	9.6	7.5	0.3	0.2	1.5
MSA[1]	11.2	9.2	0.3	0.1	1.5
U.S.	16.9	10.8	1.6	0.6	3.8

Note: Persons of Hispanic or Latino origin can be of any race; (1) Figures cover the Portland-Vancouver-Hillsboro, OR-WA Metropolitan Statistical Area—see Appendix B for areas included
Source: U.S. Census Bureau, 2011-2013 American Community Survey 3-Year Estimates

Segregation

Type	Segregation Indices[1]				Percent Change		
	1990	2000	2010	2010 Rank[2]	1990-2000	1990-2010	2000-2010
Black/White	63.2	51.8	46.0	81	-11.4	-17.2	-5.9
Asian/White	31.2	35.1	35.8	75	3.9	4.7	0.8
Hispanic/White	25.6	34.2	34.3	83	8.6	8.6	0.0

Note: All figures cover the Metropolitan Statistical Area—see Appendix B for areas included; Figures are based on an analysis of 1990, 2000, and 2010 Census Decennial Census tract data by William H. Frey, Brookings Institution and the University of Michigan Social Science Data Analysis Network. In this analysis all racial groups (whites, blacks, and asians) are non-Hispanic members of those races. Hispanics are shown as a separate category;
(1) Segregation Indices are Dissimilarity Indices that measure the degree to which the minority group is distributed differently than whites across census tracts. They range from 0 (complete integration) to 100 (complete segregation) where the value indicates the percentage of the minority group that needs to move to be distributed exactly like whites; (2) Ranges from 1 (most segregated) to 102 (least segregated); n/a not available.
Source: www.CensusScope.org

Ancestry

Area	German	Irish	English	American	Italian	Polish	French[2]	Scottish	Dutch
City	17.3	12.1	10.7	5.7	4.5	2.4	3.1	3.3	1.9
MSA[1]	19.7	11.6	11.1	5.3	3.9	2.0	3.2	3.1	2.2
U.S.	14.9	10.8	8.0	7.4	5.5	3.0	2.7	1.7	1.4

Note: Figures are the percentage of the total population reporting a particular ancestry. The nine most commonly reported ancestries in the U.S. are shown. Figures include multiple ancestries (e.g. if a person reported being Irish and Italian, they were included in both columns); (1) Figures cover the Portland-Vancouver-Hillsboro, OR-WA Metropolitan Statistical Area—see Appendix B for areas included; (2) Excludes Basque
Source: U.S. Census Bureau, 2011-2013 American Community Survey 3-Year Estimates

Foreign-Born Population

Area	Any Foreign Country	Mexico	Asia	Europe	Carribean	South America	Central America[2]	Africa	Canada
City	14.1	3.1	5.6	2.9	0.2	0.3	0.4	0.9	0.4
MSA[1]	12.5	3.8	4.4	2.4	0.1	0.3	0.4	0.4	0.5
U.S.	13.0	3.7	3.8	1.5	1.2	0.9	1.0	0.6	0.3

Note: (1) Figures cover the Portland-Vancouver-Hillsboro, OR-WA Metropolitan Statistical Area—see Appendix B for areas included; (2) Excludes Mexico.
Source: U.S. Census Bureau, 2011-2013 American Community Survey 3-Year Estimates

Marital Status

Area	Never Married	Now Married[2]	Separated	Widowed	Divorced
City	40.7	40.5	1.9	4.3	12.6
MSA[1]	31.5	49.3	1.8	4.8	12.5
U.S.	32.7	48.1	2.2	6.0	11.0

Note: Figures are percentages and cover the population 15 years of age and older; (1) Figures cover the Portland-Vancouver-Hillsboro, OR-WA Metropolitan Statistical Area—see Appendix B for areas included; (2) Excludes separated
Source: U.S. Census Bureau, 2011-2013 American Community Survey 3-Year Estimates

Disability Status

Area	All Ages	Under 18 Years Old	18 to 64 Years Old	65 Years and Over
City	12.1	4.1	10.3	37.6
MSA[1]	11.9	4.1	10.1	36.6
U.S.	12.3	4.1	10.2	36.3

Note: Figures show percent of the civilian noninstitutionalized population that reported having a disability. Disability status is determined from from six types of difficulty: vision, hearing, cognitive, ambulatory, self-care, and independent living. For children under 5 years old, hearing and vision difficulty are used to determine disability status. For children between the ages of 5 and 14, disability status is determined from hearing, vision, cognitive, ambulatory, and self-care difficulties. For people aged 15 years and older, they are considered to have a disability if they have difficulty with any one of the six difficulty types; (1) Figures cover the Portland-Vancouver-Hillsboro, OR-WA Metropolitan Statistical Area—see Appendix B for areas included.
Source: U.S. Census Bureau, 2011-2013 American Community Survey 3-Year Estimates

Age

Area	Under Age 5	Age 5–19	Age 20–34	Age 35–44	Age 45–54	Age 55–64	Age 65–74	Age 75–84	Age 85+	Median Age
City	5.8	15.0	26.6	16.7	12.9	12.2	6.3	2.9	1.7	36.4
MSA[1]	6.2	19.2	21.3	14.6	13.8	12.7	7.1	3.4	1.7	37.3
U.S.	6.4	19.9	20.7	12.9	14.1	12.3	7.6	4.2	1.9	37.4

Note: (1) Figures cover the Portland-Vancouver-Hillsboro, OR-WA Metropolitan Statistical Area—see Appendix B for areas included
Source: U.S. Census Bureau, 2011-2013 American Community Survey 3-Year Estimates

Gender

Area	Males	Females	Males per 100 Females
City	298,719	304,328	98.2
MSA[1]	1,130,628	1,157,386	97.7
U.S.	154,451,010	159,410,713	96.9

Note: (1) Figures cover the Portland-Vancouver-Hillsboro, OR-WA Metropolitan Statistical Area—see Appendix B for areas included
Source: U.S. Census Bureau, 2011-2013 American Community Survey 3-Year Estimates

Religious Groups by Family

Area	Catholic	Baptist	Non-Den.	Methodist[2]	Lutheran	LDS[3]	Pentecostal	Presbyterian[4]	Muslim[5]	Judaism
MSA[1]	10.6	2.3	4.5	1.0	1.6	3.8	2.0	1.0	0.1	0.3
U.S.	19.1	9.3	4.0	4.0	2.3	2.0	1.9	1.6	0.8	0.7

Note: Figures are the number of adherents as a percentage of the total population; (1) Figures cover the Portland-Vancouver-Hillsboro, OR-WA Metropolitan Statistical Area—see Appendix B for areas included; (2) Methodist/Pietist; (3) Latter Day Saints; (4) Reformed; (5) Figures are estimates
Source: Association of Statisticians of American Religious Bodies, 2010 U.S. Religion Census: Religious Congregations & Membership Study

Religious Groups by Tradition

Area	Catholic	Evangelical Protestant	Mainline Protestant	Other Tradition	Black Protestant	Orthodox
MSA[1]	10.6	11.7	3.7	5.2	0.2	0.3
U.S.	19.1	16.2	7.3	4.3	1.6	0.3

Note: Figures are the number of adherents as a percentage of the total population; (1) Figures cover the Portland-Vancouver-Hillsboro, OR-WA Metropolitan Statistical Area—see Appendix B for areas included
Source: Association of Statisticians of American Religious Bodies, 2010 U.S. Religion Census: Religious Congregations & Membership Study

ECONOMY

Gross Metropolitan Product

Area	2012	2013	2014	2015	Rank[2]
MSA[1]	147.0	153.8	161.5	171.5	20

Note: Figures are in billions of dollars; (1) Figures cover the Portland-Vancouver-Hillsboro, OR-WA Metropolitan Statistical Area—see Appendix B for areas included; (2) Rank is based on 2015 data and ranges from 1 to 363
Source: The U.S. Conference of Mayors, U.S. Metro Economies: GMP and Employment 2013-2015, June 2014

Economic Growth

Area	2010-12 (%)	2013 (%)	2014 (%)	2015 (%)	Rank[2]
MSA[1]	4.9	3.2	3.5	4.3	19
U.S.	2.1	2.0	2.3	3.2	–

Note: Figures are real gross metropolitan product (GMP) growth rates and represent annual average percent change; (1) Figures cover the Portland-Vancouver-Hillsboro, OR-WA Metropolitan Statistical Area—see Appendix B for areas included; (2) Rank is based on 2015 data and ranges from 1 to 363
Source: The U.S. Conference of Mayors, U.S. Metro Economies: GMP and Employment 2013-2015, June 2014

Metropolitan Area Exports

Area	2008	2009	2010	2011	2012	2013	Rank[2]
MSA[1]	19,477.1	15,482.4	18,544.9	20,875.7	20,337.7	17,606.8	20

Note: Figures are in millions of dollars; (1) Figures cover the Portland-Vancouver-Hillsboro, OR-WA Metropolitan Statistical Area—see Appendix B for areas included; (2) Rank is based on 2013 data and ranges from 1 to 387
Source: U.S. Department of Commerce, International Trade Administration, Office of Trade & Industry Information, Manufacturing & Services, data extracted April 3, 2015

Building Permits

Area	Single-Family			Multi-Family			Total		
	2013	2014	Pct. Chg.	2013	2014	Pct. Chg.	2013	2014	Pct. Chg.
City	763	792	3.8	2,992	4,224	41.2	3,755	5,016	33.6
MSA[1]	5,717	5,462	-4.5	6,013	6,894	14.7	11,730	12,356	5.3
U.S.	620,802	634,597	2.2	370,020	411,766	11.3	990,822	1,046,363	5.6

Note: (1) Figures cover the Portland-Vancouver-Hillsboro, OR-WA Metropolitan Statistical Area—see Appendix B for areas included; Figures represent new, privately-owned housing units authorized (unadjusted data); All permit data are based on estimates with imputation.
Source: U.S. Census Bureau, Manufacturing, Mining, and Construction Statistics, Building Permits, 2013, 2014

Bankruptcy Filings

Area	Business Filings			Nonbusiness Filings		
	2013	2014	% Chg.	2013	2014	% Chg.
Multnomah County	74	49	-33.8	2,429	2,213	-8.9
U.S.	33,212	26,983	-18.8	1,038,720	909,812	-12.4

Note: Business filings include Chapter 7, Chapter 11, Chapter 12, and Chapter 13; Nonbusiness filings include Chapter 7, Chapter 11, and Chapter 13
Source: Administrative Office of the U.S. Courts, Business and Nonbusiness Bankruptcy, County Cases Commenced by Chapter of the Bankruptcy Code, During the 12- Month Period Ending December 31, 2013 and Business and Nonbusiness Bankruptcy, County Cases Commenced by Chapter of the Bankruptcy Code, During the 12- Month Period Ending December 31, 2014

Housing Vacancy Rates

Area	Gross Vacancy Rate[2] (%)			Year-Round Vacancy Rate[3] (%)			Rental Vacancy Rate[4] (%)			Homeowner Vacancy Rate[5] (%)		
	2012	2013	2014	2012	2013	2014	2012	2013	2014	2012	2013	2014
MSA[1]	7.0	6.5	6.3	6.6	6.1	6.2	5.0	3.1	3.6	1.9	1.2	1.3
U.S.	13.8	13.6	13.4	10.8	10.7	10.4	8.7	8.3	7.6	2.0	2.0	1.9

Note: (1) Figures cover the Portland-Vancouver-Hillsboro, OR-WA Metropolitan Statistical Area—see Appendix B for areas included; (2) The percentage of the total housing inventory that is vacant; (3) The percentage of the housing inventory (excluding seasonal units) that is year-round vacant; (4) The percentage of rental inventory that is vacant for rent; (5) The percentage of homeowner inventory that is vacant for sale
Source: U.S. Census Bureau, Housing Vacancies and Homeownership Annual Statistics: 2014

INCOME

Income

Area	Per Capita ($)	Median Household ($)	Average Household ($)
City	31,812	52,421	73,563
MSA[1]	29,978	57,732	76,085
U.S.	27,884	52,176	72,897

Note: (1) Figures cover the Portland-Vancouver-Hillsboro, OR-WA Metropolitan Statistical Area—see Appendix B for areas included
Source: U.S. Census Bureau, 2011-2013 American Community Survey 3-Year Estimates

Household Income Distribution

Area	Percent of Households Earning							
	Under $15,000	$15,000 -24,999	$25,000 -34,999	$35,000 -49,999	$50,000 -74,999	$75,000 -99,000	$100,000 -149,999	$150,000 and up
City	14.9	9.7	10.0	13.5	16.7	12.4	13.1	9.7
MSA[1]	11.0	9.3	9.4	13.6	18.8	13.7	14.5	9.7
U.S.	13.0	10.9	10.3	13.6	17.9	11.9	12.7	9.6

Note: (1) Figures cover the Portland-Vancouver-Hillsboro, OR-WA Metropolitan Statistical Area—see Appendix B for areas included
Source: U.S. Census Bureau, 2011-2013 American Community Survey 3-Year Estimates

Poverty Rate

Area	All Ages	Under 18 Years Old	18 to 64 Years Old	65 Years and Over
City	18.5	23.7	18.3	10.9
MSA[1]	14.2	18.5	13.8	8.0
U.S.	15.9	22.4	14.8	9.5

Note: Figures are percentage of people whose income during the past 12 months was below the poverty level;
(1) Figures cover the Portland-Vancouver-Hillsboro, OR-WA Metropolitan Statistical Area—see Appendix B for areas included
Source: U.S. Census Bureau, 2011-2013 American Community Survey 3-Year Estimates

EMPLOYMENT

Labor Force and Employment

Area	Civilian Labor Force			Workers Employed		
	Dec. 2013	Dec. 2014	% Chg.	Dec. 2013	Dec. 2014	% Chg.
City	336,471	345,730	2.8	317,062	327,696	3.4
MSA[1]	1,185,566	1,215,428	2.5	1,108,886	1,143,702	3.1
U.S.	154,408,000	155,521,000	0.7	144,423,000	147,190,000	1.9

Note: Data is not seasonally adjusted and covers workers 16 years of age and older; (1) Figures cover the Portland-Vancouver-Hillsboro, OR-WA Metropolitan Statistical Area—see Appendix B for areas included
Source: Bureau of Labor Statistics, Local Area Unemployment Statistics

Unemployment Rate

Area	2014											
	Jan.	Feb.	Mar.	Apr.	May	Jun.	Jul.	Aug.	Sep.	Oct.	Nov.	Dec.
City	6.4	6.6	6.4	5.8	5.7	5.9	6.0	6.0	5.5	5.6	5.5	5.2
MSA[1]	7.0	7.2	6.9	6.3	6.2	6.3	6.5	6.5	6.0	6.1	6.1	5.9
U.S.	7.0	7.0	6.8	5.9	6.1	6.3	6.5	6.3	5.7	5.5	5.5	5.4

Note: Data is not seasonally adjusted and covers workers 16 years of age and older; (1) Figures cover the Portland-Vancouver-Hillsboro, OR-WA Metropolitan Statistical Area—see Appendix B for areas included
Source: Bureau of Labor Statistics, Local Area Unemployment Statistics

Employment by Occupation

Occupation Classification	City (%)	MSA[1] (%)	U.S. (%)
Management, Business, Science, and Arts	45.0	39.5	36.2
Natural Resources, Construction, and Maintenance	5.0	7.6	9.0
Production, Transportation, and Material Moving	10.0	11.9	12.1
Sales and Office	21.2	23.9	24.4
Service	18.7	17.2	18.3

Note: Figures cover employed civilians 16 years of age and older; (1) Figures cover the Portland-Vancouver-Hillsboro, OR-WA Metropolitan Statistical Area—see Appendix B for areas included
Source: U.S. Census Bureau, 2011-2013 American Community Survey 3-Year Estimates

Employment by Industry

Sector	MSA[1]		U.S.
	Number of Employees	Percent of Total	Percent of Total
Construction	53,400	4.9	4.4
Education and Health Services	159,800	14.6	15.5
Financial Activities	65,100	5.9	5.7
Government	150,500	13.7	15.8
Information	24,200	2.2	2.0
Leisure and Hospitality	108,100	9.9	10.3
Manufacturing	118,900	10.9	8.7
Mining and Logging	1,100	0.1	0.6
Other Services	38,200	3.5	4.0
Professional and Business Services	165,300	15.1	13.8
Retail Trade	117,900	10.8	11.4
Transportation, Warehousing, and Utilities	38,100	3.5	3.9
Wholesale Trade	54,300	5.0	4.2

Note: Figures are non-farm employment as of December 2014. Figures are not seasonally adjusted and include workers 16 years of age and older; (1) Figures cover the Portland-Vancouver-Hillsboro, OR-WA Metropolitan Statistical Area—see Appendix B for areas included
Source: Bureau of Labor Statistics, Current Employment Statistics, Employment, Hours, and Earnings

Occupations with Greatest Projected Employment Growth: 2012 – 2022

Occupation[1]	2012 Employment	2022 Projected Employment	Numeric Employment Change	Percent Employment Change
Retail Salespersons	55,160	62,550	7,390	13.4
Combined Food Preparation and Serving Workers, Including Fast Food	35,480	42,020	6,540	18.4
Registered Nurses	30,680	35,640	4,960	16.2
Waiters and Waitresses	27,760	32,690	4,930	17.8
Janitors and Cleaners, Except Maids and Housekeeping Cleaners	24,200	28,670	4,470	18.4
Bookkeeping, Accounting, and Auditing Clerks	26,030	30,280	4,250	16.3
Customer Service Representatives	22,630	26,520	3,890	17.2
Medical Secretaries	12,380	16,170	3,790	30.6
Farmworkers and Laborers, Crop, Nursery, and Greenhouse	20,290	24,010	3,720	18.4
Secretaries and Administrative Assistants, Except Legal, Medical, and Executive	22,400	26,100	3,700	16.5

Note: Projections cover Oregon; (1) Sorted by numeric employment change
Source: www.projectionscentral.com, State Occupational Projections, 2012–2022 Long-Term Projections

Fastest Growing Occupations: 2012 – 2022

Occupation[1]	2012 Employment	2022 Projected Employment	Numeric Employment Change	Percent Employment Change
Skincare Specialists	300	470	170	57.2
Computer Numerically Controlled Machine Tool Programmers, Metal and Plastic	460	680	220	47.2
Roofers	1,960	2,740	780	39.5
Brickmasons and Blockmasons	460	640	180	38.9
Physician Assistants	930	1,290	360	38.7
Insulation Workers, Floor, Ceiling, and Wall	450	620	170	38.7
Fence Erectors	420	570	150	38.3
Diagnostic Medical Sonographers	470	650	180	38.2
Market Research Analysts and Marketing Specialists	2,390	3,290	900	37.8
Helpers—Brickmasons, Blockmasons, Stonemasons, and Tile and Marble Setters	270	380	110	37.4

Note: Projections cover Oregon; (1) Sorted by percent employment change and excludes occupations with numeric employment change less than 100
Source: www.projectionscentral.com, State Occupational Projections, 2012–2022 Long-Term Projections

Average Wages

Occupation	$/Hr.	Occupation	$/Hr.
Accountants and Auditors	32.74	Maids and Housekeeping Cleaners	11.94
Automotive Mechanics	20.59	Maintenance and Repair Workers	20.32
Bookkeepers	19.25	Marketing Managers	52.74
Carpenters	20.89	Nuclear Medicine Technologists	40.06
Cashiers	11.91	Nurses, Licensed Practical	24.14
Clerks, General Office	16.34	Nurses, Registered	41.08
Clerks, Receptionists/Information	14.05	Nursing Assistants	13.90
Clerks, Shipping/Receiving	15.53	Packers and Packagers, Hand	12.01
Computer Programmers	35.50	Physical Therapists	38.57
Computer Systems Analysts	42.01	Postal Service Mail Carriers	24.92
Computer User Support Specialists	23.81	Real Estate Brokers	41.83
Cooks, Restaurant	11.62	Retail Salespersons	13.04
Dentists	73.12	Sales Reps., Exc. Tech./Scientific	32.68
Electrical Engineers	42.95	Sales Reps., Tech./Scientific	38.75
Electricians	35.00	Secretaries, Exc. Legal/Med./Exec.	17.62
Financial Managers	52.99	Security Guards	15.19
First-Line Supervisors/Managers, Sales	19.22	Surgeons	n/a
Food Preparation Workers	11.00	Teacher Assistants	14.50
General and Operations Managers	51.85	Teachers, Elementary School	28.50
Hairdressers/Cosmetologists	14.59	Teachers, Secondary School	28.60
Internists	102.98	Telemarketers	12.59
Janitors and Cleaners	12.93	Truck Drivers, Heavy/Tractor-Trailer	19.88
Landscaping/Groundskeeping Workers	14.39	Truck Drivers, Light/Delivery Svcs.	16.94
Lawyers	58.93	Waiters and Waitresses	11.45

Note: Wage data covers the Portland-Vancouver-Hillsboro, OR-WA Metropolitan Statistical Area—see Appendix B for areas included; Hourly wages for elementary/secondary school teachers and teacher assistants were calculated by the editors from annual wage data assuming a 40 hour work week; n/a not available.
Source: Bureau of Labor Statistics, Metro Area Occupational Employment and Wage Estimates, May 2014

TAXES

State Corporate Income Tax Rates

State	Tax Rate (%)	Income Brackets ($)	Num. of Brackets	Financial Institution Tax Rate (%)[a]	Federal Income Tax Ded.
Oregon	6.6 - 7.6 (w)	1 million	2	6.6 - 7.6 (w)	No

Note: Tax rates as of January 1, 2015; (a) Rates listed are the corporate income tax rate applied to financial institutions or excise taxes based on income. Some states have other taxes based upon the value of deposits or shares; (w) Oregon's minimum tax for C corporations depends on the Oregon sales of the filing group. The minimum tax ranges from $150 for corporations with sales under $500,000, up to $100,000 for companies with sales of $100 million or above.
Source: Federation of Tax Administrators, "State Corporate Income Tax Rates, 2015"

State Individual Income Tax Rates

State	Tax Rate (%)	Income Brackets ($)	Num. of Brackets	Personal Exempt. ($)[1]		Fed. Inc. Tax Ded.
				Single	Dependents	
Oregon (a)	5.0 - 9.9	3,350 -125,000 (b)	4	194 (c)	194 (c)	Yes (n)

Note: Tax rates as of January 1, 2015; Local- and county-level taxes are not included; n/a not applicable; (1) Married joint filers generally receive double the single exemption; (a) 17 states have statutory provision for automatically adjusting to the rate of inflation the dollar values of the income tax brackets, standard deductions, and/or personal exemptions. Massachusetts, Michigan, and Nebraska index the personal exemption only. Oregon does not index the income brackets for $125,000 and over. Maine has suspended indexing for 2014 and 2015; (b) For joint returns, taxes are twice the tax on half the couple's income; (c) The personal exemption takes the form of a tax credit instead of a deduction; (n) The deduction for federal income tax is limited to $5,000 for individuals and $10,000 for joint returns in Missouri and Montana, and to $6,350 for all filers in Oregon.
Source: Federation of Tax Administrators, "State Individual Income Tax Rates, 2015"

Various State and Local Tax Rates

State	State and Local Sales and Use (%)	State Sales and Use (%)	Gasoline[1] (¢/gal.)	Cigarette[2] ($/pack)	Spirits[3] ($/gal.)	Wine[4] ($/gal.)	Beer[5] ($/gal.)
Oregon	None	None	31.07	1.31	22.72 (g)	0.67	0.08

Note: All tax rates as of January 1, 2015; (1) The American Petroleum Institute has developed a methodology for determining the average tax rate on a gallon of fuel. Rates may include any of the following: excise taxes, environmental fees, storage tank fees, other fees or taxes, general sales tax, and local taxes. In states where gasoline is subject to the general sales tax, or where the fuel tax is based on the average sale price, the average rate determined by API is sensitive to changes in the price of gasoline. States that fully or partially apply general sales taxes to gasoline: CA, CO, GA, IL, IN, MI, NY; (2) The federal excise tax of $1.0066 per pack and local taxes are not included; (3) Rates are those applicable to off-premise sales of 40% alcohol by volume (a.b.v.) distilled spirits in 750ml containers. Local excise taxes are excluded; (4) Rates are those applicable to off-premise sales of 11% a.b.v. non-carbonated wine in 750ml containers; (5) Rates are those applicable to off-premise sales of 4.7% a.b.v. beer in 12 ounce containers; (g) States where the government controls sales. In these "control states," products are subject to ad valorem mark-up and excise taxes. The excise tax rate is calculated using a methodology developed by the Distilled Spirits Council of the United States.
Source: Tax Foundation, 2015 Facts & Figures: How Does Your State Compare?

State Business Tax Climate Index Rankings

State	Overall Rank	Corporate Tax Index Rank	Individual Income Tax Index Rank	Sales Tax Index Rank	Unemployment Insurance Tax Index Rank	Property Tax Index Rank
Oregon	12	36	31	4	30	15

Note: The index is a measure of how each state's tax laws affect economic performance. The lower the rank, the more favorable a state's tax system is for business. States without a given tax are given a ranking of 1. The scores/rankings for the District of Columbia do not affect other states. The 2015 index represents the tax climate as of July 1, 2014.
Source: Tax Foundation, State Business Tax Climate Index 2015

COMMERCIAL REAL ESTATE

Office Market

Market Area	Inventory (sq. ft.)	Vacancy Rate (%)	Under Construction (sq. ft.)	YTD Net Absorption (sq. ft.)	Total Average Asking Rent ($/sq. ft./year)
Portland	53,503,692	10.9	469,828	-53,419	22.07
National	4,745,108,508	14.3	71,190,461	51,084,126	27.40

Source: Newmark Grubb Knight Frank, National Office Market Report, 4th Quarter 2014

Industrial/Warehouse/R&D Market

Market Area	Inventory (sq. ft.)	Vacancy Rate (%)	Under Construction (sq. ft.)	YTD Net Absorption (sq. ft.)	Total Average Asking Rent ($/sq. ft./year)
Portland	262,876,140	5.9	5,330,824	3,983,606	5.80
National	14,238,613,765	7.2	134,387,407	185,246,438	5.64

Source: Newmark Grubb Knight Frank, National Industrial Market Report, 4th Quarter 2014

COMMERCIAL UTILITIES

Typical Monthly Electric Bills

Area	Commercial Service ($/month)		Industrial Service ($/month)	
	1,500 kWh	40 kW demand 14,000 kWh	1,000 kW demand 200,000 kWh	50,000 kW demand 32,500,000 kWh
City	176	1,299	20,892	2,083,747
Average[1]	201	1,653	26,124	2,639,743

Note: Figures are based on annualized 2014 rates; (1) Average based on 180 utilities surveyed
Source: Edison Electric Institute, Typical Bills and Average Rates Report, Summer 2014

TRANSPORTATION

Means of Transportation to Work

Area	Car/Truck/Van		Public Transportation			Bicycle	Walked	Other Means	Worked at Home
	Drove Alone	Car-pooled	Bus	Subway	Railroad				
City	58.0	9.1	9.4	0.8	0.2	6.1	5.9	2.8	7.6
MSA[1]	70.9	9.7	4.7	0.6	0.3	2.3	3.6	1.7	6.4
U.S.	76.4	9.6	2.6	1.8	0.6	0.6	2.8	1.3	4.3

Note: Figures are percentages and cover workers 16 years of age and older; (1) Figures cover the Portland-Vancouver-Hillsboro, OR-WA Metropolitan Statistical Area—see Appendix B for areas included
Source: U.S. Census Bureau, 2011-2013 American Community Survey 3-Year Estimates

Travel Time to Work

Area	Less Than 10 Minutes	10 to 19 Minutes	20 to 29 Minutes	30 to 44 Minutes	45 to 59 Minutes	60 to 89 Minutes	90 Minutes or More
City	9.2	31.1	26.3	21.1	6.1	4.2	1.9
MSA[1]	11.5	29.3	23.2	21.6	7.9	4.5	1.9
U.S.	13.3	29.7	20.9	20.2	7.7	5.7	2.6

Note: Figures are percentages and include workers 16 years old and over; (1) Figures cover the Portland-Vancouver-Hillsboro, OR-WA Metropolitan Statistical Area—see Appendix B for areas included
Source: U.S. Census Bureau, 2011-2013 American Community Survey 3-Year Estimates

Travel Time Index

Area	1985	1990	1995	2000	2005	2010	2011
Urban Area[1]	1.08	1.13	1.21	1.29	1.30	1.28	1.28
Average[2]	1.09	1.14	1.16	1.19	1.23	1.18	1.18

Note: Travel Time Index—the ratio of travel time in the peak period to the travel time at free-flow conditions. For example, a value of 1.30 indicates a 20-minute free-flow trip takes 26 minutes in the peak. Free-flow speeds (60 mph on freeways and 35 mph on principal arterials) are used as the comparison threshold; (1) Covers the Portland OR-WA urban area; (2) average of 498 urban areas
Source: Texas Transportation Institute, Urban Mobility Report 2012, December 2012

Public Transportation

Agency Name / Mode of Transportation	Vehicles Operated in Maximum Service	Annual Unlinked Passenger Trips (in thous.)	Annual Passenger Miles (in thous.)
Tri-County Metropolitan Transportation District of Oregon (Tri-Met)			
Bus (directly operated)	505	58,662.0	230,817.7
Demand Response (purchased transportation)	223	929.6	9,200.4
Demand Response Taxi (purchased transportation)	52	108.2	1,072.6
Hybrid Rail (purchased transportation)	4	441.9	3,552.6
Light Rail (directly operated)	104	39,174.4	216,270.1

Source: Federal Transit Administration, National Transit Database, 2013

Air Transportation

Airport Name and Code / Type of Service	Passenger Airlines[1]	Passenger Enplanements	Freight Carriers[2]	Freight (lbs.)
Portland International (PDX)				
Domestic service (U.S. carriers - 2014)	23	7,626,002	17	198,210,129
International service (U.S. carriers - 2013)	6	181,063	4	4,285,064

Note: (1) Includes all U.S.-based major, minor and commuter airlines that carried at least one passenger during the year; (2) Includes all U.S.-based airlines and freight carriers that transported at least one lb. of freight during the year.
Source: Bureau of Transportation Statistics, The Intermodal Transportation Database, Air Carriers: T-100 Domestic Market (U.S. Carriers), 2014; Bureau of Transportation Statistics, The Intermodal Transportation Database, Air Carriers: T-100 International Market (U.S. Carriers), 2013

Other Transportation Statistics

Major Highways:	I-5; I-80
Amtrak Service:	Yes
Major Waterways/Ports:	Port of Portland

Source: Amtrak.com; Google Maps

BUSINESSES

Major Business Headquarters

Company Name	Rankings	
	Fortune[1]	Forbes[2]
Precision Castparts Corp.	322	-

Note: (1) Fortune 500—companies that produce a 10-K are ranked 1 to 500 based on 2013 revenue; (2) all private companies with at least $2 billion in annual revenue through the end of their most current fiscal year are ranked 1 to 221; companies listed are headquartered in the city; dashes indicate no ranking
Source: Fortune, "Fortune 500," June 16, 2014; Forbes, "America's Largest Private Companies," November 5, 2014

Fast-Growing Businesses

According to *Inc.*, Portland is home to three of America's 500 fastest-growing private companies: **Vacasa** (#9); **The Clymb** (#103); **Revant** (#429). Criteria: must be an independent, privately-held, for-profit, U.S. corporation, proprietorship or partnership; revenues must be at least $100,000 in 2010 and $2 million in 2013; must have four-year operating/sales history. Holding companies, regulated banks, and utilities were excluded. *Inc., "America's 500 Fastest-Growing Private Companies," September 2014*

According to Deloitte, Portland is home to three of North America's 500 fastest-growing high-technology companies: **Puppet Labs** (#42); **Janrain** (#73); **Smarsh** (#403). Companies are ranked by percentage growth in revenue over a five-year period. Criteria for inclusion: company must be headquartered within North America; must own proprietary intellectual property or proprietary technology that contributes to a significant portion of the company's operating revenue, or devote a significant proportion of revenues to research and development of technology; must have been in business for a minumum of five years with 2009 operating revenues of at least $50,000 USD/CD and 2013 operating revenues of at least $5 million USD/CD. *Deloitte Touche Tohmatsu, 2014 Technology Fast 500[TM]*

Minority- and Women-Owned Businesses

Group	All Firms		Firms with Paid Employees			
	Firms	Sales ($000)	Firms	Sales ($000)	Employees	Payroll ($000)
Asian	4,409	982,920	1,095	854,499	7,902	154,402
Black	2,050	146,144	186	108,651	1,439	33,879
Hispanic	1,952	346,578	284	291,780	2,322	66,974
Women	20,883	3,929,473	2,911	3,374,648	22,742	661,114
All Firms	65,461	95,850,826	17,854	93,584,358	362,826	15,868,330

Note: Figures cover firms located in the city; minority- and women-owned business are defined as firms in which the corresponding group own 51% or more of the stock or equity of the company
Source: U.S. Census Bureau, 2007 Economic Census, Survey of Business Owners (2012 Survey of Business Owners data will be released starting in June 2015)

**HOTELS &
CONVENTION
CENTERS**

Hotels/Motels

Area	5 Star		4 Star		3 Star		2 Star		1 Star		Not Rated	
	Num.	Pct.[3]	Num.	Pct.[3]	Num.	Pct.[3]	Num.	Pct.[3]	Num.	Pct.[3]	Num.	Pct.[3]
City[1]	1	0.5	13	6.0	62	28.6	123	56.7	6	2.8	12	5.5
Total[2]	166	0.9	1,264	7.0	5,718	31.8	9,340	52.0	411	2.3	1,070	6.0

Note: (1) Figures cover Portland and vicinity; (2) Figures cover all 100 cities in this book; (3) Percentage of hotels which have a given star rating; Star ratings are determined by expedia.com and offer an indication of the general quality of a particular hotel.
Source: expedia.com, April 2, 2015

The Portland-Vancouver-Hillsboro, OR-WA metro area is home to two of the best hotels in the U.S. according to *Travel & Leisure*: **Allison Inn & Spa**; **Heathman Hotel**. Criteria: service; location; rooms; food; and value. The list includes the top 236 hotels in the U.S. *Travel & Leisure, "T+L 500, The World's Best Hotels 2015"*

Major Convention Centers

Name	Overall Space (sq. ft.)	Exhibit Space (sq. ft.)	Meeting Space (sq. ft.)	Meeting Rooms
Oregon Convention Center	n/a	255,000	22,800	50

Note: Table includes convention centers located in the Portland-Vancouver-Hillsboro, OR-WA metro area; n/a not available
Source: Original research

Living Environment

COST OF LIVING

Cost of Living Index

Composite Index	Groceries	Housing	Utilities	Trans-portation	Health Care	Misc. Goods/Services
124.8	114.1	160.2	91.0	111.6	114.2	115.9

Note: The Cost of Living Index measures regional differences in the cost of consumer goods and services, excluding taxes and non-consumer expenditures, for professional and managerial households in the top income quintile. It is based on more than 50,000 prices covering almost 60 different items for which prices are collected three times a year by chambers of commerce, economic development organizations or university applied economic centers in each participating urban area. The numbers shown should be read as a percentage above or below the national average of 100. For example, a value of 115.4 in the groceries column indicates that grocery prices are 15.4% higher than the national average. Small differences in the index numbers should not be interpreted as significant; Figures cover the Portland OR urban area.
Source: The Council for Community and Economic Research, ACCRA Cost of Living Index, 2014

Grocery Prices

Area[1]	T-Bone Steak ($/pound)	Frying Chicken ($/pound)	Whole Milk ($/half gal.)	Eggs ($/dozen)	Orange Juice ($/64 oz.)	Coffee ($/11.5 oz.)
City[2]	10.13	2.23	1.98	2.09	3.90	5.42
Avg.	10.40	1.37	2.40	1.99	3.46	4.27
Min.	8.48	0.93	1.37	1.30	2.83	2.99
Max.	14.20	2.44	3.62	4.02	6.42	6.96

Note: (1) Values for the local area are compared with the average, minimum and maximum values for all 308 areas in the Cost of Living Index; (2) Figures cover the Portland OR urban area; **T-Bone Steak** *(price per pound);* **Frying Chicken** *(price per pound, whole fryer);* **Whole Milk** *(half gallon carton);* **Eggs** *(price per dozen, Grade A, large);* **Orange Juice** *(64 oz. Tropicana or Florida Natural);* **Coffee** *(11.5 oz. can, vacuum-packed, Maxwell House, Hills Bros, or Folgers).*
Source: The Council for Community and Economic Research, ACCRA Cost of Living Index, 2014

Housing and Utility Costs

Area[1]	New Home Price ($)	Apartment Rent ($/month)	All Electric ($/month)	Part Electric ($/month)	Other Energy ($/month)	Telephone ($/month)
City[2]	404,703	2,196	-	80.86	74.95	25.01
Avg.	305,838	919	181.00	93.66	73.14	27.95
Min.	183,142	480	112.00	42.06	23.42	17.16
Max.	1,358,576	3,851	594.00	180.03	440.99	40.42

Note: (1) Values for the local area are compared with the average, minimum and maximum values for all 308 areas in the Cost of Living Index; (2) Figures cover the Portland OR urban area; **New Home Price** *(2,400 sf living area, 8,000 sf lot, in urban area with full utilities);* **Apartment Rent** *(950 sf 2 bedroom/1.5 or 2 bath, unfurnished, excluding all utilities except water);* **All Electric** *(average monthly cost for an all-electric home);* **Part Electric** *(average monthly cost for a part-electric home);* **Other Energy** *(average monthly cost for natural gas, fuel oil, coal, wood, and any other forms of energy except electricity);* **Telephone** *(price includes basic monthly rate for a private residential line plus additional local usage charges incurred by a family of four).*
Source: The Council for Community and Economic Research, ACCRA Cost of Living Index, 2014

Health Care, Transportation, and Other Costs

Area[1]	Doctor ($/visit)	Dentist ($/visit)	Optometrist ($/visit)	Gasoline ($/gallon)	Beauty Salon ($/visit)	Men's Shirt ($)
City[2]	131.34	104.55	110.90	3.84	44.20	29.59
Avg.	102.86	87.89	97.66	3.44	34.37	26.74
Min.	67.47	65.78	51.18	3.00	17.43	12.79
Max.	173.50	150.14	235.00	4.33	64.28	49.50

Note: (1) Values for the local area are compared with the average, minimum and maximum values for all 308 areas in the Cost of Living Index; (2) Figures cover the Portland OR urban area; **Doctor** *(general practitioners routine exam of an established patient);* **Dentist** *(adult teeth cleaning and periodic oral examination);* **Optometrist** *(full vision eye exam for established adult patient);* **Gasoline** *(one gallon regular unleaded, national brand, including all taxes, cash price at self-service pump if available);* **Beauty Salon** *(woman's shampoo, trim, and blow-dry);* **Men's Shirt** *(cotton/polyester dress shirt, pinpoint weave, long sleeves).*
Source: The Council for Community and Economic Research, ACCRA Cost of Living Index, 2014

HOUSING

House Price Index (HPI)

Area	National Ranking[2]	Quarterly Change (%)	One-Year Change (%)	Five-Year Change (%)
MSA[1]	39	1.44	9.03	12.08
U.S.[3]	–	1.35	4.91	11.59

Note: The HPI is a weighted repeat sales index. It measures average price changes in repeat sales or refinancings on the same properties. This information is obtained by reviewing repeat mortgage transactions on single-family properties whose mortgages have been purchased or securitized by Fannie Mae or Freddie Mac in January 1975; (1) Portland-Vancouver-Hillsboro Metropolitan Statistical Area—see Appendix B for areas included; (2) Rankings are based on annual percentage change for all metro areas containing at least 15,000 transactions over the last 10 years and ranges from 1 to 275; (3) figures based on a weighted average of Census Division estimates using a seasonally adjusted, purchase-only index; all figures are for the period ending December 31, 2014
Source: Federal Housing Finance Agency, House Price Index, February 26, 2015

Median Single-Family Home Prices

Area	2012	2013	2014p	Percent Change 2013 to 2014
MSA[1]	232.9	265.5	286.0	7.7
U.S. Average	177.2	197.4	209.0	5.9

Note: Figures are median sales prices of existing single-family homes in thousands of dollars; (p) preliminary; n/a not available; (1) Portland-Vancouver-Hillsboro, OR-WA Metropolitan Statistical Area—see Appendix B for areas included
Source: National Association of Realtors, Median Sales Price of Existing Single-Family Homes for Metropolitan Areas, 4th Quarter 2014

Qualifying Income Based on Median Sales Price of Existing Single-Family Homes

Area	With 5% Down ($)	With 10% Down ($)	With 20% Down ($)
MSA[1]	63,487	60,146	53,463
U.S. Average	45,863	43,449	38,621

Note: Figures are preliminary; Qualifying income is based on a mortgage rate of 4.0%. Monthly principal and interest payment is limited to 25% of income; n/a not available; (1) Portland-Vancouver-Hillsboro, OR-WA Metropolitan Statistical Area—see Appendix B for areas included
Source: National Association of Realtors, Qualifying Income Based on Median Sales Price of Existing Single-Family Homes for Metropolitan Areas, 4th Quarter 2014

Median Apartment Condo-Coop Home Prices

Area	2012	2013	2014p	Percent Change 2013 to 2014
MSA[1]	149.8	179.3	187.6	4.6
U.S. Average	173.7	194.9	205.1	5.2

Note: Figures are median sales prices of existing apartment condo-coop homes in thousands of dollars; (p) preliminary; n/a not available; (1) Portland-Vancouver-Hillsboro, OR-WA Metropolitan Statistical Area—see Appendix B for areas included
Source: National Association of Realtors, Median Sales Price of Existing Apartment Condo-Coop Homes for Metropolitan Areas, 4th Quarter 2014

Gross Monthly Rent

Area	Under $200	$200 -299	$300 -499	$500 -749	$750 -999	$1,000 -1,499	$1,500 and up	Median ($)
City	1.9	2.9	3.9	17.8	31.3	27.6	14.7	929
MSA[1]	1.3	2.0	3.1	16.1	33.4	30.7	13.5	951
U.S.	1.7	3.2	7.8	22.1	24.3	26.0	14.9	900

Note: Figures are percentages except for Median; Gross rent is the contract rent plus the estimated average monthly cost of utilities (electricity, gas, and water and sewer) and fuels (oil, coal, kerosene, wood, etc.) if these are paid by the renter (or paid for the renter by someone else); (1) Figures cover the Portland-Vancouver-Hillsboro, OR-WA Metropolitan Statistical Area—see Appendix B for areas included
Source: U.S. Census Bureau, 2011-2013 American Community Survey 3-Year Estimates

Homeownership Rate

Area	2007 (%)	2008 (%)	2009 (%)	2010 (%)	2011 (%)	2012 (%)	2013 (%)	2014 (%)
MSA[1]	61.2	62.6	64.0	63.7	63.7	63.9	60.9	59.8
U.S.	68.1	67.8	67.4	66.9	66.1	65.4	65.1	64.5

Note: (1) Figures cover the Portland-Vancouver-Hillsboro, OR-WA Metropolitan Statistical Area—see Appendix B for areas included
Source: U.S. Census Bureau, Housing Vacancies and Homeownership Annual Statistics: 2014

Year Housing Structure Built

Area	2010 or Later	2000 -2009	1990 -1999	1980 -1989	1970 -1979	1960 -1969	1950 -1959	1940 -1949	Before 1940	Median Year
City	0.7	12.1	8.2	5.5	11.6	9.5	12.6	9.1	30.7	1958
MSA[1]	0.9	16.5	18.8	11.3	18.2	9.1	7.4	5.1	12.6	1979
U.S.	0.9	15.0	13.9	13.8	15.8	11.0	10.9	5.4	13.3	1976

Note: Figures are percentages except for Median Year; (1) Figures cover the Portland-Vancouver-Hillsboro, OR-WA Metropolitan Statistical Area—see Appendix B for areas included
Source: U.S. Census Bureau, 2011-2013 American Community Survey 3-Year Estimates

HEALTH

Health Risk Data

Category	MSA[1] (%)	U.S. (%)
Adults aged 18–64 who have any kind of health care coverage	81.5	79.6
Adults who reported being in good or excellent health	84.5	83.1
Adults who are current smokers	15.9	19.6
Adults who are heavy drinkers[2]	7.4	6.1
Adults who are binge drinkers[3]	17.4	16.9
Adults who are overweight (BMI 25.0 - 29.9)	34.4	35.8
Adults who are obese (BMI 30.0 - 99.8)	25.9	27.6
Adults who participated in any physical activities in the past month	84.5	77.1
Adults 50+ who have ever had a sigmoidoscopy or colonoscopy	71.9	67.3
Women aged 40+ who have had a mammogram within the past two years	76.0	74.0
Men aged 40+ who have had a PSA test within the past two years	37.3	45.2
Adults aged 65+ who have had flu shot within the past year	59.7	60.1
Adults who always wear a seatbelt	98.2	93.8

Note: Data as of 2012 unless otherwise noted; (1) Figures cover the Portland-Vancouver-Beaverton, OR-WA Metropolitan Statistical Area—see Appendix B for areas included; (2) Heavy drinkers are classified as males having more than two drinks per day or females having more than one drink per day; (3) Binge drinkers are classified as males having five or more drinks on one occasion or females having four or more drinks on one occasion
Source: Centers for Disease Control and Prevention, Behaviorial Risk Factor Surveillance System, SMART: Selected Metropolitan/Micropolitan Area Risk Trends, 2012 (Note: the CDC has discontinued this dataset but will be releasing a replacement in late 2015)

Chronic Health Indicators

Category	MSA[1] (%)	U.S. (%)
Adults who have ever been told they had a heart attack	3.3	4.5
Adults who have ever been told they had a stroke	2.6	2.9
Adults who have been told they currently have asthma	9.6	8.9
Adults who have ever been told they have arthritis	24.4	25.7
Adults who have ever been told they have diabetes[2]	8.9	9.7
Adults who have ever been told they had skin cancer	5.5	5.7
Adults who have ever been told they had any other types of cancer	6.3	6.5
Adults who have ever been told they have COPD	4.9	6.2
Adults who have ever been told they have kidney disease	2.9	2.5
Adults who have ever been told they have a form of depression	21.9	18.0

Note: Data as of 2012 unless otherwise noted; (1) Figures cover the Portland-Vancouver-Beaverton, OR-WA Metropolitan Statistical Area—see Appendix B for areas included; (2) Figures do not include pregnancy-related, borderline, or pre-diabetes
Source: Centers for Disease Control and Prevention, Behaviorial Risk Factor Surveillance System, SMART: Selected Metropolitan/Micropolitan Area Risk Trends, 2012 (Note: the CDC has discontinued this dataset but will be releasing a replacement in late 2015)

Mortality Rates for the Top 10 Causes of Death in the U.S.

ICD-10[a] Sub-Chapter	ICD-10[a] Code	Age-Adjusted Mortality Rate[1] per 100,000 population	
		County[2]	U.S.
Malignant neoplasms	C00-C97	173.6	166.2
Ischaemic heart diseases	I20-I25	73.9	105.7
Other forms of heart disease	I30-I51	53.7	49.3
Chronic lower respiratory diseases	J40-J47	44.7	42.1
Organic, including symptomatic, mental disorders	F01-F09	48.6	38.1
Cerebrovascular diseases	I60-I69	41.9	37.0
Other external causes of accidental injury	W00-X59	35.5	26.9
Other degenerative diseases of the nervous system	G30-G31	32.9	25.6
Diabetes mellitus	E10-E14	25.1	21.3
Hypertensive diseases	I10-I15	18.6	19.4

Note: (a) ICD-10 = International Classification of Diseases 10th Revision; (1) Mortality rates are a three year average covering 2011-2013; (2) Figures cover Multnomah County
Source: Centers for Disease Control and Prevention, National Center for Health Statistics. Compressed Mortality File 1999-2013 on CDC WONDER Online Database, released October 2014. Data are compiled from the Compressed Mortality File 1999-2013, Series 20 No. 2S, 2014.

Mortality Rates for Selected Causes of Death

ICD-10[a] Sub-Chapter	ICD-10[a] Code	Age-Adjusted Mortality Rate[1] per 100,000 population	
		County[2]	U.S.
Assault	X85-Y09	3.1	5.2
Diseases of the liver	K70-K76	14.7	13.2
Human immunodeficiency virus (HIV) disease	B20-B24	2.4	2.2
Influenza and pneumonia	J09-J18	9.9	15.4
Intentional self-harm	X60-X84	15.8	12.5
Malnutrition	E40-E46	*0.8	0.9
Obesity and other hyperalimentation	E65-E68	2.3	1.8
Renal failure	N17-N19	6.8	13.1
Transport accidents	V01-V99	6.5	11.7
Viral hepatitis	B15-B19	4.7	2.2

Note: (a) ICD-10 = International Classification of Diseases 10th Revision; (1) Mortality rates are a three year average covering 2011-2013; (2) Figures cover Multnomah County; (*) Unreliable data as per CDC
Source: Centers for Disease Control and Prevention, National Center for Health Statistics. Compressed Mortality File 1999-2013 on CDC WONDER Online Database, released October 2014. Data are compiled from the Compressed Mortality File 1999-2013, Series 20 No. 2S, 2014.

Health Insurance Coverage

Area	With Health Insurance	With Private Health Insurance	With Public Health Insurance	Without Health Insurance	Population Under Age 18 Without Health Insurance
City	84.6	67.3	26.6	15.4	4.1
MSA[1]	86.1	70.0	26.9	13.9	5.7
U.S.	85.2	65.2	31.0	14.8	7.3

Note: Figures are percentages that cover the civilian noninstitutionalized population; (1) Figures cover the Portland-Vancouver-Hillsboro, OR-WA Metropolitan Statistical Area—see Appendix B for areas included
Source: U.S. Census Bureau, 2011-2013 American Community Survey 3-Year Estimates

Number of Medical Professionals

Area[1]	MDs[2]	DOs[2,3]	Dentists	Podiatrists	Chiropractors	Optometrists
Local (number)	4,382	229	687	40	486	153
Local (rate[4])	577.5	30.2	89.7	5.2	63.4	20.0
U.S. (rate[4])	270.0	20.2	63.1	5.7	25.2	14.9

Note: Data as of 2013 unless noted; (1) Local data covers Multnomah County; (2) Data as of 2012 and includes all active, non-federal physicians; (3) Doctor of Osteopathic Medicine; (4) rate per 100,000 population
Source: U.S. Department of Health and Human Services, Health Resources and Services Administration, Bureau of Health Professions, Area Resource File (ARF) 2013-2014

Best Hospitals

According to *U.S. News*, the Portland-Vancouver-Hillsboro, OR-WA metro area is home to one of the best hospitals in the U.S.: **Oregon Health and Science University Hospital** (5 specialties). The hospital listed was nationally ranked in at least one adult specialty. Only 144 hospitals nationwide were nationally ranked in one or more specialties. Seventeen hospitals in the U.S. made the Honor Roll with high scores in at least six specialties. *U.S. News Online, "America's Best Children's Hospitals 2014-15"*

According to *U.S. News*, the Portland-Vancouver-Hillsboro, OR-WA metro area is home to one of the best children's hospitals in the U.S.: **Doernbecher Children's Hospital at OHSU** (10 specialties). The hospital listed was highly ranked in at least one pediatric specialty. Eighty-nine children's hospitals in the U.S. were nationally ranked in at least one specialty. Ten children's hospitals in the U.S. made the Honor Roll with high scores in at least three specialties. *U.S. News Online, "America's Best Children's Hospitals 2014-15"*

EDUCATION

Public School District Statistics

District Name	Schls	Pupils	Pupil/ Teacher Ratio	Minority Pupils[1] (%)	Free Lunch Eligible[2] (%)	IEP[3] (%)
Centennial School District 28J	10	6,167	23.0	49.0	63.4	15.9
David Douglas School District 40	14	10,818	22.2	55.6	68.1	14.2
Parkrose School District 3	6	3,428	23.0	63.9	64.9	14.8
Portland School District 1J	86	46,748	19.2	43.9	37.7	16.0

Note: Table includes school districts with 2,000 or more students; (1) Percentage of students that are not non-Hispanic white; (2) Percentage of students that are eligible for the free lunch program; (3) Percentage of students that have an Individualized Education Program.
Source: U.S. Department of Education, National Center for Education Statistics, Common Core of Data, Local Education Agency (School District) Universe Survey: School Year 2012-2013; U.S. Department of Education, National Center for Education Statistics, Common Core of Data, Public Elementary/Secondary School Universe Survey: School Year 2012-2013

Highest Level of Education

Area	Less than H.S.	H.S. Diploma	Some College, No Deg.	Associate Degree	Bachelor's Degree	Master's Degree	Prof. School Degree	Doctorate Degree
City	9.1	17.2	22.3	7.0	26.4	12.3	3.6	2.1
MSA[1]	9.2	22.0	25.4	8.6	21.9	9.0	2.3	1.5
U.S.	13.7	28.0	21.2	7.9	18.2	7.7	1.9	1.3

Note: Figures cover persons age 25 and over; (1) Figures cover the Portland-Vancouver-Hillsboro, OR-WA Metropolitan Statistical Area—see Appendix B for areas included
Source: U.S. Census Bureau, 2011-2013 American Community Survey 3-Year Estimates

Educational Attainment by Race

Area	High School Graduate or Higher (%)					Bachelor's Degree or Higher (%)				
	Total	White	Black	Asian	Hisp.[2]	Total	White	Black	Asian	Hisp.[2]
City	90.9	93.8	87.2	75.4	62.5	44.4	48.1	16.6	36.0	20.6
MSA[1]	90.8	92.7	87.8	84.6	61.2	34.8	35.7	21.0	44.5	14.8
U.S.	86.3	88.3	83.1	85.7	64.0	29.1	30.4	18.8	50.7	13.7

Note: Figures shown cover persons 25 years old and over; (1) Figures cover the Portland-Vancouver-Hillsboro, OR-WA Metropolitan Statistical Area—see Appendix B for areas included; (2) People of Hispanic origin can be of any race
Source: U.S. Census Bureau, 2011-2013 American Community Survey 3-Year Estimates

School Enrollment by Grade and Control

Area	Preschool (%)		Kindergarten (%)		Grades 1 - 4 (%)		Grades 5 - 8 (%)		Grades 9 - 12 (%)	
	Public	Private	Public	Private	Public	Private	Public	Private	Public	Private
City	35.1	64.9	83.8	16.2	88.7	11.3	90.9	9.1	86.9	13.1
MSA[1]	38.1	61.9	83.4	16.6	89.6	10.4	90.8	9.2	91.9	8.1
U.S.	57.7	42.3	87.9	12.1	89.9	10.1	90.0	10.0	90.7	9.3

Note: Figures shown cover persons 3 years old and over; (1) Figures cover the Portland-Vancouver-Hillsboro, OR-WA Metropolitan Statistical Area—see Appendix B for areas included
Source: U.S. Census Bureau, 2011-2013 American Community Survey 3-Year Estimates

Average Salaries of Public School Classroom Teachers

Area	2013-14		2014-15		Percent Change 2013-14 to 2014-15	Percent Change 2004-05 to 2014-15
	Dollars	Rank[1]	Dollars	Rank[1]		
OREGON	58,638	14	59,811	13	2.00	23.8
U.S. Average	56,610	–	57,379	–	1.36	20.8

Note: (1) State rank ranges from 1 to 51 where 1 indicates highest salary.
Source: National Education Association, Rankings & Estimates: Rankings of the States 2014 and Estimates of School Statistics 2015, March 2015

Higher Education

Four-Year Colleges			Two-Year Colleges			Medical Schools[1]	Law Schools[2]	Voc/ Tech[3]
Public	Private Non-profit	Private For-profit	Public	Private Non-profit	Private For-profit			
2	15	6	1	1	11	1	1	1

Note: Figures cover institutions located within the city limits and include main campuses only; (1) includes schools accredited by the Liaison Committee on Medical Education and the American Osteopathic Association's Commission on Osteopathic College Accreditation; (2) includes ABA-accredited schools, schools with provisional ABA accreditation, and state accredited schools; (3) includes all schools with programs that are less than 2 years.
Source: National Center for Education Statistics, Integrated Postsecondary Education System (IPEDS), 2013-14; Association of American Medical Colleges, Member List, May 1, 2015; American Osteopathic Association, Member List, May 1, 2015; Law School Admission Council, Official Guide to ABA-Approved Law Schools Online, May 1, 2015; Wikipedia, List of Medical Schools in the United States, May 1, 2015; Wikipedia, List of Law Schools in the United States, May 1, 2015

According to *U.S. News & World Report*, the Portland-Vancouver-Hillsboro, OR-WA metro area is home to three of the best liberal arts colleges in the U.S.: **Lewis & Clark College** (#77); **Reed College 1** (#77); **Linfield College** (#124). The indicators used to capture academic quality fall into a number of categories: assessment by administrators at peer institutions; retention of students; faculty resources; student selectivity; financial resources; alumni giving; high school counselor ratings of colleges; and graduation rate. *U.S. News & World Report, "America's Best Colleges 2015"*

According to *U.S. News & World Report*, the Portland-Vancouver-Hillsboro, OR-WA metro area is home to one of the top 100 law schools in the U.S.: **Lewis & Clark College (Northwestern)** (#94). The rankings are based on a weighted average of 12 measures of quality: peer assessment score; assessment score by lawyers/judges; median LSAT scores; median undergrad GPA; acceptance rate; employment rates for graduates; placement success; bar passage rate; faculty resources; expenditures per student; student/faculty ratio; and library resources. *U.S. News & World Report, "America's Best Graduate Schools, Law, 2016"*

According to *U.S. News & World Report*, the Portland-Vancouver-Hillsboro, OR-WA metro area is home to one of the top 75 medical schools for research in the U.S.: **Oregon Health and Science University** (#31). The rankings are based on a weighted average of 11 measures of quality: quality assessment; peer assessment score; assessment score by residency directors; research activity; total research activity; average research activity per faculty member; student selectivity; median MCAT total score; median undergraduate GPA; acceptance rate; and faculty resources. *U.S. News & World Report, "America's Best Graduate Schools, Medical, 2016"*

PRESIDENTIAL ELECTION

2012 Presidential Election Results

Area	Obama (%)	Romney (%)	Other (%)
Multnomah County	75.3	20.7	4.0
U.S.	51.0	47.2	1.8

Note: Results may not add to 100% due to rounding
Source: Dave Leip's Atlas of U.S. Presidential Elections

EMPLOYERS

Major Employers

Company Name	Industry
Children's Creative Learning Center	Child day care services
Clackamas Community College	Community college
Coho Distributing	Liquor
Con-Way Enterprise Services	Accounting, auditing, and bookkeeping
Legacy Emanuel Hospital and Health Center	General medical and surgical hospitals
Nike	Rubber and plastics footwear
Oregon Health & Science University	Colleges and universities
PCC Structurals	Aircraft parts and equipment, nec
Portland Adventist Medical Center	General medical and surgical hospitals
Portland Community College	Community college
Portland State University	Colleges and universities
Providence Health & Services - Oregon	Skilled nursing care facilities
School Dist 1 Multnomah County	Public elementary and secondary schools
Shilo Management Corp.	Motels
Southwest Washington Medical Center	General medical and surgical hospitals
Stancorp Mortgage Investors	Life insurance
SW Washington Hospital	General medical and surgical hospitals
Tektronix	Instruments to measure elasticity
The Evergreen Aviation and Space Museum	Museums and art galleries
Veterans Health Administration	Administration of veterans' affairs

Note: Companies shown are located within the Portland-Vancouver-Hillsboro, OR-WA Metropolitan Statistical Area.
Source: Hoovers.com; Wikipedia

PUBLIC SAFETY

Crime Rate

Area	All Crimes	Violent Crimes				Property Crimes		
		Murder	Forcible Rape	Robbery	Aggrav. Assault	Burglary	Larceny -Theft	Motor Vehicle Theft
City	5,347.6	2.3	38.4	150.5	291.6	677.7	3,647.1	539.9
Suburbs[1]	2,490.7	1.1	28.2	46.0	92.9	402.9	1,709.7	209.9
Metro[2]	3,242.3	1.4	30.9	73.5	145.2	475.2	2,219.4	296.8
U.S.	3,098.6	4.5	25.2	109.1	229.1	610.0	1,899.4	221.3

Note: Figures are crimes per 100,000 population; (1) All areas within the metro area that are located outside the city limits; (2) Figures cover the Portland-Vancouver-Hillsboro, OR-WA Metropolitan Statistical Area—see Appendix B for areas included
Source: FBI Uniform Crime Reports, 2013

Hate Crimes

Area	Number of Quarters Reported	Number of Incidents per Bias Motivation						
		Race	Religion	Sexual Orientation	Ethnicity	Disability	Gender	Gender Identity
City	3	1	1	3	1	0	0	0
U.S.	4	2,871	1,031	1,233	655	83	18	31

Source: Federal Bureau of Investigation, Hate Crime Statistics 2013

Identity Theft Consumer Complaints

Area	Complaints	Complaints per 100,000 Population	Rank[2]
MSA[1]	3,685	159.2	7
U.S.	332,646	104.3	-

Note: (1) Figures cover the Portland-Vancouver-Hillsboro, OR-WA Metropolitan Statistical Area—see Appendix B for areas included; (2) Rank ranges from 1 to 380 where 1 indicates greatest number of identity theft complaints per 100,000 population
Source: Federal Trade Commission, Consumer Sentinel Network Data Book for January–December 2014

Fraud and Other Consumer Complaints

Area	Complaints	Complaints per 100,000 Population	Rank[2]
MSA[1]	10,508	454.0	55
U.S.	2,250,205	705.7	-

Note: (1) Figures cover the Portland-Vancouver-Hillsboro, OR-WA Metropolitan Statistical Area—see Appendix B for areas included; (2) Rank ranges from 1 to 380 where 1 indicates greatest number of identity theft complaints per 100,000 population
Source: Federal Trade Commission, Consumer Sentinel Network Data Book for January–December 2014

RECREATION

Culture

Dance[1]	Theatre[1]	Instrumental Music[1]	Vocal Music[1]	Series and Festivals	Museums and Art Galleries[2]	Zoos and Aquariums[3]
6	6	12	2	6	67	1

Note: (1) Professional perfoming groups; (2) Based on organizations with SIC code 8412; (3) AZA-accredited
Source: The Grey House Performing Arts Directory, 2015-16; Association of Zoos & Aquariums, AZA Member Zoos & Aquariums, April 2015; www.AccuLeads.com, April 2015

Professional Sports Teams

Team Name	League	Year Established
Portland Timbers	Major League Soccer (MLS)	2011
Portland Trail Blazers	National Basketball Association (NBA)	1970

Note: Includes teams located in the Portland-Vancouver-Hillsboro, OR-WA Metropolitan Statistical Area.
Source: Wikipedia, Major Professional Sports Teams of the United States and Canada, April 2015

CLIMATE

Average and Extreme Temperatures

Temperature	Jan	Feb	Mar	Apr	May	Jun	Jul	Aug	Sep	Oct	Nov	Dec	Yr.
Extreme High (°F)	65	71	83	93	100	102	107	107	105	92	73	64	107
Average High (°F)	45	50	56	61	68	73	80	79	74	64	53	46	62
Average Temp. (°F)	39	43	48	52	58	63	68	68	63	55	46	41	54
Average Low (°F)	34	36	39	42	48	53	57	57	52	46	40	36	45
Extreme Low (°F)	-2	-3	19	29	29	39	43	44	34	26	13	6	-3

Note: Figures cover the years 1926-1992
Source: National Climatic Data Center, International Station Meteorological Climate Summary, 9/96

Average Precipitation/Snowfall/Humidity

Precip./Humidity	Jan	Feb	Mar	Apr	May	Jun	Jul	Aug	Sep	Oct	Nov	Dec	Yr.
Avg. Precip. (in.)	5.5	4.2	3.8	2.4	2.0	1.5	0.5	0.9	1.7	3.0	5.5	6.6	37.5
Avg. Snowfall (in.)	3	1	1	Tr	Tr	0	0	0	0	0	1	2	7
Avg. Rel. Hum. 7am (%)	85	86	86	84	80	78	77	81	87	90	88	87	84
Avg. Rel. Hum. 4pm (%)	75	67	60	55	53	50	45	45	49	61	74	79	59

Note: Figures cover the years 1926-1992; Tr = Trace amounts (<0.05 in. of rain; <0.5 in. of snow)
Source: National Climatic Data Center, International Station Meteorological Climate Summary, 9/96

Weather Conditions

Temperature			Daytime Sky			Precipitation		
5°F & below	32°F & below	90°F & above	Clear	Partly cloudy	Cloudy	0.01 inch or more precip.	0.1 inch or more snow/ice	Thunder-storms
< 1	37	11	67	116	182	152	4	7

Note: Figures are average number of days per year and cover the years 1926-1992
Source: National Climatic Data Center, International Station Meteorological Climate Summary, 9/96

HAZARDOUS WASTE

Superfund Sites

Portland has two hazardous waste sites on the EPA's Superfund Final National Priorities List: **McCormick & Baxter Creosoting Co. (Portland Plant); Portland Harbor**. There are a total of 1,322 Superfund sites on the list in the U.S. *U.S. Environmental Protection Agency, Final National Priorities List, April 14, 2015*

AIR & WATER QUALITY

Air Quality Trends: Ozone

	2004	2005	2006	2007	2008	2009	2010	2011	2012	2013
MSA[1]	0.060	0.059	0.067	0.058	0.062	0.064	0.056	0.056	0.059	0.053

Note: (1) Data covers the Portland-Vancouver-Hillsboro, OR-WA Metropolitan Statistical Area—see Appendix B for areas included. The values shown are the composite ozone concentration averages among trend sites based on the highest fourth daily maximum 8-hour concentration in parts per million. These trends are based on sites having an adequate record of monitoring data during the trend period. Data from exceptional events are included.
Source: U.S. Environmental Protection Agency, Air Quality Monitoring Information, "Air Quality Trends by City, 2000-2013"

Air Quality Index

Area	Percent of Days when Air Quality was...[2]					AQI Statistics[2]	
	Good	Moderate	Unhealthy for Sensitive Groups	Unhealthy	Very Unhealthy	Maximum	Median
MSA[1]	77.3	20.5	1.9	0.3	0.0	153	36

Note: (1) Data covers the Portland-Vancouver-Hillsboro, OR-WA Metropolitan Statistical Area—see Appendix B for areas included; (2) Based on 365 days with AQI data in 2014. Air Quality Index (AQI) is an index for reporting daily air quality. EPA calculates the AQI for five major air pollutants regulated by the Clean Air Act: ground-level ozone, particle pollution (aka particulate matter), carbon monoxide, sulfur dioxide, and nitrogen dioxide. The AQI runs from 0 to 500. The higher the AQI value, the greater the level of air pollution and the greater the health concern. There are six AQI categories: "Good" AQI is between 0 and 50. Air quality is considered satisfactory; "Moderate" AQI is between 51 and 100. Air quality is acceptable; "Unhealthy for Sensitive Groups" When AQI values are between 101 and 150, members of sensitive groups may experience health effects; "Unhealthy" When AQI values are between 151 and 200 everyone may begin to experience health effects; "Very Unhealthy" AQI values between 201 and 300 trigger a health alert; "Hazardous" AQI values over 300 trigger warnings of emergency conditions (not shown).
Source: U.S. Environmental Protection Agency, Air Quality Index Report, 2014

Air Quality Index Pollutants

Area	Percent of Days when AQI Pollutant was...[2]					
	Carbon Monoxide	Nitrogen Dioxide	Ozone	Sulfur Dioxide	Particulate Matter 2.5	Particulate Matter 10
MSA[1]	0.0	1.6	41.6	0.0	56.7	0.0

Note: (1) Data covers the Portland-Vancouver-Hillsboro, OR-WA Metropolitan Statistical Area—see Appendix B for areas included; (2) Based on 365 days with AQI data in 2014. The Air Quality Index (AQI) is an index for reporting daily air quality. EPA calculates the AQI for five major air pollutants regulated by the Clean Air Act: ground-level ozone, particle pollution (also known as particulate matter), carbon monoxide, sulfur dioxide, and nitrogen dioxide. The AQI runs from 0 to 500. The higher the AQI value, the greater the level of air pollution and the greater the health concern.
Source: U.S. Environmental Protection Agency, Air Quality Index Report, 2014

Maximum Air Pollutant Concentrations: Particulate Matter, Ozone, CO and Lead

	Particulate Matter 10 (ug/m³)	Particulate Matter 2.5 Wtd AM (ug/m³)	Particulate Matter 2.5 24-Hr (ug/m³)	Ozone (ppm)	Carbon Monoxide (ppm)	Lead (ug/m³)
MSA[1] Level	43	9.1	56	0.059	2	n/a
NAAQS[2]	150	15	35	0.075	9	0.15
Met NAAQS[2]	Yes	Yes	No	Yes	Yes	n/a

Note: (1) Data covers the Portland-Vancouver-Hillsboro, OR-WA Metropolitan Statistical Area—see Appendix B for areas included; Data from exceptional events are included; (2) National Ambient Air Quality Standards; ppm = parts per million; ug/m³ = micrograms per cubic meter; n/a not available.
Concentrations: Particulate Matter 10 (coarse particulate)—highest second maximum 24-hour concentration; Particulate Matter 2.5 Wtd AM (fine particulate)—highest weighted annual mean concentration; Particulate Matter 2.5 24-Hour (fine particulate)—highest 98th percentile 24-hour concentration; Ozone—highest fourth daily maximum 8-hour concentration; Carbon Monoxide—highest second maximum non-overlapping 8-hour concentration; Lead—maximum running 3-month average
Source: U.S. Environmental Protection Agency, Air Quality Monitoring Information, "Air Quality Statistics by City, 2013"

Maximum Air Pollutant Concentrations: Nitrogen Dioxide and Sulfur Dioxide

	Nitrogen Dioxide AM (ppb)	Nitrogen Dioxide 1-Hr (ppb)	Sulfur Dioxide AM (ppb)	Sulfur Dioxide 1-Hr (ppb)	Sulfur Dioxide 24-Hr (ppb)
MSA[1] Level	10	33	n/a	5	n/a
NAAQS[2]	53	100	30	75	140
Met NAAQS[2]	Yes	Yes	n/a	Yes	n/a

Note: (1) Data covers the Portland-Vancouver-Hillsboro, OR-WA Metropolitan Statistical Area—see Appendix B for areas included; Data from exceptional events are included; (2) National Ambient Air Quality Standards; ppm = parts per million; ug/m^3 = micrograms per cubic meter; n/a not available.
Concentrations: Nitrogen Dioxide AM—highest arithmetic mean concentration; Nitrogen Dioxide 1-Hr—highest 98th percentile 1-hour daily maximum concentration; Sulfur Dioxide AM—highest annual mean concentration; Sulfur Dioxide 1-Hr—highest 99th percentile 1-hour daily maximum concentration; Sulfur Dioxide 24-Hr—highest second maximum 24-hour concentration
Source: U.S. Environmental Protection Agency, Air Quality Monitoring Information, "Air Quality Statistics by City, 2013"

Drinking Water

Water System Name	Pop. Served	Primary Water Source Type	Violations[1] Health Based	Violations[1] Monitoring/ Reporting
Portland Water Bureau	564,600	Surface	0	0

Note: (1) Based on violation data from January 1, 2014 to December 31, 2014 (includes unresolved violations from earlier years)
Source: U.S. Environmental Protection Agency, Office of Ground Water and Drinking Water, Safe Drinking Water Information System (based on data extracted January 27, 2015)

Provo, Utah

Background

Provo is situated on the Provo River at a site that was once under the waters of Lake Bonneville in a prehistoric period. Year after year, Provo enjoys one of the country's highest employment rates, a growing high-tech economy, a minuscule crime rate, and a magnificent natural environment. The seat of Utah County, it lies at the base of the steep Wasatch Mountains, with Provo Peak rising to a height of 11,054 feet just east of the city, making Provo convenient to many of Utah's famed ski areas and to the Uinta National Forest.

The Spanish missionaries Francisco Silvestre Velez de Escalante and Francisco Atanasio Dominguez, exploring for a more direct route from present-day New Mexico to California, were probably the first Europeans to view the area, but they did not stay long or establish a permanent mission. They did, however, note that the area could easily be irrigated and developed into an important agricultural settlement. Etienne Prevot, a Canadian trapper and explorer, likewise visited but did not settle, though he too remarked on the beauty and potential of the site. They also noted the presence of the site's original inhabitants, the Ute Indians, who held an important fish festival on the river every spring.

Permanent European settlement of Provo is strongly linked to Mormon history. In 1849, John S. Higbee, with 30 families in a wagon train, left the larger Salt Lake City community to move north. As they arrived at the site, they confronted a group of Ute, with whom white settlers had already been in some conflict. A short-lived peace agreement gave way to further conflict and a series of battles, after which the Indians agreed to resettlement. Peace ensued, and Provo was not subject to long periods of Indian hostilities as were many other young Western towns.

Irrigation has been central to Provo's success, and in the very year of Higbee's arrival, two large canals were dug, taking water from the Provo River. Thereafter, grain mills were constructed to serve the needs of nearby farmers. Important rail links were completed in the 1870s connecting Provo to Salt Lake City and to the Union Pacific System, and giving impetus to the region's agricultural and mining industries.

Provo's growth then took off, with an electric generating plant built in 1890, and in 1914, an interurban commuter rail service established between Provo and Salt Lake City. The town had become a major regional industrial center, with ironworks, flourmills, and brickyards. Today, industries include computer hardware and software, food processing, clothing, and electronic equipment.

Provo's industrial dynamism and creativity is reflected in the careers of two of its favorite sons. Dr. Harvey Fletcher, who was associated with Bell Laboratories, was the inventor of many aids to the deaf and hearing-impaired, and was an important early leader of the National Acoustic Association. Philo T. Farnsworth, born in Beaver, Utah, but raised in Provo, was a college student in 1924 when he developed the fundamental concepts of television at the age of 18.

Provo is home to Farnsworth's alma mater, Brigham Young University, a private university operated by The Church of Jesus Christ of Latter-day Saints. The school was founded in 1875 and has earned national respect for everything from its football team and undergraduate liberal arts program to its graduate programs in business and law. The Provo Tabernacle that was destroyed by fire in 2010 is being rebuilt.

In 2001, Provo resident Larry H. Miller donated the Larry H. Miller Field to Brigham Young University. Initially, the stadium hosted the Provo Angels minor league professional baseball team, but the stadium in recent years has been used as a training and competitive facility by other teams, including the Brigham Young Cougars. In 2009, the city of Provo implemented CITYWATCH, a city-wide emergency notification system. The Utah Valley Convention Center was completed in early 2012.

The climate of Provo is semi-arid continental. Summers are generally hot and dry. Winters are cold but not severe. Precipitation is generally light, with most of the rain falling in the spring.

Rankings

General Rankings

- Provo was selected as one the best places to live in America by *Outside Magazine*. The city ranked #2. Criteria included nearby adventure, healthy eating options, bike lanes, green spaces, number of outfitters and bike shops, miles of trails, median income, and unemployment rate. *Outside Magazine, "Outside's Best 16 Best Places to Live in the U.S. 2014," September 2014*

- In their second annual survey, analysts for the small- and mid-sized city lifestyle site Livability.com looked at data for more than 2,000 U.S. cities to determine the rankings for Livability's "Top 100 Best Places to Live" in 2015. Provo ranked #35. Criteria: vibrant economy; low cost of living; abundant lifestyle amenities. *Livability.com, "Top 100 Best Places to Live 2015"*

Business/Finance Rankings

- Based on the Bureau of Labor Statistics (BLS) quarterly reports on employment and wages over fourth-quarter 2011–2012, researchers at 24/7 Wall Street listed the Provo metro area as the #5 metro area for wage growth. *247wallst.com, "American Cities Where Wages Are Soaring," July 15, 2013*

- The business website 24/7 Wall Street drew on Brookings Institution research on 50 advanced industries to identify the proportion of workers in the nation's largest metropolitan areas that were employed in jobs requiring knowledge in the science, technology, engineering, or math (STEM) fields. The Provo metro area was #12. *247wallst.com, "15 Cities with the Most High-Tech Jobs," March 13, 2015*

- *Forbes* ranked the largest metro areas in the U.S. in terms of the "Best Cities for Young Professionals." The Provo metro area ranked #7 out of 15. Criteria: job growth; unemployment rate; median salary of college graduates age 24 to 34; cost of living; number of small businesses per capita; number of large companies; percentage of population 25 years of age and older with college degrees. *Forbes.com, "America's 15 Best Cities for Young Professionals," August 18, 2014*

- Provo was ranked #5 out of 100 metro areas in terms of economic performance (#1 = best) during the recession and recovery from trough quarter through the second quarter of 2013. Criteria: percent change in employment; percentage point change in unemployment rate; percent change in gross metropolitan product; percent change in House Price Index. *Brookings Institution, MetroMonitor: Tracking Economic Recession and Recovery in America's 100 Largest Metropolitan Areas, September 2013*

- The finance site *24/7 Wall St.* identified the metropolitan areas that have the smallest and largest pay disparities between men and women, comparing the median earnings for the past 12 months of both men and women working full-time in the country's 100 largest metropolitan statistical areas. Of the ten worst-paying metros for women, the Provo metro area ranked #1. *24/7 Wall St., "The Best (and Worst) Paying Cities for Women," March 6, 2015*

- The Provo metro area appeared on the Milken Institute "2013 Best Performing Cities" list. Rank: #3 out of 200 large metro areas. Criteria: job growth; wage and salary growth; high-tech output growth. *Milken Institute, "Best-Performing Cities 2014," January 2015*

- *Forbes* ranked the 200 most populous metro areas to determine the nation's "Best Places for Business and Careers." The Provo metro area was ranked #3. Criteria: costs (business and living); job growth (past and projected); income growth; educational attainment (college and high school); projected economic growth; cultural and recreational opportunities; net migration patterns; number of highly ranked colleges. *Forbes, "The Best Places for Business and Careers 2014," July 23, 2014*

Children/Family Rankings

- *Forbes* analyzed data on the 100 largest metropolitan areas in the United States to compile its 2014 list of the ten "Best Cities for Raising a Family." The Provo metro area was ranked #10. Criteria: median income; overall cost of living; housing affordability; commuting delays; percentage of families owning homes; crime rate; education quality (mainly test scores). *Forbes, "The Best Cities for Raising a Family," April 16, 2014*

Education Rankings

- Personal finance website *WalletHub* analyzed the 150 largest U.S. metropolitan statistical areas to determine where the most educated Americans are choosing to settle. Criteria: educational attainment; percentage of workers with jobs in computer, engineering, and science fields; quality and size of each metro area's universities. Provo was ranked #4 (#1 = most educated city). *www.WalletHub.com, "2014's Most and Least Educated Cities*

- Provo was identified as one of "Smartest Cities in America" by the brain-training website *Lumosity* using data from three million of its own users. The metro area ranked #17 out of 50. Criteria: users' brain performance index scores, considering core cognitive abilities such as memory, processing speed, flexibility, attention and problem-solving. *Lumosity, " Smartest Cities in America," June 25, 2013*

Environmental Rankings

- The Weather Channel determined the nation's snowiest cities, based on the National Oceanic and Atmospheric Administration's 30-year average snowfall data. Among cities with a population of at least 100,000, the #11-ranked city was Provo *weather.com, America's 20 Snowiest Major Cities, February 3, 2014*

- The Provo metro area came in at #114 for the relative comfort of its climate on Sperling's list of "chill cities," as measured by the Sperling Heat Index. All 361 metro areas are included. Criteria included daytime high temperatures, nighttime low temperatures, dew point, and relative humidity at the high temperatures. *www.bertsperling.com, "Sperling's Chill Cities," July 18, 2013*

- Sperling's BestPlaces assessed 379 metropolitan areas of the United States for the likelihood of dangerously extreme weather events or earthquakes. In general the Southeast and South-Central regions have the highest risk of weather extremes and earthquakes, while the Pacific Northwest enjoys the lowest risk. Of the least risky metropolitan areas, the Provo metro area was ranked #29. *www.bestplaces.net, "Safest Places from Natural Disasters," April 2011*

Food/Drink Rankings

- For the Gallup-Healthways Well-Being Index, researchers interviewed at least 300 adults in each of 189 metropolitan areas on residents' access to affordable fresh produce. The Provo metro area was found to be among the top ten communities for affordable produce accessibility. *www.gallup.com, "In Anchorage, Access to Fruits and Vegetables Remains Lowest," April 8, 2014*

Health/Fitness Rankings

- The Gallup-Healthways Well-Being Index tracks Americans' optimism about their communities in addition to their satisfaction with the metro areas in which they live. Gallup researchers asked at least 300 adult residents in each of 189 U.S. metropolitan areas whether their metro was improving. The Provo metro area placed among the top ten in the percentage of residents who were optimistic about their metro area. *www.gallup.com, "City Satisfaction Highest in Fort Collins-Loveland, Colo.," April 11, 2014*

- For the Gallup-Healthways Well-Being Index, researchers asked at least 300 adult residents in each of 189 U.S. metropolitan areas how satisfied they were with the metro area in which they lived. The Provo metro area was among the top ten for residents' satisfaction. *www.gallup.com, "City Satisfaction Highest in Fort Collins-Loveland, Colo.," April 11, 2014*

• The Provo metro area appeared in the 2013 Gallup-Healthways Well-Being Index. The area ranked #1 out of 189. The Gallup-Healthways Well-Being Index score is an average of six sub-indexes, which individually examine life evaluation, emotional health, work environment, physical health, healthy behaviors, and access to basic necessities. Results are based on telephone interviews conducted as part of the Gallup-Healthways Well-Being Index survey January 2–December 29, 2012, and January 2–December 30, 2013, with a random sample of 531,630 adults, aged 18 and older, living in metropolitan areas in the 50 U.S. states and the District of Columbia. *Gallup-Healthways, "State of American Well-Being," March 25, 2014*

Real Estate Rankings

• The Provo metro area was identified as one of the top 20 housing markets to invest in for 2015 by *Forbes*. The area ranked #2. Criteria: strong population and job growth; relatively low home prices which are below equilibrium home price (EHP). The EHP is what the average price for a market should be, if speculation, weird distortions in local income, and other factors (like the housing collapse) weren't present in the market. *Forbes.com, "Best Buy Cities: Where to Invest in Housing in 2015," January 9, 2015*

• Provo was ranked #95 out of 275 metro areas in terms of house price appreciation in 2014 (#1 = highest rate). *Federal Housing Finance Agency, House Price Index, 4th Quarter 2014*

• Provo was ranked #204 out of 226 metro areas in terms of housing affordability in 2014 by the National Association of Home Builders (#1 = most affordable). The NAHB-Wells Fargo Housing Opportunity Index (HOI) for a given area is defined as the share of homes sold in that area that would have been affordable to a family earning the local median income, based on standard mortgage underwriting criteria. *National Association of Home Builders®, NAHB-Wells Fargo Housing Opportunity Index, 4th Quarter 2014*

Safety Rankings

• Farmers Insurance, in partnership with Sperling's BestPlaces, ranked metro areas in the U.S. and identified the "Most Secure Places to Live." The Provo metro area ranked #12 out of the top 20 in the mid-size city category (150,000 to 500,000 residents). Criteria: economic stability; crime statistics; extreme weather; risk of natural disasters; housing depreciation; foreclosures; air quality; environmental hazards; life expectancy; motor vehicle fatalities; and employment numbers. *Farmers Insurance Group of Companies, "Most Secure U.S. Places to Live in the U.S.," June 25, 2013*

• The National Insurance Crime Bureau ranked 380 metro areas in the U.S. in terms of per capita rates of vehicle theft. The Provo metro area ranked #326 (#1 = highest rate). Criteria: number of vehicle theft offenses per 100,000 inhabitants in 2012. *National Insurance Crime Bureau, "Hot Spots 2012," June 26, 2013*

Seniors/Retirement Rankings

• From its Best Cities for Successful Aging indexes, the Milken Institute generated rankings for metropolitan areas, weighing data in eight categories—health care, wellness, living arrangements, transportation, financial characteristics, education and employment opportunities, community engagement, and overall livability. The Provo metro area was ranked #3 overall in the large metro area category. *Milken Institute, "Best Cities for Successful Aging, 2014"*

Women/Minorities Rankings

• *24/7 Wall St.* compared median earnings over a 12-month period for men and women who worked full-time, year-round, and employment composition by sector to identify the worst-paying cities for women. Of the largest 100 U.S. metropolitan areas, Provo was ranked #1 in pay disparity. *24/7 Wall St., "The Worst-Paying Cities for Women," March 8, 2013*

Miscellaneous Rankings

- According to the World Giving Index, the United States is the fifth most generous nation in the world. The finance and lifestyle site NerdWallet looked for the U.S. cities that topped the list in donating money and time to good causes. The Provo metro area proved to be the #1-ranked metro area, judged by culture of volunteerism, depth of commitment in terms of volunteer hours per year, and monetary contributions. *www.nerdwallet.com, "Most Generous Cities," September 22, 2013*

- The National Alliance to End Homelessness ranked the 100 most populous metro areas in terms the rate of homelessness. The Provo metro area ranked #98. Criteria: number of homeless people per 10,000 population in 2011. *National Alliance to End Homelessness, The State of Homelessness in America 2012*

Business Environment

CITY FINANCES

City Government Finances

Component	2012 ($000)	2012 ($ per capita)
Total Revenues	155,825	1,385
Total Expenditures	155,218	1,380
Debt Outstanding	115,062	1,023
Cash and Securities[1]	119,057	1,058

Note: (1) Cash and security holdings of a government at the close of its fiscal year, including those of its dependent agencies, utilities, and liquor stores.
Source: U.S Census Bureau, State & Local Government Finances 2012

City Government Revenue by Source

Source	2012 ($000)	2012 ($ per capita)
General Revenue		
From Federal Government	7,235	64
From State Government	4,190	37
From Local Governments	333	3
Taxes		
Property	14,417	128
Sales and Gross Receipts	23,634	210
Personal Income	0	0
Corporate Income	0	0
Motor Vehicle License	0	0
Other Taxes	1,122	10
Current Charges	29,743	264
Liquor Store	0	0
Utility	68,510	609
Employee Retirement	0	0

Source: U.S Census Bureau, State & Local Government Finances 2012

City Government Expenditures by Function

Function	2012 ($000)	2012 ($ per capita)	2012 (%)
General Direct Expenditures			
Air Transportation	1,585	14	1.0
Corrections	0	0	0.0
Education	0	0	0.0
Employment Security Administration	0	0	0.0
Financial Administration	3,604	32	2.3
Fire Protection	8,311	74	5.4
General Public Buildings	2,997	27	1.9
Governmental Administration, Other	2,011	18	1.3
Health	0	0	0.0
Highways	10,267	91	6.6
Hospitals	0	0	0.0
Housing and Community Development	5,466	49	3.5
Interest on General Debt	4,453	40	2.9
Judicial and Legal	2,534	23	1.6
Libraries	3,731	33	2.4
Parking	0	0	0.0
Parks and Recreation	26,653	237	17.2
Police Protection	15,167	135	9.8
Public Welfare	0	0	0.0
Sewerage	5,686	51	3.7
Solid Waste Management	3,286	29	2.1
Veterans' Services	0	0	0.0
Liquor Store	0	0	0.0
Utility	57,139	508	36.8
Employee Retirement	0	0	0.0

Source: U.S Census Bureau, State & Local Government Finances 2012

DEMOGRAPHICS

Population Growth

Area	1990 Census	2000 Census	2010 Census	Population Growth (%) 1990-2000	Population Growth (%) 2000-2010
City	87,148	105,166	112,488	20.7	7.0
MSA[1]	269,407	376,774	526,810	39.9	39.8
U.S.	248,709,873	281,421,906	308,745,538	13.2	9.7

Note: (1) Figures cover the Provo-Orem, UT Metropolitan Statistical Area—see Appendix B for areas included
Source: U.S. Census Bureau, Census 1990, 2000, 2010

Household Size

Area	One	Two	Three	Four	Five	Six	Seven or More	Average Household Size
City	14.0	33.1	17.7	16.3	9.0	5.6	4.3	3.30
MSA[1]	12.5	26.4	15.8	17.2	12.5	9.2	6.3	3.64
U.S.	27.7	33.6	15.7	13.1	6.0	2.3	1.5	2.64

Note: (1) Figures cover the Provo-Orem, UT Metropolitan Statistical Area—see Appendix B for areas included
Source: U.S. Census Bureau, 2011-2013 American Community Survey 3-Year Estimates

Race

Area	White Alone[2] (%)	Black Alone[2] (%)	Asian Alone[2] (%)	AIAN[3] Alone[2] (%)	NHOPI[4] Alone[2] (%)	Other Race Alone[2] (%)	Two or More Races (%)
City	87.1	0.9	3.1	0.5	1.4	3.7	3.3
MSA[1]	91.9	0.6	1.5	0.5	0.9	2.3	2.3
U.S.	73.9	12.6	5.0	0.8	0.2	4.7	2.9

Note: (1) Figures cover the Provo-Orem, UT Metropolitan Statistical Area—see Appendix B for areas included; (2) Alone is defined as not being in combination with one or more other races; (3) American Indian and Alaska Native; (4) Native Hawaiian and Other Pacific Islander
Source: U.S. Census Bureau, 2011-2013 American Community Survey 3-Year Estimates

Hispanic or Latino Origin

Area	Total (%)	Mexican (%)	Puerto Rican (%)	Cuban (%)	Other (%)
City	18.2	11.2	0.4	0.4	6.3
MSA[1]	10.8	7.1	0.2	0.1	3.4
U.S.	16.9	10.8	1.6	0.6	3.8

Note: Persons of Hispanic or Latino origin can be of any race; (1) Figures cover the Provo-Orem, UT Metropolitan Statistical Area—see Appendix B for areas included
Source: U.S. Census Bureau, 2011-2013 American Community Survey 3-Year Estimates

Segregation

Type	1990	2000	2010	2010 Rank[2]	1990-2000	1990-2010	2000-2010
Black/White	38.6	29.4	21.9	102	-9.2	-16.7	-7.5
Asian/White	32.3	31.5	28.2	94	-0.8	-4.1	-3.3
Hispanic/White	20.9	33.3	30.9	93	12.4	10.0	-2.4

Note: All figures cover the Metropolitan Statistical Area—see Appendix B for areas included; Figures are based on an analysis of 1990, 2000, and 2010 Census Decennial Census tract data by William H. Frey, Brookings Institution and the University of Michigan Social Science Data Analysis Network. In this analysis all racial groups (whites, blacks, and asians) are non-Hispanic members of those races. Hispanics are shown as a separate category;
(1) Segregation Indices are Dissimilarity Indices that measure the degree to which the minority group is distributed differently than whites across census tracts. They range from 0 (complete integration) to 100 (complete segregation) where the value indicates the percentage of the minority group that needs to move to be distributed exactly like whites; (2) Ranges from 1 (most segregated) to 102 (least segregated); n/a not available.
Source: www.CensusScope.org

Ancestry

Area	German	Irish	English	American	Italian	Polish	French[2]	Scottish	Dutch
City	10.6	5.4	23.1	4.6	2.7	0.5	2.6	4.4	1.6
MSA[1]	11.8	5.4	28.8	5.8	2.4	0.7	2.1	5.5	1.9
U.S.	14.9	10.8	8.0	7.4	5.5	3.0	2.7	1.7	1.4

Note: Figures are the percentage of the total population reporting a particular ancestry. The nine most commonly reported ancestries in the U.S. are shown. Figures include multiple ancestries (e.g. if a person reported being Irish and Italian, they were included in both columns); (1) Figures cover the Provo-Orem, UT Metropolitan Statistical Area—see Appendix B for areas included; (2) Excludes Basque
Source: U.S. Census Bureau, 2011-2013 American Community Survey 3-Year Estimates

Foreign-Born Population

Area	Percent of Population Born in								
	Any Foreign Country	Mexico	Asia	Europe	Carribean	South America	Central America[2]	Africa	Canada
City	n/a	n/a	n/a	n/a	n/a	n/a	n/a	n/a	n/a
MSA[1]	7.2	2.7	1.1	0.6	0.1	1.3	0.5	0.1	0.5
U.S.	13.0	3.7	3.8	1.5	1.2	0.9	1.0	0.6	0.3

Note: (1) Figures cover the Provo-Orem, UT Metropolitan Statistical Area—see Appendix B for areas included; (2) Excludes Mexico.
Source: U.S. Census Bureau, 2011-2013 American Community Survey 3-Year Estimates

Marital Status

Area	Never Married	Now Married[2]	Separated	Widowed	Divorced
City	46.9	44.6	0.8	2.2	5.5
MSA[1]	31.9	58.2	1.1	2.6	6.3
U.S.	32.7	48.1	2.2	6.0	11.0

Note: Figures are percentages and cover the population 15 years of age and older; (1) Figures cover the Provo-Orem, UT Metropolitan Statistical Area—see Appendix B for areas included; (2) Excludes separated
Source: U.S. Census Bureau, 2011-2013 American Community Survey 3-Year Estimates

Disability Status

Area	All Ages	Under 18 Years Old	18 to 64 Years Old	65 Years and Over
City	7.4	4.2	6.1	36.7
MSA[1]	7.2	2.9	6.6	34.7
U.S.	12.3	4.1	10.2	36.3

Note: Figures show percent of the civilian noninstitutionalized population that reported having a disability. Disability status is determined from from six types of difficulty: vision, hearing, cognitive, ambulatory, self-care, and independent living. For children under 5 years old, hearing and vision difficulty are used to determine disability status. For children between the ages of 5 and 14, disability status is determined from hearing, vision, cognitive, ambulatory, and self-care difficulties. For people aged 15 years and older, they are considered to have a disability if they have difficulty with any one of the six difficulty types; (1) Figures cover the Provo-Orem, UT Metropolitan Statistical Area—see Appendix B for areas included.
Source: U.S. Census Bureau, 2011-2013 American Community Survey 3-Year Estimates

Age

Area	Percent of Population									Median Age
	Under Age 5	Age 5–19	Age 20–34	Age 35–44	Age 45–54	Age 55–64	Age 65–74	Age 75–84	Age 85+	
City	8.7	22.6	44.7	7.5	5.4	5.2	2.7	1.9	1.1	23.6
MSA[1]	10.7	28.7	27.4	11.6	8.3	6.5	3.9	2.2	0.8	24.5
U.S.	6.4	19.9	20.7	12.9	14.1	12.3	7.6	4.2	1.9	37.4

Note: (1) Figures cover the Provo-Orem, UT Metropolitan Statistical Area—see Appendix B for areas included
Source: U.S. Census Bureau, 2011-2013 American Community Survey 3-Year Estimates

Gender

Area	Males	Females	Males per 100 Females
City	57,216	58,211	98.3
MSA[1]	277,155	273,824	101.2
U.S.	154,451,010	159,410,713	96.9

Note: (1) Figures cover the Provo-Orem, UT Metropolitan Statistical Area—see Appendix B for areas included
Source: U.S. Census Bureau, 2011-2013 American Community Survey 3-Year Estimates

Religious Groups by Family

Area	Catholic	Baptist	Non-Den.	Methodist[2]	Lutheran	LDS[3]	Pente-costal	Presby-terian[4]	Muslim[5]	Judaism
MSA[1]	1.3	0.1	0.1	0.2	<0.1	88.6	0.1	0.1	<0.1	<0.1
U.S.	19.1	9.3	4.0	4.0	2.3	2.0	1.9	1.6	0.8	0.7

Note: Figures are the number of adherents as a percentage of the total population; (1) Figures cover the Provo-Orem, UT Metropolitan Statistical Area—see Appendix B for areas included; (2) Methodist/Pietist; (3) Latter Day Saints; (4) Reformed; (5) Figures are estimates
Source: Association of Statisticians of American Religious Bodies, 2010 U.S. Religion Census: Religious Congregations & Membership Study

Religious Groups by Tradition

Area	Catholic	Evangelical Protestant	Mainline Protestant	Other Tradition	Black Protestant	Orthodox
MSA[1]	1.3	0.5	0.1	88.9	<0.1	<0.1
U.S.	19.1	16.2	7.3	4.3	1.6	0.3

Note: Figures are the number of adherents as a percentage of the total population; (1) Figures cover the Provo-Orem, UT Metropolitan Statistical Area—see Appendix B for areas included
Source: Association of Statisticians of American Religious Bodies, 2010 U.S. Religion Census: Religious Congregations & Membership Study

ECONOMY

Gross Metropolitan Product

Area	2012	2013	2014	2015	Rank[2]
MSA[1]	17.0	17.8	18.7	19.9	120

Note: Figures are in billions of dollars; (1) Figures cover the Provo-Orem, UT Metropolitan Statistical Area—see Appendix B for areas included; (2) Rank is based on 2015 data and ranges from 1 to 363
Source: The U.S. Conference of Mayors, U.S. Metro Economies: GMP and Employment 2013-2015, June 2014

Economic Growth

Area	2010-12 (%)	2013 (%)	2014 (%)	2015 (%)	Rank[2]
MSA[1]	4.1	3.7	3.4	4.6	10
U.S.	2.1	2.0	2.3	3.2	–

Note: Figures are real gross metropolitan product (GMP) growth rates and represent annual average percent change; (1) Figures cover the Provo-Orem, UT Metropolitan Statistical Area—see Appendix B for areas included; (2) Rank is based on 2015 data and ranges from 1 to 363
Source: The U.S. Conference of Mayors, U.S. Metro Economies: GMP and Employment 2013-2015, June 2014

Metropolitan Area Exports

Area	2008	2009	2010	2011	2012	2013	Rank[2]
MSA[1]	2,218.0	1,772.8	2,024.6	2,056.4	2,058.1	2,789.2	83

Note: Figures are in millions of dollars; (1) Figures cover the Provo-Orem, UT Metropolitan Statistical Area—see Appendix B for areas included; (2) Rank is based on 2013 data and ranges from 1 to 387
Source: U.S. Department of Commerce, International Trade Administration, Office of Trade & Industry Information, Manufacturing & Services, data extracted April 3, 2015

Building Permits

Area	Single-Family			Multi-Family			Total		
	2013	2014	Pct. Chg.	2013	2014	Pct. Chg.	2013	2014	Pct. Chg.
City	136	128	-5.9	51	163	219.6	187	291	55.6
MSA[1]	2,675	2,679	0.1	748	2,616	249.7	3,423	5,295	54.7
U.S.	620,802	634,597	2.2	370,020	411,766	11.3	990,822	1,046,363	5.6

Note: (1) Figures cover the Provo-Orem, UT Metropolitan Statistical Area—see Appendix B for areas included; Figures represent new, privately-owned housing units authorized (unadjusted data); All permit data are based on estimates with imputation.
Source: U.S. Census Bureau, Manufacturing, Mining, and Construction Statistics, Building Permits, 2013, 2014

Bankruptcy Filings

Area	Business Filings			Nonbusiness Filings		
	2013	2014	% Chg.	2013	2014	% Chg.
Utah County	57	43	-24.6	2,083	2,003	-3.8
U.S.	33,212	26,983	-18.8	1,038,720	909,812	-12.4

Note: Business filings include Chapter 7, Chapter 11, Chapter 12, and Chapter 13; Nonbusiness filings include Chapter 7, Chapter 11, and Chapter 13
Source: Administrative Office of the U.S. Courts, Business and Nonbusiness Bankruptcy, County Cases Commenced by Chapter of the Bankruptcy Code, During the 12- Month Period Ending December 31, 2013 and Business and Nonbusiness Bankruptcy, County Cases Commenced by Chapter of the Bankruptcy Code, During the 12- Month Period Ending December 31, 2014

Housing Vacancy Rates

Area	Gross Vacancy Rate[2] (%)			Year-Round Vacancy Rate[3] (%)			Rental Vacancy Rate[4] (%)			Homeowner Vacancy Rate[5] (%)		
	2012	2013	2014	2012	2013	2014	2012	2013	2014	2012	2013	2014
MSA[1]	n/a	n/a	n/a	n/a	n/a	n/a	n/a	n/a	n/a	n/a	n/a	n/a
U.S.	13.8	13.6	13.4	10.8	10.7	10.4	8.7	8.3	7.6	2.0	2.0	1.9

Note: (1) Figures cover the Provo-Orem, UT Metropolitan Statistical Area—see Appendix B for areas included; (2) The percentage of the total housing inventory that is vacant; (3) The percentage of the housing inventory (excluding seasonal units) that is year-round vacant; (4) The percentage of rental inventory that is vacant for rent; (5) The percentage of homeowner inventory that is vacant for sale; n/a not available
Source: U.S. Census Bureau, Housing Vacancies and Homeownership Annual Statistics: 2014

INCOME

Income

Area	Per Capita ($)	Median Household ($)	Average Household ($)
City	16,496	38,542	55,455
MSA[1]	20,470	60,215	73,641
U.S.	27,884	52,176	72,897

Note: (1) Figures cover the Provo-Orem, UT Metropolitan Statistical Area—see Appendix B for areas included
Source: U.S. Census Bureau, 2011-2013 American Community Survey 3-Year Estimates

Household Income Distribution

Area	Percent of Households Earning							
	Under $15,000	$15,000 -24,999	$25,000 -34,999	$35,000 -49,999	$50,000 -74,999	$75,000 -99,000	$100,000 -149,999	$150,000 and up
City	18.8	13.8	13.3	15.6	16.9	9.8	7.2	4.6
MSA[1]	9.4	8.4	9.0	14.5	21.6	15.0	14.5	7.8
U.S.	13.0	10.9	10.3	13.6	17.9	11.9	12.7	9.6

Note: (1) Figures cover the Provo-Orem, UT Metropolitan Statistical Area—see Appendix B for areas included
Source: U.S. Census Bureau, 2011-2013 American Community Survey 3-Year Estimates

Poverty Rate

Area	All Ages	Under 18 Years Old	18 to 64 Years Old	65 Years and Over
City	31.7	29.4	34.6	7.8
MSA[1]	14.1	12.9	15.8	5.5
U.S.	15.9	22.4	14.8	9.5

Note: Figures are percentage of people whose income during the past 12 months was below the poverty level;
(1) Figures cover the Provo-Orem, UT Metropolitan Statistical Area—see Appendix B for areas included
Source: U.S. Census Bureau, 2011-2013 American Community Survey 3-Year Estimates

EMPLOYMENT

Labor Force and Employment

Area	Civilian Labor Force			Workers Employed		
	Dec. 2013	Dec. 2014	% Chg.	Dec. 2013	Dec. 2014	% Chg.
City	61,667	63,496	3.0	59,690	61,968	3.8
MSA[1]	257,646	265,249	3.0	248,594	258,088	3.8
U.S.	154,408,000	155,521,000	0.7	144,423,000	147,190,000	1.9

Note: Data is not seasonally adjusted and covers workers 16 years of age and older; (1) Figures cover the
Provo-Orem, UT Metropolitan Statistical Area—see Appendix B for areas included
Source: Bureau of Labor Statistics, Local Area Unemployment Statistics

Unemployment Rate

Area	2014											
	Jan.	Feb.	Mar.	Apr.	May	Jun.	Jul.	Aug.	Sep.	Oct.	Nov.	Dec.
City	3.8	3.9	3.5	2.9	3.3	4.1	3.7	3.6	3.1	3.0	2.5	2.4
MSA[1]	4.1	4.2	3.9	3.2	3.4	4.0	3.8	3.7	3.2	3.1	2.7	2.7
U.S.	7.0	7.0	6.8	5.9	6.1	6.3	6.5	6.3	5.7	5.5	5.5	5.4

Note: Data is not seasonally adjusted and covers workers 16 years of age and older; (1) Figures cover the
Provo-Orem, UT Metropolitan Statistical Area—see Appendix B for areas included
Source: Bureau of Labor Statistics, Local Area Unemployment Statistics

Employment by Occupation

Occupation Classification	City (%)	MSA[1] (%)	U.S. (%)
Management, Business, Science, and Arts	40.4	39.9	36.2
Natural Resources, Construction, and Maintenance	5.4	7.5	9.0
Production, Transportation, and Material Moving	8.0	10.0	12.1
Sales and Office	26.5	26.5	24.4
Service	19.7	16.2	18.3

Note: Figures cover employed civilians 16 years of age and older; (1) Figures cover the Provo-Orem, UT
Metropolitan Statistical Area—see Appendix B for areas included
Source: U.S. Census Bureau, 2011-2013 American Community Survey 3-Year Estimates

Employment by Industry

Sector	MSA[1]		U.S.
	Number of Employees	Percent of Total	Percent of Total
Construction, Mining, and Logging	16,700	7.6	5.0
Education and Health Services	48,400	21.9	15.5
Financial Activities	6,800	3.1	5.7
Government	30,300	13.7	15.8
Information	10,200	4.6	2.0
Leisure and Hospitality	17,900	8.1	10.3
Manufacturing	18,800	8.5	8.7
Other Services	4,800	2.2	4.0
Professional and Business Services	29,600	13.4	13.8
Retail Trade	27,900	12.6	11.4
Transportation, Warehousing, and Utilities	3,300	1.5	3.9
Wholesale Trade	6,400	2.9	4.2

Note: Figures are non-farm employment as of December 2014. Figures are not seasonally adjusted and include
workers 16 years of age and older; (1) Figures cover the Provo-Orem, UT Metropolitan Statistical Area—see
Appendix B for areas included; n/a not available
Source: Bureau of Labor Statistics, Current Employment Statistics, Employment, Hours, and Earnings

Occupations with Greatest Projected Employment Growth: 2012 – 2022

Occupation[1]	2012 Employment	2022 Projected Employment	Numeric Employment Change	Percent Employment Change
Customer Service Representatives	38,930	51,740	12,810	32.9
Combined Food Preparation and Serving Workers, Including Fast Food	30,260	39,290	9,030	29.8
Retail Salespersons	43,320	52,130	8,810	20.3
Secretaries and Administrative Assistants, Except Legal, Medical, and Executive	22,760	29,380	6,620	29.1
Registered Nurses	19,160	25,160	6,000	31.4
General and Operations Managers	22,950	28,680	5,730	25.0
Office Clerks, General	26,700	31,850	5,150	19.3
Heavy and Tractor-Trailer Truck Drivers	21,170	26,300	5,130	24.2
Laborers and Freight, Stock, and Material Movers, Hand	17,700	22,700	5,000	28.3
Construction Laborers	13,470	17,950	4,480	33.2

Note: Projections cover Utah; (1) Sorted by numeric employment change
Source: www.projectionscentral.com, State Occupational Projections, 2012–2022 Long-Term Projections

Fastest Growing Occupations: 2012 – 2022

Occupation[1]	2012 Employment	2022 Projected Employment	Numeric Employment Change	Percent Employment Change
Aircraft Structure, Surfaces, Rigging, and Systems Assemblers	340	670	330	95.3
Helpers—Electricians	660	1,190	530	80.6
Helpers—Brickmasons, Blockmasons, Stonemasons, and Tile and Marble Setters	560	990	430	77.3
Brickmasons and Blockmasons	1,010	1,730	720	70.6
Biomedical Engineers	440	730	290	67.3
Painters, Transportation Equipment	310	510	200	65.9
Health Specialties Teachers, Postsecondary	2,220	3,670	1,450	65.0
Interpreters and Translators	590	940	350	59.5
Credit Counselors	610	970	360	58.8
Skincare Specialists	470	740	270	56.8

Note: Projections cover Utah; (1) Sorted by percent employment change and excludes occupations with numeric employment change less than 100
Source: www.projectionscentral.com, State Occupational Projections, 2012–2022 Long-Term Projections

Average Wages

Occupation	$/Hr.	Occupation	$/Hr.
Accountants and Auditors	31.81	Maids and Housekeeping Cleaners	9.40
Automotive Mechanics	16.78	Maintenance and Repair Workers	16.71
Bookkeepers	16.74	Marketing Managers	56.40
Carpenters	18.13	Nuclear Medicine Technologists	n/a
Cashiers	9.40	Nurses, Licensed Practical	19.71
Clerks, General Office	12.53	Nurses, Registered	27.91
Clerks, Receptionists/Information	12.05	Nursing Assistants	11.36
Clerks, Shipping/Receiving	12.56	Packers and Packagers, Hand	10.80
Computer Programmers	36.64	Physical Therapists	35.82
Computer Systems Analysts	37.74	Postal Service Mail Carriers	24.99
Computer User Support Specialists	19.41	Real Estate Brokers	n/a
Cooks, Restaurant	10.58	Retail Salespersons	12.25
Dentists	55.54	Sales Reps., Exc. Tech./Scientific	32.49
Electrical Engineers	39.85	Sales Reps., Tech./Scientific	38.50
Electricians	22.83	Secretaries, Exc. Legal/Med./Exec.	14.58
Financial Managers	54.02	Security Guards	14.09
First-Line Supervisors/Managers, Sales	18.10	Surgeons	100.95
Food Preparation Workers	9.39	Teacher Assistants	11.30
General and Operations Managers	40.93	Teachers, Elementary School	26.80
Hairdressers/Cosmetologists	12.66	Teachers, Secondary School	29.00
Internists	n/a	Telemarketers	12.88
Janitors and Cleaners	9.91	Truck Drivers, Heavy/Tractor-Trailer	23.28
Landscaping/Groundskeeping Workers	11.47	Truck Drivers, Light/Delivery Svcs.	13.67
Lawyers	57.38	Waiters and Waitresses	10.89

Note: Wage data covers the Provo-Orem, UT Metropolitan Statistical Area—see Appendix B for areas included; Hourly wages for elementary/secondary school teachers and teacher assistants were calculated by the editors from annual wage data assuming a 40 hour work week; n/a not available.
Source: Bureau of Labor Statistics, Metro Area Occupational Employment and Wage Estimates, May 2014

TAXES

State Corporate Income Tax Rates

State	Tax Rate (%)	Income Brackets ($)	Num. of Brackets	Financial Institution Tax Rate (%)[a]	Federal Income Tax Ded.
Utah	5.0 (c)	Flat rate	–	5.0 (c)	No

Note: Tax rates as of January 1, 2015; (a) Rates listed are the corporate income tax rate applied to financial institutions or excise taxes based on income. Some states have other taxes based upon the value of deposits or shares; (c) Minimum tax is $800 in California, $100 in District of Columbia, $50 in North Dakota (banks), $500 in Rhode Island, $200 per location in South Dakota (banks), $100 in Utah, $250 in Vermont.
Source: Federation of Tax Administrators, "State Corporate Income Tax Rates, 2015"

State Individual Income Tax Rates

State	Tax Rate (%)	Income Brackets ($)	Num. of Brackets	Personal Exempt. ($)[1]		Fed. Inc. Tax Ded.
				Single	Dependents	
Utah	5.0	Flat rate	1	(t)	(t)	No

Note: Tax rates as of January 1, 2015; Local- and county-level taxes are not included; n/a not applicable; (1) Married joint filers generally receive double the single exemption; (t) Utah provides a tax credit equal to 6% of the federal personal exemption amounts (and applicable standard deduction).
Source: Federation of Tax Administrators, "State Individual Income Tax Rates, 2015"

Various State and Local Tax Rates

State	State and Local Sales and Use (%)	State Sales and Use (%)	Gasoline[1] (¢/gal.)	Cigarette[2] ($/pack)	Spirits[3] ($/gal.)	Wine[4] ($/gal.)	Beer[5] ($/gal.)
Utah	6.75	5.95 (b)	24.5	1.70	12.18 (g)	(l)	0.41 (p)

*Note: All tax rates as of January 1, 2015; (1) The American Petroleum Institute has developed a methodology for determining the average tax rate on a gallon of fuel. Rates may include any of the following: excise taxes, environmental fees, storage tank fees, other fees or taxes, general sales tax, and local taxes. In states where gasoline is subject to the general sales tax, or where the fuel tax is based on the average sale price, the average rate determined by API is sensitive to changes in the price of gasoline. States that fully or partially apply general sales taxes to gasoline: CA, CO, GA, IL, IN, MI, NY; (2) The federal excise tax of $1.0066 per pack and local taxes are not included; (3) Rates are those applicable to off-premise sales of 40% alcohol by volume (a.b.v.) distilled spirits in 750ml containers. Local excise taxes are excluded; (4) Rates are those applicable to off-premise sales of 11% a.b.v. non-carbonated wine in 750ml containers; (5) Rates are those applicable to off-premise sales of 4.7% a.b.v. beer in 12 ounce containers; (b) Three states levy mandatory, statewide, local add-on sales taxes at the state level: California (1%), Utah (1.25%), and Virginia (1%). We include these in their state sales taxes; (g) States where the government controls sales. In these "control states," products are subject to ad valorem mark-up and excise taxes. The excise tax rate is calculated using a methodology developed by the Distilled Spirits Council of the United States; (l) Control states, where the government controls all sales. Products can be subject to ad valorem mark-up and excise taxes; (p) Local excise taxes are excluded.
Source: Tax Foundation, 2015 Facts & Figures: How Does Your State Compare?*

State Business Tax Climate Index Rankings

State	Overall Rank	Corporate Tax Index Rank	Individual Income Tax Index Rank	Sales Tax Index Rank	Unemployment Insurance Tax Index Rank	Property Tax Index Rank
Utah	9	5	12	19	22	4

*Note: The index is a measure of how each state's tax laws affect economic performance. The lower the rank, the more favorable a state's tax system is for business. States without a given tax are given a ranking of 1. The scores/rankings for the District of Columbia do not affect other states. The 2015 index represents the tax climate as of July 1, 2014.
Source: Tax Foundation, State Business Tax Climate Index 2015*

COMMERCIAL UTILITIES

Typical Monthly Electric Bills

Area	Commercial Service ($/month)		Industrial Service ($/month)	
	1,500 kWh	40 kW demand 14,000 kWh	1,000 kW demand 200,000 kWh	50,000 kW demand 32,500,000 kWh
City	n/a	n/a	n/a	n/a
Average[1]	201	1,653	26,124	2,639,743

*Note: Figures are based on annualized 2014 rates; (1) Average based on 180 utilities surveyed; n/a not available
Source: Edison Electric Institute, Typical Bills and Average Rates Report, Summer 2014*

TRANSPORTATION

Means of Transportation to Work

Area	Car/Truck/Van Drove Alone	Car/Truck/Van Car-pooled	Public Transportation Bus	Public Transportation Subway	Public Transportation Railroad	Bicycle	Walked	Other Means	Worked at Home
City	60.2	15.0	1.1	0.1	0.5	3.6	12.7	1.5	5.4
MSA[1]	72.4	13.5	1.2	0.2	0.3	1.3	4.2	1.1	6.0
U.S.	76.4	9.6	2.6	1.8	0.6	0.6	2.8	1.3	4.3

*Note: Figures are percentages and cover workers 16 years of age and older; (1) Figures cover the Provo-Orem, UT Metropolitan Statistical Area—see Appendix B for areas included
Source: U.S. Census Bureau, 2011-2013 American Community Survey 3-Year Estimates*

Travel Time to Work

Area	Less Than 10 Minutes	10 to 19 Minutes	20 to 29 Minutes	30 to 44 Minutes	45 to 59 Minutes	60 to 89 Minutes	90 Minutes or More
City	23.7	45.0	16.8	7.3	3.2	2.5	1.4
MSA[1]	18.2	35.2	21.0	14.6	6.0	3.5	1.5
U.S.	13.3	29.7	20.9	20.2	7.7	5.7	2.6

*Note: Figures are percentages and include workers 16 years old and over; (1) Figures cover the Provo-Orem, UT Metropolitan Statistical Area—see Appendix B for areas included
Source: U.S. Census Bureau, 2011-2013 American Community Survey 3-Year Estimates*

Travel Time Index

Area	1985	1990	1995	2000	2005	2010	2011
Urban Area[1]	1.03	1.03	1.05	1.07	1.09	1.14	1.14
Average[2]	1.09	1.14	1.16	1.19	1.23	1.18	1.18

Note: Travel Time Index—the ratio of travel time in the peak period to the travel time at free-flow conditions. For example, a value of 1.30 indicates a 20-minute free-flow trip takes 26 minutes in the peak. Free-flow speeds (60 mph on freeways and 35 mph on principal arterials) are used as the comparison threshold; (1) Covers the Provo-Orem UT urban area; (2) average of 498 urban areas
Source: Texas Transportation Institute, Urban Mobility Report 2012, December 2012

Public Transportation

Agency Name / Mode of Transportation	Vehicles Operated in Maximum Service	Annual Unlinked Passenger Trips (in thous.)	Annual Passenger Miles (in thous.)
Utah Transit Authority (UT)			
Bus (directly operated)	389	18,863.9	74,067.9
Bus (purchased transportation)	7	44.0	569.0
Commuter Bus (directly operated)	54	787.8	13,663.1
Commuter Rail (directly operated)	36	3,816.4	108,921.2
Demand Response (directly operated)	69	236.4	2,351.9
Demand Response (purchased transportation)	55	147.0	2,158.5
Light Rail (directly operated)	84	18,997.9	85,567.4
Vanpool (directly operated)	420	1,387.8	53,824.9

Source: Federal Transit Administration, National Transit Database, 2013

Air Transportation

Airport Name and Code / Type of Service	Passenger Airlines[1]	Passenger Enplanements	Freight Carriers[2]	Freight (lbs.)
Salt Lake City International (50 miles) (SLC)				
Domestic service (U.S. carriers - 2014)	29	9,938,384	21	175,955,786
International service (U.S. carriers - 2013)	8	183,850	4	879,386

Note: (1) Includes all U.S.-based major, minor and commuter airlines that carried at least one passenger during the year; (2) Includes all U.S.-based airlines and freight carriers that transported at least one lb. of freight during the year.
Source: Bureau of Transportation Statistics, The Intermodal Transportation Database, Air Carriers: T-100 Domestic Market (U.S. Carriers), 2014; Bureau of Transportation Statistics, The Intermodal Transportation Database, Air Carriers: T-100 International Market (U.S. Carriers), 2013

Other Transportation Statistics

Major Highways:	I-15
Amtrak Service:	Yes
Major Waterways/Ports:	None

Source: Amtrak.com; Google Maps

BUSINESSES

Major Business Headquarters

Company Name	Rankings	
	Fortune[1]	Forbes[2]
No companies listed	-	-

Note: (1) Fortune 500—companies that produce a 10-K are ranked 1 to 500 based on 2013 revenue; (2) all private companies with at least $2 billion in annual revenue through the end of their most current fiscal year are ranked 1 to 221; companies listed are headquartered in the city; dashes indicate no ranking
Source: Fortune, "Fortune 500," June 16, 2014; Forbes, "America's Largest Private Companies," November 5, 2014

Fast-Growing Businesses

According to *Inc.*, Provo is home to two of America's 500 fastest-growing private companies: **PcCareSupport** (#224); **Peak Capital Partners** (#408). Criteria: must be an independent, privately-held, for-profit, U.S. corporation, proprietorship or partnership; revenues must be at least $100,000 in 2010 and $2 million in 2013; must have four-year operating/sales history. Holding companies, regulated banks, and utilities were excluded. *Inc., "America's 500 Fastest-Growing Private Companies," September 2014*

According to *Fortune*, Provo is home to one of the 100 fastest-growing companies in the world: **Nu Skin Enterprises** (#68). Companies were ranked by their revenue growth rate; their EPS growth rate; and their three-year annualized total return to investors for the period ending June 30, 2014. Criteria for inclusion: a company, foreign or domestic, must trade on a major U.S. stock exchange; must file quarterly reports with the SEC; must have a minimum market capitalization of $250 million; must have a stock price of at least $5 on June 30, 2014; must have been trading continuously since June 30, 2010; must have revenue and net income for the four quarters ended on or before April 30, 2014, of at least $50 million and $10 million, respectively; and must have posted a compound annual growth in revenue and earnings per share of at least 20% annually over the three years ending on or before April 30, 2014. Real estate investment trusts, limited-liability companies, limited parterships, business development companies, closed end investment firms, and companies that lost money in the quarter ending April 30, 2014 were excluded. *Fortune, "100 Fastest-Growing Companies," August 28, 2014*

According to Deloitte, Provo is home to one of North America's 500 fastest-growing high-technology companies: **Ancestry.com** (#490). Companies are ranked by percentage growth in revenue over a five-year period. Criteria for inclusion: company must be headquartered within North America; must own proprietary intellectual property or proprietary technology that contributes to a significant portion of the company's operating revenue, or devote a significant proportion of revenues to research and development of technology; must have been in business for a minumum of five years with 2009 operating revenues of at least $50,000 USD/CD and 2013 operating revenues of at least $5 million USD/CD. *Deloitte Touche Tohmatsu, 2014 Technology Fast 500*[TM]

Minority- and Women-Owned Businesses

Group	All Firms		Firms with Paid Employees			
	Firms	Sales ($000)	Firms	Sales ($000)	Employees	Payroll ($000)
Asian	189	51,957	48	49,027	413	9,948
Black	(s)	(s)	(s)	(s)	(s)	(s)
Hispanic	414	24,262	27	15,576	148	2,668
Women	2,309	248,081	261	213,343	2,417	63,401
All Firms	8,505	7,588,728	2,162	7,349,176	69,888	2,113,241

Note: Figures cover firms located in the city; minority- and women-owned business are defined as firms in which the corresponding group own 51% or more of the stock or equity of the company; (s) estimates are suppressed when publication standards are not met
Source: U.S. Census Bureau, 2007 Economic Census, Survey of Business Owners (2012 Survey of Business Owners data will be released starting in June 2015)

HOTELS & CONVENTION CENTERS

Hotels/Motels

Area	5 Star		4 Star		3 Star		2 Star		1 Star		Not Rated	
	Num.	Pct.[3]	Num.	Pct.[3]	Num.	Pct.[3]	Num.	Pct.[3]	Num.	Pct.[3]	Num.	Pct.[3]
City[1]	0	0.0	1	1.2	24	28.6	54	64.3	1	1.2	4	4.8
Total[2]	166	0.9	1,264	7.0	5,718	31.8	9,340	52.0	411	2.3	1,070	6.0

Note: (1) Figures cover Provo and vicinity; (2) Figures cover all 100 cities in this book; (3) Percentage of hotels which have a given star rating; Star ratings are determined by expedia.com and offer an indication of the general quality of a particular hotel.
Source: expedia.com, April 2, 2015

Major Convention Centers

Name	Overall Space (sq. ft.)	Exhibit Space (sq. ft.)	Meeting Space (sq. ft.)	Meeting Rooms
Utah Valley Convention Center	83,578	19,620	9,979	10

Note: Table includes convention centers located in the Provo-Orem, UT metro area; n/a not available
Source: Original research

Living Environment

COST OF LIVING

Cost of Living Index

Composite Index	Groceries	Housing	Utilities	Trans-portation	Health Care	Misc. Goods/ Services
91.4	99.3	84.2	85.2	96.3	92.6	94.3

Note: The Cost of Living Index measures regional differences in the cost of consumer goods and services, excluding taxes and non-consumer expenditures, for professional and managerial households in the top income quintile. It is based on more than 50,000 prices covering almost 60 different items for which prices are collected three times a year by chambers of commerce, economic development organizations or university applied economic centers in each participating urban area. The numbers shown should be read as a percentage above or below the national average of 100. For example, a value of 115.4 in the groceries column indicates that grocery prices are 15.4% higher than the national average. Small differences in the index numbers should not be interpreted as significant; Figures cover the Provo-Orem UT urban area.
Source: The Council for Community and Economic Research, ACCRA Cost of Living Index, 2014

Grocery Prices

Area[1]	T-Bone Steak ($/pound)	Frying Chicken ($/pound)	Whole Milk ($/half gal.)	Eggs ($/dozen)	Orange Juice ($/64 oz.)	Coffee ($/11.5 oz.)
City[2]	9.56	1.47	2.13	1.65	3.30	5.31
Avg.	10.40	1.37	2.40	1.99	3.46	4.27
Min.	8.48	0.93	1.37	1.30	2.83	2.99
Max.	14.20	2.44	3.62	4.02	6.42	6.96

Note: (1) Values for the local area are compared with the average, minimum and maximum values for all 308 areas in the Cost of Living Index; (2) Figures cover the Provo-Orem UT urban area; **T-Bone Steak** *(price per pound);* **Frying Chicken** *(price per pound, whole fryer);* **Whole Milk** *(half gallon carton);* **Eggs** *(price per dozen, Grade A, large);* **Orange Juice** *(64 oz. Tropicana or Florida Natural);* **Coffee** *(11.5 oz. can, vacuum-packed, Maxwell House, Hills Bros, or Folgers).*
Source: The Council for Community and Economic Research, ACCRA Cost of Living Index, 2014

Housing and Utility Costs

Area[1]	New Home Price ($)	Apartment Rent ($/month)	All Electric ($/month)	Part Electric ($/month)	Other Energy ($/month)	Telephone ($/month)
City[2]	260,061	783	-	65.05	74.80	24.80
Avg.	305,838	919	181.00	93.66	73.14	27.95
Min.	183,142	480	112.00	42.06	23.42	17.16
Max.	1,358,576	3,851	594.00	180.03	440.99	40.42

Note: (1) Values for the local area are compared with the average, minimum and maximum values for all 308 areas in the Cost of Living Index; (2) Figures cover the Provo-Orem UT urban area; **New Home Price** *(2,400 sf living area, 8,000 sf lot, in urban area with full utilities);* **Apartment Rent** *(950 sf 2 bedroom/1.5 or 2 bath, unfurnished, excluding all utilities except water);* **All Electric** *(average monthly cost for an all-electric home);* **Part Electric** *(average monthly cost for a part-electric home);* **Other Energy** *(average monthly cost for natural gas, fuel oil, coal, wood, and any other forms of energy except electricity);* **Telephone** *(price includes basic monthly rate for a private residential line plus additional local usage charges incurred by a family of four).*
Source: The Council for Community and Economic Research, ACCRA Cost of Living Index, 2014

Health Care, Transportation, and Other Costs

Area[1]	Doctor ($/visit)	Dentist ($/visit)	Optometrist ($/visit)	Gasoline ($/gallon)	Beauty Salon ($/visit)	Men's Shirt ($)
City[2]	98.95	75.26	89.10	3.13	30.99	20.62
Avg.	102.86	87.89	97.66	3.44	34.37	26.74
Min.	67.47	65.78	51.18	3.00	17.43	12.79
Max.	173.50	150.14	235.00	4.33	64.28	49.50

Note: (1) Values for the local area are compared with the average, minimum and maximum values for all 308 areas in the Cost of Living Index; (2) Figures cover the Provo-Orem UT urban area; **Doctor** *(general practitioners routine exam of an established patient);* **Dentist** *(adult teeth cleaning and periodic oral examination);* **Optometrist** *(full vision eye exam for established adult patient);* **Gasoline** *(one gallon regular unleaded, national brand, including all taxes, cash price at self-service pump if available);* **Beauty Salon** *(woman's shampoo, trim, and blow-dry);* **Men's Shirt** *(cotton/polyester dress shirt, pinpoint weave, long sleeves).*
Source: The Council for Community and Economic Research, ACCRA Cost of Living Index, 2014

HOUSING

House Price Index (HPI)

Area	National Ranking[2]	Quarterly Change (%)	One-Year Change (%)	Five-Year Change (%)
MSA[1]	95	2.06	5.66	12.34
U.S.[3]	–	1.35	4.91	11.59

Note: The HPI is a weighted repeat sales index. It measures average price changes in repeat sales or refinancings on the same properties. This information is obtained by reviewing repeat mortgage transactions on single-family properties whose mortgages have been purchased or securitized by Fannie Mae or Freddie Mac in January 1975; (1) Provo-Orem Metropolitan Statistical Area—see Appendix B for areas included; (2) Rankings are based on annual percentage change for all metro areas containing at least 15,000 transactions over the last 10 years and ranges from 1 to 275; (3) figures based on a weighted average of Census Division estimates using a seasonally adjusted, purchase-only index; all figures are for the period ending December 31, 2014
Source: Federal Housing Finance Agency, House Price Index, February 26, 2015

Median Single-Family Home Prices

Area	2012	2013	2014p	Percent Change 2013 to 2014
MSA[1]	n/a	n/a	n/a	n/a
U.S. Average	177.2	197.4	209.0	5.9

Note: Figures are median sales prices of existing single-family homes in thousands of dollars; (p) preliminary; n/a not available; (1) Provo-Orem, UT Metropolitan Statistical Area—see Appendix B for areas included
Source: National Association of Realtors, Median Sales Price of Existing Single-Family Homes for Metropolitan Areas, 4th Quarter 2014

Qualifying Income Based on Median Sales Price of Existing Single-Family Homes

Area	With 5% Down ($)	With 10% Down ($)	With 20% Down ($)
MSA[1]	n/a	n/a	n/a
U.S. Average	45,863	43,449	38,621

Note: Figures are preliminary; Qualifying income is based on a mortgage rate of 4.0%. Monthly principal and interest payment is limited to 25% of income; n/a not available; (1) Provo-Orem, UT Metropolitan Statistical Area—see Appendix B for areas included
Source: National Association of Realtors, Qualifying Income Based on Median Sales Price of Existing Single-Family Homes for Metropolitan Areas, 4th Quarter 2014

Median Apartment Condo-Coop Home Prices

Area	2012	2013	2014p	Percent Change 2013 to 2014
MSA[1]	n/a	n/a	n/a	n/a
U.S. Average	173.7	194.9	205.1	5.2

Note: Figures are median sales prices of existing apartment condo-coop homes in thousands of dollars; (p) preliminary; n/a not available; (1) Provo-Orem, UT Metropolitan Statistical Area—see Appendix B for areas included
Source: National Association of Realtors, Median Sales Price of Existing Apartment Condo-Coop Homes for Metropolitan Areas, 4th Quarter 2014

Gross Monthly Rent

Area	Under $200	$200 -299	$300 -499	$500 -749	$750 -999	$1,000 -1,499	$1,500 and up	Median ($)
City	1.8	3.0	12.0	37.4	22.0	19.1	4.8	723
MSA[1]	1.0	1.6	6.9	26.7	25.5	27.6	10.7	864
U.S.	1.7	3.2	7.8	22.1	24.3	26.0	14.9	900

Note: Figures are percentages except for Median; Gross rent is the contract rent plus the estimated average monthly cost of utilities (electricity, gas, and water and sewer) and fuels (oil, coal, kerosene, wood, etc.) if these are paid by the renter (or paid for the renter by someone else); (1) Figures cover the Provo-Orem, UT Metropolitan Statistical Area—see Appendix B for areas included
Source: U.S. Census Bureau, 2011-2013 American Community Survey 3-Year Estimates

Homeownership Rate

Area	2007 (%)	2008 (%)	2009 (%)	2010 (%)	2011 (%)	2012 (%)	2013 (%)	2014 (%)
MSA[1]	n/a	n/a	n/a	n/a	n/a	n/a	n/a	n/a
U.S.	68.1	67.8	67.4	66.9	66.1	65.4	65.1	64.5

Note: (1) Figures cover the Provo-Orem, UT Metropolitan Statistical Area—see Appendix B for areas included; n/a not available
Source: U.S. Census Bureau, Housing Vacancies and Homeownership Annual Statistics: 2014

Year Housing Structure Built

Area	2010 or Later	2000 -2009	1990 -1999	1980 -1989	1970 -1979	1960 -1969	1950 -1959	1940 -1949	Before 1940	Median Year
City	0.6	13.4	19.4	13.2	19.6	10.5	8.5	5.9	9.0	1978
MSA[1]	2.1	30.2	21.1	9.4	16.1	5.4	6.2	3.6	5.9	1992
U.S.	0.9	15.0	13.9	13.8	15.8	11.0	10.9	5.4	13.3	1976

Note: Figures are percentages except for Median Year; (1) Figures cover the Provo-Orem, UT Metropolitan Statistical Area—see Appendix B for areas included
Source: U.S. Census Bureau, 2011-2013 American Community Survey 3-Year Estimates

HEALTH

Health Risk Data

Category	MSA[1] (%)	U.S. (%)
Adults aged 18–64 who have any kind of health care coverage	79.5	79.6
Adults who reported being in good or excellent health	88.6	83.1
Adults who are current smokers	5.1	19.6
Adults who are heavy drinkers[2]	2.0	6.1
Adults who are binge drinkers[3]	6.2	16.9
Adults who are overweight (BMI 25.0 - 29.9)	31.5	35.8
Adults who are obese (BMI 30.0 - 99.8)	22.4	27.6
Adults who participated in any physical activities in the past month	85.5	77.1
Adults 50+ who have ever had a sigmoidoscopy or colonoscopy	71.4	67.3
Women aged 40+ who have had a mammogram within the past two years	65.2	74.0
Men aged 40+ who have had a PSA test within the past two years	34.3	45.2
Adults aged 65+ who have had flu shot within the past year	51.1	60.1
Adults who always wear a seatbelt	92.0	93.8

Note: Data as of 2012 unless otherwise noted; (1) Figures cover the Provo-Orem, UT Metropolitan Statistical Area—see Appendix B for areas included; (2) Heavy drinkers are classified as males having more than two drinks per day or females having more than one drink per day; (3) Binge drinkers are classified as males having five or more drinks on one occasion or females having four or more drinks on one occasion
Source: Centers for Disease Control and Prevention, Behaviorial Risk Factor Surveillance System, SMART: Selected Metropolitan/Micropolitan Area Risk Trends, 2012 (Note: the CDC has discontinued this dataset but will be releasing a replacement in late 2015)

Chronic Health Indicators

Category	MSA[1] (%)	U.S. (%)
Adults who have ever been told they had a heart attack	1.9	4.5
Adults who have ever been told they had a stroke	1.6	2.9
Adults who have been told they currently have asthma	8.0	8.9
Adults who have ever been told they have arthritis	17.2	25.7
Adults who have ever been told they have diabetes[2]	5.0	9.7
Adults who have ever been told they had skin cancer	5.2	5.7
Adults who have ever been told they had any other types of cancer	3.9	6.5
Adults who have ever been told they have COPD	3.3	6.2
Adults who have ever been told they have kidney disease	2.5	2.5
Adults who have ever been told they have a form of depression	19.1	18.0

Note: Data as of 2012 unless otherwise noted; (1) Figures cover the Provo-Orem, UT Metropolitan Statistical Area—see Appendix B for areas included; (2) Figures do not include pregnancy-related, borderline, or pre-diabetes
Source: Centers for Disease Control and Prevention, Behaviorial Risk Factor Surveillance System, SMART: Selected Metropolitan/Micropolitan Area Risk Trends, 2012 (Note: the CDC has discontinued this dataset but will be releasing a replacement in late 2015)

Mortality Rates for the Top 10 Causes of Death in the U.S.

ICD-10[a] Sub-Chapter	ICD-10[a] Code	Age-Adjusted Mortality Rate[1] per 100,000 population	
		County[2]	U.S.
Malignant neoplasms	C00-C97	120.0	166.2
Ischaemic heart diseases	I20-I25	67.2	105.7
Other forms of heart disease	I30-I51	74.4	49.3
Chronic lower respiratory diseases	J40-J47	20.3	42.1
Organic, including symptomatic, mental disorders	F01-F09	41.2	38.1
Cerebrovascular diseases	I60-I69	46.7	37.0
Other external causes of accidental injury	W00-X59	29.1	26.9
Other degenerative diseases of the nervous system	G30-G31	22.3	25.6
Diabetes mellitus	E10-E14	25.1	21.3
Hypertensive diseases	I10-I15	10.6	19.4

Note: (a) ICD-10 = International Classification of Diseases 10th Revision; (1) Mortality rates are a three year average covering 2011-2013; (2) Figures cover Utah County
Source: Centers for Disease Control and Prevention, National Center for Health Statistics. Compressed Mortality File 1999-2013 on CDC WONDER Online Database, released October 2014. Data are compiled from the Compressed Mortality File 1999-2013, Series 20 No. 2S, 2014.

Mortality Rates for Selected Causes of Death

ICD-10[a] Sub-Chapter	ICD-10[a] Code	Age-Adjusted Mortality Rate[1] per 100,000 population	
		County[2]	U.S.
Assault	X85-Y09	*1.2	5.2
Diseases of the liver	K70-K76	10.3	13.2
Human immunodeficiency virus (HIV) disease	B20-B24	Suppressed	2.2
Influenza and pneumonia	J09-J18	15.5	15.4
Intentional self-harm	X60-X84	16.8	12.5
Malnutrition	E40-E46	2.4	0.9
Obesity and other hyperalimentation	E65-E68	3.2	1.8
Renal failure	N17-N19	17.7	13.1
Transport accidents	V01-V99	7.5	11.7
Viral hepatitis	B15-B19	*0.9	2.2

Note: (a) ICD-10 = International Classification of Diseases 10th Revision; (1) Mortality rates are a three year average covering 2011-2013; (2) Figures cover Utah County; (*) Unreliable data as per CDC
Source: Centers for Disease Control and Prevention, National Center for Health Statistics. Compressed Mortality File 1999-2013 on CDC WONDER Online Database, released October 2014. Data are compiled from the Compressed Mortality File 1999-2013, Series 20 No. 2S, 2014.

Health Insurance Coverage

Area	With Health Insurance	With Private Health Insurance	With Public Health Insurance	Without Health Insurance	Population Under Age 18 Without Health Insurance
City	83.8	72.6	18.6	16.2	13.1
MSA[1]	86.7	76.5	17.6	13.3	9.1
U.S.	85.2	65.2	31.0	14.8	7.3

Note: Figures are percentages that cover the civilian noninstitutionalized population; (1) Figures cover the Provo-Orem, UT Metropolitan Statistical Area—see Appendix B for areas included
Source: U.S. Census Bureau, 2011-2013 American Community Survey 3-Year Estimates

Number of Medical Professionals

Area[1]	MDs[2]	DOs[2,3]	Dentists	Podiatrists	Chiropractors	Optometrists
Local (number)	651	79	350	19	130	53
Local (rate[4])	120.6	14.6	63.4	3.4	23.6	9.6
U.S. (rate[4])	270.0	20.2	63.1	5.7	25.2	14.9

Note: Data as of 2013 unless noted; (1) Local data covers Utah County; (2) Data as of 2012 and includes all active, non-federal physicians; (3) Doctor of Osteopathic Medicine; (4) rate per 100,000 population
Source: U.S. Department of Health and Human Services, Health Resources and Services Administration, Bureau of Health Professions, Area Resource File (ARF) 2013-2014

EDUCATION

Public School District Statistics

District Name	Schls	Pupils	Pupil/ Teacher Ratio	Minority Pupils[1] (%)	Free Lunch Eligible[2] (%)	IEP[3] (%)
Provo District	24	14,553	22.8	34.8	52.9	16.2

Note: Table includes school districts with 2,000 or more students; (1) Percentage of students that are not non-Hispanic white; (2) Percentage of students that are eligible for the free lunch program; (3) Percentage of students that have an Individualized Education Program.
Source: U.S. Department of Education, National Center for Education Statistics, Common Core of Data, Local Education Agency (School District) Universe Survey: School Year 2012-2013; U.S. Department of Education, National Center for Education Statistics, Common Core of Data, Public Elementary/Secondary School Universe Survey: School Year 2012-2013

Highest Level of Education

Area	Less than H.S.	H.S. Diploma	Some College, No Deg.	Associate Degree	Bachelor's Degree	Master's Degree	Prof. School Degree	Doctorate Degree
City	10.2	13.1	29.7	8.3	26.4	8.3	1.5	2.6
MSA[1]	6.9	17.3	28.9	10.6	25.1	7.8	1.4	2.0
U.S.	13.7	28.0	21.2	7.9	18.2	7.7	1.9	1.3

Note: Figures cover persons age 25 and over; (1) Figures cover the Provo-Orem, UT Metropolitan Statistical Area—see Appendix B for areas included
Source: U.S. Census Bureau, 2011-2013 American Community Survey 3-Year Estimates

Educational Attainment by Race

Area	High School Graduate or Higher (%)					Bachelor's Degree or Higher (%)				
	Total	White	Black	Asian	Hisp.[2]	Total	White	Black	Asian	Hisp.[2]
City	89.8	91.6	n/a	86.3	66.3	38.8	39.9	n/a	52.7	17.0
MSA[1]	93.1	94.0	81.2	91.4	69.7	36.3	36.8	40.6	57.7	17.7
U.S.	86.3	88.3	83.1	85.7	64.0	29.1	30.4	18.8	50.7	13.7

Note: Figures shown cover persons 25 years old and over; (1) Figures cover the Provo-Orem, UT Metropolitan Statistical Area—see Appendix B for areas included; (2) People of Hispanic origin can be of any race
Source: U.S. Census Bureau, 2011-2013 American Community Survey 3-Year Estimates

School Enrollment by Grade and Control

Area	Preschool (%)		Kindergarten (%)		Grades 1 - 4 (%)		Grades 5 - 8 (%)		Grades 9 - 12 (%)	
	Public	Private	Public	Private	Public	Private	Public	Private	Public	Private
City	41.2	58.8	91.5	8.5	97.1	2.9	93.0	7.0	91.6	8.4
MSA[1]	41.4	58.6	91.6	8.4	95.2	4.8	95.1	4.9	95.7	4.3
U.S.	57.7	42.3	87.9	12.1	89.9	10.1	90.0	10.0	90.7	9.3

Note: Figures shown cover persons 3 years old and over; (1) Figures cover the Provo-Orem, UT Metropolitan Statistical Area—see Appendix B for areas included
Source: U.S. Census Bureau, 2011-2013 American Community Survey 3-Year Estimates

Average Salaries of Public School Classroom Teachers

Area	2013-14		2014-15		Percent Change 2013-14 to 2014-15	Percent Change 2004-05 to 2014-15
	Dollars	Rank[1]	Dollars	Rank[1]		
UTAH	45,695	44	45,848	45	0.33	16.2
U.S. Average	56,610	–	57,379	–	1.36	20.8

Note: (1) State rank ranges from 1 to 51 where 1 indicates highest salary.
Source: National Education Association, Rankings & Estimates: Rankings of the States 2014 and Estimates of School Statistics 2015, March 2015

Higher Education

Four-Year Colleges			Two-Year Colleges			Medical Schools[1]	Law Schools[2]	Voc/ Tech[3]
Public	Private Non-profit	Private For-profit	Public	Private Non-profit	Private For-profit			
0	1	1	0	0	3	0	1	4

Note: Figures cover institutions located within the city limits and include main campuses only; (1) includes schools accredited by the Liaison Committee on Medical Education and the American Osteopathic Association's Commission on Osteopathic College Accreditation; (2) includes ABA-accredited schools, schools with provisional ABA accreditation, and state accredited schools; (3) includes all schools with programs that are less than 2 years.

Source: National Center for Education Statistics, Integrated Postsecondary Education System (IPEDS), 2013-14; Association of American Medical Colleges, Member List, May 1, 2015; American Osteopathic Association, Member List, May 1, 2015; Law School Admission Council, Official Guide to ABA-Approved Law Schools Online, May 1, 2015; Wikipedia, List of Medical Schools in the United States, May 1, 2015; Wikipedia, List of Law Schools in the United States, May 1, 2015

According to *U.S. News & World Report,* the Provo-Orem, UT metro area is home to one of the best national universities in the U.S.: **Brigham Young University-Provo** (#62). The indicators used to capture academic quality fall into a number of categories: assessment by administrators at peer institutions; retention of students; faculty resources; student selectivity; financial resources; alumni giving; high school counselor ratings of colleges; and graduation rate. *U.S. News & World Report, "America's Best Colleges 2015"*

According to *U.S. News & World Report,* the Provo-Orem, UT metro area is home to one of the top 100 law schools in the U.S.: **Brigham Young University (Clark)** (#34). The rankings are based on a weighted average of 12 measures of quality: peer assessment score; assessment score by lawyers/judges; median LSAT scores; median undergrad GPA; acceptance rate; employment rates for graduates; placement success; bar passage rate; faculty resources; expenditures per student; student/faculty ratio; and library resources. *U.S. News & World Report, "America's Best Graduate Schools, Law, 2016"*

According to *U.S. News & World Report,* the Provo-Orem, UT metro area is home to one of the top 75 business schools in the U.S.: **Brigham Young University (Marriott)** (#33). The rankings are based on a weighted average of the following nine measures: quality assessment; peer assessment; recruiter assessment; placement success; mean starting salary and bonus; student selectivity; mean GMAT and GRE scores; mean undergraduate GPA; and acceptance rate. *U.S. News & World Report, "America's Best Graduate Schools, Business, 2016"*

PRESIDENTIAL ELECTION

2012 Presidential Election Results

Area	Obama (%)	Romney (%)	Other (%)
Utah County	9.8	88.3	2.0
U.S.	51.0	47.2	1.8

Note: Results may not add to 100% due to rounding
Source: Dave Leip's Atlas of U.S. Presidential Elections

EMPLOYERS

Major Employers

Company Name	Industry
About Time Technologies	Movements, clock or watch
Ancestry.com	Communication services, nec
Brigham Young University	Colleges and universities
Brigham Young University	Libraries
City of Provo	Mayors' office
Intermountain Health Care	General medical and surgical hospitals
Morinda Holdings	Bottled and canned soft drinks
Novell	Prepackaged software
Nu Skin Enterprises United States	Drugs, proprietaries, and sundries
Nu Skin International	Toilet preparations
Phone Directories Company	Directories, phone: publish only, not printed on site
Rbm Services	Building cleaning service
TPUSA	Telemarketing services
Utah Dept of Human Services	Mental hospital, except for the mentally retarded
Utah Dept of Human Services	Intermediate care facilities
Utah Valley University	College, except junior
Wal-Mart Stores	Department stores, discount
Wasatch Summit	Management consulting services
Xango	Drugs, proprietaries, and sundries

Note: Companies shown are located within the Provo-Orem, UT Metropolitan Statistical Area.
Source: Hoovers.com; Wikipedia

PUBLIC SAFETY

Crime Rate

Area	All Crimes	Violent Crimes				Property Crimes		
		Murder	Forcible Rape	Robbery	Aggrav. Assault	Burglary	Larceny -Theft	Motor Vehicle Theft
City	2,539.8	0.9	70.1	18.0	47.9	281.3	2,029.3	92.4
Suburbs[1]	1,790.4	1.1	16.2	6.3	29.0	217.5	1,442.1	78.1
Metro[2]	1,946.5	1.1	27.4	8.7	32.9	230.8	1,564.4	81.0
U.S.	3,098.6	4.5	25.2	109.1	229.1	610.0	1,899.4	221.3

Note: Figures are crimes per 100,000 population; (1) All areas within the metro area that are located outside the city limits; (2) Figures cover the Provo-Orem, UT Metropolitan Statistical Area—see Appendix B for areas included
Source: FBI Uniform Crime Reports, 2013

Hate Crimes

Area	Number of Quarters Reported	Number of Incidents per Bias Motivation						
		Race	Religion	Sexual Orientation	Ethnicity	Disability	Gender	Gender Identity
City	4	1	0	0	0	0	0	0
U.S.	4	2,871	1,031	1,233	655	83	18	31

Source: Federal Bureau of Investigation, Hate Crime Statistics 2013

Identity Theft Consumer Complaints

Area	Complaints	Complaints per 100,000 Population	Rank[2]
MSA[1]	238	42.3	352
U.S.	332,646	104.3	-

Note: (1) Figures cover the Provo-Orem, UT Metropolitan Statistical Area—see Appendix B for areas included; (2) Rank ranges from 1 to 380 where 1 indicates greatest number of identity theft complaints per 100,000 population
Source: Federal Trade Commission, Consumer Sentinel Network Data Book for January–December 2014

Fraud and Other Consumer Complaints

Area	Complaints	Complaints per 100,000 Population	Rank[2]
MSA[1]	1,557	276.9	349
U.S.	2,250,205	705.7	-

Note: (1) Figures cover the Provo-Orem, UT Metropolitan Statistical Area—see Appendix B for areas included; (2) Rank ranges from 1 to 380 where 1 indicates greatest number of identity theft complaints per 100,000 population
Source: Federal Trade Commission, Consumer Sentinel Network Data Book for January–December 2014

RECREATION

Culture

Dance[1]	Theatre[1]	Instrumental Music[1]	Vocal Music[1]	Series and Festivals	Museums and Art Galleries[2]	Zoos and Aquariums[3]
0	0	0	0	1	3	0

Note: (1) Professional performing groups; (2) Based on organizations with SIC code 8412; (3) AZA-accredited
Source: The Grey House Performing Arts Directory, 2015-16; Association of Zoos & Aquariums, AZA Member Zoos & Aquariums, April 2015; www.AccuLeads.com, April 2015

Professional Sports Teams

Team Name	League	Year Established
No teams are located in the metro area		

Source: Wikipedia, Major Professional Sports Teams of the United States and Canada, April 2015

CLIMATE

Average and Extreme Temperatures

Temperature	Jan	Feb	Mar	Apr	May	Jun	Jul	Aug	Sep	Oct	Nov	Dec	Yr.
Extreme High (°F)	62	69	78	85	93	104	107	104	100	89	75	67	107
Average High (°F)	37	43	52	62	72	83	93	90	80	66	50	38	64
Average Temp. (°F)	28	34	41	50	59	69	78	76	65	53	40	30	52
Average Low (°F)	19	24	31	38	46	54	62	61	51	40	30	22	40
Extreme Low (°F)	-22	-14	2	15	25	35	40	37	27	16	-14	-15	-22

Note: Figures cover the years 1948-1990
Source: National Climatic Data Center, International Station Meteorological Climate Summary, 9/96

Average Precipitation/Snowfall/Humidity

Precip./Humidity	Jan	Feb	Mar	Apr	May	Jun	Jul	Aug	Sep	Oct	Nov	Dec	Yr.
Avg. Precip. (in.)	1.3	1.2	1.8	2.0	1.7	0.9	0.8	0.9	1.1	1.3	1.3	1.4	15.6
Avg. Snowfall (in.)	13	10	11	6	1	Tr	0	0	Tr	2	6	13	63
Avg. Rel. Hum. 5am (%)	79	77	71	67	66	60	53	54	60	68	75	79	67
Avg. Rel. Hum. 5pm (%)	69	59	47	38	33	26	22	23	28	40	59	71	43

Note: Figures cover the years 1948-1990; Tr = Trace amounts (<0.05 in. of rain; <0.5 in. of snow)
Source: National Climatic Data Center, International Station Meteorological Climate Summary, 9/96

Weather Conditions

Temperature			Daytime Sky			Precipitation		
5°F & below	32°F & below	90°F & above	Clear	Partly cloudy	Cloudy	0.01 inch or more precip.	0.1 inch or more snow/ice	Thunder-storms
7	128	56	94	152	119	92	38	38

Note: Figures are average number of days per year and cover the years 1948-1990
Source: National Climatic Data Center, International Station Meteorological Climate Summary, 9/96

HAZARDOUS WASTE

Superfund Sites

Provo has no sites on the EPA's Superfund Final National Priorities List. There are a total of 1,322 Superfund sites on the list in the U.S. *U.S. Environmental Protection Agency, Final National Priorities List, April 14, 2015*

AIR & WATER QUALITY

Air Quality Trends: Ozone

	2004	2005	2006	2007	2008	2009	2010	2011	2012	2013
MSA[1]	0.070	0.079	0.077	0.076	0.073	0.069	0.070	0.065	0.077	0.074

Note: (1) Data covers the Provo-Orem, UT Metropolitan Statistical Area—see Appendix B for areas included. The values shown are the composite ozone concentration averages among trend sites based on the highest fourth daily maximum 8-hour concentration in parts per million. These trends are based on sites having an adequate record of monitoring data during the trend period. Data from exceptional events are included.
Source: U.S. Environmental Protection Agency, Air Quality Monitoring Information, "Air Quality Trends by City, 2000-2013"

Air Quality Index

Area	Percent of Days when Air Quality was...[2]					AQI Statistics[2]	
	Good	Moderate	Unhealthy for Sensitive Groups	Unhealthy	Very Unhealthy	Maximum	Median
MSA[1]	74.5	23.6	1.9	0.0	0.0	120	42

Note: (1) Data covers the Provo-Orem, UT Metropolitan Statistical Area—see Appendix B for areas included; (2) Based on 365 days with AQI data in 2014. Air Quality Index (AQI) is an index for reporting daily air quality. EPA calculates the AQI for five major air pollutants regulated by the Clean Air Act: ground-level ozone, particle pollution (aka particulate matter), carbon monoxide, sulfur dioxide, and nitrogen dioxide. The AQI runs from 0 to 500. The higher the AQI value, the greater the level of air pollution and the greater the health concern. There are six AQI categories: "Good" AQI is between 0 and 50. Air quality is considered satisfactory; "Moderate" AQI is between 51 and 100. Air quality is acceptable; "Unhealthy for Sensitive Groups" When AQI values are between 101 and 150, members of sensitive groups may experience health effects; "Unhealthy" When AQI values are between 151 and 200 everyone may begin to experience health effects; "Very Unhealthy" AQI values between 201 and 300 trigger a health alert; "Hazardous" AQI values over 300 trigger warnings of emergency conditions (not shown).
Source: U.S. Environmental Protection Agency, Air Quality Index Report, 2014

Air Quality Index Pollutants

Area	Percent of Days when AQI Pollutant was...[2]					
	Carbon Monoxide	Nitrogen Dioxide	Ozone	Sulfur Dioxide	Particulate Matter 2.5	Particulate Matter 10
MSA[1]	0.0	19.2	59.7	0.0	18.9	2.2

Note: (1) Data covers the Provo-Orem, UT Metropolitan Statistical Area—see Appendix B for areas included; (2) Based on 365 days with AQI data in 2014. The Air Quality Index (AQI) is an index for reporting daily air quality. EPA calculates the AQI for five major air pollutants regulated by the Clean Air Act: ground-level ozone, particle pollution (also known as particulate matter), carbon monoxide, sulfur dioxide, and nitrogen dioxide. The AQI runs from 0 to 500. The higher the AQI value, the greater the level of air pollution and the greater the health concern.
Source: U.S. Environmental Protection Agency, Air Quality Index Report, 2014

Maximum Air Pollutant Concentrations: Particulate Matter, Ozone, CO and Lead

	Particulate Matter 10 (ug/m^3)	Particulate Matter 2.5 Wtd AM (ug/m^3)	Particulate Matter 2.5 24-Hr (ug/m^3)	Ozone (ppm)	Carbon Monoxide (ppm)	Lead (ug/m^3)
MSA[1] Level	136	12.5	82	0.077	2	n/a
NAAQS[2]	150	15	35	0.075	9	0.15
Met NAAQS[2]	Yes	Yes	No	No	Yes	n/a

Note: (1) Data covers the Provo-Orem, UT Metropolitan Statistical Area—see Appendix B for areas included; Data from exceptional events are included; (2) National Ambient Air Quality Standards; ppm = parts per million; ug/m^3 = micrograms per cubic meter; n/a not available.
Concentrations: Particulate Matter 10 (coarse particulate)—highest second maximum 24-hour concentration; Particulate Matter 2.5 Wtd AM (fine particulate)—highest weighted annual mean concentration; Particulate Matter 2.5 24-Hour (fine particulate)—highest 98th percentile 24-hour concentration; Ozone—highest fourth daily maximum 8-hour concentration; Carbon Monoxide—highest second maximum non-overlapping 8-hour concentration; Lead—maximum running 3-month average
Source: U.S. Environmental Protection Agency, Air Quality Monitoring Information, "Air Quality Statistics by City, 2013"

Maximum Air Pollutant Concentrations: Nitrogen Dioxide and Sulfur Dioxide

	Nitrogen Dioxide AM (ppb)	Nitrogen Dioxide 1-Hr (ppb)	Sulfur Dioxide AM (ppb)	Sulfur Dioxide 1-Hr (ppb)	Sulfur Dioxide 24-Hr (ppb)
MSA[1] Level	19	75	n/a	n/a	n/a
NAAQS[2]	53	100	30	75	140
Met NAAQS[2]	Yes	Yes	n/a	n/a	n/a

Note: (1) Data covers the Provo-Orem, UT Metropolitan Statistical Area—see Appendix B for areas included; Data from exceptional events are included; (2) National Ambient Air Quality Standards; ppm = parts per million; ug/m^3 = micrograms per cubic meter; n/a not available.
Concentrations: Nitrogen Dioxide AM—highest arithmetic mean concentration; Nitrogen Dioxide 1-Hr—highest 98th percentile 1-hour daily maximum concentration; Sulfur Dioxide AM—highest annual mean concentration; Sulfur Dioxide 1-Hr—highest 99th percentile 1-hour daily maximum concentration; Sulfur Dioxide 24-Hr—highest second maximum 24-hour concentration
Source: U.S. Environmental Protection Agency, Air Quality Monitoring Information, "Air Quality Statistics by City, 2013"

Drinking Water

Water System Name	Pop. Served	Primary Water Source Type	Violations[1] Health Based	Violations[1] Monitoring/ Reporting
Provo City	115,000	Purchased Surface	0	0

Note: (1) Based on violation data from January 1, 2014 to December 31, 2014 (includes unresolved violations from earlier years)
Source: U.S. Environmental Protection Agency, Office of Ground Water and Drinking Water, Safe Drinking Water Information System (based on data extracted January 27, 2015)

Reno, Nevada

Background

Dubbed the "Biggest Little City in the World," Reno is known as a mecca for tourists who want to gamble, but it is so much more. Washoes and Paiutes roamed the area before white explorers led by the famed John C. Fremont arrived in the nineteenth century. Due to the Truckee River running through it, the area became a stopping point for people hurrying to California to take advantage of the 1849 gold rush. In 1859, prospectors discovered the Comstock Lode-a massive vein of gold and silver forty miles to the south of the Truckee.

A shrewd entrepreneur by the name of Charles Fuller built a toll bridge across the river for prospectors desperate to reach the lode. He also built a hotel. Floods kept destroying Fuller's bridge, and he sold the land to Myron Lake in 1861, who constructed another bridge around which a settlement grew. Lake turned over to the Central Pacific Railroad several dozen acres of his land, on the condition that half of the transcontinental railroad would run through the area. Here, the town of Reno was founded in 1868 and named after Jesse Lee Reno, a valiant Union officer killed during the Civil War. Reno became an important shipping point for the mines of the Comstock Lode.

By 1900, the lode was in decline and Reno had to look to other commercial ventures. One was the quick divorce-a six weeks' residency requirement was approved by the state legislature in 1931. In a continuing effort to jumpstart the state's economy during the Great Depression, Nevada legalized gambling in 1931. As the number of gambling houses increased in Reno, so did its population.

The Reno Arch (on which is emblazoned the city's nickname) welcomes tourists to an array of glittering casinos and hotels. The tourist and gambling industry are still quite important to the area's commerce but other commercial ventures have been attracted to Reno's business-friendly environment, which includes no corporate or personal income taxes, nor unitary, inventory, or franchise taxes. Recently, Urban Outfitters chose Reno for its 462,000 square-foot West Coast fulfillment center. Key industries throughout the Greater Reno-Sparks-Tahoe area include manufacturing, distribution/logistics/internet fulfillment; back office/business support; financial and intangible assets; clean energy; aerospace/aviation/defense. Companies with distribution and fulfillment operations in the city include Walmart, PetSmart, Urban Outfitters, Barnes & Noble, jcp, Kmart, and Toys R Us.

The University of Nevada, Reno opened its Earthquake Engineering Laboratory in 2014. The lab makes the university's seismic simulation facility the largest in the country and the second-largest in the world. Also in the city is significant meeting space at the Reno-Sparks Convention Center, recently joined by the Reno Events Center that is part of a $65 million, two-phased project to bring special event and meeting venues to the downtown area. In addition, Reno is home to the National Bowling Stadium and the Reno-Sparks Livestock Events Center. The Reno Aces play ball under the flag of the MLB-affiliated Pacific Coast League. The city also hosts ArtTown, in which music, visual arts, film, dance, theater and historical tours are the featured highlights of the month of July. This is among the country's largest visual and performing arts festivals.

Located on a semi-arid plateau to the east of the Sierra Nevada mountains, Reno offers a generally healthy climate with short, albeit hot, summers and relatively mild winters. Temperatures can vary widely from day to night. More than half of the city's precipitation falls as a rain-snow mixture during winter. Located at the edge of the Sierra Nevada, snows can pile up but tends to melt within a few days. Reno sees relatively little rain.

Rankings

General Rankings

- Among the 50 largest U.S. cities, Reno placed #32 in Vocativ's "semi-exhaustive, mostly scientific" city Livability Index for people aged 35 and under. Average salary, unemployment rates, rents, and other living costs were considered, along with crime rates, weather, public transportation, access to music and sports, and "lifestyle metrics" such as the price of dinner at Buffalo Wild Wings and an ounce of high-quality weed. *vocative.com, "The Livability Index: The Best U.S. Cities for People 35 and Under," December 9, 2014*

- Reno was selected as one of America's best cities by *Bloomberg Businessweek*. The city ranked #42 out of 50. Criteria: leisure attributes (the number of restaurants, bars, libraries, museums, professional sports teams, and park acres by population); educational attributes (public school performance, the number of colleges, and graduate degree holders); economic factors (2011 income and June and July 2012 unemployment); crime; and air quality. *Bloomberg BusinessWeek, "America's Best Cities," September 26, 2012*

- In their second annual survey, analysts for the small- and mid-sized city lifestyle site Livability.com looked at data for more than 2,000 U.S. cities to determine the rankings for Livability's "Top 100 Best Places to Live" in 2015. Reno ranked #54. Criteria: vibrant economy; low cost of living; abundant lifestyle amenities. *Livability.com, "Top 100 Best Places to Live 2015"*

Business/Finance Rankings

- Using data from the Council for Community and Economic Research's 2013 Annual Report, NerdWallet ranked the 100 most affordable cities in America. States from the central and southern United States dominate the list. On the affordability scale, Reno ranked #57. *NerdWallet.com, "Most Affordable Cities in America," June 4, 2014*

- CareerBliss, an employment and careers website, analyzed U.S. Bureau of Labor Statistics data, more than 30,000 company reviews from employees and former employees, and job openings over a 12-month period to arrive at its list of the best and worst places in the United States to look for a job. Reno was #10 among the worst places. *CareerBliss.com, "CareerBliss 2013 Best and Worst Cities to Find a Job," January 8, 2013*

- The Reno metro area appeared on the Milken Institute "2013 Best Performing Cities" list. Rank: #167 out of 200 large metro areas. Criteria: job growth; wage and salary growth; high-tech output growth. *Milken Institute, "Best-Performing Cities 2014," January 2015*

- *Forbes* ranked the 200 most populous metro areas to determine the nation's "Best Places for Business and Careers." The Reno metro area was ranked #123. Criteria: costs (business and living); job growth (past and projected); income growth; educational attainment (college and high school); projected economic growth; cultural and recreational opportunities; net migration patterns; number of highly ranked colleges. *Forbes, "The Best Places for Business and Careers 2014," July 23, 2014*

Dating/Romance Rankings

- Of the 100 U.S. cities surveyed by *Men's Health* in its quest to identify the nation's best cities for dating and forming relationships, Reno was ranked #68 for online dating (#1 = best). *Men's Health, "The Best and Worst Cities for Online Dating," January 30, 2013*

Education Rankings

- Personal finance website *WalletHub* analyzed the 150 largest U.S. metropolitan statistical areas to determine where the most educated Americans are choosing to settle. Criteria: educational attainment; percentage of workers with jobs in computer, engineering, and science fields; quality and size of each metro area's universities. Reno was ranked #61 (#1 = most educated city). *www.WalletHub.com, "2014's Most and Least Educated Cities"*

Environmental Rankings

- The Reno metro area came in at #74 for the relative comfort of its climate on Sperling's list of "chill cities," as measured by the Sperling Heat Index. All 361 metro areas are included. Criteria included daytime high temperatures, nighttime low temperatures, dew point, and relative humidity at the high temperatures. *www.bertsperling.com, "Sperling's Chill Cities," July 18, 2013*

- Sperling's BestPlaces assessed 379 metropolitan areas of the United States for the likelihood of dangerously extreme weather events or earthquakes. In general the Southeast and South-Central regions have the highest risk of weather extremes and earthquakes, while the Pacific Northwest enjoys the lowest risk. Of the least risky metropolitan areas, the Reno metro area was ranked #66. *www.bestplaces.net, "Safest Places from Natural Disasters," April 2011*

- Reno was highlighted as one of the 25 metro areas most polluted by short-term particle pollution (24-hour PM 2.5) in the U.S. during 2011 through 2013. The area ranked #15. *American Lung Association, State of the Air 2015*

Food/Drink Rankings

- *Men's Health* ranked 100 major U.S. cities in terms of alcohol intoxication. Reno ranked #91 (#1 = most sober).Criteria: binge drinking; alcohol-related traffic accidents, arrests, and fatalities. *Men's Health, "The Drunkest Cities in America," November 19, 2013*

Health/Fitness Rankings

- *Men's Health* ranked 100 major U.S. cities in terms of the best and worst cities for men. Reno ranked #42. Criteria: thirty-three data points were examined covering health, fitness, and quality of life. *Men's Health, "The Best & Worst Cities for Men 2014," December 6, 2013*

- The Reno metro area appeared in the 2013 Gallup-Healthways Well-Being Index. The area ranked #74 out of 189. The Gallup-Healthways Well-Being Index score is an average of six sub-indexes, which individually examine life evaluation, emotional health, work environment, physical health, healthy behaviors, and access to basic necessities. Results are based on telephone interviews conducted as part of the Gallup-Healthways Well-Being Index survey January 2–December 29, 2012, and January 2–December 30, 2013, with a random sample of 531,630 adults, aged 18 and older, living in metropolitan areas in the 50 U.S. states and the District of Columbia. *Gallup-Healthways, "State of American Well-Being," March 25, 2014*

- Reno was selected as one of the "20 Most Livable U.S. Cities for Wheelchair Users" by the Christopher & Dana Reeve Foundation. The city ranked #3. Criteria: Medicaid eligibility and spending; access to physicians and rehabilitation facilities; access to fitness facilities and recreation; access to paratransit; percentage of people living with disabilities who are employed; clean air; climate. *Christopher & Dana Reeve Foundation, "20 Most Livable U.S. Cities for Wheelchair Users," July 26, 2010*

Real Estate Rankings

- Reno was ranked #4 out of 275 metro areas in terms of house price appreciation in 2014 (#1 = highest rate). *Federal Housing Finance Agency, House Price Index, 4th Quarter 2014*

- The Reno metro area was identified as one of 14 best housing markets for the next five years. Criteria: projected annualized change in home prices between the fourth quarter 2012 and the fourth quarter 2017. *The Business Insider, "The 14 Best Housing Markets for the Next Five Years," May 20, 2013*

- The Reno metro area was identified as one of the 20 best housing markets in the U.S. in 2014. The area ranked #8 out of 178 markets with a home price appreciation of 13.3%. Criteria: year-over-year change of median sales price of existing single-family homes between the 4th quarter of 2013 and the 4th quarter of 2014. *National Association of Realtors®, Median Sales Price of Existing Single-Family Homes for Metropolitan Areas, 4th Quarter 2014*

- The Reno metro area was identified as one of the 10 best condo markets in the U.S. in 2014. The area ranked #2 out of 66 markets with a price appreciation of 19.0%. Criteria: year-over-year change of median sales price of existing apartment condo-coop homes between the 4th quarter of 2013 and the 4th quarter of 2014. *National Association of Realtors®, Median Sales Price of Existing Apartment Condo-Coop Homes for Metropolitan Areas, 4th Quarter 2014*

- Reno was ranked #184 out of 226 metro areas in terms of housing affordability in 2014 by the National Association of Home Builders (#1 = most affordable). The NAHB-Wells Fargo Housing Opportunity Index (HOI) for a given area is defined as the share of homes sold in that area that would have been affordable to a family earning the local median income, based on standard mortgage underwriting criteria. *National Association of Home Builders®, NAHB-Wells Fargo Housing Opportunity Index, 4th Quarter 2014*

Safety Rankings

- In search of the nation's safest cities, Business Insider looked at the FBI's preliminary Uniform Crime Report, excluding localities with fewer than 200,000 residents. To judge by its low murder, rape, and robbery data, Reno made the 20 safest cities list, at #17. *www.businessinsider.com, "The 20 Safest Cities in America," July 25, 2013*

- Allstate ranked the 200 largest cities in America in terms of driver safety. Reno ranked #17. Allstate researchers analyzed internal property damage claims over a two-year period from January 2011 to December 2012. A weighted average of the two-year numbers determined the annual percentages. *Allstate, "Allstate America's Best Drivers Report, 2014"*

- The National Insurance Crime Bureau ranked 380 metro areas in the U.S. in terms of per capita rates of vehicle theft. The Reno metro area ranked #79 (#1 = highest rate). Criteria: number of vehicle theft offenses per 100,000 inhabitants in 2012. *National Insurance Crime Bureau, "Hot Spots 2012," June 26, 2013*

Seniors/Retirement Rankings

- From its Best Cities for Successful Aging indexes, the Milken Institute generated rankings for metropolitan areas, weighing data in eight categories—health care, wellness, living arrangements, transportation, financial characteristics, education and employment opportunities, community engagement, and overall livability. The Reno metro area was ranked #96 overall in the small metro area category. *Milken Institute, "Best Cities for Successful Aging, 2014"*

- Reno was identified as one of the most popular places to retire by *Topretirements.com*. The list reflects the 100 cities (out of 900+ total cities reviewed) that visitors to the website are most interested in for retirement. *Topretirements.com, "Most Popular Places to Retire for 2014," February 25, 2014*

Sports/Recreation Rankings

- Reno was chosen as a bicycle friendly community by the League of American Bicyclists. A "Bicycle Friendly Community" welcomes cyclists by providing safe accommodation for cycling and encouraging people to bike for transportation and recreation. There are four award levels: Platinum; Gold; Silver; and Bronze. The community achieved an award level of Bronze. *League of American Bicyclists, "Bicycle Friendly Community Master List," Fall 2013*

- Reno was chosen as one of America's best cities for bicycling. The city ranked #42 out of 50. Criteria: robust cycling infrastructure; vibrant bike culture. The editors only considered cities with populations of 95,000 or more. *Bicycling, "America's Top 50 Bike-Friendly Cities," May 23, 2012*

Women/Minorities Rankings

- *Women's Health* examined U.S. cities and identified the 100 best cities for women. Reno was ranked #41. Criteria: 30 categories were examined from obesity and breast cancer rates to commuting times and hours spent working out. *Women's Health, "Best Cities for Women 2012"*

Business Environment

CITY FINANCES

City Government Finances

Component	2012 ($000)	2012 ($ per capita)
Total Revenues	315,187	1,399
Total Expenditures	287,169	1,275
Debt Outstanding	1,242,972	5,519
Cash and Securities[1]	654,354	2,905

Note: (1) Cash and security holdings of a government at the close of its fiscal year, including those of its dependent agencies, utilities, and liquor stores.
Source: U.S Census Bureau, State & Local Government Finances 2012

City Government Revenue by Source

Source	2012 ($000)	2012 ($ per capita)
General Revenue		
From Federal Government	11,236	50
From State Government	41,296	183
From Local Governments	19,467	86
Taxes		
Property	58,749	261
Sales and Gross Receipts	41,409	184
Personal Income	0	0
Corporate Income	0	0
Motor Vehicle License	0	0
Other Taxes	21,120	94
Current Charges	71,879	319
Liquor Store	0	0
Utility	0	0
Employee Retirement	0	0

Source: U.S Census Bureau, State & Local Government Finances 2012

City Government Expenditures by Function

Function	2012 ($000)	2012 ($ per capita)	2012 (%)
General Direct Expenditures			
Air Transportation	0	0	0.0
Corrections	0	0	0.0
Education	0	0	0.0
Employment Security Administration	0	0	0.0
Financial Administration	4,109	18	1.4
Fire Protection	43,930	195	15.3
General Public Buildings	0	0	0.0
Governmental Administration, Other	16,981	75	5.9
Health	0	0	0.0
Highways	26,867	119	9.4
Hospitals	0	0	0.0
Housing and Community Development	19,531	87	6.8
Interest on General Debt	43,557	193	15.2
Judicial and Legal	9,774	43	3.4
Libraries	0	0	0.0
Parking	0	0	0.0
Parks and Recreation	10,942	49	3.8
Police Protection	53,550	238	18.6
Public Welfare	0	0	0.0
Sewerage	40,437	180	14.1
Solid Waste Management	0	0	0.0
Veterans' Services	0	0	0.0
Liquor Store	0	0	0.0
Utility	0	0	0.0
Employee Retirement	0	0	0.0

Source: U.S Census Bureau, State & Local Government Finances 2012

DEMOGRAPHICS

Population Growth

Area	1990 Census	2000 Census	2010 Census	Population Growth (%) 1990-2000	Population Growth (%) 2000-2010
City	139,950	180,480	225,221	29.0	24.8
MSA[1]	257,193	342,885	425,417	33.3	24.1
U.S.	248,709,873	281,421,906	308,745,538	13.2	9.7

Note: (1) Figures cover the Reno-Sparks, NV Metropolitan Statistical Area—see Appendix B for areas included
Source: U.S. Census Bureau, Census 1990, 2000, 2010

Household Size

Area	Persons in Household (%) One	Two	Three	Four	Five	Six	Seven or More	Average Household Size
City	34.6	32.0	13.7	10.9	5.1	2.3	1.3	2.50
MSA[1]	29.7	34.9	14.3	12.4	5.0	2.3	1.4	2.59
U.S.	27.7	33.6	15.7	13.1	6.0	2.3	1.5	2.64

Note: (1) Figures cover the Reno, NV Metropolitan Statistical Area—see Appendix B for areas included
Source: U.S. Census Bureau, 2011-2013 American Community Survey 3-Year Estimates

Race

Area	White Alone[2] (%)	Black Alone[2] (%)	Asian Alone[2] (%)	AIAN[3] Alone[2] (%)	NHOPI[4] Alone[2] (%)	Other Race Alone[2] (%)	Two or More Races (%)
City	78.6	2.8	6.5	0.9	0.8	6.9	3.4
MSA[1]	80.7	2.4	5.3	1.6	0.6	5.9	3.5
U.S.	73.9	12.6	5.0	0.8	0.2	4.7	2.9

Note: (1) Figures cover the Reno, NV Metropolitan Statistical Area—see Appendix B for areas included; (2) Alone is defined as not being in combination with one or more other races; (3) American Indian and Alaska Native; (4) Native Hawaiian and Other Pacific Islander
Source: U.S. Census Bureau, 2011-2013 American Community Survey 3-Year Estimates

Hispanic or Latino Origin

Area	Total (%)	Mexican (%)	Puerto Rican (%)	Cuban (%)	Other (%)
City	25.4	20.1	0.6	0.1	4.6
MSA[1]	22.8	18.0	0.5	0.1	4.1
U.S.	16.9	10.8	1.6	0.6	3.8

Note: Persons of Hispanic or Latino origin can be of any race; (1) Figures cover the Reno, NV Metropolitan Statistical Area—see Appendix B for areas included
Source: U.S. Census Bureau, 2011-2013 American Community Survey 3-Year Estimates

Segregation

Type	Segregation Indices[1] 1990	2000	2010	2010 Rank[2]	Percent Change 1990-2000	1990-2010	2000-2010
Black/White	n/a	n/a	n/a	n/a	n/a	n/a	n/a
Asian/White	n/a	n/a	n/a	n/a	n/a	n/a	n/a
Hispanic/White	n/a	n/a	n/a	n/a	n/a	n/a	n/a

Note: All figures cover the Metropolitan Statistical Area—see Appendix B for areas included; Figures are based on an analysis of 1990, 2000, and 2010 Census Decennial Census tract data by William H. Frey, Brookings Institution and the University of Michigan Social Science Data Analysis Network. In this analysis all racial groups (whites, blacks, and asians) are non-Hispanic members of those races. Hispanics are shown as a separate category;
(1) Segregation Indices are Dissimilarity Indices that measure the degree to which the minority group is distributed differently than whites across census tracts. They range from 0 (complete integration) to 100 (complete segregation) where the value indicates the percentage of the minority group that needs to move to be distributed exactly like whites; (2) Ranges from 1 (most segregated) to 102 (least segregated); n/a not available.
Source: www.CensusScope.org

Ancestry

Area	German	Irish	English	American	Italian	Polish	French[2]	Scottish	Dutch
City	14.1	11.8	8.0	5.1	6.4	1.6	2.8	2.2	1.7
MSA[1]	14.8	11.7	9.2	5.5	6.6	1.8	3.1	2.4	1.6
U.S.	14.9	10.8	8.0	7.4	5.5	3.0	2.7	1.7	1.4

Note: Figures are the percentage of the total population reporting a particular ancestry. The nine most commonly reported ancestries in the U.S. are shown. Figures include multiple ancestries (e.g. if a person reported being Irish and Italian, they were included in both columns); (1) Figures cover the Reno, NV Metropolitan Statistical Area—see Appendix B for areas included; (2) Excludes Basque
Source: U.S. Census Bureau, 2011-2013 American Community Survey 3-Year Estimates

Foreign-Born Population

Area	Percent of Population Born in								
	Any Foreign Country	Mexico	Asia	Europe	Carribean	South America	Central America[2]	Africa	Canada
City	17.0	8.0	5.0	1.3	0.0	0.3	1.8	0.2	0.2
MSA[1]	15.0	7.2	4.0	1.2	0.1	0.3	1.4	0.2	0.3
U.S.	13.0	3.7	3.8	1.5	1.2	0.9	1.0	0.6	0.3

Note: (1) Figures cover the Reno, NV Metropolitan Statistical Area—see Appendix B for areas included; (2) Excludes Mexico.
Source: U.S. Census Bureau, 2011-2013 American Community Survey 3-Year Estimates

Marital Status

Area	Never Married	Now Married[2]	Separated	Widowed	Divorced
City	35.8	42.1	2.3	4.8	15.0
MSA[1]	31.6	46.7	2.0	4.9	14.7
U.S.	32.7	48.1	2.2	6.0	11.0

Note: Figures are percentages and cover the population 15 years of age and older; (1) Figures cover the Reno, NV Metropolitan Statistical Area—see Appendix B for areas included; (2) Excludes separated
Source: U.S. Census Bureau, 2011-2013 American Community Survey 3-Year Estimates

Disability Status

Area	All Ages	Under 18 Years Old	18 to 64 Years Old	65 Years and Over
City	11.1	3.2	9.6	34.0
MSA[1]	11.6	3.7	9.8	33.6
U.S.	12.3	4.1	10.2	36.3

Note: Figures show percent of the civilian noninstitutionalized population that reported having a disability. Disability status is determined from from six types of difficulty: vision, hearing, cognitive, ambulatory, self-care, and independent living. For children under 5 years old, hearing and vision difficulty are used to determine disability status. For children between the ages of 5 and 14, disability status is determined from hearing, vision, cognitive, ambulatory, and self-care difficulties. For people aged 15 years and older, they are considered to have a disability if they have difficulty with any one of the six difficulty types; (1) Figures cover the Reno, NV Metropolitan Statistical Area—see Appendix B for areas included.
Source: U.S. Census Bureau, 2011-2013 American Community Survey 3-Year Estimates

Age

Area	Percent of Population									Median Age
	Under Age 5	Age 5–19	Age 20–34	Age 35–44	Age 45–54	Age 55–64	Age 65–74	Age 75–84	Age 85+	
City	6.7	19.3	24.7	12.4	13.1	11.5	7.2	3.5	1.6	34.5
MSA[1]	6.3	19.1	21.3	12.7	13.9	13.2	8.3	3.6	1.5	37.6
U.S.	6.4	19.9	20.7	12.9	14.1	12.3	7.6	4.2	1.9	37.4

Note: (1) Figures cover the Reno, NV Metropolitan Statistical Area—see Appendix B for areas included
Source: U.S. Census Bureau, 2011-2013 American Community Survey 3-Year Estimates

Gender

Area	Males	Females	Males per 100 Females
City	117,408	113,377	103.6
MSA[1]	218,347	215,262	101.4
U.S.	154,451,010	159,410,713	96.9

Note: (1) Figures cover the Reno, NV Metropolitan Statistical Area—see Appendix B for areas included
Source: U.S. Census Bureau, 2011-2013 American Community Survey 3-Year Estimates

Religious Groups by Family

Area	Catholic	Baptist	Non-Den.	Methodist[2]	Lutheran	LDS[3]	Pente-costal	Presby-terian[4]	Muslim[5]	Judaism
MSA[1]	14.3	1.5	3.2	0.9	0.8	4.6	2.0	0.4	0.1	0.2
U.S.	19.1	9.3	4.0	4.0	2.3	2.0	1.9	1.6	0.8	0.7

Note: Figures are the number of adherents as a percentage of the total population; (1) Figures cover the Reno-Sparks, NV Metropolitan Statistical Area—see Appendix B for areas included; (2) Methodist/Pietist; (3) Latter Day Saints; (4) Reformed; (5) Figures are estimates
Source: Association of Statisticians of American Religious Bodies, 2010 U.S. Religion Census: Religious Congregations & Membership Study

Religious Groups by Tradition

Area	Catholic	Evangelical Protestant	Mainline Protestant	Other Tradition	Black Protestant	Orthodox
MSA[1]	14.3	7.7	1.9	5.1	0.2	0.1
U.S.	19.1	16.2	7.3	4.3	1.6	0.3

Note: Figures are the number of adherents as a percentage of the total population; (1) Figures cover the Reno-Sparks, NV Metropolitan Statistical Area—see Appendix B for areas included
Source: Association of Statisticians of American Religious Bodies, 2010 U.S. Religion Census: Religious Congregations & Membership Study

ECONOMY

Gross Metropolitan Product

Area	2012	2013	2014	2015	Rank[2]
MSA[1]	20.4	20.9	21.7	22.8	108

Note: Figures are in billions of dollars; (1) Figures cover the Reno, NV Metropolitan Statistical Area—see Appendix B for areas included; (2) Rank is based on 2015 data and ranges from 1 to 363
Source: The U.S. Conference of Mayors, U.S. Metro Economies: GMP and Employment 2013-2015, June 2014

Economic Growth

Area	2010-12 (%)	2013 (%)	2014 (%)	2015 (%)	Rank[2]
MSA[1]	0.8	1.0	2.5	3.0	155
U.S.	2.1	2.0	2.3	3.2	–

Note: Figures are real gross metropolitan product (GMP) growth rates and represent annual average percent change; (1) Figures cover the Reno, NV Metropolitan Statistical Area—see Appendix B for areas included; (2) Rank is based on 2015 data and ranges from 1 to 363
Source: The U.S. Conference of Mayors, U.S. Metro Economies: GMP and Employment 2013-2015, June 2014

Metropolitan Area Exports

Area	2008	2009	2010	2011	2012	2013	Rank[2]
MSA[1]	1,317.0	1,233.8	1,511.9	1,687.4	2,019.0	2,117.4	97

Note: Figures are in millions of dollars; (1) Figures cover the Reno, NV Metropolitan Statistical Area—see Appendix B for areas included; (2) Rank is based on 2013 data and ranges from 1 to 387
Source: U.S. Department of Commerce, International Trade Administration, Office of Trade & Industry Information, Manufacturing & Services, data extracted April 3, 2015

Building Permits

Area	Single-Family			Multi-Family			Total		
	2013	2014	Pct. Chg.	2013	2014	Pct. Chg.	2013	2014	Pct. Chg.
City	687	858	24.9	426	699	64.1	1,113	1,557	39.9
MSA[1]	1,243	1,507	21.2	477	709	48.6	1,720	2,216	28.8
U.S.	620,802	634,597	2.2	370,020	411,766	11.3	990,822	1,046,363	5.6

Note: (1) Figures cover the Reno, NV Metropolitan Statistical Area—see Appendix B for areas included;
Figures represent new, privately-owned housing units authorized (unadjusted data); All permit data are based
on estimates with imputation.
Source: U.S. Census Bureau, Manufacturing, Mining, and Construction Statistics, Building Permits, 2013, 2014

Bankruptcy Filings

Area	Business Filings			Nonbusiness Filings		
	2013	2014	% Chg.	2013	2014	% Chg.
Washoe County	87	64	-26.4	1,615	1,454	-10.0
U.S.	33,212	26,983	-18.8	1,038,720	909,812	-12.4

Note: Business filings include Chapter 7, Chapter 11, Chapter 12, and Chapter 13; Nonbusiness filings include
Chapter 7, Chapter 11, and Chapter 13
Source: Administrative Office of the U.S. Courts, Business and Nonbusiness Bankruptcy, County Cases
Commenced by Chapter of the Bankruptcy Code, During the 12- Month Period Ending December 31, 2013 and
Business and Nonbusiness Bankruptcy, County Cases Commenced by Chapter of the Bankruptcy Code, During
the 12- Month Period Ending December 31, 2014

Housing Vacancy Rates

Area	Gross Vacancy Rate[2] (%)			Year-Round Vacancy Rate[3] (%)			Rental Vacancy Rate[4] (%)			Homeowner Vacancy Rate[5] (%)		
	2012	2013	2014	2012	2013	2014	2012	2013	2014	2012	2013	2014
MSA[1]	n/a	n/a	n/a	n/a	n/a	n/a	n/a	n/a	n/a	n/a	n/a	n/a
U.S.	13.8	13.6	13.4	10.8	10.7	10.4	8.7	8.3	7.6	2.0	2.0	1.9

Note: (1) Figures cover the Reno, NV Metropolitan Statistical Area—see Appendix B for areas included; (2) The
percentage of the total housing inventory that is vacant; (3) The percentage of the housing inventory (excluding
seasonal units) that is year-round vacant; (4) The percentage of rental inventory that is vacant for rent; (5) The
percentage of homeowner inventory that is vacant for sale; n/a not available
Source: U.S. Census Bureau, Housing Vacancies and Homeownership Annual Statistics: 2014

INCOME

Income

Area	Per Capita ($)	Median Household ($)	Average Household ($)
City	25,716	46,348	62,934
MSA[1]	28,115	51,916	70,915
U.S.	27,884	52,176	72,897

Note: (1) Figures cover the Reno, NV Metropolitan Statistical Area—see Appendix B for areas included
Source: U.S. Census Bureau, 2011-2013 American Community Survey 3-Year Estimates

Household Income Distribution

Area	Percent of Households Earning							
	Under $15,000	$15,000 -24,999	$25,000 -34,999	$35,000 -49,999	$50,000 -74,999	$75,000 -99,000	$100,000 -149,999	$150,000 and up
City	15.7	13.0	10.6	13.5	18.4	10.5	11.3	7.0
MSA[1]	12.7	11.5	10.2	13.5	19.2	11.6	13.5	7.8
U.S.	13.0	10.9	10.3	13.6	17.9	11.9	12.7	9.6

Note: (1) Figures cover the Reno, NV Metropolitan Statistical Area—see Appendix B for areas included
Source: U.S. Census Bureau, 2011-2013 American Community Survey 3-Year Estimates

Poverty Rate

Area	All Ages	Under 18 Years Old	18 to 64 Years Old	65 Years and Over
City	18.5	23.2	18.3	11.0
MSA[1]	15.5	21.3	15.0	8.2
U.S.	15.9	22.4	14.8	9.5

Note: Figures are percentage of people whose income during the past 12 months was below the poverty level;
(1) Figures cover the Reno, NV Metropolitan Statistical Area—see Appendix B for areas included
Source: U.S. Census Bureau, 2011-2013 American Community Survey 3-Year Estimates

EMPLOYMENT

Labor Force and Employment

Area	Civilian Labor Force			Workers Employed		
	Dec. 2013	Dec. 2014	% Chg.	Dec. 2013	Dec. 2014	% Chg.
City	119,781	119,949	0.1	110,144	112,134	1.8
MSA[1]	224,477	224,562	0.0	206,330	210,050	1.8
U.S.	154,408,000	155,521,000	0.7	144,423,000	147,190,000	1.9

Note: Data is not seasonally adjusted and covers workers 16 years of age and older; (1) Figures cover the
Reno, NV Metropolitan Statistical Area—see Appendix B for areas included
Source: Bureau of Labor Statistics, Local Area Unemployment Statistics

Unemployment Rate

Area	2014											
	Jan.	Feb.	Mar.	Apr.	May	Jun.	Jul.	Aug.	Sep.	Oct.	Nov.	Dec.
City	8.9	8.5	8.3	7.8	7.5	7.6	7.4	7.1	6.9	6.7	6.6	6.5
MSA[1]	9.0	8.6	8.4	7.8	7.4	7.5	7.3	7.0	6.9	6.6	6.5	6.5
U.S.	7.0	7.0	6.8	5.9	6.1	6.3	6.5	6.3	5.7	5.5	5.5	5.4

Note: Data is not seasonally adjusted and covers workers 16 years of age and older; (1) Figures cover the
Reno, NV Metropolitan Statistical Area—see Appendix B for areas included
Source: Bureau of Labor Statistics, Local Area Unemployment Statistics

Employment by Occupation

Occupation Classification	City (%)	MSA[1] (%)	U.S. (%)
Management, Business, Science, and Arts	33.0	33.1	36.2
Natural Resources, Construction, and Maintenance	6.9	7.7	9.0
Production, Transportation, and Material Moving	11.0	11.0	12.1
Sales and Office	26.8	26.8	24.4
Service	22.3	21.4	18.3

Note: Figures cover employed civilians 16 years of age and older; (1) Figures cover the Reno, NV Metropolitan
Statistical Area—see Appendix B for areas included
Source: U.S. Census Bureau, 2011-2013 American Community Survey 3-Year Estimates

Employment by Industry

Sector	MSA[1]		U.S.
	Number of Employees	Percent of Total	Percent of Total
Construction	10,900	5.3	4.4
Education and Health Services	24,000	11.6	15.5
Financial Activities	9,600	4.7	5.7
Government	29,600	14.4	15.8
Information	2,000	1.0	2.0
Leisure and Hospitality	35,500	17.2	10.3
Manufacturing	13,000	6.3	8.7
Mining and Logging	200	0.1	0.6
Other Services	5,800	2.8	4.0
Professional and Business Services	28,400	13.8	13.8
Retail Trade	22,700	11.0	11.4
Transportation, Warehousing, and Utilities	15,200	7.4	3.9
Wholesale Trade	9,200	4.5	4.2

Note: Figures are non-farm employment as of December 2014. Figures are not seasonally adjusted and include workers 16 years of age and older; (1) Figures cover the Reno, NV Metropolitan Statistical Area—see Appendix B for areas included
Source: Bureau of Labor Statistics, Current Employment Statistics, Employment, Hours, and Earnings

Occupations with Greatest Projected Employment Growth: 2012 – 2022

Occupation[1]	2012 Employment	2022 Projected Employment	Numeric Employment Change	Percent Employment Change
Combined Food Preparation and Serving Workers, Including Fast Food	29,300	35,950	6,650	22.7
Retail Salespersons	45,710	51,200	5,490	12.0
Carpenters	10,350	15,400	5,050	48.8
Construction Laborers	7,620	11,780	4,160	54.7
Waiters and Waitresses	37,760	41,880	4,120	10.9
Laborers and Freight, Stock, and Material Movers, Hand	18,250	21,670	3,420	18.7
Gaming Dealers	22,640	25,950	3,310	14.6
Personal Care Aides	8,020	11,090	3,070	38.2
Customer Service Representatives	16,580	19,620	3,040	18.3
Cooks, Restaurant	17,440	20,450	3,010	17.3

Note: Projections cover Nevada; (1) Sorted by numeric employment change
Source: www.projectionscentral.com, State Occupational Projections, 2012–2022 Long-Term Projections

Fastest Growing Occupations: 2012 – 2022

Occupation[1]	2012 Employment	2022 Projected Employment	Numeric Employment Change	Percent Employment Change
Helpers—Brickmasons, Blockmasons, Stonemasons, and Tile and Marble Setters	170	380	210	119.8
Helpers—Painters, Paperhangers, Plasterers, and Stucco Masons	90	200	110	113.8
Brickmasons and Blockmasons	470	970	500	104.4
Cement Masons and Concrete Finishers	1,200	2,250	1,050	87.3
Structural Iron and Steel Workers	530	980	450	86.3
Helpers—Carpenters	160	300	140	83.9
Glaziers	460	810	350	77.1
Crane and Tower Operators	280	470	190	68.5
Roofers	1,200	2,020	820	67.8
Helpers—Electricians	260	430	170	65.3

Note: Projections cover Nevada; (1) Sorted by percent employment change and excludes occupations with numeric employment change less than 100
Source: www.projectionscentral.com, State Occupational Projections, 2012–2022 Long-Term Projections

Average Wages

Occupation	$/Hr.	Occupation	$/Hr.
Accountants and Auditors	30.67	Maids and Housekeeping Cleaners	10.09
Automotive Mechanics	19.61	Maintenance and Repair Workers	18.67
Bookkeepers	19.01	Marketing Managers	45.79
Carpenters	21.98	Nuclear Medicine Technologists	n/a
Cashiers	10.42	Nurses, Licensed Practical	24.00
Clerks, General Office	17.04	Nurses, Registered	36.23
Clerks, Receptionists/Information	13.73	Nursing Assistants	13.75
Clerks, Shipping/Receiving	15.22	Packers and Packagers, Hand	10.16
Computer Programmers	37.15	Physical Therapists	44.27
Computer Systems Analysts	31.60	Postal Service Mail Carriers	24.92
Computer User Support Specialists	20.80	Real Estate Brokers	27.65
Cooks, Restaurant	12.08	Retail Salespersons	12.99
Dentists	102.52	Sales Reps., Exc. Tech./Scientific	28.94
Electrical Engineers	40.30	Sales Reps., Tech./Scientific	38.90
Electricians	27.35	Secretaries, Exc. Legal/Med./Exec.	17.84
Financial Managers	47.23	Security Guards	11.83
First-Line Supervisors/Managers, Sales	20.07	Surgeons	116.44
Food Preparation Workers	9.78	Teacher Assistants	12.80
General and Operations Managers	48.92	Teachers, Elementary School	25.40
Hairdressers/Cosmetologists	10.52	Teachers, Secondary School	24.80
Internists	n/a	Telemarketers	13.77
Janitors and Cleaners	10.58	Truck Drivers, Heavy/Tractor-Trailer	22.83
Landscaping/Groundskeeping Workers	13.08	Truck Drivers, Light/Delivery Svcs.	16.06
Lawyers	54.03	Waiters and Waitresses	9.97

Note: Wage data covers the Reno-Sparks, NV Metropolitan Statistical Area—see Appendix B for areas included; Hourly wages for elementary/secondary school teachers and teacher assistants were calculated by the editors from annual wage data assuming a 40 hour work week; n/a not available.
Source: Bureau of Labor Statistics, Metro Area Occupational Employment and Wage Estimates, May 2014

TAXES

State Corporate Income Tax Rates

State	Tax Rate (%)	Income Brackets ($)	Num. of Brackets	Financial Institution Tax Rate (%)[a]	Federal Income Tax Ded.
Nevada	None	–	–	–	–

Note: Tax rates as of January 1, 2015; (a) Rates listed are the corporate income tax rate applied to financial institutions or excise taxes based on income. Some states have other taxes based upon the value of deposits or shares.
Source: Federation of Tax Administrators, "State Corporate Income Tax Rates, 2015"

State Individual Income Tax Rates

State	Tax Rate (%)	Income Brackets ($)	Num. of Brackets	Personal Exempt. ($)[1]		Fed. Inc. Tax Ded.
				Single	Dependents	
Nevada	None	–	–	–	–	–

Note: Tax rates as of January 1, 2015; Local- and county-level taxes are not included; n/a not applicable; (1) Married joint filers generally receive double the single exemption
Source: Federation of Tax Administrators, "State Individual Income Tax Rates, 2015"

Various State and Local Tax Rates

State	State and Local Sales and Use (%)	State Sales and Use (%)	Gasoline[1] (¢/gal.)	Cigarette[2] ($/pack)	Spirits[3] ($/gal.)	Wine[4] ($/gal.)	Beer[5] ($/gal.)
Nevada	7.725	6.85	33.15	0.80	3.60 (f)	0.70	0.16

Note: All tax rates as of January 1, 2015; (1) The American Petroleum Institute has developed a methodology for determining the average tax rate on a gallon of fuel. Rates may include any of the following: excise taxes, environmental fees, storage tank fees, other fees or taxes, general sales tax, and local taxes. In states where gasoline is subject to the general sales tax, or where the fuel tax is based on the average sale price, the average rate determined by API is sensitive to changes in the price of gasoline. States that fully or partially apply general sales taxes to gasoline: CA, CO, GA, IL, IN, MI, NY; (2) The federal excise tax of $1.0066 per pack and local taxes are not included; (3) Rates are those applicable to off-premise sales of 40% alcohol by volume (a.b.v.) distilled spirits in 750ml containers. Local excise taxes are excluded; (4) Rates are those applicable to off-premise sales of 11% a.b.v. non-carbonated wine in 750ml containers; (5) Rates are those applicable to off-premise sales of 4.7% a.b.v. beer in 12 ounce containers; (f) Different rates are also applicable according to alcohol content, place of production, size of container, or place purchased (on- or off-premise or onboard airlines).
Source: Tax Foundation, 2015 Facts & Figures: How Does Your State Compare?

State Business Tax Climate Index Rankings

State	Overall Rank	Corporate Tax Index Rank	Individual Income Tax Index Rank	Sales Tax Index Rank	Unemployment Insurance Tax Index Rank	Property Tax Index Rank
Nevada	3	1	1	39	43	9

Note: The index is a measure of how each state's tax laws affect economic performance. The lower the rank, the more favorable a state's tax system is for business. States without a given tax are given a ranking of 1. The scores/rankings for the District of Columbia do not affect other states. The 2015 index represents the tax climate as of July 1, 2014.
Source: Tax Foundation, State Business Tax Climate Index 2015

COMMERCIAL UTILITIES

Typical Monthly Electric Bills

Area	Commercial Service ($/month)		Industrial Service ($/month)	
	1,500 kWh	40 kW demand 14,000 kWh	1,000 kW demand 200,000 kWh	50,000 kW demand 32,500,000 kWh
City	121	1,077	26,151	2,875,364
Average[1]	201	1,653	26,124	2,639,743

Note: Figures are based on annualized 2014 rates; (1) Average based on 180 utilities surveyed
Source: Edison Electric Institute, Typical Bills and Average Rates Report, Summer 2014

TRANSPORTATION

Means of Transportation to Work

Area	Car/Truck/Van		Public Transportation			Bicycle	Walked	Other Means	Worked at Home
	Drove Alone	Car-pooled	Bus	Subway	Railroad				
City	76.6	10.1	3.2	0.0	0.0	1.0	3.8	2.0	3.2
MSA[1]	78.1	10.4	2.4	0.0	0.0	0.7	2.7	1.9	3.8
U.S.	76.4	9.6	2.6	1.8	0.6	0.6	2.8	1.3	4.3

Note: Figures are percentages and cover workers 16 years of age and older; (1) Figures cover the Reno, NV Metropolitan Statistical Area—see Appendix B for areas included
Source: U.S. Census Bureau, 2011-2013 American Community Survey 3-Year Estimates

Travel Time to Work

Area	Less Than 10 Minutes	10 to 19 Minutes	20 to 29 Minutes	30 to 44 Minutes	45 to 59 Minutes	60 to 89 Minutes	90 Minutes or More
City	14.3	45.4	22.9	9.6	3.2	3.1	1.5
MSA[1]	12.5	39.4	25.4	14.1	3.4	3.0	2.1
U.S.	13.3	29.7	20.9	20.2	7.7	5.7	2.6

Note: Figures are percentages and include workers 16 years old and over; (1) Figures cover the Reno, NV Metropolitan Statistical Area—see Appendix B for areas included
Source: U.S. Census Bureau, 2011-2013 American Community Survey 3-Year Estimates

Travel Time Index

Area	1985	1990	1995	2000	2005	2010	2011
Urban Area[1]	n/a	n/a	n/a	n/a	n/a	n/a	n/a
Average[2]	1.09	1.14	1.16	1.19	1.23	1.18	1.18

Note: Travel Time Index—the ratio of travel time in the peak period to the travel time at free-flow conditions. For example, a value of 1.30 indicates a 20-minute free-flow trip takes 26 minutes in the peak. Free-flow speeds (60 mph on freeways and 35 mph on principal arterials) are used as the comparison threshold; (1) Data for the Reno, NV urban area was not available; (2) average of 498 urban areas
Source: Texas Transportation Institute, Urban Mobility Report 2012, December 2012

Public Transportation

Agency Name / Mode of Transportation	Vehicles Operated in Maximum Service	Annual Unlinked Passenger Trips (in thous.)	Annual Passenger Miles (in thous.)
Regional Transportation Commission of Washoe County (RTC)			
Bus (purchased transportation)	56	8,008.7	27,565.7
Commuter Bus (purchased transportation)	3	42.3	146.5
Demand Response (purchased transportation)	47	218.6	1,454.5
Demand Response Taxi (purchased transportation)	7	14.2	102.9
Vanpool (purchased transportation)	41	112.3	5,843.0

Source: Federal Transit Administration, National Transit Database, 2013

Air Transportation

Airport Name and Code / Type of Service	Passenger Airlines[1]	Passenger Enplanements	Freight Carriers[2]	Freight (lbs.)
Reno-Tahoe International (RNO)				
Domestic service (U.S. carriers - 2014)	16	1,600,929	12	80,536,465
International service (U.S. carriers - 2013)	3	664	0	0

Note: (1) Includes all U.S.-based major, minor and commuter airlines that carried at least one passenger during the year; (2) Includes all U.S.-based airlines and freight carriers that transported at least one lb. of freight during the year.
Source: Bureau of Transportation Statistics, The Intermodal Transportation Database, Air Carriers: T-100 Domestic Market (U.S. Carriers), 2014; Bureau of Transportation Statistics, The Intermodal Transportation Database, Air Carriers: T-100 International Market (U.S. Carriers), 2013

Other Transportation Statistics

Major Highways:	I-80
Amtrak Service:	Yes
Major Waterways/Ports:	None

Source: Amtrak.com; Google Maps

BUSINESSES

Major Business Headquarters

Company Name	Rankings	
	Fortune[1]	Forbes[2]
No companies listed	-	-

Note: (1) Fortune 500—companies that produce a 10-K are ranked 1 to 500 based on 2013 revenue; (2) all private companies with at least $2 billion in annual revenue through the end of their most current fiscal year are ranked 1 to 221; companies listed are headquartered in the city; dashes indicate no ranking
Source: Fortune, "Fortune 500," June 16, 2014; Forbes, "America's Largest Private Companies," November 5, 2014

Minority- and Women-Owned Businesses

Group	All Firms		Firms with Paid Employees			
	Firms	Sales ($000)	Firms	Sales ($000)	Employees	Payroll ($000)
Asian	1,242	341,194	297	269,738	2,594	65,114
Black	325	101,611	67	97,057	1,434	29,581
Hispanic	1,244	256,298	316	216,956	1,512	46,762
Women	5,893	1,267,638	926	1,088,069	6,832	244,076
All Firms	22,084	30,968,448	6,977	30,083,086	142,233	5,506,314

Note: Figures cover firms located in the city; minority- and women-owned business are defined as firms in which the corresponding group own 51% or more of the stock or equity of the company
Source: U.S. Census Bureau, 2007 Economic Census, Survey of Business Owners (2012 Survey of Business Owners data will be released starting in June 2015)

HOTELS & CONVENTION CENTERS

Hotels/Motels

Area	5 Star		4 Star		3 Star		2 Star		1 Star		Not Rated	
	Num.	Pct.[3]	Num.	Pct.[3]	Num.	Pct.[3]	Num.	Pct.[3]	Num.	Pct.[3]	Num.	Pct.[3]
City[1]	0	0.0	6	7.4	24	29.6	38	46.9	1	1.2	12	14.8
Total[2]	166	0.9	1,264	7.0	5,718	31.8	9,340	52.0	411	2.3	1,070	6.0

Note: (1) Figures cover Reno and vicinity; (2) Figures cover all 100 cities in this book; (3) Percentage of hotels which have a given star rating; Star ratings are determined by expedia.com and offer an indication of the general quality of a particular hotel.
Source: expedia.com, April 2, 2015

Major Convention Centers

Name	Overall Space (sq. ft.)	Exhibit Space (sq. ft.)	Meeting Space (sq. ft.)	Meeting Rooms
Reno-Sparks Convention Center	n/a	381,000	n/a	53

Note: Table includes convention centers located in the Reno, NV metro area; n/a not available
Source: Original research

Living Environment

COST OF LIVING

Cost of Living Index

Composite Index	Groceries	Housing	Utilities	Trans- portation	Health Care	Misc. Goods/ Services
97.0	105.8	85.8	81.7	107.3	94.6	104.2

Note: The Cost of Living Index measures regional differences in the cost of consumer goods and services, excluding taxes and non-consumer expenditures, for professional and managerial households in the top income quintile. It is based on more than 50,000 prices covering almost 60 different items for which prices are collected three times a year by chambers of commerce, economic development organizations or university applied economic centers in each participating urban area. The numbers shown should be read as a percentage above or below the national average of 100. For example, a value of 115.4 in the groceries column indicates that grocery prices are 15.4% higher than the national average. Small differences in the index numbers should not be interpreted as significant; Figures cover the Reno-Sparks NV urban area.
Source: The Council for Community and Economic Research, ACCRA Cost of Living Index, 2014

Grocery Prices

Area[1]	T-Bone Steak ($/pound)	Frying Chicken ($/pound)	Whole Milk ($/half gal.)	Eggs ($/dozen)	Orange Juice ($/64 oz.)	Coffee ($/11.5 oz.)
City[2]	10.12	1.45	2.29	1.85	3.70	4.70
Avg.	10.40	1.37	2.40	1.99	3.46	4.27
Min.	8.48	0.93	1.37	1.30	2.83	2.99
Max.	14.20	2.44	3.62	4.02	6.42	6.96

*Note: (1) Values for the local area are compared with the average, minimum and maximum values for all 308 areas in the Cost of Living Index; (2) Figures cover the Reno-Sparks NV urban area; **T-Bone Steak** (price per pound); **Frying Chicken** (price per pound, whole fryer); **Whole Milk** (half gallon carton); **Eggs** (price per dozen, Grade A, large); **Orange Juice** (64 oz. Tropicana or Florida Natural); **Coffee** (11.5 oz. can, vacuum-packed, Maxwell House, Hills Bros, or Folgers).*
Source: The Council for Community and Economic Research, ACCRA Cost of Living Index, 2014

Housing and Utility Costs

Area[1]	New Home Price ($)	Apartment Rent ($/month)	All Electric ($/month)	Part Electric ($/month)	Other Energy ($/month)	Telephone ($/month)
City[2]	248,538	930	-	80.67	72.32	19.43
Avg.	305,838	919	181.00	93.66	73.14	27.95
Min.	183,142	480	112.00	42.06	23.42	17.16
Max.	1,358,576	3,851	594.00	180.03	440.99	40.42

*Note: (1) Values for the local area are compared with the average, minimum and maximum values for all 308 areas in the Cost of Living Index; (2) Figures cover the Reno-Sparks NV urban area; **New Home Price** (2,400 sf living area, 8,000 sf lot, in urban area with full utilities); **Apartment Rent** (950 sf 2 bedroom/1.5 or 2 bath, unfurnished, excluding all utilities except water); **All Electric** (average monthly cost for an all-electric home); **Part Electric** (average monthly cost for a part-electric home); **Other Energy** (average monthly cost for natural gas, fuel oil, coal, wood, and any other forms of energy except electricity); **Telephone** (price includes basic monthly rate for a private residential line plus additional local usage charges incurred by a family of four).*
Source: The Council for Community and Economic Research, ACCRA Cost of Living Index, 2014

Health Care, Transportation, and Other Costs

Area[1]	Doctor ($/visit)	Dentist ($/visit)	Optometrist ($/visit)	Gasoline ($/gallon)	Beauty Salon ($/visit)	Men's Shirt ($)
City[2]	78.40	91.03	110.56	3.73	33.74	22.02
Avg.	102.86	87.89	97.66	3.44	34.37	26.74
Min.	67.47	65.78	51.18	3.00	17.43	12.79
Max.	173.50	150.14	235.00	4.33	64.28	49.50

*Note: (1) Values for the local area are compared with the average, minimum and maximum values for all 308 areas in the Cost of Living Index; (2) Figures cover the Reno-Sparks NV urban area; **Doctor** (general practitioners routine exam of an established patient); **Dentist** (adult teeth cleaning and periodic oral examination); **Optometrist** (full vision eye exam for established adult patient); **Gasoline** (one gallon regular unleaded, national brand, including all taxes, cash price at self-service pump if available); **Beauty Salon** (woman's shampoo, trim, and blow-dry); **Men's Shirt** (cotton/polyester dress shirt, pinpoint weave, long sleeves).*
Source: The Council for Community and Economic Research, ACCRA Cost of Living Index, 2014

HOUSING

House Price Index (HPI)

Area	National Ranking[2]	Quarterly Change (%)	One-Year Change (%)	Five-Year Change (%)
MSA[1]	4	0.27	13.11	15.60
U.S.[3]	–	1.35	4.91	11.59

Note: The HPI is a weighted repeat sales index. It measures average price changes in repeat sales or refinancings on the same properties. This information is obtained by reviewing repeat mortgage transactions on single-family properties whose mortgages have been purchased or securitized by Fannie Mae or Freddie Mac in January 1975; (1) Reno Metropolitan Statistical Area—see Appendix B for areas included; (2) Rankings are based on annual percentage change for all metro areas containing at least 15,000 transactions over the last 10 years and ranges from 1 to 275; (3) figures based on a weighted average of Census Division estimates using a seasonally adjusted, purchase-only index; all figures are for the period ending December 31, 2014
Source: Federal Housing Finance Agency, House Price Index, February 26, 2015

Median Single-Family Home Prices

Area	2012	2013	2014p	Percent Change 2013 to 2014
MSA[1]	169.7	218.4	247.5	13.3
U.S. Average	177.2	197.4	209.0	5.9

Note: Figures are median sales prices of existing single-family homes in thousands of dollars; (p) preliminary; n/a not available; (1) Reno, NV Metropolitan Statistical Area—see Appendix B for areas included
Source: National Association of Realtors, Median Sales Price of Existing Single-Family Homes for Metropolitan Areas, 4th Quarter 2014

Qualifying Income Based on Median Sales Price of Existing Single-Family Homes

Area	With 5% Down ($)	With 10% Down ($)	With 20% Down ($)
MSA[1]	57,883	54,837	48,744
U.S. Average	45,863	43,449	38,621

Note: Figures are preliminary; Qualifying income is based on a mortgage rate of 4.0%. Monthly principal and interest payment is limited to 25% of income; n/a not available; (1) Reno, NV Metropolitan Statistical Area—see Appendix B for areas included
Source: National Association of Realtors, Qualifying Income Based on Median Sales Price of Existing Single-Family Homes for Metropolitan Areas, 4th Quarter 2014

Median Apartment Condo-Coop Home Prices

Area	2012	2013	2014p	Percent Change 2013 to 2014
MSA[1]	75.7	96.6	115.0	19.0
U.S. Average	173.7	194.9	205.1	5.2

Note: Figures are median sales prices of existing apartment condo-coop homes in thousands of dollars; (p) preliminary; n/a not available; (1) Reno, NV Metropolitan Statistical Area—see Appendix B for areas included
Source: National Association of Realtors, Median Sales Price of Existing Apartment Condo-Coop Homes for Metropolitan Areas, 4th Quarter 2014

Gross Monthly Rent

Area	Under $200	$200 -299	$300 -499	$500 -749	$750 -999	$1,000 -1,499	$1,500 and up	Median ($)
City	1.1	1.5	8.1	29.0	28.4	22.2	9.7	837
MSA[1]	0.9	1.2	6.5	25.6	27.5	26.6	11.7	886
U.S.	1.7	3.2	7.8	22.1	24.3	26.0	14.9	900

Note: Figures are percentages except for Median; Gross rent is the contract rent plus the estimated average monthly cost of utilities (electricity, gas, and water and sewer) and fuels (oil, coal, kerosene, wood, etc.) if these are paid by the renter (or paid for the renter by someone else); (1) Figures cover the Reno, NV Metropolitan Statistical Area—see Appendix B for areas included
Source: U.S. Census Bureau, 2011-2013 American Community Survey 3-Year Estimates

Homeownership Rate

Area	2007 (%)	2008 (%)	2009 (%)	2010 (%)	2011 (%)	2012 (%)	2013 (%)	2014 (%)
MSA[1]	n/a	n/a	n/a	n/a	n/a	n/a	n/a	n/a
U.S.	68.1	67.8	67.4	66.9	66.1	65.4	65.1	64.5

Note: (1) Figures cover the Reno, NV Metropolitan Statistical Area—see Appendix B for areas included; n/a not available
Source: U.S. Census Bureau, Housing Vacancies and Homeownership Annual Statistics: 2014

Year Housing Structure Built

Area	2010 or Later	2000 -2009	1990 -1999	1980 -1989	1970 -1979	1960 -1969	1950 -1959	1940 -1949	Before 1940	Median Year
City	1.2	22.6	17.6	14.2	20.4	9.9	6.3	3.3	4.4	1984
MSA[1]	1.0	23.9	19.4	15.5	20.5	9.0	5.1	2.4	3.1	1986
U.S.	0.9	15.0	13.9	13.8	15.8	11.0	10.9	5.4	13.3	1976

Note: Figures are percentages except for Median Year; (1) Figures cover the Reno, NV Metropolitan Statistical Area—see Appendix B for areas included
Source: U.S. Census Bureau, 2011-2013 American Community Survey 3-Year Estimates

HEALTH

Health Risk Data

Category	MSA[1] (%)	U.S. (%)
Adults aged 18–64 who have any kind of health care coverage	71.1	79.6
Adults who reported being in good or excellent health	83.6	83.1
Adults who are current smokers	17.4	19.6
Adults who are heavy drinkers[2]	7.5	6.1
Adults who are binge drinkers[3]	17.5	16.9
Adults who are overweight (BMI 25.0 - 29.9)	35.4	35.8
Adults who are obese (BMI 30.0 - 99.8)	21.9	27.6
Adults who participated in any physical activities in the past month	82.5	77.1
Adults 50+ who have ever had a sigmoidoscopy or colonoscopy	65.4	67.3
Women aged 40+ who have had a mammogram within the past two years	69.3	74.0
Men aged 40+ who have had a PSA test within the past two years	48.5	45.2
Adults aged 65+ who have had flu shot within the past year	52.6	60.1
Adults who always wear a seatbelt	95.1	93.8

Note: Data as of 2012 unless otherwise noted; (1) Figures cover the Reno-Sparks, NV Metropolitan Statistical Area—see Appendix B for areas included; (2) Heavy drinkers are classified as males having more than two drinks per day or females having more than one drink per day; (3) Binge drinkers are classified as males having five or more drinks on one occasion or females having four or more drinks on one occasion
Source: Centers for Disease Control and Prevention, Behaviorial Risk Factor Surveillance System, SMART: Selected Metropolitan/Micropolitan Area Risk Trends, 2012 (Note: the CDC has discontinued this dataset but will be releasing a replacement in late 2015)

Chronic Health Indicators

Category	MSA[1] (%)	U.S. (%)
Adults who have ever been told they had a heart attack	3.5	4.5
Adults who have ever been told they had a stroke	1.3	2.9
Adults who have been told they currently have asthma	7.8	8.9
Adults who have ever been told they have arthritis	24.2	25.7
Adults who have ever been told they have diabetes[2]	6.4	9.7
Adults who have ever been told they had skin cancer	5.6	5.7
Adults who have ever been told they had any other types of cancer	6.4	6.5
Adults who have ever been told they have COPD	5.8	6.2
Adults who have ever been told they have kidney disease	3.3	2.5
Adults who have ever been told they have a form of depression	18.8	18.0

Note: Data as of 2012 unless otherwise noted; (1) Figures cover the Reno-Sparks, NV Metropolitan Statistical Area—see Appendix B for areas included; (2) Figures do not include pregnancy-related, borderline, or pre-diabetes
Source: Centers for Disease Control and Prevention, Behaviorial Risk Factor Surveillance System, SMART: Selected Metropolitan/Micropolitan Area Risk Trends, 2012 (Note: the CDC has discontinued this dataset but will be releasing a replacement in late 2015)

Mortality Rates for the Top 10 Causes of Death in the U.S.

ICD-10[a] Sub-Chapter	ICD-10[a] Code	Age-Adjusted Mortality Rate[1] per 100,000 population	
		County[2]	U.S.
Malignant neoplasms	C00-C97	161.7	166.2
Ischaemic heart diseases	I20-I25	131.6	105.7
Other forms of heart disease	I30-I51	33.2	49.3
Chronic lower respiratory diseases	J40-J47	49.3	42.1
Organic, including symptomatic, mental disorders	F01-F09	29.5	38.1
Cerebrovascular diseases	I60-I69	30.9	37.0
Other external causes of accidental injury	W00-X59	34.4	26.9
Other degenerative diseases of the nervous system	G30-G31	28.4	25.6
Diabetes mellitus	E10-E14	17.2	21.3
Hypertensive diseases	I10-I15	44.8	19.4

Note: (a) ICD-10 = International Classification of Diseases 10th Revision; (1) Mortality rates are a three year average covering 2011-2013; (2) Figures cover Washoe County
Source: Centers for Disease Control and Prevention, National Center for Health Statistics. Compressed Mortality File 1999-2013 on CDC WONDER Online Database, released October 2014. Data are compiled from the Compressed Mortality File 1999-2013, Series 20 No. 2S, 2014.

Mortality Rates for Selected Causes of Death

ICD-10[a] Sub-Chapter	ICD-10[a] Code	Age-Adjusted Mortality Rate[1] per 100,000 population	
		County[2]	U.S.
Assault	X85-Y09	4.4	5.2
Diseases of the liver	K70-K76	18.9	13.2
Human immunodeficiency virus (HIV) disease	B20-B24	*1.0	2.2
Influenza and pneumonia	J09-J18	18.1	15.4
Intentional self-harm	X60-X84	19.4	12.5
Malnutrition	E40-E46	Suppressed	0.9
Obesity and other hyperalimentation	E65-E68	*1.1	1.8
Renal failure	N17-N19	7.3	13.1
Transport accidents	V01-V99	9.1	11.7
Viral hepatitis	B15-B19	3.8	2.2

Note: (a) ICD-10 = International Classification of Diseases 10th Revision; (1) Mortality rates are a three year average covering 2011-2013; (2) Figures cover Washoe County; (*) Unreliable data as per CDC
Source: Centers for Disease Control and Prevention, National Center for Health Statistics. Compressed Mortality File 1999-2013 on CDC WONDER Online Database, released October 2014. Data are compiled from the Compressed Mortality File 1999-2013, Series 20 No. 2S, 2014.

Health Insurance Coverage

Area	With Health Insurance	With Private Health Insurance	With Public Health Insurance	Without Health Insurance	Population Under Age 18 Without Health Insurance
City	76.8	61.9	23.5	23.2	18.7
MSA[1]	79.6	64.4	24.8	20.4	17.0
U.S.	85.2	65.2	31.0	14.8	7.3

Note: Figures are percentages that cover the civilian noninstitutionalized population; (1) Figures cover the Reno, NV Metropolitan Statistical Area—see Appendix B for areas included
Source: U.S. Census Bureau, 2011-2013 American Community Survey 3-Year Estimates

Number of Medical Professionals

Area[1]	MDs[2]	DOs[2,3]	Dentists	Podiatrists	Chiropractors	Optometrists
Local (number)	1,153	86	274	18	108	80
Local (rate[4])	268.7	20.0	63.2	4.1	24.9	18.4
U.S. (rate[4])	270.0	20.2	63.1	5.7	25.2	14.9

Note: Data as of 2013 unless noted; (1) Local data covers Washoe County; (2) Data as of 2012 and includes all active, non-federal physicians; (3) Doctor of Osteopathic Medicine; (4) rate per 100,000 population
Source: U.S. Department of Health and Human Services, Health Resources and Services Administration, Bureau of Health Professions, Area Resource File (ARF) 2013-2014

EDUCATION

Public School District Statistics

District Name	Schls	Pupils	Pupil/ Teacher Ratio	Minority Pupils[1] (%)	Free Lunch Eligible[2] (%)	IEP[3] (%)
Washoe County School District	106	64,995	20.8	52.8	39.9	13.3

Note: Table includes school districts with 2,000 or more students; (1) Percentage of students that are not non-Hispanic white; (2) Percentage of students that are eligible for the free lunch program; (3) Percentage of students that have an Individualized Education Program.
Source: U.S. Department of Education, National Center for Education Statistics, Common Core of Data, Local Education Agency (School District) Universe Survey: School Year 2012-2013; U.S. Department of Education, National Center for Education Statistics, Common Core of Data, Public Elementary/Secondary School Universe Survey: School Year 2012-2013

Best High Schools

According to *The Daily Beast,* Reno is home to one of the best high schools in the U.S.: **The Davidson Academy of Nevada** (#34); *The Daily Beast* used six indicators culled from school surveys to compare public high schools in the U.S., with graduation and college acceptance rates weighed most heavily. Other criteria included: college-level courses/exams and SAT/ACT scores. *The Daily Beast, "Top High Schools 2014"*

Highest Level of Education

Area	Less than H.S.	H.S. Diploma	Some College, No Deg.	Associate Degree	Bachelor's Degree	Master's Degree	Prof. School Degree	Doctorate Degree
City	14.5	22.8	26.2	6.8	18.6	6.8	2.4	1.9
MSA[1]	13.7	24.1	26.6	7.6	17.9	6.5	2.2	1.5
U.S.	13.7	28.0	21.2	7.9	18.2	7.7	1.9	1.3

Note: Figures cover persons age 25 and over; (1) Figures cover the Reno, NV Metropolitan Statistical Area—see Appendix B for areas included
Source: U.S. Census Bureau, 2011-2013 American Community Survey 3-Year Estimates

Educational Attainment by Race

Area	High School Graduate or Higher (%)					Bachelor's Degree or Higher (%)				
	Total	White	Black	Asian	Hisp.[2]	Total	White	Black	Asian	Hisp.[2]
City	85.5	87.6	86.0	88.4	53.2	29.7	31.6	19.4	39.4	8.2
MSA[1]	86.3	88.1	87.8	87.7	54.5	28.0	29.4	21.3	37.8	9.2
U.S.	86.3	88.3	83.1	85.7	64.0	29.1	30.4	18.8	50.7	13.7

Note: Figures shown cover persons 25 years old and over; (1) Figures cover the Reno, NV Metropolitan Statistical Area—see Appendix B for areas included; (2) People of Hispanic origin can be of any race
Source: U.S. Census Bureau, 2011-2013 American Community Survey 3-Year Estimates

School Enrollment by Grade and Control

Area	Preschool (%)		Kindergarten (%)		Grades 1 - 4 (%)		Grades 5 - 8 (%)		Grades 9 - 12 (%)	
	Public	Private	Public	Private	Public	Private	Public	Private	Public	Private
City	63.8	36.2	89.3	10.7	93.6	6.4	93.2	6.8	96.8	3.2
MSA[1]	55.2	44.8	89.9	10.1	93.0	7.0	92.6	7.4	94.9	5.1
U.S.	57.7	42.3	87.9	12.1	89.9	10.1	90.0	10.0	90.7	9.3

Note: Figures shown cover persons 3 years old and over; (1) Figures cover the Reno, NV Metropolitan Statistical Area—see Appendix B for areas included
Source: U.S. Census Bureau, 2011-2013 American Community Survey 3-Year Estimates

Average Salaries of Public School Classroom Teachers

Area	2013-14		2014-15		Percent Change 2013-14 to 2014-15	Percent Change 2004-05 to 2014-15
	Dollars	Rank[1]	Dollars	Rank[1]		
NEVADA	55,813	20	56,703	19	1.59	30.7
U.S. Average	56,610	–	57,379	–	1.36	20.8

Note: (1) State rank ranges from 1 to 51 where 1 indicates highest salary.
Source: National Education Association, Rankings & Estimates: Rankings of the States 2014 and Estimates of School Statistics 2015, March 2015

Higher Education

Four-Year Colleges			Two-Year Colleges			Medical Schools[1]	Law Schools[2]	Voc/Tech[3]
Public	Private Non-profit	Private For-profit	Public	Private Non-profit	Private For-profit			
1	0	2	1	0	5	1	0	0

Note: Figures cover institutions located within the city limits and include main campuses only; (1) includes schools accredited by the Liaison Committee on Medical Education and the American Osteopathic Association's Commission on Osteopathic College Accreditation; (2) includes ABA-accredited schools, schools with provisional ABA accreditation, and state accredited schools; (3) includes all schools with programs that are less than 2 years.
Source: National Center for Education Statistics, Integrated Postsecondary Education System (IPEDS), 2013-14; Association of American Medical Colleges, Member List, May 1, 2015; American Osteopathic Association, Member List, May 1, 2015; Law School Admission Council, Official Guide to ABA-Approved Law Schools Online, May 1, 2015; Wikipedia, List of Medical Schools in the United States, May 1, 2015; Wikipedia, List of Law Schools in the United States, May 1, 2015

According to *U.S. News & World Report*, the Reno, NV metro area is home to one of the best national universities in the U.S.: **University of Nevada-Reno** (#194). The indicators used to capture academic quality fall into a number of categories: assessment by administrators at peer institutions; retention of students; faculty resources; student selectivity; financial resources; alumni giving; high school counselor ratings of colleges; and graduation rate. *U.S. News & World Report, "America's Best Colleges 2015"*

PRESIDENTIAL ELECTION

2012 Presidential Election Results

Area	Obama (%)	Romney (%)	Other (%)
Washoe County	50.7	47.2	2.1
U.S.	51.0	47.2	1.8

Note: Results may not add to 100% due to rounding
Source: Dave Leip's Atlas of U.S. Presidential Elections

EMPLOYERS

Major Employers

Company Name	Industry
Atlantis Casino Resort	Casino hotels
Bellagio	Casino hotels
Circus Circus Casinos - Reno	Casino hotels
City of Reno	Executive & legislative offices combined
Desert Palace	Casino hotels
Eldorado Hotel & Casino	Casino hotels
Grand Sierra Resort & Casino	Casino hotels
Harrahs Reno	Casino hotels
IGT	All other miscellaneous manufacturing
Integrity Staffing Solutions	Temporary help services
Mandalay Corp	Casino hotels
Peppermill Hotel Casino - Reno	Casino hotels
Renown Regional Medical Center	General medical and surgical hospitals
Saint Marys	General medical and surgical hospitals
Sierra Nevada Healthcare System	General medical and surgical hospitals
Silver Legacy Resort Casino	Casino hotels
Sparks Nugget	Casino hotels
Truckee Meadows Community Coll	Junior colleges
United Parcel Service	Couriers
University of Nevada-Reno	Colleges and universities
Washoe County Comptroller	Executive & legislative offices combined
Washoe County School District	Elementary and secondary schools
West Business Solutions	Telemarketing bureaus

Note: Companies shown are located within the Reno, NV Metropolitan Statistical Area.
Source: Hoovers.com; Wikipedia

PUBLIC SAFETY

Crime Rate

Area	All Crimes	Violent Crimes				Property Crimes		
		Murder	Forcible Rape	Robbery	Aggrav. Assault	Burglary	Larceny -Theft	Motor Vehicle Theft
City	3,583.6	6.0	29.2	131.1	329.8	606.7	2,107.4	373.2
Suburbs[1]	2,287.5	4.4	33.0	41.8	165.2	531.1	1,343.5	168.6
Metro[2]	2,975.1	5.2	31.0	89.2	252.5	571.2	1,748.7	277.2
U.S.	3,098.6	4.5	25.2	109.1	229.1	610.0	1,899.4	221.3

Note: Figures are crimes per 100,000 population; (1) All areas within the metro area that are located outside the city limits; (2) Figures cover the Reno, NV Metropolitan Statistical Area—see Appendix B for areas included
Source: FBI Uniform Crime Reports, 2013

Hate Crimes

Area	Number of Quarters Reported	Number of Incidents per Bias Motivation						
		Race	Religion	Sexual Orientation	Ethnicity	Disability	Gender	Gender Identity
City	2	2	1	1	0	0	0	0
U.S.	4	2,871	1,031	1,233	655	83	18	31

Source: Federal Bureau of Investigation, Hate Crime Statistics 2013

Identity Theft Consumer Complaints

Area	Complaints	Complaints per 100,000 Population	Rank[2]
MSA[1]	445	101.7	58
U.S.	332,646	104.3	-

Note: (1) Figures cover the Reno, NV Metropolitan Statistical Area—see Appendix B for areas included; (2) Rank ranges from 1 to 380 where 1 indicates greatest number of identity theft complaints per 100,000 population
Source: Federal Trade Commission, Consumer Sentinel Network Data Book for January–December 2014

Fraud and Other Consumer Complaints

Area	Complaints	Complaints per 100,000 Population	Rank[2]
MSA[1]	1,952	446.0	66
U.S.	2,250,205	705.7	-

Note: (1) Figures cover the Reno, NV Metropolitan Statistical Area—see Appendix B for areas included; (2) Rank ranges from 1 to 380 where 1 indicates greatest number of identity theft complaints per 100,000 population
Source: Federal Trade Commission, Consumer Sentinel Network Data Book for January–December 2014

RECREATION

Culture

Dance[1]	Theatre[1]	Instrumental Music[1]	Vocal Music[1]	Series and Festivals	Museums and Art Galleries[2]	Zoos and Aquariums[3]
2	1	2	1	2	19	0

Note: (1) Professional perfoming groups; (2) Based on organizations with SIC code 8412; (3) AZA-accredited
Source: The Grey House Performing Arts Directory, 2015-16; Association of Zoos & Aquariums, AZA Member Zoos & Aquariums, April 2015; www.AccuLeads.com, April 2015

Professional Sports Teams

Team Name	League	Year Established

No teams are located in the metro area
Source: Wikipedia, Major Professional Sports Teams of the United States and Canada, April 2015

CLIMATE

Average and Extreme Temperatures

Temperature	Jan	Feb	Mar	Apr	May	Jun	Jul	Aug	Sep	Oct	Nov	Dec	Yr.
Extreme High (°F)	70	75	83	89	96	103	104	105	101	91	77	70	105
Average High (°F)	45	51	56	64	73	82	91	89	81	70	55	46	67
Average Temp. (°F)	32	38	41	48	56	63	70	68	61	51	40	33	50
Average Low (°F)	19	23	26	31	38	44	49	47	40	32	25	20	33
Extreme Low (°F)	-16	-16	0	13	18	25	33	24	20	8	1	-16	-16

Note: Figures cover the years 1949-1992
Source: National Climatic Data Center, International Station Meteorological Climate Summary, 9/96

Average Precipitation/Snowfall/Humidity

Precip./Humidity	Jan	Feb	Mar	Apr	May	Jun	Jul	Aug	Sep	Oct	Nov	Dec	Yr.
Avg. Precip. (in.)	1.0	0.9	0.7	0.4	0.7	0.4	0.3	0.2	0.3	0.4	0.8	1.0	7.2
Avg. Snowfall (in.)	6	5	4	1	1	Tr	0	0	Tr	Tr	2	4	24
Avg. Rel. Hum. 7am (%)	79	77	71	61	55	51	49	55	64	72	78	80	66
Avg. Rel. Hum. 4pm (%)	51	41	34	27	26	22	19	19	22	27	41	51	32

Note: Figures cover the years 1949-1992; Tr = Trace amounts (<0.05 in. of rain; <0.5 in. of snow)
Source: National Climatic Data Center, International Station Meteorological Climate Summary, 9/96

Weather Conditions

Temperature			Daytime Sky			Precipitation		
10°F & below	32°F & below	90°F & above	Clear	Partly cloudy	Cloudy	0.01 inch or more precip.	0.1 inch or more snow/ice	Thunder-storms
14	178	50	143	139	83	50	17	14

Note: Figures are average number of days per year and cover the years 1949-1992
Source: National Climatic Data Center, International Station Meteorological Climate Summary, 9/96

HAZARDOUS WASTE

Superfund Sites

Reno has no sites on the EPA's Superfund Final National Priorities List. There are a total of 1,322 Superfund sites on the list in the U.S. *U.S. Environmental Protection Agency, Final National Priorities List, April 14, 2015*

AIR & WATER QUALITY

Air Quality Trends: Ozone

	2004	2005	2006	2007	2008	2009	2010	2011	2012	2013
MSA[1]	0.069	0.067	0.071	0.069	0.074	0.064	0.067	0.064	0.070	0.066

Note: (1) Data covers the Reno, NV Metropolitan Statistical Area—see Appendix B for areas included. The values shown are the composite ozone concentration averages among trend sites based on the highest fourth daily maximum 8-hour concentration in parts per million. These trends are based on sites having an adequate record of monitoring data during the trend period. Data from exceptional events are included.
Source: U.S. Environmental Protection Agency, Air Quality Monitoring Information, "Air Quality Trends by City, 2000-2013"

Air Quality Index

Area	Percent of Days when Air Quality was...[2]					AQI Statistics[2]	
	Good	Moderate	Unhealthy for Sensitive Groups	Unhealthy	Very Unhealthy	Maximum	Median
MSA[1]	60.0	36.7	1.1	0.8	1.4	891	47

Note: (1) Data covers the Reno, NV Metropolitan Statistical Area—see Appendix B for areas included; (2) Based on 365 days with AQI data in 2014. Air Quality Index (AQI) is an index for reporting daily air quality. EPA calculates the AQI for five major air pollutants regulated by the Clean Air Act: ground-level ozone, particle pollution (aka particulate matter), carbon monoxide, sulfur dioxide, and nitrogen dioxide. The AQI runs from 0 to 500. The higher the AQI value, the greater the level of air pollution and the greater the health concern. There are six AQI categories: "Good" AQI is between 0 and 50. Air quality is considered satisfactory; "Moderate" AQI is between 51 and 100. Air quality is acceptable; "Unhealthy for Sensitive Groups" When AQI values are between 101 and 150, members of sensitive groups may experience health effects; "Unhealthy" When AQI values are between 151 and 200 everyone may begin to experience health effects; "Very Unhealthy" AQI values between 201 and 300 trigger a health alert; "Hazardous" AQI values over 300 trigger warnings of emergency conditions (not shown).
Source: U.S. Environmental Protection Agency, Air Quality Index Report, 2014

Air Quality Index Pollutants

Area	Percent of Days when AQI Pollutant was...[2]					
	Carbon Monoxide	Nitrogen Dioxide	Ozone	Sulfur Dioxide	Particulate Matter 2.5	Particulate Matter 10
MSA[1]	0.0	3.8	59.5	0.0	26.0	10.7

Note: (1) Data covers the Reno, NV Metropolitan Statistical Area—see Appendix B for areas included;
(2) Based on 365 days with AQI data in 2014. The Air Quality Index (AQI) is an index for reporting daily air quality. EPA calculates the AQI for five major air pollutants regulated by the Clean Air Act: ground-level ozone, particle pollution (also known as particulate matter), carbon monoxide, sulfur dioxide, and nitrogen dioxide. The AQI runs from 0 to 500. The higher the AQI value, the greater the level of air pollution and the greater the health concern.
Source: U.S. Environmental Protection Agency, Air Quality Index Report, 2014

Maximum Air Pollutant Concentrations: Particulate Matter, Ozone, CO and Lead

	Particulate Matter 10 (ug/m³)	Particulate Matter 2.5 Wtd AM (ug/m³)	Particulate Matter 2.5 24-Hr (ug/m³)	Ozone (ppm)	Carbon Monoxide (ppm)	Lead (ug/m³)
MSA[1] Level	999	12.3	41	0.069	2	n/a
NAAQS[2]	150	15	35	0.075	9	0.15
Met NAAQS[2]	No	Yes	No	Yes	Yes	n/a

Note: (1) Data covers the Reno, NV Metropolitan Statistical Area—see Appendix B for areas included; Data from exceptional events are included; (2) National Ambient Air Quality Standards; ppm = parts per million; ug/m³ = micrograms per cubic meter; n/a not available.
Concentrations: Particulate Matter 10 (coarse particulate)—highest second maximum 24-hour concentration; Particulate Matter 2.5 Wtd AM (fine particulate)—highest weighted annual mean concentration; Particulate Matter 2.5 24-Hour (fine particulate)—highest 98th percentile 24-hour concentration; Ozone—highest fourth daily maximum 8-hour concentration; Carbon Monoxide—highest second maximum non-overlapping 8-hour concentration; Lead—maximum running 3-month average
Source: U.S. Environmental Protection Agency, Air Quality Monitoring Information, "Air Quality Statistics by City, 2013"

Maximum Air Pollutant Concentrations: Nitrogen Dioxide and Sulfur Dioxide

	Nitrogen Dioxide AM (ppb)	Nitrogen Dioxide 1-Hr (ppb)	Sulfur Dioxide AM (ppb)	Sulfur Dioxide 1-Hr (ppb)	Sulfur Dioxide 24-Hr (ppb)
MSA[1] Level	16	56	n/a	6	n/a
NAAQS[2]	53	100	30	75	140
Met NAAQS[2]	Yes	Yes	n/a	Yes	n/a

Note: (1) Data covers the Reno, NV Metropolitan Statistical Area—see Appendix B for areas included; Data from exceptional events are included; (2) National Ambient Air Quality Standards; ppm = parts per million; ug/m³ = micrograms per cubic meter; n/a not available.
Concentrations: Nitrogen Dioxide AM—highest arithmetic mean concentration; Nitrogen Dioxide 1-Hr—highest 98th percentile 1-hour daily maximum concentration; Sulfur Dioxide AM—highest annual mean concentration; Sulfur Dioxide 1-Hr—highest 99th percentile 1-hour daily maximum concentration; Sulfur Dioxide 24-Hr—highest second maximum 24-hour concentration
Source: U.S. Environmental Protection Agency, Air Quality Monitoring Information, "Air Quality Statistics by City, 2013"

Drinking Water

Water System Name	Pop. Served	Primary Water Source Type	Violations[1]	
			Health Based	Monitoring/ Reporting
Truckee Meadows Water Authority	311,932	Surface	0	0

Note: (1) Based on violation data from January 1, 2014 to December 31, 2014 (includes unresolved violations from earlier years)
Source: U.S. Environmental Protection Agency, Office of Ground Water and Drinking Water, Safe Drinking Water Information System (based on data extracted January 27, 2015)

Sacramento, California

Background

Sacramento is the capital of California and the seat of Sacramento County. It was named after the Sacramento River which derived its name from the word referring to the Catholic Holy Eucharist. It lies at the juncture of the Sacramento and American rivers.

A Swiss soldier, Captain John Augustus Sutter settled Sacramento in 1839, when he received permission of the Mexican government to establish a new colony which became known as New Helvetia. The 50,000-acre land grant included a wide swath of the rich and fertile valley between the two rivers, and Sutter's ranch, trading post, and agricultural projects were soon productive and profitable. When, in 1846, American troops occupied the area, Sutter was well-positioned to take advantage, and his trade soon extended well up the northern coast.

In 1948, one of Sutter's employees, a carpenter named James W. Marshall, discovered gold at the mill at Columa, and "Sutter's Mill". The discovery brought an onslaught of prospectors and the beginning of the California gold rush. The prospectors overwhelmed New Helvetia resources and the havoc that followed destroyed the economic foundation of the town. The newcomers overran Sutter's land and claimed it as their own. Sutter tried to expand his business to include mining supplies, but was only meagerly rewarded. He then ceded land along the Sacramento River to his son, who founded the town that became the city we know today.

Sacramento was a natural center for miners' needs, including housing, food, banking,transportation and necessary mining equipment. One of Sacramento's most famous entrepreneurs is Levi Strauss who sold the ultimate mining pants known as "Levi's". Sacramento's economy was booming, but it was plagued by floods, as well as fire and a cholera epidemic. The flooding has since been well controlled by dam projects, which also now supply electricity to a wide area. In 1854, John Sutter managed to fight off a daunting list of candidates, and Sacramento became California's capital.

On April 3, 1860, the legendary Pony Express carried mail from Sacramento to St. Joseph , Missouri. This team of riders relayed the mail on horseback established a new record at the time. The ten day journey of the nearly 1,800 mile trip, although unprofitable, found the attention of the federal government and helped launch of our current postal system. The honor of its fastest delivery of a package is held by Lincoln's inaugural address which beat the average time of 10 days to just eight.

The state Renaissance Revival capitol building was built in 1860. The domed granite structure is built on a sloping terrace, with a park full of trees and flowers surrounding the building. The tree-lined streets laid out in front are broad and straight, and eye-pleasing camellias decorate the scenery in random patterns.

Sutter's Fort State Historical Monument features a restoration of Sutter's original ranch and trading post, and a designated Old Sacramento Historical Area preserves many buildings from the gold rush period and thereafter. At the city's Crocker Art Museum, visitors can view an extensive collection of works by Michelangelo, Rembrandt, and Leonardo da Vinci. In October 2010, the Crocker completed a 125,000-ft. expansion.

The Wells Fargo Museum is a monument to the history of the Pony Express and the era of the gold rush. Housed in the original bank building that managed the Pony Express, staff dressed in period attire conduct tours. The museum displays include tools, gold nuggets, documents and other artifacts relevant to the Pony Express and the miners of the gold rush era.

The Woodland Opera House opened in 1896 and is on the National Register of Historic Places. When motion pictures became the preferred means of entertainment, the opera house suffered financial difficulties and closed in 1913. The boarded up building was dormant until 1971 when it was saved from demolition by Yolo County Historic Society who gave it to the state in 1980. The building underwent a total renovation in 1982, and is now a major entertainment venue.

Sacramento has a mild climate with abundant sunshine. A nearly cloud-free sky prevails throughout the summer months, which are usually dry, with warm to hot afternoons and mostly mild nights.

Rankings

Business/Finance Rankings

- Based on metro area social media reviews, the employment opinion group Glassdoor surveyed 50 of the largest U.S. metro areas on measures including compensation and benefits, satisfaction with management, business outlook, and number of employers hiring. The Sacramento metro area was ranked #17 in overall employee satisfaction. *www.glassdoor.com, "Employment Satisfaction Report Card by City," June 13, 2014*

- In a survey of economic confidence in the nation's 50 largest metropolitan areas conducted January–December 2014, the Sacramento metro area placed #22, according to Gallup's 2014 Economic Confidence Index. *Gallup, "San Jose and San Francisco Lead in Economic Confidence," March 19, 2015*

- Using data from the Council for Community and Economic Research's 2013 Annual Report, NerdWallet ranked the 100 U.S. cities with the most expensive cost of living. Cities in California and in the Northeast topped the list. Of the cities with the highest cost of living, Sacramento ranked #37. *NerdWallet.com, "Most Expensive Cities in America," June 4, 2014*

- The Brookings Institution ranked the 50 largest cities in the U.S. based on income inequality. Sacramento was ranked #27. (#1 = greatest ineqality). Criteria: the cities were ranked based on the "95/20 ratio," a figure representing the income at which a household earns more than 95 percent of all other households, divided by the income at which a household earns more than only 20 percent of all other households. *Brookings Institution, "Income Inequality in America's 50 Largest Cities, 2007-2013," March 17, 2015*

- Sacramento was ranked #28 out of 100 metro areas in terms of economic performance (#1 = best) during the recession and recovery from trough quarter through the second quarter of 2013. Criteria: percent change in employment; percentage point change in unemployment rate; percent change in gross metropolitan product; percent change in House Price Index. *Brookings Institution, MetroMonitor: Tracking Economic Recession and Recovery in America's 100 Largest Metropolitan Areas, September 2013*

- The finance site *24/7 Wall St.* identified the metropolitan areas that have the smallest and largest pay disparities between men and women, comparing the median earnings for the past 12 months of both men and women working full-time in the country's 100 largest metropolitan statistical areas. Of the ten best-paying metros for women, the Sacramento metro area ranked #3. *24/7 Wall St., "The Best (and Worst) Paying Cities for Women," March 6, 2015*

- *Forbes* reports that Sacramento was identified as one of the happiest cities to work in by CareerBliss.com, an online community for career advancement. The city ranked #2 out of 10. Criteria: work-life balance; an employee's relationship with his or her boss and co-workers; general work environment; compensation; opportunities for advancement; company culture; and resources. *Forbes.com, "The 10 Happiest and Unhappiest Cities to Work in Right Now," January 16, 2015*

- The Sacramento metro area appeared on the Milken Institute "2013 Best Performing Cities" list. Rank: #89 out of 200 large metro areas. Criteria: job growth; wage and salary growth; high-tech output growth. *Milken Institute, "Best-Performing Cities 2014," January 2015*

- *Forbes* ranked the 200 most populous metro areas to determine the nation's "Best Places for Business and Careers." The Sacramento metro area was ranked #124. Criteria: costs (business and living); job growth (past and projected); income growth; educational attainment (college and high school); projected economic growth; cultural and recreational opportunities; net migration patterns; number of highly ranked colleges. *Forbes, "The Best Places for Business and Careers 2014," July 23, 2014*

Dating/Romance Rankings

- Of the 100 U.S. cities surveyed by *Men's Health* in its quest to identify the nation's best cities for dating and forming relationships, Sacramento was ranked #38 for online dating (#1 = best). *Men's Health, "The Best and Worst Cities for Online Dating," January 30, 2013*

Education Rankings

- Personal finance website *WalletHub* analyzed the 150 largest U.S. metropolitan statistical areas to determine where the most educated Americans are choosing to settle. Criteria: educational attainment; percentage of workers with jobs in computer, engineering, and science fields; quality and size of each metro area's universities. Sacramento was ranked #26 (#1 = most educated city). *www.WalletHub.com, "2014's Most and Least Educated Cities*

- The real estate website *MovoTo.com* selected Sacramento as one of the "Nerdiest Cities in America." The city ranked #4 among the top 10 derived from data on the 50 most populous cities in the United States. Criteria: Number of annual comic book, video game, anime, and sci-fi/fantasy conventions; people per comic book store, video game store, and traditional gaming store; people per LARPing ("live action role-playing") group; people per science museum. Also factored in: distance to the nearest Renaissance faire. *MovoTo.com, "The 10 Nerdiest Cities in America," April 10, 2013*

- Sacramento was selected as one of America's most literate cities. The city ranked #38 out of the 77 largest U.S. cities. Criteria: number of booksellers; library resources; Internet resources; educational attainment; periodical publishing resources; newspaper circulation. *Central Connecticut State University, "America's Most Literate Cities, 2014," April 8, 2015*

Environmental Rankings

- The Sacramento metro area came in at #121 for the relative comfort of its climate on Sperling's list of "chill cities," as measured by the Sperling Heat Index. All 361 metro areas are included. Criteria included daytime high temperatures, nighttime low temperatures, dew point, and relative humidity at the high temperatures. *www.bertsperling.com, "Sperling's Chill Cities," July 18, 2013*

- Sperling's BestPlaces assessed 379 metropolitan areas of the United States for the likelihood of dangerously extreme weather events or earthquakes. In general the Southeast and South-Central regions have the highest risk of weather extremes and earthquakes, while the Pacific Northwest enjoys the lowest risk. Of the least risky metropolitan areas, the Sacramento metro area was ranked #47. *www.bestplaces.net, "Safest Places from Natural Disasters," April 2011*

- Sacramento was identified as one of America's dirtiest metro areas by *Forbes*. The area ranked #12 out of 20. Criteria: air quality; water quality; toxic releases; superfund sites. *Forbes, "America's 20 Dirtiest Cities," December 10, 2012*

- The U.S. Environmental Protection Agency (EPA) released a list of large U.S. metropolitan areas with the most ENERGY STAR certified buildings in 2014. The Sacramento metro area was ranked #19 out of 25. *U.S. Environmental Protection Agency, "Top Cities With the Most ENERGY STAR Certified Buildings in 2014," March 25, 2015*

- Sacramento was highlighted as one of the 25 most ozone-polluted metro areas in the U.S. during 2011 through 2013. The area ranked #5. *American Lung Association, State of the Air 2015*

- Sacramento was highlighted as one of the 25 metro areas most polluted by short-term particle pollution (24-hour PM 2.5) in the U.S. during 2011 through 2013. The area ranked #14. *American Lung Association, State of the Air 2015*

Food/Drink Rankings

- *Men's Health* ranked 100 major U.S. cities in terms of alcohol intoxication. Sacramento ranked #70 (#1 = most sober).Criteria: binge drinking; alcohol-related traffic accidents, arrests, and fatalities. *Men's Health, "The Drunkest Cities in America," November 19, 2013*

Health/Fitness Rankings

- For each of the 50 most populous metro areas in the United States, the American College of Sports Medicine's American Fitness Index evaluated infrastructure, community assets, and policies that encourage healthy and fit lifestyles, including preventive health behaviors, levels of chronic disease conditions, health care access, and community resources and policies that support physical activity. The Sacramento metro area ranked #7 for "community fitness." Personal health indicators were considered as well as community and environmental indicators. *www.americanfitnessindex.org, "ACSM American Fitness Index Health and Community Fitness Status of the 50 Largest Metropolitan Areas," May 2013*

- The Sacramento metro area was identified as one of the worst cities for bed bugs in America by pest control company Orkin. The area ranked #41 out of 50 based on the number of bed bug treatments Orkin performed from January to December 2013. *Orkin, "Chicago Tops Bed Bug Cities List for Second Year in a Row," January 16, 2014*

- Sacramento was identified as one of 15 cities with the highest increase in bed bug activity in the U.S. by pest control provider Terminix. The city ranked #1.Criteria: cities with the largest percentage gains in bed bug customer calls from January–May 2013 compared to the same time period in 2012. *Terminix, "Cities with Highest Increases in Bed Bug Activity," July 9, 2013*

- Sacramento was selected as one of the 25 fittest cities in America by *Men's Fitness Online*. It ranked #19 out of America's 50 largest cities. Criteria: fitness centers and sport stores; nutrition; sports participation; TV viewing; overweight/sedentary; junk food; air quality; geography; commute; parks and open space; city recreational facilities; access to healthcare; motivation; mayor and city initiatives; state obesity initiatives. *Men's Fitness, "The Fittest and Fattest Cities in America," March 5, 2012*

- Sacramento was identified as a "2013 Spring Allergy Capital." The area ranked #94 out of 100. Three groups of factors were used to identify the most severe cities for people with allergies during the spring season: annual pollen levels; medicine utilization; access to board-certified allergists. *Asthma and Allergy Foundation of America, "Spring Allergy Capitals 2013"*

- Sacramento was identified as a "2013 Fall Allergy Capital." The area ranked #99 out of 100. Three groups of factors were used to identify the most severe cities for people with allergies during the fall season: annual pollen levels; medicine utilization; access to board-certified allergists. *Asthma and Allergy Foundation of America, "Fall Allergy Capitals 2013"*

- Sacramento was identified as a "2013 Asthma Capital." The area ranked #65 out of the nation's 100 largest metropolitan areas. Twelve factors were used to identify the most challenging places to live for people with asthma: estimated prevalence; self-reported prevalence; crude death rate for asthma; annual pollen score; annual air quality; public smoking laws; number of board-certified asthma specialists; school inhaler access laws; rescue medication use; controller medication use; uninsured rate; poverty rate. *Asthma and Allergy Foundation of America, "Asthma Capitals 2013"*

- *Men's Health* ranked 100 major U.S. cities in terms of the best and worst cities for men. Sacramento ranked #38. Criteria: thirty-three data points were examined covering health, fitness, and quality of life. *Men's Health, "The Best & Worst Cities for Men 2014," December 6, 2013*

- Sacramento was selected as one of the best metropolitan areas for hospital care in America by *HealthGrades.com*. The rankings are based on a comprehensive study of patient death and complication rates in the nation's nearly 5,000 hospitals. Hospitals performing in the top 5% nationwide across 26 different medical procedures and diagnoses were identified. *HealthGrades.com* then ranked cities by the highest percentage of these Distinguished Hospitals for Clinical Excellence™. The Sacramento metro area ranked #41. *HealthGrades.com, "America's Top 50 Cities for Hospital Care," January 21, 2012*

- The Sacramento metro area appeared in the 2013 Gallup-Healthways Well-Being Index. The area ranked #82 out of 189. The Gallup-Healthways Well-Being Index score is an average of six sub-indexes, which individually examine life evaluation, emotional health, work environment, physical health, healthy behaviors, and access to basic necessities. Results are based on telephone interviews conducted as part of the Gallup-Healthways Well-Being Index survey January 2–December 29, 2012, and January 2–December 30, 2013, with a random sample of 531,630 adults, aged 18 and older, living in metropolitan areas in the 50 U.S. states and the District of Columbia. *Gallup-Healthways, "State of American Well-Being," March 25, 2014*

- The Sacramento metro area was identified as one of "America's Most Stressful Cities" by *Sperling's BestPlaces*. The metro area ranked #8 out of 50. Criteria: unemployment rate; suicide rate; commute time; mental health; poor rest; alcohol use; violent crime rate; property crime rate; cloudy days annually. *Sperling's BestPlaces, www.BestPlaces.net, "Stressful Cities 2012*

Real Estate Rankings

- The Sacramento metro area was identified as #10 among the ten housing markets with the highest percentage of distressed property sales, based on the findings of the housing data website RealtyTrac. Criteria included being sold "short"—for less than the outstanding mortgage balance—or in a foreclosure auction, income and poverty figures, and unemployment data. *247wallst.com, "Cities Selling the Most Distressed Homes," January 23, 2014*

- The Sacramento metro area was identified as one of the nation's 20 hottest housing markets in 2015.Criteria: median number of days homes were spending on the market in March 2015. The area ranked #20. *Realtor.com, "These Are the 20 Hottest Housing Markets in the U.S. Right Now," April 8, 2015*

- The Sacramento metro area was identified as one of the top 20 housing markets to invest in for 2015 by *Forbes*. The area ranked #19. Criteria: strong population and job growth; relatively low home prices which are below equilibrium home price (EHP). The EHP is what the average price for a market should be, if speculation, weird distortions in local income, and other factors (like the housing collapse) weren't present in the market. *Forbes.com, "Best Buy Cities: Where to Invest in Housing in 2015," January 9, 2015*

- Sacramento was ranked #67 out of 275 metro areas in terms of house price appreciation in 2014 (#1 = highest rate). *Federal Housing Finance Agency, House Price Index, 4th Quarter 2014*

- The Sacramento metro area was identified as one of the 20 best housing markets in the U.S. in 2014. The area ranked #13 out of 178 markets with a home price appreciation of 12.2%. Criteria: year-over-year change of median sales price of existing single-family homes between the 4th quarter of 2013 and the 4th quarter of 2014. *National Association of Realtors®, Median Sales Price of Existing Single-Family Homes for Metropolitan Areas, 4th Quarter 2014*

- The Sacramento metro area was identified as one of the 10 best condo markets in the U.S. in 2014. The area ranked #10 out of 66 markets with a price appreciation of 12.9%. Criteria: year-over-year change of median sales price of existing apartment condo-coop homes between the 4th quarter of 2013 and the 4th quarter of 2014. *National Association of Realtors®, Median Sales Price of Existing Apartment Condo-Coop Homes for Metropolitan Areas, 4th Quarter 2014*

- The Sacramento metro area was identified as one of the 20 least affordable housing markets in the U.S. in 2014. The area ranked #20 out of 178 markets. Criteria: whether or not a typical family could qualify for a mortgage loan on a typical home. *National Association of Realtors®, Affordability Index of Existing Single-Family Homes for Metropolitan Areas, 2014*

- Sacramento was ranked #205 out of 226 metro areas in terms of housing affordability in 2014 by the National Association of Home Builders (#1 = most affordable). The NAHB-Wells Fargo Housing Opportunity Index (HOI) for a given area is defined as the share of homes sold in that area that would have been affordable to a family earning the local median income, based on standard mortgage underwriting criteria. *National Association of Home Builders®, NAHB-Wells Fargo Housing Opportunity Index, 4th Quarter 2014*

Safety Rankings

- Symantec, in partnership with Sperling's BestPlaces, ranked the 50 largest cities in the U.S. in terms of their vulnerability to cybercrime. The city ranked #8. Criteria: number of cyberattacks and potential infections; level of Internet access; expenditures on smartphones and computer hardware/software; wireless hotspots; broadband connectivity; Internet usage; online purchases. *Symantec, "Riskiest Online Cities of 2012" February 15, 2012*

- Allstate ranked the 200 largest cities in America in terms of driver safety. Sacramento ranked #114. Allstate researchers analyzed internal property damage claims over a two-year period from January 2011 to December 2012. A weighted average of the two-year numbers determined the annual percentages. *Allstate, "Allstate America's Best Drivers Report, 2014"*

- The National Insurance Crime Bureau ranked 380 metro areas in the U.S. in terms of per capita rates of vehicle theft. The Sacramento metro area ranked #24 (#1 = highest rate). Criteria: number of vehicle theft offenses per 100,000 inhabitants in 2012. *National Insurance Crime Bureau, "Hot Spots 2012," June 26, 2013*

Seniors/Retirement Rankings

- From its Best Cities for Successful Aging indexes, the Milken Institute generated rankings for metropolitan areas, weighing data in eight categories—health care, wellness, living arrangements, transportation, financial characteristics, education and employment opportunities, community engagement, and overall livability. The Sacramento metro area was ranked #87 overall in the large metro area category. *Milken Institute, "Best Cities for Successful Aging, 2014"*

Sports/Recreation Rankings

- Sacramento was chosen as a bicycle friendly community by the League of American Bicyclists. A "Bicycle Friendly Community" welcomes cyclists by providing safe accommodation for cycling and encouraging people to bike for transportation and recreation. There are four award levels: Platinum; Gold; Silver; and Bronze. The community achieved an award level of Silver. *League of American Bicyclists, "Bicycle Friendly Community Master List," Fall 2013*

- Sacramento was chosen as one of America's best cities for bicycling. The city ranked #25 out of 50. Criteria: robust cycling infrastructure; vibrant bike culture. The editors only considered cities with populations of 95,000 or more. *Bicycling, "America's Top 50 Bike-Friendly Cities," May 23, 2012*

Women/Minorities Rankings

- To determine the best metro areas for working women, the personal finance website NerdWallet considered city size as well as relevant economic metrics—high salaries, narrow pay differential by gender, prevalence of women in the highest-paying industries, and population growth over 2010–2012. Of the large U.S. cities examined, the Sacramento metro area held the #10 position. *www.nerdwallet.com, "Best Places for Women in the Workforce," May 19, 2013*

- *Women's Health* examined U.S. cities and identified the 100 best cities for women. Sacramento was ranked #65. Criteria: 30 categories were examined from obesity and breast cancer rates to commuting times and hours spent working out. *Women's Health, "Best Cities for Women 2012"*

Miscellaneous Rankings

- According to *Condé Nast Traveler* magazine's 2013 Readers' Choice Survey of American cities, Sacramento was rated #10 (#1 = worst) among the ten most unfriendly. *www.cntraveler.com, "The Friendliest and Unfriendliest Cities in the U.S.," July 30, 2013*

- Mars Chocolate North America, the makers of COMBOS®, in partnership with Sperling's BestPlaces, ranked 50 major metro areas in terms of their "manliness." The Sacramento metro area ranked #44. Criteria: number of professional sports teams; number of nearby NASCAR tracks and racing events; manly lifestyle; concentration of manly retail stores; manly occupations per capita; salty snack sales; "Board of Manliness" rankings. *Mars Chocolate North America, "America's Manliest Cities 2012"*

- The National Alliance to End Homelessness ranked the 100 most populous metro areas in terms the rate of homelessness. The Sacramento metro area ranked #41. Criteria: number of homeless people per 10,000 population in 2011. *National Alliance to End Homelessness, The State of Homelessness in America 2012*

Business Environment

CITY FINANCES

City Government Finances

Component	2012 ($000)	2012 ($ per capita)
Total Revenues	973,892	2,088
Total Expenditures	924,050	1,981
Debt Outstanding	1,087,279	2,331
Cash and Securities[1]	1,128,754	2,420

Note: (1) Cash and security holdings of a government at the close of its fiscal year, including those of its dependent agencies, utilities, and liquor stores.
Source: U.S Census Bureau, State & Local Government Finances 2012

City Government Revenue by Source

Source	2012 ($000)	2012 ($ per capita)
General Revenue		
From Federal Government	43,626	94
From State Government	85,125	182
From Local Governments	34	0
Taxes		
Property	198,730	426
Sales and Gross Receipts	145,953	313
Personal Income	0	0
Corporate Income	0	0
Motor Vehicle License	0	0
Other Taxes	21,985	47
Current Charges	315,842	677
Liquor Store	0	0
Utility	80,973	174
Employee Retirement	8,108	17

Source: U.S Census Bureau, State & Local Government Finances 2012

City Government Expenditures by Function

Function	2012 ($000)	2012 ($ per capita)	2012 (%)
General Direct Expenditures			
Air Transportation	0	0	0.0
Corrections	0	0	0.0
Education	0	0	0.0
Employment Security Administration	0	0	0.0
Financial Administration	5,903	13	0.6
Fire Protection	87,182	187	9.4
General Public Buildings	5,598	12	0.6
Governmental Administration, Other	73,398	157	7.9
Health	17,874	38	1.9
Highways	148,341	318	16.1
Hospitals	0	0	0.0
Housing and Community Development	29,397	63	3.2
Interest on General Debt	46,425	100	5.0
Judicial and Legal	2,630	6	0.3
Libraries	12,300	26	1.3
Parking	15,376	33	1.7
Parks and Recreation	63,229	136	6.8
Police Protection	136,069	292	14.7
Public Welfare	0	0	0.0
Sewerage	20,939	45	2.3
Solid Waste Management	59,366	127	6.4
Veterans' Services	0	0	0.0
Liquor Store	0	0	0.0
Utility	91,795	197	9.9
Employee Retirement	25,914	56	2.8

Source: U.S Census Bureau, State & Local Government Finances 2012

DEMOGRAPHICS

Population Growth

Area	1990 Census	2000 Census	2010 Census	Population Growth (%) 1990-2000	Population Growth (%) 2000-2010
City	368,923	407,018	466,488	10.3	14.6
MSA[1]	1,481,126	1,796,857	2,149,127	21.3	19.6
U.S.	248,709,873	281,421,906	308,745,538	13.2	9.7

Note: (1) Figures cover the Sacramento—Arden-Arcade—Roseville, CA Metropolitan Statistical Area—see Appendix B for areas included
Source: U.S. Census Bureau, Census 1990, 2000, 2010

Household Size

Area	Persons in Household (%) One	Two	Three	Four	Five	Six	Seven or More	Average Household Size
City	33.0	29.2	14.2	11.7	5.8	3.2	2.8	2.65
MSA[1]	26.2	32.7	15.9	13.7	6.6	2.9	2.0	2.73
U.S.	27.7	33.6	15.7	13.1	6.0	2.3	1.5	2.64

Note: (1) Figures cover the Sacramento—Arden-Arcade—Roseville, CA Metropolitan Statistical Area—see Appendix B for areas included
Source: U.S. Census Bureau, 2011-2013 American Community Survey 3-Year Estimates

Race

Area	White Alone[2] (%)	Black Alone[2] (%)	Asian Alone[2] (%)	AIAN[3] Alone[2] (%)	NHOPI[4] Alone[2] (%)	Other Race Alone[2] (%)	Two or More Races (%)
City	49.8	14.1	18.6	0.8	1.4	8.4	6.9
MSA[1]	66.6	7.2	12.3	0.8	0.7	6.4	5.9
U.S.	73.9	12.6	5.0	0.8	0.2	4.7	2.9

Note: (1) Figures cover the Sacramento—Arden-Arcade—Roseville, CA Metropolitan Statistical Area—see Appendix B for areas included; (2) Alone is defined as not being in combination with one or more other races; (3) American Indian and Alaska Native; (4) Native Hawaiian and Other Pacific Islander
Source: U.S. Census Bureau, 2011-2013 American Community Survey 3-Year Estimates

Hispanic or Latino Origin

Area	Total (%)	Mexican (%)	Puerto Rican (%)	Cuban (%)	Other (%)
City	27.5	23.8	0.8	0.1	2.7
MSA[1]	20.6	17.0	0.7	0.2	2.8
U.S.	16.9	10.8	1.6	0.6	3.8

Note: Persons of Hispanic or Latino origin can be of any race; (1) Figures cover the Sacramento—Arden-Arcade—Roseville, CA Metropolitan Statistical Area—see Appendix B for areas included
Source: U.S. Census Bureau, 2011-2013 American Community Survey 3-Year Estimates

Segregation

Type	Segregation Indices[1] 1990	2000	2010	2010 Rank[2]	Percent Change 1990-2000	Percent Change 1990-2010	Percent Change 2000-2010
Black/White	55.7	57.9	56.9	46	2.2	1.2	-1.0
Asian/White	48.1	50.0	49.9	8	1.9	1.8	-0.1
Hispanic/White	37.0	40.3	38.9	71	3.3	1.9	-1.4

Note: All figures cover the Metropolitan Statistical Area—see Appendix B for areas included; Figures are based on an analysis of 1990, 2000, and 2010 Census Decennial Census tract data by William H. Frey, Brookings Institution and the University of Michigan Social Science Data Analysis Network. In this analysis all racial groups (whites, blacks, and asians) are non-Hispanic members of those races. Hispanics are shown as a separate category;
(1) Segregation Indices are Dissimilarity Indices that measure the degree to which the minority group is distributed differently than whites across census tracts. They range from 0 (complete integration) to 100 (complete segregation) where the value indicates the percentage of the minority group that needs to move to be distributed exactly like whites; (2) Ranges from 1 (most segregated) to 102 (least segregated); n/a not available.
Source: www.CensusScope.org

Ancestry

Area	German	Irish	English	American	Italian	Polish	French[2]	Scottish	Dutch
City	8.3	6.7	5.4	2.4	3.8	0.9	1.6	1.4	0.8
MSA[1]	13.2	9.7	8.8	3.7	5.3	1.5	2.6	2.0	1.3
U.S.	14.9	10.8	8.0	7.4	5.5	3.0	2.7	1.7	1.4

Note: Figures are the percentage of the total population reporting a particular ancestry. The nine most commonly reported ancestries in the U.S. are shown. Figures include multiple ancestries (e.g. if a person reported being Irish and Italian, they were included in both columns); (1) Figures cover the Sacramento—Arden-Arcade—Roseville, CA Metropolitan Statistical Area—see Appendix B for areas included; (2) Excludes Basque
Source: U.S. Census Bureau, 2011-2013 American Community Survey 3-Year Estimates

Foreign-Born Population

Area	Any Foreign Country	Mexico	Asia	Europe	Carribean	South America	Central America[2]	Africa	Canada
City	22.5	7.0	10.8	1.6	0.2	0.3	0.6	0.5	0.1
MSA[1]	18.0	4.9	8.0	2.8	0.1	0.3	0.6	0.4	0.3
U.S.	13.0	3.7	3.8	1.5	1.2	0.9	1.0	0.6	0.3

Note: (1) Figures cover the Sacramento—Arden-Arcade—Roseville, CA Metropolitan Statistical Area—see Appendix B for areas included; (2) Excludes Mexico.
Source: U.S. Census Bureau, 2011-2013 American Community Survey 3-Year Estimates

Marital Status

Area	Never Married	Now Married[2]	Separated	Widowed	Divorced
City	40.3	39.2	2.8	5.4	12.3
MSA[1]	33.2	47.2	2.4	5.4	11.7
U.S.	32.7	48.1	2.2	6.0	11.0

Note: Figures are percentages and cover the population 15 years of age and older; (1) Figures cover the Sacramento—Arden-Arcade—Roseville, CA Metropolitan Statistical Area—see Appendix B for areas included; (2) Excludes separated
Source: U.S. Census Bureau, 2011-2013 American Community Survey 3-Year Estimates

Disability Status

Area	All Ages	Under 18 Years Old	18 to 64 Years Old	65 Years and Over
City	13.2	4.1	11.5	42.1
MSA[1]	12.1	4.1	9.9	38.1
U.S.	12.3	4.1	10.2	36.3

Note: Figures show percent of the civilian noninstitutionalized population that reported having a disability. Disability status is determined from from six types of difficulty: vision, hearing, cognitive, ambulatory, self-care, and independent living. For children under 5 years old, hearing and vision difficulty are used to determine disability status. For children between the ages of 5 and 14, disability status is determined from hearing, vision, cognitive, ambulatory, and self-care difficulties. For people aged 15 years and older, they are considered to have a disability if they have difficulty with any one of the six difficulty types; (1) Figures cover the Sacramento—Arden-Arcade—Roseville, CA Metropolitan Statistical Area—see Appendix B for areas included.
Source: U.S. Census Bureau, 2011-2013 American Community Survey 3-Year Estimates

Age

Area	Under Age 5	Age 5–19	Age 20–34	Age 35–44	Age 45–54	Age 55–64	Age 65–74	Age 75–84	Age 85+	Median Age
City	7.1	19.7	24.9	13.1	12.6	11.3	6.1	3.4	1.9	34.0
MSA[1]	6.4	20.6	21.1	12.8	14.0	12.1	7.2	3.9	1.8	36.4
U.S.	6.4	19.9	20.7	12.9	14.1	12.3	7.6	4.2	1.9	37.4

Note: (1) Figures cover the Sacramento—Arden-Arcade—Roseville, CA Metropolitan Statistical Area—see Appendix B for areas included
Source: U.S. Census Bureau, 2011-2013 American Community Survey 3-Year Estimates

Gender

Area	Males	Females	Males per 100 Females
City	230,879	244,657	94.4
MSA[1]	1,075,677	1,119,301	96.1
U.S.	154,451,010	159,410,713	96.9

Note: (1) Figures cover the Sacramento—Arden-Arcade—Roseville, CA Metropolitan Statistical Area—see Appendix B for areas included
Source: U.S. Census Bureau, 2011-2013 American Community Survey 3-Year Estimates

Religious Groups by Family

Area	Catholic	Baptist	Non-Den.	Methodist[2]	Lutheran	LDS[3]	Pente-costal	Presby-terian[4]	Muslim[5]	Judaism
MSA[1]	16.2	3.2	4.0	1.8	0.8	3.4	2.0	0.8	0.8	0.3
U.S.	19.1	9.3	4.0	4.0	2.3	2.0	1.9	1.6	0.8	0.7

Note: Figures are the number of adherents as a percentage of the total population; (1) Figures cover the Sacramento—Arden-Arcade—Roseville, CA Metropolitan Statistical Area—see Appendix B for areas included; (2) Methodist/Pietist; (3) Latter Day Saints; (4) Reformed; (5) Figures are estimates
Source: Association of Statisticians of American Religious Bodies, 2010 U.S. Religion Census: Religious Congregations & Membership Study

Religious Groups by Tradition

Area	Catholic	Evangelical Protestant	Mainline Protestant	Other Tradition	Black Protestant	Orthodox
MSA[1]	16.2	11.4	2.2	5.8	0.6	0.3
U.S.	19.1	16.2	7.3	4.3	1.6	0.3

Note: Figures are the number of adherents as a percentage of the total population; (1) Figures cover the Sacramento—Arden-Arcade—Roseville, CA Metropolitan Statistical Area—see Appendix B for areas included
Source: Association of Statisticians of American Religious Bodies, 2010 U.S. Religion Census: Religious Congregations & Membership Study

ECONOMY

Gross Metropolitan Product

Area	2012	2013	2014	2015	Rank[2]
MSA[1]	97.6	100.4	104.6	110.7	33

Note: Figures are in billions of dollars; (1) Figures cover the Sacramento—Arden-Arcade—Roseville, CA Metropolitan Statistical Area—see Appendix B for areas included; (2) Rank is based on 2015 data and ranges from 1 to 363
Source: The U.S. Conference of Mayors, U.S. Metro Economies: GMP and Employment 2013-2015, June 2014

Economic Growth

Area	2010-12 (%)	2013 (%)	2014 (%)	2015 (%)	Rank[2]
MSA[1]	1.8	1.5	2.4	3.9	35
U.S.	2.1	2.0	2.3	3.2	–

Note: Figures are real gross metropolitan product (GMP) growth rates and represent annual average percent change; (1) Figures cover the Sacramento—Arden-Arcade—Roseville, CA Metropolitan Statistical Area—see Appendix B for areas included; (2) Rank is based on 2015 data and ranges from 1 to 363
Source: The U.S. Conference of Mayors, U.S. Metro Economies: GMP and Employment 2013-2015, June 2014

Metropolitan Area Exports

Area	2008	2009	2010	2011	2012	2013	Rank[2]
MSA[1]	3,608.0	3,502.0	4,070.5	4,686.0	5,194.6	5,777.1	47

Note: Figures are in millions of dollars; (1) Figures cover the Sacramento—Arden-Arcade—Roseville, CA Metropolitan Statistical Area—see Appendix B for areas included; (2) Rank is based on 2013 data and ranges from 1 to 387
Source: U.S. Department of Commerce, International Trade Administration, Office of Trade & Industry Information, Manufacturing & Services, data extracted April 3, 2015

Building Permits

Area	Single-Family			Multi-Family			Total		
	2013	2014	Pct. Chg.	2013	2014	Pct. Chg.	2013	2014	Pct. Chg.
City	232	256	10.3	27	25	-7.4	259	281	8.5
MSA[1]	3,539	3,694	4.4	650	465	-28.5	4,189	4,159	-0.7
U.S.	620,802	634,597	2.2	370,020	411,766	11.3	990,822	1,046,363	5.6

Note: (1) Figures cover the Sacramento—Arden-Arcade—Roseville, CA Metropolitan Statistical Area—see Appendix B for areas included; Figures represent new, privately-owned housing units authorized (unadjusted data); All permit data are based on estimates with imputation.
Source: U.S. Census Bureau, Manufacturing, Mining, and Construction Statistics, Building Permits, 2013, 2014

Bankruptcy Filings

Area	Business Filings			Nonbusiness Filings		
	2013	2014	% Chg.	2013	2014	% Chg.
Sacramento County	207	128	-38.2	6,736	5,064	-24.8
U.S.	33,212	26,983	-18.8	1,038,720	909,812	-12.4

Note: Business filings include Chapter 7, Chapter 11, Chapter 12, and Chapter 13; Nonbusiness filings include Chapter 7, Chapter 11, and Chapter 13
Source: Administrative Office of the U.S. Courts, Business and Nonbusiness Bankruptcy, County Cases Commenced by Chapter of the Bankruptcy Code, During the 12- Month Period Ending December 31, 2013 and Business and Nonbusiness Bankruptcy, County Cases Commenced by Chapter of the Bankruptcy Code, During the 12- Month Period Ending December 31, 2014

Housing Vacancy Rates

Area	Gross Vacancy Rate[2] (%)			Year-Round Vacancy Rate[3] (%)			Rental Vacancy Rate[4] (%)			Homeowner Vacancy Rate[5] (%)		
	2012	2013	2014	2012	2013	2014	2012	2013	2014	2012	2013	2014
MSA[1]	8.5	9.7	10.2	7.6	8.4	7.6	5.7	7.0	6.5	2.3	1.2	1.0
U.S.	13.8	13.6	13.4	10.8	10.7	10.4	8.7	8.3	7.6	2.0	2.0	1.9

Note: (1) Figures cover the Sacramento—Arden-Arcade—Roseville, CA Metropolitan Statistical Area—see Appendix B for areas included; (2) The percentage of the total housing inventory that is vacant; (3) The percentage of the housing inventory (excluding seasonal units) that is year-round vacant; (4) The percentage of rental inventory that is vacant for rent; (5) The percentage of homeowner inventory that is vacant for sale
Source: U.S. Census Bureau, Housing Vacancies and Homeownership Annual Statistics: 2014

INCOME

Income

Area	Per Capita ($)	Median Household ($)	Average Household ($)
City	24,952	48,807	64,943
MSA[1]	28,234	57,217	76,121
U.S.	27,884	52,176	72,897

Note: (1) Figures cover the Sacramento—Arden-Arcade—Roseville, CA Metropolitan Statistical Area—see Appendix B for areas included
Source: U.S. Census Bureau, 2011-2013 American Community Survey 3-Year Estimates

Household Income Distribution

Area	Percent of Households Earning							
	Under $15,000	$15,000 -24,999	$25,000 -34,999	$35,000 -49,999	$50,000 -74,999	$75,000 -99,000	$100,000 -149,999	$150,000 and up
City	16.3	11.0	10.3	13.3	18.7	11.2	11.7	7.6
MSA[1]	11.8	9.8	9.6	13.0	17.9	12.4	14.5	11.0
U.S.	13.0	10.9	10.3	13.6	17.9	11.9	12.7	9.6

Note: (1) Figures cover the Sacramento—Arden-Arcade—Roseville, CA Metropolitan Statistical Area—see Appendix B for areas included
Source: U.S. Census Bureau, 2011-2013 American Community Survey 3-Year Estimates

Poverty Rate

Area	All Ages	Under 18 Years Old	18 to 64 Years Old	65 Years and Over
City	23.2	33.6	21.3	12.1
MSA[1]	16.5	22.0	15.9	8.9
U.S.	15.9	22.4	14.8	9.5

Note: Figures are percentage of people whose income during the past 12 months was below the poverty level;
(1) Figures cover the Sacramento—Arden-Arcade—Roseville, CA Metropolitan Statistical Area—see Appendix B for areas included
Source: U.S. Census Bureau, 2011-2013 American Community Survey 3-Year Estimates

EMPLOYMENT

Labor Force and Employment

Area	Civilian Labor Force			Workers Employed		
	Dec. 2013	Dec. 2014	% Chg.	Dec. 2013	Dec. 2014	% Chg.
City	224,686	225,924	0.6	206,006	210,607	2.2
MSA[1]	1,039,207	1,046,596	0.7	959,164	980,489	2.2
U.S.	154,408,000	155,521,000	0.7	144,423,000	147,190,000	1.9

Note: Data is not seasonally adjusted and covers workers 16 years of age and older; (1) Figures cover the
Sacramento—Arden-Arcade—Roseville, CA Metropolitan Statistical Area—see Appendix B for areas included
Source: Bureau of Labor Statistics, Local Area Unemployment Statistics

Unemployment Rate

Area	2014											
	Jan.	Feb.	Mar.	Apr.	May	Jun.	Jul.	Aug.	Sep.	Oct.	Nov.	Dec.
City	8.7	8.7	8.7	7.4	7.4	7.6	8.1	7.8	7.2	7.2	7.2	6.8
MSA[1]	8.1	8.1	8.1	6.9	6.8	7.0	7.5	7.2	6.6	6.6	6.7	6.3
U.S.	7.0	7.0	6.8	5.9	6.1	6.3	6.5	6.3	5.7	5.5	5.5	5.4

Note: Data is not seasonally adjusted and covers workers 16 years of age and older; (1) Figures cover the
Sacramento—Arden-Arcade—Roseville, CA Metropolitan Statistical Area—see Appendix B for areas included
Source: Bureau of Labor Statistics, Local Area Unemployment Statistics

Employment by Occupation

Occupation Classification	City (%)	MSA[1] (%)	U.S. (%)
Management, Business, Science, and Arts	38.2	38.9	36.2
Natural Resources, Construction, and Maintenance	6.7	8.0	9.0
Production, Transportation, and Material Moving	9.0	8.4	12.1
Sales and Office	26.1	25.7	24.4
Service	20.0	19.0	18.3

Note: Figures cover employed civilians 16 years of age and older; (1) Figures cover the
Sacramento—Arden-Arcade—Roseville, CA Metropolitan Statistical Area—see Appendix B for areas included
Source: U.S. Census Bureau, 2011-2013 American Community Survey 3-Year Estimates

Employment by Industry

Sector	MSA[1]		U.S.
	Number of Employees	Percent of Total	Percent of Total
Construction	45,300	5.0	4.4
Education and Health Services	137,000	15.1	15.5
Financial Activities	49,400	5.5	5.7
Government	228,400	25.3	15.8
Information	13,700	1.5	2.0
Leisure and Hospitality	91,200	10.1	10.3
Manufacturing	35,000	3.9	8.7
Mining and Logging	500	0.1	0.6
Other Services	30,700	3.4	4.0
Professional and Business Services	121,600	13.4	13.8
Retail Trade	102,700	11.4	11.4
Transportation, Warehousing, and Utilities	24,400	2.7	3.9
Wholesale Trade	24,600	2.7	4.2

Note: Figures are non-farm employment as of December 2014. Figures are not seasonally adjusted and include workers 16 years of age and older; (1) Figures cover the Sacramento—Arden-Arcade—Roseville, CA Metropolitan Statistical Area—see Appendix B for areas included
Source: Bureau of Labor Statistics, Current Employment Statistics, Employment, Hours, and Earnings

Occupations with Greatest Projected Employment Growth: 2012 – 2022

Occupation[1]	2012 Employment	2022 Projected Employment	Numeric Employment Change	Percent Employment Change
Personal Care Aides	386,900	587,200	200,300	51.8
Combined Food Preparation and Serving Workers, Including Fast Food	286,000	362,400	76,400	26.7
Retail Salespersons	468,400	528,100	59,700	12.7
Laborers and Freight, Stock, and Material Movers, Hand	270,500	322,300	51,800	19.1
Waiters and Waitresses	246,100	290,300	44,200	18.0
Registered Nurses	254,500	297,400	42,900	16.9
General and Operations Managers	253,800	295,700	41,900	16.5
Secretaries and Administrative Assistants, Except Legal, Medical, and Executive	212,800	250,100	37,300	17.5
Cashiers	357,800	392,600	34,800	9.7
Cooks, Restaurant	116,900	150,600	33,700	28.8

Note: Projections cover California; (1) Sorted by numeric employment change
Source: www.projectionscentral.com, State Occupational Projections, 2012–2022 Long-Term Projections

Fastest Growing Occupations: 2012 – 2022

Occupation[1]	2012 Employment	2022 Projected Employment	Numeric Employment Change	Percent Employment Change
Economists	3,100	5,100	2,000	64.5
Helpers—Brickmasons, Blockmasons, Stonemasons, and Tile and Marble Setters	2,900	4,600	1,700	58.6
Brickmasons and Blockmasons	5,100	8,000	2,900	56.9
Insulation Workers, Floor, Ceiling, and Wall	1,600	2,500	900	56.3
Stonemasons	1,100	1,700	600	54.5
Insulation Workers, Mechanical	1,100	1,700	600	54.5
Personal Care Aides	386,900	587,200	200,300	51.8
Foresters	1,200	1,800	600	50.0
Terrazzo Workers and Finishers	1,100	1,600	500	45.5
Mechanical Door Repairers	1,100	1,600	500	45.5

Note: Projections cover California; (1) Sorted by percent employment change and excludes occupations with numeric employment change less than 100
Source: www.projectionscentral.com, State Occupational Projections, 2012–2022 Long-Term Projections

Average Wages

Occupation	$/Hr.	Occupation	$/Hr.
Accountants and Auditors	32.79	Maids and Housekeeping Cleaners	13.54
Automotive Mechanics	22.50	Maintenance and Repair Workers	19.83
Bookkeepers	19.80	Marketing Managers	56.13
Carpenters	22.94	Nuclear Medicine Technologists	50.94
Cashiers	12.17	Nurses, Licensed Practical	27.59
Clerks, General Office	16.11	Nurses, Registered	50.67
Clerks, Receptionists/Information	14.09	Nursing Assistants	15.59
Clerks, Shipping/Receiving	15.07	Packers and Packagers, Hand	12.78
Computer Programmers	36.53	Physical Therapists	45.28
Computer Systems Analysts	38.26	Postal Service Mail Carriers	25.51
Computer User Support Specialists	27.84	Real Estate Brokers	n/a
Cooks, Restaurant	11.34	Retail Salespersons	12.79
Dentists	88.71	Sales Reps., Exc. Tech./Scientific	31.85
Electrical Engineers	50.64	Sales Reps., Tech./Scientific	41.20
Electricians	29.07	Secretaries, Exc. Legal/Med./Exec.	17.72
Financial Managers	56.32	Security Guards	12.75
First-Line Supervisors/Managers, Sales	20.02	Surgeons	n/a
Food Preparation Workers	10.14	Teacher Assistants	14.40
General and Operations Managers	53.55	Teachers, Elementary School	32.40
Hairdressers/Cosmetologists	11.88	Teachers, Secondary School	33.30
Internists	108.61	Telemarketers	15.40
Janitors and Cleaners	12.91	Truck Drivers, Heavy/Tractor-Trailer	19.39
Landscaping/Groundskeeping Workers	13.80	Truck Drivers, Light/Delivery Svcs.	17.86
Lawyers	61.90	Waiters and Waitresses	11.79

Note: Wage data covers the Sacramento—Arden-Arcade—Roseville, CA Metropolitan Statistical Area—see Appendix B for areas included; Hourly wages for elementary/secondary school teachers and teacher assistants were calculated by the editors from annual wage data assuming a 40 hour work week; n/a not available.
Source: Bureau of Labor Statistics, Metro Area Occupational Employment and Wage Estimates, May 2014

TAXES

State Corporate Income Tax Rates

State	Tax Rate (%)	Income Brackets ($)	Num. of Brackets	Financial Institution Tax Rate (%)[a]	Federal Income Tax Ded.
California	8.84 (c)	Flat rate	1	10.84 (c)	No

Note: Tax rates as of January 1, 2015; (a) Rates listed are the corporate income tax rate applied to financial institutions or excise taxes based on income. Some states have other taxes based upon the value of deposits or shares; (c) Minimum tax is $800 in California, $100 in District of Columbia, $50 in North Dakota (banks), $500 in Rhode Island, $200 per location in South Dakota (banks), $100 in Utah, $250 in Vermont.
Source: Federation of Tax Administrators, "State Corporate Income Tax Rates, 2015"

State Individual Income Tax Rates

State	Tax Rate (%)	Income Brackets ($)	Num. of Brackets	Personal Exempt. ($)[1] Single	Dependents	Fed. Inc. Tax Ded.
California (a)	1.0 - 12.3 (f)	7,749- 519,687 (b)	9	108 (c)	333 (c)	No

Note: Tax rates as of January 1, 2015; Local- and county-level taxes are not included; n/a not applicable; (1) Married joint filers generally receive double the single exemption; (a) 17 states have statutory provision for automatically adjusting to the rate of inflation the dollar values of the income tax brackets, standard deductions, and/or personal exemptions. Massachusetts, Michigan, and Nebraska index the personal exemption only. Oregon does not index the income brackets for $125,000 and over. Maine has suspended indexing for 2014 and 2015; (b) For joint returns, taxes are twice the tax on half the couple's income; (c) The personal exemption takes the form of a tax credit instead of a deduction; (f) California imposes an additional 1% tax on taxable income over $1 million, making the maximum rate 13.3% over $1 million.
Source: Federation of Tax Administrators, "State Individual Income Tax Rates, 2015"

Various State and Local Tax Rates

State	State and Local Sales and Use (%)	State Sales and Use (%)	Gasoline[1] (¢/gal.)	Cigarette[2] ($/pack)	Spirits[3] ($/gal.)	Wine[4] ($/gal.)	Beer[5] ($/gal.)
California	8.5	7.50 (b)	45.39	0.87	3.30 (f)	0.20	0.20

Note: All tax rates as of January 1, 2015; (1) The American Petroleum Institute has developed a methodology for determining the average tax rate on a gallon of fuel. Rates may include any of the following: excise taxes, environmental fees, storage tank fees, other fees or taxes, general sales tax, and local taxes. In states where gasoline is subject to the general sales tax, or where the fuel tax is based on the average sale price, the average rate determined by API is sensitive to changes in the price of gasoline. States that fully or partially apply general sales taxes to gasoline: CA, CO, GA, IL, IN, MI, NY; (2) The federal excise tax of $1.0066 per pack and local taxes are not included; (3) Rates are those applicable to off-premise sales of 40% alcohol by volume (a.b.v.) distilled spirits in 750ml containers. Local excise taxes are excluded; (4) Rates are those applicable to off-premise sales of 11% a.b.v. non-carbonated wine in 750ml containers; (5) Rates are those applicable to off-premise sales of 4.7% a.b.v. beer in 12 ounce containers; (b) Three states levy mandatory, statewide, local add-on sales taxes at the state level: California (1%), Utah (1.25%), and Virginia (1%). We include these in their state sales taxes; (f) Different rates are also applicable according to alcohol content, place of production, size of container, or place purchased (on- or off-premise or onboard airlines).
Source: Tax Foundation, 2015 Facts & Figures: How Does Your State Compare?

State Business Tax Climate Index Rankings

State	Overall Rank	Corporate Tax Index Rank	Individual Income Tax Index Rank	Sales Tax Index Rank	Unemployment Insurance Tax Index Rank	Property Tax Index Rank
California	48	34	50	42	14	14

Note: The index is a measure of how each state's tax laws affect economic performance. The lower the rank, the more favorable a state's tax system is for business. States without a given tax are given a ranking of 1. The scores/rankings for the District of Columbia do not affect other states. The 2015 index represents the tax climate as of July 1, 2014.
Source: Tax Foundation, State Business Tax Climate Index 2015

COMMERCIAL REAL ESTATE

Office Market

Market Area	Inventory (sq. ft.)	Vacancy Rate (%)	Under Construction (sq. ft.)	YTD Net Absorption (sq. ft.)	Total Average Asking Rent ($/sq. ft./year)
Sacramento	65,899,491	20.1	173,187	668,412	22.20
National	4,745,108,508	14.3	71,190,461	51,084,126	27.40

Source: Newmark Grubb Knight Frank, National Office Market Report, 4th Quarter 2014

Industrial/Warehouse/R&D Market

Market Area	Inventory (sq. ft.)	Vacancy Rate (%)	Under Construction (sq. ft.)	YTD Net Absorption (sq. ft.)	Total Average Asking Rent ($/sq. ft./year)
Sacramento	202,645,082	10.4	839,022	3,674,182	4.79
National	14,238,613,765	7.2	134,387,407	185,246,438	5.64

Source: Newmark Grubb Knight Frank, National Industrial Market Report, 4th Quarter 2014

COMMERCIAL UTILITIES

Typical Monthly Electric Bills

Area	Commercial Service ($/month)		Industrial Service ($/month)	
	1,500 kWh	40 kW demand 14,000 kWh	1,000 kW demand 200,000 kWh	50,000 kW demand 32,500,000 kWh
City	n/a	n/a	n/a	n/a
Average[1]	201	1,653	26,124	2,639,743

Note: Figures are based on annualized 2014 rates; (1) Average based on 180 utilities surveyed; n/a not available
Source: Edison Electric Institute, Typical Bills and Average Rates Report, Summer 2014

TRANSPORTATION

Means of Transportation to Work

Area	Car/Truck/Van		Public Transportation			Bicycle	Walked	Other Means	Worked at Home
	Drove Alone	Car-pooled	Bus	Subway	Railroad				
City	71.8	12.5	3.1	0.4	0.4	2.3	3.3	1.5	4.7
MSA[1]	75.2	11.3	1.9	0.3	0.2	1.9	2.2	1.3	5.8
U.S.	76.4	9.6	2.6	1.8	0.6	0.6	2.8	1.3	4.3

Note: Figures are percentages and cover workers 16 years of age and older; (1) Figures cover the Sacramento—Arden-Arcade—Roseville, CA Metropolitan Statistical Area—see Appendix B for areas included Source: U.S. Census Bureau, 2011-2013 American Community Survey 3-Year Estimates

Travel Time to Work

Area	Less Than 10 Minutes	10 to 19 Minutes	20 to 29 Minutes	30 to 44 Minutes	45 to 59 Minutes	60 to 89 Minutes	90 Minutes or More
City	10.2	35.2	25.2	18.7	4.6	3.0	3.2
MSA[1]	11.7	30.2	22.5	21.8	6.9	3.8	3.1
U.S.	13.3	29.7	20.9	20.2	7.7	5.7	2.6

Note: Figures are percentages and include workers 16 years old and over; (1) Figures cover the Sacramento—Arden-Arcade—Roseville, CA Metropolitan Statistical Area—see Appendix B for areas included Source: U.S. Census Bureau, 2011-2013 American Community Survey 3-Year Estimates

Travel Time Index

Area	1985	1990	1995	2000	2005	2010	2011
Urban Area[1]	1.07	1.16	1.17	1.21	1.27	1.20	1.20
Average[2]	1.09	1.14	1.16	1.19	1.23	1.18	1.18

Note: Travel Time Index—the ratio of travel time in the peak period to the travel time at free-flow conditions. For example, a value of 1.30 indicates a 20-minute free-flow trip takes 26 minutes in the peak. Free-flow speeds (60 mph on freeways and 35 mph on principal arterials) are used as the comparison threshold; (1) Covers the Sacramento CA urban area; (2) average of 498 urban areas Source: Texas Transportation Institute, Urban Mobility Report 2012, December 2012

Public Transportation

Agency Name / Mode of Transportation	Vehicles Operated in Maximum Service	Annual Unlinked Passenger Trips (in thous.)	Annual Passenger Miles (in thous.)
Sacramento Regional Transit District (Sacramento RT)			
Bus (directly operated)	158	13,784.2	49,439.9
Demand Response (directly operated)	2	4.0	16.3
Light Rail (directly operated)	61	13,513.5	75,796.5

Source: Federal Transit Administration, National Transit Database, 2013

Air Transportation

Airport Name and Code / Type of Service	Passenger Airlines[1]	Passenger Enplanements	Freight Carriers[2]	Freight (lbs.)
Sacramento International (SMF)				
Domestic service (U.S. carriers - 2014)	20	4,322,997	10	63,424,413
International service (U.S. carriers - 2013)	3	1,316	0	0

Note: (1) Includes all U.S.-based major, minor and commuter airlines that carried at least one passenger during the year; (2) Includes all U.S.-based airlines and freight carriers that transported at least one lb. of freight during the year.
Source: Bureau of Transportation Statistics, The Intermodal Transportation Database, Air Carriers: T-100 Domestic Market (U.S. Carriers), 2014; Bureau of Transportation Statistics, The Intermodal Transportation Database, Air Carriers: T-100 International Market (U.S. Carriers), 2013

Other Transportation Statistics

Major Highways:	I-5; I-80
Amtrak Service:	Yes
Major Waterways/Ports:	None

Source: Amtrak.com; Google Maps

BUSINESSES

Major Business Headquarters

Company Name	Rankings	
	Fortune[1]	Forbes[2]
No companies listed	-	-

Note: (1) Fortune 500—companies that produce a 10-K are ranked 1 to 500 based on 2013 revenue; (2) all private companies with at least $2 billion in annual revenue through the end of their most current fiscal year are ranked 1 to 221; companies listed are headquartered in the city; dashes indicate no ranking
Source: Fortune, "Fortune 500," June 16, 2014; Forbes, "America's Largest Private Companies," November 5, 2014

Minority Business Opportunity

Sacramento is home to two companies which are on the *Hispanic Business* 500 list (500 largest U.S. Hispanic-owned companies based on 2012 revenue): **Martin Brothers Construction** (#168); **Informatix** (#265). Companies included must show at least 51 percent ownership by Hispanic U.S. citizens, and must maintain headquarters in one of the 50 states or Washington, D.C. *Hispanic Business, "Hispanic Business 500," June 20, 2013*

Minority- and Women-Owned Businesses

Group	All Firms		Firms with Paid Employees			
	Firms	Sales ($000)	Firms	Sales ($000)	Employees	Payroll ($000)
Asian	6,823	1,511,955	1,405	1,256,960	7,437	211,519
Black	3,069	146,794	304	102,076	1,317	33,923
Hispanic	3,156	749,077	575	642,658	4,111	155,010
Women	11,449	2,618,788	1,405	2,358,755	12,602	454,158
All Firms	35,990	43,264,498	9,054	41,954,885	174,018	7,329,867

Note: Figures cover firms located in the city; minority- and women-owned business are defined as firms in which the corresponding group own 51% or more of the stock or equity of the company
Source: U.S. Census Bureau, 2007 Economic Census, Survey of Business Owners (2012 Survey of Business Owners data will be released starting in June 2015)

HOTELS & CONVENTION CENTERS

Hotels/Motels

Area	5 Star		4 Star		3 Star		2 Star		1 Star		Not Rated	
	Num.	Pct.[3]	Num.	Pct.[3]	Num.	Pct.[3]	Num.	Pct.[3]	Num.	Pct.[3]	Num.	Pct.[3]
City[1]	0	0.0	4	2.3	49	28.0	110	62.9	4	2.3	8	4.6
Total[2]	166	0.9	1,264	7.0	5,718	31.8	9,340	52.0	411	2.3	1,070	6.0

Note: (1) Figures cover Sacramento and vicinity; (2) Figures cover all 100 cities in this book; (3) Percentage of hotels which have a given star rating; Star ratings are determined by expedia.com and offer an indication of the general quality of a particular hotel.
Source: expedia.com, April 2, 2015

Major Convention Centers

Name	Overall Space (sq. ft.)	Exhibit Space (sq. ft.)	Meeting Space (sq. ft.)	Meeting Rooms
Sacramento Convention Center	n/a	134,000	24,000	31

Note: Table includes convention centers located in the Sacramento—Arden-Arcade—Roseville, CA metro area; n/a not available
Source: Original research

Living Environment

COST OF LIVING

Cost of Living Index

Composite Index	Groceries	Housing	Utilities	Trans-portation	Health Care	Misc. Goods/ Services
112.5	116.1	117.4	114.7	110.7	111.8	106.5

Note: The Cost of Living Index measures regional differences in the cost of consumer goods and services, excluding taxes and non-consumer expenditures, for professional and managerial households in the top income quintile. It is based on more than 50,000 prices covering almost 60 different items for which prices are collected three times a year by chambers of commerce, economic development organizations or university applied economic centers in each participating urban area. The numbers shown should be read as a percentage above or below the national average of 100. For example, a value of 115.4 in the groceries column indicates that grocery prices are 15.4% higher than the national average. Small differences in the index numbers should not be interpreted as significant; Figures cover the Sacramento CA urban area.
Source: The Council for Community and Economic Research, ACCRA Cost of Living Index, 2014

Grocery Prices

Area[1]	T-Bone Steak ($/pound)	Frying Chicken ($/pound)	Whole Milk ($/half gal.)	Eggs ($/dozen)	Orange Juice ($/64 oz.)	Coffee ($/11.5 oz.)
City[2]	9.80	1.52	2.45	2.29	3.98	5.34
Avg.	10.40	1.37	2.40	1.99	3.46	4.27
Min.	8.48	0.93	1.37	1.30	2.83	2.99
Max.	14.20	2.44	3.62	4.02	6.42	6.96

*Note: (1) Values for the local area are compared with the average, minimum and maximum values for all 308 areas in the Cost of Living Index; (2) Figures cover the Sacramento CA urban area; **T-Bone Steak** (price per pound); **Frying Chicken** (price per pound, whole fryer); **Whole Milk** (half gallon carton); **Eggs** (price per dozen, Grade A, large); **Orange Juice** (64 oz. Tropicana or Florida Natural); **Coffee** (11.5 oz. can, vacuum-packed, Maxwell House, Hills Bros, or Folgers).*
Source: The Council for Community and Economic Research, ACCRA Cost of Living Index, 2014

Housing and Utility Costs

Area[1]	New Home Price ($)	Apartment Rent ($/month)	All Electric ($/month)	Part Electric ($/month)	Other Energy ($/month)	Telephone ($/month)
City[2]	371,449	1,028	-	165.81	38.42	29.74
Avg.	305,838	919	181.00	93.66	73.14	27.95
Min.	183,142	480	112.00	42.06	23.42	17.16
Max.	1,358,576	3,851	594.00	180.03	440.99	40.42

*Note: (1) Values for the local area are compared with the average, minimum and maximum values for all 308 areas in the Cost of Living Index; (2) Figures cover the Sacramento CA urban area; **New Home Price** (2,400 sf living area, 8,000 sf lot, in urban area with full utilities); **Apartment Rent** (950 sf 2 bedroom/1.5 or 2 bath, unfurnished, excluding all utilities except water); **All Electric** (average monthly cost for an all-electric home); **Part Electric** (average monthly cost for a part-electric home); **Other Energy** (average monthly cost for natural gas, fuel oil, coal, wood, and any other forms of energy except electricity); **Telephone** (price includes basic monthly rate for a private residential line plus additional local usage charges incurred by a family of four).*
Source: The Council for Community and Economic Research, ACCRA Cost of Living Index, 2014

Health Care, Transportation, and Other Costs

Area[1]	Doctor ($/visit)	Dentist ($/visit)	Optometrist ($/visit)	Gasoline ($/gallon)	Beauty Salon ($/visit)	Men's Shirt ($)
City[2]	110.82	103.23	113.80	3.75	43.78	27.65
Avg.	102.86	87.89	97.66	3.44	34.37	26.74
Min.	67.47	65.78	51.18	3.00	17.43	12.79
Max.	173.50	150.14	235.00	4.33	64.28	49.50

*Note: (1) Values for the local area are compared with the average, minimum and maximum values for all 308 areas in the Cost of Living Index; (2) Figures cover the Sacramento CA urban area; **Doctor** (general practitioners routine exam of an established patient); **Dentist** (adult teeth cleaning and periodic oral examination); **Optometrist** (full vision eye exam for established adult patient); **Gasoline** (one gallon regular unleaded, national brand, including all taxes, cash price at self-service pump if available); **Beauty Salon** (woman's shampoo, trim, and blow-dry); **Men's Shirt** (cotton/polyester dress shirt, pinpoint weave, long sleeves).*
Source: The Council for Community and Economic Research, ACCRA Cost of Living Index, 2014

HOUSING

House Price Index (HPI)

Area	National Ranking[2]	Quarterly Change (%)	One-Year Change (%)	Five-Year Change (%)
MSA[1]	67	0.91	7.14	21.20
U.S.[3]	–	1.35	4.91	11.59

Note: The HPI is a weighted repeat sales index. It measures average price changes in repeat sales or refinancings on the same properties. This information is obtained by reviewing repeat mortgage transactions on single-family properties whose mortgages have been purchased or securitized by Fannie Mae or Freddie Mac in January 1975; (1) Sacramento—Roseville—Arden-Arcade Metropolitan Statistical Area—see Appendix B for areas included; (2) Rankings are based on annual percentage change for all metro areas containing at least 15,000 transactions over the last 10 years and ranges from 1 to 275; (3) figures based on a weighted average of Census Division estimates using a seasonally adjusted, purchase-only index; all figures are for the period ending December 31, 2014
Source: Federal Housing Finance Agency, House Price Index, February 26, 2015

Median Single-Family Home Prices

Area	2012	2013	2014p	Percent Change 2013 to 2014
MSA[1]	176.8	239.5	268.7	12.2
U.S. Average	177.2	197.4	209.0	5.9

Note: Figures are median sales prices of existing single-family homes in thousands of dollars; (p) preliminary; n/a not available; (1) Sacramento—Arden-Arcade—Roseville, CA Metropolitan Statistical Area—see Appendix B for areas included
Source: National Association of Realtors, Median Sales Price of Existing Single-Family Homes for Metropolitan Areas, 4th Quarter 2014

Qualifying Income Based on Median Sales Price of Existing Single-Family Homes

Area	With 5% Down ($)	With 10% Down ($)	With 20% Down ($)
MSA[1]	59,048	55,940	49,725
U.S. Average	45,863	43,449	38,621

Note: Figures are preliminary; Qualifying income is based on a mortgage rate of 4.0%. Monthly principal and interest payment is limited to 25% of income; n/a not available; (1) Sacramento—Arden-Arcade—Roseville, CA Metropolitan Statistical Area—see Appendix B for areas included
Source: National Association of Realtors, Qualifying Income Based on Median Sales Price of Existing Single-Family Homes for Metropolitan Areas, 4th Quarter 2014

Median Apartment Condo-Coop Home Prices

Area	2012	2013	2014p	Percent Change 2013 to 2014
MSA[1]	80.6	123.0	138.9	12.9
U.S. Average	173.7	194.9	205.1	5.2

Note: Figures are median sales prices of existing apartment condo-coop homes in thousands of dollars; (p) preliminary; n/a not available; (1) Sacramento—Arden-Arcade—Roseville, CA Metropolitan Statistical Area—see Appendix B for areas included
Source: National Association of Realtors, Median Sales Price of Existing Apartment Condo-Coop Homes for Metropolitan Areas, 4th Quarter 2014

Gross Monthly Rent

Area	Under $200	$200 -299	$300 -499	$500 -749	$750 -999	$1,000 -1,499	$1,500 and up	Median ($)
City	1.3	3.0	4.5	15.9	26.8	34.2	14.3	986
MSA[1]	0.9	1.9	3.2	14.1	26.3	33.6	20.0	1,047
U.S.	1.7	3.2	7.8	22.1	24.3	26.0	14.9	900

Note: Figures are percentages except for Median; Gross rent is the contract rent plus the estimated average monthly cost of utilities (electricity, gas, and water and sewer) and fuels (oil, coal, kerosene, wood, etc.) if these are paid by the renter (or paid for the renter by someone else); (1) Figures cover the Sacramento—Arden-Arcade—Roseville, CA Metropolitan Statistical Area—see Appendix B for areas included
Source: U.S. Census Bureau, 2011-2013 American Community Survey 3-Year Estimates

Homeownership Rate

Area	2007 (%)	2008 (%)	2009 (%)	2010 (%)	2011 (%)	2012 (%)	2013 (%)	2014 (%)
MSA[1]	60.8	61.1	64.3	61.1	57.2	58.6	60.4	60.1
U.S.	68.1	67.8	67.4	66.9	66.1	65.4	65.1	64.5

Note: (1) Figures cover the Sacramento—Arden-Arcade—Roseville, CA Metropolitan Statistical Area—see Appendix B for areas included
Source: U.S. Census Bureau, Housing Vacancies and Homeownership Annual Statistics: 2014

Year Housing Structure Built

Area	2010 or Later	2000 -2009	1990 -1999	1980 -1989	1970 -1979	1960 -1969	1950 -1959	1940 -1949	Before 1940	Median Year
City	0.2	16.3	7.6	14.8	15.6	12.3	13.2	8.5	11.5	1973
MSA[1]	0.6	18.9	14.2	16.5	19.7	11.1	10.7	3.9	4.5	1980
U.S.	0.9	15.0	13.9	13.8	15.8	11.0	10.9	5.4	13.3	1976

Note: Figures are percentages except for Median Year; (1) Figures cover the Sacramento—Arden-Arcade—Roseville, CA Metropolitan Statistical Area—see Appendix B for areas included
Source: U.S. Census Bureau, 2011-2013 American Community Survey 3-Year Estimates

HEALTH

Health Risk Data

Category	MSA[1] (%)	U.S. (%)
Adults aged 18–64 who have any kind of health care coverage	81.2	79.6
Adults who reported being in good or excellent health	85.8	83.1
Adults who are current smokers	14.7	19.6
Adults who are heavy drinkers[2]	6.2	6.1
Adults who are binge drinkers[3]	16.6	16.9
Adults who are overweight (BMI 25.0 - 29.9)	36.0	35.8
Adults who are obese (BMI 30.0 - 99.8)	25.4	27.6
Adults who participated in any physical activities in the past month	84.4	77.1
Adults 50+ who have ever had a sigmoidoscopy or colonoscopy	71.9	67.3
Women aged 40+ who have had a mammogram within the past two years	82.2	74.0
Men aged 40+ who have had a PSA test within the past two years	34.6	45.2
Adults aged 65+ who have had flu shot within the past year	61.6	60.1
Adults who always wear a seatbelt	n/a	93.8

Note: Data as of 2012 unless otherwise noted; n/a not available; (1) Figures cover the Sacramento-Arden-Arcade-Roseville, CA Metropolitan Statistical Area—see Appendix B for areas included; (2) Heavy drinkers are classified as males having more than two drinks per day or females having more than one drink per day; (3) Binge drinkers are classified as males having five or more drinks on one occasion or females having four or more drinks on one occasion
Source: Centers for Disease Control and Prevention, Behaviorial Risk Factor Surveillance System, SMART: Selected Metropolitan/Micropolitan Area Risk Trends, 2012 (Note: the CDC has discontinued this dataset but will be releasing a replacement in late 2015)

Chronic Health Indicators

Category	MSA[1] (%)	U.S. (%)
Adults who have ever been told they had a heart attack	2.8	4.5
Adults who have ever been told they had a stroke	2.7	2.9
Adults who have been told they currently have asthma	10.0	8.9
Adults who have ever been told they have arthritis	24.5	25.7
Adults who have ever been told they have diabetes[2]	9.5	9.7
Adults who have ever been told they had skin cancer	5.2	5.7
Adults who have ever been told they had any other types of cancer	6.3	6.5
Adults who have ever been told they have COPD	4.6	6.2
Adults who have ever been told they have kidney disease	1.8	2.5
Adults who have ever been told they have a form of depression	10.6	18.0

Note: Data as of 2012 unless otherwise noted; (1) Figures cover the Sacramento-Arden-Arcade-Roseville, CA Metropolitan Statistical Area—see Appendix B for areas included; (2) Figures do not include pregnancy-related, borderline, or pre-diabetes
Source: Centers for Disease Control and Prevention, Behaviorial Risk Factor Surveillance System, SMART: Selected Metropolitan/Micropolitan Area Risk Trends, 2012 (Note: the CDC has discontinued this dataset but will be releasing a replacement in late 2015)

Mortality Rates for the Top 10 Causes of Death in the U.S.

ICD-10[a] Sub-Chapter	ICD-10[a] Code	Age-Adjusted Mortality Rate[1] per 100,000 population	
		County[2]	U.S.
Malignant neoplasms	C00-C97	167.6	166.2
Ischaemic heart diseases	I20-I25	106.6	105.7
Other forms of heart disease	I30-I51	39.6	49.3
Chronic lower respiratory diseases	J40-J47	40.9	42.1
Organic, including symptomatic, mental disorders	F01-F09	34.6	38.1
Cerebrovascular diseases	I60-I69	39.4	37.0
Other external causes of accidental injury	W00-X59	23.0	26.9
Other degenerative diseases of the nervous system	G30-G31	28.3	25.6
Diabetes mellitus	E10-E14	22.7	21.3
Hypertensive diseases	I10-I15	27.2	19.4

Note: (a) ICD-10 = International Classification of Diseases 10th Revision; (1) Mortality rates are a three year average covering 2011-2013; (2) Figures cover Sacramento County
Source: Centers for Disease Control and Prevention, National Center for Health Statistics. Compressed Mortality File 1999-2013 on CDC WONDER Online Database, released October 2014. Data are compiled from the Compressed Mortality File 1999-2013, Series 20 No. 2S, 2014.

Mortality Rates for Selected Causes of Death

ICD-10[a] Sub-Chapter	ICD-10[a] Code	Age-Adjusted Mortality Rate[1] per 100,000 population	
		County[2]	U.S.
Assault	X85-Y09	5.7	5.2
Diseases of the liver	K70-K76	13.5	13.2
Human immunodeficiency virus (HIV) disease	B20-B24	1.9	2.2
Influenza and pneumonia	J09-J18	17.0	15.4
Intentional self-harm	X60-X84	13.0	12.5
Malnutrition	E40-E46	0.9	0.9
Obesity and other hyperalimentation	E65-E68	1.5	1.8
Renal failure	N17-N19	5.7	13.1
Transport accidents	V01-V99	9.8	11.7
Viral hepatitis	B15-B19	4.7	2.2

Note: (a) ICD-10 = International Classification of Diseases 10th Revision; (1) Mortality rates are a three year average covering 2011-2013; (2) Figures cover Sacramento County
Source: Centers for Disease Control and Prevention, National Center for Health Statistics. Compressed Mortality File 1999-2013 on CDC WONDER Online Database, released October 2014. Data are compiled from the Compressed Mortality File 1999-2013, Series 20 No. 2S, 2014.

Health Insurance Coverage

Area	With Health Insurance	With Private Health Insurance	With Public Health Insurance	Without Health Insurance	Population Under Age 18 Without Health Insurance
City	83.8	57.3	35.5	16.2	5.8
MSA[1]	86.2	66.3	30.8	13.8	5.9
U.S.	85.2	65.2	31.0	14.8	7.3

Note: Figures are percentages that cover the civilian noninstitutionalized population; (1) Figures cover the Sacramento—Arden-Arcade—Roseville, CA Metropolitan Statistical Area—see Appendix B for areas included
Source: U.S. Census Bureau, 2011-2013 American Community Survey 3-Year Estimates

Number of Medical Professionals

Area[1]	MDs[2]	DOs[2,3]	Dentists	Podiatrists	Chiropractors	Optometrists
Local (number)	4,179	168	1,052	63	317	243
Local (rate[4])	288.5	11.6	71.9	4.3	21.7	16.6
U.S. (rate[4])	270.0	20.2	63.1	5.7	25.2	14.9

Note: Data as of 2013 unless noted; (1) Local data covers Sacramento County; (2) Data as of 2012 and includes all active, non-federal physicians; (3) Doctor of Osteopathic Medicine; (4) rate per 100,000 population
Source: U.S. Department of Health and Human Services, Health Resources and Services Administration, Bureau of Health Professions, Area Resource File (ARF) 2013-2014

Best Hospitals

According to *U.S. News*, the Sacramento—Arden-Arcade—Roseville, CA metro area is home to one of the best hospitals in the U.S.: **University of California, Davis Medical Center** (10 specialties). The hospital listed was nationally ranked in at least one adult specialty. Only 144 hospitals nationwide were nationally ranked in one or more specialties. Seventeen hospitals in the U.S. made the Honor Roll with high scores in at least six specialties. *U.S. News Online, "America's Best Children's Hospitals 2014-15"*

According to *U.S. News*, the Sacramento—Arden-Arcade—Roseville, CA metro area is home to one of the best children's hospitals in the U.S.: **University of California Davis Children's Hospital** (4 specialties). The hospital listed was highly ranked in at least one pediatric specialty. Eighty-nine children's hospitals in the U.S. were nationally ranked in at least one specialty. Ten children's hospitals in the U.S. made the Honor Roll with high scores in at least three specialties. *U.S. News Online, "America's Best Children's Hospitals 2014-15"*

EDUCATION

Public School District Statistics

District Name	Schls	Pupils	Pupil/ Teacher Ratio	Minority Pupils[1] (%)	Free Lunch Eligible[2] (%)	IEP[3] (%)
Natomas Unified	18	12,454	23.1	80.7	41.9	10.4
Robla Elementary	6	2,119	25.6	83.9	76.2	12.4
Sacramento City Unified	87	47,616	26.3	81.2	66.8	12.2

Note: Table includes school districts with 2,000 or more students; (1) Percentage of students that are not non-Hispanic white; (2) Percentage of students that are eligible for the free lunch program; (3) Percentage of students that have an Individualized Education Program.
Source: U.S. Department of Education, National Center for Education Statistics, Common Core of Data, Local Education Agency (School District) Universe Survey: School Year 2012-2013; U.S. Department of Education, National Center for Education Statistics, Common Core of Data, Public Elementary/Secondary School Universe Survey: School Year 2012-2013

Highest Level of Education

Area	Less than H.S.	H.S. Diploma	Some College, No Deg.	Associate Degree	Bachelor's Degree	Master's Degree	Prof. School Degree	Doctorate Degree
City	16.9	21.1	24.3	8.5	18.5	6.6	2.7	1.3
MSA[1]	11.9	21.8	26.3	9.6	19.7	6.9	2.4	1.4
U.S.	13.7	28.0	21.2	7.9	18.2	7.7	1.9	1.3

Note: Figures cover persons age 25 and over; (1) Figures cover the Sacramento—Arden-Arcade—Roseville, CA Metropolitan Statistical Area—see Appendix B for areas included
Source: U.S. Census Bureau, 2011-2013 American Community Survey 3-Year Estimates

Educational Attainment by Race

Area	High School Graduate or Higher (%)					Bachelor's Degree or Higher (%)				
	Total	White	Black	Asian	Hisp.[2]	Total	White	Black	Asian	Hisp.[2]
City	83.1	86.8	88.6	77.4	65.2	29.2	34.3	18.2	32.8	13.6
MSA[1]	88.1	91.0	88.4	81.9	69.5	30.4	32.0	19.3	39.7	13.7
U.S.	86.3	88.3	83.1	85.7	64.0	29.1	30.4	18.8	50.7	13.7

Note: Figures shown cover persons 25 years old and over; (1) Figures cover the Sacramento—Arden-Arcade—Roseville, CA Metropolitan Statistical Area—see Appendix B for areas included; (2) People of Hispanic origin can be of any race
Source: U.S. Census Bureau, 2011-2013 American Community Survey 3-Year Estimates

School Enrollment by Grade and Control

Area	Preschool (%)		Kindergarten (%)		Grades 1 - 4 (%)		Grades 5 - 8 (%)		Grades 9 - 12 (%)	
	Public	Private	Public	Private	Public	Private	Public	Private	Public	Private
City	69.7	30.3	90.9	9.1	93.1	6.9	93.4	6.6	90.2	9.8
MSA[1]	55.9	44.1	89.4	10.6	92.0	8.0	92.4	7.6	91.2	8.8
U.S.	57.7	42.3	87.9	12.1	89.9	10.1	90.0	10.0	90.7	9.3

Note: Figures shown cover persons 3 years old and over; (1) Figures cover the Sacramento—Arden-Arcade—Roseville, CA Metropolitan Statistical Area—see Appendix B for areas included
Source: U.S. Census Bureau, 2011-2013 American Community Survey 3-Year Estimates

Average Salaries of Public School Classroom Teachers

Area	2013-14 Dollars	2013-14 Rank[1]	2014-15 Dollars	2014-15 Rank[1]	Percent Change 2013-14 to 2014-15	Percent Change 2004-05 to 2014-15
CALIFORNIA	71,396	4	72,535	4	1.59	25.9
U.S. Average	56,610	–	57,379	–	1.36	20.8

Note: (1) State rank ranges from 1 to 51 where 1 indicates highest salary.
Source: National Education Association, Rankings & Estimates: Rankings of the States 2014 and Estimates of School Statistics 2015, March 2015

Higher Education

Four-Year Colleges Public	Four-Year Colleges Private Non-profit	Four-Year Colleges Private For-profit	Two-Year Colleges Public	Two-Year Colleges Private Non-profit	Two-Year Colleges Private For-profit	Medical Schools[1]	Law Schools[2]	Voc/ Tech[3]
1	1	3	4	0	5	1	2	7

Note: Figures cover institutions located within the city limits and include main campuses only; (1) includes schools accredited by the Liaison Committee on Medical Education and the American Osteopathic Association's Commission on Osteopathic College Accreditation; (2) includes ABA-accredited schools, schools with provisional ABA accreditation, and state accredited schools; (3) includes all schools with programs that are less than 2 years.
Source: National Center for Education Statistics, Integrated Postsecondary Education System (IPEDS), 2013-14; Association of American Medical Colleges, Member List, May 1, 2015; American Osteopathic Association, Member List, May 1, 2015; Law School Admission Council, Official Guide to ABA-Approved Law Schools Online, May 1, 2015; Wikipedia, List of Medical Schools in the United States, May 1, 2015; Wikipedia, List of Law Schools in the United States, May 1, 2015

According to *U.S. News & World Report*, the Sacramento—Arden-Arcade—Roseville, CA metro area is home to one of the best national universities in the U.S.: **University of California-Davis** (#38). The indicators used to capture academic quality fall into a number of categories: assessment by administrators at peer institutions; retention of students; faculty resources; student selectivity; financial resources; alumni giving; high school counselor ratings of colleges; and graduation rate. *U.S. News & World Report, "America's Best Colleges 2015"*

According to *U.S. News & World Report*, the Sacramento—Arden-Arcade—Roseville, CA metro area is home to one of the top 100 law schools in the U.S.: **University of California-Davis** (#31). The rankings are based on a weighted average of 12 measures of quality: peer assessment score; assessment score by lawyers/judges; median LSAT scores; median undergrad GPA; acceptance rate; employment rates for graduates; placement success; bar passage rate; faculty resources; expenditures per student; student/faculty ratio; and library resources. *U.S. News & World Report, "America's Best Graduate Schools, Law, 2016"*

According to *U.S. News & World Report*, the Sacramento—Arden-Arcade—Roseville, CA metro area is home to one of the top 75 medical schools for research in the U.S.: **University of California-Davis** (#43). The rankings are based on a weighted average of 11 measures of quality: quality assessment; peer assessment score; assessment score by residency directors; research activity; total research activity; average research activity per faculty member; student selectivity; median MCAT total score; median undergraduate GPA; acceptance rate; and faculty resources. *U.S. News & World Report, "America's Best Graduate Schools, Medical, 2016"*

According to *U.S. News & World Report*, the Sacramento—Arden-Arcade—Roseville, CA metro area is home to one of the top 75 business schools in the U.S.: **University of California-Davis** (#48). The rankings are based on a weighted average of the following nine measures: quality assessment; peer assessment; recruiter assessment; placement success; mean starting salary and bonus; student selectivity; mean GMAT and GRE scores; mean undergraduate GPA; and acceptance rate. *U.S. News & World Report, "America's Best Graduate Schools, Business, 2016"*

PRESIDENTIAL ELECTION

2012 Presidential Election Results

Area	Obama (%)	Romney (%)	Other (%)
Sacramento County	57.5	40.0	2.5
U.S.	51.0	47.2	1.8

Note: Results may not add to 100% due to rounding
Source: Dave Leip's Atlas of U.S. Presidential Elections

EMPLOYERS

Major Employers

Company Name	Industry
Air Resources Board Tstg Off	Engineers-environmental
C H W Mercy Healthcare	X-ray laboratory, including dental
CA Dept of Corrections and Rehab	Correctional institutions
Cache Creek Casino Resorts	Casino hotel
California Department of General Services	Building maintenance services, nec
California Department of Justice	Legal counsel and prosecution
California Department of Transportation	Regulation, administration of transportation
California Dept of Health Care Services	Administration of public health programs
California Employment Dev Dept	Administration of social and manpower programs
California State University Sacramento	Colleges and universities
CHW/Mercy Healthcare	Hospitals
Corrections Department	State government-correctional institutions
Dept of Transportation In Ca	Government offices-state
Employment Development Department	Government-job training/voc rehab svcs
Environmental Protection Agency	State government-environmental programs
Food & Agriculture, Calif. Dept of	Marketing and consumer service, government
Hewlett-Packard Co.	Computer hardware
Intel Corporation	Semiconductor devices (mfrs)
Kaiser Foundation Hospitals	Trusts, nec
Kaiser Permanente	Medical clinic
Los Rios Community College District	Colleges and universities
McClatchy Newspapers	Newspapers, publishing and printing
Mercy General Hospital	Hospitals
Raley's Inc.	Grocery distribution
Red Hawk Casino	Gambling establishment
Sacramento City Unified School District	Education
Sacramento Municipal Utility District	Electrical services
Sacramento Municipal Utility District	Electricity company
SBC Telecommunications	Telecommunications
Shaw Environmental & Infrastructure	Engineering services
Sutter Health Sacramento Sierra Region	Health screening service
Sutter Medical Center	Hospitals
Sutter Roseville Medical Center	General medical and surgical hospitals
UC Davis Medical Center	Hospitals
University Enterprises	Educational services
University of California, Davis	General medical and surgical hospitals
Water Resource Department	State government-environmental programs
Water Resources, California Dept of	Air, water, and solid waste management

Note: Companies shown are located within the Sacramento—Arden-Arcade—Roseville, CA Metropolitan Statistical Area.
Source: Hoovers.com; Wikipedia

Best Companies to Work For

Sacramento Municipal Utility District, headquartered in Sacramento, is among the "100 Best Places to Work in IT." To qualify, companies, both public and private, had to have a minimum of 50 IT employees and were selected based on average salary and bonus increases, the percentage of IT staffers promoted, IT staff turnover rates, training and development programs, and the percentage of women and minorities in IT staff and management positions. In addition, *Computerworld* looked at retention efforts, programs for recognizing and rewarding outstanding performances, and benefits such as flextime, elder care and child care, and reimbursement for college tuition and the cost of pursuing technology certifications. *Computerworld, "100 Best Places to Work in IT 2014"*

PUBLIC SAFETY

Crime Rate

Area	All Crimes	Violent Crimes				Property Crimes		
		Murder	Forcible Rape	Robbery	Aggrav. Assault	Burglary	Larceny -Theft	Motor Vehicle Theft
City	4,416.1	7.1	19.9	242.2	386.9	812.7	2,349.1	598.3
Suburbs[1]	2,842.6	3.3	21.6	97.4	227.6	622.0	1,550.7	320.1
Metro[2]	3,182.5	4.1	21.2	128.7	262.0	663.2	1,723.2	380.2
U.S.	3,098.6	4.5	25.2	109.1	229.1	610.0	1,899.4	221.3

Note: Figures are crimes per 100,000 population; (1) All areas within the metro area that are located outside the city limits; (2) Figures cover the Sacramento—Arden-Arcade—Roseville, CA Metropolitan Statistical Area—see Appendix B for areas included
Source: FBI Uniform Crime Reports, 2013

Hate Crimes

Area	Number of Quarters Reported	Number of Incidents per Bias Motivation						
		Race	Religion	Sexual Orientation	Ethnicity	Disability	Gender	Gender Identity
City	4	6	2	6	2	0	0	0
U.S.	4	2,871	1,031	1,233	655	83	18	31

Source: Federal Bureau of Investigation, Hate Crime Statistics 2013

Identity Theft Consumer Complaints

Area	Complaints	Complaints per 100,000 Population	Rank[2]
MSA[1]	2,198	99.2	65
U.S.	332,646	104.3	-

Note: (1) Figures cover the Sacramento—Arden-Arcade—Roseville, CA Metropolitan Statistical Area—see Appendix B for areas included; (2) Rank ranges from 1 to 380 where 1 indicates greatest number of identity theft complaints per 100,000 population
Source: Federal Trade Commission, Consumer Sentinel Network Data Book for January–December 2014

Fraud and Other Consumer Complaints

Area	Complaints	Complaints per 100,000 Population	Rank[2]
MSA[1]	10,161	458.6	47
U.S.	2,250,205	705.7	-

Note: (1) Figures cover the Sacramento—Arden-Arcade—Roseville, CA Metropolitan Statistical Area—see Appendix B for areas included; (2) Rank ranges from 1 to 380 where 1 indicates greatest number of identity theft complaints per 100,000 population
Source: Federal Trade Commission, Consumer Sentinel Network Data Book for January–December 2014

RECREATION

Culture

Dance[1]	Theatre[1]	Instrumental Music[1]	Vocal Music[1]	Series and Festivals	Museums and Art Galleries[2]	Zoos and Aquariums[3]
1	6	3	4	4	53	1

Note: (1) Professional perfoming groups; (2) Based on organizations with SIC code 8412; (3) AZA-accredited
Source: The Grey House Performing Arts Directory, 2015-16; Association of Zoos & Aquariums, AZA Member Zoos & Aquariums, April 2015; www.AccuLeads.com, April 2015

Professional Sports Teams

Team Name	League	Year Established
Sacramento Kings	National Basketball Association (NBA)	1985

Note: Includes teams located in the Sacramento—Arden-Arcade—Roseville, CA Metropolitan Statistical Area.
Source: Wikipedia, Major Professional Sports Teams of the United States and Canada, April 2015

CLIMATE

Average and Extreme Temperatures

Temperature	Jan	Feb	Mar	Apr	May	Jun	Jul	Aug	Sep	Oct	Nov	Dec	Yr.
Extreme High (°F)	70	76	88	93	105	115	114	109	108	101	87	72	115
Average High (°F)	53	60	64	71	80	87	93	91	87	78	63	53	73
Average Temp. (°F)	45	51	54	59	65	72	76	75	72	64	53	46	61
Average Low (°F)	38	41	43	46	50	55	58	58	56	50	43	38	48
Extreme Low (°F)	20	23	26	32	34	41	48	48	43	35	26	18	18

Note: Figures cover the years 1947-1990
Source: National Climatic Data Center, International Station Meteorological Climate Summary, 9/96

Average Precipitation/Snowfall/Humidity

Precip./Humidity	Jan	Feb	Mar	Apr	May	Jun	Jul	Aug	Sep	Oct	Nov	Dec	Yr.
Avg. Precip. (in.)	3.6	2.8	2.4	1.3	0.4	0.1	Tr	0.1	0.3	1.0	2.4	2.8	17.3
Avg. Snowfall (in.)	Tr	Tr	Tr	Tr	0	0	0	0	0	0	0	Tr	Tr
Avg. Rel. Hum. 7am (%)	90	88	84	78	71	67	68	73	75	80	87	90	79
Avg. Rel. Hum. 4pm (%)	70	59	51	43	36	31	28	29	31	39	57	70	45

Note: Figures cover the years 1947-1990; Tr = Trace amounts (<0.05 in. of rain; <0.5 in. of snow)
Source: National Climatic Data Center, International Station Meteorological Climate Summary, 9/96

Weather Conditions

Temperature			Daytime Sky			Precipitation		
10°F & below	32°F & below	90°F & above	Clear	Partly cloudy	Cloudy	0.01 inch or more precip.	0.1 inch or more snow/ice	Thunder-storms
0	21	73	175	111	79	58	< 1	2

Note: Figures are average number of days per year and cover the years 1947-1990
Source: National Climatic Data Center, International Station Meteorological Climate Summary, 9/96

HAZARDOUS WASTE

Superfund Sites

Sacramento has three hazardous waste sites on the EPA's Superfund Final National Priorities List: **Mather Air Force Base (AC&W Disposal Site)**; **McClellan Air Force Base (Ground Water Contamination)**; **Sacramento Army Depot**. There are a total of 1,322 Superfund sites on the list in the U.S. *U.S. Environmental Protection Agency, Final National Priorities List, April 14, 2015*

AIR & WATER QUALITY

Air Quality Trends: Ozone

	2004	2005	2006	2007	2008	2009	2010	2011	2012	2013
MSA[1]	0.081	0.089	0.094	0.080	0.089	0.083	0.077	0.078	0.082	0.071

Note: (1) Data covers the Sacramento—Arden-Arcade—Roseville, CA Metropolitan Statistical Area—see Appendix B for areas included. The values shown are the composite ozone concentration averages among trend sites based on the highest fourth daily maximum 8-hour concentration in parts per million. These trends are based on sites having an adequate record of monitoring data during the trend period. Data from exceptional events are included.
Source: U.S. Environmental Protection Agency, Air Quality Monitoring Information, "Air Quality Trends by City, 2000-2013"

Air Quality Index

Area	Percent of Days when Air Quality was...[2]					AQI Statistics[2]	
	Good	Moderate	Unhealthy for Sensitive Groups	Unhealthy	Very Unhealthy	Maximum	Median
MSA[1]	46.8	43.6	8.8	0.5	0.3	240	53

Note: (1) Data covers the Sacramento—Arden-Arcade—Roseville, CA Metropolitan Statistical Area—see Appendix B for areas included; (2) Based on 365 days with AQI data in 2014. Air Quality Index (AQI) is an index for reporting daily air quality. EPA calculates the AQI for five major air pollutants regulated by the Clean Air Act: ground-level ozone, particle pollution (aka particulate matter), carbon monoxide, sulfur dioxide, and nitrogen dioxide. The AQI runs from 0 to 500. The higher the AQI value, the greater the level of air pollution and the greater the health concern. There are six AQI categories: "Good" AQI is between 0 and 50. Air quality is considered satisfactory; "Moderate" AQI is between 51 and 100. Air quality is acceptable; "Unhealthy for Sensitive Groups" When AQI values are between 101 and 150, members of sensitive groups may experience health effects; "Unhealthy" When AQI values are between 151 and 200 everyone may begin to experience health effects; "Very Unhealthy" AQI values between 201 and 300 trigger a health alert; "Hazardous" AQI values over 300 trigger warnings of emergency conditions (not shown).
Source: U.S. Environmental Protection Agency, Air Quality Index Report, 2014

Air Quality Index Pollutants

Area	Percent of Days when AQI Pollutant was...[2]					
	Carbon Monoxide	Nitrogen Dioxide	Ozone	Sulfur Dioxide	Particulate Matter 2.5	Particulate Matter 10
MSA[1]	0.0	0.3	65.5	0.0	33.4	0.8

Note: (1) Data covers the Sacramento—Arden-Arcade—Roseville, CA Metropolitan Statistical Area—see Appendix B for areas included; (2) Based on 365 days with AQI data in 2014. The Air Quality Index (AQI) is an index for reporting daily air quality. EPA calculates the AQI for five major air pollutants regulated by the Clean Air Act: ground-level ozone, particle pollution (also known as particulate matter), carbon monoxide, sulfur dioxide, and nitrogen dioxide. The AQI runs from 0 to 500. The higher the AQI value, the greater the level of air pollution and the greater the health concern.
Source: U.S. Environmental Protection Agency, Air Quality Index Report, 2014

Maximum Air Pollutant Concentrations: Particulate Matter, Ozone, CO and Lead

	Particulate Matter 10 (ug/m^3)	Particulate Matter 2.5 Wtd AM (ug/m^3)	Particulate Matter 2.5 24-Hr (ug/m^3)	Ozone (ppm)	Carbon Monoxide (ppm)	Lead (ug/m^3)
MSA[1] Level	68	11.5	40	0.082	2	n/a
NAAQS[2]	150	15	35	0.075	9	0.15
Met NAAQS[2]	Yes	Yes	No	No	Yes	n/a

Note: (1) Data covers the Sacramento—Arden-Arcade—Roseville, CA Metropolitan Statistical Area—see Appendix B for areas included; Data from exceptional events are included; (2) National Ambient Air Quality Standards; ppm = parts per million; ug/m^3 = micrograms per cubic meter; n/a not available.
Concentrations: Particulate Matter 10 (coarse particulate)—highest second maximum 24-hour concentration; Particulate Matter 2.5 Wtd AM (fine particulate)—highest weighted annual mean concentration; Particulate Matter 2.5 24-Hour (fine particulate)—highest 98th percentile 24-hour concentration; Ozone—highest fourth daily maximum 8-hour concentration; Carbon Monoxide—highest second maximum non-overlapping 8-hour concentration; Lead—maximum running 3-month average
Source: U.S. Environmental Protection Agency, Air Quality Monitoring Information, "Air Quality Statistics by City, 2013"

Maximum Air Pollutant Concentrations: Nitrogen Dioxide and Sulfur Dioxide

	Nitrogen Dioxide AM (ppb)	Nitrogen Dioxide 1-Hr (ppb)	Sulfur Dioxide AM (ppb)	Sulfur Dioxide 1-Hr (ppb)	Sulfur Dioxide 24-Hr (ppb)
MSA[1] Level	10	50	n/a	3	n/a
NAAQS[2]	53	100	30	75	140
Met NAAQS[2]	Yes	Yes	n/a	Yes	n/a

Note: (1) Data covers the Sacramento—Arden-Arcade—Roseville, CA Metropolitan Statistical Area—see Appendix B for areas included; Data from exceptional events are included; (2) National Ambient Air Quality Standards; ppm = parts per million; ug/m^3 = micrograms per cubic meter; n/a not available.
Concentrations: Nitrogen Dioxide AM—highest arithmetic mean concentration; Nitrogen Dioxide 1-Hr—highest 98th percentile 1-hour daily maximum concentration; Sulfur Dioxide AM—highest annual mean concentration; Sulfur Dioxide 1-Hr—highest 99th percentile 1-hour daily maximum concentration; Sulfur Dioxide 24-Hr—highest second maximum 24-hour concentration
Source: U.S. Environmental Protection Agency, Air Quality Monitoring Information, "Air Quality Statistics by City, 2013"

Drinking Water

Water System Name	Pop. Served	Primary Water Source Type	Violations[1]	
			Health Based	Monitoring/ Reporting
City of Sacramento Main	486,189	Surface	0	0
Sacramento Suburban Water District	171,200	Purchased Surface	0	0

Note: (1) Based on violation data from January 1, 2014 to December 31, 2014 (includes unresolved violations from earlier years)
Source: U.S. Environmental Protection Agency, Office of Ground Water and Drinking Water, Safe Drinking Water Information System (based on data extracted January 27, 2015)

Salem, Oregon

Background

The first civilization to occupy the Willamette Valley, the geographical area surrounding Salem, were the Kalapuya Native Americans, who resided there seasonally for over 5,000 years. The Kalapuya were semi-nomadic, subsisting on the bounty of wild game and vegetation. They were master canoe-builders whose primary means of transportation was the intricate web of rivers and streams flowing through the Willamette countryside.

In the early 19th century, sailors from distant shores brought devastating diseases to the region—small pox, measles and malaria. The native population, declined from 15,000 in the 1750s, to around 600 in less than 100 years. By 1910, this number dropped to 130. In 1856, the Kalapuya were relocated to the Grande Ronde Reservation, about 30 miles west of present-day Salem; their nomadic lifestyle was over, and they were joined by 26 other tribes from the surrounding area.

The first non-native settlers to call Salem home were Methodist ministers who established the Willamette Mission, ten miles north of Salem. The Methodist Mission would later become the Oregon Institute, the first "white settlers" school west of the Missouri River. The whole community became known as the "Institute." In later years, the institute would become Willamette University. French Canadian trappers were responsible for bringing Catholicism to Oregon and, for a while, hostilities ran high between the Christian communities.

By 1843, a new influx of settlers arrived in wagons with the fervor of manifest destiny. They brought an agrarian lifestyle, planting wheat, raising sheep, and building mills for lumber. By 1851, the steamboat "Hoosier" traveled the Willamette River south to Eugene, and north to Oregon City (near Portland), providing trade and transportation to the entire Willamette Valley. Oregon achieved statehood in 1859, and Salem was the new state capital. Although Oregon entered statehood as a "free" state, it was illegal for black people to live there. One of the initial proposed candidates for Oregon's first governor was Abraham Lincoln, who turned down the job because his wife, Mary, had no interest in moving west.

The population tripled in the years between 1900 and 1920. In 1903, Salem won the moniker "The Cherry City" in recognition of its food processing industry. In 1920, the Oregon Pulp and Paper Company began operations, and Salem General Hospital opened its doors. By the time of its centennial in 1940, Salem's population topped 30,900.

Salem's most famous native son was Herbert Hoover, who occupied the White House from 1929 to 1933. Although Hoover was not born in Salem, he spent part of his childhood there. Other notable sons of the city include Senator Charles McNary, a Vice-Presidential nominee in 1940, and Hollis Hawley, a leader in the U.S. House of Representatives.

After a disasterous flood in 1964, Salem began reconstructing the downtown area as a shopping destination, and in 1970 Chemeketa Community College opened its doors. In the 1990s, Salem's roots as a lumber producer gradually waned and a new high-technology industry took root. In 1989, the computer chip manufacturer, Siltec, moved to Salem, later renamed Mitsubishi Silicon America, and the electronics giant, II Morrow, followed suit.

In 1962, Salem found itself in the spotlight when movie producers filmed the the Oscar Award-winning movie, *One Flew Over the Cuckoo's Nest,* in the Oregon State Mental Hospital. Now listed in the National Register of Historic Places, the hospital has been converted into the Oregon State Hospital Museum of Mental Health. In 2005, Oregonian writer Sarah Kershaw won a Pulitzer for her series about the discovery of 5,000 copper urns, unearthed in a seemingly forgotten, little-known storage room in the hospital. The urns contained the cremated remains of former hospital patients.

Salem is the capital of Oregon, and is located one hour west of the Cascade Mountains, and one hour east of the Pacific Ocean. In addition to the Oregon State Fair, Salem also hosts numerous festivals and tours. The historic Deepwood Estate holds an annual Jazz and winefest each year, with two sound stages and lots of local gourmet "sips and nibbles."

Like most of the Willamette Valley area, Salem has a Marine West Coast climate with some distinct characteristics of the Mediterranean climate. Rain is heaviest in late fall and throughout winter, but precipitation is spread from October until May, with a dry season from June through September. Light snowfall occurs in winter, but major snows are rare. Mostly cloudy skies, and low cloud ceilings are commonplace during the rainy season. Salem's mean annual temperature is 53.0 °F, annual precipitation is 39.64 inches, including an average 3.5 inches of snow.

Rankings

General Rankings

- In their second annual survey, analysts for the small- and mid-sized city lifestyle site Livability.com looked at data for more than 2,000 U.S. cities to determine the rankings for Livability's "Top 100 Best Places to Live" in 2015. Salem ranked #88. Criteria: vibrant economy; low cost of living; abundant lifestyle amenities. *Livability.com, "Top 100 Best Places to Live 2015"*

Business/Finance Rankings

- The Salem metro area appeared on the Milken Institute "2013 Best Performing Cities" list. Rank: #117 out of 200 large metro areas. Criteria: job growth; wage and salary growth; high-tech output growth. *Milken Institute, "Best-Performing Cities 2014," January 2015*

- *Forbes* ranked the 200 most populous metro areas to determine the nation's "Best Places for Business and Careers." The Salem metro area was ranked #98. Criteria: costs (business and living); job growth (past and projected); income growth; educational attainment (college and high school); projected economic growth; cultural and recreational opportunities; net migration patterns; number of highly ranked colleges. *Forbes, "The Best Places for Business and Careers 2014," July 23, 2014*

Dating/Romance Rankings

- Salem was selected as one of the most romantic cities in America by Amazon.com. The city ranked #16 of 20. Criteria: cities with 100,000 or more residents were ranked on their per capita sales of romance novels and relationship books, romantic comedy movies, romantic music, and sexual wellness products. *Amazon.com, "Top 20 Most Romantic Cities in America," February 5, 2015*

Education Rankings

- Personal finance website *WalletHub* analyzed the 150 largest U.S. metropolitan statistical areas to determine where the most educated Americans are choosing to settle. Criteria: educational attainment; percentage of workers with jobs in computer, engineering, and science fields; quality and size of each metro area's universities. Salem was ranked #108 (#1 = most educated city). *www.WalletHub.com, "2014's Most and Least Educated Cities*

Environmental Rankings

- The Salem metro area came in at #15 for the relative comfort of its climate on Sperling's list of "chill cities," as measured by the Sperling Heat Index. All 361 metro areas are included. Criteria included daytime high temperatures, nighttime low temperatures, dew point, and relative humidity at the high temperatures. *www.bertsperling.com, "Sperling's Chill Cities," July 18, 2013*

- Sperling's BestPlaces assessed 379 metropolitan areas of the United States for the likelihood of dangerously extreme weather events or earthquakes. In general the Southeast and South-Central regions have the highest risk of weather extremes and earthquakes, while the Pacific Northwest enjoys the lowest risk. Of the least risky metropolitan areas, the Salem metro area was ranked #7. *www.bestplaces.net, "Safest Places from Natural Disasters," April 2011*

Health/Fitness Rankings

- The Salem metro area appeared in the 2013 Gallup-Healthways Well-Being Index. The area ranked #130 out of 189. The Gallup-Healthways Well-Being Index score is an average of six sub-indexes, which individually examine life evaluation, emotional health, work environment, physical health, healthy behaviors, and access to basic necessities. Results are based on telephone interviews conducted as part of the Gallup-Healthways Well-Being Index survey January 2–December 29, 2012, and January 2–December 30, 2013, with a random sample of 531,630 adults, aged 18 and older, living in metropolitan areas in the 50 U.S. states and the District of Columbia. *Gallup-Healthways, "State of American Well-Being," March 25, 2014*

Real Estate Rankings

- Salem was ranked #73 out of 275 metro areas in terms of house price appreciation in 2014 (#1 = highest rate). *Federal Housing Finance Agency, House Price Index, 4th Quarter 2014*

- The Salem metro area was identified as one of the 20 best housing markets in the U.S. in 2014. The area ranked #17 out of 178 markets with a home price appreciation of 11.4%. Criteria: year-over-year change of median sales price of existing single-family homes between the 4th quarter of 2013 and the 4th quarter of 2014. *National Association of Realtors®, Median Sales Price of Existing Single-Family Homes for Metropolitan Areas, 4th Quarter 2014*

- Salem was ranked #124 out of 226 metro areas in terms of housing affordability in 2014 by the National Association of Home Builders (#1 = most affordable). The NAHB-Wells Fargo Housing Opportunity Index (HOI) for a given area is defined as the share of homes sold in that area that would have been affordable to a family earning the local median income, based on standard mortgage underwriting criteria. *National Association of Home Builders®, NAHB-Wells Fargo Housing Opportunity Index, 4th Quarter 2014*

Safety Rankings

- Allstate ranked the 200 largest cities in America in terms of driver safety. Salem ranked #102. Allstate researchers analyzed internal property damage claims over a two-year period from January 2011 to December 2012. A weighted average of the two-year numbers determined the annual percentages. *Allstate, "Allstate America's Best Drivers Report, 2014"*

- The National Insurance Crime Bureau ranked 380 metro areas in the U.S. in terms of per capita rates of vehicle theft. The Salem metro area ranked #77 (#1 = highest rate). Criteria: number of vehicle theft offenses per 100,000 inhabitants in 2012. *National Insurance Crime Bureau, "Hot Spots 2012," June 26, 2013*

Seniors/Retirement Rankings

- From its Best Cities for Successful Aging indexes, the Milken Institute generated rankings for metropolitan areas, weighing data in eight categories—health care, wellness, living arrangements, transportation, financial characteristics, education and employment opportunities, community engagement, and overall livability. The Salem metro area was ranked #207 overall in the small metro area category. *Milken Institute, "Best Cities for Successful Aging, 2014"*

Sports/Recreation Rankings

- Salem was chosen as a bicycle friendly community by the League of American Bicyclists. A "Bicycle Friendly Community" welcomes cyclists by providing safe accommodation for cycling and encouraging people to bike for transportation and recreation. There are four award levels: Platinum; Gold; Silver; and Bronze. The community achieved an award level of Bronze. *League of American Bicyclists, "Bicycle Friendly Community Master List," Fall 2013*

- Salem was chosen as one of America's best cities for bicycling. The city ranked #22 out of 50. Criteria: robust cycling infrastructure; vibrant bike culture. The editors only considered cities with populations of 95,000 or more. *Bicycling, "America's Top 50 Bike-Friendly Cities," May 23, 2012*

Miscellaneous Rankings

- According to the World Giving Index, the United States is the fifth most generous nation in the world. The finance and lifestyle site NerdWallet looked for the U.S. cities that topped the list in donating money and time to good causes. The Salem metro area proved to be the #11-ranked metro area, judged by culture of volunteerism, depth of commitment in terms of volunteer hours per year, and monetary contributions. *www.nerdwallet.com, "Most Generous Cities," September 22, 2013*

Business Environment

CITY FINANCES

City Government Finances

Component	2012 ($000)	2012 ($ per capita)
Total Revenues	279,462	1,807
Total Expenditures	270,872	1,752
Debt Outstanding	711,512	4,601
Cash and Securities[1]	518,733	3,355

Note: (1) Cash and security holdings of a government at the close of its fiscal year, including those of its dependent agencies, utilities, and liquor stores.
Source: U.S Census Bureau, State & Local Government Finances 2012

City Government Revenue by Source

Source	2012 ($000)	2012 ($ per capita)
General Revenue		
From Federal Government	20,657	134
From State Government	48,506	314
From Local Governments	6,859	44
Taxes		
Property	77,131	499
Sales and Gross Receipts	16,691	108
Personal Income	0	0
Corporate Income	0	0
Motor Vehicle License	0	0
Other Taxes	7,479	48
Current Charges	50,874	329
Liquor Store	0	0
Utility	28,118	182
Employee Retirement	0	0

Source: U.S Census Bureau, State & Local Government Finances 2012

City Government Expenditures by Function

Function	2012 ($000)	2012 ($ per capita)	2012 (%)
General Direct Expenditures			
Air Transportation	1,053	7	0.4
Corrections	0	0	0.0
Education	0	0	0.0
Employment Security Administration	0	0	0.0
Financial Administration	7,317	47	2.7
Fire Protection	25,287	164	9.3
General Public Buildings	0	0	0.0
Governmental Administration, Other	4,525	29	1.7
Health	1,182	8	0.4
Highways	34,889	226	12.9
Hospitals	0	0	0.0
Housing and Community Development	31,412	203	11.6
Interest on General Debt	20,870	135	7.7
Judicial and Legal	1,627	11	0.6
Libraries	4,261	28	1.6
Parking	1,688	11	0.6
Parks and Recreation	8,953	58	3.3
Police Protection	33,461	216	12.4
Public Welfare	0	0	0.0
Sewerage	29,263	189	10.8
Solid Waste Management	0	0	0.0
Veterans' Services	0	0	0.0
Liquor Store	0	0	0.0
Utility	30,002	194	11.1
Employee Retirement	0	0	0.0

Source: U.S Census Bureau, State & Local Government Finances 2012

DEMOGRAPHICS

Population Growth

Area	1990 Census	2000 Census	2010 Census	Population Growth (%) 1990-2000	Population Growth (%) 2000-2010
City	112,046	136,924	154,637	22.2	12.9
MSA[1]	278,024	347,214	390,738	24.9	12.5
U.S.	248,709,873	281,421,906	308,745,538	13.2	9.7

Note: (1) Figures cover the Salem, OR Metropolitan Statistical Area—see Appendix B for areas included
Source: U.S. Census Bureau, Census 1990, 2000, 2010

Household Size

Area	Persons in Household (%) One	Two	Three	Four	Five	Six	Seven or More	Average Household Size
City	29.7	32.1	14.9	12.6	6.6	2.7	1.5	2.59
MSA[1]	25.0	34.4	15.4	12.2	7.7	3.1	2.1	2.72
U.S.	27.7	33.6	15.7	13.1	6.0	2.3	1.5	2.64

Note: (1) Figures cover the Salem, OR Metropolitan Statistical Area—see Appendix B for areas included
Source: U.S. Census Bureau, 2011-2013 American Community Survey 3-Year Estimates

Race

Area	White Alone[2] (%)	Black Alone[2] (%)	Asian Alone[2] (%)	AIAN[3] Alone[2] (%)	NHOPI[4] Alone[2] (%)	Other Race Alone[2] (%)	Two or More Races (%)
City	80.4	1.2	3.0	0.8	1.0	8.8	4.8
MSA[1]	82.2	0.8	1.9	1.2	0.6	9.0	4.3
U.S.	73.9	12.6	5.0	0.8	0.2	4.7	2.9

Note: (1) Figures cover the Salem, OR Metropolitan Statistical Area—see Appendix B for areas included; (2) Alone is defined as not being in combination with one or more other races; (3) American Indian and Alaska Native; (4) Native Hawaiian and Other Pacific Islander
Source: U.S. Census Bureau, 2011-2013 American Community Survey 3-Year Estimates

Hispanic or Latino Origin

Area	Total (%)	Mexican (%)	Puerto Rican (%)	Cuban (%)	Other (%)
City	20.7	18.8	0.1	0.1	1.7
MSA[1]	22.6	20.7	0.2	0.0	1.7
U.S.	16.9	10.8	1.6	0.6	3.8

Note: Persons of Hispanic or Latino origin can be of any race; (1) Figures cover the Salem, OR Metropolitan Statistical Area—see Appendix B for areas included
Source: U.S. Census Bureau, 2011-2013 American Community Survey 3-Year Estimates

Segregation

Type	Segregation Indices[1] 1990	2000	2010	2010 Rank[2]	Percent Change 1990-2000	1990-2010	2000-2010
Black/White	n/a	n/a	n/a	n/a	n/a	n/a	n/a
Asian/White	n/a	n/a	n/a	n/a	n/a	n/a	n/a
Hispanic/White	n/a	n/a	n/a	n/a	n/a	n/a	n/a

Note: All figures cover the Metropolitan Statistical Area—see Appendix B for areas included; Figures are based on an analysis of 1990, 2000, and 2010 Census Decennial Census tract data by William H. Frey, Brookings Institution and the University of Michigan Social Science Data Analysis Network. In this analysis all racial groups (whites, blacks, and asians) are non-Hispanic members of those races. Hispanics are shown as a separate category;
(1) Segregation Indices are Dissimilarity Indices that measure the degree to which the minority group is distributed differently than whites across census tracts. They range from 0 (complete integration) to 100 (complete segregation) where the value indicates the percentage of the minority group that needs to move to be distributed exactly like whites; (2) Ranges from 1 (most segregated) to 102 (least segregated); n/a not available.
Source: www.CensusScope.org

Ancestry

Area	German	Irish	English	American	Italian	Polish	French[2]	Scottish	Dutch
City	19.6	11.5	11.1	4.4	3.5	1.1	3.4	2.8	2.1
MSA[1]	19.7	10.1	10.9	4.5	3.1	1.3	3.1	2.7	2.2
U.S.	14.9	10.8	8.0	7.4	5.5	3.0	2.7	1.7	1.4

Note: Figures are the percentage of the total population reporting a particular ancestry. The nine most commonly reported ancestries in the U.S. are shown. Figures include multiple ancestries (e.g. if a person reported being Irish and Italian, they were included in both columns); (1) Figures cover the Salem, OR Metropolitan Statistical Area—see Appendix B for areas included; (2) Excludes Basque
Source: U.S. Census Bureau, 2011-2013 American Community Survey 3-Year Estimates

Foreign-Born Population

Area	Percent of Population Born in								
	Any Foreign Country	Mexico	Asia	Europe	Carribean	South America	Central America[2]	Africa	Canada
City	n/a	n/a	n/a	n/a	n/a	n/a	n/a	n/a	n/a
MSA[1]	12.0	7.9	1.5	1.3	0.1	0.3	0.3	0.1	0.3
U.S.	13.0	3.7	3.8	1.5	1.2	0.9	1.0	0.6	0.3

Note: (1) Figures cover the Salem, OR Metropolitan Statistical Area—see Appendix B for areas included; (2) Excludes Mexico.
Source: U.S. Census Bureau, 2011-2013 American Community Survey 3-Year Estimates

Marital Status

Area	Never Married	Now Married[2]	Separated	Widowed	Divorced
City	32.7	44.7	2.6	5.1	14.8
MSA[1]	30.2	50.0	2.4	5.2	12.2
U.S.	32.7	48.1	2.2	6.0	11.0

Note: Figures are percentages and cover the population 15 years of age and older; (1) Figures cover the Salem, OR Metropolitan Statistical Area—see Appendix B for areas included; (2) Excludes separated
Source: U.S. Census Bureau, 2011-2013 American Community Survey 3-Year Estimates

Disability Status

Area	All Ages	Under 18 Years Old	18 to 64 Years Old	65 Years and Over
City	14.2	5.0	13.9	34.3
MSA[1]	14.2	4.9	13.2	36.2
U.S.	12.3	4.1	10.2	36.3

Note: Figures show percent of the civilian noninstitutionalized population that reported having a disability. Disability status is determined from from six types of difficulty: vision, hearing, cognitive, ambulatory, self-care, and independent living. For children under 5 years old, hearing and vision difficulty are used to determine disability status. For children between the ages of 5 and 14, disability status is determined from hearing, vision, cognitive, ambulatory, and self-care difficulties. For people aged 15 years and older, they are considered to have a disability if they have difficulty with any one of the six difficulty types; (1) Figures cover the Salem, OR Metropolitan Statistical Area—see Appendix B for areas included.
Source: U.S. Census Bureau, 2011-2013 American Community Survey 3-Year Estimates

Age

Area	Percent of Population									Median Age
	Under Age 5	Age 5–19	Age 20–34	Age 35–44	Age 45–54	Age 55–64	Age 65–74	Age 75–84	Age 85+	
City	7.4	20.9	21.6	12.9	12.5	11.7	7.1	3.8	2.1	35.0
MSA[1]	6.9	21.8	20.4	12.4	12.4	12.3	7.7	4.1	2.1	35.7
U.S.	6.4	19.9	20.7	12.9	14.1	12.3	7.6	4.2	1.9	37.4

Note: (1) Figures cover the Salem, OR Metropolitan Statistical Area—see Appendix B for areas included
Source: U.S. Census Bureau, 2011-2013 American Community Survey 3-Year Estimates

Gender

Area	Males	Females	Males per 100 Females
City	77,965	80,744	96.6
MSA[1]	196,381	200,953	97.7
U.S.	154,451,010	159,410,713	96.9

Note: (1) Figures cover the Salem, OR Metropolitan Statistical Area—see Appendix B for areas included
Source: U.S. Census Bureau, 2011-2013 American Community Survey 3-Year Estimates

Religious Groups by Family

Area	Catholic	Baptist	Non-Den.	Methodist[2]	Lutheran	LDS[3]	Pente-costal	Presby-terian[4]	Muslim[5]	Judaism
MSA[1]	16.7	2.2	3.0	1.2	1.7	3.9	3.4	0.7	<0.1	0.1
U.S.	19.1	9.3	4.0	4.0	2.3	2.0	1.9	1.6	0.8	0.7

Note: Figures are the number of adherents as a percentage of the total population; (1) Figures cover the Salem, OR Metropolitan Statistical Area—see Appendix B for areas included; (2) Methodist/Pietist; (3) Latter Day Saints; (4) Reformed; (5) Figures are estimates
Source: Association of Statisticians of American Religious Bodies, 2010 U.S. Religion Census: Religious Congregations & Membership Study

Religious Groups by Tradition

Area	Catholic	Evangelical Protestant	Mainline Protestant	Other Tradition	Black Protestant	Orthodox
MSA[1]	16.7	14.1	3.8	4.2	<0.1	<0.1
U.S.	19.1	16.2	7.3	4.3	1.6	0.3

Note: Figures are the number of adherents as a percentage of the total population; (1) Figures cover the Salem, OR Metropolitan Statistical Area—see Appendix B for areas included
Source: Association of Statisticians of American Religious Bodies, 2010 U.S. Religion Census: Religious Congregations & Membership Study

ECONOMY

Gross Metropolitan Product

Area	2012	2013	2014	2015	Rank[2]
MSA[1]	12.7	13.1	13.6	14.3	152

Note: Figures are in billions of dollars; (1) Figures cover the Salem, OR Metropolitan Statistical Area—see Appendix B for areas included; (2) Rank is based on 2015 data and ranges from 1 to 363
Source: The U.S. Conference of Mayors, U.S. Metro Economies: GMP and Employment 2013-2015, June 2014

Economic Growth

Area	2010-12 (%)	2013 (%)	2014 (%)	2015 (%)	Rank[2]
MSA[1]	-0.4	1.6	1.7	3.2	119
U.S.	2.1	2.0	2.3	3.2	–

Note: Figures are real gross metropolitan product (GMP) growth rates and represent annual average percent change; (1) Figures cover the Salem, OR Metropolitan Statistical Area—see Appendix B for areas included; (2) Rank is based on 2015 data and ranges from 1 to 363
Source: The U.S. Conference of Mayors, U.S. Metro Economies: GMP and Employment 2013-2015, June 2014

Metropolitan Area Exports

Area	2008	2009	2010	2011	2012	2013	Rank[2]
MSA[1]	331.9	325.2	453.8	508.7	437.3	414.4	232

Note: Figures are in millions of dollars; (1) Figures cover the Salem, OR Metropolitan Statistical Area—see Appendix B for areas included; (2) Rank is based on 2013 data and ranges from 1 to 387
Source: U.S. Department of Commerce, International Trade Administration, Office of Trade & Industry Information, Manufacturing & Services, data extracted April 3, 2015

Building Permits

Area	Single-Family			Multi-Family			Total		
	2013	2014	Pct. Chg.	2013	2014	Pct. Chg.	2013	2014	Pct. Chg.
City	283	270	-4.6	294	21	-92.9	577	291	-49.6
MSA[1]	646	712	10.2	304	232	-23.7	950	944	-0.6
U.S.	620,802	634,597	2.2	370,020	411,766	11.3	990,822	1,046,363	5.6

Note: (1) Figures cover the Salem, OR Metropolitan Statistical Area—see Appendix B for areas included; Figures represent new, privately-owned housing units authorized (unadjusted data); All permit data are based on estimates with imputation.
Source: U.S. Census Bureau, Manufacturing, Mining, and Construction Statistics, Building Permits, 2013, 2014

Bankruptcy Filings

Area	Business Filings			Nonbusiness Filings		
	2013	2014	% Chg.	2013	2014	% Chg.
Marion County	25	19	-24.0	1,334	1,219	-8.6
U.S.	33,212	26,983	-18.8	1,038,720	909,812	-12.4

Note: Business filings include Chapter 7, Chapter 11, Chapter 12, and Chapter 13; Nonbusiness filings include Chapter 7, Chapter 11, and Chapter 13
Source: Administrative Office of the U.S. Courts, Business and Nonbusiness Bankruptcy, County Cases Commenced by Chapter of the Bankruptcy Code, During the 12- Month Period Ending December 31, 2013 and Business and Nonbusiness Bankruptcy, County Cases Commenced by Chapter of the Bankruptcy Code, During the 12- Month Period Ending December 31, 2014

Housing Vacancy Rates

Area	Gross Vacancy Rate[2] (%)			Year-Round Vacancy Rate[3] (%)			Rental Vacancy Rate[4] (%)			Homeowner Vacancy Rate[5] (%)		
	2012	2013	2014	2012	2013	2014	2012	2013	2014	2012	2013	2014
MSA[1]	n/a	n/a	n/a	n/a	n/a	n/a	n/a	n/a	n/a	n/a	n/a	n/a
U.S.	13.8	13.6	13.4	10.8	10.7	10.4	8.7	8.3	7.6	2.0	2.0	1.9

Note: (1) Figures cover the Salem, OR Metropolitan Statistical Area—see Appendix B for areas included; (2) The percentage of the total housing inventory that is vacant; (3) The percentage of the housing inventory (excluding seasonal units) that is year-round vacant; (4) The percentage of rental inventory that is vacant for rent; (5) The percentage of homeowner inventory that is vacant for sale; n/a not available
Source: U.S. Census Bureau, Housing Vacancies and Homeownership Annual Statistics: 2014

INCOME

Income

Area	Per Capita ($)	Median Household ($)	Average Household ($)
City	22,242	44,773	58,617
MSA[1]	21,769	46,763	59,174
U.S.	27,884	52,176	72,897

Note: (1) Figures cover the Salem, OR Metropolitan Statistical Area—see Appendix B for areas included
Source: U.S. Census Bureau, 2011-2013 American Community Survey 3-Year Estimates

Household Income Distribution

Area	Percent of Households Earning							
	Under $15,000	$15,000 -24,999	$25,000 -34,999	$35,000 -49,999	$50,000 -74,999	$75,000 -99,000	$100,000 -149,999	$150,000 and up
City	15.8	11.7	12.0	15.5	18.6	11.3	10.3	4.8
MSA[1]	13.7	11.6	11.7	15.4	20.2	11.9	10.9	4.4
U.S.	13.0	10.9	10.3	13.6	17.9	11.9	12.7	9.6

Note: (1) Figures cover the Salem, OR Metropolitan Statistical Area—see Appendix B for areas included
Source: U.S. Census Bureau, 2011-2013 American Community Survey 3-Year Estimates

Poverty Rate

Area	All Ages	Under 18 Years Old	18 to 64 Years Old	65 Years and Over
City	20.5	29.5	18.9	10.2
MSA[1]	19.7	29.1	18.6	7.5
U.S.	15.9	22.4	14.8	9.5

Note: Figures are percentage of people whose income during the past 12 months was below the poverty level;
(1) Figures cover the Salem, OR Metropolitan Statistical Area—see Appendix B for areas included
Source: U.S. Census Bureau, 2011-2013 American Community Survey 3-Year Estimates

EMPLOYMENT

Labor Force and Employment

Area	Civilian Labor Force			Workers Employed		
	Dec. 2013	Dec. 2014	% Chg.	Dec. 2013	Dec. 2014	% Chg.
City	72,077	74,276	3.1	66,723	69,347	3.9
MSA[1]	180,148	185,317	2.9	166,202	172,750	3.9
U.S.	154,408,000	155,521,000	0.7	144,423,000	147,190,000	1.9

Note: Data is not seasonally adjusted and covers workers 16 years of age and older; (1) Figures cover the
Salem, OR Metropolitan Statistical Area—see Appendix B for areas included
Source: Bureau of Labor Statistics, Local Area Unemployment Statistics

Unemployment Rate

Area	2014											
	Jan.	Feb.	Mar.	Apr.	May	Jun.	Jul.	Aug.	Sep.	Oct.	Nov.	Dec.
City	8.0	8.3	8.1	7.2	7.0	7.3	7.6	7.3	6.5	6.7	6.8	6.6
MSA[1]	8.5	8.6	8.3	7.3	7.0	7.2	7.5	7.3	6.5	6.7	6.9	6.8
U.S.	7.0	7.0	6.8	5.9	6.1	6.3	6.5	6.3	5.7	5.5	5.5	5.4

Note: Data is not seasonally adjusted and covers workers 16 years of age and older; (1) Figures cover the
Salem, OR Metropolitan Statistical Area—see Appendix B for areas included
Source: Bureau of Labor Statistics, Local Area Unemployment Statistics

Employment by Occupation

Occupation Classification	City (%)	MSA[1] (%)	U.S. (%)
Management, Business, Science, and Arts	34.7	30.6	36.2
Natural Resources, Construction, and Maintenance	9.0	12.0	9.0
Production, Transportation, and Material Moving	11.0	13.0	12.1
Sales and Office	24.2	24.5	24.4
Service	21.2	19.9	18.3

Note: Figures cover employed civilians 16 years of age and older; (1) Figures cover the Salem, OR
Metropolitan Statistical Area—see Appendix B for areas included
Source: U.S. Census Bureau, 2011-2013 American Community Survey 3-Year Estimates

Employment by Industry

Sector	MSA[1]		U.S.
	Number of Employees	Percent of Total	Percent of Total
Construction	7,800	5.1	4.4
Education and Health Services	24,200	15.9	15.5
Financial Activities	7,200	4.7	5.7
Government	42,000	27.6	15.8
Information	1,000	0.7	2.0
Leisure and Hospitality	13,500	8.9	10.3
Manufacturing	11,600	7.6	8.7
Mining and Logging	1,200	0.8	0.6
Other Services	5,300	3.5	4.0
Professional and Business Services	12,600	8.3	13.8
Retail Trade	18,000	11.8	11.4
Transportation, Warehousing, and Utilities	3,900	2.6	3.9
Wholesale Trade	3,900	2.6	4.2

Note: Figures are non-farm employment as of December 2014. Figures are not seasonally adjusted and include workers 16 years of age and older; (1) Figures cover the Salem, OR Metropolitan Statistical Area—see Appendix B for areas included
Source: Bureau of Labor Statistics, Current Employment Statistics, Employment, Hours, and Earnings

Occupations with Greatest Projected Employment Growth: 2012 – 2022

Occupation[1]	2012 Employment	2022 Projected Employment	Numeric Employment Change	Percent Employment Change
Retail Salespersons	55,160	62,550	7,390	13.4
Combined Food Preparation and Serving Workers, Including Fast Food	35,480	42,020	6,540	18.4
Registered Nurses	30,680	35,640	4,960	16.2
Waiters and Waitresses	27,760	32,690	4,930	17.8
Janitors and Cleaners, Except Maids and Housekeeping Cleaners	24,200	28,670	4,470	18.4
Bookkeeping, Accounting, and Auditing Clerks	26,030	30,280	4,250	16.3
Customer Service Representatives	22,630	26,520	3,890	17.2
Medical Secretaries	12,380	16,170	3,790	30.6
Farmworkers and Laborers, Crop, Nursery, and Greenhouse	20,290	24,010	3,720	18.4
Secretaries and Administrative Assistants, Except Legal, Medical, and Executive	22,400	26,100	3,700	16.5

Note: Projections cover Oregon; (1) Sorted by numeric employment change
Source: www.projectionscentral.com, State Occupational Projections, 2012–2022 Long-Term Projections

Fastest Growing Occupations: 2012 – 2022

Occupation[1]	2012 Employment	2022 Projected Employment	Numeric Employment Change	Percent Employment Change
Skincare Specialists	300	470	170	57.2
Computer Numerically Controlled Machine Tool Programmers, Metal and Plastic	460	680	220	47.2
Roofers	1,960	2,740	780	39.5
Brickmasons and Blockmasons	460	640	180	38.9
Physician Assistants	930	1,290	360	38.7
Insulation Workers, Floor, Ceiling, and Wall	450	620	170	38.7
Fence Erectors	420	570	150	38.3
Diagnostic Medical Sonographers	470	650	180	38.2
Market Research Analysts and Marketing Specialists	2,390	3,290	900	37.8
Helpers—Brickmasons, Blockmasons, Stonemasons, and Tile and Marble Setters	270	380	110	37.4

Note: Projections cover Oregon; (1) Sorted by percent employment change and excludes occupations with numeric employment change less than 100
Source: www.projectionscentral.com, State Occupational Projections, 2012–2022 Long-Term Projections

Average Wages

Occupation	$/Hr.	Occupation	$/Hr.
Accountants and Auditors	30.82	Maids and Housekeeping Cleaners	11.45
Automotive Mechanics	20.50	Maintenance and Repair Workers	17.47
Bookkeepers	18.36	Marketing Managers	36.40
Carpenters	20.36	Nuclear Medicine Technologists	n/a
Cashiers	11.35	Nurses, Licensed Practical	22.33
Clerks, General Office	15.81	Nurses, Registered	37.43
Clerks, Receptionists/Information	13.99	Nursing Assistants	14.19
Clerks, Shipping/Receiving	14.60	Packers and Packagers, Hand	10.39
Computer Programmers	36.39	Physical Therapists	39.98
Computer Systems Analysts	37.11	Postal Service Mail Carriers	24.05
Computer User Support Specialists	24.03	Real Estate Brokers	26.23
Cooks, Restaurant	11.49	Retail Salespersons	12.94
Dentists	81.34	Sales Reps., Exc. Tech./Scientific	21.91
Electrical Engineers	45.32	Sales Reps., Tech./Scientific	39.34
Electricians	27.80	Secretaries, Exc. Legal/Med./Exec.	16.38
Financial Managers	44.82	Security Guards	13.67
First-Line Supervisors/Managers, Sales	17.97	Surgeons	n/a
Food Preparation Workers	10.78	Teacher Assistants	16.20
General and Operations Managers	42.99	Teachers, Elementary School	28.80
Hairdressers/Cosmetologists	12.30	Teachers, Secondary School	27.10
Internists	102.69	Telemarketers	10.69
Janitors and Cleaners	13.69	Truck Drivers, Heavy/Tractor-Trailer	17.54
Landscaping/Groundskeeping Workers	13.45	Truck Drivers, Light/Delivery Svcs.	18.65
Lawyers	57.07	Waiters and Waitresses	10.85

Note: Wage data covers the Salem, OR Metropolitan Statistical Area—see Appendix B for areas included;
Hourly wages for elementary/secondary school teachers and teacher assistants were calculated by the editors
from annual wage data assuming a 40 hour work week; n/a not available.
Source: Bureau of Labor Statistics, Metro Area Occupational Employment and Wage Estimates, May 2014

TAXES

State Corporate Income Tax Rates

State	Tax Rate (%)	Income Brackets ($)	Num. of Brackets	Financial Institution Tax Rate (%)[a]	Federal Income Tax Ded.
Oregon	6.6 - 7.6 (w)	1 million	2	6.6 - 7.6 (w)	No

Note: Tax rates as of January 1, 2015; (a) Rates listed are the corporate income tax rate applied to financial institutions or excise taxes based on income. Some states have other taxes based upon the value of deposits or shares; (w) Oregon's minimum tax for C corporations depends on the Oregon sales of the filing group. The minimum tax ranges from $150 for corporations with sales under $500,000, up to $100,000 for companies with sales of $100 million or above.
Source: Federation of Tax Administrators, "State Corporate Income Tax Rates, 2015"

State Individual Income Tax Rates

State	Tax Rate (%)	Income Brackets ($)	Num. of Brackets	Personal Exempt. ($)[1] Single	Personal Exempt. ($)[1] Dependents	Fed. Inc. Tax Ded.
Oregon (a)	5.0 - 9.9	3,350 -125,000 (b)	4	194 (c)	194 (c)	Yes (n)

Note: Tax rates as of January 1, 2015; Local- and county-level taxes are not included; n/a not applicable; (1) Married joint filers generally receive double the single exemption; (a) 17 states have statutory provision for automatically adjusting to the rate of inflation the dollar values of the income tax brackets, standard deductions, and/or personal exemptions. Massachusetts, Michigan, and Nebraska index the personal exemptiononly. Oregon does not index the income brackets for $125,000 and over. Maine has suspended indexing for 2014 and 2015; (b) For joint returns, taxes are twice the tax on half the couple's income; (c) The personal exemption takes the form of a tax credit instead of a deduction; (n) The deduction for federal income tax is limited to $5,000 for individuals and $10,000 for joint returns in Missouri and Montana, and to $6,350 for all filers in Oregon.
Source: Federation of Tax Administrators, "State Individual Income Tax Rates, 2015"

Various State and Local Tax Rates

State	State and Local Sales and Use (%)	State Sales and Use (%)	Gasoline[1] (¢/gal.)	Cigarette[2] ($/pack)	Spirits[3] ($/gal.)	Wine[4] ($/gal.)	Beer[5] ($/gal.)
Oregon	None	None	31.07	1.31	22.72 (g)	0.67	0.08

Note: All tax rates as of January 1, 2015; (1) The American Petroleum Institute has developed a methodology for determining the average tax rate on a gallon of fuel. Rates may include any of the following: excise taxes, environmental fees, storage tank fees, other fees or taxes, general sales tax, and local taxes. In states where gasoline is subject to the general sales tax, or where the fuel tax is based on the average sale price, the average rate determined by API is sensitive to changes in the price of gasoline. States that fully or partially apply general sales taxes to gasoline: CA, CO, GA, IL, IN, MI, NY; (2) The federal excise tax of $1.0066 per pack and local taxes are not included; (3) Rates are those applicable to off-premise sales of 40% alcohol by volume (a.b.v.) distilled spirits in 750ml containers. Local excise taxes are excluded; (4) Rates are those applicable to off-premise sales of 11% a.b.v. non-carbonated wine in 750ml containers; (5) Rates are those applicable to off-premise sales of 4.7% a.b.v. beer in 12 ounce containers; (g) States where the government controls sales. In these "control states," products are subject to ad valorem mark-up and excise taxes. The excise tax rate is calculated using a methodology developed by the Distilled Spirits Council of the United States.
Source: Tax Foundation, 2015 Facts & Figures: How Does Your State Compare?

State Business Tax Climate Index Rankings

State	Overall Rank	Corporate Tax Index Rank	Individual Income Tax Index Rank	Sales Tax Index Rank	Unemployment Insurance Tax Index Rank	Property Tax Index Rank
Oregon	12	36	31	4	30	15

Note: The index is a measure of how each state's tax laws affect economic performance. The lower the rank, the more favorable a state's tax system is for business. States without a given tax are given a ranking of 1. The scores/rankings for the District of Columbia do not affect other states. The 2015 index represents the tax climate as of July 1, 2014.
Source: Tax Foundation, State Business Tax Climate Index 2015

COMMERCIAL UTILITIES

Typical Monthly Electric Bills

Area	Commercial Service ($/month) 1,500 kWh	Commercial Service ($/month) 40 kW demand 14,000 kWh	Industrial Service ($/month) 1,000 kW demand 200,000 kWh	Industrial Service ($/month) 50,000 kW demand 32,500,000 kWh
City	176	1,299	20,892	2,083,747
Average[1]	201	1,653	26,124	2,639,743

Note: Figures are based on annualized 2014 rates; (1) Average based on 180 utilities surveyed
Source: Edison Electric Institute, Typical Bills and Average Rates Report, Summer 2014

TRANSPORTATION

Means of Transportation to Work

Area	Car/Truck/Van		Public Transportation			Bicycle	Walked	Other Means	Worked at Home
	Drove Alone	Car-pooled	Bus	Subway	Railroad				
City	75.5	11.8	1.8	0.0	0.0	1.8	4.7	0.8	3.6
MSA[1]	74.4	13.9	1.3	0.0	0.0	1.3	4.2	1.0	4.0
U.S.	76.4	9.6	2.6	1.8	0.6	0.6	2.8	1.3	4.3

Note: Figures are percentages and cover workers 16 years of age and older; (1) Figures cover the Salem, OR Metropolitan Statistical Area—see Appendix B for areas included
Source: U.S. Census Bureau, 2011-2013 American Community Survey 3-Year Estimates

Travel Time to Work

Area	Less Than 10 Minutes	10 to 19 Minutes	20 to 29 Minutes	30 to 44 Minutes	45 to 59 Minutes	60 to 89 Minutes	90 Minutes or More
City	16.6	41.9	19.3	12.2	4.0	4.2	1.8
MSA[1]	17.9	33.6	21.7	15.1	5.3	4.4	2.0
U.S.	13.3	29.7	20.9	20.2	7.7	5.7	2.6

Note: Figures are percentages and include workers 16 years old and over; (1) Figures cover the Salem, OR Metropolitan Statistical Area—see Appendix B for areas included
Source: U.S. Census Bureau, 2011-2013 American Community Survey 3-Year Estimates

Travel Time Index

Area	1985	1990	1995	2000	2005	2010	2011
Urban Area[1]	1.05	1.09	1.14	1.19	1.19	1.14	1.14
Average[2]	1.09	1.14	1.16	1.19	1.23	1.18	1.18

Note: Travel Time Index—the ratio of travel time in the peak period to the travel time at free-flow conditions. For example, a value of 1.30 indicates a 20-minute free-flow trip takes 26 minutes in the peak. Free-flow speeds (60 mph on freeways and 35 mph on principal arterials) are used as the comparison threshold; (1) Covers the Salem OR urban area; (2) average of 498 urban areas
Source: Texas Transportation Institute, Urban Mobility Report 2012, December 2012

Public Transportation

Agency Name / Mode of Transportation	Vehicles Operated in Maximum Service	Annual Unlinked Passenger Trips (in thous.)	Annual Passenger Miles (in thous.)
Salem Area Mass Transit District			
Bus (directly operated)	54	3,413.9	11,060.9
Demand Response (purchased transportation)	144	488.5	5,534.3
Vanpool (purchased transportation)	24	72.7	2,611.1

Source: Federal Transit Administration, National Transit Database, 2013

Air Transportation

Airport Name and Code / Type of Service	Passenger Airlines[1]	Passenger Enplanements	Freight Carriers[2]	Freight (lbs.)
Portland International Airport (60 miles) (PDX)				
Domestic service (U.S. carriers - 2014)	23	7,626,002	17	198,210,129
International service (U.S. carriers - 2013)	6	181,063	4	4,285,064

Note: (1) Includes all U.S.-based major, minor and commuter airlines that carried at least one passenger during the year; (2) Includes all U.S.-based airlines and freight carriers that transported at least one lb. of freight during the year.
Source: Bureau of Transportation Statistics, The Intermodal Transportation Database, Air Carriers: T-100 Domestic Market (U.S. Carriers), 2014; Bureau of Transportation Statistics, The Intermodal Transportation Database, Air Carriers: T-100 International Market (U.S. Carriers), 2013

Other Transportation Statistics

Major Highways:	I-5
Amtrak Service:	Yes
Major Waterways/Ports:	Willamette River

Source: Amtrak.com; Google Maps

BUSINESSES

Major Business Headquarters

Company Name	Rankings	
	Fortune[1]	Forbes[2]
No companies listed	-	-

Note: (1) Fortune 500—companies that produce a 10-K are ranked 1 to 500 based on 2013 revenue; (2) all private companies with at least $2 billion in annual revenue through the end of their most current fiscal year are ranked 1 to 221; companies listed are headquartered in the city; dashes indicate no ranking
Source: Fortune, "Fortune 500," June 16, 2014; Forbes, "America's Largest Private Companies," November 5, 2014

Minority- and Women-Owned Businesses

Group	All Firms		Firms with Paid Employees			
	Firms	Sales ($000)	Firms	Sales ($000)	Employees	Payroll ($000)
Asian	485	79,378	157	69,489	1,032	13,538
Black	64	4,651	3	3,390	21	569
Hispanic	716	46,836	93	36,238	374	12,267
Women	3,550	445,618	498	364,210	4,360	105,720
All Firms	12,879	12,221,548	3,852	11,898,129	65,838	2,141,130

Note: Figures cover firms located in the city; minority- and women-owned business are defined as firms in which the corresponding group own 51% or more of the stock or equity of the company
Source: U.S. Census Bureau, 2007 Economic Census, Survey of Business Owners (2012 Survey of Business Owners data will be released starting in June 2015)

**HOTELS &
CONVENTION
CENTERS**

Hotels/Motels

Area	5 Star		4 Star		3 Star		2 Star		1 Star		Not Rated	
	Num.	Pct.[3]	Num.	Pct.[3]	Num.	Pct.[3]	Num.	Pct.[3]	Num.	Pct.[3]	Num.	Pct.[3]
City[1]	0	0.0	0	0.0	16	17.6	65	71.4	4	4.4	6	6.6
Total[2]	166	0.9	1,264	7.0	5,718	31.8	9,340	52.0	411	2.3	1,070	6.0

Note: (1) Figures cover Salem and vicinity; (2) Figures cover all 100 cities in this book; (3) Percentage of hotels which have a given star rating; Star ratings are determined by expedia.com and offer an indication of the general quality of a particular hotel.
Source: expedia.com, April 2, 2015

Major Convention Centers

Name	Overall Space (sq. ft.)	Exhibit Space (sq. ft.)	Meeting Space (sq. ft.)	Meeting Rooms
Salem Convention Center	n/a	n/a	30,000	14

Note: Table includes convention centers located in the Salem, OR metro area; n/a not available
Source: Original research

Living Environment

COST OF LIVING

Cost of Living Index

Composite Index	Groceries	Housing	Utilities	Trans-portation	Health Care	Misc. Goods/Services
n/a	n/a	n/a	n/a	n/a	n/a	n/a

Note: The Cost of Living Index measures regional differences in the cost of consumer goods and services, excluding taxes and non-consumer expenditures, for professional and managerial households in the top income quintile. It is based on more than 50,000 prices covering almost 60 different items for which prices are collected three times a year by chambers of commerce, economic development organizations or university applied economic centers in each participating urban area. The numbers shown should be read as a percentage above or below the national average of 100. For example, a value of 115.4 in the groceries column indicates that grocery prices are 15.4% higher than the national average. Small differences in the index numbers should not be interpreted as significant; n/a not available.
Source: The Council for Community and Economic Research, ACCRA Cost of Living Index, 2014

Grocery Prices

Area[1]	T-Bone Steak ($/pound)	Frying Chicken ($/pound)	Whole Milk ($/half gal.)	Eggs ($/dozen)	Orange Juice ($/64 oz.)	Coffee ($/11.5 oz.)
City[2]	n/a	n/a	n/a	n/a	n/a	n/a
Avg.	10.40	1.37	2.40	1.99	3.46	4.27
Min.	8.48	0.93	1.37	1.30	2.83	2.99
Max.	14.20	2.44	3.62	4.02	6.42	6.96

Note: (1) Values for the local area are compared with the average, minimum and maximum values for all 308 areas in the Cost of Living Index; (2) Figures cover the Salem OR urban area; n/a not available; **T-Bone Steak** *(price per pound);* **Frying Chicken** *(price per pound, whole fryer);* **Whole Milk** *(half gallon carton);* **Eggs** *(price per dozen, Grade A, large);* **Orange Juice** *(64 oz. Tropicana or Florida Natural);* **Coffee** *(11.5 oz. can, vacuum-packed, Maxwell House, Hills Bros, or Folgers).*
Source: The Council for Community and Economic Research, ACCRA Cost of Living Index, 2014

Housing and Utility Costs

Area[1]	New Home Price ($)	Apartment Rent ($/month)	All Electric ($/month)	Part Electric ($/month)	Other Energy ($/month)	Telephone ($/month)
City[2]	n/a	n/a	n/a	n/a	n/a	n/a
Avg.	305,838	919	181.00	93.66	73.14	27.95
Min.	183,142	480	112.00	42.06	23.42	17.16
Max.	1,358,576	3,851	594.00	180.03	440.99	40.42

Note: (1) Values for the local area are compared with the average, minimum and maximum values for all 308 areas in the Cost of Living Index; (2) Figures cover the Salem OR urban area; n/a not available; **New Home Price** *(2,400 sf living area, 8,000 sf lot, in urban area with full utilities);* **Apartment Rent** *(950 sf 2 bedroom/1.5 or 2 bath, unfurnished, excluding all utilities except water);* **All Electric** *(average monthly cost for an all-electric home);* **Part Electric** *(average monthly cost for a part-electric home);* **Other Energy** *(average monthly cost for natural gas, fuel oil, coal, wood, and any other forms of energy except electricity);* **Telephone** *(price includes basic monthly rate for a private residential line plus additional local usage charges incurred by a family of four).*
Source: The Council for Community and Economic Research, ACCRA Cost of Living Index, 2014

Health Care, Transportation, and Other Costs

Area[1]	Doctor ($/visit)	Dentist ($/visit)	Optometrist ($/visit)	Gasoline ($/gallon)	Beauty Salon ($/visit)	Men's Shirt ($)
City[2]	n/a	n/a	n/a	n/a	n/a	n/a
Avg.	102.86	87.89	97.66	3.44	34.37	26.74
Min.	67.47	65.78	51.18	3.00	17.43	12.79
Max.	173.50	150.14	235.00	4.33	64.28	49.50

Note: (1) Values for the local area are compared with the average, minimum and maximum values for all 308 areas in the Cost of Living Index; (2) Figures cover the Salem OR urban area; n/a not available; **Doctor** *(general practitioners routine exam of an established patient);* **Dentist** *(adult teeth cleaning and periodic oral examination);* **Optometrist** *(full vision eye exam for established adult patient);* **Gasoline** *(one gallon regular unleaded, national brand, including all taxes, cash price at self-service pump if available);* **Beauty Salon** *(woman's shampoo, trim, and blow-dry);* **Men's Shirt** *(cotton/polyester dress shirt, pinpoint weave, long sleeves).*
Source: The Council for Community and Economic Research, ACCRA Cost of Living Index, 2014

HOUSING

House Price Index (HPI)

Area	National Ranking[2]	Quarterly Change (%)	One-Year Change (%)	Five-Year Change (%)
MSA[1]	73	1.24	6.72	-2.31
U.S.[3]	–	1.35	4.91	11.59

Note: The HPI is a weighted repeat sales index. It measures average price changes in repeat sales or refinancings on the same properties. This information is obtained by reviewing repeat mortgage transactions on single-family properties whose mortgages have been purchased or securitized by Fannie Mae or Freddie Mac in January 1975; (1) Salem Metropolitan Statistical Area—see Appendix B for areas included; (2) Rankings are based on annual percentage change for all metro areas containing at least 15,000 transactions over the last 10 years and ranges from 1 to 275; (3) figures based on a weighted average of Census Division estimates using a seasonally adjusted, purchase-only index; all figures are for the period ending December 31, 2014
Source: Federal Housing Finance Agency, House Price Index, February 26, 2015

Median Single-Family Home Prices

Area	2012	2013	2014p	Percent Change 2013 to 2014
MSA[1]	147.7	168.5	187.7	11.4
U.S. Average	177.2	197.4	209.0	5.9

Note: Figures are median sales prices of existing single-family homes in thousands of dollars; (p) preliminary; n/a not available; (1) Salem, OR Metropolitan Statistical Area—see Appendix B for areas included
Source: National Association of Realtors, Median Sales Price of Existing Single-Family Homes for Metropolitan Areas, 4th Quarter 2014

Qualifying Income Based on Median Sales Price of Existing Single-Family Homes

Area	With 5% Down ($)	With 10% Down ($)	With 20% Down ($)
MSA[1]	40,567	38,432	34,161
U.S. Average	45,863	43,449	38,621

Note: Figures are preliminary; Qualifying income is based on a mortgage rate of 4.0%. Monthly principal and interest payment is limited to 25% of income; n/a not available; (1) Salem, OR Metropolitan Statistical Area—see Appendix B for areas included
Source: National Association of Realtors, Qualifying Income Based on Median Sales Price of Existing Single-Family Homes for Metropolitan Areas, 4th Quarter 2014

Median Apartment Condo-Coop Home Prices

Area	2012	2013	2014p	Percent Change 2013 to 2014
MSA[1]	n/a	n/a	n/a	n/a
U.S. Average	173.7	194.9	205.1	5.2

Note: Figures are median sales prices of existing apartment condo-coop homes in thousands of dollars; (p) preliminary; n/a not available; (1) Salem, OR Metropolitan Statistical Area—see Appendix B for areas included
Source: National Association of Realtors, Median Sales Price of Existing Apartment Condo-Coop Homes for Metropolitan Areas, 4th Quarter 2014

Gross Monthly Rent

Area	Under $200	$200 -299	$300 -499	$500 -749	$750 -999	$1,000 -1,499	$1,500 and up	Median ($)
City	1.3	2.3	8.6	33.8	27.8	18.8	7.3	775
MSA[1]	1.8	2.5	7.4	34.6	27.2	19.1	7.4	777
U.S.	1.7	3.2	7.8	22.1	24.3	26.0	14.9	900

Note: Figures are percentages except for Median; Gross rent is the contract rent plus the estimated average monthly cost of utilities (electricity, gas, and water and sewer) and fuels (oil, coal, kerosene, wood, etc.) if these are paid by the renter (or paid for the renter by someone else); (1) Figures cover the Salem, OR Metropolitan Statistical Area—see Appendix B for areas included
Source: U.S. Census Bureau, 2011-2013 American Community Survey 3-Year Estimates

Homeownership Rate

Area	2007 (%)	2008 (%)	2009 (%)	2010 (%)	2011 (%)	2012 (%)	2013 (%)	2014 (%)
MSA[1]	n/a	n/a	n/a	n/a	n/a	n/a	n/a	n/a
U.S.	68.1	67.8	67.4	66.9	66.1	65.4	65.1	64.5

Note: (1) Figures cover the Salem, OR Metropolitan Statistical Area—see Appendix B for areas included; n/a not available
Source: U.S. Census Bureau, Housing Vacancies and Homeownership Annual Statistics: 2014

Year Housing Structure Built

Area	2010 or Later	2000 -2009	1990 -1999	1980 -1989	1970 -1979	1960 -1969	1950 -1959	1940 -1949	Before 1940	Median Year
City	0.4	14.5	16.4	11.9	21.9	10.1	9.5	6.1	9.1	1977
MSA[1]	1.0	14.6	18.7	10.2	23.5	10.2	7.7	4.7	9.3	1978
U.S.	0.9	15.0	13.9	13.8	15.8	11.0	10.9	5.4	13.3	1976

Note: Figures are percentages except for Median Year; (1) Figures cover the Salem, OR Metropolitan Statistical Area—see Appendix B for areas included
Source: U.S. Census Bureau, 2011-2013 American Community Survey 3-Year Estimates

HEALTH

Health Risk Data

Category	MSA[1] (%)	U.S. (%)
Adults aged 18–64 who have any kind of health care coverage	n/a	79.6
Adults who reported being in good or excellent health	n/a	83.1
Adults who are current smokers	n/a	19.6
Adults who are heavy drinkers[2]	n/a	6.1
Adults who are binge drinkers[3]	n/a	16.9
Adults who are overweight (BMI 25.0 - 29.9)	n/a	35.8
Adults who are obese (BMI 30.0 - 99.8)	n/a	27.6
Adults who participated in any physical activities in the past month	n/a	77.1
Adults 50+ who have ever had a sigmoidoscopy or colonoscopy	n/a	67.3
Women aged 40+ who have had a mammogram within the past two years	n/a	74.0
Men aged 40+ who have had a PSA test within the past two years	n/a	45.2
Adults aged 65+ who have had flu shot within the past year	n/a	60.1
Adults who always wear a seatbelt	n/a	93.8

Note: Data as of 2012 unless otherwise noted; n/a not available; (1) Figures cover the Salem, OR Metropolitan Statistical Area—see Appendix B for areas included; (2) Heavy drinkers are classified as males having more than two drinks per day or females having more than one drink per day; (3) Binge drinkers are classified as males having five or more drinks on one occasion or females having four or more drinks on one occasion
Source: Centers for Disease Control and Prevention, Behaviorial Risk Factor Surveillance System, SMART: Selected Metropolitan/Micropolitan Area Risk Trends, 2012 (Note: the CDC has discontinued this dataset but will be releasing a replacement in late 2015)

Chronic Health Indicators

Category	MSA[1] (%)	U.S. (%)
Adults who have ever been told they had a heart attack	n/a	4.5
Adults who have ever been told they had a stroke	n/a	2.9
Adults who have been told they currently have asthma	n/a	8.9
Adults who have ever been told they have arthritis	n/a	25.7
Adults who have ever been told they have diabetes[2]	n/a	9.7
Adults who have ever been told they had skin cancer	n/a	5.7
Adults who have ever been told they had any other types of cancer	n/a	6.5
Adults who have ever been told they have COPD	n/a	6.2
Adults who have ever been told they have kidney disease	n/a	2.5
Adults who have ever been told they have a form of depression	n/a	18.0

Note: Data as of 2012 unless otherwise noted; n/a not available; (1) Figures cover the Salem, OR Metropolitan Statistical Area—see Appendix B for areas included; (2) Figures do not include pregnancy-related, borderline, or pre-diabetes
Source: Centers for Disease Control and Prevention, Behaviorial Risk Factor Surveillance System, SMART: Selected Metropolitan/Micropolitan Area Risk Trends, 2012 (Note: the CDC has discontinued this dataset but will be releasing a replacement in late 2015)

Mortality Rates for the Top 10 Causes of Death in the U.S.

ICD-10[a] Sub-Chapter	ICD-10[a] Code	Age-Adjusted Mortality Rate[1] per 100,000 population	
		County[2]	U.S.
Malignant neoplasms	C00-C97	168.8	166.2
Ischaemic heart diseases	I20-I25	73.8	105.7
Other forms of heart disease	I30-I51	49.9	49.3
Chronic lower respiratory diseases	J40-J47	41.6	42.1
Organic, including symptomatic, mental disorders	F01-F09	52.3	38.1
Cerebrovascular diseases	I60-I69	40.5	37.0
Other external causes of accidental injury	W00-X59	29.0	26.9
Other degenerative diseases of the nervous system	G30-G31	25.3	25.6
Diabetes mellitus	E10-E14	30.5	21.3
Hypertensive diseases	I10-I15	14.6	19.4

Note: (a) ICD-10 = International Classification of Diseases 10th Revision; (1) Mortality rates are a three year average covering 2011-2013; (2) Figures cover Marion County
Source: Centers for Disease Control and Prevention, National Center for Health Statistics. Compressed Mortality File 1999-2013 on CDC WONDER Online Database, released October 2014. Data are compiled from the Compressed Mortality File 1999-2013, Series 20 No. 2S, 2014.

Mortality Rates for Selected Causes of Death

ICD-10[a] Sub-Chapter	ICD-10[a] Code	Age-Adjusted Mortality Rate[1] per 100,000 population	
		County[2]	U.S.
Assault	X85-Y09	2.7	5.2
Diseases of the liver	K70-K76	16.3	13.2
Human immunodeficiency virus (HIV) disease	B20-B24	Suppressed	2.2
Influenza and pneumonia	J09-J18	10.4	15.4
Intentional self-harm	X60-X84	13.6	12.5
Malnutrition	E40-E46	*0.9	0.9
Obesity and other hyperalimentation	E65-E68	3.1	1.8
Renal failure	N17-N19	6.6	13.1
Transport accidents	V01-V99	10.4	11.7
Viral hepatitis	B15-B19	4.3	2.2

Note: (a) ICD-10 = International Classification of Diseases 10th Revision; (1) Mortality rates are a three year average covering 2011-2013; (2) Figures cover Marion County; (*) Unreliable data as per CDC
Source: Centers for Disease Control and Prevention, National Center for Health Statistics. Compressed Mortality File 1999-2013 on CDC WONDER Online Database, released October 2014. Data are compiled from the Compressed Mortality File 1999-2013, Series 20 No. 2S, 2014.

Health Insurance Coverage

Area	With Health Insurance	With Private Health Insurance	With Public Health Insurance	Without Health Insurance	Population Under Age 18 Without Health Insurance
City	83.3	61.5	33.7	16.7	6.9
MSA[1]	83.5	61.4	34.9	16.5	6.7
U.S.	85.2	65.2	31.0	14.8	7.3

Note: Figures are percentages that cover the civilian noninstitutionalized population; (1) Figures cover the Salem, OR Metropolitan Statistical Area—see Appendix B for areas included
Source: U.S. Census Bureau, 2011-2013 American Community Survey 3-Year Estimates

Number of Medical Professionals

Area[1]	MDs[2]	DOs[2,3]	Dentists	Podiatrists	Chiropractors	Optometrists
Local (number)	574	39	243	14	96	50
Local (rate[4])	179.3	12.2	75.4	4.3	29.8	15.5
U.S. (rate[4])	270.0	20.2	63.1	5.7	25.2	14.9

Note: Data as of 2013 unless noted; (1) Local data covers Marion County; (2) Data as of 2012 and includes all active, non-federal physicians; (3) Doctor of Osteopathic Medicine; (4) rate per 100,000 population
Source: U.S. Department of Health and Human Services, Health Resources and Services Administration, Bureau of Health Professions, Area Resource File (ARF) 2013-2014

EDUCATION

Public School District Statistics

District Name	Schls	Pupils	Pupil/ Teacher Ratio	Minority Pupils[1] (%)	Free Lunch Eligible[2] (%)	IEP[3] (%)
Ode Head Start	n/a	21,762	n/a	35.9	n/a	0.0
Salem-Keizer School District 24J	65	40,360	22.2	49.8	51.7	16.3

Note: Table includes school districts with 2,000 or more students; (1) Percentage of students that are not non-Hispanic white; (2) Percentage of students that are eligible for the free lunch program; (3) Percentage of students that have an Individualized Education Program.
Source: U.S. Department of Education, National Center for Education Statistics, Common Core of Data, Local Education Agency (School District) Universe Survey: School Year 2012-2013; U.S. Department of Education, National Center for Education Statistics, Common Core of Data, Public Elementary/Secondary School Universe Survey: School Year 2012-2013

Highest Level of Education

Area	Less than H.S.	H.S. Diploma	Some College, No Deg.	Associate Degree	Bachelor's Degree	Master's Degree	Prof. School Degree	Doctorate Degree
City	13.4	25.2	27.2	7.6	16.2	7.3	1.9	1.2
MSA[1]	15.1	26.5	27.2	8.2	14.9	5.8	1.5	0.8
U.S.	13.7	28.0	21.2	7.9	18.2	7.7	1.9	1.3

Note: Figures cover persons age 25 and over; (1) Figures cover the Salem, OR Metropolitan Statistical Area—see Appendix B for areas included
Source: U.S. Census Bureau, 2011-2013 American Community Survey 3-Year Estimates

Educational Attainment by Race

Area	High School Graduate or Higher (%)					Bachelor's Degree or Higher (%)				
	Total	White	Black	Asian	Hisp.[2]	Total	White	Black	Asian	Hisp.[2]
City	86.6	90.1	86.7	88.0	52.3	26.6	28.4	29.9	28.5	10.7
MSA[1]	84.9	88.2	80.9	90.7	50.7	23.0	24.6	35.0	32.9	7.8
U.S.	86.3	88.3	83.1	85.7	64.0	29.1	30.4	18.8	50.7	13.7

Note: Figures shown cover persons 25 years old and over; (1) Figures cover the Salem, OR Metropolitan Statistical Area—see Appendix B for areas included; (2) People of Hispanic origin can be of any race
Source: U.S. Census Bureau, 2011-2013 American Community Survey 3-Year Estimates

School Enrollment by Grade and Control

Area	Preschool (%)		Kindergarten (%)		Grades 1 - 4 (%)		Grades 5 - 8 (%)		Grades 9 - 12 (%)	
	Public	Private	Public	Private	Public	Private	Public	Private	Public	Private
City	68.9	31.1	89.8	10.2	93.1	6.9	92.2	7.8	94.4	5.6
MSA[1]	59.1	40.9	90.5	9.5	91.3	8.7	91.2	8.8	92.1	7.9
U.S.	57.7	42.3	87.9	12.1	89.9	10.1	90.0	10.0	90.7	9.3

Note: Figures shown cover persons 3 years old and over; (1) Figures cover the Salem, OR Metropolitan Statistical Area—see Appendix B for areas included
Source: U.S. Census Bureau, 2011-2013 American Community Survey 3-Year Estimates

Average Salaries of Public School Classroom Teachers

Area	2013-14		2014-15		Percent Change 2013-14 to 2014-15	Percent Change 2004-05 to 2014-15
	Dollars	Rank[1]	Dollars	Rank[1]		
OREGON	58,638	14	59,811	13	2.00	23.8
U.S. Average	56,610	–	57,379	–	1.36	20.8

Note: (1) State rank ranges from 1 to 51 where 1 indicates highest salary.
Source: National Education Association, Rankings & Estimates: Rankings of the States 2014 and Estimates of School Statistics 2015, March 2015

Higher Education

Four-Year Colleges			Two-Year Colleges			Medical Schools[1]	Law Schools[2]	Voc/ Tech[3]
Public	Private Non-profit	Private For-profit	Public	Private Non-profit	Private For-profit			
0	2	1	1	0	3	0	1	1

Note: Figures cover institutions located within the city limits and include main campuses only; (1) includes schools accredited by the Liaison Committee on Medical Education and the American Osteopathic Association's Commission on Osteopathic College Accreditation; (2) includes ABA-accredited schools, schools with provisional ABA accreditation, and state accredited schools; (3) includes all schools with programs that are less than 2 years.
Source: National Center for Education Statistics, Integrated Postsecondary Education System (IPEDS), 2013-14; Association of American Medical Colleges, Member List, May 1, 2015; American Osteopathic Association, Member List, May 1, 2015; Law School Admission Council, Official Guide to ABA-Approved Law Schools Online, May 1, 2015; Wikipedia, List of Medical Schools in the United States, May 1, 2015; Wikipedia, List of Law Schools in the United States, May 1, 2015

According to *U.S. News & World Report*, the Salem, OR metro area is home to one of the best liberal arts colleges in the U.S.: **Willamette University** (#64). The indicators used to capture academic quality fall into a number of categories: assessment by administrators at peer institutions; retention of students; faculty resources; student selectivity; financial resources; alumni giving; high school counselor ratings of colleges; and graduation rate. *U.S. News & World Report, "America's Best Colleges 2015"*

PRESIDENTIAL ELECTION

2012 Presidential Election Results

Area	Obama (%)	Romney (%)	Other (%)
Marion County	46.7	50.2	3.1
U.S.	51.0	47.2	1.8

Note: Results may not add to 100% due to rounding
Source: Dave Leip's Atlas of U.S. Presidential Elections

EMPLOYERS

Major Employers

Company Name	Industry
City of Salem	Municipal government
Commonwealth of Massachusetts Offices	State government
Crosby's Marketplace	Food market
Dominion/Salem Harbor Station	Public utility
Excelitas Technologies Corp.	Manufacturer
Groom Construction	Service
Grosvenor Park Nursing Center	Health care
Harbor Sweets	Retail
Hawthorne Hotel	Lodging
Home Depot	Retail
Jacqueline's Gourmet Cookies	Manufacturer
Market Basket	Food market
Middle-Oak Insurance Co.	Insurance
North Shore Medical Center	Health care
Northeast Behavioral Health Services	Health care
Peabody Essex Museum	Cultural/tourism
Salem Five Savings Bank	Banking
Salem Glass	Retail
Salem State University	Higher education
Salem YMCA	Social service agency
Shaw's Supermarket	Food market
Spaulding Rehabilitation Hospital	Health care
Target	Retail
Thermal Circuits	Manufacturer
Wal-Mart	Retail

Note: Companies shown are located within the Salem, OR Metropolitan Statistical Area.
Source: Hoovers.com; Wikipedia

PUBLIC SAFETY

Crime Rate

Area	All Crimes	Violent Crimes				Property Crimes		
		Murder	Forcible Rape	Robbery	Aggrav. Assault	Burglary	Larceny -Theft	Motor Vehicle Theft
City	4,614.7	4.4	29.7	87.2	207.3	621.2	3,250.2	414.6
Suburbs[1]	2,682.3	2.9	22.0	31.6	114.7	440.0	1,868.4	202.7
Metro[2]	3,448.8	3.5	25.1	53.6	151.4	511.9	2,416.5	286.8
U.S.	3,098.6	4.5	25.2	109.1	229.1	610.0	1,899.4	221.3

Note: Figures are crimes per 100,000 population; (1) All areas within the metro area that are located outside the city limits; (2) Figures cover the Salem, OR Metropolitan Statistical Area—see Appendix B for areas included
Source: FBI Uniform Crime Reports, 2013

Hate Crimes

Area	Number of Quarters Reported	Number of Incidents per Bias Motivation						
		Race	Religion	Sexual Orientation	Ethnicity	Disability	Gender	Gender Identity
City	4	7	1	4	2	0	0	0
U.S.	4	2,871	1,031	1,233	655	83	18	31

Source: Federal Bureau of Investigation, Hate Crime Statistics 2013

Identity Theft Consumer Complaints

Area	Complaints	Complaints per 100,000 Population	Rank[2]
MSA[1]	567	141.6	14
U.S.	332,646	104.3	-

Note: (1) Figures cover the Salem, OR Metropolitan Statistical Area—see Appendix B for areas included; (2) Rank ranges from 1 to 380 where 1 indicates greatest number of identity theft complaints per 100,000 population
Source: Federal Trade Commission, Consumer Sentinel Network Data Book for January–December 2014

Fraud and Other Consumer Complaints

Area	Complaints	Complaints per 100,000 Population	Rank[2]
MSA[1]	1,427	356.4	224
U.S.	2,250,205	705.7	-

Note: (1) Figures cover the Salem, OR Metropolitan Statistical Area—see Appendix B for areas included; (2) Rank ranges from 1 to 380 where 1 indicates greatest number of identity theft complaints per 100,000 population
Source: Federal Trade Commission, Consumer Sentinel Network Data Book for January–December 2014

RECREATION

Culture

Dance[1]	Theatre[1]	Instrumental Music[1]	Vocal Music[1]	Series and Festivals	Museums and Art Galleries[2]	Zoos and Aquariums[3]
0	1	2	0	0	8	0

Note: (1) Professional perfoming groups; (2) Based on organizations with SIC code 8412; (3) AZA-accredited
Source: The Grey House Performing Arts Directory, 2015-16; Association of Zoos & Aquariums, AZA Member Zoos & Aquariums, April 2015; www.AccuLeads.com, April 2015

Professional Sports Teams

Team Name	League	Year Established

No teams are located in the metro area
Source: Wikipedia, Major Professional Sports Teams of the United States and Canada, April 2015

CLIMATE

Average and Extreme Temperatures

Temperature	Jan	Feb	Mar	Apr	May	Jun	Jul	Aug	Sep	Oct	Nov	Dec	Yr.
Extreme High (°F)	65	72	75	88	100	102	106	108	104	93	72	66	108
Average High (°F)	46	51	55	61	67	74	82	81	76	64	53	47	63
Average Temp. (°F)	39	43	46	50	55	61	66	67	62	53	45	41	52
Average Low (°F)	32	34	36	38	43	48	51	51	47	41	37	34	41
Extreme Low (°F)	-10	-4	12	23	25	32	37	36	26	23	9	-12	-12

Note: Figures cover the years 1948-1990
Source: National Climatic Data Center, International Station Meteorological Climate Summary, 9/96

Average Precipitation/Snowfall/Humidity

Precip./Humidity	Jan	Feb	Mar	Apr	May	Jun	Jul	Aug	Sep	Oct	Nov	Dec	Yr.
Avg. Precip. (in.)	6.5	4.9	4.3	2.4	2.0	1.4	0.5	0.7	1.5	3.3	6.1	6.8	40.2
Avg. Snowfall (in.)	3	1	1	Tr	Tr	0	0	0	0	Tr	Tr	2	7
Avg. Rel. Hum. 7am (%)	87	89	89	85	81	77	75	79	86	92	90	89	85
Avg. Rel. Hum. 4pm (%)	76	70	62	56	53	50	40	40	45	61	76	81	59

Note: Figures cover the years 1948-1990; Tr = Trace amounts (<0.05 in. of rain; <0.5 in. of snow)
Source: National Climatic Data Center, International Station Meteorological Climate Summary, 9/96

Weather Conditions

Temperature			Daytime Sky			Precipitation		
5°F & below	32°F & below	90°F & above	Clear	Partly cloudy	Cloudy	0.01 inch or more precip.	0.1 inch or more snow/ice	Thunder-storms
< 1	66	16	78	119	168	146	6	5

Note: Figures are average number of days per year and cover the years 1948-1990
Source: National Climatic Data Center, International Station Meteorological Climate Summary, 9/96

HAZARDOUS WASTE

Superfund Sites

Salem has no sites on the EPA's Superfund Final National Priorities List. There are a total of 1,322 Superfund sites on the list in the U.S. *U.S. Environmental Protection Agency, Final National Priorities List, April 14, 2015*

AIR & WATER QUALITY

Air Quality Trends: Ozone

	2004	2005	2006	2007	2008	2009	2010	2011	2012	2013
MSA[1]	0.062	0.063	0.075	0.060	0.066	0.069	0.057	0.057	0.063	0.055

Note: (1) Data covers the Salem, OR Metropolitan Statistical Area—see Appendix B for areas included. The values shown are the composite ozone concentration averages among trend sites based on the highest fourth daily maximum 8-hour concentration in parts per million. These trends are based on sites having an adequate record of monitoring data during the trend period. Data from exceptional events are included.
Source: U.S. Environmental Protection Agency, Air Quality Monitoring Information, "Air Quality Trends by City, 2000-2013"

Air Quality Index

Area	Percent of Days when Air Quality was...[2]					AQI Statistics[2]	
	Good	Moderate	Unhealthy for Sensitive Groups	Unhealthy	Very Unhealthy	Maximum	Median
MSA[1]	87.4	12.3	0.0	0.3	0.0	154	29

Note: (1) Data covers the Salem, OR Metropolitan Statistical Area—see Appendix B for areas included; (2) Based on 365 days with AQI data in 2014. Air Quality Index (AQI) is an index for reporting daily air quality. EPA calculates the AQI for five major air pollutants regulated by the Clean Air Act: ground-level ozone, particle pollution (aka particulate matter), carbon monoxide, sulfur dioxide, and nitrogen dioxide. The AQI runs from 0 to 500. The higher the AQI value, the greater the level of air pollution and the greater the health concern. There are six AQI categories: "Good" AQI is between 0 and 50. Air quality is considered satisfactory; "Moderate" AQI is between 51 and 100. Air quality is acceptable; "Unhealthy for Sensitive Groups" When AQI values are between 101 and 150, members of sensitive groups may experience health effects; "Unhealthy" When AQI values are between 151 and 200 everyone may begin to experience health effects; "Very Unhealthy" AQI values between 201 and 300 trigger a health alert; "Hazardous" AQI values over 300 trigger warnings of emergency conditions (not shown).
Source: U.S. Environmental Protection Agency, Air Quality Index Report, 2014

Air Quality Index Pollutants

Area	Carbon Monoxide	Nitrogen Dioxide	Ozone	Sulfur Dioxide	Particulate Matter 2.5	Particulate Matter 10
		Percent of Days when AQI Pollutant was...[2]				
MSA[1]	0.0	0.0	35.3	0.0	64.7	0.0

Note: (1) Data covers the Salem, OR Metropolitan Statistical Area—see Appendix B for areas included; (2) Based on 365 days with AQI data in 2014. The Air Quality Index (AQI) is an index for reporting daily air quality. EPA calculates the AQI for five major air pollutants regulated by the Clean Air Act: ground-level ozone, particle pollution (also known as particulate matter), carbon monoxide, sulfur dioxide, and nitrogen dioxide. The AQI runs from 0 to 500. The higher the AQI value, the greater the level of air pollution and the greater the health concern.
Source: U.S. Environmental Protection Agency, Air Quality Index Report, 2014

Maximum Air Pollutant Concentrations: Particulate Matter, Ozone, CO and Lead

	Particulate Matter 10 (ug/m^3)	Particulate Matter 2.5 Wtd AM (ug/m^3)	Particulate Matter 2.5 24-Hr (ug/m^3)	Ozone (ppm)	Carbon Monoxide (ppm)	Lead (ug/m^3)
MSA[1] Level	n/a	n/a	n/a	0.055	n/a	n/a
NAAQS[2]	150	15	35	0.075	9	0.15
Met NAAQS[2]	n/a	n/a	n/a	Yes	n/a	n/a

Note: (1) Data covers the Salem, OR Metropolitan Statistical Area—see Appendix B for areas included; Data from exceptional events are included; (2) National Ambient Air Quality Standards; ppm = parts per million; ug/m^3 = micrograms per cubic meter; n/a not available.
Concentrations: Particulate Matter 10 (coarse particulate)—highest second maximum 24-hour concentration; Particulate Matter 2.5 Wtd AM (fine particulate)—highest weighted annual mean concentration; Particulate Matter 2.5 24-Hour (fine particulate)—highest 98th percentile 24-hour concentration; Ozone—highest fourth daily maximum 8-hour concentration; Carbon Monoxide—highest second maximum non-overlapping 8-hour concentration; Lead—maximum running 3-month average
Source: U.S. Environmental Protection Agency, Air Quality Monitoring Information, "Air Quality Statistics by City, 2013"

Maximum Air Pollutant Concentrations: Nitrogen Dioxide and Sulfur Dioxide

	Nitrogen Dioxide AM (ppb)	Nitrogen Dioxide 1-Hr (ppb)	Sulfur Dioxide AM (ppb)	Sulfur Dioxide 1-Hr (ppb)	Sulfur Dioxide 24-Hr (ppb)
MSA[1] Level	n/a	n/a	n/a	n/a	n/a
NAAQS[2]	53	100	30	75	140
Met NAAQS[2]	n/a	n/a	n/a	n/a	n/a

Note: (1) Data covers the Salem, OR Metropolitan Statistical Area—see Appendix B for areas included; Data from exceptional events are included; (2) National Ambient Air Quality Standards; ppm = parts per million; ug/m^3 = micrograms per cubic meter; n/a not available.
Concentrations: Nitrogen Dioxide AM—highest arithmetic mean concentration; Nitrogen Dioxide 1-Hr—highest 98th percentile 1-hour daily maximum concentration; Sulfur Dioxide AM—highest annual mean concentration; Sulfur Dioxide 1-Hr—highest 99th percentile 1-hour daily maximum concentration; Sulfur Dioxide 24-Hr—highest second maximum 24-hour concentration
Source: U.S. Environmental Protection Agency, Air Quality Monitoring Information, "Air Quality Statistics by City, 2013"

Drinking Water

Water System Name	Pop. Served	Primary Water Source Type	Violations[1] Health Based	Violations[1] Monitoring/ Reporting
Salem Public Works	189,000	Surface	0	0

Note: (1) Based on violation data from January 1, 2014 to December 31, 2014 (includes unresolved violations from earlier years)
Source: U.S. Environmental Protection Agency, Office of Ground Water and Drinking Water, Safe Drinking Water Information System (based on data extracted January 27, 2015)

Salt Lake City, Utah

Background

One cannot disassociate Salt Lake City, Utah's largest city and state capital, from its Mormon, or Church of Jesus Christ of Latter-day Saints, origins. The city was founded by Brigham Young on July 24, 1847, as a place of refuge from mainstream ostracism for the Mormon's polygamous lifestyle.

Brigham Young decided to lead his people to a "land that nobody wanted," so they could exercise their form of worship in peace. Two scouts, Orson Pratt and Erastus Snow located the site for Brigham Young, who declared: "This is the place." The site that was to be called Salt Lake City was breathtaking. The area was bordered on the east and southwest by the dramatic peaks of the Wasatch Range, and on the northwest by the Great Salt Lake.

The land was too dry and hard for farming, but Mormon industry diverted the flow of mountain streams to irrigate the land, and the valley turned into a prosperous agricultural region. A little more than 10 years after its incorporation as a city, the U.S. government was still suspicious of its Mormon residents. Fort Douglas was erected in 1862, manned by federal troops to keep an eye on the Mormons and their polygamous practices. In 1869, the completion of the Transcontinental Railroad brought mining, industry, and other non-Mormon interests to Salt Lake City. As for polygamy, the Mormon Church made it illegal in 1890.

While mining played a major role in the early development of Salt Lake City, major industry sectors now include construction, trade, transportation, communications, finance, insurance, and real estate. The University of Utah Research Park located here occupies 320 acres adjacent to campus, and houses 53 companies and 82 academic departments where 9,700 people are employed.

Major efforts to revitalize the downtown area have been unfolding in recent years. For instance, the $1 billion City Creek Center, with residences, offices, and a mall, recently opened and occupies 20 acres. The Salt Lake City Redevelopment Agency is currently supporting the renovation of retail space that is part of the Utah Theater, a former 1918 vaudeville theater on Main Steet. The new $116 million, 2,500-seat Utah Performing Arts Center is slated for a spring 2016 opening. In addition, downtown streetcars are receiving a boost.

Salt Lake City International Airport is home to Delta Airlines' fifth-largest hub. A terminal redevelopment plan is newly underway, with a projected 2022 opening date for a new terminal and accompanying facilities.

The NBA's Utah Jazz plays at the EnergySolutions Arena. The city is also home to Real Salt Lake of Major League Soccer.

The nearby mountain ranges and the Great Salt Lake greatly influence climatic conditions. Temperatures are moderated by the lake in winter, and storm activity is enhanced by both the lake and the mountains. Salt Lake City normally has a semi-arid continental climate with four well-defined seasons. Summers are hot and dry, while winters are cold, but generally not severe. Mountains to the north and east act as a barrier to frequent invasions of cold air. Heavy fog can develop when there is a temperature inversion in winter and may persist for several days at a time.

Rankings

General Rankings

- The Salt Lake City metro area was identified as one of America's fastest-growing areas in terms of population and economy by *Forbes*. The area ranked #12 out of 20. The 100 most populous metro areas in the U.S. were evaluated on the following criteria: estimated population growth; job growth; gross metropolitan product growth; unemployment; median salaries for college-educated workers. *Forbes, "America's Fastest-Growing Cities 2015," January 27, 2015*

- Salt Lake City was selected as one of "America's Favorite Cities." The city ranked #2 in the "Quality of Life: Cleanliness" category. Respondents to an online survey were asked to rate 38 top urban destinations in the United States from a visitor's perspective. Criteria: cleanliness. *Travel + Leisure, "America's Favorite Cities 2014"*

- In their second annual survey, analysts for the small- and mid-sized city lifestyle site Livability.com looked at data for more than 2,000 U.S. cities to determine the rankings for Livability's "Top 100 Best Places to Live" in 2015. Salt Lake City ranked #18. Criteria: vibrant economy; low cost of living; abundant lifestyle amenities. *Livability.com, "Top 100 Best Places to Live 2015"*

Business/Finance Rankings

- The editors of *Kiplinger's Personal Finance Magazine* named Salt Lake City to their list of ten of the best metro areas for start-ups. The area rank #6.Criteria: well-educated workforce; low living costs for self-employed people, as measured by the Council for Community and Economic Research; a strong existing community of small business; low unemployment; low business costs. *www.kiplinger.com, "10 Great Cities for Starting a Business," October 2014*

- The finance website Wall St. Cheat Sheet reported on the prospects for high-wage job creation in the nation's largest metro areas over the next five years and ranked them accordingly, drawing on in-depth analysis by CareerBuilder and Economic Modeling Specialists International (EMSI). The Salt Lake City metro area placed #5 on the Wall St. Cheat Sheet list. *wallstcheatsheet.com, "Top 10 Cities for High-Wage Job Growth," December 8, 2013*

- The business website 24/7 Wall Street drew on Brookings Institution research on 50 advanced industries to identify the proportion of workers in the nation's largest metropolitan areas that were employed in jobs requiring knowledge in the science, technology, engineering, or math (STEM) fields. The Salt Lake City metro area was #15. *247wallst.com, "15 Cities with the Most High-Tech Jobs," March 13, 2015*

- Based on metro area social media reviews, the employment opinion group Glassdoor surveyed 50 of the largest U.S. metro areas on measures including compensation and benefits, satisfaction with management, business outlook, and number of employers hiring. The Salt Lake City metro area was ranked #5 in overall employee satisfaction. *www.glassdoor.com, "Employment Satisfaction Report Card by City," June 13, 2014*

- *Forbes* ranked the largest metro areas in the U.S. in terms of the "Best Cities for Young Professionals." The Salt Lake City metro area ranked #4 out of 15. Criteria: job growth; unemployment rate; median salary of college graduates age 24 to 34; cost of living; number of small businesses per capita; number of large companies; percentage of population 25 years of age and older with college degrees. *Forbes.com, "America's 15 Best Cities for Young Professionals," August 18, 2014*

- Salt Lake City was ranked #13 out of 100 metro areas in terms of economic performance (#1 = best) during the recession and recovery from trough quarter through the second quarter of 2013. Criteria: percent change in employment; percentage point change in unemployment rate; percent change in gross metropolitan product; percent change in House Price Index. *Brookings Institution, MetroMonitor: Tracking Economic Recession and Recovery in America's 100 Largest Metropolitan Areas, September 2013*

- Salt Lake City was identified as one of the best places for finding a job by *U.S. News & World Report*. The city ranked #2 out of 10. Criteria: strong job market. *U.S. News & World Report, "The 10 Best Cities to Find Jobs," June 17, 2013*

- Salt Lake City was identified as one of "America's Hardest-Working Towns." The city ranked #12 out of 25. Criteria: average hours worked per capita; willingness to work during personal time; number of dual income households; local employment rate. *Parade, "What is America's Hardest-Working Town?," April 15, 2012*

- Salt Lake City was identified as one of the best cities for college graduates to find work—and live. The city ranked #12 out of 15. Criteria: job availability; average salary; average rent. *CareerBuilder.com, "15 Best Cities for College Grads to Find Work—and Live," June 5, 2012*

- *Forbes* reports that Salt Lake City was identified as one of the unhappiest cities to work in by CareerBliss.com, an online community for career advancement. The city ranked #4 out of 10. Criteria: work-life balance; an employee's relationship with his or her boss and co-workers; general work environment; compensation; opportunities for advancement; company culture; and resources. *Forbes.com, "The 10 Happiest and Unhappiest Cities to Work in Right Now," January 16, 2015*

- The Salt Lake City metro area appeared on the Milken Institute "2013 Best Performing Cities" list. Rank: #6 out of 200 large metro areas. Criteria: job growth; wage and salary growth; high-tech output growth. *Milken Institute, "Best-Performing Cities 2014," January 2015*

- *Forbes* ranked the 200 most populous metro areas to determine the nation's "Best Places for Business and Careers." The Salt Lake City metro area was ranked #8. Criteria: costs (business and living); job growth (past and projected); income growth; educational attainment (college and high school); projected economic growth; cultural and recreational opportunities; net migration patterns; number of highly ranked colleges. *Forbes, "The Best Places for Business and Careers 2014," July 23, 2014*

Culture/Performing Arts Rankings

- Salt Lake City was selected as one of America's top cities for the arts. The city ranked #15 in the mid-sized city (population 100,000 to 499,999) category. Criteria: readers' top choices for arts travel destinations based on the richness and variety of visual arts sites, activities and events. *American Style, "2012 Top 25 Arts Destinations," June 2012*

Dating/Romance Rankings

- Of the 100 U.S. cities surveyed by *Men's Health* in its quest to identify the nation's best cities for dating and forming relationships, Salt Lake City was ranked #22 for online dating (#1 = best). *Men's Health, "The Best and Worst Cities for Online Dating," January 30, 2013*

Education Rankings

- *Reader's Digest* analyzed data for 120 U.S. cities to arrive at a list of "America's 10 Sharpest Cities." Researchers looked at education level, eating and exercise habits, health conditions, and sociability factors calculated to build and maintain mental alertness into the upper decades of life. Salt Lake City ranked #7 on the list. *Reader's Digest, "America's 10 Sharpest Cities," October 2012*

- Personal finance website *WalletHub* analyzed the 150 largest U.S. metropolitan statistical areas to determine where the most educated Americans are choosing to settle. Criteria: educational attainment; percentage of workers with jobs in computer, engineering, and science fields; quality and size of each metro area's universities. Salt Lake City was ranked #46 (#1 = most educated city). *www.WalletHub.com, "2014's Most and Least Educated Cities*

- Salt Lake City was selected as one of the most well-read cities in America by Amazon.com. The city ranked #14 among the top 20. Cities with populations greater than 100,000 were evaluated based on per capita sales of books, magazines and newspapers. *Amazon.com, "The 20 Most Well-Read Cities in America," May 20, 2014*

Environmental Rankings

- The Weather Channel determined the nation's snowiest cities, based on the National Oceanic and Atmospheric Administration's 30-year average snowfall data. Among cities with a population of at least 100,000, the #12-ranked city was Salt Lake City *weather.com, America's 20 Snowiest Major Cities, February 3, 2014*

- The Salt Lake City metro area came in at #71 for the relative comfort of its climate on Sperling's list of "chill cities," as measured by the Sperling Heat Index. All 361 metro areas are included. Criteria included daytime high temperatures, nighttime low temperatures, dew point, and relative humidity at the high temperatures. *www.bertsperling.com, "Sperling's Chill Cities," July 18, 2013*

- Sperling's BestPlaces assessed 379 metropolitan areas of the United States for the likelihood of dangerously extreme weather events or earthquakes. In general the Southeast and South-Central regions have the highest risk of weather extremes and earthquakes, while the Pacific Northwest enjoys the lowest risk. Of the least risky metropolitan areas, the Salt Lake City metro area was ranked #56. *www.bestplaces.net, "Safest Places from Natural Disasters," April 2011*

- *The Daily Beast* identifed the snowiest among the 100 largest U.S. cities, looking at average snowfall per month from December 2011 through March 2012 and from December 1, 2012 to December 21, 2012. Number of days with maximum and minimum temperatures of 32 degrees or less contributed to the rankings. Salt Lake City ranked #16. *The Daily Beast, "25 Snowiest Cities in America," December 21, 2012*

- The U.S. Environmental Protection Agency (EPA) released a list of large U.S. metropolitan areas with the most ENERGY STAR certified buildings in 2014. The Salt Lake City metro area was ranked #25 out of 25. *U.S. Environmental Protection Agency, "Top Cities With the Most ENERGY STAR Certified Buildings in 2014," March 25, 2015*

- The U.S. Environmental Protection Agency (EPA) released a list of mid-size U.S. metropolitan areas with the most ENERGY STAR certified buildings in 2014. The Salt Lake City metro area was ranked #5 out of 10. *U.S. Environmental Protection Agency, "Top Cities With the Most ENERGY STAR Certified Buildings in 2014," March 25, 2015*

- The Salt Lake City metro area was identified as one of the snowiest major metropolitan areas in the U.S. by *Forbes*. The metro area ranked #3 out of 10. Criteria: average annual snowfall. *Forbes, "America's Snowiest Cities," January 12, 2011*

- The U.S. Conference of Mayors and Wal-Mart Stores sponsor the Mayors' Climate Protection Awards Program. The awards recognize and honor mayors for outstanding and innovative practices that mayors are taking to increase energy efficiency in their cities, and to help curb global warming. Salt Lake City received First Place Honors in the large city category. *U.S. Conference of Mayors, "2013 Mayors' Climate Protection Awards Program," June 21, 2013*

- Salt Lake City was highlighted as one of the 25 metro areas most polluted by short-term particle pollution (24-hour PM 2.5) in the U.S. during 2011 through 2013. The area ranked #7. *American Lung Association, State of the Air 2015*

Food/Drink Rankings

- *Men's Health* ranked 100 major U.S. cities in terms of alcohol intoxication. Salt Lake City ranked #1 (#1 = most sober).Criteria: binge drinking; alcohol-related traffic accidents, arrests, and fatalities. *Men's Health, "The Drunkest Cities in America," November 19, 2013*

- Salt Lake City was selected as one of America's 10 most vegan-friendly cities. The city was ranked #7. *People for the Ethical Treatment of Animals, "Top Vegan-Friendly Cities of 2013," June 11, 2013*

Health/Fitness Rankings

- For each of the 50 most populous metro areas in the United States, the American College of Sports Medicine's American Fitness Index evaluated infrastructure, community assets, and policies that encourage healthy and fit lifestyles, including preventive health behaviors, levels of chronic disease conditions, health care access, and community resources and policies that support physical activity. The Salt Lake City metro area ranked #12 for "community fitness." Personal health indicators were considered as well as community and environmental indicators. *www.americanfitnessindex.org, "ACSM American Fitness Index Health and Community Fitness Status of the 50 Largest Metropolitan Areas," May 2013*

- Salt Lake City was identified as a "2013 Spring Allergy Capital." The area ranked #85 out of 100. Three groups of factors were used to identify the most severe cities for people with allergies during the spring season: annual pollen levels; medicine utilization; access to board-certified allergists. *Asthma and Allergy Foundation of America, "Spring Allergy Capitals 2013"*

- Salt Lake City was identified as a "2013 Fall Allergy Capital." The area ranked #92 out of 100. Three groups of factors were used to identify the most severe cities for people with allergies during the fall season: annual pollen levels; medicine utilization; access to board-certified allergists. *Asthma and Allergy Foundation of America, "Fall Allergy Capitals 2013"*

- Salt Lake City was identified as a "2013 Asthma Capital." The area ranked #52 out of the nation's 100 largest metropolitan areas. Twelve factors were used to identify the most challenging places to live for people with asthma: estimated prevalence; self-reported prevalence; crude death rate for asthma; annual pollen score; annual air quality; public smoking laws; number of board-certified asthma specialists; school inhaler access laws; rescue medication use; controller medication use; uninsured rate; poverty rate. *Asthma and Allergy Foundation of America, "Asthma Capitals 2013"*

- *Men's Health* ranked 100 major U.S. cities in terms of the best and worst cities for men. Salt Lake City ranked #18. Criteria: thirty-three data points were examined covering health, fitness, and quality of life. *Men's Health, "The Best & Worst Cities for Men 2014," December 6, 2013*

- The Salt Lake City metro area appeared in the 2013 Gallup-Healthways Well-Being Index. The area ranked #38 out of 189. The Gallup-Healthways Well-Being Index score is an average of six sub-indexes, which individually examine life evaluation, emotional health, work environment, physical health, healthy behaviors, and access to basic necessities. Results are based on telephone interviews conducted as part of the Gallup-Healthways Well-Being Index survey January 2–December 29, 2012, and January 2–December 30, 2013, with a random sample of 531,630 adults, aged 18 and older, living in metropolitan areas in the 50 U.S. states and the District of Columbia. *Gallup-Healthways, "State of American Well-Being," March 25, 2014*

Real Estate Rankings

- The Salt Lake City metro area was identified as one of the top 20 housing markets to invest in for 2015 by *Forbes*. The area ranked #12. Criteria: strong population and job growth; relatively low home prices which are below equilibrium home price (EHP). The EHP is what the average price for a market should be, if speculation, weird distortions in local income, and other factors (like the housing collapse) weren't present in the market. *Forbes.com, "Best Buy Cities: Where to Invest in Housing in 2015," January 9, 2015*

- Salt Lake City was ranked #106 out of 275 metro areas in terms of house price appreciation in 2014 (#1 = highest rate). *Federal Housing Finance Agency, House Price Index, 4th Quarter 2014*

- Salt Lake City was ranked #159 out of 226 metro areas in terms of housing affordability in 2014 by the National Association of Home Builders (#1 = most affordable). The NAHB-Wells Fargo Housing Opportunity Index (HOI) for a given area is defined as the share of homes sold in that area that would have been affordable to a family earning the local median income, based on standard mortgage underwriting criteria. *National Association of Home Builders®, NAHB-Wells Fargo Housing Opportunity Index, 4th Quarter 2014*

Safety Rankings

- Allstate ranked the 200 largest cities in America in terms of driver safety. Salt Lake City ranked #67. Allstate researchers analyzed internal property damage claims over a two-year period from January 2011 to December 2012. A weighted average of the two-year numbers determined the annual percentages. *Allstate, "Allstate America's Best Drivers Report, 2014"*

- The National Insurance Crime Bureau ranked 380 metro areas in the U.S. in terms of per capita rates of vehicle theft. The Salt Lake City metro area ranked #17 (#1 = highest rate). Criteria: number of vehicle theft offenses per 100,000 inhabitants in 2012. *National Insurance Crime Bureau, "Hot Spots 2012," June 26, 2013*

Seniors/Retirement Rankings

- From its Best Cities for Successful Aging indexes, the Milken Institute generated rankings for metropolitan areas, weighing data in eight categories—health care, wellness, living arrangements, transportation, financial characteristics, education and employment opportunities, community engagement, and overall livability. The Salt Lake City metro area was ranked #5 overall in the large metro area category. *Milken Institute, "Best Cities for Successful Aging, 2014"*

- Salt Lake City made the 2014 *Forbes* list of "25 Best Places to Retire." Criteria include: housing and living costs; tax climate for retirees; weather and air quality; crime rates; doctor availability; active-lifestyle rankings for walkability, bicycling and volunteering. *Forbes.com, "The Best Places to Retire in 2014," January 16, 2014*

- *Forbes* selected the Salt Lake City metro area as one of 25 "Best Places for a Working Retirement." Criteria: affordability; improving, above-average economies and job prospects; and a favorable tax climate for retirees. *Forbes.com, "Best Places for a Working Retirement in 2013," February 4, 2013*

Sports/Recreation Rankings

- Salt Lake City was chosen as a bicycle friendly community by the League of American Bicyclists. A "Bicycle Friendly Community" welcomes cyclists by providing safe accommodation for cycling and encouraging people to bike for transportation and recreation. There are four award levels: Platinum; Gold; Silver; and Bronze. The community achieved an award level of Silver. *League of American Bicyclists, "Bicycle Friendly Community Master List," Fall 2013*

- Salt Lake City was chosen as one of America's best cities for bicycling. The city ranked #26 out of 50. Criteria: robust cycling infrastructure; vibrant bike culture. The editors only considered cities with populations of 95,000 or more. *Bicycling, "America's Top 50 Bike-Friendly Cities," May 23, 2012*

Women/Minorities Rankings

- *Women's Health* examined U.S. cities and identified the 100 best cities for women. Salt Lake City was ranked #17. Criteria: 30 categories were examined from obesity and breast cancer rates to commuting times and hours spent working out. *Women's Health, "Best Cities for Women 2012"*

- Salt Lake City was selected as one of the gayest cities in America by *The Advocate*. The city ranked #8 out of 15. This year's criteria include points for a city's LGBT elected officials (and fractional points for the state's elected officials), points for the percentage of the population comprised by lesbian-coupled households, a point for a gay rodeo association, points for bars listed in *Out* magazine's 200 Best Bars list, a point per women's college, and points for concert performances by Mariah Carey, Pink, Lady Gaga, or the Jonas Brothers. The raw score is divided by the population to provide a ranking based on a per capita LGBT quotient. *The Advocate, "2014's Gayest Cities in America" January 6, 2014*

Miscellaneous Rankings

- Salt Lake City was selected as a 2013 Digital Cities Survey winner. The city ranked #4 in the mid-sized city (125,000 to 249,999 population) category. The survey examined and assessed how city governments are utilizing information technology to operate and deliver quality service to their customers and citizens. Survey questions focused on implementation and adoption of online service delivery; planning and governance; and the infrastructure and architecture that make the transformation to digital government possible. *Center for Digital Government, "2013 Digital Cities Survey," November 7, 2013*

- According to the World Giving Index, the United States is the fifth most generous nation in the world. The finance and lifestyle site NerdWallet looked for the U.S. cities that topped the list in donating money and time to good causes. The Salt Lake City metro area proved to be the #3-ranked metro area, judged by culture of volunteerism, depth of commitment in terms of volunteer hours per year, and monetary contributions. *www.nerdwallet.com, "Most Generous Cities," September 22, 2013*

- Market analyst Scarborough Research surveyed adults who had done volunteer work over the previous 12 months to find out where volunteers are concentrated. The Salt Lake City metro area made the list for highest volunteer participation. *Scarborough Research, "Salt Lake City, UT; Minneapolis, MN; and Des Moines, IA Lend a Helping Hand," November 27, 2012*

- Salt Lake City appeared on *Travel + Leisure's* list of America's least attractive people. Criteria: cities were selected by readers in their annual America's Favorite Cities survey. The city ranked #2 out of 10. *Travel + Leisure, "America's Most and Least Attractive People," November 2013*

- Mars Chocolate North America, the makers of COMBOS®, in partnership with Sperling's BestPlaces, ranked 50 major metro areas in terms of their "manliness." The Salt Lake City metro area ranked #26. Criteria: number of professional sports teams; number of nearby NASCAR tracks and racing events; manly lifestyle; concentration of manly retail stores; manly occupations per capita; salty snack sales; "Board of Manliness" rankings. *Mars Chocolate North America, "America's Manliest Cities 2012"*

- The National Alliance to End Homelessness ranked the 100 most populous metro areas in terms the rate of homelessness. The Salt Lake City metro area ranked #35. Criteria: number of homeless people per 10,000 population in 2011. *National Alliance to End Homelessness, The State of Homelessness in America 2012*

Business Environment

CITY FINANCES

City Government Finances

Component	2012 ($000)	2012 ($ per capita)
Total Revenues	591,281	3,171
Total Expenditures	435,444	2,336
Debt Outstanding	393,188	2,109
Cash and Securities[1]	673,590	3,613

Note: (1) Cash and security holdings of a government at the close of its fiscal year, including those of its dependent agencies, utilities, and liquor stores.
Source: U.S Census Bureau, State & Local Government Finances 2012

City Government Revenue by Source

Source	2012 ($000)	2012 ($ per capita)
General Revenue		
From Federal Government	11,758	63
From State Government	9,634	52
From Local Governments	9,320	50
Taxes		
Property	121,703	653
Sales and Gross Receipts	65,590	352
Personal Income	0	0
Corporate Income	0	0
Motor Vehicle License	0	0
Other Taxes	13,840	74
Current Charges	244,872	1,313
Liquor Store	0	0
Utility	61,921	332
Employee Retirement	0	0

Source: U.S Census Bureau, State & Local Government Finances 2012

City Government Expenditures by Function

Function	2012 ($000)	2012 ($ per capita)	2012 (%)
General Direct Expenditures			
Air Transportation	84,427	453	19.4
Corrections	0	0	0.0
Education	0	0	0.0
Employment Security Administration	0	0	0.0
Financial Administration	4,730	25	1.1
Fire Protection	35,529	191	8.2
General Public Buildings	5,812	31	1.3
Governmental Administration, Other	9,306	50	2.1
Health	0	0	0.0
Highways	41,738	224	9.6
Hospitals	0	0	0.0
Housing and Community Development	34,270	184	7.9
Interest on General Debt	14,669	79	3.4
Judicial and Legal	9,049	49	2.1
Libraries	13,410	72	3.1
Parking	0	0	0.0
Parks and Recreation	21,323	114	4.9
Police Protection	56,894	305	13.1
Public Welfare	0	0	0.0
Sewerage	14,424	77	3.3
Solid Waste Management	7,908	42	1.8
Veterans' Services	0	0	0.0
Liquor Store	0	0	0.0
Utility	52,561	282	12.1
Employee Retirement	0	0	0.0

Source: U.S Census Bureau, State & Local Government Finances 2012

DEMOGRAPHICS

Population Growth

Area	1990 Census	2000 Census	2010 Census	Population Growth (%)	
				1990-2000	2000-2010
City	159,796	181,743	186,440	13.7	2.6
MSA[1]	768,075	968,858	1,124,197	26.1	16.0
U.S.	248,709,873	281,421,906	308,745,538	13.2	9.7

Note: (1) Figures cover the Salt Lake City, UT Metropolitan Statistical Area—see Appendix B for areas included
Source: U.S. Census Bureau, Census 1990, 2000, 2010

Household Size

Area	Persons in Household (%)							Average Household Size
	One	Two	Three	Four	Five	Six	Seven or More	
City	36.1	30.4	13.9	10.0	4.8	2.6	2.3	2.48
MSA[1]	22.8	29.5	16.0	14.2	8.8	4.8	3.9	3.04
U.S.	27.7	33.6	15.7	13.1	6.0	2.3	1.5	2.64

Note: (1) Figures cover the Salt Lake City, UT Metropolitan Statistical Area—see Appendix B for areas included
Source: U.S. Census Bureau, 2011-2013 American Community Survey 3-Year Estimates

Race

Area	White Alone[2] (%)	Black Alone[2] (%)	Asian Alone[2] (%)	AIAN[3] Alone[2] (%)	NHOPI[4] Alone[2] (%)	Other Race Alone[2] (%)	Two or More Races (%)
City	73.7	2.9	5.2	1.2	2.4	11.9	2.7
MSA[1]	83.8	1.6	3.3	0.9	1.5	6.3	2.6
U.S.	73.9	12.6	5.0	0.8	0.2	4.7	2.9

Note: (1) Figures cover the Salt Lake City, UT Metropolitan Statistical Area—see Appendix B for areas included; (2) Alone is defined as not being in combination with one or more other races; (3) American Indian and Alaska Native; (4) Native Hawaiian and Other Pacific Islander
Source: U.S. Census Bureau, 2011-2013 American Community Survey 3-Year Estimates

Hispanic or Latino Origin

Area	Total (%)	Mexican (%)	Puerto Rican (%)	Cuban (%)	Other (%)
City	20.2	16.2	0.3	0.0	3.8
MSA[1]	17.1	12.8	0.3	0.1	4.0
U.S.	16.9	10.8	1.6	0.6	3.8

Note: Persons of Hispanic or Latino origin can be of any race; (1) Figures cover the Salt Lake City, UT Metropolitan Statistical Area—see Appendix B for areas included
Source: U.S. Census Bureau, 2011-2013 American Community Survey 3-Year Estimates

Segregation

Type	Segregation Indices[1]				Percent Change		
	1990	2000	2010	2010 Rank[2]	1990-2000	1990-2010	2000-2010
Black/White	44.0	38.1	39.3	93	-5.9	-4.8	1.2
Asian/White	32.0	33.3	31.0	88	1.3	-1.0	-2.3
Hispanic/White	31.4	41.2	42.9	53	9.8	11.5	1.7

Note: All figures cover the Metropolitan Statistical Area—see Appendix B for areas included; Figures are based on an analysis of 1990, 2000, and 2010 Census Decennial Census tract data by William H. Frey, Brookings Institution and the University of Michigan Social Science Data Analysis Network. In this analysis all racial groups (whites, blacks, and asians) are non-Hispanic members of those races. Hispanics are shown as a separate category;
(1) Segregation Indices are Dissimilarity Indices that measure the degree to which the minority group is distributed differently than whites across census tracts. They range from 0 (complete integration) to 100 (complete segregation) where the value indicates the percentage of the minority group that needs to move to be distributed exactly like whites; (2) Ranges from 1 (most segregated) to 102 (least segregated); n/a not available.
Source: www.CensusScope.org

Ancestry

Area	German	Irish	English	American	Italian	Polish	French[2]	Scottish	Dutch
City	10.8	6.5	16.1	4.0	2.8	1.1	1.9	3.8	2.1
MSA[1]	11.4	6.2	21.9	5.2	2.9	1.0	1.8	4.0	2.4
U.S.	14.9	10.8	8.0	7.4	5.5	3.0	2.7	1.7	1.4

Note: Figures are the percentage of the total population reporting a particular ancestry. The nine most commonly reported ancestries in the U.S. are shown. Figures include multiple ancestries (e.g. if a person reported being Irish and Italian, they were included in both columns); (1) Figures cover the Salt Lake City, UT Metropolitan Statistical Area—see Appendix B for areas included; (2) Excludes Basque
Source: U.S. Census Bureau, 2011-2013 American Community Survey 3-Year Estimates

Foreign-Born Population

Area	Percent of Population Born in								
	Any Foreign Country	Mexico	Asia	Europe	Carribean	South America	Central America[2]	Africa	Canada
City	17.5	6.7	4.1	2.4	0.3	1.0	0.7	1.0	0.4
MSA[1]	11.9	4.9	2.7	1.4	0.1	1.1	0.6	0.4	0.3
U.S.	13.0	3.7	3.8	1.5	1.2	0.9	1.0	0.6	0.3

Note: (1) Figures cover the Salt Lake City, UT Metropolitan Statistical Area—see Appendix B for areas included; (2) Excludes Mexico.
Source: U.S. Census Bureau, 2011-2013 American Community Survey 3-Year Estimates

Marital Status

Area	Never Married	Now Married[2]	Separated	Widowed	Divorced
City	41.3	41.0	1.8	4.3	11.6
MSA[1]	31.1	52.4	2.0	3.9	10.7
U.S.	32.7	48.1	2.2	6.0	11.0

Note: Figures are percentages and cover the population 15 years of age and older; (1) Figures cover the Salt Lake City, UT Metropolitan Statistical Area—see Appendix B for areas included; (2) Excludes separated
Source: U.S. Census Bureau, 2011-2013 American Community Survey 3-Year Estimates

Disability Status

Area	All Ages	Under 18 Years Old	18 to 64 Years Old	65 Years and Over
City	11.4	3.7	10.1	38.1
MSA[1]	9.1	3.4	8.2	34.5
U.S.	12.3	4.1	10.2	36.3

Note: Figures show percent of the civilian noninstitutionalized population that reported having a disability. Disability status is determined from from six types of difficulty: vision, hearing, cognitive, ambulatory, self-care, and independent living. For children under 5 years old, hearing and vision difficulty are used to determine disability status. For children between the ages of 5 and 14, disability status is determined from hearing, vision, cognitive, ambulatory, and self-care difficulties. For people aged 15 years and older, they are considered to have a disability if they have difficulty with any one of the six difficulty types; (1) Figures cover the Salt Lake City, UT Metropolitan Statistical Area—see Appendix B for areas included.
Source: U.S. Census Bureau, 2011-2013 American Community Survey 3-Year Estimates

Age

Area	Percent of Population									Median Age
	Under Age 5	Age 5–19	Age 20–34	Age 35–44	Age 45–54	Age 55–64	Age 65–74	Age 75–84	Age 85+	
City	7.4	17.7	31.0	13.4	11.2	9.4	5.2	3.1	1.5	31.7
MSA[1]	8.4	23.2	24.2	13.7	11.6	9.8	5.2	2.7	1.1	31.4
U.S.	6.4	19.9	20.7	12.9	14.1	12.3	7.6	4.2	1.9	37.4

Note: (1) Figures cover the Salt Lake City, UT Metropolitan Statistical Area—see Appendix B for areas included
Source: U.S. Census Bureau, 2011-2013 American Community Survey 3-Year Estimates

Gender

Area	Males	Females	Males per 100 Females
City	97,585	92,016	106.1
MSA[1]	564,875	559,027	101.0
U.S.	154,451,010	159,410,713	96.9

Note: (1) Figures cover the Salt Lake City, UT Metropolitan Statistical Area—see Appendix B for areas included
Source: U.S. Census Bureau, 2011-2013 American Community Survey 3-Year Estimates

Religious Groups by Family

Area	Catholic	Baptist	Non-Den.	Methodist[2]	Lutheran	LDS[3]	Pente-costal	Presby-terian[4]	Muslim[5]	Judaism
MSA[1]	8.9	0.8	0.5	0.5	0.5	58.9	0.7	0.4	0.4	0.1
U.S.	19.1	9.3	4.0	4.0	2.3	2.0	1.9	1.6	0.8	0.7

Note: Figures are the number of adherents as a percentage of the total population; (1) Figures cover the Salt Lake City, UT Metropolitan Statistical Area—see Appendix B for areas included; (2) Methodist/Pietist; (3) Latter Day Saints; (4) Reformed; (5) Figures are estimates
Source: Association of Statisticians of American Religious Bodies, 2010 U.S. Religion Census: Religious Congregations & Membership Study

Religious Groups by Tradition

Area	Catholic	Evangelical Protestant	Mainline Protestant	Other Tradition	Black Protestant	Orthodox
MSA[1]	8.9	2.6	1.3	60.1	0.1	0.5
U.S.	19.1	16.2	7.3	4.3	1.6	0.3

Note: Figures are the number of adherents as a percentage of the total population; (1) Figures cover the Salt Lake City, UT Metropolitan Statistical Area—see Appendix B for areas included
Source: Association of Statisticians of American Religious Bodies, 2010 U.S. Religion Census: Religious Congregations & Membership Study

ECONOMY

Gross Metropolitan Product

Area	2012	2013	2014	2015	Rank[2]
MSA[1]	74.8	77.7	81.2	85.9	42

Note: Figures are in billions of dollars; (1) Figures cover the Salt Lake City, UT Metropolitan Statistical Area—see Appendix B for areas included; (2) Rank is based on 2015 data and ranges from 1 to 363
Source: The U.S. Conference of Mayors, U.S. Metro Economies: GMP and Employment 2013-2015, June 2014

Economic Growth

Area	2010-12 (%)	2013 (%)	2014 (%)	2015 (%)	Rank[2]
MSA[1]	3.6	2.9	2.9	3.9	35
U.S.	2.1	2.0	2.3	3.2	–

Note: Figures are real gross metropolitan product (GMP) growth rates and represent annual average percent change; (1) Figures cover the Salt Lake City, UT Metropolitan Statistical Area—see Appendix B for areas included; (2) Rank is based on 2015 data and ranges from 1 to 363
Source: The U.S. Conference of Mayors, U.S. Metro Economies: GMP and Employment 2013-2015, June 2014

Metropolitan Area Exports

Area	2008	2009	2010	2011	2012	2013	Rank[2]
MSA[1]	7,799.0	7,783.5	10,719.2	15,579.2	15,990.0	11,867.2	26

Note: Figures are in millions of dollars; (1) Figures cover the Salt Lake City, UT Metropolitan Statistical Area—see Appendix B for areas included; (2) Rank is based on 2013 data and ranges from 1 to 387
Source: U.S. Department of Commerce, International Trade Administration, Office of Trade & Industry Information, Manufacturing & Services, data extracted April 3, 2015

Building Permits

Area	Single-Family			Multi-Family			Total		
	2013	2014	Pct. Chg.	2013	2014	Pct. Chg.	2013	2014	Pct. Chg.
City	80	95	18.8	178	245	37.6	258	340	31.8
MSA[1]	3,447	3,159	-8.4	2,081	2,159	3.7	5,528	5,318	-3.8
U.S.	620,802	634,597	2.2	370,020	411,766	11.3	990,822	1,046,363	5.6

Note: (1) Figures cover the Salt Lake City, UT Metropolitan Statistical Area—see Appendix B for areas included; Figures represent new, privately-owned housing units authorized (unadjusted data); All permit data are based on estimates with imputation.
Source: U.S. Census Bureau, Manufacturing, Mining, and Construction Statistics, Building Permits, 2013, 2014

Bankruptcy Filings

Area	Business Filings			Nonbusiness Filings		
	2013	2014	% Chg.	2013	2014	% Chg.
Salt Lake County	127	114	-10.2	6,361	5,837	-8.2
U.S.	33,212	26,983	-18.8	1,038,720	909,812	-12.4

Note: Business filings include Chapter 7, Chapter 11, Chapter 12, and Chapter 13; Nonbusiness filings include Chapter 7, Chapter 11, and Chapter 13
Source: Administrative Office of the U.S. Courts, Business and Nonbusiness Bankruptcy, County Cases Commenced by Chapter of the Bankruptcy Code, During the 12- Month Period Ending December 31, 2013 and Business and Nonbusiness Bankruptcy, County Cases Commenced by Chapter of the Bankruptcy Code, During the 12- Month Period Ending December 31, 2014

Housing Vacancy Rates

Area	Gross Vacancy Rate[2] (%)			Year-Round Vacancy Rate[3] (%)			Rental Vacancy Rate[4] (%)			Homeowner Vacancy Rate[5] (%)		
	2012	2013	2014	2012	2013	2014	2012	2013	2014	2012	2013	2014
MSA[1]	7.9	7.4	7.8	7.3	6.8	7.6	7.3	6.7	9.8	0.8	1.5	1.8
U.S.	13.8	13.6	13.4	10.8	10.7	10.4	8.7	8.3	7.6	2.0	2.0	1.9

Note: (1) Figures cover the Salt Lake City, UT Metropolitan Statistical Area—see Appendix B for areas included; (2) The percentage of the total housing inventory that is vacant; (3) The percentage of the housing inventory (excluding seasonal units) that is year-round vacant; (4) The percentage of rental inventory that is vacant for rent; (5) The percentage of homeowner inventory that is vacant for sale
Source: U.S. Census Bureau, Housing Vacancies and Homeownership Annual Statistics: 2014

INCOME

Income

Area	Per Capita ($)	Median Household ($)	Average Household ($)
City	28,892	45,774	71,057
MSA[1]	25,911	60,322	76,812
U.S.	27,884	52,176	72,897

Note: (1) Figures cover the Salt Lake City, UT Metropolitan Statistical Area—see Appendix B for areas included
Source: U.S. Census Bureau, 2011-2013 American Community Survey 3-Year Estimates

Household Income Distribution

Area	Percent of Households Earning							
	Under $15,000	$15,000 -24,999	$25,000 -34,999	$35,000 -49,999	$50,000 -74,999	$75,000 -99,000	$100,000 -149,999	$150,000 and up
City	16.3	12.2	10.9	13.3	17.6	10.5	9.6	9.5
MSA[1]	9.0	9.1	9.1	13.6	21.1	14.3	14.4	9.2
U.S.	13.0	10.9	10.3	13.6	17.9	11.9	12.7	9.6

Note: (1) Figures cover the Salt Lake City, UT Metropolitan Statistical Area—see Appendix B for areas included
Source: U.S. Census Bureau, 2011-2013 American Community Survey 3-Year Estimates

Poverty Rate

Area	All Ages	Under 18 Years Old	18 to 64 Years Old	65 Years and Over
City	20.2	25.3	19.6	12.3
MSA[1]	13.1	17.2	12.1	6.8
U.S.	15.9	22.4	14.8	9.5

Note: Figures are percentage of people whose income during the past 12 months was below the poverty level;
(1) Figures cover the Salt Lake City, UT Metropolitan Statistical Area—see Appendix B for areas included
Source: U.S. Census Bureau, 2011-2013 American Community Survey 3-Year Estimates

EMPLOYMENT

Labor Force and Employment

Area	Civilian Labor Force			Workers Employed		
	Dec. 2013	Dec. 2014	% Chg.	Dec. 2013	Dec. 2014	% Chg.
City	107,003	107,929	0.9	103,241	104,692	1.4
MSA[1]	605,373	609,378	0.7	582,348	590,573	1.4
U.S.	154,408,000	155,521,000	0.7	144,423,000	147,190,000	1.9

Note: Data is not seasonally adjusted and covers workers 16 years of age and older; (1) Figures cover the Salt Lake City, UT Metropolitan Statistical Area—see Appendix B for areas included
Source: Bureau of Labor Statistics, Local Area Unemployment Statistics

Unemployment Rate

Area	2014											
	Jan.	Feb.	Mar.	Apr.	May	Jun.	Jul.	Aug.	Sep.	Oct.	Nov.	Dec.
City	3.9	3.9	3.9	3.1	3.4	3.8	3.7	3.7	3.3	3.3	3.0	3.0
MSA[1]	4.3	4.4	4.2	3.4	3.6	4.0	3.9	3.9	3.4	3.4	3.1	3.1
U.S.	7.0	7.0	6.8	5.9	6.1	6.3	6.5	6.3	5.7	5.5	5.5	5.4

Note: Data is not seasonally adjusted and covers workers 16 years of age and older; (1) Figures cover the Salt Lake City, UT Metropolitan Statistical Area—see Appendix B for areas included
Source: Bureau of Labor Statistics, Local Area Unemployment Statistics

Employment by Occupation

Occupation Classification	City (%)	MSA[1] (%)	U.S. (%)
Management, Business, Science, and Arts	44.8	37.4	36.2
Natural Resources, Construction, and Maintenance	5.4	8.3	9.0
Production, Transportation, and Material Moving	10.6	12.0	12.1
Sales and Office	21.4	27.4	24.4
Service	17.8	14.9	18.3

Note: Figures cover employed civilians 16 years of age and older; (1) Figures cover the Salt Lake City, UT Metropolitan Statistical Area—see Appendix B for areas included
Source: U.S. Census Bureau, 2011-2013 American Community Survey 3-Year Estimates

Employment by Industry

Sector	MSA[1]		U.S.
	Number of Employees	Percent of Total	Percent of Total
Construction, Mining, and Logging	35,700	5.3	5.0
Education and Health Services	75,300	11.2	15.5
Financial Activities	52,800	7.9	5.7
Government	105,600	15.7	15.8
Information	18,500	2.8	2.0
Leisure and Hospitality	55,200	8.2	10.3
Manufacturing	54,000	8.0	8.7
Other Services	20,300	3.0	4.0
Professional and Business Services	116,200	17.3	13.8
Retail Trade	73,200	10.9	11.4
Transportation, Warehousing, and Utilities	33,200	4.9	3.9
Wholesale Trade	31,300	4.7	4.2

Note: Figures are non-farm employment as of December 2014. Figures are not seasonally adjusted and include workers 16 years of age and older; (1) Figures cover the Salt Lake City, UT Metropolitan Statistical Area—see Appendix B for areas included; n/a not available
Source: Bureau of Labor Statistics, Current Employment Statistics, Employment, Hours, and Earnings

Occupations with Greatest Projected Employment Growth: 2012 – 2022

Occupation[1]	2012 Employment	2022 Projected Employment	Numeric Employment Change	Percent Employment Change
Customer Service Representatives	38,930	51,740	12,810	32.9
Combined Food Preparation and Serving Workers, Including Fast Food	30,260	39,290	9,030	29.8
Retail Salespersons	43,320	52,130	8,810	20.3
Secretaries and Administrative Assistants, Except Legal, Medical, and Executive	22,760	29,380	6,620	29.1
Registered Nurses	19,160	25,160	6,000	31.4
General and Operations Managers	22,950	28,680	5,730	25.0
Office Clerks, General	26,700	31,850	5,150	19.3
Heavy and Tractor-Trailer Truck Drivers	21,170	26,300	5,130	24.2
Laborers and Freight, Stock, and Material Movers, Hand	17,700	22,700	5,000	28.3
Construction Laborers	13,470	17,950	4,480	33.2

Note: Projections cover Utah; (1) Sorted by numeric employment change
Source: www.projectionscentral.com, State Occupational Projections, 2012–2022 Long-Term Projections

Fastest Growing Occupations: 2012 – 2022

Occupation[1]	2012 Employment	2022 Projected Employment	Numeric Employment Change	Percent Employment Change
Aircraft Structure, Surfaces, Rigging, and Systems Assemblers	340	670	330	95.3
Helpers—Electricians	660	1,190	530	80.6
Helpers—Brickmasons, Blockmasons, Stonemasons, and Tile and Marble Setters	560	990	430	77.3
Brickmasons and Blockmasons	1,010	1,730	720	70.6
Biomedical Engineers	440	730	290	67.3
Painters, Transportation Equipment	310	510	200	65.9
Health Specialties Teachers, Postsecondary	2,220	3,670	1,450	65.0
Interpreters and Translators	590	940	350	59.5
Credit Counselors	610	970	360	58.8
Skincare Specialists	470	740	270	56.8

Note: Projections cover Utah; (1) Sorted by percent employment change and excludes occupations with numeric employment change less than 100
Source: www.projectionscentral.com, State Occupational Projections, 2012–2022 Long-Term Projections

Average Wages

Occupation	$/Hr.	Occupation	$/Hr.
Accountants and Auditors	33.89	Maids and Housekeeping Cleaners	9.48
Automotive Mechanics	18.70	Maintenance and Repair Workers	17.96
Bookkeepers	17.43	Marketing Managers	62.31
Carpenters	18.39	Nuclear Medicine Technologists	32.12
Cashiers	9.62	Nurses, Licensed Practical	22.81
Clerks, General Office	13.78	Nurses, Registered	30.51
Clerks, Receptionists/Information	12.73	Nursing Assistants	11.94
Clerks, Shipping/Receiving	14.54	Packers and Packagers, Hand	10.79
Computer Programmers	38.16	Physical Therapists	37.89
Computer Systems Analysts	35.14	Postal Service Mail Carriers	25.44
Computer User Support Specialists	21.90	Real Estate Brokers	35.96
Cooks, Restaurant	11.92	Retail Salespersons	12.82
Dentists	68.03	Sales Reps., Exc. Tech./Scientific	36.15
Electrical Engineers	43.92	Sales Reps., Tech./Scientific	48.29
Electricians	23.08	Secretaries, Exc. Legal/Med./Exec.	16.23
Financial Managers	54.45	Security Guards	14.80
First-Line Supervisors/Managers, Sales	19.38	Surgeons	n/a
Food Preparation Workers	9.67	Teacher Assistants	11.50
General and Operations Managers	46.68	Teachers, Elementary School	27.90
Hairdressers/Cosmetologists	14.02	Teachers, Secondary School	26.90
Internists	93.65	Telemarketers	12.23
Janitors and Cleaners	10.28	Truck Drivers, Heavy/Tractor-Trailer	20.09
Landscaping/Groundskeeping Workers	12.22	Truck Drivers, Light/Delivery Svcs.	15.54
Lawyers	60.92	Waiters and Waitresses	11.09

Note: Wage data covers the Salt Lake City, UT Metropolitan Statistical Area—see Appendix B for areas included; Hourly wages for elementary/secondary school teachers and teacher assistants were calculated by the editors from annual wage data assuming a 40 hour work week; n/a not available.
Source: Bureau of Labor Statistics, Metro Area Occupational Employment and Wage Estimates, May 2014

TAXES

State Corporate Income Tax Rates

State	Tax Rate (%)	Income Brackets ($)	Num. of Brackets	Financial Institution Tax Rate (%)[a]	Federal Income Tax Ded.
Utah	5.0 (c)	Flat rate	–	5.0 (c)	No

Note: Tax rates as of January 1, 2015; (a) Rates listed are the corporate income tax rate applied to financial institutions or excise taxes based on income. Some states have other taxes based upon the value of deposits or shares; (c) Minimum tax is $800 in California, $100 in District of Columbia, $50 in North Dakota (banks), $500 in Rhode Island, $200 per location in South Dakota (banks), $100 in Utah, $250 in Vermont.
Source: Federation of Tax Administrators, "State Corporate Income Tax Rates, 2015"

State Individual Income Tax Rates

State	Tax Rate (%)	Income Brackets ($)	Num. of Brackets	Personal Exempt. ($)[1]		Fed. Inc. Tax Ded.
				Single	Dependents	
Utah	5.0	Flat rate	1	(t)	(t)	No

Note: Tax rates as of January 1, 2015; Local- and county-level taxes are not included; n/a not applicable; (1) Married joint filers generally receive double the single exemption; (t) Utah provides a tax credit equal to 6% of the federal personal exemption amounts (and applicable standard deduction).
Source: Federation of Tax Administrators, "State Individual Income Tax Rates, 2015"

Various State and Local Tax Rates

State	State and Local Sales and Use (%)	State Sales and Use (%)	Gasoline[1] (¢/gal.)	Cigarette[2] ($/pack)	Spirits[3] ($/gal.)	Wine[4] ($/gal.)	Beer[5] ($/gal.)
Utah	6.85	5.95 (b)	24.5	1.70	12.18 (g)	(l)	0.41 (p)

Note: All tax rates as of January 1, 2015; (1) The American Petroleum Institute has developed a methodology for determining the average tax rate on a gallon of fuel. Rates may include any of the following: excise taxes, environmental fees, storage tank fees, other fees or taxes, general sales tax, and local taxes. In states where gasoline is subject to the general sales tax, or where the fuel tax is based on the average sale price, the average rate determined by API is sensitive to changes in the price of gasoline. States that fully or partially apply general sales taxes to gasoline: CA, CO, GA, IL, IN, MI, NY; (2) The federal excise tax of $1.0066 per pack and local taxes are not included; (3) Rates are those applicable to off-premise sales of 40% alcohol by volume (a.b.v.) distilled spirits in 750ml containers. Local excise taxes are excluded; (4) Rates are those applicable to off-premise sales of 11% a.b.v. non-carbonated wine in 750ml containers; (5) Rates are those applicable to off-premise sales of 4.7% a.b.v. beer in 12 ounce containers; (b) Three states levy mandatory, statewide, local add-on sales taxes at the state level: California (1%), Utah (1.25%), and Virginia (1%). We include these in their state sales taxes; (g) States where the government controls sales. In these "control states," products are subject to ad valorem mark-up and excise taxes. The excise tax rate is calculated using a methodology developed by the Distilled Spirits Council of the United States; (l) Control states, where the government controls all sales. Products can be subject to ad valorem mark-up and excise taxes; (p) Local excise taxes are excluded. Source: Tax Foundation, 2015 Facts & Figures: How Does Your State Compare?

State Business Tax Climate Index Rankings

State	Overall Rank	Corporate Tax Index Rank	Individual Income Tax Index Rank	Sales Tax Index Rank	Unemployment Insurance Tax Index Rank	Property Tax Index Rank
Utah	9	5	12	19	22	4

Note: The index is a measure of how each state's tax laws affect economic performance. The lower the rank, the more favorable a state's tax system is for business. States without a given tax are given a ranking of 1. The scores/rankings for the District of Columbia do not affect other states. The 2015 index represents the tax climate as of July 1, 2014. Source: Tax Foundation, State Business Tax Climate Index 2015

COMMERCIAL REAL ESTATE

Office Market

Market Area	Inventory (sq. ft.)	Vacancy Rate (%)	Under Construction (sq. ft.)	YTD Net Absorption (sq. ft.)	Total Average Asking Rent ($/sq. ft./year)
Salt Lake City	30,630,901	9.9	1,352,087	667,975	22.22
National	4,745,108,508	14.3	71,190,461	51,084,126	27.40

Source: Newmark Grubb Knight Frank, National Office Market Report, 4th Quarter 2014

Industrial/Warehouse/R&D Market

Market Area	Inventory (sq. ft.)	Vacancy Rate (%)	Under Construction (sq. ft.)	YTD Net Absorption (sq. ft.)	Total Average Asking Rent ($/sq. ft./year)
Salt Lake City	132,201,114	3.8	2,477,271	2,720,590	5.04
National	14,238,613,765	7.2	134,387,407	185,246,438	5.64

Source: Newmark Grubb Knight Frank, National Industrial Market Report, 4th Quarter 2014

COMMERCIAL UTILITIES

Typical Monthly Electric Bills

Area	Commercial Service ($/month)		Industrial Service ($/month)	
	1,500 kWh	40 kW demand 14,000 kWh	1,000 kW demand 200,000 kWh	50,000 kW demand 32,500,000 kWh
City	186	1,277	24,957	1,779,293
Average[1]	201	1,653	26,124	2,639,743

Note: Figures are based on annualized 2014 rates; (1) Average based on 180 utilities surveyed Source: Edison Electric Institute, Typical Bills and Average Rates Report, Summer 2014

TRANSPORTATION

Means of Transportation to Work

Area	Car/Truck/Van		Public Transportation			Bicycle	Walked	Other Means	Worked at Home
	Drove Alone	Car-pooled	Bus	Subway	Railroad				
City	67.1	12.8	5.3	0.2	0.3	2.9	4.9	2.7	3.7
MSA[1]	75.2	12.5	2.5	0.3	0.4	0.8	1.9	1.8	4.7
U.S.	76.4	9.6	2.6	1.8	0.6	0.6	2.8	1.3	4.3

Note: Figures are percentages and cover workers 16 years of age and older; (1) Figures cover the Salt Lake City, UT Metropolitan Statistical Area—see Appendix B for areas included
Source: U.S. Census Bureau, 2011-2013 American Community Survey 3-Year Estimates

Travel Time to Work

Area	Less Than 10 Minutes	10 to 19 Minutes	20 to 29 Minutes	30 to 44 Minutes	45 to 59 Minutes	60 to 89 Minutes	90 Minutes or More
City	14.5	44.8	21.2	11.9	3.7	2.4	1.5
MSA[1]	10.8	33.3	26.6	20.2	5.1	2.5	1.4
U.S.	13.3	29.7	20.9	20.2	7.7	5.7	2.6

Note: Figures are percentages and include workers 16 years old and over; (1) Figures cover the Salt Lake City, UT Metropolitan Statistical Area—see Appendix B for areas included
Source: U.S. Census Bureau, 2011-2013 American Community Survey 3-Year Estimates

Travel Time Index

Area	1985	1990	1995	2000	2005	2010	2011
Urban Area[1]	1.09	1.13	1.21	1.23	1.20	1.14	1.14
Average[2]	1.09	1.14	1.16	1.19	1.23	1.18	1.18

Note: Travel Time Index—the ratio of travel time in the peak period to the travel time at free-flow conditions. For example, a value of 1.30 indicates a 20-minute free-flow trip takes 26 minutes in the peak. Free-flow speeds (60 mph on freeways and 35 mph on principal arterials) are used as the comparison threshold; (1) Covers the Salt Lake City UT urban area; (2) average of 498 urban areas
Source: Texas Transportation Institute, Urban Mobility Report 2012, December 2012

Public Transportation

Agency Name / Mode of Transportation	Vehicles Operated in Maximum Service	Annual Unlinked Passenger Trips (in thous.)	Annual Passenger Miles (in thous.)
Utah Transit Authority (UTA)			
Bus (directly operated)	389	18,863.9	74,067.9
Bus (purchased transportation)	7	44.0	569.0
Commuter Bus (directly operated)	54	787.8	13,663.1
Commuter Rail (directly operated)	36	3,816.4	108,921.2
Demand Response (directly operated)	69	236.4	2,351.9
Demand Response (purchased transportation)	55	147.0	2,158.5
Light Rail (directly operated)	84	18,997.9	85,567.4
Vanpool (directly operated)	420	1,387.8	53,824.9

Source: Federal Transit Administration, National Transit Database, 2013

Air Transportation

Airport Name and Code / Type of Service	Passenger Airlines[1]	Passenger Enplanements	Freight Carriers[2]	Freight (lbs.)
Salt Lake City International (SLC)				
Domestic service (U.S. carriers - 2014)	29	9,938,384	21	175,955,786
International service (U.S. carriers - 2013)	8	183,850	4	879,386

Note: (1) Includes all U.S.-based major, minor and commuter airlines that carried at least one passenger during the year; (2) Includes all U.S.-based airlines and freight carriers that transported at least one lb. of freight during the year.
Source: Bureau of Transportation Statistics, The Intermodal Transportation Database, Air Carriers: T-100 Domestic Market (U.S. Carriers), 2014; Bureau of Transportation Statistics, The Intermodal Transportation Database, Air Carriers: T-100 International Market (U.S. Carriers), 2013

Other Transportation Statistics

Major Highways:	I-15; I-80; I-84
Amtrak Service:	Yes
Major Waterways/Ports:	None

Source: Amtrak.com; Google Maps

BUSINESSES

Major Business Headquarters

Company Name	Rankings	
	Fortune[1]	Forbes[2]
Huntsman Corporation	253	-
Sinclair Oil	-	51

Note: (1) Fortune 500—companies that produce a 10-K are ranked 1 to 500 based on 2013 revenue; (2) all private companies with at least $2 billion in annual revenue through the end of their most current fiscal year are ranked 1 to 221; companies listed are headquartered in the city; dashes indicate no ranking
Source: Fortune, "Fortune 500," June 16, 2014; Forbes, "America's Largest Private Companies," November 5, 2014

Fast-Growing Businesses

According to *Inc.*, Salt Lake City is home to five of America's 500 fastest-growing private companies: **Connexion Point** (#86); **Alliance Health** (#104); **VRx** (#124); **OnSite Care** (#339); **JayBird** (#392). Criteria: must be an independent, privately-held, for-profit, U.S. corporation, proprietorship or partnership; revenues must be at least $100,000 in 2010 and $2 million in 2013; must have four-year operating/sales history. Holding companies, regulated banks, and utilities were excluded. *Inc., "America's 500 Fastest-Growing Private Companies," September 2014*

According to *Initiative for a Competitive Inner City (ICIC)*, Salt Lake City is home to one of America's 100 fastest-growing "inner city" companies: **Red Iguana** (#82). Criteria for inclusion: company must be headquartered in or have 51 percent or more of its physical operations in an economically distressed urban area; must be an independent, for-profit corporation, partnership or proprietorship; must have 10 or more employees and have a five-year sales history that includes sales of at least $200,000 in the base year and at least $1 million in the current year with no decrease in sales over the two most recent years. This year, for the first time in the list's 16-year history, the Inner City 100 consists of 10 fast-growing businesses in 10 industry categories. Companies were ranked overall by revenue growth over the five-year period between 2009 and 2013 as well as within their respective industry categories. *Initiative for a Competitive Inner City (ICIC), "Inner City 100 Companies, 2014"*

According to Deloitte, Salt Lake City is home to two of North America's 500 fastest-growing high-technology companies: **Fusion-io** (#39); **Packsize** (#292). Companies are ranked by percentage growth in revenue over a five-year period. Criteria for inclusion: company must be headquartered within North America; must own proprietary intellectual property or proprietary technology that contributes to a significant portion of the company's operating revenue, or devote a significant proportion of revenues to research and development of technology; must have been in business for a minumum of five years with 2009 operating revenues of at least $50,000 USD/CD and 2013 operating revenues of at least $5 million USD/CD. *Deloitte Touche Tohmatsu, 2014 Technology Fast 500*[TM]

Minority Business Opportunity

Salt Lake City is home to one company which is on the *Hispanic Business* 500 list (500 largest U.S. Hispanic-owned companies based on 2012 revenue): **ProCast Marble** (#423). Companies included must show at least 51 percent ownership by Hispanic U.S. citizens, and must maintain headquarters in one of the 50 states or Washington, D.C. *Hispanic Business, "Hispanic Business 500," June 20, 2013*

Minority- and Women-Owned Businesses

Group	All Firms		Firms with Paid Employees			
	Firms	Sales ($000)	Firms	Sales ($000)	Employees	Payroll ($000)
Asian	660	136,344	201	116,339	895	21,682
Black	196	12,518	8	3,186	67	1,468
Hispanic	967	230,922	177	207,303	1,116	30,657
Women	6,000	1,493,402	889	1,367,416	7,619	238,360
All Firms	23,826	63,266,392	7,367	62,251,821	222,169	9,383,217

Note: Figures cover firms located in the city; minority- and women-owned business are defined as firms in which the corresponding group own 51% or more of the stock or equity of the company
Source: U.S. Census Bureau, 2007 Economic Census, Survey of Business Owners (2012 Survey of Business Owners data will be released starting in June 2015)

**HOTELS &
CONVENTION
CENTERS**

Hotels/Motels

Area	5 Star		4 Star		3 Star		2 Star		1 Star		Not Rated	
	Num.	Pct.[3]	Num.	Pct.[3]	Num.	Pct.[3]	Num.	Pct.[3]	Num.	Pct.[3]	Num.	Pct.[3]
City[1]	1	0.7	4	2.9	52	37.1	75	53.6	2	1.4	6	4.3
Total[2]	166	0.9	1,264	7.0	5,718	31.8	9,340	52.0	411	2.3	1,070	6.0

Note: (1) Figures cover Salt Lake City and vicinity; (2) Figures cover all 100 cities in this book; (3) Percentage of hotels which have a given star rating; Star ratings are determined by expedia.com and offer an indication of the general quality of a particular hotel.
Source: expedia.com, April 2, 2015

The Salt Lake City, UT metro area is home to six of the best hotels in the U.S. according to *Travel & Leisure*: **Montage Deer Valley**; **St. Regis Deer Valley (Park City)**; **Stein Eriksen Lodge**; **Grand America Hotel Salt Lake City**; **Hotel Monaco Salt Lake City**; **Sundance Mountain Resort**. Criteria: service; location; rooms; food; and value. The list includes the top 236 hotels in the U.S. *Travel & Leisure, "T+L 500, The World's Best Hotels 2015"*

The Salt Lake City, UT metro area is home to one of the best hotels in the world according to *Condé Nast Traveler*: **Montage Deer Valley, Park City**. The selections are based on editors' picks. The list includes the top 25 hotels in the U.S. *Condé Nast Traveler, "Gold List 2015, The Top Hotels in the World"*

Major Convention Centers

Name	Overall Space (sq. ft.)	Exhibit Space (sq. ft.)	Meeting Space (sq. ft.)	Meeting Rooms
Salt Palace Convention Center	n/a	364,500	89,810	52

Note: Table includes convention centers located in the Salt Lake City, UT metro area; n/a not available
Source: Original research

Living Environment

COST OF LIVING

Cost of Living Index

Composite Index	Groceries	Housing	Utilities	Trans-portation	Health Care	Misc. Goods/ Services
94.1	96.8	90.8	94.0	101.5	94.8	93.0

Note: The Cost of Living Index measures regional differences in the cost of consumer goods and services, excluding taxes and non-consumer expenditures, for professional and managerial households in the top income quintile. It is based on more than 50,000 prices covering almost 60 different items for which prices are collected three times a year by chambers of commerce, economic development organizations or university applied economic centers in each participating urban area. The numbers shown should be read as a percentage above or below the national average of 100. For example, a value of 115.4 in the groceries column indicates that grocery prices are 15.4% higher than the national average. Small differences in the index numbers should not be interpreted as significant; Figures cover the Salt Lake City UT urban area.
Source: The Council for Community and Economic Research, ACCRA Cost of Living Index, 2014

Grocery Prices

Area[1]	T-Bone Steak ($/pound)	Frying Chicken ($/pound)	Whole Milk ($/half gal.)	Eggs ($/dozen)	Orange Juice ($/64 oz.)	Coffee ($/11.5 oz.)
City[2]	10.69	1.40	2.28	1.66	3.71	4.98
Avg.	10.40	1.37	2.40	1.99	3.46	4.27
Min.	8.48	0.93	1.37	1.30	2.83	2.99
Max.	14.20	2.44	3.62	4.02	6.42	6.96

Note: (1) Values for the local area are compared with the average, minimum and maximum values for all 308 areas in the Cost of Living Index; (2) Figures cover the Salt Lake City UT urban area; **T-Bone Steak** *(price per pound);* **Frying Chicken** *(price per pound, whole fryer);* **Whole Milk** *(half gallon carton);* **Eggs** *(price per dozen, Grade A, large);* **Orange Juice** *(64 oz. Tropicana or Florida Natural);* **Coffee** *(11.5 oz. can, vacuum-packed, Maxwell House, Hills Bros, or Folgers).*
Source: The Council for Community and Economic Research, ACCRA Cost of Living Index, 2014

Housing and Utility Costs

Area[1]	New Home Price ($)	Apartment Rent ($/month)	All Electric ($/month)	Part Electric ($/month)	Other Energy ($/month)	Telephone ($/month)
City[2]	278,495	865	-	71.14	71.90	29.99
Avg.	305,838	919	181.00	93.66	73.14	27.95
Min.	183,142	480	112.00	42.06	23.42	17.16
Max.	1,358,576	3,851	594.00	180.03	440.99	40.42

Note: (1) Values for the local area are compared with the average, minimum and maximum values for all 308 areas in the Cost of Living Index; (2) Figures cover the Salt Lake City UT urban area; **New Home Price** *(2,400 sf living area, 8,000 sf lot, in urban area with full utilities);* **Apartment Rent** *(950 sf 2 bedroom/1.5 or 2 bath, unfurnished, excluding all utilities except water);* **All Electric** *(average monthly cost for an all-electric home);* **Part Electric** *(average monthly cost for a part-electric home);* **Other Energy** *(average monthly cost for natural gas, fuel oil, coal, wood, and any other forms of energy except electricity);* **Telephone** *(price includes basic monthly rate for a private residential line plus additional local usage charges incurred by a family of four).*
Source: The Council for Community and Economic Research, ACCRA Cost of Living Index, 2014

Health Care, Transportation, and Other Costs

Area[1]	Doctor ($/visit)	Dentist ($/visit)	Optometrist ($/visit)	Gasoline ($/gallon)	Beauty Salon ($/visit)	Men's Shirt ($)
City[2]	98.89	75.78	86.83	3.33	38.92	19.77
Avg.	102.86	87.89	97.66	3.44	34.37	26.74
Min.	67.47	65.78	51.18	3.00	17.43	12.79
Max.	173.50	150.14	235.00	4.33	64.28	49.50

Note: (1) Values for the local area are compared with the average, minimum and maximum values for all 308 areas in the Cost of Living Index; (2) Figures cover the Salt Lake City UT urban area; **Doctor** *(general practitioners routine exam of an established patient);* **Dentist** *(adult teeth cleaning and periodic oral examination);* **Optometrist** *(full vision eye exam for established adult patient);* **Gasoline** *(one gallon regular unleaded, national brand, including all taxes, cash price at self-service pump if available);* **Beauty Salon** *(woman's shampoo, trim, and blow-dry);* **Men's Shirt** *(cotton/polyester dress shirt, pinpoint weave, long sleeves).*
Source: The Council for Community and Economic Research, ACCRA Cost of Living Index, 2014

HOUSING

House Price Index (HPI)

Area	National Ranking[2]	Quarterly Change (%)	One-Year Change (%)	Five-Year Change (%)
MSA[1]	106	0.58	5.11	12.00
U.S.[3]	–	1.35	4.91	11.59

Note: The HPI is a weighted repeat sales index. It measures average price changes in repeat sales or refinancings on the same properties. This information is obtained by reviewing repeat mortgage transactions on single-family properties whose mortgages have been purchased or securitized by Fannie Mae or Freddie Mac in January 1975; (1) Salt Lake City Metropolitan Statistical Area—see Appendix B for areas included; (2) Rankings are based on annual percentage change for all metro areas containing at least 15,000 transactions over the last 10 years and ranges from 1 to 275; (3) figures based on a weighted average of Census Division estimates using a seasonally adjusted, purchase-only index; all figures are for the period ending December 31, 2014

Source: Federal Housing Finance Agency, House Price Index, February 26, 2015

Median Single-Family Home Prices

Area	2012	2013	2014p	Percent Change 2013 to 2014
MSA[1]	204.7	230.6	239.1	3.7
U.S. Average	177.2	197.4	209.0	5.9

Note: Figures are median sales prices of existing single-family homes in thousands of dollars; (p) preliminary; n/a not available; (1) Salt Lake City, UT Metropolitan Statistical Area—see Appendix B for areas included
Source: National Association of Realtors, Median Sales Price of Existing Single-Family Homes for Metropolitan Areas, 4th Quarter 2014

Qualifying Income Based on Median Sales Price of Existing Single-Family Homes

Area	With 5% Down ($)	With 10% Down ($)	With 20% Down ($)
MSA[1]	54,169	51,318	45,616
U.S. Average	45,863	43,449	38,621

Note: Figures are preliminary; Qualifying income is based on a mortgage rate of 4.0%. Monthly principal and interest payment is limited to 25% of income; n/a not available; (1) Salt Lake City, UT Metropolitan Statistical Area—see Appendix B for areas included
Source: National Association of Realtors, Qualifying Income Based on Median Sales Price of Existing Single-Family Homes for Metropolitan Areas, 4th Quarter 2014

Median Apartment Condo-Coop Home Prices

Area	2012	2013	2014p	Percent Change 2013 to 2014
MSA[1]	135.5	168.9	174.3	3.2
U.S. Average	173.7	194.9	205.1	5.2

Note: Figures are median sales prices of existing apartment condo-coop homes in thousands of dollars; (p) preliminary; n/a not available; (1) Salt Lake City, UT Metropolitan Statistical Area—see Appendix B for areas included
Source: National Association of Realtors, Median Sales Price of Existing Apartment Condo-Coop Homes for Metropolitan Areas, 4th Quarter 2014

Gross Monthly Rent

Area	Under $200	$200 -299	$300 -499	$500 -749	$750 -999	$1,000 -1,499	$1,500 and up	Median ($)
City	2.0	3.2	7.4	31.5	29.2	19.9	6.8	794
MSA[1]	1.2	1.8	4.4	20.7	32.6	29.4	10.0	904
U.S.	1.7	3.2	7.8	22.1	24.3	26.0	14.9	900

Note: Figures are percentages except for Median; Gross rent is the contract rent plus the estimated average monthly cost of utilities (electricity, gas, and water and sewer) and fuels (oil, coal, kerosene, wood, etc.) if these are paid by the renter (or paid for the renter by someone else); (1) Figures cover the Salt Lake City, UT Metropolitan Statistical Area—see Appendix B for areas included
Source: U.S. Census Bureau, 2011-2013 American Community Survey 3-Year Estimates

Homeownership Rate

Area	2007 (%)	2008 (%)	2009 (%)	2010 (%)	2011 (%)	2012 (%)	2013 (%)	2014 (%)
MSA[1]	71.8	72.0	68.8	65.5	66.4	66.9	66.8	68.2
U.S.	68.1	67.8	67.4	66.9	66.1	65.4	65.1	64.5

Note: (1) Figures cover the Salt Lake City, UT Metropolitan Statistical Area—see Appendix B for areas included
Source: U.S. Census Bureau, Housing Vacancies and Homeownership Annual Statistics: 2014

Year Housing Structure Built

Area	2010 or Later	2000 -2009	1990 -1999	1980 -1989	1970 -1979	1960 -1969	1950 -1959	1940 -1949	Before 1940	Median Year
City	0.6	6.3	5.6	8.0	13.6	9.4	15.1	10.4	31.2	1956
MSA[1]	1.5	17.0	16.4	13.3	20.2	9.0	9.9	4.0	8.6	1979
U.S.	0.9	15.0	13.9	13.8	15.8	11.0	10.9	5.4	13.3	1976

Note: Figures are percentages except for Median Year; (1) Figures cover the Salt Lake City, UT Metropolitan Statistical Area—see Appendix B for areas included
Source: U.S. Census Bureau, 2011-2013 American Community Survey 3-Year Estimates

HEALTH

Health Risk Data

Category	MSA[1] (%)	U.S. (%)
Adults aged 18–64 who have any kind of health care coverage	77.6	79.6
Adults who reported being in good or excellent health	85.8	83.1
Adults who are current smokers	12.8	19.6
Adults who are heavy drinkers[2]	4.5	6.1
Adults who are binge drinkers[3]	14.6	16.9
Adults who are overweight (BMI 25.0 - 29.9)	34.0	35.8
Adults who are obese (BMI 30.0 - 99.8)	24.3	27.6
Adults who participated in any physical activities in the past month	82.3	77.1
Adults 50+ who have ever had a sigmoidoscopy or colonoscopy	72.1	67.3
Women aged 40+ who have had a mammogram within the past two years	68.2	74.0
Men aged 40+ who have had a PSA test within the past two years	36.1	45.2
Adults aged 65+ who have had flu shot within the past year	58.8	60.1
Adults who always wear a seatbelt	93.3	93.8

Note: Data as of 2012 unless otherwise noted; (1) Figures cover the Salt Lake City, UT Metropolitan Statistical Area—see Appendix B for areas included; (2) Heavy drinkers are classified as males having more than two drinks per day or females having more than one drink per day; (3) Binge drinkers are classified as males having five or more drinks on one occasion or females having four or more drinks on one occasion
Source: Centers for Disease Control and Prevention, Behaviorial Risk Factor Surveillance System, SMART: Selected Metropolitan/Micropolitan Area Risk Trends, 2012 (Note: the CDC has discontinued this dataset but will be releasing a replacement in late 2015)

Chronic Health Indicators

Category	MSA[1] (%)	U.S. (%)
Adults who have ever been told they had a heart attack	2.4	4.5
Adults who have ever been told they had a stroke	2.1	2.9
Adults who have been told they currently have asthma	9.6	8.9
Adults who have ever been told they have arthritis	19.1	25.7
Adults who have ever been told they have diabetes[2]	7.2	9.7
Adults who have ever been told they had skin cancer	5.9	5.7
Adults who have ever been told they had any other types of cancer	4.7	6.5
Adults who have ever been told they have COPD	3.9	6.2
Adults who have ever been told they have kidney disease	3.0	2.5
Adults who have ever been told they have a form of depression	22.6	18.0

Note: Data as of 2012 unless otherwise noted; (1) Figures cover the Salt Lake City, UT Metropolitan Statistical Area—see Appendix B for areas included; (2) Figures do not include pregnancy-related, borderline, or pre-diabetes
Source: Centers for Disease Control and Prevention, Behaviorial Risk Factor Surveillance System, SMART: Selected Metropolitan/Micropolitan Area Risk Trends, 2012 (Note: the CDC has discontinued this dataset but will be releasing a replacement in late 2015)

Mortality Rates for the Top 10 Causes of Death in the U.S.

ICD-10[a] Sub-Chapter	ICD-10[a] Code	Age-Adjusted Mortality Rate[1] per 100,000 population	
		County[2]	U.S.
Malignant neoplasms	C00-C97	130.6	166.2
Ischaemic heart diseases	I20-I25	62.5	105.7
Other forms of heart disease	I30-I51	67.7	49.3
Chronic lower respiratory diseases	J40-J47	33.0	42.1
Organic, including symptomatic, mental disorders	F01-F09	55.3	38.1
Cerebrovascular diseases	I60-I69	35.3	37.0
Other external causes of accidental injury	W00-X59	34.1	26.9
Other degenerative diseases of the nervous system	G30-G31	18.7	25.6
Diabetes mellitus	E10-E14	27.7	21.3
Hypertensive diseases	I10-I15	11.5	19.4

Note: (a) ICD-10 = International Classification of Diseases 10th Revision; (1) Mortality rates are a three year average covering 2011-2013; (2) Figures cover Salt Lake County
Source: Centers for Disease Control and Prevention, National Center for Health Statistics. Compressed Mortality File 1999-2013 on CDC WONDER Online Database, released October 2014. Data are compiled from the Compressed Mortality File 1999-2013, Series 20 No. 2S, 2014.

Mortality Rates for Selected Causes of Death

ICD-10[a] Sub-Chapter	ICD-10[a] Code	Age-Adjusted Mortality Rate[1] per 100,000 population	
		County[2]	U.S.
Assault	X85-Y09	2.1	5.2
Diseases of the liver	K70-K76	12.5	13.2
Human immunodeficiency virus (HIV) disease	B20-B24	1.0	2.2
Influenza and pneumonia	J09-J18	16.0	15.4
Intentional self-harm	X60-X84	21.1	12.5
Malnutrition	E40-E46	1.4	0.9
Obesity and other hyperalimentation	E65-E68	3.0	1.8
Renal failure	N17-N19	9.9	13.1
Transport accidents	V01-V99	8.7	11.7
Viral hepatitis	B15-B19	2.1	2.2

Note: (a) ICD-10 = International Classification of Diseases 10th Revision; (1) Mortality rates are a three year average covering 2011-2013; (2) Figures cover Salt Lake County
Source: Centers for Disease Control and Prevention, National Center for Health Statistics. Compressed Mortality File 1999-2013 on CDC WONDER Online Database, released October 2014. Data are compiled from the Compressed Mortality File 1999-2013, Series 20 No. 2S, 2014.

Health Insurance Coverage

Area	With Health Insurance	With Private Health Insurance	With Public Health Insurance	Without Health Insurance	Population Under Age 18 Without Health Insurance
City	80.9	64.5	23.9	19.1	14.7
MSA[1]	84.2	71.9	20.1	15.8	11.6
U.S.	85.2	65.2	31.0	14.8	7.3

Note: Figures are percentages that cover the civilian noninstitutionalized population; (1) Figures cover the Salt Lake City, UT Metropolitan Statistical Area—see Appendix B for areas included
Source: U.S. Census Bureau, 2011-2013 American Community Survey 3-Year Estimates

Number of Medical Professionals

Area[1]	MDs[2]	DOs[2,3]	Dentists	Podiatrists	Chiropractors	Optometrists
Local (number)	3,734	124	782	59	274	134
Local (rate[4])	350.8	11.6	72.3	5.5	25.4	12.4
U.S. (rate[4])	270.0	20.2	63.1	5.7	25.2	14.9

Note: Data as of 2013 unless noted; (1) Local data covers Salt Lake County; (2) Data as of 2012 and includes all active, non-federal physicians; (3) Doctor of Osteopathic Medicine; (4) rate per 100,000 population
Source: U.S. Department of Health and Human Services, Health Resources and Services Administration, Bureau of Health Professions, Area Resource File (ARF) 2013-2014

Best Hospitals

According to *U.S. News*, the Salt Lake City, UT metro area is home to one of the best children's hospitals in the U.S.: **Primary Children's Hospital** (8 specialties). The hospital listed was highly ranked in at least one pediatric specialty. Eighty-nine children's hospitals in the U.S. were nationally ranked in at least one specialty. Ten children's hospitals in the U.S. made the Honor Roll with high scores in at least three specialties. *U.S. News Online, "America's Best Children's Hospitals 2014-15"*

EDUCATION

Public School District Statistics

District Name	Schls	Pupils	Pupil/ Teacher Ratio	Minority Pupils[1] (%)	Free Lunch Eligible[2] (%)	IEP[3] (%)
Granite District	92	69,312	23.9	44.5	64.8	12.2
Salt Lake District	42	24,680	21.4	58.4	70.8	12.4

Note: Table includes school districts with 2,000 or more students; (1) Percentage of students that are not non-Hispanic white; (2) Percentage of students that are eligible for the free lunch program; (3) Percentage of students that have an Individualized Education Program.
Source: U.S. Department of Education, National Center for Education Statistics, Common Core of Data, Local Education Agency (School District) Universe Survey: School Year 2012-2013; U.S. Department of Education, National Center for Education Statistics, Common Core of Data, Public Elementary/Secondary School Universe Survey: School Year 2012-2013

Best High Schools

According to *The Daily Beast*, Salt Lake City is home to one of the best high schools in the U.S.: **Academy for Math, Engineering & Science** (#362); *The Daily Beast* used six indicators culled from school surveys to compare public high schools in the U.S., with graduation and college acceptance rates weighed most heavily. Other criteria included: college-level courses/exams and SAT/ACT scores. *The Daily Beast, "Top High Schools 2014"*

Highest Level of Education

Area	Less than H.S.	H.S. Diploma	Some College, No Deg.	Associate Degree	Bachelor's Degree	Master's Degree	Prof. School Degree	Doctorate Degree
City	13.5	16.9	20.6	6.2	24.5	10.3	4.2	3.8
MSA[1]	10.6	23.0	26.3	8.8	20.4	7.4	2.0	1.5
U.S.	13.7	28.0	21.2	7.9	18.2	7.7	1.9	1.3

Note: Figures cover persons age 25 and over; (1) Figures cover the Salt Lake City, UT Metropolitan Statistical Area—see Appendix B for areas included
Source: U.S. Census Bureau, 2011-2013 American Community Survey 3-Year Estimates

Educational Attainment by Race

Area	High School Graduate or Higher (%)					Bachelor's Degree or Higher (%)				
	Total	White	Black	Asian	Hisp.[2]	Total	White	Black	Asian	Hisp.[2]
City	86.5	92.5	80.0	88.0	51.3	42.8	47.1	24.7	65.6	15.0
MSA[1]	89.4	92.2	82.5	82.9	62.9	31.3	32.4	22.5	50.5	12.0
U.S.	86.3	88.3	83.1	85.7	64.0	29.1	30.4	18.8	50.7	13.7

Note: Figures shown cover persons 25 years old and over; (1) Figures cover the Salt Lake City, UT Metropolitan Statistical Area—see Appendix B for areas included; (2) People of Hispanic origin can be of any race
Source: U.S. Census Bureau, 2011-2013 American Community Survey 3-Year Estimates

School Enrollment by Grade and Control

Area	Preschool (%)		Kindergarten (%)		Grades 1 - 4 (%)		Grades 5 - 8 (%)		Grades 9 - 12 (%)	
	Public	Private	Public	Private	Public	Private	Public	Private	Public	Private
City	42.8	57.2	85.4	14.6	90.1	9.9	90.0	10.0	91.7	8.3
MSA[1]	50.2	49.8	91.1	8.9	92.8	7.2	93.4	6.6	93.5	6.5
U.S.	57.7	42.3	87.9	12.1	89.9	10.1	90.0	10.0	90.7	9.3

Note: Figures shown cover persons 3 years old and over; (1) Figures cover the Salt Lake City, UT Metropolitan Statistical Area—see Appendix B for areas included
Source: U.S. Census Bureau, 2011-2013 American Community Survey 3-Year Estimates

Average Salaries of Public School Classroom Teachers

Area	2013-14		2014-15		Percent Change 2013-14 to 2014-15	Percent Change 2004-05 to 2014-15
	Dollars	Rank[1]	Dollars	Rank[1]		
UTAH	45,695	44	45,848	45	0.33	16.2
U.S. Average	56,610	–	57,379	–	1.36	20.8

Note: (1) State rank ranges from 1 to 51 where 1 indicates highest salary.
Source: National Education Association, Rankings & Estimates: Rankings of the States 2014 and Estimates of School Statistics 2015, March 2015

Higher Education

Four-Year Colleges			Two-Year Colleges			Medical Schools[1]	Law Schools[2]	Voc/ Tech[3]
Public	Private Non-profit	Private For-profit	Public	Private Non-profit	Private For-profit			
1	4	3	1	1	2	1	1	6

Note: Figures cover institutions located within the city limits and include main campuses only; (1) includes schools accredited by the Liaison Committee on Medical Education and the American Osteopathic Association's Commission on Osteopathic College Accreditation; (2) includes ABA-accredited schools, schools with provisional ABA accreditation, and state accredited schools; (3) includes all schools with programs that are less than 2 years.
Source: National Center for Education Statistics, Integrated Postsecondary Education System (IPEDS), 2013-14; Association of American Medical Colleges, Member List, May 1, 2015; American Osteopathic Association, Member List, May 1, 2015; Law School Admission Council, Official Guide to ABA-Approved Law Schools Online, May 1, 2015; Wikipedia, List of Medical Schools in the United States, May 1, 2015; Wikipedia, List of Law Schools in the United States, May 1, 2015

According to *U.S. News & World Report*, the Salt Lake City, UT metro area is home to one of the best national universities in the U.S.: **University of Utah** (#129). The indicators used to capture academic quality fall into a number of categories: assessment by administrators at peer institutions; retention of students; faculty resources; student selectivity; financial resources; alumni giving; high school counselor ratings of colleges; and graduation rate. *U.S. News & World Report, "America's Best Colleges 2015"*

According to *U.S. News & World Report*, the Salt Lake City, UT metro area is home to one of the top 100 law schools in the U.S.: **University of Utah (Quinney)** (#42). The rankings are based on a weighted average of 12 measures of quality: peer assessment score; assessment score by lawyers/judges; median LSAT scores; median undergrad GPA; acceptance rate; employment rates for graduates; placement success; bar passage rate; faculty resources; expenditures per student; student/faculty ratio; and library resources. *U.S. News & World Report, "America's Best Graduate Schools, Law, 2016"*

According to *U.S. News & World Report*, the Salt Lake City, UT metro area is home to one of the top 75 medical schools for research in the U.S.: **University of Utah** (#48). The rankings are based on a weighted average of 11 measures of quality: quality assessment; peer assessment score; assessment score by residency directors; research activity; total research activity; average research activity per faculty member; student selectivity; median MCAT total score; median undergraduate GPA; acceptance rate; and faculty resources. *U.S. News & World Report, "America's Best Graduate Schools, Medical, 2016"*

According to *U.S. News & World Report*, the Salt Lake City, UT metro area is home to one of the top 75 business schools in the U.S.: **University of Utah (Eccles)** (#70). The rankings are based on a weighted average of the following nine measures: quality assessment; peer assessment; recruiter assessment; placement success; mean starting salary and bonus; student selectivity; mean GMAT and GRE scores; mean undergraduate GPA; and acceptance rate. *U.S. News & World Report, "America's Best Graduate Schools, Business, 2016"*

PRESIDENTIAL ELECTION

2012 Presidential Election Results

Area	Obama (%)	Romney (%)	Other (%)
Salt Lake County	38.8	58.2	3.0
U.S.	51.0	47.2	1.8

Note: Results may not add to 100% due to rounding
Source: Dave Leip's Atlas of U.S. Presidential Elections

EMPLOYERS

Major Employers

Company Name	Industry
ACS Commercial Solutions	Data entry service
Alsco	Laundry and garment services, nec
Boart Longyear Company	Test boring for nonmetallic minerals
Church of Jesus Christ of LDS	Mormon Church
Comenity Capital Bank	State commercial banks
County of Salt Lake	Executive offices
EnergySolutions	Nonresidential construction, nec
Executive Office of the State of Utah	Executive offices
Granite School District Aid Association	Public elementary and secondary schools
Huntsman Corporation	Plastics materials & resins
Huntsman Holdings LLC	Polystyrene resins
Intermountain Health Care	General medical and surgical hospitals
Jordan School District	Public elementary and secondary schools
Longyear Holdings	Test boring for nonmetallic minerals
Sinclair Oil Corporation	Petroleum refining
Smith's Food & Drug Centers	Grocery stores
Sportsman's Warehouse Holdings	Hunting equipment
State of Utah	Governor's office
The University of Utah	Colleges and universities
TPUSA	Telemarketing services
University of Utah Hospitals & Clinics	General medical and surgical hospitals
Utah Department of Human Services	Administration of social and manpower programs
Zions Bancorporation	Bank holding companies

Note: Companies shown are located within the Salt Lake City, UT Metropolitan Statistical Area.
Source: Hoovers.com; Wikipedia

Best Companies to Work For

CHG Healthcare Services; O.C. Tanner, headquartered in Salt Lake City, are among "The 100 Best Companies to Work For." To pick the best companies, *Fortune* partnered with the Great Place to Work Institute. Two-thirds of a company's score is based on the results of the Institute's Trust Index survey, which is sent to a random sample of employees from each company. The questions related to attitudes about management's credibility, job satisfaction, and camaraderie. The other third of the scoring is based on the company's responses to the Institute's Culture Audit, which includes detailed questions about pay and benefit programs, and a series of open-ended questions about hiring practices, internal communication, training, recognition programs, and diversity efforts. Any company that is at least five years old with more than 1,000 U.S. employees is eligible. *Fortune, "The 100 Best Companies to Work For," 2015*

CHG Healthcare Services; Clearlink, headquartered in Salt Lake City, are among the "100 Best Places to Work in IT." To qualify, companies, both public and private, had to have a minimum of 50 IT employees and were selected based on average salary and bonus increases, the percentage of IT staffers promoted, IT staff turnover rates, training and development programs, and the percentage of women and minorities in IT staff and management positions. In addition, *Computerworld* looked at retention efforts, programs for recognizing and rewarding outstanding performances, and benefits such as flextime, elder care and child care, and reimbursement for college tuition and the cost of pursuing technology certifications. *Computerworld, "100 Best Places to Work in IT 2014"*

PUBLIC SAFETY

Crime Rate

Area	All Crimes	Violent Crimes				Property Crimes		
		Murder	Forcible Rape	Robbery	Aggrav. Assault	Burglary	Larceny -Theft	Motor Vehicle Theft
City	7,850.9	3.7	107.2	221.8	442.6	1,087.0	5,002.5	986.1
Suburbs[1]	4,075.5	1.4	47.3	57.0	167.2	600.3	2,808.9	393.5
Metro[2]	4,704.6	1.8	57.3	84.4	213.1	681.4	3,174.4	492.2
U.S.	3,098.6	4.5	25.2	109.1	229.1	610.0	1,899.4	221.3

Note: Figures are crimes per 100,000 population; (1) All areas within the metro area that are located outside the city limits; (2) Figures cover the Salt Lake City, UT Metropolitan Statistical Area—see Appendix B for areas included
Source: FBI Uniform Crime Reports, 2013

Hate Crimes

Area	Number of Quarters Reported	Number of Incidents per Bias Motivation						
		Race	Religion	Sexual Orientation	Ethnicity	Disability	Gender	Gender Identity
City	4	3	1	1	0	0	0	0
U.S.	4	2,871	1,031	1,233	655	83	18	31

Source: Federal Bureau of Investigation, Hate Crime Statistics 2013

Identity Theft Consumer Complaints

Area	Complaints	Complaints per 100,000 Population	Rank[2]
MSA[1]	770	67.5	205
U.S.	332,646	104.3	-

Note: (1) Figures cover the Salt Lake City, UT Metropolitan Statistical Area—see Appendix B for areas included; (2) Rank ranges from 1 to 380 where 1 indicates greatest number of identity theft complaints per 100,000 population
Source: Federal Trade Commission, Consumer Sentinel Network Data Book for January–December 2014

Fraud and Other Consumer Complaints

Area	Complaints	Complaints per 100,000 Population	Rank[2]
MSA[1]	4,417	387.3	160
U.S.	2,250,205	705.7	-

Note: (1) Figures cover the Salt Lake City, UT Metropolitan Statistical Area—see Appendix B for areas included; (2) Rank ranges from 1 to 380 where 1 indicates greatest number of identity theft complaints per 100,000 population
Source: Federal Trade Commission, Consumer Sentinel Network Data Book for January–December 2014

RECREATION

Culture

Dance[1]	Theatre[1]	Instrumental Music[1]	Vocal Music[1]	Series and Festivals	Museums and Art Galleries[2]	Zoos and Aquariums[3]
4	7	9	5	6	47	2

Note: (1) Professional perfoming groups; (2) Based on organizations with SIC code 8412; (3) AZA-accredited
Source: The Grey House Performing Arts Directory, 2015-16; Association of Zoos & Aquariums, AZA Member Zoos & Aquariums, April 2015; www.AccuLeads.com, April 2015

Professional Sports Teams

Team Name	League	Year Established
Real Salt Lake	Major League Soccer (MLS)	2005
Utah Jazz	National Basketball Association (NBA)	1979

Note: Includes teams located in the Salt Lake City, UT Metropolitan Statistical Area.
Source: Wikipedia, Major Professional Sports Teams of the United States and Canada, April 2015

CLIMATE

Average and Extreme Temperatures

Temperature	Jan	Feb	Mar	Apr	May	Jun	Jul	Aug	Sep	Oct	Nov	Dec	Yr.
Extreme High (°F)	62	69	78	85	93	104	107	104	100	89	75	67	107
Average High (°F)	37	43	52	62	72	83	93	90	80	66	50	38	64
Average Temp. (°F)	28	34	41	50	59	69	78	76	65	53	40	30	52
Average Low (°F)	19	24	31	38	46	54	62	61	51	40	30	22	40
Extreme Low (°F)	-22	-14	2	15	25	35	40	37	27	16	-14	-15	-22

Note: Figures cover the years 1948-1990
Source: National Climatic Data Center, International Station Meteorological Climate Summary, 9/96

Average Precipitation/Snowfall/Humidity

Precip./Humidity	Jan	Feb	Mar	Apr	May	Jun	Jul	Aug	Sep	Oct	Nov	Dec	Yr.
Avg. Precip. (in.)	1.3	1.2	1.8	2.0	1.7	0.9	0.8	0.9	1.1	1.3	1.3	1.4	15.6
Avg. Snowfall (in.)	13	10	11	6	1	Tr	0	0	Tr	2	6	13	63
Avg. Rel. Hum. 5am (%)	79	77	71	67	66	60	53	54	60	68	75	79	67
Avg. Rel. Hum. 5pm (%)	69	59	47	38	33	26	22	23	28	40	59	71	43

Note: Figures cover the years 1948-1990; Tr = Trace amounts (<0.05 in. of rain; <0.5 in. of snow)
Source: National Climatic Data Center, International Station Meteorological Climate Summary, 9/96

Weather Conditions

Temperature			Daytime Sky			Precipitation		
5°F & below	32°F & below	90°F & above	Clear	Partly cloudy	Cloudy	0.01 inch or more precip.	0.1 inch or more snow/ice	Thunder-storms
7	128	56	94	152	119	92	38	38

Note: Figures are average number of days per year and cover the years 1948-1990
Source: National Climatic Data Center, International Station Meteorological Climate Summary, 9/96

HAZARDOUS WASTE

Superfund Sites

Salt Lake City has four hazardous waste sites on the EPA's Superfund Final National Priorities List: **700 South 1600 East PCE Plume; Portland Cement (Kiln Dust 2 & 3); Utah Power & Light/American Barrel Co.; Wasatch Chemical Co. (Lot 6)**. There are a total of 1,322 Superfund sites on the list in the U.S. *U.S. Environmental Protection Agency, Final National Priorities List, April 14, 2015*

AIR & WATER QUALITY

Air Quality Trends: Ozone

	2004	2005	2006	2007	2008	2009	2010	2011	2012	2013
MSA[1]	0.072	0.084	0.082	0.081	0.075	0.074	0.072	0.074	0.079	0.076

Note: (1) Data covers the Salt Lake City, UT Metropolitan Statistical Area—see Appendix B for areas included. The values shown are the composite ozone concentration averages among trend sites based on the highest fourth daily maximum 8-hour concentration in parts per million. These trends are based on sites having an adequate record of monitoring data during the trend period. Data from exceptional events are included.
Source: U.S. Environmental Protection Agency, Air Quality Monitoring Information, "Air Quality Trends by City, 2000-2013"

Air Quality Index

Area	Percent of Days when Air Quality was...[2]					AQI Statistics[2]	
	Good	Moderate	Unhealthy for Sensitive Groups	Unhealthy	Very Unhealthy	Maximum	Median
MSA[1]	77.0	18.4	4.1	0.5	0.0	154	42

Note: (1) Data covers the Salt Lake City, UT Metropolitan Statistical Area—see Appendix B for areas included; (2) Based on 365 days with AQI data in 2014. Air Quality Index (AQI) is an index for reporting daily air quality. EPA calculates the AQI for five major air pollutants regulated by the Clean Air Act: ground-level ozone, particle pollution (aka particulate matter), carbon monoxide, sulfur dioxide, and nitrogen dioxide. The AQI runs from 0 to 500. The higher the AQI value, the greater the level of air pollution and the greater the health concern. There are six AQI categories: "Good" AQI is between 0 and 50. Air quality is considered satisfactory; "Moderate" AQI is between 51 and 100. Air quality is acceptable; "Unhealthy for Sensitive Groups" When AQI values are between 101 and 150, members of sensitive groups may experience health effects; "Unhealthy" When AQI values are between 151 and 200 everyone may begin to experience health effects; "Very Unhealthy" AQI values between 201 and 300 trigger a health alert; "Hazardous" AQI values over 300 trigger warnings of emergency conditions (not shown).
Source: U.S. Environmental Protection Agency, Air Quality Index Report, 2014

Air Quality Index Pollutants

Area	Percent of Days when AQI Pollutant was...[2]					
	Carbon Monoxide	Nitrogen Dioxide	Ozone	Sulfur Dioxide	Particulate Matter 2.5	Particulate Matter 10
MSA[1]	0.0	16.7	60.8	0.0	21.4	1.1

Note: (1) Data covers the Salt Lake City, UT Metropolitan Statistical Area—see Appendix B for areas included; (2) Based on 365 days with AQI data in 2014. The Air Quality Index (AQI) is an index for reporting daily air quality. EPA calculates the AQI for five major air pollutants regulated by the Clean Air Act: ground-level ozone, particle pollution (also known as particulate matter), carbon monoxide, sulfur dioxide, and nitrogen dioxide. The AQI runs from 0 to 500. The higher the AQI value, the greater the level of air pollution and the greater the health concern.
Source: U.S. Environmental Protection Agency, Air Quality Index Report, 2014

Maximum Air Pollutant Concentrations: Particulate Matter, Ozone, CO and Lead

	Particulate Matter 10 (ug/m³)	Particulate Matter 2.5 Wtd AM (ug/m³)	Particulate Matter 2.5 24-Hr (ug/m³)	Ozone (ppm)	Carbon Monoxide (ppm)	Lead (ug/m³)
MSA¹ Level	105	12.1	59	0.077	2	0.08
NAAQS²	150	15	35	0.075	9	0.15
Met NAAQS²	Yes	Yes	No	No	Yes	Yes

Note: (1) Data covers the Salt Lake City, UT Metropolitan Statistical Area—see Appendix B for areas included; Data from exceptional events are included; (2) National Ambient Air Quality Standards; ppm = parts per million; ug/m³ = micrograms per cubic meter; n/a not available.
Concentrations: Particulate Matter 10 (coarse particulate)—highest second maximum 24-hour concentration; Particulate Matter 2.5 Wtd AM (fine particulate)—highest weighted annual mean concentration; Particulate Matter 2.5 24-Hour (fine particulate)—highest 98th percentile 24-hour concentration; Ozone—highest fourth daily maximum 8-hour concentration; Carbon Monoxide—highest second maximum non-overlapping 8-hour concentration; Lead—maximum running 3-month average
Source: U.S. Environmental Protection Agency, Air Quality Monitoring Information, "Air Quality Statistics by City, 2013"

Maximum Air Pollutant Concentrations: Nitrogen Dioxide and Sulfur Dioxide

	Nitrogen Dioxide AM (ppb)	Nitrogen Dioxide 1-Hr (ppb)	Sulfur Dioxide AM (ppb)	Sulfur Dioxide 1-Hr (ppb)	Sulfur Dioxide 24-Hr (ppb)
MSA¹ Level	18	62	n/a	31	n/a
NAAQS²	53	100	30	75	140
Met NAAQS²	Yes	Yes	n/a	Yes	n/a

Note: (1) Data covers the Salt Lake City, UT Metropolitan Statistical Area—see Appendix B for areas included; Data from exceptional events are included; (2) National Ambient Air Quality Standards; ppm = parts per million; ug/m³ = micrograms per cubic meter; n/a not available.
Concentrations: Nitrogen Dioxide AM—highest arithmetic mean concentration; Nitrogen Dioxide 1-Hr—highest 98th percentile 1-hour daily maximum concentration; Sulfur Dioxide AM—highest annual mean concentration; Sulfur Dioxide 1-Hr—highest 99th percentile 1-hour daily maximum concentration; Sulfur Dioxide 24-Hr—highest second maximum 24-hour concentration
Source: U.S. Environmental Protection Agency, Air Quality Monitoring Information, "Air Quality Statistics by City, 2013"

Drinking Water

Water System Name	Pop. Served	Primary Water Source Type	Violations¹ Health Based	Violations¹ Monitoring/ Reporting
Salt Lake City Water System	318,506	Surface	0	0

Note: (1) Based on violation data from January 1, 2014 to December 31, 2014 (includes unresolved violations from earlier years)
Source: U.S. Environmental Protection Agency, Office of Ground Water and Drinking Water, Safe Drinking Water Information System (based on data extracted January 27, 2015)

San Diego, California

Background

San Diego is the archetypal southern California City. Located 100 miles south of Los Angeles, near the Mexican border, San Diego is characterized by sunny days, an excellent harbor, a populous citizenry that alludes to its Spanish heritage, and recreational activities based on ideal weather conditions.

San Diego was first claimed in 1542 for Spain by Juan Rodriquez Cabrillo, a Portuguese navigator in the service of the Spanish crown. The site remained uneventful until 1769, when Spanish colonizer, Gaspar de Portola, established the first European settlement in California. Accompanying de Portola was a Franciscan monk named Junipero Serra, who established the Mission Basilica San Diega de Alcala, the first of a chain of missions along the California Coast.

After San Diego fell under the U.S. flag during the Mexican War of 1846, the city existed in relative isolation, deferring status and importance to its sister cities in the north, Los Angeles and San Francisco. Even when San Francisco businessman Alonzo Horton bought 1,000 acres of land near the harbor to establish a logical and practical downtown there, San Diego remained secondary to both these cities, and saw a decrease in population from 40,000 in 1880 to 17,000 at the turn of the century.

World War II repopulated the city, when the Navy moved one of its bases from Pearl Harbor to San Diego. The naval base brought personnel and a number of related industries, such as nuclear and oceanographic research, and aviation development. In celebration of this past, the famed IMidway, a 1,000-foot World War II aircraft carrier, has undergone a $6.5 million reconstruction and has been moved to Navy Pier, where it opened in 2004 as a floating museum.

Today, San Diego is the second most populous city in California, with plenty of outdoor activities, jobs, fine educational institutions, theaters, and museums with which to attract new residents, young and old alike. San Diego's downtown redevelopment agency has transformed what was largely an abandoned downtown into a glittering showcase of waterfront skyscrapers, live-work loft developments, five-star hotels, and many cafes, restaurants, and shops. The once-industrial East Village adjacent to PETCO ballpark is now the new frontier in San Diego's downtown urban renewal.

According to recent studies, the western part of the U.S., from Seattle to the Silicon Valley, and from San Diego to Denver, is becoming the center for all the hot growth industries, namely telecommunications, biomedical products, software, and financial services. San Diego leads the country in biotechnology companies that are attracting venture capital.

The San Diego Convention Center underwent expansion in 2001 that increased exhibit space from 250,000 to 615,000 square feet. The water supply system, always a significant issue in this part of California, has been upgraded and improved in recent years. The San Diego International Airport, at present trends, will shift from serving 16 million passengers in 2004 to serving more than 27 million by 2030, and appropriate airport renovations are being discussed.

San Diego summers are cool and winters are warm in comparison with other locations along the same general latitude, due to the Pacific Ocean. A marked feature of the climate is the wide variation in temperature. In nearby valleys, for example, daytime temperatures are much warmer in summer and noticeably cooler on winter nights than in the city proper. As is usual on the Pacific Coast, nighttime and early morning cloudiness is the norm. Considerable fog occurs along the coast, especially during the winter months.

Rankings

General Rankings

- The San Diego metro area was identified as one of America's fastest-growing areas in terms of population and economy by *Forbes*. The area ranked #16 out of 20. The 100 most populous metro areas in the U.S. were evaluated on the following criteria: estimated population growth; job growth; gross metropolitan product growth; unemployment; median salaries for college-educated workers. *Forbes, "America's Fastest-Growing Cities 2015," January 27, 2015*

- Among the 50 largest U.S. cities, San Diego placed #27 in Vocativ's "semi-exhaustive, mostly scientific" city Livability Index for people aged 35 and under. Average salary, unemployment rates, rents, and other living costs were considered, along with crime rates, weather, public transportation, access to music and sports, and "lifestyle metrics" such as the price of dinner at Buffalo Wild Wings and an ounce of high-quality weed. *vocative.com, "The Livability Index: The Best U.S. Cities for People 35 and Under," December 9, 2014*

- San Diego was selected as one of America's best cities by *Bloomberg Businessweek*. The city ranked #9 out of 50. Criteria: leisure attributes (the number of restaurants, bars, libraries, museums, professional sports teams, and park acres by population); educational attributes (public school performance, the number of colleges, and graduate degree holders); economic factors (2011 income and June and July 2012 unemployment); crime; and air quality. *Bloomberg BusinessWeek, "America's Best Cities," September 26, 2012*

Business/Finance Rankings

- Measuring indicators of "tolerance"—the nonjudgmental environment that "attracts open-minded and new-thinking kinds of people"— as well as concentrations of technological and economic innovators, analysts identified the most creative American metro areas. On the resulting 2012 Creativity Index, the San Diego metro area placed #4. *www.thedailybeast.com, "Boulder, Ann Arbor, Tucson & More: 20 Most Creative U.S. Cities," June 26, 2012*

- Building on the U.S. Department of Labor's Occupational Information Network Data Collection Program, the Brookings Institution defined STEM occupations and job opportunities for STEM workers at various levels of educational attainment. The San Diego metro area was placed among the ten large metro areas with the highest demand for high-level STEM knowledge. *www.brookings.edu, "The Hidden Stem Economy," June 10, 2013*

- San Diego was the #10-ranked city in a Seedtable analysis of the world's most active cities for start-up companies, as reported by Statista. *www.statista.com, "San Francisco Has the Most Active Start-Up Scene," August 21, 2013*

- The business website 24/7 Wall Street drew on Brookings Institution research on 50 advanced industries to identify the proportion of workers in the nation's largest metropolitan areas that were employed in jobs requiring knowledge in the science, technology, engineering, or math (STEM) fields. The San Diego metro area was #10. *247wallst.com, "15 Cities with the Most High-Tech Jobs," March 13, 2015*

- Based on metro area social media reviews, the employment opinion group Glassdoor surveyed 50 of the largest U.S. metro areas on measures including compensation and benefits, satisfaction with management, business outlook, and number of employers hiring. The San Diego metro area was ranked #6 in overall employee satisfaction. *www.glassdoor.com, "Employment Satisfaction Report Card by City," June 13, 2014*

- In a survey of economic confidence in the nation's 50 largest metropolitan areas conducted January–December 2014, the San Diego metro area placed #20, according to Gallup's 2014 Economic Confidence Index. *Gallup, "San Jose and San Francisco Lead in Economic Confidence," March 19, 2015*

- Using data from the Council for Community and Economic Research's 2013 Annual Report, NerdWallet ranked the 100 U.S. cities with the most expensive cost of living. Cities in California and in the Northeast topped the list. Of the cities with the highest cost of living, San Diego ranked #20. *NerdWallet.com, "Most Expensive Cities in America," June 4, 2014*

- The Brookings Institution ranked the 50 largest cities in the U.S. based on income inequality. San Diego was ranked #32. (#1 = greatest ineqality). Criteria: the cities were ranked based on the "95/20 ratio," a figure representing the income at which a household earns more than 95 percent of all other households, divided by the income at which a household earns more than only 20 percent of all other households. *Brookings Institution, "Income Inequality in America's 50 Largest Cities, 2007-2013," March 17, 2015*

- San Diego was ranked #27 out of 100 metro areas in terms of economic performance (#1 = best) during the recession and recovery from trough quarter through the second quarter of 2013. Criteria: percent change in employment; percentage point change in unemployment rate; percent change in gross metropolitan product; percent change in House Price Index. *Brookings Institution, MetroMonitor: Tracking Economic Recession and Recovery in America's 100 Largest Metropolitan Areas, September 2013*

- Payscale.com ranked the 20 largest metro areas in terms of wage growth. The San Diego metro area ranked #1. Criteria: private-sector wage growth between the 1st quarter of 2014 and the 1st quarter of 2015. *PayScale, "Wage Trends by Metro Area," 1st Quarter, 2015*

- For its annual survey of the "Most Expensive U.S. Cities to Live In," Kiplinger applied Cost of Living Index statistics developed by the Council for Community and Economic Research to U.S. Census Bureau population and median household income data for cities with populations above 50,000. In the resulting ranking, San Diego ranked #10. *Kiplinger.com, "Most Expensive U.S. Cities to Live In," May 2014*

- San Diego was identified as one of the happiest cities for young professionals by *CareerBliss.com*, an online community for career advancement. The city ranked #5. Criteria: more than 45,000 young professionals were asked to rate key factors that affect workplace happiness including: work-life balance; compensation; company culture; overall work environment; company reputation; relationships with managers and co-workers; opportunities for growth; job resources; daily tasks; job autonomy. Young professionals are defined as having less than 10 years of work experience. *CareerBliss.com, "Happiest Cities for Young Professionals," April 26, 2013*

- The San Diego metro area appeared on the Milken Institute "2013 Best Performing Cities" list. Rank: #22 out of 200 large metro areas. Criteria: job growth; wage and salary growth; high-tech output growth. *Milken Institute, "Best-Performing Cities 2014," January 2015*

- *Forbes* ranked the 200 most populous metro areas to determine the nation's "Best Places for Business and Careers." The San Diego metro area was ranked #70. Criteria: costs (business and living); job growth (past and projected); income growth; educational attainment (college and high school); projected economic growth; cultural and recreational opportunities; net migration patterns; number of highly ranked colleges. *Forbes, "The Best Places for Business and Careers 2014," July 23, 2014*

Culture/Performing Arts Rankings

- San Diego was selected as one of America's top cities for the arts. The city ranked #17 in the big city (population 500,000 and over) category. Criteria: readers' top choices for arts travel destinations based on the richness and variety of visual arts sites, activities and events. *American Style, "2012 Top 25 Arts Destinations," June 2012*

Dating/Romance Rankings

- A *Cosmopolitan* magazine article surveyed the gender balance and other factors to arrive at a list of the best and worst cities for women to meet single guys. San Diego was #2 among the best for single women looking for dates. *www.cosmopolitan.com, "Working the Ratio," October 1, 2013*

- *Forbes* reports that the San Diego metro area made Rent.com's Best Cities for Newlyweds survey for 2013, based on Bureau of Labor Statistics and Census Bureau data on number of married couples, percentage of families with children under age six, average annual income, cost of living, and availability of rentals. *www.forbes.com, "The 10 Best Cities for Newlyweds to Live and Work In," May 30, 2013*

- Of the 100 U.S. cities surveyed by *Men's Health* in its quest to identify the nation's best cities for dating and forming relationships, San Diego was ranked #3 for online dating (#1 = best). *Men's Health, "The Best and Worst Cities for Online Dating," January 30, 2013*

- San Diego was selected as one of America's best cities for singles by the readers of *Travel + Leisure* in their annual "America's Favorite Cities" survey. The city was ranked #11 out of 20. Criteria included good-looking locals, cool shopping, and hipster-magnet coffee bars. *Travel + Leisure, "America's Best Cities for Singles," January 23, 2015*

- San Diego was selected as one of the best cities for single women by *Rent.com*. Criteria: high single male-to-female ratio. *Rent.com, "Top Cities for Single Women," March 7, 2013*

- San Diego was selected as one of the best cities for newlyweds by *Rent.com*. The city ranked #8 of 10. Criteria: cost of living; availability of rental inventory; annual mean wages; percentage of married couples; percentage of children under the age of six. *Rent.com, "10 Best Cities for Newlyweds," May 10, 2013*

- San Diego was selected as one of "America's Best Cities for Dating" by *Yahoo! Travel*. Criteria: high proportion of singles; excellent dating venues and/or stunning natural settings. *Yahoo! Travel, "America's Best Cities for Dating," February 7, 2012*

Education Rankings

- The San Diego metro area was selected as one of the world's most inventive cities by *Forbes*. The area was ranked #2 out of 15. Criteria: patent applications per capita. *Forbes, "World's 15 Most Inventive Cities," July 9, 2013*

- The San Diego metro area was selected as one of America's most innovative cities" by *The Business Insider*. The metro area was ranked #17 out of 20. Criteria: patents per capita. *The Business Insider, "The 20 Most Innovative Cities in the U.S.," February 1, 2013*

- Personal finance website *WalletHub* analyzed the 150 largest U.S. metropolitan statistical areas to determine where the most educated Americans are choosing to settle. Criteria: educational attainment; percentage of workers with jobs in computer, engineering, and science fields; quality and size of each metro area's universities. San Diego was ranked #21 (#1 = most educated city). *www.WalletHub.com, "2014's Most and Least Educated Cities*

- San Diego was selected as one of America's most literate cities. The city ranked #31 out of the 77 largest U.S. cities. Criteria: number of booksellers; library resources; Internet resources; educational attainment; periodical publishing resources; newspaper circulation. *Central Connecticut State University, "America's Most Literate Cities, 2014," April 8, 2015*

Environmental Rankings

- The San Diego metro area came in at #129 for the relative comfort of its climate on Sperling's list of "chill cities," as measured by the Sperling Heat Index. All 361 metro areas are included. Criteria included daytime high temperatures, nighttime low temperatures, dew point, and relative humidity at the high temperatures. *www.bertsperling.com, "Sperling's Chill Cities," July 18, 2013*

- Sperling's BestPlaces assessed 379 metropolitan areas of the United States for the likelihood of dangerously extreme weather events or earthquakes. In general the Southeast and South-Central regions have the highest risk of weather extremes and earthquakes, while the Pacific Northwest enjoys the lowest risk. Of the least risky metropolitan areas, the San Diego metro area was ranked #128. *www.bestplaces.net, "Safest Places from Natural Disasters," April 2011*

- The U.S. Environmental Protection Agency (EPA) released a list of large U.S. metropolitan areas with the most ENERGY STAR certified buildings in 2014. The San Diego metro area was ranked #17 out of 25. *U.S. Environmental Protection Agency, "Top Cities With the Most ENERGY STAR Certified Buildings in 2014," March 25, 2015*

Food/Drink Rankings

- *Men's Health* ranked 100 major U.S. cities in terms of alcohol intoxication. San Diego ranked #89 (#1 = most sober).Criteria: binge drinking; alcohol-related traffic accidents, arrests, and fatalities. *Men's Health, "The Drunkest Cities in America," November 19, 2013*

- San Diego was identified as one of the most vegetarian-friendly cities in America by GrubHub.com, the nation's largest food ordering service. The city ranked #3 out of 10. Criteria: percentage of vegetarian restaurants. *GrubHub.com, "Top Vegetarian-Friendly Cities," July 18, 2012*

- San Diego was selected as one of America's best cities for hamburgers by the readers of *Travel + Leisure* in their annual America's Favorite Cities survey. The city was ranked #6 out of 10. *Travel + Leisure, "America's Best Burger Cities," August 25, 2013*

- PETCO Park (San Diego Padres) was selected as one of PETA's "Top 10 Vegetarian-Friendly Major League Ballparks" for 2013. The park ranked #9. *People for the Ethical Treatment of Animals, "Top 10 Vegetarian-Friendly Major League Ballparks," June 12, 2013*

Health/Fitness Rankings

- Analysts who tracked obesity rates in the nation's largest metro areas (those with populations above one million) found that the San Diego metro area was one of the ten major metros where residents were least likely to be obese, defined as a BMI score of 30 or above. *www.gallup.com, "Boulder, Colo., Residents Still Least Likely to Be Obese," April 4, 2014*

- Analysts who tracked obesity rates in 189 of the nation's metro areas found that the San Diego metro area was one of the ten communities where residents were least likely to be obese, defined as a BMI score of 30 or above. *www.gallup.com, "Boulder, Colo., Residents Still Least Likely to Be Obese," April 4, 2014*

- For each of the 50 most populous metro areas in the United States, the American College of Sports Medicine's American Fitness Index evaluated infrastructure, community assets, and policies that encourage healthy and fit lifestyles, including preventive health behaviors, levels of chronic disease conditions, health care access, and community resources and policies that support physical activity. The San Diego metro area ranked #14 for "community fitness." Personal health indicators were considered as well as community and environmental indicators. *www.americanfitnessindex.org, "ACSM American Fitness Index Health and Community Fitness Status of the 50 Largest Metropolitan Areas," May 2013*

- The San Diego metro area was identified as one of the worst cities for bed bugs in America by pest control company Orkin. The area ranked #26 out of 50 based on the number of bed bug treatments Orkin performed from January to December 2013. *Orkin, "Chicago Tops Bed Bug Cities List for Second Year in a Row," January 16, 2014*

- San Diego was selected as one of the 25 fittest cities in America by *Men's Fitness Online*. It ranked #8 out of America's 50 largest cities. Criteria: fitness centers and sport stores; nutrition; sports participation; TV viewing; overweight/sedentary; junk food; air quality; geography; commute; parks and open space; city recreational facilities; access to healthcare; motivation; mayor and city initiatives; state obesity initiatives. *Men's Fitness, "The Fittest and Fattest Cities in America," March 5, 2012*

- San Diego was identified as a "2013 Spring Allergy Capital." The area ranked #97 out of 100. Three groups of factors were used to identify the most severe cities for people with allergies during the spring season: annual pollen levels; medicine utilization; access to board-certified allergists. *Asthma and Allergy Foundation of America, "Spring Allergy Capitals 2013"*

- San Diego was identified as a "2013 Fall Allergy Capital." The area ranked #91 out of 100. Three groups of factors were used to identify the most severe cities for people with allergies during the fall season: annual pollen levels; medicine utilization; access to board-certified allergists. *Asthma and Allergy Foundation of America, "Fall Allergy Capitals 2013"*

- San Diego was identified as a "2013 Asthma Capital." The area ranked #73 out of the nation's 100 largest metropolitan areas. Twelve factors were used to identify the most challenging places to live for people with asthma: estimated prevalence; self-reported prevalence; crude death rate for asthma; annual pollen score; annual air quality; public smoking laws; number of board-certified asthma specialists; school inhaler access laws; rescue medication use; controller medication use; uninsured rate; poverty rate. *Asthma and Allergy Foundation of America, "Asthma Capitals 2013"*

- *Men's Health* ranked 100 major U.S. cities in terms of the best and worst cities for men. San Diego ranked #14. Criteria: thirty-three data points were examined covering health, fitness, and quality of life. *Men's Health, "The Best & Worst Cities for Men 2014," December 6, 2013*

- San Diego was selected as one of the best metropolitan areas for hospital care in America by *HealthGrades.com*. The rankings are based on a comprehensive study of patient death and complication rates in the nation's nearly 5,000 hospitals. Hospitals performing in the top 5% nationwide across 26 different medical procedures and diagnoses were identified. *HealthGrades.com* then ranked cities by the highest percentage of these Distinguished Hospitals for Clinical Excellence™. The San Diego metro area ranked #29. *HealthGrades.com, "America's Top 50 Cities for Hospital Care," January 21, 2012*

- The San Diego metro area appeared in the 2013 Gallup-Healthways Well-Being Index. The area ranked #36 out of 189. The Gallup-Healthways Well-Being Index score is an average of six sub-indexes, which individually examine life evaluation, emotional health, work environment, physical health, healthy behaviors, and access to basic necessities. Results are based on telephone interviews conducted as part of the Gallup-Healthways Well-Being Index survey January 2–December 29, 2012, and January 2–December 30, 2013, with a random sample of 531,630 adults, aged 18 and older, living in metropolitan areas in the 50 U.S. states and the District of Columbia. *Gallup-Healthways, "State of American Well-Being," March 25, 2014*

- The San Diego metro area was identified as one of "America's Most Stressful Cities" by *Sperling's BestPlaces*. The metro area ranked #21 out of 50. Criteria: unemployment rate; suicide rate; commute time; mental health; poor rest; alcohol use; violent crime rate; property crime rate; cloudy days annually. *Sperling's BestPlaces, www.BestPlaces.net, "Stressful Cities 2012"*

Pet Rankings

- San Diego was selected as one of the best cities for dogs by real estate website Estately.com. The city was ranked #2. Criteria: weather; walkability; yard sizes; dog activities; meetup groups; availability of dogsitters. *Estately.com, "17 Best U.S. Cities for Dogs," May 14, 2013*

Real Estate Rankings

- Using data from the housing-market research firm RealtyTrac, Yahoo! Finance researchers listed the housing markets in which housing affordability is deteriorating most, factoring in interest rates as well as median home prices. The San Diego metro area was among the least affordable housing markets according to the percentage difference in the income required to buy a home in December 2013 as opposed to in December 2012. *news.yahoo.com, "10 Cities Where Ordinary People Can No Longer Afford Homes," March 5, 2014*

- The San Diego metro area was identified as one of the nations's 20 hottest housing markets in 2015. Criteria: listing views relative to the number of listings. The area ranked #8. *Realtor.com, "These Are the 20 Hottest Housing Markets in the U.S. Right Now," April 8, 2015*

- The San Diego metro area was identified as one of the nation's 20 hottest housing markets in 2015.Criteria: median number of days homes were spending on the market in March 2015. The area ranked #10. *Realtor.com, "These Are the 20 Hottest Housing Markets in the U.S. Right Now," April 8, 2015*

- San Diego was ranked #86 out of 275 metro areas in terms of house price appreciation in 2014 (#1 = highest rate). *Federal Housing Finance Agency, House Price Index, 4th Quarter 2014*

- The San Diego metro area was identified as one of the 10 best condo markets in the U.S. in 2014. The area ranked #9 out of 66 markets with a price appreciation of 13.2%. Criteria: year-over-year change of median sales price of existing apartment condo-coop homes between the 4th quarter of 2013 and the 4th quarter of 2014. *National Association of Realtors®, Median Sales Price of Existing Apartment Condo-Coop Homes for Metropolitan Areas, 4th Quarter 2014*

- The San Diego metro area was identified as one of the 20 least affordable housing markets in the U.S. in 2014. The area ranked #6 out of 178 markets. Criteria: whether or not a typical family could qualify for a mortgage loan on a typical home. *National Association of Realtors®, Affordability Index of Existing Single-Family Homes for Metropolitan Areas, 2014*

- San Diego was ranked #217 out of 226 metro areas in terms of housing affordability in 2014 by the National Association of Home Builders (#1 = most affordable). The NAHB-Wells Fargo Housing Opportunity Index (HOI) for a given area is defined as the share of homes sold in that area that would have been affordable to a family earning the local median income, based on standard mortgage underwriting criteria. *National Association of Home Builders®, NAHB-Wells Fargo Housing Opportunity Index, 4th Quarter 2014*

Safety Rankings

- In search of the nation's safest cities, Business Insider looked at the FBI's preliminary Uniform Crime Report, excluding localities with fewer than 200,000 residents. To judge by its low murder, rape, and robbery data, San Diego made the 20 safest cities list, at #20. *www.businessinsider.com, "The 20 Safest Cities in America," July 25, 2013*

- Symantec, in partnership with Sperling's BestPlaces, ranked the 50 largest cities in the U.S. in terms of their vulnerability to cybercrime. The city ranked #12. Criteria: number of cyberattacks and potential infections; level of Internet access; expenditures on smartphones and computer hardware/software; wireless hotspots; broadband connectivity; Internet usage; online purchases. *Symantec, "Riskiest Online Cities of 2012" February 15, 2012*

- Allstate ranked the 200 largest cities in America in terms of driver safety. San Diego ranked #112. Allstate researchers analyzed internal property damage claims over a two-year period from January 2011 to December 2012. A weighted average of the two-year numbers determined the annual percentages. *Allstate, "Allstate America's Best Drivers Report, 2014"*

- San Diego was identified as one of the safest large cities in America by CQ Press. All 32 cities with populations of 500,000 or more that reported crime rates in 2012 for murder, rape, robbery, aggravated assault, burglary, and motor vehicle thefts were ranked. The city ranked #4 out of the top 10. *CQ Press, City Crime Rankings 2014*

- The National Insurance Crime Bureau ranked 380 metro areas in the U.S. in terms of per capita rates of vehicle theft. The San Diego metro area ranked #26 (#1 = highest rate). Criteria: number of vehicle theft offenses per 100,000 inhabitants in 2012. *National Insurance Crime Bureau, "Hot Spots 2012," June 26, 2013*

Seniors/Retirement Rankings

- In addition to affordability, good employment prospects, low crime rates, and pleasant climate, the Huffington Post considered community strength, recreational opportunities, and other markers of stress-free living in its search for the best retirement destinations for those who appreciate peace and quiet. Among those on the list was San Diego. *www.huffingtonpost.com, "Best Places to Retire: 10 Most Relaxing U.S. Cities to Enjoy Your Golden Years," April 2, 2013*

- From its Best Cities for Successful Aging indexes, the Milken Institute generated rankings for metropolitan areas, weighing data in eight categories—health care, wellness, living arrangements, transportation, financial characteristics, education and employment opportunities, community engagement, and overall livability. The San Diego metro area was ranked #37 overall in the large metro area category. *Milken Institute, "Best Cities for Successful Aging, 2014"*

- San Diego was identified as one of the most popular places to retire by *Topretirements.com*. The list reflects the 100 cities (out of 900+ total cities reviewed) that visitors to the website are most interested in for retirement. *Topretirements.com, "Most Popular Places to Retire for 2014," February 25, 2014*

Sports/Recreation Rankings

- The sports site Bleacher Report named San Diego as one of the nation's top ten golf cities. Criteria included the concentration of public and private golf courses in a given city and the favored locations of PGA tour events. *BleacherReport.com, "Top 10 U.S. Cities for Golf," September 16, 2013*

- San Diego was selected as one of "America's Most Miserable Sports Cities" by *Forbes*. The city was ranked #5. Criteria: postseason losses; years since last title; ratio of cumulative seasons to championships won. Contenders were limited to cities with at least 75 total seasons of NFL, NBA, NHL and MLB play. *Forbes, "America's Most Miserable Sports Cities," July 31, 2013*

Women/Minorities Rankings

- *Women's Health* examined U.S. cities and identified the 100 best cities for women. San Diego was ranked #18. Criteria: 30 categories were examined from obesity and breast cancer rates to commuting times and hours spent working out. *Women's Health, "Best Cities for Women 2012"*

- San Diego was selected as one of the best cities for young Latinos in 2013 by mun2, a national cable television broadcast network. The city ranked #12. Criteria: U.S. cities with populations over 500,000 residents were evaluated on the following criteria: number of young latinos; jobs; friendliness; cost of living; fun. *mun2.tv, "Best Cities for Young Latinos 2013*

Miscellaneous Rankings

- The watchdog site Charity Navigator conducts an annual study of charities in the nation's major markets both to analyze statistical differences in their financial, accountability, and transparency practices and to track year-to-year variations in individual communities. The San Diego metro area was ranked #1 among the 30 metro markets. *www.charitynavigator.org, "Metro Market Study 2013," June 1, 2013*

- Business Insider reports on the 2013 Trick-or-Treat Index compiled by the real estate site Zillow, which used its own Home Value Index and Walk Score along with population density and local crime stats to determine that San Diego ranked #12 for "how much candy it gives out versus how far kids have to walk to get it." Zillow also zeroes in on the best neighborhoods in its top 20 cities. *www.businessinsider.com, "These Are the Best Cities for Trick-or-Treating," October 15, 2013*

- Mars Chocolate North America, the makers of COMBOS®, in partnership with Sperling's BestPlaces, ranked 50 major metro areas in terms of their "manliness." The San Diego metro area ranked #50. Criteria: number of professional sports teams; number of nearby NASCAR tracks and racing events; manly lifestyle; concentration of manly retail stores; manly occupations per capita; salty snack sales; "Board of Manliness" rankings. *Mars Chocolate North America, "America's Manliest Cities 2012"*

- The National Alliance to End Homelessness ranked the 100 most populous metro areas in terms the rate of homelessness. The San Diego metro area ranked #16. Criteria: number of homeless people per 10,000 population in 2011. *National Alliance to End Homelessness, The State of Homelessness in America 2012*

Business Environment

CITY FINANCES

City Government Finances

Component	2012 ($000)	2012 ($ per capita)
Total Revenues	3,140,374	2,402
Total Expenditures	3,155,570	2,414
Debt Outstanding	3,433,704	2,626
Cash and Securities[1]	8,277,836	6,332

*Note: (1) Cash and security holdings of a government at the close of its fiscal
year, including those of its dependent agencies, utilities, and liquor stores.
Source: U.S Census Bureau, State & Local Government Finances 2012*

City Government Revenue by Source

Source	2012 ($000)	2012 ($ per capita)
General Revenue		
From Federal Government	217,963	167
From State Government	148,634	114
From Local Governments	3,405	3
Taxes		
Property	587,625	449
Sales and Gross Receipts	508,942	389
Personal Income	0	0
Corporate Income	0	0
Motor Vehicle License	0	0
Other Taxes	25,674	20
Current Charges	816,713	625
Liquor Store	0	0
Utility	408,119	312
Employee Retirement	115,571	88

Source: U.S Census Bureau, State & Local Government Finances 2012

City Government Expenditures by Function

Function	2012 ($000)	2012 ($ per capita)	2012 (%)
General Direct Expenditures			
Air Transportation	2,658	2	0.1
Corrections	0	0	0.0
Education	0	0	0.0
Employment Security Administration	0	0	0.0
Financial Administration	28,379	22	0.9
Fire Protection	171,141	131	5.4
General Public Buildings	57,966	44	1.8
Governmental Administration, Other	40,499	31	1.3
Health	13,157	10	0.4
Highways	227,386	174	7.2
Hospitals	0	0	0.0
Housing and Community Development	464,784	356	14.7
Interest on General Debt	147,445	113	4.7
Judicial and Legal	34,046	26	1.1
Libraries	92,090	70	2.9
Parking	2,945	2	0.1
Parks and Recreation	233,587	179	7.4
Police Protection	300,172	230	9.5
Public Welfare	0	0	0.0
Sewerage	256,309	196	8.1
Solid Waste Management	41,451	32	1.3
Veterans' Services	0	0	0.0
Liquor Store	0	0	0.0
Utility	427,713	327	13.6
Employee Retirement	366,364	280	11.6

Source: U.S Census Bureau, State & Local Government Finances 2012

DEMOGRAPHICS

Population Growth

Area	1990 Census	2000 Census	2010 Census	Population Growth (%) 1990-2000	Population Growth (%) 2000-2010
City	1,111,048	1,223,400	1,307,402	10.1	6.9
MSA[1]	2,498,016	2,813,833	3,095,313	12.6	10.0
U.S.	248,709,873	281,421,906	308,745,538	13.2	9.7

Note: (1) Figures cover the San Diego-Carlsbad-San Marcos, CA Metropolitan Statistical Area—see Appendix B for areas included
Source: U.S. Census Bureau, Census 1990, 2000, 2010

Household Size

Area	One	Two	Three	Four	Five	Six	Seven or More	Average Household Size
City	29.0	32.4	15.7	12.8	5.7	2.5	1.9	2.73
MSA[1]	24.9	32.7	16.8	14.3	6.5	2.8	2.1	2.86
U.S.	27.7	33.6	15.7	13.1	6.0	2.3	1.5	2.64

Note: (1) Figures cover the San Diego-Carlsbad, CA Metropolitan Statistical Area—see Appendix B for areas included
Source: U.S. Census Bureau, 2011-2013 American Community Survey 3-Year Estimates

Race

Area	White Alone[2] (%)	Black Alone[2] (%)	Asian Alone[2] (%)	AIAN[3] Alone[2] (%)	NHOPI[4] Alone[2] (%)	Other Race Alone[2] (%)	Two or More Races (%)
City	64.1	6.7	16.7	0.6	0.4	6.7	4.8
MSA[1]	71.0	5.1	11.2	0.7	0.5	6.8	4.7
U.S.	73.9	12.6	5.0	0.8	0.2	4.7	2.9

Note: (1) Figures cover the San Diego-Carlsbad, CA Metropolitan Statistical Area—see Appendix B for areas included; (2) Alone is defined as not being in combination with one or more other races; (3) American Indian and Alaska Native; (4) Native Hawaiian and Other Pacific Islander
Source: U.S. Census Bureau, 2011-2013 American Community Survey 3-Year Estimates

Hispanic or Latino Origin

Area	Total (%)	Mexican (%)	Puerto Rican (%)	Cuban (%)	Other (%)
City	29.9	26.4	0.7	0.2	2.6
MSA[1]	32.7	29.1	0.7	0.2	2.7
U.S.	16.9	10.8	1.6	0.6	3.8

Note: Persons of Hispanic or Latino origin can be of any race; (1) Figures cover the San Diego-Carlsbad, CA Metropolitan Statistical Area—see Appendix B for areas included
Source: U.S. Census Bureau, 2011-2013 American Community Survey 3-Year Estimates

Segregation

Type	1990	2000	2010	2010 Rank[2]	1990-2000	1990-2010	2000-2010
Black/White	58.1	55.5	51.2	68	-2.6	-6.9	-4.3
Asian/White	47.9	49.9	48.2	13	2.0	0.3	-1.7
Hispanic/White	45.2	50.6	49.6	25	5.4	4.4	-1.0

Note: All figures cover the Metropolitan Statistical Area—see Appendix B for areas included; Figures are based on an analysis of 1990, 2000, and 2010 Census Decennial Census tract data by William H. Frey, Brookings Institution and the University of Michigan Social Science Data Analysis Network. In this analysis all racial groups (whites, blacks, and asians) are non-Hispanic members of those races. Hispanics are shown as a separate category;
(1) Segregation Indices are Dissimilarity Indices that measure the degree to which the minority group is distributed differently than whites across census tracts. They range from 0 (complete integration) to 100 (complete segregation) where the value indicates the percentage of the minority group that needs to move to be distributed exactly like whites; (2) Ranges from 1 (most segregated) to 102 (least segregated); n/a not available.
Source: www.CensusScope.org

Ancestry

Area	German	Irish	English	American	Italian	Polish	French[2]	Scottish	Dutch
City	9.3	7.6	5.9	3.2	4.1	1.8	2.1	1.4	0.9
MSA[1]	10.6	8.3	8.3	3.2	4.4	1.8	2.2	1.5	1.0
U.S.	14.9	10.8	8.0	7.4	5.5	3.0	2.7	1.7	1.4

Note: Figures are the percentage of the total population reporting a particular ancestry. The nine most commonly reported ancestries in the U.S. are shown. Figures include multiple ancestries (e.g. if a person reported being Irish and Italian, they were included in both columns); (1) Figures cover the San Diego-Carlsbad, CA Metropolitan Statistical Area—see Appendix B for areas included; (2) Excludes Basque
Source: U.S. Census Bureau, 2011-2013 American Community Survey 3-Year Estimates

Foreign-Born Population

Area	Percent of Population Born in								
	Any Foreign Country	Mexico	Asia	Europe	Carribean	South America	Central America[2]	Africa	Canada
City	26.3	9.3	12.0	2.3	0.2	0.6	0.5	0.9	0.4
MSA[1]	23.4	10.6	8.7	1.9	0.2	0.5	0.5	0.6	0.4
U.S.	13.0	3.7	3.8	1.5	1.2	0.9	1.0	0.6	0.3

Note: (1) Figures cover the San Diego-Carlsbad, CA Metropolitan Statistical Area—see Appendix B for areas included; (2) Excludes Mexico.
Source: U.S. Census Bureau, 2011-2013 American Community Survey 3-Year Estimates

Marital Status

Area	Never Married	Now Married[2]	Separated	Widowed	Divorced
City	40.7	42.8	2.0	4.6	10.0
MSA[1]	35.9	47.0	1.9	5.0	10.3
U.S.	32.7	48.1	2.2	6.0	11.0

Note: Figures are percentages and cover the population 15 years of age and older; (1) Figures cover the San Diego-Carlsbad, CA Metropolitan Statistical Area—see Appendix B for areas included; (2) Excludes separated
Source: U.S. Census Bureau, 2011-2013 American Community Survey 3-Year Estimates

Disability Status

Area	All Ages	Under 18 Years Old	18 to 64 Years Old	65 Years and Over
City	8.7	3.0	6.2	34.9
MSA[1]	9.5	2.8	7.0	35.7
U.S.	12.3	4.1	10.2	36.3

Note: Figures show percent of the civilian noninstitutionalized population that reported having a disability. Disability status is determined from from six types of difficulty: vision, hearing, cognitive, ambulatory, self-care, and independent living. For children under 5 years old, hearing and vision difficulty are used to determine disability status. For children between the ages of 5 and 14, disability status is determined from hearing, vision, cognitive, ambulatory, and self-care difficulties. For people aged 15 years and older, they are considered to have a disability if they have difficulty with any one of the six difficulty types; (1) Figures cover the San Diego-Carlsbad, CA Metropolitan Statistical Area—see Appendix B for areas included.
Source: U.S. Census Bureau, 2011-2013 American Community Survey 3-Year Estimates

Age

Area	Percent of Population									Median Age
	Under Age 5	Age 5–19	Age 20–34	Age 35–44	Age 45–54	Age 55–64	Age 65–74	Age 75–84	Age 85+	
City	6.4	18.1	27.5	13.5	13.0	10.4	6.2	3.4	1.6	33.6
MSA[1]	6.6	19.2	24.3	13.3	13.5	11.1	6.4	3.7	1.9	34.9
U.S.	6.4	19.9	20.7	12.9	14.1	12.3	7.6	4.2	1.9	37.4

Note: (1) Figures cover the San Diego-Carlsbad, CA Metropolitan Statistical Area—see Appendix B for areas included
Source: U.S. Census Bureau, 2011-2013 American Community Survey 3-Year Estimates

Gender

Area	Males	Females	Males per 100 Females
City	674,569	662,953	101.8
MSA[1]	1,595,328	1,579,985	101.0
U.S.	154,451,010	159,410,713	96.9

Note: (1) Figures cover the San Diego-Carlsbad, CA Metropolitan Statistical Area—see Appendix B for areas included
Source: U.S. Census Bureau, 2011-2013 American Community Survey 3-Year Estimates

Religious Groups by Family

Area	Catholic	Baptist	Non-Den.	Methodist[2]	Lutheran	LDS[3]	Pentecostal	Presbyterian[4]	Muslim[5]	Judaism
MSA[1]	25.9	2.0	4.8	1.1	1.0	2.3	1.0	0.9	0.7	0.5
U.S.	19.1	9.3	4.0	4.0	2.3	2.0	1.9	1.6	0.8	0.7

Note: Figures are the number of adherents as a percentage of the total population; (1) Figures cover the San Diego-Carlsbad-San Marcos, CA Metropolitan Statistical Area—see Appendix B for areas included; (2) Methodist/Pietist; (3) Latter Day Saints; (4) Reformed; (5) Figures are estimates
Source: Association of Statisticians of American Religious Bodies, 2010 U.S. Religion Census: Religious Congregations & Membership Study

Religious Groups by Tradition

Area	Catholic	Evangelical Protestant	Mainline Protestant	Other Tradition	Black Protestant	Orthodox
MSA[1]	25.9	9.8	2.4	5.2	0.4	0.3
U.S.	19.1	16.2	7.3	4.3	1.6	0.3

Note: Figures are the number of adherents as a percentage of the total population; (1) Figures cover the San Diego-Carlsbad-San Marcos, CA Metropolitan Statistical Area—see Appendix B for areas included
Source: Association of Statisticians of American Religious Bodies, 2010 U.S. Religion Census: Religious Congregations & Membership Study

ECONOMY

Gross Metropolitan Product

Area	2012	2013	2014	2015	Rank[2]
MSA[1]	177.4	182.7	190.8	201.8	17

Note: Figures are in billions of dollars; (1) Figures cover the San Diego-Carlsbad, CA Metropolitan Statistical Area—see Appendix B for areas included; (2) Rank is based on 2015 data and ranges from 1 to 363
Source: The U.S. Conference of Mayors, U.S. Metro Economies: GMP and Employment 2013-2015, June 2014

Economic Growth

Area	2010-12 (%)	2013 (%)	2014 (%)	2015 (%)	Rank[2]
MSA[1]	2.4	1.8	2.7	3.8	47
U.S.	2.1	2.0	2.3	3.2	–

Note: Figures are real gross metropolitan product (GMP) growth rates and represent annual average percent change; (1) Figures cover the San Diego-Carlsbad, CA Metropolitan Statistical Area—see Appendix B for areas included; (2) Rank is based on 2015 data and ranges from 1 to 363
Source: The U.S. Conference of Mayors, U.S. Metro Economies: GMP and Employment 2013-2015, June 2014

Metropolitan Area Exports

Area	2008	2009	2010	2011	2012	2013	Rank[2]
MSA[1]	15,855.9	13,418.6	16,464.3	17,410.5	17,183.3	17,885.5	19

Note: Figures are in millions of dollars; (1) Figures cover the San Diego-Carlsbad, CA Metropolitan Statistical Area—see Appendix B for areas included; (2) Rank is based on 2013 data and ranges from 1 to 387
Source: U.S. Department of Commerce, International Trade Administration, Office of Trade & Industry Information, Manufacturing & Services, data extracted April 3, 2015

Building Permits

Area	Single-Family			Multi-Family			Total		
	2013	2014	Pct. Chg.	2013	2014	Pct. Chg.	2013	2014	Pct. Chg.
City	821	712	-13.3	4,487	2,031	-54.7	5,308	2,743	-48.3
MSA[1]	2,565	2,487	-3.0	5,699	4,388	-23.0	8,264	6,875	-16.8
U.S.	620,802	634,597	2.2	370,020	411,766	11.3	990,822	1,046,363	5.6

Note: (1) Figures cover the San Diego-Carlsbad, CA Metropolitan Statistical Area—see Appendix B for areas included; Figures represent new, privately-owned housing units authorized (unadjusted data); All permit data are based on estimates with imputation.
Source: U.S. Census Bureau, Manufacturing, Mining, and Construction Statistics, Building Permits, 2013, 2014

Bankruptcy Filings

Area	Business Filings			Nonbusiness Filings		
	2013	2014	% Chg.	2013	2014	% Chg.
San Diego County	467	378	-19.1	11,822	9,544	-19.3
U.S.	33,212	26,983	-18.8	1,038,720	909,812	-12.4

Note: Business filings include Chapter 7, Chapter 11, Chapter 12, and Chapter 13; Nonbusiness filings include Chapter 7, Chapter 11, and Chapter 13
Source: Administrative Office of the U.S. Courts, Business and Nonbusiness Bankruptcy, County Cases Commenced by Chapter of the Bankruptcy Code, During the 12- Month Period Ending December 31, 2013 and Business and Nonbusiness Bankruptcy, County Cases Commenced by Chapter of the Bankruptcy Code, During the 12- Month Period Ending December 31, 2014

Housing Vacancy Rates

Area	Gross Vacancy Rate[2] (%)			Year-Round Vacancy Rate[3] (%)			Rental Vacancy Rate[4] (%)			Homeowner Vacancy Rate[5] (%)		
	2012	2013	2014	2012	2013	2014	2012	2013	2014	2012	2013	2014
MSA[1]	9.1	7.8	7.7	8.6	7.4	7.3	7.1	5.5	4.8	1.4	1.2	1.3
U.S.	13.8	13.6	13.4	10.8	10.7	10.4	8.7	8.3	7.6	2.0	2.0	1.9

Note: (1) Figures cover the San Diego-Carlsbad, CA Metropolitan Statistical Area—see Appendix B for areas included; (2) The percentage of the total housing inventory that is vacant; (3) The percentage of the housing inventory (excluding seasonal units) that is year-round vacant; (4) The percentage of rental inventory that is vacant for rent; (5) The percentage of homeowner inventory that is vacant for sale
Source: U.S. Census Bureau, Housing Vacancies and Homeownership Annual Statistics: 2014

INCOME

Income

Area	Per Capita ($)	Median Household ($)	Average Household ($)
City	32,658	63,258	86,740
MSA[1]	30,031	61,382	83,467
U.S.	27,884	52,176	72,897

Note: (1) Figures cover the San Diego-Carlsbad, CA Metropolitan Statistical Area—see Appendix B for areas included
Source: U.S. Census Bureau, 2011-2013 American Community Survey 3-Year Estimates

Household Income Distribution

Area	Percent of Households Earning							
	Under $15,000	$15,000 -24,999	$25,000 -34,999	$35,000 -49,999	$50,000 -74,999	$75,000 -99,000	$100,000 -149,999	$150,000 and up
City	10.8	8.8	8.3	12.1	17.0	12.8	15.6	14.7
MSA[1]	11.1	8.9	9.0	12.4	17.3	12.6	15.2	13.5
U.S.	13.0	10.9	10.3	13.6	17.9	11.9	12.7	9.6

Note: (1) Figures cover the San Diego-Carlsbad, CA Metropolitan Statistical Area—see Appendix B for areas included
Source: U.S. Census Bureau, 2011-2013 American Community Survey 3-Year Estimates

Poverty Rate

Area	All Ages	Under 18 Years Old	18 to 64 Years Old	65 Years and Over
City	15.7	21.7	14.8	9.5
MSA[1]	15.1	19.4	14.6	9.3
U.S.	15.9	22.4	14.8	9.5

Note: Figures are percentage of people whose income during the past 12 months was below the poverty level;
(1) Figures cover the San Diego-Carlsbad, CA Metropolitan Statistical Area—see Appendix B for areas included
Source: U.S. Census Bureau, 2011-2013 American Community Survey 3-Year Estimates

EMPLOYMENT

Labor Force and Employment

Area	Civilian Labor Force			Workers Employed		
	Dec. 2013	Dec. 2014	% Chg.	Dec. 2013	Dec. 2014	% Chg.
City	690,196	695,388	0.8	645,688	659,330	2.1
MSA[1]	1,541,159	1,551,683	0.7	1,436,717	1,467,071	2.1
U.S.	154,408,000	155,521,000	0.7	144,423,000	147,190,000	1.9

Note: Data is not seasonally adjusted and covers workers 16 years of age and older; (1) Figures cover the San Diego-Carlsbad, CA Metropolitan Statistical Area—see Appendix B for areas included
Source: Bureau of Labor Statistics, Local Area Unemployment Statistics

Unemployment Rate

Area	2014											
	Jan.	Feb.	Mar.	Apr.	May	Jun.	Jul.	Aug.	Sep.	Oct.	Nov.	Dec.
City	6.8	6.8	6.7	5.8	5.8	6.1	6.5	6.3	5.8	5.7	5.7	5.2
MSA[1]	7.2	7.1	7.1	6.1	6.1	6.4	6.9	6.6	6.1	6.0	6.0	5.5
U.S.	7.0	7.0	6.8	5.9	6.1	6.3	6.5	6.3	5.7	5.5	5.5	5.4

Note: Data is not seasonally adjusted and covers workers 16 years of age and older; (1) Figures cover the San Diego-Carlsbad, CA Metropolitan Statistical Area—see Appendix B for areas included
Source: Bureau of Labor Statistics, Local Area Unemployment Statistics

Employment by Occupation

Occupation Classification	City (%)	MSA[1] (%)	U.S. (%)
Management, Business, Science, and Arts	45.0	40.1	36.2
Natural Resources, Construction, and Maintenance	5.7	7.9	9.0
Production, Transportation, and Material Moving	7.1	8.3	12.1
Sales and Office	22.5	23.9	24.4
Service	19.6	19.9	18.3

Note: Figures cover employed civilians 16 years of age and older; (1) Figures cover the San Diego-Carlsbad, CA Metropolitan Statistical Area—see Appendix B for areas included
Source: U.S. Census Bureau, 2011-2013 American Community Survey 3-Year Estimates

Employment by Industry

Sector	MSA[1]		U.S.
	Number of Employees	Percent of Total	Percent of Total
Construction	63,400	4.6	4.4
Education and Health Services	191,100	13.9	15.5
Financial Activities	70,600	5.1	5.7
Government	236,600	17.2	15.8
Information	24,900	1.8	2.0
Leisure and Hospitality	178,800	13.0	10.3
Manufacturing	97,400	7.1	8.7
Mining and Logging	400	<0.1	0.6
Other Services	54,100	3.9	4.0
Professional and Business Services	237,200	17.2	13.8
Retail Trade	152,400	11.1	11.4
Transportation, Warehousing, and Utilities	27,500	2.0	3.9
Wholesale Trade	44,000	3.2	4.2

Note: Figures are non-farm employment as of December 2014. Figures are not seasonally adjusted and include workers 16 years of age and older; (1) Figures cover the San Diego-Carlsbad, CA Metropolitan Statistical Area—see Appendix B for areas included
Source: Bureau of Labor Statistics, Current Employment Statistics, Employment, Hours, and Earnings

Occupations with Greatest Projected Employment Growth: 2012 – 2022

Occupation[1]	2012 Employment	2022 Projected Employment	Numeric Employment Change	Percent Employment Change
Personal Care Aides	386,900	587,200	200,300	51.8
Combined Food Preparation and Serving Workers, Including Fast Food	286,000	362,400	76,400	26.7
Retail Salespersons	468,400	528,100	59,700	12.7
Laborers and Freight, Stock, and Material Movers, Hand	270,500	322,300	51,800	19.1
Waiters and Waitresses	246,100	290,300	44,200	18.0
Registered Nurses	254,500	297,400	42,900	16.9
General and Operations Managers	253,800	295,700	41,900	16.5
Secretaries and Administrative Assistants, Except Legal, Medical, and Executive	212,800	250,100	37,300	17.5
Cashiers	357,800	392,600	34,800	9.7
Cooks, Restaurant	116,900	150,600	33,700	28.8

Note: Projections cover California; (1) Sorted by numeric employment change
Source: www.projectionscentral.com, State Occupational Projections, 2012–2022 Long-Term Projections

Fastest Growing Occupations: 2012 – 2022

Occupation[1]	2012 Employment	2022 Projected Employment	Numeric Employment Change	Percent Employment Change
Economists	3,100	5,100	2,000	64.5
Helpers—Brickmasons, Blockmasons, Stonemasons, and Tile and Marble Setters	2,900	4,600	1,700	58.6
Brickmasons and Blockmasons	5,100	8,000	2,900	56.9
Insulation Workers, Floor, Ceiling, and Wall	1,600	2,500	900	56.3
Stonemasons	1,100	1,700	600	54.5
Insulation Workers, Mechanical	1,100	1,700	600	54.5
Personal Care Aides	386,900	587,200	200,300	51.8
Foresters	1,200	1,800	600	50.0
Terrazzo Workers and Finishers	1,100	1,600	500	45.5
Mechanical Door Repairers	1,100	1,600	500	45.5

Note: Projections cover California; (1) Sorted by percent employment change and excludes occupations with numeric employment change less than 100
Source: www.projectionscentral.com, State Occupational Projections, 2012–2022 Long-Term Projections

Average Wages

Occupation	$/Hr.	Occupation	$/Hr.
Accountants and Auditors	37.51	Maids and Housekeeping Cleaners	10.97
Automotive Mechanics	20.62	Maintenance and Repair Workers	19.46
Bookkeepers	19.99	Marketing Managers	70.12
Carpenters	21.74	Nuclear Medicine Technologists	37.17
Cashiers	10.98	Nurses, Licensed Practical	24.22
Clerks, General Office	15.79	Nurses, Registered	41.23
Clerks, Receptionists/Information	14.15	Nursing Assistants	13.66
Clerks, Shipping/Receiving	16.29	Packers and Packagers, Hand	11.08
Computer Programmers	40.29	Physical Therapists	43.10
Computer Systems Analysts	44.11	Postal Service Mail Carriers	25.62
Computer User Support Specialists	26.32	Real Estate Brokers	43.87
Cooks, Restaurant	11.89	Retail Salespersons	13.34
Dentists	82.71	Sales Reps., Exc. Tech./Scientific	27.73
Electrical Engineers	53.45	Sales Reps., Tech./Scientific	41.16
Electricians	31.91	Secretaries, Exc. Legal/Med./Exec.	18.46
Financial Managers	65.07	Security Guards	14.56
First-Line Supervisors/Managers, Sales	22.26	Surgeons	105.25
Food Preparation Workers	10.31	Teacher Assistants	14.30
General and Operations Managers	58.68	Teachers, Elementary School	31.60
Hairdressers/Cosmetologists	15.36	Teachers, Secondary School	35.00
Internists	98.53	Telemarketers	12.15
Janitors and Cleaners	12.96	Truck Drivers, Heavy/Tractor-Trailer	19.56
Landscaping/Groundskeeping Workers	13.22	Truck Drivers, Light/Delivery Svcs.	16.71
Lawyers	69.45	Waiters and Waitresses	12.44

Note: Wage data covers the San Diego-Carlsbad-San Marcos, CA Metropolitan Statistical Area—see Appendix B for areas included; Hourly wages for elementary/secondary school teachers and teacher assistants were calculated by the editors from annual wage data assuming a 40 hour work week; n/a not available.
Source: Bureau of Labor Statistics, Metro Area Occupational Employment and Wage Estimates, May 2014

TAXES

State Corporate Income Tax Rates

State	Tax Rate (%)	Income Brackets ($)	Num. of Brackets	Financial Institution Tax Rate (%)[a]	Federal Income Tax Ded.
California	8.84 (c)	Flat rate	1	10.84 (c)	No

Note: Tax rates as of January 1, 2015; (a) Rates listed are the corporate income tax rate applied to financial institutions or excise taxes based on income. Some states have other taxes based upon the value of deposits or shares; (c) Minimum tax is $800 in California, $100 in District of Columbia, $50 in North Dakota (banks), $500 in Rhode Island, $200 per location in South Dakota (banks), $100 in Utah, $250 in Vermont.
Source: Federation of Tax Administrators, "State Corporate Income Tax Rates, 2015"

State Individual Income Tax Rates

State	Tax Rate (%)	Income Brackets ($)	Num. of Brackets	Personal Exempt. ($)[1] Single	Personal Exempt. ($)[1] Dependents	Fed. Inc. Tax Ded.
California (a)	1.0 - 12.3 (f)	7,749- 519,687 (b)	9	108 (c)	333 (c)	No

Note: Tax rates as of January 1, 2015; Local- and county-level taxes are not included; n/a not applicable; (1) Married joint filers generally receive double the single exemption; (a) 17 states have statutory provision for automatically adjusting to the rate of inflation the dollar values of the income tax brackets, standard deductions, and/or personal exemptions. Massachusetts, Michigan, and Nebraska index the personal exemptiononly. Oregon does not index the income brackets for $125,000 and over. Maine has suspended indexing for 2014 and 2015; (b) For joint returns, taxes are twice the tax on half the couple's income; (c) The personal exemption takes the form of a tax credit instead of a deduction; (f) California imposes an additional 1% tax on taxable income over $1 million, making the maximum rate 13.3% over $1 million.
Source: Federation of Tax Administrators, "State Individual Income Tax Rates, 2015"

Various State and Local Tax Rates

State	State and Local Sales and Use (%)	State Sales and Use (%)	Gasoline[1] (¢/gal.)	Cigarette[2] ($/pack)	Spirits[3] ($/gal.)	Wine[4] ($/gal.)	Beer[5] ($/gal.)
California	8.0	7.50 (b)	45.39	0.87	3.30 (f)	0.20	0.20

Note: All tax rates as of January 1, 2015; (1) The American Petroleum Institute has developed a methodology for determining the average tax rate on a gallon of fuel. Rates may include any of the following: excise taxes, environmental fees, storage tank fees, other fees or taxes, general sales tax, and local taxes. In states where gasoline is subject to the general sales tax, or where the fuel tax is based on the average sale price, the average rate determined by API is sensitive to changes in the price of gasoline. States that fully or partially apply general sales taxes to gasoline: CA, CO, GA, IL, IN, MI, NY; (2) The federal excise tax of $1.0066 per pack and local taxes are not included; (3) Rates are those applicable to off-premise sales of 40% alcohol by volume (a.b.v.) distilled spirits in 750ml containers. Local excise taxes are excluded; (4) Rates are those applicable to off-premise sales of 11% a.b.v. non-carbonated wine in 750ml containers; (5) Rates are those applicable to off-premise sales of 4.7% a.b.v. beer in 12 ounce containers; (b) Three states levy mandatory, statewide, local add-on sales taxes at the state level: California (1%), Utah (1.25%), and Virginia (1%). We include these in their state sales taxes; (f) Different rates are also applicable according to alcohol content, place of production, size of container, or place purchased (on- or off-premise or onboard airlines).
Source: Tax Foundation, 2015 Facts & Figures: How Does Your State Compare?

State Business Tax Climate Index Rankings

State	Overall Rank	Corporate Tax Index Rank	Individual Income Tax Index Rank	Sales Tax Index Rank	Unemployment Insurance Tax Index Rank	Property Tax Index Rank
California	48	34	50	42	14	14

Note: The index is a measure of how each state's tax laws affect economic performance. The lower the rank, the more favorable a state's tax system is for business. States without a given tax are given a ranking of 1. The scores/rankings for the District of Columbia do not affect other states. The 2015 index represents the tax climate as of July 1, 2014.
Source: Tax Foundation, State Business Tax Climate Index 2015

COMMERCIAL REAL ESTATE

Office Market

Market Area	Inventory (sq. ft.)	Vacancy Rate (%)	Under Construction (sq. ft.)	YTD Net Absorption (sq. ft.)	Total Average Asking Rent ($/sq. ft./year)
San Diego	69,475,172	13.7	700,847	684,740	27.96
National	4,745,108,508	14.3	71,190,461	51,084,126	27.40

Source: Newmark Grubb Knight Frank, National Office Market Report, 4th Quarter 2014

Industrial/Warehouse/R&D Market

Market Area	Inventory (sq. ft.)	Vacancy Rate (%)	Under Construction (sq. ft.)	YTD Net Absorption (sq. ft.)	Total Average Asking Rent ($/sq. ft./year)
San Diego	176,436,721	6.8	0	2,660,280	9.84
National	14,238,613,765	7.2	134,387,407	185,246,438	5.64

Source: Newmark Grubb Knight Frank, National Industrial Market Report, 4th Quarter 2014

COMMERCIAL UTILITIES

Typical Monthly Electric Bills

Area	Commercial Service ($/month)		Industrial Service ($/month)	
	1,500 kWh	40 kW demand 14,000 kWh	1,000 kW demand 200,000 kWh	50,000 kW demand 32,500,000 kWh
City	344	2,729	51,722	3,472,864
Average[1]	201	1,653	26,124	2,639,743

Note: Figures are based on annualized 2014 rates; (1) Average based on 180 utilities surveyed
Source: Edison Electric Institute, Typical Bills and Average Rates Report, Summer 2014

TRANSPORTATION

Means of Transportation to Work

Area	Car/Truck/Van		Public Transportation			Bicycle	Walked	Other Means	Worked at Home
	Drove Alone	Car-pooled	Bus	Subway	Railroad				
City	74.9	9.3	3.7	0.0	0.1	0.9	3.1	1.4	6.5
MSA[1]	76.1	9.8	2.6	0.0	0.2	0.7	2.9	1.4	6.4
U.S.	76.4	9.6	2.6	1.8	0.6	0.6	2.8	1.3	4.3

Note: Figures are percentages and cover workers 16 years of age and older; (1) Figures cover the San Diego-Carlsbad, CA Metropolitan Statistical Area—see Appendix B for areas included
Source: U.S. Census Bureau, 2011-2013 American Community Survey 3-Year Estimates

Travel Time to Work

Area	Less Than 10 Minutes	10 to 19 Minutes	20 to 29 Minutes	30 to 44 Minutes	45 to 59 Minutes	60 to 89 Minutes	90 Minutes or More
City	8.5	34.7	29.0	19.7	4.0	2.5	1.6
MSA[1]	9.1	31.8	26.0	21.1	6.2	3.7	2.0
U.S.	13.3	29.7	20.9	20.2	7.7	5.7	2.6

Note: Figures are percentages and include workers 16 years old and over; (1) Figures cover the San Diego-Carlsbad, CA Metropolitan Statistical Area—see Appendix B for areas included
Source: U.S. Census Bureau, 2011-2013 American Community Survey 3-Year Estimates

Travel Time Index

Area	1985	1990	1995	2000	2005	2010	2011
Urban Area[1]	1.06	1.13	1.12	1.19	1.23	1.18	1.18
Average[2]	1.09	1.14	1.16	1.19	1.23	1.18	1.18

Note: Travel Time Index—the ratio of travel time in the peak period to the travel time at free-flow conditions. For example, a value of 1.30 indicates a 20-minute free-flow trip takes 26 minutes in the peak. Free-flow speeds (60 mph on freeways and 35 mph on principal arterials) are used as the comparison threshold; (1) Covers the San Diego CA urban area; (2) average of 498 urban areas
Source: Texas Transportation Institute, Urban Mobility Report 2012, December 2012

Public Transportation

Agency Name / Mode of Transportation	Vehicles Operated in Maximum Service	Annual Unlinked Passenger Trips (in thous.)	Annual Passenger Miles (in thous.)
San Diego Metropolitan Transit System (MTS)			
Bus (directly operated)	209	28,926.9	108,221.8
Bus (purchased transportation)	205	22,660.6	71,925.4
Commuter Bus (purchased transportation)	23	307.4	7,343.8
Demand Response (purchased transportation)	116	511.2	4,751.7
Light Rail (directly operated)	96	29,699.4	173,151.1
North San Diego County Transit District (NCTD)			
Bus (purchased transportation)	137	8,347.2	39,705.6
Commuter Rail (purchased transportation)	25	1,629.2	44,875.3
Demand Response (purchased transportation)	5	10.7	33.3
Demand Response Taxi (purchased transportation)	52	145.0	1,232.8
Hybrid Rail (purchased transportation)	6	2,000.9	18,103.0
San Diego Association of Governments (SANDAG)			
Vanpool (purchased transportation)	738	2,161.1	101,673.5

Source: Federal Transit Administration, National Transit Database, 2013

Air Transportation

Airport Name and Code / Type of Service	Passenger Airlines[1]	Passenger Enplanements	Freight Carriers[2]	Freight (lbs.)
San Diego International-Lindbergh Field (SAN)				
Domestic service (U.S. carriers - 2014)	29	8,992,800	17	135,484,335
International service (U.S. carriers - 2013)	8	100,828	1	31,759

Note: (1) Includes all U.S.-based major, minor and commuter airlines that carried at least one passenger during the year; (2) Includes all U.S.-based airlines and freight carriers that transported at least one lb. of freight during the year.
Source: Bureau of Transportation Statistics, The Intermodal Transportation Database, Air Carriers: T-100 Domestic Market (U.S. Carriers), 2014; Bureau of Transportation Statistics, The Intermodal Transportation Database, Air Carriers: T-100 International Market (U.S. Carriers), 2013

Other Transportation Statistics

Major Highways:	I-5; I-8; I-15
Amtrak Service:	Yes
Major Waterways/Ports:	San Diego Harbor

Source: Amtrak.com; Google Maps

BUSINESSES

Major Business Headquarters

Company Name	Rankings	
	Fortune[1]	Forbes[2]
Petco Animal Supplies	-	146
Qualcomm Incorporated	120	-
Sempra Energy	267	-

Note: (1) Fortune 500—companies that produce a 10-K are ranked 1 to 500 based on 2013 revenue; (2) all private companies with at least $2 billion in annual revenue through the end of their most current fiscal year are ranked 1 to 221; companies listed are headquartered in the city; dashes indicate no ranking
Source: Fortune, "Fortune 500," June 16, 2014; Forbes, "America's Largest Private Companies," November 5, 2014

Fast-Growing Businesses

According to *Inc.*, San Diego is home to nine of America's 500 fastest-growing private companies: **Multifamily Utility** (#56); **PhotoBin** (#60); **Pathway Genomics** (#173); **Tealium** (#253); **HoverCam** (#302); **Softhq** (#308); **Gold Refinery of San Diego** (#323); **Reliant Services Group** (#385); **New Venture Escrow** (#419). Criteria: must be an independent, privately-held, for-profit, U.S. corporation, proprietorship or partnership; revenues must be at least $100,000 in 2010 and $2 million in 2013; must have four-year operating/sales history. Holding companies, regulated banks, and utilities were excluded. *Inc., "America's 500 Fastest-Growing Private Companies," September 2014*

According to *Fortune*, San Diego is home to two of the 100 fastest-growing companies in the world: **Ligand Pharmaceuticals (La Jolla)** (#13); **BofI Holding** (#69). Companies were ranked by their revenue growth rate; their EPS growth rate; and their three-year annualized total return to investors for the period ending June 30, 2014. Criteria for inclusion: a company, foreign or domestic, must trade on a major U.S. stock exchange; must file quarterly reports with the SEC; must have a minimum market capitalization of $250 million; must have a stock price of at least $5 on June 30, 2014; must have been trading continuously since June 30, 2010; must have revenue and net income for the four quarters ended on or before April 30, 2014, of at least $50 million and $10 million, respectively; and must have posted a compound annual growth in revenue and earnings per share of at least 20% annually over the three years ending on or before April 30, 2014. Real estate investment trusts, limited-liability companies, limited parterships, business development companies, closed end investment firms, and companies that lost money in the quarter ending April 30, 2014 were excluded. *Fortune, "100 Fastest-Growing Companies," August 28, 2014*

According to Deloitte, San Diego is home to 18 of North America's 500 fastest-growing high-technology companies: **iboss** (#70); **TearLab Corporation** (#79); **Black Mountain Systems** (#130); **PayLease** (#154); **Arena Pharmaceuticals** (#157); **Ambit Biosciences** (#158); **DexCom** (#218); **Voxox** (#224); **TakeLessons** (#261); **Sequenom** (#283); **Mitek Systems** (#294); **Halozyme Therapeutics** (#298); **SmartDrive Systems** (#399); **Peregrine Semiconductor Corp.** (#407); **Kratos Defense & Security Solutions** (#411); **XIFIN** (#413); **RF Industries, Ltd.** (#452); **Qualcomm** (#493). Companies are ranked by percentage growth in revenue over a five-year period. Criteria for inclusion: company must be headquartered within North America;

must own proprietary intellectual property or proprietary technology that contributes to a significant portion of the company's operating revenue, or devote a significant proportion of revenues to research and development of technology; must have been in business for a minumum of five years with 2009 operating revenues of at least $50,000 USD/CD and 2013 operating revenues of at least $5 million USD/CD. *Deloitte Touche Tohmatsu, 2014 Technology Fast 500*[TM]

Minority Business Opportunity

San Diego is home to two companies which are on the *Hispanic Business* 500 list (500 largest U.S. Hispanic-owned companies based on 2012 revenue): **WSA Distributing** (#95); **Rescue Social Change Group** (#397). Companies included must show at least 51 percent ownership by Hispanic U.S. citizens, and must maintain headquarters in one of the 50 states or Washington, D.C. *Hispanic Business, "Hispanic Business 500," June 20, 2013*

San Diego is home to one company which is on the *Hispanic Business* Fastest-Growing 100 list (greatest sales growth from 2008 to 2012): **Rescue Social Change Group** (#77). Companies included must show at least 51 percent ownership by Hispanic U.S. citizens, and must maintain headquarters in one of the 50 states or Washington, D.C. In addition, companies must have minimum revenues of $200,000 for calendar year 2008. *Hispanic Business, June 20, 2013*

Minority- and Women-Owned Businesses

Group	All Firms		Firms with Paid Employees			
	Firms	Sales ($000)	Firms	Sales ($000)	Employees	Payroll ($000)
Asian	17,449	6,050,362	3,628	5,596,220	30,837	931,286
Black	4,471	415,928	365	315,648	4,011	113,382
Hispanic	16,669	2,900,814	2,376	2,375,728	17,377	429,264
Women	40,020	6,853,430	5,173	5,718,438	53,352	1,610,742
All Firms	130,519	151,762,267	32,437	146,973,850	677,509	32,704,056

Note: Figures cover firms located in the city; minority- and women-owned business are defined as firms in which the corresponding group own 51% or more of the stock or equity of the company
Source: U.S. Census Bureau, 2007 Economic Census, Survey of Business Owners (2012 Survey of Business Owners data will be released starting in June 2015)

HOTELS & CONVENTION CENTERS

Hotels/Motels

Area	5 Star		4 Star		3 Star		2 Star		1 Star		Not Rated	
	Num.	Pct.[3]	Num.	Pct.[3]	Num.	Pct.[3]	Num.	Pct.[3]	Num.	Pct.[3]	Num.	Pct.[3]
City[1]	7	1.4	42	8.7	145	29.9	227	46.8	7	1.4	57	11.8
Total[2]	166	0.9	1,264	7.0	5,718	31.8	9,340	52.0	411	2.3	1,070	6.0

Note: (1) Figures cover San Diego and vicinity; (2) Figures cover all 100 cities in this book; (3) Percentage of hotels which have a given star rating; Star ratings are determined by expedia.com and offer an indication of the general quality of a particular hotel.
Source: expedia.com, April 2, 2015

The San Diego-Carlsbad, CA metro area is home to five of the best hotels in the U.S. according to *Travel & Leisure*: **Park Hyatt Aviara Resort**; **L'Auberge Del Mar**; **Lodge at Torrey Pines**; **Rancho Valencia Resort & Spa**; **Grand Del Mar**. Criteria: service; location; rooms; food; and value. The list includes the top 236 hotels in the U.S. *Travel & Leisure, "T+L 500, The World's Best Hotels 2015"*

The San Diego-Carlsbad, CA metro area is home to one of the best hotels in the world according to *Condé Nast Traveler*: **Rancho Valencia Resort & Spa, Rancho Santa Fe**. The selections are based on editors' picks. The list includes the top 25 hotels in the U.S. *Condé Nast Traveler, "Gold List 2015, The Top Hotels in the World"*

Major Convention Centers

Name	Overall Space (sq. ft.)	Exhibit Space (sq. ft.)	Meeting Space (sq. ft.)	Meeting Rooms
San Diego Convention Center	2,600,000	615,701	204,114	72

Note: Table includes convention centers located in the San Diego-Carlsbad, CA metro area; n/a not available
Source: Original research

Living Environment

COST OF LIVING

Cost of Living Index

Composite Index	Groceries	Housing	Utilities	Trans-portation	Health Care	Misc. Goods/ Services
135.0	105.3	203.1	111.5	116.9	112.8	105.7

Note: The Cost of Living Index measures regional differences in the cost of consumer goods and services, excluding taxes and non-consumer expenditures, for professional and managerial households in the top income quintile. It is based on more than 50,000 prices covering almost 60 different items for which prices are collected three times a year by chambers of commerce, economic development organizations or university applied economic centers in each participating urban area. The numbers shown should be read as a percentage above or below the national average of 100. For example, a value of 115.4 in the groceries column indicates that grocery prices are 15.4% higher than the national average. Small differences in the index numbers should not be interpreted as significant; Figures cover the San Diego CA urban area.
Source: The Council for Community and Economic Research, ACCRA Cost of Living Index, 2014

Grocery Prices

Area[1]	T-Bone Steak ($/pound)	Frying Chicken ($/pound)	Whole Milk ($/half gal.)	Eggs ($/dozen)	Orange Juice ($/64 oz.)	Coffee ($/11.5 oz.)
City[2]	10.04	1.40	2.58	2.67	3.27	5.09
Avg.	10.40	1.37	2.40	1.99	3.46	4.27
Min.	8.48	0.93	1.37	1.30	2.83	2.99
Max.	14.20	2.44	3.62	4.02	6.42	6.96

Note: (1) Values for the local area are compared with the average, minimum and maximum values for all 308 areas in the Cost of Living Index; (2) Figures cover the San Diego CA urban area; **T-Bone Steak** *(price per pound);* **Frying Chicken** *(price per pound, whole fryer);* **Whole Milk** *(half gallon carton);* **Eggs** *(price per dozen, Grade A, large);* **Orange Juice** *(64 oz. Tropicana or Florida Natural);* **Coffee** *(11.5 oz. can, vacuum-packed, Maxwell House, Hills Bros, or Folgers).*
Source: The Council for Community and Economic Research, ACCRA Cost of Living Index, 2014

Housing and Utility Costs

Area[1]	New Home Price ($)	Apartment Rent ($/month)	All Electric ($/month)	Part Electric ($/month)	Other Energy ($/month)	Telephone ($/month)
City[2]	634,116	1,754	-	123.00	56.46	33.30
Avg.	305,838	919	181.00	93.66	73.14	27.95
Min.	183,142	480	112.00	42.06	23.42	17.16
Max.	1,358,576	3,851	594.00	180.03	440.99	40.42

Note: (1) Values for the local area are compared with the average, minimum and maximum values for all 308 areas in the Cost of Living Index; (2) Figures cover the San Diego CA urban area; **New Home Price** *(2,400 sf living area, 8,000 sf lot, in urban area with full utilities);* **Apartment Rent** *(950 sf 2 bedroom/1.5 or 2 bath, unfurnished, excluding all utilities except water);* **All Electric** *(average monthly cost for an all-electric home);* **Part Electric** *(average monthly cost for a part-electric home);* **Other Energy** *(average monthly cost for natural gas, fuel oil, coal, wood, and any other forms of energy except electricity);* **Telephone** *(price includes basic monthly rate for a private residential line plus additional local usage charges incurred by a family of four).*
Source: The Council for Community and Economic Research, ACCRA Cost of Living Index, 2014

Health Care, Transportation, and Other Costs

Area[1]	Doctor ($/visit)	Dentist ($/visit)	Optometrist ($/visit)	Gasoline ($/gallon)	Beauty Salon ($/visit)	Men's Shirt ($)
City[2]	106.91	106.67	103.63	4.08	56.71	26.86
Avg.	102.86	87.89	97.66	3.44	34.37	26.74
Min.	67.47	65.78	51.18	3.00	17.43	12.79
Max.	173.50	150.14	235.00	4.33	64.28	49.50

Note: (1) Values for the local area are compared with the average, minimum and maximum values for all 308 areas in the Cost of Living Index; (2) Figures cover the San Diego CA urban area; **Doctor** *(general practitioners routine exam of an established patient);* **Dentist** *(adult teeth cleaning and periodic oral examination);* **Optometrist** *(full vision eye exam for established adult patient);* **Gasoline** *(one gallon regular unleaded, national brand, including all taxes, cash price at self-service pump if available);* **Beauty Salon** *(woman's shampoo, trim, and blow-dry);* **Men's Shirt** *(cotton/polyester dress shirt, pinpoint weave, long sleeves).*
Source: The Council for Community and Economic Research, ACCRA Cost of Living Index, 2014

HOUSING

House Price Index (HPI)

Area	National Ranking[2]	Quarterly Change (%)	One-Year Change (%)	Five-Year Change (%)
MSA[1]	86	0.62	6.05	22.50
U.S.[3]	–	1.35	4.91	11.59

Note: The HPI is a weighted repeat sales index. It measures average price changes in repeat sales or refinancings on the same properties. This information is obtained by reviewing repeat mortgage transactions on single-family properties whose mortgages have been purchased or securitized by Fannie Mae or Freddie Mac in January 1975; (1) San Diego-Carlsbad Metropolitan Statistical Area—see Appendix B for areas included; (2) Rankings are based on annual percentage change for all metro areas containing at least 15,000 transactions over the last 10 years and ranges from 1 to 275; (3) figures based on a weighted average of Census Division estimates using a seasonally adjusted, purchase-only index; all figures are for the period ending December 31, 2014
Source: Federal Housing Finance Agency, House Price Index, February 26, 2015

Median Single-Family Home Prices

Area	2012	2013	2014p	Percent Change 2013 to 2014
MSA[1]	385.5	464.3	497.9	7.2
U.S. Average	177.2	197.4	209.0	5.9

Note: Figures are median sales prices of existing single-family homes in thousands of dollars; (p) preliminary; n/a not available; (1) San Diego-Carlsbad, CA Metropolitan Statistical Area—see Appendix B for areas included
Source: National Association of Realtors, Median Sales Price of Existing Single-Family Homes for Metropolitan Areas, 4th Quarter 2014

Qualifying Income Based on Median Sales Price of Existing Single-Family Homes

Area	With 5% Down ($)	With 10% Down ($)	With 20% Down ($)
MSA[1]	108,361	102,658	91,251
U.S. Average	45,863	43,449	38,621

Note: Figures are preliminary; Qualifying income is based on a mortgage rate of 4.0%. Monthly principal and interest payment is limited to 25% of income; n/a not available; (1) San Diego-Carlsbad, CA Metropolitan Statistical Area—see Appendix B for areas included
Source: National Association of Realtors, Qualifying Income Based on Median Sales Price of Existing Single-Family Homes for Metropolitan Areas, 4th Quarter 2014

Median Apartment Condo-Coop Home Prices

Area	2012	2013	2014p	Percent Change 2013 to 2014
MSA[1]	224.5	293.2	331.8	13.2
U.S. Average	173.7	194.9	205.1	5.2

Note: Figures are median sales prices of existing apartment condo-coop homes in thousands of dollars; (p) preliminary; n/a not available; (1) San Diego-Carlsbad, CA Metropolitan Statistical Area—see Appendix B for areas included
Source: National Association of Realtors, Median Sales Price of Existing Apartment Condo-Coop Homes for Metropolitan Areas, 4th Quarter 2014

Gross Monthly Rent

Area	Under $200	$200 -299	$300 -499	$500 -749	$750 -999	$1,000 -1,499	$1,500 and up	Median ($)
City	0.6	1.4	2.1	5.5	17.8	33.5	39.0	1,320
MSA[1]	0.6	1.5	2.3	5.2	17.5	36.8	36.1	1,282
U.S.	1.7	3.2	7.8	22.1	24.3	26.0	14.9	900

Note: Figures are percentages except for Median; Gross rent is the contract rent plus the estimated average monthly cost of utilities (electricity, gas, and water and sewer) and fuels (oil, coal, kerosene, wood, etc.) if these are paid by the renter (or paid for the renter by someone else); (1) Figures cover the San Diego-Carlsbad, CA Metropolitan Statistical Area—see Appendix B for areas included
Source: U.S. Census Bureau, 2011-2013 American Community Survey 3-Year Estimates

Homeownership Rate

Area	2007 (%)	2008 (%)	2009 (%)	2010 (%)	2011 (%)	2012 (%)	2013 (%)	2014 (%)
MSA[1]	59.6	57.1	56.4	54.4	55.2	55.4	55.0	57.4
U.S.	68.1	67.8	67.4	66.9	66.1	65.4	65.1	64.5

Note: (1) Figures cover the San Diego-Carlsbad, CA Metropolitan Statistical Area—see Appendix B for areas included
Source: U.S. Census Bureau, Housing Vacancies and Homeownership Annual Statistics: 2014

Year Housing Structure Built

Area	2010 or Later	2000 -2009	1990 -1999	1980 -1989	1970 -1979	1960 -1969	1950 -1959	1940 -1949	Before 1940	Median Year
City	0.6	10.5	11.4	18.0	22.0	13.0	12.7	4.9	6.9	1976
MSA[1]	0.6	11.9	12.3	20.0	23.7	12.6	10.8	3.8	4.3	1978
U.S.	0.9	15.0	13.9	13.8	15.8	11.0	10.9	5.4	13.3	1976

Note: Figures are percentages except for Median Year; (1) Figures cover the San Diego-Carlsbad, CA Metropolitan Statistical Area—see Appendix B for areas included
Source: U.S. Census Bureau, 2011-2013 American Community Survey 3-Year Estimates

HEALTH

Health Risk Data

Category	MSA[1] (%)	U.S. (%)
Adults aged 18–64 who have any kind of health care coverage	77.1	79.6
Adults who reported being in good or excellent health	84.2	83.1
Adults who are current smokers	10.6	19.6
Adults who are heavy drinkers[2]	8.0	6.1
Adults who are binge drinkers[3]	19.0	16.9
Adults who are overweight (BMI 25.0 - 29.9)	36.8	35.8
Adults who are obese (BMI 30.0 - 99.8)	22.3	27.6
Adults who participated in any physical activities in the past month	82.9	77.1
Adults 50+ who have ever had a sigmoidoscopy or colonoscopy	68.0	67.3
Women aged 40+ who have had a mammogram within the past two years	72.8	74.0
Men aged 40+ who have had a PSA test within the past two years	43.7	45.2
Adults aged 65+ who have had flu shot within the past year	55.1	60.1
Adults who always wear a seatbelt	n/a	93.8

Note: Data as of 2012 unless otherwise noted; n/a not available; (1) Figures cover the San Diego-Carlsbad-San Marcos, CA Metropolitan Statistical Area—see Appendix B for areas included; (2) Heavy drinkers are classified as males having more than two drinks per day or females having more than one drink per day; (3) Binge drinkers are classified as males having five or more drinks on one occasion or females having four or more drinks on one occasion
Source: Centers for Disease Control and Prevention, Behaviorial Risk Factor Surveillance System, SMART: Selected Metropolitan/Micropolitan Area Risk Trends, 2012 (Note: the CDC has discontinued this dataset but will be releasing a replacement in late 2015)

Chronic Health Indicators

Category	MSA[1] (%)	U.S. (%)
Adults who have ever been told they had a heart attack	3.2	4.5
Adults who have ever been told they had a stroke	1.7	2.9
Adults who have been told they currently have asthma	6.9	8.9
Adults who have ever been told they have arthritis	22.1	25.7
Adults who have ever been told they have diabetes[2]	9.3	9.7
Adults who have ever been told they had skin cancer	7.4	5.7
Adults who have ever been told they had any other types of cancer	5.7	6.5
Adults who have ever been told they have COPD	4.0	6.2
Adults who have ever been told they have kidney disease	2.9	2.5
Adults who have ever been told they have a form of depression	11.5	18.0

Note: Data as of 2012 unless otherwise noted; (1) Figures cover the San Diego-Carlsbad-San Marcos, CA Metropolitan Statistical Area—see Appendix B for areas included; (2) Figures do not include pregnancy-related, borderline, or pre-diabetes
Source: Centers for Disease Control and Prevention, Behaviorial Risk Factor Surveillance System, SMART: Selected Metropolitan/Micropolitan Area Risk Trends, 2012 (Note: the CDC has discontinued this dataset but will be releasing a replacement in late 2015)

Mortality Rates for the Top 10 Causes of Death in the U.S.

ICD-10[a] Sub-Chapter	ICD-10[a] Code	Age-Adjusted Mortality Rate[1] per 100,000 population	
		County[2]	U.S.
Malignant neoplasms	C00-C97	155.4	166.2
Ischaemic heart diseases	I20-I25	94.5	105.7
Other forms of heart disease	I30-I51	37.4	49.3
Chronic lower respiratory diseases	J40-J47	33.6	42.1
Organic, including symptomatic, mental disorders	F01-F09	22.9	38.1
Cerebrovascular diseases	I60-I69	32.2	37.0
Other external causes of accidental injury	W00-X59	23.3	26.9
Other degenerative diseases of the nervous system	G30-G31	38.8	25.6
Diabetes mellitus	E10-E14	19.3	21.3
Hypertensive diseases	I10-I15	18.7	19.4

Note: (a) ICD-10 = International Classification of Diseases 10th Revision; (1) Mortality rates are a three year average covering 2011-2013; (2) Figures cover San Diego County
Source: Centers for Disease Control and Prevention, National Center for Health Statistics. Compressed Mortality File 1999-2013 on CDC WONDER Online Database, released October 2014. Data are compiled from the Compressed Mortality File 1999-2013, Series 20 No. 2S, 2014.

Mortality Rates for Selected Causes of Death

ICD-10[a] Sub-Chapter	ICD-10[a] Code	Age-Adjusted Mortality Rate[1] per 100,000 population	
		County[2]	U.S.
Assault	X85-Y09	2.9	5.2
Diseases of the liver	K70-K76	11.6	13.2
Human immunodeficiency virus (HIV) disease	B20-B24	1.8	2.2
Influenza and pneumonia	J09-J18	9.6	15.4
Intentional self-harm	X60-X84	12.5	12.5
Malnutrition	E40-E46	0.6	0.9
Obesity and other hyperalimentation	E65-E68	1.7	1.8
Renal failure	N17-N19	2.8	13.1
Transport accidents	V01-V99	7.2	11.7
Viral hepatitis	B15-B19	3.4	2.2

Note: (a) ICD-10 = International Classification of Diseases 10th Revision; (1) Mortality rates are a three year average covering 2011-2013; (2) Figures cover San Diego County
Source: Centers for Disease Control and Prevention, National Center for Health Statistics. Compressed Mortality File 1999-2013 on CDC WONDER Online Database, released October 2014. Data are compiled from the Compressed Mortality File 1999-2013, Series 20 No. 2S, 2014.

Health Insurance Coverage

Area	With Health Insurance	With Private Health Insurance	With Public Health Insurance	Without Health Insurance	Population Under Age 18 Without Health Insurance
City	83.3	66.2	25.5	16.7	8.2
MSA[1]	83.2	65.4	26.6	16.8	8.4
U.S.	85.2	65.2	31.0	14.8	7.3

Note: Figures are percentages that cover the civilian noninstitutionalized population; (1) Figures cover the San Diego-Carlsbad, CA Metropolitan Statistical Area—see Appendix B for areas included
Source: U.S. Census Bureau, 2011-2013 American Community Survey 3-Year Estimates

Number of Medical Professionals

Area[1]	MDs[2]	DOs[2,3]	Dentists	Podiatrists	Chiropractors	Optometrists
Local (number)	9,523	481	2,542	126	993	508
Local (rate[4])	299.1	15.1	78.9	3.9	30.8	15.8
U.S. (rate[4])	270.0	20.2	63.1	5.7	25.2	14.9

Note: Data as of 2013 unless noted; (1) Local data covers San Diego County; (2) Data as of 2012 and includes all active, non-federal physicians; (3) Doctor of Osteopathic Medicine; (4) rate per 100,000 population
Source: U.S. Department of Health and Human Services, Health Resources and Services Administration, Bureau of Health Professions, Area Resource File (ARF) 2013-2014

Best Hospitals

According to *U.S. News*, the San Diego-Carlsbad, CA metro area is home to three of the best hospitals in the U.S.: **Scripps La Jolla Hospitals and Clinics** (8 specialties); **Scripps Mercy Hospital** (1 specialty); **UC San Diego Medical Center** (11 specialties). The hospitals listed were nationally ranked in at least one adult specialty. Only 144 hospitals nationwide were nationally ranked in one or more specialties. Seventeen hospitals in the U.S. made the Honor Roll with high scores in at least six specialties. *U.S. News Online, "America's Best Children's Hospitals 2014-15"*

According to *U.S. News*, the San Diego-Carlsbad, CA metro area is home to one of the best children's hospitals in the U.S.: **Rady Children's Hospital** (10 specialties). The hospital listed was highly ranked in at least one pediatric specialty. Eighty-nine children's hospitals in the U.S. were nationally ranked in at least one specialty. Ten children's hospitals in the U.S. made the Honor Roll with high scores in at least three specialties. *U.S. News Online, "America's Best Children's Hospitals 2014-15"*

EDUCATION

Public School District Statistics

District Name	Schls	Pupils	Pupil/ Teacher Ratio	Minority Pupils[1] (%)	Free Lunch Eligible[2] (%)	IEP[3] (%)
Del Mar Union Elementary	8	4,384	17.5	42.0	4.0	13.3
Poway Unified	37	35,196	28.2	47.6	10.1	10.8
SBC - High Tech High	5	2,276	21.4	72.9	23.0	0.0
San Diego County Office of Education	23	4,151	17.2	75.7	64.7	17.8
San Diego USD	224	130,271	19.8	76.8	55.4	11.1

Note: Table includes school districts with 2,000 or more students; (1) Percentage of students that are not non-Hispanic white; (2) Percentage of students that are eligible for the free lunch program; (3) Percentage of students that have an Individualized Education Program.
Source: U.S. Department of Education, National Center for Education Statistics, Common Core of Data, Local Education Agency (School District) Universe Survey: School Year 2012-2013; U.S. Department of Education, National Center for Education Statistics, Common Core of Data, Public Elementary/Secondary School Universe Survey: School Year 2012-2013

Best High Schools

According to *The Daily Beast*, San Diego is home to six of the best high schools in the U.S.: **Canyon Crest Academy** (#72); **Westview High School** (#127); **Torrey Pines High School** (#199); **The Preuss School UCSD (La Jolla)** (#205); **Mt. Carmel High School** (#299); **James Madison High School** (#671); *The Daily Beast* used six indicators culled from school surveys to compare public high schools in the U.S., with graduation and college acceptance rates weighed most heavily. Other criteria included: college-level courses/exams and SAT/ACT scores. *The Daily Beast, "Top High Schools 2014"*

Highest Level of Education

Area	Less than H.S.	H.S. Diploma	Some College, No Deg.	Associate Degree	Bachelor's Degree	Master's Degree	Prof. School Degree	Doctorate Degree
City	12.7	16.6	21.1	7.6	25.0	10.6	3.4	3.0
MSA[1]	14.4	19.3	22.3	9.5	21.3	8.6	2.6	2.0
U.S.	13.7	28.0	21.2	7.9	18.2	7.7	1.9	1.3

Note: Figures cover persons age 25 and over; (1) Figures cover the San Diego-Carlsbad, CA Metropolitan Statistical Area—see Appendix B for areas included
Source: U.S. Census Bureau, 2011-2013 American Community Survey 3-Year Estimates

Educational Attainment by Race

Area	High School Graduate or Higher (%)					Bachelor's Degree or Higher (%)				
	Total	White	Black	Asian	Hisp.[2]	Total	White	Black	Asian	Hisp.[2]
City	87.3	89.5	89.0	87.5	66.3	41.9	45.3	20.7	48.0	17.4
MSA[1]	85.6	86.9	89.7	87.8	64.2	34.5	35.7	21.1	45.6	14.9
U.S.	86.3	88.3	83.1	85.7	64.0	29.1	30.4	18.8	50.7	13.7

Note: Figures shown cover persons 25 years old and over; (1) Figures cover the San Diego-Carlsbad, CA Metropolitan Statistical Area—see Appendix B for areas included; (2) People of Hispanic origin can be of any race
Source: U.S. Census Bureau, 2011-2013 American Community Survey 3-Year Estimates

School Enrollment by Grade and Control

Area	Preschool (%)		Kindergarten (%)		Grades 1 - 4 (%)		Grades 5 - 8 (%)		Grades 9 - 12 (%)	
	Public	Private	Public	Private	Public	Private	Public	Private	Public	Private
City	54.5	45.5	89.9	10.1	91.9	8.1	92.1	7.9	93.7	6.3
MSA[1]	55.1	44.9	90.7	9.3	92.3	7.7	92.3	7.7	93.4	6.6
U.S.	57.7	42.3	87.9	12.1	89.9	10.1	90.0	10.0	90.7	9.3

Note: Figures shown cover persons 3 years old and over; (1) Figures cover the San Diego-Carlsbad, CA
Metropolitan Statistical Area—see Appendix B for areas included
Source: U.S. Census Bureau, 2011-2013 American Community Survey 3-Year Estimates

Average Salaries of Public School Classroom Teachers

Area	2013-14		2014-15		Percent Change 2013-14 to 2014-15	Percent Change 2004-05 to 2014-15
	Dollars	Rank[1]	Dollars	Rank[1]		
CALIFORNIA	71,396	4	72,535	4	1.59	25.9
U.S. Average	56,610	–	57,379	–	1.36	20.8

Note: (1) State rank ranges from 1 to 51 where 1 indicates highest salary.
Source: National Education Association, Rankings & Estimates: Rankings of the States 2014 and Estimates of
School Statistics 2015, March 2015

Higher Education

Four-Year Colleges			Two-Year Colleges			Medical Schools[1]	Law Schools[2]	Voc/ Tech[3]
Public	Private Non-profit	Private For-profit	Public	Private Non-profit	Private For-profit			
2	11	8	3	0	5	1	3	9

Note: Figures cover institutions located within the city limits and include main campuses only; (1) includes
schools accredited by the Liaison Committee on Medical Education and the American Osteopathic Association's
Commission on Osteopathic College Accreditation; (2) includes ABA-accredited schools, schools with
provisional ABA accreditation, and state accredited schools; (3) includes all schools with programs that are less
than 2 years.
Source: National Center for Education Statistics, Integrated Postsecondary Education System (IPEDS),
2013-14; Association of American Medical Colleges, Member List, May 1, 2015; American Osteopathic
Association, Member List, May 1, 2015; Law School Admission Council, Official Guide to ABA-Approved Law
Schools Online, May 1, 2015; Wikipedia, List of Medical Schools in the United States, May 1, 2015; Wikipedia,
List of Law Schools in the United States, May 1, 2015

According to U.S. News & World Report, the San Diego-Carlsbad, CA metro area is home to two
of the best national universities in the U.S.: **University of San Diego** (#95); **San Diego State
University** (#149). The indicators used to capture academic quality fall into a number of
categories: assessment by administrators at peer institutions; retention of students; faculty
resources; student selectivity; financial resources; alumni giving; high school counselor ratings of
colleges; and graduation rate. U.S. News & World Report, "America's Best Colleges 2015"

According to U.S. News & World Report, the San Diego-Carlsbad, CA metro area is home to one
of the top 100 law schools in the U.S.: **University of San Diego** (#71). The rankings are based on
a weighted average of 12 measures of quality: peer assessment score; assessment score by
lawyers/judges; median LSAT scores; median undergrad GPA; acceptance rate; employment rates
for graduates; placement success; bar passage rate; faculty resources; expenditures per student;
student/faculty ratio; and library resources. U.S. News & World Report, "America's Best Graduate
Schools, Law, 2016"

According to U.S. News & World Report, the San Diego-Carlsbad, CA metro area is home to one
of the top 75 business schools in the U.S.: **University of California-San Diego (Rady)** (#63).
The rankings are based on a weighted average of the following nine measures: quality assessment;
peer assessment; recruiter assessment; placement success; mean starting salary and bonus; student
selectivity; mean GMAT and GRE scores; mean undergraduate GPA; and acceptance rate. U.S.
News & World Report, "America's Best Graduate Schools, Business, 2016"

**PRESIDENTIAL
ELECTION**

2012 Presidential Election Results

Area	Obama (%)	Romney (%)	Other (%)
San Diego County	51.7	46.2	2.1
U.S.	51.0	47.2	1.8

Note: Results may not add to 100% due to rounding
Source: Dave Leip's Atlas of U.S. Presidential Elections

EMPLOYERS

Major Employers

Company Name	Industry
Barona Resort & Casino	Resort hotel
CA Dept of Housing & Comm Dev	Housing agency, government
City of San Diego	Municipal police
Elite Show Services	Help supply services
Forestry and Fire Protection, CA Dept of	Fire department, not including volunteer
Go-Staff	Temporary help service
Kaiser Foundation Hospitals	Trusts, nec
Marine Corps, United States	Marine corps
Palomar Community College District	Junior colleges
Qualcomm International	Patent buying, licensing, leasing
Risk Management Strategies	Employee programs administration
San Diego State University	Colleges and universities
Sharp Memorial Hospital	General medical and surgical hospitals
Solar Turbines Incorporated	Turbines and turbine generator sets
The Navy United States Department of	Navy
The Navy United States Department of	Medical centers
University of California, San Diego	General medical and surgical hospitals
Veterans Health Administration	Administration of veterans' affairs

Note: Companies shown are located within the San Diego-Carlsbad, CA Metropolitan Statistical Area.
Source: Hoovers.com; Wikipedia

Best Companies to Work For

Scripps Health, headquartered in San Diego, is among "The 100 Best Companies to Work For." To pick the best companies, *Fortune* partnered with the Great Place to Work Institute. Two-thirds of a company's score is based on the results of the Institute's Trust Index survey, which is sent to a random sample of employees from each company. The questions related to attitudes about management's credibility, job satisfaction, and camaraderie. The other third of the scoring is based on the company's responses to the Institute's Culture Audit, which includes detailed questions about pay and benefit programs, and a series of open-ended questions about hiring practices, internal communication, training, recognition programs, and diversity efforts. Any company that is at least five years old with more than 1,000 U.S. employees is eligible. *Fortune, "The 100 Best Companies to Work For," 2015*

Scripps Health, headquartered in San Diego, is among the "100 Best Companies for Working Mothers." Criteria: leave policies, workforce representation, benefits, child care, advancement programs, and flexibility policies. This year *Working Mother* gave particular weight to representation of women, advancement programs and flex. *Working Mother, "100 Best Companies 2014"*

Scripps Health, headquartered in San Diego, is among the "50 Best Employers for Workers Over 50." Criteria: recruiting practices; opportunities for training, education, and career development; workplace accommodations; alternative work options, such as flexible scheduling, job sharing, and phased retirement; employee health and pension benefits; and retiree benefits. Employers with at least 50 employees based in the U.S. are eligible, including for-profit companies, not-for-profit organizations, and government employers. *AARP, "2013 AARP Best Employers for Workers Over 50"*

Qualcomm; Sharp HealthCare, headquartered in San Diego, are among the "100 Best Places to Work in IT." To qualify, companies, both public and private, had to have a minimum of 50 IT employees and were selected based on average salary and bonus increases, the percentage of IT staffers promoted, IT staff turnover rates, training and development programs, and the percentage of women and minorities in IT staff and management positions. In addition, *Computerworld* looked at retention efforts, programs for recognizing and rewarding outstanding performances, and benefits such as flextime, elder care and child care, and reimbursement for college tuition and the cost of pursuing technology certifications. *Computerworld, "100 Best Places to Work in IT 2014"*

PUBLIC SAFETY

Crime Rate

Area	All Crimes	Violent Crimes				Property Crimes		
		Murder	Forcible Rape	Robbery	Aggrav. Assault	Burglary	Larceny -Theft	Motor Vehicle Theft
City	2,744.4	2.9	23.4	107.9	258.8	471.0	1,425.2	455.3
Suburbs[1]	2,392.3	1.7	19.0	86.1	209.6	410.1	1,389.7	276.2
Metro[2]	2,540.5	2.2	20.8	95.3	230.3	435.7	1,404.6	351.6
U.S.	3,098.6	4.5	25.2	109.1	229.1	610.0	1,899.4	221.3

Note: Figures are crimes per 100,000 population; (1) All areas within the metro area that are located outside the city limits; (2) Figures cover the San Diego-Carlsbad, CA Metropolitan Statistical Area—see Appendix B for areas included
Source: FBI Uniform Crime Reports, 2013

Hate Crimes

Area	Number of Quarters Reported	Number of Incidents per Bias Motivation						
		Race	Religion	Sexual Orientation	Ethnicity	Disability	Gender	Gender Identity
City	4	18	12	12	1	0	0	0
U.S.	4	2,871	1,031	1,233	655	83	18	31

Source: Federal Bureau of Investigation, Hate Crime Statistics 2013

Identity Theft Consumer Complaints

Area	Complaints	Complaints per 100,000 Population	Rank[2]
MSA[1]	2,814	87.6	96
U.S.	332,646	104.3	-

Note: (1) Figures cover the San Diego-Carlsbad, CA Metropolitan Statistical Area—see Appendix B for areas included; (2) Rank ranges from 1 to 380 where 1 indicates greatest number of identity theft complaints per 100,000 population
Source: Federal Trade Commission, Consumer Sentinel Network Data Book for January–December 2014

Fraud and Other Consumer Complaints

Area	Complaints	Complaints per 100,000 Population	Rank[2]
MSA[1]	15,025	467.9	40
U.S.	2,250,205	705.7	-

Note: (1) Figures cover the San Diego-Carlsbad, CA Metropolitan Statistical Area—see Appendix B for areas included; (2) Rank ranges from 1 to 380 where 1 indicates greatest number of identity theft complaints per 100,000 population
Source: Federal Trade Commission, Consumer Sentinel Network Data Book for January–December 2014

RECREATION

Culture

Dance[1]	Theatre[1]	Instrumental Music[1]	Vocal Music[1]	Series and Festivals	Museums and Art Galleries[2]	Zoos and Aquariums[3]
7	16	8	6	9	95	2

Note: (1) Professional perfoming groups; (2) Based on organizations with SIC code 8412; (3) AZA-accredited
Source: The Grey House Performing Arts Directory, 2015-16; Association of Zoos & Aquariums, AZA Member Zoos & Aquariums, April 2015; www.AccuLeads.com, April 2015

Professional Sports Teams

Team Name	League	Year Established
San Diego Chargers	National Football League (NFL)	1961
San Diego Padres	Major League Baseball (MLB)	1969

Note: Includes teams located in the San Diego-Carlsbad, CA Metropolitan Statistical Area.
Source: Wikipedia, Major Professional Sports Teams of the United States and Canada, April 2015

CLIMATE

Average and Extreme Temperatures

Temperature	Jan	Feb	Mar	Apr	May	Jun	Jul	Aug	Sep	Oct	Nov	Dec	Yr.
Extreme High (°F)	88	88	93	98	96	101	95	98	111	107	97	88	111
Average High (°F)	65	66	66	68	69	72	76	77	77	74	71	66	71
Average Temp. (°F)	57	58	59	62	64	67	71	72	71	67	62	58	64
Average Low (°F)	48	50	52	55	58	61	65	66	65	60	53	49	57
Extreme Low (°F)	29	36	39	44	48	51	55	58	51	43	38	34	29

Note: Figures cover the years 1948-1990
Source: National Climatic Data Center, International Station Meteorological Climate Summary, 9/96

Average Precipitation/Snowfall/Humidity

Precip./Humidity	Jan	Feb	Mar	Apr	May	Jun	Jul	Aug	Sep	Oct	Nov	Dec	Yr.
Avg. Precip. (in.)	1.9	1.4	1.7	0.8	0.2	0.1	Tr	0.1	0.2	0.4	1.2	1.4	9.5
Avg. Snowfall (in.)	Tr	0	0	0	0	0	0	0	0	0	0	Tr	Tr
Avg. Rel. Hum. 7am (%)	70	72	73	72	73	77	79	79	78	74	69	68	74
Avg. Rel. Hum. 4pm (%)	57	58	59	59	63	66	65	66	65	63	60	58	62

Note: Figures cover the years 1948-1990; Tr = Trace amounts (<0.05 in. of rain; <0.5 in. of snow)
Source: National Climatic Data Center, International Station Meteorological Climate Summary, 9/96

Weather Conditions

Temperature			Daytime Sky			Precipitation		
10°F & below	32°F & below	90°F & above	Clear	Partly cloudy	Cloudy	0.01 inch or more precip.	0.1 inch or more snow/ice	Thunder-storms
0	< 1	4	115	126	124	40	0	5

Note: Figures are average number of days per year and cover the years 1948-1990
Source: National Climatic Data Center, International Station Meteorological Climate Summary, 9/96

HAZARDOUS WASTE

Superfund Sites

San Diego has one hazardous waste site on the EPA's Superfund Final National Priorities List: **Camp Pendleton Marine Corps Base.** There are a total of 1,322 Superfund sites on the list in the U.S. *U.S. Environmental Protection Agency, Final National Priorities List, April 14, 2015*

AIR & WATER QUALITY

Air Quality Trends: Ozone

	2004	2005	2006	2007	2008	2009	2010	2011	2012	2013
MSA[1]	0.076	0.070	0.073	0.073	0.080	0.071	0.069	0.067	0.066	0.066

Note: (1) Data covers the San Diego-Carlsbad, CA Metropolitan Statistical Area—see Appendix B for areas included. The values shown are the composite ozone concentration averages among trend sites based on the highest fourth daily maximum 8-hour concentration in parts per million. These trends are based on sites having an adequate record of monitoring data during the trend period. Data from exceptional events are included.
Source: U.S. Environmental Protection Agency, Air Quality Monitoring Information, "Air Quality Trends by City, 2000-2013"

Air Quality Index

Area	Percent of Days when Air Quality was...[2]					AQI Statistics[2]	
	Good	Moderate	Unhealthy for Sensitive Groups	Unhealthy	Very Unhealthy	Maximum	Median
MSA[1]	29.9	65.2	4.7	0.3	0.0	165	58

Note: (1) Data covers the San Diego-Carlsbad, CA Metropolitan Statistical Area—see Appendix B for areas included; (2) Based on 365 days with AQI data in 2014. Air Quality Index (AQI) is an index for reporting daily air quality. EPA calculates the AQI for five major air pollutants regulated by the Clean Air Act: ground-level ozone, particle pollution (aka particulate matter), carbon monoxide, sulfur dioxide, and nitrogen dioxide. The AQI runs from 0 to 500. The higher the AQI value, the greater the level of air pollution and the greater the health concern. There are six AQI categories: "Good" AQI is between 0 and 50. Air quality is considered satisfactory; "Moderate" AQI is between 51 and 100. Air quality is acceptable; "Unhealthy for Sensitive Groups" When AQI values are between 101 and 150, members of sensitive groups may experience health effects; "Unhealthy" When AQI values are between 151 and 200 everyone may begin to experience health effects; "Very Unhealthy" AQI values between 201 and 300 trigger a health alert; "Hazardous" AQI values over 300 trigger warnings of emergency conditions (not shown).
Source: U.S. Environmental Protection Agency, Air Quality Index Report, 2014

Air Quality Index Pollutants

Area	Percent of Days when AQI Pollutant was...[2]					
	Carbon Monoxide	Nitrogen Dioxide	Ozone	Sulfur Dioxide	Particulate Matter 2.5	Particulate Matter 10
MSA[1]	0.0	5.8	41.6	0.0	48.2	4.4

Note: (1) Data covers the San Diego-Carlsbad, CA Metropolitan Statistical Area—see Appendix B for areas included; (2) Based on 365 days with AQI data in 2014. The Air Quality Index (AQI) is an index for reporting daily air quality. EPA calculates the AQI for five major air pollutants regulated by the Clean Air Act: ground-level ozone, particle pollution (also known as particulate matter), carbon monoxide, sulfur dioxide, and nitrogen dioxide. The AQI runs from 0 to 500. The higher the AQI value, the greater the level of air pollution and the greater the health concern.
Source: U.S. Environmental Protection Agency, Air Quality Index Report, 2014

Maximum Air Pollutant Concentrations: Particulate Matter, Ozone, CO and Lead

	Particulate Matter 10 (ug/m^3)	Particulate Matter 2.5 Wtd AM (ug/m^3)	Particulate Matter 2.5 24-Hr (ug/m^3)	Ozone (ppm)	Carbon Monoxide (ppm)	Lead (ug/m^3)
MSA[1] Level	214	11.1	24	0.078	7	0.01
NAAQS[2]	150	15	35	0.075	9	0.15
Met NAAQS[2]	No	Yes	Yes	No	Yes	Yes

Note: (1) Data covers the San Diego-Carlsbad, CA Metropolitan Statistical Area—see Appendix B for areas included; Data from exceptional events are included; (2) National Ambient Air Quality Standards; ppm = parts per million; ug/m^3 = micrograms per cubic meter; n/a not available.
Concentrations: Particulate Matter 10 (coarse particulate)—highest second maximum 24-hour concentration; Particulate Matter 2.5 Wtd AM (fine particulate)—highest weighted annual mean concentration; Particulate Matter 2.5 24-Hour (fine particulate)—highest 98th percentile 24-hour concentration; Ozone—highest fourth daily maximum 8-hour concentration; Carbon Monoxide—highest second maximum non-overlapping 8-hour concentration; Lead—maximum running 3-month average
Source: U.S. Environmental Protection Agency, Air Quality Monitoring Information, "Air Quality Statistics by City, 2013"

Maximum Air Pollutant Concentrations: Nitrogen Dioxide and Sulfur Dioxide

	Nitrogen Dioxide AM (ppb)	Nitrogen Dioxide 1-Hr (ppb)	Sulfur Dioxide AM (ppb)	Sulfur Dioxide 1-Hr (ppb)	Sulfur Dioxide 24-Hr (ppb)
MSA[1] Level	19	75	n/a	1	n/a
NAAQS[2]	53	100	30	75	140
Met NAAQS[2]	Yes	Yes	n/a	Yes	n/a

Note: (1) Data covers the San Diego-Carlsbad, CA Metropolitan Statistical Area—see Appendix B for areas included; Data from exceptional events are included; (2) National Ambient Air Quality Standards; ppm = parts per million; ug/m^3 = micrograms per cubic meter; n/a not available.
Concentrations: Nitrogen Dioxide AM—highest arithmetic mean concentration; Nitrogen Dioxide 1-Hr—highest 98th percentile 1-hour daily maximum concentration; Sulfur Dioxide AM—highest annual mean concentration; Sulfur Dioxide 1-Hr—highest 99th percentile 1-hour daily maximum concentration; Sulfur Dioxide 24-Hr—highest second maximum 24-hour concentration
Source: U.S. Environmental Protection Agency, Air Quality Monitoring Information, "Air Quality Statistics by City, 2013"

Drinking Water

Water System Name	Pop. Served	Primary Water Source Type	Violations[1]	
			Health Based	Monitoring/ Reporting
City of San Diego	1,326,200	Surface	0	0

Note: (1) Based on violation data from January 1, 2014 to December 31, 2014 (includes unresolved violations from earlier years)
Source: U.S. Environmental Protection Agency, Office of Ground Water and Drinking Water, Safe Drinking Water Information System (based on data extracted January 27, 2015)

San Francisco, California

Background

San Francisco is one of the most beautiful cities in the world. It is blessed with a mild climate, one of the best landlocked harbors in the world, and a strong sense of civic pride shaped by its unique history. It has been said that San Francisco is "Paris, but populated with Americans, most of them smiling."

The hilly peninsula known today as San Francisco and its bay was largely ignored by explorers during the sixteenth and seventeenth centuries. Until the 1760s, no European had seen the "Golden Gate," or the narrow strip of water leading into what was to become one of the greatest harbors in the world. However, even with the eventual discovery of that prime piece of real estate, San Francisco remained a quiet and pastoral settlement for nearly 90 years.

The discovery of gold in the Sierra Nevada foothills in 1848 changed San Francisco forever. Every hopeful adventurer from around the world docked in San Francisco, aspiring to make his fortune. San Francisco had entered its phase as a rowdy, frontier, gold-prospecting town, with plenty of bachelors, amusing themselves at the gambling houses and saloons.

When the supply of gold dwindled, many of the men went back to their native countries, but some stayed and continued to live in the ethnic neighborhoods they had created—neighborhoods that still exist today, such as Chinatown, the Italian District, and the Japan Center.

The charm of San Francisco lies in its cosmopolitan, yet cohesive, flavor. Ever mindful of its citizenry, newspapers in San Francisco range from English, Irish, Spanish, and Swiss to Chinese, Japanese, and Korean, with many community newspapers in between. In addition, the city has long been home to a significant gay community.

The San Francisco Bay Area is one of the major economic regions of the United States, with one of the highest percentages of college-educated adults in the nation, which translates into a high per-capita real income. The Bay Area is also home to 20 percent of California's environmental companies, and leads the state with the largest concentration of biotech companies. A former warehouse district in San Francisco has become the center for nearly 400 multimedia and Internet-related companies. Before the Internet crash in 2000, this industry cluster, combined with the concentration of multimedia activity in the Bay Area, had produced jobs for nearly 60,000 people. In terms of world trade, high-tech exports from the Silicon Valley area accounted for almost one-third of the nation's high-technology exports.

AT&T Park, home of the San Francisco Giants major league baseball team, was completed in 2000, and the Giants won the World Series in 2010 and again in 2012. The city offers excellent convention facilities with its Moscone Center, where a third building, Moscone West, was completed in 2003, bringing exhibit space to 770,000 square feet. The center was named for Mayor George Moscone, who championed controversial causes and who was murdered in office in 1978, along with gay activist Harvey Milk. The film, *The Times of Harvey Milk* won the 2008 Academy Award for best picture.

The Fine Arts Museums of San Francisco include the de Young, which is the city's oldest museum, and the Legion of Honor, a beautiful Beaux-arts museum that is home to Rodin's *Thinker*. In 2005, the de Young Museum reopened in a new building in Golden Gate Park, replacing an earlier structure damaged by the 1989 earthquake.

Also damaged in that quake was the main facility of the California Academy of Sciences, which oversees the Steinhart Aquarium, the Morrison Planetarium and the Natural History Museum. The California Academy of Sciences, also located in Golden Gate Park was reopened in the fall of 2008. Architect Renzo Piano designed the building to be seismically safe, green and sustainable. Dedicated to the study of art and science, the building allows outside views from nearly anywhere inside.

San Francisco is known as the "Air-Conditioned City" with cool pleasant summers and mild winters. It has greater climatic variability than any other urban area of the same size in the country. Sea fogs and associated low stratus clouds are most common in the summertime, when it is not unusual to see perched on the Golden Gate Bridge a low cloud illuminated by the sun.

Rankings

General Rankings

- The San Francisco metro area was identified as one of America's fastest-growing areas in terms of population and economy by *Forbes*. The area ranked #7 out of 20. The 100 most populous metro areas in the U.S. were evaluated on the following criteria: estimated population growth; job growth; gross metropolitan product growth; unemployment; median salaries for college-educated workers. *Forbes, "America's Fastest-Growing Cities 2015," January 27, 2015*

- Among the 50 largest U.S. cities, San Francisco placed #3 in Vocativ's "semi-exhaustive, mostly scientific" city Livability Index for people aged 35 and under. Average salary, unemployment rates, rents, and other living costs were considered, along with crime rates, weather, public transportation, access to music and sports, and "lifestyle metrics" such as the price of dinner at Buffalo Wild Wings and an ounce of high-quality weed. *vocative.com, "The Livability Index: The Best U.S. Cities for People 35 and Under," December 9, 2014*

- San Francisco was selected as one of the best places in the world to visit by *National Geographic Traveler*. The list reflects what's authentic, culturally rich, sustainable, superlative, and timely in the world of travel today. *National Geographic Traveler, "2015 Best of the World," December 2014/January 2015*

- San Francisco was selected as one of America's best cities by *Bloomberg Businessweek*. The city ranked #1 out of 50. Criteria: leisure attributes (the number of restaurants, bars, libraries, museums, professional sports teams, and park acres by population); educational attributes (public school performance, the number of colleges, and graduate degree holders); economic factors (2011 income and June and July 2012 unemployment); crime; and air quality. *Bloomberg BusinessWeek, "America's Best Cities," September 26, 2012*

- San Francisco was selected as one of "America's Favorite Cities." The city ranked #3 in the "Type of Trip: Gay-friendly Vacation" category. Respondents to an online survey were asked to rate 38 top urban destinations in the United States from a visitor's perspective. Criteria: gay-friendly. *Travel + Leisure, "America's Favorite Cities 20143"*

- San Francisco was selected as one of the "10 Best Places to Live Now" by *Men's Journal*. San Francisco ranked #5. *Men's Journal, "10 Best Places to Live Now," April 2015*

- The human resources consulting firm Mercer ranked 230 cities worldwide in terms of overall quality of life. San Francisco ranked #27. Criteria: political, social, economic, and socio-cultural factors; medical and health considerations; schools and education; public services and transportation; recreation; consumer goods; housing; and natural environment. *Mercer, "Mercer 2015 Quality of Living Survey," March 4, 2015*

- San Francisco appeared on *Travel + Leisure's* list of the ten best cities in the United States and Canada. The city was ranked #4. Criteria: activities/attractions; culture/arts; restaurants/food; people; and value. *Travel + Leisure, "The World's Best Awards 2014"*

- Based on nearly 77,000 responses, *Condé Nast Traveler* ranked its readers' favorite cities worldwide. San Francisco ranked #20. *Condé Nast Traveler, Readers' Choice Awards 2014, "Top 10 Cities in the World"*

Business/Finance Rankings

- Measuring indicators of "tolerance"—the nonjudgmental environment that "attracts open-minded and new-thinking kinds of people"— as well as concentrations of technological and economic innovators, analysts identified the most creative American metro areas. On the resulting 2012 Creativity Index, the San Francisco metro area placed #2. *www.thedailybeast.com, "Boulder, Ann Arbor, Tucson & More: 20 Most Creative U.S. Cities," June 26, 2012*

- TransUnion ranked the nation's metro areas by average credit score, calculated on the VantageScore system, developed by the three major credit-reporting bureaus—TransUnion, Experian, and Equifax. The San Francisco metro area was among the ten cities with the highest collective credit score, meaning that its residents posed the lowest average consumer credit risk. *www.usatoday.com, "Metro Areas' Average Credit Rating Revealed," February 7, 2013*

- Building on the U.S. Department of Labor's Occupational Information Network Data Collection Program, the Brookings Institution defined STEM occupations and job opportunities for STEM workers at various levels of educational attainment. The San Francisco metro area was one of the ten metro areas where workers in low-education-level STEM jobs earn the lowest relative wages. *www.brookings.edu, "The Hidden Stem Economy," June 10, 2013*

- Based on the Bureau of Labor Statistics (BLS) quarterly reports on employment and wages over fourth-quarter 2011–2012, researchers at 24/7 Wall Street listed the San Francisco metro area as the #1 metro area for wage growth. *247wallst.com, "American Cities Where Wages Are Soaring," July 15, 2013*

- San Francisco was the #1-ranked city in a Seedtable analysis of the world's most active cities for start-up companies, as reported by Statista. *www.statista.com, "San Francisco Has the Most Active Start-Up Scene," August 21, 2013*

- The business website 24/7 Wall Street drew on Brookings Institution research on 50 advanced industries to identify the proportion of workers in the nation's largest metropolitan areas that were employed in jobs requiring knowledge in the science, technology, engineering, or math (STEM) fields. The San Francisco metro area was #5. *247wallst.com, "15 Cities with the Most High-Tech Jobs," March 13, 2015*

- Based on metro area social media reviews, the employment opinion group Glassdoor surveyed 50 of the largest U.S. metro areas on measures including compensation and benefits, satisfaction with management, business outlook, and number of employers hiring. The San Francisco metro area was ranked #2 in overall employee satisfaction. *www.glassdoor.com, "Employment Satisfaction Report Card by City," June 13, 2014*

- In a survey of economic confidence in the nation's 50 largest metropolitan areas conducted January–December 2014, the San Francisco metro area placed #2, according to Gallup's 2014 Economic Confidence Index. *Gallup, "San Jose and San Francisco Lead in Economic Confidence," March 19, 2015*

- Using data from the Council for Community and Economic Research's 2013 Annual Report, NerdWallet ranked the 100 U.S. cities with the most expensive cost of living. Cities in California and in the Northeast topped the list. Of the cities with the highest cost of living, San Francisco ranked #4. *NerdWallet.com, "Most Expensive Cities in America," June 4, 2014*

- The Brookings Institution ranked the 50 largest cities in the U.S. based on income inequality. San Francisco was ranked #2. (#1 = greatest ineqality). Criteria: the cities were ranked based on the "95/20 ratio," a figure representing the income at which a household earns more than 95 percent of all other households, divided by the income at which a household earns more than only 20 percent of all other households. *Brookings Institution, "Income Inequality in America's 50 Largest Cities, 2007-2013," March 17, 2015*

- *Forbes* ranked the largest metro areas in the U.S. in terms of the "Best Cities for Young Professionals." The San Francisco metro area ranked #15 out of 15. Criteria: job growth; unemployment rate; median salary of college graduates age 24 to 34; cost of living; number of small businesses per capita; number of large companies; percentage of population 25 years of age and older with college degrees. *Forbes.com, "America's 15 Best Cities for Young Professionals," August 18, 2014*

- San Francisco was ranked #14 out of 100 metro areas in terms of economic performance (#1 = best) during the recession and recovery from trough quarter through the second quarter of 2013. Criteria: percent change in employment; percentage point change in unemployment rate; percent change in gross metropolitan product; percent change in House Price Index. *Brookings Institution, MetroMonitor: Tracking Economic Recession and Recovery in America's 100 Largest Metropolitan Areas, September 2013*

- San Francisco was identified as one of the best places for finding a job by *U.S. News & World Report*. The city ranked #10 out of 10. Criteria: strong job market. *U.S. News & World Report, "The 10 Best Cities to Find Jobs," June 17, 2013*

- Payscale.com ranked the 20 largest metro areas in terms of wage growth. The San Francisco metro area ranked #3. Criteria: private-sector wage growth between the 1st quarter of 2014 and the 1st quarter of 2015. *PayScale, "Wage Trends by Metro Area," 1st Quarter, 2015*

- For its annual survey of the "Most Expensive U.S. Cities to Live In," Kiplinger applied Cost of Living Index statistics developed by the Council for Community and Economic Research to U.S. Census Bureau population and median household income data for cities with populations above 50,000. In the resulting ranking, San Francisco ranked #3. *Kiplinger.com, "Most Expensive U.S. Cities to Live In," May 2014*

- San Francisco was identified as one of America's most frugal metro areas by *Coupons.com*. The city ranked #14 out of 25. Criteria: online coupon usage. *Coupons.com, "Top 25 Most Frugal Cities of 2013," April 10, 2014*

- San Francisco was identified as one of America's "10 Best Cities to Find Jobs" by *U.S. News & World Report*. The city ranked #10. Criteria: Bureau of labor Statistics unemployment rates; employment data from Indeed.com and juju.com. *U.S. News & World Report, "10 Best Cities to Find Jobs," June 17, 2013*

- San Francisco was identified as one of the best cities for college graduates to find work—and live. The city ranked #13 out of 15. Criteria: job availability; average salary; average rent. *CareerBuilder.com, "15 Best Cities for College Grads to Find Work—and Live," June 5, 2012*

- San Francisco was identified as one of the happiest cities for young professionals by *CareerBliss.com,* an online community for career advancement. The city ranked #2. Criteria: more than 45,000 young professionals were asked to rate key factors that affect workplace happiness including: work-life balance; compensation; company culture; overall work environment; company reputation; relationships with managers and co-workers; opportunities for growth; job resources; daily tasks; job autonomy. Young professionals are defined as having less than 10 years of work experience. *CareerBliss.com, "Happiest Cities for Young Professionals," April 26, 2013*

- The San Francisco metro area appeared on the Milken Institute "2013 Best Performing Cities" list. Rank: #1 out of 200 large metro areas. Criteria: job growth; wage and salary growth; high-tech output growth. *Milken Institute, "Best-Performing Cities 2014," January 2015*

- *Forbes* ranked the 200 most populous metro areas to determine the nation's "Best Places for Business and Careers." The San Francisco metro area was ranked #18. Criteria: costs (business and living); job growth (past and projected); income growth; educational attainment (college and high school); projected economic growth; cultural and recreational opportunities; net migration patterns; number of highly ranked colleges. *Forbes, "The Best Places for Business and Careers 2014," July 23, 2014*

- Mercer Human Resources Consulting ranked 211 urban areas worldwide in terms of cost-of-living. San Francisco ranked #74 (the lower the ranking, the higher the cost-of-living). The survey measured the comparative cost of over 200 items (such as housing, food, clothing, household goods, transportation, and entertainment) in each location. *Mercer, "2014 Cost of Living Survey," July 10, 2014*

Culture/Performing Arts Rankings

- San Francisco was selected as one of the ten best large U.S. cities in which to be a moviemaker. Of cities with a population over 400,000, the city was ranked #5. Criteria: film community; access to new films; access to equipment; cost of living; tax incentives. *MovieMaker Magazine, "Best Places to Live and Work as a Moviemaker: 2013," January 22, 2015*

- San Francisco was selected as one of America's top cities for the arts. The city ranked #4 in the big city (population 500,000 and over) category. Criteria: readers' top choices for arts travel destinations based on the richness and variety of visual arts sites, activities and events. *American Style, "2012 Top 25 Arts Destinations," June 2012*

Dating/Romance Rankings

- A *Cosmopolitan* magazine article surveyed the gender balance and other factors to arrive at a list of the best and worst cities for women to meet single guys. San Francisco was #5 among the best for single women looking for dates. *www.cosmopolitan.com, "Working the Ratio," October 1, 2013*

- CreditDonkey, a financial education website, sought out the ten best U.S. cities for newlyweds, considering the number of married couples, divorce rate, average credit score, and average number of hours worked per week in metro areas with a million or more residents. The San Francisco metro area placed #9. *www.creditdonkey.com, "Study: Best Cities for Newlyweds," November 30, 2013*

- San Francisco took the #6 spot on NerdWallet's list of best cities for singles wanting to date, based on the availability of singles; "date-friendliness," as determined by a city's walkability and the number of bars and restaurants per thousand residents; and the affordability of dating in terms of the cost of movie tickets, pizza, and wine for two. *www.nerdwallet.com, "Best Cities for Singles," February 2, 2015*

- Of the 100 U.S. cities surveyed by *Men's Health* in its quest to identify the nation's best cities for dating and forming relationships, San Francisco was ranked #5 for online dating (#1 = best). *Men's Health, "The Best and Worst Cities for Online Dating," January 30, 2013*

- San Francisco ranked #9 among cities congenial to singles, according to Kiplinger, which searched for "dating scenes as financially attractive as they are romantically promising." High percentages of unmarried people, above-average household incomes, and cost-of-living factors determined the rankings. *Kiplinger.com, "10 Best Cities for Singles," February 2014*

- San Francisco was selected as one of America's best cities for singles by the readers of *Travel + Leisure* in their annual "America's Favorite Cities" survey. The city was ranked #19 out of 20. Criteria included good-looking locals, cool shopping, and hipster-magnet coffee bars. *Travel + Leisure, "America's Best Cities for Singles," January 23, 2015*

- San Francisco was selected as one of the best cities for post grads by *Rent.com*. The city ranked #4 of 10. Criteria: millenial population; jobs per capita; unemployment rate; median rent; number of bars and restaurants; access to nightlife and entertainment. *Rent.com, "Top 10 Best Cities for Post Grads," April 3, 2015*

- San Francisco was selected as one of "America's Best Cities for Dating" by *Yahoo! Travel*. Criteria: high proportion of singles; excellent dating venues and/or stunning natural settings. *Yahoo! Travel, "America's Best Cities for Dating," February 7, 2012*

Education Rankings

- The San Francisco metro area was selected as one of the world's most inventive cities by *Forbes*. The area was ranked #3 out of 15. Criteria: patent applications per capita. *Forbes, "World's 15 Most Inventive Cities," July 9, 2013*

- Based on a Brookings Institution study, *24/7 Wall St.* identified the ten U.S. metropolitan areas with the most average patent filings per million residents between 2007 and 2011. San Francisco ranked #8. *24/7 Wall St., "America's Most Innovative Cities," February 1, 2013*

- The San Francisco metro area was selected as one of America's most innovative cities" by *The Business Insider*. The metro area was ranked #8 out of 20. Criteria: patents per capita. *The Business Insider, "The 20 Most Innovative Cities in the U.S.," February 1, 2013*

- *Fast Company* magazine measured six key components of "smart" cities and three "drivers" for each component to reveal the top ten "Smartest Cities in North America." By these complex metrics, San Francisco ranked #2. *Fastcoexist.com, "The Top 10 Smartest Cities in North America," November 15, 2013*

- *Reader's Digest* analyzed data for 120 U.S. cities to arrive at a list of "America's 10 Sharpest Cities." Researchers looked at education level, eating and exercise habits, health conditions, and sociability factors calculated to build and maintain mental alertness into the upper decades of life. San Francisco ranked #1 on the list. *Reader's Digest, "America's 10 Sharpest Cities," October 2012*

- San Francisco was identified as one of America's "smartest" metropolitan areas by *The Business Journals*. The area ranked #7 out of 10. Criteria: percentage of adults (25 and older) with high school diplomas, bachelor's degrees and graduate degrees. *The Business Journals, "Where the Brainpower Is: Exclusive U.S. Rankings, Insights," February 27, 2014*

- Personal finance website *WalletHub* analyzed the 150 largest U.S. metropolitan statistical areas to determine where the most educated Americans are choosing to settle. Criteria: educational attainment; percentage of workers with jobs in computer, engineering, and science fields; quality and size of each metro area's universities. San Francisco was ranked #14 (#1 = most educated city). *www.WalletHub.com, "2014's Most and Least Educated Cities*

- San Francisco was selected as one of America's most literate cities. The city ranked #8 out of the 77 largest U.S. cities. Criteria: number of booksellers; library resources; Internet resources; educational attainment; periodical publishing resources; newspaper circulation. *Central Connecticut State University, "America's Most Literate Cities, 2014," April 8, 2015*

Environmental Rankings

- The San Francisco metro area came in at #28 for the relative comfort of its climate on Sperling's list of "chill cities," as measured by the Sperling Heat Index. All 361 metro areas are included. Criteria included daytime high temperatures, nighttime low temperatures, dew point, and relative humidity at the high temperatures. *www.bertsperling.com, "Sperling's Chill Cities," July 18, 2013*

- Sperling's BestPlaces assessed 379 metropolitan areas of the United States for the likelihood of dangerously extreme weather events or earthquakes. In general the Southeast and South-Central regions have the highest risk of weather extremes and earthquakes, while the Pacific Northwest enjoys the lowest risk. Of the least risky metropolitan areas, the San Francisco metro area was ranked #75. *www.bestplaces.net, "Safest Places from Natural Disasters," April 2011*

- The U.S. Environmental Protection Agency (EPA) released a list of large U.S. metropolitan areas with the most ENERGY STAR certified buildings in 2014. The San Francisco metro area was ranked #5 out of 25. *U.S. Environmental Protection Agency, "Top Cities With the Most ENERGY STAR Certified Buildings in 2014," March 25, 2015*

Food/Drink Rankings

- According to Fodor's Travel, San Francisco placed #5 among the best U.S. cities for food-truck cuisine. *www.fodors.com, "America's Best Food Truck Cities," December 20, 2013*

- *Men's Health* ranked 100 major U.S. cities in terms of alcohol intoxication. San Francisco ranked #35 (#1 = most sober).Criteria: binge drinking; alcohol-related traffic accidents, arrests, and fatalities. *Men's Health, "The Drunkest Cities in America," November 19, 2013*

- San Francisco was identified as one of the most vegetarian-friendly cities in America by GrubHub.com, the nation's largest food ordering service. The city ranked #7 out of 10. Criteria: percentage of vegetarian restaurants. *GrubHub.com, "Top Vegetarian-Friendly Cities," July 18, 2012*

- AT&T Park (San Francisco Giants) was selected as one of PETA's "Top 10 Vegetarian-Friendly Major League Ballparks" for 2013. The park ranked #4. *People for the Ethical Treatment of Animals, "Top 10 Vegetarian-Friendly Major League Ballparks," June 12, 2013*

Health/Fitness Rankings

- Analysts who tracked obesity rates in the nation's largest metro areas (those with populations above one million) found that the San Francisco metro area was one of the ten major metros where residents were least likely to be obese, defined as a BMI score of 30 or above. *www.gallup.com, "Boulder, Colo., Residents Still Least Likely to Be Obese," April 4, 2014*

- For each of the 50 most populous metro areas in the United States, the American College of Sports Medicine's American Fitness Index evaluated infrastructure, community assets, and policies that encourage healthy and fit lifestyles, including preventive health behaviors, levels of chronic disease conditions, health care access, and community resources and policies that support physical activity. The San Francisco metro area ranked #4 for "community fitness." Personal health indicators were considered as well as community and environmental indicators. *www.americanfitnessindex.org, "ACSM American Fitness Index Health and Community Fitness Status of the 50 Largest Metropolitan Areas," May 2013*

- *Business Insider* reported Trulia's analysis of the 100 largest U.S. metro areas to identify the nation's best cities for weight loss, based on healthful food options, access to outdoor activities, weight-loss centers, gyms, and opportunities to bike or walk to work. San Francisco ranked #1. *Businessinsider.com, "These Are the Best US Cities for Weight loss," January 17, 2013*

- San Francisco was identified as one of the 10 most walkable cities in the U.S. by Walk Score, a Seattle-based service that rates the convenience and transit access of 10,000 neighborhoods in 3,000 cities. The area ranked #2 out of the 50 largest U.S. cities. Walk Score measures walkability by analyzing hundreds of walking routes to nearby amenities. Walk Score also measures pedestrian friendliness by analyzing population density and road metrics such as block length and intersection density. *WalkScore.com, March 20, 2014*

- The San Francisco metro area was identified as one of the worst cities for bed bugs in America by pest control company Orkin. The area ranked #19 out of 50 based on the number of bed bug treatments Orkin performed from January to December 2013. *Orkin, "Chicago Tops Bed Bug Cities List for Second Year in a Row," January 16, 2014*

- San Francisco was identified as one of 15 cities with the highest increase in bed bug activity in the U.S. by pest control provider Terminix. The city ranked #12.Criteria: cities with the largest percentage gains in bed bug customer calls from January–May 2013 compared to the same time period in 2012. *Terminix, "Cities with Highest Increases in Bed Bug Activity," July 9, 2013*

- San Francisco was selected as one of the 25 fittest cities in America by *Men's Fitness Online*. It ranked #2 out of America's 50 largest cities. Criteria: fitness centers and sport stores; nutrition; sports participation; TV viewing; overweight/sedentary; junk food; air quality; geography; commute; parks and open space; city recreational facilities; access to healthcare; motivation; mayor and city initiatives; state obesity initiatives. *Men's Fitness, "The Fittest and Fattest Cities in America," March 5, 2012*

- San Francisco was identified as a "2013 Spring Allergy Capital." The area ranked #84 out of 100. Three groups of factors were used to identify the most severe cities for people with allergies during the spring season: annual pollen levels; medicine utilization; access to board-certified allergists. *Asthma and Allergy Foundation of America, "Spring Allergy Capitals 2013"*

- San Francisco was identified as a "2013 Fall Allergy Capital." The area ranked #88 out of 100. Three groups of factors were used to identify the most severe cities for people with allergies during the fall season: annual pollen levels; medicine utilization; access to board-certified allergists. *Asthma and Allergy Foundation of America, "Fall Allergy Capitals 2013"*

- San Francisco was identified as a "2013 Asthma Capital." The area ranked #100 out of the nation's 100 largest metropolitan areas. Twelve factors were used to identify the most challenging places to live for people with asthma: estimated prevalence; self-reported prevalence; crude death rate for asthma; annual pollen score; annual air quality; public smoking laws; number of board-certified asthma specialists; school inhaler access laws; rescue medication use; controller medication use; uninsured rate; poverty rate. *Asthma and Allergy Foundation of America, "Asthma Capitals 2013"*

- *Men's Health* ranked 100 major U.S. cities in terms of the best and worst cities for men. San Francisco ranked #10. Criteria: thirty-three data points were examined covering health, fitness, and quality of life. *Men's Health, "The Best & Worst Cities for Men 2014," December 6, 2013*

- San Francisco was selected as one of the best metropolitan areas for hospital care in America by *HealthGrades.com*. The rankings are based on a comprehensive study of patient death and complication rates in the nation's nearly 5,000 hospitals. Hospitals performing in the top 5% nationwide across 26 different medical procedures and diagnoses were identified. *HealthGrades.com* then ranked cities by the highest percentage of these Distinguished Hospitals for Clinical Excellence™. The San Francisco metro area ranked #49. *HealthGrades.com, "America's Top 50 Cities for Hospital Care," January 21, 2012*

- The San Francisco metro area appeared in the 2013 Gallup-Healthways Well-Being Index. The area ranked #9 out of 189. The Gallup-Healthways Well-Being Index score is an average of six sub-indexes, which individually examine life evaluation, emotional health, work environment, physical health, healthy behaviors, and access to basic necessities. Results are based on telephone interviews conducted as part of the Gallup-Healthways Well-Being Index survey January 2–December 29, 2012, and January 2–December 30, 2013, with a random sample of 531,630 adults, aged 18 and older, living in metropolitan areas in the 50 U.S. states and the District of Columbia. *Gallup-Healthways, "State of American Well-Being," March 25, 2014*

- The San Francisco metro area was identified as one of "America's Most Stressful Cities" by *Sperling's BestPlaces*. The metro area ranked #28 out of 50. Criteria: unemployment rate; suicide rate; commute time; mental health; poor rest; alcohol use; violent crime rate; property crime rate; cloudy days annually. *Sperling's BestPlaces, www.BestPlaces.net, "Stressful Cities 2012*

Pet Rankings

- San Francisco was selected as one of the best cities for dogs by real estate website Estately.com. The city was ranked #5. Criteria: weather; walkability; yard sizes; dog activities; meetup groups; availability of dogsitters. *Estately.com, "17 Best U.S. Cities for Dogs," May 14, 2013*

Real Estate Rankings

- Using data from the housing-market research firm RealtyTrac, Yahoo! Finance researchers listed the housing markets in which housing affordability is deteriorating most, factoring in interest rates as well as median home prices. The San Francisco metro area was among the least affordable housing markets according to the percentage difference in the income required to buy a home in December 2013 as opposed to in December 2012. *news.yahoo.com, "10 Cities Where Ordinary People Can No Longer Afford Homes," March 5, 2014*

- The San Francisco metro area was identified as one of the nation's 20 hottest housing markets in 2015.Criteria: median number of days homes were spending on the market in March 2015. The area ranked #2. *Realtor.com, "These Are the 20 Hottest Housing Markets in the U.S. Right Now," April 8, 2015*

- San Francisco was ranked #11 out of 275 metro areas in terms of house price appreciation in 2014 (#1 = highest rate). *Federal Housing Finance Agency, House Price Index, 4th Quarter 2014*

- The San Francisco metro area was identified as one of the 20 least affordable housing markets in the U.S. in 2014. The area ranked #4 out of 178 markets. Criteria: whether or not a typical family could qualify for a mortgage loan on a typical home. *National Association of Realtors®, Affordability Index of Existing Single-Family Homes for Metropolitan Areas, 2014*

- San Francisco was ranked #226 out of 226 metro areas in terms of housing affordability in 2014 by the National Association of Home Builders (#1 = most affordable). The NAHB-Wells Fargo Housing Opportunity Index (HOI) for a given area is defined as the share of homes sold in that area that would have been affordable to a family earning the local median income, based on standard mortgage underwriting criteria. *National Association of Home Builders®, NAHB-Wells Fargo Housing Opportunity Index, 4th Quarter 2014*

Safety Rankings

- Symantec, in partnership with Sperling's BestPlaces, ranked the 50 largest cities in the U.S. in terms of their vulnerability to cybercrime. The city ranked #3. Criteria: number of cyberattacks and potential infections; level of Internet access; expenditures on smartphones and computer hardware/software; wireless hotspots; broadband connectivity; Internet usage; online purchases. *Symantec, "Riskiest Online Cities of 2012" February 15, 2012*

- Farmers Insurance, in partnership with Sperling's BestPlaces, ranked metro areas in the U.S. and identified the "Most Secure Places to Live." The San Francisco metro area ranked #8 out of the top 20 in the large metro area category (500,000 or more residents). Criteria: economic stability; crime statistics; extreme weather; risk of natural disasters; housing depreciation; foreclosures; air quality; environmental hazards; life expectancy; motor vehicle fatalities; and employment numbers. *Farmers Insurance Group of Companies, "Most Secure U.S. Places to Live in the U.S.," June 25, 2013*

- Allstate ranked the 200 largest cities in America in terms of driver safety. San Francisco ranked #190. Allstate researchers analyzed internal property damage claims over a two-year period from January 2011 to December 2012. A weighted average of the two-year numbers determined the annual percentages. *Allstate, "Allstate America's Best Drivers Report, 2014"*

- The National Insurance Crime Bureau ranked 380 metro areas in the U.S. in terms of per capita rates of vehicle theft. The San Francisco metro area ranked #4 (#1 = highest rate). Criteria: number of vehicle theft offenses per 100,000 inhabitants in 2012. *National Insurance Crime Bureau, "Hot Spots 2012," June 26, 2013*

Seniors/Retirement Rankings

- From its Best Cities for Successful Aging indexes, the Milken Institute generated rankings for metropolitan areas, weighing data in eight categories—health care, wellness, living arrangements, transportation, financial characteristics, education and employment opportunities, community engagement, and overall livability. The San Francisco metro area was ranked #17 overall in the large metro area category. *Milken Institute, "Best Cities for Successful Aging, 2014"*

Sports/Recreation Rankings

- According to the personal finance website NerdWallet, the San Francisco metro area, at #5, is one of the nation's top dozen metro areas for sports fans. Criteria included the presence of all four major sports—MLB, NFL, NHL, and NBA, fan enthusiasm (as measured by game attendance), ticket affordability, and "sports culture," that is, number of sports bars. *www.nerdwallet.com, "Best Cities for Sports Fans," May 5, 2013*

- San Francisco was chosen as a bicycle friendly community by the League of American Bicyclists. A "Bicycle Friendly Community" welcomes cyclists by providing safe accommodation for cycling and encouraging people to bike for transportation and recreation. There are four award levels: Platinum; Gold; Silver; and Bronze. The community achieved an award level of Gold. *League of American Bicyclists, "Bicycle Friendly Community Master List," Fall 2013*

- San Francisco was selected as one of the most playful cities in the U.S. by KaBOOM! The organization's Playful City USA initiative honors cities and towns across the nation for a vision, plan and commitment to creating an agenda for play. Criteria: creating a local play commission or task force; designing an annual action plan for play; conducting a play space audit; outlining a financial investment in play for the current fiscal year; and proclaiming and celebrating an annual "play day." *KaBOOM! National Campaign for Play, "2013 Playful City USA Communities"*

- San Francisco was chosen as one of America's best cities for bicycling. The city ranked #8 out of 50. Criteria: robust cycling infrastructure; vibrant bike culture. The editors only considered cities with populations of 95,000 or more. *Bicycling, "America's Top 50 Bike-Friendly Cities," May 23, 2012*

Transportation Rankings

- Business Insider presented a Walk Score ranking of public transportation in 316 U.S. cities and thousands of city neighborhoods in which San Francisco earned the #2-ranked "Transit Score," awarded for frequency, type of route, and distance between stops. *www.businessinsider.com, "The US Cities with the Best Public Transportation Systems," January 30, 2014*

- More U.S. households choose not to have a car in 2012 than in prior years, according to a study by the University of Michigan Transportation Research Institute. The business website 24/7 Wall Street examined that study, along with a 2010 Census Special Report to arrive at its ranking of cities in which the fewest households had a vehicle. San Francisco held the #5 position. *247wallst.com, "Cities Where No One Wants to Drive," February 6, 2014*

- San Francisco was identified as one of the most congested metro areas in the U.S. The area ranked #2 out of 10. Criteria: yearly delay per auto commuter in hours. *Texas A&M Transportation Institute, "2012 Urban Mobility Report," December 2012*

- The San Francisco metro area appeared on *Forbes* list of places with the most extreme commutes. The metro area ranked #1 out of 10. Criteria: average travel time; percentage of mega commuters. Mega-commuters travel more than 90 minutes and 50 miles each way to work. *Forbes.com, "The Cities with the Most Extreme Commutes," March 5, 2013*

Women/Minorities Rankings

- The Daily Beast surveyed the nation's cities for highest percentage of singles and lowest divorce rate, plus other measures, to determine "emotional intelligence"—happiness, confidence, kindness—which, researchers say, has a strong correlation with people's satisfaction with their romantic relationships. San Francisco placed #3. *www.thedailybeast.com, "Best Cities to Find Love and Stay in Love," February 14, 2014*

- To determine the best metro areas for working women, the personal finance website NerdWallet considered city size as well as relevant economic metrics—high salaries, narrow pay differential by gender, prevalence of women in the highest-paying industries, and population growth over 2010–2012. Of the large U.S. cities examined, the San Francisco metro area held the #2 position. *www.nerdwallet.com, "Best Places for Women in the Workforce," May 19, 2013*

- *Women's Health* examined U.S. cities and identified the 100 best cities for women. San Francisco was ranked #11. Criteria: 30 categories were examined from obesity and breast cancer rates to commuting times and hours spent working out. *Women's Health, "Best Cities for Women 2012"*

- San Francisco was selected as one of the gayest cities in America by *The Advocate*. The city ranked #11 out of 15. This year's criteria include points for a city's LGBT elected officials (and fractional points for the state's elected officials), points for the percentage of the population comprised by lesbian-coupled households, a point for a gay rodeo association, points for bars listed in *Out* magazine's 200 Best Bars list, a point per women's college, and points for concert performances by Mariah Carey, Pink, Lady Gaga, or the Jonas Brothers. The raw score is divided by the population to provide a ranking based on a per capita LGBT quotient. *The Advocate, "2014's Gayest Cities in America" January 6, 2014*

- San Francisco was selected as one of the best cities for young Latinos in 2013 by mun2, a national cable television broadcast network. The city ranked #15. Criteria: U.S. cities with populations over 500,000 residents were evaluated on the following criteria: number of young latinos; jobs; friendliness; cost of living; fun. *mun2.tv, "Best Cities for Young Latinos 2013*

Miscellaneous Rankings

- *Travel + Leisure* invited readers to rate cities on indicators such as aloofness, "smarty-pants residents," highbrow cultural offerings, high-end shopping, artisanal coffeehouses, conspicuous eco-consciousness, and more in order to identify the nation's snobbiest cities. Cities large and small made the list; among them was San Francisco, at #1. *www.travelandleisure.com, "America's Snobbiest Cities, June 2013*

- The watchdog site Charity Navigator conducts an annual study of charities in the nation's major markets both to analyze statistical differences in their financial, accountability, and transparency practices and to track year-to-year variations in individual communities. The San Francisco metro area was ranked #5 among the 30 metro markets. *www.charitynavigator.org, "Metro Market Study 2013," June 1, 2013*

- Ink Army reported on a survey by the website TotalBeauty calculating the number of tattoo shops per 100,000 residents in order to determine the U.S. cities with the most tattoo acceptance. San Francisco took the #7 slot. *inkarmy.com, "Most Tattoo Friendly Cities in the United States," November 1, 2013*

- Business Insider reports on the 2013 Trick-or-Treat Index compiled by the real estate site Zillow, which used its own Home Value Index and Walk Score along with population density and local crime stats to determine that San Francisco ranked #1 for "how much candy it gives out versus how far kids have to walk to get it." Zillow also zeroes in on the best neighborhoods in its top 20 cities. *www.businessinsider.com, "These Are the Best Cities for Trick-or-Treating," October 15, 2013*

- The Harris Poll's Happiness Index survey revealed that of the top ten U.S. markets, the San Francisco metro area residents ranked #10 in happiness. Criteria included strong assent to positive statements and strong disagreement with negative ones, and degree of agreement with a series of statements about respondents' personal relationships and general outlook. The online survey was conducted between July 14 and July 30, 2013. *www.harrisinteractive.com, "Dallas/Fort Worth Is "Happiest" City among America's Top Ten Markets," September 4, 2013*

- Market analyst Scarborough Research surveyed adults who had done volunteer work over the previous 12 months to find out where volunteers are concentrated. The San Francisco metro area made the list for highest volunteer participation. *Scarborough Research, "Salt Lake City, UT; Minneapolis, MN; and Des Moines, IA Lend a Helping Hand," November 27, 2012*

- San Francisco was selected as one of the best travel desinations in the world during Thanksgiving by *Fodor's Travel*. Criteria: attractions; history; events. *Fodors.com, "10 Best Thanksgiving Destinations for 2013," October 18, 2013*

- San Francisco was selected as one of America's funniest cities by the Humor Research Lab at the University of Colorado. The city ranked #9 out of 10. Criteria: frequency of visits to comedy websites; number of comedy clubs per square mile; traveling comedians' ratings of each city's comedy-club audiences; number of famous comedians born in each city per capita; number of famous funny tweeters living in each city per capita; number of comedy radio stations available in each city; frequency of humor-related web searches originating in each city. *The New York Times, "So These Professors Walk Into a Comedy Club…," April 20, 2014*

- San Francisco appeared on *Travel + Leisure's* list of America's most attractive people. Criteria: cities were selected by readers in their annual America's Favorite Cities survey. The city ranked #1 out of 10. *Travel + Leisure, "America's Most and Least Attractive People," November 2013*

- Mars Chocolate North America, the makers of COMBOS®, in partnership with Sperling's BestPlaces, ranked 50 major metro areas in terms of their "manliness." The San Francisco metro area ranked #49. Criteria: number of professional sports teams; number of nearby NASCAR tracks and racing events; manly lifestyle; concentration of manly retail stores; manly occupations per capita; salty snack sales; "Board of Manliness" rankings. *Mars Chocolate North America, "America's Manliest Cities 2012"*

- San Francisco was selected as one of the most tattooed cities in America by *Lovelyish.com*. The city was ranked #7. Criteria: number of tattoo shops per capita. *Lovelyish.com, "Top Ten: Most Tattooed Cities in America," October 17, 2012*

- San Francisco was selected as one of "America's Best Cities for Hipsters" by *Travel + Leisure*. The city was ranked #1 out of 20. Criteria: live music; coffee bars; independent boutiques; best microbrews; offbeat and tech-savvy locals. *Travel + Leisure, "America's Best Cities for Hipsters," November 2013*

- The National Alliance to End Homelessness ranked the 100 most populous metro areas in terms the rate of homelessness. The San Francisco metro area ranked #12. Criteria: number of homeless people per 10,000 population in 2011. *National Alliance to End Homelessness, The State of Homelessness in America 2012*

Business Environment

CITY FINANCES

City Government Finances

Component	2012 ($000)	2012 ($ per capita)
Total Revenues	8,266,722	10,266
Total Expenditures	8,828,177	10,963
Debt Outstanding	13,075,219	16,238
Cash and Securities[1]	21,752,110	27,013

Note: (1) Cash and security holdings of a government at the close of its fiscal year, including those of its dependent agencies, utilities, and liquor stores.
Source: U.S Census Bureau, State & Local Government Finances 2012

City Government Revenue by Source

Source	2012 ($000)	2012 ($ per capita)
General Revenue		
From Federal Government	261,500	325
From State Government	1,615,454	2,006
From Local Governments	478,984	595
Taxes		
Property	1,449,627	1,800
Sales and Gross Receipts	687,899	854
Personal Income	0	0
Corporate Income	0	0
Motor Vehicle License	0	0
Other Taxes	708,694	880
Current Charges	1,687,909	2,096
Liquor Store	0	0
Utility	664,844	826
Employee Retirement	327,821	407

Source: U.S Census Bureau, State & Local Government Finances 2012

City Government Expenditures by Function

Function	2012 ($000)	2012 ($ per capita)	2012 (%)
General Direct Expenditures			
Air Transportation	416,257	517	4.7
Corrections	157,187	195	1.8
Education	0	0	0.0
Employment Security Administration	0	0	0.0
Financial Administration	42,152	52	0.5
Fire Protection	241,079	299	2.7
General Public Buildings	13,089	16	0.1
Governmental Administration, Other	116,812	145	1.3
Health	864,566	1,074	9.8
Highways	221,806	275	2.5
Hospitals	858,517	1,066	9.7
Housing and Community Development	241,553	300	2.7
Interest on General Debt	403,855	502	4.6
Judicial and Legal	75,492	94	0.9
Libraries	84,143	104	1.0
Parking	134,644	167	1.5
Parks and Recreation	242,871	302	2.8
Police Protection	377,911	469	4.3
Public Welfare	484,543	602	5.5
Sewerage	270,708	336	3.1
Solid Waste Management	0	0	0.0
Veterans' Services	0	0	0.0
Liquor Store	0	0	0.0
Utility	2,144,624	2,663	24.3
Employee Retirement	979,558	1,216	11.1

Source: U.S Census Bureau, State & Local Government Finances 2012

DEMOGRAPHICS

Population Growth

Area	1990 Census	2000 Census	2010 Census	Population Growth (%) 1990-2000	Population Growth (%) 2000-2010
City	723,959	776,733	805,235	7.3	3.7
MSA[1]	3,686,592	4,123,740	4,335,391	11.9	5.1
U.S.	248,709,873	281,421,906	308,745,538	13.2	9.7

Note: (1) Figures cover the San Francisco-Oakland-Fremont, CA Metropolitan Statistical Area—see Appendix B for areas included
Source: U.S. Census Bureau, Census 1990, 2000, 2010

Household Size

Area	Persons in Household (%) One	Two	Three	Four	Five	Six	Seven or More	Average Household Size
City	38.4	33.1	13.0	9.1	3.5	1.5	1.4	2.31
MSA[1]	28.4	31.5	16.3	13.8	5.9	2.4	1.7	2.67
U.S.	27.7	33.6	15.7	13.1	6.0	2.3	1.5	2.64

Note: (1) Figures cover the San Francisco-Oakland-Hayward, CA Metropolitan Statistical Area—see Appendix B for areas included
Source: U.S. Census Bureau, 2011-2013 American Community Survey 3-Year Estimates

Race

Area	White Alone[2] (%)	Black Alone[2] (%)	Asian Alone[2] (%)	AIAN[3] Alone[2] (%)	NHOPI[4] Alone[2] (%)	Other Race Alone[2] (%)	Two or More Races (%)
City	49.5	5.8	33.4	0.4	0.4	6.1	4.4
MSA[1]	54.3	8.0	23.8	0.5	0.7	7.4	5.4
U.S.	73.9	12.6	5.0	0.8	0.2	4.7	2.9

Note: (1) Figures cover the San Francisco-Oakland-Hayward, CA Metropolitan Statistical Area—see Appendix B for areas included; (2) Alone is defined as not being in combination with one or more other races; (3) American Indian and Alaska Native; (4) Native Hawaiian and Other Pacific Islander
Source: U.S. Census Bureau, 2011-2013 American Community Survey 3-Year Estimates

Hispanic or Latino Origin

Area	Total (%)	Mexican (%)	Puerto Rican (%)	Cuban (%)	Other (%)
City	15.3	7.6	0.6	0.2	6.9
MSA[1]	21.8	14.7	0.7	0.2	6.3
U.S.	16.9	10.8	1.6	0.6	3.8

Note: Persons of Hispanic or Latino origin can be of any race; (1) Figures cover the San Francisco-Oakland-Hayward, CA Metropolitan Statistical Area—see Appendix B for areas included
Source: U.S. Census Bureau, 2011-2013 American Community Survey 3-Year Estimates

Segregation

Type	Segregation Indices[1] 1990	2000	2010	2010 Rank[2]	Percent Change 1990-2000	Percent Change 1990-2010	Percent Change 2000-2010
Black/White	67.0	65.7	62.0	34	-1.3	-5.0	-3.7
Asian/White	45.8	46.7	46.6	18	0.9	0.8	-0.1
Hispanic/White	43.7	49.7	49.6	26	6.0	5.9	-0.1

Note: All figures cover the Metropolitan Statistical Area—see Appendix B for areas included; Figures are based on an analysis of 1990, 2000, and 2010 Census Decennial Census tract data by William H. Frey, Brookings Institution and the University of Michigan Social Science Data Analysis Network. In this analysis all racial groups (whites, blacks, and asians) are non-Hispanic members of those races. Hispanics are shown as a separate category;
(1) Segregation Indices are Dissimilarity Indices that measure the degree to which the minority group is distributed differently than whites across census tracts. They range from 0 (complete integration) to 100 (complete segregation) where the value indicates the percentage of the minority group that needs to move to be distributed exactly like whites; (2) Ranges from 1 (most segregated) to 102 (least segregated); n/a not available.
Source: www.CensusScope.org

Ancestry

Area	German	Irish	English	American	Italian	Polish	French[2]	Scottish	Dutch
City	7.9	7.9	4.9	2.8	5.0	1.7	2.2	1.4	0.9
MSA[1]	8.5	7.9	6.3	2.9	5.3	1.5	2.0	1.6	0.9
U.S.	14.9	10.8	8.0	7.4	5.5	3.0	2.7	1.7	1.4

Note: Figures are the percentage of the total population reporting a particular ancestry. The nine most commonly reported ancestries in the U.S. are shown. Figures include multiple ancestries (e.g. if a person reported being Irish and Italian, they were included in both columns); (1) Figures cover the San Francisco-Oakland-Hayward, CA Metropolitan Statistical Area—see Appendix B for areas included; (2) Excludes Basque
Source: U.S. Census Bureau, 2011-2013 American Community Survey 3-Year Estimates

Foreign-Born Population

Area	Percent of Population Born in								
	Any Foreign Country	Mexico	Asia	Europe	Carribean	South America	Central America[2]	Africa	Canada
City	35.8	2.8	22.9	4.7	0.2	1.1	2.9	0.3	0.6
MSA[1]	29.8	5.6	16.3	2.9	0.1	1.0	2.5	0.6	0.4
U.S.	13.0	3.7	3.8	1.5	1.2	0.9	1.0	0.6	0.3

Note: (1) Figures cover the San Francisco-Oakland-Hayward, CA Metropolitan Statistical Area—see Appendix B for areas included; (2) Excludes Mexico.
Source: U.S. Census Bureau, 2011-2013 American Community Survey 3-Year Estimates

Marital Status

Area	Never Married	Now Married[2]	Separated	Widowed	Divorced
City	46.5	38.1	1.6	5.1	8.6
MSA[1]	36.0	47.3	1.9	5.2	9.6
U.S.	32.7	48.1	2.2	6.0	11.0

Note: Figures are percentages and cover the population 15 years of age and older; (1) Figures cover the San Francisco-Oakland-Hayward, CA Metropolitan Statistical Area—see Appendix B for areas included; (2) Excludes separated
Source: U.S. Census Bureau, 2011-2013 American Community Survey 3-Year Estimates

Disability Status

Area	All Ages	Under 18 Years Old	18 to 64 Years Old	65 Years and Over
City	10.5	1.7	6.9	38.2
MSA[1]	9.6	2.7	7.0	33.5
U.S.	12.3	4.1	10.2	36.3

Note: Figures show percent of the civilian noninstitutionalized population that reported having a disability. Disability status is determined from from six types of difficulty: vision, hearing, cognitive, ambulatory, self-care, and independent living. For children under 5 years old, hearing and vision difficulty are used to determine disability status. For children between the ages of 5 and 14, disability status is determined from hearing, vision, cognitive, ambulatory, and self-care difficulties. For people aged 15 years and older, they are considered to have a disability if they have difficulty with any one of the six difficulty types; (1) Figures cover the San Francisco-Oakland-Hayward, CA Metropolitan Statistical Area—see Appendix B for areas included.
Source: U.S. Census Bureau, 2011-2013 American Community Survey 3-Year Estimates

Age

Area	Percent of Population									Median Age
	Under Age 5	Age 5–19	Age 20–34	Age 35–44	Age 45–54	Age 55–64	Age 65–74	Age 75–84	Age 85+	
City	4.5	10.8	28.4	16.4	13.7	12.2	7.1	4.6	2.3	38.6
MSA[1]	5.8	17.3	21.6	14.8	14.7	12.5	7.3	4.0	2.0	38.6
U.S.	6.4	19.9	20.7	12.9	14.1	12.3	7.6	4.2	1.9	37.4

Note: (1) Figures cover the San Francisco-Oakland-Hayward, CA Metropolitan Statistical Area—see Appendix B for areas included
Source: U.S. Census Bureau, 2011-2013 American Community Survey 3-Year Estimates

Gender

Area	Males	Females	Males per 100 Females
City	420,456	406,170	103.5
MSA[1]	2,199,538	2,255,873	97.5
U.S.	154,451,010	159,410,713	96.9

Note: (1) Figures cover the San Francisco-Oakland-Hayward, CA Metropolitan Statistical Area—see Appendix B for areas included
Source: U.S. Census Bureau, 2011-2013 American Community Survey 3-Year Estimates

Religious Groups by Family

Area	Catholic	Baptist	Non-Den.	Methodist[2]	Lutheran	LDS[3]	Pente-costal	Presby-terian[4]	Muslim[5]	Judaism
MSA[1]	20.8	2.5	2.5	2.0	0.6	1.6	1.2	1.1	1.2	0.9
U.S.	19.1	9.3	4.0	4.0	2.3	2.0	1.9	1.6	0.8	0.7

Note: Figures are the number of adherents as a percentage of the total population; (1) Figures cover the San Francisco-Oakland-Fremont, CA Metropolitan Statistical Area—see Appendix B for areas included; (2) Methodist/Pietist; (3) Latter Day Saints; (4) Reformed; (5) Figures are estimates
Source: Association of Statisticians of American Religious Bodies, 2010 U.S. Religion Census: Religious Congregations & Membership Study

Religious Groups by Tradition

Area	Catholic	Evangelical Protestant	Mainline Protestant	Other Tradition	Black Protestant	Orthodox
MSA[1]	20.8	6.2	3.8	5.2	1.1	0.7
U.S.	19.1	16.2	7.3	4.3	1.6	0.3

Note: Figures are the number of adherents as a percentage of the total population; (1) Figures cover the San Francisco-Oakland-Fremont, CA Metropolitan Statistical Area—see Appendix B for areas included
Source: Association of Statisticians of American Religious Bodies, 2010 U.S. Religion Census: Religious Congregations & Membership Study

ECONOMY

Gross Metropolitan Product

Area	2012	2013	2014	2015	Rank[2]
MSA[1]	360.4	379.4	395.6	417.8	7

Note: Figures are in billions of dollars; (1) Figures cover the San Francisco-Oakland-Hayward, CA Metropolitan Statistical Area—see Appendix B for areas included; (2) Rank is based on 2015 data and ranges from 1 to 363
Source: The U.S. Conference of Mayors, U.S. Metro Economies: GMP and Employment 2013-2015, June 2014

Economic Growth

Area	2010-12 (%)	2013 (%)	2014 (%)	2015 (%)	Rank[2]
MSA[1]	3.8	4.1	2.6	3.7	54
U.S.	2.1	2.0	2.3	3.2	–

Note: Figures are real gross metropolitan product (GMP) growth rates and represent annual average percent change; (1) Figures cover the San Francisco-Oakland-Hayward, CA Metropolitan Statistical Area—see Appendix B for areas included; (2) Rank is based on 2015 data and ranges from 1 to 363
Source: The U.S. Conference of Mayors, U.S. Metro Economies: GMP and Employment 2013-2015, June 2014

Metropolitan Area Exports

Area	2008	2009	2010	2011	2012	2013	Rank[2]
MSA[1]	20,470.4	16,040.3	21,355.4	23,573.8	23,031.7	25,305.3	10

Note: Figures are in millions of dollars; (1) Figures cover the San Francisco-Oakland-Hayward, CA Metropolitan Statistical Area—see Appendix B for areas included; (2) Rank is based on 2013 data and ranges from 1 to 387
Source: U.S. Department of Commerce, International Trade Administration, Office of Trade & Industry Information, Manufacturing & Services, data extracted April 3, 2015

Building Permits

Area	Single-Family			Multi-Family			Total		
	2013	2014	Pct. Chg.	2013	2014	Pct. Chg.	2013	2014	Pct. Chg.
City	54	35	-35.2	4,420	2,676	-39.5	4,474	2,711	-39.4
MSA[1]	3,659	3,716	1.6	7,263	6,285	-13.5	10,922	10,001	-8.4
U.S.	620,802	634,597	2.2	370,020	411,766	11.3	990,822	1,046,363	5.6

Note: (1) Figures cover the San Francisco-Oakland-Hayward, CA Metropolitan Statistical Area—see Appendix B for areas included; Figures represent new, privately-owned housing units authorized (unadjusted data); All permit data are based on estimates with imputation.
Source: U.S. Census Bureau, Manufacturing, Mining, and Construction Statistics, Building Permits, 2013, 2014

Bankruptcy Filings

Area	Business Filings			Nonbusiness Filings		
	2013	2014	% Chg.	2013	2014	% Chg.
San Francisco County	113	89	-21.2	980	694	-29.2
U.S.	33,212	26,983	-18.8	1,038,720	909,812	-12.4

Note: Business filings include Chapter 7, Chapter 11, Chapter 12, and Chapter 13; Nonbusiness filings include Chapter 7, Chapter 11, and Chapter 13
Source: Administrative Office of the U.S. Courts, Business and Nonbusiness Bankruptcy, County Cases Commenced by Chapter of the Bankruptcy Code, During the 12- Month Period Ending December 31, 2013 and Business and Nonbusiness Bankruptcy, County Cases Commenced by Chapter of the Bankruptcy Code, During the 12- Month Period Ending December 31, 2014

Housing Vacancy Rates

Area	Gross Vacancy Rate[2] (%)			Year-Round Vacancy Rate[3] (%)			Rental Vacancy Rate[4] (%)			Homeowner Vacancy Rate[5] (%)		
	2012	2013	2014	2012	2013	2014	2012	2013	2014	2012	2013	2014
MSA[1]	6.9	6.5	5.9	6.8	6.4	5.9	3.2	3.9	3.2	1.0	1.1	0.4
U.S.	13.8	13.6	13.4	10.8	10.7	10.4	8.7	8.3	7.6	2.0	2.0	1.9

Note: (1) Figures cover the San Francisco-Oakland-Hayward, CA Metropolitan Statistical Area—see Appendix B for areas included; (2) The percentage of the total housing inventory that is vacant; (3) The percentage of the housing inventory (excluding seasonal units) that is year-round vacant; (4) The percentage of rental inventory that is vacant for rent; (5) The percentage of homeowner inventory that is vacant for sale
Source: U.S. Census Bureau, Housing Vacancies and Homeownership Annual Statistics: 2014

INCOME

Income

Area	Per Capita ($)	Median Household ($)	Average Household ($)
City	48,861	74,559	110,996
MSA[1]	41,528	76,767	109,045
U.S.	27,884	52,176	72,897

Note: (1) Figures cover the San Francisco-Oakland-Hayward, CA Metropolitan Statistical Area—see Appendix B for areas included
Source: U.S. Census Bureau, 2011-2013 American Community Survey 3-Year Estimates

Household Income Distribution

Area	Percent of Households Earning							
	Under $15,000	$15,000 -24,999	$25,000 -34,999	$35,000 -49,999	$50,000 -74,999	$75,000 -99,000	$100,000 -149,999	$150,000 and up
City	13.4	8.0	6.7	8.7	13.4	10.4	15.8	23.7
MSA[1]	9.6	7.6	6.8	9.9	15.1	11.7	17.0	22.3
U.S.	13.0	10.9	10.3	13.6	17.9	11.9	12.7	9.6

Note: (1) Figures cover the San Francisco-Oakland-Hayward, CA Metropolitan Statistical Area—see Appendix B for areas included
Source: U.S. Census Bureau, 2011-2013 American Community Survey 3-Year Estimates

Poverty Rate

Area	All Ages	Under 18 Years Old	18 to 64 Years Old	65 Years and Over
City	14.2	14.0	14.1	15.2
MSA[1]	11.7	14.1	11.5	9.0
U.S.	15.9	22.4	14.8	9.5

Note: Figures are percentage of people whose income during the past 12 months was below the poverty level; (1) Figures cover the San Francisco-Oakland-Hayward, CA Metropolitan Statistical Area—see Appendix B for areas included
Source: U.S. Census Bureau, 2011-2013 American Community Survey 3-Year Estimates

EMPLOYMENT

Labor Force and Employment

Area	Civilian Labor Force			Workers Employed		
	Dec. 2013	Dec. 2014	% Chg.	Dec. 2013	Dec. 2014	% Chg.
City	522,913	540,603	3.4	498,846	520,640	4.4
MD[1]	945,703	977,381	3.3	902,803	942,144	4.4
U.S.	154,408,000	155,521,000	0.7	144,423,000	147,190,000	1.9

Note: Data is not seasonally adjusted and covers workers 16 years of age and older; (1) Figures cover the San Francisco-Redwood City-South San Francisco, CA Metropolitan Division—see Appendix B for areas included
Source: Bureau of Labor Statistics, Local Area Unemployment Statistics

Unemployment Rate

Area	2014											
	Jan.	Feb.	Mar.	Apr.	May	Jun.	Jul.	Aug.	Sep.	Oct.	Nov.	Dec.
City	5.0	4.9	4.9	4.1	4.2	4.3	4.6	4.5	4.1	4.1	4.1	3.7
MD[1]	4.9	4.8	4.8	4.0	4.1	4.3	4.6	4.4	4.1	4.0	4.0	3.6
U.S.	7.0	7.0	6.8	5.9	6.1	6.3	6.5	6.3	5.7	5.5	5.5	5.4

Note: Data is not seasonally adjusted and covers workers 16 years of age and older; (1) Figures cover the San Francisco-Redwood City-South San Francisco, CA Metropolitan Division—see Appendix B for areas included
Source: Bureau of Labor Statistics, Local Area Unemployment Statistics

Employment by Occupation

Occupation Classification	City (%)	MSA[1] (%)	U.S. (%)
Management, Business, Science, and Arts	52.2	46.5	36.2
Natural Resources, Construction, and Maintenance	3.9	6.4	9.0
Production, Transportation, and Material Moving	5.3	7.4	12.1
Sales and Office	21.3	22.5	24.4
Service	17.3	17.3	18.3

Note: Figures cover employed civilians 16 years of age and older; (1) Figures cover the San Francisco-Oakland-Hayward, CA Metropolitan Statistical Area—see Appendix B for areas included
Source: U.S. Census Bureau, 2011-2013 American Community Survey 3-Year Estimates

Employment by Industry

Sector	MD[1]		U.S.
	Number of Employees	Percent of Total	Percent of Total
Construction	35,300	3.4	4.4
Education and Health Services	131,300	12.6	15.5
Financial Activities	72,800	7.0	5.7
Government	123,200	11.8	15.8
Information	56,000	5.4	2.0
Leisure and Hospitality	136,400	13.1	10.3
Manufacturing	36,100	3.5	8.7
Mining and Logging	100	<0.1	0.6
Other Services	41,100	3.9	4.0
Professional and Business Services	258,000	24.8	13.8
Retail Trade	84,900	8.1	11.4
Transportation, Warehousing, and Utilities	40,800	3.9	3.9
Wholesale Trade	26,300	2.5	4.2

Note: Figures are non-farm employment as of December 2014. Figures are not seasonally adjusted and include workers 16 years of age and older; (1) Figures cover the San Francisco-Redwood City-South San Francisco, CA Metropolitan Division—see Appendix B for areas included
Source: Bureau of Labor Statistics, Current Employment Statistics, Employment, Hours, and Earnings

Occupations with Greatest Projected Employment Growth: 2012 – 2022

Occupation[1]	2012 Employment	2022 Projected Employment	Numeric Employment Change	Percent Employment Change
Personal Care Aides	386,900	587,200	200,300	51.8
Combined Food Preparation and Serving Workers, Including Fast Food	286,000	362,400	76,400	26.7
Retail Salespersons	468,400	528,100	59,700	12.7
Laborers and Freight, Stock, and Material Movers, Hand	270,500	322,300	51,800	19.1
Waiters and Waitresses	246,100	290,300	44,200	18.0
Registered Nurses	254,500	297,400	42,900	16.9
General and Operations Managers	253,800	295,700	41,900	16.5
Secretaries and Administrative Assistants, Except Legal, Medical, and Executive	212,800	250,100	37,300	17.5
Cashiers	357,800	392,600	34,800	9.7
Cooks, Restaurant	116,900	150,600	33,700	28.8

Note: Projections cover California; (1) Sorted by numeric employment change
Source: www.projectionscentral.com, State Occupational Projections, 2012–2022 Long-Term Projections

Fastest Growing Occupations: 2012 – 2022

Occupation[1]	2012 Employment	2022 Projected Employment	Numeric Employment Change	Percent Employment Change
Economists	3,100	5,100	2,000	64.5
Helpers—Brickmasons, Blockmasons, Stonemasons, and Tile and Marble Setters	2,900	4,600	1,700	58.6
Brickmasons and Blockmasons	5,100	8,000	2,900	56.9
Insulation Workers, Floor, Ceiling, and Wall	1,600	2,500	900	56.3
Stonemasons	1,100	1,700	600	54.5
Insulation Workers, Mechanical	1,100	1,700	600	54.5
Personal Care Aides	386,900	587,200	200,300	51.8
Foresters	1,200	1,800	600	50.0
Terrazzo Workers and Finishers	1,100	1,600	500	45.5
Mechanical Door Repairers	1,100	1,600	500	45.5

Note: Projections cover California; (1) Sorted by percent employment change and excludes occupations with numeric employment change less than 100
Source: www.projectionscentral.com, State Occupational Projections, 2012–2022 Long-Term Projections

Average Wages

Occupation	$/Hr.	Occupation	$/Hr.
Accountants and Auditors	42.23	Maids and Housekeeping Cleaners	16.90
Automotive Mechanics	26.07	Maintenance and Repair Workers	25.10
Bookkeepers	24.04	Marketing Managers	86.40
Carpenters	31.17	Nuclear Medicine Technologists	54.17
Cashiers	13.01	Nurses, Licensed Practical	29.61
Clerks, General Office	19.40	Nurses, Registered	61.63
Clerks, Receptionists/Information	17.28	Nursing Assistants	19.20
Clerks, Shipping/Receiving	17.84	Packers and Packagers, Hand	13.17
Computer Programmers	50.37	Physical Therapists	50.54
Computer Systems Analysts	50.86	Postal Service Mail Carriers	26.78
Computer User Support Specialists	34.05	Real Estate Brokers	40.04
Cooks, Restaurant	14.21	Retail Salespersons	15.30
Dentists	90.43	Sales Reps., Exc. Tech./Scientific	29.54
Electrical Engineers	56.55	Sales Reps., Tech./Scientific	48.03
Electricians	41.67	Secretaries, Exc. Legal/Med./Exec.	21.58
Financial Managers	85.60	Security Guards	15.87
First-Line Supervisors/Managers, Sales	23.94	Surgeons	94.79
Food Preparation Workers	11.58	Teacher Assistants	17.50
General and Operations Managers	72.35	Teachers, Elementary School	33.10
Hairdressers/Cosmetologists	18.36	Teachers, Secondary School	35.00
Internists	80.03	Telemarketers	15.57
Janitors and Cleaners	14.03	Truck Drivers, Heavy/Tractor-Trailer	22.44
Landscaping/Groundskeeping Workers	18.40	Truck Drivers, Light/Delivery Svcs.	19.39
Lawyers	82.65	Waiters and Waitresses	12.63

Note: Wage data covers the San Francisco-San Mateo-Redwood City, CA Metropolitan Division—see Appendix B for areas included; Hourly wages for elementary/secondary school teachers and teacher assistants were calculated by the editors from annual wage data assuming a 40 hour work week; n/a not available.
Source: Bureau of Labor Statistics, Metro Area Occupational Employment and Wage Estimates, May 2014

TAXES

State Corporate Income Tax Rates

State	Tax Rate (%)	Income Brackets ($)	Num. of Brackets	Financial Institution Tax Rate (%)[a]	Federal Income Tax Ded.
California	8.84 (c)	Flat rate	1	10.84 (c)	No

Note: Tax rates as of January 1, 2015; (a) Rates listed are the corporate income tax rate applied to financial institutions or excise taxes based on income. Some states have other taxes based upon the value of deposits or shares; (c) Minimum tax is $800 in California, $100 in District of Columbia, $50 in North Dakota (banks), $500 in Rhode Island, $200 per location in South Dakota (banks), $100 in Utah, $250 in Vermont.
Source: Federation of Tax Administrators, "State Corporate Income Tax Rates, 2015"

State Individual Income Tax Rates

State	Tax Rate (%)	Income Brackets ($)	Num. of Brackets	Personal Exempt. ($)[1]		Fed. Inc. Tax Ded.
				Single	Dependents	
California (a)	1.0 - 12.3 (f)	7,749- 519,687 (b)	9	108 (c)	333 (c)	No

Note: Tax rates as of January 1, 2015; Local- and county-level taxes are not included; n/a not applicable; (1) Married joint filers generally receive double the single exemption; (a) 17 states have statutory provision for automatically adjusting to the rate of inflation the dollar values of the income tax brackets, standard deductions, and/or personal exemptions. Massachusetts, Michigan, and Nebraska index the personal exemption only. Oregon does not index the income brackets for $125,000 and over. Maine has suspended indexing for 2014 and 2015; (b) For joint returns, taxes are twice the tax on half the couple's income; (c) The personal exemption takes the form of a tax credit instead of a deduction; (f) California imposes an additional 1% tax on taxable income over $1 million, making the maximum rate 13.3% over $1 million.
Source: Federation of Tax Administrators, "State Individual Income Tax Rates, 2015"

Various State and Local Tax Rates

State	State and Local Sales and Use (%)	State Sales and Use (%)	Gasoline[1] (¢/gal.)	Cigarette[2] ($/pack)	Spirits[3] ($/gal.)	Wine[4] ($/gal.)	Beer[5] ($/gal.)
California	8.75	7.50 (b)	45.39	0.87	3.30 (f)	0.20	0.20

Note: All tax rates as of January 1, 2015; (1) The American Petroleum Institute has developed a methodology for determining the average tax rate on a gallon of fuel. Rates may include any of the following: excise taxes, environmental fees, storage tank fees, other fees or taxes, general sales tax, and local taxes. In states where gasoline is subject to the general sales tax, or where the fuel tax is based on the average sale price, the average rate determined by API is sensitive to changes in the price of gasoline. States that fully or partially apply general sales taxes to gasoline: CA, CO, GA, IL, IN, MI, NY; (2) The federal excise tax of $1.0066 per pack and local taxes are not included; (3) Rates are those applicable to off-premise sales of 40% alcohol by volume (a.b.v.) distilled spirits in 750ml containers. Local excise taxes are excluded; (4) Rates are those applicable to off-premise sales of 11% a.b.v. non-carbonated wine in 750ml containers; (5) Rates are those applicable to off-premise sales of 4.7% a.b.v. beer in 12 ounce containers; (b) Three states levy mandatory, statewide, local add-on sales taxes at the state level: California (1%), Utah (1.25%), and Virginia (1%). We include these in their state sales taxes; (f) Different rates are also applicable according to alcohol content, place of production, size of container, or place purchased (on- or off-premise or onboard airlines).
Source: Tax Foundation, 2015 Facts & Figures: How Does Your State Compare?

State Business Tax Climate Index Rankings

State	Overall Rank	Corporate Tax Index Rank	Individual Income Tax Index Rank	Sales Tax Index Rank	Unemployment Insurance Tax Index Rank	Property Tax Index Rank
California	48	34	50	42	14	14

Note: The index is a measure of how each state's tax laws affect economic performance. The lower the rank, the more favorable a state's tax system is for business. States without a given tax are given a ranking of 1. The scores/rankings for the District of Columbia do not affect other states. The 2015 index represents the tax climate as of July 1, 2014.
Source: Tax Foundation, State Business Tax Climate Index 2015

COMMERCIAL REAL ESTATE

Office Market

Market Area	Inventory (sq. ft.)	Vacancy Rate (%)	Under Construction (sq. ft.)	YTD Net Absorption (sq. ft.)	Total Average Asking Rent ($/sq. ft./year)
Oakland/East Bay	72,691,218	14.9	0	-683,681	25.33
San Francisco	83,626,709	4.4	3,573,744	1,594,368	62.59
National	4,745,108,508	14.3	71,190,461	51,084,126	27.40

Source: Newmark Grubb Knight Frank, National Office Market Report, 4th Quarter 2014

Industrial/Warehouse/R&D Market

Market Area	Inventory (sq. ft.)	Vacancy Rate (%)	Under Construction (sq. ft.)	YTD Net Absorption (sq. ft.)	Total Average Asking Rent ($/sq. ft./year)
Oakland/East Bay	265,171,739	7.0	2,251,412	4,403,523	8.49
National	14,238,613,765	7.2	134,387,407	185,246,438	5.64

Source: Newmark Grubb Knight Frank, National Industrial Market Report, 4th Quarter 2014

COMMERCIAL UTILITIES

Typical Monthly Electric Bills

Area	Commercial Service ($/month)		Industrial Service ($/month)	
	1,500 kWh	40 kW demand 14,000 kWh	1,000 kW demand 200,000 kWh	50,000 kW demand 32,500,000 kWh
City	299	2,473	42,294	3,279,227
Average[1]	201	1,653	26,124	2,639,743

Note: Figures are based on annualized 2014 rates; (1) Average based on 180 utilities surveyed
Source: Edison Electric Institute, Typical Bills and Average Rates Report, Summer 2014

TRANSPORTATION

Means of Transportation to Work

Area	Car/Truck/Van		Public Transportation			Bicycle	Walked	Other Means	Worked at Home
	Drove Alone	Car-pooled	Bus	Subway	Railroad				
City	36.7	7.3	22.4	6.7	1.3	3.7	10.2	4.6	7.1
MSA[1]	60.6	10.0	7.7	5.9	1.0	1.9	4.4	2.3	6.1
U.S.	76.4	9.6	2.6	1.8	0.6	0.6	2.8	1.3	4.3

Note: Figures are percentages and cover workers 16 years of age and older; (1) Figures cover the San Francisco-Oakland-Hayward, CA Metropolitan Statistical Area—see Appendix B for areas included
Source: U.S. Census Bureau, 2011-2013 American Community Survey 3-Year Estimates

Travel Time to Work

Area	Less Than 10 Minutes	10 to 19 Minutes	20 to 29 Minutes	30 to 44 Minutes	45 to 59 Minutes	60 to 89 Minutes	90 Minutes or More
City	4.9	21.5	21.8	28.3	11.2	10.0	2.4
MSA[1]	7.8	24.9	19.0	24.2	11.2	9.9	3.0
U.S.	13.3	29.7	20.9	20.2	7.7	5.7	2.6

Note: Figures are percentages and include workers 16 years old and over; (1) Figures cover the San Francisco-Oakland-Hayward, CA Metropolitan Statistical Area—see Appendix B for areas included
Source: U.S. Census Bureau, 2011-2013 American Community Survey 3-Year Estimates

Travel Time Index

Area	1985	1990	1995	2000	2005	2010	2011
Urban Area[1]	1.18	1.25	1.23	1.26	1.31	1.22	1.22
Average[2]	1.09	1.14	1.16	1.19	1.23	1.18	1.18

Note: Travel Time Index—the ratio of travel time in the peak period to the travel time at free-flow conditions. For example, a value of 1.30 indicates a 20-minute free-flow trip takes 26 minutes in the peak. Free-flow speeds (60 mph on freeways and 35 mph on principal arterials) are used as the comparison threshold; (1) Covers the San Francisco-Oakland CA urban area; (2) average of 498 urban areas
Source: Texas Transportation Institute, Urban Mobility Report 2012, December 2012

Public Transportation

Agency Name / Mode of Transportation	Vehicles Operated in Maximum Service	Annual Unlinked Passenger Trips (in thous.)	Annual Passenger Miles (in thous.)
San Francisco Municipal Railway (MUNI)			
Bus (directly operated)	388	97,180.9	222,183.7
Cable Car (directly operated)	27	6,813.3	8,497.2
Demand Response (purchased transportation)	112	582.6	3,135.9
Demand Response Taxi (purchased transportation)	1,478	277.8	686.8
Light Rail (directly operated)	131	45,358.8	129,329.4
Streetcar Rail (directly operated)	24	8,390.3	12,372.3
Trolleybus (directly operated)	213	65,247.6	95,481.5
San Francisco Bay Area Rapid Transit District (BART)			
Heavy Rail (directly operated)	534	126,546.5	1,649,251.2

Source: Federal Transit Administration, National Transit Database, 2013

Air Transportation

Airport Name and Code / Type of Service	Passenger Airlines[1]	Passenger Enplanements	Freight Carriers[2]	Freight (lbs.)
San Francisco International (SFO)				
Domestic service (U.S. carriers - 2014)	26	17,733,061	17	104,946,994
International service (U.S. carriers - 2013)	9	1,880,671	7	42,819,338

Note: (1) Includes all U.S.-based major, minor and commuter airlines that carried at least one passenger during the year; (2) Includes all U.S.-based airlines and freight carriers that transported at least one lb. of freight during the year.
Source: Bureau of Transportation Statistics, The Intermodal Transportation Database, Air Carriers: T-100 Domestic Market (U.S. Carriers), 2014; Bureau of Transportation Statistics, The Intermodal Transportation Database, Air Carriers: T-100 International Market (U.S. Carriers), 2013

Other Transportation Statistics

Major Highways:	I-80
Amtrak Service:	Bus connection
Major Waterways/Ports:	Port of San Francisco

Source: Amtrak.com; Google Maps

BUSINESSES

Major Business Headquarters

Company Name	Rankings	
	Fortune[1]	Forbes[2]
Bechtel	-	4
Levi Strauss & Co	-	86
McKesson	15	-
PG&E Corporation	183	-
The Charles Schwab Corporation	459	-
The Gap	178	-
URS Corporation	256	-
Wells Fargo	29	-
Wilbur-Ellis	-	153

Note: (1) Fortune 500—companies that produce a 10-K are ranked 1 to 500 based on 2013 revenue; (2) all private companies with at least $2 billion in annual revenue through the end of their most current fiscal year are ranked 1 to 221; companies listed are headquartered in the city; dashes indicate no ranking
Source: Fortune, "Fortune 500," June 16, 2014; Forbes, "America's Largest Private Companies," November 5, 2014

Fast-Growing Businesses

According to *Inc.*, San Francisco is home to 14 of America's 500 fastest-growing private companies: **Dolls Kill** (#33); **Bizness Apps** (#58); **Inkling** (#105); **Twilio** (#139); **LiveRamp** (#144); **PresenceLearning** (#146); **6 Pack Fitness** (#181); **Levitate Media** (#237); **LiveRail** (#243); **Lending Club** (#248); **Six Spoke Media** (#369); **Tracker Corp** (#468); **Build Group** (#477); **Maven Recruiting Group** (#487). Criteria: must be an independent, privately-held, for-profit, U.S. corporation, proprietorship or partnership; revenues must be at least $100,000 in 2010 and $2 million in 2013; must have four-year operating/sales history. Holding companies, regulated banks, and utilities were excluded. *Inc., "America's 500 Fastest-Growing Private Companies," September 2014*

According to *Fortune*, San Francisco is home to one of the 100 fastest-growing companies in the world: **RPX** (#92). Companies were ranked by their revenue growth rate; their EPS growth rate; and their three-year annualized total return to investors for the period ending June 30, 2014. Criteria for inclusion: a company, foreign or domestic, must trade on a major U.S. stock exchange; must file quarterly reports with the SEC; must have a minimum market capitalization of $250 million; must have a stock price of at least $5 on June 30, 2014; must have been trading continuously since June 30, 2010; must have revenue and net income for the four quarters ended on or before April 30, 2014, of at least $50 million and $10 million, respectively; and must have posted a compound annual growth in revenue and earnings per share of at least 20% annually over the three years ending on or before April 30, 2014. Real estate investment trusts, limited-liability companies, limited parterships, business development companies, closed end investment firms, and companies that lost money in the quarter ending April 30, 2014 were excluded. *Fortune, "100 Fastest-Growing Companies," August 28, 2014*

According to Deloitte, San Francisco is home to 25 of North America's 500 fastest-growing high-technology companies: **Twilio** (#3); **Kabam** (#6); **New Relic** (#19); **Grammarly.com** (#55); **Prosper Marketplace** (#57); **Sharethrough** (#72); **BrightRoll** (#81); **Trulia** (#91); **Sojern** (#108); **Splunk** (#119); **Marin Software** (#127); **MuleSoft** (#131); **Yelp** (#144); **Zynga** (#168); **InsideView Technologies** (#171); **Scribd** (#207); **Recommind** (#250); **Medivation** (#306); **Vendini** (#335); **salesforce.com** (#412); **Fluidigm Corporation** (#417); **WideOrbit** (#429); **Riverbed Technology** (#441); **Tagged** (#463); **Servicesource International** (#475). Companies are ranked by percentage growth in revenue over a five-year period. Criteria for inclusion: company must be headquartered within North America; must own proprietary intellectual property or proprietary technology that contributes to a significant portion of the company's operating revenue, or devote a significant proportion of revenues to research and development of technology; must have been in business for a minumum of five years with 2009 operating revenues of at least $50,000 USD/CD and 2013 operating revenues of at least $5 million USD/CD. *Deloitte Touche Tohmatsu, 2014 Technology Fast 500™*

Minority Business Opportunity

San Francisco is home to one company which is on the *Black Enterprise* Asset Manager 15 list (15 largest asset management firms based on assets under management): **Progress Investment Management Co.** (#4). Criteria: company must have been operational in previous calendar year and be at least 51% black-owned. *Black Enterprise, B.E. 100s, 2014*

San Francisco is home to one company which is on the *Black Enterprise* Private Equity 15 list (15 largest private equity firms based on capital under management): **MacFarlane Partners** (#2). Criteria: company must be operational in previous calendar year and be at least 51% black-owned. *Black Enterprise, B.E. 100s, 2014*

San Francisco is home to one company which is on the *Hispanic Business* 500 list (500 largest U.S. Hispanic-owned companies based on 2012 revenue): **Yerba Buena Engineering & Construction** (#152). Companies included must show at least 51 percent ownership by Hispanic U.S. citizens, and must maintain headquarters in one of the 50 states or Washington, D.C. *Hispanic Business, "Hispanic Business 500," June 20, 2013*

San Francisco is home to one company which is on the *Hispanic Business* Fastest-Growing 100 list (greatest sales growth from 2008 to 2012): **Yerba Buena Engineering & Construction** (#33). Companies included must show at least 51 percent ownership by Hispanic U.S. citizens, and must maintain headquarters in one of the 50 states or Washington, D.C. In addition, companies must have minimum revenues of $200,000 for calendar year 2008. *Hispanic Business, June 20, 2013*

Minority- and Women-Owned Businesses

Group	All Firms		Firms with Paid Employees			
	Firms	Sales ($000)	Firms	Sales ($000)	Employees	Payroll ($000)
Asian	25,236	7,638,482	5,880	6,735,069	40,988	1,405,707
Black	2,788	261,763	301	192,245	2,502	75,355
Hispanic	6,915	986,789	989	757,813	6,421	265,414
Women	31,639	5,268,560	4,628	4,186,663	30,502	1,133,912
All Firms	105,030	161,709,354	25,356	156,979,583	511,507	34,727,580

Note: Figures cover firms located in the city; minority- and women-owned business are defined as firms in which the corresponding group own 51% or more of the stock or equity of the company
Source: U.S. Census Bureau, 2007 Economic Census, Survey of Business Owners (2012 Survey of Business Owners data will be released starting in June 2015)

HOTELS & CONVENTION CENTERS

Hotels/Motels

Area	5 Star		4 Star		3 Star		2 Star		1 Star		Not Rated	
	Num.	Pct.[3]	Num.	Pct.[3]	Num.	Pct.[3]	Num.	Pct.[3]	Num.	Pct.[3]	Num.	Pct.[3]
City[1]	7	1.8	48	12.7	109	28.8	162	42.7	19	5.0	34	9.0
Total[2]	166	0.9	1,264	7.0	5,718	31.8	9,340	52.0	411	2.3	1,070	6.0

Note: (1) Figures cover San Francisco and vicinity; (2) Figures cover all 100 cities in this book; (3) Percentage of hotels which have a given star rating; Star ratings are determined by expedia.com and offer an indication of the general quality of a particular hotel.
Source: expedia.com, April 2, 2015

The San Francisco-Redwood City-South San Francisco, CA metro area is home to nine of the best hotels in the U.S. according to *Travel & Leisure*: **Ritz-Carlton, Half Moon Bay**; **Four Seasons Hotel San Francisco**; **Hotel Vitale**; **Mandarin Oriental, San Francisco**; **Ritz-Carlton, San Francisco**; **Scarlet Huntington**; **St. Regis San Francisco**; **Taj Campton Place**; **Cavallo Point-The Lodge at the Golden Gate**. Criteria: service; location; rooms; food; and value. The list includes the top 236 hotels in the U.S. *Travel & Leisure, "T+L 500, The World's Best Hotels 2015"*

The San Francisco-Redwood City-South San Francisco, CA metro area is home to two of the best hotels in the world according to *Condé Nast Traveler*: **Ritz-Carlton, Half Moon Bay**; **Hotel Vitale**. The selections are based on editors' picks. The list includes the top 25 hotels in the U.S. *Condé Nast Traveler, "Gold List 2015, The Top Hotels in the World"*

Major Convention Centers

Name	Overall Space (sq. ft.)	Exhibit Space (sq. ft.)	Meeting Space (sq. ft.)	Meeting Rooms
Concourse Exhibition Center at Showplace Square	125,000	125,000	n/a	n/a
Moscone Convention Center	1,346,000	441,960	159,980	69

Note: Table includes convention centers located in the San Francisco-Oakland-Hayward, CA metro area; n/a not available
Source: Original research

Living Environment

COST OF LIVING

Cost of Living Index

Composite Index	Groceries	Housing	Utilities	Trans-portation	Health Care	Misc. Goods/ Services
166.9	123.5	302.4	101.7	110.4	118.9	116.2

Note: The Cost of Living Index measures regional differences in the cost of consumer goods and services, excluding taxes and non-consumer expenditures, for professional and managerial households in the top income quintile. It is based on more than 50,000 prices covering almost 60 different items for which prices are collected three times a year by chambers of commerce, economic development organizations or university applied economic centers in each participating urban area. The numbers shown should be read as a percentage above or below the national average of 100. For example, a value of 115.4 in the groceries column indicates that grocery prices are 15.4% higher than the national average. Small differences in the index numbers should not be interpreted as significant; Figures cover the San Francisco CA urban area.
Source: The Council for Community and Economic Research, ACCRA Cost of Living Index, 2014

Grocery Prices

Area[1]	T-Bone Steak ($/pound)	Frying Chicken ($/pound)	Whole Milk ($/half gal.)	Eggs ($/dozen)	Orange Juice ($/64 oz.)	Coffee ($/11.5 oz.)
City[2]	10.74	1.72	2.81	3.15	4.34	5.78
Avg.	10.40	1.37	2.40	1.99	3.46	4.27
Min.	8.48	0.93	1.37	1.30	2.83	2.99
Max.	14.20	2.44	3.62	4.02	6.42	6.96

*Note: (1) Values for the local area are compared with the average, minimum and maximum values for all 308 areas in the Cost of Living Index; (2) Figures cover the San Francisco CA urban area; **T-Bone Steak** (price per pound); **Frying Chicken** (price per pound, whole fryer); **Whole Milk** (half gallon carton); **Eggs** (price per dozen, Grade A, large); **Orange Juice** (64 oz. Tropicana or Florida Natural); **Coffee** (11.5 oz. can, vacuum-packed, Maxwell House, Hills Bros, or Folgers).*
Source: The Council for Community and Economic Research, ACCRA Cost of Living Index, 2014

Housing and Utility Costs

Area[1]	New Home Price ($)	Apartment Rent ($/month)	All Electric ($/month)	Part Electric ($/month)	Other Energy ($/month)	Telephone ($/month)
City[2]	920,224	3,072	-	118.94	71.93	24.12
Avg.	305,838	919	181.00	93.66	73.14	27.95
Min.	183,142	480	112.00	42.06	23.42	17.16
Max.	1,358,576	3,851	594.00	180.03	440.99	40.42

*Note: (1) Values for the local area are compared with the average, minimum and maximum values for all 308 areas in the Cost of Living Index; (2) Figures cover the San Francisco CA urban area; **New Home Price** (2,400 sf living area, 8,000 sf lot, in urban area with full utilities); **Apartment Rent** (950 sf 2 bedroom/1.5 or 2 bath, unfurnished, excluding all utilities except water); **All Electric** (average monthly cost for an all-electric home); **Part Electric** (average monthly cost for a part-electric home); **Other Energy** (average monthly cost for natural gas, fuel oil, coal, wood, and any other forms of energy except electricity); **Telephone** (price includes basic monthly rate for a private residential line plus additional local usage charges incurred by a family of four).*
Source: The Council for Community and Economic Research, ACCRA Cost of Living Index, 2014

Health Care, Transportation, and Other Costs

Area[1]	Doctor ($/visit)	Dentist ($/visit)	Optometrist ($/visit)	Gasoline ($/gallon)	Beauty Salon ($/visit)	Men's Shirt ($)
City[2]	127.18	117.15	120.63	3.73	60.47	33.81
Avg.	102.86	87.89	97.66	3.44	34.37	26.74
Min.	67.47	65.78	51.18	3.00	17.43	12.79
Max.	173.50	150.14	235.00	4.33	64.28	49.50

*Note: (1) Values for the local area are compared with the average, minimum and maximum values for all 308 areas in the Cost of Living Index; (2) Figures cover the San Francisco CA urban area; **Doctor** (general practitioners routine exam of an established patient); **Dentist** (adult teeth cleaning and periodic oral examination); **Optometrist** (full vision eye exam for established adult patient); **Gasoline** (one gallon regular unleaded, national brand, including all taxes, cash price at self-service pump if available); **Beauty Salon** (woman's shampoo, trim, and blow-dry); **Men's Shirt** (cotton/polyester dress shirt, pinpoint weave, long sleeves).*
Source: The Council for Community and Economic Research, ACCRA Cost of Living Index, 2014

HOUSING

House Price Index (HPI)

Area	National Ranking[2]	Quarterly Change (%)	One-Year Change (%)	Five-Year Change (%)
MD[1]	11	1.37	11.15	33.82
U.S.[3]	–	1.35	4.91	11.59

Note: The HPI is a weighted repeat sales index. It measures average price changes in repeat sales or refinancings on the same properties. This information is obtained by reviewing repeat mortgage transactions on single-family properties whose mortgages have been purchased or securitized by Fannie Mae or Freddie Mac in January 1975; (1) San Francisco-Redwood City-South San Francisco Metropolitan Division—see Appendix B for areas included; (2) Rankings are based on annual percentage change for all metro areas containing at least 15,000 transactions over the last 10 years and ranges from 1 to 275; (3) figures based on a weighted average of Census Division estimates using a seasonally adjusted, purchase-only index; all figures are for the period ending December 31, 2014
Source: Federal Housing Finance Agency, House Price Index, February 26, 2015

Median Single-Family Home Prices

Area	2012	2013	2014p	Percent Change 2013 to 2014
MSA[1]	543.8	669.6	737.6	10.2
U.S. Average	177.2	197.4	209.0	5.9

Note: Figures are median sales prices of existing single-family homes in thousands of dollars; (p) preliminary; n/a not available; (1) San Francisco-Oakland-Hayward, CA Metropolitan Statistical Area—see Appendix B for areas included
Source: National Association of Realtors, Median Sales Price of Existing Single-Family Homes for Metropolitan Areas, 4th Quarter 2014

Qualifying Income Based on Median Sales Price of Existing Single-Family Homes

Area	With 5% Down ($)	With 10% Down ($)	With 20% Down ($)
MSA[1]	163,256	154,663	137,478
U.S. Average	45,863	43,449	38,621

Note: Figures are preliminary; Qualifying income is based on a mortgage rate of 4.0%. Monthly principal and interest payment is limited to 25% of income; n/a not available; (1) San Francisco-Oakland-Hayward, CA Metropolitan Statistical Area—see Appendix B for areas included
Source: National Association of Realtors, Qualifying Income Based on Median Sales Price of Existing Single-Family Homes for Metropolitan Areas, 4th Quarter 2014

Median Apartment Condo-Coop Home Prices

Area	2012	2013	2014p	Percent Change 2013 to 2014
MSA[1]	393.8	517.4	580.1	12.1
U.S. Average	173.7	194.9	205.1	5.2

Note: Figures are median sales prices of existing apartment condo-coop homes in thousands of dollars; (p) preliminary; n/a not available; (1) San Francisco-Oakland-Hayward, CA Metropolitan Statistical Area—see Appendix B for areas included
Source: National Association of Realtors, Median Sales Price of Existing Apartment Condo-Coop Homes for Metropolitan Areas, 4th Quarter 2014

Gross Monthly Rent

Area	Under $200	$200 -299	$300 -499	$500 -749	$750 -999	$1,000 -1,499	$1,500 and up	Median ($)
City	1.4	4.4	5.0	8.1	9.2	22.5	49.4	1,487
MSA[1]	0.9	3.0	3.5	5.6	11.2	31.3	44.5	1,412
U.S.	1.7	3.2	7.8	22.1	24.3	26.0	14.9	900

Note: Figures are percentages except for Median; Gross rent is the contract rent plus the estimated average monthly cost of utilities (electricity, gas, and water and sewer) and fuels (oil, coal, kerosene, wood, etc.) if these are paid by the renter (or paid for the renter by someone else); (1) Figures cover the San Francisco-Oakland-Hayward, CA Metropolitan Statistical Area—see Appendix B for areas included
Source: U.S. Census Bureau, 2011-2013 American Community Survey 3-Year Estimates

Homeownership Rate

Area	2007 (%)	2008 (%)	2009 (%)	2010 (%)	2011 (%)	2012 (%)	2013 (%)	2014 (%)
MSA[1]	58.0	56.4	57.3	58.0	56.1	53.2	55.2	54.6
U.S.	68.1	67.8	67.4	66.9	66.1	65.4	65.1	64.5

Note: (1) Figures cover the San Francisco-Oakland-Hayward, CA Metropolitan Statistical Area—see Appendix B for areas included
Source: U.S. Census Bureau, Housing Vacancies and Homeownership Annual Statistics: 2014

Year Housing Structure Built

Area	2010 or Later	2000 -2009	1990 -1999	1980 -1989	1970 -1979	1960 -1969	1950 -1959	1940 -1949	Before 1940	Median Year
City	0.4	7.3	4.1	5.0	7.1	8.1	9.3	10.2	48.5	1942
MSA[1]	0.5	8.4	7.9	10.7	15.5	13.3	14.6	8.5	20.5	1965
U.S.	0.9	15.0	13.9	13.8	15.8	11.0	10.9	5.4	13.3	1976

Note: Figures are percentages except for Median Year; (1) Figures cover the San Francisco-Oakland-Hayward, CA Metropolitan Statistical Area—see Appendix B for areas included
Source: U.S. Census Bureau, 2011-2013 American Community Survey 3-Year Estimates

HEALTH

Health Risk Data

Category	MSA[1] (%)	U.S. (%)
Adults aged 18–64 who have any kind of health care coverage	84.5	79.6
Adults who reported being in good or excellent health	86.6	83.1
Adults who are current smokers	11.3	19.6
Adults who are heavy drinkers[2]	6.0	6.1
Adults who are binge drinkers[3]	18.9	16.9
Adults who are overweight (BMI 25.0 - 29.9)	30.6	35.8
Adults who are obese (BMI 30.0 - 99.8)	19.1	27.6
Adults who participated in any physical activities in the past month	82.5	77.1
Adults 50+ who have ever had a sigmoidoscopy or colonoscopy	64.6	67.3
Women aged 40+ who have had a mammogram within the past two years	78.7	74.0
Men aged 40+ who have had a PSA test within the past two years	38.4	45.2
Adults aged 65+ who have had flu shot within the past year	64.6	60.1
Adults who always wear a seatbelt	n/a	93.8

Note: Data as of 2012 unless otherwise noted; n/a not available; (1) Figures cover the San Francisco-San Mateo-Redwood City, CA—see Appendix B for areas included; (2) Heavy drinkers are classified as males having more than two drinks per day or females having more than one drink per day; (3) Binge drinkers are classified as males having five or more drinks on one occasion or females having four or more drinks on one occasion
Source: Centers for Disease Control and Prevention, Behaviorial Risk Factor Surveillance System, SMART: Selected Metropolitan/Micropolitan Area Risk Trends, 2012 (Note: the CDC has discontinued this dataset but will be releasing a replacement in late 2015)

Chronic Health Indicators

Category	MSA[1] (%)	U.S. (%)
Adults who have ever been told they had a heart attack	n/a	4.5
Adults who have ever been told they had a stroke	n/a	2.9
Adults who have been told they currently have asthma	10.7	8.9
Adults who have ever been told they have arthritis	21.3	25.7
Adults who have ever been told they have diabetes[2]	8.2	9.7
Adults who have ever been told they had skin cancer	4.4	5.7
Adults who have ever been told they had any other types of cancer	6.6	6.5
Adults who have ever been told they have COPD	3.0	6.2
Adults who have ever been told they have kidney disease	1.5	2.5
Adults who have ever been told they have a form of depression	10.9	18.0

Note: Data as of 2012 unless otherwise noted; n/a not available; (1) Figures cover the San Francisco-San Mateo-Redwood City, CA—see Appendix B for areas included; (2) Figures do not include pregnancy-related, borderline, or pre-diabetes
Source: Centers for Disease Control and Prevention, Behaviorial Risk Factor Surveillance System, SMART: Selected Metropolitan/Micropolitan Area Risk Trends, 2012 (Note: the CDC has discontinued this dataset but will be releasing a replacement in late 2015)

Mortality Rates for the Top 10 Causes of Death in the U.S.

ICD-10[a] Sub-Chapter	ICD-10[a] Code	Age-Adjusted Mortality Rate[1] per 100,000 population	
		County[2]	U.S.
Malignant neoplasms	C00-C97	143.7	166.2
Ischaemic heart diseases	I20-I25	66.4	105.7
Other forms of heart disease	I30-I51	28.0	49.3
Chronic lower respiratory diseases	J40-J47	20.7	42.1
Organic, including symptomatic, mental disorders	F01-F09	19.8	38.1
Cerebrovascular diseases	I60-I69	34.2	37.0
Other external causes of accidental injury	W00-X59	26.3	26.9
Other degenerative diseases of the nervous system	G30-G31	29.0	25.6
Diabetes mellitus	E10-E14	11.8	21.3
Hypertensive diseases	I10-I15	26.5	19.4

Note: (a) ICD-10 = International Classification of Diseases 10th Revision; (1) Mortality rates are a three year average covering 2011-2013; (2) Figures cover San Francisco County
Source: Centers for Disease Control and Prevention, National Center for Health Statistics. Compressed Mortality File 1999-2013 on CDC WONDER Online Database, released October 2014. Data are compiled from the Compressed Mortality File 1999-2013, Series 20 No. 2S, 2014.

Mortality Rates for Selected Causes of Death

ICD-10[a] Sub-Chapter	ICD-10[a] Code	Age-Adjusted Mortality Rate[1] per 100,000 population	
		County[2]	U.S.
Assault	X85-Y09	5.3	5.2
Diseases of the liver	K70-K76	10.0	13.2
Human immunodeficiency virus (HIV) disease	B20-B24	7.0	2.2
Influenza and pneumonia	J09-J18	13.9	15.4
Intentional self-harm	X60-X84	9.1	12.5
Malnutrition	E40-E46	*0.4	0.9
Obesity and other hyperalimentation	E65-E68	*0.7	1.8
Renal failure	N17-N19	6.6	13.1
Transport accidents	V01-V99	3.7	11.7
Viral hepatitis	B15-B19	3.3	2.2

Note: (a) ICD-10 = International Classification of Diseases 10th Revision; (1) Mortality rates are a three year average covering 2011-2013; (2) Figures cover San Francisco County; (*) Unreliable data as per CDC
Source: Centers for Disease Control and Prevention, National Center for Health Statistics. Compressed Mortality File 1999-2013 on CDC WONDER Online Database, released October 2014. Data are compiled from the Compressed Mortality File 1999-2013, Series 20 No. 2S, 2014.

Health Insurance Coverage

Area	With Health Insurance	With Private Health Insurance	With Public Health Insurance	Without Health Insurance	Population Under Age 18 Without Health Insurance
City	89.7	70.9	27.2	10.3	3.4
MSA[1]	88.5	71.9	26.4	11.5	4.8
U.S.	85.2	65.2	31.0	14.8	7.3

Note: Figures are percentages that cover the civilian noninstitutionalized population; (1) Figures cover the San Francisco-Oakland-Hayward, CA Metropolitan Statistical Area—see Appendix B for areas included
Source: U.S. Census Bureau, 2011-2013 American Community Survey 3-Year Estimates

Number of Medical Professionals

Area[1]	MDs[2]	DOs[2,3]	Dentists	Podiatrists	Chiropractors	Optometrists
Local (number)	6,491	88	1,168	86	304	199
Local (rate[4])	782.3	10.6	138.9	10.2	36.1	23.7
U.S. (rate[4])	270.0	20.2	63.1	5.7	25.2	14.9

Note: Data as of 2013 unless noted; (1) Local data covers San Francisco County; (2) Data as of 2012 and includes all active, non-federal physicians; (3) Doctor of Osteopathic Medicine; (4) rate per 100,000 population
Source: U.S. Department of Health and Human Services, Health Resources and Services Administration, Bureau of Health Professions, Area Resource File (ARF) 2013-2014

Best Hospitals

According to *U.S. News*, the San Francisco-Redwood City-South San Francisco, CA metro area is home to one of the best hospitals in the U.S.: **UCSF Medical Center** (Honor Roll/11 specialties). The hospital listed was nationally ranked in at least one adult specialty. Only 144 hospitals nationwide were nationally ranked in one or more specialties. Seventeen hospitals in the U.S. made the Honor Roll with high scores in at least six specialties. *U.S. News Online, "America's Best Children's Hospitals 2014-15"*

According to *U.S. News*, the San Francisco-Redwood City-South San Francisco, CA metro area is home to one of the best children's hospitals in the U.S.: **UCSF Benioff Children's Hospital** (10 specialties). The hospital listed was highly ranked in at least one pediatric specialty. Eighty-nine children's hospitals in the U.S. were nationally ranked in at least one specialty. Ten children's hospitals in the U.S. made the Honor Roll with high scores in at least three specialties. *U.S. News Online, "America's Best Children's Hospitals 2014-15"*

EDUCATION

Public School District Statistics

District Name	Schls	Pupils	Pupil/ Teacher Ratio	Minority Pupils[1] (%)	Free Lunch Eligible[2] (%)	IEP[3] (%)
San Francisco USD	126	56,970	19.8	89.2	46.7	12.0

Note: Table includes school districts with 2,000 or more students; (1) Percentage of students that are not non-Hispanic white; (2) Percentage of students that are eligible for the free lunch program; (3) Percentage of students that have an Individualized Education Program.
Source: U.S. Department of Education, National Center for Education Statistics, Common Core of Data, Local Education Agency (School District) Universe Survey: School Year 2012-2013; U.S. Department of Education, National Center for Education Statistics, Common Core of Data, Public Elementary/Secondary School Universe Survey: School Year 2012-2013

Highest Level of Education

Area	Less than H.S.	H.S. Diploma	Some College, No Deg.	Associate Degree	Bachelor's Degree	Master's Degree	Prof. School Degree	Doctorate Degree
City	13.5	13.1	15.2	5.3	32.1	13.5	4.9	2.4
MSA[1]	12.1	17.1	19.1	6.9	27.0	11.7	3.6	2.5
U.S.	13.7	28.0	21.2	7.9	18.2	7.7	1.9	1.3

Note: Figures cover persons age 25 and over; (1) Figures cover the San Francisco-Oakland-Hayward, CA Metropolitan Statistical Area—see Appendix B for areas included
Source: U.S. Census Bureau, 2011-2013 American Community Survey 3-Year Estimates

Educational Attainment by Race

Area	High School Graduate or Higher (%)					Bachelor's Degree or Higher (%)				
	Total	White	Black	Asian	Hisp.[2]	Total	White	Black	Asian	Hisp.[2]
City	86.5	94.5	86.0	76.4	73.6	52.9	66.5	23.4	41.4	29.5
MSA[1]	87.9	91.2	89.8	85.3	67.9	44.8	49.3	23.4	50.5	18.4
U.S.	86.3	88.3	83.1	85.7	64.0	29.1	30.4	18.8	50.7	13.7

Note: Figures shown cover persons 25 years old and over; (1) Figures cover the San Francisco-Oakland-Hayward, CA Metropolitan Statistical Area—see Appendix B for areas included; (2) People of Hispanic origin can be of any race
Source: U.S. Census Bureau, 2011-2013 American Community Survey 3-Year Estimates

School Enrollment by Grade and Control

Area	Preschool (%)		Kindergarten (%)		Grades 1 - 4 (%)		Grades 5 - 8 (%)		Grades 9 - 12 (%)	
	Public	Private	Public	Private	Public	Private	Public	Private	Public	Private
City	35.0	65.0	70.4	29.6	71.2	28.8	69.6	30.4	77.7	22.3
MSA[1]	40.8	59.2	83.4	16.6	86.0	14.0	86.0	14.0	88.3	11.7
U.S.	57.7	42.3	87.9	12.1	89.9	10.1	90.0	10.0	90.7	9.3

Note: Figures shown cover persons 3 years old and over; (1) Figures cover the San Francisco-Oakland-Hayward, CA Metropolitan Statistical Area—see Appendix B for areas included
Source: U.S. Census Bureau, 2011-2013 American Community Survey 3-Year Estimates

Average Salaries of Public School Classroom Teachers

Area	2013-14		2014-15		Percent Change 2013-14 to 2014-15	Percent Change 2004-05 to 2014-15
	Dollars	Rank[1]	Dollars	Rank[1]		
CALIFORNIA	71,396	4	72,535	4	1.59	25.9
U.S. Average	56,610	–	57,379	–	1.36	20.8

Note: (1) State rank ranges from 1 to 51 where 1 indicates highest salary.
Source: National Education Association, Rankings & Estimates: Rankings of the States 2014 and Estimates of School Statistics 2015, March 2015

Higher Education

Four-Year Colleges			Two-Year Colleges			Medical Schools[1]	Law Schools[2]	Voc/ Tech[3]
Public	Private Non-profit	Private For-profit	Public	Private Non-profit	Private For-profit			
3	9	3	1	0	3	1	4	4

Note: Figures cover institutions located within the city limits and include main campuses only; (1) includes schools accredited by the Liaison Committee on Medical Education and the American Osteopathic Association's Commission on Osteopathic College Accreditation; (2) includes ABA-accredited schools, schools with provisional ABA accreditation, and state accredited schools; (3) includes all schools with programs that are less than 2 years.
Source: National Center for Education Statistics, Integrated Postsecondary Education System (IPEDS), 2013-14; Association of American Medical Colleges, Member List, May 1, 2015; American Osteopathic Association, Member List, May 1, 2015; Law School Admission Council, Official Guide to ABA-Approved Law Schools Online, May 1, 2015; Wikipedia, List of Medical Schools in the United States, May 1, 2015; Wikipedia, List of Law Schools in the United States, May 1, 2015

According to *U.S. News & World Report,* the San Francisco-Redwood City-South San Francisco, CA metro division is home to one of the best national universities in the U.S.: **University of San Francisco** (#106). The indicators used to capture academic quality fall into a number of categories: assessment by administrators at peer institutions; retention of students; faculty resources; student selectivity; financial resources; alumni giving; high school counselor ratings of colleges; and graduation rate. *U.S. News & World Report, "America's Best Colleges 2015"*

According to *U.S. News & World Report,* the San Francisco-Redwood City-South San Francisco, CA metro division is home to one of the top 100 law schools in the U.S.: **University of California (Hastings)** (#59). The rankings are based on a weighted average of 12 measures of quality: peer assessment score; assessment score by lawyers/judges; median LSAT scores; median undergrad GPA; acceptance rate; employment rates for graduates; placement success; bar passage rate; faculty resources; expenditures per student; student/faculty ratio; and library resources. *U.S. News & World Report, "America's Best Graduate Schools, Law, 2016"*

According to *U.S. News & World Report,* the San Francisco-Redwood City-South San Francisco, CA metro division is home to one of the top 75 medical schools for research in the U.S.: **University of California-San Francisco** (#3). The rankings are based on a weighted average of 11 measures of quality: quality assessment; peer assessment score; assessment score by residency directors; research activity; total research activity; average research activity per faculty member; student selectivity; median MCAT total score; median undergraduate GPA; acceptance rate; and faculty resources. *U.S. News & World Report, "America's Best Graduate Schools, Medical, 2016"*

PRESIDENTIAL ELECTION

2012 Presidential Election Results

Area	Obama (%)	Romney (%)	Other (%)
San Francisco County	83.4	13.3	3.3
U.S.	51.0	47.2	1.8

Note: Results may not add to 100% due to rounding
Source: Dave Leip's Atlas of U.S. Presidential Elections

EMPLOYERS

Major Employers

Company Name	Industry
All Hallows Preservation	Apartment building operators
AT&T Corp.	Telephone communication, except radio
AT&T Services	Telephone communication, except radio
California Pacific Medical Center	General medical and surgical hospitals
City & County of San Francisco	General medical and surgical hospitals
City & County of San Francisco	Public welfare administration: nonoperating, govt.
Edy's Grand Ice Cream	Ice cream and ice milk
Franklin Templeton Services	Investment advice
Lawrence Berkeley National Laboratory	Supply agency, government
Lawrence Berkeley National Laboratory	Noncommercial research organizations
Lawrence Livermore National Laboratory	Noncommercial research organizations
Menlo Worldwide Forwarding	Letter delivery, private air
Oracle America	Minicomputers
Oracle Systems Corporation	Prepackaged software
Pacific Gas and Electric Company	Electric and other services combined
PACPIZZA	Pizzeria, chain
San Francisco Community College District	Colleges and universities
University of California, Berkeley	University
Veterans Health Administration	Administration of veterans' affairs
Wells Fargo Bank	National commercial banks

Note: Companies shown are located within the San Francisco-Oakland-Hayward, CA Metropolitan Statistical Area.
Source: Hoovers.com; Wikipedia

Best Companies to Work For

Kimpton Hotels & Restaurants; Twitter; salesforce, headquartered in San Francisco, are among "The 100 Best Companies to Work For." To pick the best companies, *Fortune* partnered with the Great Place to Work Institute. Two-thirds of a company's score is based on the results of the Institute's Trust Index survey, which is sent to a random sample of employees from each company. The questions related to attitudes about management's credibility, job satisfaction, and camaraderie. The other third of the scoring is based on the company's responses to the Institute's Culture Audit, which includes detailed questions about pay and benefit programs, and a series of open-ended questions about hiring practices, internal communication, training, recognition programs, and diversity efforts. Any company that is at least five years old with more than 1,000 U.S. employees is eligible. *Fortune, "The 100 Best Companies to Work For," 2015*

Kimpton Hotels & Restaurants; McKesson, headquartered in San Francisco, are among the "100 Best Places to Work in IT." To qualify, companies, both public and private, had to have a minimum of 50 IT employees and were selected based on average salary and bonus increases, the percentage of IT staffers promoted, IT staff turnover rates, training and development programs, and the percentage of women and minorities in IT staff and management positions. In addition, *Computerworld* looked at retention efforts, programs for recognizing and rewarding outstanding performances, and benefits such as flextime, elder care and child care, and reimbursement for college tuition and the cost of pursuing technology certifications. *Computerworld, "100 Best Places to Work in IT 2014"*

Williams-Sonoma, Inc, headquartered in San Francisco, is among the "Top Companies for Executive Women." To be named to the list, companies with a minimum of two women on the board complete a comprehensive application that focuses on the number of women in senior ranks. In addition to assessing corporate programs and policies dedicated to advancing women, NAFE examined the number of women in each company overall, in senior management, and on its board of directors, paying particular attention to the number of women with profit-and-loss responsibility. *National Association for Female Executives, "2015 NAFE Top 50 Companies for Executive Women"*

PUBLIC SAFETY

Crime Rate

Area	All Crimes	Violent Crimes				Property Crimes		
		Murder	Forcible Rape	Robbery	Aggrav. Assault	Burglary	Larceny -Theft	Motor Vehicle Theft
City	6,642.3	5.8	19.3	503.9	318.2	711.3	4,380.5	703.5
Suburbs[1]	2,375.5	1.5	17.9	77.4	154.4	429.3	1,471.9	223.1
Metro[2]	4,626.3	3.7	18.7	302.4	240.8	578.0	3,006.2	476.5
U.S.	3,098.6	4.5	25.2	109.1	229.1	610.0	1,899.4	221.3

Note: Figures are crimes per 100,000 population; (1) All areas within the metro area that are located outside the city limits; (2) Figures cover the San Francisco-Redwood City-South San Francisco, CA Metropolitan Division—see Appendix B for areas included
Source: FBI Uniform Crime Reports, 2013

Hate Crimes

Area	Number of Quarters Reported	Number of Incidents per Bias Motivation						
		Race	Religion	Sexual Orientation	Ethnicity	Disability	Gender	Gender Identity
City	4	7	3	13	1	0	0	0
U.S.	4	2,871	1,031	1,233	655	83	18	31

Source: Federal Bureau of Investigation, Hate Crime Statistics 2013

Identity Theft Consumer Complaints

Area	Complaints	Complaints per 100,000 Population	Rank[2]
MSA[1]	5,060	112.0	38
U.S.	332,646	104.3	-

Note: (1) Figures cover the San Francisco-Oakland-Hayward, CA Metropolitan Statistical Area—see Appendix B for areas included; (2) Rank ranges from 1 to 380 where 1 indicates greatest number of identity theft complaints per 100,000 population
Source: Federal Trade Commission, Consumer Sentinel Network Data Book for January–December 2014

Fraud and Other Consumer Complaints

Area	Complaints	Complaints per 100,000 Population	Rank[2]
MSA[1]	20,557	455.2	53
U.S.	2,250,205	705.7	-

Note: (1) Figures cover the San Francisco-Oakland-Hayward, CA Metropolitan Statistical Area—see Appendix B for areas included; (2) Rank ranges from 1 to 380 where 1 indicates greatest number of identity theft complaints per 100,000 population
Source: Federal Trade Commission, Consumer Sentinel Network Data Book for January–December 2014

RECREATION

Culture

Dance[1]	Theatre[1]	Instrumental Music[1]	Vocal Music[1]	Series and Festivals	Museums and Art Galleries[2]	Zoos and Aquariums[3]
27	26	13	18	25	162	3

Note: (1) Professional perfoming groups; (2) Based on organizations with SIC code 8412; (3) AZA-accredited
Source: The Grey House Performing Arts Directory, 2015-16; Association of Zoos & Aquariums, AZA Member Zoos & Aquariums, April 2015; www.AccuLeads.com, April 2015

Professional Sports Teams

Team Name	League	Year Established
Golden State Warriors	National Basketball Association (NBA)	1962
Oakland Athletics	Major League Baseball (MLB)	1968
Oakland Raiders	National Football League (NFL)	1960
San Francisco 49ers	National Football League (NFL)	1946
San Francisco Giants	Major League Baseball (MLB)	1958

Note: Includes teams located in the San Francisco-Oakland-Hayward, CA Metropolitan Statistical Area.
Source: Wikipedia, Major Professional Sports Teams of the United States and Canada, April 2015

CLIMATE

Average and Extreme Temperatures

Temperature	Jan	Feb	Mar	Apr	May	Jun	Jul	Aug	Sep	Oct	Nov	Dec	Yr.
Extreme High (°F)	72	77	85	92	97	106	105	98	103	99	85	75	106
Average High (°F)	56	59	61	64	66	70	71	72	73	70	63	56	65
Average Temp. (°F)	49	52	53	56	58	61	63	63	64	61	55	50	57
Average Low (°F)	42	44	45	47	49	52	53	54	54	51	47	42	49
Extreme Low (°F)	26	30	31	36	39	43	44	45	41	37	31	24	24

Note: Figures cover the years 1948-1990
Source: National Climatic Data Center, International Station Meteorological Climate Summary, 9/96

Average Precipitation/Snowfall/Humidity

Precip./Humidity	Jan	Feb	Mar	Apr	May	Jun	Jul	Aug	Sep	Oct	Nov	Dec	Yr.
Avg. Precip. (in.)	4.3	3.1	2.9	1.4	0.3	0.1	Tr	Tr	0.2	1.0	2.5	3.4	19.3
Avg. Snowfall (in.)	Tr	Tr	Tr	0	0	0	0	0	0	0	0	Tr	Tr
Avg. Rel. Hum. 7am (%)	86	85	82	79	78	77	81	83	83	83	85	86	82
Avg. Rel. Hum. 4pm (%)	67	65	63	61	61	60	60	62	60	60	64	68	63

Note: Figures cover the years 1948-1990; Tr = Trace amounts (<0.05 in. of rain; <0.5 in. of snow)
Source: National Climatic Data Center, International Station Meteorological Climate Summary, 9/96

Weather Conditions

Temperature			Daytime Sky			Precipitation		
10°F & below	32°F & below	90°F & above	Clear	Partly cloudy	Cloudy	0.01 inch or more precip.	0.1 inch or more snow/ice	Thunder-storms
0	6	4	136	130	99	63	< 1	5

Note: Figures are average number of days per year and cover the years 1948-1990
Source: National Climatic Data Center, International Station Meteorological Climate Summary, 9/96

HAZARDOUS WASTE

Superfund Sites

San Francisco has one hazardous waste site on the EPA's Superfund Final National Priorities List: **Treasure Island Naval Air Station - Hunters Point Annex**. There are a total of 1,322 Superfund sites on the list in the U.S. *U.S. Environmental Protection Agency, Final National Priorities List, April 14, 2015*

AIR & WATER QUALITY

Air Quality Trends: Ozone

	2004	2005	2006	2007	2008	2009	2010	2011	2012	2013
MSA[1]	0.063	0.058	0.066	0.059	0.067	0.066	0.063	0.062	0.059	0.058

Note: (1) Data covers the San Francisco-Oakland-Hayward, CA Metropolitan Statistical Area—see Appendix B for areas included. The values shown are the composite ozone concentration averages among trend sites based on the highest fourth daily maximum 8-hour concentration in parts per million. These trends are based on sites having an adequate record of monitoring data during the trend period. Data from exceptional events are included.
Source: U.S. Environmental Protection Agency, Air Quality Monitoring Information, "Air Quality Trends by City, 2000-2013"

Air Quality Index

Area	Percent of Days when Air Quality was...[2]					AQI Statistics[2]	
	Good	Moderate	Unhealthy for Sensitive Groups	Unhealthy	Very Unhealthy	Maximum	Median
MSA[1]	56.4	41.6	1.9	0.0	0.0	119	48

Note: (1) Data covers the San Francisco-Oakland-Hayward, CA Metropolitan Statistical Area—see Appendix B for areas included; (2) Based on 365 days with AQI data in 2014. Air Quality Index (AQI) is an index for reporting daily air quality. EPA calculates the AQI for five major air pollutants regulated by the Clean Air Act: ground-level ozone, particle pollution (aka particulate matter), carbon monoxide, sulfur dioxide, and nitrogen dioxide. The AQI runs from 0 to 500. The higher the AQI value, the greater the level of air pollution and the greater the health concern. There are six AQI categories: "Good" AQI is between 0 and 50. Air quality is considered satisfactory; "Moderate" AQI is between 51 and 100. Air quality is acceptable; "Unhealthy for Sensitive Groups" When AQI values are between 101 and 150, members of sensitive groups may experience health effects; "Unhealthy" When AQI values are between 151 and 200 everyone may begin to experience health effects; "Very Unhealthy" AQI values between 201 and 300 trigger a health alert; "Hazardous" AQI values over 300 trigger warnings of emergency conditions (not shown).
Source: U.S. Environmental Protection Agency, Air Quality Index Report, 2014

Air Quality Index Pollutants

Area	Percent of Days when AQI Pollutant was...[2]					
	Carbon Monoxide	Nitrogen Dioxide	Ozone	Sulfur Dioxide	Particulate Matter 2.5	Particulate Matter 10
MSA[1]	0.0	5.2	18.6	0.0	76.2	0.0

Note: (1) Data covers the San Francisco-Oakland-Hayward, CA Metropolitan Statistical Area—see Appendix B for areas included; (2) Based on 365 days with AQI data in 2014. The Air Quality Index (AQI) is an index for reporting daily air quality. EPA calculates the AQI for five major air pollutants regulated by the Clean Air Act: ground-level ozone, particle pollution (also known as particulate matter), carbon monoxide, sulfur dioxide, and nitrogen dioxide. The AQI runs from 0 to 500. The higher the AQI value, the greater the level of air pollution and the greater the health concern.
Source: U.S. Environmental Protection Agency, Air Quality Index Report, 2014

Maximum Air Pollutant Concentrations: Particulate Matter, Ozone, CO and Lead

	Particulate Matter 10 (ug/m^3)	Particulate Matter 2.5 Wtd AM (ug/m^3)	Particulate Matter 2.5 24-Hr (ug/m^3)	Ozone (ppm)	Carbon Monoxide (ppm)	Lead (ug/m^3)
MSA[1] Level	42	12.8	32	0.069	3	0.22
NAAQS[2]	150	15	35	0.075	9	0.15
Met NAAQS[2]	Yes	Yes	Yes	Yes	Yes	No

Note: (1) Data covers the San Francisco-Oakland-Hayward, CA Metropolitan Statistical Area—see Appendix B for areas included; Data from exceptional events are included; (2) National Ambient Air Quality Standards; ppm = parts per million; ug/m^3 = micrograms per cubic meter; n/a not available.
Concentrations: Particulate Matter 10 (coarse particulate)—highest second maximum 24-hour concentration; Particulate Matter 2.5 Wtd AM (fine particulate)—highest weighted annual mean concentration; Particulate Matter 2.5 24-Hour (fine particulate)—highest 98th percentile 24-hour concentration; Ozone—highest fourth daily maximum 8-hour concentration; Carbon Monoxide—highest second maximum non-overlapping 8-hour concentration; Lead—maximum running 3-month average
Source: U.S. Environmental Protection Agency, Air Quality Monitoring Information, "Air Quality Statistics by City, 2013"

Maximum Air Pollutant Concentrations: Nitrogen Dioxide and Sulfur Dioxide

	Nitrogen Dioxide AM (ppb)	Nitrogen Dioxide 1-Hr (ppb)	Sulfur Dioxide AM (ppb)	Sulfur Dioxide 1-Hr (ppb)	Sulfur Dioxide 24-Hr (ppb)
MSA[1] Level	17	60	n/a	17	n/a
NAAQS[2]	53	100	30	75	140
Met NAAQS[2]	Yes	Yes	n/a	Yes	n/a

Note: (1) Data covers the San Francisco-Oakland-Hayward, CA Metropolitan Statistical Area—see Appendix B for areas included; Data from exceptional events are included; (2) National Ambient Air Quality Standards; ppm = parts per million; ug/m^3 = micrograms per cubic meter; n/a not available.
Concentrations: Nitrogen Dioxide AM—highest arithmetic mean concentration; Nitrogen Dioxide 1-Hr—highest 98th percentile 1-hour daily maximum concentration; Sulfur Dioxide AM—highest annual mean concentration; Sulfur Dioxide 1-Hr—highest 99th percentile 1-hour daily maximum concentration; Sulfur Dioxide 24-Hr—highest second maximum 24-hour concentration
Source: U.S. Environmental Protection Agency, Air Quality Monitoring Information, "Air Quality Statistics by City, 2013"

Drinking Water

Water System Name	Pop. Served	Primary Water Source Type	Violations[1]	
			Health Based	Monitoring/ Reporting
San Francisco Intl Airport	103,423	Purchased Surface	0	0
San Francisco Public Utilities	2,400,000	Purchased Surface	n/a	n/a

Note: (1) Based on violation data from January 1, 2014 to December 31, 2014 (includes unresolved violations from earlier years)
Source: U.S. Environmental Protection Agency, Office of Ground Water and Drinking Water, Safe Drinking Water Information System (based on data extracted January 27, 2015)

San Jose, California

Background

Like many cities in the valleys of northern California, San Jose is an abundant cornucopia of wine grapes and produce. Situated only seven miles from the southernmost tip of San Francisco Bay, San Jose is flanked by the Santa Cruz Mountains to the west, and the Mount Hamilton arm of the Diablo Range to the east. The Coyote and Guadalupe rivers gently cut through this landscape, carrying water only in the spring.

San Jose was founded on November 29, 1777, by Spanish colonizers, and can rightfully claim to be the oldest civic settlement in California. Like its present-day role, San Jose was established by the Spanish to be a produce and cattle supplier to the nearby communities and presidios of San Francisco and Monterey.

After U.S. troops wrested the territory of California from Mexican rule, San Jose became its state capital. At the same time, the city served as a supply base to gold prospectors.

Today, San Jose retains much of its history. As in the past, it is still a major shipping and processing center for agricultural produce. Also, San Jose produces some of the best table wines in the country. To remind its citizens of its Spanish heritage, a replica of the Mission of Santa Clara stands on the grounds of the University of Santa Clara.

Due to annexation of surrounding communities after World War II, the population of San Jose has increased more than tenfold. With the additional industries of NASA research, and electronic components and motors production to attract people to the area, San Jose is rapidly becoming a family-oriented community of housing developments and shopping malls.

During the 1990s, San Jose was home to more than half of Silicon Valley's leading semiconductor, networking, and telecommunications companies, giving it the nickname "Capital of Silicon Valley." The newly renovated downtown became headquarters for a number of major developers of computer software.

In the new century, San Jose suffered from the downturn in electronics and computer industries, but the city has developed numerous strategies, including economic incentives and redevelopment programs to solve unemployment and ensure that the city remains economically healthy and grows into the future.

The HP Pavilion, home of the San Jose Sharks hockey team, is one of the most active venues for events in the world, selling the most tickets to non-sporting events of any venue in the United States.

San Jose enjoys a Mediterranean, or dry summer subtropical, climate. The rain that does fall comes mostly during the months of November through March. Severe winter storms with gale winds and heavy rain occur occasionally. The summer weather is dominated by night and morning stratus clouds along with sea breezes blowing from the cold waters of the bay. During the winter months fog is common, causing difficult flying conditions. Inversions causing pollution are not common during the summer months, but become more frequent during the fall and winter.

Rankings

General Rankings

- The San Jose metro area was identified as one of America's fastest-growing areas in terms of population and economy by *Forbes*. The area ranked #17 out of 20. The 100 most populous metro areas in the U.S. were evaluated on the following criteria: estimated population growth; job growth; gross metropolitan product growth; unemployment; median salaries for college-educated workers. *Forbes, "America's Fastest-Growing Cities 2015," January 27, 2015*

- Among the 50 largest U.S. cities, San Jose placed #26 in Vocativ's "semi-exhaustive, mostly scientific" city Livability Index for people aged 35 and under. Average salary, unemployment rates, rents, and other living costs were considered, along with crime rates, weather, public transportation, access to music and sports, and "lifestyle metrics" such as the price of dinner at Buffalo Wild Wings and an ounce of high-quality weed. *vocative.com, "The Livability Index: The Best U.S. Cities for People 35 and Under," December 9, 2014*

- San Jose was selected as one of America's best cities by *Bloomberg Businessweek*. The city ranked #33 out of 50. Criteria: leisure attributes (the number of restaurants, bars, libraries, museums, professional sports teams, and park acres by population); educational attributes (public school performance, the number of colleges, and graduate degree holders); economic factors (2011 income and June and July 2012 unemployment); crime; and air quality. *Bloomberg BusinessWeek, "America's Best Cities," September 26, 2012*

Business/Finance Rankings

- Measuring indicators of "tolerance"—the nonjudgmental environment that "attracts open-minded and new-thinking kinds of people"— as well as concentrations of technological and economic innovators, analysts identified the most creative American metro areas. On the resulting 2012 Creativity Index, the San Jose metro area placed #12. *www.thedailybeast.com, "Boulder, Ann Arbor, Tucson & More: 20 Most Creative U.S. Cities," June 26, 2012*

- TransUnion ranked the nation's metro areas by average credit score, calculated on the VantageScore system, developed by the three major credit-reporting bureaus—TransUnion, Experian, and Equifax. The San Jose metro area was among the ten cities with the highest collective credit score, meaning that its residents posed the lowest average consumer credit risk. *www.usatoday.com, "Metro Areas' Average Credit Rating Revealed," February 7, 2013*

- Building on the U.S. Department of Labor's Occupational Information Network Data Collection Program, the Brookings Institution defined STEM occupations and job opportunities for STEM workers at various levels of educational attainment. The San Jose metro area was placed among the ten large metro areas with the highest demand for high-level STEM knowledge. *www.brookings.edu, "The Hidden Stem Economy," June 10, 2013*

- The business website 24/7 Wall Street drew on Brookings Institution research on 50 advanced industries to identify the proportion of workers in the nation's largest metropolitan areas that were employed in jobs requiring knowledge in the science, technology, engineering, or math (STEM) fields. The San Jose metro area was #1. *247wallst.com, "15 Cities with the Most High-Tech Jobs," March 13, 2015*

- Based on metro area social media reviews, the employment opinion group Glassdoor surveyed 50 of the largest U.S. metro areas on measures including compensation and benefits, satisfaction with management, business outlook, and number of employers hiring. The San Jose metro area was ranked #1 in overall employee satisfaction. *www.glassdoor.com, "Employment Satisfaction Report Card by City," June 13, 2014*

- In a survey of economic confidence in the nation's 50 largest metropolitan areas conducted January–December 2014, the San Jose metro area placed #1, according to Gallup's 2014 Economic Confidence Index. *Gallup, "San Jose and San Francisco Lead in Economic Confidence," March 19, 2015*

- Using data from the Council for Community and Economic Research's 2013 Annual Report, NerdWallet ranked the 100 U.S. cities with the most expensive cost of living. Cities in California and in the Northeast topped the list. Of the cities with the highest cost of living, San Jose ranked #6. *NerdWallet.com, "Most Expensive Cities in America," June 4, 2014*

- The Brookings Institution ranked the 50 largest cities in the U.S. based on income inequality. San Jose was ranked #25. (#1 = greatest ineqality). Criteria: the cities were ranked based on the "95/20 ratio," a figure representing the income at which a household earns more than 95 percent of all other households, divided by the income at which a household earns more than only 20 percent of all other households. *Brookings Institution, "Income Inequality in America's 50 Largest Cities, 2007-2013," March 17, 2015*

- *Forbes* ranked the largest metro areas in the U.S. in terms of the "Best Cities for Young Professionals." The San Jose metro area ranked #11 out of 15. Criteria: job growth; unemployment rate; median salary of college graduates age 24 to 34; cost of living; number of small businesses per capita; number of large companies; percentage of population 25 years of age and older with college degrees. *Forbes.com, "America's 15 Best Cities for Young Professionals," August 18, 2014*

- San Jose was ranked #1 out of 100 metro areas in terms of economic performance (#1 = best) during the recession and recovery from trough quarter through the second quarter of 2013. Criteria: percent change in employment; percentage point change in unemployment rate; percent change in gross metropolitan product; percent change in House Price Index. *Brookings Institution, MetroMonitor: Tracking Economic Recession and Recovery in America's 100 Largest Metropolitan Areas, September 2013*

- For its annual survey of the "Most Expensive U.S. Cities to Live In," Kiplinger applied Cost of Living Index statistics developed by the Council for Community and Economic Research to U.S. Census Bureau population and median household income data for cities with populations above 50,000. In the resulting ranking, San Jose ranked #4. *Kiplinger.com, "Most Expensive U.S. Cities to Live In," May 2014*

- San Jose was identified as one of the happiest cities for young professionals by *CareerBliss.com*, an online community for career advancement. The city ranked #1. Criteria: more than 45,000 young professionals were asked to rate key factors that affect workplace happiness including: work-life balance; compensation; company culture; overall work environment; company reputation; relationships with managers and co-workers; opportunities for growth; job resources; daily tasks; job autonomy. Young professionals are defined as having less than 10 years of work experience. *CareerBliss.com, "Happiest Cities for Young Professionals," April 26, 2013*

- The San Jose metro area appeared on the Milken Institute "2013 Best Performing Cities" list. Rank: #4 out of 200 large metro areas. Criteria: job growth; wage and salary growth; high-tech output growth. *Milken Institute, "Best-Performing Cities 2014," January 2015*

- *Forbes* ranked the 200 most populous metro areas to determine the nation's "Best Places for Business and Careers." The San Jose metro area was ranked #32. Criteria: costs (business and living); job growth (past and projected); income growth; educational attainment (college and high school); projected economic growth; cultural and recreational opportunities; net migration patterns; number of highly ranked colleges. *Forbes, "The Best Places for Business and Careers 2014," July 23, 2014*

Dating/Romance Rankings

- A *Cosmopolitan* magazine article surveyed the gender balance and other factors to arrive at a list of the best and worst cities for women to meet single guys. San Jose was #7 among the best for single women looking for dates. *www.cosmopolitan.com, "Working the Ratio," October 1, 2013*

- *Forbes* reports that the San Jose metro area made Rent.com's Best Cities for Newlyweds survey for 2013, based on Bureau of Labor Statistics and Census Bureau data on number of married couples, percentage of families with children under age six, average annual income, cost of living, and availability of rentals. *www.forbes.com, "The 10 Best Cities for Newlyweds to Live and Work In," May 30, 2013*

- CreditDonkey, a financial education website, sought out the ten best U.S. cities for newlyweds, considering the number of married couples, divorce rate, average credit score, and average number of hours worked per week in metro areas with a million or more residents. The San Jose metro area placed #2. *www.creditdonkey.com, "Study: Best Cities for Newlyweds," November 30, 2013*

- Of the 100 U.S. cities surveyed by *Men's Health* in its quest to identify the nation's best cities for dating and forming relationships, San Jose was ranked #43 for online dating (#1 = best). *Men's Health, "The Best and Worst Cities for Online Dating," January 30, 2013*

- San Jose was selected as one of the best cities for single women by *Rent.com*. Criteria: high single male-to-female ratio. *Rent.com, "Top Cities for Single Women," March 7, 2013*

- San Jose was selected as one of the best cities for newlyweds by *Rent.com*. The city ranked #6 of 10. Criteria: cost of living; availability of rental inventory; annual mean wages; percentage of married couples; percentage of children under the age of six. *Rent.com, "10 Best Cities for Newlyweds," May 10, 2013*

Education Rankings

- Based on a Brookings Institution study, *24/7 Wall St.* identified the ten U.S. metropolitan areas with the most average patent filings per million residents between 2007 and 2011. San Jose ranked #1. *24/7 Wall St., "America's Most Innovative Cities," February 1, 2013*

- The San Jose metro area was selected as one of America's most innovative cities" by *The Business Insider*. The metro area was ranked #1 out of 20. Criteria: patents per capita. *The Business Insider, "The 20 Most Innovative Cities in the U.S.," February 1, 2013*

- San Jose was identified as one of America's "smartest" metropolitan areas by *The Business Journals*. The area ranked #5 out of 10. Criteria: percentage of adults (25 and older) with high school diplomas, bachelor's degrees and graduate degrees. *The Business Journals, "Where the Brainpower Is: Exclusive U.S. Rankings, Insights," February 27, 2014*

- Personal finance website *WalletHub* analyzed the 150 largest U.S. metropolitan statistical areas to determine where the most educated Americans are choosing to settle. Criteria: educational attainment; percentage of workers with jobs in computer, engineering, and science fields; quality and size of each metro area's universities. San Jose was ranked #7 (#1 = most educated city). *www.WalletHub.com, "2014's Most and Least Educated Cities*

- The real estate website *MovoTo.com* selected San Jose as one of the "Nerdiest Cities in America." The city ranked #9 among the top 10 derived from data on the 50 most populous cities in the United States. Criteria: Number of annual comic book, video game, anime, and sci-fi/fantasy conventions; people per comic book store, video game store, and traditional gaming store; people per LARPing ("live action role-playing") group; people per science museum. Also factored in: distance to the nearest Renaissance faire. *MovoTo.com, "The 10 Nerdiest Cities in America," April 10, 2013*

- San Jose was selected as one of America's most literate cities. The city ranked #39 out of the 77 largest U.S. cities. Criteria: number of booksellers; library resources; Internet resources; educational attainment; periodical publishing resources; newspaper circulation. *Central Connecticut State University, "America's Most Literate Cities, 2014," April 8, 2015*

Environmental Rankings

- The San Jose metro area came in at #48 for the relative comfort of its climate on Sperling's list of "chill cities," as measured by the Sperling Heat Index. All 361 metro areas are included. Criteria included daytime high temperatures, nighttime low temperatures, dew point, and relative humidity at the high temperatures. *www.bertsperling.com, "Sperling's Chill Cities," July 18, 2013*

- Sperling's BestPlaces assessed 379 metropolitan areas of the United States for the likelihood of dangerously extreme weather events or earthquakes. In general the Southeast and South-Central regions have the highest risk of weather extremes and earthquakes, while the Pacific Northwest enjoys the lowest risk. Of the least risky metropolitan areas, the San Jose metro area was ranked #69. *www.bestplaces.net, "Safest Places from Natural Disasters," April 2011*

- San Jose was identified as one of America's dirtiest metro areas by *Forbes*. The area ranked #8 out of 20. Criteria: air quality; water quality; toxic releases; superfund sites. *Forbes, "America's 20 Dirtiest Cities," December 10, 2012*

- The U.S. Environmental Protection Agency (EPA) released a list of large U.S. metropolitan areas with the most ENERGY STAR certified buildings in 2014. The San Jose metro area was ranked #22 out of 25. *U.S. Environmental Protection Agency, "Top Cities With the Most ENERGY STAR Certified Buildings in 2014," March 25, 2015*

- The U.S. Environmental Protection Agency (EPA) released a list of mid-size U.S. metropolitan areas with the most ENERGY STAR certified buildings in 2014. The San Jose metro area was ranked #2 out of 10. *U.S. Environmental Protection Agency, "Top Cities With the Most ENERGY STAR Certified Buildings in 2014," March 25, 2015*

- San Jose was highlighted as one of the 25 metro areas most polluted by year-round particle pollution (Annual PM 2.5) in the U.S. during 2011 through 2013. The area ranked #7. *American Lung Association, State of the Air 2015*

- San Jose was highlighted as one of the 25 metro areas most polluted by short-term particle pollution (24-hour PM 2.5) in the U.S. during 2011 through 2013. The area ranked #6. *American Lung Association, State of the Air 2015*

Food/Drink Rankings

- *Men's Health* ranked 100 major U.S. cities in terms of alcohol intoxication. San Jose ranked #46 (#1 = most sober).Criteria: binge drinking; alcohol-related traffic accidents, arrests, and fatalities. *Men's Health, "The Drunkest Cities in America," November 19, 2013*

- San Jose was identified as one of the most vegetarian-friendly cities in America by GrubHub.com, the nation's largest food ordering service. The city ranked #2 out of 10. Criteria: percentage of vegetarian restaurants. *GrubHub.com, "Top Vegetarian-Friendly Cities," July 18, 2012*

Health/Fitness Rankings

- Analysts who tracked obesity rates in the nation's largest metro areas (those with populations above one million) found that the San Jose metro area was one of the ten major metros where residents were least likely to be obese, defined as a BMI score of 30 or above. *www.gallup.com, "Boulder, Colo., Residents Still Least Likely to Be Obese," April 4, 2014*

- Analysts who tracked obesity rates in 189 of the nation's metro areas found that the San Jose metro area was one of the ten communities where residents were least likely to be obese, defined as a BMI score of 30 or above. *www.gallup.com, "Boulder, Colo., Residents Still Least Likely to Be Obese," April 4, 2014*

- For each of the 50 most populous metro areas in the United States, the American College of Sports Medicine's American Fitness Index evaluated infrastructure, community assets, and policies that encourage healthy and fit lifestyles, including preventive health behaviors, levels of chronic disease conditions, health care access, and community resources and policies that support physical activity. The San Jose metro area ranked #10 for "community fitness." Personal health indicators were considered as well as community and environmental indicators. *www.americanfitnessindex.org, "ACSM American Fitness Index Health and Community Fitness Status of the 50 Largest Metropolitan Areas," May 2013*

- The San Jose metro area was identified as one of the worst cities for bed bugs in America by pest control company Orkin. The area ranked #19 out of 50 based on the number of bed bug treatments Orkin performed from January to December 2013. *Orkin, "Chicago Tops Bed Bug Cities List for Second Year in a Row," January 16, 2014*

- San Jose was selected as one of the 25 fittest cities in America by *Men's Fitness Online*. It ranked #14 out of America's 50 largest cities. Criteria: fitness centers and sport stores; nutrition; sports participation; TV viewing; overweight/sedentary; junk food; air quality; geography; commute; parks and open space; city recreational facilities; access to healthcare; motivation; mayor and city initiatives; state obesity initiatives. *Men's Fitness, "The Fittest and Fattest Cities in America," March 5, 2012*

- San Jose was identified as a "2013 Spring Allergy Capital." The area ranked #88 out of 100. Three groups of factors were used to identify the most severe cities for people with allergies during the spring season: annual pollen levels; medicine utilization; access to board-certified allergists. *Asthma and Allergy Foundation of America, "Spring Allergy Capitals 2013"*

- San Jose was identified as a "2013 Fall Allergy Capital." The area ranked #95 out of 100. Three groups of factors were used to identify the most severe cities for people with allergies during the fall season: annual pollen levels; medicine utilization; access to board-certified allergists. *Asthma and Allergy Foundation of America, "Fall Allergy Capitals 2013"*

- San Jose was identified as a "2013 Asthma Capital." The area ranked #88 out of the nation's 100 largest metropolitan areas. Twelve factors were used to identify the most challenging places to live for people with asthma: estimated prevalence; self-reported prevalence; crude death rate for asthma; annual pollen score; annual air quality; public smoking laws; number of board-certified asthma specialists; school inhaler access laws; rescue medication use; controller medication use; uninsured rate; poverty rate. *Asthma and Allergy Foundation of America, "Asthma Capitals 2013"*

- *Men's Health* ranked 100 major U.S. cities in terms of the best and worst cities for men. San Jose ranked #3. Criteria: thirty-three data points were examined covering health, fitness, and quality of life. *Men's Health, "The Best & Worst Cities for Men 2014," December 6, 2013*

- The San Jose metro area appeared in the 2013 Gallup-Healthways Well-Being Index. The area ranked #5 out of 189. The Gallup-Healthways Well-Being Index score is an average of six sub-indexes, which individually examine life evaluation, emotional health, work environment, physical health, healthy behaviors, and access to basic necessities. Results are based on telephone interviews conducted as part of the Gallup-Healthways Well-Being Index survey January 2–December 29, 2012, and January 2–December 30, 2013, with a random sample of 531,630 adults, aged 18 and older, living in metropolitan areas in the 50 U.S. states and the District of Columbia. *Gallup-Healthways, "State of American Well-Being," March 25, 2014*

- The San Jose metro area was identified as one of "America's Most Stressful Cities" by *Sperling's BestPlaces*. The metro area ranked #45 out of 50. Criteria: unemployment rate; suicide rate; commute time; mental health; poor rest; alcohol use; violent crime rate; property crime rate; cloudy days annually. *Sperling's BestPlaces, www.BestPlaces.net, "Stressful Cities 2012*

Real Estate Rankings

- The San Jose metro area appeared on Realtor.com's list of the hottest housing markets to watch in 2015. Criteria: strong housing growth; affordable prices; and fast-paced sales. *Realtor.com®, "Top 10 Hot Housing Markets to Watch in 2015," December 4, 2014*

- Using data from the housing-market research firm RealtyTrac, Yahoo! Finance researchers listed the housing markets in which housing affordability is deteriorating most, factoring in interest rates as well as median home prices. The San Jose metro area was among the least affordable housing markets according to the percentage difference in the income required to buy a home in December 2013 as opposed to in December 2012. *news.yahoo.com, "10 Cities Where Ordinary People Can No Longer Afford Homes," March 5, 2014*

- The San Jose metro area was identified as one of the nation's 20 hottest housing markets in 2015.Criteria: median number of days homes were spending on the market in March 2015. The area ranked #1. *Realtor.com, "These Are the 20 Hottest Housing Markets in the U.S. Right Now," April 8, 2015*

- San Jose was ranked #21 out of 275 metro areas in terms of house price appreciation in 2014 (#1 = highest rate). *Federal Housing Finance Agency, House Price Index, 4th Quarter 2014*

- The San Jose metro area was identified as one of the 20 least affordable housing markets in the U.S. in 2014. The area ranked #1 out of 178 markets. Criteria: whether or not a typical family could qualify for a mortgage loan on a typical home. *National Association of Realtors®, Affordability Index of Existing Single-Family Homes for Metropolitan Areas, 2014*

- San Jose was ranked #220 out of 226 metro areas in terms of housing affordability in 2014 by the National Association of Home Builders (#1 = most affordable). The NAHB-Wells Fargo Housing Opportunity Index (HOI) for a given area is defined as the share of homes sold in that area that would have been affordable to a family earning the local median income, based on standard mortgage underwriting criteria. *National Association of Home Builders®, NAHB-Wells Fargo Housing Opportunity Index, 4th Quarter 2014*

Safety Rankings

- Symantec, in partnership with Sperling's BestPlaces, ranked the 50 largest cities in the U.S. in terms of their vulnerability to cybercrime. The city ranked #13. Criteria: number of cyberattacks and potential infections; level of Internet access; expenditures on smartphones and computer hardware/software; wireless hotspots; broadband connectivity; Internet usage; online purchases. *Symantec, "Riskiest Online Cities of 2012" February 15, 2012*

- Farmers Insurance, in partnership with Sperling's BestPlaces, ranked metro areas in the U.S. and identified the "Most Secure Places to Live." The San Jose metro area ranked #7 out of the top 20 in the large metro area category (500,000 or more residents). Criteria: economic stability; crime statistics; extreme weather; risk of natural disasters; housing depreciation; foreclosures; air quality; environmental hazards; life expectancy; motor vehicle fatalities; and employment numbers. *Farmers Insurance Group of Companies, "Most Secure U.S. Places to Live in the U.S.," June 25, 2013*

- Allstate ranked the 200 largest cities in America in terms of driver safety. San Jose ranked #151. Allstate researchers analyzed internal property damage claims over a two-year period from January 2011 to December 2012. A weighted average of the two-year numbers determined the annual percentages. *Allstate, "Allstate America's Best Drivers Report, 2014"*

- San Jose was identified as one of the safest large cities in America by CQ Press. All 32 cities with populations of 500,000 or more that reported crime rates in 2012 for murder, rape, robbery, aggravated assault, burglary, and motor vehicle thefts were ranked. The city ranked #8 out of the top 10. *CQ Press, City Crime Rankings 2014*

- The National Insurance Crime Bureau ranked 380 metro areas in the U.S. in terms of per capita rates of vehicle theft. The San Jose metro area ranked #9 (#1 = highest rate). Criteria: number of vehicle theft offenses per 100,000 inhabitants in 2012. *National Insurance Crime Bureau, "Hot Spots 2012," June 26, 2013*

Seniors/Retirement Rankings

- From its Best Cities for Successful Aging indexes, the Milken Institute generated rankings for metropolitan areas, weighing data in eight categories—health care, wellness, living arrangements, transportation, financial characteristics, education and employment opportunities, community engagement, and overall livability. The San Jose metro area was ranked #65 overall in the large metro area category. *Milken Institute, "Best Cities for Successful Aging, 2014"*

Sports/Recreation Rankings

- San Jose was chosen as a bicycle friendly community by the League of American Bicyclists. A "Bicycle Friendly Community" welcomes cyclists by providing safe accommodation for cycling and encouraging people to bike for transportation and recreation. There are four award levels: Platinum; Gold; Silver; and Bronze. The community achieved an award level of Bronze. *League of American Bicyclists, "Bicycle Friendly Community Master List," Fall 2013*

- San Jose was chosen as one of America's best cities for bicycling. The city ranked #29 out of 50. Criteria: robust cycling infrastructure; vibrant bike culture. The editors only considered cities with populations of 95,000 or more. *Bicycling, "America's Top 50 Bike-Friendly Cities," May 23, 2012*

Women/Minorities Rankings

- The Daily Beast surveyed the nation's cities for highest percentage of singles and lowest divorce rate, plus other measures, to determine "emotional intelligence"—happiness, confidence, kindness—which, researchers say, has a strong correlation with people's satisfaction with their romantic relationships. San Jose placed #24. *www.thedailybeast.com, "Best Cities to Find Love and Stay in Love," February 14, 2014*

- To determine the best metro areas for working women, the personal finance website NerdWallet considered city size as well as relevant economic metrics—high salaries, narrow pay differential by gender, prevalence of women in the highest-paying industries, and population growth over 2010–2012. Of the large U.S. cities examined, the San Jose metro area held the #3 position. *www.nerdwallet.com, "Best Places for Women in the Workforce," May 19, 2013*

- *Women's Health* examined U.S. cities and identified the 100 best cities for women. San Jose was ranked #2. Criteria: 30 categories were examined from obesity and breast cancer rates to commuting times and hours spent working out. *Women's Health, "Best Cities for Women 2012"*

- San Jose was selected as one of the best cities for young Latinos in 2013 by mun2, a national cable television broadcast network. The city ranked #13. Criteria: U.S. cities with populations over 500,000 residents were evaluated on the following criteria: number of young latinos; jobs; friendliness; cost of living; fun. *mun2.tv, "Best Cities for Young Latinos 2013*

Miscellaneous Rankings

- Business Insider reports on the 2013 Trick-or-Treat Index compiled by the real estate site Zillow, which used its own Home Value Index and Walk Score along with population density and local crime stats to determine that San Jose ranked #4 for "how much candy it gives out versus how far kids have to walk to get it." Zillow also zeroes in on the best neighborhoods in its top 20 cities. *www.businessinsider.com, "These Are the Best Cities for Trick-or-Treating," October 15, 2013*

- The National Alliance to End Homelessness ranked the 100 most populous metro areas in terms the rate of homelessness. The San Jose metro area ranked #7. Criteria: number of homeless people per 10,000 population in 2011. *National Alliance to End Homelessness, The State of Homelessness in America 2012*

- The financial education website CreditDonkey compiled a list of the ten "best" cities of the future, based on percentage of housing built in 1990 or later, population change since 2010, and construction jobs as a percentage of population. Also considered were two more futuristic criteria: number of DeLorean cars available for purchase and number of spaceport companies and proposed spaceports. San Jose was scored #7. *www.creditDonkey.com, "In the Future, Almost All of America's 'Best' Cities Will Be on the West Coast, Report Says," February 14, 2014*

Business Environment

CITY FINANCES

City Government Finances

Component	2012 ($000)	2012 ($ per capita)
Total Revenues	1,753,154	1,853
Total Expenditures	1,741,437	1,841
Debt Outstanding	5,924,630	6,263
Cash and Securities[1]	7,086,202	7,491

Note: (1) Cash and security holdings of a government at the close of its fiscal year, including those of its dependent agencies, utilities, and liquor stores.
Source: U.S Census Bureau, State & Local Government Finances 2012

City Government Revenue by Source

Source	2012 ($000)	2012 ($ per capita)
General Revenue		
From Federal Government	51,212	54
From State Government	65,387	69
From Local Governments	150	0
Taxes		
Property	449,503	475
Sales and Gross Receipts	288,172	305
Personal Income	0	0
Corporate Income	0	0
Motor Vehicle License	0	0
Other Taxes	125,743	133
Current Charges	596,190	630
Liquor Store	0	0
Utility	28,472	30
Employee Retirement	3,537	4

Source: U.S Census Bureau, State & Local Government Finances 2012

City Government Expenditures by Function

Function	2012 ($000)	2012 ($ per capita)	2012 (%)
General Direct Expenditures			
Air Transportation	91,135	96	5.2
Corrections	0	0	0.0
Education	0	0	0.0
Employment Security Administration	0	0	0.0
Financial Administration	0	0	0.0
Fire Protection	122,185	129	7.0
General Public Buildings	0	0	0.0
Governmental Administration, Other	98,836	104	5.7
Health	1,835	2	0.1
Highways	79,197	84	4.5
Hospitals	0	0	0.0
Housing and Community Development	43,499	46	2.5
Interest on General Debt	261,476	276	15.0
Judicial and Legal	0	0	0.0
Libraries	29,809	32	1.7
Parking	6,705	7	0.4
Parks and Recreation	89,615	95	5.1
Police Protection	251,179	266	14.4
Public Welfare	0	0	0.0
Sewerage	115,881	123	6.7
Solid Waste Management	142,090	150	8.2
Veterans' Services	0	0	0.0
Liquor Store	0	0	0.0
Utility	23,580	25	1.4
Employee Retirement	289,810	306	16.6

Source: U.S Census Bureau, State & Local Government Finances 2012

DEMOGRAPHICS

Population Growth

Area	1990 Census	2000 Census	2010 Census	Population Growth (%)	
				1990-2000	2000-2010
City	784,324	894,943	945,942	14.1	5.7
MSA[1]	1,534,280	1,735,819	1,836,911	13.1	5.8
U.S.	248,709,873	281,421,906	308,745,538	13.2	9.7

Note: (1) Figures cover the San Jose-Sunnyvale-Santa Clara, CA Metropolitan Statistical Area—see Appendix B for areas included
Source: U.S. Census Bureau, Census 1990, 2000, 2010

Household Size

Area	Persons in Household (%)							Average Household Size
	One	Two	Three	Four	Five	Six	Seven or More	
City	19.7	27.6	18.7	18.2	8.7	3.6	3.4	3.12
MSA[1]	21.6	29.2	18.6	17.4	7.7	2.9	2.6	2.94
U.S.	27.7	33.6	15.7	13.1	6.0	2.3	1.5	2.64

Note: (1) Figures cover the San Jose-Sunnyvale-Santa Clara, CA Metropolitan Statistical Area—see Appendix B for areas included
Source: U.S. Census Bureau, 2011-2013 American Community Survey 3-Year Estimates

Race

Area	White Alone[2] (%)	Black Alone[2] (%)	Asian Alone[2] (%)	AIAN[3] Alone[2] (%)	NHOPI[4] Alone[2] (%)	Other Race Alone[2] (%)	Two or More Races (%)
City	45.8	3.0	32.9	0.7	0.4	12.5	4.7
MSA[1]	50.6	2.6	32.1	0.5	0.4	9.4	4.5
U.S.	73.9	12.6	5.0	0.8	0.2	4.7	2.9

Note: (1) Figures cover the San Jose-Sunnyvale-Santa Clara, CA Metropolitan Statistical Area—see Appendix B for areas included; (2) Alone is defined as not being in combination with one or more other races; (3) American Indian and Alaska Native; (4) Native Hawaiian and Other Pacific Islander
Source: U.S. Census Bureau, 2011-2013 American Community Survey 3-Year Estimates

Hispanic or Latino Origin

Area	Total (%)	Mexican (%)	Puerto Rican (%)	Cuban (%)	Other (%)
City	33.4	29.1	0.4	0.2	3.7
MSA[1]	27.7	23.7	0.4	0.1	3.5
U.S.	16.9	10.8	1.6	0.6	3.8

Note: Persons of Hispanic or Latino origin can be of any race; (1) Figures cover the San Jose-Sunnyvale-Santa Clara, CA Metropolitan Statistical Area—see Appendix B for areas included
Source: U.S. Census Bureau, 2011-2013 American Community Survey 3-Year Estimates

Segregation

Type	Segregation Indices[1]				Percent Change		
	1990	2000	2010	2010 Rank[2]	1990-2000	1990-2010	2000-2010
Black/White	43.2	41.6	40.9	89	-1.7	-2.4	-0.7
Asian/White	38.8	43.4	45.0	25	4.6	6.1	1.6
Hispanic/White	47.9	50.7	47.6	36	2.9	-0.2	-3.1

Note: All figures cover the Metropolitan Statistical Area—see Appendix B for areas included; Figures are based on an analysis of 1990, 2000, and 2010 Census Decennial Census tract data by William H. Frey, Brookings Institution and the University of Michigan Social Science Data Analysis Network. In this analysis all racial groups (whites, blacks, and asians) are non-Hispanic members of those races. Hispanics are shown as a separate category;
(1) Segregation Indices are Dissimilarity Indices that measure the degree to which the minority group is distributed differently than whites across census tracts. They range from 0 (complete integration) to 100 (complete segregation) where the value indicates the percentage of the minority group that needs to move to be distributed exactly like whites; (2) Ranges from 1 (most segregated) to 102 (least segregated); n/a not available.
Source: www.CensusScope.org

Ancestry

Area	German	Irish	English	American	Italian	Polish	French[2]	Scottish	Dutch
City	5.9	4.8	4.1	1.8	4.2	0.9	1.3	0.9	0.7
MSA[1]	7.1	5.6	5.2	2.2	4.5	1.2	1.6	1.1	0.8
U.S.	14.9	10.8	8.0	7.4	5.5	3.0	2.7	1.7	1.4

Note: Figures are the percentage of the total population reporting a particular ancestry. The nine most commonly reported ancestries in the U.S. are shown. Figures include multiple ancestries (e.g. if a person reported being Irish and Italian, they were included in both columns); (1) Figures cover the San Jose-Sunnyvale-Santa Clara, CA Metropolitan Statistical Area—see Appendix B for areas included; (2) Excludes Basque
Source: U.S. Census Bureau, 2011-2013 American Community Survey 3-Year Estimates

Foreign-Born Population

Area	Percent of Population Born in								
	Any Foreign Country	Mexico	Asia	Europe	Carribean	South America	Central America[2]	Africa	Canada
City	38.7	10.3	23.5	2.1	0.1	0.5	1.1	0.6	0.4
MSA[1]	36.8	8.2	22.8	2.9	0.1	0.6	0.9	0.5	0.5
U.S.	13.0	3.7	3.8	1.5	1.2	0.9	1.0	0.6	0.3

Note: (1) Figures cover the San Jose-Sunnyvale-Santa Clara, CA Metropolitan Statistical Area—see Appendix B for areas included; (2) Excludes Mexico.
Source: U.S. Census Bureau, 2011-2013 American Community Survey 3-Year Estimates

Marital Status

Area	Never Married	Now Married[2]	Separated	Widowed	Divorced
City	34.6	50.9	1.9	4.5	8.2
MSA[1]	32.6	53.1	1.7	4.4	8.1
U.S.	32.7	48.1	2.2	6.0	11.0

Note: Figures are percentages and cover the population 15 years of age and older; (1) Figures cover the San Jose-Sunnyvale-Santa Clara, CA Metropolitan Statistical Area—see Appendix B for areas included; (2) Excludes separated
Source: U.S. Census Bureau, 2011-2013 American Community Survey 3-Year Estimates

Disability Status

Area	All Ages	Under 18 Years Old	18 to 64 Years Old	65 Years and Over
City	8.3	2.6	5.9	36.0
MSA[1]	7.7	2.4	5.2	33.1
U.S.	12.3	4.1	10.2	36.3

Note: Figures show percent of the civilian noninstitutionalized population that reported having a disability. Disability status is determined from from six types of difficulty: vision, hearing, cognitive, ambulatory, self-care, and independent living. For children under 5 years old, hearing and vision difficulty are used to determine disability status. For children between the ages of 5 and 14, disability status is determined from hearing, vision, cognitive, ambulatory, and self-care difficulties. For people aged 15 years and older, they are considered to have a disability if they have difficulty with any one of the six difficulty types; (1) Figures cover the San Jose-Sunnyvale-Santa Clara, CA Metropolitan Statistical Area—see Appendix B for areas included.
Source: U.S. Census Bureau, 2011-2013 American Community Survey 3-Year Estimates

Age

Area	Percent of Population									Median Age
	Under Age 5	Age 5–19	Age 20–34	Age 35–44	Age 45–54	Age 55–64	Age 65–74	Age 75–84	Age 85+	
City	6.8	19.7	22.0	15.4	14.3	10.8	6.0	3.5	1.4	35.8
MSA[1]	6.7	19.5	21.4	15.2	14.6	10.9	6.4	3.6	1.6	36.5
U.S.	6.4	19.9	20.7	12.9	14.1	12.3	7.6	4.2	1.9	37.4

Note: (1) Figures cover the San Jose-Sunnyvale-Santa Clara, CA Metropolitan Statistical Area—see Appendix B for areas included
Source: U.S. Census Bureau, 2011-2013 American Community Survey 3-Year Estimates

Gender

Area	Males	Females	Males per 100 Females
City	495,022	488,753	101.3
MSA[1]	951,310	942,011	101.0
U.S.	154,451,010	159,410,713	96.9

Note: (1) Figures cover the San Jose-Sunnyvale-Santa Clara, CA Metropolitan Statistical Area—see Appendix B for areas included
Source: U.S. Census Bureau, 2011-2013 American Community Survey 3-Year Estimates

Religious Groups by Family

Area	Catholic	Baptist	Non-Den.	Methodist[2]	Lutheran	LDS[3]	Pente-costal	Presby-terian[4]	Muslim[5]	Judaism
MSA[1]	26.0	1.4	4.3	1.1	0.6	1.4	1.2	0.7	1.0	0.7
U.S.	19.1	9.3	4.0	4.0	2.3	2.0	1.9	1.6	0.8	0.7

Note: Figures are the number of adherents as a percentage of the total population; (1) Figures cover the San Jose-Sunnyvale-Santa Clara, CA Metropolitan Statistical Area—see Appendix B for areas included; (2) Methodist/Pietist; (3) Latter Day Saints; (4) Reformed; (5) Figures are estimates
Source: Association of Statisticians of American Religious Bodies, 2010 U.S. Religion Census: Religious Congregations & Membership Study

Religious Groups by Tradition

Area	Catholic	Evangelical Protestant	Mainline Protestant	Other Tradition	Black Protestant	Orthodox
MSA[1]	26.0	8.2	2.5	6.9	0.1	0.4
U.S.	19.1	16.2	7.3	4.3	1.6	0.3

Note: Figures are the number of adherents as a percentage of the total population; (1) Figures cover the San Jose-Sunnyvale-Santa Clara, CA Metropolitan Statistical Area—see Appendix B for areas included
Source: Association of Statisticians of American Religious Bodies, 2010 U.S. Religion Census: Religious Congregations & Membership Study

ECONOMY

Gross Metropolitan Product

Area	2012	2013	2014	2015	Rank[2]
MSA[1]	173.9	182.7	192.2	203.2	16

Note: Figures are in billions of dollars; (1) Figures cover the San Jose-Sunnyvale-Santa Clara, CA Metropolitan Statistical Area—see Appendix B for areas included; (2) Rank is based on 2015 data and ranges from 1 to 363
Source: The U.S. Conference of Mayors, U.S. Metro Economies: GMP and Employment 2013-2015, June 2014

Economic Growth

Area	2010-12 (%)	2013 (%)	2014 (%)	2015 (%)	Rank[2]
MSA[1]	5.2	4.3	3.7	3.9	35
U.S.	2.1	2.0	2.3	3.2	–

Note: Figures are real gross metropolitan product (GMP) growth rates and represent annual average percent change; (1) Figures cover the San Jose-Sunnyvale-Santa Clara, CA Metropolitan Statistical Area—see Appendix B for areas included; (2) Rank is based on 2015 data and ranges from 1 to 363
Source: The U.S. Conference of Mayors, U.S. Metro Economies: GMP and Employment 2013-2015, June 2014

Metropolitan Area Exports

Area	2008	2009	2010	2011	2012	2013	Rank[2]
MSA[1]	27,048.6	21,405.8	26,333.0	26,712.1	26,687.7	23,413.1	13

Note: Figures are in millions of dollars; (1) Figures cover the San Jose-Sunnyvale-Santa Clara, CA Metropolitan Statistical Area—see Appendix B for areas included; (2) Rank is based on 2013 data and ranges from 1 to 387
Source: U.S. Department of Commerce, International Trade Administration, Office of Trade & Industry Information, Manufacturing & Services, data extracted April 3, 2015

Building Permits

Area	Single-Family			Multi-Family			Total		
	2013	2014	Pct. Chg.	2013	2014	Pct. Chg.	2013	2014	Pct. Chg.
City	274	384	40.1	3,429	4,061	18.4	3,703	4,445	20.0
MSA[1]	1,870	1,861	-0.5	5,894	8,176	38.7	7,764	10,037	29.3
U.S.	620,802	634,597	2.2	370,020	411,766	11.3	990,822	1,046,363	5.6

Note: (1) Figures cover the San Jose-Sunnyvale-Santa Clara, CA Metropolitan Statistical Area—see Appendix B for areas included; Figures represent new, privately-owned housing units authorized (unadjusted data); All permit data are based on estimates with imputation.
Source: U.S. Census Bureau, Manufacturing, Mining, and Construction Statistics, Building Permits, 2013, 2014

Bankruptcy Filings

Area	Business Filings			Nonbusiness Filings		
	2013	2014	% Chg.	2013	2014	% Chg.
Santa Clara County	199	147	-26.1	4,248	3,173	-25.3
U.S.	33,212	26,983	-18.8	1,038,720	909,812	-12.4

Note: Business filings include Chapter 7, Chapter 11, Chapter 12, and Chapter 13; Nonbusiness filings include Chapter 7, Chapter 11, and Chapter 13
Source: Administrative Office of the U.S. Courts, Business and Nonbusiness Bankruptcy, County Cases Commenced by Chapter of the Bankruptcy Code, During the 12- Month Period Ending December 31, 2013 and Business and Nonbusiness Bankruptcy, County Cases Commenced by Chapter of the Bankruptcy Code, During the 12- Month Period Ending December 31, 2014

Housing Vacancy Rates

Area	Gross Vacancy Rate[2] (%)			Year-Round Vacancy Rate[3] (%)			Rental Vacancy Rate[4] (%)			Homeowner Vacancy Rate[5] (%)		
	2012	2013	2014	2012	2013	2014	2012	2013	2014	2012	2013	2014
MSA[1]	3.8	5.0	4.7	3.7	4.9	4.5	3.8	3.0	2.9	0.9	0.6	0.6
U.S.	13.8	13.6	13.4	10.8	10.7	10.4	8.7	8.3	7.6	2.0	2.0	1.9

Note: (1) Figures cover the San Jose-Sunnyvale-Santa Clara, CA Metropolitan Statistical Area—see Appendix B for areas included; (2) The percentage of the total housing inventory that is vacant; (3) The percentage of the housing inventory (excluding seasonal units) that is year-round vacant; (4) The percentage of rental inventory that is vacant for rent; (5) The percentage of homeowner inventory that is vacant for sale
Source: U.S. Census Bureau, Housing Vacancies and Homeownership Annual Statistics: 2014

INCOME

Income

Area	Per Capita ($)	Median Household ($)	Average Household ($)
City	34,059	80,609	104,333
MSA[1]	41,294	90,434	120,427
U.S.	27,884	52,176	72,897

Note: (1) Figures cover the San Jose-Sunnyvale-Santa Clara, CA Metropolitan Statistical Area—see Appendix B for areas included
Source: U.S. Census Bureau, 2011-2013 American Community Survey 3-Year Estimates

Household Income Distribution

Area	Percent of Households Earning							
	Under $15,000	$15,000 -24,999	$25,000 -34,999	$35,000 -49,999	$50,000 -74,999	$75,000 -99,000	$100,000 -149,999	$150,000 and up
City	8.1	7.2	7.2	10.1	14.7	12.2	18.0	22.5
MSA[1]	7.2	6.4	6.4	8.9	13.8	11.6	18.6	27.0
U.S.	13.0	10.9	10.3	13.6	17.9	11.9	12.7	9.6

Note: (1) Figures cover the San Jose-Sunnyvale-Santa Clara, CA Metropolitan Statistical Area—see Appendix B for areas included
Source: U.S. Census Bureau, 2011-2013 American Community Survey 3-Year Estimates

Poverty Rate

Area	All Ages	Under 18 Years Old	18 to 64 Years Old	65 Years and Over
City	12.6	15.3	11.8	10.8
MSA[1]	10.6	12.6	10.1	9.0
U.S.	15.9	22.4	14.8	9.5

Note: Figures are percentage of people whose income during the past 12 months was below the poverty level;
(1) Figures cover the San Jose-Sunnyvale-Santa Clara, CA Metropolitan Statistical Area—see Appendix B for areas included
Source: U.S. Census Bureau, 2011-2013 American Community Survey 3-Year Estimates

EMPLOYMENT

Labor Force and Employment

Area	Civilian Labor Force			Workers Employed		
	Dec. 2013	Dec. 2014	% Chg.	Dec. 2013	Dec. 2014	% Chg.
City	523,072	539,145	3.1	490,669	512,941	4.5
MSA[1]	1,006,995	1,039,234	3.2	949,768	992,810	4.5
U.S.	154,408,000	155,521,000	0.7	144,423,000	147,190,000	1.9

Note: Data is not seasonally adjusted and covers workers 16 years of age and older; (1) Figures cover the San Jose-Sunnyvale-Santa Clara, CA Metropolitan Statistical Area—see Appendix B for areas included
Source: Bureau of Labor Statistics, Local Area Unemployment Statistics

Unemployment Rate

Area	2014											
	Jan.	Feb.	Mar.	Apr.	May	Jun.	Jul.	Aug.	Sep.	Oct.	Nov.	Dec.
City	6.5	6.5	6.5	5.5	5.6	5.8	6.2	6.0	5.5	5.4	5.4	4.9
MSA[1]	6.0	6.0	6.0	5.1	5.1	5.3	5.7	5.4	5.0	5.0	4.9	4.5
U.S.	7.0	7.0	6.8	5.9	6.1	6.3	6.5	6.3	5.7	5.5	5.5	5.4

Note: Data is not seasonally adjusted and covers workers 16 years of age and older; (1) Figures cover the San Jose-Sunnyvale-Santa Clara, CA Metropolitan Statistical Area—see Appendix B for areas included
Source: Bureau of Labor Statistics, Local Area Unemployment Statistics

Employment by Occupation

Occupation Classification	City (%)	MSA[1] (%)	U.S. (%)
Management, Business, Science, and Arts	41.4	49.0	36.2
Natural Resources, Construction, and Maintenance	7.9	6.9	9.0
Production, Transportation, and Material Moving	10.4	8.4	12.1
Sales and Office	22.3	20.4	24.4
Service	18.0	15.4	18.3

Note: Figures cover employed civilians 16 years of age and older; (1) Figures cover the San Jose-Sunnyvale-Santa Clara, CA Metropolitan Statistical Area—see Appendix B for areas included
Source: U.S. Census Bureau, 2011-2013 American Community Survey 3-Year Estimates

Employment by Industry

| Sector | MSA[1] | | U.S. |
	Number of Employees	Percent of Total	Percent of Total
Construction	40,000	3.9	4.4
Education and Health Services	153,700	14.8	15.5
Financial Activities	36,000	3.5	5.7
Government	96,600	9.3	15.8
Information	70,900	6.8	2.0
Leisure and Hospitality	92,700	8.9	10.3
Manufacturing	161,900	15.6	8.7
Mining and Logging	300	<0.1	0.6
Other Services	25,900	2.5	4.0
Professional and Business Services	214,700	20.7	13.8
Retail Trade	90,800	8.8	11.4
Transportation, Warehousing, and Utilities	16,100	1.6	3.9
Wholesale Trade	37,600	3.6	4.2

Note: Figures are non-farm employment as of December 2014. Figures are not seasonally adjusted and include workers 16 years of age and older; (1) Figures cover the San Jose-Sunnyvale-Santa Clara, CA Metropolitan Statistical Area—see Appendix B for areas included
Source: Bureau of Labor Statistics, Current Employment Statistics, Employment, Hours, and Earnings

Occupations with Greatest Projected Employment Growth: 2012 – 2022

Occupation[1]	2012 Employment	2022 Projected Employment	Numeric Employment Change	Percent Employment Change
Personal Care Aides	386,900	587,200	200,300	51.8
Combined Food Preparation and Serving Workers, Including Fast Food	286,000	362,400	76,400	26.7
Retail Salespersons	468,400	528,100	59,700	12.7
Laborers and Freight, Stock, and Material Movers, Hand	270,500	322,300	51,800	19.1
Waiters and Waitresses	246,100	290,300	44,200	18.0
Registered Nurses	254,500	297,400	42,900	16.9
General and Operations Managers	253,800	295,700	41,900	16.5
Secretaries and Administrative Assistants, Except Legal, Medical, and Executive	212,800	250,100	37,300	17.5
Cashiers	357,800	392,600	34,800	9.7
Cooks, Restaurant	116,900	150,600	33,700	28.8

Note: Projections cover California; (1) Sorted by numeric employment change
Source: www.projectionscentral.com, State Occupational Projections, 2012–2022 Long-Term Projections

Fastest Growing Occupations: 2012 – 2022

Occupation[1]	2012 Employment	2022 Projected Employment	Numeric Employment Change	Percent Employment Change
Economists	3,100	5,100	2,000	64.5
Helpers—Brickmasons, Blockmasons, Stonemasons, and Tile and Marble Setters	2,900	4,600	1,700	58.6
Brickmasons and Blockmasons	5,100	8,000	2,900	56.9
Insulation Workers, Floor, Ceiling, and Wall	1,600	2,500	900	56.3
Stonemasons	1,100	1,700	600	54.5
Insulation Workers, Mechanical	1,100	1,700	600	54.5
Personal Care Aides	386,900	587,200	200,300	51.8
Foresters	1,200	1,800	600	50.0
Terrazzo Workers and Finishers	1,100	1,600	500	45.5
Mechanical Door Repairers	1,100	1,600	500	45.5

Note: Projections cover California; (1) Sorted by percent employment change and excludes occupations with numeric employment change less than 100
Source: www.projectionscentral.com, State Occupational Projections, 2012–2022 Long-Term Projections

Average Wages

Occupation	$/Hr.	Occupation	$/Hr.
Accountants and Auditors	44.69	Maids and Housekeeping Cleaners	14.64
Automotive Mechanics	24.99	Maintenance and Repair Workers	22.42
Bookkeepers	23.84	Marketing Managers	90.33
Carpenters	29.18	Nuclear Medicine Technologists	57.46
Cashiers	12.19	Nurses, Licensed Practical	28.63
Clerks, General Office	19.36	Nurses, Registered	58.57
Clerks, Receptionists/Information	17.32	Nursing Assistants	16.50
Clerks, Shipping/Receiving	17.31	Packers and Packagers, Hand	11.96
Computer Programmers	45.20	Physical Therapists	48.82
Computer Systems Analysts	52.16	Postal Service Mail Carriers	26.71
Computer User Support Specialists	36.30	Real Estate Brokers	40.86
Cooks, Restaurant	12.92	Retail Salespersons	13.40
Dentists	75.07	Sales Reps., Exc. Tech./Scientific	35.32
Electrical Engineers	61.65	Sales Reps., Tech./Scientific	54.47
Electricians	35.29	Secretaries, Exc. Legal/Med./Exec.	21.31
Financial Managers	79.99	Security Guards	14.33
First-Line Supervisors/Managers, Sales	23.58	Surgeons	113.16
Food Preparation Workers	11.48	Teacher Assistants	15.50
General and Operations Managers	74.72	Teachers, Elementary School	34.40
Hairdressers/Cosmetologists	11.55	Teachers, Secondary School	36.10
Internists	110.04	Telemarketers	14.43
Janitors and Cleaners	13.63	Truck Drivers, Heavy/Tractor-Trailer	22.34
Landscaping/Groundskeeping Workers	15.69	Truck Drivers, Light/Delivery Svcs.	18.59
Lawyers	96.75	Waiters and Waitresses	12.02

Note: Wage data covers the San Jose-Sunnyvale-Santa Clara, CA Metropolitan Statistical Area—see Appendix B for areas included; Hourly wages for elementary/secondary school teachers and teacher assistants were calculated by the editors from annual wage data assuming a 40 hour work week; n/a not available.
Source: Bureau of Labor Statistics, Metro Area Occupational Employment and Wage Estimates, May 2014

TAXES

State Corporate Income Tax Rates

State	Tax Rate (%)	Income Brackets ($)	Num. of Brackets	Financial Institution Tax Rate (%)[a]	Federal Income Tax Ded.
California	8.84 (c)	Flat rate	1	10.84 (c)	No

Note: Tax rates as of January 1, 2015; (a) Rates listed are the corporate income tax rate applied to financial institutions or excise taxes based on income. Some states have other taxes based upon the value of deposits or shares; (c) Minimum tax is $800 in California, $100 in District of Columbia, $50 in North Dakota (banks), $500 in Rhode Island, $200 per location in South Dakota (banks), $100 in Utah, $250 in Vermont.
Source: Federation of Tax Administrators, "State Corporate Income Tax Rates, 2015"

State Individual Income Tax Rates

State	Tax Rate (%)	Income Brackets ($)	Num. of Brackets	Personal Exempt. ($)[1]		Fed. Inc. Tax Ded.
				Single	Dependents	
California (a)	1.0 - 12.3 (f)	7,749- 519,687 (b)	9	108 (c)	333 (c)	No

Note: Tax rates as of January 1, 2015; Local- and county-level taxes are not included; n/a not applicable; (1) Married joint filers generally receive double the single exemption; (a) 17 states have statutory provision for automatically adjusting to the rate of inflation the dollar values of the income tax brackets, standard deductions, and/or personal exemptions. Massachusetts, Michigan, and Nebraska index the personal exemptiononly. Oregon does not index the income brackets for $125,000 and over. Maine has suspended indexing for 2014 and 2015; (b) For joint returns, taxes are twice the tax on half the couple's income; (c) The personal exemption takes the form of a tax credit instead of a deduction; (f) California imposes an additional 1% tax on taxable income over $1 million, making the maximum rate 13.3% over $1 million.
Source: Federation of Tax Administrators, "State Individual Income Tax Rates, 2015"

Various State and Local Tax Rates

State	State and Local Sales and Use (%)	State Sales and Use (%)	Gasoline[1] (¢/gal.)	Cigarette[2] ($/pack)	Spirits[3] ($/gal.)	Wine[4] ($/gal.)	Beer[5] ($/gal.)
California	8.75	7.50 (b)	45.39	0.87	3.30 (f)	0.20	0.20

Note: All tax rates as of January 1, 2015; (1) The American Petroleum Institute has developed a methodology for determining the average tax rate on a gallon of fuel. Rates may include any of the following: excise taxes, environmental fees, storage tank fees, other fees or taxes, general sales tax, and local taxes. In states where gasoline is subject to the general sales tax, or where the fuel tax is based on the average sale price, the average rate determined by API is sensitive to changes in the price of gasoline. States that fully or partially apply general sales taxes to gasoline: CA, CO, GA, IL, IN, MI, NY; (2) The federal excise tax of $1.0066 per pack and local taxes are not included; (3) Rates are those applicable to off-premise sales of 40% alcohol by volume (a.b.v.) distilled spirits in 750ml containers. Local excise taxes are excluded; (4) Rates are those applicable to off-premise sales of 11% a.b.v. non-carbonated wine in 750ml containers; (5) Rates are those applicable to off-premise sales of 4.7% a.b.v. beer in 12 ounce containers; (b) Three states levy mandatory, statewide, local add-on sales taxes at the state level: California (1%), Utah (1.25%), and Virginia (1%). We include these in their state sales taxes; (f) Different rates are also applicable according to alcohol content, place of production, size of container, or place purchased (on- or off-premise or onboard airlines).
Source: Tax Foundation, 2015 Facts & Figures: How Does Your State Compare?

State Business Tax Climate Index Rankings

State	Overall Rank	Corporate Tax Index Rank	Individual Income Tax Index Rank	Sales Tax Index Rank	Unemployment Insurance Tax Index Rank	Property Tax Index Rank
California	48	34	50	42	14	14

Note: The index is a measure of how each state's tax laws affect economic performance. The lower the rank, the more favorable a state's tax system is for business. States without a given tax are given a ranking of 1. The scores/rankings for the District of Columbia do not affect other states. The 2015 index represents the tax climate as of July 1, 2014.
Source: Tax Foundation, State Business Tax Climate Index 2015

COMMERCIAL REAL ESTATE

Office Market

Market Area	Inventory (sq. ft.)	Vacancy Rate (%)	Under Construction (sq. ft.)	YTD Net Absorption (sq. ft.)	Total Average Asking Rent ($/sq. ft./year)
Silicon Valley	68,888,109	9.8	9,951,581	1,610,486	37.44
National	4,745,108,508	14.3	71,190,461	51,084,126	27.40

Source: Newmark Grubb Knight Frank, National Office Market Report, 4th Quarter 2014

Industrial/Warehouse/R&D Market

Market Area	Inventory (sq. ft.)	Vacancy Rate (%)	Under Construction (sq. ft.)	YTD Net Absorption (sq. ft.)	Total Average Asking Rent ($/sq. ft./year)
Silicon Valley	218,847,089	9.6	383,180	648,232	15.96
National	14,238,613,765	7.2	134,387,407	185,246,438	5.64

Source: Newmark Grubb Knight Frank, National Industrial Market Report, 4th Quarter 2014

COMMERCIAL UTILITIES

Typical Monthly Electric Bills

Area	Commercial Service ($/month)		Industrial Service ($/month)	
	1,500 kWh	40 kW demand 14,000 kWh	1,000 kW demand 200,000 kWh	50,000 kW demand 32,500,000 kWh
City	299	2,473	42,294	3,279,227
Average[1]	201	1,653	26,124	2,639,743

Note: Figures are based on annualized 2014 rates; (1) Average based on 180 utilities surveyed
Source: Edison Electric Institute, Typical Bills and Average Rates Report, Summer 2014

TRANSPORTATION

Means of Transportation to Work

Area	Car/Truck/Van		Public Transportation			Bicycle	Walked	Other Means	Worked at Home
	Drove Alone	Car-pooled	Bus	Subway	Railroad				
City	77.2	11.1	2.6	0.2	0.8	0.9	1.6	1.6	4.0
MSA[1]	76.3	10.4	2.3	0.2	1.1	1.8	2.0	1.5	4.5
U.S.	76.4	9.6	2.6	1.8	0.6	0.6	2.8	1.3	4.3

Note: Figures are percentages and cover workers 16 years of age and older; (1) Figures cover the San Jose-Sunnyvale-Santa Clara, CA Metropolitan Statistical Area—see Appendix B for areas included
Source: U.S. Census Bureau, 2011-2013 American Community Survey 3-Year Estimates

Travel Time to Work

Area	Less Than 10 Minutes	10 to 19 Minutes	20 to 29 Minutes	30 to 44 Minutes	45 to 59 Minutes	60 to 89 Minutes	90 Minutes or More
City	6.6	27.6	25.8	24.8	7.5	5.7	1.9
MSA[1]	8.4	29.4	25.5	22.2	7.3	5.4	1.9
U.S.	13.3	29.7	20.9	20.2	7.7	5.7	2.6

Note: Figures are percentages and include workers 16 years old and over; (1) Figures cover the San Jose-Sunnyvale-Santa Clara, CA Metropolitan Statistical Area—see Appendix B for areas included
Source: U.S. Census Bureau, 2011-2013 American Community Survey 3-Year Estimates

Travel Time Index

Area	1985	1990	1995	2000	2005	2010	2011
Urban Area[1]	1.17	1.23	1.21	1.28	1.29	1.24	1.24
Average[2]	1.09	1.14	1.16	1.19	1.23	1.18	1.18

Note: Travel Time Index—the ratio of travel time in the peak period to the travel time at free-flow conditions. For example, a value of 1.30 indicates a 20-minute free-flow trip takes 26 minutes in the peak. Free-flow speeds (60 mph on freeways and 35 mph on principal arterials) are used as the comparison threshold; (1) Covers the San Jose CA urban area; (2) average of 498 urban areas
Source: Texas Transportation Institute, Urban Mobility Report 2012, December 2012

Public Transportation

Agency Name / Mode of Transportation	Vehicles Operated in Maximum Service	Annual Unlinked Passenger Trips (in thous.)	Annual Passenger Miles (in thous.)
Santa Clara Valley Transportation Authority (VTA)			
Bus (directly operated)	360	32,404.6	166,423.9
Bus (purchased transportation)	11	341.4	1,320.9
Demand Response (purchased transportation)	240	732.8	8,205.0
Light Rail (directly operated)	56	10,742.3	58,102.9

Source: Federal Transit Administration, National Transit Database, 2013

Air Transportation

Airport Name and Code / Type of Service	Passenger Airlines[1]	Passenger Enplanements	Freight Carriers[2]	Freight (lbs.)
San Jose International (SJC)				
Domestic service (U.S. carriers - 2014)	26	4,442,038	12	49,088,789
International service (U.S. carriers - 2013)	5	72,472	1	45,500

Note: (1) Includes all U.S.-based major, minor and commuter airlines that carried at least one passenger during the year; (2) Includes all U.S.-based airlines and freight carriers that transported at least one lb. of freight during the year.
Source: Bureau of Transportation Statistics, The Intermodal Transportation Database, Air Carriers: T-100 Domestic Market (U.S. Carriers), 2014; Bureau of Transportation Statistics, The Intermodal Transportation Database, Air Carriers: T-100 International Market (U.S. Carriers), 2013

Other Transportation Statistics

Major Highways:	I-80
Amtrak Service:	Yes
Major Waterways/Ports:	None

Source: Amtrak.com; Google Maps

BUSINESSES

Major Business Headquarters

Company Name	Rankings	
	Fortune[1]	Forbes[2]
Cisco Systems	55	-
Fry's Electronics	-	211
Sanmina	432	-
eBay	180	-

Note: (1) Fortune 500—companies that produce a 10-K are ranked 1 to 500 based on 2013 revenue; (2) all private companies with at least $2 billion in annual revenue through the end of their most current fiscal year are ranked 1 to 221; companies listed are headquartered in the city; dashes indicate no ranking Source: Fortune, "Fortune 500," June 16, 2014; Forbes, "America's Largest Private Companies," November 5, 2014

Fast-Growing Businesses

According to *Fortune*, San Jose is home to two of the 100 fastest-growing companies in the world: **PDF Solutions** (#27); **TiVo** (#73). Companies were ranked by their revenue growth rate; their EPS growth rate; and their three-year annualized total return to investors for the period ending June 30, 2014. Criteria for inclusion: a company, foreign or domestic, must trade on a major U.S. stock exchange; must file quarterly reports with the SEC; must have a minimum market capitalization of $250 million; must have a stock price of at least $5 on June 30, 2014; must have been trading continuously since June 30, 2010; must have revenue and net income for the four quarters ended on or before April 30, 2014, of at least $50 million and $10 million, respectively; and must have posted a compound annual growth in revenue and earnings per share of at least 20% annually over the three years ending on or before April 30, 2014. Real estate investment trusts, limited-liability companies, limited parterships, business development companies, closed end investment firms, and companies that lost money in the quarter ending April 30, 2014 were excluded. *Fortune, "100 Fastest-Growing Companies," August 28, 2014*

According to Deloitte, San Jose is home to nine of North America's 500 fastest-growing high-technology companies: **Apigee** (#5); **Malwarebytes** (#76); **GainSpan Corporation** (#97); **InvenSense** (#169); **NeuroSky** (#231); **Ubiquiti Networks** (#235); **Vormetric** (#380); **Cavium** (#387); **Vocera Communications** (#471). Companies are ranked by percentage growth in revenue over a five-year period. Criteria for inclusion: company must be headquartered within North America; must own proprietary intellectual property or proprietary technology that contributes to a significant portion of the company's operating revenue, or devote a significant proportion of revenues to research and development of technology; must have been in business for a minumum of five years with 2009 operating revenues of at least $50,000 USD/CD and 2013 operating revenues of at least $5 million USD/CD. *Deloitte Touche Tohmatsu, 2014 Technology Fast 500*[TM]

Minority Business Opportunity

San Jose is home to two companies which are on the *Hispanic Business* 500 list (500 largest U.S. Hispanic-owned companies based on 2012 revenue): **RW Garcia Co.** (#160); **Acosta Sheet Metal Mfg. Co.** (#292). Companies included must show at least 51 percent ownership by Hispanic U.S. citizens, and must maintain headquarters in one of the 50 states or Washington, D.C. *Hispanic Business, "Hispanic Business 500," June 20, 2013*

San Jose is home to one company which is on the *Hispanic Business* Fastest-Growing 100 list (greatest sales growth from 2008 to 2012): **RW Garcia Co.** (#88). Companies included must show at least 51 percent ownership by Hispanic U.S. citizens, and must maintain headquarters in one of the 50 states or Washington, D.C. In addition, companies must have minimum revenues of $200,000 for calendar year 2008. *Hispanic Business, June 20, 2013*

Minority- and Women-Owned Businesses

Group	All Firms		Firms with Paid Employees			
	Firms	Sales ($000)	Firms	Sales ($000)	Employees	Payroll ($000)
Asian	22,088	6,238,740	4,226	5,444,558	29,969	875,716
Black	(s)	(s)	(s)	(s)	(s)	(s)
Hispanic	10,140	1,326,830	1,665	1,040,989	11,274	278,501
Women	22,000	2,791,388	2,535	2,134,168	18,394	543,361
All Firms	71,553	100,139,638	16,163	97,406,346	351,572	22,132,495

Note: Figures cover firms located in the city; minority- and women-owned business are defined as firms in which the corresponding group own 51% or more of the stock or equity of the company; (s) estimates are suppressed when publication standards are not met
Source: U.S. Census Bureau, 2007 Economic Census, Survey of Business Owners (2012 Survey of Business Owners data will be released starting in June 2015)

HOTELS & CONVENTION CENTERS

Hotels/Motels

Area	5 Star		4 Star		3 Star		2 Star		1 Star		Not Rated	
	Num.	Pct.[3]	Num.	Pct.[3]	Num.	Pct.[3]	Num.	Pct.[3]	Num.	Pct.[3]	Num.	Pct.[3]
City[1]	2	0.7	21	7.6	97	34.9	127	45.7	1	0.4	30	10.8
Total[2]	166	0.9	1,264	7.0	5,718	31.8	9,340	52.0	411	2.3	1,070	6.0

Note: (1) Figures cover San Jose and vicinity; (2) Figures cover all 100 cities in this book; (3) Percentage of hotels which have a given star rating; Star ratings are determined by expedia.com and offer an indication of the general quality of a particular hotel.
Source: expedia.com, April 2, 2015

Major Convention Centers

Name	Overall Space (sq. ft.)	Exhibit Space (sq. ft.)	Meeting Space (sq. ft.)	Meeting Rooms
San Jose McEnery Convention Center	425,000	143,000	n/a	31

Note: Table includes convention centers located in the San Jose-Sunnyvale-Santa Clara, CA metro area; n/a not available
Source: Original research

Living Environment

COST OF LIVING

Cost of Living Index

Composite Index	Groceries	Housing	Utilities	Trans-portation	Health Care	Misc. Goods/ Services
150.0	119.8	245.3	125.8	111.4	116.7	106.7

Note: The Cost of Living Index measures regional differences in the cost of consumer goods and services, excluding taxes and non-consumer expenditures, for professional and managerial households in the top income quintile. It is based on more than 50,000 prices covering almost 60 different items for which prices are collected three times a year by chambers of commerce, economic development organizations or university applied economic centers in each participating urban area. The numbers shown should be read as a percentage above or below the national average of 100. For example, a value of 115.4 in the groceries column indicates that grocery prices are 15.4% higher than the national average. Small differences in the index numbers should not be interpreted as significant; Figures cover the San Jose CA urban area.
Source: The Council for Community and Economic Research, ACCRA Cost of Living Index, 2014

Grocery Prices

Area[1]	T-Bone Steak ($/pound)	Frying Chicken ($/pound)	Whole Milk ($/half gal.)	Eggs ($/dozen)	Orange Juice ($/64 oz.)	Coffee ($/11.5 oz.)
City[2]	11.28	1.43	2.53	2.53	4.11	6.32
Avg.	10.40	1.37	2.40	1.99	3.46	4.27
Min.	8.48	0.93	1.37	1.30	2.83	2.99
Max.	14.20	2.44	3.62	4.02	6.42	6.96

*Note: (1) Values for the local area are compared with the average, minimum and maximum values for all 308 areas in the Cost of Living Index; (2) Figures cover the San Jose CA urban area; **T-Bone Steak** (price per pound); **Frying Chicken** (price per pound, whole fryer); **Whole Milk** (half gallon carton); **Eggs** (price per dozen, Grade A, large); **Orange Juice** (64 oz. Tropicana or Florida Natural); **Coffee** (11.5 oz. can, vacuum-packed, Maxwell House, Hills Bros, or Folgers).*
Source: The Council for Community and Economic Research, ACCRA Cost of Living Index, 2014

Housing and Utility Costs

Area[1]	New Home Price ($)	Apartment Rent ($/month)	All Electric ($/month)	Part Electric ($/month)	Other Energy ($/month)	Telephone ($/month)
City[2]	813,571	1,778	-	178.34	70.10	26.98
Avg.	305,838	919	181.00	93.66	73.14	27.95
Min.	183,142	480	112.00	42.06	23.42	17.16
Max.	1,358,576	3,851	594.00	180.03	440.99	40.42

*Note: (1) Values for the local area are compared with the average, minimum and maximum values for all 308 areas in the Cost of Living Index; (2) Figures cover the San Jose CA urban area; **New Home Price** (2,400 sf living area, 8,000 sf lot, in urban area with full utilities); **Apartment Rent** (950 sf 2 bedroom/1.5 or 2 bath, unfurnished, excluding all utilities except water); **All Electric** (average monthly cost for an all-electric home); **Part Electric** (average monthly cost for a part-electric home); **Other Energy** (average monthly cost for natural gas, fuel oil, coal, wood, and any other forms of energy except electricity); **Telephone** (price includes basic monthly rate for a private residential line plus additional local usage charges incurred by a family of four).*
Source: The Council for Community and Economic Research, ACCRA Cost of Living Index, 2014

Health Care, Transportation, and Other Costs

Area[1]	Doctor ($/visit)	Dentist ($/visit)	Optometrist ($/visit)	Gasoline ($/gallon)	Beauty Salon ($/visit)	Men's Shirt ($)
City[2]	110.69	113.79	129.54	3.82	50.49	25.17
Avg.	102.86	87.89	97.66	3.44	34.37	26.74
Min.	67.47	65.78	51.18	3.00	17.43	12.79
Max.	173.50	150.14	235.00	4.33	64.28	49.50

*Note: (1) Values for the local area are compared with the average, minimum and maximum values for all 308 areas in the Cost of Living Index; (2) Figures cover the San Jose CA urban area; **Doctor** (general practitioners routine exam of an established patient); **Dentist** (adult teeth cleaning and periodic oral examination); **Optometrist** (full vision eye exam for established adult patient); **Gasoline** (one gallon regular unleaded, national brand, including all taxes, cash price at self-service pump if available); **Beauty Salon** (woman's shampoo, trim, and blow-dry); **Men's Shirt** (cotton/polyester dress shirt, pinpoint weave, long sleeves).*
Source: The Council for Community and Economic Research, ACCRA Cost of Living Index, 2014

HOUSING

House Price Index (HPI)

Area	National Ranking[2]	Quarterly Change (%)	One-Year Change (%)	Five-Year Change (%)
MSA[1]	21	1.21	10.28	37.27
U.S.[3]	–	1.35	4.91	11.59

Note: The HPI is a weighted repeat sales index. It measures average price changes in repeat sales or refinancings on the same properties. This information is obtained by reviewing repeat mortgage transactions on single-family properties whose mortgages have been purchased or securitized by Fannie Mae or Freddie Mac in January 1975; (1) San Jose-Sunnyvale-Santa Clara Metropolitan Statistical Area—see Appendix B for areas included; (2) Rankings are based on annual percentage change for all metro areas containing at least 15,000 transactions over the last 10 years and ranges from 1 to 275; (3) figures based on a weighted average of Census Division estimates using a seasonally adjusted, purchase-only index; all figures are for the period ending December 31, 2014
Source: Federal Housing Finance Agency, House Price Index, February 26, 2015

Median Single-Family Home Prices

Area	2012	2013	2014p	Percent Change 2013 to 2014
MSA[1]	645.0	780.0	860.0	10.3
U.S. Average	177.2	197.4	209.0	5.9

Note: Figures are median sales prices of existing single-family homes in thousands of dollars; (p) preliminary; n/a not available; (1) San Jose-Sunnyvale-Santa Clara, CA Metropolitan Statistical Area—see Appendix B for areas included
Source: National Association of Realtors, Median Sales Price of Existing Single-Family Homes for Metropolitan Areas, 4th Quarter 2014

Qualifying Income Based on Median Sales Price of Existing Single-Family Homes

Area	With 5% Down ($)	With 10% Down ($)	With 20% Down ($)
MSA[1]	187,890	178,001	158,223
U.S. Average	45,863	43,449	38,621

Note: Figures are preliminary; Qualifying income is based on a mortgage rate of 4.0%. Monthly principal and interest payment is limited to 25% of income; n/a not available; (1) San Jose-Sunnyvale-Santa Clara, CA Metropolitan Statistical Area—see Appendix B for areas included
Source: National Association of Realtors, Qualifying Income Based on Median Sales Price of Existing Single-Family Homes for Metropolitan Areas, 4th Quarter 2014

Median Apartment Condo-Coop Home Prices

Area	2012	2013	2014p	Percent Change 2013 to 2014
MSA[1]	n/a	n/a	n/a	n/a
U.S. Average	173.7	194.9	205.1	5.2

Note: Figures are median sales prices of existing apartment condo-coop homes in thousands of dollars; (p) preliminary; n/a not available; (1) San Jose-Sunnyvale-Santa Clara, CA Metropolitan Statistical Area—see Appendix B for areas included
Source: National Association of Realtors, Median Sales Price of Existing Apartment Condo-Coop Homes for Metropolitan Areas, 4th Quarter 2014

Gross Monthly Rent

Area	Under $200	$200 -299	$300 -499	$500 -749	$750 -999	$1,000 -1,499	$1,500 and up	Median ($)
City	0.9	2.2	3.1	4.9	8.4	32.7	47.8	1,470
MSA[1]	0.7	1.6	2.7	3.9	7.1	29.9	54.1	1,576
U.S.	1.7	3.2	7.8	22.1	24.3	26.0	14.9	900

Note: Figures are percentages except for Median; Gross rent is the contract rent plus the estimated average monthly cost of utilities (electricity, gas, and water and sewer) and fuels (oil, coal, kerosene, wood, etc.) if these are paid by the renter (or paid for the renter by someone else); (1) Figures cover the San Jose-Sunnyvale-Santa Clara, CA Metropolitan Statistical Area—see Appendix B for areas included
Source: U.S. Census Bureau, 2011-2013 American Community Survey 3-Year Estimates

Homeownership Rate

Area	2007 (%)	2008 (%)	2009 (%)	2010 (%)	2011 (%)	2012 (%)	2013 (%)	2014 (%)
MSA[1]	57.6	54.6	57.2	58.9	60.4	58.6	56.4	56.4
U.S.	68.1	67.8	67.4	66.9	66.1	65.4	65.1	64.5

Note: (1) Figures cover the San Jose-Sunnyvale-Santa Clara, CA Metropolitan Statistical Area—see Appendix B for areas included
Source: U.S. Census Bureau, Housing Vacancies and Homeownership Annual Statistics: 2014

Year Housing Structure Built

Area	2010 or Later	2000 -2009	1990 -1999	1980 -1989	1970 -1979	1960 -1969	1950 -1959	1940 -1949	Before 1940	Median Year
City	0.5	10.3	10.1	13.7	25.2	19.3	12.4	3.2	5.3	1974
MSA[1]	0.6	9.7	10.4	12.9	22.7	18.7	15.7	4.2	5.1	1973
U.S.	0.9	15.0	13.9	13.8	15.8	11.0	10.9	5.4	13.3	1976

Note: Figures are percentages except for Median Year; (1) Figures cover the San Jose-Sunnyvale-Santa Clara, CA Metropolitan Statistical Area—see Appendix B for areas included
Source: U.S. Census Bureau, 2011-2013 American Community Survey 3-Year Estimates

HEALTH

Health Risk Data

Category	MSA[1] (%)	U.S. (%)
Adults aged 18–64 who have any kind of health care coverage	82.5	79.6
Adults who reported being in good or excellent health	88.2	83.1
Adults who are current smokers	9.6	19.6
Adults who are heavy drinkers[2]	4.3	6.1
Adults who are binge drinkers[3]	16.4	16.9
Adults who are overweight (BMI 25.0 - 29.9)	33.0	35.8
Adults who are obese (BMI 30.0 - 99.8)	15.9	27.6
Adults who participated in any physical activities in the past month	83.6	77.1
Adults 50+ who have ever had a sigmoidoscopy or colonoscopy	72.3	67.3
Women aged 40+ who have had a mammogram within the past two years	82.7	74.0
Men aged 40+ who have had a PSA test within the past two years	31.4	45.2
Adults aged 65+ who have had flu shot within the past year	54.1	60.1
Adults who always wear a seatbelt	n/a	93.8

Note: Data as of 2012 unless otherwise noted; n/a not available; (1) Figures cover the San Jose-Sunnyvale-Santa Clara, CA Metropolitan Statistical Area—see Appendix B for areas included; (2) Heavy drinkers are classified as males having more than two drinks per day or females having more than one drink per day; (3) Binge drinkers are classified as males having five or more drinks on one occasion or females having four or more drinks on one occasion
Source: Centers for Disease Control and Prevention, Behaviorial Risk Factor Surveillance System, SMART: Selected Metropolitan/Micropolitan Area Risk Trends, 2012 (Note: the CDC has discontinued this dataset but will be releasing a replacement in late 2015)

Chronic Health Indicators

Category	MSA[1] (%)	U.S. (%)
Adults who have ever been told they had a heart attack	3.8	4.5
Adults who have ever been told they had a stroke	n/a	2.9
Adults who have been told they currently have asthma	8.4	8.9
Adults who have ever been told they have arthritis	17.2	25.7
Adults who have ever been told they have diabetes[2]	7.4	9.7
Adults who have ever been told they had skin cancer	4.1	5.7
Adults who have ever been told they had any other types of cancer	3.9	6.5
Adults who have ever been told they have COPD	2.7	6.2
Adults who have ever been told they have kidney disease	2.9	2.5
Adults who have ever been told they have a form of depression	11.3	18.0

Note: Data as of 2012 unless otherwise noted; n/a not available; (1) Figures cover the San Jose-Sunnyvale-Santa Clara, CA Metropolitan Statistical Area—see Appendix B for areas included; (2) Figures do not include pregnancy-related, borderline, or pre-diabetes
Source: Centers for Disease Control and Prevention, Behaviorial Risk Factor Surveillance System, SMART: Selected Metropolitan/Micropolitan Area Risk Trends, 2012 (Note: the CDC has discontinued this dataset but will be releasing a replacement in late 2015)

Mortality Rates for the Top 10 Causes of Death in the U.S.

ICD-10[a] Sub-Chapter	ICD-10[a] Code	Age-Adjusted Mortality Rate[1] per 100,000 population	
		County[2]	U.S.
Malignant neoplasms	C00-C97	132.5	166.2
Ischaemic heart diseases	I20-I25	71.7	105.7
Other forms of heart disease	I30-I51	21.5	49.3
Chronic lower respiratory diseases	J40-J47	24.0	42.1
Organic, including symptomatic, mental disorders	F01-F09	10.3	38.1
Cerebrovascular diseases	I60-I69	25.3	37.0
Other external causes of accidental injury	W00-X59	17.2	26.9
Other degenerative diseases of the nervous system	G30-G31	44.1	25.6
Diabetes mellitus	E10-E14	22.1	21.3
Hypertensive diseases	I10-I15	29.7	19.4

Note: (a) ICD-10 = International Classification of Diseases 10th Revision; (1) Mortality rates are a three year average covering 2011-2013; (2) Figures cover Santa Clara County
Source: Centers for Disease Control and Prevention, National Center for Health Statistics. Compressed Mortality File 1999-2013 on CDC WONDER Online Database, released October 2014. Data are compiled from the Compressed Mortality File 1999-2013, Series 20 No. 2S, 2014.

Mortality Rates for Selected Causes of Death

ICD-10[a] Sub-Chapter	ICD-10[a] Code	Age-Adjusted Mortality Rate[1] per 100,000 population	
		County[2]	U.S.
Assault	X85-Y09	3.1	5.2
Diseases of the liver	K70-K76	10.0	13.2
Human immunodeficiency virus (HIV) disease	B20-B24	0.7	2.2
Influenza and pneumonia	J09-J18	13.0	15.4
Intentional self-harm	X60-X84	8.2	12.5
Malnutrition	E40-E46	*0.3	0.9
Obesity and other hyperalimentation	E65-E68	1.1	1.8
Renal failure	N17-N19	1.6	13.1
Transport accidents	V01-V99	5.8	11.7
Viral hepatitis	B15-B19	2.3	2.2

Note: (a) ICD-10 = International Classification of Diseases 10th Revision; (1) Mortality rates are a three year average covering 2011-2013; (2) Figures cover Santa Clara County; (*) Unreliable data as per CDC
Source: Centers for Disease Control and Prevention, National Center for Health Statistics. Compressed Mortality File 1999-2013 on CDC WONDER Online Database, released October 2014. Data are compiled from the Compressed Mortality File 1999-2013, Series 20 No. 2S, 2014.

Health Insurance Coverage

Area	With Health Insurance	With Private Health Insurance	With Public Health Insurance	Without Health Insurance	Population Under Age 18 Without Health Insurance
City	86.3	66.6	26.6	13.7	4.5
MSA[1]	88.5	72.3	23.9	11.5	3.9
U.S.	85.2	65.2	31.0	14.8	7.3

Note: Figures are percentages that cover the civilian noninstitutionalized population; (1) Figures cover the San Jose-Sunnyvale-Santa Clara, CA Metropolitan Statistical Area—see Appendix B for areas included
Source: U.S. Census Bureau, 2011-2013 American Community Survey 3-Year Estimates

Number of Medical Professionals

Area[1]	MDs[2]	DOs[2,3]	Dentists	Podiatrists	Chiropractors	Optometrists
Local (number)	7,175	135	1,972	109	703	436
Local (rate[4])	389.7	7.3	105.4	5.8	37.6	23.3
U.S. (rate[4])	270.0	20.2	63.1	5.7	25.2	14.9

Note: Data as of 2013 unless noted; (1) Local data covers Santa Clara County; (2) Data as of 2012 and includes all active, non-federal physicians; (3) Doctor of Osteopathic Medicine; (4) rate per 100,000 population
Source: U.S. Department of Health and Human Services, Health Resources and Services Administration, Bureau of Health Professions, Area Resource File (ARF) 2013-2014

Best Hospitals

According to *U.S. News*, the San Jose-Sunnyvale-Santa Clara, CA metro area is home to one of the best hospitals in the U.S.: **Stanford Hospital and Clinics** (12 specialties). The hospital listed was nationally ranked in at least one adult specialty. Only 144 hospitals nationwide were nationally ranked in one or more specialties. Seventeen hospitals in the U.S. made the Honor Roll with high scores in at least six specialties. *U.S. News Online, "America's Best Children's Hospitals 2014-15"*

According to *U.S. News*, the San Jose-Sunnyvale-Santa Clara, CA metro area is home to one of the best children's hospitals in the U.S.: **Lucile Packard Children's Hospital at Stanford** (9 specialties). The hospital listed was highly ranked in at least one pediatric specialty. Eighty-nine children's hospitals in the U.S. were nationally ranked in at least one specialty. Ten children's hospitals in the U.S. made the Honor Roll with high scores in at least three specialties. *U.S. News Online, "America's Best Children's Hospitals 2014-15"*

EDUCATION

Public School District Statistics

District Name	Schls	Pupils	Pupil/ Teacher Ratio	Minority Pupils[1] (%)	Free Lunch Eligible[2] (%)	IEP[3] (%)
Alum Rock Union Elementary	29	12,659	19.5	97.8	98.6	10.2
Berryessa Union Elementary	14	7,980	23.4	94.8	28.1	9.9
Cambrian	5	3,373	24.4	53.1	13.6	11.4
Campbell Union High	7	7,373	23.3	59.2	5.7	10.1
East Side Union High	22	26,297	24.1	92.7	34.7	9.4
Evergreen Elementary	18	13,375	25.3	92.5	25.4	7.4
Franklin-mckinley Elementary	20	10,703	25.5	98.5	59.9	8.6
Moreland Elementary	6	4,477	22.4	71.9	26.4	9.7
Mount Pleasant Elementary	5	2,540	23.7	97.0	58.4	14.4
Oak Grove Elementary	20	11,372	25.8	80.7	36.0	9.9
San Jose USD	53	33,184	22.6	74.1	37.4	9.9
Santa Clara County Office of Education	21	8,770	18.9	85.6	51.6	21.8
Union Elementary	9	5,298	24.0	45.9	10.3	9.4

Note: Table includes school districts with 2,000 or more students; (1) Percentage of students that are not non-Hispanic white; (2) Percentage of students that are eligible for the free lunch program; (3) Percentage of students that have an Individualized Education Program.
Source: U.S. Department of Education, National Center for Education Statistics, Common Core of Data, Local Education Agency (School District) Universe Survey: School Year 2012-2013; U.S. Department of Education, National Center for Education Statistics, Common Core of Data, Public Elementary/Secondary School Universe Survey: School Year 2012-2013

Highest Level of Education

Area	Less than H.S.	H.S. Diploma	Some College, No Deg.	Associate Degree	Bachelor's Degree	Master's Degree	Prof. School Degree	Doctorate Degree
City	17.5	18.3	18.9	7.7	23.3	10.7	1.6	1.9
MSA[1]	13.5	15.7	17.4	7.1	25.5	14.8	2.6	3.3
U.S.	13.7	28.0	21.2	7.9	18.2	7.7	1.9	1.3

Note: Figures cover persons age 25 and over; (1) Figures cover the San Jose-Sunnyvale-Santa Clara, CA Metropolitan Statistical Area—see Appendix B for areas included
Source: U.S. Census Bureau, 2011-2013 American Community Survey 3-Year Estimates

Educational Attainment by Race

Area	High School Graduate or Higher (%)					Bachelor's Degree or Higher (%)				
	Total	White	Black	Asian	Hisp.[2]	Total	White	Black	Asian	Hisp.[2]
City	82.5	85.2	92.6	84.0	64.0	37.6	36.2	27.8	49.7	12.1
MSA[1]	86.5	88.2	92.5	89.0	65.2	46.2	43.7	29.2	61.2	13.6
U.S.	86.3	88.3	83.1	85.7	64.0	29.1	30.4	18.8	50.7	13.7

Note: Figures shown cover persons 25 years old and over; (1) Figures cover the San Jose-Sunnyvale-Santa Clara, CA Metropolitan Statistical Area—see Appendix B for areas included; (2) People of Hispanic origin can be of any race
Source: U.S. Census Bureau, 2011-2013 American Community Survey 3-Year Estimates

School Enrollment by Grade and Control

Area	Preschool (%)		Kindergarten (%)		Grades 1 - 4 (%)		Grades 5 - 8 (%)		Grades 9 - 12 (%)	
	Public	Private	Public	Private	Public	Private	Public	Private	Public	Private
City	44.4	55.6	82.5	17.5	89.5	10.5	89.7	10.3	89.9	10.1
MSA[1]	35.4	64.6	83.2	16.8	87.7	12.3	87.6	12.4	89.1	10.9
U.S.	57.7	42.3	87.9	12.1	89.9	10.1	90.0	10.0	90.7	9.3

Note: Figures shown cover persons 3 years old and over; (1) Figures cover the San Jose-Sunnyvale-Santa Clara, CA Metropolitan Statistical Area—see Appendix B for areas included
Source: U.S. Census Bureau, 2011-2013 American Community Survey 3-Year Estimates

Average Salaries of Public School Classroom Teachers

Area	2013-14		2014-15		Percent Change 2013-14 to 2014-15	Percent Change 2004-05 to 2014-15
	Dollars	Rank[1]	Dollars	Rank[1]		
CALIFORNIA	71,396	4	72,535	4	1.59	25.9
U.S. Average	56,610	–	57,379	–	1.36	20.8

Note: (1) State rank ranges from 1 to 51 where 1 indicates highest salary.
Source: National Education Association, Rankings & Estimates: Rankings of the States 2014 and Estimates of School Statistics 2015, March 2015

Higher Education

Four-Year Colleges			Two-Year Colleges			Medical Schools[1]	Law Schools[2]	Voc/ Tech[3]
Public	Private Non-profit	Private For-profit	Public	Private Non-profit	Private For-profit			
1	1	2	2	0	1	0	1	4

Note: Figures cover institutions located within the city limits and include main campuses only; (1) includes schools accredited by the Liaison Committee on Medical Education and the American Osteopathic Association's Commission on Osteopathic College Accreditation; (2) includes ABA-accredited schools, schools with provisional ABA accreditation, and state accredited schools; (3) includes all schools with programs that are less than 2 years.
Source: National Center for Education Statistics, Integrated Postsecondary Education System (IPEDS), 2013-14; Association of American Medical Colleges, Member List, May 1, 2015; American Osteopathic Association, Member List, May 1, 2015; Law School Admission Council, Official Guide to ABA-Approved Law Schools Online, May 1, 2015; Wikipedia, List of Medical Schools in the United States, May 1, 2015; Wikipedia, List of Law Schools in the United States, May 1, 2015

According to U.S. News & World Report, the San Jose-Sunnyvale-Santa Clara, CA metro area is home to one of the best national universities in the U.S.: **Stanford University** (#4). The indicators used to capture academic quality fall into a number of categories: assessment by administrators at peer institutions; retention of students; faculty resources; student selectivity; financial resources; alumni giving; high school counselor ratings of colleges; and graduation rate. U.S. News & World Report, "America's Best Colleges 2015"

According to U.S. News & World Report, the San Jose-Sunnyvale-Santa Clara, CA metro area is home to two of the top 100 law schools in the U.S.: **Stanford University** (#2); **Santa Clara University** (#94). The rankings are based on a weighted average of 12 measures of quality: peer assessment score; assessment score by lawyers/judges; median LSAT scores; median undergrad GPA; acceptance rate; employment rates for graduates; placement success; bar passage rate; faculty resources; expenditures per student; student/faculty ratio; and library resources. U.S. News & World Report, "America's Best Graduate Schools, Law, 2016"

According to U.S. News & World Report, the San Jose-Sunnyvale-Santa Clara, CA metro area is home to one of the top 75 medical schools for research in the U.S.: **Stanford University** (#2). The rankings are based on a weighted average of 11 measures of quality: quality assessment; peer assessment score; assessment score by residency directors; research activity; total research activity; average research activity per faculty member; student selectivity; median MCAT total score; median undergraduate GPA; acceptance rate; and faculty resources. U.S. News & World Report, "America's Best Graduate Schools, Medical, 2016"

According to U.S. News & World Report, the San Jose-Sunnyvale-Santa Clara, CA metro area is home to one of the top 75 business schools in the U.S.: **Stanford University** (#1). The rankings are based on a weighted average of the following nine measures: quality assessment; peer assessment; recruiter assessment; placement success; mean starting salary and bonus; student selectivity; mean GMAT and GRE scores; mean undergraduate GPA; and acceptance rate. U.S. News & World Report, "America's Best Graduate Schools, Business, 2016"

PRESIDENTIAL ELECTION

2012 Presidential Election Results

Area	Obama (%)	Romney (%)	Other (%)
Santa Clara County	69.9	27.6	2.5
U.S.	51.0	47.2	1.8

Note: Results may not add to 100% due to rounding
Source: Dave Leip's Atlas of U.S. Presidential Elections

EMPLOYERS

Major Employers

Company Name	Industry
Apple	Radio and tv communications equipment
Cisco Systems	Data conversion equipment, media-to-media: computer
City of San Jose	Executive offices
Cypress Semiconductor International	Semiconductor devices
e4e	Business services, nec
Hadco Santa Clara	Printed circuit boards
Hewlett-Packard Company	Computer (hardware) development
Hewlett-Packard Company	Electronic computers
Hitachi Global Storage Technologies	Computer storage devices
Intel Corporation	Semiconductors and related devices
Juniper Networks	Computer peripheral equipment, nec
LSI Corporation	Semiconductors and related devices
Mormon Church	Churches, temples, and shrines
Rosendin Electric	Electrical work
San Jose State University	Colleges and universities
Seagate Technology	Computer storage devices
Stanford Hospital and Clinics	General medical and surgical hospitals
The Leland Stanford Junior University	General medical and surgical hospitals
Veterans Health Administration	General medical and surgical hospitals

Note: Companies shown are located within the San Jose-Sunnyvale-Santa Clara, CA Metropolitan Statistical Area.
Source: Hoovers.com; Wikipedia

Best Companies to Work For

Adobe Systems; Cadence; Cisco, headquartered in San Jose, are among "The 100 Best Companies to Work For." To pick the best companies, *Fortune* partnered with the Great Place to Work Institute. Two-thirds of a company's score is based on the results of the Institute's Trust Index survey, which is sent to a random sample of employees from each company. The questions related to attitudes about management's credibility, job satisfaction, and camaraderie. The other third of the scoring is based on the company's responses to the Institute's Culture Audit, which includes detailed questions about pay and benefit programs, and a series of open-ended questions about hiring practices, internal communication, training, recognition programs, and diversity efforts. Any company that is at least five years old with more than 1,000 U.S. employees is eligible. *Fortune, "The 100 Best Companies to Work For," 2015*

Cisco, headquartered in San Jose, is among the "100 Best Companies for Working Mothers." Criteria: leave policies, workforce representation, benefits, child care, advancement programs, and flexibility policies. This year *Working Mother* gave particular weight to representation of women, advancement programs and flex. *Working Mother, "100 Best Companies 2014"*

Cisco, headquartered in San Jose, is among the "Best Companies for Multicultural Women." *Working Mother* selected 25 companies based on a detailed application completed by public and private firms based in the United States, excluding government agencies, companies in the human resources field and non-autonomous divisions. Companies supplied data about the hiring, pay, and promotion of multicultural employees. Applications focused on representation of multicultural women, recruitment, retention and advancement programs, and company culture. *Working Mother, "2014 Best Companies for Multicultural Women"*

Cisco, headquartered in San Jose, is among the "Top Companies for Executive Women." To be named to the list, companies with a minimum of two women on the board complete a comprehensive application that focuses on the number of women in senior ranks. In addition to assessing corporate programs and policies dedicated to advancing women, NAFE examined the number of women in each company overall, in senior management, and on its board of directors, paying particular attention to the number of women with profit-and-loss responsibility. *National Association for Female Executives, "2015 NAFE Top 50 Companies for Executive Women"*

PUBLIC SAFETY

Crime Rate

Area	All Crimes	Violent Crimes				Property Crimes		
		Murder	Forcible Rape	Robbery	Aggrav. Assault	Burglary	Larceny -Theft	Motor Vehicle Theft
City	2,895.2	3.8	27.2	110.4	182.6	521.4	1,250.9	798.9
Suburbs[1]	2,311.4	2.1	15.6	47.5	104.8	410.5	1,477.0	254.0
Metro[2]	2,613.9	3.0	21.6	80.1	145.1	467.9	1,359.9	536.3
U.S.	3,098.6	4.5	25.2	109.1	229.1	610.0	1,899.4	221.3

Note: Figures are crimes per 100,000 population; (1) All areas within the metro area that are located outside the city limits; (2) Figures cover the San Jose-Sunnyvale-Santa Clara, CA Metropolitan Statistical Area—see Appendix B for areas included
Source: FBI Uniform Crime Reports, 2013

Hate Crimes

Area	Number of Quarters Reported	Number of Incidents per Bias Motivation						
		Race	Religion	Sexual Orientation	Ethnicity	Disability	Gender	Gender Identity
City	4	6	2	6	1	0	0	0
U.S.	4	2,871	1,031	1,233	655	83	18	31

Source: Federal Bureau of Investigation, Hate Crime Statistics 2013

Identity Theft Consumer Complaints

Area	Complaints	Complaints per 100,000 Population	Rank[2]
MSA[1]	1,628	84.8	105
U.S.	332,646	104.3	-

Note: (1) Figures cover the San Jose-Sunnyvale-Santa Clara, CA Metropolitan Statistical Area—see Appendix B for areas included; (2) Rank ranges from 1 to 380 where 1 indicates greatest number of identity theft complaints per 100,000 population
Source: Federal Trade Commission, Consumer Sentinel Network Data Book for January–December 2014

Fraud and Other Consumer Complaints

Area	Complaints	Complaints per 100,000 Population	Rank[2]
MSA[1]	7,506	391.0	152
U.S.	2,250,205	705.7	-

Note: (1) Figures cover the San Jose-Sunnyvale-Santa Clara, CA Metropolitan Statistical Area—see Appendix B for areas included; (2) Rank ranges from 1 to 380 where 1 indicates greatest number of identity theft complaints per 100,000 population
Source: Federal Trade Commission, Consumer Sentinel Network Data Book for January–December 2014

RECREATION

Culture

Dance[1]	Theatre[1]	Instrumental Music[1]	Vocal Music[1]	Series and Festivals	Museums and Art Galleries[2]	Zoos and Aquariums[3]
2	8	5	1	0	37	1

Note: (1) Professional perfoming groups; (2) Based on organizations with SIC code 8412; (3) AZA-accredited
Source: The Grey House Performing Arts Directory, 2015-16; Association of Zoos & Aquariums, AZA Member Zoos & Aquariums, April 2015; www.AccuLeads.com, April 2015

Professional Sports Teams

Team Name	League	Year Established
San Jose Earthquakes	Major League Soccer (MLS)	1996
San Jose Sharks	National Hockey League (NHL)	1991

Note: Includes teams located in the San Jose-Sunnyvale-Santa Clara, CA Metropolitan Statistical Area.
Source: Wikipedia, Major Professional Sports Teams of the United States and Canada, April 2015

CLIMATE

Average and Extreme Temperatures

Temperature	Jan	Feb	Mar	Apr	May	Jun	Jul	Aug	Sep	Oct	Nov	Dec	Yr.
Extreme High (°F)	76	82	83	95	103	104	105	101	105	100	87	76	105
Average High (°F)	57	61	63	67	70	74	75	75	76	72	65	58	68
Average Temp. (°F)	50	53	55	58	61	65	66	67	66	63	56	50	59
Average Low (°F)	42	45	46	48	51	55	57	58	57	53	47	42	50
Extreme Low (°F)	21	26	30	32	38	43	45	47	41	33	29	23	21

Note: Figures cover the years 1945-1993
Source: National Climatic Data Center, International Station Meteorological Climate Summary, 9/96

Average Precipitation/Snowfall/Humidity

Precip./Humidity	Jan	Feb	Mar	Apr	May	Jun	Jul	Aug	Sep	Oct	Nov	Dec	Yr.
Avg. Precip. (in.)	2.7	2.3	2.2	0.9	0.3	0.1	Tr	Tr	0.2	0.7	1.7	2.3	13.5
Avg. Snowfall (in.)	Tr	Tr	Tr	0	0	0	0	0	0	0	0	Tr	Tr
Avg. Rel. Hum. 7am (%)	82	82	80	76	74	73	77	79	79	79	81	82	79
Avg. Rel. Hum. 4pm (%)	62	59	56	52	53	54	58	58	55	54	59	63	57

Note: Figures cover the years 1945-1993; Tr = Trace amounts (<0.05 in. of rain; <0.5 in. of snow)
Source: National Climatic Data Center, International Station Meteorological Climate Summary, 9/96

Weather Conditions

Temperature			Daytime Sky			Precipitation		
10°F & below	32°F & below	90°F & above	Clear	Partly cloudy	Cloudy	0.01 inch or more precip.	0.1 inch or more snow/ice	Thunder-storms
0	5	5	106	180	79	57	< 1	6

Note: Figures are average number of days per year and cover the years 1945-1993
Source: National Climatic Data Center, International Station Meteorological Climate Summary, 9/96

HAZARDOUS WASTE

Superfund Sites

San Jose has one hazardous waste site on the EPA's Superfund Final National Priorities List: **Lorentz Barrel & Drum Co.** There are a total of 1,322 Superfund sites on the list in the U.S. *U.S. Environmental Protection Agency, Final National Priorities List, April 14, 2015*

AIR & WATER QUALITY

Air Quality Trends: Ozone

	2004	2005	2006	2007	2008	2009	2010	2011	2012	2013
MSA[1]	0.072	0.066	0.080	0.068	0.074	0.072	0.074	0.066	0.065	0.064

Note: (1) Data covers the San Jose-Sunnyvale-Santa Clara, CA Metropolitan Statistical Area—see Appendix B for areas included. The values shown are the composite ozone concentration averages among trend sites based on the highest fourth daily maximum 8-hour concentration in parts per million. These trends are based on sites having an adequate record of monitoring data during the trend period. Data from exceptional events are included.
Source: U.S. Environmental Protection Agency, Air Quality Monitoring Information, "Air Quality Trends by City, 2000-2013"

Air Quality Index

Area	Percent of Days when Air Quality was...[2]					AQI Statistics[2]	
	Good	Moderate	Unhealthy for Sensitive Groups	Unhealthy	Very Unhealthy	Maximum	Median
MSA[1]	73.7	24.9	1.1	0.3	0.0	154	41

Note: (1) Data covers the San Jose-Sunnyvale-Santa Clara, CA Metropolitan Statistical Area—see Appendix B for areas included; (2) Based on 365 days with AQI data in 2014. Air Quality Index (AQI) is an index for reporting daily air quality. EPA calculates the AQI for five major air pollutants regulated by the Clean Air Act: ground-level ozone, particle pollution (aka particulate matter), carbon monoxide, sulfur dioxide, and nitrogen dioxide. The AQI runs from 0 to 500. The higher the AQI value, the greater the level of air pollution and the greater the health concern. There are six AQI categories: "Good" AQI is between 0 and 50. Air quality is considered satisfactory; "Moderate" AQI is between 51 and 100. Air quality is acceptable; "Unhealthy for Sensitive Groups" When AQI values are between 101 and 150, members of sensitive groups may experience health effects; "Unhealthy" When AQI values are between 151 and 200 everyone may begin to experience health effects; "Very Unhealthy" AQI values between 201 and 300 trigger a health alert; "Hazardous" AQI values over 300 trigger warnings of emergency conditions (not shown).
Source: U.S. Environmental Protection Agency, Air Quality Index Report, 2014

Air Quality Index Pollutants

Area	Percent of Days when AQI Pollutant was...[2]					
	Carbon Monoxide	Nitrogen Dioxide	Ozone	Sulfur Dioxide	Particulate Matter 2.5	Particulate Matter 10
MSA[1]	0.0	3.0	61.9	0.0	34.5	0.5

Note: (1) Data covers the San Jose-Sunnyvale-Santa Clara, CA Metropolitan Statistical Area—see Appendix B for areas included; (2) Based on 365 days with AQI data in 2014. The Air Quality Index (AQI) is an index for reporting daily air quality. EPA calculates the AQI for five major air pollutants regulated by the Clean Air Act: ground-level ozone, particle pollution (also known as particulate matter), carbon monoxide, sulfur dioxide, and nitrogen dioxide. The AQI runs from 0 to 500. The higher the AQI value, the greater the level of air pollution and the greater the health concern.
Source: U.S. Environmental Protection Agency, Air Quality Index Report, 2014

Maximum Air Pollutant Concentrations: Particulate Matter, Ozone, CO and Lead

	Particulate Matter 10 (ug/m³)	Particulate Matter 2.5 Wtd AM (ug/m³)	Particulate Matter 2.5 24-Hr (ug/m³)	Ozone (ppm)	Carbon Monoxide (ppm)	Lead (ug/m³)
MSA[1] Level	53	11.9	35	0.071	2	0.12
NAAQS[2]	150	15	35	0.075	9	0.15
Met NAAQS[2]	Yes	Yes	Yes	Yes	Yes	Yes

Note: (1) Data covers the San Jose-Sunnyvale-Santa Clara, CA Metropolitan Statistical Area—see Appendix B for areas included; Data from exceptional events are included; (2) National Ambient Air Quality Standards; ppm = parts per million; ug/m³ = micrograms per cubic meter; n/a not available.
Concentrations: Particulate Matter 10 (coarse particulate)—highest second maximum 24-hour concentration; Particulate Matter 2.5 Wtd AM (fine particulate)—highest weighted annual mean concentration; Particulate Matter 2.5 24-Hour (fine particulate)—highest 98th percentile 24-hour concentration; Ozone—highest fourth daily maximum 8-hour concentration; Carbon Monoxide—highest second maximum non-overlapping 8-hour concentration; Lead—maximum running 3-month average
Source: U.S. Environmental Protection Agency, Air Quality Monitoring Information, "Air Quality Statistics by City, 2013"

Maximum Air Pollutant Concentrations: Nitrogen Dioxide and Sulfur Dioxide

	Nitrogen Dioxide AM (ppb)	Nitrogen Dioxide 1-Hr (ppb)	Sulfur Dioxide AM (ppb)	Sulfur Dioxide 1-Hr (ppb)	Sulfur Dioxide 24-Hr (ppb)
MSA[1] Level	15	52	n/a	10	n/a
NAAQS[2]	53	100	30	75	140
Met NAAQS[2]	Yes	Yes	n/a	Yes	n/a

Note: (1) Data covers the San Jose-Sunnyvale-Santa Clara, CA Metropolitan Statistical Area—see Appendix B for areas included; Data from exceptional events are included; (2) National Ambient Air Quality Standards; ppm = parts per million; ug/m³ = micrograms per cubic meter; n/a not available.
Concentrations: Nitrogen Dioxide AM—highest arithmetic mean concentration; Nitrogen Dioxide 1-Hr—highest 98th percentile 1-hour daily maximum concentration; Sulfur Dioxide AM—highest annual mean concentration; Sulfur Dioxide 1-Hr—highest 99th percentile 1-hour daily maximum concentration; Sulfur Dioxide 24-Hr—highest second maximum 24-hour concentration
Source: U.S. Environmental Protection Agency, Air Quality Monitoring Information, "Air Quality Statistics by City, 2013"

Drinking Water

Water System Name	Pop. Served	Primary Water Source Type	Violations[1] Health Based	Monitoring/ Reporting
San Jose Water Company	998,000	Surface	0	0

Note: (1) Based on violation data from January 1, 2014 to December 31, 2014 (includes unresolved violations from earlier years)
Source: U.S. Environmental Protection Agency, Office of Ground Water and Drinking Water, Safe Drinking Water Information System (based on data extracted January 27, 2015)

Santa Rosa, California

Background

Santa Rosa is located 55 miles north of San Francisco and is in the county seat of Sonoma County and home to one-third of the county's residents. The city is part of both the San Francisco Bay Area and the region known as California's wine country. The popularity of the vineyards, especially among tourists, has helped the city evolve from a small farming town during the California gold rush to a thriving, modern city known for its climate, location and natural beauty.

During the early days of European exploration, the area that is now Santa Rosa was a homestead for wealthy and prominent families, both under Mexican and Spanish rule. In 1852, the Mexican-American War ended and the territory of California became part of the United States. Also around this time, the California Gold Rush brought large numbers of new settlers to the area. As the gold rush waned, explorers found they could make more money farming than they could digging for gold. The community began to grow, and the city was officially incorporated 1868. That same year, the first railroad line reached the city helping Santa Rosa's population to increase tenfold in just seven years. During the twentieth century, population began to level off, and Santa Rosa settled into a medium-sized city that affords residents the benefits of living in a larger urban center.

The city recently completed a Sonoma-Marin Area Rail transit (SMART) station downtown, and is planning another in North Santa Rosa. The new transit access points are expected to enhance pedestrian-friendly neighborhoods.

The city has long hoped to reunify its Old Courthouse Square, creating a large plaza and closing a block of Mendocino Avenue to traffic, but recently delayed the project in order to focus on other municipal priorities such as a four-year planning effort to annex 620 acres. Health care facilities were on the move in 2013, with Kaiser Permanente launching plans to build a new medical hub, and Sutter Medical Center constructing an 80,000 square-foot medical office building in Santa Rosa.

Largely as a result of the city's natural beauty and highly regarded vineyards, Santa Rosa has become a popular destination for tourists. Situated between the Sonoma and Napa Valleys, it's an ideal destination for wine enthusiasts. In addition to wine production, major attractions in Santa Rosa include the Luther Burbank Home and Gardens, the Redwood Empire Ice Arena, the Sonoma County Museum, and the 6th Street Playhouse. The city is also home to the Charles M. Schulz Museum and Research Center, which celebrates the life and work of the Peanuts comic strip. Schulz lived in Santa Rosa for over 30 years, and in 2000, the city renamed its airport "Charles M. Schulz Sonoma County Airport." The airport is served by Alaska Airlines, with destinations that include San Diego, Los Angeles, Portland and Seattle.

Institutions of higher learning in the city include the University of San Francisco Santa Rosa, Empire College and Santa Rosa Junior College.

The city has the same comfortable northern California climate as other Bay Area cities with hot, but not uncomfortable, average temperatures and low humidity. This climate is enjoyed not only by the city's residents and visitors, but also is ideal for wine grape production. The majority of the city's precipitation falls during the spring and winter months, when temperatures are generally much cooler.

Rankings

General Rankings

- In their second annual survey, analysts for the small- and mid-sized city lifestyle site Livability.com looked at data for more than 2,000 U.S. cities to determine the rankings for Livability's "Top 100 Best Places to Live" in 2015. Santa Rosa ranked #78. Criteria: vibrant economy; low cost of living; abundant lifestyle amenities. *Livability.com, "Top 100 Best Places to Live 2015"*

Business/Finance Rankings

- The Santa Rosa metro area appeared on the Milken Institute "2013 Best Performing Cities" list. Rank: #121 out of 200 large metro areas. Criteria: job growth; wage and salary growth; high-tech output growth. *Milken Institute, "Best-Performing Cities 2014," January 2015*

- *Forbes* ranked the 200 most populous metro areas to determine the nation's "Best Places for Business and Careers." The Santa Rosa metro area was ranked #138. Criteria: costs (business and living); job growth (past and projected); income growth; educational attainment (college and high school); projected economic growth; cultural and recreational opportunities; net migration patterns; number of highly ranked colleges. *Forbes, "The Best Places for Business and Careers 2014," July 23, 2014*

Education Rankings

- Personal finance website *WalletHub* analyzed the 150 largest U.S. metropolitan statistical areas to determine where the most educated Americans are choosing to settle. Criteria: educational attainment; percentage of workers with jobs in computer, engineering, and science fields; quality and size of each metro area's universities. Santa Rosa was ranked #41 (#1 = most educated city). *www.WalletHub.com, "2014's Most and Least Educated Cities*

Environmental Rankings

- The Santa Rosa metro area came in at #26 for the relative comfort of its climate on Sperling's list of "chill cities," as measured by the Sperling Heat Index. All 361 metro areas are included. Criteria included daytime high temperatures, nighttime low temperatures, dew point, and relative humidity at the high temperatures. *www.bertsperling.com, "Sperling's Chill Cities," July 18, 2013*

- Sperling's BestPlaces assessed 379 metropolitan areas of the United States for the likelihood of dangerously extreme weather events or earthquakes. In general the Southeast and South-Central regions have the highest risk of weather extremes and earthquakes, while the Pacific Northwest enjoys the lowest risk. Of the least risky metropolitan areas, the Santa Rosa metro area was ranked #104. *www.bestplaces.net, "Safest Places from Natural Disasters," April 2011*

Health/Fitness Rankings

- The Santa Rosa metro area appeared in the 2013 Gallup-Healthways Well-Being Index. The area ranked #27 out of 189. The Gallup-Healthways Well-Being Index score is an average of six sub-indexes, which individually examine life evaluation, emotional health, work environment, physical health, healthy behaviors, and access to basic necessities. Results are based on telephone interviews conducted as part of the Gallup-Healthways Well-Being Index survey January 2–December 29, 2012, and January 2–December 30, 2013, with a random sample of 531,630 adults, aged 18 and older, living in metropolitan areas in the 50 U.S. states and the District of Columbia. *Gallup-Healthways, "State of American Well-Being," March 25, 2014*

Real Estate Rankings

- Using data from the housing-market research firm RealtyTrac, Yahoo! Finance researchers listed the housing markets in which housing affordability is deteriorating most, factoring in interest rates as well as median home prices. The Santa Rosa metro area was among the least affordable housing markets according to the percentage difference in the income required to buy a home in December 2013 as opposed to in December 2012. *news.yahoo.com, "10 Cities Where Ordinary People Can No Longer Afford Homes," March 5, 2014*

- The Santa Rosa metro area was identified as one of the nations's 20 hottest housing markets in 2015. Criteria: listing views relative to the number of listings. The area ranked #5. *Realtor.com, "These Are the 20 Hottest Housing Markets in the U.S. Right Now," April 8, 2015*

- The Santa Rosa metro area was identified as one of the nation's 20 hottest housing markets in 2015.Criteria: median number of days homes were spending on the market in March 2015. The area ranked #3. *Realtor.com, "These Are the 20 Hottest Housing Markets in the U.S. Right Now," April 8, 2015*

- Santa Rosa was ranked #31 out of 275 metro areas in terms of house price appreciation in 2014 (#1 = highest rate). *Federal Housing Finance Agency, House Price Index, 4th Quarter 2014*

- Santa Rosa was ranked #218 out of 226 metro areas in terms of housing affordability in 2014 by the National Association of Home Builders (#1 = most affordable). The NAHB-Wells Fargo Housing Opportunity Index (HOI) for a given area is defined as the share of homes sold in that area that would have been affordable to a family earning the local median income, based on standard mortgage underwriting criteria. *National Association of Home Builders®, NAHB-Wells Fargo Housing Opportunity Index, 4th Quarter 2014*

Safety Rankings

- Allstate ranked the 200 largest cities in America in terms of driver safety. Santa Rosa ranked #119. Allstate researchers analyzed internal property damage claims over a two-year period from January 2011 to December 2012. A weighted average of the two-year numbers determined the annual percentages. *Allstate, "Allstate America's Best Drivers Report, 2014"*

- The National Insurance Crime Bureau ranked 380 metro areas in the U.S. in terms of per capita rates of vehicle theft. The Santa Rosa metro area ranked #174 (#1 = highest rate). Criteria: number of vehicle theft offenses per 100,000 inhabitants in 2012. *National Insurance Crime Bureau, "Hot Spots 2012," June 26, 2013*

Seniors/Retirement Rankings

- From its Best Cities for Successful Aging indexes, the Milken Institute generated rankings for metropolitan areas, weighing data in eight categories—health care, wellness, living arrangements, transportation, financial characteristics, education and employment opportunities, community engagement, and overall livability. The Santa Rosa metro area was ranked #170 overall in the small metro area category. *Milken Institute, "Best Cities for Successful Aging, 2014"*

Women/Minorities Rankings

- To determine the best metro areas for working women, the personal finance website NerdWallet considered city size as well as relevant economic metrics—high salaries, narrow pay differential by gender, prevalence of women in the highest-paying industries, and population growth over 2010–2012. Of the small U.S. cities examined, the Santa Rosa metro area held the #5 position. *www.nerdwallet.com, "Best Places for Women in the Workforce," May 19, 2013*

Business Environment

CITY FINANCES

City Government Finances

Component	2012 ($000)	2012 ($ per capita)
Total Revenues	303,628	1,809
Total Expenditures	306,581	1,827
Debt Outstanding	483,062	2,879
Cash and Securities[1]	301,492	1,797

Note: (1) Cash and security holdings of a government at the close of its fiscal year, including those of its dependent agencies, utilities, and liquor stores.
Source: U.S Census Bureau, State & Local Government Finances 2012

City Government Revenue by Source

Source	2012 ($000)	2012 ($ per capita)
General Revenue		
From Federal Government	9,822	59
From State Government	14,627	87
From Local Governments	73	0
Taxes		
Property	43,406	259
Sales and Gross Receipts	65,961	393
Personal Income	0	0
Corporate Income	0	0
Motor Vehicle License	0	0
Other Taxes	10,139	60
Current Charges	96,038	572
Liquor Store	0	0
Utility	41,504	247
Employee Retirement	0	0

Source: U.S Census Bureau, State & Local Government Finances 2012

City Government Expenditures by Function

Function	2012 ($000)	2012 ($ per capita)	2012 (%)
General Direct Expenditures			
Air Transportation	0	0	0.0
Corrections	0	0	0.0
Education	0	0	0.0
Employment Security Administration	0	0	0.0
Financial Administration	7,963	47	2.6
Fire Protection	28,612	170	9.3
General Public Buildings	0	0	0.0
Governmental Administration, Other	24,037	143	7.8
Health	2,264	13	0.7
Highways	28,901	172	9.4
Hospitals	0	0	0.0
Housing and Community Development	8,378	50	2.7
Interest on General Debt	17,705	106	5.8
Judicial and Legal	1,994	12	0.7
Libraries	0	0	0.0
Parking	4,694	28	1.5
Parks and Recreation	17,667	105	5.8
Police Protection	43,434	259	14.2
Public Welfare	0	0	0.0
Sewerage	57,621	343	18.8
Solid Waste Management	0	0	0.0
Veterans' Services	0	0	0.0
Liquor Store	0	0	0.0
Utility	56,254	335	18.3
Employee Retirement	0	0	0.0

Source: U.S Census Bureau, State & Local Government Finances 2012

DEMOGRAPHICS

Population Growth

Area	1990 Census	2000 Census	2010 Census	Population Growth (%) 1990-2000	Population Growth (%) 2000-2010
City	123,297	147,595	167,815	19.7	13.7
MSA[1]	388,222	458,614	483,878	18.1	5.5
U.S.	248,709,873	281,421,906	308,745,538	13.2	9.7

Note: (1) Figures cover the Santa Rosa-Petaluma, CA Metropolitan Statistical Area—see Appendix B for areas included
Source: U.S. Census Bureau, Census 1990, 2000, 2010

Household Size

Area	Persons in Household (%) One	Two	Three	Four	Five	Six	Seven or More	Average Household Size
City	28.9	32.1	15.3	13.2	6.9	1.6	2.0	2.67
MSA[1]	28.3	34.2	15.2	13.2	5.8	1.7	1.5	2.60
U.S.	27.7	33.6	15.7	13.1	6.0	2.3	1.5	2.64

Note: (1) Figures cover the Santa Rosa, CA Metropolitan Statistical Area—see Appendix B for areas included
Source: U.S. Census Bureau, 2011-2013 American Community Survey 3-Year Estimates

Race

Area	White Alone[2] (%)	Black Alone[2] (%)	Asian Alone[2] (%)	AIAN[3] Alone[2] (%)	NHOPI[4] Alone[2] (%)	Other Race Alone[2] (%)	Two or More Races (%)
City	74.6	2.4	4.9	1.8	0.7	11.2	4.5
MSA[1]	78.1	1.6	3.9	1.2	0.3	10.8	4.1
U.S.	73.9	12.6	5.0	0.8	0.2	4.7	2.9

Note: (1) Figures cover the Santa Rosa, CA Metropolitan Statistical Area—see Appendix B for areas included;
(2) Alone is defined as not being in combination with one or more other races; (3) American Indian and Alaska Native; (4) Native Hawaiian and Other Pacific Islander
Source: U.S. Census Bureau, 2011-2013 American Community Survey 3-Year Estimates

Hispanic or Latino Origin

Area	Total (%)	Mexican (%)	Puerto Rican (%)	Cuban (%)	Other (%)
City	30.2	26.2	0.6	0.0	3.4
MSA[1]	25.5	21.7	0.5	0.1	3.2
U.S.	16.9	10.8	1.6	0.6	3.8

Note: Persons of Hispanic or Latino origin can be of any race; (1) Figures cover the Santa Rosa, CA Metropolitan Statistical Area—see Appendix B for areas included
Source: U.S. Census Bureau, 2011-2013 American Community Survey 3-Year Estimates

Segregation

Type	Segregation Indices[1] 1990	2000	2010	2010 Rank[2]	Percent Change 1990-2000	Percent Change 1990-2010	Percent Change 2000-2010
Black/White	n/a	n/a	n/a	n/a	n/a	n/a	n/a
Asian/White	n/a	n/a	n/a	n/a	n/a	n/a	n/a
Hispanic/White	n/a	n/a	n/a	n/a	n/a	n/a	n/a

Note: All figures cover the Metropolitan Statistical Area—see Appendix B for areas included; Figures are based on an analysis of 1990, 2000, and 2010 Census Decennial Census tract data by William H. Frey, Brookings Institution and the University of Michigan Social Science Data Analysis Network. In this analysis all racial groups (whites, blacks, and asians) are non-Hispanic members of those races. Hispanics are shown as a separate category;
(1) Segregation Indices are Dissimilarity Indices that measure the degree to which the minority group is distributed differently than whites across census tracts. They range from 0 (complete integration) to 100 (complete segregation) where the value indicates the percentage of the minority group that needs to move to be distributed exactly like whites; (2) Ranges from 1 (most segregated) to 102 (least segregated); n/a not available.
Source: www.CensusScope.org

Ancestry

Area	German	Irish	English	American	Italian	Polish	French[2]	Scottish	Dutch
City	12.6	11.0	9.3	4.5	8.0	1.4	3.4	2.5	1.6
MSA[1]	14.1	12.6	10.7	4.5	9.2	1.8	3.5	2.5	1.7
U.S.	14.9	10.8	8.0	7.4	5.5	3.0	2.7	1.7	1.4

Note: Figures are the percentage of the total population reporting a particular ancestry. The nine most commonly reported ancestries in the U.S. are shown. Figures include multiple ancestries (e.g. if a person reported being Irish and Italian, they were included in both columns); (1) Figures cover the Santa Rosa, CA Metropolitan Statistical Area—see Appendix B for areas included; (2) Excludes Basque
Source: U.S. Census Bureau, 2011-2013 American Community Survey 3-Year Estimates

Foreign-Born Population

Area	Any Foreign Country	Mexico	Asia	Europe	Carribean	South America	Central America[2]	Africa	Canada
City	18.8	10.8	3.5	1.3	0.1	0.3	0.9	1.0	0.4
MSA[1]	16.8	9.6	2.8	2.0	0.0	0.3	0.9	0.6	0.3
U.S.	13.0	3.7	3.8	1.5	1.2	0.9	1.0	0.6	0.3

Note: (1) Figures cover the Santa Rosa, CA Metropolitan Statistical Area—see Appendix B for areas included; (2) Excludes Mexico.
Source: U.S. Census Bureau, 2011-2013 American Community Survey 3-Year Estimates

Marital Status

Area	Never Married	Now Married[2]	Separated	Widowed	Divorced
City	34.3	44.0	2.2	5.6	13.9
MSA[1]	32.2	46.6	2.0	5.4	13.7
U.S.	32.7	48.1	2.2	6.0	11.0

Note: Figures are percentages and cover the population 15 years of age and older; (1) Figures cover the Santa Rosa, CA Metropolitan Statistical Area—see Appendix B for areas included; (2) Excludes separated
Source: U.S. Census Bureau, 2011-2013 American Community Survey 3-Year Estimates

Disability Status

Area	All Ages	Under 18 Years Old	18 to 64 Years Old	65 Years and Over
City	11.9	3.4	9.5	38.1
MSA[1]	11.1	3.1	8.5	33.4
U.S.	12.3	4.1	10.2	36.3

Note: Figures show percent of the civilian noninstitutionalized population that reported having a disability. Disability status is determined from from six types of difficulty: vision, hearing, cognitive, ambulatory, self-care, and independent living. For children under 5 years old, hearing and vision difficulty are used to determine disability status. For children between the ages of 5 and 14, disability status is determined from hearing, vision, cognitive, ambulatory, and self-care difficulties. For people aged 15 years and older, they are considered to have a disability if they have difficulty with any one of the six difficulty types; (1) Figures cover the Santa Rosa, CA Metropolitan Statistical Area—see Appendix B for areas included.
Source: U.S. Census Bureau, 2011-2013 American Community Survey 3-Year Estimates

Age

Area	Under Age 5	Age 5–19	Age 20–34	Age 35–44	Age 45–54	Age 55–64	Age 65–74	Age 75–84	Age 85+	Median Age
City	6.1	20.0	20.2	13.1	14.1	12.7	7.0	4.3	2.4	37.8
MSA[1]	5.5	18.5	19.5	12.2	14.5	14.6	8.6	4.4	2.2	40.5
U.S.	6.4	19.9	20.7	12.9	14.1	12.3	7.6	4.2	1.9	37.4

Note: (1) Figures cover the Santa Rosa, CA Metropolitan Statistical Area—see Appendix B for areas included
Source: U.S. Census Bureau, 2011-2013 American Community Survey 3-Year Estimates

Gender

Area	Males	Females	Males per 100 Females
City	84,919	85,574	99.2
MSA[1]	241,429	249,628	96.7
U.S.	154,451,010	159,410,713	96.9

Note: (1) Figures cover the Santa Rosa, CA Metropolitan Statistical Area—see Appendix B for areas included
Source: U.S. Census Bureau, 2011-2013 American Community Survey 3-Year Estimates

Religious Groups by Family

Area	Catholic	Baptist	Non-Den.	Methodist[2]	Lutheran	LDS[3]	Pentecostal	Presbyterian[4]	Muslim[5]	Judaism
MSA[1]	22.3	1.4	1.5	0.9	1.0	1.9	0.7	0.9	0.5	0.4
U.S.	19.1	9.3	4.0	4.0	2.3	2.0	1.9	1.6	0.8	0.7

Note: Figures are the number of adherents as a percentage of the total population; (1) Figures cover the Santa Rosa-Petaluma, CA Metropolitan Statistical Area—see Appendix B for areas included; (2) Methodist/Pietist; (3) Latter Day Saints; (4) Reformed; (5) Figures are estimates
Source: Association of Statisticians of American Religious Bodies, 2010 U.S. Religion Census: Religious Congregations & Membership Study

Religious Groups by Tradition

Area	Catholic	Evangelical Protestant	Mainline Protestant	Other Tradition	Black Protestant	Orthodox
MSA[1]	22.3	5.3	2.4	4.8	<0.1	0.3
U.S.	19.1	16.2	7.3	4.3	1.6	0.3

Note: Figures are the number of adherents as a percentage of the total population; (1) Figures cover the Santa Rosa-Petaluma, CA Metropolitan Statistical Area—see Appendix B for areas included
Source: Association of Statisticians of American Religious Bodies, 2010 U.S. Religion Census: Religious Congregations & Membership Study

ECONOMY

Gross Metropolitan Product

Area	2012	2013	2014	2015	Rank[2]
MSA[1]	20.3	20.9	21.9	23.0	104

Note: Figures are in billions of dollars; (1) Figures cover the Santa Rosa, CA Metropolitan Statistical Area—see Appendix B for areas included; (2) Rank is based on 2015 data and ranges from 1 to 363
Source: The U.S. Conference of Mayors, U.S. Metro Economies: GMP and Employment 2013-2015, June 2014

Economic Growth

Area	2010-12 (%)	2013 (%)	2014 (%)	2015 (%)	Rank[2]
MSA[1]	0.4	1.6	2.9	3.3	102
U.S.	2.1	2.0	2.3	3.2	–

Note: Figures are real gross metropolitan product (GMP) growth rates and represent annual average percent change; (1) Figures cover the Santa Rosa, CA Metropolitan Statistical Area—see Appendix B for areas included; (2) Rank is based on 2015 data and ranges from 1 to 363
Source: The U.S. Conference of Mayors, U.S. Metro Economies: GMP and Employment 2013-2015, June 2014

Metropolitan Area Exports

Area	2008	2009	2010	2011	2012	2013	Rank[2]
MSA[1]	1,117.8	880.1	992.4	1,132.2	1,059.1	1,044.8	154

Note: Figures are in millions of dollars; (1) Figures cover the Santa Rosa, CA Metropolitan Statistical Area—see Appendix B for areas included; (2) Rank is based on 2013 data and ranges from 1 to 387
Source: U.S. Department of Commerce, International Trade Administration, Office of Trade & Industry Information, Manufacturing & Services, data extracted April 3, 2015

Building Permits

Area	Single-Family			Multi-Family			Total		
	2013	2014	Pct. Chg.	2013	2014	Pct. Chg.	2013	2014	Pct. Chg.
City	138	184	33.3	347	64	-81.6	485	248	-48.9
MSA[1]	453	419	-7.5	593	244	-58.9	1,046	663	-36.6
U.S.	620,802	634,597	2.2	370,020	411,766	11.3	990,822	1,046,363	5.6

Note: (1) Figures cover the Santa Rosa, CA Metropolitan Statistical Area—see Appendix B for areas included;
Figures represent new, privately-owned housing units authorized (unadjusted data); All permit data are based
on estimates with imputation.
Source: U.S. Census Bureau, Manufacturing, Mining, and Construction Statistics, Building Permits, 2013, 2014

Bankruptcy Filings

Area	Business Filings			Nonbusiness Filings		
	2013	2014	% Chg.	2013	2014	% Chg.
Sonoma County	43	48	11.6	1,258	930	-26.1
U.S.	33,212	26,983	-18.8	1,038,720	909,812	-12.4

Note: Business filings include Chapter 7, Chapter 11, Chapter 12, and Chapter 13; Nonbusiness filings include
Chapter 7, Chapter 11, and Chapter 13
Source: Administrative Office of the U.S. Courts, Business and Nonbusiness Bankruptcy, County Cases
Commenced by Chapter of the Bankruptcy Code, During the 12- Month Period Ending December 31, 2013 and
Business and Nonbusiness Bankruptcy, County Cases Commenced by Chapter of the Bankruptcy Code, During
the 12- Month Period Ending December 31, 2014

Housing Vacancy Rates

Area	Gross Vacancy Rate[2] (%)			Year-Round Vacancy Rate[3] (%)			Rental Vacancy Rate[4] (%)			Homeowner Vacancy Rate[5] (%)		
	2012	2013	2014	2012	2013	2014	2012	2013	2014	2012	2013	2014
MSA[1]	n/a	n/a	n/a	n/a	n/a	n/a	n/a	n/a	n/a	n/a	n/a	n/a
U.S.	13.8	13.6	13.4	10.8	10.7	10.4	8.7	8.3	7.6	2.0	2.0	1.9

Note: (1) Figures cover the Santa Rosa, CA Metropolitan Statistical Area—see Appendix B for areas included;
(2) The percentage of the total housing inventory that is vacant; (3) The percentage of the housing inventory
(excluding seasonal units) that is year-round vacant; (4) The percentage of rental inventory that is vacant for
rent; (5) The percentage of homeowner inventory that is vacant for sale; n/a not available
Source: U.S. Census Bureau, Housing Vacancies and Homeownership Annual Statistics: 2014

INCOME

Income

Area	Per Capita ($)	Median Household ($)	Average Household ($)
City	29,133	58,908	76,326
MSA[1]	32,554	61,479	83,455
U.S.	27,884	52,176	72,897

Note: (1) Figures cover the Santa Rosa, CA Metropolitan Statistical Area—see Appendix B for areas included
Source: U.S. Census Bureau, 2011-2013 American Community Survey 3-Year Estimates

Household Income Distribution

Area	Percent of Households Earning							
	Under $15,000	$15,000 -24,999	$25,000 -34,999	$35,000 -49,999	$50,000 -74,999	$75,000 -99,000	$100,000 -149,999	$150,000 and up
City	8.6	9.8	9.1	14.8	19.9	12.9	14.5	10.5
MSA[1]	8.5	10.0	8.7	13.4	18.1	12.6	16.2	12.6
U.S.	13.0	10.9	10.3	13.6	17.9	11.9	12.7	9.6

Note: (1) Figures cover the Santa Rosa, CA Metropolitan Statistical Area—see Appendix B for areas included
Source: U.S. Census Bureau, 2011-2013 American Community Survey 3-Year Estimates

Poverty Rate

Area	All Ages	Under 18 Years Old	18 to 64 Years Old	65 Years and Over
City	13.2	17.7	12.8	7.0
MSA[1]	12.2	16.1	12.4	6.3
U.S.	15.9	22.4	14.8	9.5

Note: Figures are percentage of people whose income during the past 12 months was below the poverty level;
(1) Figures cover the Santa Rosa, CA Metropolitan Statistical Area—see Appendix B for areas included
Source: U.S. Census Bureau, 2011-2013 American Community Survey 3-Year Estimates

EMPLOYMENT

Labor Force and Employment

Area	Civilian Labor Force			Workers Employed		
	Dec. 2013	Dec. 2014	% Chg.	Dec. 2013	Dec. 2014	% Chg.
City	87,121	87,301	0.2	81,415	82,474	1.3
MSA[1]	253,990	254,794	0.3	239,042	242,150	1.3
U.S.	154,408,000	155,521,000	0.7	144,423,000	147,190,000	1.9

Note: Data is not seasonally adjusted and covers workers 16 years of age and older; (1) Figures cover the
Santa Rosa, CA Metropolitan Statistical Area—see Appendix B for areas included
Source: Bureau of Labor Statistics, Local Area Unemployment Statistics

Unemployment Rate

Area	2014											
	Jan.	Feb.	Mar.	Apr.	May	Jun.	Jul.	Aug.	Sep.	Oct.	Nov.	Dec.
City	7.0	7.0	7.0	5.9	5.8	6.1	6.6	6.3	5.7	5.7	5.9	5.5
MSA[1]	6.3	6.3	6.3	5.3	5.2	5.5	5.9	5.6	5.1	5.2	5.3	5.0
U.S.	7.0	7.0	6.8	5.9	6.1	6.3	6.5	6.3	5.7	5.5	5.5	5.4

Note: Data is not seasonally adjusted and covers workers 16 years of age and older; (1) Figures cover the
Santa Rosa, CA Metropolitan Statistical Area—see Appendix B for areas included
Source: Bureau of Labor Statistics, Local Area Unemployment Statistics

Employment by Occupation

Occupation Classification	City (%)	MSA[1] (%)	U.S. (%)
Management, Business, Science, and Arts	34.1	35.9	36.2
Natural Resources, Construction, and Maintenance	9.4	9.9	9.0
Production, Transportation, and Material Moving	11.1	9.5	12.1
Sales and Office	26.1	24.6	24.4
Service	19.4	20.1	18.3

Note: Figures cover employed civilians 16 years of age and older; (1) Figures cover the Santa Rosa, CA
Metropolitan Statistical Area—see Appendix B for areas included
Source: U.S. Census Bureau, 2011-2013 American Community Survey 3-Year Estimates

Employment by Industry

Sector	MSA[1]		U.S.
	Number of Employees	Percent of Total	Percent of Total
Construction	10,300	5.3	4.4
Education and Health Services	32,600	16.8	15.5
Financial Activities	7,600	3.9	5.7
Government	31,800	16.4	15.8
Information	2,700	1.4	2.0
Leisure and Hospitality	24,300	12.5	10.3
Manufacturing	20,200	10.4	8.7
Mining and Logging	300	0.2	0.6
Other Services	6,700	3.5	4.0
Professional and Business Services	20,000	10.3	13.8
Retail Trade	25,200	13.0	11.4
Transportation, Warehousing, and Utilities	4,400	2.3	3.9
Wholesale Trade	7,900	4.1	4.2

Note: Figures are non-farm employment as of December 2014. Figures are not seasonally adjusted and include workers 16 years of age and older; (1) Figures cover the Santa Rosa, CA Metropolitan Statistical Area—see Appendix B for areas included
Source: Bureau of Labor Statistics, Current Employment Statistics, Employment, Hours, and Earnings

Occupations with Greatest Projected Employment Growth: 2012 – 2022

Occupation[1]	2012 Employment	2022 Projected Employment	Numeric Employment Change	Percent Employment Change
Personal Care Aides	386,900	587,200	200,300	51.8
Combined Food Preparation and Serving Workers, Including Fast Food	286,000	362,400	76,400	26.7
Retail Salespersons	468,400	528,100	59,700	12.7
Laborers and Freight, Stock, and Material Movers, Hand	270,500	322,300	51,800	19.1
Waiters and Waitresses	246,100	290,300	44,200	18.0
Registered Nurses	254,500	297,400	42,900	16.9
General and Operations Managers	253,800	295,700	41,900	16.5
Secretaries and Administrative Assistants, Except Legal, Medical, and Executive	212,800	250,100	37,300	17.5
Cashiers	357,800	392,600	34,800	9.7
Cooks, Restaurant	116,900	150,600	33,700	28.8

Note: Projections cover California; (1) Sorted by numeric employment change
Source: www.projectionscentral.com, State Occupational Projections, 2012–2022 Long-Term Projections

Fastest Growing Occupations: 2012 – 2022

Occupation[1]	2012 Employment	2022 Projected Employment	Numeric Employment Change	Percent Employment Change
Economists	3,100	5,100	2,000	64.5
Helpers—Brickmasons, Blockmasons, Stonemasons, and Tile and Marble Setters	2,900	4,600	1,700	58.6
Brickmasons and Blockmasons	5,100	8,000	2,900	56.9
Insulation Workers, Floor, Ceiling, and Wall	1,600	2,500	900	56.3
Stonemasons	1,100	1,700	600	54.5
Insulation Workers, Mechanical	1,100	1,700	600	54.5
Personal Care Aides	386,900	587,200	200,300	51.8
Foresters	1,200	1,800	600	50.0
Terrazzo Workers and Finishers	1,100	1,600	500	45.5
Mechanical Door Repairers	1,100	1,600	500	45.5

Note: Projections cover California; (1) Sorted by percent employment change and excludes occupations with numeric employment change less than 100
Source: www.projectionscentral.com, State Occupational Projections, 2012–2022 Long-Term Projections

Average Wages

Occupation	$/Hr.	Occupation	$/Hr.
Accountants and Auditors	34.61	Maids and Housekeeping Cleaners	13.96
Automotive Mechanics	23.44	Maintenance and Repair Workers	22.42
Bookkeepers	21.37	Marketing Managers	64.87
Carpenters	29.72	Nuclear Medicine Technologists	n/a
Cashiers	12.52	Nurses, Licensed Practical	24.38
Clerks, General Office	17.87	Nurses, Registered	49.36
Clerks, Receptionists/Information	16.81	Nursing Assistants	15.35
Clerks, Shipping/Receiving	16.40	Packers and Packagers, Hand	10.94
Computer Programmers	37.30	Physical Therapists	43.46
Computer Systems Analysts	37.04	Postal Service Mail Carriers	25.51
Computer User Support Specialists	27.87	Real Estate Brokers	50.54
Cooks, Restaurant	12.49	Retail Salespersons	13.49
Dentists	89.30	Sales Reps., Exc. Tech./Scientific	29.47
Electrical Engineers	48.52	Sales Reps., Tech./Scientific	45.85
Electricians	33.78	Secretaries, Exc. Legal/Med./Exec.	19.44
Financial Managers	55.30	Security Guards	14.70
First-Line Supervisors/Managers, Sales	21.77	Surgeons	114.81
Food Preparation Workers	10.87	Teacher Assistants	13.30
General and Operations Managers	55.98	Teachers, Elementary School	23.70
Hairdressers/Cosmetologists	11.54	Teachers, Secondary School	32.50
Internists	113.18	Telemarketers	13.12
Janitors and Cleaners	13.77	Truck Drivers, Heavy/Tractor-Trailer	21.96
Landscaping/Groundskeeping Workers	15.00	Truck Drivers, Light/Delivery Svcs.	17.73
Lawyers	77.19	Waiters and Waitresses	12.08

Note: Wage data covers the Santa Rosa-Petaluma, CA Metropolitan Statistical Area—see Appendix B for areas included; Hourly wages for elementary/secondary school teachers and teacher assistants were calculated by the editors from annual wage data assuming a 40 hour work week; n/a not available.
Source: Bureau of Labor Statistics, Metro Area Occupational Employment and Wage Estimates, May 2014

TAXES

State Corporate Income Tax Rates

State	Tax Rate (%)	Income Brackets ($)	Num. of Brackets	Financial Institution Tax Rate (%)[a]	Federal Income Tax Ded.
California	8.84 (c)	Flat rate	1	10.84 (c)	No

Note: Tax rates as of January 1, 2015; (a) Rates listed are the corporate income tax rate applied to financial institutions or excise taxes based on income. Some states have other taxes based upon the value of deposits or shares; (c) Minimum tax is $800 in California, $100 in District of Columbia, $50 in North Dakota (banks), $500 in Rhode Island, $200 per location in South Dakota (banks), $100 in Utah, $250 in Vermont.
Source: Federation of Tax Administrators, "State Corporate Income Tax Rates, 2015"

State Individual Income Tax Rates

State	Tax Rate (%)	Income Brackets ($)	Num. of Brackets	Personal Exempt. ($)[1] Single	Personal Exempt. ($)[1] Dependents	Fed. Inc. Tax Ded.
California (a)	1.0 - 12.3 (f)	7,749- 519,687 (b)	9	108 (c)	333 (c)	No

Note: Tax rates as of January 1, 2015; Local- and county-level taxes are not included; n/a not applicable; (1) Married joint filers generally receive double the single exemption; (a) 17 states have statutory provision for automatically adjusting to the rate of inflation the dollar values of the income tax brackets, standard deductions, and/or personal exemptions. Massachusetts, Michigan, and Nebraska index the personal exemption only. Oregon does not index the income brackets for $125,000 and over. Maine has suspended indexing for 2014 and 2015; (b) For joint returns, taxes are twice the tax on half the couple's income; (c) The personal exemption takes the form of a tax credit instead of a deduction; (f) California imposes an additional 1% tax on taxable income over $1 million, making the maximum rate 13.3% over $1 million.
Source: Federation of Tax Administrators, "State Individual Income Tax Rates, 2015"

Various State and Local Tax Rates

State	State and Local Sales and Use (%)	State Sales and Use (%)	Gasoline[1] (¢/gal.)	Cigarette[2] ($/pack)	Spirits[3] ($/gal.)	Wine[4] ($/gal.)	Beer[5] ($/gal.)
California	8.75	7.50 (b)	45.39	0.87	3.30 (f)	0.20	0.20

Note: All tax rates as of January 1, 2015; (1) The American Petroleum Institute has developed a methodology for determining the average tax rate on a gallon of fuel. Rates may include any of the following: excise taxes, environmental fees, storage tank fees, other fees or taxes, general sales tax, and local taxes. In states where gasoline is subject to the general sales tax, or where the fuel tax is based on the average sale price, the average rate determined by API is sensitive to changes in the price of gasoline. States that fully or partially apply general sales taxes to gasoline: CA, CO, GA, IL, IN, MI, NY; (2) The federal excise tax of $1.0066 per pack and local taxes are not included; (3) Rates are those applicable to off-premise sales of 40% alcohol by volume (a.b.v.) distilled spirits in 750ml containers. Local excise taxes are excluded; (4) Rates are those applicable to off-premise sales of 11% a.b.v. non-carbonated wine in 750ml containers; (5) Rates are those applicable to off-premise sales of 4.7% a.b.v. beer in 12 ounce containers; (b) Three states levy mandatory, statewide, local add-on sales taxes at the state level: California (1%), Utah (1.25%), and Virginia (1%). We include these in their state sales taxes; (f) Different rates are also applicable according to alcohol content, place of production, size of container, or place purchased (on- or off-premise or onboard airlines).
Source: Tax Foundation, 2015 Facts & Figures: How Does Your State Compare?

State Business Tax Climate Index Rankings

State	Overall Rank	Corporate Tax Index Rank	Individual Income Tax Index Rank	Sales Tax Index Rank	Unemployment Insurance Tax Index Rank	Property Tax Index Rank
California	48	34	50	42	14	14

Note: The index is a measure of how each state's tax laws affect economic performance. The lower the rank, the more favorable a state's tax system is for business. States without a given tax are given a ranking of 1. The scores/rankings for the District of Columbia do not affect other states. The 2015 index represents the tax climate as of July 1, 2014.
Source: Tax Foundation, State Business Tax Climate Index 2015

COMMERCIAL UTILITIES

Typical Monthly Electric Bills

Area	Commercial Service ($/month)		Industrial Service ($/month)	
	1,500 kWh	40 kW demand 14,000 kWh	1,000 kW demand 200,000 kWh	50,000 kW demand 32,500,000 kWh
City	299	2,473	42,294	3,279,227
Average[1]	201	1,653	26,124	2,639,743

Note: Figures are based on annualized 2014 rates; (1) Average based on 180 utilities surveyed
Source: Edison Electric Institute, Typical Bills and Average Rates Report, Summer 2014

TRANSPORTATION

Means of Transportation to Work

Area	Car/Truck/Van Drove Alone	Car/Truck/Van Car-pooled	Bus	Subway	Railroad	Bicycle	Walked	Other Means	Worked at Home
City	78.9	10.0	1.8	0.0	0.0	1.1	3.4	1.0	3.8
MSA[1]	76.5	9.7	1.7	0.0	0.0	1.0	3.2	1.3	6.6
U.S.	76.4	9.6	2.6	1.8	0.6	0.6	2.8	1.3	4.3

Note: Figures are percentages and cover workers 16 years of age and older; (1) Figures cover the Santa Rosa, CA Metropolitan Statistical Area—see Appendix B for areas included
Source: U.S. Census Bureau, 2011-2013 American Community Survey 3-Year Estimates

Travel Time to Work

Area	Less Than 10 Minutes	10 to 19 Minutes	20 to 29 Minutes	30 to 44 Minutes	45 to 59 Minutes	60 to 89 Minutes	90 Minutes or More
City	14.6	42.8	19.2	12.8	3.9	4.3	2.6
MSA[1]	15.5	33.6	19.7	15.3	5.8	6.5	3.5
U.S.	13.3	29.7	20.9	20.2	7.7	5.7	2.6

Note: Figures are percentages and include workers 16 years old and over; (1) Figures cover the Santa Rosa, CA Metropolitan Statistical Area—see Appendix B for areas included
Source: U.S. Census Bureau, 2011-2013 American Community Survey 3-Year Estimates

Travel Time Index

Area	1985	1990	1995	2000	2005	2010	2011
Urban Area[1]	n/a	n/a	n/a	n/a	n/a	n/a	n/a
Average[2]	1.09	1.14	1.16	1.19	1.23	1.18	1.18

Note: Travel Time Index—the ratio of travel time in the peak period to the travel time at free-flow conditions. For example, a value of 1.30 indicates a 20-minute free-flow trip takes 26 minutes in the peak. Free-flow speeds (60 mph on freeways and 35 mph on principal arterials) are used as the comparison threshold; (1) Data for the Santa Rosa, CA urban area was not available; (2) average of 498 urban areas
Source: Texas Transportation Institute, Urban Mobility Report 2012, December 2012

Public Transportation

Agency Name / Mode of Transportation	Vehicles Operated in Maximum Service	Annual Unlinked Passenger Trips (in thous.)	Annual Passenger Miles (in thous.)
City of Santa Rosa (Santa Rosa CityBus)			
Bus (directly operated)	25	2,808.6	7,751.8
Bus (purchased transportation)	1	7.6	32.6
Demand Response (purchased transportation)	13	52.9	232.1
Sonoma County Transit			
Bus (directly operated)	3	24.9	230.9
Bus (purchased transportation)	38	1,339.7	12,445.9
Demand Response (purchased transportation)	25	39.1	442.4

Source: Federal Transit Administration, National Transit Database, 2013

Air Transportation

Airport Name and Code / Type of Service	Passenger Airlines[1]	Passenger Enplanements	Freight Carriers[2]	Freight (lbs.)
San Francisco International (SFO)				
Domestic service (U.S. carriers - 2014)	26	17,733,061	17	104,946,994
International service (U.S. carriers - 2013)	9	1,880,671	7	42,819,338

Note: (1) Includes all U.S.-based major, minor and commuter airlines that carried at least one passenger during the year; (2) Includes all U.S.-based airlines and freight carriers that transported at least one lb. of freight during the year.
Source: Bureau of Transportation Statistics, The Intermodal Transportation Database, Air Carriers: T-100 Domestic Market (U.S. Carriers), 2014; Bureau of Transportation Statistics, The Intermodal Transportation Database, Air Carriers: T-100 International Market (U.S. Carriers), 2013

Other Transportation Statistics

Major Highways:	SR-101
Amtrak Service:	Yes
Major Waterways/Ports:	Near Pacific Ocean

Source: Amtrak.com; Google Maps

BUSINESSES

Major Business Headquarters

Company Name	Rankings	
	Fortune[1]	Forbes[2]
No companies listed	-	-

Note: (1) Fortune 500—companies that produce a 10-K are ranked 1 to 500 based on 2013 revenue; (2) all private companies with at least $2 billion in annual revenue through the end of their most current fiscal year are ranked 1 to 221; companies listed are headquartered in the city; dashes indicate no ranking
Source: Fortune, "Fortune 500," June 16, 2014; Forbes, "America's Largest Private Companies," November 5, 2014

Fast-Growing Businesses

According to *Inc.*, Santa Rosa is home to one of America's 500 fastest-growing private companies: **Moore Heating & Air Conditioning** (#261). Criteria: must be an independent, privately-held, for-profit, U.S. corporation, proprietorship or partnership; revenues must be at least $100,000 in 2010 and $2 million in 2013; must have four-year operating/sales history. Holding companies, regulated banks, and utilities were excluded. *Inc., "America's 500 Fastest-Growing Private Companies," September 2014*

Minority Business Opportunity

Santa Rosa is home to one company which is on the *Hispanic Business* 500 list (500 largest U.S. Hispanic-owned companies based on 2012 revenue): **La Tortilla Factory** (#105). Companies included must show at least 51 percent ownership by Hispanic U.S. citizens, and must maintain headquarters in one of the 50 states or Washington, D.C. *Hispanic Business, "Hispanic Business 500," June 20, 2013*

Minority- and Women-Owned Businesses

Group	All Firms		Firms with Paid Employees			
	Firms	Sales ($000)	Firms	Sales ($000)	Employees	Payroll ($000)
Asian	940	333,168	366	312,314	3,629	88,405
Black	227	12,020	5	(w)	20 - 99	(w)
Hispanic	1,426	200,083	292	168,578	1,663	39,761
Women	4,729	584,397	809	451,876	4,642	108,130
All Firms	16,481	12,004,937	4,634	11,346,756	66,419	2,829,125

Note: Figures cover firms located in the city; minority- and women-owned business are defined as firms in which the corresponding group own 51% or more of the stock or equity of the company; (w) withheld to avoid disclosing data for individual companies
Source: U.S. Census Bureau, 2007 Economic Census, Survey of Business Owners (2012 Survey of Business Owners data will be released starting in June 2015)

HOTELS & CONVENTION CENTERS

Hotels/Motels

Area	5 Star		4 Star		3 Star		2 Star		1 Star		Not Rated	
	Num.	Pct.[3]	Num.	Pct.[3]	Num.	Pct.[3]	Num.	Pct.[3]	Num.	Pct.[3]	Num.	Pct.[3]
City[1]	0	0.0	12	14.1	30	35.3	37	43.5	0	0.0	6	7.1
Total[2]	166	0.9	1,264	7.0	5,718	31.8	9,340	52.0	411	2.3	1,070	6.0

Note: (1) Figures cover Santa Rosa and vicinity; (2) Figures cover all 100 cities in this book; (3) Percentage of hotels which have a given star rating; Star ratings are determined by expedia.com and offer an indication of the general quality of a particular hotel.
Source: expedia.com, April 2, 2015

The Santa Rosa, CA metro area is home to eight of the best hotels in the U.S. according to *Travel & Leisure*: **Calistoga Ranch; Solage Calistoga; Farmhouse Inn; Hotel Healdsburg; Auberge du Soleil; Carneros Inn; Meadowood Napa Valley; Vintage Inn**. Criteria: service; location; rooms; food; and value. The list includes the top 236 hotels in the U.S. *Travel & Leisure, "T+L 500, The World's Best Hotels 2015"*

Major Convention Centers

Name	Overall Space (sq. ft.)	Exhibit Space (sq. ft.)	Meeting Space (sq. ft.)	Meeting Rooms

There are no major convention centers located in the metro area
Source: Original research

Living Environment

COST OF LIVING

Cost of Living Index

Composite Index	Groceries	Housing	Utilities	Trans-portation	Health Care	Misc. Goods/Services
n/a	n/a	n/a	n/a	n/a	n/a	n/a

Note: The Cost of Living Index measures regional differences in the cost of consumer goods and services, excluding taxes and non-consumer expenditures, for professional and managerial households in the top income quintile. It is based on more than 50,000 prices covering almost 60 different items for which prices are collected three times a year by chambers of commerce, economic development organizations or university applied economic centers in each participating urban area. The numbers shown should be read as a percentage above or below the national average of 100. For example, a value of 115.4 in the groceries column indicates that grocery prices are 15.4% higher than the national average. Small differences in the index numbers should not be interpreted as significant; n/a not available.
Source: The Council for Community and Economic Research, ACCRA Cost of Living Index, 2014

Grocery Prices

Area[1]	T-Bone Steak ($/pound)	Frying Chicken ($/pound)	Whole Milk ($/half gal.)	Eggs ($/dozen)	Orange Juice ($/64 oz.)	Coffee ($/11.5 oz.)
City[2]	n/a	n/a	n/a	n/a	n/a	n/a
Avg.	10.40	1.37	2.40	1.99	3.46	4.27
Min.	8.48	0.93	1.37	1.30	2.83	2.99
Max.	14.20	2.44	3.62	4.02	6.42	6.96

Note: (1) Values for the local area are compared with the average, minimum and maximum values for all 308 areas in the Cost of Living Index; (2) Figures cover the Santa Rosa CA urban area; n/a not available; **T-Bone Steak** *(price per pound);* **Frying Chicken** *(price per pound, whole fryer);* **Whole Milk** *(half gallon carton);* **Eggs** *(price per dozen, Grade A, large);* **Orange Juice** *(64 oz. Tropicana or Florida Natural);* **Coffee** *(11.5 oz. can, vacuum-packed, Maxwell House, Hills Bros, or Folgers).*
Source: The Council for Community and Economic Research, ACCRA Cost of Living Index, 2014

Housing and Utility Costs

Area[1]	New Home Price ($)	Apartment Rent ($/month)	All Electric ($/month)	Part Electric ($/month)	Other Energy ($/month)	Telephone ($/month)
City[2]	n/a	n/a	n/a	n/a	n/a	n/a
Avg.	305,838	919	181.00	93.66	73.14	27.95
Min.	183,142	480	112.00	42.06	23.42	17.16
Max.	1,358,576	3,851	594.00	180.03	440.99	40.42

Note: (1) Values for the local area are compared with the average, minimum and maximum values for all 308 areas in the Cost of Living Index; (2) Figures cover the Santa Rosa CA urban area; n/a not available; **New Home Price** *(2,400 sf living area, 8,000 sf lot, in urban area with full utilities);* **Apartment Rent** *(950 sf 2 bedroom/1.5 or 2 bath, unfurnished, excluding all utilities except water);* **All Electric** *(average monthly cost for an all-electric home);* **Part Electric** *(average monthly cost for a part-electric home);* **Other Energy** *(average monthly cost for natural gas, fuel oil, coal, wood, and any other forms of energy except electricity);* **Telephone** *(price includes basic monthly rate for a private residential line plus additional local usage charges incurred by a family of four).*
Source: The Council for Community and Economic Research, ACCRA Cost of Living Index, 2014

Health Care, Transportation, and Other Costs

Area[1]	Doctor ($/visit)	Dentist ($/visit)	Optometrist ($/visit)	Gasoline ($/gallon)	Beauty Salon ($/visit)	Men's Shirt ($)
City[2]	n/a	n/a	n/a	n/a	n/a	n/a
Avg.	102.86	87.89	97.66	3.44	34.37	26.74
Min.	67.47	65.78	51.18	3.00	17.43	12.79
Max.	173.50	150.14	235.00	4.33	64.28	49.50

Note: (1) Values for the local area are compared with the average, minimum and maximum values for all 308 areas in the Cost of Living Index; (2) Figures cover the Santa Rosa CA urban area; n/a not available; **Doctor** *(general practitioners routine exam of an established patient);* **Dentist** *(adult teeth cleaning and periodic oral examination);* **Optometrist** *(full vision eye exam for established adult patient);* **Gasoline** *(one gallon regular unleaded, national brand, including all taxes, cash price at self-service pump if available);* **Beauty Salon** *(woman's shampoo, trim, and blow-dry);* **Men's Shirt** *(cotton/polyester dress shirt, pinpoint weave, long sleeves).*
Source: The Council for Community and Economic Research, ACCRA Cost of Living Index, 2014

HOUSING

House Price Index (HPI)

Area	National Ranking[2]	Quarterly Change (%)	One-Year Change (%)	Five-Year Change (%)
MSA[1]	31	1.35	9.59	24.69
U.S.[3]	–	1.35	4.91	11.59

Note: The HPI is a weighted repeat sales index. It measures average price changes in repeat sales or refinancings on the same properties. This information is obtained by reviewing repeat mortgage transactions on single-family properties whose mortgages have been purchased or securitized by Fannie Mae or Freddie Mac in January 1975; (1) Santa Rosa Metropolitan Statistical Area—see Appendix B for areas included; (2) Rankings are based on annual percentage change for all metro areas containing at least 15,000 transactions over the last 10 years and ranges from 1 to 275; (3) figures based on a weighted average of Census Division estimates using a seasonally adjusted, purchase-only index; all figures are for the period ending December 31, 2014
Source: Federal Housing Finance Agency, House Price Index, February 26, 2015

Median Single-Family Home Prices

Area	2012	2013	2014p	Percent Change 2013 to 2014
MSA[1]	n/a	n/a	n/a	n/a
U.S. Average	177.2	197.4	209.0	5.9

Note: Figures are median sales prices of existing single-family homes in thousands of dollars; (p) preliminary; n/a not available; (1) Santa Rosa, CA Metropolitan Statistical Area—see Appendix B for areas included
Source: National Association of Realtors, Median Sales Price of Existing Single-Family Homes for Metropolitan Areas, 4th Quarter 2014

Qualifying Income Based on Median Sales Price of Existing Single-Family Homes

Area	With 5% Down ($)	With 10% Down ($)	With 20% Down ($)
MSA[1]	n/a	n/a	n/a
U.S. Average	45,863	43,449	38,621

Note: Figures are preliminary; Qualifying income is based on a mortgage rate of 4.0%. Monthly principal and interest payment is limited to 25% of income; n/a not available; (1) Santa Rosa, CA Metropolitan Statistical Area—see Appendix B for areas included
Source: National Association of Realtors, Qualifying Income Based on Median Sales Price of Existing Single-Family Homes for Metropolitan Areas, 4th Quarter 2014

Median Apartment Condo-Coop Home Prices

Area	2012	2013	2014p	Percent Change 2013 to 2014
MSA[1]	n/a	n/a	n/a	n/a
U.S. Average	173.7	194.9	205.1	5.2

Note: Figures are median sales prices of existing apartment condo-coop homes in thousands of dollars; (p) preliminary; n/a not available; (1) Santa Rosa, CA Metropolitan Statistical Area—see Appendix B for areas included
Source: National Association of Realtors, Median Sales Price of Existing Apartment Condo-Coop Homes for Metropolitan Areas, 4th Quarter 2014

Gross Monthly Rent

Area	Under $200	$200 -299	$300 -499	$500 -749	$750 -999	$1,000 -1,499	$1,500 and up	Median ($)
City	0.7	2.2	2.9	4.0	17.5	39.8	32.8	1,254
MSA[1]	0.7	2.2	3.3	5.5	15.6	39.6	33.0	1,257
U.S.	1.7	3.2	7.8	22.1	24.3	26.0	14.9	900

Note: Figures are percentages except for Median; Gross rent is the contract rent plus the estimated average monthly cost of utilities (electricity, gas, and water and sewer) and fuels (oil, coal, kerosene, wood, etc.) if these are paid by the renter (or paid for the renter by someone else); (1) Figures cover the Santa Rosa, CA Metropolitan Statistical Area—see Appendix B for areas included
Source: U.S. Census Bureau, 2011-2013 American Community Survey 3-Year Estimates

Homeownership Rate

Area	2007 (%)	2008 (%)	2009 (%)	2010 (%)	2011 (%)	2012 (%)	2013 (%)	2014 (%)
MSA[1]	n/a	n/a	n/a	n/a	n/a	n/a	n/a	n/a
U.S.	68.1	67.8	67.4	66.9	66.1	65.4	65.1	64.5

Note: (1) Figures cover the Santa Rosa, CA Metropolitan Statistical Area—see Appendix B for areas included; n/a not available
Source: U.S. Census Bureau, Housing Vacancies and Homeownership Annual Statistics: 2014

Year Housing Structure Built

Area	2010 or Later	2000 -2009	1990 -1999	1980 -1989	1970 -1979	1960 -1969	1950 -1959	1940 -1949	Before 1940	Median Year
City	0.3	14.4	13.9	17.3	23.2	12.4	7.4	5.1	5.8	1978
MSA[1]	0.4	11.2	13.5	18.6	21.7	11.3	8.8	5.3	9.3	1977
U.S.	0.9	15.0	13.9	13.8	15.8	11.0	10.9	5.4	13.3	1976

Note: Figures are percentages except for Median Year; (1) Figures cover the Santa Rosa, CA Metropolitan Statistical Area—see Appendix B for areas included
Source: U.S. Census Bureau, 2011-2013 American Community Survey 3-Year Estimates

HEALTH

Health Risk Data

Category	MSA[1] (%)	U.S. (%)
Adults aged 18–64 who have any kind of health care coverage	n/a	79.6
Adults who reported being in good or excellent health	n/a	83.1
Adults who are current smokers	n/a	19.6
Adults who are heavy drinkers[2]	n/a	6.1
Adults who are binge drinkers[3]	n/a	16.9
Adults who are overweight (BMI 25.0 - 29.9)	n/a	35.8
Adults who are obese (BMI 30.0 - 99.8)	n/a	27.6
Adults who participated in any physical activities in the past month	n/a	77.1
Adults 50+ who have ever had a sigmoidoscopy or colonoscopy	n/a	67.3
Women aged 40+ who have had a mammogram within the past two years	n/a	74.0
Men aged 40+ who have had a PSA test within the past two years	n/a	45.2
Adults aged 65+ who have had flu shot within the past year	n/a	60.1
Adults who always wear a seatbelt	n/a	93.8

Note: Data as of 2012 unless otherwise noted; n/a not available; (1) Figures cover the Santa Rosa, CA Metropolitan Statistical Area—see Appendix B for areas included; (2) Heavy drinkers are classified as males having more than two drinks per day or females having more than one drink per day; (3) Binge drinkers are classified as males having five or more drinks on one occasion or females having four or more drinks on one occasion
Source: Centers for Disease Control and Prevention, Behaviorial Risk Factor Surveillance System, SMART: Selected Metropolitan/Micropolitan Area Risk Trends, 2012 (Note: the CDC has discontinued this dataset but will be releasing a replacement in late 2015)

Chronic Health Indicators

Category	MSA[1] (%)	U.S. (%)
Adults who have ever been told they had a heart attack	n/a	4.5
Adults who have ever been told they had a stroke	n/a	2.9
Adults who have been told they currently have asthma	n/a	8.9
Adults who have ever been told they have arthritis	n/a	25.7
Adults who have ever been told they have diabetes[2]	n/a	9.7
Adults who have ever been told they had skin cancer	n/a	5.7
Adults who have ever been told they had any other types of cancer	n/a	6.5
Adults who have ever been told they have COPD	n/a	6.2
Adults who have ever been told they have kidney disease	n/a	2.5
Adults who have ever been told they have a form of depression	n/a	18.0

Note: Data as of 2012 unless otherwise noted; n/a not available; (1) Figures cover the Santa Rosa, CA Metropolitan Statistical Area—see Appendix B for areas included; (2) Figures do not include pregnancy-related, borderline, or pre-diabetes
Source: Centers for Disease Control and Prevention, Behaviorial Risk Factor Surveillance System, SMART: Selected Metropolitan/Micropolitan Area Risk Trends, 2012 (Note: the CDC has discontinued this dataset but will be releasing a replacement in late 2015)

Mortality Rates for the Top 10 Causes of Death in the U.S.

ICD-10[a] Sub-Chapter	ICD-10[a] Code	Age-Adjusted Mortality Rate[1] per 100,000 population	
		County[2]	U.S.
Malignant neoplasms	C00-C97	156.6	166.2
Ischaemic heart diseases	I20-I25	86.8	105.7
Other forms of heart disease	I30-I51	37.8	49.3
Chronic lower respiratory diseases	J40-J47	37.4	42.1
Organic, including symptomatic, mental disorders	F01-F09	17.0	38.1
Cerebrovascular diseases	I60-I69	35.7	37.0
Other external causes of accidental injury	W00-X59	18.3	26.9
Other degenerative diseases of the nervous system	G30-G31	42.0	25.6
Diabetes mellitus	E10-E14	17.9	21.3
Hypertensive diseases	I10-I15	17.0	19.4

Note: (a) ICD-10 = International Classification of Diseases 10th Revision; (1) Mortality rates are a three year average covering 2011-2013; (2) Figures cover Sonoma County
Source: Centers for Disease Control and Prevention, National Center for Health Statistics. Compressed Mortality File 1999-2013 on CDC WONDER Online Database, released October 2014. Data are compiled from the Compressed Mortality File 1999-2013, Series 20 No. 2S, 2014.

Mortality Rates for Selected Causes of Death

ICD-10[a] Sub-Chapter	ICD-10[a] Code	Age-Adjusted Mortality Rate[1] per 100,000 population	
		County[2]	U.S.
Assault	X85-Y09	2.1	5.2
Diseases of the liver	K70-K76	13.6	13.2
Human immunodeficiency virus (HIV) disease	B20-B24	1.6	2.2
Influenza and pneumonia	J09-J18	8.6	15.4
Intentional self-harm	X60-X84	11.1	12.5
Malnutrition	E40-E46	Suppressed	0.9
Obesity and other hyperalimentation	E65-E68	1.4	1.8
Renal failure	N17-N19	3.7	13.1
Transport accidents	V01-V99	5.8	11.7
Viral hepatitis	B15-B19	3.6	2.2

Note: (a) ICD-10 = International Classification of Diseases 10th Revision; (1) Mortality rates are a three year average covering 2011-2013; (2) Figures cover Sonoma County
Source: Centers for Disease Control and Prevention, National Center for Health Statistics. Compressed Mortality File 1999-2013 on CDC WONDER Online Database, released October 2014. Data are compiled from the Compressed Mortality File 1999-2013, Series 20 No. 2S, 2014.

Health Insurance Coverage

Area	With Health Insurance	With Private Health Insurance	With Public Health Insurance	Without Health Insurance	Population Under Age 18 Without Health Insurance
City	84.3	63.1	32.5	15.7	7.9
MSA[1]	85.7	68.0	30.1	14.3	6.9
U.S.	85.2	65.2	31.0	14.8	7.3

Note: Figures are percentages that cover the civilian noninstitutionalized population; (1) Figures cover the Santa Rosa, CA Metropolitan Statistical Area—see Appendix B for areas included
Source: U.S. Census Bureau, 2011-2013 American Community Survey 3-Year Estimates

Number of Medical Professionals

Area[1]	MDs[2]	DOs[2,3]	Dentists	Podiatrists	Chiropractors	Optometrists
Local (number)	1,226	60	425	30	177	74
Local (rate[4])	249.8	12.2	85.8	6.1	35.7	14.9
U.S. (rate[4])	270.0	20.2	63.1	5.7	25.2	14.9

Note: Data as of 2013 unless noted; (1) Local data covers Sonoma County; (2) Data as of 2012 and includes all active, non-federal physicians; (3) Doctor of Osteopathic Medicine; (4) rate per 100,000 population
Source: U.S. Department of Health and Human Services, Health Resources and Services Administration, Bureau of Health Professions, Area Resource File (ARF) 2013-2014

EDUCATION

Public School District Statistics

District Name	Schls	Pupils	Pupil/ Teacher Ratio	Minority Pupils[1] (%)	Free Lunch Eligible[2] (%)	IEP[3] (%)
Rincon Valley Union Elementary	9	3,373	21.8	41.6	29.3	18.3
Roseland Elementary	4	2,442	23.1	96.6	79.4	10.0
Santa Rosa Elementary	13	5,197	18.7	71.3	56.0	11.9
Santa Rosa High	19	11,233	22.1	57.6	37.2	13.3

Note: Table includes school districts with 2,000 or more students; (1) Percentage of students that are not non-Hispanic white; (2) Percentage of students that are eligible for the free lunch program; (3) Percentage of students that have an Individualized Education Program.
Source: U.S. Department of Education, National Center for Education Statistics, Common Core of Data, Local Education Agency (School District) Universe Survey: School Year 2012-2013; U.S. Department of Education, National Center for Education Statistics, Common Core of Data, Public Elementary/Secondary School Universe Survey: School Year 2012-2013

Highest Level of Education

Area	Less than H.S.	H.S. Diploma	Some College, No Deg.	Associate Degree	Bachelor's Degree	Master's Degree	Prof. School Degree	Doctorate Degree
City	14.3	20.6	25.9	9.2	18.9	6.8	3.0	1.2
MSA[1]	12.9	20.5	25.6	9.1	20.6	7.2	2.8	1.2
U.S.	13.7	28.0	21.2	7.9	18.2	7.7	1.9	1.3

Note: Figures cover persons age 25 and over; (1) Figures cover the Santa Rosa, CA Metropolitan Statistical Area—see Appendix B for areas included
Source: U.S. Census Bureau, 2011-2013 American Community Survey 3-Year Estimates

Educational Attainment by Race

Area	High School Graduate or Higher (%)					Bachelor's Degree or Higher (%)				
	Total	White	Black	Asian	Hisp.[2]	Total	White	Black	Asian	Hisp.[2]
City	85.7	90.1	82.0	80.9	58.3	29.9	32.5	22.5	40.4	9.6
MSA[1]	87.1	90.8	83.3	84.3	57.9	31.9	34.2	29.4	43.8	10.5
U.S.	86.3	88.3	83.1	85.7	64.0	29.1	30.4	18.8	50.7	13.7

Note: Figures shown cover persons 25 years old and over; (1) Figures cover the Santa Rosa, CA Metropolitan Statistical Area—see Appendix B for areas included; (2) People of Hispanic origin can be of any race
Source: U.S. Census Bureau, 2011-2013 American Community Survey 3-Year Estimates

School Enrollment by Grade and Control

Area	Preschool (%)		Kindergarten (%)		Grades 1 - 4 (%)		Grades 5 - 8 (%)		Grades 9 - 12 (%)	
	Public	Private	Public	Private	Public	Private	Public	Private	Public	Private
City	50.5	49.5	91.4	8.6	97.1	2.9	97.3	2.7	90.8	9.2
MSA[1]	45.9	54.1	87.3	12.7	92.0	8.0	92.1	7.9	90.9	9.1
U.S.	57.7	42.3	87.9	12.1	89.9	10.1	90.0	10.0	90.7	9.3

Note: Figures shown cover persons 3 years old and over; (1) Figures cover the Santa Rosa, CA Metropolitan Statistical Area—see Appendix B for areas included
Source: U.S. Census Bureau, 2011-2013 American Community Survey 3-Year Estimates

Average Salaries of Public School Classroom Teachers

Area	2013-14		2014-15		Percent Change 2013-14 to 2014-15	Percent Change 2004-05 to 2014-15
	Dollars	Rank[1]	Dollars	Rank[1]		
CALIFORNIA	71,396	4	72,535	4	1.59	25.9
U.S. Average	56,610	–	57,379	–	1.36	20.8

Note: (1) State rank ranges from 1 to 51 where 1 indicates highest salary.
Source: National Education Association, Rankings & Estimates: Rankings of the States 2014 and Estimates of School Statistics 2015, March 2015

Higher Education

Four-Year Colleges			Two-Year Colleges			Medical Schools[1]	Law Schools[2]	Voc/ Tech[3]
Public	Private Non-profit	Private For-profit	Public	Private Non-profit	Private For-profit			
0	1	0	1	0	1	0	1	1

Note: Figures cover institutions located within the city limits and include main campuses only; (1) includes schools accredited by the Liaison Committee on Medical Education and the American Osteopathic Association's Commission on Osteopathic College Accreditation; (2) includes ABA-accredited schools, schools with provisional ABA accreditation, and state accredited schools; (3) includes all schools with programs that are less than 2 years.
Source: National Center for Education Statistics, Integrated Postsecondary Education System (IPEDS), 2013-14; Association of American Medical Colleges, Member List, May 1, 2015; American Osteopathic Association, Member List, May 1, 2015; Law School Admission Council, Official Guide to ABA-Approved Law Schools Online, May 1, 2015; Wikipedia, List of Medical Schools in the United States, May 1, 2015; Wikipedia, List of Law Schools in the United States, May 1, 2015

PRESIDENTIAL ELECTION

2012 Presidential Election Results

Area	Obama (%)	Romney (%)	Other (%)
Sonoma County	70.8	26.0	3.2
U.S.	51.0	47.2	1.8

Note: Results may not add to 100% due to rounding
Source: Dave Leip's Atlas of U.S. Presidential Elections

EMPLOYERS

Major Employers

Company Name	Industry
Agilent Technologies	Manufacturer
Amy's Kitchen	Restaurant
AT&T	Telecommunications
Exchange Bank	Finance
G&G Supermarket	Grocery
Hansel Auto Group	Auto dealer
Home Depot	Retail
JDS Uniphase Corporation	Communications
Kaiser Permanente	Insurance
Kendall-Jackson Wine Estate	Winery
Korbel	Champagne
Lucky	Supermarket
Mary's Pizza Shack	Restaurant
Medtronic Cardio Vascular	Healthcare
Pacific Gas & Electric Company	Utility company
Petaluma Acquisition	Poultry processing
River Rock Casino	Gambling
Safeway	Supermarket
St Joseph Health System	Healthcare
State Farm Insurance	Insurance
Sutter Medical Center of Santa Rosa	Healthcare
Walmart Stores	Retail
Wells Fargo & Company	Finance

Note: Companies shown are located within the Santa Rosa, CA Metropolitan Statistical Area.
Source: Hoovers.com; Wikipedia

PUBLIC SAFETY

Crime Rate

Area	All Crimes	Violent Crimes				Property Crimes		
		Murder	Forcible Rape	Robbery	Aggrav. Assault	Burglary	Larceny -Theft	Motor Vehicle Theft
City	2,358.9	1.7	24.5	61.2	227.9	371.9	1,491.6	180.1
Suburbs[1]	1,841.3	1.9	26.0	42.4	313.6	360.7	969.4	127.4
Metro[2]	2,020.8	1.8	25.5	48.9	283.9	364.5	1,150.4	145.7
U.S.	3,098.6	4.5	25.2	109.1	229.1	610.0	1,899.4	221.3

Note: Figures are crimes per 100,000 population; (1) All areas within the metro area that are located outside the city limits; (2) Figures cover the Santa Rosa, CA Metropolitan Statistical Area—see Appendix B for areas included
Source: FBI Uniform Crime Reports, 2013

Hate Crimes

Area	Number of Quarters Reported	Number of Incidents per Bias Motivation						
		Race	Religion	Sexual Orientation	Ethnicity	Disability	Gender	Gender Identity
City	4	0	1	2	0	0	0	0
U.S.	4	2,871	1,031	1,233	655	83	18	31

Source: Federal Bureau of Investigation, Hate Crime Statistics 2013

Identity Theft Consumer Complaints

Area	Complaints	Complaints per 100,000 Population	Rank[2]
MSA[1]	361	72.9	168
U.S.	332,646	104.3	-

Note: (1) Figures cover the Santa Rosa, CA Metropolitan Statistical Area—see Appendix B for areas included; (2) Rank ranges from 1 to 380 where 1 indicates greatest number of identity theft complaints per 100,000 population
Source: Federal Trade Commission, Consumer Sentinel Network Data Book for January–December 2014

Fraud and Other Consumer Complaints

Area	Complaints	Complaints per 100,000 Population	Rank[2]
MSA[1]	2,074	419.0	107
U.S.	2,250,205	705.7	-

Note: (1) Figures cover the Santa Rosa, CA Metropolitan Statistical Area—see Appendix B for areas included; (2) Rank ranges from 1 to 380 where 1 indicates greatest number of identity theft complaints per 100,000 population
Source: Federal Trade Commission, Consumer Sentinel Network Data Book for January–December 2014

RECREATION

Culture

Dance[1]	Theatre[1]	Instrumental Music[1]	Vocal Music[1]	Series and Festivals	Museums and Art Galleries[2]	Zoos and Aquariums[3]
0	1	2	0	3	9	1

Note: (1) Professional perfoming groups; (2) Based on organizations with SIC code 8412; (3) AZA-accredited
Source: The Grey House Performing Arts Directory, 2015-16; Association of Zoos & Aquariums, AZA Member Zoos & Aquariums, April 2015; www.AccuLeads.com, April 2015

Professional Sports Teams

Team Name	League	Year Established
No teams are located in the metro area		

Source: Wikipedia, Major Professional Sports Teams of the United States and Canada, April 2015

CLIMATE

Average and Extreme Temperatures

Temperature	Jan	Feb	Mar	Apr	May	Jun	Jul	Aug	Sep	Oct	Nov	Dec	Yr.
Extreme High (°F)	69	72	83	89	99	102	103	105	109	94	85	73	109
Average High (°F)	56	61	65	69	74	79	81	84	84	75	65	58	71
Average Temp. (°F)	46	50	51	55	60	63	65	66	65	60	52	47	57
Average Low (°F)	35	38	36	41	45	47	49	47	46	44	39	35	42
Extreme Low (°F)	24	26	25	29	32	36	41	40	36	32	28	23	23

Note: Figures cover the years 1948-1990
Source: National Climatic Data Center, International Station Meteorological Climate Summary, 9/96

Average Precipitation/Snowfall/Humidity

Precip./Humidity	Jan	Feb	Mar	Apr	May	Jun	Jul	Aug	Sep	Oct	Nov	Dec	Yr.
Avg. Precip. (in.)	5.6	6.2	4.5	0.7	0.9	0.1	0.0	0.0	0.0	2.3	4.7	4.0	29.0
Avg. Snowfall (in.)	n/a	n/a	n/a	0	0	0	0	0	0	0	n/a	n/a	n/a
Avg. Rel. Hum. (%)	85	74	70	69	68	63	71	68	66	74	81	82	73

Note: Figures cover the years 1948-1990
Source: National Climatic Data Center, International Station Meteorological Climate Summary, 9/96

Weather Conditions

Temperature			Daytime Sky			Precipitation		
0°F & below	32°F & below	90°F & above	Clear	Partly cloudy	Cloudy	0.01 inch or more precip.	0.1 inch or more snow/ice	Thunder-storms
0	43	30	n/a	n/a	n/a	n/a	n/a	2

Note: Figures are average number of days per year and cover the years 1948-1990
Source: National Climatic Data Center, International Station Meteorological Climate Summary, 9/96

HAZARDOUS WASTE

Superfund Sites

Santa Rosa has no sites on the EPA's Superfund Final National Priorities List. There are a total of 1,322 Superfund sites on the list in the U.S. *U.S. Environmental Protection Agency, Final National Priorities List, April 14, 2015*

AIR & WATER QUALITY

Air Quality Trends: Ozone

	2004	2005	2006	2007	2008	2009	2010	2011	2012	2013
MSA[1]	0.053	0.049	0.053	0.054	0.058	0.052	0.054	0.050	0.050	0.055

Note: (1) Data covers the Santa Rosa, CA Metropolitan Statistical Area—see Appendix B for areas included. The values shown are the composite ozone concentration averages among trend sites based on the highest fourth daily maximum 8-hour concentration in parts per million. These trends are based on sites having an adequate record of monitoring data during the trend period. Data from exceptional events are included.
Source: U.S. Environmental Protection Agency, Air Quality Monitoring Information, "Air Quality Trends by City, 2000-2013"

Air Quality Index

Area	Percent of Days when Air Quality was...[2]					AQI Statistics[2]	
	Good	Moderate	Unhealthy for Sensitive Groups	Unhealthy	Very Unhealthy	Maximum	Median
MSA[1]	87.9	12.1	0.0	0.0	0.0	81	35

Note: (1) Data covers the Santa Rosa, CA Metropolitan Statistical Area—see Appendix B for areas included; (2) Based on 365 days with AQI data in 2014. Air Quality Index (AQI) is an index for reporting daily air quality. EPA calculates the AQI for five major air pollutants regulated by the Clean Air Act: ground-level ozone, particle pollution (aka particulate matter), carbon monoxide, sulfur dioxide, and nitrogen dioxide. The AQI runs from 0 to 500. The higher the AQI value, the greater the level of air pollution and the greater the health concern. There are six AQI categories: "Good" AQI is between 0 and 50. Air quality is considered satisfactory; "Moderate" AQI is between 51 and 100. Air quality is acceptable; "Unhealthy for Sensitive Groups" When AQI values are between 101 and 150, members of sensitive groups may experience health effects; "Unhealthy" When AQI values are between 151 and 200 everyone may begin to experience health effects; "Very Unhealthy" AQI values between 201 and 300 trigger a health alert; "Hazardous" AQI values over 300 trigger warnings of emergency conditions (not shown).
Source: U.S. Environmental Protection Agency, Air Quality Index Report, 2014

Air Quality Index Pollutants

Area	Percent of Days when AQI Pollutant was...[2]					
	Carbon Monoxide	Nitrogen Dioxide	Ozone	Sulfur Dioxide	Particulate Matter 2.5	Particulate Matter 10
MSA[1]	0.0	0.0	54.0	0.0	45.2	0.8

Note: (1) Data covers the Santa Rosa, CA Metropolitan Statistical Area—see Appendix B for areas included; (2) Based on 365 days with AQI data in 2014. The Air Quality Index (AQI) is an index for reporting daily air quality. EPA calculates the AQI for five major air pollutants regulated by the Clean Air Act: ground-level ozone, particle pollution (also known as particulate matter), carbon monoxide, sulfur dioxide, and nitrogen dioxide. The AQI runs from 0 to 500. The higher the AQI value, the greater the level of air pollution and the greater the health concern.
Source: U.S. Environmental Protection Agency, Air Quality Index Report, 2014

Maximum Air Pollutant Concentrations: Particulate Matter, Ozone, CO and Lead

	Particulate Matter 10 (ug/m³)	Particulate Matter 2.5 Wtd AM (ug/m³)	Particulate Matter 2.5 24-Hr (ug/m³)	Ozone (ppm)	Carbon Monoxide (ppm)	Lead (ug/m³)
MSA[1] Level	30	8.5	23	0.055	1	n/a
NAAQS[2]	150	15	35	0.075	9	0.15
Met NAAQS[2]	Yes	Yes	Yes	Yes	Yes	n/a

Note: (1) Data covers the Santa Rosa, CA Metropolitan Statistical Area—see Appendix B for areas included; Data from exceptional events are included; (2) National Ambient Air Quality Standards; ppm = parts per million; ug/m³ = micrograms per cubic meter; n/a not available.
Concentrations: Particulate Matter 10 (coarse particulate)—highest second maximum 24-hour concentration; Particulate Matter 2.5 Wtd AM (fine particulate)—highest weighted annual mean concentration; Particulate Matter 2.5 24-Hour (fine particulate)—highest 98th percentile 24-hour concentration; Ozone—highest fourth daily maximum 8-hour concentration; Carbon Monoxide—highest second maximum non-overlapping 8-hour concentration; Lead—maximum running 3-month average
Source: U.S. Environmental Protection Agency, Air Quality Monitoring Information, "Air Quality Statistics by City, 2013"

Maximum Air Pollutant Concentrations: Nitrogen Dioxide and Sulfur Dioxide

	Nitrogen Dioxide AM (ppb)	Nitrogen Dioxide 1-Hr (ppb)	Sulfur Dioxide AM (ppb)	Sulfur Dioxide 1-Hr (ppb)	Sulfur Dioxide 24-Hr (ppb)
MSA[1] Level	9	37	n/a	n/a	n/a
NAAQS[2]	53	100	30	75	140
Met NAAQS[2]	Yes	Yes	n/a	n/a	n/a

Note: (1) Data covers the Santa Rosa, CA Metropolitan Statistical Area—see Appendix B for areas included; Data from exceptional events are included; (2) National Ambient Air Quality Standards; ppm = parts per million; ug/m³ = micrograms per cubic meter; n/a not available.
Concentrations: Nitrogen Dioxide AM—highest arithmetic mean concentration; Nitrogen Dioxide 1-Hr—highest 98th percentile 1-hour daily maximum concentration; Sulfur Dioxide AM—highest annual mean concentration; Sulfur Dioxide 1-Hr—highest 99th percentile 1-hour daily maximum concentration; Sulfur Dioxide 24-Hr—highest second maximum 24-hour concentration
Source: U.S. Environmental Protection Agency, Air Quality Monitoring Information, "Air Quality Statistics by City, 2013"

Drinking Water

Water System Name	Pop. Served	Primary Water Source Type	Violations[1]	
			Health Based	Monitoring/ Reporting
City of Santa Rosa	157,985	Ground	0	0

Note: (1) Based on violation data from January 1, 2014 to December 31, 2014 (includes unresolved violations from earlier years)
Source: U.S. Environmental Protection Agency, Office of Ground Water and Drinking Water, Safe Drinking Water Information System (based on data extracted January 27, 2015)

Seattle, Washington

Background

Believe it or not, the virgin hinterlands and wide curving arch of Elliot Bay of present-day Seattle were once named New York. The city was renamed Seattle in 1853, for the Native American Indian Chief Seattle, two years after its first five families from Illinois had settled into the narrow strip of land between Puget Sound and Lake Washington.

The lush, green forests of the "Emerald City," created by the infamously frequent rains and its many natural waterways, gave birth to Seattle's first major industry—lumber. However, this industry also bred a society of bearded, rabble-rousing bachelors. To alleviate that problem, Asa Mercer, president of the Territorial University, which later became the University of Washington, trekked back east and recruited marriageable women. Among those "Mercer girls" was Ms. Mercer herself. Seattle was settling down.

Today, the city does not rely on lumber as its major industry, but now boasts commercial aircraft production and missile research, due to the presence of Boeing on the outskirts of the city.

In addition, importing and exporting is a major revenue source. As the closest U.S. mainland port to Asia, Seattle has become a key trade center for goods such as cars, forest products, electronic equipment, bananas, and petroleum products. The city and it surrounding region is also home to the headquarters of Amazon.com, Nordstrom, Starbucks, Costco and Nintendo.

On the technology front, Seattle seems to be moving in the direction of becoming the next Silicon Valley. It is predominantly a software town dominated by Microsoft in nearby Redmond, with its more than 30,000 employees. Early in 2003 Corbis, the online photo-archive company, moved its headquarters to the city's historic Pioneer Square. And an increase in the rise of young firms brings the feeling that the city is ready for more expansion and innovation.

The Seattle Seaport Terminal Project is actually comprised of a number of small-and-large-scale projects designed to improve the port's facilities for businesses, passengers, residents, and tourists. One phase of the project, a major renovation of Terminal 5, cost some $265 million and was completed by 1998. Other construction has included a Cruise Ship Terminal improvement, completed in 2000. More than $2 billion has been invested in port facilities improvements over the past fifteen years, and approximately that much again is expected to be invested in coming years.

Seattle has undergone a cultural and commercial reemergence of its downtown. Tourists and locals are drawn by luxury hotels, restaurants, a 16-screen movie theater, and other entertainment-oriented businesses, and the first in a nationwide chain of Game Works, computerized playgrounds for adults. In Center City Seattle, an estimated $761.6 million in development projects were completed in 2006, and more are currently under construction. Football's Seattle Seahawks are Super Bowl XLVIII champions.

The arts are a vital part of Seattle life. The world-famous Seattle Opera, now performing in a state-of-the-art hall dedicated in 2003, is perhaps best-known for its summer presentations of Wagner's *Ring* cycle. The Seattle Philharmonic Orchestra celebrated its 50th anniversary in 2004; its annual Bushnell Concerto Competition features promising new area musicians. The Seattle Museum recently constructed Olympic Sculpture Park, which turned disused waterfront property into a permanent green space with plantings native to Puget Sound. The Seattle Museum of Flight's remarkable collection—the largest on the West Coast—includes a Concorde, donated by British Airways, and the Boeing 707 used as Air Force One by presidents from Eisenhower to Nixon.

Seattle has a distinctly marine climate. The city's location on Puget Sound and between two mountain ranges ensures a mild climate year round, with only moderate variations in temperature. Summers are generally sunny and, while winters are rainy, most of the rain falls between October and March. In 2010, Seattle was the sixth busiest port in the United States.

Rankings

General Rankings

- The Seattle metro area was identified as one of America's fastest-growing areas in terms of population and economy by *Forbes*. The area ranked #5 out of 20. The 100 most populous metro areas in the U.S. were evaluated on the following criteria: estimated population growth; job growth; gross metropolitan product growth; unemployment; median salaries for college-educated workers. *Forbes, "America's Fastest-Growing Cities 2015," January 27, 2015*

- Among the 50 largest U.S. cities, Seattle placed #7 in Vocativ's "semi-exhaustive, mostly scientific" city Livability Index for people aged 35 and under. Average salary, unemployment rates, rents, and other living costs were considered, along with crime rates, weather, public transportation, access to music and sports, and "lifestyle metrics" such as the price of dinner at Buffalo Wild Wings and an ounce of high-quality weed. *vocative.com, "The Livability Index: The Best U.S. Cities for People 35 and Under," December 9, 2014*

- Seattle was selected as one of America's best cities by *Bloomberg Businessweek*. The city ranked #2 out of 50. Criteria: leisure attributes (the number of restaurants, bars, libraries, museums, professional sports teams, and park acres by population); educational attributes (public school performance, the number of colleges, and graduate degree holders); economic factors (2011 income and June and July 2012 unemployment); crime; and air quality. *Bloomberg BusinessWeek, "America's Best Cities," September 26, 2012*

- The human resources consulting firm Mercer ranked 230 cities worldwide in terms of overall quality of life. Seattle ranked #44. Criteria: political, social, economic, and socio-cultural factors; medical and health considerations; schools and education; public services and transportation; recreation; consumer goods; housing; and natural environment. *Mercer, "Mercer 2015 Quality of Living Survey," March 4, 2015*

- The U.S. Conference of Mayors and Waste Management sponsor the City Livability Awards Program. The awards recognize and honor mayors for exemplary leadership in developing and implementing specific programs that improve the quality of life in America's cities. Seattle was one of 17 second round finalists in the large cities (population 100,000 or more) category. *U.S. Conference of Mayors, "2015 City Livability Awards"*

Business/Finance Rankings

- Measuring indicators of "tolerance"—the nonjudgmental environment that "attracts open-minded and new-thinking kinds of people"— as well as concentrations of technological and economic innovators, analysts identified the most creative American metro areas. On the resulting 2012 Creativity Index, the Seattle metro area placed #4. *www.thedailybeast.com, "Boulder, Ann Arbor, Tucson & More: 20 Most Creative U.S. Cities," June 26, 2012*

- The personal finance site NerdWallet scored the nation's 50 largest American cities according to how friendly a business climate they offer to would-be entrepreneurs. Criteria included access to funding, human capital, local economy, and business-friendliness as judged by small business owners. On the resulting list of most welcoming cities, Seattle ranked #8. *www.nerdwallet.com, "Best Cities to Start a Business," May 7, 2014*

- Recognizing the sizeable percentage of American workers who are self-employed, NerdWallet editors assessed the country's cities according to percentage of freelancers, median rental costs, and affordability of median healthcare costs. By these criteria, Seattle placed #9 among the best cities for independent workers. *www.nerdwallet.com, "Best Cities for Freelancers," February 25, 2014*

- TransUnion ranked the nation's metro areas by average credit score, calculated on the VantageScore system, developed by the three major credit-reporting bureaus—TransUnion, Experian, and Equifax. The Seattle metro area was among the ten cities with the highest collective credit score, meaning that its residents posed the lowest average consumer credit risk. *www.usatoday.com, "Metro Areas' Average Credit Rating Revealed," February 7, 2013*

- Building on the U.S. Department of Labor's Occupational Information Network Data Collection Program, the Brookings Institution defined STEM occupations and job opportunities for STEM workers at various levels of educational attainment. The Seattle metro area was placed among the ten large metro areas with the highest demand for high-level STEM knowledge. *www.brookings.edu, "The Hidden Stem Economy," June 10, 2013*

- Seattle was the #6-ranked city in a Seedtable analysis of the world's most active cities for start-up companies, as reported by Statista. *www.statista.com, "San Francisco Has the Most Active Start-Up Scene," August 21, 2013*

- The business website 24/7 Wall Street drew on Brookings Institution research on 50 advanced industries to identify the proportion of workers in the nation's largest metropolitan areas that were employed in jobs requiring knowledge in the science, technology, engineering, or math (STEM) fields. The Seattle metro area was #2. *247wallst.com, "15 Cities with the Most High-Tech Jobs," March 13, 2015*

- Based on metro area social media reviews, the employment opinion group Glassdoor surveyed 50 of the largest U.S. metro areas on measures including compensation and benefits, satisfaction with management, business outlook, and number of employers hiring. The Seattle metro area was ranked #7 in overall employee satisfaction. *www.glassdoor.com, "Employment Satisfaction Report Card by City," June 13, 2014*

- In a survey of economic confidence in the nation's 50 largest metropolitan areas conducted January–December 2014, the Seattle metro area placed #7, according to Gallup's 2014 Economic Confidence Index. *Gallup, "San Jose and San Francisco Lead in Economic Confidence," March 19, 2015*

- Using data from the Council for Community and Economic Research's 2013 Annual Report, NerdWallet ranked the 100 U.S. cities with the most expensive cost of living. Cities in California and in the Northeast topped the list. Of the cities with the highest cost of living, Seattle ranked #30. *NerdWallet.com, "Most Expensive Cities in America," June 4, 2014*

- The Brookings Institution ranked the 50 largest cities in the U.S. based on income inequality. Seattle was ranked #18. (#1 = greatest ineqality). Criteria: the cities were ranked based on the "95/20 ratio," a figure representing the income at which a household earns more than 95 percent of all other households, divided by the income at which a household earns more than only 20 percent of all other households. *Brookings Institution, "Income Inequality in America's 50 Largest Cities, 2007-2013," March 17, 2015*

- *Forbes* ranked the largest metro areas in the U.S. in terms of the "Best Cities for Young Professionals." The Seattle metro area ranked #13 out of 15. Criteria: job growth; unemployment rate; median salary of college graduates age 24 to 34; cost of living; number of small businesses per capita; number of large companies; percentage of population 25 years of age and older with college degrees. *Forbes.com, "America's 15 Best Cities for Young Professionals," August 18, 2014*

- Seattle was ranked #15 out of 100 metro areas in terms of economic performance (#1 = best) during the recession and recovery from trough quarter through the second quarter of 2013. Criteria: percent change in employment; percentage point change in unemployment rate; percent change in gross metropolitan product; percent change in House Price Index. *Brookings Institution, MetroMonitor: Tracking Economic Recession and Recovery in America's 100 Largest Metropolitan Areas, September 2013*

- Seattle was identified as one of the best places for finding a job by *U.S. News & World Report*. The city ranked #6 out of 10. Criteria: strong job market. *U.S. News & World Report, "The 10 Best Cities to Find Jobs," June 17, 2013*

- Payscale.com ranked the 20 largest metro areas in terms of wage growth. The Seattle metro area ranked #5. Criteria: private-sector wage growth between the 1st quarter of 2014 and the 1st quarter of 2015. *PayScale, "Wage Trends by Metro Area," 1st Quarter, 2015*

- The Seattle metro area was identified as one of the most debt-ridden places in America by the finance site Credit.com. The metro area was ranked #4. Criteria: residents' average personal debt load and average credit scores. *Credit.com, "The Most Debt-Ridden Cities," May 1, 2014*

- Seattle was identified as one of America's "10 Best Cities to Find Jobs" by *U.S. News & World Report*. The city ranked #6. Criteria: Bureau of labor Statistics unemployment rates; employment data from Indeed.com and juju.com. *U.S. News & World Report, "10 Best Cities to Find Jobs," June 17, 2013*

- Seattle was identified as one of the best cities for college graduates to find work—and live. The city ranked #14 out of 15. Criteria: job availability; average salary; average rent. *CareerBuilder.com, "15 Best Cities for College Grads to Find Work—and Live," June 5, 2012*

- The Seattle metro area appeared on the Milken Institute "2013 Best Performing Cities" list. Rank: #11 out of 200 large metro areas. Criteria: job growth; wage and salary growth; high-tech output growth. *Milken Institute, "Best-Performing Cities 2014," January 2015*

- *Forbes* ranked the 200 most populous metro areas to determine the nation's "Best Places for Business and Careers." The Seattle metro area was ranked #9. Criteria: costs (business and living); job growth (past and projected); income growth; educational attainment (college and high school); projected economic growth; cultural and recreational opportunities; net migration patterns; number of highly ranked colleges. *Forbes, "The Best Places for Business and Careers 2014," July 23, 2014*

- Mercer Human Resources Consulting ranked 211 urban areas worldwide in terms of cost-of-living. Seattle ranked #153 (the lower the ranking, the higher the cost-of-living). The survey measured the comparative cost of over 200 items (such as housing, food, clothing, household goods, transportation, and entertainment) in each location. *Mercer, "2014 Cost of Living Survey," July 10, 2014*

Culture/Performing Arts Rankings

- Seattle was selected as one of America's top cities for the arts. The city ranked #8 in the big city (population 500,000 and over) category. Criteria: readers' top choices for arts travel destinations based on the richness and variety of visual arts sites, activities and events. *American Style, "2012 Top 25 Arts Destinations," June 2012*

Dating/Romance Rankings

- *Forbes* reports that the Seattle metro area made Rent.com's Best Cities for Newlyweds survey for 2013, based on Bureau of Labor Statistics and Census Bureau data on number of married couples, percentage of families with children under age six, average annual income, cost of living, and availability of rentals. *www.forbes.com, "The 10 Best Cities for Newlyweds to Live and Work In," May 30, 2013*

- Seattle took the #10 spot on NerdWallet's list of best cities for singles wanting to date, based on the availability of singles; "date-friendliness," as determined by a city's walkability and the number of bars and restaurants per thousand residents; and the affordability of dating in terms of the cost of movie tickets, pizza, and wine for two. *www.nerdwallet.com, "Best Cities for Singles," February 2, 2015*

- Of the 100 U.S. cities surveyed by *Men's Health* in its quest to identify the nation's best cities for dating and forming relationships, Seattle was ranked #8 for online dating (#1 = best). *Men's Health, "The Best and Worst Cities for Online Dating," January 30, 2013*

- Seattle was selected as one of the best cities for single women by *Rent.com*. Criteria: high single male-to-female ratio. *Rent.com, "Top Cities for Single Women," March 7, 2013*

- Seattle was selected as one of the best cities for newlyweds by *Rent.com*. The city ranked #2 of 10. Criteria: cost of living; availability of rental inventory; annual mean wages; percentage of married couples; percentage of children under the age of six. *Rent.com, "10 Best Cities for Newlyweds," May 10, 2013*

- Seattle was selected as one of the best cities for post grads by *Rent.com*. The city ranked #7 of 10. Criteria: millenial population; jobs per capita; unemployment rate; median rent; number of bars and restaurants; access to nightlife and entertainment. *Rent.com, "Top 10 Best Cities for Post Grads," April 3, 2015*

- Seattle was selected as one of "America's Best Cities for Dating" by *Yahoo! Travel*. Criteria: high proportion of singles; excellent dating venues and/or stunning natural settings. *Yahoo! Travel, "America's Best Cities for Dating," February 7, 2012*

Education Rankings

- The Seattle metro area was selected as one of the world's most inventive cities by *Forbes*. The area was ranked #13 out of 15. Criteria: patent applications per capita. *Forbes, "World's 15 Most Inventive Cities," July 9, 2013*

- The Seattle metro area was selected as one of America's most innovative cities" by *The Business Insider*. The metro area was ranked #11 out of 20. Criteria: patents per capita. *The Business Insider, "The 20 Most Innovative Cities in the U.S.," February 1, 2013*

- *Fast Company* magazine measured six key components of "smart" cities and three "drivers" for each component to reveal the top ten "Smartest Cities in North America." By these complex metrics, Seattle ranked #1. *Fastcoexist.com, "The Top 10 Smartest Cities in North America," November 15, 2013*

- *Reader's Digest* analyzed data for 120 U.S. cities to arrive at a list of "America's 10 Sharpest Cities." Researchers looked at education level, eating and exercise habits, health conditions, and sociability factors calculated to build and maintain mental alertness into the upper decades of life. Seattle ranked #4 on the list. *Reader's Digest, "America's 10 Sharpest Cities," October 2012*

- Personal finance website *WalletHub* analyzed the 150 largest U.S. metropolitan statistical areas to determine where the most educated Americans are choosing to settle. Criteria: educational attainment; percentage of workers with jobs in computer, engineering, and science fields; quality and size of each metro area's universities. Seattle was ranked #6 (#1 = most educated city). *www.WalletHub.com, "2014's Most and Least Educated Cities*

- Seattle was selected as one of the most well-read cities in America by Amazon.com. The city ranked #4 among the top 20. Cities with populations greater than 100,000 were evaluated based on per capita sales of books, magazines and newspapers. *Amazon.com, "The 20 Most Well-Read Cities in America," May 20, 2014*

- The real estate website *MovoTo.com* selected Seattle as one of the "Nerdiest Cities in America." The city ranked #3 among the top 10 derived from data on the 50 most populous cities in the United States. Criteria: Number of annual comic book, video game, anime, and sci-fi/fantasy conventions; people per comic book store, video game store, and traditional gaming store; people per LARPing ("live action role-playing") group; people per science museum. Also factored in: distance to the nearest Renaissance faire. *MovoTo.com, "The 10 Nerdiest Cities in America," April 10, 2013*

- Seattle was selected as one of America's most literate cities. The city ranked #3 out of the 77 largest U.S. cities. Criteria: number of booksellers; library resources; Internet resources; educational attainment; periodical publishing resources; newspaper circulation. *Central Connecticut State University, "America's Most Literate Cities, 2014," April 8, 2015*

Environmental Rankings

- The Seattle metro area came in at #8 for the relative comfort of its climate on Sperling's list of "chill cities," as measured by the Sperling Heat Index. All 361 metro areas are included. Criteria included daytime high temperatures, nighttime low temperatures, dew point, and relative humidity at the high temperatures. *www.bertsperling.com, "Sperling's Chill Cities," July 18, 2013*

- Sperling's BestPlaces assessed 379 metropolitan areas of the United States for the likelihood of dangerously extreme weather events or earthquakes. In general the Southeast and South-Central regions have the highest risk of weather extremes and earthquakes, while the Pacific Northwest enjoys the lowest risk. Of the least risky metropolitan areas, the Seattle metro area was ranked #8. *www.bestplaces.net, "Safest Places from Natural Disasters," April 2011*

- *The Daily Beast* identifed the snowiest among the 100 largest U.S. cities, looking at average snowfall per month from December 2011 through March 2012 and from December 1, 2012 to December 21, 2012. Number of days with maximum and minimum temperatures of 32 degrees or less contributed to the rankings. Seattle ranked #23. *The Daily Beast, "25 Snowiest Cities in America," December 21, 2012*

- The U.S. Environmental Protection Agency (EPA) released a list of large U.S. metropolitan areas with the most ENERGY STAR certified buildings in 2014. The Seattle metro area was ranked #13 out of 25. *U.S. Environmental Protection Agency, "Top Cities With the Most ENERGY STAR Certified Buildings in 2014," March 25, 2015*

- Seattle was highlighted as one of the 25 metro areas most polluted by short-term particle pollution (24-hour PM 2.5) in the U.S. during 2011 through 2013. The area ranked #18. *American Lung Association, State of the Air 2015*

Food/Drink Rankings

- According to Fodor's Travel, Seattle placed #18 among the best U.S. cities for food-truck cuisine. *www.fodors.com, "America's Best Food Truck Cities," December 20, 2013*

- *Men's Health* ranked 100 major U.S. cities in terms of alcohol intoxication. Seattle ranked #27 (#1 = most sober).Criteria: binge drinking; alcohol-related traffic accidents, arrests, and fatalities. *Men's Health, "The Drunkest Cities in America," November 19, 2013*

- Seattle was identified as one of the most vegetarian-friendly cities in America by GrubHub.com, the nation's largest food ordering service. The city ranked #1 out of 10. Criteria: percentage of vegetarian restaurants. *GrubHub.com, "Top Vegetarian-Friendly Cities," July 18, 2012*

- Seattle was selected as one of America's 10 most vegan-friendly cities. The city was ranked #6. *People for the Ethical Treatment of Animals, "Top Vegan-Friendly Cities of 2013," June 11, 2013*

- Safeco Field (Seattle Mariners) was selected as one of PETA's "Top 10 Vegetarian-Friendly Major League Ballparks" for 2013. The park ranked #6. *People for the Ethical Treatment of Animals, "Top 10 Vegetarian-Friendly Major League Ballparks," June 12, 2013*

Health/Fitness Rankings

- Analysts who tracked obesity rates in the nation's largest metro areas (those with populations above one million) found that the Seattle metro area was one of the ten major metros where residents were least likely to be obese, defined as a BMI score of 30 or above. *www.gallup.com, "Boulder, Colo., Residents Still Least Likely to Be Obese," April 4, 2014*

- For each of the 50 most populous metro areas in the United States, the American College of Sports Medicine's American Fitness Index evaluated infrastructure, community assets, and policies that encourage healthy and fit lifestyles, including preventive health behaviors, levels of chronic disease conditions, health care access, and community resources and policies that support physical activity. The Seattle metro area ranked #8 for "community fitness." Personal health indicators were considered as well as community and environmental indicators. *www.americanfitnessindex.org, "ACSM American Fitness Index Health and Community Fitness Status of the 50 Largest Metropolitan Areas," May 2013*

- *Business Insider* reported Trulia's analysis of the 100 largest U.S. metro areas to identify the nation's best cities for weight loss, based on healthful food options, access to outdoor activities, weight-loss centers, gyms, and opportunities to bike or walk to work. Seattle ranked #10. *Businessinsider.com, "These Are the Best US Cities for Weight loss," January 17, 2013*

- Seattle was identified as one of the 10 most walkable cities in the U.S. by Walk Score, a Seattle-based service that rates the convenience and transit access of 10,000 neighborhoods in 3,000 cities. The area ranked #8 out of the 50 largest U.S. cities. Walk Score measures walkability by analyzing hundreds of walking routes to nearby amenities. Walk Score also measures pedestrian friendliness by analyzing population density and road metrics such as block length and intersection density. *WalkScore.com, March 20, 2014*

- The Seattle metro area was identified as one of the worst cities for bed bugs in America by pest control company Orkin. The area ranked #18 out of 50 based on the number of bed bug treatments Orkin performed from January to December 2013. *Orkin, "Chicago Tops Bed Bug Cities List for Second Year in a Row," January 16, 2014*

- Seattle was selected as one of the 25 fittest cities in America by *Men's Fitness Online*. It ranked #6 out of America's 50 largest cities. Criteria: fitness centers and sport stores; nutrition; sports participation; TV viewing; overweight/sedentary; junk food; air quality; geography; commute; parks and open space; city recreational facilities; access to healthcare; motivation; mayor and city initiatives; state obesity initiatives. *Men's Fitness, "The Fittest and Fattest Cities in America," March 5, 2012*

- Seattle was identified as a "2013 Spring Allergy Capital." The area ranked #93 out of 100. Three groups of factors were used to identify the most severe cities for people with allergies during the spring season: annual pollen levels; medicine utilization; access to board-certified allergists. *Asthma and Allergy Foundation of America, "Spring Allergy Capitals 2013"*

- Seattle was identified as a "2013 Fall Allergy Capital." The area ranked #84 out of 100. Three groups of factors were used to identify the most severe cities for people with allergies during the fall season: annual pollen levels; medicine utilization; access to board-certified allergists. *Asthma and Allergy Foundation of America, "Fall Allergy Capitals 2013"*

- Seattle was identified as a "2013 Asthma Capital." The area ranked #99 out of the nation's 100 largest metropolitan areas. Twelve factors were used to identify the most challenging places to live for people with asthma: estimated prevalence; self-reported prevalence; crude death rate for asthma; annual pollen score; annual air quality; public smoking laws; number of board-certified asthma specialists; school inhaler access laws; rescue medication use; controller medication use; uninsured rate; poverty rate. *Asthma and Allergy Foundation of America, "Asthma Capitals 2013"*

- *Men's Health* ranked 100 major U.S. cities in terms of the best and worst cities for men. Seattle ranked #1. Criteria: thirty-three data points were examined covering health, fitness, and quality of life. *Men's Health, "The Best & Worst Cities for Men 2014," December 6, 2013*

- Seattle was selected as one of the best metropolitan areas for hospital care in America by *HealthGrades.com*. The rankings are based on a comprehensive study of patient death and complication rates in the nation's nearly 5,000 hospitals. Hospitals performing in the top 5% nationwide across 26 different medical procedures and diagnoses were identified. *HealthGrades.com* then ranked cities by the highest percentage of these Distinguished Hospitals for Clinical Excellence™. The Seattle metro area ranked #35. *HealthGrades.com, "America's Top 50 Cities for Hospital Care," January 21, 2012*

- The Seattle metro area appeared in the 2013 Gallup-Healthways Well-Being Index. The area ranked #32 out of 189. The Gallup-Healthways Well-Being Index score is an average of six sub-indexes, which individually examine life evaluation, emotional health, work environment, physical health, healthy behaviors, and access to basic necessities. Results are based on telephone interviews conducted as part of the Gallup-Healthways Well-Being Index survey January 2–December 29, 2012, and January 2–December 30, 2013, with a random sample of 531,630 adults, aged 18 and older, living in metropolitan areas in the 50 U.S. states and the District of Columbia. *Gallup-Healthways, "State of American Well-Being," March 25, 2014*

- The Seattle metro area was identified as one of "America's Most Stressful Cities" by *Sperling's BestPlaces*. The metro area ranked #9 out of 50. Criteria: unemployment rate; suicide rate; commute time; mental health; poor rest; alcohol use; violent crime rate; property crime rate; cloudy days annually. *Sperling's BestPlaces, www.BestPlaces.net, "Stressful Cities 2012*

- Seattle was selected as one of the "20 Most Livable U.S. Cities for Wheelchair Users" by the Christopher & Dana Reeve Foundation. The city ranked #1. Criteria: Medicaid eligibility and spending; access to physicians and rehabilitation facilities; access to fitness facilities and recreation; access to paratransit; percentage of people living with disabilities who are employed; clean air; climate. *Christopher & Dana Reeve Foundation, "20 Most Livable U.S. Cities for Wheelchair Users," July 26, 2010*

Pet Rankings

- Seattle was selected as the best city for dogs in the northwestern U.S. by *Dog Fancy*. Criteria: dog-friendly open spaces and dog parks; events celebrating dogs and their owners; vet-to-dog ratios; abundant pet supply and other services; municipal laws that support and protect all pets. *Dog Fancy, "DogTown USA 2013," June 18, 2013*

- Seattle was selected as one of the best cities for dogs by real estate website Estately.com. The city was ranked #3. Criteria: weather; walkability; yard sizes; dog activities; meetup groups; availability of dogsitters. *Estately.com, "17 Best U.S. Cities for Dogs," May 14, 2013*

Real Estate Rankings

- On the list compiled by Penske Truck Rental, the Seattle metro area was named the #6 moving destination in 2014, based on one-way consumer truck rental reservations made through Penske's website and reservations call center. *blog.gopenske.com, "Penske Truck Rental's 2014 Top Moving Destinations List," February 4, 2015*

- Using data from the housing-market research firm RealtyTrac, Yahoo! Finance researchers listed the housing markets in which housing affordability is deteriorating most, factoring in interest rates as well as median home prices. The Seattle metro area was among the least affordable housing markets according to the percentage difference in the income required to buy a home in December 2013 as opposed to in December 2012. *news.yahoo.com, "10 Cities Where Ordinary People Can No Longer Afford Homes," March 5, 2014*

- The Seattle metro area was identified as one of the nation's 20 hottest housing markets in 2015.Criteria: median number of days homes were spending on the market in March 2015. The area ranked #5. *Realtor.com, "These Are the 20 Hottest Housing Markets in the U.S. Right Now," April 8, 2015*

- Seattle was ranked #49 out of 275 metro areas in terms of house price appreciation in 2014 (#1 = highest rate). *Federal Housing Finance Agency, House Price Index, 4th Quarter 2014*

- The Seattle metro area was identified as one of the 20 least affordable housing markets in the U.S. in 2014. The area ranked #14 out of 178 markets. Criteria: whether or not a typical family could qualify for a mortgage loan on a typical home. *National Association of Realtors®, Affordability Index of Existing Single-Family Homes for Metropolitan Areas, 2014*

- Seattle was ranked #199 out of 226 metro areas in terms of housing affordability in 2014 by the National Association of Home Builders (#1 = most affordable). The NAHB-Wells Fargo Housing Opportunity Index (HOI) for a given area is defined as the share of homes sold in that area that would have been affordable to a family earning the local median income, based on standard mortgage underwriting criteria. *National Association of Home Builders®, NAHB-Wells Fargo Housing Opportunity Index, 4th Quarter 2014*

Safety Rankings

- Symantec, in partnership with Sperling's BestPlaces, ranked the 50 largest cities in the U.S. in terms of their vulnerability to cybercrime. The city ranked #2. Criteria: number of cyberattacks and potential infections; level of Internet access; expenditures on smartphones and computer hardware/software; wireless hotspots; broadband connectivity; Internet usage; online purchases. *Symantec, "Riskiest Online Cities of 2012" February 15, 2012*

- Allstate ranked the 200 largest cities in America in terms of driver safety. Seattle ranked #173. Allstate researchers analyzed internal property damage claims over a two-year period from January 2011 to December 2012. A weighted average of the two-year numbers determined the annual percentages. *Allstate, "Allstate America's Best Drivers Report, 2014"*

- Seattle was identified as one of the least disaster-proof places in the U.S. in terms of its vulnerability to natural and non-natural disasters. The city ranked #2 out of 5. Rankings are based on the U.S. Center for Disease Control's Cities Readiness Initiative (CRI). As part of the CRI, the CDC and state public health personnel assess local emergency-management plans, protocols and capabilities for 72 Metropolitan Statistical Areas and four non-MSA large cities. *Forbes, "America's Most and Least Disaster-Proof Cities," December 12, 2011*

- Seattle was identified as one of the safest large cities in America by CQ Press. All 32 cities with populations of 500,000 or more that reported crime rates in 2012 for murder, rape, robbery, aggravated assault, burglary, and motor vehicle thefts were ranked. The city ranked #9 out of the top 10. *CQ Press, City Crime Rankings 2014*

- The National Insurance Crime Bureau ranked 380 metro areas in the U.S. in terms of per capita rates of vehicle theft. The Seattle metro area ranked #13 (#1 = highest rate). Criteria: number of vehicle theft offenses per 100,000 inhabitants in 2012. *National Insurance Crime Bureau, "Hot Spots 2012," June 26, 2013*

Seniors/Retirement Rankings

- From its Best Cities for Successful Aging indexes, the Milken Institute generated rankings for metropolitan areas, weighing data in eight categories—health care, wellness, living arrangements, transportation, financial characteristics, education and employment opportunities, community engagement, and overall livability. The Seattle metro area was ranked #48 overall in the large metro area category. *Milken Institute, "Best Cities for Successful Aging, 2014"*

- Seattle was identified as one of the most popular places to retire by *Topretirements.com*. The list reflects the 100 cities (out of 900+ total cities reviewed) that visitors to the website are most interested in for retirement. *Topretirements.com, "Most Popular Places to Retire for 2014," February 25, 2014*

Sports/Recreation Rankings

- Seattle was selected as one of "America's Most Miserable Sports Cities" by *Forbes*. The city was ranked #1. Criteria: postseason losses; years since last title; ratio of cumulative seasons to championships won. Contenders were limited to cities with at least 75 total seasons of NFL, NBA, NHL and MLB play. *Forbes, "America's Most Miserable Sports Cities," July 31, 2013*

- Seattle was chosen as a bicycle friendly community by the League of American Bicyclists. A "Bicycle Friendly Community" welcomes cyclists by providing safe accommodation for cycling and encouraging people to bike for transportation and recreation. There are four award levels: Platinum; Gold; Silver; and Bronze. The community achieved an award level of Gold. *League of American Bicyclists, "Bicycle Friendly Community Master List," Fall 2013*

- Seattle was chosen as one of America's best cities for bicycling. The city ranked #10 out of 50. Criteria: robust cycling infrastructure; vibrant bike culture. The editors only considered cities with populations of 95,000 or more. *Bicycling, "America's Top 50 Bike-Friendly Cities," May 23, 2012*

Transportation Rankings

- Business Insider presented a Walk Score ranking of public transportation in 316 U.S. cities and thousands of city neighborhoods in which Seattle earned the #7-ranked "Transit Score," awarded for frequency, type of route, and distance between stops. *www.businessinsider.com, "The US Cities with the Best Public Transportation Systems," January 30, 2014*

- More U.S. households choose not to have a car in 2012 than in prior years, according to a study by the University of Michigan Transportation Research Institute. The business website 24/7 Wall Street examined that study, along with a 2010 Census Special Report to arrive at its ranking of cities in which the fewest households had a vehicle. Seattle held the #10 position. *247wallst.com, "Cities Where No One Wants to Drive," February 6, 2014*

- Seattle was identified as one of the most congested metro areas in the U.S. The area ranked #9 out of 10. Criteria: yearly delay per auto commuter in hours. *Texas A&M Transportation Institute, "2012 Urban Mobility Report," December 2012*

- The Seattle metro area appeared on *Forbes* list of places with the most extreme commutes. The metro area ranked #10 out of 10. Criteria: average travel time; percentage of mega commuters. Mega-commuters travel more than 90 minutes and 50 miles each way to work. *Forbes.com, "The Cities with the Most Extreme Commutes," March 5, 2013*

Women/Minorities Rankings

- The Daily Beast surveyed the nation's cities for highest percentage of singles and lowest divorce rate, plus other measures, to determine "emotional intelligence"—happiness, confidence, kindness—which, researchers say, has a strong correlation with people's satisfaction with their romantic relationships. Seattle placed #9. *www.thedailybeast.com, "Best Cities to Find Love and Stay in Love," February 14, 2014*

- 24/7 Wall St. compared median earnings over a 12-month period for men and women who worked full-time, year-round, and employment composition by sector to identify the worst-paying cities for women. Of the largest 100 U.S. metropolitan areas, Seattle was ranked #10 in pay disparity. *24/7 Wall St., "The Worst-Paying Cities for Women," March 8, 2013*

- *Women's Health* examined U.S. cities and identified the 100 best cities for women. Seattle was ranked #13. Criteria: 30 categories were examined from obesity and breast cancer rates to commuting times and hours spent working out. *Women's Health, "Best Cities for Women 2012"*

- Seattle was selected as one of the gayest cities in America by *The Advocate*. The city ranked #3 out of 15. This year's criteria include points for a city's LGBT elected officials (and fractional points for the state's elected officials), points for the percentage of the population comprised by lesbian-coupled households, a point for a gay rodeo association, points for bars listed in *Out* magazine's 200 Best Bars list, a point per women's college, and points for concert performances by Mariah Carey, Pink, Lady Gaga, or the Jonas Brothers. The raw score is divided by the population to provide a ranking based on a per capita LGBT quotient. *The Advocate, "2014's Gayest Cities in America" January 6, 2014*

Miscellaneous Rankings

- Seattle was selected as a 2013 Digital Cities Survey winner. The city ranked #4 in the large city (250,000 or more population) category. The survey examined and assessed how city governments are utilizing information technology to operate and deliver quality service to their customers and citizens. Survey questions focused on implementation and adoption of online service delivery; planning and governance; and the infrastructure and architecture that make the transformation to digital government possible. *Center for Digital Government, "2013 Digital Cities Survey," November 7, 2013*

- *Travel + Leisure* invited readers to rate cities on indicators such as aloofness, "smarty-pants residents," highbrow cultural offerings, high-end shopping, artisanal coffeehouses, conspicuous eco-consciousness, and more in order to identify the nation's snobbiest cities. Cities large and small made the list; among them was Seattle, at #5. *www.travelandleisure.com, "America's Snobbiest Cities, June 2013*

- Of the American metro areas that allow medical or recreational use of marijuana, the Seattle metro area was identified by CNBC editors as one of the most livable for marijuana lovers. Criteria included the Sperling's BestPlaces assessment of marijuana-friendly cities in terms of sound economy, cultural diversity, and a healthy population, plus cost-of-living index and high-quality schools. *www.cnbc.com, "The Best Cities to Live for Marijuana Lovers," February 5, 2014*

- The watchdog site Charity Navigator conducts an annual study of charities in the nation's major markets both to analyze statistical differences in their financial, accountability, and transparency practices and to track year-to-year variations in individual communities. The Seattle metro area was ranked #20 among the 30 metro markets. *www.charitynavigator.org, "Metro Market Study 2013," June 1, 2013*

- Business Insider reports on the 2013 Trick-or-Treat Index compiled by the real estate site Zillow, which used its own Home Value Index and Walk Score along with population density and local crime stats to determine that Seattle ranked #5 for "how much candy it gives out versus how far kids have to walk to get it." Zillow also zeroes in on the best neighborhoods in its top 20 cities. *www.businessinsider.com, "These Are the Best Cities for Trick-or-Treating," October 15, 2013*

- Market analyst Scarborough Research surveyed adults who had done volunteer work over the previous 12 months to find out where volunteers are concentrated. The Seattle metro area made the list for highest volunteer participation. *Scarborough Research, "Salt Lake City, UT; Minneapolis, MN; and Des Moines, IA Lend a Helping Hand," November 27, 2012*

- Seattle was selected as one of the 10 best run cities in America by *24/7 Wall St*. The city ranked #7. Criteria: the 100 largest cities in the U.S. were ranked in terms of economy, job market, crime, and the welfare of its residents. *24/7 Wall St., "The Best and Worst Run Cities in America," January 15, 2013*

- Seattle was selected as one of America's funniest cities by the Humor Research Lab at the University of Colorado. The city ranked #10 out of 10. Criteria: frequency of visits to comedy websites; number of comedy clubs per square mile; traveling comedians' ratings of each city's comedy-club audiences; number of famous comedians born in each city per capita; number of famous funny tweeters living in each city per capita; number of comedy radio stations available in each city; frequency of humor-related web searches originating in each city. *The New York Times, "So These Professors Walk Into a Comedy Club...," April 20, 2014*

- Seattle appeared on *Travel + Leisure's* list of America's most attractive people. Criteria: cities were selected by readers in their annual America's Favorite Cities survey. The city ranked #9 out of 10. *Travel + Leisure, "America's Most and Least Attractive People," November 2013*

- Mars Chocolate North America, the makers of COMBOS®, in partnership with Sperling's BestPlaces, ranked 50 major metro areas in terms of their "manliness." The Seattle metro area ranked #41. Criteria: number of professional sports teams; number of nearby NASCAR tracks and racing events; manly lifestyle; concentration of manly retail stores; manly occupations per capita; salty snack sales; "Board of Manliness" rankings. *Mars Chocolate North America, "America's Manliest Cities 2012"*

- Seattle was selected as one of "America's Best Cities for Hipsters" by *Travel + Leisure*. The city was ranked #11 out of 20. Criteria: live music; coffee bars; independent boutiques; best microbrews; offbeat and tech-savvy locals. *Travel + Leisure, "America's Best Cities for Hipsters," November 2013*

- The National Alliance to End Homelessness ranked the 100 most populous metro areas in terms the rate of homelessness. The Seattle metro area ranked #8. Criteria: number of homeless people per 10,000 population in 2011. *National Alliance to End Homelessness, The State of Homelessness in America 2012*

- The financial education website CreditDonkey compiled a list of the ten "best" cities of the future, based on percentage of housing built in 1990 or later, population change since 2010, and construction jobs as a percentage of population. Also considered were two more futuristic criteria: number of DeLorean cars available for purchase and number of spaceport companies and proposed spaceports. Seattle was scored #3. *www.creditDonkey.com, "In the Future, Almost All of America's 'Best' Cities Will Be on the West Coast, Report Says," February 14, 2014*

Business Environment

CITY FINANCES

City Government Finances

Component	2012 ($000)	2012 ($ per capita)
Total Revenues	2,836,795	4,661
Total Expenditures	2,807,836	4,613
Debt Outstanding	4,163,648	6,841
Cash and Securities[1]	2,572,947	4,227

Note: (1) Cash and security holdings of a government at the close of its fiscal year, including those of its dependent agencies, utilities, and liquor stores.
Source: U.S Census Bureau, State & Local Government Finances 2012

City Government Revenue by Source

Source	2012 ($000)	2012 ($ per capita)
General Revenue		
From Federal Government	53,288	88
From State Government	132,286	217
From Local Governments	7,585	12
Taxes		
Property	397,437	653
Sales and Gross Receipts	452,057	743
Personal Income	0	0
Corporate Income	0	0
Motor Vehicle License	4,665	8
Other Taxes	59,366	98
Current Charges	551,705	906
Liquor Store	0	0
Utility	945,577	1,554
Employee Retirement	42,122	69

Source: U.S Census Bureau, State & Local Government Finances 2012

City Government Expenditures by Function

Function	2012 ($000)	2012 ($ per capita)	2012 (%)
General Direct Expenditures			
Air Transportation	0	0	0.0
Corrections	1	< 1	< 0.1
Education	5,009	8	0.2
Employment Security Administration	0	0	0.0
Financial Administration	10,681	18	0.4
Fire Protection	128,764	212	4.6
General Public Buildings	5,786	10	0.2
Governmental Administration, Other	29,780	49	1.1
Health	6,373	10	0.2
Highways	190,606	313	6.8
Hospitals	0	0	0.0
Housing and Community Development	28,706	47	1.0
Interest on General Debt	67,983	112	2.4
Judicial and Legal	27,125	45	1.0
Libraries	43,808	72	1.6
Parking	8,928	15	0.3
Parks and Recreation	151,557	249	5.4
Police Protection	174,096	286	6.2
Public Welfare	102,873	169	3.7
Sewerage	191,841	315	6.8
Solid Waste Management	169,571	279	6.0
Veterans' Services	0	0	0.0
Liquor Store	0	0	0.0
Utility	1,015,281	1,668	36.2
Employee Retirement	134,393	221	4.8

Source: U.S Census Bureau, State & Local Government Finances 2012

DEMOGRAPHICS

Population Growth

Area	1990 Census	2000 Census	2010 Census	Population Growth (%) 1990-2000	Population Growth (%) 2000-2010
City	516,262	563,374	608,660	9.1	8.0
MSA[1]	2,559,164	3,043,878	3,439,809	18.9	13.0
U.S.	248,709,873	281,421,906	308,745,538	13.2	9.7

Note: (1) Figures cover the Seattle-Tacoma-Bellevue, WA Metropolitan Statistical Area—see Appendix B for areas included
Source: U.S. Census Bureau, Census 1990, 2000, 2010

Household Size

Area	One	Two	Three	Four	Five	Six	Seven or More	Average Household Size
City	41.3	33.2	12.2	8.7	2.9	1.0	0.8	2.12
MSA[1]	28.9	33.5	15.9	13.3	5.1	2.0	1.2	2.54
U.S.	27.7	33.6	15.7	13.1	6.0	2.3	1.5	2.64

Note: (1) Figures cover the Seattle-Tacoma-Bellevue, WA Metropolitan Statistical Area—see Appendix B for areas included
Source: U.S. Census Bureau, 2011-2013 American Community Survey 3-Year Estimates

Race

Area	White Alone[2] (%)	Black Alone[2] (%)	Asian Alone[2] (%)	AIAN[3] Alone[2] (%)	NHOPI[4] Alone[2] (%)	Other Race Alone[2] (%)	Two or More Races (%)
City	70.0	7.6	14.0	0.7	0.3	1.8	5.7
MSA[1]	72.7	5.6	11.8	0.9	0.8	2.4	5.7
U.S.	73.9	12.6	5.0	0.8	0.2	4.7	2.9

Note: (1) Figures cover the Seattle-Tacoma-Bellevue, WA Metropolitan Statistical Area—see Appendix B for areas included; (2) Alone is defined as not being in combination with one or more other races; (3) American Indian and Alaska Native; (4) Native Hawaiian and Other Pacific Islander
Source: U.S. Census Bureau, 2011-2013 American Community Survey 3-Year Estimates

Hispanic or Latino Origin

Area	Total (%)	Mexican (%)	Puerto Rican (%)	Cuban (%)	Other (%)
City	6.8	4.3	0.4	0.2	1.9
MSA[1]	9.3	6.8	0.5	0.1	1.9
U.S.	16.9	10.8	1.6	0.6	3.8

Note: Persons of Hispanic or Latino origin can be of any race; (1) Figures cover the Seattle-Tacoma-Bellevue, WA Metropolitan Statistical Area—see Appendix B for areas included
Source: U.S. Census Bureau, 2011-2013 American Community Survey 3-Year Estimates

Segregation

Type	Segregation Indices[1] 1990	2000	2010	2010 Rank[2]	Percent Change 1990-2000	1990-2010	2000-2010
Black/White	56.5	52.4	49.1	72	-4.1	-7.4	-3.3
Asian/White	36.8	37.6	37.6	69	0.8	0.8	0.0
Hispanic/White	22.3	30.4	32.8	87	8.1	10.5	2.4

Note: All figures cover the Metropolitan Statistical Area—see Appendix B for areas included; Figures are based on an analysis of 1990, 2000, and 2010 Census Decennial Census tract data by William H. Frey, Brookings Institution and the University of Michigan Social Science Data Analysis Network. In this analysis all racial groups (whites, blacks, and asians) are non-Hispanic members of those races. Hispanics are shown as a separate category;
(1) Segregation Indices are Dissimilarity Indices that measure the degree to which the minority group is distributed differently than whites across census tracts. They range from 0 (complete integration) to 100 (complete segregation) where the value indicates the percentage of the minority group that needs to move to be distributed exactly like whites; (2) Ranges from 1 (most segregated) to 102 (least segregated); n/a not available.
Source: www.CensusScope.org

Ancestry

Area	German	Irish	English	American	Italian	Polish	French[2]	Scottish	Dutch
City	16.4	11.4	11.0	3.4	4.4	2.4	3.3	3.1	1.8
MSA[1]	16.6	10.9	10.4	4.5	3.7	1.9	3.2	2.8	1.8
U.S.	14.9	10.8	8.0	7.4	5.5	3.0	2.7	1.7	1.4

Note: Figures are the percentage of the total population reporting a particular ancestry. The nine most commonly reported ancestries in the U.S. are shown. Figures include multiple ancestries (e.g. if a person reported being Irish and Italian, they were included in both columns); (1) Figures cover the Seattle-Tacoma-Bellevue, WA Metropolitan Statistical Area—see Appendix B for areas included; (2) Excludes Basque
Source: U.S. Census Bureau, 2011-2013 American Community Survey 3-Year Estimates

Foreign-Born Population

Area	Any Foreign Country	Mexico	Asia	Europe	Carribean	South America	Central America[2]	Africa	Canada
							Percent of Population Born in		
City	18.3	1.4	9.8	2.6	0.2	0.3	0.4	2.4	0.9
MSA[1]	17.2	2.5	8.5	2.8	0.1	0.4	0.5	1.3	0.8
U.S.	13.0	3.7	3.8	1.5	1.2	0.9	1.0	0.6	0.3

Note: (1) Figures cover the Seattle-Tacoma-Bellevue, WA Metropolitan Statistical Area—see Appendix B for areas included; (2) Excludes Mexico.
Source: U.S. Census Bureau, 2011-2013 American Community Survey 3-Year Estimates

Marital Status

Area	Never Married	Now Married[2]	Separated	Widowed	Divorced
City	44.2	39.5	1.4	4.0	10.9
MSA[1]	32.4	49.5	1.6	4.4	12.0
U.S.	32.7	48.1	2.2	6.0	11.0

Note: Figures are percentages and cover the population 15 years of age and older; (1) Figures cover the Seattle-Tacoma-Bellevue, WA Metropolitan Statistical Area—see Appendix B for areas included; (2) Excludes separated
Source: U.S. Census Bureau, 2011-2013 American Community Survey 3-Year Estimates

Disability Status

Area	All Ages	Under 18 Years Old	18 to 64 Years Old	65 Years and Over
City	9.1	2.4	6.8	34.0
MSA[1]	10.9	3.6	9.1	35.7
U.S.	12.3	4.1	10.2	36.3

Note: Figures show percent of the civilian noninstitutionalized population that reported having a disability. Disability status is determined from from six types of difficulty: vision, hearing, cognitive, ambulatory, self-care, and independent living. For children under 5 years old, hearing and vision difficulty are used to determine disability status. For children between the ages of 5 and 14, disability status is determined from hearing, vision, cognitive, ambulatory, and self-care difficulties. For people aged 15 years and older, they are considered to have a disability if they have difficulty with any one of the six difficulty types; (1) Figures cover the Seattle-Tacoma-Bellevue, WA Metropolitan Statistical Area—see Appendix B for areas included.
Source: U.S. Census Bureau, 2011-2013 American Community Survey 3-Year Estimates

Age

Area	Under Age 5	Age 5–19	Age 20–34	Age 35–44	Age 45–54	Age 55–64	Age 65–74	Age 75–84	Age 85+	Median Age
					Percent of Population					
City	5.3	13.1	30.1	15.7	12.7	11.7	6.4	3.1	1.8	35.9
MSA[1]	6.4	18.4	22.4	14.5	14.6	12.3	6.6	3.3	1.6	37.0
U.S.	6.4	19.9	20.7	12.9	14.1	12.3	7.6	4.2	1.9	37.4

Note: (1) Figures cover the Seattle-Tacoma-Bellevue, WA Metropolitan Statistical Area—see Appendix B for areas included
Source: U.S. Census Bureau, 2011-2013 American Community Survey 3-Year Estimates

Gender

Area	Males	Females	Males per 100 Females
City	316,940	319,330	99.3
MSA[1]	1,772,064	1,781,242	99.5
U.S.	154,451,010	159,410,713	96.9

Note: (1) Figures cover the Seattle-Tacoma-Bellevue, WA Metropolitan Statistical Area—see Appendix B for areas included
Source: U.S. Census Bureau, 2011-2013 American Community Survey 3-Year Estimates

Religious Groups by Family

Area	Catholic	Baptist	Non-Den.	Methodist[2]	Lutheran	LDS[3]	Pente-costal	Presby-terian[4]	Muslim[5]	Judaism
MSA[1]	12.3	2.2	5.0	1.2	2.1	3.3	2.8	1.4	0.5	0.5
U.S.	19.1	9.3	4.0	4.0	2.3	2.0	1.9	1.6	0.8	0.7

Note: Figures are the number of adherents as a percentage of the total population; (1) Figures cover the Seattle-Tacoma-Bellevue, WA Metropolitan Statistical Area—see Appendix B for areas included; (2) Methodist/Pietist; (3) Latter Day Saints; (4) Reformed; (5) Figures are estimates
Source: Association of Statisticians of American Religious Bodies, 2010 U.S. Religion Census: Religious Congregations & Membership Study

Religious Groups by Tradition

Area	Catholic	Evangelical Protestant	Mainline Protestant	Other Tradition	Black Protestant	Orthodox
MSA[1]	12.3	11.9	4.7	5.9	0.4	0.4
U.S.	19.1	16.2	7.3	4.3	1.6	0.3

Note: Figures are the number of adherents as a percentage of the total population; (1) Figures cover the Seattle-Tacoma-Bellevue, WA Metropolitan Statistical Area—see Appendix B for areas included
Source: Association of Statisticians of American Religious Bodies, 2010 U.S. Religion Census: Religious Congregations & Membership Study

ECONOMY

Gross Metropolitan Product

Area	2012	2013	2014	2015	Rank[2]
MSA[1]	258.8	269.5	279.8	293.8	12

Note: Figures are in billions of dollars; (1) Figures cover the Seattle-Tacoma-Bellevue, WA Metropolitan Statistical Area—see Appendix B for areas included; (2) Rank is based on 2015 data and ranges from 1 to 363
Source: The U.S. Conference of Mayors, U.S. Metro Economies: GMP and Employment 2013-2015, June 2014

Economic Growth

Area	2010-12 (%)	2013 (%)	2014 (%)	2015 (%)	Rank[2]
MSA[1]	4.0	2.8	2.3	3.1	134
U.S.	2.1	2.0	2.3	3.2	–

Note: Figures are real gross metropolitan product (GMP) growth rates and represent annual average percent change; (1) Figures cover the Seattle-Tacoma-Bellevue, WA Metropolitan Statistical Area—see Appendix B for areas included; (2) Rank is based on 2015 data and ranges from 1 to 363
Source: The U.S. Conference of Mayors, U.S. Metro Economies: GMP and Employment 2013-2015, June 2014

Metropolitan Area Exports

Area	2008	2009	2010	2011	2012	2013	Rank[2]
MSA[1]	46,911.2	36,942.3	35,409.6	41,117.5	50,301.7	56,686.4	4

Note: Figures are in millions of dollars; (1) Figures cover the Seattle-Tacoma-Bellevue, WA Metropolitan Statistical Area—see Appendix B for areas included; (2) Rank is based on 2013 data and ranges from 1 to 387
Source: U.S. Department of Commerce, International Trade Administration, Office of Trade & Industry Information, Manufacturing & Services, data extracted April 3, 2015

Building Permits

Area	Single-Family			Multi-Family			Total		
	2013	2014	Pct. Chg.	2013	2014	Pct. Chg.	2013	2014	Pct. Chg.
City	822	898	9.2	5,855	6,547	11.8	6,677	7,445	11.5
MSA[1]	8,773	8,665	-1.2	10,744	13,288	23.7	19,517	21,953	12.5
U.S.	620,802	634,597	2.2	370,020	411,766	11.3	990,822	1,046,363	5.6

Note: (1) Figures cover the Seattle-Tacoma-Bellevue, WA Metropolitan Statistical Area—see Appendix B for areas included; Figures represent new, privately-owned housing units authorized (unadjusted data); All permit data are based on estimates with imputation.
Source: U.S. Census Bureau, Manufacturing, Mining, and Construction Statistics, Building Permits, 2013, 2014

Bankruptcy Filings

Area	Business Filings			Nonbusiness Filings		
	2013	2014	% Chg.	2013	2014	% Chg.
King County	218	185	-15.1	5,624	4,752	-15.5
U.S.	33,212	26,983	-18.8	1,038,720	909,812	-12.4

Note: Business filings include Chapter 7, Chapter 11, Chapter 12, and Chapter 13; Nonbusiness filings include Chapter 7, Chapter 11, and Chapter 13
Source: Administrative Office of the U.S. Courts, Business and Nonbusiness Bankruptcy, County Cases Commenced by Chapter of the Bankruptcy Code, During the 12- Month Period Ending December 31, 2013 and Business and Nonbusiness Bankruptcy, County Cases Commenced by Chapter of the Bankruptcy Code, During the 12- Month Period Ending December 31, 2014

Housing Vacancy Rates

Area	Gross Vacancy Rate[2] (%)			Year-Round Vacancy Rate[3] (%)			Rental Vacancy Rate[4] (%)			Homeowner Vacancy Rate[5] (%)		
	2012	2013	2014	2012	2013	2014	2012	2013	2014	2012	2013	2014
MSA[1]	8.1	6.9	6.9	8.0	6.6	6.7	5.7	4.3	4.4	2.3	1.7	1.2
U.S.	13.8	13.6	13.4	10.8	10.7	10.4	8.7	8.3	7.6	2.0	2.0	1.9

Note: (1) Figures cover the Seattle-Tacoma-Bellevue, WA Metropolitan Statistical Area—see Appendix B for areas included; (2) The percentage of the total housing inventory that is vacant; (3) The percentage of the housing inventory (excluding seasonal units) that is year-round vacant; (4) The percentage of rental inventory that is vacant for rent; (5) The percentage of homeowner inventory that is vacant for sale
Source: U.S. Census Bureau, Housing Vacancies and Homeownership Annual Statistics: 2014

INCOME

Income

Area	Per Capita ($)	Median Household ($)	Average Household ($)
City	42,929	65,454	92,113
MSA[1]	35,186	66,750	88,361
U.S.	27,884	52,176	72,897

Note: (1) Figures cover the Seattle-Tacoma-Bellevue, WA Metropolitan Statistical Area—see Appendix B for areas included
Source: U.S. Census Bureau, 2011-2013 American Community Survey 3-Year Estimates

Household Income Distribution

Area	Percent of Households Earning							
	Under $15,000	$15,000 -24,999	$25,000 -34,999	$35,000 -49,999	$50,000 -74,999	$75,000 -99,000	$100,000 -149,999	$150,000 and up
City	12.3	7.5	8.2	11.3	16.4	12.2	15.7	16.5
MSA[1]	9.4	7.7	8.2	12.1	18.0	13.5	16.9	14.3
U.S.	13.0	10.9	10.3	13.6	17.9	11.9	12.7	9.6

Note: (1) Figures cover the Seattle-Tacoma-Bellevue, WA Metropolitan Statistical Area—see Appendix B for areas included
Source: U.S. Census Bureau, 2011-2013 American Community Survey 3-Year Estimates

Poverty Rate

Area	All Ages	Under 18 Years Old	18 to 64 Years Old	65 Years and Over
City	14.4	15.9	14.1	14.6
MSA[1]	12.0	15.9	11.3	8.8
U.S.	15.9	22.4	14.8	9.5

Note: Figures are percentage of people whose income during the past 12 months was below the poverty level;
(1) Figures cover the Seattle-Tacoma-Bellevue, WA Metropolitan Statistical Area—see Appendix B for areas included
Source: U.S. Census Bureau, 2011-2013 American Community Survey 3-Year Estimates

EMPLOYMENT

Labor Force and Employment

Area	Civilian Labor Force			Workers Employed		
	Dec. 2013	Dec. 2014	% Chg.	Dec. 2013	Dec. 2014	% Chg.
City	403,307	409,272	1.5	386,941	393,826	1.8
MD[1]	1,535,809	1,556,437	1.3	1,463,517	1,489,804	1.8
U.S.	154,408,000	155,521,000	0.7	144,423,000	147,190,000	1.9

Note: Data is not seasonally adjusted and covers workers 16 years of age and older; (1) Figures cover the
Seattle-Bellevue-Everett, WA Metropolitan Division—see Appendix B for areas included
Source: Bureau of Labor Statistics, Local Area Unemployment Statistics

Unemployment Rate

Area	2014											
	Jan.	Feb.	Mar.	Apr.	May	Jun.	Jul.	Aug.	Sep.	Oct.	Nov.	Dec.
City	4.2	4.4	4.3	3.7	3.9	4.4	4.4	4.3	4.2	4.0	4.1	3.8
MD[1]	5.0	5.1	5.1	4.3	4.5	5.0	5.0	4.8	4.6	4.5	4.6	4.3
U.S.	7.0	7.0	6.8	5.9	6.1	6.3	6.5	6.3	5.7	5.5	5.5	5.4

Note: Data is not seasonally adjusted and covers workers 16 years of age and older; (1) Figures cover the
Seattle-Bellevue-Everett, WA Metropolitan Division—see Appendix B for areas included
Source: Bureau of Labor Statistics, Local Area Unemployment Statistics

Employment by Occupation

Occupation Classification	City (%)	MSA[1] (%)	U.S. (%)
Management, Business, Science, and Arts	55.2	42.7	36.2
Natural Resources, Construction, and Maintenance	3.4	7.6	9.0
Production, Transportation, and Material Moving	5.8	10.2	12.1
Sales and Office	19.3	22.7	24.4
Service	16.2	16.8	18.3

Note: Figures cover employed civilians 16 years of age and older; (1) Figures cover the
Seattle-Tacoma-Bellevue, WA Metropolitan Statistical Area—see Appendix B for areas included
Source: U.S. Census Bureau, 2011-2013 American Community Survey 3-Year Estimates

Employment by Industry

Sector	MD[1]		U.S.
	Number of Employees	Percent of Total	Percent of Total
Construction	81,500	5.2	4.4
Education and Health Services	204,600	12.9	15.5
Financial Activities	86,700	5.5	5.7
Government	209,500	13.3	15.8
Information	91,600	5.8	2.0
Leisure and Hospitality	148,900	9.4	10.3
Manufacturing	169,900	10.7	8.7
Mining and Logging	700	<0.1	0.6
Other Services	57,300	3.6	4.0
Professional and Business Services	236,100	14.9	13.8
Retail Trade	171,800	10.9	11.4
Transportation, Warehousing, and Utilities	51,000	3.2	3.9
Wholesale Trade	70,900	4.5	4.2

Note: Figures are non-farm employment as of December 2014. Figures are not seasonally adjusted and include workers 16 years of age and older; (1) Figures cover the Seattle-Bellevue-Everett, WA Metropolitan Division—see Appendix B for areas included
Source: Bureau of Labor Statistics, Current Employment Statistics, Employment, Hours, and Earnings

Occupations with Greatest Projected Employment Growth: 2012 – 2022

Occupation[1]	2012 Employment	2022 Projected Employment	Numeric Employment Change	Percent Employment Change
Software Developers, Applications	53,200	67,380	14,180	26.7
Retail Salespersons	104,060	118,020	13,960	13.4
Carpenters	36,640	49,230	12,590	34.4
Registered Nurses	54,550	65,210	10,660	19.6
Combined Food Preparation and Serving Workers, Including Fast Food	56,700	67,250	10,550	18.6
Janitors and Cleaners, Except Maids and Housekeeping Cleaners	43,100	52,040	8,940	20.8
Bookkeeping, Accounting, and Auditing Clerks	44,950	53,480	8,530	19.0
Secretaries and Administrative Assistants, Except Legal, Medical, and Executive	42,100	50,210	8,110	19.3
Construction Laborers	22,740	30,730	7,990	35.1
Waiters and Waitresses	42,250	50,130	7,880	18.7

Note: Projections cover Washington; (1) Sorted by numeric employment change
Source: www.projectionscentral.com, State Occupational Projections, 2012–2022 Long-Term Projections

Fastest Growing Occupations: 2012 – 2022

Occupation[1]	2012 Employment	2022 Projected Employment	Numeric Employment Change	Percent Employment Change
Massage Therapists	9,230	13,640	4,410	47.8
Nursing Instructors and Teachers, Postsecondary	1,230	1,800	570	46.0
Mechanical Door Repairers	580	840	260	45.3
Fence Erectors	1,200	1,720	520	43.2
Reinforcing Iron and Rebar Workers	940	1,320	380	40.5
Cement Masons and Concrete Finishers	2,460	3,450	990	40.4
Roofers	5,000	7,000	2,000	39.9
Engine and Other Machine Assemblers	1,090	1,530	440	39.9
Brickmasons and Blockmasons	960	1,340	380	39.8
Helpers—Brickmasons, Blockmasons, Stonemasons, and Tile and Marble Setters	410	570	160	39.7

Note: Projections cover Washington; (1) Sorted by percent employment change and excludes occupations with numeric employment change less than 100
Source: www.projectionscentral.com, State Occupational Projections, 2012–2022 Long-Term Projections

Average Wages

Occupation	$/Hr.	Occupation	$/Hr.
Accountants and Auditors	37.33	Maids and Housekeeping Cleaners	12.07
Automotive Mechanics	22.27	Maintenance and Repair Workers	21.05
Bookkeepers	20.90	Marketing Managers	68.07
Carpenters	26.09	Nuclear Medicine Technologists	42.69
Cashiers	13.31	Nurses, Licensed Practical	25.95
Clerks, General Office	16.27	Nurses, Registered	40.52
Clerks, Receptionists/Information	15.67	Nursing Assistants	15.24
Clerks, Shipping/Receiving	17.89	Packers and Packagers, Hand	13.77
Computer Programmers	57.58	Physical Therapists	40.65
Computer Systems Analysts	49.01	Postal Service Mail Carriers	25.61
Computer User Support Specialists	28.74	Real Estate Brokers	42.63
Cooks, Restaurant	13.08	Retail Salespersons	14.35
Dentists	88.07	Sales Reps., Exc. Tech./Scientific	35.28
Electrical Engineers	50.78	Sales Reps., Tech./Scientific	43.16
Electricians	34.96	Secretaries, Exc. Legal/Med./Exec.	19.95
Financial Managers	59.47	Security Guards	16.33
First-Line Supervisors/Managers, Sales	22.25	Surgeons	104.00
Food Preparation Workers	11.93	Teacher Assistants	15.90
General and Operations Managers	63.37	Teachers, Elementary School	29.50
Hairdressers/Cosmetologists	18.24	Teachers, Secondary School	31.10
Internists	98.11	Telemarketers	13.49
Janitors and Cleaners	14.27	Truck Drivers, Heavy/Tractor-Trailer	22.18
Landscaping/Groundskeeping Workers	16.23	Truck Drivers, Light/Delivery Svcs.	17.66
Lawyers	63.11	Waiters and Waitresses	14.45

Note: Wage data covers the Seattle-Bellevue-Everett, WA Metropolitan Division—see Appendix B for areas included; Hourly wages for elementary/secondary school teachers and teacher assistants were calculated by the editors from annual wage data assuming a 40 hour work week; n/a not available.
Source: Bureau of Labor Statistics, Metro Area Occupational Employment and Wage Estimates, May 2014

TAXES

State Corporate Income Tax Rates

State	Tax Rate (%)	Income Brackets ($)	Num. of Brackets	Financial Institution Tax Rate (%)[a]	Federal Income Tax Ded.
Washington	None	–	–	–	–

Note: Tax rates as of January 1, 2015; (a) Rates listed are the corporate income tax rate applied to financial institutions or excise taxes based on income. Some states have other taxes based upon the value of deposits or shares.
Source: Federation of Tax Administrators, "State Corporate Income Tax Rates, 2015"

State Individual Income Tax Rates

State	Tax Rate (%)	Income Brackets ($)	Num. of Brackets	Personal Exempt. ($)[1] Single	Dependents	Fed. Inc. Tax Ded.
Washington	None	–	–	–	–	–

Note: Tax rates as of January 1, 2015; Local- and county-level taxes are not included; n/a not applicable;
(1) Married joint filers generally receive double the single exemption
Source: Federation of Tax Administrators, "State Individual Income Tax Rates, 2015"

Various State and Local Tax Rates

State	State and Local Sales and Use (%)	State Sales and Use (%)	Gasoline[1] (¢/gal.)	Cigarette[2] ($/pack)	Spirits[3] ($/gal.)	Wine[4] ($/gal.)	Beer[5] ($/gal.)
Washington	9.5	6.50	37.5	3.025	35.22 (j)(k)	0.87	0.26 (p)

Note: All tax rates as of January 1, 2015; (1) The American Petroleum Institute has developed a methodology for determining the average tax rate on a gallon of fuel. Rates may include any of the following: excise taxes, environmental fees, storage tank fees, other fees or taxes, general sales tax, and local taxes. In states where gasoline is subject to the general sales tax, or where the fuel tax is based on the average sale price, the average rate determined by API is sensitive to changes in the price of gasoline. States that fully or partially apply general sales taxes to gasoline: CA, CO, GA, IL, IN, MI, NY; (2) The federal excise tax of $1.0066 per pack and local taxes are not included; (3) Rates are those applicable to off-premise sales of 40% alcohol by volume (a.b.v.) distilled spirits in 750ml containers. Local excise taxes are excluded; (4) Rates are those applicable to off-premise sales of 11% a.b.v. non-carbonated wine in 750ml containers; (5) Rates are those applicable to off-premise sales of 4.7% a.b.v. beer in 12 ounce containers; (j) Includes sales taxes specific to alcoholic beverages; (k) Includes the retail (17%) and distributor (10%) license fees, converted into a gallonage excise tax rate; (p) Local excise taxes are excluded.
Source: Tax Foundation, 2015 Facts & Figures: How Does Your State Compare?

State Business Tax Climate Index Rankings

State	Overall Rank	Corporate Tax Index Rank	Individual Income Tax Index Rank	Sales Tax Index Rank	Unemployment Insurance Tax Index Rank	Property Tax Index Rank
Washington	11	28	6	46	19	23

Note: The index is a measure of how each state's tax laws affect economic performance. The lower the rank, the more favorable a state's tax system is for business. States without a given tax are given a ranking of 1. The scores/rankings for the District of Columbia do not affect other states. The 2015 index represents the tax climate as of July 1, 2014.
Source: Tax Foundation, State Business Tax Climate Index 2015

COMMERCIAL REAL ESTATE

Office Market

Market Area	Inventory (sq. ft.)	Vacancy Rate (%)	Under Construction (sq. ft.)	YTD Net Absorption (sq. ft.)	Total Average Asking Rent ($/sq. ft./year)
Seattle	109,367,271	12.0	4,059,506	2,090,252	29.89
National	4,745,108,508	14.3	71,190,461	51,084,126	27.40

Source: Newmark Grubb Knight Frank, National Office Market Report, 4th Quarter 2014

Industrial/Warehouse/R&D Market

Market Area	Inventory (sq. ft.)	Vacancy Rate (%)	Under Construction (sq. ft.)	YTD Net Absorption (sq. ft.)	Total Average Asking Rent ($/sq. ft./year)
Seattle	287,168,423	5.1	3,822,210	3,852,632	7.20
National	14,238,613,765	7.2	134,387,407	185,246,438	5.64

Source: Newmark Grubb Knight Frank, National Industrial Market Report, 4th Quarter 2014

COMMERCIAL UTILITIES

Typical Monthly Electric Bills

Area	Commercial Service ($/month)		Industrial Service ($/month)	
	40 kW demand 5,000 kWh	500 kW demand 100,000 kWh	5,000 kW demand 1,500,000 kWh	70,000 kW demand 50,000,000 kWh
City	382	7,150	97,981	2,888,362

Note: Figures are based on rates in effect January 2, 2014
Source: Memphis Light, Gas and Water, 2014 Utility Bill Comparisons for Selected U.S. Cities

TRANSPORTATION

Means of Transportation to Work

| Area | Car/Truck/Van | | Public Transportation | | | Bicycle | Walked | Other Means | Worked at Home |
	Drove Alone	Car-pooled	Bus	Subway	Railroad				
City	51.0	8.6	18.6	0.4	0.1	3.7	9.3	1.6	6.7
MSA[1]	70.0	10.2	8.0	0.2	0.4	1.0	3.6	1.2	5.4
U.S.	76.4	9.6	2.6	1.8	0.6	0.6	2.8	1.3	4.3

Note: Figures are percentages and cover workers 16 years of age and older; (1) Figures cover the Seattle-Tacoma-Bellevue, WA Metropolitan Statistical Area—see Appendix B for areas included
Source: U.S. Census Bureau, 2011-2013 American Community Survey 3-Year Estimates

Travel Time to Work

Area	Less Than 10 Minutes	10 to 19 Minutes	20 to 29 Minutes	30 to 44 Minutes	45 to 59 Minutes	60 to 89 Minutes	90 Minutes or More
City	8.4	27.4	24.6	25.8	8.5	3.9	1.5
MSA[1]	8.9	25.2	22.1	24.9	9.8	6.7	2.4
U.S.	13.3	29.7	20.9	20.2	7.7	5.7	2.6

Note: Figures are percentages and include workers 16 years old and over; (1) Figures cover the Seattle-Tacoma-Bellevue, WA Metropolitan Statistical Area—see Appendix B for areas included
Source: U.S. Census Bureau, 2011-2013 American Community Survey 3-Year Estimates

Travel Time Index

Area	1985	1990	1995	2000	2005	2010	2011
Urban Area[1]	1.12	1.26	1.28	1.29	1.31	1.26	1.26
Average[2]	1.09	1.14	1.16	1.19	1.23	1.18	1.18

Note: Travel Time Index—the ratio of travel time in the peak period to the travel time at free-flow conditions. For example, a value of 1.30 indicates a 20-minute free-flow trip takes 26 minutes in the peak. Free-flow speeds (60 mph on freeways and 35 mph on principal arterials) are used as the comparison threshold; (1) Covers the Seattle WA urban area; (2) average of 498 urban areas
Source: Texas Transportation Institute, Urban Mobility Report 2012, December 2012

Public Transportation

Agency Name / Mode of Transportation	Vehicles Operated in Maximum Service	Annual Unlinked Passenger Trips (in thous.)	Annual Passenger Miles (in thous.)
King County Department of Transportation (KC Metro)			
Bus (directly operated)	951	97,702.5	484,205.1
Bus (purchased transportation)	33	1,007.0	3,811.0
Demand Response (purchased transportation)	323	1,103.4	11,838.6
Demand Response Taxi (purchased transportation)	45	86.4	772.9
Streetcar Rail (directly operated)	3	760.9	653.5
Trolleybus (directly operated)	131	19,008.0	35,187.0
Vanpool (directly operated)	1,342	3,523.8	73,144.8

Source: Federal Transit Administration, National Transit Database, 2013

Air Transportation

Airport Name and Code / Type of Service	Passenger Airlines[1]	Passenger Enplanements	Freight Carriers[2]	Freight (lbs.)
Seattle-Tacoma International (SEA)				
Domestic service (U.S. carriers - 2014)	20	16,003,997	21	197,852,690
International service (U.S. carriers - 2013)	9	982,200	9	20,220,474

Note: (1) Includes all U.S.-based major, minor and commuter airlines that carried at least one passenger during the year; (2) Includes all U.S.-based airlines and freight carriers that transported at least one lb. of freight during the year.
Source: Bureau of Transportation Statistics, The Intermodal Transportation Database, Air Carriers: T-100 Domestic Market (U.S. Carriers), 2014; Bureau of Transportation Statistics, The Intermodal Transportation Database, Air Carriers: T-100 International Market (U.S. Carriers), 2013

Other Transportation Statistics

Major Highways:	I-50; I-90
Amtrak Service:	Yes
Major Waterways/Ports:	Puget Sound; Port of Seattle

Source: Amtrak.com; Google Maps

BUSINESSES

Major Business Headquarters

Company Name	Rankings	
	Fortune[1]	Forbes[2]
Alaska Air Group	482	-
Amazon.com	35	-
Expeditors International of Washington	425	-
Nordstrom	224	-
Starbucks Corporation	196	-

Note: (1) Fortune 500—companies that produce a 10-K are ranked 1 to 500 based on 2013 revenue; (2) all private companies with at least $2 billion in annual revenue through the end of their most current fiscal year are ranked 1 to 221; companies listed are headquartered in the city; dashes indicate no ranking Source: Fortune, "Fortune 500," June 16, 2014; Forbes, "America's Largest Private Companies," November 5, 2014

Fast-Growing Businesses

According to *Inc.*, Seattle is home to three of America's 500 fastest-growing private companies: **TUNE** (#88); **Level 11** (#391); **Spoken Communications** (#413). Criteria: must be an independent, privately-held, for-profit, U.S. corporation, proprietorship or partnership; revenues must be at least $100,000 in 2010 and $2 million in 2013; must have four-year operating/sales history. Holding companies, regulated banks, and utilities were excluded. *Inc., "America's 500 Fastest-Growing Private Companies," September 2014*

According to *Initiative for a Competitive Inner City (ICIC)*, Seattle is home to three of America's 100 fastest-growing "inner city" companies: **True Fabrications** (#43); **QuoteWizard** (#44); **Capelli's Gentlemen's Barbershop** (#86). Criteria for inclusion: company must be headquartered in or have 51 percent or more of its physical operations in an economically distressed urban area; must be an independent, for-profit corporation, partnership or proprietorship; must have 10 or more employees and have a five-year sales history that includes sales of at least $200,000 in the base year and at least $1 million in the current year with no decrease in sales over the two most recent years. This year, for the first time in the list's 16-year history, the Inner City 100 consists of 10 fast-growing businesses in 10 industry categories. Companies were ranked overall by revenue growth over the five-year period between 2009 and 2013 as well as within their respective industry categories. *Initiative for a Competitive Inner City (ICIC), "Inner City 100 Companies, 2014"*

According to Deloitte, Seattle is home to 11 of North America's 500 fastest-growing high-technology companies: **Mixpo** (#87); **Tableau Software** (#100); **Skytap** (#105); **Zillow** (#116); **Moz** (#167); **Redfin** (#185); **NanoString Technologies** (#282); **QuoteWizard** (#304); **Airbiquity** (#305); **Amazon.com** (#383); **LabConnect** (#421). Companies are ranked by percentage growth in revenue over a five-year period. Criteria for inclusion: company must be headquartered within North America; must own proprietary intellectual property or proprietary technology that contributes to a significant portion of the company's operating revenue, or devote a significant proportion of revenues to research and development of technology; must have been in business for a minumum of five years with 2009 operating revenues of at least $50,000 USD/CD and 2013 operating revenues of at least $5 million USD/CD. *Deloitte Touche Tohmatsu, 2014 Technology Fast 500*[TM]

Minority Business Opportunity

Seattle is home to one company which is on the *Black Enterprise* Asset Manager 15 list (15 largest asset management firms based on assets under management): **Pugh Capital Management** (#11). Criteria: company must have been operational in previous calendar year and be at least 51% black-owned. *Black Enterprise, B.E. 100s, 2014*

Minority- and Women-Owned Businesses

Group	All Firms		Firms with Paid Employees			
	Firms	Sales ($000)	Firms	Sales ($000)	Employees	Payroll ($000)
Asian	7,280	3,022,401	2,324	2,848,877	14,852	410,796
Black	2,767	218,684	232	146,863	2,114	48,604
Hispanic	1,883	(s)	319	(s)	(s)	(s)
Women	22,412	3,661,712	3,508	2,959,994	25,983	866,463
All Firms	73,997	110,631,598	20,729	107,961,786	416,268	22,731,747

Note: Figures cover firms located in the city; minority- and women-owned business are defined as firms in which the corresponding group own 51% or more of the stock or equity of the company; (s) estimates are suppressed when publication standards are not met
Source: U.S. Census Bureau, 2007 Economic Census, Survey of Business Owners (2012 Survey of Business Owners data will be released starting in June 2015)

**HOTELS &
CONVENTION
CENTERS**

Hotels/Motels

Area	5 Star		4 Star		3 Star		2 Star		1 Star		Not Rated	
	Num.	Pct.[3]	Num.	Pct.[3]	Num.	Pct.[3]	Num.	Pct.[3]	Num.	Pct.[3]	Num.	Pct.[3]
City[1]	2	0.8	27	11.2	81	33.5	108	44.6	7	2.9	17	7.0
Total[2]	166	0.9	1,264	7.0	5,718	31.8	9,340	52.0	411	2.3	1,070	6.0

Note: (1) Figures cover Seattle and vicinity; (2) Figures cover all 100 cities in this book; (3) Percentage of hotels which have a given star rating; Star ratings are determined by expedia.com and offer an indication of the general quality of a particular hotel.
Source: expedia.com, April 2, 2015

The Seattle-Bellevue-Everett, WA metro area is home to five of the best hotels in the U.S. according to *Travel & Leisure*: **Four Seasons Hotel Seattle**; **Hotel 1000**; **Inn at the Market**; **The Fairmont Olympic Hotel**; **Willows Lodge**. Criteria: service; location; rooms; food; and value. The list includes the top 236 hotels in the U.S. *Travel & Leisure, "T+L 500, The World's Best Hotels 2015"*

The Seattle-Bellevue-Everett, WA metro area is home to one of the best hotels in the world according to *Condé Nast Traveler*: **Four Seasons Hotel Seattle**. The selections are based on editors' picks. The list includes the top 25 hotels in the U.S. *Condé Nast Traveler, "Gold List 2015, The Top Hotels in the World"*

Major Convention Centers

Name	Overall Space (sq. ft.)	Exhibit Space (sq. ft.)	Meeting Space (sq. ft.)	Meeting Rooms
Meydenbaur Center	n/a	36,000	12,000	n/a
Seattle Center Exhibition Hall	n/a	34,000	n/a	n/a
Washington State Convention & Trade Center	n/a	205,700	57,000	61

Note: Table includes convention centers located in the Seattle-Tacoma-Bellevue, WA metro area; n/a not available
Source: Original research

Living Environment

COST OF LIVING

Cost of Living Index

Composite Index	Groceries	Housing	Utilities	Trans-portation	Health Care	Misc. Goods/Services
126.5	111.4	164.8	98.5	118.0	116.5	113.2

Note: The Cost of Living Index measures regional differences in the cost of consumer goods and services, excluding taxes and non-consumer expenditures, for professional and managerial households in the top income quintile. It is based on more than 50,000 prices covering almost 60 different items for which prices are collected three times a year by chambers of commerce, economic development organizations or university applied economic centers in each participating urban area. The numbers shown should be read as a percentage above or below the national average of 100. For example, a value of 115.4 in the groceries column indicates that grocery prices are 15.4% higher than the national average. Small differences in the index numbers should not be interpreted as significant; Figures cover the Seattle WA urban area.
Source: The Council for Community and Economic Research, ACCRA Cost of Living Index, 2014

Grocery Prices

Area[1]	T-Bone Steak ($/pound)	Frying Chicken ($/pound)	Whole Milk ($/half gal.)	Eggs ($/dozen)	Orange Juice ($/64 oz.)	Coffee ($/11.5 oz.)
City[2]	11.38	1.72	1.97	2.02	3.78	5.48
Avg.	10.40	1.37	2.40	1.99	3.46	4.27
Min.	8.48	0.93	1.37	1.30	2.83	2.99
Max.	14.20	2.44	3.62	4.02	6.42	6.96

*Note: (1) Values for the local area are compared with the average, minimum and maximum values for all 308 areas in the Cost of Living Index; (2) Figures cover the Seattle WA urban area; **T-Bone Steak** (price per pound); **Frying Chicken** (price per pound, whole fryer); **Whole Milk** (half gallon carton); **Eggs** (price per dozen, Grade A, large); **Orange Juice** (64 oz. Tropicana or Florida Natural); **Coffee** (11.5 oz. can, vacuum-packed, Maxwell House, Hills Bros, or Folgers).*
Source: The Council for Community and Economic Research, ACCRA Cost of Living Index, 2014

Housing and Utility Costs

Area[1]	New Home Price ($)	Apartment Rent ($/month)	All Electric ($/month)	Part Electric ($/month)	Other Energy ($/month)	Telephone ($/month)
City[2]	472,833	1,821	173.00	-	-	25.95
Avg.	305,838	919	181.00	93.66	73.14	27.95
Min.	183,142	480	112.00	42.06	23.42	17.16
Max.	1,358,576	3,851	594.00	180.03	440.99	40.42

*Note: (1) Values for the local area are compared with the average, minimum and maximum values for all 308 areas in the Cost of Living Index; (2) Figures cover the Seattle WA urban area; **New Home Price** (2,400 sf living area, 8,000 sf lot, in urban area with full utilities); **Apartment Rent** (950 sf 2 bedroom/1.5 or 2 bath, unfurnished, excluding all utilities except water); **All Electric** (average monthly cost for an all-electric home); **Part Electric** (average monthly cost for a part-electric home); **Other Energy** (average monthly cost for natural gas, fuel oil, coal, wood, and any other forms of energy except electricity); **Telephone** (price includes basic monthly rate for a private residential line plus additional local usage charges incurred by a family of four).*
Source: The Council for Community and Economic Research, ACCRA Cost of Living Index, 2014

Health Care, Transportation, and Other Costs

Area[1]	Doctor ($/visit)	Dentist ($/visit)	Optometrist ($/visit)	Gasoline ($/gallon)	Beauty Salon ($/visit)	Men's Shirt ($)
City[2]	103.22	119.44	139.00	3.78	55.89	22.52
Avg.	102.86	87.89	97.66	3.44	34.37	26.74
Min.	67.47	65.78	51.18	3.00	17.43	12.79
Max.	173.50	150.14	235.00	4.33	64.28	49.50

*Note: (1) Values for the local area are compared with the average, minimum and maximum values for all 308 areas in the Cost of Living Index; (2) Figures cover the Seattle WA urban area; **Doctor** (general practitioners routine exam of an established patient); **Dentist** (adult teeth cleaning and periodic oral examination); **Optometrist** (full vision eye exam for established adult patient); **Gasoline** (one gallon regular unleaded, national brand, including all taxes, cash price at self-service pump if available); **Beauty Salon** (woman's shampoo, trim, and blow-dry); **Men's Shirt** (cotton/polyester dress shirt, pinpoint weave, long sleeves).*
Source: The Council for Community and Economic Research, ACCRA Cost of Living Index, 2014

HOUSING

House Price Index (HPI)

Area	National Ranking[2]	Quarterly Change (%)	One-Year Change (%)	Five-Year Change (%)
MD[1]	49	0.31	8.22	10.57
U.S.[3]	–	1.35	4.91	11.59

Note: The HPI is a weighted repeat sales index. It measures average price changes in repeat sales or refinancings on the same properties. This information is obtained by reviewing repeat mortgage transactions on single-family properties whose mortgages have been purchased or securitized by Fannie Mae or Freddie Mac in January 1975; (1) Seattle-Bellevue-Everett Metropolitan Division—see Appendix B for areas included; (2) Rankings are based on annual percentage change for all metro areas containing at least 15,000 transactions over the last 10 years and ranges from 1 to 275; (3) figures based on a weighted average of Census Division estimates using a seasonally adjusted, purchase-only index; all figures are for the period ending December 31, 2014

Source: Federal Housing Finance Agency, House Price Index, February 26, 2015

Median Single-Family Home Prices

Area	2012	2013	2014p	Percent Change 2013 to 2014
MSA[1]	300.4	336.3	356.6	6.0
U.S. Average	177.2	197.4	209.0	5.9

Note: Figures are median sales prices of existing single-family homes in thousands of dollars; (p) preliminary; n/a not available; (1) Seattle-Tacoma-Bellevue, WA Metropolitan Statistical Area—see Appendix B for areas included

Source: National Association of Realtors, Median Sales Price of Existing Single-Family Homes for Metropolitan Areas, 4th Quarter 2014

Qualifying Income Based on Median Sales Price of Existing Single-Family Homes

Area	With 5% Down ($)	With 10% Down ($)	With 20% Down ($)
MSA[1]	77,354	73,282	65,140
U.S. Average	45,863	43,449	38,621

Note: Figures are preliminary; Qualifying income is based on a mortgage rate of 4.0%. Monthly principal and interest payment is limited to 25% of income; n/a not available; (1) Seattle-Tacoma-Bellevue, WA Metropolitan Statistical Area—see Appendix B for areas included

Source: National Association of Realtors, Qualifying Income Based on Median Sales Price of Existing Single-Family Homes for Metropolitan Areas, 4th Quarter 2014

Median Apartment Condo-Coop Home Prices

Area	2012	2013	2014p	Percent Change 2013 to 2014
MSA[1]	n/a	n/a	n/a	n/a
U.S. Average	173.7	194.9	205.1	5.2

Note: Figures are median sales prices of existing apartment condo-coop homes in thousands of dollars; (p) preliminary; n/a not available; (1) Seattle-Tacoma-Bellevue, WA Metropolitan Statistical Area—see Appendix B for areas included

Source: National Association of Realtors, Median Sales Price of Existing Apartment Condo-Coop Homes for Metropolitan Areas, 4th Quarter 2014

Gross Monthly Rent

Area	Under $200	$200 -299	$300 -499	$500 -749	$750 -999	$1,000 -1,499	$1,500 and up	Median ($)
City	1.7	3.7	3.9	9.3	23.7	31.7	26.1	1,104
MSA[1]	1.3	2.3	3.0	10.5	24.4	35.0	23.5	1,102
U.S.	1.7	3.2	7.8	22.1	24.3	26.0	14.9	900

Note: Figures are percentages except for Median; Gross rent is the contract rent plus the estimated average monthly cost of utilities (electricity, gas, and water and sewer) and fuels (oil, coal, kerosene, wood, etc.) if these are paid by the renter (or paid for the renter by someone else); (1) Figures cover the Seattle-Tacoma-Bellevue, WA Metropolitan Statistical Area—see Appendix B for areas included

Source: U.S. Census Bureau, 2011-2013 American Community Survey 3-Year Estimates

Homeownership Rate

Area	2007 (%)	2008 (%)	2009 (%)	2010 (%)	2011 (%)	2012 (%)	2013 (%)	2014 (%)
MSA[1]	62.8	61.3	61.2	60.9	60.7	60.4	61.0	61.3
U.S.	68.1	67.8	67.4	66.9	66.1	65.4	65.1	64.5

Note: (1) Figures cover the Seattle-Tacoma-Bellevue, WA Metropolitan Statistical Area—see Appendix B for areas included
Source: U.S. Census Bureau, Housing Vacancies and Homeownership Annual Statistics: 2014

Year Housing Structure Built

Area	2010 or Later	2000 -2009	1990 -1999	1980 -1989	1970 -1979	1960 -1969	1950 -1959	1940 -1949	Before 1940	Median Year
City	1.3	15.3	8.0	7.6	9.0	9.2	11.4	9.5	28.6	1961
MSA[1]	1.3	16.9	15.9	15.4	15.2	11.5	7.9	4.8	11.0	1980
U.S.	0.9	15.0	13.9	13.8	15.8	11.0	10.9	5.4	13.3	1976

Note: Figures are percentages except for Median Year; (1) Figures cover the Seattle-Tacoma-Bellevue, WA Metropolitan Statistical Area—see Appendix B for areas included
Source: U.S. Census Bureau, 2011-2013 American Community Survey 3-Year Estimates

HEALTH

Health Risk Data

Category	MD[1] (%)	U.S. (%)
Adults aged 18–64 who have any kind of health care coverage	82.4	79.6
Adults who reported being in good or excellent health	86.2	83.1
Adults who are current smokers	14.9	19.6
Adults who are heavy drinkers[2]	6.6	6.1
Adults who are binge drinkers[3]	17.8	16.9
Adults who are overweight (BMI 25.0 - 29.9)	34.9	35.8
Adults who are obese (BMI 30.0 - 99.8)	23.8	27.6
Adults who participated in any physical activities in the past month	84.5	77.1
Adults 50+ who have ever had a sigmoidoscopy or colonoscopy	73.1	67.3
Women aged 40+ who have had a mammogram within the past two years	73.0	74.0
Men aged 40+ who have had a PSA test within the past two years	32.6	45.2
Adults aged 65+ who have had flu shot within the past year	60.7	60.1
Adults who always wear a seatbelt	96.8	93.8

Note: Data as of 2012 unless otherwise noted; (1) Figures cover the Seattle-Bellevue-Everett, WA Metropolitan Division—see Appendix B for areas included; (2) Heavy drinkers are classified as males having more than two drinks per day or females having more than one drink per day; (3) Binge drinkers are classified as males having five or more drinks on one occasion or females having four or more drinks on one occasion
Source: Centers for Disease Control and Prevention, Behaviorial Risk Factor Surveillance System, SMART: Selected Metropolitan/Micropolitan Area Risk Trends, 2012 (Note: the CDC has discontinued this dataset but will be releasing a replacement in late 2015)

Chronic Health Indicators

Category	MD[1] (%)	U.S. (%)
Adults who have ever been told they had a heart attack	2.9	4.5
Adults who have ever been told they had a stroke	2.1	2.9
Adults who have been told they currently have asthma	8.3	8.9
Adults who have ever been told they have arthritis	21.9	25.7
Adults who have ever been told they have diabetes[2]	7.8	9.7
Adults who have ever been told they had skin cancer	5.6	5.7
Adults who have ever been told they had any other types of cancer	6.4	6.5
Adults who have ever been told they have COPD	3.9	6.2
Adults who have ever been told they have kidney disease	2.6	2.5
Adults who have ever been told they have a form of depression	21.3	18.0

Note: Data as of 2012 unless otherwise noted; (1) Figures cover the Seattle-Bellevue-Everett, WA Metropolitan Division—see Appendix B for areas included; (2) Figures do not include pregnancy-related, borderline, or pre-diabetes
Source: Centers for Disease Control and Prevention, Behaviorial Risk Factor Surveillance System, SMART: Selected Metropolitan/Micropolitan Area Risk Trends, 2012 (Note: the CDC has discontinued this dataset but will be releasing a replacement in late 2015)

Mortality Rates for the Top 10 Causes of Death in the U.S.

ICD-10[a] Sub-Chapter	ICD-10[a] Code	Age-Adjusted Mortality Rate[1] per 100,000 population	
		County[2]	U.S.
Malignant neoplasms	C00-C97	148.9	166.2
Ischaemic heart diseases	I20-I25	79.4	105.7
Other forms of heart disease	I30-I51	30.5	49.3
Chronic lower respiratory diseases	J40-J47	30.3	42.1
Organic, including symptomatic, mental disorders	F01-F09	22.5	38.1
Cerebrovascular diseases	I60-I69	30.3	37.0
Other external causes of accidental injury	W00-X59	24.1	26.9
Other degenerative diseases of the nervous system	G30-G31	40.7	25.6
Diabetes mellitus	E10-E14	18.3	21.3
Hypertensive diseases	I10-I15	17.2	19.4

Note: (a) ICD-10 = International Classification of Diseases 10th Revision; (1) Mortality rates are a three year average covering 2011-2013; (2) Figures cover King County
Source: Centers for Disease Control and Prevention, National Center for Health Statistics. Compressed Mortality File 1999-2013 on CDC WONDER Online Database, released October 2014. Data are compiled from the Compressed Mortality File 1999-2013, Series 20 No. 2S, 2014.

Mortality Rates for Selected Causes of Death

ICD-10[a] Sub-Chapter	ICD-10[a] Code	Age-Adjusted Mortality Rate[1] per 100,000 population	
		County[2]	U.S.
Assault	X85-Y09	2.4	5.2
Diseases of the liver	K70-K76	11.3	13.2
Human immunodeficiency virus (HIV) disease	B20-B24	1.4	2.2
Influenza and pneumonia	J09-J18	8.9	15.4
Intentional self-harm	X60-X84	12.2	12.5
Malnutrition	E40-E46	0.8	0.9
Obesity and other hyperalimentation	E65-E68	1.7	1.8
Renal failure	N17-N19	6.5	13.1
Transport accidents	V01-V99	5.9	11.7
Viral hepatitis	B15-B19	2.8	2.2

Note: (a) ICD-10 = International Classification of Diseases 10th Revision; (1) Mortality rates are a three year average covering 2011-2013; (2) Figures cover King County
Source: Centers for Disease Control and Prevention, National Center for Health Statistics. Compressed Mortality File 1999-2013 on CDC WONDER Online Database, released October 2014. Data are compiled from the Compressed Mortality File 1999-2013, Series 20 No. 2S, 2014.

Health Insurance Coverage

Area	With Health Insurance	With Private Health Insurance	With Public Health Insurance	Without Health Insurance	Population Under Age 18 Without Health Insurance
City	88.6	76.6	20.6	11.4	4.9
MSA[1]	87.2	72.7	24.5	12.8	5.3
U.S.	85.2	65.2	31.0	14.8	7.3

Note: Figures are percentages that cover the civilian noninstitutionalized population; (1) Figures cover the Seattle-Tacoma-Bellevue, WA Metropolitan Statistical Area—see Appendix B for areas included
Source: U.S. Census Bureau, 2011-2013 American Community Survey 3-Year Estimates

Number of Medical Professionals

Area[1]	MDs[2]	DOs[2,3]	Dentists	Podiatrists	Chiropractors	Optometrists
Local (number)	9,316	276	2,065	129	863	401
Local (rate[4])	463.8	13.7	100.9	6.3	42.2	19.6
U.S. (rate[4])	270.0	20.2	63.1	5.7	25.2	14.9

Note: Data as of 2013 unless noted; (1) Local data covers King County; (2) Data as of 2012 and includes all active, non-federal physicians; (3) Doctor of Osteopathic Medicine; (4) rate per 100,000 population
Source: U.S. Department of Health and Human Services, Health Resources and Services Administration, Bureau of Health Professions, Area Resource File (ARF) 2013-2014

Best Hospitals

According to *U.S. News*, the Seattle-Bellevue-Everett, WA metro area is home to one of the best hospitals in the U.S.: **University of Washington Medical Center** (Honor Roll/13 specialties). The hospital listed was nationally ranked in at least one adult specialty. Only 144 hospitals nationwide were nationally ranked in one or more specialties. Seventeen hospitals in the U.S. made the Honor Roll with high scores in at least six specialties. *U.S. News Online, "America's Best Children's Hospitals 2014-15"*

According to *U.S. News*, the Seattle-Bellevue-Everett, WA metro area is home to one of the best children's hospitals in the U.S.: **Seattle Children's Hospital** (10 specialties). The hospital listed was highly ranked in at least one pediatric specialty. Eighty-nine children's hospitals in the U.S. were nationally ranked in at least one specialty. Ten children's hospitals in the U.S. made the Honor Roll with high scores in at least three specialties. *U.S. News Online, "America's Best Children's Hospitals 2014-15"*

EDUCATION

Public School District Statistics

District Name	Schls	Pupils	Pupil/ Teacher Ratio	Minority Pupils[1] (%)	Free Lunch Eligible[2] (%)	IEP[3] (%)
Seattle School District #1	104	50,655	18.2	56.0	33.1	13.2

Note: Table includes school districts with 2,000 or more students; (1) Percentage of students that are not non-Hispanic white; (2) Percentage of students that are eligible for the free lunch program; (3) Percentage of students that have an Individualized Education Program.
Source: U.S. Department of Education, National Center for Education Statistics, Common Core of Data, Local Education Agency (School District) Universe Survey: School Year 2012-2013; U.S. Department of Education, National Center for Education Statistics, Common Core of Data, Public Elementary/Secondary School Universe Survey: School Year 2012-2013

Highest Level of Education

Area	Less than H.S.	H.S. Diploma	Some College, No Deg.	Associate Degree	Bachelor's Degree	Master's Degree	Prof. School Degree	Doctorate Degree
City	6.8	11.7	17.0	6.8	34.5	15.0	4.9	3.4
MSA[1]	8.3	21.3	23.1	9.1	24.3	9.7	2.4	1.7
U.S.	13.7	28.0	21.2	7.9	18.2	7.7	1.9	1.3

Note: Figures cover persons age 25 and over; (1) Figures cover the Seattle-Tacoma-Bellevue, WA Metropolitan Statistical Area—see Appendix B for areas included
Source: U.S. Census Bureau, 2011-2013 American Community Survey 3-Year Estimates

Educational Attainment by Race

Area	High School Graduate or Higher (%)					Bachelor's Degree or Higher (%)				
	Total	White	Black	Asian	Hisp.[2]	Total	White	Black	Asian	Hisp.[2]
City	93.2	96.8	81.7	82.0	79.8	57.8	64.3	22.2	47.8	39.2
MSA[1]	91.7	93.7	87.4	86.1	70.6	38.1	39.1	20.3	47.9	18.6
U.S.	86.3	88.3	83.1	85.7	64.0	29.1	30.4	18.8	50.7	13.7

Note: Figures shown cover persons 25 years old and over; (1) Figures cover the Seattle-Tacoma-Bellevue, WA Metropolitan Statistical Area—see Appendix B for areas included; (2) People of Hispanic origin can be of any race
Source: U.S. Census Bureau, 2011-2013 American Community Survey 3-Year Estimates

School Enrollment by Grade and Control

Area	Preschool (%)		Kindergarten (%)		Grades 1 - 4 (%)		Grades 5 - 8 (%)		Grades 9 - 12 (%)	
	Public	Private	Public	Private	Public	Private	Public	Private	Public	Private
City	34.9	65.1	73.8	26.2	78.1	21.9	77.7	22.3	79.1	20.9
MSA[1]	42.6	57.4	82.2	17.8	88.9	11.1	89.0	11.0	91.2	8.8
U.S.	57.7	42.3	87.9	12.1	89.9	10.1	90.0	10.0	90.7	9.3

Note: Figures shown cover persons 3 years old and over; (1) Figures cover the Seattle-Tacoma-Bellevue, WA Metropolitan Statistical Area—see Appendix B for areas included
Source: U.S. Census Bureau, 2011-2013 American Community Survey 3-Year Estimates

Average Salaries of Public School Classroom Teachers

Area	2013-14 Dollars	2013-14 Rank[1]	2014-15 Dollars	2014-15 Rank[1]	Percent Change 2013-14 to 2014-15	Percent Change 2004-05 to 2014-15
WASHINGTON	52,969	23	53,714	23	1.41	17.5
U.S. Average	56,610	–	57,379	–	1.36	20.8

Note: (1) State rank ranges from 1 to 51 where 1 indicates highest salary.
Source: National Education Association, Rankings & Estimates: Rankings of the States 2014 and Estimates of School Statistics 2015, March 2015

Higher Education

Four-Year Colleges Public	Four-Year Colleges Private Non-profit	Four-Year Colleges Private For-profit	Two-Year Colleges Public	Two-Year Colleges Private Non-profit	Two-Year Colleges Private For-profit	Medical Schools[1]	Law Schools[2]	Voc/ Tech[3]
4	8	4	0	0	1	1	2	7

Note: Figures cover institutions located within the city limits and include main campuses only; (1) includes schools accredited by the Liaison Committee on Medical Education and the American Osteopathic Association's Commission on Osteopathic College Accreditation; (2) includes ABA-accredited schools, schools with provisional ABA accreditation, and state accredited schools; (3) includes all schools with programs that are less than 2 years.
Source: National Center for Education Statistics, Integrated Postsecondary Education System (IPEDS), 2013-14; Association of American Medical Colleges, Member List, May 1, 2015; American Osteopathic Association, Member List, May 1, 2015; Law School Admission Council, Official Guide to ABA-Approved Law Schools Online, May 1, 2015; Wikipedia, List of Medical Schools in the United States, May 1, 2015; Wikipedia, List of Law Schools in the United States, May 1, 2015

According to *U.S. News & World Report*, the Seattle-Bellevue-Everett, WA metro division is home to one of the best national universities in the U.S.: **University of Washington** (#48). The indicators used to capture academic quality fall into a number of categories: assessment by administrators at peer institutions; retention of students; faculty resources; student selectivity; financial resources; alumni giving; high school counselor ratings of colleges; and graduation rate. *U.S. News & World Report, "America's Best Colleges 2015"*

According to *U.S. News & World Report*, the Seattle-Bellevue-Everett, WA metro division is home to one of the top 100 law schools in the U.S.: **University of Washington** (#28). The rankings are based on a weighted average of 12 measures of quality: peer assessment score; assessment score by lawyers/judges; median LSAT scores; median undergrad GPA; acceptance rate; employment rates for graduates; placement success; bar passage rate; faculty resources; expenditures per student; student/faculty ratio; and library resources. *U.S. News & World Report, "America's Best Graduate Schools, Law, 2016"*

According to *U.S. News & World Report*, the Seattle-Bellevue-Everett, WA metro division is home to one of the top 75 medical schools for research in the U.S.: **University of Washington** (#10). The rankings are based on a weighted average of 11 measures of quality: quality assessment; peer assessment score; assessment score by residency directors; research activity; total research activity; average research activity per faculty member; student selectivity; median MCAT total score; median undergraduate GPA; acceptance rate; and faculty resources. *U.S. News & World Report, "America's Best Graduate Schools, Medical, 2016"*

According to *U.S. News & World Report*, the Seattle-Bellevue-Everett, WA metro division is home to one of the top 75 business schools in the U.S.: **University of Washington (Foster)** (#23). The rankings are based on a weighted average of the following nine measures: quality assessment; peer assessment; recruiter assessment; placement success; mean starting salary and bonus; student selectivity; mean GMAT and GRE scores; mean undergraduate GPA; and acceptance rate. *U.S. News & World Report, "America's Best Graduate Schools, Business, 2016"*

PRESIDENTIAL ELECTION

2012 Presidential Election Results

Area	Obama (%)	Romney (%)	Other (%)
King County	68.8	28.8	2.3
U.S.	51.0	47.2	1.8

Note: Results may not add to 100% due to rounding
Source: Dave Leip's Atlas of U.S. Presidential Elections

EMPLOYERS

Major Employers

Company Name	Industry
City of Tacoma	Switching and terminal services
Costco Wholesale Corporation	Miscellaneous general merchandise stores
County of Snohomish	Bureau of public roads
Evergreen Healthcare	General medical and surgical hospitals
Harborview Medical Center	General medical and surgical hospitals
King County Public Hospital Dist No. 2	Hospital and health services consultant
Microsoft Corporation	Prepackaged software
Prologix Distribution Services (West)	General merchandise, non-durable
R U Corporation	American restaurant
SNC-Lavalin Constructors	Heavy construction, nec
Social & Health Svcs, Washington Dept of	General medical and surgical hospitals
Swedish Health Services	General medical and surgical hospitals
T-Mobile USA	Radio, telephone communication
The Boeing Company	Airplanes, fixed or rotary wing
Tulalip Resort Casino	Casino hotel
United States Department of the Army	Medical centers
University of Washington	Colleges and universities
Virginia Mason Medical Center	General medical and surgical hospitals
Virginia Mason Medical Center	Clinic, operated by physicians
Virginia Mason Seattle Main Clinic	Clinic, operated by physicians

Note: Companies shown are located within the Seattle-Tacoma-Bellevue, WA Metropolitan Statistical Area.
Source: Hoovers.com; Wikipedia

Best Companies to Work For

Nordstrom; Perkins Coie, headquartered in Seattle, are among "The 100 Best Companies to Work For." To pick the best companies, *Fortune* partnered with the Great Place to Work Institute. Two-thirds of a company's score is based on the results of the Institute's Trust Index survey, which is sent to a random sample of employees from each company. The questions related to attitudes about management's credibility, job satisfaction, and camaraderie. The other third of the scoring is based on the company's responses to the Institute's Culture Audit, which includes detailed questions about pay and benefit programs, and a series of open-ended questions about hiring practices, internal communication, training, recognition programs, and diversity efforts. Any company that is at least five years old with more than 1,000 U.S. employees is eligible. *Fortune, "The 100 Best Companies to Work For," 2015*

Moss Adams, headquartered in Seattle, is among the "100 Best Companies for Working Mothers." Criteria: leave policies, workforce representation, benefits, child care, advancement programs, and flexibility policies. This year *Working Mother* gave particular weight to representation of women, advancement programs and flex. *Working Mother, "100 Best Companies 2014"*

Perkins Coie LLP, headquartered in Seattle, is among the "50 Best Employers for Workers Over 50." Criteria: recruiting practices; opportunities for training, education, and career development; workplace accommodations; alternative work options, such as flexible scheduling, job sharing, and phased retirement; employee health and pension benefits; and retiree benefits. Employers with at least 50 employees based in the U.S. are eligible, including for-profit companies, not-for-profit organizations, and government employers. *AARP, "2013 AARP Best Employers for Workers Over 50"*

Avanade, headquartered in Seattle, is among the "100 Best Places to Work in IT." To qualify, companies, both public and private, had to have a minimum of 50 IT employees and were selected based on average salary and bonus increases, the percentage of IT staffers promoted, IT staff turnover rates, training and development programs, and the percentage of women and minorities in IT staff and management positions. In addition, *Computerworld* looked at retention efforts, programs for recognizing and rewarding outstanding performances, and benefits such as flextime, elder care and child care, and reimbursement for college tuition and the cost of pursuing technology certifications. *Computerworld, "100 Best Places to Work in IT 2014"*

Moss Adams, headquartered in Seattle, is among the "Top Companies for Executive Women." To be named to the list, companies with a minimum of two women on the board complete a comprehensive application that focuses on the number of women in senior ranks. In addition to assessing corporate programs and policies dedicated to advancing women, NAFE examined the number of women in each company overall, in senior management, and on its board of directors, paying particular attention to the number of women with profit-and-loss responsibility. *National Association for Female Executives, "2015 NAFE Top 50 Companies for Executive Women"*

PUBLIC SAFETY

Crime Rate

Area	All Crimes	Violent Crimes				Property Crimes		
		Murder	Forcible Rape	Robbery	Aggrav. Assault	Burglary	Larceny -Theft	Motor Vehicle Theft
City	6,166.8	3.0	23.8	249.1	308.8	1,148.7	3,763.0	670.5
Suburbs[1]	3,691.4	1.6	30.0	69.3	96.2	729.1	2,310.5	454.7
Metro[2]	4,264.0	1.9	28.6	110.9	145.3	826.2	2,646.5	504.6
U.S.	3,098.6	4.5	25.2	109.1	229.1	610.0	1,899.4	221.3

Note: Figures are crimes per 100,000 population; (1) All areas within the metro area that are located outside the city limits; (2) Figures cover the Seattle-Bellevue-Everett, WA Metropolitan Division—see Appendix B for areas included
Source: FBI Uniform Crime Reports, 2013

Hate Crimes

Area	Number of Quarters Reported	Number of Incidents per Bias Motivation						
		Race	Religion	Sexual Orientation	Ethnicity	Disability	Gender	Gender Identity
City	4	50	14	14	6	3	2	0
U.S.	4	2,871	1,031	1,233	655	83	18	31

Source: Federal Bureau of Investigation, Hate Crime Statistics 2013

Identity Theft Consumer Complaints

Area	Complaints	Complaints per 100,000 Population	Rank[2]
MSA[1]	7,473	207.0	2
U.S.	332,646	104.3	-

Note: (1) Figures cover the Seattle-Tacoma-Bellevue, WA Metropolitan Statistical Area—see Appendix B for areas included; (2) Rank ranges from 1 to 380 where 1 indicates greatest number of identity theft complaints per 100,000 population
Source: Federal Trade Commission, Consumer Sentinel Network Data Book for January–December 2014

Fraud and Other Consumer Complaints

Area	Complaints	Complaints per 100,000 Population	Rank[2]
MSA[1]	16,884	467.7	41
U.S.	2,250,205	705.7	-

Note: (1) Figures cover the Seattle-Tacoma-Bellevue, WA Metropolitan Statistical Area—see Appendix B for areas included; (2) Rank ranges from 1 to 380 where 1 indicates greatest number of identity theft complaints per 100,000 population
Source: Federal Trade Commission, Consumer Sentinel Network Data Book for January–December 2014

RECREATION

Culture

Dance[1]	Theatre[1]	Instrumental Music[1]	Vocal Music[1]	Series and Festivals	Museums and Art Galleries[2]	Zoos and Aquariums[3]
8	12	9	6	13	105	2

Note: (1) Professional performing groups; (2) Based on organizations with SIC code 8412; (3) AZA-accredited
Source: The Grey House Performing Arts Directory, 2015-16; Association of Zoos & Aquariums, AZA Member Zoos & Aquariums, April 2015; www.AccuLeads.com, April 2015

Professional Sports Teams

Team Name	League	Year Established
Seattle Mariners	Major League Baseball (MLB)	1977
Seattle Seahawks	National Football League (NFL)	1976
Seattle Sounders FC	Major League Soccer (MLS)	2009

Note: Includes teams located in the Seattle-Tacoma-Bellevue, WA Metropolitan Statistical Area.
Source: Wikipedia, Major Professional Sports Teams of the United States and Canada, April 2015

CLIMATE

Average and Extreme Temperatures

Temperature	Jan	Feb	Mar	Apr	May	Jun	Jul	Aug	Sep	Oct	Nov	Dec	Yr.
Extreme High (°F)	64	70	75	85	93	96	98	99	98	89	74	63	99
Average High (°F)	44	48	52	57	64	69	75	74	69	59	50	45	59
Average Temp. (°F)	39	43	45	49	55	61	65	65	60	52	45	41	52
Average Low (°F)	34	36	38	41	46	51	54	55	51	45	39	36	44
Extreme Low (°F)	0	1	11	29	28	38	43	44	35	28	6	6	0

Note: Figures cover the years 1948-1990
Source: National Climatic Data Center, International Station Meteorological Climate Summary, 9/96

Average Precipitation/Snowfall/Humidity

Precip./Humidity	Jan	Feb	Mar	Apr	May	Jun	Jul	Aug	Sep	Oct	Nov	Dec	Yr.
Avg. Precip. (in.)	5.7	4.2	3.7	2.4	1.7	1.4	0.8	1.1	1.9	3.5	5.9	5.9	38.4
Avg. Snowfall (in.)	5	2	1	Tr	Tr	0	0	0	0	Tr	1	3	13
Avg. Rel. Hum. 7am (%)	83	83	84	83	80	79	79	84	87	88	85	85	83
Avg. Rel. Hum. 4pm (%)	76	69	63	57	54	54	49	51	57	68	76	79	63

Note: Figures cover the years 1948-1990; Tr = Trace amounts (<0.05 in. of rain; <0.5 in. of snow)
Source: National Climatic Data Center, International Station Meteorological Climate Summary, 9/96

Weather Conditions

Temperature			Daytime Sky			Precipitation		
5°F & below	32°F & below	90°F & above	Clear	Partly cloudy	Cloudy	0.01 inch or more precip.	0.1 inch or more snow/ice	Thunder-storms
< 1	38	3	57	121	187	157	8	8

Note: Figures are average number of days per year and cover the years 1948-1990
Source: National Climatic Data Center, International Station Meteorological Climate Summary, 9/96

HAZARDOUS WASTE

Superfund Sites

Seattle has four hazardous waste sites on the EPA's Superfund Final National Priorities List: **Harbor Island (Lead); Lockheed West Seattle; Lower Duwamish Waterway; Pacific Sound Resources.** There are a total of 1,322 Superfund sites on the list in the U.S. *U.S. Environmental Protection Agency, Final National Priorities List, April 14, 2015*

AIR & WATER QUALITY

Air Quality Trends: Ozone

	2004	2005	2006	2007	2008	2009	2010	2011	2012	2013
MSA[1]	0.064	0.054	0.065	0.059	0.056	0.061	0.056	0.053	0.059	0.052

Note: (1) Data covers the Seattle-Tacoma-Bellevue, WA Metropolitan Statistical Area—see Appendix B for areas included. The values shown are the composite ozone concentration averages among trend sites based on the highest fourth daily maximum 8-hour concentration in parts per million. These trends are based on sites having an adequate record of monitoring data during the trend period. Data from exceptional events are included.
Source: U.S. Environmental Protection Agency, Air Quality Monitoring Information, "Air Quality Trends by City, 2000-2013"

Air Quality Index

Area	Percent of Days when Air Quality was...[2]					AQI Statistics[2]	
	Good	Moderate	Unhealthy for Sensitive Groups	Unhealthy	Very Unhealthy	Maximum	Median
MSA[1]	66.0	32.3	1.6	0.0	0.0	133	43

Note: (1) Data covers the Seattle-Tacoma-Bellevue, WA Metropolitan Statistical Area—see Appendix B for areas included; (2) Based on 365 days with AQI data in 2014. Air Quality Index (AQI) is an index for reporting daily air quality. EPA calculates the AQI for five major air pollutants regulated by the Clean Air Act: ground-level ozone, particle pollution (aka particulate matter), carbon monoxide, sulfur dioxide, and nitrogen dioxide. The AQI runs from 0 to 500. The higher the AQI value, the greater the level of air pollution and the greater the health concern. There are six AQI categories: "Good" AQI is between 0 and 50. Air quality is considered satisfactory; "Moderate" AQI is between 51 and 100. Air quality is acceptable; "Unhealthy for Sensitive Groups" When AQI values are between 101 and 150, members of sensitive groups may experience health effects; "Unhealthy" When AQI values are between 151 and 200 everyone may begin to experience health effects; "Very Unhealthy" AQI values between 201 and 300 trigger a health alert; "Hazardous" AQI values over 300 trigger warnings of emergency conditions (not shown).
Source: U.S. Environmental Protection Agency, Air Quality Index Report, 2014

Air Quality Index Pollutants

Area	Percent of Days when AQI Pollutant was...[2]					
	Carbon Monoxide	Nitrogen Dioxide	Ozone	Sulfur Dioxide	Particulate Matter 2.5	Particulate Matter 10
MSA[1]	0.0	18.9	36.2	0.0	44.9	0.0

Note: (1) Data covers the Seattle-Tacoma-Bellevue, WA Metropolitan Statistical Area—see Appendix B for areas included; (2) Based on 365 days with AQI data in 2014. The Air Quality Index (AQI) is an index for reporting daily air quality. EPA calculates the AQI for five major air pollutants regulated by the Clean Air Act: ground-level ozone, particle pollution (also known as particulate matter), carbon monoxide, sulfur dioxide, and nitrogen dioxide. The AQI runs from 0 to 500. The higher the AQI value, the greater the level of air pollution and the greater the health concern.
Source: U.S. Environmental Protection Agency, Air Quality Index Report, 2014

Maximum Air Pollutant Concentrations: Particulate Matter, Ozone, CO and Lead

	Particulate Matter 10 (ug/m^3)	Particulate Matter 2.5 Wtd AM (ug/m^3)	Particulate Matter 2.5 24-Hr (ug/m^3)	Ozone (ppm)	Carbon Monoxide (ppm)	Lead (ug/m^3)
MSA[1] Level	28	12.2	34	0.059	1	n/a
NAAQS[2]	150	15	35	0.075	9	0.15
Met NAAQS[2]	Yes	Yes	Yes	Yes	Yes	n/a

Note: (1) Data covers the Seattle-Tacoma-Bellevue, WA Metropolitan Statistical Area—see Appendix B for areas included; Data from exceptional events are included; (2) National Ambient Air Quality Standards; ppm = parts per million; ug/m^3 = micrograms per cubic meter; n/a not available.
Concentrations: Particulate Matter 10 (coarse particulate)—highest second maximum 24-hour concentration; Particulate Matter 2.5 Wtd AM (fine particulate)—highest weighted annual mean concentration; Particulate Matter 2.5 24-Hour (fine particulate)—highest 98th percentile 24-hour concentration; Ozone—highest fourth daily maximum 8-hour concentration; Carbon Monoxide—highest second maximum non-overlapping 8-hour concentration; Lead—maximum running 3-month average
Source: U.S. Environmental Protection Agency, Air Quality Monitoring Information, "Air Quality Statistics by City, 2013"

Maximum Air Pollutant Concentrations: Nitrogen Dioxide and Sulfur Dioxide

	Nitrogen Dioxide AM (ppb)	Nitrogen Dioxide 1-Hr (ppb)	Sulfur Dioxide AM (ppb)	Sulfur Dioxide 1-Hr (ppb)	Sulfur Dioxide 24-Hr (ppb)
MSA[1] Level	n/a	n/a	n/a	n/a	n/a
NAAQS[2]	53	100	30	75	140
Met NAAQS[2]	n/a	n/a	n/a	n/a	n/a

Note: (1) Data covers the Seattle-Tacoma-Bellevue, WA Metropolitan Statistical Area—see Appendix B for areas included; Data from exceptional events are included; (2) National Ambient Air Quality Standards; ppm = parts per million; ug/m^3 = micrograms per cubic meter; n/a not available.
Concentrations: Nitrogen Dioxide AM—highest arithmetic mean concentration; Nitrogen Dioxide 1-Hr—highest 98th percentile 1-hour daily maximum concentration; Sulfur Dioxide AM—highest annual mean concentration; Sulfur Dioxide 1-Hr—highest 99th percentile 1-hour daily maximum concentration; Sulfur Dioxide 24-Hr—highest second maximum 24-hour concentration
Source: U.S. Environmental Protection Agency, Air Quality Monitoring Information, "Air Quality Statistics by City, 2013"

Drinking Water

Water System Name	Pop. Served	Primary Water Source Type	Violations[1]	
			Health Based	Monitoring/ Reporting
Seattle Public Utilities	836,000	Surface	0	0

Note: (1) Based on violation data from January 1, 2014 to December 31, 2014 (includes unresolved violations from earlier years)

Source: U.S. Environmental Protection Agency, Office of Ground Water and Drinking Water, Safe Drinking Water Information System (based on data extracted January 27, 2015)

Spokane, Washington

Background

Spokane, located on the Spokane River in western Washington State is approximately 20 miles from the Idaho border. It is the largest city in Spokane County, as well as the second most populous city in the state, after Seattle. The city was originally known as a railroad hub at the end of the nineteenth century, but it has since evolved into a modern, business-friendly city, and an urban center for the surrounding areas.

The area that is now Spokane was originally settled in 1871, and known as Spokan Falls, after the Spokane Native American tribe. The tribe originally settled in the area because of the abundance of salmon in the Spokane River. The first European settlement in the area was primarily a fur-trading post. Army Camp Spokane was established 56 miles northwest of the city to protect the settlement, and the construction of the Northern Pacific Railway. The railway reached the colony in 1881, bringing a wave of new European settlers to the area. The city of was officially incorporated as Spokan in 1881. It became Spokane in 1891.

The city's development was slowed somewhat by a large fire in 1889 that destroyed 27 blocks of the downtown area. The damage was widespread because a technical failure cut off water pressure to the firefighters' hoses. The construction of a railroad yard in 1892 by the Great Northern Railroad after the fire was instrumental in the city's recovery. For most of the twentieth century, Spokane was known primarily as a transportation hub for the region. That image began to change when the city hosted the 1974 World's Fair, pushing Spokane, then the smallest city to host a World's Fair, into the modern twentieth century. Many of the structures and improvements completed for the fair are still standing today. The exposition was held at Riverfront Park, which also hosted the U.S. Pavilion, the Looff Carousel, and the Great Northern Railway clock tower, a testament to the city's railroad days.

Today, Spokane benefits from the migration to urban living that is sweeping other US cities, as well as its proximity to natural resources such as lakes, mountains, and the river. A concerted effort to draw business and economic to the downtown has resulted in such developments as Kendall Yards, located along the river, a multi-year effort to bring in retail, residents, and other commercial activity. In 2014, the Centennial Trail through Kendall Yards, which draws runners, walkers and cyclists along the upper banks of the Spokane River, was given the Livable Community Award from Futurewise, a Seattle-based organization working to protect the state's natural attributes while, as the organization says, "keeping our communities great places to live."

Meantime, attention is being directed to the Riverfront Park, the city's number one tourist draw. The park, with its pavilions, shelters, and even IMAX theater, will undergo scrutiny as a master planning process launched in 2014 takes it into the future.

Transportation in the city is served by the Spokane Transit Authority (STA), which operates numerous buses and is contemplating a corridor for future high performance transit, possibly light rail, as part of its Capital Improvement Program 2013–2018.

Major attractions in Spokane include the Spokane Falls in the heart of Riverfront Park, Manito Park and Botanical Gardens, the John A. Finch Arboretum, and the Northwest Museum of Arts and Culture. Each year, the city hosts a diverse mix of sports, music and cultural festivals. Hoopfest, which was started in 1989, is the world's largest 3-on-3 basketball tournament, attracting more than 7,000 teams. The Spokane International Film Festival enlivens the winter cultural season.

Major institutes of higher learning in the city include Gonzaga University, Whitworth University, and the Community College of Spokane. The University of Washington operates a Spokane campus, where first-year medical students have the option of doing their studies.

Spokane has a typical four-season climate. Summers are generally hot and dry, while winters are cold with snowfall and other precipitation that can be heavy at times. Spokane generally has a more stable climate than other cities in the northwest because it is shielded by mountain ranges that prevent it from being influenced by the Pacific Ocean to the west and harsh Arctic winds originating in the north.

Rankings

Business/Finance Rankings

- The Spokane metro area appeared on the Milken Institute "2013 Best Performing Cities" list. Rank: #138 out of 200 large metro areas. Criteria: job growth; wage and salary growth; high-tech output growth. *Milken Institute, "Best-Performing Cities 2014," January 2015*

- *Forbes* ranked the 200 most populous metro areas to determine the nation's "Best Places for Business and Careers." The Spokane metro area was ranked #128. Criteria: costs (business and living); job growth (past and projected); income growth; educational attainment (college and high school); projected economic growth; cultural and recreational opportunities; net migration patterns; number of highly ranked colleges. *Forbes, "The Best Places for Business and Careers 2014," July 23, 2014*

Education Rankings

- Personal finance website *WalletHub* analyzed the 150 largest U.S. metropolitan statistical areas to determine where the most educated Americans are choosing to settle. Criteria: educational attainment; percentage of workers with jobs in computer, engineering, and science fields; quality and size of each metro area's universities. Spokane was ranked #35 (#1 = most educated city). *www.WalletHub.com, "2014's Most and Least Educated Cities*

Environmental Rankings

- The Spokane metro area came in at #20 for the relative comfort of its climate on Sperling's list of "chill cities," as measured by the Sperling Heat Index. All 361 metro areas are included. Criteria included daytime high temperatures, nighttime low temperatures, dew point, and relative humidity at the high temperatures. *www.bertsperling.com, "Sperling's Chill Cities," July 18, 2013*

- Sperling's BestPlaces assessed 379 metropolitan areas of the United States for the likelihood of dangerously extreme weather events or earthquakes. In general the Southeast and South-Central regions have the highest risk of weather extremes and earthquakes, while the Pacific Northwest enjoys the lowest risk. Of the least risky metropolitan areas, the Spokane metro area was ranked #6. *www.bestplaces.net, "Safest Places from Natural Disasters," April 2011*

- *The Daily Beast* identifed the snowiest among the 100 largest U.S. cities, looking at average snowfall per month from December 2011 through March 2012 and from December 1, 2012 to December 21, 2012. Number of days with maximum and minimum temperatures of 32 degrees or less contributed to the rankings. Spokane ranked #5. *The Daily Beast, "25 Snowiest Cities in America," December 21, 2012*

- Spokane was highlighted as one of the cleanest metro areas for ozone air pollution in the U.S. during 2011 through 2013. The list represents cities with no monitored ozone air pollution in unhealthful ranges. *American Lung Association, State of the Air 2015*

Health/Fitness Rankings

- The Spokane metro area appeared in the 2013 Gallup-Healthways Well-Being Index. The area ranked #66 out of 189. The Gallup-Healthways Well-Being Index score is an average of six sub-indexes, which individually examine life evaluation, emotional health, work environment, physical health, healthy behaviors, and access to basic necessities. Results are based on telephone interviews conducted as part of the Gallup-Healthways Well-Being Index survey January 2–December 29, 2012, and January 2–December 30, 2013, with a random sample of 531,630 adults, aged 18 and older, living in metropolitan areas in the 50 U.S. states and the District of Columbia. *Gallup-Healthways, "State of American Well-Being," March 25, 2014*

Real Estate Rankings

- Spokane was ranked #133 out of 275 metro areas in terms of house price appreciation in 2014 (#1 = highest rate). *Federal Housing Finance Agency, House Price Index, 4th Quarter 2014*

- Spokane was ranked #58 out of 226 metro areas in terms of housing affordability in 2014 by the National Association of Home Builders (#1 = most affordable). The NAHB-Wells Fargo Housing Opportunity Index (HOI) for a given area is defined as the share of homes sold in that area that would have been affordable to a family earning the local median income, based on standard mortgage underwriting criteria. *National Association of Home Builders®, NAHB-Wells Fargo Housing Opportunity Index, 4th Quarter 2014*

Safety Rankings

- Allstate ranked the 200 largest cities in America in terms of driver safety. Spokane ranked #71. Allstate researchers analyzed internal property damage claims over a two-year period from January 2011 to December 2012. A weighted average of the two-year numbers determined the annual percentages. *Allstate, "Allstate America's Best Drivers Report, 2014"*

- The National Insurance Crime Bureau ranked 380 metro areas in the U.S. in terms of per capita rates of vehicle theft. The Spokane metro area ranked #7 (#1 = highest rate). Criteria: number of vehicle theft offenses per 100,000 inhabitants in 2012. *National Insurance Crime Bureau, "Hot Spots 2012," June 26, 2013*

Seniors/Retirement Rankings

- From its Best Cities for Successful Aging indexes, the Milken Institute generated rankings for metropolitan areas, weighing data in eight categories—health care, wellness, living arrangements, transportation, financial characteristics, education and employment opportunities, community engagement, and overall livability. The Spokane metro area was ranked #51 overall in the large metro area category. *Milken Institute, "Best Cities for Successful Aging, 2014"*

- The AARP named Spokane one of the "10 Best Places to Live on $100 a Day." Analysts looked at 200 cities to arrive at their 10-best list. Criteria includes: cost of living; quality-of-life; arts and culture; educational institutions; restaurants; community life; health care; natural setting; sunny days per year; and overall vibe. *AARP The Magazine, "10 Best Places to Live on $100 a Day," July 2012*

- Spokane was identified as one of the most popular places to retire by *Topretirements.com*. The list reflects the 100 cities (out of 900+ total cities reviewed) that visitors to the website are most interested in for retirement. *Topretirements.com, "Most Popular Places to Retire for 2014," February 25, 2014*

Sports/Recreation Rankings

- Spokane was chosen as a bicycle friendly community by the League of American Bicyclists. A "Bicycle Friendly Community" welcomes cyclists by providing safe accommodation for cycling and encouraging people to bike for transportation and recreation. There are four award levels: Platinum; Gold; Silver; and Bronze. The community achieved an award level of Bronze. *League of American Bicyclists, "Bicycle Friendly Community Master List," Fall 2013*

Transportation Rankings

- NerdWallet surveyed average annual car insurance premiums in 125 U.S. cities to identify the least expensive U.S. cities in which to insure a car. Locations without no-fault insurance laws was a strong determinant. Spokane came in at #9 for the least expensive rates. *www.nerdwallet.com, "Best Cities for Cheap Car Insurance," February 3, 2014*

Miscellaneous Rankings

- Market analyst Scarborough Research surveyed adults who had done volunteer work over the previous 12 months to find out where volunteers are concentrated. The Spokane metro area made the list for highest volunteer participation. *Scarborough Research, "Salt Lake City, UT; Minneapolis, MN; and Des Moines, IA Lend a Helping Hand," November 27, 2012*

Business Environment

CITY FINANCES

City Government Finances

Component	2012 ($000)	2012 ($ per capita)
Total Revenues	395,803	1,895
Total Expenditures	395,587	1,894
Debt Outstanding	189,920	909
Cash and Securities[1]	488,705	2,339

Note: (1) Cash and security holdings of a government at the close of its fiscal year, including those of its dependent agencies, utilities, and liquor stores.
Source: U.S Census Bureau, State & Local Government Finances 2012

City Government Revenue by Source

Source	2012 ($000)	2012 ($ per capita)
General Revenue		
From Federal Government	11,209	54
From State Government	29,410	141
From Local Governments	6,180	30
Taxes		
Property	60,887	291
Sales and Gross Receipts	66,408	318
Personal Income	0	0
Corporate Income	0	0
Motor Vehicle License	0	0
Other Taxes	6,947	33
Current Charges	160,789	770
Liquor Store	0	0
Utility	33,195	159
Employee Retirement	1,968	9

Source: U.S Census Bureau, State & Local Government Finances 2012

City Government Expenditures by Function

Function	2012 ($000)	2012 ($ per capita)	2012 (%)
General Direct Expenditures			
Air Transportation	505	2	0.1
Corrections	1,068	5	0.3
Education	0	0	0.0
Employment Security Administration	0	0	0.0
Financial Administration	1,500	7	0.4
Fire Protection	37,478	179	9.5
General Public Buildings	813	4	0.2
Governmental Administration, Other	7,357	35	1.9
Health	413	2	0.1
Highways	36,606	175	9.3
Hospitals	0	0	0.0
Housing and Community Development	10,160	49	2.6
Interest on General Debt	8,982	43	2.3
Judicial and Legal	9,759	47	2.5
Libraries	8,119	39	2.1
Parking	504	2	0.1
Parks and Recreation	19,328	93	4.9
Police Protection	42,570	204	10.8
Public Welfare	3,937	19	1.0
Sewerage	54,198	259	13.7
Solid Waste Management	63,436	304	16.0
Veterans' Services	0	0	0.0
Liquor Store	0	0	0.0
Utility	27,327	131	6.9
Employee Retirement	21,921	105	5.5

Source: U.S Census Bureau, State & Local Government Finances 2012

DEMOGRAPHICS

Population Growth

Area	1990 Census	2000 Census	2010 Census	Population Growth (%) 1990-2000	Population Growth (%) 2000-2010
City	178,202	195,629	208,916	9.8	6.8
MSA[1]	361,364	417,939	471,221	15.7	12.7
U.S.	248,709,873	281,421,906	308,745,538	13.2	9.7

Note: (1) Figures cover the Spokane, WA Metropolitan Statistical Area—see Appendix B for areas included
Source: U.S. Census Bureau, Census 1990, 2000, 2010

Household Size

Area	Persons in Household (%) One	Two	Three	Four	Five	Six	Seven or More	Average Household Size
City	34.4	34.2	13.2	11.3	4.4	1.6	0.9	2.33
MSA[1]	28.9	37.1	13.7	12.0	5.3	1.9	1.2	2.46
U.S.	27.7	33.6	15.7	13.1	6.0	2.3	1.5	2.64

Note: (1) Figures cover the Spokane-Spokane Valley, WA Metropolitan Statistical Area—see Appendix B for areas included
Source: U.S. Census Bureau, 2011-2013 American Community Survey 3-Year Estimates

Race

Area	White Alone[2] (%)	Black Alone[2] (%)	Asian Alone[2] (%)	AIAN[3] Alone[2] (%)	NHOPI[4] Alone[2] (%)	Other Race Alone[2] (%)	Two or More Races (%)
City	87.7	2.6	2.9	1.5	0.3	0.9	4.0
MSA[1]	89.4	1.8	2.1	1.7	0.3	0.9	3.7
U.S.	73.9	12.6	5.0	0.8	0.2	4.7	2.9

Note: (1) Figures cover the Spokane-Spokane Valley, WA Metropolitan Statistical Area—see Appendix B for areas included; (2) Alone is defined as not being in combination with one or more other races; (3) American Indian and Alaska Native; (4) Native Hawaiian and Other Pacific Islander
Source: U.S. Census Bureau, 2011-2013 American Community Survey 3-Year Estimates

Hispanic or Latino Origin

Area	Total (%)	Mexican (%)	Puerto Rican (%)	Cuban (%)	Other (%)
City	5.5	3.6	0.2	0.1	1.7
MSA[1]	4.7	3.3	0.2	0.1	1.1
U.S.	16.9	10.8	1.6	0.6	3.8

Note: Persons of Hispanic or Latino origin can be of any race; (1) Figures cover the Spokane-Spokane Valley, WA Metropolitan Statistical Area—see Appendix B for areas included
Source: U.S. Census Bureau, 2011-2013 American Community Survey 3-Year Estimates

Segregation

Type	Segregation Indices[1] 1990	2000	2010	2010 Rank[2]	Percent Change 1990-2000	1990-2010	2000-2010
Black/White	n/a	n/a	n/a	n/a	n/a	n/a	n/a
Asian/White	n/a	n/a	n/a	n/a	n/a	n/a	n/a
Hispanic/White	n/a	n/a	n/a	n/a	n/a	n/a	n/a

Note: All figures cover the Metropolitan Statistical Area—see Appendix B for areas included; Figures are based on an analysis of 1990, 2000, and 2010 Census Decennial Census tract data by William H. Frey, Brookings Institution and the University of Michigan Social Science Data Analysis Network. In this analysis all racial groups (whites, blacks, and asians) are non-Hispanic members of those races. Hispanics are shown as a separate category;
(1) Segregation Indices are Dissimilarity Indices that measure the degree to which the minority group is distributed differently than whites across census tracts. They range from 0 (complete integration) to 100 (complete segregation) where the value indicates the percentage of the minority group that needs to move to be distributed exactly like whites; (2) Ranges from 1 (most segregated) to 102 (least segregated); n/a not available.
Source: www.CensusScope.org

Ancestry

Area	German	Irish	English	American	Italian	Polish	French[2]	Scottish	Dutch
City	22.0	13.5	10.6	5.3	5.1	1.8	3.4	2.7	1.8
MSA[1]	23.1	13.4	11.0	5.5	4.7	1.8	3.6	2.9	1.9
U.S.	14.9	10.8	8.0	7.4	5.5	3.0	2.7	1.7	1.4

Note: Figures are the percentage of the total population reporting a particular ancestry. The nine most commonly reported ancestries in the U.S. are shown. Figures include multiple ancestries (e.g. if a person reported being Irish and Italian, they were included in both columns); (1) Figures cover the Spokane-Spokane Valley, WA Metropolitan Statistical Area—see Appendix B for areas included; (2) Excludes Basque
Source: U.S. Census Bureau, 2011-2013 American Community Survey 3-Year Estimates

Foreign-Born Population

Area	Percent of Population Born in								
	Any Foreign Country	Mexico	Asia	Europe	Carribean	South America	Central America[2]	Africa	Canada
City	n/a	n/a	n/a	n/a	n/a	n/a	n/a	n/a	n/a
MSA[1]	5.4	0.4	1.9	2.0	0.0	0.1	0.1	0.3	0.4
U.S.	13.0	3.7	3.8	1.5	1.2	0.9	1.0	0.6	0.3

Note: (1) Figures cover the Spokane-Spokane Valley, WA Metropolitan Statistical Area—see Appendix B for areas included; (2) Excludes Mexico.
Source: U.S. Census Bureau, 2011-2013 American Community Survey 3-Year Estimates

Marital Status

Area	Never Married	Now Married[2]	Separated	Widowed	Divorced
City	34.3	42.6	1.7	5.9	15.6
MSA[1]	29.8	49.4	1.4	5.6	13.8
U.S.	32.7	48.1	2.2	6.0	11.0

Note: Figures are percentages and cover the population 15 years of age and older; (1) Figures cover the Spokane-Spokane Valley, WA Metropolitan Statistical Area—see Appendix B for areas included; (2) Excludes separated
Source: U.S. Census Bureau, 2011-2013 American Community Survey 3-Year Estimates

Disability Status

Area	All Ages	Under 18 Years Old	18 to 64 Years Old	65 Years and Over
City	15.6	5.0	14.1	39.9
MSA[1]	14.9	5.0	13.0	38.9
U.S.	12.3	4.1	10.2	36.3

Note: Figures show percent of the civilian noninstitutionalized population that reported having a disability. Disability status is determined from from six types of difficulty: vision, hearing, cognitive, ambulatory, self-care, and independent living. For children under 5 years old, hearing and vision difficulty are used to determine disability status. For children between the ages of 5 and 14, disability status is determined from hearing, vision, cognitive, ambulatory, and self-care difficulties. For people aged 15 years and older, they are considered to have a disability if they have difficulty with any one of the six difficulty types; (1) Figures cover the Spokane-Spokane Valley, WA Metropolitan Statistical Area—see Appendix B for areas included.
Source: U.S. Census Bureau, 2011-2013 American Community Survey 3-Year Estimates

Age

Area	Percent of Population									Median Age
	Under Age 5	Age 5–19	Age 20–34	Age 35–44	Age 45–54	Age 55–64	Age 65–74	Age 75–84	Age 85+	
City	7.1	17.9	24.6	11.9	12.4	12.1	7.2	4.6	2.3	35.3
MSA[1]	6.1	19.6	20.8	11.9	13.7	13.5	8.2	4.4	1.8	38.0
U.S.	6.4	19.9	20.7	12.9	14.1	12.3	7.6	4.2	1.9	37.4

Note: (1) Figures cover the Spokane-Spokane Valley, WA Metropolitan Statistical Area—see Appendix B for areas included
Source: U.S. Census Bureau, 2011-2013 American Community Survey 3-Year Estimates

Gender

Area	Males	Females	Males per 100 Females
City	102,789	107,087	96.0
MSA[1]	264,607	268,120	98.7
U.S.	154,451,010	159,410,713	96.9

Note: (1) Figures cover the Spokane-Spokane Valley, WA Metropolitan Statistical Area—see Appendix B for areas included
Source: U.S. Census Bureau, 2011-2013 American Community Survey 3-Year Estimates

Religious Groups by Family

Area	Catholic	Baptist	Non-Den.	Methodist[2]	Lutheran	LDS[3]	Pentecostal	Presbyterian[4]	Muslim[5]	Judaism
MSA[1]	13.1	1.9	4.3	1.0	2.9	5.2	2.9	1.5	0.1	0.2
U.S.	19.1	9.3	4.0	4.0	2.3	2.0	1.9	1.6	0.8	0.7

Note: Figures are the number of adherents as a percentage of the total population; (1) Figures cover the Spokane, WA Metropolitan Statistical Area—see Appendix B for areas included; (2) Methodist/Pietist; (3) Latter Day Saints; (4) Reformed; (5) Figures are estimates
Source: Association of Statisticians of American Religious Bodies, 2010 U.S. Religion Census: Religious Congregations & Membership Study

Religious Groups by Tradition

Area	Catholic	Evangelical Protestant	Mainline Protestant	Other Tradition	Black Protestant	Orthodox
MSA[1]	13.1	12.4	4.9	6.3	0.1	0.2
U.S.	19.1	16.2	7.3	4.3	1.6	0.3

Note: Figures are the number of adherents as a percentage of the total population; (1) Figures cover the Spokane, WA Metropolitan Statistical Area—see Appendix B for areas included
Source: Association of Statisticians of American Religious Bodies, 2010 U.S. Religion Census: Religious Congregations & Membership Study

ECONOMY

Gross Metropolitan Product

Area	2012	2013	2014	2015	Rank[2]
MSA[1]	19.3	19.9	20.5	21.5	112

Note: Figures are in billions of dollars; (1) Figures cover the Spokane-Spokane Valley, WA Metropolitan Statistical Area—see Appendix B for areas included; (2) Rank is based on 2015 data and ranges from 1 to 363
Source: The U.S. Conference of Mayors, U.S. Metro Economies: GMP and Employment 2013-2015, June 2014

Economic Growth

Area	2010-12 (%)	2013 (%)	2014 (%)	2015 (%)	Rank[2]
MSA[1]	1.6	1.9	1.4	2.9	172
U.S.	2.1	2.0	2.3	3.2	–

Note: Figures are real gross metropolitan product (GMP) growth rates and represent annual average percent change; (1) Figures cover the Spokane-Spokane Valley, WA Metropolitan Statistical Area—see Appendix B for areas included; (2) Rank is based on 2015 data and ranges from 1 to 363
Source: The U.S. Conference of Mayors, U.S. Metro Economies: GMP and Employment 2013-2015, June 2014

Metropolitan Area Exports

Area	2008	2009	2010	2011	2012	2013	Rank[2]
MSA[1]	894.8	662.2	727.4	761.4	873.5	862.4	172

Note: Figures are in millions of dollars; (1) Figures cover the Spokane-Spokane Valley, WA Metropolitan Statistical Area—see Appendix B for areas included; (2) Rank is based on 2013 data and ranges from 1 to 387
Source: U.S. Department of Commerce, International Trade Administration, Office of Trade & Industry Information, Manufacturing & Services, data extracted April 3, 2015

Building Permits

Area	Single-Family			Multi-Family			Total		
	2013	2014	Pct. Chg.	2013	2014	Pct. Chg.	2013	2014	Pct. Chg.
City	321	223	-30.5	142	296	108.5	463	519	12.1
MSA[1]	1,299	1,135	-12.6	335	825	146.3	1,634	1,960	20.0
U.S.	620,802	634,597	2.2	370,020	411,766	11.3	990,822	1,046,363	5.6

Note: (1) Figures cover the Spokane-Spokane Valley, WA Metropolitan Statistical Area—see Appendix B for areas included; Figures represent new, privately-owned housing units authorized (unadjusted data); All permit data are based on estimates with imputation.
Source: U.S. Census Bureau, Manufacturing, Mining, and Construction Statistics, Building Permits, 2013, 2014

Bankruptcy Filings

Area	Business Filings			Nonbusiness Filings		
	2013	2014	% Chg.	2013	2014	% Chg.
Spokane County	51	30	-41.2	1,786	1,654	-7.4
U.S.	33,212	26,983	-18.8	1,038,720	909,812	-12.4

Note: Business filings include Chapter 7, Chapter 11, Chapter 12, and Chapter 13; Nonbusiness filings include Chapter 7, Chapter 11, and Chapter 13
Source: Administrative Office of the U.S. Courts, Business and Nonbusiness Bankruptcy, County Cases Commenced by Chapter of the Bankruptcy Code, During the 12- Month Period Ending December 31, 2013 and Business and Nonbusiness Bankruptcy, County Cases Commenced by Chapter of the Bankruptcy Code, During the 12- Month Period Ending December 31, 2014

Housing Vacancy Rates

Area	Gross Vacancy Rate[2] (%)			Year-Round Vacancy Rate[3] (%)			Rental Vacancy Rate[4] (%)			Homeowner Vacancy Rate[5] (%)		
	2012	2013	2014	2012	2013	2014	2012	2013	2014	2012	2013	2014
MSA[1]	n/a	n/a	n/a	n/a	n/a	n/a	n/a	n/a	n/a	n/a	n/a	n/a
U.S.	13.8	13.6	13.4	10.8	10.7	10.4	8.7	8.3	7.6	2.0	2.0	1.9

Note: (1) Figures cover the Spokane-Spokane Valley, WA Metropolitan Statistical Area—see Appendix B for areas included; (2) The percentage of the total housing inventory that is vacant; (3) The percentage of the housing inventory (excluding seasonal units) that is year-round vacant; (4) The percentage of rental inventory that is vacant for rent; (5) The percentage of homeowner inventory that is vacant for sale; n/a not available
Source: U.S. Census Bureau, Housing Vacancies and Homeownership Annual Statistics: 2014

INCOME

Income

Area	Per Capita ($)	Median Household ($)	Average Household ($)
City	23,781	41,200	55,686
MSA[1]	24,924	48,116	61,566
U.S.	27,884	52,176	72,897

Note: (1) Figures cover the Spokane-Spokane Valley, WA Metropolitan Statistical Area—see Appendix B for areas included
Source: U.S. Census Bureau, 2011-2013 American Community Survey 3-Year Estimates

Household Income Distribution

Area	Percent of Households Earning							
	Under $15,000	$15,000 -24,999	$25,000 -34,999	$35,000 -49,999	$50,000 -74,999	$75,000 -99,000	$100,000 -149,999	$150,000 and up
City	17.1	13.6	12.6	14.2	18.0	11.7	8.3	4.6
MSA[1]	14.3	11.7	11.6	14.2	19.3	12.6	10.7	5.7
U.S.	13.0	10.9	10.3	13.6	17.9	11.9	12.7	9.6

Note: (1) Figures cover the Spokane-Spokane Valley, WA Metropolitan Statistical Area—see Appendix B for areas included
Source: U.S. Census Bureau, 2011-2013 American Community Survey 3-Year Estimates

Poverty Rate

Area	All Ages	Under 18 Years Old	18 to 64 Years Old	65 Years and Over
City	19.5	23.3	20.2	10.5
MSA[1]	16.0	19.3	16.6	8.1
U.S.	15.9	22.4	14.8	9.5

Note: Figures are percentage of people whose income during the past 12 months was below the poverty level; (1) Figures cover the Spokane-Spokane Valley, WA Metropolitan Statistical Area—see Appendix B for areas included
Source: U.S. Census Bureau, 2011-2013 American Community Survey 3-Year Estimates

EMPLOYMENT

Labor Force and Employment

Area	Civilian Labor Force			Workers Employed		
	Dec. 2013	Dec. 2014	% Chg.	Dec. 2013	Dec. 2014	% Chg.
City	99,937	101,944	2.0	92,391	93,991	1.7
MSA[1]	249,497	253,873	1.8	229,979	233,898	1.7
U.S.	154,408,000	155,521,000	0.7	144,423,000	147,190,000	1.9

Note: Data is not seasonally adjusted and covers workers 16 years of age and older; (1) Figures cover the Spokane-Spokane Valley, WA Metropolitan Statistical Area—see Appendix B for areas included
Source: Bureau of Labor Statistics, Local Area Unemployment Statistics

Unemployment Rate

Area	2014											
	Jan.	Feb.	Mar.	Apr.	May	Jun.	Jul.	Aug.	Sep.	Oct.	Nov.	Dec.
City	8.0	8.6	7.9	6.8	7.0	6.6	7.0	7.3	6.8	6.8	7.1	7.8
MSA[1]	8.5	8.8	8.2	6.9	6.9	6.5	6.9	7.2	6.7	6.7	7.1	7.9
U.S.	7.0	7.0	6.8	5.9	6.1	6.3	6.5	6.3	5.7	5.5	5.5	5.4

Note: Data is not seasonally adjusted and covers workers 16 years of age and older; (1) Figures cover the Spokane-Spokane Valley, WA Metropolitan Statistical Area—see Appendix B for areas included
Source: Bureau of Labor Statistics, Local Area Unemployment Statistics

Employment by Occupation

Occupation Classification	City (%)	MSA[1] (%)	U.S. (%)
Management, Business, Science, and Arts	34.7	35.3	36.2
Natural Resources, Construction, and Maintenance	7.1	8.1	9.0
Production, Transportation, and Material Moving	11.0	11.3	12.1
Sales and Office	25.7	26.1	24.4
Service	21.5	19.2	18.3

Note: Figures cover employed civilians 16 years of age and older; (1) Figures cover the Spokane-Spokane Valley, WA Metropolitan Statistical Area—see Appendix B for areas included
Source: U.S. Census Bureau, 2011-2013 American Community Survey 3-Year Estimates

Employment by Industry

Sector	MSA[1]		U.S.
	Number of Employees	Percent of Total	Percent of Total
Construction, Mining, and Logging	10,800	4.6	5.0
Education and Health Services	49,100	20.8	15.5
Financial Activities	14,300	6.1	5.7
Government	40,400	17.1	15.8
Information	3,100	1.3	2.0
Leisure and Hospitality	21,100	9.0	10.3
Manufacturing	16,900	7.2	8.7
Other Services	9,700	4.1	4.0
Professional and Business Services	24,000	10.2	13.8
Retail Trade	28,800	12.2	11.4
Transportation, Warehousing, and Utilities	7,100	3.0	3.9
Wholesale Trade	10,400	4.4	4.2

Note: Figures are non-farm employment as of December 2014. Figures are not seasonally adjusted and include workers 16 years of age and older; (1) Figures cover the Spokane-Spokane Valley, WA Metropolitan Statistical Area—see Appendix B for areas included; n/a not available
Source: Bureau of Labor Statistics, Current Employment Statistics, Employment, Hours, and Earnings

Occupations with Greatest Projected Employment Growth: 2012 – 2022

Occupation[1]	2012 Employment	2022 Projected Employment	Numeric Employment Change	Percent Employment Change
Software Developers, Applications	53,200	67,380	14,180	26.7
Retail Salespersons	104,060	118,020	13,960	13.4
Carpenters	36,640	49,230	12,590	34.4
Registered Nurses	54,550	65,210	10,660	19.6
Combined Food Preparation and Serving Workers, Including Fast Food	56,700	67,250	10,550	18.6
Janitors and Cleaners, Except Maids and Housekeeping Cleaners	43,100	52,040	8,940	20.8
Bookkeeping, Accounting, and Auditing Clerks	44,950	53,480	8,530	19.0
Secretaries and Administrative Assistants, Except Legal, Medical, and Executive	42,100	50,210	8,110	19.3
Construction Laborers	22,740	30,730	7,990	35.1
Waiters and Waitresses	42,250	50,130	7,880	18.7

Note: Projections cover Washington; (1) Sorted by numeric employment change
Source: www.projectionscentral.com, State Occupational Projections, 2012–2022 Long-Term Projections

Fastest Growing Occupations: 2012 – 2022

Occupation[1]	2012 Employment	2022 Projected Employment	Numeric Employment Change	Percent Employment Change
Massage Therapists	9,230	13,640	4,410	47.8
Nursing Instructors and Teachers, Postsecondary	1,230	1,800	570	46.0
Mechanical Door Repairers	580	840	260	45.3
Fence Erectors	1,200	1,720	520	43.2
Reinforcing Iron and Rebar Workers	940	1,320	380	40.5
Cement Masons and Concrete Finishers	2,460	3,450	990	40.4
Roofers	5,000	7,000	2,000	39.9
Engine and Other Machine Assemblers	1,090	1,530	440	39.9
Brickmasons and Blockmasons	960	1,340	380	39.8
Helpers—Brickmasons, Blockmasons, Stonemasons, and Tile and Marble Setters	410	570	160	39.7

Note: Projections cover Washington; (1) Sorted by percent employment change and excludes occupations with numeric employment change less than 100
Source: www.projectionscentral.com, State Occupational Projections, 2012–2022 Long-Term Projections

Average Wages

Occupation	$/Hr.	Occupation	$/Hr.
Accountants and Auditors	29.41	Maids and Housekeeping Cleaners	10.98
Automotive Mechanics	21.09	Maintenance and Repair Workers	18.08
Bookkeepers	18.66	Marketing Managers	52.77
Carpenters	23.53	Nuclear Medicine Technologists	35.89
Cashiers	12.08	Nurses, Licensed Practical	21.72
Clerks, General Office	14.69	Nurses, Registered	35.14
Clerks, Receptionists/Information	13.93	Nursing Assistants	12.71
Clerks, Shipping/Receiving	15.46	Packers and Packagers, Hand	11.56
Computer Programmers	26.47	Physical Therapists	38.63
Computer Systems Analysts	34.89	Postal Service Mail Carriers	24.97
Computer User Support Specialists	22.37	Real Estate Brokers	n/a
Cooks, Restaurant	12.06	Retail Salespersons	14.27
Dentists	95.08	Sales Reps., Exc. Tech./Scientific	25.66
Electrical Engineers	41.46	Sales Reps., Tech./Scientific	n/a
Electricians	28.19	Secretaries, Exc. Legal/Med./Exec.	16.31
Financial Managers	47.12	Security Guards	13.32
First-Line Supervisors/Managers, Sales	22.00	Surgeons	n/a
Food Preparation Workers	10.77	Teacher Assistants	12.90
General and Operations Managers	46.30	Teachers, Elementary School	29.20
Hairdressers/Cosmetologists	13.64	Teachers, Secondary School	30.30
Internists	76.87	Telemarketers	11.51
Janitors and Cleaners	13.73	Truck Drivers, Heavy/Tractor-Trailer	19.94
Landscaping/Groundskeeping Workers	13.07	Truck Drivers, Light/Delivery Svcs.	17.33
Lawyers	47.57	Waiters and Waitresses	12.73

*Note: Wage data covers the Spokane, WA Metropolitan Statistical Area—see Appendix B for areas included;
Hourly wages for elementary/secondary school teachers and teacher assistants were calculated by the editors
from annual wage data assuming a 40 hour work week; n/a not available.*
Source: Bureau of Labor Statistics, Metro Area Occupational Employment and Wage Estimates, May 2014

TAXES

State Corporate Income Tax Rates

State	Tax Rate (%)	Income Brackets ($)	Num. of Brackets	Financial Institution Tax Rate (%)[a]	Federal Income Tax Ded.
Washington	None	–	–	–	–

*Note: Tax rates as of January 1, 2015; (a) Rates listed are the corporate income tax rate applied to financial
institutions or excise taxes based on income. Some states have other taxes based upon the value of deposits or
shares.*
Source: Federation of Tax Administrators, "State Corporate Income Tax Rates, 2015"

State Individual Income Tax Rates

State	Tax Rate (%)	Income Brackets ($)	Num. of Brackets	Personal Exempt. ($)[1]		Fed. Inc. Tax Ded.
				Single	Dependents	
Washington	None	–	–	–	–	–

*Note: Tax rates as of January 1, 2015; Local- and county-level taxes are not included; n/a not applicable;
(1) Married joint filers generally receive double the single exemption*
Source: Federation of Tax Administrators, "State Individual Income Tax Rates, 2015"

Various State and Local Tax Rates

State	State and Local Sales and Use (%)	State Sales and Use (%)	Gasoline[1] (¢/gal.)	Cigarette[2] ($/pack)	Spirits[3] ($/gal.)	Wine[4] ($/gal.)	Beer[5] ($/gal.)
Washington	8.7	6.50	37.5	3.025	35.22 (j)(k)	0.87	0.26 (p)

Note: All tax rates as of January 1, 2015; (1) The American Petroleum Institute has developed a methodology for determining the average tax rate on a gallon of fuel. Rates may include any of the following: excise taxes, environmental fees, storage tank fees, other fees or taxes, general sales tax, and local taxes. In states where gasoline is subject to the general sales tax, or where the fuel tax is based on the average sale price, the average rate determined by API is sensitive to changes in the price of gasoline. States that fully or partially apply general sales taxes to gasoline: CA, CO, GA, IL, IN, MI, NY; (2) The federal excise tax of $1.0066 per pack and local taxes are not included; (3) Rates are those applicable to off-premise sales of 40% alcohol by volume (a.b.v.) distilled spirits in 750ml containers. Local excise taxes are excluded; (4) Rates are those applicable to off-premise sales of 11% a.b.v. non-carbonated wine in 750ml containers; (5) Rates are those applicable to off-premise sales of 4.7% a.b.v. beer in 12 ounce containers; (j) Includes sales taxes specific to alcoholic beverages; (k) Includes the retail (17%) and distributor (10%) license fees, converted into a gallonage excise tax rate; (p) Local excise taxes are excluded.
Source: Tax Foundation, 2015 Facts & Figures: How Does Your State Compare?

State Business Tax Climate Index Rankings

State	Overall Rank	Corporate Tax Index Rank	Individual Income Tax Index Rank	Sales Tax Index Rank	Unemployment Insurance Tax Index Rank	Property Tax Index Rank
Washington	11	28	6	46	19	23

Note: The index is a measure of how each state's tax laws affect economic performance. The lower the rank, the more favorable a state's tax system is for business. States without a given tax are given a ranking of 1. The scores/rankings for the District of Columbia do not affect other states. The 2015 index represents the tax climate as of July 1, 2014.
Source: Tax Foundation, State Business Tax Climate Index 2015

COMMERCIAL UTILITIES

Typical Monthly Electric Bills

Area	Commercial Service ($/month)		Industrial Service ($/month)	
	1,500 kWh	40 kW demand 14,000 kWh	1,000 kW demand 200,000 kWh	50,000 kW demand 32,500,000 kWh
City	189	1,458	20,554	1,784,521
Average[1]	201	1,653	26,124	2,639,743

Note: Figures are based on annualized 2014 rates; (1) Average based on 180 utilities surveyed
Source: Edison Electric Institute, Typical Bills and Average Rates Report, Summer 2014

TRANSPORTATION

Means of Transportation to Work

Area	Car/Truck/Van		Public Transportation			Bicycle	Walked	Other Means	Worked at Home
	Drove Alone	Car-pooled	Bus	Subway	Railroad				
City	76.0	9.9	4.0	0.0	0.0	0.6	3.7	0.6	5.2
MSA[1]	76.7	10.5	2.5	0.0	0.0	0.5	3.0	0.9	5.9
U.S.	76.4	9.6	2.6	1.8	0.6	0.6	2.8	1.3	4.3

Note: Figures are percentages and cover workers 16 years of age and older; (1) Figures cover the Spokane-Spokane Valley, WA Metropolitan Statistical Area—see Appendix B for areas included
Source: U.S. Census Bureau, 2011-2013 American Community Survey 3-Year Estimates

Travel Time to Work

Area	Less Than 10 Minutes	10 to 19 Minutes	20 to 29 Minutes	30 to 44 Minutes	45 to 59 Minutes	60 to 89 Minutes	90 Minutes or More
City	16.2	40.0	23.3	14.5	2.7	1.7	1.5
MSA[1]	15.1	34.4	24.1	17.4	4.7	2.5	1.7
U.S.	13.3	29.7	20.9	20.2	7.7	5.7	2.6

Note: Figures are percentages and include workers 16 years old and over; (1) Figures cover the Spokane-Spokane Valley, WA Metropolitan Statistical Area—see Appendix B for areas included
Source: U.S. Census Bureau, 2011-2013 American Community Survey 3-Year Estimates

Travel Time Index

Area	1985	1990	1995	2000	2005	2010	2011
Urban Area[1]	1.07	1.10	1.13	1.17	1.12	1.12	1.12
Average[2]	1.09	1.14	1.16	1.19	1.23	1.18	1.18

Note: Travel Time Index—the ratio of travel time in the peak period to the travel time at free-flow conditions. For example, a value of 1.30 indicates a 20-minute free-flow trip takes 26 minutes in the peak. Free-flow speeds (60 mph on freeways and 35 mph on principal arterials) are used as the comparison threshold; (1) Covers the Spokane WA-ID urban area; (2) average of 498 urban areas
Source: Texas Transportation Institute, Urban Mobility Report 2012, December 2012

Public Transportation

Agency Name / Mode of Transportation	Vehicles Operated in Maximum Service	Annual Unlinked Passenger Trips (in thous.)	Annual Passenger Miles (in thous.)
Spokane Transit Authority (STA)			
Bus (directly operated)	114	11,087.0	47,944.9
Demand Response (directly operated)	57	251.3	1,902.1
Demand Response (purchased transportation)	48	231.8	1,657.6
Vanpool (directly operated)	98	241.3	6,084.7

Source: Federal Transit Administration, National Transit Database, 2013

Air Transportation

Airport Name and Code / Type of Service	Passenger Airlines[1]	Passenger Enplanements	Freight Carriers[2]	Freight (lbs.)
Spokane International (GEG)				
Domestic service (U.S. carriers - 2014)	20	1,444,816	10	71,530,437
International service (U.S. carriers - 2013)	2	371	2	1,026,168

Note: (1) Includes all U.S.-based major, minor and commuter airlines that carried at least one passenger during the year; (2) Includes all U.S.-based airlines and freight carriers that transported at least one lb. of freight during the year.
Source: Bureau of Transportation Statistics, The Intermodal Transportation Database, Air Carriers: T-100 Domestic Market (U.S. Carriers), 2014; Bureau of Transportation Statistics, The Intermodal Transportation Database, Air Carriers: T-100 International Market (U.S. Carriers), 2013

Other Transportation Statistics

Major Highways:	I-90
Amtrak Service:	Yes
Major Waterways/Ports:	Spokane River

Source: Amtrak.com; Google Maps

BUSINESSES

Major Business Headquarters

Company Name	Rankings	
	Fortune[1]	Forbes[2]
No companies listed	-	-

Note: (1) Fortune 500—companies that produce a 10-K are ranked 1 to 500 based on 2013 revenue; (2) all private companies with at least $2 billion in annual revenue through the end of their most current fiscal year are ranked 1 to 221; companies listed are headquartered in the city; dashes indicate no ranking
Source: Fortune, "Fortune 500," June 16, 2014; Forbes, "America's Largest Private Companies," November 5, 2014

Fast-Growing Businesses

According to *Inc.*, Spokane is home to one of America's 500 fastest-growing private companies: **etailz** (#313). Criteria: must be an independent, privately-held, for-profit, U.S. corporation, proprietorship or partnership; revenues must be at least $100,000 in 2010 and $2 million in 2013; must have four-year operating/sales history. Holding companies, regulated banks, and utilities were excluded. *Inc.*, *"America's 500 Fastest-Growing Private Companies," September 2014*

Minority- and Women-Owned Businesses

Group	All Firms		Firms with Paid Employees			
	Firms	Sales ($000)	Firms	Sales ($000)	Employees	Payroll ($000)
Asian	495	167,237	156	149,698	1,911	23,628
Black	(s)	(s)	(s)	(s)	(s)	(s)
Hispanic	281	128,907	54	125,522	597	18,453
Women	4,421	550,598	614	461,612	4,457	117,083
All Firms	18,014	18,131,041	5,413	17,567,352	99,629	3,666,612

Note: Figures cover firms located in the city; minority- and women-owned business are defined as firms in which the corresponding group own 51% or more of the stock or equity of the company; (s) estimates are suppressed when publication standards are not met
Source: U.S. Census Bureau, 2007 Economic Census, Survey of Business Owners (2012 Survey of Business Owners data will be released starting in June 2015)

HOTELS & CONVENTION CENTERS

Hotels/Motels

Area	5 Star		4 Star		3 Star		2 Star		1 Star		Not Rated	
	Num.	Pct.[3]	Num.	Pct.[3]	Num.	Pct.[3]	Num.	Pct.[3]	Num.	Pct.[3]	Num.	Pct.[3]
City[1]	0	0.0	3	3.4	26	29.5	54	61.4	1	1.1	4	4.5
Total[2]	166	0.9	1,264	7.0	5,718	31.8	9,340	52.0	411	2.3	1,070	6.0

Note: (1) Figures cover Spokane and vicinity; (2) Figures cover all 100 cities in this book; (3) Percentage of hotels which have a given star rating; Star ratings are determined by expedia.com and offer an indication of the general quality of a particular hotel.
Source: expedia.com, April 2, 2015

Major Convention Centers

Name	Overall Space (sq. ft.)	Exhibit Space (sq. ft.)	Meeting Space (sq. ft.)	Meeting Rooms
Spokane Convention Center	164,307	100,160	35,732	23

Note: Table includes convention centers located in the Spokane-Spokane Valley, WA metro area; n/a not available
Source: Original research

Living Environment

COST OF LIVING

Cost of Living Index

Composite Index	Groceries	Housing	Utilities	Trans-portation	Health Care	Misc. Goods/ Services
95.4	91.6	87.5	79.0	103.1	111.8	104.1

Note: The Cost of Living Index measures regional differences in the cost of consumer goods and services, excluding taxes and non-consumer expenditures, for professional and managerial households in the top income quintile. It is based on more than 50,000 prices covering almost 60 different items for which prices are collected three times a year by chambers of commerce, economic development organizations or university applied economic centers in each participating urban area. The numbers shown should be read as a percentage above or below the national average of 100. For example, a value of 115.4 in the groceries column indicates that grocery prices are 15.4% higher than the national average. Small differences in the index numbers should not be interpreted as significant; Figures cover the Spokane WA urban area.
Source: The Council for Community and Economic Research, ACCRA Cost of Living Index, 2014

Grocery Prices

Area[1]	T-Bone Steak ($/pound)	Frying Chicken ($/pound)	Whole Milk ($/half gal.)	Eggs ($/dozen)	Orange Juice ($/64 oz.)	Coffee ($/11.5 oz.)
City[2]	10.80	1.51	1.89	1.93	3.00	4.55
Avg.	10.40	1.37	2.40	1.99	3.46	4.27
Min.	8.48	0.93	1.37	1.30	2.83	2.99
Max.	14.20	2.44	3.62	4.02	6.42	6.96

*Note: (1) Values for the local area are compared with the average, minimum and maximum values for all 308 areas in the Cost of Living Index; (2) Figures cover the Spokane WA urban area; **T-Bone Steak** (price per pound); **Frying Chicken** (price per pound, whole fryer); **Whole Milk** (half gallon carton); **Eggs** (price per dozen, Grade A, large); **Orange Juice** (64 oz. Tropicana or Florida Natural); **Coffee** (11.5 oz. can, vacuum-packed, Maxwell House, Hills Bros, or Folgers).*
Source: The Council for Community and Economic Research, ACCRA Cost of Living Index, 2014

Housing and Utility Costs

Area[1]	New Home Price ($)	Apartment Rent ($/month)	All Electric ($/month)	Part Electric ($/month)	Other Energy ($/month)	Telephone ($/month)
City[2]	274,248	740	-	55.87	77.90	22.09
Avg.	305,838	919	181.00	93.66	73.14	27.95
Min.	183,142	480	112.00	42.06	23.42	17.16
Max.	1,358,576	3,851	594.00	180.03	440.99	40.42

*Note: (1) Values for the local area are compared with the average, minimum and maximum values for all 308 areas in the Cost of Living Index; (2) Figures cover the Spokane WA urban area; **New Home Price** (2,400 sf living area, 8,000 sf lot, in urban area with full utilities); **Apartment Rent** (950 sf 2 bedroom/1.5 or 2 bath, unfurnished, excluding all utilities except water); **All Electric** (average monthly cost for an all-electric home); **Part Electric** (average monthly cost for a part-electric home); **Other Energy** (average monthly cost for natural gas, fuel oil, coal, wood, and any other forms of energy except electricity); **Telephone** (price includes basic monthly rate for a private residential line plus additional local usage charges incurred by a family of four).*
Source: The Council for Community and Economic Research, ACCRA Cost of Living Index, 2014

Health Care, Transportation, and Other Costs

Area[1]	Doctor ($/visit)	Dentist ($/visit)	Optometrist ($/visit)	Gasoline ($/gallon)	Beauty Salon ($/visit)	Men's Shirt ($)
City[2]	126.67	97.88	118.51	3.59	30.50	22.41
Avg.	102.86	87.89	97.66	3.44	34.37	26.74
Min.	67.47	65.78	51.18	3.00	17.43	12.79
Max.	173.50	150.14	235.00	4.33	64.28	49.50

*Note: (1) Values for the local area are compared with the average, minimum and maximum values for all 308 areas in the Cost of Living Index; (2) Figures cover the Spokane WA urban area; **Doctor** (general practitioners routine exam of an established patient); **Dentist** (adult teeth cleaning and periodic oral examination); **Optometrist** (full vision eye exam for established adult patient); **Gasoline** (one gallon regular unleaded, national brand, including all taxes, cash price at self-service pump if available); **Beauty Salon** (woman's shampoo, trim, and blow-dry); **Men's Shirt** (cotton/polyester dress shirt, pinpoint weave, long sleeves).*
Source: The Council for Community and Economic Research, ACCRA Cost of Living Index, 2014

HOUSING

House Price Index (HPI)

Area	National Ranking[2]	Quarterly Change (%)	One-Year Change (%)	Five-Year Change (%)
MSA[1]	133	-0.72	4.34	-5.75
U.S.[3]	–	1.35	4.91	11.59

Note: The HPI is a weighted repeat sales index. It measures average price changes in repeat sales or refinancings on the same properties. This information is obtained by reviewing repeat mortgage transactions on single-family properties whose mortgages have been purchased or securitized by Fannie Mae or Freddie Mac in January 1975; (1) Spokane-Spokane Valley Metropolitan Statistical Area—see Appendix B for areas included; (2) Rankings are based on annual percentage change for all metro areas containing at least 15,000 transactions over the last 10 years and ranges from 1 to 275; (3) figures based on a weighted average of Census Division estimates using a seasonally adjusted, purchase-only index; all figures are for the period ending December 31, 2014
Source: Federal Housing Finance Agency, House Price Index, February 26, 2015

Median Single-Family Home Prices

Area	2012	2013	2014p	Percent Change 2013 to 2014
MSA[1]	169.5	174.2	178.3	2.4
U.S. Average	177.2	197.4	209.0	5.9

Note: Figures are median sales prices of existing single-family homes in thousands of dollars; (p) preliminary; n/a not available; (1) Spokane-Spokane Valley, WA Metropolitan Statistical Area—see Appendix B for areas included
Source: National Association of Realtors, Median Sales Price of Existing Single-Family Homes for Metropolitan Areas, 4th Quarter 2014

Qualifying Income Based on Median Sales Price of Existing Single-Family Homes

Area	With 5% Down ($)	With 10% Down ($)	With 20% Down ($)
MSA[1]	38,875	36,829	32,736
U.S. Average	45,863	43,449	38,621

Note: Figures are preliminary; Qualifying income is based on a mortgage rate of 4.0%. Monthly principal and interest payment is limited to 25% of income; n/a not available; (1) Spokane-Spokane Valley, WA Metropolitan Statistical Area—see Appendix B for areas included
Source: National Association of Realtors, Qualifying Income Based on Median Sales Price of Existing Single-Family Homes for Metropolitan Areas, 4th Quarter 2014

Median Apartment Condo-Coop Home Prices

Area	2012	2013	2014p	Percent Change 2013 to 2014
MSA[1]	n/a	n/a	n/a	n/a
U.S. Average	173.7	194.9	205.1	5.2

Note: Figures are median sales prices of existing apartment condo-coop homes in thousands of dollars; (p) preliminary; n/a not available; (1) Spokane-Spokane Valley, WA Metropolitan Statistical Area—see Appendix B for areas included
Source: National Association of Realtors, Median Sales Price of Existing Apartment Condo-Coop Homes for Metropolitan Areas, 4th Quarter 2014

Gross Monthly Rent

Area	Under $200	$200 -299	$300 -499	$500 -749	$750 -999	$1,000 -1,499	$1,500 and up	Median ($)
City	2.4	4.2	11.9	34.6	25.5	17.5	3.9	732
MSA[1]	1.7	3.6	10.9	32.9	28.0	18.3	4.7	757
U.S.	1.7	3.2	7.8	22.1	24.3	26.0	14.9	900

Note: Figures are percentages except for Median; Gross rent is the contract rent plus the estimated average monthly cost of utilities (electricity, gas, and water and sewer) and fuels (oil, coal, kerosene, wood, etc.) if these are paid by the renter (or paid for the renter by someone else); (1) Figures cover the Spokane-Spokane Valley, WA Metropolitan Statistical Area—see Appendix B for areas included
Source: U.S. Census Bureau, 2011-2013 American Community Survey 3-Year Estimates

Homeownership Rate

Area	2007 (%)	2008 (%)	2009 (%)	2010 (%)	2011 (%)	2012 (%)	2013 (%)	2014 (%)
MSA[1]	n/a	n/a	n/a	n/a	n/a	n/a	n/a	n/a
U.S.	68.1	67.8	67.4	66.9	66.1	65.4	65.1	64.5

Note: (1) Figures cover the Spokane-Spokane Valley, WA Metropolitan Statistical Area—see Appendix B for areas included; n/a not available
Source: U.S. Census Bureau, Housing Vacancies and Homeownership Annual Statistics: 2014

Year Housing Structure Built

Area	2010 or Later	2000 -2009	1990 -1999	1980 -1989	1970 -1979	1960 -1969	1950 -1959	1940 -1949	Before 1940	Median Year
City	0.6	8.7	8.3	8.5	15.0	6.7	15.2	9.8	27.2	1959
MSA[1]	1.0	15.4	14.2	10.7	19.2	7.1	11.1	6.2	15.2	1975
U.S.	0.9	15.0	13.9	13.8	15.8	11.0	10.9	5.4	13.3	1976

Note: Figures are percentages except for Median Year; (1) Figures cover the Spokane-Spokane Valley, WA Metropolitan Statistical Area—see Appendix B for areas included
Source: U.S. Census Bureau, 2011-2013 American Community Survey 3-Year Estimates

HEALTH

Health Risk Data

Category	MSA[1] (%)	U.S. (%)
Adults aged 18–64 who have any kind of health care coverage	77.5	79.6
Adults who reported being in good or excellent health	85.1	83.1
Adults who are current smokers	18.4	19.6
Adults who are heavy drinkers[2]	8.1	6.1
Adults who are binge drinkers[3]	17.2	16.9
Adults who are overweight (BMI 25.0 - 29.9)	32.1	35.8
Adults who are obese (BMI 30.0 - 99.8)	28.9	27.6
Adults who participated in any physical activities in the past month	79.5	77.1
Adults 50+ who have ever had a sigmoidoscopy or colonoscopy	69.8	67.3
Women aged 40+ who have had a mammogram within the past two years	70.8	74.0
Men aged 40+ who have had a PSA test within the past two years	40.1	45.2
Adults aged 65+ who have had flu shot within the past year	59.1	60.1
Adults who always wear a seatbelt	97.5	93.8

Note: Data as of 2012 unless otherwise noted; (1) Figures cover the Spokane, WA Metropolitan Statistical Area—see Appendix B for areas included; (2) Heavy drinkers are classified as males having more than two drinks per day or females having more than one drink per day; (3) Binge drinkers are classified as males having five or more drinks on one occasion or females having four or more drinks on one occasion
Source: Centers for Disease Control and Prevention, Behaviorial Risk Factor Surveillance System, SMART: Selected Metropolitan/Micropolitan Area Risk Trends, 2012 (Note: the CDC has discontinued this dataset but will be releasing a replacement in late 2015)

Chronic Health Indicators

Category	MSA[1] (%)	U.S. (%)
Adults who have ever been told they had a heart attack	3.5	4.5
Adults who have ever been told they had a stroke	2.5	2.9
Adults who have been told they currently have asthma	10.8	8.9
Adults who have ever been told they have arthritis	30.0	25.7
Adults who have ever been told they have diabetes[2]	9.2	9.7
Adults who have ever been told they had skin cancer	5.5	5.7
Adults who have ever been told they had any other types of cancer	6.7	6.5
Adults who have ever been told they have COPD	7.2	6.2
Adults who have ever been told they have kidney disease	3.7	2.5
Adults who have ever been told they have a form of depression	21.6	18.0

Note: Data as of 2012 unless otherwise noted; (1) Figures cover the Spokane, WA Metropolitan Statistical Area—see Appendix B for areas included; (2) Figures do not include pregnancy-related, borderline, or pre-diabetes
Source: Centers for Disease Control and Prevention, Behaviorial Risk Factor Surveillance System, SMART: Selected Metropolitan/Micropolitan Area Risk Trends, 2012 (Note: the CDC has discontinued this dataset but will be releasing a replacement in late 2015)

Mortality Rates for the Top 10 Causes of Death in the U.S.

ICD-10[a] Sub-Chapter	ICD-10[a] Code	Age-Adjusted Mortality Rate[1] per 100,000 population	
		County[2]	U.S.
Malignant neoplasms	C00-C97	171.3	166.2
Ischaemic heart diseases	I20-I25	84.4	105.7
Other forms of heart disease	I30-I51	42.1	49.3
Chronic lower respiratory diseases	J40-J47	54.4	42.1
Organic, including symptomatic, mental disorders	F01-F09	32.1	38.1
Cerebrovascular diseases	I60-I69	41.1	37.0
Other external causes of accidental injury	W00-X59	46.9	26.9
Other degenerative diseases of the nervous system	G30-G31	44.6	25.6
Diabetes mellitus	E10-E14	24.7	21.3
Hypertensive diseases	I10-I15	16.9	19.4

Note: (a) ICD-10 = International Classification of Diseases 10th Revision; (1) Mortality rates are a three year average covering 2011-2013; (2) Figures cover Spokane County
Source: Centers for Disease Control and Prevention, National Center for Health Statistics. Compressed Mortality File 1999-2013 on CDC WONDER Online Database, released October 2014. Data are compiled from the Compressed Mortality File 1999-2013, Series 20 No. 2S, 2014.

Mortality Rates for Selected Causes of Death

ICD-10[a] Sub-Chapter	ICD-10[a] Code	Age-Adjusted Mortality Rate[1] per 100,000 population	
		County[2]	U.S.
Assault	X85-Y09	3.4	5.2
Diseases of the liver	K70-K76	16.5	13.2
Human immunodeficiency virus (HIV) disease	B20-B24	*0.7	2.2
Influenza and pneumonia	J09-J18	12.3	15.4
Intentional self-harm	X60-X84	15.9	12.5
Malnutrition	E40-E46	1.3	0.9
Obesity and other hyperalimentation	E65-E68	2.2	1.8
Renal failure	N17-N19	7.0	13.1
Transport accidents	V01-V99	8.8	11.7
Viral hepatitis	B15-B19	3.0	2.2

Note: (a) ICD-10 = International Classification of Diseases 10th Revision; (1) Mortality rates are a three year average covering 2011-2013; (2) Figures cover Spokane County; (*) Unreliable data as per CDC
Source: Centers for Disease Control and Prevention, National Center for Health Statistics. Compressed Mortality File 1999-2013 on CDC WONDER Online Database, released October 2014. Data are compiled from the Compressed Mortality File 1999-2013, Series 20 No. 2S, 2014.

Health Insurance Coverage

Area	With Health Insurance	With Private Health Insurance	With Public Health Insurance	Without Health Insurance	Population Under Age 18 Without Health Insurance
City	85.4	60.9	36.0	14.6	5.5
MSA[1]	86.2	64.4	34.8	13.8	6.0
U.S.	85.2	65.2	31.0	14.8	7.3

Note: Figures are percentages that cover the civilian noninstitutionalized population; (1) Figures cover the Spokane-Spokane Valley, WA Metropolitan Statistical Area—see Appendix B for areas included
Source: U.S. Census Bureau, 2011-2013 American Community Survey 3-Year Estimates

Number of Medical Professionals

Area[1]	MDs[2]	DOs[2,3]	Dentists	Podiatrists	Chiropractors	Optometrists
Local (number)	1,292	93	353	23	133	88
Local (rate[4])	271.6	19.5	73.6	4.8	27.7	18.4
U.S. (rate[4])	270.0	20.2	63.1	5.7	25.2	14.9

Note: Data as of 2013 unless noted; (1) Local data covers Spokane County; (2) Data as of 2012 and includes all active, non-federal physicians; (3) Doctor of Osteopathic Medicine; (4) rate per 100,000 population
Source: U.S. Department of Health and Human Services, Health Resources and Services Administration, Bureau of Health Professions, Area Resource File (ARF) 2013-2014

EDUCATION

Public School District Statistics

District Name	Schls	Pupils	Pupil/ Teacher Ratio	Minority Pupils[1] (%)	Free Lunch Eligible[2] (%)	IEP[3] (%)
East Valley School District (Spokane)	9	4,567	19.6	20.8	43.8	14.1
Spokane School District	62	29,032	17.5	28.8	49.8	14.1
West Valley School District (Spokane)	11	3,841	20.0	19.8	43.9	14.0

Note: Table includes school districts with 2,000 or more students; (1) Percentage of students that are not non-Hispanic white; (2) Percentage of students that are eligible for the free lunch program; (3) Percentage of students that have an Individualized Education Program.
Source: U.S. Department of Education, National Center for Education Statistics, Common Core of Data, Local Education Agency (School District) Universe Survey: School Year 2012-2013; U.S. Department of Education, National Center for Education Statistics, Common Core of Data, Public Elementary/Secondary School Universe Survey: School Year 2012-2013

Best High Schools

According to *The Daily Beast*, Spokane is home to two of the best high schools in the U.S.: **Lewis and Clark High School** (#649); **North Central High School** (#748); *The Daily Beast* used six indicators culled from school surveys to compare public high schools in the U.S., with graduation and college acceptance rates weighed most heavily. Other criteria included: college-level courses/exams and SAT/ACT scores. *The Daily Beast, "Top High Schools 2014"*

Highest Level of Education

Area	Less than H.S.	H.S. Diploma	Some College, No Deg.	Associate Degree	Bachelor's Degree	Master's Degree	Prof. School Degree	Doctorate Degree
City	9.2	26.1	25.8	10.4	17.6	7.4	2.3	1.3
MSA[1]	7.7	27.0	27.0	11.4	17.4	6.7	1.8	1.0
U.S.	13.7	28.0	21.2	7.9	18.2	7.7	1.9	1.3

Note: Figures cover persons age 25 and over; (1) Figures cover the Spokane-Spokane Valley, WA Metropolitan Statistical Area—see Appendix B for areas included
Source: U.S. Census Bureau, 2011-2013 American Community Survey 3-Year Estimates

Educational Attainment by Race

Area	High School Graduate or Higher (%)					Bachelor's Degree or Higher (%)				
	Total	White	Black	Asian	Hisp.[2]	Total	White	Black	Asian	Hisp.[2]
City	90.8	91.8	85.4	76.7	81.1	28.5	29.5	18.0	24.3	20.8
MSA[1]	92.3	93.0	84.0	82.9	80.4	26.9	27.6	15.7	27.5	18.8
U.S.	86.3	88.3	83.1	85.7	64.0	29.1	30.4	18.8	50.7	13.7

Note: Figures shown cover persons 25 years old and over; (1) Figures cover the Spokane-Spokane Valley, WA Metropolitan Statistical Area—see Appendix B for areas included; (2) People of Hispanic origin can be of any race
Source: U.S. Census Bureau, 2011-2013 American Community Survey 3-Year Estimates

School Enrollment by Grade and Control

Area	Preschool (%)		Kindergarten (%)		Grades 1 - 4 (%)		Grades 5 - 8 (%)		Grades 9 - 12 (%)	
	Public	Private	Public	Private	Public	Private	Public	Private	Public	Private
City	32.1	67.9	83.1	16.9	87.9	12.1	93.5	6.5	93.5	6.5
MSA[1]	40.4	59.6	84.1	15.9	89.6	10.4	90.9	9.1	93.0	7.0
U.S.	57.7	42.3	87.9	12.1	89.9	10.1	90.0	10.0	90.7	9.3

Note: Figures shown cover persons 3 years old and over; (1) Figures cover the Spokane-Spokane Valley, WA Metropolitan Statistical Area—see Appendix B for areas included
Source: U.S. Census Bureau, 2011-2013 American Community Survey 3-Year Estimates

Average Salaries of Public School Classroom Teachers

Area	2013-14		2014-15		Percent Change 2013-14 to 2014-15	Percent Change 2004-05 to 2014-15
	Dollars	Rank[1]	Dollars	Rank[1]		
WASHINGTON	52,969	23	53,714	23	1.41	17.5
U.S. Average	56,610	–	57,379	–	1.36	20.8

Note: (1) State rank ranges from 1 to 51 where 1 indicates highest salary.
Source: National Education Association, Rankings & Estimates: Rankings of the States 2014 and Estimates of School Statistics 2015, March 2015

Higher Education

Four-Year Colleges			Two-Year Colleges			Medical Schools[1]	Law Schools[2]	Voc/Tech[3]
Public	Private Non-profit	Private For-profit	Public	Private Non-profit	Private For-profit			
0	3	0	2	0	3	0	1	3

Note: Figures cover institutions located within the city limits and include main campuses only; (1) includes schools accredited by the Liaison Committee on Medical Education and the American Osteopathic Association's Commission on Osteopathic College Accreditation; (2) includes ABA-accredited schools, schools with provisional ABA accreditation, and state accredited schools; (3) includes all schools with programs that are less than 2 years.
Source: National Center for Education Statistics, Integrated Postsecondary Education System (IPEDS), 2013-14; Association of American Medical Colleges, Member List, May 1, 2015; American Osteopathic Association, Member List, May 1, 2015; Law School Admission Council, Official Guide to ABA-Approved Law Schools Online, May 1, 2015; Wikipedia, List of Medical Schools in the United States, May 1, 2015; Wikipedia, List of Law Schools in the United States, May 1, 2015

PRESIDENTIAL ELECTION

2012 Presidential Election Results

Area	Obama (%)	Romney (%)	Other (%)
Spokane County	45.6	51.6	2.8
U.S.	51.0	47.2	1.8

Note: Results may not add to 100% due to rounding
Source: Dave Leip's Atlas of U.S. Presidential Elections

EMPLOYERS

Major Employers

Company Name	Industry
92nd Air Refueling Wing, & Fairchild AFB	Military
Central Valley School District	Education
City of Spokane	Government
Community College of Spokane	Education
Deaconess Medical Center	Healthcare
Gonzaga University	Education
Northern Quest Resort & Casino	Hotel/casino
Providence Sacred Heart Medical Center	Healthcare
Rockwood Clinic PS	Healthcare
Spokane County	Government
Spokane Public Schools	Education
State of Washington	Government
URM Stores	Distribution
Walmart	Retail
West Corp.	Customer service

Note: Companies shown are located within the Spokane-Spokane Valley, WA Metropolitan Statistical Area.
Source: Hoovers.com; Wikipedia

PUBLIC SAFETY

Crime Rate

Area	All Crimes	Violent Crimes				Property Crimes		
		Murder	Forcible Rape	Robbery	Aggrav. Assault	Burglary	Larceny -Theft	Motor Vehicle Theft
City	10,008.9	5.2	79.2	247.2	355.6	1,856.1	6,372.5	1,093.0
Suburbs[1]	3,607.3	2.8	26.7	43.3	87.8	779.1	2,348.3	319.4
Metro[2]	6,113.6	3.7	47.3	123.1	192.7	1,200.7	3,923.8	622.2
U.S.	3,098.6	4.5	25.2	109.1	229.1	610.0	1,899.4	221.3

Note: Figures are crimes per 100,000 population; (1) All areas within the metro area that are located outside the city limits; (2) Figures cover the Spokane-Spokane Valley, WA Metropolitan Statistical Area—see Appendix B for areas included
Source: FBI Uniform Crime Reports, 2013

Hate Crimes

Area	Number of Quarters Reported	Number of Incidents per Bias Motivation						
		Race	Religion	Sexual Orientation	Ethnicity	Disability	Gender	Gender Identity
City	3	1	0	1	0	0	0	0
U.S.	4	2,871	1,031	1,233	655	83	18	31

Source: Federal Bureau of Investigation, Hate Crime Statistics 2013

Identity Theft Consumer Complaints

Area	Complaints	Complaints per 100,000 Population	Rank[2]
MSA[1]	484	90.3	89
U.S.	332,646	104.3	-

Note: (1) Figures cover the Spokane-Spokane Valley, WA Metropolitan Statistical Area—see Appendix B for areas included; (2) Rank ranges from 1 to 380 where 1 indicates greatest number of identity theft complaints per 100,000 population
Source: Federal Trade Commission, Consumer Sentinel Network Data Book for January–December 2014

Fraud and Other Consumer Complaints

Area	Complaints	Complaints per 100,000 Population	Rank[2]
MSA[1]	2,595	484.4	29
U.S.	2,250,205	705.7	-

Note: (1) Figures cover the Spokane-Spokane Valley, WA Metropolitan Statistical Area—see Appendix B for areas included; (2) Rank ranges from 1 to 380 where 1 indicates greatest number of identity theft complaints per 100,000 population
Source: Federal Trade Commission, Consumer Sentinel Network Data Book for January–December 2014

RECREATION

Culture

Dance[1]	Theatre[1]	Instrumental Music[1]	Vocal Music[1]	Series and Festivals	Museums and Art Galleries[2]	Zoos and Aquariums[3]
0	3	1	0	1	15	0

Note: (1) Professional perfoming groups; (2) Based on organizations with SIC code 8412; (3) AZA-accredited
Source: The Grey House Performing Arts Directory, 2015-16; Association of Zoos & Aquariums, AZA Member Zoos & Aquariums, April 2015; www.AccuLeads.com, April 2015

Professional Sports Teams

Team Name	League	Year Established
No teams are located in the metro area		

Source: Wikipedia, Major Professional Sports Teams of the United States and Canada, April 2015

CLIMATE

Average and Extreme Temperatures

Temperature	Jan	Feb	Mar	Apr	May	Jun	Jul	Aug	Sep	Oct	Nov	Dec	Yr.
Extreme High (°F)	59	61	71	90	96	100	103	108	98	86	67	56	108
Average High (°F)	31	39	47	57	66	74	83	82	72	58	42	33	57
Average Temp. (°F)	26	32	38	46	55	62	69	68	60	48	35	28	47
Average Low (°F)	20	25	29	35	42	50	55	54	46	37	29	22	37
Extreme Low (°F)	-24	-22	-7	17	24	33	37	35	24	11	-21	-25	-25

Note: Figures cover the years 1948-1990
Source: National Climatic Data Center, International Station Meteorological Climate Summary, 9/96

Average Precipitation/Snowfall/Humidity

Precip./Humidity	Jan	Feb	Mar	Apr	May	Jun	Jul	Aug	Sep	Oct	Nov	Dec	Yr.
Avg. Precip. (in.)	2.3	1.6	1.5	1.1	1.5	1.3	0.6	0.7	0.8	1.2	2.2	2.4	17.0
Avg. Snowfall (in.)	16	8	4	1	Tr	Tr	0	0	0	Tr	6	15	51
Avg. Rel. Hum. 7am (%)	85	85	80	72	68	64	56	59	69	81	87	88	74
Avg. Rel. Hum. 4pm (%)	79	70	55	43	41	36	27	28	34	51	75	83	52

Note: Figures cover the years 1948-1990; Tr = Trace amounts (<0.05 in. of rain; <0.5 in. of snow)
Source: National Climatic Data Center, International Station Meteorological Climate Summary, 9/96

Weather Conditions

Temperature			Daytime Sky			Precipitation		
5°F & below	32°F & below	90°F & above	Clear	Partly cloudy	Cloudy	0.01 inch or more precip.	0.1 inch or more snow/ice	Thunder-storms
9	140	18	78	135	152	113	37	11

Note: Figures are average number of days per year and cover the years 1948-1990
Source: National Climatic Data Center, International Station Meteorological Climate Summary, 9/96

HAZARDOUS WASTE

Superfund Sites

Spokane has six hazardous waste sites on the EPA's Superfund Final National Priorities List: **Colbert Landfill; Fairchild Air Force Base (4 Waste Areas); General Electric Co. (Spokane Shop); Greenacres Landfill; North Market Street; Northside Landfill.** There are a total of 1,322 Superfund sites on the list in the U.S. *U.S. Environmental Protection Agency, Final National Priorities List, April 14, 2015*

AIR & WATER QUALITY

Air Quality Trends: Ozone

	2004	2005	2006	2007	2008	2009	2010	2011	2012	2013
MSA[1]	0.065	0.063	0.066	0.064	0.058	0.057	0.058	0.056	0.063	0.062

Note: (1) Data covers the Spokane-Spokane Valley, WA Metropolitan Statistical Area—see Appendix B for areas included. The values shown are the composite ozone concentration averages among trend sites based on the highest fourth daily maximum 8-hour concentration in parts per million. These trends are based on sites having an adequate record of monitoring data during the trend period. Data from exceptional events are included.
Source: U.S. Environmental Protection Agency, Air Quality Monitoring Information, "Air Quality Trends by City, 2000-2013"

Air Quality Index

Area	Percent of Days when Air Quality was...[2]					AQI Statistics[2]	
	Good	Moderate	Unhealthy for Sensitive Groups	Unhealthy	Very Unhealthy	Maximum	Median
MSA[1]	80.0	19.5	0.5	0.0	0.0	105	35

Note: (1) Data covers the Spokane-Spokane Valley, WA Metropolitan Statistical Area—see Appendix B for areas included; (2) Based on 365 days with AQI data in 2014. Air Quality Index (AQI) is an index for reporting daily air quality. EPA calculates the AQI for five major air pollutants regulated by the Clean Air Act: ground-level ozone, particle pollution (aka particulate matter), carbon monoxide, sulfur dioxide, and nitrogen dioxide. The AQI runs from 0 to 500. The higher the AQI value, the greater the level of air pollution and the greater the health concern. There are six AQI categories: "Good" AQI is between 0 and 50. Air quality is considered satisfactory; "Moderate" AQI is between 51 and 100. Air quality is acceptable; "Unhealthy for Sensitive Groups" When AQI values are between 101 and 150, members of sensitive groups may experience health effects; "Unhealthy" When AQI values are between 151 and 200 everyone may begin to experience health effects; "Very Unhealthy" AQI values between 201 and 300 trigger a health alert; "Hazardous" AQI values over 300 trigger warnings of emergency conditions (not shown).
Source: U.S. Environmental Protection Agency, Air Quality Index Report, 2014

Air Quality Index Pollutants

Area	Percent of Days when AQI Pollutant was...[2]					
	Carbon Monoxide	Nitrogen Dioxide	Ozone	Sulfur Dioxide	Particulate Matter 2.5	Particulate Matter 10
MSA[1]	0.8	0.0	24.1	0.0	60.8	14.2

Note: (1) Data covers the Spokane-Spokane Valley, WA Metropolitan Statistical Area—see Appendix B for areas included; (2) Based on 365 days with AQI data in 2014. The Air Quality Index (AQI) is an index for reporting daily air quality. EPA calculates the AQI for five major air pollutants regulated by the Clean Air Act: ground-level ozone, particle pollution (also known as particulate matter), carbon monoxide, sulfur dioxide, and nitrogen dioxide. The AQI runs from 0 to 500. The higher the AQI value, the greater the level of air pollution and the greater the health concern.
Source: U.S. Environmental Protection Agency, Air Quality Index Report, 2014

Maximum Air Pollutant Concentrations: Particulate Matter, Ozone, CO and Lead

	Particulate Matter 10 (ug/m^3)	Particulate Matter 2.5 Wtd AM (ug/m^3)	Particulate Matter 2.5 24-Hr (ug/m^3)	Ozone (ppm)	Carbon Monoxide (ppm)	Lead (ug/m^3)
MSA[1] Level	68	9.2	31	0.062	2	n/a
NAAQS[2]	150	15	35	0.075	9	0.15
Met NAAQS[2]	Yes	Yes	Yes	Yes	Yes	n/a

Note: (1) Data covers the Spokane-Spokane Valley, WA Metropolitan Statistical Area—see Appendix B for areas included; Data from exceptional events are included; (2) National Ambient Air Quality Standards; ppm = parts per million; ug/m^3 = micrograms per cubic meter; n/a not available.
Concentrations: Particulate Matter 10 (coarse particulate)—highest second maximum 24-hour concentration; Particulate Matter 2.5 Wtd AM (fine particulate)—highest weighted annual mean concentration; Particulate Matter 2.5 24-Hour (fine particulate)—highest 98th percentile 24-hour concentration; Ozone—highest fourth daily maximum 8-hour concentration; Carbon Monoxide—highest second maximum non-overlapping 8-hour concentration; Lead—maximum running 3-month average
Source: U.S. Environmental Protection Agency, Air Quality Monitoring Information, "Air Quality Statistics by City, 2013"

Maximum Air Pollutant Concentrations: Nitrogen Dioxide and Sulfur Dioxide

	Nitrogen Dioxide AM (ppb)	Nitrogen Dioxide 1-Hr (ppb)	Sulfur Dioxide AM (ppb)	Sulfur Dioxide 1-Hr (ppb)	Sulfur Dioxide 24-Hr (ppb)
MSA[1] Level	n/a	n/a	n/a	n/a	n/a
NAAQS[2]	53	100	30	75	140
Met NAAQS[2]	n/a	n/a	n/a	n/a	n/a

Note: (1) Data covers the Spokane-Spokane Valley, WA Metropolitan Statistical Area—see Appendix B for areas included; Data from exceptional events are included; (2) National Ambient Air Quality Standards; ppm = parts per million; ug/m^3 = micrograms per cubic meter; n/a not available.
Concentrations: Nitrogen Dioxide AM—highest arithmetic mean concentration; Nitrogen Dioxide 1-Hr—highest 98th percentile 1-hour daily maximum concentration; Sulfur Dioxide AM—highest annual mean concentration; Sulfur Dioxide 1-Hr—highest 99th percentile 1-hour daily maximum concentration; Sulfur Dioxide 24-Hr—highest second maximum 24-hour concentration
Source: U.S. Environmental Protection Agency, Air Quality Monitoring Information, "Air Quality Statistics by City, 2013"

Drinking Water

Water System Name	Pop. Served	Primary Water Source Type	Violations[1] Health Based	Violations[1] Monitoring/ Reporting
City of Spokane	227,455	Ground	0	0

Note: (1) Based on violation data from January 1, 2014 to December 31, 2014 (includes unresolved violations from earlier years)
Source: U.S. Environmental Protection Agency, Office of Ground Water and Drinking Water, Safe Drinking Water Information System (based on data extracted January 27, 2015)

Appendix A: Comparative Statistics

Population Growth: City

City	1990 Census	2000 Census	2010 Census	Population Growth (%)	
				1990-2000	2000-2010
Albuquerque, NM	388,375	448,607	545,852	15.5	21.7
Anchorage, AK	226,338	260,283	291,826	15.0	12.1
Ann Arbor, MI	111,018	114,024	113,934	2.7	-0.1
Athens, GA	86,561	100,266	115,452	15.8	15.1
Atlanta, GA	394,092	416,474	420,003	5.7	0.8
Austin, TX	499,053	656,562	790,390	31.6	20.4
Billings, MT	81,812	89,847	104,170	9.8	15.9
Boise City, ID	144,317	185,787	205,671	28.7	10.7
Boston, MA	574,283	589,141	617,594	2.6	4.8
Boulder, CO	87,737	94,673	97,385	7.9	2.9
Cape Coral, FL	75,507	102,286	154,305	35.5	50.9
Cedar Rapids, IA	110,829	120,758	126,326	9.0	4.6
Charleston, SC	96,102	96,650	120,083	0.6	24.2
Charlotte, NC	428,283	540,828	731,424	26.3	35.2
Chicago, IL	2,783,726	2,896,016	2,695,598	4.0	-6.9
Clarksville, TN	78,569	103,455	132,929	31.7	28.5
Colorado Springs, CO	283,798	360,890	416,427	27.2	15.4
Columbia, MO	71,069	84,531	108,500	18.9	28.4
Columbus, OH	648,656	711,470	787,033	9.7	10.6
Dallas, TX	1,006,971	1,188,580	1,197,816	18.0	0.8
Davenport, IA	95,705	98,359	99,685	2.8	1.3
Denver, CO	467,153	554,636	600,158	18.7	8.2
Des Moines, IA	193,569	198,682	203,433	2.6	2.4
Durham, NC	151,737	187,035	228,330	23.3	22.1
El Paso, TX	515,541	563,662	649,121	9.3	15.2
Erie, PA	108,718	103,717	101,786	-4.6	-1.9
Eugene, OR	118,073	137,893	156,185	16.8	13.3
Fargo, ND	74,372	90,599	105,549	21.8	16.5
Fayetteville, NC	118,247	121,015	200,564	2.3	65.7
Fort Collins, CO	89,555	118,652	143,986	32.5	21.4
Fort Wayne, IN	205,671	205,727	253,691	0.0	23.3
Fort Worth, TX	448,311	534,694	741,206	19.3	38.6
Gainesville, FL	90,519	95,447	124,354	5.4	30.3
Grand Rapids, MI	189,145	197,800	188,040	4.6	-4.9
Green Bay, WI	96,466	102,313	104,057	6.1	1.7
Greensboro, NC	193,389	223,891	269,666	15.8	20.4
Honolulu, HI	376,465	371,657	337,256	-1.3	-9.3
Houston, TX	1,697,610	1,953,631	2,099,451	15.1	7.5
Huntsville, AL	161,842	158,216	180,105	-2.2	13.8
Indianapolis, IN	730,993	781,870	820,445	7.0	4.9
Jacksonville, FL	635,221	735,617	821,784	15.8	11.7
Kansas City, MO	434,967	441,545	459,787	1.5	4.1
Lafayette, LA	104,735	110,257	120,623	5.3	9.4
Las Vegas, NV	261,374	478,434	583,756	83.0	22.0
Lexington, KY	225,366	260,512	295,803	15.6	13.5
Lincoln, NE	193,629	225,581	258,379	16.5	14.5
Little Rock, AR	177,519	183,133	193,524	3.2	5.7
Los Angeles, CA	3,487,671	3,694,820	3,792,621	5.9	2.6
Louisville, KY	269,160	256,231	597,337	-4.8	133.1
Lubbock, TX	187,170	199,564	229,573	6.6	15.0
Madison, WI	193,451	208,054	233,209	7.5	12.1
Manchester, NH	99,567	107,006	109,565	7.5	2.4
McAllen, TX	86,145	106,414	129,877	23.5	22.0
Miami, FL	358,843	362,470	399,457	1.0	10.2
Midland, TX	89,358	94,996	111,147	6.3	17.0

Table continued on next page.

City	1990 Census	2000 Census	2010 Census	Population Growth (%)	
				1990-2000	2000-2010
Minneapolis, MN	368,383	382,618	382,578	3.9	0.0
Nashville, TN	488,364	545,524	601,222	11.7	10.2
New Orleans, LA	496,938	484,674	343,829	-2.5	-29.1
New York, NY	7,322,552	8,008,278	8,175,133	9.4	2.1
Oklahoma City, OK	445,065	506,132	579,999	13.7	14.6
Omaha, NE	371,972	390,007	408,958	4.8	4.9
Orlando, FL	161,172	185,951	238,300	15.4	28.2
Oxnard, CA	143,271	170,358	197,899	18.9	16.2
Palm Bay, FL	62,587	79,413	103,190	26.9	29.9
Peoria, IL	114,341	112,936	115,007	-1.2	1.8
Philadelphia, PA	1,585,577	1,517,550	1,526,006	-4.3	0.6
Phoenix, AZ	989,873	1,321,045	1,445,632	33.5	9.4
Pittsburgh, PA	369,785	334,563	305,704	-9.5	-8.6
Portland, OR	485,833	529,121	583,776	8.9	10.3
Providence, RI	160,734	173,618	178,042	8.0	2.5
Provo, UT	87,148	105,166	112,488	20.7	7.0
Raleigh, NC	226,841	276,093	403,892	21.7	46.3
Reno, NV	139,950	180,480	225,221	29.0	24.8
Richmond, VA	202,783	197,790	204,214	-2.5	3.2
Roanoke, VA	96,415	94,911	97,032	-1.6	2.2
Rochester, MN	74,151	85,806	106,769	15.7	24.4
Sacramento, CA	368,923	407,018	466,488	10.3	14.6
Salem, OR	112,046	136,924	154,637	22.2	12.9
Salt Lake City, UT	159,796	181,743	186,440	13.7	2.6
San Antonio, TX	997,258	1,144,646	1,327,407	14.8	16.0
San Diego, CA	1,111,048	1,223,400	1,307,402	10.1	6.9
San Francisco, CA	723,959	776,733	805,235	7.3	3.7
San Jose, CA	784,324	894,943	945,942	14.1	5.7
Santa Rosa, CA	123,297	147,595	167,815	19.7	13.7
Savannah, GA	138,038	131,510	136,286	-4.7	3.6
Seattle, WA	516,262	563,374	608,660	9.1	8.0
Sioux Falls, SD	102,262	123,975	153,888	21.2	24.1
Spokane, WA	178,202	195,629	208,916	9.8	6.8
Springfield, IL	108,997	111,454	116,250	2.3	4.3
Tallahassee, FL	128,014	150,624	181,376	17.7	20.4
Tampa, FL	279,960	303,447	335,709	8.4	10.6
Topeka, KS	121,197	122,377	127,473	1.0	4.2
Tulsa, OK	367,241	393,049	391,906	7.0	-0.3
Tyler, TX	77,653	83,650	96,900	7.7	15.8
Virginia Beach, VA	393,069	425,257	437,994	8.2	3.0
Washington, DC	606,900	572,059	601,723	-5.7	5.2
Wichita, KS	313,693	344,284	382,368	9.8	11.1
Wilmington, NC	64,609	75,838	106,476	17.4	40.4
Winston-Salem, NC	168,139	185,776	229,617	10.5	23.6
Worcester, MA	169,759	172,648	181,045	1.7	4.9
U.S.	248,709,873	281,421,906	308,745,538	13.2	9.7

Source: U.S. Census Bureau, Census 2010, 2000, 1990

Population Growth: Metro Area

Metro Area	1990 Census	2000 Census	2010 Census	Population Growth (%) 1990-2000	2000-2010
Albuquerque, NM	599,416	729,649	887,077	21.7	21.6
Anchorage, AK	266,021	319,605	380,821	20.1	19.2
Ann Arbor, MI	282,937	322,895	344,791	14.1	6.8
Athens, GA	136,025	166,079	192,541	22.1	15.9
Atlanta, GA	3,069,411	4,247,981	5,268,860	38.4	24.0
Austin, TX	846,217	1,249,763	1,716,289	47.7	37.3
Billings, MT	121,499	138,904	158,050	14.3	13.8
Boise City, ID	319,596	464,840	616,561	45.4	32.6
Boston, MA	4,133,895	4,391,344	4,552,402	6.2	3.7
Boulder, CO	208,898	269,758	294,567	29.1	9.2
Cape Coral, FL	335,113	440,888	618,754	31.6	40.3
Cedar Rapids, IA	210,640	237,230	257,940	12.6	8.7
Charleston, SC	506,875	549,033	664,607	8.3	21.1
Charlotte, NC	1,024,331	1,330,448	1,758,038	29.9	32.1
Chicago, IL	8,182,076	9,098,316	9,461,105	11.2	4.0
Clarksville, TN	189,277	232,000	273,949	22.6	18.1
Colorado Springs, CO	409,482	537,484	645,613	31.3	20.1
Columbia, MO	122,010	145,666	172,786	19.4	18.6
Columbus, OH	1,405,176	1,612,694	1,836,536	14.8	13.9
Dallas, TX	3,989,294	5,161,544	6,371,773	29.4	23.4
Davenport, IA	368,151	376,019	379,690	2.1	1.0
Denver, CO	1,666,935	2,179,296	2,543,482	30.7	16.7
Des Moines, IA	416,346	481,394	569,633	15.6	18.3
Durham, NC	344,646	426,493	504,357	23.7	18.3
El Paso, TX	591,610	679,622	800,647	14.9	17.8
Erie, PA	275,603	280,843	280,566	1.9	-0.1
Eugene, OR	282,912	322,959	351,715	14.2	8.9
Fargo, ND	153,296	174,367	208,777	13.7	19.7
Fayetteville, NC	297,422	336,609	366,383	13.2	8.8
Fort Collins, CO	186,136	251,494	299,630	35.1	19.1
Fort Wayne, IN	354,435	390,156	416,257	10.1	6.7
Fort Worth, TX	3,989,294	5,161,544	6,371,773	29.4	23.4
Gainesville, FL	191,263	232,392	264,275	21.5	13.7
Grand Rapids, MI	645,914	740,482	774,160	14.6	4.5
Green Bay, WI	243,698	282,599	306,241	16.0	8.4
Greensboro, NC	540,257	643,430	723,801	19.1	12.5
Honolulu, HI	836,231	876,156	953,207	4.8	8.8
Houston, TX	3,767,335	4,715,407	5,946,800	25.2	26.1
Huntsville, AL	293,047	342,376	417,593	16.8	22.0
Indianapolis, IN	1,294,217	1,525,104	1,756,241	17.8	15.2
Jacksonville, FL	925,213	1,122,750	1,345,596	21.4	19.8
Kansas City, MO	1,636,528	1,836,038	2,035,334	12.2	10.9
Lafayette, LA	208,740	239,086	273,738	14.5	14.5
Las Vegas, NV	741,459	1,375,765	1,951,269	85.5	41.8
Lexington, KY	348,428	408,326	472,099	17.2	15.6
Lincoln, NE	229,091	266,787	302,157	16.5	13.3
Little Rock, AR	535,034	610,518	699,757	14.1	14.6
Los Angeles, CA	11,273,720	12,365,627	12,828,837	9.7	3.7
Louisville, KY	1,055,973	1,161,975	1,283,566	10.0	10.5
Lubbock, TX	229,940	249,700	284,890	8.6	14.1
Madison, WI	432,323	501,774	568,593	16.1	13.3
Manchester, NH	336,073	380,841	400,721	13.3	5.2
McAllen, TX	383,545	569,463	774,769	48.5	36.1
Miami, FL	4,056,100	5,007,564	5,564,635	23.5	11.1
Midland, TX	106,611	116,009	136,872	8.8	18.0

Table continued on next page.

Metro Area	1990 Census	2000 Census	2010 Census	Population Growth (%) 1990-2000	Population Growth (%) 2000-2010
Minneapolis, MN	2,538,834	2,968,806	3,279,833	16.9	10.5
Nashville, TN	1,048,218	1,311,789	1,589,934	25.1	21.2
New Orleans, LA	1,264,391	1,316,510	1,167,764	4.1	-11.3
New York, NY	16,845,992	18,323,002	18,897,109	8.8	3.1
Oklahoma City, OK	971,042	1,095,421	1,252,987	12.8	14.4
Omaha, NE	685,797	767,041	865,350	11.8	12.8
Orlando, FL	1,224,852	1,644,561	2,134,411	34.3	29.8
Oxnard, CA	669,016	753,197	823,318	12.6	9.3
Palm Bay, FL	398,978	476,230	543,376	19.4	14.1
Peoria, IL	358,552	366,899	379,186	2.3	3.3
Philadelphia, PA	5,435,470	5,687,147	5,965,343	4.6	4.9
Phoenix, AZ	2,238,480	3,251,876	4,192,887	45.3	28.9
Pittsburgh, PA	2,468,289	2,431,087	2,356,285	-1.5	-3.1
Portland, OR	1,523,741	1,927,881	2,226,009	26.5	15.5
Providence, RI	1,509,789	1,582,997	1,600,852	4.8	1.1
Provo, UT	269,407	376,774	526,810	39.9	39.8
Raleigh, NC	541,081	797,071	1,130,490	47.3	41.8
Reno, NV	257,193	342,885	425,417	33.3	24.1
Richmond, VA	949,244	1,096,957	1,258,251	15.6	14.7
Roanoke, VA	268,465	288,309	308,707	7.4	7.1
Rochester, MN	141,945	163,618	186,011	15.3	13.7
Sacramento, CA	1,481,126	1,796,857	2,149,127	21.3	19.6
Salem, OR	278,024	347,214	390,738	24.9	12.5
Salt Lake City, UT	768,075	968,858	1,124,197	26.1	16.0
San Antonio, TX	1,407,745	1,711,703	2,142,508	21.6	25.2
San Diego, CA	2,498,016	2,813,833	3,095,313	12.6	10.0
San Francisco, CA	3,686,592	4,123,740	4,335,391	11.9	5.1
San Jose, CA	1,534,280	1,735,819	1,836,911	13.1	5.8
Santa Rosa, CA	388,222	458,614	483,878	18.1	5.5
Savannah, GA	258,060	293,000	347,611	13.5	18.6
Seattle, WA	2,559,164	3,043,878	3,439,809	18.9	13.0
Sioux Falls, SD	153,500	187,093	228,261	21.9	22.0
Spokane, WA	361,364	417,939	471,221	15.7	12.7
Springfield, IL	189,550	201,437	210,170	6.3	4.3
Tallahassee, FL	259,096	320,304	367,413	23.6	14.7
Tampa, FL	2,067,959	2,395,997	2,783,243	15.9	16.2
Topeka, KS	210,257	224,551	233,870	6.8	4.2
Tulsa, OK	761,019	859,532	937,478	12.9	9.1
Tyler, TX	151,309	174,706	209,714	15.5	20.0
Virginia Beach, VA	1,449,389	1,576,370	1,671,683	8.8	6.0
Washington, DC	4,122,914	4,796,183	5,582,170	16.3	16.4
Wichita, KS	511,111	571,166	623,061	11.7	9.1
Wilmington, NC	200,124	274,532	362,315	37.2	32.0
Winston-Salem, NC	361,091	421,961	477,717	16.9	13.2
Worcester, MA	709,728	750,963	798,552	5.8	6.3
U.S.	248,709,873	281,421,906	308,745,538	13.2	9.7

Note: Figures cover the Metropolitan Statistical Area (MSA)—see Appendix B for areas included
Source: U.S. Census Bureau, Census 2010, 2000, 1990

Household Size: City

City	Persons in Household (%)							Average Household Size
	One	Two	Three	Four	Five	Six	Seven or More	
Albuquerque, NM	32.4	32.8	15.3	11.5	5.0	2.2	0.8	2.46
Anchorage, AK	26.3	33.1	17.1	13.0	5.7	2.6	2.2	2.77
Ann Arbor, MI	38.3	34.0	13.2	9.0	3.1	1.9	0.5	2.24
Athens, GA	34.3	33.9	14.6	11.5	3.4	1.5	0.8	2.63
Atlanta, GA	46.6	29.9	11.2	7.5	2.9	1.3	0.7	2.26
Austin, TX	33.8	33.1	14.8	10.7	4.7	1.6	1.2	2.46
Billings, MT	32.3	35.5	13.8	10.5	5.9	1.3	0.8	2.38
Boise City, ID	30.6	35.0	16.4	11.1	4.5	1.9	0.6	2.39
Boston, MA	37.7	31.4	14.8	9.7	3.9	1.6	1.0	2.37
Boulder, CO	33.1	36.1	16.0	10.3	3.7	0.7	0.2	2.26
Cape Coral, FL	22.0	41.5	15.7	11.2	6.5	1.8	1.2	2.87
Cedar Rapids, IA	33.0	34.9	13.7	11.7	3.9	1.7	1.1	2.39
Charleston, SC	36.8	35.9	14.1	9.3	2.9	0.5	0.4	2.28
Charlotte, NC	31.5	31.4	16.0	12.6	5.5	2.0	1.1	2.56
Chicago, IL	36.7	28.0	14.1	10.6	5.8	2.6	2.2	2.59
Clarksville, TN	22.0	32.0	19.2	15.5	6.8	2.3	2.0	2.72
Colorado Springs, CO	29.1	34.1	15.0	13.3	5.4	2.1	1.1	2.53
Columbia, MO	33.1	32.9	15.3	12.8	4.2	1.4	0.3	2.37
Columbus, OH	36.7	30.8	14.7	9.8	4.9	1.9	1.3	2.41
Dallas, TX	34.6	28.4	14.0	11.5	6.6	3.0	2.0	2.62
Davenport, IA	34.5	31.7	15.6	9.6	5.7	1.5	1.3	2.44
Denver, CO	40.6	31.5	12.0	8.3	4.2	2.0	1.4	2.30
Des Moines, IA	32.3	29.9	16.2	11.0	6.5	2.4	1.8	2.48
Durham, NC	34.2	33.8	14.4	10.9	4.0	2.0	0.7	2.35
El Paso, TX	23.2	26.6	18.9	16.6	8.9	3.6	2.2	3.01
Erie, PA	36.6	32.0	14.0	9.8	4.3	1.5	1.9	2.33
Eugene, OR	33.0	36.1	15.6	9.4	3.9	1.3	0.7	2.30
Fargo, ND	36.3	34.4	15.0	8.4	4.4	1.3	0.3	2.18
Fayetteville, NC	29.6	35.1	17.0	11.7	4.5	1.3	0.8	2.48
Fort Collins, CO	26.2	36.5	19.0	11.7	4.6	1.5	0.6	2.46
Fort Wayne, IN	33.1	30.6	16.1	11.5	5.3	2.3	1.1	2.46
Fort Worth, TX	27.1	28.4	15.2	15.0	8.3	3.5	2.4	2.87
Gainesville, FL	37.7	35.3	14.9	9.1	1.9	1.0	0.1	2.35
Grand Rapids, MI	33.1	31.5	13.7	11.8	5.8	2.3	1.7	2.51
Green Bay, WI	32.8	33.9	13.5	11.9	4.7	1.7	1.5	2.38
Greensboro, NC	33.9	33.2	15.0	11.2	4.4	1.5	0.8	2.34
Honolulu, HI	33.9	30.9	14.6	10.3	4.6	2.6	3.1	2.59
Houston, TX	32.2	29.3	15.0	11.8	7.0	2.7	2.1	2.70
Huntsville, AL	37.1	33.0	13.8	9.9	4.2	1.2	0.8	2.31
Indianapolis, IN	34.1	31.9	14.7	10.8	5.0	2.2	1.2	2.50
Jacksonville, FL	31.2	33.2	16.4	11.7	4.7	1.6	1.3	2.62
Kansas City, MO	36.3	32.9	13.6	10.2	4.3	1.6	1.1	2.38
Lafayette, LA	35.2	32.6	14.8	11.4	4.3	0.7	1.0	2.40
Las Vegas, NV	28.7	31.4	15.2	13.0	6.6	3.0	2.1	2.78
Lexington, KY	32.8	33.9	15.7	11.2	4.0	1.7	0.6	2.37
Lincoln, NE	31.1	35.2	14.2	11.3	5.1	2.0	1.0	2.38
Little Rock, AR	38.1	35.0	13.7	8.3	3.5	0.7	0.7	2.44
Los Angeles, CA	30.3	27.9	15.4	13.2	7.1	3.2	2.8	2.84
Louisville, KY	32.8	32.5	15.4	11.8	4.9	1.7	0.9	2.43
Lubbock, TX	29.5	33.1	15.2	13.4	5.1	2.3	1.3	2.55
Madison, WI	37.1	35.0	13.3	9.9	3.1	1.2	0.5	2.20
Manchester, NH	32.7	34.8	14.4	10.9	4.8	1.4	0.9	2.36
McAllen, TX	21.9	25.1	18.8	15.5	11.1	5.0	2.6	3.20
Miami, FL	36.5	30.3	15.4	10.3	4.2	1.8	1.4	2.66

le continued on next page.

City	Persons in Household (%)							Average Household Size
	One	Two	Three	Four	Five	Six	Seven or More	
Midland, TX	24.3	32.7	18.4	13.5	6.7	2.6	1.9	2.80
Minneapolis, MN	40.0	32.4	11.4	8.9	3.8	1.6	1.9	2.27
Nashville, TN	36.8	32.2	13.8	10.3	4.0	1.6	1.1	2.41
New Orleans, LA	40.6	29.9	14.4	8.5	4.2	1.3	1.1	2.35
New York, NY	33.1	27.6	16.1	12.4	6.0	2.6	2.2	2.66
Oklahoma City, OK	31.1	32.2	15.4	11.4	6.1	2.4	1.4	2.57
Omaha, NE	33.9	31.8	13.7	10.7	6.1	2.1	1.7	2.47
Orlando, FL	37.7	32.9	13.6	10.5	3.4	1.2	0.6	2.41
Oxnard, CA	14.7	21.9	16.7	18.4	12.5	6.8	8.9	3.93
Palm Bay, FL	26.4	37.5	16.2	10.2	5.8	2.0	1.9	2.76
Peoria, IL	36.7	31.2	13.1	10.7	4.5	2.5	1.2	2.37
Philadelphia, PA	40.0	27.3	14.7	9.9	4.7	2.0	1.4	2.58
Phoenix, AZ	28.8	30.2	15.0	13.0	6.8	3.4	2.7	2.83
Pittsburgh, PA	41.3	33.2	12.7	8.1	3.2	0.9	0.6	2.14
Portland, OR	35.1	33.8	14.4	10.0	3.8	1.7	1.2	2.34
Providence, RI	30.8	27.0	18.5	14.3	5.9	1.9	1.5	2.67
Provo, UT	14.0	33.1	17.7	16.3	9.0	5.6	4.3	3.30
Raleigh, NC	33.1	32.0	15.4	12.4	4.4	1.8	0.8	2.43
Reno, NV	34.6	32.0	13.7	10.9	5.1	2.3	1.3	2.50
Richmond, VA	40.6	31.4	14.7	8.0	3.6	1.0	0.7	2.34
Roanoke, VA	36.7	33.3	15.1	9.3	3.2	1.0	1.4	2.27
Rochester, MN	31.7	33.5	13.6	12.6	5.6	1.7	1.3	2.45
Sacramento, CA	33.0	29.2	14.2	11.7	5.8	3.2	2.8	2.65
Salem, OR	29.7	32.1	14.9	12.6	6.6	2.7	1.5	2.59
Salt Lake City, UT	36.1	30.4	13.9	10.0	4.8	2.6	2.3	2.48
San Antonio, TX	28.5	29.1	16.5	13.2	7.4	3.0	2.3	2.82
San Diego, CA	29.0	32.4	15.7	12.8	5.7	2.5	1.9	2.73
San Francisco, CA	38.4	33.1	13.0	9.1	3.5	1.5	1.4	2.31
San Jose, CA	19.7	27.6	18.7	18.2	8.7	3.6	3.4	3.12
Santa Rosa, CA	28.9	32.1	15.3	13.2	6.9	1.6	2.0	2.67
Savannah, GA	35.4	31.6	15.3	9.3	5.1	2.1	1.1	2.54
Seattle, WA	41.3	33.2	12.2	8.7	2.9	1.0	0.8	2.12
Sioux Falls, SD	29.6	36.4	14.3	10.6	5.4	2.5	1.2	2.43
Spokane, WA	34.4	34.2	13.2	11.3	4.4	1.6	0.9	2.33
Springfield, IL	37.3	33.0	14.3	9.1	3.6	1.8	0.9	2.24
Tallahassee, FL	32.7	34.3	17.9	10.4	3.2	1.0	0.5	2.34
Tampa, FL	37.4	31.3	14.7	10.6	3.9	1.3	0.9	2.40
Topeka, KS	36.1	33.1	12.4	10.1	4.5	2.3	1.5	2.35
Tulsa, OK	34.8	32.5	14.0	10.3	5.1	2.1	1.2	2.38
Tyler, TX	32.7	32.0	16.5	11.2	3.4	2.0	2.1	2.49
Virginia Beach, VA	24.2	34.1	18.5	14.1	6.1	1.8	1.2	2.64
Washington, DC	44.7	30.1	12.1	7.6	3.4	1.3	0.8	2.21
Wichita, KS	32.5	32.0	14.1	11.6	5.8	2.2	1.8	2.53
Wilmington, NC	36.3	35.1	14.9	10.4	2.1	0.7	0.4	2.20
Winston-Salem, NC	34.8	32.0	13.9	11.3	4.4	2.5	1.1	2.43
Worcester, MA	32.4	29.7	16.3	12.4	6.1	1.9	1.2	2.52
U.S.	27.7	33.6	15.7	13.1	6.0	2.3	1.5	2.64

U.S. Census Bureau, 2011-2013 American Community Survey 3-Year Estimates

Household Size: Metro Area

Metro Area	Persons in Household (%)							Average Household Size
	One	Two	Three	Four	Five	Six	Seven or More	
Albuquerque, NM	29.5	33.8	15.3	12.1	5.6	2.5	1.2	2.59
Anchorage, AK	25.2	34.1	16.7	13.0	5.8	2.8	2.3	2.80
Ann Arbor, MI	31.2	34.3	14.6	12.6	4.8	1.6	0.8	2.44
Athens, GA	29.2	34.5	15.7	13.2	4.6	1.7	1.1	2.70
Atlanta, GA	26.6	31.4	16.6	14.8	6.5	2.5	1.5	2.78
Austin, TX	27.8	33.1	15.9	13.5	6.1	2.3	1.4	2.68
Billings, MT	29.8	37.1	13.4	11.5	5.6	1.5	1.0	2.44
Boise City, ID	24.1	34.7	15.5	13.9	6.8	3.0	1.8	2.71
Boston, MA	28.4	32.5	16.3	14.4	5.8	1.8	0.9	2.54
Boulder, CO	28.2	36.1	15.4	13.2	5.1	1.5	0.6	2.44
Cape Coral, FL	28.1	43.7	11.9	9.6	4.2	1.7	0.8	2.64
Cedar Rapids, IA	29.4	36.1	13.9	12.9	5.0	1.7	1.0	2.45
Charleston, SC	28.3	35.3	16.7	12.5	4.8	1.6	0.8	2.58
Charlotte, NC	26.7	33.8	17.0	13.5	5.9	2.1	1.1	2.66
Chicago, IL	28.5	29.9	15.8	14.2	7.1	2.8	1.8	2.73
Clarksville, TN	22.1	32.9	18.6	14.4	7.1	2.9	2.0	2.72
Colorado Springs, CO	25.7	35.0	15.6	14.2	6.0	2.3	1.2	2.63
Columbia, MO	30.3	34.7	16.0	12.4	4.6	1.4	0.5	2.42
Columbus, OH	29.4	33.2	15.6	12.9	5.7	2.0	1.1	2.55
Dallas, TX	25.2	30.8	16.6	15.0	7.5	3.0	1.8	2.80
Davenport, IA	31.4	35.2	14.1	11.3	5.4	1.6	1.1	2.42
Denver, CO	29.6	33.3	15.0	12.8	5.5	2.3	1.4	2.56
Des Moines, IA	27.0	34.2	15.9	13.6	6.2	2.0	1.1	2.52
Durham, NC	30.7	35.7	15.0	11.7	4.4	1.7	0.7	2.43
El Paso, TX	21.4	25.9	19.1	17.2	9.8	4.0	2.8	3.13
Erie, PA	30.2	35.4	14.6	11.8	5.1	1.8	1.1	2.44
Eugene, OR	29.4	38.0	15.2	10.3	4.4	1.6	1.0	2.39
Fargo, ND	31.8	34.4	15.2	11.4	5.1	1.7	0.5	2.34
Fayetteville, NC	28.0	32.5	18.3	12.9	5.6	1.6	1.1	2.60
Fort Collins, CO	25.4	39.4	16.1	12.2	4.7	1.6	0.7	2.45
Fort Wayne, IN	29.0	32.7	16.0	12.8	5.8	2.3	1.2	2.54
Fort Worth, TX	25.2	30.8	16.6	15.0	7.5	3.0	1.8	2.80
Gainesville, FL	32.8	35.9	15.2	10.7	3.5	1.1	0.7	2.47
Grand Rapids, MI	24.8	34.4	15.5	14.2	7.2	2.6	1.3	2.65
Green Bay, WI	27.6	36.5	14.2	13.7	5.5	1.6	1.0	2.47
Greensboro, NC	28.6	35.2	16.1	12.2	5.0	1.8	1.0	2.47
Honolulu, HI	23.7	30.1	17.1	14.1	7.2	3.4	4.3	3.04
Houston, TX	24.4	29.9	16.9	15.3	8.1	3.2	2.1	2.91
Huntsville, AL	29.3	34.6	15.9	12.7	5.0	1.4	0.9	2.50
Indianapolis, IN	28.6	33.3	15.8	13.2	5.9	2.2	1.0	2.58
Jacksonville, FL	28.4	34.9	16.2	12.5	5.1	1.8	1.0	2.65
Kansas City, MO	28.7	34.0	15.3	12.9	5.8	2.1	1.2	2.54
Lafayette, LA	27.9	32.2	17.8	12.9	5.8	2.1	1.3	2.63
Las Vegas, NV	27.8	32.0	15.4	13.1	6.7	3.2	2.0	2.79
Lexington, KY	29.6	35.0	16.0	12.2	4.5	1.9	0.7	2.45
Lincoln, NE	29.5	35.8	14.2	11.8	5.5	2.1	1.0	2.43
Little Rock, AR	29.7	36.6	15.4	11.4	4.8	1.4	0.6	2.58
Los Angeles, CA	24.9	28.1	16.4	15.4	8.3	3.7	3.2	3.03
Louisville, KY	29.2	34.3	15.8	12.9	5.3	1.7	0.8	2.51
Lubbock, TX	27.7	33.8	15.5	13.4	5.9	2.3	1.5	2.61
Madison, WI	30.2	36.7	14.6	11.8	4.3	1.7	0.7	2.37
Manchester, NH	25.3	35.7	16.0	14.8	5.8	1.5	1.0	2.56
McAllen, TX	15.9	23.7	17.8	17.4	13.0	6.7	5.6	3.60
Miami, FL	29.1	32.1	16.3	13.3	5.7	2.1	1.3	2.81

Table continued on next page.

Metro Area	Persons in Household (%)							Average Household Size
	One	Two	Three	Four	Five	Six	Seven or More	
Midland, TX	24.2	32.9	17.4	14.0	7.1	2.4	1.9	2.81
Minneapolis, MN	27.9	33.8	15.0	13.8	6.0	2.1	1.3	2.54
Nashville, TN	28.2	34.1	15.7	13.2	5.6	1.9	1.2	2.60
New Orleans, LA	31.4	32.5	16.3	11.8	5.3	1.6	1.1	2.56
New York, NY	28.1	28.9	16.9	14.7	6.8	2.6	1.9	2.75
Oklahoma City, OK	28.7	33.9	15.6	12.5	6.0	2.2	1.2	2.60
Omaha, NE	28.8	33.7	14.5	12.8	6.6	2.2	1.4	2.56
Orlando, FL	26.5	35.1	16.5	13.1	5.7	1.9	1.1	2.82
Oxnard, CA	20.7	30.5	17.3	16.0	8.3	3.7	3.5	3.08
Palm Bay, FL	30.5	39.9	13.4	10.0	4.1	1.1	1.0	2.48
Peoria, IL	29.8	36.0	13.6	12.5	5.0	2.0	1.1	2.45
Philadelphia, PA	29.7	31.2	16.4	13.5	6.0	2.1	1.2	2.63
Phoenix, AZ	26.8	34.8	14.3	12.7	6.4	3.0	2.1	2.76
Pittsburgh, PA	32.4	35.3	14.9	11.4	4.2	1.2	0.6	2.33
Portland, OR	27.6	34.6	15.7	13.0	5.6	2.0	1.5	2.57
Providence, RI	29.6	32.9	16.6	13.5	5.1	1.6	0.9	2.49
Provo, UT	12.5	26.4	15.8	17.2	12.5	9.2	6.3	3.64
Raleigh, NC	25.9	32.7	17.0	15.2	6.1	2.0	1.1	2.65
Reno, NV	29.7	34.9	14.3	12.4	5.0	2.3	1.4	2.59
Richmond, VA	28.6	34.1	16.6	13.2	5.1	1.7	0.8	2.60
Roanoke, VA	29.3	37.4	15.2	11.2	4.4	1.2	1.1	2.37
Rochester, MN	27.7	36.1	13.9	13.6	5.9	1.7	1.2	2.51
Sacramento, CA	26.2	32.7	15.9	13.7	6.6	2.9	2.0	2.73
Salem, OR	25.0	34.4	15.4	12.2	7.7	3.1	2.1	2.72
Salt Lake City, UT	22.8	29.5	16.0	14.2	8.8	4.8	3.9	3.04
San Antonio, TX	25.4	30.9	16.7	14.1	7.4	3.0	2.3	2.86
San Diego, CA	24.9	32.7	16.8	14.3	6.5	2.8	2.1	2.86
San Francisco, CA	28.4	31.5	16.3	13.8	5.9	2.4	1.7	2.67
San Jose, CA	21.6	29.2	18.6	17.4	7.7	2.9	2.6	2.94
Santa Rosa, CA	28.3	34.2	15.2	13.2	5.8	1.7	1.5	2.60
Savannah, GA	28.4	33.9	16.1	13.3	5.4	2.1	1.0	2.64
Seattle, WA	28.9	33.5	15.9	13.3	5.1	2.0	1.2	2.54
Sioux Falls, SD	26.9	36.5	14.2	12.2	6.3	2.5	1.4	2.53
Spokane, WA	28.9	37.1	13.7	12.0	5.3	1.9	1.2	2.46
Springfield, IL	31.3	35.1	15.5	10.7	4.8	1.8	0.9	2.36
Tallahassee, FL	28.9	35.0	18.0	11.8	4.0	1.5	0.9	2.46
Tampa, FL	32.0	36.0	14.3	10.9	4.2	1.5	0.9	2.49
Topeka, KS	29.9	36.0	13.2	11.7	5.4	2.3	1.6	2.46
Tulsa, OK	28.1	34.4	15.6	12.5	5.9	2.2	1.3	2.55
Tyler, TX	26.7	34.9	15.6	12.3	5.9	2.5	2.1	2.65
Virginia Beach, VA	26.2	34.3	17.8	12.9	5.8	1.8	1.1	2.62
Washington, DC	27.3	30.6	16.7	14.6	6.6	2.7	1.5	2.73
Wichita, KS	29.3	33.4	14.3	12.5	6.2	2.6	1.6	2.59
Wilmington, NC	30.3	36.8	15.7	11.9	3.4	1.3	0.6	2.41
Winston-Salem, NC	29.3	35.7	15.2	12.0	4.6	2.2	0.9	2.49
Worcester, MA	26.6	32.6	17.2	14.9	6.0	2.0	0.8	2.60
U.S.	27.7	33.6	15.7	13.1	6.0	2.3	1.5	2.64

Note: Figures cover the Metropolitan Statistical Area (MSA)—see Appendix B for areas included
Source: U.S. Census Bureau, 2011-2013 American Community Survey 3-Year Estimates

Race: City

City	White Alone[1] (%)	Black Alone[1] (%)	Asian Alone[1] (%)	AIAN[2] Alone[1] (%)	NHOPI[3] Alone[1] (%)	Other Race Alone[1] (%)	Two or More Races (%)
Albuquerque, NM	72.0	3.5	2.6	4.2	0.1	13.7	3.9
Anchorage, AK	65.9	6.0	8.4	6.7	2.1	1.4	9.5
Ann Arbor, MI	73.7	7.4	14.4	0.2	0.0	0.5	3.7
Athens, GA	65.5	26.4	4.3	0.2	0.0	1.5	2.1
Atlanta, GA	40.5	52.8	3.7	0.2	0.0	1.0	1.7
Austin, TX	74.9	7.7	6.6	0.6	0.1	6.8	3.3
Billings, MT	89.0	1.1	1.1	4.4	0.1	1.7	2.7
Boise City, ID	89.6	1.2	3.6	0.7	0.2	1.4	3.4
Boston, MA	53.4	25.2	9.1	0.4	0.0	7.5	4.5
Boulder, CO	89.4	0.8	4.5	0.2	0.0	2.0	3.0
Cape Coral, FL	91.0	3.4	1.8	0.4	0.0	2.1	1.4
Cedar Rapids, IA	87.3	6.5	1.7	0.3	0.0	1.1	3.1
Charleston, SC	71.8	24.4	1.4	0.2	0.1	0.5	1.6
Charlotte, NC	52.0	35.1	5.3	0.4	0.1	4.4	2.7
Chicago, IL	48.4	31.7	5.8	0.3	0.0	11.5	2.3
Clarksville, TN	66.5	22.7	2.2	1.0	0.4	2.2	5.0
Colorado Springs, CO	80.2	6.2	2.9	0.6	0.3	5.0	4.8
Columbia, MO	79.5	9.7	5.6	0.2	0.0	0.8	4.2
Columbus, OH	61.6	27.7	4.4	0.2	0.0	2.3	3.7
Dallas, TX	58.5	24.6	3.0	0.2	0.0	11.6	2.1
Davenport, IA	81.1	11.3	2.3	0.3	0.0	1.4	3.5
Denver, CO	75.0	9.9	3.5	1.0	0.1	7.0	3.4
Des Moines, IA	77.7	10.5	5.0	0.3	0.1	3.2	3.2
Durham, NC	48.6	40.2	4.8	0.6	0.1	2.5	3.2
El Paso, TX	83.2	3.6	1.2	0.5	0.2	9.1	2.2
Erie, PA	75.6	15.8	2.3	0.4	0.0	1.9	4.0
Eugene, OR	85.7	1.4	4.2	1.1	0.4	2.6	4.5
Fargo, ND	89.6	3.0	2.7	1.4	0.0	0.5	2.7
Fayetteville, NC	47.3	41.1	2.8	0.9	0.5	2.5	4.9
Fort Collins, CO	89.6	1.2	2.9	0.4	0.2	2.0	3.7
Fort Wayne, IN	73.9	16.1	3.3	0.3	0.1	2.8	3.4
Fort Worth, TX	66.2	18.7	3.6	0.8	0.2	7.5	3.0
Gainesville, FL	65.5	23.0	6.8	0.3	0.1	1.0	3.3
Grand Rapids, MI	69.5	20.8	1.9	0.4	0.0	2.7	4.6
Green Bay, WI	82.4	3.8	4.5	2.8	0.0	2.6	3.9
Greensboro, NC	49.1	41.6	3.9	0.4	0.1	2.6	2.2
Honolulu, HI	18.0	1.9	54.2	0.1	8.1	0.7	17.1
Houston, TX	58.2	23.1	6.2	0.4	0.0	10.1	2.0
Huntsville, AL	62.3	31.0	2.1	0.5	0.1	1.2	2.9
Indianapolis, IN	61.5	27.8	2.2	0.3	0.0	5.4	2.8
Jacksonville, FL	60.4	30.5	4.4	0.3	0.1	1.0	3.3
Kansas City, MO	59.7	28.5	2.6	0.5	0.2	4.8	3.6
Lafayette, LA	64.2	30.9	2.0	0.3	0.0	0.7	1.8
Las Vegas, NV	65.3	11.6	6.6	0.6	0.6	10.9	4.4
Lexington, KY	76.2	14.6	3.6	0.3	0.0	2.9	2.5
Lincoln, NE	86.8	4.1	4.1	0.7	0.1	1.2	3.1
Little Rock, AR	51.6	42.3	3.0	0.3	0.0	1.1	1.6
Los Angeles, CA	52.4	9.1	11.4	0.5	0.2	22.8	3.5
Louisville, KY	71.1	22.7	2.3	0.1	0.0	0.8	2.9
Lubbock, TX	77.6	8.0	2.3	0.6	0.1	8.1	3.4
Madison, WI	79.9	7.2	8.0	0.4	0.0	1.5	3.0
Manchester, NH	85.8	4.7	4.5	0.1	0.0	2.4	2.5
McAllen, TX	87.9	0.8	2.6	0.5	0.0	6.8	1.4
Miami, FL	75.4	19.8	1.0	0.2	0.0	2.6	1.1

...le continued on next page.

City	White Alone[1] (%)	Black Alone[1] (%)	Asian Alone[1] (%)	AIAN[2] Alone[1] (%)	NHOPI[3] Alone[1] (%)	Other Race Alone[1] (%)	Two or More Races (%)
Midland, TX	79.0	7.8	1.6	0.3	0.1	9.1	2.0
Minneapolis, MN	66.2	17.9	5.8	1.4	0.0	3.8	4.8
Nashville, TN	60.9	28.4	3.2	0.3	0.1	4.9	2.3
New Orleans, LA	34.1	59.8	3.0	0.3	0.0	1.5	1.4
New York, NY	43.7	24.7	13.2	0.4	0.1	14.9	3.1
Oklahoma City, OK	68.0	14.2	4.2	3.1	0.0	3.9	6.6
Omaha, NE	76.2	12.9	2.8	0.6	0.0	4.5	2.9
Orlando, FL	59.3	27.6	3.6	0.3	0.0	6.5	2.7
Oxnard, CA	73.8	2.8	8.0	0.9	0.2	10.5	3.8
Palm Bay, FL	75.3	17.6	1.4	0.5	0.0	2.0	3.3
Peoria, IL	62.5	27.1	5.3	0.5	0.0	1.2	3.4
Philadelphia, PA	41.4	43.0	6.6	0.3	0.1	6.0	2.6
Phoenix, AZ	76.6	6.8	3.2	2.0	0.2	8.4	2.8
Pittsburgh, PA	66.6	24.9	5.0	0.2	0.0	0.4	2.9
Portland, OR	77.8	6.1	7.6	0.7	0.5	2.9	4.4
Providence, RI	50.7	16.1	6.6	1.1	0.1	21.6	3.8
Provo, UT	87.1	0.9	3.1	0.5	1.4	3.7	3.3
Raleigh, NC	60.3	29.6	4.4	0.2	0.1	3.2	2.1
Reno, NV	78.6	2.8	6.5	0.9	0.8	6.9	3.4
Richmond, VA	43.4	49.0	2.2	0.3	0.0	1.5	3.6
Roanoke, VA	64.9	27.1	2.1	0.4	0.2	0.8	4.5
Rochester, MN	82.4	6.5	6.9	0.2	0.0	1.0	3.0
Sacramento, CA	49.8	14.1	18.6	0.8	1.4	8.4	6.9
Salem, OR	80.4	1.2	3.0	0.8	1.0	8.8	4.8
Salt Lake City, UT	73.7	2.9	5.2	1.2	2.4	11.9	2.7
San Antonio, TX	76.2	6.9	2.4	0.7	0.1	10.9	2.7
San Diego, CA	64.1	6.7	16.7	0.6	0.4	6.7	4.8
San Francisco, CA	49.5	5.8	33.4	0.4	0.4	6.1	4.4
San Jose, CA	45.8	3.0	32.9	0.7	0.4	12.5	4.7
Santa Rosa, CA	74.6	2.4	4.9	1.8	0.7	11.2	4.5
Savannah, GA	41.9	53.4	1.7	0.3	0.1	0.8	1.7
Seattle, WA	70.0	7.6	14.0	0.7	0.3	1.8	5.7
Sioux Falls, SD	86.1	4.6	2.2	2.8	0.0	2.3	2.1
Spokane, WA	87.7	2.6	2.9	1.5	0.3	0.9	4.0
Springfield, IL	75.1	19.2	2.4	0.2	0.0	0.7	2.3
Tallahassee, FL	56.6	35.8	3.9	0.3	0.0	1.2	2.3
Tampa, FL	64.0	25.9	3.9	0.3	0.1	2.9	3.0
Topeka, KS	78.2	10.6	1.4	1.0	0.0	2.7	6.1
Tulsa, OK	66.4	15.1	2.5	4.2	0.1	4.2	7.5
Tyler, TX	69.3	23.9	2.1	0.4	0.0	2.5	1.8
Virginia Beach, VA	68.3	19.3	6.5	0.3	0.1	1.2	4.3
Washington, DC	40.2	49.4	3.6	0.3	0.0	4.0	2.5
Wichita, KS	76.0	11.3	4.8	1.0	0.0	2.6	4.4
Wilmington, NC	75.4	19.6	1.7	0.4	0.0	1.5	1.2
Winston-Salem, NC	58.6	34.4	1.9	0.2	0.2	2.7	1.9
Worcester, MA	72.2	12.7	6.5	0.3	0.1	4.2	4.1
U.S.	73.9	12.6	5.0	0.8	0.2	4.7	2.9

Note: (1) Alone is defined as not being in combination with one or more other races; (2) American Indian and Alaska Native; (3) Native Hawaiian and Other Pacific Islander
Source: U.S. Census Bureau, 2011-2013 American Community Survey 3-Year Estimates

Race: Metro Area

Metro Area	White Alone[1] (%)	Black Alone[1] (%)	Asian Alone[1] (%)	AIAN[2] Alone[1] (%)	NHOPI[3] Alone[1] (%)	Other Race Alone[1] (%)	Two or More Races (%)
Albuquerque, NM	71.8	2.8	1.9	5.5	0.1	14.1	3.8
Anchorage, AK	70.3	4.8	6.7	6.4	1.7	1.3	8.8
Ann Arbor, MI	74.4	12.2	8.1	0.2	0.0	1.0	4.2
Athens, GA	73.4	19.5	3.4	0.3	0.0	1.4	2.0
Atlanta, GA	56.2	32.9	5.1	0.3	0.0	3.4	2.2
Austin, TX	78.6	7.3	4.9	0.5	0.1	5.7	2.9
Billings, MT	90.7	0.8	0.8	3.9	0.1	1.4	2.4
Boise City, ID	91.6	0.7	2.0	0.6	0.2	2.1	2.8
Boston, MA	78.1	7.8	6.9	0.2	0.0	4.1	2.9
Boulder, CO	88.3	1.0	4.1	0.5	0.1	3.2	2.9
Cape Coral, FL	84.1	8.3	1.6	0.4	0.0	3.9	1.7
Cedar Rapids, IA	91.4	3.7	1.6	0.4	0.0	0.8	2.1
Charleston, SC	67.3	27.2	1.7	0.4	0.1	1.2	2.2
Charlotte, NC	69.4	22.1	3.0	0.4	0.0	3.0	2.1
Chicago, IL	66.7	17.0	5.9	0.2	0.0	7.9	2.2
Clarksville, TN	73.0	18.5	1.7	0.6	0.4	1.6	4.2
Colorado Springs, CO	81.6	5.8	2.7	0.6	0.3	3.8	5.1
Columbia, MO	82.8	8.3	4.0	0.1	0.1	0.8	3.9
Columbus, OH	78.0	14.4	3.2	0.2	0.0	1.3	2.9
Dallas, TX	69.6	15.0	5.6	0.5	0.1	6.5	2.7
Davenport, IA	86.4	7.3	1.8	0.3	0.0	1.8	2.5
Denver, CO	81.9	5.6	3.8	0.8	0.1	4.4	3.5
Des Moines, IA	87.5	4.8	3.4	0.2	0.1	1.8	2.3
Durham, NC	62.8	26.8	4.5	0.5	0.0	2.7	2.7
El Paso, TX	82.1	3.4	1.1	0.6	0.2	10.4	2.2
Erie, PA	88.1	7.0	1.3	0.3	0.0	0.9	2.4
Eugene, OR	88.4	1.0	2.6	1.1	0.3	2.4	4.3
Fargo, ND	91.5	2.2	2.0	1.1	0.0	0.4	2.6
Fayetteville, NC	51.5	36.0	2.1	2.3	0.3	2.4	5.3
Fort Collins, CO	90.8	0.8	2.0	0.5	0.1	2.7	3.1
Fort Wayne, IN	82.2	10.3	2.4	0.3	0.1	2.0	2.7
Fort Worth, TX	69.6	15.0	5.6	0.5	0.1	6.5	2.7
Gainesville, FL	71.5	19.2	5.1	0.3	0.1	1.0	2.8
Grand Rapids, MI	86.1	6.5	2.2	0.5	0.0	1.9	2.9
Green Bay, WI	89.4	2.2	2.5	2.0	0.0	1.3	2.6
Greensboro, NC	65.6	26.1	3.2	0.5	0.0	2.5	2.0
Honolulu, HI	21.5	2.6	43.1	0.2	9.3	1.0	22.4
Houston, TX	65.7	17.2	6.9	0.4	0.1	7.6	2.2
Huntsville, AL	71.5	22.0	2.2	0.6	0.1	1.1	2.5
Indianapolis, IN	77.6	14.6	2.2	0.2	0.0	2.9	2.4
Jacksonville, FL	70.8	21.5	3.5	0.3	0.1	0.9	2.9
Kansas City, MO	79.1	12.5	2.5	0.5	0.1	2.5	2.9
Lafayette, LA	70.8	24.4	1.4	0.4	0.0	0.6	2.2
Las Vegas, NV	64.9	10.7	9.0	0.6	0.7	9.8	4.4
Lexington, KY	81.5	11.1	2.5	0.2	0.0	2.3	2.3
Lincoln, NE	88.2	3.6	3.6	0.7	0.1	1.1	2.8
Little Rock, AR	72.6	22.6	1.5	0.3	0.0	1.0	1.9
Los Angeles, CA	56.1	6.8	15.0	0.5	0.3	17.7	3.7
Louisville, KY	80.8	14.0	1.7	0.1	0.0	1.0	2.4
Lubbock, TX	79.9	6.9	1.9	0.5	0.1	7.6	3.2
Madison, WI	87.2	4.5	4.2	0.3	0.0	1.4	2.3
Manchester, NH	90.6	2.3	3.4	0.1	0.0	1.4	2.2
McAllen, TX	92.3	0.6	1.0	0.3	0.0	5.0	0.7
Miami, FL	71.7	21.3	2.4	0.2	0.0	2.5	1.9

continued on next page.

Metro Area	White Alone[1] (%)	Black Alone[1] (%)	Asian Alone[1] (%)	AIAN[2] Alone[1] (%)	NHOPI[3] Alone[1] (%)	Other Race Alone[1] (%)	Two or More Races (%)
Midland, TX	81.1	6.5	1.5	0.4	0.1	8.8	1.8
Minneapolis, MN	81.2	7.4	5.9	0.6	0.0	1.8	3.0
Nashville, TN	77.7	15.3	2.3	0.3	0.0	2.5	1.9
New Orleans, LA	58.5	34.7	2.8	0.4	0.0	1.9	1.6
New York, NY	59.5	17.2	10.2	0.3	0.0	10.1	2.8
Oklahoma City, OK	74.5	10.1	2.9	3.7	0.1	2.6	6.1
Omaha, NE	84.3	7.7	2.3	0.5	0.1	2.6	2.5
Orlando, FL	71.7	16.1	4.1	0.3	0.1	4.8	2.9
Oxnard, CA	77.7	1.8	6.9	0.6	0.1	8.4	4.3
Palm Bay, FL	83.4	10.2	2.1	0.2	0.1	1.3	2.6
Peoria, IL	85.8	9.2	2.1	0.2	0.0	0.7	2.0
Philadelphia, PA	68.1	20.8	5.2	0.2	0.0	3.2	2.4
Phoenix, AZ	80.5	5.1	3.4	2.2	0.2	5.6	2.9
Pittsburgh, PA	87.5	8.2	1.9	0.1	0.0	0.3	1.9
Portland, OR	82.1	2.9	6.0	0.8	0.5	3.6	4.0
Providence, RI	83.6	5.4	2.8	0.4	0.0	5.1	2.7
Provo, UT	91.9	0.6	1.5	0.5	0.9	2.3	2.3
Raleigh, NC	69.7	20.3	4.7	0.4	0.0	2.8	2.2
Reno, NV	80.7	2.4	5.3	1.6	0.6	5.9	3.5
Richmond, VA	62.0	30.2	3.3	0.4	0.0	1.5	2.5
Roanoke, VA	82.3	12.8	1.7	0.2	0.1	0.4	2.5
Rochester, MN	89.5	3.6	3.9	0.2	0.0	0.7	2.1
Sacramento, CA	66.6	7.2	12.3	0.8	0.7	6.4	5.9
Salem, OR	82.2	0.8	1.9	1.2	0.6	9.0	4.3
Salt Lake City, UT	83.8	1.6	3.3	0.9	1.5	6.3	2.6
San Antonio, TX	78.8	6.5	2.2	0.6	0.1	8.7	3.1
San Diego, CA	71.0	5.1	11.2	0.7	0.5	6.8	4.7
San Francisco, CA	54.3	8.0	23.8	0.5	0.7	7.4	5.4
San Jose, CA	50.6	2.6	32.1	0.5	0.4	9.4	4.5
Santa Rosa, CA	78.1	1.6	3.9	1.2	0.3	10.8	4.1
Savannah, GA	60.9	33.5	2.2	0.3	0.1	0.9	2.3
Seattle, WA	72.7	5.6	11.8	0.9	0.8	2.4	5.7
Sioux Falls, SD	89.5	3.3	1.5	2.1	0.0	1.7	1.8
Spokane, WA	89.4	1.8	2.1	1.7	0.3	0.9	3.7
Springfield, IL	84.0	11.5	1.7	0.2	0.0	0.6	2.0
Tallahassee, FL	61.0	32.9	2.4	0.3	0.0	1.4	2.0
Tampa, FL	79.5	12.0	3.0	0.4	0.1	2.5	2.6
Topeka, KS	85.5	6.1	0.9	1.2	0.0	1.6	4.6
Tulsa, OK	72.7	8.0	1.9	6.9	0.1	2.4	8.0
Tyler, TX	76.7	18.1	1.3	0.3	0.0	2.1	1.5
Virginia Beach, VA	60.4	30.9	3.6	0.3	0.1	1.1	3.6
Washington, DC	56.0	25.4	9.5	0.3	0.1	5.1	3.6
Wichita, KS	82.7	7.5	3.3	0.9	0.0	1.9	3.7
Wilmington, NC	80.0	15.1	1.1	0.5	0.0	1.7	1.6
Winston-Salem, NC	77.1	17.6	1.4	0.3	0.1	2.0	1.5
Worcester, MA	85.9	4.2	3.9	0.2	0.0	3.1	2.7
U.S.	73.9	12.6	5.0	0.8	0.2	4.7	2.9

Note: (1) Figures cover the Metropolitan Statistical Area (MSA)—see Appendix B for areas included; (1) Alone is defined as not being in combination with one or more other races; (2) American Indian and Alaska Native; (3) Native Hawaiian & Other Pacific Islander
Source: U.S. Census Bureau, 2011-2013 American Community Survey 3-Year Estimates

Hispanic Origin: City

City	Hispanic or Latino (%)	Mexican (%)	Puerto Rican (%)	Cuban (%)	Other Hispanic or Latino (%)
Albuquerque, NM	46.9	26.2	0.5	0.6	19.6
Anchorage, AK	8.3	4.5	1.2	0.2	2.3
Ann Arbor, MI	4.4	2.2	0.2	0.1	1.9
Athens, GA	10.6	7.2	0.4	0.4	2.7
Atlanta, GA	5.3	2.8	0.7	0.4	1.5
Austin, TX	33.9	28.5	0.6	0.5	4.3
Billings, MT	5.5	3.9	0.4	0.0	1.1
Boise City, ID	7.6	6.3	0.2	0.1	1.1
Boston, MA	18.5	1.1	5.0	0.4	12.0
Boulder, CO	8.3	5.9	0.3	0.3	1.8
Cape Coral, FL	19.1	1.9	5.3	5.6	6.3
Cedar Rapids, IA	3.7	2.9	0.2	0.0	0.6
Charleston, SC	2.9	1.0	1.0	0.4	0.7
Charlotte, NC	13.4	5.2	1.0	0.3	6.7
Chicago, IL	29.1	21.8	3.8	0.3	3.2
Clarksville, TN	10.2	5.2	2.8	0.1	2.1
Colorado Springs, CO	17.1	11.2	0.9	0.2	4.7
Columbia, MO	3.6	2.1	0.4	0.5	0.7
Columbus, OH	5.8	3.5	0.7	0.1	1.4
Dallas, TX	41.8	37.2	0.4	0.2	4.0
Davenport, IA	8.1	7.1	0.3	0.1	0.6
Denver, CO	31.2	26.3	0.6	0.2	4.0
Des Moines, IA	12.4	9.8	0.2	0.1	2.2
Durham, NC	13.8	8.2	0.7	0.3	4.6
El Paso, TX	79.7	75.7	1.1	0.3	2.7
Erie, PA	6.8	1.0	5.1	0.2	0.5
Eugene, OR	8.3	6.5	0.3	0.1	1.4
Fargo, ND	2.9	2.0	0.2	0.1	0.6
Fayetteville, NC	11.1	4.1	3.8	0.3	2.9
Fort Collins, CO	10.6	7.4	0.8	0.1	2.3
Fort Wayne, IN	8.3	6.4	0.4	0.1	1.4
Fort Worth, TX	34.5	31.1	0.7	0.1	2.6
Gainesville, FL	10.1	1.1	2.5	2.8	3.8
Grand Rapids, MI	15.0	9.0	1.5	0.3	4.2
Green Bay, WI	12.3	9.4	1.4	0.1	1.5
Greensboro, NC	7.4	4.5	0.5	0.2	2.2
Honolulu, HI	6.0	1.6	2.1	0.1	2.1
Houston, TX	43.8	33.0	0.5	0.3	9.9
Huntsville, AL	5.8	3.9	0.8	0.1	1.0
Indianapolis, IN	9.7	7.2	0.5	0.1	1.9
Jacksonville, FL	8.2	1.8	2.7	1.0	2.7
Kansas City, MO	10.0	7.6	0.4	0.3	1.6
Lafayette, LA	4.4	2.0	0.3	0.2	2.0
Las Vegas, NV	31.7	24.5	0.9	0.9	5.3
Lexington, KY	6.9	5.1	0.5	0.2	1.2
Lincoln, NE	6.7	5.0	0.2	0.1	1.4
Little Rock, AR	5.9	4.1	0.2	0.0	1.5
Los Angeles, CA	48.6	32.5	0.5	0.3	15.3
Louisville, KY	4.8	2.2	0.3	1.4	0.9
Lubbock, TX	33.6	29.3	0.2	0.0	4.0
Madison, WI	6.9	4.9	0.8	0.2	1.0
Manchester, NH	8.1	2.6	2.2	0.1	3.2
McAllen, TX	84.8	80.5	0.4	0.1	3.8
Miami, FL	70.3	2.0	3.3	34.4	30.6
land, TX	39.9	37.9	0.1	0.3	1.7

...ble continued on next page.

City	Hispanic or Latino (%)	Mexican (%)	Puerto Rican (%)	Cuban (%)	Other Hispanic or Latino (%)
Minneapolis, MN	10.1	6.4	0.4	0.2	3.1
Nashville, TN	10.1	6.1	0.6	0.4	3.1
New Orleans, LA	5.4	1.2	0.4	0.3	3.5
New York, NY	28.8	3.9	8.9	0.5	15.5
Oklahoma City, OK	18.3	15.6	0.3	0.1	2.3
Omaha, NE	13.3	10.6	0.3	0.1	2.3
Orlando, FL	27.7	2.7	14.8	1.5	8.7
Oxnard, CA	73.8	69.7	0.4	0.1	3.6
Palm Bay, FL	13.6	1.2	6.9	1.6	3.8
Peoria, IL	5.4	4.2	0.3	0.0	0.8
Philadelphia, PA	13.0	1.1	8.6	0.2	3.1
Phoenix, AZ	40.6	37.4	0.5	0.3	2.4
Pittsburgh, PA	2.5	0.9	0.6	0.2	0.9
Portland, OR	9.6	7.5	0.3	0.2	1.5
Providence, RI	40.0	1.9	8.1	0.3	29.7
Provo, UT	18.2	11.2	0.4	0.4	6.3
Raleigh, NC	11.3	5.1	1.1	0.3	4.8
Reno, NV	25.4	20.1	0.6	0.1	4.6
Richmond, VA	6.3	2.1	0.6	0.1	3.6
Roanoke, VA	5.7	1.8	0.7	0.3	3.0
Rochester, MN	5.5	4.0	0.4	0.1	0.9
Sacramento, CA	27.5	23.8	0.8	0.1	2.7
Salem, OR	20.7	18.8	0.1	0.1	1.7
Salt Lake City, UT	20.2	16.2	0.3	0.0	3.8
San Antonio, TX	63.0	57.1	1.0	0.2	4.6
San Diego, CA	29.9	26.4	0.7	0.2	2.6
San Francisco, CA	15.3	7.6	0.6	0.2	6.9
San Jose, CA	33.4	29.1	0.4	0.2	3.7
Santa Rosa, CA	30.2	26.2	0.6	0.0	3.4
Savannah, GA	5.7	2.7	1.1	0.2	1.7
Seattle, WA	6.8	4.3	0.4	0.2	1.9
Sioux Falls, SD	4.9	2.5	0.1	0.0	2.3
Spokane, WA	5.5	3.6	0.2	0.1	1.7
Springfield, IL	2.5	1.7	0.2	0.0	0.6
Tallahassee, FL	6.6	1.5	1.5	1.5	2.2
Tampa, FL	22.6	2.5	7.4	6.5	6.2
Topeka, KS	13.7	12.0	0.4	0.1	1.2
Tulsa, OK	14.6	12.2	0.5	0.1	1.8
Tyler, TX	22.8	20.8	0.2	0.1	1.8
Virginia Beach, VA	7.2	2.3	2.4	0.2	2.3
Washington, DC	9.9	1.4	0.6	0.3	7.6
Wichita, KS	15.9	14.3	0.5	0.1	1.1
Wilmington, NC	5.2	3.2	0.4	0.1	1.4
Winston-Salem, NC	15.5	11.0	1.3	0.2	3.1
Worcester, MA	20.6	0.9	12.4	0.2	7.1
U.S.	16.9	10.8	1.6	0.6	3.8

Note: Persons of Hispanic or Latino origin can be of any race
Source: U.S. Census Bureau, 2011-2013 American Community Survey 3-Year Estimates

Hispanic Origin: Metro Area

Metro Area	Hispanic or Latino (%)	Mexican (%)	Puerto Rican (%)	Cuban (%)	Other Hispanic or Latino (%)
Albuquerque, NM	47.4	25.6	0.4	0.4	21.0
Anchorage, AK	7.3	4.1	1.1	0.2	2.0
Ann Arbor, MI	4.3	2.2	0.3	0.1	1.7
Athens, GA	8.2	5.6	0.5	0.3	1.9
Atlanta, GA	10.5	6.0	1.0	0.4	3.1
Austin, TX	31.7	26.9	0.6	0.4	3.9
Billings, MT	4.9	3.8	0.3	0.0	0.8
Boise City, ID	12.8	10.9	0.3	0.1	1.5
Boston, MA	9.7	0.6	2.7	0.2	6.1
Boulder, CO	13.6	10.8	0.3	0.2	2.3
Cape Coral, FL	18.9	5.8	4.2	3.5	5.4
Cedar Rapids, IA	2.6	1.8	0.1	0.0	0.6
Charleston, SC	5.3	2.9	0.8	0.1	1.4
Charlotte, NC	9.4	4.5	0.9	0.3	3.7
Chicago, IL	21.2	16.8	2.1	0.2	2.1
Clarksville, TN	7.9	4.4	1.7	0.1	1.7
Colorado Springs, CO	15.3	9.5	1.1	0.2	4.5
Columbia, MO	3.1	1.9	0.3	0.3	0.6
Columbus, OH	3.7	2.2	0.5	0.1	0.9
Dallas, TX	27.8	23.7	0.6	0.2	3.3
Davenport, IA	8.0	7.2	0.3	0.1	0.4
Denver, CO	22.7	18.1	0.5	0.1	3.9
Des Moines, IA	6.9	5.1	0.2	0.1	1.4
Durham, NC	11.3	6.9	0.6	0.2	3.5
El Paso, TX	81.2	77.4	1.0	0.2	2.6
Erie, PA	3.6	0.7	2.4	0.1	0.5
Eugene, OR	7.8	6.3	0.3	0.1	1.2
Fargo, ND	2.7	2.0	0.2	0.1	0.4
Fayetteville, NC	10.6	4.1	3.7	0.3	2.5
Fort Collins, CO	10.8	8.1	0.4	0.1	2.2
Fort Wayne, IN	6.1	4.6	0.4	0.1	1.0
Fort Worth, TX	27.8	23.7	0.6	0.2	3.3
Gainesville, FL	8.5	1.4	2.3	2.0	2.8
Grand Rapids, MI	8.8	6.0	0.8	0.3	1.7
Green Bay, WI	6.6	4.6	0.8	0.1	1.0
Greensboro, NC	7.8	5.5	0.6	0.2	1.5
Honolulu, HI	8.9	2.6	3.1	0.1	3.1
Houston, TX	35.9	27.7	0.5	0.3	7.3
Huntsville, AL	4.9	3.5	0.6	0.1	0.7
Indianapolis, IN	6.2	4.5	0.3	0.1	1.3
Jacksonville, FL	7.4	1.7	2.4	0.9	2.5
Kansas City, MO	8.5	6.5	0.3	0.2	1.4
Lafayette, LA	3.4	1.8	0.2	0.1	1.3
Las Vegas, NV	29.7	22.7	1.0	1.1	5.0
Lexington, KY	5.6	4.2	0.4	0.1	0.9
Lincoln, NE	6.0	4.5	0.2	0.1	1.2
Little Rock, AR	4.9	3.7	0.2	0.0	1.0
Los Angeles, CA	44.8	34.9	0.5	0.4	9.0
Louisville, KY	4.2	2.2	0.3	0.7	0.9
Lubbock, TX	33.8	29.8	0.2	0.0	3.7
Madison, WI	5.4	4.0	0.5	0.1	0.9
Manchester, NH	5.6	1.8	1.5	0.1	2.2
McAllen, TX	90.9	88.4	0.2	0.1	2.2
ㅡmi, FL	42.2	2.4	3.7	18.2	17.8
ㅡ, TX	40.1	37.8	0.3	0.2	1.7

continued on next page.

Metro Area	Hispanic or Latino (%)	Mexican (%)	Puerto Rican (%)	Cuban (%)	Other Hispanic or Latino (%)
Minneapolis, MN	5.5	3.7	0.3	0.1	1.4
Nashville, TN	6.7	4.2	0.5	0.2	1.7
New Orleans, LA	8.1	1.8	0.5	0.6	5.2
New York, NY	23.2	3.0	6.4	0.7	13.1
Oklahoma City, OK	11.9	10.0	0.3	0.1	1.6
Omaha, NE	9.4	7.4	0.3	0.1	1.6
Orlando, FL	26.7	3.4	13.5	1.9	7.9
Oxnard, CA	41.2	36.6	0.5	0.2	3.9
Palm Bay, FL	8.7	1.5	3.4	1.1	2.7
Peoria, IL	3.1	2.3	0.3	0.0	0.4
Philadelphia, PA	8.3	1.7	4.3	0.2	2.1
Phoenix, AZ	29.8	26.8	0.6	0.2	2.2
Pittsburgh, PA	1.4	0.5	0.4	0.0	0.5
Portland, OR	11.2	9.2	0.3	0.1	1.5
Providence, RI	10.9	0.7	3.6	0.1	6.5
Provo, UT	10.8	7.1	0.2	0.1	3.4
Raleigh, NC	10.3	5.9	1.0	0.3	3.1
Reno, NV	22.8	18.0	0.5	0.1	4.1
Richmond, VA	5.4	1.8	1.0	0.2	2.4
Roanoke, VA	3.4	1.3	0.4	0.3	1.3
Rochester, MN	4.0	3.0	0.3	0.1	0.6
Sacramento, CA	20.6	17.0	0.7	0.2	2.8
Salem, OR	22.6	20.7	0.2	0.0	1.7
Salt Lake City, UT	17.1	12.8	0.3	0.1	4.0
San Antonio, TX	54.4	48.9	1.0	0.2	4.3
San Diego, CA	32.7	29.1	0.7	0.2	2.7
San Francisco, CA	21.8	14.7	0.7	0.2	6.3
San Jose, CA	27.7	23.7	0.4	0.1	3.5
Santa Rosa, CA	25.5	21.7	0.5	0.1	3.2
Savannah, GA	5.5	2.8	1.1	0.2	1.3
Seattle, WA	9.3	6.8	0.5	0.1	1.9
Sioux Falls, SD	3.7	1.9	0.1	0.0	1.7
Spokane, WA	4.7	3.3	0.2	0.1	1.1
Springfield, IL	2.0	1.4	0.1	0.0	0.4
Tallahassee, FL	6.2	1.9	1.2	1.1	2.0
Tampa, FL	17.0	3.5	5.6	3.3	4.6
Topeka, KS	9.3	8.1	0.4	0.0	0.9
Tulsa, OK	8.7	7.2	0.4	0.1	1.1
Tyler, TX	18.0	16.3	0.2	0.1	1.4
Virginia Beach, VA	5.8	2.0	1.8	0.2	1.8
Washington, DC	14.4	2.2	0.9	0.3	11.0
Wichita, KS	11.9	10.6	0.4	0.1	0.8
Wilmington, NC	5.6	4.0	0.5	0.2	0.9
Winston-Salem, NC	9.6	6.7	0.7	0.2	2.0
Worcester, MA	9.9	0.7	5.8	0.1	3.3
U.S.	16.9	10.8	1.6	0.6	3.8

Note: Persons of Hispanic or Latino origin can be of any race; Figures cover the Metropolitan Statistical Area (MSA)—see Appendix B for areas included
Source: U.S. Census Bureau, 2011-2013 American Community Survey 3-Year Estimates

Age: City

City	Percent of Population							
	Under Age 5	Age 5–19	Age 20–34	Age 35–44	Age 45–54	Age 55–64	Age 65–74	Age 75–84
Albuquerque, NM	6.7	19.3	23.1	12.7	13.3	12.0	7.1	4.0
Anchorage, AK	7.5	20.5	25.4	12.9	14.0	11.7	5.2	2.2
Ann Arbor, MI	4.2	19.5	37.9	9.5	9.2	9.5	5.5	3.1
Athens, GA	5.9	21.3	36.8	10.3	8.8	8.2	5.0	2.5
Atlanta, GA	6.2	16.3	30.7	14.8	12.3	9.6	5.7	3.0
Austin, TX	6.8	18.1	31.0	15.4	12.1	9.3	4.2	2.1
Billings, MT	6.6	18.7	21.6	12.0	13.3	12.9	7.8	4.7
Boise City, ID	5.9	18.7	23.9	13.3	13.9	12.6	6.5	3.4
Boston, MA	5.4	15.9	34.9	12.4	11.3	9.6	5.6	3.2
Boulder, CO	3.9	19.8	36.0	10.7	10.5	9.4	5.4	2.7
Cape Coral, FL	5.7	19.8	14.8	12.3	14.5	14.2	10.9	5.4
Cedar Rapids, IA	6.9	19.3	23.3	12.4	12.8	12.1	6.6	4.5
Charleston, SC	6.2	15.6	30.0	12.1	11.6	11.7	7.5	3.6
Charlotte, NC	7.4	20.3	24.6	15.5	13.3	10.0	5.1	2.7
Chicago, IL	6.8	18.3	27.3	14.2	12.4	10.2	5.9	3.3
Clarksville, TN	9.2	21.4	30.4	13.3	10.9	7.7	4.2	2.1
Colorado Springs, CO	7.1	20.3	23.6	12.4	13.8	11.4	6.4	3.6
Columbia, MO	6.2	20.2	36.1	10.0	9.9	8.8	4.4	2.9
Columbus, OH	7.7	18.6	29.1	13.5	12.2	10.1	5.0	2.7
Dallas, TX	8.1	20.2	26.4	14.0	12.4	9.8	5.1	2.8
Davenport, IA	7.2	19.8	23.1	12.2	12.8	12.4	6.5	3.7
Denver, CO	7.0	16.3	28.6	15.3	11.7	10.5	5.8	3.1
Des Moines, IA	8.0	20.2	24.5	12.8	12.8	10.9	6.0	3.3
Durham, NC	7.5	18.5	28.1	14.3	12.0	10.3	5.4	2.5
El Paso, TX	7.9	23.3	22.4	12.5	12.5	10.0	6.2	3.9
Erie, PA	7.0	19.8	24.3	11.5	12.8	11.4	6.6	4.2
Eugene, OR	4.7	17.8	28.7	11.9	11.3	12.2	7.2	3.8
Fargo, ND	6.4	18.0	32.8	11.1	10.9	10.2	4.8	3.7
Fayetteville, NC	8.4	19.6	28.7	11.6	11.5	9.8	5.7	3.7
Fort Collins, CO	5.5	19.6	33.0	11.5	11.7	9.8	5.0	2.5
Fort Wayne, IN	7.5	21.1	21.4	12.5	13.0	11.8	6.6	4.0
Fort Worth, TX	8.6	23.2	23.4	14.3	12.5	9.3	4.8	2.6
Gainesville, FL	4.5	17.7	43.9	8.4	8.0	9.1	4.2	3.0
Grand Rapids, MI	7.9	20.0	28.0	11.8	10.9	10.0	5.2	3.8
Green Bay, WI	7.7	19.1	24.3	11.8	13.3	11.8	5.8	4.0
Greensboro, NC	6.5	19.6	25.1	12.8	12.9	11.1	6.5	4.0
Honolulu, HI	5.4	14.9	22.7	12.6	13.5	13.0	8.3	6.0
Houston, TX	7.8	20.1	25.8	14.0	12.6	10.2	5.5	2.9
Huntsville, AL	6.2	18.5	22.8	12.0	14.7	11.7	7.7	4.5
Indianapolis, IN	7.5	19.9	24.2	13.0	13.4	11.3	5.9	3.3
Jacksonville, FL	7.0	18.9	23.2	13.1	14.1	12.0	6.8	3.4
Kansas City, MO	7.2	18.7	24.1	13.2	13.6	11.8	6.4	3.5
Lafayette, LA	5.5	19.4	26.8	11.7	13.2	11.5	6.6	4.0
Las Vegas, NV	6.8	20.5	20.6	14.2	13.6	11.3	7.7	4.1
Lexington, KY	6.3	18.3	26.9	13.3	12.9	11.2	6.2	3.2
Lincoln, NE	7.0	19.7	27.4	12.0	11.7	11.0	6.0	3.6
Little Rock, AR	6.8	18.4	23.1	13.6	13.1	12.4	7.0	3.7
Los Angeles, CA	6.5	18.7	25.4	14.8	13.3	10.5	5.9	3.4
Louisville, KY	6.7	19.1	21.2	12.8	14.2	12.8	7.0	4.3
Lubbock, TX	7.1	21.7	29.2	10.5	11.1	9.5	5.8	4.0
Madison, WI	5.7	16.6	34.9	11.5	11.2	10.1	5.3	3.1
Manchester, NH	5.6	17.6	24.2	14.0	13.8	11.8	7.0	3.8
Allen, TX	7.5	24.4	21.3	13.9	11.8	10.1	6.4	3.0
FL	6.3	14.4	23.2	14.8	14.2	11.2	7.9	5.5

continued on next page.

City	Percent of Population							
	Under Age 5	Age 5–19	Age 20–34	Age 35–44	Age 45–54	Age 55–64	Age 65–74	Age 75–84
Midland, TX	8.5	21.8	23.7	12.0	12.2	11.0	5.4	3.7
Minneapolis, MN	6.9	17.2	31.8	13.3	11.9	10.4	4.8	2.3
Nashville, TN	7.1	17.4	27.2	13.8	12.9	11.1	5.8	3.3
New Orleans, LA	6.3	17.3	26.3	12.4	13.5	12.8	6.5	3.4
New York, NY	6.6	17.2	25.1	14.0	13.3	11.3	6.8	3.9
Oklahoma City, OK	8.0	19.9	24.1	12.6	12.7	11.5	6.2	3.5
Omaha, NE	7.4	20.5	23.7	12.3	13.1	11.5	6.2	3.7
Orlando, FL	7.3	16.8	29.0	14.9	12.8	9.4	5.4	3.1
Oxnard, CA	8.6	22.8	25.2	13.5	11.8	9.4	5.0	2.8
Palm Bay, FL	5.9	19.4	17.0	11.1	16.3	13.7	9.3	5.2
Peoria, IL	7.1	21.5	23.8	11.8	11.3	11.4	6.8	3.8
Philadelphia, PA	6.9	18.7	26.4	12.2	12.6	11.1	6.5	3.9
Phoenix, AZ	7.7	22.1	23.2	14.2	13.5	10.2	5.3	2.6
Pittsburgh, PA	5.0	16.4	30.9	10.4	11.4	12.0	6.7	4.5
Portland, OR	5.8	15.0	26.6	16.7	12.9	12.2	6.3	2.9
Providence, RI	5.9	23.0	30.3	12.1	11.1	8.9	4.5	2.5
Provo, UT	8.7	22.6	44.7	7.5	5.4	5.2	2.7	1.9
Raleigh, NC	6.9	20.1	27.7	15.2	12.3	9.1	4.9	2.6
Reno, NV	6.7	19.3	24.7	12.4	13.1	11.5	7.2	3.5
Richmond, VA	6.4	16.3	30.4	11.5	12.4	11.8	6.0	3.5
Roanoke, VA	7.3	16.7	21.8	13.0	13.9	13.1	7.3	4.0
Rochester, MN	7.4	19.4	22.6	12.5	13.4	11.3	6.9	4.4
Sacramento, CA	7.1	19.7	24.9	13.1	12.6	11.3	6.1	3.4
Salem, OR	7.4	20.9	21.6	12.9	12.5	11.7	7.1	3.8
Salt Lake City, UT	7.4	17.7	31.0	13.4	11.2	9.4	5.2	3.1
San Antonio, TX	7.4	21.8	23.7	13.0	12.9	10.3	6.1	3.5
San Diego, CA	6.4	18.1	27.5	13.5	13.0	10.4	6.2	3.4
San Francisco, CA	4.5	10.8	28.4	16.4	13.7	12.2	7.1	4.6
San Jose, CA	6.8	19.7	22.0	15.4	14.3	10.8	6.0	3.5
Santa Rosa, CA	6.1	20.0	20.2	13.1	14.1	12.7	7.0	4.3
Savannah, GA	6.8	19.8	27.6	11.0	11.6	10.7	6.7	3.8
Seattle, WA	5.3	13.1	30.1	15.7	12.7	11.7	6.4	3.1
Sioux Falls, SD	8.2	18.4	25.0	12.6	12.9	11.7	5.9	3.4
Spokane, WA	7.1	17.9	24.6	11.9	12.4	12.1	7.2	4.6
Springfield, IL	6.3	18.5	20.7	11.6	14.1	13.7	7.6	4.5
Tallahassee, FL	5.1	19.8	39.0	9.9	9.2	8.6	4.5	2.7
Tampa, FL	6.1	19.2	24.4	13.6	14.3	11.1	6.0	3.8
Topeka, KS	7.6	19.1	21.5	11.5	13.1	12.4	7.3	4.9
Tulsa, OK	7.6	19.6	23.1	12.0	13.0	12.0	6.8	4.0
Tyler, TX	6.2	20.4	25.0	11.5	11.0	10.8	7.1	5.4
Virginia Beach, VA	6.7	19.1	24.2	13.1	14.2	11.2	6.5	3.4
Washington, DC	6.1	14.5	31.6	13.7	12.0	10.7	6.2	3.5
Wichita, KS	8.0	20.8	22.2	12.2	13.1	11.6	6.3	3.8
Wilmington, NC	4.9	18.0	27.6	11.6	12.1	12.1	7.5	4.4
Winston-Salem, NC	7.3	20.9	22.4	12.7	12.9	11.1	6.8	4.3
Worcester, MA	6.8	19.8	25.5	12.0	13.0	10.9	6.1	3.6
U.S.	6.4	19.9	20.7	12.9	14.1	12.3	7.6	4.2

Source: U.S. Census Bureau, 2011-2013 American Community Survey 3-Year Estimates

Age: Metro Area

Metro Area	Percent of Population							
	Under Age 5	Age 5–19	Age 20–34	Age 35–44	Age 45–54	Age 55–64	Age 65–74	Age 75–84
Albuquerque, NM	6.5	20.1	21.2	12.5	13.8	12.7	7.7	4.0
Anchorage, AK	7.5	21.1	23.9	13.0	14.2	12.0	5.3	2.3
Ann Arbor, MI	5.3	20.2	26.6	12.2	13.1	11.7	6.4	3.1
Athens, GA	5.7	21.4	28.6	11.6	11.5	10.3	6.5	3.1
Atlanta, GA	6.9	21.8	20.6	15.2	14.6	11.0	6.1	2.8
Austin, TX	7.1	20.6	25.0	15.4	13.0	10.2	5.3	2.5
Billings, MT	6.3	19.1	19.3	12.1	14.1	13.8	8.0	4.7
Boise City, ID	7.0	22.7	20.4	13.5	13.1	11.4	7.0	3.4
Boston, MA	5.6	18.6	21.4	13.1	15.1	12.5	7.3	4.2
Boulder, CO	5.3	19.9	23.7	13.3	14.1	12.5	6.5	3.2
Cape Coral, FL	5.1	16.2	16.0	10.9	12.8	14.1	14.0	7.8
Cedar Rapids, IA	6.3	20.4	19.8	12.8	14.2	12.4	7.4	4.7
Charleston, SC	6.6	18.9	23.3	12.8	13.8	12.2	7.5	3.5
Charlotte, NC	6.7	21.0	19.9	14.9	14.5	11.4	6.9	3.4
Chicago, IL	6.5	20.7	21.1	13.7	14.2	11.8	6.7	3.7
Clarksville, TN	8.8	21.4	27.1	12.8	11.4	9.1	5.5	2.9
Colorado Springs, CO	7.0	21.4	22.7	12.6	14.0	11.6	6.4	3.3
Columbia, MO	6.1	20.0	31.1	11.1	11.7	10.4	5.3	3.0
Columbus, OH	6.8	20.4	22.1	13.8	14.0	11.7	6.5	3.4
Dallas, TX	7.4	22.4	21.4	14.7	14.0	10.4	5.7	2.8
Davenport, IA	6.3	19.5	18.8	12.1	14.0	13.5	8.5	4.8
Denver, CO	6.7	19.9	21.9	14.7	14.1	11.9	6.4	3.1
Des Moines, IA	7.3	21.0	21.2	13.8	13.7	11.4	6.4	3.5
Durham, NC	6.3	19.1	23.6	13.6	13.2	12.0	7.0	3.6
El Paso, TX	8.2	24.3	22.4	12.8	12.1	9.6	5.7	3.5
Erie, PA	5.9	19.8	20.2	11.7	14.0	13.6	7.8	4.9
Eugene, OR	5.0	17.8	22.3	11.4	12.8	14.4	9.1	4.8
Fargo, ND	6.8	19.6	28.3	11.9	11.9	10.7	5.4	3.6
Fayetteville, NC	8.5	21.2	26.0	12.4	12.2	10.1	5.7	3.0
Fort Collins, CO	5.6	19.1	24.6	12.0	13.0	12.9	7.5	3.8
Fort Wayne, IN	7.1	21.8	19.6	12.6	13.7	12.4	7.0	4.0
Fort Worth, TX	7.4	22.4	21.4	14.7	14.0	10.4	5.7	2.8
Gainesville, FL	5.5	18.2	31.3	10.3	11.3	11.5	6.7	3.6
Grand Rapids, MI	6.8	21.7	21.0	12.3	14.0	11.9	6.7	3.8
Green Bay, WI	6.5	20.1	19.5	12.7	15.2	12.8	7.1	4.1
Greensboro, NC	6.0	20.0	19.8	13.4	14.3	12.5	7.9	4.4
Honolulu, HI	6.5	17.7	23.1	12.7	13.0	11.9	7.8	4.7
Houston, TX	7.7	22.4	22.0	14.3	13.6	10.8	5.6	2.6
Huntsville, AL	6.1	19.8	20.4	13.0	15.8	12.1	7.4	4.0
Indianapolis, IN	7.0	21.1	20.5	13.6	14.4	11.7	6.6	3.6
Jacksonville, FL	6.3	19.5	20.7	13.1	14.7	12.7	7.7	3.8
Kansas City, MO	6.9	20.7	20.0	13.3	14.3	12.2	7.0	3.8
Lafayette, LA	7.1	20.8	22.1	12.3	14.0	11.8	6.7	3.8
Las Vegas, NV	6.7	20.1	21.6	14.4	13.5	11.4	7.6	3.5
Lexington, KY	6.3	19.3	23.6	13.4	13.6	11.9	6.7	3.5
Lincoln, NE	6.8	20.3	25.4	11.9	12.3	11.5	6.3	3.7
Little Rock, AR	6.8	20.0	21.9	13.0	13.4	11.9	7.5	4.0
Los Angeles, CA	6.4	20.0	22.6	14.2	14.0	10.9	6.4	3.6
Louisville, KY	6.3	19.5	19.7	13.2	14.7	13.1	7.6	4.2
Lubbock, TX	7.1	21.7	26.9	11.0	11.6	10.2	6.3	4.0
Madison, WI	6.0	18.8	24.2	12.9	14.0	12.3	6.6	3.6
Manchester, NH	5.7	19.5	18.6	13.5	16.8	13.2	7.1	4.0
McAllen, TX	9.6	27.8	21.2	13.2	10.4	8.0	5.4	3.2
ʹmi, FL	5.7	17.8	19.6	13.6	14.9	11.9	8.3	5.5

...le continued on next page.

Metro Area	Percent of Population							
	Under Age 5	Age 5–19	Age 20–34	Age 35–44	Age 45–54	Age 55–64	Age 65–74	Age 75–84
Midland, TX	8.2	22.1	23.1	11.9	12.9	11.2	5.5	3.5
Minneapolis, MN	6.7	20.4	21.0	13.4	15.0	12.0	6.4	3.5
Nashville, TN	6.7	20.0	21.8	14.0	14.3	11.8	6.7	3.4
New Orleans, LA	6.4	19.0	21.8	12.6	14.4	13.1	7.4	3.9
New York, NY	6.2	18.9	21.2	13.6	14.7	12.0	7.3	4.2
Oklahoma City, OK	7.2	20.5	22.8	12.6	13.1	11.7	6.9	3.7
Omaha, NE	7.4	21.2	21.5	12.9	13.7	11.7	6.3	3.6
Orlando, FL	6.0	19.6	22.2	13.6	14.1	11.3	7.4	4.0
Oxnard, CA	6.5	21.3	20.0	12.9	14.6	12.0	7.0	3.8
Palm Bay, FL	4.8	16.6	16.1	10.7	15.8	14.6	11.3	7.5
Peoria, IL	6.4	19.7	19.3	12.4	13.7	13.2	8.1	4.9
Philadelphia, PA	6.1	19.5	20.5	12.6	14.8	12.6	7.4	4.4
Phoenix, AZ	7.0	21.3	21.1	13.5	13.0	11.0	7.6	4.0
Pittsburgh, PA	5.1	17.3	18.7	11.8	15.0	14.6	8.8	5.9
Portland, OR	6.2	19.2	21.3	14.6	13.8	12.7	7.1	3.4
Providence, RI	5.3	18.9	20.0	12.6	15.2	13.0	7.8	4.6
Provo, UT	10.7	28.7	27.4	11.6	8.3	6.5	3.9	2.2
Raleigh, NC	6.8	21.6	20.7	15.7	14.6	10.7	5.9	2.8
Reno, NV	6.3	19.1	21.3	12.7	13.9	13.2	8.3	3.6
Richmond, VA	6.0	19.4	20.6	13.3	14.9	12.8	7.4	3.7
Roanoke, VA	5.6	17.9	17.4	12.8	14.7	14.4	9.4	5.2
Rochester, MN	7.0	20.3	19.2	12.3	14.5	12.5	7.5	4.6
Sacramento, CA	6.4	20.6	21.1	12.8	14.0	12.1	7.2	3.9
Salem, OR	6.9	21.8	20.4	12.4	12.4	12.3	7.7	4.1
Salt Lake City, UT	8.4	23.2	24.2	13.7	11.6	9.8	5.2	2.7
San Antonio, TX	7.1	22.1	21.7	13.2	13.3	10.9	6.6	3.5
San Diego, CA	6.6	19.2	24.3	13.3	13.5	11.1	6.4	3.7
San Francisco, CA	5.8	17.3	21.6	14.8	14.7	12.5	7.3	4.0
San Jose, CA	6.7	19.5	21.4	15.2	14.6	10.9	6.4	3.6
Santa Rosa, CA	5.5	18.5	19.5	12.2	14.5	14.6	8.6	4.4
Savannah, GA	6.9	20.0	23.7	12.7	13.1	11.4	7.1	3.6
Seattle, WA	6.4	18.4	22.4	14.5	14.6	12.3	6.6	3.3
Sioux Falls, SD	7.8	20.6	22.0	13.0	13.5	11.7	6.0	3.5
Spokane, WA	6.1	19.6	20.8	11.9	13.7	13.5	8.2	4.4
Springfield, IL	6.1	19.4	18.8	12.4	14.7	13.9	7.9	4.4
Tallahassee, FL	5.5	19.3	28.2	11.6	12.3	11.9	6.6	3.3
Tampa, FL	5.5	17.6	18.6	12.6	14.6	13.2	9.5	5.8
Topeka, KS	6.6	20.4	18.0	11.6	14.1	13.7	8.4	4.9
Tulsa, OK	7.0	20.8	20.1	12.7	13.6	12.3	7.7	4.2
Tyler, TX	7.0	21.1	20.8	12.0	12.6	11.7	8.1	4.8
Virginia Beach, VA	6.4	19.6	23.6	12.3	14.3	11.7	6.9	3.7
Washington, DC	6.7	19.4	22.1	14.6	14.9	11.5	6.3	3.0
Wichita, KS	7.5	21.7	20.5	12.0	13.5	12.2	6.7	4.0
Wilmington, NC	5.5	18.2	22.0	13.0	13.5	13.0	8.8	4.5
Winston-Salem, NC	6.1	19.9	18.1	13.3	14.7	12.9	8.4	4.7
Worcester, MA	5.6	20.0	18.8	13.2	16.1	12.9	7.2	4.1
U.S.	6.4	19.9	20.7	12.9	14.1	12.3	7.6	4.2

Note: Figures cover the Metropolitan Statistical Area (MSA)—see Appendix B for areas included
Source: U.S. Census Bureau, 2011-2013 American Community Survey 3-Year Estimates

Segregation

Area	Black/White Index[1]	Black/White Rank[2]	Asian/White Index[1]	Asian/White Rank[2]	Hispanic/White Index[1]	Hispanic/White Rank[2]
Albuquerque, NM	30.9	99	28.5	93	36.4	79
Anchorage, AK	n/a	n/a	n/a	n/a	n/a	n/a
Ann Arbor, MI	n/a	n/a	n/a	n/a	n/a	n/a
Athens, GA	n/a	n/a	n/a	n/a	n/a	n/a
Atlanta, GA	59.0	41	48.5	10	49.5	27
Austin, TX	50.1	70	41.2	49	43.2	51
Billings, MT	n/a	n/a	n/a	n/a	n/a	n/a
Boise City, ID	30.2	101	27.6	95	36.2	80
Boston, MA	64.0	27	45.4	23	59.6	5
Boulder, CO	n/a	n/a	n/a	n/a	n/a	n/a
Cape Coral, FL	61.6	35	25.3	96	40.2	63
Cedar Rapids, IA	n/a	n/a	n/a	n/a	n/a	n/a
Charleston, SC	41.5	88	33.4	84	39.8	66
Charlotte, NC	53.8	56	43.6	34	47.6	35
Chicago, IL	76.4	3	44.9	26	56.3	10
Clarksville, TN	n/a	n/a	n/a	n/a	n/a	n/a
Colorado Springs, CO	39.3	92	24.1	98	30.3	95
Columbia, MO	n/a	n/a	n/a	n/a	n/a	n/a
Columbus, OH	62.2	33	43.3	35	41.5	59
Dallas, TX	56.6	48	46.6	19	50.3	24
Davenport, IA	n/a	n/a	n/a	n/a	n/a	n/a
Denver, CO	62.6	31	33.4	83	48.8	31
Des Moines, IA	51.6	66	35.5	76	46.7	40
Durham, NC	48.1	75	44.0	30	48.0	33
El Paso, TX	30.7	100	22.2	100	43.3	50
Erie, PA	n/a	n/a	n/a	n/a	n/a	n/a
Eugene, OR	n/a	n/a	n/a	n/a	n/a	n/a
Fargo, ND	n/a	n/a	n/a	n/a	n/a	n/a
Fayetteville, NC	n/a	n/a	n/a	n/a	n/a	n/a
Fort Collins, CO	n/a	n/a	n/a	n/a	n/a	n/a
Fort Wayne, IN	n/a	n/a	n/a	n/a	n/a	n/a
Fort Worth, TX	56.6	48	46.6	19	50.3	24
Gainesville, FL	n/a	n/a	n/a	n/a	n/a	n/a
Grand Rapids, MI	64.3	26	43.2	37	50.4	23
Green Bay, WI	n/a	n/a	n/a	n/a	n/a	n/a
Greensboro, NC	54.7	53	47.7	14	41.1	61
Honolulu, HI	36.9	95	42.1	44	31.9	91
Houston, TX	61.4	36	50.4	7	52.5	18
Huntsville, AL	n/a	n/a	n/a	n/a	n/a	n/a
Indianapolis, IN	66.4	15	41.6	47	47.3	37
Jacksonville, FL	53.1	59	37.5	71	27.6	98
Kansas City, MO	61.2	39	38.4	65	44.4	48
Lafayette, LA	n/a	n/a	n/a	n/a	n/a	n/a
Las Vegas, NV	37.6	94	28.8	92	42.0	58
Lexington, KY	n/a	n/a	n/a	n/a	n/a	n/a
Lincoln, NE	n/a	n/a	n/a	n/a	n/a	n/a
Little Rock, AR	58.8	42	39.7	59	39.7	68
Los Angeles, CA	67.8	10	48.4	12	62.2	2
Louisville, KY	58.1	43	42.2	43	38.7	73
Lubbock, TX	n/a	n/a	n/a	n/a	n/a	n/a
Madison, WI	49.6	71	44.2	29	40.1	65
Manchester, NH	n/a	n/a	n/a	n/a	n/a	n/a
McAllen, TX	40.7	90	46.7	17	39.2	69
___i, FL	64.8	23	34.2	80	57.4	8
___, TX	n/a	n/a	n/a	n/a	n/a	n/a

continued on next page.

Area	Black/White		Asian/White		Hispanic/White	
	Index[1]	Rank[2]	Index[1]	Rank[2]	Index[1]	Rank[2]
Minneapolis, MN	52.9	60	42.8	39	42.5	54
Nashville, TN	56.2	49	41.0	51	47.9	34
New Orleans, LA	63.9	28	48.6	9	38.3	74
New York, NY	78.0	2	51.9	3	62.0	3
Oklahoma City, OK	51.4	67	39.2	60	47.0	38
Omaha, NE	61.3	38	36.3	74	48.8	30
Orlando, FL	50.7	69	33.9	81	40.2	64
Oxnard, CA	39.9	91	31.2	87	54.6	13
Palm Bay, FL	47.2	79	20.6	101	25.0	101
Peoria, IL	n/a	n/a	n/a	n/a	n/a	n/a
Philadelphia, PA	68.4	9	42.3	42	55.1	12
Phoenix, AZ	43.6	86	32.7	85	49.3	28
Pittsburgh, PA	65.8	17	52.4	2	28.6	97
Portland, OR	46.0	81	35.8	75	34.3	83
Providence, RI	53.5	57	40.1	55	60.1	4
Provo, UT	21.9	102	28.2	94	30.9	93
Raleigh, NC	42.1	87	46.7	16	37.1	76
Reno, NV	n/a	n/a	n/a	n/a	n/a	n/a
Richmond, VA	52.4	63	43.9	32	44.9	46
Roanoke, VA	n/a	n/a	n/a	n/a	n/a	n/a
Rochester, MN	n/a	n/a	n/a	n/a	n/a	n/a
Sacramento, CA	56.9	46	49.9	8	38.9	71
Salem, OR	n/a	n/a	n/a	n/a	n/a	n/a
Salt Lake City, UT	39.3	93	31.0	88	42.9	53
San Antonio, TX	49.0	73	38.3	66	46.1	43
San Diego, CA	51.2	68	48.2	13	49.6	25
San Francisco, CA	62.0	34	46.6	18	49.6	26
San Jose, CA	40.9	89	45.0	25	47.6	36
Santa Rosa, CA	n/a	n/a	n/a	n/a	n/a	n/a
Savannah, GA	n/a	n/a	n/a	n/a	n/a	n/a
Seattle, WA	49.1	72	37.6	69	32.8	87
Sioux Falls, SD	n/a	n/a	n/a	n/a	n/a	n/a
Spokane, WA	n/a	n/a	n/a	n/a	n/a	n/a
Springfield, IL	n/a	n/a	n/a	n/a	n/a	n/a
Tallahassee, FL	n/a	n/a	n/a	n/a	n/a	n/a
Tampa, FL	56.2	50	35.3	78	40.7	62
Topeka, KS	n/a	n/a	n/a	n/a	n/a	n/a
Tulsa, OK	56.6	47	42.6	40	45.3	45
Tyler, TX	n/a	n/a	n/a	n/a	n/a	n/a
Virginia Beach, VA	47.8	76	34.3	79	32.2	90
Washington, DC	62.3	32	38.9	64	48.3	32
Wichita, KS	58.0	44	46.5	20	42.3	56
Wilmington, NC	n/a	n/a	n/a	n/a	n/a	n/a
Winston-Salem, NC	n/a	n/a	n/a	n/a	n/a	n/a
Worcester, MA	52.6	61	45.8	22	52.7	17

Note: Figures are based on an analysis of 1990, 2000, and 2010 Census Decennial Census tract data by William H. Frey, Brookings Institution and the University of Michigan Social Science Data Analysis Network. In this analysis all racial groups (whites, blacks, and asians) are non-Hispanic members of those races. Hispanics are shown as a separate category; All figures cover the Metropolitan Statistical Area (see Appendix B for areas included); (1) Segregation Indices are Dissimilarity Indices that measure the degree to which the minority group is distributed differently than whites across census tracts. They range from 0 (complete integration) to 100 (complete [segregation) where the value indicates the percentage of the minority group that needs to move to be distributed exactly like whites; (2) Ranges from 1 (most segregated) to 102 (least segregated); n/a not available.
Source: www.CensusScope.org

Religious Groups by Family

Area[1]	Catholic	Baptist	Non-Den.	Methodist[2]	Lutheran	LDS[3]	Pentecostal	Presbyterian[4]	Muslim[5]	Judaism
Albuquerque, NM	27.2	3.8	4.2	1.5	1.0	2.4	1.5	1.1	0.2	0.3
Anchorage, AK	6.9	5.0	6.4	1.4	1.9	5.1	1.9	0.7	0.2	0.1
Ann Arbor, MI	12.4	2.2	1.6	3.1	2.9	0.9	1.9	3.0	1.3	0.9
Athens, GA	4.4	16.3	2.3	8.4	0.4	0.8	2.8	2.0	0.4	0.2
Atlanta, GA	7.5	17.5	6.9	7.9	0.5	0.8	2.6	1.8	0.8	0.6
Austin, TX	16.0	10.3	4.5	3.6	2.0	1.2	0.8	1.1	1.2	0.3
Billings, MT	12.1	2.5	3.8	2.1	6.1	4.9	4.1	1.8	<0.1	0.1
Boise City, ID	8.0	2.9	4.2	2.1	1.2	15.9	2.3	0.6	0.1	0.1
Boston, MA	44.4	1.2	1.0	1.0	0.4	0.4	0.6	1.6	0.4	1.4
Boulder, CO	20.1	2.4	4.8	1.8	3.1	3.0	0.5	2.0	0.1	0.8
Cape Coral, FL	16.2	5.0	3.0	2.5	1.2	0.5	4.4	1.4	0.9	0.2
Cedar Rapids, IA	18.8	2.4	3.0	7.3	11.3	0.9	1.8	3.3	0.5	0.1
Charleston, SC	6.2	12.4	7.1	10.0	1.1	1.0	2.0	2.4	0.2	0.3
Charlotte, NC	5.9	17.3	6.8	8.6	1.3	0.8	3.3	4.5	0.2	0.3
Chicago, IL	34.2	3.2	4.5	1.9	3.0	0.4	1.2	1.9	3.3	0.8
Clarksville, TN	4.1	30.9	2.3	6.2	0.6	1.5	1.8	1.1	0.1	<0.1
Colorado Springs, CO	8.4	4.3	7.4	2.4	2.0	3.0	1.1	2.1	0.1	0.1
Columbia, MO	6.6	14.7	5.4	4.3	1.7	1.4	1.1	2.3	0.3	0.3
Columbus, OH	11.8	5.3	3.6	4.7	2.4	0.7	2.0	2.0	0.8	0.5
Dallas, TX	13.3	18.7	7.8	5.3	0.8	1.2	2.2	1.0	2.4	0.4
Davenport, IA	14.9	5.0	2.7	5.3	8.7	0.8	1.4	3.0	0.9	0.1
Denver, CO	16.1	3.0	4.6	1.7	2.1	2.4	1.2	1.6	0.6	0.6
Des Moines, IA	13.6	4.8	3.3	7.0	8.2	1.0	2.4	3.0	0.3	0.3
Durham, NC	5.1	13.9	5.6	8.1	0.5	0.8	1.4	2.5	0.5	0.6
El Paso, TX	43.2	3.8	5.0	0.9	0.3	1.6	1.4	0.2	0.1	0.2
Erie, PA	33.5	2.2	1.7	5.7	3.0	0.6	2.2	2.1	0.7	0.2
Eugene, OR	6.2	3.1	1.9	0.9	1.4	3.7	3.3	0.6	0.1	0.4
Fargo, ND	17.4	0.4	0.5	3.3	32.5	0.6	1.5	1.9	0.1	<0.1
Fayetteville, NC	2.6	14.1	10.5	6.2	0.2	1.4	4.9	2.1	0.2	<0.1
Fort Collins, CO	11.8	2.2	6.4	4.4	3.5	3.0	4.7	1.9	0.1	<0.1
Fort Wayne, IN	14.2	6.1	6.8	5.1	8.5	0.4	1.5	1.7	0.3	0.1
Fort Worth, TX	13.3	18.7	7.8	5.3	0.8	1.2	2.2	1.0	2.4	0.4
Gainesville, FL	7.6	12.3	4.3	6.4	0.5	1.0	3.5	1.1	1.1	0.4
Grand Rapids, MI	17.2	1.7	8.4	3.1	2.1	0.6	1.1	10.0	1.1	0.1
Green Bay, WI	42.0	0.7	3.4	2.2	12.7	0.4	0.6	1.0	0.1	0.1
Greensboro, NC	2.7	12.8	7.4	9.9	0.7	0.8	2.5	3.2	0.6	0.4
Honolulu, HI	18.2	1.9	2.2	0.8	0.3	5.1	4.2	1.5	<0.1	0.1
Houston, TX	17.1	16.0	7.3	4.9	1.1	1.1	1.5	0.9	2.7	0.4
Huntsville, AL	4.0	27.6	3.2	7.5	0.7	1.2	1.2	1.7	0.2	0.2
Indianapolis, IN	10.5	10.3	7.2	5.0	1.7	0.7	1.6	1.7	0.2	0.4
Jacksonville, FL	9.9	18.5	7.8	4.5	0.7	1.1	1.9	1.6	0.6	0.4
Kansas City, MO	12.7	13.2	5.2	5.9	2.3	2.5	2.6	1.6	0.3	0.4
Lafayette, LA	47.0	14.8	4.0	2.6	0.2	0.4	2.9	0.2	0.1	0.1
Las Vegas, NV	18.1	3.0	3.1	0.4	0.7	6.4	1.5	0.2	0.1	0.3
Lexington, KY	6.8	24.9	2.4	5.9	0.4	1.1	2.1	1.4	0.1	0.3
Lincoln, NE	14.8	2.4	1.9	7.2	11.3	1.2	1.4	3.9	0.2	0.2
Little Rock, AR	4.5	25.9	6.1	7.3	0.5	0.9	2.9	0.9	0.1	0.1
Los Angeles, CA	33.8	2.8	3.6	1.1	0.7	1.7	1.8	0.9	0.7	1.0
Louisville, KY	13.7	25.1	1.7	3.7	0.6	0.8	1.0	1.2	0.5	0.4
Lubbock, TX	13.4	22.4	7.3	6.6	0.5	1.4	1.9	0.8	1.8	0.1
Madison, WI	21.8	1.1	1.6	3.7	12.8	0.5	0.4	2.2	0.5	0.5
Manchester, NH	31.2	1.4	2.4	1.2	0.5	0.6	0.5	2.0	0.3	0.5
McAllen, TX	34.7	4.5	2.8	1.3	0.4	1.3	1.2	0.2	1.0	<0.1
⸳⸳⸳, FL	18.6	5.4	4.2	1.3	0.5	0.5	1.8	0.7	0.9	1.6
⸳⸳⸳ TX	22.4	25.3	8.8	4.2	0.7	1.2	1.6	1.9	3.7	<0.1

continued on next page.

Area[1]	Catholic	Baptist	Non-Den.	Methodist[2]	Lutheran	LDS[3]	Pentecostal	Presbyterian[4]	Muslim[5]	Judaism
Minneapolis, MN	21.7	2.5	3.0	2.8	14.5	0.6	1.8	1.9	0.4	0.7
Nashville, TN	4.1	25.3	5.8	6.1	0.4	0.8	2.2	2.1	0.4	0.2
New Orleans, LA	31.6	8.4	3.7	2.7	0.8	0.6	2.1	0.5	0.5	0.5
New York, NY	36.9	1.9	1.8	1.3	0.8	0.4	0.9	1.1	2.3	4.8
Oklahoma City, OK	6.4	25.4	7.1	10.6	0.7	1.3	3.2	1.0	0.2	0.1
Omaha, NE	21.6	4.6	1.8	3.9	7.9	1.8	1.3	2.3	0.5	0.4
Orlando, FL	13.2	7.0	5.7	3.0	0.9	1.0	3.2	1.4	1.3	0.3
Oxnard, CA	28.2	1.9	4.1	1.1	1.5	2.5	1.3	0.7	0.4	0.7
Palm Bay, FL	11.9	6.5	5.3	4.0	1.2	1.0	1.0	1.3	0.8	0.1
Peoria, IL	11.5	5.5	5.3	5.0	6.1	0.5	1.5	2.8	5.2	0.1
Philadelphia, PA	33.5	3.9	2.9	3.0	1.9	0.3	0.9	2.1	1.3	1.4
Phoenix, AZ	13.4	3.5	5.2	1.0	1.6	6.1	2.9	0.6	0.2	0.3
Pittsburgh, PA	32.8	2.3	2.8	5.7	3.4	0.4	1.1	4.7	0.3	0.7
Portland, OR	10.6	2.3	4.5	1.0	1.6	3.8	2.0	1.0	0.1	0.3
Providence, RI	47.0	1.4	1.2	0.8	0.5	0.3	0.6	1.0	0.1	0.7
Provo, UT	1.3	0.1	0.1	0.2	<0.1	88.6	0.1	0.1	<0.1	<0.1
Raleigh, NC	9.2	12.1	6.0	6.7	0.9	0.9	2.3	2.3	0.9	0.3
Reno, NV	14.3	1.5	3.2	0.9	0.8	4.6	2.0	0.4	0.1	0.2
Richmond, VA	6.0	19.9	5.5	6.1	0.6	1.0	1.8	2.1	2.8	0.4
Roanoke, VA	3.7	22.4	4.6	7.3	1.4	1.1	2.8	2.5	2.2	0.3
Rochester, MN	23.4	1.7	4.7	4.9	21.1	1.1	1.3	2.9	0.3	0.2
Sacramento, CA	16.2	3.2	4.0	1.8	0.8	3.4	2.0	0.8	0.8	0.3
Salem, OR	16.7	2.2	3.0	1.2	1.7	3.9	3.4	0.7	<0.1	0.1
Salt Lake City, UT	8.9	0.8	0.5	0.5	0.5	58.9	0.7	0.4	0.4	0.1
San Antonio, TX	28.4	8.5	6.0	3.1	1.7	1.4	1.3	0.8	1.0	0.2
San Diego, CA	25.9	2.0	4.8	1.1	1.0	2.3	1.0	0.9	0.7	0.5
San Francisco, CA	20.8	2.5	2.5	2.0	0.6	1.6	1.2	1.1	1.2	0.9
San Jose, CA	26.0	1.4	4.3	1.1	0.6	1.4	1.2	0.7	1.0	0.7
Santa Rosa, CA	22.3	1.4	1.5	0.9	1.0	1.9	0.7	0.9	0.5	0.4
Savannah, GA	7.1	19.7	6.9	8.9	1.6	1.0	2.4	1.0	0.2	0.8
Seattle, WA	12.3	2.2	5.0	1.2	2.1	3.3	2.8	1.4	0.5	0.5
Sioux Falls, SD	14.9	3.0	1.5	3.9	21.4	0.7	1.1	6.2	0.3	0.1
Spokane, WA	13.1	1.9	4.3	1.0	2.9	5.2	2.9	1.5	0.1	0.2
Springfield, IL	15.6	11.7	2.7	6.8	5.6	0.8	5.0	2.0	1.6	0.2
Tallahassee, FL	4.8	16.1	6.8	9.2	0.5	1.0	2.2	1.6	0.9	0.4
Tampa, FL	10.9	7.1	3.8	3.5	1.0	0.6	2.1	1.0	1.3	0.5
Topeka, KS	12.8	9.1	4.1	7.3	3.6	1.5	2.0	1.7	0.1	0.1
Tulsa, OK	5.8	22.9	7.6	9.2	0.8	1.2	3.3	1.3	0.3	0.3
Tyler, TX	12.2	33.6	9.0	6.4	0.6	1.2	5.1	0.7	0.4	0.1
Virginia Beach, VA	6.4	11.6	6.2	5.3	0.7	0.9	1.9	2.0	2.1	0.4
Washington, DC	14.5	7.3	4.9	4.5	1.3	1.2	1.1	1.4	2.4	1.2
Wichita, KS	14.5	13.5	3.2	7.2	1.8	1.4	2.0	1.7	0.2	<0.1
Wilmington, NC	6.2	14.5	4.6	8.5	0.9	1.0	1.1	2.5	0.3	0.1
Winston-Salem, NC	3.6	17.5	9.4	12.4	0.7	0.7	2.6	2.2	0.3	0.1
Worcester, MA	38.4	1.2	1.8	1.0	0.9	0.3	1.1	2.1	0.1	0.5
U.S.	19.1	9.3	4.0	4.0	2.3	2.0	1.9	1.6	0.8	0.7

Note: Figures are the number of adherents as a percentage of the total population; (1) Figures cover the Metropolitan Statistical Area—see Appendix B for areas included; (2) Methodist/Pietist; (3) Latter Day Saints; (4) Reformed; (5) Figures are estimates
Source: Association of Statisticians of American Religious Bodies, 2010 U.S. Religion Census: Religious Congregations & Membership Study

Religious Groups by Tradition

Area	Catholic	Evangelical Protestant	Mainline Protestant	Other Tradition	Black Protestant	Orthodox
Albuquerque, NM	27.2	11.3	3.3	3.9	0.2	0.2
Anchorage, AK	6.9	15.7	3.6	6.8	0.3	0.6
Ann Arbor, MI	12.4	7.3	7.5	3.8	1.6	0.3
Athens, GA	4.4	21.1	9.8	1.7	2.5	0.1
Atlanta, GA	7.5	26.1	9.8	2.9	3.2	0.3
Austin, TX	16.0	16.1	6.3	3.9	1.4	0.1
Billings, MT	12.1	13.7	8.2	5.2	0.1	0.1
Boise City, ID	8.0	13.0	4.4	16.7	<0.1	0.1
Boston, MA	44.4	3.2	4.5	3.4	0.2	1.1
Boulder, CO	20.1	9.8	6.5	4.9	<0.1	0.2
Cape Coral, FL	16.2	14.3	4.6	2.0	0.3	0.2
Cedar Rapids, IA	18.8	13.7	17.5	2.0	0.2	0.2
Charleston, SC	6.2	19.7	11.2	1.9	7.3	0.1
Charlotte, NC	5.9	27.6	13.3	1.7	2.8	0.5
Chicago, IL	34.2	9.8	5.1	5.1	2.1	0.9
Clarksville, TN	4.1	35.4	7.3	1.7	2.4	<0.1
Colorado Springs, CO	8.4	15.2	5.4	3.7	0.4	0.1
Columbia, MO	6.6	19.9	10.5	2.3	0.5	0.1
Columbus, OH	11.8	11.9	9.5	3.1	1.1	0.3
Dallas, TX	13.3	28.3	7.0	4.8	1.8	0.2
Davenport, IA	14.9	11.4	15.1	2.4	1.6	0.1
Denver, CO	16.1	11.1	4.5	4.6	0.4	0.3
Des Moines, IA	13.6	12.4	16.8	1.9	0.9	0.1
Durham, NC	5.1	19.4	11.7	2.9	3.1	0.1
El Paso, TX	43.2	10.9	1.3	2.1	0.2	0.1
Erie, PA	33.5	8.4	11.7	1.6	0.9	0.3
Eugene, OR	6.2	9.7	3.4	5.5	0.1	0.1
Fargo, ND	17.4	10.7	30.8	0.9	<0.1	<0.1
Fayetteville, NC	2.6	26.7	7.9	1.8	4.3	0.1
Fort Collins, CO	11.8	18.8	5.9	4.0	<0.1	0.1
Fort Wayne, IN	14.2	24.6	9.2	1.0	2.4	0.2
Fort Worth, TX	13.3	28.3	7.0	4.8	1.8	0.2
Gainesville, FL	7.6	20.4	7.0	4.2	2.2	0.1
Grand Rapids, MI	17.2	20.7	7.6	2.2	1.1	0.2
Green Bay, WI	42.0	14.1	8.1	0.6	<0.1	<0.1
Greensboro, NC	2.7	23.2	14.0	2.2	2.6	0.1
Honolulu, HI	18.2	9.7	2.9	8.4	<0.1	<0.1
Houston, TX	17.1	24.9	6.7	4.9	1.3	0.2
Huntsville, AL	4.0	33.3	9.7	1.9	1.8	0.1
Indianapolis, IN	10.5	18.3	9.6	1.7	1.9	0.3
Jacksonville, FL	9.9	27.1	5.7	2.9	4.2	0.3
Kansas City, MO	12.7	20.6	10.0	3.7	2.6	0.1
Lafayette, LA	47.0	12.8	3.2	0.8	9.3	0.1
Las Vegas, NV	18.1	7.7	1.4	7.6	0.4	0.4
Lexington, KY	6.8	28.3	10.3	1.7	2.1	0.2
Lincoln, NE	14.8	14.8	16.2	2.0	0.1	0.1
Little Rock, AR	4.5	33.9	8.2	1.7	3.5	0.1
Los Angeles, CA	33.8	9.0	2.4	4.6	0.9	0.6
Louisville, KY	13.7	24.5	7.1	2.0	3.0	0.1
Lubbock, TX	13.4	31.5	8.6	4.0	0.7	0.1
Madison, WI	21.8	7.3	15.4	2.3	0.1	0.1
Manchester, NH	31.2	5.1	4.4	1.8	<0.1	0.7
McAllen, TX	34.7	9.7	1.9	2.4	<0.1	<0.1
Miami, FL	18.6	11.4	2.5	3.5	1.7	0.3
Midland, TX	22.4	35.5	7.2	5.4	1.0	<0.1

Table continued on next page.

Area	Catholic	Evangelical Protestant	Mainline Protestant	Other Tradition	Black Protestant	Orthodox
Minneapolis, MN	21.7	12.9	14.5	2.3	0.5	0.2
Nashville, TN	4.1	33.0	8.0	1.7	3.4	0.5
New Orleans, LA	31.6	12.7	4.0	2.1	3.0	0.1
New York, NY	36.9	4.0	4.1	8.4	1.2	1.0
Oklahoma City, OK	6.4	39.1	9.9	2.8	1.9	0.2
Omaha, NE	21.6	12.1	10.8	3.3	1.5	0.1
Orlando, FL	13.2	17.8	4.8	3.3	1.2	0.3
Oxnard, CA	28.2	8.9	2.7	4.5	0.2	0.2
Palm Bay, FL	11.9	14.0	5.7	2.0	1.0	0.2
Peoria, IL	11.5	18.9	11.1	6.2	0.9	0.1
Philadelphia, PA	33.5	6.3	8.9	3.7	1.8	0.4
Phoenix, AZ	13.4	13.2	2.6	7.8	0.2	0.3
Pittsburgh, PA	32.8	7.4	13.8	2.1	0.9	0.7
Portland, OR	10.6	11.7	3.7	5.2	0.2	0.3
Providence, RI	47.0	2.8	4.7	1.6	0.1	0.6
Provo, UT	1.3	0.5	0.1	88.9	<0.1	<0.1
Raleigh, NC	9.2	19.9	10.1	3.3	1.7	0.2
Reno, NV	14.3	7.7	1.9	5.1	0.2	0.1
Richmond, VA	6.0	23.7	13.3	4.6	2.4	0.2
Roanoke, VA	3.7	31.7	13.2	4.0	1.2	0.2
Rochester, MN	23.4	19.0	21.1	2.1	<0.1	0.1
Sacramento, CA	16.2	11.4	2.2	5.8	0.6	0.3
Salem, OR	16.7	14.1	3.8	4.2	<0.1	<0.1
Salt Lake City, UT	8.9	2.6	1.3	60.1	0.1	0.5
San Antonio, TX	28.4	17.0	5.0	3.2	0.4	0.1
San Diego, CA	25.9	9.8	2.4	5.2	0.4	0.3
San Francisco, CA	20.8	6.2	3.8	5.2	1.1	0.7
San Jose, CA	26.0	8.2	2.5	6.9	0.1	0.4
Santa Rosa, CA	22.3	5.3	2.4	4.8	<0.1	0.3
Savannah, GA	7.1	25.1	9.5	2.6	8.6	0.1
Seattle, WA	12.3	11.9	4.7	5.9	0.4	0.4
Sioux Falls, SD	14.9	12.9	28.1	1.2	0.1	0.1
Spokane, WA	13.1	12.4	4.9	6.3	0.1	0.2
Springfield, IL	15.6	21.5	11.7	3.2	2.1	0.1
Tallahassee, FL	4.8	21.9	6.4	3.0	9.2	0.2
Tampa, FL	10.9	13.6	5.2	3.1	1.2	0.8
Topeka, KS	12.8	15.5	12.9	1.8	2.8	<0.1
Tulsa, OK	5.8	34.6	11.3	2.2	1.6	0.1
Tyler, TX	12.2	45.5	7.4	1.7	4.1	<0.1
Virginia Beach, VA	6.4	18.0	9.4	4.0	2.3	0.3
Washington, DC	14.5	12.4	8.8	5.9	2.3	0.6
Wichita, KS	14.5	20.7	11.1	2.4	1.9	0.2
Wilmington, NC	6.2	20.4	10.8	1.7	3.1	0.1
Winston-Salem, NC	3.6	29.2	15.7	1.3	2.3	0.3
Worcester, MA	38.4	4.7	5.4	2.4	0.1	1.0
U.S.	19.1	16.2	7.3	4.3	1.6	0.3

Note: Figures are the number of adherents as a percentage of the total population; (1) Figures cover the Metropolitan Statistical Area—see Appendix B for areas included; Source: Association of Statisticians of American Religious Bodies, 2010 U.S. Religion Census: Religious Congregations & Membership Study

Ancestry: City

City	German	Irish	English	American	Italian	Polish	French[1]	Scottish	Dutch
Albuquerque, NM	10.4	7.4	6.7	4.0	3.2	1.2	2.0	1.7	1.0
Anchorage, AK	16.7	10.1	8.6	5.7	3.2	1.8	2.8	3.0	1.7
Ann Arbor, MI	18.0	10.0	10.2	5.4	5.0	6.6	3.2	2.9	2.4
Athens, GA	9.2	7.9	9.1	8.6	2.5	1.8	1.5	3.2	0.7
Atlanta, GA	5.9	5.2	6.7	7.4	2.1	1.2	1.4	2.2	0.6
Austin, TX	12.8	8.4	8.3	4.2	3.0	1.6	3.0	2.2	0.9
Billings, MT	26.2	12.1	9.8	14.5	3.7	2.0	3.2	2.4	1.8
Boise City, ID	18.0	10.5	14.2	6.9	4.6	1.8	2.5	3.8	2.2
Boston, MA	4.7	14.6	5.0	6.0	8.0	2.6	1.9	1.3	0.5
Boulder, CO	22.4	14.0	12.9	5.1	6.6	4.1	4.4	3.1	2.0
Cape Coral, FL	18.9	14.5	8.6	9.9	11.1	4.5	3.3	1.4	1.0
Cedar Rapids, IA	37.0	15.7	8.8	5.3	2.2	1.8	2.8	1.8	1.8
Charleston, SC	12.0	11.4	11.4	13.9	4.2	2.1	2.7	3.2	1.0
Charlotte, NC	9.7	7.7	7.4	5.2	3.4	1.8	1.5	2.2	0.7
Chicago, IL	7.4	7.5	2.2	2.0	4.0	6.0	0.9	0.6	0.6
Clarksville, TN	13.6	11.5	6.9	7.0	3.3	2.5	2.2	1.6	1.3
Colorado Springs, CO	22.4	13.0	10.2	5.8	5.8	2.4	3.0	2.9	2.1
Columbia, MO	27.2	13.3	11.3	5.3	3.9	2.5	3.1	2.9	1.7
Columbus, OH	20.2	11.6	6.7	5.4	5.3	2.2	1.9	1.5	1.0
Dallas, TX	5.9	4.4	5.0	3.2	1.4	0.9	1.4	1.1	0.5
Davenport, IA	31.6	15.0	6.4	6.3	2.3	2.4	2.2	1.1	2.3
Denver, CO	14.9	10.1	7.8	3.3	4.2	2.5	2.5	2.2	1.4
Des Moines, IA	21.1	11.8	7.5	5.2	3.5	1.2	2.0	1.7	3.3
Durham, NC	6.8	5.5	7.5	4.3	2.7	1.6	1.3	1.8	0.8
El Paso, TX	3.5	2.9	1.7	4.2	1.0	0.4	0.6	0.4	0.2
Erie, PA	24.3	15.7	5.1	2.9	11.5	11.6	1.8	0.8	1.3
Eugene, OR	19.0	13.3	12.0	4.9	4.2	2.6	3.7	2.8	2.2
Fargo, ND	40.1	9.6	5.1	2.1	1.4	2.5	3.1	1.6	1.1
Fayetteville, NC	10.4	7.5	5.0	5.2	2.6	1.4	1.4	1.8	0.6
Fort Collins, CO	26.3	14.2	11.6	4.1	6.8	3.6	3.9	2.9	2.6
Fort Wayne, IN	26.7	9.3	6.8	11.3	2.6	2.2	3.5	1.5	1.6
Fort Worth, TX	8.9	7.1	5.4	6.8	1.9	1.2	1.5	1.5	0.7
Gainesville, FL	11.5	10.6	8.4	4.2	5.9	3.0	2.5	2.5	1.0
Grand Rapids, MI	15.3	8.9	6.8	3.2	3.0	7.0	3.0	1.3	15.0
Green Bay, WI	33.0	8.8	3.4	4.0	2.1	9.8	5.0	0.9	4.0
Greensboro, NC	7.4	5.8	7.9	5.6	2.3	1.1	1.1	2.1	0.6
Honolulu, HI	4.3	3.2	2.8	1.5	2.0	0.6	1.3	0.9	0.4
Houston, TX	5.3	3.7	3.9	3.8	1.6	0.9	1.7	0.9	0.5
Huntsville, AL	10.7	8.8	9.6	9.9	2.7	1.0	1.9	2.3	1.0
Indianapolis, IN	16.2	10.0	6.5	7.5	2.1	1.5	1.8	1.6	1.1
Jacksonville, FL	9.6	9.7	8.2	6.0	4.0	1.6	2.1	1.8	0.8
Kansas City, MO	17.4	11.7	7.5	9.4	3.3	1.4	2.2	1.6	1.3
Lafayette, LA	9.2	6.6	5.9	7.7	3.4	0.7	20.1	1.3	0.7
Las Vegas, NV	9.8	8.2	5.7	3.8	6.2	2.3	2.2	1.3	0.7
Lexington, KY	13.6	12.5	11.5	15.1	3.2	1.3	2.0	2.6	1.2
Lincoln, NE	40.0	13.4	9.4	4.6	2.0	2.6	2.8	1.7	2.0
Little Rock, AR	8.1	7.4	7.6	6.3	1.4	0.7	1.6	1.9	0.6
Los Angeles, CA	4.3	3.7	3.1	3.0	2.6	1.6	1.2	0.8	0.5
Louisville, KY	16.4	12.4	8.5	14.7	2.4	0.8	2.0	1.5	1.2
Lubbock, TX	11.8	8.0	7.4	7.5	1.7	0.9	1.6	1.5	0.9
Madison, WI	33.3	13.3	8.8	3.0	4.2	5.2	2.7	1.7	2.1
Manchester, NH	7.1	19.5	9.3	3.4	8.0	4.8	17.4	1.9	0.5
McAllen, TX	4.3	2.6	2.8	2.5	1.4	0.2	3.1	0.3	0.4
Miami, FL	2.0	1.5	1.1	4.7	2.3	0.8	0.8	0.3	0.3
Midland, TX	11.6	8.3	7.1	6.5	1.2	0.6	1.3	1.5	0.8
Minneapolis, MN	22.2	10.7	5.8	2.3	2.3	3.9	2.9	1.4	1.4

Table continued on next page.

City	German	Irish	English	American	Italian	Polish	French[1]	Scottish	Dutch
Nashville, TN	9.2	8.9	8.1	7.7	2.4	1.0	2.0	1.9	0.9
New Orleans, LA	6.8	6.0	4.2	3.4	4.1	0.8	6.2	1.0	0.4
New York, NY	3.0	4.7	1.7	4.5	6.8	2.5	0.8	0.4	0.3
Oklahoma City, OK	12.7	9.5	7.2	7.2	1.6	0.9	2.1	1.9	1.2
Omaha, NE	27.4	14.6	7.1	3.5	4.7	4.1	2.4	1.2	1.7
Orlando, FL	7.9	6.5	5.6	7.4	3.7	1.5	1.5	1.3	0.7
Oxnard, CA	4.1	3.4	2.4	1.5	1.7	0.5	0.9	0.6	0.5
Palm Bay, FL	14.2	12.1	10.9	12.1	8.7	3.2	3.3	1.9	1.1
Peoria, IL	20.5	9.4	7.3	5.0	3.2	2.0	1.9	1.3	0.9
Philadelphia, PA	7.2	11.8	2.6	2.5	7.9	3.4	0.7	0.6	0.4
Phoenix, AZ	11.8	8.1	6.2	4.2	4.0	2.2	1.9	1.4	1.1
Pittsburgh, PA	19.6	16.3	5.0	3.9	12.7	7.5	1.6	1.6	0.7
Portland, OR	17.3	12.1	10.7	5.7	4.5	2.4	3.1	3.3	1.9
Providence, RI	3.3	8.5	3.9	2.6	9.9	1.8	3.1	1.1	0.4
Provo, UT	10.6	5.4	23.1	4.6	2.7	0.5	2.6	4.4	1.6
Raleigh, NC	9.9	8.1	9.9	10.0	3.8	1.8	1.7	2.5	0.9
Reno, NV	14.1	11.8	8.0	5.1	6.4	1.6	2.8	2.2	1.7
Richmond, VA	7.3	6.7	8.5	4.0	2.5	1.0	1.6	1.9	0.6
Roanoke, VA	11.2	10.1	10.1	11.8	2.2	1.2	2.0	1.6	1.4
Rochester, MN	32.4	10.2	6.2	4.3	1.9	3.8	2.7	1.1	2.1
Sacramento, CA	8.3	6.7	5.4	2.4	3.8	0.9	1.6	1.4	0.8
Salem, OR	19.6	11.5	11.1	4.4	3.5	1.1	3.4	2.8	2.1
Salt Lake City, UT	10.8	6.5	16.1	4.0	2.8	1.1	1.9	3.8	2.1
San Antonio, TX	8.5	4.6	4.0	3.8	1.9	1.1	1.5	0.9	0.5
San Diego, CA	9.3	7.6	5.9	3.2	4.1	1.8	2.1	1.4	0.9
San Francisco, CA	7.9	7.9	4.9	2.8	5.0	1.7	2.2	1.4	0.9
San Jose, CA	5.9	4.8	4.1	1.8	4.2	0.9	1.3	0.9	0.7
Santa Rosa, CA	12.6	11.0	9.3	4.5	8.0	1.4	3.4	2.5	1.6
Savannah, GA	6.1	6.5	5.5	4.2	2.2	1.3	1.4	1.6	0.6
Seattle, WA	16.4	11.4	11.0	3.4	4.4	2.4	3.3	3.1	1.8
Sioux Falls, SD	36.8	10.8	4.6	3.9	1.1	1.6	2.4	0.8	7.2
Spokane, WA	22.0	13.5	10.6	5.3	5.1	1.8	3.4	2.7	1.8
Springfield, IL	23.5	13.8	9.1	6.6	5.3	2.1	2.1	1.5	1.1
Tallahassee, FL	9.8	9.7	8.8	4.3	4.5	2.1	1.9	2.3	0.9
Tampa, FL	8.7	8.0	5.8	5.7	6.0	1.9	2.0	1.5	1.0
Topeka, KS	26.0	13.6	10.2	4.9	2.8	1.0	3.2	2.0	1.8
Tulsa, OK	13.5	11.2	8.7	8.2	1.8	1.0	2.5	2.2	1.5
Tyler, TX	9.0	9.2	8.2	7.1	2.3	0.8	2.5	1.6	0.9
Virginia Beach, VA	13.2	11.4	9.3	14.1	6.1	2.9	2.6	2.3	1.1
Washington, DC	6.6	6.5	5.2	2.7	3.8	2.1	1.4	1.4	0.5
Wichita, KS	21.6	10.3	8.2	8.7	1.8	0.9	2.3	1.8	1.5
Wilmington, NC	10.9	9.7	10.2	21.4	4.5	1.6	2.1	3.8	1.4
Winston-Salem, NC	8.8	6.0	9.2	5.2	2.4	1.2	1.4	2.6	0.8
Worcester, MA	3.1	15.9	4.8	3.0	9.6	4.5	7.6	1.2	0.4
U.S.	14.9	10.8	8.0	7.4	5.5	3.0	2.7	1.7	1.4

Note: Figures are the percentage of the total population reporting a particular ancestry. The nine most commonly reported ancestries in the U.S. are shown. Figures include multiple ancestries (e.g. if a person reported being Irish and Italian, they were included in both columns); (1) Excludes Basque
Source: U.S. Census Bureau, 2011-2013 American Community Survey 3-Year Estimates

Ancestry: Metro Area

Metro Area	German	Irish	English	American	Italian	Polish	French[1]	Scottish	Dutch
Albuquerque, NM	10.6	7.2	6.8	4.8	3.1	1.5	1.8	1.6	1.0
Anchorage, AK	18.1	10.8	8.7	5.6	3.2	1.9	3.0	3.0	1.8
Ann Arbor, MI	20.8	11.1	10.3	7.6	5.0	6.7	3.1	2.7	2.0
Athens, GA	9.3	8.9	9.7	13.0	2.5	1.3	1.6	2.9	0.7
Atlanta, GA	7.5	7.6	7.4	10.2	2.5	1.3	1.5	1.7	0.8
Austin, TX	14.6	8.7	8.8	5.1	3.0	1.6	2.8	2.2	1.0
Billings, MT	28.1	11.8	10.0	15.2	3.1	1.9	3.0	2.6	2.0
Boise City, ID	17.0	8.8	13.9	10.4	3.3	1.5	2.2	3.2	2.0
Boston, MA	6.3	23.4	10.5	4.9	14.8	3.7	5.7	2.5	0.6
Boulder, CO	22.4	13.6	13.5	5.5	5.8	3.8	4.0	3.4	2.3
Cape Coral, FL	15.5	11.9	9.0	13.6	7.7	3.5	3.1	1.5	1.3
Cedar Rapids, IA	40.7	16.4	9.2	6.3	2.0	1.5	2.7	1.6	2.1
Charleston, SC	11.4	10.4	9.0	13.5	3.6	1.7	2.6	2.6	1.0
Charlotte, NC	12.0	9.2	8.3	10.1	3.7	1.8	1.6	2.3	1.0
Chicago, IL	15.4	11.8	4.4	3.0	7.1	9.3	1.5	1.0	1.3
Clarksville, TN	12.4	10.5	8.2	13.2	3.0	2.0	1.8	1.9	1.3
Colorado Springs, CO	22.2	13.2	10.1	6.3	5.4	2.6	3.2	2.9	2.1
Columbia, MO	27.4	13.5	11.5	6.5	3.5	1.9	3.0	2.8	1.5
Columbus, OH	25.5	14.0	9.4	8.1	5.5	2.3	2.2	2.1	1.7
Dallas, TX	10.3	8.2	7.5	6.9	2.2	1.1	2.0	1.7	0.9
Davenport, IA	28.7	14.8	8.6	6.6	2.7	2.2	2.3	1.5	2.1
Denver, CO	19.7	11.9	9.9	5.1	5.3	2.7	2.8	2.4	1.6
Des Moines, IA	28.5	13.8	9.4	5.5	3.2	1.4	2.3	1.6	3.9
Durham, NC	9.4	7.9	10.6	7.0	3.0	2.0	1.9	2.3	0.9
El Paso, TX	3.3	2.6	1.6	3.9	1.0	0.4	0.6	0.4	0.2
Erie, PA	28.9	17.7	8.3	4.7	12.4	12.1	1.8	1.6	1.5
Eugene, OR	19.0	13.6	12.0	5.9	4.2	2.3	3.4	3.0	2.3
Fargo, ND	39.8	8.4	4.5	2.1	1.3	2.7	3.2	1.2	1.1
Fayetteville, NC	9.4	7.5	5.2	7.9	2.8	1.2	1.3	1.9	0.8
Fort Collins, CO	28.2	13.9	12.6	4.7	5.8	3.1	4.0	3.1	2.5
Fort Wayne, IN	30.4	9.1	7.7	12.4	2.5	2.3	3.5	1.6	1.6
Fort Worth, TX	10.3	8.2	7.5	6.9	2.2	1.1	2.0	1.7	0.9
Gainesville, FL	12.7	11.2	9.8	6.1	4.8	2.5	2.6	2.2	1.3
Grand Rapids, MI	21.5	11.1	9.9	5.1	3.2	6.9	3.7	1.9	20.6
Green Bay, WI	38.4	9.6	3.6	4.4	2.5	10.4	4.9	0.9	5.0
Greensboro, NC	9.0	7.0	9.6	10.2	2.3	0.9	1.3	2.1	0.8
Honolulu, HI	5.2	4.0	3.3	1.5	2.0	0.8	1.1	0.8	0.6
Houston, TX	8.7	6.0	5.4	4.9	2.1	1.3	2.3	1.2	0.7
Huntsville, AL	10.1	9.0	9.3	14.7	2.1	1.0	1.8	2.0	0.9
Indianapolis, IN	20.4	11.7	9.1	9.8	2.6	1.9	2.1	2.0	1.7
Jacksonville, FL	11.2	11.4	9.6	8.4	4.8	2.1	2.6	2.3	1.0
Kansas City, MO	23.1	13.4	10.1	8.3	3.4	1.8	2.6	2.0	1.5
Lafayette, LA	8.0	4.6	4.2	10.7	2.5	0.4	21.0	0.7	0.3
Las Vegas, NV	10.5	8.2	6.1	4.2	6.0	2.4	2.1	1.4	0.9
Lexington, KY	14.1	12.6	11.9	19.0	2.9	1.3	1.9	2.7	1.2
Lincoln, NE	41.3	13.1	9.2	4.8	2.0	2.5	2.8	1.7	2.1
Little Rock, AR	10.9	10.4	10.2	10.5	1.7	0.9	2.2	2.0	1.1
Los Angeles, CA	6.0	4.9	4.3	3.5	3.0	1.3	1.4	1.0	0.7
Louisville, KY	18.7	12.8	9.5	18.1	2.3	1.0	2.1	1.8	1.2
Lubbock, TX	11.8	8.4	7.2	8.0	1.5	0.8	1.6	1.6	0.9
Madison, WI	40.3	13.7	8.8	3.6	3.3	4.8	2.7	1.5	2.0
Manchester, NH	8.1	21.2	13.3	4.3	9.7	4.8	14.7	3.2	0.9
McAllen, TX	2.6	1.3	1.2	1.6	0.6	0.2	0.9	0.3	0.2
Miami, FL	5.2	5.1	3.3	6.1	5.4	2.2	1.4	0.7	0.5
Midland, TX	11.3	8.2	6.9	6.3	1.1	0.6	1.3	1.8	0.9
Minneapolis, MN	32.4	11.9	5.9	3.5	2.8	4.7	3.7	1.3	1.6

Table continued on next page.

Metro Area	German	Irish	English	American	Italian	Polish	French[1]	Scottish	Dutch
Nashville, TN	10.8	11.0	10.3	14.0	2.6	1.2	2.2	2.3	1.0
New Orleans, LA	10.8	8.5	4.9	6.2	8.9	0.7	14.3	1.0	0.5
New York, NY	7.2	10.7	3.1	4.7	13.7	4.2	1.1	0.7	0.6
Oklahoma City, OK	14.1	11.2	8.3	9.1	1.7	1.0	2.2	1.9	1.5
Omaha, NE	32.0	15.2	8.6	4.4	4.6	4.0	2.5	1.3	2.0
Orlando, FL	10.4	8.5	7.2	8.8	5.1	2.3	2.2	1.6	0.9
Oxnard, CA	11.6	8.7	8.3	3.6	5.1	1.9	2.5	1.9	1.1
Palm Bay, FL	15.8	14.0	11.1	11.9	8.5	3.3	3.4	2.4	1.7
Peoria, IL	31.1	12.6	10.0	8.4	4.3	2.3	2.6	1.8	1.7
Philadelphia, PA	16.4	20.1	7.5	3.8	14.0	5.3	1.5	1.3	1.0
Phoenix, AZ	14.4	9.4	8.3	6.4	4.6	2.6	2.3	1.7	1.4
Pittsburgh, PA	28.6	19.1	8.3	4.6	16.4	9.0	1.9	1.9	1.3
Portland, OR	19.7	11.6	11.1	5.3	3.9	2.0	3.2	3.1	2.2
Providence, RI	5.1	18.7	11.1	3.3	15.4	4.2	11.1	1.9	0.5
Provo, UT	11.8	5.4	28.8	5.8	2.4	0.7	2.1	5.5	1.9
Raleigh, NC	11.1	10.0	11.2	11.7	4.6	2.2	1.9	2.8	1.2
Reno, NV	14.8	11.7	9.2	5.5	6.6	1.8	3.1	2.4	1.6
Richmond, VA	9.7	8.7	11.8	8.5	3.6	1.6	1.9	2.2	0.8
Roanoke, VA	14.5	12.4	13.0	15.1	2.5	1.4	2.1	2.0	1.3
Rochester, MN	38.3	10.9	6.2	4.4	1.6	3.4	2.6	1.1	2.4
Sacramento, CA	13.2	9.7	8.8	3.7	5.3	1.5	2.6	2.0	1.3
Salem, OR	19.7	10.1	10.9	4.5	3.1	1.3	3.1	2.7	2.2
Salt Lake City, UT	11.4	6.2	21.9	5.2	2.9	1.0	1.8	4.0	2.4
San Antonio, TX	12.1	5.9	5.5	4.4	2.0	1.6	1.9	1.2	0.6
San Diego, CA	10.6	8.3	8.3	3.2	4.4	1.8	2.2	1.5	1.0
San Francisco, CA	8.5	7.9	6.3	2.9	5.3	1.5	2.0	1.6	0.9
San Jose, CA	7.1	5.6	5.2	2.2	4.5	1.2	1.6	1.1	0.8
Santa Rosa, CA	14.1	12.6	10.7	4.5	9.2	1.8	3.5	2.5	1.7
Savannah, GA	9.5	9.5	7.8	7.3	2.8	1.5	1.9	2.0	0.9
Seattle, WA	16.6	10.9	10.4	4.5	3.7	1.9	3.2	2.8	1.8
Sioux Falls, SD	40.2	10.4	4.7	4.4	1.1	1.4	2.2	0.8	7.8
Spokane, WA	23.1	13.4	11.0	5.5	4.7	1.8	3.6	2.9	1.9
Springfield, IL	25.7	14.5	10.4	8.0	5.6	2.0	2.1	1.8	1.4
Tallahassee, FL	9.8	9.9	8.8	5.9	4.0	1.6	2.0	2.5	1.1
Tampa, FL	12.9	11.6	8.6	9.7	7.7	3.0	2.9	1.8	1.2
Topeka, KS	29.7	14.4	10.3	6.8	2.6	1.3	3.2	2.0	1.9
Tulsa, OK	15.0	12.5	8.6	9.4	1.9	1.0	2.5	2.0	1.7
Tyler, TX	10.5	11.1	9.2	9.4	1.9	1.0	3.1	2.0	1.2
Virginia Beach, VA	10.9	9.5	9.6	11.0	4.5	2.0	2.2	2.1	1.0
Washington, DC	10.6	9.4	7.6	4.9	4.5	2.3	1.7	1.8	0.8
Wichita, KS	25.7	11.4	9.0	10.3	1.9	1.1	2.6	2.1	1.9
Wilmington, NC	11.8	11.3	11.3	19.5	4.6	2.0	2.2	3.0	1.2
Winston-Salem, NC	12.3	8.0	10.3	11.8	2.1	1.1	1.3	2.4	1.1
Worcester, MA	6.6	20.2	10.5	4.3	13.4	6.5	14.6	2.3	0.8
U.S.	14.9	10.8	8.0	7.4	5.5	3.0	2.7	1.7	1.4

Note: Figures are the percentage of the total population reporting a particular ancestry. The nine most commonly reported ancestries in the U.S. are shown. Figures include multiple ancestries (e.g. if a person reported being Irish and Italian, they were included in both columns); Figures cover the Metropolitan Statistical Area—see Appendix B for areas included; (1) Excludes Basque
Source: U.S. Census Bureau, 2011-2013 American Community Survey 3-Year Estimates

Foreign-Born Population: City

City	Percent of Population Born in								
	Any Foreign Country	Mexico	Asia	Europe	Carribean	South America	Central America[1]	Africa	Canada
Albuquerque, NM	10.6	6.0	2.2	1.0	0.4	0.4	0.3	0.2	0.2
Anchorage, AK	9.4	0.9	5.6	1.1	0.4	0.3	0.2	0.3	0.3
Ann Arbor, MI	17.2	0.7	10.7	3.2	0.1	0.6	0.3	0.7	0.7
Athens, GA	n/a	n/a	n/a	n/a	n/a	n/a	n/a	n/a	n/a
Atlanta, GA	7.8	1.4	2.7	1.3	0.6	0.4	0.3	0.7	0.1
Austin, TX	18.3	8.7	5.0	1.2	0.4	0.5	1.6	0.6	0.3
Billings, MT	n/a	n/a	n/a	n/a	n/a	n/a	n/a	n/a	n/a
Boise City, ID	7.4	1.4	3.3	1.5	0.0	0.1	0.3	0.4	0.4
Boston, MA	26.9	0.5	6.7	3.6	7.9	2.2	3.0	2.6	0.4
Boulder, CO	9.7	1.8	3.6	3.0	0.1	0.4	0.1	0.1	0.4
Cape Coral, FL	n/a	n/a	n/a	n/a	n/a	n/a	n/a	n/a	n/a
Cedar Rapids, IA	n/a	n/a	n/a	n/a	n/a	n/a	n/a	n/a	n/a
Charleston, SC	n/a	n/a	n/a	n/a	n/a	n/a	n/a	n/a	n/a
Charlotte, NC	15.3	2.9	4.2	1.5	1.0	1.3	2.6	1.6	0.2
Chicago, IL	21.4	9.7	4.6	3.8	0.4	1.0	0.9	0.8	0.2
Clarksville, TN	n/a	n/a	n/a	n/a	n/a	n/a	n/a	n/a	n/a
Colorado Springs, CO	8.2	2.5	2.1	1.7	0.3	0.4	0.5	0.4	0.3
Columbia, MO	n/a	n/a	n/a	n/a	n/a	n/a	n/a	n/a	n/a
Columbus, OH	11.1	1.8	3.9	0.9	0.3	0.4	0.4	3.3	0.1
Dallas, TX	24.4	16.8	2.6	0.8	0.1	0.4	2.0	1.4	0.2
Davenport, IA	n/a	n/a	n/a	n/a	n/a	n/a	n/a	n/a	n/a
Denver, CO	15.8	9.0	2.8	1.4	0.2	0.4	0.5	1.2	0.3
Des Moines, IA	n/a	n/a	n/a	n/a	n/a	n/a	n/a	n/a	n/a
Durham, NC	14.6	4.5	3.6	1.1	0.4	0.7	2.5	1.4	0.3
El Paso, TX	24.9	22.2	1.0	0.5	0.2	0.3	0.4	0.1	0.1
Erie, PA	n/a	n/a	n/a	n/a	n/a	n/a	n/a	n/a	n/a
Eugene, OR	7.9	2.0	3.5	1.1	0.1	0.2	0.2	0.2	0.4
Fargo, ND	n/a	n/a	n/a	n/a	n/a	n/a	n/a	n/a	n/a
Fayetteville, NC	5.9	0.6	2.2	1.0	0.7	0.4	0.8	0.2	0.0
Fort Collins, CO	6.1	1.2	2.5	1.2	0.1	0.4	0.2	0.2	0.3
Fort Wayne, IN	7.8	2.4	2.9	1.1	0.2	0.3	0.5	0.4	0.2
Fort Worth, TX	17.8	11.5	3.2	0.7	0.2	0.4	0.8	0.7	0.2
Gainesville, FL	12.5	0.4	5.3	1.5	2.1	1.9	0.3	0.6	0.4
Grand Rapids, MI	9.6	3.2	1.9	0.7	0.6	0.2	1.7	0.8	0.5
Green Bay, WI	n/a	n/a	n/a	n/a	n/a	n/a	n/a	n/a	n/a
Greensboro, NC	10.4	2.3	3.5	0.9	0.4	0.8	0.7	1.7	0.2
Honolulu, HI	27.8	0.2	23.2	1.1	0.1	0.2	0.0	0.1	0.3
Houston, TX	28.0	13.1	5.5	1.1	0.6	1.0	5.3	1.2	0.2
Huntsville, AL	6.3	1.7	2.0	0.9	0.4	0.2	0.2	0.7	0.1
Indianapolis, IN	8.3	3.4	2.0	0.5	0.3	0.2	0.8	1.0	0.1
Jacksonville, FL	9.6	0.5	3.7	1.7	1.4	1.0	0.6	0.5	0.2
Kansas City, MO	7.7	2.4	2.1	0.7	0.4	0.3	0.4	1.1	0.1
Lafayette, LA	n/a	n/a	n/a	n/a	n/a	n/a	n/a	n/a	n/a
Las Vegas, NV	21.3	10.1	5.1	1.5	0.8	0.8	2.0	0.4	0.4
Lexington, KY	9.0	2.7	3.3	0.8	0.2	0.3	0.5	0.8	0.2
Lincoln, NE	7.6	1.4	3.8	1.0	0.1	0.2	0.3	0.6	0.1
Little Rock, AR	n/a	n/a	n/a	n/a	n/a	n/a	n/a	n/a	n/a
Los Angeles, CA	38.6	13.9	11.1	2.4	0.3	1.1	8.6	0.7	0.3
Louisville, KY	6.9	1.0	2.2	0.9	1.4	0.2	0.2	1.0	0.1
Lubbock, TX	5.9	2.3	2.0	0.6	0.1	0.2	0.2	0.4	0.1
Madison, WI	10.8	2.0	5.8	1.3	0.1	0.5	0.2	0.6	0.3
Manchester, NH	13.2	1.3	4.2	2.2	1.3	1.2	0.5	1.3	1.1
McAllen, TX	n/a	n/a	n/a	n/a	n/a	n/a	n/a	n/a	n/a
Miami, FL	57.0	1.0	1.0	1.7	32.7	7.8	12.2	0.2	0.2

Table continued on next page.

City	Percent of Population Born in								
	Any Foreign Country	Mexico	Asia	Europe	Carribean	South America	Central America[1]	Africa	Canada
Midland, TX	n/a	n/a	n/a	n/a	n/a	n/a	n/a	n/a	n/a
Minneapolis, MN	15.0	3.0	3.8	1.1	0.2	1.6	0.6	4.4	0.2
Nashville, TN	12.0	3.1	3.6	0.9	0.4	0.5	1.6	1.7	0.2
New Orleans, LA	5.9	0.4	2.2	0.7	0.2	0.4	1.7	0.2	0.1
New York, NY	37.3	2.2	10.4	5.7	10.4	5.1	1.5	1.6	0.3
Oklahoma City, OK	12.5	6.9	3.2	0.4	0.1	0.2	1.0	0.4	0.1
Omaha, NE	9.9	4.4	2.4	0.6	0.2	0.2	1.0	1.0	0.1
Orlando, FL	18.4	1.3	2.9	1.3	5.7	5.6	0.7	0.5	0.3
Oxnard, CA	n/a	n/a	n/a	n/a	n/a	n/a	n/a	n/a	n/a
Palm Bay, FL	n/a	n/a	n/a	n/a	n/a	n/a	n/a	n/a	n/a
Peoria, IL	n/a	n/a	n/a	n/a	n/a	n/a	n/a	n/a	n/a
Philadelphia, PA	12.4	0.5	4.9	2.2	2.1	0.8	0.5	1.3	0.1
Phoenix, AZ	20.1	13.1	3.0	1.5	0.3	0.4	0.8	0.7	0.4
Pittsburgh, PA	7.9	0.1	4.4	1.9	0.2	0.3	0.1	0.7	0.1
Portland, OR	14.1	3.1	5.6	2.9	0.2	0.3	0.4	0.9	0.4
Providence, RI	29.6	0.5	4.7	2.1	10.2	1.6	7.3	2.9	0.2
Provo, UT	n/a	n/a	n/a	n/a	n/a	n/a	n/a	n/a	n/a
Raleigh, NC	13.1	3.0	3.7	1.2	0.8	0.9	1.8	1.5	0.3
Reno, NV	17.0	8.0	5.0	1.3	0.0	0.3	1.8	0.2	0.2
Richmond, VA	6.5	1.1	1.2	0.7	0.3	0.4	1.9	0.8	0.1
Roanoke, VA	n/a	n/a	n/a	n/a	n/a	n/a	n/a	n/a	n/a
Rochester, MN	12.6	1.7	5.1	1.4	0.2	0.4	0.1	3.0	0.5
Sacramento, CA	22.5	7.0	10.8	1.6	0.2	0.3	0.6	0.5	0.1
Salem, OR	n/a	n/a	n/a	n/a	n/a	n/a	n/a	n/a	n/a
Salt Lake City, UT	17.5	6.7	4.1	2.4	0.3	1.0	0.7	1.0	0.4
San Antonio, TX	14.1	9.7	2.2	0.6	0.2	0.2	0.8	0.3	0.1
San Diego, CA	26.3	9.3	12.0	2.3	0.2	0.6	0.5	0.9	0.4
San Francisco, CA	35.8	2.8	22.9	4.7	0.2	1.1	2.9	0.3	0.6
San Jose, CA	38.7	10.3	23.5	2.1	0.1	0.5	1.1	0.6	0.4
Santa Rosa, CA	18.8	10.8	3.5	1.3	0.1	0.3	0.9	1.0	0.4
Savannah, GA	5.7	1.7	1.2	0.7	0.4	0.6	0.2	0.4	0.2
Seattle, WA	18.3	1.4	9.8	2.6	0.2	0.3	0.4	2.4	0.9
Sioux Falls, SD	n/a	n/a	n/a	n/a	n/a	n/a	n/a	n/a	n/a
Spokane, WA	n/a	n/a	n/a	n/a	n/a	n/a	n/a	n/a	n/a
Springfield, IL	n/a	n/a	n/a	n/a	n/a	n/a	n/a	n/a	n/a
Tallahassee, FL	7.9	0.4	2.8	0.9	2.0	0.8	0.3	0.6	0.2
Tampa, FL	15.2	1.0	3.2	1.5	5.8	1.6	1.1	0.6	0.2
Topeka, KS	n/a	n/a	n/a	n/a	n/a	n/a	n/a	n/a	n/a
Tulsa, OK	10.1	5.6	2.2	0.6	0.1	0.2	0.8	0.3	0.1
Tyler, TX	n/a	n/a	n/a	n/a	n/a	n/a	n/a	n/a	n/a
Virginia Beach, VA	8.6	0.3	4.7	1.5	0.6	0.5	0.4	0.5	0.2
Washington, DC	14.2	0.4	2.7	2.6	1.4	1.3	3.1	2.2	0.3
Wichita, KS	10.5	4.7	3.8	0.5	0.1	0.2	0.3	0.7	0.1
Wilmington, NC	n/a	n/a	n/a	n/a	n/a	n/a	n/a	n/a	n/a
Winston-Salem, NC	10.7	5.6	1.5	0.8	0.4	0.5	1.4	0.2	0.1
Worcester, MA	21.8	0.4	5.8	4.2	3.1	2.4	0.9	4.8	0.2
U.S.	13.0	3.7	3.8	1.5	1.2	0.9	1.0	0.6	0.3

Note: (1) Excludes Mexico
Source: U.S. Census Bureau, 2011-2013 American Community Survey 3-Year Estimates

Foreign-Born Population: Metro Area

Metro Area	Any Foreign Country	Mexico	Asia	Europe	Carribean	South America	Central America[1]	Africa	Canada
Albuquerque, NM	9.6	6.0	1.6	0.8	0.3	0.3	0.3	0.1	0.1
Anchorage, AK	8.1	0.7	4.5	1.2	0.3	0.2	0.2	0.3	0.3
Ann Arbor, MI	11.4	0.6	6.5	1.9	0.2	0.5	0.5	0.6	0.5
Athens, GA	7.5	2.6	2.6	0.7	0.2	0.4	0.7	0.2	0.1
Atlanta, GA	13.2	3.1	3.9	1.2	1.5	0.9	1.0	1.3	0.2
Austin, TX	14.8	7.3	3.7	1.1	0.3	0.4	1.1	0.5	0.3
Billings, MT	n/a	n/a	n/a	n/a	n/a	n/a	n/a	n/a	n/a
Boise City, ID	6.6	2.8	1.6	1.1	0.0	0.2	0.2	0.2	0.3
Boston, MA	16.9	0.2	5.3	3.3	3.0	1.8	1.4	1.4	0.5
Boulder, CO	10.5	3.7	3.2	2.3	0.1	0.3	0.3	0.3	0.4
Cape Coral, FL	15.1	2.7	1.2	2.2	4.4	1.8	1.6	0.1	1.0
Cedar Rapids, IA	n/a	n/a	n/a	n/a	n/a	n/a	n/a	n/a	n/a
Charleston, SC	5.2	1.4	1.3	1.0	0.3	0.4	0.4	0.1	0.2
Charlotte, NC	9.4	2.4	2.2	1.1	0.6	0.8	1.3	0.7	0.2
Chicago, IL	17.8	7.0	4.7	3.9	0.3	0.6	0.5	0.5	0.2
Clarksville, TN	n/a	n/a	n/a	n/a	n/a	n/a	n/a	n/a	n/a
Colorado Springs, CO	7.1	1.8	2.0	1.7	0.3	0.3	0.4	0.3	0.3
Columbia, MO	n/a	n/a	n/a	n/a	n/a	n/a	n/a	n/a	n/a
Columbus, OH	6.9	0.9	2.6	0.8	0.2	0.2	0.2	1.6	0.2
Dallas, TX	17.5	9.1	4.3	0.8	0.2	0.5	1.3	1.0	0.2
Davenport, IA	4.7	1.6	1.4	0.7	0.1	0.1	0.1	0.5	0.1
Denver, CO	12.1	5.5	2.9	1.5	0.1	0.4	0.4	0.9	0.3
Des Moines, IA	7.6	1.9	2.5	1.4	0.0	0.2	0.5	0.9	0.1
Durham, NC	12.1	3.7	3.3	1.3	0.3	0.5	1.8	0.9	0.3
El Paso, TX	25.8	23.4	0.9	0.4	0.2	0.2	0.4	0.1	0.1
Erie, PA	4.1	0.1	1.4	1.6	0.2	0.1	0.1	0.4	0.1
Eugene, OR	5.8	1.8	2.0	0.9	0.0	0.2	0.2	0.1	0.4
Fargo, ND	5.1	0.1	2.4	0.8	0.0	0.1	0.0	1.2	0.3
Fayetteville, NC	5.3	0.9	1.7	0.9	0.6	0.3	0.7	0.2	0.1
Fort Collins, CO	5.3	1.8	1.6	1.0	0.0	0.3	0.2	0.2	0.2
Fort Wayne, IN	5.6	1.6	2.1	0.9	0.1	0.2	0.3	0.2	0.2
Fort Worth, TX	17.5	9.1	4.3	0.8	0.2	0.5	1.3	1.0	0.2
Gainesville, FL	9.9	0.5	3.7	1.4	1.7	1.4	0.3	0.5	0.4
Grand Rapids, MI	6.4	1.8	1.8	1.0	0.3	0.2	0.5	0.4	0.3
Green Bay, WI	4.4	1.9	1.4	0.4	0.2	0.1	0.2	0.1	0.1
Greensboro, NC	8.4	2.8	2.6	0.7	0.2	0.4	0.5	0.9	0.2
Honolulu, HI	19.3	0.2	15.8	0.7	0.1	0.2	0.1	0.1	0.3
Houston, TX	22.3	9.8	5.3	1.0	0.5	1.0	3.3	1.0	0.3
Huntsville, AL	5.2	1.5	1.9	0.8	0.3	0.1	0.1	0.4	0.1
Indianapolis, IN	6.0	1.9	1.9	0.6	0.2	0.2	0.4	0.6	0.1
Jacksonville, FL	7.9	0.4	2.9	1.6	1.1	0.8	0.4	0.4	0.2
Kansas City, MO	6.4	2.1	2.0	0.6	0.2	0.2	0.4	0.6	0.1
Lafayette, LA	n/a	n/a	n/a	n/a	n/a	n/a	n/a	n/a	n/a
Las Vegas, NV	21.8	9.0	6.7	1.7	0.9	0.7	1.8	0.6	0.4
Lexington, KY	6.7	2.1	2.3	0.7	0.2	0.2	0.4	0.5	0.2
Lincoln, NE	6.8	1.2	3.3	0.9	0.1	0.2	0.3	0.5	0.1
Little Rock, AR	3.8	1.3	1.4	0.4	0.0	0.1	0.3	0.1	0.1
Los Angeles, CA	33.8	13.2	12.4	1.7	0.3	0.9	4.3	0.5	0.3
Louisville, KY	5.1	1.0	1.5	0.7	0.8	0.2	0.2	0.6	0.1
Lubbock, TX	5.6	2.6	1.7	0.5	0.1	0.2	0.2	0.3	0.1
Madison, WI	6.9	1.7	3.0	1.0	0.1	0.3	0.2	0.4	0.2
Manchester, NH	8.8	0.7	3.0	1.7	0.7	0.9	0.4	0.6	1.0
McAllen, TX	n/a	n/a	n/a	n/a	n/a	n/a	n/a	n/a	n/a
Miami, FL	38.5	1.1	2.0	2.3	20.4	7.6	4.2	0.4	0.6

Table continued on next page.

Metro Area	Percent of Population Born in								
	Any Foreign Country	Mexico	Asia	Europe	Carribean	South America	Central America[1]	Africa	Canada
Midland, TX	n/a	n/a	n/a	n/a	n/a	n/a	n/a	n/a	n/a
Minneapolis, MN	9.7	1.4	3.9	1.1	0.1	0.5	0.4	2.0	0.2
Nashville, TN	7.3	2.0	2.2	0.7	0.2	0.3	0.8	0.8	0.2
New Orleans, LA	7.1	0.6	2.0	0.6	0.7	0.4	2.5	0.2	0.1
New York, NY	28.5	1.7	8.0	4.7	6.5	4.3	1.9	1.2	0.2
Oklahoma City, OK	8.1	4.0	2.3	0.4	0.1	0.2	0.6	0.4	0.1
Omaha, NE	6.9	2.8	2.0	0.6	0.1	0.1	0.6	0.6	0.1
Orlando, FL	16.2	1.4	2.9	1.6	4.9	3.7	0.9	0.5	0.4
Oxnard, CA	22.6	13.1	5.3	1.6	0.1	0.6	1.2	0.2	0.5
Palm Bay, FL	8.6	0.5	1.8	1.9	2.2	0.9	0.6	0.2	0.6
Peoria, IL	3.6	0.6	1.8	0.6	0.1	0.2	0.0	0.1	0.1
Philadelphia, PA	9.9	0.9	4.0	2.0	1.1	0.5	0.4	0.9	0.1
Phoenix, AZ	14.4	7.9	2.9	1.4	0.2	0.3	0.5	0.4	0.7
Pittsburgh, PA	3.5	0.1	1.7	1.0	0.1	0.1	0.1	0.2	0.1
Portland, OR	12.5	3.8	4.4	2.4	0.1	0.3	0.4	0.4	0.5
Providence, RI	12.9	0.2	2.1	4.4	1.8	1.0	1.6	1.4	0.2
Provo, UT	7.2	2.7	1.1	0.6	0.1	1.3	0.5	0.1	0.5
Raleigh, NC	11.6	3.1	3.8	1.1	0.5	0.7	1.1	0.9	0.3
Reno, NV	15.0	7.2	4.0	1.2	0.1	0.3	1.4	0.2	0.3
Richmond, VA	7.2	0.8	2.6	1.1	0.4	0.4	1.1	0.6	0.1
Roanoke, VA	4.7	0.6	1.5	0.8	0.6	0.1	0.5	0.5	0.1
Rochester, MN	7.3	1.1	2.9	0.9	0.1	0.2	0.1	1.6	0.3
Sacramento, CA	18.0	4.9	8.0	2.8	0.1	0.3	0.6	0.4	0.3
Salem, OR	12.0	7.9	1.5	1.3	0.1	0.3	0.3	0.1	0.3
Salt Lake City, UT	11.9	4.9	2.7	1.4	0.1	1.1	0.6	0.4	0.3
San Antonio, TX	11.8	7.8	1.9	0.7	0.1	0.3	0.6	0.3	0.1
San Diego, CA	23.4	10.6	8.7	1.9	0.2	0.5	0.5	0.6	0.4
San Francisco, CA	29.8	5.6	16.3	2.9	0.1	1.0	2.5	0.6	0.4
San Jose, CA	36.8	8.2	22.8	2.9	0.1	0.6	0.9	0.5	0.5
Santa Rosa, CA	16.8	9.6	2.8	2.0	0.0	0.3	0.9	0.6	0.3
Savannah, GA	5.9	1.4	1.8	0.8	0.5	0.4	0.2	0.5	0.2
Seattle, WA	17.2	2.5	8.5	2.8	0.1	0.4	0.5	1.3	0.8
Sioux Falls, SD	n/a	n/a	n/a	n/a	n/a	n/a	n/a	n/a	n/a
Spokane, WA	5.4	0.4	1.9	2.0	0.0	0.1	0.1	0.3	0.4
Springfield, IL	3.3	0.2	1.6	0.6	0.2	0.1	0.0	0.5	0.1
Tallahassee, FL	6.3	0.6	1.9	0.8	1.3	0.6	0.3	0.4	0.2
Tampa, FL	12.7	1.4	2.5	2.3	3.1	1.6	0.7	0.4	0.7
Topeka, KS	n/a	n/a	n/a	n/a	n/a	n/a	n/a	n/a	n/a
Tulsa, OK	5.9	2.9	1.5	0.5	0.1	0.2	0.4	0.2	0.1
Tyler, TX	n/a	n/a	n/a	n/a	n/a	n/a	n/a	n/a	n/a
Virginia Beach, VA	6.2	0.4	2.7	1.1	0.5	0.3	0.5	0.5	0.2
Washington, DC	21.9	0.8	7.8	1.9	1.1	2.3	4.6	3.1	0.2
Wichita, KS	7.4	3.2	2.6	0.5	0.1	0.2	0.2	0.5	0.1
Wilmington, NC	5.3	1.9	0.9	1.0	0.2	0.2	0.7	0.1	0.2
Winston-Salem, NC	6.8	3.3	1.1	0.6	0.2	0.3	0.9	0.2	0.1
Worcester, MA	10.6	0.3	3.2	2.3	1.0	1.3	0.5	1.4	0.5
U.S.	13.0	3.7	3.8	1.5	1.2	0.9	1.0	0.6	0.3

Note: Figures cover the Metropolitan Statistical Area—see Appendix B for areas included; (1) Excludes Mexico
Source: U.S. Census Bureau, 2011-2013 American Community Survey 3-Year Estimates

Marital Status: City

City	Never Married	Now Married[1]	Separated	Widowed	Divorced
Albuquerque, NM	35.7	43.1	1.9	5.2	14.0
Anchorage, AK	35.3	47.4	1.6	3.6	12.1
Ann Arbor, MI	55.8	31.9	0.7	3.6	8.2
Athens, GA	56.8	29.6	1.4	4.3	7.8
Atlanta, GA	54.0	27.3	2.4	5.4	10.9
Austin, TX	43.6	39.1	2.4	3.4	11.5
Billings, MT	30.5	45.8	1.3	6.7	15.7
Boise City, ID	33.1	47.2	0.9	4.8	14.1
Boston, MA	56.6	28.3	2.9	4.3	7.9
Boulder, CO	55.7	32.8	0.7	2.7	8.1
Cape Coral, FL	24.6	52.6	2.3	6.9	13.6
Cedar Rapids, IA	34.5	45.8	1.9	6.2	11.6
Charleston, SC	42.5	38.5	2.5	5.3	11.2
Charlotte, NC	39.9	42.3	3.1	4.6	10.1
Chicago, IL	48.9	34.5	2.5	5.4	8.6
Clarksville, TN	28.1	52.8	3.3	3.9	12.0
Colorado Springs, CO	29.3	51.0	2.0	4.6	12.9
Columbia, MO	51.5	35.5	1.2	3.3	8.5
Columbus, OH	43.8	36.5	2.6	4.5	12.5
Dallas, TX	40.9	39.6	3.5	4.8	11.2
Davenport, IA	35.4	42.5	1.5	6.4	14.1
Denver, CO	41.8	38.5	2.3	4.4	13.0
Des Moines, IA	34.7	43.1	2.2	6.0	14.0
Durham, NC	41.8	40.2	2.8	4.6	10.6
El Paso, TX	31.9	47.0	3.8	5.7	11.6
Erie, PA	43.5	35.9	3.0	6.4	11.2
Eugene, OR	43.2	37.1	1.4	5.2	13.1
Fargo, ND	43.6	41.3	1.2	4.4	9.4
Fayetteville, NC	32.5	45.7	4.0	5.4	12.4
Fort Collins, CO	44.0	42.3	0.7	3.4	9.6
Fort Wayne, IN	34.4	44.0	1.7	6.1	13.9
Fort Worth, TX	33.9	46.1	3.0	4.6	12.5
Gainesville, FL	62.2	24.0	2.0	3.9	7.8
Grand Rapids, MI	44.8	36.7	2.6	5.3	10.6
Green Bay, WI	37.4	44.0	1.5	5.2	11.9
Greensboro, NC	41.3	39.5	3.0	5.4	10.8
Honolulu, HI	36.7	44.5	1.4	7.3	10.2
Houston, TX	39.5	41.5	3.5	4.8	10.6
Huntsville, AL	35.7	42.0	2.5	6.0	13.8
Indianapolis, IN	39.0	39.5	2.4	5.3	13.8
Jacksonville, FL	34.5	42.9	2.7	5.8	14.1
Kansas City, MO	39.0	39.6	2.4	5.6	13.3
Lafayette, LA	40.6	39.1	2.5	6.1	11.8
Las Vegas, NV	33.1	43.3	3.1	5.5	15.0
Lexington, KY	38.1	43.2	1.8	4.5	12.4
Lincoln, NE	37.5	45.8	1.3	4.3	11.1
Little Rock, AR	39.0	39.1	2.6	5.5	13.8
Los Angeles, CA	45.7	38.2	2.9	4.7	8.5
Louisville, KY	35.3	42.0	2.7	6.5	13.6
Lubbock, TX	40.1	41.2	2.2	5.2	11.3
Madison, WI	48.3	37.6	1.2	3.5	9.4
Manchester, NH	38.0	40.2	2.1	5.5	14.3
McAllen, TX	29.9	52.1	3.6	5.9	8.5
Miami, FL	41.0	34.2	4.6	6.6	13.6
Midland, TX	30.3	51.6	1.9	5.4	10.9
Minneapolis, MN	51.8	33.2	1.7	3.3	10.0

Table continued on next page.

City	Never Married	Now Married[1]	Separated	Widowed	Divorced
Nashville, TN	40.4	39.1	2.6	5.1	12.9
New Orleans, LA	48.8	30.1	3.0	6.1	12.1
New York, NY	44.1	38.6	3.4	5.7	8.1
Oklahoma City, OK	31.9	47.3	2.5	5.5	12.9
Omaha, NE	36.8	43.7	1.8	5.5	12.2
Orlando, FL	43.9	33.8	3.6	5.3	13.5
Oxnard, CA	38.3	45.5	2.7	4.4	9.1
Palm Bay, FL	27.2	47.5	3.1	8.3	13.9
Peoria, IL	41.8	40.5	1.2	6.3	10.2
Philadelphia, PA	52.2	28.7	3.4	6.7	9.0
Phoenix, AZ	38.9	41.7	2.5	4.2	12.7
Pittsburgh, PA	51.2	30.9	2.3	6.5	9.0
Portland, OR	40.7	40.5	1.9	4.3	12.6
Providence, RI	54.7	28.6	3.3	4.7	8.6
Provo, UT	46.9	44.6	0.8	2.2	5.5
Raleigh, NC	42.4	40.5	2.8	3.9	10.3
Reno, NV	35.8	42.1	2.3	4.8	15.0
Richmond, VA	52.0	25.7	4.3	6.0	12.1
Roanoke, VA	34.7	39.5	3.0	7.4	15.3
Rochester, MN	32.3	51.3	1.3	4.8	10.3
Sacramento, CA	40.3	39.2	2.8	5.4	12.3
Salem, OR	32.7	44.7	2.6	5.1	14.8
Salt Lake City, UT	41.3	41.0	1.8	4.3	11.6
San Antonio, TX	36.1	42.8	3.3	5.4	12.4
San Diego, CA	40.7	42.8	2.0	4.6	10.0
San Francisco, CA	46.5	38.1	1.6	5.1	8.6
San Jose, CA	34.6	50.9	1.9	4.5	8.2
Santa Rosa, CA	34.3	44.0	2.2	5.6	13.9
Savannah, GA	45.2	31.7	2.8	7.0	13.4
Seattle, WA	44.2	39.5	1.4	4.0	10.9
Sioux Falls, SD	34.0	48.4	1.3	5.0	11.4
Spokane, WA	34.3	42.6	1.7	5.9	15.6
Springfield, IL	34.4	41.2	1.8	7.5	15.1
Tallahassee, FL	55.8	30.0	1.5	3.6	9.2
Tampa, FL	41.6	36.6	3.1	5.7	13.0
Topeka, KS	31.3	44.3	1.9	6.4	16.1
Tulsa, OK	33.5	42.9	2.7	6.0	15.0
Tyler, TX	34.0	42.3	3.2	7.4	13.1
Virginia Beach, VA	31.6	49.5	2.7	4.8	11.4
Washington, DC	57.5	26.0	2.3	4.7	9.6
Wichita, KS	31.9	46.9	2.2	5.7	13.3
Wilmington, NC	42.9	37.5	2.9	5.1	11.7
Winston-Salem, NC	40.0	40.1	3.1	6.4	10.4
Worcester, MA	43.8	35.5	2.8	6.3	11.6
U.S.	32.7	48.1	2.2	6.0	11.0

Note: Figures are percentages and cover the population 15 years of age and older; (1) Excludes separated
Source: U.S. Census Bureau, 2011-2013 American Community Survey 3-Year Estimates

Marital Status: Metro Area

Metro Area	Never Married	Now Married[1]	Separated	Widowed	Divorced
Albuquerque, NM	33.9	45.4	1.8	5.3	13.6
Anchorage, AK	33.4	49.0	1.6	3.7	12.3
Ann Arbor, MI	41.8	43.8	1.0	4.3	9.1
Athens, GA	44.7	39.4	1.6	5.4	8.9
Atlanta, GA	34.4	47.4	2.3	4.8	11.2
Austin, TX	35.9	47.4	2.1	3.6	11.0
Billings, MT	27.5	50.1	1.3	6.4	14.7
Boise City, ID	27.5	53.8	1.2	4.8	12.6
Boston, MA	36.4	47.3	1.9	5.4	9.0
Boulder, CO	37.2	47.7	1.1	3.5	10.6
Cape Coral, FL	26.0	50.3	2.1	8.2	13.4
Cedar Rapids, IA	28.8	51.7	1.7	6.0	11.7
Charleston, SC	33.7	45.9	3.2	5.9	11.2
Charlotte, NC	31.6	49.6	3.0	5.5	10.2
Chicago, IL	36.4	46.9	1.9	5.6	9.1
Clarksville, TN	26.8	54.2	2.7	5.1	11.2
Colorado Springs, CO	28.1	53.9	1.8	4.3	11.9
Columbia, MO	43.3	42.0	1.6	3.8	9.2
Columbus, OH	33.6	47.5	2.0	5.1	11.8
Dallas, TX	31.4	50.4	2.5	4.5	11.2
Davenport, IA	28.7	50.3	1.3	6.9	12.8
Denver, CO	31.9	49.5	1.8	4.3	12.5
Des Moines, IA	28.7	53.2	1.6	5.0	11.5
Durham, NC	37.2	45.4	2.3	4.9	10.1
El Paso, TX	32.5	47.4	3.9	5.4	10.9
Erie, PA	34.7	46.6	2.3	6.4	10.0
Eugene, OR	33.3	45.1	1.6	5.9	14.1
Fargo, ND	37.9	47.2	1.0	4.5	9.3
Fayetteville, NC	31.6	47.6	3.7	5.3	11.8
Fort Collins, CO	33.6	50.9	1.0	4.0	10.5
Fort Wayne, IN	29.8	50.1	1.5	5.8	12.7
Fort Worth, TX	31.4	50.4	2.5	4.5	11.2
Gainesville, FL	46.0	37.2	1.9	5.2	9.8
Grand Rapids, MI	31.5	52.4	1.3	4.8	10.0
Green Bay, WI	30.2	53.4	1.0	5.2	10.2
Greensboro, NC	32.1	47.4	3.3	6.2	11.0
Honolulu, HI	33.8	50.2	1.3	6.2	8.6
Houston, TX	32.9	49.6	2.8	4.5	10.1
Huntsville, AL	29.7	50.5	2.0	5.7	12.1
Indianapolis, IN	31.3	48.8	1.8	5.3	12.9
Jacksonville, FL	31.2	46.8	2.4	5.8	13.8
Kansas City, MO	29.7	50.3	1.8	5.6	12.6
Lafayette, LA	33.1	46.2	2.7	6.1	11.9
Las Vegas, NV	33.6	44.7	2.7	5.2	13.9
Lexington, KY	33.4	47.1	2.2	4.9	12.5
Lincoln, NE	35.6	48.3	1.2	4.2	10.7
Little Rock, AR	30.5	48.0	2.1	5.7	13.6
Los Angeles, CA	39.8	44.0	2.6	5.0	8.6
Louisville, KY	30.6	47.4	2.1	6.4	13.4
Lubbock, TX	37.0	44.3	2.3	5.4	11.0
Madison, WI	35.4	49.1	1.2	4.3	10.0
Manchester, NH	30.5	51.3	1.4	5.0	11.9
McAllen, TX	31.5	52.4	4.1	5.1	6.8
Miami, FL	34.3	43.0	3.1	6.9	12.7
Midland, TX	29.6	52.8	1.8	5.1	10.6
Minneapolis, MN	32.9	51.2	1.3	4.4	10.1

Table continued on next page.

Metro Area	Never Married	Now Married[1]	Separated	Widowed	Divorced
Nashville, TN	30.8	49.4	2.0	5.4	12.4
New Orleans, LA	37.3	41.5	2.5	6.6	12.1
New York, NY	37.9	45.5	2.6	6.0	8.0
Oklahoma City, OK	29.9	49.3	2.2	5.8	12.8
Omaha, NE	31.4	50.9	1.5	5.2	11.1
Orlando, FL	35.0	44.9	2.6	5.5	12.0
Oxnard, CA	32.2	50.4	1.9	5.1	10.4
Palm Bay, FL	26.6	48.0	2.3	8.6	14.5
Peoria, IL	29.6	51.7	1.3	6.3	11.0
Philadelphia, PA	37.3	44.9	2.3	6.4	9.0
Phoenix, AZ	33.3	47.5	1.9	5.0	12.3
Pittsburgh, PA	31.6	48.5	2.0	8.1	9.8
Portland, OR	31.5	49.3	1.8	4.8	12.5
Providence, RI	35.0	45.3	2.0	6.5	11.2
Provo, UT	31.9	58.2	1.1	2.6	6.3
Raleigh, NC	31.7	51.7	2.8	4.4	9.5
Reno, NV	31.6	46.7	2.0	4.9	14.7
Richmond, VA	34.5	45.5	2.9	6.0	11.2
Roanoke, VA	26.5	51.7	2.3	7.1	12.4
Rochester, MN	28.1	56.2	1.1	5.1	9.5
Sacramento, CA	33.2	47.2	2.4	5.4	11.7
Salem, OR	30.2	50.0	2.4	5.2	12.2
Salt Lake City, UT	31.1	52.4	2.0	3.9	10.7
San Antonio, TX	32.6	47.7	2.8	5.4	11.5
San Diego, CA	35.9	47.0	1.9	5.0	10.3
San Francisco, CA	36.0	47.3	1.9	5.2	9.6
San Jose, CA	32.6	53.1	1.7	4.4	8.1
Santa Rosa, CA	32.2	46.6	2.0	5.4	13.7
Savannah, GA	34.5	44.4	2.4	5.9	12.8
Seattle, WA	32.4	49.5	1.6	4.4	12.0
Sioux Falls, SD	30.9	52.6	1.1	5.0	10.4
Spokane, WA	29.8	49.4	1.4	5.6	13.8
Springfield, IL	30.2	48.1	1.7	6.8	13.2
Tallahassee, FL	43.0	39.6	1.9	4.5	11.1
Tampa, FL	30.1	46.2	2.4	7.4	13.9
Topeka, KS	26.7	52.0	1.4	6.2	13.7
Tulsa, OK	27.2	51.1	2.1	6.1	13.5
Tyler, TX	27.2	50.8	2.6	7.1	12.2
Virginia Beach, VA	33.6	46.6	3.0	5.5	11.2
Washington, DC	36.2	48.2	2.3	4.4	9.0
Wichita, KS	28.7	51.2	1.7	5.8	12.6
Wilmington, NC	33.4	47.0	2.7	5.5	11.4
Winston-Salem, NC	29.5	50.0	2.9	6.6	11.1
Worcester, MA	33.3	47.8	1.9	5.9	11.0
U.S.	32.7	48.1	2.2	6.0	11.0

Note: Figures are percentages and cover the population 15 years of age and older; Figures cover the Metropolitan Statistical Area—see Appendix B for areas included; (1) Excludes separated
Source: U.S. Census Bureau, 2011-2013 American Community Survey 3-Year Estimates

Disability Status: City

City	All Ages	Under 18 Years Old	18 to 64 Years Old	65 Years and Over
Albuquerque, NM	12.8	4.0	10.8	39.2
Anchorage, AK	9.8	2.9	9.1	37.5
Ann Arbor, MI	6.6	2.0	4.7	27.6
Athens, GA	9.9	2.9	8.6	34.5
Atlanta, GA	11.4	3.3	9.6	39.4
Austin, TX	9.2	4.3	8.1	35.5
Billings, MT	13.8	5.0	11.6	36.8
Boise City, ID	11.3	4.1	9.4	36.0
Boston, MA	12.0	5.5	9.3	42.2
Boulder, CO	6.7	1.4	5.4	25.4
Cape Coral, FL	12.8	2.9	10.6	31.9
Cedar Rapids, IA	11.4	5.2	9.2	33.5
Charleston, SC	10.1	2.9	7.8	32.9
Charlotte, NC	8.8	3.1	7.5	34.5
Chicago, IL	11.0	3.4	9.0	40.7
Clarksville, TN	13.8	5.8	14.2	42.8
Colorado Springs, CO	12.0	4.2	10.8	36.2
Columbia, MO	9.4	2.9	8.1	34.7
Columbus, OH	12.2	5.3	10.9	40.2
Dallas, TX	9.4	2.9	8.0	38.1
Davenport, IA	10.9	2.9	9.7	33.2
Denver, CO	9.8	2.7	8.1	35.7
Des Moines, IA	12.9	4.4	12.8	33.6
Durham, NC	9.7	2.9	8.4	36.6
El Paso, TX	12.6	3.6	10.6	45.3
Erie, PA	18.1	9.3	16.7	40.5
Eugene, OR	13.2	4.6	10.3	39.5
Fargo, ND	9.1	2.2	8.2	28.9
Fayetteville, NC	13.8	3.9	13.1	41.9
Fort Collins, CO	7.5	1.9	5.9	33.2
Fort Wayne, IN	12.3	4.7	10.9	36.0
Fort Worth, TX	10.6	3.4	10.1	39.8
Gainesville, FL	9.4	4.5	7.2	38.6
Grand Rapids, MI	12.6	4.9	11.1	39.1
Green Bay, WI	13.3	3.5	12.4	38.4
Greensboro, NC	9.7	2.6	7.8	33.8
Honolulu, HI	11.1	2.5	7.2	33.5
Houston, TX	10.1	3.7	8.5	38.3
Huntsville, AL	13.2	4.2	11.0	37.7
Indianapolis, IN	13.2	5.3	12.2	39.0
Jacksonville, FL	12.6	4.2	11.2	38.1
Kansas City, MO	12.6	3.9	11.7	36.1
Lafayette, LA	12.3	4.8	10.9	34.1
Las Vegas, NV	12.7	3.9	11.2	36.6
Lexington, KY	11.5	4.6	9.4	38.0
Lincoln, NE	9.5	3.0	7.6	34.1
Little Rock, AR	12.0	3.2	10.4	36.8
Los Angeles, CA	9.7	2.7	7.2	39.4
Louisville, KY	15.1	5.9	13.7	38.9
Lubbock, TX	13.7	5.2	12.1	42.4
Madison, WI	8.5	3.7	6.7	31.0
Manchester, NH	13.3	5.7	11.1	37.1
McAllen, TX	12.2	4.4	9.6	48.7
Miami, FL	12.4	3.1	8.8	38.8
Midland, TX	11.9	4.4	9.7	44.0

Table continued on next page.

City	All Ages	Under 18 Years Old	18 to 64 Years Old	65 Years and Over
Minneapolis, MN	10.3	4.6	9.2	35.0
Nashville, TN	11.3	3.5	9.8	37.9
New Orleans, LA	13.9	4.7	12.4	40.3
New York, NY	10.3	3.2	7.7	36.8
Oklahoma City, OK	13.0	4.5	11.7	40.9
Omaha, NE	10.9	3.9	9.6	34.3
Orlando, FL	9.5	4.5	7.5	35.4
Oxnard, CA	10.5	4.4	9.1	41.1
Palm Bay, FL	14.5	3.5	12.3	38.2
Peoria, IL	11.7	4.7	10.1	33.6
Philadelphia, PA	15.9	6.4	14.5	41.7
Phoenix, AZ	9.5	3.2	8.5	35.7
Pittsburgh, PA	14.0	5.6	11.4	37.7
Portland, OR	12.1	4.1	10.3	37.6
Providence, RI	11.8	4.3	10.9	40.8
Provo, UT	7.4	4.2	6.1	36.7
Raleigh, NC	7.8	3.6	6.1	32.9
Reno, NV	11.1	3.2	9.6	34.0
Richmond, VA	15.7	7.1	14.0	41.3
Roanoke, VA	17.6	7.0	16.6	39.0
Rochester, MN	9.4	2.5	7.7	30.4
Sacramento, CA	13.2	4.1	11.5	42.1
Salem, OR	14.2	5.0	13.9	34.3
Salt Lake City, UT	11.4	3.7	10.1	38.1
San Antonio, TX	13.9	5.2	12.3	44.9
San Diego, CA	8.7	3.0	6.2	34.9
San Francisco, CA	10.5	1.7	6.9	38.2
San Jose, CA	8.3	2.6	5.9	36.0
Santa Rosa, CA	11.9	3.4	9.5	38.1
Savannah, GA	13.1	4.1	11.0	40.5
Seattle, WA	9.1	2.4	6.8	34.0
Sioux Falls, SD	10.0	2.3	9.3	31.7
Spokane, WA	15.6	5.0	14.1	39.9
Springfield, IL	16.1	6.0	15.1	36.2
Tallahassee, FL	8.9	4.2	6.9	35.9
Tampa, FL	12.9	5.1	11.2	38.4
Topeka, KS	16.5	3.6	16.4	39.1
Tulsa, OK	14.1	5.2	13.0	36.8
Tyler, TX	12.5	4.9	10.1	35.2
Virginia Beach, VA	10.0	3.9	7.9	34.0
Washington, DC	11.2	5.1	9.0	34.6
Wichita, KS	12.5	3.5	11.2	39.3
Wilmington, NC	13.7	4.6	10.7	40.9
Winston-Salem, NC	11.0	3.8	9.3	34.1
Worcester, MA	13.7	5.9	11.6	41.5
U.S.	12.3	4.1	10.2	36.3

Note: Figures show percent of the civilian noninstitutionalized population that reported having a disability. Disability status is determined from from six types of difficulty: vision, hearing, cognitive, ambulatory, self-care, and independent living. For children under 5 years old, hearing and vision difficulty are used to determine disability status. For children between the ages of 5 and 14, disability status is determined from hearing, vision, cognitive, ambulatory, and self-care difficulties. For people aged 15 years and older, they are considered to have a disability if they have difficulty with any one of the six difficulty types.
Source: U.S. Census Bureau, 2011-2013 American Community Survey 3-Year Estimates

Disability Status: Metro Area

Metro Area	All Ages	Under 18 Years Old	18 to 64 Years Old	65 Years and Over
Albuquerque, NM	13.3	4.0	11.6	38.6
Anchorage, AK	10.2	3.0	9.5	38.1
Ann Arbor, MI	8.6	2.7	6.8	30.8
Athens, GA	11.4	3.2	9.8	36.8
Atlanta, GA	9.9	3.3	8.7	35.1
Austin, TX	9.5	4.0	8.5	33.1
Billings, MT	14.1	5.5	11.9	37.1
Boise City, ID	11.6	4.5	10.0	36.2
Boston, MA	10.5	4.0	7.9	33.7
Boulder, CO	8.3	2.9	7.0	26.7
Cape Coral, FL	14.2	3.6	10.8	29.8
Cedar Rapids, IA	10.5	4.8	8.4	29.5
Charleston, SC	11.4	3.5	9.6	35.7
Charlotte, NC	11.0	3.5	9.5	35.7
Chicago, IL	9.8	3.1	7.8	35.1
Clarksville, TN	13.9	5.1	14.1	38.9
Colorado Springs, CO	11.6	4.3	10.7	34.1
Columbia, MO	10.2	3.7	9.1	33.0
Columbus, OH	11.9	4.7	10.4	36.7
Dallas, TX	9.5	3.3	8.2	35.8
Davenport, IA	11.6	3.8	9.1	33.6
Denver, CO	9.3	3.2	7.8	32.4
Des Moines, IA	10.1	3.1	9.2	31.9
Durham, NC	10.5	3.1	8.7	33.9
El Paso, TX	12.6	3.7	11.1	46.2
Erie, PA	14.8	6.7	12.6	36.8
Eugene, OR	15.6	5.4	13.1	37.9
Fargo, ND	9.4	2.8	8.1	32.0
Fayetteville, NC	13.8	4.3	13.4	43.2
Fort Collins, CO	9.4	2.8	7.4	30.7
Fort Wayne, IN	11.8	4.8	10.1	35.2
Fort Worth, TX	9.5	3.3	8.2	35.8
Gainesville, FL	11.0	3.7	8.6	37.0
Grand Rapids, MI	11.4	4.5	9.8	34.2
Green Bay, WI	10.9	3.7	9.2	33.0
Greensboro, NC	12.0	3.5	10.2	34.7
Honolulu, HI	10.6	3.0	7.6	34.1
Houston, TX	9.6	3.5	8.4	37.0
Huntsville, AL	12.2	3.5	10.2	37.8
Indianapolis, IN	12.1	4.7	10.7	36.4
Jacksonville, FL	12.7	4.4	10.8	36.6
Kansas City, MO	11.6	3.6	10.2	35.3
Lafayette, LA	13.8	5.0	12.5	40.7
Las Vegas, NV	11.7	3.8	10.2	35.2
Lexington, KY	12.8	4.8	11.1	38.2
Lincoln, NE	9.5	2.9	7.5	34.0
Little Rock, AR	14.0	5.4	12.4	38.5
Los Angeles, CA	9.3	2.7	6.8	36.5
Louisville, KY	14.4	5.3	12.8	38.3
Lubbock, TX	14.1	5.4	12.3	43.0
Madison, WI	9.4	4.0	7.4	30.7
Manchester, NH	10.8	4.6	8.8	33.1
McAllen, TX	13.6	6.0	12.0	50.3
Miami, FL	10.9	2.9	7.5	34.6
Midland, TX	12.1	4.8	9.9	44.6

Table continued on next page.

Metro Area	All Ages	Under 18 Years Old	18 to 64 Years Old	65 Years and Over
Minneapolis, MN	9.2	3.5	7.6	30.7
Nashville, TN	11.5	3.8	10.0	36.7
New Orleans, LA	13.9	5.5	11.7	40.0
New York, NY	9.8	3.1	7.3	33.6
Oklahoma City, OK	13.3	4.3	11.8	40.3
Omaha, NE	10.3	3.6	9.0	33.3
Orlando, FL	11.2	4.4	8.9	35.0
Oxnard, CA	10.2	3.9	7.8	35.2
Palm Bay, FL	15.3	3.9	12.0	34.7
Peoria, IL	10.9	3.9	8.4	32.6
Philadelphia, PA	12.1	4.5	10.0	34.3
Phoenix, AZ	10.3	3.2	8.5	32.6
Pittsburgh, PA	14.0	5.1	11.0	35.1
Portland, OR	11.9	4.1	10.1	36.6
Providence, RI	13.0	4.6	10.7	35.5
Provo, UT	7.2	2.9	6.6	34.7
Raleigh, NC	8.4	3.3	6.9	32.2
Reno, NV	11.6	3.7	9.8	33.6
Richmond, VA	12.1	4.4	10.1	35.5
Roanoke, VA	14.8	5.1	12.6	35.2
Rochester, MN	9.0	2.7	7.0	29.9
Sacramento, CA	12.1	4.1	9.9	38.1
Salem, OR	14.2	4.9	13.2	36.2
Salt Lake City, UT	9.1	3.4	8.2	34.5
San Antonio, TX	13.3	4.8	11.7	42.2
San Diego, CA	9.5	2.8	7.0	35.7
San Francisco, CA	9.6	2.7	7.0	33.5
San Jose, CA	7.7	2.4	5.2	33.1
Santa Rosa, CA	11.1	3.1	8.5	33.4
Savannah, GA	11.5	3.2	9.8	37.3
Seattle, WA	10.9	3.6	9.1	35.7
Sioux Falls, SD	9.6	2.9	8.5	31.6
Spokane, WA	14.9	5.0	13.0	38.9
Springfield, IL	14.1	6.2	12.4	34.6
Tallahassee, FL	11.0	4.6	8.9	35.4
Tampa, FL	14.0	4.5	11.2	34.6
Topeka, KS	14.6	3.9	13.8	35.7
Tulsa, OK	14.4	4.8	13.1	38.7
Tyler, TX	13.1	5.2	11.2	34.6
Virginia Beach, VA	10.9	3.9	9.1	33.7
Washington, DC	8.0	2.8	6.3	30.6
Wichita, KS	12.1	3.9	10.6	37.6
Wilmington, NC	13.7	4.2	11.3	37.7
Winston-Salem, NC	13.1	4.7	11.1	34.8
Worcester, MA	11.7	5.0	9.5	34.3
U.S.	12.3	4.1	10.2	36.3

Note: Figures show percent of the civilian noninstitutionalized population that reported having a disability. Disability status is determined from from six types of difficulty: vision, hearing, cognitive, ambulatory, self-care, and independent living. For children under 5 years old, hearing and vision difficulty are used to determine disability status. For children between the ages of 5 and 14, disability status is determined from hearing, vision, cognitive, ambulatory, and self-care difficulties. For people aged 15 years and older, they are considered to have a disability if they have difficulty with any one of the six difficulty types; Figures cover the Metropolitan Statistical Area—see Appendix B for areas included

Source: U.S. Census Bureau, 2011-2013 American Community Survey 3-Year Estimates

Male/Female Ratio: City

City	Males	Females	Males per 100 Females
Albuquerque, NM	269,222	285,083	94.4
Anchorage, AK	151,980	146,404	103.8
Ann Arbor, MI	58,168	58,005	100.3
Athens, GA	56,490	62,221	90.8
Atlanta, GA	220,467	220,597	99.9
Austin, TX	434,273	428,603	101.3
Billings, MT	51,432	55,776	92.2
Boise City, ID	104,867	107,013	98.0
Boston, MA	304,699	332,926	91.5
Boulder, CO	51,017	50,854	100.3
Cape Coral, FL	79,085	82,607	95.7
Cedar Rapids, IA	62,690	65,432	95.8
Charleston, SC	59,351	66,304	89.5
Charlotte, NC	371,347	403,086	92.1
Chicago, IL	1,318,892	1,393,100	94.7
Clarksville, TN	69,555	71,073	97.9
Colorado Springs, CO	215,263	218,356	98.6
Columbia, MO	54,336	58,880	92.3
Columbus, OH	395,555	414,832	95.4
Dallas, TX	621,146	618,122	100.5
Davenport, IA	49,731	51,590	96.4
Denver, CO	317,325	317,360	100.0
Des Moines, IA	101,802	104,769	97.2
Durham, NC	113,327	126,339	89.7
El Paso, TX	324,421	346,637	93.6
Erie, PA	49,740	51,343	96.9
Eugene, OR	77,877	80,292	97.0
Fargo, ND	55,020	55,454	99.2
Fayetteville, NC	99,138	103,438	95.8
Fort Collins, CO	73,780	75,195	98.1
Fort Wayne, IN	122,638	131,968	92.9
Fort Worth, TX	377,614	399,898	94.4
Gainesville, FL	60,742	65,911	92.2
Grand Rapids, MI	92,894	97,664	95.1
Green Bay, WI	51,307	53,316	96.2
Greensboro, NC	130,638	145,673	89.7
Honolulu, HI	170,480	174,427	97.7
Houston, TX	1,083,898	1,078,370	100.5
Huntsville, AL	89,776	93,926	95.6
Indianapolis, IN	402,096	431,804	93.1
Jacksonville, FL	405,350	430,737	94.1
Kansas City, MO	225,947	238,501	94.7
Lafayette, LA	59,888	63,109	94.9
Las Vegas, NV	301,119	294,787	102.1
Lexington, KY	149,904	155,094	96.7
Lincoln, NE	132,892	132,578	100.2
Little Rock, AR	93,837	102,598	91.5
Los Angeles, CA	1,914,874	1,937,942	98.8
Louisville, KY	292,181	313,248	93.3
Lubbock, TX	116,283	120,205	96.7
Madison, WI	118,531	121,770	97.3
Manchester, NH	55,100	55,068	100.1
McAllen, TX	66,239	68,893	96.1
Miami, FL	207,228	206,916	100.2
Midland, TX	58,026	61,145	94.9

Table continued on next page.

City	Males	Females	Males per 100 Females
Minneapolis, MN	198,752	194,909	102.0
Nashville, TN	302,021	321,874	93.8
New Orleans, LA	177,685	192,080	92.5
New York, NY	3,975,566	4,365,556	91.1
Oklahoma City, OK	295,559	304,485	97.1
Omaha, NE	209,768	219,013	95.8
Orlando, FL	120,322	129,452	92.9
Oxnard, CA	102,516	98,864	103.7
Palm Bay, FL	47,695	56,485	84.4
Peoria, IL	54,981	60,833	90.4
Philadelphia, PA	730,467	816,303	89.5
Phoenix, AZ	745,057	743,612	100.2
Pittsburgh, PA	148,248	157,751	94.0
Portland, OR	298,719	304,328	98.2
Providence, RI	86,711	91,428	94.8
Provo, UT	57,216	58,211	98.3
Raleigh, NC	203,584	219,614	92.7
Reno, NV	117,408	113,377	103.6
Richmond, VA	100,088	110,365	90.7
Roanoke, VA	46,584	51,070	91.2
Rochester, MN	53,066	56,258	94.3
Sacramento, CA	230,879	244,657	94.4
Salem, OR	77,965	80,744	96.6
Salt Lake City, UT	97,585	92,016	106.1
San Antonio, TX	675,440	708,276	95.4
San Diego, CA	674,569	662,953	101.8
San Francisco, CA	420,456	406,170	103.5
San Jose, CA	495,022	488,753	101.3
Santa Rosa, CA	84,919	85,574	99.2
Savannah, GA	67,265	74,521	90.3
Seattle, WA	316,940	319,330	99.3
Sioux Falls, SD	80,030	80,518	99.4
Spokane, WA	102,789	107,087	96.0
Springfield, IL	56,324	60,684	92.8
Tallahassee, FL	89,007	96,668	92.1
Tampa, FL	170,731	178,698	95.5
Topeka, KS	61,217	66,694	91.8
Tulsa, OK	191,759	203,450	94.3
Tyler, TX	46,121	53,283	86.6
Virginia Beach, VA	218,702	226,859	96.4
Washington, DC	299,718	333,449	89.9
Wichita, KS	190,463	194,691	97.8
Wilmington, NC	51,873	58,206	89.1
Winston-Salem, NC	109,996	124,235	88.5
Worcester, MA	87,241	95,145	91.7
U.S.	154,451,010	159,410,713	96.9

Source: U.S. Census Bureau, 2011-2013 American Community Survey 3-Year Estimates

Male/Female Ratio: Metro Area

Metro Area	Males	Females	Males per 100 Females
Albuquerque, NM	443,025	457,019	96.9
Anchorage, AK	200,581	191,444	104.8
Ann Arbor, MI	173,332	178,013	97.4
Athens, GA	94,417	101,892	92.7
Atlanta, GA	2,648,950	2,801,341	94.6
Austin, TX	918,435	914,909	100.4
Billings, MT	79,631	83,411	95.5
Boise City, ID	318,282	320,228	99.4
Boston, MA	2,250,752	2,392,619	94.1
Boulder, CO	153,103	152,181	100.6
Cape Coral, FL	316,615	329,066	96.2
Cedar Rapids, IA	129,627	132,007	98.2
Charleston, SC	341,017	356,099	95.8
Charlotte, NC	1,115,779	1,179,924	94.6
Chicago, IL	4,652,858	4,861,354	95.7
Clarksville, TN	135,821	134,884	100.7
Colorado Springs, CO	335,926	333,190	100.8
Columbia, MO	81,563	86,820	93.9
Columbus, OH	956,827	988,980	96.7
Dallas, TX	3,301,095	3,393,794	97.3
Davenport, IA	188,146	194,300	96.8
Denver, CO	1,318,148	1,329,879	99.1
Des Moines, IA	290,333	299,670	96.9
Durham, NC	252,398	272,977	92.5
El Paso, TX	405,065	423,307	95.7
Erie, PA	138,217	142,462	97.0
Eugene, OR	174,253	180,485	96.5
Fargo, ND	109,338	108,318	100.9
Fayetteville, NC	182,311	192,352	94.8
Fort Collins, CO	154,721	155,883	99.3
Fort Wayne, IN	206,410	215,343	95.9
Fort Worth, TX	3,301,095	3,393,794	97.3
Gainesville, FL	130,829	137,730	95.0
Grand Rapids, MI	496,436	509,598	97.4
Green Bay, WI	155,064	155,643	99.6
Greensboro, NC	353,362	382,528	92.4
Honolulu, HI	491,583	483,100	101.8
Houston, TX	3,076,211	3,104,755	99.1
Huntsville, AL	211,831	218,536	96.9
Indianapolis, IN	944,327	986,738	95.7
Jacksonville, FL	670,928	707,065	94.9
Kansas City, MO	1,000,116	1,039,202	96.2
Lafayette, LA	231,522	243,048	95.3
Las Vegas, NV	1,003,453	993,918	101.0
Lexington, KY	237,743	246,503	96.4
Lincoln, NE	155,726	154,585	100.7
Little Rock, AR	348,536	369,164	94.4
Los Angeles, CA	6,433,666	6,602,204	97.4
Louisville, KY	610,951	641,909	95.2
Lubbock, TX	148,268	151,160	98.1
Madison, WI	308,430	312,225	98.8
Manchester, NH	199,795	203,184	98.3
McAllen, TX	393,607	411,890	95.6
Miami, FL	2,796,261	2,963,665	94.4
Midland, TX	74,592	75,892	98.3

Table continued on next page.

Metro Area	Males	Females	Males per 100 Females
Minneapolis, MN	1,691,801	1,731,624	97.7
Nashville, TN	843,798	883,814	95.5
New Orleans, LA	595,635	631,894	94.3
New York, NY	9,588,708	10,250,992	93.5
Oklahoma City, OK	640,103	657,728	97.3
Omaha, NE	437,416	448,403	97.5
Orlando, FL	1,088,197	1,133,645	96.0
Oxnard, CA	414,557	420,323	98.6
Palm Bay, FL	267,572	279,831	95.6
Peoria, IL	186,544	194,515	95.9
Philadelphia, PA	2,905,084	3,111,882	93.4
Phoenix, AZ	2,151,086	2,175,269	98.9
Pittsburgh, PA	1,144,050	1,216,496	94.0
Portland, OR	1,130,628	1,157,386	97.7
Providence, RI	775,445	826,242	93.9
Provo, UT	277,155	273,824	101.2
Raleigh, NC	580,255	608,423	95.4
Reno, NV	218,347	215,262	101.4
Richmond, VA	595,906	636,733	93.6
Roanoke, VA	149,362	160,766	92.9
Rochester, MN	103,661	106,336	97.5
Sacramento, CA	1,075,677	1,119,301	96.1
Salem, OR	196,381	200,953	97.7
Salt Lake City, UT	564,875	559,027	101.0
San Antonio, TX	1,100,400	1,134,484	97.0
San Diego, CA	1,595,328	1,579,985	101.0
San Francisco, CA	2,199,538	2,255,873	97.5
San Jose, CA	951,310	942,011	101.0
Santa Rosa, CA	241,429	249,628	96.7
Savannah, GA	175,117	186,378	94.0
Seattle, WA	1,772,064	1,781,242	99.5
Sioux Falls, SD	119,034	118,946	100.1
Spokane, WA	264,607	268,120	98.7
Springfield, IL	101,637	110,147	92.3
Tallahassee, FL	181,396	191,849	94.6
Tampa, FL	1,379,741	1,468,026	94.0
Topeka, KS	114,781	119,775	95.8
Tulsa, OK	467,985	485,135	96.5
Tyler, TX	103,615	110,914	93.4
Virginia Beach, VA	834,506	863,039	96.7
Washington, DC	2,860,283	3,001,035	95.3
Wichita, KS	314,540	320,772	98.1
Wilmington, NC	128,681	135,148	95.2
Winston-Salem, NC	311,623	335,810	92.8
Worcester, MA	455,895	468,049	97.4
U.S.	154,451,010	159,410,713	96.9

Note: Figures cover the Metropolitan Statistical Area (MSA)—see Appendix B for areas included
Source: U.S. Census Bureau, 2011-2013 American Community Survey 3-Year Estimates

Gross Metropolitan Product

MSA[1]	2012	2013	2014	2015	Rank[2]
Albuquerque, NM	38.8	39.9	41.5	43.3	62
Anchorage, AK	28.6	29.3	30.4	31.8	83
Ann Arbor, MI	19.3	19.8	20.6	21.6	111
Athens, GA	6.8	7.1	7.4	7.7	224
Atlanta, GA	294.0	306.2	321.1	339.9	10
Austin, TX	98.7	104.4	110.6	117.5	31
Billings, MT	8.5	8.7	8.9	9.4	205
Boise City, ID	27.5	28.3	29.5	31.1	85
Boston, MA	336.2	347.0	361.2	379.4	9
Boulder, CO	20.3	21.1	21.8	22.9	107
Cape Coral, FL	20.9	21.9	23.1	24.6	95
Cedar Rapids, IA	14.8	15.3	15.8	16.5	142
Charleston, SC	31.0	31.9	33.3	35.2	74
Charlotte, NC	125.2	131.7	138.1	146.3	22
Chicago, IL	571.0	588.6	611.5	641.0	3
Clarksville, TN	11.8	11.8	12.2	12.7	167
Colorado Springs, CO	28.0	28.6	29.6	31.2	84
Columbia, MO	7.3	7.6	7.8	8.3	219
Columbus, OH	99.8	102.8	106.4	112.1	32
Dallas, TX	418.6	440.1	464.7	491.4	6
Davenport, IA	18.6	18.9	19.5	20.4	116
Denver, CO	167.9	174.8	182.6	192.6	18
Des Moines, IA	42.1	44.0	45.6	47.9	57
Durham, NC	39.7	41.5	43.6	46.3	58
El Paso, TX	29.6	29.9	31.1	32.6	78
Erie, PA	10.0	10.1	10.3	10.8	186
Eugene, OR	12.2	12.6	13.0	13.6	160
Fargo, ND	13.2	13.9	14.5	15.3	146
Fayetteville, NC	18.7	18.8	19.4	20.3	117
Fort Collins, CO	12.4	12.8	13.3	14.0	155
Fort Wayne, IN	19.0	19.5	20.3	21.2	115
Fort Worth, TX	418.6	440.1	464.7	491.4	6
Gainesville, FL	10.5	10.7	11.1	11.6	174
Grand Rapids, MI	35.3	36.8	39.0	40.9	65
Green Bay, WI	15.9	16.4	17.1	17.9	133
Greensboro, NC	36.9	38.1	39.4	41.4	64
Honolulu, HI	56.6	57.8	59.8	62.2	51
Houston, TX	449.7	467.5	496.1	523.2	4
Huntsville, AL	21.7	22.1	22.9	24.1	99
Indianapolis, IN	112.8	116.5	120.8	126.5	27
Jacksonville, FL	62.3	65.1	68.1	71.9	47
Kansas City, MO	113.8	117.2	121.3	127.5	26
Lafayette, LA	17.7	17.8	18.8	19.6	123
Las Vegas, NV	95.6	98.7	103.2	109.5	34
Lexington, KY	23.9	24.8	25.7	27.1	90
Lincoln, NE	15.9	16.5	17.4	18.3	130
Little Rock, AR	34.4	35.5	36.9	38.7	68
Los Angeles, CA	765.7	792.2	822.9	865.2	2
Louisville, KY	63.8	66.6	69.0	72.5	46
Lubbock, TX	10.9	11.3	11.7	12.1	172
Madison, WI	38.0	39.3	41.0	43.2	63
Manchester, NH	22.2	22.4	23.2	24.3	98
McAllen, TX	16.0	16.6	17.4	18.4	128
Miami, FL	274.1	284.9	298.8	315.6	11
Midland, TX	16.2	17.9	20.0	21.3	114
Minneapolis, MN	218.5	228.6	237.6	249.8	13

Table continued on next page.

MSA[1]	2012	2013	2014	2015	Rank[2]
Nashville, TN	91.1	96.3	100.8	106.2	35
New Orleans, LA	80.2	83.7	87.4	91.0	40
New York, NY	1,335.1	1,386.0	1,433.2	1,500.4	1
Oklahoma City, OK	63.3	65.0	67.7	70.5	49
Omaha, NE	51.9	52.9	55.0	57.8	52
Orlando, FL	106.1	110.7	117.0	124.5	28
Oxnard, CA	39.1	39.7	41.3	43.5	61
Palm Bay, FL	18.1	18.5	19.1	20.2	118
Peoria, IL	21.3	21.5	22.1	23.0	104
Philadelphia, PA	364.0	375.3	387.7	406.2	8
Phoenix, AZ	201.7	210.9	221.0	234.5	14
Pittsburgh, PA	123.6	126.7	130.9	137.1	24
Portland, OR	147.0	153.8	161.5	171.5	20
Providence, RI	69.5	71.5	74.2	77.5	44
Provo, UT	17.0	17.8	18.7	19.9	120
Raleigh, NC	61.4	63.7	67.4	71.8	48
Reno, NV	20.4	20.9	21.7	22.8	108
Richmond, VA	70.1	72.2	75.0	78.7	43
Roanoke, VA	13.7	14.1	14.5	15.1	148
Rochester, MN	9.7	10.0	10.3	10.9	184
Sacramento, CA	97.6	100.4	104.6	110.7	33
Salem, OR	12.7	13.1	13.6	14.3	152
Salt Lake City, UT	74.8	77.7	81.2	85.9	42
San Antonio, TX	92.0	95.1	99.9	105.4	36
San Diego, CA	177.4	182.7	190.8	201.8	17
San Francisco, CA	360.4	379.4	395.6	417.8	7
San Jose, CA	173.9	182.7	192.2	203.2	16
Santa Rosa, CA	20.3	20.9	21.9	23.0	104
Savannah, GA	14.1	14.6	15.1	15.9	145
Seattle, WA	258.8	269.5	279.8	293.8	12
Sioux Falls, SD	16.6	17.7	18.4	19.4	125
Spokane, WA	19.3	19.9	20.5	21.5	112
Springfield, IL	10.0	10.0	10.3	10.7	190
Tallahassee, FL	13.4	13.7	14.2	14.9	150
Tampa, FL	119.9	125.7	131.7	139.0	23
Topeka, KS	9.9	10.0	10.2	10.6	192
Tulsa, OK	47.9	48.5	50.5	52.9	54
Tyler, TX	9.4	9.7	10.1	10.5	194
Virginia Beach, VA	85.2	87.3	90.0	93.8	39
Washington, DC	447.0	458.1	475.5	501.7	5
Wichita, KS	29.4	29.7	30.7	32.3	82
Wilmington, NC	15.4	16.1	17.0	18.0	132
Winston-Salem, NC	23.0	23.5	24.3	25.4	92
Worcester, MA	30.5	31.5	32.6	34.0	75

Note: Figures are in billions of dollars; (1) Metropolitan Statistical Area—see Appendix B for areas included; (2) Rank is based on 2015 data and ranges from 1 to 363.
Source: The U.S. Conference of Mayors, U.S. Metro Economies: GMP and Employment 2013-2015, June 2014

Economic Growth

Area	2010-12 (%)	2013 (%)	2014 (%)	2015 (%)	Rank[2]
Albuquerque, NM	0.6	1.2	2.2	2.7	220
Anchorage, AK	1.6	1.1	1.1	3.7	54
Ann Arbor, MI	1.4	1.2	2.6	2.9	172
Athens, GA	0.2	2.8	2.1	2.7	220
Atlanta, GA	2.6	2.7	3.3	3.9	35
Austin, TX	5.1	4.6	3.9	4.7	8
Billings, MT	4.2	1.0	1.6	2.7	220
Boise City, ID	1.3	1.5	2.7	3.4	88
Boston, MA	2.2	1.9	2.5	3.0	155
Boulder, CO	3.7	2.4	1.9	2.9	172
Cape Coral, FL	1.3	3.4	3.8	4.3	19
Cedar Rapids, IA	1.4	1.4	1.7	2.7	220
Charleston, SC	3.5	1.6	2.7	3.6	61
Charlotte, NC	3.3	3.8	3.3	3.9	35
Chicago, IL	2.2	1.8	2.3	2.9	172
Clarksville, TN	3.6	-1.1	1.2	2.8	194
Colorado Springs, CO	2.1	0.7	1.8	3.1	134
Columbia, MO	2.8	3.3	1.2	3.3	102
Columbus, OH	2.9	1.7	1.9	3.3	102
Dallas, TX	3.8	3.7	3.3	4.5	14
Davenport, IA	1.8	0.2	1.9	2.5	254
Denver, CO	2.1	2.8	2.6	3.8	47
Des Moines, IA	2.9	2.3	2.1	3.1	134
Durham, NC	-0.4	3.1	3.5	4.1	25
El Paso, TX	2.4	-0.3	1.9	3.1	134
Erie, PA	3.1	-0.1	1.1	2.0	321
Eugene, OR	1.8	1.6	1.8	2.9	172
Fargo, ND	4.3	3.4	2.5	3.9	35
Fayetteville, NC	0.8	-0.9	1.4	2.4	270
Fort Collins, CO	2.5	1.8	2.0	3.3	102
Fort Wayne, IN	2.4	1.6	2.7	2.5	254
Fort Worth, TX	3.8	3.7	3.3	4.5	14
Gainesville, FL	-0.3	1.3	2.0	2.3	285
Grand Rapids, MI	3.9	3.0	4.4	2.9	172
Green Bay, WI	1.3	1.9	2.4	3.1	134
Greensboro, NC	2.1	1.8	2.1	3.1	134
Honolulu, HI	2.3	0.8	1.8	1.9	332
Houston, TX	4.8	2.8	3.5	4.8	6
Huntsville, AL	0.4	0.6	2.1	3.3	102
Indianapolis, IN	2.5	2.1	2.1	2.8	194
Jacksonville, FL	1.4	3.2	3.0	3.5	74
Kansas City, MO	1.8	1.5	1.9	3.2	119
Lafayette, LA	-3.6	-1.3	2.9	3.8	47
Las Vegas, NV	1.3	1.8	2.9	4.0	29
Lexington, KY	0.9	2.2	2.2	3.5	74
Lincoln, NE	2.3	2.4	3.8	2.8	194
Little Rock, AR	1.4	1.7	2.5	3.0	155
Los Angeles, CA	2.1	2.3	2.3	3.3	102
Louisville, KY	3.2	3.0	2.0	3.1	134
Lubbock, TX	0.8	2.7	1.0	1.9	332
Madison, WI	1.9	1.9	2.8	3.2	119
Manchester, NH	1.7	0.1	2.1	2.9	172
McAllen, TX	1.5	2.0	2.5	4.6	10
Miami, FL	2.4	2.7	3.2	3.6	61
Midland, TX	10.3	8.5	7.1	8.4	1
Minneapolis, MN	3.2	3.2	2.4	3.2	119

Table continued on next page.

Area	2010-12 (%)	2013 (%)	2014 (%)	2015 (%)	Rank[2]
Nashville, TN	4.5	4.2	3.1	3.4	88
New Orleans, LA	0.8	3.9	2.2	3.0	155
New York, NY	1.3	2.7	1.8	2.6	239
Oklahoma City, OK	2.4	1.3	2.0	2.9	172
Omaha, NE	1.5	0.3	2.4	3.1	134
Orlando, FL	2.4	3.0	4.1	4.4	16
Oxnard, CA	1.8	0.5	2.2	3.6	61
Palm Bay, FL	-1.7	0.7	1.8	3.6	61
Peoria, IL	8.7	-0.4	1.2	2.5	254
Philadelphia, PA	1.3	1.8	1.7	2.7	220
Phoenix, AZ	2.6	3.3	3.2	4.0	29
Pittsburgh, PA	2.8	1.3	1.7	2.6	239
Portland, OR	4.9	3.2	3.5	4.3	19
Providence, RI	1.0	1.7	2.1	2.5	254
Provo, UT	4.1	3.7	3.4	4.6	10
Raleigh, NC	2.3	2.3	4.1	4.5	14
Reno, NV	0.8	1.0	2.5	3.0	155
Richmond, VA	2.1	1.6	2.3	2.8	194
Roanoke, VA	1.4	1.1	1.1	2.3	285
Rochester, MN	0.3	0.8	1.7	3.3	102
Sacramento, CA	1.8	1.5	2.4	3.9	35
Salem, OR	-0.4	1.6	1.7	3.2	119
Salt Lake City, UT	3.6	2.9	2.9	3.9	35
San Antonio, TX	3.8	1.8	3.0	4.0	29
San Diego, CA	2.4	1.8	2.7	3.8	47
San Francisco, CA	3.8	4.1	2.6	3.7	54
San Jose, CA	5.2	4.3	3.7	3.9	35
Santa Rosa, CA	0.4	1.6	2.9	3.3	102
Savannah, GA	2.3	1.9	2.1	3.1	134
Seattle, WA	4.0	2.8	2.3	3.1	134
Sioux Falls, SD	2.7	4.3	2.0	3.3	102
Spokane, WA	1.6	1.9	1.4	2.9	172
Springfield, IL	-0.3	-0.9	1.0	1.8	339
Tallahassee, FL	-0.8	1.3	1.9	2.8	194
Tampa, FL	2.3	3.5	3.1	3.6	61
Topeka, KS	1.4	-0.7	0.8	2.3	285
Tulsa, OK	1.4	0.2	2.1	3.3	102
Tyler, TX	1.7	2.2	1.2	3.9	35
Virginia Beach, VA	1.2	1.0	1.5	2.2	301
Washington, DC	1.1	1.2	2.1	3.4	88
Wichita, KS	2.6	-0.2	1.6	3.4	88
Wilmington, NC	1.3	3.1	3.7	4.1	25
Winston-Salem, NC	-0.7	0.8	1.7	2.8	194
Worcester, MA	0.9	1.8	1.8	2.3	285
U.S.	2.1	2.0	2.3	3.2	–

Note: Figures are real gross metropolitan product (GMP) growth rates and represent annual average percent change.(1) Metropolitan Statistical Area—see Appendix B for areas included; (2) Rank is based on 2015 data and ranges from 1 to 363
Source: The U.S. Conference of Mayors, U.S. Metro Economies: GMP and Employment 2013-2015, June 2014

Metropolitan Area Exports

Area	2008	2009	2010	2011	2012	2013	Rank[2]
Albuquerque, NM	474.9	357.6	519.9	951.9	1,790.6	1,389.6	129
Anchorage, AK	245.8	213.9	n/a	n/a	416.4	518.0	211
Ann Arbor, MI	1,084.6	903.4	1,050.8	1,129.5	1,053.4	1,156.2	145
Athens, GA	171.4	214.6	194.6	221.6	229.7	286.0	271
Atlanta, GA	14,432.9	13,405.9	15,009.7	17,229.1	18,169.1	18,827.9	18
Austin, TX	7,405.5	5,963.7	8,867.8	8,626.3	8,976.6	8,870.8	38
Billings, MT	88.6	70.7	86.7	102.1	141.4	139.8	326
Boise City, ID	3,851.2	2,849.7	3,647.7	4,131.5	4,088.2	3,657.9	68
Boston, MA	22,955.2	18,972.6	21,804.5	22,292.8	21,234.8	22,212.8	14
Boulder, CO	891.7	727.2	1,058.7	946.7	1,128.0	1,046.0	153
Cape Coral, FL	282.8	237.5	298.0	305.1	509.8	442.6	225
Cedar Rapids, IA	909.9	734.8	749.5	880.8	889.1	930.2	161
Charleston, SC	2,005.5	1,455.7	2,120.0	2,299.4	2,429.8	3,464.3	71
Charlotte, NC	5,036.3	4,133.4	5,424.6	6,253.3	6,322.6	10,684.1	31
Chicago, IL	35,554.7	28,196.6	33,672.0	39,522.4	40,568.0	44,910.6	6
Clarksville, TN	311.4	158.4	238.3	328.8	326.3	315.9	263
Colorado Springs, CO	1,932.4	1,281.1	1,193.1	1,118.7	1,044.6	1,065.4	149
Columbia, MO	234.8	211.1	255.6	281.6	296.6	423.9	230
Columbus, OH	3,881.8	2,872.7	3,554.4	4,327.5	5,488.6	5,731.4	48
Dallas, TX	22,503.7	19,881.8	22,500.4	26,648.7	27,820.9	27,596.0	9
Davenport, IA	5,255.0	3,542.6	4,792.8	6,725.9	7,926.1	7,141.2	42
Denver, CO	4,633.5	4,309.8	4,990.9	3,771.3	3,355.8	3,618.4	69
Des Moines, IA	1,034.6	782.3	767.9	970.1	1,183.2	1,279.4	138
Durham, NC	2,688.4	2,656.1	2,736.6	2,640.3	2,723.2	2,971.7	80
El Paso, TX	9,390.5	7,748.0	10,315.9	11,615.9	12,796.9	14,359.7	22
Erie, PA	1,861.9	1,407.8	1,063.3	1,577.7	1,854.2	1,808.1	106
Eugene, OR	781.3	314.4	415.5	464.5	482.2	476.0	218
Fargo, ND	677.2	465.9	548.6	730.8	785.9	817.9	175
Fayetteville, NC	300.4	218.4	260.1	307.7	322.3	344.0	251
Fort Collins, CO	631.5	584.0	694.1	812.7	861.7	986.1	157
Fort Wayne, IN	1,142.8	916.8	1,059.2	1,283.8	1,353.5	1,441.8	127
Fort Worth, TX	22,503.7	19,881.8	22,500.4	26,648.7	27,820.9	27,596.0	9
Gainesville, FL	285.5	233.2	277.7	305.1	348.6	295.0	270
Grand Rapids, MI	2,993.7	2,408.5	2,474.0	2,791.9	3,156.4	5,314.8	53
Green Bay, WI	622.1	496.1	669.9	1,023.2	1,031.6	914.8	163
Greensboro, NC	3,687.9	3,168.6	4,007.8	4,054.1	4,281.9	4,278.3	61
Honolulu, HI	546.0	357.9	439.5	375.3	306.3	323.2	257
Houston, TX	80,015.1	65,820.9	80,569.7	104,457.0	110,298.0	114,963.0	1
Huntsville, AL	1,079.3	1,136.5	986.8	1,293.3	1,491.5	1,518.7	123
Indianapolis, IN	8,590.0	8,030.9	9,446.7	9,560.7	10,436.0	9,747.5	34
Jacksonville, FL	1,973.5	1,634.4	1,940.5	2,385.2	2,595.0	2,467.8	91
Kansas City, MO	7,799.7	5,888.9	7,374.1	7,958.9	7,880.8	8,012.1	41
Lafayette, LA	762.7	657.0	488.1	655.9	726.0	1,261.8	139
Las Vegas, NV	1,167.7	1,022.7	1,187.8	1,667.6	1,811.5	2,008.2	100
Lexington, KY	2,490.6	2,260.2	2,400.4	2,170.5	2,462.1	2,294.0	92
Lincoln, NE	733.4	682.8	722.7	922.1	904.7	818.4	174
Little Rock, AR	1,411.0	1,693.8	790.2	892.4	2,418.9	2,497.5	90
Los Angeles, CA	59,985.6	51,528.4	62,167.6	72,688.9	75,007.5	76,305.7	3
Louisville, KY	5,662.1	5,316.1	6,187.8	6,756.6	7,706.7	8,898.0	36
Lubbock, TX	1,016.6	530.4	772.8	966.9	657.9	536.8	209
Madison, WI	1,595.5	1,571.6	1,906.5	1,958.1	2,168.7	2,292.1	93
Manchester, NH	2,005.6	1,743.0	2,612.1	2,494.1	1,634.9	1,445.8	126
McAllen, TX	4,578.5	3,736.1	4,527.1	4,676.1	5,198.5	5,265.5	54
Miami, FL	33,411.5	31,175.0	35,866.9	43,129.9	47,858.7	41,771.5	7
Midland, TX	93.5	75.6	87.2	81.1	104.4	164.1	316
Minneapolis, MN	25,212.2	20,096.7	23,192.8	26,189.1	25,155.7	23,747.5	12

Table continued on next page.

Area	2008	2009	2010	2011	2012	2013	Rank[2]
Nashville, TN	5,259.5	4,406.6	5,748.5	5,878.7	6,402.1	8,702.8	39
New Orleans, LA	12,664.5	10,145.1	13,964.9	20,336.9	24,359.5	30,030.9	8
New York, NY	95,244.3	69,990.3	85,081.2	105,102.0	102,298.0	106,923.0	2
Oklahoma City, OK	1,233.8	987.6	1,196.1	1,592.8	1,574.6	1,581.7	120
Omaha, NE	2,317.1	1,924.4	2,079.4	2,658.0	3,529.3	4,255.9	62
Orlando, FL	3,388.0	2,947.1	3,453.6	3,230.0	3,850.6	3,227.7	76
Oxnard, CA	2,579.1	2,483.8	2,611.2	2,919.8	2,854.6	2,893.9	82
Palm Bay, FL	782.6	555.5	858.3	1,162.8	982.3	984.3	158
Peoria, IL	14,230.0	7,846.5	11,104.0	15,182.3	17,838.0	12,184.5	25
Philadelphia, PA	21,683.2	19,067.4	22,710.0	26,155.8	22,991.6	24,929.2	11
Phoenix, AZ	12,623.6	7,947.5	9,342.7	10,914.4	10,834.3	11,473.5	27
Pittsburgh, PA	11,309.0	8,343.0	12,160.7	15,165.5	14,134.7	10,444.4	32
Portland, OR	19,477.1	15,482.4	18,544.9	20,875.7	20,337.7	17,606.8	20
Providence, RI	5,382.0	5,392.0	5,791.9	7,139.1	5,830.8	6,609.0	44
Provo, UT	2,218.0	1,772.8	2,024.6	2,056.4	2,058.1	2,789.2	83
Raleigh, NC	2,076.7	1,799.5	1,912.4	2,254.4	2,308.1	2,280.6	95
Reno, NV	1,317.0	1,233.8	1,511.9	1,687.4	2,019.0	2,117.4	97
Richmond, VA	5,162.4	4,096.8	4,606.5	5,072.8	4,328.1	4,337.2	60
Roanoke, VA	669.3	582.4	709.8	659.8	716.6	746.5	182
Rochester, MN	938.2	779.7	984.5	842.6	1,023.7	1,061.0	151
Sacramento, CA	3,608.0	3,502.0	4,070.5	4,686.0	5,194.6	5,777.1	47
Salem, OR	331.9	325.2	453.8	508.7	437.3	414.4	232
Salt Lake City, UT	7,799.0	7,783.5	10,719.2	15,579.2	15,990.0	11,867.2	26
San Antonio, TX	5,049.5	4,390.0	6,416.2	10,506.5	14,010.2	19,287.6	16
San Diego, CA	15,855.9	13,418.6	16,464.3	17,410.5	17,183.3	17,885.5	19
San Francisco, CA	20,470.4	16,040.3	21,355.4	23,573.8	23,031.7	25,305.3	10
San Jose, CA	27,048.6	21,405.8	26,333.0	26,712.1	26,687.7	23,413.1	13
Santa Rosa, CA	1,117.8	880.1	992.4	1,132.2	1,059.1	1,044.8	154
Savannah, GA	3,598.5	2,724.7	3,459.1	4,140.2	4,116.5	5,436.4	52
Seattle, WA	46,911.2	36,942.3	35,409.6	41,117.5	50,301.7	56,686.4	4
Sioux Falls, SD	234.1	202.8	330.3	457.8	439.5	433.0	229
Spokane, WA	894.8	662.2	727.4	761.4	873.5	862.4	172
Springfield, IL	86.8	87.0	148.6	158.0	99.5	97.5	350
Tallahassee, FL	119.1	108.1	117.8	118.1	130.8	122.5	337
Tampa, FL	7,153.5	6,463.6	6,633.6	7,736.7	7,190.0	6,673.0	43
Topeka, KS	446.2	441.8	478.1	483.2	265.0	303.3	265
Tulsa, OK	2,878.1	2,441.1	2,741.8	3,123.6	3,578.9	3,818.0	65
Tyler, TX	147.1	130.1	184.4	249.6	221.1	219.6	302
Virginia Beach, VA	2,278.8	2,004.5	2,450.7	2,594.6	2,735.0	2,539.2	88
Washington, DC	9,879.4	9,226.1	11,082.9	10,237.9	14,609.7	16,225.0	21
Wichita, KS	6,845.9	4,954.8	5,512.0	4,169.2	4,250.3	3,785.5	66
Wilmington, NC	1,138.8	1,078.6	1,161.9	951.6	923.5	766.7	179
Winston-Salem, NC	1,855.1	1,741.5	1,554.6	1,268.3	1,148.1	1,660.1	117
Worcester, MA	2,863.5	2,035.9	2,355.7	2,397.0	2,966.2	3,393.6	73

Note: Figures are in millions of dollars; (1) Metropolitan Statistical Area—see Appendix B for areas included; (2) Rank is based on 2013 data and ranges from 1 to 387; n/a not available
Source: U.S. Department of Commerce, International Trade Administration, Office of Trade & Industry Information, Manufacturing & Services, data extracted April 3, 2015

Building Permits: City

City	Single-Family			Multi-Family			Total		
	2013	2014	Pct. Chg.	2013	2014	Pct. Chg.	2013	2014	Pct. Chg.
Albuquerque, NM	434	1,110	155.8	1,040	306	-70.6	1,474	1,416	-3.9
Anchorage, AK	475	572	20.4	58	198	241.4	533	770	44.5
Ann Arbor, MI	27	22	-18.5	198	2	-99.0	225	24	-89.3
Athens, GA	143	116	-18.9	351	422	20.2	494	538	8.9
Atlanta, GA	473	545	15.2	5,070	3,960	-21.9	5,543	4,505	-18.7
Austin, TX	2,573	2,800	8.8	9,261	6,642	-28.3	11,834	9,442	-20.2
Billings, MT	481	473	-1.7	558	132	-76.3	1,039	605	-41.8
Boise City, ID	498	467	-6.2	222	793	257.2	720	1,260	75.0
Boston, MA	34	48	41.2	2,527	2,793	10.5	2,561	2,841	10.9
Boulder, CO	89	104	16.9	789	504	-36.1	878	608	-30.8
Cape Coral, FL	492	663	34.8	6	0	-100.0	498	663	33.1
Cedar Rapids, IA	242	325	34.3	245	124	-49.4	487	449	-7.8
Charleston, SC	576	600	4.2	351	378	7.7	927	978	5.5
Charlotte, NC	n/a	n/a	n/a	n/a	n/a	n/a	n/a	n/a	n/a
Chicago, IL	448	536	19.6	2,577	5,214	102.3	3,025	5,750	90.1
Clarksville, TN	779	850	9.1	580	137	-76.4	1,359	987	-27.4
Colorado Springs, CO	n/a	n/a	n/a	n/a	n/a	n/a	n/a	n/a	n/a
Columbia, MO	631	444	-29.6	378	739	95.5	1,009	1,183	17.2
Columbus, OH	770	724	-6.0	3,565	2,918	-18.1	4,335	3,642	-16.0
Dallas, TX	1,075	1,181	9.9	7,559	6,675	-11.7	8,634	7,856	-9.0
Davenport, IA	114	90	-21.1	16	30	87.5	130	120	-7.7
Denver, CO	1,284	1,710	33.2	4,586	4,248	-7.4	5,870	5,958	1.5
Des Moines, IA	184	116	-37.0	559	167	-70.1	743	283	-61.9
Durham, NC	1,112	1,154	3.8	2,636	360	-86.3	3,748	1,514	-59.6
El Paso, TX	2,271	2,021	-11.0	1,408	777	-44.8	3,679	2,798	-23.9
Erie, PA	2	3	50.0	0	0	-	2	3	50.0
Eugene, OR	182	224	23.1	733	808	10.2	915	1,032	12.8
Fargo, ND	509	377	-25.9	1,146	1,793	56.5	1,655	2,170	31.1
Fayetteville, NC	437	346	-20.8	288	77	-73.3	725	423	-41.7
Fort Collins, CO	612	742	21.2	779	410	-47.4	1,391	1,152	-17.2
Fort Wayne, IN	n/a	n/a	n/a	n/a	n/a	n/a	n/a	n/a	n/a
Fort Worth, TX	3,321	3,121	-6.0	2,334	2,802	20.1	5,655	5,923	4.7
Gainesville, FL	63	67	6.3	240	263	9.6	303	330	8.9
Grand Rapids, MI	59	75	27.1	96	128	33.3	155	203	31.0
Green Bay, WI	71	70	-1.4	105	110	4.8	176	180	2.3
Greensboro, NC	354	415	17.2	614	814	32.6	968	1,229	27.0
Honolulu, HI	n/a	n/a	n/a	n/a	n/a	n/a	n/a	n/a	n/a
Houston, TX	5,198	5,398	3.8	8,845	14,906	68.5	14,043	20,304	44.6
Huntsville, AL	1,000	897	-10.3	306	977	219.3	1,306	1,874	43.5
Indianapolis, IN	562	572	1.8	671	554	-17.4	1,233	1,126	-8.7
Jacksonville, FL	1,844	2,106	14.2	709	1,196	68.7	2,553	3,302	29.3
Kansas City, MO	703	656	-6.7	827	2,078	151.3	1,530	2,734	78.7
Lafayette, LA	n/a	n/a	n/a	n/a	n/a	n/a	n/a	n/a	n/a
Las Vegas, NV	1,517	1,453	-4.2	0	0	-	1,517	1,453	-4.2
Lexington, KY	676	687	1.6	223	538	141.3	899	1,225	36.3
Lincoln, NE	844	854	1.2	531	938	76.6	1,375	1,792	30.3
Little Rock, AR	356	338	-5.1	252	441	75.0	608	779	28.1
Los Angeles, CA	1,144	1,668	45.8	7,248	9,596	32.4	8,392	11,264	34.2
Louisville, KY	938	964	2.8	1,289	1,449	12.4	2,227	2,413	8.4
Lubbock, TX	938	888	-5.3	1,039	1,161	11.7	1,977	2,049	3.6
Madison, WI	217	235	8.3	1,018	1,445	41.9	1,235	1,680	36.0
Manchester, NH	49	104	112.2	38	10	-73.7	87	114	31.0
McAllen, TX	374	412	10.2	145	196	35.2	519	608	17.1
Miami, FL	115	72	-37.4	4,371	3,714	-15.0	4,486	3,786	-15.6

Table continued on next page.

City	Single-Family			Multi-Family			Total		
	2013	2014	Pct. Chg.	2013	2014	Pct. Chg.	2013	2014	Pct. Chg.
Midland, TX	732	917	25.3	1,092	636	-41.8	1,824	1,553	-14.9
Minneapolis, MN	146	138	-5.5	3,176	1,821	-42.7	3,322	1,959	-41.0
Nashville, TN	1,824	2,538	39.1	2,142	3,829	78.8	3,966	6,367	60.5
New Orleans, LA	736	574	-22.0	159	452	184.3	895	1,026	14.6
New York, NY	402	541	34.6	17,593	19,346	10.0	17,995	19,887	10.5
Oklahoma City, OK	3,609	3,306	-8.4	804	1,155	43.7	4,413	4,461	1.1
Omaha, NE	1,567	1,306	-16.7	1,003	1,147	14.4	2,570	2,453	-4.6
Orlando, FL	1,037	915	-11.8	1,850	1,934	4.5	2,887	2,849	-1.3
Oxnard, CA	94	71	-24.5	276	431	56.2	370	502	35.7
Palm Bay, FL	157	162	3.2	0	0	-	157	162	3.2
Peoria, IL	147	51	-65.3	6	0	-100.0	153	51	-66.7
Philadelphia, PA	632	756	19.6	2,183	3,217	47.4	2,815	3,973	41.1
Phoenix, AZ	1,673	1,608	-3.9	1,458	3,530	142.1	3,131	5,138	64.1
Pittsburgh, PA	100	89	-11.0	0	249	-	100	338	238.0
Portland, OR	763	792	3.8	2,992	4,224	41.2	3,755	5,016	33.6
Providence, RI	16	14	-12.5	26	13	-50.0	42	27	-35.7
Provo, UT	136	128	-5.9	51	163	219.6	187	291	55.6
Raleigh, NC	1,662	1,318	-20.7	2,138	3,337	56.1	3,800	4,655	22.5
Reno, NV	687	858	24.9	426	699	64.1	1,113	1,557	39.9
Richmond, VA	106	182	71.7	743	369	-50.3	849	551	-35.1
Roanoke, VA	65	35	-46.2	161	14	-91.3	226	49	-78.3
Rochester, MN	323	352	9.0	44	134	204.5	367	486	32.4
Sacramento, CA	232	256	10.3	27	25	-7.4	259	281	8.5
Salem, OR	283	270	-4.6	294	21	-92.9	577	291	-49.6
Salt Lake City, UT	80	95	18.8	178	245	37.6	258	340	31.8
San Antonio, TX	2,102	2,270	8.0	16	3,368	20,950.0	2,118	5,638	166.2
San Diego, CA	821	712	-13.3	4,487	2,031	-54.7	5,308	2,743	-48.3
San Francisco, CA	54	35	-35.2	4,420	2,676	-39.5	4,474	2,711	-39.4
San Jose, CA	274	384	40.1	3,429	4,061	18.4	3,703	4,445	20.0
Santa Rosa, CA	138	184	33.3	347	64	-81.6	485	248	-48.9
Savannah, GA	265	341	28.7	18	23	27.8	283	364	28.6
Seattle, WA	822	898	9.2	5,855	6,547	11.8	6,677	7,445	11.5
Sioux Falls, SD	1,025	842	-17.9	986	1,036	5.1	2,011	1,878	-6.6
Spokane, WA	321	223	-30.5	142	296	108.5	463	519	12.1
Springfield, IL	81	89	9.9	46	137	197.8	127	226	78.0
Tallahassee, FL	293	271	-7.5	648	632	-2.5	941	903	-4.0
Tampa, FL	686	712	3.8	1,168	1,843	57.8	1,854	2,555	37.8
Topeka, KS	84	86	2.4	2	28	1,300.0	86	114	32.6
Tulsa, OK	436	402	-7.8	164	963	487.2	600	1,365	127.5
Tyler, TX	271	268	-1.1	0	12	-	271	280	3.3
Virginia Beach, VA	733	688	-6.1	929	520	-44.0	1,662	1,208	-27.3
Washington, DC	333	288	-13.5	2,922	3,901	33.5	3,255	4,189	28.7
Wichita, KS	536	550	2.6	200	182	-9.0	736	732	-0.5
Wilmington, NC	n/a	n/a	n/a	n/a	n/a	n/a	n/a	n/a	n/a
Winston-Salem, NC	476	514	8.0	502	269	-46.4	978	783	-19.9
Worcester, MA	53	88	66.0	8	16	100.0	61	104	70.5
U.S.	620,802	634,597	2.2	370,020	411,766	11.3	990,822	1,046,363	5.6

Note: Figures represent new, privately-owned housing units authorized (unadjusted data); All permit data are based on estimates with imputation
Source: U.S. Census Bureau, Manufacturing, Mining, and Construction Statistics, Building Permits, 2013, 2014

Building Permits: Metro Area

Metro Area	Single-Family			Multi-Family			Total		
	2013	2014	Pct. Chg.	2013	2014	Pct. Chg.	2013	2014	Pct. Chg.
Albuquerque, NM	1,456	2,128	46.2	1,150	415	-63.9	2,606	2,543	-2.4
Anchorage, AK	500	671	34.2	76	216	184.2	576	887	54.0
Ann Arbor, MI	394	385	-2.3	364	185	-49.2	758	570	-24.8
Athens, GA	698	502	-28.1	381	428	12.3	1,079	930	-13.8
Atlanta, GA	14,824	16,984	14.6	9,473	9,699	2.4	24,297	26,683	9.8
Austin, TX	8,941	11,515	28.8	11,911	8,434	-29.2	20,852	19,949	-4.3
Billings, MT	974	517	-46.9	1,128	134	-88.1	2,102	651	-69.0
Boise City, ID	3,522	3,481	-1.2	843	1,702	101.9	4,365	5,183	18.7
Boston, MA	4,953	4,991	0.8	7,068	7,033	-0.5	12,021	12,024	0.0
Boulder, CO	591	560	-5.2	1,034	811	-21.6	1,625	1,371	-15.6
Cape Coral, FL	2,531	3,112	23.0	645	983	52.4	3,176	4,095	28.9
Cedar Rapids, IA	625	644	3.0	324	237	-26.9	949	881	-7.2
Charleston, SC	3,779	4,144	9.7	1,638	2,011	22.8	5,417	6,155	13.6
Charlotte, NC	8,792	11,306	28.6	5,217	7,231	38.6	14,009	18,537	32.3
Chicago, IL	7,261	7,723	6.4	4,366	7,956	82.2	11,627	15,679	34.8
Clarksville, TN	1,256	1,276	1.6	586	231	-60.6	1,842	1,507	-18.2
Colorado Springs, CO	2,885	2,662	-7.7	702	1,011	44.0	3,587	3,673	2.4
Columbia, MO	836	663	-20.7	396	751	89.6	1,232	1,414	14.8
Columbus, OH	3,495	3,497	0.1	4,868	3,547	-27.1	8,363	7,044	-15.8
Dallas, TX	21,224	22,550	6.2	16,686	18,868	13.1	37,910	41,418	9.3
Davenport, IA	510	458	-10.2	107	197	84.1	617	655	6.2
Denver, CO	6,965	8,064	15.8	8,510	7,703	-9.5	15,475	15,767	1.9
Des Moines, IA	3,307	2,952	-10.7	1,614	1,484	-8.1	4,921	4,436	-9.9
Durham, NC	1,969	2,167	10.1	2,725	420	-84.6	4,694	2,587	-44.9
El Paso, TX	2,613	2,260	-13.5	1,484	783	-47.2	4,097	3,043	-25.7
Erie, PA	258	166	-35.7	209	155	-25.8	467	321	-31.3
Eugene, OR	506	506	0.0	743	810	9.0	1,249	1,316	5.4
Fargo, ND	1,395	1,242	-11.0	1,698	2,524	48.6	3,093	3,766	21.8
Fayetteville, NC	1,269	1,012	-20.3	621	77	-87.6	1,890	1,089	-42.4
Fort Collins, CO	1,489	1,627	9.3	888	871	-1.9	2,377	2,498	5.1
Fort Wayne, IN	960	883	-8.0	75	362	382.7	1,035	1,245	20.3
Fort Worth, TX	21,224	22,550	6.2	16,686	18,868	13.1	37,910	41,418	9.3
Gainesville, FL	558	536	-3.9	242	263	8.7	800	799	-0.1
Grand Rapids, MI	1,319	2,273	72.3	162	898	454.3	1,481	3,171	114.1
Green Bay, WI	719	641	-10.8	551	363	-34.1	1,270	1,004	-20.9
Greensboro, NC	1,416	1,470	3.8	616	1,162	88.6	2,032	2,632	29.5
Honolulu, HI	1,137	875	-23.0	1,504	703	-53.3	2,641	1,578	-40.2
Houston, TX	34,542	38,315	10.9	16,791	25,426	51.4	51,333	63,741	24.2
Huntsville, AL	1,944	1,784	-8.2	306	1,033	237.6	2,250	2,817	25.2
Indianapolis, IN	5,014	4,965	-1.0	3,137	3,041	-3.1	8,151	8,006	-1.8
Jacksonville, FL	6,281	6,299	0.3	1,077	1,482	37.6	7,358	7,781	5.7
Kansas City, MO	4,229	4,170	-1.4	3,303	4,031	22.0	7,532	8,201	8.9
Lafayette, LA	1,399	2,224	59.0	155	138	-11.0	1,554	2,362	52.0
Las Vegas, NV	7,067	6,809	-3.7	1,506	3,227	114.3	8,573	10,036	17.1
Lexington, KY	1,335	1,319	-1.2	319	569	78.4	1,654	1,888	14.1
Lincoln, NE	1,052	1,052	0.0	535	942	76.1	1,587	1,994	25.6
Little Rock, AR	1,681	1,514	-9.9	814	568	-30.2	2,495	2,082	-16.6
Los Angeles, CA	7,509	8,300	10.5	17,689	18,650	5.4	25,198	26,950	7.0
Louisville, KY	2,551	2,390	-6.3	1,466	1,621	10.6	4,017	4,011	-0.1
Lubbock, TX	1,009	975	-3.4	1,039	1,161	11.7	2,048	2,136	4.3
Madison, WI	1,212	1,243	2.6	1,754	2,562	46.1	2,966	3,805	28.3
Manchester, NH	468	464	-0.9	99	504	409.1	567	968	70.7
McAllen, TX	2,545	2,840	11.6	749	633	-15.5	3,294	3,473	5.4
Miami, FL	6,369	5,791	-9.1	13,552	9,468	-30.1	19,921	15,259	-23.4

Table continued on next page.

Metro Area	Single-Family			Multi-Family			Total		
	2013	2014	Pct. Chg.	2013	2014	Pct. Chg.	2013	2014	Pct. Chg.
Midland, TX	732	920	25.7	1,092	636	-41.8	1,824	1,556	-14.7
Minneapolis, MN	7,174	6,689	-6.8	4,859	4,736	-2.5	12,033	11,425	-5.1
Nashville, TN	7,020	9,075	29.3	3,869	5,869	51.7	10,889	14,944	37.2
New Orleans, LA	2,441	2,440	0.0	175	551	214.9	2,616	2,991	14.3
New York, NY	10,139	11,799	16.4	29,685	36,185	21.9	39,824	47,984	20.5
Oklahoma City, OK	6,359	5,959	-6.3	1,146	1,911	66.8	7,505	7,870	4.9
Omaha, NE	3,039	2,639	-13.2	1,425	1,553	9.0	4,464	4,192	-6.1
Orlando, FL	9,222	9,806	6.3	6,341	6,309	-0.5	15,563	16,115	3.5
Oxnard, CA	430	536	24.7	571	778	36.3	1,001	1,314	31.3
Palm Bay, FL	1,349	1,241	-8.0	24	45	87.5	1,373	1,286	-6.3
Peoria, IL	538	835	55.2	80	55	-31.3	618	890	44.0
Philadelphia, PA	6,252	6,379	2.0	4,965	7,252	46.1	11,217	13,631	21.5
Phoenix, AZ	12,959	11,557	-10.8	5,778	8,784	52.0	18,737	20,341	8.6
Pittsburgh, PA	3,251	3,082	-5.2	1,312	1,108	-15.5	4,563	4,190	-8.2
Portland, OR	5,717	5,462	-4.5	6,013	6,894	14.7	11,730	12,356	5.3
Providence, RI	1,465	1,441	-1.6	509	334	-34.4	1,974	1,775	-10.1
Provo, UT	2,675	2,679	0.1	748	2,616	249.7	3,423	5,295	54.7
Raleigh, NC	8,034	7,680	-4.4	3,397	3,967	16.8	11,431	11,647	1.9
Reno, NV	1,243	1,507	21.2	477	709	48.6	1,720	2,216	28.8
Richmond, VA	3,555	3,181	-10.5	1,450	1,131	-22.0	5,005	4,312	-13.8
Roanoke, VA	476	425	-10.7	209	86	-58.9	685	511	-25.4
Rochester, MN	594	621	4.5	44	211	379.5	638	832	30.4
Sacramento, CA	3,539	3,694	4.4	650	465	-28.5	4,189	4,159	-0.7
Salem, OR	646	712	10.2	304	232	-23.7	950	944	-0.6
Salt Lake City, UT	3,447	3,159	-8.4	2,081	2,159	3.7	5,528	5,318	-3.8
San Antonio, TX	5,827	6,220	6.7	301	4,112	1,266.1	6,128	10,332	68.6
San Diego, CA	2,565	2,487	-3.0	5,699	4,388	-23.0	8,264	6,875	-16.8
San Francisco, CA	3,659	3,716	1.6	7,263	6,285	-13.5	10,922	10,001	-8.4
San Jose, CA	1,870	1,861	-0.5	5,894	8,176	38.7	7,764	10,037	29.3
Santa Rosa, CA	453	419	-7.5	593	244	-58.9	1,046	663	-36.6
Savannah, GA	1,517	1,857	22.4	233	354	51.9	1,750	2,211	26.3
Seattle, WA	8,773	8,665	-1.2	10,744	13,288	23.7	19,517	21,953	12.5
Sioux Falls, SD	1,330	1,134	-14.7	1,079	1,196	10.8	2,409	2,330	-3.3
Spokane, WA	1,299	1,135	-12.6	335	825	146.3	1,634	1,960	20.0
Springfield, IL	276	300	8.7	64	155	142.2	340	455	33.8
Tallahassee, FL	628	628	0.0	652	632	-3.1	1,280	1,260	-1.6
Tampa, FL	7,314	7,267	-0.6	4,838	5,119	5.8	12,152	12,386	1.9
Topeka, KS	272	285	4.8	10	30	200.0	282	315	11.7
Tulsa, OK	3,008	3,022	0.5	717	1,511	110.7	3,725	4,533	21.7
Tyler, TX	373	377	1.1	0	12	-	373	389	4.3
Virginia Beach, VA	4,104	3,766	-8.2	3,273	1,949	-40.5	7,377	5,715	-22.5
Washington, DC	13,274	12,411	-6.5	10,759	12,393	15.2	24,033	24,804	3.2
Wichita, KS	1,163	1,177	1.2	341	337	-1.2	1,504	1,514	0.7
Wilmington, NC	3,141	1,367	-56.5	916	841	-8.2	4,057	2,208	-45.6
Winston-Salem, NC	1,001	1,424	42.3	502	661	31.7	1,503	2,085	38.7
Worcester, MA	1,164	1,274	9.5	177	110	-37.9	1,341	1,384	3.2
U.S.	620,802	634,597	2.2	370,020	411,766	11.3	990,822	1,046,363	5.6

Note: Figures cover the Metropolitan Statistical Area—see Appendix B for areas included; Figures represent new, privately-owned housing units authorized (unadjusted data); All permit data are based on estimates with imputation
Source: U.S. Census Bureau, Manufacturing, Mining, and Construction Statistics, Building Permits, 2013, 2014

Housing Vacancy Rates

Metro Area[1]	Gross Vacancy Rate[2] (%)			Year-Round Vacancy Rate[3] (%)			Rental Vacancy Rate[4] (%)			Homeowner Vacancy Rate[5] (%)		
	2012	2013	2014	2012	2013	2014	2012	2013	2014	2012	2013	2014
Albuquerque, NM	7.1	8.4	8.6	6.5	7.7	7.3	5.1	7.8	7.5	2.2	2.4	1.9
Anchorage, AK	n/a	n/a	n/a	n/a	n/a	n/a	n/a	n/a	n/a	n/a	n/a	n/a
Ann Arbor, MI	n/a	n/a	n/a	n/a	n/a	n/a	n/a	n/a	n/a	n/a	n/a	n/a
Athens, GA	n/a	n/a	n/a	n/a	n/a	n/a	n/a	n/a	n/a	n/a	n/a	n/a
Atlanta, GA	12.5	12.4	11.0	12.2	11.8	10.3	10.6	10.2	8.8	2.6	2.1	2.5
Austin, TX	12.7	12.5	12.4	11.9	11.9	11.6	9.6	12.1	10.9	1.3	1.1	0.8
Billings, MT	n/a	n/a	n/a	n/a	n/a	n/a	n/a	n/a	n/a	n/a	n/a	n/a
Boise City, ID	n/a	n/a	n/a	n/a	n/a	n/a	n/a	n/a	n/a	n/a	n/a	n/a
Boston, MA	8.6	7.8	9.2	6.9	6.2	6.4	5.9	6.8	4.9	1.3	1.1	0.8
Boulder, CO	n/a	n/a	n/a	n/a	n/a	n/a	n/a	n/a	n/a	n/a	n/a	n/a
Cape Coral, FL	n/a	n/a	n/a	n/a	n/a	n/a	n/a	n/a	n/a	n/a	n/a	n/a
Cedar Rapids, IA	n/a	n/a	n/a	n/a	n/a	n/a	n/a	n/a	n/a	n/a	n/a	n/a
Charleston, SC	n/a	n/a	n/a	n/a	n/a	n/a	n/a	n/a	n/a	n/a	n/a	n/a
Charlotte, NC	8.0	9.3	7.9	7.7	8.7	7.8	6.4	6.4	6.0	1.3	3.5	1.7
Chicago, IL	10.8	10.5	10.3	10.6	10.3	10.2	9.7	10.9	9.1	2.8	2.8	2.6
Clarksville, TN	n/a	n/a	n/a	n/a	n/a	n/a	n/a	n/a	n/a	n/a	n/a	n/a
Colorado Springs, CO	n/a	n/a	n/a	n/a	n/a	n/a	n/a	n/a	n/a	n/a	n/a	n/a
Columbia, MO	n/a	n/a	n/a	n/a	n/a	n/a	n/a	n/a	n/a	n/a	n/a	n/a
Columbus, OH	13.7	9.8	10.2	13.7	9.8	9.9	8.3	6.3	7.0	2.3	1.1	1.7
Dallas, TX	8.7	9.0	9.2	8.4	8.8	9.0	9.2	8.2	9.8	2.1	1.9	1.5
Davenport, IA	n/a	n/a	n/a	n/a	n/a	n/a	n/a	n/a	n/a	n/a	n/a	n/a
Denver, CO	6.3	6.3	6.1	5.9	5.5	5.1	4.7	5.3	3.3	1.5	1.2	0.8
Des Moines, IA	n/a	n/a	n/a	n/a	n/a	n/a	n/a	n/a	n/a	n/a	n/a	n/a
Durham, NC	n/a	n/a	n/a	n/a	n/a	n/a	n/a	n/a	n/a	n/a	n/a	n/a
El Paso, TX	4.3	8.8	9.3	4.3	8.6	8.4	8.2	7.9	9.2	0.1	2.9	1.5
Erie, PA	n/a	n/a	n/a	n/a	n/a	n/a	n/a	n/a	n/a	n/a	n/a	n/a
Eugene, OR	n/a	n/a	n/a	n/a	n/a	n/a	n/a	n/a	n/a	n/a	n/a	n/a
Fargo, ND	n/a	n/a	n/a	n/a	n/a	n/a	n/a	n/a	n/a	n/a	n/a	n/a
Fayetteville, NC	n/a	n/a	n/a	n/a	n/a	n/a	n/a	n/a	n/a	n/a	n/a	n/a
Fort Collins, CO	n/a	n/a	n/a	n/a	n/a	n/a	n/a	n/a	n/a	n/a	n/a	n/a
Fort Wayne, IN	n/a	n/a	n/a	n/a	n/a	n/a	n/a	n/a	n/a	n/a	n/a	n/a
Fort Worth, TX	8.7	9.0	9.2	8.4	8.8	9.0	9.2	8.2	9.8	2.1	1.9	1.5
Gainesville, FL	n/a	n/a	n/a	n/a	n/a	n/a	n/a	n/a	n/a	n/a	n/a	n/a
Grand Rapids, MI	8.8	7.2	6.5	6.4	6.2	5.8	5.6	5.1	3.7	2.4	2.5	1.6
Green Bay, WI	n/a	n/a	n/a	n/a	n/a	n/a	n/a	n/a	n/a	n/a	n/a	n/a
Greensboro, NC	12.1	12.5	11.4	12.0	12.4	10.9	7.6	9.6	8.6	3.5	3.0	2.0
Honolulu, HI	10.2	10.9	12.3	8.8	8.6	10.2	6.3	6.0	5.6	1.3	0.9	1.1
Houston, TX	9.8	9.6	8.9	9.4	9.0	8.4	11.4	10.0	8.6	1.9	2.3	1.3
Huntsville, AL	n/a	n/a	n/a	n/a	n/a	n/a	n/a	n/a	n/a	n/a	n/a	n/a
Indianapolis, IN	10.5	9.2	8.8	9.5	8.7	8.7	11.1	10.9	10.9	1.8	1.5	2.2
Jacksonville, FL	15.4	14.2	16.6	14.4	12.7	14.0	11.7	8.4	11.1	1.9	1.5	2.6
Kansas City, MO	10.5	10.8	9.0	10.3	10.4	8.6	11.2	10.1	9.5	1.6	2.0	1.5
Lafayette, LA	n/a	n/a	n/a	n/a	n/a	n/a	n/a	n/a	n/a	n/a	n/a	n/a
Las Vegas, NV	16.2	16.6	14.3	15.0	15.5	13.4	12.8	14.1	10.1	3.4	3.0	2.9
Lexington, KY	n/a	n/a	n/a	n/a	n/a	n/a	n/a	n/a	n/a	n/a	n/a	n/a
Lincoln, NE	n/a	n/a	n/a	n/a	n/a	n/a	n/a	n/a	n/a	n/a	n/a	n/a
Little Rock, AR	n/a	n/a	n/a	n/a	n/a	n/a	n/a	n/a	n/a	n/a	n/a	n/a
Los Angeles, CA	6.2	6.2	5.8	5.9	5.7	5.5	4.9	4.2	4.6	1.3	1.2	0.8
Louisville, KY	10.6	11.0	10.3	10.6	11.0	9.8	7.2	7.8	5.5	2.4	0.8	2.2
Lubbock, TX	n/a	n/a	n/a	n/a	n/a	n/a	n/a	n/a	n/a	n/a	n/a	n/a
Madison, WI	n/a	n/a	n/a	n/a	n/a	n/a	n/a	n/a	n/a	n/a	n/a	n/a
Manchester, NH	n/a	n/a	n/a	n/a	n/a	n/a	n/a	n/a	n/a	n/a	n/a	n/a
McAllen, TX	n/a	n/a	n/a	n/a	n/a	n/a	n/a	n/a	n/a	n/a	n/a	n/a
Miami, FL	20.1	20.2	19.6	10.1	10.3	10.4	8.2	6.7	7.0	0.9	1.7	1.8

Table continued on next page.

Metro Area[1]	Gross Vacancy Rate[2] (%)			Year-Round Vacancy Rate[3] (%)			Rental Vacancy Rate[4] (%)			Homeowner Vacancy Rate[5] (%)		
	2012	2013	2014	2012	2013	2014	2012	2013	2014	2012	2013	2014
Midland, TX	n/a	n/a	n/a	n/a	n/a	n/a	n/a	n/a	n/a	n/a	n/a	n/a
Minneapolis, MN	5.8	5.7	5.7	5.2	5.1	5.3	5.3	5.4	4.4	1.2	0.9	1.4
Nashville, TN	8.7	6.6	7.0	8.2	6.4	6.7	8.4	5.3	4.0	1.6	0.9	2.4
New Orleans, LA	13.6	13.3	13.0	13.4	12.7	12.3	15.9	11.1	8.5	2.9	1.9	1.6
New York, NY	9.8	9.5	9.2	8.4	8.1	7.9	6.4	5.4	4.6	2.2	2.1	1.6
Oklahoma City, OK	12.8	13.0	13.4	12.6	12.6	12.9	10.2	8.7	10.1	2.5	2.0	1.7
Omaha, NE	8.3	7.5	7.7	7.9	6.5	7.0	9.5	6.1	5.5	1.2	1.3	1.8
Orlando, FL	21.2	20.5	18.8	14.3	15.5	15.2	18.5	14.7	14.6	2.2	2.8	3.1
Oxnard, CA	5.5	7.4	8.4	4.6	5.6	8.1	2.3	5.3	2.5	0.5	1.7	2.1
Palm Bay, FL	n/a	n/a	n/a	n/a	n/a	n/a	n/a	n/a	n/a	n/a	n/a	n/a
Peoria, IL	n/a	n/a	n/a	n/a	n/a	n/a	n/a	n/a	n/a	n/a	n/a	n/a
Philadelphia, PA	10.2	10.4	10.2	9.8	10.2	10.0	12.6	11.6	9.7	1.9	1.6	2.0
Phoenix, AZ	16.6	18.4	17.5	9.8	11.5	11.3	10.3	9.7	9.7	2.7	2.4	2.9
Pittsburgh, PA	14.4	12.7	12.2	14.1	12.5	11.7	6.4	7.8	6.1	1.3	1.7	1.2
Portland, OR	7.0	6.5	6.3	6.6	6.1	6.2	5.0	3.1	3.6	1.9	1.2	1.3
Providence, RI	13.8	12.3	13.2	10.9	8.9	9.9	8.0	6.6	6.8	2.9	2.3	1.6
Provo, UT	n/a	n/a	n/a	n/a	n/a	n/a	n/a	n/a	n/a	n/a	n/a	n/a
Raleigh, NC	8.5	7.3	6.4	8.2	7.2	6.4	8.8	6.9	5.3	1.9	1.8	0.6
Reno, NV	n/a	n/a	n/a	n/a	n/a	n/a	n/a	n/a	n/a	n/a	n/a	n/a
Richmond, VA	13.8	14.5	11.8	13.0	13.6	11.5	17.5	11.4	12.0	1.4	2.4	1.9
Roanoke, VA	n/a	n/a	n/a	n/a	n/a	n/a	n/a	n/a	n/a	n/a	n/a	n/a
Rochester, MN	n/a	n/a	n/a	n/a	n/a	n/a	n/a	n/a	n/a	n/a	n/a	n/a
Sacramento, CA	8.5	9.7	10.2	7.6	8.4	7.6	5.7	7.0	6.5	2.3	1.2	1.0
Salem, OR	n/a	n/a	n/a	n/a	n/a	n/a	n/a	n/a	n/a	n/a	n/a	n/a
Salt Lake City, UT	7.9	7.4	7.8	7.3	6.8	7.6	7.3	6.7	9.8	0.8	1.5	1.8
San Antonio, TX	11.3	9.0	8.6	10.4	8.3	8.2	9.0	9.1	7.3	2.7	1.4	1.2
San Diego, CA	9.1	7.8	7.7	8.6	7.4	7.3	7.1	5.5	4.8	1.4	1.2	1.3
San Francisco, CA	6.9	6.5	5.9	6.8	6.4	5.9	3.2	3.9	3.2	1.0	1.1	0.4
San Jose, CA	3.8	5.0	4.7	3.7	4.9	4.5	3.8	3.0	2.9	0.9	0.6	0.6
Santa Rosa, CA	n/a	n/a	n/a	n/a	n/a	n/a	n/a	n/a	n/a	n/a	n/a	n/a
Savannah, GA	n/a	n/a	n/a	n/a	n/a	n/a	n/a	n/a	n/a	n/a	n/a	n/a
Seattle, WA	8.1	6.9	6.9	8.0	6.6	6.7	5.7	4.3	4.4	2.3	1.7	1.2
Sioux Falls, SD	n/a	n/a	n/a	n/a	n/a	n/a	n/a	n/a	n/a	n/a	n/a	n/a
Spokane, WA	n/a	n/a	n/a	n/a	n/a	n/a	n/a	n/a	n/a	n/a	n/a	n/a
Springfield, IL	n/a	n/a	n/a	n/a	n/a	n/a	n/a	n/a	n/a	n/a	n/a	n/a
Tallahassee, FL	n/a	n/a	n/a	n/a	n/a	n/a	n/a	n/a	n/a	n/a	n/a	n/a
Tampa, FL	20.8	18.4	18.3	14.2	12.1	11.5	13.0	9.2	8.4	2.0	2.1	2.4
Topeka, KS	n/a	n/a	n/a	n/a	n/a	n/a	n/a	n/a	n/a	n/a	n/a	n/a
Tulsa, OK	13.3	12.0	11.0	12.8	11.5	10.5	9.5	10.5	9.7	2.4	2.4	1.2
Tyler, TX	n/a	n/a	n/a	n/a	n/a	n/a	n/a	n/a	n/a	n/a	n/a	n/a
Virginia Beach, VA	10.8	9.6	9.4	9.5	8.7	8.4	8.7	7.0	6.6	2.9	2.5	2.0
Washington, DC	8.1	8.3	7.8	7.9	8.2	7.5	6.4	7.2	6.7	1.3	1.3	1.4
Wichita, KS	n/a	n/a	n/a	n/a	n/a	n/a	n/a	n/a	n/a	n/a	n/a	n/a
Wilmington, NC	n/a	n/a	n/a	n/a	n/a	n/a	n/a	n/a	n/a	n/a	n/a	n/a
Winston-Salem, NC	n/a	n/a	n/a	n/a	n/a	n/a	n/a	n/a	n/a	n/a	n/a	n/a
Worcester, MA	10.3	10.8	11.0	9.5	8.6	6.8	3.7	6.4	4.5	2.4	3.1	1.9
U.S.	13.8	13.6	13.4	10.8	10.7	10.4	8.7	8.3	7.6	2.0	2.0	1.9

Note: (1) Metropolitan Statistical Area—see Appendix B for areas included; (2) The percentage of the total housing inventory that is vacant; (3) The percentage of the housing inventory (excluding seasonal units) that is year-round vacant; (4) The percentage of rental inventory that is vacant for rent; (5) The percentage of homeowner inventory that is vacant for sale; n/a not available
Source: U.S. Census Bureau, Housing Vacancies and Homeownership Annual Statistics: 2014

Bankruptcy Filings

City	Area Covered	Business Filings			Nonbusiness Filings		
		2013	2014	% Chg.	2013	2014	% Chg.
Albuquerque, NM	Bernalillo County	64	50	-21.9	1,668	1,399	-16.1
Anchorage, AK	Anchorage Borough	19	17	-10.5	268	210	-21.6
Ann Arbor, MI	Washtenaw County	22	16	-27.3	939	848	-9.7
Athens, GA	Clarke County	18	7	-61.1	383	381	-0.5
Atlanta, GA	Fulton County	256	161	-37.1	5,143	5,080	-1.2
Austin, TX	Travis County	141	112	-20.6	1,062	838	-21.1
Billings, MT	Yellowstone County	13	17	30.8	296	263	-11.1
Boise City, ID	Ada County	60	47	-21.7	1,494	1,177	-21.2
Boston, MA	Suffolk County	30	31	3.3	946	764	-19.2
Boulder, CO	Boulder County	46	33	-28.3	708	544	-23.2
Cape Coral, FL	Lee County	79	74	-6.3	1,833	1,619	-11.7
Cedar Rapids, IA	Linn County	10	5	-50.0	407	347	-14.7
Charleston, SC	Charleston County	22	29	31.8	480	448	-6.7
Charlotte, NC	Mecklenburg County	70	63	-10.0	1,653	1,326	-19.8
Chicago, IL	Cook County	794	569	-28.3	35,315	33,968	-3.8
Clarksville, TN	Montgomery County	14	14	0.0	773	808	4.5
Colorado Springs, CO	El Paso County	51	40	-21.6	2,641	2,126	-19.5
Columbia, MO	Boone County	8	10	25.0	577	419	-27.4
Columbus, OH	Franklin County	82	82	0.0	5,271	4,806	-8.8
Dallas, TX	Dallas County	310	379	22.3	5,162	4,779	-7.4
Davenport, IA	Scott County	22	12	-45.5	357	379	6.2
Denver, CO	Denver County	126	69	-45.2	2,829	2,203	-22.1
Des Moines, IA	Polk County	55	39	-29.1	1,110	978	-11.9
Durham, NC	Durham County	12	18	50.0	575	533	-7.3
El Paso, TX	El Paso County	82	68	-17.1	2,108	2,035	-3.5
Erie, PA	Erie County	17	13	-23.5	664	491	-26.1
Eugene, OR	Lane County	29	18	-37.9	1,174	1,025	-12.7
Fargo, ND	Cass County	12	9	-25.0	292	257	-12.0
Fayetteville, NC	Cumberland County	12	12	0.0	838	822	-1.9
Fort Collins, CO	Larimer County	49	29	-40.8	1,077	857	-20.4
Fort Wayne, IN	Allen County	35	19	-45.7	2,101	1,710	-18.6
Fort Worth, TX	Tarrant County	214	177	-17.3	4,694	4,302	-8.4
Gainesville, FL	Alachua County	30	15	-50.0	297	314	5.7
Grand Rapids, MI	Kent County	86	55	-36.0	1,841	1,532	-16.8
Green Bay, WI	Brown County	28	20	-28.6	776	731	-5.8
Greensboro, NC	Guilford County	65	32	-50.8	880	782	-11.1
Honolulu, HI	Honolulu County	54	44	-18.5	1,231	1,057	-14.1
Houston, TX	Harris County	388	300	-22.7	5,462	4,832	-11.5
Huntsville, AL	Madison County	40	35	-12.5	1,425	1,334	-6.4
Indianapolis, IN	Marion County	119	85	-28.6	5,633	4,942	-12.3
Jacksonville, FL	Duval County	137	106	-22.6	3,773	2,917	-22.7
Kansas City, MO	Jackson County	61	45	-26.2	3,110	2,916	-6.2
Lafayette, LA	Lafayette Parish	20	40	100.0	495	516	4.2
Las Vegas, NV	Clark County	408	327	-19.9	10,814	8,554	-20.9
Lexington, KY	Fayette County	40	39	-2.5	1,010	942	-6.7
Lincoln, NE	Lancaster County	22	20	-9.1	804	771	-4.1
Little Rock, AR	Pulaski County	49	23	-53.1	2,456	2,455	0.0
Los Angeles, CA	Los Angeles County	1,456	1,212	-16.8	37,662	29,341	-22.1
Louisville, KY	Jefferson County	66	65	-1.5	3,579	3,353	-6.3
Lubbock, TX	Lubbock County	25	12	-52.0	253	177	-30.0
Madison, WI	Dane County	47	40	-14.9	1,199	991	-17.3
Manchester, NH	Hillsborough County	69	78	13.0	942	750	-20.4
McAllen, TX	Hidalgo County	47	45	-4.3	627	649	3.5
Miami, FL	Miami-Dade County	379	266	-29.8	16,145	14,486	-10.3
Midland, TX	Midland County	8	8	0.0	49	53	8.2

Table continued on next page.

City	Area Covered	Business Filings			Nonbusiness Filings		
		2013	2014	% Chg.	2013	2014	% Chg.
Minneapolis, MN	Hennepin County	106	110	3.8	3,267	2,625	-19.7
Nashville, TN	Davidson County	78	70	-10.3	3,434	3,124	-9.0
New Orleans, LA	Orleans Parish	40	45	12.5	704	674	-4.3
New York, NY	Bronx County	69	43	-37.7	2,389	2,057	-13.9
New York, NY	Kings County	196	140	-28.6	2,790	2,484	-11.0
New York, NY	New York County	248	301	21.4	1,470	1,110	-24.5
New York, NY	Queens County	127	145	14.2	3,719	3,058	-17.8
New York, NY	Richmond County	39	29	-25.6	863	725	-16.0
Oklahoma City, OK	Oklahoma County	56	57	1.8	2,452	2,365	-3.5
Omaha, NE	Douglas County	62	44	-29.0	1,788	1,514	-15.3
Orlando, FL	Orange County	354	192	-45.8	5,776	5,383	-6.8
Oxnard, CA	Ventura County	101	84	-16.8	2,483	1,935	-22.1
Palm Bay, FL	Brevard County	58	49	-15.5	1,992	1,581	-20.6
Peoria, IL	Peoria County	13	8	-38.5	676	631	-6.7
Philadelphia, PA	Philadelphia County	103	89	-13.6	3,129	2,879	-8.0
Phoenix, AZ	Maricopa County	705	545	-22.7	15,679	13,283	-15.3
Pittsburgh, PA	Allegheny County	129	88	-31.8	2,807	2,209	-21.3
Portland, OR	Multnomah County	74	49	-33.8	2,429	2,213	-8.9
Providence, RI	Providence County	70	46	-34.3	2,207	1,830	-17.1
Provo, UT	Utah County	57	43	-24.6	2,083	2,003	-3.8
Raleigh, NC	Wake County	138	110	-20.3	1,927	1,823	-5.4
Reno, NV	Washoe County	87	64	-26.4	1,615	1,454	-10.0
Richmond, VA	Richmond city	11	25	127.3	951	1,009	6.1
Roanoke, VA	Roanoke city	6	5	-16.7	387	307	-20.7
Rochester, MN	Olmsted County	12	2	-83.3	252	224	-11.1
Sacramento, CA	Sacramento County	207	128	-38.2	6,736	5,064	-24.8
Salem, OR	Marion County	25	19	-24.0	1,334	1,219	-8.6
Salt Lake City, UT	Salt Lake County	127	114	-10.2	6,361	5,837	-8.2
San Antonio, TX	Bexar County	157	124	-21.0	2,696	2,497	-7.4
San Diego, CA	San Diego County	467	378	-19.1	11,822	9,544	-19.3
San Francisco, CA	San Francisco County	113	89	-21.2	980	694	-29.2
San Jose, CA	Santa Clara County	199	147	-26.1	4,248	3,173	-25.3
Santa Rosa, CA	Sonoma County	43	48	11.6	1,258	930	-26.1
Savannah, GA	Chatham County	42	24	-42.9	1,517	1,390	-8.4
Seattle, WA	King County	218	185	-15.1	5,624	4,752	-15.5
Sioux Falls, SD	Minnehaha County	25	13	-48.0	391	379	-3.1
Spokane, WA	Spokane County	51	30	-41.2	1,786	1,654	-7.4
Springfield, IL	Sangamon County	20	12	-40.0	649	551	-15.1
Tallahassee, FL	Leon County	53	44	-17.0	441	427	-3.2
Tampa, FL	Hillsborough County	185	206	11.4	4,632	3,876	-16.3
Topeka, KS	Shawnee County	15	7	-53.3	926	854	-7.8
Tulsa, OK	Tulsa County	56	53	-5.4	1,838	1,656	-9.9
Tyler, TX	Smith County	20	14	-30.0	312	307	-1.6
Virginia Beach, VA	Virginia Beach city	40	31	-22.5	1,779	1,712	-3.8
Washington, DC	District of Columbia	67	68	1.5	756	706	-6.6
Wichita, KS	Sedgwick County	74	43	-41.9	1,873	1,597	-14.7
Wilmington, NC	New Hanover County	33	22	-33.3	429	295	-31.2
Winston-Salem, NC	Forsyth County	24	21	-12.5	622	574	-7.7
Worcester, MA	Worcester County	46	52	13.0	1,860	1,561	-16.1
U.S.	U.S.	33,212	26,983	-18.8	1,038,720	909,812	-12.4

Note: Business filings include Chapter 7, Chapter 11, Chapter 12, and Chapter 13; Nonbusiness filings include Chapter 7, Chapter 11, and Chapter 13
Source: Administrative Office of the U.S. Courts, Business and Nonbusiness Bankruptcy, County Cases Commenced by Chapter of the Bankruptcy Code, During the 12- Month Period Ending December 31, 2013 and Business and Nonbusiness Bankruptcy, County Cases Commenced by Chapter of the Bankruptcy Code, During the 12- Month Period Ending December 31, 2014

Income: City

City	Per Capita ($)	Median Household ($)	Average Household ($)
Albuquerque, NM	26,403	46,668	63,418
Anchorage, AK	35,769	76,159	96,249
Ann Arbor, MI	34,905	53,458	77,948
Athens, GA	18,885	31,884	49,581
Atlanta, GA	36,091	46,783	82,895
Austin, TX	32,091	54,331	77,898
Billings, MT	27,024	47,196	64,341
Boise City, ID	27,616	46,757	65,336
Boston, MA	33,565	52,465	80,025
Boulder, CO	37,315	57,012	88,752
Cape Coral, FL	22,251	48,095	59,217
Cedar Rapids, IA	27,993	51,338	66,289
Charleston, SC	32,832	52,066	75,238
Charlotte, NC	31,262	51,271	78,433
Chicago, IL	27,979	46,014	70,505
Clarksville, TN	21,017	46,100	55,585
Colorado Springs, CO	28,854	53,619	72,046
Columbia, MO	26,555	42,945	66,161
Columbus, OH	23,998	43,441	56,932
Dallas, TX	27,380	42,026	69,885
Davenport, IA	23,740	45,323	57,396
Denver, CO	33,654	50,728	75,906
Des Moines, IA	23,359	44,830	57,515
Durham, NC	28,758	48,046	69,050
El Paso, TX	19,895	41,657	58,012
Erie, PA	18,383	32,672	43,093
Eugene, OR	25,688	40,628	59,964
Fargo, ND	29,475	45,227	65,810
Fayetteville, NC	22,842	44,770	55,955
Fort Collins, CO	28,766	53,435	72,215
Fort Wayne, IN	22,911	42,309	55,904
Fort Worth, TX	24,059	51,168	67,578
Gainesville, FL	19,235	31,584	47,358
Grand Rapids, MI	20,358	39,308	51,270
Green Bay, WI	24,054	42,088	57,746
Greensboro, NC	25,496	40,415	60,551
Honolulu, HI	30,378	59,490	77,842
Houston, TX	27,328	44,451	71,474
Huntsville, AL	29,649	47,575	68,995
Indianapolis, IN	23,722	41,154	57,910
Jacksonville, FL	24,870	45,978	62,959
Kansas City, MO	26,546	44,613	61,958
Lafayette, LA	28,454	45,317	67,042
Las Vegas, NV	24,945	48,676	66,092
Lexington, KY	29,203	47,977	70,104
Lincoln, NE	26,047	48,329	64,180
Little Rock, AR	28,976	44,911	68,114
Los Angeles, CA	27,345	47,812	75,509
Louisville, KY	26,043	43,963	62,879
Lubbock, TX	23,537	43,413	60,480
Madison, WI	31,208	51,833	70,350
Manchester, NH	26,965	52,462	63,747
McAllen, TX	21,205	40,651	65,383
Miami, FL	21,416	30,126	52,271
Midland, TX	34,306	63,819	94,266
Minneapolis, MN	31,616	49,777	72,720

Table continued on next page.

City	Per Capita ($)	Median Household ($)	Average Household ($)
Nashville, TN	26,976	45,542	63,645
New Orleans, LA	26,348	35,837	60,632
New York, NY	31,746	51,526	82,008
Oklahoma City, OK	25,085	45,073	63,367
Omaha, NE	26,700	47,275	65,560
Orlando, FL	25,083	42,026	57,912
Oxnard, CA	20,438	59,465	75,180
Palm Bay, FL	20,122	41,540	51,765
Peoria, IL	25,937	42,214	62,309
Philadelphia, PA	21,902	36,222	53,661
Phoenix, AZ	23,367	45,775	63,762
Pittsburgh, PA	27,159	39,527	60,305
Portland, OR	31,812	52,421	73,563
Providence, RI	21,500	36,700	58,248
Provo, UT	16,496	38,542	55,455
Raleigh, NC	30,174	54,088	74,854
Reno, NV	25,716	46,348	62,934
Richmond, VA	26,307	39,469	60,519
Roanoke, VA	23,049	37,710	51,923
Rochester, MN	32,709	62,105	79,970
Sacramento, CA	24,952	48,807	64,943
Salem, OR	22,242	44,773	58,617
Salt Lake City, UT	28,892	45,774	71,057
San Antonio, TX	22,311	45,253	60,746
San Diego, CA	32,658	63,258	86,740
San Francisco, CA	48,861	74,559	110,996
San Jose, CA	34,059	80,609	104,333
Santa Rosa, CA	29,133	58,908	76,326
Savannah, GA	19,928	36,144	49,971
Seattle, WA	42,929	65,454	92,113
Sioux Falls, SD	27,527	51,099	66,919
Spokane, WA	23,781	41,200	55,686
Springfield, IL	28,023	47,571	63,512
Tallahassee, FL	23,752	39,868	57,997
Tampa, FL	28,945	41,927	68,704
Topeka, KS	23,305	40,323	55,106
Tulsa, OK	27,071	41,162	63,845
Tyler, TX	26,733	43,239	66,559
Virginia Beach, VA	31,665	64,771	82,655
Washington, DC	45,851	66,950	102,656
Wichita, KS	24,236	44,532	60,298
Wilmington, NC	29,410	41,724	66,019
Winston-Salem, NC	24,319	38,566	60,142
Worcester, MA	23,935	44,553	60,978
U.S.	27,884	52,176	72,897

Source: U.S. Census Bureau, 2011-2013 American Community Survey 3-Year Estimates

Income: Metro Area

Metro Area	Per Capita ($)	Median Household ($)	Average Household ($)
Albuquerque, NM	25,525	47,754	64,396
Anchorage, AK	34,228	74,830	93,213
Ann Arbor, MI	33,495	58,254	81,651
Athens, GA	21,588	39,291	57,764
Atlanta, GA	28,166	55,295	76,582
Austin, TX	31,255	60,443	82,338
Billings, MT	27,609	50,472	66,897
Boise City, ID	23,630	48,755	63,335
Boston, MA	38,552	72,543	98,859
Boulder, CO	37,871	69,260	93,227
Cape Coral, FL	26,690	46,587	66,302
Cedar Rapids, IA	29,230	56,875	71,523
Charleston, SC	27,162	51,580	68,685
Charlotte, NC	27,924	51,264	72,780
Chicago, IL	30,787	60,140	82,611
Clarksville, TN	21,868	46,183	58,156
Colorado Springs, CO	29,097	57,110	75,630
Columbia, MO	26,893	48,302	67,075
Columbus, OH	28,576	53,914	72,580
Dallas, TX	29,110	57,630	80,048
Davenport, IA	27,302	50,868	65,946
Denver, CO	33,364	62,229	83,895
Des Moines, IA	30,477	60,410	76,654
Durham, NC	30,332	51,565	75,434
El Paso, TX	18,563	40,595	56,031
Erie, PA	24,092	44,639	59,400
Eugene, OR	23,915	41,936	57,134
Fargo, ND	29,135	52,391	69,495
Fayetteville, NC	21,837	44,185	55,886
Fort Collins, CO	30,422	57,316	74,915
Fort Wayne, IN	24,763	48,377	62,511
Fort Worth, TX	29,110	57,630	80,048
Gainesville, FL	24,234	41,211	60,668
Grand Rapids, MI	25,405	52,348	67,685
Green Bay, WI	27,301	52,442	67,946
Greensboro, NC	24,211	42,822	59,885
Honolulu, HI	30,002	71,728	89,208
Houston, TX	28,849	56,889	81,822
Huntsville, AL	29,792	54,838	74,829
Indianapolis, IN	27,356	51,601	70,125
Jacksonville, FL	27,340	51,016	70,192
Kansas City, MO	29,429	55,664	73,931
Lafayette, LA	25,649	46,222	65,919
Las Vegas, NV	25,354	50,498	67,454
Lexington, KY	28,014	49,044	69,062
Lincoln, NE	27,029	51,337	67,656
Little Rock, AR	25,562	48,472	64,010
Los Angeles, CA	28,785	58,569	84,766
Louisville, KY	26,931	50,039	67,010
Lubbock, TX	23,840	44,523	62,415
Madison, WI	32,231	59,981	77,083
Manchester, NH	34,090	69,024	87,185
McAllen, TX	14,274	33,845	49,333
Miami, FL	26,619	46,982	70,524
Midland, TX	33,571	63,581	92,348
Minneapolis, MN	33,687	66,489	85,723

Table continued on next page.

Metro Area	Per Capita ($)	Median Household ($)	Average Household ($)
Nashville, TN	27,929	51,825	71,398
New Orleans, LA	26,502	45,592	65,898
New York, NY	35,258	65,253	95,316
Oklahoma City, OK	26,164	49,552	67,160
Omaha, NE	28,664	55,901	72,996
Orlando, FL	24,095	47,119	64,638
Oxnard, CA	32,489	75,536	97,897
Palm Bay, FL	26,305	47,076	62,678
Peoria, IL	27,894	52,544	68,367
Philadelphia, PA	32,069	60,683	83,695
Phoenix, AZ	26,247	51,923	70,448
Pittsburgh, PA	29,593	51,059	68,999
Portland, OR	29,978	57,732	76,085
Providence, RI	29,778	55,313	74,418
Provo, UT	20,470	60,215	73,641
Raleigh, NC	30,770	61,390	81,319
Reno, NV	28,115	51,916	70,915
Richmond, VA	29,784	57,646	76,580
Roanoke, VA	26,610	48,673	63,727
Rochester, MN	32,088	62,638	80,275
Sacramento, CA	28,234	57,217	76,121
Salem, OR	21,769	46,763	59,174
Salt Lake City, UT	25,911	60,322	76,812
San Antonio, TX	24,742	51,401	68,839
San Diego, CA	30,031	61,382	83,467
San Francisco, CA	41,528	76,767	109,045
San Jose, CA	41,294	90,434	120,427
Santa Rosa, CA	32,554	61,479	83,455
Savannah, GA	25,036	48,852	65,120
Seattle, WA	35,186	66,750	88,361
Sioux Falls, SD	27,867	55,755	70,171
Spokane, WA	24,924	48,116	61,566
Springfield, IL	29,517	54,500	70,117
Tallahassee, FL	24,467	45,683	62,453
Tampa, FL	26,573	45,492	63,858
Topeka, KS	25,376	49,442	62,629
Tulsa, OK	26,110	48,184	65,783
Tyler, TX	24,846	46,436	65,051
Virginia Beach, VA	28,389	57,148	73,663
Washington, DC	42,965	89,605	115,614
Wichita, KS	25,197	49,943	64,352
Wilmington, NC	28,107	48,645	67,933
Winston-Salem, NC	24,548	43,042	60,886
Worcester, MA	30,579	62,221	79,777
U.S.	27,884	52,176	72,897

Note: Figures cover the Metropolitan Statistical Area (MSA)—see Appendix B for areas included
Source: U.S. Census Bureau, 2011-2013 American Community Survey 3-Year Estimates

Household Income Distribution: City

City	Under $15,000	$15,000 -24,999	$25,000 -34,999	$35,000 -49,999	$50,000 -74,999	$75,000 -99,000	$100,000 -149,999	$150,000 and up
Albuquerque, NM	15.2	12.1	11.3	13.9	18.0	11.4	11.4	6.7
Anchorage, AK	5.5	6.2	6.3	12.9	18.1	15.2	19.1	16.7
Ann Arbor, MI	16.5	9.4	9.6	11.8	15.7	10.4	13.9	12.8
Athens, GA	28.6	13.2	11.7	12.4	14.0	8.3	6.6	5.4
Atlanta, GA	20.5	10.8	9.5	11.2	15.1	9.2	10.4	13.3
Austin, TX	12.5	9.5	10.2	14.3	17.7	11.6	13.2	11.0
Billings, MT	14.5	12.3	10.3	15.0	18.4	11.5	11.2	6.7
Boise City, ID	13.7	11.5	12.1	15.5	17.1	11.6	10.6	7.8
Boston, MA	19.8	9.9	7.2	11.1	15.0	10.5	13.5	13.0
Boulder, CO	16.7	9.2	8.9	10.4	14.7	9.8	12.5	17.9
Cape Coral, FL	11.2	11.9	12.8	16.1	21.6	11.7	9.8	5.0
Cedar Rapids, IA	12.2	9.8	11.5	14.8	19.3	13.4	12.5	6.3
Charleston, SC	17.2	9.4	9.3	12.2	17.2	11.6	11.6	11.5
Charlotte, NC	12.4	10.1	11.5	14.8	17.8	10.6	11.9	11.0
Chicago, IL	18.0	11.6	10.6	12.8	16.1	10.4	10.8	9.7
Clarksville, TN	13.4	10.8	12.1	17.6	23.2	11.2	8.7	2.9
Colorado Springs, CO	10.6	11.1	10.5	14.2	18.7	12.8	13.5	8.8
Columbia, MO	19.5	12.2	10.0	13.9	14.7	9.6	11.3	9.0
Columbus, OH	16.8	12.0	11.7	15.5	18.6	10.9	9.8	4.7
Dallas, TX	16.3	13.2	12.4	14.9	16.6	8.5	8.9	9.3
Davenport, IA	14.9	12.2	12.1	15.5	18.1	11.9	11.6	3.6
Denver, CO	14.6	10.4	10.7	13.5	16.6	11.3	11.4	11.4
Des Moines, IA	14.8	11.8	12.1	15.9	20.3	11.8	9.5	4.0
Durham, NC	13.4	12.3	12.3	13.9	17.0	10.9	11.1	9.1
El Paso, TX	17.2	13.7	11.7	15.6	17.3	9.9	9.2	5.4
Erie, PA	22.9	16.7	12.6	16.9	15.2	8.7	5.0	2.0
Eugene, OR	22.0	11.3	11.3	14.0	17.2	8.1	10.0	6.2
Fargo, ND	13.7	11.5	12.8	16.2	18.1	10.7	9.7	7.4
Fayetteville, NC	14.5	11.0	12.7	17.5	20.9	10.7	8.7	4.0
Fort Collins, CO	13.8	11.2	8.6	13.5	17.3	13.1	13.4	9.2
Fort Wayne, IN	15.3	13.0	12.8	16.6	18.8	10.6	9.1	3.8
Fort Worth, TX	13.5	11.0	10.9	13.4	19.3	12.4	12.1	7.4
Gainesville, FL	28.1	12.4	13.4	12.7	15.2	7.8	6.3	4.1
Grand Rapids, MI	18.7	13.4	12.0	17.2	18.3	9.5	7.7	3.1
Green Bay, WI	16.2	11.9	13.3	17.2	19.1	10.4	6.9	4.8
Greensboro, NC	16.3	13.9	13.4	15.3	16.7	9.5	8.7	6.3
Honolulu, HI	11.8	8.3	8.6	13.2	19.8	13.1	14.1	11.3
Houston, TX	15.7	13.1	11.6	14.3	15.9	9.5	9.7	10.2
Huntsville, AL	15.5	11.9	10.2	13.9	15.8	10.6	12.9	9.2
Indianapolis, IN	17.3	13.0	12.5	15.2	17.6	10.4	9.1	4.9
Jacksonville, FL	15.1	11.7	11.5	14.9	18.6	11.0	10.8	6.3
Kansas City, MO	16.6	11.8	11.5	14.7	17.9	10.7	10.4	6.4
Lafayette, LA	18.5	12.4	9.4	14.3	14.6	9.9	12.0	8.9
Las Vegas, NV	12.9	11.3	11.3	15.6	18.8	11.8	11.0	7.3
Lexington, KY	15.6	11.1	10.4	14.4	16.7	10.8	12.1	8.8
Lincoln, NE	13.1	11.0	11.6	15.8	18.5	12.0	11.4	6.6
Little Rock, AR	16.9	13.3	10.4	13.9	15.8	10.0	10.0	9.7
Los Angeles, CA	15.9	12.3	10.4	13.0	15.8	10.2	11.3	11.0
Louisville, KY	16.4	12.8	11.7	14.5	17.4	10.7	9.9	6.6
Lubbock, TX	16.8	12.8	12.2	14.1	17.5	10.9	9.5	6.2
Madison, WI	14.3	10.1	10.3	13.7	18.0	12.0	12.9	8.7
Manchester, NH	13.0	11.1	11.0	12.6	21.0	12.8	13.0	5.3
McAllen, TX	20.0	14.3	10.3	13.5	14.8	9.8	10.2	7.1
Miami, FL	26.9	16.4	12.5	12.8	12.5	6.3	6.6	6.0

Table continued on next page.

City	Percent of Households Earning							
	Under $15,000	$15,000 -24,999	$25,000 -34,999	$35,000 -49,999	$50,000 -74,999	$75,000 -99,000	$100,000 -149,999	$150,000 and up
Midland, TX	8.4	8.7	8.6	12.9	19.2	12.7	15.9	13.5
Minneapolis, MN	17.0	10.7	9.3	13.2	16.3	11.5	12.5	9.7
Nashville, TN	13.8	12.2	12.2	16.0	18.3	11.0	9.8	6.7
New Orleans, LA	24.8	13.8	10.5	12.5	13.7	8.4	8.7	7.6
New York, NY	17.0	10.9	9.1	11.6	15.6	10.7	12.4	12.6
Oklahoma City, OK	14.4	12.0	12.4	15.5	17.7	11.1	10.7	6.3
Omaha, NE	14.0	12.3	11.8	14.3	18.4	11.5	10.6	7.1
Orlando, FL	15.0	14.7	12.8	16.1	18.8	8.6	8.4	5.6
Oxnard, CA	8.0	10.0	8.7	14.9	20.1	14.3	15.1	8.9
Palm Bay, FL	13.6	14.1	14.4	15.6	20.6	11.4	7.6	2.6
Peoria, IL	17.6	13.8	11.2	13.7	15.2	11.5	10.9	6.1
Philadelphia, PA	23.4	13.6	11.7	13.8	15.4	9.0	8.2	5.0
Phoenix, AZ	15.0	12.1	11.4	15.1	17.5	10.9	10.9	7.2
Pittsburgh, PA	20.9	13.1	11.6	13.2	16.8	9.2	8.2	7.0
Portland, OR	14.9	9.7	10.0	13.5	16.7	12.4	13.1	9.7
Providence, RI	25.7	12.7	9.9	12.6	15.4	8.6	8.3	6.7
Provo, UT	18.8	13.8	13.3	15.6	16.9	9.8	7.2	4.6
Raleigh, NC	11.1	8.9	10.9	14.6	19.4	12.2	12.7	10.0
Reno, NV	15.7	13.0	10.6	13.5	18.4	10.5	11.3	7.0
Richmond, VA	21.5	11.8	11.9	14.9	16.2	8.9	8.0	6.8
Roanoke, VA	17.5	15.4	14.0	14.4	19.0	8.9	6.9	3.9
Rochester, MN	9.4	8.6	8.9	13.2	18.9	14.8	15.3	10.9
Sacramento, CA	16.3	11.0	10.3	13.3	18.7	11.2	11.7	7.6
Salem, OR	15.8	11.7	12.0	15.5	18.6	11.3	10.3	4.8
Salt Lake City, UT	16.3	12.2	10.9	13.3	17.6	10.5	9.6	9.5
San Antonio, TX	15.3	12.5	11.6	15.2	18.7	10.3	10.3	6.2
San Diego, CA	10.8	8.8	8.3	12.1	17.0	12.8	15.6	14.7
San Francisco, CA	13.4	8.0	6.7	8.7	13.4	10.4	15.8	23.7
San Jose, CA	8.1	7.2	7.2	10.1	14.7	12.2	18.0	22.5
Santa Rosa, CA	8.6	9.8	9.1	14.8	19.9	12.9	14.5	10.5
Savannah, GA	22.6	14.3	11.5	15.4	17.1	8.2	6.7	4.3
Seattle, WA	12.3	7.5	8.2	11.3	16.4	12.2	15.7	16.5
Sioux Falls, SD	9.7	10.4	12.3	16.5	20.0	13.4	10.9	6.9
Spokane, WA	17.1	13.6	12.6	14.2	18.0	11.7	8.3	4.6
Springfield, IL	16.3	11.1	11.0	14.0	17.9	11.2	11.5	7.0
Tallahassee, FL	22.6	11.9	10.8	14.2	15.3	9.2	9.1	6.8
Tampa, FL	18.8	13.0	11.5	13.1	15.6	8.6	9.5	9.9
Topeka, KS	16.1	13.1	14.3	16.0	18.1	10.2	8.3	4.0
Tulsa, OK	16.7	13.4	12.8	15.1	17.5	8.5	8.7	7.4
Tyler, TX	14.8	14.0	12.0	15.2	17.6	9.5	9.2	7.6
Virginia Beach, VA	7.2	6.7	8.7	13.8	21.6	14.5	16.4	11.2
Washington, DC	15.0	7.6	6.8	10.1	14.5	10.4	15.6	19.9
Wichita, KS	14.2	12.9	12.6	15.0	18.3	11.5	10.2	5.4
Wilmington, NC	17.7	12.9	12.7	13.9	16.9	8.5	9.2	8.0
Winston-Salem, NC	17.9	14.9	13.4	14.3	15.6	8.3	8.7	6.8
Worcester, MA	19.1	12.0	10.3	13.3	17.5	10.3	10.7	6.8
U.S.	13.0	10.9	10.3	13.6	17.9	11.9	12.7	9.6

Source: U.S. Census Bureau, 2011-2013 American Community Survey 3-Year Estimates

Household Income Distribution: Metro Area

Metro Area	Percent of Households Earning							
	Under $15,000	$15,000 -24,999	$25,000 -34,999	$35,000 -49,999	$50,000 -74,999	$75,000 -99,000	$100,000 -149,999	$150,000 and up
Albuquerque, NM	15.0	12.1	11.1	13.6	18.1	11.3	11.6	7.3
Anchorage, AK	6.2	6.7	6.4	12.2	18.6	15.4	19.0	15.5
Ann Arbor, MI	12.6	9.5	9.7	12.4	15.4	11.8	15.3	13.3
Athens, GA	21.7	12.7	11.3	13.2	15.5	10.0	9.2	6.7
Atlanta, GA	11.9	9.8	10.0	13.7	18.5	12.0	13.4	10.7
Austin, TX	10.3	8.7	9.2	13.7	18.1	12.8	15.1	12.2
Billings, MT	13.2	11.4	10.4	14.5	19.1	12.7	12.0	6.8
Boise City, ID	12.3	11.2	11.9	15.6	20.2	12.1	10.4	6.3
Boston, MA	10.7	7.8	7.2	10.1	15.7	12.6	17.5	18.5
Boulder, CO	10.9	8.0	7.8	11.3	15.4	12.2	16.3	18.2
Cape Coral, FL	12.0	12.5	12.6	16.0	18.9	10.7	9.8	7.4
Cedar Rapids, IA	10.0	9.1	10.7	13.5	20.2	14.7	14.3	7.5
Charleston, SC	13.6	10.6	10.1	14.1	19.2	12.4	12.0	8.1
Charlotte, NC	12.5	10.8	10.9	14.6	18.1	11.7	12.0	9.4
Chicago, IL	11.6	9.4	9.1	12.3	17.6	12.8	14.7	12.5
Clarksville, TN	13.6	11.8	12.1	16.2	21.5	11.6	9.0	4.1
Colorado Springs, CO	9.4	10.0	9.8	14.1	19.3	13.4	14.5	9.7
Columbia, MO	16.5	11.5	10.2	13.6	17.1	11.6	11.3	8.2
Columbus, OH	12.4	10.1	10.2	13.8	18.7	12.2	13.4	9.2
Dallas, TX	10.4	9.5	10.1	13.5	18.3	12.1	14.5	11.6
Davenport, IA	12.0	10.7	11.4	15.0	19.8	12.4	12.3	6.5
Denver, CO	9.7	8.5	9.1	12.8	18.4	13.2	15.5	12.8
Des Moines, IA	9.7	8.6	9.7	13.3	19.9	14.4	15.2	9.2
Durham, NC	13.0	11.3	10.6	13.7	17.3	10.9	12.2	11.0
El Paso, TX	17.7	13.9	12.2	15.5	17.4	9.7	8.7	4.9
Erie, PA	15.3	12.5	11.5	15.9	18.5	11.7	9.7	4.8
Eugene, OR	17.5	12.9	11.9	14.7	18.5	10.5	9.2	4.7
Fargo, ND	11.5	10.5	11.6	14.3	19.3	12.6	12.5	7.6
Fayetteville, NC	15.0	12.1	12.5	15.8	19.8	11.4	9.3	4.2
Fort Collins, CO	10.7	10.6	9.7	13.2	18.7	13.4	14.1	9.7
Fort Wayne, IN	11.9	11.4	11.8	16.5	20.4	12.4	10.6	5.0
Fort Worth, TX	10.4	9.5	10.1	13.5	18.3	12.1	14.5	11.6
Gainesville, FL	20.7	11.4	11.9	13.3	16.2	10.3	9.1	7.1
Grand Rapids, MI	10.8	10.7	11.2	14.9	20.7	12.8	12.4	6.5
Green Bay, WI	10.9	10.8	10.8	15.0	20.6	13.4	12.0	6.6
Greensboro, NC	15.3	13.1	12.5	15.2	17.7	10.8	9.7	5.6
Honolulu, HI	8.5	6.3	7.0	11.7	18.9	14.2	19.1	14.5
Houston, TX	11.3	10.2	9.8	13.0	17.2	11.8	13.8	12.9
Huntsville, AL	12.5	9.8	10.2	13.5	16.7	12.1	15.2	10.3
Indianapolis, IN	12.3	10.6	10.7	14.7	18.8	12.4	12.6	7.9
Jacksonville, FL	13.1	10.6	10.6	14.5	19.2	11.7	12.0	8.1
Kansas City, MO	11.3	9.6	10.1	14.1	18.7	13.2	13.9	9.1
Lafayette, LA	16.8	12.5	10.4	13.4	15.8	11.4	11.8	7.9
Las Vegas, NV	11.5	10.7	11.5	15.6	19.9	12.2	11.3	7.2
Lexington, KY	14.8	10.9	11.0	14.1	17.2	11.8	12.4	7.9
Lincoln, NE	12.2	10.3	11.0	15.2	18.8	12.7	12.5	7.2
Little Rock, AR	13.4	12.0	11.2	14.7	18.8	12.1	11.4	6.4
Los Angeles, CA	11.8	10.2	9.1	12.3	16.7	11.8	14.3	13.7
Louisville, KY	13.5	11.3	10.6	14.5	18.9	12.3	11.9	6.9
Lubbock, TX	15.9	12.7	12.0	14.4	17.4	11.0	10.2	6.6
Madison, WI	10.2	8.6	9.7	13.4	19.3	13.8	15.4	9.6
Manchester, NH	8.1	8.3	8.2	11.6	17.4	14.3	18.8	13.4
McAllen, TX	24.0	15.5	11.5	14.2	15.1	8.5	7.7	3.4
Miami, FL	14.9	12.2	11.1	14.1	17.2	10.4	11.1	9.0

Table continued on next page.

Metro Area	Percent of Households Earning							
	Under $15,000	$15,000 -24,999	$25,000 -34,999	$35,000 -49,999	$50,000 -74,999	$75,000 -99,000	$100,000 -149,999	$150,000 and up
Midland, TX	8.0	8.7	9.6	13.3	17.9	13.0	16.3	13.2
Minneapolis, MN	8.8	8.0	8.2	12.2	18.6	14.4	17.1	12.6
Nashville, TN	11.3	10.8	10.9	15.2	19.0	12.4	12.0	8.5
New Orleans, LA	17.1	12.0	11.0	13.3	16.4	10.8	11.3	8.1
New York, NY	12.2	9.0	8.1	10.7	15.5	11.8	15.5	17.2
Oklahoma City, OK	12.9	11.1	11.4	15.0	18.8	12.1	11.6	7.0
Omaha, NE	10.8	9.8	10.2	13.9	19.6	13.4	13.7	8.5
Orlando, FL	12.5	12.0	12.5	15.5	19.0	10.9	10.7	6.8
Oxnard, CA	7.2	7.7	7.1	11.1	16.5	13.6	18.4	18.3
Palm Bay, FL	12.9	11.8	12.3	15.6	19.0	11.1	11.1	6.2
Peoria, IL	11.3	10.8	10.6	14.5	19.0	13.6	13.5	6.6
Philadelphia, PA	12.1	9.3	8.8	12.0	16.9	12.3	15.3	13.3
Phoenix, AZ	11.8	10.7	10.8	14.7	18.7	12.2	12.8	8.5
Pittsburgh, PA	13.2	11.6	10.8	13.3	18.6	12.1	12.3	8.0
Portland, OR	11.0	9.3	9.4	13.6	18.8	13.7	14.5	9.7
Providence, RI	13.6	10.4	9.1	12.6	17.3	12.3	14.4	10.3
Provo, UT	9.4	8.4	9.0	14.5	21.6	15.0	14.5	7.8
Raleigh, NC	9.2	8.2	9.8	13.4	18.4	13.0	15.6	12.3
Reno, NV	12.7	11.5	10.2	13.5	19.2	11.6	13.5	7.8
Richmond, VA	10.9	8.7	9.5	13.9	19.0	12.9	14.8	10.2
Roanoke, VA	12.6	12.2	11.8	14.6	19.7	12.2	10.8	6.2
Rochester, MN	8.9	8.3	9.0	13.5	19.1	15.4	15.4	10.5
Sacramento, CA	11.8	9.8	9.6	13.0	17.9	12.4	14.5	11.0
Salem, OR	13.7	11.6	11.7	15.4	20.2	11.9	10.9	4.4
Salt Lake City, UT	9.0	9.1	9.1	13.6	21.1	14.3	14.4	9.2
San Antonio, TX	12.7	11.0	10.3	14.6	18.9	11.9	12.4	8.1
San Diego, CA	11.1	8.9	9.0	12.4	17.3	12.6	15.2	13.5
San Francisco, CA	9.6	7.6	6.8	9.9	15.1	11.7	17.0	22.3
San Jose, CA	7.2	6.4	6.4	8.9	13.8	11.6	18.6	27.0
Santa Rosa, CA	8.5	10.0	8.7	13.4	18.1	12.6	16.2	12.6
Savannah, GA	14.8	11.3	10.0	14.8	18.2	12.0	11.4	7.5
Seattle, WA	9.4	7.7	8.2	12.1	18.0	13.5	16.9	14.3
Sioux Falls, SD	8.8	9.2	11.3	15.6	20.2	15.4	12.5	7.1
Spokane, WA	14.3	11.7	11.6	14.2	19.3	12.6	10.7	5.7
Springfield, IL	12.7	10.0	9.9	13.8	18.3	13.2	13.9	8.4
Tallahassee, FL	17.5	11.4	10.9	13.9	17.5	11.0	11.0	6.8
Tampa, FL	14.1	12.9	12.0	15.1	18.0	10.7	10.3	7.0
Topeka, KS	12.2	10.9	12.0	15.5	19.7	12.7	11.7	5.3
Tulsa, OK	13.5	11.5	11.4	15.2	19.1	11.3	11.2	6.8
Tyler, TX	13.2	12.5	12.8	14.2	18.4	11.9	10.3	6.7
Virginia Beach, VA	10.3	8.9	9.8	14.2	19.9	13.4	14.6	8.9
Washington, DC	6.4	5.2	5.5	9.2	15.7	13.2	20.0	24.9
Wichita, KS	12.1	11.6	11.2	15.2	19.4	12.6	12.3	5.6
Wilmington, NC	13.8	11.2	11.7	14.6	18.0	11.6	11.8	7.3
Winston-Salem, NC	15.0	13.3	13.0	14.9	17.7	10.5	9.7	5.9
Worcester, MA	10.8	9.7	8.8	11.6	17.1	13.4	16.2	12.4
U.S.	13.0	10.9	10.3	13.6	17.9	11.9	12.7	9.6

Note: Figures cover the Metropolitan Statistical Area (MSA)—see Appendix B for areas included
Source: Source: U.S. Census Bureau, 2011-2013 American Community Survey 3-Year Estimates

Poverty Rate: City

City	All Ages	Under 18 Years Old	18 to 64 Years Old	65 Years and Over
Albuquerque, NM	18.6	26.1	17.9	8.1
Anchorage, AK	7.7	10.6	7.0	4.2
Ann Arbor, MI	24.1	13.7	28.9	6.1
Athens, GA	36.9	37.0	40.2	11.6
Atlanta, GA	25.4	38.7	22.9	16.9
Austin, TX	19.0	26.6	17.7	8.9
Billings, MT	15.2	19.6	14.8	10.2
Boise City, ID	15.9	18.9	16.6	6.3
Boston, MA	22.1	30.3	20.5	19.7
Boulder, CO	23.8	8.8	29.2	6.0
Cape Coral, FL	14.9	21.3	14.6	7.9
Cedar Rapids, IA	12.4	14.4	12.9	6.5
Charleston, SC	20.1	26.0	20.4	10.1
Charlotte, NC	17.7	24.4	16.2	9.8
Chicago, IL	23.5	35.0	20.6	17.6
Clarksville, TN	18.1	26.7	15.5	7.9
Colorado Springs, CO	14.1	19.1	13.3	8.2
Columbia, MO	25.1	20.5	28.8	6.2
Columbus, OH	22.5	33.0	20.4	10.6
Dallas, TX	24.4	38.1	20.2	15.9
Davenport, IA	17.8	26.9	16.1	8.5
Denver, CO	18.7	28.3	16.9	11.2
Des Moines, IA	20.0	30.6	17.8	8.3
Durham, NC	20.6	27.6	19.6	11.0
El Paso, TX	21.7	30.4	18.3	18.6
Erie, PA	28.1	43.7	25.4	13.9
Eugene, OR	26.7	23.9	31.0	8.7
Fargo, ND	16.7	15.6	18.4	6.9
Fayetteville, NC	18.2	26.1	16.2	10.4
Fort Collins, CO	18.5	11.4	22.2	6.1
Fort Wayne, IN	20.5	31.0	18.5	8.2
Fort Worth, TX	20.1	27.8	17.4	12.9
Gainesville, FL	36.4	30.7	40.3	10.8
Grand Rapids, MI	27.1	37.4	26.1	9.9
Green Bay, WI	18.5	26.4	16.6	12.9
Greensboro, NC	20.4	27.1	19.8	11.0
Honolulu, HI	12.3	16.8	11.9	9.4
Houston, TX	23.3	36.3	19.5	14.4
Huntsville, AL	17.6	26.5	17.0	6.8
Indianapolis, IN	21.6	32.4	19.3	10.6
Jacksonville, FL	18.0	26.5	16.2	10.2
Kansas City, MO	19.8	30.0	17.9	9.8
Lafayette, LA	19.1	26.4	18.4	9.9
Las Vegas, NV	18.6	27.1	17.0	9.9
Lexington, KY	18.5	21.8	19.2	8.2
Lincoln, NE	16.3	19.8	16.9	5.7
Little Rock, AR	18.5	26.9	17.4	8.0
Los Angeles, CA	22.9	33.5	20.5	16.3
Louisville, KY	18.9	27.9	17.3	10.1
Lubbock, TX	21.4	26.8	21.7	7.7
Madison, WI	20.2	22.7	21.7	4.4
Manchester, NH	15.4	23.9	14.0	9.1
McAllen, TX	28.0	36.0	24.5	26.9
Miami, FL	30.3	44.9	25.8	31.8
Midland, TX	10.3	15.0	8.2	10.4

Table continued on next page.

City	All Ages	Under 18 Years Old	18 to 64 Years Old	65 Years and Over
Minneapolis, MN	22.4	30.1	21.1	14.6
Nashville, TN	19.0	30.9	16.6	8.9
New Orleans, LA	28.1	41.5	25.9	16.7
New York, NY	21.0	30.3	18.4	19.0
Oklahoma City, OK	18.9	28.3	16.9	8.3
Omaha, NE	17.6	25.3	16.1	8.8
Orlando, FL	20.9	33.8	17.5	15.0
Oxnard, CA	17.1	26.7	14.0	9.0
Palm Bay, FL	19.3	32.6	17.6	7.2
Peoria, IL	24.9	37.7	22.7	9.8
Philadelphia, PA	27.2	37.5	25.4	17.3
Phoenix, AZ	23.4	34.1	20.7	11.1
Pittsburgh, PA	22.8	31.8	22.5	13.4
Portland, OR	18.5	23.7	18.3	10.9
Providence, RI	31.1	43.2	28.2	19.4
Provo, UT	31.7	29.4	34.6	7.8
Raleigh, NC	16.1	23.0	14.8	7.2
Reno, NV	18.5	23.2	18.3	11.0
Richmond, VA	26.2	40.1	24.0	15.9
Roanoke, VA	21.7	32.1	20.7	10.4
Rochester, MN	10.1	10.7	10.5	6.8
Sacramento, CA	23.2	33.6	21.3	12.1
Salem, OR	20.5	29.5	18.9	10.2
Salt Lake City, UT	20.2	25.3	19.6	12.3
San Antonio, TX	20.5	29.5	18.1	12.8
San Diego, CA	15.7	21.7	14.8	9.5
San Francisco, CA	14.2	14.0	14.1	15.2
San Jose, CA	12.6	15.3	11.8	10.8
Santa Rosa, CA	13.2	17.7	12.8	7.0
Savannah, GA	26.7	41.8	24.3	11.5
Seattle, WA	14.4	15.9	14.1	14.6
Sioux Falls, SD	11.6	15.7	10.6	7.6
Spokane, WA	19.5	23.3	20.2	10.5
Springfield, IL	19.7	29.6	19.0	7.6
Tallahassee, FL	29.8	27.1	33.0	8.7
Tampa, FL	22.7	31.9	20.6	17.6
Topeka, KS	20.6	29.0	20.2	8.0
Tulsa, OK	20.1	31.0	18.0	9.5
Tyler, TX	20.8	29.9	19.5	11.6
Virginia Beach, VA	8.7	13.7	7.4	5.8
Washington, DC	18.8	28.5	17.1	14.0
Wichita, KS	18.3	26.8	16.4	8.7
Wilmington, NC	22.0	30.5	22.8	7.5
Winston-Salem, NC	25.7	39.9	23.4	9.3
Worcester, MA	23.3	33.9	21.1	14.9
U.S.	15.9	22.4	14.8	9.5

Note: Figures are percentage of people whose income during the past 12 months was below the poverty level
Source: U.S. Census Bureau, 2011-2013 American Community Survey 3-Year Estimates

Poverty Rate: Metro Area

Metro Area	All Ages	Under 18 Years Old	18 to 64 Years Old	65 Years and Over
Albuquerque, NM	19.3	27.2	18.2	9.9
Anchorage, AK	8.2	11.1	7.5	4.3
Ann Arbor, MI	16.6	16.5	18.4	6.0
Athens, GA	27.0	26.1	30.1	10.1
Atlanta, GA	16.3	23.0	14.6	9.6
Austin, TX	15.0	19.4	14.4	6.8
Billings, MT	12.8	16.3	12.4	9.1
Boise City, ID	16.2	20.7	15.7	8.9
Boston, MA	10.6	13.2	10.0	8.9
Boulder, CO	14.5	13.2	16.3	5.9
Cape Coral, FL	16.0	27.1	16.3	6.8
Cedar Rapids, IA	10.0	11.7	10.1	6.6
Charleston, SC	16.1	23.1	14.9	8.9
Charlotte, NC	15.5	21.4	14.3	9.0
Chicago, IL	14.5	20.9	13.0	9.4
Clarksville, TN	17.8	25.8	15.5	8.8
Colorado Springs, CO	12.1	16.1	11.4	7.3
Columbia, MO	20.1	17.9	22.7	6.9
Columbus, OH	15.2	21.2	14.2	7.3
Dallas, TX	15.1	21.8	13.1	9.1
Davenport, IA	13.0	20.2	12.0	6.5
Denver, CO	12.6	17.6	11.5	7.3
Des Moines, IA	11.5	15.3	10.8	6.7
Durham, NC	17.9	23.2	18.0	7.5
El Paso, TX	23.6	32.7	19.8	19.4
Erie, PA	17.0	26.0	15.6	9.3
Eugene, OR	22.0	25.2	24.4	8.5
Fargo, ND	13.0	12.4	14.3	6.3
Fayetteville, NC	18.1	25.7	16.0	10.9
Fort Collins, CO	14.0	13.0	16.1	5.0
Fort Wayne, IN	15.9	24.3	14.3	6.5
Fort Worth, TX	15.1	21.8	13.1	9.1
Gainesville, FL	25.5	25.1	28.4	9.8
Grand Rapids, MI	14.2	18.9	13.9	6.4
Green Bay, WI	11.4	15.2	10.3	9.0
Greensboro, NC	18.7	26.2	17.8	10.1
Honolulu, HI	9.9	13.5	9.3	7.2
Houston, TX	16.8	24.7	14.3	10.5
Huntsville, AL	13.6	19.1	12.8	7.6
Indianapolis, IN	14.7	20.8	13.5	7.5
Jacksonville, FL	15.2	21.2	14.3	8.4
Kansas City, MO	12.9	18.5	11.9	6.5
Lafayette, LA	17.6	23.7	15.9	13.1
Las Vegas, NV	16.3	23.5	15.0	9.2
Lexington, KY	16.9	20.8	17.0	8.5
Lincoln, NE	14.7	17.5	15.4	5.6
Little Rock, AR	15.1	20.7	14.4	7.6
Los Angeles, CA	17.4	24.7	15.7	12.2
Louisville, KY	15.1	21.9	13.9	8.8
Lubbock, TX	20.3	26.5	20.2	7.7
Madison, WI	12.8	14.9	13.3	5.4
Manchester, NH	9.3	13.2	8.5	5.9
McAllen, TX	35.5	46.7	30.2	26.5
Miami, FL	17.7	24.6	16.0	15.2
Midland, TX	9.5	13.0	8.0	9.4

Table continued on next page.

Metro Area	All Ages	Under 18 Years Old	18 to 64 Years Old	65 Years and Over
Minneapolis, MN	10.7	13.9	10.1	7.1
Nashville, TN	14.3	20.8	13.0	8.0
New Orleans, LA	19.4	28.3	17.7	12.1
New York, NY	14.5	20.5	13.0	11.8
Oklahoma City, OK	15.8	22.0	14.9	8.0
Omaha, NE	12.7	17.8	11.4	7.7
Orlando, FL	16.6	24.0	15.4	9.6
Oxnard, CA	11.6	17.4	10.3	7.0
Palm Bay, FL	14.6	22.8	14.5	7.4
Peoria, IL	13.9	20.7	13.0	6.8
Philadelphia, PA	13.4	18.2	12.7	9.0
Phoenix, AZ	17.4	25.2	16.1	8.0
Pittsburgh, PA	12.5	18.1	12.0	8.0
Portland, OR	14.2	18.5	13.8	8.0
Providence, RI	13.9	19.8	12.8	9.9
Provo, UT	14.1	12.9	15.8	5.5
Raleigh, NC	12.3	17.2	11.1	7.2
Reno, NV	15.5	21.3	15.0	8.2
Richmond, VA	12.6	17.4	12.0	7.6
Roanoke, VA	13.7	19.4	13.2	8.2
Rochester, MN	9.0	10.4	8.7	7.6
Sacramento, CA	16.5	22.0	15.9	8.9
Salem, OR	19.7	29.1	18.6	7.5
Salt Lake City, UT	13.1	17.2	12.1	6.8
San Antonio, TX	16.8	24.2	14.9	10.6
San Diego, CA	15.1	19.4	14.6	9.3
San Francisco, CA	11.7	14.1	11.5	9.0
San Jose, CA	10.6	12.6	10.1	9.0
Santa Rosa, CA	12.2	16.1	12.4	6.3
Savannah, GA	17.9	27.1	16.3	8.6
Seattle, WA	12.0	15.9	11.3	8.8
Sioux Falls, SD	9.8	12.7	9.0	7.8
Spokane, WA	16.0	19.3	16.6	8.1
Springfield, IL	15.8	24.6	14.6	6.6
Tallahassee, FL	22.3	25.1	23.7	8.5
Tampa, FL	16.1	23.2	15.6	9.4
Topeka, KS	14.5	20.1	14.3	6.3
Tulsa, OK	15.0	21.9	13.6	8.6
Tyler, TX	17.4	24.3	15.9	11.3
Virginia Beach, VA	12.7	18.9	11.4	7.0
Washington, DC	8.4	10.9	7.8	7.1
Wichita, KS	15.1	21.8	13.6	7.9
Wilmington, NC	18.0	24.6	18.0	8.7
Winston-Salem, NC	18.8	29.0	17.2	9.4
Worcester, MA	12.1	16.8	11.2	8.5
U.S.	15.9	22.4	14.8	9.5

Note: Figures are percentage of people whose income during the past 12 months was below the poverty level;
Figures cover the Metropolitan Statistical Area—see Appendix B for areas included
Source: U.S. Census Bureau, 2011-2013 American Community Survey 3-Year Estimates

Employment by Industry

Metro Area[1]	(A)	(B)	(C)	(D)	(E)	(F)	(G)	(H)	(I)	(J)	(K)	(L)	(M)	(N)
Albuquerque, NM	5.6	n/a	16.0	4.7	21.7	2.0	10.4	4.3	n/a	3.1	15.0	11.5	2.7	3.1
Anchorage, AK	n/a	5.5	16.5	4.7	20.0	2.5	10.5	1.3	2.1	3.9	11.6	12.3	6.3	2.7
Ann Arbor, MI	1.7	n/a	12.4	3.6	38.1	2.3	7.0	6.6	n/a	3.1	13.1	8.0	1.6	2.4
Athens, GA	n/a	n/a	n/a	n/a	33.1	n/a	10.5	n/a	n/a	n/a	7.7	11.3	n/a	n/a
Atlanta, GA	n/a	4.0	12.2	6.4	12.8	3.5	10.3	6.0	0.1	3.8	18.4	11.1	5.5	6.1
Austin, TX	5.4	n/a	11.8	5.7	18.4	2.8	11.4	6.2	n/a	4.3	16.4	10.9	1.8	5.0
Billings, MT	n/a	n/a	17.0	n/a	11.7	n/a	12.5	n/a	n/a	n/a	10.4	n/a	n/a	n/a
Boise City, ID	6.2	n/a	15.1	5.6	15.9	1.5	9.2	8.7	n/a	3.6	14.1	12.2	3.2	4.7
Boston, MA[4]	3.3	n/a	22.6	8.1	11.4	3.2	9.6	4.7	n/a	3.8	19.0	8.6	2.3	3.3
Boulder, CO	2.8	n/a	12.9	4.2	20.0	4.6	10.3	9.9	n/a	3.2	18.2	9.7	1.0	3.1
Cape Coral, FL	8.9	n/a	11.4	4.9	16.8	1.3	16.4	2.2	n/a	4.1	12.7	16.5	2.0	2.9
Cedar Rapids, IA	5.6	n/a	14.2	7.6	11.8	3.3	8.0	14.3	n/a	3.7	9.0	12.0	6.5	4.0
Charleston, SC	4.9	n/a	11.4	4.2	19.2	1.6	12.7	7.7	n/a	4.1	15.3	12.3	4.2	2.5
Charlotte, NC	5.0	n/a	10.3	7.6	14.1	2.3	10.9	9.2	n/a	3.4	16.3	11.6	4.3	5.0
Chicago, IL[2]	n/a	3.1	15.7	6.8	11.7	2.0	9.4	7.7	<0.1	4.3	18.6	10.2	5.2	5.3
Clarksville, TN	3.6	n/a	13.0	3.5	22.7	1.3	12.4	11.3	n/a	3.4	10.4	13.2	2.7	n/a
Colorado Springs, CO	5.3	n/a	13.1	6.1	18.6	2.6	12.2	4.5	n/a	5.9	15.8	12.1	1.8	2.0
Columbia, MO	n/a	n/a	n/a	n/a	31.5	n/a	n/a	n/a	n/a	n/a	n/a	11.9	n/a	n/a
Columbus, OH	3.5	n/a	14.4	7.3	16.2	1.7	9.5	6.7	n/a	3.8	17.5	10.4	4.9	4.2
Dallas, TX[2]	5.4	n/a	12.2	9.1	11.8	2.9	9.6	7.0	n/a	3.3	18.6	10.1	3.8	6.2
Davenport, IA	n/a	n/a	n/a	n/a	n/a	n/a	n/a	n/a	n/a	n/a	n/a	n/a	n/a	n/a
Denver, CO	6.9	n/a	12.6	7.2	13.9	3.2	10.8	4.8	n/a	3.9	17.8	9.9	3.9	5.0
Des Moines, IA	5.0	n/a	13.6	15.7	12.9	1.9	8.3	5.7	n/a	4.0	13.1	11.5	3.1	5.2
Durham, NC	2.3	n/a	20.3	4.7	22.8	1.4	8.8	10.3	n/a	3.5	12.5	8.7	1.5	3.3
El Paso, TX	4.2	n/a	14.0	4.0	23.2	2.0	10.9	5.7	n/a	3.2	10.7	13.7	4.8	3.7
Erie, PA	3.1	n/a	21.7	4.9	12.3	0.9	10.3	17.0	n/a	4.6	7.7	12.2	2.5	2.8
Eugene, OR	n/a	3.7	15.7	4.8	20.3	2.3	10.0	8.6	0.6	3.2	10.2	14.2	2.4	4.0
Fargo, ND	5.8	n/a	15.3	7.5	13.5	2.3	10.4	7.3	n/a	3.8	11.3	12.4	3.7	6.6
Fayetteville, NC	3.5	n/a	11.4	3.0	31.0	1.1	12.0	6.1	n/a	3.6	9.6	13.3	3.6	1.9
Fort Collins, CO	6.5	n/a	10.2	4.2	24.2	1.7	12.4	8.4	n/a	3.7	12.8	11.4	2.0	2.6
Fort Wayne, IN	4.3	n/a	18.2	5.4	10.2	1.4	9.0	16.3	n/a	5.2	9.9	10.7	4.2	5.1
Fort Worth, TX[2]	7.3	n/a	12.6	5.7	13.3	1.3	10.8	9.7	n/a	3.7	11.6	11.6	7.6	4.8
Gainesville, FL	3.3	n/a	18.0	4.6	31.4	1.1	10.8	3.2	n/a	3.2	9.6	10.7	2.1	2.1
Grand Rapids, MI	3.6	n/a	16.3	4.8	8.9	1.0	8.5	20.0	n/a	4.1	15.1	9.4	2.7	5.6
Green Bay, WI	4.0	n/a	13.4	7.0	12.6	1.3	9.5	16.7	n/a	4.6	11.5	10.3	4.6	4.5
Greensboro, NC	3.7	n/a	13.8	5.0	12.9	1.4	9.1	15.1	n/a	3.6	14.6	10.8	4.7	5.2
Honolulu, HI	5.2	n/a	13.4	4.5	21.4	1.6	14.6	2.4	n/a	4.5	14.2	10.6	4.7	3.1
Houston, TX	n/a	7.0	12.0	5.0	12.8	1.1	9.7	8.6	3.9	3.5	15.7	10.3	4.6	5.8
Huntsville, AL	3.6	n/a	9.4	2.8	22.5	1.2	8.6	10.7	n/a	3.2	22.6	11.4	1.4	2.7
Indianapolis, IN	n/a	4.3	14.4	6.2	12.8	1.7	9.9	9.0	0.1	4.4	15.6	11.0	6.2	4.7
Jacksonville, FL	n/a	5.2	14.9	9.7	11.9	1.4	12.0	4.4	0.1	3.5	15.8	12.2	5.2	3.7
Kansas City, MO	4.3	n/a	13.7	7.2	14.2	2.8	9.7	7.0	n/a	4.0	16.7	10.7	4.5	5.1
Lafayette, LA	n/a	4.9	13.3	5.6	11.9	1.3	9.6	9.1	10.3	3.1	10.4	12.9	3.1	4.6
Las Vegas, NV	n/a	5.4	9.3	4.9	10.9	1.1	31.1	2.4	<0.1	2.9	13.1	12.1	4.3	2.4
Lexington, KY	4.0	n/a	12.7	3.5	18.9	2.1	10.6	11.4	n/a	3.3	14.6	11.3	4.0	3.6
Lincoln, NE	4.1	n/a	15.8	7.9	21.6	1.4	9.2	7.6	n/a	3.7	9.7	11.0	5.9	2.1
Little Rock, AR	4.9	n/a	14.8	5.9	20.5	1.9	9.2	5.8	n/a	4.6	12.7	11.2	4.1	4.3
Los Angeles, CA[2]	n/a	2.8	17.8	4.9	13.2	4.6	10.9	8.4	0.1	3.5	14.3	10.1	3.9	5.3
Louisville, KY	4.4	n/a	13.3	7.1	12.5	1.5	10.2	11.6	n/a	3.8	13.2	10.3	7.6	4.4
Lubbock, TX	4.5	n/a	16.0	5.5	21.1	2.7	12.4	3.5	n/a	4.0	7.9	13.4	3.8	5.0
Madison, WI	3.8	n/a	11.7	6.0	22.9	3.8	8.3	8.8	n/a	4.8	12.5	11.0	2.4	3.9
Manchester, NH[3]	4.5	n/a	19.8	7.2	10.9	2.7	8.3	7.1	n/a	4.7	14.8	12.9	2.6	4.5
McAllen, TX	4.0	n/a	26.3	3.6	22.7	0.9	8.8	2.5	n/a	2.5	6.3	15.7	3.4	3.2
Miami, FL[2]	n/a	3.3	15.4	6.9	12.5	1.7	11.9	3.4	<0.1	4.5	14.1	13.5	6.0	6.6
Midland, TX	30.2	n/a	7.1	4.7	9.6	0.9	9.0	4.1	n/a	3.2	9.9	10.3	4.7	6.3
Minneapolis, MN	3.6	n/a	16.0	7.6	13.0	2.1	8.9	10.1	n/a	4.2	16.0	9.8	3.6	5.1

Table continued on next page.

Metro Area[1]	(A)	(B)	(C)	(D)	(E)	(F)	(G)	(H)	(I)	(J)	(K)	(L)	(M)	(N)
Nashville, TN	4.1	n/a	15.4	6.3	12.7	2.3	10.6	8.9	n/a	4.2	15.4	10.8	4.6	4.8
New Orleans, LA	n/a	5.2	16.0	4.9	13.0	1.5	14.7	5.3	1.4	4.1	13.1	11.6	5.1	4.2
New York, NY[2]	3.5	n/a	19.7	8.9	13.5	3.5	9.3	3.1	n/a	4.3	16.0	10.4	3.6	4.2
Oklahoma City, OK	n/a	4.4	14.3	5.3	20.4	1.3	10.2	6.0	3.4	3.6	13.1	10.9	2.7	4.4
Omaha, NE	5.0	n/a	16.1	8.8	13.5	2.3	9.4	6.5	n/a	3.6	14.6	11.0	5.7	3.6
Orlando, FL	n/a	5.1	12.1	6.3	10.5	2.1	20.9	3.5	<0.1	3.3	16.4	12.7	3.1	3.9
Oxnard, CA	n/a	4.6	13.8	6.2	15.1	1.9	11.9	10.2	0.4	3.3	12.2	13.9	2.2	4.4
Palm Bay, FL	5.0	n/a	16.8	3.7	14.2	0.9	12.2	10.0	n/a	4.0	15.0	13.5	1.7	2.7
Peoria, IL	4.4	n/a	19.3	4.3	11.9	1.2	9.7	15.0	n/a	4.4	11.2	10.4	4.1	4.1
Philadelphia, PA[2]	2.3	n/a	29.7	6.3	13.9	1.5	9.7	3.9	n/a	4.4	13.2	8.4	3.9	2.7
Phoenix, AZ	n/a	5.1	14.6	8.7	12.7	1.8	10.6	6.1	0.2	3.5	16.8	12.3	3.6	4.1
Pittsburgh, PA	n/a	4.6	20.9	5.9	10.3	1.6	9.5	7.7	1.1	4.4	14.8	11.5	4.0	3.8
Portland, OR	n/a	4.9	14.6	5.9	13.7	2.2	9.9	10.9	0.1	3.5	15.1	10.8	3.5	5.0
Providence, RI[3]	n/a	3.6	22.0	6.1	12.6	1.8	10.8	9.1	<0.1	4.7	11.7	11.4	2.5	3.6
Provo, UT	7.6	n/a	21.9	3.1	13.7	4.6	8.1	8.5	n/a	2.2	13.4	12.6	1.5	2.9
Raleigh, NC	5.7	n/a	11.7	4.7	16.4	3.3	11.1	5.5	n/a	4.1	19.8	11.5	2.1	4.0
Reno, NV	n/a	5.3	11.6	4.7	14.4	1.0	17.2	6.3	0.1	2.8	13.8	11.0	7.4	4.5
Richmond, VA	5.2	n/a	14.4	7.7	17.4	1.2	9.2	4.8	n/a	4.8	15.8	11.8	3.3	4.3
Roanoke, VA	5.0	n/a	16.4	5.2	13.9	1.0	8.4	10.3	n/a	4.7	13.3	11.4	5.7	4.5
Rochester, MN	3.4	n/a	39.5	2.4	11.2	1.7	8.4	9.4	n/a	3.2	5.1	10.8	2.7	2.3
Sacramento, CA	n/a	5.0	15.1	5.5	25.3	1.5	10.1	3.9	0.1	3.4	13.4	11.4	2.7	2.7
Salem, OR	n/a	5.1	15.9	4.7	27.6	0.7	8.9	7.6	0.8	3.5	8.3	11.8	2.6	2.6
Salt Lake City, UT	5.3	n/a	11.2	7.9	15.7	2.8	8.2	8.0	n/a	3.0	17.3	10.9	4.9	4.7
San Antonio, TX	n/a	4.9	15.5	8.6	17.2	2.3	11.9	4.7	0.9	3.6	12.8	11.5	2.7	3.5
San Diego, CA	n/a	4.6	13.9	5.1	17.2	1.8	13.0	7.1	<0.1	3.9	17.2	11.1	2.0	3.2
San Francisco, CA[2]	n/a	3.4	12.6	7.0	11.8	5.4	13.1	3.5	<0.1	3.9	24.8	8.1	3.9	2.5
San Jose, CA	n/a	3.9	14.8	3.5	9.3	6.8	8.9	15.6	<0.1	2.5	20.7	8.8	1.6	3.6
Santa Rosa, CA	n/a	5.3	16.8	3.9	16.4	1.4	12.5	10.4	0.2	3.5	10.3	13.0	2.3	4.1
Savannah, GA	3.6	n/a	14.5	3.8	13.9	1.2	14.4	9.8	n/a	4.3	12.1	12.2	6.5	3.9
Seattle, WA[2]	n/a	5.2	12.9	5.5	13.3	5.8	9.4	10.7	<0.1	3.6	14.9	10.9	3.2	4.5
Sioux Falls, SD	4.9	n/a	20.4	10.9	9.1	1.8	9.1	9.4	n/a	3.2	9.0	13.0	3.7	5.5
Spokane, WA	4.6	n/a	20.8	6.1	17.1	1.3	9.0	7.2	n/a	4.1	10.2	12.2	3.0	4.4
Springfield, IL	3.6	n/a	18.2	6.3	26.9	1.5	9.5	2.7	n/a	5.7	9.3	11.1	2.0	3.1
Tallahassee, FL	3.6	n/a	11.9	4.1	35.2	2.2	10.8	1.6	n/a	5.3	11.3	11.1	1.1	1.9
Tampa, FL	n/a	4.8	15.6	8.4	12.6	2.1	11.5	5.0	<0.1	3.7	16.7	13.0	2.4	4.1
Topeka, KS	5.2	n/a	16.3	6.7	24.4	1.3	7.5	6.4	n/a	3.8	11.4	10.0	3.9	3.0
Tulsa, OK	n/a	5.0	15.5	5.1	13.4	1.7	9.0	11.7	1.8	3.8	13.5	11.3	4.7	3.6
Tyler, TX	6.5	n/a	22.7	4.4	13.4	2.3	11.0	5.6	n/a	4.0	9.0	13.2	4.5	3.3
Virginia Beach, VA	4.5	n/a	13.8	5.0	20.7	1.5	10.9	7.3	n/a	4.8	13.8	11.9	3.2	2.7
Washington, DC[2]	4.5	n/a	12.8	4.4	22.9	2.5	9.6	1.3	n/a	6.3	22.7	8.7	2.4	2.0
Wichita, KS	5.5	n/a	15.6	3.7	13.5	1.5	10.2	17.7	n/a	3.2	11.4	11.2	3.3	3.1
Wilmington, NC	5.4	n/a	12.0	4.9	19.2	2.4	14.8	4.9	n/a	3.9	12.5	14.2	2.4	3.4
Winston-Salem, NC	3.5	n/a	20.5	5.0	12.7	0.9	9.6	12.0	n/a	3.7	13.7	11.1	3.9	3.4
Worcester, MA[3]	3.3	n/a	23.3	5.1	15.8	1.2	8.4	9.8	n/a	3.7	9.7	11.3	4.5	3.8
U.S.	5.0	4.4	15.5	5.7	15.8	2.0	10.3	8.7	0.6	4.0	13.8	11.4	3.9	4.2

Note: All figures are percentages covering non-farm employment as of December 2014 and are not seasonally adjusted;
(1) Figures cover the Metropolitan Statistical Area (MSA) except where noted. See Appendix B for areas included; (2) Metropolitan Division; (3) New England City and Town Area; (4) New England City and Town Area Division; (A) Construction, Mining, and Logging (some areas report Construction separate from Mining and Logging); (B) Construction; (C) Education and Health Services; (D) Financial Activities; (E) Government; (F) Information; (G) Leisure and Hospitality; (H) Manufacturing; (I) Mining and Logging; (J) Other Services; (K) Professional and Business Services; (L) Retail Trade; (M) Transportation and Utilities; (N) Wholesale Trade; n/a not available
Source: Bureau of Labor Statistics, Current Employment Statistics, Employment, Hours, and Earnings

Labor Force, Employment and Job Growth: City

City	Civilian Labor Force			Workers Employed		
	Dec. 2013	Dec. 2014	% Chg.	Dec. 2013	Dec. 2014	% Chg.
Albuquerque, NM	269,058	268,681	-0.1	253,374	255,366	0.8
Anchorage, AK	161,364	162,186	0.5	153,539	154,675	0.7
Ann Arbor, MI	61,458	62,527	1.7	58,959	60,807	3.1
Athens, GA	58,098	58,233	0.2	54,164	54,791	1.2
Atlanta, GA	230,075	232,034	0.9	211,965	215,889	1.9
Austin, TX	520,901	531,265	2.0	501,106	515,399	2.9
Billings, MT	56,312	56,686	0.7	54,003	54,802	1.5
Boise City, ID	115,170	115,344	0.2	110,221	111,964	1.6
Boston, MA	349,305	356,708	2.1	330,598	340,962	3.1
Boulder, CO	59,422	59,883	0.8	56,735	58,038	2.3
Cape Coral, FL	80,176	82,969	3.5	75,135	78,825	4.9
Cedar Rapids, IA	71,883	71,495	-0.5	68,424	68,269	-0.2
Charleston, SC	66,385	68,271	2.8	63,572	65,182	2.5
Charlotte, NC	421,260	425,392	1.0	398,670	408,035	2.3
Chicago, IL	1,358,761	1,361,612	0.2	1,237,219	1,278,994	3.4
Clarksville, TN	56,955	56,613	-0.6	53,150	53,062	-0.2
Colorado Springs, CO	215,051	214,044	-0.5	200,273	203,493	1.6
Columbia, MO	65,992	67,687	2.6	63,612	65,689	3.3
Columbus, OH	435,341	440,795	1.3	412,078	424,206	2.9
Dallas, TX	628,877	644,851	2.5	594,858	618,008	3.9
Davenport, IA	51,448	51,607	0.3	48,411	48,548	0.3
Denver, CO	364,755	371,168	1.8	343,595	356,126	3.6
Des Moines, IA	111,116	113,143	1.8	104,874	107,217	2.2
Durham, NC	127,698	128,389	0.5	121,870	123,469	1.3
El Paso, TX	291,236	288,097	-1.1	272,823	274,124	0.5
Erie, PA	45,629	45,264	-0.8	42,213	42,773	1.3
Eugene, OR	77,207	78,708	1.9	72,364	74,184	2.5
Fargo, ND	63,513	65,858	3.7	61,885	64,193	3.7
Fayetteville, NC	74,063	72,860	-1.6	69,330	69,164	-0.2
Fort Collins, CO	86,406	87,583	1.4	82,460	84,643	2.6
Fort Wayne, IN	119,899	120,503	0.5	112,064	113,482	1.3
Fort Worth, TX	386,122	393,410	1.9	366,908	377,987	3.0
Gainesville, FL	63,864	65,155	2.0	60,490	62,150	2.7
Grand Rapids, MI	97,774	99,110	1.4	90,984	94,402	3.8
Green Bay, WI	55,640	55,446	-0.3	51,059	52,867	3.5
Greensboro, NC	137,883	137,084	-0.6	129,397	130,458	0.8
Honolulu, HI	460,385	469,161	1.9	442,022	452,749	2.4
Houston, TX	1,132,953	1,158,089	2.2	1,077,239	1,113,785	3.4
Huntsville, AL	90,673	89,429	-1.4	85,404	84,932	-0.6
Indianapolis, IN	425,221	430,205	1.2	396,167	404,120	2.0
Jacksonville, FL	429,171	434,184	1.2	401,740	410,048	2.1
Kansas City, MO	244,157	252,292	3.3	227,582	238,398	4.8
Lafayette, LA	64,366	66,367	3.1	61,853	63,005	1.9
Las Vegas, NV	288,653	293,421	1.7	263,230	272,820	3.6
Lexington, KY	169,676	164,945	-2.8	161,353	159,074	-1.4
Lincoln, NE	153,110	153,680	0.4	148,712	149,851	0.8
Little Rock, AR	92,969	93,816	0.9	87,363	89,201	2.1
Los Angeles, CA	2,001,203	2,023,204	1.1	1,820,275	1,862,132	2.3
Louisville, KY	380,412	374,238	-1.6	355,415	357,039	0.5
Lubbock, TX	123,688	124,204	0.4	118,815	120,508	1.4
Madison, WI	148,233	151,368	2.1	142,540	146,937	3.1
Manchester, NH	62,090	62,556	0.8	59,058	60,098	1.8
McAllen, TX	63,415	63,736	0.5	59,732	60,846	1.9
Miami, FL	204,318	209,288	2.4	190,542	196,787	3.3
Midland, TX	71,357	76,671	7.4	69,168	74,970	8.4

Table continued on next page.

City	Civilian Labor Force			Workers Employed		
	Dec. 2013	Dec. 2014	% Chg.	Dec. 2013	Dec. 2014	% Chg.
Minneapolis, MN	226,735	226,378	-0.2	217,650	219,575	0.9
Nashville, TN	353,381	351,800	-0.4	336,639	335,389	-0.4
New Orleans, LA	173,364	179,735	3.7	163,628	167,131	2.1
New York, NY	4,082,835	4,121,481	0.9	3,766,200	3,865,586	2.6
Oklahoma City, OK	302,302	300,796	-0.5	289,357	291,008	0.6
Omaha, NE	228,426	229,167	0.3	220,129	221,984	0.8
Orlando, FL	147,553	151,977	3.0	139,444	144,840	3.9
Oxnard, CA	100,705	99,409	-1.3	92,898	92,730	-0.2
Palm Bay, FL	49,117	49,484	0.7	45,486	46,412	2.0
Peoria, IL	55,482	54,130	-2.4	50,191	50,552	0.7
Philadelphia, PA	683,240	682,563	-0.1	624,523	639,820	2.4
Phoenix, AZ	729,162	750,178	2.9	683,046	707,507	3.6
Pittsburgh, PA	155,623	155,259	-0.2	146,953	148,458	1.0
Portland, OR	336,471	345,730	2.8	317,062	327,696	3.4
Providence, RI	86,679	85,407	-1.5	78,364	79,120	1.0
Provo, UT	61,667	63,496	3.0	59,690	61,968	3.8
Raleigh, NC	225,384	230,215	2.1	215,331	221,676	2.9
Reno, NV	119,781	119,949	0.1	110,144	112,134	1.8
Richmond, VA	110,682	111,203	0.5	103,904	105,357	1.4
Roanoke, VA	49,677	49,641	-0.1	46,779	47,151	0.8
Rochester, MN	60,497	60,446	-0.1	58,346	58,757	0.7
Sacramento, CA	224,686	225,924	0.6	206,006	210,607	2.2
Salem, OR	72,077	74,276	3.1	66,723	69,347	3.9
Salt Lake City, UT	107,003	107,929	0.9	103,241	104,692	1.4
San Antonio, TX	665,217	676,837	1.7	633,279	652,731	3.1
San Diego, CA	690,196	695,388	0.8	645,688	659,330	2.1
San Francisco, CA	522,913	540,603	3.4	498,846	520,640	4.4
San Jose, CA	523,072	539,145	3.1	490,669	512,941	4.5
Santa Rosa, CA	87,121	87,301	0.2	81,415	82,474	1.3
Savannah, GA	63,923	64,485	0.9	58,614	59,872	2.1
Seattle, WA	403,307	409,272	1.5	386,941	393,826	1.8
Sioux Falls, SD	94,854	96,535	1.8	91,799	93,526	1.9
Spokane, WA	99,937	101,944	2.0	92,391	93,991	1.7
Springfield, IL	58,425	58,602	0.3	54,132	55,356	2.3
Tallahassee, FL	96,950	99,198	2.3	91,539	94,333	3.1
Tampa, FL	182,483	184,674	1.2	171,471	175,032	2.1
Topeka, KS	63,322	63,837	0.8	60,042	61,045	1.7
Tulsa, OK	194,398	193,757	-0.3	185,103	186,890	1.0
Tyler, TX	48,500	49,440	1.9	45,914	47,496	3.4
Virginia Beach, VA	229,693	228,187	-0.7	218,263	218,127	-0.1
Washington, DC	371,236	382,019	2.9	343,031	353,654	3.1
Wichita, KS	185,773	187,025	0.7	175,819	178,296	1.4
Wilmington, NC	55,703	55,690	0.0	52,580	53,198	1.2
Winston-Salem, NC	110,060	109,175	-0.8	103,650	104,072	0.4
Worcester, MA	89,535	91,328	2.0	82,975	86,013	3.7
U.S.	154,408,000	155,521,000	0.7	144,423,000	147,190,000	1.9

Note: Data is not seasonally adjusted and covers workers 16 years of age and older
Source: Bureau of Labor Statistics, Local Area Unemployment Statistics

Labor Force, Employment and Job Growth: Metro Area

Metro Area[1]	Civilian Labor Force			Workers Employed		
	Dec. 2013	Dec. 2014	% Chg.	Dec. 2013	Dec. 2014	% Chg.
Albuquerque, NM	415,650	414,520	-0.3	389,105	391,974	0.7
Anchorage, AK	206,084	206,927	0.4	194,694	196,055	0.7
Ann Arbor, MI	184,281	186,936	1.4	175,187	180,678	3.1
Athens, GA	94,913	95,298	0.4	88,840	90,012	1.3
Atlanta, GA	2,791,270	2,815,375	0.9	2,598,666	2,647,261	1.9
Austin, TX	1,032,725	1,052,087	1.9	988,473	1,016,673	2.9
Billings, MT	85,366	85,903	0.6	81,779	82,995	1.5
Boise City, ID	312,188	313,572	0.4	296,477	300,918	1.5
Boston, MA[4]	1,520,594	1,552,222	2.1	1,443,823	1,488,588	3.1
Boulder, CO	175,574	177,034	0.8	167,341	171,184	2.3
Cape Coral, FL	304,065	315,307	3.7	285,502	299,521	4.9
Cedar Rapids, IA	144,731	144,082	-0.4	137,729	137,538	-0.1
Charleston, SC	338,882	348,192	2.7	321,313	329,245	2.5
Charlotte, NC	1,174,230	1,184,609	0.9	1,099,106	1,125,541	2.4
Chicago, IL[2]	3,758,317	3,777,331	0.5	3,450,135	3,567,076	3.4
Clarksville, TN	108,531	107,539	-0.9	100,928	101,055	0.1
Colorado Springs, CO	317,531	315,991	-0.5	295,202	299,942	1.6
Columbia, MO	97,963	100,486	2.6	94,189	97,265	3.3
Columbus, OH	1,020,830	1,034,102	1.3	966,006	994,183	2.9
Dallas, TX[2]	2,331,802	2,392,061	2.6	2,210,843	2,296,944	3.9
Davenport, IA	194,454	194,082	-0.2	181,649	182,541	0.5
Denver, CO	1,470,470	1,497,400	1.8	1,386,478	1,437,876	3.7
Des Moines, IA	334,297	340,970	2.0	319,616	326,880	2.3
Durham, NC	270,301	271,289	0.4	256,766	259,905	1.2
El Paso, TX	350,534	346,011	-1.3	326,299	327,831	0.5
Erie, PA	133,865	132,990	-0.7	124,960	126,617	1.3
Eugene, OR	168,275	171,408	1.9	156,388	160,322	2.5
Fargo, ND	126,236	131,007	3.8	122,617	127,473	4.0
Fayetteville, NC	146,200	142,889	-2.3	134,082	133,752	-0.2
Fort Collins, CO	173,690	175,415	1.0	164,957	169,324	2.6
Fort Wayne, IN	203,906	205,369	0.7	191,667	194,314	1.4
Fort Worth, TX[2]	1,177,281	1,198,013	1.8	1,117,300	1,150,482	3.0
Gainesville, FL	134,410	137,132	2.0	127,340	130,889	2.8
Grand Rapids, MI	531,709	541,925	1.9	502,841	521,839	3.8
Green Bay, WI	168,435	171,803	2.0	158,852	164,440	3.5
Greensboro, NC	357,367	353,721	-1.0	332,708	335,400	0.8
Honolulu, HI	460,385	469,161	1.9	442,022	452,749	2.4
Houston, TX	3,210,505	3,280,203	2.2	3,045,705	3,148,828	3.4
Huntsville, AL	209,521	206,534	-1.4	197,294	196,222	-0.5
Indianapolis, IN	981,345	996,479	1.5	922,753	942,497	2.1
Jacksonville, FL	706,767	715,342	1.2	663,622	677,314	2.1
Kansas City, MO	1,071,183	1,107,078	3.4	1,011,658	1,055,730	4.4
Lafayette, LA	226,804	234,554	3.4	217,493	221,842	2.0
Las Vegas, NV	1,005,346	1,023,287	1.8	918,649	952,117	3.6
Lexington, KY	263,030	255,792	-2.8	249,550	246,382	-1.3
Lincoln, NE	179,125	179,760	0.4	173,816	175,145	0.8
Little Rock, AR	335,097	338,366	1.0	315,108	321,765	2.1
Los Angeles, CA[2]	4,988,880	5,047,001	1.2	4,562,492	4,667,406	2.3
Louisville, KY	629,438	626,503	-0.5	590,084	597,380	1.2
Lubbock, TX	153,418	153,908	0.3	147,248	149,220	1.3
Madison, WI	368,745	376,562	2.1	353,230	364,184	3.1
Manchester, NH[3]	114,919	115,941	0.9	109,798	111,785	1.8
McAllen, TX	337,227	336,129	-0.3	305,062	310,751	1.9
Miami, FL[2]	1,292,935	1,322,890	2.3	1,205,792	1,245,316	3.3
Midland, TX	89,915	96,559	7.4	87,140	94,394	8.3

Table continued on next page.

Metro Area[1]	Civilian Labor Force			Workers Employed		
	Dec. 2013	Dec. 2014	% Chg.	Dec. 2013	Dec. 2014	% Chg.
Minneapolis, MN	1,904,505	1,905,506	0.1	1,824,770	1,843,783	1.0
Nashville, TN	901,839	896,903	-0.5	857,621	854,219	-0.4
New Orleans, LA	581,922	603,346	3.7	552,417	564,490	2.2
New York, NY[2]	6,959,013	7,017,636	0.8	6,466,641	6,611,164	2.2
Oklahoma City, OK	648,737	646,136	-0.4	620,148	624,543	0.7
Omaha, NE	476,219	478,096	0.4	458,544	462,809	0.9
Orlando, FL	1,177,275	1,211,468	2.9	1,106,175	1,149,268	3.9
Oxnard, CA	432,764	427,575	-1.2	401,909	401,181	-0.2
Palm Bay, FL	254,921	256,415	0.6	236,334	241,147	2.0
Peoria, IL	187,911	184,654	-1.7	171,896	173,229	0.8
Philadelphia, PA[2]	970,794	971,041	0.0	895,703	916,043	2.3
Phoenix, AZ	2,080,302	2,140,674	2.9	1,953,680	2,023,418	3.6
Pittsburgh, PA	1,200,870	1,195,363	-0.5	1,130,540	1,141,244	0.9
Portland, OR	1,185,566	1,215,428	2.5	1,108,886	1,143,702	3.1
Providence, RI[3]	680,750	675,936	-0.7	625,230	634,087	1.4
Provo, UT	257,646	265,249	3.0	248,594	258,088	3.8
Raleigh, NC	618,124	629,675	1.9	586,865	604,111	2.9
Reno, NV	224,477	224,562	0.0	206,330	210,050	1.8
Richmond, VA	648,143	651,865	0.6	612,891	621,055	1.3
Roanoke, VA	159,624	159,655	0.0	151,479	152,525	0.7
Rochester, MN	115,978	116,698	0.6	111,656	113,108	1.3
Sacramento, CA	1,039,207	1,046,596	0.7	959,164	980,489	2.2
Salem, OR	180,148	185,317	2.9	166,202	172,750	3.9
Salt Lake City, UT	605,373	609,378	0.7	582,348	590,573	1.4
San Antonio, TX	1,078,143	1,096,505	1.7	1,025,485	1,056,403	3.0
San Diego, CA	1,541,159	1,551,683	0.7	1,436,717	1,467,071	2.1
San Francisco, CA[2]	945,703	977,381	3.3	902,803	942,144	4.4
San Jose, CA	1,006,995	1,039,234	3.2	949,768	992,810	4.5
Santa Rosa, CA	253,990	254,794	0.3	239,042	242,150	1.3
Savannah, GA	170,618	172,492	1.1	158,457	161,896	2.2
Seattle, WA[2]	1,535,809	1,556,437	1.3	1,463,517	1,489,804	1.8
Sioux Falls, SD	140,284	142,640	1.7	136,077	138,463	1.8
Spokane, WA	249,497	253,873	1.8	229,979	233,898	1.7
Springfield, IL	109,228	109,836	0.6	101,716	104,024	2.3
Tallahassee, FL	185,716	189,921	2.3	175,128	180,393	3.0
Tampa, FL	1,413,617	1,430,638	1.2	1,327,059	1,355,252	2.1
Topeka, KS	119,934	120,948	0.8	114,262	116,056	1.6
Tulsa, OK	464,674	463,735	-0.2	441,252	445,953	1.1
Tyler, TX	101,802	103,643	1.8	96,086	99,397	3.4
Virginia Beach, VA	836,154	829,722	-0.8	788,797	787,936	-0.1
Washington, DC[2]	2,566,590	2,576,993	0.4	2,436,513	2,459,715	1.0
Wichita, KS	307,119	309,464	0.8	291,865	295,832	1.4
Wilmington, NC	132,318	131,612	-0.5	123,743	125,184	1.2
Winston-Salem, NC	310,079	306,441	-1.2	290,747	291,862	0.4
Worcester, MA[3]	340,358	348,073	2.3	318,232	329,698	3.6
U.S.	154,408,000	155,521,000	0.7	144,423,000	147,190,000	1.9

Note: Data is not seasonally adjusted and covers workers 16 years of age and older; (1) Figures cover the Metropolitan Statistical Area (MSA) except where noted. See Appendix B for areas included; (2) Metropolitan Division; (3) New England City and Town Area; (4) New England City and Town Area Division
Source: Bureau of Labor Statistics, Local Area Unemployment Statistics

Unemployment Rate: City

City	2014											
	Jan.	Feb.	Mar.	Apr.	May	Jun.	Jul.	Aug.	Sep.	Oct.	Nov.	Dec.
Albuquerque, NM	6.3	6.2	6.1	5.5	5.7	6.6	6.4	6.0	5.7	5.5	5.3	5.0
Anchorage, AK	5.4	5.7	5.5	5.3	5.2	5.6	5.0	4.9	4.9	4.7	4.8	4.6
Ann Arbor, MI	4.1	4.3	4.3	3.7	4.4	4.5	5.2	4.1	3.8	3.3	3.0	2.8
Athens, GA	6.8	6.8	6.9	6.3	7.0	8.0	8.2	7.6	6.9	6.4	6.1	5.9
Atlanta, GA	8.0	8.0	7.9	7.2	7.8	8.3	8.6	8.3	7.5	7.4	7.1	7.0
Austin, TX	4.1	4.0	3.8	3.3	3.6	3.9	4.0	3.9	3.6	3.4	3.3	3.0
Billings, MT	4.5	4.3	4.4	3.5	3.3	3.9	3.6	3.6	3.3	3.2	3.4	3.3
Boise City, ID	4.8	4.6	4.4	4.1	3.9	4.1	4.0	4.1	3.7	3.4	3.3	2.9
Boston, MA	5.9	5.5	5.2	4.9	5.3	5.8	5.9	5.5	5.5	4.8	4.7	4.4
Boulder, CO	5.0	5.1	4.8	4.2	4.0	4.5	4.4	3.8	3.3	3.3	3.5	3.1
Cape Coral, FL	6.5	6.4	6.4	5.7	6.1	6.3	6.6	6.5	5.9	5.6	5.5	5.0
Cedar Rapids, IA	5.4	5.2	5.0	4.4	4.3	4.5	4.6	4.5	4.4	4.0	4.2	4.5
Charleston, SC	4.5	4.3	4.2	3.8	4.4	5.1	5.2	5.5	5.1	4.8	4.8	4.5
Charlotte, NC	5.5	5.6	5.4	4.8	5.3	5.4	5.7	5.5	4.8	4.6	4.4	4.1
Chicago, IL	9.3	9.3	8.5	7.7	7.7	7.9	8.1	7.6	6.9	6.8	6.5	6.1
Clarksville, TN	6.6	6.7	6.7	6.0	6.6	7.6	7.9	7.6	6.9	6.9	6.7	6.3
Colorado Springs, CO	7.4	7.2	7.2	6.5	5.8	6.1	5.9	5.5	5.0	4.7	4.9	4.9
Columbia, MO	4.2	4.6	4.6	3.7	4.1	4.7	4.4	4.2	3.7	3.1	3.3	3.0
Columbus, OH	6.0	5.7	5.3	4.3	4.6	5.0	5.1	4.8	4.5	4.1	4.1	3.8
Dallas, TX	5.8	5.8	5.5	5.0	5.3	5.5	5.6	5.5	5.0	4.7	4.6	4.2
Davenport, IA	6.6	6.4	6.2	5.4	5.5	5.9	5.9	5.7	5.6	5.4	5.6	5.9
Denver, CO	6.2	6.1	6.0	5.2	4.8	4.9	4.7	4.5	4.1	3.9	4.0	4.1
Des Moines, IA	6.4	6.2	6.0	5.1	4.8	4.8	4.8	4.9	4.6	4.6	4.7	5.2
Durham, NC	4.7	4.8	4.7	4.1	4.7	4.8	5.2	4.9	4.2	4.2	4.1	3.8
El Paso, TX	6.7	6.7	6.3	5.7	5.9	6.4	6.5	6.3	5.8	5.5	5.3	4.9
Erie, PA	8.2	8.3	8.1	6.6	7.1	7.1	7.5	7.1	6.1	5.7	5.8	5.5
Eugene, OR	6.9	6.8	6.7	5.9	5.9	6.5	6.9	6.8	6.0	5.9	5.9	5.7
Fargo, ND	3.0	2.9	2.9	2.5	2.2	2.7	2.3	2.3	2.1	2.0	2.2	2.5
Fayetteville, NC	6.6	6.8	6.5	5.7	6.5	6.6	7.2	6.9	5.9	5.6	5.5	5.1
Fort Collins, CO	5.3	5.3	5.0	4.4	3.9	4.2	4.1	3.8	3.4	3.3	3.4	3.4
Fort Wayne, IN	6.6	6.9	6.6	5.6	5.9	6.0	6.9	6.0	5.5	5.6	6.0	5.8
Fort Worth, TX	5.4	5.4	5.2	4.6	4.9	5.3	5.4	5.2	4.7	4.4	4.3	3.9
Gainesville, FL	5.5	5.4	5.3	4.5	5.2	5.9	6.2	5.8	5.3	4.9	5.0	4.6
Grand Rapids, MI	7.3	7.6	7.5	6.0	6.9	7.1	8.2	6.5	5.8	5.2	4.9	4.8
Green Bay, WI	6.6	7.0	6.7	5.8	5.6	5.7	5.5	5.1	4.8	4.6	4.7	4.7
Greensboro, NC	6.5	6.4	6.2	5.6	6.3	6.4	6.9	6.5	5.5	5.2	5.1	4.8
Honolulu, HI	4.4	4.2	4.1	4.0	4.0	4.6	4.1	3.9	4.1	3.9	3.9	3.5
Houston, TX	5.3	5.2	5.0	4.4	4.8	5.1	5.2	5.0	4.6	4.3	4.2	3.8
Huntsville, AL	6.7	7.1	6.8	5.7	6.0	6.9	7.1	6.4	5.6	5.4	5.2	5.0
Indianapolis, IN	6.8	7.3	7.0	6.3	6.5	6.4	6.6	6.6	6.0	6.1	6.3	6.1
Jacksonville, FL	6.8	6.9	6.8	6.2	6.6	6.8	7.1	7.1	6.4	6.0	6.0	5.6
Kansas City, MO	7.3	7.5	7.4	6.1	7.0	6.8	7.5	7.2	6.6	6.0	5.7	5.5
Lafayette, LA	4.6	4.0	4.4	4.0	5.0	5.7	5.9	6.0	5.5	5.6	5.5	5.1
Las Vegas, NV	9.0	8.6	8.6	8.2	8.0	8.3	8.3	7.8	7.6	7.3	7.2	7.0
Lexington, KY	5.6	6.0	5.8	4.8	5.1	5.2	5.1	4.6	4.2	3.9	4.0	3.6
Lincoln, NE	3.5	3.4	3.2	2.8	2.9	3.1	3.1	2.7	2.6	2.4	2.2	2.5
Little Rock, AR	6.3	6.2	5.8	5.3	5.6	5.6	5.9	5.6	5.3	4.9	4.8	4.9
Los Angeles, CA	9.5	9.2	9.0	8.2	8.4	8.7	9.5	9.1	8.5	8.4	8.3	8.0
Louisville, KY	7.4	7.7	7.4	6.2	6.4	6.4	6.2	5.8	5.3	4.8	4.9	4.6
Lubbock, TX	4.2	4.2	4.0	3.4	3.8	4.5	4.6	4.1	3.7	3.5	3.4	3.0
Madison, WI	3.9	4.2	4.1	3.5	3.8	4.1	3.9	3.6	3.4	3.2	3.2	2.9
Manchester, NH	5.5	5.4	5.3	4.8	4.5	4.7	4.5	4.4	4.2	4.0	4.1	3.9
McAllen, TX	6.3	6.2	6.0	5.4	5.7	6.1	6.2	6.0	5.4	5.0	4.8	4.5
Miami, FL	6.9	7.3	7.7	7.3	7.4	7.1	7.3	7.7	7.2	6.5	6.0	6.0
Midland, TX	3.2	3.2	3.0	2.6	2.9	3.1	3.1	2.9	2.8	2.6	2.4	2.2

Table continued on next page.

City	2014											
	Jan.	Feb.	Mar.	Apr.	May	Jun.	Jul.	Aug.	Sep.	Oct.	Nov.	Dec.
Minneapolis, MN	4.6	4.5	4.4	3.7	3.7	4.1	3.9	3.7	3.5	3.0	3.0	3.0
Nashville, TN	4.8	5.0	5.1	4.5	5.0	5.4	5.7	5.6	5.1	4.9	4.9	4.7
New Orleans, LA	6.4	5.8	6.1	5.5	6.5	7.6	8.0	8.2	7.9	7.5	7.4	7.0
New York, NY	8.3	8.5	8.1	7.1	7.3	7.2	7.6	7.1	6.5	6.6	6.6	6.2
Oklahoma City, OK	4.6	4.5	4.2	3.5	3.9	4.2	3.9	3.8	3.7	3.6	3.4	3.3
Omaha, NE	4.3	4.1	4.1	3.4	3.4	3.8	3.8	3.4	3.2	3.1	3.0	3.1
Orlando, FL	5.8	5.8	5.7	5.2	5.5	5.5	5.9	5.8	5.4	5.2	5.1	4.7
Oxnard, CA	8.1	7.9	7.7	6.6	6.6	6.9	7.7	7.6	7.1	7.0	7.2	6.7
Palm Bay, FL	7.8	7.8	7.9	7.4	7.5	7.7	7.8	7.5	6.9	6.7	6.9	6.2
Peoria, IL	9.5	9.4	8.7	7.2	7.7	7.9	8.2	8.0	7.2	7.1	7.1	6.6
Philadelphia, PA	9.2	9.0	8.8	7.5	8.5	8.4	8.8	8.4	7.3	7.0	6.8	6.3
Phoenix, AZ	6.5	6.3	6.3	5.6	5.9	6.4	6.5	6.6	6.2	6.0	5.8	5.7
Pittsburgh, PA	6.3	6.2	6.1	5.0	6.0	6.0	6.4	6.1	5.0	4.8	4.8	4.4
Portland, OR	6.4	6.6	6.4	5.8	5.7	5.9	6.0	6.0	5.5	5.6	5.5	5.2
Providence, RI	10.9	10.3	10.2	9.3	9.2	8.8	9.4	9.0	8.3	7.8	7.7	7.4
Provo, UT	3.8	3.9	3.5	2.9	3.3	4.1	3.7	3.6	3.1	3.0	2.5	2.4
Raleigh, NC	4.7	4.8	4.7	4.2	4.8	4.8	5.1	4.9	4.2	4.1	4.0	3.7
Reno, NV	8.9	8.5	8.3	7.8	7.5	7.6	7.4	7.1	6.9	6.7	6.6	6.5
Richmond, VA	6.7	6.6	6.5	5.8	6.2	6.4	6.6	6.6	6.0	5.5	5.4	5.3
Roanoke, VA	6.5	6.4	6.2	5.6	5.9	6.2	6.2	6.5	5.6	5.1	5.2	5.0
Rochester, MN	4.4	4.4	4.4	3.6	3.4	3.6	3.4	3.1	2.9	2.6	2.7	2.8
Sacramento, CA	8.7	8.7	8.7	7.4	7.4	7.6	8.1	7.8	7.2	7.2	7.2	6.8
Salem, OR	8.0	8.3	8.1	7.2	7.0	7.3	7.6	7.3	6.5	6.7	6.8	6.6
Salt Lake City, UT	3.9	3.9	3.9	3.1	3.4	3.8	3.7	3.7	3.3	3.3	3.0	3.0
San Antonio, TX	5.1	5.1	4.8	4.2	4.5	4.9	5.0	4.7	4.4	4.1	3.9	3.6
San Diego, CA	6.8	6.8	6.7	5.8	5.8	6.1	6.5	6.3	5.8	5.7	5.7	5.2
San Francisco, CA	5.0	4.9	4.9	4.1	4.2	4.3	4.6	4.5	4.1	4.1	4.1	3.7
San Jose, CA	6.5	6.5	6.5	5.5	5.6	5.8	6.2	6.0	5.5	5.4	5.4	4.9
Santa Rosa, CA	7.0	7.0	7.0	5.9	5.8	6.1	6.6	6.3	5.7	5.7	5.9	5.5
Savannah, GA	8.5	8.3	8.6	7.3	8.1	9.0	9.3	8.8	7.9	7.4	6.9	7.2
Seattle, WA	4.2	4.4	4.3	3.7	3.9	4.4	4.4	4.3	4.2	4.0	4.1	3.8
Sioux Falls, SD	3.7	3.7	3.7	3.1	2.9	2.8	2.6	2.7	2.6	2.6	2.8	3.1
Spokane, WA	8.0	8.6	7.9	6.8	7.0	6.6	7.0	7.3	6.8	6.8	7.1	7.8
Springfield, IL	7.5	7.7	7.1	5.7	6.0	6.4	6.8	6.5	5.9	5.8	6.0	5.5
Tallahassee, FL	5.9	5.8	5.7	5.2	5.8	6.3	6.6	6.3	5.7	5.3	5.4	4.9
Tampa, FL	6.3	6.2	6.2	5.6	5.9	6.1	6.4	6.3	5.8	5.6	5.6	5.2
Topeka, KS	6.0	6.1	5.9	4.9	5.0	5.3	5.5	5.3	4.8	4.5	4.5	4.4
Tulsa, OK	5.1	5.0	4.7	3.9	4.4	4.5	4.2	4.1	4.0	3.9	3.7	3.5
Tyler, TX	5.9	5.8	5.4	4.7	5.0	5.4	5.5	5.1	5.0	4.7	4.5	3.9
Virginia Beach, VA	5.3	5.3	5.2	4.6	5.0	5.1	5.2	5.2	4.8	4.6	4.5	4.4
Washington, DC	8.1	8.1	7.9	7.2	7.4	8.0	8.1	8.1	8.0	7.7	7.6	7.4
Wichita, KS	6.2	6.2	6.0	5.2	5.5	6.0	6.4	5.8	5.4	5.0	4.8	4.7
Wilmington, NC	6.2	6.1	5.7	4.9	5.3	5.5	5.9	5.7	4.9	4.7	4.5	4.5
Winston-Salem, NC	6.1	6.1	6.0	5.3	6.0	6.2	6.5	6.1	5.0	4.8	4.8	4.7
Worcester, MA	8.1	7.7	7.4	6.7	7.1	7.6	7.8	7.1	7.0	6.1	6.1	5.8
U.S.	7.0	7.0	6.8	5.9	6.1	6.3	6.5	6.3	5.7	5.5	5.5	5.4

Note: Data is not seasonally adjusted and covers workers 16 years of age and older; All figures are percentages
Source: Bureau of Labor Statistics, Local Area Unemployment Statistics

Unemployment Rate: Metro Area

Metro Area[1]	2014											
	Jan.	Feb.	Mar.	Apr.	May	Jun.	Jul.	Aug.	Sep.	Oct.	Nov.	Dec.
Albuquerque, NM	6.9	6.7	6.6	6.1	6.3	7.2	7.1	6.6	6.2	5.9	5.8	5.4
Anchorage, AK	6.2	6.5	6.3	6.0	5.8	6.2	5.6	5.4	5.4	5.2	5.4	5.3
Ann Arbor, MI	5.0	5.3	5.2	4.5	5.3	5.5	6.3	5.0	4.6	4.1	3.6	3.3
Athens, GA	6.5	6.5	6.5	5.9	6.6	7.4	7.7	7.1	6.4	6.0	5.7	5.5
Atlanta, GA	7.1	7.1	7.0	6.4	6.9	7.3	7.6	7.3	6.7	6.5	6.1	6.0
Austin, TX	4.6	4.6	4.4	3.8	4.1	4.4	4.5	4.4	4.1	3.8	3.7	3.4
Billings, MT	4.6	4.4	4.5	3.6	3.4	3.9	3.7	3.6	3.3	3.2	3.6	3.4
Boise City, ID	5.7	5.4	5.2	4.7	4.4	4.6	4.6	4.7	4.2	4.0	4.2	4.0
Boston, MA[4]	5.6	5.3	5.0	4.6	4.8	5.3	5.3	4.9	5.0	4.4	4.3	4.1
Boulder, CO	5.1	5.2	5.0	4.2	4.0	4.3	4.2	3.8	3.4	3.3	3.4	3.3
Cape Coral, FL	6.3	6.2	6.1	5.5	6.0	6.3	6.7	6.6	6.0	5.6	5.4	5.0
Cedar Rapids, IA	5.7	5.5	5.3	4.5	4.3	4.5	4.5	4.5	4.3	4.0	4.1	4.5
Charleston, SC	5.3	5.3	5.0	4.5	5.1	5.8	6.0	6.3	5.9	5.7	5.6	5.4
Charlotte, NC	6.6	6.6	6.3	5.7	6.2	6.3	6.6	6.5	5.7	5.5	5.3	5.0
Chicago, IL[2]	8.8	8.8	8.1	7.1	7.0	7.3	7.4	6.9	6.2	6.1	5.8	5.6
Clarksville, TN	7.2	7.4	7.3	6.4	6.9	7.5	7.8	7.3	6.7	6.5	6.4	6.0
Colorado Springs, CO	7.6	7.4	7.3	6.5	5.9	6.2	6.0	5.5	5.0	4.8	5.0	5.1
Columbia, MO	4.6	5.1	4.8	3.8	4.1	4.7	4.7	4.3	3.7	3.2	3.4	3.2
Columbus, OH	6.1	5.8	5.3	4.4	4.6	5.1	5.2	4.8	4.4	4.2	4.1	3.9
Dallas, TX[2]	5.6	5.6	5.4	4.8	5.0	5.3	5.4	5.2	4.8	4.5	4.4	4.0
Davenport, IA	7.6	7.4	7.0	5.7	5.9	6.0	6.3	5.9	6.0	5.8	5.8	5.9
Denver, CO	6.1	6.1	5.9	5.2	4.8	4.9	4.8	4.5	4.0	3.9	4.0	4.0
Des Moines, IA	5.1	4.9	4.8	4.1	3.9	4.1	4.0	4.1	3.9	4.0	3.8	4.1
Durham, NC	5.3	5.3	5.2	4.5	5.1	5.2	5.6	5.4	4.7	4.6	4.5	4.2
El Paso, TX	7.3	7.2	6.8	6.2	6.5	7.0	7.1	6.8	6.3	5.9	5.7	5.3
Erie, PA	7.5	7.5	7.3	5.9	6.2	6.4	6.6	6.2	5.2	4.9	5.0	4.8
Eugene, OR	7.8	7.9	7.7	6.9	6.6	7.0	7.3	7.3	6.6	6.7	6.7	6.5
Fargo, ND	3.5	3.5	3.3	2.8	2.4	2.9	2.6	2.5	2.2	2.1	2.2	2.7
Fayetteville, NC	8.5	8.6	8.2	7.4	8.0	8.2	8.7	8.4	7.2	7.0	6.9	6.4
Fort Collins, CO	5.6	5.6	5.3	4.5	4.1	4.3	4.2	3.9	3.4	3.4	3.5	3.5
Fort Wayne, IN	6.2	6.4	6.2	5.2	5.5	5.5	6.5	5.5	5.0	5.2	5.5	5.4
Fort Worth, TX[2]	5.6	5.5	5.3	4.7	4.9	5.3	5.4	5.2	4.7	4.5	4.4	4.0
Gainesville, FL	5.6	5.5	5.4	4.7	5.2	5.6	5.9	5.7	5.1	4.8	4.9	4.6
Grand Rapids, MI	5.7	6.0	5.9	4.6	5.3	5.4	6.3	4.9	4.4	4.0	3.8	3.7
Green Bay, WI	6.1	6.4	6.2	5.3	5.0	5.2	5.1	4.8	4.3	4.1	4.3	4.3
Greensboro, NC	7.2	7.2	6.9	6.2	6.7	6.9	7.2	6.9	5.9	5.7	5.6	5.2
Honolulu, HI	4.4	4.2	4.1	4.0	4.0	4.6	4.1	3.9	4.1	3.9	3.9	3.5
Houston, TX	5.5	5.4	5.2	4.6	4.9	5.3	5.4	5.1	4.7	4.4	4.3	4.0
Huntsville, AL	6.8	7.2	6.8	5.7	6.0	6.8	6.9	6.5	5.6	5.4	5.1	5.0
Indianapolis, IN	6.1	6.5	6.2	5.4	5.7	5.7	5.8	5.7	5.2	5.4	5.6	5.4
Jacksonville, FL	6.5	6.5	6.5	5.9	6.2	6.4	6.8	6.7	6.1	5.8	5.7	5.3
Kansas City, MO	6.3	6.6	6.3	5.1	5.8	5.7	6.1	5.7	5.4	4.9	4.8	4.6
Lafayette, LA	4.9	4.3	4.7	4.2	5.1	5.9	6.1	6.2	5.8	5.8	5.8	5.4
Las Vegas, NV	8.8	8.5	8.4	8.0	7.8	8.0	8.0	7.6	7.4	7.1	7.0	7.0
Lexington, KY	5.9	6.3	6.0	4.9	5.3	5.3	5.3	4.7	4.3	4.0	4.1	3.7
Lincoln, NE	3.6	3.5	3.3	2.8	2.9	3.2	3.2	2.8	2.6	2.4	2.3	2.6
Little Rock, AR	6.5	6.3	5.8	5.2	5.6	5.6	5.8	5.4	5.2	4.8	4.8	4.9
Los Angeles, CA[2]	9.0	8.7	8.5	7.8	8.0	8.2	9.0	8.6	8.1	8.0	7.9	7.5
Louisville, KY	7.0	7.3	7.0	5.8	6.1	6.1	5.9	5.6	5.1	4.8	4.9	4.6
Lubbock, TX	4.3	4.3	4.1	3.5	3.8	4.5	4.7	4.2	3.8	3.5	3.4	3.0
Madison, WI	4.6	4.9	4.8	4.0	4.0	4.2	4.0	3.8	3.5	3.3	3.4	3.3
Manchester, NH[3]	5.0	5.0	4.8	4.3	4.2	4.3	4.1	4.0	3.9	3.6	3.8	3.6
McAllen, TX	10.2	9.7	9.3	8.4	8.3	9.3	9.5	9.1	8.0	7.3	7.7	7.6
Miami, FL[2]	6.9	7.1	7.5	6.9	7.1	6.9	7.1	7.3	6.8	6.3	5.8	5.9
Midland, TX	3.2	3.2	3.1	2.6	2.9	3.2	3.2	2.9	2.8	2.6	2.4	2.2

Table continued on next page.

Metro Area[1]	2014											
	Jan.	Feb.	Mar.	Apr.	May	Jun.	Jul.	Aug.	Sep.	Oct.	Nov.	Dec.
Minneapolis, MN	4.9	4.9	4.8	3.9	3.7	4.0	3.9	3.6	3.5	3.0	3.1	3.2
Nashville, TN	5.0	5.2	5.3	4.6	5.1	5.7	6.0	5.8	5.3	5.1	5.0	4.8
New Orleans, LA	5.8	5.2	5.5	5.0	5.9	6.9	7.2	7.4	7.1	6.9	6.8	6.4
New York, NY[2]	7.7	7.8	7.5	6.5	6.7	6.7	7.1	6.7	6.2	6.2	6.1	5.8
Oklahoma City, OK	4.7	4.7	4.3	3.6	4.1	4.3	4.0	3.9	3.7	3.7	3.5	3.3
Omaha, NE	4.4	4.3	4.2	3.5	3.5	3.9	3.9	3.5	3.3	3.1	3.1	3.2
Orlando, FL	6.3	6.3	6.2	5.7	5.9	6.1	6.4	6.3	5.8	5.5	5.5	5.1
Oxnard, CA	7.5	7.3	7.1	6.1	6.1	6.4	7.0	7.0	6.6	6.4	6.6	6.2
Palm Bay, FL	7.6	7.5	7.4	6.7	7.0	7.0	7.3	7.3	6.7	6.4	6.4	6.0
Peoria, IL	8.9	9.1	8.4	6.6	6.8	7.0	7.3	7.0	6.2	6.2	6.3	6.2
Philadelphia, PA[2]	8.3	8.2	8.0	6.8	7.6	7.6	8.0	7.7	6.6	6.4	6.2	5.7
Phoenix, AZ	6.3	6.2	6.2	5.5	5.8	6.2	6.3	6.4	6.0	5.8	5.6	5.5
Pittsburgh, PA	6.7	6.6	6.4	5.1	5.7	5.9	6.2	5.9	4.9	4.6	4.7	4.5
Portland, OR	7.0	7.2	6.9	6.3	6.2	6.3	6.5	6.5	6.0	6.1	6.1	5.9
Providence, RI[3]	9.4	9.0	8.7	7.7	7.5	7.2	7.7	7.3	6.8	6.3	6.3	6.2
Provo, UT	4.1	4.2	3.9	3.2	3.4	4.0	3.8	3.7	3.2	3.1	2.7	2.7
Raleigh, NC	5.3	5.3	5.2	4.6	5.1	5.2	5.5	5.3	4.6	4.4	4.3	4.1
Reno, NV	9.0	8.6	8.4	7.8	7.4	7.5	7.3	7.0	6.9	6.6	6.5	6.5
Richmond, VA	5.9	5.9	5.8	5.2	5.5	5.7	5.8	5.8	5.3	5.0	4.9	4.7
Roanoke, VA	5.7	5.7	5.5	4.8	5.2	5.4	5.5	5.6	5.0	4.7	4.6	4.5
Rochester, MN	4.8	4.8	4.7	3.9	3.4	3.6	3.5	3.1	2.9	2.6	2.7	3.1
Sacramento, CA	8.1	8.1	8.1	6.9	6.8	7.0	7.5	7.2	6.6	6.6	6.7	6.3
Salem, OR	8.5	8.6	8.3	7.3	7.0	7.2	7.5	7.3	6.5	6.7	6.9	6.8
Salt Lake City, UT	4.3	4.4	4.2	3.4	3.6	4.0	3.9	3.9	3.4	3.4	3.1	3.1
San Antonio, TX	5.2	5.2	4.9	4.3	4.6	4.9	5.0	4.8	4.5	4.2	4.0	3.7
San Diego, CA	7.2	7.1	7.1	6.1	6.1	6.4	6.9	6.6	6.1	6.0	6.0	5.5
San Francisco, CA[2]	4.9	4.8	4.8	4.0	4.1	4.3	4.6	4.4	4.1	4.0	4.0	3.6
San Jose, CA	6.0	6.0	6.0	5.1	5.1	5.3	5.7	5.4	5.0	5.0	4.9	4.5
Santa Rosa, CA	6.3	6.3	6.3	5.3	5.2	5.5	5.9	5.6	5.1	5.2	5.3	5.0
Savannah, GA	7.4	7.3	7.4	6.5	7.1	7.6	7.9	7.6	6.8	6.6	6.1	6.1
Seattle, WA[2]	5.0	5.1	5.1	4.3	4.5	5.0	5.0	4.8	4.6	4.5	4.6	4.3
Sioux Falls, SD	3.5	3.5	3.5	2.9	2.8	2.7	2.4	2.5	2.5	2.4	2.6	2.9
Spokane, WA	8.5	8.8	8.2	6.9	6.9	6.5	6.9	7.2	6.7	6.7	7.1	7.9
Springfield, IL	7.3	7.5	6.9	5.3	5.6	5.8	6.1	5.9	5.4	5.4	5.5	5.3
Tallahassee, FL	6.0	5.9	5.9	5.2	5.8	6.1	6.5	6.3	5.7	5.4	5.4	5.0
Tampa, FL	6.5	6.4	6.4	5.7	6.1	6.2	6.5	6.4	5.9	5.7	5.7	5.3
Topeka, KS	5.6	5.8	5.4	4.4	4.6	4.9	5.0	4.8	4.4	4.1	4.1	4.0
Tulsa, OK	5.4	5.2	4.8	4.1	4.6	4.7	4.4	4.3	4.2	4.1	4.0	3.8
Tyler, TX	6.1	6.0	5.6	4.9	5.1	5.4	5.5	5.2	5.0	4.7	4.6	4.1
Virginia Beach, VA	6.2	6.1	5.9	5.3	5.7	5.8	5.9	5.9	5.5	5.2	5.2	5.0
Washington, DC[2]	5.4	5.5	5.4	4.8	5.2	5.4	5.5	5.5	5.1	4.8	4.7	4.6
Wichita, KS	5.8	5.8	5.6	4.9	5.1	5.5	6.0	5.4	5.0	4.7	4.5	4.4
Wilmington, NC	7.2	7.1	6.5	5.7	6.1	6.2	6.5	6.2	5.4	5.2	5.1	4.9
Winston-Salem, NC	6.5	6.5	6.3	5.6	6.1	6.2	6.5	6.3	5.4	5.2	5.1	4.8
Worcester, MA[3]	7.3	7.1	6.8	6.0	6.1	6.4	6.6	6.2	6.0	5.4	5.4	5.3
U.S.	7.0	7.0	6.8	5.9	6.1	6.3	6.5	6.3	5.7	5.5	5.5	5.4

Note: Data is not seasonally adjusted and covers workers 16 years of age and older; All figures are percentages; (1) Figures cover the Metropolitan Statistical Area (MSA) except where noted. See Appendix B for areas included; (2) Metropolitan Division; (3) New England City and Town Area; (4) New England City and Town Area Division
Source: Bureau of Labor Statistics, Local Area Unemployment Statistics

Average Hourly Wages: Occupations A – C

Metro Area[1]	Accountants/ Auditors	Automotive Mechanics	Book- keepers	Carpenters	Cashiers	Clerks, Gen. Office	Clerks, Recep./Info.
Albuquerque, NM	30.53	19.82	17.21	18.35	10.07	12.62	12.30
Anchorage, AK	38.15	23.62	21.70	31.91	12.05	20.64	15.67
Ann Arbor, MI	29.52	18.68	18.55	26.96	10.51	15.37	13.17
Athens, GA	27.70	17.29	15.39	14.66	9.12	12.14	12.72
Atlanta, GA	37.98	19.46	18.75	20.59	9.33	13.71	13.81
Austin, TX	32.55	18.74	19.22	18.19	10.31	16.13	13.51
Billings, MT	29.56	20.43	16.29	19.33	10.05	14.68	13.27
Boise City, ID	31.21	19.95	16.67	16.83	10.18	13.70	12.93
Boston, MA[4]	39.60	23.35	22.08	29.83	10.63	18.04	15.35
Boulder, CO	36.66	20.61	18.94	19.33	11.16	19.42	14.09
Cape Coral, FL	32.71	19.81	16.61	18.60	9.83	13.22	13.00
Cedar Rapids, IA	29.57	17.30	17.24	19.96	9.12	16.12	12.75
Charleston, SC	28.39	19.80	16.44	18.76	9.48	12.52	13.73
Charlotte, NC	36.72	20.80	18.06	17.22	9.38	13.83	13.58
Chicago, IL[2]	35.71	21.80	19.50	30.94	10.55	15.74	14.16
Clarksville, TN	27.33	19.77	15.70	17.69	9.16	13.49	11.35
Colorado Springs, CO	31.59	20.26	16.46	21.37	10.46	15.97	13.32
Columbia, MO	31.60	17.20	18.81	21.09	9.36	14.08	12.60
Columbus, OH	33.16	18.54	20.54	21.88	9.74	15.02	12.95
Dallas, TX[2]	37.39	20.77	19.04	14.87	9.56	16.19	13.04
Davenport, IA	31.93	18.18	16.18	22.41	9.51	14.33	12.53
Denver, CO	37.01	20.60	19.12	20.42	10.56	17.84	15.02
Des Moines, IA	33.01	19.91	17.48	20.80	9.38	16.03	13.65
Durham, NC	36.57	18.65	18.91	18.57	9.55	14.16	13.64
El Paso, TX	28.34	15.87	15.25	13.88	8.96	12.73	10.04
Erie, PA	28.00	15.20	14.38	18.87	8.90	13.44	11.24
Eugene, OR	29.42	17.85	17.43	21.32	10.76	14.38	13.22
Fargo, ND	27.33	19.01	17.41	18.55	9.65	12.99	12.50
Fayetteville, NC	32.71	17.05	15.84	16.03	9.27	12.96	11.43
Fort Collins, CO	30.38	20.72	17.74	19.23	10.12	15.89	13.73
Fort Wayne, IN	31.40	18.64	16.30	19.02	9.03	12.71	13.08
Fort Worth, TX[2]	34.66	19.75	18.03	15.44	9.96	15.42	12.59
Gainesville, FL	29.10	18.61	16.71	16.67	9.19	12.50	11.65
Grand Rapids, MI	30.22	18.74	17.52	20.67	9.34	15.12	14.25
Green Bay, WI	30.01	19.28	17.07	21.98	8.91	14.66	13.82
Greensboro, NC	33.47	19.53	17.37	15.00	9.02	12.48	12.78
Honolulu, HI	29.42	21.49	18.39	34.11	10.72	15.52	13.84
Houston, TX	39.99	19.38	19.12	16.69	9.70	16.52	12.97
Huntsville, AL	34.54	17.01	17.38	16.42	9.01	11.37	12.05
Indianapolis, IN	33.67	22.69	18.45	21.30	9.36	14.01	13.37
Jacksonville, FL	32.77	18.31	17.44	15.42	9.38	13.05	12.94
Kansas City, MO	32.02	19.02	18.37	23.43	9.72	14.93	13.85
Lafayette, LA	32.05	18.85	17.31	17.64	9.07	11.76	11.09
Las Vegas, NV	30.63	19.99	18.00	23.76	10.72	15.19	12.91
Lexington, KY	32.60	16.37	17.23	18.86	9.18	14.41	12.93
Lincoln, NE	30.36	19.48	16.08	15.99	9.29	11.75	12.79
Little Rock, AR	31.83	16.88	17.02	16.60	9.06	12.07	11.45
Los Angeles, CA[2]	36.68	18.59	20.19	26.08	10.49	15.32	14.37
Louisville, KY	29.75	17.38	17.21	18.27	9.45	14.15	12.88
Lubbock, TX	31.54	16.42	14.49	15.54	8.84	14.34	11.31
Madison, WI	33.54	18.96	18.53	26.80	9.47	16.01	13.45
Manchester, NH[3]	34.98	20.55	19.94	22.05	9.43	17.02	13.61
McAllen, TX	29.71	15.33	14.22	14.17	9.10	11.99	9.71
Miami, FL[2]	33.67	17.39	17.29	16.85	9.44	13.81	12.67
Midland, TX	37.18	23.24	19.42	17.94	10.45	17.65	13.86

Table continued on next page.

Metro Area[1]	Accountants/ Auditors	Automotive Mechanics	Book-keepers	Carpenters	Cashiers	Clerks, Gen. Office	Clerks, Recep./Info.
Minneapolis, MN	33.66	19.29	19.40	25.79	10.39	15.99	14.21
Nashville, TN	33.06	19.39	18.33	16.83	9.69	15.41	13.95
New Orleans, LA	30.95	19.11	17.27	18.71	9.09	11.95	12.10
New York, NY[2]	46.51	20.77	21.12	32.32	10.63	15.49	14.92
Oklahoma City, OK	32.22	19.09	16.90	17.16	9.21	13.54	13.08
Omaha, NE	33.29	19.98	17.17	18.19	9.20	13.17	12.95
Orlando, FL	31.76	18.27	16.61	16.98	9.30	13.27	12.79
Oxnard, CA	36.91	20.91	21.42	24.04	11.80	15.59	13.92
Palm Bay, FL	31.02	17.49	16.28	15.44	9.52	14.05	13.21
Peoria, IL	36.00	17.24	16.77	24.90	9.64	14.05	12.57
Philadelphia, PA[2]	37.07	19.79	19.77	26.27	10.10	16.50	13.49
Phoenix, AZ	31.92	20.45	17.99	19.02	10.25	15.98	13.20
Pittsburgh, PA	32.36	17.79	17.24	22.79	9.21	14.44	12.57
Portland, OR	32.74	20.59	19.25	20.89	11.91	16.34	14.05
Providence, RI[3]	37.07	19.06	18.81	21.67	10.22	16.17	14.27
Provo, UT	31.81	16.78	16.74	18.13	9.40	12.53	12.05
Raleigh, NC	32.43	21.65	18.04	16.10	9.26	14.05	13.55
Reno, NV	30.67	19.61	19.01	21.98	10.42	17.04	13.73
Richmond, VA	35.28	20.20	18.64	18.87	9.38	14.75	13.28
Roanoke, VA	32.34	16.30	16.80	15.59	9.47	13.46	12.15
Rochester, MN	30.62	17.81	19.08	20.47	9.47	14.44	12.09
Sacramento, CA	32.79	22.50	19.80	22.94	12.17	16.11	14.09
Salem, OR	30.82	20.50	18.36	20.36	11.35	15.81	13.99
Salt Lake City, UT	33.89	18.70	17.43	18.39	9.62	13.78	12.73
San Antonio, TX	33.59	18.94	17.96	17.92	9.58	15.01	11.89
San Diego, CA	37.51	20.62	19.99	21.74	10.98	15.79	14.15
San Francisco, CA[2]	42.23	26.07	24.04	31.17	13.01	19.40	17.28
San Jose, CA	44.69	24.99	23.84	29.18	12.19	19.36	17.32
Santa Rosa, CA	34.61	23.44	21.37	29.72	12.52	17.87	16.81
Savannah, GA	34.28	21.01	17.36	20.03	9.50	13.20	13.21
Seattle, WA[2]	37.33	22.27	20.90	26.09	13.31	16.27	15.67
Sioux Falls, SD	30.61	19.04	14.98	16.81	9.41	11.65	12.21
Spokane, WA	29.41	21.09	18.66	23.53	12.08	14.69	13.93
Springfield, IL	31.43	19.61	19.85	22.18	9.67	n/a	13.07
Tallahassee, FL	26.61	16.97	16.12	19.58	9.31	12.01	11.78
Tampa, FL	33.01	18.87	16.07	16.31	9.42	13.31	13.08
Topeka, KS	27.87	17.35	16.16	18.40	8.88	14.19	12.20
Tulsa, OK	32.20	18.18	17.09	15.76	9.21	13.41	12.93
Tyler, TX	33.97	21.27	17.66	15.54	9.11	14.60	11.40
Virginia Beach, VA	34.29	20.37	17.41	18.66	9.20	14.10	12.41
Washington, DC[2]	41.96	24.13	21.90	22.41	10.61	17.86	14.91
Wichita, KS	31.23	18.25	16.89	17.35	9.15	13.29	12.49
Wilmington, NC	34.46	20.81	16.38	16.74	9.17	13.12	11.94
Winston-Salem, NC	32.70	19.81	17.41	16.62	8.93	13.87	12.81
Worcester, MA[3]	36.25	19.23	19.10	23.74	10.35	15.93	15.08

Notes: (1) Figures cover the Metropolitan Statistical Area (MSA) except where noted. See Appendix B for areas included; (2) Metropolitan Division; (3) New England City and Town Area; (4) New England City and Town Area Division; n/a not available
Source: Bureau of Labor Statistics, May 2014 Metro Area Occupational Employment and Wage Estimates

Average Hourly Wages: Occupations C – E

Metro Area	Clerks, Ship./Rec.	Computer Programmers	Computer Systems Analysts	Comp. User Support Specialists	Cooks, Restaurant	Dentists	Electrical Engineers
Albuquerque, NM	14.19	47.67	35.95	21.40	10.54	90.64	51.12
Anchorage, AK	18.30	38.79	37.89	25.59	14.45	105.67	53.37
Ann Arbor, MI	18.11	33.36	39.04	20.08	11.24	88.92	46.61
Athens, GA	14.88	26.72	28.85	19.61	9.20	n/a	37.44
Atlanta, GA	14.24	47.23	39.53	25.60	11.41	91.62	42.31
Austin, TX	13.79	42.31	38.17	24.07	10.96	82.77	52.24
Billings, MT	13.31	27.50	35.04	21.03	10.31	73.25	36.65
Boise City, ID	13.54	31.15	37.77	20.70	9.81	85.84	44.74
Boston, MA[4]	17.40	42.97	42.53	31.18	13.84	87.92	50.23
Boulder, CO	15.58	45.70	42.22	26.32	11.59	89.92	47.38
Cape Coral, FL	12.90	45.16	40.73	19.77	11.59	50.97	32.32
Cedar Rapids, IA	15.78	33.92	36.20	20.36	10.03	102.47	40.70
Charleston, SC	14.81	35.48	33.17	23.47	11.26	88.43	36.59
Charlotte, NC	15.20	40.21	43.76	24.76	10.79	92.52	47.05
Chicago, IL[2]	15.77	35.72	40.12	26.17	11.37	62.67	45.60
Clarksville, TN	16.19	24.00	36.80	18.85	9.70	n/a	36.18
Colorado Springs, CO	14.48	37.28	46.56	23.66	11.63	100.65	50.76
Columbia, MO	13.19	30.91	36.36	18.16	10.06	70.98	n/a
Columbus, OH	13.57	34.92	38.29	24.48	11.45	91.59	37.92
Dallas, TX[2]	14.53	39.61	41.45	23.89	11.58	107.16	44.24
Davenport, IA	14.59	33.42	n/a	19.16	10.14	n/a	40.87
Denver, CO	16.05	46.46	46.48	27.55	11.63	79.78	46.18
Des Moines, IA	17.45	34.60	38.43	22.06	9.90	92.50	33.13
Durham, NC	15.05	38.84	42.10	26.85	10.04	77.76	42.12
El Paso, TX	11.36	36.58	32.53	21.75	9.26	107.28	45.16
Erie, PA	13.92	29.66	33.79	19.39	9.72	87.57	41.52
Eugene, OR	15.02	27.98	36.63	21.02	11.04	92.36	42.35
Fargo, ND	15.12	27.39	n/a	22.53	11.61	87.72	40.55
Fayetteville, NC	14.62	36.84	39.11	23.26	9.25	106.04	38.58
Fort Collins, CO	13.49	43.50	42.95	25.95	11.24	67.22	46.14
Fort Wayne, IN	13.07	32.59	32.07	20.13	9.83	85.46	36.45
Fort Worth, TX[2]	14.49	39.65	42.08	23.54	11.18	80.18	45.23
Gainesville, FL	14.56	28.74	37.02	19.84	10.17	93.12	33.07
Grand Rapids, MI	14.92	33.48	33.93	24.39	10.28	103.95	40.50
Green Bay, WI	15.31	33.82	33.58	21.09	10.31	104.38	31.93
Greensboro, NC	14.81	36.97	40.19	22.57	10.07	114.43	45.78
Honolulu, HI	16.27	33.81	38.30	23.78	12.56	83.04	41.55
Houston, TX	14.63	37.77	49.51	27.66	10.61	83.10	52.03
Huntsville, AL	15.12	43.72	42.61	22.75	9.92	89.18	47.11
Indianapolis, IN	14.65	32.36	35.84	25.76	10.90	56.85	40.58
Jacksonville, FL	15.15	36.13	36.86	21.05	11.36	81.76	40.80
Kansas City, MO	15.03	35.03	37.81	24.88	10.77	75.41	44.15
Lafayette, LA	14.93	25.02	31.63	22.34	9.84	39.93	n/a
Las Vegas, NV	16.42	38.46	38.43	24.36	14.21	62.06	42.42
Lexington, KY	15.05	28.97	36.61	16.06	10.77	84.48	41.85
Lincoln, NE	15.40	31.15	32.72	19.91	10.95	94.10	45.32
Little Rock, AR	14.19	33.28	33.64	21.92	9.72	98.56	41.75
Los Angeles, CA[2]	14.56	43.18	45.36	26.63	11.48	70.52	53.36
Louisville, KY	15.49	30.08	32.91	21.82	10.48	76.18	39.58
Lubbock, TX	13.02	28.20	34.05	18.18	9.46	67.89	35.65
Madison, WI	15.00	37.01	33.61	23.21	11.16	89.41	38.63
Manchester, NH[3]	14.98	30.68	38.89	24.08	12.12	94.00	43.36
McAllen, TX	10.83	32.26	30.92	17.82	9.80	106.15	42.65
Miami, FL[2]	13.34	45.10	48.37	24.29	11.87	77.55	43.09
Midland, TX	n/a	37.84	33.98	22.48	11.31	74.78	n/a

Table continued on next page.

Metro Area	Clerks, Ship./Rec.	Computer Programmers	Computer Systems Analysts	Comp. User Support Specialists	Cooks, Restaurant	Dentists	Electrical Engineers
Minneapolis, MN	16.57	38.76	42.18	25.81	12.03	91.00	44.80
Nashville, TN	14.52	37.14	35.56	22.31	10.66	82.20	37.82
New Orleans, LA	15.60	34.05	30.86	22.56	11.06	102.62	50.88
New York, NY[2]	16.99	43.94	48.44	29.01	13.41	74.04	47.29
Oklahoma City, OK	15.23	32.75	36.34	20.86	10.38	73.03	40.37
Omaha, NE	15.13	39.24	36.34	23.50	11.15	74.64	36.31
Orlando, FL	13.49	36.45	41.93	20.75	11.81	96.90	42.16
Oxnard, CA	16.02	48.02	49.88	24.80	12.52	59.61	51.41
Palm Bay, FL	13.03	44.22	36.29	24.22	10.53	67.43	41.57
Peoria, IL	14.99	30.57	44.75	23.18	10.97	n/a	46.47
Philadelphia, PA[2]	16.71	41.28	45.48	25.98	12.29	86.68	46.36
Phoenix, AZ	15.64	39.60	43.35	24.36	11.20	64.84	49.47
Pittsburgh, PA	15.68	33.59	35.62	24.09	11.56	73.25	42.15
Portland, OR	15.53	35.50	42.01	23.81	11.62	73.12	42.95
Providence, RI[3]	15.60	37.19	37.62	24.00	12.07	81.94	45.59
Provo, UT	12.56	36.64	37.74	19.41	10.58	55.54	39.85
Raleigh, NC	14.37	39.08	41.91	24.93	10.73	100.91	40.24
Reno, NV	15.22	37.15	31.60	20.80	12.08	102.52	40.30
Richmond, VA	15.59	38.24	40.17	25.49	11.00	71.36	41.94
Roanoke, VA	13.48	41.29	35.35	21.65	10.04	91.70	41.55
Rochester, MN	15.64	44.65	31.04	23.50	12.35	97.47	42.60
Sacramento, CA	15.07	36.53	38.26	27.84	11.34	88.71	50.64
Salem, OR	14.60	36.39	37.11	24.03	11.49	81.34	45.32
Salt Lake City, UT	14.54	38.16	35.14	21.90	11.92	68.03	43.92
San Antonio, TX	13.54	38.96	37.89	21.15	10.09	84.92	43.18
San Diego, CA	16.29	40.29	44.11	26.32	11.89	82.71	53.45
San Francisco, CA[2]	17.84	50.37	50.86	34.05	14.21	90.43	56.55
San Jose, CA	17.31	45.20	52.16	36.30	12.92	75.07	61.65
Santa Rosa, CA	16.40	37.30	37.04	27.87	12.49	89.30	48.52
Savannah, GA	17.97	n/a	35.28	26.00	10.28	106.56	45.37
Seattle, WA[2]	17.89	57.58	49.01	28.74	13.08	88.07	50.78
Sioux Falls, SD	13.74	27.33	31.92	17.72	10.99	76.94	38.62
Spokane, WA	15.46	26.47	34.89	22.37	12.06	95.08	41.46
Springfield, IL	15.39	32.75	47.97	21.52	11.18	n/a	41.27
Tallahassee, FL	12.10	28.15	42.25	17.87	10.68	104.55	43.20
Tampa, FL	13.49	35.31	38.92	22.25	11.91	84.08	43.77
Topeka, KS	20.25	34.10	30.26	21.04	9.42	89.78	n/a
Tulsa, OK	15.41	32.24	37.74	23.20	10.75	71.50	39.11
Tyler, TX	13.28	29.42	31.67	20.99	10.26	85.74	53.16
Virginia Beach, VA	15.57	31.62	38.76	23.31	11.30	74.67	39.15
Washington, DC[2]	16.60	44.45	49.88	28.89	12.93	72.78	52.36
Wichita, KS	14.73	33.11	36.89	16.61	9.70	88.39	41.58
Wilmington, NC	13.97	40.02	38.53	22.05	10.64	96.76	55.91
Winston-Salem, NC	14.75	37.18	41.46	21.38	10.04	99.23	44.38
Worcester, MA[3]	16.82	40.41	42.44	26.87	12.25	94.14	45.39

Notes: (1) Figures cover the Metropolitan Statistical Area (MSA) except where noted. See Appendix B for areas included; (2) Metropolitan Division; (3) New England City and Town Area; (4) New England City and Town Area Division; n/a not available
Source: Bureau of Labor Statistics, May 2014 Metro Area Occupational Employment and Wage Estimates

Average Hourly Wages: Occupations E – I

Metro Area	Electricians	Financial Managers	First-Line Supervisors/ Mgrs., Sales	Food Preparation Workers	General/ Operations Managers	Hairdressers/ Cosmetologists	Internists
Albuquerque, NM	20.63	52.39	17.47	10.11	47.54	12.41	n/a
Anchorage, AK	37.67	57.37	20.58	11.77	52.07	15.62	87.17
Ann Arbor, MI	34.13	52.36	21.31	10.91	58.44	12.74	n/a
Athens, GA	21.17	52.53	18.71	9.46	44.55	13.01	n/a
Atlanta, GA	22.92	64.95	20.49	9.97	58.17	13.23	125.05
Austin, TX	22.44	65.24	20.91	10.58	57.92	16.16	n/a
Billings, MT	28.93	55.25	19.30	9.55	47.00	18.62	n/a
Boise City, ID	22.22	48.15	18.16	9.20	39.82	11.79	n/a
Boston, MA[4]	32.26	65.97	22.79	12.12	69.66	15.82	97.42
Boulder, CO	22.87	66.19	24.57	10.82	62.75	15.89	101.78
Cape Coral, FL	18.53	51.28	21.86	9.84	55.15	15.98	99.55
Cedar Rapids, IA	27.91	58.49	19.19	9.99	47.50	11.92	n/a
Charleston, SC	21.15	53.06	19.67	10.77	48.40	12.98	95.46
Charlotte, NC	19.05	73.64	21.93	10.08	62.61	14.14	n/a
Chicago, IL[2]	35.99	62.95	20.26	10.17	53.12	13.44	74.91
Clarksville, TN	19.36	29.83	18.14	10.10	39.05	11.03	n/a
Colorado Springs, CO	22.45	66.96	23.33	10.18	54.42	12.65	n/a
Columbia, MO	24.83	49.17	18.87	9.20	34.34	14.11	n/a
Columbus, OH	22.22	62.76	17.92	10.72	54.06	12.37	87.88
Dallas, TX[2]	19.95	67.69	22.06	9.68	66.25	12.48	82.59
Davenport, IA	29.18	46.43	17.65	9.68	42.34	11.50	n/a
Denver, CO	23.46	73.42	20.81	10.87	64.10	13.60	104.45
Des Moines, IA	26.17	60.19	18.93	9.49	51.39	15.76	102.12
Durham, NC	19.86	63.65	20.19	11.24	66.10	12.94	n/a
El Paso, TX	18.67	48.33	20.84	8.55	50.94	8.93	118.46
Erie, PA	25.09	48.18	19.36	10.85	48.75	11.84	n/a
Eugene, OR	29.10	43.83	18.18	10.61	40.22	12.34	n/a
Fargo, ND	26.64	50.52	20.34	12.29	50.18	14.31	n/a
Fayetteville, NC	19.38	56.53	18.43	9.70	59.24	12.81	n/a
Fort Collins, CO	22.15	61.03	20.77	11.18	47.71	12.67	n/a
Fort Wayne, IN	26.12	50.86	18.86	9.87	53.12	10.88	n/a
Fort Worth, TX[2]	20.19	59.62	23.34	9.79	56.63	12.43	102.25
Gainesville, FL	18.32	64.77	18.84	9.99	55.68	13.03	113.85
Grand Rapids, MI	22.61	48.24	19.28	10.13	53.57	12.90	38.10
Green Bay, WI	23.51	50.91	17.79	10.23	47.34	11.41	122.85
Greensboro, NC	18.85	60.86	20.92	9.23	62.90	13.38	110.75
Honolulu, HI	31.86	48.00	22.63	10.93	49.10	18.81	91.52
Houston, TX	23.54	71.19	22.25	9.79	66.54	14.67	82.70
Huntsville, AL	21.89	59.17	20.18	8.61	64.51	12.68	n/a
Indianapolis, IN	26.18	54.52	20.39	9.13	55.79	13.67	122.48
Jacksonville, FL	20.58	64.14	19.99	10.04	58.38	15.99	107.64
Kansas City, MO	27.72	58.18	19.61	9.82	52.19	12.54	112.97
Lafayette, LA	21.25	42.95	18.38	8.85	57.52	11.58	n/a
Las Vegas, NV	27.13	49.10	20.58	13.01	49.24	11.31	84.91
Lexington, KY	21.06	47.58	18.05	10.39	44.05	14.22	84.01
Lincoln, NE	21.64	63.78	17.32	9.17	51.18	11.26	n/a
Little Rock, AR	22.27	53.33	16.62	9.12	43.64	12.53	103.98
Los Angeles, CA[2]	28.71	73.35	20.59	9.99	61.38	13.23	84.61
Louisville, KY	24.69	50.81	18.04	9.97	46.38	12.56	95.90
Lubbock, TX	19.63	51.82	21.88	9.29	50.12	10.76	n/a
Madison, WI	26.74	54.80	18.79	10.16	53.76	13.91	122.70
Manchester, NH[3]	24.92	56.64	21.18	13.27	57.08	12.97	n/a
McAllen, TX	15.82	45.16	20.37	8.91	40.70	12.47	n/a
Miami, FL[2]	25.09	66.96	20.92	10.53	65.16	12.07	95.49
Midland, TX	22.50	71.96	25.03	10.84	62.58	15.33	n/a

Table continued on next page.

Metro Area	Electricians	Financial Managers	First-Line Supervisors/ Mgrs., Sales	Food Preparation Workers	General/ Operations Managers	Hairdressers/ Cosmetolo-gists	Internists
Minneapolis, MN	29.39	64.61	19.66	12.02	54.47	12.93	107.43
Nashville, TN	22.65	52.35	19.69	9.33	55.29	14.48	82.28
New Orleans, LA	23.93	49.32	19.47	8.67	52.92	12.40	116.99
New York, NY[2]	36.31	90.14	24.85	12.00	77.14	16.02	88.73
Oklahoma City, OK	22.89	48.69	19.01	9.33	49.86	10.94	89.29
Omaha, NE	23.27	65.65	21.01	9.11	53.30	13.54	94.13
Orlando, FL	18.52	62.39	19.97	10.60	55.63	11.82	105.54
Oxnard, CA	27.04	57.20	21.66	11.67	58.42	12.46	99.51
Palm Bay, FL	19.63	58.11	19.96	10.24	56.20	13.29	n/a
Peoria, IL	29.24	54.23	17.75	9.78	47.99	9.58	113.32
Philadelphia, PA[2]	31.88	75.01	24.43	10.99	66.30	13.51	100.69
Phoenix, AZ	21.77	56.97	19.42	10.37	52.50	12.16	84.25
Pittsburgh, PA	26.48	67.54	21.36	10.08	55.92	11.92	103.20
Portland, OR	35.00	52.99	19.22	11.00	51.85	14.59	102.98
Providence, RI[3]	24.15	63.15	22.35	11.05	64.63	13.60	90.20
Provo, UT	22.83	54.02	18.10	9.39	40.93	12.66	n/a
Raleigh, NC	18.56	60.35	20.97	9.86	65.27	14.38	114.03
Reno, NV	27.35	47.23	20.07	9.78	48.92	10.52	n/a
Richmond, VA	22.42	64.04	21.49	9.63	59.09	16.57	96.24
Roanoke, VA	20.74	57.00	20.41	9.37	52.94	13.69	85.77
Rochester, MN	31.43	50.08	18.30	10.90	41.83	14.36	n/a
Sacramento, CA	29.07	56.32	20.02	10.14	53.55	11.88	108.61
Salem, OR	27.80	44.82	17.97	10.78	42.99	12.30	102.69
Salt Lake City, UT	23.08	54.45	19.38	9.67	46.68	14.02	93.65
San Antonio, TX	21.23	61.53	22.05	9.76	54.74	12.44	n/a
San Diego, CA	31.91	65.07	22.26	10.31	58.68	15.36	98.53
San Francisco, CA[2]	41.67	85.60	23.94	11.58	72.35	18.36	80.03
San Jose, CA	35.29	79.99	23.58	11.48	74.72	11.55	110.04
Santa Rosa, CA	33.78	55.30	21.77	10.87	55.98	11.54	113.18
Savannah, GA	22.22	60.86	16.71	10.03	43.56	11.24	n/a
Seattle, WA[2]	34.96	59.47	22.25	11.93	63.37	18.24	98.11
Sioux Falls, SD	21.56	63.66	21.93	9.32	60.49	14.51	117.25
Spokane, WA	28.19	47.12	22.00	10.77	46.30	13.64	76.87
Springfield, IL	32.10	47.83	18.50	10.13	46.32	19.15	63.16
Tallahassee, FL	18.66	52.43	20.41	9.56	56.30	13.10	n/a
Tampa, FL	19.04	62.50	21.17	10.01	62.54	13.63	105.04
Topeka, KS	24.24	50.04	19.33	8.97	42.57	13.24	n/a
Tulsa, OK	22.46	54.15	18.57	9.22	50.31	11.63	98.48
Tyler, TX	19.66	53.28	19.90	9.03	54.59	14.38	n/a
Virginia Beach, VA	22.14	57.19	19.47	9.99	57.52	16.63	81.30
Washington, DC[2]	27.07	71.05	22.49	10.93	69.97	16.97	n/a
Wichita, KS	23.64	42.88	19.10	8.85	49.24	12.55	123.92
Wilmington, NC	19.73	53.29	20.77	9.61	57.79	12.69	n/a
Winston-Salem, NC	24.18	64.03	20.02	9.74	60.54	13.99	n/a
Worcester, MA[3]	31.42	53.53	22.14	10.87	56.52	16.28	n/a

Notes: (1) Figures cover the Metropolitan Statistical Area (MSA) except where noted. See Appendix B for areas included; (2) Metropolitan Division; (3) New England City and Town Area; (4) New England City and Town Area Division; n/a not available
Source: Bureau of Labor Statistics, May 2014 Metro Area Occupational Employment and Wage Estimates

Average Hourly Wages: Occupations J – N

Metro Area	Janitors/ Cleaners	Landscapers	Lawyers	Maids/ House- keepers	Main- tenance Repairers	Marketing Managers	Nuclear Medicine Techs
Albuquerque, NM	10.84	11.39	43.13	9.06	17.34	43.67	35.06
Anchorage, AK	13.96	15.76	57.05	11.80	22.16	43.16	n/a
Ann Arbor, MI	14.49	13.30	66.46	10.25	19.27	56.03	33.16
Athens, GA	10.90	13.31	48.77	9.44	16.76	52.97	n/a
Atlanta, GA	11.63	12.39	66.91	9.24	18.51	65.68	35.15
Austin, TX	10.70	11.84	63.59	9.32	17.30	68.82	35.23
Billings, MT	12.51	11.85	35.98	10.18	15.40	n/a	n/a
Boise City, ID	10.63	12.63	50.07	10.54	15.46	51.47	n/a
Boston, MA[4]	15.55	16.67	72.96	13.80	22.05	67.44	37.99
Boulder, CO	13.26	13.43	59.33	9.78	18.72	70.60	37.63
Cape Coral, FL	11.93	11.41	42.74	10.18	16.36	54.42	31.55
Cedar Rapids, IA	13.76	13.01	49.81	10.03	21.56	55.01	n/a
Charleston, SC	10.36	11.51	48.27	9.55	18.73	50.87	33.40
Charlotte, NC	10.29	11.30	59.02	8.90	18.67	66.37	33.35
Chicago, IL[2]	13.87	13.49	60.77	11.62	20.70	59.32	35.08
Clarksville, TN	10.97	11.95	38.00	9.53	18.16	36.81	n/a
Colorado Springs, CO	12.21	12.34	53.13	9.60	17.93	66.67	n/a
Columbia, MO	12.44	11.28	55.59	9.62	16.07	50.54	n/a
Columbus, OH	12.46	12.19	56.31	10.05	19.08	63.69	32.86
Dallas, TX[2]	10.05	11.91	69.58	9.34	17.74	68.82	33.63
Davenport, IA	12.36	12.55	53.98	9.97	17.80	43.57	n/a
Denver, CO	11.61	13.64	65.99	10.24	19.12	67.90	38.70
Des Moines, IA	11.57	15.15	60.72	10.23	17.75	60.13	32.20
Durham, NC	11.28	13.65	51.42	10.30	20.29	76.12	n/a
El Paso, TX	9.89	10.00	71.19	8.55	13.50	57.93	n/a
Erie, PA	10.59	11.18	50.10	8.87	15.52	54.91	n/a
Eugene, OR	12.54	14.20	42.01	10.36	18.32	33.62	n/a
Fargo, ND	12.69	11.47	49.31	9.46	17.41	53.29	n/a
Fayetteville, NC	10.17	10.01	48.40	8.53	15.92	n/a	28.39
Fort Collins, CO	11.76	13.24	66.59	9.99	17.29	67.14	n/a
Fort Wayne, IN	11.12	11.69	62.69	8.71	19.18	47.72	30.53
Fort Worth, TX[2]	10.54	11.63	56.57	9.40	16.75	56.57	34.54
Gainesville, FL	10.63	10.90	48.54	9.86	17.14	62.12	n/a
Grand Rapids, MI	11.84	12.17	46.77	10.06	17.89	44.94	n/a
Green Bay, WI	11.92	13.42	41.62	9.78	18.70	51.21	n/a
Greensboro, NC	9.70	11.75	60.88	9.04	19.02	62.43	31.89
Honolulu, HI	12.01	14.13	50.53	15.83	20.38	44.45	42.17
Houston, TX	10.06	11.35	78.40	9.07	18.00	73.12	34.42
Huntsville, AL	10.21	10.31	66.26	8.33	19.40	63.98	24.87
Indianapolis, IN	12.18	11.68	53.41	9.10	18.03	52.22	34.40
Jacksonville, FL	11.55	12.18	52.18	9.35	17.52	57.64	35.62
Kansas City, MO	12.23	12.79	63.28	9.66	17.70	57.69	33.60
Lafayette, LA	9.81	10.85	48.67	8.66	18.33	35.31	27.19
Las Vegas, NV	14.03	12.39	60.83	15.39	22.63	55.16	36.22
Lexington, KY	11.24	11.28	48.19	9.28	16.48	45.66	n/a
Lincoln, NE	10.82	12.17	52.83	9.26	18.90	46.17	31.55
Little Rock, AR	10.17	10.77	46.55	8.60	15.42	52.58	31.74
Los Angeles, CA[2]	13.07	13.57	82.27	12.17	20.92	68.97	48.08
Louisville, KY	10.99	12.11	46.23	9.28	18.81	54.06	28.80
Lubbock, TX	10.11	11.28	65.52	8.78	15.46	57.30	35.94
Madison, WI	12.11	13.38	51.62	10.06	19.03	51.71	n/a
Manchester, NH[3]	11.79	16.75	60.87	10.39	20.69	50.53	n/a
McAllen, TX	10.24	9.75	52.56	8.56	11.44	n/a	n/a
Miami, FL[2]	10.25	11.04	71.66	9.97	15.64	52.20	35.69
Midland, TX	11.45	14.20	n/a	10.06	20.01	67.96	n/a

Table continued on next page.

Metro Area	Janitors/ Cleaners	Landscapers	Lawyers	Maids/ House-keepers	Main-tenance Repairers	Marketing Managers	Nuclear Medicine Techs
Minneapolis, MN	12.90	14.13	64.40	10.77	21.40	63.45	36.95
Nashville, TN	10.76	12.02	57.91	9.85	18.10	47.41	29.91
New Orleans, LA	11.24	10.71	64.02	9.66	17.75	52.86	31.41
New York, NY[2]	15.81	15.96	80.56	17.82	21.32	86.43	40.07
Oklahoma City, OK	10.49	12.31	50.19	9.20	16.73	44.40	33.51
Omaha, NE	11.42	12.68	47.82	9.43	18.04	51.81	31.60
Orlando, FL	10.25	11.57	70.01	9.98	15.68	54.52	35.88
Oxnard, CA	14.13	13.29	74.13	11.15	19.73	71.68	47.69
Palm Bay, FL	11.28	11.76	47.11	10.32	16.43	60.20	32.09
Peoria, IL	11.53	13.40	61.57	10.26	18.12	56.35	32.53
Philadelphia, PA[2]	13.68	15.11	66.04	11.72	20.02	80.96	35.05
Phoenix, AZ	10.94	11.61	60.06	9.99	17.50	57.16	37.02
Pittsburgh, PA	12.33	12.49	66.20	10.27	19.11	70.82	28.46
Portland, OR	12.93	14.39	58.93	11.94	20.32	52.74	40.06
Providence, RI[3]	13.84	14.21	56.50	12.18	19.61	62.61	40.69
Provo, UT	9.91	11.47	57.38	9.40	16.71	56.40	n/a
Raleigh, NC	10.01	11.64	61.58	9.28	18.62	65.26	32.48
Reno, NV	10.58	13.08	54.03	10.09	18.67	45.79	n/a
Richmond, VA	10.74	12.31	61.69	9.84	18.58	66.50	31.36
Roanoke, VA	10.62	11.97	56.54	9.07	16.31	69.20	31.39
Rochester, MN	13.91	13.55	48.97	10.88	18.71	59.53	n/a
Sacramento, CA	12.91	13.80	61.90	13.54	19.83	56.13	50.94
Salem, OR	13.69	13.45	57.07	11.45	17.47	36.40	n/a
Salt Lake City, UT	10.28	12.22	60.92	9.48	17.96	62.31	32.12
San Antonio, TX	10.45	12.21	60.15	9.40	15.50	52.16	32.74
San Diego, CA	12.96	13.22	69.45	10.97	19.46	70.12	37.17
San Francisco, CA[2]	14.03	18.40	82.65	16.90	25.10	86.40	54.17
San Jose, CA	13.63	15.69	96.75	14.64	22.42	90.33	57.46
Santa Rosa, CA	13.77	15.00	77.19	13.96	22.42	64.87	n/a
Savannah, GA	10.21	10.35	45.27	8.65	18.60	46.64	n/a
Seattle, WA[2]	14.27	16.23	63.11	12.07	21.05	68.07	42.69
Sioux Falls, SD	11.01	12.41	49.13	9.11	16.04	53.54	26.13
Spokane, WA	13.73	13.07	47.57	10.98	18.08	52.77	35.89
Springfield, IL	13.55	14.52	51.79	10.22	19.49	41.03	35.33
Tallahassee, FL	10.15	10.80	51.85	9.18	14.86	41.02	n/a
Tampa, FL	10.50	11.19	56.02	9.46	15.83	55.62	36.51
Topeka, KS	11.82	13.09	38.39	9.01	18.03	60.82	n/a
Tulsa, OK	10.55	11.43	68.76	9.24	17.33	48.13	28.15
Tyler, TX	9.79	10.75	55.31	8.46	16.32	n/a	n/a
Virginia Beach, VA	10.54	11.80	58.75	9.86	17.20	54.08	31.30
Washington, DC[2]	12.72	13.10	77.76	12.18	21.78	74.74	37.71
Wichita, KS	11.51	12.29	46.25	9.00	16.84	57.47	n/a
Wilmington, NC	10.22	11.32	47.06	9.61	18.53	51.98	n/a
Winston-Salem, NC	9.50	11.96	67.84	8.74	18.25	60.61	34.61
Worcester, MA[3]	14.97	15.31	58.44	11.17	20.59	60.16	n/a

Notes: (1) Figures cover the Metropolitan Statistical Area (MSA) except where noted. See Appendix B for areas included; (2) Metropolitan Division; (3) New England City and Town Area; (4) New England City and Town Area Division; n/a not available
Source: Bureau of Labor Statistics, May 2014 Metro Area Occupational Employment and Wage Estimates

Average Hourly Wages: Occupations N – R

Metro Area	Nurses, Licensed Practical	Nurses, Registered	Nursing Assistants	Packers/ Packagers	Physical Therapists	Postal Mail Carriers	R.E. Brokers
Albuquerque, NM	23.04	32.08	13.56	9.38	42.05	25.32	n/a
Anchorage, AK	25.37	41.46	17.75	13.44	48.61	25.82	42.45
Ann Arbor, MI	22.53	33.45	14.39	10.01	38.02	25.07	n/a
Athens, GA	19.18	29.28	10.65	10.21	39.78	23.71	n/a
Atlanta, GA	19.12	31.27	11.22	11.08	39.00	25.21	54.71
Austin, TX	22.40	31.42	11.92	11.54	36.27	25.51	56.11
Billings, MT	19.04	31.34	12.31	11.20	35.01	25.15	22.10
Boise City, ID	20.09	29.51	11.14	12.24	36.62	24.83	n/a
Boston, MA[4]	26.04	43.69	14.98	11.46	39.63	26.31	60.84
Boulder, CO	22.06	34.99	13.61	10.50	35.24	25.32	31.66
Cape Coral, FL	20.35	30.64	12.52	9.31	44.59	24.80	22.86
Cedar Rapids, IA	18.31	25.86	11.88	8.96	33.84	25.01	n/a
Charleston, SC	19.89	31.98	11.57	10.97	38.61	24.42	27.17
Charlotte, NC	19.74	28.49	11.21	10.95	38.61	24.80	30.80
Chicago, IL[2]	23.40	35.35	12.34	11.25	38.00	25.38	47.43
Clarksville, TN	18.91	27.70	12.03	9.71	37.99	24.87	n/a
Colorado Springs, CO	21.39	31.03	12.49	10.75	36.99	25.15	n/a
Columbia, MO	18.14	27.18	11.68	9.72	32.87	24.69	n/a
Columbus, OH	20.22	31.29	12.03	11.41	36.56	24.53	40.25
Dallas, TX[2]	23.73	34.57	12.31	10.63	47.84	25.37	n/a
Davenport, IA	18.17	26.30	11.75	11.01	34.98	24.40	n/a
Denver, CO	23.98	34.76	14.69	11.03	36.46	25.20	40.15
Des Moines, IA	19.74	27.38	12.29	9.98	36.71	25.06	n/a
Durham, NC	22.08	32.29	12.43	10.10	36.88	24.86	29.05
El Paso, TX	21.28	31.21	10.30	9.13	46.97	24.27	n/a
Erie, PA	19.14	27.49	12.45	11.44	37.54	24.01	n/a
Eugene, OR	22.53	38.61	13.86	10.83	42.09	24.68	32.09
Fargo, ND	18.22	29.24	13.58	10.53	34.16	24.49	n/a
Fayetteville, NC	19.54	29.96	11.07	9.20	38.19	24.55	18.48
Fort Collins, CO	21.75	31.50	13.68	9.53	34.13	25.41	30.37
Fort Wayne, IN	19.31	25.50	11.11	10.68	38.43	25.11	n/a
Fort Worth, TX[2]	22.81	34.32	11.86	11.20	40.58	25.27	42.75
Gainesville, FL	20.12	29.16	10.93	9.58	37.82	24.31	n/a
Grand Rapids, MI	19.55	28.62	12.70	9.88	37.45	24.45	n/a
Green Bay, WI	18.61	28.57	12.59	11.68	40.13	24.11	n/a
Greensboro, NC	20.09	29.50	10.67	9.81	34.96	24.58	21.37
Honolulu, HI	23.19	43.39	14.28	10.66	38.79	26.41	72.67
Houston, TX	23.39	36.30	12.21	10.79	43.09	24.92	56.32
Huntsville, AL	17.96	27.18	11.48	10.90	39.13	24.20	29.62
Indianapolis, IN	20.40	30.02	12.27	10.65	39.56	24.58	47.92
Jacksonville, FL	20.15	30.30	11.49	9.70	45.60	25.15	n/a
Kansas City, MO	19.27	30.18	12.02	11.86	36.91	24.73	n/a
Lafayette, LA	17.44	28.28	9.35	9.76	34.68	25.04	26.33
Las Vegas, NV	25.70	39.82	16.84	11.10	68.02	25.25	57.87
Lexington, KY	18.81	28.46	12.21	9.95	38.70	25.07	n/a
Lincoln, NE	18.46	26.80	12.07	10.19	35.07	24.98	n/a
Little Rock, AR	18.20	29.00	11.10	9.47	37.53	24.64	n/a
Los Angeles, CA[2]	24.02	45.26	14.15	10.44	42.21	26.10	48.11
Louisville, KY	19.16	29.21	12.16	10.55	38.60	24.57	n/a
Lubbock, TX	21.03	29.11	11.44	8.57	40.80	25.31	n/a
Madison, WI	21.50	35.93	13.89	15.33	37.19	24.91	21.81
Manchester, NH[3]	24.35	32.53	14.74	10.52	36.56	25.52	n/a
McAllen, TX	22.31	31.38	9.65	9.22	45.05	24.89	n/a
Miami, FL[2]	20.67	30.72	11.29	9.44	34.48	25.43	n/a
Midland, TX	21.64	31.16	12.46	12.63	36.67	25.43	n/a

Table continued on next page.

Metro Area	Nurses, Licensed Practical	Nurses, Registered	Nursing Assistants	Packers/ Packagers	Physical Therapists	Postal Mail Carriers	R.E. Brokers
Minneapolis, MN	21.36	36.33	14.48	11.53	36.46	24.83	n/a
Nashville, TN	18.71	28.51	11.12	10.64	38.94	25.03	n/a
New Orleans, LA	19.51	31.38	11.00	10.63	40.05	24.54	n/a
New York, NY[2]	25.00	41.35	16.33	11.24	43.86	25.71	56.08
Oklahoma City, OK	19.06	28.17	11.01	11.72	37.49	24.88	n/a
Omaha, NE	19.68	28.70	12.39	10.15	35.03	24.99	n/a
Orlando, FL	19.09	29.53	11.66	10.63	41.89	25.19	55.07
Oxnard, CA	25.10	41.29	14.21	11.19	41.46	25.87	n/a
Palm Bay, FL	20.37	29.36	11.54	9.56	42.97	24.96	25.52
Peoria, IL	20.98	27.02	11.51	11.30	37.14	24.78	n/a
Philadelphia, PA[2]	23.83	35.66	14.18	11.30	39.61	25.18	57.53
Phoenix, AZ	25.13	35.15	13.85	11.08	40.31	25.45	n/a
Pittsburgh, PA	19.95	30.03	13.28	12.20	39.16	25.07	n/a
Portland, OR	24.14	41.08	13.90	12.01	38.57	24.92	41.83
Providence, RI[3]	24.48	36.37	13.65	10.71	39.30	25.21	26.78
Provo, UT	19.71	27.91	11.36	10.80	35.82	24.99	n/a
Raleigh, NC	21.05	28.98	11.64	10.62	35.90	24.64	27.57
Reno, NV	24.00	36.23	13.75	10.16	44.27	24.92	27.65
Richmond, VA	19.13	30.66	11.41	11.78	39.91	24.19	54.12
Roanoke, VA	19.04	28.45	11.55	9.55	50.52	24.57	n/a
Rochester, MN	22.02	31.56	14.89	10.59	39.81	25.51	n/a
Sacramento, CA	27.59	50.67	15.59	12.78	45.28	25.51	n/a
Salem, OR	22.33	37.43	14.19	10.39	39.98	24.05	26.23
Salt Lake City, UT	22.81	30.51	11.94	10.79	37.89	25.44	35.96
San Antonio, TX	20.65	31.91	11.64	10.73	41.87	25.09	32.39
San Diego, CA	24.22	41.23	13.66	11.08	43.10	25.62	43.87
San Francisco, CA[2]	29.61	61.63	19.20	13.17	50.54	26.78	40.04
San Jose, CA	28.63	58.57	16.50	11.96	48.82	26.71	40.86
Santa Rosa, CA	24.38	49.36	15.35	10.94	43.46	25.51	50.54
Savannah, GA	18.62	29.37	10.62	9.38	42.35	25.20	21.46
Seattle, WA[2]	25.95	40.52	15.24	13.77	40.65	25.61	42.63
Sioux Falls, SD	16.88	26.30	11.64	10.65	32.70	24.51	38.96
Spokane, WA	21.72	35.14	12.71	11.56	38.63	24.97	n/a
Springfield, IL	18.68	30.04	12.42	10.89	32.64	24.54	n/a
Tallahassee, FL	19.21	27.68	10.98	9.23	40.52	24.74	n/a
Tampa, FL	20.11	30.68	11.61	9.28	37.77	25.12	20.90
Topeka, KS	19.49	30.01	11.19	13.93	43.51	24.04	n/a
Tulsa, OK	19.13	28.79	10.94	10.21	39.09	24.94	n/a
Tyler, TX	20.58	28.16	9.85	11.68	44.11	25.16	n/a
Virginia Beach, VA	18.87	28.99	11.40	10.44	39.89	25.11	35.85
Washington, DC[2]	23.48	36.65	13.53	10.19	39.93	25.08	39.18
Wichita, KS	19.17	25.37	11.26	9.63	36.33	24.75	n/a
Wilmington, NC	19.14	27.14	10.78	9.87	43.24	24.02	27.20
Winston-Salem, NC	19.86	29.33	11.23	11.20	39.34	24.21	24.66
Worcester, MA[3]	26.14	43.44	14.74	10.31	37.04	24.65	n/a

Notes: (1) Figures cover the Metropolitan Statistical Area (MSA) except where noted. See Appendix B for areas included; (2) Metropolitan Division; (3) New England City and Town Area; (4) New England City and Town Area Division; n/a not available
Source: Bureau of Labor Statistics, May 2014 Metro Area Occupational Employment and Wage Estimates

Average Hourly Wages: Occupations R – T

Metro Area	Retail Salespersons	Sales Reps., Except Tech./Scien.	Sales Reps., Tech./Scien.	Secretaries, Exc. Leg./ Med./Exec.	Security Guards	Surgeons	Teacher Assistants
Albuquerque, NM	11.93	25.47	32.08	15.01	13.09	n/a	9.80
Anchorage, AK	12.99	28.46	37.22	16.96	14.72	n/a	17.70
Ann Arbor, MI	12.87	34.07	37.02	17.93	16.86	n/a	13.70
Athens, GA	10.84	25.40	26.49	15.47	13.58	n/a	8.80
Atlanta, GA	12.20	30.23	38.88	17.11	11.76	119.43	10.60
Austin, TX	13.21	31.05	39.30	16.04	12.59	102.01	10.50
Billings, MT	13.67	25.53	n/a	14.85	11.70	n/a	13.70
Boise City, ID	12.38	28.69	30.79	14.58	13.16	n/a	11.90
Boston, MA[4]	12.52	40.91	46.95	21.58	15.10	123.81	14.50
Boulder, CO	14.72	38.65	36.38	17.54	15.25	103.98	15.50
Cape Coral, FL	11.99	26.37	43.19	14.95	11.25	n/a	13.30
Cedar Rapids, IA	12.01	32.42	39.84	14.48	n/a	n/a	13.10
Charleston, SC	11.27	29.99	34.28	15.48	13.90	131.24	11.10
Charlotte, NC	12.45	34.71	41.36	17.12	11.54	122.15	11.00
Chicago, IL[2]	12.51	34.23	36.30	17.77	14.44	121.53	13.70
Clarksville, TN	12.04	22.17	44.78	13.70	14.07	n/a	11.00
Colorado Springs, CO	13.47	32.60	36.45	15.92	13.45	113.24	11.90
Columbia, MO	10.41	25.25	32.47	14.86	12.17	n/a	11.50
Columbus, OH	11.64	32.86	40.03	16.63	12.42	108.75	13.10
Dallas, TX[2]	12.97	36.59	35.52	16.76	13.07	107.42	10.90
Davenport, IA	12.90	29.86	32.49	15.06	11.86	113.22	11.90
Denver, CO	12.90	34.55	47.66	18.22	14.70	115.12	13.30
Des Moines, IA	13.39	35.00	37.34	16.84	17.65	104.00	10.80
Durham, NC	11.52	30.76	48.15	17.74	12.61	114.66	12.50
El Paso, TX	11.34	21.16	37.74	13.05	10.13	116.07	11.00
Erie, PA	11.42	27.80	30.04	14.02	11.21	122.52	10.20
Eugene, OR	13.26	23.83	37.87	16.13	12.67	n/a	13.10
Fargo, ND	13.08	30.35	38.20	16.52	11.74	n/a	14.30
Fayetteville, NC	10.63	23.83	n/a	14.89	16.12	n/a	10.00
Fort Collins, CO	12.51	28.50	33.51	16.40	11.03	102.71	12.70
Fort Wayne, IN	11.68	28.94	47.60	15.93	15.50	n/a	11.20
Fort Worth, TX[2]	12.49	34.57	35.89	14.87	13.96	123.79	9.20
Gainesville, FL	11.27	24.02	37.49	14.25	11.33	124.14	9.50
Grand Rapids, MI	12.13	29.54	40.88	15.68	10.68	n/a	12.70
Green Bay, WI	11.50	31.92	38.67	16.31	11.69	n/a	13.60
Greensboro, NC	12.57	36.10	34.25	15.84	11.25	n/a	10.80
Honolulu, HI	12.09	22.95	34.42	18.61	13.23	n/a	13.10
Houston, TX	12.65	37.04	45.99	16.42	12.12	106.03	10.10
Huntsville, AL	11.95	29.32	44.28	17.41	12.99	n/a	8.90
Indianapolis, IN	12.37	33.02	44.66	16.78	13.24	n/a	11.00
Jacksonville, FL	11.63	27.56	37.64	15.06	10.72	111.20	12.70
Kansas City, MO	11.83	32.28	47.71	16.22	14.14	118.85	11.60
Lafayette, LA	11.55	27.68	33.19	14.63	11.78	70.64	10.30
Las Vegas, NV	12.87	30.00	42.07	17.97	13.08	126.61	15.50
Lexington, KY	12.15	26.55	32.51	16.26	10.14	108.58	14.90
Lincoln, NE	11.58	26.81	31.96	15.94	15.82	n/a	12.10
Little Rock, AR	13.22	27.97	31.22	14.56	12.32	95.23	9.60
Los Angeles, CA[2]	12.89	30.21	40.43	18.49	12.86	119.27	14.20
Louisville, KY	11.81	32.36	46.31	15.70	12.33	n/a	14.10
Lubbock, TX	11.44	27.57	37.38	13.80	11.53	n/a	9.50
Madison, WI	12.15	30.12	35.85	17.54	11.61	119.57	12.80
Manchester, NH[3]	12.05	31.88	43.36	15.85	13.39	n/a	13.00
McAllen, TX	10.10	23.55	n/a	12.11	10.48	n/a	10.90
Miami, FL[2]	11.35	26.12	34.36	14.84	10.96	n/a	11.60
Midland, TX	16.03	31.12	38.87	15.96	13.54	n/a	8.80

Table continued on next page.

Metro Area	Retail Salespersons	Sales Reps., Except Tech./Scien.	Sales Reps., Tech./Scien.	Secretaries, Exc. Leg./ Med./Exec.	Security Guards	Surgeons	Teacher Assistants
Minneapolis, MN	11.58	36.90	48.32	19.12	14.70	n/a	15.40
Nashville, TN	13.10	29.39	36.34	15.64	14.21	n/a	11.50
New Orleans, LA	12.46	31.07	41.18	15.49	14.39	116.86	11.40
New York, NY[2]	12.88	37.87	49.43	19.19	15.53	104.98	14.10
Oklahoma City, OK	12.60	28.10	34.62	14.86	13.95	114.86	9.00
Omaha, NE	12.29	28.11	34.71	15.91	13.87	n/a	10.30
Orlando, FL	11.53	27.45	35.16	15.27	11.32	n/a	11.80
Oxnard, CA	12.76	n/a	46.05	18.59	15.68	121.08	14.70
Palm Bay, FL	12.10	25.05	39.33	14.49	11.97	112.98	11.60
Peoria, IL	11.80	26.80	32.35	14.79	14.82	n/a	11.30
Philadelphia, PA[2]	13.03	33.11	52.02	17.66	12.30	n/a	12.60
Phoenix, AZ	11.97	28.59	44.41	16.47	13.71	117.17	11.80
Pittsburgh, PA	12.62	31.62	38.90	15.77	11.77	114.66	11.30
Portland, OR	13.04	32.68	38.75	17.62	15.19	n/a	14.50
Providence, RI[3]	12.95	32.08	41.03	18.15	13.03	125.75	14.80
Provo, UT	12.25	32.49	38.50	14.58	14.09	100.95	11.30
Raleigh, NC	11.72	29.57	48.22	16.55	12.95	n/a	11.00
Reno, NV	12.99	28.94	38.90	17.84	11.83	116.44	12.80
Richmond, VA	12.17	34.63	45.81	16.69	13.10	113.16	11.40
Roanoke, VA	11.93	28.59	36.15	15.72	10.76	94.20	11.60
Rochester, MN	12.67	27.65	34.68	18.13	12.53	n/a	12.30
Sacramento, CA	12.79	31.85	41.20	17.72	12.75	n/a	14.40
Salem, OR	12.94	21.91	39.34	16.38	13.67	n/a	16.20
Salt Lake City, UT	12.82	36.15	48.29	16.23	14.80	n/a	11.50
San Antonio, TX	12.78	32.89	36.78	15.32	11.61	116.16	11.20
San Diego, CA	13.34	27.73	41.16	18.46	14.56	105.25	14.30
San Francisco, CA[2]	15.30	29.54	48.03	21.58	15.87	94.79	17.50
San Jose, CA	13.40	35.32	54.47	21.31	14.33	113.16	15.50
Santa Rosa, CA	13.49	29.47	45.85	19.44	14.70	114.81	13.30
Savannah, GA	11.45	28.34	29.44	16.68	13.44	n/a	9.90
Seattle, WA[2]	14.35	35.28	43.16	19.95	16.33	104.00	15.90
Sioux Falls, SD	12.95	27.44	47.04	13.39	12.84	n/a	10.80
Spokane, WA	14.27	25.66	n/a	16.31	13.32	n/a	12.90
Springfield, IL	12.00	25.58	38.91	17.31	20.37	92.52	11.10
Tallahassee, FL	10.95	25.49	35.94	14.52	12.86	124.29	12.30
Tampa, FL	12.17	31.31	34.58	14.85	10.62	121.64	10.40
Topeka, KS	11.31	29.02	41.78	14.44	10.57	n/a	11.30
Tulsa, OK	12.77	29.62	37.57	14.36	13.21	79.73	11.00
Tyler, TX	12.78	26.77	51.68	14.99	13.71	n/a	11.70
Virginia Beach, VA	11.55	29.08	41.92	15.72	13.77	119.18	12.10
Washington, DC[2]	12.20	36.98	52.11	20.79	18.20	103.94	14.40
Wichita, KS	13.03	32.52	41.09	14.76	12.44	122.05	12.30
Wilmington, NC	12.47	27.18	41.51	15.70	11.87	n/a	11.90
Winston-Salem, NC	12.84	28.37	n/a	16.42	12.91	n/a	10.70
Worcester, MA[3]	12.12	33.20	43.15	19.49	13.56	126.96	14.00

Notes: (1) Figures cover the Metropolitan Statistical Area (MSA) except where noted. See Appendix B for areas included; (2) Metropolitan Division; (3) New England City and Town Area; (4) New England City and Town Area Division; n/a not available
Source: Bureau of Labor Statistics, May 2014 Metro Area Occupational Employment and Wage Estimates

Average Hourly Wages: Occupations T – Z

Metro Area	Teachers, Elementary School	Teachers, Secondary School	Tele-marketers	Truck Driv., Heavy/ Trac. Trail.	Truck Drivers, Light	Waiters/ Waitresses
Albuquerque, NM	21.10	22.80	10.63	18.93	14.78	10.44
Anchorage, AK	33.20	33.30	n/a	26.53	18.71	13.45
Ann Arbor, MI	28.10	29.90	n/a	19.35	16.82	11.24
Athens, GA	26.10	27.70	n/a	21.06	16.84	8.47
Atlanta, GA	25.90	26.90	14.51	20.07	16.69	9.20
Austin, TX	23.00	23.70	11.84	18.81	17.42	9.85
Billings, MT	24.10	26.70	13.17	23.71	17.24	9.33
Boise City, ID	24.50	24.20	12.08	18.12	14.55	8.96
Boston, MA[4]	35.30	36.10	14.91	23.78	17.42	13.88
Boulder, CO	26.90	27.30	12.13	21.50	16.76	11.02
Cape Coral, FL	23.80	24.60	10.01	17.41	15.51	9.55
Cedar Rapids, IA	24.70	24.60	10.64	20.70	16.51	8.78
Charleston, SC	24.50	25.50	9.50	20.52	14.54	9.67
Charlotte, NC	21.20	21.70	13.37	19.22	15.72	9.95
Chicago, IL[2]	29.70	36.30	13.61	23.57	18.56	10.38
Clarksville, TN	27.40	26.40	n/a	15.19	13.62	8.80
Colorado Springs, CO	22.10	22.40	11.94	18.92	14.73	9.56
Columbia, MO	n/a	n/a	n/a	19.81	14.74	9.61
Columbus, OH	30.20	30.50	11.19	20.65	16.53	10.34
Dallas, TX[2]	25.40	26.10	14.68	20.00	15.74	10.42
Davenport, IA	25.60	29.00	10.88	19.82	15.19	9.85
Denver, CO	25.60	27.10	14.69	22.34	16.52	10.01
Des Moines, IA	26.10	26.60	14.55	21.57	17.04	8.69
Durham, NC	20.70	21.60	12.38	18.04	17.96	9.57
El Paso, TX	24.40	24.70	10.43	17.44	12.44	8.85
Erie, PA	26.60	26.00	n/a	17.45	17.12	8.76
Eugene, OR	26.40	26.20	n/a	19.12	17.16	11.02
Fargo, ND	25.20	24.00	9.84	19.73	15.83	10.07
Fayetteville, NC	19.50	19.60	n/a	15.03	15.83	8.73
Fort Collins, CO	23.60	23.80	13.69	16.93	17.08	10.10
Fort Wayne, IN	24.30	24.80	10.23	18.83	15.78	9.69
Fort Worth, TX[2]	26.00	26.60	11.23	18.98	15.83	9.08
Gainesville, FL	22.10	24.40	9.39	14.27	15.92	9.80
Grand Rapids, MI	34.10	29.30	13.61	18.10	15.91	9.81
Green Bay, WI	25.50	24.90	12.96	19.44	15.69	8.96
Greensboro, NC	21.20	21.70	10.97	19.10	15.60	9.23
Honolulu, HI	26.30	26.80	12.13	20.79	14.96	14.19
Houston, TX	25.40	25.90	12.37	23.01	16.33	10.78
Huntsville, AL	24.50	24.60	n/a	17.32	14.71	9.69
Indianapolis, IN	25.00	26.30	16.03	22.03	17.09	10.53
Jacksonville, FL	24.60	24.80	10.16	19.07	16.18	10.17
Kansas City, MO	23.00	24.00	12.75	21.28	16.69	9.66
Lafayette, LA	24.10	24.80	n/a	18.12	14.34	8.98
Las Vegas, NV	25.20	25.60	13.83	21.71	16.57	11.33
Lexington, KY	25.00	25.20	13.05	20.97	15.77	9.24
Lincoln, NE	25.70	25.90	11.10	n/a	14.00	8.75
Little Rock, AR	22.40	24.30	8.66	18.54	13.70	8.31
Los Angeles, CA[2]	34.60	35.30	13.05	20.06	16.61	11.81
Louisville, KY	27.20	26.90	12.12	21.09	17.94	9.46
Lubbock, TX	22.00	23.20	n/a	18.50	15.05	9.39
Madison, WI	24.90	27.10	12.56	21.52	15.95	11.31
Manchester, NH[3]	26.90	26.60	15.41	19.39	15.72	11.23
McAllen, TX	24.10	25.40	10.52	16.33	11.43	9.42
Miami, FL[2]	24.60	28.60	11.87	17.57	14.33	10.36
Midland, TX	24.30	24.80	n/a	22.62	15.44	10.06

Table continued on next page.

Metro Area	Teachers, Elementary School	Teachers, Secondary School	Tele-marketers	Truck Driv., Heavy/ Trac. Trail.	Truck Drivers, Light	Waiters/ Waitresses
Minneapolis, MN	31.10	31.70	14.88	21.88	18.21	9.24
Nashville, TN	25.00	25.00	13.27	19.95	15.94	8.95
New Orleans, LA	23.80	25.10	14.37	19.52	16.85	9.73
New York, NY[2]	36.20	38.20	15.89	22.71	18.22	13.21
Oklahoma City, OK	19.70	20.90	10.22	18.92	15.91	9.72
Omaha, NE	22.70	23.70	10.99	19.87	14.70	8.79
Orlando, FL	22.70	22.30	10.88	18.65	15.77	10.52
Oxnard, CA	33.30	33.30	16.20	22.71	18.52	11.45
Palm Bay, FL	21.10	21.50	10.27	16.39	14.19	10.45
Peoria, IL	22.70	30.00	12.20	18.58	16.70	10.16
Philadelphia, PA[2]	32.00	31.50	14.12	21.75	17.00	10.19
Phoenix, AZ	21.00	23.60	11.67	20.02	16.12	10.41
Pittsburgh, PA	27.70	29.40	13.19	20.51	16.15	9.45
Portland, OR	28.50	28.60	12.59	19.88	16.94	11.45
Providence, RI[3]	33.50	32.60	16.78	19.94	18.33	9.95
Provo, UT	26.80	29.00	12.88	23.28	13.67	10.89
Raleigh, NC	21.70	22.30	17.13	20.09	15.93	9.98
Reno, NV	25.40	24.80	13.77	22.83	16.06	9.97
Richmond, VA	26.60	27.40	12.40	19.39	15.86	10.39
Roanoke, VA	22.50	23.30	15.62	18.42	16.08	10.16
Rochester, MN	26.60	26.50	n/a	21.57	15.86	8.39
Sacramento, CA	32.40	33.30	15.40	19.39	17.86	11.79
Salem, OR	28.80	27.10	10.69	17.54	18.65	10.85
Salt Lake City, UT	27.90	26.90	12.23	20.09	15.54	11.09
San Antonio, TX	27.10	27.70	10.63	18.18	14.56	9.36
San Diego, CA	31.60	35.00	12.15	19.56	16.71	12.44
San Francisco, CA[2]	33.10	35.00	15.57	22.44	19.39	12.63
San Jose, CA	34.40	36.10	14.43	22.34	18.59	12.02
Santa Rosa, CA	23.70	32.50	13.12	21.96	17.73	12.08
Savannah, GA	26.70	23.60	14.79	18.16	13.78	9.66
Seattle, WA[2]	29.50	31.10	13.49	22.18	17.66	14.45
Sioux Falls, SD	20.40	20.20	14.22	20.16	15.48	8.70
Spokane, WA	29.20	30.30	11.51	19.94	17.33	12.73
Springfield, IL	29.30	30.30	15.10	18.92	14.56	9.49
Tallahassee, FL	20.50	20.60	13.57	15.64	15.75	10.54
Tampa, FL	21.30	21.60	12.64	16.66	16.98	10.26
Topeka, KS	24.20	24.40	n/a	18.40	15.87	8.48
Tulsa, OK	22.50	22.50	10.63	20.67	15.12	9.09
Tyler, TX	21.50	23.10	n/a	18.50	15.84	9.01
Virginia Beach, VA	27.80	28.10	11.94	18.63	16.64	11.46
Washington, DC[2]	33.00	33.80	11.65	20.74	18.52	11.74
Wichita, KS	21.50	22.90	11.47	18.16	14.14	8.87
Wilmington, NC	19.60	19.90	9.73	17.23	14.51	9.14
Winston-Salem, NC	20.60	20.90	15.27	19.53	15.87	9.27
Worcester, MA[3]	31.90	33.00	15.33	24.01	18.22	11.70

Notes: (1) Figures cover the Metropolitan Statistical Area (MSA) except where noted. See Appendix B for areas included; (2) Metropolitan Division; (3) New England City and Town Area; (4) New England City and Town Area Division; Hourly wages for elementary and secondary school teachers were calculated by the editors from annual wage data assuming a 40 hour work week; n/a not available
Source: Bureau of Labor Statistics, May 2014 Metro Area Occupational Employment and Wage Estimates

Means of Transportation to Work: City

City	Car/Truck/Van		Public Transportation			Bicycle	Walked	Other Means	Worked at Home
	Drove Alone	Car-pooled	Bus	Subway	Railroad				
Albuquerque, NM	79.6	9.7	1.7	0.0	0.1	1.3	2.1	1.5	3.8
Anchorage, AK	74.4	12.1	2.2	0.0	0.0	1.2	3.4	2.8	4.0
Ann Arbor, MI	57.4	5.9	10.3	0.1	0.0	5.1	14.4	0.5	6.3
Athens, GA	76.3	9.6	3.1	0.0	0.0	1.7	5.1	1.6	2.5
Atlanta, GA	68.5	7.5	6.2	3.0	0.1	0.9	4.9	1.2	7.7
Austin, TX	73.3	10.3	3.9	0.0	0.1	1.6	2.6	1.5	6.6
Billings, MT	78.5	10.5	1.1	0.0	0.0	1.2	3.6	0.9	4.1
Boise City, ID	78.9	7.6	0.7	0.0	0.0	2.5	3.2	1.4	5.6
Boston, MA	38.7	6.5	13.5	17.6	1.4	1.9	14.8	1.9	3.6
Boulder, CO	51.3	5.2	9.0	0.1	0.0	10.8	10.5	1.6	11.5
Cape Coral, FL	83.2	9.3	0.5	0.0	0.0	0.4	0.8	1.5	4.4
Cedar Rapids, IA	81.9	8.9	1.2	0.0	0.0	0.5	3.0	1.2	3.3
Charleston, SC	76.5	6.5	2.2	0.0	0.0	2.5	5.8	1.5	4.9
Charlotte, NC	76.1	10.2	3.5	0.3	0.1	0.2	2.2	1.4	6.0
Chicago, IL	50.0	8.9	14.2	11.0	1.8	1.4	6.7	1.7	4.3
Clarksville, TN	84.0	9.2	0.9	0.0	0.0	0.1	2.8	1.1	1.9
Colorado Springs, CO	79.5	10.3	0.9	0.0	0.0	0.6	2.1	1.3	5.3
Columbia, MO	76.3	10.4	1.0	0.0	0.0	1.6	6.0	1.0	3.7
Columbus, OH	80.1	8.8	3.2	0.0	0.0	0.8	2.9	1.0	3.3
Dallas, TX	76.6	11.2	3.3	0.3	0.4	0.2	1.9	1.8	4.3
Davenport, IA	85.4	7.5	0.8	0.0	0.0	0.4	2.2	1.2	2.6
Denver, CO	69.6	8.8	6.0	0.6	0.2	2.4	4.8	1.3	6.3
Des Moines, IA	81.3	10.4	1.4	0.0	0.0	0.3	2.8	1.0	2.8
Durham, NC	73.8	11.7	4.2	0.0	0.0	1.1	3.2	1.5	4.4
El Paso, TX	79.2	11.3	2.0	0.0	0.0	0.1	2.0	2.5	2.8
Erie, PA	74.9	10.5	4.5	0.0	0.0	0.4	5.7	1.5	2.3
Eugene, OR	65.7	8.2	3.9	0.0	0.0	8.0	7.0	0.9	6.4
Fargo, ND	80.8	8.4	1.0	0.0	0.0	1.0	4.7	1.3	2.8
Fayetteville, NC	81.7	8.9	0.8	0.1	0.0	0.1	5.0	1.0	2.4
Fort Collins, CO	71.2	7.9	1.3	0.0	0.0	7.4	4.0	1.3	6.8
Fort Wayne, IN	84.5	8.4	0.9	0.0	0.0	0.4	1.3	1.1	3.4
Fort Worth, TX	81.9	11.1	0.7	0.0	0.2	0.2	1.2	1.6	3.2
Gainesville, FL	64.3	8.9	7.9	0.0	0.0	6.6	5.1	2.7	4.5
Grand Rapids, MI	75.2	11.5	3.7	0.0	0.0	0.9	3.2	0.7	4.9
Green Bay, WI	79.3	9.9	1.6	0.0	0.0	0.8	3.4	2.2	2.9
Greensboro, NC	81.3	8.9	1.8	0.0	0.0	0.3	2.1	1.2	4.2
Honolulu, HI	57.5	12.6	12.1	0.0	0.0	1.9	8.9	3.5	3.5
Houston, TX	75.7	12.1	4.2	0.1	0.1	0.6	2.1	1.8	3.4
Huntsville, AL	86.0	6.8	0.4	0.0	0.0	0.2	1.5	2.2	2.8
Indianapolis, IN	81.5	10.0	2.2	0.0	0.0	0.4	2.1	1.0	2.7
Jacksonville, FL	80.3	10.0	1.9	0.0	0.0	0.4	1.2	1.5	4.6
Kansas City, MO	79.5	9.3	3.3	0.0	0.0	0.4	2.2	1.2	4.0
Lafayette, LA	81.2	10.1	0.8	0.0	0.0	1.1	2.4	1.5	2.9
Las Vegas, NV	78.1	11.4	3.9	0.0	0.0	0.4	1.7	1.4	3.0
Lexington, KY	79.2	9.3	1.7	0.0	0.0	1.2	3.8	0.8	4.0
Lincoln, NE	81.1	9.1	1.4	0.0	0.0	1.8	2.7	0.7	3.2
Little Rock, AR	84.8	8.9	1.3	0.0	0.0	0.1	1.3	0.9	2.7
Los Angeles, CA	67.2	9.8	10.2	0.6	0.1	1.1	3.7	1.6	5.7
Louisville, KY	82.1	8.2	3.0	0.0	0.0	0.3	2.3	1.3	2.8
Lubbock, TX	82.9	10.0	0.8	0.0	0.0	0.6	2.2	0.9	2.6
Madison, WI	63.5	8.3	9.0	0.0	0.0	5.2	9.5	0.7	3.8
Manchester, NH	80.6	10.2	1.3	0.1	0.0	0.2	3.4	0.8	3.4
McAllen, TX	74.0	9.7	0.6	0.0	0.0	0.2	0.9	8.0	6.8
Miami, FL	68.9	9.6	10.4	0.7	0.3	0.9	4.7	1.2	3.3

Table continued on next page.

City	Car/Truck/Van		Public Transportation			Bicycle	Walked	Other Means	Worked at Home
	Drove Alone	Car-pooled	Bus	Subway	Railroad				
Midland, TX	83.3	11.2	0.2	0.0	0.0	0.2	1.0	1.7	2.5
Minneapolis, MN	62.2	8.2	11.9	0.4	0.4	3.9	6.5	1.1	5.4
Nashville, TN	80.1	9.9	2.1	0.0	0.1	0.3	2.1	1.1	4.4
New Orleans, LA	70.0	9.7	6.3	0.0	0.0	2.8	5.0	2.4	3.7
New York, NY	22.0	4.7	11.4	42.8	1.7	1.0	10.2	2.3	4.0
Oklahoma City, OK	81.8	11.6	0.5	0.0	0.0	0.2	1.6	0.9	3.3
Omaha, NE	81.2	10.1	1.5	0.0	0.0	0.2	2.7	0.9	3.3
Orlando, FL	79.2	7.9	5.2	0.0	0.0	0.6	2.2	1.5	3.5
Oxnard, CA	72.6	20.5	1.3	0.0	0.1	0.7	1.3	1.0	2.5
Palm Bay, FL	83.6	10.5	0.2	0.1	0.0	0.7	1.2	1.4	2.4
Peoria, IL	81.3	8.8	3.4	0.0	0.0	0.5	2.9	0.8	2.4
Philadelphia, PA	50.1	8.9	18.2	4.9	2.8	2.1	8.5	1.6	3.0
Phoenix, AZ	75.0	12.0	3.5	0.1	0.1	0.7	1.9	2.1	4.7
Pittsburgh, PA	55.7	9.7	16.2	0.3	0.0	1.8	11.1	1.6	3.8
Portland, OR	58.0	9.1	9.4	0.8	0.2	6.1	5.9	2.8	7.6
Providence, RI	59.7	11.7	7.7	0.1	0.9	1.2	11.2	3.1	4.4
Provo, UT	60.2	15.0	1.1	0.1	0.5	3.6	12.7	1.5	5.4
Raleigh, NC	79.3	9.6	2.1	0.0	0.0	0.5	1.9	1.2	5.3
Reno, NV	76.6	10.1	3.2	0.0	0.0	1.0	3.8	2.0	3.2
Richmond, VA	70.1	10.9	5.4	0.1	0.0	2.1	5.2	1.6	4.7
Roanoke, VA	80.4	9.3	3.2	0.1	0.0	0.1	2.8	1.3	2.8
Rochester, MN	74.6	11.0	5.4	0.1	0.0	0.7	4.1	0.9	3.1
Sacramento, CA	71.8	12.5	3.1	0.4	0.4	2.3	3.3	1.5	4.7
Salem, OR	75.5	11.8	1.8	0.0	0.0	1.8	4.7	0.8	3.6
Salt Lake City, UT	67.1	12.8	5.3	0.2	0.3	2.9	4.9	2.7	3.7
San Antonio, TX	79.2	11.0	3.4	0.0	0.0	0.3	1.9	1.0	3.2
San Diego, CA	74.9	9.3	3.7	0.0	0.1	0.9	3.1	1.4	6.5
San Francisco, CA	36.7	7.3	22.4	6.7	1.3	3.7	10.2	4.6	7.1
San Jose, CA	77.2	11.1	2.6	0.2	0.8	0.9	1.6	1.6	4.0
Santa Rosa, CA	78.9	10.0	1.8	0.0	0.0	1.1	3.4	1.0	3.8
Savannah, GA	76.5	10.3	3.4	0.0	0.0	1.7	4.0	0.9	3.3
Seattle, WA	51.0	8.6	18.6	0.4	0.1	3.7	9.3	1.6	6.7
Sioux Falls, SD	84.5	8.1	1.0	0.0	0.0	0.5	2.4	1.3	2.3
Spokane, WA	76.0	9.9	4.0	0.0	0.0	0.6	3.7	0.6	5.2
Springfield, IL	80.1	9.9	1.9	0.2	0.0	0.2	3.4	0.8	3.5
Tallahassee, FL	81.4	7.9	2.4	0.0	0.0	0.9	3.0	1.1	3.2
Tampa, FL	78.7	8.2	2.5	0.0	0.0	1.4	2.4	1.6	5.1
Topeka, KS	80.3	12.3	1.0	0.0	0.0	0.3	2.1	1.2	2.8
Tulsa, OK	81.7	10.6	1.0	0.0	0.0	0.2	1.8	1.3	3.4
Tyler, TX	82.0	10.3	0.3	0.0	0.0	0.2	1.7	2.2	3.2
Virginia Beach, VA	82.0	8.2	0.7	0.1	0.0	0.6	2.5	1.1	4.7
Washington, DC	33.1	5.8	16.5	21.6	0.4	4.0	12.6	1.4	4.5
Wichita, KS	84.8	8.7	0.6	0.0	0.0	0.3	1.4	1.1	3.0
Wilmington, NC	76.4	9.4	1.5	0.0	0.0	1.6	3.4	1.7	6.1
Winston-Salem, NC	81.1	8.2	2.0	0.0	0.0	0.1	2.2	2.1	4.3
Worcester, MA	74.2	11.1	2.6	0.2	0.5	0.3	6.4	1.1	3.5
U.S.	76.4	9.6	2.6	1.8	0.6	0.6	2.8	1.3	4.3

Note: Figures are percentages and cover workers 16 years of age and older
Source: U.S. Census Bureau, 2011-2013 American Community Survey 3-Year Estimates

Means of Transportation to Work: Metro Area

Metro Area	Car/Truck/Van		Public Transportation			Bicycle	Walked	Other Means	Worked at Home
	Drove Alone	Car-pooled	Bus	Subway	Railroad				
Albuquerque, NM	80.0	9.6	1.3	0.0	0.3	1.0	1.9	1.6	4.4
Anchorage, AK	73.8	12.4	2.0	0.0	0.0	1.0	3.1	3.5	4.3
Ann Arbor, MI	73.0	7.7	5.2	0.0	0.0	2.0	6.2	0.7	5.3
Athens, GA	80.1	8.9	1.9	0.0	0.0	1.1	3.4	1.3	3.3
Atlanta, GA	77.9	10.4	2.2	0.7	0.1	0.2	1.4	1.3	5.8
Austin, TX	76.0	10.6	2.2	0.0	0.1	0.9	1.9	1.4	6.9
Billings, MT	78.7	10.8	1.0	0.0	0.0	0.9	3.5	1.0	4.0
Boise City, ID	79.0	8.7	0.4	0.0	0.0	1.1	2.0	1.9	6.8
Boston, MA	68.5	7.5	4.1	5.7	2.0	0.9	5.4	1.3	4.5
Boulder, CO	64.1	8.0	5.5	0.0	0.0	4.4	5.1	1.8	11.1
Cape Coral, FL	77.8	11.1	1.1	0.0	0.0	0.7	1.0	2.6	5.7
Cedar Rapids, IA	82.8	8.2	0.8	0.0	0.0	0.3	2.7	1.1	4.0
Charleston, SC	80.5	9.2	1.5	0.0	0.0	0.9	2.7	0.9	4.3
Charlotte, NC	80.2	10.0	1.6	0.1	0.1	0.1	1.4	1.1	5.3
Chicago, IL	70.9	8.5	4.7	3.6	3.1	0.6	3.1	1.1	4.2
Clarksville, TN	81.2	9.9	0.7	0.0	0.0	0.1	4.1	1.6	2.3
Colorado Springs, CO	77.5	10.4	0.7	0.0	0.0	0.4	4.1	1.1	5.8
Columbia, MO	78.4	10.7	0.8	0.0	0.0	1.1	4.5	1.0	3.5
Columbus, OH	82.5	8.0	1.7	0.0	0.0	0.4	2.2	1.0	4.2
Dallas, TX	80.8	10.2	1.0	0.2	0.3	0.2	1.2	1.4	4.8
Davenport, IA	84.4	8.4	0.9	0.0	0.0	0.3	1.8	1.2	3.0
Denver, CO	75.9	9.0	3.7	0.4	0.2	1.0	2.2	1.2	6.4
Des Moines, IA	84.0	8.5	0.8	0.0	0.0	0.2	1.7	0.8	4.0
Durham, NC	73.6	10.7	4.2	0.0	0.0	1.0	3.2	1.7	5.5
El Paso, TX	78.7	11.3	1.7	0.0	0.0	0.1	2.4	2.8	3.0
Erie, PA	80.1	9.5	1.8	0.0	0.0	0.3	3.8	1.0	3.4
Eugene, OR	70.9	10.0	2.8	0.0	0.0	4.5	4.7	0.8	6.3
Fargo, ND	81.1	8.3	0.8	0.0	0.0	0.7	4.3	1.0	3.7
Fayetteville, NC	83.3	9.2	0.7	0.0	0.0	0.2	3.4	1.2	2.1
Fort Collins, CO	74.3	8.3	1.0	0.0	0.0	4.3	3.0	1.5	7.6
Fort Wayne, IN	84.9	7.8	0.6	0.0	0.0	0.4	1.3	1.0	4.0
Fort Worth, TX	80.8	10.2	1.0	0.2	0.3	0.2	1.2	1.4	4.8
Gainesville, FL	73.4	9.7	4.3	0.0	0.0	3.3	3.1	1.8	4.4
Grand Rapids, MI	82.1	9.3	1.4	0.0	0.0	0.5	2.0	0.7	3.9
Green Bay, WI	82.4	8.2	0.7	0.0	0.0	0.4	2.7	1.2	4.3
Greensboro, NC	82.8	9.5	1.0	0.0	0.0	0.2	1.6	0.9	4.0
Honolulu, HI	64.4	14.8	8.0	0.0	0.0	1.2	5.2	2.9	3.5
Houston, TX	79.9	10.9	2.4	0.0	0.0	0.3	1.4	1.5	3.5
Huntsville, AL	86.9	7.7	0.3	0.1	0.0	0.1	1.1	1.3	2.6
Indianapolis, IN	83.7	8.9	1.1	0.0	0.0	0.3	1.6	0.9	3.6
Jacksonville, FL	80.8	9.8	1.3	0.0	0.0	0.6	1.2	1.4	4.9
Kansas City, MO	83.2	9.0	1.2	0.0	0.0	0.2	1.3	0.9	4.2
Lafayette, LA	82.7	10.8	0.5	0.0	0.0	0.4	1.9	1.6	2.1
Las Vegas, NV	78.9	10.6	3.7	0.0	0.0	0.3	1.8	1.6	2.9
Lexington, KY	80.3	9.7	1.2	0.0	0.0	0.8	3.2	0.7	4.1
Lincoln, NE	81.2	8.9	1.3	0.0	0.0	1.6	2.7	0.7	3.7
Little Rock, AR	85.5	9.0	0.7	0.0	0.0	0.1	1.1	0.9	2.8
Los Angeles, CA	73.9	10.1	5.4	0.3	0.2	0.9	2.7	1.3	5.1
Louisville, KY	83.8	8.5	1.8	0.0	0.0	0.2	1.7	1.0	3.0
Lubbock, TX	82.9	10.0	0.7	0.0	0.0	0.5	2.1	1.0	2.7
Madison, WI	74.0	8.6	4.4	0.0	0.0	2.4	5.3	0.7	4.5
Manchester, NH	81.6	8.4	0.7	0.1	0.1	0.1	2.2	0.8	6.1
McAllen, TX	78.9	11.0	0.2	0.0	0.0	0.1	1.2	4.0	4.5
Miami, FL	77.9	9.6	3.6	0.2	0.2	0.6	1.8	1.3	4.8

Table continued on next page.

| Metro Area | Car/Truck/Van | | Public Transportation | | | Bicycle | Walked | Other Means | Worked at Home |
	Drove Alone	Car-pooled	Bus	Subway	Railroad				
Midland, TX	82.9	10.4	0.2	0.0	0.0	0.1	0.8	2.3	3.3
Minneapolis, MN	78.4	8.4	4.2	0.1	0.2	0.9	2.2	0.8	4.9
Nashville, TN	82.5	9.4	1.1	0.0	0.1	0.2	1.3	0.9	4.5
New Orleans, LA	79.1	10.3	2.4	0.0	0.0	1.1	2.5	2.0	2.6
New York, NY	50.5	6.8	7.9	18.6	3.6	0.6	6.1	1.9	4.1
Oklahoma City, OK	83.1	10.2	0.5	0.0	0.0	0.3	1.6	1.0	3.2
Omaha, NE	83.1	9.5	0.9	0.0	0.0	0.2	1.9	0.9	3.6
Orlando, FL	80.7	9.4	2.0	0.0	0.0	0.5	1.2	1.6	4.6
Oxnard, CA	76.7	12.7	0.9	0.0	0.3	0.7	2.0	1.0	5.6
Palm Bay, FL	82.7	8.5	0.6	0.0	0.0	0.6	1.1	1.9	4.6
Peoria, IL	84.4	8.7	1.2	0.0	0.0	0.3	2.0	0.6	2.7
Philadelphia, PA	73.3	7.8	5.5	1.7	2.3	0.7	3.8	0.9	4.0
Phoenix, AZ	76.5	11.3	2.1	0.0	0.0	0.9	1.5	1.9	5.8
Pittsburgh, PA	77.5	8.9	4.8	0.2	0.0	0.3	3.4	1.2	3.7
Portland, OR	70.9	9.7	4.7	0.6	0.3	2.3	3.6	1.7	6.4
Providence, RI	80.6	8.7	1.8	0.1	0.9	0.3	3.2	1.1	3.3
Provo, UT	72.4	13.5	1.2	0.2	0.3	1.3	4.2	1.1	6.0
Raleigh, NC	80.5	9.4	1.0	0.0	0.0	0.2	1.3	1.2	6.4
Reno, NV	78.1	10.4	2.4	0.0	0.0	0.7	2.7	1.9	3.8
Richmond, VA	81.8	8.9	1.5	0.0	0.0	0.5	1.6	1.1	4.6
Roanoke, VA	83.2	8.6	1.3	0.0	0.0	0.1	2.3	1.1	3.4
Rochester, MN	75.9	11.2	3.7	0.0	0.0	0.5	3.3	0.9	4.4
Sacramento, CA	75.2	11.3	1.9	0.3	0.2	1.9	2.2	1.3	5.8
Salem, OR	74.4	13.9	1.3	0.0	0.0	1.3	4.2	1.0	4.0
Salt Lake City, UT	75.2	12.5	2.5	0.3	0.4	0.8	1.9	1.8	4.7
San Antonio, TX	79.3	11.0	2.3	0.0	0.0	0.2	1.8	1.1	4.3
San Diego, CA	76.1	9.8	2.6	0.0	0.2	0.7	2.9	1.4	6.4
San Francisco, CA	60.6	10.0	7.7	5.9	1.0	1.9	4.4	2.3	6.1
San Jose, CA	76.3	10.4	2.3	0.2	1.1	1.8	2.0	1.5	4.5
Santa Rosa, CA	76.5	9.7	1.7	0.0	0.0	1.0	3.2	1.3	6.6
Savannah, GA	82.1	8.9	1.8	0.0	0.0	0.7	2.2	1.0	3.5
Seattle, WA	70.0	10.2	8.0	0.2	0.4	1.0	3.6	1.2	5.4
Sioux Falls, SD	84.1	8.0	0.7	0.0	0.0	0.4	2.3	1.2	3.4
Spokane, WA	76.7	10.5	2.5	0.0	0.0	0.5	3.0	0.9	5.9
Springfield, IL	81.8	10.1	1.2	0.1	0.0	0.2	2.4	0.9	3.3
Tallahassee, FL	82.1	9.7	1.4	0.0	0.0	0.5	1.9	1.1	3.3
Tampa, FL	80.8	9.0	1.2	0.0	0.0	0.8	1.5	1.4	5.2
Topeka, KS	81.5	11.7	0.6	0.0	0.0	0.2	1.8	0.8	3.3
Tulsa, OK	83.5	9.9	0.6	0.0	0.0	0.2	1.4	1.1	3.4
Tyler, TX	83.0	10.2	0.3	0.0	0.0	0.1	1.4	1.6	3.3
Virginia Beach, VA	81.3	8.4	1.7	0.0	0.0	0.4	2.7	1.2	4.2
Washington, DC	66.0	9.9	5.5	7.9	0.7	0.8	3.3	0.9	4.9
Wichita, KS	85.2	8.4	0.4	0.0	0.0	0.3	1.5	1.0	3.2
Wilmington, NC	77.5	11.1	0.9	0.0	0.0	0.9	2.0	1.6	6.1
Winston-Salem, NC	83.4	8.9	0.8	0.0	0.0	0.1	1.4	1.3	4.0
Worcester, MA	82.1	8.7	0.7	0.2	0.6	0.1	2.9	0.6	4.1
U.S.	76.4	9.6	2.6	1.8	0.6	0.6	2.8	1.3	4.3

Note: Figures are percentages and cover workers 16 years of age and older; (1) Figures cover the Metropolitan Statistical Area—see Appendix B for areas included
Source: U.S. Census Bureau, 2011-2013 American Community Survey 3-Year Estimates

Travel Time to Work: City

City	Less Than 10 Minutes	10 to 19 Minutes	20 to 29 Minutes	30 to 44 Minutes	45 to 59 Minutes	60 to 89 Minutes	90 Minutes or More
Albuquerque, NM	11.5	36.8	28.7	16.5	3.1	2.0	1.4
Anchorage, AK	15.3	44.4	22.1	12.0	2.8	1.4	1.9
Ann Arbor, MI	15.3	45.0	18.4	12.5	5.0	3.3	0.5
Athens, GA	17.8	48.7	16.6	8.2	3.3	3.5	1.9
Atlanta, GA	9.0	31.4	27.6	19.4	6.1	4.3	2.3
Austin, TX	10.6	33.9	24.5	21.4	5.0	3.1	1.5
Billings, MT	19.6	51.2	19.2	5.0	1.8	1.2	2.0
Boise City, ID	17.3	44.9	24.2	9.7	1.3	1.3	1.3
Boston, MA	7.9	22.0	20.2	28.6	10.6	8.7	1.9
Boulder, CO	20.8	42.7	16.2	11.4	4.9	2.5	1.5
Cape Coral, FL	7.2	25.3	19.5	30.1	11.0	4.6	2.3
Cedar Rapids, IA	20.2	47.4	17.1	10.1	2.1	1.8	1.3
Charleston, SC	14.7	35.3	26.5	16.5	3.6	2.4	1.1
Charlotte, NC	10.4	31.0	25.4	23.0	5.5	2.8	2.0
Chicago, IL	5.2	18.1	18.6	29.2	13.6	11.6	3.6
Clarksville, TN	12.7	34.5	27.0	15.7	5.4	4.0	0.7
Colorado Springs, CO	13.3	38.3	27.2	14.5	2.7	2.5	1.5
Columbia, MO	21.6	52.7	12.7	7.7	3.0	1.3	1.1
Columbus, OH	10.0	34.5	31.1	18.6	3.1	1.5	1.2
Dallas, TX	9.0	29.0	22.8	25.2	7.3	4.8	2.0
Davenport, IA	17.5	48.1	22.3	7.0	2.5	1.7	1.0
Denver, CO	9.9	30.2	24.8	23.1	6.5	3.9	1.5
Des Moines, IA	16.0	41.7	26.6	10.9	2.5	1.3	1.0
Durham, NC	11.3	42.0	23.4	15.9	3.3	2.4	1.7
El Paso, TX	8.8	34.0	28.9	21.2	3.6	2.0	1.5
Erie, PA	21.3	50.1	16.4	7.7	2.2	1.6	0.7
Eugene, OR	17.5	50.6	19.9	7.2	1.9	2.1	0.8
Fargo, ND	22.4	56.4	13.7	3.6	1.2	1.9	1.0
Fayetteville, NC	15.1	41.6	23.7	12.3	3.2	2.1	2.0
Fort Collins, CO	17.9	45.2	18.5	10.7	3.2	2.7	1.9
Fort Wayne, IN	11.8	42.6	28.4	11.3	2.7	1.6	1.5
Fort Worth, TX	9.3	29.1	23.1	23.1	8.1	5.6	1.7
Gainesville, FL	18.0	53.7	16.3	8.7	1.8	0.9	0.6
Grand Rapids, MI	16.9	42.2	23.5	9.6	3.4	2.9	1.4
Green Bay, WI	16.2	51.0	17.5	8.8	3.1	2.1	1.2
Greensboro, NC	12.6	45.9	21.9	13.6	2.2	1.8	2.1
Honolulu, HI	8.4	35.9	24.7	22.0	5.0	3.2	0.8
Houston, TX	8.6	27.9	23.5	25.6	7.2	5.5	1.7
Huntsville, AL	15.4	44.0	24.9	12.1	1.6	1.1	1.0
Indianapolis, IN	11.1	30.3	29.4	21.1	4.4	2.6	1.1
Jacksonville, FL	7.8	30.1	30.9	22.3	4.9	2.7	1.3
Kansas City, MO	12.4	34.6	26.9	19.4	3.7	1.8	1.1
Lafayette, LA	18.1	44.6	17.6	11.5	1.8	3.3	3.0
Las Vegas, NV	7.1	26.1	29.2	28.5	4.5	2.8	1.8
Lexington, KY	13.0	43.0	25.0	13.0	2.9	2.0	1.1
Lincoln, NE	16.2	47.2	23.2	8.2	2.5	1.8	1.0
Little Rock, AR	13.6	41.3	30.0	10.4	2.4	1.6	0.8
Los Angeles, CA	7.2	24.3	20.3	26.9	9.5	8.6	3.2
Louisville, KY	10.2	33.1	30.2	19.0	3.8	2.2	1.4
Lubbock, TX	20.4	58.3	12.7	4.9	1.9	1.1	0.7
Madison, WI	15.0	41.4	25.0	12.5	3.1	2.3	0.7
Manchester, NH	13.2	40.6	21.0	13.7	4.8	4.2	2.6
McAllen, TX	17.2	43.8	21.7	10.6	2.5	1.2	3.0
Miami, FL	7.1	26.6	27.0	25.8	7.2	4.4	2.0
Midland, TX	18.3	47.2	16.8	11.4	1.6	2.7	2.0

Table continued on next page.

City	Less Than 10 Minutes	10 to 19 Minutes	20 to 29 Minutes	30 to 44 Minutes	45 to 59 Minutes	60 to 89 Minutes	90 Minutes or More
Minneapolis, MN	8.6	34.9	29.7	19.2	3.9	2.5	1.2
Nashville, TN	8.9	31.0	28.0	23.7	5.1	2.2	1.2
New Orleans, LA	10.5	34.9	25.5	19.3	4.3	3.6	1.8
New York, NY	4.3	13.6	14.5	27.7	15.4	17.9	6.6
Oklahoma City, OK	13.1	36.7	29.0	16.1	2.4	1.4	1.3
Omaha, NE	14.9	42.9	26.5	11.7	1.7	1.3	0.9
Orlando, FL	8.3	34.0	26.1	20.5	5.3	3.1	2.6
Oxnard, CA	9.2	34.1	25.8	21.1	4.5	3.3	2.1
Palm Bay, FL	7.4	26.9	30.4	22.9	5.4	3.9	3.2
Peoria, IL	16.5	46.6	24.2	7.2	2.2	2.4	0.9
Philadelphia, PA	6.3	20.7	20.0	27.2	12.7	9.6	3.5
Phoenix, AZ	9.1	29.2	25.0	25.4	6.6	3.4	1.4
Pittsburgh, PA	10.2	33.2	25.6	21.1	5.6	3.1	1.2
Portland, OR	9.2	31.1	26.3	21.1	6.1	4.2	1.9
Providence, RI	15.5	42.4	18.9	12.4	4.3	4.5	2.0
Provo, UT	23.7	45.0	16.8	7.3	3.2	2.5	1.4
Raleigh, NC	11.9	35.9	27.2	17.6	4.1	2.1	1.2
Reno, NV	14.3	45.4	22.9	9.6	3.2	3.1	1.5
Richmond, VA	12.0	38.4	25.7	15.5	3.9	2.5	2.0
Roanoke, VA	14.3	48.5	21.4	10.7	2.3	1.7	1.1
Rochester, MN	20.6	56.6	11.9	5.6	2.0	2.2	1.1
Sacramento, CA	10.2	35.2	25.2	18.7	4.6	3.0	3.2
Salem, OR	16.6	41.9	19.3	12.2	4.0	4.2	1.8
Salt Lake City, UT	14.5	44.8	21.2	11.9	3.7	2.4	1.5
San Antonio, TX	10.5	31.7	27.6	20.9	4.7	2.8	1.8
San Diego, CA	8.5	34.7	29.0	19.7	4.0	2.5	1.6
San Francisco, CA	4.9	21.5	21.8	28.3	11.2	10.0	2.4
San Jose, CA	6.6	27.6	25.8	24.8	7.5	5.7	1.9
Santa Rosa, CA	14.6	42.8	19.2	12.8	3.9	4.3	2.6
Savannah, GA	14.1	40.0	25.9	13.7	3.7	1.5	1.1
Seattle, WA	8.4	27.4	24.6	25.8	8.5	3.9	1.5
Sioux Falls, SD	16.2	53.8	20.9	4.6	1.7	2.0	0.8
Spokane, WA	16.2	40.0	23.3	14.5	2.7	1.7	1.5
Springfield, IL	20.4	51.3	17.6	6.5	1.5	1.3	1.3
Tallahassee, FL	15.8	43.8	24.2	12.1	1.7	1.4	0.9
Tampa, FL	12.6	33.5	23.9	19.2	6.1	3.2	1.7
Topeka, KS	18.7	55.0	14.6	7.0	1.2	2.3	1.2
Tulsa, OK	16.3	43.7	24.7	10.9	1.9	1.4	1.1
Tyler, TX	21.5	44.2	16.8	11.4	2.5	1.4	2.2
Virginia Beach, VA	11.2	32.5	26.0	21.3	5.4	2.4	1.3
Washington, DC	5.7	19.9	23.0	31.2	11.0	6.8	2.4
Wichita, KS	14.3	47.2	25.3	9.8	1.5	1.1	0.8
Wilmington, NC	18.9	49.5	18.0	7.8	2.7	1.8	1.3
Winston-Salem, NC	14.8	47.3	20.6	10.6	3.0	2.1	1.5
Worcester, MA	12.7	38.8	19.8	15.5	5.8	5.2	2.0
U.S.	13.3	29.7	20.9	20.2	7.7	5.7	2.6

Note: Figures are percentages and include workers 16 years old and over
Source: U.S. Census Bureau, 2011-2013 American Community Survey 3-Year Estimates

Travel Time to Work: Metro Area

Metro Area	Less Than 10 Minutes	10 to 19 Minutes	20 to 29 Minutes	30 to 44 Minutes	45 to 59 Minutes	60 to 89 Minutes	90 Minutes or More
Albuquerque, NM	11.9	32.4	25.7	19.7	5.5	3.1	1.7
Anchorage, AK	15.0	41.1	20.7	11.8	4.5	4.4	2.4
Ann Arbor, MI	12.2	34.8	23.3	18.2	6.6	3.8	1.0
Athens, GA	14.2	40.8	21.2	13.4	4.1	3.7	2.6
Atlanta, GA	8.0	23.5	20.4	24.9	11.8	8.5	2.9
Austin, TX	10.8	28.9	22.2	23.0	8.2	5.0	2.0
Billings, MT	18.2	43.6	22.6	9.0	2.4	1.7	2.5
Boise City, ID	14.4	34.8	26.3	17.6	3.8	2.0	1.2
Boston, MA	10.4	23.8	18.4	24.2	11.1	9.2	2.8
Boulder, CO	15.7	34.5	21.1	16.7	6.3	4.0	1.6
Cape Coral, FL	8.4	27.5	20.7	26.4	9.4	4.9	2.7
Cedar Rapids, IA	20.0	38.7	20.5	13.3	4.0	2.4	1.2
Charleston, SC	10.5	30.1	24.3	22.9	7.7	3.0	1.4
Charlotte, NC	10.6	29.7	22.8	22.9	8.2	4.0	2.0
Chicago, IL	9.0	22.5	18.8	24.8	11.7	9.9	3.2
Clarksville, TN	15.9	32.6	24.3	16.3	5.6	4.0	1.1
Colorado Springs, CO	13.0	35.4	25.9	16.7	4.5	2.9	1.6
Columbia, MO	17.6	47.4	18.1	11.4	3.4	1.1	1.0
Columbus, OH	11.7	30.3	26.7	21.5	5.6	2.9	1.4
Dallas, TX	9.9	26.5	21.2	24.8	9.8	5.9	1.9
Davenport, IA	17.6	38.5	24.3	13.0	3.5	2.0	1.2
Denver, CO	9.1	26.1	23.8	25.4	8.7	5.0	1.9
Des Moines, IA	15.8	36.6	27.6	14.5	3.0	1.5	1.0
Durham, NC	11.1	35.3	24.2	19.0	6.0	2.9	1.4
El Paso, TX	9.6	32.3	27.8	22.0	4.0	2.6	1.6
Erie, PA	19.8	38.9	21.8	13.4	3.2	1.8	1.1
Eugene, OR	17.0	43.5	21.7	11.0	2.8	2.6	1.3
Fargo, ND	21.3	49.4	16.8	7.5	1.9	2.1	1.0
Fayetteville, NC	12.6	35.1	25.4	18.3	4.2	2.5	2.0
Fort Collins, CO	16.0	38.5	19.8	13.8	5.1	4.5	2.3
Fort Wayne, IN	13.1	36.5	29.5	14.0	3.9	1.5	1.5
Fort Worth, TX	9.9	26.5	21.2	24.8	9.8	5.9	1.9
Gainesville, FL	13.4	40.3	23.3	16.1	3.7	2.1	1.0
Grand Rapids, MI	15.5	35.0	24.3	16.1	4.9	2.5	1.6
Green Bay, WI	17.2	40.4	22.5	13.2	3.6	1.9	1.2
Greensboro, NC	12.3	38.4	24.0	16.6	4.5	2.1	2.1
Honolulu, HI	9.9	25.8	20.5	25.5	9.3	6.9	2.3
Houston, TX	8.6	24.9	20.8	25.4	10.6	7.6	2.1
Huntsville, AL	11.9	33.7	26.9	19.8	4.5	2.0	1.3
Indianapolis, IN	11.9	27.5	24.4	23.9	7.5	3.5	1.4
Jacksonville, FL	9.2	27.6	26.3	23.7	7.8	3.9	1.5
Kansas City, MO	13.2	31.3	24.7	21.3	5.9	2.3	1.2
Lafayette, LA	16.6	34.2	19.7	17.1	4.4	3.6	4.4
Las Vegas, NV	8.3	29.0	29.5	24.6	4.3	2.6	1.8
Lexington, KY	14.8	37.4	23.8	16.4	4.2	2.0	1.4
Lincoln, NE	16.2	44.0	24.0	10.2	2.8	1.8	1.0
Little Rock, AR	12.9	33.3	24.1	19.7	6.0	2.8	1.2
Los Angeles, CA	8.1	26.2	20.4	24.8	9.1	8.3	3.1
Louisville, KY	10.6	30.4	27.7	21.3	5.6	2.9	1.4
Lubbock, TX	20.0	52.5	15.6	7.5	2.3	1.2	0.8
Madison, WI	16.2	33.2	24.4	17.5	4.8	2.7	1.1
Manchester, NH	11.8	30.0	21.1	19.1	8.3	6.8	2.8
McAllen, TX	13.7	38.2	24.0	17.3	2.7	1.8	2.2
Miami, FL	7.5	24.9	23.2	27.5	9.0	5.9	2.0
Midland, TX	17.8	44.9	18.2	12.1	2.0	2.7	2.4

Table continued on next page.

Metro Area	Less Than 10 Minutes	10 to 19 Minutes	20 to 29 Minutes	30 to 44 Minutes	45 to 59 Minutes	60 to 89 Minutes	90 Minutes or More
Minneapolis, MN	10.9	28.2	24.9	22.8	7.7	4.1	1.3
Nashville, TN	9.8	27.6	22.7	23.7	9.4	5.0	1.7
New Orleans, LA	11.3	30.8	21.7	20.7	7.4	5.7	2.4
New York, NY	7.8	19.9	16.6	23.6	12.0	14.0	6.1
Oklahoma City, OK	14.1	32.9	25.6	19.1	4.6	2.2	1.6
Omaha, NE	14.5	37.2	26.7	15.7	3.2	1.6	1.0
Orlando, FL	7.2	27.6	23.7	25.4	9.6	4.5	2.0
Oxnard, CA	13.6	31.3	20.8	19.3	6.5	5.5	2.8
Palm Bay, FL	12.5	32.3	24.9	18.8	5.5	3.8	2.3
Peoria, IL	16.6	35.1	26.0	15.4	3.3	2.2	1.3
Philadelphia, PA	10.1	25.5	20.5	23.1	10.4	7.5	2.8
Phoenix, AZ	9.9	27.2	23.4	24.8	8.6	4.6	1.5
Pittsburgh, PA	12.5	27.6	21.5	21.7	9.0	5.8	1.9
Portland, OR	11.5	29.3	23.2	21.6	7.9	4.5	1.9
Providence, RI	13.0	31.8	21.9	18.2	7.0	5.4	2.6
Provo, UT	18.2	35.2	21.0	14.6	6.0	3.5	1.5
Raleigh, NC	10.5	29.4	25.5	22.4	7.3	3.3	1.7
Reno, NV	12.5	39.4	25.4	14.1	3.4	3.0	2.1
Richmond, VA	9.3	31.1	27.0	21.8	5.9	2.9	2.0
Roanoke, VA	13.8	36.0	24.5	16.4	5.1	3.0	1.2
Rochester, MN	19.4	42.6	19.1	11.2	3.6	2.5	1.5
Sacramento, CA	11.7	30.2	22.5	21.8	6.9	3.8	3.1
Salem, OR	17.9	33.6	21.7	15.1	5.3	4.4	2.0
Salt Lake City, UT	10.8	33.3	26.6	20.2	5.1	2.5	1.4
San Antonio, TX	10.9	28.9	25.0	22.2	7.0	3.9	2.0
San Diego, CA	9.1	31.8	26.0	21.1	6.2	3.7	2.0
San Francisco, CA	7.8	24.9	19.0	24.2	11.2	9.9	3.0
San Jose, CA	8.4	29.4	25.5	22.2	7.3	5.4	1.9
Santa Rosa, CA	15.5	33.6	19.7	15.3	5.8	6.5	3.5
Savannah, GA	10.1	30.2	28.1	21.5	6.6	2.3	1.2
Seattle, WA	8.9	25.2	22.1	24.9	9.8	6.7	2.4
Sioux Falls, SD	17.1	45.0	23.9	8.8	2.4	1.8	1.1
Spokane, WA	15.1	34.4	24.1	17.4	4.7	2.5	1.7
Springfield, IL	17.1	41.7	23.6	12.4	2.4	1.7	1.1
Tallahassee, FL	11.9	34.0	25.4	20.4	5.2	2.1	1.0
Tampa, FL	10.6	28.2	22.9	22.6	9.0	4.9	1.7
Topeka, KS	15.9	42.6	20.8	12.3	3.9	3.1	1.4
Tulsa, OK	14.7	34.2	25.7	17.5	4.4	2.2	1.2
Tyler, TX	15.8	35.1	21.1	18.6	3.7	3.0	2.7
Virginia Beach, VA	10.7	32.7	23.9	20.9	6.7	3.5	1.5
Washington, DC	6.3	19.5	17.9	25.7	13.8	12.5	4.4
Wichita, KS	16.7	39.1	25.3	14.2	2.6	1.3	0.8
Wilmington, NC	12.9	40.1	22.5	15.0	4.4	3.0	2.1
Winston-Salem, NC	12.6	35.7	24.3	17.9	4.9	2.6	2.0
Worcester, MA	12.5	26.8	19.7	20.5	9.6	7.9	2.9
U.S.	13.3	29.7	20.9	20.2	7.7	5.7	2.6

Note: Figures are percentages and include workers 16 years old and over; Figures cover the Metropolitan Statistical Area—see Appendix B for areas included
Source: U.S. Census Bureau, 2011-2013 American Community Survey 3-Year Estimates

2012 Presidential Election Results

City	Area Covered	Obama	Romney	Other
Albuquerque, NM	Bernalillo County	55.6	39.3	5.1
Anchorage, AK	Districts 18 – 32	41.5	54.5	4.0
Ann Arbor, MI	Washtenaw County	67.0	31.3	1.7
Athens, GA	Clarke County	63.3	34.4	2.4
Atlanta, GA	Fulton County	64.3	34.5	1.2
Austin, TX	Travis County	60.1	36.2	3.6
Billings, MT	Yellowstone County	38.4	58.9	2.8
Boise City, ID	Ada County	42.7	54.0	3.2
Boston, MA	Suffolk County	77.6	20.8	1.6
Boulder, CO	Boulder County	69.7	27.9	2.4
Cape Coral, FL	Lee County	41.4	57.9	0.7
Cedar Rapids, IA	Linn County	57.9	40.2	1.9
Charleston, SC	Charleston County	50.4	48.0	1.6
Charlotte, NC	Mecklenburg County	60.7	38.2	1.1
Chicago, IL	Cook County	74.0	24.6	1.3
Clarksville, TN	Montgomery County	44.0	54.5	1.5
Colorado Springs, CO	El Paso County	38.1	59.4	2.5
Columbia, MO	Boone County	50.2	47.1	2.7
Columbus, OH	Franklin County	60.1	38.4	1.5
Dallas, TX	Dallas County	57.1	41.7	1.2
Davenport, IA	Scott County	56.1	42.4	1.5
Denver, CO	Denver County	73.5	24.4	2.1
Des Moines, IA	Polk County	56.1	42.0	1.9
Durham, NC	Durham County	75.8	23.0	1.2
El Paso, TX	El Paso County	65.6	33.0	1.3
Erie, PA	Erie County	57.4	41.3	1.3
Eugene, OR	Lane County	59.7	36.4	3.9
Fargo, ND	Cass County	47.0	49.9	3.1
Fayetteville, NC	Cumberland County	59.4	39.7	0.9
Fort Collins, CO	Larimer County	51.4	45.8	2.7
Fort Wayne, IN	Allen County	40.9	57.6	1.5
Fort Worth, TX	Tarrant County	41.4	57.1	1.4
Gainesville, FL	Alachua County	57.9	40.5	1.6
Grand Rapids, MI	Kent County	45.5	53.4	1.0
Green Bay, WI	Brown County	48.6	50.4	1.0
Greensboro, NC	Guilford County	57.7	41.2	1.1
Honolulu, HI	Honolulu County	68.9	29.8	1.3
Houston, TX	Harris County	49.4	49.3	1.3
Huntsville, AL	Madison County	40.0	58.6	1.4
Indianapolis, IN	Marion County	60.2	38.1	1.7
Jacksonville, FL	Duval County	47.8	51.4	0.8
Kansas City, MO	Jackson County	58.7	39.7	1.6
Lafayette, LA	Lafayette Parish	32.2	65.9	1.9
Las Vegas, NV	Clark County	56.4	41.9	1.8
Lexington, KY	Fayette County	49.3	48.3	2.3
Lincoln, NE	Lancaster County	49.0	49.3	1.7
Little Rock, AR	Pulaski County	54.7	43.3	2.0
Los Angeles, CA	Los Angeles County	68.6	29.1	2.3
Louisville, KY	Jefferson County	54.8	43.7	1.4
Lubbock, TX	Lubbock County	28.8	69.6	1.6
Madison, WI	Dane County	71.1	27.6	1.3
Manchester, NH	Hillsborough County	49.7	48.6	1.6
McAllen, TX	Hidalgo County	70.4	28.6	1.0
Miami, FL	Miami-Dade County	61.6	37.9	0.4
Midland, TX	Midland County	18.6	80.1	1.4
Minneapolis, MN	Hennepin County	62.3	35.3	2.4

Table continued on next page.

City	Area Covered	Obama	Romney	Other
Nashville, TN	Davidson County	58.4	39.9	1.7
New Orleans, LA	Orleans Parish	80.3	17.7	2.0
New York, NY	Bronx County	91.4	8.1	0.5
New York, NY	Kings County	82.0	16.9	1.1
New York, NY	New York County	83.7	14.9	1.3
New York, NY	Queens County	79.1	19.9	1.0
New York, NY	Richmond County	50.7	48.1	1.2
Oklahoma City, OK	Oklahoma County	41.7	58.3	0.0
Omaha, NE	Douglas County	47.2	51.4	1.4
Orlando, FL	Orange County	58.7	40.4	0.9
Oxnard, CA	Ventura County	51.7	46.1	2.2
Palm Bay, FL	Brevard County	43.1	55.8	1.1
Peoria, IL	Peoria County	51.3	46.9	1.8
Philadelphia, PA	Philadelphia County	85.3	14.0	0.7
Phoenix, AZ	Maricopa County	43.1	54.9	2.0
Pittsburgh, PA	Allegheny County	56.6	42.2	1.2
Portland, OR	Multnomah County	75.3	20.7	4.0
Providence, RI	Providence County	66.5	31.6	1.9
Provo, UT	Utah County	9.8	88.3	2.0
Raleigh, NC	Wake County	54.9	43.5	1.6
Reno, NV	Washoe County	50.7	47.2	2.1
Richmond, VA	Richmond City	77.0	21.4	1.6
Roanoke, VA	Roanoke City	59.1	37.6	3.3
Rochester, MN	Olmsted County	50.2	47.0	2.7
Sacramento, CA	Sacramento County	57.5	40.0	2.5
Salem, OR	Marion County	46.7	50.2	3.1
Salt Lake City, UT	Salt Lake County	38.8	58.2	3.0
San Antonio, TX	Bexar County	51.6	47.0	1.4
San Diego, CA	San Diego County	51.7	46.2	2.1
San Francisco, CA	San Francisco County	83.4	13.3	3.3
San Jose, CA	Santa Clara County	69.9	27.6	2.5
Santa Rosa, CA	Sonoma County	70.8	26.0	3.2
Savannah, GA	Chatham County	55.5	43.5	1.0
Seattle, WA	King County	68.8	28.8	2.3
Sioux Falls, SD	Minnehaha County	45.3	52.7	2.0
Spokane, WA	Spokane County	45.6	51.6	2.8
Springfield, IL	Sangamon County	44.6	53.3	2.1
Tallahassee, FL	Leon County	61.3	37.6	1.1
Tampa, FL	Hillsborough County	52.8	46.2	1.0
Topeka, KS	Shawnee County	48.0	49.7	2.2
Tulsa, OK	Tulsa County	36.3	63.7	0.0
Tyler, TX	Smith County	26.1	73.0	1.0
Virginia Beach, VA	Virginia Beach City	48.0	50.5	1.6
Washington, DC	District of Columbia	91.1	7.1	1.8
Wichita, KS	Sedgwick County	39.0	58.7	2.3
Wilmington, NC	New Hanover County	47.0	51.5	1.5
Winston-Salem, NC	Forsyth County	53.0	45.8	1.1
Worcester, MA	Worcester County	53.7	44.5	1.8
U.S.	U.S.	51.0	47.2	1.8

Note: Results are percentages and may not add to 100% due to rounding
Source: Dave Leip's Atlas of U.S. Presidential Elections

House Price Index (HPI)

Metro Area[1]	National Ranking[3]	Quarterly Change (%)	One-Year Change (%)	Five-Year Change (%)
Albuquerque, NM	187	0.19	3.13	-4.10
Anchorage, AK	248	-1.16	1.26	7.37
Ann Arbor, MI	75	-0.13	6.59	18.50
Athens, GA	82	-0.57	6.20	-2.89
Atlanta, GA	40	0.55	8.87	2.55
Austin, TX	18	1.20	10.57	27.37
Billings, MT	154	-1.43	3.86	11.67
Boise City, ID	65	0.31	7.45	8.86
Boston, MA[2]	91	1.10	5.92	9.51
Boulder, CO	34	1.67	9.27	19.39
Cape Coral, FL	14	4.12	10.98	30.10
Cedar Rapids, IA	213	-0.19	2.22	2.64
Charleston, SC	60	0.93	7.63	4.92
Charlotte, NC	114	1.14	4.86	2.39
Chicago, IL[2]	99	0.58	5.46	-3.39
Clarksville, TN	n/r	n/a	2.66	1.19
Colorado Springs, CO	147	-0.33	4.01	4.01
Columbia, MO	210	-0.91	2.44	6.37
Columbus, OH	124	-0.12	4.51	4.48
Dallas, TX[2]	32	1.10	9.51	17.75
Davenport, IA	241	-1.18	1.56	4.99
Denver, CO	24	1.73	10.18	24.67
Des Moines, IA	144	1.09	4.06	5.16
Durham, NC	141	-0.26	4.16	3.18
El Paso, TX	222	-0.06	1.99	-0.86
Erie, PA	n/r	n/a	-3.32	3.79
Eugene, OR	135	-0.05	4.33	-0.31
Fargo, ND	70	-0.71	6.81	19.60
Fayetteville, NC	270	-1.16	-0.38	-3.72
Fort Collins, CO	63	0.78	7.53	19.30
Fort Wayne, IN	224	1.30	1.96	3.73
Fort Worth, TX[2]	74	0.28	6.65	11.53
Gainesville, FL	n/r	n/a	4.19	-12.63
Grand Rapids, MI	69	-0.38	6.97	10.95
Green Bay, WI	177	-0.55	3.36	-1.17
Greensboro, NC	233	1.38	1.79	-1.71
Honolulu, HI	97	1.94	5.54	20.20
Houston, TX	13	0.87	11.02	23.21
Huntsville, AL	125	0.99	4.51	-1.26
Indianapolis, IN	155	-0.31	3.85	3.89
Jacksonville, FL	51	1.61	8.13	-0.80
Kansas City, MO	117	0.34	4.69	1.41
Lafayette, LA	153	1.69	3.88	6.75
Las Vegas, NV	6	1.44	12.66	23.87
Lexington, KY	152	-0.24	3.88	1.74
Lincoln, NE	164	0.87	3.67	9.23
Little Rock, AR	225	1.15	1.94	2.82
Los Angeles, CA[2]	56	1.22	7.85	21.79
Louisville, KY	161	0.90	3.72	4.39
Lubbock, TX	143	0.37	4.07	11.65
Madison, WI	192	0.19	2.95	1.61
Manchester, NH	166	-0.16	3.65	-0.77
McAllen, TX	n/r	n/a	8.85	6.64
Miami, FL[2]	7	2.71	12.17	21.88
Midland, TX	n/r	n/a	8.78	40.53

Table continued on next page.

Metro Area[1]	National Ranking[3]	Quarterly Change (%)	One-Year Change (%)	Five-Year Change (%)
Minneapolis, MN	108	-0.26	5.11	5.36
Nashville, TN	58	1.18	7.74	12.51
New Orleans, LA	127	0.86	4.43	6.89
New York, NY[2]	175	0.37	3.47	0.02
Oklahoma City, OK	72	1.86	6.73	10.20
Omaha, NE	180	0.02	3.30	5.32
Orlando, FL	26	3.18	9.84	5.81
Oxnard, CA	77	0.71	6.55	17.96
Palm Bay, FL	43	3.61	8.69	7.88
Peoria, IL	231	0.08	1.83	1.89
Philadelphia, PA[2]	194	0.41	2.90	0.63
Phoenix, AZ	68	1.15	7.05	21.42
Pittsburgh, PA	138	-0.68	4.17	11.17
Portland, OR	39	1.44	9.03	12.08
Providence, RI	129	0.12	4.42	-2.37
Provo, UT	95	2.06	5.66	12.34
Raleigh, NC	93	0.29	5.78	4.43
Reno, NV	4	0.27	13.11	15.60
Richmond, VA	132	0.90	4.36	-3.34
Roanoke, VA	184	1.59	3.27	-5.01
Rochester, MN	169	0.17	3.62	3.05
Sacramento, CA	67	0.91	7.14	21.20
Salem, OR	73	1.24	6.72	-2.31
Salt Lake City, UT	106	0.58	5.11	12.00
San Antonio, TX	96	0.35	5.61	11.65
San Diego, CA	86	0.62	6.05	22.50
San Francisco, CA[2]	11	1.37	11.15	33.82
San Jose, CA	21	1.21	10.28	37.27
Santa Rosa, CA	31	1.35	9.59	24.69
Savannah, GA	236	-1.71	1.64	-6.77
Seattle, WA[2]	49	0.31	8.22	10.57
Sioux Falls, SD	113	1.17	4.90	9.95
Spokane, WA	133	-0.72	4.34	-5.75
Springfield, IL	212	0.44	2.37	6.80
Tallahassee, FL	220	-1.36	2.06	-10.88
Tampa, FL	46	1.25	8.46	8.55
Topeka, KS	253	1.01	1.05	0.94
Tulsa, OK	140	0.12	4.16	3.12
Tyler, TX	n/r	n/a	3.73	5.11
Virginia Beach, VA	123	1.84	4.52	-5.15
Washington, DC[2]	94	1.48	5.71	13.58
Wichita, KS	198	0.19	2.85	1.16
Wilmington, NC	103	-1.02	5.25	-8.59
Winston-Salem, NC	215	0.83	2.17	-4.09
Worcester, MA	157	0.78	3.83	-0.11
U.S.[4]	–	1.35	4.91	11.59

Note: The HPI is a weighted repeat sales index. It measures average price changes in repeat sales or refinancings on the same properties. This information is obtained by reviewing repeat mortgage transactions on single-family properties whose mortgages have been purchased or securitized by Fannie Mae or Freddie Mac in January 1975; (1) figures cover the Metropolitan Statistical Area (MSA) unless noted otherwise—see Appendix B for areas included; (2) Metropolitan Division—see Appendix B for areas included; (3) Rankings are based on annual percentage change, for all MSAs containing at least 15,000 transactions over the last 10 years and ranges from 1 to 275; (4) figures based on a weighted division average; all figures are for the period ended December 31, 2014; n/a not available; n/r not ranked
Source: Federal Housing Finance Agency, House Price Index, February 26, 2015

Homeownership Rate

Metro Area	2007	2008	2009	2010	2011	2012	2013	2014
Albuquerque, NM	70.5	68.2	65.7	65.5	67.1	62.8	65.9	64.4
Anchorage, AK	n/a	n/a	n/a	n/a	n/a	n/a	n/a	n/a
Ann Arbor, MI	n/a	n/a	n/a	n/a	n/a	n/a	n/a	n/a
Athens, GA	n/a	n/a	n/a	n/a	n/a	n/a	n/a	n/a
Atlanta, GA	66.4	67.5	67.7	67.2	65.8	62.1	61.6	61.6
Austin, TX	66.4	65.5	64.0	65.8	58.4	60.1	59.6	61.1
Billings, MT	n/a	n/a	n/a	n/a	n/a	n/a	n/a	n/a
Boise City, ID	n/a	n/a	n/a	n/a	n/a	n/a	n/a	n/a
Boston, MA	64.8	66.2	65.5	66.0	65.5	66.0	66.3	62.8
Boulder, CO	n/a	n/a	n/a	n/a	n/a	n/a	n/a	n/a
Cape Coral, FL	n/a	n/a	n/a	n/a	n/a	n/a	n/a	n/a
Cedar Rapids, IA	n/a	n/a	n/a	n/a	n/a	n/a	n/a	n/a
Charleston, SC	n/a	n/a	n/a	n/a	n/a	n/a	n/a	n/a
Charlotte, NC	66.5	65.4	66.1	66.1	63.6	58.3	58.9	58.1
Chicago, IL	69.0	68.4	69.2	68.2	67.7	67.1	68.2	66.3
Clarksville, TN	n/a	n/a	n/a	n/a	n/a	n/a	n/a	n/a
Colorado Springs, CO	n/a	n/a	n/a	n/a	n/a	n/a	n/a	n/a
Columbia, MO	n/a	n/a	n/a	n/a	n/a	n/a	n/a	n/a
Columbus, OH	66.1	61.2	61.5	62.2	59.7	60.7	60.5	60.0
Dallas, TX	60.9	60.9	61.6	63.8	62.6	61.8	59.9	57.7
Davenport, IA	n/a	n/a	n/a	n/a	n/a	n/a	n/a	n/a
Denver, CO	69.5	66.9	65.3	65.7	63.0	61.8	61.0	61.9
Des Moines, IA	n/a	n/a	n/a	n/a	n/a	n/a	n/a	n/a
Durham, NC	n/a	n/a	n/a	n/a	n/a	n/a	n/a	n/a
El Paso, TX	68.2	64.8	63.8	70.1	72.0	67.4	69.3	66.7
Erie, PA	n/a	n/a	n/a	n/a	n/a	n/a	n/a	n/a
Eugene, OR	n/a	n/a	n/a	n/a	n/a	n/a	n/a	n/a
Fargo, ND	n/a	n/a	n/a	n/a	n/a	n/a	n/a	n/a
Fayetteville, NC	n/a	n/a	n/a	n/a	n/a	n/a	n/a	n/a
Fort Collins, CO	n/a	n/a	n/a	n/a	n/a	n/a	n/a	n/a
Fort Wayne, IN	n/a	n/a	n/a	n/a	n/a	n/a	n/a	n/a
Fort Worth, TX	60.9	60.9	61.6	63.8	62.6	61.8	59.9	57.7
Gainesville, FL	n/a	n/a	n/a	n/a	n/a	n/a	n/a	n/a
Grand Rapids, MI	78.6	77.6	75.6	76.4	76.4	76.9	73.7	71.6
Green Bay, WI	n/a	n/a	n/a	n/a	n/a	n/a	n/a	n/a
Greensboro, NC	62.1	68.0	70.7	68.8	62.7	64.9	67.9	68.1
Honolulu, HI	58.8	57.2	57.6	54.9	54.1	56.1	57.9	58.2
Houston, TX	64.5	64.8	63.6	61.4	61.3	62.1	60.5	60.4
Huntsville, AL	n/a	n/a	n/a	n/a	n/a	n/a	n/a	n/a
Indianapolis, IN	75.9	75.0	71.0	68.8	68.3	67.1	67.5	66.9
Jacksonville, FL	70.9	72.1	72.6	70.0	68.0	66.6	69.9	65.3
Kansas City, MO	71.3	70.2	69.5	68.8	68.5	65.1	65.6	66.1
Lafayette, LA	n/a	n/a	n/a	n/a	n/a	n/a	n/a	n/a
Las Vegas, NV	60.5	60.3	59.0	55.7	52.9	52.6	52.8	53.2
Lexington, KY	n/a	n/a	n/a	n/a	n/a	n/a	n/a	n/a
Lincoln, NE	n/a	n/a	n/a	n/a	n/a	n/a	n/a	n/a
Little Rock, AR	n/a	n/a	n/a	n/a	n/a	n/a	n/a	n/a
Los Angeles, CA	52.3	52.1	50.4	49.7	50.1	49.9	48.7	49.0
Louisville, KY	67.2	67.9	67.7	63.4	61.7	63.3	64.5	68.9
Lubbock, TX	n/a	n/a	n/a	n/a	n/a	n/a	n/a	n/a
Madison, WI	n/a	n/a	n/a	n/a	n/a	n/a	n/a	n/a
Manchester, NH	n/a	n/a	n/a	n/a	n/a	n/a	n/a	n/a
McAllen, TX	n/a	n/a	n/a	n/a	n/a	n/a	n/a	n/a
Miami, FL	66.6	66.0	67.1	63.8	64.2	61.8	60.1	58.8
Midland, TX	n/a	n/a	n/a	n/a	n/a	n/a	n/a	n/a
Minneapolis, MN	70.7	69.9	70.9	71.2	69.1	70.8	71.7	69.7

Table continued on next page.

Metro Area	2007	2008	2009	2010	2011	2012	2013	2014
Nashville, TN	70.0	71.3	71.8	70.4	69.6	64.9	63.9	67.1
New Orleans, LA	67.8	68.0	68.2	66.9	63.9	62.4	61.4	60.6
New York, NY	53.8	52.6	51.7	51.6	50.9	51.5	50.6	50.7
Oklahoma City, OK	68.2	69.5	69.0	70.0	69.6	67.3	67.6	65.7
Omaha, NE	67.9	72.5	73.1	73.2	71.6	72.4	70.6	68.7
Orlando, FL	71.8	70.5	72.4	70.8	68.6	68.0	65.5	62.3
Oxnard, CA	71.4	71.7	73.1	67.1	67.0	66.1	66.8	64.5
Palm Bay, FL	n/a	n/a	n/a	n/a	n/a	n/a	n/a	n/a
Peoria, IL	n/a	n/a	n/a	n/a	n/a	n/a	n/a	n/a
Philadelphia, PA	73.1	71.8	69.7	70.7	69.7	69.5	69.1	67.0
Phoenix, AZ	70.8	70.2	69.8	66.5	63.3	63.1	62.2	61.9
Pittsburgh, PA	73.6	73.2	71.7	70.4	70.3	67.9	68.3	69.1
Portland, OR	61.2	62.6	64.0	63.7	63.7	63.9	60.9	59.8
Providence, RI	64.1	63.9	61.7	61.0	61.3	61.7	60.1	61.6
Provo, UT	n/a	n/a	n/a	n/a	n/a	n/a	n/a	n/a
Raleigh, NC	72.8	70.7	65.7	65.9	66.7	67.7	65.5	65.5
Reno, NV	n/a	n/a	n/a	n/a	n/a	n/a	n/a	n/a
Richmond, VA	72.7	72.4	72.2	68.1	65.2	67.0	65.4	72.6
Roanoke, VA	n/a	n/a	n/a	n/a	n/a	n/a	n/a	n/a
Rochester, MN	n/a	n/a	n/a	n/a	n/a	n/a	n/a	n/a
Sacramento, CA	60.8	61.1	64.3	61.1	57.2	58.6	60.4	60.1
Salem, OR	n/a	n/a	n/a	n/a	n/a	n/a	n/a	n/a
Salt Lake City, UT	71.8	72.0	68.8	65.5	66.4	66.9	66.8	68.2
San Antonio, TX	62.4	66.1	69.8	70.1	66.5	67.5	70.1	70.2
San Diego, CA	59.6	57.1	56.4	54.4	55.2	55.4	55.0	57.4
San Francisco, CA	58.0	56.4	57.3	58.0	56.1	53.2	55.2	54.6
San Jose, CA	57.6	54.6	57.2	58.9	60.4	58.6	56.4	56.4
Santa Rosa, CA	n/a	n/a	n/a	n/a	n/a	n/a	n/a	n/a
Savannah, GA	n/a	n/a	n/a	n/a	n/a	n/a	n/a	n/a
Seattle, WA	62.8	61.3	61.2	60.9	60.7	60.4	61.0	61.3
Sioux Falls, SD	n/a	n/a	n/a	n/a	n/a	n/a	n/a	n/a
Spokane, WA	n/a	n/a	n/a	n/a	n/a	n/a	n/a	n/a
Springfield, IL	n/a	n/a	n/a	n/a	n/a	n/a	n/a	n/a
Tallahassee, FL	n/a	n/a	n/a	n/a	n/a	n/a	n/a	n/a
Tampa, FL	72.9	70.5	68.3	68.3	68.3	67.0	65.3	64.9
Topeka, KS	n/a	n/a	n/a	n/a	n/a	n/a	n/a	n/a
Tulsa, OK	66.7	66.8	67.8	64.2	64.4	66.5	64.1	65.3
Tyler, TX	n/a	n/a	n/a	n/a	n/a	n/a	n/a	n/a
Virginia Beach, VA	66.0	63.9	63.5	61.4	62.3	62.0	63.3	64.1
Washington, DC	69.2	68.1	67.2	67.3	67.6	66.9	66.0	65.0
Wichita, KS	n/a	n/a	n/a	n/a	n/a	n/a	n/a	n/a
Wilmington, NC	n/a	n/a	n/a	n/a	n/a	n/a	n/a	n/a
Winston-Salem, NC	n/a	n/a	n/a	n/a	n/a	n/a	n/a	n/a
Worcester, MA	67.8	68.5	64.4	64.1	65.8	61.9	63.3	62.5
U.S.	68.1	67.8	67.4	66.9	66.1	65.4	65.1	64.5

Note: Figures are percentages and cover the Metropolitan Statistical Area—see Appendix B for areas included
Source: U.S. Census Bureau, Housing Vacancies and Homeownership Annual Statistics: 2014

Year Housing Structure Built: City

City	2010 or Later	2000 -2009	1990 -1999	1980 -1989	1970 -1979	1960 -1969	1950 -1959	1940 -1949	Before 1940	Median Year
Albuquerque, NM	0.6	18.3	15.1	15.1	20.5	10.5	12.4	4.5	3.1	1980
Anchorage, AK	0.6	13.8	11.2	24.4	29.5	12.2	6.3	1.7	0.4	1980
Ann Arbor, MI	0.1	8.0	10.1	10.9	16.4	18.9	13.7	6.9	14.9	1968
Athens, GA	0.8	18.3	19.5	19.3	17.9	10.4	6.2	3.1	4.5	1984
Atlanta, GA	1.2	24.9	10.8	8.4	8.6	13.4	12.3	6.8	13.7	1974
Austin, TX	1.5	22.7	16.2	21.1	19.0	8.1	5.8	2.7	3.0	1985
Billings, MT	1.4	14.7	10.3	11.6	20.1	10.1	16.1	6.7	8.8	1974
Boise City, ID	0.7	12.6	22.2	14.6	22.4	7.7	8.0	4.7	7.0	1980
Boston, MA	0.5	6.8	3.8	5.8	7.2	7.9	7.5	5.8	54.7	<1940
Boulder, CO	1.2	9.8	9.8	16.9	23.6	18.2	9.1	2.1	9.3	1975
Cape Coral, FL	0.5	43.3	14.4	22.7	11.9	5.9	0.8	0.3	0.2	1996
Cedar Rapids, IA	1.0	14.7	14.8	6.4	14.3	13.2	13.1	5.2	17.3	1971
Charleston, SC	1.4	24.7	12.8	13.1	10.9	10.9	7.1	4.3	14.7	1982
Charlotte, NC	1.3	25.2	20.7	15.7	13.6	10.3	7.1	3.0	3.2	1988
Chicago, IL	0.4	8.7	4.4	3.9	6.9	9.8	12.3	8.3	45.3	1946
Clarksville, TN	3.9	28.4	21.2	13.3	13.0	9.1	5.9	2.5	2.7	1992
Colorado Springs, CO	0.9	18.3	15.1	19.6	18.9	11.2	7.6	2.2	6.2	1982
Columbia, MO	1.1	25.9	18.7	13.4	13.5	13.1	5.6	2.6	6.0	1987
Columbus, OH	1.0	12.8	14.9	13.2	15.6	13.3	11.5	5.2	12.5	1975
Dallas, TX	1.1	12.5	9.3	17.4	19.6	14.6	13.4	6.3	5.8	1975
Davenport, IA	0.4	8.7	7.5	6.3	11.9	12.6	14.5	17.2	20.8	1958
Denver, CO	1.3	13.8	6.9	8.5	14.0	11.9	16.0	7.0	20.6	1965
Des Moines, IA	0.9	7.4	7.4	6.8	12.7	10.9	16.9	8.9	28.1	1958
Durham, NC	2.1	20.9	18.9	17.5	11.0	11.2	7.8	4.7	5.9	1985
El Paso, TX	2.8	16.9	12.8	14.8	18.3	12.9	12.7	4.1	4.7	1979
Erie, PA	0.2	3.8	2.9	4.3	9.5	8.0	19.2	11.4	40.7	1948
Eugene, OR	0.9	13.4	17.8	8.7	22.6	13.7	9.3	6.0	7.7	1976
Fargo, ND	2.2	18.5	20.0	14.0	16.7	7.3	8.1	2.2	11.1	1983
Fayetteville, NC	1.9	16.8	17.7	16.9	19.2	14.4	8.6	2.6	1.9	1982
Fort Collins, CO	0.9	20.3	21.7	17.4	20.4	8.0	3.4	2.0	5.8	1986
Fort Wayne, IN	0.3	6.7	14.1	12.5	14.6	16.6	12.3	7.0	15.9	1969
Fort Worth, TX	1.9	27.1	11.2	15.2	10.7	9.3	12.3	5.8	6.5	1984
Gainesville, FL	0.4	15.5	15.9	19.3	22.7	12.6	7.4	2.5	3.8	1981
Grand Rapids, MI	0.3	5.1	6.0	6.7	8.4	10.3	17.3	9.2	36.7	1952
Green Bay, WI	0.6	6.6	10.1	11.6	16.2	12.1	16.1	7.8	18.9	1966
Greensboro, NC	0.8	15.2	18.7	17.1	16.7	12.1	10.0	4.3	5.1	1981
Honolulu, HI	0.9	7.1	8.2	10.6	26.5	22.2	13.4	5.6	5.4	1971
Houston, TX	1.4	15.8	9.3	13.7	24.6	14.5	11.3	5.0	4.5	1976
Huntsville, AL	1.8	15.0	11.6	14.6	16.3	22.7	11.0	3.3	3.7	1976
Indianapolis, IN	0.6	10.6	12.7	11.8	13.4	13.6	13.9	7.1	16.2	1969
Jacksonville, FL	0.9	20.9	14.4	16.2	14.3	11.0	11.7	5.4	5.2	1981
Kansas City, MO	0.5	11.4	8.7	8.5	12.1	14.9	15.2	7.1	21.6	1964
Lafayette, LA	1.4	14.0	11.2	17.8	21.0	15.6	11.0	4.1	4.0	1977
Las Vegas, NV	1.1	24.1	32.4	17.8	11.0	7.3	4.9	1.1	0.4	1992
Lexington, KY	1.2	17.4	16.3	14.2	16.3	13.4	10.0	3.4	7.6	1979
Lincoln, NE	0.9	16.5	15.0	11.0	15.8	10.8	12.0	3.3	14.8	1976
Little Rock, AR	0.8	11.8	14.9	18.8	20.3	12.5	9.3	4.6	7.0	1978
Los Angeles, CA	0.6	6.6	5.7	10.2	13.6	14.2	18.0	10.5	20.6	1961
Louisville, KY	0.4	13.0	10.9	6.7	14.1	13.8	15.3	7.4	18.4	1966
Lubbock, TX	1.9	16.5	11.7	15.0	18.7	15.0	13.4	4.7	3.1	1977
Madison, WI	1.3	17.1	13.3	10.6	15.1	12.1	12.2	4.7	13.6	1975
Manchester, NH	0.2	6.1	6.2	14.4	10.5	7.2	9.0	7.7	38.6	1954
McAllen, TX	2.2	27.3	19.0	20.2	17.1	6.2	5.2	1.1	1.9	1989
Miami, FL	1.2	20.1	5.9	7.7	13.1	10.0	16.1	15.3	10.5	1968
Midland, TX	1.8	11.2	9.5	22.4	17.1	12.3	19.4	4.4	1.8	1977

Table continued on next page.

City	2010 or Later	2000 -2009	1990 -1999	1980 -1989	1970 -1979	1960 -1969	1950 -1959	1940 -1949	Before 1940	Median Year
Minneapolis, MN	0.5	7.4	3.4	6.5	9.3	7.6	9.8	7.8	47.7	1943
Nashville, TN	1.1	15.8	11.9	17.3	16.7	13.8	12.0	5.0	6.4	1978
New Orleans, LA	1.5	8.6	3.9	7.8	14.3	10.6	12.5	10.4	30.3	1957
New York, NY	0.6	6.3	3.6	4.5	7.2	12.5	13.7	10.3	41.3	1948
Oklahoma City, OK	2.1	14.5	9.8	15.5	17.1	14.1	11.3	6.3	9.2	1975
Omaha, NE	0.5	5.7	10.0	10.3	17.6	14.9	12.9	5.5	22.6	1966
Orlando, FL	0.4	24.7	17.4	18.2	13.4	8.1	10.5	3.9	3.5	1986
Oxnard, CA	0.4	14.1	10.3	11.0	21.2	21.0	15.0	4.5	2.6	1973
Palm Bay, FL	0.1	29.4	15.1	37.4	12.4	3.8	1.5	0.1	0.2	1989
Peoria, IL	0.9	9.2	7.5	6.0	15.8	13.3	15.8	9.4	22.0	1962
Philadelphia, PA	0.4	3.6	2.8	4.1	7.0	10.9	16.5	15.5	39.1	1947
Phoenix, AZ	0.7	18.0	16.2	18.8	20.7	9.6	10.6	3.3	2.1	1982
Pittsburgh, PA	0.3	3.8	2.9	4.5	5.8	7.8	13.2	9.1	52.6	<1940
Portland, OR	0.7	12.1	8.2	5.5	11.6	9.5	12.6	9.1	30.7	1958
Providence, RI	0.1	5.8	3.9	5.6	7.9	6.9	9.0	7.9	52.8	<1940
Provo, UT	0.6	13.4	19.4	13.2	19.6	10.5	8.5	5.9	9.0	1978
Raleigh, NC	1.7	28.6	21.4	18.4	10.9	8.4	5.4	2.3	3.0	1991
Reno, NV	1.2	22.6	17.6	14.2	20.4	9.9	6.3	3.3	4.4	1984
Richmond, VA	0.8	5.8	4.7	6.1	11.7	12.8	16.1	9.3	32.8	1955
Roanoke, VA	0.1	6.2	5.7	6.8	13.4	13.0	19.5	11.5	23.8	1958
Rochester, MN	1.3	19.9	15.1	13.4	13.7	13.2	10.9	4.4	8.1	1980
Sacramento, CA	0.2	16.3	7.6	14.8	15.6	12.3	13.2	8.5	11.5	1973
Salem, OR	0.4	14.5	16.4	11.9	21.9	10.1	9.5	6.1	9.1	1977
Salt Lake City, UT	0.6	6.3	5.6	8.0	13.6	9.4	15.1	10.4	31.2	1956
San Antonio, TX	1.3	18.6	12.6	17.4	17.5	11.3	10.3	5.5	5.6	1980
San Diego, CA	0.6	10.5	11.4	18.0	22.0	13.0	12.7	4.9	6.9	1976
San Francisco, CA	0.4	7.3	4.1	5.0	7.1	8.1	9.3	10.2	48.5	1942
San Jose, CA	0.5	10.3	10.1	13.7	25.2	19.3	12.4	3.2	5.3	1974
Santa Rosa, CA	0.3	14.4	13.9	17.3	23.2	12.4	7.4	5.1	5.8	1978
Savannah, GA	1.9	10.6	7.6	10.4	15.5	13.2	15.6	7.5	17.7	1967
Seattle, WA	1.3	15.3	8.0	7.6	9.0	9.2	11.4	9.5	28.6	1961
Sioux Falls, SD	3.1	21.9	15.4	11.5	16.0	8.5	9.0	5.1	9.5	1982
Spokane, WA	0.6	8.7	8.3	8.5	15.0	6.7	15.2	9.8	27.2	1959
Springfield, IL	0.2	9.5	13.1	10.6	14.7	14.8	11.3	7.6	18.2	1969
Tallahassee, FL	1.0	20.3	17.9	18.2	18.5	10.8	8.0	3.5	1.8	1984
Tampa, FL	1.4	19.9	10.9	13.0	11.4	12.6	15.9	6.0	8.8	1976
Topeka, KS	0.5	8.4	8.4	10.8	14.0	17.6	15.6	7.1	17.8	1965
Tulsa, OK	0.7	6.4	8.0	14.3	21.9	14.4	16.9	7.8	9.7	1971
Tyler, TX	1.7	17.7	9.7	15.8	17.6	12.4	14.5	6.4	4.2	1977
Virginia Beach, VA	0.9	11.5	14.2	28.6	22.2	13.2	6.5	1.6	1.2	1982
Washington, DC	1.0	8.7	3.1	4.6	8.2	12.4	13.4	13.0	35.7	1951
Wichita, KS	0.6	11.5	12.4	12.1	13.8	8.8	20.8	8.9	11.1	1970
Wilmington, NC	0.7	16.0	22.9	15.5	10.7	9.3	8.1	6.2	10.5	1983
Winston-Salem, NC	0.7	14.7	11.4	12.6	15.5	15.7	14.3	6.0	9.1	1973
Worcester, MA	0.6	4.8	4.5	9.1	9.0	6.3	10.0	8.3	47.4	1943
U.S.	0.9	15.0	13.9	13.8	15.8	11.0	10.9	5.4	13.3	1976

Note: Figures are percentages except for Median Year
Source: U.S. Census Bureau, 2011-2013 American Community Survey 3-Year Estimates

Year Housing Structure Built: Metro Area

Metro Area	2010 or Later	2000 -2009	1990 -1999	1980 -1989	1970 -1979	1960 -1969	1950 -1959	1940 -1949	Before 1940	Median Year
Albuquerque, NM	0.7	19.4	17.8	17.2	18.6	9.4	9.9	3.7	3.3	1983
Anchorage, AK	1.0	19.1	12.8	24.7	25.5	9.9	5.0	1.5	0.5	1983
Ann Arbor, MI	0.4	14.4	16.3	10.9	16.8	12.8	11.1	5.2	12.0	1975
Athens, GA	0.8	20.2	20.2	18.7	17.4	9.6	5.5	2.7	5.0	1985
Atlanta, GA	0.9	26.9	22.6	18.2	13.1	8.0	5.1	2.1	3.3	1990
Austin, TX	2.4	30.7	19.4	19.1	14.3	5.5	4.1	2.0	2.6	1991
Billings, MT	1.5	16.1	11.2	12.1	21.1	8.3	12.9	5.7	11.1	1976
Boise City, ID	1.2	27.9	22.2	10.4	18.1	5.4	5.1	3.7	5.9	1991
Boston, MA	0.6	8.1	7.2	10.6	11.0	10.4	11.2	5.7	35.2	1958
Boulder, CO	0.8	13.9	19.9	17.0	21.9	11.8	5.3	1.7	7.7	1981
Cape Coral, FL	0.5	34.4	17.9	21.8	15.8	5.5	2.8	0.6	0.7	1992
Cedar Rapids, IA	1.2	16.2	15.8	6.7	14.3	11.4	11.0	4.4	19.0	1973
Charleston, SC	1.7	26.5	15.9	17.4	15.6	9.3	6.0	2.8	4.7	1987
Charlotte, NC	1.4	26.2	20.4	14.9	12.6	9.2	7.2	3.5	4.6	1989
Chicago, IL	0.4	11.9	10.9	8.9	14.0	12.0	13.5	5.9	22.4	1967
Clarksville, TN	3.0	23.7	21.3	12.9	14.7	10.2	6.9	2.6	4.8	1988
Colorado Springs, CO	1.3	21.1	16.6	18.5	17.9	10.1	6.9	1.9	5.7	1984
Columbia, MO	1.0	23.2	19.2	14.2	17.8	12.2	4.9	2.2	5.3	1985
Columbus, OH	1.0	15.5	16.6	12.1	14.5	12.2	10.8	4.3	12.9	1977
Dallas, TX	1.7	23.2	16.6	19.6	15.5	9.5	7.7	3.1	3.0	1986
Davenport, IA	0.8	8.2	7.8	6.8	14.5	13.9	14.1	10.8	23.2	1961
Denver, CO	0.9	18.6	15.7	15.2	19.0	10.4	10.0	3.1	7.2	1980
Des Moines, IA	2.2	18.6	14.8	8.9	14.3	9.4	10.1	4.9	16.8	1976
Durham, NC	1.9	20.5	19.7	17.5	13.1	10.7	7.1	4.0	5.5	1985
El Paso, TX	3.1	18.6	14.1	15.8	17.6	11.6	11.2	3.7	4.3	1981
Erie, PA	0.4	7.1	9.0	8.6	14.4	9.8	15.3	8.1	27.3	1960
Eugene, OR	0.8	12.5	16.0	9.5	23.0	14.2	9.4	7.1	7.6	1975
Fargo, ND	2.4	20.7	16.5	11.4	18.1	7.6	9.2	2.8	11.2	1981
Fayetteville, NC	3.0	20.9	20.2	16.4	16.9	11.4	6.9	2.2	2.1	1986
Fort Collins, CO	1.5	20.3	20.7	14.3	21.6	8.3	4.0	2.2	7.3	1985
Fort Wayne, IN	0.9	11.4	14.9	11.5	14.7	13.8	10.8	5.9	16.0	1972
Fort Worth, TX	1.7	23.2	16.6	19.6	15.5	9.5	7.7	3.1	3.0	1986
Gainesville, FL	0.7	19.4	20.9	20.6	18.8	9.2	5.7	1.7	3.1	1986
Grand Rapids, MI	0.6	13.8	16.3	12.3	14.2	9.9	11.4	5.1	16.3	1975
Green Bay, WI	1.3	16.1	16.5	11.4	15.7	9.7	9.7	4.9	14.7	1977
Greensboro, NC	1.0	16.2	19.1	15.3	15.7	11.5	10.2	5.0	6.1	1981
Honolulu, HI	1.2	11.1	12.6	12.8	24.9	19.0	11.1	4.1	3.3	1975
Houston, TX	2.3	25.3	14.6	16.1	19.7	9.4	6.8	3.0	2.7	1985
Huntsville, AL	2.6	21.8	19.8	15.7	12.8	14.2	7.4	2.4	3.4	1986
Indianapolis, IN	1.3	17.3	16.7	10.7	13.3	11.6	11.1	5.1	12.9	1977
Jacksonville, FL	1.1	24.4	16.9	17.9	13.8	8.9	8.8	4.0	4.1	1986
Kansas City, MO	0.6	15.1	14.4	12.4	15.7	12.5	12.5	4.8	11.9	1975
Lafayette, LA	2.5	17.9	13.9	16.7	18.2	11.7	9.2	4.3	5.7	1981
Las Vegas, NV	1.3	34.3	27.9	15.3	12.5	5.2	2.6	0.7	0.3	1995
Lexington, KY	1.2	18.9	17.7	13.9	16.0	11.5	8.8	3.3	8.8	1981
Lincoln, NE	1.1	16.8	15.0	10.6	16.1	10.3	11.1	3.3	15.7	1976
Little Rock, AR	2.3	19.6	19.0	16.8	17.7	10.2	7.2	3.4	3.9	1985
Los Angeles, CA	0.5	7.0	7.6	12.6	16.5	15.9	19.0	8.8	12.2	1966
Louisville, KY	0.7	15.0	13.9	9.3	16.3	12.4	12.6	6.3	13.4	1973
Lubbock, TX	1.8	16.4	12.4	15.1	17.8	14.1	13.5	5.2	3.7	1978
Madison, WI	1.1	18.0	15.6	11.0	16.3	10.0	9.3	3.8	14.9	1977
Manchester, NH	0.4	10.4	9.9	20.9	15.8	9.6	7.2	3.8	22.0	1975
McAllen, TX	2.4	31.3	23.6	18.4	12.6	4.8	3.6	1.6	1.8	1993
Miami, FL	0.5	14.1	14.8	20.0	21.9	12.8	10.4	3.2	2.3	1980
Midland, TX	2.6	12.4	12.1	22.5	16.0	11.2	16.7	4.2	2.2	1980

Table continued on next page.

Metro Area	2010 or Later	2000 -2009	1990 -1999	1980 -1989	1970 -1979	1960 -1969	1950 -1959	1940 -1949	Before 1940	Median Year
Minneapolis, MN	0.7	15.2	14.7	14.7	15.5	10.0	10.2	4.1	14.9	1977
Nashville, TN	1.6	22.0	18.9	16.1	14.9	10.3	7.7	3.3	5.2	1985
New Orleans, LA	1.2	13.1	9.6	14.6	19.4	13.4	10.1	5.9	12.8	1974
New York, NY	0.6	7.4	6.0	7.8	9.9	13.8	16.5	9.3	28.7	1957
Oklahoma City, OK	2.1	16.3	11.0	15.8	18.4	13.3	10.6	5.5	7.0	1977
Omaha, NE	1.5	15.4	12.5	10.3	15.6	12.2	9.7	4.2	18.5	1973
Orlando, FL	0.9	26.8	21.3	22.0	13.8	6.5	5.8	1.4	1.7	1990
Oxnard, CA	0.4	11.3	10.8	16.7	23.2	20.6	10.5	2.9	3.6	1975
Palm Bay, FL	0.6	20.2	16.3	25.7	13.8	15.4	6.5	0.8	0.9	1985
Peoria, IL	0.7	10.0	8.4	5.8	17.8	12.8	16.2	8.8	19.6	1964
Philadelphia, PA	0.6	8.5	9.0	10.1	12.4	12.4	16.0	9.1	21.8	1962
Phoenix, AZ	0.9	28.1	20.8	18.2	17.2	6.8	5.4	1.5	1.0	1990
Pittsburgh, PA	0.5	6.6	7.7	7.5	12.1	11.1	16.8	9.6	28.1	1957
Portland, OR	0.9	16.5	18.8	11.3	18.2	9.1	7.4	5.1	12.6	1979
Providence, RI	0.4	6.8	7.9	10.4	12.3	10.5	11.7	6.8	33.3	1958
Provo, UT	2.1	30.2	21.1	9.4	16.1	5.4	6.2	3.6	5.9	1992
Raleigh, NC	2.0	30.3	25.6	16.6	10.5	6.4	4.1	1.8	2.8	1993
Reno, NV	1.0	23.9	19.4	15.5	20.5	9.0	5.1	2.4	3.1	1986
Richmond, VA	1.3	16.0	15.2	16.0	16.8	10.9	9.9	4.3	9.6	1979
Roanoke, VA	0.6	12.3	12.7	13.3	17.6	12.3	12.4	6.1	12.7	1974
Rochester, MN	1.1	19.2	14.7	11.6	13.9	10.9	8.8	4.0	15.9	1977
Sacramento, CA	0.6	18.9	14.2	16.5	19.7	11.1	10.7	3.9	4.5	1980
Salem, OR	1.0	14.6	18.7	10.2	23.5	10.2	7.7	4.7	9.3	1978
Salt Lake City, UT	1.5	17.0	16.4	13.3	20.2	9.0	9.9	4.0	8.6	1979
San Antonio, TX	2.2	24.1	14.7	16.1	15.9	9.5	8.1	4.5	4.9	1984
San Diego, CA	0.6	11.9	12.3	20.0	23.7	12.6	10.8	3.8	4.3	1978
San Francisco, CA	0.5	8.4	7.9	10.7	15.5	13.3	14.6	8.5	20.5	1965
San Jose, CA	0.6	9.7	10.4	12.9	22.7	18.7	15.7	4.2	5.1	1973
Santa Rosa, CA	0.4	11.2	13.5	18.6	21.7	11.3	8.8	5.3	9.3	1977
Savannah, GA	1.7	23.8	15.8	14.8	12.8	8.6	8.9	4.7	8.8	1984
Seattle, WA	1.3	16.9	15.9	15.4	15.2	11.5	7.9	4.8	11.0	1980
Sioux Falls, SD	2.7	22.3	15.9	10.1	15.1	7.7	8.3	4.8	13.1	1981
Spokane, WA	1.0	15.4	14.2	10.7	19.2	7.1	11.1	6.2	15.2	1975
Springfield, IL	0.6	10.8	13.7	10.0	16.2	13.3	11.8	7.0	16.5	1971
Tallahassee, FL	0.9	20.2	21.6	20.1	16.7	8.4	6.5	2.9	2.7	1986
Tampa, FL	1.0	17.3	14.3	21.3	21.7	11.0	8.7	2.0	2.8	1982
Topeka, KS	0.5	10.3	11.3	11.0	16.5	15.3	11.6	5.6	17.8	1970
Tulsa, OK	1.3	15.3	12.1	15.1	20.5	11.2	11.3	5.7	7.6	1977
Tyler, TX	1.7	20.1	15.2	18.0	17.6	10.2	9.3	4.3	3.6	1983
Virginia Beach, VA	1.2	13.9	14.7	19.4	16.3	12.7	10.6	5.4	5.8	1980
Washington, DC	1.2	15.7	14.3	16.6	15.1	12.9	10.0	5.5	8.7	1979
Wichita, KS	0.9	12.8	13.9	12.2	14.1	8.3	18.4	7.2	12.3	1973
Wilmington, NC	1.1	22.4	25.1	16.3	12.2	7.4	5.8	3.8	5.8	1989
Winston-Salem, NC	0.8	16.8	17.4	14.7	15.9	12.5	10.2	5.0	6.7	1980
Worcester, MA	0.6	9.0	9.1	12.6	11.4	8.4	10.6	6.0	32.2	1961
U.S.	0.9	15.0	13.9	13.8	15.8	11.0	10.9	5.4	13.3	1976

Note: Figures are percentages except for Median Year; Figures cover the Metropolitan Statistical Area—see Appendix B for areas included
Source: U.S. Census Bureau, 2011-2013 American Community Survey 3-Year Estimates

Highest Level of Education: City

City	Less than H.S.	H.S. Diploma	Some College, No Deg.	Associate Degree	Bachelors Degree	Masters Degree	Profess. School Degree	Doctorate Degree
Albuquerque, NM	10.8	23.3	24.4	8.0	18.7	10.2	2.3	2.3
Anchorage, AK	7.5	24.5	27.3	8.3	20.3	8.4	2.4	1.3
Ann Arbor, MI	3.7	8.5	12.6	4.8	28.7	24.4	6.4	10.9
Athens, GA	13.6	22.6	20.2	4.8	19.0	11.9	2.5	5.3
Atlanta, GA	11.1	19.5	16.6	4.6	28.3	12.9	4.8	2.2
Austin, TX	12.9	16.4	19.5	5.3	29.3	11.5	2.8	2.2
Billings, MT	7.4	29.5	26.8	7.3	20.1	5.8	2.0	1.1
Boise City, ID	5.9	20.5	25.8	9.0	24.7	10.2	2.4	1.6
Boston, MA	15.2	22.2	14.4	4.4	24.0	12.6	4.3	2.9
Boulder, CO	3.5	7.2	11.8	3.9	35.3	23.7	5.1	9.6
Cape Coral, FL	9.0	38.9	23.6	7.9	13.5	5.2	1.0	0.8
Cedar Rapids, IA	7.1	27.5	24.1	10.9	20.4	7.0	1.7	1.1
Charleston, SC	6.9	18.5	18.4	7.4	30.4	11.1	4.4	2.9
Charlotte, NC	11.4	19.8	21.1	7.2	27.9	9.5	2.2	1.0
Chicago, IL	18.6	23.3	18.1	5.6	20.7	9.4	2.9	1.4
Clarksville, TN	8.6	29.0	28.9	9.4	16.6	6.0	0.8	0.8
Colorado Springs, CO	6.7	20.9	25.0	10.7	22.3	11.1	1.9	1.3
Columbia, MO	6.4	14.5	18.3	5.7	30.8	14.0	4.0	6.3
Columbus, OH	11.8	26.4	21.9	6.9	21.7	8.1	1.8	1.4
Dallas, TX	25.8	22.0	18.1	4.6	18.5	7.3	2.7	1.1
Davenport, IA	10.0	30.1	21.4	12.1	18.1	6.1	1.4	0.7
Denver, CO	13.9	18.2	18.4	5.3	26.9	11.5	3.9	1.9
Des Moines, IA	12.3	31.1	22.2	9.2	17.8	5.2	1.4	0.8
Durham, NC	13.2	16.3	18.6	5.7	24.7	12.8	3.7	4.9
El Paso, TX	22.7	23.5	23.4	7.5	15.6	5.5	1.2	0.7
Erie, PA	13.6	41.7	16.0	7.1	14.7	5.0	0.8	1.1
Eugene, OR	6.1	18.8	29.0	7.8	22.0	10.6	2.5	3.2
Fargo, ND	5.5	19.8	23.3	12.8	26.0	7.8	2.7	2.2
Fayetteville, NC	9.3	24.8	30.8	10.9	16.0	6.0	1.2	1.1
Fort Collins, CO	4.7	14.0	20.5	9.1	31.8	13.7	2.4	3.8
Fort Wayne, IN	12.2	28.5	24.7	9.4	16.9	6.2	1.4	0.8
Fort Worth, TX	20.2	24.4	23.1	5.7	17.7	6.7	1.2	0.9
Gainesville, FL	8.3	20.6	18.1	10.4	21.8	11.2	3.7	5.8
Grand Rapids, MI	15.4	24.0	23.4	7.2	19.4	7.7	1.7	1.2
Green Bay, WI	13.1	33.5	19.6	10.6	17.2	4.3	1.1	0.6
Greensboro, NC	11.7	22.7	22.3	6.5	23.8	9.5	1.9	1.5
Honolulu, HI	12.0	24.6	19.3	9.0	22.4	8.2	2.6	1.9
Houston, TX	23.8	22.6	19.0	4.6	18.6	7.4	2.4	1.5
Huntsville, AL	9.9	20.5	23.0	7.8	24.1	11.0	1.9	1.9
Indianapolis, IN	15.2	29.2	21.2	7.1	17.9	6.7	1.8	1.0
Jacksonville, FL	12.1	29.4	23.3	9.6	17.8	5.5	1.5	0.8
Kansas City, MO	12.0	26.0	23.3	6.8	20.0	8.4	2.3	1.1
Lafayette, LA	13.6	25.2	22.9	5.4	21.6	7.0	2.3	1.8
Las Vegas, NV	17.0	29.2	24.4	7.7	14.2	5.2	1.6	0.7
Lexington, KY	10.9	20.6	20.5	7.4	23.3	10.8	3.5	3.1
Lincoln, NE	6.9	22.2	23.3	10.9	23.8	8.3	1.9	2.7
Little Rock, AR	9.4	25.2	21.7	5.2	23.7	8.9	3.9	2.0
Los Angeles, CA	25.2	19.6	18.0	5.9	20.9	6.6	2.6	1.2
Louisville, KY	13.1	29.9	22.8	7.3	15.7	8.0	2.0	1.3
Lubbock, TX	14.6	24.5	25.9	6.2	18.3	6.7	2.1	1.7
Madison, WI	5.1	15.9	17.2	8.1	29.4	15.5	3.9	5.0
Manchester, NH	12.9	32.7	18.8	9.3	18.4	6.1	0.8	0.9
McAllen, TX	27.3	19.7	20.6	5.9	18.5	5.0	2.3	0.7
Miami, FL	28.0	29.9	11.9	6.9	14.4	5.1	3.0	0.8
Midland, TX	18.3	22.9	27.4	6.0	18.2	5.4	1.3	0.4

Table continued on next page.

City	Less than H.S.	H.S. Diploma	Some College, No Deg.	Associate Degree	Bachelors Degree	Masters Degree	Profess. School Degree	Doctorate Degree
Minneapolis, MN	11.4	16.9	18.2	6.6	29.3	11.7	3.8	2.3
Nashville, TN	13.3	24.6	20.6	5.8	22.9	8.4	2.5	2.0
New Orleans, LA	15.5	23.5	22.3	4.4	19.5	8.4	4.2	2.2
New York, NY	20.1	24.4	14.4	6.3	20.6	9.9	3.0	1.4
Oklahoma City, OK	15.6	25.2	24.4	6.5	18.9	6.4	2.0	1.0
Omaha, NE	12.4	23.3	24.2	6.8	21.6	7.7	2.6	1.4
Orlando, FL	11.1	25.1	19.0	11.1	22.5	7.9	2.2	1.1
Oxnard, CA	34.7	21.2	20.4	7.8	11.7	3.1	0.7	0.4
Palm Bay, FL	13.7	32.3	24.2	12.0	12.0	5.1	0.4	0.3
Peoria, IL	11.8	26.9	19.8	9.2	19.9	8.6	2.7	1.2
Philadelphia, PA	18.6	34.2	17.8	5.1	14.3	6.6	2.2	1.3
Phoenix, AZ	19.4	23.7	22.8	7.6	17.2	6.5	1.9	0.9
Pittsburgh, PA	8.8	29.2	16.7	8.0	18.8	11.3	3.5	3.7
Portland, OR	9.1	17.2	22.3	7.0	26.4	12.3	3.6	2.1
Providence, RI	26.7	22.5	16.7	5.3	15.2	7.8	3.0	2.9
Provo, UT	10.2	13.1	29.7	8.3	26.4	8.3	1.5	2.6
Raleigh, NC	10.5	16.3	19.1	7.1	31.1	11.1	2.7	2.0
Reno, NV	14.5	22.8	26.2	6.8	18.6	6.8	2.4	1.9
Richmond, VA	18.2	23.2	18.8	5.0	21.2	9.3	2.8	1.4
Roanoke, VA	17.7	30.2	21.7	7.4	14.3	6.1	1.9	0.8
Rochester, MN	6.3	21.1	19.8	11.0	24.9	9.7	4.6	2.7
Sacramento, CA	16.9	21.1	24.3	8.5	18.5	6.6	2.7	1.3
Salem, OR	13.4	25.2	27.2	7.6	16.2	7.3	1.9	1.2
Salt Lake City, UT	13.5	16.9	20.6	6.2	24.5	10.3	4.2	3.8
San Antonio, TX	18.8	25.6	23.3	7.1	16.2	6.3	1.7	0.9
San Diego, CA	12.7	16.6	21.1	7.6	25.0	10.6	3.4	3.0
San Francisco, CA	13.5	13.1	15.2	5.3	32.1	13.5	4.9	2.4
San Jose, CA	17.5	18.3	18.9	7.7	23.3	10.7	1.6	1.9
Santa Rosa, CA	14.3	20.6	25.9	9.2	18.9	6.8	3.0	1.2
Savannah, GA	14.0	29.5	24.0	5.1	17.5	6.7	1.9	1.4
Seattle, WA	6.8	11.7	17.0	6.8	34.5	15.0	4.9	3.4
Sioux Falls, SD	9.1	27.5	20.4	10.5	21.8	7.4	1.9	1.4
Spokane, WA	9.2	26.1	25.8	10.4	17.6	7.4	2.3	1.3
Springfield, IL	9.1	26.6	22.4	7.6	20.3	10.0	2.8	1.2
Tallahassee, FL	7.7	16.4	19.2	9.1	26.0	13.8	3.9	3.9
Tampa, FL	13.5	26.6	18.2	7.8	20.7	8.4	3.2	1.7
Topeka, KS	12.1	32.3	22.7	6.5	16.7	6.7	2.0	1.0
Tulsa, OK	13.1	25.3	23.4	7.8	20.2	6.6	2.5	1.1
Tyler, TX	15.6	21.1	24.7	9.1	18.6	6.9	2.7	1.3
Virginia Beach, VA	6.0	22.9	27.4	10.0	21.9	8.8	2.0	1.0
Washington, DC	11.4	18.2	13.9	3.0	23.0	18.1	8.5	3.9
Wichita, KS	12.4	26.8	26.2	6.3	19.0	7.1	1.4	0.9
Wilmington, NC	10.7	19.3	20.0	9.9	25.9	9.8	2.4	2.1
Winston-Salem, NC	15.6	24.4	20.6	6.5	20.3	8.1	2.5	2.0
Worcester, MA	15.3	29.7	16.9	8.3	18.4	8.1	1.7	1.6
U.S.	13.7	28.0	21.2	7.9	18.2	7.7	1.9	1.3

Note: Figures cover persons age 25 and over
Source: U.S. Census Bureau, 2011-2013 American Community Survey 3-Year Estimates

Highest Level of Education: Metro Area

Metro Area	Less than H.S.	H.S. Diploma	Some College, No Deg.	Associate Degree	Bachelors Degree	Masters Degree	Profess. School Degree	Doctorate Degree
Albuquerque, NM	12.5	25.1	24.2	8.1	16.9	9.2	2.0	2.0
Anchorage, AK	7.5	26.2	28.1	8.4	18.8	7.6	2.2	1.2
Ann Arbor, MI	5.8	16.2	19.9	6.7	24.9	16.3	4.4	5.8
Athens, GA	14.1	26.5	20.6	5.2	17.1	10.4	2.5	3.7
Atlanta, GA	12.2	24.8	20.8	7.1	22.7	8.9	2.2	1.3
Austin, TX	11.8	19.3	21.5	6.5	26.9	9.9	2.3	1.7
Billings, MT	7.7	31.1	26.6	7.1	19.4	5.2	1.9	0.9
Boise City, ID	10.0	25.2	26.7	8.3	20.4	6.8	1.6	1.0
Boston, MA	9.2	24.3	15.6	7.2	24.3	13.4	3.2	2.8
Boulder, CO	6.2	12.6	17.2	5.6	31.1	18.1	3.4	5.7
Cape Coral, FL	13.2	32.5	21.5	7.8	15.8	6.2	1.9	1.2
Cedar Rapids, IA	6.5	28.9	23.2	12.4	20.1	6.5	1.6	0.9
Charleston, SC	11.5	25.8	22.4	8.8	20.1	7.9	2.0	1.3
Charlotte, NC	13.2	25.4	21.8	8.4	21.6	7.3	1.5	0.9
Chicago, IL	13.2	25.0	20.2	6.8	21.3	9.7	2.5	1.2
Clarksville, TN	11.4	31.2	26.9	8.9	14.7	5.3	1.0	0.6
Colorado Springs, CO	6.1	21.5	26.1	11.3	21.5	10.6	1.7	1.3
Columbia, MO	6.3	20.1	19.6	6.7	27.5	11.8	3.4	4.5
Columbus, OH	9.9	29.2	20.5	7.2	21.4	8.4	2.0	1.4
Dallas, TX	15.9	22.8	22.9	6.6	21.3	7.9	1.6	1.0
Davenport, IA	9.9	31.0	23.2	10.5	17.0	6.6	1.2	0.7
Denver, CO	10.1	20.8	21.8	7.7	25.5	10.3	2.5	1.4
Des Moines, IA	7.3	26.4	21.1	10.1	25.1	7.0	1.9	1.1
Durham, NC	12.4	19.4	18.1	6.3	22.8	12.3	3.7	5.0
El Paso, TX	25.2	23.8	22.8	7.3	14.3	5.0	1.0	0.7
Erie, PA	9.6	40.8	16.3	8.1	16.3	6.3	1.4	1.2
Eugene, OR	8.6	25.5	29.8	8.3	16.8	7.4	1.7	1.9
Fargo, ND	5.6	22.0	23.5	13.7	25.0	6.7	1.8	1.7
Fayetteville, NC	11.0	27.3	29.1	10.9	14.7	5.4	0.9	0.7
Fort Collins, CO	5.4	18.6	23.6	8.9	27.2	11.6	2.1	2.7
Fort Wayne, IN	10.7	31.5	23.6	9.4	16.1	6.4	1.5	0.7
Fort Worth, TX	15.9	22.8	22.9	6.6	21.3	7.9	1.6	1.0
Gainesville, FL	8.8	22.6	20.0	10.6	20.3	9.6	3.7	4.4
Grand Rapids, MI	10.1	28.4	22.9	8.9	19.6	7.5	1.6	0.9
Green Bay, WI	9.4	34.0	19.8	11.5	18.2	5.3	1.2	0.6
Greensboro, NC	14.9	28.6	21.6	7.9	18.3	6.5	1.3	1.0
Honolulu, HI	9.5	26.4	21.7	10.3	21.2	7.4	2.3	1.4
Houston, TX	18.6	23.7	21.6	6.3	19.5	7.1	1.9	1.3
Huntsville, AL	11.0	23.6	22.2	7.8	22.5	10.2	1.3	1.5
Indianapolis, IN	11.2	29.6	20.8	7.7	19.9	7.5	2.0	1.2
Jacksonville, FL	10.8	28.6	23.4	9.5	19.0	6.2	1.6	0.9
Kansas City, MO	9.1	26.6	23.4	7.5	21.4	8.8	2.1	1.0
Lafayette, LA	19.5	35.0	20.1	5.3	14.1	4.1	1.1	0.8
Las Vegas, NV	15.9	29.5	25.0	7.5	14.8	5.0	1.5	0.7
Lexington, KY	12.3	24.7	20.6	7.4	20.6	9.4	2.8	2.3
Lincoln, NE	6.6	22.8	23.1	11.3	23.5	8.1	1.9	2.6
Little Rock, AR	10.9	31.0	23.6	6.2	18.3	6.8	1.9	1.3
Los Angeles, CA	21.5	20.0	19.9	7.1	20.6	7.2	2.4	1.3
Louisville, KY	12.2	31.0	22.4	7.7	16.1	7.5	1.9	1.1
Lubbock, TX	16.2	25.5	25.3	6.1	17.3	6.3	1.8	1.5
Madison, WI	5.7	23.1	19.7	9.8	24.6	11.1	3.0	2.9
Manchester, NH	8.9	27.3	18.6	9.6	23.0	9.9	1.3	1.4
McAllen, TX	37.8	24.0	17.6	4.4	11.5	3.4	1.0	0.4
Miami, FL	15.8	27.9	18.4	8.8	18.6	6.8	2.7	1.2
Midland, TX	18.3	23.4	27.0	6.3	17.6	5.8	1.3	0.4

Table continued on next page.

Metro Area	Less than H.S.	H.S. Diploma	Some College, No Deg.	Associate Degree	Bachelors Degree	Masters Degree	Profess. School Degree	Doctorate Degree
Minneapolis, MN	7.0	22.9	21.5	9.8	25.9	9.1	2.4	1.4
Nashville, TN	12.2	29.1	21.1	6.3	20.7	7.3	1.9	1.5
New Orleans, LA	15.3	29.3	23.1	5.6	16.9	5.9	2.6	1.2
New York, NY	14.9	25.9	15.7	6.6	21.7	10.8	2.9	1.5
Oklahoma City, OK	12.7	27.5	24.8	6.8	18.6	6.7	1.8	1.2
Omaha, NE	9.1	25.3	24.4	8.2	21.8	7.9	2.2	1.1
Orlando, FL	12.4	28.4	21.0	9.8	19.0	6.7	1.6	1.0
Oxnard, CA	17.0	19.1	23.8	8.8	19.8	7.9	2.3	1.3
Palm Bay, FL	10.3	28.5	23.5	11.4	16.5	7.4	1.4	1.1
Peoria, IL	8.8	31.8	23.3	9.8	17.7	6.5	1.4	0.7
Philadelphia, PA	10.9	30.8	17.8	6.6	20.5	9.3	2.5	1.7
Phoenix, AZ	13.6	23.9	25.1	8.4	18.7	7.5	1.8	1.1
Pittsburgh, PA	7.9	35.3	16.6	9.5	18.9	8.4	2.0	1.5
Portland, OR	9.2	22.0	25.4	8.6	21.9	9.0	2.3	1.5
Providence, RI	15.4	28.1	18.3	8.6	18.2	8.3	1.8	1.3
Provo, UT	6.9	17.3	28.9	10.6	25.1	7.8	1.4	2.0
Raleigh, NC	10.4	19.8	19.0	8.5	27.6	10.8	2.0	2.0
Reno, NV	13.7	24.1	26.6	7.6	17.9	6.5	2.2	1.5
Richmond, VA	12.7	26.7	21.0	6.9	20.5	8.9	2.1	1.3
Roanoke, VA	13.2	30.4	21.8	8.5	17.1	6.5	1.6	1.0
Rochester, MN	6.4	26.3	21.2	11.8	21.4	7.8	3.3	1.8
Sacramento, CA	11.9	21.8	26.3	9.6	19.7	6.9	2.4	1.4
Salem, OR	15.1	26.5	27.2	8.2	14.9	5.8	1.5	0.8
Salt Lake City, UT	10.6	23.0	26.3	8.8	20.4	7.4	2.0	1.5
San Antonio, TX	16.6	25.8	23.6	7.5	17.2	6.8	1.6	1.0
San Diego, CA	14.4	19.3	22.3	9.5	21.3	8.6	2.6	2.0
San Francisco, CA	12.1	17.1	19.1	6.9	27.0	11.7	3.6	2.5
San Jose, CA	13.5	15.7	17.4	7.1	25.5	14.8	2.6	3.3
Santa Rosa, CA	12.9	20.5	25.6	9.1	20.6	7.2	2.8	1.2
Savannah, GA	11.9	27.9	23.5	7.0	18.9	7.6	1.9	1.4
Seattle, WA	8.3	21.3	23.1	9.1	24.3	9.7	2.4	1.7
Sioux Falls, SD	8.2	29.1	20.7	11.4	21.2	6.5	1.7	1.1
Spokane, WA	7.7	27.0	27.0	11.4	17.4	6.7	1.8	1.0
Springfield, IL	7.9	29.1	22.8	8.0	20.1	8.7	2.3	1.1
Tallahassee, FL	10.8	23.8	20.3	8.3	21.1	10.6	2.6	2.6
Tampa, FL	12.0	30.8	21.1	9.5	17.3	6.4	1.8	1.0
Topeka, KS	9.2	34.1	23.8	6.8	17.1	6.6	1.6	0.9
Tulsa, OK	11.5	30.0	23.8	8.6	18.0	5.7	1.6	0.8
Tyler, TX	15.1	25.4	25.5	9.3	17.0	5.2	1.7	0.8
Virginia Beach, VA	9.9	26.1	26.0	9.0	18.3	8.1	1.6	1.0
Washington, DC	9.8	19.2	17.4	5.6	25.0	15.8	4.3	2.9
Wichita, KS	10.4	27.6	26.5	7.2	19.3	7.0	1.2	0.8
Wilmington, NC	10.7	23.6	23.3	9.3	22.2	7.5	2.0	1.5
Winston-Salem, NC	16.0	29.9	20.9	7.9	16.9	5.8	1.5	1.1
Worcester, MA	10.5	29.8	18.3	9.0	19.7	9.5	1.6	1.5
U.S.	13.7	28.0	21.2	7.9	18.2	7.7	1.9	1.3

Note: Figures cover persons age 25 and over; Figures cover the Metropolitan Statistical Area—see Appendix B for areas included
Source: U.S. Census Bureau, 2011-2013 American Community Survey 3-Year Estimates

School Enrollment by Grade and Control: City

City	Preschool (%)		Kindergarten (%)		Grades 1 - 4 (%)		Grades 5 - 8 (%)		Grades 9 - 12 (%)	
	Public	Private	Public	Private	Public	Private	Public	Private	Public	Private
Albuquerque, NM	57.0	43.0	90.0	10.0	89.8	10.2	88.3	11.7	88.8	11.2
Anchorage, AK	41.1	58.9	91.3	8.7	92.5	7.5	93.1	6.9	91.4	8.6
Ann Arbor, MI	23.9	76.1	85.8	14.2	91.1	8.9	84.4	15.6	89.4	10.6
Athens, GA	67.4	32.6	84.6	15.4	93.5	6.5	90.1	9.9	89.3	10.7
Atlanta, GA	55.1	44.9	81.2	18.8	84.3	15.7	83.7	16.3	78.2	21.8
Austin, TX	47.4	52.6	87.8	12.2	91.3	8.7	90.2	9.8	92.6	7.4
Billings, MT	45.4	54.6	90.3	9.7	94.6	5.4	91.2	8.8	91.2	8.8
Boise City, ID	52.4	47.6	92.8	7.2	92.6	7.4	93.3	6.7	92.8	7.2
Boston, MA	53.1	46.9	85.0	15.0	86.9	13.1	85.9	14.1	87.0	13.0
Boulder, CO	24.7	75.3	85.4	14.6	86.0	14.0	86.2	13.8	93.2	6.8
Cape Coral, FL	64.1	35.9	94.4	5.6	94.1	5.9	95.7	4.3	93.0	7.0
Cedar Rapids, IA	55.7	44.3	87.6	12.4	85.5	14.5	89.3	10.7	87.9	12.1
Charleston, SC	39.3	60.7	79.4	20.6	77.8	22.2	72.7	27.3	82.1	17.9
Charlotte, NC	42.2	57.8	90.3	9.7	90.1	9.9	88.6	11.4	90.0	10.0
Chicago, IL	65.1	34.9	82.8	17.2	85.5	14.5	86.8	13.2	88.4	11.6
Clarksville, TN	67.0	33.0	96.4	3.6	94.5	5.5	94.8	5.2	90.8	9.2
Colorado Springs, CO	59.5	40.5	89.5	10.5	93.0	7.0	93.4	6.6	93.1	6.9
Columbia, MO	38.3	61.7	83.9	16.1	84.4	15.6	80.2	19.8	94.3	5.7
Columbus, OH	55.0	45.0	89.8	10.2	88.8	11.2	88.0	12.0	88.0	12.0
Dallas, TX	70.4	29.6	89.5	10.5	92.3	7.7	89.6	10.4	90.7	9.3
Davenport, IA	66.4	33.6	86.2	13.8	91.1	8.9	86.9	13.1	91.1	8.9
Denver, CO	58.9	41.1	88.4	11.6	88.7	11.3	86.8	13.2	90.2	9.8
Des Moines, IA	69.9	30.1	89.1	10.9	91.5	8.5	90.3	9.7	91.6	8.4
Durham, NC	51.4	48.6	86.5	13.5	91.2	8.8	89.5	10.5	92.1	7.9
El Paso, TX	81.6	18.4	94.1	5.9	95.0	5.0	94.3	5.7	96.7	3.3
Erie, PA	42.7	57.3	86.3	13.7	87.7	12.3	89.3	10.7	85.2	14.8
Eugene, OR	36.0	64.0	81.2	18.8	85.8	14.2	87.3	12.7	90.9	9.1
Fargo, ND	57.7	42.3	82.5	17.5	79.1	20.9	88.3	11.7	85.1	14.9
Fayetteville, NC	72.2	27.8	90.7	9.3	89.6	10.4	89.6	10.4	90.0	10.0
Fort Collins, CO	31.5	68.5	92.1	7.9	90.1	9.9	90.1	9.9	97.4	2.6
Fort Wayne, IN	52.6	47.4	80.8	19.2	84.5	15.5	81.1	18.9	87.7	12.3
Fort Worth, TX	62.7	37.3	92.6	7.4	93.6	6.4	92.2	7.8	93.8	6.2
Gainesville, FL	56.4	43.6	69.8	30.2	86.0	14.0	87.5	12.5	89.3	10.7
Grand Rapids, MI	67.9	32.1	81.1	18.9	79.5	20.5	86.8	13.2	85.9	14.1
Green Bay, WI	79.4	20.6	87.0	13.0	88.9	11.1	91.6	8.4	90.5	9.5
Greensboro, NC	57.9	42.1	91.9	8.1	92.4	7.6	90.4	9.6	91.6	8.4
Honolulu, HI	41.3	58.7	86.7	13.3	81.9	18.1	80.8	19.2	74.1	25.9
Houston, TX	66.5	33.5	91.4	8.6	92.8	7.2	93.1	6.9	92.8	7.2
Huntsville, AL	40.1	59.9	83.3	16.7	86.0	14.0	85.0	15.0	88.0	12.0
Indianapolis, IN	43.0	57.0	83.6	16.4	89.2	10.8	89.1	10.9	88.0	12.0
Jacksonville, FL	58.5	41.5	86.1	13.9	83.7	16.3	84.6	15.4	84.5	15.5
Kansas City, MO	53.3	46.7	84.4	15.6	84.5	15.5	85.3	14.7	88.0	12.0
Lafayette, LA	52.9	47.1	80.2	19.8	82.3	17.7	73.9	26.1	76.0	24.0
Las Vegas, NV	50.7	49.3	86.9	13.1	92.9	7.1	91.9	8.1	94.7	5.3
Lexington, KY	46.1	53.9	82.5	17.5	85.7	14.3	87.6	12.4	88.2	11.8
Lincoln, NE	48.0	52.0	81.7	18.3	84.3	15.7	83.6	16.4	88.1	11.9
Little Rock, AR	60.3	39.7	86.8	13.2	80.1	19.9	73.1	26.9	81.2	18.8
Los Angeles, CA	61.5	38.5	86.7	13.3	89.1	10.9	88.8	11.2	89.5	10.5
Louisville, KY	50.2	49.8	84.6	15.4	82.5	17.5	81.3	18.7	82.1	17.9
Lubbock, TX	65.9	34.1	89.1	10.9	93.5	6.5	94.5	5.5	95.8	4.2
Madison, WI	44.4	55.6	89.5	10.5	92.4	7.6	88.5	11.5	94.1	5.9
Manchester, NH	41.7	58.3	75.4	24.6	92.1	7.9	89.4	10.6	95.7	4.3
McAllen, TX	82.0	18.0	86.6	13.4	96.1	3.9	93.7	6.3	94.8	5.2
Miami, FL	59.3	40.7	81.2	18.8	85.6	14.4	90.6	9.4	89.5	10.5
Midland, TX	42.0	58.0	77.3	22.7	87.5	12.5	85.9	14.1	88.8	11.2

Table continued on next page.

City	Preschool (%)		Kindergarten (%)		Grades 1 - 4 (%)		Grades 5 - 8 (%)		Grades 9 - 12 (%)	
	Public	Private	Public	Private	Public	Private	Public	Private	Public	Private
Minneapolis, MN	59.5	40.5	86.2	13.8	88.6	11.4	86.7	13.3	89.9	10.1
Nashville, TN	60.3	39.7	87.5	12.5	88.3	11.7	81.9	18.1	82.1	17.9
New Orleans, LA	60.2	39.8	77.7	22.3	81.5	18.5	78.2	21.8	81.2	18.8
New York, NY	54.4	45.6	79.1	20.9	83.3	16.7	82.8	17.2	83.2	16.8
Oklahoma City, OK	68.4	31.6	92.1	7.9	91.0	9.0	91.5	8.5	91.5	8.5
Omaha, NE	57.1	42.9	81.1	18.9	85.1	14.9	86.1	13.9	86.8	13.2
Orlando, FL	54.2	45.8	82.0	18.0	91.0	9.0	92.2	7.8	91.9	8.1
Oxnard, CA	74.8	25.2	94.1	5.9	93.9	6.1	94.6	5.4	93.3	6.7
Palm Bay, FL	47.0	53.0	93.4	6.6	89.6	10.4	87.1	12.9	86.4	13.6
Peoria, IL	70.8	29.2	78.5	21.5	83.1	16.9	74.6	25.4	85.3	14.7
Philadelphia, PA	57.0	43.0	82.1	17.9	81.3	18.7	79.4	20.6	81.7	18.3
Phoenix, AZ	57.3	42.7	92.8	7.2	94.1	5.9	94.1	5.9	93.7	6.3
Pittsburgh, PA	63.0	37.0	81.6	18.4	80.4	19.6	78.0	22.0	79.1	20.9
Portland, OR	35.1	64.9	83.8	16.2	88.7	11.3	90.9	9.1	86.9	13.1
Providence, RI	71.3	28.7	79.1	20.9	89.7	10.3	88.3	11.7	86.5	13.5
Provo, UT	41.2	58.8	91.5	8.5	97.1	2.9	93.0	7.0	91.6	8.4
Raleigh, NC	35.4	64.6	90.4	9.6	90.8	9.2	89.6	10.4	92.2	7.8
Reno, NV	63.8	36.2	89.3	10.7	93.6	6.4	93.2	6.8	96.8	3.2
Richmond, VA	54.7	45.3	82.3	17.7	86.2	13.8	85.3	14.7	89.7	10.3
Roanoke, VA	58.2	41.8	93.3	6.7	95.2	4.8	91.5	8.5	95.9	4.1
Rochester, MN	45.7	54.3	82.8	17.2	83.6	16.4	83.9	16.1	91.1	8.9
Sacramento, CA	69.7	30.3	90.9	9.1	93.1	6.9	93.4	6.6	90.2	9.8
Salem, OR	68.9	31.1	89.8	10.2	93.1	6.9	92.2	7.8	94.4	5.6
Salt Lake City, UT	42.8	57.2	85.4	14.6	90.1	9.9	90.0	10.0	91.7	8.3
San Antonio, TX	69.3	30.7	90.3	9.7	93.1	6.9	92.2	7.8	93.6	6.4
San Diego, CA	54.5	45.5	89.9	10.1	91.9	8.1	92.1	7.9	93.7	6.3
San Francisco, CA	35.0	65.0	70.4	29.6	71.2	28.8	69.6	30.4	77.7	22.3
San Jose, CA	44.4	55.6	82.5	17.5	89.5	10.5	89.7	10.3	89.9	10.1
Santa Rosa, CA	50.5	49.5	91.4	8.6	97.1	2.9	97.3	2.7	90.8	9.2
Savannah, GA	73.0	27.0	89.4	10.6	92.7	7.3	87.8	12.2	82.5	17.5
Seattle, WA	34.9	65.1	73.8	26.2	78.1	21.9	77.7	22.3	79.1	20.9
Sioux Falls, SD	57.5	42.5	86.7	13.3	87.5	12.5	92.1	7.9	90.7	9.3
Spokane, WA	32.1	67.9	83.1	16.9	87.9	12.1	93.5	6.5	93.5	6.5
Springfield, IL	67.8	32.2	80.3	19.7	85.3	14.7	85.8	14.2	83.9	16.1
Tallahassee, FL	55.3	44.7	91.6	8.4	90.8	9.2	89.0	11.0	90.8	9.2
Tampa, FL	54.6	45.4	91.9	8.1	90.2	9.8	87.2	12.8	90.8	9.2
Topeka, KS	72.1	27.9	97.5	2.5	89.2	10.8	89.3	10.7	88.6	11.4
Tulsa, OK	71.7	28.3	89.3	10.7	89.4	10.6	85.7	14.3	86.3	13.7
Tyler, TX	68.3	31.7	98.2	1.8	92.8	7.2	89.8	10.2	88.6	11.4
Virginia Beach, VA	33.2	66.8	85.9	14.1	90.1	9.9	91.1	8.9	93.3	6.7
Washington, DC	73.9	26.1	88.4	11.6	81.6	18.4	81.6	18.4	83.2	16.8
Wichita, KS	69.3	30.7	84.0	16.0	86.6	13.4	86.6	13.4	83.2	16.8
Wilmington, NC	55.9	44.1	90.4	9.6	86.8	13.2	77.6	22.4	87.7	12.3
Winston-Salem, NC	53.8	46.2	90.1	9.9	91.9	8.1	91.9	8.1	93.2	6.8
Worcester, MA	75.0	25.0	95.3	4.7	92.3	7.7	91.3	8.7	89.9	10.1
U.S.	57.7	42.3	87.9	12.1	89.9	10.1	90.0	10.0	90.7	9.3

Note: Figures shown cover persons 3 years old and over
Source: U.S. Census Bureau, 2011-2013 American Community Survey 3-Year Estimates

School Enrollment by Grade and Control: Metro Area

Metro Area	Preschool (%)		Kindergarten (%)		Grades 1 - 4 (%)		Grades 5 - 8 (%)		Grades 9 - 12 (%)	
	Public	Private	Public	Private	Public	Private	Public	Private	Public	Private
Albuquerque, NM	61.8	38.2	89.1	10.9	90.7	9.3	89.4	10.6	89.7	10.3
Anchorage, AK	47.7	52.3	89.9	10.1	91.0	9.0	90.8	9.2	90.9	9.1
Ann Arbor, MI	51.7	48.3	87.1	12.9	89.6	10.4	88.4	11.6	89.7	10.3
Athens, GA	67.9	32.1	88.5	11.5	93.3	6.7	89.8	10.2	87.4	12.6
Atlanta, GA	54.0	46.0	87.6	12.4	90.5	9.5	89.9	10.1	90.6	9.4
Austin, TX	50.2	49.8	88.8	11.2	92.2	7.8	92.2	7.8	93.5	6.5
Billings, MT	44.8	55.2	91.7	8.3	95.0	5.0	90.4	9.6	89.5	10.5
Boise City, ID	47.1	52.9	90.3	9.7	92.9	7.1	94.1	5.9	93.6	6.4
Boston, MA	42.9	57.1	86.2	13.8	90.1	9.9	89.1	10.9	86.8	13.2
Boulder, CO	42.9	57.1	92.9	7.1	90.1	9.9	91.7	8.3	95.2	4.8
Cape Coral, FL	59.9	40.1	94.5	5.5	94.1	5.9	91.5	8.5	93.6	6.4
Cedar Rapids, IA	59.5	40.5	86.0	14.0	87.0	13.0	90.4	9.6	90.5	9.5
Charleston, SC	44.5	55.5	84.8	15.2	88.3	11.7	88.2	11.8	89.8	10.2
Charlotte, NC	46.7	53.3	90.9	9.1	91.3	8.7	90.3	9.7	90.9	9.1
Chicago, IL	57.7	42.3	86.0	14.0	88.5	11.5	89.1	10.9	90.9	9.1
Clarksville, TN	71.4	28.6	94.8	5.2	90.8	9.2	92.3	7.7	90.2	9.8
Colorado Springs, CO	62.2	37.8	90.7	9.3	93.3	6.7	92.9	7.1	93.4	6.6
Columbia, MO	38.3	61.7	87.7	12.3	88.0	12.0	84.4	15.6	92.3	7.7
Columbus, OH	50.7	49.3	87.7	12.3	89.3	10.7	89.2	10.8	89.1	10.9
Dallas, TX	56.4	43.6	89.9	10.1	92.6	7.4	92.2	7.8	92.4	7.6
Davenport, IA	66.9	33.1	90.5	9.5	91.2	8.8	90.6	9.4	93.1	6.9
Denver, CO	56.1	43.9	90.4	9.6	92.9	7.1	91.6	8.4	92.6	7.4
Des Moines, IA	62.1	37.9	88.8	11.2	91.0	9.0	91.5	8.5	91.5	8.5
Durham, NC	45.1	54.9	88.7	11.3	91.2	8.8	90.2	9.8	90.7	9.3
El Paso, TX	84.6	15.4	95.2	4.8	95.9	4.1	95.3	4.7	97.2	2.8
Erie, PA	45.0	55.0	85.8	14.2	88.1	11.9	90.2	9.8	88.5	11.5
Eugene, OR	53.0	47.0	83.8	16.2	89.4	10.6	89.7	10.3	92.8	7.2
Fargo, ND	62.9	37.1	87.3	12.7	86.0	14.0	90.7	9.3	89.3	10.7
Fayetteville, NC	70.0	30.0	91.7	8.3	91.5	8.5	91.2	8.8	91.7	8.3
Fort Collins, CO	38.2	61.8	86.5	13.5	91.5	8.5	90.6	9.4	95.9	4.1
Fort Wayne, IN	47.5	52.5	76.8	23.2	82.1	17.9	79.2	20.8	88.2	11.8
Fort Worth, TX	56.4	43.6	89.9	10.1	92.6	7.4	92.2	7.8	92.4	7.6
Gainesville, FL	50.0	50.0	77.7	22.3	86.1	13.9	88.6	11.4	87.7	12.3
Grand Rapids, MI	64.2	35.8	84.5	15.5	84.2	15.8	85.7	14.3	87.2	12.8
Green Bay, WI	73.2	26.8	84.1	15.9	89.0	11.0	91.3	8.7	92.6	7.4
Greensboro, NC	58.2	41.8	90.6	9.4	91.5	8.5	91.2	8.8	90.3	9.7
Honolulu, HI	39.7	60.3	84.0	16.0	82.6	17.4	79.0	21.0	75.1	24.9
Houston, TX	59.0	41.0	89.8	10.2	93.5	6.5	94.0	6.0	93.6	6.4
Huntsville, AL	44.8	55.2	85.5	14.5	87.5	12.5	88.1	11.9	88.8	11.2
Indianapolis, IN	47.0	53.0	83.1	16.9	88.9	11.1	90.0	10.0	89.3	10.7
Jacksonville, FL	54.8	45.2	86.2	13.8	85.8	14.2	87.2	12.8	86.5	13.5
Kansas City, MO	52.6	47.4	85.7	14.3	88.5	11.5	88.7	11.3	89.7	10.3
Lafayette, LA	58.7	41.3	81.0	19.0	79.6	20.4	77.6	22.4	78.4	21.6
Las Vegas, NV	55.8	44.2	90.3	9.7	93.4	6.6	94.5	5.5	95.3	4.7
Lexington, KY	46.6	53.4	84.5	15.5	85.8	14.2	86.5	13.5	87.2	12.8
Lincoln, NE	49.2	50.8	79.1	20.9	83.6	16.4	83.3	16.7	88.8	11.2
Little Rock, AR	60.1	39.9	87.5	12.5	86.1	13.9	85.7	14.3	87.3	12.7
Los Angeles, CA	59.0	41.0	87.9	12.1	90.3	9.7	90.6	9.4	91.8	8.2
Louisville, KY	49.9	50.1	85.8	14.2	84.3	15.7	83.2	16.8	84.1	15.9
Lubbock, TX	65.4	34.6	88.7	11.3	93.0	7.0	94.1	5.9	94.8	5.2
Madison, WI	53.4	46.6	90.9	9.1	90.8	9.2	90.0	10.0	94.9	5.1
Manchester, NH	38.3	61.7	74.7	25.3	90.6	9.4	90.2	9.8	91.1	8.9
McAllen, TX	91.8	8.2	94.9	5.1	97.9	2.1	97.8	2.2	97.7	2.3
Miami, FL	49.0	51.0	82.2	17.8	86.3	13.7	88.1	11.9	87.7	12.3
Midland, TX	46.0	54.0	81.5	18.5	90.2	9.8	87.9	12.1	89.3	10.7

Table continued on next page.

Metro Area	Preschool (%)		Kindergarten (%)		Grades 1 - 4 (%)		Grades 5 - 8 (%)		Grades 9 - 12 (%)	
	Public	Private	Public	Private	Public	Private	Public	Private	Public	Private
Minneapolis, MN	54.8	45.2	86.2	13.8	87.5	12.5	88.8	11.2	91.4	8.6
Nashville, TN	51.8	48.2	88.4	11.6	89.3	10.7	86.2	13.8	85.3	14.7
New Orleans, LA	55.4	44.6	75.9	24.1	77.4	22.6	76.1	23.9	76.0	24.0
New York, NY	49.5	50.5	81.6	18.4	86.5	13.5	86.6	13.4	86.1	13.9
Oklahoma City, OK	73.1	26.9	89.9	10.1	91.2	8.8	91.7	8.3	92.0	8.0
Omaha, NE	56.3	43.7	84.5	15.5	86.6	13.4	87.6	12.4	87.5	12.5
Orlando, FL	51.0	49.0	87.6	12.4	89.1	10.9	88.9	11.1	91.2	8.8
Oxnard, CA	53.3	46.7	90.2	9.8	91.1	8.9	90.2	9.8	90.2	9.8
Palm Bay, FL	51.4	48.6	90.0	10.0	89.9	10.1	87.8	12.2	90.0	10.0
Peoria, IL	62.4	37.6	85.6	14.4	86.4	13.6	86.5	13.5	91.1	8.9
Philadelphia, PA	43.1	56.9	79.9	20.1	84.8	15.2	83.9	16.1	83.7	16.3
Phoenix, AZ	57.4	42.6	92.2	7.8	92.9	7.1	94.2	5.8	94.1	5.9
Pittsburgh, PA	47.8	52.2	85.7	14.3	87.9	12.1	87.9	12.1	89.7	10.3
Portland, OR	38.1	61.9	83.4	16.6	89.6	10.4	90.8	9.2	91.9	8.1
Providence, RI	51.1	48.9	85.8	14.2	90.0	10.0	90.4	9.6	87.8	12.2
Provo, UT	41.4	58.6	91.6	8.4	95.2	4.8	95.1	4.9	95.7	4.3
Raleigh, NC	36.9	63.1	88.3	11.7	89.7	10.3	88.7	11.3	91.5	8.5
Reno, NV	55.2	44.8	89.9	10.1	93.0	7.0	92.6	7.4	94.9	5.1
Richmond, VA	40.0	60.0	88.4	11.6	89.9	10.1	91.0	9.0	92.0	8.0
Roanoke, VA	50.7	49.3	92.9	7.1	92.3	7.7	90.7	9.3	95.5	4.5
Rochester, MN	58.9	41.1	86.3	13.7	87.0	13.0	87.6	12.4	92.3	7.7
Sacramento, CA	55.9	44.1	89.4	10.6	92.0	8.0	92.4	7.6	91.2	8.8
Salem, OR	59.1	40.9	90.5	9.5	91.3	8.7	91.2	8.8	92.1	7.9
Salt Lake City, UT	50.2	49.8	91.1	8.9	92.8	7.2	93.4	6.6	93.5	6.5
San Antonio, TX	65.5	34.5	91.1	8.9	92.3	7.7	92.7	7.3	93.6	6.4
San Diego, CA	55.1	44.9	90.7	9.3	92.3	7.7	92.3	7.7	93.4	6.6
San Francisco, CA	40.8	59.2	83.4	16.6	86.0	14.0	86.0	14.0	88.3	11.7
San Jose, CA	35.4	64.6	83.2	16.8	87.7	12.3	87.6	12.4	89.1	10.9
Santa Rosa, CA	45.9	54.1	87.3	12.7	92.0	8.0	92.1	7.9	90.9	9.1
Savannah, GA	62.2	37.8	88.6	11.4	88.7	11.3	85.9	14.1	83.5	16.5
Seattle, WA	42.6	57.4	82.2	17.8	88.9	11.1	89.0	11.0	91.2	8.8
Sioux Falls, SD	55.8	44.2	88.7	11.3	87.9	12.1	91.7	8.3	90.8	9.2
Spokane, WA	40.4	59.6	84.1	15.9	89.6	10.4	90.9	9.1	93.0	7.0
Springfield, IL	68.9	31.1	89.0	11.0	88.9	11.1	88.0	12.0	87.3	12.7
Tallahassee, FL	63.3	36.7	86.1	13.9	90.8	9.2	87.6	12.4	88.7	11.3
Tampa, FL	57.6	42.4	88.3	11.7	89.4	10.6	88.8	11.2	91.5	8.5
Topeka, KS	72.4	27.6	91.6	8.4	88.2	11.8	88.1	11.9	89.8	10.2
Tulsa, OK	69.8	30.2	89.7	10.3	89.9	10.1	88.4	11.6	88.8	11.2
Tyler, TX	70.7	29.3	95.0	5.0	93.6	6.4	91.5	8.5	89.8	10.2
Virginia Beach, VA	54.3	45.7	87.4	12.6	90.5	9.5	91.2	8.8	93.3	6.7
Washington, DC	40.7	59.3	84.3	15.7	88.3	11.7	88.1	11.9	89.0	11.0
Wichita, KS	67.2	32.8	85.3	14.7	87.8	12.2	88.2	11.8	87.0	13.0
Wilmington, NC	53.6	46.4	90.3	9.7	90.2	9.8	88.1	11.9	92.6	7.4
Winston-Salem, NC	52.5	47.5	90.4	9.6	90.8	9.2	91.3	8.7	93.6	6.4
Worcester, MA	60.5	39.5	89.4	10.6	92.7	7.3	91.4	8.6	91.2	8.8
U.S.	57.7	42.3	87.9	12.1	89.9	10.1	90.0	10.0	90.7	9.3

Note: Figures shown cover persons 3 years old and over; Figures cover the Metropolitan Statistical Area—see Appendix B for areas included
Source: U.S. Census Bureau, 2011-2013 American Community Survey 3-Year Estimates

Educational Attainment by Race: City

City	High School Graduate or Higher (%)					Bachelor's Degree or Higher (%)				
	Total	White	Black	Asian	Hisp.[1]	Total	White	Black	Asian	Hisp.[1]
Albuquerque, NM	89.2	91.4	90.8	82.8	80.2	33.6	37.3	30.3	44.9	18.6
Anchorage, AK	92.5	95.9	86.0	76.0	87.8	32.4	37.8	22.4	22.0	22.9
Ann Arbor, MI	96.3	97.1	89.7	96.8	89.0	70.4	70.9	40.5	85.0	55.5
Athens, GA	86.4	90.3	80.0	91.5	53.0	38.7	50.5	10.5	69.9	9.9
Atlanta, GA	88.9	96.5	82.0	96.8	76.8	48.2	74.1	23.3	82.5	42.0
Austin, TX	87.1	89.0	88.1	92.0	64.6	45.8	49.0	21.6	67.8	19.6
Billings, MT	92.6	93.5	n/a	n/a	82.6	29.0	30.3	n/a	n/a	12.5
Boise City, ID	94.1	95.0	n/a	82.1	81.4	38.9	39.4	n/a	50.2	17.9
Boston, MA	84.8	91.7	80.1	77.2	65.4	43.8	59.1	17.9	47.5	16.7
Boulder, CO	96.5	97.6	n/a	96.0	70.0	73.6	75.8	n/a	68.2	39.1
Cape Coral, FL	91.0	91.2	93.1	79.5	76.0	20.6	20.9	11.2	24.5	17.3
Cedar Rapids, IA	92.9	93.3	87.8	95.3	67.8	30.3	30.3	18.9	65.2	10.9
Charleston, SC	93.1	96.7	81.3	n/a	89.4	48.7	58.8	15.5	n/a	32.2
Charlotte, NC	88.6	92.0	87.6	84.8	58.9	40.6	51.4	23.7	54.7	15.6
Chicago, IL	81.4	85.4	82.0	85.9	60.0	34.4	45.5	18.0	57.6	12.9
Clarksville, TN	91.4	92.9	88.0	84.2	86.2	24.1	26.4	16.6	26.3	18.7
Colorado Springs, CO	93.3	95.0	91.7	86.1	79.2	36.6	39.2	22.9	35.9	16.4
Columbia, MO	93.6	94.7	86.3	91.4	81.1	55.2	58.1	24.8	74.3	42.6
Columbus, OH	88.2	90.3	85.1	86.1	61.6	33.0	37.8	17.6	61.5	16.2
Dallas, TX	74.2	74.6	82.9	84.1	45.4	29.6	37.2	16.0	58.9	8.4
Davenport, IA	90.0	91.8	82.9	69.1	70.8	26.4	27.9	10.6	41.5	11.4
Denver, CO	86.1	88.5	87.3	76.8	60.8	44.1	49.4	23.9	46.8	11.0
Des Moines, IA	87.7	89.9	85.1	68.7	57.4	25.3	27.4	15.5	20.9	7.1
Durham, NC	86.8	87.9	87.2	90.9	42.1	46.1	57.3	30.3	72.5	12.7
El Paso, TX	77.3	77.6	92.0	89.6	72.2	23.0	22.8	27.9	48.4	18.6
Erie, PA	86.4	88.7	80.3	51.7	70.4	21.6	23.7	11.2	20.7	6.9
Eugene, OR	93.9	94.6	96.3	95.5	68.5	38.3	38.8	31.3	57.3	18.0
Fargo, ND	94.5	95.5	83.5	87.0	77.3	38.7	38.9	36.7	55.8	14.6
Fayetteville, NC	90.7	93.1	88.7	81.2	89.6	24.2	27.9	19.9	34.0	16.6
Fort Collins, CO	95.3	96.1	87.5	96.0	75.7	51.7	52.8	23.5	65.2	25.9
Fort Wayne, IN	87.8	91.0	81.6	61.7	57.6	25.3	27.6	13.7	27.7	12.6
Fort Worth, TX	79.8	81.0	85.9	78.9	53.0	26.6	30.6	16.8	36.2	9.4
Gainesville, FL	91.7	94.4	85.4	87.8	93.1	42.5	48.6	18.9	69.7	43.3
Grand Rapids, MI	84.6	88.2	75.7	69.5	50.0	30.0	35.4	11.7	32.4	9.0
Green Bay, WI	86.9	88.4	89.6	73.8	47.5	23.2	24.7	6.7	21.5	7.0
Greensboro, NC	88.3	92.4	86.4	61.2	58.8	36.7	47.2	23.6	29.1	12.2
Honolulu, HI	88.0	96.6	95.6	84.6	93.1	35.0	51.5	33.0	33.3	27.0
Houston, TX	76.2	75.8	85.0	84.8	52.8	30.0	34.3	19.7	56.3	10.7
Huntsville, AL	90.1	92.9	84.1	90.2	71.4	38.9	45.3	22.8	57.1	24.1
Indianapolis, IN	84.8	87.5	83.8	81.2	52.9	27.3	32.5	15.1	51.5	8.7
Jacksonville, FL	87.9	89.6	84.7	85.1	84.3	25.7	28.4	16.5	44.8	23.6
Kansas City, MO	88.0	92.2	83.3	76.6	64.9	31.9	40.0	14.9	42.0	15.1
Lafayette, LA	86.4	91.8	73.4	85.9	74.3	32.8	39.4	14.8	55.7	27.4
Las Vegas, NV	83.0	85.6	85.8	89.5	59.2	21.7	23.1	16.8	39.0	7.4
Lexington, KY	89.1	91.4	84.9	88.7	53.0	40.7	44.2	18.5	73.0	14.2
Lincoln, NE	93.1	94.9	88.3	77.7	62.4	36.7	38.2	18.1	37.8	13.8
Little Rock, AR	90.6	93.9	86.1	92.8	70.7	38.4	50.2	20.0	62.8	15.5
Los Angeles, CA	74.8	79.1	86.2	89.5	51.2	31.3	36.6	23.0	51.7	9.8
Louisville, KY	86.9	88.0	83.5	78.3	74.3	27.0	29.3	16.1	56.0	21.0
Lubbock, TX	85.4	88.2	81.0	90.3	67.1	28.8	31.2	12.1	73.9	9.8
Madison, WI	94.9	96.2	87.7	88.0	78.5	53.7	55.3	23.2	67.4	32.2
Manchester, NH	87.1	88.6	76.2	66.3	65.1	26.3	26.9	11.0	32.5	10.5
McAllen, TX	72.7	73.6	n/a	94.8	68.1	26.5	26.2	n/a	65.9	22.3
Miami, FL	72.0	73.4	66.3	80.4	68.7	23.3	25.7	10.4	58.5	19.3
Midland, TX	81.7	84.1	80.6	79.4	61.4	25.4	27.8	15.6	43.1	9.1

Table continued on next page.

City	High School Graduate or Higher (%)					Bachelor's Degree or Higher (%)				
	Total	White	Black	Asian	Hisp.[1]	Total	White	Black	Asian	Hisp.[1]
Minneapolis, MN	88.6	94.1	75.5	74.7	53.4	47.0	55.9	16.5	45.2	15.8
Nashville, TN	86.7	90.1	85.6	79.0	56.7	35.7	41.0	24.3	51.2	12.9
New Orleans, LA	84.5	94.8	78.9	66.8	74.1	34.2	60.7	16.2	33.9	31.9
New York, NY	79.9	86.6	80.6	74.3	64.2	34.9	46.3	21.4	41.1	15.7
Oklahoma City, OK	84.4	86.0	88.2	78.4	47.3	28.3	31.4	18.5	35.6	8.4
Omaha, NE	87.6	90.6	83.8	73.9	46.7	33.3	36.3	17.7	52.0	10.2
Orlando, FL	88.9	92.3	81.4	90.7	82.6	33.7	39.6	17.2	59.7	23.4
Oxnard, CA	65.3	62.2	86.9	87.9	51.8	15.9	14.6	19.4	32.1	8.2
Palm Bay, FL	86.3	88.7	77.7	90.2	82.3	17.9	18.4	14.9	25.4	15.3
Peoria, IL	88.2	91.1	79.0	93.8	67.6	32.4	35.8	11.4	79.3	15.2
Philadelphia, PA	81.4	86.7	80.7	67.6	62.6	24.4	34.5	13.6	33.6	11.4
Phoenix, AZ	80.6	82.3	86.2	83.8	56.7	26.5	28.0	16.5	51.2	8.7
Pittsburgh, PA	91.2	92.7	85.9	92.7	86.8	37.3	42.3	14.8	78.1	48.2
Portland, OR	90.9	93.8	87.2	75.4	62.5	44.4	48.1	16.6	36.0	20.6
Providence, RI	73.3	80.3	74.9	66.8	56.4	28.8	40.9	17.1	39.1	7.8
Provo, UT	89.8	91.6	n/a	86.3	66.3	38.8	39.9	n/a	52.7	17.0
Raleigh, NC	89.5	92.7	89.0	83.0	47.2	47.0	56.8	29.5	43.8	13.2
Reno, NV	85.5	87.6	86.0	88.4	53.2	29.7	31.6	19.4	39.4	8.2
Richmond, VA	81.8	90.2	74.0	88.7	46.0	34.7	55.9	13.6	62.0	14.4
Roanoke, VA	82.3	85.2	77.4	56.1	51.2	23.0	27.9	11.3	25.5	7.4
Rochester, MN	93.7	95.1	77.8	88.9	71.5	41.8	42.2	24.4	53.4	26.1
Sacramento, CA	83.1	86.8	88.6	77.4	65.2	29.2	34.3	18.2	32.8	13.6
Salem, OR	86.6	90.1	86.7	88.0	52.3	26.6	28.4	29.9	28.5	10.7
Salt Lake City, UT	86.5	92.5	80.0	88.0	51.3	42.8	47.1	24.7	65.6	15.0
San Antonio, TX	81.2	82.6	88.5	84.1	72.4	25.1	26.4	22.6	52.1	14.4
San Diego, CA	87.3	89.5	89.0	87.5	66.3	41.9	45.3	20.7	48.0	17.4
San Francisco, CA	86.5	94.5	86.0	76.4	73.6	52.9	66.5	23.4	41.4	29.5
San Jose, CA	82.5	85.2	92.6	84.0	64.0	37.6	36.2	27.8	49.7	12.1
Santa Rosa, CA	85.7	90.1	82.0	80.9	58.3	29.9	32.5	22.5	40.4	9.6
Savannah, GA	86.0	91.4	81.6	79.4	62.2	27.4	38.8	16.4	45.9	26.4
Seattle, WA	93.2	96.8	81.7	82.0	79.8	57.8	64.3	22.2	47.8	39.2
Sioux Falls, SD	90.9	93.4	68.0	69.8	56.1	32.5	34.1	14.8	39.3	13.0
Spokane, WA	90.8	91.8	85.4	76.7	81.1	28.5	29.5	18.0	24.3	20.8
Springfield, IL	90.9	92.1	84.2	94.0	90.1	34.4	36.9	17.2	69.9	40.7
Tallahassee, FL	92.3	96.3	85.1	93.6	90.0	47.5	56.6	28.3	78.0	41.9
Tampa, FL	86.5	89.5	79.3	85.4	76.3	33.9	40.2	13.4	54.7	18.8
Topeka, KS	87.9	89.4	81.3	85.7	61.6	26.4	28.2	11.4	63.1	9.4
Tulsa, OK	86.9	89.0	87.5	78.6	53.2	30.4	34.7	16.6	41.0	8.5
Tyler, TX	84.4	84.5	84.9	96.6	46.5	29.6	33.0	16.2	55.4	6.5
Virginia Beach, VA	94.0	95.1	90.6	92.0	92.6	33.7	35.5	24.7	39.8	21.9
Washington, DC	88.6	96.6	82.7	90.1	70.0	53.5	85.9	23.5	75.2	40.1
Wichita, KS	87.6	89.2	88.4	75.4	58.7	28.3	30.5	16.6	30.3	11.6
Wilmington, NC	89.3	92.6	79.4	72.1	54.6	40.1	47.0	13.3	42.5	17.4
Winston-Salem, NC	84.4	85.3	85.2	87.4	41.4	32.9	40.4	18.1	63.0	8.4
Worcester, MA	84.7	87.2	88.2	71.4	66.5	29.8	32.9	20.4	30.9	11.8
U.S.	86.3	88.3	83.1	85.7	64.0	29.1	30.4	18.8	50.7	13.7

Note: Figures shown cover persons 25 years old and over; (1) People of Hispanic origin can be of any race
Source: U.S. Census Bureau, 2011-2013 American Community Survey 3-Year Estimates

Educational Attainment by Race: Metro Area

Metro Area	High School Graduate or Higher (%)					Bachelor's Degree or Higher (%)				
	Total	White	Black	Asian	Hisp.[1]	Total	White	Black	Asian	Hisp.[1]
Albuquerque, NM	87.5	89.9	91.1	83.9	77.7	30.1	33.8	30.6	44.5	16.4
Anchorage, AK	92.5	95.2	86.0	75.9	88.1	29.7	33.5	21.9	21.7	22.6
Ann Arbor, MI	94.2	95.1	89.2	96.0	83.6	51.5	53.4	23.1	80.4	30.4
Athens, GA	85.9	88.7	78.2	88.7	53.6	33.5	39.0	10.9	63.1	10.3
Atlanta, GA	87.8	89.0	88.4	86.5	60.0	35.1	38.7	27.4	52.9	15.6
Austin, TX	88.2	89.7	89.0	92.1	67.1	40.8	42.6	24.1	65.8	17.8
Billings, MT	92.3	92.9	n/a	n/a	79.7	27.4	28.3	n/a	n/a	11.5
Boise City, ID	90.0	90.9	91.0	83.3	63.2	29.9	30.3	25.3	48.4	10.4
Boston, MA	90.8	93.5	81.6	84.6	69.3	43.7	45.9	23.8	57.7	19.6
Boulder, CO	93.8	95.1	86.8	95.0	62.3	58.3	60.0	38.1	69.9	21.8
Cape Coral, FL	86.8	89.1	73.1	86.0	63.2	25.0	26.5	12.6	34.9	11.9
Cedar Rapids, IA	93.5	93.8	87.9	96.3	75.0	29.1	28.7	19.2	69.5	18.1
Charleston, SC	88.5	91.8	81.1	81.6	69.4	31.4	38.2	13.7	34.3	20.9
Charlotte, NC	86.8	88.6	85.1	85.3	59.1	31.2	33.8	22.0	52.3	14.6
Chicago, IL	86.8	89.9	85.3	90.1	61.9	34.8	38.1	20.2	62.2	12.4
Clarksville, TN	88.6	89.3	86.2	84.5	81.9	21.6	23.0	14.8	32.5	15.8
Colorado Springs, CO	93.9	95.3	92.8	84.3	82.1	35.1	37.2	22.6	35.2	17.1
Columbia, MO	93.7	94.4	89.0	90.5	81.2	47.2	48.5	24.6	72.2	37.5
Columbus, OH	90.1	91.2	85.6	89.3	66.7	33.2	34.4	19.7	67.2	19.7
Dallas, TX	84.1	85.3	88.8	88.0	55.2	31.9	33.4	23.7	55.9	11.0
Davenport, IA	90.1	91.3	81.2	82.7	68.0	25.5	25.9	14.4	58.2	12.4
Denver, CO	89.9	91.5	89.5	84.7	66.3	39.7	41.7	25.3	46.7	13.0
Des Moines, IA	92.7	94.0	85.8	82.2	61.0	35.1	36.3	16.9	43.3	14.1
Durham, NC	87.6	89.8	85.1	90.1	47.5	43.7	50.1	26.2	74.8	12.3
El Paso, TX	74.8	75.4	92.6	90.6	69.5	21.0	20.9	28.3	48.9	16.7
Erie, PA	90.4	91.6	79.7	66.3	75.1	25.1	26.0	11.8	39.3	10.9
Eugene, OR	91.4	92.2	94.2	87.3	69.5	27.9	28.2	30.0	45.7	14.2
Fargo, ND	94.4	95.2	82.5	85.9	80.4	35.2	35.6	27.0	48.7	11.1
Fayetteville, NC	89.0	90.8	88.0	81.3	85.2	21.7	24.1	18.9	29.4	15.9
Fort Collins, CO	94.6	95.6	85.4	95.9	74.1	43.6	44.4	18.4	60.3	21.2
Fort Wayne, IN	89.3	91.4	81.8	68.6	60.4	24.8	25.9	14.6	33.7	12.6
Fort Worth, TX	84.1	85.3	88.8	88.0	55.2	31.9	33.4	23.7	55.9	11.0
Gainesville, FL	91.2	93.2	83.6	89.3	90.7	38.1	41.1	16.1	70.2	42.2
Grand Rapids, MI	89.9	91.7	79.0	71.4	60.6	29.6	31.0	13.3	36.5	12.3
Green Bay, WI	90.6	91.5	85.6	81.1	54.2	25.3	25.6	17.5	35.4	14.8
Greensboro, NC	85.1	86.9	84.7	68.6	52.6	27.1	29.4	21.1	34.0	10.5
Honolulu, HI	90.5	96.7	96.3	87.6	90.9	32.2	44.2	28.2	33.1	21.6
Houston, TX	81.4	82.1	87.8	86.2	58.2	29.9	30.8	24.4	53.9	12.0
Huntsville, AL	89.0	90.2	85.9	88.7	68.8	35.5	37.9	26.0	53.8	24.3
Indianapolis, IN	88.8	90.5	84.8	86.1	59.1	30.6	32.7	17.6	57.3	13.5
Jacksonville, FL	89.2	90.4	84.8	87.0	85.2	27.7	29.7	17.0	46.1	25.3
Kansas City, MO	90.9	92.7	85.9	83.1	66.0	33.4	36.0	17.1	50.3	15.8
Lafayette, LA	80.5	84.3	69.3	60.9	64.5	20.0	22.7	11.1	24.0	15.6
Las Vegas, NV	84.1	86.3	86.8	87.9	61.8	22.1	23.1	16.5	35.2	8.6
Lexington, KY	87.7	89.2	84.8	88.9	52.5	35.1	36.9	17.7	72.2	13.1
Lincoln, NE	93.4	94.9	88.4	77.7	63.4	36.1	37.3	18.7	38.1	14.9
Little Rock, AR	89.1	90.3	86.0	88.6	70.0	28.3	30.1	20.4	56.2	12.9
Los Angeles, CA	78.5	81.1	88.3	87.2	57.4	31.6	33.3	24.1	49.9	10.9
Louisville, KY	87.8	88.5	84.2	82.0	71.0	26.6	27.7	16.8	55.8	18.9
Lubbock, TX	83.8	86.6	79.1	90.6	63.9	27.0	29.0	11.6	73.3	8.7
Madison, WI	94.3	95.3	86.7	87.4	70.0	41.7	41.9	22.0	62.8	25.0
Manchester, NH	91.1	91.8	81.9	85.0	70.1	35.5	35.2	26.7	57.2	16.9
McAllen, TX	62.2	62.4	77.0	94.3	58.2	16.2	15.8	28.8	65.0	13.9
Miami, FL	84.2	85.7	79.1	87.1	77.3	29.2	31.7	17.2	49.7	23.8
Midland, TX	81.7	83.9	80.7	81.5	61.3	25.0	27.1	15.1	47.0	9.6

Table continued on next page.

Metro Area	High School Graduate or Higher (%)					Bachelor's Degree or Higher (%)				
	Total	White	Black	Asian	Hisp.[1]	Total	White	Black	Asian	Hisp.[1]
Minneapolis, MN	93.0	95.3	81.5	79.9	64.7	38.8	40.5	20.0	43.7	18.3
Nashville, TN	87.8	89.3	85.2	83.7	60.3	31.4	32.7	24.1	50.0	12.9
New Orleans, LA	84.7	89.1	78.6	70.9	72.9	26.6	32.5	15.3	35.2	20.3
New York, NY	85.1	89.6	82.7	82.3	67.5	36.8	41.7	22.2	52.9	16.5
Oklahoma City, OK	87.3	88.6	89.2	80.9	54.1	28.2	29.8	20.2	41.3	10.0
Omaha, NE	90.9	92.8	85.5	77.5	53.0	33.0	34.3	19.9	50.9	12.1
Orlando, FL	87.6	89.5	83.1	85.6	79.2	28.3	29.9	19.1	47.6	18.9
Oxnard, CA	83.0	84.0	93.0	91.5	59.7	31.3	31.3	33.6	55.2	11.3
Palm Bay, FL	89.7	91.0	79.2	85.6	85.2	26.4	27.1	15.6	38.9	23.7
Peoria, IL	91.2	92.3	79.6	93.6	72.5	26.3	26.3	11.7	78.3	15.8
Philadelphia, PA	89.1	91.9	84.3	82.2	67.8	33.9	37.7	18.0	53.5	15.4
Phoenix, AZ	86.4	87.8	88.6	86.9	62.9	29.0	29.8	22.5	53.3	10.5
Pittsburgh, PA	92.1	92.6	87.9	89.0	85.3	30.8	31.1	16.8	71.0	36.1
Portland, OR	90.8	92.7	87.8	84.6	61.2	34.8	35.7	21.0	44.5	14.8
Providence, RI	84.6	86.3	77.0	78.7	63.0	29.5	30.9	19.2	44.5	12.1
Provo, UT	93.1	94.0	81.2	91.4	69.7	36.3	36.8	40.6	57.7	17.7
Raleigh, NC	89.6	91.9	86.4	90.5	51.5	42.4	46.1	26.6	66.7	15.0
Reno, NV	86.3	88.1	87.8	87.7	54.5	28.0	29.4	21.3	37.8	9.2
Richmond, VA	87.3	90.5	81.3	87.5	62.6	32.7	38.2	18.7	59.0	18.0
Roanoke, VA	86.8	88.1	80.5	80.6	62.0	26.2	27.5	15.0	57.4	8.3
Rochester, MN	93.6	94.4	79.2	88.4	71.4	34.2	33.9	25.0	52.1	23.3
Sacramento, CA	88.1	91.0	88.4	81.9	69.5	30.4	32.0	19.3	39.7	13.7
Salem, OR	84.9	88.2	80.9	90.7	50.7	23.0	24.6	35.0	32.9	7.8
Salt Lake City, UT	89.4	92.2	82.5	82.9	62.9	31.3	32.4	22.5	50.5	12.0
San Antonio, TX	83.4	84.7	89.9	82.4	73.2	26.5	27.7	24.7	48.7	14.9
San Diego, CA	85.6	86.9	89.7	87.8	64.2	34.5	35.7	21.1	45.6	14.9
San Francisco, CA	87.9	91.2	89.8	85.3	67.9	44.8	49.3	23.4	50.5	18.4
San Jose, CA	86.5	88.2	92.5	89.0	65.2	46.2	43.7	29.2	61.2	13.6
Santa Rosa, CA	87.1	90.8	83.3	84.3	57.9	31.9	34.2	29.4	43.8	10.5
Savannah, GA	88.1	90.1	84.5	83.0	69.0	29.8	33.9	19.8	45.6	25.4
Seattle, WA	91.7	93.7	87.4	86.1	70.6	38.1	39.1	20.3	47.9	18.6
Sioux Falls, SD	91.8	93.6	69.5	71.3	58.4	30.6	31.6	15.1	37.4	14.5
Spokane, WA	92.3	93.0	84.0	82.9	80.4	26.9	27.6	15.7	27.5	18.8
Springfield, IL	92.1	93.0	83.2	91.1	89.0	32.2	33.2	17.7	61.4	41.4
Tallahassee, FL	89.2	93.0	81.5	91.9	80.8	36.9	42.7	22.5	73.6	32.9
Tampa, FL	88.0	89.2	83.6	84.2	77.3	26.6	27.0	18.4	48.7	18.4
Topeka, KS	90.8	91.9	82.5	84.2	65.9	26.1	27.2	12.1	59.3	10.3
Tulsa, OK	88.5	89.7	88.2	82.3	58.0	26.1	28.1	18.0	37.5	10.8
Tyler, TX	84.9	85.1	85.7	94.5	45.9	24.8	26.7	14.5	53.6	5.8
Virginia Beach, VA	90.1	92.6	84.8	89.5	84.1	29.0	32.9	18.9	43.7	20.2
Washington, DC	90.2	93.1	89.6	90.5	66.1	48.1	55.6	31.0	62.2	23.6
Wichita, KS	89.6	90.9	87.7	76.5	62.4	28.3	29.7	16.7	30.3	12.1
Wilmington, NC	89.3	92.1	79.3	77.8	55.8	33.2	37.2	13.1	44.4	13.4
Winston-Salem, NC	84.0	84.8	84.5	79.8	47.0	25.4	26.6	18.3	48.0	9.3
Worcester, MA	89.5	90.9	87.8	82.5	67.6	32.4	32.9	23.4	53.3	14.3
U.S.	86.3	88.3	83.1	85.7	64.0	29.1	30.4	18.8	50.7	13.7

Note: Figures shown cover persons 25 years old and over; Figures cover the Metropolitan Statistical Area—see Appendix B for areas included; (1) People of Hispanic origin can be of any race
Source: U.S. Census Bureau, 2011-2013 American Community Survey 3-Year Estimates

Cost of Living Index

Urban Area	Composite	Groceries	Housing	Utilities	Transp.	Health	Misc.
Albuquerque, NM[1]	92.7	89.8	82.6	89.1	99.9	97.8	99.4
Anchorage, AK	125.7	112.6	154.1	98.9	107.0	139.0	121.8
Ann Arbor, MI	101.7	85.8	112.7	106.6	105.0	99.2	97.0
Athens, GA	n/a	n/a	n/a	n/a	n/a	n/a	n/a
Atlanta, GA	94.9	91.2	87.1	92.0	102.0	102.5	99.6
Austin, TX	92.9	84.0	86.0	91.1	97.2	99.4	99.8
Billings, MT	n/a	n/a	n/a	n/a	n/a	n/a	n/a
Boise City, ID	93.2	85.6	86.7	87.9	103.7	103.8	97.3
Boston, MA	139.1	125.5	175.3	144.3	104.1	126.1	129.7
Boulder, CO	n/a	n/a	n/a	n/a	n/a	n/a	n/a
Cape Coral, FL	97.4	91.9	93.2	98.1	109.1	98.1	98.3
Cedar Rapids, IA	91.6	86.5	82.1	102.2	94.6	101.5	95.2
Charleston, SC	99.8	104.9	88.8	113.5	95.7	103.0	103.4
Charlotte, NC	95.4	101.6	83.7	106.6	98.4	98.2	97.0
Chicago, IL	114.8	98.1	135.3	98.9	124.1	97.7	109.2
Clarksville, TN	n/a	n/a	n/a	n/a	n/a	n/a	n/a
Colorado Springs, CO	95.7	93.5	94.4	101.0	94.4	102.4	95.6
Columbia, MO	95.6	91.3	88.3	98.0	94.3	101.7	102.1
Columbus, OH	86.9	86.5	77.1	96.4	96.2	95.1	87.2
Dallas, TX	95.6	92.3	75.5	106.9	102.2	99.1	106.2
Davenport, IA	95.4	86.6	100.2	85.5	111.2	94.9	92.1
Denver, CO	103.8	93.4	115.5	101.3	94.8	103.7	103.0
Des Moines, IA	90.0	85.2	85.4	89.5	96.1	93.6	92.8
Durham, NC	92.3	100.4	80.2	83.5	98.6	101.7	97.5
El Paso, TX	91.2	90.8	84.0	87.2	97.5	89.9	96.1
Erie, PA	97.8	97.5	94.8	97.1	100.5	94.6	99.9
Eugene, OR	n/a	n/a	n/a	n/a	n/a	n/a	n/a
Fargo, ND	93.5	97.6	83.6	89.4	95.6	111.8	97.4
Fayetteville, NC	n/a	n/a	n/a	n/a	n/a	n/a	n/a
Fort Collins, CO	n/a	n/a	n/a	n/a	n/a	n/a	n/a
Fort Wayne, IN	91.3	82.5	85.0	89.5	104.3	95.8	94.7
Fort Worth, TX	97.1	93.6	85.6	99.6	101.8	104.1	103.9
Gainesville, FL	98.7	97.3	94.1	106.1	104.1	101.2	98.1
Grand Rapids, MI	92.7	84.4	77.6	99.4	106.6	91.8	100.9
Green Bay, WI	93.3	86.4	83.9	101.2	99.5	106.1	96.9
Greensboro, NC[2]	88.1	98.0	69.5	100.3	85.3	102.9	94.0
Honolulu, HI	168.3	154.7	262.4	171.4	126.5	111.3	123.1
Houston, TX	98.8	79.5	107.3	103.2	95.4	96.4	100.2
Huntsville, AL	94.2	89.4	79.1	103.7	98.7	96.2	103.2
Indianapolis, IN	91.6	85.5	80.9	91.3	99.4	115.7	96.1
Jacksonville, FL	94.9	95.2	83.3	105.7	104.7	85.1	98.4
Kansas City, MO	98.9	95.6	91.7	110.6	98.2	96.3	102.9
Lafayette, LA	95.9	90.5	101.5	87.8	104.1	84.8	94.6
Las Vegas, NV	100.4	96.5	99.7	85.3	100.9	103.4	106.4
Lexington, KY	89.4	86.1	75.6	101.0	97.9	94.3	94.1
Lincoln, NE	89.3	87.6	75.6	92.3	96.6	95.0	96.3
Little Rock, AR	97.9	89.2	96.6	110.3	93.3	83.9	102.5
Los Angeles, CA	129.8	102.8	196.8	108.0	111.0	109.5	104.8
Louisville, KY	91.0	85.3	81.6	87.2	101.0	91.2	98.1
Lubbock, TX	89.2	90.4	81.4	78.4	95.0	95.6	95.0
Madison, WI	105.2	90.5	110.4	104.2	106.1	123.9	104.2
Manchester, NH	120.2	98.5	137.9	122.7	101.2	117.7	121.9
McAllen, TX	87.9	83.3	78.8	99.9	94.6	88.6	90.5
Miami, FL	107.2	99.9	118.0	95.7	110.4	104.4	104.3
Midland, TX	99.4	88.3	100.2	93.2	104.7	95.0	103.7
Minneapolis, MN	109.7	115.4	116.5	97.8	103.6	98.9	109.4

Table continued on next page.

Urban Area	Composite	Groceries	Housing	Utilities	Transp.	Health	Misc.
Nashville, TN	87.3	87.8	74.3	87.0	94.1	81.4	95.8
New Orleans, LA	98.4	97.9	95.1	91.3	100.0	103.2	102.1
New York, NY	170.7	118.7	320.3	124.0	111.9	110.3	119.2
Oklahoma City, OK	89.9	87.8	82.2	91.6	98.9	98.1	91.7
Omaha, NE	86.9	84.3	78.4	91.1	96.6	100.6	87.6
Orlando, FL	96.0	96.7	78.6	104.4	98.5	99.3	105.6
Oxnard, CA	n/a	n/a	n/a	n/a	n/a	n/a	n/a
Palm Bay, TX	n/a	n/a	n/a	n/a	n/a	n/a	n/a
Peoria, IL	99.2	89.0	100.0	95.9	108.2	95.8	100.8
Philadelphia, PA	120.8	112.8	141.9	128.2	105.1	100.0	114.3
Phoenix, AZ	95.6	93.4	96.2	97.6	95.5	95.8	95.4
Pittsburgh, PA	93.6	94.2	79.3	94.9	104.2	100.9	99.1
Portland, OR	117.1	102.7	142.3	96.6	115.1	117.2	110.1
Providence, RI	125.2	106.9	138.8	133.1	104.2	118.2	128.4
Provo, UT	95.5	88.3	87.1	91.0	111.3	93.1	100.8
Raleigh, NC	93.3	101.7	76.1	105.7	97.8	101.7	96.6
Reno, NV	89.8	90.1	88.1	73.0	103.1	93.3	90.4
Richmond, VA	101.4	98.2	89.4	107.6	99.7	106.5	110.1
Roanoke, VA	999.0	91.0	89.3	98.9	91.3	96.7	89.7
Rochester, MN	100.6	95.9	99.3	101.8	101.9	104.8	102.0
Sacramento, CA	999.0	116.1	117.4	114.7	110.7	111.8	106.5
Salem, OR	n/a	n/a	n/a	n/a	n/a	n/a	n/a
Salt Lake City, UT	94.1	88.4	90.0	84.2	98.8	96.7	100.5
San Antonio, TX	88.4	81.4	79.5	82.6	95.5	93.7	96.6
San Diego, CA	129.4	101.6	199.0	97.7	113.3	109.7	104.5
San Francisco, CA	160.8	119.2	293.5	95.0	114.9	119.9	116.4
San Jose, CA	148.6	110.4	255.6	123.2	112.1	114.6	106.5
Santa Rosa, CA	n/a	n/a	n/a	n/a	n/a	n/a	n/a
Savannah, GA	92.5	91.2	71.5	111.5	102.0	100.1	99.2
Seattle, WA	118.6	102.6	140.1	97.0	118.3	118.9	114.7
Sioux Falls, SD	97.1	86.3	92.5	107.1	93.7	101.3	102.8
Spokane, WA	95.6	91.8	88.4	91.2	99.5	109.8	100.5
Springfield, IL	999.0	95.4	80.4	76.8	101.5	105.1	87.2
Tallahassee, FL	98.1	99.2	98.2	88.7	101.1	101.4	98.6
Tampa, FL	92.8	92.7	78.4	93.9	102.3	95.6	99.8
Topeka, KS	93.4	87.5	91.4	84.0	94.3	91.8	100.2
Tulsa, OK	88.0	85.5	65.0	96.5	96.3	95.5	100.3
Tyler, TX	999.0	93.0	95.8	94.0	96.3	90.7	96.6
Virginia Beach, VA[3]	n/a	n/a	n/a	n/a	n/a	n/a	n/a
Washington, DC	139.4	107.9	247.5	104.1	105.6	98.6	96.6
Wichita, KS	91.6	88.2	75.6	107.7	96.9	94.8	98.2
Wilmington, NC	98.2	104.8	84.9	107.8	97.8	107.4	102.0
Winston-Salem, NC	999.0	102.4	66.8	105.9	96.5	106.5	97.8
Worcester, MA[4]	104.2	94.3	97.7	117.6	103.8	123.4	106.6
U.S.	100.0	100.0	100.0	100.0	100.0	100.0	100.0

Note: The Cost of Living Index measures regional differences in the cost of consumer goods and services, excluding taxes and non-consumer expenditures, for professional and managerial households in the top income quintile. It is based on more than 50,000 prices covering almost 60 different items for which prices are collected three times a year by chambers of commerce, economic development organizations or university applied economic centers in each participating urban area. The numbers shown should be read as a percentage above or below the national average of 100. For example, a value of 115.4 in the groceries column indicates that grocery prices are 15.4% higher than the national average. Small differences in the index numbers should not be interpreted as significant. In cases where data is not available for the city, data for the metro area or for a neighboring city has been provided and noted as follows: (1) Rio Rancho, NM; (2) Winston-Salem, NC; (3) Hampton Roads-SE Virginia; (4) Fitchburg-Leominster, MA
Source: The Council for Community and Economic Research (formerly ACCRA), Cost of Living Index, 2014

Grocery Prices

Urban Area	T-Bone Steak ($/pound)	Frying Chicken ($/pound)	Whole Milk ($/half gal.)	Eggs ($/dozen)	Orange Juice ($/64 oz.)	Coffee ($/11.5 oz.)
Albuquerque, NM[1]	10.88	1.06	2.52	2.04	3.48	4.79
Anchorage, AK	11.85	1.39	2.53	2.29	4.54	5.49
Ann Arbor, MI	10.58	1.17	2.22	1.80	3.05	3.75
Athens, GA	n/a	n/a	n/a	n/a	n/a	n/a
Atlanta, GA	11.61	1.26	2.45	1.80	3.48	4.84
Austin, TX	9.82	1.09	2.18	1.95	3.22	3.79
Billings, MT	n/a	n/a	n/a	n/a	n/a	n/a
Boise City, ID	8.98	1.29	1.72	1.35	3.52	4.75
Boston, MA	11.29	1.76	2.79	2.72	3.92	4.75
Boulder, CO	n/a	n/a	n/a	n/a	n/a	n/a
Cape Coral, FL	11.36	1.42	2.83	2.11	3.84	4.12
Cedar Rapids, IA	9.85	1.41	2.32	1.88	3.20	3.97
Charleston, SC	11.45	1.44	2.72	1.98	3.72	4.48
Charlotte, NC	10.21	1.37	2.62	1.92	3.41	3.98
Chicago, IL	10.81	1.54	1.93	1.87	3.88	5.43
Clarksville, TN	n/a	n/a	n/a	n/a	n/a	n/a
Colorado Springs, CO	10.56	1.09	2.00	2.07	3.14	4.64
Columbia, MO	10.36	1.28	2.46	1.95	3.28	4.15
Columbus, OH	11.65	1.11	2.06	1.86	3.20	4.55
Dallas, TX	9.53	1.35	2.34	1.81	4.01	4.09
Davenport, IA	9.49	1.52	2.43	1.89	3.15	4.28
Denver, CO	10.29	1.35	2.05	2.10	3.66	5.13
Des Moines, IA	9.21	1.55	2.24	1.88	3.11	4.16
Durham, NC	9.90	1.32	2.58	2.09	3.46	4.01
El Paso, TX	10.65	1.30	2.26	1.78	3.22	4.43
Erie, PA	10.11	1.63	2.19	1.90	3.45	4.08
Eugene, OR	n/a	n/a	n/a	n/a	n/a	n/a
Fargo, ND	10.26	1.83	2.96	2.01	3.50	4.35
Fayetteville, NC	n/a	n/a	n/a	n/a	n/a	n/a
Fort Collins, CO	n/a	n/a	n/a	n/a	n/a	n/a
Fort Wayne, IN	10.26	1.10	2.06	1.77	3.58	4.84
Fort Worth, TX	10.05	1.13	2.01	1.89	3.53	4.12
Gainesville, FL	11.14	1.47	2.83	1.99	3.57	3.78
Grand Rapids, MI	11.49	1.13	2.36	1.92	3.30	3.78
Green Bay, WI	10.99	1.63	2.48	1.76	3.19	3.96
Greensboro, NC[2]	11.31	1.34	2.69	2.08	3.34	3.89
Honolulu, HI	11.62	2.42	3.62	3.58	4.92	6.96
Houston, TX	8.77	1.09	2.12	1.83	3.08	3.88
Huntsville, AL	10.87	1.30	2.37	1.98	3.29	4.15
Indianapolis, IN	9.97	1.20	2.17	1.78	3.30	3.97
Jacksonville, FL	10.84	1.45	2.75	1.92	3.39	3.96
Kansas City, MO	10.45	1.82	2.44	2.04	3.57	3.93
Lafayette, LA	9.74	1.15	2.75	1.84	3.45	3.67
Las Vegas, NV	8.83	1.61	2.17	2.02	3.95	4.81
Lexington, KY	10.90	1.21	2.36	1.93	3.54	4.28
Lincoln, NE	10.03	1.18	2.49	1.71	3.63	4.84
Little Rock, AR	10.46	1.13	2.17	1.78	3.22	4.02
Los Angeles, CA	9.88	1.53	2.51	2.46	3.20	5.09
Louisville, KY	9.26	1.04	2.06	1.84	3.24	4.51
Lubbock, TX	9.75	1.16	2.69	2.13	3.21	3.86
Madison, WI	10.55	1.67	2.38	1.75	3.44	4.45
Manchester, NH	9.61	1.43	2.11	1.96	2.96	3.60
McAllen, TX	9.47	1.02	2.42	1.79	3.03	3.34
Miami, FL	10.50	1.62	2.82	2.17	3.26	3.42
Midland, TX	10.45	1.16	2.06	1.82	3.08	3.70

Table continued on next page.

Urban Area	T-Bone Steak ($/pound)	Frying Chicken ($/pound)	Whole Milk ($/half gal.)	Eggs ($/dozen)	Orange Juice ($/64 oz.)	Coffee ($/11.5 oz.)
Minneapolis, MN	14.20	1.80	2.23	1.91	3.83	4.66
Nashville, TN	10.75	1.28	2.07	1.91	3.24	4.04
New Orleans, LA	10.80	1.14	2.54	2.08	3.38	3.60
New York, NY	11.75	1.60	2.06	2.49	4.32	4.73
Oklahoma City, OK	10.13	1.18	2.32	1.80	3.47	4.06
Omaha, NE	10.11	1.29	2.27	1.85	3.38	4.15
Orlando, FL	11.07	1.45	2.69	1.92	3.55	4.09
Oxnard, CA	n/a	n/a	n/a	n/a	n/a	n/a
Palm Bay, TX	n/a	n/a	n/a	n/a	n/a	n/a
Peoria, IL	9.99	1.02	2.31	2.00	3.40	4.31
Philadelphia, PA	10.95	1.70	2.24	2.47	3.84	4.05
Phoenix, AZ	10.45	1.99	1.83	2.06	3.61	4.76
Pittsburgh, PA	11.35	1.56	2.13	1.82	3.41	4.08
Portland, OR	10.13	2.23	1.98	2.09	3.90	5.42
Providence, RI	11.24	1.58	2.95	2.69	3.57	4.89
Provo, UT	9.56	1.47	2.13	1.65	3.30	5.31
Raleigh, NC	10.94	1.39	2.48	2.14	3.52	4.07
Reno, NV	10.12	1.45	2.29	1.85	3.70	4.70
Richmond, VA	9.82	1.46	2.26	1.90	3.24	4.02
Roanoke, VA	9.76	1.11	2.30	1.94	3.12	3.89
Rochester, MN	n/a	n/a	n/a	n/a	n/a	n/a
Sacramento, CA	9.80	1.52	2.45	2.29	3.98	5.34
Salem, OR	n/a	n/a	n/a	n/a	n/a	n/a
Salt Lake City, UT	10.69	1.40	2.28	1.66	3.71	4.98
San Antonio, TX	9.29	1.35	2.47	2.17	2.96	3.76
San Diego, CA	10.04	1.40	2.58	2.67	3.27	5.09
San Francisco, CA	10.74	1.72	2.81	3.15	4.34	5.78
San Jose, CA	11.28	1.43	2.53	2.53	4.11	6.32
Santa Rosa, CA	n/a	n/a	n/a	n/a	n/a	n/a
Savannah, GA	10.66	1.42	2.72	1.82	3.20	4.15
Seattle, WA	11.38	1.72	1.97	2.02	3.78	5.48
Sioux Falls, SD	10.05	1.89	2.40	1.81	3.10	4.24
Spokane, WA	10.80	1.51	1.89	1.93	3.00	4.55
Springfield, IL	10.04	1.29	2.31	1.95	3.03	3.80
Tallahassee, FL	n/a	n/a	n/a	n/a	n/a	n/a
Tampa, FL	10.60	1.43	2.69	2.04	3.38	3.56
Topeka, KS	10.30	1.49	2.43	1.90	3.31	4.34
Tulsa, OK	10.30	1.19	2.40	1.95	3.67	3.55
Tyler, TX	9.48	1.12	2.78	2.03	3.26	3.44
Virginia Beach, VA[3]	10.03	1.19	2.47	1.88	3.70	3.85
Washington, DC	11.28	1.69	2.67	2.13	3.57	4.79
Wichita, KS	9.39	1.44	2.24	1.69	3.39	3.86
Wilmington, NC	10.14	1.46	2.72	2.11	3.32	3.96
Winston-Salem, NC	11.31	1.34	2.69	2.08	3.34	3.89
Worcester, MA[4]	9.78	1.45	1.82	1.82	2.96	3.48
Average*	10.40	1.37	2.40	1.99	3.46	4.27
Minimum*	8.48	0.93	1.37	1.30	2.83	2.99
Maximum*	14.20	2.44	3.62	4.02	6.42	6.96

*Note: **T-Bone Steak** (price per pound); **Frying Chicken** (price per pound, whole fryer); **Whole Milk** (half gallon carton); **Eggs** (price per dozen, Grade A, large); **Orange Juice** (64 oz. Tropicana or Florida Natural); **Coffee** (11.5 oz. can, vacuum-packed, Maxwell House, Hills Bros, or Folgers); (*) Values for the local area are compared with the average, minimum, and maximum values for all 308 areas in the Cost of Living Index report; n/a not available; In cases where data is not available for the city, data for the metro area or for a neighboring city has been provided and noted as follows: (1) Rio Rancho, NM; (2) Winston-Salem, NC; (3) Hampton Roads-SE Virginia; (4) Fitchburg-Leominster, MA*
Source: The Council for Community and Economic Research (formerly ACCRA), Cost of Living Index, 2014

Housing and Utility Costs

Urban Area	New Home Price ($)	Apartment Rent ($/month)	All Electric ($/month)	Part Electric ($/month)	Other Energy ($/month)	Telephone ($/month)
Albuquerque, NM[1]	234,773	747	-	103.86	59.10	22.15
Anchorage, AK	493,524	1,280	-	82.78	85.24	26.34
Ann Arbor, MI	357,512	1,013	-	112.83	70.62	27.02
Athens, GA	n/a	n/a	n/a	n/a	n/a	n/a
Atlanta, GA	286,196	948	-	92.54	62.77	25.06
Austin, TX	239,151	1,037	-	103.58	41.87	35.66
Billings, MT	n/a	n/a	n/a	n/a	n/a	n/a
Boise City, ID	266,916	730	-	83.64	65.94	24.98
Boston, MA	487,661	1,940	-	106.16	122.55	38.25
Boulder, CO	n/a	n/a	n/a	n/a	n/a	n/a
Cape Coral, FL	260,323	925	165.00	-	-	19.97
Cedar Rapids, IA	266,293	752	-	100.61	69.98	29.99
Charleston, SC	263,355	1,078	202.00	-	-	28.92
Charlotte, NC	253,000	859	175.00	-	-	31.26
Chicago, IL	428,069	1,149	-	86.13	79.96	30.02
Clarksville, TN	n/a	n/a	n/a	n/a	n/a	n/a
Colorado Springs, CO	285,348	963	-	73.42	61.97	31.64
Columbia, MO	272,145	751	-	88.84	66.60	29.28
Columbus, OH	231,144	821	-	81.41	76.30	27.99
Dallas, TX	214,204	825	-	126.22	50.81	28.15
Davenport, IA	320,560	747	-	75.39	70.86	24.52
Denver, CO	377,658	1,158	-	96.13	68.50	27.60
Des Moines, IA	277,543	638	-	76.85	71.31	28.50
Durham, NC	220,534	794	169.00	-	-	20.50
El Paso, TX	244,332	930	-	99.97	39.65	26.95
Erie, PA	261,665	735	-	89.20	81.87	21.95
Eugene, OR	n/a	n/a	n/a	n/a	n/a	n/a
Fargo, ND	247,098	820	-	66.58	71.58	29.95
Fayetteville, NC	n/a	n/a	n/a	n/a	n/a	n/a
Fort Collins, CO	n/a	n/a	n/a	n/a	n/a	n/a
Fort Wayne, IN	242,584	620	-	69.95	68.49	30.99
Fort Worth, TX	228,573	1,332	-	125.46	51.44	23.97
Gainesville, FL	275,745	890	-	124.58	44.11	27.78
Grand Rapids, MI	224,700	801	-	87.26	75.22	25.98
Green Bay, WI	258,349	659	-	77.19	73.74	35.08
Greensboro, NC[2]	203,576	620	170.00	-	-	31.73
Honolulu, HI	752,644	2,975	498.00	-	-	28.95
Houston, TX	273,623	1,427	-	116.14	41.72	30.15
Huntsville, AL	229,687	836	151.00	-	-	35.51
Indianapolis, IN	233,436	903	-	81.78	83.73	25.68
Jacksonville, FL	229,363	1,069	170.00	-	-	32.75
Kansas City, MO	281,080	824	-	91.74	70.92	34.11
Lafayette, LA	272,388	907	-	95.47	49.71	28.73
Las Vegas, NV	334,773	911	-	133.02	49.81	18.66
Lexington, KY	207,741	848	-	68.99	67.19	32.67
Lincoln, NE	227,531	727	-	71.46	85.52	26.84
Little Rock, AR	298,117	777	-	81.80	63.66	39.30
Los Angeles, CA	574,972	2,289	-	112.12	69.90	33.30
Louisville, KY	236,192	808	-	52.85	71.13	29.18
Lubbock, TX	241,638	811	-	81.85	44.15	24.01
Madison, WI	367,067	911	-	103.82	84.76	23.99
Manchester, NH	376,734	1,309	-	107.64	98.01	36.12
McAllen, TX	227,081	768	-	139.08	38.11	21.01
Miami, FL	357,091	1,300	164.00	-	-	27.70
Midland, TX	252,485	1,281	-	115.55	42.96	24.95

Table continued on next page.

Urban Area	New Home Price ($)	Apartment Rent ($/month)	All Electric ($/month)	Part Electric ($/month)	Other Energy ($/month)	Telephone ($/month)
Minneapolis, MN	343,961	1,118	-	85.84	74.83	25.07
Nashville, TN	211,580	870	-	97.85	63.67	24.50
New Orleans, LA	285,368	908	-	90.13	40.75	26.23
New York, NY	936,793	2,221	-	127.59	111.72	30.33
Oklahoma City, OK	246,396	779	-	81.43	66.90	28.01
Omaha, NE	236,764	732	-	83.52	77.29	26.68
Orlando, FL	274,673	889	190.00	-	-	28.88
Oxnard, CA	n/a	n/a	n/a	n/a	n/a	n/a
Palm Bay, TX	n/a	n/a	n/a	n/a	n/a	n/a
Peoria, IL	334,061	698	-	93.06	63.51	29.18
Philadelphia, PA	406,468	1,283	-	121.67	65.97	38.50
Phoenix, AZ	283,722	827	188.00	-	-	21.32
Pittsburgh, PA	241,321	986	-	94.00	87.20	25.98
Portland, OR	404,703	2,196	-	80.86	74.95	25.01
Providence, RI	386,111	1,394	-	102.86	103.42	36.19
Provo, UT	260,061	783	-	65.05	74.80	24.80
Raleigh, NC	236,443	713	-	91.07	63.74	32.22
Reno, NV	248,538	930	-	80.67	72.32	19.43
Richmond, VA	260,500	867	-	88.12	77.82	34.01
Roanoke, VA	281,983	746	178.00	-	-	25.25
Rochester, MN	n/a	n/a	n/a	n/a	n/a	n/a
Sacramento, CA	371,449	1,028	-	165.81	38.42	29.74
Salem, OR	n/a	n/a	n/a	n/a	n/a	n/a
Salt Lake City, UT	278,495	865	-	71.14	71.90	29.99
San Antonio, TX	225,397	855	-	96.27	37.03	25.51
San Diego, CA	634,116	1,754	-	123.00	56.46	33.30
San Francisco, CA	920,224	3,072	-	118.94	71.93	24.12
San Jose, CA	813,571	1,778	-	178.34	70.10	26.98
Santa Rosa, CA	n/a	n/a	n/a	n/a	n/a	n/a
Savannah, GA	198,491	767	164.00	-	-	33.80
Seattle, WA	472,833	1,821	173.00	-	-	25.95
Sioux Falls, SD	299,389	755	-	78.88	68.21	35.59
Spokane, WA	274,248	740	-	55.87	77.90	22.09
Springfield, IL	250,588	722	-	84.90	63.73	17.16
Tallahassee, FL	n/a	n/a	n/a	n/a	n/a	n/a
Tampa, FL	212,792	843	161.00	-	-	32.47
Topeka, KS	249,762	808	-	82.02	77.34	22.99
Tulsa, OK	197,493	592	-	79.44	58.96	32.13
Tyler, TX	268,261	1,071	-	121.67	44.31	24.72
Virginia Beach, VA[3]	270,044	968	-	90.92	70.55	34.99
Washington, DC	784,280	1,973	-	78.99	84.64	27.32
Wichita, KS	220,755	678	-	92.01	70.07	36.77
Wilmington, NC	285,525	708	172.00	-	-	29.98
Winston-Salem, NC	203,576	620	170.00	-	-	31.73
Worcester, MA[4]	314,699	991	-	91.53	120.26	29.33
Average*	305,838	919	181.00	93.66	73.14	27.95
Minimum*	183,142	480	112.00	42.06	23.42	17.16
Maximum*	1,358,576	3,851	594.00	180.03	440.99	40.42

*Note: **New Home Price** (2,400 sf living area, 8,000 sf lot, in urban area with full utilities); **Apartment Rent** (950 sf 2 bedroom/1.5 or 2 bath, unfurnished, excluding all utilities except water); **All Electric** (average monthly cost for an all-electric home); **Part Electric** (average monthly cost for a part-electric home); **Other Energy** (average monthly cost for natural gas, fuel oil, coal, wood, and any other forms of energy except electricity); **Telephone** (price includes basic monthly rate for a private residential line plus additional local usage charges incurred by a family of four); (*) Values for the local area are compared with the average, minimum, and maximum values for all 308 areas in the Cost of Living Index report; n/a not available; In cases where data is not available for the city, data for the metro area or for a neighboring city has been provided noted as follows: (1) Rio Rancho, NM; (2) Winston-Salem, NC; (3) Hampton Roads-SE Virginia; (4) Fitchburg-Leominster, MA Source: The Council for Community and Economic Research (formerly ACCRA), Cost of Living Index, 2014*

Health Care, Transportation, and Other Costs

Urban Area	Doctor ($/visit)	Dentist ($/visit)	Optometrist ($/visit)	Gasoline ($/gallon)	Beauty Salon ($/visit)	Men's Shirt ($)
Albuquerque, NM[1]	96.44	93.30	99.33	3.28	25.89	33.77
Anchorage, AK	167.20	129.47	164.89	3.76	48.53	27.39
Ann Arbor, MI	102.40	90.29	89.73	3.50	34.04	22.67
Athens, GA	n/a	n/a	n/a	n/a	n/a	n/a
Atlanta, GA	97.13	100.61	83.70	3.44	42.80	24.27
Austin, TX	89.86	91.64	122.67	3.33	41.49	29.72
Billings, MT	n/a	n/a	n/a	n/a	n/a	n/a
Boise City, ID	123.82	83.40	110.75	3.48	28.39	30.38
Boston, MA	149.67	105.07	121.77	3.60	50.67	40.32
Boulder, CO	n/a	n/a	n/a	n/a	n/a	n/a
Cape Coral, FL	107.90	92.31	93.93	3.58	39.87	23.17
Cedar Rapids, IA	127.22	76.53	119.95	3.27	36.04	20.67
Charleston, SC	108.95	101.00	97.24	3.31	35.29	33.13
Charlotte, NC	100.20	90.87	118.61	3.46	36.30	24.22
Chicago, IL	94.00	96.67	91.53	4.16	42.33	22.05
Clarksville, TN	n/a	n/a	n/a	n/a	n/a	n/a
Colorado Springs, CO	115.00	90.05	107.03	3.32	34.60	23.58
Columbia, MO	118.50	87.62	76.89	3.19	31.20	25.84
Columbus, OH	103.46	79.79	59.89	3.54	32.33	24.90
Dallas, TX	100.80	86.99	102.48	3.36	39.23	31.16
Davenport, IA	93.34	95.40	98.33	3.43	28.25	28.39
Denver, CO	120.48	85.30	99.71	3.46	36.43	29.58
Des Moines, IA	115.93	77.19	83.75	3.32	28.41	18.52
Durham, NC	92.23	83.08	119.00	3.51	44.25	20.23
El Paso, TX	83.67	79.14	75.22	3.31	32.50	24.55
Erie, PA	83.59	80.79	95.25	3.19	41.26	36.26
Eugene, OR	n/a	n/a	n/a	n/a	n/a	n/a
Fargo, ND	146.17	92.47	79.17	3.30	27.40	26.75
Fayetteville, NC	n/a	n/a	n/a	n/a	n/a	n/a
Fort Collins, CO	n/a	n/a	n/a	n/a	n/a	n/a
Fort Wayne, IN	86.33	82.00	85.28	3.52	22.37	22.66
Fort Worth, TX	98.71	97.50	90.58	3.44	44.90	35.77
Gainesville, FL	88.61	99.78	82.72	3.49	35.00	20.65
Grand Rapids, MI	90.90	78.31	84.00	3.41	34.78	22.59
Green Bay, WI	138.69	84.75	63.17	3.32	29.65	35.70
Greensboro, NC[2]	125.36	82.29	99.82	3.44	35.67	36.54
Honolulu, HI	110.28	92.34	142.51	4.21	52.93	37.57
Houston, TX	82.15	83.51	86.81	3.29	49.10	25.91
Huntsville, AL	80.83	90.64	108.06	3.35	31.92	30.07
Indianapolis, IN	97.32	86.70	86.96	3.45	29.63	30.41
Jacksonville, FL	67.47	91.07	74.07	3.41	57.78	21.33
Kansas City, MO	99.61	86.63	95.86	3.37	27.37	40.23
Lafayette, LA	75.97	76.38	72.87	3.20	33.93	28.99
Las Vegas, NV	114.52	88.96	98.47	3.57	49.06	43.20
Lexington, KY	85.60	83.67	73.13	3.40	39.80	38.14
Lincoln, NE	110.11	77.67	94.67	3.38	27.95	30.96
Little Rock, AR	92.19	66.00	81.67	3.33	41.33	31.51
Los Angeles, CA	97.18	108.13	124.85	4.01	63.24	27.74
Louisville, KY	87.77	87.47	82.00	3.69	32.80	30.67
Lubbock, TX	102.87	78.39	98.87	3.18	35.33	29.71
Madison, WI	158.67	92.44	61.00	3.44	43.78	27.44
Manchester, NH	144.42	103.07	99.49	3.45	37.50	27.89
McAllen, TX	71.67	68.33	68.22	3.23	29.11	19.16
Miami, FL	101.25	96.00	92.50	3.63	53.00	22.99
Midland, TX	96.00	86.00	99.00	3.30	35.00	15.08

Table continued on next page.

Urban Area	Doctor ($/visit)	Dentist ($/visit)	Optometrist ($/visit)	Gasoline ($/gallon)	Beauty Salon ($/visit)	Men's Shirt ($)
Minneapolis, MN	127.48	83.29	80.70	3.42	33.73	28.37
Nashville, TN	80.53	78.65	67.17	3.33	31.13	23.67
New Orleans, LA	81.90	96.78	73.45	3.29	44.67	22.43
New York, NY	108.70	112.67	92.65	3.72	58.68	26.11
Oklahoma City, OK	85.39	99.85	98.73	3.09	36.21	27.03
Omaha, NE	129.98	73.06	97.32	3.23	28.05	19.90
Orlando, FL	84.90	83.18	63.41	3.42	45.04	25.52
Oxnard, CA	n/a	n/a	n/a	n/a	n/a	n/a
Palm Bay, TX	n/a	n/a	n/a	n/a	n/a	n/a
Peoria, IL	97.38	74.95	94.46	3.52	24.99	25.38
Philadelphia, PA	118.19	92.59	102.22	3.60	52.14	40.74
Phoenix, AZ	105.67	98.33	76.00	3.42	25.00	21.66
Pittsburgh, PA	101.66	86.88	107.00	3.65	34.71	25.50
Portland, OR	131.34	104.55	110.90	3.84	44.20	29.59
Providence, RI	149.00	97.78	127.22	3.60	40.00	37.21
Provo, UT	98.95	75.26	89.10	3.13	30.99	20.62
Raleigh, NC	94.33	102.23	97.06	3.45	35.43	21.43
Reno, NV	78.40	91.03	110.56	3.73	33.74	22.02
Richmond, VA	100.07	97.80	118.13	3.28	45.00	19.96
Roanoke, VA	76.92	99.07	77.67	3.15	31.46	15.33
Rochester, MN	n/a	n/a	n/a	n/a	n/a	n/a
Sacramento, CA	110.82	103.23	113.80	3.75	43.78	27.65
Salem, OR	n/a	n/a	n/a	n/a	n/a	n/a
Salt Lake City, UT	98.89	75.78	86.83	3.33	38.92	19.77
San Antonio, TX	96.30	84.33	87.56	3.32	34.15	32.08
San Diego, CA	106.91	106.67	103.63	4.08	56.71	26.86
San Francisco, CA	127.18	117.15	120.63	3.73	60.47	33.81
San Jose, CA	110.69	113.79	129.54	3.82	50.49	25.17
Santa Rosa, CA	n/a	n/a	n/a	n/a	n/a	n/a
Savannah, GA	110.33	81.99	71.91	3.36	35.32	23.38
Seattle, WA	103.22	119.44	139.00	3.78	55.89	22.52
Sioux Falls, SD	114.70	84.04	107.03	3.34	28.62	23.71
Spokane, WA	126.67	97.88	118.51	3.59	30.50	22.41
Springfield, IL	129.22	82.72	82.91	3.49	35.79	17.19
Tallahassee, FL	n/a	n/a	n/a	n/a	n/a	n/a
Tampa, FL	85.10	76.28	92.33	3.40	32.07	22.35
Topeka, KS	87.70	79.95	127.53	3.22	27.33	31.73
Tulsa, OK	106.78	73.80	78.86	3.11	33.89	22.11
Tyler, TX	78.96	84.22	97.50	3.27	41.93	27.84
Virginia Beach, VA[3]	115.08	98.11	92.11	3.34	38.87	24.74
Washington, DC	87.41	89.46	70.67	3.57	51.29	27.45
Wichita, KS	95.75	79.28	134.52	3.28	39.50	37.09
Wilmington, NC	125.22	96.67	108.61	3.48	34.44	41.18
Winston-Salem, NC	125.36	82.29	99.82	3.44	35.67	36.54
Worcester, MA[4]	154.80	98.73	108.75	3.99	32.11	26.60
Average*	102.86	87.89	97.66	3.44	34.37	26.74
Minimum*	67.47	65.78	51.18	3.00	17.43	12.79
Maximum*	173.50	150.14	235.00	4.33	64.28	49.50

Note: **Doctor** (general practitioners routine exam of an established patient); **Dentist** (adult teeth cleaning and periodic oral examination); **Optometrist** (full vision eye exam for established adult patient); **Gasoline** (one gallon regular unleaded, national brand, including all taxes, cash price at self-service pump if available); **Beauty Salon** (woman's shampoo, trim, and blow-dry); **Men's Shirt** (cotton/polyester dress shirt, pinpoint weave, long sleeves); (*) Values for the local area are compared with the average, minimum, and maximum values for all 308 areas in the Cost of Living Index report; n/a not available; In cases where data is not available for the city, data for the metro area or for a neighboring city has been provided and noted as follows: (1) Rio Rancho, NM; (2) Winston-Salem, NC; (3) Hampton Roads-SE Virginia; (4) Fitchburg-Leominster, MA
Source: The Council for Community and Economic Research (formerly ACCRA), Cost of Living Index, 2014

Number of Medical Professionals

City	Area Covered	MDs[1]	DOs[1,2]	Dentists	Podiatrists	Chiropractors	Optometrists
Albuquerque, NM	Bernalillo County	419.0	19.9	74.7	8.1	22.8	15.9
Anchorage, AK	Anchorage (B) Borough	310.4	27.5	104.1	4.3	46.7	24.2
Ann Arbor, MI	Washtenaw County	1,145.7	33.0	150.7	5.4	22.3	15.0
Athens, GA	Clarke County	278.5	9.1	54.5	5.0	19.8	17.3
Atlanta, GA	Fulton County	482.4	10.0	65.1	4.1	47.1	13.9
Austin, TX	Travis County	295.7	15.9	64.2	4.9	30.1	15.1
Billings, MT	Yellowstone County	339.7	19.8	83.1	7.1	32.5	24.0
Boise City, ID	Ada County	278.3	20.5	79.7	3.4	50.7	17.8
Boston, MA	Suffolk County	1,350.0	12.4	174.2	8.6	14.3	29.2
Boulder, CO	Boulder County	361.4	23.2	91.5	4.5	67.0	23.2
Cape Coral, FL	Lee County	178.3	26.4	45.4	7.4	26.3	13.3
Cedar Rapids, IA	Linn County	191.0	17.2	68.5	7.4	53.2	16.2
Charleston, SC	Charleston County	780.4	23.5	102.2	5.1	41.8	19.0
Charlotte, NC	Mecklenburg County	301.1	9.2	64.8	3.3	30.7	13.3
Chicago, IL	Cook County	408.2	21.6	79.9	10.9	24.6	17.6
Clarksville, TN	Montgomery County	107.9	19.4	40.6	2.2	15.2	14.1
Colorado Springs, CO	El Paso County	185.2	27.4	96.6	3.8	37.8	21.8
Columbia, MO	Boone County	755.7	40.9	59.1	5.3	27.5	22.8
Columbus, OH	Franklin County	405.5	60.6	82.2	6.5	22.7	24.4
Dallas, TX	Dallas County	308.9	19.6	74.5	3.9	31.8	12.0
Davenport, IA	Scott County	220.9	50.3	67.4	3.5	158.9	15.2
Denver, CO	Denver County	562.1	25.7	65.4	6.6	30.7	14.3
Des Moines, IA	Polk County	227.5	106.5	64.8	9.7	44.3	22.1
Durham, NC	Durham County	1,121.1	12.0	70.8	5.2	16.0	14.2
El Paso, TX	El Paso County	175.4	13.8	37.0	3.6	8.1	7.8
Erie, PA	Erie County	170.6	100.4	62.6	11.4	35.7	15.0
Eugene, OR	Lane County	242.3	11.6	64.9	2.8	26.4	16.6
Fargo, ND	Cass County	413.2	10.2	71.1	3.7	57.0	28.2
Fayetteville, NC	Cumberland County	197.8	17.0	91.0	5.2	10.4	17.8
Fort Collins, CO	Larimer County	231.3	24.1	74.9	4.1	49.6	19.9
Fort Wayne, IN	Allen County	251.1	17.7	58.0	5.0	18.4	21.5
Fort Worth, TX	Tarrant County	172.7	37.6	53.1	4.1	22.8	13.5
Gainesville, FL	Alachua County	857.7	24.6	158.3	4.7	25.7	12.6
Grand Rapids, MI	Kent County	298.9	54.2	67.2	4.8	28.0	21.7
Green Bay, WI	Brown County	227.3	19.0	64.8	3.5	38.9	17.7
Greensboro, NC	Guilford County	257.1	7.8	53.7	4.1	14.4	10.3
Honolulu, HI	Honolulu County	323.5	13.7	90.1	2.9	16.2	21.0
Houston, TX	Harris County	297.8	9.5	61.8	4.5	20.6	17.6
Huntsville, AL	Madison County	263.4	10.5	54.7	3.7	21.9	17.6
Indianapolis, IN	Marion County	423.9	16.4	78.5	6.1	14.6	17.3
Jacksonville, FL	Duval County	340.5	23.5	69.5	7.6	21.4	14.8
Kansas City, MO	Jackson County	275.2	59.9	77.6	5.7	39.0	16.9
Lafayette, LA	Lafayette Parish	356.7	5.7	63.6	3.9	29.8	13.8
Las Vegas, NV	Clark County	172.1	25.1	56.2	3.6	19.1	11.6
Lexington, KY	Fayette County	676.8	27.8	127.8	7.8	21.4	17.5
Lincoln, NE	Lancaster County	216.7	9.5	90.8	4.4	36.3	19.8
Little Rock, AR	Pulaski County	680.6	11.3	69.2	4.3	17.9	17.4
Los Angeles, CA	Los Angeles County	281.9	10.6	77.4	5.7	26.2	15.1
Louisville, KY	Jefferson County	461.3	12.2	93.6	7.8	27.7	12.7
Lubbock, TX	Lubbock County	360.7	16.8	51.0	3.1	16.2	14.8
Madison, WI	Dane County	567.3	16.5	65.1	4.9	40.2	18.6
Manchester, NH	Hillsborough County	231.5	21.9	74.1	4.7	23.5	17.1
McAllen, TX	Hidalgo County	107.1	2.8	24.2	1.1	8.4	6.0
Miami, FL	Miami-Dade County	320.3	15.4	56.6	8.9	16.8	11.5
Midland, TX	Midland County	161.1	4.8	49.4	2.6	15.1	11.8
Minneapolis, MN	Hennepin County	479.3	13.6	87.3	3.7	63.9	18.0

Table continued on next page.

City	Area Covered	MDs[1]	DOs[1,2]	Dentists	Podiatrists	Chiropractors	Optometrists
Nashville, TN	Davidson County	602.2	9.2	71.3	3.9	20.8	13.5
New Orleans, LA	Orleans Parish	714.0	13.2	62.8	3.4	7.1	6.1
New York, NY	New York City County	460.1	13.9	81.1	12.3	14.6	13.8
Oklahoma City, OK	Oklahoma County	387.9	41.3	93.3	4.9	24.7	17.7
Omaha, NE	Douglas County	511.9	24.1	83.2	4.5	35.2	17.3
Orlando, FL	Orange County	274.5	19.5	44.4	4.0	23.4	12.2
Oxnard, CA	Ventura County	218.0	8.5	79.8	5.1	34.2	14.9
Palm Bay, FL	Brevard County	214.5	18.6	54.9	6.5	24.1	14.7
Peoria, IL	Peoria County	501.6	39.0	67.9	7.4	45.1	18.6
Philadelphia, PA	Philadelphia County	506.8	42.2	65.2	16.8	14.9	14.7
Phoenix, AZ	Maricopa County	235.5	32.1	62.8	5.8	33.1	13.6
Pittsburgh, PA	Allegheny County	609.7	35.6	86.2	10.4	39.7	18.0
Portland, OR	Multnomah County	577.5	30.2	89.7	5.2	63.4	20.0
Providence, RI	Providence County	454.6	16.0	58.2	9.7	18.2	17.5
Provo, UT	Utah County	120.6	14.6	63.4	3.4	23.6	9.6
Raleigh, NC	Wake County	267.7	7.5	65.2	3.1	24.1	15.7
Reno, NV	Washoe County	268.7	20.0	63.2	4.1	24.9	18.4
Richmond, VA	Richmond City	668.9	16.1	122.0	9.8	6.5	12.1
Roanoke, VA	Roanoke City	493.5	41.9	60.7	14.2	14.2	22.3
Rochester, MN	Olmsted County	2,262.2	53.7	80.4	6.0	36.9	17.4
Sacramento, CA	Sacramento County	288.5	11.6	71.9	4.3	21.7	16.6
Salem, OR	Marion County	179.3	12.2	75.4	4.3	29.8	15.5
Salt Lake City, UT	Salt Lake County	350.8	11.6	72.3	5.5	25.4	12.4
San Antonio, TX	Bexar County	315.8	18.7	76.9	5.3	14.8	13.7
San Diego, CA	San Diego County	299.1	15.1	78.9	3.9	30.8	15.8
San Francisco, CA	San Francisco County	782.3	10.6	138.9	10.2	36.1	23.7
San Jose, CA	Santa Clara County	389.7	7.3	105.4	5.8	37.6	23.3
Santa Rosa, CA	Sonoma County	249.8	12.2	85.8	6.1	35.7	14.9
Savannah, GA	Chatham County	343.0	17.3	62.1	6.5	16.5	12.9
Seattle, WA	King County	463.8	13.7	100.9	6.3	42.2	19.6
Sioux Falls, SD	Minnehaha County	333.3	22.2	51.7	5.0	52.3	20.0
Spokane, WA	Spokane County	271.6	19.5	73.6	4.8	27.7	18.4
Springfield, IL	Sangamon County	578.2	14.1	67.8	5.0	33.7	21.1
Tallahassee, FL	Leon County	259.6	8.5	36.9	3.9	18.8	17.7
Tampa, FL	Hillsborough County	315.7	25.5	50.7	5.0	23.3	11.4
Topeka, KS	Shawnee County	209.6	23.5	59.9	5.6	24.1	26.3
Tulsa, OK	Tulsa County	274.4	104.0	65.5	3.7	36.1	20.1
Tyler, TX	Smith County	362.0	23.7	56.3	6.5	24.0	14.8
Virginia Beach, VA	Virginia Beach City	250.6	12.3	70.1	6.9	25.8	14.0
Washington, DC	District of Columbia	767.7	15.1	116.0	8.2	7.4	13.2
Wichita, KS	Sedgwick County	255.6	37.7	54.9	2.6	37.3	24.3
Wilmington, NC	New Hanover County	354.8	21.5	71.8	6.6	32.4	17.8
Winston-Salem, NC	Forsyth County	606.8	28.2	60.3	6.1	14.4	16.6
Worcester, MA	Worcester County	354.7	18.0	65.0	6.3	20.0	17.2
U.S.	U.S.	270.0	20.2	63.1	5.7	25.2	14.9

Note: All figures are rates per 100,000 population; Data as of 2013 unless noted; (1) Data as of 2012; (2) Doctor of Osteopathic Medicine; Source: U.S. Department of Health and Human Services, Health Resources and Services Administration, Bureau of Health Professions, Area Resource File (ARF) 2013-2014

Health Insurance Coverage: City

City	With Health Insurance	With Private Health Insurance	With Public Health Insurance	Without Health Insurance	Population Under Age 18 Without Health Insurance
Albuquerque, NM	84.2	59.5	35.2	15.8	6.2
Anchorage, AK	83.1	67.9	23.9	16.9	11.1
Ann Arbor, MI	93.8	85.9	17.5	6.2	2.9
Athens, GA	82.4	66.8	23.1	17.6	9.5
Atlanta, GA	81.7	61.6	27.6	18.3	7.1
Austin, TX	80.3	64.5	22.3	19.7	9.3
Billings, MT	83.3	65.1	30.8	16.7	10.4
Boise City, ID	86.4	72.9	24.5	13.6	7.0
Boston, MA	95.0	65.9	36.4	5.0	1.6
Boulder, CO	92.0	85.0	14.2	8.0	7.1
Cape Coral, FL	79.6	56.1	35.9	20.4	10.5
Cedar Rapids, IA	91.5	74.6	29.4	8.5	3.6
Charleston, SC	87.2	73.4	24.8	12.8	8.7
Charlotte, NC	81.7	63.8	25.2	18.3	7.4
Chicago, IL	80.2	52.4	33.9	19.8	4.7
Clarksville, TN	86.4	69.3	29.8	13.6	4.5
Colorado Springs, CO	86.0	69.3	28.4	14.0	6.9
Columbia, MO	91.1	80.9	18.2	8.9	5.6
Columbus, OH	84.5	62.6	29.4	15.5	7.1
Dallas, TX	69.6	44.9	30.5	30.4	15.9
Davenport, IA	88.4	68.1	32.5	11.6	5.1
Denver, CO	83.4	60.8	30.0	16.6	8.9
Des Moines, IA	89.0	63.0	37.8	11.0	3.5
Durham, NC	82.4	64.4	26.0	17.6	8.5
El Paso, TX	73.7	48.3	32.7	26.3	12.7
Erie, PA	89.2	56.6	45.7	10.8	3.1
Eugene, OR	85.6	68.1	28.8	14.4	5.0
Fargo, ND	89.6	78.2	21.7	10.4	5.3
Fayetteville, NC	86.0	65.3	34.5	14.0	5.0
Fort Collins, CO	89.8	79.8	18.7	10.2	3.7
Fort Wayne, IN	82.8	60.7	31.5	17.2	10.9
Fort Worth, TX	75.9	54.3	27.7	24.1	12.9
Gainesville, FL	82.9	69.3	20.6	17.1	7.1
Grand Rapids, MI	86.8	59.5	38.2	13.2	2.4
Green Bay, WI	87.4	61.6	36.4	12.6	6.7
Greensboro, NC	83.1	63.0	28.7	16.9	6.2
Honolulu, HI	93.2	75.8	31.5	6.8	2.6
Houston, TX	71.4	46.4	30.7	28.6	15.2
Huntsville, AL	84.2	68.5	29.4	15.8	4.8
Indianapolis, IN	82.6	58.0	33.8	17.4	8.4
Jacksonville, FL	82.6	61.5	30.9	17.4	8.4
Kansas City, MO	82.6	63.3	28.6	17.4	8.2
Lafayette, LA	82.7	63.8	28.9	17.3	4.0
Las Vegas, NV	76.7	58.7	27.3	23.3	16.6
Lexington, KY	86.4	71.9	24.0	13.6	5.7
Lincoln, NE	88.4	74.4	23.9	11.6	6.0
Little Rock, AR	84.2	63.2	31.2	15.8	5.7
Los Angeles, CA	74.9	48.7	31.8	25.1	9.0
Louisville, KY	85.6	65.7	32.1	14.4	4.7
Lubbock, TX	81.7	63.0	28.0	18.3	9.6
Madison, WI	92.5	80.5	21.9	7.5	2.9
Manchester, NH	85.5	64.4	31.3	14.5	3.6
McAllen, TX	65.3	40.2	29.5	34.7	18.8
Miami, FL	66.2	33.2	36.1	33.8	12.4
Midland, TX	79.4	66.2	22.1	20.6	16.3

Table continued on next page.

City	With Health Insurance	With Private Health Insurance	With Public Health Insurance	Without Health Insurance	Population Under Age 18 Without Health Insurance
Minneapolis, MN	87.8	65.1	29.9	12.2	7.0
Nashville, TN	83.1	63.1	28.5	16.9	7.6
New Orleans, LA	81.8	52.2	37.1	18.2	5.3
New York, NY	86.0	54.0	39.6	14.0	4.1
Oklahoma City, OK	79.5	58.9	30.4	20.5	10.3
Omaha, NE	85.8	67.0	28.7	14.2	6.2
Orlando, FL	76.3	55.2	26.8	23.7	12.3
Oxnard, CA	75.6	48.1	34.2	24.4	10.4
Palm Bay, FL	82.8	55.9	38.8	17.2	8.6
Peoria, IL	88.7	61.0	39.2	11.3	2.0
Philadelphia, PA	85.5	54.4	41.1	14.5	5.1
Phoenix, AZ	77.1	51.5	32.0	22.9	14.7
Pittsburgh, PA	90.1	69.7	32.4	9.9	3.8
Portland, OR	84.6	67.3	26.6	15.4	4.1
Providence, RI	80.4	50.3	36.3	19.6	5.8
Provo, UT	83.8	72.6	18.6	16.2	13.1
Raleigh, NC	84.4	69.3	22.7	15.6	8.9
Reno, NV	76.8	61.9	23.5	23.2	18.7
Richmond, VA	82.4	58.5	33.2	17.6	4.3
Roanoke, VA	83.4	57.7	35.9	16.6	4.8
Rochester, MN	92.7	78.9	25.8	7.3	4.8
Sacramento, CA	83.8	57.3	35.5	16.2	5.8
Salem, OR	83.3	61.5	33.7	16.7	6.9
Salt Lake City, UT	80.9	64.5	23.9	19.1	14.7
San Antonio, TX	78.8	56.7	31.7	21.2	10.3
San Diego, CA	83.3	66.2	25.5	16.7	8.2
San Francisco, CA	89.7	70.9	27.2	10.3	3.4
San Jose, CA	86.3	66.6	26.6	13.7	4.5
Santa Rosa, CA	84.3	63.1	32.5	15.7	7.9
Savannah, GA	78.5	56.2	31.7	21.5	8.8
Seattle, WA	88.6	76.6	20.6	11.4	4.9
Sioux Falls, SD	88.9	74.7	24.8	11.1	5.9
Spokane, WA	85.4	60.9	36.0	14.6	5.5
Springfield, IL	88.2	66.4	36.1	11.8	3.5
Tallahassee, FL	85.8	72.8	20.9	14.2	5.0
Tampa, FL	81.9	57.3	32.0	18.1	8.2
Topeka, KS	84.5	64.6	33.8	15.5	7.2
Tulsa, OK	78.4	56.3	32.6	21.6	10.7
Tyler, TX	78.5	58.9	30.5	21.5	12.2
Virginia Beach, VA	89.3	79.7	21.1	10.7	4.3
Washington, DC	93.4	69.6	35.1	6.6	2.6
Wichita, KS	83.8	64.4	29.7	16.2	7.0
Wilmington, NC	83.3	65.2	30.3	16.7	5.7
Winston-Salem, NC	81.7	58.2	33.6	18.3	7.0
Worcester, MA	95.1	61.5	43.1	4.9	1.4
U.S.	85.2	65.2	31.0	14.8	7.3

Note: Figures are percentages that cover the civilian noninstitutionalized population
Source: U.S. Census Bureau, 2011-2013 American Community Survey 3-Year Estimates

Health Insurance Coverage: Metro Area

Metro Area	With Health Insurance	With Private Health Insurance	With Public Health Insurance	Without Health Insurance	Population Under Age 18 Without Health Insurance
Albuquerque, NM	83.8	58.3	36.1	16.2	6.6
Anchorage, AK	82.3	66.6	24.6	17.7	11.6
Ann Arbor, MI	92.7	81.3	22.9	7.3	2.8
Athens, GA	83.8	67.2	25.1	16.2	7.2
Atlanta, GA	81.2	64.9	24.3	18.8	9.6
Austin, TX	81.9	68.0	22.0	18.1	9.9
Billings, MT	83.7	67.1	29.4	16.3	10.3
Boise City, ID	84.7	68.1	27.2	15.3	7.4
Boston, MA	95.6	76.8	30.1	4.4	1.7
Boulder, CO	89.4	79.2	18.8	10.6	6.8
Cape Coral, FL	79.2	56.0	40.4	20.8	13.2
Cedar Rapids, IA	92.9	77.5	28.3	7.1	2.9
Charleston, SC	83.4	66.6	28.0	16.6	9.3
Charlotte, NC	83.8	65.7	27.5	16.2	7.0
Chicago, IL	86.0	66.1	28.7	14.0	4.0
Clarksville, TN	85.7	68.7	29.6	14.3	6.5
Colorado Springs, CO	87.1	72.0	26.7	12.9	6.7
Columbia, MO	90.6	79.0	20.4	9.4	4.8
Columbus, OH	88.3	70.7	27.2	11.7	5.3
Dallas, TX	78.1	60.8	24.3	21.9	12.9
Davenport, IA	90.5	73.0	32.6	9.5	3.8
Denver, CO	85.3	69.4	24.5	14.7	8.9
Des Moines, IA	92.3	76.7	27.1	7.7	3.4
Durham, NC	85.2	68.6	26.7	14.8	7.8
El Paso, TX	72.2	45.7	33.0	27.8	13.2
Erie, PA	91.3	69.2	36.5	8.7	2.5
Eugene, OR	85.0	64.5	34.7	15.0	5.9
Fargo, ND	91.3	80.0	22.0	8.7	4.8
Fayetteville, NC	85.7	64.0	34.1	14.3	5.1
Fort Collins, CO	88.2	75.1	24.0	11.8	6.4
Fort Wayne, IN	85.2	66.7	28.4	14.8	10.0
Fort Worth, TX	78.1	60.8	24.3	21.9	12.9
Gainesville, FL	84.2	68.1	25.9	15.8	8.4
Grand Rapids, MI	90.3	73.8	28.7	9.7	3.4
Green Bay, WI	91.3	72.3	29.9	8.7	4.0
Greensboro, NC	83.4	62.2	31.2	16.6	7.8
Honolulu, HI	94.3	78.9	29.4	5.7	2.7
Houston, TX	76.5	57.1	25.6	23.5	13.3
Huntsville, AL	87.2	72.9	27.0	12.8	3.4
Indianapolis, IN	86.5	68.6	28.0	13.5	6.7
Jacksonville, FL	84.2	65.3	30.0	15.8	8.0
Kansas City, MO	86.9	72.4	25.3	13.1	6.7
Lafayette, LA	83.5	62.0	31.8	16.5	4.4
Las Vegas, NV	77.8	61.8	24.9	22.2	15.7
Lexington, KY	87.1	71.5	25.8	12.9	4.8
Lincoln, NE	89.2	76.0	23.4	10.8	5.5
Little Rock, AR	85.8	65.6	31.7	14.2	4.8
Los Angeles, CA	79.2	56.0	29.5	20.8	8.4
Louisville, KY	87.3	70.5	29.3	12.7	5.2
Lubbock, TX	80.9	61.5	28.7	19.1	10.4
Madison, WI	93.0	81.0	23.6	7.0	3.5
Manchester, NH	90.0	75.5	24.7	10.0	3.0
McAllen, TX	63.4	30.9	37.0	36.6	17.3
Miami, FL	74.9	51.1	31.1	25.1	13.0
Midland, TX	77.5	64.9	21.1	22.5	21.6

Table continued on next page.

Metro Area	With Health Insurance	With Private Health Insurance	With Public Health Insurance	Without Health Insurance	Population Under Age 18 Without Health Insurance
Minneapolis, MN	91.8	77.5	24.8	8.2	5.1
Nashville, TN	86.4	68.7	27.1	13.6	5.8
New Orleans, LA	83.4	58.5	33.5	16.6	4.5
New York, NY	87.2	64.8	31.8	12.8	4.4
Oklahoma City, OK	82.7	64.4	29.1	17.3	9.3
Omaha, NE	89.0	74.0	25.5	11.0	5.1
Orlando, FL	79.2	59.5	28.4	20.8	12.1
Oxnard, CA	83.8	66.4	26.9	16.2	7.6
Palm Bay, FL	83.2	62.3	37.7	16.8	10.9
Peoria, IL	90.6	72.1	32.3	9.4	3.2
Philadelphia, PA	90.1	71.8	30.0	9.9	4.1
Phoenix, AZ	82.6	61.5	31.0	17.4	12.0
Pittsburgh, PA	92.1	75.4	32.5	7.9	3.1
Portland, OR	86.1	70.0	26.9	13.9	5.7
Providence, RI	91.2	70.4	33.5	8.8	3.5
Provo, UT	86.7	76.5	17.6	13.3	9.1
Raleigh, NC	85.8	71.9	22.3	14.2	7.7
Reno, NV	79.6	64.4	24.8	20.4	17.0
Richmond, VA	87.6	73.0	25.7	12.4	5.5
Roanoke, VA	88.5	69.8	32.1	11.5	4.2
Rochester, MN	92.8	79.2	26.3	7.2	5.2
Sacramento, CA	86.2	66.3	30.8	13.8	5.9
Salem, OR	83.5	61.4	34.9	16.5	6.7
Salt Lake City, UT	84.2	71.9	20.1	15.8	11.6
San Antonio, TX	80.6	61.0	30.1	19.4	10.0
San Diego, CA	83.2	65.4	26.6	16.8	8.4
San Francisco, CA	88.5	71.9	26.4	11.5	4.8
San Jose, CA	88.5	72.3	23.9	11.5	3.9
Santa Rosa, CA	85.7	68.0	30.1	14.3	6.9
Savannah, GA	81.2	64.2	27.0	18.8	8.9
Seattle, WA	87.2	72.7	24.5	12.8	5.3
Sioux Falls, SD	90.6	78.2	23.1	9.4	4.6
Spokane, WA	86.2	64.4	34.8	13.8	6.0
Springfield, IL	90.8	71.9	33.0	9.2	2.9
Tallahassee, FL	85.8	69.6	26.0	14.2	6.9
Tampa, FL	82.4	59.6	34.6	17.6	9.2
Topeka, KS	88.0	71.6	31.1	12.0	6.2
Tulsa, OK	82.6	63.7	30.4	17.4	9.2
Tyler, TX	78.9	59.4	30.7	21.1	13.8
Virginia Beach, VA	87.9	73.8	26.2	12.1	4.6
Washington, DC	88.4	76.7	21.4	11.6	5.0
Wichita, KS	86.5	69.6	27.8	13.5	6.2
Wilmington, NC	83.3	66.6	30.1	16.7	7.2
Winston-Salem, NC	84.7	63.3	33.4	15.3	6.1
Worcester, MA	95.5	73.6	33.6	4.5	1.7
U.S.	85.2	65.2	31.0	14.8	7.3

Note: Figures are percentages that cover the civilian noninstitutionalized population; Figures cover the Metropolitan Statistical Area (MSA)—see Appendix B for areas included
Source: U.S. Census Bureau, 2011-2013 American Community Survey 3-Year Estimates

Crime Rate: City

City	All Crimes	Violent Crimes				Property Crimes		
		Murder	Forcible Rape	Robbery	Aggrav. Assault	Burglary	Larceny-Theft	Motor Vehicle Theft
Albuquerque, NM	6,244.7	6.6	78.7	187.4	502.2	1,307.3	3,624.2	538.4
Anchorage, AK	4,831.1	4.7	136.2	174.3	497.9	440.1	3,287.6	290.2
Ann Arbor, MI	2,373.3	2.6	41.1	42.0	125.9	351.0	1,730.3	80.5
Athens, GA	3,727.9	1.7	30.8	104.1	199.8	805.0	2,424.2	162.3
Atlanta, GA	7,326.7	18.6	23.3	523.9	657.4	1,316.6	3,804.3	982.7
Austin, TX	5,213.1	3.0	25.3	88.8	246.4	762.4	3,834.8	252.5
Billings, MT	5,532.4	3.7	36.2	75.1	218.9	917.4	3,779.2	501.8
Boise City, ID	2,492.0	1.4	57.4	21.0	200.2	384.9	1,727.7	99.4
Boston, MA	3,555.5	6.1	43.3	290.2	442.8	480.9	2,042.1	250.1
Boulder, CO	3,078.9	0.0	37.0	38.9	136.1	595.2	2,174.5	97.2
Cape Coral, FL	2,185.2	1.8	4.3	24.5	89.9	491.2	1,484.8	88.7
Cedar Rapids, IA	3,963.7	3.1	35.8	70.0	195.9	759.5	2,668.6	230.9
Charleston, SC	2,690.9	5.5	22.8	56.6	96.7	239.8	2,142.2	127.4
Charlotte, NC	4,257.4	7.0	27.5	215.5	358.0	768.7	2,659.1	221.6
Chicago, IL	n/a	15.2	n/a	434.3	n/a	653.4	2,407.5	464.5
Clarksville, TN	3,357.9	4.1	57.7	79.0	372.9	700.6	2,036.4	107.1
Colorado Springs, CO	4,601.6	6.0	84.8	95.8	247.4	854.4	2,871.1	442.1
Columbia, MO	4,167.1	4.4	58.5	97.7	202.5	613.5	3,045.7	144.9
Columbus, OH	6,885.1	11.0	71.7	411.9	163.7	1,926.0	3,841.9	459.0
Dallas, TX	4,828.9	11.4	43.3	334.8	274.3	1,156.6	2,420.2	588.4
Davenport, IA	4,813.7	2.0	86.4	164.0	389.9	943.7	2,993.1	234.7
Denver, CO	4,283.3	6.2	79.2	174.4	370.0	757.8	2,358.5	537.3
Des Moines, IA	5,323.8	5.3	43.4	101.7	344.3	1,114.3	3,304.9	409.9
Durham, NC[1]	5,089.5	8.9	26.7	261.1	429.2	1,394.1	2,670.6	298.9
El Paso, TX	2,660.0	1.5	25.9	67.2	276.4	260.6	1,911.6	116.8
Erie, PA	3,635.4	3.0	59.5	173.6	217.2	1,008.8	2,076.1	97.2
Eugene, OR	5,250.5	0.0	42.9	123.0	87.7	971.0	3,642.3	383.6
Fargo, ND	3,289.8	2.7	63.9	52.2	282.6	631.0	2,108.0	149.4
Fayetteville, NC	6,631.8	12.3	32.1	289.3	243.9	1,619.1	4,123.5	311.6
Fort Collins, CO	2,775.4	0.0	38.0	24.7	175.3	353.8	2,090.4	93.3
Fort Wayne, IN	4,221.0	12.2	37.3	175.4	147.6	940.3	2,756.8	151.5
Fort Worth, TX	4,903.7	6.1	66.3	159.2	328.6	1,053.9	2,985.5	304.0
Gainesville, FL	4,575.4	4.7	49.0	122.4	460.5	586.1	3,159.8	192.7
Grand Rapids, MI	3,929.6	8.9	42.9	246.3	395.4	847.7	2,256.6	131.8
Green Bay, WI	3,019.8	1.9	49.5	75.2	349.2	547.1	1,903.8	93.2
Greensboro, NC	4,648.8	9.7	25.1	177.6	306.4	1,063.9	2,886.4	179.7
Honolulu, HI	n/a	n/a	n/a	n/a	n/a	n/a	n/a	n/a
Houston, TX	6,049.3	9.8	28.3	453.6	471.0	1,088.4	3,374.8	623.5
Huntsville, AL	5,804.4	13.0	47.1	211.7	544.0	1,019.8	3,588.3	380.5
Indianapolis, IN	6,478.9	15.2	77.2	446.9	693.2	1,581.4	3,076.4	588.7
Jacksonville, FL	4,523.0	11.0	53.4	168.4	387.5	835.8	2,880.4	186.5
Kansas City, MO	6,554.5	21.3	81.0	357.0	800.4	1,377.4	2,996.5	920.9
Lafayette, LA	6,835.8	6.5	13.8	220.4	462.7	1,034.0	4,857.8	240.7
Las Vegas, NV	3,954.9	6.5	47.0	271.4	433.2	985.4	1,769.3	442.2
Lexington, KY	4,338.3	5.8	43.4	151.3	105.9	833.8	2,928.9	269.2
Lincoln, NE	3,866.0	1.9	53.1	79.2	235.8	531.8	2,849.8	114.4
Little Rock, AR	9,273.6	17.7	60.3	478.2	850.6	1,922.0	5,397.7	547.1
Los Angeles, CA	2,639.2	6.5	19.7	203.3	196.6	405.5	1,436.9	370.8
Louisville, KY	4,831.3	7.2	23.8	212.6	299.4	1,031.1	2,955.5	301.7
Lubbock, TX	5,627.3	2.1	37.0	163.1	566.7	1,096.4	3,406.4	355.6
Madison, WI	3,551.4	2.1	31.3	122.1	209.1	569.8	2,512.8	104.3
Manchester, NH	4,475.1	3.6	82.4	267.2	323.3	809.7	2,844.8	144.0
McAllen, TX	4,108.9	1.5	4.4	61.0	58.8	393.6	3,416.3	173.3
Miami, FL	6,183.9	17.0	22.9	529.6	612.3	954.4	3,590.2	457.5

Table continued on next page.

City	All Crimes	Violent Crimes				Property Crimes		
		Murder	Forcible Rape	Robbery	Aggrav. Assault	Burglary	Larceny -Theft	Motor Vehicle Theft
Midland, TX	2,896.3	4.1	18.0	51.5	212.7	464.6	2,011.3	134.1
Minneapolis, MN	5,905.0	9.1	97.2	468.4	444.5	1,161.3	3,327.1	397.5
Nashville, TN	4,888.0	5.5	68.7	253.4	712.5	883.0	2,776.6	188.3
New Orleans, LA	4,639.0	41.4	46.7	301.8	396.5	849.6	2,434.6	568.4
New York, NY	2,314.8	4.0	13.2	228.3	378.4	197.8	1,404.6	88.5
Oklahoma City, OK	6,194.2	10.2	74.4	196.8	544.6	1,324.9	3,369.6	673.7
Omaha, NE	5,071.3	9.9	43.3	168.9	354.1	825.5	2,945.1	724.6
Orlando, FL	7,425.8	6.7	49.8	226.3	631.8	1,376.2	4,732.3	402.8
Oxnard, CA	2,825.8	7.4	4.9	161.9	147.1	480.8	1,696.0	327.7
Palm Bay, FL	2,307.7	2.9	20.1	41.2	367.8	495.3	1,270.2	110.2
Peoria, IL	4,483.7	13.8	20.7	237.2	404.5	968.5	2,671.8	167.3
Philadelphia, PA	4,540.8	15.9	82.3	486.9	514.2	670.1	2,398.5	372.9
Phoenix, AZ	4,631.9	7.9	42.3	215.2	366.5	1,114.9	2,462.0	423.1
Pittsburgh, PA	4,000.2	14.6	25.4	310.8	383.6	706.4	2,359.3	200.2
Portland, OR	5,347.6	2.3	38.4	150.5	291.6	677.7	3,647.1	539.9
Providence, RI	5,080.9	6.7	54.2	204.0	358.3	1,021.9	2,897.9	537.8
Provo, UT	2,539.8	0.9	70.1	18.0	47.9	281.3	2,029.3	92.4
Raleigh, NC	3,455.3	2.8	18.4	141.0	230.1	735.9	2,162.7	164.3
Reno, NV	3,583.6	6.0	29.2	131.1	329.8	606.7	2,107.4	373.2
Richmond, VA	4,713.2	17.4	20.2	293.2	292.7	853.7	2,795.2	440.7
Roanoke, VA	5,004.7	9.2	44.9	145.0	267.5	641.3	3,713.0	183.8
Rochester, MN	2,527.5	0.0	45.6	49.2	100.3	391.2	1,847.3	93.9
Sacramento, CA	4,416.1	7.1	19.9	242.2	386.9	812.7	2,349.1	598.3
Salem, OR	4,614.7	4.4	29.7	87.2	207.3	621.2	3,250.2	414.6
Salt Lake City, UT	7,850.9	3.7	107.2	221.8	442.6	1,087.0	5,002.5	986.1
San Antonio, TX	6,345.7	5.1	47.4	156.6	421.6	1,060.9	4,184.2	469.9
San Diego, CA	2,744.4	2.9	23.4	107.9	258.8	471.0	1,425.2	455.3
San Francisco, CA	6,642.3	5.8	19.3	503.9	318.2	711.3	4,380.5	703.5
San Jose, CA	2,895.2	3.8	27.2	110.4	182.6	521.4	1,250.9	798.9
Santa Rosa, CA	2,358.9	1.7	24.5	61.2	227.9	371.9	1,491.6	180.1
Savannah, GA	3,957.9	12.8	20.8	176.0	152.2	903.5	2,384.4	308.2
Seattle, WA	6,166.8	3.0	23.8	249.1	308.8	1,148.7	3,763.0	670.5
Sioux Falls, SD	3,441.0	1.9	85.3	41.4	264.6	537.9	2,346.8	163.2
Spokane, WA	10,008.9	5.2	79.2	247.2	355.6	1,856.1	6,372.5	1,093.0
Springfield, IL	6,046.8	3.4	60.5	244.6	706.4	1,107.8	3,782.7	141.5
Tallahassee, FL	5,041.5	5.8	84.8	205.1	445.1	1,103.3	2,964.3	233.2
Tampa, FL	3,108.3	8.0	22.2	165.1	401.6	555.1	1,799.0	157.4
Topeka, KS	5,544.9	8.6	25.8	134.4	309.4	967.1	3,655.2	444.5
Tulsa, OK	6,287.7	15.2	94.6	252.0	608.4	1,504.4	3,207.6	605.6
Tyler, TX	4,490.5	5.0	43.0	53.0	274.9	824.7	3,110.0	179.9
Virginia Beach, VA	2,652.8	3.8	31.1	67.5	59.7	312.2	2,079.9	98.7
Washington, DC	5,793.0	15.9	60.8	566.2	576.1	512.6	3,574.6	486.8
Wichita, KS	6,175.4	3.9	63.1	121.1	604.9	1,017.6	3,851.4	513.3
Wilmington, NC	5,618.8	6.3	35.1	228.0	349.6	1,482.2	3,215.7	301.8
Winston-Salem, NC	6,055.3	6.4	33.9	186.2	378.3	1,646.7	3,544.8	259.1
Worcester, MA	4,354.8	4.9	12.0	263.3	673.7	1,044.4	2,139.0	217.5
U.S.	3,098.6	4.5	25.2	109.1	229.1	610.0	1,899.4	221.3

Note: Figures are crimes per 100,000 population in 2013 except where noted; n/a not available; (1) 2012 data
Source: FBI Uniform Crime Reports, 2013

Crime Rate: Suburbs

Suburbs[1]	All Crimes	Violent Crimes				Property Crimes		
		Murder	Forcible Rape	Robbery	Aggrav. Assault	Burglary	Larceny -Theft	Motor Vehicle Theft
Albuquerque, NM	3,575.1	4.6	38.9	56.0	589.9	886.3	1,754.3	245.0
Anchorage, AK	7,133.4	6.6	72.9	39.7	291.4	529.9	5,808.7	384.2
Ann Arbor, MI	2,418.0	3.4	58.8	47.4	242.4	464.5	1,482.3	119.3
Athens, GA	2,766.6	0.0	19.4	11.6	141.0	539.4	1,953.0	102.2
Atlanta, GA	3,398.5	4.7	19.2	125.5	165.3	763.9	2,040.0	279.9
Austin, TX	1,964.6	2.5	21.6	23.3	146.3	341.6	1,349.4	79.8
Billings, MT	1,868.7	0.0	17.5	5.3	115.7	380.4	1,155.2	194.6
Boise City, ID	1,644.6	0.7	43.8	9.0	143.2	340.9	1,034.1	72.9
Boston, MA	2,119.7	1.8	29.0	82.0	251.7	370.1	1,291.6	93.6
Boulder, CO	2,202.8	1.0	59.8	16.4	134.9	298.8	1,579.7	112.3
Cape Coral, FL	2,640.5	4.5	29.0	109.0	260.8	603.9	1,497.8	135.6
Cedar Rapids, IA	1,222.7	0.0	20.7	6.7	81.5	309.8	742.5	61.5
Charleston, SC	3,688.7	7.5	29.6	74.2	286.8	705.4	2,321.0	264.2
Charlotte, NC	2,895.6	4.2	20.4	57.7	207.7	638.6	1,850.1	116.9
Chicago, IL	n/a	1.8	n/a	59.7	n/a	299.3	1,392.6	82.8
Clarksville, TN	2,365.5	6.0	36.8	36.8	132.0	602.3	1,460.3	91.5
Colorado Springs, CO	1,921.2	6.6	52.7	19.0	173.5	429.3	1,115.3	124.8
Columbia, MO	2,504.6	0.0	19.6	28.5	222.7	331.3	1,793.8	108.7
Columbus, OH	2,783.7	1.6	24.5	49.9	64.8	593.9	1,979.6	69.3
Dallas, TX	2,583.7	2.2	24.0	54.8	103.5	504.5	1,722.1	172.7
Davenport, IA	2,160.6	1.8	20.2	28.4	209.6	362.8	1,486.7	51.1
Denver, CO	2,691.8	2.9	44.7	48.6	136.8	369.5	1,866.6	222.9
Des Moines, IA	1,810.8	0.8	17.7	9.3	119.0	314.9	1,261.7	87.4
Durham, NC[2]	2,848.2	2.1	16.6	38.9	120.7	845.7	1,724.3	99.8
El Paso, TX	1,953.6	1.2	36.9	24.0	185.8	364.8	1,238.2	102.7
Erie, PA	2,065.8	0.6	16.1	29.5	81.8	386.3	1,509.2	42.3
Eugene, OR	2,815.7	2.0	18.7	23.8	101.6	512.1	1,956.3	201.2
Fargo, ND	1,783.6	0.9	19.8	9.9	79.2	357.4	1,217.3	99.0
Fayetteville, NC	3,979.7	2.8	12.0	103.1	271.2	1,273.2	2,173.3	144.1
Fort Collins, CO	1,985.6	1.2	48.8	17.5	106.7	243.0	1,503.9	64.5
Fort Wayne, IN	1,651.3	1.8	17.1	30.7	56.7	320.8	1,147.3	76.8
Fort Worth, TX	3,047.6	2.8	21.3	65.1	169.9	563.3	2,057.7	167.6
Gainesville, FL	2,558.8	2.8	36.8	57.7	361.3	560.0	1,455.5	84.8
Grand Rapids, MI	1,866.4	0.9	71.9	22.4	115.7	348.5	1,248.4	58.7
Green Bay, WI	1,511.6	0.0	11.6	12.5	45.3	216.2	1,190.9	35.2
Greensboro, NC	3,276.5	1.7	14.3	64.8	158.6	924.9	1,967.1	145.0
Honolulu, HI	n/a	n/a	n/a	n/a	n/a	n/a	n/a	n/a
Houston, TX	2,983.4	3.9	20.1	116.2	204.2	631.7	1,770.7	236.6
Huntsville, AL	2,385.9	1.2	40.0	30.0	166.6	522.9	1,507.0	118.1
Indianapolis, IN	1,134.2	1.7	13.8	33.0	n/a	345.7	1,608.4	136.0
Jacksonville, FL	2,490.1	1.1	23.9	40.6	237.4	435.7	1,666.2	85.2
Kansas City, MO	2,890.6	3.3	30.6	45.4	156.6	469.2	1,926.0	259.5
Lafayette, LA	3,019.1	4.5	19.2	68.1	285.0	717.5	1,718.5	206.4
Las Vegas, NV	2,951.8	3.6	28.5	122.6	294.6	720.0	1,475.8	306.6
Lexington, KY	3,366.8	3.3	28.2	64.8	75.3	687.6	2,404.0	103.5
Lincoln, NE	1,550.7	0.0	21.7	4.3	63.1	269.7	1,148.3	43.5
Little Rock, AR	4,175.7	4.0	33.3	62.0	301.9	996.1	2,534.9	243.5
Los Angeles, CA	2,709.0	4.8	16.1	144.8	222.7	528.1	1,392.9	399.6
Louisville, KY	1,826.6	2.4	18.9	53.6	n/a	531.2	1,776.8	140.4
Lubbock, TX	2,175.1	6.4	44.5	3.2	184.4	518.3	1,279.9	138.3
Madison, WI	1,802.0	1.6	23.5	19.0	79.8	251.1	1,379.8	47.2
Manchester, NH	1,882.3	2.0	31.0	30.3	69.5	258.9	1,439.1	51.4
McAllen, TX	3,955.7	2.9	28.0	56.5	231.5	860.9	2,581.5	194.4
Miami, FL	4,571.9	7.1	32.4	187.8	328.8	675.8	3,049.9	290.1

Table continued on next page.

Suburbs[1]	All Crimes	Violent Crimes				Property Crimes		
		Murder	Forcible Rape	Robbery	Aggrav. Assault	Burglary	Larceny -Theft	Motor Vehicle Theft
Midland, TX	3,001.3	3.0	9.0	20.9	226.7	656.3	1,781.1	304.3
Minneapolis, MN	2,475.7	1.7	27.5	48.5	99.7	341.5	1,812.6	144.3
Nashville, TN	2,412.8	2.2	27.9	36.2	275.4	419.6	1,556.2	95.3
New Orleans, LA	3,183.0	9.2	16.8	77.4	233.8	539.4	2,145.6	160.9
New York, NY	1,772.8	2.0	7.7	86.8	115.7	287.2	1,182.9	90.5
Oklahoma City, OK	2,980.6	2.3	34.5	33.6	157.5	681.2	1,880.4	191.1
Omaha, NE	2,327.4	1.1	33.7	28.4	153.0	423.2	1,473.3	214.7
Orlando, FL	3,523.1	3.6	40.5	110.3	338.5	820.1	2,033.1	177.0
Oxnard, CA	1,928.3	3.0	11.8	43.7	94.8	350.4	1,293.6	131.0
Palm Bay, FL	3,558.1	3.8	57.4	95.7	389.6	724.9	2,157.8	128.9
Peoria, IL	1,874.2	2.3	23.0	21.5	149.1	401.0	1,238.0	39.3
Philadelphia, PA	2,740.7	5.5	32.4	143.4	309.1	356.8	1,774.1	119.4
Phoenix, AZ	-1,815.2	3.3	22.8	63.2	178.3	531.2	2,093.0	n/a
Pittsburgh, PA	1,872.0	2.5	14.1	49.7	160.4	316.4	1,270.5	58.4
Portland, OR	2,490.7	1.1	28.2	46.0	92.9	402.9	1,709.7	209.9
Providence, RI	2,398.8	2.0	41.1	65.1	194.3	487.6	1,460.8	148.0
Provo, UT	1,790.4	1.1	16.2	6.3	29.0	217.5	1,442.1	78.1
Raleigh, NC	1,979.2	2.7	9.6	27.5	84.4	489.1	1,292.3	73.6
Reno, NV	2,287.5	4.4	33.0	41.8	165.2	531.1	1,343.5	168.6
Richmond, VA	2,210.8	3.9	20.0	49.0	92.5	361.0	1,591.1	93.4
Roanoke, VA	1,616.7	3.3	25.3	14.5	90.4	223.1	1,192.1	67.9
Rochester, MN	997.4	0.0	14.8	2.0	69.0	280.9	590.3	40.4
Sacramento, CA	2,842.6	3.3	21.6	97.4	227.6	622.0	1,550.7	320.1
Salem, OR	2,682.3	2.9	22.0	31.6	114.7	440.0	1,868.4	202.7
Salt Lake City, UT	4,075.5	1.4	47.3	57.0	167.2	600.3	2,808.9	393.5
San Antonio, TX	2,511.9	3.8	25.9	27.3	127.9	510.2	1,687.4	129.5
San Diego, CA	2,392.3	1.7	19.0	86.1	209.6	410.1	1,389.7	276.2
San Francisco, CA	2,375.5	1.5	17.9	77.4	154.4	429.3	1,471.9	223.1
San Jose, CA	2,311.4	2.1	15.6	47.5	104.8	410.5	1,477.0	254.0
Santa Rosa, CA	1,841.3	1.9	26.0	42.4	313.6	360.7	969.4	127.4
Savannah, GA	2,349.7	4.6	14.5	65.5	149.3	555.2	1,450.2	110.4
Seattle, WA	3,691.4	1.6	30.0	69.3	96.2	729.1	2,310.5	454.7
Sioux Falls, SD	1,075.2	0.0	26.3	1.3	58.8	339.2	583.3	66.3
Spokane, WA	3,607.3	2.8	26.7	43.3	87.8	779.1	2,348.3	319.4
Springfield, IL	2,951.5	32.6	91.5	67.3	271.5	483.0	1,330.0	675.5
Tallahassee, FL	2,919.3	3.2	33.1	35.8	352.9	617.9	1,788.6	87.8
Tampa, FL	3,131.4	3.8	32.2	80.4	252.2	628.5	1,981.3	153.0
Topeka, KS	1,903.2	1.9	15.0	3.8	173.6	423.2	1,175.9	109.8
Tulsa, OK	2,054.8	0.7	33.9	17.5	148.5	442.7	1,256.7	154.7
Tyler, TX	2,198.5	2.6	11.9	22.2	158.7	642.7	1,218.8	141.7
Virginia Beach, VA	3,558.7	8.0	33.6	97.9	214.7	611.3	2,425.9	167.2
Washington, DC	2,188.1	2.6	19.2	93.8	117.5	261.4	1,525.3	168.3
Wichita, KS	2,436.9	2.8	35.1	12.4	171.5	491.4	1,605.3	118.5
Wilmington, NC	2,737.9	1.3	16.7	28.9	132.1	656.9	1,806.4	95.6
Winston-Salem, NC	2,696.6	1.9	14.9	44.0	178.8	805.8	1,540.8	110.3
Worcester, MA	1,888.6	0.7	36.6	31.8	207.5	368.2	1,170.2	73.5
U.S.	3,098.6	4.5	25.2	109.1	229.1	610.0	1,899.4	221.3

Note: Figures are crimes per 100,000 population in 2013 except where noted; n/a not available; (1) All areas within the metro area that are located outside the city limits; (2) 2012 data
Source: FBI Uniform Crime Reports, 2013

Crime Rate: Metro Area

Metro Area[1]	All Crimes	Violent Crimes				Property Crimes		
		Murder	Forcible Rape	Robbery	Aggrav. Assault	Burglary	Larceny -Theft	Motor Vehicle Theft
Albuquerque, NM	5,226.0	5.9	63.5	137.3	535.7	1,146.7	2,910.6	426.4
Anchorage, AK	4,941.6	4.8	133.2	167.9	488.0	444.4	3,408.6	294.7
Ann Arbor, MI	2,403.2	3.1	52.9	45.6	203.9	427.0	1,564.3	106.5
Athens, GA	3,351.4	1.0	26.3	67.9	176.8	701.0	2,239.7	138.8
Atlanta, GA	3,719.9	5.9	19.5	158.1	205.6	809.1	2,184.4	337.4
Austin, TX	3,449.8	2.8	23.3	53.3	192.0	534.0	2,485.7	158.7
Billings, MT	4,264.6	2.4	29.7	51.0	183.2	731.6	2,871.2	395.5
Boise City, ID	1,925.0	0.9	48.3	13.0	162.1	355.5	1,263.5	81.7
Boston, MA[2]	2,595.6	3.2	33.8	151.0	315.0	406.8	1,540.4	145.4
Boulder, CO	2,493.1	0.6	52.2	23.8	135.3	397.0	1,776.8	107.3
Cape Coral, FL	2,527.1	3.8	22.9	87.9	218.2	575.9	1,494.6	123.9
Cedar Rapids, IA	2,560.4	1.5	28.1	37.6	137.3	529.2	1,682.6	144.2
Charleston, SC	3,510.2	7.2	28.4	71.0	252.8	622.1	2,289.0	239.7
Charlotte, NC	3,385.4	5.2	23.0	114.4	261.8	685.4	2,141.0	154.6
Chicago, IL[2]	n/a	6.8	n/a	198.7	n/a	430.7	1,769.2	224.4
Clarksville, TN	2,883.5	5.0	47.7	58.8	257.8	653.6	1,761.0	99.7
Colorado Springs, CO	3,643.2	6.2	73.4	68.4	221.0	702.4	2,243.3	328.7
Columbia, MO	3,620.5	2.9	45.7	75.0	209.1	520.7	2,634.1	133.0
Columbus, OH	4,541.3	5.7	44.7	205.0	107.2	1,164.8	2,777.7	236.3
Dallas, TX[2]	3,209.0	4.7	29.4	132.8	151.1	686.1	1,916.5	288.4
Davenport, IA	2,864.5	1.8	37.8	64.4	257.4	516.9	1,886.4	99.8
Denver, CO	3,075.3	3.7	53.0	78.9	193.0	463.1	1,985.1	298.6
Des Moines, IA	3,032.5	2.3	26.7	41.4	197.4	592.9	1,972.2	199.5
Durham, NC[3]	3,867.3	5.2	21.2	139.9	261.0	1,095.0	2,154.6	190.3
El Paso, TX	2,523.7	1.4	28.0	58.9	258.9	280.7	1,781.6	114.1
Erie, PA	2,630.1	1.4	31.7	81.3	130.5	610.1	1,713.0	62.0
Eugene, OR	3,898.7	1.1	29.5	67.9	95.4	716.2	2,706.3	282.3
Fargo, ND	2,536.8	1.8	41.9	31.1	180.9	494.2	1,662.7	124.2
Fayetteville, NC	5,400.4	7.9	22.7	202.9	256.6	1,458.5	3,217.9	233.8
Fort Collins, CO	2,360.8	0.6	43.7	20.9	139.3	295.7	1,782.5	78.2
Fort Wayne, IN	3,195.4	8.0	29.2	117.7	111.3	693.0	2,114.5	121.7
Fort Worth, TX[2]	3,682.2	3.9	36.7	97.3	224.1	731.0	2,375.0	214.3
Gainesville, FL	3,502.5	3.7	42.5	88.0	407.7	572.2	2,253.0	135.3
Grand Rapids, MI	2,256.2	2.4	66.4	64.7	168.6	442.8	1,438.8	72.5
Green Bay, WI	2,018.4	0.6	24.3	33.6	147.4	327.4	1,430.4	54.7
Greensboro, NC	3,793.1	4.7	18.3	107.3	214.3	977.2	2,313.2	158.1
Honolulu, HI	n/a	n/a	n/a	n/a	n/a	n/a	n/a	n/a
Houston, TX	4,047.8	5.9	22.9	233.3	296.8	790.3	2,327.6	370.9
Huntsville, AL	3,839.4	6.2	43.0	107.2	327.0	734.2	2,391.9	229.7
Indianapolis, IN	3,468.6	7.6	41.5	213.8	n/a	885.4	2,249.6	333.7
Jacksonville, FL	3,724.4	7.1	41.9	118.2	328.5	678.6	2,403.5	146.7
Kansas City, MO	3,722.8	7.4	42.1	116.2	302.8	675.5	2,169.2	409.7
Lafayette, LA	4,006.3	5.0	17.8	107.5	330.9	799.3	2,530.4	215.2
Las Vegas, NV	3,694.8	5.7	42.2	232.8	397.3	916.5	1,693.2	407.0
Lexington, KY	3,979.7	4.9	37.8	119.3	94.6	779.8	2,735.2	208.0
Lincoln, NE	3,526.4	1.6	48.5	68.3	210.5	493.4	2,600.3	104.0
Little Rock, AR	5,567.3	7.7	40.7	175.6	451.6	1,248.9	3,316.4	326.4
Los Angeles, CA[2]	2,682.0	5.4	17.5	167.5	212.6	480.6	1,410.0	388.5
Louisville, KY	3,430.4	4.9	21.6	138.5	n/a	798.0	2,405.9	226.5
Lubbock, TX	4,905.4	3.0	38.6	129.7	486.8	975.5	2,961.7	310.2
Madison, WI	2,479.7	1.8	26.5	58.9	129.9	374.6	1,818.7	69.3
Manchester, NH	2,590.9	2.5	45.1	95.1	138.9	409.4	1,823.3	76.7
McAllen, TX	3,981.2	2.7	24.0	57.2	202.7	783.3	2,720.3	190.9
Miami, FL[2]	4,828.3	8.7	30.9	242.2	373.9	720.1	3,135.8	316.7

Table continued on next page.

Metro Area[1]	All Crimes	Violent Crimes				Property Crimes		
		Murder	Forcible Rape	Robbery	Aggrav. Assault	Burglary	Larceny -Theft	Motor Vehicle Theft
Midland, TX	2,918.9	3.9	16.0	44.9	215.7	505.8	1,961.8	170.8
Minneapolis, MN	2,868.9	2.5	35.5	96.7	139.2	435.5	1,986.2	173.3
Nashville, TN	3,314.2	3.4	42.8	115.3	434.6	588.3	2,000.6	129.2
New Orleans, LA	3,626.0	19.0	25.9	145.7	283.3	633.8	2,233.5	284.9
New York, NY[2]	2,093.6	3.2	11.0	170.6	271.2	234.3	1,314.1	89.3
Oklahoma City, OK	4,458.6	5.9	52.8	108.7	335.5	977.3	2,565.3	413.1
Omaha, NE	3,632.6	5.3	38.3	95.2	248.6	614.6	2,173.4	457.2
Orlando, FL	3,960.2	3.9	41.5	123.3	371.3	882.4	2,335.4	202.3
Oxnard, CA	2,144.6	4.0	10.1	72.2	107.4	381.8	1,390.5	178.4
Palm Bay, FL	3,321.0	3.6	50.3	85.4	385.5	681.4	1,989.5	125.3
Peoria, IL	2,668.8	5.8	22.3	87.2	226.9	573.8	1,674.6	78.3
Philadelphia, PA[2]	4,062.9	13.1	69.1	395.7	459.7	586.9	2,232.8	305.6
Phoenix, AZ	392.3	4.8	29.5	115.3	242.8	731.0	2,219.4	n/a
Pittsburgh, PA	2,149.4	4.1	15.5	83.7	189.5	367.2	1,412.4	76.9
Portland, OR	3,242.3	1.4	30.9	73.5	145.2	475.2	2,219.4	296.8
Providence, RI	2,697.8	2.5	42.6	80.6	212.6	547.1	1,621.0	191.4
Provo, UT	1,946.5	1.1	27.4	8.7	32.9	230.8	1,564.4	81.0
Raleigh, NC	2,502.6	2.7	12.7	67.8	136.0	576.6	1,600.9	105.8
Reno, NV	2,975.1	5.2	31.0	89.2	252.5	571.2	1,748.7	277.2
Richmond, VA	2,639.5	6.2	20.0	90.8	126.8	445.4	1,797.4	152.9
Roanoke, VA	2,682.4	5.1	31.5	55.6	146.1	354.6	1,985.1	104.4
Rochester, MN	1,792.2	0.0	30.8	26.5	85.3	338.2	1,243.2	68.2
Sacramento, CA	3,182.5	4.1	21.2	128.7	262.0	663.2	1,723.2	380.2
Salem, OR	3,448.8	3.5	25.1	53.6	151.4	511.9	2,416.5	286.8
Salt Lake City, UT	4,704.6	1.8	57.3	84.4	213.1	681.4	3,174.4	492.2
San Antonio, TX	4,874.8	4.6	39.1	107.0	308.9	849.6	3,226.3	339.3
San Diego, CA	2,540.5	2.2	20.8	95.3	230.3	435.7	1,404.6	351.6
San Francisco, CA[2]	4,626.3	3.7	18.7	302.4	240.8	578.0	3,006.2	476.5
San Jose, CA	2,613.9	3.0	21.6	80.1	145.1	467.9	1,359.9	536.3
Santa Rosa, CA	2,020.8	1.8	25.5	48.9	283.9	364.5	1,150.4	145.7
Savannah, GA	3,381.8	9.8	18.6	136.4	151.2	778.7	2,049.7	237.4
Seattle, WA[2]	4,264.0	1.9	28.6	110.9	145.3	826.2	2,646.5	504.6
Sioux Falls, SD	2,658.9	1.2	65.8	28.1	196.6	472.2	1,763.8	131.2
Spokane, WA	6,113.6	3.7	47.3	123.1	192.7	1,200.7	3,923.8	622.2
Springfield, IL	4,661.8	16.5	74.4	165.3	511.8	828.2	2,685.2	380.4
Tallahassee, FL	3,976.4	4.5	58.9	120.1	398.8	859.7	2,374.2	160.2
Tampa, FL	3,128.6	4.3	31.0	90.8	270.5	619.5	1,959.0	153.6
Topeka, KS	3,890.6	5.5	20.9	75.0	247.7	720.1	2,528.9	292.5
Tulsa, OK	3,794.1	6.7	58.8	113.8	337.5	879.0	2,058.3	340.0
Tyler, TX	3,254.1	3.7	26.2	36.4	212.2	726.5	2,089.8	159.3
Virginia Beach, VA	3,320.0	6.9	32.9	89.9	173.9	532.5	2,334.8	149.2
Washington, DC[2]	2,685.6	4.4	24.9	158.9	180.8	296.1	1,808.1	212.3
Wichita, KS	4,704.4	3.5	52.1	78.3	434.4	810.6	2,967.6	358.0
Wilmington, NC	3,936.0	3.4	24.4	111.7	222.6	1,000.1	2,392.5	181.4
Winston-Salem, NC	3,911.7	3.5	21.8	95.4	251.0	1,110.0	2,265.8	164.2
Worcester, MA	2,419.0	1.6	31.3	81.6	307.8	513.7	1,378.6	104.5
U.S.	3,098.6	4.5	25.2	109.1	229.1	610.0	1,899.4	221.3

Note: Figures are crimes per 100,000 population in 2013 except where noted; n/a not available; (1) Figures cover the Metropolitan Statistical Area except where noted; (2) Metropolitan Division (MD); (3) 2012 data
Source: FBI Uniform Crime Reports, 2013

Temperature & Precipitation: Yearly Averages and Extremes

City	Extreme Low (°F)	Average Low (°F)	Average Temp. (°F)	Average High (°F)	Extreme High (°F)	Average Precip. (in.)	Average Snow (in.)
Albuquerque, NM	-17	43	57	70	105	8.5	11
Anchorage, AK	-34	29	36	43	85	15.7	71
Ann Arbor, MI	-21	39	49	58	104	32.4	41
Athens, GA	-8	52	62	72	105	49.8	2
Atlanta, GA	-8	52	62	72	105	49.8	2
Austin, TX	-2	58	69	79	109	31.1	1
Billings, MT	-32	36	47	59	105	14.6	59
Boise City, ID	-25	39	51	63	111	11.8	22
Boston, MA	-12	44	52	59	102	42.9	41
Boulder, CO	-25	37	51	64	103	15.5	63
Cape Coral, FL	26	65	75	84	103	53.9	0
Cedar Rapids, IA	-34	36	47	57	105	34.4	33
Charleston, SC	6	55	66	76	104	52.1	1
Charlotte, NC	-5	50	61	71	104	42.8	6
Chicago, IL	-27	40	49	59	104	35.4	39
Clarksville, TN	-17	49	60	70	107	47.4	11
Colorado Springs, CO	-24	36	49	62	99	17.0	48
Columbia, MO	-20	44	54	64	111	40.6	25
Columbus, OH	-19	42	52	62	104	37.9	28
Dallas, TX	-2	56	67	77	112	33.9	3
Davenport, IA	-24	40	50	60	108	31.8	33
Denver, CO	-25	37	51	64	103	15.5	63
Des Moines, IA	-24	40	50	60	108	31.8	33
Durham, NC	-9	48	60	71	105	42.0	8
El Paso, TX	-8	50	64	78	114	8.6	6
Erie, PA	-18	41	49	57	100	40.5	83
Eugene, OR	-12	42	53	63	108	47.3	7
Fargo, ND	-36	31	41	52	106	19.6	40
Fayetteville, NC	-9	48	60	71	105	42.0	8
Fort Collins, CO	-25	37	51	64	103	15.5	63
Fort Wayne, IN	-22	40	50	60	106	35.9	33
Fort Worth, TX	-1	55	66	76	113	32.3	3
Gainesville, FL	10	58	69	79	102	50.9	Trace
Grand Rapids, MI	-22	38	48	57	102	34.7	73
Green Bay, WI	-31	34	44	54	99	28.3	46
Greensboro, NC	-8	47	58	69	103	42.5	10
Honolulu, HI	52	70	77	84	94	22.4	0
Houston, TX	7	58	69	79	107	46.9	Trace
Huntsville, AL	-11	50	61	71	104	56.8	4
Indianapolis, IN	-23	42	53	62	104	40.2	25
Jacksonville, FL	7	58	69	79	103	52.0	0
Kansas City, MO	-23	44	54	64	109	38.1	21
Lafayette, LA	8	57	68	78	103	58.5	Trace
Las Vegas, NV	8	53	67	80	116	4.0	1
Lexington, KY	-21	45	55	65	103	45.1	17
Lincoln, NE	-33	39	51	62	108	29.1	27
Little Rock, AR	-5	51	62	73	112	50.7	5
Los Angeles, CA	27	55	63	70	110	11.3	Trace
Louisville, KY	-20	46	57	67	105	43.9	17
Lubbock, TX	-16	47	60	74	110	18.4	10
Madison, WI	-37	35	46	57	104	31.1	42
Manchester, NH	-33	34	46	57	102	36.9	63
McAllen, TX	16	65	74	83	106	25.8	Trace
Miami, FL	30	69	76	83	98	57.1	0
Midland, TX	-11	50	64	77	116	14.6	4

Table continued on next page.

City	Extreme Low (°F)	Average Low (°F)	Average Temp. (°F)	Average High (°F)	Extreme High (°F)	Average Precip. (in.)	Average Snow (in.)
Minneapolis, MN	-34	35	45	54	105	27.1	52
Nashville, TN	-17	49	60	70	107	47.4	11
New Orleans, LA	11	59	69	78	102	60.6	Trace
New York, NY	-2	47	55	62	104	47.0	23
Oklahoma City, OK	-8	49	60	71	110	32.8	10
Omaha, NE	-23	40	51	62	110	30.1	29
Orlando, FL	19	62	72	82	100	47.7	Trace
Oxnard, CA	27	51	60	68	105	12.0	0
Palm Bay, FL	21	65	74	82	100	50.5	0
Peoria, IL	-26	41	51	61	113	35.4	23
Philadelphia, PA	-7	45	55	64	104	41.4	22
Phoenix, AZ	17	59	72	86	122	7.3	Trace
Pittsburgh, PA	-18	41	51	60	103	37.1	43
Portland, OR	-3	45	54	62	107	37.5	7
Providence, RI	-13	42	51	60	104	45.3	35
Provo, UT	-22	40	52	64	107	15.6	63
Raleigh, NC	-9	48	60	71	105	42.0	8
Reno, NV	-16	33	50	67	105	7.2	24
Richmond, VA	-8	48	58	69	105	43.0	13
Roanoke, VA	-11	46	57	67	105	40.8	23
Rochester, MN	-40	34	44	54	102	29.4	47
Sacramento, CA	18	48	61	73	115	17.3	Trace
Salem, OR	-12	41	52	63	108	40.2	7
Salt Lake City, UT	-22	40	52	64	107	15.6	63
San Antonio, TX	0	58	69	80	108	29.6	1
San Diego, CA	29	57	64	71	111	9.5	Trace
San Francisco, CA	24	49	57	65	106	19.3	Trace
San Jose, CA	21	50	59	68	105	13.5	Trace
Santa Rosa, CA	23	42	57	71	109	29.0	n/a
Savannah, GA	3	56	67	77	105	50.3	Trace
Seattle, WA	0	44	52	59	99	38.4	13
Sioux Falls, SD	-36	35	46	57	110	24.6	38
Spokane, WA	-25	37	47	57	108	17.0	51
Springfield, IL	-24	44	54	63	112	34.9	21
Tallahassee, FL	6	56	68	79	103	63.3	Trace
Tampa, FL	18	63	73	82	99	46.7	Trace
Topeka, KS	-26	43	55	66	110	34.4	21
Tulsa, OK	-8	50	61	71	112	38.9	10
Tyler, TX	-2	56	67	77	112	33.9	3
Virginia Beach, VA	-3	51	60	69	104	44.8	8
Washington, DC	-5	49	58	67	104	39.5	18
Wichita, KS	-21	45	57	68	113	29.3	17
Wilmington, NC	0	53	64	74	104	55.0	2
Winston-Salem, NC	-8	47	58	69	103	42.5	10
Worcester, MA	-13	38	47	56	99	47.6	62

Source: National Climatic Data Center, International Station Meteorological Climate Summary, 9/96

Weather Conditions

City	Temperature			Daytime Sky			Precipitation		
	10°F & below	32°F & below	90°F & above	Clear	Partly cloudy	Cloudy	0.01 inch or more precip.	1.0 inch or more snow/ice	Thunder-storms
Albuquerque, NM	4	114	65	140	161	64	60	9	38
Anchorage, AK	n/a	194	n/a	50	115	200	113	49	2
Ann Arbor, MI	n/a	136	12	74	134	157	135	38	32
Athens, GA	1	49	38	98	147	120	116	3	48
Atlanta, GA	1	49	38	98	147	120	116	3	48
Austin, TX	< 1	20	111	105	148	112	83	1	41
Billings, MT	n/a	149	29	75	163	127	97	41	27
Boise City, ID	n/a	124	45	106	133	126	91	22	14
Boston, MA	n/a	97	12	88	127	150	253	48	18
Boulder, CO	24	155	33	99	177	89	90	38	39
Cape Coral, FL	n/a	n/a	115	93	220	52	110	0	92
Cedar Rapids, IA	n/a	156	16	89	132	144	109	28	42
Charleston, SC	< 1	33	53	89	162	114	114	1	59
Charlotte, NC	1	65	44	98	142	125	113	3	41
Chicago, IL	n/a	132	17	83	136	146	125	31	38
Clarksville, TN	5	76	51	98	135	132	119	8	54
Colorado Springs, CO	21	161	18	108	157	100	98	33	49
Columbia, MO	17	108	36	99	127	139	110	17	52
Columbus, OH	n/a	118	19	72	137	156	136	29	40
Dallas, TX	1	34	102	108	160	97	78	2	49
Davenport, IA	n/a	137	26	99	129	137	106	25	46
Denver, CO	24	155	33	99	177	89	90	38	39
Des Moines, IA	n/a	137	26	99	129	137	106	25	46
Durham, NC	n/a	n/a	39	98	143	124	110	3	42
El Paso, TX	1	59	106	147	164	54	49	3	35
Erie, PA	n/a	124	3	57	128	180	165	55	36
Eugene, OR	n/a	n/a	15	75	115	175	136	4	3
Fargo, ND	n/a	180	15	81	145	139	100	38	31
Fayetteville, NC	n/a	n/a	39	98	143	124	110	3	42
Fort Collins, CO	24	155	33	99	177	89	90	38	39
Fort Wayne, IN	n/a	131	16	75	140	150	131	31	39
Fort Worth, TX	1	40	100	123	136	106	79	3	47
Gainesville, FL	n/a	n/a	77	88	196	81	119	0	78
Grand Rapids, MI	n/a	146	11	67	119	179	142	57	34
Green Bay, WI	n/a	163	7	86	125	154	120	40	33
Greensboro, NC	3	85	32	94	143	128	113	5	43
Honolulu, HI	n/a	n/a	23	25	286	54	98	0	7
Houston, TX	n/a	n/a	96	83	168	114	101	1	62
Huntsville, AL	2	66	49	70	118	177	116	2	54
Indianapolis, IN	19	119	19	83	128	154	127	24	43
Jacksonville, FL	< 1	16	83	86	181	98	114	1	65
Kansas City, MO	22	110	39	112	134	119	103	17	51
Lafayette, LA	< 1	21	86	99	150	116	113	< 1	73
Las Vegas, NV	< 1	37	134	185	132	48	27	2	13
Lexington, KY	11	96	22	86	136	143	129	17	44
Lincoln, NE	n/a	145	40	108	135	122	94	19	46
Little Rock, AR	1	57	73	110	142	113	104	4	57
Los Angeles, CA	0	< 1	5	131	125	109	34	0	1
Louisville, KY	8	90	35	82	143	140	125	15	45
Lubbock, TX	5	93	79	134	150	81	62	8	48
Madison, WI	n/a	161	14	88	119	158	118	38	40
Manchester, NH	n/a	171	12	87	131	147	125	32	19
McAllen, TX	n/a	n/a	116	86	180	99	72	0	27
Miami, FL	n/a	n/a	55	48	263	54	128	0	74

Table continued on next page.

City	Temperature			Daytime Sky			Precipitation		
	10°F & below	32°F & below	90°F & above	Clear	Partly cloudy	Cloudy	0.01 inch or more precip.	1.0 inch or more snow/ice	Thunder-storms
Midland, TX	1	62	102	144	138	83	52	3	38
Minneapolis, MN	n/a	156	16	93	125	147	113	41	37
Nashville, TN	5	76	51	98	135	132	119	8	54
New Orleans, LA	0	13	70	90	169	106	114	1	69
New York, NY	n/a	n/a	18	85	166	114	120	11	20
Oklahoma City, OK	5	79	70	124	131	110	80	8	50
Omaha, NE	n/a	139	35	100	142	123	97	20	46
Orlando, FL	n/a	n/a	90	76	208	81	115	0	80
Oxnard, CA	0	1	2	114	155	96	34	< 1	1
Palm Bay, FL	n/a	n/a	59	75	228	62	124	0	73
Peoria, IL	n/a	127	27	89	127	149	115	22	49
Philadelphia, PA	5	94	23	81	146	138	117	14	27
Phoenix, AZ	0	10	167	186	125	54	37	< 1	23
Pittsburgh, PA	n/a	121	8	62	137	166	154	42	35
Portland, OR	n/a	37	11	67	116	182	152	4	7
Providence, RI	n/a	117	9	85	134	146	123	21	21
Provo, UT	n/a	128	56	94	152	119	92	38	38
Raleigh, NC	n/a	n/a	39	98	143	124	110	3	42
Reno, NV	14	178	50	143	139	83	50	17	14
Richmond, VA	3	79	41	90	147	128	115	7	43
Roanoke, VA	4	89	31	90	152	123	119	11	35
Rochester, MN	n/a	165	9	87	126	152	114	40	41
Sacramento, CA	0	21	73	175	111	79	58	< 1	2
Salem, OR	n/a	66	16	78	119	168	146	6	5
Salt Lake City, UT	n/a	128	56	94	152	119	92	38	38
San Antonio, TX	n/a	n/a	112	97	153	115	81	1	36
San Diego, CA	0	< 1	4	115	126	124	40	0	5
San Francisco, CA	0	6	4	136	130	99	63	< 1	5
San Jose, CA	0	5	5	106	180	79	57	< 1	6
Santa Rosa, CA	n/a	43	30	n/a	365	n/a	n/a	n/a	2
Savannah, GA	< 1	29	70	97	155	113	111	< 1	63
Seattle, WA	n/a	38	3	57	121	187	157	8	8
Sioux Falls, SD	n/a	n/a	n/a	95	136	134	n/a	n/a	n/a
Spokane, WA	n/a	140	18	78	135	152	113	37	11
Springfield, IL	19	111	34	96	126	143	111	18	49
Tallahassee, FL	< 1	31	86	93	175	97	114	1	83
Tampa, FL	n/a	n/a	85	81	204	80	107	< 1	87
Topeka, KS	20	123	45	110	128	127	96	15	54
Tulsa, OK	6	78	74	117	141	107	88	8	50
Tyler, TX	1	34	102	108	160	97	78	2	49
Virginia Beach, VA	< 1	53	33	89	149	127	115	5	38
Washington, DC	2	71	34	84	144	137	112	9	30
Wichita, KS	13	110	63	117	132	116	87	13	54
Wilmington, NC	< 1	42	46	96	150	119	115	1	47
Winston-Salem, NC	3	85	32	94	143	128	113	5	43
Worcester, MA	n/a	141	4	81	144	140	131	32	23

Note: Figures are average number of days per year
Source: National Climatic Data Center, International Station Meteorological Climate Summary, 9/96

Air Quality Index

MSA[1] (Days[2])	Percent of Days when Air Quality was...					AQI Statistics	
	Good	Moderate	Unhealthy for Sensitive Groups	Unhealthy	Very Unhealthy	Maximum	Median
Albuquerque, NM (365)	64.1	35.3	0.5	0.0	0.0	105	47
Anchorage, AK (365)	67.4	29.0	2.7	0.5	0.3	231	34
Ann Arbor, MI (365)	71.0	28.8	0.3	0.0	0.0	106	41
Athens, GA (358)	70.1	29.9	0.0	0.0	0.0	92	41
Atlanta, GA (365)	38.4	58.9	2.5	0.0	0.3	214	54
Austin, TX (365)	71.8	28.2	0.0	0.0	0.0	93	42
Billings, MT (365)	81.4	16.4	2.2	0.0	0.0	125	27
Boise City, ID (365)	87.9	11.8	0.0	0.3	0.0	156	37
Boston, MA (365)	58.1	41.9	0.0	0.0	0.0	97	47
Boulder, CO (362)	84.3	15.2	0.6	0.0	0.0	126	41
Cape Coral, FL (365)	88.5	11.5	0.0	0.0	0.0	81	35
Cedar Rapids, IA (365)	61.6	35.3	3.0	0.0	0.0	149	44
Charleston, SC (365)	80.8	19.2	0.0	0.0	0.0	74	39
Charlotte, NC (365)	69.3	30.7	0.0	0.0	0.0	100	45
Chicago, IL (365)	16.4	79.2	4.1	0.3	0.0	155	62
Clarksville, TN (365)	75.1	24.9	0.0	0.0	0.0	87	42
Colorado Springs, CO (365)	84.9	14.8	0.3	0.0	0.0	104	42
Columbia, MO (214)	96.3	3.7	0.0	0.0	0.0	71	35
Columbus, OH (365)	62.2	37.5	0.3	0.0	0.0	102	45
Dallas, TX (365)	53.2	43.0	3.8	0.0	0.0	132	49
Davenport, IA (365)	33.2	65.8	1.1	0.0	0.0	111	56
Denver, CO (365)	45.2	51.8	2.7	0.3	0.0	152	51
Des Moines, IA (365)	79.7	20.3	0.0	0.0	0.0	91	37
Durham, NC (365)	86.0	14.0	0.0	0.0	0.0	84	37
El Paso, TX (365)	55.3	43.6	0.8	0.3	0.0	158	48
Erie, PA (359)	65.5	34.5	0.0	0.0	0.0	99	43
Eugene, OR (365)	69.6	25.8	4.7	0.0	0.0	135	39
Fargo, ND (365)	89.9	9.9	0.3	0.0	0.0	113	33
Fayetteville, NC (314)	78.0	22.0	0.0	0.0	0.0	80	41
Fort Collins, CO (365)	74.2	24.7	1.1	0.0	0.0	116	45
Fort Wayne, IN (365)	52.6	45.8	1.6	0.0	0.0	147	49
Fort Worth, TX (365)	53.2	43.0	3.8	0.0	0.0	132	49
Gainesville, FL (364)	93.4	6.6	0.0	0.0	0.0	64	33
Grand Rapids, MI (365)	71.2	28.5	0.3	0.0	0.0	121	40
Green Bay, WI (365)	68.8	29.0	2.2	0.0	0.0	114	40
Greensboro, NC (363)	79.3	20.7	0.0	0.0	0.0	87	42
Honolulu, HI (360)	97.5	2.2	0.0	0.3	0.0	195	27
Houston, TX (365)	43.6	54.5	1.9	0.0	0.0	150	53
Huntsville, AL (338)	88.8	11.2	0.0	0.0	0.0	87	36
Indianapolis, IN (365)	35.3	56.4	7.9	0.3	0.0	191	58
Jacksonville, FL (365)	70.1	29.0	0.8	0.0	0.0	106	43
Kansas City, MO (365)	26.6	58.9	14.5	0.0	0.0	150	61
Lafayette, LA (364)	62.9	37.1	0.0	0.0	0.0	96	44.5
Las Vegas, NV (365)	46.3	51.8	1.6	0.3	0.0	158	51
Lexington, KY (365)	80.8	19.2	0.0	0.0	0.0	83	40
Lincoln, NE (265)	90.2	9.4	0.4	0.0	0.0	109	34
Little Rock, AR (365)	63.8	35.9	0.3	0.0	0.0	108	43
Los Angeles, CA (365)	6.8	69.0	20.8	3.3	0.0	187	76
Louisville, KY (365)	30.1	61.9	7.9	0.0	0.0	145	56
Lubbock, TX (265)	87.5	12.5	0.0	0.0	0.0	100	28
Madison, WI (365)	72.6	27.1	0.3	0.0	0.0	112	40
Manchester, NH (365)	92.3	7.4	0.3	0.0	0.0	109	36
McAllen, TX (365)	75.3	24.7	0.0	0.0	0.0	88	37
Miami, FL (365)	74.0	25.2	0.8	0.0	0.0	123	43

Table continued on next page.

MSA[1] (Days[2])	Percent of Days when Air Quality was...					AQI Statistics	
	Good	Moderate	Unhealthy for Sensitive Groups	Unhealthy	Very Unhealthy	Maximum	Median
Midland, TX (n/a)	n/a	n/a	n/a	n/a	n/a	n/a	n/a
Minneapolis, MN (365)	60.0	39.5	0.5	0.0	0.0	130	46
Nashville, TN (365)	61.1	38.4	0.5	0.0	0.0	119	45
New Orleans, LA (365)	53.2	43.8	3.0	0.0	0.0	132	48
New York, NY (365)	38.9	58.1	2.7	0.3	0.0	161	54
Oklahoma City, OK (365)	66.0	34.0	0.0	0.0	0.0	100	45
Omaha, NE (365)	61.4	37.8	0.8	0.0	0.0	114	44
Orlando, FL (365)	85.5	14.2	0.3	0.0	0.0	106	38
Oxnard, CA (365)	49.0	49.0	1.9	0.0	0.0	124	51
Palm Bay, FL (365)	89.3	10.7	0.0	0.0	0.0	77	36
Peoria, IL (365)	62.7	29.6	6.6	1.1	0.0	185	43
Philadelphia, PA (365)	25.2	70.7	3.6	0.5	0.0	152	57
Phoenix, AZ (365)	8.5	66.0	20.3	3.6	1.6	825	77
Pittsburgh, PA (365)	29.6	65.5	4.7	0.3	0.0	155	58
Portland, OR (365)	77.3	20.5	1.9	0.3	0.0	153	36
Providence, RI (365)	74.0	25.8	0.3	0.0	0.0	121	42
Provo, UT (365)	74.5	23.6	1.9	0.0	0.0	120	42
Raleigh, NC (365)	70.4	29.6	0.0	0.0	0.0	84	42
Reno, NV (365)	60.0	36.7	1.1	0.8	1.4	891	47
Richmond, VA (365)	79.7	20.0	0.3	0.0	0.0	104	41
Roanoke, VA (365)	82.5	17.3	0.3	0.0	0.0	108	38
Rochester, MN (365)	85.5	14.2	0.3	0.0	0.0	103	35
Sacramento, CA (365)	46.8	43.6	8.8	0.5	0.3	240	53
Salem, OR (365)	87.4	12.3	0.0	0.3	0.0	154	29
Salt Lake City, UT (365)	77.0	18.4	4.1	0.5	0.0	154	42
San Antonio, TX (365)	60.0	39.2	0.8	0.0	0.0	125	46
San Diego, CA (365)	29.9	65.2	4.7	0.3	0.0	165	58
San Francisco, CA (365)	56.4	41.6	1.9	0.0	0.0	119	48
San Jose, CA (365)	73.7	24.9	1.1	0.3	0.0	154	41
Santa Rosa, CA (365)	87.9	12.1	0.0	0.0	0.0	81	35
Savannah, GA (365)	69.9	29.6	0.5	0.0	0.0	114	43
Seattle, WA (365)	66.0	32.3	1.6	0.0	0.0	133	43
Sioux Falls, SD (363)	83.5	16.3	0.3	0.0	0.0	104	36
Spokane, WA (365)	80.0	19.5	0.5	0.0	0.0	105	35
Springfield, IL (365)	93.4	6.6	0.0	0.0	0.0	78	31
Tallahassee, FL (365)	69.6	30.1	0.0	0.3	0.0	157	42
Tampa, FL (365)	64.1	35.6	0.3	0.0	0.0	112	45
Topeka, KS (365)	89.9	9.9	0.3	0.0	0.0	105	35
Tulsa, OK (365)	65.8	34.2	0.0	0.0	0.0	97	43
Tyler, TX (365)	96.2	3.8	0.0	0.0	0.0	84	31
Virginia Beach, VA (365)	77.8	22.2	0.0	0.0	0.0	87	40
Washington, DC (365)	57.5	41.4	1.1	0.0	0.0	129	48
Wichita, KS (365)	80.8	18.4	0.8	0.0	0.0	140	39
Wilmington, NC (365)	86.6	13.4	0.0	0.0	0.0	77	36
Winston-Salem, NC (365)	70.1	29.9	0.0	0.0	0.0	91	44
Worcester, MA (365)	83.0	17.0	0.0	0.0	0.0	100	36

Note: The Air Quality Index (AQI) is an index for reporting daily air quality. EPA calculates the AQI for five major air pollutants regulated by the Clean Air Act: ground-level ozone, particle pollution (also known as particulate matter), carbon monoxide, sulfur dioxide, and nitrogen dioxide. The AQI runs from 0 to 500. The higher the AQI value, the greater the level of air pollution and the greater the health concern. There are six AQI categories: "Good" The AQI is between 0 and 50. Air quality is considered satisfactory; "Moderate" The AQI is between 51 and 100. Air quality is acceptable; "Unhealthy for Sensitive Groups" When AQI values are between 101 and 150, members of sensitive groups may experience health effects; "Unhealthy" When AQI values are between 151 and 200 everyone may begin to experience health effects; "Very Unhealthy" AQI values between 201 and 300 trigger a health alert; "Hazardous" AQI values over 300 trigger health warnings of emergency conditions; Data covers the entire county unless noted otherwise; (1) Data covers the Metropolitan Statistical Area—see Appendix B for areas included; (2) Number of days with AQI data in 2014
Source: U.S. Environmental Protection Agency, Air Quality Index Report, 2014

Air Quality Index Pollutants

MSA[1] (Days[2])	Percent of Days when AQI Pollutant was...					
	Carbon Monoxide	Nitrogen Dioxide	Ozone	Sulfur Dioxide	Particulate Matter 2.5	Particulate Matter 10
Albuquerque, NM (365)	0.0	1.1	57.3	0.8	20.0	20.8
Anchorage, AK (365)	0.3	0.0	14.8	0.0	55.1	29.9
Ann Arbor, MI (365)	0.0	0.0	38.1	0.0	61.9	0.0
Athens, GA (358)	0.0	0.0	21.8	0.0	78.2	0.0
Atlanta, GA (365)	0.0	1.1	22.2	0.0	76.7	0.0
Austin, TX (365)	0.0	3.6	40.3	0.0	55.9	0.3
Billings, MT (365)	0.0	0.0	0.0	43.8	56.2	0.0
Boise City, ID (365)	0.3	18.4	63.0	0.0	10.4	7.9
Boston, MA (365)	0.0	4.4	21.9	0.8	72.3	0.5
Boulder, CO (362)	0.0	0.0	92.0	0.0	7.7	0.3
Cape Coral, FL (365)	0.0	0.0	55.9	0.0	42.7	1.4
Cedar Rapids, IA (365)	0.0	0.0	23.0	15.9	60.3	0.8
Charleston, SC (365)	0.0	0.8	23.3	0.3	75.6	0.0
Charlotte, NC (365)	0.0	2.2	40.0	0.0	57.8	0.0
Chicago, IL (365)	0.0	3.3	7.4	2.5	81.1	5.8
Clarksville, TN (365)	0.0	0.0	48.2	2.2	49.6	0.0
Colorado Springs, CO (365)	0.0	0.0	86.6	11.2	2.2	0.0
Columbia, MO (214)	0.0	0.0	100.0	0.0	0.0	0.0
Columbus, OH (365)	0.0	4.9	26.0	0.3	68.5	0.3
Dallas, TX (365)	0.0	6.8	41.9	0.3	50.1	0.8
Davenport, IA (365)	0.0	0.0	6.6	0.0	64.1	29.3
Denver, CO (365)	0.0	26.8	46.3	0.3	23.3	3.3
Des Moines, IA (365)	0.0	7.4	28.8	0.0	63.0	0.8
Durham, NC (365)	0.0	0.0	50.7	0.5	48.8	0.0
El Paso, TX (365)	0.0	9.9	32.1	0.0	55.3	2.7
Erie, PA (359)	0.0	0.3	33.4	0.0	66.0	0.3
Eugene, OR (365)	0.0	0.0	26.0	0.0	74.0	0.0
Fargo, ND (365)	0.0	2.2	59.7	0.0	32.1	6.0
Fayetteville, NC (314)	0.0	0.0	40.8	0.0	59.2	0.0
Fort Collins, CO (365)	0.0	0.0	95.1	0.0	4.1	0.8
Fort Wayne, IN (365)	0.0	0.8	13.4	0.5	85.2	0.0
Fort Worth, TX (365)	0.0	6.8	41.9	0.3	50.1	0.8
Gainesville, FL (364)	0.0	0.0	51.4	0.0	48.6	0.0
Grand Rapids, MI (365)	0.0	0.0	31.8	0.0	68.2	0.0
Green Bay, WI (365)	0.0	0.0	34.5	12.1	53.4	0.0
Greensboro, NC (363)	0.0	0.0	40.5	2.8	56.7	0.0
Honolulu, HI (360)	0.0	0.3	52.5	1.7	38.9	6.7
Houston, TX (365)	0.0	5.8	22.2	0.8	65.8	5.5
Huntsville, AL (338)	0.0	0.0	60.7	0.0	22.8	16.6
Indianapolis, IN (365)	0.0	1.4	12.3	23.8	62.2	0.3
Jacksonville, FL (365)	0.0	1.1	32.9	7.9	58.1	0.0
Kansas City, MO (365)	0.0	2.2	14.0	26.8	54.8	2.2
Lafayette, LA (364)	0.0	0.0	22.8	0.0	76.9	0.3
Las Vegas, NV (365)	0.0	1.4	58.1	0.0	37.3	3.3
Lexington, KY (365)	0.0	12.3	39.7	0.0	47.9	0.0
Lincoln, NE (265)	0.0	0.0	67.5	0.0	32.5	0.0
Little Rock, AR (365)	0.0	3.0	27.1	0.0	69.9	0.0
Los Angeles, CA (365)	1.1	4.9	33.7	0.0	58.9	1.4
Louisville, KY (365)	0.0	0.8	9.0	17.8	72.3	0.0
Lubbock, TX (265)	0.0	0.0	0.0	0.0	100.0	0.0
Madison, WI (365)	0.0	0.0	37.8	0.0	61.9	0.3
Manchester, NH (365)	0.0	0.0	82.7	0.0	17.3	0.0
McAllen, TX (365)	0.0	0.0	27.7	0.0	71.5	0.8
Miami, FL (365)	0.0	2.7	26.3	0.0	71.0	0.0

Table continued on next page.

MSA[1] (Days[2])	Percent of Days when AQI Pollutant was...					
	Carbon Monoxide	Nitrogen Dioxide	Ozone	Sulfur Dioxide	Particulate Matter 2.5	Particulate Matter 10
Midland, TX (n/a)	n/a	n/a	n/a	n/a	n/a	n/a
Minneapolis, MN (365)	0.0	2.2	22.5	0.8	72.6	1.9
Nashville, TN (365)	0.0	5.5	23.0	0.3	71.2	0.0
New Orleans, LA (365)	0.0	1.4	28.8	10.4	59.5	0.0
New York, NY (365)	0.0	20.8	23.0	0.3	55.9	0.0
Oklahoma City, OK (365)	0.0	6.3	49.9	0.0	42.2	1.6
Omaha, NE (365)	0.0	0.0	30.4	4.9	45.2	19.5
Orlando, FL (365)	0.0	0.5	56.4	0.0	43.0	0.0
Oxnard, CA (365)	0.0	0.3	48.8	0.0	49.0	1.9
Palm Bay, FL (365)	0.0	0.0	62.5	0.0	37.5	0.0
Peoria, IL (365)	0.0	0.0	33.7	20.3	46.0	0.0
Philadelphia, PA (365)	0.0	0.8	18.4	0.3	80.5	0.0
Phoenix, AZ (365)	0.0	1.6	19.7	0.0	20.5	58.1
Pittsburgh, PA (365)	0.0	0.3	10.4	10.4	78.9	0.0
Portland, OR (365)	0.0	1.6	41.6	0.0	56.7	0.0
Providence, RI (365)	0.0	9.3	38.6	0.0	51.5	0.5
Provo, UT (365)	0.0	19.2	59.7	0.0	18.9	2.2
Raleigh, NC (365)	0.0	5.2	40.3	0.0	54.5	0.0
Reno, NV (365)	0.0	3.8	59.5	0.0	26.0	10.7
Richmond, VA (365)	0.0	8.5	48.5	1.4	41.6	0.0
Roanoke, VA (365)	0.3	2.7	30.4	0.0	66.6	0.0
Rochester, MN (365)	0.0	0.0	49.9	0.8	49.3	0.0
Sacramento, CA (365)	0.0	0.3	65.5	0.0	33.4	0.8
Salem, OR (365)	0.0	0.0	35.3	0.0	64.7	0.0
Salt Lake City, UT (365)	0.0	16.7	60.8	0.0	21.4	1.1
San Antonio, TX (365)	0.0	4.1	37.5	0.0	58.1	0.3
San Diego, CA (365)	0.0	5.8	41.6	0.0	48.2	4.4
San Francisco, CA (365)	0.0	5.2	18.6	0.0	76.2	0.0
San Jose, CA (365)	0.0	3.0	61.9	0.0	34.5	0.5
Santa Rosa, CA (365)	0.0	0.0	54.0	0.0	45.2	0.8
Savannah, GA (365)	0.0	0.0	9.9	25.5	64.7	0.0
Seattle, WA (365)	0.0	18.9	36.2	0.0	44.9	0.0
Sioux Falls, SD (363)	0.0	0.6	60.3	0.0	34.7	4.4
Spokane, WA (365)	0.8	0.0	24.1	0.0	60.8	14.2
Springfield, IL (365)	0.0	0.0	86.0	2.7	11.2	0.0
Tallahassee, FL (365)	0.0	0.0	23.8	0.0	76.2	0.0
Tampa, FL (365)	0.0	0.5	35.9	5.8	57.8	0.0
Topeka, KS (365)	0.0	0.0	79.2	0.0	14.8	6.0
Tulsa, OK (365)	0.0	0.5	45.8	0.3	52.9	0.5
Tyler, TX (365)	0.0	0.5	99.5	0.0	0.0	0.0
Virginia Beach, VA (365)	0.0	5.2	42.2	4.7	47.9	0.0
Washington, DC (365)	0.0	5.8	37.3	0.0	57.0	0.0
Wichita, KS (365)	0.0	6.3	66.8	0.0	14.8	12.1
Wilmington, NC (365)	0.0	0.0	45.8	5.5	48.8	0.0
Winston-Salem, NC (365)	0.0	3.0	33.7	0.0	63.3	0.0
Worcester, MA (365)	0.0	5.8	58.9	0.0	34.2	1.1

Note: The Air Quality Index (AQI) is an index for reporting daily air quality. EPA calculates the AQI for five major air pollutants regulated by the Clean Air Act: ground-level ozone, particle pollution (also known as particulate matter), carbon monoxide, sulfur dioxide, and nitrogen dioxide. The AQI runs from 0 to 500. The higher the AQI value, the greater the level of air pollution and the greater the health concern; (1) Data covers the Metropolitan Statistical Area—see Appendix B for areas included; (2) Number of days with AQI data in 2014 Source: U.S. Environmental Protection Agency, Air Quality Index Report, 2014

Air Quality Trends: Ozone

MSA[1]	2004	2005	2006	2007	2008	2009	2010	2011	2012	2013
Albuquerque, NM	0.071	0.074	0.071	0.070	0.066	0.065	0.066	0.070	0.070	0.068
Anchorage, AK	n/a	n/a	n/a	n/a	n/a	n/a	n/a	n/a	n/a	n/a
Ann Arbor, MI	0.071	0.083	0.076	0.077	0.069	0.065	0.066	0.077	0.085	0.065
Athens, GA	0.078	0.082	0.086	0.083	0.077	0.067	0.073	0.075	0.071	0.060
Atlanta, GA	0.081	0.085	0.092	0.091	0.080	0.072	0.074	0.078	0.077	0.065
Austin, TX	0.081	0.081	0.083	0.073	0.072	0.073	0.072	0.074	0.075	0.070
Billings, MT	n/a	n/a	n/a	n/a	n/a	n/a	n/a	n/a	n/a	n/a
Boise City, ID	n/a	n/a	n/a	n/a	n/a	n/a	n/a	n/a	n/a	n/a
Boston, MA	0.075	0.082	0.077	0.081	0.072	0.070	0.069	0.066	0.068	0.067
Boulder, CO	0.068	0.076	0.082	0.085	0.076	0.073	0.072	0.076	0.076	0.079
Cape Coral, FL	0.072	0.070	0.070	0.069	0.068	0.062	0.064	0.062	0.063	0.065
Cedar Rapids, IA	0.063	0.073	0.065	0.076	0.063	0.061	0.064	0.064	0.071	0.060
Charleston, SC	0.072	0.073	0.071	0.065	0.069	0.059	0.067	0.066	0.063	0.059
Charlotte, NC	0.078	0.085	0.084	0.088	0.081	0.067	0.076	0.078	0.076	0.064
Chicago, IL	0.067	0.083	0.069	0.079	0.064	0.065	0.069	0.071	0.081	0.067
Clarksville, TN	n/a	n/a	n/a	n/a	n/a	n/a	n/a	n/a	n/a	n/a
Colorado Springs, CO	0.070	0.077	0.072	0.072	0.070	0.060	0.068	0.074	0.075	0.074
Columbia, MO	n/a	n/a	n/a	n/a	n/a	n/a	n/a	n/a	n/a	n/a
Columbus, OH	0.075	0.085	0.077	0.081	0.073	0.070	0.074	0.078	0.079	0.068
Dallas, TX	0.087	0.093	0.089	0.081	0.077	0.080	0.076	0.085	0.083	0.078
Davenport, IA	0.064	0.071	0.065	0.072	0.061	0.061	0.061	0.059	0.069	0.066
Denver, CO	0.068	0.075	0.080	0.079	0.075	0.070	0.072	0.078	0.080	0.080
Des Moines, IA	0.051	0.072	0.064	0.069	0.059	0.061	0.064	0.063	0.070	0.059
Durham, NC	0.072	0.079	0.073	0.077	0.075	0.064	0.072	0.070	0.068	0.058
El Paso, TX	0.074	0.077	0.077	0.074	0.074	0.068	0.068	0.069	0.067	0.066
Erie, PA	0.074	0.086	0.077	0.084	0.074	0.069	0.075	0.072	0.082	0.068
Eugene, OR	0.066	0.068	0.073	0.060	0.059	0.065	0.058	0.059	0.061	0.055
Fargo, ND	0.056	0.061	0.065	0.055	0.055	0.057	0.063	0.057	0.063	0.059
Fayetteville, NC	0.075	0.088	0.073	0.081	0.075	0.066	0.072	0.075	0.069	0.062
Fort Collins, CO	0.069	0.076	0.077	0.074	0.071	0.066	0.072	0.073	0.077	0.074
Fort Wayne, IN	0.071	0.081	0.072	0.079	0.068	0.065	0.067	0.071	0.076	0.062
Fort Worth, TX	0.087	0.093	0.089	0.081	0.077	0.080	0.076	0.085	0.083	0.078
Gainesville, FL	0.075	0.073	0.075	0.078	0.069	0.056	0.069	0.064	0.064	0.062
Grand Rapids, MI	0.070	0.083	0.082	0.085	0.068	0.069	0.068	0.076	0.080	0.068
Green Bay, WI	0.072	0.084	0.072	0.084	0.064	0.068	0.072	0.068	0.083	0.067
Greensboro, NC	0.074	0.078	0.075	0.082	0.084	0.068	0.074	0.071	0.076	0.062
Honolulu, HI	0.046	0.042	0.040	0.033	0.041	0.048	0.047	0.046	0.043	0.047
Houston, TX	0.092	0.087	0.090	0.079	0.074	0.079	0.078	0.082	0.081	0.074
Huntsville, AL	0.077	0.075	0.079	0.082	0.073	0.066	0.071	0.072	0.076	0.064
Indianapolis, IN	0.071	0.080	0.076	0.081	0.070	0.070	0.068	0.071	0.075	0.063
Jacksonville, FL	0.074	0.072	0.074	0.073	0.069	0.061	0.067	0.066	0.060	0.057
Kansas City, MO	0.066	0.082	0.085	0.076	0.067	0.068	0.068	0.074	0.082	0.066
Lafayette, LA	n/a	n/a	n/a	n/a	n/a	n/a	n/a	n/a	n/a	n/a
Las Vegas, NV	0.078	0.082	0.081	0.081	0.074	0.072	0.071	0.074	0.077	0.073
Lexington, KY	0.064	0.078	0.070	0.079	0.070	0.064	0.070	0.074	0.078	0.061
Lincoln, NE	0.056	0.056	0.056	0.054	0.051	0.053	0.050	0.053	0.058	0.055
Little Rock, AR	0.073	0.083	0.083	0.081	0.068	0.072	0.072	0.078	0.078	0.067
Los Angeles, CA	0.088	0.083	0.088	0.084	0.088	0.085	0.073	0.077	0.078	0.074
Louisville, KY	0.071	0.083	0.076	0.083	0.074	0.068	0.075	0.081	0.085	0.065
Lubbock, TX	n/a	n/a	n/a	n/a	n/a	n/a	n/a	n/a	n/a	n/a
Madison, WI	0.065	0.079	0.066	0.079	0.064	0.063	0.062	0.068	0.074	0.067
Manchester, NH	n/a	n/a	n/a	n/a	n/a	n/a	n/a	n/a	n/a	n/a
McAllen, TX	0.070	0.069	0.060	0.055	0.058	0.060	0.065	0.062	0.061	0.055
Miami, FL	0.063	0.064	0.074	0.066	0.067	0.062	0.064	0.060	0.062	0.061
Midland, TX	n/a	n/a	n/a	n/a	n/a	n/a	n/a	n/a	n/a	n/a
Minneapolis, MN	0.062	0.073	0.068	0.073	0.059	0.062	0.065	0.064	0.069	0.065

Table continued on next page.

MSA[1]	2004	2005	2006	2007	2008	2009	2010	2011	2012	2013
Nashville, TN	0.072	0.078	0.078	0.083	0.072	0.064	0.073	0.071	0.077	0.065
New Orleans, LA	0.076	0.076	0.078	0.079	0.070	0.073	0.075	0.073	0.072	0.064
New York, NY	0.079	0.091	0.087	0.086	0.080	0.071	0.081	0.081	0.079	0.071
Oklahoma City, OK	0.072	0.076	0.081	0.073	0.071	0.072	0.071	0.082	0.078	0.070
Omaha, NE	0.069	0.073	0.071	0.066	0.058	0.060	0.063	0.061	0.073	0.061
Orlando, FL	0.074	0.080	0.078	0.075	0.069	0.064	0.068	0.072	0.069	0.063
Oxnard, CA	0.084	0.080	0.081	0.075	0.079	0.079	0.074	0.074	0.071	0.068
Palm Bay, FL	0.067	0.070	0.076	0.068	0.068	0.063	0.064	0.066	0.065	0.063
Peoria, IL	0.064	0.075	0.069	0.078	0.064	0.061	0.064	0.068	0.072	0.062
Philadelphia, PA	0.080	0.088	0.083	0.086	0.082	0.069	0.082	0.082	0.081	0.067
Phoenix, AZ	0.073	0.078	0.078	0.073	0.076	0.069	0.072	0.076	0.076	0.073
Pittsburgh, PA	0.074	0.085	0.077	0.078	0.075	0.068	0.075	0.072	0.079	0.070
Portland, OR	0.060	0.059	0.067	0.058	0.062	0.064	0.056	0.056	0.059	0.053
Providence, RI	0.081	0.087	0.082	0.084	0.078	0.068	0.076	0.075	0.077	0.076
Provo, UT	0.070	0.079	0.077	0.076	0.073	0.069	0.070	0.065	0.077	0.074
Raleigh, NC	0.076	0.083	0.074	0.081	0.078	0.067	0.072	0.075	0.073	0.061
Reno, NV	0.069	0.067	0.071	0.069	0.074	0.064	0.067	0.064	0.070	0.066
Richmond, VA	0.076	0.082	0.082	0.081	0.082	0.065	0.078	0.076	0.076	0.064
Roanoke, VA	0.071	0.076	0.076	0.076	0.071	0.064	0.073	0.067	0.070	0.057
Rochester, MN	n/a	n/a	n/a	n/a	n/a	n/a	n/a	n/a	n/a	n/a
Sacramento, CA	0.081	0.089	0.094	0.080	0.089	0.083	0.077	0.078	0.082	0.071
Salem, OR	0.062	0.063	0.075	0.060	0.066	0.069	0.057	0.057	0.063	0.055
Salt Lake City, UT	0.072	0.084	0.082	0.081	0.075	0.074	0.072	0.074	0.079	0.076
San Antonio, TX	0.085	0.082	0.083	0.071	0.075	0.070	0.072	0.075	0.079	0.076
San Diego, CA	0.076	0.070	0.073	0.073	0.080	0.071	0.069	0.067	0.066	0.066
San Francisco, CA	0.063	0.058	0.066	0.059	0.067	0.066	0.063	0.062	0.059	0.058
San Jose, CA	0.072	0.066	0.080	0.068	0.074	0.072	0.074	0.066	0.065	0.064
Santa Rosa, CA	0.053	0.049	0.053	0.054	0.058	0.052	0.054	0.050	0.050	0.055
Savannah, GA	0.071	0.068	0.069	0.065	0.067	0.062	0.065	0.065	0.063	0.059
Seattle, WA	0.064	0.054	0.065	0.059	0.056	0.061	0.056	0.053	0.059	0.052
Sioux Falls, SD	n/a	n/a	n/a	n/a	n/a	n/a	n/a	n/a	n/a	n/a
Spokane, WA	0.065	0.063	0.066	0.064	0.058	0.057	0.058	0.056	0.063	0.062
Springfield, IL	n/a	n/a	n/a	n/a	n/a	n/a	n/a	n/a	n/a	n/a
Tallahassee, FL	0.071	0.070	0.071	0.072	0.071	0.058	0.066	0.065	0.066	0.061
Tampa, FL	0.074	0.075	0.074	0.076	0.075	0.064	0.067	0.071	0.066	0.066
Topeka, KS	n/a	n/a	n/a	n/a	n/a	n/a	n/a	n/a	n/a	n/a
Tulsa, OK	0.071	0.080	0.082	0.072	0.071	0.071	0.071	0.083	0.084	0.070
Tyler, TX	0.081	0.083	0.082	0.077	0.072	0.075	0.072	0.078	0.076	0.071
Virginia Beach, VA	0.075	0.078	0.074	0.077	0.078	0.065	0.074	0.075	0.069	0.065
Washington, DC	0.080	0.083	0.086	0.084	0.078	0.067	0.081	0.080	0.079	0.067
Wichita, KS	0.060	0.076	0.077	0.065	0.068	0.073	0.075	0.079	0.081	0.071
Wilmington, NC	0.070	0.075	0.072	0.071	0.063	0.060	0.062	0.064	0.064	0.064
Winston-Salem, NC	0.075	0.077	0.077	0.080	0.079	0.067	0.078	0.073	0.076	0.063
Worcester, MA	0.074	0.085	0.077	0.089	0.081	0.077	0.070	0.065	0.070	0.067

Note: (1) Data covers the Metropolitan Statistical Area—see Appendix B for areas included; n/a not available. The values shown are the composite ozone concentration averages among trend sites based on the highest fourth daily maximum 8-hour concentration in parts per million. These trends are based on sites having an adequate record of monitoring data during the trend period. Data from exceptional events are included.
Source: U.S. Environmental Protection Agency, Air Quality Monitoring Information, "Air Quality Trends by City, 2000-2013"

Maximum Air Pollutant Concentrations: Particulate Matter, Ozone, CO and Lead

Metro Aea	PM 10 (ug/m³)	PM 2.5 Wtd AM (ug/m³)	PM 2.5 24-Hr (ug/m³)	Ozone (ppm)	Carbon Monoxide (ppm)	Lead (ug/m³)
Albuquerque, NM	155	8.7	19	0.072	1	0.01
Anchorage, AK	120	6.4	28	n/a	4	n/a
Ann Arbor, MI	n/a	8.6	19	0.066	n/a	n/a
Athens, GA	n/a	9.7	28	0.06	n/a	n/a
Atlanta, GA	34	9.7	20	0.071	1	0.01
Austin, TX	57	7.2	24	0.07	0	n/a
Billings, MT	n/a	n/a	n/a	n/a	n/a	n/a
Boise City, ID	99	13	89	0.074	1	n/a
Boston, MA	50	9	23	0.073	1	n/a
Boulder, CO	51	7.1	23	0.079	n/a	n/a
Cape Coral, FL	49	5.8	15	0.066	n/a	n/a
Cedar Rapids, IA	55	9.5	22	0.06	1	n/a
Charleston, SC	34	7.1	16	0.059	n/a	n/a
Charlotte, NC	45	8.9	18	0.067	2	n/a
Chicago, IL	121	11.3	27	0.075	1	0.1
Clarksville, TN	26	9.8	22	0.064	n/a	n/a
Colorado Springs, CO	52	6	18	0.074	2	n/a
Columbia, MO	n/a	n/a	n/a	0.062	n/a	n/a
Columbus, OH	41	10.2	24	0.073	1	0.01
Dallas, TX	93	10.6	26	0.085	2	0.08
Davenport, IA	154	10.4	26	0.06	1	n/a
Denver, CO	97	8.2	23	0.085	3	0.02
Des Moines, IA	45	9	22	0.059	1	n/a
Durham, NC	24	7.8	18	0.062	n/a	n/a
El Paso, TX	233	10.8	30	0.073	3	0.03
Erie, PA	31	12.2	26	0.068	1	n/a
Eugene, OR	42	9.8	41	0.056	n/a	n/a
Fargo, ND	62	6.7	18	0.059	0	n/a
Fayetteville, NC	27	8.8	19	0.062	n/a	n/a
Fort Collins, CO	55	6.8	18	0.082	1	n/a
Fort Wayne, IN	n/a	9.5	20	0.062	2	n/a
Fort Worth, TX	93	10.6	26	0.085	2	0.08
Gainesville, FL	n/a	6.9	16	0.062	n/a	n/a
Grand Rapids, MI	29	9	19	0.068	1	0.06
Green Bay, WI	n/a	n/a	n/a	0.068	n/a	n/a
Greensboro, NC	26	8.7	19	0.062	n/a	n/a
Honolulu, HI	39	6.2	13	0.051	1	0
Houston, TX	80	11.3	27	0.084	2	0.01
Huntsville, AL	37	8.6	16	0.064	n/a	n/a
Indianapolis, IN	56	11.5	25	0.069	2	0.02
Jacksonville, FL	47	6.3	16	0.06	1	n/a
Kansas City, MO	95	9.9	22	0.071	2	0.01
Lafayette, LA	74	7.9	18	0.066	n/a	n/a
Las Vegas, NV	169	10.1	26	0.082	3	0.01
Lexington, KY	25	9.4	20	0.061	n/a	n/a
Lincoln, NE	n/a	8.1	20	0.055	n/a	n/a
Little Rock, AR	61	11	29	0.07	1	n/a
Los Angeles, CA	91	12.5	30	0.094	3	0.1
Louisville, KY	36	11.4	23	0.068	1	n/a
Lubbock, TX	n/a	n/a	n/a	n/a	n/a	n/a
Madison, WI	29	9.3	23	0.067	n/a	n/a
Manchester, NH	18	7.5	14	0.068	0	n/a
McAllen, TX	88	n/a	n/a	0.055	n/a	n/a
Miami, FL	62	5.8	14	0.068	1	n/a
Midland, TX	n/a	n/a	n/a	n/a	n/a	n/a

Table continued on next page.

Metro Aea	PM 10 (ug/m³)	PM 2.5 Wtd AM (ug/m³)	PM 2.5 24-Hr (ug/m³)	Ozone (ppm)	Carbon Monoxide (ppm)	Lead (ug/m³)
Minneapolis, MN	70	10.2	23	0.067	3	0.11
Nashville, TN	29	10.1	20	0.068	1	n/a
New Orleans, LA	52	7.9	18	0.071	n/a	0.08
New York, NY	43	10.7	31	0.078	2	0.01
Oklahoma City, OK	62	9.4	21	0.073	1	n/a
Omaha, NE	91	11	24	0.066	2	0.13
Orlando, FL	62	6.3	16	0.065	1	n/a
Oxnard, CA	143	9.3	23	0.077	n/a	n/a
Palm Bay, FL	54	5.8	21	0.063	n/a	n/a
Peoria, IL	n/a	n/a	n/a	0.066	n/a	0.01
Philadelphia, PA	64	11.5	31	0.073	2	0.04
Phoenix, AZ	510	10.6	42	0.079	3	0.04
Pittsburgh, PA	65	12	31	0.078	2	0.22
Portland, OR	43	9.1	56	0.059	2	n/a
Providence, RI	41	8.5	22	0.079	1	n/a
Provo, UT	136	12.5	82	0.077	2	n/a
Raleigh, NC	27	10.6	22	0.062	1	n/a
Reno, NV	999	12.3	41	0.069	2	n/a
Richmond, VA	30	8.1	19	0.066	1	0
Roanoke, VA	n/a	n/a	n/a	0.057	1	n/a
Rochester, MN	n/a	7.9	21	0.064	n/a	n/a
Sacramento, CA	68	11.5	40	0.082	2	n/a
Salem, OR	n/a	n/a	n/a	0.055	n/a	n/a
Salt Lake City, UT	105	12.1	59	0.077	2	0.08
San Antonio, TX	71	8.3	26	0.083	n/a	0.02
San Diego, CA	214	11.1	24	0.078	7	0.01
San Francisco, CA	42	12.8	32	0.069	3	0.22
San Jose, CA	53	11.9	35	0.071	2	0.12
Santa Rosa, CA	30	8.5	23	0.055	1	n/a
Savannah, GA	n/a	9	18	0.059	n/a	n/a
Seattle, WA	28	12.2	34	0.059	1	n/a
Sioux Falls, SD	55	8.9	23	0.067	1	n/a
Spokane, WA	68	9.2	31	0.062	2	n/a
Springfield, IL	n/a	n/a	n/a	0.062	n/a	n/a
Tallahassee, FL	n/a	7.9	20	0.062	n/a	n/a
Tampa, FL	49	6.5	15	0.07	1	0.49
Topeka, KS	54	8.4	20	0.066	n/a	n/a
Tulsa, OK	67	9.3	21	0.072	1	0.01
Tyler, TX	n/a	n/a	n/a	0.071	n/a	n/a
Virginia Beach, VA	21	7.7	18	0.068	1	n/a
Washington, DC	32	9.3	23	0.072	3	0
Wichita, KS	84	9.5	22	0.071	1	n/a
Wilmington, NC	n/a	6.6	15	0.064	n/a	n/a
Winston-Salem, NC	26	8.3	20	0.066	2	n/a
Worcester, MA	47	7.2	18	0.068	1	n/a
NAAQS[1]	150	15	35	0.075	9	0.15

Note: Data from exceptional events are included; Data covers the Metropolitan Statistical Area—see Appendix B for areas included; (1) National Ambient Air Quality Standards; ppm = parts per million; ug/m³ = micrograms per cubic meter; n/a not available Concentrations: Particulate Matter 10 (coarse particulate)—highest second maximum 24-hour concentration; Particulate Matter 2.5 Wtd AM (fine particulate)—highest weighted annual mean concentration; Particulate Matter 2.5 24-Hour (fine particulate)—highest 98th percentile 24-hour concentration; Ozone—highest fourth daily maximum 8-hour concentration; Carbon Monoxide—highest second maximum non-overlapping 8-hour concentration; Lead—maximum running 3-month average Source: U.S. Environmental Protection Agency, Air Quality Monitoring Information, "Air Quality Statistics by City, 2013"

Maximum Air Pollutant Concentrations: Nitrogen Dioxide and Sulfur Dioxide

Metro Area	Nitrogen Dioxide AM (ppb)	Nitrogen Dioxide 1-Hr (ppb)	Sulfur Dioxide AM (ppb)	Sulfur Dioxide 1-Hr (ppb)	Sulfur Dioxide 24-Hr (ppb)
Albuquerque, NM	12	45	n/a	4	n/a
Anchorage, AK	n/a	n/a	n/a	n/a	n/a
Ann Arbor, MI	n/a	n/a	n/a	n/a	n/a
Athens, GA	n/a	n/a	n/a	n/a	n/a
Atlanta, GA	9	43	n/a	9	n/a
Austin, TX	5	n/a	n/a	5	n/a
Billings, MT	n/a	n/a	n/a	48	n/a
Boise City, ID	11	n/a	n/a	n/a	n/a
Boston, MA	18	50	n/a	31	n/a
Boulder, CO	n/a	n/a	n/a	n/a	n/a
Cape Coral, FL	n/a	n/a	n/a	n/a	n/a
Cedar Rapids, IA	n/a	n/a	n/a	25	n/a
Charleston, SC	7	37	n/a	15	n/a
Charlotte, NC	8	39	n/a	8	n/a
Chicago, IL	21	64	n/a	73	n/a
Clarksville, TN	n/a	n/a	n/a	28	n/a
Colorado Springs, CO	n/a	n/a	n/a	58	n/a
Columbia, MO	n/a	n/a	n/a	n/a	n/a
Columbus, OH	n/a	n/a	n/a	13	n/a
Dallas, TX	12	49	n/a	16	n/a
Davenport, IA	7	39	n/a	15	n/a
Denver, CO	24	68	n/a	38	n/a
Des Moines, IA	9	37	n/a	1	n/a
Durham, NC	n/a	n/a	n/a	6	n/a
El Paso, TX	14	56	n/a	9	n/a
Erie, PA	6	36	n/a	12	n/a
Eugene, OR	n/a	n/a	n/a	n/a	n/a
Fargo, ND	4	36	n/a	n/a	n/a
Fayetteville, NC	n/a	n/a	n/a	n/a	n/a
Fort Collins, CO	n/a	n/a	n/a	n/a	n/a
Fort Wayne, IN	n/a	n/a	n/a	6	n/a
Fort Worth, TX	12	49	n/a	16	n/a
Gainesville, FL	n/a	n/a	n/a	n/a	n/a
Grand Rapids, MI	n/a	n/a	n/a	9	n/a
Green Bay, WI	n/a	n/a	n/a	76	n/a
Greensboro, NC	n/a	n/a	n/a	n/a	n/a
Honolulu, HI	3	23	n/a	9	n/a
Houston, TX	13	58	n/a	35	n/a
Huntsville, AL	n/a	n/a	n/a	n/a	n/a
Indianapolis, IN	12	44	n/a	78	n/a
Jacksonville, FL	8	38	n/a	60	n/a
Kansas City, MO	13	48	n/a	156	n/a
Lafayette, LA	n/a	n/a	n/a	n/a	n/a
Las Vegas, NV	14	n/a	n/a	7	n/a
Lexington, KY	7	44	n/a	18	n/a
Lincoln, NE	n/a	n/a	n/a	n/a	n/a
Little Rock, AR	10	47	n/a	7	n/a
Los Angeles, CA	23	71	n/a	12	n/a
Louisville, KY	11	43	n/a	117	n/a
Lubbock, TX	n/a	n/a	n/a	n/a	n/a
Madison, WI	n/a	n/a	n/a	8	n/a
Manchester, NH	n/a	n/a	n/a	5	n/a
McAllen, TX	n/a	n/a	n/a	n/a	n/a
Miami, FL	8	44	n/a	3	n/a
Midland, TX	n/a	n/a	n/a	n/a	n/a

Table continued on next page.

Metro Area	Nitrogen Dioxide AM (ppb)	Nitrogen Dioxide 1-Hr (ppb)	Sulfur Dioxide AM (ppb)	Sulfur Dioxide 1-Hr (ppb)	Sulfur Dioxide 24-Hr (ppb)
Minneapolis, MN	9	43	n/a	15	n/a
Nashville, TN	10	42	n/a	10	n/a
New Orleans, LA	6	46	n/a	181	n/a
New York, NY	22	62	n/a	22	n/a
Oklahoma City, OK	9	46	n/a	3	n/a
Omaha, NE	n/a	n/a	n/a	56	n/a
Orlando, FL	5	34	n/a	3	n/a
Oxnard, CA	9	37	n/a	n/a	n/a
Palm Bay, FL	n/a	n/a	n/a	n/a	n/a
Peoria, IL	n/a	n/a	n/a	195	n/a
Philadelphia, PA	17	52	n/a	15	n/a
Phoenix, AZ	25	63	n/a	9	n/a
Pittsburgh, PA	11	40	n/a	81	n/a
Portland, OR	10	33	n/a	5	n/a
Providence, RI	10	43	n/a	62	n/a
Provo, UT	19	75	n/a	n/a	n/a
Raleigh, NC	n/a	n/a	n/a	6	n/a
Reno, NV	16	56	n/a	6	n/a
Richmond, VA	8	41	n/a	30	n/a
Roanoke, VA	6	35	n/a	n/a	n/a
Rochester, MN	n/a	n/a	n/a	n/a	n/a
Sacramento, CA	10	50	n/a	3	n/a
Salem, OR	n/a	n/a	n/a	n/a	n/a
Salt Lake City, UT	18	62	n/a	31	n/a
San Antonio, TX	5	35	n/a	15	n/a
San Diego, CA	19	75	n/a	1	n/a
San Francisco, CA	17	60	n/a	17	n/a
San Jose, CA	15	52	n/a	10	n/a
Santa Rosa, CA	9	37	n/a	n/a	n/a
Savannah, GA	n/a	n/a	n/a	93	n/a
Seattle, WA	n/a	n/a	n/a	n/a	n/a
Sioux Falls, SD	5	34	n/a	3	n/a
Spokane, WA	n/a	n/a	n/a	n/a	n/a
Springfield, IL	n/a	n/a	n/a	12	n/a
Tallahassee, FL	n/a	n/a	n/a	n/a	n/a
Tampa, FL	5	34	n/a	68	n/a
Topeka, KS	n/a	n/a	n/a	n/a	n/a
Tulsa, OK	8	38	n/a	48	n/a
Tyler, TX	3	17	n/a	n/a	n/a
Virginia Beach, VA	8	41	n/a	52	n/a
Washington, DC	13	64	n/a	10	n/a
Wichita, KS	9	40	n/a	6	n/a
Wilmington, NC	n/a	n/a	n/a	45	n/a
Winston-Salem, NC	6	37	n/a	5	n/a
Worcester, MA	12	48	n/a	8	n/a
NAAQS[1]	53	100	30	75	140

Note: Data from exceptional events are included; Data covers the Metropolitan Statistical Area—see Appendix B for areas included; (1) National Ambient Air Quality Standards; ppb = parts per billion; n/a not available
Concentrations: Nitrogen Dioxide AM—highest arithmetic mean concentration; Nitrogen Dioxide 1-Hr—highest 98th percentile 1-hour daily maximum concentration; Sulfur Dioxide AM—highest annual mean concentration; Sulfur Dioxide 1-Hr—highest 99th percentile 1-hour daily maximum concentration; Sulfur Dioxide 24-Hr—highest second maximum 24-hour concentration
Source: U.S. Environmental Protection Agency, Air Quality Monitoring Information, "Air Quality Statistics by City, 2013"

Appendix B: Metropolitan Area Definitions

Metropolitan Statistical Areas (MSA), Metropolitan Divisions (MD), New England City and Town Areas (NECTA), and New England City and Town Area Divisions (NECTAD)

Note: In February 2013, the Office of Management and Budget (OMB) announced changes to metropolitan and micropolitan statistical area definitions. Both current and historical definitions are shown below. If the change only affected the name of the metro area, the counties included were not repeated.

Albuquerque, NM MSA
Bernalillo, Sandoval, Torrance, and Valencia Counties

Anchorage, AK MSA
Anchorage Municipality and Matanuska-Susitna Borough

Ann Arbor, MI MSA
Washtenaw County

Athens-Clarke County, GA MSA
Clarke, Madison, Oconee, and Oglethorpe Counties

Atlanta-Sandy Springs-Roswell, GA MSA
Barrow, Bartow, Butts, Carroll, Cherokee, Clayton, Cobb, Coweta, Dawson, DeKalb, Douglas, Fayette, Forsyth, Fulton, Gwinnett, Haralson, Heard, Henry, Jasper, Lamar, Meriwether, Morgan, Newton, Paulding, Pickens, Pike, Rockdale, Spalding, and Walton Counties
Previously Atlanta-Sandy Springs-Marietta, GA MSA
Barrow, Bartow, Butts, Carroll, Cherokee, Clayton, Cobb, Coweta, Dawson, DeKalb, Douglas, Fayette, Forsyth, Fulton, Gwinnett, Haralson, Heard, Henry, Jasper, Lamar, Meriwether, Newton, Paulding, Pickens, Pike, Rockdale, Spalding, and Walton Counties

Austin-Round Rock, TX MSA
Previously Austin-Round Rock-San Marcos, TX MSA
Bastrop, Caldwell, Hays, Travis, and Williamson Counties

Billings, MT MSA
Carbon and Yellowstone Counties

Boise City, ID MSA
Previously Boise City-Nampa, ID MSA
Ada, Boise, Canyon, Gem, and Owyhee Counties

Boston, MA

Boston-Cambridge-Newton, MA-NH MSA
Peviously Boston-Cambridge-Quincy, MA-NH MSA
Essex, Middlesex, Norfolk, Plymouth, and Suffolk Counties, MA; Rockingham and Strafford Counties, NH

Boston, MA MD
Previously Boston-Quincy, MA MD
Norfolk, Plymouth, and Suffolk Counties

Boston-Cambridge-Nashua, MA-NH NECTA
Includes 157 cities and towns in Massachusetts and 34 cities and towns in New Hampshire
Previously Boston-Cambridge-Quincy, MA-NH NECTA
Includes 155 cities and towns in Massachusetts and 38 cities and towns in New Hampshire

Boston-Cambridge-Newton, MA NECTA Division
Includes 92 cities and towns in Massachusetts
Previously Boston-Cambridge-Quincy, MA NECTA Division
Includes 97 cities and towns in Massachusetts

Boulder, CO MSA
Boulder County

Cape Coral-Fort Myers, FL MSA
Lee County

Cedar Rapids, IA, MSA
Benton, Jones, and Linn Counties

Charleston-North Charleston, SC MSA
Previously Charleston-North Charleston- Summerville, SC MSA
Berkeley, Charleston, and Dorchester Counties

Charlotte-Concord-Gastonia, NC-SC MSA
Cabarrus, Gaston, Iredell, Lincoln, Mecklenburg, Rowan, and Union Counties, NC; Chester, Lancaster, and York Counties, SC
Previously Charlotte-Gastonia-Rock Hill, NC-SC MSA
Anson, Cabarrus, Gaston, Mecklenburg, and Union Counties, NC; York County, SC

Chicago, IL

Chicago-Naperville-Elgin, IL-IN-WI MSA
Previously Chicago-Joliet-Naperville, IL-IN-WI MSA
Cook, DeKalb, DuPage, Grundy, Kane, Kendall, Lake, McHenry, and Will Counties, IL; Jasper, Lake, Newton, and Porter Counties, IN; Kenosha County, WI

Chicago-Naperville-Arlington Heights, IL MD
Cook, DuPage, Grundy, Kendall, McHenry, and Will Counties
Previously Chicago-Joliet-Naperville, IL MD
Cook, DeKalb, DuPage, Grundy, Kane, Kendall, McHenry, and Will Counties

Lake County-Kenosha County, IL-WI MD
Lake County, IL; Kenosha County, WI

Clarksville, TN-KY MSA
Mongomery and Stewart Counties, TN; Christian and Trigg Counties, KY

Colorado Springs, CO MSA
El Paso and Teller Counties

Columbia, MO MSA
Boone and Howard Counties

Columbus, OH MSA
Delaware, Fairfield, Franklin, Licking, Madison, Morrow, Pickaway, and Union Counties

Dallas, TX

Dallas-Fort Worth-Arlington, TX MSA
Collin, Dallas, Denton, Ellis, Hunt, Johnson, Kaufman, Parker, Rockwall, Tarrant, and Wise Counties

Dallas-Plano-Irving, TX MD
Collin, Dallas, Denton, Ellis, Hunt, Kaufman, and Rockwall Counties

Davenport-Moline-Rock Island, IA-IL MSA
Henry, Mercer, and Rock Island Counties, IA; Scott County, IL

Denver-Aurora-Lakewood, CO MSA
Previously Denver-Aurora-Broomfield, CO MSA
Adams, Arapahoe, Broomfield, Clear Creek, Denver, Douglas, Elbert, Gilpin, Jefferson, and Park Counties

Des Moines-West Des Moines, IA MSA
Dallas, Guthrie, Madison, Polk, and Warren Counties

Durham-Chapel Hill, NC MSA
Chatham, Durham, Orange, and and Person Counties

El Paso, TX MSA
El Paso County

Erie, PA MSA
Erie County

Eugene, OR MSA
Previously Eugene-Springfield, OR MSA
Lane County

Fargo, ND-MN MSA
Cass County, ND; Clay County, MN

Fayetteville, NC MSA
Cumberland, and Hoke Counties

Fort Collins, CO MSA
Previously Fort Collins-Loveland, CO MSA
Larimer County

Fort Wayne, IN MSA
Allen, Wells, and Whitley Counties

Fort Worth, TX

Dallas-Fort Worth-Arlington, TX MSA
Collin, Dallas, Denton, Ellis, Hunt, Johnson, Kaufman, Parker, Rockwall, Tarrant, and Wise Counties

Fort Worth-Arlington, TX MD
Hood, Johnson, Parker, Somervell, Tarrant, and Wise Counties

Gainesville, FL MSA
Alachua, and Gilchrist Counties

Grand Rapids-Wyoming, MI MSA
Barry, Kent, Montcalm, and Ottawa Counties

Green Bay, WI MSA
Brown, Kewaunee, and Oconto Counties

Greensboro-High Point, NC MSA
Guilford, Randolph, and Rockingham Counties

Honolulu, HI MSA
Honolulu County

Houston-The Woodlands-Sugar Land-Baytown, TX MSA
Austin, Brazoria, Chambers, Fort Bend, Galveston, Harris, Liberty, Montgomery, and Waller Counties
Previously Houston-Sugar Land-Baytown, TX MSA
Austin, Brazoria, Chambers, Fort Bend, Galveston, Harris, Liberty, Montgomery, San Jacinto, and Waller Counties

Huntsville, AL MSA
Limestone and Madison Counties

Indianapolis-Carmel, IN MSA
Boone, Brown, Hamilton, Hancock, Hendricks, Johnson, Marion, Morgan, Putnam, and Shelby Counties

Jacksonville, FL MSA
Baker, Clay, Duval, Nassau, and St. Johns Counties

Kansas City, MO-KS MSA
Franklin, Johnson, Leavenworth, Linn, Miami, and Wyandotte Counties, KS; Bates, Caldwell, Cass, Clay, Clinton, Jackson, Lafayette, Platte, and Ray Counties, MO

Lafayette, LA MSA
Acadia, Iberia, Lafayette, St. Martin, and Vermilion Parishes

Las Vegas-Henderson-Paradise, NV MSA
Previously Las Vegas-Paradise, NV MSA
Clark County

Lexington-Fayette, KY MSA
Bourbon, Clark, Fayette, Jessamine, Scott, and Woodford Counties

Lincoln, NE MSA
Lancaster and Seward Counties

Little Rock-North Little Rock-Conway, AR MSA
Faulkner, Grant, Lonoke, Perry, Pulaski and Saline Counties, AR

Los Angeles, CA

Los Angeles-Long Beach-Anaheim, CA MSA
Previously Los Angeles-Long Beach-Santa Ana, CA MSA
Los Angeles and Orange Counties

Los Angeles-Long Beach-Glendale, CA MD
Los Angeles County

Anaheim-Santa Ana-Irvine, CA MD
Previously Santa Ana-Anaheim-Irvine, CA MD
Orange County

Louisville/Jefferson, KY-IN MSA
Clark, Floyd, Harrison, Scott, and Washington Counties, IN; Bullitt, Henry, Jefferson, Oldham, Shelby, Spencer, and Trimble Counties, KY

Lubbock, TX MSA
Crosby, Lubbock, and Lynn Counties

Madison, WI MSA
Columbia, Dane, and Iowa Counties

Manchester, NH

Manchester-Nashua, NH MSA
Hillsborough County

Manchester, NH NECTA
Includes 11 cities and towns in New Hampshire
Previously Manchester, NH NECTA
Includes 9 cities and towns in New Hampshire

McAllen-Edinburg-Mission, TX
Hidalgo County

Miami, FL

Miami-Fort Lauderdale-West Palm Beach, FL MSA
Previously Miami-Fort Lauderdale-Pompano Beach, FL MSA
Broward, Miami-Dade, and Palm Beach Counties

Miami-Miami Beach-Kendall, FL MD
Miami-Dade County

Midland, TX MSA
Martin, and Midland Counties

Minneapolis-St. Paul-Bloomington, MN-WI MSA
Anoka, Carver, Chisago, Dakota, Hennepin, Isanti, Le Sueur, Mille Lacs, Ramsey, Scott, Sherburne, Sibley, Washington, and Wright Counties, MN; Pierce and St. Croix Counties, WI

Nashville-Davidson-Murfreesboro-Franklin, TN MSA
Cannon, Cheatham, Davidson, Dickson, Hickman, Macon, Robertson, Rutherford, Smith, Sumner, Trousdale, Williamson, and Wilson Counties

New Orleans-Metarie-Kenner, LA MSA
Jefferson, Orleans, Plaquemines, St. Bernard, St. Charles, St. James, St. John the Baptist, and St. Tammany Parish
Previously New Orleans-Metarie-Kenner, LA MSA
Jefferson, Orleans, Plaquemines, St. Bernard, St. Charles, St. John the Baptist, and St. Tammany Parish

New York, NY

New York-Newark-Jersey City, NY-NJ-PA MSA
Bergen, Essex, Hudson, Hunterdon, Middlesex, Monmouth, Morris, Ocean, Passaic, Somerset, Sussex, and Union Counties, NJ; Bronx, Dutchess, Kings, Nassau, New York, Orange, Putnam, Queens, Richmond, Rockland, Suffolk, and Westchester Counties, NY; Pike County, PA
Previously New York-Northern New Jersey-Long Island, NY-NJ-PA MSA
Bergen, Essex, Hudson, Hunterdon, Middlesex, Monmouth, Morris, Ocean, Passaic, Somerset, Sussex, and Union Counties, NJ; Bronx, Kings, Nassau, New York, Putnam, Queens, Richmond, Rockland, Suffolk, and Westchester Counties, NY; Pike County, PA

New York-Jersey City-White Plains, NY-NJ MD
Bergen, Hudson, Middlesex, Monmouth, Ocean, and Passaic Counties, NJ; Bronx, Kings, New York, Putnam, Queens, Richmond, Rockland, and Westchester Counties, NY
Previously New York-Wayne-White Plains, NY-NJ MD
Bergen, Hudson, and Passaic Counties, NJ; Bronx, Kings, New York, Putnam, Queens, Richmond, Rockland, and Westchester Counties, NY

Nassau-Suffolk, NY MD
Nassau and Suffolk Counties

Oklahoma City, OK MSA
Canadian, Cleveland, Grady, Lincoln, Logan, McClain, and Oklahoma Counties

Omaha-Council Bluffs, NE-IA MSA
Harrison, Mills, and Pottawattamie Counties, IA; Cass, Douglas, Sarpy, Saunders, and Washington Counties, NE

Orlando-Kissimmee-Sanford, FL MSA
Lake, Orange, Osceola, and Seminole Counties

Oxnard-Thousand Oaks-Ventura, CA MSA
Ventura County

Palm Bay-Melbourne-Titusville, FL MSA
Brevard County

Peoria, IL MSA
Marshall, Peoria, Stark, Tazewell, and Woodford Counties

Philadelphia, PA

Philadelphia-Camden-Wilmington, PA-NJ-DE-MD MSA
New Castle County, DE; Cecil County, MD; Burlington, Camden, Gloucester, and Salem Counties, NJ; Bucks, Chester, Delaware, Montgomery, and Philadelphia Counties, PA

Philadelphia, PA MD
Delaware and Philadelphia Counties
Previously Philadelphia, PA MD
Bucks, Chester, Delaware, Montgomery, and Philadelphia Counties

Phoenix-Mesa-Scottsdale, AZ MSA
Previously Phoenix-Mesa-Glendale, AZ MSA
Maricopa and Pinal Counties

Pittsburgh, PA MSA
Allegheny, Armstrong, Beaver, Butler, Fayette, Washington, and Westmoreland Counties

Portland-Vancouver-Hillsboro, OR-WA MSA
Clackamas, Columbia, Multnomah, Washington, and Yamhill Counties, OR; Clark and Skamania Counties, WA

Providence, RI

Providence-New Bedford-Fall River, RI-MA MSA
Previously Providence-New Bedford-Fall River, RI-MA MSA
Bristol County, MA; Bristol, Kent, Newport, Providence, and Washington Counties, RI

Providence-Warwick, RI-MA NECTA
Includes 12 cities and towns in Massachusetts and 36 cities and towns in Rhode Island
Previously Providence-Fall River-Warwick, RI-MA NECTA
Includes 12 cities and towns in Massachusetts and 37 cities and towns in Rhode Island

Provo-Orem, UT MSA
Juab and Utah Counties

Raleigh, NC MSA
Previously Raleigh-Cary, NC MSA
Franklin, Johnston, and Wake Counties

Reno, NV MSA
Previously Reno-Sparks, NV MSA
Storey and Washoe Counties

Richmond, VA MSA
Amelia, Caroline, Charles City, Chesterfield, Dinwiddie, Goochland, Hanover, Henrico, King William, New Kent, Powhatan, Prince George, and Sussex Counties; Colonial Heights, Hopewell, Petersburg, and Richmond Cities

Roanoke, VA MSA
Roanoke and Salem cities; Botetourt, Craig, Franklin, and Roanoke Counties

Rochester, MN MSA
Dodge, Fillmore, Olmsted, and Wabasha Counties

Sacramento—Roseville—Arden-Arcade, CA MSA
El Dorado, Placer, Sacramento, and Yolo Counties

Salem, OR MSA
Marion and Polk Counties

Salt Lake City, UT MSA
Salt Lake and Tooele Counties

San Antonio-New Braunfels, TX MSA
Atascosa, Bandera, Bexar, Comal, Guadalupe, Kendall, Medina, and Wilson Counties

San Diego-Carlsbad, CA MSA
Previously San Diego-Carlsbad-San Marcos, CA MSA
San Diego County

San Francisco, CA

San Francisco-Oakland-Hayward, CA MSA
Previously San Francisco-Oakland- Fremont, CA MSA
Alameda, Contra Costa, Marin, San Francisco, and San Mateo
Counties

San Francisco-Redwood City-South San Francisco, CA MD
San Francisco and San Mateo Counties

Previously San Francisco-San Mateo-Redwood City, CA MD
Marin, San Francisco, and San Mateo Counties

San Jose-Sunnyvale-Santa Clara, CA MSA
San Benito and Santa Clara Counties

Santa Rosa, CA MSA
Previously Santa Rosa-Petaluma, CA MSA
Sonoma County

Savannah, GA MSA
Bryan, Chatham, and Effingham Counties

Seattle, WA

Seattle-Tacoma-Bellevue, WA MSA
King, Pierce, and Snohomish Counties

Seattle-Bellevue-Everett, WA MD
King and Snohomish Counties

Sioux Falls, SD MSA
Lincoln, McCook, Minnehaha, and Turner Counties

Spokane-Spokane Valley, WA MSA
Pend Oreille, Spokane, and Stevens Counties
Previously Spokane, WA MSA
Spokane County

Springfield, IL MSA
Menard and Sangamon Counties

Tallahassee, FL MSA
Gadsden, Jefferson, Leon, and Wakulla Counties

Tampa-St. Petersburg-Clearwater, FL MSA
Hernando, Hillsborough, Pasco, and Pinellas Counties

Topeka, KS MSA
Jackson, Jefferson, Osage, Shawnee, and Wabaunsee Counties

Tulsa, OK MSA
Creek, Okmulgee, Osage, Pawnee, Rogers, Tulsa, and Wagoner
Counties

Tyler, TX MSA
Smith County

Virginia Beach-Norfolk-Newport News, VA-NC MSA
Currituck County, NC; Chesapeake, Hampton, Newport News,
Norfolk, Poquoson, Portsmouth, Suffolk, Virginia Beach and
Williamsburg cities, VA; Gloucester, Isle of Wight, James City,
Mathews, Surry, and York Counties, VA

Washington, DC

Washington-Arlington-Alexandria, DC-VA-MD-WV MSA
District of Columbia; Calvert, Charles, Frederick, Montgomery, and
Prince George's Counties, MD; Alexandria, Fairfax, Falls Church,
Fredericksburg, Manassas Park, and Manassas cities, VA; Arlington,
Clarke, Culpepper, Fairfax, Fauquier, Loudoun, Prince William,
Rappahannock, Spotsylvania, Stafford, and Warren Counties, VA;
Jefferson County, WV
Previously Washington-Arlington-Alexandria, DC-VA-MD-WV MSA
District of Columbia; Calvert, Charles, Frederick, Montgomery, and
Prince George's Counties, MD; Alexandria, Fairfax, Falls Church,
Fredericksburg, Manassas Park, and Manassas cities, VA; Arlington,
Clarke, Fairfax, Fauquier, Loudoun, Prince William, Spotsylvania,
Stafford, and Warren Counties, VA; Jefferson County, WV

Washington-Arlington-Alexandria, DC-VA-MD-WV MD
District of Columbia; Calvert, Charles, and Prince George's Counties,
MD; Alexandria, Fairfax, Falls Church, Fredericksburg, Manassas
Park, and Manassas cities, VA; Arlington, Clarke, Culpepper, Fairfax,
Fauquier, Loudoun, Prince William, Rappahannock, Spotsylvania,
Stafford, and Warren Counties, VA; Jefferson County, WV
Previously Washington-Arlington-Alexandria, DC-VA-MD-WV MD
District of Columbia; Calvert, Charles, and Prince George's Counties,
MD; Alexandria, Fairfax, Falls Church, Fredericksburg, Manassas
Park, and Manassas cities, VA; Arlington, Clarke, Fairfax, Fauquier,
Loudoun, Prince William, Spotsylvania, Stafford, and Warren
Counties, VA; Jefferson County, WV

Wichita, KS MSA
Butler, Harvey, Kingman, Sedgwick, and Sumner Counties

Wilmington, NC MSA
New Hanover and Pender Counties

Winston-Salem, NC MSA
Davidson, Davie, Forsyth, Stokes, and Yadkin Counties

Worcester, MA

Worcester, MA-CT MSA
Windham County, CT; Worcester County, MA
Previously Worcester, MA MSA
Worcester County

Worcester, MA-CT NECTA
Includes 40 cities and towns in Massachusetts and 8 cities and towns
in Connecticut
Previously Worcester, MA-CT NECTA
Includes 37 cities and towns in Massachusetts and 3 cities and towns
in Connecticut

Appendix C: Government Type and Primary County

This appendix includes the government structure of each place included in this book. It also includes the county or county equivalent in which each place is located. If a place spans more that one county, the county in which the majority of the population resides is shown.

Albuquerque, NM
Government Type: City
County: Bernalillo

Anchorage, AK
Government Type: Municipality
Borough: Anchorage

Ann Arbor, MI
Government Type: City
County: Washtenaw

Athens, GA
Government Type: Consolidated
   city-county
County: Clarke

Atlanta, GA
Government Type: City
County: Fulton

Austin, TX
Government Type: City
County: Travis

Billings, MT
Government Type: City
County: Yellowstone

Boise City, ID
Government Type: City
County: Ada

Boston, MA
Government Type: City
County: Suffolk

Boulder, CO
Government Type: City
County: Boulder

Cape Coral, FL
Government Type: City
County: Lee

Cedar Rapids, IA
Government Type: City
County: Linn

Charleston, SC
Government Type: City
County: Charleston

Charlotte, NC
Government Type: City
County: Mecklenburg

Chicago, IL
Government Type: City
County: Cook

Clarksville, TN
Government Type: City
County: Montgomery

Colorado Springs, CO
Government Type: City
County: El Paso

Columbia, MO
Government Type: City
County: Boone

Columbus, OH
Government Type: City
County: Franklin

Dallas, TX
Government Type: City
County: Dallas

Davenport, IA
Government Type: City
County: Scott

Denver, CO
Government Type: City
County: Denver

Des Moines, IA
Government Type: City
County: Polk

Durham, NC
Government Type: City
County: Durham

El Paso, TX
Government Type: City
County: El Paso

Erie, PA
Government Type: City
County: Erie

Eugene, OR
Government Type: City
County: Lane

Fargo, ND
Government Type: City
County: Cass

Fayetteville, NC
Government Type: City
County: Cumberland

Fort Collins, CO
Government Type: City
County: Larimer

Fort Wayne, IN
Government Type: City
County: Allen

Fort Worth, TX
Government Type: City
County: Tarrant

Gainesville, FL
Government Type: City
County: Alachua

Grand Rapids, MI
Government Type: City
County: Kent

Green Bay, WI
Government Type: City
County: Brown

Greensboro, NC
Government Type: City
County: Guilford

Honolulu, HI
Government Type: Census Designated Place
   (CDP)
County: Honolulu

Houston, TX
Government Type: City
County: Harris

Huntsville, AL
Government Type: City
County: Madison

Indianapolis, IN
Government Type: City
County: Marion

Jacksonville, FL
Government Type: City
County: Duval

Kansas City, MO
Government Type: City
County: Jackson

Lafayette, LA
Government Type: City
Parish: Lafayette

Las Vegas, NV
Government Type: City
County: Clark

Lexington, KY
Government Type: Consolidated city-county
County: Fayette

Lincoln, NE
Government Type: City
County: Lancaster

Little Rock, AR
Government Type: City
County: Pulaski

Los Angeles, CA
Government Type: City
County: Los Angeles

Louisville, KY
Government Type: Consolidated city-county
County: Jefferson

Lubbock, TX
Government Type: City
County: Lubbock

Madison, WI
Government Type: City
County: Dane

Manchester, NH
Government Type: City
County: Hillsborough

McAllen, TX
Government Type: City
County: Hidalgo

Miami, FL
Government Type: City
County: Miami-Dade

Midland, TX
Government Type: City
County: Midland

Minneapolis, MN
Government Type: City
County: Hennepin

Nashville, TN
Government Type: Consolidated city-county
County: Davidson

New Orleans, LA
Government Type: City
Parish: Orleans

New York, NY
Government Type: City
Counties: Bronx; Kings; New York; Queens;
    Staten Island

Oklahoma City, OK
Government Type: City
County: Oklahoma

Omaha, NE
Government Type: City
County: Douglas

Orlando, FL
Government Type: City
County: Orange

Oxnard, CA
Government Type: City
County: Ventura

Palm Bay, FL
Government Type: City
County: Brevard

Peoria, IL
Government Type: City
County: Peoria

Philadelphia, PA
Government Type: City
County: Philadelphia

Phoenix, AZ
Government Type: City
County: Maricopa

Pittsburgh, PA
Government Type: City
County: Allegheny

Portland, OR
Government Type: City
County: Multnomah

Providence, RI
Government Type: City
County: Providence

Provo, UT
Government Type: City
County: Utah

Raleigh, NC
Government Type: City
County: Wake

Reno, NV
Government Type: City
County: Washoe

Richmond, VA
Government Type: Independent city
County: Richmond city

Roanoke, VA
Government Type: Independent city
County: Roanoke city

Rochester, MN
Government Type: City
County: Olmsted

Sacramento, CA
Government Type: City
County: Sacramento

Salem, OR
Government Type: City
County: Marion

Salt Lake City, UT
Government Type: City
County: Salt Lake

San Antonio, TX
Government Type: City
County: Bexar

San Diego, CA
Government Type: City
County: San Diego

San Francisco, CA
Government Type: City
County: San Francisco

San Jose, CA
Government Type: City
County: Santa Clara

Santa Rosa, CA
Government Type: City
County: Sonoma

Savannah, GA
Government Type: City
County: Chatham

Seattle, WA
Government Type: City
County: King

Sioux Falls, SD
Government Type: City
County: Minnehaha

Spokane, WA
Government Type: City
County: Spokane

Springfield, IL
Government Type: City
County: Sangamon

Tallahassee, FL
Government Type: City
County: Leon

Tampa, FL
Government Type: City
County: Hillsborough

Topeka, KS
Government Type: City
County: Shawnee

Tulsa, OK
Government Type: City
County: Tulsa

Tyler, TX
Government Type: City
County: Smith

Virginia Beach, VA
Government Type: Independent city
County: Virginia Beach city

Washington, DC
Government Type: City
County: District of Columbia

Wichita, KS
Government Type: City
County: Sedgwick

Wilmington, NC
Government Type: City
County: New Hanover

Winston-Salem, NC
Government Type: City
County: Forsyth

Worcester, MA
Government Type: City
County: Worcester

Appendix D: Chambers of Commerce

Albuquerque, NM
Albuquerque Chamber of Commerce
P.O. Box 25100
Albuquerque, NM 87125
Phone: (505) 764-3700
Fax: (505) 764-3714
www.abqchamber.com

Albuquerque Economic Development Dept
851 University Blvd SE
Suite 203
Albuquerque, NM 87106
Phone: (505) 246-6200
Fax: (505) 246-6219
www.cabq.gov/econdev

Anchorage, AK
Anchorage Chamber of Commerce
1016 W Sixth Avenue
Suite 303
Anchorage, AK 99501
Phone: (907) 272-2401
Fax: (907) 272-4117
www.anchoragechamber.org

Anchorage Economic Development
Department
900 W 5th Avenue
Suite 300
Anchorage, AK 99501
Phone: (907) 258-3700
Fax: (907) 258-6646
www.aedcweb.com/aedcdig

Ann Arbor, MI
Ann Arbor Area Chamber of Commerce
115 West Huron
3rd Floor
Ann Arbor, MI 48104
Phone: (734) 665-4433
Fax: (734) 665-4191
www.annarborchamber.org

Ann Arbor Economic Development
Department
201 S Division
Suite 430
Ann Arbor, MI 48104
Phone: (734) 761-9317
www.annarborspark.org

Athens, GA
Athens Area Chamber of Commerce
246 W Hancock Avenue
Athens, GA 30601
Phone: (706) 549-6800
Fax: (706) 549-5636
www.aacoc.org

Athens-Clarke Economic Development
150 E. Hancock Avenue
P.O. Box 1692
Athens, GA 30603
Phone: (706) 613-3810
Fax: (706) 613-3812
www.athensbusiness.org/contact.aspx

Atlanta, GA
Metro Atlanta Chamber of Commerce
235 Andrew Young International Blvd NW
Atlanta, GA 30303
Phone: (404) 880-9000
Fax: (404) 586-8464
www.metroatlantachamber.com/contact_us.html

Austin, TX
Greater Austin Chamber of Commerce
210 Barton Springs Road
Suite 400
Austin, TX 78704
Phone: (512) 478-9383
Fax: (512) 478-6389
www.austin-chamber.org

Billings, MT
Billings Area Chamber of Commerce
815 S 27th St
Billings, MT 59101
Phone: (406) 245-4111
Fax: (406) 2457333
www.billingschamber.com

Boise City, ID
Boise Metro Chamber of Commerce
250 S 5th Street
Suite 800
Boise City, ID 83701
Phone: (208) 472-5200
Fax: (208) 472-5201
www.boisechamber.org

Boston, MA
Greater Boston Chamber of Commerce
265 Franklin Street
12th Floor
Boston, MA 02110
Phone: (617) 227-4500
Fax: (617) 227-7505
www.bostonchamber.com

Boulder, CO
Boulder Chamber of Commerce
2440 Pearl Street
Boulder, CO 80302
Phone: (303) 442-1044
Fax: (303) 938-8837
www.boulderchamber.com

City of Boulder Economic Vitality Program
P.O. Box 791
Boulder, CO 80306
Phone: (303) 441-3090
www.bouldercolorado.gov

Cape Coral, FL
Chamber of Commerce of Cape Coral
2051 Cape Coral Parkway East
Cape Coral, FL 33904
Phone: (239) 549-6900
Fax: (239) 549-9609
www.capecoralchamber.com

Cedar Rapids, IA
Cedar Rapids Chamber of Commerce
424 First Avenue NE
Cedar Rapids, IA 52401
Phone: (319) 398-5317
Fax: (319) 398-5228
www.cedarrapids.org

Cedar Rapids Economic Development
50 Second Avenue Bridge
Sixth Floor
Cedar Rapids, IA 52401-1256
Phone: (319) 286-5041
Fax: (319) 286-5141
www.cedar-rapids.org

Charleston, SC
Charleston Metro Chamber of Commerce
P.O. Box 975
Charleston, SC 29402
Phone: (843) 577-2510
www.charlestonchamber.net

Charlotte, NC
Charlotte Chamber of Commerce
330 S Tryon Street
P.O. Box 32785
Charlotte, NC 28232
Phone: (704) 378-1300
Fax: (704) 374-1903
www.charlottechamber.com

Charlotte Regional Partnership
1001 Morehead Square Drive
Suite 200
Charlotte, NC 28203
Phone: (704) 347-8942
Fax: (704) 347-8981
www.charlotteusa.com

Chicago, IL
Chicagoland Chamber of Commerce
200 E Randolph Street
Suite 2200
Chicago, IL 60601-6436
Phone: (312) 494-6700
Fax: (312) 861-0660
www.chicagolandchamber.org

City of Chicago Department of Planning
and Development
City Hall, Room 1000
121 North La Salle Street
Chicago, IL 60602
Phone: (312) 744-4190
Fax: (312) 744-2271
www.egov.cityofchicago.org

Clarksville, TN
Clarksville Area Chamber of Commerce
25 Jefferson Street
Suite 300
Clarksville, TN 37040
Phone: (931) 647-2331
www.clarksvillechamber.com

Colorado Springs, CO
Greater Colorado Springs Chamber of
Commerce
6 S. Tejon Street
Suite 700
Colorado Springs, CO 80903
Phone: (719) 635-1551
Fax: (719) 635-1571
www.gcsco.wliinc3.com

Greater Colorado Springs Economic
Development Corp
90 South Cascade Avenue
Suite 1050
Colorado Springs, CO 80903
Phone: (719) 471-8183
Fax: (719) 471-9733
www.coloradosprings.org

Columbia, MO
Columbia Chamber of Commerce
300 South Providence Rd.
PO Box 1016
Columbia, MO 65205-1016
Phone: (573) 874-1132
Fax: (573) 443-3986
www.columbiamochamber.com

Columbus, OH
Greater Columbus Chamber
37 North High Street
Columbus, OH 43215
Phone: (614) 221-1321
Fax: (614) 221-1408
www.columbus.org

Dallas, TX
City of Dallas Economic Development
Department
1500 Marilla Street
5C South
Dallas, TX 75201
Phone: (214) 670-1685
Fax: (214) 670-0158
www.dallas-edd.org

Greater Dallas Chamber of Commerce
700 North Pearl Street
Suite1200
Dallas, TX 75201
Phone: (214) 746-6600
Fax: (214) 746-6799
www.dallaschamber.org

Davenport, IA
Quad Cities Chamber
331 W. 3rd St.,
Davenport, IA 52801
Phone: (563) 322-1706
www.quadcitieschamber.com

Denver, CO
Denver Metro Chamber of Commerce
1445 Market Street
Denver, CO 80202
Phone: (303) 534-8500
Fax: (303) 534-3200
www.denverchamber.org

Downtown Denver Partnership
511 16th Street
Suite 200
Denver, CO 80202
Phone: (303) 534-6161
Fax: (303) 534-2803
www.downtowndenver.com

Des Moines, IA
Des Moines Downtown Chamber
301 Grand Ave
Des Moines, IA 50309
Phone: (515) 309-3229
www.desmoinesdowtownchamber.com

Greater Des Moines Partnership
700 Locust Street
Suite 100
Des Moines, IA 50309
Phone: (515) 286-4950
Fax: (515) 286-4974
www.desmoinesmetro.com

Durham, NC
Durham Chamber of Commerce
PO Box 3829
Durham, NC 27702
Phone: (919) 682-2133
Fax: (919) 688-8351
www.durhamchamber.org

North Carolina Institute of Minority
Economic Development
114 W Parish Street
Durham, NC 27701
Phone: (919) 956-8889
Fax: (919) 688-7668
www.ncimed.com

El Paso, TX
City of El Paso Department of Economic
Development
2 Civic Center Plaza
El Paso, TX 79901
Phone: (915) 541-4000
Fax: (915) 541-1316
www.elpasotexas.gov

Greater El Paso Chamber of Commerce
10 Civic Center Plaza
El Paso, TX 79901
Phone: (915) 534-0500
Fax: (915) 534-0510
www.elpaso.org

Erie, PA
Erie Regional Chamber and Growth
Partnership
208 E. Bayfront Parkway
Suite 100
Erie, PA 16507
Phone: (814) 454-7191
www.eriepa.com

Eugene, OR
Eugene Area Chamber of Commerce
1401 Williamette Street
Eugene, OR 97401
Phone: (541) 484-1314
Fax: (541) 484-4942
www.eugenechamber.com

Fargo, ND
Chamber of Commerce of Fargo Moorhead
202 First Avenue North
Fargo, ND 56560
Phone: (218) 233-1100
Fax: (218) 233-1200
www.fmchamber.com

Greater Fargo-Moorhead Economic
Development Corporation
51 Broadway, Suite 500
Fargo, ND 58102
Phone: (701) 364-1900
Fax: (701) 293-7819
www.gfmedc.com

Fayetteville, NC
Fayetteville Regional Chamber
1019 Hay Street
Fayetteville, NC 28305
Phone: (910) 483-8133
Fax: (910) 483-0263
www.fayettevillencchamber.org

Fort Collins, CO
Fort Collins Chamber of Commerce
225 South Meldrum
Fort Collins, CO 80521
Phone: (970) 482-3746
Fax: (970) 482-3774
www.fcchamber.org

Fort Wayne, IN
City of Fort Wayne Economic Development
1 Main St
1 Main Street
Fort Wayne, IN 46802
Phone: (260) 427-1111
Fax: (260) 427-1375
www.cityoffortwayne.org

Greater Fort Wayne Chamber of Commerce
826 Ewing Street
Fort Wayne, IN 46802
Phone: (260) 424-1435
Fax: (260) 426-7232
www.fwchamber.org

Fort Worth, TX
City of Fort Worth Economic Development
City Hall
900 Monroe Street, Suite 301
Fort Worth, TX 76102
Phone: (817) 392-6103
Fax: (817) 392-2431
www.fortworthgov.org

Fort Worth Chamber of Commerce
777 Taylor Street
Suite 900
Fort Worth, TX 76102-4997
Phone: (817) 336-2491
Fax: (817) 877-4034
www.fortworthchamber.com

Gainesville, FL
Gainesville Area Chamber of Commerce
300 East University Avenue
Suite 100
Gainesville, FL 32601
Phone: (352) 334-7100
Fax: (352) 334-7141
www.gainesvillechamber.com

Grand Rapids, MI
Grands Rapids Area Chamber of Commerce
111 Pearl Street N.W.
Grand Rapids, MI 49503
Phone: (616) 771-0300
Fax: (616) 771-0318
www.grandrapids.org

Green Bay, WI
Economic Development
100 N Jefferson St
Room 202
Green Bay, WI 54301
Phone: (920) 448-3397
Fax: (920) 448-3063
www.ci.green-bay.wi.us

Green Bay Area Chamber of Commerce
300 N. Broadway
Suite 3A
Green Bay, WI 54305-1660
Phone: (920) 437-8704
Fax: (920) 593-3468
www.titletown.org

Greensboro, NC
Greensboro Area Chamber of Commerce
342 N Elm St.
Greensboro, NC 27401
Phone: (336) 387-8301
Fax: (336) 275-9299
www.greensboro.org

Honolulu, HI
The Chamber of Commerce of Hawaii
1132 Bishop Street
Suite 402
Honolulu, HI 96813
Phone: (808) 545-4300
Fax: (808) 545-4369
www.cochawaii.com

Houston, TX
Greater Houston Partnership
1200 Smith Street
Suite 700
Houston, TX 77002-4400
Phone: (713) 844-3600
Fax: (713) 844-0200
www.houston.org

Huntsville, AL
Chamber of Commerce of
Huntsville/Madison County
225 Church Street
Huntsville, AL 35801
Phone: (256) 535-2000
Fax: (256) 535-2015
www.huntsvillealabamausa.com

Indianapolis, IN
Greater Indianapolis Chamber of Commerce
111 Monument Circle
Suite 1950
Indianapolis, IN 46204
Phone: (317) 464-2222
Fax: (317) 464-2217
www.indychamber.com

The Indy Partnership
111 Monument Circle
Suite 1800
Indianapolis, IN 46204
Phone: (317) 236-6262
Fax: (317) 236-6275
www.indypartnership.com

Jacksonville, FL
Jacksonville Chamber of Commerce
3 Independent Drive
Jacksonville, FL 32202
Phone: (904) 366-6600
Fax: (904) 632-0617
www.myjaxchamber.com

Kansas City, MO
Greater Kansas City Chamber of Commerce
2600 Commerce Tower
911 Main Street
Kansas City, MO 64105
Phone: (816) 221-2424
Fax: (816) 221-7440
www.kcchamber.com

Kansas City Area Development Council
2600 Commerce Tower
911 Main Street
Kansas City, MO 64105
Phone: (816) 221-2121
Fax: (816) 842-2865
www.thinkkc.com

Lafayette, LA
Greater Lafayette Chamber of Commerce
804 East Saint Mary Blvd.
Lafayette, LA 70503
Phone: (337) 233-2705
Fax: (337) 234-8671
www.lafchamber.org

Las Vegas, NV
Las Vegas Chamber of Commerce
6671 Las Vegas Blvd South
Suite 300
Las Vegas, NV 89119
Phone: (702) 735-1616
Fax: (702) 735-0406
www.lvchamber.org

Las Vegas Office of Business Development
400 Stewart Avenue
City Hall
Las Vegas, NV 89101
Phone: (702) 229-6011
Fax: (702) 385-3128
www.lasvegasnevada.gov

Lexington, KY
Greater Lexington Chamber of Commerce
330 East Main Street
Suite 100
Lexington, KY 40507
Phone: (859) 254-4447
Fax: (859) 233-3304
www.commercelexington.com

Lexington Downtown Development
Authority
101 East Vine Street
Suite 500
Lexington, KY 40507
Phone: (859) 425-2296
Fax: (859) 425-2292
www.lexingtondda.com

Lincoln, NE
Lincoln Chamber of Commerce
1135 M Street
Suite 200
Lincoln, NE 68508
Phone: (402) 436-2350
Fax: (402) 436-2360
www.lcoc.com

Little Rock, AR
Little Rock Regional Chamber of
Commerce
One Chamber Plaza
Little Rock, AR 72201-1618
Phone: (501) 374-2001
www.littlerockchamber.com

Los Angeles, CA
Los Angeles Area Chamber of Commerce
350 South Bixel Street
Los Angeles, CA 90017
Phone: (213) 580-7500
Fax: (213) 580-7511
www.lachamber.org

Los Angeles County Economic
Development Corporation
444 South Flower Street
34th Floor
Los Angeles, CA 90071
Phone: (213) 622-4300
Fax: (213) 622-7100
www.laedc.org

Louisville, KY
The Greater Louisville Chamber of
Commerce
614 West Main Street
Suite 6000
Louisville, KY 40202
Phone: (502) 625-0000
Fax: (502) 625-0010
www.greaterlouisville.com

Lubbock, TX
Lubbock Chamber of Commerce
1500 Broadway
Suite 101
Lubbock, TX 79401
Phone: (806) 761-7000
Fax: (806) 761-7013
www.lubbockchamber.com

Madison, WI
Greater Madison Chamber of Commerce
615 East Washington Avenue
P.O. Box 71
Madison, WI 53701-0071
Phone: (608) 256-8348
Fax: (608) 256-0333
www.greatermadisonchamber.com

Manchester, NH
Greater Manchester Chamber of Commerce
889 Elm Street
Manchester, NH 03101
Phone: (603) 666-6600
Fax: (603) 626-0910
www.manchester-chamber.org

Manchester Economic Development Office
One City Hall Plaza
Manchester, NH 03101
Phone: (603) 624-6505
Fax: (603) 624-6308
www.yourmanchesternh.com

Miami, FL
Greater Miami Chamber of Commerce
1601 Biscayne Boulevard
Ballroom Level
Miami, FL 33132-1260
Phone: (305) 350-7700
Fax: (305) 374-6902
www.greatermiami.com

The Beacon Council
80 Southwest 8th Street
Suite 2400
Miami, FL 33130
Phone: (305) 579-1300
Fax: (305) 375-0271
www.beaconcouncil.com

Midland, TX
Midland Chamber of Commerce
109 N. Main
Midland, TX 79701
Phone: (432) 683-3381
Fax: (432) 686-3556
www.midlandtxchamber.com

Minneapolis, MN
Minneapolis Community Development
Agency
Crown Roller Mill
105 5th Avenue South, Suite 200
Minneapolis, MN 55401
Phone: (612) 673-5095
Fax: (612) 673-5100
www.ci.minneapolis.mn.us

Minneapolis Regional Chamber
81 South Ninth Street
Suite 200
Minneapolis, MN 55402
Phone: (612) 370-9100
Fax: (612) 370-9195
www.minneapolischamber.org

Nashville, TN
Nashville Area Chamber of Commerce
211 Commerce Street
Suite 100
Nashville, TN 37201
Phone: (615) 743-3000
Fax: (615) 256-3074
www.nashvillechamber.cm

Tennessee Valley Authority Economic
Development Corp.
P.O. Box 292409
Nashville, TN 37229-2409
Phone: (615) 232-6225
www.tvaed.com

New Orleans, LA
New Orleans Chamber of Commerce
1515 Poydras St
Suite 1010
New Orleans, LA 70112
Phone: (504) 799-4260
Fax: (504) 799-4259
www.neworleanschamber.org

New York, NY
New York City Economic Development
Corporation
110 William Street
New York, NY 10038
Phone: (212) 619-5000
www.nycedc.com

The Partnership for New York City
One Battery Park Plaza
5th Floor
New York, NY 10004
Phone: (212) 493-7400
Fax: (212) 344-3344
www.pfnyc.org

Oklahoma City, OK
Greater Oklahoma City Chamber of
Commerce
123 Park Avenue
Oklahoma City, OK 73102
Phone: (405) 297-8900
Fax: (405) 297-8916
www.okcchamber.com

Omaha, NE
Omaha Chamber of Commerce
1301 Harney Street
Omaha, NE 68102
Phone: (402) 346-5000
Fax: (402) 346-7050
www.omahachamber.org

Orlando, FL
Metro Orlando Economic Development
Commission of Mid-Florida
301 East Pine Street
Suite 900
Orlando, FL 32801
Phone: (407) 422-7159
Fax: (407) 425.6428
www.orlandoedc.com

Orlando Regional Chamber of Commerce
75 South Ivanhoe Boulevard
PO Box 1234
Orlando, FL 32802
Phone: (407) 425-1234
Fax: (407) 839-5020
www.orlando.org

Oxnard, CA
Oxnard Chamber of Commerce
400 E Esplanade Drive
Suite 302
Oxnard, CA 93036
Phone: (805) 983-6118
Fax: (805) 604-7331
www.oxnardchamber.org

Palm Bay, FL
Greater Palm Bay Chamber of Commerce
4100 Dixie Highway NE
Palm Bay, FL 32905
Phone: (321) 951-9998
www.greaterpalmbaychamber.com

Peoria, IL
Peoria Area Chamber
100 SW Water St.
Peoria, IL 61602
Phone: (309) 495-5900
www.peoriachamber.org

Philadelphia, PA
Greater Philadelphia Chamber of
Commerce
200 South Broad Street
Suite 700
Philadelphia, PA 19102
Phone: (215) 545-1234
Fax: (215) 790-3600
www.greaterphilachamber.com

Phoenix, AZ
Greater Phoenix Chamber of Commerce
201 North Central Avenue
27th Floor
Phoenix, AZ 85073
Phone: (602) 495-2195
Fax: (602) 495-8913
www.phoenixchamber.com

Greater Phoenix Economic Council
2 North Central Avenue
Suite 2500
Phoenix, AZ 85004
Phone: (602) 256-7700
Fax: (602) 256-7744
www.gpec.org

Pittsburgh, PA
Allegheny County Industrial Development
Authority
425 6th Avenue
Suite 800
Pittsburgh, PA 15219
Phone: (412) 350-1067
Fax: (412) 642-2217
www.alleghenycounty.us

Greater Pittsburgh Chamber of Commerce
425 6th Avenue
12th Floor
Pittsburgh, PA 15219
Phone: (412) 392-4500
Fax: (412) 392-4520
www.alleghenyconference.org

Portland, OR
Portland Business Alliance
200 SW Market Street
Suite 1770
Portland, OR 97201
Phone: (503) 224-8684
Fax: (503) 323-9186
www.portlandalliance.com

Providence, RI
Greater Providence Chamber of Commerce
30 Exchange Terrace
Fourth Floor
Providence, RI 02903
Phone: (401) 521-5000
Fax: (401) 351-2090
www.provchamber.com

Rhode Island Economic Development
Corporation
Providence City Hall
25 Dorrance Street
Providence, RI 02903
Phone: (401) 421-7740
Fax: (401) 751-0203
www.providenceri.com

Provo, UT
Provo-Orem Chamber of Commerce
51 South University Avenue
Suite 215
Provo, UT 84601
Phone: (801) 851-2555
Fax: (801) 851-2557
www.thechamber.org

Raleigh, NC
Greater Raleigh Chamber of Commerce
800 South Salisbury Street
Raleigh, NC 27601-2978
Phone: (919) 664-7000
Fax: (919) 664-7099
www.raleighchamber.org

Reno, NV
Greater Reno-Sparks Chamber of
Commerce
1 East First Street
16th Floor
Reno, NV 89505
Phone: (775) 337-3030
Fax: (775) 337-3038
www.reno-sparkschamber.org

The Chamber Reno-Sparks-Northern
Nevada
449 S. Virginia St.
2nd Floor
Reno, NV 89501
Phone: (775) 636-9550
www.thechambernv.org

Richmond, VA
Greater Richmond Chamber
600 East Main Street
Suite 700
Richmond, VA 23219
Phone: (804) 648-1234
www.grcc.com

Greater Richmond Partnership
901 East Byrd Street
Suite 801
Richmond, VA 23219-4070
Phone: (804) 643-3227
Fax: (804) 343-7167
www.grpva.com

Roanoke, VA
Roanoke Regional Chamber of Commerce
210 S. Jefferson St.
Roanoke, VA 24011-1702
Phone: (540) 983-0700
Fax: (540) 983-0723
www.roanokechamber.org

Rochester, MN
Rochester Area Chamber of Commerce
220 South Broadway
Suite 100
Rochester, MN 55904
Phone: (507) 288-1122
Fax: (507) 282-8960
www.rochestermnchamber.com

Sacramento, CA
Sacramento Metro Chamber of Commerce
One Capitol Mall
Suite 300
Sacramento, CA 95814
Phone: (916) 552-6800
Fax: (916) 443-2672
www.metrochamber.org

Salem, OR
Salem Area Chamber of Commerce
1110 Commercial Street NE
Salem, OR 97301
Phone: (503) 581-1466
Fax: (503) 581-0972
www.salemchamber.org

Salt Lake City, UT
Department of Economic Development
451 South State Street
Room 345
Salt Lake City, UT 84111
Phone: (801) 535-6306
Fax: (801) 535-6331
www.slcgov.com/mayor/ED

Salt Lake Chamber
175 E. University Blvd. (400 S)
Suite 600
Salt Lake City, UT 84111
Phone: (801) 364-3631
www.slchamber.com

San Antonio, TX
San Antonio Economic Development
Department
P.O. Box 839966
San Antonio, TX 78283-3966
Phone: (210) 207-8080
Fax: (210) 207-8151
www.sanantonio.gov/edd

The Greater San Antonio Chamber of
Commerce
602 E. Commerce Street
San Antonio, TX 78205
Phone: (210) 229-2100
Fax: (210) 229-1600
www.sachamber.org

San Diego, CA
San Diego Economic Development
Corporation
401 B Street
Suite 1100
San Diego, CA 92101
Phone: (619) 234-8484
Fax: (619) 234-1935
www.sandiegobusiness.org

San Diego Regional Chamber of Commerce
402 West Broadway
Suite 1000
San Diego, CA 92101-3585
Phone: (619) 544-1300
Fax: (619) 744-7481
www.sdchamber.org

San Francisco, CA
San Francisco Chamber of Commerce
235 Montgomery Street
12th Floor
San Francisco, CA 94104
Phone: (415) 392-4520
Fax: (415) 392-0485
www.sfchamber.com

San Jose, CA
Office of Economic Development
60 South Market Street
Suite 470
San Jose, CA 95113
Phone: (408) 277-5880
Fax: (408) 277-3615
www.sba.gov

San Jose-Silicon Valley Chamber of
Commerce
310 South First Street
San Jose, CA 95113
Phone: (408) 291-5250
Fax: (408) 286-5019
www.sjchamber.com

Santa Rosa, CA
Santa Rosa Chamber of Commerce
1260 North Dutton Avenue
Suite 272
Santa Rosa, CA 95401
Phone: (707) 545-1414
www.santarosachamber.com

Savannah, GA
Economic Development Authority
131 Hutchinson Island Road
4th Floor
Savannah, GA 31421
Phone: (912) 447-8450
Fax: (912) 447-8455
www.seda.org

Savannah Chamber of Commerce
101 E. Bay Street
Savannah, GA 31402
Phone: (912) 644-6400
Fax: (912) 644-6499
www.savannahchamber.com

Seattle, WA
Greater Seattle Chamber of Commerce
1301 Fifth Avenue
Suite 2500
Seattle, WA 98101
Phone: (206) 389-7200
Fax: (206) 389-7288
www.seattlechamber.com

Sioux Falls, SD
Sioux Falls Area Chamber of Commerce
200 N. Phillips Avenue
Suite 102
Sioux Falls, SD 57104
Phone: (605) 336-1620
Fax: (605) 336-6499
www.siouxfallschamber.com

Spokane, WA
Greater Spokane
801 W Riverside
Suite 100
Spokane, WA 99201
Phone: (509) 624-1393
Fax: (509) 747-0077
www.spokanechamber.org

Springfield, IL
The Greater Springfield Chamber of
Commerce
1011 S. Second St.
Springfield, IL 62704
Phone: (217) 525-1173
Fax: (217) 525-8768
www.gscc.org

Tallahassee, FL
Greater Tallahassee Chamber of Commerce
300 E. Park Avenue
PO Box 1638
Tallahassee, FL 32301
Phone: (850) 224-8116
Fax: (850) 561-3860
www.talchamber.com

Tampa, FL
Greater Tampa Chamber of Commerce
P.O. Box 420
Tampa, FL 33601-0420
Phone: (813) 276-9401
Fax: (813) 229-7855
www.tampachamber.com

Topeka, KS
Greater Topeka Chamber of Commerce/GO
Topeka
120 SE Sixth Avenue
Suite 110
Topeka, KS 66603
Phone: (785) 234-2644
Fax: (785) 234-8656
www.topekachamber.org

Tulsa, OK
Tulsa Regional Chamber
1 West 3rd Street
Suite 100
Tulsa, OK 74103
Phone: (918) 585-1201
Fax: (918) 585-8016
www.tulsachamber.com

Tyler, TX
Tyler Area Chamber of Commerce
315 N. Broadway Ave.
Suite 100
Tyler, TX 75702
Phone: (800) 235-5712
Fax: (903) 593-2746
www.tylertexas.com

Virginia Beach, VA
Hampton Roads Chamber of Commerce
500 East Main St
Suite 700
Virginia Beach, VA 23510
Phone: (757) 664-2531
www.hamptonroadschamber.com

Washington, DC
District of Columbia Chamber of
Commerce
1213 K Street NW
Washington, DC 20005
Phone: (202) 347-7201
Fax: (202) 638-6762
www.dcchamber.org

District of Columbia Office of Planning and
Economic Development
J.A. Wilson Building
1350 Pennsylvania Ave NW, Suite 317
Washington, DC 20004
Phone: (202) 727-6365
Fax: (202) 727-6703
www.dcbiz.dc.gov

Wichita, KS
City of Wichita Economic Development
Department
City Hall, 12th Floor
455 North Main Street
Wichita, KS 67202
Phone: (316) 268-4524
Fax: (316) 268-4656
www.wichitagov.org

Wichita Metro Chamber of Commerce
350 West Douglas Avenue
Wichita, KS 67202
Phone: (316) 265-7771
www.wichitachamber.org

Wilmington, NC
Wilmington Chamber of Commerce
One Estell Lee Place
Wilmington, NC 28401
Phone: (910) 762-2611
www.wilmingtonchamber.org

Winston-Salem, NC
Winston-Salem Chamber of Commerce
411 West Fourth Street
Suite 211
Winston-Salem, NC 27101
Phone: (336) 728-9200
www.winstonsalem.com

Worcester, MA
Worcester Regional Chamber of Commerce
446 Main St.
Suite 200
Worcester, MA 01608
Phone: (508) 753-2924
Fax: (508) 754-8560
www.worcesterchamber.org

Appendix E: State Departments of Labor

Alabama
Alabama Department of Labor
P.O. Box 303500
Montgomery, AL 36130-3500
Phone: (334) 242-3072
www.Alalabor.state.al.us

Alaska
Dept of Labor and Workforce Devel.
P.O. Box 11149
Juneau, AK 99822-2249
Phone: (907) 465-2700
www.labor.state.AK.us

Arizona
Arizona Industrial Commission
800 West Washington Street
Phoenix, AZ 85007
Phone: (602) 542-4515
www.ica.state.AZ.us

Arkansas
Department of Labor
10421 West Markham
Little Rock, AR 72205
Phone: (501) 682-4500
www.Arkansas.gov/labor

California
Labor and Workforce Development
445 Golden Gate Ave., 10th Floor
San Francisco, CA 94102
Phone: (916) 263-1811
www.labor.CA.gov

Colorado
Dept of Labor and Employment
633 17th St., 2nd Floor
Denver, CO 80202-3660
Phone: (888) 390-7936
www.COworkforce.com

Connecticut
Department of Labor
200 Folly Brook Blvd.
Wethersfield, CT 06109-1114
Phone: (860) 263-6000
www.CT.gov/dol

Delaware
Department of Labor
4425 N. Market St., 4th Floor
Wilmington, DE 19802
Phone: (302) 451-3423
www.Delawareworks.com

District of Columbia
Employment Services Department
614 New York Ave., NE, Suite 300
Washington, DC 20002
Phone: (202) 671-1900
www.DOES.DC.gov

Florida
Agency for Workforce Innovation
The Caldwell Building
107 East Madison St. Suite 100
Tallahassee, FL 32399-4120
Phone: (800) 342-3450
www.Floridajobs.org

Georgia
Department of Labor
Sussex Place, Room 600
148 Andrew Young Intl Blvd., NE
Atlanta, GA 30303
Phone: (404) 656-3011
www.dol.state.GA.us

Hawaii
Dept of Labor & Industrial Relations
830 Punchbowl Street
Honolulu, HI 96813
Phone: (808) 586-8842
wwwHawaii.gov/labor

Idaho
Department of Labor
317 W. Main St.
Boise, ID 83735-0001
Phone: (208) 332-3579
www.labor.Idaho.gov

Illinois
Department of Labor
160 N. LaSalle Street, 13th Floor
Suite C-1300
Chicago, IL 60601
Phone: (312) 793-2800
www.state.IL.us/agency/idol

Indiana
Indiana Government Center South
402 W. Washington Street
Room W195
Indianapolis, IN 46204
Phone: (317) 232-2655
www.IN.gov/labor

Iowa
Iowa Workforce Development
1000 East Grand Avenue
Des Moines, IA 50319-0209
Phone: (515) 242-5870
www.Iowaworkforce.org/labor

Kansas
Department of Labor
401 S.W. Topeka Blvd.
Topeka, KS 66603-3182
Phone: (785) 296-5000
www.dol.KS.gov

Kentucky
Philip Anderson, Commissioner
Department of Labor
1047 U.S. Hwy 127 South, Suite 4
Frankfort, KY 40601-4381
Phone: (502) 564-3070
www.labor.KY.gov

Louisiana
Department of Labor
P.O. Box 94094
Baton Rouge, LA 70804-9094
Phone: (225) 342-3111
www.LAworks.net

Maine
Department of Labor
45 Commerce Street
Augusta, ME 04330
Phone: (207) 623-7900
www.state.ME.us/labor

Maryland
Department of Labor and Industry
500 N. Calvert Street
Suite 401
Baltimore, MD 21202
Phone: (410) 767-2357
www.dllr.state.MD.us

Massachusetts
Dept of Labor & Work Force Devel.
One Ashburton Place
Room 2112
Boston, MA 02108
Phone: (617) 626-7100
www.Mass.gov/eolwd

Michigan
Dept of Labor & Economic Growth
P.O. Box 30004
Lansing, MI 48909
Phone: (517) 335-0400
www.Michigan.gov/cis

Minnesota
Dept of Labor and Industry
443 Lafayette Road North
Saint Paul, MN 55155
Phone: (651) 284-5070
www.doli.state.MN.us

Mississippi
Dept of Employment Security
P.O. Box 1699
Jackson, MS 39215-1699
Phone: (601) 321-6000
www.mdes.MS.gov

Missouri
Labor and Industrial Relations
P.O. Box 599
3315 W. Truman Boulevard
Jefferson City, MO 65102-0599
Phone: (573) 751-7500
www.dolir.MO.gov/lirc

Montana
Dept of Labor and Industry
P.O. Box 1728
Helena, MT 59624-1728
Phone: (406) 444-9091
www.dli.MT.gov

Nebraska
Department of Labor
550 South 16th Street
Box 94600
Lincoln, NE 68509-4600
Phone: (402) 471-9000
www.Nebraskaworkforce.com

Nevada
Dept of Business and Industry
555 E. Washington Ave.
Suite 4100
Las Vegas, NV 89101-1050
Phone: (702) 486-2650
www.laborcommissioner.com

New Hampshire
Department of Labor
State Office Park South
95 Pleasant Street
Concord, NH 03301
Phone: (603) 271-3176
www.labor.state.NH.us

New Jersey
Department of Labor
John Fitch Plaza, 13th Floor
Suite D
Trenton, NJ 08625-0110
Phone: (609) 777-3200
lwd.dol.state.nj.us/labor

New Mexico
Department of Labor
401 Broadway, NE
Albuquerque, NM 87103-1928
Phone: (505) 841-8450
www.dol.state.NM.us

New York
Department of Labor
State Office Bldg. # 12
W.A. Harriman Campus
Albany, NY 12240
Phone: (518) 457-5519
www.labor.state.NY.us

North Carolina
Department of Labor
4 West Edenton Street
Raleigh, NC 27601-1092
Phone: (919) 733-7166
www.nclabor.com

North Dakota
Department of Labor
State Capitol Building
600 East Boulevard, Dept 406
Bismark, ND 58505-0340
Phone: (701) 328-2660
www.nd.gov/labor

Ohio
Department of Commerce
77 South High Street, 22nd Floor
Columbus, OH 43215
Phone: (614) 644-2239
www.com.state.OH.us

Oklahoma
Department of Labor
4001 N. Lincoln Blvd.
Oklahoma City, OK 73105-5212
Phone: (405) 528-1500
www.state.OK.us/~okdol

Oregon
Bureau of Labor and Industries
800 NE Oregon St., #32
Portland, OR 97232
Phone: (971) 673-0761
www.Oregon.gov/boli

Pennsylvania
Dept of Labor and Industry
1700 Labor and Industry Bldg
7th and Forster Streets
Harrisburg, PA 17120
Phone: (717) 787-5279
www.dli.state.PA.us

Rhode Island
Department of Labor and Training
1511 Pontiac Avenue
Cranston, RI 02920
Phone: (401) 462-8000
www.dlt.state.RI.us

South Carolina
Dept of Labor, Licensing & Regulations
P.O. Box 11329
Columbia, SC 29211-1329
Phone: (803) 896-4300
www.llr.state.SC.us

South Dakota
Department of Labor
700 Governors Drive
Pierre, SD 57501-2291
Phone: (605) 773-3682
www.state.SD.us

Tennessee
Dept of Labor & Workforce Development
Andrew Johnson Tower
710 James Robertson Pkwy
Nashville, TN 37243-0655
Phone: (615) 741-6642
www.state.TN.us/labor-wfd

Texas
Texas Workforce Commission
101 East 15th St.
Austin, TX 78778
Phone: (512) 475-2670
www.twc.state.TX.us

Utah
Utah Labor Commission
P.O. Box 146610
Salt Lake City, UT 84114-6610
Phone: (801) 530-6800
Laborcommission.Utah.gov

Vermont
Department of Labor
5 Green Mountain Drive
P.O. Box 488
Montpelier, VT 05601-0488
Phone: (802) 828-4000
www.labor.verMont.gov

Virginia
Dept of Labor and Industry
Powers-Taylor Building
13 S. 13th Street
Richmond, VA 23219
Phone: (804) 371-2327
www.doli.Virginia.gov

Washington
Dept of Labor and Industries
P.O. Box 44001
Olympia, WA 98504-4001
Phone: (360) 902-4200
www.lni.WA.gov

West Virginia
Division of Labor
State Capitol Complex, Building #6
1900 Kanawha Blvd.
Charleston, WV 25305
Phone: (304) 558-7890
www.labor.state.WV.us

Wisconsin
Dept of Workforce Development
201 E. Washington Ave., #A400
P.O. Box 7946
Madison, WI 53707-7946
Phone: (608) 266-6861
www.dwd.state.WI.us

Wyoming
Department of Employment
1510 East Pershing Blvd.
Cheyenne, WY 82002
Phone: (307) 777-7261
www.doe.state.WY.us

Source: U.S. Department of Labor

Grey House Publishing

Grey House Publishing

2015 Title List
Visit www.GreyHouse.com for Product Information, Table of Contents, and Sample Pages.

General Reference
An African Biographical Dictionary
America's College Museums
American Environmental Leaders: From Colonial Times to the Present
Encyclopedia of African-American Writing
Encyclopedia of Constitutional Amendments
Encyclopedia of Gun Control & Gun Rights
An Encyclopedia of Human Rights in the United States
Encyclopedia of Invasions & Conquests
Encyclopedia of Prisoners of War & Internment
Encyclopedia of Religion & Law in America
Encyclopedia of Rural America
Encyclopedia of the Continental Congress
Encyclopedia of the United States Cabinet, 1789-2010
Encyclopedia of War Journalism
Encyclopedia of Warrior Peoples & Fighting Groups
The Environmental Debate: A Documentary History
The Evolution Wars: A Guide to the Debates
From Suffrage to the Senate: America's Political Women
Global Terror & Political Risk Assessment
Media & Communications 1900-2020
Nations of the World
Political Corruption in America
Privacy Rights in the Digital Era
The Religious Right: A Reference Handbook
Speakers of the House of Representatives, 1789-2009
This is Who We Were: 1880-1900
This is Who We Were: A Companion to the 1940 Census
This is Who We Were: In the 1910s
This is Who We Were: In the 1920s
This is Who We Were: In the 1940s
This is Who We Were: In the 1950s
This is Who We Were: In the 1960s
This is Who We Were: In the 1970s
U.S. Land & Natural Resource Policy
The Value of a Dollar 1600-1865: Colonial Era to the Civil War
The Value of a Dollar: 1860-2014
Working Americans 1770-1869 Vol. IX: Revolutionary War to the Civil War
Working Americans 1880-1999 Vol. I: The Working Class
Working Americans 1880-1999 Vol. II: The Middle Class
Working Americans 1880-1999 Vol. III: The Upper Class
Working Americans 1880-1999 Vol. IV: Their Children
Working Americans 1880-2015 Vol. V: Americans At War
Working Americans 1880-2005 Vol. VI: Women at Work
Working Americans 1880-2006 Vol. VII: Social Movements
Working Americans 1880-2007 Vol. VIII: Immigrants
Working Americans 1880-2009 Vol. X: Sports & Recreation
Working Americans 1880-2010 Vol. XI: Inventors & Entrepreneurs
Working Americans 1880-2011 Vol. XII: Our History through Music
Working Americans 1880-2012 Vol. XIII: Education & Educators
World Cultural Leaders of the 20th & 21st Centuries

Education Information
Charter School Movement
Comparative Guide to American Elementary & Secondary Schools
Complete Learning Disabilities Directory
Educators Resource Directory
Special Education: A Reference Book for Policy and Curriculum Development

Health Information
Comparative Guide to American Hospitals
Complete Directory for Pediatric Disorders
Complete Directory for People with Chronic Illness
Complete Directory for People with Disabilities
Complete Mental Health Directory
Diabetes in America: Analysis of an Epidemic
Directory of Drug & Alcohol Residential Rehab Facilities
Directory of Health Care Group Purchasing Organizations
Directory of Hospital Personnel
HMO/PPO Directory
Medical Device Register
Older Americans Information Directory

Business Information
Complete Television, Radio & Cable Industry Directory
Directory of Business Information Resources
Directory of Mail Order Catalogs
Directory of Venture Capital & Private Equity Firms
Environmental Resource Handbook
Food & Beverage Market Place
Grey House Homeland Security Directory
Grey House Performing Arts Directory
Grey House Safety & Security Directory
Grey House Transportation Security Directory
Hudson's Washington News Media Contacts Directory
New York State Directory
Rauch Market Research Guides
Sports Market Place Directory

Statistics & Demographics
American Tally
America's Top-Rated Cities
America's Top-Rated Smaller Cities
America's Top-Rated Small Towns & Cities
Ancestry & Ethnicity in America
The Asian Databook
Comparative Guide to American Suburbs
The Hispanic Databook
Profiles of America
"Profiles of" Series – State Handbooks
Weather America

Financial Ratings Series
TheStreet Ratings' Guide to Bond & Money Market Mutual Funds
TheStreet Ratings' Guide to Common Stocks
TheStreet Ratings' Guide to Exchange-Traded Funds
TheStreet Ratings' Guide to Stock Mutual Funds
TheStreet Ratings' Ultimate Guided Tour of Stock Investing
Weiss Ratings' Consumer Guides
Weiss Ratings' Guide to Banks
Weiss Ratings' Guide to Credit Unions
Weiss Ratings' Guide to Health Insurers
Weiss Ratings' Guide to Life & Annuity Insurers
Weiss Ratings' Guide to Property & Casualty Insurers

Bowker's Books In Print® Titles
American Book Publishing Record® Annual
American Book Publishing Record® Monthly
Books In Print®
Books In Print® Supplement
Books Out Loud™
Bowker's Complete Video Directory™
Children's Books In Print®
El-Hi Textbooks & Serials In Print®
Forthcoming Books®
Large Print Books & Serials™
Law Books & Serials In Print™
Medical & Health Care Books In Print™
Publishers, Distributors & Wholesalers of the US™
Subject Guide to Books In Print®
Subject Guide to Children's Books In Print®

Canadian General Reference
Associations Canada
Canadian Almanac & Directory
Canadian Environmental Resource Guide
Canadian Parliamentary Guide
Canadian Venture Capital & Private Equity Firms
Financial Services Canada
Governments Canada
Health Guide Canada
The History of Canada
Libraries Canada
Major Canadian Cities

2015 Title List

Visit www.SalemPress.com for Product Information, Table of Contents, and Sample Pages.

Science, Careers & Mathematics

Ancient Creatures: Unearthed
Applied Science
Applied Science: Engineering & Mathematics
Applied Science: Science & Medicine
Applied Science: Technology
Biomes and Ecosystems
Careers in Business
Careers in Chemistry
Careers in Communications & Media
Careers in Environment & Conservation
Careers in Healthcare
Careers in Hospitality & Tourism
Careers in Human Services
Careers in Law, Criminal Justice & Emergency Services
Careers in Physics
Careers in Technology Services & Repair
Computer Technology Innovators
Contemporary Biographies in Business
Contemporary Biographies in Chemistry
Contemporary Biographies in Communications & Media
Contemporary Biographies in Environment & Conservation
Contemporary Biographies in Healthcare
Contemporary Biographies in Hospitality & Tourism
Contemporary Biographies in Law & Criminal Justice
Contemporary Biographies in Physics
Earth Science
Earth Science: Earth Materials & Resources
Earth Science: Earth's Surface and History
Earth Science: Physics & Chemistry of the Earth
Earth Science: Weather, Water & Atmosphere
Encyclopedia of Energy
Encyclopedia of Environmental Issues
Encyclopedia of Environmental Issues: Atmosphere and Air Pollution
Encyclopedia of Environmental Issues: Ecology and Ecosystems
Encyclopedia of Environmental Issues: Energy and Energy Use
Encyclopedia of Environmental Issues: Policy and Activism
Encyclopedia of Environmental Issues: Preservation/Wilderness Issues
Encyclopedia of Environmental Issues: Water and Water Pollution
Encyclopedia of Global Resources
Encyclopedia of Global Warming
Encyclopedia of Mathematics & Society
Encyclopedia of Mathematics & Society: Engineering, Tech, Medicine
Encyclopedia of Mathematics & Society: Great Mathematicians
Encyclopedia of Mathematics & Society: Math & Social Sciences
Encyclopedia of Mathematics & Society: Math Development/Concepts
Encyclopedia of Mathematics & Society: Math in Culture & Society
Encyclopedia of Mathematics & Society: Space, Science, Environment
Encyclopedia of the Ancient World
Forensic Science
Geography Basics
Internet Innovators
Inventions and Inventors
Magill's Encyclopedia of Science: Animal Life
Magill's Encyclopedia of Science: Plant life
Notable Natural Disasters
Principles of Chemistry
Science and Scientists
Solar System
Solar System: Great Astronomers
Solar System: Study of the Universe
Solar System: The Inner Planets
Solar System: The Moon and Other Small Bodies
Solar System: The Outer Planets
Solar System: The Sun and Other Stars
World Geography

Literature

American Ethnic Writers
Classics of Science Fiction & Fantasy Literature
Critical Insights: Authors
Critical Insights: New Literary Collection Bundles
Critical Insights: Themes
Critical Insights: Works
Critical Survey of Drama
Critical Survey of Graphic Novels: Heroes & Super Heroes
Critical Survey of Graphic Novels: History, Theme & Technique
Critical Survey of Graphic Novels: Independents/Underground Classics
Critical Survey of Graphic Novels: Manga
Critical Survey of Long Fiction
Critical Survey of Mystery & Detective Fiction
Critical Survey of Mythology and Folklore: Heroes and Heroines
Critical Survey of Mythology and Folklore: Love, Sexuality & Desire
Critical Survey of Mythology and Folklore: World Mythology
Critical Survey of Poetry
Critical Survey of Poetry: American Poets
Critical Survey of Poetry: British, Irish & Commonwealth Poets
Critical Survey of Poetry: Cumulative Index
Critical Survey of Poetry: European Poets
Critical Survey of Poetry: Topical Essays
Critical Survey of Poetry: World Poets
Critical Survey of Shakespeare's Sonnets
Critical Survey of Short Fiction
Critical Survey of Short Fiction: American Writers
Critical Survey of Short Fiction: British, Irish, Commonwealth Writers
Critical Survey of Short Fiction: Cumulative Index
Critical Survey of Short Fiction: European Writers
Critical Survey of Short Fiction: Topical Essays
Critical Survey of Short Fiction: World Writers
Cyclopedia of Literary Characters
Holocaust Literature
Introduction to Literary Context: American Poetry of the 20th Century
Introduction to Literary Context: American Post-Modernist Novels
Introduction to Literary Context: American Short Fiction
Introduction to Literary Context: English Literature
Introduction to Literary Context: Plays
Introduction to Literary Context: World Literature
Magill's Literary Annual 2015
Magill's Survey of American Literature
Magill's Survey of World Literature
Masterplots
Masterplots II: African American Literature
Masterplots II: American Fiction Series
Masterplots II: British & Commonwealth Fiction Series
Masterplots II: Christian Literature
Masterplots II: Drama Series
Masterplots II: Juvenile & Young Adult Literature, Supplement
Masterplots II: Nonfiction Series
Masterplots II: Poetry Series
Masterplots II: Short Story Series
Masterplots II: Women's Literature Series
Notable African American Writers
Notable American Novelists
Notable Playwrights
Notable Poets
Recommended Reading: 500 Classics Reviewed
Short Story Writers

2015 Title List

Visit www.SalemPress.com for Product Information, Table of Contents, and Sample Pages.

History and Social Science

The 2000s in America
50 States
African American History
Agriculture in History
American First Ladies
American Heroes
American Indian Culture
American Indian History
American Indian Tribes
American Presidents
American Villains
America's Historic Sites
Ancient Greece
The Bill of Rights
The Civil Rights Movement
The Cold War
Countries, Peoples & Cultures
Countries, Peoples & Cultures: Central & South America
Countries, Peoples & Cultures: Central, South & Southeast Asia
Countries, Peoples & Cultures: East & South Africa
Countries, Peoples & Cultures: East Asia & the Pacific
Countries, Peoples & Cultures: Eastern Europe
Countries, Peoples & Cultures: Middle East & North Africa
Countries, Peoples & Cultures: North America & the Caribbean
Countries, Peoples & Cultures: West & Central Africa
Countries, Peoples & Cultures: Western Europe
Defining Documents: American Revolution (1754-1805)
Defining Documents: Civil War (1860-1865)
Defining Documents: Emergence of Modern America (1868-1918)
Defining Documents: Exploration & Colonial America (1492-1755)
Defining Documents: Manifest Destiny (1803-1860)
Defining Documents: Post-War 1940s (1945-1949)
Defining Documents: Reconstruction (1865-1880)
Defining Documents: The 1920s
Defining Documents: The 1930s
Defining Documents: The American West (1836-1900)
Defining Documents: The Ancient World (2700 B.C.E.-50 C.E.)
Defining Documents: The Middle Ages (524-1431)
Defining Documents: World War I
Defining Documents: World War II (1939-1946)
The Eighties in America
Encyclopedia of American Immigration
Encyclopedia of Flight
Encyclopedia of the Ancient World
The Fifties in America
The Forties in America
Great Athletes
Great Athletes: Baseball
Great Athletes: Basketball
Great Athletes: Boxing & Soccer
Great Athletes: Cumulative Index
Great Athletes: Football
Great Athletes: Golf & Tennis
Great Athletes: Olympics
Great Athletes: Racing & Individual Sports
Great Events from History: 17th Century
Great Events from History: 18th Century
Great Events from History: 19th Century
Great Events from History: 20th Century (1901-1940)
Great Events from History: 20th Century (1941-1970)
Great Events from History: 20th Century (1971-2000)
Great Events from History: Ancient World
Great Events from History: Cumulative Indexes
Great Events from History: Gay, Lesbian, Bisexual, Transgender Events
Great Events from History: Middle Ages
Great Events from History: Modern Scandals
Great Events from History: Renaissance & Early Modern Era

Great Lives from History: 17th Century
Great Lives from History: 18th Century
Great Lives from History: 19th Century
Great Lives from History: 20th Century
Great Lives from History: African Americans
Great Lives from History: Ancient World
Great Lives from History: Asian & Pacific Islander Americans
Great Lives from History: Cumulative Indexes
Great Lives from History: Incredibly Wealthy
Great Lives from History: Inventors & Inventions
Great Lives from History: Jewish Americans
Great Lives from History: Latinos
Great Lives from History: Middle Ages
Great Lives from History: Notorious Lives
Great Lives from History: Renaissance & Early Modern Era
Great Lives from History: Scientists & Science
Historical Encyclopedia of American Business
Immigration in U.S. History
Magill's Guide to Military History
Milestone Documents in African American History
Milestone Documents in American History
Milestone Documents in World History
Milestone Documents of American Leaders
Milestone Documents of World Religions
Musicians & Composers 20th Century
The Nineties in America
The Seventies in America
The Sixties in America
Survey of American Industry and Careers
The Thirties in America
The Twenties in America
United States at War
U.S.A. in Space
U.S. Court Cases
U.S. Government Leaders
U.S. Laws, Acts, and Treaties
U.S. Legal System
U.S. Supreme Court
Weapons and Warfare
World Conflicts: Asia and the Middle East

Health

Addictions & Substance Abuse
Adolescent Health
Cancer
Complementary & Alternative Medicine
Genetics & Inherited Conditions
Health Issues
Infectious Diseases & Conditions
Magill's Medical Guide
Psychology & Behavioral Health
Psychology Basics

Current Biography
Current Biography Cumulative Index 1946-2013
Current Biography Monthly Magazine
Current Biography Yearbook: 2003
Current Biography Yearbook: 2004
Current Biography Yearbook: 2005
Current Biography Yearbook: 2006
Current Biography Yearbook: 2007
Current Biography Yearbook: 2008
Current Biography Yearbook: 2009
Current Biography Yearbook: 2010
Current Biography Yearbook: 2011
Current Biography Yearbook: 2012
Current Biography Yearbook: 2013
Current Biography Yearbook: 2014
Current Biography Yearbook: 2015

Core Collections
Children's Core Collection
Fiction Core Collection
Middle & Junior High School Core
Public Library Core Collection: Nonfiction
Senior High Core Collection

The Reference Shelf
Aging in America
American Military Presence Overseas
The Arab Spring
The Brain
The Business of Food
Conspiracy Theories
The Digital Age
Dinosaurs
Embracing New Paradigms in Education
Faith & Science
Families: Traditional and New Structures
The Future of U.S. Economic Relations: Mexico, Cuba, and Venezuela
Global Climate Change
Graphic Novels and Comic Books
Immigration in the U.S.
Internet Safety
Marijuana Reform
The News and its Future
The Paranormal
Politics of the Ocean
Reality Television
Representative American Speeches: 2008-2009
Representative American Speeches: 2009-2010
Representative American Speeches: 2010-2011
Representative American Speeches: 2011-2012
Representative American Speeches: 2012-2013
Representative American Speeches: 2013-2014
Representative American Speeches: 2014-2015
Revisiting Gender
Robotics
Russia
Social Networking
Social Services for the Poor
Space Exploration & Development
Sports in America
The Supreme Court
The Transformation of American Cities
U.S. Infrastructure
U.S. National Debate Topic: Surveillance
U.S. National Debate Topic: The Ocean
U.S. National Debate Topic: Transportation Infrastructure
Whistleblowers

Readers' Guide
Abridged Readers' Guide to Periodical Literature
Readers' Guide to Periodical Literature

Indexes
Index to Legal Periodicals & Books
Short Story Index
Book Review Digest

Sears List
Sears List of Subject Headings
Sears: Lista de Encabezamientos de Materia

Facts About Series
Facts About American Immigration
Facts About China
Facts About the 20th Century
Facts About the Presidents
Facts About the World's Languages

Nobel Prize Winners
Nobel Prize Winners: 1901-1986
Nobel Prize Winners: 1987-1991
Nobel Prize Winners: 1992-1996
Nobel Prize Winners: 1997-2001

World Authors
World Authors: 1995-2000
World Authors: 2000-2005

Famous First Facts
Famous First Facts
Famous First Facts About American Politics
Famous First Facts About Sports
Famous First Facts About the Environment
Famous First Facts: International Edition

American Book of Days
The American Book of Days
The International Book of Days

Junior Authors & Illustrators
Tenth Book of Junior Authors & Illustrations

Monographs
The Barnhart Dictionary of Etymology
Celebrate the World
Guide to the Ancient World
Indexing from A to Z
The Poetry Break
Radical Change: Books for Youth in a Digital Age

Wilson Chronology
Wilson Chronology of Asia and the Pacific
Wilson Chronology of Human Rights
Wilson Chronology of Ideas
Wilson Chronology of the Arts
Wilson Chronology of the World's Religions
Wilson Chronology of Women's Achievements

Grey House Publishing | Salem Press | H.W. Wilson | 4919 Route, 22 PO Box 56, Amenia NY 12501-0056